The Mortal Messiah

From Bethlehem to Calvary

Book I

Bruce R. McConkie

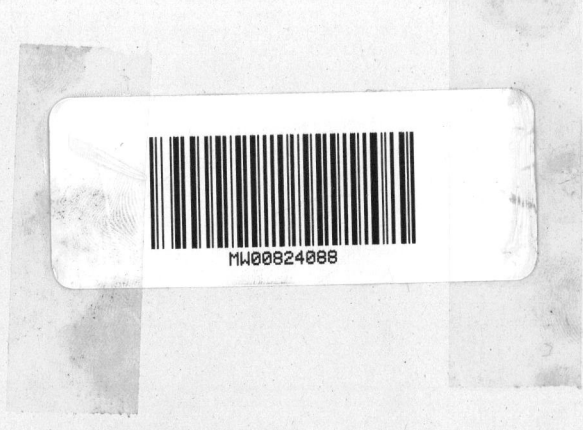

Deseret Book Company
Salt Lake City, Utah

Vol. 1 ISBN 0-87747-784-1 (hardbound)
ISBN 0-87579-403-3 (softbound)

Library of Congress Cataloging-in-Publication Data

McConkie, Bruce R.
The mortal Messiah: from Bethlehem to Calvary.

Includes index.
1. Jesus Christ—Biography. 2. Christian biography—Palestine.
3. Judaism—History—Post-exilic period, 586 B.C.–210 A.D.
I. Title.
BT301.2.M16 232.9'01 79-19606

Printed in the United States of America

10 9 8 7 6 5 4 3 2

I believe in Christ, he is my King;
With all my heart to him I'll sing;
I'll raise my voice in praise and joy,
In grand amens my tongue employ.

I believe in Christ, he is God's Son;
On earth to dwell his soul did come;
He healed the sick, the dead he raised,
Good works were his, his name be praised.

I believe in Christ, O blessed name,
As Mary's Son he came to reign
'Mid mortal men, his earthly kin,
To save them from the woes of sin.

I believe in Christ, who marked the path,
Who did gain all his Father hath,
Who said to men: "Come follow me,
That ye, my friends, with God may be."

I believe in Christ—my Lord, my God—
My feet he plants on gospel sod;
I'll worship him with all my might;
He is the source of truth and light.

I believe in Christ, he ransoms me;
From Satan's grasp he sets me free,
And I shall live with joy and love
In his eternal courts above.

I believe in Christ, he stands supreme;
From him I'll gain my fondest dream;
And while I strive through grief and pain,
His voice is heard: "Ye shall obtain."

I believe in Christ; so come what may,
With him I'll stand in that great day
When on this earth he comes again,
To rule among the sons of men.

—Bruce R. McConkie

THE MESSIANIC TRILOGY

The forerunner of this work is *The Promised Messiah: The First Coming of Christ,* which deals with the Messianic prophecies. This work, *The Mortal Messiah: From Bethlehem to Calvary,* is a Life of Christ published in four books. These four books contain the following:

BOOK I

Section I *A Root Out of Dry Ground*
Section II *Jesus' Years of Preparation*
Section III *Jesus' Early Judean Ministry*

BOOK II

Section IV *Jesus Begins the Great Galilean Ministry*
Section V *The Twelve, The Sermon on The Mount, and Rising Pharisaic Opposition*
Section VI *The Continuing Galilean Ministry*

BOOK III

Section VII *The Galilean Ministry Reaches Its Peak*
Section VIII *The Later Judean Ministry*
Section IX *The Perean Ministry*
Section X *From the Anointing to the Royal Reign*

BOOK IV

Section XI *The Paschal Feast, The Private Prayers and Sermons, and Gethsemane*
Section XII *The Trials, The Cross, and The Tomb*
Section XIII *He Riseth; He Ministereth; He Ascendeth*

The concluding work in this whole series will be *The Millennial Messiah: The Second Coming of the Son of Man.*

ABBREVIATIONS

Scriptural references are abbreviated in a standard and self-identifying way. Other books are cited by author and title except for the following:

Commentary I	Bruce R. McConkie, *Doctrinal New Testament Commentary.* Vol. 1, *The Gospels.* Bookcraft, 1965.
Edersheim	Alfred Edersheim, *The Life and Times of Jesus the Messiah.* 1883.
Farrar	F. W. Farrar, *The Life of Christ.* London: Cassell & Co., Ltd., 1874.
Geikie	Cunningham Geikie, *The Life and Words of Christ.* 1886.
Hymns	*Hymns, The Church of Jesus Christ of Latter-day Saints.* 1948.
JST	Joseph Smith Translation (Inspired Version) of the Bible.
Mormon Doctrine	Bruce R. McConkie, *Mormon Doctrine,* 2nd ed. Bookcraft, 1966.
Sketches	Alfred Edersheim, *Sketches of Jewish Social Life in the Days of Christ.* 1876.
Talmage	James E. Talmage, *Jesus the Christ.* 1915.
Teachings	Joseph Fielding Smith, comp., *Teachings of the Prophet Joseph Smith.* 1938.
Temple	Alfred Edersheim, *The Temple: Its Ministry and Services As They Were at the Time of Jesus Christ.*

CONTENTS

Chapter 14

Chapter 15

Chapter 16

SECTION II

JESUS' YEARS OF PREPARATION

Chapter 17

SECTION III

JESUS' EARLY JUDEAN MINISTRY

Chapter 26

Chapter 27

Chapter 28

Chapter 29

Chapter 30

PREFACE

My original intent, as this opus and its companion volumes took form in my mind, was to write two volumes—one dealing with the Messianic prophecies and the First Coming of the Messiah; the other with the prophetic utterances and revealed realities relative to his Second Coming. I had not dared even to think of assuming the prerogative of writing an account of the life of the greatest Person ever to walk the dusty paths of planet Earth. After all, I reasoned, I already had in print a nearly nine-hundred-page doctrinal commentary on the four Gospels, which in the very nature of things dealt primarily with the doings and sayings of Him who is eternal as he dwelt among men in mortal guise.

I knew, of course, that no man has and no man can write a *Life of Christ* in the true sense of the word, for two very good and sufficient reasons:

1. The data to do so does not exist. The material is simply not available. We do not know how he spent his youth, who his friends were, what part he played in church and civic affairs, how he conducted himself within the framework of the Jewish family system, and hosts of other things. Though we know a great deal about the historical and social circumstances of his day, very little authentic information is available of his actual life from either secular or spiritual sources. What Matthew, Mark, Luke, and John put in their Gospel accounts was written as their testimony of a

small part of his divine doings. Personal items are scarcely mentioned. The Gospels contain only that portion of our Lord's words, and only those glimpses of selected acts and deeds, which the Spirit knew beforehand should be preserved for presentation to the unbelieving and skeptical masses of men into whose hands the New Testament would come. Even God will not pour more knowledge and light and intelligence and understanding into human souls than they are prepared to accept. Such would be and is contrary to his whole plan for the advancement and growth and ultimate perfection of his children.

2. No mortal man, no matter how gifted he may be in literary craftsmanship, and no matter how highly endowed he may be with that spiritual insight which puts the words and acts of men into a true eternal perspective—no mortal, I say, can write the biography of a God. A biography is but the projection through the eyes of a penman of what the writer *believes* were the acts and what he *feels* were the thoughts and emotions of another man who had like feelings with his own. How, then, can any mortal plumb the depths of the feelings, or understand in full the doings, of an Eternal Being? How can one of limited talent tell, in true perspective, the whole story of Him who has all talent, and tell it in such a way that other dustlike creatures will catch the vision and rejoice in the portrayal?

It is not mere chance that the ancient inspired writers did not write a *Life of Our Lord.* Even they could not have done so; and if they had been so magnificently and gloriously endowed as to be able to record and analyze the infinitely complex character of an Infinite and Eternal Being, still none of us, their fellow dust-low creatures, would have been qualified to understand to the full what was written. Indeed, such is the spiritual degeneracy that is spread out over carnal and fallen man, that many things that might have been written about him would have had an adverse effect upon the minds of the doubting souls destined to dwell on earth after his day.

Just as the sealed portion of the Book of Mormon cannot be understood by men until they exercise faith like unto the brother of Jared, so the real *Life of Our Lord* cannot be written, and could not be understood if it were written, until men attain the spiritual stature to stand the effulgent brilliance that would shine forth from such a work if all things relative to him and his mortal doings were set forth in pristine perfection. All of this means that the true *Life of Christ* must be written by the spirit of revelation and of prophecy, and cannot come forth until that millennial day when men, like the brother of Jared, have a perfect knowledge that God can show them all things. Only then will they be able to believe and rejoice in the heavenly account.

For our day and time, and for this dispensation of grace, all we can do is write a study relative to his life. We can take those slivers of knowledge of him that have been preserved to us, add to them the revealed truths made manifest through latter-day revelation, use our best literary skill and organizational ability, sift out the speculative fabrications of uninspired authors, and come up with a near-biography which, hopefully, will do credit to his holy name. Our present study relative to the life of him who was perfect—a study based on the best light and knowledge now available—will be far from perfect. But any deficiencies will be those of the intellect and not of the heart, for in our heart we know he was divine, and we desire to present him in such a light as to please him and his Father.

In addition to all this, I have a deep and profound respect for *Jesus the Christ,* the scholarly work of Elder James E. Talmage, one of my most prominent predecessors. Why, I thought, should I step into the most difficult of all fields of gospel writing—that of composing something akin to a *Life of Christ?* But as I pondered and prayed and put into words, in the first volume of this series, the true meaning of the many Messianic messages, as I gained a working knowledge of what the makers of words and the coiners of phrases in Christendom had presumed to write about him of whom they know so little, and as I envisioned more fully the faithless and uninspired nature of almost everything that worldly men have recorded about the marvelous works and message of him who is known to us by revelation, there came into my heart an overpowering desire to put into words, as best I might, for all to read, what we believe and know about the greatest life ever lived.

Further, I knew, as do all who have studied the sources and toiled through the voluminous tomes of many authors, that my friend and colleague who gave us *Jesus the Christ* did not attempt to bring forth a near-biography that partakes of as many elements of a life of Christ as is possible. His work, like my *Doctrinal New Testament Commentary—The Gospels,* is in large measure a commentary about and an explanation of the teachings of the Master. It follows the pattern of his day, interweaving with well-chosen words a true and sound perspective of those things with which he was privileged to deal. His work is profound and sound and should be studied by every member of the true Church. But I think I hear his voice, vocal and penetrating above those of all others qualified to speak in the specialized field here involved, saying, "Now is the time to build on the foundations I laid some seventy years ago, using the added knowledge that has since come by research and revelation, and to pen a companion volume to the one I was privileged to write."

Such in any event is the labor I have undertaken in this work—*The Mortal Messiah: From Bethlehem to Calvary.* As to its value, I say only that it is what it is, and it will stand or fall on its own merit; nor do I think what is here recorded is the beginning and the end. It too is but an opening door. Others who follow will find the errors and deficiencies that always and ever attend every mortal work, will correct them, and, building upon whatever foundations then exist, will write greater and better works on the same subject. But if perchance this work leads some soul—or, the Lord willing, many souls—to love and follow him of whom it speaks, it will have fulfilled the desires and hopes of the author, who himself knows and testifies of the divine Sonship and of the perfect ministry of the Mortal Messiah.

I am deeply indebted—more than I can express—to Velma Harvey, a most able and efficient secretary, for much wise counsel, for many thoughtful suggestions, and for handling the myriad matters presented in such a work as this.

SECTION I

A ROOT OUT OF DRY GROUND

A ROOT OUT OF DRY GROUND

"He shall grow up before him as a tender plant, and as a root out of a dry ground." (Isa. 53:2.)

Our Lord, King Messiah—born of Mary and begotten by Elohim—grew up before his Father as a Tender Plant; as a Vine of whose fruit men may eat and never hunger more; as a Tree from whose branches the fruit of eternal life may be plucked.

But he grew up also as a Root out of dry ground; as a Vine in arid and sterile soil; as a Tree for which there was little soil and sun and water in the dry garden where he had been planted by his Father.

Our Lord, King Messiah, grew up in the arid soil of a spiritually degenerate society—in a Holy City that had become like Egypt and Sodom; among a people who chose darkness rather than light because their deeds were evil; and in the midst of a people who had a form of godliness but denied the power thereof.

He grew up to sit on a throne honored only in memory; as part of a subject people who wore a Roman yoke and were ruled by an Idumean despot; as part of the only nation under heaven who would crucify their King.

He grew up in the arid and sterile soil of a Judaism where the priesthood was bought and sold; where his Father's house had become a den of thieves; where sacrifices and feasts and fasts and Sabbaths all testified of a then-unknown Jehovah.

As a prelude to studying his growth, we must analyze the soil in which he grew. If ever a divine and tender plant grew up in dry ground, it was he who one day would say, "Every plant, which my heavenly Father hath not planted, shall be rooted up." (Matt. 15:13.)

Chapter I

"COME . . . LEARN OF ME"

Come drink of the waters of life;
Come feast on the good word of God;
Come eat of the manna from heav'n;
Come bask in the light of the Lord.

Come hear him speak peace to the storm;
Come see him give sight to the blind;
Come watch him heal legs that are lame;
Come view him give life to the dead.

Come feel of his Spirit anew;
Come hear what he says to all men;
Come walk in the way he commands;
Come learn of the One who is God.

—Bruce R. McConkie

The Father Commands: "Hear Ye Him!"

"This is my beloved Son, in whom I am well pleased; hear ye him." (Matt. 17:5.)

The Shekinah, a visible manifestation of the Divine Presence, the bright and shining cloud—which rested upon Moses in the holy mount, and out of which a Voice spoke from between the cherubim in the Holy of Holies—this sacred covering that surrounded the Presence of Deity, once more was manifest in Israel. A bright cloud, sent from heaven, overshadowed the angelic visitants who ministered to their mortal Kinsman, and a voice spake, the same voice that had said of old, "Thou art my Son; this day have I begotten thee." (Ps. 2:7.) The glory and power and Spirit, shining forth from the divine cloud, had come again, and the command was: "*Hear ye Him.*"

This was the day of the Son, the dispensation of crucifixion and martyrdom, the hour of atonement. This was the day when the bright and shining cloud that shielded the Personage from men was to be lifted, and all men were to see God in the person of his Son. After four thousand weary years, as promised by all the holy prophets since the world began, the ransom was to be paid by One without sin. The Promised Messiah now ministered as the Mortal Messiah, and his Father commanded all men: "*Hear ye Him.*"

Ancient Israel followed the cloud by day and the pillar of fire by night. Enoch hearkened to the voice from heaven, "Get ye upon the mount Simeon." There he beheld the heavens open, was clothed upon with glory, and "saw the Lord." (Moses 7:1-4.) Moses spent forty days amid the thunders and lightnings and fires of Sinai. There he received the holy law, written by the finger of God on tables of stone. Moriancumer talked with the Lord for three hours, and the voice came out of the cloud. (Ether 2.) It had ever been thus anciently—the Shekinah rested where the Lord's chosen people were; the power, glory, and Spirit of the Almighty was shown forth among those whom God had chosen out of the world; the Voice spake from the cloud, declaring truth, testifying, pointing the way. And now the Son himself, introduced by the Voice out of the cloud, dwelt among men, and they were commanded: "*Hear ye Him.*"

"God, who at sundry times and in divers manners spake in time past unto the fathers by the prophets," so the Apostle announced, "hath in these last days spoken unto us by his

Son." (Heb. 1:1-2.) God spoke by and through the Son. The words of the Father fell from the lips of the Son. "My doctrine is not mine, but his that sent me," Jesus said. "If any man will do his will, he shall know of the doctrine, whether it be of God, or whether I speak of myself." (John 7:16-17.) That God whom it is life eternal to know was revealing himself through his Son. "He that hath seen me hath seen the Father" (John 14:9) was the divine pronouncement. Is it any wonder, then, when the Shekinah once again was seen on earth, that the Voice, speaking from the heavenly cloud of light surrounding the Divine Presence, proclaimed the heaven-sent message—*Hear ye Him!*

Who is this Jesus of whom the Father saith, "Hear ye him"? Whence came he, and of what import is his message?

Jesus our Lord—born in Bethlehem, crucified on Calvary—lived the only perfect life ever known on planet Earth, or, for that matter, on any of the worlds without number created by him and his Father.

He was and is the Firstborn, the first spirit child born to the Eternal Father. In that spirit realm of light and glory he advanced and progressed and became like the Father in power and might and dominion. He was and is the Great Jehovah. Under the Father he was and is the Creator of all things from the beginning, and he was chosen in the councils of eternity to be the Redeemer and Savior.

When the time came for him to gain his mortal body and undergo the probationary experiences of mortality, he was born on this earth. He came here to dwell as a mortal, subject to the testing experiences that are the common lot of all mankind. He lived and breathed as all men do; he ate and drank as his needs required; he wielded the carpenter's saw, toiled in the fields of grain, and slept on the barren Palestinian soil. His experiences were like those of his Israelite kinsmen. Upon him the rains fell; around him the snows swirled. He was hungry, cold, tired, sick, and afflicted, as all men are; and when he died, his eternal spirit left its tenement of clay, as is the case with all of Adam's race. He was a man, a mortal man, a son of Adam, and God his Father saw fit to let him live as other men live, experience as they experience, sorrow and suffer as they do, and overcome as they must, if they are ever to return to the Divine Presence where joy and peace and eternal glory abound.

But he came from God and was born as his Son, inheriting from his Father the power of immortality. He came with the talents and abilities and spiritual endowments that he possessed in that eternal world where the spirit children of a gracious Father await the day of their mortal probation. He came with the spiritual talent to attune his soul to the Infinite so that he could think and speak and act in complete harmony with the mind and will of him whose Son he was. There was more than just a spark of divinity in his dust-created body. He was God's Son, the Only Begotten in the flesh. His native capacity exceeded that of any other person who ever lived. Not only could he alone work out the infinite and eternal atonement, because he possessed the power of immortality, but he alone could also do the other things that he did while in mortality—all because of his own preeminent preexistent stature, because of the talents and abilities he there possessed, and which were still his as he walked among mortal men.

Jesus our Lord was both a mortal man and a Divine Son. All men were his brethren and he was like them in appearance. Their ills and ailments were as his. But he alone was the Offspring of God in the flesh, and he alone came to earth with talents and insights that exceeded those of Adam and Enoch and Noah and Abraham. Though he was mortal, he retained his Godship. He was the only perfect Being ever to grace this lowly orb.

This Jesus of whom we now speak, and of whose mortal experiences we shall write in this work, was the greatest *man* who ever lived. In addition to the fact that he is "the Lord Omnipotent who reigneth, who was, and is from all eternity to all eternity," spoken of by King Benjamin (Mosiah 3:5), he is also the Suffering Servant of Isaiah (Isa. 53). Our challenge, as we attempt to paint a true picture of the Mortal Messiah, is to show him as a man; as a pilgrim far removed from his heavenly home; as the earthbound Christ, who lives and acts and is as other men—our challenge is to view him as a man, but with it all, a man of superlative talents and abilities, a man who reflected the light of heaven in every word and act.

"Though he were a Son," Paul tells us, as he confesses and certifies that our Lord is the Offspring of the Most High, "yet learned he obedience by the things which he suffered." That is, though God was his Father, he nonetheless was a mortal who suffered and struggled and obeyed. "And being made perfect," Paul continues, "he became the author of eternal salvation unto all them that obey him." (Heb. 5:8-9.) Thus, the Lord Jesus—having kept the whole law, having lived a perfect life, a life without sin—attained eternal perfection, a state of eternal glory like that of his Father. Because of his dual nature he became the Author (or, better, the Cause) of eternal salvation, meaning of both immortality and eternal life.

As to Jesus our Lord and the message he heralds to all who will hear, these things we know, and of them we are commanded to teach and testify:

1. That he who was born of Mary in Bethlehem of Judea; who dwelt and preached in Palestine; who healed the sick, opened the blind eyes, and caused the lame to leap; who stilled the storms and walked on the waters; who commanded the tomb-encased corpse to come forth, and it was done; who was condemned, scourged, and crucified; who died between two thieves at a place called Calvary; who came forth from a borrowed grave, on the third day, in glorious immortality—that this Jesus, who is both Christ and King, is, in fact, the Son of the living God.

2. That he who did all this did also, by virtue of his divine Sonship, work out the infinite and eternal atonement whereby all men are raised in immortality, while those who believe and obey come forth in the resurrection to inherit

eternal life; and that he, as the Word of God, the Spokesman of the Father, has and does present to the world the message of salvation, the plan of salvation, the gospel of Christ whereby this eternal life, the greatest of all the gifts of God, may be gained.

These things we know, for the Holy Spirit of God has revealed them to the spirit within us. We are living witnesses of him whose we are and by whom salvation comes. And we feel impelled to speak out, boldly, of him and his laws, and all that he has done for us, and all that he expects of us. This decision was not left to us: it is his will, and we are simply acting as his agent in teaching and testifying to all men everywhere those things which we verily believe and know to be true.

The Son Invites: "Come, . . . Learn of Me"

Jesus said: "Come, . . . learn of me" (Matt. 11:28-30)[1]—and learn we must, if we are ever to become like him and attain that kingdom where he and his Father dwell in celestial splendor.

"Learn of me!" Learn of the Lord Jesus Christ! Learn of him who is the Firstborn of the Father, the Great Jehovah, the Creator of worlds without number. Learn of him who is the God of Israel, the Promised Messiah, our Savior and Redeemer. Learn of him who dwelt in mortality for a scant thirty-four years; who set a perfect example for his brethren; who climaxed his earthly work in Gethsemane, at Golgotha, and before an open tomb.

Whence, then, comes our knowledge, and to what sources do we turn to learn truths about him whose name is Truth? As to his eternal existence and the things that he has done in ages past and will do in eons yet unborn, we have the Holy Scriptures and the inspired utterances of those whose Spirit-guided words come from the ultimate source of all truth. As to his ministry on planet earth, we have the four Gospels, the accounts in Third Nephi, sections 45 and 93 in the Doctrine and Covenants, and a few slivers of information in other parts of the Standard Works. As to all things connected with him, we should ponder and pray about that which is known, and then welcome the spirit of enlightenment and understanding that it is within our power to receive.

There is, of course, no such thing as a perfect biography of the Man Jesus, no such thing even as a sound and sane and proper biography. Neither I nor anyone else, with the knowledge presently available and with the literary craftsmanship with which writers of our generation have been blessed, could write such a work. Known facts about his mortal life are so fragmentary; the silence that broods over long periods of his earth life is so unbroken; what Matthew, Mark, Luke, and John chose to record was so selective and partial—that no one can even outline a chronological account of his life, or begin to show how his character and attributes became what they were. Recognized scholars have not so much as agreed upon a harmony of the four Gospels, nor can we expect them to do so with the data now available.

Biographies often reflect the feelings and sentiments, sometimes even the whims and idiosyncrasies, of those who write them. Authors are often prone to put their own proclivities and personality quirks into the pictures they paint of their subjects. Source materials, particularly for people long since departed to other realms, are often far from accurate. Tradition and speculation soon overshadow the fragments of reality that are known. How could a heavy tome on the life of Enoch or Ezra, on Melchizedek or Moriancumer, be other than a fictional accumulation of the fantasies of a fertile brain and a fluid pen? The known facts about any of these, and about Jethro and Joshua, about Joseph and Jeremiah, about Jesus himself, and about thousands of others who deserve an immortal remembrance in the hearts of succeeding generations, are so slight that any biography of the traditional sort must of necessity be largely imagination.

Unless and until more is known of Jesus and his life, it is

not only unwise but impossible to write a reality-based biographical dissertation about him. This work, thus, is not a biography in the traditional sense; it is not a life of our Lord of the sort that sectarians write; it is not a volume that puts words in the divine mouth, or assumes thoughts that may have been in his mind, or records with sinaitic finality emotions with which he may have been filled on great occasions. Insofar as finite limitations allow, it does not interlace the facts preserved in Holy Writ with the traditions of the fathers; it does not weave into the account the words of uninspired literary craftsmen, whose joy has always been to speculate what they would have done and therefore what Jesus did, in the various events of which we have knowledge; it does not draw out of the ethereal blue those personal fantasies—all of which taken together bring to full gestation and untimely birth the various biographies now extant about the greatest life ever lived.

This work is more of a commentary than a biography, more of an analysis of known events in his life than an exposition of his feelings and personality. Such biographical data, and such logical assumptions as fit in with his known character, can scarcely be avoided, nor is there any attempt so to do. There cannot help but be in this work, or in any work about any man written by any person, some things that are speculation and opinion. No biography, near-biography, or biography-type writing can possibly avoid this, and those who read any such compositions should be acutely aware that such is the case. Such awareness should be particularly keen when a devout person reads any biographical assumptions or recitations that deal with him who is our Lord.

In my judgment, those scriptural writers who have preserved for us the verities we do, in fact, know about him have so written their accounts as to omit, deliberately and designedly, nearly all of the personal items that would enable later biographers to portray his personality and personal affairs to the full. He is the Son of God; some things he had in common with his fellow mortals; other characteristics and abilities were his only; none of the rest of us have them, nor can we envision completely what they were or how they developed. We may suppose that an all-wise Father designed it so, and that he has permitted us to have available only those things with which we can equate and which are an example and an encouragement to us. We are not dealing with a mortal man in the full and unrestricted sense of the word when we write of him who inherited the power of immortality from that Man of Holiness who is the Immortal One. As he neared the end of his own Gospel account, the Beloved John said, "Many other signs truly did Jesus in the presence of his disciples, which are not written in this book: But these are written, that ye might believe that Jesus is the Christ, the Son of God; and that believing ye might have life through his name." (John 20:30-31.) Our approach and purpose will be the same as that of our ancient colleague.

We shall, accordingly, in this work talk about known family relations; known personality traits; known locales of labor and routes of travel; known facts about the character, perfections, and attributes that Jesus possessed; and beyond these limitations, we shall seek not to go. Much that is written will, of course, be in the nature of commentary; it will be akin to commentary, not the pure doctrinal commentary found in my *Doctrinal New Testament Commentary: The Gospels*, but commentary that teaches doctrines in the unique settings in which the utterances were given. We shall not strive to portray a rounded picture relative to each doctrine presented, but simply to expound and understand the portions of eternal truth that Jesus gave to the particular peoples who were then and there the hearers of his gracious words.

Doctrines and principles are the same under all circumstances. Truth is eternal. The principles of the everlasting gospel do not vary; they are the same in all ages and among all people. The Lord does not walk in crooked paths, nor vary from that which he hath said, nor alter the course in which men must walk to return to that far-off home whence they came. All men, in all ages, in all parts of our planet, must believe and obey the same doctrines and ordinances to gain salvation.

But a knowledge of the circumstances and conditions under which Jesus expounded these principles of perfection to his fellow mortals will enable us more perfectly to perceive the profound nature of the truths themselves. What better setting is there for the proclamation, "I am the light of the world," than when the great golden lamp-stands in the temple are blazing forth their light as part of the Feast of Tabernacles? How better can he teach that he brings living water that quenches all thirst forever, and which is therefore a well springing up unto everlasting life, than when the woman of Samaria stoops to draw water for him from Jacob's Well? What teaching as to the nature and kind of bodies possessed by resurrected beings can equal that in the Upper Room, when he comes through the wall, eats food before his disciples, and permits them to feel the nail marks in his hands and feet and thrust their hands into the spear wound in his side? Truly a knowledge of the events in the life of Jesus enables us more fully to comprehend the doctrines he taught!

We have in our possession only a few brief words that fell from the lips of the Son of God while he dwelt in mortality. The time needed to read them is measured in minutes. And yet he spoke enough to fill libraries and to provide a lifetime of reading and more. We know from the Gospel accounts a few of the travels and troubles and trials of the Man who bore his Father's image and who did all things well. We know enough about him to envision what a perfect man should be and to have the hope of eternal life kindled in our souls. But "there are also many other things which Jesus did," says his intimate friend and confidant, the Beloved John, "the which, if they should be written every one, I suppose that even the world itself could not contain the books that should be written." (John 21:25.) Hyperbole? Perhaps. But regardless, what we have heard from His lips is but a stanza of a poetic gospel whose verses are without number; and what we have seen him do is but a glimpse of the acts and wonders that roll endlessly across the eternal screen where the acts of all beings are viewed.

To write a biography when only one-tenth of one percent of the background information is available would be foolhardy. To comment about and put into their perspective and relationship to us those choice and heaven-like gems that we do have is a work worthy of the mightiest pen, the keenest mind, and the deepest spiritual insight known to man. Someday a perfect biography will be forthcoming, written of course by the spirit of revelation. For the present we must content ourselves with what we have, and what we can envision, with the limited insight that is ours. Perhaps that in itself is a manifestation of the divine will. We have what we have, and we can comprehend what we can comprehend. If we knew more, it would be all to the good; yet, mayhap, we have all we are entitled to have and all we are capable of receiving.

We cannot but suppose that an Omnipotent wisdom has drawn a curtain of discreet silence over the childhood and youth of Mary's son; over the young manhood and growing experiences of him who was reared in Galilee and learned the carpenter's trade in Joseph's shop; over his family relationship and the endearing friendships that developing and maturing manhood so keenly cherishes; over the social and familial relationships that formed the basis of that Jewish culture in which an all-wise Father had sent him to dwell. Perhaps, after all, we have received all that we in our present state of spiritual maturity are prepared and qualified to receive. Perhaps, as we ponder what is recorded in this work, *The Mortal Messiah: From Bethlehem to Calvary*, we shall find enough to give us that guidance so devoutly desired and needed by those who love their Lord and who seek to impress his image upon their own countenances.

We do not have all gospel truths, but we do have the fulness of the everlasting gospel, meaning we have all of the laws, doctrines, principles, and ordinances needed to save and exalt us with a fulness of eternal glory hereafter. Similarly, we do not know all things about the life of our Lord, of the sayings of this greatest of the seers, or of the mighty works that he did in Judea and Perea and Galilee. But we do know enough about him to bask in the eternal light that proceeds from his presence, to see divinity inscribed on every feature and manifest in every act, and to know that if we heed his call, "Follow thou me" (2 Ne. 31:10), we can become like him and go where he is. With this assurance we are prepared to launch boldly into the glorious study at hand.

As we seek to learn of our Lord, we need guidance. He said: "Come unto me, all ye that labour and are heavy laden, and I will give you rest. Take my yoke upon you, and learn of me; for I am meek and lowly in heart: and ye shall find rest unto your souls. For my yoke is easy, and my burden is light." (Matt. 11:28-30.)

Learn of Him, whose roots sink deep as eternity! Learn what he was like while yet a spirit Son of an exalted Father. Learn of his valiance and progression in preexistence, of his creative enterprises, of the worlds without number that rolled into existence at his word. Learn of his power, might, and dominion in that day when he was chosen and became the Lamb slain from the foundation of the world. Learn of his foreordained ministry to redeem and to ransom and to save.

Learn of Him, of whom we know so little! Learn of the revelation of his holy gospel to the sons of men. Learn that all men everywhere, be they whosoever they are, whether Jew or Gentile, bond or free, black or white, all of the family of that Adam who begat us, all are to call upon God in the name of the Son forevermore. Learn that beginning with Adam, righteous mortals, by the revelations of the Holy Spirit to the spirits within them, have known of his divine Sonship. Learn that all of these Messianic ministers who preceded him in life have testified of his coming, and that all who have come thereafter have had the testimony of Jesus interwoven into the very fibers and sinews of their souls. Learn that it is he who appeared to the partriarchs, who is the God of Abraham and Israel, and who is the source of truth and light among all of us lowly creatures who dwell here below.

Learn of Him—the Man nobody knows! Learn that he was born of Mary in the City of David which is called Bethlehem. Learn that he received not of the fulness at the first, but grew from grace to grace, experiencing, feeling, undergoing all the needed probations of mortality. Learn that he was in all points tempted, like as we are, yet remaining without sin. Learn of the wondrous works that he wrought, how he healed earth's sin-sick souls by the power of his everlasting word. Learn that he sweat great drops of blood from every pore, so great was his anguish and sorrow for the sins of his people. Learn that he was lifted up upon the cross, crucified on Calvary, that he might thereby lay down his life, preparatory to taking it up again in immortal glory. Learn that he gained the victory over the grave, redeemed the faithful from their spiritual fall, and has now ascended up on high, where he sits on the right hand of the Father, reigning with almighty power. Learn that he has come again in our day to men whom he has called to be prophets, as of old, that he has set up his kingdom anew, and that in a not far distant day he shall return in all the glory of his Father's kingdom, to reign personally among us mortals for a thousand years.

All this learning, this weight of wondrous wisdom, this knowledge of truths beyond carnal comprehension, all is available to those who will pay the scholar's price. True it is that gospel scholarship is seldom sought in today's world, and that even many of those few who do so seek have little knowledge of the available source material or of how to read those volumes whose contents are known and understood only by the power of the Spirit.

"Understandest thou what thou readest?" inquired Philip

of the eunuch from the court of Candace. "How can I, except some man should guide me?" came the reply. (Acts 8:30-31.) Certain things men may learn for themselves, and that they are expected so to do by a divine providence, none can doubt. But after the alphabet has been learned, after fluency in reading has been acquired, after the source books have been identified by name and by title, still the seeker after spiritual truths must do his research subject to the eternal law which says, "The things of God knoweth no man, but the Spirit of God," and that "the natural man receiveth not the things of the Spirit of God: for they are foolishness unto him: neither can he know them, because they are spiritually discerned." (1 Cor. 2:11-14.)

Jesus Saith: "Come Unto Me"

Learn of Him! But do it in the way he has provided and by compliance with the laws that enable the desired knowledge to flow to the truth-seeking soul. How is this done, and whence comes that sure knowledge which is the testimony of him who is Lord of all?

"Come unto me," he says to all who labor in the libraries of the world. "Come unto me" is his invitation to all who are burdened with the weight of ignorance and intolerance. "Come unto me" and I will open the books; "Come unto me" and I will lift the gloom of darkness and uncertainty from your minds; "Come unto me" and I will remove the crushing weight of ignorance and doubt, and ye shall find rest to your souls.

"Come unto me" and "take my yoke upon you"—be as I am, join my Church, bear the burdens of my ministry, keep my commandments. "Come unto me" and the light of my everlasting word shall illumine your souls; "Come unto me" and ye shall receive the gift of the Holy Ghost, and he shall bear record to thee of the Father, and of me, and of all things that were and are and shall be, for he is a witness and a revealer of all truth.

"Come unto me" and receive my Spirit, and then shall ye have power to learn of me. This is the great and grand secret. This is the course that is provided for us and for all men, and it is provided in the wisdom of him who knoweth all things. This is the sole and only way to learn of Christ within the full sense and meaning of his tender and solicitous invitation. "No man can know that Jesus is the Lord, but by the Holy Ghost."[2] Little slivers of truth come to all who seek to know; occasional flashes of lightning give glimpses of the eternal realities that are hidden by the gloom and darkness of unbelief. But to learn and know those truths which reveal the Son of Man in his majesty and beauty and that prepare the truth seeker to be one with his Lord, such rays of the noonday sun shine forth only upon those who gain the enlightening companionship of the Holy Spirit.

It is with this understanding, then, that we open the eternal records and, having broken hearts and contrite spirits, begin to learn of our Lord. If we study, pray, ponder, and obey, as required by his eternal law, perchance it will then be with us as it was with Lehi: we shall see One descending out of the midst of heaven whose luster is above that of the sun at noonday. Perchance he will give us, as he gave Lehi, a book, bidding us also to read and learn the wonders of his ways. And then perchance, when we have read and seen for ourselves, we too will exclaim many great things unto him whose we are, such as:

"Great and marvelous are thy works, O Lord God Almighty! Thy throne is high in the heavens, and thy power, and goodness, and mercy are over all the inhabitants of the earth: and, because thou art merciful, thou wilt not suffer those who come unto thee that they shall perish!" (1 Ne. 1:14.)

Jesus Saith: "Follow Thou Me"

We all need our heroes, our patterns and guides. If we choose evil exemplars, we become evil ourselves because we adopt their ways. Everyone imitates someone else; all of us learn what we know from other people. If all instruction and education ceased, if all patterns of living were taken away, civilization would cease in one generation, and all of earth's inhabitants would sink to a state of barbarism.

Providentially a gracious Father endows all his children with the Light of Christ, that righteous power and influence which proceeds forth from the presence of God to fill the immensity of space. Part of this enlightening spirit is the universal gift of conscience; it causes unlearned and untaught people to do what is right by instinct. But a gracious Father has also sent noble spirits and good men among all peoples to teach that measure of truth which they are able to bear, and to set such an example as their fellow mortals are capable of following. These are the prophets and seers, the poets and philosophers, the sages and wise men, the leaders and influential persons found among all nations and kindreds. And a gracious Father sent one Supreme Pattern and guide to be a light and an example for all men of all ages; he sent his Son. Christ is our Pattern, our Exemplar, the great Prototype of all that is good and right and edifying.

"What manner of men ought ye to be?" So asked our great Exemplar of his Nephite disciples. His own answer: "Verily I say unto you, even as I am." (3 Ne. 27:27.) Manifestly, if we emulate him so that his way of life becomes ours, we shall qualify for the same glory and exaltation that is his, for "when he shall appear, we shall be like him." (1 Jn. 3:2.)

In the final analysis, our purpose in learning of our Lord is to gain that knowledge, insight, and desire which will cause us to become like him—all in harmony with his divine promise: "Ye shall have fulness of joy; and ye shall sit down in the kingdom of my Father; yea, your joy shall be full, even as the Father hath given me fulness of joy; and ye shall be even as I am, and I am even as the Father; and the Father and I are one." (3 Ne. 28:10.)

NOTES

1. This invitation is always issued when the Lord has a people on earth. In every dispensation people have been invited to learn of Christ. For our day the invitation is: "Learn of me, and listen to my words; walk in the meekness of my Spirit, and you shall have peace in me. I am Jesus Christ; I came by the will of the Father, and I do his will." (D&C 19:23-24.)

2. This is Joseph Smith's inspired rendition of Paul's statement in 1 Corinthians 12:3. (*Teachings*, p. 223.)

BEFORE BETHLEHEM

Our birth is but a sleep and a forgetting:
The Soul that rises with us, our life's Star,
Hath had elsewhere its setting,
And cometh from afar:
Not in entire forgetfulness,
And not in utter nakedness,
But trailing clouds of glory do we come
From God, who is our home.

—*William Wordsworth*[1]

Man—In the Beginning with God

Our blessed Lord, who as Mary's son dwelt among us for a short span, is truly the Man nobody knows. Those, in particular, whose knowledge of him is bounded by Bethlehem where he was born and Calvary where he died, have no intelligent way to put in a proper perspective even those slivers of light and knowledge which have been preserved for us by the Gospel authors. Before we even attempt to view and envision the events of his mortal life, we must have an acute awareness of certain eternal verities. These are:

1. *The Father is an exalted Person.*

It is a philosophical impossibility to believe that the Man

Jesus is the Son of God in the literal and full sense of the word if we suppose that his Father is a spirit essence or power that fills the immensity of space and is everywhere and nowhere in particular present, and if we believe that God is an immaterial, uncreated Being without body, parts, or passions, as the creeds of Christendom recite.[2] To know and understand Christ and his mission and ministry, we must know certain basic things about that Progenitor whence he sprang.

God himself is the First Man and the Father of all men. In the pure language, spoken by Adam, the name of the Father is *Man of Holiness*, which means he is a holy Man; and when the scriptures speak of Deity creating man in his own image, they are to be understood as literal renditions of that which in reality occurred. "God himself . . . is an exalted man, and sits enthroned in yonder heavens," the Prophet Joseph Smith said.[3] "The Father has a body of flesh and bones as tangible as man's" (D&C 130:22) is the scriptural assertion. When Paul says the Son is the brightness of his Father's glory, "and the express image of his person" (Heb. 1:3), he is certifying that the Risen Lord—who ate and drank with the apostles after he rose from the dead, and into whose riven side they had thrust their hands—had a resurrected body of the same sort and kind possessed by the exalted Father.

2. *Christ and all men are spirit children of the Father.*

God lives in the family unit. He is our Father in heaven—the literal and personal Father of the spirits of all men. He begat us; we are the offspring of Heavenly Parents; we have an Eternal Father and an Eternal Mother. We were born as spirits, and we dwelt in the presence of our Eternal Parents; we lived before our mortal birth. As spirits we were in all respects as we are now save only that we were not housed in mortal bodies as is the present circumstance. Christ was the Firstborn of all the heavenly host; Lucifer was a son of the morning; each of us came into being as conscious identities in our appointed order; and Christ is our Elder Brother.

3. *The spirit children of the Father were subject to his laws.*

In his infinite wisdom and goodness, the Eternal Father ordained laws by obedience to which his spirit children could advance and progress and eventually obtain the high reward of eternal life. These laws are the good news conveyed by God to his spirit progeny; they are the plan of salvation; they are the gospel of the Father. Paul called them "the gospel of God, . . . Concerning his Son Jesus Christ our Lord." (Rom. 1:1-3.) With reference to them, Joseph Smith said: "God himself, finding he was in the midst of spirits and glory, because he was more intelligent, saw proper to institute laws whereby the rest could have a privilege to advance like himself."[4]

Manifestly, there were no laws but God's laws in that eternal world; every law ordained and established by him was good; and obedience and conformity to any of his laws moved the obedient person (Christ included) along the path to glory and exaltation.

Similarly, failure to obey a given law denied such failing person the blessing and advancement that otherwise would have resulted, and disobedience imposed the penalties prescribed for such a rebellious course.

4. *All spirits were endowed with agency in preexistence.*

An all-wise Father endowed his spirit children with agency—the freedom and ability to choose good or evil—while they yet dwelt in his presence. Unless there are opposites—good and evil, virtue and vice, right and wrong—and unless intelligent beings are free to choose; free to obey or disobey; free to do good and work righteousness, or to walk in evil paths—unless this freedom exists, there can be no advancement and progression; no joy as contrasted with sorrow; no talents of one kind or another as contrasted with their absence; no eternal salvation as contrasted with eternal damnation. There can be no light unless there is darkness; no heat unless there is cold; no up unless there is down; no right unless there is left; no life unless there is death; and so on through all the realm of created and existent things. Opposites and agency are essential to existence and to progression. Without them there would be nothing.[5]

5. *Spirits developed an infinite variety and degree of talents while yet in preexistence.*

Being subject to law, and having their agency, all the spirits of men, while yet in the Eternal Presence, developed aptitudes, talents, capacities, and abilities of every sort, kind, and degree. During the long expanse of life which then was, an infinite variety of talents and abilities came into being. As the ages rolled, no two spirits remained alike. Mozart became a musician; Einstein centered his interest in mathematics; Michelangelo turned his attention to painting. Cain was a liar, a schemer, a rebel who maintained a close affinity to Lucifer. Abraham and Moses and all of the prophets sought and obtained the talent for spirituality. Mary and Eve were two of the greatest of all the spirit daughters of the Father. The whole house of Israel, known and segregated out from their fellows, was inclined toward spiritual things. And so it went through all the hosts of heaven, each individual developing such talents and abilities as his soul desired.

The Lord endowed us all with agency; he gave us laws that would enable us to advance and progress and become like him; and he counseled and exhorted us to pursue the course leading to glory and exaltation. He himself was the embodiment and personification of all good things. Every desirable characteristic and trait dwelt in him in its eternal fulness. All of his obedient children started to become like him in one way or another. There was as great a variety and degree of talent and ability among us there as there is among us here. Some excelled in one way, others in another. The Firstborn excelled all of us in all things.

6. *Spirit children have the capacity to become like their Eternal Father.*

We are members of the family of the Eternal Father. He is a glorified and exalted and eternal Being, having a resurrected body of flesh and bones. His name is God, and the kind of life he lives is God's life. His name is also Eternal, and the name of the kind of life he lives is eternal life. Eternal life is God's life, and God's life is eternal life. We are commanded to be perfect as he is perfect and to advance and progress until we become like him, or in other words, until we gain eternal life. Thus Joseph Smith said, "You have got to learn how to be Gods yourselves, and to be kings and priests to God, the same as all Gods have done before you, namely, by going from one small degree to another, and from a small capacity to a great one; from grace to grace, from exaltation to exaltation, until you attain to the resurrection of the dead, and are able to dwell in everlasting burnings, and to sit in glory, as do those who sit enthroned in everlasting power." (*Teachings*, pp. 346-47.) Christ our Lord has so obtained, thus enabling him to say to the faithful: "Ye shall be even as I am, and I am even as the Father." (3 Ne. 28:10.)

7. *Mortal life is an essential step leading to eternal life.*

According to the terms and conditions of the Father's plan, his spirit children must dwell on earth as mortals for two reasons:

a. To gain mortal bodies, bodies of flesh and bones, bodies subject to disease and death, bodies that could and would be raised in immortality, becoming bodies of flesh and bones, through an infinite and eternal atoning sacrifice;

b. To undergo a probationary, testing experience, one in which it would be determined whether each of the Father's spirit children would overcome the world, rise above carnal things, and love and serve that Being who made them, or whether they would live after the manner of the world, live as the generality of mankind do, and thus fail to gain eternal life.

Mortality paves the way for immortality, and eternal life is reserved for those who believe and obey. Is it any wonder, then, that when the great plan was presented to us in the councils of eternity, "the morning stars sang together, and all the sons of God shouted for joy"? (Job 38:7.) The morning stars were those who were noble and great in preexistence, the Lord Jesus himself being chief among them and bearing the title "the bright and morning star" (Rev. 22:16), which brings us to the realization that a mortal probation was as essential for the Firstborn as for all those subsequently born among heaven's hosts.

8. *Mortal life is simply a projection of preexistent life.*

Birth and death are simply events that occur in the course of continuing life. We are born, which means the spirit passes from preexistence into a mortal body, there to dwell for a time and a season. We die, meaning the spirit steps out of its tenement of clay and enters a spirit world, there to await the day of the resurrection. Meanwhile the body returns to the dust whence it came, there to await that same day when mortality shall put on immortality and corruption shall put on incorruption.

When we die, our spirits continue to live. We take with us into the spirit realm every truth, every trait, every characteristic we enjoyed and possessed as mortals. And further: "Whatever principle of intelligence we attain unto in this life, it will rise with us in the resurrection. And if a person gains more knowledge and intelligence in this life through his diligence and obedience than another, he will have so much the advantage in the world to come." (D&C 130: 18-19.)

Similarly, when we pass from preexistence to mortality, we bring with us the traits and talents there developed. True, we forget what went before because we are here being tested, but the capacities and abilities that then were ours are yet resident within us. Mozart is still a musician; Einstein retains his mathematical abilities; Michelangelo his artistic talent; Abraham, Moses, and the prophets their spiritual talents and abilities. Cain still lies and schemes. And all men with their infinitely varied talents and personalities pick up the course of progression where they left it off when they left the heavenly realms.

Michael the archangel, standing second only to Christ among the spirits destined to dwell on earth, came to Eden's vales with all the sense, wisdom, and judgment that he had gained in preexistence. He came as a son of God, into an Edenic state from which he soon fell, bringing with him the desires, inclinations, aptitudes, and talents developed during long years of obedience in the Divine Presence. He came endowed with every gift and grace that rightfully was his. His life on earth was but a projection and a continuation of that life which was his before the foundations of his future abode had even been laid.

And as with Adam, so with all men: all bring with them what was then theirs; all build in mortality upon the foundation laid in premortality. Abraham, who by obedience and devotion became one of the noble and great in preexistence, came into mortality with every talent and capacity that then was his. He was foreordained to be the father of the faithful. "I know him," the Lord said of Abraham, "that he will command his children and his household after him, and they shall keep the way of the Lord, to do justice and judgment; that the Lord may bring upon Abraham that which he hath spoken of him." (Gen. 18:19.)

Jeremiah was chosen before he was born; before he came forth out of the womb, the Lord ordained him, and sanctified him, and called him to be a prophet; before he drew a mortal breath his mission was known and prepared—all because of the special talents and powers he came to have while yet a spirit being. (Jer. 1:5.)

And Christ our Lord, Firstborn of the Father, mightiest of all the spirit host, a Man like unto his Father, was also chosen and foreordained and anointed to come into mortality and do the very work that he then accomplished. Before he took upon himself flesh and blood he was the Great Jehovah, the Eternal One, Great I AM. He stood next to the Father, and became, at the Father's fiat, the Creator of all things from the beginning. Worlds without number rolled into their orbits at his word. He was the Word of God's power, the Messenger of salvation, the One who executed the divine will in all immensity. When such a life is projected from its eternal home into our mortal sphere, can anyone suppose that it could be other than the greatest life ever lived?

Jesus—God Before the World Was

Mortal life does not stand alone. It can only be understood when it is related to the premortality that went before and the immortality that will come after. If we know who Abraham and Jeremiah were in preexistence, we can understand the spiritual stature that was theirs while they dwelt on earth, while they lived apart from their heavenly associates, and we can also see how it is that they have now entered into their exaltation and, sitting upon thrones, are not angels but gods.[6]

And so it is with the greatest life ever lived. It was what it was because the Spirit housed in the body provided by Mary was the greatest of all the primeval hosts. Before Bethlehem, before the Holy Land, before the earth itself, before the universe and the whole sidereal heavens, before all things, was Christ our Lord. He who was to breath his first breath of mortal life in a little-known Judean village was the Eternal One whose goings forth had been from of old, from everlasting. Bethlehem was not the beginning. It was simply a way station along an eternal course. And he who found rest in a stable because there was no room in the inns was simply abiding with the animals for a moment as he rested from those creative enterprises by which he made the worlds and all things that in them are.

A Holy Being who was God yesterday remains as God today, and will continue in the same exalted state tomorrow. The course of the Gods is one eternal round; it does not vary. They are now as they were then, and they shall yet be as they have ever been. If it were not so they would not be exalted, for exaltation consists in being the same unchangeable being from everlasting to everlasting. Thus Paul said: "Jesus Christ the same yesterday, and to day, and for ever." (Heb. 13:8.) And Moroni, speaking of "the God of Abraham, and the God of Isaac, and the God of Jacob; . . . that same God who created the heavens and the earth, and all things that in them are," taught the same truth. He said: "God is the same yesterday, today, and forever, and in him there is no variableness neither shadow of changing." (Morm. 9:11, 9.) This unchanging, everlasting, eternal way of life—a way of life in which the same character, perfections, and attributes are always present—is the kind of life lived by both the Father and the Son, for they are one in powers and perfections.

Who, then, was Jesus before he was born of Mary to begin his mortal pilgrimage? Truly, he was God in the full sense of the word. He possessed all of the attributes of godliness in their fulness and perfection. He was perfect; he was like unto God. As the angelic visitant said to King Benjamin, he was "the Lord Omnipotent who reigneth, who was, and is from all eternity to all eternity," concerning whom the eternal decree was: "The time cometh, and is not far distant, that with power" he "shall come down from heaven among the children of men, and shall dwell in a tabernacle of clay." (Mosiah 3:5.)

"I was in the beginning with the Father, and am the Firstborn," he said to Joseph Smith. (D&C 93:21.) And of his high and exalted status—from the day of his birth as the First Son of his Father to the time he came forth in glorious immortality—Paul extols: He "is the image of the invisible God, the firstborn of every creature: For by him were all things created, that are in heaven, and that are in earth, visible and invisible, whether they be thrones, or dominions, or principalities, or powers: all things were created by him, and for him: And he is before all things, and by him all things consist. And he is the head of the body, the church: who is the beginning, the firstborn from the dead; that in all things he might have the preeminence. For it pleased the Father that in him should all fulness dwell." (Col. 1:15-19.) He was truly "like unto God." (Abr. 3:24.)

To Abraham and the ancients he revealed himself by the exalted and ineffable name, Jehovah—the Great I AM, the I AM THAT I AM, the Eternal One. He was the God of Israel who performed all the mighty works among that chosen race. But the thing about him which, above all else, crystallizes in our minds his high and exalted status and the infinite powers he possessed is the fact that he was the Creator of all things—this earth, all worlds, the universe, the sidereal heavens, worlds without number. By all this it is perfectly clear that our Lord prepared for his mortal probation by performing infinitely great acts through an eternity of time.

How long did Adam and Abraham and Jeremiah (and all men!) spend in preparing to take the test of a mortal probation? What ages and eons and eternities passed away while Christ dwelt in the Eternal Presence and did the work then assigned him? How can we measure infinite duration in finite terms? To such questions we have no definitive answers. Suffice it to say, the passage of time was infinite from man's viewpoint. We have an authentic account, which can be accepted as true, that life has been going on in this system for almost 2,555,000,000 years.[7] Presumably this system is the universe (or whatever scientific term is applicable) created by the Father through the instrumentality of the Son.

In attempting to give a concept of what is involved in the expression "worlds without number," the scripture says, "were it possible that man could number the particles of the earth, yea, millions of earths like this, it would not be a beginning to the number" of the Lord's creations. (Moses 7:30.) In terms of time, as we speak of time, the duration involved in such creative enterprises is beyond finite comprehension. Preexistence lasted for a duration beyond our power to understand, and during all the time then involved, the Firstborn and all those who came after him were preparing to take the tests of this mortal probation. But in this case, he attained the status of God and exercised creative powers and was like his Father before he chose Bethlehem as the place of his birth.

These revealed truths about our Lord's premortal life have come to us so we will know and understand (among other things) that what he did in scarcely more than three decades of mortal life was not just chance. He was not an ordinary man. He was the great Creator housed in a tabernacle of clay. He was the Eternal Jehovah ministering among men. He was God's Almighty Son doing the things his Father sent him to do. He inherited from the Father of his mortal body the powers and characteristics of his Perfect Parent. He was placed in a position to excel all men. He was the God of Israel taking his place and receiving his lot and inheritance among that chosen people. He was the Only Begotten of the Father, the only Son born into mortality as the Offspring of an Immortal Being. He was both God and the Son of God. He was the Promised Messiah. No ordinary standards, no mortal measuring rods set forth his mortal stature and greatness. If we know and understand all these things we are in a position to learn of him as a mortal, as a Man among men, as a God housed in clay, as earth's Chief Citizen working out his own salvation, and as God's Son doing the things for his fellowmen that no other could ever do.

NOTES

1. "Ode: Intimations of Immortality." These words of the poet Wordsworth, well known among Latter-day Saints because of their inspired recitation of the doctrine of preexistence, a doctrine soon to be revealed to a latter-day prophet, were, interestingly, written in 1805, the very year of the birth of Joseph Smith, the prophet through whom the pure knowledge of preexistence was to come.

2. False creeds make false churches. There is no salvation in believing a lie. Every informed, inspired, and discerning person is revolted by the absurdities and scripture-defying pronouncements in the creeds of Christendom, whose chief function is to define and set forth the nature and kind of Being that God is. The same Lord Jesus who walked the dusty lanes of Palestine also appeared in glory, standing at the right hand of his Father, in a grove of trees in western New York, in the spring of 1820, to usher in the dispensation of the fulness of times. He then commanded his chief latter-day witness, Joseph Smith, to join none of the churches then upon the earth, because "they were all wrong," and "all their creeds were an abomination in his sight." (JS-H 1:17-19.) By way of illustration, let us note the following creedal concepts from the doctrinal foundation of the Church of England:

(a) From the "Articles of Religion," article I, entitled *Of Faith in the Holy Trinity:* "There is but one living and true God everlasting, without body, parts, or passions; of infinite power, wisdom, and goodness; the Maker, and Preserver of all things both visible and invisible. And in unity of this Godhead there be three Persons, of one substance, power, and eternity; the Father, the Son, and the Holy Ghost." (*Book of Common Prayer,* p. 685.)

(b) In *The Creed,* which is said or sung each time Holy Communion (the Lord's Supper) is administered, we find such assertions as: "Jesus Christ, . . . God of God, Light of Light, Very God of very God, Begotten not made, Being of one substance with the Father, . . . was incarnate by the Holy Ghost of the Virgin Mary." And: "The Holy Ghost, The Lord and giver of life." (Ibid., pp. 291-92.)

(c) In the *Apostles Creed,* which is said on thirty-nine Sundays each year, it is recited that "Jesus Christ . . . was conceived by the Holy Ghost." (Ibid., p. 52.)

(d) The *Creed of Saint Athanasius,* which is "sung or said . . . by the Minister and people standing," on Christmas, Easter, and a total of thirteen Sundays each year, and which is, if we may paraphrase Nephi's language, "most abominable above all other creeds" (1 Ne. 13:5), is here set forth in its entirety:

Whosoever would be saved: needeth before all things to hold fast the Catholick Faith.
Which Faith except a man keep whole and undefiled: without doubt he will perish eternally.
Now the Catholick Faith is this: that we worship one God in Trinity, and the Trinity in Unity;
Neither confusing the Persons: nor dividing the Substance.
For there is one Person of the Father, another of the Son: another of the Holy Ghost;
But the Godhead of the Father, and of the Son, and of the Holy Ghost is all one: the glory equal, the majesty co-eternal.
Such as the Father is, such is the Son: and such is the Holy Ghost;
The Father uncreated, the Son uncreated: the Holy Ghost uncreated;
The Father infinite, the Son infinite: the Holy Ghost infinite;
The Father eternal, the Son eternal: the Holy Ghost eternal;
And yet there are not three eternals: but one eternal;
As also there are not three uncreated, nor three infinites: but one infinite, and one uncreated.
So likewise the Father is almighty, the Son almighty: the Holy Ghost almighty;
And yet there are not three almighties: but one almighty.
So the Father is God, the Son God: the Holy Ghost God;
And yet there are not three Gods: but one God.
So the Father is Lord, the Son Lord: the Holy Ghost Lord;
And yet there are not three Lords: but one Lord.
For like as we are compelled by the Christian verity: to confess each Person by himself to be both God and Lord;
So are we forbidden by the Catholick Religion: to speak of three Gods or three Lords.
The Father is made of none: nor created, nor begotten.
The Son is of the Father alone: not made, nor created, but begotten.
The Holy Ghost is of the Father and the Son: not made, nor created, nor begotten, but proceeding.
There is therefore one Father, not three Fathers; one Son, not three Sons: one Holy Ghost, not three Holy Ghosts.
And in this Trinity there is no before or after: no greater or less;
But all three Persons are co-eternal together: and co-equal.
So that in all ways, as is aforesaid: both the Trinity is to be worshipped in Unity, and the Unity in Trinity.
He therefore that would be saved: let him thus think of the Trinity.
Furthermore it is necessary to eternal salvation: that he also believe faithfully the Incarnation of our Lord Jesus Christ.
Now the right Faith is that we believe and confess: that our Lord Jesus Christ, the Son of God, is both God and Man.
He is God, of the Substance of the Father, begotten before the worlds: and he is Man, of the Substance of his Mother, born in the world;
Perfect God: perfect Man, of reasoning soul and human flesh subsisting;
Equal to the Father as touching his Godhead: less than the Father as touching his Manhood.
Who although he be God and Man: yet he is not two, but is one Christ;
One, however, not by conversion of Godhead into flesh: but by taking of Manhood into God;
One altogether: not by confusion of Substance, but by unity of Person.

For as reasoning soul and flesh is one man: so God and Man is one Christ;
Who suffered for our salvation: descended into hell, rose again from the dead;
Ascended into heaven, sat down at the right hand of the Father: from whence he shall come to judge the quick and the dead.
At whose coming all men must rise again with their bodies: and shall give account for their own deeds.
And they that have done good will go into life eternal: they that have done evil into eternal fire.
This is the Catholick Faith: which except a man do faithfully and stedfastly believe, he cannot be saved.
Glory be to the Father, and to the Son: and to the Holy Ghost;
As it was in the beginning, is now, and ever shall be: world without end. Amen. (Ibid., pp. 68-71.)

It was of these creeds, and their kindred, as found in all the sects of Christendom and in one manner and form or another in all the churches of men, whether professing to be Christian or pagan, of which Jeremiah prophesied when he said that gathered Israel in the last days, having come again to know their God by revelation, would say: "Surely our fathers have inherited lies, vanity, and things wherein there is no profit. Shall a man make gods unto himself, and they are no gods?" (Jer. 16:10-21.)

3. This statement, as it fell from the lips of the seer of latter days, is found in the King Follett Discourse, the greatest sermon ever delivered by the Prophet Joseph Smith. The context is as follows: "God himself was once as we are now, and is an exalted man, and sits enthroned in yonder heavens! That is the great secret. If the veil were rent today, and the great God who holds this world in its orbit, and who upholds all worlds and all things by his power, was to make himself visible,—I say, if you were to see him today, you would see him like a man in form—like yourselves in all the person, image, and very form as a man; for Adam was created in the very fashion, image and likeness of God, and received instruction from, and walked, talked and conversed with him, as one man talks and communes with another." (*Teachings*, p. 345.)

4. Continuing this same thought, the Prophet also said: "The relationship we have with God places us in a situation to advance in knowledge. He has power to institute laws to instruct the weaker intelligences, that they may be exalted with himself, so that they might have one glory upon another, and all that knowledge, power, glory, and intelligence, which is requisite in order to save them." (*Teachings*, p. 354.)

5. Lehi's reasoning as to opposites and agency, as found in 2 Nephi 2, surpasses anything else of its kind in the whole realm of secular and scriptural writing. His conclusion is that without these things, "all things must have vanished away."

6. This concept that some of the children of our Father have already become gods is a sound doctrinal reality. In a measure and to a degree they have already become like Christ, who is the Prototype of all saved beings. As Paul expressed it, they have become "perfect" and have come "unto the measure of the stature of the fulness of Christ." (Eph. 4:13.) This high status is now enjoyed by all of the prophets and righteous saints who were with Christ in his resurrection. Abraham, Isaac, and Jacob, as examples and prototypes, whose attainments stand as a pattern of all others similarly situated, are specifically named by revelation as having already attained Godhood. (D&C 132:29-39.)

7. All of the prophets who have seen within the veil have known many things that were never preserved and passed on to their posterity and to the residue of men. Joseph Smith and the early brethren in this dispensation knew much that we do not know and will not know until we attain the same spiritual stature that was theirs. This matter of how long eternity has been going on in our portion of created things is one of these matters. The sliver of information that has been preserved for us is found in an epistle of W. W. Phelps, written on Christmas day, 1844, and published to the Church in the *Times and Seasons*. Brother Phelps speaks of "Jesus Christ, whose goings forth, as the prophets said, have been from of old, from eternity," in what is a clear allusion to Micah's prophecy that Bethlehem shall be the birthplace of our Lord. "Out of thee [Bethlehem Ephratah] shall come forth unto me that is to be ruler in Israel; whose goings forth have been from of old, from everlasting," the Lord said through that ancient prophet. (Micah 5:2.) Then, in an interpolative explanation of what is meant by "from eternity," or "from everlasting," Brother Phelps says, "And that eternity [the one during which Christ's doings have been known], agreeable

to the records found in the catacombs of Egypt, has been going on in this system [not this world], almost two thousand five hundred and fifty-five millions of years." (*Times and Seasons* 5:758.) That is to say, the papyrus from which the Prophet Joseph translated the Book of Abraham, to whom the Lord gave a knowledge of his infinite creations, also contained this expression relative to what apparently is the universe in which we live, which universe has been created by the Father through the instrumentality of the Son. The time mentioned has no reference, as some have falsely supposed, to the period of this earth's existence.

THE PROMISED MESSIAH

Lo, I come: in the volume of the book it is written of me, I delight to do thy will, O my God: yea, thy law is within my heart. (Ps. 40:7-8.)[1]

True Messianic Concepts

Our Lord—blessed be his name—was the Messiah in ages past ("I am Messiah, the King of Zion, the Rock of Heaven," he said to Enoch [Moses 7:53]). Ministering among men as Mary's son, he continued to act in all the glory and dignity of his Messianic might; and he yet serves in that same office, as John the Baptist witnessed when he conferred the Aaronic Priesthood upon mortals "in the name of Messiah." (D&C 13.)

I have written elsewhere, in *The Promised Messiah: The First Coming of Christ,* about the Messianic prophecies.[2] In a very real sense it is an introduction to this life of our Lord, *The Mortal Messiah: From Bethlehem to Calvary.* Knowing who the Mortal Messiah once was; knowing what he did in ages past; knowing what he was destined to do in the days of his mortal probation; knowing his present state of reenthroned glory and omnipotence as he sits with his Father on the blazing throne of God—a vision of all this puts us in a position to understand what he actually did when he dwelt among us lowly mortals. True Messianic concepts may well be summarized under three headings:

1. Who he was before the foundations of the earth were laid, and his position and standing in the eternal scheme of things;

2. What he was destined to do as a mortal to put into full operation the terms and conditions of the Father's plan; and

3. Various circumstances and events that were to occur incident to and in the course of his mortal pilgrimage.

As to his status, glory, and dominion in the midst of eternity, before the earth was made or mortal men were, we must come to know—

That there is a God in heaven who is infinite and eternal; who has a body of flesh and bones as tangible as man's, and who is in fact a resurrected, glorified, perfected, and exalted Man; who has all power, all might, and all dominion, and who knows all things; and who in the ultimate and full sense is the Creator, Upholder, and Preserver of all things, both this earth and all worlds, the sidereal heavens, and all things that in them are;

That the Great God, by whom all things are and for whom all things are created, is the personal and literal Father of the spirits of all men, of which number the Messiah was the Firstborn; and that our Primal Parent ordained and established the plan of salvation whereby all his spirit children, Christ included, had power to advance and progress and become like him;

That in the premortal sphere, by obedience to law, the Firstborn advanced and progressed and became like the Father in power and intelligence, and became, under the Father, the Creator of all things, meaning that he was the Executive Officer who brought to pass the Father's creative enterprises;

That the Messiah then was the Great Jehovah, the Eternal One, the Lord Omnipotent, and was God in his own right;

That when the Father presented his plan for the salvation of his children; when the nature and purpose of our mortal probation was set forth; when it was known that a

Redeemer would be needed to ransom men from temporal and spiritual death; and when the cry went forth, "Whom shall I send," the future Messiah stepped forth and said, "Here am I, send me" (Abr. 3:24-27; Moses 4:1-4)[3];

That he was then chosen and foreordained to be the Lamb slain from the foundation of the world; that he was then selected to be the Son of God, the Only Begotten in the flesh, the One Person who would come into mortality with the power of immortality, thus having power to work out the infinite and eternal atonement;

That the gospel of salvation was then named for him and he became the Savior and Redeemer, the God of Israel, the Holy One of Israel, the Word of God, the great Judge, the Lawgiver, the Father of the righteous of all ages.

If we come to know all those things which appertain to the premortal life and being of the Messiah—his position in the eternal scheme of things—then his mortal ministry takes on an entirely different perspective. What he did and was, as God, before the world was, is the basis for what he did and was, as a mortal, far removed from the throne and glory that once was his.

As to the crowning purpose of the mortal ministry of the second member of the Eternal Godhead, the ancient believers were well instructed. From Adam, the first man, to John, the last legal administrator of the old order, to a greater or lesser degree, depending on their faith and righteousness, the ancient saints knew—

That Adam, attended by his lovely consort Eve, fell from that state of immortality in which they lived when first clothed with flesh and bones; that they thereby became mortal and brought temporal and spiritual death into the world, for themselves and their posterity; and that in their mortal state they were able to bear the souls of men, thus providing bodies for the spirit children of the Father, and thus themselves becoming the parents of the human race;

That a Deliverer, a Savior, a Redeemer—a Messiah!—(who is Christ) must come to ransom men from the temporal and spiritual death brought upon them by the fall of Adam; that the deliverance, the salvation, the redemption to be wrought by him would abolish death, bring immortality to all men, and make eternal life available to all the obedient;

That through this great redemption—this infinite and eternal atonement—the Messiah would reconcile fallen and sinful man to God; would mediate between man and his Maker; would intercede for the penitent before the Father's throne; would justify them, adopt them, free them from prison, and make them joint-heirs with himself of all the glory and dominion that are to be.

These realities relative to our status as the children of the Father; relative to the position of Christ in the eternal scheme of things; relative to the infinitely wondrous and eternally effective sacrifice he wrought—these realities are the heart and core of revealed religion. The Father created us and all things, and ordained and established his eternal plan, the gospel of God, so that we might become as he is. For this we worship and serve him with all our power. The Son redeemed us and put into operation the provisions of the Father's plan. And for this we worship and serve him also with all our hearts.

There are no concepts of revealed religion, no doctrines of the everlasting gospel, no views on any subject, that have ever entered the heart of man that compare, even in slight degree, with these Messiah-centered truths. These verities are the doctrine that salvation is in the Messiah; that by him redemption cometh; and that he is the resurrection and the life. His Father's name is Man of Holiness, and he was destined to be, and is, the Son of Man of Holiness, the great Deliverer, without whose atoning sacrifice the very purposes of creation would have vanished away.

As to the various circumstances and events of his mortal pilgrimage, which were foreknown and foretaught by the prophets who preceded him—as to these, their number and extent are sufficient to identify without question the One Life to which they apply. There have been, there are, and there will be other mortals of whose earthly missions small slivers of truth are manifest in advance. Joseph Smith and Moses were identified and foreknown by name centuries before they came to dwell on earth. Columbus and Cyrus had their work cut out for them long before their mortal probations, and because their labors were destined to affect the Lord's people, they were made known to prophets in advance. But the Man Jesus is the only one whose birth and life and ministry and death and resurrection were taught in such detail by the Messianic witnesses of old that it is almost as though his history was written in advance. Various of these Messianic utterances are analyzed in *The Promised Messiah: The First Coming of Christ,* and those applicable to this present work will be considered in the pages that follow. However, so that our approach in studying the only perfect life ever lived will be what it should be, we shall here recite enough to indicate the detail, extent, and import of those Messianic prophecies which deal with our Lord's mortal experiences.

Inspired men, hundreds and thousands of years before his birth, speaking by the power of the Holy Ghost, telling what God had revealed to them, taught and prophesied such things as these:

A mighty prophet would prepare the way before him. As the voice of one crying in the wilderness of unbelief, this forerunner would cry repentance and administer baptism in water to believing souls; and as the crowning act of his life, this prophet would baptize the Son of God, see the Holy Ghost descend upon him like a dove, and bear witness that he was the Lamb of God who should save the world.

The Promised Messiah would be conceived by the power of the Holy Ghost, God would be his Father, and his mother would be called Mary. She would be a virgin, pure, choice, favored above all womankind.

He would be born in Bethlehem. A new star and many other signs and wonders in heaven would herald the event, and it would occur six hundred years from the time Lehi left

Jerusalem. He would be the seed of Eve, a descendant of Noah, the seed of Abraham, a branch of Israel, the Son of David.

He was to bear the names Emmanuel, Jesus, Christ, Messiah, King, Lord, and God. He was to be the Redeemer and Savior, and the Holy One of Israel, who would live without sin. He was to be known as Jesus Christ, the Son of God, the Father of heaven and earth, the Creator of all things from the beginning.

He was to flee into Egypt and be called back to his homeland. He was to dwell in Nazareth and be called a Nazarene. He was to be baptized to fulfill all righteousness, and the ordinance would take place in Bethabara beyond Jordan, at which time the Holy Ghost would descend upon him in the sign of a dove.

He was to come down from heaven, dwell in a tabernacle of clay, work mighty miracles, heal the sick, raise the dead, cause the lame to walk and the blind to see, cure all manner of diseases, and cast out devils. He was to suffer temptations and pain, hunger, thirst, and fatigue, and in his greatest ordeal he would bleed great drops of blood from every pore.

He was to teach the gospel, carry the lambs of his flock in his arms, speak in parables to the unbelieving, call twelve apostles and others, and send his message to the Gentiles. At a triumphal hour he was to ride into Jerusalem on an ass amid cries of "Hosanna to the Son of David."

He was to be persecuted for righteousness' sake; to bear the infirmities of the people; to be a man of sorrows and acquainted with grief; to be rejected by his people; to be betrayed for thirty pieces of silver by his own familiar friend; to be judged of men, lifted up upon a cross, and crucified by wicked hands; to die, be with the wicked in his death, find interment in a tomb of a wealthy person, rise again the third day, and bring to pass the resurrection of all men. No bone of his body was to be broken, though his flesh was to be pierced and nails were to be driven into his hands and feet. And so on and so on and so on.

To persons unacquainted with the Messianic prophecies, it may seem as though these words are a recitation made after the events, a recitation of what we now know to have occurred. They are, in fact, a partial summary only of some of the things the prophets foretold concerning him. This concept that his birth and life and ministry were all foreknown, foreordained, and foretaught is essential to an understanding of the things he did. Truly, he did not act of himself alone, but guided by the Spirit, he did ever those things which his Father directed.

Jewish Messianic Concepts

What were the Jewish concepts concerning that promised Prophet, that prophet who would be raised up by the Lord and given Messianic power, and who would be like unto Moses?

They should have been, in every respect and detail, the same as those of the saints who preceded them; and they would have been exactly the same concepts held by their righteous forebears if it had not been for the wickedness, rebellion, apostasy, and spiritual darkness that was almost everywhere present in the meridian of time. The Jewish Hebrews then dwelling in Canaan had the scriptures—"and they are they which testify of me." (John 5:39.)

It was a Jewish psalmist who prophesied that the Son would be begotten by God and worshipped by the people; that he would bear testimony of his Father in the congregation of the people; and that he would sit on his Father's right hand, as a priest forever, until all his enemies were overthrown. It was a Jewish prophet who said the Child, born of a virgin, would be the mighty God, the everlasting Father, the Prince of Peace, and that he would reign on David's throne. It was a Jewish prophet who proclaimed that the Lord Jehovah, in whom is everlasting strength, would live and die, and that his dead body would come forth from the grave. For that matter it was Moses, the man of God whom they revered, who set up the whole system of sacrificial offerings wherein the blood of animals—animals without spot or blemish—was shed in similitude of the coming sacrifice of the Lamb of God. It was a Jewish prophet who spoke of the Suffering Servant who would be despised and rejected; who would be a Man of Sorrows and acquainted with grief; who would bear our griefs, carry our sorrows, and be stricken, smitten, and afflicted by men; who would be wounded for our transgressions and bear the sins of many; who would heal us with his stripes; who would make his soul an offering for sin, and pour out his soul unto death; who would justify many, and make intercession for the transgressors; and so on and so on and so on.

All the Jewish prophets were Messianic prophets; many of their prophetic declarations were preserved in the scriptures then extant; and had that same Spirit which rested upon the prophets rested also upon the Jews of Jesus' day, then the people in that meridian period would have known the truth about their Messiah. They would have known that his kingdom was not of this world; that his mission was to bring life and immortality to light through the gospel; that he came to bring immortality and eternal life to men; that he was the resurrection and the life; and that his atoning sacrifice was the rock foundation upon which the house of salvation is built. That they did not know these things, and that such was not the case, brings us now to a consideration of what Jesus' contemporaries did in fact anticipate in the way of a Deliverer, and hence to an understanding of why they reacted to Jesus in the way the New Testament authors recite.

Israel became a kingdom when Samuel anointed Saul, in 1095 B.C., to rule and reign, in power and might, among and over the Lord's chosen people. Three decades later David received the same divine anointing. There then followed ten years of struggle and intrigue and war, culminating in the deaths of Saul and Jonathan. Thereupon, in 1055 B.C.—forty years after Saul had begun the process of imposing kingly designed burdens upon the people whose only previous King had been Jehovah himself—David ascended the throne of Judah; yet another seven years was to elapse before he became king and ruler of all Israel. But with the ascendancy of the son of Jesse, the Bethlehemite, to the throne of Israel, there was ushered in such a reign of power and might and dominion and supremacy as was scarcely known among the mighty nations of the day. Israel's enemies were defeated, slain, imprisoned, and made to serve their Hebrew masters. For forty years David's word was law and blood flowed when any dared oppose him. For another forty years Solomon, his son, reigned in such splendor and supremacy that for a thousand years the house of Jacob would look back with wonder and nationalistic pride at the kingdom and glory of their early rulers.

As king followed king, and war and bloodshed prevailed everywhere; as one king caused Israel to worship Jehovah, and the next commanded them to bow before Baal; as prophets came and went, and were persecuted and slain for the witness born in their Redeemer's name; as the kingdom of Israel, composed of ten of the tribes, went into Assyrian bondage in the days of Shalmanezer (about 721 B.C.); as the people of Judah, after Lehi left Jerusalem, were carried captive into Babylon by Nebuchadnezzar; as the Jews returned from Babylon under Zerubbabel in 536 B.C., and again under Ezra and Nehemiah nearly eighty years later; as all the wars and sorrows continued to sweep over Jewry, down to the days of Jesus; as all these things, and myriads more, came to pass during this long millennium of their history—yet the hope and expectancy of people always faced forward to a day of deliverance, to a Deliverer, to a Messiah.

In large measure and at many times, particularly from the day of Malachi, whose prophecies were forthcoming between 397 and 317 B.C., darkness prevailed in Israel. They had the scriptures; the priesthood remained; they kept the law of Moses to a degree; but their interests were upon the letter and not the spirit of the law. It comes, therefore, as no surprise to find that all Israel in the days of Jesus were looking for a temporal Deliverer, for a Messiah born in the lineage of Abraham and David, who, sitting on the throne of their greatest king, would free them from personal and national bondage and vanquish their enemies. They looked for a preeminent Judahite ruler—for the scepter was not to depart from David's Judah until Shiloh came—who would throw off the Roman yoke and scatter the legions of the Caesars as David had caused the Philistines to flee when one small pebble from his sling felled the mighty Goliath.

Such a Deliverer, such a Messiah, as they envisioned, would not only restore the kingdom to Israel, but would also return the dispersed of that great nation to their original inheritance in their promised Canaan. All Israel again would find residence on the soil that once was theirs. It would yet be as when Joshua drove out the cursed races who worshipped Baal, who burned their children in the fires of Moloch, and who sacrificed to devils. This glorious concept of the gathering of Israel, proclaimed by all the prophets, cherished by the downcast and downtrodden of Jacob for generations, was truly part of their common Messianic hope. So ingrained was it, and so assured were the chosen people of its fulfillment in Messiah's day, that, as Edersheim observes, "Every devout Jew prayed, day by day: 'Proclaim by Thy loud trumpet our deliverance, and *raise up a banner to gather our dispersed, and gather us together from the four ends of the earth.* Blessed be Thou, O Lord! *Who gatherest the outcasts of Thy people Israel.'* That prayer included in its generality also the lost ten tribes. So, for example, the prophecy was rendered: 'They hasten hither, like a bird out of Egypt,'—referring to Israel of old; 'and like a dove out of the land of Assyria'—referring to the ten tribes. And thus even these wanderers, so long lost, were to be reckoned in the field of the Good Shepherd."[4]

This Jewish hope and full expectancy that their Messiah would "recover the remnant of his people, which shall be left, from Assyria, and from Egypt, and from Pathros, and from Cush, and from Elam, and from Shinar, and from Hamath, and from the islands of the sea"; that he would "assemble the outcasts of Israel, and gather together the dispersed of Judah from the four corners of the earth"; and that they should "fly upon the shoulders of the Philistines," as they came (Isa. 11), was more than a vaporous dream of the night. It was the nationalistic hope that had kept them alive as a distinct people in spite of century after century of enslavement and slaughter. So fully was it a part of their religion, their worship, and their way of life that even the apostles of the Lamb, after they knew with a perfect knowledge that their Risen Lord was indeed the Promised Messiah; after they knew that his kingdom was not of this world; after they knew full well that he had no intention of throwing off the Roman yoke and of doing all the things their Jewish fellows supposed the Messiah would do—after all this, as they stood with him on Olivet, outside Jerusalem's walls, they asked that which was yet uppermost in their minds, the one great concern that still weighed in upon them: "Lord, wilt thou at this time restore again the kingdom to Israel?" His answer ended forever the Messianic hope that their era was the one appointed for the gathering of Israel, that the promised kingdom would be in their day. "It is not for you to know the times or the seasons, which the Father hath put in his own power," he replied. Their work was to be worldwide; it was to be of a scope and nature that even they had not yet envisioned; they were to preach the gospel to every creature; and there would yet be a future day, a millennial day, when the Millennial Messiah—"this same Jesus, which is taken up from you into heaven"—would come again to fulfill all that the prophets of old had promised. (Acts 1:6-11.)

Messiah's kingdom, in the full and complete sense of the word, was to be a millennial kingdom. Only then would the "living waters . . . go out from Jerusalem," according to the promise; only then would "the Lord" reign as "king over all the earth." (Zech. 14:8-9.) For their meridian-day Messiah was to be the Suffering Servant; the Teacher without peer; the Sinless One who would redeem and ransom and save; who would abolish death, and bring "life and immortality to light through the gospel" (2 Tim. 1:10); who would lay down his life, according to the flesh, and take it again, by the power of the Spirit, that all men might "be raised in immortality unto eternal life, even as many as would believe" (D&C 29:43).

He truly shall yet reign as King of kings and Lord of lords, and "the kingdoms of this world" shall "become the kingdoms of our Lord, and of his Christ." (Rev. 11:15.) But all the hopes of temporal rule, when he *first* came among men, were false and groundless. "My kingdom is not of this world: if my kingdom were of this world, then would my servants fight" (John 18:36), was his mortal proclamation. The day when he shall reign on the throne of David, slay the Goliaths of the world, and drive the Philistines from Israel's door is reserved for his *second* appearance. All the hopes of Jewish Israel that their Promised Messiah, like Moses and David, would free their lands, as it were, from the "modern" Canaanites, Hittites, Amorites, Perizzites, Hivites, and Jebusites were to fade away. Neither the wealth and wisdom of Solomon nor the might and glory of David were then to be restored, nor was Israel to gather in from her long dispersion to the standard he would then raise.

'What think ye of the Messiah,' Jesus asked certain Pharisees. "Whose son is he?" Their reply, using words that were but a summary of what was in the minds of the generality of the people, acclaimed: 'He is the son of David; he shall free us from our captors; he shall brake the hated Gentile yoke; he shall gather in our dispersed brethren; we shall become a mighty nation again.' But Jesus spoke not of the millennial kingdom, which was millenniums away; their concern should have been centered in his meridian ministry, which brought salvation to them. "Whose son is he?" If the Mortal Messiah was to be a temporal ruler only, how then was he God's Son, as even David attested in proclaiming that one Lord said to another Lord, 'Sit thou on my right hand, until that future day when all things spoken by all the prophets concerning thee and all Israel shall be fulfilled.' Is it any wonder that "no man was able to answer him a word, neither durst any man from that day forth ask him any more questions"? (Matt. 22:41-46.)

And yet we must not generalize to the point of assuming there were none among the Jews who knew and understood the mission and ministry of the Anointed One who would deliver and redeem. Our Lord—called *Christ* in the Greek and *Messiah* or *Messias* in the Hebrew—was known and recognized and worshipped by many of his Jewish kinsmen while he yet dwelt among them. There is no doubt that "all the people"—chanting in a frenzy of hate and derision, "His blood be on us, and on our children" as Pilate sought to free the Prisoner (Matt. 27:24-26)—were representative of the thought and feeling of a nation. But within the nation, and among the diverse parties and sects, there were those who loved light more than darkness, and who sought blessings from him of whom the hate-filled mob cried, "Crucify him, crucify him." (Luke 23:21.)

There were those who had sufficient spiritual insight to know that the Messiah was the Great Jehovah, and that born of woman he would deliver fallen men from their corrupt and carnal state and make them fit candidates for eternal salvation. Elisabeth, the Levite wife, while her womb contained the Messiah's forerunner, acclaimed Mary as the mother of the Lord. (Luke 1:41-45.) Simeon, a just and devout Jew who waited for the Consolation of Israel, learned from the Holy Ghost that he should not see death until he had seen the Lord's Messiah; and it became his blessed privilege to take the Child Jesus in his arms and to bless him and to prophesy of his mission in Israel. (Luke 2:25-35.) Anna the Jewess, a prophetess mighty in faith and good works, also saw and believed and testified. (Luke 2:36-38.) John the Baptist, our Lord's Jewish forerunner, answering the priests and Levites who asked, "Who art thou," replied,

"I am not the Christ"; and then of that Messiah whose shoe's latchet he felt unworthy to unloose, the Baptist testified, "Behold the Lamb of God, which taketh away the sin of the world." (John 1:19-36.)

Andrew, a Jew, brother to Simon Peter, introduced Peter himself to the gospel with the salutation, "We have found the Messias." (John 1:37-41.) Jewish Philip bore a like witness, and Jewish Nathanael, speaking to the Messiah mouth to mouth, affirmed, "Rabbi, thou art the Son of God; thou art the King of Israel." (John 1:41-51.) Peter, Jewish to the hilt, as were all the Twelve, testified before his fellow apostles and to the Lord Jesus: 'Thou art the Messiah, the Son of the Living God,' after which witness Jesus began to show the disciples how he should suffer and die and rise again the third day. (Matt. 16:13-21.) Martha, as Jewish as mortal women can be, who with her sister Mary knew that had Jesus been present, their brother Lazarus would not have died, spoke for herself and her Jewish sister in saying: 'I believe that thou art the Messiah, the Son of God, which should come into the world.' (John 11:1-46.)

All these and many others are named as Messianic witnesses in Holy Writ. Such accounts are but samples and illustrations. Among the Jewish people there were many who understood the scriptures, who knew their true meanings, and who believed in him of whom they testify. Indeed, it was "a very great multitude" of Jewish believers, on the occasion of our Lord's triumphal entry into Jerusalem, who cried out to their Messiah, 'Save, we beseech thee,' "Hosanna to the Son of David," and whose witness was: "Blessed is he that cometh in the name of the Lord; Hosanna in the highest." (Matt. 21:1-11.) And it was Jewish converts who became living torches on Roman walls; whose flesh was torn by wild beasts in orgies of slaughter in Roman arenas; whose bodies were hewn and slashed with gladiatorial swords; who welcomed crucifixion and death rather than bring dishonor to the Messianic name that they as Christians chose to bear. Whatever we may say of the Messianic hopes and knowledge of the generality of the Jews, the basic reality remains unchanged that there were those who believed, and that all men had power to believe, and would have believed, had they not chosen darkness rather than light because their deeds were evil.

NOTES

1. These Messianic words, as first spoken by David, are in a context that marvelously summarizes the nature of Messiah's ministry. Of the coming Christ the Psalmist said: "Sacrifice and offering thou didst not desire; mine ears hast thou opened: burnt offering and sin offering hast thou not required. Then said I, Lo, I come: in the volume of the book it is written of me, I delight to do thy will, O my God: yea, thy law is within my heart. I have preached righteousness in the great congregation: lo, I have not refrained my lips, O Lord, thou knowest. I have not hid thy righteousness within my heart; I have declared thy faithfulness and thy salvation: I have not concealed thy lovingkindness and thy truth from the great congregation. . . . Let all those that seek thee rejoice and be glad in thee: let such as love thy salvation say continually, The Lord be magnified." (Psalm 40:6-10, 16.)

That these words foretold the Messiah's approach in presenting the message of his Father is perfectly clear. Their use by Paul in his theological discourse to the Hebrews dramatizes that the Messiah came to end sacrifices and center the attention of all true believers in the sacrifice he made of his own body. In showing how Israel's ancient sacrifices were "a shadow of good things to come" and would in due course be done away, Paul uses the Psalmic words here involved in this way: "When he [the Messiah] cometh into the world, he saith, Sacrifice and offering thou wouldest not, but a body hast thou prepared me: In burnt offerings and sacrifices for sin thou hast had no pleasure. Then said I, Lo, I come (in the volume of the book it is written of me,) to do thy will, O God."

Paul then shows that the first sacrifices, those offered anciently, were done away when God established the second, the sacrifice of the body of his Son. Of the will and purpose of Deity in so ordaining, the inspired record says: "By the which will we are sanctified through the offering of the body of Jesus Christ once for all." (Heb. 10:1-10.)

2. For twice as many years as the two thousand of the so-called Christian era, believing persons looked forward for salvation to the then future atonement of the Messiah. Even as we now look back with rejoicing to what has been done by Deity, our forebears looked forward in joyful anticipation to what he would do in the day of his mortality. To envision how he deals with men, it is of surpassing import to know the Messianic teachings and promises given the saints during the first four thousand years of the earth's temporal continuance. To summarize the truths in this field, as they were revealed to and known by those who lived before our Lord placed himself in the hands of men, is the purpose of *The Promised Messiah: The First Coming of Christ* (Deseret Book, 1978).

3. One of the saddest examples of a misconceived and twisted knowledge of an otherwise glorious concept is the all-too-common heresy that there were two plans of salvation; that the Father (presumptively at a loss to know what to do) asked others for proposals; that Christ offered a plan involving agency and Lucifer proposed a plan denying agency; that the Father chose between them; and that Lucifer, his plan being rejected, rebelled, and then there was war in heaven.

Even a cursory knowledge of the overall scheme of things reassures spiritually discerning persons that all things center in the Father; that the plan of salvation which he designed was to save his children, Christ included; and that neither Christ nor Lucifer could of themselves save anyone. As Jesus said: "The Son can do nothing of himself. . . . I can of mine own self do nothing." (John 5:19, 30.)

There is, of course, a sense in which we may refer to Lucifer's proposed modifications of the Father's plan as Lucifer's plan, and Christ made the Father's plan his own by adoption. But what is basically important in this respect is to know that the power to save is vested in the Father, and that he originated, ordained, created, and established his own plan; that he announced it to his children; and that he then asked for a volunteer to be the Redeemer, the Deliverer, the Messiah, who would put the eternal plan of the Eternal Father into eternal operation.

4. Edersheim 1:78. Italics added. In another passage Edersheim says: "Perhaps the most valuable element in Rabbinic commentation on Messianic times is that in which, as so frequently, it is explained, that all the miracles and deliverances of Israel's past would be re-enacted, only in a much wider manner, in the days of the Messiah. . . . It is in this sense that we would understand the two sayings of the Talmud: 'All the prophets prophesied only of the days of the Messiah,' and 'The world was created only for the Messiah.' " (Edersheim 1:162-63.)

FOUR MILLENNIUMS OF TRUE WORSHIP

Thou shalt worship the Lord thy God,
and him only shalt thou serve.
(Luke 4:8.)[1]

True Worship Before the Flood

True and heaven-sent worship has been found on earth from the day of the first man to the present moment whenever and wherever men have been willing to hearken to their Maker. Christianity did not originate in the so-called Christian era. Our Lord did not bring it for the first time when he came to dwell on earth. Pure religion and approved worship have been with us from the beginning.

In the beginning that God who created man, male and female, in his own likeness and image; in the beginning the Eternal Father, by whom all things are, and who placed his son, Adam, and his daughter, Eve, in Eden; in the beginning the great Creator whose Beloved and Chosen Son was foreordained to be the Redeemer and Savior; in the beginning this Holy Being, as it was his right to do, commanded all men "that they should love and serve him, the only living and true God, and that he should be the only being whom they should worship." (D&C 20:18-19.)

The divine decree—"Thou shalt love the Lord thy God with all thy heart, with all thy might, mind, and strength; and in the name of Jesus Christ thou shalt serve him" (D&C

59:5) —is as old as the human race. An angelic ministrant, speaking by the power of the Holy Ghost, delivered to Adam the heaven-sent word: "Thou shalt do all that thou doest in the name of the Son, and thou shalt repent and call upon God in the name of the Son forevermore." (Moses 5:8.) Line upon line and precept upon precept, our first father was counseled from on high until he gained the fulness of the everlasting gospel, which gospel is the good news, the glad tidings, that all men may be saved if they keep the commandments of the Lord.

True worship consists in obeying the laws and ordinances of the gospel. It consists in believing in Christ, in joining the true Church, in being born again, in keeping the commandments after baptism, in acquiring the attributes of godliness, in doing all the things that must be done to gain eternal life in our Father's kingdom. True worship consists in emulating the thoughts and words and deeds of the Holy Messiah, so that men, following him and becoming like him, may reign with him in everlasting glory. True worship is the chief and major concern of man. God speaks, revelations are forthcoming, apostles and prophets labor out their days, the gifts of the Spirit are poured out upon the faithful, miracles are wrought, and the hand of the Lord is seen in all things—all to the end that men may worship the Father in spirit and in truth.

True worship is always and everlastingly the same. Truth does not vary, and God does not change. We are saved today by obedience to the same eternal laws that have saved men in all ages past and that will save them in all ages future.[2] The Author and Finisher of our faith is the same yesterday, today, and forever. In him there is no variableness, neither shadow of turning. Salvation always comes by obedience to the laws and ordinances of the everlasting gospel, the gospel that has existed with God from all eternity and that will continue to crown his unchangeable goodness toward his creatures forever.

Some have supposed that God dealt differently with the

ancient patriarchs than he did with men in the Christian era, or that he requires more of us in this age of supposed enlightenment than he did of those in the early ages of man's life on earth. Nothing could be further from the truth. Some of the mightiest and noblest spirits of all the hosts of heaven were sent to earth in the early gospel dispensations. Michael, known in his mortal ministry as Adam, in preexistence stood next to the Lord Jehovah himself in power, might, dominion, and intelligence; and Gabriel, who dwelt among men as Noah, was but a hair's breadth behind the first man in possession of godly graces. We can scarcely conceive of the high spiritual endowments of Enoch and all his city, true saints who qualified to flee the bounds of this earth and dwell in an appointed heaven without tasting death.

Let us look at each of the great patriarchs who presided as high priests over the Lord's people during the 1,656 years from the fall of Adam to the flood of Noah. These noble and great souls worshipped the Father in spirit and in truth and, with the hosts of faithful saints in each of their days, have long since gone on to glory and exaltation in the mansions that are prepared. For instance:

Adam, standing as the presiding high priest over all the earth for all ages, offered sacrifices of the firstlings of his flocks in similitude of the sacrifice of the Only Begotten of the Father.

Seth, who was like unto Adam in all things and could only be distinguished from him by their differences in age, performed baptisms by immersion for the remission of sins.

Enos laid on hands for the gift of the Holy Ghost and confirmed believing and obedient persons as members of the Church of Jesus Christ as it was then constituted.

Cainan conferred the holy priesthood upon his fellow mortals and ordained them to offices in that holy order which is without beginning of days or end of years.

Mahalaleel entered that order of the priesthood which is named the new and everlasting covenant of marriage and taught his children to go and do likewise.

Jared preached the gospel, prophesied of the coming Messiah, and testified that salvation was and is and is to come in and through the atoning blood of Christ, the Lord Omnipotent.

Enoch received revelations and visions, saw the Lord, and kept the law of Christ so fully and completely that he and all his city were translated.

Methuselah saw the future, prophesied by the power of the Holy Ghost, and dwelt in righteousness on earth for more years than any of the descendants of Adam of whom we have record.

Lamech enjoyed the gifts of the Spirit and rejoiced in that testimony of Jesus which is the spirit of prophecy.

Noah, going forth as a legal administrator and holding the same priesthood possessed by Enoch and his forebears, taught faith in the Lord Jesus Christ, repentance, baptism, and the receipt of the Holy Ghost, telling his wicked and adulterous generation that unless they accepted the gospel, the floods would come in upon them and misery would be their doom.

All these—and they comprise the patriarchal chain from Adam to Noah—and the saints over whom they presided in their days had the fulness of the everlasting gospel and dwelt in righteousness upon earth all the days of their appointed probation.[3] Souls were just as precious in that day as in any day, and a gracious God gave his laws to all who would accept them.

True Worship from Noah to Moses

When father Noah entered the ark, he took the holy priesthood with him. When the rains descended and the floods came; when the fountains of the mighty deep broke forth, sweeping from the earth all living things save those that were in the ark; when the Lord cleansed and baptized the very earth itself, the man Noah was a mighty prophet, a preacher of righteousness, a legal administrator who represented his God. Noah entered the ark as a member of the Church of Jesus Christ, as a saint in the congregation of Zion, and when he stepped forth onto dry ground one year and seventeen days later, there was no change in his status. He was still the Lord's agent; he still held the priesthood; the gospel was still on earth. True worship continued.

One of Noah's first acts after the flood was to build an altar and offer sacrifices in similitude of the coming sacrifice of the Lamb of God. After his day the gospel continued as it had after Adam's day. Each was the father of all living in his day, and their faithful descendants hearkened to their words and continued to worship Him who is eternal. Thus, pure religion was preserved through the flood, and men continued to work out their salvation as they had before the wicked and ungodly were destroyed in earth's one great deluge.

Our knowledge of prophets and peoples who had the gospel between Noah and Moses is somewhat sketchy. According to the best chronologies, from the flood in 2348 B.C. to the exodus from Egypt in 1491 B.C., there were 857 intervening years. We do know that whenever any person or group of people possessed the higher priesthood, they had the fulness of the gospel and were therefore worshipping the Lord according to the approved pattern.[4] We know that from the flood to the birth of Abraham was 352 years, during which time there were ten generations of men. These were: Noah, Shem, Arphaxad, Salah, Eber, Peleg, Reu, Serug, Nahor, Terah, and Abram (who became Abraham). How many of these remained true and faithful to the covenant of salvation made with their fathers we do not know. Terah, the father of Abraham, lived under apostate conditions and worshipped false gods. After Abraham came Isaac, Jacob, Joseph, Ephraim and Manasseh, and the children of Israel in general, who as a nation were burdened by Egyptian bondage, and among whom Moses was born in 1571 B.C.

It would appear that the gospel continued to operate to some degree, perhaps only in a fragmentary form, among the enslaved descendants of Jacob, in spite of the enticements of Egypt and the cruel overlordship and persecutions imposed by their Egyptian rulers. It is true that Moses received his priesthood from a non-Israelite source, but when he came to deliver his nation from Pharaoh, the record speaks of others who were elders of Israel and who well may have been priesthood bearers. It describes a people who, though in bondage, had an effective organization of their own, and it tells how they demanded of Pharaoh the privilege of journeying into the wilderness so they might offer sacrifices to Jehovah. It would seem that they had preserved at least some of the teachings of their fathers, and that some degree of true worship continued among them. In any event there were those on earth among whom the priesthood and true worship had remained. Abraham received the priesthood from Melchizedek, "who received it through the lineage of his fathers, even till Noah." (D&C 84:14.)[5] Thus there is a direct priesthood line from Adam to Abraham without a break.

There were also in the days of Abraham other nations and peoples of whom we know nothing—except that they dwelt on earth and worshipped the true God—who also held the priesthood. Through these nations the priesthood descended to Jethro, who conferred it upon his son-in-law Moses. The revealed account speaks of one Esaias, of whose ministry we know nothing, except that he received the priesthood under the hand of God (meaning, apparently, by special dispensation); that he lived in the days of Abraham and was blessed by him; and that he conferred the priesthood upon Gad. From Gad it descended by successive and authoritative conferrals to Jeremy, Elihu, Caleb, and Jethro, and then to the great lawgiver, Moses. (D&C 84:6-15.)

From such inspired writings as have been preserved to us, we are led to believe that the high points of true worship from the assuaging of the flood to the ministry of Moses occurred under the leadership of Melchizedek and in the days of Abraham, Isaac, Jacob, and Joseph. This man Melchizedek, than whom none of the ancients were greater, reigned as king in Shiloam, which is Salem, and which we suppose was Jeru-Salem. His people had all gone astray, reveling in unrighteousness and every form of evil. By faith and mighty works Melchizedek reclaimed them, brought them back to the cause of Christ, established peace among them, and was called by them the prince of peace, the king of heaven, and the king of peace. When but a child he feared God, stopped the mouths of lions, and quenched the violence of fire. His people wrought righteousness and sought the blessing of translation and to find an inheritance in Enoch's city. He it was, as priest of the Most High God, who conferred the priesthood upon Abraham, who blessed the father of the faithful, and who received tithes from him. Because he was such a great high priest, the Church in ancient days, to avoid the too-frequent repetition of the name of the divine Son, called the priesthood itself in his name: *The Melchizedek Priesthood.* That there have been few high points in history to compare with the pinnacles of pure worship attained in the days of Melchizedek none can doubt.[6]

Abraham is everywhere revered as the father of the faithful and the friend of God. Whatever patriarchal lines may have been for the first 2,008 years of man's life on this earth, with the advent of Abraham in 1996 B.C., the Lord centered all things in his friend from Ur. From that day onward as long as time should roll or the earth should stand, the decree was that faithful spirits (in the main), those who would believe God and work righteousness, would come to earth as Abraham's seed. Those not of his literal bloodline who accept the gospel are adopted into his family, become his seed, and rise up and bless him as their father. With Abraham, and then with Isaac, and then with Jacob, the Lord made the covenant that their seed would continue, both in the world and out of the world, as innumerable as the sand upon the seashore or as the stars in heaven for multitude. This is the promise of eternal increase that is made in connection with celestial marriage, and that has been restored in modern times. It was restored by Elias and Elijah: by Elias, "who committed the dispensation of the gospel of Abraham," under which commission all who enter into celestial marriage receive the promise that in them and in their seed after them shall all generations be blessed; and by Elijah, who brought back the sealing power so that once again legal administrators could seal on earth and have it bound eternally in the heavens.[7]

These are in fact "the promises made to the fathers" that have been planted "in the hearts of the children." (D&C 2:1-3.) "I give unto thee a promise," Jehovah said to Abraham, that "in thy seed after thee (that is to say, the literal seed, or the seed of the body) shall all the families of the earth be blessed, even with the blessings of the Gospel, which are the blessings of salvation, even of life eternal." (Abr. 2:11.) Eternal life grows out of celestial marriage, out of the continuation of the family unit in eternity, and out of the inheritance of eternal increase. And thus, of all those who enter this order of matrimony, our revelation says: "This promise"—the promise of eternal increase, the promise of exaltation, the promise made to Abraham, the promise that has been planted in the hearts of all faithful members of the Church in this day—"This promise is yours also, because ye are of Abraham, and the promise was made unto Abraham." With reference to the promise, the Lord then says, "By this law is the continuation of the works of my Father, wherein he glorifieth himself," and then he adds this divine exhortation: "Go ye, therefore, and do the works of Abraham; enter ye into my law and ye shall be saved." (D&C 132:31-32.)

Joseph, the son of Jacob, who was sold by his envious and conniving brothers to the Ishmaelites for twenty pieces of silver (appropriately a lesser price than the thirty pieces of silver given Judas for betraying Jesus), was by them sold in Egypt to Potiphar, captain of Pharaoh's guard. This Joseph, who is described as being like his latter-day counterpart of the same name—Joseph Smith, Jr., who heads our dispensation—became one of the greatest prophets. His prophecies deal primarily with Moses, who was to deliver Israel from Egypt; with the Nephites and Lamanites, his descendants, who were to inhabit an American promised land; and with Joseph Smith and the restoration of the gospel in the latter days. (2 Ne. 3-4; JST, Gen. 50.)

Thus, only one conclusion can be reached for the period from Noah to Moses: heaven-sent worship was on earth, and pure religion ruled in the hearts of the saints.

True Worship in Ancient Israel

True worship among the chosen people rose to the heights and dropped to the depths during the fifteen hundred years of Israelite history that preceded the ministry of the Mortal Messiah. There were times when the house of Jacob climbed Sinai and found God; times when they were conquered by the world in the valley of Megiddo; times when they wandered through the wilderness of Idumea in search of truth; times when, without living water to drink, they perished in the deserts of Edom.

Nor did all Israel always travel together in one course. Worship among them was as varied as life itself; all degrees and kinds of conduct were shown forth at one time or another. Some of our fathers worshipped the Lord with a pure heart and a contrite spirit; others bowed before Baal, burned their children in the fires of Moloch, and found more pleasure in the deceptions of Jezebel than in the exhortations of Elijah. There were faithful maidens who could persuade a Naaman to dip seven times in Jordan and come up free from leprosy, according to the word of Elisha the man of God; and there were also selfish and grasping Gehazis who sought to enrich themselves by selling the gifts of God, and upon whom the leprosy of sin was permanently attached.

There were prophets and there were evil men among the Lord's people. Moses spoke with the Lord face to face, as a man speaketh with his friend, while Korah, Dathan, and Abiram, preferring the fleshpots of Egypt to the austerity of the gospel, led a rebellion against the great lawgiver. And there was opposition from without the fold as well as from within. Nehemiah rebuilt the walls of Jerusalem with a sword in one hand and a trowel in the other as Sanballat and the Arabians mocked and opposed at every turn. It was no easier to come off triumphant in the warfare of life in those days than it is in these; Israel's whole history was one of trial and testing. When they served the Lord, they prospered; when they rebelled, evil and desolation and death attended them.

Israel grew from a small group of some 70 souls into a great nation while sojourning in Egypt. When they came out of bondage there were 600,000, and more, men of war in age from twenty years old and upwards. Counting wives and children and others, the Israelites who went through the Red Sea—while the waters congealed as a wall on the right hand and on the left—numbered in the millions. We suppose they had retained fragments and portions of their ancient religion, portions of that which came down to them from the patriarchs, in spite of their enslavement by the Pharaohs. But it seems clear that the fulness of the gospel, at least in its beauty and perfection, came to them anew under the hands of Moses. Because Moses held the higher or Melchizedek Priesthood, he had the fulness of the gospel: he could thereby lay on hands for the gift of the Holy Ghost and confer upon men the power to sanctify their souls; he could thereby perform celestial marriages, which open the door to eternal life; and he could thereby seal people up unto eternal life with callings and elections made sure, so that they had an absolute guarantee of arising in the resurrection in a state of glory and honor and immortality and eternal life.

When Israel, as a people and as a whole, failed to live in harmony with the law of Christ as contained in the fulness of his everlasting gospel, the Lord "in his wrath" withdrew the fulness of his law from them. Because "they hardened their hearts" and would not "enter into his rest while in the wilderness, which rest is the fulness of his glory, . . . he took Moses out of their midst, and the Holy Priesthood also." (D&C 84:19-28.) That is, he took the Melchizedek Priesthood, which administers the gospel, out of their midst in the sense that it did not continue and pass from one priesthood holder to another in the normal and usual sense of the word. The keys of the priesthood were taken away with Moses so that any future priesthood ordinations required special divine authorization. But in place of the higher priesthood the Lord gave a lesser order, and in place of the fulness of the gospel he gave a preparatory gospel—the law of carnal commandments, the law of Moses—to serve as a schoolmaster to bring them, after a long day of trial and testing, back to the law of Christ in its fulness.[8] There is the fulness of the gospel, and there is the preparatory gospel. There is the full law of Christ, and there is a partial law of Christ. The Mosaic system was the partial law, a portion of the mind and will of Jehovah, a strict and severe testing arrangement that would qualify those who obeyed its terms and conditions to receive the eternal fulness when the Messiah came to deliver and to restore it.

Whenever any individual or any selected groups in Israel qualified for more light and greater blessings than were found in the law of Moses, the Lord gave them the law of Christ in its fulness. Such was the case among the Nephites for six hundred continuous years. They kept the law of Moses "because of the commandments," even though it had "become dead" unto them. But they also had the Melchizedek Priesthood and the fulness of the gospel. They believed in Christ and were "reconciled to God," and all things were theirs. (2 Ne. 25:23-27; Alma 13.) We know this same state of superior enlightenment existed at many other times and places in Israel. There were at many times, and may have been at all times, prophets and righteous men in Israel who held this higher order of priesthood. Joseph

Smith said, "All the prophets had the Melchizedek Priesthood and were ordained by God himself" (*Teachings,* p. 181), meaning they received that holy order by special dispensation. Elijah, for instance, was the very prophet chosen to bring back the keys of the sealing power in our day. (*Teachings,* pp. 172, 330, 335-41.)

With the advent of a lesser law in Israel, there came also a lesser priesthood to administer the inferior order. Aaron and his sons, and the Levites in general, received the Aaronic or Levitical order. By the power and authority of this preparatory priesthood—this priesthood of Elias which is a forerunner to prepare the way for the higher order—all of the ordinances and rites and performances of the Mosaic system were administered from the days of Aaron to the coming of John. It was the priesthood that governed Israel temporally whenever they were willing to submit to the rule of Deity, and the high priests who governed in their religious affairs were high priests of the Aaronic order.

Messiah's advent brought back again the Melchizedek Priesthood and placed it over the kingdom so that future direction and governance came from that source. With the restoration of the higher priesthood came the restoration of the higher law. Again men had the everlasting fulness. Again they could perfect their souls and enter into that rest which is the fulness of the glory of the Lord. As Paul stated to his Hebrew brethren, brethren who knew and practiced priesthood performances and understood the need for proper authority in all that they did: "If therefore perfection were by the Levitical priesthood, (for under it the people received the law,) what further need was there that another priest should rise after the order of Melchisedec, and not be called after the order of Aaron?" He is here showing how Christ, who was "called of God an high priest after the order of Melchisedec," brought back the gospel to replace the law of Moses. "For the priesthood being changed," he continues, "there is made of necessity a change also of the law." (Heb. 5:10; 7:11-12.)

Our conclusion, then, is that during all her long, wearisome, wandering history, Israel (or at least portions of that chosen race) worshipped the Lord in the true and proper sense of the word, either as possessors of the fulness of the gospel or while in subjection to the inferior and lesser order, which nonetheless came from God and was founded upon as many true principles as the people were willing to accept.

True Worship Among the Jews

In evaluating both the presence and the practice of true worship among the Jews, we must walk lightly and tread in winding paths, paths that are poorly marked and difficult to discern, paths that crisscross in a maze of diverse and differing directions. Many of the Jews in that day followed the form of true worship. They had the revealed pattern before them, and they adhered to it rigidly, with a fixity of purpose seldom seen among any people. A few of them enjoyed also the true spirit that is appointed to be the companion of true worship. But among their leaders and spreading out among the generality of the people, their worship embraced only the form of godliness. They went through the rituals and performances; they overstepped the mark in many things, Sabbath observance being chief among them; and they perverted and twisted so many basic principles that the Spirit of the Lord could not find lodgment in their souls. But with it all, the light still burned in some quarters in Israel; sacrifices were still offered by legal administrators upon divinely consecrated altars; the temple was still the Father's house, however much they had made it a den of thieves; and there were those prepared to receive their Messiah when he came even though the clamoring crowds chanted their cries of crucifixion.

Our Lord's conversation with the woman of Samaria at Jacob's Well gives a clear insight into the quality and kind of worship then extant. The woman—who was living in adultery and devoid of the true spirit of inspiration, and who was concerned more with form than with substance, as was the case with that whole adulterous society of ritualistic worshippers, yet who perceived Jesus to be a prophet—said: "Our fathers worshipped in this mountain; and ye say, that in Jerusalem is the place where men ought to worship."

Knowing that it is not where, but who and how we worship that counts; knowing that the whole Jerusalem-centered system of ritualistic performances would soon be fulfilled; knowing that his Jewish compatriots would soon be scattered to the four winds, Jesus replied: "Woman, believe me, the hour cometh, when ye shall neither in this mountain, nor yet at Jerusalem, worship the Father." These words began to put the subject back into perspective; it is the Father in whom true worship centers. Then came the prophetic words: "Ye worship ye know not what: we know what we worship: for salvation is of the Jews." (John 4:5-22.) The Samaritans had lost the knowledge of God, but it had been retained by the Jews. They knew that God was their Father, and the sweet incenses burned in their ordinances ascended to him.

If an inspired, modern-day Mormon, placed in a like situation, had been speaking today—not to a Samaritan but to a sectarian who believed the creeds of Christendom, creeds that convert the true God into a confused spirit nothingness that fills immensity—the forthcoming words might have been: 'Ye worship ye know not what: we know what we worship: for salvation is of the Latter-day Saints.'

"*We know what we worship!*" A true knowledge of God is the true foundation upon which true worship and true religion rest. Other peoples anciently worshipped gods of wood and stone fashioned by men's hands. The Greeks placed a stone Diana in a majestic temple, above Mars Hill, in their Athenian acropolis. Before this statue and in this pagan temple, itself one of the architectural marvels of the world, they performed such acts of worship and generated such feelings of adoration as one can develop for an inanimate work of art.[9] In contrast the Jews knew their God was a personal being, a glorified and exalted Man, an Eternal Father.

Many modern Christians worship a Trinity defined as being three Gods in one; as a spirit essence that fills the immensity of space; as a power and influence that has neither body, parts, nor passions; and is in fact as impersonal as Diana and all her kindred images. No doubt they generate such feelings of reverence, awe, and adoration as one can for such an impersonal nothingness. In contrast, the Latter-day Saints worship the God of the Jews.

Having announced that the Jews knew what they worshipped, meaning they were operating within the framework of true worship, our Lord said: "Salvation is of the Jews." That is to say, the Jews knew God was their Father; they looked forward to a Jewish Messiah and Deliverer who would reign forever on the throne of Jewish David; they had the holy scriptures, the words of the prophets, the guideposts for the lives of men; and they followed the law of Moses, the highest revealed standards then had among men. Salvation was available only to those who lived by pure and perfect Jewish standards, the standards set forth by the prophets.

Then came the perfect counsel that was needed for that day and for ours: "But the hour cometh, and now is, when the true worshippers shall worship the Father in spirit and in truth: for the Father seeketh such to worship him." And for an accurate rendition of the actual words then spoken, we now turn to the Joseph Smith Translation: "For unto such hath God promised his Spirit," the account says, "And they who worship him, must worship in spirit and in truth." (John 4:23; JST, John 4:26.) And therein lay the problem. Though the door was open that would have enabled them to worship the Father in spirit and in truth, and to receive thereby the sanctifying influence of the Holy Ghost in their lives, most of the Jews failed so to do. To them the Mortal Messiah—and no man could come unto the Father but by him—was a stumbling block. Because they rejected him and his mission, true worship ceased and the whole nation, scattered and peeled, meted out and trodden down, became a hiss and a byword wherever they sought to lay their heads.

But, for our present purposes, suffice it to say that true worship was found on earth during all of the first four millenniums of that mortality which began with Adam's fall. For four thousand years—nearly a million and a half days—the mind and will of the Lord had been manifest among men. Over two hundred thousand weekly Sabbaths had passed, each providing an occasion and an opportunity to deal more particularly with spiritual things. Prophets and preachers of righteousness had given as much of the mind and will of the Lord as men in their various days would receive. All things from the beginning had pointed to one supreme and transcendent event: the coming and mortal ministry of the Eternal Messiah.

NOTES

1. These words, quoted from a source not now found in the Bible, were spoken by Jesus to the arch-tempter when that evil spirit sought the soul of him who "was in all points tempted like as we are, yet [who remained] without sin." (Heb. 4:15.) It is evident they were part of some text then extant, and it is even more evident that they constitute the perfect summary of the real and true meaning of the whole body of revealed writ. Man was created so that he might worship the Lord because by so doing fallen mortals become as their Eternal Progenitor.

2. Joseph Smith spoke at extended length, on numerous occasions, reasoning along the same lines as here set forth, to show that the Lord "set the ordinances to be the same forever and ever." (*Teachings*, p. 168.) One brief reference to these teachings will here suffice: "The gospel has always been the same; the ordinances to fulfill its requirements, the same, and the officers to officiate, the same; and the signs and fruits resulting from the promises, the same; therefore, as Noah was a preacher of righteousness he must have been baptized and ordained to the priesthood by the laying on of the hands, etc." (*Teachings*, p. 264.)

3. One of the high points in the ministerial and worshipful experiences of the ancient patriarchs occurred in 3077 B.C., three years before Adam's spirit took leave of his mortal tenement. On that occasion, Adam "called Seth, Enos, Cainan, Mahalaleel, Jared, Enoch, and Methuselah, who were all high priests, with the residue of his posterity who were righteous, into the valley of Adam-ondi-Ahman, and there bestowed upon them his last blessing." Lamech, who was born in 3130 B.C., certainly would have been included in the unnamed "posterity." It was on this occasion that "the Lord [Christ] appeared unto them, and they rose up and blessed Adam, and called him Michael, the prince, the archangel. And the Lord administered comfort unto Adam, and said unto him: I have set thee to be at the head; a multitude of nations shall come of thee, and thou art a prince over them forever. And Adam stood up in the midst of the congregation; and, notwithstanding he was bowed down with age, being full of the Holy Ghost, predicted whatsoever should befall his posterity unto the latest generation." (D&C 107:53-56.) This certainly was one of the crowning worship services of all history, a service in which the righteous saints assembled to pay their devotions; and the Lord Jesus Christ himself, more than three millenniums before his mortal birth, came to speak to the people and to bless the great head of the human race.

4. "This greater priesthood administereth the gospel and holdeth the key of the

mysteries of the kingdom," our revelation says. Also: This "priesthood continueth in the church of God in all generations." (D&C 84:17-19.) These statements, as their context shows, refer to the authority, organization, and doctrine found on earth from Adam to Moses. Thus, whenever the Melchizedek Priesthood is found among men, there also is the Church of Jesus Christ and the fulness of the gospel; and wherever the gospel and the Church are found, there also is the priesthood. Any one of these is inseparable from each of the others. It is a knowledge of this and other similar truths that enables us to know, from the very sketchy and fragmentary accounts available to us, what the ancient saints actually possessed.

5. These words of scripture seem to say that there was more than one generation between Melchizedek and Noah, which means that the tradition from apocryphal sources that Melchizedek was Shem the son of Noah cannot be true.

6. Alma 13:14-19; D&C 84:13-14; 107:1-4; JST, Gen. 14:17-40; Heb. 7:1-4; 11:33-34; *Teachings,* pp. 322-23. Our King James Version of the Bible speaks of Melchizedek as being "without father, without mother, without descent, having neither beginning of days, nor end of life; but made like unto the Son of God; abideth a priest continually" (Heb. 7:3-4), as though he were some unique and mystical character apart from the races of men. The Joseph Smith Translation perfects the obviously imperfect King James passage in this way: "For this Melchizedek was ordained a priest after the order of the Son of God, which order was without father, without mother, without descent, having neither beginning of days, nor end of life. And all those who are ordained unto this priesthood are made like unto the Son of God, abiding a priest continually." (JST, Heb. 7:3.) In this connection it should be noted that the Joseph Smith Translation renditions in the fourteenth chapter of Genesis recite some of the greatest and most glorious concepts in any revelation relative to this "order of the Son of God," this Melchizedek Priesthood as we call it. (JST, Gen. 14:17-40.)

7. D&C 110:12-16; 132:29-32; Abr. 2:6-11; Gen. 17:1-4; 23:15-18; 26:1-5; 28:10-15.

8. Galatians 3. This chapter, contrary to the views that prevail in modern Christendom, shows how Abraham had the gospel, how in the day of Moses the lesser law "was added because of transgressions," how this law was to continue until the Messiah came, and how "the law was our schoolmaster to bring us unto Christ."

9. It was of this temple and this statue, in all their artistry and magnificence, that Paul said to the Epicurean and Stoic philosophers: "God that made the world and all things therein, seeing that he is Lord of heaven and earth, dwelleth not in temples made with hands; Neither is worshipped with men's hands, as though he needed any thing, seeing he giveth to all life, and breath, and all things." (Acts 17:24-25.) Would it be amiss to give a modern paraphrase of Paul's words, a paraphrase pointed not at those who worship Diana, but at those who suppose that "God is a spirit," as the King James Version erroneously says in the Jacob's Well passage? Would it be amiss if the passage said: "God that made the world and all things therein, seeing that he is Lord of heaven and earth, is not a congeries of laws floating like a fog in the universe; he is not the unclothed, indivisible, uncreated, impersonal spirit essence defined in the creeds of Christendom; for what adoration and what true worship (including the essential element of emulation) can there be for impersonal laws, as though man should pray: O thou great law of gravity grant me this my petition"?

THE LAW OF MOSES

My servant Moses . . . who is faithful
in all mine house. With him will I speak
mouth to mouth, even apparently,
and not in dark speeches; and the
similitude of the Lord shall he behold. . . .
(Num. 12:7-8.)

And there arose not a prophet since in
Israel like unto Moses, whom the Lord
knew face to face, In all signs and
wonders, which the Lord sent him to do.
(Deut. 34:10-11.)[1]

Jesus Lived the Law of Moses

We cannot portray, with any degree of sense and wisdom, the deeds done by the Mortal Messiah, nor can we envision the true meaning of much that he taught, unless we know what was involved in the law and system that was given to men to prepare the way for his coming. That system was the law of Moses—the law, on the one hand, that for fifteen hundred burdensome years had been the whip and the scourge in the hands of the Almighty to bring recalcitrant Israel repeatedly back to their proper standards; the law, on the other hand, that had shown forth bright rays of divine light for that blessed millennium and a half during which men were privileged to live in harmony with its uplifting standards.

Jesus was born among a people and in a home where the law of Moses was the rule and standard by which all things were measured. During his young and maturing years he was taught its precepts; he learned all that appertained to it; and he conformed in every respect to its rituals and provisions. When he was eight days old he was circumcised, according to the law, so that the mark of Moses, the man of God, and of Abraham, the friend of God, might ever thereafter be found in his flesh. When the days of Mary's purification according to the law of Moses were accomplished, she and Joseph took the newborn baby to the temple to present him to the Lord. At the age of twelve he became a son of the law, attended the regular feasts, and began to assume the responsibilities of the maturing males of the chosen race. It was at that age, at the Feast of the Passover, that he confounded the wise men in the temple and made to Mary the famous statement "Wist ye not that I must be about my Father's business" (Luke 2:49), indicating that even then the divine truth had come to him that he was one set apart from his fellows because God was his Father.

We can rest assured that our Lord was present many times when the morning and evening sacrifices were offered; that he went up to Jerusalem to keep the Feast of Tabernacles and to worship in the holy convocations that were recurring times of rejoicing under the Mosaic system; that he rejoiced with his kindred on the Day of Atonement and made it an occasion to draw near to his Father; that he went many times to the temple, which he revered as his Father's house, to ponder and pray and worship. To the growing boy, the eager and inquiring youth, the maturing man, and the teaching Rabbi, the law that had so long been a light to the paths of his forebears was also a light to his.

We must gaze back to the day of Moses and of Aaron; we must look upon the performances and ordinances of the Levitical law, during the fifteen hundred years it was in force in Israel; we must hear the voices of the prophets and teachers who were subject to the Mosaic system; we must know what the ancients had and were—all this if we are to catch the true vision of what Jesus was; if we are to learn why he taught as he did; if we are to understand why he reacted as he did to both friend and foe. This we shall do as we lay the foundation for the study of his life.

The Divinity of the Law of Moses

It is axiomatic, an obvious truism, that all things have their opposites and that nothing can be understood or known except as it relates to other similar or diverse things. The beauties and blessings of one system of conduct or of one way of life can only be envisioned to the full when both compared and contrasted with other systems or ways in the same field. We must both compare and contrast the law of Moses with the gospel of Christ, and each of them with other lesser systems of worship, if we are to see how the Mosaic system fits into the eternal scheme of things.

To have the whole picture before us, we might well divide individuals, groups, races, and nations into four classes or types:

1. *There are those whose consciences are seared with a hot iron, who rebel against light and decency, who revel in unrighteousness, and who seek to live and rule in outright wickedness.*

Such are the Gadianton robbers of the Nephites, the marauding bands of ancient Palestine, and the thieves and robbers of every society. Such are the Genghis Khans, the Caesars, and the war lords of China and other nations whose lives consist of plundering, ravaging, and destroying. Such are the ancient mystery religions, the sex-centered worship of Ashtoreth, and the witchcraft, necromancy, astrology, and outright Satan worship of both ancient and modern peoples. Such also are the empire-building nations of history—Egyptians, Assyrians, Babylonians, Persians, Greeks, Romans, Barbarians, many of the kingdoms and empires of Europe and Asia, the anti-Christs among the Jaredites, and the degenerate Lamanites of Hebrew descent: all these are peoples and nations led by godless wretches whose aim is to enslave and rule their fellowmen. All these are without God in the world: their course is one of carnality and evil; they are not neutral in the warfare between good and evil; they affirmatively defy the good and espouse the evil. Their religion is the religion of Satan; they serve on his errand and further his purposes. They are purely and simply in opposition to all that is good and decent among men. To put them in perspective, theologically speaking, we might say that all these are the telestial mortals among us.

2. *There are those who seek to do good and to live by standards of decency and integrity; who heed the voice of conscience; who believe that a man's word should be his bond; and who maintain that men should organize and govern themselves so as to better their social circumstances and assure to each person freedom of conscience and the rights to life, liberty, and the pursuit of happiness.*

Such are the ideals at least of the great religions of the world—Christian, Jewish, Islam, Buddhism, Confucianism, Shintoism, or what have you—all seek to better and uplift man; all seek to assure him of whatever they conceive salvation to be. Such are the temperance societies, the welfare organizations, the freedom foundations, the schools and universities among free peoples. Such also are the benevolent dictatorships, the kindly monarchies, and the republics of both the Old and New Worlds.

None of these is pure religion; none embraces within its fold true worship; but all are founded, in general, on right principles; all operate for the betterment and uplift of fallen man.

Theologically speaking, these might be said to be terrestrial in nature. They are good for man; they advance him in the scale of progression; they help the downtrodden and better the status of those in need. But they can neither save nor exalt a human soul; they neither embrace nor follow a course of pure and perfect worship.

3. *Above these peoples and nations come those who have the preparatory gospel—the law of Moses!—the principles of revealed truth that put them in the course leading to eternal life in our Father's kingdom.*

Such was the righteous portion of the house of Israel from the day of Moses to the coming of John; such was the righteous or Nephite portion of father Lehi's seed on the American continent. Be it known that not all Israel kept the law of Moses. There were clusters and groups and whole tribes and nations that for generations at a time wallowed in dire and awful apostasy and denied themselves the blessings that might have been theirs. And be it known that not all of father Lehi's children walked in the path charted for them by their noble parent. Laman and Lemuel and their seed (with some notable exceptions) sought that which was evil and kept not the law of Moses.

But what we must have clearly before us is that the law of Moses as such was a higher and more perfect order of worship than any system of worship other than the fulness of the everlasting gospel. That is to say, the law of Moses was a higher and better and more nearly perfect system of worship than modern Catholic and sectarian Christianity, to say nothing of the fact that it surpassed Mohammedanism, Buddhism, and all other forms of worship. This is so because those who lived the law of Moses had revelation, were led by prophets, held the priesthood, and did the things that started them in the direction of the celestial kingdom. This superiority of the law of Moses will become apparent as we set forth the principles and practices upon which it was based. Theologically speaking, those who received and lived the law of Moses might be said to have been walking in a celestial course, to have been taking some of the initial steps leading to eternal life, to have been preparing themselves for that eternal fulness out of which eternal life comes.

4. *Finally we come to those who have the fulness of the everlasting gospel; who have the law of Christ in all its beauty and perfection; who are the true saints, the saints of the living God; who hold the holy priesthood; who enjoy the gift of the Holy Ghost; who have been born again and are in process of sanctifying their souls; who have the gifts of the Spirit; who receive revelations and see within the veil; who work miracles, open blind eyes, unstop deaf ears, and cause lame men to leap; and who have power to seal righteous souls up to eternal life in the everlasting realms of Him who is Eternal.*

Such are the citizens of the true kingdom, in whatever age is involved; such are members of the only true and living church on earth, in whatever age is involved; such are the faithful among the Latter-day Saints. Theologically speaking, those who believe and obey the everlasting fulness of saving truth might be said to be earth's celestial souls, souls who will receive back again in the resurrection the same body that was a natural body, which perfected body will be able to stand the glory of a celestial kingdom.

Moses and Christ—Their Laws Compared

We shall now compare the law of Moses with the fulness of the gospel. In doing so we must be aware that both of them come from God and are the laws of Christ.

We say, and our scriptures so certify, that there are two gospels, two laws, two revealed systems that Jehovah has given his people. One gospel is called the everlasting gospel, the fulness of the gospel, the gospel of Christ. It is the plan of salvation, by conformity to which man can gain the fulness of reward in that kingdom which is everlasting. The other gospel is the preparatory gospel, the partial gospel, the lesser gospel. It is the law of Moses by conformity to which men qualify, either in this life or the next, to receive that eternal fulness out of which eternal life grows. Both gospels are good news from God (as the very word *gospel* signifies), but one is greater than the other: one contains sufficient power and knowledge to save and exalt here and now, while the other prepares men to receive that future fulness which alone gives the guarantee of salvation.

We say, and our scriptures also so certify, that there are two priesthoods, two systems that authorize man to represent his Maker and to act in his place and stead in ministering salvation to mortals. One priesthood is the priesthood after the order of the Son of God; it is the Melchizedek Priesthood, the higher or greater priesthood, the holy order, the priesthood that administers the fulness of the gospel and has power to seal men up unto eternal life. The other priesthood is the Aaronic Priesthood, the Levitical Priesthood, the lower or lesser priesthood, the priesthood that administers the law of Moses.

Joseph Smith was asked, "Was the Priesthood of Melchizedek taken away when Moses died?" He replied: "All Priesthood is Melchizedek, but there are different portions or degrees of it. That portion which brought Moses to speak with God face to face was taken away; but that which brought the ministry of angels remained." (*Teachings,* pp. 180-81.) In other words, there is only one priesthood, but it comes in degrees; it is given partially or it is conferred in its fulness; it comes as the order of Aaron or as the order of Melchizedek. In this same sense, there is only one gospel, one law, one system of salvation, and it comes in degrees. It is all the law of Christ. Salvation comes from no other source. He gives to men as much of his law as they are able to bear. If they can only bear up under the burdens of the lesser system, the schooling system, the preparatory gospel, that is all they receive. Men are given according to their desires and their deeds.

Even today with the fulness of the gospel we have not received all of the light and knowledge that Enoch and many of the ancients possessed. We do, of course, have all the keys and powers ever had by any peoples and hence are able to assure worthy people of the fulness of reward in our Father's kingdom. Historically, the fulness of the gospel and the fulness of the priesthood came first; the law of Moses and the partial priesthood came second. The law of Moses was added to the gospel and the lesser priesthood was added to the greater. There are restrictions and limitations in the lesser system that are not present in the gospel itself. All of the saints from Adam to Moses had the fulness of the priesthood and the fulness of the law of Christ. Those from Moses to John had the lesser orders, the lesser priesthood and the lesser gospel, except of course when groups and portions of the people (such as the Nephites) qualified for the higher law and power.

To gain the celestial kingdom, the Lord says: Ye must be "sanctified through the law which I have given unto you, even the law of Christ," which law is the fulness of the gospel. The revealed word specifies that those who "abide the law of a terrestrial kingdom" shall obtain a terrestrial glory, and that those who "abide the law of a telestial kingdom" shall obtain a telestial glory. No such requirement is set forth for gaining a celestial glory. Instead, the revelation says that those who so obtain must be "*able* to abide the law of a celestial kingdom." (D&C 88:21-24.) In other words, salvation in the celestial kingdom will come to all who are *able* to live the full law of Christ, even though they did not have opportunity so to do in the course of a mortal probation. Thus, all those who kept the law of Moses, who lived the law of the preparatory gospel to the full, thus establishing that they were able to live the Lord's law, will in due course gain a celestial inheritance. All of the great and eternal truths found in the law of Moses are also part and portion of the fulness of the gospel, in the same sense that all of the powers of the Aaronic Priesthood are embraced within the Melchizedek Priesthood.

It should come as no surprise to learn that the law of Moses includes such basic and eternal verities as these:

Under the law, the people had "the first and great commandment," which is, "Thou shalt love the Lord thy God with all thy heart, and with all thy soul, and with all thy mind"; they had also the second great commandment, which is "like unto" the first: "Thou shalt love thy neighbour as thyself." So spake Jesus in answer to the query, "Which is the great commandment in the law?" And having so stated, our Lord added, "On these two commandments hang all the law and the prophets." (Matt. 22:35-40.) That is to say, all of the gospel of salvation, all of the ancient law given to Moses, all of the prophetic counsel of all the inspired men of all the ages—all of it is anchored and grounded upon these two eternal verities: love of the true God and love of one's fellowmen.

The words used to codify these laws did not originate with the Lord Jesus during his mortal ministry. The two commandments were not an outpouring of his superior wisdom; they were not a new and superlative summary of the mind and will of the Lord; they were, rather, a direct quotation from the law of Moses. Moses said them and Jesus quoted them. It was Moses who said: "Hear, O Israel: The Lord our God is one Lord: And thou shalt love the Lord thy God with all thine heart, and with all thy soul, and with all thy might"; and having so said, it was Moses who commanded Israel to teach these words diligently unto their children, to talk of them as they sat in their houses and as they walked by the way, when they lay down and when they rose up, and also that they should bind them for a sign upon their hands, let them be continually before their eyes, and write them upon the posts of their houses and the gates to their dwelling places. (Deut. 6:4-9.) And it was Moses who said, in the Lord's name, "Thou shalt love thy neighbour as thyself." (Lev. 19:18.) It is indeed difficult to conceive how a greater emphasis could have been put on these basic truths than was placed upon them by Moses, the man of God.

We have stated that those who kept the law of Moses were heirs of eternal life, an eternal verity that Jesus confirmed in this conversation. Our Lord was asked,

"Master, what shall I do to inherit eternal life?" He responded: "What is written in the law? how readest thou?" which is tantamount to saying, 'If you want eternal life, keep the law of Moses.' His interrogator replied: "Thou shalt love the Lord thy God with all thy heart, and with all thy soul, and with all thy strength, and with all thy mind; and thy neighbour as thyself." If there was anything that all Israel knew about the law of Moses and the teachings of all the prophets, it was that to gain salvation, they must love their God and their fellowmen. And so Jesus affirmed: "Thou hast answered right: this do, and thou shalt live." 'Keep these commandments which came through Moses, and thou shalt have eternal life.' It was at this point that our Lord's tempter, desiring to justify himself, asked, "Who is my neighbour?" and the Master Teacher replied with the parable of the good Samaritan. (Luke 10:25-37.)

Upon the foundation of the first and second commandments, we place the Ten Commandments, that Israelite code of revealed law that is so highly esteemed that it has become the basic legal code for nearly all those who accept the Christian way of life. The Lord revealed the Ten Commandments to Moses twice, the first time as part of the gospel, the second time as part of the law of Moses, with the only substantive difference between the two revealed accounts being the reason for keeping the Sabbath day holy. Under the gospel the Sabbath day commemorated the creation; under the Mosaic system, the deliverance from Egypt with a mighty hand and a stretched-out arm.

The Ten Commandments—decreeing as they do that the saints shall have no gods before the Lord; that they shall neither make nor worship any graven images; that they shall not take the name of God in vain; that they shall keep holy the Sabbath; that they shall honor their father and mother; that they shall not kill, nor commit adultery, nor steal, nor bear false witness, nor covet—all of these are part of the law of Moses as they are part of the gospel.[2] And it was to these commandments that Jesus turned to give answer to the query, "Good Master, what good thing shall I do, that I may have eternal life?" Having replied, "If thou wilt enter into life, keep the commandments," and then being asked, "Which?" Jesus particularized by saying: "Thou shalt do no murder, Thou shalt not commit adultery, Thou shalt not steal, Thou shalt not bear false witness, Honour thy father and thy mother: and, Thou shalt love thy neighbour as thyself." (Matt. 19:16-19.) And thus again the witness is born that by keeping the law of Moses men go forward on the charted course toward eternal life.

As an integral part of the whole law of Moses; as an essential part of every rite and performance of the Mosaic system; as a spoken or implied part of every commandment given to Israel; as a unifying thread woven into the whole tapestry of their society; as a divine decree, echoing and reechoing like the thunders of Sinai—stands the great Mosaic message: Keep the commandments. Keep the commandments and be blessed; disobey and be cursed. The repetitively stated Nephite declaration—"Inasmuch as ye shall keep my commandments ye shall prosper in the land; but inasmuch as ye will not keep my commandments ye shall be cut off from my presence" (2 Ne. 1:20)—was but an echo of what Moses and the prophets had been telling Israel for generations.

"And now, Israel," Moses proclaimed, "what doth the Lord thy God require of thee, but to fear the Lord thy God, to walk in all his ways, and to love him, and to serve the Lord thy God with all thy heart and with all thy soul, To keep the commandments of the Lord, and his statutes, which I command thee this day for thy good?" Thereupon Moses acclaims the might and glory of the Lord, recounts some of his wondrous works, and says: "Therefore thou shalt love the Lord thy God, and keep his charge, and his statutes, and his judgments, and his commandments, alway." The blessings to accrue by obedience and the curses to befall from disobedience are then enumerated in graphic detail. (Deut. 10:12-22; 11; 27; 28.)

Perhaps nothing shows the divine approval enjoyed by ancient Israel—and therefore the divine nature of their law, by obedience to which they gained such great things—than the endless miracles and wonders wrought among them by the power of God. The Lord by his angel went before the camps of Israel in a cloud by day and a pillar of fire by night, that they might know he was near and had a personal interest in preserving them. (Ex. 13:20-22; 14:19-24; 23:20-25; Deut. 1:33.) Lest they perish in the wilderness for want of food, the Lord, for forty years, rained bread from heaven upon them. This manna—by which no other people before or since has ever been fed, coming as it did by the opening of the heavens—certified to all who tasted its delicious flavor that as man doth not live by bread alone, even so his spiritual life depends upon receiving every word that proceedeth out of the mouth of God. Temporal food and spiritual food come from the same source, and both are essential to the full and complete life of the soul. (Ex. 16:1-36; Deut. 8:1-4.)

What indicates divine approval more than the receipt of personal and continuing revelation? Under the Mosaic system, direct revelation was given; the voice of a living, personal, speaking God was heard; angels ministered to men. God was not, as he is in Christendom today, an unknown spirit essence; he was a living reality. Many of these revelations came to the high priest of the Aaronic order, by means of the Urim and Thummim, which he carried in the breastplate of judgment when he went in before the Lord. (Ex. 28:30.)

As a result of the sacrificial offerings of Aaron and his sons and the consequent devotion and worship of the people, the Lord Jehovah promised to dwell among the children of Israel and to be their God, thus leading to that close personal relationship which existed between the Lord and his people when he dwelt personally in Zion. (Ex. 29:38-46; Moses 7:16.)

All of this—and much more that could be set forth—

shows the greatness and dignity of the law of Moses. This law was no mean or low system, either of theology or of ethics. That it exceeded what is had among sectarian Christians today is shown by the fact that the Lord wrought miracles and poured out wonders upon its faithful adherents. What Moses had was ennobling and uplifting. It was part of the law of Christ. Its essence and tenor is summed up perfectly in the words of Micah: "What doth the Lord require of thee, but to do justly, and to love mercy, and to walk humbly with thy God?" (Micah 6:8.)

Moses and Christ—Their Laws Contrasted

By obedience to his law, by heeding his voice, by keeping his gospel covenant, Israel had power to become "a peculiar treasure" unto the Lord above all people, to become "a kingdom of priests, and an holy nation." (Ex. 19:5-6; Deut. 7:6; 14:1-2.) This they failed to do. The gospel offered to them was not "mixed with faith in them that heard it." (Heb. 4:2.) In its place came the law of Moses, a law that was "added because of transgressions." (Gal. 3:19.) As Abinadi expresses it, "They were a stiffnecked people, quick to do iniquity, and slow to remember the Lord their God; Therefore there was a law given them, yea, a law of performances and of ordinances, a law which they were to observe strictly from day to day, to keep them in remembrance of God and their duty towards him." (Mosiah 13:29-30.)

As we have seen, many of the great and eternal truths of the gospel remained and were the rock foundation upon which the law was built. Men were still to worship and serve the Lord; they were still to love their neighbors as themselves; and the Ten Commandments retained their efficacy, virtue, and force; but under the law of Moses severe penalties were added for disobedience. The element of fear as well as of love became a dominant incentive in doing the things that must be done if salvation is to be won. Under the law of the gospel men are commanded to honor the Sabbath day and keep it holy. If they keep this commandment, they are blessed; if they heed it not, the promised blessings pass them by. But under the law of Moses a penalty was added for dishonoring the Sabbath, and that penalty was death. Extreme? Severe? So it would seem to us, but the Lord was taking a nation of bondsmen and slaves and turning them into kings and priests. It required strict obedience to his laws, and the sooner the rebels were sloughed off the sooner the whole nation would walk in paths of righteousness.

There are, in fact, a great host of offenses, set forth primarily in Exodus and Leviticus, for which the law decreed either excommunication or death as the penalty. Israelites were excommunicated, for instance, for eating any manner of fat from oxen, sheep, or goats, or for eating the blood of birds or beasts. The death penalty was imposed for murder, adultery, and various sexual perversions; it was decreed for blasphemy, witchcraft, and sacrificing to false gods; even those who either cursed or smote father or mother, and the sons of Aaron who drank wine or strong drink before entering the tabernacle of the congregation, were to be put to death. The whole tone and tenor of the Mosaic system may be summed up in the decree: "Thou shalt give life for life, Eye for eye, tooth for tooth, hand for hand, foot for foot, Burning for burning, wound for wound, stripe for stripe." (Ex. 21:23-25.) An illustration of the severity with which the divine decrees were applied anciently is seen in the slaying of Nadab and Abihu by the Lord. "There went out fire from the Lord, and devoured them," the account says, because they offered "strange fire" upon the altar; that is, these sons of Aaron performed a sacrificial ordinance of their own devising. (Lev. 10:1-2.)[3]

The contrast between the benevolent influence exerted by Christianity and the severe near-compulsion of the law of Moses is nowhere better illustrated than in the sayings of Jesus. Coming as he did to lift Israel from the level of the law to the high standard of the gospel, it was our Lord's wont to say: "Ye have heard that it was said by them of old time," such and such, "But I say unto you," this and this. In this way he extended the ancient definition of adultery to include looking upon a woman in lust; he condemned the ancient practice of giving "a writing of divorcement," and set forth a marital standard that is higher than the one even now required in the Church, a standard that labels as adultery and fornication the marrying of certain divorced persons. He revoked the power to swear oaths and in place of the ancient law, "An eye for an eye, a tooth for a tooth," he counseled, "That ye resist not evil: but whosoever shall smite thee on thy right cheek, turn to him the other also." And the Mosaic standard, "Thou shalt love thy neighbour, and hate thine enemy," became "Love your enemies, bless them that curse you, do good to them that hate you, and pray for them which despitefully use you, and persecute you." (Matt. 5.)

Our conclusion, then, is:

1. That the law of Moses is superior to every law except the gospel;

2. That those who lived its terms and conditions thereby charted a course leading to eternal life;

3. That it prepares men for the fulness of revealed truth; and

4. That the gospel itself is far greater than the ancient law of Moses.

NOTES

1. We must not lose sight of the high and exalted place of Moses in the divine program. He ranks with Adam and Enoch; he has the spiritual stature of Noah and Abraham; and he stands with Melchizedek and Moriancumer in faith and devotion. How fitting it is that the law that was to govern the Lord's people for one-fourth of the entire period from the fall of man to the Second Coming of the Messiah should come through this son of Amram and Jochebed. It is no wonder that Holy Writ speaks of him in words like these: "Moses was caught up into an exceedingly high mountain, And he saw God face to face, and he talked with him, and the glory of God was upon Moses; therefore Moses could endure his presence. And God spake unto Moses, saying: Behold, . . . thou art my son; wherefore look, and I will show thee the workmanship of mine hands. . . . And I have a work for thee, Moses, my son; and thou art in the similitude of mine Only Begotten." (Moses 1:1-6.)

2. The account in Exodus (Ex. 20:1-17) sets forth the Ten Commandments as part of the gospel. The account in Deuteronomy (Deut. 5:1-21), given later and written anew by the finger of God on a second set of tablets of stone, is the account that governed those under the law of Moses. It is of more than passing interest that the direction to Israel to keep the Sabbath in commemoration of the day of their deliverance from Egypt had the

effect of changing the day of the week on which the Sabbath was kept each succeeding year. Christmas comes on a different day of the week each year for us, and so did the weekly Sabbaths in ancient Israel: A full consideration of this is found in *Sunday—The True Sabbath of God* by Samuel Walter Gamble, a Methodist minister.

3. The death of these priests for performing an unauthorized ordinance gives us insight into how the Lord deals with those of his people, at least, who do that which he has not authorized them to do. Certainly in principle, and to some degree the same condemnation, in a spiritual sense, rests upon all ministers who perform unauthorized ordinances.

JERUSALEM—THE HOLY CITY

Beautiful for situation, the joy of the whole earth, is mount Zion, . . . the city of the great King. God is known in her palaces. . . . Jerusalem . . . the city of the great King.
(Ps. 48:2-3; Matt. 5:35.)[1]

Enoch's Zion—the City of Holiness

Holy cities, sacred sites, dwelling places set apart—symbols of celestial rest—such are the capital cities of the saints in all ages. Always the Lord has a Zion, a Jerusalem, a City of Holiness, a place from which his word and his law can go forth; a place to which all men can look to receive guidance from on high; a place where apostles and prophets give counsel to their fellowmen; a place where living oracles commune with the Infinite and speak forth his mind and announce his will. In every age the Lord gathers his people; in every age the saints come together to worship the Father in the name of the Son; in every age there is a capital city, a city of refuge, a City of Holiness, a Zion of God—a sacred site from which he can send forth his word and govern his people. Such is Jerusalem—Old Jerusalem, New Jerusalem, Jerusalem of the ages.

Up to now, through all of earth's long years, there has been one time, one time only, when the Lord's system of capital cities has worked perfectly. Such was in the day of Enoch, the seventh from Adam. In that holy day, so faithful were the saints that the Lord, the Great Jehovah, "came and dwelt with his people," even as he will in the millennial era that is to be. In that holy day, the saints "dwelt in righteousness," even as they shall when the Lord comes again to dwell among mortals. "And the Lord called his people ZION, because they were of one heart and one mind, and dwelt in righteousness; and there were no poor among them. And Enoch . . . built a city that was called the City of Holiness, even ZION. . . . And Enoch and all his people walked with God, and he dwelt in the midst of Zion; and it came to pass that Zion was not, for God received it up into his own bosom; and from thence went forth the saying, ZION IS FLED." (Moses 7:16-21, 69.)

Zion is taken up into heaven! And "this is Zion—THE PURE IN HEART," and the pure in heart shall see God. (D&C 97:16-21.) The Lord's people—and it is the people who were named Zion—went where he was; the inhabitants of the City of Holiness ascended up on high; their purity and perfection prepared them for the divine presence.

Thereafter, from the time when the people whose name was Zion were translated until the day of the great deluge, the converted saints had no earthly city to which they could gather. And so, as the divine record recites, for "generation upon generation" the faithful saints were translated and taken up into heaven to associate with others of like spiritual caliber in that Zion which God had taken into his own bosom. "The Holy Ghost fell on many," the account says, "and they were caught up by the powers of heaven into Zion." (Moses 7:24-27.)

Righteous men, after the flood—knowing what had happened to their faithful counterparts before the flood; knowing that those who held the holy priesthood had "power, by faith, . . . to stand in the presence of God"; knowing that if

God had gathered some into a translated realm, he might be prevailed upon to gather others also—"men having this faith, coming up unto this order of God, were translated and taken up into heaven." (JST, Gen. 14:25-32.)

Melchizedek Creates His Zion—Ancient Jerusalem

Righteous men, after the flood, not only sought an inheritance in Enoch's Zion, but also began the process of building their own City of Holiness on earth; and this brings us to the first scriptural mention of Salem, of Jeru-Salem, of Jerusalem. In reciting what Enoch and his people had gained through faith and by the power of the priesthood, the scripture says: "And now, Melchizedek was a priest of this order; therefore he obtained peace in Salem, and was called the Prince of peace. And his people wrought righteousness, and obtained heaven, and sought for the city of Enoch which God had before taken, separating it from the earth, having reserved it unto the latter days, or the end of the world. . . . And this Melchizedek, having thus established righteousness, was called the king of heaven by his people, or, in other words, the King of peace." (JST, Gen. 14:33-36.)

Abraham, who received his priesthood from Melchizedek, was one of those who sought for the heavenly city. "He looked for a city," Paul says, "which hath foundations, whose builder and maker is God." Isaac and Jacob, heirs of the promises made to Abraham, also sought an inheritance in the heavenly city. But it was not their privilege so to obtain.

Theirs was a different mortal mission; and though they declared "plainly" that they sought such a reward, yet they knew it was not to be, and "confessed that they were strangers and pilgrims on the earth." Their reward was postponed to a future day, for God "hath prepared for them a city," as he has for all those who serve him with like faith and zeal. (Heb. 11:8-16.)

In the true and full sense of the word *Zion* and *Jerusalem* are probably synonymous terms. Enoch built Zion, a City of Holiness, and Melchizedek, reigning as king and ministering as priest of the Most High God, sought to make Jerusalem, his capital city, into another Zion. As we have seen, Melchizedek himself was called by his people the Prince of peace, the King of peace, and the King of heaven, for Jerusalem had become a heaven to them. And interestingly, according to the linguistic scholars and specialists, Salem means *peace*, and Jerusalem means *city of peace*, or *sacred Salem*, and Isaiah's designation of Jerusalem as the holy city is said to mean, literally translated, the *city of holiness.*[2]

That Jerusalem came nearer in Melchizedek's day to becoming in truth and in fact a Zion of God than it has in any of its long and tumultuous history is perfectly clear. Indeed, after Melchizedek's day we lose track of what transpired in and relative to this sacred spot, which had started out to be an abode for the righteous, and we know little more of its history until Israelite times. Joshua found the city in the hands of the Jebusites, and he and others who followed made war upon its inhabitants, but it was not until David's day that it became an Israelite city. David made it his capital; Solomon built the temple in it; the ark of God rested there; the Shekinah rested in the Holy of Holies; the whole system of Levitical sacrifices centered in its hallowed areas; and it was called Zion, or Mount Zion. Isaiah called it the Holy City, and the Psalmist proclaimed: "In Judah is God known: his name is great in Israel. In Salem also is his tabernacle, and his dwelling place in Zion." (Ps. 76:1-2.) Jerusalem had become and ever thereafter would remain the center of Israelite and Jewish worship. Truly, as it is written: "The Lord loveth the gates of Zion more than all the dwellings of Jacob. Glorious things are spoken of thee, O city of God. . . . And of Zion it shall be said, This and that man was born in her: and the highest himself shall establish her. The Lord shall count, when he writeth up the people, that this man was born there." (Ps. 87.)

The Jewish Jerusalem of Jesus' Day

Out of all this there arose a general concept and feeling, both in ancient Israel and in Jewish Israel, that the place of worship was almost as important as the very God to whom reverential adoration was given. The chosen people came to feel that the place where the great altar was built, the land whereon the temple stood, and the city wherein these sacred structures were found were as essential to true worship as the very manner and form in which they paid their devotions to the Most High. Jacob's descendants were almost as concerned about where they worshipped as with who received their devotions and how they were extended. Jehovah was the God of Jerusalem; Jerusalem, with its temple, was the focal point of all their religious devotions; it was Jehovah himself who had so decreed; and whenever Israel, either those of old or the Jews of Jesus' day, were in line of their duty, they turned to their capital city for spiritual refreshment.

It was no idle expression when, near Sychar at Jacob's Well, the woman of Samaria, recognizing Jesus as the Jew that he was, said: "Our fathers worshipped in this mountain; and ye say, that in Jerusalem is the place where men ought to worship." Nor was the reply of the Incarnate Jehovah—who once centered the worship of his people in the Holy City, but who would soon fulfill his ancient law and command all men to worship the Father in spirit and in truth in all places—nor was his reply anything short of an endorsement of the existing practice and a prophetic pronouncement as to the future, when he said: "Woman, believe me, the hour cometh, when ye shall neither in this mountain, nor yet at Jerusalem, worship the Father." (John 4:5-25.)

This city where the Jews worshipped in the day of Jesus, and from which holy place true worship was soon to go forth to all cities in all lands, is not an unknown quantity. We know what life was like within its precincts. Our knowledge comes from reliable sources, both secular and profane. Written accounts and archeological unearthings are numerous and authentic. We may not be able to paint as complete and detailed a picture as we can of, say, Korea's Seoul, or Thailand's Bangkok, or Indonesia's Djakarta—all cities that are far removed and socially distinct from our western civilization—but we have no trouble piecing enough together to envision with a certainty that borders on complete knowledge the way people lived in that day, both in Jerusalem and in all Palestine.

We know their way of worship and system of religious rites; their governmental structure and the names and duties of their legislative, executive, and judicial officers; their social structure, including their customs, practices, mores, legends, and folklore. We know their business practices, their commercial customs, their monetary system, the trades they plied, the crops they grew. We know the kind of houses they lived in, the sources of their water, the way they disposed of their garbage and refuse, and the degree of sanitation that prevailed among them. We know about their architectural abilities, their palaces and public buildings, the walls that surrounded their cities, and the gates by which they came and went. We know enough about the roads they built so that we can imagine ourselves traveling on them; enough about their beasts of burden and modes of transportation so that we could duplicate them; enough about their weapons and system of warfare to depict them in paintings and replay them in dramas. We know the diseases with which they were afflicted, the state of their healing arts, their quarantine regulations, the general status of their health, and how they buried their dead. We know what foods they ate, what beverages they drank, how they cooked, the clothes they wore, and the jewelry with which they adorned themselves. We know the language they spoke, the degree of their literary craftsmanship, the educational standards of all classes, and the effect upon them of Greek and Roman and other Gentile cultures. These and a host of related matters all were preserved in the records of the past and have been set forth for us by competent and able historians. They will be considered by us as occasions require.

Blessed Canaan, sacred spot, land of the ancient saints, has as its capital city Jerusalem, the city of Jewish delight; the Holy Land is crowned with the Holy City. Stretched out as a garden of choice land, this Canaan of old, this Palestine of the Hebrews, provided the trade routes between the great nations of antiquity. Toward the south and west lay Egypt and the fertile valley of the Nile; to the north and east lay the rich stretches of Mesopotamia and the Tigris and Euphrates rivers—the Nile pouring its life-giving fluids into the Mediterranean Sea, and the great rivers of Mesopotamia joining hands to feed the Persian Gulf. Palestine was anchored, as it were, to all the wealth of Egypt and her Pharaohs, on the one hand, and to the kingdoms that held sway, from time to time, in Syria, Assyria, and Babylonia, on the other hand. It was to be expected—nay, it was inevitable, greed and conquest being what they are—that the armies of these lands and kingdoms would invade the places where Moses had placed the house of Jacob.

Palestine was truly a land flowing with milk and honey. It had been such in the days of Abraham and Melchizedek; its wealth had been tapped by the Amorites and Hittites and assorted Gentile tribes in the pre-Israelite days; and it was still to be found in abundance when Joshua and Caleb and their fellow spies crossed over Jordan to survey the land. During all of Israel's long history, ten thousand shepherds led their sheep beside still waters in fruitful valleys, while their cattle browsed and fattened on a thousand hills. And it was through these same valleys and over these same hills that the armies of Assyria, of Babylon, and of Egypt ravaged and pillaged from generation to generation as envious Gentiles coveted the wealth and crops of Jehovah's people.

It was a land sanctified by a sacrificial struggle on Mount Moriah; by a bush that burned and was not consumed; by a voice that commanded, "Put off thy shoes from off thy feet, for the place whereon thou standest is holy ground" (Ex. 3:5); by the faith of a widow in Zarepath whose son rose from the dead because she hearkened to the words of a Tishbite prophet. It was a land choice and favored, a promised land, a land selected and saved as a habitation for Israel. And Jerusalem was its crowning jewel.

Jerusalem itself is a mountain city, a city founded amid and upon the Judean hills, a city built upon the mountains. When, in due course, the true saints build the promised temple there, then the scripture will be fulfilled that says that Judah shall "flee unto Jerusalem, unto the mountains of the Lord's house." (D&C 133:13.) It was founded upon land awarded by lot to Benjamin, although adjacent Bethlehem was part of the inheritance of Judah.

Deep ravines on three sides made it easy to defend in olden times. On the east is the valley of Kidron, or valley of Jehoshaphat. Over the brook Kidron are the Garden of Gethsemane, the Mount of Olives, and the road to Bethany and Jericho. There also was the ancient village of Siloam. On the south is the valley of Hinnom, one of the most evil spots in a land that should have been holy.[3] Another ravine, the Tyropoeon Valley, is on the west. Mount Zion is probably the hill just south of the southwest corner of the city wall.[4] And the place of greatest interest within those sacred walls was the Temple of Herod.

In the days of Jesus, the walled portion of the city encompassed some three hundred acres of houses and streets and markets and shops. Perhaps 200,000 to 250,000 Palestinians dwelt within its walls and immediate environs. Tacitus speaks of a population of 600,000; at the time of the Passover this number rose to between 2,000,000 and 3,000,000. Ecclesiastically speaking, persons living outside the walls were counted as inhabitants of the city, and at Passover time great numbers of Jews camped outside the city proper, but within the limits of a Sabbath day's journey. Josephus says that 1,100,000 men perished in Jerusalem when Titus and the legions from Rome wrought vengeance upon the nation that crucified their King. But whatever the actual number of its inhabitants, Jerusalem of the Jews, in Jesus' day, was truly a city of greatness and magnificence.

Among its citizens were artisans of every kind. In its shops and at its bazaars could be purchased goods from every nation. Its palaces, academies, and synagogues were places of renown, and the learned and mighty of all nations could tread its streets with the same satisfaction found in Rome or any of the great metropolises of the day. But in addition to all that was had elsewhere, Jerusalem was the center of such true religion and heaven-approved worship as was then found on earth.

Contrasting its then state with that which prevailed a millennium before, when David and Solomon had first made it an Israelite capital, Edersheim says: "If the dust of ten centuries could have been wiped from the eyelids of those sleepers, and one of them who thronged Jerusalem in the highday of its glory, during the reign of King Solomon, had returned to its streets, he would scarcely have recognized the once familiar city. Then, as now, a Jewish king reigned, who bore undivided rule over the whole land; then, as now, the city was filled with riches and adorned with palaces and architectural monument; then, as now, Jerusalem was crowded with strangers from all lands. Solomon and Herod were each the last Jewish king over the Land of Promise; Solomon and Herod, each, built the Temple. But with the son of David began, and with the Idumean ended, 'the kingdom'; or rather, having fulfilled its mission, it gave place to the spiritual world-kingdom of 'David's greater Son.' The sceptre departed from Judah to where the nations were to gather under its sway. And the Temple which Solomon built was the first. In it the Shekhinah dwelt visibly. The Temple which Herod reared was the last. The ruins of its burning, which the torch of the Romans had kindled, were never to be restored. Herod was not the antitype, he was the Barabbas, of David's Royal Son." (Edersheim 1:111.)

However, our chief concerns are not in the social, governmental, and cultural conditions of Jewish life in the meridian of time, important as these are to an understanding of the Life we are to consider. It is not the palaces and markets, not the kings and soldiers, not the schools and pedagogy that will set the stage for Messiah's ministry. His work will deal with the things of the Spirit. Our chief interest, then, is in the spiritual state of the people, their religious life, their understanding of the Messianic message delivered to them by the ancient prophets, and—above all!—their personal spiritual stature and the degree to which they kept the commandments and were in a condition to receive the guidance of the Holy Spirit.

That they were dull of hearing and slow to perceive the truth was proclaimed by the Lord Jesus as he spoke in irony and in sorrow of the city where he came to reign as King but was rejected by his own. "It cannot be that a prophet perish out of Jerusalem," he said. "O Jerusalem, Jerusalem, which killest the prophets, and stonest them that are sent unto thee; how often would I have gathered thy children together, as a hen doth gather her brood under her wings, and ye would not! Behold, your house is left unto you desolate." (Luke 13:31-35.)

And again: "He beheld the city, and wept over it, Saying, If thou hadst known, even thou, at least in this thy day, the things which belong unto thy peace! but now they are hid from thine eyes. For the days shall come upon thee, that thine enemies shall cast a trench about thee, and compass thee round, and keep thee in on every side, And shall lay thee even with the ground, and thy children within thee; and they shall not leave in thee one stone upon another; because thou knewest not the time of thy visitation." (Luke 19:41-45.)

The depths to which Jerusalem had sunk are seen in the words of the Beloved John, who, identifying it as "the great city, . . . where also our Lord was crucified," said that "spiritually [it] is called Sodom and Egypt." (Rev. 11:8.)

The Jerusalem of the Future

"Jerusalem shall be trodden down of the Gentiles," Jesus said, "until the times of the Gentiles be fulfilled." (Luke 21:24.)[5] Jerusalem—glorious and perfect in the days of Abraham and Melchizedek; Jerusalem—like Enoch's Zion for a time and a season some four thousand years ago; Jerusalem—then lost to our sight for a millennium, and until David took it from the Jebusites; Jerusalem—in Israelite hands for another millennium; Jerusalem—where kings reigned and prophets preached for a thousand Israelite years; Jerusalem—where our Lord ministered, was rejected by his own, and found death upon the cross; Jerusalem—a city of saints and a city of devils: this Jerusalem, Jesus says, "shall be trodden down of the Gentiles!"

And so for two millenniums the Gentiles have held sway in Jehovah's Jerusalem. Completely destroyed by Titus in A.D. 70, it was restored by Hadrian in A.D. 135 and became a Roman colony. He erected a temple to Jupiter Capitolinus on the very site where once the temple to Jehovah had stood. Two centuries later, in 336, wicked Constantine, an evil emperor who made apostasy and false worship reputable, erected a so-called Christian church on the supposed site of the holy sepulchre. Thereafter the sacred soil passed from the hands of apostate Christians into the hands of apostate pagans; it was retaken by the Crusaders in 1099, retaken by "nonbelievers" in 1187, and passed back and forth among various groups of them until 1917, when it was taken by British troops under General Allenby. The modern walls were built in 1542; on the site of Solomon's Temple now stands the Muslim temple known as the Dome of the Rock. Christians, Mohammedans, and Jews now dwell together under a tenuous and oft-interrupted peace, and the Holy City continues to be trodden down of the Gentiles. And, be it noted, even Jews are Gentiles when they believe not the truth.

But it shall not ever be thus. Darkness flees before light.

A new day is dawning. Already, in the language of Isaiah of old, the cry is going forth: "Awake, awake; put on thy strength, O Zion; put on thy beautiful garments, O Jerusalem, the holy city." What does it mean for Zion to put on her strength, and to what people was Isaiah making reference? Joseph Smith answers: "He had reference to those whom God should call in the last days, who should hold the power of priesthood to bring again Zion, and the redemption of Israel; and to put on her strength is to put on the authority of the priesthood, which she, Zion, has a right to by lineage; also to return to that power which she had lost." And when that day comes, again in Isaiah's language, "there shall no more come into [Jerusalem] the uncircumcised and the unclean," for it will be a day of righteousness, a day when men shall be cleansed in the waters of baptism.

Addressing himself further to the city he loved, Isaiah says: "Shake thyself from the dust; arise, and sit down, O Jerusalem: loose thyself from the bands of thy neck, O captive daughter of Zion." Question: "What are we to understand by Zion loosing herself from the bands of her neck?" The Prophet's answer: "We are to understand that the scattered remnants are exhorted to return to the Lord from whence they have fallen; which if they do, the promise of the Lord is that he will speak to them, or give them revelation. . . . The bands of her neck are the curses of God upon her, or the remnants of Israel in their scattered condition among the Gentiles."

As to what shall transpire relative to Israel and Jerusalem in the promised day of restoration, Isaiah says in the Lord's name: "My people shall know my name; therefore they shall know in that day that I am he that doth speak: behold, it is I." Jehovah shall be known again. Revelation shall commence anew. "How beautiful upon the mountains are the feet of him that bringeth good tidings, that publisheth peace; that bringeth good tidings of good, that publisheth salvation; that saith unto Zion, Thy God reigneth! Thy watchmen shall lift up the voice; with the voice together shall they sing: for they shall see eye to eye, when the Lord shall bring again Zion. Break forth into joy, sing together, ye waste places of Jerusalem: for the Lord hath comforted his people, he hath redeemed Jerusalem." (Isa. 52:1-10; D&C 113:7-10.)

In the great day of restoration—a day that has commenced, but in which many things yet remain to be restored—there will finally be two world capitals, both called Zion, both called Jerusalem. One shall be the seat of government, the other the spiritual capital of the world, "for out of Zion shall go forth the law, and the word of the Lord from Jerusalem." (Isa. 2:1-5.) That is to say, Jerusalem of old shall be restored, built up anew in glory and beauty, according to the promises, and also, another Jerusalem, a New Jerusalem, shall be established. Moroni tells us "of the New Jerusalem, which should come down out of heaven," and of "the holy sanctuary of the Lord." He says that Ether wrote both of this New Jerusalem, which should be upon the American continent, and of the restoration of the Jerusalem in the Old World, the one whence Lehi came. "And there shall be a new heaven and a new earth," the account says; "and they shall be like unto the old save the old have passed away, and all things have become new. And then cometh the New Jerusalem; and blessed are they who dwell therein, for it is they whose garments are white through the blood of the Lamb. . . . And then also cometh the Jerusalem of old; and the inhabitants thereof, blessed are they, for they have been washed in the blood of the Lamb; and they are they who were scattered and gathered in from the four quarters of the earth, and from the north countries, and are partakers of the fulfilling of the covenant which God made with their father, Abraham." (Ether 13:1-12; 3 Ne. 20:22; 21:23-24.)

That the New Jerusalem, the latter-day Zion, the Zion to which Enoch and his city shall return, shall be in Jackson County, Missouri, has been set forth plainly in latter-day revelation. (D&C 84:1-4.) Of this millennial Zion, the New Testament apostle says: "And I saw a new heaven and a new earth: for the first heaven and the first earth were passed away; and there was no more sea. And I John saw the holy city, new Jerusalem, coming down from God out of heaven, prepared as a bride adorned for her husband. And I heard a great voice out of heaven saying, Behold, the tabernacle of God is with men, and he will dwell with them, and they shall be his people, and God himself shall be with them, and be their God. And God shall wipe away all tears from their eyes; and there shall be no more death, neither sorrow, nor crying, neither shall there be any more pain: for the former things are passed away." (Rev. 21:1-4.)

To complete our vision of the concept of holy cities, as the New Testament account records, there will also be a day, a celestial day, when this earth becomes a heaven in the full, complete, and eternal sense, when the celestial New Jerusalem shall be with men. It was John, also, who saw this "holy Jerusalem, descending out of heaven from God, Having the glory of God." This is the city having twelve gates and twelve foundations, "and in them the names of the twelve apostles of the Lamb." This is the city with streets of pure gold, "as it were transparent glass." Of it John says: "And I saw no temple therein: for the Lord God Almighty and the Lamb are the temple of it. And the city had no need of the sun, neither of the moon, to shine in it: for the glory of God did lighten it, and the Lamb is the light thereof. And the nations of them which are saved shall walk in the light of it: and the kings of the earth do bring their glory and honour into it. And the gates of it shall not be shut at all by day: for there shall be no night there. And they shall bring the glory and honour of the nations into it. And there shall in no wise enter into it any thing that defileth, neither whatsoever worketh abomination, or maketh a lie: but they which are written in the Lamb's book of life." (Rev. 21:10-27.)

NOTES

1. The Great King is the Lord—the Lord Jehovah, the Lord Jesus.
2. These word usages, which so closely parallel divine terminology where Zion itself is

concerned, are set forth in the article on Jerusalem in *The New Bible Dictionary*, p. 615.

3. The valley of Hinnom was the scene of some of the most horrifying and abominable practices ever to defile Israel. It was here that Solomon built places for the worship of Molech; it was here that infant sacrifices were sponsored by those wicked kings, Ahaz and Manasseh; it was here that Josiah spread human bones and other corruptions; it was here (in Jesus' day) that garbage, dead animals, and human corpses were burned. This valley was both the cesspool of Jerusalem and the place where continuing fires burned the refuse of the city, giving rise to the use of the term *Ge Hinnom* or *Gehenna,* or land of Hinnom, as the symbol for the eternal fires of hell.

4. This same name, Mount Zion—as it is associated with the New Jerusalem—is the place where the Lamb shall stand at his Second coming with 144,000 high priests; it is located in Jackson County, Missouri. (Rev. 14:1; D&C 133:17-25.)

5. The times of the Gentiles is that time or era, that expanse of time or years, during which the gospel goes to the Gentiles on a preferential basis. In Jesus' day the gospel was offered first to his Jewish kinsmen; only later was it preached in Gentile ears. In our day it has been restored to Gentiles, meaning to non-Jewish people—people, however, who are of the house of Israel. It now is being taught on a preferential basis to Gentiles or non-Jewish people, for, as Paul said, "blindness in part is happened to Israel, until the fulness of the Gentiles be come in." (Rom. 11:25.)

The restoration of the gospel foreshadows the end of the Gentile era and the ushering in of the Jewish era. Our revelations say that after the remnant of Jerusalem's Jews have been scattered in all nations, an event that has long since occurred, "they shall be gathered again." They are, however, to remain in their scattered state "until the times of the Gentiles be fulfilled. . . . And when the times of the Gentiles is come in, a light shall break forth among them that sit in darkness, and it shall be the fulness of my gospel. But they [the generality of the scattered Jews] receive it not; for they perceive not the light, and they turn their hearts from me because of the precepts of men. And in that generation shall the times of the Gentiles be fulfilled." (D&C 45:24-29.) That the Jews, a few of them, are now beginning to believe the restored gospel and are returning to their true Messiah is well known. The times of the Gentiles shall soon be fulfilled, and the times of the Jews once again shall come into being.

Chapter 7

JEHOVAH'S HOLY HOUSES

The Lord, whom ye seek, shall suddenly come to his temple. (Mal. 3:1.)[1]

The Law of Temple Worship

What is a temple? It is a house of the Lord; a house for Deity that is built on earth; a house prepared by the saints as a dwelling place for the Most High, in the most literal sense of the word; a house where a personal God personally comes. It is a holy sanctuary, set apart from the world, wherein the saints of God prepare to meet their Lord; where the pure in heart shall see God, according to the promises; where those teachings are given and those ordinances performed which prepare the saints for that eternal life which consists of dwelling with the Father and being like him and his Son. The teachings and ordinances here involved embrace the mysteries of the kingdom and are not now and never have been heralded to the world, nor can they be understood except by those who worship the Father in spirit and in truth, and who have attained that spiritual stature which enables men to know God and Jesus Christ, whom he hath sent.

When the Lord comes from heaven to the earth, as he

does more frequently than is supposed, where does he make his visitations? Those whom he visits know the answer; he comes to one of his houses. Whenever the Great Jehovah visits his people, he comes, suddenly as it were, to his temple. If he has occasion to come when he has no house on earth, his visit is made on a mountain, in a grove, in a wilderness area, or at some location apart from the tumults and contentions of carnal men; and in that event the place of his appearance becomes a temporary temple, a site used by him in place of the house his people would normally have prepared.

Why have temples? They are built by the tithing and sacrifice of the Lord's people; they are dedicated and given to him; they become his earthly houses; in them the mysteries of the kingdom are revealed; in them the pure in heart see God; in them men are sealed up unto eternal life—all to the end that man may become as his Maker, and live and reign forever in the heavenly Jerusalem, as part of the general assembly and Church of the Firstborn, where God and Christ are the judge of all. Of temples the Lord says: "Therein are the keys of the holy priesthood ordained, that you may receive honor and glory." In them, he says, his saints shall receive washings, anointings, baptisms, revelations, oracles, conversations, statutes, judgments, endowments, and sealings. In them are held solemn assemblies. In them the fulness of the priesthood is received and the patriarchal order conferred upon men. In them the family unit is made eternal. Because of them life eternal is available. With temples men can be exalted; without them there is no exaltation. (D&C 124:28-40; 131:1-4; 132:1-33.)

When and where have there been temples on earth? We know the answer to this question in principle, but we do not know the specific times and places. Our revelation on temples tells us that the blessings conferred through their use are essential to the "foundation of Zion," that is, to the setting up of congregations of saints who shall be pure in heart; that through their use, "glory, honor, and endowment" shall be conferred upon all the inhabitants of Zion; and that these blessings are to come only "by the ordinance of my holy house, which my people are *always* commanded to build unto my holy name." (D&C 124:39. Italics added.) That is to say, whenever the Lord has had a people on earth, from the days of Adam to the present moment, he has always commanded them to build temples so that they could be taught how to gain eternal life, and so that all of the ordinances of salvation and exaltation could be performed for and on their behalf.

Temples constructed before the flood of Noah were obviously destroyed in that great deluge; those built by the Jaredites and Nephites are buried in the jungles and lost in the wildernesses of the Americas; apostate versions of true temples are being uncovered by archeologists in many places, including perhaps the pyramids of Egypt and the Americas; but such slivers of truth about ancient temples as the world now has are found in the accounts relative to Israel's tabernacle and the subsequent houses of the Lord built in Jerusalem. It is of them we shall now speak more particularly.

Temples in Ancient Israel

One of the first things Israel did when freed from Egyptian bondage was to set up a tent or tabernacle as a house or place where Moses and Aaron and the elders of the people could commune with Jehovah. This tabernacle—in reality a portable temple—became more elaborate as rapidly as the seed of Jacob gained the means and had the time to perfect its construction. Detailed directions came to Moses by revelation as to the materials to be used, the ornamentation for its curtains and parts, and the manner and form of worship attending its use.

The tabernacle complex consisted of a large rectangular court in the western part of which stood a small building or tabernacle. In the eastern part of the court were an altar for the offering of sacrifices and a laver for priestly washings. All Israel had access to the court wherein these burnt offerings were made. The tabernacle proper was divided into two parts, the holy place and the most holy place, or Holy of Holies; and the Holy of Holies was separated from the holy place by the veil of the temple. A curtain or screen also hung at the entrance to the holy place. The tabernacle proper was made of delicate tapestries decorated with cherubim and spread on wooden frames covered with gold. In the holy place there was the altar of incense, the golden candlestick, and the table of shewbread. In the Holy of Holies was placed the ark of the covenant with its mercy seat and with the two golden-winged cherubim at the sides.

All that was part of, or placed in, or performed in the tabernacle was symbolical of Christ and his atoning sacrifice. The sacrifices on the great altar in the court were performed in similitude of the coming sacrifice of the Lamb of God, and each detailed step in their performance bore record in one way or another of something concerning the infinite sacrifice of Israel's Promised Messiah. Light from the seven candles on the golden candlestick shone forth as a reminder of him who is the Light of the world; clouds of odors rising from the altar of incense were as the prayers of the saints before the throne of God ("golden vials full of odours, which are the prayers of the saints," John says in Rev. 5:8); and the shewbread, the bread on display, the bread of the Presence, bore record that there in the temple was found the Presence of God. These loaves of bread, twelve in number, one for each of the tribes of Israel, spread out on "the table of the bread of the Presence," were both an acknowledgment that Jehovah gave life and nourishment to Israel and a witness that Israel was grateful for the goodness of their God to them.

But it was in the Holy of Holies that the most perfect symbolism was found. There was placed the ark of the covenant, a chest of acacia wood in which rested the stone tablets on which were written the Ten Commandments. The presence of these sacred stones, the commandments having been written by the finger of God, was a constant reminder to Israel of their covenant to worship and serve him who had delivered them from bondage, and that they should have no God before him. On top of the ark rested the mercy seat, a cover of pure gold, symbolizing to the mind that because of the atonement yet to be wrought, repentant souls would find mercy before the eternal throne. The mercy seat, serving as it were as the throne of God, was a symbol of his forgiveness and of his goodness and grace in providing mercy through his atonement. Once each year, on the Day of Atonement, the high priest entered the Holy of Holies, thus testifying anew to all the people that mercy might be theirs through the great propitiatory sacrifice that was to be. And the two cherubim—overshadowing the mercy seat with their wings—bore record that the ark itself was the very throne of God set up among his people and that Jehovah did in fact dwell in his house and was among them.

Once the tabernacle was prepared according to the divine plan; once this sacred sanctuary was set up as a house of the Lord; once a holy temple was again available in Israel—then Jehovah honored his word and used the sacred building and the holy place and the Holy of Holies as his own earthly house. To this place he came down to commune with Moses and give commandments to his people. When Moses, for instance, complained, saying, "I am not able to bear all this people alone, because it is too heavy for me," the Lord replied: "Gather unto me seventy men of the elders of Israel, whom thou knowest to be the elders of the people, and officers over them; and bring them unto the tabernacle of the congregation, that they may stand there with thee. And I will come down and talk with thee there: and I will take of the spirit which is upon thee, and will put it upon them; and they shall bear the burden of the people with thee, that thou bear it not thyself alone." As was his wont, Moses hearkened to the voice of his Lord. He "went out, and told the people the words of the Lord, and gathered the seventy men of the elders of the people, and set them round about the tabernacle. And the Lord came down in a cloud, and spake unto him, and took of the spirit that was upon him, and gave it unto the seventy elders: and it came to pass, that, when the spirit rested upon them, they prophesied, and did not cease." (Num. 11.)[2]

Truly, in that day, the Shekinah rested in the Holy of Holies, and God was with his people.

As far as we know, all temples in Israel from Moses to Solomon were of the portable-tabernacle type. But after David had secured and established the temporal kingdom, with all the power and prestige of an oriental court, he collected the materials so that his son Solomon could build a house to Jehovah. That house—Solomon's Temple—patterned after the tabernacle of the congregation and used for the same purposes, was one of the earth's then most magnificent and costly buildings. The courtyard contained the sacrificial altar, thirty feet square and fifteen feet high, and the molten sea, a bronze basin, fifteen feet in diameter and seven and a half feet in height, resting on the backs of twelve oxen, one for each tribe, as is the case also in all modern temples. That this sea was a baptismal font for the living is perfectly clear, even as its modern counterparts are fonts or seas wherein baptisms are performed for the dead.[3] The holy place and the Holy of Holies contained the same items that once were found in the same sacred places in the tabernacle, except that Solomon's Temple had ten golden candlesticks rather than the one in the Temple of Moses. The Urim and Thummim was kept in the Holy of Holies in Solomon's Temple, which may also have been the case in the older and less ornate building after which it was patterned. And, of course, the divine presence, the Shekinah, yet rested where it had of old, insomuch that "fire came down from heaven, and consumed the burnt offering and the sacrifices; and the glory of the Lord filled the house," and the Lord appeared to Solomon in a dream. (2 Chron. 7.)

Solomon's Temple was destroyed by the Babylonians

under Nebuchadnezzar, shortly after Lehi left Jerusalem. It was rebuilt some seventy years later by Zerubbabel and was dedicated in 516 B.C. However, there never again was that same rich and plenteous outpouring of Divine grace that once had set Israel apart from all peoples. Zerubbabel's Temple did not contain the ark of the covenant and the tablets of the Decalogue; the mercy seat was no more; and the cherubim no longer bore visible testimony that the throne of God was in the midst of his people. All these things had been lost; and the Urim and Thummim, the ultimate symbol of divine grace—for by it revelations came—had been taken away. The spirit of prophecy, the fire from heaven, the cloud surrounding the Divine Presence were seldom seen in those and later days.

Ordinances of the House of the Lord

We do not have a complete knowledge of what ordinances were performed in ancient temples, and if we did it would not be our privilege to delineate the doings of our brethren of old with any degree of particularity. Nor, for that matter, can we set forth the things that transpire in modern temples. Ordinances performed in the Lord's sanctuaries, though not secret, are of such a sacred nature as to be reserved for the eyes and ears and hearts of those only whose attained spiritual maturity prepares them to receive the mysteries of the kingdom. Temple ordinances, whether ancient or modern, are not published to the world; their sacred nature witnesses that they should not be bandied about by brutish persons; that which is spiritual and sacred must not be held up to mockery, or be made the object of raillery by carnal men.

We can, however, speak in general terms of what is done in temples; we can name the ordinances and tell their purpose and intent; and we can quote from the scriptures such passages as speak in guarded and reserved terms of those things which are reserved for the faithful only. And based on what has been revealed and is preserved to us and on what we know about the purpose and use of latter-day temples, we can reach some reasonable conclusions as to what was involved in their ancient usage.

We know that Mosaic temples were used for the offering of sacrifices and various related performances of the law of carnal commandments. It is clear that the molten sea was for baptisms and that the laver was for ritualistic washings. In commanding his saints of latter days to build him a house, the Lord asked: "How shall your washings be acceptable unto me, except ye perform them in a house which ye have built to my name?" Then he said: "For, for this cause [that Israel's washings might be acceptable] I commanded Moses that he should build a tabernacle, that they should bear it with them in the wilderness, and [for the same reason] to build a house in the land of promise." Then the Lord speaks of anointings, endowments, and other temple ordinances—all in a context that shows that what we now have is patterned after the rites and ceremonies of our ancestors. (D&C 124:37-41.)

Isaiah's call to ancient Israel—"Wash you, make you clean; put away the evil of your doings from before mine eyes; cease to do evil; Learn to do well"—was an invitation to partake of and implement the cleansing ordinances of the temple. (Isa. 1:16-17.) The Lord's promise to gathered Israel in the latter days—"Then will I sprinkle clean water upon you, and ye shall be clean: from all your filthiness, and from all your idols, will I cleanse you"—has reference to the same things as do the words of revelation that say: "Cleanse your hands and your feet before me, that I may make you clean; That I may testify unto your Father, and your God, and my God, that you are clean from the blood of this wicked generation." (Ezek. 36:25; D&C 88:74-75.)

Joseph Smith tells us that "all things" pertaining to our dispensation "should be conducted precisely in accordance with the preceding dispensations," and that the Lord "set the ordinances to be the same forever and ever." He says the same ordinances are revealed anew in one dispensation after another. (*Teachings,* p. 168.) We know that celestial marriage is the crowning ordinance of the house of the Lord today and assume it must have been so also in days gone by. For instance, "David's wives and concubines were given unto him of me, by the hand of Nathan, my servant, and others of the prophets who had the keys of this power," the Lord says. (D&C 132:39.) This same thing would have been true relative to the marriage discipline among all the faithful of Israel. We cannot, therefore, escape the conclusion that then, as now, temples were the places where those higher ordinances were performed which lead to glory and honor everlasting.

Herod's Temple

This is the temple Jesus knew. It is the one in which Gabriel and Zacharias conversed relative to him who should prepare the way before the Lord. It is the one in which Jesus was taken as an infant. Here at the age of twelve he confounded the wise men. From it he drove the moneychangers, and in its courts his voice was raised day after day as he acclaimed in word and by deed his own divine Sonship. It was of this house that he spoke when he said that not one stone should be left upon another. It was an integral part of his life and played a major role in his death. False witnesses swore he had said he would destroy the temple and raise it again in three days. It was the seat of the Great Sanhedrin that condemned him to death, and its veil, separating the holy place from the Holy of Holies, was the one rent from top to bottom when he voluntarily gave up the ghost and went to preach to the spirits in prison. And to it, after his demise, Peter and John resorted when they commanded the man, lame from his mother's womb, to rise up and walk; and when he found he could do so, he leaped for joy, praising God.

This temple—the last divinely approved sanctuary of the

Jewish dispensation—was refurbished by Herod the Great commencing in 20 B.C. It had been built in the days of Ezra, and was defiled and cleansed again in the days of the Maccabees, and was raised to new heights of grandeur. Its construction was still going forward when Jesus blessed its courts with his presence, and it was not completed in every respect until A.D. 64, just six years before its destruction. Built on a larger and grander scale than anything of the past, as far as the building itself was concerned, it yet never gained a fraction of the spiritual preeminence of its predecessors. The Shekinah—the visible manifestation of the presence of the Lord—never filled its Holy of Holies and the divine cloud never overshadowed its courts. Angels did minister before its altars, visions were seen by some of its priests, and the spirit of prophecy rested upon some who worshipped within its portals. But the great divine outpouring of grace and goodness and miracles that so filled the houses of Moses and Solomon, and to a lesser extent that of Zerubbabel, were absent. Jesus himself foretold its destruction, and his words were made a living reality by the flames and venom of Rome in A.D. 70—thus ending Jewish sacrifices and their form of temple worship forever.

Herod's Temple[4]—built by as evil and corrupt a tyrant as ever wore a crown—was an enlargement and a perfection of those houses of the Lord after which it was patterned. Solomon's Temple, though magnificent and costly, was small in comparison; and the Temple of Zerubbabel, larger but less elaborate than that of Solomon, was far from the magnificent masterpiece built by the Jewish Idumean who bore the title "king of the Jews." In its construction, which had gone on for forty-six years by the time of Jesus' ministry, a thousand vehicles transported the stone, a thousand priests supervised the work, and ten thousand skilled laborers wrought wonders with the costly materials. Built of marble and gold, the house of worship itself probably surpassed any of the architectural marvels of that or any day. Certainly Rome and Greece and Egypt had nothing to compare with it. And a Jewish proverb kept alive their tradition: "He that has not seen the Temple of Herod, has never known what beauty is."

To all of this there attaches a certain fitness of things as well as a touch of irony. This was the temple where the Son of God ministered—and what is more fitting than for temple building to reach its pinnacle in the day when his voice was heard within its walls? But this was also a temple built by an evil ruler—a Jew, yes, but an Idumean Jew, one who was half Idumean and half Samaritan, one whose lineage was impure, one who was apparently a descendant of Edom who is Esau—whose interest was not to serve Jehovah and see true rites performed, but to court popularity with the people and to satisfy an almost lustful desire to build monuments of splendor and renown. And yet, perhaps, there is even a certain fitness about this, for the very temple that he built in wickedness and that was turned into a den of thieves by those who used it was in its final destruction, when not one stone was left upon another, left to serve as a symbol of the destruction of all the evils of those who crucified their Lord.

Temples, of course, whether made by righteous or evil hands, do not of themselves establish the truth or falsity of the religious systems under which they flourish. The Parthenon—the chief temple of Athena on the Acropolis at Athens, where her gold and ivory statue sat anciently—was also one of the architectural marvels of the ages. But it was the very building of which Paul spoke, having reference to the pagan idol housed therein, when on Mars' Hill he said: "God that made the world and all things therein, seeing that he is Lord of heaven and earth, dwelleth not in temples made with hands; Neither is worshipped with men's hands, as though he needed any thing, seeing he giveth to all life, and breath, and all things." (Acts 17:22-31.) Temples as such do not prove the divinity of a system of religion, but without them there is no true order of worship. When built among those who have the priesthood and who enjoy the spirit of revelation, they are in fact the Lord's houses, and when such peoples are true and faithful—and such was not the case among the Jews of Jesus' day—the Divine Presence rests upon and the Person of the Lord is seen within these holy houses.

Herod's Temple was a true temple. It bore the stamp of divine approval, and true ordinances, performed by legal administrators who had been called of God as was Aaron, were performed in its courts, on its altars, and in the Holy of Holies itself. The priests who ministered in this house of the Lord held the Aaronic or Levitical Priesthood, and on occasional instances, as when Gabriel visited Zacharias, they saw within the veil. The problem of worship among the Jews was not the lack of a temple; it was not that they had departed from the true ordinances; it was not that baptism and sacrifices were unknown among them. They had the form and knew the manner in which they should worship. Their problem was one of substance: they had the form of godliness, but they denied the power thereof; they were wading through ritualistic performances whose true meanings they no longer comprehended. That faith, hope, charity, and love which prepares men for the acceptance of revealed truth no longer was found in sufficient measure to enable them to see in Jesus their true Messiah, in spite of the fact that all the ordinances of Herod's Temple bore record of this Man from Galilee.

But the temple itself, the foundations, walls, and courts, the altars, fires, and veils—all these were as they should be. The ark of the covenant with its mercy seat, the stone tablets whereon the Decalogue was written, the Urim and Thummim, and the cherubim overshadowing the throne of God, as it were—all these were absent. But so had they been in the divinely approved Temple of Zerubbabel. If there was a brazen sea, or its equivalent, for baptisms, we do not know it. Probably there was not, as witness the need for the son of Zacharias to baptize in Jordan near Bethabara. Yet the sacrificial ordinances could and did go forward, as properly they should have done; the holy incense still ascended to the

Lord; and the holy lights still shone forth from the candles in the holy place.

Drawings of the temple, based on recorded accounts and archeological unearthings, agree in general as to the arrangements of the walls, gates, porches, courts, and altars. However, all independent researchers have come up with differing views on many points, and all are faced with problems they cannot solve. No doubt this is as it should be, and there is no reason to suppose that the things of God—the washings, anointings, endowments, sealings, marriages, "conversations," and the like, which our revelations tell us were performed in the temples of old—shall ever be discovered by the wisdom of men.

According to the best data available, the wall surrounding the temple grounds—and the wall and everything therein, in the full sense of the word, is accounted to be the temple—was 5,085 feet long, just 195 feet short of a full mile. Some stones in these walls measured from 20 to 40 feet in length and weighed more than a hundred tons each. Within the nearly and approximately rectangular space so enclosed, scores and hundreds of thousands of worshippers at a time could easily and conveniently assemble. The number 210,000 is given as the attendance figure for those assembling to worship in the great court at one time. The four principal gates to the temple area were in the west wall, where the Tyropoeon Valley lies. There was also one gate on the north, and another on the east, where the Kidron Valley runs, and there were two on the south.

Just inside the four walls were porches, that is, cloisters or halls. Over this porch area was a flat roof, supported by three rows of Corinthian pillars, each pillar being cut from a single block of marble, and each being 37½ feet high. The Royal Porch on the south was supported by 160 pillars arranged in four rows of 40 pillars each. Solomon's Porch was on the east. In all of the porches it was the custom for the people to meet and have gospel discussions, and there may even have been benches or seats in them. In one of them the young Jesus, when but twelve years of age, was found by Joseph and Mary disputing with the doctors and wise men; in all of them our Lord taught his doctrine from time to time; and Solomon's Porch is singled out by name as the place, during the Feast of Dedication, where he affirmed in plainness the doctrine of the divine Sonship, saying, "I and my Father are one." (John 10:30.) It was in these sacred porches—cloisters or halls, if you will—where the early saints met, "continuing daily with one accord in the temple, . . . Praising God," and seeking to learn and do his will. (Acts 2:46-47.) The porches themselves, architecturally speaking, were among the finest features of the temple, and spiritually speaking, were the centers—for the true significance of the sacrificial ordinances was in large part lost—where most of the temple-truth came forth that was taught in Jesus' day.

Within the walls and their porches was the court of the Gentiles, an area, paved with marble, to which all people were welcome, both Jew and Gentile. Proper reverence and decorum were expected of all, and there were signs, in Greek and Latin, warning Gentiles not to enter the temple building itself on pain of death. It was in this public court that oxen, sheep, and doves were sold for sacrificial purposes, and from it our Lord, in anger, drove those who he said had turned his Father's house into a den of thieves.

As to the temple building proper, it contained the court of women with its chests for charitable contributions, in which place Jesus probably made his comments about the widow's mite. It contained the court of Israel and of the priests, in which stood the great altar of unhewn stones, which was 48 feet square at the bottom and 36 feet at the top, and which rose 15 feet in height. In the temple also was the holy place, containing the table of the shewbread, the golden candlestick, and the altar of incense. And finally, with a veil separating it from the holy place, in it stood the Holy of Holies, a sanctuary 30 feet square, a sanctuary now empty except for a large stone—occupying the place where the ark, the mercy seat, and the cherubim should have been—and on which stone the high priest sprinkled the blood each year on the Day of Atonement. In overall dimensions the temple proper, including the steps and a "porch" on each side, was 150 feet square. Its foundations rested on immense blocks of white marble covered with gold, each block being, according to Josephus, 67 ½ by 9 feet. The abbreviated recitations here given, though sufficient for our purposes, cannot begin to set forth the grandeur and magnificence and the architectural perfections of this holy house, a house that was truly one of the greatest buildings of any age and that also was truly a house of the Lord.

It is one thing to have a temple building of grandeur and architectural perfection, one built of all the costly materials that the wealth of kingdoms can produce, and quite another to have one in which the Spirit of God dwells in full measure. Though both may be houses of and for the Almighty, one far exceeds the other in eternal worth and glory as Edersheim so aptly says: "To the devout and earnest Jew the second Temple must, 'in comparison of' 'the house in her first glory,' have indeed appeared 'as nothing.' True, in architectural splendour the second, as restored by Herod, far surpassed the first Temple. But, unless faith had recognized in Jesus of Nazareth 'the Desire of all nations,' who should 'fill this house with glory,' it would have been difficult to draw other than sad comparisons. Confessedly, the real elements of Temple-glory no longer existed. The Holy of Holies was quite empty, the ark of the covenant, with the cherubim, the tables of the law, the book of the covenant, Aaron's rod that budded, and the pot of manna, were no longer in the sanctuary. The fire that had descended from heaven upon the altar was extinct. What was far more solemn, the visible presence of God in the Shechinah was wanting. Nor could the will of God be now ascertained through the Urim and Thummim, nor even the high-priest be anointed with the holy oil, its very composition being unknown." (*Temple*, pp. 61-62.) And thus is it ever when the Lord's people fail to walk faithfully in the light they have received. Though they continue to enjoy all their lessened spiritual capacity permits, that which once was theirs and which might still rest in power upon them is withheld.

For fifteen hundred years—while wandering in the wilderness near the borders of their promised land; while walking in the course set by their inspired judges; while wearing the yoke forged upon them by their despotic kings; while faced with Assyrian overlordship or led captive into Babylon; while freed from bondage and returned to Jerusalem's hills; while faced with the tyranny of Antiochus Epiphanes, or suffering through the era of the Maccabees; while plundered by Rome or ruled by Antipater, the Idumean, and all the Herods that sprang from him; and even while the very Son of God ministered among them—for all those long years the temple was the center of Jewish religion.

To the temple every devout person turned for spiritual refreshment, and from it streams of living water flowed. To it the hosts of Israel came to celebrate their great religious feasts. In its courts sacrifices were made, sins were forgiven, and souls were sanctified. Within its porches the truths of salvation were taught; and within its walls the faithful assembled to renew their covenants and offer their vows and sacraments to the Most High. On its altars legal administrators burned the offerings that were slain in similitude of the sacrifice of the Son of God. Behind its veil and in its Holy of Holies, once each year, the high priest made atonement for the sins of the people, and on occasion fire descended from heaven to consume the offerings on its altars, and the Divine Presence, the Shekinah, dwelt visibly between the cherubim. There is no way of overstating or overdramatizing the place and power of the temple in the lives of the Jewish people.

"Wherever a Roman, a Greek, or an Asiatic might wander, he could take his gods with him, or find rites kindred to his own. It was far otherwise with the Jew. He had only one Temple, that in Jerusalem; only one God, Him who had once throned there between the Cherubim, and Who was still King over Zion. That Temple was the only place where a God-appointed, pure priesthood could offer acceptable sacrifices, whether for forgiveness of sin, or for fellowship with God. Here, in the impenetrable gloom of the innermost sanctuary, which the High-Priest alone might enter once a year for most solemn expiation, had stood the Ark, the leader of the people into the Land of Promise, and the footstool on which the Shechinah had rested. From that golden altar rose the sweet cloud of incense, symbol of Israel's accepted prayers; that seven-branched candlestick shed its perpetual light, indicative of the brightness of God's Covenant Presence; on that table, as it were before the face of Jehovah, was laid, week by week, 'the Bread of the Face,' a constant sacrificial meal which Israel offered unto God, and wherewith God in turn fed His chosen priesthood. On the great blood-sprinkled altar of sacrifice smoked the daily and festive burnt-offerings, brought by all Israel, and for all Israel, wherever scattered; while the vast courts of the Temple were thronged not only by native Palestinians, but literally by 'Jews out of every nation under heaven.' Around this Temple gathered the sacred memories of the past; to it clung the yet brighter hopes of the future. The history of Israel and all their prospects were intertwined with their religion; so that it may be said that without their religion they had no history, and without their history no religion. Thus, history, patriotism, religion, and hope alike pointed to Jerusalem and the Temple as the centre of Israel's unity." (Edersheim 1:3-4.)

But all this was soon to end. True sacrificial ordinances could be performed only in similitude of the Eternal Sacrifice which was to be. When the Lamb of God—the Eternal Paschal Lamb—permitted himself to be sacrificed for the sins of the world, the need for sacrificial similitudes pointing to and pre-figuring his atoning sacrifice were no longer needed. And when the need for sacrifices ceased, the need for sacrificial altars and sacrificial sites ceased also. All the temples of all the ages up to then had been constructed as sanctuaries in which burnt offerings should be made. They were the true centers of worship for the ancient saints, but their purposes were now accomplished and their usefulness as sacrificial sanctuaries was at an end. The temples of the future, the houses of the Lord which were yet to be, the holy sanctuaries to which the saints of the future would turn, these would be constructed according to the needs of the new dispensation.

And so it was that Herod's Temple died—not in peace and serenity surrounded by children and loved ones; not with the calmness and assurance that attends the passing of the faithful; not with the hope of a better life that lives in the hearts of the saints—but Herod's Temple died in agony; died of internal corruption and pain; died with a sword at its throat and while ravaged by wild beasts; died with the burning conscience that foresees the sulfurous fires of gehenna; died in terror under the hand of Titus. And it was even denied a decent burial: in its expiring agonies its sanctuaries were looted, its gold and treasures became the booty of war, and, according to the promises, not one stone was left upon another. If a stele of stone had been placed on the once sacred ground—the ground where the struggle for life brought only death—it would have borne some such inscription as this: "Slain in A.D. 70—Along with 1,100,000 of the men of Israel, whose worship center it was—By Roman Gentiles—As befits a heavenly house that had been desecrated and turned into a den of thieves by those in whose custody it had been placed."

Jewish Temples of the Future

The Jewish Temple—named for hated Herod, an Idumean Jew, one of the most dissolute and evil rulers ever to work iniquity among the chosen people—was utterly destroyed, as well it should have been, in that day when

Jerusalem began to be trodden down of the Gentiles. But when the fulness of the Gentiles is come in, and the Jews once again believe in the true Messiah and worship the Father in his name, there will once again be a temple in Jerusalem—a temple named for their beloved Lord, Jesus of Nazareth, a Galilean Jew, the only perfect Man of all the chosen race.

Herod's Temple became dust because the Jewish nation, whose house of worship it was, rejected their Messiah and chose to walk in their own wayward course. A house of the Lord—the Lord Jesus Christ, the Messiah of the Jews—shall rise again in Jerusalem, perhaps on the very site where the ancient holy house stood, because the remnants of Judah shall accept their King, believe his gospel, and walk in his paths. A holy temple, the house of the Lord—a sacred sanctuary with its Holy of Holies where the Divine Presence, the Shekinah of old, shall once more be manifest to Israel—shall be built in Old Jerusalem. It shall be built by the Jews: Jews who believe in Christ; Jews who are converted to the truth; Jews who are members of The Church of Jesus Christ of Latter-day Saints; Jews who hold again the powers and priesthoods possessed by their ancestors. The keys and powers whereby temples are built vest in the President of the Church, the presiding high priest among the Lord's latter-day people. These keys, first conferred by angelic ministrants—Moses, Elijah, Elias, and others—upon Joseph Smith and Oliver Cowdery, have come down in direct succession and rest upon and are exercised by the prophet of God on earth, the one who, as it were, wears the mantle of Joseph Smith. And so it is that the Jews shall build their temple, and the Jews who do it will be Mormons; they will be Jews who are the converted and baptized saints of the latter days.

In a discourse on the Second Coming of Christ, given April 6, 1843, the Prophet Joseph Smith said: "Judah must return, Jerusalem must be rebuilt, and the temple, and water come out from under the temple, and the waters of the Dead

Sea be healed. It will take some time to rebuild the walls of the city and the temple, &c.; and all this must be done before the Son of Man will make His appearance." (*Teachings,* p. 286.) In a revelation to Joseph Smith, given November 3, 1831, the Lord said: "Let them . . . who are among the Gentiles flee unto Zion," which was then being established in America. "And let them who be of Judah flee unto Jerusalem, unto the mountains of the Lord's house." (D&C 133:12-13.) That is to say, let the Jews gather in their own Jerusalem, a city built upon four hills or mountains, a city in whose mountains they shall build the house of the Lord in due course.[5]

These modern prophetic words, about the return of Judah and the building of a temple in Jerusalem, make allusion to other ancient prophetic words that set forth with great clarity that the Jews shall yet build such a house in Old Jerusalem. We shall now note what three of the prophets of Judah—Malachi, Zechariah, and Ezekiel—have said in this respect.

Malachi, in speaking of the Second Coming of the Messiah, asks: "Who may abide the day of his coming? and who shall stand when he appeareth?" Of that glorious day this ancient prophet then says of the Lord: "He shall sit as a refiner and purifier of silver: and he shall purify the sons of Levi, and purge them as gold and silver, that they may offer unto the Lord an offering in righteousness. Then shall the offering of Judah and Jerusalem be pleasant unto the Lord, as in the days of old, and as in former years." (Mal. 3:1-6.) Shall the sons of Levi, those ancient Levitical ministers, offer sacrifices again, at the Second Coming, "as in the days of old, and as in former years"? We shall speak more particularly of this in the next chapter as we analyze the Mosaic system of sacrifices that was to operate in the day of Jesus. For our present purposes we need only observe that when John the Baptist conferred the Aaronic Priesthood again upon mortals, he alluded to these very words of Malachi by saying that this newly restored Aaronic order "shall never be taken again from the earth, until the sons of Levi do offer again an offering unto the Lord in righteousness." (D&C 13:1.)

Zechariah, also speaking of our Lord's return in power and great glory—"the Lord my God shall come, and all the saints with thee"—said: "And it shall be in that day, that living waters shall go out from Jerusalem; half of them toward the former [eastern] sea, and half of them toward the hinder [western] sea: in summer and in winter shall it be. And the Lord shall be king over all the earth: in that day shall there be one Lord, and his name one." This is the millennial day when the Lord reigns personally upon the earth, and when, as the Prophet said, "water" shall "come out from under the temple." Zechariah continues: "And it shall come to pass, that every one that is left of all the nations which came against Jerusalem [most of the people will have been destroyed in the wars and desolations incident to the Second Coming] shall even go up from year to year to worship the King, the Lord of hosts, and to keep the feast of tabernacles," which feast, anciently, was centered in and around the temple and its ceremonies. Also, Zechariah says—and here we have mention both of the temple and of sacrifices— "In that day shall there be upon the bells of the horses, HOLINESS UNTO THE LORD; and the pots in the Lord's house [the temple] shall be like the bowls before the altar. Yea, every pot in Jerusalem and in Judah [he is speaking of Old Jerusalem and the land of Judah, not the American New Jerusalem] shall be holiness unto the Lord of hosts: and all they that sacrifice [are not these the sons of Levi?] shall come and take of them, and seethe therein: and in that day there shall be no more the Canaanite in the house of the Lord of hosts." (Zech. 14.) With reference to this last restriction as to who may enter the house of the Lord, it should be remembered that anciently anyone was free to enter the court of the Gentiles, a permission that will be revoked in that millennial day when all are converted to the truth.

Ezekiel has much more to say about Judah's latter-day

house than either of his fellow prophets, or perhaps than all of Israel's other prophets combined. Twelve of the forty-eight chapters in the book of Ezekiel deal with the general subject here involved. In chapter 37 is the glorious vision of the resurrection in which Israel's dry bones come out of their graves; breath enters each person; sinews and flesh and skin take on a newness of life; the whole house of Israel lives again; they arise, stand upon their feet, and march as a very great army; and then—in resurrected glory—they inherit the land promised to Abraham and his seed forever. Associated with this is the coming forth of the Stick of Joseph—the Book of Mormon—in the hands of latter-day Ephraim, to join with the Stick of Judah—the Bible—the two volumes of holy scripture being destined to take the message of salvation to all Israel.

Then, as Ezekiel records, the Lord says: "Behold, I will take the children of Israel from among the heathen, whither they be gone, and will gather them on every side, and bring them into their own land." They shall return to their ancient Palestine, the very land where the feet of their fathers were planted.

"And I will make them one nation in the land upon the mountains of Israel; and one king shall be king to them all: and they shall be no more two nations, neither shall they be divided into two kingdoms any more at all." Rehoboam shall not reign in Judah and Jeroboam in Ephraim. They shall have one King, the Lord of hosts, who reigns personally upon the earth; the day of the divided kingdom, of two nations of the chosen people, shall cease. Israel shall be one.

"Neither shall they defile themselves any more with their idols, nor with their detestable things, nor with any of their transgressions: but I will save them out of all their dwellingplaces, wherein they have sinned, and will cleanse them: so shall they be my people, and I will be their God." At long last, after worshipping false gods, the gods of the creeds; after following the evil and detestable practices of carnal men; after being in an apostate and degenerate state for centuries—their ancient Lord will save them. They will be cleansed by baptism; once again they will be the Lord's people, and he will be their God.

"And David my servant shall be king over them; and they all shall have one shepherd: they shall also walk in my judgments, and observe my statutes, and do them. And they shall dwell in the land that I have given unto Jacob my servant, wherein your fathers have dwelt; and they shall dwell therein, even they, and their children, and their children's children for ever: and my servant David shall be their prince for ever." What shall happen to Israel, both Judah and Ephraim? They shall be one nation and have one King, even David, who is Christ, and he shall reign over them forever. He is the one Lord and the one Shepherd over all the earth. They shall walk in his statues and in his judgments; they shall keep his commandments and live his gospel precepts. And where shall they dwell? In the land given unto Jacob, old Canaan, the Jewish Palestine, the Holy Land where also our Lord lived during mortality. And how long shall they abide there? They and their children, and their children's children, shall dwell there forever. The meek shall inherit the earth. This is not to say that there are not other lands of promise, and that the American land of Joseph shall not become the inheritance of Nephites and that portion of latter-day Israel, in the main, which is now in the restored kingdom; but it is to say that the Israel of Ezekiel's day, which was Jewish, shall dwell in the land of old Jerusalem, where their temple will be built.

"Moreover I will make a covenant of peace with them; it shall be an everlasting covenant with them: and I will place them, and multiply them, and will set my sanctuary in the midst of them for evermore. My tabernacle also shall be with them: yea, I will be their God, and they shall be my people. And the heathen shall know that I the Lord do sanctify Israel, when my sanctuary shall be in the midst of them for evermore." The covenant of peace, the everlasting covenant, is the gospel—the gospel of the Lord Jesus Christ, the gospel restored through Joseph Smith and his associates. It contains that plan of salvation which requires the building of temples so that all the ordinances of salvation and exaltation may be performed for the living and the dead. In the very nature of things the Lord's sanctuary, his temple, will stand in the midst of his congregations; otherwise they would not be his people. We have, then, an express prophecy of the building of the Lord's sanctuary, not alone in Jackson County where the New Jerusalem will be built, but in Old Jerusalem, in the land of Judah, among and for the people who descended from those who worshipped there in Solomon's Temple, in Zerubbabel's Temple, and in Herod's Temple.

Having laid this foundation relative to the conversion and glory of latter-day Israel, with particular emphasis upon the Jewish portion of that people, Ezekiel, in chapters 38 and 39, tells of the wars and desolations incident to the Second Coming. Then in chapters 40 through 48 he devotes himself to the details, and they are most specific, of what has come to be called Ezekiel's Temple. Worldly scholars, not knowing the purposes of the Lord where his people are concerned; not understanding the doctrine of the gathering of Israel in the last days; not being aware that the gospel was to be restored in the latter days; not knowing that temples are essential to the salvation of men no matter what age they live in—worldly scholars have assumed that Ezekiel's Temple was not and will not be built. The truth is that its construction lies ahead. No doubt some of the recitations relative to it are figurative, though it is clear that some sacrificial ordinances are yet to be performed.

It is clear that Ezekiel's Temple, to be built by the Jews in Jerusalem, is destined for millennial use. In chapter 43, for instance, the Lord calls it, specifically, "the place of my throne, and the place of the soles of my feet, where I will dwell in the midst of the children of Israel for ever." That is to say, it will be the place of his throne during the Millennium when he dwells among the house of Israel, and it was the place where the soles of his feet trod when he dwelt on earth as a mortal. In this same chapter he says his house shall be built "upon the top of the mountain." In chapter 47 we find the statements to which the Prophet alluded when he said the water would "come out from under the temple, and the waters of the Dead Sea be healed." Ezekiel's language is: "Waters issued out from under the threshold of the house eastward. . . . These waters issue out toward the east country, and go down into the desert, and go into the sea: which being brought forth into the sea, the waters shall be healed." Ezekiel's concluding expression, relative to Old Jerusalem where the temple shall stand, is: "And the name of the city from that day shall be, The Lord is there."

NOTES

1. When the Lord comes—be it in time's meridian, at his Second Coming, or whensoever—he always comes to his temple, for temples are his dwelling places on earth. Accordingly, Malachi's Messianic utterance, though part of a recitation of what is to be in latter days, when only those who are prepared shall "abide the day of his coming," has application also, in principle, to his mortal ministry. The Lord Jehovah came to his temple in Jerusalem; came to cleanse and purify it, at least to the extent of casting out the money-changers and evil men who were making merchandise therein; even as he shall come to cleanse the earth and destroy the wicked when he comes again to his temple to usher in the millennial era.

2. The episode here recited is, of course, the calling of the Seventy, and their responsibility, then as now, was "to act in the name of the Lord," under proper direction, "in building up the church and regulating all the affairs of the same." (D&C 107:34.)

3. There was no baptism for the dead until after the visit of the slain Messiah to the spirits in prison and his proclamation of liberty to the captives there imprisoned. Baptism for the living, as is becoming increasingly clear even in apostate Christendom, has prevailed among mortals in all ages, including those which antedated the ministry of John the Baptist.

4. The part played by Herod's Temple in the social, cultural, and religious life of the Jews of Jerusalem, those of Palestine, and those scattered abroad is seen in these words of Edersheim: "The Temple itself," he says, "which, from a small building, little larger than an ordinary church, in the time of Solomon, had become that great and glorious House which excited the admiration of the foreigner, and kindled the enthusiasm of every son of Israel. At the time of Christ it had been already forty-six years in building, and workmen were still, and for a long time, engaged on it. But what a heterogeneous crowd thronged its porches and courts! Hellenists; scattered wanderers from the most distant parts of the earth—east, west, north, and south; Galileans, quick of temper and uncouth of Jewish speech; Judeans and Jerusalemites; white-robed Priests and Levites; Temple officials; broad-phylacteried, wide-fringed Pharisees, and courtly, ironical Sadducees; and, in the outer court, curious Gentiles! Some had come to worship; others to pay vows, or bring offerings, or to seek purification; some to meet friends, and discourse on religious subjects in those colonnaded porches, which ran round the Sanctuary; or else to have their questions answered, or their causes heard and decided, by the smaller Sanhedrin of twenty-

three, that sat in the entering of the gate or by the Great Sanhedrin. The latter no longer occupied the Hall of Hewn Stones, Gazith, but met in some chamber attached to those 'shops' or booths, on the Temple Mount, which belonged to the High-Priestly family of Ananias, and where such profitable trade was driven by those who, in their cupidity and covetousness, were worthy successors of the sons of Eli. In the Court of the Gentiles (or in its porches) sat the official money-changers, who for a fixed discount changed all foreign coins into those of the Sanctuary. Here also was that great mart for sacrificial animals, and all that was requisite for offerings. How the simple, earnest country people, who came to pay vows, or bring offerings for purifying, must have wondered, and felt oppressed in that atmosphere of strangely blended religious rigorism and utter worldliness; and how they must have been taxed, imposed upon, and treated with utmost curtness, nay, rudeness, by those who laughed at their boorishness, and despised them as cursed, ignorant country people, little better than heathens, or, for that matter, than brute beasts. Here also there lay about a crowd of noisy beggars, unsightly from disease, and clamorous for help. And close by passed the luxurious scion of the High-Priestly families; the proud, intensely self-conscious Teacher of the Law, respectfully followed by his disciples; and the quick-witted, subtle Scribe. These were men who, on Sabbaths and feast-days, would come out on the Temple-terrace to teach the people, or condescend to answer their questions; who in the Synagogues would hold their puzzled hearers spell-bound by their traditional lore and subtle argumentation, or tickle the fancy of the entranced multitude, that thronged every available space, by their ingenious frivolities, their marvellous legends, or their clever sayings; but who would, if occasion required, quell an opponent by well-poised questions, or crush him beneath the sheer weight of authority. Yet others were there who, despite the utterly lowering influence which the frivolities of the prevalent religion, and the elaborate trifling of its endless observances, must have exercised on the moral and religious feelings of all—perhaps, because of them—turned aside, and looked back with loving gaze to the spiritual promises of the past, and forward with longing expectancy to the near 'consolation of Israel,' waiting for it in prayerful fellowship, and with bright, heaven-granted gleams of its dawning lift amidst the encircling gloom." (Edersheim 1:114-15.)

5. There will also be, of course, a latter-day temple in the New Jerusalem on the American continent. (D&C 84:1-5.)

MOSAIC SACRIFICES IN JESUS' DAY

Why dost thou offer sacrifices unto the Lord? (Moses 5:6.)

Gospel Sacrifices—Past and Future

All things bear record of Christ—things which are in heaven above, and in the earth beneath, and in the waters under the earth—all bear record of the Lord; of his creative power; of his redeeming grace; of his goodness and mercy unto us. From the dead dust of the deserts to the living light of the heavenly luminaries; from the amoeba in its primordial ooze to the sons of God who reign in immortal glory; from the lowest to the highest, and from the least unto the greatest—things, both animate and inanimate, bear record of Him whose we are and by whom we have life and breath and all things.

All gospel ordinances, all the religious rites revealed from heaven, all of the performances and formalisms of the law of Moses—all bear witness of Christ, all are ordained in such a way, all are performed in such a manner as to symbolize something about him and his ministry. And those ordinances and performances which teach the truths relative to his infinite and eternal atonement are the most important and perfect of them all. The three ordinances that excel in this respect are baptism, the sacrament, and sacrifice, with the sacrificial rites setting forth the best similitudes of the three.

Baptisms, in all ages, are performed by immersion in water in similitude of the death, burial, and resurrection of Christ. When baptized persons are buried with Christ in baptism, they die as to the carnal things of this world. When they come forth from their watery grave, it is with a newness of life; they are, as it were, "resurrected" to a continuing mortal life of righteousness. The elements of water, blood, and spirit, which were present in the atonement, are also the elements that are present in every baptism. Thus, every baptismal ordinance centers attention in the atonement, in the very atonement by virtue of which the ordinance of baptism gains efficacy, virtue, and force.

The sacramental emblems, the bread and wine or water, are administered by Aaronic authority in similitude of and in remembrance of the broken flesh and spilt blood of our Redeemer. By this sacred ordinance the saints of God renew the covenant previously made in the waters of baptism; by it they covenant anew to keep the commandments and are promised, in return, the companionship of the Holy Spirit in this life and eternal life in the realms ahead. And, similarly, when proper sacrifices were made—and throughout Israelite history these were also performed by Aaronic authority and were in similitude of the atoning sacrifice of the Son—they also were occasions for renewing the covenant of salvation that had been made in the waters of baptism. Sacrifices before the coming of the Messiah and the sacramental ordinance thereafter each served the same purpose in the great and eternal scheme of things.

Sacrifices were first performed as gospel ordinances. They antedated Moses and his law; they were administered by Melchizedek authority; and Adam was the first legal administrator to use the similitudes involved. He and Eve were commanded by the Lord "that they should worship the Lord their God, and should offer the firstlings of their flocks, for an offering unto the Lord." Manifestly this commandment contained the divine instructions as to how and in what manner the newly revealed ordinances should be performed; and when Adam, acting pursuant to revelation, conformed to the divine will, an angel descended and asked: "Why dost thou offer sacrifices unto the Lord?" Adam replied: "I know not, save the Lord commanded me." Thereupon the angel revealed the great underlying principle that pertains to all true sacrificial ordinances: "This thing is a similitude of the sacrifice of the Only Begotten of the Father, which is full of grace and truth. Wherefore, thou shalt do all that thou doest in the name of the Son, and thou shalt repent and call upon God in the name of the Son forevermore." (Moses 5:5-8.)

From that Adamic day until our Lord shed his own blood in sacrifice for the sins of the world, the sacrificial system remained in force among his people. Whenever and wherever there were legal administrators who had the truth, sacrifices were offered that prefigured the coming sacrifice of the Lamb of God. So fundamental and basic were these ordinances to the true system of worship, and so ingrained were they in every devout person, that they continued among apostate groups. Even though men changed the ordinances and broke the everlasting covenant, most of them still retained sacrifices and burnt offerings in one form or another. Not knowing that the true sacrificial system was first revealed to the first man; not knowing that it continued without variation among faithful people; and not knowing that it was then imitated in one perverted form or another among apostate peoples, it has been assumed, falsely, that it is a performance that each evolving nation has developed for itself. Edersheim, interestingly, is not far from the truth when he sets forth the view that sacrificial performances came by instinct to Adam's seed. "We might argue from their universality," he says, "that, along with the acknowledgment of a Divine power, the dim remembrance of a happy past, and the hope of a happier future, sacrifices belonged to the primeval traditions which mankind inherited from Paradise. To sacrifice seems as 'natural' to man as to pray; the one indicates what he feels about himself, the other what he feels about God. The one means a felt need of propitiation; the other a felt sense of dependence." (*Temple,* pp. 106-7.)

But the fact is that sacrificial offerings were revealed gospel ordinances. For over twenty-five hundred years, from Adam to Moses, all those who had the gospel also offered sacrifices. When the Mosaic law was added to the gospel system, then for nearly fifteen hundred years these ordinances—changed, expanded upon, and set forth in meticulous detail—were performed as part of the Mosaic system.

When the Lamb of God, in Gethsemane and at Golgotha, worked out the infinite and eternal atonement and permitted himself to be slain for the sins of the world, it was intended that the sacrificial ordinances prefiguring that most transcendent of all events should cease. No one has set forth why this was destined to be with the clarity and plainness found in the words of the prophet Amulek. "According to the great plan of the Eternal God," he said, "there must be an atonement made, or else all mankind must unavoidably perish. . . . It is expedient that there should be a great and last sacrifice; yea, not a sacrifice of man, neither of beast, neither of any manner of fowl; for it shall not be a human sacrifice; but it must be an infinite and eternal sacrifice. . . . and then shall there be, or it is expedient there should be, a stop to the shedding of blood; then shall the law of Moses be fulfilled; yea, it shall be all fulfilled, every jot and tittle, and none shall have passed away. And behold, this is the whole meaning of the law, every whit pointing to that great and last sacrifice; and that great and last sacrifice will be the Son of God, yea, infinite and eternal." (Alma 34:9-14.)

Appearing in resurrected glory to his Nephite kinsmen, our Lord affirmed the end of the old order and announced the beginning of the new one. "By me redemption cometh," he said, "and in me is the law of Moses fulfilled. . . . And ye shall offer up unto me no more the shedding of blood." It is the Lord Jesus who is the Lord Jehovah who is speaking, which means that the sacrifices of old were offered to Christ. "Yea, your sacrifices and your burnt offerings shall be done away, for I will accept none of your sacrifices and your burnt offerings. And ye shall offer for a sacrifice unto me a broken heart and a contrite spirit." (3 Ne. 9:17-20.)

It was during this American ministry that our Lord instituted in the New World, as he had done in Jerusalem and the Old World, the sacramental ordinance in which broken bread was eaten in remembrance of his body, and wine was drunk in remembrance of his blood. From that blessed day onward the sacrament replaced sacrifices except that as part of the restitution of all things—and then on a limited basis only—blood sacrifices will be offered again. It was of these future sacrificial ordinances that Malachi prophesied, in a setting descriptive of the Second Coming of the Son of Man, that the returning Lord would "purify the sons of Levi, . . . that they may offer unto the Lord an offering in righteousness." Of this offering, to be made in "Judah and Jerusalem," the prophecy says it shall be "pleasant unto the Lord, as in the days of old, and as in former years." (Mal. 3:1-5.) It was to these sacrifices that Ezekiel alluded when he set forth the nature and use of the temple yet to be built in Jerusalem. And so that they might be performed by Levites who once again were legal administrators, John the Baptist, a Levite whose right it was to offer sacrifices anciently, and who was in fact the last Levitical priest to hold the keys of the ministry, brought back the ancient order of Aaron, saying to Joseph Smith and Oliver Cowdery, as he did so, that "this shall never be taken again from the earth, until the sons of Levi do offer again an offering unto the Lord in righteousness." (D&C 13.)[1]

The Sacrifices in Herod's Temple

In this our day—which we, in our self-conceived conceit, are pleased to designate as an age of enlightenment and intellectual achievement—we look with some revulsion upon religious rites that call for the slaying of lambs and fowl and the sprinkling of their blood in a particular and specified way. In our modern sophistication we suppose we have risen above the seeming barbarism of those sacrificial ordinances which called for the slaying of oxen and sheep and red heifers; which called for a scapegoat to carry the sins of the people into a wilderness area; and which imposed the stench and dung and filth of dying beasts upon those who sought to commune with Deity in holy places. We are pleased to replace the daily sacrifices with the weekly sacramental ordinances; to partake of the emblems of his broken flesh and spilt blood rather than to burn the firstlings of our flocks upon altars of stone; to renew the covenant made in the waters of baptism by partaking of bread and water in the quiet of a chapel rather than by burning the flesh of animals amid the death noises and bleating that accompanied sacrificial ordinances.

But whatever our oversophisticated sensitivities lead us to assume, the facts remain that sacrifices were instituted by the mild and merciful Jesus; that they were set forth, in a manner and in a form, to bear witness of his atoning sacrifice; that they were as essential to the salvation of men anciently as the sacrament is to ours today; and that they were performed with divine authority, by legal administrators, for the whole of that four thousand years which extended from the day the first man was cast out of his garden home to the day when our Lord's forerunner baptized in Jordan near Bethabara. In contrast there have been only two or three hundred years during which legal administrators, empowered from on high, have performed sacramental ordinances that were in fact binding on earth and sealed in the heavens.

Unless we have more than a superficial knowledge of what was involved in the sacrificial ordinances; unless we know why and how the Lord dealt with his people through this type of formalism; unless we catch the vision of the similitudes of sacrifice—and in many respects they are better than those found in the sacrament—we can never understand the life and ministry of the Man Jesus as fully as we should. And we are now speaking not just of a dim and general awareness that sacrifices are performed in similitude of the sacrifice of the Son of God, who is full of grace and truth, but of an awareness of enough of the details and rituals to envision how and in what manner they bore testimony of him whose life we study.

We need not extract from the writings of Moses, the man of God, all that is set forth relative to sacrificial performances. Volumes might be written in exposition of what the ancient lawgiver recorded, to say nothing of the manner in which his counsel was followed or perverted, as the case may be, both in Israel and among those who knew not the Mosaic system. We shall, rather, turn to the sacrificial offerings that the Jews made on the great altar in the holy temple in Jerusalem at the time of Jesus. These are the ordinances Jesus learned as he grew up in his Jewish home. They are the ones that should have introduced his Jewish brethren to their Lord and King. Unfortunately for most of his brethren, however, they had lost the true and correct understanding of the sacred rites. Though they performed by rote and to the best of their ability what had come down to them from their fathers; though they were strict and vigilant in conforming to the divine will as they understood it—and the ordinances themselves were virtually identical with those of former days—the unfortunate reality was that they had only the form and not the substance. They had a form of godliness, but were far removed from the eternal power that should have been present; the true meaning and intent of the rites did not register in their sin-filled hearts.

There are, of course, many commentaries, plus shelves of dry tomes, that deal with the sacrificial systems of old. We shall limit our quotations, however, to one author, Alfred Edersheim, a sectarian of faith and understanding who wrote a century ago and who had the sense and insight to recognize Jesus as the Messiah and to seek to extol him for what he in fact was, God's own Son. In his scholarly work *The Temple—Its Ministry and Services as They Were at the Time of Christ,* he exhibits a remarkably sound view of the principles and doctrines underlying the law of sacrifice, a view that is especially commendable since he did not have the Book of Mormon and latter-day revelation to keep him on the true course. As to the procedures and intricate mechanics of the ritualistic performances themselves, they can be deciphered by any competent scholar who will dredge his way through the surprisingly voluminous Jewish source material.

We shall now speak, in an abbreviated and digested way, of both the doctrine and the performances; of the law of sacrifice itself and the sacrificial rites based thereon; of the principles that are eternal and of the procedures that change with the variant circumstances. As to the procedures, those mentioned are the ones operative in Herod's Temple in Jesus' day. With deliberate intent we shall not record a hundredth—nay, not a thousandth—part of the unbelievably complex rituals and formalisms.

First we will note the order and meaning of those Mosaic rites that are sacrificial in nature. One basic principle is set out in these words: "The sacrifices of the Old Testament were *symbolical* and *typical.* An outward observance without any real inward meaning is only a ceremony. But a rite which has a present spiritual meaning is a *symbol;* and if, besides, it also points to a future reality, conveying at the same time, by anticipation, the blessing that is yet to appear, it is a *type.* Thus the Old Testament sacrifices were not only symbols, nor yet merely predictions by fact (as prophecy is a prediction by words), but they already conveyed to the believing Israelite the blessing that was to flow from the future reality to which they pointed." (*Temple*, p. 106. Italiacs added.) That is to say, believing Israel then knew, and believing Israel of old had always known, that in the symbolical and typical ordinances performed by their authorized priests there was immediate forgiveness, mediation, and that at-one-ment with God which is part of atonement.

Another basic concept is given thus: "The fundamental idea of sacrifice in the Old Testament is that of substitution, which again seems to imply everything else—atonement and redemption, vicarious punishment and forgiveness." (*Temple,* p. 107.) Sacrificial ordinances were performed by "a mediatorial priesthood," a conclusion that accords with the revealed word to Joseph Smith that Moses "was ordained by the hand of angels to be a mediator of this first covenant, (the law.)" (JST, Gal. 3:19-20.) "All this was *symbolical* (of man's need, God's mercy, and his covenant), and *typical,* till He should come to whom it all pointed, and who had all along given reality to it; He whose Priesthood was perfect, and who on a perfect altar brought a perfect sacrifice, once for all—a perfect Substitute, and a perfect Mediator." (*Temple,* p. 108.)

One other basic concept must be set forth. When Israel became the Lord's people, it was by covenant. The Lord revealed his mind and his will to Moses. "And Moses came and told the people all the words of the Lord, and all the judgments: and all the people answered with one voice, and said, All the words which the Lord hath said will we do." Then Moses wrote all the words in a book, built an altar and offered sacrifices, took the blood of the oxen, and sprinkled half of it on the altar and half on the people. Then he said: "Behold the blood of the covenant, which the Lord hath made with you concerning all these words." (Ex. 24.) Israel was thus in fellowship with their God; they had attained at-one-ment. The sacrificial system then became the arrangement whereby this covenant could be renewed and the chosen people could reinstate themselves in grace whenever they fell therefrom. "On the ground of this covenant-sacrifice all others rested. These were, then, either sacrifices of communion with God, or else intended to restore that communion when it had been disturbed or dimmed through sin and trespass: sacrifices *in* communion, or *for* communion with God. To the former class belong the burnt- and the peace-offerings; to the latter, the sin- and trespass-offerings." (*Temple,* p. 108.)

Sacrifices were of two kinds—bloody and unbloody, the latter group including meat and drink offerings, the first sheaf at the Passover, the two loaves at Pentecost, and the shewbread. Bloody sacrifices were made with oxen, sheep, goats, turtledoves, and young pigeons. There were eleven occasions for public sacrifices and five for private sacrifices;[2] some were said to be most holy, others less holy. Always they were made with something that belonged to the offerer. All animal sacrifices were to be free of blemishes, and salt was always added as a symbol of incorruption. The sacrificial animals were always slain by the priests, and "the death of the sacrifice was only a means towards an end, that end being the shedding and sprinkling of the blood, by which the atonement was really made."

When men offered private sacrifices the formalities included, in most instances, the laying on of hands on the animal while sins were confessed and a prayer offered. Words of the prayer were to this effect: "I entreat, O Jehovah: I have sinned, I have done perversely, I have rebelled, I have committed (naming the sin, trespass, or, in the case of a burnt-offering, the breach of positive or negative command); but I return in repentance, and let this be for my atonement." (*Temples,* pp. 109-15.)

Did the Jewish worshippers in the day of Jesus know that their sacrificial ordinances were part of an atoning process? That the blood of animals was being shed so they could gain forgiveness of sins? That the animal or fowl—slain for the sins of men, as it were—was but a substitute, a symbol, a type of him who should bear the sins of all men? The answers are in the affirmative. Contrary to what is found in some sweeping and superficial pronouncements, the fact is that they did know and they did understand; at least the knowledge was had by many of them, for Jewry, as is the case with Christendom, was fragmented and there were many divergent views on all basic doctrines. However, the Messianic problem in Jesus' day was one of the Person to whom the similitudes pointed rather than the fact of their so doing. As to the fact that the principles themselves were known and understood by the spiritually literate among them, there are many quotations from rabbinical and related sources that say such things as:

"The soul of every creature is bound up in its blood; therefore I gave it to atone for the soul of man—that one soul should come and atone for the other."

"One soul is substitute for the other."

"I gave the soul for you on the altar, that the soul of the animal should be an atonement for the soul of the man."

"The offerer, as it were, puts away his sins from himself, and transfers them upon the living animal."

"As often as any one sins with his soul, whether from haste or malice, he puts away his sin from himself, and places it upon the head of his sacrifice, and it is an atonement for him."

"After the prayer of confession (connected with the imposition of hands) the sins of the children of Israel lay on the sacrifice (of the Day of Atonement)."

"Properly speaking, the blood of the sinner should have been shed, and his body burned, as those of the sacrifices. But the Holy One—blessed be He!—accepted our sacrifice from us as redemption and atonement. Behold the full grace which Jehovah—blessed be He!—has shown to man! In His compassion and in the fulness of His grace He accepted the soul of the animal instead of his soul, that through it there might be an atonement."

"He that brought a sacrifice [was] required to come to the knowledge that that sacrifice was his redemption." (*Temple,* pp. 119-20.)

Having set forth the doctrine that sacrifices were offered—(1) as a means of maintaining communion with Deity; as a renewed seal of man's acceptance of the covenant God made with Moses; as a reaffirmation on the part of the Lord's people that they would keep his statutes and judgments (and burnt offerings and peace offerings were for these purposes); and (2) that they were "intended to restore that communion when it had been dimmed or disturbed"; that through them an atonement was made for sin; that they were the recurring means of receiving freedom from the burdens of iniquity (and sin offerings and trespass offerings were for these purposes)—we now come to a consideration of these four types of sacrifices:

1. *The burnt offering.*

This offering symbolized "the entire surrender unto God, whether of the individual or of the congregation, and His acceptance thereof." It was a "sacrifice of devotion and service. Thus day by day it formed the regular morning and evening service in the Temple, while on the sabbaths, new moons, and festivals additional burnt-offerings followed the ordinary worship. There the covenant people brought the covenant-sacrifice, and the multitude of offerings indicated, as it were, the fulness, richness, and joyousness of their self-surrender." (*Temple,* pp. 126-27.)

2. *The sin offering.*

"This is the most important of all sacrifices [from an individual standpoint]. It made atonement for the *person* of the offender, whereas the trespass-offering only atoned for one special offence. Hence sin-offerings were brought on festive occasions for the whole people, but never trespass-offerings. In fact, the trespass-offering may be regarded as representing ransom for a special wrong, while the sin-offering symbolized general redemption. Both sacrifices applied only to sins 'through ignorance,' in opposition to those done 'presumptuously' (or 'with a high hand'). For the latter the law provided no atonement, but held out 'a certain fearful looking for of judgment, and fiery indignation.' . . . In reference both to sin- and to trespass-offerings, the Rabbinical principle must be kept in view—that they only atoned in case of real repentance. . . . Neither oil nor frankincense were to be brought with a sin-offering. There was nothing joyous about it. It represented a terrible necessity, for which God, in his wondrous grace, had made provision." (*Temple,* pp. 128-30.)

One rare and unusual sin offering must be noted. It was of a red heifer, one pure in color "upon which never came yoke," and it was to cleanse any in Israel from "Levitical defilement," from "defilement by the dead." The chief thing distinguishing it from all other sacrifices was "that it was a sacrifice offered once for all (at least so long as its ashes lasted); that its blood was sprinkled, not on the altar, but outside the camp towards the sanctuary; and that it was wholly burnt, along with cedarwood, as the symbol of imperishable existence, [with] hyssop, as that of purification from corruption, and [with] 'scarlet,' which from its colour was the emblem of life. Thus the sacrifice of highest life, brought as a sin offering, and, so far as possible, once for all, was in its turn accompanied by the symbols of imperishable existence, freedom from corruption, and fulness of life, so as yet more to intensify its significance. But even this is not all. The gathered ashes with running water were sprinkled on the third and seventh days on that which was to be purified. Assuredly, if death meant 'the wages of sin,' this purification pointed, in all its details, to 'the gift of God,' which is 'eternal life,' through the sacrifice of Him in whom is the fulness of life." (*Temple,* p. 349.)

3. *The trespass offering.*

This was offered to clear a person from specific instances of wrongdoing, "for certain transgressions committed through ignorance, or else, according to Jewish tradition, where a man afterwards voluntarily confessed himself guilty." (*Temple,* p. 133.)

4. *The peace offering.*

"The most joyous of all sacrifices was the peace-offering, or, as from its derivation it might also be rendered, the offering of completion. This was, indeed, a season of happy fellowship with the Covenant God, in which He condescended to become Israel's Guest at the sacrificial meal, even as He was always their Host. . . . It is this sacrifice which is so frequently referred to in the Book of Psalms as the grateful homage of a soul justified and accepted before God." (*Temple,* p. 134.) Appropriately, for instance, Solomon at the dedication of the temple offered 22,000 oxen and 120,000 sheep as a peace offering. (1 Kgs. 8:63.)

There is much to say about sacrifices as they were from Moses to Zacharias, who begat John, nearly all of which is beyond the scope and need of this work. We cannot, however, leave this portion of our study without referring to the Day of Atonement; the day when all Israel was commanded to look to the Lord for remission of sins; the day when the high priest, who sat in Aaron's seat, mediated between Israel and their King—all according to the directions given by Moses, the man of God. "The most solemn of all sacrifices were those of the Day of Atonement, when the high-priest, arrayed in his linen garments, stood before the Lord Himself within the Most Holy Place to make an atonement." (*Temple,* p. 132.) On this day, once each year, the high priest entered the Holy of Holies, spoke the ineffable name, sprinkled the blood of the covenant, and performed the expiatory rites by which the Lord's people were cleansed from sin.

Without going into all the preparations for and complexities of the performances undertaken on the Day of Atonement—and they were complex, numerous, and burdensome—but simply as a means of getting a feeling relative to sacrifice as such, let us set forth a portion of what transpired on this day of days. "From Numbers 29:7-11 it appears that the offerings on the Day of Atonement were really of a threefold kind—'*the continual burnt offering,*' that is, the daily morning and evening sacrifices, with their meat- and drink-offerings; *the festive sacrifices of the day,* consisting for the high-priest and the priesthood, of 'a ram for a burnt-offering,' and for the people of one young bullock, one ram, and seven lambs of the first year (with their meat-offerings) for a burnt-sacrifice, and one kid of the goats for a sin-offering; and, thirdly, and chiefly, *the peculiar expiatory sacrifices of the day,* which were a young bullock as a sin-offering for the high-priest, his house, and the sons of Aaron, and another sin-offering for the people, consisting of two goats, one of which was to be killed and its blood sprinkled, as directed, while the other was to be sent away into the wilderness, bearing 'all the iniquities of the children of Israel, and all their transgressions in all their sins' which had been confessed 'over him,' and laid upon him by the high priest." (*Temple,* p. 306.)

As to the sin offering for himself, and the uttering of the ineffable name, Edersheim says of the high priest: "He then laid both his hands upon the head of the bullock, and confessed as follows:—'Ah, JEHOVAH! I have committed iniquity; I have transgressed; I have sinned—I and my house. Oh, then, JEHOVAH, I entreat Thee, cover over (atone for, let there be atonement for) the iniquities, the transgressions, and the sins which I have committed, transgressed, and sinned before Thee, I and my house—even as it is written in the law of Moses, Thy servant: "For, on that day will He cover over (atone) for you to make you clean; from all your transgressions before JEHOVAH ye shall be cleansed." ' It will be noticed that in this solemn confession the name JEHOVAH occurred three times. Other three times was it pronounced in the confession which the high priest made over the same bullock for the priesthood; a seventh time was it uttered when he cast the lot as to which of the two goats was to be 'for JEHOVAH;' and once again he spoke it three times in the confession over the so-called 'scape-goat' which bore the sins of the people. All these *ten* times the high-priest pronounced the very name of JEHOVAH, and, as he spoke it, those who stood near cast themselves with their faces on the ground, while the multitude responded: 'Blessed be the Name; the glory of His kingdom is for ever and ever.' "

Thereafter the two goats were brought forth, the lots were cast, and one was chosen to bear the inscription, "la-

JEHOVAH," for Jehovah, the other "la-Azazel," for Azazel (an expression translated "scapegoat" in our Bible). The goat bearing the name of Jehovah was sacrificed; the one chosen as the scapegoat, after all the sins of the people were placed upon him, was to be set free in a wilderness place to carry off the sins and iniquities of the Lord's people. In the course of the various sacrifices the high priest sprinkled the blood of the bullock and the goat according to the ritualistic pattern. (*Temple,* pp. 310-16.)

"By these expiatory sprinklings the high priest had cleansed the sanctuary in all its parts from the defilement of the priesthood and the worshippers. The Most Holy Place, the veil, the Holy Place, the altar of incense, and the altar of burnt-offering were now clean alike, so far as the priesthood and as the people were concerned; and in their relationship to the sanctuary both priests and worshippers were atoned for. So far as the law could give it, there was now again free access for all; or, to put it otherwise, the continuance of typical sacrificial communion with God was once more restored and secured. Had it not been for these services, it would have been impossible for priests and people to offer sacrifices, and so to obtain the forgiveness of sins, or to have fellowship with God. But the consciences were not yet free from a sense of personal guilt and sin. That remained to be done through the 'scape-goat.' . . .

"Most solemn as the services had hitherto been, the worshippers would chiefly think with awe of the high-priest going into the immediate presence of God, coming out thence alive, and securing for them by the blood the continuance of the Old Testament privileges of sacrifices and of access unto God through them. What now took place concerned them, if possible, even more nearly. Their own personal guilt and sins were now to be removed from them, and that in a symbolical rite, at one and the same time the most mysterious and the most significant of all. All this while the 'scape-goat,' with the 'scarlet tongue,' telling of the guilt it was to bear, had stood looking eastwards, confronting the people, and waiting for the terrible load which it was to carry away 'unto a land not inhabited.' Laying both his hands on the head of this goat, the high-priest now confessed and pleaded: 'Ah, JEHOVAH! they have committed iniquity; they have transgressed; they have sinned—Thy people, the house of Israel. Oh, then, JEHOVAH! cover over (atone for), I intreat Thee, upon their iniquities, their transgressions, and their sins, which they have wickedly committed, transgressed, and sinned before Thee—Thy people, the house of Israel. As it is written in the law of Moses, Thy servant, saying: "For on that day shall it be covered over (atoned) for you, to make you clean from all your sins before JEHOVAH ye shall be cleansed." ' And while the prostrate multitude worshipped at the name of Jehovah, the high-priest turned his face towards them as he uttered the last words, '*Ye shall be cleansed!*' as if to declare to them the absolution and remission of their sins." (*Temple*, pp. 316-18.)

Sacrifices—Both Mortal and Eternal

Our Lord was born to die. He came into the world to die upon the cross for the sins of the world. The Lamb of God came to be sacrificed. He came to shed his blood on an eternal altar not made with hands. He came to sprinkle his redeeming blood upon his saints so they might be pure and spotless before him. Did he kneel by a rock—a natural altar—as he sweat great drops of blood in Gethsemane? Was the blood of the Lamb of God sprinkled upon an earthly altar and in a Most Holy Place, as it were? Perhaps; but be that as it may, the eternal reality is that he came to die; he came as a Lamb slain from the foundation of the world as it were, to shed his blood for his brethren. He came to bear their sins, to carry them as Azazel to a land apart. He came as the great and Eternal High Priest to rend the veil of the temple, that all men might enter the Holy of Holies and dwell forever in the Divine Presence. He came as the living Paschal Lamb to put a divine seal upon all the sacrifices, all the burnt offerings, all the sin offerings, all the trespass offerings, all the peace offerings ever offered by either Melchizedek or Aaronic authority since the world began. He came to fulfill the law that he himself had given to Moses, to bring redemption, to atone for the sins of the world. He came as the Lamb of God. He was appointed unto death, and all else incident to his mortal probation was truly incidental.

Did he speak as no man before or since has ever spoken? Was he the Master Teacher, the greatest Rabbi of them all? Did the lame leap when he spoke? the blind eyes see when he willed it? the deaf hear at a whisper from him? Did the decaying and stinking corpse of his friend from Bethany live again because he said, "Lazarus, come forth"? Did wondrous words and wondrous works flow from him as a stream? Was his life perfect in all respects as befits the Holy One of Israel? So be it. All this, and more, is as it is. Never was there such a man as this man. But underlying it all, like a great foundation upon which a Holy Temple is built, is the eternal reality that the chief and foremost achievement in the life of God's Son was his death—his death as a sacrifice for sin, the death in which he made his soul an offering for sin.

We shall trace his travels as best we may. We shall hear his words to the extent our ears are open. We shall rejoice with the sick souls who rise in health from their cots of pain. We shall partake of his feelings as he is glorified by his Father on the Holy Mount, and as he sorrows for the sins of his people. We shall weep with him over doomed Jerusalem. We shall seek to think what he thought, to speak as he spoke, to act as he acted, to feel as he felt—such of necessity must be in studying his life. But underlying it all will be the spoken and unspoken message: He came to die; he must go up to Jerusalem, and suffer many things, and be killed, and be raised again the third day; he must lay down his life of himself because his Father wills it; and he must make his soul an offering for sin, for he is the Lamb of God.

Whatever else he did is all to the good. It prepares men

for the one supreme act of his life. Because he spoke and lived as he did, men are able to believe he was the Son of God; and because he was the Son of God, his atoning sacrifice has efficacy, virtue, and force in time and in eternity.

That we may now have an acute awareness of how our Lord's eternal sacrifice crowned all the sacrifices of the past; that we may know how the types and shadows of the Mosaic system took on form and substance in Christ; that we may see how the work of the mediator of the old covenant ended, and how that of the Mediator of the new covenant began, we shall turn to our theological friend, Paul. He wrote to the Hebrews. His message was that Christ came in fulfillment of the Mosaic sacrificial system; that the old covenant was now fulfilled; and that all Israel and all men must now look to the great and Eternal High Priest if they are to enter into the eternal Holy of Holies and dwell with God and Christ and the prophets and apostles of all the ages.

Paul's epistle to the Hebrews takes on a whole new meaning when it is read and studied with an understanding of the sacrificial system and the temple rites that prevailed in the day of Jesus. Our apostolic friend begins his epistle—as it is the nature and disposition of a true apostle to do—by announcing that the Great Elohim, the God to whom the Hebrews prayed in times past, sent his Son into the world; that the Son was in the express image of the Father's person; and that he came as promised in the holy scriptures. The Son is identified by name as the Man Jesus—the Captain of their salvation, who came to destroy death—who "took on him the seed of Abraham," so that "in all things" being "made like unto his brethren, . . . he might be a merciful and faithful high priest in things pertaining to God, to make reconciliation for the sins of the people. For in that he himself hath suffered being tempted, he is able to succour them that are tempted." (Heb. 2:16-18.) As we have seen, the high priests in Israel, on the Day of Atonement and at other times, through their sacrificial offerings made "reconciliation for the sins of the people." That is, by the shedding and sprinkling of the blood of bullocks and goats an atonement was wrought and the sins of the people were forgiven. It is this same prerogative that Paul is now claiming for another of Abraham's seed.

With this introduction Paul issues this invitation to his Hebrew brethren: "Consider the Apostle and High Priest of our profession, Christ Jesus." (Heb. 3:1.) That is, even as the high priests in Israel made reconciliation for the sins of the people, let us now consider the High Priest of the gospel, of our profession, of the new covenant, and see wherein he also made reconciliation through his blood for the sins of men. Paul then sets forth how and why Christ's position was greater than that of Moses, the man of God, and tells how their fathers, lacking faith, rejected Jehovah's gospel and were not able, under the law, to enter into the rest of the Lord, which rest is the fulness of his glory.

Having shown from the scriptures that Israel did not and could not enter the Lord's rest under the law, Paul then turns to Christ as the means of so obtaining. "Seeing then that we have a great high priest," he says, "that is passed into the heavens, Jesus the Son of God, let us hold fast our profession." Let us hold fast to Christ and his gospel, for he has entered into the heavens and can guide us in so doing, which thing the high priests of the Aaronic order could not do. "For we have not an high priest which cannot be touched with the feeling of our infirmities; but was in all points tempted like as we are, yet without sin." Our High Priest, the High Priest of the gospel, having suffered, having felt infirmities, having been tempted in all points like as we are, he will understand our like situation and make intercession for us. "Let us therefore come boldly unto the throne of grace" as the high priests of old turned to the Holy of Holies wherein was the throne of God with its mercy seat, "that we may obtain mercy, and find grace to help in time of need." (Heb. 4:14-16.)

With the principle now set forth that the new gospel

covenant—"our profession"—has also its High Priest; that the new religion has come to supplant the old, which former system was a type and shadow of things to come; that the High Priest of the new order is Christ Jesus who has ascended into heaven—Paul makes a pointed comparison of the mortal offerings of the Aaronic high priests and the eternal offering of the High Priest who came after the order of Melchizedek. "For every high priest taken from among men," he says, having reference to the high priests of the Aaronic order who served on the Day of Atonement and at other times, "is ordained for men in things pertaining to God, that he may offer both gifts and sacrifices for sins." The sacrifices offered by the ancient legal administrators were for the remission of sins. Like baptism and the sacrament, they had cleansing power; sin and iniquity were burned away upon the altars where they were offered. If it had not been so, what a direful and calamitous state rebellious and sinful Israel would have been in.

But such was God's gracious system; and of a high priest who had such a delegation of authority, Paul continues, such a one "can have compassion on the ignorant, and on them that are out of the way; for that he himself also is compassed with infirmity." Transgressions made in ignorance and those for which there was full repentance were forgiven through the sacrifices. "And by reason hereof," by reason of his own infirmities and sins, such a high priest "ought, as for the people, so also for himself, to offer for sins." We have seen that the high priest went first into the Holy of Holies to cleanse himself and thereafter to cleanse the people so that it would be, as with the priest, so with the people.

"And no man taketh this honour unto himself, but he that is called of God, as was Aaron." None but God can forgive sins; any man, of himself, who attempts such a high spiritual labor fails. Either God does it or he authorizes someone to act on his behalf. Anciently the one so authorized was Aaron, and those thereafter endowed with this priestly power were those who were called as had been their worthy ancestor. Hence Paul's need to establish the authority of the Son of God himself to act in the sin-remitting capacity here involved. "So also Christ glorified not himself to be made an high priest." He did not assume the prerogative of ministering in that high and exalted status; the power to make reconciliation and forgive sins did not originate with him; it was conferred upon him by his Father, as Paul shows by quoting these words spoken to Christ by the Father: "Thou art my Son, to day have I begotten thee. As he saith also in another place, Thou art a priest for ever after the order of Melchisedec."

And so we have an Eternal High Priest, one whose priesthood and service continue forever. The old high priests of the Aaronic order served, each in turn, for a time and a season. Each entered the Holy of Holies on one day each year during their tenure in the high and holy office that was theirs. But now there is an Eternal High Priest, who came after the order of Melchizedek; he continueth ever. Of him the account testifies: "In the days of his flesh," while he dwelt in mortality and before he became immortal, "when he had offered up prayers and supplications with strong crying and tears unto him that was able to save him from death"—when, as an Intercessor, he had prayed for his brethren; when, on his own behalf, he had pleaded that if it were possible, he might not drink the bitter cup, as he took upon himself the sins of the world—"and was heard in that he feared." That is, the Father heard the prayer and declined to remove the cup. The answer was: "Though he were a Son, yet learned he obedience by the things which he suffered." 'Though he were a Son yet he learned of obedience its terrible costs and glorious rewards by the things which he suffered, for he knew how to obey.' In agony he drank the dregs of the bitter cup, sweat great drops of blood from every pore, suffered more than it is possible for man to suffer except it be unto death, and thereby performed the appointed sacrificial labor. "And being made perfect, he became the author [the cause] of eternal salvation unto all them that obey him," and the Messianic promise was fulfilled relative to him, being "called of God an high priest after the order of Melchisedec." (Heb. 5:1-10.)

At this point in his Spirit-guided epistle to the Hebrews—to those who practiced the sacrificial ordinances and who did know or should have known their significance—Paul says there are many things he would like to tell them of the Eternal High Priest if they were not "dull of hearing." (Heb. 5:11.) He does exhort the Hebrew saints to "go on unto perfection" and not to turn back from their newly found profession, lest "they crucify to themselves the Son of God afresh, and put him to an open shame," thus becoming sons of perdition. He says God is not unmindful of their "labour of love" as they have "ministered to the saints," and he exhorts them to endure "unto the end."

Then he turns back to their ancient Hebrew history; speaks of Abraham, whom they revered, and of the promises of the Lord to him; tells how Abraham was promised, with an oath, that he and his seed, including all who become his seed by faith, repentance, and baptism, should be blessed forever—"even with the blessings of the Gospel, which are the blessings of salvation, even of life eternal" (Abr. 2:10-11)[3]—and then he exhorts the Hebrews to "lay hold upon the hope set before us: Which hope we have as an anchor of the soul, both sure and stedfast, and which entereth into that within the veil; Whither the forerunner is for us entered, even Jesus, made an high priest for ever after the order of Melchisedec." (Heb. 6:1-20.) Paul's exhortation is that the Hebrews should lay hold upon the hope of eternal life promised them as the seed of Abraham. This hope, he says, will be an anchor to their souls and will prepare them to enter within the veil—to pass through the veil of the temple, even as it is in temples today, in similitude of entering the presence of God—which is made possible because of the sacrifice of the Eternal High Priest, Jesus our Forerunner, who as a priest forever after the order of Melchizedek has already passed through the veil.

In this setting, as the Hebrew readers think on Abraham—their patriarch, progenitor, and friend—Paul turns their minds to one who presided over the father of the faithful and to whom their great progenitor was in subjection. He speaks of the man Melchizedek, "who met Abraham returning from the slaughter of the kings, and blessed him." He speaks of the priesthood of the man Melchizedek, a priesthood that that mighty man conferred upon Abraham, and that preceded and is greater than the priestly powers given later to Aaron and his seed. "For this Melchizedek was ordained a priest after the order of the Son of God, which order was without father, without mother, without descent, having neither beginning of days, nor end of life. And all those who are ordained unto this priesthood are made like unto the Son of God, abiding a priest continually." (JST, Heb. 7:1-3.)

Then follows an argument that cannot be gainsaid. It is that Melchizedek and Abraham held an eternal priesthood that was not confined to any one lineage and was not gained by Levitical descent. This priesthood is the power whereby men gain endless life, which is eternal life, which is exaltation within the veil. It preceded the Levitical order, which order came because of father and mother and was conferred only upon those who descended from Aaron and Levi. In contrast to the higher order, as he had already shown, this lesser priesthood did not prepare men to enter the rest of the Lord; and also, while this Levitical priesthood was in active operation, yet Messianic prophecies were made that another Priest would rise after the order of Melchizedek. Paul's argument is that since perfection came not by the Levitical priesthood which administered the law of Moses, and since there was to be another Priest come after the higher order of Melchizedek, it follows that with the change of priesthood there would be a change of the law also, and that the new law was the gospel. He notes that Christ, who came "after the similitude of Melchisedec," was not of the tribe of Levi but of Judah; that he received his priesthood with an oath, which was not the case with the Levitical priests; and that the oath was a declaration in the Lord's name that he, Jesus, would be a priest forever, that is, that his priesthood would continue in time and in eternity. "By so much was Jesus made a surety of a better testament," Paul says.

Then our apostolic author gets back to the matter of sacrifices and temple ordinances. "And they [the Aaronic high priests of Levitical descent] truly were many priests, because they were not suffered to continue by reason of death." They were born and died, they came and went, one succeeded another, as is the common lot of mortals as pertaining to all the positions to be filled in this life. "But this man [Jesus, who received the Melchizedek Priesthood, which is not confined to those of the lineage of Levi], because he continueth ever, hath an unchangeable priesthood. Wherefore he is able also to save them to the uttermost that come unto God by him, seeing he ever liveth to make intercession for them." And even at this time the intercessory prayers continue to ascend to the Father, as the Eternal High Priest pleads: "Father, behold the sufferings and death of him who did no sin, in whom thou wast well pleased; behold the blood of thy Son which was shed, the blood of him whom thou gavest that thyself might be glorified; Wherefore, Father, spare these my brethren that believe on my name, that they may come unto me and have everlasting life." (D&C 45:4-5.) Paul continues: "For such an high priest became us, who is holy, harmless, undefiled, separate from sinners, and made higher than the heavens; Who needeth not daily, as those high priests, to offer up sacrifice, first for his own sins, and then for the people's: for this he did once, when he offered up himself. For the law maketh men high priests which have infirmity; but the word of the oath, which was since the law, maketh the Son, who is consecrated for evermore." (Heb. 7.)

Thus far Paul has taught the principles involved. He has shown that Israel failed to enter into eternal glory through the law alone. He has shown that salvation did not come by the law of Moses alone. He has shown that the Messianic High Priest was needed to sacrifice himself for the sins of the people. Now he is prepared to show how each performance of the Mosaic sacrificial system bore record of and pointed to the great and eternal sacrifice of the promised High Priest. "We have such an high priest," he says, "who is set on the right hand of the throne of the Majesty in the heavens." He is "a minister of the sanctuary, and of the true tabernacle, which the Lord pitched, and not man." There is, as it were, an eternal sanctuary, an eternal tabernacle in the heavens above, after which the tabernacle of Moses was patterned; the one was temporal, the other spiritual. "For every high priest is ordained to offer gifts and sacrifices: wherefore it is of necessity that this man have somewhat also to offer. For if he were on earth, he should not be a priest [for he was not of the house of Levi], seeing that there are priests that offer gifts according to the law." But, be it noted, these Levitical priests, these sons of Aaron, these mortal ministers who receive their priesthood because of lineage, who gain their power because of father and mother, as it were, these priests "serve unto the example and shadow of heavenly things, as Moses was admonished of God when he was about to make the tabernacle: for, See, saith he, that thou make all things according to the pattern shewed to thee in the mount." All that Moses ordained in the way of sacrificial performances; all that had been done in Israel in this respect for fifteen hundred years; all the oxen and sheep and goats that had been given as gifts to the Lord to be slain on his altars; all the offerings burned on these altars; all the blood shed and sprinkled in the rituals of the law—all of these things were but a shadow of what was to be; all of them typified and bore record of the Eternal High Priest. Manifestly the tabernacles and the temples in which they were performed must be built according to the heavenly pattern.

And now, because the Eternal High Priest has made his sacrifice, he has "obtained a more excellent ministry, by how much also he is the mediator of a better covenant [the gospel], which was established upon better promises. For if that first covenant [the law of Moses] had been faultless, then should no place have been sought for the second." At this point our inspired writer quotes Jeremiah's prophetic assurance that the Lord would make a new covenant with the house of Israel—a gospel covenant to replace the law—and that part of the new covenant was the promise: "I will be merciful to their unrighteousness, and their sins and their iniquities will I remember no more." (Heb. 8.)

As of the Mosaic covenant, whose terms and conditions were kept in force by Aaron's priestly sons, it is written: "Then verily the first covenant had also ordinances of divine service." The Lord's hand was in what came to Moses; his law was of divine origin. And this covenant had also "a worldly sanctuary. For there was a tabernacle made; the first, wherein was the candlestick, and the table, and the shewbread; which is called the sanctuary." This was the Holy Place, set off from the courts by a covering or veil; and the same arrangement prevailed in the temple of Jesus' day. "And after the second veil [which was in reality the veil of the temple], the tabernacle which is called the Holiest of all [the Holy of Holies]; Which had the golden censer, and the ark of the covenant overlaid round about with gold, wherein was the golden pot that had manna, and Aaron's rod that budded, and the tables of the covenant." The ark, the manna, Aaron's rod, the tables whereon the Decalogue was written, and the Urim and Thummim—none of these remained in Herod's Temple, the Holy of Holies containing only a rock whereon the high priest sprinkled the blood on the Day of Atonement. "And over it [the ark, stand] the cherubims of glory shadowing the mercyseat; of which we cannot now speak particularly." (Paul is here limiting himself as to what he will write openly about those sacred things which go on in temples.)

"Now when these things were thus ordained," when all these things were in order, "the priests went always [continually, from day to day] into the first tabernacle [the Holy

Place], accomplishing the service of God. But into the second [the Holy of Holies] went the high priest alone once every year [on the Day of Atonement], not without blood, which he offered for himself, and for the errors of the people." The blood of the bullock and the goat were sprinkled in the Holy of Holies as the earthly high priest atoned for the sins of the people.

With the sacrificial services of the temple thus summarized, and with specific mention being made of the sprinkling of the blood in the Holy of Holies on the Day of Atonement, Paul now says: "The Holy Ghost this signifying, that the way into the holiest of all was not yet made manifest, while as the first tabernacle was yet standing: Which was a figure for the time then present, in which were offered both gifts and sacrifices, that could not make him that did the service perfect, as pertaining to the conscience; Which stood only in meats and drinks, and divers washings, and carnal ordinances, imposed on them until the time of reformation." That is to say: The Holy Ghost bore record—to Paul, to Moses, to all who would hear—that all of these Mosaic performances were but a figure, a type and a shadow, a similitude of what was to be. They of themselves and standing alone did not admit Israel into the Holiest Place, which is heaven itself. The sacrificial service was not to be perfected until Christ's atonement was brought to pass, and all of the offerings, washings, and divers ordinances simply pointed toward the time of reformation, the time when Christ would come with the new covenant, at which time these sacrifices and performances would be done away. (Heb. 9:1-10.)

Now our apostolic friend turns from what was in Moses' day to what Jesus did to fulfill the law and bring in "the time of reformation." "But Christ being come an high priest of good things to come," he says, "by a greater and more perfect tabernacle, not made with hands, that is to say, not of this building; Neither by the blood of goats and calves, but by his own blood he entered in once into the holy place, having obtained eternal redemption for us." As the earthly high priests, once each year, entered into the Holy of Holies to cleanse the people with the blood of their sacrifices, so Christ, once for all, entered the eternal Holy of Holies and through the shedding of his own blood made forgiveness of sins possible for all men. "For if the blood of bulls and of goats, and the ashes of an heifer sprinkling the unclean, sanctifieth to the purifying of the flesh [this is the red heifer whose ashes were sprinkled upon those defiled by contact with death]: How much more shall the blood of Christ, who through the eternal Spirit offered himself without spot to God, purge your conscience from dead works to serve the living God?"

"And for this cause," because of our Lord's atonement, "he is the mediator of the new testament [covenant], that by means of death [his own], for the redemption of the transgressions that were under the first testament [covenant]"—that is, Christ's death gave efficacy and validity to the sacrificial performances made under the Mosaic system; if he had not been slain for the sins of the world there would have been no forgiveness as a result of the ordinances performed by the high priests of the Aaronic order; and, hence, through his atonement "they which are called," whether in Moses' day or in his own, "receive the promise of eternal inheritance." All men in all ages are saved through the atoning blood of Christ the Lord Omnipotent; any ordinance in any age, past, present, or future, is efficacious only because of that atonement and in no other way.

"For where a testament [covenant] is," Paul continues, "there must also of necessity be the death of the testator. For a testament [covenant] is of force after men are dead: otherwise it is of no strength at all while the testator liveth." The gospel covenant was not and could not be put into force and operation without the death of Christ. Except for his atoning sacrifice there would be neither immortality nor eternal life. If there were no atonement, there would be no forgiveness of sins, no reconciliation with God, no validity to baptism, no eternal marriage, no sanctified souls. If there were no atonement, the purposes of creation would have failed. The gospel covenant would have had "no strength at all" without the death of the testator.

"Whereupon neither the first testament [the old covenant made with Moses] was dedicated without blood. For when Moses had spoken every precept to all the people according to the law, he took the blood of calves and of goats, with water, and scarlet wool, and hyssop, and sprinkled both the book, and all the people, Saying, This is the blood of the testament [covenant] which God hath enjoined unto you. Moreover he sprinkled with blood both the tabernacle, and all the vessels of the ministry. And almost all things are by the law purged with blood; and without shedding of blood is no remission." How perfectly did Jehovah make blood sacrifices the type of the sacrifice that he himself should make for the cleansing and purifying of those who believe in him!

"It was therefore necessary that the patterns of things in the heavens should be purified with these; but the heavenly things themselves with better sacrifices than these." That is to say, the tabernacle and all its appurtenances, patterned as they were after what was in heaven, were purified by the sprinkling of blood; but they who shall dwell in heaven itself must be purified with an eternal sacrifice, that of Christ. "For Christ is not entered into the holy places made with hands, which are the figures of the true; but into heaven itself, now to appear in the presence of God for us." Our Lord did not enter the Holy Place and the Holy of Holies in offering his sacrifice—these places are only figures of the true heavenly tabernacle; but he entered into heaven itself there to make intercession forever for us.

"Nor yet that he should offer himself often, as the high priest entereth into the holy place every year with blood of others; For then must he often have suffered since the foundation of the world: but now once in the end of the world hath he appeared to put away sin by the sacrifice of himself.

And as it is appointed unto men once to die, but after this the judgment: So Christ was once offered to bear the sins of many; and unto them that look for him shall he appear the second time without sin unto salvation. For the law having a shadow of good things to come, and not the very image of the things, can never with those sacrifices which they offered year by year continually make the comers thereunto perfect." Again the announcement is made that perfection does not come by the Levitical priesthood, for its ordinances were only a shadow of what was to be. "For then would they not have ceased to be offered? because that the worshippers once purged should have had no more conscience of sins. But in those sacrifices there is a remembrance again made of sins every year. For it is not possible that the blood of bulls and of goats should take away sins." (Heb. 9:11-10:2.)

At this point Paul quotes a Messianic prophecy that contrasts the sacrifices of the law with the sacrifice of the "body" prepared for the Messiah, and explains that the Lord taketh away the old sacrifices "that he may establish the second. By the which will we are sanctified through the offering of the body of Jesus Christ once for all. And every priest standeth daily ministering and offering oftentimes the same sacrifices, which can never take away sins: But this man, after he had offered one sacrifice for sins for ever, sat down on the right hand of God; From henceforth expecting till his enemies be made his footstool. For by one offering he hath perfected for ever them that are sanctified."

Lest any reader should think that the apostle was simply drawing interesting analogies or comparing systems which by chance had analogous patterns, Paul says that the Holy Ghost was a witness of the truth of his interpretations. He refers again to Jeremiah's prophecy about the new covenant whereby sins and iniquities will no longer be remembered and then says: "Now where remission of these is, there is no more offering for sin." (Heb. 10:3-18.)

After all these explanations, not a few of which are repetitious in nature, the author of the epistle to the Hebrews applies the doctrine taught to his hearers with these words of exhortation: "Having therefore, brethren, boldness to enter into the holiest by the blood of Jesus, By a new and living way, which he hath consecrated for us, through the veil, that is to say, his flesh; And having an high priest over the house of God; Let us draw near with a true heart in full assurance of faith, having our hearts sprinkled from an evil conscience, and our bodies washed with pure water. Let us hold fast the profession of our faith without wavering."

Coupled with this exhortation is a warning that "if we sin wilfully after that we have received the knowledge of the truth, there remaineth no more sacrifice for sins, But a certain fearful looking for of judgment and fiery indignation, which shall devour the adversaries. He that despised Moses' law died without mercy under two or three witnesses: Of how much sorer punishment, suppose ye, shall he be thought worthy, who hath trodden under foot the Son of God, and hath counted the blood of the covenant, wherewith he was sanctified, an unholy thing, and hath done despite unto the Spirit of grace?" (Heb. 10:19-29.)

There follows the great discourse on faith, some further exhortations and promises of eternal reward, and then a return to the purpose of the epistle, that of proving to the Hebrews, by their own sacrificial performances, that Jesus is the Lamb of God whose atoning sacrifice taketh away the sins of the world. "We have an altar, whereof they have no right to eat which serve the tabernacle. For the bodies of those beasts, whose blood is brought into the sanctuary by the high priest for sin, are burned without the camp. Wherefore Jesus also, that he might sanctify the people with his own blood, suffered without the gate. Let us go forth therefore unto him without the camp, bearing his reproach. For here have we no continuing city, but we seek one to come. By him therefore let us offer the sacrifice of praise to God continually, that is, the fruit of our lips giving thanks to his name. But to do good and to communicate forget not: for with such sacrifices God is well pleased." (Heb. 11-13.)

It may seem, in a life of Christ, that we have been unnecessarily prolix and have gone into too much detail relative to the sacrifices of Jesus' day, as well as to their purpose and meaning. To the contrary, this very omission is one of the great deficiencies of most of what is written about our Lord in modern times. Paul thought it of sufficient moment to give forth such statements as we have now quoted, and the reality is that no one can really understand our Lord's life and sayings without a knowledge of the religious system in which he was reared and which was designed to introduce him and bear record of his ministry. The law of sacrifice is the introduction of the Lord Jesus Christ to the world.

It was a desolating day when Herod's Temple died. It was a sad and sorrowful day for the Jews when sacrifices ceased, for with their passing went also the last vestige of the true religious performances that prevailed among them. Without these they had left less than a shell of godliness. Had they turned to the Eternal Temple and to the Eternal Sacrifice, all would have been well with them, but as it is, we can only say, with Peter: "Repent ye therefore, and be converted, that your sins may be blotted out, when the times of refreshing shall come from the presence of the Lord; And he shall send Jesus Christ, which before was preached unto you: Whom the heaven must receive until the times of restitution of all things, which God hath spoken by the mouth of all his holy prophets since the world began." (Acts 3:19-21.) The times of restitution commenced in the spring of 1820, and the times of refreshing, when the earth shall be renewed and receive its paradisiacal glory, are not far distant.

NOTES

1. In speaking of the restoration of all things, as promised by all the holy prophets since the world began, and after quoting Malachi's promise that the Lord, at his Second Coming, would purify the sons of Levi so that once again they could and would offer anew unto him their ancient sacrifices, the Prophet Joseph Smith said: "It is generally supposed that sacrifice was entirely done away when the Great Sacrifice [i.e.,] the sacrifice of the Lord Jesus was offered up, and that there will be no necessity for the ordinance of sacrifice in [the] future; but those who assert this are certainly not acquainted with the duties, privileges and authority of the Priesthood, or with the Prophets." The authority of the priest-

hood here referred to is the thing that John the Baptist brought back on May 15, 1829, and the knowledge of what the prophets have left us includes, among other things, the teachings of Malachi, Zechariah, and Ezekiel as these are set forth in chapter 7 herein.

Joseph Smith continues: "The offering of sacrifice has ever been connected and forms a part of the duties of the Priesthood. It began with the Priesthood, and will be continued until after the coming of Christ, from generation to generation. We frequently have mention made of the offering of sacrifice by the servants of the Most High in ancient days, prior to the law of Moses; which ordinances will be continued when the Priesthood is restored with all its authority, power and blessings." The frequent references to sacrifices performed by Melchizedek authority include those of Adam, Abraham and the patriarchs, and all those performed among the American Hebrews known as Nephites, for among them there were no Levites and the detailed performances of the law of Moses, such as the daily sacrifice, were not undertaken. The restoration of the priesthood to perform, once again, the type of ordinances that were part of the ancient gospel dispensations has reference to the revelation of all things incident to these holy performances, which restoration is still future.

"These sacrifices, as well as every ordinance belonging to the Priesthood, will, when the Temple of the Lord shall be built, and the sons of Levi be purified, be fully restored and attended to in all their powers, ramifications, and blessings. This ever did and ever will exist when the powers of the Melchizedek Priesthood are sufficiently manifest; else how can the restitution of all things spoken of by the Holy Prophets are brought to pass. It is not to be understood that the law of Moses will be established again with all its rites and variety of ceremonies; this has never been spoken of by the prophets; but those things which existed prior to Moses' day, namely, sacrifice, will be continued.

"It may be asked by some, what necessity for sacrifice, since the Great Sacrifice was offered? In answer to which, if repentance, baptism, and faith existed prior to the days of Christ, what necessity for them since that time?" (*Teachings*, pp. 172-73.)

2. The *public sacrifices* were "the daily sacrifices; the additional for the Sabbath; for the New Moon; the Passover sacrifices; the lamb when the sheaf was waved; the Pentecostal sacrifices; those brought with the two first loaves; New Year's; Atonement Day sacrifices; those on the first day of, and those on the octave of 'Tabernacles.' *Private sacrifices* they classify as those on account of sins by word or deed; those on account of what concerned the body (such as various defilements); those on account of property (firstlings, tithes); those on account of festive seasons; and those on account of vows or promises." (*Temple*, p. 111.)

3. It should be noted that all who receive the gospel are called by Abraham's name and are accounted his seed.

JEWISH FEASTS IN JESUS' DAY

When he was come into Galilee, the Galileans received him, having seen all the things that he did at Jerusalem at the feast: for they also went unto the feast. . . . After this there was a feast of the Jews; and Jesus went up to Jerusalem. (John 4:45; 5:1.)

The Nature of Jewish Feasts

Jesus used the Jewish feasts as the ideal and perfect occasions to proclaim his divine Sonship, to dramatize the great and eternal truths concerning himself in such ways that they never would be forgotten, and to work miracles and bless his fellowmen. We may suppose also that he used them as occasions of personal worship and communion with his Father, for such was the very purpose for which they had been established, and it was his wont, as a Jew, to keep his own law, until the time that he himself fulfilled and revoked it.

Many sweet and lovely episodes of his life occurred at the feasts. Some of his most profound doctrine was taught to the worshipful throngs who assembled to keep the feasts; and miracles, beyond compare, were wrought by his hands at those solemn and sacred times. The Jewish feasts were part of the life of Jesus. We see him at the Feast of the Passover, when but twelve years of age, confounding the wise and the learned. He was there because "his parents went to Jerusalem every year at the feast of the passover." (Luke 2:41-52.) We hear him tell Peter and John to prepare the Passover so that he and the Twelve could eat thereof. We hear his brethren—Mary's other sons, who did not then believe—chide him with the challenge to go to the Feast of Tabernacles and work further miracles, and we hear his reply that they should go now and he will come later. We see the Jews, astonished at his absence, seeking him at the feast. About the midst of the feast, we find him teaching in the temple; and then, "In the last day, that great day of the feast," as the priest takes water from the stream of Siloam, in a golden vessel, and pours it upon the altar, we hear his dramatic pronouncement: "If any man thirst, let him come unto me, and drink. He that believeth on me, as the scripture hath said, out of his belly shall flow rivers of living water." (John 7:1-39.)

As we place Jesus in the setting of the Jewish feasts, where he so logically is found and so naturally fits; as we envision that these feasts were part of the great schooling system, part of the way of worship of devout Jews, and were, therefore, imposed upon Jesus by his guardians and by the social pressure of his day; as we realize that he was acquainted with them and participated in their rituals, we must keep foremost in our thoughts the central performances undertaken at them. All of the feasts were occasions for the offering of sacrifices: public sacrifices for the spiritual well-being and salvation of the whole congregation, and private sacrifices for the forgiveness of personal sins and the reconciliation of true worshippers with their God. Sacrificial offerings; offerings made on the great altar, thirty by thirty feet square at the top; sacrifices in which blood was shed as a symbol of reconciliation; sacrifices made in similitude of Him who mingled with the festive throngs at those very feasts, seeking to do them good, while their rulers sought to do him ill—these were the center of Jewish religious worship. They were ordinances of salvation, and without them, as far as that day was concerned, men could not gain an inheritance with Him who dwells behind the veil.

There were three great feasts—the Feast of the Passover, the Feast of Pentecost, and the Feast of Tabernacles. All Israelite males were commanded to appear three times a year before the Lord in his sanctuary, meaning that attendance at these three feasts was obligatory, and all were to go up to Jerusalem to worship the King, the Lord of Hosts, to purify themselves before him, and to carry back to their various cities and farms the spirit of festive worship in which they had participated. Women were welcome—and we find Mary accompanying Joseph, at least when their twelve-year-old son taught in the temple—though they were not required to attend.

These feasts, in ancient times, had a great unifying effect upon the people, both religiously, politically, and socially. Without them the self-willed tribes might have divided themselves into a dozen kingdoms, each going its own way, to the destruction of Israel as a people and as a nation. By the time of Jesus, however, it was no longer possible for all males—scattered among many nations, as they were—to go up three times a year to the City of God. Instead twenty-four courses of lay attendants were appointed to stand in the temple as representatives of all the people; attendance at the feasts became something that could be delegated, as it were.

These great feasts were times for festive offerings, a form of private sacrifices, as distinguished from the public sacrifices for the whole congregation. They were occasions for making freewill offerings for the poor and the Levites. At them and at other feasts there was a holy convocation, or gathering together for sacred purposes; there was rest, either from all work or from all servile work, as the case may be; and certain special sacrifices, depending upon the occasion, were offered for the whole congregation.

We shall now make such reference as must needs be to

the feasts here named and to the others—the Feast of Esther or Purim, and the Feast of the Dedication of the Temple—that also played a vital part in Jewish worship.

The Feast of the Passover

By Feast of the Passover we mean the Passover itself, which fell on the 14th of Nisan, and also the Feast of Unleavened Bread, which lasted from Nisan 15 through 21. Though separate feasts, they were considered to be one, and they both commemorated the Exodus from Egyptian bondage. Our chief interest in them, as we study the life of our Lord, is to learn why and how and in what manner they were kept by the Jews in Jesus' day, and for that matter how the Lord Jesus himself kept this greatest of all Jewish feasts. This latter we shall set forth more particularly when we recline with Jesus and the Twelve, in a place apart from the throngs, to eat the Paschal Supper, and see how naturally and easily the sacrament of the Lord's Supper grew out of it.

But as to the Passover proper, and as to the Feast of Unleavened Bread, which was part and portion of the over-all festival—what were they, whence and why did they come, and what purpose did they serve? Without question the Passover season was the most joyous and glorious time of Jewish and Israelitish worship. Israel was born when Jacob's name was changed and when that faithful patriarch began to have seed. Her numbers were a mere seventy when she saved herself from famine by going down into Egypt. There she prospered until there arose a new king who knew not Joseph. Then came slavery, bondage, toil. Then were her male children slain and her young men scourged. Then did they find their own straw to make the bricks for Pharaoh's palaces and cities. Then were they downtrodden physically, socially, culturally, spiritually. Now, after four centuries, numbering more than two million souls, they cried mightily unto the Lord for deliverance. And the Great I AM, the God of Abraham, Isaac, and Jacob, their fathers, sent them a Moses.

Miracles were wrought; plagues were poured out; Pharaoh hardened his heart; the burdens on Jacob's seed increased; until finally, in their dire extremity, the Lord in his wrath chose to slay the firstborn of Pharaoh who sat on his throne, the firstborn of the governors who hated his people, the firstborn of the taskmasters whose whips cut the flesh of the chosen seed, the firstborn in every Egyptian family in all the land, and the firstborn of all their cattle. Let these hosts die, he decreed, and die they did, for they had defied God and said by the mouth of Pharaoh, 'Who is Jehovah that I and my people should give heed unto him?'

Then, in his mercy and goodness, lest the destroying angel slay any of the chosen seed, the Lord provided a Passover, a way of escape for his people. Later, in the wilderness, as their priestly rituals were perfected, he added to this the Feast of Unleavened Bread. That all Israel might know and remember and ponder that the Lord Jehovah, who delivered them from Egyptian bondage, was their Messiah, their Christ and the One who would shed his blood for the sins of the world, the angel of death was commanded to pass over the houses on whose doors and lintels the blood of a sacrificial lamb had been sprinkled. Israel was to be saved by the blood of the lamb.

In each Israelite house a young lamb or kid, a male of the first year and one without blemish, was selected and slain. The head of each house, using a sprig of hyssop, sprinkled blood on the doorposts and on the lintel; the lamb or kid was roasted whole; not a bone was broken; and it was eaten, in haste, along with unleavened bread and bitter herbs.

No uncircumcised male, none in whose flesh the symbol of the Abrahamic covenant was not found, was to partake, but each male who did partake was to stand with his loins girt, his staff in his hand, and his shoes on his feet. Any of the uneaten flesh was to be burned. In later generations this Egyptian Passover became a permanent Passover with such changes and perfections in the ritualistic arrangements as better suited the accustomed and established order of religious services.

Israel was a people, the Lord's people, from the day Jacob and Leah had Reuben. She became a nation, a dependent nation, while dwelling in Goshen and living under Egyptian sovereignty, and she went into bondage and slavery when the fortunes of war put Egypt in unfriendly hands. But she was born as a free nation when Jehovah removed the heavy hand of Egypt, and she was redeemed from a state of slavery when the Great Jehovah led her through the Red Sea—first into a wilderness, and then into a fruitful land flowing with milk and honey. Israel became a free people, a free nation, a new kingdom on that first Passover night, and ever thereafter the Passover festivities were a birthday celebration, but—and this was the whole center and heart of the occasion—a celebration in which Christ and his redeeming ministry were brought over and over again to the attention of all those who subjected themselves to the rituals of this chief feast.

In the day of Jesus, both public and private sacrifices were made, and the paschal lambs were slain for each family or group, each of such units containing from ten to twenty persons. Jesus and the Twelve made up a group of thirteen, which dropped to an even twelve when evil Judas withdrew. When Nero sat in Caesar's seat a count was made of the number of lambs slain in Jerusalem at one Passover: the total, 256,000. On the basis of a minimum of ten in each group, this meant a Passover population for the holy city of 2,560,000. Josephus placed it that year at 2,700,200, and there were times when the assembled hosts numbered not less than 3,000,000.

Rabbi Gamaliel, the teacher of Paul, said: "Whoever does not explain three things in the Passover has not fulfilled the duty incumbent on him. These three things are: the Passover lamb, the unleavened bread, and the bitter herbs. *The Passover lamb* means that God passed over the blood-sprinkled place on the houses of our fathers in Egypt; *the un-*

leavened bread means that our fathers were delivered out of Egypt (in haste); and *the bitter herbs* mean that the Egyptians made bitter the lives of our fathers in Egypt." (*Temple,* p. 237.)

Paul, who was taught from on high as well as being the pupil of Gamaliel, knew more about the Passover than did his rabbinical instructor. In administering a severe rebuke to the sinning saints of Corinth, the apostle says: "Your glorying is not good." Then he asks: "Know ye not that a little leaven leaveneth the whole lump?" That is, if you have in your heart the spirit of the gospel, it will influence you to pursue a course of righteousness, but if you still have in your heart the spirit of the world, your conduct will be after the manner of the world. "Purge out therefore the old leaven"—forsake the world and cast away the evil inclinations of your souls—"that ye may be a new lump"—that ye may be born again, be a new creature of the Holy Ghost, live in a newness of life—"as ye are unleavened"—that is, live in righteousness because ye are no longer leavened with the unrighteousness of the world. "For even Christ our passover is sacrificed for us," meaning that all this is possible because the Eternal Paschal Lamb has wrought the atoning sacrifice for us. "Therefore let us keep the feast, not with old leaven, neither with the leaven of malice and wickedness; but with the unleavened bread of sincerity and truth." (1 Cor. 5:6-8.) With the offering of the Eternal Sacrifice the Passover ceases except in the sense that the true saints adopt the true principles upon which it was based, and so purge the leaven of wickedness out of their souls and eat forever of the unleavened bread of truth and righteousness.

The Feast of Unleavened Bread was an occasion in Israel for joy and rejoicing. The bread itself was called "the bread of affliction," to remind Israel of the sorrows and sufferings of their Egyptian bondage (Deut. 12:1-8), but the emphasis was not upon the afflictions of the past but upon the joys of the present and the future. Israel had been delivered from bondage through the Passover, and the eating of unleavened bread for seven days did more to remind them that the fulness of the earth was now theirs than to unduly emphasize the afflictions that once were theirs.

On the first day of the feast (the second day of the Passover) there was a holy convocation, and the first ripe sheaf of grain was presented to the Lord. It was the feast of spring, with all the joy and rebirth that goes with the season. On each day of the feast, following the regular morning sacrifice, burnt offerings were made wherein the people surrendered their will to the will of the Lord, and sin offerings were made as an atonement for their sins. On the concluding day there was a solemn assembly. All in all it is difficult to imagine how a festive period could have been devised, under the Mosaic system, that would have done more to bring spirituality and blessings into the lives of the people than did the performances and worship of the Passover period. And that the Lord participated in them to the full we shall set forth in due course.[1]

Everything connected with the Passover period, from Nisan 14 through 21, is so dramatic, so filled with symbolism, so designed to center the attention of the Lord's people in the great and eternal truths of salvation that even today, when the Passover is past and we no longer need, to the extent our forebears did, to ponder its place in the plan of salvation, we are still prone to use its happenings to teach various related truths and principles. Thoughtful Christians may well reason, as many of them have, along such lines as these:

The Passover is a type of deliverance from the slavery of sin; from the bondage of the world; from the Pharaohs of greed and power and lust. It is the passing over of the angel of spiritual death so that the darkness of unbelief is replaced by the light of the gospel. It is a deliverance from the doom we deserve for our sins; from the spiritual death that awaits the wicked; from the outer darkness of Egypt and Sodom and Sheol—because the blood of Christ has been applied to us by faith. By sprinkling our Lord's blood upon the doorposts of our hearts and upon the lintels of our souls, we set our dwellings apart from the world; we make open and visible confession of our allegiance to Him whose blood has eternal saving power; we set ourselves apart from the Egyptians, the Sodomites, and the seekers after Sheol; and we place ourselves with the believing portion of mankind. As each family group ate their paschal lamb and drank of the cup of blessing, so must we eat the flesh and drink the blood of the Lord Jesus. As the Passover was useless unless eaten, so must we live godly lives in Christ, and openly certify our love for him by keeping his commandments. As it was eaten with bitter herbs, so must we eat our Passover with the bitter herbs of confession and repentance. As ancient Israel ate their Passover girt for a journey, shod with sandals, with a staff in their hands, so must modern Israel dress for their journey; so must they clothe themselves with the robes of righteousness, as they journey from Idumea to Zion, from Babylon to Palestine. As they, in the face of all the power and influence of Egypt, prepared to follow Moses wherever he led them, so must we follow our modern Moses through the Red Sea of doubt, into the wilderness of trials, and finally over the Jordan to that Promised Land where Abraham, Isaac, and Jacob and all the saints now dwell, there to rest in glory.

Truly the saints today can slay their own paschal lambs, eat their own unleavened bread, keep their own Passover, and serve Him whom their forebears served during that millennium and a half when the original Feast of the Passover was kept with joy and rejoicing!

The Feast of Pentecost

Pentecost had its beginning in the Passover, and the Passover had its ending, seven weeks later, in Pentecost; the two feasts are tied together, with the one growing out of the other. At the Passover, on the first day of the Feast of Unleavened Bread, Israel presented the Passover sheaf to the

Lord. With ritualistic ceremony they harvested the first of the barley crop, threshed the heads of grain, parched the grain, and ground it into fine flour. One omer (just over five pints) of fine flour was chosen, and oil and frankincense were added; the mixture was then waved before the Lord, and a portion was burned on the altar. This was the beginning of the harvest, which would be climaxed fifty days later at Pentecost. The Passover began on Nisan 14 (early April) with the beginning of the harvest of barley, and Pentecost came on Sivan 6 (about the end of May) with the start of the harvest of wheat. They were the harvest festivals of Israel.

On the day of Pentecost—called also the Feast of Harvest, the Day of First Fruits, and the Feast of Weeks—Israel was to hold a holy convocation and do no servile work. All males were to appear before the Lord in his sanctuary, and the appointed sacrifices and offerings were to be made. The order of worship and the performances attending it are generally conceded to be as follows:

1. On the days preceding the feast, the pilgrim bands—"Jews, devout men, out of every nation under heaven" (Acts 2:5)—joyously assembled at Jerusalem, at the Holy City, the City of the Great King, the site of the Lord's House. What a glorious thing it is for the faithful to go up to Zion, the city of their God!

2. Also before the appointed day, attended by the appointed ceremonial recitations and performances, sheaves of wheat were reaped and the grain was harvested, parched, ground into flour, and sifted through twelve sieves. The night before, the two wave loaves, each of leavened bread and weighing together more than ten pounds, were baked.

3. The great altar was cleansed, all things were arranged for the rites to follow, and about midnight the temple gates were opened so the priests could examine the animals brought by the people for burnt offerings and for peace offerings.

4. With the dawn came the regular morning sacrifice and the assembling of great throngs of worshippers at the temple.

Devout Jews took seriously Jehovah's decree that the adult males of his kingdom should appear before him in his sanctuary three times each year.

5. Then came the appointed festive offerings. These were, first, one kid of the goats, for a sin offering, made with proper imposition of hands, confession of sin, and sprinkling of blood; and then, the burnt offerings, consisting of two young bullocks, one ram, and seven lambs of the first year, along with their appropriate meat offerings.

6. At this point, the Levites chanted the Hallel, Psalms 113 to 118, to the accompaniment of a flute and the singing voices of Levite children, and the people either repeated or responded to the psalms of praise as they did at the Feast of the Passover.

7. "Then came the peculiar offering of the day—that of the two wave-loaves, with their accompanying sacrifices. These consisted of seven lambs of the first year, without blemish, one young bullock, and two rams for a burnt-offering, with their appropriate meat-offerings; and then 'one kid of the goats for a sin-offering, and two lambs of the first year for a sacrifice of peace-offerings.' " These are not to be confused with the festive offerings. The two lambs were waved, while yet alive, along with the wave loaves, and their principal parts were again waved after being slain.

8. "After the ceremony of the wave-loaves, the people brought their own freewill-offerings, each as the Lord had prospered him—the afternoon and evening being spent in the festive meal, to which the stranger, the poor, and the Levite were bidden as the Lord's welcome guests."

9. There was of course the evening sacrifice, and in practice, because of the great number of freewill offerings, it generally took up to a week to offer them all. (*Temple*, pp. 249-67.)

Jewish tradition, having apparent foundation in fact, held that as the Passover commemorated the deliverance from Egypt, so Pentecost commemorated the wondrous outpouring of divine grace that occurred fifty days later when with his own finger—the same finger that had touched the sixteen stones for Moriancumer—the Great Jehovah wrote his law on tablets of stone and gave them to Moses the man of God. What is more to the point is that our Lord was crucified as part of the Passover, and that the Holy Spirit of God came in power on the Day of Pentecost. For forty days after his resurrection Jesus continued to minister among the Twelve as a resurrected Being. Then he ascended to his Father, leaving them with instructions to tarry in Jerusalem until they were endowed with power from on high. Ten days later, "when the day of Pentecost was fully come," the apostles, with Matthias now one of their number, and perhaps other believers, "were all with one accord in one place. And suddenly there came a sound from heaven as of a rushing mighty wind, and it filled all the house where they were sitting."

Were they in the temple at the time, and was the house where they were sitting one of the porches where Jesus had so often sat to teach and expound? Opinions may vary, but such is not improbable. The "house," wherever it was, was open to the public, for great hosts—of whom three thousand were converted and baptized—rushed to hear and see and feel the miracle. How many houses there were, aside from the house of the Lord, where three or ten or scores of thousands could readily assemble is open to question. Further, the place where Jerusalem's throngs were found on a feast day was in the great court that surrounded the holy sanctuary. But an even more compelling question is: Where else would the Jewish apostles and their followers have gone on a Jewish feast day than to the Lord's holy sanctuary? They, as yet—for the gift of the Holy Ghost had not taken hold of their minds—felt subject to the law that called for every male to appear before the Lord in his sanctuary on that day. Would they have been keeping the commandment and standing in the line of their duty, as they then understood it, or would they have been elsewhere, plotting, as it were, against what they had always known to be the established order? For that matter, it was their wont, on all days, to make the temple their center of worship. Habits change gradually. Jesus and the Twelve had worshipped in the temple while the Lord dwelt among them. Each one of them, time after time, had made the required appearance at the appointed place.

Further, after Jesus "was parted from them, and carried up into heaven," the Twelve "worshipped him, and returned to Jerusalem with great joy: And were continually in the temple, praising and blessing God." (Luke 24:49-53.) And even after the Day of Pentecost, their numbers swelled by the three thousand Pentecostal baptisms, the record says: "And they, continuing daily with one accord in the temple, and breaking bread from house to house, did eat their meat with gladness and singleness of heart, Praising God, and having favour with all the people." (Acts 2:46-47.) Later still, Peter and John, while walking through the gate called Beautiful, healed the man lame from his mother's womb, causing the "Gentile" mobs, then in the court of the Gentiles, to cause their arrest and imprisonment. Indeed, we might well ask: If fire was to come down from heaven again, as it had done in Solomon's Temple, where else would it come than to the house used by the Lord as his own?

But wherever the miracle occurred, it was the ushering in of the day of miracles and revelation that always attends the true saints. For, "there appeared unto them cloven tongues like as of fire, and it sat upon each of them." It was as though the fires on the stony altars of the dying dispensation were now ignited in the mellowed hearts of the Saints. "And they were all filled with the Holy Ghost, and began to speak with other tongues, as the Spirit gave them utterance. . . . Now when this was noised abroad, the multitude came together, and were confounded, because that every man heard them speak in his own language." The apostles spoke in Aramaic, with their Galilean and Palestinian dialects, and all men, be they whosoever they might be and speaking whatsoever language was theirs, heard and understood.

"And they were all amazed and marvelled, saying one to another, Behold, are not all these which speak Galileans? And how hear we every man in our own tongue, wherein we were born?" (Acts 2:1-13.) How fitting it was that, while the sacrificial fires yet burned on the altar of sacrifice, living fire should come down from heaven to burn forever in the hearts of those who were to sacrifice their lives in the cause of truth and righteousness.

The Feast of Tabernacles

Taking our cues and quotations from Edersheim (*Temple,* pp. 268-87), but tempering his views with the added light and knowledge revealed in the dispensation of the fulness of times, we shall now turn to the Feast of Tabernacles, "the most joyous of all festive seasons in Israel." As we have heretofore seen, this is the one great Jewish-Israelitish feast that was not abolished forever when He who gave the law also fulfilled that which had come from Him. As the prophets have said, it shall be celebrated again during the Millennium, when the sons of Levi, in purity and worthiness, at the direction of the Melchizedek authority that governs the Church of God in all ages, shall offer again an offering unto the Lord in righteousness. Our present major concern, however, is to see how and in what manner this feast bore record of Jesus and to see how he himself used it during his mortal ministry to show the people what witness they were in fact bearing through its sacred and holy rituals.

Of Passover, Pentecost, and Tabernacles—the three annual festive occasions when Jehovah commanded all male Israelites to appear before him in his holy sanctuary in Jerusalem, and not to come empty handed—it is appropriately said: "If the beginning of the harvest had pointed back to the birth of Israel in their Exodus from Egypt, and forward to the true Passover-sacrifice in the future; if the corn-harvest was connected with the giving of the law on Mount Sinai in the past, and the outpouring of the Holy

Spirit on the Day of Pentecost; the harvest-thanksgiving of the Feast of Tabernacles reminded Israel, on the one hand, of their dwelling in booths in the wilderness, while, on the other hand, it pointed to the final harvest when Israel's mission should be completed, and all nations gathered unto the Lord." (*Temple,* p. 269.)

Thus the Feast of Tabernacles is called also the Feast of Booths, for Israel dwelt in booths or huts when she first came out of Egypt, and the Feast of Ingathering, for by Tishri 15, when the seven-day feast began (the September-October period), the whole harvest, with its corn and wine and oil, had been stored for the winter ahead. To envision how Jewish Israel worshipped in the days of Jesus, it will be instructive to summarize what was done at this feast. As with all feasts, it was a period of worship and spiritual refreshment, a time to renew covenants and return unto the Lord with full purpose of heart. In this case, however, the feast began four days after the Day of Atonement, "in which the sin of Israel had been removed, and its covenant relation to God restored. Thus a sanctified nation could keep a holy feast of harvest joy unto the Lord, just as in the truest sense it will be in that day," spoken of by the prophets, when "every one that is left of all the nations . . . shall even go up from year to year to worship the King, the Lord of hosts, and to keep the feast of tabernacles," when millennial righteousness will be such that "Holiness unto the Lord" will be inscribed on almost all things. (Zech. 14:16-21; *Temple*, pp. 271-72.)

Joyous festivities marked the Feast of Tabernacles; the "ingathering" spirit prevailed; without their harvests Israel would perish for want of bread; and famine was a constant threat. How natural that they should rejoice in what the Lord had given them—from the soil and the rain and the sun! And how natural that Jehovah would expect of them thanksgiving and rejoicing for the bounties that flowed from his hands! Thus we hear him say: "Thou shalt observe the feast of tabernacles seven days, after that thou hast gathered in thy corn and thy wine: And thou shalt rejoice in thy feast, thou, and thy son, and thy daughter, and thy manservant, and thy maidservant, and the Levite, the stranger, and the fatherless, and the widow, that are within thy gates." Why? "Because the Lord thy God shall bless thee in all thine increase, and in all the works of thine hands, therefore thou shalt surely rejoice." Then, as to the three great feasts—Passover, Pentecost, and Tabernacles—the Lord said of all who went up to Jerusalem to keep them: "And they shall not appear before the Lord empty: Every man shall give as he is able, according to the blessing of the Lord thy God which he hath given thee." (Deut. 16:13-17.) And at these festive occasions, both those who gave and those who received would have occasion to rejoice. "Votive, freewill, and peace-offerings would mark their gratitude to God, and at the meal which ensued the poor, the stranger, the Levite, and the homeless would be welcome guests, for the Lord's sake." (*Temple,* p. 272.)

In the day of Jesus, as had been the case since the day of Moses, all male Israel, at Tabernacle-time, left their houses of wood and stone and dwelt in huts or booths made of the boughs of living trees. For one week, except in very heavy rain, they ate, slept, prayed, studied, and lived in these temporary abodes. Women, the sick and their attendants, slaves, infants dependent on their mothers, and some away on pious duties were exempt. "When ye have gathered in the fruit of the land," was the decree the Lord had given them, "ye shall keep a feast unto the Lord seven days: on the first day shall be a sabbath, and on the eighth day shall be a sabbath." The eighth day, the Octave of the feast, was, strictly speaking, not part of the feast itself, but served as an added day of worship. "And ye shall take you on the first day the boughs of goodly trees, branches of palm trees, and the boughs of thick trees, and willows of the brook; and ye shall rejoice before the Lord your God seven days." The use of these boughs and branches in the rejoicing rites shall be set forth shortly. "And ye shall keep it a feast unto the Lord seven days in the year. It shall be a statute for ever in your generations: ye shall celebrate it in the seventh month. Ye shall dwell in booths seven days; all that are Israelites born shall dwell in booths: That your generations may know that I made the children of Israel to dwell in booths, when I brought them out of the land of Egypt: I am the Lord your God." (Lev. 23:39-43.) Surely there were those among them who realized thereby, not alone that their tent-type life in escaping from Egypt was a temporary arrangement as they traveled en route to a promised land, but that all men are strangers and pilgrims on earth, en route to a more enduring abode, a home, not made with hands, that is eternal in the heavens.

We have heretofore dealt, sufficiently for our needs—in connection with Passover and with Pentecost and with Mosaic sacrificial performances as such—with the sacrificial system of worship. We are aware of how sins are forgiven, how covenants are made, how vows are kept, how God is blessed and glorified, and how spiritual refreshment comes through sacrificial offerings. We need here merely point out the unique and peculiar nature of the sacrifices required at the Feast of Tabernacles, and to remind ourselves that sacrifices as such—whether public or private, and whether offered as burnt offerings, sin offerings, trespass offerings, or peace offerings—were at the heart and core of ritualistic religion in those days.

Burnt offerings—the sacrifices of devotion and service, which symbolized the entire surrender of the people to Jehovah and his acceptance of them—were more numerous during the Feast of Tabernacles than at any of the other festivals. On each of the seven days, two rams and 14 lambs were offered; on the first day 13 bullocks were also offered, with this number being diminished by one each day, so that seven only were offered on the seventh day. Thus 182 burnt offerings, each with its proper meat and drink offering, sent their sweet savor up to Jehovah during this period. In addition, one kid was offered for a sin offering on each day; and on the Octave day, seven lambs, one ram, and one bullock were offered as burnt offerings, plus one kid as a sin offering. All of these were in addition to the continual burnt offerings, their meat and drink offerings, and all of the private offerings of the hosts of devout worshippers. Our purpose in setting this forth is simply to show that the Feast of Tabernacles should have been and was the great period both of thanksgiving and of rededication.

Now let us go back to "the boughs of goodly trees, branches of palm trees, and the boughs of thick trees, and willows of the brook," which the people were to take and use as they rejoiced before the Lord. In the day of Jesus—and we must assume such was the case from the beginning of the feast—these were carried in the hands of the people. Since the use to which they were put is the same as that of the white handkerchiefs, when the Hosanna Shout is given at temple dedications and certain other solemn assemblies in latter-day Israel, we shall note particularly the rabbinical regulations relative to them. "The Rabbis ruled, that 'the fruit of the goodly trees' meant the *aethrog,* or citron, and 'the boughs of thick trees' the myrtle, provided it had 'not more berries than leaves.' The *aethrogs* must be without blemish or deficiency of any kind; the palm branches at least three handbreadths high, and fit to be shaken; and each branch fresh, entire, unpolluted, and not taken from any idolatrous grove. Every worshipper carried the *aethrog* in his left hand, and in his right the *lulav,* or palm, with myrtle and willow branch on either side of it, tied together on the outside with its own kind, though in the inside it might be fastened even with gold thread. There can be no doubt that the *lulav* was intended to remind Israel of the different stages of their wilderness journey, as represented by the different vegetation—the palm branches recalling the valley and plains, the 'boughs of thick trees,' the bushes on the mountain heights, and the willows those brooks from which God had given his people drink; while the *aethrog* was to remind them of the fruits of the good land which the Lord had given them. The *lulav* was used in the Temple on each of the seven festive days, even children, if they were able to shake it, being bound to carry one."

The use of these *lulavs* was in this manner: On each of the seven days of the feast, "while the morning sacrifice was being prepared, a priest, accompanied by a joyous procession with music, went down to the Pool of Siloam, whence he drew water into a golden pitcher." Amid much pageantry this water was carried back to the great altar; and when the wine of the drink offering was poured out, so was the water from Siloam, as part of an elaborate ceremony. "As soon as the wine and the water were being poured out, the temple music began, and the 'Hallel' was sung. . . . When the choir came to these words, 'O give thanks to the Lord,' and again when they sang, 'O work then now salvation, Jehovah;' and once more at the close, 'O give thanks unto the Lord,' all the worshippers shook their *lulavs* towards the altar. When, therefore, the multitudes from Jerusalem, on meeting Jesus, 'cut down branches from the trees, and strewed them in the way, and . . . cried, saying, O then, work now salvation to the Son of David!' they applied, in reference to Christ, what was regarded as one of the chief ceremonies of the Feast of Tabernacles, praying that God would from 'the highest' heavens manifest and send that salvation in connection with the Son of David, which was symbolised by the pouring out of the water." (*Temple*, pp. 274-79.)

In the cries of praise and adoration—given each day for seven days, as the temple throngs waved their palm branches toward the great altar, and consisting of a three-times-repeated expression of glorious exultation—we see the pattern for the Hosanna Shout as it has been revealed anew and is now given, also on special and sacred occasions. In our day, while waving white handkerchiefs with each word or phrase of praise, united Israel exults:

Hosanna, Hosanna, Hosanna,
To God and the Lamb;

Hosanna, Hosanna, Hosanna,
To God and the Lamb;
Hosanna, Hosanna, Hosanna,
To God and the Lamb;
Amen, Amen, Amen!

However, at the Feast of Tabernacles, in addition to the daily Hosanna Shout, which followed and grew out of the offering of the daily sacrifice, there was yet another shout—a Great Hosanna, a Hosanna of Hosannas—which was given on one day only, following the festive sacrifices, and on "that great day of the feast." The setting for the Great Hosanna was the ceremonial circuiting of the altar by those appointed so to do. "On every one of the seven days the priests formed in procession, and made the circuit of the altar, singing: 'O then, now work salvation, Jehovah! O Jehovah, give prosperity!' But on the seventh, 'that great day of the feast,' they made the circuit of the altar seven times, remembering how the walls of Jericho had fallen in similar circumstances, and anticipating how, by the direct interposition of God, the walls of heathenism would fall before Jehovah, and the land lie open for his people to go in and possess it." This time, on the day called by the Rabbis "Day of the Great Hosanna," "Day of Willows," and "Day of Beating the Branches," amid their cries of praise to Jehovah, the worshipping throngs waved their *lulavs* with such vigor that "all the leaves were shaken off the willow boughs, and the palm branches beaten in pieces by the side of the altar." Such was the climactic moment of the Hosanna Shout in the Feast of Tabernacles. (*Temple,* pp. 280-81.)

Similitudes of the Feast of Tabernacles

There are in the Feast of Tabernacles more ceremonies that center in Christ, more similitudes that tell of his life and ministry, and more types and shadows that testify of him and his redeeming sacrifice than in any of the other feasts. In a general sense, the Feast of Tabernacles has all that the other feasts had, and a great deal more that is unique, distinctive, and reserved for this most joyous of all festive occasions.

The chief and most important symbolism in all the feasts was that shown forth through the sacrificial ordinances. These bore record of the coming sacrifice of the Lamb of God and taught the people how redemption came and how sins were to be remitted by the sprinkling of his blood. At the Feast of Tabernacles the number of public sacrifices was multiplied, and we may suppose that in practice—because the Day of Atonement had just cleansed and sanctified the people, and because of the especially joyous nature of the feast—there were more private sacrifices, more votive offerings, more freewill offerings than at any other time.

We are aware of the reasons Israel dwelt in booths at this season and of their rejoicing over the harvests reaped; and we see in these things a type of man's pilgrimage through the wilderness of the world and of the eternal rejoicing that will attend the harvest of the souls of men. We have noted how the Hosanna Shout spoke praise to Jehovah and how its very words were interpreted by the multitudes to apply to the Son of David as he made his triumphal entry into Jerusalem as they spread palm branches in the way. We need not pursue further what is clear to all who are spiritually literate, except to show how two of the special ceremonies of the feast bore record of Christ and were used by him to dramatize and announce the fulfillment of the figures found in them. One of these is the pouring out of the water, which preceded the Hosanna Shout, and the other is the illumination of the temple. Both of these ceremonies are said to be post-Mosaic and post-Exilic, that is, to have been added after the day of the great lawgiver and after the return from Babylon. This may be true; if so, it is an indication of continuing revelation to the Lord's people; or, it may be that the rites, though not mentioned in Holy Writ, were part of the ceremonies from the beginning. In any event they were a vital part of valid and approved performances in the day of Jesus. He was acquainted with them and used them for his own purposes.

As we have seen, the priests poured the water from Siloam on the altar after the daily morning sacrifice and before the festive offerings, and as a prelude to the waving of palm branches in the Hosanna Shout. Of this pouring of the water it is said: "Its main and real application was to the future outpouring of the Holy Spirit, as predicted—probably in allusion to this very rite—by Isaiah the prophet. Thus the Talmud says distinctly: 'Why is the name of it called, The drawing out of water? Because of the pouring out of the Holy Spirit, according to what is said: "With joy shall ye draw water out of the wells of salvation."' Hence, also, the feast and the peculiar joyousness of it are alike designated as those of 'the drawing out of water;' for, according to the same Rabbinical authorities, the Holy Spirit dwells in man only through joy."

Now with this concept before us—that Israel by the power of the Spirit was to draw waters from the wells of salvation, and that such was symbolized by the rite then in progress—and with the Hosanna Shout ringing in our ears, let us see what happened in the life of Jesus on the seventh day of the feast. "It was on that day, after the priest had returned from Siloam with his golden pitcher, and for the last time poured its contents to the base of the altar; after the 'Hallel' had been sung to the sound of the flute, the people responding and worshipping as the priests three times drew the threefold blasts from their silver trumpets—just when the interest of the people had been raised to its highest pitch, that, from amidst the mass of worshippers, who were waving towards the altar quite a forest of leafy branches as the last words of Psalm 118 were chanted—a voice was raised which resounded through the Temple, startled the multitude, and carried fear and hatred to the hearts of their leaders. It was Jesus, who 'stood and cried, saying, If any man thirst, let him come unto me, and drink.' Then by faith in him should each one truly become like the Pool of Siloam, and from his inmost being, 'flow rivers of living water.' 'This spake he of the Spirit, which they that believe on him should receive.' (John 7:37-39.) Thus the significance of the rite, in which they had just taken part, was not only fully explained, but the mode of its fulfilment pointed out." (*Temple,* pp. 279-81.)

At the close of the first day of the feast—amid hymns and songs of praise; with instrumental music accompanying and trumpets blowing repeated blasts; as dancers held flaming torches in their hands; and amid pageantry that was itself ritualistic—four of the sons of Levi lighted the four great golden candelabras. "The light shining out of the Temple into the darkness around, and lighting up every court in Jerusalem, must have been intended as a symbol not only of the Shechinah which once filled the Temple, but of that 'great light' which 'the people that walked in darkness' were to see, and which was to shine 'upon them that dwell in the land of the shadow of death.'" (*Temple,* p. 285.) Surely, Master Teacher that he was, the shining forth of this light from the temple was the occasion for Jesus, at that very feast, to say: "I am the light of the world: he that followeth me shall not walk in darkness, but shall have the light of life." (John 8:12.)

So much for the similitudes of the past. But what of the future? The Feast of Tabernacles is both past and future. What wondrous types and figures, what sacred similitudes and symbolisms, will yet be given at the Feast of Tabernacles that is to be? Surely, whatever they are—fitted to the then-existing needs, as they will be—they will testify of a Lord who came, of a Christ who is risen, and of a King who reigns. And it is not without significance that when the Beloved John saw in vision the hosts of Israel and of all men worshipping God in millennial peace and in celestial glory, he saw a renewed scene, before the throne of God, of what had been prefigured around the altar in Herod's Temple. "After this I beheld, and, lo, a great multitude, which no man could number, of all nations, and kindreds, and people, and tongues, stood before the throne, and before the Lamb, clothed with white robes, and palms in their hands; And cried with a loud voice, saying, Salvation to our God which sitteth upon the throne, and unto the Lamb." These are they who are "before the throne of God, and serve him day and night in his temple." And "the Lamb which is in the midst of the throne shall feed them, and shall lead them unto living fountains of waters." (Rev. 7.)

Other Feasts, Fasts, and Formalities

Passover, Pentecost, and Tabernacles—each with its sacred symbolism; each with its redeeming power; each serving as a shadow of better things to come—these were the three great feasts of Jewish Israel, the triennial times when all adult males were to appear before the Lord, in the holy sanctuary, and there renew their covenants and receive anew a remission of their sins. But if there are greater feasts, there must needs be lesser ones: there cannot be the blazing light of the sun at its zenith unless there is also the lesser light of the dawning day or the calming glow of an approaching twilight, and what we must not forget is that the lesser light also guides our footsteps and the lesser feasts also feed our souls.

Each New Moon—of which there were twelve or thirteen each year, as the case may be[2]—was a festive day marked by the offering of special sacrifices,[3] the blowing of trumpets, and a joyous spirit of rededication. It was also an occasion for state banquets, for family feasts, and one, like the Sabbath, when trade and handicraft work ceased. It was with the Day of the New Moon as it was with all else that Israel had: by offering in sacrifice the firstlings of their flocks and the firstfruits of their harvests, all of their flocks and the whole of their harvests became holy before the Lord; and so by sanctifying the first day of the month, the whole lunar period became one of rejoicing and thanksgiving. Religion was truly a way of life with Jewish Israel; their whole course of conduct was religious in nature, worshipful in character, and Jehovah-centered in fact.

"Scarcely any other festive season could have left so continuous an impress on the religious life of Israel as the 'New Moons.' Recurring at the beginning of every month, and marking it, the solemn proclamation of the day, by—'It is sanctified,' was intended to give a hallowed character to each month, while the blowing of the priests' trumpets and the special sacrifices brought, would summon, as it were, the Lord's host to offer their tribute unto their exalted King, and thus bring themselves into 'remembrance' before Him. . . .

"In the law of God only these two things are enjoined in the observance of the 'New Moon'—the 'blowing of trumpets' and special festive sacrifices. Of old the 'blowing of trumpets' had been the signal for Israel's host on their march through the wilderness, as it afterwards summoned them to warfare, and proclaimed or marked days of public rejoicing, and feasts, as well as the 'beginnings of their months.' The object of it is expressly stated to have been 'for a memorial,' that they might 'be remembered before Jehovah,' it being specially added: 'I am Jehovah your God.' It was, so to speak, the host of God assembled, waiting for their Leader; the people of God united to proclaim their King. At the blast of the priests' trumpets they ranged themselves, as it were, under his banner and before his throne, and this symbolical confession and proclamation of him as 'Jehovah their God,' brought them before him to be 'remembered' and 'saved.' And so every season of 'blowing the trumpets,' whether at New Moons, at the Feast of Trumpets or New Year's Day, at other festivals, in the Sabbatical and Year of Jubilee, or in the time of war, was a public acknowledgment of Jehovah as King. Accordingly we find the same symbols adopted in the figurative language of the New Testament. As of old the sound of the trumpet summoned the congregation before the Lord at the door of the Tabernacle, so 'His elect' shall be summoned by the sound of the trumpet in the day of Christ's coming, and not only the living, but those also who had 'slept'—'the dead in Christ.' Similarly, the heavenly hosts are marshalled to the war of successive judgments, till, as 'the seventh angel sounded,' Christ is proclaimed King Universal: 'The kingdoms of this world are become the kingdoms of our Lord, and of his Christ, and he shall reign for ever and ever.' "[4]

On the first day of the seventh month, *Tishri,* the New Moon festival became the Feast of Trumpets, or the Day of Blowing of Trumpets, when horns and trumpets were blown—not merely during the offering of sacrifices as on the regular New Moon festivals, but all day long in Jerusalem, when additional sacrifices were prescribed,[5] and when a holy convocation was held. This was New Year's Day, the first day of the civil year. It preceded the Day of Atonement by ten days, during which time the people were expected to repent, as a condition precedent to the remission of sins that came when the high priest made an atonement for them and sprinkled the redeeming blood in the Holy of Holies.

In the day of Jesus there were three other festive seasons that are not mentioned in the law of Moses, but that were an established part of the worship system to which our Lord was subject. These feasts, brought into being by the spirit of inspiration as it had rested upon the recognized leaders of the people, were established to commemorate great historical events rather than to typify gospel truths. Hence, no special rites and sacrifices were prescribed.

The Feast of Purim commemorated the preservation of the Jews in Persia from the massacre planned by Haman in the days of Esther and Ahasuerus. It lasted two days and included the reading of the book of Esther, the cursing of Haman and all idolaters, and the blessing of Mordecai and all Israelites. It was an occasion of great merriment and rejoicing, and is believed by some to be the "feast of the Jews" to which Jesus went when he healed "the impotent man" at the pool of Bethesda. (John 5:1-9.)[6]

The Feast of Dedication commemorated the cleansing and rededication of Zerubbabel's Temple in 164 B.C., when Judas Maccabaeus freed the Jews from Syro-Grecian domination. It was patterned after the Feast of Tabernacles to the extent that it lasted eight days, included the illumination of the temple, the singing of the Hallel on each day, and the waving of palm branches toward the altar in the Hosanna Shout. It was during this feast that the Lord Jesus, having healed the man who was blind from birth, having announced himself as the Good Shepherd, and having taught plainly that he would die for the people, made the great proclamation: "I and my Father are one." (John 9, 10.)

There were eight times each year when selected families were privileged to bring wood to the temple for sacrificial use, and a ninth, the Feast of Wood Offering, when all the people—"even proselytes, slaves, Nethinim, and bastards, but notably the priests and Levites"—were so privileged. "On this occasion (as on the Day of Atonement) the maidens went dressed in white, to dance and sing in the vineyards around Jerusalem, when an opportunity was offered to young men to select their companions for life." (*Temple*, pp. 336-38.)

Feasting is one form of worship and fasting another; both are so ordained as to bring the Lord's people into communion with him, so that he can bless them for their goodness and purity of heart. From Adam's day to ours, whenever and wherever the true saints have dwelt on earth, the law of the fast has been interwoven into their system of worship. If we had the records of all the dispensations from the beginning, we would find in them the same type of recitation found in the Nephite scripture: "And the church did meet together oft, to fast and to pray, and to speak one with another concerning the welfare of their souls." (Moro. 6:5.)

And so it was with the Jews in the day of Jesus. Fasting was a basic and integral part of their way of worship. The Day of Atonement was a fast day; so also was the first day of the Feast of Purim, which was called the Fast of Esther. Besides these two, there were four other great fasts: one, "in memory of the taking of Jerusalem by Nebuchadnezzar and the interruption of the daily sacrifice"; another, "kept on account of the destruction of the first (and afterwards of the second) Temple"; still another, "in memory of the slaughter of Gedaliah and his associates at Mizpah," as set out in Jeremiah 41; and fourth, commemorating the day on which "the siege of Jerusalem by Nebuchadnezzar commenced." Further: "It was customary to fast *twice a week,* between the Paschal week and Pentecost, and between the Feast of Tabernacles and that of the Dedication of the Temple. The days appointed for this purpose were the Monday and the Thursday of each week—because, according to tradition, Moses went up Mount Sinai the second time to receive the Tables of the Law on a Thursday, and came down again on a Monday." (*Temple,* pp. 339-40.) From Passover to Pentecost was seven weeks, and from Tabernacles to Dedication was about ten weeks, the two periods thus adding about thirty-four fast days to the Jewish calendar of fasts, bringing to a total of about forty the number of formal fast days in each year. In addition there were such private fasts for private purposes as devout persons felt they should hold, all of which adds up to a far heavier fasting schedule than is commonly followed in the true Church as it is now constituted.

When the whole sacrificial system, plus the ritualistic formalities of the various feasts, plus the rituals attending the formal fasts are all viewed together, we have a reasonably comprehensive picture of at least the formal side of Jewish worship in our Lord's day. We have heretofore summarized their rites and formalisms where sacrifices and feasts are concerned. These words relative to fasts complete the picture: "On public fasts, the practice was to bring the ark which contained the rolls of the law from the synagogue into the streets, and to strew ashes upon it. The people all appeared covered with sackcloth and ashes. Ashes were publicly strewn on the heads of the elders and judges. Then one more venerable than the rest would address the people, his sermon being based on such an admonition as this: 'My brethren, it is not said of the men of Nineveh, that God had respect to their sackcloth or their fasting, but that "God saw their works, that they turned from their evil way." Similarly, it is written in the "traditions" of the prophets: "Rend your heart, and not your garments, and turn unto Jehovah your God."' An aged man, whose heart and home 'God had emptied,' that he might give himself wholly to prayer, was chosen to lead the devotions. Confession of sin and prayer mingled with the penitential Psalms. In Jerusalem they gathered at the eastern gate, and seven times as the voice of prayer ceased, they bade the priests 'blow!' and they blew with horns and their priests' trumpets. In other towns, they only blew horns. After prayer, the people retired to the cemeteries to mourn and weep. In order to be a proper fast, it must be continued from one sundown till after the next, when the stars appeared, and for about twenty-six hours the most rigid abstinence from all food and drink was enjoined." (*Temple,* pp. 340-41.)

Our Lord fasted for forty days at the beginning of his ministry, although he and his disciples deliberately did not conform to the burdensome and ritualistic fasting formalities of the day. Instead, in some of the strong language he was wont to use, he condemned the hypocritical and self-seeking level to which the fasting of his day had degenerated.

NOTES

1. See chapters 22, 29, 30, and 95 through 101 in this work, *The Mortal Messiah.*

2. Israel's calendar was lunar, and the advent of each New Moon—a determination made by observing the lunar phases—became a matter of great moment to them. The calendar was kept in balance by inserting a thirteenth month in the year from time to time. The mean duration of the Jewish month was 29 days, 12 hours, 44 minutes, and 3½ seconds; the year itself consisted of 354 days, 8 hours, 48 minutes, and 38 seconds. In a nineteen-year period it took the insertion of seven lunar months to keep the calendar in accordance with the Julian.

3. In addition to the daily sacrifice, the offering included two bullocks, a ram, and seven lambs as a burnt offering, with meat offerings and drink offerings, and a kid as a sin offering. (Num. 28:11-15.) And as on all festive occasions there were also the private offerings of the people.

4. *Temple,* pp. 288-91; Num. 10:1-10; 28:11-15; Matt. 24:31; 1 Cor. 15:52; 1 Thess. 4:16; Rev. 8:2; 10:7; 11:15.

5. In addition to the daily sacrifice and the eleven victims offered at all other New Moon festivals, a young bullock, a ram, and seven lambs of the first year were offered with their accustomed meat offerings, and a kid for a sin offering. (Num. 29:1-6.)

6. In chapter 38 we take the view, as does President J. Reuben Clark, that it was the Feast of the Passover. Elder James E. Talmage skirts the issue and expresses no view one way or the other.

JEWISH SYNAGOGUES IN JESUS' DAY

Organize yourselves; prepare every
needful thing; and establish a house,
even a house of prayer, a house of
fasting, a house of faith, a house
of learning, a house of glory, a house of
order, a house of God; That your
incomings may be in the name of the
Lord; that your outgoings may be in the
name of the Lord; that all your
salutations may be in the name of the
Lord, with uplifted hands unto
the Most High. (D&C 88:119-120.)[1]

The Law of Synagogue Worship

What is a synagogue? In the proper and true and full sense, it is a congregation of saints who worship the Father, in the name of the Son, by the power of the Holy Spirit. It is a congregation of people, of true believers; an assemblage of the saints, of those who have received the truths of heaven by revelation and are trying to apply them to their lives. Just as Zion is the pure in heart, so the synagogue is the saints of God. Zion is people, and the synagogue is people.

But Zion is also a place, one where the pure in heart congregate; and a synagogue is also a place, a house of worship, a building where the worshippers of the true God assemble to pay their devotions to the Most High. In the very nature of things, the term *synagogue* came to refer to the building in which the Lord's people assembled to praise his name and seek his grace. It became a house of worship comparable to the ward meetinghouses and the stake tabernacles found in latter-day Israel. When the people who are Zion lose their purity in heart, and when the congregation that is a true synagogue departs from the faith, all that is left is the house or place where they communed with their Maker. The Spirit may depart, but the building remains. It is looked upon as the synagogue and is so considered by all who see it. Such were the synagogues of which the New Testament speaks.

The word *synagogue* itself is of Greek origin and means to bring together or assemble; it is used in the Septuagint for the Assembly of Israel. It is thus the scriptural designation given, especially from exilic times, to the congregations of true believers, although there have been synagogues or congregations or assemblies of saints from the beginning. Adam assembled his righteous posterity in the valley of Adam-ondi-Ahman, possibly in a house built to hold them; Enoch and others of the preachers of righteousness who lived before the flood presided over congregations of true saints; and Shem, Melchizedek, Abraham, and others of the patriarchs did likewise after the day when the earth was cleansed by water. Moses and the prophets, Aaron and his sons, and various of the Levites and other Israelites continued so to do all down through Jewish history.

We do not know what kinds of temples the saints had before the flood. Our knowledge is limited to the fact that the gospel and its ordinances are always the same, and are always administered in the same way and according to the same terms and conditions; that those who lived anciently were as much entitled to endowments and sealings and washings and anointings and conversations in holy places as we are; and that the Lord has told us that he always, and in all ages, commands his people to build a house to his "holy name." (D&C 124:39.)

Similarly, we do not know what kinds of buildings were used as synagogues before the flood, or during patriarchal times, or while Israel dwelt in Egypt, or during the period of the First Commonwealth, which extended from the Exodus to the Babylonian captivity. Since there were congregations of true worshippers in those days, it follows that they built, as directed by the spirit of inspiration, such facilities as fitted their needs. We do know from secular and archeological sources that synagogues were built during the entire period of the Second Commonwealth, which extended from the captivity of the Jews in Babylonia to the destruction of their temple in A.D. 70. The Book of Mormon tells us that the Nephites had temples and sanctuaries and synagogues "which were built after the manner of the Jews." (2 Ne. 26:26; Alma 16:13.) It is clear from this, since Lehi and Ishmael and their families left Jerusalem just before that great city was overrun by Nebuchadnezzar, that there were synagogues in Jewish Israel before that people was taken into Babylonia. Jews since the destruction of their temple have, of course, continued to build and use synagogues.

Based on the records of the past, and knowing the divinely approved practice of the true Church in modern times, we conclude that synagogues are essential to salvation; that is to say, the Lord's people always and ever must build holy houses in which they can worship him whose they are. Otherwise the great blessings of the gospel will not flow to them in such an abundant measure as to prepare them for celestial rest.

The Manner of Worship in Jewish Synagogues

Whatever the nature of synagogues may have been for the first four thousand years of planet Earth's temporal continuance, our present interest is in what they were like and how they were used in the day the Mortal Messiah dwelt among men. Pure religion, as it once came from the Eternal Fountain, had long since been muddied with the silt and dross of disobedient men; and the synagogues, where streams of living water should have flown, had become stagnant pools full of filth and disease.

These synagogues—those in Judea and Galilee and Perea and in all the places where Jewish Israel dwelt in the first decades of the Christian era—were built in prominent places: on the highest ground, at the corners of streets, or at the entrance to chief squares. Sacred symbols, such as the seven-branched candlestick or a pot of manna, were often carved on the lintels. The synagogues contained seating room for the worshippers, an ark or chest containing the rolls of the law, and a platform with a pulpit or lectern. They were consecrated by prayer, and rules of decorum were imposed upon worshippers, including decency and cleanliness of dress and reverence in demeanor. The church buildings of the early Christians were patterned after them. It is said that there were between 460 and 480 synagogues in Jerusalem at the time it was burned by the torch of Titus. Assuming a normal city population of 600,000, this means somewhat more than 1250 worshippers for each synagogue, a not improbable circumstance.

Synagogues were not used for the offering of sacrifices, but they were used for nearly all other forms of worship—for prayers, funerals, weddings, circumcisions, musical presentations, scriptural readings, sermons, and lectures, as schools for young children, and as places of general assembly and social intercourse. It is apparent from several New Testament accounts that they sometimes were the centers of religious contention and debates. Judicial bodies met in them, and penalties of beating and scourging were carried out within their walls.

Synagogue worship did not fall into a rigid mold. There was a needed elasticity in the approved services, and the ruler of the synagogue exercised the prerogative of altering the services as special needs arose, of inviting whom he would to offer prayers, and of calling on such guest readers and preachers as he chose. It was then as it is now: the over-all objective was the teaching of the people; then, as now, the purpose was to learn the Lord's law and to gain the encouragement needed to keep his commandments. The basic pattern of synagogue worship in the day of Jesus, and thus the one with which he was familiar and in which he participated, was as follows:

1. *Two opening prayers or "benedictions" were offered.* Those in use two thousand years ago were:

"I. Blessed be Thou, O Lord, King of the world, Who formest the light and createst the darkness, Who makest peace and createst everything; Who, in mercy, givest light to the earth and to those who dwell upon it, and in Thy goodness day by day and every day renewest the works of creation. Blessed be the Lord our God for the glory of His handiwork and for the light-giving lights which He has made for His praise. Selah! Blessed be the Lord our God, Who hath formed the lights."

"II. With great love hast Thou loved us, O Lord our God, and with much overflowing pity hast Thou pitied us, our Father and our King. For the sake of our fathers who trusted in Thee, and Thou taughtest them the statutes of life, have mercy upon us and teach us. Enlighten our eyes in Thy law; cause our hearts to cleave to Thy commandments; unite our hearts to love and fear Thy name, and we shall not be put to shame, world without end. For Thou art a God Who preparest salvation, and us hast Thou chosen from among all nations and tongues, and hast in truth brought us near to Thy great Name—Selah—that we may lovingly praise Thee and Thy Oneness. Blessed be the Lord Who in love chose His people Israel." (*Sketches,* pp. 269-70.)

2. *Then came the Shema.* This consisted of the reading of three passages of scripture from Deuteronomy and Numbers that were considered credal in nature; that is, they expressed the basic belief of the Jews concerning the Lord and their

relationship to him, and the need on their part to keep his statutes and judgments as a condition precedent to the receipt of his blessings. The initial word in the passage that begins "Hear, O Israel," is *Shema;* hence the name applied to the scriptures involved. The three passages were:

"Hear, O Israel: The Lord our God is one Lord: And thou shalt love the Lord thy God with all thine heart, and with all thy soul, and with all thy might. And these words, which I command thee this day, shall be in thine heart: And thou shalt teach them diligently unto thy children, and shalt talk of them when thou sittest in thine house, and when thou walkest by the way, and when thou liest down, and when thou risest up. And thou shalt bind them for a sign upon thine hand, and they shall be as frontlets between thine eyes. And thou shalt write them upon the posts of thy house, and on thy gates." (Deut. 6:4-9.)

"And it shall come to pass, if ye shall hearken diligently unto my commandments which I command you this day, to love the Lord your God, and to serve him with all your heart and with all your soul, That I will give you the rain of your land in his due season, the first rain and the latter rain, that thou mayest gather in thy corn, and thy wine, and thine oil. And I will send grass in thy fields for thy cattle, that thou mayest eat and be full. Take heed to yourselves, that your heart be not deceived, and ye turn aside, and serve other gods, and worship them; And then the Lord's wrath be kindled against you, and he shut up the heaven, that there be no rain, and that the land yield not her fruit; and lest ye perish quickly from off the good land which the Lord giveth you. Therefore shall ye lay up these my words in your heart and in your soul, and bind them for a sign upon your hand, that they may be as frontlets between your eyes. And ye shall teach them your children, speaking of them when thou sittest in thine house, and when thou walkest by the way, when thou liest down, and when thou risest up. And thou shalt write them upon the door posts of thine house, and upon thy gates: That your days may be multiplied, and the days of your children, in the land which the Lord sware unto your fathers to give them, as the days of heaven upon the earth." (Deut. 11:13-21.)

"And the Lord spake unto Moses, saying, Speak unto the children of Israel, and bid them that they make them fringes in the borders of their garments throughout their generations, and that they put upon the fringe of the borders a ribband of blue: And it shall be unto you for a fringe, that ye may look upon it, and remember all the commandments of the Lord, and do them; and that ye seek not after your own heart and your own eyes, after which ye use to go a whoring: That ye may remember, and do all my commandments, and be holy unto your God. I am the Lord your God, which brought you out of the land of Egypt, to be your God: I am the Lord your God." (Num. 15:37-41.)

3. *Next came the prayers after the Shema.*

"True it is, that Thou art Jehovah our God and the God of our fathers, our King and the King of our fathers, our Saviour and the Saviour of our fathers, our Creator, the Rock of our salvation, our Help and our Deliverer. Thy name is from everlasting, and there is no God beside Thee. A new song did they that were delivered sing to Thy Name by the seashore; together did all praise and own Thee King, and say, Jehovah shall reign world without end! Blessed be the Lord Who saveth Israel!"

Next: "O Lord our God! cause us to lie down in peace, and raise us up again to life, O our King! Spread over us the tabernacle of Thy peace; strengthen us before Thee in Thy good counsel, and deliver us for Thy Name's sake. Be Thou for protection round about us; keep far from us the enemy, the pestilence, the sword, famine, and affliction. Keep Satan from before and from behind us, and hide us in the shadow of Thy wings, for Thou art a God Who helpest and deliverest us; and Thou, O God, art a gracious and merciful King. Keep Thou our going out and our coming in, for life and for peace, from henceforth and for ever." (*Sketches,* p. 271.)

4. *Then came nineteen eulogies, benedictions, or supplications.* The first three and the last three—and we shall quote these six—were fixed and formalized in the day of Jesus. In his day other petitions, extemporaneous in nature, were inserted between the two groups of three, thus giving rise to the endless repetitions and long prayers so offensive to our Lord. The six formal eulogies were as follows:

"I. 'Blessed be the Lord our God and the God of our fathers, the God of Abraham, the God of Isaac, and the God of Jacob; the great, the mighty, and the terrible God; the Most High God, Who showeth mercy and kindness, Who createth all things, Who remembereth the gracious promises to the fathers, and bringeth a Saviour to their children's children, for His own Name's sake, in love. O King, Helper, Saviour, and Shield! Blessed art Thou, O Jehovah, the Shield of Abraham.'

"II. 'Thou, O Lord, art mighty for ever; Thou, Who quickenest the dead, art mighty to save. In Thy mercy Thou preservest the living; Thou quickenest the dead; in Thine abundant pity Thou bearest up those who fall, and healest those who are diseased, and loosest those who are bound, and fulfillest Thy faithful word to those who sleep in the dust. Who is like unto Thee, Lord of strength, and who can be compared to Thee, Who killest and makest alive, and causest salvation to spring forth? And faithful art Thou to give life unto the dead. Blessed be Thou, Jehovah, Who quickenest the dead!"

"III. 'Thou art holy, and Thy Name is holy; and the holy ones praise Thee every day. Selah! Blessed art Thou, Jehovah God, the Holy One!' "

At this point there were thirteen other eulogies, and then the following three:

"XVII. 'Take gracious pleasure, O Jehovah our God, in Thy people Israel, and in their prayers. Accept the burnt-offerings of Israel, and their prayers, with Thy good pleasure; and may the services of Thy people Israel be ever acceptable unto Thee. And oh that our eyes may see it, as

Thou turnest in mercy to Zion! Blessed be Thou, O Jehovah, Who restoreth His Shechinah to Zion!'

"XVIII. 'We praise Thee, because Thou art Jehovah our God, and the God of our fathers, for ever and ever. Thou art the Rock of our life, the Shield of our salvation, from generation to generation. We laud Thee, and declare Thy praise for our lives which are kept within Thine hand, and for our souls which are committed unto Thee, and for Thy wonders which are with us every day, and Thy wondrous deeds and Thy goodnesses, which are at all seasons—evening, morning, and mid-day. Thou gracious One, Whose compassions never end; Thou pitying One, Whose grace never ceaseth—for ever do we put our trust in Thee! And for all this Thy Name, O our King, be blessed and extolled always, for ever and ever! And all living bless Thee—Selah—and praise Thy Name in truth, O God, our Salvation and our Help. Blessed art Thou, Jehovah; Thy Name is the gracious One, to Whom praise is due.'

"XIX. 'Oh bestow on Thy people Israel great peace, for ever; for Thou art King and Lord of all peace, and it is good in Thine eyes to bless Thy people Israel with praise at all times and in every hour. Blessed art Thou, Jehovah, Who blesseth His people Israel with peace." (*Sketches,* pp. 273-75.)

All of these prayers were given by one person, with the congregation responding by an "Amen." The normal procedure was for the one appointed to give the prayers and recite the Shema also to be the one who read from the prophets. If this procedure was followed in Capernaum on that Sabbath when our Lord read the prophecy of Isaiah relative to Himself and announced its fulfillment in Him, then Jesus himself gave, on that occasion, the foregoing prayers. A careful analysis will show many things in these prayers that were fulfilled in the mortal ministry of him of whom we testify.

5. *At this point the Aaronic blessing was pronounced,* either by a priest or by someone appointed to represent him.

This blessing was:

"The Lord bless thee, and keep thee: The Lord make his face shine upon thee, and be gracious unto thee: The Lord lift up his countenance upon thee, and give thee peace." (Num. 6:24-26.)

6. *Then came the reading of the law.* That is, selected readings were taken from the Pentateuch, composed of the five books of Moses, which was considered to be the law. On the Sabbath seven persons were called upon to read from the law, and on other days a lesser number. The first and the last reader also offered a benediction.

7. *Next came a lesson from the prophets,* meaning that someone read from and expounded upon a selected prophetic passage. This is what our Lord did when in Capernaum he opened the book and found in Isaiah the passage pertaining to himself, which he then read and expounded.

8. *Finally, there was a sermon or address.* No doubt this was the portion of the service when Jesus and Paul and the early disciples found occasion to preach Christ, and that salvation which comes through him, to the Jewish worshippers in the synagogues of Palestine, Ephesus, Corinth, and elsewhere.

How Jesus Used Jewish Synagogues

There can be little room for doubt that the Lord Jesus while a child went to school in a synagogue in Nazareth. We know he grew up in subjection to Mary and Joseph, and synagogue schooling was a way of life for all of the young and rising generation. Nor can there be any doubt that during his formative and maturing years our Lord worshipped in various synagogues, even as he also went to Jerusalem and mingled with the worshipping throngs in the temple courts at Passover time. He was a Jew, brought up in subjection to Jewish law and Jewish tradition, and these included making the synagogue a living part of one's being.

We do know that from the day he began his ministry

until he voluntarily laid down his life, the temple and the various synagogues became his bases of operation. In them he taught and read and preached; in them he testified, exhorted, and rebuked; in them he healed the sick and wrought endless miracles; in them the Divine Light was shown forth with a heavenly radiance that left no place for the shadows of darkness then enshrouding a fallen nation.

Our New Testament accounts themselves do not recite the mode and manner of worship carried out in the synagogues in our Lord's day in the Land of Jesus; nor is it needful that they should do so. Those to whom the Gospels and the Acts of the Apostles were first written were already familiar with the songs and sermons, with the prayers and preachments, and with the rites and readings presented so repetitiously in those Jewish houses of worship and learning. What we have recounted in this respect has come from nonscriptural but authentic sources. Our scriptures simply say that the Savior taught or healed or read or preached in the synagogues, and it is left for us to conclude—and there is no alternative but to do so—that his doings and sayings within the sacred walls of necessity fitted into the regular order supervised by the rulers of the synagogues and with which those then and there assembled were familiar.

He taught in the synagogues because that is where people went to be taught, to hear sermons, and to learn how and in what manner they might draw near to Jehovah. And he healed the sick in the synagogues because that is where devout people, people with faith to be healed, came to seek blessings from the Source of all that is good. Those who first received the scriptural words of the apostles Matthew and John and of the disciples Mark and Luke would expect to read that Jesus taught and healed in the synagogues because those were the places where such things should have been done in the society and under the circumstances then prevailing.

When the day of Jesus' ministry arrived, he was first baptized by John in Jordan. There the Holy Ghost descended in quiet serenity like a dove. Then he was led of the Spirit into the wilderness, where he fasted for forty days, was tempted of the devil, and overcame the world as it were. Then he was ready to preach; then he was ready to heal.

As Matthew records it: "From that time Jesus began to preach. . . . And Jesus went about all Galilee, teaching in their synagogues, and preaching the gospel of the kingdom, and healing all manner of sickness and all manner of disease among the people." (Matt. 4:17-23.) Also: "And Jesus went about all the cities and villages, teaching in their synagogues, and preaching the gospel of the kingdom, and healing every sickness and every disease among the people." (Matt. 9:35; 13:54-58; Mark 6:1-6.)

Mark says our Lord called Zebedee's sons from their nets, and that he and they went straightway into Capernaum, where Jesus "on the sabbath day . . . entered into the synagogue, and taught. . . . And there was in their synagogue a man with an unclean spirit," which evil spirit forsook his ill-gotten abode at Jesus' word. Thereafter, "he preached in their synagogues throughout all Galilee, and cast out devils." (Mark 1:16-39; Luke 4:31-44.)

Luke gives this account of the commencement of his ministry: "And he taught in their synagogues, being glorified of all. And he came to Nazareth, where he had been brought up: and, as his custom was, he went into the synagogue on the sabbath day, and stood up for to read." This day in Nazareth was the one on which he announced his divine Sonship by saying in the synagogue that he came in fulfillment of Isaiah's great Messianic prophecy about preaching the gospel, healing the brokenhearted, and setting the captive free. (Luke 4:15-30.) And so it was that day in and day out, Sabbath after Sabbath, throughout his whole ministry, he sought out congregations of hearers, who were assembled, as was the norm of the day, in places where preachments should be given, and he there gave food and drink to those who hungered and thirsted after righteousness.

It was in a synagogue on the Sabbath that he was asked,

"Is it lawful to heal on the sabbath days?" to which he responded, "It is lawful to do well on the sabbath days"; then, so that his answer would be forever implanted in the hearts of his hearers, he said to one with a withered hand, "Stretch forth thine hand," and he doing so was healed instantly. (Matt. 12:9-13; Luke 13:9-17.) It was in a synagogue in Capernaum, upon whose lintel archeologists have found carved a pot of manna, that he preached his great sermon on the bread of life, showing that the manna given to their fathers was but a type of the living bread that should come down from heaven, "that a man may eat thereof, and not die." (John 6:50.) We need not say more along this line except to note that, when questioned by the high priest, Jesus answered, "I spake openly to the world; I ever taught in the synagogue, and in the temple, whither the Jews always resort." (John 18:19-20.)

Until the day of Jesus, except for the temple itself, Jewish synagogues were the only divinely approved houses of worship in the Old World. But as the Jewish people began the process of rejecting their Jewish Messiah, the true spirit of worship began to withdraw itself from those houses in which the revealed truths of the past had been taught with at least a measurable degree of understanding. As the people became polarized—a few believing in Jesus, the great masses rejecting his divine Messiahship—the Pharisees and rulers of the synagogues decreed that all who believed in Christ "should be put out of the synagogue." (John 9:22; 12:42-43; 16:2.) The schooling, the social intercourse, the religious teachings of the people—these were to be denied them.

In process of time the synagogues became houses of hate and persecution rather than houses of learning and true worship. Jesus told the Twelve and other true believers: "Beware of men: for they will deliver you up to the councils, and they will scourge you in their synagogues." (Matt. 10:17; 23:34; Mark 13:9.) In those sacred spots where sermons had attested to the saving power of the Promised Messiah, cries of anguish would now be heard from the lips of true believers as the scourgers' lash cut their flesh. Paul himself, "breathing out threatenings and slaughter against the disciples of the Lord," took letters from the high priest addressed to the rulers of the synagogues in Damascus, reciting "that if he found any of this way, whether they were men or women, he might bring them bound unto Jerusalem." (Acts 9:1-2.) In an open confession of his sins, Paul later said, "Lord . . . I imprisoned and beat in every synagogue them that believed on thee." (Acts 22:19; 26:11.) By rejecting Jesus and opposing the truth, the congregation of Israel became the congregation of unbelief, of hatred, of evil, of Lucifer. They became, as the scripture recites, "the synagogue of Satan." (Rev. 2:9; 3:9.)

NOTES

1. These words appertain to the building of the Kirtland Temple, which temple was a synagogue; that is to say, the Kirtland Temple was not a temple in the full and true sense of the word; it was not a sanctuary set apart from the world; it was not designed for the performance of those endowments, ordinances, and sealings which open the door to eternal salvation for the living and the dead—for, in the day of its building, these things had not yet been revealed in this dispensation. The Lord's House in Kirtland was a temple in the sense that it was a House of the Lord, one to which he and his servants came, but it was also, in a manner of speaking, a synagogue, meaning a House of the Lord where true worshippers came to worship the Father in Spirit and in truth.

Chapter 11

JEWISH SABBATHS IN JESUS' DAY

The sabbath was made for man, and
not man for the sabbath: Therefore the
Son of man is Lord also
of the sabbath. . . .

Is it lawful to do good on the sabbath
days, or to do evil? to save life, or to
kill? (Mark 2:27-28; 3:4.)

The Law of Sabbath Worship

We do not overstate our case when we say that the Jewish system of Sabbath observance that prevailed in the day of Jesus was ritualistic, degenerate, and almost unbelievably absurd, a system filled with fanatical restrictions. Nor do we think that this is a conclusion upon which reasonable minds can differ, once the facts are in and the evidence is weighed.

Their system of Sabbath worship clearly shows how a great and important concept can be preserved even though it is twisted and perverted in the hands of uninspired teachers. To see why our Jewish brethren in the meridian of time placed such emphasis on Sabbath observance, we need but record the true order of such worship that has prevailed among the Lord's people from the beginning. This we have done, in brief form, in chapter 21 of *The Promised Messiah: The First Coming of Christ.* For our purposes now, as a prelude to a recitation of what prevailed in our Lord's day, we shall simply summarize some of the basic principles.

Those whose souls are touched by the Holy Spirit and who understand the hand-dealings of the Almighty with his earthly children know that Sabbath observance is essential to salvation, and that those who keep this day holy, in the manner and way Deity designed, shall be guided along the path leading to salvation in the celestial kingdom of heaven. Again, we are not overstating the case, nor are we reaching a conclusion without scriptural warrant.

The Lord our Heavenly Father created us; ordained the plan and system whereunder we could advance and progress and become like him; placed us in this mortal sphere, where we are subject to all of the lusts and passions of the flesh; and decreed that if we would overcome the world and live godly lives in spite of earth and hell, he would save us in his everlasting presence. While here, we must deal with temporal things and be subject to Satan's enticements. Unless we somehow manage to turn from worldly matters and put first in our lives the things of God's kingdom, we shall fail the test and lose our souls.

We need help, constant help—help from day to day, help all the time. Such is given through the gospel and by the Holy Spirit. And the Sabbath day is one of the chief arrangements whereby this spiritual help is made available. That Holy Being who prepared the test we are now taking, in his infinite wisdom, knew—and so arranged—that if we would devote one day in seven exclusively to spiritual things, we would have power to conduct ourselves in such a way as to save our souls. Hence came the Sabbath.

The true Sabbath is a day of worship, a day for spiritual refreshment, a day to learn the laws of the Lord, a day to renew our covenants, a day to pay our devotions to the Most High. The true Sabbath is a day to remember the Lord and his goodness to us, a day to read and ponder his holy word, a day to confess our sins, a day to strengthen each other, and to visit the fatherless and the widows in their affliction. The true Sabbath is a day of preaching and testifying, a day of fasting and prayer, a day of rejoicing and thanksgiving, a day to partake of the good things of the Spirit and to sanctify our souls. The true Sabbath is essential to salvation, and those who use it to the full, according to the divine intent, shall attain celestial rest.

In the very nature of things, true Sabbath worship precludes worldly activities. Hence on that day we rest from all servile work; we lay our temporal pursuits aside for the moment; we refrain from recreational activities; we let our crops and our herds fend for themselves and our shops and our factories remain closed and idle; we leave the fish in the streams and the golf clubs in the locker room. Except for the preparation of modest meals, or the pulling of the ox from the mire, as it were, on this the Lord's day, we do no other things except to worship the Lord in spirit and in truth. Such was the law of the Sabbath among the ancestors of the Jews, and such is that law among us.

It should come as no surprise, then, to find this law singled out as a sign between the Lord and his people. Its proper observance always has identified and always will identify the true saints, and its desecration and improper observance always has revealed and always will reveal those who are not the Lord's people and who are not feeding their souls spiritually according to the plan of the great Creator.

It should come as no surprise to find the Lord, by the mouth of Moses, decreeing death to those who desecrate his holy day, or to hear him promise Israel that if they would hallow the Sabbath, "As I commanded your fathers . . . Then shall there enter into the gates of this city kings and princes sitting upon the throne of David, riding in chariots and on horses, they, and their princes, the men of Judah, and the inhabitants of Jerusalem: and this city shall remain for ever." (Jer. 17:20-27.)

We need not, for our present purposes, pursue further the matter of the true law of the Sabbath. It suffices for us to know that few things in the gospel are more important, and for us to be aware of the original philosophy that preceded the perversions of Jesus' day. The Sabbath as such was no less important among the Jews in that day than it had ever been. If properly kept, it could have led to the fulness of the blessings of the gospel. That those then living in the fading light of the past still knew, in principle, that it was important beyond expression is perfectly clear from the records of the day. The issue is that they chose to keep and observe its law in such a way that their very observance was itself a desecration.

The Jews and Their Sabbath

Jewish worship in the day of Jesus—with its inordinate emphasis on formalisms, on rituals, on performances, on the letter rather than the spirit of the law—revolved around four centers:

1. *The temple,* Jehovah's holy house, the place where Deity revealed himself, and to which he called all Israel to come and serve and worship him;

2. *Sacrificial offerings* performed in similitude of the sacrifice of the Promised Messiah, performed as types and shadows of the sacrifice of the Eternal High Priest, who, entering himself within the heavenly veil, was able to lead all others into the Divine Presence;

3. Those *feasts or festivals* when the faithful, in person or represented by delegates, appeared before the Lord in Jerusalem, at the temple, to worship, sacrifice, and receive a renewed outpouring of divine grace; and

4. *Sabbath observance,* which included attendance at worship services in the synagogues, plus conformity to the rabbinically imposed restrictions of rest, which turned what should have been a day of spiritual refreshment into one of drudgery and unneeded and often unheeded self-denial.

As to the temple—it was still the Lord's house, though it had been defiled in large measure by wicked men, so much so that the Divine Presence no longer rested between the cherubim in the Holy of Holies.

As to sacrifice—they were still performed by Aaronic authority, though the priestly administrators and the people generally no longer saw in them the great spiritual symbolisms that made them such an important part of the worship of their fathers.

As to the feasts—they still assembled Israel to the city of the Great King, where true worship and divinely approved ordinances could be performed, but they had degenerated into occasions of revelry and debate, and the worship that should have attended them left much to be desired.

As to Sabbath observance—this was a field in which all Jewry had gone wild, a true principle, out of which a sane practice should have grown but which was so altered, twisted, and perverted that what should have been a holy day had become a blasphemous mockery. The synagogue services had some merit, to which reference has been made in chapter 10, but all else that then attended these dehallowed days came from beneath and not from above.

"Ye Shall Do No Servile Work Therein"

Of his holy day—"the sabbath of the Lord thy God"—Jehovah commanded: "In it thou shalt not do any work, thou, nor thy son, nor thy daughter, thy manservant, nor thy maidservant, nor thy cattle, nor thy stranger that is within thy gates." (Ex. 20:10.)

Such was the divine decree, but the practical problem was—what is work? What physical acts might be done by members of the chosen race, or their slaves, or their cattle, without incurring the wrath of Him who was jealous of his name and who visited the iniquity of the fathers upon the children unto the third and fourth generation among those that hated him?

Sowing and reaping are clearly work. But suppose only a few seeds are scattered on unploughed land, is such an act sinful? If oxen bear a yoke and pull a plough, it is work, but if they only carry the weight of a rope, what then? Is it permissible to set a broken arm, to give medicine to sick persons, or for a lame man to use his crutches? Can an author write a page, a single line, or even one letter from the alphabet? Is it permissible to read, or walk, or boil water, or what have you, and if so, how limited or extensive may the exertions be? If a man stumbles and falls, must he lie prone until the Sabbath's end? How heavy a burden may he bear without breaking the divine decree? These and ten thousand other tickish, petty questions occupied the time of the brightest minds in all Jewry, and the answers they gave and the rules they adopted can scarcely be believed.

Jewish law in Jesus' day forbade thirty-nine chief or principal types of work. These were: (1) sowing, (2) ploughing, (3) reaping, (4) binding sheaves, (5) threshing, (6) winnowing, (7) sifting (selecting), (8) grinding, (9) sifting in a sieve, (10) kneading, (11) baking—all of which restrictions had to do with the preparation of bread; (12) shearing the wool, (13) washing it, (14) beating it, (15) dyeing it, (16) spinning, (17) putting it on the weaver's beam, (18) making two thrum threads, (19) weaving two threads, (20) separating two threads, (21) making a knot, (22) undoing a knot, (23) sewing two stitches, (24) tearing in order to sew two stitches—all of which restrictions had to do with dress; (25) catching deer, (26) killing, (27) skinning, (28) salting it, (29) preparing its skin, (30) scraping off its hair, (31) cutting it up, (32) writing two letters, (33) scraping in order to write two letters—all of which are connected with hunting and writing; (34) building, (35) pulling down, (36) extinguishing fire, (37) lighting fire, (38) beating with the hammer, and (39) carrying from one possession into the other—all of which appertain to the work necessary for a private house. Each of these thirty-nine principal prohibitions contained within itself numerous related items that were banned on the Sabbath day.

Jewish tractates of Jesus' day set forth chapter after chapter of detailed explanations and illustrations relative to these thirty-nine principal types of prohibited work. For instance: Scattering two seeds was sowing; sweeping away or breaking a single clod was ploughing; plucking one blade of grass was sin; watering fruit or removing a withered leaf was forbidden; picking fruit, or even lifting it from the ground, was reaping; cutting a mushroom was a double sin, one both of harvesting and of sowing, for a new one would grow in place of the old; fishing, or anything that put an end to life, ranked with harvesting; rubbing ears of corn together, or anything else connected with food, was classed as binding of sheaves.

"If a woman were to roll wheat to take away the husks, she would be guilty of sifting with a sieve. If she were rubbing the ends of the stalks, she would be guilty of threshing. If she were cleansing what adheres to the side of a stalk, she would be guilty of sifting. If she were bruising the stalk, she would be guilty of grinding. If she were throwing it up in her hands, she would be guilty of winnowing. Distinctions like the following are made: A radish may be dipped into salt, but not left in it too long, since this would be to make pickle. A new dress might be put on, irrespective of the danger that in so doing it might be torn. Mud on the dress might be crushed in the hand and shaken off, but the dress must not be rubbed (for fear of affecting the material). If a person took a bath, opinions are divided, whether the whole body should be dried at once, or limb after limb. If water had fallen on the dress, some allowed the dress to be shaken but not wrung; others, to be wrung but not shaken. One Rabbi allowed to spit into the handkerchief, and that although it may necessitate the compressing of what had been wetted; but there is a grave discussion whether it was lawful to spit on the ground, and then to rub it with the foot, because thereby the earth may be scratched. It may, however, be done on stones. In the labour of grinding would be included such an act as crushing salt. To sweep, or to water the ground, would involve the same sin as beating out the corn. To lay on a plaster would be a grievous sin; to scratch out a big letter, leaving room for two small ones, would be a sin, but to write one big letter occupying the room of two small letters was no sin. To change one letter to another might imply a double sin. And so on through endless details!" (Edersheim 2:783.)

What constituted a burden that might not be carried on the Sabbath day? By the mouth of Jeremiah the Lord had said: "Take heed to yourselves, and bear no burden on the sabbath day, nor bring it in by the gates of Jerusalem: Neither carry forth a burden out of your houses on the sabbath day, neither do ye any work, but hallow ye the sabbath day, as I commanded your fathers." (Jer. 17:21-22.)

To the followers of rabbinism this meant: Carry no burden greater than the weight of a fig and no food larger than the size of an olive. Anything, however trifling, that could be put to practical use was a burden. "Thus, two horse's hairs might be made into a birdtrap; a scrap of clean paper into a custom-house notice; a small piece of paper written upon might be converted into a wrapper for a small flagon. In all these cases, therefore, transport would involve sin. Similarly, ink sufficient to write two letters, wax enough to fill up a small hole, even a pebble with which you might aim at a little bird, or a small piece of broken earthenware with which you might stir the coals, would be 'burdens!'" (Edersheim 2:784.)

"It was forbidden to write two letters, either with the right hand or the left, whether of the same size or of different sizes, or with different inks, or in different languages, or with any pigment; with ruddle, gum, vitriol, or anything that can make marks; or even to write two letters, one on each side of a corner of two walls, or on two leaves of a writing-tablet, if they could be read together, or to write them on the body. But they might be written on any dark fluid, on the sap of a fruit-tree, on road-dust, on sand, or on anything in which the writing did not remain. If they were written with the hand turned upside down, or with the foot, or the mouth, or the elbow, or if one letter were added to another previously made, or other letters traced over, or if a person designed to write the letter and only wrote two, or if he wrote one letter on the ground and one on the wall, or on two walls, or on two pages of a book, so that they could not be read together, it was not illegal. If a person, through forgetfulness, wrote two characters at different times, one in the morning, the other, perhaps towards evening, it was a question among the Rabbis whether he had or had not broken the Sabbath." (Geikie, pp. 448-49.)

What if a house or its contents caught fire on the Sabbath? To put out a fire and save a building or its contents was clearly work. However, one might rescue from the fire the scriptures and the phylacteries and the cases that contained them, but liturgical pieces, though they contained the name of Deity, were to be left to the flames. Only the food and drink needed for the Sabbath might be rescued, except that "if the food were in a cupboard or basket the whole might be carried out. Similarly, all utensils needed for the Sabbath meal, but of dress only what was absolutely necessary, might be saved, it being, however, provided, that a person might put on a dress, save it, go back and put on another, and so on." (Edersheim 2:784-85.)

How far might one carry a burden on the Sabbath day? The set distance was an ordinary Sabbath day's journey, which extended two thousand cubits from one's dwelling. But out of practical necessity and by the use of legal fictions this distance might be extended. For instance, if groups of houses could be somehow defined as one dwelling, then burdens could be carried between them. Each house opening onto a private court was, of course, a private dwelling, and so it was unlawful to carry things from one to another on the Sabbath. If, however, all of the families would deposit, before the Sabbath, some food in the common court, a connection would thus be established among them all so that they could be considered one dwelling, and all difficulties about carrying burdens from one to the other would be removed. Or if a man deposited, on Friday, food for two meals, at a distance of two thousand cubits from his dwelling, he thereby constituted that place his dwelling, and on the Sabbath he could carry burdens an extra two thousand cubits. Or if a beam, a wire, or a rope were placed across a blind alley or a narrow street, this made all the houses thereon one dwelling "so that everything was lawful there which a man might do on the Sabbath in his own house." (Edersheim 2:777.)

Practice of the healing arts was work and therefore could not be done on the Sabbath. Broken bones could not be set; surgical operations were not allowed; emetics could not be given. "A plaster might be worn, provided its object was to prevent the wound from getting worse, not to heal it, for that would have been a work. Ornaments which could not easily be taken off might be worn in one's courtyard. Similarly, a person might go about with wadding in his ear, but not with false teeth nor with a gold plug in the tooth. If the wadding fell out of the ear, it could not be replaced. Some, indeed, thought that its healing virtues lay in the oil in which it had been soaked, and which had dried up, but others ascribed them to the warmth of the wadding itself. In either case there was danger of healing—of doing anything for the purpose of a cure—and hence wadding might not be put into the ear on the Sabbath, although if worn before it might be continued. Again, as regarded false teeth: they might fall out, and the wearer might then lift and carry them, which would be sinful on the Sabbath. But anything which formed part of the ordinary dress of a person might be worn also on the Sabbath, and children whose ears were being bored might have a plug put into the hole. It was also allowed to go about on crutches, or with a wooden leg, and children might have bells on their dresses; but it was prohibited to walk on stilts, or to carry any heathen amulet." (Edersheim 2:782.)

Although remedies could not be used for the curing of the sick, certain acts could be performed if there was "actual danger to life." Thus: "If on the Sabbath a wall had fallen on a person, and it were doubtful whether he was under the ruins or not, whether he was alive or dead, a Jew or Gentile, it would be duty to clear away the rubbish sufficiently to find the body. If life were not extinct, the labour would have to be continued; but if the person were dead nothing further should be done to extricate the body." (Edersheim 2:787.)

To kindle a fire on the Sabbath day was forbidden. Food must be prepared, lights kindled, and vessels washed before sunset on Friday. Ovens could not be kept warm for Sabbath use, and there were scores of regulations relative to food that might be eaten. For instance: "If a hen had laid on the Sabbath, the egg was forbidden, because, evidently, it could not have been destined on a weekday for eating, since it was not yet laid, and did not exist; while if the hen had been kept, not for laying but for fattening, the egg might be eaten as forming part of the hen that had fallen off!" (Edersheim 2:787.)

If an object was thrown into the air and caught again with the same hand, it was sin; if caught with the other hand, there was a division of opinion; if caught in the mouth and eaten, there was no guilt because the object no longer existed. "If it rained, and the water which fell from the sky were carried, there was no sin in it; but if the rain had run down from a wall it would involve sin. If a person were in one place, and his hand filled with fruit stretched into another, and the Sabbath overtook him in this attitude, he would have to drop the fruit, since if he withdrew his full hand from one locality into another, he would be carrying a burden on the Sabbath." (Edersheim 2:779.)

We need not go further in our analysis of the degenerate system of Sabbath observance imposed by the Rabbis upon Jesus, Joseph, Mary, Peter, James, John, and all the Jews of their day. We must state pointedly, however, that what is here recited is only a sample, a small sample—not so much as a thousandth part—of what then existed.[1] Obviously the mere recitation of such regulations as these should suffice to show the apostate nature of that Jewish system of worship which was so caustically condemned by Him who said: "Ye made the commandment of God of none effect by your tradition." (Matt. 15:6.)

We must also state that however absurd and lacking in spirituality these Jewish Sabbath regulations seem to us, they were of deep and sincere concern to those who had submitted themselves to that rule of priestcraft out of which they grew. In this connection, there were even times in their long history when they submitted to slavery and death rather than wage war on the Sabbath, although in the days of the Second Commonwealth it had been established that defensive military acts were permissible.[2]

In the light of all this it will come as no surprise—as we hereafter set forth how the Rabbis and those who sat in Aaron's seat opposed the great High Priest who ministered among them—to find religious bigots thirsting for Innocent Blood because the Son of Man defies their traditions and claims Lordship over the Sabbath itself.

NOTES

1. These comments about Jewish Sabbath observance and the illustrations set forth are digested from Edersheim, pages 775-87, and from Geikie, pages 448-50, both of which authors, in turn, digested their material from the Mishnah. The English version of the Mishnah, used in this work by the present author, takes thirty-seven solid pages of fine print to set forth the detailed policies and illustrations that governed Sabbath observance in ancient Jewry (Mishnah, pp. 100-136), plus special Sabbath regulations recited in connection with the feasts and other matters.

2. Josephus gives us an account of how the Jews were persuaded to wage defensive war on the Sabbath. It happened in the day of Mattathias, father of the great Judas Maccabeus. At that time the Syrian king, Antiochus IV (Epiphanes), had forbidden the Jewish religion. Mattathias led a revolt and with some insurgents fled from Jerusalem into the nearby deserts. The pursuing and attacking Syrians "fought against them on the Sabbath-day, and they burnt them as they were in the caves, without resistance, and without so much as stopping up the entrances of the caves. And they avoided to defend themselves on that day, because they were not willing to break in upon the honour they owed the Sabbath, even in such distresses; for our law requires that we rest upon that day. There were about a thousand, with their wives and children, who were smothered and died in these caves: but many of those that escaped joined themselves to Mattathias, and appointed him to be their ruler, who taught them to fight even on the Sabbath-day; and told them that unless they would do so, they would become their own enemies, by observing the law [so rigorously,] while their adversaries would still assault them on this day, and they would not then defend themselves; and that nothing could then hinder but they must all perish without fighting. This speech persuaded them; and this rule continues among us to this day, that if there be a necessity, we may fight on Sabbath-days." (Josephus, *Antiquities*, Book 12, chapter 6.)

Chapter 12

JEWISH FAMILY LIFE IN JESUS' DAY

Our fathers have told us [the things of God]. We will not hide them from their children, shewing to the generation to come the praises of the Lord, and his strength, and his wonderful works that he hath done.

For he established a testimony in Jacob, and appointed a law in Israel, which he commanded our fathers, that they should make them known to their children:

That the generation to come might know them, even the children which should be born; who should arise and declare them to their children:

That they might set their hope in God, and not forget the works of God, but keep his commandments. (Ps. 78:3-7.)

The Law of Family Worship

All things center in the family, and the family is the center of all things. Salvation itself is a family affair and consists of the continuation of the family unit in eternity. God himself is exalted and omnipotent because he is a Father, and his kingdoms and dominions are composed of his children over whom he rules in equity and justice forever. The whole system of salvation, of revelation, of religion, of worship—all that comes from Deity for the benefit of man—is tied into a divine patriarchal system. If any of us gain the fulness of reward in our Father's kingdom, it will be because we enter into family relationships that are eternal in nature; it will be because we have perfected our own patriarchal family units. These concepts are part of the very foundation upon which true religion rests.

True worship is a family affair. God deals with and through families, righteous families, faithful families, families who will believe and obey. The whole object and end of true religion is to enable a man to become—through celestial marriage—an eternal father in his own right, and to enable a woman to become an eternal mother. It is thus inevitable—it could not be otherwise—that God, who is our Father, deals with chosen and favored families in making his mind and will and purposes known to mortals.

Adam, our first father, received the gospel, became the presiding patriarch over all the earth for all ages, and presided over all of the Lord's earthly affairs during his mortal probation. The congregation of saints in his and succeeding days—or in other words, the Church—was organized on a family or patriarchal basis. From his day to the time of the flood, the Church was a family organization; the priesthood went from father to son; the gospel was taught by parents to their children, and then by children to their children and their children's children.

After our first parents had received the gospel; after they had learned by revelation of the future atonement of the

Only Begotten; after they knew about the redemption, with its immortality for all men, and its eternal life for the obedient, the record says: "And Adam and Eve blessed the name of God, and they made all things known unto their sons and their daughters." (Moses 5:6-12.)

After they knew that to gain salvation men must believe in Christ, repent of their sins, be baptized, receive the gift of the Holy Ghost, and thereafter keep the commandments of God; after they knew that "the Son of God hath atoned for original guilt, wherein the sins of the parents cannot be answered upon the heads of the children"; after they knew that as children "begin to grow up, sin conceiveth in their hearts, and they taste the bitter, that they may know to prize the good"; after they had received the divine commandments relative to this whole system of salvation, then the Lord commanded: "Teach it unto your children." Also: "I give unto you a commandment, to teach these things freely unto your children." That is to say: The fathers were to teach the doctrines of salvation to their children, that all members of the family unit—knowing the truth—might, through obedience, become heirs of salvation. It was imperative that children learn that "no unclean thing can dwell" in the presence of God, and that all men "must be born again" if they are to enter "the kingdom of heaven." (Moses 6:51-62.)

After the flood it was the same. The Church was a family organization and the gospel was taught by fathers to their children. The great Abrahamic covenant—renewed first with Isaac, then with Jacob, and then extended to all the seed of Abraham—was a family covenant, a covenant of eternal increase, through celestial marriage. "Abraham received promises concerning his seed, and of the fruit of his loins," our revelation recites, "which were to continue so long as they were in the world: and as touching Abraham and his seed, out of the world they should continue; both in the world and out of the world should they continue as innumerable as the stars; or, if ye were to count the sand upon the seashore ye could not number them." (D&C 132:30.) Of

Abraham the Lord said: "I know him, that he will command his children and his household after him, and they shall keep the way of the Lord, to do justice and judgment." (Gen. 18:19.)

The house or family of Israel, who are the descendants of the sons of Jacob, was the Lord's chosen family throughout their long history. That his mind and his purposes might be known among them, parents were commanded to teach his law to their children, generation upon generation. "These words, which I command thee this day," Moses said, as he summarized the law to Israel, "shall be in thine heart: And thou shalt teach them diligently unto thy children, and shalt talk of them when thou sittest in thine house, and when thou walkest by the way, and when thou liest down, and when thou risest up."[1]

In principle the Nephites did the same thing, as we see from these words of King Benjamin: "And ye will not suffer your children that they go hungry, or naked; neither will ye suffer that they transgress the laws of God, and fight and quarrel one with another, and serve the devil, who is the master of sin, or who is the evil spirit which hath been spoken of by our fathers, he being an enemy to all righteousness. But ye will teach them to walk in the ways of truth and soberness; ye will teach them to love one another, and to serve one another." (Mosiah 4:14-15.)

When our Lord removed the restriction that limited gospel blessings to the house of Israel—"Go not into the way of the Gentiles, and into any city of the Samaritans enter ye not: But go rather to the lost sheep of the house of Israel" (Matt. 10:5-6) was his initial command to the Twelve—and sent the message of salvation to all men, he was simply enlarging the chosen family. He was putting into active operation the promise that he, as Jehovah, had made aforetime to Abraham: "As many as receive this Gospel shall be called after thy name, and shall be accounted thy seed, and shall rise up and bless thee, as their father." (Abr. 2:10.)

Those who receive the gospel take upon themselves the

name of Christ; they are adopted as his sons and his daughters; they become members of his family; he is their new Father. Hence, Paul's statement that those who "have been baptized into Christ have put on Christ. There is neither Jew nor Greek, there is neither bond nor free, there is neither male nor female: for ye are all one in Christ Jesus. And if ye be Christ's, then are ye Abraham's seed, and heirs according to the promise." (Gal. 3:27-29.) And the members of the family of Abraham and of Christ have the same obligation that has always rested upon members of the chosen family: "to bring up your children in light and truth." (D&C 93:40.)[2] "And they shall also teach their children to pray, and to walk uprightly before the Lord." (D&C 68:28.)

Jewish and Gentile Families

In his infinite wisdom, having compassion and solicitude for the welfare of his Son, the Father sent the Lord Jesus into a Jewish home, into a Jewish family circle. In such an environment the Infant Messiah would receive tender and loving care and be exposed to the best teaching and training available in any mortal family unit. Even God's own Son—as he stretched and turned in his swaddling clothes; as he waited to be weaned; as he learned to walk and talk and feed himself; as he learned to read and write and memorize; as he partook of the varied experiences that are the common lot of all who undergo a mortal probation—even he would be influenced by his environment and would be preserved from the defilements of paganism because the home in which he dwelt was Jewish.

The law of family worship, the system revealed by the Great Jehovah to enable his people to gain exaltation through the continuation of the family unit in eternity, was known, in part at least, to the Jews of Jesus' day and in the true sense of the word to no other Old World people. Jewish families, therefore, had a religious foundation and a spiritual status totally unknown among the Gentiles. As a result, those families among them which were pious and devout—whose members looked for the Consolation of Israel and who sought to live by the high standards found in the law and in the prophets—such families lived lives of decency and morality. Husbands and wives were faithful to each other, scriptural study and daily prayer were part of the rituals of life, and the family members lived honest, sober, and upright lives. Such was the environment prevailing in the family circle in which God placed his Son.

In contrast, family life among the Gentiles was defiled, corrupt, devoid of decency, and of such a low order as scarcely to be worthy of the name. "Strange as it may sound," Edersheim says, "it is strictly true that, beyond the boundaries of Israel, it would be scarcely possible to speak with any propriety of family life, or even of the family, as we understand these terms. . . . Few of those who have learned to admire classical antiquity have a full conception of any one phase in its social life—whether of the position of woman, the relation of the sexes, slavery, the education of children, their relation to their parents, or the state of public morality. Fewer still have combined all these features into one picture, and that not merely as exhibited by the lower orders, or even among the higher classes, but as fully owned and approved by those whose names have descended in the admiration of ages as the thinkers, the sages, the poets, the historians, and the statesmen of antiquity. Assuredly, St. Paul's description of the ancient world in the first and second chapters of his Epistle to the Romans must have appeared to those who lived in the midst of it as Divine even in its tenderness, delicacy, and charity; the full picture under bright sunlight would have been scarcely susceptible of exhibition. For such a world there was only one alternative—either the judgment of Sodom, or the mercy of the Gospel and the healing of the Cross."[3]

It is evident—self-evident!—that any nation or people having any reasonable degree of understanding relative to the true status and position of the family in the eternal scheme of things would be unique, separate, distinct, peculiar, a people set apart. And so it was with the Jews of Jesus' day. There was no race and no kindred like them among all the peoples of the earth. They were Jews of Abrahamic ancestry, and all others were Gentiles, lesser breeds without the law.

True, their knowledge was incomplete, and the full glory of perfect familial relationships had been lost among them. But they had been born in the family of Israel; the traditions of their fathers still lingered in their homes; and they did have the holy scriptures, wherein the Abrahamic covenant and the chosen status of Israel were extolled. They were, indeed, a unique people, a peculiar people, a people set apart from all others. Their family-centered way of life, their religious traditions, their social customs all combined to separate them, to make them a people without peer. As Edersheim says: "It may be safely asserted, that the grand distinction, which divided all mankind into Jews and Gentiles, was not only religious, but also social. [Albeit, let us here insert, the social grew out of the religious.] However near the cities of the heathen to those of Israel, however frequent and close the intercourse between the two parties, no one could have entered a Jewish town or village without feeling, so to speak, in quite another world. The aspects of the streets, the building and arrangement of the houses, the municipal and religious rule, the manners and customs of the people, their habits and ways—above all, the family life, stood in marked contrast to what would be seen elsewhere. On every side there was evidence that religion here was not merely a creed, nor a set of observances, but that it pervaded every relationship, and dominated every phase of life." (*Sketches*, p. 86.)

As we view Jewish families and Gentile families, is it any wonder that the Son of God came among the Jews? Though they would take his life in due course, because of priestcraft and iniquity, yet divine providence required an environment and a social and religious climate that would enable him to grow to maturity, unstained, preserved physically and spiritually, so that he could do his appointed work before he laid down his life as our Savior and Redeemer.

How Jewish Families Lived

In Jesus' day the Jews had their temple, their synagogues, and their homes, and around them their whole life revolved. Three times each year faithful men appeared before the Lord in his sanctuary—and would not Jesus, who kept his Father's law, have been among them?—there, by sacrifice, to recommit themselves to Jehovah and to receive anew a remission of their sins.

Many people frequented the sacred courts to teach and be taught and to partake of the spirit of worship that centered in the Holy of Holies.

Every Sabbath and on certain feast days, the faithful—and would not Jesus have been among them?—came to the synagogue to pray, to hear the word of the Lord taught, and to receive the exhortations so important even to the most spiritual of men. But the home was something else—day in and day out, week after week, month added to month, and one year following another; the home was the place where true worship was taught and practiced. Every Jewish home was itself a house of worship, a house of prayer, and—shall we not say it—a house of God.

And Jesus our Lord was nursed and suckled in a Jewish home; he played within its walls as a child; he was guided by a Jewish mother and a Jewish foster father as he learned the customs and discipline and way of life of the race of which he was a part. In the real and practical sense it was his first and chief house of worship. It is true that he went up to the temple when twelve years of age and undoubtedly three times each year from then until the time his active ministry began. It is true that he worshipped as a youth and in his maturing years in Jewish synagogues; we know that during his ministry he used them as teaching centers, as the sites for miracles, and as the reverent and sacred houses of worship that they in fact were.

But we cannot see our Lord in proper perspective unless we see him in the home of Joseph and Mary; unless we know what he was taught within those private walls; unless we are aware of the practices and rituals that were there impressed upon his receptive and truth-seeking mind. Jesus was the Son of God and dwelt among men with native endowments without equal, but he was also a product, as we all are, of his environment; and his Father chose to place him in the care and custody, during his formative years, of Jewish Joseph and Jewish Mary and their Jewish home with all its Jewish teachings, practices, and ways of worship.

Joseph and Mary lived in modest circumstances. They offered in sacrifice, when Jesus was presented in the temple, "a pair of turtledoves, or two young pigeons," rather than the more expensive lamb. (Luke 2:21-24.) What happened to the gifts of "gold, and frankincense, and myrrh" that came to the "young child" we do not know. (Matt. 2:11.) Perhaps they sustained the family during their exile in Egypt; perhaps they were divided among relatives and others of modest means. Their home in Nazareth would have been small, without running water and other amenities common in even the poorer homes today. Such furniture as they possessed would have been well made; their clothing would have been of homespun Galilean wool; and as to their food, the principal fare would have been the meat and vegetables and fruits grown and raised so abundantly in the hills of Galilee. Perhaps they had occasional foods and articles of adornment that were imported.

We can scarcely question that as other sons and daughters came, they lived in close and intimate quarters, with limited amounts of this world's goods, the children sharing food and exchanging clothes as their needs required. Certainly the whole family lived in lesser circumstances of opulence than generally prevails in homes located in the developed nations today. There were wealthy people in

Nazareth and other Palestinian communities whose houses were mansions by any standards, but we have no reason to suppose that the home of Joseph and Mary was in any way pretentious. The Father of the Son placed his Eternal Offspring in modest circumstances: the Prince who was to be King was neither born nor reared in a palace. How fitting it was, rather, that the One who was to ascend above all others should be cradled in a manger and reared in a carpenter's home.

But it is the spirit and teachings, the love and harmony, not the wood and mortar and chairs, that make a true home. And in those things that are important, the home provided by the just and faithful husband of Mary excelled. Perhaps there neither was nor has been one like it in all Israel. Family life being what it is, and having the impact that it does upon the children who are reared in the family circle, surely the Father of us all, who also was the Father of One only in mortality, would have chosen that family circle which was preeminent above all others as the environment for his Only Begotten Son.

When we describe Jewish family life in the day of Jesus, our choice of words strays into the field of the superlatives. The plain fact is that there were not then and have not been since—except among the meridian saints and among the Latter-day Saints, both of which peoples enjoyed a home life hallowed by eternal marriage and all that grows out of it—there were not then and have not been since families like the ancient Jewish families. Such were not found among the Gentiles of Jesus' day and are not found among the Christians of modern Christendom, nor among the modern Jews. Those ancient members of Jacob's house still had the priesthood of Almighty God; they still centered their whole social structure in the revealed word that had come from Moses and the prophets; they had in fact preserved their unique and peculiar status among men by preserving the family teachings and customs, all of which raised family life to a state of excellence seldom excelled even by their righteous forebears. True, Rabbinism, which sought to override the spirit of the law with traditionalism and the worship of the letter, often made void some of the highest family principles. But the Lord's system of familial relationships had been revealed and was known to the people, and among the truly pious and devout the true principles were in active operation.

Men married at sixteen or seventeen years of age, almost never later than twenty; and women at a somewhat younger age, often when not older than fourteen. These ages applied to all, Joseph and Mary included.[4] Children were esteemed to be a heritage from the Lord and were devoutly desired. Birth control was unknown among the Jews, and parents rejoiced in large families and numerous progeny. From the days of Moses, if a man died having no child, his brother was obligated to marry "the wife of the dead," and raise up seed unto his deceased brother, "that his name be not put out of Israel." (Deut. 25:5-10.)[5] There were special provisions for avoiding this responsibility so that the widow could marry another, which was the very thing that made possible the marriage of Ruth and Boaz, through whose lineage our Lord was born. (Ruth 4.)

Mothers taught their children almost from the moment of birth; at least the tutorial processes began by the time infant lips began to lisp their first words and phrases. The Psalms and prayers were used as lullabies. At the age of two years children were weaned, with the occasion being celebrated by a feast. When the children reached about three years of age fathers began to assume their Mosaically imposed obligation to teach them, not nursery rhymes, but verses of scripture, benedictions, and wise sayings. Formal schooling began at five or six, with the Bible as the text. This scriptural study began with Leviticus, extended out to the whole of the Pentateuch, went thence to the Prophets, and finally to the Hagiographa, that portion of the Bible not in the law and the prophets. The children learned to read and write and to memorize the chants of the Levites, those

Psalms which were part of festive celebrations, and the historical recitations that were part of family devotions. At sixteen or seventeen boys were sent to academies taught by the Rabbis. It is no wonder that Jewish Paul was able to say to Jewish Timothy: "From a child thou hast known the holy scriptures, which are able to make thee wise unto salvation." (2 Tim. 3:15.)[6] Such was the heritage of all Jewish children of the day.

But the educational system imposed upon Jewish children was more, far more, than formal schooling arrangements. It was part and portion of their way of life. They learned from what was done as well as from what was said. All male children were circumcised at eight days. A spirit of religion and devotion pervaded every home. Private prayers were offered both morning and evening. Before every meal they washed and prayed, and after every repast they gave thanks. There were frequent special family feasts. Every Sabbath was a holy and sanctified day on which they rested from their labors, worshipped at the synagogue, kept a Sabbath light burning in the home, adorned their homes, ate their best food, and bestowed upon each child the blessing of Israel.

Devout fathers wore phylacteries during prayer (the Pharisees wore them all day long), and these contained parchments whereon were written these four passages from the scriptures: Exodus 13:1-10, Exodus 13:11-16, Deuteronomy 6:4-9, and Deuteronomy 11:13-21. On the doorpost of the home of every devout Jew hung the Mezuzah, which contained a parchment whereon was written, in twenty-two lines, Deuteronomy 6:4-9 and 11:13-21, as both of these passages command. The Shema, composed of Deuteronomy 6:4-9, Deuteronomy 11:13-21, and Numbers 15:37-41, was repeated twice each day by every male. Family prayers were the order of the day in all homes.

Israel's deliverance from Egyptian bondage was recited, formally and in a question-and-answer dialogue, as each family ate the paschal lamb during the Feast of the Passover.

The morning and evening sacrifices and all of the special drama and ritual and ceremony that was part of all the great feasts had the effect of dramatically rehearsing the basic doctrines revealed by Jehovah to his people. On every Sabbath and twice during the week Moses and the prophets were read in the synagogues.

Every pious home had either portions or all of the Old Testament; it is difficult to believe that in the home where our Lord was reared there would have been anything less than the whole of that body of revealed writ which was then available to anyone. There were even little parchment rolls for children that contained such scripture as the Shema, the Hallel, the history of the creation and of the flood, and the first eight chapters of Leviticus.

Jewish homes, Jewish family life, the rearing of Jewish children, indeed, the whole Jewish way of life was founded upon Jewish theology. Jehovah's command to children—so basic that it was decree number five in the Decalogue itself—was: "Honour thy father and thy mother: that thy days may be long upon the land which the Lord thy God giveth thee." (Ex. 20:12.) Jehovah's command to parents—so basic that the Jews carried it in their phylacteries, hung it in their Mezuzahs, recited it twice daily in their Shema—was: 'Bring up thy children in light and in truth.' And that which was to be taught was theological; it was the holy scriptures; it was the mind and will and voice of the Lord to his people. And this is what separated the Jews from all other people.

"In the days of Christ," Edersheim says, "the pious Jew had no other knowledge, neither sought nor cared for any other—in fact, denounced it—than that of the law of God. At the outset, let it be remembered that, in heathenism, theology, or rather mythology, had no influence whatever on thinking or life—was literally submerged under their waves. To the pious Jew, on the contrary, the knowledge of God was everything; and to prepare for or impart that knowledge was the sum total, the sole object of his education. This was the life of his soul—the better, and only true life, to which all else as well as the life of the body were merely subservient, as means towards an end. His religion consisted of two things: knowledge of God, which by a series of inferences, one from the other, ultimately resolved itself into theology, as they understood it; and service, which again consisted of the proper observance of all that was prescribed by God, and of works of charity towards men—the latter, indeed, going beyond the bound of what was strictly due (the *Chovoth*) into special merit or 'righteousness' (*Zedakah*). But as service presupposed knowledge, theology was again at the foundation of all, and also the crown of all, which conferred the greatest merit. This is expressed or implied in almost innumerable passages of Jewish writings. Let one suffice, not only because it sounds more rationalistic, but because it is to this day repeated each morning in his prayers by every Jew: 'These are the things of which a man eats the fruit in this world, but their possession continueth for the next world: to honour father and mother, pious works, peacemaking between man and man, and the study of the law, which is equivalent to them all.' " (*Sketches,* pp. 124-25.)

NOTES

1. Deut. 6:4-9. See also Deut. 6:20-25; 4:9-10; 11:19; 31:10-13. Special provision was also made in the law of Moses that parents should teach their children all things appertaining to the Passover and their deliverance from Egyptian bondage. (Ex. 12:26-27; 13:8, 14.)

2. In this connection how comforting is the scriptural assurance: "Train up a child in the way he should go: and when he is old, he will not depart from it." (Prov. 22:6.)

3. *Sketches,* pp. 123-24. Lest we forget, in the passage to which Edersheim refers, Paul is condemning the Jews for their iniquities and for doing the very things they know will damn the Gentiles. Among other things the apostle says that because the Gentiles rejected the true knowledge of God and worshipped idols, "God also gave them up to uncleanness through the lusts of their own hearts, to dishonour their own bodies between themselves." Also that he "gave them up unto vile affections: for even their women did change the natural use [of their bodies] into that which is against nature: And likewise also the men, leaving the natural use of the woman, burned in their lust one toward another; men with men working that which is unseemly, and receiving in themselves that recompence of their error which was meet. And even as they did not like to retain God in their knowledge, God gave them over to a reprobate mind, to do those things which are not convenient; Being filled with all unrighteousness, fornication, wickedness, covetousness, maliciousness; full of envy, murder, debate, deceit, malignity; whisperers, Backbiters, haters of God, despiteful, proud, boasters, inventors of evil things, disobedient to parents, Without understanding, covenantbreakers, without natural affection, implacable, unmerciful: Who knowing the judgment of God, that they which commit such things are worthy of death, not only do the same, but have pleasure in them that do them." (Rom. 1:18-32.) The second chapter of

Romans carries on with the theme. Our purpose in setting it out here is to make it clear beyond question that there is no exaggeration in the sweeping denunciation of the degraded state of morality and family life among the non-Jewish people.

4. The common concept—shown in pictures and dramatized in fictional renditions of what fertile minds assume may have happened in the lives of members of the Holy Family—that Joseph was an old man when he took Mary as his bride is patently false. This traditional notion arises from two things: (1) The fact that Joseph apparently had died by the time of the crucifixion; at least on that occasion our Lord asked the Beloved Disciple to care for Mary, which John thereafter did. (John 19:25-27.) (2) False traditions which maintain that Mary was a virgin forever, had no sexual association with Joseph, and bore him no children. The only logical circumstances under which Joseph could have been substantially older than Mary would have been one in which he was taking her as a second wife after the death of a previous spouse, or one in which he and Mary were entering into a polygamous marriage. As Edersheim says: "Polygamy . . . undoubtedly was in force at the time of our Lord." (*Temple*, p. 142.) There is no reason to believe that either of these conditions prevailed, and we are left to conclude that Joseph was certainly not older than twenty years when he took Mary as his wife, and she was at least fourteen, perhaps fifteen or sixteen.

5. Manifestly this system of marriage discipline, revealed by Jehovah to Moses, could only prevail in a day when plural marriage was a divinely approved order.

6. This rabbinical declaration, taken from the Mishnah, "quaintly maps out," as Edersheim expresses it, the different periods of Jewish life: "At five years of age, reading of the Bible; at ten years, learning the Mishnah; at thirteen years, bound to the commandments; at fifteen years, the study of the Talmud; at eighteen years, marriage; at twenty, the pursuit of trade or business (active life); at thirty years, full vigour; at forty, maturity of reason; at fifty, for counsel; at sixty, commencement of agedness; at seventy, grey age; at eighty advanced old age; at ninety, bowed down; at a hundred, as if he were dead and gone, and taken from the world." (*Sketches*, p. 105.)

JEWISH APOSTASY IN JESUS' DAY

This is an evil generation. (Luke 11:29.)

Ye are the children of them
which killed the prophets. Fill ye up then
the measure of your fathers. Ye serpents,
ye generation of vipers,
how can ye escape the damnation of hell?
(Matt. 23:31-33.)

Apostasy through the Ages

Adam and Eve—our first parents, our common ancestors, the mother and father of all living—had the fulness of the everlasting gospel. They received the plan of salvation from God himself, it being "declared by holy angels sent forth from the presence of God, and by his own voice, and by the gift of the Holy Ghost." (Moses 5:58.) They saw God, knew his laws, entertained angels, received revelations, beheld visions, and were in tune with the Infinite. They exercised faith in the Lord Jesus Christ; repented of their sins; were baptized in similitude of the death, burial, and resurrection of the Promised Messiah; and received the gift of the Holy Ghost. They were endowed with power from on high, were sealed in the new and everlasting covenant of marriage, and received the fulness of the ordinances of the house of the Lord.

After baptism, and after celestial marriage, they walked in paths of truth and righteousness, kept the commandments, and endured to the end. Having charted for themselves a course leading to eternal life, they pressed forward with a steadfastness in Christ—believing, obeying, conforming, consecrating, sacrificing—until their calling and election was made sure and they were sealed up unto eternal life.

And they taught all these things unto their children. They preached the gospel in plainness and perfection to all their numerous progeny. They made known the laws and ordinances of salvation—all to the end that the sons of men might believe and obey and come to know the joy of their redemption, "and the eternal life which God giveth unto all the obedient." (Moses 5:11.)

But, alas, sorrow rather than salvation lay ahead for many of the seed of mighty Michael and his lovely consort Eve. Many who were the seed of their bodies apostatized; they departed from the truth; they left the faith of their fathers; they turned from light to darkness, from righteousness to wickedness, from God to Satan. Apostasy consists of two things:

1. *Believing false doctrine.* "And all those who preach false doctrines, . . . wo, wo, wo be unto them, saith the Lord God Almighty, for they shall be thrust down to hell!"

2. *Living after the manner of the world.* "And all those who commit whoredoms, and pervert the right way of the Lord, wo, wo, wo be unto them, saith the Lord God Almighty, for they shall be thrust down to hell!" (2 Ne. 28:15.)

And so, from the very beginning, "Satan came among them, . . . and he commanded them, saying: Believe it not; and they believed it not, and they loved Satan more than God. And men began from that time forth to be carnal, sensual, and devilish." (Moses 5:11-13.) Thus apostasy began; men fell away from the truth even in the day of righteous Adam; men turned to carnal and ungodly practices even in the day when there were living witnesses to tell them of Eden's beauty, of the fall and promised redemption, and of angelic ministrations and heavenly revelations of the mind and will of Him whose they and we are.

Cain, a first generation son of the first man, rejected the gospel, refused to hearken to Adam, and loved Satan more than God. In his carnal and fallen state, Cain "rejected the greater counsel which was had from God," coveted the flocks of Abel, made a covenant with Satan, slew his righteous brother, and gloried in his wickedness. Others followed his course, and apostasy, rebellion, and wickedness became the established order of that and all succeeding days. (Moses 5.)

In Enoch's day there were great wars and rebellions; wickedness was so great in Noah's day that a merciful God swept the wicked and ungodly into a watery grave; Abraham's father worshipped idols; the whole city in which Melchizedek dwelt had departed from the truth; and all the Gentile nations in the days of ancient Israel were outside the pale of saving grace.

Apostasy has been and is the prevailing social and religious state of most men in all ages from Adam's to ours. The devil is not dead: Lucifer lives as surely as God does; he slays others but has not himself been slain. His influence covers the earth and has done so since the fall of man. He seeks to damn men, and "wide is the gate, and broad is the way, that leadeth to destruction." (Matt. 7:13.) Of our own day it is written: "Darkness covereth the earth, and gross darkness the minds of the people, and all flesh has become corrupt before my face." (D&C 112:23.) Also: "The whole world lieth in sin, and groaneth under darkness and under the bondage of sin." (D&C 84:49.) The war that began in heaven is continuing here among mortals, and up to this point most of the victories have been won by the enemy of all righteousness.

Apostasy in Ancient Israel

Israel—the Lord's own people, his own peculiar treasure, a people favored above all the nations of the earth—spent her entire history, as a people, wavering between true and false religion. Like a great pendulum the people swung back and forth between the true worship of Jehovah and the paying of devotions to Baal and all the gods of the degenerate nations in whose custody they found their promised land. The righteousness of parents was swallowed up in the wickedness of their children, with the children's children turning back to the standard of their grandparents. Eli served the Lord, and his sons served Baal. One king kept the feasts and commanded obedience to the law of Moses; the next honored the priests of Baal and worshipped the queen of heaven; and yet the next cut down the groves and destroyed the altars of the heathen. And so it went generation after generation.

Knowing the plagues God had poured out upon Egypt; having seen the waters of the Red Sea part to free them from Pharaoh; seeing the pillar of fire that gave protection by night and the cloud that went before them by day; hearing the rolling thunders and seeing the burning fires that rested on Sinai when the Lord came down to talk with Moses; eating daily the bread that miraculously came down from heaven; brandishing swords and staves that put to flight armies of aliens; seeing the earth open and swallow those who opposed Moses; living and walking, as it were, in the light of daily miracles—yet, in the midst of all this, Israel murmured and forsook the Lord. From time to time her people made a golden calf; they longed for the fleshpots of Egypt; their children were sacrificed in the fires of Molech; the daily sacrifices were done away; the Israelite hosts came not up to Jerusalem to keep the Feast of Tabernacles; they worshipped gods of wood and stone; they bowed before idols that neither hear nor see nor speak; and they kept not the law of Moses, the man of God.

As Moses' mortal ministry neared its end, he assembled all Israel and "commanded the people, saying, Keep all the commandments which I command you this day." Thereupon he summarized the blessings of obedience and set forth the cursings of apostasy. Among the curses, plagues, diseases, and torments that should come upon them if they chose disobedience was the assurance that the Lord would destroy their nation by bringing upon them fierce and relentless warriors; that in the siege of their cities delicate Hebrew women would eat their own children; and that the chosen people would be scattered "among all people, from the one end of the earth even unto the other," where they would "serve other gods," which neither they nor their fathers had known, and that they would no longer enjoy the light of heaven in which their fathers had basked. (Deut. 27—33.) That these dire calamities befell them—when Benhadad, king of Syria, besieged Samaria (2 Kgs. 6:26-29); and again when Nebuchadnezzar laid Jerusalem low (Lam. 4:10); and yet again when Titus overthrew the Holy City and tore apart the temple stone by stone—is well known.

As a means of impressing upon the people both the blessings of obedience and the cursings of disobedience, Joshua, as Moses had aforetime commanded, assembled all Israel in the valley between Mount Gerizim and Mount Ebal. Six of the tribes were over against Mount Gerizim to bless the people and the other six against Mount Ebal to respond to the cursings. The Levites then read, one by one, the cursings and the blessings, and the respective groups, speaking for all the house of Israel, gave a solemn response of "Amen," thus binding the whole nation to seek righteousness and shun evil. The concluding statement of this solemn rededication to Jehovah was: "Cursed be he that confirmeth not all the words of this law to do them." (Deut. 27:9-26. See also Josh. 8:32-35.)

We need make no attempt in this present work to recite all that befell ancient Israel because of apostasy and rebellion against the Lord. Let it suffice for our purposes—and we are only laying a foundation for a consideration of that apostasy which culminated in the crucifying of a God—let it suffice simply to point to three passages from Holy Writ.

The first of these involves the final overthrow of Jerusalem by Nebuchadnezzar in the day of Zedekiah, who, though a puppet ruler, had rebelled against Babylonia. "Moreover all the chief of the priests, and the people, transgressed very much after all the abominations of the heathen; and polluted the house of the Lord which he had hallowed in Jerusalem. And the Lord God of their fathers sent to them by his messengers, rising up betimes, and sending; because he had compassion on his people, and on his dwelling place: But they mocked the messengers of God, and despised his words, and misused his prophets, until the wrath of the Lord arose against his people, till there was no remedy. Therefore he brought upon them the king of the Chaldees, who slew their young men with the sword in the house of their sanctuary, and had no compassion upon young man or maiden, old man, or him that stooped for age: he gave them all into his hand." This was the day when the house of the Lord was burned, the walls of Jerusalem broken down, and those who escaped the sword were carried captive to Babylon. (2 Chr. 36:9-23.)[1]

Next, without any exposition, for the meaning is clear from the words themselves, we quote this language from the Psalms: "They did not destroy the nations, concerning whom the Lord commanded them: But were mingled among the heathen, and learned their works. And they served their idols: which were a snare unto them. Yea, they sacrificed their sons and their daughters unto devils, And shed innocent blood, even the blood of their sons and of their daughters, whom they sacrificed unto the idols of Canaan: and the land was polluted with blood. Thus were they defiled with their own works, and went a whoring with their own inventions. Therefore was the wrath of the Lord kindled against his people, insomuch that he abhorred his own inheritance. And he gave them into the hand of the heathen;

and they that hated them ruled over them. Their enemies also oppressed them, and they were brought into subjection under their hand. Many times did he deliver them; but they provoked him with their counsel, and were brought low for their iniquity." (Ps. 106:34-43.)

And third, these words of Isaiah deserve thoughtful consideration, for they not only describe the apostate condition of ancient Israel, but also have application to those who lived in the day of Jesus. "Ah sinful nation," Isaiah intones, "a people laden with iniquity, a seed of evildoers, children that are corrupters: they have forsaken the Lord, they have provoked the Holy One of Israel unto anger, they are gone away backward. . . . Except the Lord of hosts had left unto us a very small remnant, we should have been as Sodom, and we should have been like unto Gomorrah." (Isa. 1:4-9.)

Apostasy Among the Jews

Except for "a very small remnant"; except for a few priests and Levites who sat in Aaron's seat and offered sacrifices as required by the law of Moses; except for a rugged Peter, a visionary John, a guileless Nathanael; except for a believing Mary and a testifying Martha, a submissive Elisabeth, and a zealous Zacharias; except for the untutored and unlearned common people, who received Him gladly because they had not been contaminated by the scribes and Rabbis; except for a relatively few people, "a very small remnant," who would believe on Mary's Son—except for such as these, all the Jews of Jesus' day were apostate.

In that day, chosen and hallowed by Him who is holy as the day for his Son to make flesh his tabernacle; in that day when the light and glory of God should shine forth in the Person of his Beloved Son; in that day when the Lord Omnipotent, who was, and is, from all eternity to all eternity, would minister among his people; in that day when the infinite and eternal atonement should be wrought; in that day—above all days from creation's morn to the hour of the crucifixion—apostasy reigned among the sons of Adam.

It was a day not as Isaiah had said of ancient Israel, that "except" for "a very small remnant" they "should have been as Sodom, and . . . like unto Gomorrah" (Isa. 1:9), but a day when even Jerusalem, their capital city, was identified by John as "the great city, which spiritually is called Sodom and Egypt, where also our Lord was crucified." (Rev. 11:8.)[2] Israel of Isaiah's day, who, except for a few righteous among them, would have become "as Sodom," had now, in Jesus' day, degenerated spiritually until in prophetic language, in spite of the few believing souls among them, they had become both "Sodom and Egypt."

Theirs was no ordinary apostasy. It was not the apostasy of the Amorites and the Philistines who were born to darkness and had never known any course except that of astrology and witchcraft and the sodomic vices. Nor was it the apostasy of a Jeroboam or a Jezebel who openly rejected the God of Israel and swore allegiance to Baal, awful and wicked as such a course was. But the Jewish apostasy in the days of Jesus was one in which they had the greatest measure of truth then possessed by any people, and yet they rejected the Stone, the Cornerstone, upon which their whole religious structure was built. It was an apostasy among a people who actually had the Aaronic Priesthood. It was an apostasy among a people who had "the gospel of repentance and of baptism, and the remission of sins, and the law of carnal commandments, which the Lord in his wrath caused to continue with the house of Aaron among the children of Israel until John" who baptized Jesus. (D&C 84:26-27.)

It was an apostasy among a people who searched the scriptures, who memorized the Messianic prophecies, who knew that the hour of his coming was upon them, and who yet rejected him—though he raised the dead and created loaves and fishes out of nothing, as it were. Theirs was a refined, cultured, congenial apostasy, if we may use such terms to identify those who love darkness more than light because their deeds are evil. Theirs was an apostasy that followed truth in name, but not in deed; one in which they worshipped the true God with their lips, while their hearts were full of adultery and lasciviousness; an apostasy in which light and darkness were so intermixed that the resultant twilight kept even devout men and women from turning to the dawning brilliance of the new day.

Why the Jews of Jesus' Day Were Apostate

Why, of all people, were the generality of the Jews of Jesus' day so completely apostate? Why were they so dulled and insensitive spiritually that they failed to see in Jesus the fulfillment of all their Messianic dreams? How came they to be so hardened and cruel, so lacking in common compassion, that they would cry, "Crucify him, crucify him," as they berated the One who they all knew had opened blind eyes, unstopped deaf ears, and even reanimated cold corpses?

Three reasons are germain to the issues here raised:

1. Since Jesus our Lord came into the world for the express purpose of dying upon the cross for the sins of the world, it follows that a Divine Providence placed him among a people, and in a religious and political climate, where the chief object and end of his mortal sojourn could and would be brought to pass. He came to die; he must be slain; his destiny was to be hanged upon a tree; and the cross was prepared for his crucifixion from the foundation of the world, as it were. It follows that he must live and minister among those who would reject him. He must incur the hatred of those whose spiritual depravity would devise and condone his death. Can we reach any conclusion except that a Divine Providence sent to earth in that day, as part of Jewish Israel, the very spirits who would so harden their hearts as to desire and seek his death?

We are not saying they were foreordained to a course of hatred and murder, only that they were the kind of spirits—the kind of mortals—who found it easy to work wickedness and spread darkness. Like Ahaz and Jezebel, like Pilate and Herod, like Laman and Lemuel, like Antiochus Epiphanes who sacrificed swine on the holy altar, like the wicked and ungodly of all races and places, they found it easy to fight the truth because of their native inclinations to walk in a worldly course. Such was their spiritual inheritance, though, as with all men, it was within their power, at any time, to save themselves by repentance and righteousness.

2. These Jews of Jesus' day—through whose instrumentality, and by means of whose social and political pressure, Roman nails were driven through the hands and feet of Him who came to save them—were apostate for exactly and precisely the same reason that men in all ages have fought the truth. That reason is, they loved darkness rather than light, because their deeds were evil; they chose to live after the manner of the world, and to dull their spiritual senses with lust and adultery and greed, because such were the desires of their hearts; like Cain, they loved Satan more than God, meaning they chose to follow the course charted for them by Satan, who is the God of this world. Apostasy is the result of unrighteousness. No one ever forsakes or rejects the truth who is guided by the power of the Holy Ghost, and the Spirit will not dwell in an unclean tabernacle.

3. But there was something unique about Jewish apostasy in the meridian day. It grew out of one of the most resolute attempts ever made by men to live what they assumed was the will of Jehovah. It grew out of what their Nephite kinsmen, long before, had called "looking beyond the mark." "The Jews were a stiffnecked people," Nephi's brother said, "and they despised the words of plainness, and killed the prophets, and sought for things that they could not understand." These words, spoken concerning the Jews of Jacob's day, applied in full measure also to their descendants in Jesus' day. "Wherefore, because of their blindness, which blindness came by looking beyond the mark, they must needs fall; for God hath taken away his plainness from them, and delivered unto them many things which they can-

not understand, because they desired it. And because they desired it God hath done it, that they may stumble."

This matter of a devout and seemingly religious people becoming spiritually blind "by looking beyond the mark" illustrates perfectly how true and saving religion can become a damning burden. For generations that went before, and then in the day of our Lord's ministry, his Israelite brethren, by "looking beyond the mark," turned the truth of heaven into a system that led them to hell. That is to say, they took the plain and simple things of pure religion and added to them a host of their own interpretations; they embellished them with added rites and performances; and they took a happy, joyous way of worship and turned it into a restrictive, curtailing, depressive system of rituals and performances. The living spirit of the Lord's law became in their hands the dead letter of Jewish ritualism.

To the true order of Sabbath worship they added so many restrictions and performances that what should have been a day of rejoicing and rededication become a gloomy burden. To the true concept about their Messiah, they added the idea of a temporal ruler, so that the Deliverer who was sent to redeem them from death, hell, the devil, and endless torment was pictured as an earthly king with a sword like Caesar's in his hand. With their true system of sacrificial offerings they interwove such greedy practices that their conduct made of the Father's house a den of thieves. And so it went—through one doctrine and performance after another, their additions to what the Lord intended turned pure religion into anything but what it was intended to be. And so Jacob, by way of prophecy, was able to say that "by the stumbling of the Jews they will reject the stone upon which they might build and have safe foundation." (Jacob 4:14-15.)

But whatever the causes, the fact is that darkness covered the land of Palestine in that day and gross darkness filled the hearts of the generality of the people. The fires that should have been eternal had burned out, and the light of heaven no longer guided the people. Spiritual darkness shrouded the nation. So degenerate and wicked were the inhabitants of the land that Jacob, speaking prophetically, said: "Christ . . . should come among the Jews, among those who are the more wicked part of the world." Those who had once walked in the light now stumbled in the darkness. "And they"—Jews of Abrahamic descent; Jews who knew the words of Moses; Jews for whom Joshua had stopped the sun; Jews who had slain one Goliath after another through their long history; these Jews, "the more wicked part of the world"!—"they shall crucify him—for thus it behooveth our God, and there is none other nation on earth that would crucify their God. For should the mighty miracles be wrought among other nations they would repent, and know that he be their God." So prophesied Jacob. Then he gave his explanation as to why the Jews had sunk to such a low level. "Because of priestcrafts and iniquities," he said, "they at Jerusalem will stiffen their necks against him, that he be crucified. Wherefore, because of their iniquities, destructions, famines, pestilences, and bloodshed shall come upon them; and they who shall not be destroyed shall be scattered among all nations." (2 Ne. 10:3-6.)

Priestcrafts and iniquities! And the effects that flow from them! What a lesson modern Christendom, those who should be the Lord's people today, can learn from the Jews, those who should have been the Lord's people yesterday!

NOTES

1. This accords with the prophecy of Jeremiah that says: "Because your fathers have forsaken me, saith the Lord, and have walked after other gods, and have served them, and have worshipped them, and have forsaken me, and have not kept my law; And ye have done worse than your fathers; for, behold, ye walk every one after the imagination of his evil heart, that they may not hearken unto me: Therefore will I cast you out of this land into a land that ye know not, neither ye nor your fathers; and there shall ye serve other gods day and night; where I will not shew you favour." (Jer. 16:11-13.)

2. Edersheim speaks of the "painful evidence [which] comes to us of the luxuriousness of Jerusalem at that time, and of the moral corruption to which it led." He points to "the recorded covert lascivious expressions used by the men, which gives a lamentable picture of the state of morals of many in the city, and the notices of the indecent dress worn not only by women, but even by the corrupt High-Priestly youths." He speaks of "the dignity of the Jerusalemites; of the wealth which they lavished on their marriages; of the ceremony

which insisted on repeated invitations to the guests to a banquet, and that men inferior in rank would not be bidden to it; of the dress in which they appeared; the manner in which the dishes were served, the wine in white crystal vases; and the punishment of the cook who had failed in his duty, and which was to be commensurate to the dignity of the party." (Edersheim 1:131-32.) As the weepings and tears of her King attest, the "Holy City" had become in his day a sodomic den.

JEWISH SECTS AND BELIEFS IN JESUS' DAY

Now I beseech you, brethren, by the
name of our Lord Jesus Christ, that
ye all speak the same thing, and that there
be no divisions among you; but that ye
be perfectly joined together
in the same mind and in the
same judgment. . . . Is Christ divided?
(1 Cor. 1:10-13.)

What did the Ancient Jews Believe?

All of the ancient Jews who were faithful believed either all or part of the gospel—the gospel of Jehovah, the gospel of the Messiah, the gospel of Christ, the gospel that is the plan of salvation, the gospel that Jesus restored and taught in his day, the everlasting gospel (God does not change!), the same gospel restored in our day through Joseph Smith.

Beginning with Abraham, the father of the Jews; going on down through Isaac, and Jacob, and Joseph, and Ephraim; including Moses and the prophets; considering particularly the kingdom of Judah, which was taken into Babylonian captivity, and then permitted to return and rebuild their temple in Jerusalem—all these Jews, who were faithful, believed either the fulness of the gospel or the preparatory gospel, as the case may be, depending on the degree of their faith and allegiance to the Lord.

Whenever there were legal administrators among them who held the Melchizedek Priesthood, the people had the fulness of the gospel, the same as we do, and, be it remembered, all the prophets held this high and holy order of divine authority. Our best illustration of this is the Nephite people, who both kept the law of Moses and rejoiced in the fulness of the gospel.

The mere presence of the higher priesthood, of itself and in its nature, means that the fulness of the gospel is present. The fulness of the gospel consists in the possession of the Melchizedek Priesthood and the enjoyment of the gift of the Holy Ghost, which gift is conferred by the power of this higher priesthood. The fulness of the gospel consists of all the laws, ordinances, doctrines, powers, and truths needed to assure mortals of a fulness of salvation, which is eternal life in the kingdom of God.

Whenever there were legal administrators among them who held only the Aaronic Priesthood, the people had only the preparatory gospel, the lesser law, the Mosaic law, the law of sacrifices and performances and carnal commandments. The presence of the Aaronic Priesthood, without the Melchizedek Priesthood, so that the lesser order holds rule and sway because there is no greater, means that the preparatory gospel only is present. This gospel, which includes faith and repentance and baptism, is to prepare men to receive the gift of the Holy Ghost and the higher ordinances of salvation, and therefore to prepare them for the fulness of the gospel and the fulness of salvation.

In the day when Jesus began his ministry there were no prophets or righteous men who held the Melchizedek Priesthood. Indeed, our Lord came to restore this higher order. John the Baptist held the Aaronic Priesthood, baptized by immersion in Jordan for the remission of sins, and promised that One would come after, the latchet of whose shoes he felt unworthy to unloose, who would baptize with fire and with the Holy Ghost.

Thus, the Jews in Jesus' day had the preparatory gospel—at least some of those among them did who were faithful; and the Jews of that day looked forward to the receipt of the fulness of the gospel with the advent of their Messiah—at least those did who were faithful. As we are aware, the generality of the people were apostate in their feelings, did not understand the purpose of the preparatory gospel that their priests administered, and failed to receive the fulness of the saving power when it came in the person of the One whose gospel it is.

What Did the Jews in Jesus' Day Believe?

There was no united Jewish religion in our Lord's day any more than there is a united Christianity in our day. It does not suffice to speak of what the Jews believed or how they lived or what their social circumstances were any more than it does to utter similar generalities with reference to modern Christendom. There are Christian churches, so-called, that define a Christian as a person who believes the three basic creeds: the Apostles Creed, the Nicene Creed, and the Athanasian Creed. There are those who say that none are Christians except those who believe in the Trinity as set out in these weather-worn documents from an uninspired past, meaning those who believe that the Father, Son, and Holy Ghost are a spirit essence or power that fills the immensity of space and is everywhere and nowhere in particular present. There are Christians, so-called, who suppose that revelation has ceased, that visions are a thing of the past, that miracles are done away, that apostles and prophets are no longer needed.

On the other hand, there are followers of Christ who believe that the creeds of Christendom are an abomination in the sight of the Lord; that the Father and the Son are personal beings having bodies of flesh and bones as tangible as man's, and that the Holy Ghost is a personage of Spirit; and that without revelation, visions, miracles, priesthood, apostles and prophets, and every gift and grace enjoyed and possessed by the ancients, man does not have the pure gospel and cannot be saved in the kingdom of God.

As with us Christians, so with those Jews. There were Jewish cults, Jewish sects, and Jewish doctrinal aberrations in the day of Jesus. There were those who believed in a resurrection and those who did not; those who believed in angels and visions and revelations and those who did not; those who looked for a Messiah who would be a temporal despot and those who saw in the lowly Nazarene the fulfillment of the Messianic prophecies.

And the very fact that these divisions of thought and conduct existed is of itself proof conclusive of the prevailing apostasy. Paul asked, "Is Christ divided?" In Jewish parlance, and fitted to their circumstances, the query would have been: "Is Jehovah divided? Does he say one thing to the Pharisees, another to the Sadducees, and yet another to the Essenes?"

To study our Lord's life in a setting of reality, we must know about the major sects and cults and doctrinal perversities that prevailed in the minds of those to whom he attempted to teach his gospel and proclaim his own divine Sonship.

Jewish Sects, Parties, and Denominations

We shall note those sects, parties, and denominations—and certain officers who served in connection with them—whose beliefs and activities had a direct bearing on the mortal ministry of the Promised Messiah. Those cults and the cultists who comprised them; those Palestinian persons of affluence and influence; those Jewish patriots and Roman rulers, plus their bootlicking sycophants; those teachers and molders of religious and political thinking in the day of the Natural Heir to David's throne—all of them lumped together—formed the social and cultural and religious milieu in which Jesus ministered and from which his converts came. Their influence upon the inhabitants of the Holy Land influenced in turn what he said and did, where he went, and whom he gathered into his fold. Since the words and works of Jesus were not wrought in a vacuum and cannot be understood as an isolated phenomenon, since no happening in the Gospel accounts is perfectly understood apart from its Jewish setting, and since an understanding of the Christian church in the meridian of time presupposes a knowledge of Jewish history and culture, with which it is inseparably joined by innumerable threads, we shall make a necessary but brief comment about the following peoples and groups:

1. *The Jewish High Priest.*

If Aaron, Israel's first high priest, had returned to his beloved Palestine to observe conditions generally; if, with Eleazar and Ithamar, his priestly sons, he had come into Herod's Temple in the day of Jesus to compare its rites and performances with those that he and they administered in the forerunner of that house of worship; if he had stood in the court of the majestic house of the Lord that crowned Jerusalem, and had looked upon the giant altar and compared the proceedings there with what he did in the tabernacle of the congregation; but, more importantly, if he had contrasted the vain and degenerate and wicked lives of those who then sat in his seat, with the righteousness and godly walk of their ancestors, many generations before, we may suppose he would have been sick at heart and would have felt like lamenting over doomed Jerusalem and its twice doomed temple, even as Jesus himself would soon do. The Jewish high priests of Jesus' day were a far cry from their counterparts in the days of Israel's genesis.

Aaron, who held the Melchizedek Priesthood and qualified by purity of heart, along with Nadab and Abihu and seventy of the elders of Israel, to see the God of that chosen people, was called of God to preside over the lesser priesthood, which ever thereafter would bear his name. He was the presiding bishop of the Church, as it were, and the office was ordained of God to be hereditary, to go from father to son, and to be the rightful inheritance of the oldest man in direct descent among the sons of Aaron.[1] And so it was in the early generations. But in the days of the kings of Israel and Judah, high priests were sometimes installed and banished from office by the unrighteousness of the occupant of the throne, and by the days of Jesus such appointments and removals were made by Gentile overlords as a matter of political expediency and without reference to the lineage of the Levite involved. As a consequence, the high priests were of the same low spiritual stature as the Herods and Pilates who appointed them. But what concerns us is that they wielded great political and religious influence, that they molded public sentiment, and that their conduct became a pattern for Jews in general.

It is worthy of note that these, shall we say, illegitimate sons of Aaron were considered nonetheless to be Jehovah's representatives, that they were subject to secular powers and engaged in political connivings that were outside the bounds of their priestly callings, and that they were a symbol or standard around which the people would rally either to worship or to crucify.

It is also worthy of note that they wielded considerable influence; were overly endowed with this world's goods; received their offices, in some instances, by crime and bribery; and were subject to the mandates and murderous designs of the Great Sanhedrin. They were "high priests by investiture" and not "high priests by anointing," as had been their forebears; and though they could still simulate and wear the breastplate, the Urim and Thummim that Aaron and his original successors once carried upon their breasts had long since been taken from their ungodly hands, and with the loss of these holy interpreters had gone also, in large measure, the spirit of prophecy and revelation.

These high priests did, however, still hold the Aaronic

Priesthood; they still performed sacrificial rites with all the similitudes and symbols that had always attended these sacred ordinances; and they still directed appropriate worship at the great feasts and made atonement for the people on that one day each year when they entered the Holy of Holies and pronounced the Ineffable Name ten times.

As to the two despicable priestly rulers who sought the blood of the Guiltless One and who joined in the conspiracy that carried him to the cross, Edersheim says: "St. Luke significantly joins together, as the highest religious authority in the land, the names of Annas and Caiaphas. The former had been appointed by Quirinius. After holding the Pontificate for nine years, he was deposed, and succeeded by others, of whom the fourth was his son-in-law Caiaphas. The character of the High-Priests during the whole of that period is described in the Talmud in terrible language. And although there is no evidence that 'the house of Annas' was guilty of the same gross self-indulgence, violence, luxury, and even public indecency, as some of their successors, they are included in the woes pronounced on the corrupt leaders of the priesthood, whom the Sanctuary is represented as bidding depart from the sacred precincts, which their presence defiled. It deserves notice, that the special sin with which the house of Annas is charged is that of 'whispering'—or hissing like vipers—which seems to refer to private influence on the judges in their administration of justice, whereby 'morals were corrupted, judgment perverted, and the Shekhinah withdrawn from Israel.' " (Edersheim 1:263.)

2. *Priests and Levites.*

We know that the Aaronic Priesthood itself has been the same from its beginning to the present, meaning that we now have what John the Baptist had, and he possessed what Aaron himself held. We know that in the Aaronic Priesthood today there are four offices—deacon, teacher, priest, and bishop. But we cannot determine from the Old and New Testament accounts what offices there were in the lesser priesthood in previous ages. The priesthood itself is power and authority; the offices in the priesthood are appointments to use the priesthood for specified purposes. When the purposes change for which priesthood is needed and used, it may well be that the offices themselves are changed. From the day of Aaron to the building of Solomon's Temple, for instance, the Levites transported the tabernacle of the congregation and had special care for the ark of the covenant. These functions were no longer needed when the House of the Lord became a permanent rather than a portable dwelling place. Functions that once were laid upon the Levites were no longer needed, and it may well be that the offices in their Levitical Order of priesthood also underwent changes.

In Aaron's day, he and his son were priests. Aaron himself—and his firstborn after him, from generation to generation—was the presiding priest; in this capacity he carried the designation of high priest, and served as the equivalent of the presiding bishop. The other members of the tribe of Levi also held the Aaronic Priesthood, or, as it is also called, the Levitical Priesthood, but they did not hold the office of priest. In the scriptural accounts they are simply called Levites. The offices they held are not named, although the duties assigned them are described. These duties were to assist Aaron's sons in transporting and caring for the tabernacle of the congregation and in various performances in the temple. Their services were comparable to those of deacons and teachers today. Our deacons and teachers cannot baptize or administer the sacrament, and the Levites, although they did some menial work connected with sacrifices, such as preparing the altar and gathering the wood, did not perform the sacrifices themselves. We assume they did not baptize and that this ordinance was left for the priests only. We know there were judges anciently and that a bishop is a common judge in Israel, and so we conclude that the present office is comparable to the ancient one.

Under the Mosaic system the Levites were scattered among the other tribes and received no landed inheritances of the sort distributed by lot to their fellow tribes. All the other tribes paid tithes to the Levites, and they in turn tithed their tithes for the support of the priests. Since our deacons—holding the Aaronic or Levitical Priesthood, as they do—are appointed to teach the gospel, and to warn, expound, and exhort, and to invite all to come to Christ; since our teachers are to watch over the Church always and to be with and strengthen the members; since they are to see that there is no iniquity in the Church and that all the members do their duty; since our priests are to visit in the homes of the members and exhort them to pray vocally and in secret and attend to all family duties, we assume their counterparts anciently—indeed, there can be little question on the matter—had similar responsibilities. It is certainly not an exaggeration to say that the priests and Levites were a sanctifying and uplifting influence on the people generally and that they were looked upon as the Lord's servants and were treated accordingly.

In the day of Jesus, the priests and Levites, whose numbers were comparatively great, administered in the sacrificial services, performed the various rituals at the feasts, cared for the temple, and were expected to be learned in the law. If nothing else, they were an ever-present witness and symbol that the Lord's priesthood was on earth and that men should turn to Jehovah for strength and guidance. That they failed to give that guidance which would have led the people to believe in their true Messiah, when as a mortal he ministered among them, shows the depths to which the Jewish social and religious structure had sunk and justifies the assertion that their priesthood had been perverted into priestcraft. The sons of Levi of that day had become impure. But in the providence of Him whose servants they should have been, the promise is that in the last days he will purify them again that once more they may perform those duties assigned to them in the priestly order which has come down from Aaron.

3. *Scribes.*

"In trying to picture to ourselves New Testament scenes,

the figure most prominent, next to those of the chief actors, is that of the *Scribe.* He seems ubiquitous; we meet him in Jerusalem, in Judea, and even in Galilee. Indeed, he is indispensable, not only in Babylon, which may have been the birthplace of his order, but among the 'dispersion' also. Everywhere he appears as the mouthpiece and representative of the people; he pushes to the front, the crowd respectfully giving way, and eagerly hanging on his utterances, as those of a recognised authority. He has been solemnly ordained by the laying on of hands; and is the *Rabbi,* 'my great one,' Master, *amplitudo.* He puts questions; he urges objections; he expects full explanations and respectful demeanour. Indeed, his hyper-ingenuity in questioning has become a proverb. There is not measure of his dignity, nor yet limit to his importance. He is the 'lawyer,' the 'well-plastered pit,' filled with the water of knowledge 'out of which not a drop can escape,' in opposition to the 'weeds of untilled soil' of ignorance. He is the Divine aristocrat, among the vulgar herd of rude and profane 'country people,' who 'know not the Law' and are 'cursed.' More than that, his order constitutes the ultimate authority on all questions of faith and practice; he is 'the Exegete of the Laws,' the 'teacher of the Law,' and along with 'the chief priests' and 'elders' a judge in the ecclesiastical tribunals, whether of the capital or in the provinces. Although generally appearing in company with 'the Pharisees,' he is not necessarily one of them—for they represent a religious party, while he has a status, and holds an office. In short, he is the *Talmid* or learned student, the *Chakham* or sage, whose honour is to be great in the future world. Each Scribe outweighed all the common people, who must accordingly pay him every honour. Nay, they were honoured of God Himself, and their praises proclaimed by the angels; and in heaven also, each of them would hold the same rank and distinction as on earth. Such was to be the respect paid to their sayings, that they were to be absolutely believed, even if they were to declare that to be at the right hand which was at the left, or *vice versa.*" (Edersheim 1:93-94.)

Israel's divine guidance as a nation began with Moses, the man of God. He spoke and the issue was determined. His voice was the voice of Jehovah. Thereafter there were judges and prophets who had scribes to record their sayings and memorialize their doings, but always the divine word was available for the asking and the mind of the Lord was revealed for the seeking. In post-exilic days the prophetic word began to decrease and the position of the scribe, as the one in whose hands the divine word was found, grew in importance. Ezra was both a prophet and a scribe. After his day, through an evolving course, as inspired utterances were less frequent, the understanding and interpretation of the seeric sayings of the past became more important and the position of the scribes took on a new meaning, until finally their influence excelled all others in molding religious thought and practice.

This same course—for Lucifer has no new ideas, but merely applies what he already knows to new situations—has been followed in apostate Christendom. When there were no longer apostles and inspired men to give the Lord's message and word to living men, the world turned to interpreters—to scholars, to doctors of divinity, to theologians, to professors of religion—to set forth what they thought or imagined the divine word of former days meant. In the opening of our dispensation the Lord, after saying that the creeds of Christendom were "an abomination in his sight" (and these creeds were the interpretations and conclusions of the scribes, as it were), then said that "those professors" (meaning all who, like the scribes, had by their interpretations and teachings perverted the truth and made it of none effect) "were all corrupt." Then he said, paraphrasing Isaiah, "they draw near to me with their lips, but their hearts are far from me, they teach for doctrines the commandments of men, having a form of godliness, but they deny the power thereof." (JS-H 1:19.) This same charge—shall we say curse? yes, for so it is—was the one hurled by the Lord Jesus against the "scribes and Pharisees" of his day, quoting also the same root text from Isaiah. (Matt. 15:1-9; Mark 7:1-9; Isa. 29:13.)

By the time of Jesus, the Jewish scribes, exalted and revered by the people, had become the chief creators and upholders of priestcraft; they had become the devisers of doctrines that condoned and upheld iniquity—and it should be remembered that, according to the prophetic word, it was "because of priestcrafts and iniquities" that our Lord was "crucified." (2 Ne. 10:5.) The scribes had become and were the enemies of Christ. They were the ones who added to the law of Moses those detailed performances and perversions which made the law of no effect. They were the ones approved to explain and teach the law and to make decisions under it. There was a tradition that they alone understood the whole law, and their words came to have more impact and import than the law itself. It is as though they were the law. They were required to learn by heart the oral law, and they spent their time teaching others and disputing among themselves. They were, in effect, false ministers, false teachers, and false prophets, all of which gives great meaning to the scriptural comment that Jesus "taught . . . as one having authority, and not as the scribes." (Matt. 7:29.)

No group had greater influence over the people than they did. Nearly all the judges came from their ranks; they made up almost the whole teaching force of the nation, and they were well represented on the Sanhedrin. No priest could attain a position of prominence and influence unless he was also a scribe. They are the ones spoken of as the lawyers and teachers of the law. In New Testament times, the terms *lawyer* and *scribe* were synonymous. Most of the scribes were also Pharisees, but as a body they were distinct from them. Of them Jesus said: "All their works they do for to be seen of men: they make broad their phylacteries, and enlarge the borders of their garments, And love the uppermost rooms at feasts, and the chief seats in the synagogues, And greetings in the markets, and to be called of men, Rabbi, Rabbi." They are the ones upon whom he heaped perhaps the severest woes ever uttered by him, including the excoriating declaration, "Ye serpents, ye generation of vipers, how can ye escape the damnation of hell?" (Matt. 23.) They were a class who could have been a blessing to the people, for they were privileged to be teachers; but, in fact, they became a cursing, for they taught not the truth. "And all those who preach false doctrines, . . . and pervert the right way of the Lord, wo, wo, wo be unto them, saith the Lord God Almighty, for they shall be thrust down to hell!" (2 Ne. 28:15.)

4. *Rabbis.*

Jesus' counsel to his disciples that they should not be called Rabbi—"for one is your Master, even Christ; and all ye are brethren" (Matt. 23:8)—was itself a condemnation both of the false adulation heaped on the uninspired teachers of the day and a denunciation of Rabbinism itself, that is, of the great body of theological absurdities that had come into being through the warped interpretations of those who were looked upon as lights to the people. As occasion requires, and as we deal with the various vagaries of Jewish theology, we shall see the revolting absurdities imposed by Rabbinism upon a religion that once had divine approval. For the present we need only note that in Jesus' day all scribes were considered to be Rabbis, for the title was merely one of respect that was given by the Jews to all of their doctors and teachers. But the title was not limited to those self-appointed embodiments of all wisdom. Christ and John the Baptist, for instance, were both addressed by respectful persons by rabbinical titles. Different degrees of honor were intended as people used the term *Rab,* meaning master; *Rabbi,* my master; and *Rabboni,* my lord and master, this last and most exalted of all the titles being the one used by Mary outside the open tomb as she bowed before the risen Master. It will suffice for our present purposes merely to be aware that all that was said of the scribes applies in part at least to the Rabbis, and that this latter group must bear much of the responsibility for creating the climate and preparing the way for the crucifixion of a God. What an awesome responsibility one assumes when he chooses to teach false doctrine![2]

5. *Pharisees, Sadducees, Essenes, and Nazarites.*

These all, in effect, were politico-religious sects or parties. Theoretically their bases were religious and their differences doctrinal; in fact, they were also political and social and cultural. They came into being in post-exilic historical settings of anguish and political oppression, and each of them exercised a leavening and sometimes controlling influence in Jewish Israel.

The Pharisees, of whom there were only between six thousand and seven thousand in the day of Jesus, had by all odds the greatest influence over Jewish thought and practice. The bulk of the common people believed as they did and conformed to some extent to their practices. Their number included the scribes, whose self-appointed mission was to tempt, berate, and deride the Son of God; and their doctrine was Rabbinism, that maze of Jewish absurdity which turned living truth into dead letter and imposed such burdens upon men that none but deluded fanatics could bear them in full. Paul was a Pharisee; so also were Gamaliel, Nicodemus, and the Arimathean called Joseph, in whose tomb our Lord was laid.

As best we can determine, from those educated guesses which historians are pleased to call historical facts, the Pharisees were those who continued the work of Ezra in collating, memorizing, and interpreting the law and all the commandments therein recorded. Apparently they began as a distinct group with political influence as the Hasidaeans back in the days of the high priest Onanias III, who was deposed by Antiochus Epiphanes in the second century B.C. Their name signifies "God's loyal ones," and they were traditionally known as "the separated ones." Under John

Hyrcanus (134-104 B.C.) they had great political power, and from that time onward they maintained a dominating position in the Sanhedrin. Such was true in the day when that body condemned our Lord.

Our special interest in the Pharisees centers in what they believed and taught and practiced in that day when the Lord Jesus had one confrontation after another with them. A knowledge of their opinions and practices in that day when our Lord was restoring the gospel again is almost essential to an understanding of the Christianity that then came into being. In that day their interest was not, as it had once been, in keeping or interpreting the law of Moses, in the true sense of the word. Rather, they then had created a new law, an oral law—the portion of the Talmud called the Mishna or "second law"; it is a law founded on tradition instead of revelation, a law that they esteemed to be of greater worth than the Torah, or law of Moses itself. A digest of Jewish traditions as well as a compendium of the ritualistic performances of the law, it was made up of formalistic minutae; of the need for washings before they could eat bread; of the requirement to bathe following a trip to the market; and of the practice of washing cups, pots, and brazen vessels. It included fasting twice a week (on Mondays and Thursdays) between the Paschal week and Pentecost, and between the Feast of Tabernacles and that of the Dedication of the Temple. Their observance of the law of tithing was punctilious beyond belief, even going to the point of refusing to buy food from or to eat food in the homes of non-Pharisees, lest the food should not have been tithed; and so on and so on and so on. And out of these beliefs and practices there grew up among them a feeling of proud self-righteousness, which dulled their spirits and closed their minds against the truths Jesus offered them.

Theologically speaking, the Pharisees believed in the unity and holiness of God, the election of Israel, life after death, the resurrection from the dead, the ministering of angels, and some among them at least in the continuation of the family unit in eternity. They were extreme advocates of the doctrine of observing the Sabbath day, to which doctrine they had appended thirty-nine principal species of prohibited acts on that day. Most of their religious emphasis, however, was on ethical principles rather than doctrinal concepts.

It was not easy to be a Pharisee, but perhaps that was part of the Pharisees' appeal to a people who believed that life never was intended to be easy. In any event they wielded the greatest religious power of any group in our Lord's day.

The Sadducees, fewer in number than their Pharisaic opponents, claimed only four thousand adherents in the day Jesus walked among men. But they were the aristocracy of the nation—the priests and rulers, the wealthy and influential, the consorters with Herod and the friends of Caesar.

Jewish legend places their beginning with Zadok, whose family ministered at the altar in the Lord's house; and among their number was found the presiding high priest, the one who, alone among all his kindred priests, went annually to commune with the Most High in the most holy place. After Cyrus opened the prison that was Babylon and sent Zerubbabel and the others back to the once Holy City to build Jehovah's house again, the remnant of Zadok stood foremost among the priestly families, ministering again, as was their right by lineage, in the sacred sacrificial offerings.

They grew into a reactionary politico-religious organization as part of an insurgent movement against the Maccabean party in the second century B.C. In their veins, at the time of John and Jesus and their apostolic colleagues, flowed the purest Jewish blood of the nation. The whole thrust of their not-too-popular party was one of opposition to the Pharisees and the oral law with all its ritualistic formalities. For them, the temple—not the synagogues, which were dominated by the Pharisees, the Rabbis, and the scribes—was the center of a religious system whose true significance they no longer understood. Being satisfied with life as it then was, they had little interest in the coming of a Messianic Deliverer, though the Sadducean sacrifices they offered on the great altar were in similitude of his promised atoning sacrifice. When Titus set the Roman torch to the temple in A.D. 70, wrenching each separate stone from the ancient foundation, the Sadducees died as a party; from then on Judaism centered in the synagogue and not the temple.

"But this priestly aristocracy were by no means the most zealous for the sanctuary from which they drew their honours and wealth. They . . . had even sought to turn parts of the Temple into a splendid family mansion. They had coquetted and debased their offices to win favour with the Ptolemies and the Syrian kings; they had held back, in half Greek irreligiousness, from taking a vigorous part in the glorious Maccabean struggle, and now [in the day of Jesus] truckled to heathen procurators, or with a half heathen king, to preserve their honours and vested interests. To please Herod, they had admitted Simon Boethus, the Alexandrian, the father of the king's young wife, to the high priesthood, from which a strict Jew, Jesus the son of Phabi, had been expelled to make room for him. They had even shown frank and hearty submission and loyalty to Rome.

"The nation, with its chosen religious leaders, the Pharisees—the representatives of the 'Saints' who had conquered in the great war of religious independence—never forgot the faint-heartedness and treachery of the priestly nobility in that magnificent struggle. Their descent might secure its members hereditary possession of the dignified offices of the Church, and there might still be a charm in their historical names; but they were regarded with open distrust and dislike by the nation and the Pharisees alike, and had to make many concessions to Pharisaic rules to protect themselves from actual violence.

"The strict fanatical heads of the Synagogue and leaders of the people, and the cold and polished Temple aristocracy, were thus bitterly opposed, and it added to the keenest of the dislike that the dreams by the Rabbinical, or Pharisaic party, of a restored theocracy, could only be realized through the existing organization of the priesthood, of which the indifferent Sadducees had the control." (Geikie, pp. 538-39.)

Theologically, the Sadducees found little to please them in the beliefs of the Pharisaically inclined masses. Strange as it may seem among a people who praised Jehovah with their lips and had his law written on scrolls of papyrus that were everywhere available for study and scholastic analysis, the Sadducees did not believe in a resurrection. They denied the reality of a future state in which rewards and punishments would be meted out as a result of good or evil acts performed by mortal men. They scoffed at the Pharisaic concepts of the immortality of the soul, and believed neither in preexistence nor the ministering of angels nor the existence of spirits. They did not believe in foreordination or that Divine Providence ruled in the lives of men, but did lay stress on the fact that men had freedom of choice as to good and evil, and concluded that whatever happened in one's life was the direct result of the exercise of such agency.[3]

But in nothing was the difference between Pharisees and Sadducees more marked than in the contrast between the Pharisaic Messianic hope and the Sadducean rejection of or at least indifference to this nationalistic concept. "The Pharisees, as the hereditary representatives of puritans who had delivered the nation in the great struggle against Syria, looked forward with touching though fanatical yearning, to the realization of the prophecies of Daniel, which, as they understood them, promised that Israel, under the Messiah, and with it, themselves, should be raised 'to dominion, and glory, and a kingdom; that all peoples, nations, and languages should serve Him, and that His kingdom should be everlasting.'[4] They believed that this national triumph would be inaugurated so soon as Israel, on its part, carried out to the full the requirements of the ceremonial laws, as expounded in their traditions. It was a matter of formal covenant, in which the truth and righteousness—that is, the justice, of Jehovah were involved. . .

"To this dream of the future, the Sadducees opposed a stolid and contemptuous indifference. Enjoying the honours and good things of the world, they had no taste for a revolution which should introduce, they knew not what, in place of a state of things with which they were quite contented. Their fathers had had no such ideas, and the sons ridiculed them. They not only laughed aside the Pharisaic idea of righteousness, as identified with a life of minute and endless observance, but fell back on the Mosaic Law, and mocked at the Messianic hope from which the zeal of their rivals had sprung. . . .

"The nation zealously supported the Pharisees. The spirit of the age was against the Sadducees. The multitude disliked to hear that what the Maccabeans had defended with their blood was uncanonical. They yielded cheerfully to the heavy yoke of the Pharisaic Rabbis, for, the more burdensome the duties required, the greater the future reward for performance. The Pharisees, moreover, were part of the people, mingled habitually with them as their spiritual guides, and were the examples of exact obedience to their own precepts. Their Messianic dreams were of national glory, and thus the crowd saw in them the representatives of their own fondest aspirations. The Sadducees—isolated, haughty, harsh, and unnational—were hated: their rivals honoured and followed. The extravagances and the hypocrisy of some might be ridiculed, but they were the accepted popular leaders.

"Indeed, apart from all other considerations, the fact that the Sadducees supported zealously every government in turn, was enough to set the people against them. Instead of this, the Pharisees shared and fostered the patriotic and religious abhorrence of the Roman supremacy, and were sworn enemies of the hated Herodian family. The result was that, in the words of Josephus, 'the Pharisees had such an influence with the people, that nothing could be done about divine worship, prayers, or sacrifices, except according to their wishes and rules, for the community believed they sought only the loftiest and worthiest aims alike in word and deed. The Sadducees were few in number; and though they belonged to the highest ranks, had so little influence, that when elected to office, they were forced to comply with the ritual of the Pharisees from fear of the people.' " (Geikie, pp. 541-42.)

If the Pharisees were a "generation of vipers" who could not "escape the damnation of hell" (Matt. 23:33), as Jesus said (and they were), and if the Sadducees used their political influence to bring about our Lord's crucifixion, thus consigning themselves to the same depths of damnation (and so it was), they both had a bedfellow whose departure from the truth and whose apostate practices equaled and even surpassed those of these two more influential sects. We speak of the *Essenes.* In number—there were some four thousand of them in Jesus' day—they were as numerous as the Sadducees. Their influence among the people, however, was slight, and they are not so much as mentioned by name in the New Testament. It was to the Pharisees that the masses turned for religious guidance, and it was to the Sadducees that the people bowed where their sacrificial system was concerned and where their relationships to the Caesars and the Herods were involved.

The Essenes drew into their fold the utter and complete fanatics of the nation. Many of them lived in colonies apart from their fellow Jews, held their property under a communal system, ate at a common table, and lived a rigid agrarian type life, full of ceremonialism. Some were celibates, "the precursors of the Christian monks," Geikie says.

Their doctrine was as far afield from reality as is common in the more freakish cults of Christendom. Their aim in life was to keep the law of Moses, which they studied day and night every day. "To blaspheme the name of Moses was the highest crime, punishable with death, and to give up his Books was a treachery which no Essene would commit, even under the agonies of torture or death." The Dead Sea Scrolls, of relatively modern discovery, were apparently kept by ancient colonies of these super-separatists from the mainstream of Jewish life.

They had their own synagogues, were pacifists, ate no animal food (since the law said, "Thou shalt not kill"), bathed their whole bodies before each meal, and took terrible oaths of secrecy to conceal their doctrines and "the secret names of the angels, which were known to the brotherhood, and gave him who learned them power, by pronouncing them, to draw down these awful beings from heaven."

"They were rigid Predestinarians, believing that all things, in the course of nature and in the life of man, are fixed by fate. When there was no moral freedom, it was idle either to preach or teach, and so they did neither." They did, however, profess to have the gift of prophecy, and were called in, from time to time, by the Herods and others to interpret dreams and give meaning to various superstitions. "The Essenes came in contact with the people," Geikie says, "as healers, prophets, dream-interpreters, and exorcists, not as teachers or preachers." (Geikie, pp. 252-57.) They were, it would seem, not far removed from the sorcerers, astrologers, and magicians of the ancient courts of Babylon and Egypt.

Historians have been wont to ascribe to the Essenes an influence and status wholly disproportionate to that which, in fact, was theirs. Since there are some high moral and ethical principles in their writings, they have been referred to as heralds of that Christianity which was to be. In this connection there has been some intellectual consternation in some quarters to discover in the documents of the Essenes some of the very concepts Jesus gave forth in his teachings, all of which simply means that gospel truths have been revealed in dispensations past and preserved in garbled form among those who have forsaken the full truth.[5]

At least from the days of Moses, both men and women in Israel were privileged to take vows setting themselves apart to serve the Lord in some special way for an appointed period. Such persons, while subject to their vows, were called *Nazarites.* Frequently the period of penance and pondering and worship and devotion was for thirty days. In the case of Samson it was for life, and John the Baptist is considered by some to have had the same lifetime obligation. As set out in Numbers 6:1-21, those so separating themselves unto the Lord, for whatever period was involved, must abstain from wine and strong drink and the eating of grapes or anything coming from the vine tree. They must let their hair grow and avoid any Levitical uncleanness. At the end of their period of separation, they shaved their heads and offered burnt offerings, sin offerings, peace offerings, and meat and drink offerings, with all their attendant formalities. Even Paul, as a temporizing gesture to the partially converted Jewish-Christians in Jerusalem—and after the law of Moses, including the law of sacrifice and the law of the Nazarite, had been done away—participated in these vows and the offerings made incident thereto. (Acts 21:23-26.)

In the days of Jesus, before he fulfilled the law of Moses and ended the offering of sacrifices, Nazarites were present in his congregations and were exerting an influence for good among the people. Their vows were personal matters and their worship a personal attempt to draw near to the Lord, as distinguished from the ascetic brotherhood found in the false worship of the Essenes.

NOTES

1. The office of presiding bishop in the Church today is a hereditary office, designed and intended to go from father to son in the appointed lineage. The Lord, however, up to this point has not revealed the lineage, but undoubtedly will do so at some time in the future, perhaps when the millennial era is ushered in. Speaking of the presiding bishop of the Church, the Lord says: "And if they be literal descendants of Aaron they have a legal right to the bishopric, if they are the firstborn among the sons of Aaron; For the firstborn holds the right of the presidency over this priesthood, and the keys or authority of the same. No man has a legal right to this office, to hold the keys of this priesthood, except he be a literal descendant and the firstborn of Aaron." (D&C 68:16-18.)

2. All scribes were Rabbis, but not all Rabbis were scribes. Jesus and other teachers were Rabbis, but most assuredly they were not scribes. In chapter 6, "The Rabbis at the Time of Christ, and Their Ideas Respecting the Messiah," in *The Life of Christ* by Cunningham Geikie, we find this analysis of the station, influence, and ministry of those Rabbis who also were scribes: "If the most important figures in the society of Christ's day were the Pharisees, it was because they were [that is, among them were most of] the Rabbis, or teachers of the Law. As such they received superstitious honour, which was, indeed, the great motive, with many, to court the title, or join the party.

"The Rabbis were classed with Moses, the patriarchs, and the prophets, and claimed equal reverence. Jacob and Joseph were both said to have been Rabbis. The Targum of Jonathan substitutes Rabbis, or Scribes, for the word 'prophets,' where it occurs. Josephus speaks of the prophets of Saul's day as Rabbis. In the Jerusalem Targum all the patriarchs are learned Rabbis. . . . They were to be dearer to Israel than father or mother, because parents [as they falsely supposed] avail only in this world, but the Rabbi for ever. They were set above kings, for is it not written, 'Through me kings reign?' Their entrance into a house brought a blessing; to live or to eat with them was the highest good fortune. To dine with a Rabbi was as if to enjoy the splendour of heavenly majesty. . . .

"To learn a single verse, or even a single letter, from a Rabbi could be repaid only by the profoundest respect. . . . The table of the Rabbi was nobler than that of kings; and his crown more glorious than theirs.

". . . The Mishna declares that it is a greater crime to speak anything to their discredit than to speak against the words of the Law. The words of the Rabbis are to be held as worth more than the words of the prophets. . . .

"Heresy, which would be fatal to the blind unanimity which was their political strength, could only be excluded by rigidly denouncing the least departure from their precepts. The Law and the Prophets must, therefore, be understood only in the sense of their traditions. . . .

"Yet, in form, the Law received boundless honour. Every saying of the Rabbis had to be based on some words of it, which were, however, explained in their own way. The spirit of the times, the wild fanaticism of the people, and their own bias, tended, alike, to make them set value only on ceremonies and worthless externalisms, to the utter neglect of the spirit of the sacred writings. Still, it was owned that the Law needed no confirmation, while the words of the Rabbis did.

"So far as the Roman authority under which they lived left them free, the Jews willingly put all power in the hands of the Rabbis. They or their nominees filled every office, from the highest in the priesthood to the lowest in the community. They were the casuists, the teachers, the priests, the judges, the magistrates, and the physicians of the nation. But their authority went still further, for, by the Rabbinical laws, nearly everything in daily life needed their counsel and aid. No one could be born, circumcised, brought up, educated, betrothed, married, or buried—no one could celebrate the Sabbath or other feasts, or begin a business, or make a contract, or kill a beast for food, or even bake bread, without the advice or presence of a Rabbi. The words of Christ respecting binding and loosing, were a Rabbinical proverb: they bound and they loosed as they thought fit. What they loosed was permitted—what they bound was forbidden. They were the brain, the eyes, the ears, the nerves, the muscles of the people, who were mere children apart from them. . . .

"They were Pharisees as to their party, and Rabbis in their relations to the Law. That one who came, not indeed, to destroy the Law and the Prophets, but to free them from the perversions of Rabbinical theology, should have been met by the bitterest hatred and a cruel death, was only an illustration of the sad truth, to which every age was borne witness, that ecclesiastical bodies who have the power to persecute, identify even the abuses of their system with the defense of religion, and are capable of any crime in their blind intolerance." (Geikie, pp. 52-55.)

3. "The Sadducees uniformly fell back on the letter of the Law, the prescriptive rights of the Temple, and the glory of the priesthood; the Pharisees, on the other hand, took their stand on the authority of the Rabbinical traditions, the value of sacred acts apart from the interposition of the priest, and advocated popular interests generally.

"The contrast between the spirit of the two parties showed itself prominently in the harsh tenacity with which the Temple aristocracy held to the letter of the Mosaic Law in its penalties, as opposed to the milder spirit in which the Pharisees interpreted them, in accordance with the spirit of the times. The Pharisees, for example, explained the Mosaic demand—an eye for an eye and a tooth for a tooth—metaphorically, and allowed recompense to be made in money, but the Sadducees required exact compliance. The Sadducees required that the widow should literally spit in the face of the brother-in-law who refused her the levirate marriage rights, but it was enough for the Pharisees that she spat on the ground before him. The Pharisees permitted the carcass of a beast that had died to be used for any other purpose than food, to save loss to the owner, but the Sadducees denounced the penalties of uncleanness on so lax a practice. They sternly required that a false witness be put to death, according to the letter of the Law, even if his testimony had done the accused no injury, and many did not even shrink from carrying out the reasoning of the Rabbis, that, as two witnesses were always required to condemn the accused, both witnesses should always be executed when any perjury had been committed in the case." (Geikie, p. 540.)

4. Geikie here paraphrased Daniel 7:14, a passage which in fact refers to the Second Coming of the Messiah and his receipt back from the Ancient of Days, who is Adam, of the keys of the earthly kingdom, preparatory to the millennial reign of peace and righteousness.

5. Of those who suppose, in all sincerity, that they are following the course prescribed by Moses or any of the spiritual giants who went before, our revelation, identifying those who shall inherit a telestial kingdom, says: "These are they who are of Paul, and of Apollos, and of Cephas. These are they who say they are some of one and some of another—some of Christ and some of John, and some of Moses, and some of Elias, and some of Esaias, and some of Isaiah, and some of Enoch; But received not the gospel, neither the testimony of Jesus, neither the prophets, neither the everlasting covenant." (D&C 76:99-101.) It is not enough, Essene-like, to die for Moses and his law; it is living and obeying, not defending and dying, that leads to salvation.

JEWISH SCRIPTURE IN JESUS' DAY

Search the scriptures; for in them ye think ye have eternal life: and they are they which testify of me. (John 5:39.)

All things must be fulfilled, which were written in the law of Moses, and in the prophets, and in the psalms, concerning me. Then opened he their understanding, that they might understand the scriptures. (Luke 24:44-45.)

Scriptures Guide Men to Salvation

We have in the Holy Scriptures—those inspired and canonized utterances of the holy prophets; those heaven-sent fragments from the records of eternity; those words and phrases spoken by the power of the Holy Ghost—we have in these sacred writings the plan and the pattern, the laws and the requirements, the gospel recitations, that will guide us to eternal life in our Father's kingdom. They chart the course we must pursue to gain peace in this life and glory and honor in the life to come.

We are not saved by the scriptures as such. In the beginning the plan of salvation was "declared by holy angels sent forth from the presence of God, and by his own voice, and by the gift of the Holy Ghost." (Moses 5:58.) The laws and truths so declared were recorded, and such of them as we now have are called the Holy Scriptures. They tell how all men—not the ancients only—may hear the voice of God, entertain angelic messengers, and enjoy the outpourings of the Holy Spirit. The Holy Scriptures are given to guide men to that state of spiritual enlightenment and perfection attained by those of old who worked out their salvation.

"The holy scriptures," Paul told his beloved Timothy, "are able to make thee wise unto salvation through faith which is in Christ Jesus." The scriptures open the door; they mark the course we must pursue; they identify the strait and narrow path; they testify of Christ and his laws; they engender faith; their worth cannot be overstated. But once the path is revealed, men must walk therein to gain the desired eternal reward. Thus, "All scripture," Paul continues, "is given by inspiration of God, and is profitable for doctrine, for reproof, for correction, for instruction in righteousness: That the man of God may be perfect, throughly furnished unto all good works." (2 Tim. 3:15-17.)

The law of the Lord is perfect,
  Converting the soul:
The testimony of the Lord is sure,
  Making wise the simple.

The statutes of the Lord are right,
  Rejoicing the heart:
The commandment of the Lord is pure,
  Enlightening the eyes.

The fear of the Lord is clean,
  Enduring for ever:

The judgments of the Lord
  Are true and righteous altogether.

More to be desired are they than gold,
  Yea, than much fine gold:
Sweeter also than honey and the honeycomb.

Moreover by them is thy servant warned:
And in keeping of them There is great reward.
—Psalm 19:7-11

In the full and complete sense, every word spoken by the power of the Holy Ghost is scripture. It is "the will of the Lord, . . . the mind of the Lord, . . . the word of the Lord, . . . the voice of the Lord, and the power of God unto salvation." (D&C 68:4.) It could not be otherwise, for the Holy Ghost is God, is one with the Father and the Son, and is their witness and revelator. His words are their words whether he speaks them personally or impresses the thoughts upon the minds of men so they find utterance by mortal tongues.

But the scriptures of which we now speak consist of those inspired statements of holy men which have been preserved for the guidance of all men and which find general acceptance by faithful people. This canonical reservoir of revealed writ varies in size and dimensions from one time to another and as between one people and another. One nation in one age has a small library of sacred writings, another in a more blessed day has many shelves stacked high with what the Lord has said to many prophets. As a general rule, the more sacred parts of Holy Writ, such as the sealed portion of the Book of Mormon, are withheld from those of lesser spiritual stature. And oftimes that which is available has been muddied by the carelessness or unbelief or defiant rebellion of those in whose custody the sacred records have rested at any given time, as witness the plain and precious parts of Genesis not found in modern Bibles but restored by revelation in the Pearl of Great Price.

Further, there is the practical matter of interpretation

and of equating and of comparing the written word with the continuing stream of oral utterances that, because the speaking voice has been inspired from on high, are themselves also scripture. Principles revealed in one day must be applied to new situations in another time; the ancient scriptures must live again in the lives of those into whose hands they fall; someone must tell what the word of God, given anciently, means today.

It takes an inspired man to understand and interpret an inspired utterance. No one but a prophet can envision the true and full meaning of prophetic words. Any person of normal mentality can absorb some of the intended meaning from the scriptures, but no one can plumb the depths unless enlightened by the same power that gave the revealed truths in the first instance. Hence, "no prophecy of the scripture is of any private interpretation," as Peter said. Why? Because "the prophecy came not in old time by the will of man: but holy men of God spake as they were moved by the Holy Ghost." (2 Pet. 1:20-21.) Similarly, holy men of God, as moved upon by the Holy Ghost, are the only ones who can make authoritative and complete statements as to the meaning and application of revealed truth.

And therein lies the problem. Such scriptures as were available to our Jewish brethren in the day of our Lord were completely buried under the private interpretations of the Rabbis.

Inspired men were few and far between in that day. Men did not look to living prophets to tell what dead prophets meant by their prophetic words. It was a day when the school of Hillel debated with the school of Shammai, and neither of them came anywhere near the truth. When our Lord and his associates came, speaking with authority, "and not as the scribes" (Matt. 7:29), it was more than a shock: it was the ax of revealed truth and of inspired interpretation chopping down the vines of tradition that encumbered the vineyard of scriptural learning.

Ancient Jewish Scriptures

When Jesus said, "Search the scriptures" (John 5:39); when "the voices of the prophets" (Acts 13:27) were heard, as it were, and the writings of Moses were "read in the synagogues every sabbath day" (Acts 15:21); when Paul spoke of "the holy scriptures, which are able to make thee wise unto salvation" (2 Tim. 3:15), to what books of Holy Writ did they have reference?

Adam and his posterity kept a book of remembrance in which sacred things were recorded. Seth, Enos, Cainan, Mahalaleel, Jared, Enoch, Methuselah, Lamech, and Noah, and all the holy men who lived before the flood wrote down what the Lord said to each of them. Shem and Melchizedek, Abraham and his descendants, and the mighty men of old—who saw God, heard his voice, entertained his messengers, saw within the veil, and knew the mysteries of the kingdom by revelation—all these were the proud possessors of authoritative writings long since lost among the children of men. In due course, as part of the restoration of all things—which Peter promises shall include all things "which God hath spoken by the mouth of all his holy prophets since the world began" (Acts 3:21)—we shall receive again the Book of Enoch, the Book of Joseph, the remainder of the Book of Abraham, plus unnumbered and unknown volumes. No revealed truth, no sacred scripture, no recorded revelation is ever permanently lost; what God has said to one person, he will say to another, and what was known in one age shall come forth again. The more truth a gracious God can give to his people, the better he and they like it.

But the Jews of Jesus' day, even as the sectarians in our day, were denied the blessing of having the fulness of revealed truth to read in their homes and preach in their synagogues. They did have enough to teach them of their Messiah and to direct their feet in the path leading to greater light and added revelation, but the inspiration rained from heaven no longer filled the reservoirs of revelation as had been the case among their fathers. They had the Old Testament, probably more of it than is found in our modern versions, but certainly only a fraction of what should have been compiled upon its pages.

We have every reason to believe that the full and pure accounts that tell of the revelation of the gospel to Adam and Noah, of their baptism and the priesthood they held, and of the Lord's extended dealings with them, as such accounts have been revealed anew through Joseph Smith, were not extant among the Jews in Jesus' day. At least there is no intimation in the teachings of Jesus or in the New Testament writings that the knowledge in these original accounts was then available to the people. It does seem clear, however, that the book of Genesis, as they had it, contained more than does the same record in the King James Version of the Bible. For instance, Jesus, in teaching that he, as Jehovah, was "before Abraham," said: "Your father Abraham rejoiced to see my day: and he saw it, and was glad" (John 8:56-58), no record of which ancient vision is found in Genesis. That Abraham did have such a vision was revealed to Joseph Smith, and he inserted the account in the Inspired Version.[1] It was the unvarying practice of Jesus, when quoting scripture, to take his words from those accounts with which his hearers were or should have been familiar. We must suppose he followed this course in this instance.

An even more conclusive reason to believe that the Jewish Genesis excelled the Christian Genesis is seen in the writings of Paul. He quoted and paraphrased a number of scriptures and referred to some historical facts, which are not in the Bible of Christendom, but which original sources have been restored by the great prophet of latter days. The clearest of these is his reference in Hebrews to ancient worthies "who through faith subdued kingdoms, wrought righteousness, obtained promises, stopped the mouths of lions, Quenched the violence of fire, escaped the edge of the sword, out of weakness were made strong, waxed valiant in fight, [and] turned to flight the armies of the aliens." (Heb. 11:33-34.) This language is, of course, a paraphrase, a quotation, and a summary of what Genesis once contained relative to Melchizedek, which makes it perfectly clear that the Melchizedek material was still in Genesis when Paul wrote to his Hebrew brethren.[2] Paul's statements about "God" preaching "before the gospel unto Abraham" (Gal. 3:8) and his explanations as to how and in what manner Moses was the mediator of the old covenant also show a more extended biblical background than is available to modern writers.[3] There seems, thus, to be little doubt that although the Jews did not have a full and perfect book of Genesis, they did have a better and more accurate one than modern Christendom possesses.

As far as we know, the other prophetic writings and Psalms, had among the Jews in the meridian of time, were substantially the same as those we now have, although, yet again, what is now extant is far less than what once was. The Hebrews on the American continent found on the brass plates of Laban sayings and writings of Joseph who was sold into Egypt, of Moses and Isaiah, of Zenos, Zenock, and Neum, and possibly of Abraham, and perhaps of many unnamed prophets, none of which seem to have been preserved through the Babylonian exile and down to our Lord's day.[4] At least there are no allusions or intimations in the New Testament accounts or the writings of contemporary historians that the Jews then had these precious gems of celestial truth, which would have been theirs had they been in complete harmony with the divine will.

The Old Testament of Jesus' Day

We have come to call the Jewish scriptures the Old Testament, meaning, as men have falsely supposed, that it is a record of Deity's dealings with a people subject to an old testament, an old covenant, a lesser law, which antedated and was less than that Christianity revealed by the Son of

God. The New Testament is supposed to contain the accounts relative to the new covenant, which superseded, fulfilled, and to some degree at least abolished what went before. In fact, both testaments or covenants deal with the eternal principles and truths that make up the everlasting gospel, the gospel of salvation, which is both an old, a present, a new, and a future covenant; it is the new and everlasting covenant. More than a third of the time period covered by the Old Testament was one in which the lesser law was "added" to the higher principles of revealed religion. Many of the ancients, though subject to the law of Moses, continued to live the higher law that had, in fact, antedated everything revealed to Moses and Aaron and their successors. The Old Testament scriptural accounts deal with both the higher gospel truths and the formalities and rigid requirements of the lesser law of Moses.

In the day of Jesus, though there were Hebrew or Aramaic copies of the scripture in usage, the Old Testament of the people, the one used generally, the one quoted by Jesus and Paul and the New Testament authors, was the Septuagint. This Greek version of Holy Writ—commonly referred to as the LXX, because according to tradition it had been translated from Hebrew into Greek by about seventy scholars—was by no means a perfect reflection of the mind and will of Him from whom scripture comes. It contained all of our present Old Testament, plus many apocryphal books, and much license had been taken by the translators. It was completed more than two hundred years before the Christian era, and many of its passages contained gross mistakes, while others presented clarifications of the Hebrew originals. Edersheim says that the "free handling of the text" by Hellenistic translators resulted in "a strenuous effort . . . to banish all anthropomorphisms, as inconsistent with their ideas of Deity." (Edersheim 1:28.)

It was of these ancient scriptures, in their original form and before they fell into evil hands, that an angel said to Nephi: "The book that thou beholdest is a record of the

Jews, which contains the covenants of the Lord, which he hath made unto the house of Israel." Then the angel, speaking more particularly of the New Testament, continued: "Thou hast beheld that the book proceeded forth from the mouth of a Jew; and when it proceeded forth from the mouth of a Jew it contained the plainness of the gospel of the Lord, of whom the twelve apostles bear record." After these scriptures went forth "in purity," they came into the hands of "a great and abominable church, which is most abominable above all other churches." Of this ill-spawned and devil-built perverter of true religion, the angel said: "They have taken away from the gospel of the Lamb many parts which are plain and most precious; and also many covenants of the Lord have they taken away." (1 Ne. 13:23-26.) That is to say, both the Old and the New Testaments found among men in our day have been subject to the deletions, perversions, and alterations of persons whose interests were not compatible with those of the prophets and apostles whose words they dared to twist.

But in addition to LXX—which includes many apocryphal writings—and to the scriptural versions in their own language, the Jews had studied the pseudepigraphic books. As to the Apocrypha, as it is now constituted—and there have been many different selections of apocryphal books over the years—we have these revealed words: "There are many things contained therein that are true, and it is mostly translated correctly." And also: "There are many things contained therein that are not true, which are interpolations by the hands of men." Those who are "enlightened by the Spirit shall obtain benefit" from studying it. (D&C 91:1-6.) Those not so gifted will do better devoting their attention to the scriptures that have greater worth. Apocryphal writings are quoted in the Jewish Talmud.

Other Jewish writings, purporting to be scripture but which never attained either canonical or apocryphal authenticity, because their authors are assumed to be unknown, are called, collectively, the pseudepigrapha. These pseudepigraphic writings contain a remarkable intermixture of truth and error. They do talk about many things found in latter-day revelation that are not otherwise recorded in either the Bible or Apocrypha. Two of these pseudepigraphic books purport to be the writings of Enoch, of whom the world knows almost nothing. Because Jude in his New Testament book quotes from the writings of Enoch the prophecy that "the Lord cometh with ten thousands of his saints, To execute judgment upon" the ungodly (Jude 1:14-15),[5] let us here refer to some of the doctrines found in this so-called Book of Enoch, writings that were known and studied by the Jews in the day Jesus ministered among them.

In the pseudepigraphic writings of Enoch we find visions, prophecies, exhortations, and doctrinal expositions relative to the Second Coming and the Millennium; the names and functions of the seven angels (including Raphael, Michael, and Gabriel); the separation of the spirits of righteous and wicked men as they await the day of judgment; the coming judgment of the wicked; the attainment of salvation by the righteous and elect; the bringing of the Son of Man before "the head of days" (meaning, obviously, the Ancient of Days); the resurrection of the dead and the separation by the Judge of the righteous and the wicked; the translation of Enoch; preexistence and the creation of the souls of all men before the foundation of the world; the war in heaven and the casting out of Satan; the dividing of the eight-thousand-year history of the earth into the first six thousand years, to be followed by one thousand years of rest, after which would come another one thousand years, and then the end; a list of beatitudes, not far removed in wisdom from those of Jesus himself; personal responsibility for sin; the salvation of animals; the state of eternal life for those who keep the commandments; and much, much more.[6]

It will be observed that the matters here recited, though taught in part and by inference in the canonical scriptures of that and our day, are in fact known only in plainness and purity by latter-day revelation. It is far more than coincidence that doctrines attributed to Enoch in the pseudepigraphic writings are the very ones the Lord saw fit to restore in plainness in our dispensation. Unfortunately, the whole of these ancient writings cannot be accepted as the mind and will and voice of Him from whom revelation comes. As with the study of the apocryphal books, so it is with the study of the pseudepigraphic writings: the seeker after revealed wisdom must be guided by the power of the Holy Spirit.

The Old Testament vs. the Talmud

Our Jewish brethren in Jesus' day were blessed with an ample library of inspired writing. They had the Old Testament in a better and more complete form than is now had in Christendom. As we have set forth, after that volume of sacred writing left their hands—during the Dark Ages, when darkness covered the earth and gross darkness the minds of the people—many of the covenants of the Lord were taken from it by evil men who worked for another Master.

Our Jewish brethren in that day had also the numerous apocryphal and pseudepigraphic books, which they believed and accepted on more or less the same basis as those Old Testament writings to which we now attach canonical authenticity. It must be remembered that much found in these latter works was the interpolation of men, was not true scripture, and could and did lead men astray.

But what our Jewish brethren did not have was communion with the heavens; they did not have a prophet to interpret the prophecies; they no longer received revelations; for them the canon of scripture was full. And be it known that whenever a people believe the canon of scripture is complete; whenever they try to feed themselves spiritually upon the prophetic word of the past alone; whenever they are without prophets and apostles to give them the living word; whenever they cease to receive new revelations—then they are no longer capable of interpreting and understanding past revelations. The prophecies of the past can only be understood by living prophets who are endowed with power from on high and whose minds are enlightened by the same Holy Spirit who authored the ancient word. People without revelation take the only course open to them: they turn to interpreters, to scribes, to ministers, to theologians, who tell them what the ancient word meant, making their determination on the basis of intellectuality rather than spirituality.

When the prophets and apostles of the Christian era no longer ministered among men, religionists turned to uninspired men for guidance; they wrote creeds and devised doctrines; they created new ordinances and changed old ones; and they came up with a new religion called by the old name, which had little resemblance to the primitive pattern. And when, after their return from Babylonian exile, the Jews ran out of prophets and no longer had living oracles to reveal and interpret the mind of Jehovah, they turned to scribes and teachers, to Rabbis and politically appointed high priests to tell them what the Lord meant when he said thus and so to Moses and the prophets.

And thus came the Midrash, the Mishnah, the Gemara, and the Talmud, which had the effect of nullifying true religion and sending a whole nation to spiritual destruction and to temporal banishment in a new Babylon, composed of all the nations of the earth, from which bondage they will not be freed until they hear again the voice of their Messiah, as he calls scattered Israel to return to his fold.

After the Jews came back to Jerusalem and their ancient land holdings in Palestine, through the good offices of Cyrus the Persian; after they no longer walked in that heavenly light which rests only upon those who listen to a prophet's voice and hear the word of God; and feeling the need to apply their ancient law to new conditions—they developed gradually, over the centuries, a whole new (and apostate!) system of religious government. Scribes, who once had been keepers of the records and copiers of the scrolls, became interpreters of the law and teachers of the people. And as uninspired men almost never agree on the meaning of scriptural passages, there soon grew up schools and sects and cults, one Rabbi or teacher vying with another, and one voice saying, as it were, Lo here is Christ, and another, Lo there. In the days of Herod the Great, the two most influential rabbinical schools were those of Hillel and Shammai, who agreed or disagreed on points both great and small as suited their fancies, their prejudices, and their nationalistic leanings. To illustrate how devoid they were of the Spirit of the Lord, we need only note that in one deliberative assembly, in order to gain approval of eighteen decrees designed to prevent all intercourse with the Gentiles, the Shammaites first murdered a number of the Hillelites.

For their own purposes of study and usage, the Jews divided the Old Testament into three parts: (1) *the law,* which consists of the Pentateuch, or five books of Moses—Genesis, Exodus, Leviticus, Numbers, and Deuteronomy; (2) *the prophets,* including the former prophets (Joshua, Judges, Samuel, and Kings), and the latter prophets (Isaiah, Jeremiah, Ezekiel, and the twelve so-called minor prophets); and (3) *the writings,* which includes Psalms, Proverbs, Job, and the rest of the book. In the very nature of things, the law was deemed the most important part of the scriptures; therein were the laws and formalities governing their whole system of worship.

Having need to interpret and apply the law to changing conditions, the scribes, no longer guided by revelation, turned to these words in Exodus: "And the Lord said unto Moses, Write thou these words: for after the tenor of these words I have made a covenant with thee and with Israel." (Ex. 34:27.) From them and some related passages, they posited the proposition that there was both a written law, which was found in the Books of Moses, and an oral law, which had been handed down from mouth to mouth. These originally were assumed to be of equal import, but since changes can be supported more easily by tradition that comes down by word of mouth than by the fixed language of divine decrees written by the finger of Jehovah on tablets of stone, the oral law gradually began to take precedence. In other words, tradition triumphed over the scriptures, leading Jesus to make the caustic comment: "Ye made the commandment of God of none effect by your tradition." (Matt. 15:6.)

The oral law was set forth in preaching and by way of oral commentaries that told what the written law was supposed to mean. These spoken interpretations—themselves the traditions of the fathers—were called the Midrash. When they in turn were written down, they became the Mishnah, or Second Law, which took precedence over the scriptures because they explained and applied them. The Midrash was the study and investigation that created the traditions and enabled the Jews to depart from their Mosaic moorings. The Mishnah was the formal, authoritative compilation of these traditions.

By adding the New Testament to their canon of scripture, the Christians changed and altered their whole course of conduct and way of life after our Lord's mortal ministry. By adding the Mishnah to their Old Testament, the Jews—as they prepared the dry ground out of which the Living Root would grow—also changed their whole course of conduct and way of life, becoming thereby the priest-ridden people who would reject and slay their Savior.

What does the Mishnah contain? In size it is almost three times as large as the New Testament; in literary style and craftsmanship it is as far removed from the New Testament as are the mediocre scribblings of untutored students from Shakespeare; and as to subject matter, it deals with rituals and traditions and with all of those priestly procedures which turned a once joyous religion into a millstone of despair. It is, for instance, the source of the Sabbath laws and restrictions set forth in chapter 11 herein.

The Torah (the Law) embraced both the written law and the oral law, the latter itself being also written in the Mishnah, thus making the Mishnah the repository of the culture, religion, and traditions of the people. It is a deposit of four centuries of religious and cultural development in Palestine. In its present form it came into being during the two hundred years before and the two hundred years following our Lord's mortal life, and without question it held a tighter grip on the minds of men when Jesus was here than it has at any other time.

As now published, the Mishnah is divided into six main sections, which are further divided into sixty-three tractates or subsections, which in turn are divided into verses. The subjects covered embrace the whole range of pentateuchal legislation, and the approach is to present the opinions of various sages and Rabbis, many of which are contradictory, and all of which are devoid of inspiration.

But the Mishnah contains only a portion of the traditions of the elders. The balance is contained in the two Talmuds or Gemaras—the Jerusalem Talmud and the Babylon Talmud. These Talmuds are commentaries on the Mishnah; phrase by phrase and thought by thought, they analyze and interpret the Mishnic recordings. Authoritatively collected and edited, they contain discussions, illustrations, explanations, and additions to the Mishnah. "If we imagine," Edersheim says, "something combining law reports, a Rabbinical 'Hansard,' and notes of a theological debating club—all thoroughly Oriental, full of digressions, anecdotes, quaint sayings, fancies, legends, and too often of what, from its profanity, superstition, and even obscenity, could scarcely be quoted, we may form some general idea of what the Talmud is." (Edersheim 1:103.)

This, then, was the state of religious understanding and scholarship among our Jewish brethren in Jesus' day. They had the scriptures, which was all well and good, but for want of inspiration they could not understand them and did not apply them to their lives. They had the apocryphal and pseudepigraphic writings, which in large measure led them astray. They had lost the theology of the past and were reveling instead in the traditions of the elders. Edersheim summarizes their religious and cultural state in these words:

"In truth, Rabbinism, as such, had no system of theology: only what ideas, conjectures, or fancies the Haggadah [that which was said by the elders] yielded concerning God, Angels, demons, man, his future destiny and present position, and Israel, with its past history and coming glory. Accordingly, by the side of what is noble and pure, what a terrible mass of utter incongruities, of conflicting statements and too often debasing superstitions, the outcome of ignorance and narrow nationalism; of legendary colouring of Biblical narratives and scenes, profane, coarse, and degrading to them; the Almighty Himself and His Angels taking part in the conversations of Rabbis, and the discussions of Academies; nay, forming a kind of heavenly Sanhedrin, which occasionally requires the aid of an earthly Rabbi. The miraculous merges into the ridiculous, and even the revolting. Miraculous cures, miraculous supplies, miraculous help, all for the glory of great Rabbis, who by a look or word can kill, and restore to life. At their bidding the eyes of a rival fall out, and are again inserted. Nay, such was the veneration due to Rabbis, that R. Joshua used to kiss the stone on which R. Eliezer had sat and lectured, saying: 'This stone is like Mount Sinai, and he who sat on it like the Ark.' Modern ingenuity has, indeed, striven to suggest deeper symbolical meanings for such stories. It should [however] own the terrible contrast existing side by side: Hebrewism and Judaism, the Old Testament and traditionalism; and it should recognise its deeper cause in the absence of that element of spiritual and inner life which Christ has brought. Thus as between the two—the old and the new—it may be fearlessly asserted that, as regards their substance and spirit, there is not a difference, but a total divergence, of fundamental principle between Rabbinism and the New Testament, so that comparison between them is not possible. Here there is absolute contrariety." (Edersheim 1:106-7.)

Truly, the time was upon them when it would take God's own Son—if they would heed his voice—to save them from the religious and cultural degeneracy into which their whole nation had sunk! What a fearful thing it is to depart from the living God, from the scriptures that flow from the pens of his prophets, and from the living oracles whom the Lord seeks to send to all who will heed their words, and to turn instead to the traditions of men!

NOTES

1. After Abraham, who then had no seed and whose wife Sarah was past the childbearing age, was told that his seed should be as the stars of heaven in number and should possess the land of Canaan, the restored scriptural account says: "Abram [for his name had not yet been changed] said, Lord God, how wilt thou give me this land for an everlasting inheritance? And the Lord said, Though thou wast dead, yet am I not able to give it thee? And if thou shalt die, yet thou shalt possess it, for the day cometh, that the Son of Man shall live; but how can he live if he be not dead? he must first be quickened. And it came to pass, that Abram looked forth and saw the days of the Son of Man, and was glad, and his soul found rest, and he believed in the Lord; and the Lord counted it unto him for righteousness." (JST, Gen. 15:1-12.)

2. We have no greater passage on the power and authority of the holy priesthood, nor one that shows better the great spiritual insight of the Prophet Joseph Smith, than the one here involved. It not only contains words and phrases reciting that "Melchizedek was a man of faith, who wrought righteousness; and when a child he feared God, and stopped the mouths of lions, and quenched the violence of fire," and says that in the priesthood is the power "to put at defiance the armies of nations" and tells how Melchizedek's people "wrought righteousness, and obtained heaven," but also tells of Enoch and his city, of the laws governing the translation of the righteous, and of the return of Zion in "the latter days, or the end of the world." (JST, Gen. 14:25-40.)

3. "Moses," Paul says, as he tells things that are not recorded in our present Old Testament, "was ordained by the hand of angels to be a mediator of this first covenant, (the law.) Now this mediator was not a mediator of the new covenant; but there is one mediator of the new covenant, who is Christ." (JST, Gal. 3:19-20.)

4. The beginning point for those desiring to research this matter is found in the Book of Mormon references to the named individuals.

5. Jude also, in the brief twenty-five verses of his one-chapter New Testament book, speaks of Michael contending for the body of Moses (verse 9), which is an allusion to the pseudepigraphic book The Assumption of Moses. This book tells of Moses' translation and his ascent as a fiery angel into heaven. (R. H. Charles, *The Apocrypha and Pseudepigrapha of the Old Testament in English* 2:407-24.) From the Book of Mormon and other sources we are led to believe that Moses was translated so he could return, in his body, before the day of resurrection, along with translated Elijah, to give the keys of the priesthood to our Lord on the mount of transfiguration. See *Mormon Doctrine,* 2nd ed., pp. 515-16.

6. Charles, *op cit.,* 2:163-281, 425-69.

Chapter 16

THE SOIL IN WHICH THE ROOT WAS PLANTED

He shall grow up before him as a tender plant, and as a root out of a dry ground. (Isa. 53:2.)

Omnipotence Prepares the Way

A God is coming to earth to dwell as a mortal among men. His mission: to do that which he alone can do; to work out the infinite and eternal atonement and bring to pass the immortality and eternal life of the offspring of the Father on worlds without number; to do that which never again, in an eternity of time, shall ever occur among the mortals who dwell on this or any of the numberless earths of their creating.

A God is coming to earth, and all things incident to this birth and life and ministry and death and resurrection and ascension to eternal glory are foreknown and foreprepared. He is to be sired by an Immortal Father, to be conceived in a mortal womb, to be born in Bethlehem, to be cradled in a manger, to be the natural heir of David, upon whose throne he shall reign. A new star is to arise in the firmament to signal his birth, and heavenly choirs, composed of the harmonious voices of angels, are to herald his coming. His mother is to be a virgin, a holy and pure vessel of the house and lineage of Solomon and David and Jesse and Boaz. She is to live in Nazareth of Galilee, to travel to Jerusalem's environs for the birth, to go into Egypt with the young child, to return to her home village, and to have other sons and daughters from her carpenter husband.

A God is coming to earth. He is to be visited by the wise men from the East and to be preserved from Herod's sword, though all those two years of age and under in all the coasts of Bethlehem are to have their innocent blood poured out upon the arid soil of Caanan. He is to grow up in subjection to his earthly parents; to know, when twelve years of age, of his divine Sonship; to minister for three and a half years among his Jewish kinsmen; and then to die upon the cross for the sins of the world.

A God is coming to earth. He is to be baptized in Jordan at Bethabara by John, and the Holy Ghost is to descend upon him, as his Father acclaims that he is God's Son. He is to preach the gospel, heal the sick, raise the dead, and call apostles and seventies to carry his message to the world and to testify of his divinity. He is to be rejected, reviled, spit upon, scourged, and crucified. He is to stand dumb before his accusers, but to bear testimony of his own divine Sonship before the faithful. He is to give up his life voluntarily, to lie three days in a borrowed tomb, to preach to the spirits in prison, to come forth in glorious immortality, to perfect his work, and to ascend up on high.

A God is coming to earth and we can scarce record a thousandth or a ten thousandth of the things he was destined to do, the words he was destined to speak, the people he was destined to heal—all of which things were known in advance and were foretold by one prophet or another on one continent or on another. Zechariah said he would ride upon the colt of an ass into Jerusalem while being acclaimed by the multitudes; that he would be betrayed for thirty pieces of silver, which would be used to purchase a potter's field; that his hands and feet and side would be wounded; and that the Jews would look upon him whom they had pierced, while Isaiah said he would pour out his soul unto death and make his grave with the rich, and so on and so on, through literally hundreds and thousands of detailed prophecies that these and hosts of prophets foreknew and foretold—all of which must be fulfilled at the appointed time. *The Promised Messiah: The First Coming of Christ* is a more than six-hundred-page analysis of the Messianic prophecies and their fulfillment.

But what more particularly concerns us here is that a God is coming to earth to fulfill all that was promised by all of the prophets during four thousand years of prophetic utterances. All must be in readiness for his Advent. Nothing must be left to chance. There must be no failure, not so much as one jot or one tittle of the inspired accounts. No "T" must be left uncrossed; no "I" must be left undotted; every comma and period must be where it is designed to be. The divine life must conform to the divine and foreordained pattern.

A God is coming to earth and everything connected with his birth and life and ministry and resurrection and ascension to eternal glory—everything!—must be perfect. It must conform to what the prophets have foreseen, foreknown, and foretold.

Mortal Mary must be living in her Galilean home. Joseph must have his carpenter shop in Nazareth. Augustus Caesar must command the Jews to go to their homelands to be taxed. Mary and Joseph must go to Bethlehem; there must be no room in the inns; the angelic choirs must be trained and be in readiness; the whole sidereal heavens must be awaiting the rise of a blazing new star. And we speak not alone of the spiritual preparations, but of the bringing to pass of *all* the temporal circumstances that were needed. The Jewish culture must be at a low ebb, and the Jewish religion but a space away from the gates of hell. Palestine must wear a Roman yoke and the sword of Caesar must be in the hands of Herod and Pilate.

Can we suppose anything was left to chance? Were not

the shepherds on the Judean hills chosen and prepared in advance so that their spiritually attuned ears could hear the angelic choirs? Did not the Spirit guide the wise men to travel from their eastern home with the gold and myrrh and frankincense? And what of Herod—was he not destined to reign as king of the Jews? Did not the Lord know in advance that this Idumean despot would have already shed so much blood, including that of wives and children, that the slaughter of all the babies near Bethlehem would scarce add more blood to his red hands or blacken any further the evil heart that kept his then degenerating body a step from its own grave?

Can we do aught but conclude that the people, the land, the government, the religious hierarchy, the evil rulers, the adulterous sign seekers, the priests and Pharisees and Rabbis, the Sadducees and Herodians—yes, and the sprinkling of truly spiritual people among that degenerate generation of Jews—can we do aught but conclude that all this was prepared in advance?

Mary and Martha and Lazarus were sent to earth at that time to be his friends, in whose house he could escape the barbs and revilings of his enemies. Peter and James and John were prepared from before the foundations of the world to be his chief apostles. Judas was where the betrayer must be. Caiaphas and Pilate and Herod and the Roman soldiers were all in their appointed places. The Caesars in Rome, the Rabbis in Jerusalem, the scribes in their schools, the priests before the altar, the Hellenists with their intellectual approaches, the common people, some of whom heard him gladly—all were in their appointed places. John, now conceived in Elisabeth's womb, would soon stand on the banks of Jordan crying repentance and baptizing the contrite.

Truly Omnipotent Wisdom had left nothing to chance. A God was coming into the world, and the world must be ready for his Advent.

From Cyrus to Herod

Brief mention must be madc of the centuries of Jewish life in which the culture and religion of Jesus' day were molded and formed. From Abraham to the going down into Egypt, the Hebrew people had the light of the gospel. How dim that light became under the Pharaohs who knew not Joseph is seen by the spiritually sick state of the people who four hundred years later followed Moses out of Egypt, through the Red Sea, and who were then led by Joshua into the land of the Canaanites, Hittites, Amorites, Perizzites, Hivites, and Jebusites. Under the judges and kings, periods of rebellion and of righteousness followed each other as a pendulum swings from one extreme to the other. With the destruction of Jerusalem by Nebuchadnezzar, shortly after Lehi left that City of David, and with the taking of the Jews into Babylon, the Hebrew way of life that had prevailed for more than a thousand years came to an abrupt and final end.

The first group of exiles, some fifty thousand in number, returned in 536 B.C. under Zerubbabel, who built again the House of the Lord. This was a day when there were still prophets in Israel; Daniel was yet alive; Haggai and Zechariah were there to encourage completion of the temple. Nehemiah, Ezra, and Malachi would yet stand in the prophetic office. But with it all, the ex-exiles were no longer what they had once been as a people; they had brought back from Babylon much that was foreign and idolatrous. Worldly customs and dogmas would never again be thrown off in their entirety by the succeeding generations of the chosen people, and, with Malachi, prophetic guidance—at least of the kind and quality known among their fathers—would cease.

After Nehemiah's day, the Jewish nation became a province of Syria, although the people maintained a certain allegiance to Persia until that empire was overthrown by Alexander the Great in 332 B.C. The Syrian governors adopted the practice of ruling the nation by high priests whom they appointed. This placed both civil and ecclesiastical rule in the hands of priests who were chosen, not by the Lord, not because they were the sons of Aaron, but by foreign and worldly overlords whose interests were not spiritual but temporal. That the Levites as a priestly class continued to serve by right of lineage and to administer in sacrificial and other matters is clear, but the overlordship and civil rule of the nation was now vested in unclean hands; and it never again would escape from the clutches of those who served a different master than had the high priests of old. This means that the office of high priest was bought and sold; that one man murdered another to gain the coveted seat; and that it was gained and dispensed like any overlordship among the Gentiles, without any divine guidance or approval.

When Persia fell at the hands of Alexander, the Macedonians imposed their rule upon the Jews. After the death of Alexander, Palestine became subject to Egypt, then to Syria, and again to Egypt. These were days of sorrow and war and intrigue. Ungodly murderers ministered in priestly offices. They are important to our present purposes simply to show that for centuries the world and all that is wicked and evil had been imposed upon the Jewish people, and that those of Jesus' day were walking in the paths charted for them by generations of their fathers.

In the beginning of the second century B.C., the Syrian Antiochus IV (Epiphanes) became master of Palestine. If ever there were dark days for the Jews, this was the time. Jerusalem was twice overrun, and thousands were slaughtered and sold into slavery each time. The religion of the Jews was forbidden, a great swine was offered in sacrifice on the altar in the temple, the daily sacrifice was discontinued, the temple was dedicated to Jupiter Olympus, and pagan images and offerings defiled its courts. Antiochus forbade the reading of the law, and tortured and slew those who persisted in their form of worship, and by 168 B.C. Jerusalem was left nearly desolate.

At this dark hour, in the providences of the Lord, the

house of Mattathias, called the Maccabees, began to rally their Jewish compatriots against the Syrian armies. One of the sons, Judas Maccabeus, routed the Syrians in one engagement after another, became a national hero, restored the daily sacrifice and the service of the temple, and became governor of Judea, thus starting a dynasty, the Asmonean, which ruled for 126 years.

The Feast of Dedication—attended by Jesus when he announced himself as the Good Shepherd, and said: "I and my Father are one. . . . I am the Son of God" (John 10)—was instituted in the days of Judas Maccabeus as the temple was rededicated after its vile desecration by Antiochus Epiphanes. And it was into the mouth of the Maccabean hero—"truly God's Hammer," Edersheim says of him—that Longfellow put these words:

> Antiochus,
> At every step thou takest there is left
> A bloody footprint in the street, by which
> The avenging wrath of God will track thee out!
> It is enough. Go to the sutler's tents:
> Those of you who are men, put on such armor
> As ye may find; those of you who are women,
> Buckle that armor on; and for the watchword
> Whisper, or cry aloud, "The Help of God."

This Asmonean rule continued until Jerusalem was taken by Pompey and the Jews were made tributary to Rome. Then it was that Antipater of Idumea was appointed by Julius Caesar to be procurator of Judea, thus starting the new dynasty that was to lay its heavy hand upon Jesus and those who followed the new revelation that he brought from his Father. Herod the Great, the son of Antipater, through the influence of Mark Antony and his own hefty sword, which was wielded with zeal in many battles, acquired the Jewish throne upon which he sat, bathed in blood, until John was born to fulfill the old dispensation and Jesus came to give life to the new one. These two prophets were born shortly before Herod's death, and one of the last acts of madness of this then-demented ruler was the slaughter of the innocents in Bethlehem in a vain attempt to destroy the true King.

The World That Awaited Our Lord

God sent his Son to overcome the world—the world of carnality and evil; the world of lust and lewdness and license; the world of hate and sin, of war and murder, of wickedness and ungodliness. The Son of Righteousness came to bring righteousness and peace. And when he came, the world had sunk into a lower abyss than at any time since all flesh, being corrupt and evil, save eight souls only, had been drowned in the waters of Noah.

There had been pockets of wickedness and kingdoms of evil-doers in many places after Noah's day. Upon the cities of the plains—Sodom, Gomorrah, Admah, and Zeboim—in order that their wicked practices should cease, the Lord rained fire and brimstone and salt and burning, so that all the people were slain and their lands left utterly desolate. The Amorites and their ilk—whose ways were ways of wickedness, of astrology, witchcraft, necromancy, and sexual debauchery—were destroyed to make way for the chosen seed. Egypt, Assyria, Babylon, Persia, Greece, and all the kingdoms of the world had ruled by blood and the sword, by torture and death. But always there had been a leaven of righteousness, a kingdom devoted to goodness, a few people who loved the Lord and sought his face. Abraham and his seed had been a leavening and preserving influence among the nations. As few as ten righteous souls in Sodom would have saved the city from the brimstone of death.

But now, in the time set apart for our Lord's coming, corruptions and evils were everywhere. A few righteous souls—a Zacharias here, an Elisabeth there—stayed, as it were, the plagues of destruction, but the wickedness of the world was everywhere and the stench of sin covered the earth. Even the covenant people, in the main, had gone astray. No longer were they a leaven to the worldly lump; subject to their priestcrafts, they would soon be in a state where they would crucify a God. Naught but a new day of righteousness and light, ushered in by one greater than the prophets, could bring hope again to men.

Such moral and ethical standards as are found among heathen people can only come from two sources: either they are remnants of gospel truths that have been handed down from those who possessed the light of heaven, or they come by the promptings of that Spirit, the light of Christ, which enlighteneth every man born into the world. Such intuitive guidance is called conscience. In the meridian of time the heathen nations were far removed timewise from ancestors who had the true standards of decency and morality, and the consciences of the people generally were so seared with the hot iron of wickedness that there were few, if any, moral standards among them.

As a summary of "the degraded morality taught by heathen sages, and legalized by the most enlightened heathen states" of ancient times, we quote these words of Edward Usher: "Socrates taught that Greeks should regard all mankind, except their own countrymen, as natural enemies; Aristotle and Cicero taught that the forgiveness of injuries is cowardly and mean; Zeno and Cato taught that there is no distinction of degree, aggravation, or heinousness in crimes; Plato taught that excessive drinking was allowable during the festival of Bacchus; Aristotle taught that deformed or infirm children ought to be destroyed; Cicero taught that fornication is in no instance wrong; Plato taught that a community of women would conduce to good, and that soldiers ought not to be restrained from even the grossest indulgence; Menander taught that a lie was better than a hurtful truth; and Zeno and Cato recommended suicide by their example, while other philosophers inculcated it in precept. And Solon enacted that sensuality was irreproachable, except when practised by a slave; several states of Greece legalized unnatural lust, and encouraged it by public statutes; philosophers and legislators sanctioned the grossest indecency, drunkenness, and lewdness during the festivals of Bacchus, Cybele, and Ceres; and Rome was distinguished by licentious divorces, and procuring of abortions, the exposing of infants, the nuisance of public stews, the sports of gladiators, the maltreatment of slaves, etc., all of which were sanctioned or connived at by both sages and legislators. Such was the state of morals among the ancient heathen." (John Fleetwood, *The Life of Our Saviour Jesus Christ*, 1862, p. 20.)

Writing of this same period, and viewing the same irreligious—even depraved—beliefs and practices, Geikie says: "The religions of antiquity had lost their vitality, and become effete forms, without influence on the heart. Philosophy was the consolation of a few—the amusement or fashion of others; but of no weight as a moral force among men at large. On its best side, that of Stoicism, it had much that was lofty, but its highest teaching was resignation to fate, and it offered only the hurtful consolation of pride in virtue, without an idea of humiliation for vice. On its worst side—that of Epicureanism—it exalted self-indulgence as the highest end. Faith in the great truths of natural religion was well-nigh extinct. Sixty-three years before the birth of Christ, Julius Caesar, at that time the Chief Pontiff of Rome, and, as such, the highest functionary of the state religion, and the official authority in religious questions, openly proclaimed, in his speech in the Senate, in reference to Catiline and his fellow-conspirators—that there was no such thing as a future life; no immortality of the soul. He opposed the execution of the accused on the ground that their crimes deserved the severest punishments, and that, therefore, they should be kept alive to endure them, since death was in reality an escape from suffering, not an evil. 'Death,' said he, 'is a rest from troubles to those in grief and misery, not a punishment; it ends all the evils of life; for there is neither care nor joy beyond it.'

"Neither was there any one to condemn such a sentiment even from such lips. Cato, the ideal Roman, a man whose aim it was to 'fulfil all righteousness,' in the sense in which he understood it, passed it over with a few words of light banter; and Cicero, who was also present, did not care to give either assent or dissent, but left the question open, as one which might be decided either way, at pleasure.

"Morality was entirely divorced from religion, as may be readily judged by the fact, that the most licentious rites had their temples, and male and female ministrants. In Juvenal's words, 'the Syrian Orontes had flowed into the Tiber,' and it brought with it the appalling immorality of the East. Doubtless, here and there, throughout the empire, the light of holy tradition still burned on the altars of many a household; but it availed nothing against the thick moral night that had settled over the earth at large. The advent of Christ was the breaking of the 'dayspring from on high' through a gloom that had been gathering for ages; a great light dawning on a world which lay in darkness, and in the shadow of death." (Geikie, p. 20.)

The Roman Yoke on Jewish Religion

The Jewish religion, with its worship of one God; the faith of their fathers, as handed down to them from Moses and the prophets; the whole way of life of the chosen people—all these, in a dark day in 63 B.C., were placed forever under the yoke of Rome. No law in Israel was more strictly enforced than the one that closed the Holy of Holies to all but one man, the high priest, who could pass through the veil into that hallowed spot on one day only each year.

Then came Pompey and the conquering legions of Rome. He and his staff, defying the strictest decree of Jehovah, entered the Holy of Holies. These Godless Gentiles, who lived and died by the sword, desecrated the House of the Lord, profaned its most holy sanctuary, and let it be known thereby that from that hour Jewish worship was subject to Roman rule. And that rule, written in blood and enforced by one emperor and king after another, continued until Titus took the temple apart stone by stone and the whole Jewish nation was scattered in all the nations of the earth. Indeed, in the just over one hundred years from the accession of Herod the Great to the destruction of Jerusalem by Titus, the Roman rulers appointed twenty-seven successive high priests to sit in Aaron's seat, in a priestly office that should have been hereditary and should have lasted in each instance for the whole lifetime of its occupant.

Herod was a Gentile who pretended to be a Jew. His ancestry stemmed back to Abraham through Esau, who is Edom, but his religious beliefs were Jewish, and his way of life worldly, even Satanic. His half-Jew, half-Gentile stance was a convenient one for him to take in controlling his kingdom. He built again the temple in Jerusalem, constructing it with a magnificence beyond that of either Solomon or Zerubbabel. But he also built a temple to Augustus in Caesarea, wherein was placed a statue of the emperor as Olympian Zeus. He placed over the great gate of the temple in Jerusalem a massive golden eagle as a symbol of Roman dominion. He built a number of towns, inhabited by Gentiles, as a means of tempering Jewish nationalism. At a later time Pilate introduced images of the emperor into Jerusalem, and even a statue of Caligula was placed in the temple itself.

It is true that under the Roman rule the Jews were granted numerous concessions, such as the right to observe the Sabbath as they chose, except that they could not (legally, that is) impose the death penalties for violations as Moses had once done. And it was to the Romans that they turned to have a Man crucified who, they said, according to their law, was worthy of death.

We shall not here particularize further as to the supremacy of the Roman world over the Jewish world. It suffices for the present to know that Caesar took precedence over Christ, through all Canaan and the civilized world, in all things both temporal and spiritual. Roman tolerance with all religions, however, was proverbial. The rulers from the land of the Tiber accepted and revered—nay, oftimes worshipped—the gods of all the conquered lands. Caesar felt no compunction in granting freedom of religion to Christ so long as it did not hinder or deter the purposes of absolute autocracy as found in the hands of the emperor. The forces against free religion that led a Jew to Calvary were not of Roman origin, though it took the iron hand of Roman authority to drive the nails and raise the cross.

As occasion requires, we shall hereafter weave into our account of the life of a Jew who was born into both a Roman and a Jewish world—and who came to save them both—such commentary about social patterns, education, trade, agriculture, fishing, business and enterprises, and local customs and life as seems appropriate. We shall speak of Palestinian roads, of the Jewish Sanhedrin, of the levirate laws of marriage, and of the Mosaic manner of divorce. We shall concern ourselves with the Herodians, Hellenists, and Publicans; with the Galileans, Pereans, and Judeans; with the various Herods and their evil ways—all as the unfolding needs of the greatest story ever told seem to warrant. As we begin this story it suffices to know that Rome ruled Jerusalem and that worldly influence abounded in Judaism itself. It was the type of a world, the kind of a social structure, the very governmental arrangement, the level of decency among the people—and all else—that Omnipotent Wisdom chose as proper for the birth and ministry and death of his Son. It could not have been otherwise; all things were to be done in the wisdom of him who knoweth all things.

The Signs of the Times

The signs of the times: what are they? It depends on what signs we are talking about and what times we are considering; it depends on what period of time is involved and what great event is being ushered in. When the signs of the times, for our day, are fulfilled and all things are come to pass which were of old foretold, the Son of Man will come in power and great glory to usher in millennial peace. When Jesus asked the Pharisees and Sadducees, "Can ye not discern the signs of the times," he referred to the signs and wonders attesting his divine Sonship, signs that were everywhere manifest before them. (Matt. 16:1-4.) In like manner we might say that the signs of the times, as pertaining to the birth of the Savior, were poured out upon the people to whom he was destined to come. Deity never sends a portentous or wondrous happening without heralding its coming and preparing the way for its occurrence. That the Jews of our Lord's day were to some extent reading the signs presaging his coming and ministry is clear from the universal ferment of Messianic expectancy to be found on every hand.

Not the least of the signs of Messiah's first coming were the religious, social, cultural, and governmental conditions existing in Palestine and elsewhere in the latter years of Herod's reign. The Messiah was to come as the Son of David, a Jew of the Jews, in a dark and dreary day; and his mission was to deliver his people, redeem the nation, triumph over the world, and reign as King of kings.

He was to be planted in arid soil; to grow up as a tender plant, as a root out of dry ground. Babylonia, Persia, Egypt, Syria, Greece, and Rome—each in turn—had ploughed in the fields of Palestine. Each had reaped harvests without dunging the land. The early rains of revelation and the latter rains of prophetic guidance had not watered the soil for centuries. The thistles and weeds and briers of sin encumbered the vineyards. There was a famine of hearing the word of the Lord.

The first Adam brought his own environment and was born into a garden of beauty and peace; the second Adam was born into an apostate world and a degenerate social order. He came to dwell among a people who drew near to the Lord with their lips, but whose hearts were far from him.

He came to be a Jew in a day when the Jewish society could provide no nutrient for his soul.

Jesus was a Jew; he was of the tribe of Judah. David, the Jew, was his father, and Mary, the Jewess, his mother. He grew up in a Jewish home, spoke the Jewish Aramaic of his day, learned Jewish customs and traditions, studied in Jewish schools, read Jewish scripture, attended Jewish synagogues, and participated in Jewish worship. From Bethlehem to Calvary, he was a Jew of the Jews.

He ministered among the Jews, called Jews to repentance, baptized Jews, ordained Jews to priesthood offices, and left twelve Jews to carry on his work among men. From a mortal standpoint he was the product of the Jewish system, which in turn was the product, in large measure, of everything that had happened to that people from Nebuchadnezzar to Herod. As Jesus ministered and taught among his Jewish kinsmen, he did so with their background, using the colloquialisms with which they were familiar and the illustrations they understood.

How well he did we shall now see as we meet him in Bethlehem, as we stay at his side till he climbs the hill of Calvary, as we see him, on Olivet, ascend to his Father, there to reign with everlasting power until that great day—the year of his redeemed—when he shall come again in all the glory of his Father's kingdom.

Blessed be his holy name!

SECTION II

JESUS' YEARS OF PREPARATION

JESUS' YEARS OF PREPARATION

The Only Begotten of the Father . . .
came and dwelt in the flesh. . . . he
received not of the fulness at the first,
but received grace for grace.
(D&C 93:11-12.)

Even a God—when clothed in mortal flesh; when as Adam's Son he dwells among his fellowmen; when here on earth to work out his own salvation—even a God receives not of the fulness of the Father at the first. Even he must be subject to the vicissitudes and trials of mortality; even he must be tried and tested to the full; even he must overcome the world.

And so we see him—during his years of preparation—as he makes himself ready for the work that he only can do.

We see Gabriel come to Zacharias, to Mary, and to Joseph, proclaiming to each in turn a portion of the glad tidings of His birth. We learn who shall declare his generation and whose Son he shall be.

Then, lo, he is born of Mary; heavenly manifestations attend. He is circumcised, named, and taken into Egypt to escape the vengeance of Herod.

We see him called out of Egypt and grow up in Nazareth; we hear him testify, when but twelve years of age, of his own divine Sonship. He continues to grow in stature and wisdom, and in favor with God and man.

Then John comes, preaching in power and preparing a people to receive Him. He is baptized in Jordan; the Holy Ghost descends upon him; he is led by the Spirit into the wilderness to be with God for forty days. Thereafter Lucifer comes, tempting, testing, fighting against God.

Our Lord triumphs. He has made flesh his tabernacle; he has attained physical and spiritual maturity. The years of his preparation are fulfilled, and the hour of his ministry has arrived.

"Hear ye him!"

Chapter 17

GABRIEL COMES TO ZACHARIAS

Gabriel, make this man to understand the vision. . . .

Whiles I was speaking in prayer, even the man Gabriel, whom I had seen in the vision at the beginning, being caused to fly swiftly, touched me about the time of the evening oblation.

And he informed me, and talked with me, and said, . . . I am now come forth to give thee skill and understanding. (Dan. 8:16, 9:21-22.)

"He Shall Prepare the Way Before Me"
(Malachi 3:1)[1]

One such as he must not come unannounced!

When God's own Son leaves his eternal throne and makes flesh his tabernacle, all the legates of the skies must herald his coming!

When the Promised Messiah takes upon himself the form of a man, so that he may abolish death, and bring life and immortality to light through his gospel,[2] mortal men are entitled to receive the word from the lips of an authorized witness.

The Mortal Messiah must be identified to his fellow mortals. His servants must prepare the way before him—make ready the manger, prepare the bridal chamber, sweep clean the temple courts, frame the cross, prepare the tomb, and, above all, testify to the people of the divinity of the One sent among them by his Father.

The providences of the Lord do not call for the heavens to rend, or the mountains to melt, or the earth to shake. His way is to send living witnesses to testify: 'Behold, the Lamb of God, who taketh away the sins of the world. This is he of whom all the prophets have testified. Believe in him; hear his word; walk in his paths and be saved.'

His kinsman, John, must be in the appointed place, at the proper time, to bear the witness he was sent to bear. Faithful Anna and saintly Simeon must be in the court of the Holy House when the Consolation of Israel is presented before the Lord as Moses commanded. The voices of the forerunners and the witnesses, of the Eliases and those who prepare the way, must be heard. His word, given through Malachi, must be fulfilled: "Behold, I will send my messenger, and he shall prepare the way before me: and the Lord, whom ye seek, shall suddenly come." (Mal. 3:1.)

And how fitting that his chief forerunner—than whom there has been no greater prophet born of woman—should precede him in birth, precede him in his ministry, precede him in death, and precede him in his future Second Advent. As the voice of one crying in the wilderness of unbelief, John came to prepare the way before his Lord in this life; and then, laying down his life for the testimony of Jesus that was his, he went as a forerunner into the paradise of God to announce that He whose mission it was to free the captives would soon be there to open the prison doors. And with a divine fitness and propriety, the resurrected John has raised his voice again to mortals in our day, preparing the way for the coming of Him who shall this time rend the heavens, and melt the mountains, and shake the earth when his presence is again revealed.

And how fitting that the same angelic ministrant who came to the mother of our Lord came also to the father of John—in each instance proclaiming a miraculous conception and the birth of a foreordained prophet.

Zacharias—His Ministry and Mission

There were many widows in Israel when Elijah sealed the heavens for "three years and six months, when great famine was throughout all the land," but only to one—the widow of Zarephath—was Elijah sent, that he might command her "barrel of meal" to "not waste," and her "cruse of oil" to not fail, "until the day that the Lord sendeth rain upon the earth." And there were, no doubt, many widows whose children died, but she alone had her son raised from death by the man of God. (Luke 4:25-26; 1 Kgs. 17.)

There were also many lepers in Israel in the day of Elisha the prophet, "and none of them was cleansed, saving Naaman the Syrian," who swallowed his pride, believed the promise given him, and washed seven times in the dirty waters of Jordan, as Elisha commanded. (Luke 4:27; 2 Kgs. 5.)

So also was it with Zacharias, who fathered the forerunner of the Messiah. There were many priests in Israel in his day, many lineal descendants of Aaron—between twenty thousand and twenty-four thousand of them—whose right it was to offer temporal sacrifices in similitude of the eternal sacrifice of their expected Deliverer. But none of these saw the angelic face and none received the heaven-sent message of comfort and hope save only Zacharias of Hebron, who, with his wife, Elisabeth, walked blamelessly before the Lord.

It was a day when the priestly office, once held by Aaron's worthy sons, was now held by their unworthy descendants. Pride, disbelief, dishonesty, violence, immorality, and even the shedding of innocent blood—all these prevailed and were more common than not among those who should have been lights to the people. Few of the priests envisioned to any real degree the true significance of the sacred ordinances it was their privilege to perform.

David, a thousand years before, had divided the priests into twenty-four courses, or houses, or families. Only four of these had returned from Babylon, but the balance had been reconstituted, and they lived in thirteen towns, mostly near Jerusalem. Those of each course went up to that city twice a year, in rotation, for six days and two Sabbaths each time, to serve in the temple. While there they lived in the temple, their wives and families remaining in their home villages.

Priestly duties were many and varied. They were teachers of the law, instructors of the people, and the judges and magistrates of their communities. They examined all cases of ceremonial uncleanness and watched over all of the affairs of the temple. "It was their awful and peculiar honour to 'come near the Lord.' None but they could minister before Him, in the Holy Place where He manifested His presence: none others could 'come nigh the vessels of the sanctuary or the altar.' It was death for any one not a priest to usurp these sacred prerogatives. They offered the morning and evening incense; trimmed the lamps of the golden candlestick, and filled them with oil; set out the shewbread weekly; kept up the fire on the great altar in front of the Temple; removed the ashes of the sacrifices; took part in the slaying and cutting up of victims, and especially in the sprinkling of their blood; and laid the offerings of all kinds on the altar." (Geikie, p. 65.)

These duties, with all that they include and imply, plus the host of other normal functions applicable to all priests, were part of the ministry of Zacharias, and indeed it was in the performance of some of them that the Lord manifested to this son of Aaron his higher and more noble mission. Zacharias, like the son he was to sire, was foreordained to bring the Lord's forerunner into mortality. And Zacharias, in this life, walked uprightly before the Lord and manifested a faith in Jehovah not found among his fellow priests. As with the widow of Zarephath and as with Naaman of Syria, John's father was singled out from the thousand score and more priests for the work that was his. Angels do not minister unto carnal and godless souls; it is those who seek, by righteousness, the blessings of heaven who are permitted to see within the veil.

Zacharias's mission was to bear an even greater son and to endow that offspring with the talents and abilities that would enable him to prepare the way before the Lord. How well he did this is now written in the records of eternity. As it happens, both Zacharias and his son were called upon, in the providences of the Lord, to lay down their lives as part of the missions assigned them from on high; both died because of the mad anxieties of demented kings. "When Herod's edict went forth to destroy the young children," as the Prophet Joseph Smith taught, "John was about six months older than Jesus, and came under this hellish edict, and Zacharias caused his mother to take him into the mountains, where he was raised on locusts and wild honey. When his father refused to disclose his hiding place, and being the officiating high priest at the Temple that year, [he] was slain by Herod's order, between the porch and the altar, as Jesus said." (*Teachings*, p. 261; Matt. 23:35.)

Zacharias Ministers in the Temple
(*Luke 1:5-10; JST, Luke 1:8-9*)

Twice each year, in April and October, the priests of the course of Abia, named for Abijah, traveled from their village homes to the House of the Lord in Jerusalem, there to take their week-long turns at performing those sacred rites and ordinances which for fifteen hundred years had been the center of Israel's worship. One of these priests, Zacharias, whose wife, Elisabeth, was both barren and past the childbearing age, dwelt in a village in the hill country of

Judea, believed to be Hebron. It was the very locale where Abraham had lived with Sarah, who also was both barren and past the childbearing age when the Lord himself saw fit to tell the Father of the Faithful that his beloved Sarah would conceive and bear Isaac, through whom the blessings of the Abrahamic covenant would continue.

It was October, the autumn of the year, when Zacharias left his beloved Elisabeth—both of them being in the autumn of their lives—to travel the some twenty lonely miles to Jerusalem. At least it was the custom to leave family members at home, for the priests dwelt in the temple itself during their week-long ministry. But perhaps he went with other priests of his course, and if so, as was common among them in that era of great expectation, they would have discussed the Consolation of Israel who was to come and deliver his people.

As nearly as we can determine, the month was October and the year was 6 B.C.[3] Herod the Great, who died in 4 B.C., was winding up his long and evil and bloody reign. Gentile by birth, Jewish by belief, and ruling with Roman authorization, Herod lived in the day in which the scepter was departing from Judah to make way for the coming of Shiloh. And what would have been more natural than for the priests traveling to the temple to perform sacrifices in similitude of that Shiloh whom they expected, and longing for release from Roman rule, to discuss their long-expected Deliverer.

In any event, Zacharias arrived at the temple and walked worthily through its sacred portals, for both he and the daughter of Aaron who stood as his wife were "righteous before God, walking in all the commandments and ordinances of the Lord blameless." With his fellow priests, he then drew lots, as was the custom, so that each of the sons of Aaron serving that week might be assigned his duties. There was one service, favored above all others, that a priest to whose lot it fell might perform but once in a lifetime. It was the burning of incense on the altar of incense in the Holy Place, near the Holy of Holies where the very presence of Jehovah came on occasion. And, lo, this time the lot fell to Zacharias; he was chosen of the Lord to perform the great mediatorial service in which the smoke of the incense, ascending to heaven, would symbolize the prayers of all Israel ascending to the divine throne. That Zacharias was to be the central figure in the temple, through this service, all the assembled worshippers knew; and that heaven itself was to respond with divine approval shining forth, they would soon learn.

In the court of the priests stood the great altar of unhewn stones whereon the sacred sacrifices were offered; this was open to the view of the people. Entrance was gained to the Holy Place through two great gold-plated doors. In this sanctuary were the two tables—one of marble, one of gold—on which the priests laid the candlestick with its seven lamps and, most importantly, the altar of incense.

It was into this sacred sanctuary that Zacharias went, accompanied by another priest who bore burning coals taken from the altar of sacrifice; these he spread upon the altar of incense and then withdrew. It then became the privilege of Elisabeth's husband to sprinkle the incense on the burning coals, that the ascending smoke and the odor might typify the ascending prayers of all Israel. This performance is also but a type of what John saw in heavenly vision and recorded in these words: "And another angel came and stood at the altar, having a golden censer; and there was given unto him much incense, that he should offer it with the prayers of all saints upon the golden altar which was before the throne. And the smoke of the incense, which came with the prayers of the saints, ascended up before God out of the angel's hand." (Rev. 8:3-4.)[4]

What prayers did Zacharias make on this occasion? Certainly not, as so many have assumed, prayers that Elisabeth should bear a son, though such in days past had been the subject of the priest's faith-filled importunings. This was not the occasion for private, but for public prayers. He was acting for and on behalf of all Israel, not for himself and

Elisabeth alone. And Israel's prayer was for redemption, for deliverance from the Gentile yoke, for the coming of their Messiah, for freedom from sin. The prayers of the one who burned the incense were the prelude to the sacrificial offering itself, which was made to bring the people in tune with the Infinite, through the forgiveness of sins and the cleansing of their lives. "And the whole multitude of the people were praying without at the time of incense"—all praying, with one heart and one mind, the same things that were being expressed formally, and officially, by the one whose lot it was to sprinkle the incense in the Holy Place. The scene was thus set for the miraculous event that was to be.

"Thou Shalt Call His Name John"
(*Luke 1:11-13*)

As the clouds of sweet incense ascend heavenward, and as the prayers of Zacharias come up into the ears of the Lord of the whole earth—and we cannot but feel that his prayers on this occasion were guided by the Spirit and uttered with a reverence, in an awe, and with a deep feeling of spirituality that is seldom equaled—as his expressions of thanksgiving and his petitions for blessings and good things reach their climax, just at this moment the veil is rent. Gabriel stands before him.[5]

At the right of the altar, near the Holy of Holies, where Jehovah himself would stand if he came personally, there stands Gabriel, the archangel next in authority to mighty Michael.

After so many years, as a herald of things to come, an angel's voice is heard again. Once more in Israel, as it had been almost always in olden times, the angelic visage is clearly seen in vision. Soon angels will be coming to others, many others, and the long night of darkness will pass. And soon God's own Son will minister among men and have his person identified by a heavenly voice. Revelation is commencing anew in Israel; the prospects are bright for a great outpouring of gospel truth, and a humble priest, who has even been denied seed to bear his priesthood after him, is the recipient of the heaven-sent message. A new day is dawning in Israel.

Zacharias is troubled, fearful, but such is a normal reaction; so also were those of old in like circumstances. His reaction is simply that of Father Jacob, who, seeing the vision of the ladder reaching up into heaven, with angels ascending and descending, exclaimed: "How dreadful is this place! this is none other but the house of God, and this is the gate of heaven." (Gen. 28:10-22.) To calm his troubled mind, the angel speaks: "Fear not, Zacharias: for thy prayer is heard." 'And the Lord shall grant thy petition: The Consolation of Israel truly shall come; he shall deliver and redeem his people; and, lo, the time is at hand, for thou hast been chosen to be the father of the one who shall prepare the way before him.' "And thy wife Elisabeth shall bear thee a son, and thou shalt call his name John."

Gabriel Announces the Mission of John

(*Luke 1:14-25*)

Gabriel continues to speak: 'Thou shalt have joy and rejoicing in thy son; and many shall rejoice at his birth, for what is done this day shall be in their hearts, and they shall remember it with gladness and tell it to others. And John shall be great in the sight of the Lord, of whom he shall testify; and he shall drink neither wine nor strong drink, for it shall be with him as though he were a Nazarite for life, for he shall be as one who has vowed a vow and been set apart for a special work all the days of his life.

'And he shall be filled with the Holy Ghost, even from within his mother's womb, so that before he is born the Holy Ghost shall come upon him, and he shall leap as it were for joy at the presence of the mother of his Lord.

'And many of the children of Israel shall he turn to the Lord their God, for he shall cry repentance, and baptize for the remission of sins, and cause many to follow the Lamb of God who taketh away the sins of the world. And he shall go before the Lord, who is Christ, in the spirit and power of Elias, preparing the way, making the rough places smooth and the crooked straight. He shall even turn the hearts of those disobedient ones, who are the children of the prophets, back to their just fathers, who foresaw this day and prophesied of it, and the hearts of the fathers shall rejoice that their children on earth believe in that Messiah whose life and labors they foresaw.

'And through all that he does, he shall make ready a people prepared for the Lord, and this people shall then follow their Messiah and be saved.'

Gabriel ceased to speak. Zacharias in wonder and amazement—perhaps overwhelmed that all this could happen to persons as aged as he and Elisabeth, perhaps guided by the Spirit in what he asked—said to the heavenly visitant, as if in a spirit of unbelief: 'How shall I know that these things shall come to pass?'

Why did he need a sign? Does not the word of one who stands in the presence of God suffice? May it not be that the main purpose of his query was to provide an occasion for "the man Gabriel" to do the thing that would cause those then present, and all who heard the account thereafter, to know that the hand of the Lord was in the doings of the day? If Zacharias had come out of the Holy Place, given the usual benediction to the people, and then said that he had seen an angel and that his barren wife, though well stricken in years, should bear a son, and then had she in fact done so, it would have been a dramatic thing. But how much more impressive did it become when Zacharias came out *both deaf and dumb,* so that he could not speak or give the usual benediction to the people there assembled, and—be it noted—so that he could not hear what the others said, even more than nine months later, when the young John was brought on the eighth day in to the temple to be circumcised. On that occasion those who were present had to make signs to the deaf

Zacharias before he could signify in writing what his son's name should be.

Immediately after the happenings of this unprecedented day—the day on which angelic ministrants commenced again to commune with their fellow mortals—Elisabeth conceived, and she rejoiced that the Lord had taken away the reproach of barrenness, for, from the day Rachel said "Give me children, or else I die" (Gen. 30:1), so it was considered in Israel.

Then Elisabeth retired from public view until the day that Mary, herself then also with child, visited her in the hill country village of Hebron.

NOTES

1. Under each subheading, where they apply, we shall hereafter place the citations from the Gospels in which the matters under consideration are set forth by Matthew, Mark, Luke, and/or John, as the case may be. When more than one New Testament author speaks of the same event, the citations will be listed in their assumed order of importance. Then, in that subsection, direct quotations, recorded within double quotation marks (". . . ."), will not be identified by a scriptural reference. Single quotation marks ('. . . .') will be used to set off and identify paraphrasing and interpreting quotes that give the meaning and thought content of what the speaker is saying or teaching.

2. Paul says, in Philippians 2:7-8, that Christ "took upon him the form of a servant, and was made in the likeness of men." Also, that he was "found in fashion as a man." The apostle also says, in 2 Timothy 1:10, that Christ "hath abolished death, and hath brought life and immortality to light through the gospel." These two passages are the ones alluded to and paraphrased in the text. Except in cases of special need, we shall not hereafter use quotation marks or give footnotes identifying the source of scriptural or other inspired statements that are paraphrased, summarized, alluded to, or in some instances quoted verbatim. All such will be considered part of the running text. When passages themselves are being analyzed (except those cited under the subsection headings), they will be identified in the usual way.

3. The date, which it is difficult to determine, affects the time of our Lord's birth, which problem is considered in footnote 2 of chapter 20 herein.

4. David spoke of this matter in these words: "Let my prayer be set forth before thee as incense; and the lifting up of my hands as the evening sacrifice." (Ps. 141:2.)

5. Why Gabriel? Why not Michael or Raphael or one of the host of unnamed angels who from time to time have parted the veil to converse with their fellow servants in mortality? Clearly there is an angelic hierarchy—a heavenly hierarchy—as well as an earthly hierarchy. Some angels take precedence over and give direction to others; it is no different in the heavenly church than in the earthly; there are those who give direction and others who go at their behest.

Michael, the archangel, the greatest of all, the one who stands next to Christ, is the one who led Jehovah's hosts when there was war in heaven and the devil and his angels were cast out; and he it is who shall again lead the armies of righteousness in the great battles ahead when all things relative to the salvation of men shall be completed. As commander-in-chief, he will have others, from general to private, serving under him. He came to earth as Adam, and the "angels are under the direction of Michael or Adam, who acts under the direction of the Lord." (*Teachings,* pp. 167-69.)

Adam, who is Michael, holds the keys of the priesthood "from generation to generation," and "Noah, who is Gabriel . . . stands next in authority to Adam in the Priesthood." (*Teachings,* p. 157.) What could be more fitting, then, than for Michael, who presides over the angels and directs their labors, to send Gabriel, his next in command, to announce to the mortals involved those things they needed to know concerning the Promised Messiah and his Elias?

It may even be that, as Michael is in charge of all things (under Christ), so Gabriel is in charge (under Michael) of those angelic ministrations which speak of Messiah's coming, and that either he or those serving under him make the necessary visitations to mortals. In this connection it was "the man Gabriel" himself who came to Daniel to tell that worthy one of the coming of "Messiah the Prince" who would "make reconciliation for iniquity" and "bring in everlasting righteousness." (Dan. 9:20-27.) Contrary to the sectarian traditions, it is Michael, not Gabriel, who shall sound the trump of the Lord in the last days as part of the great winding-up scene.

THE ANNUNCIATION TO MARY

Behold, a virgin shall conceive, and bear a son, and shall call his name Immanuel. (Isa. 7:14.)

And I beheld the city of Nazareth; and in the city of Nazareth I beheld a virgin, and she was exceedingly fair and white. . . . [Yea], A virgin, most beautiful and fair above all other virgins. (1 Ne. 13-15.)

"Knowest Thou the Condescension of God?"

(*1 Nephi 11:16*)

John is now conceived in Elisabeth's womb; the son of Zacharias will soon be born; our Lord's forerunner, destined to be six months his senior, shall soon breathe the breath of life. The words of Gabriel are coming to pass, and soon the Son of God must be sired, conceived, born, and laid in a manger.

But how can a God be born into mortality? How can the Eternal One take upon himself flesh and blood, and let himself be fashioned as a Man? A child—any child, including the Child—must have progenitors; he must have parents, both a father and a mother. Gabriel will soon tell the Virgin of Galilee that she shall be the mother. As to the father—he is Elohim. The Son of God shall have God as his Father; it is just that simple, and it could not be otherwise. The doctrine of the divine Sonship lies at the foundation of true religion; without it, Christ becomes just another man, a great moral teacher, or what have you, without power to ransom, to redeem, and to save.

Having seen in vision—more than six hundred years before the events themselves transpired—the city of Nazareth and a gracious and beautiful virgin therein, Nephi was asked by an angel: "Knowest thou the condescension of God?" He responded by saying he knew of the Lord's love for his children, but not the full answer to the profound query framed by angelic lips. Then the angel answered his own question by saying: "Behold, the virgin whom thou seest is the mother of the Son of God, after the manner of the flesh." That is to say, the condescension of God lies in the fact that he, an exalted Being, steps down from his eternal throne to become the Father of a mortal Son, a Son born "after the manner of the flesh."

Immediately after hearing these words, Nephi saw that the virgin "was carried away in the Spirit; and after she had been carried away in the Spirit for the space of a time," Nephi saw "the virgin again, bearing a child in her arms." Thereupon the angel said: "Behold the Lamb of God, yea, even the Son of the Eternal Father!" To be "carried away in the Spirit" means to be transported bodily from one location to another, as witness the fact that Nephi, at the very time he beheld these visions, had been "caught away in the Spirit of the Lord" and taken bodily "into an exceeding high mountain," which he never "had before seen," and upon which he "never had before" set his "foot." (1 Ne. 11:1, 13-21.)

Without overstepping the bounds of propriety by saying more than is appropriate, let us say this: God the Almighty; the Maker and Preserver and Upholder of all things; the

Omnipotent One; he by whom the sidereal heavens came into being, who made the universe and all that therein is; he by whose word we are, who is the Author of that life which has been going on in this system for nigh unto 2,555,000,000 years;[1] God the Almighty, who once dwelt on an earth of his own and has now ascended the throne of eternal power to reign in everlasting glory;[2] who has a glorified and exalted body, a body of flesh and bones as tangible as man's; who reigns in equity and justice over the endless billions of his spirit children who inhabit the worlds without number that roll into being at his word—God the Almighty, who is infinite and eternal, elects, in his fathomless wisdom, to beget a Son, an Only Son, the Only Begotten in the flesh.

God, who is infinite and immortal, condescends to step down from his throne, to join with one who is finite and mortal in bringing forth, "after the manner of the flesh," the Mortal Messiah.

"Who Shall Declare His Generation?"

(*Matthew 1:1-17; Luke 3:23-38; JST, Luke 3:30-31, 45*)

If God, who is eternal, steps down from his high and holy place to beget an Only Begotten Son "after the manner of the flesh," who can know it? How can such wondrous knowledge be given to carnal men? It may be easy to find someone who would claim to be the mother, but how can her selection for such an exalted position of motherhood be known for sure? Who shall declare Messiah's generation?

True, he cometh in the fulness of his own time to fulfill all that has been spoken—concerning that coming and ministry—by the mouths of all the holy prophets since the world began; he cometh to merit all the praise and adoration and thanksgiving and reverence and worship that has foredwelt in the hearts of the righteous of all preceding ages; he cometh to make flesh his tabernacle, to take upon himself the form of men, and to do the will of the Father whose Son he is. But who shall declare his generation? Who knows his genesis? Or who can tell whence and how he came? Who are his parents? When God has a Son, how can this be known among mortal men?

Matthew identifies his Gospel as "The book of the generation of Jesus Christ, the son of David, the son of Abraham." Then he gives a genealogy down to "Joseph the husband of Mary, of whom was born Jesus, who is called Christ." Luke begins with this same Joseph and traces the genealogy back to "Adam, which was the son of God," or, as the Joseph Smith Translation has it, to "Adam, who was formed of God, and [was] the first man upon the earth."

Matthew's and Luke's accounts seemingly do not agree, though, in fact, the two of them taken together give a perfect picture of what is involved. Both purport to give the genealogy of Joseph, whose bloodline is not involved, but who was of the royal lineage. It is generally agreed that Matthew's account gives the royal lineage and therefore records names of those whose right it was to sit on David's throne, and that Luke's record contains the personal pedigree of Mary's husband. Matthew says Joseph was a son of Jacob, and Luke says that he was a son of Heli. It appears, however, that Jacob and Heli were brothers and that Heli was the father of Joseph and Jacob the father of Mary, making Joseph and Mary first cousins with the same ancestral lines. How fitting it is that the New Testament should preserve both a royal and a personal pedigree of these two, so that there could be no question, either by blood or by kingly right, as to the noble and exalted status of the Son of David. "Had Judah been a free and independent nation, ruled by her rightful sovereign, Joseph the carpenter would have been her crowned king; and his lawful successor to the throne would have been Jesus of Nazareth, the King of the Jews." (Talmage, p. 87.)

But our question still remains: "Who shall declare his generation?" (Isa. 53:8.) And the answer is: Since we are dealing with spiritual things, which can only be known by the power of the Holy Spirit, no one can declare the generation of "Jesus, who is called Christ," except by the power of the Holy Ghost. "No man can say [know] that Jesus is the Lord, but by the Holy Ghost." (1 Cor. 12:3.)[3] There is no other way. When the theologians of our day deny the divine Sonship, they are thereby testifying that the Holy Ghost does not speak by their mouths, and that they are, as a consequence, false prophets.

And so it is that Matthew, who, in all the majesty of his apostolic office, took it upon himself to set forth our Lord's ancestry, proceeds to speak of his birth to a virgin, as we shall hereafter recite.

Gabriel Comes to Mary
(*Luke 1:26-38; JST, Luke 1:28-29, 34-35*)

Angels, Alma says, come to men, women, and children to impart the word of God. (Alma 32:23.) And never was there a case when angelic ministration was more deserved, or served a greater purpose, or was manifest in a sweeter and more tender way, than when Gabriel, who stands in the presence of God, came to Mary to announce her divine call to be the mother of the Son of God. She at the time dwelt in Nazareth, a city of Galilee, located some eighty miles northward from the Holy City and the Holy Temple, where last the angelic form had been seen and the angelic voice heard.

Mary was espoused to Joseph, meaning she had made a formal contract of marriage with him that yet had to be completed in a second ceremony before they would commence living together as husband and wife. She was, however, considered by their law to be his wife; the contract could be broken only by a formal "bill of divorcement," and any infidelity on her part would be classed as adultery, for which Jehovah had of old decreed death as the penalty.

Faithful Jews prayed in their homes three times daily—at the time of the morning offering, at noon, and at the time of the evening sacrifice. Perhaps at such a time (for the veil grows thin when prayers flow from the heart) the man Gabriel "came in" to her humble home. She was alone; her spiritual eyes were open; and she saw the minister from heaven. He spoke: "Hail, thou virgin, who art highly favoured of the Lord. The Lord is with thee, for thou art chosen and blessed among women."[4]

Understandably the humble, perhaps even shy and timid, Maid of Nazareth was troubled by such lavish praise from one sent from the other world and who spoke only the truth. Sensing her feelings, Gabriel continued: "Fear not, Mary: for thou hast found favour with God. And, behold, thou shalt conceive in thy womb, and bring forth a son, and shalt call his name Jesus."

Jesus, blessed name—signifying *Jehovah is salvation*—her Son to be a Savior! Had she ever hoped or thought that the Messiah, expected by her people, would be born as her Son? Had the Spirit, even before Gabriel came, whispered any message of hope or comfort or expectancy to the soul of one so attuned to spiritual things as she was?

But there was more, telling her in plain words the status and mission and dominion of him who was to be her Son: "He shall be great, and shall be called the Son of the Highest: and the Lord God shall give unto him the throne of his father David: And he shall reign over the house of Jacob for ever; and of his kingdom there shall be no end."

"The Son of the Highest"—the Supreme God shall be his Father! "The throne of his father David"—the symbol of all Jewish hope and triumph and glory and freedom and deliverance! An eternal kingdom—the kingdom of our God and of his Christ, and they shall reign forever and ever!

Mary asked, "How shall this be, seeing I know not a man?" Obviously she could, at the proper time, know Joseph, and he could be the father of all her children, not just those who would come after the Firstborn. She knew that. But already the concept was framed in her mind that the promised Son was not to originate from any power on earth. This offspring was to be himself almighty—God's Almighty

Son. How and by what means and through whose instrumentality does such a conception come?

Gabriel explains: "The Holy Ghost shall come upon thee, and the power of the Highest shall overshadow thee: therefore also that holy thing [better, that holy child] which shall be born of thee shall be called the Son of God."

Again the answer is perfect. There is a power beyond man's. When God is involved, he uses his minister, the Holy Ghost, to overshadow the future mother and to carry her away in the Spirit. She shall conceive by the power of the Holy Ghost, and God himself shall be the sire. It is his Son of whom Gabriel is speaking. A son is begotten by a father: whether on earth or in heaven it is the same.

The great message has been spoken. One who stands in the Divine Presence has brought the great announcement to the one who will hold the Divine Presence in her bosom. Now Gabriel speaks to Mary of personal things: "And, behold, thy cousin Elisabeth, she hath also conceived a son in her old age: and this is the sixth month with her, who was called barren. For with God nothing shall be impossible."

This news was to be a sign to Mary of the truth of the greater message that had preceded it. Elisabeth, stricken in years and past the childbearing age, was to have a child, because with God nothing is impossible, even as Sarah, also stricken in years and past the childbearing age, was promised a son by the Lord, who said: "Is any thing too hard for the Lord?" (Gen. 18:14.) Gabriel's announcement about Elisabeth was unspoken counsel to Mary to go and receive comfort and help from her cousin, whom she no doubt loved and revered—the inference is that Mary's mother was dead—and who, being herself with child in a miraculous manner, could speak peace to the young virgin's heart as no other mortal could.

Then Mary gave the answer that ranks, in submissive obedience and divine conformity, along with the one given by the Beloved and Chosen One in the councils of eternity. When he was chosen to be the Redeemer and to put into operation the terms and conditions of his Father's plan, he said: "Father, thy will be done, and the glory be thine forever." (Moses 4:2.) Mary said simply: "Behold the handmaid of the Lord; be it unto me according to thy word." Gabriel then departed.

Having so spoken, Mary contented herself until the divine conception had come to pass, and then she arose and went in haste to her cousin Elisabeth, a hundred and more miles hence in Hebron of Judea.

Mary Visits Elisabeth

(*Luke 1:39-45; JST, Luke 1:43-44*)

There is high drama here. We can scarce conceive how deep the emotions were, or what anxieties and fears bore in upon the tender feelings of Mary and Elisabeth. Nor can we envision how Joseph felt as he learned his betrothed was with child by another, or how subdued and chastened, yet how exalted and exulting, Zacharias was as he pondered what had happened to him in the Holy Place.

Zacharias could no longer speak or hear. He had doubted for a moment the angelic voice, and the penalty of his disbelief rested heavily upon him. For more than nine months he was shut out completely from the normal communion and the usual intercourse with his Judean friends. We suppose he went about his priestly duties as best he could, even journeying back to the temple after a six-month interval, for his assigned week of ceremonial service. No doubt he wrote, for Elisabeth to read, the account of the angel who stood between the golden altar of incense and the seven-branched candlesticks, and proclaimed that she and he would bring forth the one to prepare the way for the great Messiah. And now Elisabeth, with child in her advanced years, needed special care and attention. The trials of life and the testing and anxieties of mortality surely were increasing in the life of this pious priest who yet continued as theretofore to walk blamelessly before the Lord.

Elisabeth—a daughter of Aaron, highly endowed spiritually, rich in faith—she too was being tested and tried and purified. With child in her advanced years, facing problems foreign to younger women who bear children, emotionally troubled, fearing to face her friends of years, she "hid herself five months," to return to normal associations just before Mary's visit. That she was overwhelmed at the honor that was hers to bear the soul of him who would prepare the way for Israel's King, we can well imagine. That the fruit of her womb was so important in the Lord's plan, and that Gabriel himself came to announce the conception, was almost beyond human comprehension. Faithful Elisabeth was being tested and rewarded.

Joseph—a just man, one who loved the Lord and waited for the Consolation of Israel—what a refiner's fire he must have gone through during the weeks and months before Gabriel spoke peace to his soul! Mary—his beloved, the one to whom he had given a writing of espousement, the fairest and most spiritually endowed of all the virgins of the land—his espoused wife, she was with child by another! Joy and gladness, thanksgiving and the sound of melody—once these had filled his soul. Now there was despondency and despair. What should he do? Surely he could not make her a public example. She must not bear the onus of adultery. Yes, instead, he would put her away privily; he would ease her burden as best he could.

And Mary—what of her? Should her testing be any easier, her mortal trials lessened, because she carried in her womb the Son of the Highest? Should she be free from the burdens borne by Sarah and Miriam—whose very name in Hebrew she bore—and by the other great women of Abrahamic lineage? Nay, rather, should not her burdens be greater? Whenever was there a great prophet—Moses, Elijah, Isaiah, Nephi, Joseph Smith—who was not tested to the full? Whenever were the women who stood by their sides freed from the tests and trials of mortality? The greater the prophet, the more severe the test! The nobler the woman, the more she is called to bear! It was the Son of God who descended below all things that he might rise to heights unknown. It was his mother who was subjected to the most trying of all circumstances that she too might ascend the throne of eternal power, as had Rebecca and Rachel and her ancestors of old.

And so we find Mary, about fifteen years of age and inexperienced in meeting the trials of life, under contract to marry one she loved, but with child by the power of the Holy Ghost. We find her in a city of Galilee—rough, rugged, untempered Galilee—where a self-righteous people were quick to condemn, ever ready to punish; where the tongue of gossip would cut her tender feelings to the bone; where she would become a hiss and a byword among her friends and relatives, for she had (as they would view it) committed the sin next only in wickedness to murder. Those among whom she dwelt would no more believe her strange tale that an angel had come to her—angels no longer came to mortals, everyone knew that!—or that the Almighty himself was the Father of that which was in her womb; they would no more believe these claims than they would believe the testimony of the fruit of her womb when he testified in their own city that he was the Messiah of whom Isaiah had spoken.[5]

What course, then, was open to the young virgin? Where could she go for the help and comfort and guidance she so much needed? Had not Gabriel pointed the way? 'Go to thy cousin Elisabeth,' he said. 'She will comfort and sustain thee. She also is with child in a miraculous way—she will understand. She is wise and experienced. She will counsel and help you, and the Lord will give you power to overcome.'

Thus we find Mary facing the trials of life—there would be others, as her Son ministered among men; as he hung on the cross; as he lay in a borrowed tomb; yes, there would be others, and her present troubles were but the beginning of sorrows—but we find her facing her problems and, of her own choice, fleeing to the side of Elisabeth. The distance was more than one hundred miles. No doubt she walked; at least she was in poor circumstances and could have ill afforded other means of travel. Certainly she was accompanied—a sister and brother and other family members or relatives, perhaps; she would not, in wisdom, have gone alone, camping out, and facing the ever-present threat of thieves and robbers. But whatever the arrangements may have been, the journey was completed. Elisabeth was no longer in seclusion, and Mary "entered into the house of Zacharias, and saluted Elisabeth."

Then came the miracle. When the trials are past and the humble suppliant has remained true to every covenant and trust, the Lord speaks. Thus, "it came to pass, that, when Elisabeth heard the salution of Mary, the babe leaped in her womb; and Elisabeth was filled with the Holy Ghost."

Elisabeth was filled with the Holy Ghost—the same Holy Spirit who spake by the mouth of all the holy prophets; the same power from on high that fell on Peter in the coasts of Caesarea Philippi, when he said: "Thou art the Christ, the Son of the living God" (Matt. 16:13-16); the same Comforter whose companionship would be offered to all the saints on the day of Pentecost—the Holy Ghost came upon Elisabeth! She became a living witness, by revelation, of what Gabriel had said to Mary.

And the Holy Ghost fell also upon the unborn baby, for Elisabeth's whole being was filled with that divine power. It is always a miracle when the Holy Ghost rests upon a mortal person, and that very fact makes the recipient a prophet. But it is more than a miracle when the Spirit enlightens the mind and quickens the intellect of a human soul who is yet in his mother's womb; and shall we not conclude that such a recipient of divine truth is more than a prophet? So the Baptist would be designated by our Lord in due course.

It was, on this sacred occasion, as though the unborn John—who in life would say: "Behold the Lamb of God, which taketh away the sin of the world" (John 1:29)—was bearing testimony before birth, by the mouth of his mother, the only mouth that could then frame his words.

Then Elisabeth—speaking for herself and for her unborn infant, and echoing the sentiments in Zacharias's heart, for he too believed—repeated to Mary what she had already heard from the lips of Gabriel: "Blessed art thou among women, and blessed is the fruit of thy womb." Then she asked, and the question itself was a testimony: "And why is it, that this blessing is upon me, that the mother of my Lord should come to me?" By way of explanation, Elisabeth continued her prophetic words: "For, lo, as soon as the voice of thy salutation sounded in mine ears, the babe leaped in my womb for joy.[6] And blessed art thou who believed, for those things which were told thee by the angel of the Lord, shall be fulfilled." Mary had believed Gabriel and all that he had told her concerning the divine conception of her Son, and relative to his birth, life, ministry, and mission.

Would it be amiss to here interject a pleasing historical fact: There were here assembled, as it were, the first Christians of Jesus' day, and they were holding their first meeting. Mary and Elisabeth, both true believers, were present, and they preached the sermons. John, in the flesh in his mother's womb, also a believer, let his witness be heard. We suppose Zacharias was there and that he could feel the spirit of the meeting, though for the moment and until John was born, his lips were sealed and his ears were stopped. Those who traveled with Mary—probably unbelievers and non-Christians, as it were—may also have witnessed the scene and felt the spirit of the participants. Needless to say, the account preserved for us by Luke—and his source must have been the blessed Virgin herself—is abbreviated and does not tell all that was spoken between the two cousins, whose sons were to change the history of the world.

Mary, however, was now in good hands. Elisabeth was wise and she could help, and what was more important, the Lord had now revealed to Elisabeth—and how often revelation comes to the woman Rebecca as well as to the man Isaac—that Mary was the one who should bear the Son of

God. There was another witness; Mary no longer had to bear the burden alone. Now if only Joseph could also know—and that too was soon to be.

The Magnificat

(*Luke 1:46-56; JST, Luke 1:46, 48-49*)

Elisabeth, as moved upon by the Holy Ghost, pays homage to Mary as the mother of the Son of God, an homage that was deserved and true and continues to this day as the perfect testimony of the goodness and grace of her who was foreordained to bear God's Son.

Then Mary responds. Her words are inspired from the same source; she also is filled with the Holy Ghost, and the utterance she makes, like that of her cousin before her, is the voice of the Lord heard through her lips. Mary's words—appropriately—pay homage to the Father, for it was by and through him that the conception of her Son had taken place, and that she, a virgin, should bear a Son.[7]

Psalmic utterances of praise and thanksgiving had always been in the highest tradition of the Israelite people. The Psalms of David and Solomon and Moses and others, preserved in the Old Testament, are still read and sung in the churches of Christendom. Great psalmic utterances of Nephi are found in the Book of Mormon. Miriam, a prophetess, the sister of Aaron, led the women of Israel in a psalm of rejoicing after they had passed through the Red Sea. Deborah, a prophetess, who judged Israel in her day, sang a great hymn of praise when the Lord, through her instrumentality, slew Sisera and saved Israel from the king of Canaan. Hannah, the mother of Samuel, burst forth in a great accolade of praise when she delivered her son to Eli. And now Mary, filled with the same Spirit and exhibiting a profound knowledge of Old Testament history and Hebrew idiom and concepts, gives forth one of the great psalms of praise of all time.

My soul doth magnify the Lord,
And my spirit rejoiceth in God my Savior.
For he hath regarded the low estate of his handmaiden:
For, behold, from henceforth all generations shall call me
blessed.

For he who is mighty hath done to me great things;
And I will magnify his holy name,
For his mercy on those who fear him
From generation to generation.

He hath shewed strength with his arm;
He hath scattered the proud in the imagination of their
hearts.
He hath put down the mighty from their high seats;
And exalted them of low degree.

He hath filled the hungry with good things;
And the rich he hath sent empty away.
He hath holpen his servant Israel,
In remembrance of his mercy,
And he spake to our fathers,
To Abraham, and to his seed for ever.

The condescension of God has been manifest; our Lord's generation is declared. Gabriel has counseled Mary, and Elisabeth has comforted her. The Holy Ghost has fallen upon two great women and one unborn child. Wondrous things have been spoken, and now it remains but for Joseph, the carpenter of Galilee, to hear from heaven the divine message, and the heart of Mary will then be at peace.

NOTES

1. See footnote 7 of chapter 2.
2. See footnote 3 of chapter 2.
3. It was the Prophet Joseph Smith who changed the word *say* to *know* in this verse. (*Teachings*, p. 223.)
4. Can we speak too highly of her whom the Lord has blessed above all women? There

was only one Christ, and there is only one Mary. Each was noble and great in preexistence, and each was foreordained to the ministry he or she performed. We cannot but think that the Father would choose the greatest female spirit to be the mother of his Son, even as he chose the male spirit like unto him to be the Savior. This is not to say that we should give any heed or credence to the false doctrines that say that Mary has been assumed bodily into heaven; that she is an intercessor who hears prayers and pleads with her Son on behalf of those who pray to her; or that she should be esteemed as co-redemptrix with the Redeemer—all of which are part of a great system of worship that did not originate in the courts on high. As our spirits recoil from these perversions of true religion, we should nonetheless maintain a balanced view and hold up Mary with that proper high esteem which is hers.

5. Nor would Mary's story have been believed any more than was Joseph Smith's when he—about the same age as Mary was at the time—announced that the Father and the Son had visited him to usher in a new gospel dispensation. Visions and revelations (to the carnally minded) were things of the past; everyone knew that!

6. Our revelation, hearkening back to the sacred events here recited, describes Elisabeth's son as "John, whom God raised up, being filled with the Holy Ghost from his mother's womb." (D&C 84:27.) From the scriptural accounts it is clear that this means, not alone from the time he came forth out of the womb, but from the time that he as a conscious identity, the spirit having entered the body, was yet encased therein.

7. The virgin birth must not be confused with the so-called immaculate conception. "From the moment of her conception, Mary, the mother of our Lord, in the false Catholic view of things, is deemed to have been free from the stain of original sin. This supposed miraculous event is called the doctrine of the *immaculate conception.* After reciting the universal prevalence of so-called original sin, Cardinal Gibbons says: 'The Church, however, declares that the Blessed Virgin Mary was exempted from the stain of original sin by the merits of our Savior Jesus Christ; and that, consequently, she was never for an instant subject to the dominion of Satan. This is what is meant by the doctrine of the Immaculate Conception.' (James Cardinal Gibbons, *The Faith of Our Fathers,* p. 220.) The virgin birth has reference to the birth of Christ and is a true doctrine; the immaculate conception has reference to the birth of Mary and is a false doctrine." (*Mormon Doctrine,* 2nd ed., pp. 375-76.)

THE ANNUNCIATION TO JOSEPH

And he shall be called
Jesus Christ, the Son of God,
The Father of heaven and earth,
The Creator of all things from the beginning;
And his mother shall be called Mary.
(Mosiah 3:8.)

"Whose Son Is He?"

(*Matthew 1:18*)

We have spoken of the condescension of God in begetting a Mortal Son; we have identified those Spirit-guided persons who have power to declare the generation of a Divine Being, one of whom is Matthew; and we now take up his witness as to whence and by what means our Lord obtained mortality. Having recited the generations of mortals from Abraham down to "Joseph the husband of Mary, of whom was born Jesus, who is called Christ," a recitation that appears to be the royal line of Mary's husband, Matthew comes to the heart of the matter by saying: "Now the birth of Jesus Christ was on this wise: When as his mother Mary was espoused to Joseph, before they came together, she was found with child of the Holy Ghost."

The issue is thus squarely set. Mary is the mother, a fact

no one questions. But what does it mean to be "with child of the Holy Ghost"? Who is the Father of Mary's Son?

We suppose those in Christendom who believe the creeds are here faced with an insurmountable obstacle. Those creeds clearly recite—if such a word may be used to describe the maze of conflicting language found in them—and the doctrines based on those creeds clearly recite, that God is a spirit essence who or which fills the immensity of space, and who or which is everywhere and nowhere in particular present. They speak of an immanent, indwelling presence in all immensity; of three Gods in one, who are without body, parts, or passions; of a spirit being (if he may so be called), in whom we live and move and have our being; and, in saying that God is a spirit, the creeds intertwine the Father, Son, and Holy Ghost into one being, essence, or power, in which none of the three can be separated from the others. Each designation is said to be a variant manifestation of the same force or law or power or whatever. Those so asserting, and we suppose so believing, are at great pains to specify that there is nothing personal, in an anthropomorphic sense, about the God or Gods they worship; that all scriptural statements to the contrary are simply accounts that were so written for teaching purposes; and that their clear meanings must be spiritualized away in this more enlightened day.

We suppose, therefore, that those so believing have difficulty in determining the paternity of the Man of Galilee. We do know that they sometimes interpret the expression "with child of the Holy Ghost" to mean that the Holy Ghost was the Father of Christ, which from their standpoint presents no particular problem because they envision no difference between or among the Father, Son, and Holy Ghost anyway.

To those, however, who know that the Godhead is composed of three separate and distinct personages, who are one in spirit and power, the issue takes on quite a different aspect. The Father is a personage of tabernacle; he has a body of flesh and bones as tangible as man's; he is in one place at one time; he lives and moves and has a being; his influence is spread through all immensity, but he is a personal Being in whose image man is created, and he is the Father of the spirits of all men. The Son was a personage of spirit, the firstborn of the Father, for that infinitely long period before he was born into mortality; since his resurrection he has been and will continue to be an exalted and perfected Holy Man, in form, appearance, and image like his Father, who also is a resurrected personage. The Holy Ghost is a personage of spirit, a spirit man, an individual, whose power and influence, however, is felt throughout all immensity, as is the power and influence of the Father and the Son. The Father, Son, and Holy Ghost are all male personages.

The Son, existing first as a spirit man, was born into mortality as a mortal man; and he has now risen in the resurrection as an immortal man. As far as this life is concerned, he was born of Mary and of Elohim; he came here as the offspring of that Holy Man who is literally our Father in heaven. He was born in mortality in the literal and full sense as the Son of God. He is the Son of his Father in the same sense that all mortals are the sons and daughters of their fathers.

Matthew's statement "with child of the Holy Ghost" means Mary was with child by the power of the Holy Ghost, not that the Holy Ghost was the parent of the fruit of her womb. Matthew's words have the same meaning as those used by Gabriel to Mary: "The Holy Ghost shall come upon thee, and the power of the Highest shall overshadow thee." (Luke 1:35.) They have the same meaning as those used by Alma in one of his great Messianic prophecies: "The Son of God cometh upon the face of the earth," he said. "And behold, he shall be born of Mary, . . . she being a virgin, a precious and chosen vessel, who shall be overshadowed and conceive by the power of the Holy Ghost, and bring forth a son, yea, even the Son of God." (Alma 7:9-10.)

As far as those who understand the scriptures and the plan of salvation are concerned, the issue is not "Whose Son is he?"—for that is well established: he is the Son of God, born in the manner we have set forth. The issue is, Was the child in Mary's womb the Son who had been sired by the Father? Had Elohim and Mary joined together to bring into mortality the One who would abolish death and bring life and immortality to light through the gospel? Was this child to be the Savior, the Redeemer, the Deliverer, the King of Israel?

This was the problem that confronted Joseph, the carpenter of Galilee. To it he must find the answer—for his own sake, for Mary's, and for the sake of all who would thereafter hear his witness.

Gabriel Comes to Joseph in a Dream
(*Matthew 1:19-25*)

When Mary told Joseph that she was with child by the power of the Holy Ghost, his reaction was one not only of shock, of sorrow, and of dismay, but also of disbelief. His soul had yet to feel the flames of the refiner's fire before so great a spiritual truth could rest easily in his heart; as with all men, his faith and his willingness to submit to the divine will in all things must be tested.

For Mary it was no easy thing to tell the man she loved that their relationship was different from that of other faithful couples. And yet Gabriel himself had brought the word! When she recited to Joseph what the aerial ambassador had told her, great and wondrous as the promises were, it must yet have been as a sword piercing her soul, a sword that would wound her feelings time and again, until that day when she, at the foot of a cross, would weep for the Son whom she had brought into the world.

For Joseph it was the beginning of a period of agony and uncertainty. That he wanted to believe Mary, but did not, is shown by his determination "to put her away privily" with as little embarrassment as possible. He planned to give her a letter of divorce in the presence of two witnesses only, as the law permitted, rather than to make the dissolution of their contract to marry a matter of public knowledge and possible gossip. It must have been at this point that Mary sped hastily to Hebron to find comfort in the arms of Elisabeth.

Joseph pondered and prayed. Was Mary with child by the power of the Holy Ghost or in some other way? As to the true father of the unborn child, Mary knew; Elisabeth knew; Zacharias knew. They all gained their testimonies by revelation, and Joseph must now learn for himself in the same way. As we have seen, there is no way for anyone—neither Joseph, nor Mary, nor any living soul—to know and declare the generation of the Son of God, except by the whisperings of the Holy Spirit. Joseph must learn by powers beyond those exercised by mortal men that Mary's child was God's Son. Until this happened, their marriage could not be completed and their union consummated; until this occurred the Holy Family could not be perfected according to the divine plan. This knowledge must come to Joseph to prepare him to provide proper paternal influence in Mary's home during the infant and maturing years of the Son whose Father is above.

It was at this point of hope and faith that Joseph prevailed with the Lord. His prayers were answered. "The angel of the Lord appeared unto him in a dream."[1] His message: "Joseph, thou son of David"—for Joseph, like Mary, was of the house and lineage of Israel's greatest king—"Fear not to take unto thee Mary thy wife: for that which is conceived in her is [by the power] of the Holy Ghost. And she shall bring forth a son, and thou shalt call his name Jesus: for he shall save his people from their sins."

Joseph now knew! Doubt fled. The circle of true believers was growing. He had the same testimony, from the same source, as did Mary and Elisabeth and Zacharias; and, according to their law, in the mouths of two or three witnesses shall every word be established. The Lord was providing his witnesses, and soon the whole nation and the whole world would be bound to believe, and that at the peril of their salvation. How often Joseph bore the special witness that was his we do not know, but that he remained true to every trust and that he performed the mission assigned him by the Lord, there can be no doubt.

At this point Matthew—whose habit it was to note the fulfillment of the Messianic prophecies—says that all these things were done to fulfill Isaiah's promise that a virgin would bring forth a son named Emmanuel, which means "God with us," or in other words that the Son would be God in mortal flesh. "Then Joseph being raised from sleep did as the angel of the Lord had bidden him, and took unto him his wife: And knew her not till she had brought forth her firstborn son: and he called his name Jesus."

We may well suppose that Mary told Joseph of her condition; that she then went to Elisabeth; that Joseph struggled with his problem for nearly three months, being fully tested; that Gabriel brought the word; that Joseph sent word to Mary of his conversion; that she returned again in haste and joy; that immediately the second part of the marriage ceremony was performed; and that Joseph, to preserve the virginity of the one who bore God's Child, refrained from sexual association with her until after Jesus came forth as her child.

John Is Born

(*Luke 1:57-63*)

Zacharias is tiring of the curse he bears; Elisabeth's time has come; Mary, in her condition, to avoid the spotlight that would attend John's birth—because of his miraculous conception in Elisabeth's old age—and to be again with her beloved Joseph, has returned to Nazareth, and so now John the Baptist is born. Elisabeth's cousins and neighbors, knowing of the heavenly visitant who announced the coming of the Lord's Elias, and knowing of the great mercy the Lord had poured out upon Zacharias's wife, rejoiced with her at the blessed birth. The man child who would join Moses and the prophets, among earth's greatest souls, was now on earth. It but remained for his Lord to come, and soon the glory of the new dispensation would begin to shine forth in Israel and in all the world.

> John, than which man a sadder or a greater
> Not till this day, has been of woman born,
> John, like some iron peak by the Creator
> Fired with the red glow of the rushing morn—
>
> This when the sun shall rise and overcome it
> Stands in his shining desolate and bare,
> Yet not the less the inexorable summit
> Flamed him his signal to the happier air.[2]

Now the man child must be circumcised; it is God's law, in force since Abraham, a token, written in the flesh, of his people. "And I will establish a covenant of circumcision with thee," he had said to Abraham, "and it shall be my covenant between me and thee, and thy seed after thee, in their generations; that thou mayest know for ever that children are not accountable before me until they are eight years old." (JST, Gen. 17:11.) Little children are not accountable, but they must be brought up in the nurture and admonition of the Lord, so that when they become accountable, they will continue to walk in his paths and be saved. Circumcision is the token, cut into the flesh so that it can never be removed or forgotten, that their parents have subjected them, in advance and by proxy as it were, to the Abrahamic covenant, the covenant that assures the faithful of eternal increase, of a progeny as numerous as the sands upon the seashore or as the stars in heaven for multitude.

"By circumcision," Edersheim says, "the child had, as it were, laid upon it the yoke of the Law, with all of duty and privilege which this implied. . . . It was, so tradition has it, as if the father had acted sacrificially as High-Priest, offering his child to God in gratitude and love; and it symbolised this deeper moral truth, that man must by his own act complete what God had first instituted." The rite itself probably commenced with "a benediction," and after it had been performed "the child received his name in a prayer," offered along these lines: "Our God, and the God of our fathers, raise up this child to his father and mother, and let his name be called in Israel Zacharias, the son of Zacharias. Let his father rejoice in the issue of his loins, and his mother in the fruit of her womb," all in harmony with the various scriptures, such as: "Thy father and thy mother shall be glad, and she that bare thee shall rejoice," which scriptures were recited, along with other petitions and expressions of thanks, as part of the prayer. (Edersheim 1:157-58; Prov. 23:25.)

It was a common practice to name a firstborn son after the father. When the officiators attempted to do so in this case, Elisabeth said: "Not so; but he shall be called John." They remonstrated with her: surely she wanted to follow the custom and pattern of their fathers; surely she wanted to honor the name of the sire. "There is none of thy kindred that is called by this name," they said. "And they made signs to his father"—indicating he was deaf as well as dumb—"how he would have him called." The child's father then wrote on a tablet: "His name is John," *Jochanan,* meaning "the grace or mercy of Jehovah," in John's case the one who would go forth to proclaim the goodness and grace of the Lord and the great plan of mercy that made salvation available to the penitent.

The Benedictus

(*Luke 1:64-80; JST, Luke 1:67-78*)

Struck dumb at Gabriel's word, Zacharias was unable to give the blessing and benediction to the waiting worshippers on that fateful day in the temple in Jerusalem. Now, with the naming of John, probably in his own home in Hebron, the tongue of the dumb is loosed, and his first words are cries of praise and exultation and benediction. He picks up where he left off more than nine months before, only this time the Holy Spirit rests mightily upon him, and his hymn of praise rises to glorious heights of grandeur. Zacharias's old-words were expressions of doubt and unbelief; his new-words come forth in tones of rapture and faith. In the interval, he has mellowed; he has confessed his sin of unbelief; he has communed with the Lord; and he is now pliantly submissive.

Filled with the Holy Ghost, speaking as with the tongue of angels, using language and thoughts found in the numerous Jewish benedictions that he had learned as a priest—thus showing how one dispensation slips easily into the next—the ancient priest burst forth with these words:

Blessed be the Lord God of Israel;
For he hath visited and redeemed his people,
And hath raised up an horn of salvation for us,
In the house of his servant David,
As he spake by the mouth of his holy prophets,
Ever since the world began,
That we should be saved from our enemies,
And from the hand of all who hate us;
To perform the mercy promised to our fathers,
And to remember his holy covenant;
The oath which he sware to our father Abraham,
That he would grant unto us,
That we, being delivered out of the hand of our enemies,
Might serve him without fear,
In holiness and righteousness before him,
All the days of our lives.

And thou, child, shalt be called the prophet of the Highest,
For thou shalt go before the face of the Lord
To prepare his ways,
To give knowledge of salvation unto his people,
By baptism for the remission of their sins,
Through the tender mercy of our God;
Whereby the day-spring from on high hath visited us,
To give light to them who sit in darkness

And the shadow of death;
To guide our feet into the way of peace.

And so, even before the old dispensation died, the first dawning rays of the new day were beginning to pierce the darkness of the past. Miracles had come again: the wondrous miracle of angelic visitation; of miraculous births; of the gift of prophecy; of God's Holy Spirit dwelling again in the hearts of men; of the Shekinah seeking entrance, as it were, to the Holy of Holies.

Gabriel had come to Zacharias, and he knew it and Elisabeth knew it and the worshippers in the temple knew it. Gabriel had come to Mary and been seen by Joseph, and they knew it. One child was born and another was already in a virgin's womb.

He was coming! The way was being prepared even before the forerunner—who must still grow and wax strong in the Spirit and wait in the deserts of Hebron for his showing to Israel—before he should cry out in Bethabara, before he should introduce the Lamb of God.

The glad tidings so far received were being heralded forth; fear was falling on those who heard the accounts, and the whole hill country of Judea, to say nothing of the mountains and valleys of Galilee—all were ablaze with the new knowledge, at the doings of the Almighty among his people.

Men were laying up the happenings of the hour in their hearts. As to John they were saying: "What manner of child shall this be!" As to the Promised Messiah, they were asking: 'When will he come?' There was an aura of expectancy. Things were building up to a climax. The forerunner had come; when would the Messiah show himself? When would the Dayspring from on high visit his people, to give light to them that sit in darkness and in the shadow of death, and to guide their feet in the way of peace?

"Surely I come quickly."

"Even so, come, Lord Jesus." (Rev. 22:20.)

NOTES

1. It was a dream and yet the angel was there. The line between dreams and visions is not clearly drawn. Lehi said: "Behold, I have dreamed a dream, or, in other words, I have seen a vision." (1 Ne. 8:2.) In general, a vision comes when one is awake, a dream while one sleeps. They may be the same, or they may differ, as the case may be. In this instance the clear inference is that the angel was there in person, as he had been when he conversed, first with Zacharias and then with Mary. It is, of course, implicit in the whole account that the angel involved was Gabriel, he having the assignment, as we suppose, to transmit the knowledge of the Savior to those immediately involved.

2. Frank W. Gunsaulus, *The Man of Galilee,* p. 27.

JESUS IS BORN

Upon Judea's Plains

I stood upon Judea's plains
And heard celestial sounds and strains;
I heard an angel, free from sin,
Announce the birth of David's kin.

On shepherds watching sheep by night
There came a shining, glorious light,
As holy choirs from heaven's dome
Saw God's own Son make clay his home.

And voices sweet sang this reprise:
"To God on high, let praise arise;
And peace, good will to men on earth;
This is the day of Jesus' birth."

To me there came this witness sure:
He is God's Son, supreme and pure,
To earth he came, my soul to save,
From sin and death and from the grave.
—Bruce R. McConkie

Joseph and Mary Go to Bethlehem

(*Luke 2:1-5; JST, Luke 2:1*)

Mary—in whose womb the Child was growing, within whose flesh the Eternal One was in process of making flesh his tabernacle—dwelt in love and peace in Nazareth of Galilee. She was sheltered and steadied by the kind arm of Joseph, her husband, for the marriage was now completed; Joseph had obeyed the command of Gabriel and taken the young virgin as his wife. His name and his influence now gave comfort to the one who would soon be a mother, to the one who would bear a Son, conceived under the most unusual circumstances ever known on earth. With Joseph's name and comforting assurances she no longer feared the gossip and shame that otherwise might have attended her forthcoming ordeal.

But Bethlehem, more than eighty dusty, dreary miles away, was the destined place for the birth of the great Deliverer. So it was written by the prophets; so it must be. Out of this small place, insignificant among the villages of Judea, must come Him whose goings forth have been from of old, from everlasting. Mary knew this and Joseph knew it; both had seen an angel; both knew, by means beyond mortal comprehension, that the Holy Thing that was in her was to "be called the Son of the Highest," who should rule on the throne of David his father forever. They must go to Bethlehem and there attend to the coming forth of a Son, lest any of the Messianic prophecies, by so much as a hair's breadth, should fail.

And so to Bethlehem they went. Was it to be taxed? Yes, for Octavian—the great Caesar Augustus—had so decreed All the world must be taxed; Rome is supreme; even the chosen people must bow to the rod of Rome, silence their hatred, swallow their pride, and obey the imperial will. Caesar speaks and the world trembles. For the Palestinian part of the world, Herod will attend to the details. He is the sycophant who licks Caesar's boots for that part of the earth;

he will humor the Jews in their traditions and let them be counted and enrolled on the taxing lists in their own cities; he will decree that they return for this purpose to the tribal areas of their ancestors. Joseph and Mary—both descendants of David, both of the tribe of Judah—must enroll in the land of Judah and in the City of David, in Bethlehem.

They went to Bethlehem because they had no choice: Caesar had spoken, and Herod was echoing the word. But this was only the occasion, the vehicle, the excuse, as it were. They would have moved heaven and earth, if need be, to place themselves in the City of David when the hour arrived for the coming of the Son of David. We cannot suppose that a considerate and loving husband, having a wife big with child, would cause her to walk, or ride a slow stepping donkey, or traverse in any manner the dusty roads of Palestine, camping out overnight as they traveled—all as the hour of her confinement approached—unless there was a reason. Joseph and Mary were going to Bethlehem for a purpose. It was the one and only place where the Messiah could be born, and we cannot but suppose that they knew it and acted wittingly.

As to why they did not reside in this city of Judah in the first instance, we can only say that the providences of the Lord called for them to live in Nazareth where Joseph carpentered for a living. Jesus was to be a Nazarene; so also was it written. And as to why they did not leave Nazareth earlier, we are left to assume that Divine Providence planned a late arrival, an arrival when there would be no room in the inns, when the new baby would be brought forth under the most humble circumstances.

Jesus Is Born in a Stable

(*3 Nephi 1:4-14; Luke 2:6-7; JST, Luke 2:7*)

As Caesar was shuffling souls around in the Old World, and as Herod was carrying out the whims and fiats of the Roman tyrant—both unwittingly preparing the way for the birth of a King whose kingdom would break in pieces all other kingdoms and bring the whole world under righteous rule—as these things went forward in the lands of which we speak, other like commotions were in progress in the New World.

Among the Nephites in the Americas the same anxieties and expectancies prevailed as to the coming of the Son of God in the flesh as were found in the home country of the Jews. The Nephite prophets had told them plainly that the Messiah would come in six hundred years from the time that Lehi left Jerusalem. According to their calculations, the time was at hand; but among them, as among their Old World kindred, there were unbelievers who opposed and fought the truth. It is the way of the wicked to shut out light and truth and to reject the Author of them.

Unbelieving Nephites were saying that the time of the Messiah's coming was past, that the signs promised by the prophets had failed, and that the beliefs of the members of the church were pious nonsense. These rebellious and spiritually illiterate persons made "a great uproar throughout the land; and the people who believed began to be very sorrowful, lest by any means those things which had been spoken might not come to pass." The saints fasted and prayed and watched; the unbelievers set a day apart on which they would slay the saints unless the signs were manifest; and Nephi prayed mightily all the day long for the safety and deliverance of his people.

Then, in wondrous glory, the voice of the Lord came unto him, speaking these words: "Lift up your head and be of good cheer; for behold, the time is at hand, and on this night shall the sign be given, and on the morrow come I into the world, to show unto the world that I will fulfill all that which I have caused to be spoken by the mouth of my holy prophets. Behold, I come unto my own, to fulfill all things which I have made known unto the children of men from the foundation of the world, and to do the will, both of the Father and of the Son—of the Father because of me, and of the Son because of my flesh. And behold, the time is at hand, and this night shall the sign be given."[1]

And that night the sign was given, as we shall hereafter note; and that night the Son of God came into the world in Bethlehem of Judea. Of this most important of all births, Luke says simply: "And she brought forth her firstborn son, and wrapped him in swaddling clothes, and laid him in a manger, because there was none to give room for them in the inns."[2]

No room in the inns! Hospitality was universal, freely extended, and everywhere to be found. People in all walks of life took strangers into their homes, fed them, washed their feet, and cared for their beasts of burden. It was a way of life. No one can fault the Jewish practice of caring for travelers, whether they were kinfolk or strangers. Had Joseph and Mary come days earlier, they might have found lodgment in the home of a relative, a friend, or a hospitable stranger, any one of whom would have summoned a midwife and prepared a cradle for the Coming One. Had they even arrived earlier in the day, there would have been a place in the rooms or inns rather than in the court, where those beasts were tethered among whom the Coming One came.

No room in the inn—not an inn of western or modern make, but a *kahn* or place of lodgment for strangers, a *caravanserai* or place where caravans or companies of travelers bedded down for the night. It may have been a large, bare building, built of rough stones, surrounding an open court in which animals could be tied up for the night. A foot or two above this courtyard were the small recesses or "low small rooms with no front wall" where the humans tethered themselves.[3]

Of these rooms Farrar says: "They are, of course, perfectly public; everything that takes place in them is visible to every person in the kahn. They are also totally devoid of even the most ordinary furniture. The traveller may bring his own carpet if he likes, may sit cross-legged upon it for his meals, and may lie upon it at night. As a rule, too, he must bring his own food, attend to his own cattle, and draw his own water from the neighbouring spring. He would neither expect nor require attendance, and would pay only the merest trifle for the advantage of shelter, safety, and a floor on which to lie. But if he chanced to arrive late, and the *leewans* [rooms] were all occupied by earlier guests, he would have no choice but to be content with such accommodation as he could find in the court-yard below, and secure for himself and his family such small amount of cleanliness and decency as are compatible with an unoccupied corner on the filthy area, which he would be obliged to share with horses, mules, and camels. The litter, the closeness, the unpleasant smell of the crowded animals, the unwelcome intrusion of the pariah dogs, the necessary society of the very lowest hangers-on of the caravanserai, are adjuncts to such a position which can only be realised by any traveller in the East who happens to have been placed in similar circumstances." (Farrar, p. 4.)

In the area of Bethlehem, sometimes the whole kahn, sometimes only the portion where the animals were kept, was located within a large cave, of which there are many in the area. But unless or until some of the saints—and such a thing is by no means improbable or beyond the realm of expectancy—see in a dream or a vision the inn where Joseph and Mary and Jesus spent that awesome night, we can only speculate as to the details.

For the present also, we have no way of knowing how or in what manner the Babe of Bethlehem was delivered. Was there a midwife among the travelers who heard the cries of travail and came to Mary's aid? Did Mary alone wrap the swaddling clothes around her infant Son, or were there other hands to help? How were her needs cared for? Needless to say, the Gospel narratives are silent on these and a lifetime of personal matters relative to the greatest life ever lived. All we can now know—perhaps all we need to know—is that he was born in the lowest conceivable circumstances.

Though heaven was his habitation and earth his footstool, he chose to lie as an infant in a manger, surrounded by horses and camels and mules. Though he laid the foundations of the earth, and worlds without number had rolled into orbit at his word, he chose to come into mortality among the beasts of the field. Though he had worn a kingly crown in the eternal courts on high, he chose to breathe as his first mortal breath the stench of a stable. Though he would one day come forth—born then in glorious immortality—with all power in heaven and on earth, for now, as the helpless child of a peasant girl, he chose to begin the days of his probation as none of Adam's race had ever done before. And there, even in such a birth, he was rejected by his people, symbolically at least, for none in the recesses and rooms of the inn had seen fit to make room for a weary woman, great with child, who needed above all at that hour the kind hands and skill of those who had attended her cousin Elisabeth in more fortuitous circumstances.

But with it all, a God had come into mortality, inheriting from his mother the power of mortality and from his Father the power of immortality. Soon the infinite and eternal atonement—sought and desired by the righteous for four thousand years—would be a living reality. Soon all that had been hoped and promised and foreseen would come to pass. Is it any wonder that angelic choirs, even now, were awaiting the cue to sing forth great anthems of praise, some of which would be heard by shepherd ears on the nearby Judean hills!

Heavenly Manifestations Attend His Birth

(*Luke 2:8-20; JST, Luke 2:12; 3 Nephi 1:15-20*)

The Messiah has come, not yet to minister among men, but first to grow up as a Tender Plant in the dry ground of Palestine. When he applies to John for baptism, his forerunner will tell all Israel who he is, and apostolic witnesses will shortly thereafter begin to proclaim his divine Sonship in every city and village of that land which shall be called holy because he was born in it. But even now, while he yet lies in a manger in a stable, shall not the word begin to go forth? Is it not requisite that his fellow mortals begin to hear of his birth and to ponder its eternal import in their souls? If the infant's birth is divine, no doubt his ministry three decades later will also measure up to heaven's standards.

And Divine Providence so decreed. The birth in Bethlehem shall be known; the coming of God's Son is no secret; as soon and as often as men can receive the word, it will be given to them. For scattered Israel, separated by half a world from the sacred happenings of that hour, the word will come with sidereal majesty, so that every man among them must believe it or face the loss of his soul. For homebound Israel, found in the surrounding fields and villages and cities, the word will come—as all gospel truths come—by the mouths of messengers who have first received their errand from the Lord, and have then been sent to tell it to their fellowmen. Those in the land where he is born and shall minister are to hear the message in the normal way because the day in which it comes to them is the day of their salvation. Those who live on the isles of the sea will see the sign of his birth written in the heavens, and they will then be expected to turn to the living oracles among them to hear the message of salvation designed for their ears. But for both the Jews and the Nephites, and for all Israel, and for all men, since he came from heaven, naught but heaven can herald the message. And such, as we shall now see, was the case.

In the Americas, Nephi had heard the voice—"the time is at hand, and on this night shall the sign be given, and on the morrow come I into the world"—and on that night the sign was given, "for behold, at the going down of the sun there was no darkness." The people were astonished. Fear fell upon them, and many fell to the earth "and became as if they were dead. . . . And it came to pass that there was no darkness in all that night, but it was as light as though it was mid-day. And it came to pass that the sun did rise in the morning again, according to its proper order; and they knew that it was the day that the Lord should be born, because of the sign which had been given."

There was no excuse for any of the inhabitants of the New World not to know of the coming of their Messiah. Samuel the Lamanite had prophesied that there would be no darkness during the night of his birth, and the promised sign had now been seen by all. When else was there ever a night when the brightness of noonday prevailed over whole continents from the going down of the sun on one day to its rising on the next?

In the Old World the message came from heaven in a different way. In the fields of Bethlehem, not far from Jerusalem and the Temple of Jehovah, there were shepherds watching their flocks by night. These were not ordinary shepherds nor ordinary flocks. The sheep there being herded—nay, not herded, but watched over, cared for with love and devotion—were destined for sacrifice on the great altar in the Lord's House, in similitude of the eternal sacrifice of Him who that wondrous night lay in a stable, perhaps among sheep of lesser destiny. And the shepherds—for whom the veil was then rent: surely they were in spiritual stature like Simeon and Anna and Zacharias and Elisabeth and Joseph and the growing group of believing souls who were coming to know, by revelation, that the Lord's Christ was now on earth. As there were many widows in Israel, and only to the one in Zarephath was Elijah sent, so there were many shepherds in Palestine, but only to those who watched over the temple flocks did the herald angel come; only they heard the heavenly choir. As Luke's idyllic language has it: "And, lo, the angel of the Lord came upon them, and the glory of the Lord shone round about them: and they were sore afraid."

"The glory of the Lord!"—a part of that ancient glory, the Shekinah, which had of old rested in the Holy of Holies and which soon would shine forth on the Holy Mount where Peter, James, and John, and Jesus would be the only mortals present!

"Sore afraid!"—holy fear; the fear of the Lord; the fear felt by Mary and by Zacharias when Gabriel came to each of them from the presence of God; the fear that leads to spiritual progression; the fear that enlarges the soul, as it is written: "The glory of the Lord is risen upon thee, . . . and thine heart shall fear, and be enlarged." (Isa. 60:1, 5.)

> *And the angel said unto them, Fear not: for, behold, I bring you good tidings of great joy, which shall be to all people. For unto you is born this day in the city of David a Saviour, which is Christ the Lord. And this shall be a sign unto you; Ye shall find the babe wrapped in swaddling clothes, lying in a manger.*

His message delivered, the angel—was it Gabriel again?—ceased to speak; the shepherds must heed the heavenly voice, find the Savior, and then commence the infinitely great and eternally important work of taking the "good tidings of great joy . . . to all people." How they will tell the message to their wives and children! How they will explain it to their neighbors and friends, and even to strangers! How they will gather the people in the courts of the temple, at the time of the morning and evening sacrifice—when the very sheep they had cared for so tenderly are attaining their divine destiny on the holy altar—and tell their fellow Jews what they have heard from heaven! And how Anna and Simeon and other devout souls, who also wait for the Consolation of Israel, will rejoice!

But wait—the heavens are still opened to them. There is now not one angel, but many. The whole heavens resound. The music, written by celestial souls for a celestial choir and sung by celestial voices with celestial fervor, rings from one end of heaven to the other. They praise the Lord; they sing of his goodness and grace; they tell of what his arm hath done; they speak of the tree upon which he shall hang; they exult at the open door of an empty tomb; they tell of prison doors being opened, and of ransomed souls rising to eternal glory. Then in a crescendo of climax comes this glorious benediction:

Glory to God in the highest, and on earth peace, good will toward men.

Then the shepherds find the Child and begin to make known what God has revealed to them. "But Mary kept all these things, and pondered them in her heart," awaiting the day when she too will bear witness of all that she feels and believes and knows concerning the Son of David, who was born in the city of David, and who came to reign on the throne of David forever.

NOTES

1. These words, spoken in the name of the Lord Jesus, are sometimes used, erroneously, as an argument that the Spirit Christ was not in the body being prepared in Mary's womb, and that therefore the spirit does not enter the body until the moment of birth, when the mother's offspring first breathes the breath of life. This is not true.

As amply attested by the writings and teachings of President Brigham Young and others, the spirit enters the body at the time of quickening, whenever that is, and remains in the developing body until the time of birth. In a formal doctrinal statement the First Presidency of the Church (Joseph F. Smith, Anthon H. Lund, and John R. Winder) have said: "The body of man enters upon its career as a tiny germ or embryo, which becomes an infant, quickened at a certain stage by the spirit whose tabernacle it is, and the child, after being born, develops into a man." (Cited, *Mormon Doctrine,* 2nd ed., p. 17.)

With reference to the words here spoken by the Lord Jesus on the night of his birth, we must understand that someone else, speaking by what is called divine investiture of authority, is speaking the words in the first person as though he were the Lord, when in fact he is only speaking in the Lord's name. In many revelations the Son speaks in this same way as though he were the Father. For an extended analysis of this matter, see *The Promised Messiah: The First Coming of Christ,* chapter 4.

2. What is the date of our Lord's birth? This is one of those fascinating problems about which the wise and the learned delight to debate. There are scholars, of repute and renown, who place his natal day in every year from 1 B.C. to 7 B.C., with 4 B.C. being the prevailing view, if we may be permitted to conclude that there is a prevailing view. How much the answer really matters is itself a fair question, since the problem is one, in part at least, of determining whether there have been errors made in the creation of our present dating system.

We do not believe it is possible with the present state of our knowledge—including that which is known both in and out of the Church—to state with finality when the natal day of the Lord Jesus actually occurred. Elder James E. Talmage takes the view that he was born on April 6, 1 B.C., basing his conclusion on Doctrine and Covenants 20:1, which speaks of the day on which the Church was organized, saying it was "one thousand eight hundred and thirty years since the coming of our Lord and Saviour Jesus Christ in the flesh." April 6 is then named as the specific day for the formal organization. Elder Talmage notes the Book of Mormon chronology, which says that the Lord Jesus would be born six hundred years after Lehi left Jerusalem. (Talmage, pp. 102-4.)

Elder Hyrum M. Smith of the Council of the Twelve wrote in the *Doctrine and Covenants Commentary:* "The organization of the Church in the year 1830 is hardly to be regarded as giving divine authority to the commonly accepted calendar. There are reasons for believing that those who, a long time after our Savior's birth, tried to ascertain the correct time, erred in their calculations, and that the Nativity occurred four years before our era, or in the year of Rome 750. All that this Revelation means to say is that the Church was organized in the year commonly accepted as 1830, A.D." Rome 750 is equivalent, as indicated, to 4 B.C.

President J. Reuben Clark, Jr., in *Our Lord of the Gospels*, a scholarly and thoughtful work, says in his preface that many scholars "fix the date of the Savior's birth at the end of 5 B.C., or the beginning or early part of 4 B.C." He then quotes the explanation of Doctrine and Covenants 20:1 as found in the *Commentary*, notes that it has been omitted in a later edition, and says: "I am not proposing any date as the true date. But in order to be as helpful to students as I could, I have taken as the date of the Savior's birth the date now accepted by many scholars,—late 5 B.C., or early 4 B.C., because Bible Commentaries and the writings of scholars are frequently keyed upon that chronology and because I believe that so to do will facilitate and make easier the work of those studying the life and works of the Savior from sources using this accepted chronology." This is the course being followed in this present work, which means, for instance, that Gabriel came to Zacharias in October of 6 B.C.; that he came to Mary in March or April of 5 B.C.; that John was born in June of 5 B.C.; and that Jesus was born in December 5 B.C., or from January to April in 4 B.C.

To illustrate how the scholars go about determining the day of Christ's Nativity, we quote the following from Edersheim: "The first and most certain date is that of the death of Herod the Great. Our Lord was born *before* the death of Herod, and, as we judge from the Gospel-history, very shortly before that event. Now the year of Herod's death has been ascertained with, we may say, absolute certainty, as shortly before the Passover of the year 750 A.U.C., which corresponds to about the 12th of April of the year 4 before Christ, according to our common reckoning. More particularly, shortly before the death of Herod there was a lunar eclipse which, it is astronomically ascertained, occurred on the night from the 12th to the 13th of March of the year 4 before Christ. Thus the death of Herod must have taken place between the 12th of March and the 12th of April—or, say, about the end of March. Again, the Gospel-history necessitates an interval of, at the least, seven or eight weeks before that date for the birth of Christ (we have to insert the purification of the Virgin—at the earliest, six weeks after the Birth—The Visit of the Magi, and the murder of the children at Bethlehem, and, at any rate, some days more before the death of Herod). Thus the birth of Christ could not have possibly occurred after the beginning of February 4 B.C., and most likely several weeks earlier." (Edersheim 2:704.)

We should add that if the slaughter of the Innocents by Herod occurred not weeks but a year or so after our Lord's birth, as some have concluded from the recitation in Matthew 2, then this whole reasoning of Edersheim would be extended an appreciable period, so that Christ could have been born on April 6 of 5 B.C. We repeat, as President Clark repeated, that this is not a settled issue. Perhaps also it does not matter too much as long as we have an accepted framework of time within which to relate the actual events of his life, and one that gives us a reasonably accurate view of when those events took place.

3. For an explanation of the word *katalyma*, which was translated *inn* in the King James Version but was rendered as *inns* in the Joseph Smith Translation, see chapter 95. In the only other place where this word is found in the New Testament, it was translated as *guestchamber*. There is no real English equivalent.

FROM BETHLEHEM TO EGYPT

For unto us a child is born, unto us a son is given. (Isa. 9:6.)

He is thy Lord; and worship thou him. (Ps. 45:11.)

Jesus Is Circumcised and Named

(Luke 2:21)

Mary's son was a Jew of the tribe of Judah into whose flesh the sign of Abraham must be cut. He must be circumcised. When eight days old, neither before nor after, this sacred rite must be performed. The Seed of Abraham must have written in his flesh the token of the covenant that he himself, as Jehovah, had made with Abraham his father. As the Giver of the covenant he must also be the heir of its obligations and of its blessings; and as we noted at the circumcision of John, the Abrahamic covenant is one of eternal increase and exaltation for all of the faithful.

Through circumcision the male children in Israel become subject to the law. And Jesus, one of these children, though he came to fulfill the law, came also to obey all of its requirements; even he will conform to the law, as each event in his life requires, until that day when it shall be nailed with him to the cross, there to die, so that a new law can rise with him as he comes forth from the tomb in a newness of life. We might even be permitted to indulge the thought that Christ's blood, first shed at circumcision, was to keep the old Mosaic law, while that same blood, shed in Gethsemane and at Calvary, was to abolish the old law and bring in the new—the new law that would ever thereafter govern all men.

We do not know where or under what circumstances Jesus was circumcised. It could have been in the house in Bethlehem where Joseph and Mary now lived, or, sensing a need to gain the inspiration of a hallowed place, they could have gone the six miles to the temple in Jerusalem. But following the rite our Lord was given his mortal name. "Thou shalt call his name Jesus," were the words of Gabriel to Joseph. 'Thou, Joseph, shall give Mary's son the name Jesus, for thou art the head of the house.'

Why this name? It was a common name among the Jews then, and it has become a sacred and holy name now among all the faithful. It derives from *Hoshea,* which means *salvation;* from *Joshua,* meaning *salvation is Jehovah;* from *Jeshua* (Jesus), meaning *Jehovah is salvation.* Our Lord was so named because, as Gabriel said, "he shall save his people from their sins."

Jesus Is Presented in the Temple

(*Luke 2:22-24, 39*)

Jesus is now at least forty-one days old; the Holy Family are yet living in Bethlehem; and Joseph and Mary and "their" Son go to Jerusalem to the temple. They have two reasons: The child Jesus, as the firstborn son, must be redeemed; and Mary, having born a son, must be purified. Such was the law, to which in all points the Holy Family conformed.

When Jehovah slew the firstborn in all the homes in Egypt, from the firstborn of Pharaoh in his palace to the firstborn of the basest serf in the lowliest hovel in the land,

and when he saved alive the firstborn in every family in Israel, on whose door the saving blood had been sprinkled, he took in payment, that his goodness might be remembered to all generations, the firstborn of all the Israelites. These would be his ministers; when the sacrificial rites and other holy ordinances were performed, it would be the firstborn in every family who would minister before Jehovah. Had this provision remained in force, Jesus would have been, like Zacharias, a priest in the temple.

But later, the Levites, as a reward for special devotion and valiance, were chosen, as a tribe, to serve in the place and stead of the firstborn in all of the families of all of the tribes. These latter were to be redeemed, each individually, from their obligation of a life of priestly service by the payment of five shekels of the sanctuary. This sum Joseph paid to redeem "his" Son, and thus was accomplished the first purpose for their visit to the Holy House.

Now Mary must undergo the rite of purification; she must become ceremonially clean. For this the law requires the offering of a lamb for a burnt offering (that is, a sacrifice of service and devotion, of worship and self-surrender to the Lord) and also the offering of a turtledove or young pigeon as a sin offering (that is, as its name implies, a sacrifice for the remission of personal sins that had been committed through ignorance). Those too poor to pay for a lamb—and such was the case with Mary—could substitute another turtledove or young pigeon.

On this occasion Mary entered the Court of the Women; dropped the price of her sacrifice into one of the thirteen trumpet-shaped chests; heard the sound of the organ, announcing that incense was about to be kindled on the Golden Altar; made her way, as one for whom a special sacrifice was being offered, to a place near the Sanctuary; and there, while the ordinance was performed, offered up the unspoken prayers of praise and thanksgiving of a grateful heart. Thus she became Levitically clean.

And so Luke says: "And when they had performed all

things according to the law of the Lord, they returned into Galilee, to their own city of Nazareth."

Simeon and Anna Testify of Christ
(*Luke 2:25-38; JST, Luke 2:35-36*)

One by one—one of a city and two of a family, as it were—the circle of living witnesses of the Lord's Christ is enlarging. Others besides those involved in the birth of Jesus and of his forerunner are receiving the divine witness and being called to share the burdens always imposed upon those who know truth by the power of the Holy Spirit. Simeon and Anna are now added to the list of true believers. Had they, forty days before in those same temple courts, heard the excited words of the shepherds who saw the angel and heard the heavenly choir? Had they, "waiting for the consolation of Israel," hoped to see him in the flesh, perhaps even when his "parents" came to redeem him from the priests and to purify his mother as the law required?

This much we know: "It was revealed" unto Simeon "by the Holy Ghost, that he should not see death, before he had seen the Lord's Christ. And he came by the Spirit into the temple." This makes Simeon a prophet; he is receiving revelation; he knows what none can know except they gain it from the same Source. Luke says he was "just and devout, . . . and the Holy Ghost was upon him." He took the Child "in his arms, and blessed God, and said, Lord, now lettest thou thy servant depart in peace, according to thy word: For mine eyes have seen thy salvation, Which thou hast prepared before the face of all people; A light to lighten the Gentiles, and the glory of thy people Israel." Even now, as the first recorded testimony borne by mortal lips is heard in the courts of the Lord's Holy House, the announcement is made that salvation comes through Christ for all people; true, he is the glory of his people Israel, but he also came to bring light to the Gentiles and salvation to all people.

Then Simeon blessed Joseph and Mary, and said to

Mary: "Behold, this child is set for the fall and rising again of many in Israel; and for a sign which shall be spoken against; (Yea, a sword shall pierce through thy own soul also,) that the thoughts of many hearts may be revealed." Would that we knew all else that he spoke, including the words of blessing pronounced upon the couple in whose custody the Child was placed. Always—as we shall see throughout this whole work—there was more uttered orally to those who then lived, usually far more, than was recorded and preserved for those who should thereafter hear the accounts. At least we know that Simeon foresaw that Jesus and his message would divide the house of Israel; that men would rise or fall as they accepted or rejected his words; that he was a sign or standard around which the righteous would rally; and that Mary, who now had joy in the growing life of the infant Son, would soon be pierced with the sword of sorrow as she saw him during his waning hours on the cross of Calvary.

At this instant, Anna, a faithful widow of great age, who like the widow of Zarephath had been set apart from all the widows of Israel, came in. She bore a like testimony, for women are not one whit behind men in the receipt of spiritual gifts. She knew that Jesus was the Lord. This knowledge she would take to her grave, and this knowledge would still be with her when she saw his face again, as he ministered among the righteous in the paradise of God; there he would greet her and bless her for the witness she bore when he was yet in Mary's arms. But for now, while she yet dwelt on earth, she gave thanks unto the Lord, "and spake of him to all them that looked for redemption in Jerusalem." The witness of truth was going forth, and the seeds were being planted, from which a crop would yet be harvested, when some thirty years later his voice would call men to the kingdom he was then establishing among men.

"And Joseph and his mother marvelled at those things which were spoken of him." Though they had both seen Gabriel, and though they both knew of the divine Sonship of the Child, yet the magnitude and glory of his mortal ministry and the greatness of the work he would do among men would dawn upon them gradually.

Wise Men from the East Seek Christ

(*Matthew 2:1-12; JST, Matthew 3:2-6; 3 Nephi 1:21-22*)

We know that Joseph's family stayed in Bethlehem until Jesus, then more than forty days old, was presented in the temple, where Simeon and Anna acclaimed his divine Sonship. Luke, who makes no mention of the coming of the wise men from the East nor of the flight into Egypt, tells us that immediately after the temple appearance the Holy Family went to Nazareth. According to the chronology we are following—and it is the same followed by President J. Reuben Clark, Jr., in *Our Lord of the Gospels*—Jesus was born in December of 5 B.C., he was circumcised in January of 4 B.C., he was presented in the temple in February, 4 B.C., and the family probably returned to Nazareth that same month. The visit of the Magi, the flight into Egypt, and the slaughter of the Innocents, also, are all presumed to have been in February of 4 B.C. The events incident to them, of course, took place in Bethlehem.

No reason is given why Joseph took his family the 180 miles or so—on foot, by donkey, or however—from Bethlehem to Nazareth and back. Perhaps they had decided to live in the land of their ancestors, near the sacred events that already had become so much a part of their very being. Their brief return visit in Nazareth may have been to close the carpentry shop and to take leave of friends and loved ones. We have already noted the view that Zacharias was slain by Herod's order when he refused to reveal the hiding place of the child John. Since we have no reason to believe that Herod's assassins were slaying children as far away as Hebron, this gives rise to the thought that Zacharias and Elisabeth may also have chosen Bethlehem for their home. Perhaps Mary and Elisabeth desired to be near each other. It does appear that when the Holy Family returned from Egypt, Joseph intended to settle again in Bethlehem, but was sent instead by angelic decree to Nazareth.

But whatever their immediate plans were, eternal purposes were at work. There was a planned and programmed course for the newborn Messiah to follow; there was a foreordained destiny as to where he lived, and what he did, and how he was received by those among whom he had made flesh his tabernacle. From the eternal perspective, those of whom we speak must be in Bethlehem so that Jesus might be worshipped by the wise men from the East; so that the Innocents of Bethlehem might be slaughtered, at Herod's word; and so that the custodians of the Child might take him into Egypt, at an angel's word—all with a view to fulfilling the Messianic prophecies about the new star that should arise, about Rachel's weeping for her children, and about the Lord calling his Son out of Egypt.

There has been more speculation about, and more legends created concerning, the so-called Magi who visited Joseph and Mary in their house in Bethlehem than about almost any other biblical event. There is an air of mystery here that appeals to the speculative mind, and the fictional accounts—as to who they were, whence they came, and the symbolical meaning of all that they did—fill many volumes.

They are presumed to be kings because of the richness of their gifts; it is said they were Gentiles, showing that all nations bowed before the newborn King; it is thought they were masters of some astrological cult that could divine great happenings from the stars. They are even named, identified, and described; their ages are given, and the color of their skin; and one can, or could in times past, at least, even view their skulls, crowned with jewels, in a cathedral in Cologne. They are thought to have dealt in magic, to be magicians of a sort, and they have become great heroes of the mystical and unknown.

And the type of speculation that surrounds the men themselves applies in a degree to the star they followed. It is supposed to be a comet or a blazing new light coming from a conjunction of Jupiter and Saturn in the constellation of Pisces, or something else. Astronomers, tinged somewhat with astrology, have a field day here. And then all of it is tied back into Balaam's prophecy—"There shall come a Star out of Jacob" (Num. 24:17)—he, Balaam, being assumed to be one of the greatest Magi of them all.

As to the wise men and their stated purpose, all we learn from Matthew—and he alone records the account—is that "there came wise men from the east to Jerusalem." Their question was: "Where is he that is born King of the Jews?" Why did they ask? "We have seen his star in the east," they said, "and are come to worship him."

Who were they? We do not know, nor does anyone. How many were there? Two or more; perhaps three, perhaps twelve, or twenty; maybe a whole congregation. They may have come together; they may have come alone, or in groups.

As to the men themselves, one thing is clear. They had prophetic insight. It was with them as it had been with saintly Simeon: the Lord had revealed to them, as it were, that they should not taste death until they had seen and worshipped the Christ. They knew the King of the Jews had been born, and they knew that a new star was destined to arise and had arisen in connection with that birth. The probability is they were themselves Jews who lived, as millions of Jews then did, in one of the nations to the East. It was the Jews, not the Gentiles, who were acquainted with the scriptures and who were waiting with anxious expectation for the coming of a King. And that King was to come to them first; he was to deliver his message to them before it went to the Gentile world, and his first witnesses were to come from his own kinsmen, from the house of Israel, not from the Gentile nations, not from the nations composed of those who knew not God and who cared nothing for the spirit of prophecy and revelation found among the Lord's people.

As to the star, there is nothing mysterious about it. The Magi, if so they are to be designated, were not reading portents in the skies nor divining the destinies of men by the movement of celestial bodies in the sidereal heavens. The new star was simply a new star of the sort we are familiar with. No doubt it exhibited an unusual brilliance, so as to attract special attention and so as to give guidance to those who walked in its light, but it was, nonetheless, a star. There was among the Jews of that day a prophecy that such a star would arise at the time of Messiah's coming, and these men who came to Jerusalem in search of that Holy Person had seen and identified the star by the spirit of inspiration. Edersheim quotes from the ancient Jewish writings relative to the prophetic knowledge then had as to such a Messianic star. One such writing says: "A star shall come out of Jacob. . . . The star shall shine forth from the East, and this is the Star of the Messiah." Another said that "a Star in the East was to appear two years before the birth of the Messiah." (Edersheim 1:211-12.)

That these traditions were true, we know from the Book of Mormon account. Samuel the Lamanite prophesied that at our Lord's birth "great lights in heaven" should appear; that during a whole night it should remain light, "And behold, there shall a new star arise, such an one as ye never have beheld; and this also shall be a sign unto you." (Hel. 14:2-6.) The fulfillment of this prophecy is stated in these simple words: "And it came to pass also that a new star did appear, according to the word."

The appearance of these wise men, whose credibility was not questioned, sent a tide of concern through all Jerusalem that grew into a flood of paranoiac proportions in the palace itself. "Herod the Great, who, after a life of splendid misery and criminal success, had now sunk into the jealous decrepitude of his savage old age, was residing in his new palace in Zion, when, half maddened as he was already by the crimes of his past career, he was thrown into a fresh paroxysm of alarm and anxiety by the visit of some Eastern Magi, bearing the strange intelligence that they had seen in the East the star of a new-born king of the Jews, and had come to worship him. Herod, a mere Idumæan usurper, a more than suspected apostate, the detested tyrant over an unwilling people, the sacrilegious plunderer of the tomb of David—Herod, a descendant of the despised Ishmael and the hated Esau, heard the tidings with a terror and indignation which it was hard to dissimulate. The grandson of one who, as was believed, had been a mere servitor in a temple at Ascalon, and who in his youth had been carried off by Edomite brigands, he well knew how worthless were his pretensions to an historic throne which he held solely by successful adventure. But his craft equalled his cruelty, and finding that all Jerusalem shared his suspense, he summoned to his palace the leading priests and theologians of the Jews—perhaps the relics of that Sanhedrin which he had long reduced to a despicable shadow—to inquire of them where the Messiah was to be born. He received the ready and confident answer that Bethlehem was the town indicated for that honour by the prophecy of Micah. Concealing, therefore, his desperate intention, he dispatched the wise men to Bethlehem, bidding them to let him know as soon as they had found the child, that he too might come and do him reverence." (Farrar, pp. 19-20.)

Guided by the light of the star, but guided even more surely by the light of that Spirit which had directed their steps from the beginning, the wise men found "the young child with Mary his mother" in the house where the Holy Family then dwelt. There is no indication whether Joseph was present, although it is presumed he was. There they worshipped the Lord Jesus, gave him "gold, and frankincense, and myrrh. And being warned of God in a dream that they should not return to Herod, they departed into their own country another way." They were still receiving revelation and guidance from on high.

And thus ends our sure knowledge of the wise men from the East. The Lord guided them to Jerusalem; they bore a witness before Herod that would not have been heeded had it come from a Simeon or an Anna, or from simple shepherds, claiming to have seen an angel and to have heard angelic choirs; and they returned to their homeland, still guided from beyond the veil and basking in the light of Him in whose presence they had knelt. We can assume they went back to their own people to testify—as Simeon and Anna had gone out among their own people—that the King of Israel, the Light to lighten the Gentiles, now dwelt upon earth. Truly, there is a divine providence attending the witness that is now beginning to go forth of the birth of a King who three short decades hence shall ask, first, Israel, and then all men, to let him reign in their hearts.

Herod Slays the Innocents
(*Matthew 2:13-18; JST, Matthew 3:13-14*)

We come now to one of the crowning acts of infamy and evil of Herod's infamous and evil reign, and yet the blood he is now to shed will scarce add to the crimson pool that stinks and smells at his palace door. "His whole career was red with the blood of murder. He had massacred priests and nobles; he had decimated the Sanhedrin; he had caused the High Priest, his brother-in-law, the young and noble Aristobulus, to be drowned in pretended sport before his eyes; he had ordered the strangulation of his favorite wife, the beautiful Asmonæan princess Mariamne, though she seems to have been the only human being whom he passionately loved. His sons Alexander, Aristobulus, and Antipater—his uncle Joseph—Antigonus and Alexander, the uncle and father of his wife—his mother-in-law Alexandra—his kinsman Cortobanus—his friends Dositheus and Gadias, were but a few of the multitudes who fell victims to his sanguinary, suspicious, and guilty terrors. His brother Pheroras and his son Archelaus barely and narrowly escaped execution by his orders. Neither the blooming youth of the prince Aristobulus nor the white hairs of the king Hyrcanus had protected them from his fawning and treacherous fury. Deaths by strangulation, deaths by burning, deaths by being cleft asunder, deaths by secret assassination, confessions forced by unutterable torture, acts of insolent and inhuman lust, mark the annals of a reign which was so cruel that, in the energetic language of the Jewish ambassadors to the Emperor Augustus, 'the survivors during his lifetime were even more miserable than the sufferers.' . . . Every dark and brutal instinct of his character seemed to acquire fresh intensity as his life drew towards its close. Haunted by the spectres of his murdered wife and murdered sons, agitated by the conflicting furies of remorse and blood, the pitiless monster, as Josephus calls him, was seized in his last days by a black and bitter ferocity, which broke out against all with whom he came in contact." (Farrar, pp. 32-33.)

Augustus Caesar himself said of Herod: "It is better to be Herod's pig than his son," which in the language spoken was a pun, and meant that since Herod was a Jew, he could not kill and eat his pig and it would therefore be safer than his son. Truly, it is as though the most fiendish and bloody occupant ever to sit on David's throne was its occupant in the very day when He came whose throne it was, and who would in due course reign in righteousness thereon.

And so, in this setting, the angel commanded Joseph: "Arise, and take the young child and his mother, and flee into Egypt, and be thou there until I bring thee word: for Herod will seek the young child to destroy him."

They fled by night. Then Herod in his hate and bitterness, acting as though Satan himself possessed his soul, went forth "and slew all the children that were in Bethlehem, and in all the coasts thereof, from two years old and under, according to the time which he had diligently inquired of the wise men."[1]

How the work of slaughter went forward we do not know. Recognizing Herod's penchant for intrigue and secrecy, and recalling that the soldiers slew Zacharias because he would not reveal the desert hiding place of the infant John, we assume that the children were ferreted out by assassins and informers, who went as Judases in disguise. Both Edersheim and Farrar conclude that the number slain did not exceed twenty. But whatever the number, the cries of weeping parents, relatives, and friends—in fulfillment of Jeremiah's prophecy concerning Rachel and her children—ascended up to the Lord, by whom they will be replayed in Herod's ears when he is brought before the bar of the Great Jehovah to give account of the deeds done in the flesh.

"Out of Egypt Have I Called My Son"

(*Matthew 2:15, 19-23; JST, Matthew 3:19, 22*)

How wondrous are the similitudes and the shadows used by the Lord to teach the great truths of his eternal plan!

How aptly he has chosen the ordinances and guided the historical happenings that testify and bear record of those things upon which the minds of men should dwell!

Lehi says to Laman: "O that thou mightest be like unto this river, continually running into the fountain of all righteousness!" and to Lemuel: "O that thou mightest be like unto this valley, firm and steadfast, and immovable in keeping the commandments of the Lord!" (1 Nephi 2:9-10)—hoping that his eldest sons, as they drink from the river and dwell in the valley, will remember the eternal truths for which they have been made a symbol.

Jacob gives his son Joseph a coat of many colors; a blood-stained coat remnant is later taken to Jacob with the false tale that its owner has been destroyed by wild beasts; and Jacob, as he handles the part of the garment that "was preserved and had not decayed," prophesies: "Even as this remnant of garment of my son hath been preserved, so shall a remnant of the seed of my son be preserved by the hand of God, and be taken unto himself, while the remainder of the seed of Joseph shall perish, even as the remnant of his garment" (Alma 46:24)—all to the end that whenever the seed of Joseph think upon the coat, upon the sale of their ancestor to the Ishmaelites, and upon the wondrous work he wrought in Egypt, they will rejoice also in the goodness of the Lord to his seed in the latter days.

Moses raises a brazen serpent on a pole before all Israel, even as the Son of God shall be lifted up, so that "as many" of those bitten by the poisonous serpents "as should look upon that serpent should live, even so as many as should look upon the Son of God with faith, having a contrite spirit, might live, even unto that life which is eternal" (Hel. 8:13-15)—all with a purpose of centering the hearts of the people upon the atoning sacrifice of the Son of God.

Abraham takes Isaac, his only begotten son, up upon Mount Moriah, there to sacrifice him at the Lord's command; and Isaac, reputed by Jewish tradition to be thirty-seven years of age at the time, submits willingly to his father's will—all as "a similitude of God and his Only Begotten Son." (Jacob 4:5.)

And now Joseph, as directed by an angel, takes Jesus into Egypt for a short season, "that it might be fulfilled which was spoken of the Lord by the prophet, saying, Out of Egypt have I called my son"—all to the end that whenever Israel remembers how God had delivered them with a mighty hand from the bondage of Egypt, they will think also that the Son of God was called out of Egypt to deliver them from the bondage of sin.

All Israel went down into Egypt to save themselves from death by famine, even as the infant Jesus was taken down into Egypt to save him from an assassin's sword. As the Lord's chosen people came out of Egypt into a land of promise to receive his law and walk in his paths, so his Beloved and Chosen came out of Egypt into that same promised land to dispense the new law and invite the chosen seed to walk in the appointed course.

In the minds of ancient Israel there was no greater miracle than their mighty deliverance from Egypt: a deliverance made possible by an outpouring of plagues upon Pharaoh's people; a deliverance assured by the saving power of a wall of water on the right hand and a wall of water on the left, as Moses led them through the Red Sea; a deliverance made effective because the Lord rained bread from heaven upon them lest they die from famine.

But now, in the minds of all men, there should be the thought of an even greater deliverance: a deliverance from the chains of sin; a deliverance from death, hell, the devil, and endless torment; a deliverance from mortality to immortality; a deliverance from spiritual death to eternal life—all through the great Deliverer, who like Israel of old overcame the Egypt of the world to dwell in the promised land.

And so Joseph, having saved Jesus by taking him into Egypt, now brings him back to Palestine that he might bring salvation to all men. Again it is at angelic direction. Herod the wicked king is dead; that much Joseph learns from the angel. He returns to Palestine, with the apparent purpose of settling in Bethlehem. Then he learns what the angel had not divulged: Archelaus reigns in Judea, "in the room of his father Herod." And so, warned again in a dream—and how providential it was that Joseph was spiritually attuned to the Infinite—"he came and dwelt in a city called Nazareth: that it might be fulfilled which was spoken by the prophets, He shall be called a Nazarene."

Jesus, the Lord of Life, has now taken upon himself mortal life. His conception, his birth, his circumcision, his flight into Egypt, his return to Nazareth—all have followed the foreordained plan. His forerunner is now growing up in the deserts of Judea. His witnesses—Zacharias, Elisabeth, Mary, Joseph, the shepherds, Simeon, Anna, the wise men from the East, and many who have believed on their words—all are letting it be known, "to all them that look for redemption," that the day of the Deliverer is at hand. It now remains but for him to mature and prepare, in Nazareth or elsewhere as his Father intends.

NOTES

1. Children are counted as being two years of age until they attain their third birthday. Apparently the decree of slaughter included all those who were two years of age and younger. Since Matthew expressly states, twice in the account, that the age of slaughter was determined by the time the wise men saw the star, which event coincided with the birth of the King, it appears the young Jesus could have been as old as two years and some months at this time. The usually accepted chronology makes him two or three months old. If his birth were placed a year or more back from December, 5 B.C., it would mean that the Holy Family stayed in Nazareth for the added period before returning to Bethlehem, which of course is a distinct possibility.

FROM INFANCY TO MANHOOD

Jesus . . . made himself of no reputation, and took upon him the form of a servant, and was made in the likeness of men: And being found in fashion as a man, he humbled himself, and became obedient unto death, even the death of the cross. (Philip. 2:5-8.)

And he received not of the fulness at first, but continued from grace to grace, until he received a fulness. (D&C 93:13.)

Jesus Grows from Infancy to Manhood

(JST, Matthew 3:24-26; Luke 2:40, 51-52.)

Jesus walked the same road from infancy to manhood that has been trod by every adult mortal, from first to last, who ever breathed the breath of life. There is only one way for a mortal to be born, to grow to maturity, to pass into the great beyond; and we are left to suppose that every law of mortal life applied to the mortal Son of the mortal Mary.

Our Lord's physical body, conceived in Mary's womb,

partook of Mary's nature; mortal genes, if you will, passed from mother to Son. His features, stature, and general appearance were passed on as much by his mortal mother as by his immortal Father. He was as much the product of the mother who bare him as were her other children. As a babe he began to grow, normally and naturally, and there was nothing supernatural about it. He learned to crawl, to walk, to run. He spoke his first word, cut his first tooth, took his first step—the same as other children do. He learned to speak; he played with toys like those of his brothers and sisters; and he played with them and with the neighbor children. He went to sleep at night and he awoke with the morning light. He took exercise, and his muscles were strong because he used them. During his ministry we see him walk long dusty miles, climb mountains, drive evil men—with force—from his Father's House.

We cannot do other than believe he was subject to disease and illness on the same basis as we all are. We know he was hungry, weary, and sorrowful; that his eyes were keen, his ears alert, and his tongue fluent. We know he seemed to his enemies as but another man, that he had to be singled out and identified with a traitor's kiss, and that he felt the stabbing pain of the Roman nails in his hands and feet the same as any mortal would. We cannot state too plainly that as a man he felt what other men feel, did what other men do, had the same appetites and passions as others have—all because he had been sent into mortality by his Father to be a mortal.

And as with our Lord's physical growth and development, so with his mental and spiritual progression. He learned to speak, to read, to write; he memorized passages of scripture, and he pondered their deep and hidden meanings. He was taught in the home by Mary, then by Joseph, as was the custom of the day. Jewish traditions and the provisions of the Torah were discussed daily in his presence. He learned the Shema, reverenced the Mezuzah, and participated in prayers, morning, noon, and night. Beginning at five or six he went to school, and certainly continued to do so until he came a son of the law at twelve years of age.

On Sabbaths and on week days he attended the synagogue, heard the prayers and sermons, and felt the spirit of the occasion. He participated in the regular worship during the feasts, particularly at Passover time. Indeed, the whole Jewish way of life was itself a teaching system, one that made the Jews a unique and peculiar people, a people set apart from all the nations of the Gentiles. It is also apparent that Jesus learned much from nature—from observing the lilies of the field, the birds of the air, and the foxes that have holes for homes.

It seems perfectly clear that our Lord grew mentally and spiritually on the same basis that he developed physically. In each case he obeyed the laws of experience and of learning, and the rewards flowed to him. The real issue of concern is not that he grew and developed and matured—all in harmony with the established order of things, as is the case with all men—but that he was so highly endowed with talents and abilities, so spiritually sensitive, so in tune with the Infinite, that his learning and wisdom soon excelled that of all his fellows. His knowledge came to him quickly and easily, because he was building—as is the case with all men—upon the foundations laid in preexistence. He brought with him from that eternal world the talents and capacities, the inclinations to conform and obey, and the ability to recognize truth that he had there acquired. Mozart had musical ability at the age of six that only a handful of men have ever gained in a whole lifetime. Jesus, when yet a child, had spiritual talents that no other man in a hundred lifetimes could obtain.

Further: In his study, and in the learning process, he was guided from on high in a way that none other has ever been. Being without sin—being clean and pure and spotless—he was entitled to the constant companionship of the Holy Spirit, the Spirit that will not dwell in an unclean tabernacle, the Spirit that, conversely, always and everlastingly dwells with the righteous. The Holy Ghost is a revelator and a sanctifier. Anyone who receives the Holy Ghost receives revelations; anyone who obtains the companionship of the Holy Spirit is sanctified. Of the Lord Jesus the scripture says: "God giveth not the Spirit by measure unto him" (John 3:34), which is to say that he enjoyed, at all times, the fulness of that light and guidance and power which comes by the power of the Holy Ghost to the faithful.

With reference to Jesus' early years—those before he went to the temple at the age of twelve to discuss the doctrines of salvation with the Rabbis—Luke tells us: "And the child grew, and waxed strong in spirit, filled with wisdom: and the grace of God was upon him." We shall glimpse the wisdom here named when we assay to determine what was in the mind of the young lad as he traveled to Jerusalem, as he participated in the Passover, and as he, remaining behind, conversed with the learned of the land. As our discussion shall then show, we cannot escape the conclusion that the knowledge then manifest in the temple had been gained gradually during the years that went before.

With reference to Jesus' latter years of preparation—those between twelve and thirty—Luke says: "And Jesus increased in wisdom and stature, and in favour with God and man." Of the developing and maturing years of our Lord's life, Matthew tells us:

> *And it came to pass that Jesus grew up with his brethren, and waxed strong, and waited upon the Lord for the time of his ministry to come. And he served under his father, and he spake not as other men, neither could he be taught; for he needed not that any man should teach him. And after many years, the hour of his ministry drew nigh.*

This wondrous exposition—"he needed not that any man should teach him"—applies to a degree to all of the prophets of all of the ages. They are taught from on high. A single glimpse beyond the veil reveals more of heaven and its laws than all the sermons of uninspired preachers combined. One flash of inspiration is worth more than all the causistry of the

Mishnah. All the traditions of the Talmud sink into darkness before one ray of revealed truth. There is no substitute for the gift of the Holy Ghost.

One day soon, the people of Nazareth, among whom he matured and by whom he was known, will ask: "Whence hath this man this wisdom?" And the answer, though not then given, will be: 'In the same way as all the prophets. He labored and studied and struggled; he treasured up words of light and truth; he pondered the scriptures—all under the influence of the Holy Spirit of God, which came to him without measure and without limit, because he was clean and pure and upright.'

The Passover Journey to Jerusalem

(*Luke 2:41-42*)

Jesus, now twelve, a son of the law, goes with Joseph and Mary from Nazareth to Jerusalem to keep the Passover. It is April of A.D. 8. His parents went every year, and Jesus may have been with them on some or all of these prior occasions. But this year is different: he is now a son of the law; his voice can legally be heard, and he is about to raise it among the doctors of the law, whose self-assumed wisdom knows no bounds, as they suppose.

This appearance in the temple is the sole New Testament record of any of our Lord's acts in the thirty years from Bethlehem to Bethabara. The Gospels are not biographies of Jesus; they are a collection of faith-promoting accounts from the Savior's ministry that, if believed, will induce receptive souls to come unto Christ and partake of his goodness.

President J. Reuben Clark, Jr.—than whom the Church has produced no greater scholar on all matters pertaining to the life of our Lord—has written a small booklet, less than one hundred pages, *Wist Ye Not That I Must Be About My Father's Business,* in which he traces Jesus' steps from Nazareth to Jerusalem and tells of the sacrifices in the temple; of the slaying of the Paschal lamb; of the eating of the Passover meal; of the Feast of Unleavened Bread; and of the doings of Jesus in the temple courts with the doctors. We have heretofore discussed the offering of sacrifices and the keeping of the feasts, and it is now our purpose, through the eyes of President Clark, to place Jesus in the sacrificial and festive setting of the Passover, in order to determine how much he then knew of his divine mission and the extent of the spiritual insight that already was his.

Joseph, Mary, Jesus, and their fellow worshippers from Nazareth begin their pilgrimage to Jerusalem. "As we think of them moving slowly down into the valley with their donkeys laden with necessary supplies," President Clark says, "picking their way among the boulders that strewed the path, we cannot escape wondering what were the thoughts of Jesus. That He was exceeding wise, the experience in the Temple shows. But was this wisdom earthborn from His studies, or did He have also a spiritual memory that brought to Him a recollection of all that had before happened, and a vision to show what was thereafter to happen along this road to Jerusalem, a road richer in incidents of God's dealings with His children, than any other road on the face of the earth? . . .

"One wonders if, as He came to Nain, He saw a vision of His future miracle of kindness there. . . .

"When He came to the neighborhood of Jezreel, did He see in vision the disastrous defeat of Josiah on the plain of Esdraelon by Pharaoh Necho, at Megiddo, a defeat so terrible and worked so deeply into the Hebrew heart, that John speaks of the great last battle as Armageddon—'the Hill of Megiddo?' Or did He see the earlier conflict in the time of the Judges, when Barak, Deborah the prophetess guiding, defeated Sisera, leading the forces of Jabin, on that same plain of Esdraelon, and did He see again the deed of Jael afterwards? And did there also come before Him the iniquities and tragic fate of Ahab and Jezebel, and the Lord's vengeance worked through Elijah against the priests of Baal, and the flight of Elijah to Carmel, the passing of the Lord before Elijah in the 'still small voice'? For Jesus was the Lord who spoke to and commanded His ancient prophets."

Then, in the course of a recitation of many other great events in Israel's history, President Clark—no longer using questions, but making affirmative declarations—says: "What must have been the feelings of the young Jesus as he looked at this present magnificence and then recalled the past, and (it seems it must be) visioned the future! . . . for we must believe there was with Him a spiritual recollection, a divine knowledge, of the past. . . . As Jesus looked at all these, . . . there must have crowded in upon his consciousness the scenes of the actual events."

As the pilgrims pass Jacob's Well, the question is asked: "As at twelve He now beheld the well, did He vision the future meeting with the woman [of Samaria] and His sermon on the living water?" And finally, as they come near to their destination, President Clark says: "We must believe that Joseph and Mary, and the youth Jesus, of the royal lineage of David, had awaiting them somewhere a joyous welcome from friends honored in the chance to give them food and shelter. One cannot escape the question whether they went on to Bethany, eastward of Jerusalem, for their lodgings, to the home where in the years to come Jesus spent so many happy hours in a home that loved and honored Him.

"Did the youth Jesus know the youth Lazarus, and the maidens, Mary and Martha?

"Or did they go to Bethlehem, where twelve years before the Messiah was born in a manger?"[1]

Jesus Participates in the Passover

In chapter 8 we considered the Mosaic sacrificial performances of Jesus' day, and in chapter 9, the Jewish feasts of that day, including the Feast of the Passover. We need not here repeat the rites and performances—intricate and detailed almost beyond belief—that appertain to their sacrifices and feasts. President Clark, of course, summarizes them in the work from which we now quote. From time to time in the course of his summary, he comes again to the concept, which seems to weigh heavily upon him, that even then, the deacon-age Jesus—scarce younger, however, than Joseph Smith, or Moroni, or Nephi, and perhaps not any younger at all than Samuel, when the Lord used these youths for his purposes—even then he was heir to the visions of eternity on a continuing basis. From various places out of long recitations about the sacrifices and the Passover, we take these words of President Clark:

"One can but ponder what the thoughts of Jesus were as He watched all this preparation for the sacrifice. Had He then the foresight of the preparation for His Last Supper, preceding His own crucifixion, such foresight as He had in the garden when He prayed: 'Father, if thou be willing, remove this cup from me: nevertheless not my will, but thine, be done.' Did He recall the day, generations before, that He gave commandment to Adam to offer sacrifice, when, under His direction, the angel told Adam the purpose of sacrifice: 'This thing is a similitude of the sacrifice of the Only Begotten of the Father, which is full of grace and truth.'...

"Again the thought thrusts itself upon us—what could have been the Youth's thoughts as He came into all this? As He crossed the Royal Bridge, did He see the morning of His arraignments; as He came in among the money changers, did He see how He cleansed the Temple of them, first at the beginning and again at the end of His public ministry?...

"Again, we can but wonder what thoughts passed through the mind of the divinely begotten Youth as He saw all this, and realized, as He must, that all of it was, in some measure, symbolic of the sacrifice He Himself was to make. His mortal eyes must have been dazzled by the pomp and splendor of it all; His mortal mind could hardly have escaped some confusion. But His spiritual eyes and intelligence must have looked through it all, and have seen to the very foundations of all its meanings—the Fall, the death, spiritual and temporal, the Gospel plan to redeem from the spiritual death, His own atonement to redeem from the temporal death. He knew the truth: 'For as in Adam all die, even so in Christ shall all be made alive.' . . .

"So Joseph and Jesus, tired after a long day of standing on the marble pavement of the Temple—it would be particularly wearisome for country folk—and laden with the lamb for the evening Paschal supper (which Joseph would carry on his shoulder) would prepare to wend their way through the city streets, and it may be out into the country, back to where Mary and the friends with whom they would later eat the Paschal meal were awaiting their return.

"So Jesus, bodily wearied by the long day during which he too may have fasted, trudged alongside Joseph as they left the Temple enclosure on their way to eat the Paschal supper. . . .

"Scholars believe that this was Jesus' first visit to the Passover; but there is nothing in the scriptural record specifically so stating, and the conclusion is apparently founded upon the fact, already alluded to, that at twelve years a boy became 'a son of the law' subject to the fasts and under obligation to attend the feasts.

"On the other hand, we have the fact that Jesus' 'parents went to Jerusalem every year at the feast of the passover,' and if they were so faithful in performing this commandment, one may well assume they would follow the other command of the Lord to instruct their children [more children than Jesus would be involved], at the Paschal supper, in the meaning of the ceremony, and this they could not do if Jesus [and the others] were not present at the Paschal feast.

"So, with all deference to the scholars, one may be bold to suggest that Jesus had several times before partaken of the Paschal meal in Jerusalem, and so, as He now went wearily to their lodgings, He looked eagerly forward to the eating of the satisfying supper, with its accompanying spiritual experiences. For nothing must be eaten after the offering of the evening sacrifice until the Passover meal.

"But here also, as at every incident in this whole ceremonial, one cannot escape pondering how much of the past was in Jesus' mind. . . .

"One cannot forego again wondering what might have passed through the mind of the youth Jesus. Did He know that this day was the pre-anniversary of the day, some twenty-one years thence, when He should be again in parts of these precincts, that He would be hurried and harried from Annas to Caiaphas, then to the illegal gathering of the elders, to the Sanhedrin, to Pilate, to Herod, and back to Pilate, and then to Calvary and crucifixion; did He now know the scorn, the envy, the malice, the murderous hate that drove forward the High Priest, the chief priests, the elders, and all the Council, and indeed the whole maddened multitude in their demand for His crucifixion; did He see Pilate wash his hands before the seething, cursing mass, and hear Pilate say: 'I am innocent of the blood of this just person,' and hear the people shout their own terrible penalty in reply: 'His blood be on us, and on our children'; did He now sense the agony of spirit in the Garden, and of His body on the cross—did He know and see all this which twenty-one years thence was to happen on this very day and, in part, in these very purlieus? Did His own mission, His own destiny, His own sacrifice, His own atonement rise before Him as a vision of Himself, the Son of God? . . .

"Still again we must wonder whether, as the shadows lengthened and the sun sank in the west, while the full moon rose from the Jordan, as Joseph and Jesus again plodded, after another long day, to their lodgings in the city, in Bethany, or it may be in Bethlehem, did the Youth see and know, on this pre-anniversary of a day yet to come, the grief He was to suffer, the spiritual and physical agony He was to endure, the death that was to come to Him, as He was sacrificed as the Lamb of God to atone for the transgression of Adam, for, by the Fall and through the Atonement man was to meet his destiny?"[2]

In their original setting, these quotations from President Clark are interlaced with long descriptions and explanations of the festive procedures followed at the Passover, and the Feast of Unleavened Bread that followed and was in large measure part of the Paschal feast itself. In more than a dozen instances President Clark asks whether or asserts positively that we must believe that the young Jesus—even then, and though but twelve years of age—had past- and prevision of those things which had been in Israel and would be in the life of Israel's Chief Citizen. This approach, so ably followed by him whom we are quoting—though necessarily speculative, as so many of the biographical pronouncements concerning Jesus must be—is an ideal pattern. We shall feel free to walk in the same path as we consider the mortal doings of the Son of an immortal Father.

Jesus, Now Twelve, Teaches in the Temple
(*Luke 2:43-50*)

After the first two days of the feast the pilgrims were free to return to their villages and cities and resume their temporal pursuits. Either then, or when the whole week was past, Joseph and Mary, with their other children and kinsmen, their friends and fellow worshippers, began the journey back to Nazareth. The spirit of rejoicing and exultation poured out through the Passover period rested upon them; there was thanksgiving in their hearts for the testimonies that were theirs, and for the goodness of Jehovah to his people Israel.

But Jesus was not with them. He, now a son of the law—with deliberation; stirred by the spirit of Passover worship of which he had been a part; recognizing in the sacrificial similitudes his own coming sacrifice; knowing his divine destiny; moved upon by the Holy Spirit, who was his monitor and guide—Jesus, unbeknown to his parents, remained behind. Thinking he was in the company, his parents did not miss him until nightfall. Then, anxious, troubled, worried for his well-being, they hastened back to the Holy City. For three long, wearisome days, days of prayer and self-reproach, they sought him—perhaps in Bethlehem and Bethany, and in all the places and among all the people known to him in Jerusalem—and then, in the one place where they should have looked first, in his Father's house, they found him. He was seated among the doctors, the Rabbis, the scribes, the learned teachers, "both hearing them, and asking them questions. And all that heard him were astonished at his understanding and answers."

Jesus was at home in his Father's House. He felt at ease; the spirit of wisdom and understanding rested mightily upon him. We suppose he had many conversations with many people within the sacred walls of the temple. He was on his own home ground, and in these very courts he would yet make some of the most profound and soul-saving declarations ever to fall from mortal lips. And it was now, as it would be then, he was master of the situation.

We wonder what subjects he talked about. The Paschal celebration was on everyone's minds. Did he speak of the Paschal lambs slain in similitude of the sacrifice of the Lamb of God who should take away the sins of the world? Surely Mary, by now, had told him of his birth and of the miracles that attended. Did he ask the wise men of Israel about the Son, born of a virgin, who should reign forever on the throne of David? Surely he felt the divine necessity to begin to let people know of his divine mission. Did he then inquire as to when the Messiah should come and how he should be known?

Truth is sent forth line upon line, precept upon precept, here a little and there a little. We cannot doubt that the youthful Jesus—as Simeon and Anna and the wise men of the East, and all the others, had already done—was himself now beginning to teach and to testify. His formal and legal ministry cannot begin for another eighteen years. For the time being he is to go back to Nazareth and be subject to Joseph and Mary. He is to mature and grow in the Spirit and find favor with God and man. He is to partake of the normal life of Jewish men, doing what they did, enjoying the familial associations that were part of their culture, and gaining all the experiences he would need for the arduous hours of his formal ministry.

We do not even know that he lived all those intervening years in Nazareth; he was surely not subject to Joseph and Mary, eating at their table and sleeping in their house, during his more mature years. Perhaps he dwelt in Bethany, in the city of Mary and Martha and Lazarus, for a time, or in Bethlehem where he first came into this life.

We cannot believe that he was silent all those years. He spoke at twelve; was his tongue then tied until he was thirty? If he felt the need to be about his Father's business as soon as he became a son of the law, would he feel that urgency any less as he continued to mature and grow in wisdom and stature and learn even more of his Father's will?

But back to the temple. Finding him among the learned, teaching and being taught, his parents, strangely, were amazed. Had they forgotten the miracle of his birth, and had they not observed the talents and abilities that so precociously were his? Mary, not Joseph, gently chided: "Son, why hast thou thus dealt with us? behold, thy father and I have sought thee sorrowing." In the family circle, subject to the family discipline of the day, Joseph was deemed to be the father of all Mary's children, Jesus included. Mary here so says; others at a later time will call him, derogatorily, the carpenter's son. There is a sweet family tenderness here in Mary's reference to Joseph as the father of Jesus.

Jesus, however, is now ministering in the temple as his real Father's Son, not as a member of Joseph's household. "How is it that ye sought me?" he asks. "Wist ye not that I must be about my Father's business?" His Father's business is to bring to pass the immortality and eternal life of man, both of which will come to pass through the atoning sacrifice that Jesus will make as the climax of his ministry. But that is twenty-one years away; for now he must return to Nazareth and be subject to those into whose custody he has been placed. Luke says these custodians "understood not the saying which he spake unto them," meaning that even they, though they knew the miracle of his birth and had full knowledge of his true Father, found it difficult to comprehend the greatness of his wisdom and his rapid growth toward the full stature of that man-God status that was his. He was going from grace to grace, from one level of intelligence to another, from a lesser to a higher degree. Soon he would inherit all power in heaven and on earth. His growth, even at twelve, had attained such proportions that it is little wonder Joseph and Mary were amazed and could not comprehend the full significance of his sayings.

NOTES

1. J. Reuben Clark, *Wist Ye Not That I Must Be About My Father's Business?* (Salt Lake City: Relief Society Magazine, n.d.), pp. 9-17.

2. Ibid., pp. 23-70 *passim.*

Chapter 23

JOHN PREPARES THE WAY

Behold, I will send my messenger, and
he shall prepare the way before me.
(Mal. 3:1.)

Prepare ye the way of the Lord, . . . And
the glory of the Lord shall be revealed.
(Isa. 40:3, 5.)

John Receives the Word of God

(Luke 3:1-2)

As the dawn comes before the day, so John comes before Jesus. The long night of rituals and rites; of performances; of sacrifices and blood; of bleating sheep cringing near an altar, awaiting the sacrificial knife; of a law that decrees an eye for an eye and a tooth for a tooth—the long night of Mosaic formalisms is drawing to its close.

Faint rays of morning light break forth in the eastern sky. John is coming from the deserts of Hebron. A voice is crying: 'Prepare ye the way; make His paths straight; the time is at hand; soon He, whose the kingdom is, shall walk among us. I, John, am his Elias.' Soon the sun in its splendor shall rise over the mountains, and the valleys of life shall be ablaze with that Light which is the glory of Israel, and which shall also lighten the Gentiles.

It is summer time. We are in Judea. The year is A.D. 26. In six months Jesus will begin his ministry, but for now the day belongs to John. All eyes focus on him; for a brief period the kingdom will rest with him alone. He will prepare the way. Six months older than Jesus, John is now about thirty years of age. He will preach and teach and cry repentance for half a year, and then in January, A.D. 27, he will baptize the Son of God in the murky waters of a river that flows from the Sea of Galilee to the Sea of Death and Desolation.

After so doing, he will continue to teach. A month later we shall hear him say he is not the Christ, and still later that Jesus is the Lamb of God. Indeed, for nearly a year after, until November or December of A.D. 27, his voice will still be heard, inviting all who will to follow his cousin who now, in the full blaze of his Messiahship, is everywhere teaching and working miracles. Then he will be imprisoned by Antipas, the evil Herod who had married his brother Philip's wife, and been condemned therefor by the son of Zacharias. Seven or eight months later, in the summer of A.D. 28, John, still in Herod's prison, will send messengers to Jesus to ask, "Art thou he that should come? or look we for another?" (Luke 7:20)—having in mind that those messengers will be converted and thereafter follow Him whose shoe's latchet the Baptist felt unworthy to unloose.

Finally, after languishing for a full year in prison, and in the winter of A.D. 29, we shall see the headsman's ax sever the Baptist's head so that it can be carried on a charger and given to an evil woman, while his spirit goes to the Paradise of God and his innocent blood joins the innocent blood of all the martyrs, to unite with theirs in crying unto the Lord until he avenges that blood on earth.

John came in a day of spiritual darkness and apostasy. The world was ruled by Rome, and Rome was the world. Everything that was carnal, sensual, and devilish was enshrined—it is not too strong a statement to say worshipped—as part of the imperial way of life. Adultery, incest, abortion, all were a way of life among the Romans. There were no accepted standards of morality and decency, and little or no belief in the immortality of the soul. All the gods of all the nations of the empire were reverenced and worshipped in the capital city, and the emperor and others were deified and adored as gods. Sacrifices were offered on the great altar in Herod's Temple to the emperor and for the well-being of the empire. The Jews themselves—in general and as a people—no longer walked in the light that once was theirs. If ever there was a need for a voice to cry out in the wilderness of wickedness, calling upon all men to repent and turn to the Lord, this was the day. If ever there was a voice—prepared in preexistence, schooled in the home of faithful Levites, and tested and made ready in the deserts of Judea—that was prepared to proclaim the word, to mark the way, to say to all, 'This is the path, come and walk therein; here is the Messiah, follow him,' that voice was John's.

Luke identifies the time and describes the day by the simple expedient of naming those who held temporal and spiritual rule over the people:

Tiberius Caesar, an evil and wicked wretch who walked in all the ways of the Caesars who went before and the Caesars who came after, and who ruled with all the despotism of Augustus and reveled in all the vices of Caligula, sat securely on the throne of the world. Rome ruled the world, and the world was wickedness.

Pontius Pilate, an evil Roman underling who chose, knowingly, to send an Innocent Man to the cross, lest Tiberius hear the rumor that Jesus claimed to be the King of the Jews, was governor of Judea. The scepter, now departed from Judah, left the chosen people in Gentile hands, and the Gentile hands strangled the Jewish religion.

Herod Antipas, an evil ruler whose lusts and incestuous life fitted the pattern of the Herods, and who chose to slay the innocent forerunner of the Lord rather than be embarrassed before his court, was Tetrarch of Galilee, and he, ruling in lust and evil, invited a satanic gloom of spiritual darkness to cover his kingdom.

Philip the tetrarch, though a milder and more humane ruler than Antipas, yet carried in his veins the blood of Herod the Idumean, and was a symbol of the worldliness that lay upon Jewish Israel. Though less evil than his brother, his rule was far from that which is inspired from above.

Luke speaks also of "Annas and Caiaphas being the high priests," which is itself an announcement of the spiritual degeneracy of the nation. In olden times high priests were called of God; not so in these days. Annas had been appointed by Quirinius, and we may suppose he had such influence with the Lord as Quirinius was able to confer, which was not enough, however, to keep him from being deposed by Valerius Gratus (Pilate's predecessor), who then named Caiaphas to the presiding position. He was deposed in due course by Vitellius in A.D. 37. Caiaphas was the son-in-law of Annas, and both of them exercised power and influence with the people.

What concerns us above all else as to the coming of John, however, is that he came with power and authority. He first received his errand from the Lord. His was no ordinary message, and he was no unauthorized witness. He was called of God and sent by him, and he represented Deity in the words that he spoke and the baptisms he performed. He was a legal administrator whose words and acts were binding on earth and in heaven, and his hearers were bound, at the peril of their salvation, to believe his words and heed his counsels.

Luke says: "The word of God came unto John the son of Zacharias in the wilderness." Later John is to say: "He that sent me to baptize with water, the same said unto me," such and such things. (John 1:33.) Who sent him we do not know. We do know that "he was baptized while he was yet in his childhood [meaning, when he was eight years of age], and was ordained by the angel of God at the time he was eight days old unto this power [note it well, not to the Aaronic Priesthood, but] to overthrow the kingdom of the Jews, and to make straight the way of the Lord before the face of his people, to prepare them for the coming of the Lord, in whose hand is given all power." (D&C 84:24.) We do not know when he received the Aaronic Priesthood, but obviously it came to him after his baptism, at whatever age was proper, and before he was sent by one whom he does not name to preach and baptize with water.

We know John was in the desert, for a period of trial and testing and training—perhaps not much different from Jesus' forty days of fasting and testing in the wilderness, as he began his ministry—but we do not know much else about his early life. The New Testament is not a biography of Jesus, let alone of John. The idea that our Lord's forerunner was a Nazarite for life, had never cut his hair or married, and that he lived always in the deserts is speculation that cannot be true.

We can think of no good reason why the Lord would send one of his servants off into the deserts for thirty years to prepare him for the ministry. Men are prepared to serve their fellowmen by associating with them and by learning of their foibles and idiosyncracies and how they will react to spoken counsel and proffered help.

It is true John did not drink wine or strong drink; that he went into the desert for a testing period before his ministry; that while there he ate locusts and wild honey; and that he came forth among the people wearing what was in their minds the prophetic garb, raiment woven from camel's hair, held in place by a leather girdle. We suppose this mode of dress was simply to alert the people to his prophetic status, for the period of his ministry was to be short, and he needed to attract as much attention as possible. That he was married, had children, and lived as normal a life as his ministerial assignments permitted, we cannot doubt.

John Preaches Repentance and Baptizes

(*Matthew 3:1-6; JST, Matthew 3:29, 32; Mark 1:1-6; JST, Mark 1:4; Luke 3:3-6*)

And so John came as come he must. He came before the Lord, "in the spirit and power of Elias," as Gabriel promised, "to make ready a people prepared for the Lord." (Luke 1:17.) His coming, as Mark has it, was "the beginning of the gospel of Jesus Christ, the Son of God"—meaning that John proclaimed the good news about Christ and salvation; that he laid the foundation and started the work; that he called the first group of true believers; and that, in reality, he set up the kingdom of God—meaning the Church of Jesus Christ—again on earth.[1] John brought the first converts into The Church of Jesus Christ of the Meridian of Time. He laid the foundations upon which the Lord Jesus and the apostles built. He was the messenger, promised by Malachi, who should go before the Lord's face to prepare the way before him. His was the voice, promised by Isaiah, that should say, "Prepare ye the way of the Lord, make his paths straight."

What does a forerunner or an Elias do to prepare a people for Him who shall come after? He calls people to repentance and baptizes them in water "for the remission of sins," which freedom from sin is actually obtained when the repentant person receives the baptism of fire and of the Holy Ghost. This was the mission of John. He acted in the power and authority of the Aaronic Priesthood.[2] A forerunner preaches "the preparatory gospel"; the One who comes after preaches the fulness of the gospel. "The preparatory gospel . . . is the gospel of repentance and of baptism, and the remission of sins." (D&C 84:26-27.) This is the gospel administered by the law of Moses; it was as far as John's authority went.

No one is ever prepared for the Lord while he remains in his sins. The Lord does not save people in their sins, but from their sins. The plan of salvation is designed to enable men to free themselves from sin so they can, as clean and spotless beings, enter the presence of Him who is without sin. No one is ever prepared for the Lord until he confesses and forsakes his sins, until he repents, until he is baptized for the remission of sins. And the fact that John was to prepare "a people" for the Lord means that a people—composed of a host of individuals—had to set their houses in order, be baptized by him, and await patiently the coming of Him who would give them the Holy Ghost. When they received the baptism of the Holy Ghost, sin and evil would be burned out of their souls as though by fire, and being thus clean, they would be fit candidates to be with the Lord—they would be prepared for the Lord.

John, Preaching in Power, Prepares a People

(*Luke 3:7-14; JST, Luke 3:12-14, 17-20; Matthew 3:7-10; JST, Matthew 3:35-37*)

No voice like John's had been heard in Israel since the days of the prophets. Isaiah and Lehi had thundered forth such damning imprecations and spoken with such divine finality. But who for centuries had come forth, as the voice of one crying in the wilderness of wickedness, with such a call for repentance as came from the tongue of John? Here at last was a man who spoke with authority. He came in the Lord's name, speaking as he was moved upon by the Holy Ghost. The Spirit gave him utterance. So persuasive were his words, so compelling his logic, so sound his doctrine, that all Israel flocked together to hear the message. They came from Jerusalem; they assembled from all Judea; they gathered from all the regions round about Jordan. Here was a man, a voice, a message—spoken in the Spirit and with power—that sank into the hearts of men with convincing and converting power. Great hosts confessed their sins and were baptized in Jordan.

Among his hearers, among those who fell under the spell of his voice, were "many of the Pharisees and Sadducees."

Even they, feeling the great swell of emotion that accompanied his words, and being swept along by a great tide of popular approval, came to be baptized. But an inspired priest does not baptize an unrepentant person. Baptism is of no avail without repentance, and contrition, and confession, and a compelling determination to walk ever after in a newness of life.

"O generation of vipers, who hath warned you to flee from the wrath to come?" demanded the voice that read the hearts of men and knew of the damning influence of these leaders of the people. His words were scarcely less of a rebuke than would be those of another voice in another day, which would say to the same hypocrites: "Ye serpents, ye generation of vipers, how can ye escape the damnation of hell?" (Matt. 23:33.) But even for these there was this hope: "Repent, therefore, and bring forth fruits meet for repentance," John commanded. 'Repent first, be baptized second, and then will you be fit candidates to receive the Spirit from him who cometh after me.'

And further: 'Think not that ye are above the law of repentance; that ye keep the law of Moses and need not change your lives; that ye will be saved by the rituals and performances to which you have bound yourselves.' "Think not to say within yourselves, We are the children of Abraham, and we only have power to bring seed unto our father Abraham." Think not to say, "We have kept the commandments of God, and none can inherit the promises but the children of Abraham; for I say unto you, That God is able of these stones to raise up children unto Abraham." Know this: God is able "of these stony Gentiles—these dogs—to raise up children unto Abraham." (*Teachings*, p. 319.)

Having invited these self-sufficient, self-righteous, self-saving souls to repent, the incisive and blunt-speaking John then gave them this warning: 'Even if you do not repent and save yourselves, know this: The ax is laid at the root of the trees—the tree of formalism and Mosaic performances; the tree that saves only the seed of Abraham; the tree of dead and evil works; all the trees that cumber the vineyard of the Lord—and every tree which bringeth not forth good fruit is hewn down, and cast into the fire.'

Hearing John's denunciation of their self-appointed leaders, perhaps fearing lest they too might be hewn down and cast into the fire, those who were repentant and had been baptized asked: "What shall we do then?" 'What course is expected of us? How shall we conduct our affairs, lest these evils come upon us also?'

He answers: 'Bear one another's burdens; help the poor; feed the hungry; clothe the naked; live as becometh saints—this is all part of your baptismal covenant. He that hath two coats, let him impart to him that hath none, and he that hath meat, let him do likewise.' And to the soldiers, many of whom must have been the Gentile troops garrisoned among them, he counseled: 'Your military rank does not give you the right to be cruel or inhuman to your fellowmen. Do violence to no man, neither accuse any falsely; and be content with your wages.'

Truly, here was a prophet again in Israel.

John Announces the Coming of Christ

(*Luke 3:15-18; JST, Luke 3:4-11; Matthew 3:11-12; JST, Matthew 3:34, 38-40; Mark 1:7-8; JST, Mark 1:6*)

With such a man and such a message, at this time of Messianic expectancy, it comes as no surprise to read in Luke that "all men mused in their hearts of John, whether he were the Christ, or not." What greater words would one expect from the lips of the Deliverer of Israel than were here being spoken by this John? What more could any man do to set in order the affairs of the earthly kingdom than was being done by this prophet-garbed preacher from the wilderness of Judea? Was he, indeed, the Promised Messiah?

And yet he had said he was a forerunner, an Elias, a voice, one coming before to prepare the way for one greater.

He must say it again, and again and again and again. He was not the Messiah, but he was his kin, and he would become his friend. And as of now, he would do the assigned work: he would prepare the way; cost what it might in time and toil and sacrifice, he would prepare the way. No man must mistake him for the Messiah.

But he must be accepted for what he was; otherwise men would not accept the one of whom he came to testify. "Why is it that ye receive not the preaching of him whom God hath sent?" he asked. "If ye receive not this in your hearts, ye receive not me; and if ye receive not me, ye receive not him of whom I am sent to bear record; and for your sins ye have no cloak."

"I indeed baptize you with water; but one mightier than I cometh, the latchet of whose shoes I am not worthy to unloose." "He shall not only baptize you with water, but with fire, and the Holy Ghost." 'I am not the Messiah, for the Messiah shall baptize with fire; he it is who shall cleanse and perfect the lives of men; he shall sanctify their souls and prepare them for eternal life. He is Christ, the great Judge.' "He shall reap the earth and harvest the ripened sheaves. With the winnowing fan of judgment, he shall separate the wicked chaff from the righteous wheat, gathering the wheat into the celestial garner and burning the chaff in the depths of hell; his threshing-floor is the whole earth." (*Commentary* 1:121.)

John's voice was one of doctrine and of testimony. He proclaimed the divine Sonship of the Coming One, testified that He was to be the Holy Messiah, and invited all men to come unto Him and be saved. And these are the words which he spake:

> *The voice of one crying in the wilderness, Prepare ye the way of the Lord, and make his paths straight.*
>
> *For behold, and lo, he shall come, as it is written in the book of the prophets, to take away the sins of the world, and to bring salvation unto the heathen nations, to gather*

together those who are lost, who are of the sheepfold of Israel;

Yea, even the dispersed and afflicted; and also to prepare the way, and make possible the preaching of the gospel unto the Gentiles;

And to be a light unto all who sit in darkness, unto the uttermost parts of the earth; to bring to pass the resurrection from the dead, and to ascend up on high, to dwell on the right hand of the Father, Until the fulness of time, and the law and the testimony shall be sealed, and the keys of the kingdom shall be delivered up again unto the Father;

To administer justice unto all; to come down in judgment upon all, and to convince all the ungodly of their ungodly deeds, which they have committed; and all this in the day that he shall come;

For it is a day of power; yea, every valley shall be filled, and every mountain and hill shall be brought low; the crooked shall be made straight, and the rough ways made smooth;

And all flesh shall see the salvation of God.

These words, inserted in the ancient record by the Prophet Joseph Smith as the spirit of revelation rested upon him, contain such a wondrous outpouring of light and understanding that they give an entirely new perspective as to how and in what manner the gospel was preached in the meridian of time. John was not, as our King James Version leaves us to assume, taking Isaiah's Messianic utterances relative to the Second Coming and applying them to the First Coming. Rather, he gave an inspired summary of the mission and ministry and work of the Promised Messiah as it pertained to both of his comings and as it affected all men of all nations. The Deliverer will come, not as a Temporal King, but to atone for the sins of the world, to bring salvation to Jew and Gentile alike, to gather Israel, to make possible the preaching of the gospel to the Gentiles, to bring to pass the resurrection, to return in glory to his Father, and to reign with almighty power. Then in the fulness of time he shall come again to administer justice and judgment unto all and to condemn the ungodly for all their evil deeds; and this shall be the day when every valley shall be exalted and every mountain shall be made low.

"And many other things in his exhortation preached he unto the people," for he was indeed a prophet—yea, more than a prophet—and He who followed after, according to the promises, was the Messiah, the very Christ, the One in whom all fulness and perfection dwells. Blessed be John who prepared the way, and blessed be He who came to fulfill all things spoken of him by his forerunner.

NOTES

1. This matter of whether John set up the kingdom and started the Church is so fundamental, so basic to an understanding of how the Lord and his servants operated in the meridian of time, and so little known and understood in the world, that we take occasion here to quote the following extracts from a sermon of the Prophet Joseph Smith: "Some say the kingdom of God was not set up on the earth until the day of Pentecost, and that John did not preach the baptism of repentance for the remission of sins. But I say, in the name of the Lord, that the kingdom of God was set up on the earth from the days of Adam to the present time, whenever there has been a righteous man on earth unto whom God revealed His word and gave power and authority to administer in His name. And where there is a priest of God—a minister who has power and authority from God to administer in the ordinances of the gospel and officiate in the priesthood of God—there is the kingdom of God. . . .

"Where did the kingdom of God begin? Where there is no kingdom of God there is no salvation. What constitutes the kingdom of God? Where there is a prophet, a priest, or a righteous man unto whom God gives His oracles, there is the kingdom of God; and where the oracles of God are not, there the kingdom of God is not. . . .

"As touching the Gospel and baptism that John preached, I would say that John came preaching the Gospel for the remission of sins; he had his authority from God, and the oracles of God were with him, and the kingdom of God for a season seemed to rest with John alone. . . .

"But, says one, the kingdom of God could not be set up in the days of John, for John said the kingdom was at hand. But I would ask if it could be any nearer to them than to be in the hands of John. The people need not wait for the days of Pentecost to find the kingdom of God, for John had it with him, and he came forth from the wilderness crying out, 'Repent ye, for the kingdom of heaven is nigh at hand,' as much as to say, 'Out here I have got the kingdom of God, and you can get it, and I am coming after you; and if you don't receive it, you will be damned;' and the scriptures represent that all Jerusalem went out unto John's baptism. There was a legal administrator, and those that were baptized were subjects for a king; and also the laws and oracles of God were there; therefore the kingdom of God was there; for no man could have better authority to administer than John; and our Savior submitted to that authority Himself, by being baptized by John; therefore the kingdom of God was set up on the earth, even in the days of John. . . .

"It is evident that the kingdom of God was on the earth, and John prepared subjects for the kingdom, by preaching the Gospel to them and baptizing them, and he prepared the way before the Savior, or came as a forerunner, and prepared subjects for the preaching of

Christ; and Christ preached through Jerusalem on the same ground where John had preached; and when the apostles were raised up, they worked in Jerusalem." (*Teachings,* pp. 271-75.)

2. "I went into the woods to inquire of the Lord, by prayer, His will concerning me," the Prophet Joseph Smith said, "and I saw an angel, and he laid his hands upon my head, and ordained me to a Priest after the order of Aaron, and to hold the keys of this Priesthood, which office was to preach repentance and baptism for the remission of sins, and also to baptize. But I was informed that this office did not extend to the laying on of hands for the giving of the Holy Ghost; that that office was a greater work, and was to be given afterward; but that my ordination was a preparatory work, or a going before, which was the spirit of Elias; for the spirit of Elias was a going before to prepare the way for the greater, which was the case with John the Baptist. He came crying through the wilderness, 'Prepare ye the way of the Lord, make his paths straight.' And they were informed, if they could receive it, it was the spirit of Elias; and John was very particular to tell the people, he was not that Light, but was sent to bear witness of that Light.

"He told the people that his mission was to preach repentance and baptize with water; but it was He that should come after him that should baptize with fire and the Holy Ghost." (*Teachings,* p. 335.)

Chapter 24

JOHN BAPTIZES JESUS

And I looked and beheld the Redeemer
of the world; . . . and I also beheld
the prophet who should prepare
the way before him. And the Lamb of God
went forth and was baptized of him;
and after he was baptized, I beheld the
heavens open, and the Holy Ghost
come down out of heaven and
abide upon him in the form of a dove.
(1 Ne. 11:27.)

Baptism Anciently

We cannot understand "the baptism of John"—why multitudes flocked to him to receive the sacred ordinance; why even the Lord Jesus insisted on immersion at his hands—unless we know how the law of baptism operated both anciently and among the Jews in his day.

It is commonly believed, as we suppose, that baptism originated with John; that fired with heavenly zeal, he cried repentance, and baptized—by immersion, sprinkling, pouring, or what have you—for the remission of sins; that such was a new beginning, a new ordinance, a new rite that was then accepted by the so-called first Christians, and by them made a part of the new dispensation. Such a concept has little comparison to the truth. There was a man called John; he did preach with heavenly zeal, and he did baptize repentant persons. But he did not originate the ordinance of baptism; it neither began nor ended with the son of Zacharias.

Baptism is an eternal ordinance, an everlasting rite, a continuing requirement in God's kingdom, and it was practiced by the Jews before John ever came on the scene to minister for a short season among men. He was no more the originator of baptism than he was of faith or repentance or sacrifice or any of the other laws in which he believed or the ordinances in which he participated. It is true that the Jews today no longer perform baptisms, just as they have ceased their sacrificial rites, but it was not so anciently, and it had not been so from the beginning.

Baptism and sacrifice both began with Adam. We have seen how the angelic ministrant revealed to him that his sacrificial performances were in "similitude of the sacrifice of the Only Begotten of the Father." (Moses 5:7.) We must also remember that God, "by his own voice," taught Adam about faith, repentance, baptism, and the gift of the Holy Ghost, and "that Adam cried unto the Lord, and he was caught away by the Spirit of the Lord, and was carried down into the water, and was laid under the water, and was brought forth out of the water. And thus he was baptized, and the Spirit of God descended upon him, and thus he was born of the Spirit, and became quickened in the inner man. And he heard a voice out of heaven, saying: Thou art baptized with fire, and with the Holy Ghost." (Moses 6:51-66.)

From that day onward baptism was the great initiatory ordinance into the earthly kingdom. All of the prophets of all of the ages both baptized others and were themselves baptized. Isaiah tells of the whole "house of Jacob" coming forth "out of the waters of Judah, or out of the waters of baptism." (1 Ne. 20:1.) Paul says "all our fathers" were "baptized unto Moses." They "did all eat the same spiritual meat," he says, "and did all drink the same spiritual drink: for they drank of that spiritual Rock that followed them: and that Rock was Christ." (1 Cor. 10:1-4.) From the time Lehi left Jerusalem until the resurrected Lord ministered among his seed six hundred years later, we find the whole Nephite people performing baptisms for faithful and repentant souls.

Whenever the Lord's people on either continent enjoyed the fulness of the everlasting gospel, this means that they had faith in Christ, repented of their sins, were baptized for the remission of sins, and had the gift of the Holy Ghost. Whenever they were restricted to the lesser law, the law of Moses, and thus had only the preparatory gospel, they still exercised faith, sought repentance, and subjected themselves to baptism in water, but were unable to obtain the right to the constant companionship of the Holy Spirit.

Baptism Among the Jews in John's Day

Baptism was an established way of life among faithful Jews in John's day. We do not suppose that all of the Jews of that day were baptized, for apostasy was rife and rebellion was common. But among the chosen seed there certainly were many faithful people who were baptized on the same basis as they offered sacrifices. "The Levitical Priesthood is forever hereditary—fixed on the head of Aaron and his sons forever, and was in active operation down to Zacharias the father of John." (*Teachings,* p. 319.) This is the priesthood that has power to baptize in water. "Zacharias was a priest of God, and officiating in the Temple, and John was a priest after his father, and held the keys of the Aaronic Priesthood, and was called of God to preach the Gospel of the kingdom of God." (*Teachings,* p. 273.) John himself "was baptized while he was yet in his childhood." (D&C 84:28.) It goes without saying that Zacharias and his fellow priests were baptized. We cannot do other than believe that Elisabeth, Mary, Joseph, Simeon, Anna, the shepherds who heard the heavenly choirs, and hosts of others who waited patiently for the Consolation of Israel had also partaken of this sacred ordinance, all before the ministry of John ever began.

Edersheim says that the baptismal ordinance administered by John was not new. "Hitherto the Law had it," he says, "that those who had contracted Levitical defilement were to immerse before offering sacrifice. Again, it was prescribed that such Gentiles as became 'proselytes of righteousness,' or 'proselytes of the Covenant,' were to be admitted to full participation in the privileges of Israel by the threefold rites of circumcision, baptism, and sacrifice—the immersion being, as it were, the acknowledgment and symbolic removal of moral defilement, corresponding to that of Levitical uncleanness." Our knowledge of the real purpose of baptism lets us know that it was not simply to remove Levitical defilement, as such had been defined by the Rabbis, but was in fact for the remission of sins. What the Edersheim statement does is establish the fact that baptism was common among the people before the ministry of John. In this connection, Edersheim quotes this significant passage from the Talmud: "A man who is guilty of sin, and makes confession, and does not turn from it, to whom is he like? To a man who has in his hand a defiling reptile, who, even if he immerses in all the waters of the world, his baptism avails him nothing; but let him cast it from his hand, and if he immerses in only forty seah of water, immediately his baptism avails him." (Edersheim 1:273.) That is to say: Baptism without repentance is of no avail. Even those who wrote the Talmud knew that.

As to how baptisms were performed for proselytes, Edersheim says: "The person to be baptized, having cut his hair and nails, undressed completely, made fresh profession of his faith before what were designated 'the fathers of the baptism,' and then immersed completely, so that every part of the body was touched by the water. The rite would, of course, be accompanied by exhortations and benedictions. . . .

"It was indeed a great thing when . . . a stranger sought shelter under the wings of the Shekhinah, and the change of condition which he underwent was regarded as complete. . . . As he stepped out of these waters he was considered as 'born anew'—in the language of the Rabbis, as if he were 'a little child just born.' . . . The past, with all that had belonged to it, was past, and he was a new man—the old, with its defilements, was buried in the waters of baptism." (Edersheim 2:745-46.)

The issue with reference to baptisms performed in the day of John was not whether people should be baptized—no one was questioning that; people everywhere had been and were being immersed in water by priestly administrators for the remission of sins. The issue was: Is John the one sent of God to baptize and thereby to prepare a people for the Promised Messiah. Any baptisms performed by the priests of Aaron, according to the patterns of the past, were ordinances of the old dispensation. And a new day was now dawning, a forerunner of the future was baptizing, an Elias of the Messias was immersing people in water—and the issue was, in Jesus' words: "The baptism of John, whence was it? from heaven, or of men?"

Jesus answered his own question by saying: "John came unto you in the way of righteousness." (Matt. 21:25-32.) And of John, Luke records: "And all the people that heard him, and the publicans, justified God, being baptized with the baptism of John. But the Pharisees and lawyers rejected the counsel of God against themselves, being not baptized of him." (Luke 7:29-30.)

John came as the last legal administrator of the old dispensation; he overthrew the kingdom of the Jews, and he ushered in a new day. He was, as pertaining to the new kingdom, "the only legal administrator in the affairs of the kingdom there was then on the earth, and holding the keys of power. The Jews had to obey his instructions or be damned by their own law." (*Teachings,* p. 276.) It was now his baptism—"the baptism of John"—that counted, not any other. As it was among the Nephites when the Lord took a new dispensation to them, the Jews had to be baptized over again. John was the new head, for the moment, of the earthly kingdom; they must turn to him. He was now baptizing, and it was his baptism that was binding on earth and in heaven.[1]

The Baptism at Bethabara

(*Matthew 3:13-17; JST, Matthew 3:42-46; Luke 3:21-23a; JST, Luke 3:28; Mark 1:9-11; JST, Mark 1:9*)

All Christendom believes, as we suppose, that Jesus was baptized by John with water taken from Jordan. How and why and in what manner the ordinance was performed is a matter of the widest speculation, and, in many quarters, of almost total misunderstanding. In a great cathedral in Curitiba, Brazil, for instance, there is a stained-glass window depicting the baptism by John of the Lord Jesus. John is standing on dry ground on Jordan's bank; Jesus is standing ankle deep in the water itself; and John is pouring a handful of water from a cup onto the divine head.[2] How much nearer the truth it would be if the picture had been chosen from the following:

Comes now John to Jordan on the crowning day of his life, the day when he, called and appointed and foreordained so to do, shall baptize the Son of God. Jesus is nearing the close of his long journey from Nazareth to Bethabara, to the spot on Jordan where John is preaching and baptizing. It is a clear, calm day; none of the storm clouds that will one day overshadow the Divine Presence have made their appearance; this is a day of peace and divine acceptance, a day when even the Father's voice will be heard by mortal man. Multitudes throng the banks of the Jordan. John preaches, as was his wont; he cries repentance, and the Spirit of the Lord leads confessing and contrite souls to ask for baptism. John stands waist deep in the water, in a cove, where the current is quiet and the water calm. The new converts make their way to him, and one by one he immerses them in the water. He speaks to each soul a few words signifying his authority and the sacred nature of the holy ordinance here performed. The Lord is pleased with the foundations of the kingdom that are being laid.

Other activities occupy their time for a season. John, again on the bank, picks up the train of thought found in his earlier sermons. There are questions and answers. Believers feel fed by the Spirit; their souls are enlarged; it is good for them to be there. Unbelievers feel hate and resentment in their hearts, and animosity and bitterness show forth from their countenances. The crowd is smaller than it was—some have departed for their homes—but a faithful few still hang on every word. There is a momentary lull in the continuing expressions of doctrine and of testimony. One of dignity and majesty appears on the bank; he has come unexpected and unheralded. He steps forth from the throng. John stands still, and a wave of recognition floods his soul. It is He; this is the day; the hour has arrived. All eyes are on the two inspired men. The Holy One speaks: 'I am he of whom thou hast borne witness. I have come to be baptized.'

John is overwhelmed, subdued. In reverential awe he feels unworthy of the honor to baptize such a one. "I have need to be baptized of thee, and comest thou to me?" he says, not quite having prepared himself for the privilege and the vision that are about to be.

Jesus answers: "Suffer me to be baptized of thee, for thus it becometh us to fulfil all righteousness."

Then John goes down into the water; Jesus follows. John, probably raising his right arm to the square, speaks some such words as these:

> *'Jesus, thou Son of the Most High God: Having authority given me by him who called me and sent me and said unto me, Thou shalt baptize the Holy Messiah, even the Lamb of God, who taketh away the sins of the world, I now baptize thee in the name of the Father, and of the Son, and of the Holy Ghost. Amen.'*[3]

Then carefully, reverentially, he places Jesus under the water, and brings him forth out of the water—the immersion in the murky waters of Jordan is complete—and, lo, John sees the heavens open and the Holy Ghost descend in bodily form, in serenity and peace, like a dove.[4] The sign of the dove is given, and the voice of the Father—graciously pleased that his Son has been baptized—speaks, and is heard by John's spiritually attuned ears and by the ears of all present who are in tune. It says:

"This is my beloved Son, in whom I am well pleased. Hear ye him."

"Hear ye him!" The Father testifies of the Son; he introduces him to the world; and he commands: *"Hear ye him!"*

Why Jesus Was Baptized

He who was holy—who did no sin, in whose mouth was no guile, whose every thought and word and deed was perfect—even he came to John to be baptized. Why? Not for the remission of sins, for he had none; not to court popularity with the people who revered John, for his message was to stand or fall on its own merit; not because he needed spiritual regeneration, for the Spirit he had with him always—but he came to be baptized "to fulfil all righteousness," that is, to accomplish all that was required of him according to the terms and conditions of his Father's plan.

"And now, if the Lamb of God, he being holy, should have need to be baptized by water, to fulfil all righteousness," Nephi acclaimed, "O then, how much more need have we, being unholy, to be baptized, yea, even by water!"

Then Nephi asks how the Lamb of God, he being holy and needing no remission of sins, fulfilled all righteousness by being immersed in Jordan by John. His answer falls into five parts, and Jesus was baptized for these reasons:

1. *To signify his humility before the Father;* to show that "according to the flesh he humbleth himself before the

Father." He is God's Almighty Son; he made the worlds; the sidereal heavens rolled into existence at his word; he has all power in heaven and on earth—and yet, as a perfect pattern of humility, he wades out into a dirty stream, whose waters are scarcely fit for human consumption, and permits a rugged, unpolished man from the desert to immerse him in baptism, because such is the law of the Lord.

2. *As a covenant of obedience;* he "witnesseth unto the Father that he would be obedient unto him in keeping his commandments." He came not to do his own will, but the will of the Father, who sent him. He was no more free of constraint and control than is any man. He walked the course set out for him because it was his Father's will, and he was under covenant, made in the waters of baptism, to do the will of the Father.

3. *To receive the gift of the Holy Ghost;* that is to say, to conform to the law that gave him the right to the constant companionship of that member of the Godhead. As we are aware, this was a formality only in his case, for he being holy and without sin, the Spirit was his companion always. At baptism he simply went through the form that is required for all men, and that he should have done so is manifest by the fact that "the Holy Ghost descended upon him in the form of a dove."

4. *To gain an inheritance in the celestial kingdom;* that is, his baptism "showeth unto the children of men the straightness of the path, and the narrowness of the gate, by which they should enter, he having set the example before them." In other words, though he is the King of the kingdom, though he authors and proclaims his Father's plan of salvation, though he ordains and establishes the laws governing all things, yet he cannot enter the kingdom of heaven without baptism.

5. *As an example to all men;* to mark the course and chart the way; to show them the path they must follow. "And he said unto the children of men: Follow thou me. Wherefore, my beloved brethren," Nephi says, "can we

follow Jesus save we shall be willing to keep the commandments of the Father?" (2 Ne. 31:5-12.)

And so it is that the Lord Jesus is baptized—to save himself and to mark the path in which all others must walk to gain the same salvation. And so it is that the miraculously born son of Zacharias, fresh from communing with the Lord in the desert, leads the Mortal Messiah down into the Jordan and immerses him in the murky water, from which watery womb he shall come forth, receive the gift of the Holy Ghost, and go forth preaching and teaching. And so it is that he shall tread his way up the Holy Mount, on which his Father's voice shall once again be heard to say: "This is my beloved Son, in whom I am well pleased; hear ye him" (Matt. 17:5); and so it is that he shall descend from the mount and continue his ministry, finally submitting to crucifixion at the hands of evil men—all "to fulfil all righteousness."

NOTES

1. A somewhat analogous situation existed in the early days of this dispensation. Some new converts, having been baptized in other churches, felt they did not need to be baptized over again as members of the newly established kingdom of God on earth. In language that is applicable, in large measure, to the Jewish situation, the Lord said: "Behold, I say unto you that all old covenants have I caused to be done away in this thing; and this is a new and an everlasting covenant, even that which was from the beginning. Wherefore, although a man should be baptized an hundred times it availeth him nothing, for you cannot enter in at the strait gate by the law of Moses, neither by your dead works. For it is because of your dead works that I have caused this last covenant and this church to be built up unto me, even as in days of old. Wherefore, enter ye in at the gate, as I have commanded, and seek not to counsel your God." (D&C 22:1-4.)

2. In this same cathedral, in the stained-glass portrayal behind the altar, may be seen Mary, our Lord's mother, sitting as it were on a throne. On either side, with outstretched arms toward her, and holding jointly a crown, stand the Father and the Son. They are placing the crown on Mary's head. About the Holy Virgin flutters a dove, which is, no doubt, intended to be the Holy Spirit.

3. The words of the baptismal prayer have not been the same in all dispensations and for all people. It appears that the words spoken fit the needs and circumstances of the moment. When Alma took Helam into the waters of Mormon, he first cried out, "O Lord, pour out thy Spirit upon thy servant, that he may do this work with holiness of heart." Then, "the Spirit of the Lord was upon him, and he said: Helam, I baptize thee, having authority from the Almighty God, as a testimony that ye have entered into a covenant to serve him until you are dead as to the mortal body; and may the Spirit of the Lord be poured out upon you; and may he grant unto you eternal life, through the redemption of Christ, whom he has prepared from the foundation of the world." (Mosiah 18:12-13.)

4. All four Gospel authors record that the Spirit descended "like a dove"; Luke adds that he also came in "bodily shape"; and the Book of Mormon accounts say he came "in

the form of a dove." (1 Ne. 11:27; 2 Ne. 31:8.) Joseph Smith said that John "led the Son of God into the waters of baptism, and had the privilege of beholding the Holy Ghost descend in the form of a dove, or rather in the sign of the dove, in witness of that administration."

Then the Prophet gives this explanation: "The sign of the dove was instituted before the creation of the world, a witness for the Holy Ghost, and the devil cannot come in the sign of a dove. The Holy Ghost is a personage, and is in the form of a personage. It does not confine itself to the form of the dove, but in sign of the dove. The Holy Ghost cannot be transformed into a dove; but the sign of a dove was given to John to signify the truth of the deed, as the dove is an emblem or token of truth and innocence." (*Teachings*, pp. 275-76.) It thus appears that John witnessed the sign of the dove, that he saw the Holy Ghost descend in the "bodily shape" of the personage that he is, and that the descent was "like a dove."

Chapter 25

THE TEMPTATION OF JESUS

I will prove you in all things, whether you will abide in my covenant, even unto death, that you may be found worthy. (D&C 98:14.)

Lucifer and the Law of Temptation

Jesus, as our evangelical authors tell us, was led by the Spirit into the wilderness to be tempted of the devil. As we shall see, however, he went into the wilderness, as guided by the Spirit, to be with God. Then, after forty days of fasting, prayer, and divine communion—and in connection with certain great spiritual experiences that then came to him—he was visited by the devil who came tempting, enticing, seeking to destroy the house of faith in which Jesus dwelt.

These recitations—that Jesus, the Son of God was tempted—give rise to speculation and wonderment as to how and why and whether he, a divine being, could be tempted. Theologians speculate as to whether he was peccable, that is, capable of being tempted and liable to commit sin, because of his human nature, or whether he was impeccable, that is, not liable to sin and thus one who was free from sin or stain, because of his divine nature. In reality there neither is nor should there be any great mystery here.

Our Lord, as a mortal, was subject to the same laws of trial and testing that govern all mortals. An understanding of the laws governing temptation, and the reasons trials exist, will show why, after Jesus went into the wilderness to commune with God, who is the Author of all righteousness, he then came out to face Lucifer, the enemy of all righteousness.

This mortal life is a probationary estate; one in which every accountable soul must be tried and tested; one in which every man must be subject to the wiles and enticements of Lucifer; one in which all men must choose to worship the Lord, by keeping his commandments, or to follow Satan, by living after the manner of the world. Worship God or submit to Satan—succinctly stated, that is all that life is about. The Lord is worshipped when men adhere to his standards and emulate his way of life. "Be holy, for I am holy," saith the Lord. (Lev. 11:45.) The devil is worshipped when men adhere to his standards and emulate his way of life; when they are carnal, sensual, and devilish; when they forget the Lord and live after the manner of the world; "for he seeketh that all men might be miserable like unto himself." (2 Ne. 2:27.)

Men must have a choice; they must be able to choose; there must be opposites; they must have agency; they must be free to worship the Lord or to follow Satan. All this is imperative. It is inherent in the whole plan of salvation. And unless men have the agency to choose to do good and work righteousness—and, in fact, do so—they cannot be saved. There is no other way.

"It must needs be"—that is, it is mandatory; it must be; it is part of the whole system of progression and salvation, and there is no other way to bring salvation to pass—"It must needs be, that there is an opposition in all things." So says Lehi. "If not so," he continues, "righteousness could not be brought to pass, neither wickedness, neither holiness nor misery, neither good nor bad." If there were no opposites, nothing could exist. There can be no light without darkness; no life without death; no heat without cold; no virtue without vice; no sense without insensibility. There can be no righteousness without wickedness; no joy without sorrow; no reward without punishment; no salvation without damnation. If these things did not exist—that is, if there were no opposites; if there were no opposition in all things; if there were no agency; if men were not free to choose one course or another—such would, as Lehi says, "destroy the wisdom of God and his eternal purposes," and, indeed, should such be the case, and it is impossible that it could be, then "all things must have vanished away." (2 Ne. 2:11-13.)

If there is a God, there is also a devil. It is the Lord who invites and entices men, by his Spirit—the light of Christ—to choose the right; it is the devil who invites and entices men to choose evil works rather than good. The enticements of the devil are temptation, and temptation is, and "must needs be," an essential part of the plan of salvation. Through it are provided the allurements and worldly things that men must overcome in order to progress and gain that eternal life which is the opposite of eternal damnation.

Hence, there is—and must be—a devil, and he is the father of lies and of wickedness. He and the fallen angels who followed him are spirit children of the Father. As Christ is the Firstborn of the Father in the spirit, so Lucifer is a son of the morning, one of those born in the morning of preexistence. He is a spirit man, a personage, an entity, comparable in form and appearance to any of the spirit children of the Eternal Father. He was the source of opposition among the spirit hosts before the world was made; he rebelled in preexistence against the Father and the Son, and he sought even then to destroy the agency of man. He and his followers were cast down to earth, and they are forever denied mortal bodies. And he, here on earth, along with all who follow him—both his spirit followers and the mortals who hearken to his enticements—is continuing the war that commenced in heaven.

There is, then, a law of temptation. It involves the Eternal Christ, by whose power Lucifer fell as lightning from heaven, and it involves the mortal Jesus, who was subject to the wiles of the spirit Lucifer as he dwelt as a man among men. And that our blessed Lord came off triumphant on earth as he did in heaven, we all know, for which ministry of triumph and glory we praise his name forever.

Jesus Communes with God in the Wilderness
(*Matthew 4:1-2; JST, Matthew 4:1-2; Mark 1:12-13; JST, Mark 1:10-11; Luke 4:1*)

After his baptism by John in Jordan at Bethabara, two things happened in the life of our Lord that always come to pass in the lives of those faithful people who find their own Bethabaras and are immersed in their own Jordans by the legal administrators of their day: (1) the Spirit of God descended upon him with power, though in his case that Spirit had ever guided his thoughts and words and acts, and (2) greater temptations confronted him than had ever been the case before.

After baptism of water comes the baptism of fire. After baptism—when converted souls commit themselves to the Lord's cause; when they covenant to forsake the world and serve the Lord—the devil tries even harder to lead them astray. Then it is that they are tested in all things to see if they will abide in the gospel covenant, even unto death, that they may be found worthy of a celestial inheritance.

Also, after his baptism Jesus did what every person who is born of the Spirit should do: he withdrew from the thronging masses of humanity to a place apart to commune with God. Matthew's account, as he originally wrote it, says: "Then"—that is, following his baptism—"Jesus was led up of the Spirit, into the wilderness, to be with God. And when he had fasted forty days and forty nights, and had communed with God, he was afterwards an hungered, and was left to be tempted of the devil." Mark tells us he "was with the wild beasts; and the angels ministered unto him." Nothing more of this forty-day period is recorded, but we cannot do other than conclude it was a time of rejoicing and spiritual refreshment beyond anything ever experienced by mortal man on earth.

Enoch "was high and lifted up, even in the bosom of the Father, and of the Son of Man," and he beheld marvelous visions beyond anything that the mind of man can conceive. He saw all the spirits that God had created, the nations of mortal men, the coming of Christ and his crucifixion, the Second Coming of the Son of Man, the millennial era, and many other things that are not recorded. (Moses 6 and 7.) The brother of Jared talked for three hours at one time with the Lord and learned many of the wonders of eternity, which are so far beyond mortal comprehension that the Lord has not permitted them to be translated in our day. (Ether 2-4.) Moses saw worlds without number and their inhabitants, and confronted and withstood Satan face to face. (Moses 1.) Paul was caught up into the third heaven and saw wondrous things, "and heard unspeakable words, which it is not lawful for a man to utter." (2 Cor. 12:1-4.) Joseph Smith saw the Father and the Son and the vision of the degrees of glory. (JS-H 1; D&C 76; 137.) Great hosts of faithful people, in tune with the Infinite, have seen and heard the mysteries of the kingdom, things that are "only to be seen and understood by the power of the Holy Spirit, which God bestows on those who love him, and purify themselves before him; To whom he grants this privilege of seeing and knowing for themselves; That through the power and manifestation of the Spirit, while in the flesh, they may be able to bear his presence in the world of glory." (D&C 76:114-118.)

If all these things, and more, happened in the lives of the prophets, what should we expect to find in the life of the greatest Prophet? If there are eternal laws by obedience to which men see visions and commune with the Infinite, what glorious communion with heaven should we find in the life of the one who obeyed all the laws ever given to mortals? If the veil has been rent for lesser men, and they have seen inconceivable glories and heard unspeakable words, what should we suppose was seen and heard by the greatest Man? Surely the spiritual stature of the Man Jesus was such that for forty days the lions and wild beasts treated him as they did Daniel. Surely the visions of eternity were opened to his view as they were to Paul and Joseph Smith. Surely he saw all that was seen by Enoch and Moses and Moriancumer. Surely there was purpose and preparation, refinement and testing, growth and development, during this period when our Lord's body was made subject to his spirit. Fasting and prayer and pondering and visions and revelations prepare men for the ministry, and it was no different, except in degree, where the preparation of the Lord Jesus was concerned.

The Temptation

(*Matthew 4:3-11; JST, Matthew 4:5-6, 8-9; Luke 4:2-13; JST, Luke 4:2, 5-6, 9*)

When man is communing with his Maker, he is not subject to temptation; when angels are ministering to him and he is under the spell of their angelic influence, he is not subject to temptation; when the Holy Spirit rests mightily upon him and the visions of eternity are open to his view, he is not subject to temptation. For forty days Jesus pondered upon the things of the Spirit, poured out his soul to his Father in prayer, sought diligently to receive revelations and see visions, was ministered to by angels, and was enwrapt in the visions of eternity—during all of which time he was not subject to temptation. We may also suppose that during this period he was "with God" in the literal sense of the word, and that the Father visited him.

As the period of edification and spiritual enlightenment drew to its close, as the visions and spiritual experiences ceased—except for two that we shall note shortly—and as Jesus prepared to go back into the normal mortal way of life, with angels no longer at his side and his eyes not open to the unending visions of eternity, then the devil came to entice, to trap, to tempt. Three times he tried and three times he failed, after which "he departed from him for a season," or, as it may be rendered, "till a fitting opportunity."

Jesus was "an hungered." For forty days and forty nights no morsel of food entered his mouth, no drop of water wet his parched lips or dripped down his throat. His extended fast left him weak physically. His body cried out for food, and he needed the strength that comes from a full stomach. His spiritual experiences were, for the moment, drawing to their close. The Divine Providence that calls upon men to fast and pray also expects them to end their fasts and cease their prayers and to take care of their physical needs. Men must eat bread or die, and the time had now come for Jesus to break his fast and to eat, perhaps the berries or locusts or wild honey that was available, and to drink refreshing draughts, perhaps from the nearby spring.

But first "the tempter came to him"—and we must assert that this was a personal appearance, one in which the spirit Lucifer, who was cast out of heaven for rebellion, came in person and spoke to Jesus face to face. It was no mere placing of thoughts in his mind, but an open and spoken conversation; "the tempter came to him" and said: "If thou be the Son of God, command these stones be made bread."

Why not? Had not Jehovah provided manna—which is bread from heaven—to all Israel, six days each week, for forty years, lest they die of hunger in the wilderness? Was it not the will of the Father that his Son now eat and regain his physical strength? And if Israel was fed by bread from heaven, when no other food was available, why would not Israel's Chief Citizen receive food in the same way? What would be wrong with duplicating for one day a miracle that had occurred on more than twelve thousand days when Moses and Aaron led Israel from Egypt to the very Jordan in whose waters he had but recently been immersed?

Actually there was no reason, save one, why food should not have been provided miraculously, which shows how devilishly devised the tempting challenge was—and for aught we know it may have been so provided at a later time. The one reason was: Lucifer had made the providing of food for Jesus' hungry body a test of his divinity. "If thou be the Son of God," do this thing. It was as though he had said: 'Cut off your arm and restore it, and then I will believe you are the Son of God and have the power you seem to think you have.' Of course he could turn stones into bread; in less than two months he would turn water into wine in Cana; and not long thereafter, on two separate occasions, he would multiply loaves and fishes so that thousands could eat, which is to say, he would make food out of the elements that surround us.

But here Lucifer was challenging him to glory in his divinity and to prostitute his powers. He was demanding that he prove something that needed no proof. Jesus knew and Satan knew—both had perfect knowledge on the point—that our Lord was the Son of God. There was no need to prove it by turning stones into bread, even though he had the power, and even though the time was at hand when it was proper for him to eat and be filled. Indeed, if he had yielded to Lucifer, turning the stones into bread, it would have indicated a doubt in his own mind of his divinity; it would have shown he felt a need to prove that which needed no proof.

Jesus answered: "It is written, Man shall not live by bread alone, but by every word that proceedeth out of the mouth of God." Of all the inspired words ever recorded by the prophets who preceded him, these few constituted the perfect rebuke to the rebel Lucifer. They are taken from the very sentence in which Moses reminded Israel of the bread from heaven, as it were, with which they had been fed for forty years. "Thou shalt remember all the way which the Lord thy God led thee these forty years in the wilderness," Moses said, "to humble thee, and to prove thee, to know what was in thine heart, whether thou wouldest keep his commandments, or no"—all of which is a type of the fasting and struggle of Jesus for forty days in the wilderness of his fast. Then came to Israel, by the mouth of Moses, the divine pronouncement: "And he humbled thee, and suffered thee to hunger, and fed thee with manna, which thou knewest not, neither did thy fathers know; that he might make thee know that man doth not live by bread only, but by every word that proceedeth out of the mouth of the Lord doth man live." (Deut. 8:2-3.)

That is, even as Israel relied upon Jehovah for their daily bread, lest they die physically, so they must rely upon him for the word of God, which is spiritual bread, lest they die spiritually. Neither temporal nor spiritual bread, standing alone, will suffice; man must eat of both to live; and in the eternal sense, the word of God, which is the bread from heaven in the full sense, is the more important. Those who make the search for earthly bread their chief concern lose sight of eternal values, fail to feed their spirits, die spiritually, and lose their souls. By choosing from the whole Old Testament the very words that show the relative worth of bread from the earth and bread from heaven, Jesus' triumph over Lucifer is complete. He, as the Son of God, chooses the bread from heaven and will find earthly food when his circumstances permit. He is master over the flesh; his appetites will be kept within the bounds set by divine standards.

We now come to one of the two remaining great spiritual experiences that were part of the period of fasting and testing to which Jesus was subject. "Then Jesus was taken up into the holy city, and the Spirit setteth him on the pinnacle of the temple," we learn from the Joseph Smith Translation. The Spirit did it, not the devil; how unthinkable it is that Lucifer would have power to transport the Son of God, or anyone for that matter, to a place of his choosing! He has no such power! Jesus was placed on the appointed pinnacle by the Spirit!

Other prophets had been and would be transported bodily from place to place by the power of the Spirit. Ezekiel was lifted up and carried by the Spirit. (Ezek. 8:2-3.) Nephi "was caught away in the Spirit of the Lord, yea, into an exceeding high mountain," upon which he "never had before" set his "foot." (1 Ne. 11:1.) Mary herself "was carried away in the Spirit," at the time of the conception of Jesus. (1 Ne. 11:19-21.) Nephi the son of Helaman "was taken by the Spirit and conveyed away out of the midst" of those who sought to imprison him, and thus "he did go forth in the Spirit, from multitude to multitude, declaring the word of God." (Hel. 10:16-17.) After Philip baptized the eunuch, "the Spirit of the Lord caught [him] away," and he was carried to Azotus. (Acts 8:39-40.) It is not an unheard-of thing for the Lord, by the power of the Spirit, to transport mortals from place to place; and it would appear that Jesus was to have all the experiences enjoyed in mortality by any of the prophets who went before or who came after, excepting only that he was not translated and taken into heaven without tasting death as some had been and would be.

Why the Spirit took him to the pinnacle of the temple is not stated. Perhaps it was to show him the throngs of worshippers and let him see anew the sacrifices being offered in similitude of his coming sacrifice. In any event, "Then the devil came unto him and said, If thou be the Son of God, cast thyself down, for it is written, He shall give his angels charge concerning thee, and in their hands they shall bear thee up, lest at any time thou dash thy foot against a stone."

Here was a new temptation, more subtle than the first. Lucifer was now quoting scripture, a Messianic prophecy, which must be fulfilled. Perhaps Jesus could control his appetites and overcome the flesh, so be it; but would he dare refuse to conform to a Messianic prophecy? Jesus had chosen, by refusing to turn stones into bread, to put spiritual things ahead of temporal things, and so now Lucifer tempts him with reference to a spiritual matter: If our Lord is choosing to put the things of God's kingdom ahead of the things of this world, then let him cast himself down, for he will then fulfill a scripture and triumph before the people in a spiritual field.

'If thou be the Son of God,' the tempter says, 'then cast thyself down in the midst of the worshipping throng. If thou art the Messiah, surely thou wilt fulfill this Messianic prophecy; how else can it be fulfilled but by you on this occasion? And what a beginning for thy ministry! All men shall hear of the marvelous thing thou hast done! They will flock to hear your message, and you will be able to accomplish what you were sent to do! This is the very thing the Messiah must do to prove his divinity, and it must be done to commence your ministry. If thou be the Son of God, thou wilt surely cast thyself down. Now, do it now; this is the time; this is your great hour!'

Jesus replied: "It is written again, Thou shalt not tempt the Lord thy God." And again the answer was perfect. First, it was his witness that he was the Son of God: 'Thou shalt not tempt me, for I am the Lord thy God. I am the God of Israel; I am the Messiah; I am the Son of God.' Next, his quotation came from a context that forbids asking the Lord to perform miracles to prove he is the true God. Moses said: "Ye shall not tempt the Lord your God, as ye tempted him in Massah." (Deut. 17:1-7.) And it was at Massah that the children of Israel, dying of thirst and perishing for want of water, as they supposed, demanded of Moses that he prove that the Lord was with them by providing water for them and their cattle. It was then that Moses smote the rock and the water gushed out, "because they tempted the Lord, saying, Is the Lord among us, or not?" (Ex. 17:1-17.) For the second time our Lord's victory over Lucifer was total and triumphant. Seductive as the appeal was, he would not yield; his divinity was not to be proved by a plunge from the temple pinnacle, nor was his ministry to be announced by any such dramatic occurrence. He was his own witness, and the people, as in all ages, must come and hear a prophet's voice and choose for themselves whether to believe or to rebel.

After this, "again, Jesus was in the Spirit"—in the second spiritual experience to which we made reference—"and it taketh him up into an exceeding high mountain, and showeth him all the kingdoms of the world and the glory of them. And the devil came unto him again, and said, All these things will I give unto thee, If thou wilt fall down and worship me. Then said Jesus unto him, Get thee hence, Satan; for it is written, Thou shalt worship the Lord thy God, and him only shalt thou serve." Thereupon Satan left him for a season.

In theory this should have been the least of all the temptations Lucifer could make to the Messiah. So here is the great Roman empire with Tiberius at its head; here are armies and navies and palaces and stately buildings; here are legions of men ready to bow the knee or draw the bow at a word from their ruler; here are the cattle and crops and vineyards on a thousand hills and in ten thousand valleys; here is the whole wealth of the whole world, plus all the power that goes with it—what of it?

Why offer a handful of dust, as it were, to him who created the earth, the universe, and the sidereal heavens, and whose destiny is to inherit, possess, and receive all things, and to have all power in heaven and on earth? Why should the Creator of all things be tempted, when a usurper who has momentary control over a few of them offers his handful back in return for obeisance and worship? But this is only the theory.

In practical reality this must have been the crowning test of the three. Jesus was a mortal man, and every mortal has planted in his heart the desire for wealth and power. One of the great purposes of mortality is to bridle this desire and to keep it under control.

Cain slays Abel to gain his flocks and herds; Esau sells his birthright for a mess of pottage; Joseph's brothers sell him to the Ishmaelites for a few pieces of silver; Judas plants the traitor's kiss for thirty pieces of silver; Ananias and Saphira hold back a part of the price of their property, and lose their souls in the process—such has always been the way with mortals. Women sell their virtue for a few baubles;

politicians sell their souls to be elected to office; generals sell the lives of their soldiers to satisfy their vanity; merchants sell their integrity for a few paltry pence—such is the way of the world. And since our Lord's temptations were real and a part of his necessary trials and tests, we cannot do other than suppose that all the kingdoms and wealth and power of Satan's world must have seemed desirable to him. Men have the potential of becoming joint-heirs with him of all that his Father hath, and yet they sell their souls for naught. Why should he be subject to any less testing?

How apt are these words, quoted from Andrewes by Farrar: "There are some that will say that we are never tempted with kingdoms. It may well be, for it needs not be, when less will serve. It was Christ only that was thus tempted; in Him lay an heroical mind that could not be tempted with small matters. But with us it is nothing so, for we esteem more basely of ourselves. We set our wares at a very easy price; he [Lucifer] may buy us even dagger-cheap. He need never carry us so high as the mount. The pinnacle is high enough; yea, the lowest steeple in all the town would serve the turn. Or let him but carry us to the leads and gutters of our own houses; nay, let us but stand in our windows or our doors, if he will give us so much as we can there see, he will tempt us throughly; we will accept it, and thank him too. . . . A matter of half-a-crown, or ten groats, a pair of shoes, or some such trifle, will bring us on our knees to the devil." (Farrar, p. 105.)

Why Jesus Was Tempted

Jesus was tempted—if we may so say—to fulfill all righteousness. It was part of the eternal plan. It gave him the experiences he needed to work out his own salvation, and it prepared him to sit in judgment upon his erring brethren, who, in a lesser degree, are tried and tested as he was.

We have said his temptations were real. Whether we can understand how and why the things he underwent were real and genuine temptations is of no great moment; that we know he was called upon to choose the right in the hardest and most difficult situations ever imposed upon mortals will perhaps suffice. That his temptations were over and above those of any other person is shown from the Messianic prophecy: "Lo, he shall suffer temptations, and pain of body, hunger, thirst, and fatigue, even more than man can suffer, except it be unto death." (Mosiah 3:7.) Of the temptations he suffered, after those of which we have here spoken, and before the trial in Gethsemane, he said to the Twelve: "Ye are they which have continued with me in my temptations." (Luke 22:28.)

Paul, as in so many other matters, is our best New Testament source of doctrinal exposition as to the temptations and sufferings of our Lord. To the Hebrews he wrote:

"It became him, for whom are all things, and by whom are all things, in bringing many sons unto glory, to make the captain of their salvation perfect through sufferings....

"Wherefore in all things it behoved him to be made like unto his brethren, that he might be a merciful and faithful high priest in things pertaining to God, to make reconciliation for the sins of the people. For in that he himself hath suffered being tempted, he is able to succour them that are tempted....

"Seeing then that we have a great high priest, that is passed into the heavens, Jesus the Son of God, let us hold fast our profession. For we have not an high priest which cannot be touched with the feeling of our infirmities; but was in all points tempted like as we are, yet without sin....

"Though he were a Son, yet learned he obedience by the things which he suffered; And being made perfect, he became the author of eternal salvation unto all them that obey him." (Heb. 2:10, 17-14; 4:14-15; 5:8-9.)

The first Adam, yielding to temptation, brought death and sin into the world; the Second Adam, overcoming temptation, brought life and righteousness to men, because he overcame the world. Having been baptized and having come off triumphant in the war with Satan, he is now prepared to go forth on the greatest ministry ever wrought among men.

SECTION III

JESUS' EARLY JUDEAN MINISTRY

JESUS' EARLY JUDEAN MINISTRY

"The word which God sent unto the children of Israel, preaching peace by Jesus Christ: (he is Lord of all:)

"That word, I say, ye know, which was published throughout all Judæa, and began from Galilee, after the baptism which John preached;

"How God anointed Jesus of Nazareth with the Holy Ghost and with power: who went about doing good, and healing all that were oppressed of the devil; for God was with him.

"And we are witnesses of all things which he did both in the land of the Jews, and in Jerusalem." (Acts 10:36-39.)

MANNA

Come drink of the waters of life;
Come feast on the good word of God;
Come drink from the cup of the Lord;
Come eat of his heaven-sent bread.

Come buy without money or price
That meat which gives life to the soul;
And eat at the table where seers
Have spoken the mind of the Lord.

Come drink, saith the Spirit to all;
Drink deep of those waters that fall

Like rain on the parched desert soil
Which heaven sends down for the soul.

Come feast on the manna from heaven
That falls like the dew of the morn;
Come feed in the pastures so green;
Find place with the sheep of the Lord.

Drink deep from the rivers that flow,
Direct from our great Fountain Head;
Rejoice in the waters so pure
Which he sendeth forth among men.

Drink deep of the fruit of the vine;
Eat now for salvation is free;
Drink wine on the lees well refined;
Eat now, for the time is at hand!

—*Bruce R. McConkie*

JOHN ACCOMPLISHES HIS MISSION

John saw and bore record
of the fulness of my glory.
(D&C 93:6.)

Two Men Called John

Two men called John sit together on the banks of the Jordan at the place called Bethabara. Both are devout and righteous souls who, like Simeon and Anna and many others, have been waiting for the Consolation of Israel; both believe the Messianic prophecies and desire to ally themselves with the Deliverer and Savior of whom they speak; both were foreordained for the ministries that are theirs; and both have the spiritual stature, acquired long before mortal birth, to recognize truth and comprehend the mysteries of the kingdom.

They talk of the hosts of Jews from all walks of life who are repenting and being baptized for the remission of sins. They discuss the words of their prophets and the hopes of their nation. As devout Jews they rejoice that the Promised Messiah is at hand. They marvel at the miracle wrought but a short time before in these very waters when one came to fulfill all righteousness by being baptized therein. They speak of the opening of the heavens and the descent—in calmness and serenity, like a dove—of the Holy Spirit of God; and their souls vibrate as they recount again the majesty of the occasion when the voice from heaven acclaimed: "This is my beloved Son, in whom I am well pleased. Hear ye him." These are true believers whose names shall be forever enshrined in the hearts of all like-minded souls who come after.

One of these men called John, at this point in their eternal association, is acting as a teacher, the other as a disciple. The teacher is the son of Elisabeth and Zacharias, and his miraculous conception, birth, name, and ministry as the Lord's forerunner were all foretold by Gabriel. He is now just past thirty-one years of age and has been preaching and teaching and baptizing for a year and a half. He is destined to do more teaching, to be imprisoned by Herod, to be slain, and then as a resurrected personage to restore in the latter days the Aaronic Priesthood. The disciple is the son of Zebedee and the brother of James. Probably a young man, scarce out of his teens, he is destined to be an apostle of the Lord Jesus Christ, to serve with Peter and James in the First Presidency, and to write the Gospel of John, the Book of Revelation, and three New Testament epistles. He is to become the Beloved Disciple and the Revelator, to be translated, and also to come again in the latter days, along with Peter and James, to restore the Melchizedek Priesthood.

John the Baptist also is destined to write of the gospel of that Lord whose witness he is, but his account, perhaps because it contains truths and concepts that the saints and the world are not yet prepared to receive, has so far not been given to men. On May 6, 1833, however, the Lord did reveal to Joseph Smith eleven verses of the Baptist's writings, and promised that "the fulness of the record of John" would be revealed when the faith of men entitled them to receive it. (D&C 93:6-18.)

From what has been revealed of the writings of the Baptist, and from what John the Apostle has written in his Gospel, it is clear that John the Apostle had before him the writings of John the Baptist when he wrote his Gospel. John 1:1-38 and John 3:23-36 are quoted or paraphrased from that which was first written by the Baptist, a reality that will be perfectly clear to all as we consider their content and message in detail. We shall now begin such a consideration.

John the Baptist—Our Lord's Witness

(*John 1:1-12; JST, John 1:1-10, 15; D&C 93:6-10*)

John the Baptist, as we are aware, was "filled with the Holy Ghost from his mother's womb"; "was ordained by the angel of God at the time he was eight days old unto this power, to overthrow the kingdom of the Jews, and to make straight the way of the Lord before the face of his people, to prepare them for the coming of the Lord"; and "was baptized while he was yet in his childhood." (D&C 84:27-28.) This we learn from latter-day revelation. Our New Testament account tells us that the son of Zacharias was in the desert, apart from men, as he prepared for his ministry. John himself speaks of someone who sent him to baptize with water and who told him he would see the Holy Spirit descend upon the Son of God and remain upon him. Jesus said John was a prophet and more than a prophet. As we are aware, he held the Aaronic Priesthood and the keys thereof while in mortality, both of which he restored to Joseph Smith and Oliver Cowdery in modern times.

Now, how much would such a man know about the plan of salvation, about the mysteries of the kingdom, about the divine mission of the one whose witness he was? Surely he would rank with the apostles and prophets of his age in greatness and spiritual stature, and from such fragmentary accounts of his doings and sayings as have come down to us, we are of the opinion that he did.

What visions, what revelations, what rending of the heavens enabled our Baptist friend to write of the Lord Jesus such things as these: "I saw his glory, that he was in the beginning, before the world was"—leading us to surmise that he saw, as Enoch and Abraham and Moses had each seen, a vision of preexistence and the spirits of men there assembled. "Therefore, in the beginning the Word was, for he was the Word, even the messenger of salvation—The light and the Redeemer of the world; the Spirit of truth, who came into the world, because the world was made by him, and in him was the life of men and the light of men."

These words rank with those of the greatest of the prophets. How aptly did John the Apostle distill their meaning in the beginning of his Gospel: "In the beginning was the Word, and the Word was with God, and the Word was God," and so forth; and even how much more profound is the thought as it comes to us as perfected by the Prophet Joseph Smith: "In the beginning was the gospel preached through the Son. And the gospel was the word, and the word was with the Son, and the Son was with God, and the Son was of God." Also: "In him was the gospel, and the gospel was the life, and the life was the light of men; And the light shineth in the world, and the world perceiveth it not."

At this point the Gospel account acclaims: "There was a man sent from God, whose name was John. The same came into the world for a witness, to bear witness of the light, to bear record of the gospel through the Son, unto all, that through him men might believe." John knew and understood the gospel and the plan of salvation. He came, and he knew he came, so that all men might believe in the Son and be saved. The depth and breadth and height of his teachings compare with those of Enoch and Moses and Joseph Smith.

"He was not that light," the account continues, "but came to bear witness of that light, Which was the true light, which lighteth every men who cometh into the world; Even the Son of God." Christ is the Light, the one to whom all men must turn for salvation; the word and the truth that comes from him will save men. All of his prophets, even John, send forth only a reflection of the greater light. "The words were made by him; men were made by him"—meaning as he acted by divine investiture of authority from his

Father—"all things were made by him, and through him, and of him," the Baptist said.

"The Word Was Made Flesh"

(*John 1:13-14, 16-18; JST, John 1:12-19; D&C 93:11-17*)

"And I, John," says the son of Zacharias, "bear record that I beheld his glory, as the glory of the Only Begotten of the Father, full of grace and truth, even the Spirit of truth, which came and dwelt in the flesh, and dwelt among us."

When this vision came and how much more the Baptist saw—and wrote—remains to be revealed. As he preached, month by month, to the throngs that came to him, the visions he had seen and the revelations he had received and the impressions borne in upon his soul by that Spirit which attended him from his mother's womb—all these must have been referred to and explained and quoted to the people. And his beloved disciple John, the future apostle, must have heard them orally even as he later received them on papyrus.

Of Jesus' birth the account now available says: "He was born, not of blood, nor of the will of the flesh, nor of the will of man, but of God." That is: 'Jesus was born, but not as other men are—not of blood—not of a mortal father who had flesh and blood; he was born—not of the will of the flesh—for no mortal appetite or desire was involved; other men are conceived because of the love between parents, but Jesus had no mortal father; he was born—not by the will of man—but because his Eternal Father willed it. As the Eternal Word, he was made flesh to fulfill eternal purposes.'

"For in the beginning was the Word, even the Son, who is made flesh, and sent unto us by the will of the Father," the holy account continues. "And as many as believe on his name shall receive of his fulness. And of his fulness have all we received, even immortality and eternal life, through his grace."

And then, his forerunner John being the last legal administrator of the old Mosaic dispensation and the first administrator sent of God in the new Christian dispensation, how appropriate it is that the revealed record contrasts the two systems. "For the law was given through Moses, but life and truth came through Jesus Christ. For the law was after a carnal commandment, to the administration of death; but the gospel was after the power of an endless life, through Jesus Christ, the Only Begotten Son, who is in the bosom of the Father." We cannot believe other than that all these things were explained and taught on the banks of the Jordan, even as they should be known and taught today.

"And I, John"—it is the Baptist speaking!—"saw that he received not of the fulness at the first, but received grace for grace; And he received not of the fulness at first, but continued from grace to grace, until he received a fulness; And thus he was called the Son of God, because he received not of the fulness at the first. And I, John, bear record"—and here comes the account of what the Baptist saw as he brought the Lord Jesus up out of the waters of Jordan—"and lo, the heavens were opened, and the Holy Ghost descended upon him in the form of a dove, and sat upon him, and there came a voice out of heaven saying: This is my beloved Son." This same John, looking forward to that day when Jesus would be raised in glorious immortality to receive that—and more—which was his before the world was, testified: "And I, John, bear record that he received a fulness of the glory of the Father; And he received all power, both in heaven and on earth, and the glory of the Father was with him, for he dwelt in him."

One other truth, known of old and revealed anew in plainness in our day, we must record: "And no man hath seen God at any time, except he hath borne record of the Son; for except it is through him no man can be saved."

How the cobwebs of the past are swept away when inspired men speak and write! How the fountains of truth pour out the waters of life when prophets of God are available to regulate the flow! How wondrous it is that we know as much as we do of that which was known anciently to two men called John!

And what a perspective it gives us of the mortal ministry of our Lord to know that all these things were known—and testimony was borne of them—even before he started his formal ministry. No doubt Jesus had done much informal teaching over the years, as he did when twelve years of age in his Father's House, and he may even have healed the sick and worked other miracles on special occasions. But his formal ministry, an account of which Divine Providence has preserved for us in the Gospels, began after his baptism, after his temptation, and, be it noted, after his forerunner had testified of him to the full to all who would listen.

Thus, as far as his formal ministry is concerned, at least, before Jesus taught the saving truths of his gospel; before he worked miracles; before he ministered comfort to the comfortless and gave hope to the downcast; before he called apostles and seventies; before any of the great events of his ministry were performed—before all this—the witness had gone forth; the testimony had been born; gospel truths had been taught; the people had been prepared for the Lord; the forerunner had done his work. The time had now come to transfer the responsibility for the kingdom, as it were, from John to Jesus.

John: Our Lord's Elias

(*John 1:19-28; JST, John 1:21-22, 26-28*)

There was a tradition among the Jews, so we learn from the Talmud, that when the Messiah came he would cry repentance, and the new kingdom would be ushered in by a great movement of reformation. John's preaching was so persuasive—so powerful was the word of testimony that God had given him—that great hosts flocked to him from Jerusalem and all Judea. Believing souls were repenting; baptisms in great numbers were being performed; and a special people was being prepared for a new kingdom. Could this be the Messiah? Was John the one for whom the whole nation had so long waited? If he was not the Messiah, who then was he? And why was he baptizing and setting up a new organization among the people?

Accounts of his ministry—no doubt garbled and confused accounts, for they would have been carried by unbelievers who found fault and who sought to discredit the great movement now sweeping the nation—accounts of his ministry reached the scribes and leaders of Jewish thought. Even the Sanhedrin itself is assumed to have been concerned. These leaders—in effect the false ministers of the false sects of the day—would not deign to go and hear the teachings of an unlearned prophet, one who had not been trained for the ministry. But they would make inquiry; they would send a deputation, chosen from among the Pharisees; they would send priests and Levites to find out what was going on. Indeed, the movement had such popular appeal that they had no choice; they must know who this disturber was, who was disrupting their kingdom and their system of religion and worship.

There was also among the Jews a prevailing doctrine relative to Elijah (Elias), whose coming must precede that of Messiah, and also a prevailing doctrine relative to Elias, who should restore all things—their kingdom and glory and the truths and powers they once possessed. Portions of these doctrines remain to this day among devout Jews who set a special chair for Elijah at their Passover meals. The Jews of Jesus' day had scriptural passages relative to Elias and his ministry that we do not have, but even then their understanding of Elias and his mission was no more accurate than their knowledge of Messias and his mission.

And so the deputation came to John to propound three great questions, which he answered plainly and forthrightly:

1. "*Who art thou? . . . Art thou Elias?*" In answer, "he confessed, and denied not that he was Elias. . . . And they asked him, saying; How then art thou Elias? And he said, I am not that Elias who was to restore all things."

'Yes; I am Elias. I am sent to go before the Lord in the spirit and power of Elias. My mission is to turn the hearts of the disobedient to the wisdom of the just, and to make ready a people prepared for the Lord. I am his forerunner; I hold the priesthood of Elias. But I am not that Elias who was to restore all things; his mission is greater than mine. I am sent to prepare the way for him.'

2. *Art thou that prophet like unto Moses whose coming is promised?* Moses, the man of God, than whom there has not been so great a prophet in all Israel, had left this promise to his people: "The Lord thy God will raise up unto thee a Prophet from the midst of thee, of thy brethren, like unto me; unto him ye shall hearken. . . . [For thus saith the Lord]: I will raise them up a Prophet from among their brethren, like unto thee [Moses], and will put my words in his mouth; and he shall speak unto them all that I shall command him. And it shall come to pass, that whosoever will not hearken unto my words which he shall speak in my name, I will require it of him." (Deut. 18:15-19.)

This, of course, is a Messianic prophecy, and the one like unto Moses was the Messiah and not another, though it was falsely assumed by many, in the day of which we speak, that Moses' words had reference to someone else, identified only as "that prophet." John's answer came in the negative; he was not "that prophet."

3. *Art thou the Christ?* His answer: "I am not the Christ." Further: 'Christ, who is preferred before me, is already among you, and he is the Son of God.'

Having been so answered, the Pharisaic priests and Levites, who had yet to give answer to those in whose employ they served, had yet another question:

"*Why baptizest thou then, if thou be not the Christ, nor Elias who was to restore all things, neither that prophet?*" John answered: "I baptize with water, but there standeth one among you, whom ye know not; He it is of whom I bear record. He is that prophet, even Elias, who, coming after me, is preferred before me, whose shoe's latchet I am not worthy to unloose, or whose place I am not able to fill; for he shall baptize, not only with water, but with fire, and with the Holy Ghost."

And so it is that the way was prepared. John will continue to preach and baptize for nearly a year. But he has now prepared the way; an organized body of worshippers is awaiting the Messiah; John has borne the testimony he was sent to bear; and tomorrow and the day following we shall see him in process, as he continues to teach and testify, of turning over the kingdom to Jesus and of saying to his own disciples: 'Follow thou him!'

Chapter 27

JESUS BEGINS HIS MINISTRY

He went forth ministering unto the people, in power and great glory; and the multitudes were gathered together to hear him. (1 Ne. 11:28.)

"Behold the Lamb of God"

(John 1:29-34; JST, John 1:30-32, 34)

Jesus is back from communing with his Father in the wilderness; his forty days and forty nights of fasting and prayer and spiritual experiences have been woven into the bones and sinews of his very being. He has now resisted the wiles of Satan, come off triumphant in temptations that were infinitely greater than any other person could have born, and overcome the world. He is now prepared to minister—formally and officially, using all his time, talents, and abilities—among his fellowmen. All that now remains is for his forerunner to make the great climactic pronouncement of Jesus' divine Sonship, and that the son of Zacharias is now prepared to do.

John has already told the deputation from Jerusalem that he, the son of Zacharias, is neither the Christ, nor Elias of the restoration, nor "that prophet" of whom Moses spoke, who, in fact, had they known it, was the Messiah. He has also told them that he is Elias the forerunner; that he has come to prepare a people for the Lord; and that the Lord, who is God's Son, the very Christ, now ministers among them, with power not only to baptize in water, as he, John, is doing, but also to baptize with fire and the Holy Ghost. The word has gone to the leaders of the people, and it is official. The deputation has come from the Sanhedrin, and has returned to report. The highest legal body of their people will now discuss the report and be apprised—however they may react—that a legal administrator, who had obvious power and authority, has told them in plain words that the Nazarene is the Messiah.

Our Lord's Elias—standing on the banks of the Jordan at the site called Bethabara, in the presence of Jesus but newly back from the wilderness, and in the presence of all the people—is now prepared to make the formal pronouncement.

What words of preparation and background he used we do not know; no doubt this great and formal introduction was the climax of a persuasive and powerful sermon. But when it came, it was in these words: "*Behold the Lamb of God, which taketh away the sin of the world.*" *The Lamb of God!* He that taketh away the sin of the world! How fitting that John, a priest, who, like his father before him, had offered lambs in sacrifice on the great altar—to atone for the sins of repentant Israel—should now introduce his Master as the Lamb of God, as the one whose coming sacrifice would give efficacy, virtue, and force to all the sacrifices of the past and make freedom from sin available to all men!

This pronouncement—and surely the words spoken were chosen by the Holy Ghost, whose guidance was ever with John—surely this majestic declaration stirred in the hearts of his hearers a remembrance of Isaiah's Messianic teachings about the Lord's Suffering Servant who should come. John may even have quoted from Israel's Messianic prophet, as he had done in announcing that he himself was the voice of one crying in the wilderness: "Prepare ye the way of the Lord, make straight in the desert a highway for our God. . . . And the glory of the Lord shall be revealed." (Isa. 40:3-5.)

The Lamb of God! To be slain for the sins of the world! The Lord's Suffering Servant! The Promised Messiah!

Had not Isaiah said, "He hath borne our griefs, and carried our sorrows"? Were we not promised that he would be "wounded for our transgressions" and "bruised for our iniquities," and that "with his stripes we are healed"? Did not Isaiah say, "The Lord hath laid on him the iniquity of us all," and that "he is brought as a lamb to the slaughter"? The Lamb of God, brought as a lamb to the slaughter!

Does not the Messianic prophecy say, "He was cut off out of the land of the living: for the transgression of my people was he stricken"? Is it not written that "it pleased the Lord to bruise him," and that he should "make his soul an offering for sin"? Was he not to "see the travail of his soul," and to "justify many; for he shall bear their iniquities"? Were not these Isaiah's words: "He hath poured out his soul unto death; . . . and he bare the sin of many, and made intercession for the transgressors"? (Isa. 53.)

Surely John's formal introduction—"Behold the Lamb of God, which taketh away the sin of the world"—crystallized, in the minds of receptive hearers, the whole purpose of four thousand years of sacrifices, all performed in similitude of the sacrifice of the Only Begotten of the Father.

But John also "bare record of him unto the people, saying, This is he of whom I said; After me cometh a man who is preferred before me; for he was before me, and I knew him, and that he should be made manifest to Israel; therefore am I come baptizing with water. And John bare record, saying: When he was baptized of me, I saw the Spirit descending from heaven like a dove, and it abode upon him. And I knew him; for he who sent me to baptize with water, the same said unto me; Upon whom thou shalt see the Spirit descending, and remaining on him, the same is he who baptizeth with the Holy Ghost."

John, having so testified, must now see to it that his disciples—all those baptized by him for the remission of sins—turn to Jesus and receive the promised baptism of the Holy Ghost. He must invite his followers to forsake him, as it were, and follow the one whom he had been sent to introduce.

John's Disciples Follow Jesus
(John 1:35-40)

John, who bore testimony of Jesus, did so for one reason and one reason only: he was seeking to persuade men to believe in Christ, to come unto him, to accept him as the Son of God, and to be saved by obedience to the laws and ordinances of his gospel. When John baptized for the remission of sins, he was not seeking disciples who would follow him, except as he guided them to the one who should come after. Indeed, the very remission of sins that he promised could not come until they received the Holy Ghost—the baptism of fire—which burns sin and evil out of a human soul as though by fire. John's whole purpose was to persuade his disciples to follow, not himself, but the Lord Jesus whose witness he was.

Thus, on the day after the great pronouncement in which he introduced Jesus and testified of his divinity, John was standing, still on Jordan's bank, with two of his disciples. Jesus walked nearby, and John said to his disciples—Andrew, the brother of Simon Peter, and John, the future apostle and revelator—"Behold the Lamb of God!" We do not know what preceded or followed these words; it may well be they were accompanied by explanations relative to John's own ministry—his ministry as the Elias of Preparation—and that also of Jesus, who came as the Elias of Restoration for that day. In any event the two disciples left John and followed Jesus—which was the whole intent and design and purpose of John where they and all of his disciples were concerned.

And this raises a question of great import. Why did Andrew and John leave their Baptist friend—whose doctrines they believed, whose words thrilled their souls, and who had himself baptized each of them in Jordan—to follow another whom as yet they did not even know? What force impels these or any seekers of religious truth to forsake family and friends and possessions and to go they know not where, at the behest of others whom they do not know, but whose words they believe? The answer: they have what we call a testimony; they know in their souls of the truth of the Lord's work; and they are willing to forsake all else to follow the new light that has been kindled in their souls.

What is this thing that we call a testimony? It is the revealed knowledge that Jesus is the Lord; that he is the Son of the living God; that he was crucified for the sins of the world; that he has brought life and immortality to light through his gospel; that his is the only name given under heaven whereby men may be saved; and that his church and kingdom, in whatever age is involved, is the one place where salvation may be found. Such a testimony comes from the Holy Ghost, and from no other source. "By the power of the Holy Ghost ye may know the truth of all things." (Moro. 10:5.)

When the Holy Spirit of God speaks to the spirit within a man—revealing truth, certifying that Jesus is the Savior—the person so blessed has a testimony. This witness comes whenever a person obeys the law upon which its receipt is predicated. "And the Spirit shall be given unto you by the prayer of faith." (D&C 42:14.) When a prophet or righteous man speaks by the power of the Holy Ghost, the Holy Ghost carries his words into the hearts of all who are in tune with the Spirit and bears record to such persons that the words spoken are true. The hearers, thus receiving truth from the Spirit, gain testimonies for themselves. Hence Paul's statement, "It pleased God by the foolishness of preaching to save them that believe." (1 Cor. 1:21.)

And so we find John bearing testimony by the power of the Holy Ghost that Jesus is the Lamb of God, the Savior of the world, whose atoning sacrifice frees men from an eternal burden of sin, and we find Andrew and John—themselves also in tune—receiving the witness in their hearts and knowing for themselves of the truth of what John said. With this knowledge they now have no choice. They must leave John and follow Jesus, for Jesus is the Lord. And so follow him they do.

Jesus, looking upon them, asks, "What seek ye?" They reply, "Rabbi, . . . where dwellest thou?" Jesus says, "Come and see." And they go and abide with Jesus that day, as their question indicates it was their desire to do. What they talked about that day we do not know, but when the day was over they knew, as they had aforetime learned from John, that he was the Messiah. They had determined henceforth to follow him, and they were ready to go out and bear testimony of his divine Sonship and enlist others in his cause.

The transfer of disciples from John to Jesus is now underway; the circle of loyalty toward the forerunner is being enlarged to take in the One who was to come, and we cannot but suppose that thousands of other devout and believing souls left the Baptist to follow the One whom he had baptized.

Jesus Calls Other Disciples

(*John 1:41-51; JST, John 1:42, 44*)

Now the processes of conversion are beginning. Andrew and John have come into the fold. They know Jesus is the Lord—they have heard his voice and believed his words. Andrew now does what every new convert should do: he seeks out the members of his family so they too may receive the saving truths of the gospel. And so Andrew "findeth his own brother Simon," and says: "We have found the Messias." It is just that simple: there was no long period of growth and development; he did not need to hear many sermons and see many miracles; it is not something that he grew into gradually. Andrew knew whereof he spoke, and he knew it the very day he left John and followed Jesus. 'We have found the Christ; he is the Messiah; God's Son has come; he is the Deliverer; John testified of him; and we now bear record that John's witness is true.'

And so Andrew brought Simon—Simon Peter!—unto Jesus. Jesus said: "Thou art Simon, the son of Jona, thou shalt be called Cephas." This new name—"which is, by interpretation, a seer, or a stone"—forecast what was to be in the life of Andrew's brother, who was destined to be, under the Lord, the chief officer of the perfected church and kingdom, the foundations of which were then being laid. Peter, the Rock and the Seer, who would yet hold the keys of the kingdom of heaven; Peter, to whom the Lord would one day say that the gates of hell should never prevail against the rock of revelation and the seership of eternal vision—Peter has now come into the fold.

Whether Peter was one of the Baptist's disciples we do not know, nor do we know how much of the witness of the Lord's Elias he had heard. Having been found by Andrew and having come to Jesus, he was taught the gospel. His soul was open and he believed the message. He too knew, immediately and by instinct, as it were, of the divine Sonship of him whom he now chose to follow. The completeness and surety of the initial conversion of John and Andrew and Peter is attested to in these words of scripture: "And they were fishermen. And they straightway left all, and followed Jesus." Such is the mark of valiant souls who know whereof they speak. These disciples had testimonies of the truth and divinity of the work from the very day they met and were taught by the Lord Jesus. Thereafter they would be fed spiritually by his teachings and his deeds, but from the beginning they were forsaking all to follow him. Even their daily bread and that of their families must somehow be supplied by other means; they are laying down their nets to commence a work that will make them fishers of men.

On the next day, Jesus and his three disciples go into Galilee to a city called Bethsaida. There Jesus himself finds Philip, and says, "Follow me," which means that our Lord and the others told Philip all that had transpired in recent days. They taught him the gospel, told him of the Baptist's teachings and testimony, and, each in turn, bore personal testimony of Jesus' divine Sonship and of the Messianic ministry that was now commencing. Philip believes, not simply because two words are spoken to him, but because the message of salvation is expounded in plainness and by the power of the Spirit. His bosom burns within him, and he knows as the others know.

What then? Philip, being converted, finds Nathanael—who is believed to be Bartholomew, the apostle—and says, "We have found him, of whom Moses in the law, and the prophets, did write, Jesus of Nazareth, the son of Joseph." Moses and the prophets wrote of the Messiah. Philip has gained his testimony, and he is now bearing it to his friend Nathanael. New converts seek out their friends, that they too may receive the light of heaven that has come into their souls. Philip calls Jesus "the son of Joseph," even as Mary said to the young lad in the temple, "Thy father and I have sought thee sorrowing," meaning that Joseph was assumed by those who knew the family to be the father of Him whose Father was divine.

Nathanael's response quotes a derogatory proverb of the day. "Can there any good thing come out of Nazareth?" he asks. Philip's response is the persuasive comment: "Come and see." Whatever else Philip said, his explanations were sufficiently influential to cause Nathanael to accept his invitation. They go to Jesus, who says of the newly found disciple, "Behold an Israelite indeed, in whom is no guile!"

Reacting quite naturally, Nathanael asks, "Whence knowest thou me?" Jesus' response is an exhibition of the gift of seership, the gift to see and have a complete awareness of events in the past, present, or future that transpire out of sight of the viewer. "Nathanael had undergone some surpassing spiritual experience while praying, or meditating, or worshiping under a fig tree. The Lord and giver of all things spiritual, though absent in body, had been present with Nathanael in spirit." (*Commentary* 1:134.) In answer to Nathanael's question, Jesus says: "Before that Philip called thee, when thou wast under the fig tree, I saw thee."

Perhaps our Lord went on to reveal to the future apostle what had actually taken place under the fig tree; and certainly, as Philip and Nathanael had traveled together to the place where Jesus was, there had been extended discussion of the testimony of the Baptist, of the reactions of Andrew and John and Simon, and of Philip himself. All this, coupled with Jesus' seeric declaration, caused the guileless Nathanael to formulate in words what already he had been phrasing in his heart: "Rabbi, thou art the Son of God; thou art the King of Israel." The fifth new convert had been added to our Lord's entourage as he prepared to go from Bethsaida, on the shores of the Sea of Galilee, to Cana, where he would change water into wine. Nathanael now knew as the others knew of the divinity of Him whom they had chosen to follow.

"Because I said unto thee, I saw thee under the fig tree, believest thou?" Jesus asked of his newest disciple, though in fact that was only the crowning cause of the testimony. Then he gave him this promise: "Thou shalt see greater things than these." He was to see greater things than he had seen under the fig tree, and have a greater manifestation of the gift of seership than Jesus had just shown forth. "Verily, verily, I say unto you," our Lord continued, "Hereafter ye shall see heaven open, and the angels of God ascending and descending upon the Son of man." When and under what circumstances this prophetic utterance was fulfilled, we do not know; we have only the ever-present assurance that all things that this Man ever spake came to pass according to his word.

Jesus here calls himself the Son of Man—not in allusion, as is falsely supposed by the scholars of sectarianism, to his humanity, as inherited from Mary, but he calls himself the Son of Man because God, who is his Father, is a Holy Man. "In the language of Adam, Man of Holiness is his name, and the name of his Only Begotten is the Son of Man, even Jesus Christ." (Moses 6:57.)

All of those whom he has so far called as his special disciples, as his traveling companions, as those who are to forsake all and follow him in his ministry, as those who one day will be called to the holy apostleship—all of these have borne testimony that they know he is divine. They have said he is the Messias; he is the one of whom Moses and the prophets wrote; he is the Son of God; he is the King of Israel. This has been their witness. Now Jesus speaks forth his own testimony of himself. He is the Son of Man, the Son of Man of Holiness, the Son of that Holy Being whom their fathers worshipped in Jehovah's name.

Truly Jesus' ministry has begun. He is teaching the gospel. He is calling disciples to forsake all and follow him. He is accepting their Spirit-born witness that he is God's Son, and he is adding his own testimony that their words are true, saying in his own words, 'I am the Son of Man, the Son of God. Follow thou me.'

JESUS BEGINS HIS MIRACLES

The Lord Omnipotent . . . shall go forth amongst men, working mighty miracles, such as healing the sick, raising the dead, causing the lame to walk, the blind to receive their sight, and the deaf to hear, and curing all manner of diseases. (Mosiah 3:5.)

Miracles—Their Nature and Occurrence

Jesus is in Cana of Galilee at a wedding feast. At his mother's earnest entreaty he turns water into wine; about one hundred fifty gallons of water become wine of delicious taste and superior quality, excelling whatever else the guests had been drinking.

It is a miracle, the first public miracle of a great ministry of miracles. Shortly, at his word, the lame shall leap, the blind see, and the ears of the deaf shall be unstopped. We shall soon see the sick healed, paralyzed bodies regain their vigor, and lepers cleansed. He will multiply loaves and fishes, calm storms, and walk on water. He will curse a fig tree, restore a severed ear, and even say to a rotting and stinking corpse: 'Arise; be made whole; live again!'

The Lord Jesus—the Lord of life—is going forth to heal

the sick, cast out devils, and raise the dead, and to perform such marvelous miracles that none who know of them—except those who love darkness rather than light because their deeds are evil—can do aught but say: 'Truly, this is God's Son; he is the Messiah. Let us follow him, and he will save us!'

One by one we shall see him perform his mighty works, and—though we know he is God's Son—yet we shall marvel at the deeds he will do. But as a prelude we must be reminded of the law of miracles and tell ourselves anew of the marvelous way in which the Lord always and everlastingly deals with his people.

What then are miracles, and how are they wrought?

Miracles defy full definition; they are manifestations of the power of God in the lives of men. That which was a miracle yesterday may be commonplace today, and some of the most common events are the greatest miracles. Birth and life and existence—these are miracles, and yet few so consider them. Death is a miracle, as is resurrection, and what is a greater miracle than the cleansing of a sin-sick soul through repentance and the receipt of the Holy Spirit?

We ordinarily think of miracles as those signs and wonders and marvels which God does for his people because they have faith in him, and which they cannot do for themselves. More often than not these performances seem to transcend natural laws, though in fact they are always in complete harmony with them, and are simply the manifestations of higher laws not generally known to mortal men.

Miracles are part of the gospel of the Lord Jesus Christ. They are one of the chief characteristics of true believers. Where they are found, there are the Lord's people; where they are not found, there the Lord's people are not. They are the signs that Deity gives to identify those who have faith. Faith is power, the power of God. Unless men have power, among other things, to perform miracles, they do not have faith.

God is a God of miracles; everlastingly, always, and

without exception, he performs miracles among his people. The decree is that signs shall follow them that believe; unless the signs are present, the beliefs involved are not founded on the Rock of Eternal Truth, who is Christ. God is an "unchangeable Being," a Being "with whom is no variableness, neither shadow of turning"—if it were not so "he would cease to be God," which he cannot do. And because he is "the same yesterday, today, and forever," miracles are always found among those who have faith. (Morm. 9; James 1:17; *Mormon Doctrine*, 2nd ed., pp. 506-8.)

Adam, as Michael, took part in the creation of the earth; and what is a greater miracle than to take unorganized matter and so arrange it that life in all its forms and varieties—including man—can dwell on the planet thus provided for mortal habitation? "Through faith [which is power, God's power] the worlds [this world and all others] were framed by the word of God." (Heb. 11:3.)

And if the earth was made by faith; if great mountains and small streams came into being by God's power; if seas and dry lands took their place because of faith; if storms and tempests and all the elements were set in being by the miracle of creation, why not continue to control and govern all these things by the same power? What is more natural than to see Enoch and Moriancumer move mountains and turn rivers out of their courses? Why should we think it impossible for Moses to part the Red Sea so that its waters congeal into walls on the right hand and on the left? Or what question should arise because Joshua stops the sun, or Jesus stills the storm or walks on the water? Where there is faith, all needed miracles are forthcoming.

Melchizedek, while yet a child, closes the mouths of lions and quenches the violence of fire; Moses and Aaron pour out plagues upon Pharaoh and his people, even to the point of slaying the firstborn in every Egyptian family; Elijah calls down fire from heaven to destroy his enemies, and multiplies the meal and the oil of a widow, whose son he raises from death; and so on and so on and so on. All these miracles—

and they are but samples of what has been—are performed in the name of Christ, by the power of Christ, because men had faith and because signs always follow those who believe.

And it is so obvious that it scarce needs stating, that if the Lord's prophets are dividing seas and stopping the sun, they are also healing the sick and opening the eyes of the blind. For instance: "There were great and marvelous works wrought by the disciples of Jesus, insomuch that they did heal the sick, and raise the dead, and cause the lame to walk, and the blind to receive their sight, and the deaf to hear; and all manner of miracles did they work among the children of men; and in nothing did they work miracles save it were in the name of Jesus." (4 Ne. 1:5.)

And it also scarce needs stating, so obvious is the fact, that the Son of God in his mortal ministry, sent as he was to labor among men and to save that which was lost, was destined to perform more miracles and work more wonders than any of the prophets who went before or who shall come after. In this, as in all things, he is the pattern.

The Marriage Feast in Cana of Galilee

(*John 2:1-2; JST, John 2:1*)

Jesus and his disciples—Andrew, John, Simon Peter, Philip, and Nathanael-Bartholomew, five noble souls who one day will be apostles—are in Bethsaida on the shores of the Sea of Galilee. The newly called followers of the Messiah are basking in the glory of his presence and in the new light of testimony that has come into their lives. They are all, both Jesus and the disciples, "called" to a marriage and to a marriage feast in nearby Cana—Cana of Galilee, a little village whose name is everywhere known for one reason and one reason only: our Lord performed his first public miracle there.

The Blessed Mary seems to be in charge of the festive portions of the wedding celebration, but no mention is made of Joseph, giving rise to the assumption that he has now passed on to that paradise where the righteous find peace and rest. John's account says the disciples were called, without indicating by whom or on what authority. Shall we not say—since Jesus' ministry has now begun and nothing must be permitted to interfere with it—that their presence was required, that one or more of them was an essential part of the proceedings that ever thereafter would be remembered for the miracle that was then to occur. Scholars generally feel that some member of the Holy Family was being married, and that Mary was supervising and guiding what went on.

Marriages and all that attended them had a significance and an import among the Jews that bespoke the divine origin of the sacred ordinance. They and their fathers believed that a proper marriage in the house of Israel had eternal implications. In Jesus' day there was a formal betrothal ceremony, after which the parties—as pertaining to inheritance, adultery, and the need for a formal divorce—were considered as married, except that they did not live together as husband and wife until after the later and second ceremony.

Devout persons fasted and confessed their sins before marriage and believed they gained a forgiveness of sins by entering the holy order of matrimony. They even had an allegory among them that "God Himself had spoken the words of blessing over the cup at the union of our first parents, when Michael and Gabriel acted as groomsmen, and the angelic choir sang the wedding hymn." (Edersheim 1:353.)

On the evening of the marriage, the bride was taken in a bridal procession to her husband's home. It was customary for friends and neighbors and onlookers to join the procession. A formal ceremony was performed; a legal instrument was signed; the required washings were performed and benedictions spoken; the cup was filled, blessed, and drunk; and the marriage supper commenced. The marriage feast lasted from a day to a week or more, with a governor of the feast acting as master of ceremonies.

Jesus' attendance at the marriage in Cana and his participation in the marriage festivities—whatever the reason and whatever the part he played—puts a divine stamp of approval upon marriage and its attendant festivities. Those who forbid marriage to any portion of their adherents are not of God. Also, at the very beginning of his ministry, it dramatized the course his ministerial service would take. Whereas John, the last legal administrator of the Old Order, had come fasting, praying, obeying the letter of the law, a prophet of the traditional mien, garbed in garments made of camel's hair—our Lord, the great Prophet of the New Order, came eating and drinking and associating with his fellows in a friendly and easy manner. His was to be a ministry among and with people, a ministry to touch the lives of men in ways in which they had never been touched before. And indeed, where better could he begin his ministry of public miracles than at a wedding feast, and upon an occasion when joy and rejoicing were in every heart?

Jesus Turns Water into Wine

(*John 2:3-12; JST, John 2:4, 9, 11*)

Every hour of every day somewhere on earth the Lord turns water into wine. By his power, pursuant to the laws he has ordained, men prepare the soil and plant the vine; from the good earth, from the rains that fall, and from the light of the sun, the vine takes nutrient, grows, and bears fruit; men dung it and dig about it and prune it, and the fruit matures and ripens; they harvest the crop and process it in the wine vat; and it comes out as wine on the lees well refined. It is a miracle. He who has given a law unto all things provides the way and the means; the water and the elements that could turn into raisins become wine instead. Life in all its forms is a miracle, and the transmutation, as it were, of one substance into another is a part and portion of earthly existence.

But in March of A.D. 27 in Cana, an obscure village of

Galilee that would not even be known today, had not this event occurred there, the Lord of life—who is the very one who gave a law unto all things, by which they grow and are and change—he who is the Lord Jesus, turned water into wine, in an instant, suddenly as it were, by laws known to him but unknown to us. It was a miracle, the first of his public miracles.

"The miracles of Christ were miracles addressed," Farrar says, "not to a cold and skeptic curiosity, but to a loving and humble faith. They needed not the acuteness of the impostor, or the self-assertion of the thaumaturge. They were indeed the signs—almost, we had said, the accidental signs—of his divine mission; but their primary object was the alleviation of human suffering, or the illustration of sacred truths, or, as in this instance, the increase of innocent joy. An obscure village, an ordinary wedding, a humble home, a few faithful peasant guests—such a scene, and no splendid amphitheatre or stately audience, beheld one of Christ's greatest miracles of power." (Farrar, pp. 127-28.)

At some point in the wedding festivities, apparently after the joyous feast had gone on for some time, "the mother of Jesus saith unto him, They have no wine." That she felt some obligation to the assembled guests none can doubt, and that she expected her Son to do something about it is also clear. Perhaps Jesus himself, at this particular marriage supper, had a personal obligation to look out for the well-being of the guests and see that they wanted for nothing. Eastern hospitality was of such a nature that it would be a matter of great embarrassment to those in charge of the festivities if the needs of the guests went unheeded.

But we are left to surmise what Mary expected Jesus to do, and it is not unreasonable to conclude that she wanted him to use his divine power. She knew God was his Father; she knew of the angelic message sent at his birth, and of the heavenly choirs that sang hosannas to his name; she had heard the testimony of Simeon and Anna in the temple; she had seen the wise men from the East and heard their witness; she knew of the angelic direction Joseph had received; and she had received the gentle rebuke, "Wist ye not that I must be about my Father's business?" when she and Joseph found their twelve-year-old teaching in the temple. Of all this we are certain.

And we cannot avoid the conclusion that between Jesus' twelfth and thirtieth years there were many marvelous and miraculous things of which Mary knew. There is no reason to believe there was a spiritual drought of eighteen years, a period when all that was divine and heaven-guided should be obscured. Nor can we avoid believing that Mary was made aware of the mission and testimony of John—her first cousin once removed, the son of her confidante and counselor, Elisabeth, the one whose birth Gabriel had also heralded.

Surely she would have been told of her Son's baptism—if indeed she was not present—and of the descent of the Holy Ghost upon him, and of the voice from heaven which said: "This is my beloved Son, in whom I am well pleased. Hear ye him." She may already have learned of Jesus' forty days in the wilderness and of the spiritual experiences and the temptations incident to them. And we would suppose that accounts of the conversion of the first disciples had reached her. The five who were with Jesus at the marriage would have sought her out to recount how they knew that the fruit of her womb was, as Philip expressed it, "Him of whom Moses in the law, and the prophets, did write," or as Nathanael testified, "The Son of God . . . the King of Israel."

In this setting, how can we do other than suppose that Mary expected her Son to provide the wine that would assure the success of the celebration then under way.

Jesus' reply seems to contain—as did his words as a twelve-year-old in the temple—a mild reproof. "Woman," he said—a form of salutation that was respectful according to the language and customs of the day, a form of salutation that he would again use as he beheld her at the foot of the cross and was lovingly putting her in the care and keeping of his beloved John—"Woman," he said, "what have I to do with thee? mine hour is not yet come." It is as though he said: 'Please, I am no longer placed in your care. No longer am I subject to the guidance of an earthly mother. My ministry has commenced. I am on my Father's business, and I must make the choices. I will determine when the hour is ripe to perform miracles, to preach, to do all that I am sent to do.'

His mother, understanding, knowing him and his ways, aware of their relationship, and receiving his gentle reproof, yet having perfect confidence in him and knowing her request was right and would be granted, said to the servants: "Whatsoever he saith unto you, do it."

Now it was the practice of the Jews—pharisaically imposed and rabbinically endorsed—to wash, for ritualistic and purification purposes, their hands before and after eating and also to wash the vessels used. The regulations and procedures, set out in the Mishnah and Talmud, were burdensome, unrealistic, and detailed. In the house in Cana six waterpots of stone were available for this purpose. Apparently they were empty, but each, when full, may have held as much as twenty-five gallons, making as much as one hundred fifty gallons of water available for the ritualistic performances of that abode.

Jesus said to the servants, "Fill the waterpots with water." They filled them to the brim. "Draw out now, and bear unto the governor of the feast," he said; and they did so.

Tasting "the water that was made wine," and not knowing whence it came, though the servants knew, the governor said to the bridegroom: "Every man at the beginning doth set forth good wine; and when men have well drunk, then that which is worse: but thou hast kept the good wine until now."

We can well imagine the sense of reverential awe that came into the hearts of the revelers as the servants let it be known what Mary's Son had done. And we can suppose that all the villagers wondered and asked, as they heard the account, 'What manner of man is this? We thought he was a carpenter of Nazareth; can he be the Messiah, as some say?' John says that by this act, Jesus "manifested forth his glory; and his disciples believed on him." Miracles follow faith, and miracles strengthen faith.

Jesus turned water into wine. Did he speak out or merely will it so? No matter; it is the deed that counts. He who but shortly before had refused to turn stones into bread to feed his own famished soul, and that for good and sufficient reasons, now provided sweet nectar for others that they might add to their already sated pleasures, as they rejoiced with a bride and a bridegroom in their newfound happiness. Ought we not also to turn the ordinary waters of life—the ritualistic and mundane washings and performances that go with mortality—into the wine of righteousness and joy that dwells in the hearts of those whose lives are purified?

After the wedding feast Jesus, Mary, her other sons, and the five disciples went to Capernaum, where they stayed until time to go to the Feast of the Passover in Jerusalem, which our Lord must needs attend and where his ministry was to take a turn and gain a prominence that none but he could now foresee.

JESUS MINISTERS AT THE PASSOVER

I am become a stranger unto my brethren, and an alien unto my mother's children. For the zeal of thine house hath eaten me up; and the reproaches of them that reproached thee are fallen upon me. (Ps. 69:8-9.)[1]

Jesus Attends the Feast of the Passover

(*John 2:12-13*)

Our Blessed Lord, after turning water into wine at the wedding celebration in Cana—which was in March of A.D. 27, according to the chronology we are using—chose for himself a city of residence, a home base as it were for the years of his active ministry. That city was Capernaum. Matthew says he "dwelt" there, that it was "his own city." (Matt. 4:13; 9:1.)

We are left to suppose that Mary and her other sons also now lived in this beautiful spot on the shores of the Sea of Galilee; at least they traveled with Jesus from Cana to Capernaum after the wedding feast. We know it was the home of Peter and Andrew, and of James and John, and that it was the place where Matthew sat as a collector of customs. It may be that on the occasion of this visit—for Jesus traveled much and abode in many places during the years of his ministry, and indeed had no permanent place to lay his head—it may be that he stayed with his family members. On later occasions it was his wont to stay with Peter.

Capernaum itself, in the days of Jesus, lay amid the wealth and prosperity of Palestine. The fertility of the plain of Gennesarct was legendary; the district itself was spoken of as "the garden of God" and as "paradise." It was here that Capernaum and numerous other cities, all exceeding fifteen thousand in population, were located. The Sea of Galilee, otherwise called the Lake of Gennesaret, was plied by four thousand boats. Industry, agriculture, and commerce thrived in all the cities there located.

Jesus' choice of Capernaum as the city of his abode placed him in the mainstream of Galilean life, in the midst of a people—part Jewish, part Gentile—where he, as the Light sent forth "to lighten the Gentiles," could fulfill Isaiah's Messianic utterance: 'In the land of Zebulun and of Naphtali, beyond Jordan, in Galilee of the Gentiles, the people that walk in darkness shall see a great light; they that dwell in the land of the shadow of death, upon them shall the light shine.' (Isa. 9:1-2.)

And shine it did, as shine it must, for a short season, following which Capernaum, then exalted to heaven, would be brought down to hell. "For if the mighty works, which have been done in thee," Jesus would soon say, "had been done in Sodom, it would have remained until this day." (Matt. 11:23-24.) Today we do not so much as know the site of ancient Capernaum.

But Jesus' stay in Capernaum on this occasion was brief. John says that "he, and his mother, and his brethren, and his disciples"—including, at least, Peter, Andrew, John, Philip, and Nathanael-Bartholomew—"continued there not many days." It would appear that the whole group of them then "went up to Jerusalem" with Jesus, because "the Jews' passover was at hand." Perhaps Jesus, during his brief stay there, had some opportunity to preach and teach in the streets; certainly any Sabbaths would have seen him in the synagogue teaching doctrine, bearing testimony, and working miracles. But the Passover, and the Feast of Unleavened Bread, which was linked with it, was now to receive the chief attention of the little group. In the year A.D. 27 these festive events covered the period April 11 to 18.

This Passover time—the first of four during Jesus' mortal ministry—was a glorious time of festivity and worship when every faithful male in Israel, if he could possibly arrange it, presented himself before the Lord in the Holy Temple in the Holy City. As the First of the Faithful, Jesus must do his duty and go to worship in his Father's House.

There again, as when first he went up at the age of twelve, and as when he attended during all the years of his preparation, he will mingle with the worshipping throngs and feel the spirit of a people set apart from all nations because they worship Jehovah and sacrifice to his holy name. There, as is his wont, he will keep the feast, eat the paschal lamb, and renew his covenant to serve God and keep his commandments—all in connection with the sacrificial offerings that will be made, legally and officially, by those holding the Priesthood of Aaron.

But this time—with holy zeal, for was it not written, "The zeal of thine house hath eaten me up"?—this time he himself, the future Paschal Lamb, will minister as none others had before done in that house which his Father still owns, but which has been desecrated by designing and sinful men whose hearts are set on money and carnal things rather than upon the great sacrificial ceremonies that would have freed them from their sins.

Jesus Cleanseth His Father's House

(*John 2:14-17*)

Arriving in Jerusalem to keep the Feast of the Passover, Jesus and his friends found their way to the Holy Temple, as all who came up to the Holy City to worship the King, the Lord of Hosts, at that season must needs do. He and his disciples came to his Father's House, to the House of the Most High God, to the house where all Israel had been commanded to worship the Father in the name of the Son by the power of the Holy Ghost. He and they came to join in worship of the Supreme Being, to place themselves in tune with the Infinite, to renew their covenants, and (in the case of all save the Sinless One who led the group) to receive a remission of their sins through the sacrificial ordinances that would be performed by those legal administrators who sat in Aaron's seat.

His Father's House! Outwardly a house of glory and honor, with solid gold covering the great marble stones of the inner temple building; the great altar of unhewn stones in daily use; the holy place, containing the table for the Bread of the Presence, the golden candlestick, and the altar of incense, in constant use; the veil and the Holy of Holies, into which the high priest went each year to make an atonement for the sins of the people, as it should be—outwardly, in architecture and form and magnificence, his Father's House was, for that day and time, as it should have been.

But inwardly it was full of ravening wolves, as it were, of greedy souls who made merchandise of sacred things, and whose hearts were sealed against the true meanings and purpose of the sacred ceremonies designed for that holy place. It is no wonder that the Shekinah no longer rested in the Holy of Holies, nor would it have done so even if the ark of the covenant—with the tables from Sinai, the Urim and Thummim (as we suppose), the mercy seat of pure gold, and the Cherubim—had been present as of old. It was to this spiritual wickedness that a righteously indignant Son of God now addressed himself.

Having passed through the vendor-crowded streets where hawkers of wares sought to profit from the traveling worshippers; having been enticed to buy salt and oil and wine and all else for sacrifices; having been offered clay dishes and ovens for the Passover lamb; having faced the higher prices made possible by the tourist trade, Jesus and his group came into the outer court, the Court of the Gentiles. There they looked upon a scene of unholy merchandising that desecrated the temple and testified against those who were engaged in its money-grubbing practices. There they saw the moneychangers, those who examined sacrificial animals for a fee, the sellers of sheep, and the hawkers of oxen and doves. The noise and the haggling destroyed every vestige of reverence; the lowing of cattle and the bleating of sheep drowned out the priestly performances nearby; and the filth and stench of the barnyard so overpowered the senses that arriving pilgrims soon lost the desire to worship the Lord in Spirit and in truth. It was a scene of desecration, of physical filth, and of spiritual degeneracy.

Moneychangers in the temple of the Lord! Greed and avarice and sharp dealing replacing the spirit of true worship! True it was that each year all Israel, both Jews and proselytes—women, slaves, and minors excepted—had to pay the atonement money to ransom their souls. This temple-tribute of half a shekel, payable only in the shekel of the Sanctuary, gave rise to a thriving and profitable exchange business. Palestinian, Roman, Grecian, Egyptian, Tyrian, and Persian coins, among others, were in common circulation in the Holy Land. Money-changing involved weighing the coins, taking deductions for loss of weight, arguing, debating, disputing, bargaining, oftentimes using scales of questionable accuracy. Tables piled high with coins of all denominations and nations were the stock in trade of those who charged a fixed fee, and more, in the lucrative enterprise.

For a fee those who brought their own sacrificial animals had them examined at the temple for Levitical fitness. All that was needed for meat offerings and drink offerings was for sale within the sacred walls. Oxen, sheep, and doves could be purchased outright. There is a record of Baba ben

Buta bringing in three thousand sheep at one time for sale in the Court of the Gentiles. Great herds of cattle and tiers of wickers filled with flocks of doves were more the rule than the exception. A courtyard, paved with marble, that could accommodate two hundred and ten thousand people had ample room for the needed sacrificial animals, for those who bought and sold, and for those who weighed and haggled as coins exchanged hands.

Profits earned or extorted through all this sacrifice-related merchandising went both to individuals and to the temple officials. Sums paid for the items needed for meat and drink offerings went directly to the temple; others paid rent for the use of temple space. Even a temple market, referred to as the bazaars of the sons of Annas, occupied part of the space in the court. Annas was, of course, the high priest before whom Jesus would stand in three years during another Passover season. There was considerable popular resentment against the sons of Annas and their temple merchandising. "From the unrighteousness of the traffic carried on in these Bazaars, and the greed of their owners," Edersheim says, "the 'Temple-market' was at the time most unpopular." Because of the prevalent abuses, he says, it is "no wonder that, in the figurative language of the Talmud, the Temple is represented as crying out against them: 'Go hence, ye sons of Eli, ye defile the Temple of Jehovah!' " (Edersheim 1:371-72.)[2]

This popular feeling relative to the merchandising practices that desecrated the temple enables us to see why there was no popular outcry when Jesus drove out the cattle and the money-changers. Aside from the fact that the targets of his indignation had their mouths closed by their own guilty consciences, the cleansing act performed by our Lord seems to have met with popular appeal among the people.

We have no doubt that the eyes of many were upon Jesus when he entered the Temple Court. It was as though the Lord whom they sought had "suddenly come to his temple." He was there in person, the Incarnate Jehovah, not to "purify the sons of Levi" (Mal. 3:1-3), as he would do at his Second Coming, but to drive out both the men and beasts whose filth and dung desecrated the Holy Place.

We are confident that word of his coming had preceded him. John's testimony that Jesus was the Lamb of God had not been borne in a corner. All Jerusalem had heard the word. The testimonies of his own disciples had surely been noised about, and the Galilean pilgrims who came to the Passover would not have hesitated to speak of the water that became wine.

And so, as the center of attraction, with many waiting and wondering what this new Rabbi would do, he who eighteen years before had said, within these same walls, that he must be about his Father's business, now engaged in that business with vigor and vengeance.

Sickened by the stench and the filth, repulsed by the jangling and haggling as paltry coins were exchanged, saddened by the complete absence of spirituality with which the chosen people should have been so richly endowed, the Son of Him whose house these evil miscreants then desecrated "made a scourge of small cords." Then, filled with indignant justice, his righteous anger blazing forth in physical strength, he of whom Moses had said, "The Lord is a man of war" (Ex. 15:3), this Galilean from Nazareth, drove out the sheep and the oxen and those in whose custody they lowed and bleated.

To the keepers of the doves he commanded: "Take these things hence." With force and violence he overturned the tables of the moneychangers, scattering their ill-gotten coins amid the dirt and dung on the marble floor. To those who bought and sold, who haggled in the temple bazaars, and whose hearts were set on laying up treasures on earth rather than in heaven, with a voice of authority he decreed: *"Make not my Father's house an house of merchandise."*

Truly, as Peter and John and Andrew and Philip and Nathanael and all his disciples saw this open and bold ushering in of our Lord's Messianic ministry, they rejoiced in what he did and remembered the Messianic words of Israel's greatest king: *"The zeal of thine house hath eaten me up."*

"My Father's house!" "Thine house," O God, *'for thou art my Father.'* When but a lad of twelve, when a mature man of thirty—during all the years of his life and ministry—Jesus, freely, openly, publicly, to all men, be they devoted disciples or sinning scribes, was bold to announce that God was his Father. Even the cleansing and purifying of the house Herod had built for the Hebrews became an occasion for such a solemn declaration. Jesus was God's Son. He knew it, and he wanted all men to gain the same sure knowledge.

Jesus Foretells His Own Death and Resurrection

(*John 2:18-25; JST, John 2:22, 24*)

Jesus has driven the cattle and sheep from the Court of the Gentiles; the cages of doves have been removed from the sacred site; the coins and scales of the bankers, who contended over the weight of their coins, are lying in the rubble; and the temple bazaars of the sons of Annas the high priest are in shambles. Merchandising in the temple has ceased, and profits are no longer flowing into the pockets of the rapacious and priest-appointed merchants who plied their wares among the Passover throngs. Indeed, their flocks and herds are scattered, their coins lost, and their merchandise destroyed. The loss to individuals and to the temple treasury itself is of giant proportion.

And yet there is no public outcry. No Roman soldiers have come to keep the peace. No one calls for Jesus' arrest. No one even berates him for causing a disturbance or for destroying the property of the merchants. One thing only happens. The leaders of the people and the officials of the temple ask, "What sign shewest thou unto us, seeing that thou doest these things?" There is no resistance, no seeming bitterness over financial loss—just an inquiry as to why he has overstepped his bounds and cleansed the temple when it is their responsibility to regulate all that therein transpires.

Why this mild reaction on the part of those whose property has been destroyed and whose functions have been assumed? We have already noted that there was popular support for the cleansing of the Temple Court; the dealings of the sons of Annas were known by the common people to be corrupt. But there was a greater reason. In the persuasive and well-chosen words of Canon Farrar, it is summarized in these words:

"Why did not this multitude of ignorant pilgrims resist? Why did these greedy chafferers content themselves with dark scowls and muttered maledictions, while they suffered their oxen and sheep to be chased into the streets and themselves ejected, and their money flung rolling on the floor, by one who was then young and unknown, and in the garb of despised Galilee? Why, in the same way we might ask, did Saul suffer Samuel to beard him in the very presence of his army? Why did David abjectly obey the orders of Joab? Why did Ahab not dare to arrest Elijah at the door of Naboth's vineyard? *Because sin is weakness;* because there is in the world nothing so abject as a guilty conscience, nothing so invincible as the sweeping tide of a Godlike indignation against all that is base and wrong. How could these paltry sacrilegious buyers and sellers, conscious of wrong-doing, oppose that scathing rebuke, or face the lightnings of those eyes that were kindled by an outraged holiness? When Phinehas the priest was zealous for the Lord of Hosts, and drove his javelin through the bodies of the prince of Simeon and the Midianitish woman with one glorious thrust, why did not guilty Israel avenge that splendid murder? Why did not every man of the tribe of Simeon become a *Goel* to the dauntless assassin? Because Vice cannot stand for one moment before Virtue's uplifted arm. Base and grovelling as they were, these money-mongering Jews felt in all that remnant of their souls which was not yet eaten away by infidelity and avarice, that the Son of Man was right.

"Nay, even the Priests and Pharisees, and Scribes and Levites, devoured as they were by pride and formalism, could not condemn an act which might have been performed by a Nehemiah or a Judas Maccabæus, and which agreed with all that was purest and best in their traditions. But when they had heard of this deed, or witnessed it, and had time to recover from the breathless mixture of admiration, disgust, and astonishment which it inspired, they came to Jesus, and though they did not dare to condemn what He had done, yet half indignantly asked Him for some sign that he had a right to act thus." (Farrar, pp. 144-46.)

Show us a sign! 'What proof can you offer that you are entitled to cleanse the courts of the temple?' The mere fact that they asked such a question shows that doubt and fear were rising in their minds: 'What if this Man really is the Messiah, as his disciples say?'

But the Lord and his prophets do not perform miracles to prove their divine appointments and priestly powers. Signs follow faith, and faith precedes the miracle. It is a wicked and adulterous generation that seeks for a sign. For them there is only one sign—"The sign of the prophet Jonas: For as Jonas was three days and three nights in the whale's belly; so shall the Son of man be three days and three nights in the heart of the earth." (Matt. 12:38-40.)

That is to say, for the wicked and ungodly, for those without faith, for those who reject the words of the prophets, there is only one sign: *the work itself.* Prophets are known by their fruits. If "the church is built upon my gospel," Jesus said to the Nephites, "then will the Father show forth his own works in it." (3 Ne. 27:10.) There are to be no signs—meaning no miracles or gifts of the Spirit—for unbelievers. They are left to pursue their own course now, but in a future day they shall know that Jesus rose again the third day and is the Son of God. His resurrection is the sign; it proves his divine Sonship and testifies of the power resident in him to cleanse the temple or do all else that his Father commands.

And so, "Jesus answered and said unto them, Destroy this temple, and in three days I will raise it up." The sign of the prophet Jonas! The only sign for wicked men! The sign that proves the work is true when it is everlastingly too late, everlastingly too late for those who seek for signs in a day when they should seek for faith, that signs might follow!

'Crucify me; destroy this body; place me in the Arimathean's tomb; and, lo, in three days I shall rise again, rise in glorious immortality, rise to judgment. This shall be your sign.'

Whether Jesus, in his answer, said more than the bare words quoted by John we do not know; but this we do know: those to whom he spoke, despite their false pretensions, knew exactly what he meant. They knew that to destroy the temple meant to take the life of the Nazarene, and that his promise to "raise it up" in three days meant that his dead body would come forth in immortality on the third day.

It may well be that one of the very reasons Jesus cleansed the temple was so he could say—in this setting, using a figure, and with words that would never be forgotten—that he would be slain and would come forth in the resurrection on the third day. In any event, his spoken word, so dramatically phrased, was not forgotten. Three years later a false witness, hoping to see him crucified on a Roman cross, would testify: "We heard him say, I will destroy this temple that is made with hands, and within three days I will build another made without hands." (Mark 14:58.) And a reviling scoffer, glorying in the agony of our Lord's crucifixion and awaiting the death that all felt was near, taunted the Cleanser of the Temple by saying: "Ah, thou that destroyest the temple, and buildest it in three days, Save thyself, and come down from the cross." (Mark 15:29-30.) And yet again, while his body lay in the tomb, a Jewish spokesman, hearkening back to our Lord's declaration made at this memorable Passover, would say to Pilate: "Sir, we remember that that deceiver said, while he was yet alive, After three days I will rise again" (Matt. 27:63), with reference to which Canon Farrar so aptly says: "Now there is no trace that Jesus had *ever* used any such words distinctly to them; and unless they had heard the saying from Judas, or unless it had been repeated by common rumour derived from the Apostles—*i.e.,* unless the 'we remember' was a distinct falsehood—they could have been referring to no other occasion than this." (Farrar, p. 149.)

And yet their immediate response to Jesus was: "Forty and six years was this temple in building, and wilt thou rear it up in three days?"[3] At this point in the record John says simply: "But he spake of the temple of his body."

After his resurrection—and the sign proving he was God's Son, the sign proving he had power to cleanse the temple, was the fact of resurrection—his disciples remembered the teachings of this day and believed all of the words Jesus had spoken unto them.

At this Passover Jesus performed many miracles, none of which are named or described in the Gospel accounts. John says simply that "many believed on his name, when they saw the miracles which he did." But Jesus, knowing "all things," including the fact that faith founded solely on miracles leaves much to be desired, "did not commit himself unto them." He sought no motley throng who followed because the sick are healed and the dead raised. His disciples must, like Peter, gain the witness of his divine Sonship by the power of the Holy Ghost. And this revealed knowledge was to come to many in the years ahead.

NOTES

1. John quotes the portion of these Messianic words that apply to the cleansing of the temple by our Lord during the First Passover of his ministry. The disciples, John says, saw in them a Messianic prophecy of the zeal of their Messiah toward his Father's House. The further pronouncement—relative to the Messiah's "brethren" and to his "mother's children"—is also of particular note at this time when Jesus has just attended a wedding celebration with his mother and the other children in her family, and when he has traveled with Mary and his brethren from Cana to Capernaum. The words "my mother's children" are a clear promise that Mary would have other children in addition to the Firstborn. It is the Catholic view that those mentioned in the New Testament as being brothers and sisters of Jesus were the children of Joseph by a former marriage and that the Blessed Virgin had but one offspring. To show that this could not be, it is merely necessary to ask: How could Jesus be the heir to the throne of David—through Joseph, as the New Testament genealogies recite—if Joseph had elder sons? Other like questions might be: What became of the motherless brothers and sisters when Joseph and Mary went to Bethlehem and then

into Egypt? And why is there no mention of them on such occasions as the Passover trip to Jerusalem when Jesus was twelve? To those who esteem marriage as being ordained of God, and who, with Paul, believe that "marriage is honourable in all, and the bed undefiled" (Heb. 13:4), there is nothing indelicate or inappropriate in the Mother of the Son of God having other children by Joseph, her legal and lawful husband.

2. Of special interest is this further comment of Edersheim: "These Temple-Bazaars, the property, and one of the principal sources of income, of the family of Annas, were the scene of the purification of the Temple by Jesus; and in the private *locale* attached to these very Bazaars, where the Sanhedrin held its meetings at the time, the final condemnation of Jesus may have been planned, if not actually pronounced." (Edersheim 1:372.)

3. It is April of A.D. 27, and forty-six years have already gone into the building of Herod's Temple. It will not be completed until A.D. 63, just seven years before the soldiers of Titus will tear it apart, stone by stone, as they acquire the gold that now covers the marble blocks.

Chapter 30

NICODEMUS VISITS JESUS

Marvel not that all mankind, yea, men
and women, all nations, kindreds,
tongues and people, must be
born again; yea, born of God, changed from
their carnal and fallen state, to a state
of righteousness, being redeemed of God,
becoming his sons and daughters;
And thus they become new creatures;
and unless they do this, they can in nowise
inherit the kingdom of God.
(Mosiah 27:25-26.)[1]

Jesus' Ministry Divides the People

Our Friend and Brother, the Lord Jesus—and blessed be he—has now spent about two months in his active and formal ministry among men. As nearly as we can tell—and this is the chronology followed by President J. Reuben Clark, Jr.—Jesus was baptized by John in Jordan in January, A.D. 27; his forty days of fasting, prayer, and worship in the wilderness were in January and February (possibly continuing into March); probably he began to teach and call disciples (Andrew, Simon, and others) in February, not later than in March; and in March in Cana came the first public miracle, the changing of water into wine. Now it is Passover time, April 11-18, and the place is Jerusalem, the Holy City.

Our Lord has driven from the Temple Court the sacrificial animals, probably numbering in the thousands; has used a scourge of small cords upon the carnal men who made merchandise in his Father's House; and has extended his own arm of healing to bless and cure many—and all Jerusalem is aware of the miracles he has done. Up to this point in the scriptural accounts there is no record of what he has said in any sermon or of what he did in the performance of any miracle, except the one in Cana. All this now is to change.

Perhaps he began his ministry when he was baptized by his kinsman; perhaps it was when he overcame temptation and viewed the wonders of eternity while in the wilderness; perhaps it was when he taught and called disciples. No matter. But when he openly confronted the priestly powers of the whole nation; when he announced that God was his Father, and that he would be slain and rise again the third day; and when he confirmed—proved, if you will—his right so to act and teach by performing many miracles, then his ministry became the matter of chief concern to all the people in all Palestine. No longer were his deeds done in a corner. No longer could anyone say: 'He is only a Galilean, a Nazarene, someone from a place out of which ariseth no prophet.'

At this Passover Jesus made his ministry the thing that would be uppermost in all minds for the three long years of that ministry, until the fourth Passover, when he would crown his work in Gethsemane, at Golgotha, and before an open tomb.

At this Passover, Jesus divided the people. He began the process of assembling the goats, to be damned, on his left hand, and the sheep, to be saved, on his right.

At this Passover, he incurred the undying enmity of the rulers of the people. Ever thereafter they would plot and scheme and seek to defame his character and mission and to bring about his death.

But at this Passover also, people began to flock to his standard because of his gracious words and his mighty miracles. Many began to believe the reports they had heard of a voice from heaven at his baptism; of a miracle performed in an obscure Galilean city; of disciples who testified openly that he was David's Son, the one of whom Moses and the prophets had written, the Promised Messiah.

And this brings us to Nicodemus—a Pharisee, a ruler of the Jews, one of the Great Sanhedrin—who came to Jesus by night to learn about this new Rabbi whose miracles bore testimony that he had divine power. In effect Nicodemus wanted to investigate the gospel in secret, lest his associates turn against him and his worldly influence wane. His discipleship does not compare with a Peter, who drew his sword in the Master's defense, or of a Thomas—unwisely and somewhat slanderously referred to as Doubting Thomas—who was willing to face persecution for the cause, and once said to the others of the Twelve: "Let us also go, that we may die with him" (John 11:16); or a Stephen, who was stoned to death for saying he saw 'the heavens opened, and the Son of man standing on the right hand of God" (Acts 7:51-60).

But at least he came, and it is apparent that he thereafter believed in Christ and supported the gospel cause. Indeed, as Edersheim says: "It must have been a mighty power of conviction to break down prejudice so far as to lead this old Sanhedrist to acknowledge a Galilean, untrained in the Schools, as a Teacher come from God, and to repair to Him for direction on, perhaps, the most delicate and important point in Jewish theology. But, even so, we cannot wonder that he should have wished to shroud his first visit in the utmost possible secrecy. It was a most compromising step for a Sanhedrist to take. With that first bold purgation of the Temple a deadly feud between Jesus and the Jewish authorities had begun, . . . and it needed not the experience and wisdom of an aged Sanhedrist to forecast the end." (Edersheim 1:381.)

We are left to assume that following his interview with Jesus, the processes of conversion continued to operate in the life of Nicodemus. On one occasion, when the officers of the Sanhedrin excused themselves for their inability to arrest Jesus, Nicodemus asked his fellow rulers: "Doth our law judge any man, before it hear him, and know what he doeth?" (John 7:45-53.) And after Joseph of Arimathea had obtained the body of the Crucified One, Nicodemus "brought a mixture of myrrh and aloes, about an hundred pound weight" (John 19:38-42) for use in preparing the body for burial.

Jesus Teaches: Fallen Man Must Be Born Again

(*John 3:1-12*)

John tells us that Nicodemus came to Jesus by night, and we are left to assume the meeting took place in a house owned or occupied by John in Jerusalem.[2] If so, the interview may well have taken place in the guest chamber on the roof, which would have been accessible via outside stairs. John was either present or Jesus recounted to him what was said. The scriptural account is clearly a digest and recitation of the chief points made in what has come to be called our Lord's first great recorded discourse.

"Rabbi," said Nicodemus in a solemn and respectful way, "we know"—perhaps indicating that he and others of the Sanhedrin had like feelings—"that thou art a teacher come from God." This pronouncement is in effect a testimony. It was clear to every unprejudiced mind that Rabbi Jesus was more than an ordinary teacher. He came from God! "For," Nicodemus continued, "no man can do these miracles that thou doest, except God be with him." If only all his fellow Sanhedrists, and the people generally, had known and remembered this simple test. Those who work miracles of the sort performed by Jesus bear the stamp of divine approval. And if a man both raises the dead and says he is the Son of God, it must of necessity be so, for a dishonest man could not wield the power that says to a decaying corpse: 'Arise and live again, because I will it.'

Jesus' answer was blunt, concise, and apparently not responsive, leading to the assumption that Nicodemus had more to say than has been preserved in the holy record. "Verily, verily, I say unto thee," Jesus said—and note that our Lord is not quoting scripture, not speaking in the name of another as the prophets of old did, but is speaking in his own name, as the Author of truth—"I say unto thee," he says, "Except a man be born again, he cannot see the kingdom of God."

Man must be born again; he must receive the promptings of the Spirit; he must turn from darkness to light; he must die as to carnal things and live again as to the things of righteousness; he must rise from spiritual death and go forth in spiritual life—all this if he is to "see" the truth; if he is to gain a testimony; if he is to know where the truth is and the course he must pursue to gain peace here and eternal reward hereafter.

If ever there were a people or a nation in need of spiritual rebirth, it was the Jewish assemblage of Jesus' day. If ever there were those in darkness who needed the light of heaven to shine in their souls, it was these children of the prophets who now dwelt in the shadow of death. If ever there were a kindred or a kingdom that needed to rise from the degeneracy of the present, as they sought for the glory of the past, it was those among whom God had sent his Son. And as that Son turned the early events of his ministry into a *cause celèbre,* which would come to the attention of all Israel, he chose to speak of being born again. One man must be born again to see the kingdom of God. All men must receive the spiritual rebirth if the people and the nation are to bask in the light of divine favor as had their fathers.

Nicodemus, himself a teacher and a leader of the people,

one who should have been guiding them toward the spiritual rebirth they so much needed, should have known they could not save themselves by continuing in the Herodian course of darkness and rebellion. If the people were to rise again to the heights attained by some under Moses and Joshua, and in the days of Samuel and of David and of Isaiah, they must once more live in the Spirit as the ancients had. If the Shekinah was to rest visibly in the Lord's Holy House, as it did in the days of Moses and Solomon, there must once again be people fit and worthy to enter the divine presence. But Nicodemus did not know; as an appointed teacher of spiritual truths, he himself was in spiritual darkness. "How can a man be born when he is old?" he asked. "Can he enter the second time into his mother's womb, and be born?"

To these foolish questions, which showed a complete lack of understanding of the great moral issues involved, Jesus gave the eternal reply that has been the basis of salvation for men and nations in all ages. Again he spoke solemnly in his own name: "Except a man be born of water and of the Spirit, he cannot enter into the kingdom of God."

Such is the plan of salvation for all men in all ages. Adam fell and brought death—both temporal death and spiritual death—into the world. The effects of his fall passed upon all men; all die temporally, and all are subject to spiritual death. Spiritual death is to die as pertaining to the things of the Spirit, as pertaining to things of righteousness. If men are to live again as pertaining to the things of righteousness, they must receive a spiritual rebirth.

Beginning in the days of Adam, the Lord's word has gone forth among his people "that all men, everywhere, must repent, or they can in nowise inherit the kingdom of God, for no unclean thing can dwell there, or dwell in his presence." By the mouths of Adam and Enoch and prophets in all ages, these words of the Lord have been taught, "That by reason of transgression cometh the fall, which fall bringeth death, and inasmuch as ye were born into the world by water, and blood, and the spirit, which I have made, and so became of dust a living soul, even so ye must be born again into the kingdom of heaven, of water, and of the Spirit, and be cleansed by blood, even the blood of mine Only Begotten; that ye might be sanctified from all sin, and enjoy the words of eternal life in this world, and eternal life in the world to come, even immortal glory."

In all ages past the Lord's people had been taught these things, and to them had been appended this divine proclamation: "This is the plan of salvation unto all men, through the blood of mine Only Begotten, who shall come in the meridian of time." (Moses 6:57-62.)

We suppose that Jesus taught these wondrous truths to the inquiring Sanhedrist, either in the same or similar words. Such a doctrine is the natural prelude to the testimony he was about to bear of himself, that as the Only Begotten of the Father he had come to bring salvation. We do know that he said, "That which is born of the flesh is flesh," meaning that people are born into this world of water and blood and the Spirit, and so become of dust living souls; and we do know that he said: "And that which is born of the Spirit is spirit," meaning that men must be born again of the Spirit if they are to be alive as to spiritual things, and therefore qualify for that spiritual or eternal life reserved for the faithful. And that this second birth, this rebirth, this birth into the kingdom of heaven, is through the waters of baptism, comes by the power of the Holy Ghost, and is possible because of the cleansing power of the blood of Christ is apparent to all. Hence, Jesus says, "Marvel not," Nicodemus, "that I said unto thee, Ye must be born again." The doctrine is so basic, so fundamental, so much at the bedrock of the house of salvation, that he and all men must believe and understand it if they are to gain the promised rewards.

"The wind bloweth where it listeth," Jesus continued—perhaps as they felt the cool refreshment of the night breeze as it gusted and whispered through the dark streets of Jerusalem—"and thou hearest the sound thereof, but canst not tell whence it cometh, and whither it goeth"—for such is the way with the gentle zephyrs, who knoweth their source or their destiny. Then came the gospel verity that grew out of the illustration: "So is every one that is born of the Spirit."

"How can these things be?" Nicodemus asked. 'How can the water of baptism, and the Spirit of the Lord, and the blood of the Only Begotten, constitute a birth into the kingdom of heaven? How can the serene and calm influence of the Spirit—the still small voice, as it were—descend, as from nowhere, upon a human soul?'

"Art thou a master of Israel, and knowest not these things?" comes the reply. 'Art thou an appointed teacher, a guide and a light to the people, a member of the Great Sanhedrin itself, and thou knowest not that spiritual rebirth is the very beginning of righteousness, and that until men are born again they are not so much as on the path leading to eternal life?' Was there just a touch of irony in our Lord's response?

Then in tones of solemn adjuration, as it were, the greatest Rabbi of them all bore testimony of the truths taught by him and by his disciples. "We speak that we do know," he said—as with all the prophets, they were sure of the truths they proclaimed—"and testify that we have seen; and ye receive not our witness." Only those who are alive spiritually can comprehend the deep and hidden meanings of those things spoken by the power of the Spirit; the light may shine in the darkness, but those who choose darkness rather than light comprehend it not.

"If I have told you earthly things, and ye believe not, how shall ye believe, if I tell you of heavenly things." 'If I have told you the simple, basic truths about being born again; if I have told you the first principles—faith, repentance, baptism, and the receipt of the Holy Ghost—and ye believe not, how shall ye either believe or understand if I tell you the "wonders of eternity," "the hidden mysteries of my kingdom," the "things which eye has not seen, nor ear heard, nor yet have entered into the heart of man"?' (*Commentary* 1:142.)

Jesus Testifies: I Am the Messiah, the Son of God, the Only Begotten
(*John 3:13-21; JST, John 3:13, 18, 21-22*)

If all men everywhere must be born again; if they must be born of water and of the Spirit and be cleansed by the blood of the Only Begotten; if they must put off the natural man and become new creatures by the power of the Holy Ghost; if they must taste the good things of the Spirit; if they must believe in the Messiah and accept him as their Savior—all to the end that they may enjoy the words of eternal life here and now and be inheritors of eternal glory hereafter—then the great questions are: Who is the Messiah? Where shall he be found? How is he to be recognized? And what must men do to accept him?

Jesus has a ready answer, the one and only true answer, which he now vouchsafes to Nicodemus. "No man hath ascended up to heaven," he says, "but he that came down from heaven, even the Son of man which is in heaven." Here, then, is one of the "heavenly things" that none can see but those whose spiritual eyes are open, and none can hear but those whose spiritual ears are attuned to the Infinite. It is: 'I am the Messiah, who has come down from heaven. I am the Son of Man of Holiness who is in heaven; and I shall yet ascend to be with God who is my Father.' And if we look upon Nicodemus with a critical eye because he failed to grasp the infinite wonder of this heavenly truth, how much more shall we despair for the hosts of sectarians who, with the New Testament scriptures before them, fail to accept the Son as the Only Begotten in the full and literal sense of the word.

"And as Moses lifted up the serpent in the wilderness," our Lord continues, "even so must the Son of man be lifted up: That whosoever believeth in him should not perish, but have eternal life."

Moses, in the wilderness, when the Lord sent "fiery serpents" among them, so that many people in Israel were bitten and died, made a serpent of brass and put it upon a pole. Then all who were bitten by the poisonous creeping things and who looked, in faith, upon the brazen serpent, lived; the others died. Why? Because Moses was commanded of God so to do, and the thing was an ordinance in Israel—an ordinance performed in similitude of the fact that the Promised Messiah would be lifted up upon the cross, and all who looked to him in faith would live; the others would die. Nephi the son of Helaman, speaking of Moses to his Hebrew brethren, asked: "Did he not bear record that the Son of God should come?" In answer, this ancient American prophet said: "As he [Moses] lifted up the brazen serpent in the wilderness, even so shall he be lifted up who should come. And as many as should look upon that serpent should live, even so as many as should look upon the Son of God with faith, having a contrite spirit, might live, even unto that life which is eternal." (Hel. 8:13-15; Num. 21:4-9.)

Eternal life—life in the highest heaven; the kind of life enjoyed by Deity himself; life reserved for those who receive, inherit, and possess all things—this glorious type and kind of everlasting existence comes to those who believe in the Son of Man! How is it brought to pass? In answer Jesus speaks what is considered by many to be the most glorious and wondrous single verse of scripture ever to fall from the lips of God or man: *"For God so loved the world, that he gave his only begotten Son, that whosoever believeth in him should not perish, but have everlasting life."*[3]

God so loved the world! The Father sent the Son! He is the Only Begotten! Believe in him and gain eternal life! "For God sent not his Son into the world to condemn the world; but that the world through him might be saved." Salvation is in Christ. "He who believeth on him is not condemned; but he who believeth not is condemned already, because he hath not believed on the name of the only Begotten Son of God, which before was preached by the mouth of the holy prophets; for they testified of me."

How could Nicodemus or anyone misunderstand these

teachings? Our Lord is speaking in the early days of his ministry. He is using plain, simple, and forceful language. The doctrine is strong. No parables are involved; nothing is hidden with imagery or in similitudes. He is saying plainly that men must believe in him; that he is the Son of God, the Promised Messiah, the Only Begotten of the Father, the One of whom Moses and the prophets testified. He is saying that men must repent and be baptized in water; that they must receive the companionship of the Holy Spirit and be born again.

It is plain and clear beyond question. Why, then, do not men believe? He answers: "And this is the condemnation, that light is come into the world, and men loved darkness rather than light, because their deeds were evil. For every one that doeth evil hateth the light, neither cometh to the light, lest his deeds should be reproved. But he who loveth truth, cometh to the light, that his deeds may be made manifest. And he who obeyeth the truth, the works which he doeth they are of God."

Jesus has spoken. These are his words. This is his testimony of the doctrine taught and of his own divine Sonship. We shall see these truths accepted by many, and this witness borne by his disciples, as we follow the feet of the Son of God along the dusty lanes of Palestine, and as we hear his voice speaking in private to his disciples and in public to all men.

How glorious is the Voice from heaven!

NOTES

1. These words, more definitive and expressive even than those spoken to Nicodemus, were spoken by the Spirit Lord Jesus to Alma the son of Alma, about a hundred years before our Lord's mortal birth. They are preceded in the Book of Mormon account by Alma's declaration: "I have repented of my sins, and have been redeemed of the Lord; behold I am born of the Spirit." (Mosiah 27:24.) Alma had, of course, been baptized of water in his youth, and the occasion of which he here speaks was the actual receipt by him of the Holy Spirit, without which no man ever receives the new birth.

2. Such ownership is inferred from John 19:27.

3. Similarly, our Lord "so loved the world that he gave his own life, that as many as would believe might become the sons of God." (D&C 34:3.)

JOHN (THE BAPTIST) AND JESUS MINISTER IN JUDEA

Believe on the Lord Jesus Christ, and thou shalt be saved. (Acts 16:31.)

Jesus Preaches and Baptizes in Judea
(*John 3:22; 4:1-3; JST, John 4:2-4; Matthew 4:12; Mark 1:14; Luke 4:14*)

Jesus came to Jerusalem at Passover time—when all Israel was present, either in person or through appointed representatives—to announce publicly and officially, before the rulers and the people, that he, the Promised Messiah, was now among them and that his ministry had commenced. With thunderous and righteous indignation he cleansed the temple and proclaimed his coming death and resurrection, thus affirming that he himself was the Messiah who had life in himself because God was his Father. All this he did openly and before all the people, and we cannot doubt that his acts and deeds were known to most of the two and a half to three million people who crowded into the city and its environs at this most sacred time.

To selected souls—Nicodemus and his own disciples among them—he spoke even more plainly. Men must be born again; repentance and faith in Christ are essential to salvation; he had come down from heaven to atone for the sins of the world; it was of him that Moses and all the prophets had spoken; he was God's Son, the Only Begotten of the Father. It was there, spoken in plain and clear Aramaic. He had announced his divine commission and had done it in the spiritual capital of Jewish Israel. It was done formally; he spoke officially; his voice was the voice of his Father; and his words would stand as a witness in time and in eternity.

Having so done, our Lord's work in Jerusalem, for the moment, was accomplished. With the departing pilgrims, who would carry an account of his doings and sayings to the chosen seed everywhere, he and his disciples also left the Holy City. Their destiny: the villages and cities of Judea, from Beersheba and Moladah in the south, to Masada and Engedi on the Dead Sea, to Joppa in the northwest and Jericho in the northeast. Their mission and purpose: to preach the gospel of the kingdom and to baptize repentant souls. For how long? For nine full months, until December of A.D. 27, at which time—having, as Peter expressed it, preached "throughout all Judea" that "word which God sent unto the children of Israel" (Acts 10:34-43)—he and his disciples went through Samaria (where the conversation at Jacob's Well took place) and into Galilee.

It is not our good fortune to possess a day-by-day account, or even a week-by-week or month-by-month summary, of what Jesus did and said in the days of his flesh. We are sure that his waking hours were filled with wise words and good deeds, his sleeping hours with the dreams of heaven and the visions of eternity, for he was serving on a mission. He was sent by his Father to preach the gospel, heal the sick, and perform the ordinances of salvation. To those whom he has called in these last days, his instructions are: "Thou shalt send forth my word unto the ends of the earth. Contend thou, therefore, morning by morning; and day after day let thy warning voice go forth; and when the night cometh let not the inhabitants of the earth slumber, because of thy speech." (D&C 112:4-5) We cannot assume that he imposed any less standard than this upon himself during his own ministry. But it is only an isolated word here and a healing miracle there that has been preserved for us by the evangelical authors.

As to the early Judean ministry, John says only that "Jesus and his disciples"—and they must by now have included more than Peter, John, Andrew, Philip, and Nathanael; perhaps women also were among them—"tarried" and baptized in "the land of Judea." Nine months gave them time to tarry long enough in each locale so that all those who dwelt there would hear the word and be accountable for their reaction to it. No doubt many of the seeds sown would be harvested by the apostles and seventies as they thereafter went forth proclaiming the same gospel and baptizing by the same power.

After naming "all Judea" as the place where Jesus "published" the glad tidings of salvation, Peter tells "how God anointed Jesus of Nazareth with the Holy Ghost and with power: who went about doing good, and healing all that were oppressed of the devil; for God was with him." (Acts 10:37-38.) The early Judean ministry thus would have been like the later great Galilean ministry, concerning which we know far more, as shall hereafter appear.

Whenever the gospel is preached by legal administrators having power and authority from on high; whenever ministers possess the power of the priesthood and are guided by the Holy Spirit; whenever those professing to be apostles and prophets do in fact hold these high and holy callings, they always both preach and baptize. Jesus was no exception. He preached the gospel and baptized repentant souls.

Jesus performed baptisms in water for the remission of sins, and he did it on the same basis and in the same way that his forerunner John performed the same sacred ordinance. When John first came, baptizing by immersion in the river Jordan, he taught that the one who was coming after him—the one mightier than he; the one whose shoes the Baptist was not worthy to bear—that such a one would baptize with the Holy Ghost and with fire.

This baptism of fire and of the Holy Ghost, which the Son of God was destined to perform, is not the baptism of which we now speak; such was to come and did come later. While Jesus was with the disciples, he did not give them the gift of the Holy Ghost, so they could have at that time the constant companionship of that member of the Godhead. It was after he ascended to his Father—it was, in fact, on the day of Pentecost—that the Holy Spirit descended in power upon those whom Jesus had called out of the world and into his earthly kingdom. But at this time, in the early days of his early Judean ministry, Jesus and his disciples performed the same baptismal ordinance that John the Baptist was still performing. One of the things this means is that Jesus had already conferred the priesthood upon his newly called disciples.

And so we find our evangelist friend, John, commenting upon the events of that day in these words: "When therefore the Pharisees had heard that Jesus made and baptized more disciples than John, They sought more diligently some means that they might put him to death; for many received John as a prophet, but they believed not on Jesus.[1] Now the Lord knew this, though he himself baptized not so many as his disciples; For he suffered them for an example, preferring one another."[2]

John Continues to Baptize and Prepare the Way

(John 3:23-26; JST, John 3:27)

It is now a full year since John the Baptist began his public ministry; since he cried repentance in the wilderness of Judea; since he reprehended the Jewish multitudes, calling them a generation of vipers; since he immersed repentant souls in the Holy River, promising them a remission of their sins and the future receipt of the Holy Ghost under the hands of Him whose forerunner the Baptist was. It is a full year since the Lord's forerunner first bore public witness that the mighty Messiah would soon walk among them, and that he would baptize them with the Holy Ghost and with fire.

It is now at least six months—probably seven, and possibly eight—since the son of Zacharias baptized the Son of God. And it is five or six months since the appointed Elias bore fervent witness that Jesus was the Lamb of God, which taketh away the sins of the world. And during all this time the promised forerunner has continued to prepare the way for the Promised Messiah.

There is nothing incongruous or unexpected in finding the one who was to prepare the way continuing to prepare a people for their Lord until that day when the one of whom the witness was borne had been identified in every mind as the one who should come. John was expected to continue to invite repentant persons to forsake the world and come unto that Christ whose witness he was. And John was doing just that. He was preaching and baptizing at Aenon near Salim—a location now unknown to us—"because there was much water there," and all valid baptisms must be performed by immersion.

Jesus and his disciples were baptizing in Judea, no doubt in many locations, for all Judea was hearing the word from the mouth of the one whose word it was. John's influence as a figure of public renown, as the center of a great national movement of popular appeal, was on the wane; that of Jesus was waxing great; and though many still came to John, multitudes flocked to Jesus.

Two reasons identify the basis for this shift in public opinion: the word of truth and salvation was with the Source of truth and the Author of salvation, as it should have been; and when John made converts, he sent them to Jesus. Whereas the forerunner had once baptized in the name of Him who should come and had made ready a congregation to receive the Lord, he now baptized in the name of Him who had come and invited his converts to join the congregation of his Leader. The converts were Christ's. The gathered sheep belonged to the Shepherd. John claimed no personal preference. He was a servant, and his glory was to serve the Master.

But it is not surprising to find some of John's disciples feeling that their teacher was deserving of more attention and honor than he was receiving. And so, when a dispute arose between them and "the Jews"—or as the better translations read, "a Jew"—"about purifying," they took the matter to John. It seems clear that the dispute involved the purifying power of baptism and whether John's baptism actually brought remission of sins.

To a caviling, disputing, contentious theologian of that day, an obvious point of debate would have been: How can John's baptism be for the remission of sins when those who receive it must have a second baptism of the Holy Ghost so that sin and evil and dross will be burned out of their souls as though by fire? How are men actually purified by baptism? Is baptism in water for the remission of sins, or is the purifying power of the Holy Spirit needed to cleanse a human soul? However the contention was phrased, John's disciples called it to the attention of the Baptist, saying: "Rabbi, he who was with thee beyond Jordan, to whom thou bearest witness, behold, the same baptizeth, and he receiveth of all people who come unto him." With these words the stage is set for John to bear one of his greatest witnesses of the one whose way he prepared.

John Reaffirms His Witness of Christ

(*John 3:27-36; JST, John 3:32-36*)

Comes now the blessed Baptist—the son of Zacharias and Elisabeth, named John by the angel Gabriel; our Lord's forerunner and witness, who also immersed him in Jordan—to bear, as far as our scriptures record, his final glorious testimony of Jesus. He will continue as a free man to speak and baptize for another four or five months, until November or December of A.D. 27; then he will be imprisoned by Herod. He will languish in the dungeons of Machaerus for more than a year, perhaps fifteen months, before Herod's headsman, at the word of almighty Antipas, will send him to a martyr's grave, from which he shall come forth, with Christ, to receive glory and honor in the kingdom that is prepared.

We can be sure that wherever he met people, and as long as he had breath, his burning witness of one greater than he was given freely, boldly, and with prophetic zeal. We know that he sent disciples to hear Jesus while he himself was restrained in the dungeons of the fortress where Herod had chosen to imprison him. But what he is now to say is his last witness to find place in the scriptures that have come to us. He whose "little light" is being "swallowed up in the boundless Dawn" (Farrar, p. 156), this stern and impassioned prophet from Hebron and the Judean deserts, speaking by the power of the Holy Ghost—which gift he possessed from his mother's womb—is opening his mouth to bear one of the most eloquent and powerful testimonies to find place in Holy Writ.

Whether he answered his disciples' queries about the purifying power of baptism, we do not know, nor does it matter. Many revelations unravel the baptismal mysteries, and many prophets have expounded upon the purifying power of the Holy Ghost. Let the disputants search the scriptures and find their answers. But there was only one Baptist, sent—as the voice of one crying in the wilderness of doubt and disbelief—to prepare the way before the Son of the Highest. John must be true to his trust and bear the witness that was his alone to proclaim. And the acceptance of that witness would provide answer for all lesser problems and solve all doctrinal controversies. Thus with the voice of testimony and of doctrine the Baptist proclaimed:

> *A man can receive nothing, except it be given him from heaven. Ye yourselves bear me witness, that I said, I am not the Christ, but that I am sent before him. He that hath the bride is the bridegroom: but the friend of the bridegroom, which standeth and heareth him, rejoiceth greatly*

because of the bridegroom's voice: this my joy there is fulfilled.

'I, John, came only as the promised Elias, but he came as the holy Messiah, of whom all the prophets have testified. Each of us has received only as the Father has given unto us—he to be the Lamb of God who taketh away the sin of the world, I to announce his coming and to prepare the way before him. It is not given to me to do his work, for he, as the Son of an immortal Father, is greater than I. Ye yourselves are witnesses that I have always said I was not the Christ, only his forerunner. He is the Bridegroom; I, his servant, am as the friend of the bridegroom, the one sent to make arrangements for the wedding. My reward is to be near him, to hear his voice, to know my mission was successful; in this my joy is full.'

He must increase, but I must decrease. He who cometh from above is above all; he who is of the earth is earthly, and speaketh of the earth; he who cometh from heaven is above all.

'His mission is beginning, mine ending; he must increase, I decrease. My counsel is: Forsake me; follow him; he is the Light of the world who teaches the truth and makes salvation available to all men. He is the Lord Omnipotent who, coming from his Father in heaven, is superior to all men; I am as other men, of the earth.'

And what he hath seen and heard, that he testifieth; and but few men receive his testimony. He who hath received his testimony hath set to his seal that God is true.

'But though he is the very Son of God, and though he carries the very message his Father sent him to deliver, yet few men receive his testimony. Those who do believe his witness and obey his counsels, however, have a seal placed upon them; they are sealed up unto eternal life in the everlasting kingdom of the Father.'

For he whom God hath sent, speaketh the words of God; for God giveth him not the Spirit by measure, for he dwelleth in him, even the fulness.

'And the Son, whom the Father hath sent, speaks the words of the Father because the Spirit of God is not apportioned to him; he enjoys it in full measure, and it is by this means that the Father dwelleth in him. Yea, and the Father loveth the Son and hath given all things into his hands—all power, all wisdom, all truth, all judgment, and the fulness of every godly attribute.'

> *The Father loveth the Son, and hath given all things into his hand. And he who believeth on the Son hath ever lasting life; and shall receive of his fulness. But he who believeth not the Son, shall not receive of his fulness; for the wrath of God is upon him.*

'Now those who believe in Jesus as the Son, who believe so fully and completely as to abide in his counsels, shall have everlasting life, even exaltation in the highest heaven of the Father's kingdom. They shall then receive of his fulness, even all power, both in heaven and on earth, and the glory of the Father shall be with them, for he shall dwell in them. But those who believe not on the Son shall fail to gain eternal life and shall not receive of his fulness, for the wrath of God is upon them.' (*Commentary* 1:147-48.)

Such is the last recorded witness of the one chosen from all the spirit hosts of heaven to prepare the way before the Son of God, to bear record of his divine Sonship, to invite all men to flock to his standard that they might be saved with him in the kingdom of his Father.

Herod Imprisons John

(*Matthew 4:12; 14:3-5; JST, Matthew 4:11; Mark 6:17-20; JST, Mark 6:21; Luke 3:19-20*)

There is no New Testament account of any act or word of either Jesus or John from the summer of A.D. 27, when the Baptist bore his wondrous witness, to November or December of that year, when Herod Antipas reached forth the Roman arm of power and imprisoned the son of Zacharias. We know only that Jesus and his disciples were tarrying and teaching in the villages and cities of Judea, and we must assume that John also continued his labors with unwearying diligence.

Herod the Great—an Idumean Jew; a Jew as to religion, a pagan as to practice; the mad monster who ordered the slaughter of the Innocents in all the coasts of Bethlehem; a polygamist who had ten wives—passed on both his murderous proclivities and his religious superstitions to his son Herod Antipas, who governed Galilee and Perea in the days of John and Jesus. Lechery and lust were a way of life with the Herods, and Antipas, like his father before him, felt free to take and reject wives at will. Divorcing his first wife, he married Herodias, the wife of his half-brother Philip (not Philip the tetrarch). Herodias, the mother of Salome by Philip, was a granddaughter of the original Herod, and so married, in turn, her uncle Philip and her uncle Antipas. Under Jewish law the marriage of Herod Antipas and Herodias was scandalous, incestuous, and adulterous, and was so viewed by the people.

Herod Antipas, conceived in sin, reared in the household of sin, himself the servant of sin, trumpeted his sinful lusts before all Israel by endorsing and practicing—openly and defiantly—the abominations of adultery and incest. Such a course could not go unreproved. John the Baptist had been sent to cry repentance; he had power to baptize for the remission of sins; and a Herod on his throne was no different from any man. All men—high or low, kings and slaves, Jews and Gentiles, everyone—must repent or they will be damned, and all men are entitled to hear the warning voice from the lips of a legal administrator.

If John commanded the publicans to exact no greater taxes than they were appointed to collect; if he commanded the soldiers to do violence to no man, to accuse none falsely, and to be content with their wages; if the common people were called to forsake lesser sins, how much greater is the need to rebuke the ruler in his palace who flaunts the sanctity of the moral law and the holiness of the family unit!

There is nothing in the prophetic nature that admits of the fear of men, whether they be kings on their thrones or generals before their armies. As Samuel rebuked David before his armies, and as Elijah called down curses upon Ahab and Jezebel in the house of the king, so John must confront Herod Antipas and his ill-gotten marriage partner. They must needs be called to repentance.

And so, apparently in a face-to-face encounter, the voice sent to cry repentance in a wilderness of sin, the voice of John, reproved Herod for all the evils he had done, and also said: "It is not lawful for thee to have thy brother's wife." The gauntlet had been hurled; the issue was set; Herod and Herodias must repent or be damned. John was a legal administrator, and he had delivered his message.

Herodias demanded the death of John, and Herod agreed. But in the providences of the Lord, there were yet further tests and added spiritual experiences for the forerunner of the Son. At a future time, Herodias, Salome, and Herod—an unholy trio—would gape upon the severed head of the Baptist as it was paraded before the drunken nobles of Herod's court. But for now, the Baptist had yet to drink the dregs of the bitter cup that an all-wise Father had placed in his hands. He must drain the cup and do all he was sent to do; he must yet suffer to the full for the testimony of Jesus. He must languish for more than a year in the dungeons of Machaerus.

Thus, when Herod "would have put [John] to death, he feared the multitude, because they counted him as a prophet," and so the decree, for the present, was one of imprisonment only. Not only did Herod fear the multitude, but he also personally feared John. He knew that John "was a just man, and a holy man, and one who feared God and observed to worship him." There must have been some stirring in Herod's soul, some desire to rise above the iniquities of his court and to live by higher standards, for the record says that when he heard of John, "he did many things for him, and heard him gladly." How often it is that adulterers and sinners of the vilest sort, knowing in their hearts that their course is evil, turn to religion of one kind or another, seeking to find peace of mind of some sort. Yet how often, as with Herod, the seeds of repentance die in the stony soil of sin where they are first sown.

Why was John imprisoned? It was with him as with all the prophets. Satan sought to silence his tongue, by death if possible, by imprisonment in any event; and the Lord permitted that evil one to triumph for a season, as part of the refining processes that would cleanse and perfect the life of his servant. The Baptist's imprisonment was "but a part of that merciful fire in which He is purging away the dross from the seven-times-refined gold of a spirit which shall be worthy of eternal bliss." (Farrar, p. 220.)

From an earthly perspective, three motives appear for the course Antipas chose to take. For one, with the fires of conscience burning at her vitals, and having an implacable hatred against one who had held her up to popular contempt and ridicule, Herodias sought his imprisonment and death. For another, and Josephus is the source of this view: "The Tetrarch was afraid that his absolute influence over the people, who seemed disposed to carry out whatever he advised, might lead to a rebellion. This circumstance is also indicated in the remark of St. Matthew, that Herod was afraid to put the Baptist to death on account of the people's opinion of him." (Edersheim 1:657.) And finally, there can be little doubt that pharisaic intrigue played its part. The Pharisees, those masters of deceit and of opposition to revealed truth, opposed Jesus and had broken with John, who bore witness of Jesus. The clear inference is that they used their persuasive powers to make Herod their tool of terror against John, just as they would make Rome their weapon to crucify the one greater than John, when the Lord Jesus was led as a lamb to the slaughter. (Edersheim 1:657-58.)

"To St. John Baptist imprisonment must have been a deadlier thing" than to most of the suffering seers and prophetic messengers who fell into like dungeons of despair, "for in the free wild life of the hermit he had lived in constant communion with the sights and sounds of nature, had breathed with delight and liberty the free winds of the wilderness. To a child of freedom and of passion, to a rugged, untamed spirit like that of John, a prison was worse than death. For the palms of Jericho and the balsams of Engedi, for the springing of the beautiful gazelles amid the mountain solitudes, and the reflection of the moonlight on the mysterious waves of the Salt Lake, he had nothing now but the chilly damps and cramping fetters of a dungeon, and the brutalities of such a jailor as a tetrarch like Antipas would have kept in a fortress like Makor [Machaerus]. In that black prison, among its lava streams and basaltic rocks, which were tenanted in reality by far worse demons of human brutality and human vice than the 'goats' and 'satyrs' and doleful creatures believed by Jewish legend to haunt its whole environment, we cannot wonder if the eye of the caged eagle began to film." (Farrar, p. 220.) Such is the eloquent language of Farrar.

From our vantage point, however, we know that the eye of the caged eagle did not begin to film. Rather, a wondrous and glorious event took place that brightened the caged eagle's eyes and enabled him to see out of the darkness of the dungeon, and beyond the confines of the earthlike prison, whereon all pilgrims from God's presence dwell for a moment. The veil was rent; the heavens were opened; angelic ministrants from the courts of glory hied themselves to the prison called earth, and to the dungeons of Herod, to speak peace to the weary and tried soul of the one who prepared the way before the Son of God. In majestic simplicity, the inspired record says: "And now Jesus knew that John was cast into prison, and he sent angels, and, behold, they came and ministered unto him."

Jesus did it! John was not forgotten by him. No more are any of those who suffer for his name's sake. Though heaven's Lord dwelt in a tabernacle of clay, yet the angelic legions were subject to his will, and he—in his love and in his pity and in his mercy—sent some of them to his friend and forerunner.

We cannot doubt that the heavens were rent after John had overcome the world. Faith precedes the miracle. After John had risen in his own mind from the bottomless pit of despair, he was prepared to ascend on angelic wings to heights beyond the skies.

His mortal work was done. As with Joseph and Hyrum in Carthage Jail, one thing only remained to be done: the sealing of his own testimony with his own blood. And that, as we shall hereafter see, was destined to be.

Prophets die that prophets may live, and through it all souls are saved and God is glorified. So be it.

NOTES

1. "That is, they accepted John as a prophet in an emotional, unreasoning way, much as the world today believes in the prophets of old. If they had accepted John in the full gospel sense, they would have also believed in Jesus as the Messiah, for such was the burden of John's message to them." (*Commentary* 1:148.)

2. Jesus was the great Exemplar—in the life that he lived, the teachings he taught, the miracles he wrought, the ordinances he performed; indeed, in all things that pertain to life and godliness. Without question he also performed all other gospel ordinances. We know he ordained the members of the Twelve. (John 15:16.) President Joseph Fielding Smith suggests that Peter, James, and John received their endowments from Jesus on the Mount of Transfiguration. (*Doctrines of Salvation* 2:165.)

JESUS TAKES THE GOSPEL TO SAMARIA

Unto him that keepeth my
commandments I will give the mysteries
of my kingdom, and the same
shall be in him a well of living water,
springing up unto everlasting life.
(D&C 63:23.)

Jesus Journeys to Sychar in Samaria
(John 4:4-6; JST, John 4:2, 6-7)

"I must needs go through Samaria," Jesus said to his disciples, as he and they prepared to leave Judea and go to Galilee. Having embittered the Pharisees with his bold doctrines to the point that "they sought more diligently some means that they might put him to death," and knowing that his mission in Judea, for the moment, was completed, Jesus chose to go back to Galilee, to the land of his youth, to the rugged and hilly homeland where friends and kinsmen dwelt, there to launch his great Galilean ministry.

But why take the dangerous and robber-infested route through Samaria? It was the Jewish practice to go the long way around, through Perea, for the Samaritans were a hated race whose customs were abhorred and whose traditions were shunned. True, "the direct road to Galilee ran through the half-heathen country of Samaria," but this "road was proverbially unsafe for Jewish passengers, either returning from Jerusalem or going to it, for it passed through the border districts where the feuds of the two rival peoples raged most fiercely. The paths among the hills of Akrabbim, leading into Samaria, had often been wet with the blood of Jew or Samaritan, for they were the scene of constant raids and forays. . . . The pilgrims from Galilee to the feasts were often molested, and sometimes even attacked and scattered, with more or less slaughter; each act of violence bringing speedy reprisals from the population of Jerusalem and Judea, on the one side, and of Galilee on the other; the villages of the border districts, as most easily reached, bearing the brunt of the feud, in smoking cottages, and indiscriminate massacre of young and old." (Geikie, p. 361.)

Why, then, did Jesus feel compelled to go through Samaria? Superficially, some have supposed it was to avoid Perea, that part of Palestinian soil which was subject to Herod Antipas, who had now imprisoned John, and who—thanks to pharisaic intrigue—apparently opposed Jesus for himself and because he was the friend and colleague of the Baptist. Perhaps with Herod's soldiers on the alert to arrest for treason any who gathered followers—whether religious or political—there were perils connected with Perean travel, and they may have been, in Jesus' case, more serious than those through Samaria. We must conclude, however, that Jesus, though merely en route to Galilee for a greater work, chose to utilize his time and to bear witness of his divinity to the Samaritans. That is, Jesus went to Samaria to preach the gospel, to tell that spiritually benighted race that he was the Messiah whom they sought, and that salvation is in him. His message is the same for all people, Jew and Gentile alike, and the Samaritans were a racial mixture, half-Israelite and half-Gentile.[1] They must hear his voice; the Everlasting Word must speak to them in person.

As to the religion of the Samaritans, it was "a spurious Judaism," Edersheim says, "consisting of a mixture of their former [pagan] superstitions with Jewish doctrines and rites." They had once built their own temple on Mount Gerizim, and they claimed their own high priest and their own priestly administrators. "In the troublous times of Antiochus IV. Epiphanes, the Samaritans escaped the fate of the Jews by repudiating all connection with Israel, and dedicating their temple to Jupiter. . . . In 130 B.C. John Hyrcanus destroyed the Temple on Mount Gerizim, which was never rebuilt." (Edersheim 1:396-98.)[2]

The Samaritans were a half-Jewish, half-heathen race who practiced a form of worship of Jehovah and who looked for a Messiah who was to come. Their religious sensitivities were not so highly refined as were those of the Jews, but they were nonetheless children of the Father of us all, and his Son chose to preach the gospel of salvation to them beginning in Sychar.

And so our Lord and his missionary companions go from Judea to Samaria—from northern Judea, where he and they were teaching and baptizing, to Jacob's Well near Sychar, a distance of some twenty miles. Their travels are through a rugged, hilly area; even in December the Palestinian weather is hot. Jesus is thirsty, hungry, weary.[3] He rests in the shade of the alcove that protects the well while his disciples go another half mile or so into the city to obtain food.

Jesus Offers Living Water to All Men

(*John 4:7-15; JST, John 4:11, 15-16*)

Jesus is alone on ground hallowed by the feet of the great patriarch Jacob, who is Israel and whose descendants are the chosen people, of whom Jesus is one. Here is the parcel of ground that Jacob gave to his son Joseph; here is the well—seven or eight feet in diameter and one hundred fifty feet deep—that the father of all Israel dug to provide life-giving draughts to his family and cattle. On either side are Ebal and Gerizim, mountains of ancient fame, and nearby is the tomb of Joseph, whose bones were carried out of Egypt.

What ponderings as to the past, and what meditations of the present and the future, our Lord now has on this sacred spot, we can only surmise.

His moment of solitude soon ends. A woman of Samaria—alone and unattended, carrying a pitcher on her head, with a long cord to lower and raise the vessel—comes to draw water from her ancestor's well. Jesus speaks. "Give me to drink," he says. And, be it noted, to have the very conversation that he is now commencing is one of the chief reasons he chose to travel through Samaria, as he made his way to his homeland of Galilee.

"How is it that thou, being a Jew, askest drink of me, which am a woman of Samaria?" the woman responds, "for the Jews have no dealings with the Samaritans." To give drink to a thirsty traveler was, in that day and in that part of the earth, a cardinal rule of proper human conduct. To drink water is to live; to thirst for its life-giving properties is to die. All people in Palestine, Jew and Samaritan alike, gave water to their neighbors as the need arose. But the woman here is so taken back by the request of a Jew that she hesitates to comply with a basic rule of their society.

Time was when the Jews cursed the Samaritans in their synagogues, refused to accept them as proselytes, accused them of worshipping idols, said that to eat their bread was like eating swine's flesh, and taught that they would be denied a resurrection. Even Jesus spoke of a Samaritan as a stranger, or more accurately, an alien. These feelings were not now so intense, as witness the fact that the disciples were then in Sychar to obtain Samaritan food, but much of the old hatreds remained. Why then was this Jew asking a Samaritan for a drink?

"If thou knewest the gift of God"—the gift of his Son ("For God so loved the world, that he gave his only begotten Son, that whosoever believeth in him should not perish, but have everlasting life"—John 3:16)[4]—"and who it is that saith to thee, Give me to drink; thou wouldest have asked of him, and he would have given thee living water."

Living water! "For the thirsty and choking traveler in a desert wilderness to find water, is to find life, to find an escape from agonizing death; similarly, the weary pilgrim traveling through the wilderness of mortality saves himself eternally by drinking from the wells of living water found in the gospel.

"Living water is the words of eternal life, the message of salvation, the truths about God and his kingdom; it is the doctrines of the gospel. Those who thirst are invited to come unto Christ and drink. Where there are prophets of God, there will be found rivers of living water, wells filled with eternal truths, springs bubbling forth their life-giving draughts that save from spiritual death." (*Commentary* 1:151-52.)

For the sin-laden woman of Samaria, Jesus' words have little meaning. Her spiritual understanding is dimmed almost to darkness because she has chosen adultery as a way of life. "The things of God knoweth no man, but the Spirit of God. . . . The natural man receiveth not the things of the Spirit of God: for they are foolishness unto him: neither can he know them, because they are spiritually discerned." (1 Cor. 2:11-14.) Her response can deal only with literal water; the things of the Spirit are beyond her comprehension.

"Sir, thou hast nothing to draw with," she says, "and the well is deep: from whence then hast thou that living water?" As though living water could be found in a dead well! As though spiritual things can be understood by a carnal mind! "Art thou greater than our father Jacob, which gave us the well, and drank thereof himself, and his children, and his cattle?" Her claim to prophetic ancestry but dramatizes the reality that even the wicked and ungodly have religious instincts that they seek to satisfy by forms of worship that do not interfere with their carnal courses.

The stage is set, all is in readiness, and the Master Teacher is now prepared to teach the perfect lesson, to deliver the message of how salvation comes to thirsty and water-hungry mortals. They must drink the draughts of eternal truth; these only will give life to the spirit; these eternal wells, full of eternal water, will make available eternal life. As the parched and swollen tongues of desert travelers are refreshed with water drawn from the wells of earth, so the thirsting spirit lives again when living water is poured into the soul. Hence, Jesus' answer is:

Whosoever shall drink of this well, shall thirst again; But whosoever drinketh of the water which I shall give him shall never thirst; but the water that I shall give him shall be in him a well of water springing up into everlasting life.

But the woman, still blinded by her sins, fails to hear the message. Still thinking only of the things of this world, as is the way with carnal people, she says: "Sir, give me this water, that I thirst not, neither come hither to draw."

Jesus Invites Men to Worship the Father

(*John 4:16-24; JST, John 4:26*)

Jesus taught the woman of Samaria that she must come to him and receive the living water that refreshes and enlivens the spirit and leads the spiritually refreshed person to eternal life. His teachings were beyond the level of her spiritual understanding. She remained in darkness. He now uses her to find other truth seekers for him, and he does it by shocking her with a demonstration of his divine power, so that, perchance, even yet she will come to an understanding of the message he is sent to deliver. "Go, call thy husband, and come hither," he directs. "I have no husband," she replies. Jesus says, "Thou hast well said, I have no husband: For thou hast had five husbands; and he whom thou now hast is not thy husband: in that saidst thou truly."

A light begins to dawn. This is no ordinary man; not only does he speak of a strange water, living water, but he also reveals those things which can only be known by divine power. "Sir, I perceive that thou art a prophet," the woman says.

This, then, is her opportunity. This Jew is a prophet; he

can solve the centuries-old dispute between the Samaritans and the Jews. True Israelite worship centers in a temple. Jerusalem has its House of Herod with its great altar and its Holy of Holies; the Samaritan temple on Mount Gerizim was destroyed more than one hundred fifty years ago. Now, here at the foot of that Samaritan place of worship, the woman ventures to say: "Our fathers worshipped in this mountain; and ye say, that in Jerusalem is the place where men ought to worship."

"Woman, believe me," comes the response, "the hour cometh, when ye shall neither in this mountain, nor yet at Jerusalem, worship the Father," which is to say: The places where men built the temples of the past shall no longer be the only centers of approved worship. The old order changeth; there ariseth a new covenant, a new gospel; the temples of the future are the bodies of the saints;[5] and the sacrifices of the future are a broken heart and a contrite spirit.[6] The true believers of the future shall worship in all places and at all times, not just when sacrificial fires burn on Gerizim and in Jerusalem.

"Ye worship ye know not what." Samaritan worship was a strange intermixture of pagan and Israelite doctrine. Centuries before they had added the worship of Jehovah to the worship of their numerous idols; now this higher form of worship had become the dominant force in their way of worship, and their rituals and performances were dominantly Mosaic in nature, but still their worship was both Jewish and pagan all wrapped in one.[7]

"We know what we worship," Jesus continued, "for salvation is of the Jews." As between Jerusalem and Mount Gerizim; as between the Jews and the Samaritans; as between a people who accepted all of the Old Testament, and another that believed only the Pentateuch; as was the case with the Samaritans—the Jews were right and the Samaritans were wrong. The Jews knew what they worshipped, and such knowledge was not had by the Samaritans. Jesus had no hesitancy in telling would-be worshippers that their system of religion was wrong. Though the Jews were apostate, as a people, yet they did have the scriptures; they did search the writings of the prophets; their priests were still legal administrators; they had the knowledge of God to a degree; and salvation was to come through them to the world. Their Messiah was to be the Savior of the world. And so Jesus, the foundation again having been laid, makes the great proclamation:

> *But the hour cometh, and now is, when the true worshippers shall worship the Father in spirit and in truth: for the Father seeketh such to worship him. For unto such hath God promised his Spirit* [not God is a Spirit, as our King James Version erroneously records]—*And they who worship him, must worship in spirit and in truth.*

Jesus Saith: I AM THE MESSIAH

(*John 4:25-30; JST, John 4:28*)

> *We know that there is a God in heaven, who is infinite and eternal, from everlasting to everlasting the same unchangeable God, the framer of heaven and earth, and all things which are in them; And that he created man, male and female, after his own image and in his own likeness, created he them; And gave unto them commandments that they should love and serve him, the only living and true God, and that he should be the only being whom they should worship.* (D&C 20:17-19.)

Praise ye the Father. Worship the Father. Come unto the Father. He is God above all. Worship him in spirit and in truth. Such is his will. But do it in and through Christ who is the Messiah.

The number one truth—in all eternity—is that God is our Father, the Creator of us and all things, whom we must worship in spirit and in truth to gain salvation. Jesus has now, at Jacob's Well, proclaimed this eternal verity. It is the beginning of all true religion.

The number two truth—in all eternity—is that the Son of

God is the Messiah, the Redeemer, through whose atoning sacrifice immortality and eternal life are brought to pass. Having testified of the Father, our Lord must now bear witness of the Son. The woman, still not comprehending the pearls of great price that are dropping from the mouth of a Jew, says: "I know that Messias cometh, which is called Christ: when he is come, he will tell us all things."[8] She could not believe this unknown Jew; if only the Messiah would come, if only he were here, all problems would be solved!

> *Jesus said unto her, I who speak unto thee am the Messias.*

She had his witness of the Father; now he bore record of himself. He knew who he was. In the temple when but twelve years of age, he had so certified, in the statements about his Father's business. He had accepted the testimonies of John the Baptist and of his disciples. Nicodemus had heard him refer to himself as the Only Begotten of the Father. He was the Messiah; he knew it; and he knew it was his mission so to testify to all who would hear, whether they were receptive or, as this Samaritan woman, had sealed hearts and unbelieving blood.

How much else Jesus said to this woman we do not know. At this point in the dialogue, John's account says the disciples returned from Sychar with food to eat. They marveled that Jesus talked with the woman—a conversation that he and not she had initiated, for it violated the customs of the day for a Rabbi to speak in public with a woman, to say nothing of a Samaritan woman, and least of all a woman of easy virtue. Yet their reserve was such and his command of the situation so complete that none asked, "What seekest thou: or, Why talkest thou with her?"

With the arrival of the disciples, the woman left, leaving, in her excitement, her water pot. In the city she said to the men, "Come, see a man, which told me all things that ever I did." No doubt her report was a great exaggeration, but Jesus may well have told her other things about her life than those which pertained to her marital state. She had heard him say he was the Messiah, and so she said to the people in the city: "Is not this the Christ?"

"Then they went out of the city," as Jesus had planned and foreseen, "and came unto him." He had preached to one unreceptive person with such power and effect that he now had a congregation of many receptive souls, all anxious to hear the marvelous message about which one of their own number spoke so positively.

"He That Reapeth Receiveth Wages"

(*John 4:31-42; JST, John 4:40*)

After the woman, whose name we do not even know, departed for Sychar, the disciples made ready their food. When it was offered to Jesus, he said: "I have meat to eat that ye know not of," which caused the disciples to ask one another: "Hath any man brought him ought to eat?"

To this Jesus said: "My meat is to do the will of him that sent me, and to finish his work." The preaching of the gospel; the spread of eternal truth; the establishment of the earthly kingdom; the onward rolling of the great cause of truth and righteousness among men—these become the work, the all-consuming passion, of those who are endowed with power from on high. It becomes their meat and their drink; it takes all their strength; it embraces every waking word and thought. Those who are called to divine service are expected to serve with all their hearts, might, mind, and strength. Temporal needs sink into oblivion. The work becomes their meat and drink and breath and life. Jesus' meat was to do the work of his Father.

Now the multitudes are arriving. "Say not ye, There are yet four months, and then cometh harvest?" Jesus asks. That is, it is late December, possibly early January, and in four months the barley harvest will begin in Palestine. But as Jesus had spoken of living water and spiritual meat, he is now speaking of a harvest, not of barley, but of human souls.

"Lift up your eyes, and look on the fields; for they are white already to harvest." Surely this was a sample of what the prophet Joel had foreseen: "Put ye in the sickle, for the harvest is ripe," he said, as he spoke of the "multitudes in the valley of decision" (Joel 3:12-14), the hosts of men who must decide whether they will be gathered with the Lord's harvest into his kingdom or be left for the day when the tares and the grain that are not harvested shall be burned.

"And he that reapeth receiveth wages, and gathereth fruit unto life eternal," Jesus continued, "that both he that soweth and he that reapeth may rejoice together." The Lord pays his servants. Those who sow and those who harvest in his fields receive wages. They receive eternal life for themselves in that kingdom which is eternal; such a reward is the wages that are provided.[9]

"And herein is that saying true, One soweth, and another reapeth. I have sent you to reap that whereon ye bestowed no labor; the prophets have labored, and ye have entered into their labors." The work of saving souls is a great cooperative enterprise: one sows and another reaps. Isaiah and the prophets foretold the coming of a Messiah and the setting up of his earthly kingdom; they sowed the seeds of faith in the hearts of all who should read and believe their words, and the disciples who were with Jesus in his ministry reaped in the fields planted by their fellow servants of old. The Nephite prophets sowed the seeds of faith and righteousness in the Book of Mormon, and we go out, in our day, to reap the harvest, so that we and our Nephite brethren can rejoice together in that great day when all are safely gathered into the Eternal Granaries.

Jesus preached to those who thus came out to hear him, and he went, at their importuning, into the city, where he abode two days ministering among the people. Many believed because of the testimony of the woman. "And many more believed because of his own word," and they testified: "We have heard him ourselves, and know that this is indeed the Christ, the Saviour of the world."

Truly, the gospel was preached in Samaria. Seeds were sown and a harvest reaped. And at a later date, apostles and seventies and other missionaries would yet reap in the same fields. Jesus' stay there lasted only a few days, but the results of his ministry shall endure to all generations. And we cannot but hope that the woman who first met him at the well of the ancient patriarch was among those who forsook the world, had their sins washed away in the waters of baptism, kept the commandments thereafter, and received an eternal inheritance with the saved and exalted of all ages.

NOTES

1. "When the Ten Tribes were transported to Assyria more than seven centuries before the Christian era, Samaria was repeopled by heathen colonists from other Assyrian provinces. These pagan peoples, intermixing somewhat with scattered remnants of Israel, founded the race of despised and hated Samaritans of Jesus' day. As a nation, they claimed Jacob as their father and maintained they were inheritors of the blessings of the chosen seed. Their religion, partially pagan in nature, accepted the Pentateuch, but rejected the prophets and the psalms. In the day of Jesus they were friendly to Herod and Rome, but bitter toward the Jews, a feeling fully reciprocated by their Jewish kindred." (*Commentary* 1:151.)

2. "The political enmity and religious separation between the Jews and Samaritans account for their mutual jealousy. On all public occasions the Samaritans took the part hostile to the Jews, while they seized every opportunity of injuring and insulting them. Thus, in the time of Antiochus III they sold many Jews into slavery. Afterwards they sought to mislead the Jews at a distance, to whom the beginning of every month (so important to the Jewish festive arrangements) was intimated by beacon fires, by kindling spurious signals. We also read that they tried to desecrate the Temple on the eve of the Passover; and that they waylaid and killed pilgrims on their road to Jerusalem. The Jews retaliated by treating the Samaritans with every mark of contempt; by accusing them of falsehood, folly, and irreligion; and, what they felt most keenly, by disowning them as of the same race or religion, and this in the most offensive terms of assumed superiority and self-righteous fanaticism." (Edersheim 1:399.)

3. "Here we view one of the most human scenes of the Master's whole ministry. The Lord of heaven, who created and controls all things, having made clay his tabernacle, is physically tired, weary, hungry, and thirsty, following his long journey from Judea. He who had power to draw food and drink from the elements, who could have transported himself at will to any location, sought rest and refreshments at Jacob's Well. In all things he was subjecting himself to the proper experiences of mortality." (*Commentary* 1:151.)

4. Farrar, p. 159, footnote 2; Edersheim 1:399-403; Luke 17:18.

5. "Know ye not that ye are the temple of God, and that the Spirit of God dwelleth in you?" (1 Cor. 3:16.)

6. "And ye shall offer up unto me no more the shedding of blood; yea, your sacrifices and your burnt offerings shall be done away, for I will accept none of your sacrifices and your burnt offerings. And ye shall offer for a sacrifice unto me a broken heart and a contrite spirit." (3 Ne. 9:19-20.) "Present your bodies a living sacrifice, holy, acceptable unto God, which is your reasonable service." (Rom. 12:1.)

7. We might liken Samaritan worship to that of the Aztecs or the Mayas, after those ancient peoples had been conquered by Cortez and the other Spanish generals. Their conquerors imposed Christianity in the form of Catholicism upon them, and the result was

a strange admixture of religious form and thought, which over the years has taken on more and more of the basics of Catholicism and less and less of the paganism of the past.

8. With the Samaritans it was as with the Jews, they anxiously awaited the advent of the Messiah. "They looked for the coming of a Messiah, in Whom the promise would be fulfilled, that the Lord God would raise up a Prophet from the midst of them, like unto Moses, in Whom his words were to be, and unto Whom they should hearken. Thus, while, in some respects, access to them would be more difficult than to His own countrymen, yet in others Jesus would find there a soil better prepared for the Divine Seed, or, at least, less encumbered by the thistles and tares of traditionalism and Pharisaic bigotry." (Edersheim 1:403.)

9. "For behold the field is white already to harvest; and lo, he that thrusteth in his sickle with his might, the same layeth up in store that he perisheth not, but bringeth salvation to his soul." (D&C 4:4.) "Whoso desireth to reap, let him thrust in his sickle with his might, and reap while the day lasts, that he may treasure up for his soul everlasting salvation in the kingdom of God." (D&C 6:3.)

INDEX

Divine investiture of authority, 349 n. 1
Doctrines, same, all men must obey, 11-12
Dove, Holy Ghost descended like, 401, 402, 403-4 n. 4
Dreams and visions, 338 n. 1

Earth, new, and new heaven, 95-96
Edersheim, Alfred, 130-31
Education: of Jewish children, 223-24; of Christ, 368-69
Egypt: Israel's deliverance from, 161-62, 365; flight of Holy Family to, 362, 364-65
Elias, 57; John the Baptist's work as, 386, 432-33
Elijah, 57, 303
Elisabeth, 46, 320-21; Gabriel tells Mary of, 319; Mary's visit to, 322-24; Holy Ghost fell upon, 323; recognized Mary as Lord's mother, 324
Elisha, 303
Enoch: city of, 84; pseudepigraphic writings of, 274-75; visions seen by, 409
Epicureanism, 291
Epiphanes, 287
Essenes, 260-61
Esther, 183
Eternal increase, 56-57, 215
Eternal life: inheriting, 75-76, 77; bringing to pass of, 477
Eulogies, formal, offered in synagogues, 194-95
Example: men's tendency to follow, 17-18; Christ's baptism set, 402-3
Ezekiel, 118-22

Faith, miracles are sign of, 446
Family: all things center in, 214; Jewish, Christ was sent to, 217; state of, among Jews, 217-18, 222-26; state of, among Gentiles, 218
Fanaticism among Essenes, 260-61
Fast days, formal, in Israel, 184-86
Fasting for forty days, 411
Feasts, Jewish: Christ's involvement in, 158-59; were occasions for sacrifice, 159-60; three great, 160-81; lesser, 181-86
Fig tree, Christ saw Nathanael under, 442-43
Firstborn, Christ is 5, 21
Forerunner, John the Baptist's role as, 302-3, 386
Forgiveness of sins, prerogative of, 144-45
Fulness: Christ received not, at first, 299, 367, 430; of Christ, men may receive, 429

Gabriel, 52, 301; appearance of, to Zacharias, 308-10; position of, in angelic hierarchy, 311-12 n. 5; appearance of, to Mary, 318-19
Galilee, people of, 322
Genealogy of Christ, 315-16
Genesis, book of, possessed by Jews, 270-71
Gentiles: time of, 97 n. 5; court of, in Herod's Temple, 111; family life among, 218; utter corruption of, 226 n. 3
Glory, assignment to degrees of, 74
God: visible manifestation of, 3-4; words of, were spoken through Christ, 5; Christ is Only Begotten Son of, 6; is an exalted man, 20-21, 35; begot spirits of men, 21, 35; is embodiment of all good, 23; men can become like, 23-24; does not change, 51, 447; modern conceptions of, 64; is not mere spirit essence, 66 n. 9; visits men in temples, 98-99, 122 n. 1; sent his Son into world, 142; knowledge about, was of greatest importance to Jews, 225-26; is Christ's literal Father, 314; condescension of, 314-15; Christ entered wilderness to commune with, 408; so loved the world that he gave his Son, 477; existence of, 500
Godhead, nature of, 329-30
Godhood: of Christ, 27-30; of prophets and righteous saints, 32 n. 6
Good men without true religion, 70-71
Gospel: principles of, do not vary, 11; fulness of, 13-14, 72; scholarship in truths of, 15; was named for Christ, 36; among children of Israel, 54-55, 59; fulness of, was withdrawn from Israel, 59-61; preparatory, 60, 71-72; fulness of, compared to Mosaic law, 72-73, 80-81; is covenant of peace, 120-21; became new law, 147-48; all who receive, become Abraham's seed, 157 n. 3, 216; Adam taught, to his

God is revealed through, 5; mortal experiences of, 5-7, 38-39; was God's Son, 6, 314; worked out infinite atonement, 7-8; invites men to learn of him, 8; man's knowledge of, is limited, 12-13, 20; invites men to come unto him, 16-17; set perfect example, 18; foreordination of, 26, 36, 284-85; godhood of, 27-30; advanced by obeying laws, 35; detailed prophecies concerning life of, 38-40; millennial reign of, 44-45; lived Mosaic law, 68; second coming of, 117-22; will reign over Israel, 120; all things bear record of, 124; fulfilled Mosaic law, 127, 151-52; came into world to die, 140-41; was in God's express image, 142; as High Priest, 143-44; intercessory prayers of, 148; taught in synagogues, 197-99; taking name of, upon oneself, 216-17; was born to Jewish family, 217, 219-20; rejection of, was necessary, 236; earthly ministry of, 282-85, 295-96; came to overcome world, 289; received not fulness at first, 299, 367, 430; preparation of, for ministry, 299-300, 370; coming of, should be announced by angels, 301-2; genealogy of, 315-16; Gabriel announces pending birth of, 318-19; parents of, 330; birth of, 343, 345, 429; signs accompanying birth of, 346-49, 359; date of birth of, 349-50 n. 2; meaning of name of, 352; redemption of, according to Israel's law, 352-53; Simeon and Anna testify of, 354-55; physical growth of, 367-68; possible feelings of, on journey to Jerusalem for Passover, 372-76; was found in temple, 378; had to be about his Father's business, 379-80; John the Baptist prophesied of, 390-91; baptism of, 400-403, 430; was capable of being tempted, 405-6; was hungry in desert, 411; divinity of, needed no proof, 412; Satan tempted, to cast himself down from temple, 414-15; Spirit carried, to mountain, 415; Satan tempted, with wealth of world, 416-17; reasons for tempting of, 417-19; glory of, John the Baptist beheld, 429; events preceding formal ministry of, 431; formal introduction of, by John the Baptist, 435-36; John the Baptist testifies of, 437-38, 485-87; disciples left John the Baptist to follow, 438-40, 483; calls his disciples, 440-44; turns water into wine, 450-54; dwells in Capernaum, 455-56; travels to Jerusalem for Passover, 456-57; drives moneychangers from temple, 461; spoke of raising temple in three days, 464-66; beginning of formal ministry of, 468-70, 479; Nicodemus' visit to, 470-71; men must believe in, to be saved, 478; preached throughout Judea, 480-81; performed baptisms, 481-82; declares himself as Messiah, 501; meat of, was to do God's will, 502

Jesus Christ, teachings of: understanding setting of, 12; on being born of water and the Spirit, 473; on living water, 496-98; on harvest of souls, 502-3

Jethro, 55

Jews: prophets of, 40-41; looked for Messiah as temporal deliverer, 43-44; many, recognized and worshipped Christ, 46-47; true worship among, 62; rejected Christ, 64; had form of godliness but denied power, 109; importance of temples to, 113-14; converted to Mormonism, shall rebuild temple, 116; feasts of, Christ used, 158-159; Sabbath observance among, 201, 205-11; four centers of worship among, 204-5; family life among, 217-18, 222-26; education of, 223-24; apostasy among, in Christ's day, 234-39; ancient, beliefs of, 241-42; divisions among, as to beliefs, 244, 276-77; brief secular history of, 286-88; subjection of, to Roman rule, 292-94; Christ ministered and taught among, 296; baptism among, 396-97; marriage customs of, 449-50. *See also* Israel

John the Baptist: recognized Christ, 47; was Christ's forerunner, 302-3; Gabriel announces birth of, to Zacharias, 309-10; leaped in his mother's womb, 323; birth of, 333; naming of, 335; ministry of, 382; had authority from God, 384, 398-99; underwent period of testing in desert, 385; laid foundations for Christ's work, 386-87; many flocked

The Mortal Messiah

From Bethlehem to Calvary

Book II

The Mortal Messiah

From Bethlehem to Calvary
Book II

Bruce R. McConkie

Deseret Book Company
Salt Lake City, Utah
1980

Vol. 2 ISBN 0-87747-803-1 (hardbound)
ISBN 0-87579-404-1 (softbound)

Library of Congress Cataloging-in-Publication Data

McConkie, Bruce R.
The mortal Messiah.

Includes indexes.
1. Jesus Christ—Biography. 2. Christian biography—Palestine.
3. Judaism—History—Post-exilic period, 586 B.C.–210 A.D.
I. Title.
BT301.2.M16 232.9'01 79-19606

Printed in the United States of America

10 9 8 7 6 5 4 3 2

THE MESSIANIC TRILOGY

The forerunner of this work is *The Promised Messiah: The First Coming of Christ*, which deals with the Messianic Prophecies. This work, *The Mortal Messiah: From Bethlehem to Calvary*, is a Life of Christ published in four books. This is Book II.

BOOK II

Section IV *Jesus Begins the Great Galilean Ministry*
Section V *The Twelve, The Sermon on the Mount, and Rising Pharisaic Opposition*
Section VI *The Continuing Galilean Ministry*

The other books on the Life of Christ are published separately as follows:

BOOK I

Section I *A Root Out of Dry Ground*
Section II *Jesus' Years of Preparation*
Section III *Jesus' Early Judean Ministry*

BOOK III

Section VII *The Galilean Ministry Reaches Its Peak*
Section VIII *The Later Judean Ministry*
Section IX *The Perean Ministry*
Section X *From the Anointing to the Royal Reign*

BOOK IV

Section XI *The Paschal Feast, The Private Prayers and Sermons, and Gethsemane*
Section XII *The Trials, The Cross, and The Tomb*
Section XIII *He Riseth; He Ministereth; He Ascendeth*

The concluding work in this whole series will be *The Millennial Messiah: The Second Coming of the Son of Man.*

ABBREVIATIONS

Scriptural references are abbreviated in a standard and self-identifying way. Other books are cited by author and title except for the following:

Commentary I	Bruce R. McConkie, *Doctrinal New Testament Commentary*. Vol. 1, *The Gospels*. Bookcraft, 1965.
Edersheim	Alfred Edersheim, *The Life and Times of Jesus the Messiah*. 1883.
Farrar	F. W. Farrar, *The Life of Christ*. London: Cassell & Co., Ltd., 1874.
Geikie	Cunningham Geikie, *The Life and Words of Christ*. 1886.
Hymns	*Hymns, The Church of Jesus Christ of Latter-day Saints*. 1948.
JST	Joseph Smith Translation (Inspired Version) of the Bible.
Mormon Doctrine	Bruce R. McConkie, *Mormon Doctrine*, 2nd ed. Bookcraft, 1966.
Sketches	Alfred Edersheim, *Sketches of Jewish Social Life in the Days of Christ*. 1876.
Talmage	James E. Talmage, *Jesus the Christ*. 1915.
Teachings	Joseph Fielding Smith, comp., *Teachings of the Prophet Joseph Smith*. 1938.
Temple	Alfred Edersheim, *The Temple: Its Ministry and Services As They Were at the Time of Jesus Christ*.

CONTENTS

SECTION IV

JESUS BEGINS THE GREAT GALILEAN MINISTRY

Chapter 33

Chapter 34

Chapter 35

Chapter 36

Chapter 50

Chapter 51

Chapter 52

Chapter 53

Chapter 59

SECTION IV

JESUS BEGINS THE GREAT GALILEAN MINISTRY

JESUS BEGINS THE GREAT GALILEAN MINISTRY

We believe that through the Atonement of Christ, all mankind may be saved, by obedience to the laws and ordinances of the Gospel. (Article of Faith 3.)

Jesus—a Preacher of Righteousness, a Mighty Minister, a Man of God—now goes forth into Galilee, where, on their streets and in their synagogues, he preaches the gospel of the kingdom: that salvation comes by him and is gained by those who believe and obey.

He brings forth a new gospel dispensation; calls sinners to repentance; applies the Messianic prophecies to himself; and calls Peter, Andrew, James, John, and Matthew to follow him.

He heals a nobleman's son; casts an evil spirit out of a demoniac; cleanses a leper; forgives sins; heals a paralytic, and an impotent man, and one with a withered hand.

Above all—while at the Passover in Jerusalem—he proclaims his divine Sonship; makes himself "equal with God"; promises to take the gospel to the dead; announces that men are resurrected, judged, and assigned their glory, by the Son; and expounds the divine law of witnesses.

He is rejected by his own in Nazareth, and because he says God is his Father, and because he violates the rabbinical sabbath rules, the Pharisees spy upon him and join with the Herodians to plot his death.

Our Lord's ministry is now well under way, and the proceedings of the present are a precursor of the future. The Son of God ministers among men, and the sons of Lucifer seek to destroy him.

JESUS PREACHES THE GOSPEL IN GALILEE

This is the gospel which I have given
unto you—
that I came into the world
to do the will of my Father,
because my Father sent me.
And my Father sent me
that I might be lifted up
upon the cross; and after that
I had been lifted up upon the cross,
that I might draw all men unto me. . . .
Now this is the commandment: Repent,
all ye ends of the earth,
and come unto me and be baptized
in my name,
that ye may be sanctified
by the reception of the Holy Ghost,
that ye may stand spotless before me
at the last day.
Verily, verily, I say unto you,
this is my gospel.
(3 Ne. 27:13-14, 20-21.)

"Repent Ye, and Believe the Gospel"

(*Mark 1:14-15; Matthew 4:17; Luke 4:14-15; JST, Luke 4:15, John 4:43-45*)

We come now to the three verses in the Synoptic Gospels that set the tone for everything that came from the pens of the synoptic authors: Matthew, Mark, and Luke. The message they contain applies also to all that is recorded in the gospel of the Beloved John.

We were with Jesus at Bethabara when he was baptized by John. We saw the heavens open and the Holy Spirit of God descend in bodily form to rest upon him. We went with him into the wilderness when he fasted and communed with his Father for forty days, and then overcame the wiles of the archtempter. We saw angels minister to him; heard John identify him as the Lamb of God, which taketh away the sin of the world; and heard him call Andrew and Simon, Philip and Nathanael, and John to follow him.

We attended the wedding celebration in Cana, drank the sweet wine that once was water, and then went with him to the Feast of the Passover in the Holy City. There, in thunderous yet righteous indignation, wielding a whip made of small cords, he drove the moneychangers from the Court of the Gentiles, overturned their tables of greed, and freed the animals and fowls that desecrated his Father's House.

We sat in reverent awe as he taught Nicodemus about spiritual rebirth and the salvation that results therefrom, and heard him say with his own lips that he was the Only Begotten of the Father and that whosoever believeth in him should not perish but have everlasting life.

Then we traveled and tarried with him for about nine months, through all the cities and villages of Judea, as he proclaimed his own divine Sonship and poured words of eternal life into the ears of his Jewish hearers. We are aware of John the Baptist's great pronouncement, made at Aenon near Salim, that all who believe in the Son shall have everlasting life; and we know that our Lord's Forerunner is now languishing in a vile and evil dungeon in a fortress near a palace where Herod Antipas revels in lustful splendor.

Only a few days ago we arose early to walk with him through rugged hill country, from northern Judea to Sychar in Samaria, where Jacob's Well is found. There, at the well and in the city, we continued to hear the words of wisdom and truth that none but he have ever spoken, and then we traveled on with him into his own Galilee.

Except for the accounts of his baptism and the temptation that followed, all that we have seen and heard and felt has come to us from John's Gospel. In all of it John was either present in person or received firsthand accounts from others, including the Lord Jesus himself. But now, after nearly a year of his active ministry, and with only about three months left before his Second Passover, we are turning also to the synoptic accounts to learn of him of whom we are already so much in awe.

And for the first time we find recorded, in plain and clear language, exactly what Jesus is doing as he goes forth to do the will of him whose servant he is. We come to the three verses that set the tone and give meaning and perspective to all that is written in all of the Gospels.

Jesus is going back to his homeland, to the land of his childhood and youth and maturing years, to the place of which he himself "testified, that a prophet hath no honour in his own country." But he is going back "in the power of the Spirit" to a people who "received him, having seen all the things that he did at Jerusalem at the feast: for they also went unto the feast." This time "a fame of him" will spread "through all the regions round about"; and as he teaches in their synagogues, he will be "glorified of all who believed on his name." Whereas he was once without honor in his own country, now, for a season at least, many will flock to him, and all will know of the wonderful works he is doing.

In the three verses of which we speak, Matthew says: "From that time Jesus began to preach, and to say, Repent: for the kingdom of heaven is at hand"; and Mark says: "Jesus came into Galilee, preaching the gospel of the kingdom of God, And saying, The time is fulfilled, and the kingdom of God is at hand: repent ye, and believe the gospel."

In these verses we find the key that opens the door to an understanding of all of Jesus' teachings. In Galilee—and elsewhere and everywhere—he invited men to believe and repent; to believe in him as the Son of God and to repent of their sins; to accept the gospel that he preached and to become members of his earthly kingdom. Jesus preached the gospel; and unless and until this dawns upon us, we will not and cannot understand his ministry among men. Jesus preached the gospel—nothing more and nothing less.

What is the gospel? The gospel of the kingdom? And what is the kingdom of heaven that is now at hand?

The gospel is the plan of salvation, the plan ordained and established by the Father to enable his spirit children to advance and progress and become like him. It is all of the laws, truths, rites, ordinances, and performances by conformity to which men can save themselves with eternal exaltation in the mansions on high. It is the system that enables the sons of God to become gods. "It is the power of God unto salvation to every one that believeth." (Rom. 1:16.)

The gospel is the glad tidings of great joy that salvation is in Christ; that a gracious God has provided a Savior for his children; that fallen man can be ransomed from temporal and spiritual death. It is: "That he came into the world, even Jesus, to be crucified for the world, and to bear the sins of the world, and to sanctify the world, and to cleanse it from all unrighteousness; That through him all might be saved whom the Father had put into his power and made by him." (D&C 76:40-41.) It is: "That the Son of God hath atoned for original guilt," so that little children "are whole from the foundation of the world" (Moses 6:54), and that all who will repent and become as their little children shall be saved.

The gospel "is the plan of salvation unto all men, through the blood of [God's] Only Begotten." It recognizes that "all men, everywhere, must repent, or they can in nowise inherit the kingdom of God, for no unclean thing can dwell there, or dwell in his presence." (Moses 6:57-62.) It consists of hearkening unto the voice of God and believing in his Only Begotten; of forsaking the world and repenting of one's sins; of being baptized in water for the remission of sins; of receiving the gift of the Holy Ghost, so that the newly born saint may be sanctified and become pure and spotless; and of then enduring to the end and working the works of righteousness all one's days. "And this is my gospel—repentance and baptism by water, and then cometh the baptism of fire and the Holy Ghost, even the Comforter, which showeth all things, and teacheth the peaceable things of the kingdom." (D&C 39:6.)

Such is the gospel, the gospel of the kingdom of God, the gospel which admits men to the kingdom of God on earth—which is the Church—and to the kingdom of God in heaven—which is the celestial kingdom. When Jesus said, "The kingdom of heaven is at hand," he was announcing that the kingdom of God on earth, which is the Church of Jesus Christ, was then organized again among men.[1]

When Jesus preached the gospel, over and over again he said such things as these: 'The God of your fathers, who was worshipped by Abraham and Moses and all the holy prophets, hath sent me; I am his Son, by whom salvation comes. As I said unto Nicodemus, I am the Only Begotten; and as I said unto the woman of Samaria, I am the Messiah. Come unto me; believe in me; keep my commandments; join my church; be baptized and I will give you the Holy Ghost; walk in the paths of righteousness and my blood shall cleanse you from all sin. And having enjoyed the words of eternal life in this world, ye shall be inheritors of eternal life, even immortal glory in the world to come.'

Jesus did not come among men simply to teach ethical principles, to give parables, to present a higher and better way of life to downtrodden humanity. That he did all this, and more, none doubt. But Jesus came among men to atone for the sins of the world, to make salvation available through the shedding of his blood, and to teach those gospel laws by obedience to which all men can be saved in the kingdom of God. Jesus preached the gospel; so it is written, and so it is.

The Gospel accounts are not, and do not pretend to be, definitive expositions of the saving truths that comprise the gospel, nor do they pretend to record the doctrinal teachings of the Lord Jesus. Rather, they are fragmentary accounts of selected sayings and a few of his doings. "The Synoptic narratives"—Matthew, Mark, and Luke—are, as Edersheim expresses it, only "brief historical summaries, with here and there special episodes or reports of teaching inserted." (Edersheim 1:422-23.)

With these realities before us, we will be able to put the episodes and reports in their proper perspective and to learn why each one has been preserved for us. Parables, healings, teachings, sermons—all that our Lord said and did—can only be understood when considered in their relationship to that gospel—the fulness of the everlasting gospel—which Jesus came to teach.

Jesus Heals the Nobleman's Son

(*John 4:46-54; JST, John 4:55-56*)

Miracles are part of the gospel. Signs follow those that believe. Where the doctrines of salvation are taught in purity and perfection, where there are believing souls who accept these truths and make them a part of their lives, and where devout souls accept Jesus as their Lord and serve him to the best of their ability, there will always be miracles. Such ever attend the preaching of the gospel to receptive and conforming people. Miracles stand as a sign and a witness of the truth and divinity of the Lord's work. Where there are miracles, there is the gospel, the Church, the kingdom, and the hope of salvation. Where there are no signs and miracles, none of these desired blessings will be found. These realizations prepare us to consider the episodes and reports that have been preserved for us in the Gospels.

And so Jesus, coming back into Galilee, to a people many of whom are for the moment receptive and friendly, goes to Cana. His fame has preceded him; indeed, part of his fame had its beginning in this very Galilean village, for it was here that water became wine at his word. But now the Galileans also have in mind what he had done at the Feast of the Passover; and we cannot discount the possibility—shall we not say probability—that the glad tidings of his doings, of nine months' duration, through all Judea, have also come to their attention. He is being hailed by many for what he says he is, the One sent to teach and heal.

While Jesus was in Cana, perhaps staying at the home of Nathanael, there came to him from Capernaum, some twenty miles away, a nobleman whose son "was at the point of death." That this nobleman was an officer, either civil or military, in the court of Herod Antipas is reasonably certain; at least the word used by John to describe him is the same one Josephus and others used repetitiously to refer to officers in the service of that evil tyrant. In any event, the nobleman besought Jesus "that he would come down, and heal his son." What words of earnest entreaty were used we do not know. Their import must have been to induce the Master to travel to the bedside of the dying son, a thing that Jesus had no intention of doing.

To this assumption that the personal presence of the Healer was required to effect a cure, Jesus said: "Except ye see signs and wonders, ye will not believe." 'Except ye see me come and lay my hands on the head of your son, as ye are aware I have done to others, ye will not believe that he shall be healed. Do ye not know that it is written of me, "He sent his word, and healed them"?' (Ps. 107:20.) In spite of this gentle rebuke, the nobleman continued to plead: "Sir, come down ere my child die."

Having thus tested the growing faith of the influential suppliant, and finding that he knew in his heart that Jesus had power to heal those who lay at death's door, our Lord said: "Go thy way; thy son liveth." There was to be no gradual cure; distance meant nothing where the exercise of healing power was involved. Jesus spoke, and the event transpired. Without further assurance, knowing only that this Man's words must all be fulfilled, the nobleman "believed the word that Jesus had spoken unto him, and he went his way."

Whereas he had come in haste, anxious and perturbed, importuning and pleading that Jesus travel to Capernaum and heal his son, now, at peace within himself, he remained overnight in or near Cana. The next day as he traveled homeward he met his servants, who said, "Thy son liveth," and he learned that the fever had left him at the very hour when Jesus had spoken those same blessed words.

This is the first healing miracle that is set forth in detail in the Gospels. Those performed at the Feast of the Passover and throughout all Judea are not described or explained. This miracle—the second performed in Cana—adds a new dimension to Jesus' healing ministry that we have not seen up to this point. It is in fact a dual miracle: one that healed the body of the absent son, and one that cured unbelief and planted faith in the heart of the present father.

With reference to the dying boy, it bears witness that the Divine Healer is not limited by geographical location; that he speaks and disease flees; that the whereabouts of the suffering suppliant is of no moment; that God governs all things; that his power is everywhere. With reference to the father who sought the divine intervention, it bears witness that the growth of faith in the heart of an earthbound pilgrim, and the healing, as it were, of the soul of man, is as great a miracle as—nay, a far greater miracle than—the healing of the physical body.

Having heard the gospel taught, and believing that the Teacher could work miracles, the father came to Jesus. 'Come down to Capernaum and heal my son,' he pleaded. By declining to go down—as though his personal presence was required for a miracle!—Jesus tested the faith of the father; and finding that it remained unshaken, he healed the child at a word. The father, without more and before word came from his servants, knew that the healing power had operated and that his son lived. When this was confirmed a day later, John says: "Himself believed, and his whole house." We have seen, thus, the miracle of healing a disease-ridden body and the healing of a truth-seeking soul; we have seen a physical cure that raised a boy from the doors of death, and a spiritual cure that enabled a man to shake off the disease of unbelief that leads to spiritual death. Truly the Master Healer uses his power in a perfect way for the blessing and benefit of his mortal brethren!

NOTE

1. When the Lord called laborers into the vineyard in this dispensation and sent them out to do again what he had done in the day of his ministry, among other things he commanded them: "Open your mouths and they shall be filled, saying: Repent, repent, and prepare ye the way of the Lord, and make his paths straight; for the kingdom of heaven is at hand; Yea, repent and be baptized, every one of you, for a remission of your sins; yea, be baptized even by water, and then cometh the baptism of fire and of the Holy Ghost. Behold, verily, verily, I say unto you, this is my gospel; and remember that they shall have faith in me or they can in nowise be saved; And upon this rock I will build my church." (D&C 33:10-13.) "And ye shall go forth baptizing with water, saying: Repent ye, repent ye, for the kingdom of heaven is at hand." (D&C 42:7.)

JESUS FULFILLS THE MESSIANIC PROPHECIES

Did not Moses prophesy unto them
concerning the coming of the Messiah,
and that God should redeem his people?
Yea, and even all the prophets who
have prophesied
ever since the world began—
have they not spoken more or less
concerning these things?
Have they not said that God himself
should come down among the children of men,
and take upon him the form of man,
and go forth in mighty power
upon the face of the earth?
(Mosiah 13:33-34.)[1]

To him give all the prophets witness,
that through his name whosoever
believeth in him
shall receive remission of sins.
(Acts 10:43.)[2]

Messianic Prophecies: Their Nature and Purpose[3]

We stand in old Jerusalem—the Holy City—the chosen spot where prophets teach Jehovah's word, and where, all too often, they die for the testimony of Jesus that is theirs. Isaiah is here—it is seven and a half centuries before Christ—and we hear him say: 'Rejoice, O Israel, for unto us a Child is born; unto us a Son is given. He is the Messiah, the Mighty God, the Prince of Peace. Behold, a virgin shall conceive; she shall bear this Son; and his name shall be called Immanuel, which means, God is with us, for God himself shall dwell as a Mortal Man.' This we hear and much more.

Then we stand on a Judean plain, a few short miles from the Holy City, where we see and hear such marvelous things that our bosom burns with living fire. We hear an angel, free from sin, announce the birth of David's kin. We hear the heavens resound as angelic choirs give glory to God and sing of peace among men of good will on earth. A Child is born; a Son makes flesh his tabernacle. His mother is none other than the Blessed Virgin of whom Isaiah and Nephi prophesied. It is as though we are seeing again what we saw before through prophetic eyes. Such is the nature of Messianic prophecies.

Again we mingle with the saints of old and hear their prophets speak in loving tones of the Messiah who is to come. Micah pictures for his hearers the little town of Bethlehem. 'Thou, Bethlehem Ephratah,' he says, 'out of thee shall come the Promised Messiah; though thou art little and insignificant among the cities of Judah, yet thy name shall be forever linked with the Lord Omnipotent, the Eternal God, for he shall be born in thee.'

We hear Jeremiah foretell the sorrow and lamentation that will be when Rachel weeps for the slain innocents in the days of Herod; we hear Hosea tell of the flight into Egypt so the Blessed Child will escape the sword that seeks his life; and we hear another prophetic voice testify: 'When he comes out of Egypt, he will go to Nazareth of Galilee, there to mature and grow and prepare; and ever thereafter he shall be called a Nazarene.'

Then we go to Bethlehem, find the caravanserie where the Eternal One lies in a manger, in that part of the camping place where the cattle are tethered. We see the flight into Egypt; and we rejoice at his return to the sacred home provided by Joseph and Mary among the Nazarenes. Again it is as though we had seen it all before; and so we had, for we had heard the Messianic utterances and known their meaning. And such is the nature of Messianic prophecies that those who go before know as surely and fully of the truth and divinity of that which is to be as do those who come after.

We see Jesus baptized at Bethabara in Jordan; we behold the heavens open and the Holy Spirit of God descend upon him, in bodily shape, with all the serenity and calmness of a dove. We hear his Forerunner's testimony: 'This is the Lamb of God, the Redeemer of the world, he who shall take upon himself the sins of all men on conditions of repentance'—and with it all we are not in Palestine; we are not standing on the banks of the Jordan; it is not January in A.D. 27. All that we see and hear is shown to us more than six hundred years before its destined occurrence, for we are with Nephi. We have been carried by the Spirit into an exceedingly high mountain where we behold in vision the very things that one day shall be when he who is the Spirit Lord shall become a mortal man.

Nor are we in any way surprised when we see it all over again, when Jesus comes to John to be baptized of him to fulfill all righteousness. The preview is the same as the performance. And such, be it known, is the nature of Messianic prophecies.

By the spirit of prophecy and revelation, as the visions of eternity rolled before them, and with a seeric insight known only to those who walk in the light of the Spirit, the ancient saints and their prophets and seers were as well informed about Christ and his ministry, as are those of us who have come after. Their Messianic prophecies were as powerful and persuasive, and as filled with the doctrines of salvation, as are our Messianic testimonies. The only difference is that they spoke of what was revealed to them in advance, and we speak of what has been revealed to us after the events.

Messianic prophecies foretell all things that men must know concerning the Lord Jesus and his mortal ministry; all things concerning his birth and ministry and death; all things concerning his teachings and miracles and healing power; all things concerning the ransom he paid and the atonement he wrought; all things concerning all of these matters which men must know to cleanse their souls through his atoning blood. Messianic prophecies reveal Christ and his ministry and the salvation that is in him—before his coming.

We speak thus, with the illustrations here recited, to lay a foundation for the gracious words Jesus is about to speak in the synagogue in Nazareth of Galilee. Our Lord has come out of Judea, through Samaria, to Cana. While there he healed the son of the nobleman, though the dying boy was twenty miles away in Capernaum. Everywhere he has preached the gospel, and now he is in the synagogue on the Sabbath, and he is about to apply, in effect, all of the Messianic prophecies to himself.

Jesus Applies the Messianic Prophecies to Himself

(*Luke 4:16-22*)

Now we are with Jesus in Nazareth—a place of blessed memory to him—the Galilean city where he was subject to Joseph and Mary; the city founded in the hills and mountains of Galilee, from whose heights the Light of the World is now sending forth his rays; the city where he is known, where he learned the carpenter's trade, where he went to school and sat in the synagogue on the Sabbath.

He has come from Cana, where he turned water into

wine and where, at his spoken word, a boy in Capernaum received life and vitality and retreated from death's open door. His fame has preceded him; his fellow Nazarenes know of the Cana-Capernaum miracle, of what he did at the Feast of the Passover, of the miracles that were part of his early Judean ministry. He is no longer just one of a motley crowd; he has stepped forth as the Leader of men; he has disciples who follow in his footsteps and testify of his divinity; and he has begun to assume prerogatives that not even the great High Priest would dare to assume. None but he—none who came before, and none who followed after—had with violence driven the priestly courtiers from the temple courts, as though he himself were greater than the temple and all its ministers. None but he controlled the elements with such ease and had such wondrous power over disease and life and death. Nothing that Jesus shall do hereafter can be done in a corner; his light can never be hidden under a bushel; the eyes of all men shall be upon him as long as he lives; and his words are those which shall be prized above all others.

With Jesus we go to the synagogue on the Sabbath. Such is his custom, such is ours, and such is the custom of all the faithful in Israel. Synagogue worship is as mandatory as anything can be in the lives of the chosen people in this meridian day. Synagogues are sacred places where Jewish Israel resorts to pay their devotions to the Most High and to praise his name in sermon and prayer. In them we do not joke or laugh or eat or do aught that is irreverent or that detracts from the true spirit of worship. And it is worthy of note that what prevailed in synagogues anciently is what should prevail in our houses of worship today, for the Christian practice of frequent worship—of sermon and song and prayer and scriptural reading, in buildings set apart for such purposes—grew out of the Jewish dispensation that preceded ours. The apostles built upon the foundations of the past as they devised the procedures for their new day.

As we enter the stone synagogue, we admire the ornamentation over the lintel; perhaps it is "a seven-branched candlestick, an open flower between two Paschal lambs, or vine-leaves with bunches of grapes, or, as at Capernaum, a pot of manna between representations of Aaron's rod."[4] We observe the holy chest—a movable ark, as it were—in which the sacred rolls of the Law and the Prophets are kept. The holy lamp is burning, "in imitation of the undying light in the Temple." Before the ark are the seats of honor where the rulers of the synagogue sit, facing the people. There is a place for the one who is to lead the devotions and a desk from which the Law is read. It is all familiar and well suited to the needs and circumstances of the day.

As we seat ourselves, it is with full anticipation that the ruler of the synagogue will call on Jesus to deliver a discourse. Whenever "some great Rabbi, or famed preacher, or else a distinguished stranger, is known to be in the town," it is the custom to invite him to preach to the people. The "institution of preaching" is a way of life among the Jews, and popular preachers are sought for, and are given complete freedom to expound and teach, using "parables, stories, allegories, witticisms, strange and foreign words, absurd legends, in short, anything that might startle an audience." We anticipate that, as is the custom, "at the close of his address, the preacher" will refer "to the great Messianic hope of Israel," but little do we realize the power and import of the Messianic proclamation that is to be made this day.

The synagogue service commences. There are two prayers, then the reciting of the *Shema*—the three passages from the Pentateuch, in which the worshippers take upon themselves the yoke of the kingdom—and then another prayer. Then come eighteen eulogies or benedictions and yet other prayers. After these liturgical formalities, the minister takes out a roll of the Law, and seven persons are called upon to read successive portions. "A descendant of Aaron was always called up first to the reading; then followed a Levite, and afterwards five ordinary Israelites. . . . The reading of the Law was both preceded and followed by brief Benedictions."

It is now time for the reading of a section from the Prophets and for the discourse of the day. This is the portion of the service that we know that Jesus personally participated in. He "stood up for to read," Luke says, "And there was delivered unto him the book of the prophet Esaias." After the reading came the sermon. If, however, he followed the practice of the day, his participation involved more than reading from the Prophets and discoursing as he chose. "The person who read in the synagogue the portion from the Prophets, was also expected to conduct the devotions, at least in greater part," meaning, "part of the *Shema,* and the whole of the Eulogies."

If Jesus, as was the custom, and as other readers of the Prophets and preachers of the sermon would have done—if Jesus participated in full, he would have read such expressions as: "Thou art Jehovah, our God, and the God of our fathers, our King, and the King of our fathers, our Saviour, and the Saviour of our fathers, our Creator, the Rock of our Salvation, our Help and our Deliverer. Thy name is from everlasting, and there is no God beside Thee." "Blessed art Thou, Jehovah, Who quickenest the dead!" "Thou art Holy, and Thy name is Holy. Selah. Blessed art Thou Jehovah God, the Holy One." Such a participation on his part would in fact have fitted perfectly into the Messianic pronouncement he was about to make, for Jehovah was the Messiah, and the salvation promised Israel and all men by the One was the salvation that would be brought to pass by the Other.

But this we do know. Standing before the people, Jesus read from Isaiah one of the greatest of the sayings of that Messianic prophet. Probably he read in Hebrew—such was the practice—and then translated or "targumed" the passage into Aramaic. The targums were the oral translations or paraphrases of the written Hebrew. This would also account for the differences between Isaiah's record in the Old Testament, and the statements as given by Jesus and recorded by Luke.

The Spirit of the Lord is upon me, because he hath anointed me to preach the gospel to the poor; he hath sent me to heal the brokenhearted, to preach deliverance to the captives, and recovering of sight to the blind, to set at liberty them that are bruised, To preach the acceptable year of the Lord.

Such were the words he read. Then he sat down—as the custom was—to deliver the discourse. All eyes were upon him, and he began by saying unto them:

This day is this scripture fulfilled in your ears.

Thereafter, many "gracious words . . . proceeded out of his mouth," to which all present bore witness. What these words were we do not know, but in the very nature of things we can rest assured that they were a sermon on the text he had read. Providentially, we do know what Isaiah's words mean and how they apply to the One who read them that day in Nazareth, in the synagogue where he had worshipped as a youth, and among the people whom he knew and whose faces were familiar to him.

The Spirit of the Lord is upon me. Isaiah said: "The Spirit of the Lord God is upon me."[5] Being pure and without sin, Jesus always and ever possessed that Spirit which will not dwell in an unclean tabernacle, but which, conversely, always abides with those whose houses of clay make a fit abode for such a celestial presence. Further, the Holy Spirit descended upon him, like a dove, when he was baptized by John, which John was the one who also testified, as we have seen, that "God giveth not his Spirit by measure unto him." It is no wonder, then, as we have also seen, that when he came into Galilee it was "in the power of the Spirit."

He hath anointed me to preach the gospel to the poor. Isaiah has it: "The Lord hath anointed me to preach good tidings unto the meek." The Messiah comes in power; he is anointed, commissioned from on high; he comes in his Father's name, to do his Father's will, because his Father sent him; he speaks, not of himself, but of his Father. And his glorious message—it is the everlasting gospel, the plan of salvation; it is the glad tidings of great joy that salvation is in Christ, that man shall gain the victory over the grave, that he has power to gain eternal life. And to whom does the message go? To the meek, to the God-fearing, to those who seek righteousness; and they, in general, are the poor among men.

He hath sent me to heal the brokenhearted. "He hath sent me to bind up the brokenhearted," Isaiah says. 'I am come to heal and to save. Let those whose spirits are depressed come unto me, and I will give them peace. Are there those who are crushed with the weight of their sins, who carry burdens of despair—let them come unto me. I will bear their burdens if they will repent. Though my own heart be broken, yet shall all those who believe in me be healed. I shall heal men spiritually even as you have seen me heal them physically.'

He hath sent me . . . to preach deliverance to the captives. "He hath sent me . . . to proclaim liberty to the captives." Messiah is a preacher; his words deliver men from the captivity of sin and the bondage of iniquity. He proclaims liberty to the sin-shackled soul. By his word—the everlasting gospel that he preaches—men in mortality and those in the spirit prison are made free.

He hath sent me . . . to preach . . . recovering of sight to the blind. There is no parallel passage in Isaiah, although the thought fits into the over-all sense and meaning acclaimed by ancient Israel's Messianic seer in the utterance he made. That is to say: Jesus, as he "targumed" Isaiah's meaning from Hebrew to Aramaic, did what only inspired interpreters can do: he expanded the words and interpreted the meaning of the original utterance. 'I am sent by the Father—not only to proclaim how deliverance from sin may be found, but to preach the recovering of spiritual sight to those who are blind spiritually. Through me they shall see out of obscurity, and out of darkness.' If a parallel passage for these added words is needed, it may be found in Isaiah's prophecy about the latter-day coming forth of the Book of

Mormon, for the promise is that through "the words of the book . . . the eyes of the blind shall see out of obscurity, and out of darkness." (Isa. 29:8.)

He hath sent me . . . to set at liberty them that are bruised. "He hath sent me . . . to proclaim . . . the opening of the prison to them that are bound." The prisoners shall go free! Messiah shall make it possible. Those who are bruised and bound and beaten and shackled in the dungeons of hell shall come forth. The word has gone forth; the prison doors shall open—be it for the prisoners of sin in this life, or, as another prophet has called them, the "prisoners of hope" in the life to come. (Zech. 9:12.) "Let the dead speak forth anthems of eternal praise to the King Immanuel, who hath ordained, before the world was, that which would enable us to redeem them out of their prison; for the prisoners shall go free." (D&C 128:22.)

He hath sent me . . . to preach the acceptable year of the Lord. "He hath sent me . . . to proclaim the acceptable year of the Lord." The acceptable year of the Lord! It is the year and the time when Messiah comes; when salvation is made available; when men have opportunity to learn what they must do to be saved in his everlasting kingdom. 'I now proclaim to you: This is the year; this is the set time; salvation is near; I am he; my word is truth; come and walk in the light of the Lord. Now is the time and the day of your salvation; this is the acceptable year.'

Then, by way of climax, having taught the doctrine with gracious words that could not be refuted, Jesus attests:

This day is this scripture fulfilled in your ears.

That is to say: 'I have read from Isaiah; I have set forth the meaning of his words; I have taught the doctrine. Now I testify that these words—and therefore all Messianic prophecies—are fulfilled in me; they apply to me; I am the one of whom the prophets spoke; I am he; I am the Messiah.'

Where such a witness is born, there are only two possible responses. One is complete acceptance, the other complete rejection. No one can argue with a testimony; it is not a debatable issue. It is there to be accepted or to be rejected. Jesus taught and testified, and as the full meaning of his gracious words sank into their hearts, his Nazarene friends made their choice. This Jesus they knew and had known from his infancy and youth. How can he be the Son of God? How can he be the Messiah? Their voice—to their eternal sorrow—was one of rejection, which they summarized in these words: "Is not this Joseph's son?" 'How then can he be the Messiah? We know him; he is one of us.'

The word fell on stony ground and found no soil in which to grow, and the seeds died without sprouting. It was a sad, dark day for Nazareth.

Jesus Is Rejected at Nazareth

(*Luke 4:23-30*)

As the spirit of rejection contained in their words—"Is not this Joseph's son?"—became the consensus of the synagogue throng, Jesus, feeling their reaction, turned from his proclamation of joy and deliverance to a proclamation of sorrow and damnation. That which might have been theirs was passing them by. And yet, opposed as they were to his claim of Messiahship, they could not explain away the reports of the wonders he had performed in Cana and Capernaum and Judea. 'We know he cannot be the Messiah—for he is Joseph's son—but what of the miracles? Can it be that he has performed them? And if the reports are true, why doesn't he show us, his friends and associates of many years, the same signs and wonders he has shown others?'

Jesus, reading their thoughts and feeling the sense of the meeting, yet remaining in complete command of the situation, continued his sermon. "Ye will surely say unto me this proverb, Physician, heal thyself: whatsoever we have heard done in Capernaum, do also here in thy country," he said. 'You have performed miracles in Cana and Capernaum, but none here, and yet you are a native of Nazareth. Why can't we see a sign, some great exhibition of your purported power? Don't you know that charity begins at home, that unless the physician heals himself of his own diseases we cannot believe he has power to heal others?' (*Commentary* 1:162.)

With bitter irony Jesus responds to the thoughts in their minds. "No prophet is accepted in his own country," he says. And as illustrations of blessings being withheld from the chosen people (the Nazarenes, as it were) and given to foreigners (those of other cities in Palestine, in this case), he referred to two accounts from Israel's history: that of Elijah, who blessed the Phoenician widow of Zarephath, and that of Elisha, who cleansed a Gentile of Syria.

After Elijah sealed the heavens that there was neither dew nor rain, but according to his word; after the brook Cherith, whereof he drank, failed for want of water; and after the ravens no longer brought him bread and flesh to eat, the Lord sent him to Zarephath in Zidon, to a widow woman, who was commanded to sustain him. Traveling thence, Elijah found the woman gathering two sticks for a fire, that she might take her last handful of meal and her last drops of oil and make them into a cake for herself and her son. Then she and her offspring faced certain death by starvation.

"Make me thereof a little cake first, and bring it unto me, and after make for thee and for thy son. For thus saith the Lord God of Israel, The barrel of meal shall not waste, neither shall the cruse of oil fail, until the day that the Lord sendeth rain upon the earth." The woman obeyed. Elijah's words were fulfilled. "And the barrel of meal wasted not, neither did the cruse of oil fail," and they all ate thereof for many days. And as though this were not enough, when the woman's son died, Elijah called him back from death, and his spirit came into his body again. All this was done for a woman of Phoenicia—who probably was not even of the house of Israel—because she had faith. (1 Kgs. 17.)

Naaman, a mighty man and captain of all the armies of Syria, was a leper. His wife had a servant, an Israelite maid who had been taken captive from her homeland. She said: "Would God my lord were with the prophet that is in Samaria! for he would recover him of his leprosy." Naaman in due course went down to Israel and was told by a messenger sent by Elisha: "Go and wash in Jordan seven times, and thy flesh shall come again to thee, and thou shalt be clean." Doing so, he became clean—a miracle wrought at a distance, as it were, somewhat like the healing of the nobleman's son by Jesus. (2 Kgs. 5.)

Elijah the prophet, who was taken up into heaven without tasting death, and Elisha, who poured water upon the hands of Elijah and upon whom his master's mantle fell—these mighty prophets, whose works were known to every Jew in Jesus' day—their miracles were performed selectively, for special individuals, not for the suffering hosts of their day. Where there is faith, there is the miracle; where there is no faith, no miracle is wrought. And if the prophets of old went outside the fold of Israel to find those worthy of their ministry, so Jesus would go outside Nazareth to find receptive souls who would believe in him and receive the blessings that he came to bestow. Should the people of Nazareth desire to see the wondrous works done elsewhere, then let them accept Him who now preached in their synagogue, and they too would receive the blessings of heaven. These things, in his infinite wisdom, Jesus taught them that day; from his more extended remarks, Luke has preserved for us these words:

> *But I tell you of a truth, many widows were in Israel in the days of Elias, when the heaven was shut up three years and six months, when great famine was throughout all the land; But unto none of them was Elias sent, save unto Sarepta, a city of Sidon, unto a woman that was a widow. And many lepers were in Israel in the time of Eliseus the prophet; and none of them was cleansed, saving Naaman the Syrian.*

Anger welled up in the hearts of his fellow Nazarenes.

Lucifer, not Jehovah, was their lord, as Jesus would one day tell the Jews in Jerusalem. Though they had given lip service—that very day, in that very synagogue—to the worship of Jehovah, yet they now, "filled with wrath," as Luke says, cast that very Jehovah out of their midst. They "thrust him out of the city"; they "led him unto the brow of the hill whereon their city was built." Why? "That they might cast him down headlong." The spirit of murder was in their hearts, and they sought the death of Jesus. His words they could not answer, his testimony they could not refute, but his voice—as they supposed—his voice they could silence.

Jesus had come unto his own, and his own received him not! The leaders of the people rejected his words when he preached in the temple at Passover time. The common people of Nazareth hardened their hearts against his words when he spoke to them in their synagogue. And so it would be throughout his whole ministry; save for a few believing souls, he was "despised and rejected of men" (Isa. 53:3); and eventually *his own* would lead him before Roman overlords, as they raised their voices in chants of "Crucify him, Crucify him."

How he escaped the wrath and murderous designs of the Nazarene mob is not recorded. Luke says simply: "But he passing through the midst of them went his way." "Perhaps His silence, perhaps the calm nobleness of His bearing, perhaps the dauntless innocence of His gaze overawed them. Apart from anything supernatural, there seems to have been in the presence of Jesus a spell of mystery and majesty which even His most ruthless and hardened enemies acknowledged, and before which they involuntarily bowed. It was to this that He owed His escape when the maddened Jews in the Temple took up stones to stone Him; it was this that made the bold and bigoted officers of the Sanhedrin unable to arrest Him as He taught in public during the Feast of Tabernacles at Jerusalem; it was this that made the armed band of His enemies, at His mere look, fall before Him to the ground in the Garden of Gethsemane. Suddenly, quietly,

He asserted His freedom, waved aside His captors, and overawing them by His simple glance, passed through their midst unharmed. Similar events have occurred in history, and continue still to occur. There is something in defenceless and yet dauntless dignity that calms even the fury of a mob. 'They stood—stopped—inquired—were ashamed—fled—separated.' " (Farrar, p. 175.)

But now the Son of God would go elsewhere to continue his ministry.

NOTES

1. These are the words of Abinadi, spoken 150 years before our Lord's mortal birth.
2. This is the testimony of Peter, gained shortly after the crucifixion.
3. An extended analysis of the Messianic prophecies is found in *The Promised Messiah: The First Coming of Christ,* a companion volume to this work.
4. This data on synagogues is digested from Edersheim 1:430-50. See also chapter 10 of *The Mortal Messiah* (Book I).
5. All of the quotations are taken from Isa. 61:1-2.

THE GALILEAN MINISTERS IN GALILEE

The land of Zebulun and the land of Naphtali,
. . . by the way of the sea,
beyond Jordan, in Galilee of the nations.
The people that walked in darkness
have seen a great light:
they that dwell in the land of the
shadow of death,
upon them hath the light shined.
(Isa. 9:1-2.)[1]

Jesus Dwells in Capernaum

(*Matthew 4:13-16; JST, Matthew 4:12; Luke 4:31-32*)

Palestine—Old Canaan—the Holy Land—the land where Jesus dwelt!

We find the Holy One of Israel, now dwelling in mortality, living among his Israelite kinsmen in the chosen land, the land promised them by Abraham their father. We find the Son of God dwelling among the chosen seed; among those to whose fathers the prophets had ministered in olden times; among those to whom the Law and the Prophets were as well known as is the light of the sun or as is the falling of the rain to men in general. We find the Holy Messiah dwelling and doing and speaking and being—all as recorded in the Messianic utterances of the prophets who went before.

And how fittingly it all falls into place. Jesus' every word and act and movement weaves itself into a majestic tapestry, a work of art that was before planned by his Father, and whose beauty was revealed—a segment here and a golden thread there—to the prophets and saints who preceded our Lord in life.

He was born in Bethlehem—the City of David, the spot beloved by Israel's greatest king—for he was the Son of David, heir to his throne, the one on whose shoulders the government would rest. He was the King who should reign in righteousness, the one who should open and no man shut, and upon whom the Lord would hang all the glory of his Father's house. His birth must be where kings are born, in the City of David.

He grew to maturity, subject to Joseph and Mary, in an obscure Galilean village. In his youth he was exposed to the wholesome rugged life of the farm and the pasture and the shop. Obscure Nazareth preserved his obscurity until the time of his showing to Israel arrived. The manners and ways of a village set apart from the marts of trade and the centers of civilization enabled him to learn the way of the swallow and to rejoice in the beauties of the lilies.

Now his ministry is upon him. With a zeal scarce hinted at in the lives of others, he must now be about his Father's business. Where shall his dwelling be? Nazareth no longer serves his needs; the obscurity of the past must flee before the light he now sheds forth. He cannot live in Jerusalem, where priests and scribes and Pharisees and Sanhedrinists—whose influence is great—seek his life and plot his death. He will visit that Sodom-like city from time to time and testify to its people; and finally, he will go there, deliberately and consciously, to suffer many things of the elders and chief priests and scribes, and to be killed, and to rise again the third day. But for the next twenty-seven months or so of his life, he needs a home base from which he can work and whence his word can go forth.

And so—rejected at Nazareth—he now turns, as the Messianic prophecies foretold, to Capernaum, that city of sin on the shores of the Sea of Galilee. He leaves the ancient land of Zebulon, where Nazareth is, to live in the land of Naphtali. He has there a nobleman friend whose son he healed; it is the city of Peter's in-laws, and the future chief apostle himself has a home there. But what is more important, it is a logical center from which to travel to the cities and villages that must hear his voice and see his face; and the throngs of travelers who pass through it will hear of his words and his miracles and carry back to their home peoples the wondering queries of earnest truth-seekers.

Matthew tells us that "leaving Nazareth, he came and dwelt in Capernaum" to fulfill the Messianic word, which promises that a great light shall shine upon those who dwell in that part of "Galilee of the Gentiles." Luke says he went to Capernaum, entered their synagogue, taught them on the Sabbath day—perhaps precisely as he had done in Nazareth—and that "they were astonished at his doctrine: for his word was with power." His doctrine was the gospel; he spoke by the power of the Holy Ghost; and it was the light of his everlasting word that was shown forth, in Galilee, in all of Palestine, and in all nations and among all peoples where he or those sent of him should teach and minister.

"I Will Make You Fishers of Men"

(Luke 5:1-11; JST, Luke 5:2, 10; Matthew 4:18-22; JST, Matthew 4:18-21; Mark 1:16-20; JST, Mark 1:18)

About one year has passed since Andrew and Peter and the Beloved John (as well as Philip and Nathanael) all came to know that Jesus was the Christ, the Son of the living God. It was Andrew who then said to Peter: "We have found the Messias." It was Philip who then said: "We have found him, of whom Moses in the law, and the prophets did write." And it was Nathanael who then testified: "Rabbi, thou art the Son of God; thou art the King of Israel."

Since then all of these brethren have been with Jesus in much of his ministry. They saw the water become wine, the moneychangers flee from the temple, the miracles wrought at the Passover and throughout all Judea. They know what Jesus said to Nicodemus and the woman of Samaria, nor is the episode involving the nobleman's son hidden from them. They were present or at least know what he said in the synagogue in Nazareth. By now they have spent hundreds, perhaps thousands, of hours conversing with and listening to the Master.

How much does a zealous convert learn about the gospel during his first year in the Church? How much would these brethren of apostolic stature learn as they ate and slept and walked and lived with the Master Teacher for weeks and months at a time? How many miracles had they witnessed? How many times and in what variety of ways had they heard him say he was the Messiah? We do not know when James (the brother of John) joined the group, but it is clear his knowledge and testimony was like that of the others.

These brethren were not novices; the gospel message was not new to them. They had testimonies of the truth and divinity of the work, and the resultant desires to serve God and keep his commandments were firmly planted in their hearts. But with it all, they still needed bread to fill their own bellies, fish to fill the mouths of their wives and children, money to support their families. They had not as yet been called into a full-time ministry; they were not yet living the law of consecration, under which all that they had and were was dedicated to the building up of the kingdom and the rolling forth of the work of Him whose special witnesses they would soon become.

It is in this setting, then, and with this understanding, that we find the brothers Andrew and Peter, and the sons of Zebedee, James and John, plying their trade as fishers of fish on the Sea of Galilee. Jesus their Lord comes into view on the shore. Seeing Peter and Andrew "casting a net into the sea," he said: "I am he of whom it is written by the prophets; follow me, and I will make you fishers of men." Probably he said more—perhaps much more; no doubt it would have recalled their numerous experiences with him of the past year. As to what happened, the inspired account says, "And they, believing on his words"—no doubt meaning all the words he had spoken to them over the months—"left their net, and straightway followed him."

Soon thereafter, he came upon James and John, in their father's ship, mending their nets. Jesus issued the call, "and straightway they left their father Zebedee in the ship with the hired servants, and went after him." These four apostles-to-be were preparing for their holy calling. No doubt they already were elders in the Melchizedek Priesthood—at least we know that at a much earlier time they were performing baptisms, which requires at least the Aaronic Priesthood, but now they were forsaking all to follow the Master. They were going forth on full-time missions; they were consecrating their time and means and talents to a greater work. They were to be fishers of men.

Luke gives us either a more amplified account of these calls or a recitation of a miraculous event that occurred immediately thereafter. Each of the two sets of brothers, in their own ships, had fished all night, as the custom was, and had caught nothing. It was morning; the ships were anchored, and the fishermen were ashore, washing their nets. Crowds so pressed in upon Jesus that he entered Peter's ship and asked him to "thrust out a little from the land." Then Jesus "sat down, and taught the people out of the ship." Again we do not know what he said, only that he preached the gospel.

When his sermon was ended, Jesus instructed Peter: "Launch out into the deep, and let down your nets for a draught." This Peter did, though he had toiled all night and caught nothing. Immediately, miraculously, the nets were so full that they broke; with the help of James and John, both ships were filled, "so that they began to sink." Those who live by the law of consecration have their just needs and wants supplied, by divine power if need be.

Peter, falling at Jesus' knees, said: "Depart from me; for I am a sinful man, O Lord," so great was his astonishment "at the draught of fishes which they had taken." It was as though he had said: 'I am unworthy of this honor. A sinner such as I is not fit company for "the King, the Lord of hosts." Depart from me, that another more deserving may see thy countenance and behold thy person.' (*Commentary* 1:166.)

Jesus' response was kind and encouraging: "Fear not; from henceforth thou shalt catch men." A new day had dawned for Peter, James, John—the future First Presidency of the Church—and for Andrew, one of the Twelve. "And when they had brought their ships to land, they forsook all, and followed him."

That Glorious Sabbath in Capernaum

(*Mark 1:21-34; Luke 4:31-41; JST, Luke 4:38; Matthew 8:14-17*)

A day in the life of our Lord: one glorious, wondrous day in Capernaum, his own city; a Sabbath day—a day of mighty preaching, of doctrine that astonished, of casting out an unclean devil in the synagogue; a day when Peter's mother-in-law was raised from her sick bed, and when a congregation of persons, possessed by evil spirits and suffering from divers diseases, came to partake of the goodness of Him who "took our infirmities, and bare our sicknesses"!

It was the Sabbath. He entered into the synagogue. No doubt Simon and Andrew, and James and John, the two sets of brothers, were with him; as devout Jews they all knew their Sabbath place, and that place was in the synagogue of the Lord, the place where Jehovah was worshipped according to the best light and knowledge then found among mortals. What a favored and choice congregation assembled here in Capernaum, in the house of worship where archaeologists have found the ornamentation over the lintel, consisting of a pot of manna between representations of Aaron's rod; in the stone building where four future apostles and their families paid their devotions. And on this particular Sabbath the Son of God himself was to address the congregation. Word most assuredly had spread through the city of the claims he had made and the gracious words he had spoken so recently in the synagogue in Nazareth. Who would not have crowded into the rectangular building to hear the word of truth and breathe the spirit of worship on such a day?

After the liturgical and formal parts of the day's worship, Jesus speaks. Neither Mark nor Luke tell us what he said, though they both recount the effect of the sermon on the hearers. They tell us "his word was with power"; that the congregation was "astonished at his doctrine"—as well they might be when one of such stature and fame arises to announce he is the Messiah and that salvation comes by him, as he had done in Nazareth; and that he "taught them as one that had authority, and not as the scribes." Many believing souls must have been in the congregation, as witness what happened that evening in Capernaum; at least no tumult of opposition arose, and no one sought to put him to death, as had been the case among those of the city where once he dwelt.

Yet there was one in the synagogue upon whom the sermon had an astonishing effect; one who was so filled with animus and hatred that he welcomed into his body an unclean devil from the blackness of hell; one who was possessed by an unclean spirit who took complete control of all mortal functions. By the mouth of the man, the demon who hated both the truth and Him who is its author cried out: "Let us alone; what have we to do with thee, thou Jesus of Nazareth? art thou come to destroy us? I know thee who thou art, the Holy One of God."

Jesus' response was immediate, authoritative, unbending. He rebuked the devil. "Hold thy peace, and come out of him," he said, for the Son of Man neither sought nor accepted testimony of his divinity from an evil source. What matter it if "the devils also believe, and tremble"? (James 2:19.) What converting power attends the witness of Lucifer that Christ is the Holy One? Testimony should be borne by the power of the Holy Ghost or remain unspoken. What does it matter what the rebels from Sheol think or know about the laws of righteousness? Can a fountain bring forth both sweet and bitter water at the same place?

When the command came, this angel of the devil, this son of perdition, this unclean spirit, who like Lucifer his master was in opposition to all righteousness—this unclean spirit had no choice but to obey. With one final burst of hatred and venom, the unclean devil tore the man, threw him in agony in their midst, cried out with a loud and defiant voice, and then came out of his ill-gotten tenement.

The man was left limp and weak, but in a state to receive strength and light. The devil joined his fellow rebels who are continuing on earth the war commenced in heaven. And the people were amazed. Questioning among themselves, some asked: "What thing is this? what new doctrine is this? for with authority commandeth he even the unclean spirits, and they do obey him." Others acclaimed: "What a word is this! for with authority and power he commandeth the unclean spirits, and they come out." Is it any wonder that "the fame of him went out into every place of the country round about," and that all Galilee heard of his doctrine, his Messianic claims, and his power even over unclean spirits?

However much it may run counter to the carnal mind to read of men possessed of devils, and of other men who cast them out, such is one of the realities of mortal life. One-third of the hosts of heaven—all spirit children of our Eternal Father who is God—were cast out of heaven for rebellion. As angels of the devil and as sons of him who is Perdition, they stalk the earth, seeking whom they may destroy. Their condemnation: they are denied bodies; for them there is no further progression; they are miserable and seek the misery of all mankind; they are damned souls, without hope, forever. If, as, and when—subject to the restrictions and laws of our gracious God—they can gain temporary tenancy in a tenement of clay, they take up their habitation in the bodies of others.

We do not know how or under what circumstances such tenancy is permitted. That all things are governed and controlled by law, we do know; and we are left to suppose that in the day when the Incarnate Jehovah came among men, there must have been more persons who were susceptible to spirit possession than has been the case in other days. Perhaps somehow many of the Jews of that day—zealous, religiously inclined, yet going beyond the mark where spiritual things are concerned—got themselves into a state where evil spirits could enter their bodies. We do know from the Messianic utterance—"And he shall cast out devils, or the evil spirits which dwell in the hearts of men" (Mosiah 3:6)—that Jesus was destined, as he did, to cast out devils, and that this power was given to his apostles and seventies and, of course, is in the true church today.

After the synagogue service, He who had not where to lay his head, who—during the days of his active ministry at least—had no home of his own, went with Simon and Andrew to their abode to partake of the festive Sabbath meal. Such feasts at family gatherings were the most joyous occasions of the week. James and John were also guests in Peter's home on this memorable day.

Mark tells us that "Simon's wife's mother lay sick of a fever, and anon they tell him of her." Luke says she "was taken with a great fever; and they besought him for her." Jesus' specially selected disciples were married men with wives and children and families of their own, as his specially called servants should be in all ages. This is a household of faith; it is Peter's dwelling place; and all who dwell with him love the Lord and seek to walk uprightly before him. That they should importune the Master to heal one of their number is the most natural thing in the world.

And that Jesus should respond is what we all expect. He stood over her, rebuked the fever, took her by the hand, and lifted her up. "Immediately the fever left her, and she ministered unto them." What a joyous occasion this must have been. As the little group partook of the bounties of life, they also feasted spiritually; as they ate bread and fish, they rejoiced in the spiritual food set forth in the sermon of the morning; as they thought about the healed demoniac, there stood ministering to their every need a woman whose body but moments before had burned with fever. What marvels were being wrought in Israel!

Nor were the day's labors completed. From the morning session in the synagogue to the going down of the sun, the word went forth; all Capernaum heard what Jesus had preached; all learned that even the unclean devils departed at his word.

People began assembling at Peter's home. "All the city was gathered together at the door." Included with them were their sick and afflicted and diseased. Some were carried on litters; others were supported by loving arms; those with diseases of every sort came in faith, assured that miraculous cures awaited them. At evening after sunset, Jesus "laid his hands on every one of them, and healed them." And at his word, the devils came out of many, saying, "Thou art Christ the Son of God," and he rebuked them and "suffered them not to speak: for they knew that he was Christ."

Jesus Tours and Preaches in Galilee

(*Matthew 4:23-25; JST, Matthew 4:22; Mark 1:35-39; Luke 4:42-44; JST, Luke 4:42*)

When the night came the labors of the day ceased; the wise words and healing power stopped for a moment. Needed sleep and rest were sought, but not for long. "In the morning, rising up a great while before day, he went out, and departed into a solitary place, and there prayed."

How often Jesus prays! If it were not a basic tenet of true

religion that private prayers are personal; that they are between the earthly suppliant and the Divine Father; that they should be known only by him who speaks and Him who hears—if it were not for these things, we would covet a knowledge of what the Son of the Father said to the Father of the Son on this and numerous other occasions. We can suppose that the voice of prayer poured out words of thanksgiving for the grace and guidance of that Capernaum Sabbath, which is scarcely over, and sought wisdom and direction for the continuing labors that lay ahead.

Jesus did not remain long in the desert solitude. Simon and the disciples followed after him. "All men seek for thee," Peter said, as the multitudes came pleading and importuning that he remain with them.

They, however, had heard the word. His voice had testified in their synagogue; the witness of his divine Sonship had been borne in their presence; he had preached the gospel, opened the door to further investigation, and demonstrated his power by the healings and the miracles. The responsibility was now theirs to obtain baptism, to join the sheepfold of the Good Shepherd, and to live as becometh saints. Jesus must go elsewhere and give others a like opportunity.

"I must preach the kingdom of God to other cities also," he said, "For therefore am I sent." And preach it he did, in Galilee (except for a brief attendance at his second Passover), for almost two years, for about twenty-one months. By then it will be October, A.D. 29, and he will go to the Feast of Tabernacles to commence his later Judean ministry. But now he is starting his first tour of Galilee, preaching, healing, doing good, and working righteousness. Those with diseases and torments are healed; the lunatics and the paralytics are made well; devils are cast out; and multitudes follow him, "from Galilee, and from Decapolis, and from Jerusalem, and from Judæa, and from beyond Jordan." His fame knows no limit, and men flock to him from every political jurisdiction.

Truly this is that which Nephi foresaw. "I . . . beheld the Lamb of God going forth among the children of men," he said. "And I beheld multitudes of people who were sick, and who were afflicted with all manner of diseases, and with devils and unclean spirits; and . . . they were healed by the power of the Lamb of God; and the devils and the unclean spirits were cast out." (1 Ne. 11:31.)

NOTE

1. The marginal reading for the introductory portion of this Messianic prophecy is: "In the former time he brought into contempt the land of Zebulon and the land of Naphtali, but in the latter time hath he made it glorious," meaning that in the coming day when the Lord Jesus would dwell there, it would be glorious because the light of his countenance would shine upon the people.

JESUS USES MIRACLES TO SPREAD THE WORK

Jesus was touched with a feeling
of their infirmities. Those cries pierced
to His inmost heart;
the groans and sighs of all that
collective misery
filled His whole soul with pity.
His heart bled for them;
He suffered with them;
their agonies were His;
so that the Evangelist St. Matthew
recalls in this place,
with a slight difference of language,
the words of Isaiah,
"Surely He bore our griefs and carried
our sorrow." (Farrar, p. 182.)[1]

A New Dimension to Jesus' Miracles

Miracles stand out as one of the chief identifying characteristics of the mortal ministry of the Messiah. His Messianic witnesses—Isaiah, Nephi, King Benjamin, and others—

spoke plainly of the throngs who would be healed by his word. We have now seen these throngs in Judea and throughout all Galilee. All of Palestine knows that here is a man who heals the sick in such a measure as was never before known in Israel. The raising of great multitudes from their beds of affliction and the casting out of many unclean spirits from many contorted and abused souls cannot be hidden from the people. Nor was it intended that it should be. Jesus' miracles bore testimony of his divinity and to the truth of the words he spoke.

Primarily, however, our Lord in his ministry is preaching the gospel of the kingdom; he is announcing to all men what they must do to gain peace in this life and eternal life in the world to come; he is proclaiming that a gracious Father ordained and established a plan of salvation that will enable the whole family of earth to advance and progress and become like their Creator; he is testifying that he is the Promised Messiah, the Savior and Redeemer, through whom salvation comes. "Whoso believeth in me, and is baptized, the same shall be saved; and they are they who shall inherit the kingdom of God. And whoso believeth not in me, and is not baptized, shall be damned." (3 Ne. 11:33-34.) This is his message; this summarizes what men must believe and what they must do. Jesus came to save sinners, and salvation comes through repentance and baptism and continued devotion to the truth. Unless we keep this perspective clearly before us, we will not and cannot keep in their perspective the disjointed collection of episodes from his life that have been preserved in the inspired writings now extant.

The miracles he is constantly performing are visible evidences in the eyes of all, believers and nonbelievers alike, that he has more than mortal power. They are proof, as it were, that his words are true. Can a deceiver and false teacher open blind eyes and unstop deaf ears? Miracles and true teachings always go hand in hand; signs follow those that believe—in their purity and perfection—the truths of the everlasting gospel.

We have little conception of the number of healings Jesus wrought. Multitudes thronged his way day after day, bringing their diseased and deformed, their lame and decrepit, their deaf and their blind. All these were healed as faith and desire warranted. Even their dead were subject to Jesus' will.

No attempt is made by the Gospel authors to record Jesus' many miracles. Only selected samples are set forth in the scriptures. The obvious plan of the inspired authors is to preserve illustrations of his purposes and powers, and surely the wide variety of healings and miraculous performances that they chose to record do attest to his power and control over all things.

After that glorious Sabbath in Capernaum when he cast out devils and healed all manner of diseases and torments, we find him touring throughout all Galilee "healing all manner of sickness and all manner of disease among the people." About three months pass, during which period the synoptists select, for analysis and exposition, only two of his miracles. These are the healing of a leper somewhere in Galilee and the healing of one sick with palsy when Jesus comes back to Capernaum.

Both of these manifestations of divine power add a new dimension, not so far seen, to his miraculous performances: the healing of the leper because of the nature of the disease, the secrecy he enjoined upon the recipient of his blessing, and the stipulation that the healed person conform to the provisions of the law of Moses; and the curing of the paralytic because it was preceded by a forgiveness of sins, showing that Jesus was Jehovah, who alone can forgive sins. Each of these miracles was performed not alone for the benefit and blessing of the suffering Israelite whose body was affected, but as a witness to the growing group of opponents that he whom they opposed came from God and had divine power. The wicked and rebellious in Israel, word upon word and miracle after miracle, were being left without excuse; their sins were being bound securely upon their own heads; the Light they were rejecting was shining forth everywhere in word and in deed.

He Heals a Leper

(*Mark 1:40-45; JST, Mark 1:40; Luke 5:12-16; JST, Luke 5:14; Matthew 8:2-4; JST, Matthew 8:2*)

Healings there have been in profuse abundance, but none—up to this point and as far as we know—has involved a leper, "a man full of leprosy." None has dealt with a body and soul plagued with a living death, one whose body was in process of rotting, decaying, and returning to the dust to gain merciful surcease from the torments of the flesh. Before the Second Coming, "the Lord God will send forth flies upon the face of the earth, which shall take hold of the inhabitants thereof, and shall eat their flesh, and shall cause maggots to come in upon them; . . . and their flesh shall fall from off their bones, and their eyes from their sockets." (D&C 29:18-19.) Before and at the time of his First Coming, there were many in Israel who were lepers, possessors of such a vile and degenerating disease that they were anathema to everyone and a curse to themselves. Except for the extent of the coming latter-day plague, it can scarcely be worse than the hell and torment and physical affliction suffered by the lepers of Jesus' day.

Leprosy is an evil and wicked disease. "The symptoms and the effects of this disease are very loathsome. There comes a white swelling or scab, with a change of the color of the hair . . . from its natural hue to yellow; then the appearance of a taint going deeper than the skin, or raw flesh appearing in the swelling. Then it spreads and attacks the cartilaginous portions of the body. The nails loosen and drop off, the gums are absorbed, and the teeth decay and fall out; the breath is a stench, the nose decays; fingers, hands, feet, may be lost, or the eyes eaten out. The human beauty has gone into corruption, and the patient feels that he is being eaten as by a fiend, who consumes him slowly in a long remorseless meal that will not end until he be destroyed. He is shut out from his fellows. As they approach he must cry, 'Unclean! unclean!' that all humanity may be warned from his precincts. He must abandon wife and child. He must go to live with other lepers, in disheartening view of miseries similar to his own. He must dwell in dismantled houses or in the tombs."[2]

"It began with little specks on the eyelids, and on the palms of the hand, and gradually spread over different parts of the body, bleaching the hair white wherever it showed itself, crusting the affected parts with shining scales, and causing swellings and sores. From the skin it slowly ate its way through the tissues, to the bones and joints and even to the marrow, rotting the whole body piecemeal. The lungs, the organs of speech and hearing, and the eyes were attacked in turn, till, at last, consumption or dropsy brought welcome death." (Geikie, pp. 390-91.)

Leprosy in biblical times, in addition to its desolating physical effects, was looked upon as the symbol of sin and uncleanness, signifying that as this evil disease ate away and destroyed the physical body, so sin eats away and corrupts the spiritual side of man. This did not mean that the disease borne by any individual attested that he was a worse sinner than his fellows, only that the disease itself was a symbol of the ills that will befall the ungodly and rebellious. It had been chosen as such a symbol, however, because it was considered to be the worst of all diseases, one that could not be cured except by direct divine intervention. There were instances in the Old Testament—Miriam, Gehazi, and Uzziah—in which rebellious persons were cursed with leprosy as a punishment for their evil deed.

And so we find the Galilean, preaching the gospel in his beloved Galilee, in an unnamed city, when a man "full of leprosy" —one in the last stages of the plague; one who is affected from head to toes, in all parts of his body; one for whom a dropsical death is not far distant—who, seeing Jesus, falls on his face, worships him, and says: "Lord, if thou wilt, thou canst make me clean."

Here is a man of faith. There is no question as to whether Jesus can heal him—only will the Great Healer use his power in this case. Indeed, here is man of great faith, for it would take an almost unbounded spiritual assurance to have the confidence of a restoration of health from a disease so dread. And was it not the recognized teaching of all the Rabbis of the day that leprosy was incurable? For such an affliction to leave the flesh of man had scarcely been heard of since the day of Naaman the Syrian.

Jesus is compassionate. With no thought of the Levitical uncleanness that results from touching a leper, he reaches forth his hand, touches the suffering suppliant—which physical contact is mentioned by all three of the synoptists—and, almost as the echo of the entreaty, says: "I will; be thou clean."[3] Immediately, instantaneously, as it were, the leper is cleansed, his leprosy departs, and the miracle is wrought. Nothing is too hard for the Lord.

There were times when Jesus deliberately performed miracles to attract attention and to force, as it were, unbelieving hearers to give credence to his words. On this occasion, for reasons not recited, he chose to give a pointed charge to the cleansed leper to "tell no man" of the healing that had come to him. "See thou say nothing to any man," he commanded, "but go thy way, shew thyself to the priest, and offer for thy cleansing those things which Moses commanded, for a testimony unto them."

It may be that at this time, when men were flocking to him in such great numbers, further fame and notoriety would have hindered him in his travels and preaching; or that such a notable miracle would fan the flames of persecution that already were beginning to burn with an intense flame; or that if the priests in the temple in Jerusalem—whence the cleansed leper must now go to seek Levitical cleanness—knew the source of the healing power, it would have been difficult to obtain the ceremonial absolution required.

Jesus, at this point, was still requiring his converts to

keep the law of Moses. After his passion and crucifixion it would be different; then "the law of commandments contained in ordinances" would be "abolished in his flesh" (Eph. 2:15); then "the handwriting of ordinances, or better, "the bond written in ordinances," would be nailed "to his cross." (Col. 2:14.) But now the healed leper must report to the priest, be shaved and examined, be quarantined for seven days, wash his clothes, offer the required sacrifices, and have the blood sprinkled and all the rites performed as set forth in Leviticus 14.

But the great thing that had happened to him was too good to keep. "He went out, and began to publish it much, and to blaze abroad the matter, insomuch that Jesus could no more openly enter into the city, but was without in desert places: and they came to him from every quarter." He, however, "withdrew himself into the wilderness, and prayed."

He Forgives and Heals One Sick with Palsy

(Mark 2:1-12; JST, Mark 2:1-3, 7, 9; Luke 5:17-26; JST, Luke 5:19-20, 23-24; Matthew 9:2-8; JST, Matthew 9:2, 4-6, 8)

Jesus is now back in Capernaum after a long Galilean tour of teaching and healing. The flames of his fame—fanned by his words, fed by the flow of miracles—are blazing forth in every part of Palestine. Never was a man's name on as many Palestinian tongues as is this Man's. His doctrine, his deeds, his doings—all that he says and every good thing that he does—are discussed in every home, at every festive meal, in every synagogue. The believing among the sick and the penitent among the afflicted seek him with a hope of being healed; those who hunger and thirst after righteousness hang on his every word and find peace to their souls as they live in harmony with his teachings; the rulers and the rebellious rate him as an evil troublemaker and seek ways to entrap and defame and even to slay him.

In Capernaum he stays with Peter, and he is now in the

home of that chief of his apostolic witnesses. Throngs crowd around. The house, apparently a large one, is filled; the living quarters, the guest chamber, the bedrooms, all are crowded with people; and throngs of others are massed around the door and out into the street. Scribes and Pharisees and "doctors of the law" have assembled there "out of every town of Galilee, and Judea, and Jerusalem." Jesus is seated, as the custom is, and is teaching his hearers. Mark, who records what he learned from Peter, and whose account of the wondrous happenings we are about to witness is the most complete, says: "He preached the word unto them." Jesus is preaching the gospel; he is speaking of his Father, of the plan of salvation, of the atoning sacrifice upon which all else rests; he is setting forth the need to repent and be baptized and receive the Holy Ghost and to work the works of righteousness. He is preaching the everlasting word, the word of truth and salvation, the word of the gospel. Such is the course he will follow everywhere.

Four men approach the house. They are carrying a litter or pallet whereon lies one sick of the palsy, one who is paralyzed, who cannot speak, and who of himself is helpless; yet he is a man of faith who has made known his desire to be deposited in the Divine Presence that perchance the one in whom his faith is centered will exercise his healing power in the paralyzed one's behalf. Unable to pass through the throng with their human burden, the four men ascend to the roof, probably by the usual outside stairs found on nearly every house. On the roof they do what is neither difficult nor uncommon; they make an opening in the thatch-type roof, and through it they lower the suffering suppliant into the presence of Jesus.

Our Lord ceases his sermon; all eyes are upon him and the paralytic, whose eyes make the entreaty that his voice cannot. Here, as planned by a Providence that foreknows all things, is a teaching situation seldom equaled in the annals of the Lord's dealings with his people. Before Jesus lies one sick of the palsy who has faith to be healed, and who seeks the blessed word that will make him well. The scribes and the Pharisees and the doctors are all present to see and become witnesses of the power of God. Shall our Lord go forward with the healing, as he has done in many other instances, and as we might suppose he would do now?

Jesus' choice is not to do so. Here also is a man, lying on a litter, who is qualified and entitled, by faith, to have his sins remitted. No verbal request, either for healing or for forgiveness, has been made to the Master; yet the desire of the incapacitated one is apparent. Jesus knows exactly what ought to be done. The man should be healed and forgiven; his faith has prepared him for both blessings. If Jesus should say to him first, 'Be thou made whole,' and then, 'Thy sins are forgiven thee,' the miraculous performance would be another example of his divine power—of which there already was an uncounted number—and the physically decrepit person would, of course, be healed physically and spiritually. Such is a possible course of procedure.

On the other hand, if Jesus should first forgive the man's sins—since none but God can forgive sins—such an act would be an announcement that he was God; then, if he commanded the sick person to rise up and walk, it would be proof that his claim to divinity was true. The teaching situation is ideally prepared, and the Master Teacher knows the course to pursue.

"Son, be of good cheer," he says. And what greater cheer and joy can come into a human heart than that which results from a remission of sins, from an assurance that one is free from earth stains, free from the bondage and sorrow that binds all sin-shackled souls? Then come the glad tidings: "Thy sins be forgiven thee," which act in itself is a greater blessing than to be made whole physically, for all men will attain physical perfection in the resurrection, but only those who are free from sin will go on, in that day, to eternal life in the kingdom of God. As part of the announced freedom from sin for the paralyzed one, Jesus then commands: "Go thy way and sin no more."

The great drama is being acted out by the greatest Dramatist of them all. Jesus has forgiven a man's sins. Luke's account puts the blessed words in the present tense: "Man, thy sins are forgiven thee." Immediately rebellion wells up in the hearts of the ever-present rebels. "Why doth this man thus speak blasphemies?" they think. "Who can forgive sins but God only?"

In part, their thinking is correct. None but God can forgive sins, and if this man is not God, then the words he has spoken are blasphemy, and according to divine law, the penalty for such is death. If, however, this man is the Messiah, then the prerogative he has assumed is proper, and it is within his province to loose on earth and have it loosed eternally in the heavens. Messiah can forgive sins because Messiah is God.

Before viewing the remainder of the drama here opening to our view, we must remind ourselves of how the law of forgiveness operates, for the Lord, who himself ordained the laws, is also himself bound to uphold and sustain and conform to them. The Lord forgives sins, but he does it in harmony with the laws he ordained before the world was.

All men sin and fall short of the glory of God; all need repentance; all need forgiveness; and all can become free from sin by obedience to the laws and ordinances that comprise the cleansing process. For those who have not accepted the gospel—the everlasting word that Jesus was this day preaching in Peter's house—the course of forgiveness is to believe in the Lord Jesus Christ, to repent, to be baptized by immersion for the remission of sins, and to receive the gift of the Holy Ghost by the laying on of hands. The Holy Ghost is a sanctifier, and those who receive the baptism of fire have sin and evil burned out of their souls as though by fire.

For those whose sins have thus been remitted and who sin after baptism—as all baptized souls do—the path to forgiveness consists of repenting and renewing the covenant made in the waters of baptism. Godly sorrow for sin, complete abandonment of the wrongful acts, confession to the

Lord and to the church officers where need be, restitution if such is possible, and renewed obedience—these are all part of the cleansing process for those who, after baptism, fall from the strait and narrow path leading to eternal life. By doing these things and by then partaking worthily of the sacrament, so that the Spirit of the Lord will come again into the lives of the penitent persons, members of the kingdom gain forgiveness of sins.

We are not told whether the paralytic here forgiven by Jesus was a member of the Church or not. The overwhelming probability is that he was, and that Jesus was now forgiving his sins anew, as he did many times to Joseph Smith and the early elders of his latter-day kingdom.[4] "Where members of the Church are concerned, there is a very close connection between manifestations of healing grace and the forgiveness of sins. When the elders administer to faithful saints, the promise is: 'And the prayer of faith shall save the sick, and the Lord shall raise him up; and if he have committed sins, they shall be forgiven him.' (James 5:15.) The very fact that a member of the kingdom has matured in the gospel to the point that he has power through faith in Christ to be healed, means that he also has so lived that he is entitled to have his sins remitted. Since all men repeatedly sin they must all gain successive remissions of their sins, otherwise none would eventually stand pure and spotless before the Lord and thus be worthy of a celestial inheritance." (*Commentary* 1:179.)

Now let us return to the worldly wise who reasoned in their hearts that Jesus' act of forgiveness was blasphemy. For that matter, they reasoned, how could anyone know if the paralytic's sins were remitted? Forgiveness of sins is not something that can be seen or felt or tasted by an outside observer. And weren't the only provisions for forgiveness accomplished by the priests through the sin offerings, the trespass offerings, and the other sacrificial performances, especially those on the day of atonement?

"Wherefore is it that ye think evil in your hearts?" Jesus

asked, for he knew their thoughts. "Why reason ye these things in your hearts? Is it not easier to say to the sick of the palsy, Thy sins be forgiven thee; than to say, Arise, and take up thy bed and walk?" His logic was perfect. 'Does it require more power to forgive sins than to make the sick rise up and walk?' Then came the healing word: "But, that ye may know that the Son of Man hath power upon earth to forgive sins, I said it. And he said unto the sick of the palsy, I say unto thee, Arise, and take up thy couch, and go unto thy house."

Thereupon strength came into the limbs and legs and organs of the paralyzed one. Speech returned; full physical capacity, for his age and circumstances, came again. He obeyed the divine counsel, took up his couch, and went his way, rejoicing and glorifying God.

And what of the others who were present? The proof of Messiahship could not be controverted. He who claimed to forgive sins—which all agreed none but God could do—had proved his divine power by turning the living death of palsy into the joyous life of physical health and spiritual cleanness. Following this display of power, the polarization of the people increased. All were amazed; the doctors of the law were, as such lawyers almost always are, unconvinced, disbelieving, rebellious. Yet "many glorified God, saying, We never saw the power of God after this manner."

Jesus had accomplished that which he set out to do.

NOTES

1. Though Canon Farrar wrote these eloquent words with reference to the multitudes who came to Peter's home to be healed on that glorious Sabbath evening in Capernaum, they apply in principle to all of our Lord's healings. Isaiah's actual Messianically spoken words were: "Surely he hath borne our griefs, and carried our sorrows" (Isa. 53:4); and what Matthew said was: "Himself took our infirmities, and bare our sicknesses" (Matt. 8:17). Isaiah's clear meaning is that the Messiah takes upon himself the sins—and hence the griefs and sorrows, for these come because of sin—of all men on condition of repentance. Matthew simply assumes his apostolic prerogative to give added meaning to Isaiah's words by applying them—properly—to the physical healings that are a type and pattern of the spiritual healings wrought through the infinite and eternal atonement of Him who ransoms men both temporally and spiritually.

2. Quoted from Deems, *Light of the Nations,* p. 185. See *Commentary* 1:173-74.

3. As to Jesus' touching the leper, Farrar says: "It was a glorious violation of the *letter* of the Law, which attached ceremonial pollution to a leper's touch; but it was at the same

time a glorious illustration of the *spirit* of the Law, which was that mercy is better than sacrifice. The hand of Jesus was not polluted by touching the leper's body, but the leper's whole body was cleansed by the touch of that holy hand. It was even thus that He touched our sinful nature, and yet remained without spot of sin." (Farrar, p. 208.)

4. D&C 29:3; 36:1; 50:36; 60:7; 62:3; 64:3; 108:1; 110:5.

JESUS BRINGS A NEW GOSPEL DISPENSATION

Behold, I say unto you
that all old covenants have I caused
to be done away
in this thing; and this is a new
and an everlasting covenant,
even that which was from the beginning.
Wherefore, although a man should be baptized
an hundred times it availeth
him nothing, for you cannot enter in
at the strait gate by the law of Moses,
neither by your dead works.
For it is because of your dead works
that I have caused this last covenant
and this church to be built up unto me,
even as in days of old.
Wherefore, enter ye in at the gate,
as I have commanded,
and seek not to counsel your God.
(D&C 22:1-4.)[1]

Jesus Calls Sinners to Repentance

(*Mark 2:13-17; JST, Mark 2:11; Luke 5:27-32; JST, Luke 5:27; Matthew 9:9-13; JST, Matthew 9:10, 13*)

Jesus is in process of restoring the gospel for his day and dispensation. So far we have seen him reveal new doctrine, call and ordain new officers, approve the baptism of John, and perform like baptisms of his own. We are aware that his new converts have the promise that in due course they will receive the gift of the Holy Ghost, which will guide them into all truth. We know that he will continue to reveal doctrine, to expound eternal truths, and to call officers to govern the affairs of his earthly kingdom. In due course he will call his Twelve special witnesses and give them the keys of the kingdom, so they can regulate all things incident thereto, to say nothing of having power to bind on earth and seal in heaven.

At the moment, however, we are with him as he calls Matthew, attends a feast in that publican's home, and speaks of his mission to call sinners to repentance. As an outgrowth of this episode we shall hear him tell why the wine of new revelation cannot be poured into the old bottles of Mosaic formalism. The place of our present happening is near Capernaum, on the Sea of Galilee.

Matthew is a publican, and publicans, as a group, are a vile, corrupt, and evil lot. They are classed with sinners and harlots. Even Jesus, in speaking of a brother caught in trespass who rebels against the discipline of the Church, says: "Let him be unto thee as an heathen man and a publican." (Matt. 18:17.) And a famous Gentile rejoinder to the question "Which are the worst kind of wild beasts?" is: "On the mountains, bears and lions; in cities, publicans and pettifoggers." The Jews had a proverb: "Take not a wife out of the family where there is a publican, for they are all publicans." (Farrar, p. 188, n. 1.)

Publicans are tax collectors; they represent Rome and are a symbol of the tyranny and oppression of the Gentile yoke. Partiality, avarice, greed, exacting more than is lawful, and petty oppression are deemed, in the public mind, to be a way of life with them. "The rabbis ranked them as cutthroats and robbers, as social outcasts, as religiously half-excommunicated." (*Commentary* 1:181.) It is assumed their wealth comes from rapine and their business is the business of extortioners.

It is to this class of people that Matthew belongs. Manifestly the claims made against them are exaggerated and do not apply to all individual tax collectors. And we know nothing of Matthew's way of life before he forsook all to follow Jesus. It is assumed that he forsook great wealth, even as Lehi and his family did when they went out from Jerusalem to be led of the Lord to their promised land, now known as America.

Matthew may have been a bright light among associates, most of whom were greedy and extortionate, or, if there were faults in his character, we must assume he repented in sackcloth and ashes before his call to the ministry. The earlier calls, also on the shores of the Galilean sea, of Simon and Andrew and of James and John were calls of men whose association with Jesus had extended over a long period. Those brethren were probably as well versed in the new theology and the new way of life as any then living in Galilee. It is natural to assume that Matthew had a similar background; his association with the Master must have been considerable before his call. Was he present that day in the synagogue when the demoniac was healed? Had he traveled with Jesus through the cities and towns of Galilee, hearing his words and seeing his miracles? Was he crowded into Peter's home when the Son of Man chose to remit the sins of the paralytic and then commanded him to take up his bed and walk? All we know is that after Jesus left the home of Peter, having there taught the word and healed the paralytic, he went to the seaside. The multitude followed, and he continued to teach; precious words yet poured forth from his lips to find lodgment in receptive ears.

There on the seashore he saw Matthew the publican, called also "Levi the son of Alpheus, sitting at the place where they receive tribute, as was customary in those days." Jesus said, "Follow me. And he left all, rose up, and followed him." Truly, as the scripture saith, "the gifts and calling of God are without repentance" (Rom. 11:29), meaning the Lord takes a Paul, an Alma, or a Matthew, as he chooses, because that called servant was prepared and foreordained from the premortal eternities to perform the labors to which the call extends. Manifestly all such do repent and make themselves worthy in all respects for the divine labor that is then theirs.

Sometime after his call, Matthew appoints a great feast in his house in honor of Jesus; perhaps also it is a farewell feast for his fellow publicans, for they are there in great numbers. Matthew himself says "many publicans and sinners came and sat down" with Jesus and his disciples. The social outcasts of society are celebrating—sinners being among them—and the Son of God and his newly called disciples sit in their midst, eat the food, and partake of the hospitality. Beholding such a scene, the scribes and Pharisees murmur. Why, they query, do Jesus and his disciples eat and drink with publicans and sinners? The questions are put to the disciples, but the answers come from Him who sets the tone of those festivities which we must believe he found enjoyable.

"They that be whole need not a physician, but they that are sick," he says. Such is the proverb of the day, which Jesus here uses with a veiled sarcasm, as though he had said, 'You self-righteous Pharisees think you have no need of my healing doctrine, and so I go to these sick publicans and sinners to make them whole.' Actually, of course, no one needed a physician more than the spiritually sick Pharisees.

"But go ye and learn what that meaneth, I will have mercy, and not sacrifice: for I am not come to call the righteous, but sinners to repentance." The Pharisaic religion was one of ritualistic forms, of rules and ceremonies, of rites and sacrifices; it was a religion that held them aloof from publicans and sinners. Jesus is here telling them that if they knew that mercy, love, charity, and all the attributes of godliness were more important than their ritualistic performances, they too would eat and drink with sinners and seek to do good to all men.

Truly, Jesus came to save sinners; and if he can take a Paul, an Alma, and a Matthew from their lowly spiritual states and raise them to apostolic and prophetic stature, surely he can pour out good things on the spiritual publicans of the world, to the end that all who will repent shall find salvation in his Father's kingdom.

Jesus Brings New Revelation to a New Church

(*Matthew 9:14-17; JST, Matthew 9:15, 18-21; Mark 2:18-22; JST, Mark 2:16-17; Luke 5:33-39; JST, Luke 5:36*)

At this point, as the feast continues in the home of the now spiritually refreshed publican Levi-Matthew, the disciples of John the Baptist add their voices of complaint to those of the scribes and Pharisees. "While he was thus teaching"—that is, at the very moment when Jesus asserted that he had come to call sinners to repentance; to call them from their old Mosaic way of life to a new gospel order—the disciples of John, who also had preached a new order of repentance and a new baptism for the remission of sins, came to him and asked: "Why do we and the Pharisees fast oft, but thy disciples fast not?"

Fasting was a fetish with the Pharisees. There were times when they fasted twice a week, regularly, religiously, and with holy zeal, as they supposed.[2] They paid tithes with such scrupulous attention to detail that they even gave a tenth part of the herbs that grew in pots on their windowsills. They attended to every sacrificial detail with such ritualistic attention that scarcely a single drop of blood was sprinkled other than at the appointed place. And John's disciples—for their master was cut in the Pharisaic mold, and had in fact been sent to wind up the affairs of the dying dispensation of

Mosaic formalisms—partook of some of the characteristics of their Pharisaic kinsmen. They fasted—perhaps as religiously as the Pharisees themselves, for the last accepted adherents to the old order were expected to live that law to the full, that it might be fulfilled in glory as the day approached when it would be replaced in full by the new gospel order.

Fasting as such is not to be condemned. In its place, and within the bounds set by Him who incorporated it as part of his eternal system, it is to be commended. Mortals can never attain the unity with Deity that it is their privilege to gain without fasting and prayer. Whether the Pharisaic fasts met with divine approval is quite another thing, however. Their fathers had been condemned for fasting for evil purposes. "Behold, ye fast for strife and debate, and to smite with the fist of wickedness," Isaiah had said to them. "Ye shall not fast as ye do this day, to make your voice to be heard on high," he had said. "Is it such a fast that I have chosen?" the Lord Jehovah asked of his people.

And that they might know the standards attending the true law of the fast, Jehovah had said to them: "Is not this the fast that I have chosen? to loose the bands of wickedness, to undo the heavy burdens, and to let the oppressed go free, and that ye break every yoke? Is it not to deal thy bread to the hungry, and that thou bring the poor that are cast out to thy house? when thou seest the naked, that thou cover him; and that thou hide not thyself from thine own flesh?" (Isa. 58.) How far removed the Pharisaic fasts were from these standards is clear to all who have studied the gospel accounts.

How apt, then, was Jesus' reply to John's disciples, disciples who were devout, who had been properly baptized, and who should now be following Jesus rather than John, as John himself had taught them. "Can the children of the bridechamber fast, while the bridegroom is with them?" he asked. His answer: "As long as they have the bridegroom with them, they cannot fast." Jesus, the Bridegroom, is with them; why should they mourn or fast? Is it not, rather, a time to rejoice? And are not Jesus' words a needed reminder and a gentle rebuke to John's disciples? Do they not remember that John himself—knowing that Jesus baptized more disciples than did the Baptist—had said that he, John, was the friend of the Bridegroom, whose joy was full because he heard the Bridegroom's voice? Have they forgotten that John testified that he must decrease while the Bridegroom increased? Why then—and this is the rebuke, if such there be in Jesus' reply—why then did not John's disciples forsake the imprisoned Baptist and follow the One whose way their master had prepared?

Then, with seeric insight—seeing what was to be more than two years hence; seeing what would be when one without sin hung on a cross between two sinners—Jesus said: "But the days will come, when the bridegroom shall be taken away from them, and then shall they fast in those days." But their fast will not be to smite with the fist of wickedness, but, rather, to draw near unto that Lord who has gone, for a moment, from them, but who will return in power and great glory at the appointed time.

At this point, the Pharisees interjected themselves again into the discussion. Knowing that John—who fasted as they did, and who to that extent was a man who followed their system—had baptized for the remission of sins, they assayed to make themselves the equal or superior of John by asking: "Why will ye not receive us with our baptism, seeing we keep the whole law?" They did all that John did, as they supposed, and they did more; they had *all* the rites and ordinances and performances and rituals handed down from Moses of old; and they kept them, so they thought.

"But Jesus said unto them, Ye keep not the law. If ye had kept the law, ye would have received me, for I am he who gave the law." No man can truly keep the law of Moses without believing in Christ, for that was the whole intent and purpose and design of the law. Jehovah gave it to help his people believe in the Messiah who was to come, who would, as the Lamb of God, sacrifice himself for the sins of the world. Men may go through the rites and performances of the law; they may exalt its letter and kill its spirit; they may think they keep the law of Moses—but they do not and cannot unless and until they know that all that they are doing centers in Christ and that he is the Savior. In that event they would receive him when he comes, for he is the Lord Jehovah who gave the law. How pointedly and expressly, without reservation or qualification, over and over again, the Lord Jesus testifies of his Messiahship!

"I receive not you with your baptism, because it profiteth you nothing," he continues. "For when that which is new is come, the old is ready to be put away." 'I have come with the new order; all old covenants have I caused to be done away; the new baptism of John and the baptism which I perform is a new and an everlasting covenant, even that which was from the beginning. Your baptism profiteth nothing because it is now performed without authority; John is the legal administrator of your dying dispensation. Though you should be baptized an hundred times, it availeth you nothing, for you cannot enter in at the strait gate by the law of Moses, neither by your dead works. When the new law comes the old law leaves. When the gospel, which was from the beginning, is restored, the law of Moses is fulfilled. It is because your works are dead works that I am bringing a new covenant. I am come to build up my church as in days of old, for my church has been on earth, from time to time, even before Moses. Wherefore, enter ye in at the gate, as I have commanded, and seek not to counsel your God.'

These things spoke Jesus in plainness. Then he added this parable: "No man putteth a piece of a new garment upon an old; if otherwise, then both the new maketh a rent, and the piece that was taken out of the new agreeth not with the old. And no man putteth new wine into old bottles; else the new wine will burst the bottles, and be spilled, and the bottles shall perish. But new wine must be put into new bottles; and both are preserved."

"What, new baptism in an old church, new revelation in a dying kingdom, new doctrine in an apostate organization! Could Jesus add Christian ordinances, with their spirit and power, to the dead formalism and ritual of the Mosaic procedures? Could new wine be put in old bottles (animal skins used as containers) without breaking the bottles and losing both the old and the new?" (*Commentary* 1:186.)[3] Jesus came to restore, not just to reform. His mission was to fulfill the old order and commence the new; he came to tramp out the dying embers of Mosaic performances and ignite the living flames of the gospel fire in the hearts of men.

We suppose that Jesus now said something more to John's disciples about their obligation to leave the dead past and come to the living present; yet he spoke to them with more tenderness and compassion than he did to the Pharisees, for John's followers were in process of preparing themselves to receive the One of whom John had testified. "No man also having drunk old wine straightway desireth new," Jesus said to them, "for he saith, The old is better." That is: 'In following John, who was sent of my Father to prepare the way before me, you have conformed to the law of Moses. Now, however, a greater than Moses is here, even the Messiah, and as John taught, you must now follow him, even though it is difficult for you to "straightway" turn from your old teachings and accept the new.' (*Commentary* 1:186.)

Thus Jesus called a lowly publican to a station of apostolic excellence; thus he taught that he came to call sinners to repentance; thus he rejected Pharisaic baptisms and claims of righteousness-born-of-the-law; thus he invited John's disciples to complete their conversion and follow him; and thus he testified that as the Messiah he had come to restore the gospel and build the city of salvation on a new foundation, not within the crumbling walls of an ancient order whose sun had set.

NOTES

1. This is a revelation given to the Prophet Joseph Smith in April 1830, just after the organization of The Church of Jesus Christ of Latter-day Saints. Some persons who had already been baptized in the sectarian churches of the day desired to enter the newly established church and kingdom of God on earth without rebaptism. This is the Lord's answer to them. The new kingdom was being established, "even as in days of old," and the same principles as applied then were still in force. There must be new revelation, new divine authority, new officers, just as it was when Jesus came to replace the old Mosaic order in his day.

2. "Private fasts would, of course, depend on individuals, but the strict Pharisees were wont to fast every Monday and Thursday during the weeks intervening between the Passover and Pentecost, and again, between the Feast of Tabernacles and that of the Dedication of the Temple. It is to this practice that the Pharisee in the parable refers [Luke 18:12] when boasting: 'I fast twice in the week.' " (Edersheim, *The Temple,* pp. 197-98.)

3. "He told them, in words of yet deeper significance, though expressed, as so often, in the homeliest metaphors, that his religion is, as it were, a robe entirely new, not a patch of unteazled cloth upon an old robe, serving only to make worse its original rents; that it is not new wine, put in all its fresh fermenting, expansive strength, into old and worn wine-skins, and so serving only to burst the wine-skins and be lost, but *new* wine in *fresh* wine-skins. The new spirit was to be embodied in wholly renovated forms; the new freedom was to be untrammelled by obsolete and long meaningless limitations; the spiritual doctrine was to be sundered for ever from the elaborate externalism of cancelled ordinances." (Farrar, p. 267.)

THE SECOND PASSOVER OF JESUS' MINISTRY

My Father worketh hitherto, and I work. . . .
God was his Father. . . .
The Father loveth the Son. . . .
All men should honour the Son,
even as they honour the Father. . . .
The Father hath . . . given to the Son to have life
in himself. . . . the Father hath sent me. . . .
I am come in my Father's name.
(John 5:1-47.)[1]

Jesus Heals a Man on the Sabbath

(*John 5:1-16; JST, John 5:3, 6, 9*)

We are with Jesus in Jerusalem. It is Passover time, the second such feast of his ministry, and his disciples are with him, for they, like he, are under obligation, imposed by Jehovah, to appear three times each year before the Lord in the temple. Our Gospel author, John in this case, does not name the feast, and many volumes have been written to sustain one view or another as to what feast it is.

And we repeat that no one is able to make a harmony of the Gospels or to list chronologically the events of Jesus' life.

Matthew, Mark, Luke, and John did not do it, and the accounts they have left us do not agree among themselves. Every reputable scholar who has made an independent study of the issues involved has found himself at loggerheads, in large or small part, with every other analyst. In this present work we are following—primarily but not entirely—the chronology of President J. Reuben Clark, Jr., who often disagrees with Elder James E. Talmage, just as Edersheim does with Farrar, or as Mark does with Luke, or as every independent analyst does with some or all of his fellows. Choices must be made; every writer must make his own, and it is doubtful if any author—nay, it is a surety that no author—has made right choices in all cases.

As to the present feast, suffice it to say that it fits as well into the chronology here as elsewhere, and it is logical to assume that Jesus—as yet not subject to the total harassment of scribes, Pharisees, and Sanhedrinists—would appear again in the Passover crowds to make the doctrinal declarations relative to him and his Father that we are about to hear.

It is the Sabbath, that holy day when servile work ceases and the children of Jehovah—those who have become his sons and his daughters through the waters of baptism—assemble to worship the Lord and renew their covenants. But worship of the Father, in spirit and in truth, is almost a thing of the past among them. Those who use the sacred Sabbath to gain spiritual refreshment are few in number. In the true and eternal sense, the Sabbath is universally desecrated among them through disuse, through failure to use it as a day for confessing their sins in the holy convocations, and through neglecting to partake of the spiritual food prepared on that day, by a gracious God, to give to all those who hunger and thirst after righteousness.

But oh, how the rigid religious formalists have compensated for their Sabbath failures and desecrations! In place of the holy and hallowed day that should have been, theirs is a Sabbath of ritualistic restrictions that defy sense and mock reason. The absurdities of Sabbath observance—shall we call it a temporal observance that replaced the spiritual worship that should have been?—these absurdities, referred to in chapter 11 herein, all were assumed to center in the decree of Deity: "In it thou shalt not do any work." (Ex. 20:10.) This was something the scribes and Pharisees could get their teeth into. Worship in spirit and in truth might be beyond their spiritual capacity, for the things of God are known only by the power of the Spirit, but carrying no burden on the Sabbath day—that was another matter. Burdens could be seen and weighed and defined and anathematized. If a man picked up sticks on the Sabbath, he could be stoned. If he carried his couch of affliction, he could be damned. Man was made for the Sabbath, and for the Sabbath he must live. This was what set the Jews apart from all mankind, and so set apart they would remain; or, at least such was what they assumed and how they felt.

And so on this particular Passover Sabbath, we see Jesus near the sheep market, at the side of the pool Bethesda, which means "House of Mercy." By this pool—evidently a mineral spring of some sort whose waters bubbled intermittently as escaping gases broke the surface—there stands a large structure with five porches. "In these lay a great many impotent folk," some blind, others halt, paralytic, or withered, all "waiting for the moving of the water." No doubt these waters had—as hot mineral springs do in our day—some curative and healing powers, which gave rise to a legend, among the superstitious and spiritually illiterate Jews, that "an angel went down at a certain season into the pool, and troubled the water," and that "whosoever then first after the troubling of the water stepped in was made whole of whatsoever disease he had."

On a pallet on one of the porches lies an impotent man, lame with paralysis, who has so suffered for thirty-eight years, almost as long as the whole history of Israel from the going through of the Red Sea to the crossing of Jordan. Jesus sees the paralytic sufferer, knows how long he has been thus, and picks him out from all the rest—for reasons best known to himself, but unquestionably involving the man's faith and spiritual stature—as the object of his divine healing power. With a heart full of compassion, our Galilean Friend asks: "Wilt thou be made whole?"

Not knowing the source of the inquiry; unaware that it was the Son of God who spoke; not realizing that the questioning voice came from Him who had cleansed lepers, cast out devils, and healed all manner of diseases, the impotent man answered: "Sir, I have no man, when the water is troubled, to put me into the pool: but while I am coming, another steppeth down before me."

Without more ado, Jesus says: "Rise, take up thy bed, and walk." "It was spoken in an accent that none could disobey. The manner of the Speaker, His voice, His mandate, thrilled like an electric spark through the withered limbs and the shattered constitution, enfeebled by a lifetime of suffering and sin. After thirty-eight years of prostration, the man instantly rose, lifted up his pallet, and began to walk. In glad amazement he looked round to see and to thank his unknown benefactor; but the crowd was large, and Jesus, anxious to escape the unspiritual excitement which would fain have regarded him as a thaumaturge alone, had quietly slipped away from observation." (Farrar, p. 286.)

A miracle is thus wrought, such a one as is seldom seen. After thirty-eight years of paralytic impotence, a man known to have spent long hours on a pallet in the porches by the pool of Bethesda—desiring and hoping and praying to be healed—in an instant arises; full strength comes into his whole body; he walks—yea, more: he carries his bed. He is seen by the multitude, many of whom no doubt rejoice with him at the new vigor and vitality exuding from every pore of his once pain-ridden flesh.

But what do the leaders of Jewry see? Is it a wondrous work of manifest goodness? No, not in any manner of speaking. What they see is a man, unlearned and ignorant in the niceties of their legalistic restrictions attending Sabbath life, desecrating that holy day, as they suppose, by bearing a burden thereon. "It is the sabbath day," thunders the Pharisaic voice, "it is not lawful for thee to carry thy bed." 'Let it lie in the street; discard it; sit thou here until the morrow; no matter the inconvenience—but carry this bed of straw, this blanket, upon which you are wont to lie, never!'

And their words, spoken not so much against the healed one as against the One who healed, shall testify forever, before the judgment bar, of the degeneracy and baseness of their religion. How awful it is when true religion sinks into superstition; when the witch hunters in search of heresy find it—not in a departure from the ancient doctrinal moorings, but in the breaking of their own petty formalisms.

In reply, rejoicing in his newfound health, the packer of the pallet says: "He that made me whole"—he who wrought this wondrous miracle; he who is a great prophet and has such wondrous power with God that at his word I walk—"the same said unto me, Take up thy bed, and walk." 'Come, rejoice with me, for a great miracle has been wrought.'

But they, as part of their inquisitorial machinations, pried still further: "What man is that which said unto thee, Take up thy bed, and walk?" Not: 'Who has worked this miracle? Who has such power with God? What mighty prophet is in our midst? Is he not the Messiah; or, will he not lead us to the Deliverer?' No; nothing of this sort; only—'Who hath counseled thee to break the Sabbath, for which offense our law says a man is worthy of death.'

Strangely, at the moment, the healed one knew not who his benefactor was. Only after Jesus found him in the temple later—we suppose worshipping and thanking the Lord for his new health—did the man from Bethesda's porches learn the source of his blessing. Jesus then said to him, "Behold, thou art made whole: sin no more, lest a worse thing come unto thee"—not meaning to teach that disease and affliction are always the result of sin, only that in this case the man had disobeyed some law that caused his affliction of long standing to imprison his body.

Thereafter the man told the Jews it was Jesus who had healed him—not, we assume, out of any malice toward the Master, but in the hope that the name of Jesus would be revered for the good deed he had done. After all, it was Jesus who selected, from among many blind and halt and withered and diseased persons, the single one to be healed; and surely he would have chosen the one whose spiritual worth caused him to merit the blessing. And it is not too much to suppose that the man and others whom he could influence joined the Church and were true to all subsequent trusts.

At this point in his account, John tells us: "Therefore did the Jews persecute Jesus, and sought to slay him, because he had done these things on the sabbath day."

What had he done? He had spoken a few words—perhaps a dozen in all—which in itself was certainly no more work than the long sermons delivered each Sabbath in the synagogues by the Rabbis. What work had Jesus done, unless the fact of healing itself was to be construed as work because divine power was exercised to change the body of the afflicted person?

The Sabbath healing of the impotent man clearly was an excuse, not a reason, for the forthcoming persecution. When men thirst for the blood of the prophets, it is not because of a reasoned judgment, arrived at by judicial deliberations. Persecution is carried out under the spell of emotion and hatred. And the voice of emotion on this day is crying: 'Here is the Son of God. Satan knows it, and he is our master. We must rid the nation of this menace at all costs; he will destroy our craft. Slay him. Crucify him. His blood be upon us and our children.'

Jesus Proclaims His Divine Sonship

(*John 5:17-24*)

What answer will Jesus give to the charge—absurd and unrealistic as it is—that he, the Lord of the Sabbath, has violated his own holy day by working thereon? In fact, he has carried no burden nor performed any servile service; he has not even overstepped any of the rigid rabbinic restrictions, not so much as the lifting of a finger on that day when men must cease from their labors. If it is a Sabbath violation to exercise the power of faith—and such is done by words and mental exertion only; if he is an accessory to the offense of another in that he said, "Take up thy bed, and walk," thus defying the scribal code of Sabbath formalisms, then, yes, he is showing contempt for the legalisms of the lawyers and the prohibitions of the doctors.

But, no matter, his concern is not to debate Sabbath rules. He has healed a man and gained a congregation of hearers; now he will bear to them a testimony that will open or close the door of salvation, depending upon its acceptance or rejection. For the purposes at hand, we will assume, as he himself seems to have done, that he has worked on that day when no work is to be done. To the charges of the Jewish leaders that he has violated their Sabbath, he says: "My Father worketh hitherto, and I work."

'True, this is the Sabbath; true, I have worked on this holy day. I have spoken healing words; and my Father, who is God, has done the work—it is his power by which the impotent man is healed. I have worked on the Sabbath, and my Father has worked on the Sabbath; is it not proper to do the Lord's work on the Lord's day? There is an eternal and unending law of work that is greater than the Sabbath. My Father and I both work everlastingly; our creative and redemptive labors go on forever for innumerable hosts on worlds without number. Why should the mere healing of one suffering soul cause such consternation among you?'

There was no misunderstanding on anyone's part as to this bold proclamation. Jesus is admitting Sabbath disobedience and adding blasphemy (as they suppose) to his arraignable offenses. "Therefore the Jews sought the more to kill him, because he not only had broken the sabbath, but said also that God was his Father, making himself equal with God."

"Equal with God!"—awful blasphemy or awesome truth!—one or the other. There is no middle ground, no room for compromise; there are no principles to compose: either Jesus is divine or he is blaspheming!

"Equal with God!"—not, as yet, in the infinite and eternal sense, but in the sense of being one with him, of being his natural heir, destined to receive, inherit, and possess all that the Father hath.

"Equal with God!"—not that he was then reigning in glory and exaltation over all the works which their hands had made, but in the sense that he was God's Son, upon whom the Father had placed his own name and to whom he had given glory and honor and power.

Then in solemn tones came words of infinite import, words whose full meaning can only be understood by the power of the Spirit—and shall we not suppose that one of the purposes of the Bethesda healing was to gain a congregation and set the stage for such a heaven-inspired statement as this?—then came from the lips of Jesus, who had a perfect knowledge of his divine paternity, this proclamation:

"The Son can do nothing of himself" ('I am come in my Father's name; aside from him I have no power; it was his power that healed the impotent man; all that I do has his approval') "but what he seeth the Father do" ('and further, I do only what I have seen the Father do, for he has revealed all his doing to me; I have seen his works') "for what things soever he doeth, these also doeth the Son likewise" ('and I do what he does, he heals the sick and so do I; I tread in his tracks for I am his Son.')[2]

"For the Father loveth the Son" (because the Son obeys the Father) "and sheweth him all things that himself doeth" ('I have seen in vision all the works of the Father; I have seen what he did in ages past; what he does even now; and he has manifest to me his future works, even "all things that himself doeth') "and he will shew him greater works than these, that ye may marvel" ('and the Father will manifest, through me, greater works than the healing of the impotent man, causing you to marvel that one who ministers among you can perform such infinite and eternal works').

Then Jesus alluded to these greater works which he would do in his Father's name—the atoning sacrifice, the resurrection, the very day of judgment itself—by saying: "For as the Father raiseth up the dead, and quickeneth them; even so the Son quickeneth whom he will." 'By the power of the Father all men shall come forth in immortality, but it is I who shall bring it to pass. It is I who shall call the dust from the graves to form again a habitation for the spirits of men; I shall quicken whom I will, when I will; by me the resurrection cometh; I am the Resurrection and the Life.'

"For the Father judgeth no man, but hath committed all judgment unto the Son." 'And when all men have passed from death to life, they shall stand before me—before the pleasing bar of the Great Jehovah—to be judged according to the deeds done in the flesh; for the Father hath committed all judgment into my hands. He, himself, judgeth no man; but my judgment shall be his judgment.'

And all this is to be "that all men should honour the Son, even as they honour the Father. He that honoureth not the Son honoureth not the Father which hath sent him." 'Beware therefore how ye treat me. Because I shall work out the infinite and eternal atonement; because I shall break the bands of death and gain the victory over the grave; because all men shall stand before me to be judged, you should honor me as you honor the Father, whose Son I am, and whose power makes all this possible. And if you do not honor me, you do not honor the Father, who you say is your God, because the Father hath sent me: I am his Son, and I do Only what he commands—all in his name and by his power.'[3]

Jesus' proclamation of his divine Sonship; his plain statements that God is his Father; his witness that he and his Father both work, he doing the Father's work here on earth; his acts and words that made him equal with God; his declarations that the Father had revealed all things to him, and that he of himself could do nothing; his assertion that the Father loved him; his doctrinal teachings that the resurrection itself comes because of him, and that he it is who shall judge all men; his command to men to honor him as they honor the Father, coupled with the decree that those who do not honor the Son do not honor the Father—all this leads to one glorious conclusion. It is: Salvation is in Christ. He is the One to whom we must look to gain eternal life. He is the Author and Finisher of our faith. He is our Redeemer, Savior, Lord, and King.

And so, having taught all that we have here recited, and no doubt much more to the same effect—for the Gospel authors only give extracts and digests of his numerous sayings—this blessed Lord Jesus then said: "He that heareth my word, and believeth on him that sent me, hath everlasting life, and shall not come into condemnation; but is passed from death unto life." 'He who believes and obeys my words, who believeth in me and my Father, shall have exaltation and shall not be damned; yea, such already have passed from spiritual death to spiritual life, for they have been born again.'

Jesus Saves the Living and the Dead

(*John 5:25-30; JST, John 5:29-31*)

We have heard such a sermon as seldom has been preached on earth or in heaven; our ears have caught the words spoken by the Son of God that he is the Savior of all men. Jesus has announced his divine Sonship and centered the whole plan of salvation in his person. All men who believe in him shall be saved; those who reject him shall be damned. But what of those who never hear a whisper of his name while they dwell as mortals? What of the nations and kingdoms of the past whose inhabitants never heard of Christ and the salvation that is in him? Is there no hope for those who have not been privileged to listen to a prophet's voice and hear the word of God?

Having assured the living that eternal life is theirs if they believe his word and live his law; having announced his status as the Judge of all, this Jesus, to whom nothing is impossible, enlarges the vision of all who will see and announces how even the dead can obtain an inheritance with him and his Father. "The hour is coming, and now is" (it is to be in this very age in which you live, he says), "when the dead shall hear the voice of the Son of God: and they that hear shall live." 'I shall preach the gospel to the dead, to those in the spirit prison; I shall visit them; they shall hear my voice; and those who believe and obey shall be saved. They shall be judged according to men in the flesh, but live according to God in the spirit. My Father is no respecter of persons; those who do not have opportunity to hear the word of truth in this life shall get it in an appointed time between death and the resurrection.'[4]

We suppose that our Lord's Jewish detractors by this time are completely overawed. How could it be otherwise, so comprehensive are the concepts of which he speaks, so infinite their application! But Jesus continues: "For as the Father hath life in himself; so hath he given to the Son to have life in himself." 'The Father is an immortal, exalted, resurrected being, who cannot die. He is the Creator of the lives of men. Life dwells in him independently; he has life in himself; all things live because of him. He is the source of life, and the one who upholds, preserves, and continues it. And he has given this same power to the Son; the Son inherits from the Father; an immortal Father passes on to his mortal Son the power of immortality; it comes as a natural inheritance.'

"And hath given him authority to execute judgment also," Jesus continues, "because he is the Son of man." Why will Jesus be the Judge of the living and the dead? Because he is the Son of Man of Holiness—the Son of an Immortal Man, a Holy Man, who is God—because he is the Son of God who has received the power to do all things, from his Father whose right it is to grant such infinite power.

Marvel not at this: for the hour is coming, in the which all that are in the graves shall hear his voice, And shall come forth; they who have done good, in the resurrection of the just; and they who have done evil, in the resurrection of the unjust. And shall all be judged of the Son of Man. For as I hear, I judge, and my judgment is just; For I can of mine own self do nothing; because I seek not mine own will, but the will of the Father who hath sent me.

Strong doctrine this! 'I, Jesus, shall call forth all that are in their graves, but every man in his own order. All shall live again; the resurrection is as universal as death; as all men die, through Adam, so all shall live again, through me. But some shall come forth in the resurrection of the just to receive eternal life; others shall come forth in the resurrection of the unjust to receive eternal damnation. All shall be judged by me and assigned their places in the realms that are prepared, and my judgment shall be just because I shall conform to the will of my Father who sent me.'[5]

Jesus Obeys the Divine Law of Witnesses

(*John 5:31-47; JST, John 5:32-35, 37-39, 41, 46*)

Seldom, if ever, has such plain and powerful and persuasive witness been borne of the divine Sonship of the Lord Jesus as has just fallen from his own lips. 'God is my Father; I am his Son; I am equal with him. I give eternal life to those who believe in me. Even the dead shall hear my voice and be judged by my law. I have life in myself and shall atone for the sins of the world. I shall open the graves of all men, call them forth in immortality, judge them, and assign them an inheritance in the worlds to be. I do the will of my Father who sent me, and all men should honor me as they honor my Father.'

Seldom, if ever, has so much been said in words as few as the Mortal Messiah is here saying to his own nation. The word has been given; the truth has been spoken; the testimony has been borne; and now—in the providences of the One who sent his Son to say these very things—the responsibility rests with the hearers to believe or disbelieve, to obey or disobey, to come unto Christ or continue in their "Gentile" ways.

How shall these Jews who hear his voice and see the wonders wrought by his hand—how shall they know if he has spoken the truth? Are they at liberty to consider him to be a confused babbler whose mind is deranged? Or an unfortunate soul possessed by demons who speak by his mouth? Or a sincere—though deluded and deceived—false prophet who speaks without divine approval? Are they bound to believe the words of this Galilean troublemaker who breaks their Sabbath and castigates their priests and scribes? Must they believe his message simply because he says it is so?

Jesus has delivered his message; a spirit of disbelief envelops the whole congregation of hearers. He has spoken by the power of the Spirit, but their souls have not been quickened by that same divine influence. Now he must tell them that pursuant to their own law—the divine law of witnesses given by Jehovah to their fathers—they must either accept his words or be damned. This law, as they well know, is that the Lord always sends his word by witnesses who testify of its truth and divinity; that one witness alone, though he speaks the truth, is not enough to bind his hearers; that two or more witnesses always unite their voices to make the divinely borne testimony binding on earth and sealed everlastingly in the heavens; and that, thus, in the mouth of two or three witnesses every word shall be established.[6]

> *If I bear witness of myself, yet my witness is true. For I am not alone; there is another who bearest witness of me, and I know that the testimony which he giveth of me is true. Ye sent unto John, and he bare witness also unto the truth. And he received not his testimony of man, but of God, and ye yourselves say that he is a prophet, therefore ye ought to receive his testimony. These things I say that ye*

might be saved. He was a burning and a shining light, and ye were willing for a season to rejoice in his light.

John and Jesus—missionary companions, as it were—both taught the same truths and bore the same witness. Jesus was not alone. There was another, the son of Zacharias, who received his own testimony from God, and who bore it, unequivocally, with fire and fervor, for he was a burning and shining light. There was nothing hidden or secret about John's witness. "Behold, the Lamb of God, which taketh away the sin of the world," he said. (John 1:29.) These very Jews had received John as a prophet. How then can they reject his testimony? And if that testimony was the same as Jesus bore, how can the words of Him of whom John testified be rejected? Jesus did not stand alone; John was his companion, and the Jews, by their own law, were bound to believe the message and accept the Messenger.

> *But I have a greater witness than the testimony of John; for the works which the Father hath given me to finish, the same works that I do, bear witness of me, that the Father hath sent me. And the Father himself who sent me, hath borne witness of me. And verily I testify unto you, that ye have never heard his voice at any time, nor seen his shape; For ye have not his word abiding in you; and him whom he hath sent, ye believe not.*

But there is more. The Father himself—that Holy Being whose shape they have not seen; that Holy Man who has a body of flesh and bones—has also borne witness of the Son. By his own voice, heard on the banks of Jordan, the Father had said, "This is my beloved Son, in whom I am well pleased. Hear ye him." (JST, Matt. 3:46.) By the power of the Holy Ghost, shed forth upon Anna and Simeon and Nathanael and Philip and a host of others, the Father had planted his witness of the divinity of his Son in receptive human hearts.

All these testimonies—borne by Jesus, by John, by the Father, by those upon whom the Holy Spirit rested, and by the miracles that Jesus wrought—all were current and up to date; they were the living witnesses, borne by living persons, in the living present. To them Jesus now added all the testimonies and all the witnesses found in holy writ.

> *Search the scriptures; for in them ye think ye have eternal life: and they are they which testify of me.*[7]

That is to say: 'Ye think ye shall inherit eternal life because of Moses and his law, but search the scriptures and learn that they testify of me and the salvation which I bring. I am the Messiah. Learn what is said about me in the Psalms and the prophets; know that all the prophets spoke of me and my ministry.'[8]

Prejudice and passion and pettiness, these three—born of unreasoning emotion—are the things that destroy men's souls. "And ye will not come to me that ye might have life, lest ye should honor me," Jesus said.

'Lest ye should honor me!' How petty; how childish; how unworthy of the seed of Abraham! Forsake salvation rather than rise above the emotional prejudices that say: 'A Galilean Carpenter cannot be the Son of God. Everyone knows he is Joseph's son; and further, no good thing cometh out of Galilee.'

"I receive not honour from men." 'Think not that ye can honor me; who among you can add to what my Father has already given me? What wealth can you give to the One whose all things are? What degrees can you confer that will add educational luster to the Author or Truth who knows all things by the power of the Spirit? What political power or influence can men add to him who already sways the universe by his voice?'

"But I know you, that ye have not the love of God in you." Jesus knew their hearts; also, they had not the love of God in them, because they did not love his Son. 'He that loveth the Father loveth also the Son; none love either the Father or the Son unless they keep their commandments.'

"I am come in my Father's name, and ye receive me not: if another shall come in his own name, him ye will receive."

Jesus bears his Father's name and is empowered, thus, to speak in the first person as though he were the Father.[9] Carnal men who come in their own name, having no divine message to deliver, find ready acceptance from other carnal men.

"How can ye believe, which receive honour one of another, and seek not the honour that cometh from God only?" A desire to know the truth precedes a testimony. Men must seek the honors—revelations, visions, companionship of the Holy Spirit, and the like—which it is the Father's good pleasure to confer; otherwise such are not obtained. As long as men's hearts are centered on the things of the world and the honors of men, they never seek the blessings of eternity with that fervor and devotion which leads to the receipt of spiritual gifts. What greater honor can a man receive than that which comes from God? Is it not glory and honor in the celestial kingdom that all true believers seek?

> *Do not think that I will accuse you to the Father; there is Moses who accuseth you, in whom ye trust. For had ye believed Moses, ye would have believed me: for he wrote of me. But if ye believe not his writings, how shall ye believe my words?*

The Lord and his prophets are one, and no one can believe in Christ and reject his prophets. "Believe in Christ and deny him not," Nephi said, "for by denying him ye also deny the prophets and the law." (2 Ne. 25:28.) And those who truly believe the words of the prophets believe also in Christ, for it is he of whom all the prophets testify.[10]

And all these things spake Jesus in Jerusalem, at the Feast of the Passover, after he healed the impotent man at the pool of Bethesda; and many other things did he say that bore witness that he is the Son of God by whom salvation comes, and that all men must come unto him and worship the Father in his name if they are to gain eternal life and sit down with Abraham, Isaac, and Jacob in the kingdom of God.

NOTES

1. The views of the modern religious-atheists—who profess to believe in Christ but say he never personally claimed to be divine—to the contrary notwithstanding, we find Jesus, everywhere and always, as in this case, attesting to the personal relationship between him and the great Elohim.

2. The great concept set forth in John 5:19-20 is beyond human comprehension. It is the doctrine that "Jesus is the replica of his Father—thinking, saying, doing, achieving, attaining, as the Father has done before." (*Commentary* 1:191.) That all of this is infinite in scope and universal in application is seen from the Prophet Joseph Smith's Spirit-guided utterances in the King Follett sermon. "It is the first principle of the Gospel to know for a certainty the Character of God," the Prophet said, "and to know that we may converse with him as one man converses with another, and that he was once a man like us; yea, that God himself, the Father of us all, dwelt on an earth, the same as Jesus Christ himself did; and I will show it from the Bible. . . .

"What did Jesus say? . . .The Scriptures inform us that Jesus said, As the Father hath power in Himself, even so hath the Son power—to do what? Why, what the Father did. The answer is obvious—in a manner to lay down His body and take it up again. Jesus, what are you going to do? To lay down my life as my Father did, and take it up again. Do we believe it? If you do not believe it, you do not believe the Bible. . . .

"What did Jesus do? Why; I do the things I saw my Father do when worlds came rolling into existence. My Father worked out his kingdom with fear and trembling, and I must do the same; and when I get my kingdom, I shall present it to my Father, so that he may obtain kingdom upon kingdom, and it will exalt him in glory. He will then take a higher exaltation, and I will take his place, and thereby become exalted myself. So that Jesus treads in the tracks of his Father, and inherits what God did before; and God is thus glorified and exalted in the salvation and exaltation of all his children. It is plain beyond disputation, and you thus learn some of the first principles of the Gospel, about which so much hath been said." (*Teachings of the Prophet Joseph Smith*, pp. 345-48.)

3."Two exalted personages, the Father and the Son, are one—one in purpose, plan, and power; one as to character, perfections, and attributes; one in all things; and therefore one in the receipt of worship and honor. In the true sense no one can believe in or know the one without having the same belief and knowledge of the other; nor can one be accepted and the other rejected. They are one." (*Commentary* 1:192-93.)

4. This visit of the Messiah to the spirits in prison—which occurred while his body lay in the Arimathean's tomb—was one in which he preached the gospel, organized his church, and sent forth his representatives to teach the truths of salvation to the hosts of the dead. There is scarcely a more glorious doctrine than that of salvation for the dead. All those who die without a knowledge of the gospel, who would have received it with all their hearts, shall receive it in the spirit world, and, having obeyed its laws, shall be heirs of full salvation. In reality, " 'God is not the God of the dead, but of the living' (Matt. 22:32), for all live unto him; all are alive in his eyes, whether their spirits are temporarily housed in mortal tabernacles or imprisoned in the spirit sphere awaiting the day of the resurrection. And the salvation of all men—living or dead (as men count death)—is centered in and comes because of the Son." (*Commentary* 1:193.)

5. "John 5:29 is the verse Joseph Smith and Sidney Rigdon were studying and pondering—in the course of their work on the Inspired Version of the Bible—when the eyes of their understanding were opened and they received the vision of the degrees of glory (D&C 76). This vision and other revelations teach that "salvation grows automatically out of the resurrection, and the coming forth in the resurrection constitutes the receipt of whatever degree of salvation has been earned. By one degree of obedience or another, all men, in this life, develop either celestial, terrestrial, or telestial bodies (or in the case of those destined to be sons of perdition, bodies of a baser sort). In the resurrection all men receive back again 'the same body which was a natural body,' whether it be celestial, terrestrial, or what have you. That body is then quickened by the glory attending its particular type, and the person receiving the body then goes automatically, as it were, to the kingdom

of glory where that degree of glory is found. (D&C 76; 88:16-33; 1 Cor. 15:35-38; *Mormon Doctrine*, pp. 573-579.)" (*Commentary* 1:196.)

6. 2 Cor. 13:1; Deut. 17:6; 19:15; Matt. 18:15-16; John 8:12-29.

7. "Man's hope of gaining salvation is in direct proportion to his knowledge of God and the laws of salvation. No man can be saved in ignorance of Jesus Christ and the laws of the gospel. Man is saved no faster than he gains knowledge of God and the saving truths recorded in the scriptures. A fountain cannot rise above its source; a people cannot live laws of which they are ignorant, nor believe in a Christ about whom they know little or nothing. The Lord expects his people to learn the doctrines of salvation. 'Search these commandments' (D&C 1:37), is a decree which applies in principle to all revelations of all ages." (*Commentary* 1:201.)

8. "Who bears testimony that Jesus is indeed the Christ?

"(1) Jesus himself, repeatedly, bluntly, plainly, over and over again testified of his own divine Sonship;

"(2) His Father, by his own voice out of heaven, by personally coming to earth to introduce the Son, and by sending the Holy Ghost to speak to the spirits of the contrite;

"(3) The Holy Ghost, the Spirit member of the Godhead, whose mission is to bear record of the Father and the Son;

"(4) The works performed by Jesus in his mortal ministry, including his miracles, teachings, resurrection, and atoning sacrifice which made immortality and eternal life a reality;

"(5) Prophets and apostles of all ages—Moses, John, Peter, Nephi, Joseph Smith, the elders of Israel, a great host which no man can number; and

"(6) The scriptures and recorded revelations of the past and present." (*Commentary* 1:198-99.)

9. It is on this basis—that of divine investiture of authority—that some scriptures call Christ the Father. Other passages call him the Father in the sense of Creator or of being the Father of those—born again as they are—who believe the gospel. See *Mormon Doctrine*, 2nd ed., p. 130.

10. "Though the Jews trusted in Moses, they were damned for rejecting the great lawgiver's testimony concerning the Messiah. Similarly, though modern sectarians trust in Peter, falsely supposing they believe what that ancient apostle taught, they shall be damned for refusing to accept Peter's testimony about the restoration of all things in the last days. (Acts 3:19-21.) In the same sense that Moses stands as the accuser of the Jews, so Peter, James, and John and the apostles of old will stand as the accusers of an apostate Christendom. . . . Similarly, if men today believed in Christ and the apostles of old, they also would believe in Joseph Smith, the Book of Mormon, and the restoration of the gospel. (*Mormon Doctrine*, pp. 75-77.)" (*Commentary* 1:202.)

JESUS: "LORD . . . OF THE SABBATH"

Thus saith the Lord; Take heed
to yourselves, and bear no burden
on the sabbath day, nor bring it in
by the gates of Jerusalem;
Neither carry forth a burden
out of your houses on the sabbath day,
neither do ye any work,
but hallow ye the sabbath day,
as I commanded your fathers. . . .
And it shall come to pass,
if ye diligently hearken unto me,
saith the Lord, to bring in
no burden through the gates
of this city on the sabbath day,
but hallow the sabbath day,
to do no work therein;
Then shall there enter into the gates
of this city kings and princes
sitting upon the throne of David,
riding in chariots and on horses,

they, and their princes,
the men of Judah, and the inhabitants
of Jerusalem: and this city
shall remain for ever. . . .
But if ye will not hearken unto me
to hallow the sabbath day,
and not to bear a burden, even entering
in at the gates of Jerusalem
on the sabbath day; then will I kindle
a fire in the gates thereof,
and it shall devour the palaces
of Jerusalem, and it shall not
be quenched. (Jer. 17:21-27.)[1]

"The Sabbath Was Made for Man"

(*Matthew 12:1-8; JST, Matthew 12:4; Mark 2:23-28; JST, Mark 2:22, 26-27; Luke 6:1-5*)

Jesus is back in Galilee with his disciples; the Passover is past; the little band has walked the wearisome miles from Jerusalem to the rugged hill country where he loved so much to be. Behind them in the capital of Jewry are the rulers of the people—the leading Rabbis, the scribes, the Sanhedrinists—smarting under the rebukes received from Jesus at the Passover; debating the doctrines delivered in the Bethesda sermon; and stirring up animosity and hatred against him, both on the pretext of Sabbath desecration and because he made himself equal with God.

Again, here in Galilee, the Sabbath issue arises to plague Jesus and his disciples and to hinder the spread of truth. 'How can this man be a true prophet if he and those who follow him violate our sacred Sabbath laws? Many among our fathers laid down their lives rather than raise the sword, even in self-defense, on the Sabbath. If a man breaks our laws, defies our traditions, desecrates our holy day, how can he be a leader, a light, or a guide among us?' So went their reasoning. No matter that he went about doing good and working miracles! This matter of Sabbath observance was of overriding import; it took precedence over all else; had not the scribes and Pharisees so ordained?[2]

Thus we see Jesus and his friends walking "through the corn fields on the sabbath day." They are hungry; his disciples pluck the ears of corn, rub them in their hands, and eat the grains of barley. In Palestine the barley harvest begins immediately after the Passover. Jesus himself makes no attempt to satisfy his own hunger; only the disciples are engaged in the act, which on any other day would have been proper in the Pharisaic eye. "When thou comest into the standing corn of thy neighbour, then thou mayest pluck the ears with thine hand; but thou shalt not move a sickle unto thy neighbour's standing corn." (Deut. 23:25.) It was the divine intent that any in Israel—for they were all brethren, and all things were the Lord's—might freely satisfy his hunger by eating his neighbor's grain.

By this one Sabbath-performed act, our Lord's fellow travelers were guilty of two violations, not of biblical, but of Rabbinic law. They had both reaped and harvested. The plucking of the ears of corn constituted reaping, and the rubbing off of the husks fell under the sabbatical prohibition against sifting in a sieve, threshing, sifting out fruit, grinding, or fanning. Each of these sins merited punishment and required a sin offering on the great altar in the house of the Lord in Jerusalem.

Spying eyes—viewing, we suppose, with prosecutorial pleasure—observed the two sins, which they could argue were capital offenses. Perhaps these peering Pharisees were following to see if the disciples of the New Order would walk more than the two thousand cubits allowed by the Rabbinic restrictions on the Sabbath day; perhaps they hoped to witness the sins of harvesting and threshing. Seeing what they did, they complained to Jesus: "Thy disciples do that which is not lawful to do upon the sabbath day."

The charge was lodged, not against Jesus, but against his

friends. When they had accused him of violating the Sabbath by healing the impotent man at Bethesda, he admitted the charge and testified that both he and his Father worked on that day, and that without God's approval he could not have commanded the man, who for thirty-eight years had taken no step and lifted no burden, to arise, carry his couch, and walk. But this time his response was one of defense and vindication. His disciples had done no wrong, he said. Even by their own traditions Sabbath observance was superseded by a higher law in proper cases.

"Have ye not read so much as this"—'with all your learning has it not come to your attention'—"what David did, when himself was an hungered, and they which were with him; How he went into the house of God, and did take and eat the shewbread, and gave also to them that were with him; which it is not lawful to eat but for the priests alone?" 'Surely even you know'—is there not a touch of irony here?—'even you know that your law calls for men to eat on the Sabbath, and that danger to life and being on the Lord's errand supersede the Sabbath law. Since David was guiltless in taking the very Bread of the Presence from off the holy table, think ye that my disciples will be condemned for rubbing a few grains of barley in their hands to make them more palatable?'

And further: "Have ye not read in the law, how that on the Sabbath days the priests in the temple profane the Sabbath, and [even] ye say they are blameless?" 'Do not the priests labor for many hours in offering sacrifices on the Sabbath day? And yet ye yourselves say they are blameless.' "But I say unto you, That in this place is one greater than the temple." 'As the priests who serve in the temple are blameless because their labors on the Sabbath day are for the salvation of men, so are my disciples, who serve me, blameless, for I am the Living Temple, through whom salvation comes.'

"If their own Rabbis had laid it down that there was 'no Sabbatism in the Temple;' that the priests on the Sabbath might hew the wood, and light the fires, and place hot fresh-baked shewbread on the table, and slay double victims, and circumcise children, and thus in every way violate the rules of the Sopherim about the Sabbath, and yet be blameless—nay, if in acting thus they were breaking the Sabbath at the bidding of the very Law which ordains the Sabbath—then if the Temple excuse *them,* ought not something greater than the Temple to excuse these? And there was something greater than the Temple here." (Farrar, pp. 336-37.)

"But if ye had known what this meaneth," Jesus continued, drawing his quotation from Hosea, "I will have mercy, and not sacrifice, ye would not have condemned the guiltless."

To ancient Israel—bound down with tradition; buried in formalism; following the letter and not the spirit of the law; not envisioning the meaning, nor the symbolism, nor the purport of their sacrifices—the Lord Jehovah, by the mouth of Hosea, proclaimed: "I desired mercy, and not sacrifice; and the knowledge of God more than burnt offerings." (Hosea 6:6.)

Micah, struggling to combat the same "form of godliness" that was devoid of the true spirit of worship, was even more severe in his denunciations—not, of course, of the true order of sacrifice, but of its perverted substitutes. A denunciation of false baptisms performed without authority is no condemnation of true ones done at the Lord's behest. "Wherewith shall I come before the Lord, and bow myself before the high God?" Micah asks. "Shall I come before him with burnt offerings, with calves of a year old? Will the Lord be pleased with thousands of rams, or with ten thousands of rivers of oil?" Is it sacrifices performed as an end in themselves that please him? "Shall I give my firstborn for my transgression, the fruit of my body for the sin of my soul?" he asks, alluding to the knowledge had by the ancients that the Firstborn of the Father, the fruit of the body of the great God, would be offered as a sacrifice for sin. "He hath shewed thee, O man, what is good; and what doth the Lord require of thee, but to do justly, and to love mercy, and to walk humbly with thy God?" (Micah 6:6-8.)

There is a higher law. Mercy is greater than sacrifice. The "letter," as it were, of sacrificial performances, or of Sabbath observance, or of tithe paying, or of keeping the Word of Wisdom, or of any act or performance, "killeth"; only the spirit giveth "life." Sabbath restrictions are not to be compared with Sabbath acts involving mercy and goodness and grace. The lesser law is superseded by the higher. "The Sabbath was expressly designed for mercy, and therefore not only might all acts of mercy be blamelessly performed thereon, but such acts would be more pleasing to God than all the insensate and self-satisfied scrupulosities which had turned a rich blessing into a burden and a snare." (Farrar, p. 337.)

"In truth, the reason why David was blameless in eating the shewbread was the same as that which made the Sabbath-labour of the priests lawful. The Sabbath-Law was not one merely of rest, but of rest for worship. The Service of the Lord was the object in view. The priests worked on the Sabbath, because this service was the object of the Sabbath; and David was allowed to eat of the shewbread, not because there was danger to life from starvation, but because he pleaded that he was on the service of the Lord and needed this provision. The disciples, when following the Lord, were similarly on the service of the Lord; ministering to Him was more than ministering in the Temple, for He was greater than the Temple. If the Pharisees had believed this, they would not have questioned their conduct, nor in so doing have themselves infringed that higher law which enjoined mercy, not sacrifice." (Edersheim 2:58.)

Wherefore the Sabbath was given unto man for a day of rest; and also that man should glorify God, and not that man should not eat;

For the Son of man made the Sabbath day, therefore the Son of man is Lord also of the Sabbath.

The Sabbath day—wondrous, glorious day! A day of

rest; a day of peace; a day of worship; a day to glorify God! The Sabbath day—a time to offer to the Lord the sacrifice of a broken heart and a contrite spirit; a time to pay our devotions to the Most High, to offer up our sacraments, and to confess our sins! "And on this day thou shalt do none other thing, only let thy food be prepared with singleness of heart that thy fasting may be perfect, or, in other words, that thy joy may be full." (D&C 59:13.)

"For the Son of man made the Sabbath day." 'I am the God of Israel, the great Jehovah, your Messiah, the one who made the Sabbath day, giving it to Moses on Sinai; therefore, I am Lord also of the Sabbath and can specify in my own name what constitutes proper Sabbath observance.' (*Commentary* 1:204-5.)

Thus, Jesus tied the Sabbath into his own divine Sonship. And we must know—as the scribes, Pharisees, and Sanhedrinists who opposed him knew—that by objecting to his Sabbath conduct, or that of his disciples, they were in fact objecting to his Messiahship.

Jesus Heals a Withered Hand on the Sabbath

(*Matthew 12:9-15; JST, Matthew 12:13; Mark 3:1-6; Luke 6:6-11*)

On yet another Galilean Sabbath, Jesus enters a synagogue, as is his wont, and teaches the people. Would that we knew what words he spoke! Spies are present. "Henceforth, at every turn and every period of His career—in the cornfields, in synagogues, in feasts, during journeys, at Capernaum, at Magdala, in Perea, at Bethany—we find Him dogged, watched, impeded, reproached, questioned, tempted, insulted, conspired against by these representatives of the leading authorities of His nation, of whom we are repeatedly told that they were not natives of the place, but 'certain which came from Jerusalem.' " (Farrar, p. 334.)

He has aforetime healed in synagogues on the Sabbath, and but recently has vindicated his disciples for harvesting and threshing a few grains of barley on that holy day. His enemies, however, at the direction of the Jewish leaders in Jerusalem, are building up a case against him. By the sheer weight of the evidence, by accumulating numerous instances of supposed wrongdoing, they seek to justify their murderous designs. Will he heal on this Sabbath as he has done on others?

There is in the synagogue a man with a withered hand, an underdeveloped hand, a hand without strength or facility, hanging on an arm and a wrist that may not have been wholly normal. Whether the man is there of his own accord to worship with his fellow Galileans, or was enticed to come as an unwitting dupe, that the guile-filled Pharisees might have aught with which to challenge the Master Healer, is not apparent. Perhaps it is the latter, for the Pharisees, "that they might accuse him," ask: "Is it lawful to heal on the sabbath days?"

This question, proposed by captious scribes and quarrelsome Pharisees, seems simple enough to us; but in their cultural and social circumstances it grew out of a maze of Rabbinic debate, uncertainty, and absurdity. Indeed: "So much unclearness prevails as to the Jewish views about healing on the Sabbath, that some connected information on the subject seems needful. We have already seen, that in their view only actual danger to life warranted a breach of the Sabbath-Law. But this opened a large field for discussion. Thus, according to some, disease of the ear, according to some throat-disease, while, according to others, such a disease as angina, involved danger, and superseded the Sabbath-Law. All applications to the outside of the body were forbidden on the Sabbath. As regarded internal remedies, such substances as were used in health, but had also a remedial effect, might be taken, although here also there was a way of evading the Law. A person suffering from toothache might not gargle his mouth with vinegar, but he might use an ordinary toothbrush and dip it in vinegar. The Gemara here adds, that gargling was lawful, if the substance was afterwards swallowed. It further explains, that affections extending from the lips, or else from the throat, inwards, may be attended to, being regarded as dangerous. Quite a number of these are enumerated, showing, that either the Rabbis were very lax in applying their canon about mortal diseases, or else that they reckoned in their number not a few which we would not regard as such. External lesions also might be attended to, if they involved danger to life. Similarly, medical aid might be called in, if a person had swallowed a piece of glass; a splinter might be removed from the eye, and even a thorn from the body." (Edersheim 2:59-60.)

But Jesus rises above the dust of Rabbinic battles; he is not concerned with their petty prohibitions, their childish rules, their endless debates. "What man shall there be among you," he asks, "that shall have one sheep, and if it fall into a pit on the sabbath day, will he not lay hold on it, and lift it out?" On this point also the Rabbinic debates raged; was it lawful to save the sheep, or not? In practice the people found ways of doing so. And so Jesus continues, "How much then is a man better than a sheep? Wherefore it is lawful to do well on the sabbath days."

At this point Jesus says to the man with the withered hand, "Stand forth," which he does. To the spies from Jerusalem, he rephrases their own tempting accusation: "Is it lawful to do good on the sabbath days, or to do evil? to save life, or to kill?" If their answer is affirmative, how can they condemn Jesus for Sabbath healings? If it is negative, they are condoning murder by neglect. They hold their peace and say nothing.

Then Jesus "looked round about on them with anger," his soul stirred with righteous indignation, he being "grieved for the hardness of their hearts," and he said to the man, "Stretch forth thine hand." The man obeyed, and his hand was restored; it became whole like unto the other one.

Among the Godfearing and the righteous such a miracle would have raised shouts of praise and thanksgiving that God dealt so graciously with suffering mortals. Not so among these enemies of Him who came down from heaven to heal men physically and to save them spiritually. Rather, "they were filled with madness" and took counsel with the hated Herodians—those half-apostate Jews who dealt traitorously toward their own people, and who stood for all that Roman tyranny imposed upon the chosen race—they took counsel with such misdirected recreants as to how they might destroy him. It was the ages-old scene of enemies forgetting their own differences and joining hands to fight the truth and Him who is its source.

While they held their council, planning how to destroy him, Jesus withdrew, leaving them to their own evil devices. His time had not yet come; much preaching lay ahead, and many miracles were yet to be wrought.

Some Gentiles Hear and Believe and Are Healed

(*Matthew 12:15-21; Mark 3:7-12*)

To what extent did Jesus preach and minister and heal among the Gentiles? Was the Holy One of Israel, while incarnate among men, destined to proclaim his message in other than Israelite ears?

As a general principle, we know from many passages that he was sent only to the lost sheep of the house of Israel; that during his lifetime he limited his preaching, and that of his disciples, to the members of the one chosen race; and that even after his resurrection, the other sheep whom he visited were Israelitish Nephites, not Gentiles whose blood lineage came from other than Abraham, Isaac, and Jacob. (See *Commentary* 1:207-9; 325; 488.)

There are, of course, many Old Testament prophecies, as Paul's writings so amply attest, that foretell the taking of the message of salvation to the Gentiles. One of these that is purely Messianic comes to us from the pen of Isaiah and contains these words: "Behold my servant, whom I uphold; mine elect, in whom my soul delighteth; I have put my spirit upon him: he shall bring forth judgment to the Gentiles. He shall not cry, nor lift up, nor cause his voice to be heard in the street. A bruised reed shall he not break, and the smoking flax shall he not quench: he shall bring forth judgment unto truth. He shall not fail nor be discouraged, till he have set judgment in the earth: and the isles shall wait for his law." (Isa. 42:1-4.)

Matthew sees in what Jesus now does at least a partial fulfillment of Isaiah's prophecy. While the Herodians and Pharisees sit in council devising ways and means to destroy him, Jesus departs, apparently into the Decapolis area, to continue his preaching and healing ministry among a more receptive people. And those to whom he goes are in large measure Gentiles. Mark tells us whence they came. He says multitudes came from Galilee, and from Judea, and from Jerusalem. In addition, multitudes came from Idumea, and from beyond Jordan, and from Tyre and Sidon—all areas measurably inhabited by Gentiles. Being on the shore of the Sea of Galilee, and because the throngs press upon him in such great numbers, seeking just to touch his person, Jesus has his disciples provide a small ship to remove him from the press of the people. Through it all he teaches much, heals many, and casts out numerous unclean spirits. Those by whose mouths unclean spirits spoke testified, "Thou art the Son of God," and Jesus charged them "that they should not make him known." As his custom was, he desired no witness from devils, only from those whose testimony came from on high.

It is to Matthew that we turn to learn the identity of many in the surging throngs. He tells us that all this happened in fulfillment of Isaiah's Messianic prophecy, which he quotes in a paraphrased or targumed form, concluding with the affirmation: "And in his name shall the Gentiles trust."

Truly, Jesus came to "shew judgment to the Gentiles" as well as to gather in the lost sheep of Israel. Though his great commission was not to raise his voice in Gentile ears nor to strive personally to bring them into the Israelite fold, yet as

Jew and Gentile mingled in the multitudes who sought his goodness, many Gentiles would believe and his healing power would bless them. Many of the bruised reeds who were weak in faith, and the smoking flax who were afflicted in body—whom Jesus taught and healed—were of Gentile blood. As Matthew testified, Jesus here labored with those outside the fold of Jacob, and his labors prefigured the great Gentile harvest that one day would sweep the world.

NOTES

1. It should come as no surprise to find that an apostate people, with this and numerous other Old Testament sabbatical injunctions before them—being devoid as they were of the Spirit of the Lord—had turned the worship of a holy being into the worship of what they esteemed to be a holy day. Jewish Sabbath observance in Jesus' day—founded upon and growing out of prophetic utterances, such as this one from Jeremiah—was not all bad; within it lay the potential of true worship; its fault came because of the quenching of the Spirit and the igniting of the fires of rigid formalism.

"The Judaism of that day substituted empty forms and meaningless ceremonies for true righteousness; it mistook uncharitable exclusiveness for genuine purity; it delighted to sun itself in the injustice of an imagined favouritism from which it would fain have shut out all God's other children; it was so profoundly hypocritical as not even to recognise its own hypocrisy; it never thought so well of itself as when it was crushing the broken reed and trampling out the last spark from the smoking flax; it thanked God for the demerits which it took for virtues, and fancied that He could be pleased with a service in which there was neither humility, nor truthfulness, nor loyalty, nor love." (Farrar, p. 330.)

2. See chapter 11 (Book I) for a brief summary of Jewish Sabbath practices. "The Sabbath was a Mosaic, nay, even a primeval institution, and it had become the most distinctive and the most passionately reverenced of all the ordinances which separated the Jews from the Gentiles as a peculiar people. It was at once the sign of their exclusive privileges, and the centre of their barren formalism. Their traditions, their patriotism, even their obstinacy, were all enlisted in its scrupulous maintenance. . . . They had suffered themselves on that day to lose battles, to be cut in pieces by their enemies, to see Jerusalem itself imperilled and captured. Its observance had been fenced round by the most painfully minute, the most ludicrously insignificant restrictions. . . . According to the pedantic school of Shammai, no one on the Sabbath might comfort the sick or enliven the sorrowful. Even the preservation of life was a breaking of the Sabbath; and, on the other hand, even to kill a flea was as bad as to kill a camel. Had not the command to 'do no manner of work upon the Sabbath day' been most absolute and most emphatic? had not Moses himself and all the congregation caused the son of Shelomith to be stoned to death for merely gathering sticks upon it? had not the Great Synagogue itself drawn up the thirty-nine *abhoth* [primary rules] and quite innumerable *toldoth* [derivative rules], or prohibitions of labours which violated it in the first or in the second degree?" (Farrar, pp. 330-32.)

SECTION V

THE TWELVE, THE SERMON ON THE MOUNT, AND THE RISING PHARISAIC OPPOSITION

THE TWELVE, THE SERMON ON THE MOUNT, AND RISING PHARISAIC OPPOSITION

Thou, O God, hast prepared
of thy goodness for the poor.
The Lord gave the word:
great was the company
of those that published it.
(Ps. 68:10-11.)

Jesus now calls unto him the Twelve—holy men; men of faith and valor; men who will serve and suffer and bleed and die for him—and upon them he confers the holy apostleship. From henceforth they shall be his special witnesses, to teach his doctrine and testify of his divine Sonship before all men.

To them—and to a great multitude—he preached the Sermon on the Mount. The Lord gave the word! Such a sermon as none but he could preach fell from his lips.

And great was the company of those that published it! Jesus, the Twelve, Mary Magdalene and other faithful women, a great host of disciples—all traveling through every city and village of Galilee—spread the word that salvation is in Christ and that all men must come unto him, repent of their sins, and keep his commandments, to gain peace in this world and eternal life in the world to come.

Jesus heals the son of a Gentile centurion, and accepts an anointing from a repentant sinner in Simon's house; he raises from death a widow's son near Nain; he acclaims John the Baptist as one than whom there is no greater prophet; and he casts a demon out of one who is deaf and blind, thus also opening his eyes and unstopping his ears.

Then the spies from the Sanhedrin launch their assaults anew. He is accused of being Satan incarnate, of casting out devils, and of performing miracles by the power of Beelzebub, the prince of devils.

He excoriates his adversaries; speaks of pardoning grace and the unpardonable sin; condemns those who seek signs, identifying them as adulterers; and extends the limits of his family to include all those who do the will of his Father who is in heaven.

The Lord gave the word! His preachers—a great and mighty host—did and do publish it to all men everywhere. It is the word of salvation, his everlasting gospel.

JESUS CHOOSES THE TWELVE

Mine apostles, the Twelve,
which were with me in my ministry
at Jerusalem,
shall stand at my right hand
at the day of my coming
in a pillar of fire,
being clothed with robes
of righteousness,
with crowns upon their heads,
in glory even as I am. (D&C 29:12.)[1]

Apostles: Their Position and Powers

Jesus is now going to call the Twelve: twelve men who will be his witnesses; who will bear, with him, the burdens of the kingdom; who will accept martyrdom and defy the rulers of the world; and who, save Judas the traitor and John the Beloved, shall seal their testimonies with their own blood.

The day has arrived and the hour is at hand to build, on the foundation he has laid, that glorious structure: the Church and kingdom of God on earth. A year and a half has elapsed since he was baptized by John, since his formal ministry began. It is the summer of A.D. 28; in less than two years (April of A.D. 30) he will finish his mortal labors, ascend unto his Father, and leave the Twelve to preach the gospel in all the world and to build up that church and kingdom which will administer salvation to all who believe and obey.

Truly, "God hath set some in the church" to be living witnesses of the truth and divinity of the work; to regulate all the affairs of the kingdom; to serve, by their very presence, as conclusive proof that the Lord's hand is in his earthly work. Who and what identifies the true church? The Holy Book responds: "First apostles, secondarily prophets, thirdly teachers"—such is the divine order of priority—"after that miracles, then gifts of healings, helps, governments, diversities of tongues." (1 Cor. 12:28.)

Truly, the Lord has given "some, apostles; and some, prophets; and some, evangelists; and some, pastors and teachers; For the perfecting of the saints, for the work of the ministry, for the edifying of the body of Christ: Till we all come in the unity of the faith." These officers, as the Holy Book also records, are placed in the true church, "That we henceforth be no more children, tossed to and fro, and carried about with every wind of doctrine, by the sleight of men, and cunning craftiness, whereby they lie in wait to deceive." These agents of the Lord, "speaking the truth in love," guide and direct the Lord's affairs on earth. (Eph. 4:11-15.)

Truly, where there are apostles and prophets, called of God and endowed with power from on high, there is the true church and kingdom; and where these are not, there the Lord's work is not established among men. And so we come to that point in time when Jesus, setting up anew for his day and dispensation the organization designed to administer salvation to mortals, is prepared to call the Twelve.

Apostles of the Lord Jesus Christ—mighty men of faith; pillars of personal righteousness; chosen spirits who were before ordained to walk with Christ, teach his doctrine, and testify of his divine Sonship!

These are they whom Lehi saw—following one whose "luster was above that of the sun at noon-day"—they whose own "brightness did exceed that of the stars in the firmament. And they came down and went forth upon the face of the earth." (1 Ne. 1:9-11.) These are they who were among "the noble and great ones" seen by Abraham, who were chosen to be rulers before they were "born." (Abr. 3:22-23.) As with Jeremiah, their fellow servant—before they were formed "in the belly," and before they came "forth out of the womb"—the Lord had known them, and "sanctified" them, and "ordained" them to be prophets and apostles "unto the nations." (Jer. 1:5.) There was no happenstance in their calls; they had been foreordained by Him who knows all things and who had prepared them from all eternity to be his ministers in the meridian day.

Witnesses of the Redeemer—humble folk; weak and simple Galileans, unlearned in Rabbinic lore; but men who could be taught from on high, whose souls will vibrate as the revelations of eternity pour in upon them!

How aptly it is written of them, and of Heaven's emissaries in all ages: "Ye see your calling, brethren, how that not many wise men after the flesh, not many mighty, not many noble, are called: But God hath chosen the foolish things of the world to confound the wise; and God hath chosen the weak things of the world to confound the things which are mighty; And base things of the world, and things which are despised, hath God chosen, yea, and things which are not, to bring to nought things that are: That no flesh should glory in his presence." (1 Cor. 1:26-29.)

His apostolic friends—men who will walk with him through his mortal trials; who will feel the scourge and carry a cross; who are appointed unto suffering and persecution and death!

"I think that God hath set forth us the apostles last, as it were appointed to death: for we are made a spectacle unto the world, and to angels, and to men. We are fools for Christ's sake, but ye are wise in Christ; we are weak, but ye are strong; ye are honourable, but we are despised. Even unto this present hour we both hunger, and thirst, and are naked, and are buffeted, and have no certain dwelling place; And labour, working with our own hands: being reviled, we bless; being persecuted, we suffer it: Being defamed, we intreat: we are made as the filth of the world, and are the offscouring of all things unto this day." (1 Cor. 4:9-13.)

Noble souls—unknown, unlearned, and unlettered now, as it were; but men who, as the world's greatest crusaders, will attain endless fame and receive eternal renown; whose names shall be engraved forever in the walls of the Holy City!

As there are twelve tribes in Israel, so there are twelve apostles for all Israel and the world; as Jehovah gave his saving truths to the twelve sons of Jacob and their seed, throughout their generations, so Jesus is placing in the hands of his twelve friends the saving truths and powers for their day; and as the names of the twelve tribes of Israel are written on the twelve gates of the Holy Jerusalem, which shall descend from God out of heaven, so are the names of the twelve apostles of the Lamb written on the twelve foundations of the walls of that celestial city. (Rev. 21:10-14.) Surely it shall be with the Jewish Twelve as it is with the Nephite Twelve—and as it shall be with the latter-day Twelve, as also with all the saints who are true and faithful: "Behold, they are righteous forever; for because of their faith in the Lamb of God their garments are made white in his blood." (1 Ne. 12:10.)

The Twelve Apostles of the Lamb—legal administrators who shall in due course hold the keys of the kingdom; who shall have power to bind on earth and seal in heaven; who shall stand in the place and stead of the Lord Jesus when he returns to his Father to reign in eternal glory forever!

The Twelve Apostles of the Lamb—the choicest and noblest spirits available to the God of Heaven to do his work in that day; the friends of his Son; those who shall see visions, receive revelations, and work wonders—such are the ministers whom Jesus is about to choose, to ordain, and to instruct! What a glorious day this is in the cause of truth and righteousness!

Jesus Calls Eleven Galileans and One Judean

(*Mark 3:13-21; JST, Mark 3:16; Matthew 10:2-4; Luke 6:12-16*)

When the servants of the Lord go forth to choose others to labor on the Lord's errand and to engage in his ministry, they have one goal and one only: to find those whom the Lord has already chosen to serve in whatever capacities are involved. Their constant prayer on those occasions is: "Lord, show unto thy servants whom thou hast chosen to do this work or fill these offices." All of the legal administrators in the earthly kingdom "must be called of God, by prophecy, and by the laying on of hands, by those who are in authority, to preach the Gospel and administer in the ordinances thereof." (A of F 5.)

It is the Lord's work and not man's, and the Lord knows whom he wants to serve in all places in his kingdom. No man, of himself, can build up the kingdom; it is only when the earthly servants get the spirit of revelation, and do thereby the things the Lord wants done, that the work prospers to the full. And as with us, so also with the Lord Jesus, who came not to do his own will, but that of his Father who sent him. We heard him say at the Passover in Jerusalem after healing the impotent man at the pool of Bethesda: "I can of mine own self do nothing; . . . because I seek not mine own will, but the will of the Father which hath sent me." (John 5:30.)

Now Jesus is to choose the Twelve—the holy apostles who were foreordained in the councils of eternity to tread in his tracks and bear witness of his name in all the world—the Twelve whose spiritual talents, developed before they were born, will enable them to build up the kingdom and withstand the pressures of the world. Whom shall he choose? He must find those whom Nephi saw in vision six hundred years before; he must select those whom he himself first called to this high and holy ministry when he and they mingled among the noble and great spirits, seen by Abraham, who were destined to be the Lord's rulers among mortal men. These foreordained ones must be found; there must be no mistakes made.

Thus we see Jesus (for the time for calling the Twelve is now) go out alone into a mountain to pray. All night long his petitions ascend to his Father; during the long hours of darkness he communes with the one who sent him and whose will he came to do. He needed—as we need during the long and dark days of life—direction from on high. He received answer to his prayer; and someday, perhaps, when our spiritual capacity enables us to know and feel what else was involved in this and other prayers of the Son of God, we shall gain that knowledge. For now, we know only that "when it was day, he called unto him his disciples: and of them he chose twelve, whom also he named apostles."

All true believers are disciples; all who keep his commandments and who follow him as he follows his Father are his disciples; the apostles, as here designated, are those chosen disciples who are ordained to the office of apostle in the Melchizedek Priesthood and who receive and use the keys of the kingdom of God on earth. There are or may be disciples without number, but those acting in the holy apostleship are twelve in number at any given time; they are the governing officers over the disciples.

Those chosen by Jesus on this memorable morning are named, as a group, four times in the New Testament—by Matthew, by Mark, and twice by Luke, once in his Gospel and once in the Acts of the Apostles. No two of these listings give the same order of seniority, and in some instances the name applied to the same person varies. All of the lists place Peter first, and the three that mention Judas place him last. The account in Acts lists only the eleven, as Judas by then had served his purpose and sealed his traitorous conduct with a suicidal death.

From other sources we know that Peter, James, and John

were the preeminent three, and were in fact the First Presidency of the Church in that day, although we have no way of knowing whether they served as a separate quorum apart from the others of the Twelve as is the case today. They may well have done, since "the keys of the kingdom" that they restored in this dispensation "belong always unto the Presidency of the High Priesthood" (D&C 81:2), meaning they are always, in all dispensations, held by the First Presidency of the Church.

Our present knowledge of the original Twelve is scanty; some things cannot be other than speculative at this time, and a true understanding of their lives and ministries—of their kinships and works, of the sermons they preached and the miracles they wrought—must await the day when all things are revealed.[2] It may be that all of them wrote Gospels that someday will come forth for the enlightenment and salvation of men, Gospels that will come forth in a day when men are prepared, by faith and good works, and have attained the spiritual stature to be worthy to study their holy words.

Without falling into the not-uncommon trap of creating a whole personality, or of pontificating a complete life-style, or of naming with finality all of the characteristics and attributes of a person, simply because we have a known sliver of information about him, we can with some assurance note at least the following about the Twelve whom Jesus called. We shall take Mark's order of seniority, since he was the disciple of Peter and is believed to have set forth views and feelings and factual knowledge received personally from the Chief Apostle.

1. *Simon Peter.*

This noble soul—chief of the apostles, valiant, courageous, conforming; as rugged and forceful as Elijah, who called down fire from heaven, and slew the priests of Baal with the sword; as submissive and spiritual as Samuel, who attuned his ear to hear the voice of God—Simon Peter was called by Jesus to preside over the earthly kingdom, to lay the foundation and build up that church which alone would administer salvation for that day and dispensation.

We shall see him in many settings: forsaking all to follow Jesus; testifying of his divine Sonship in the coast of Caesarea Philippi; severing the ear of Malchus with a sword in Gethsemane; denying that he knows who Christ is in the courtyard of Caiaphas, the high priest; accusing the Jews, to their face, of murdering the Lord; penning the most sublime language in the New Testament; being crucified, head downward, for the testimony of Jesus that was his; coming in resurrected glory in 1829 to restore priesthood and keys and call men again to the holy apostleship.

He is described as being "generous, impetuous, wavering, noble, timid," of being "thoroughly human," and of having a "most lovable disposition." He was all this and more. There has seldom been such a mighty man as he on earth. "It would be hard to tell," says one analyst, "whether most of his fervour flowed through the outlet of adoration or activity. His full heart put force and promptitude into every movement. Is his Master encompassed by fierce ruffians?—Peter's ardour flashes in his ready sword, and converts the Galilean boatman into the soldier instantaneous. Is there a rumor of a resurrection from Joseph's tomb?—John's nimbler foot distances his older friend; but Peter's eagerness outruns the serene love of John, and past the gazing disciple he rushes breathless into the vacant sepulchre. Is the risen Saviour on the strand?—his comrades secure the net, and turn the vessel's head for shore; but Peter plunges over the vessel's side, and struggling through the waves, in his dripping coat falls down at his Master's feet. Does Jesus say, 'Bring of the fish ye have caught?'—ere any one could anticipate the word, Peter's brawny arm is lugging the weltering net with its glittering spoil ashore, and every eager movement unwittingly is answering beforehand the question of the Lord, 'Simon, lovest thou me?' And that fervour is the best, which, like Peter's, and as occasion requires, can ascend in ecstatic ascriptions of adoration and praise, or follow

Christ to prison and to death; which can concentrate itself on feats of heroic devotion, or distribute itself in the affectionate assiduities of a miscellaneous industry." (Dr. Hamilton, cited in Farrar, pp. 195-96.)

2. *James.*

The whims of chance and the happenstance of history leave us little knowledge that is unique and personal about the second man in seniority in that earthly kingdom of the One who chose and placed in their order those whom he had foreordained unto those very positions in the councils of eternity. James and his brother John, their father Zebedee, and Simon and Andrew were partners in a prosperous fishing business. They owned boats and employed servants. They forsook all to follow Jesus, and James was the first apostolic martyr in the meridian dispensation. He was beheaded by Herod Agrippa just before the Passover in A.D. 44. With Peter, his file leader, and John, his brother, he served in the Council of Three whose destiny called them to preside over the others of the Twelve and over the whole earthly kingdom of their Lord. It was these three who alone were present when Jesus raised the daughter of Jairus from death; they alone of the Twelve ascended the Mount of Transfiguration to receive keys and powers from Elias, Moses, and Jesus, and to hear the Heavenly Voice acclaim that the Beloved Son was then dwelling on earth; they were the ones chosen to be nearby when the sins of all men were laden on the Nazarene's back as he sweat great drops of blood in Gethsemane; and it was they, in June 1829, who ministered with life-giving power to their mortal fellowservants.

3. *John.*

We come now to John: to John the disciple of the Baptist—who forsook the forerunner, to follow Him of whom the witness said, "Behold the Lamb of God, which taketh away the sin of the world" (John 1:29); to John the Beloved—the disciple whom Jesus loved, and who, at the last supper, leaned on the Master's breast; to John the Revelator—who was banished to Patmos where he saw the visions of eternity and wrote the book of Revelation; to John—the author of the Gospel of that name, a gospel oriented to the saints, and of three other New Testament epistles; to John—generally esteemed to be a mystic, though he and James are called by Jesus Boanerges, or Sons of Thunder, because they were rugged and forceful characters, like Elijah, who would have called down fire from heaven upon their enemies; to John—the translated one, who alone of all the Twelve chose to live on earth until the Second Coming that he might bring souls unto salvation; to John—an apostle of love, than whom there have been few greater on earth. He is known to us for his inspired writings, his heavenly visions, and his incomparable centuries-long missionary work. It was he to whom Jesus, hanging in agony upon the cross, entrusted the care of the Blessed Virgin, and who enjoyed as close an intimacy with the Lord as any man who ever lived.

4. *Andrew.*

In the veins of Andrew surged the same believing blood that made his brother Peter a valiant witness of the truth. They were sons of Jona, fishing partners, and friends of Zebedee's children. Andrew and John the apostle were disciples of the Baptist, who, believing his witness of the Messiah, forsook the son of Zacharias to follow Jesus. After one day with our Lord, Andrew gained a witness of his divinity, found his brother, the future president of the Church, and said: "We have found the Messias." (John 1:41.) Andrew was with Peter when the Lord found them casting a net into the still Galilean waters, and said: "Follow me, and I will make you fishers of men." (Matt. 4:19.) He is mentioned in connection with several New Testament episodes and, according to tradition, was crucified at Patrae in Achaia.

5. *Philip.*

Jesus found Philip, apparently searched for him, at Bethsaida, the city where Andrew and Peter then lived. This early-found disciple was with Jesus at the marriage feast in Cana and is mentioned several other times. His most noted conversation of which we have record was the plea, "Lord, shew us the Father, and it sufficeth us," in reply to which he received the mild rebuke: "Have I been so long time with you, and yet hast thou not known me, Philip? he that hath seen me hath seen the Father; and how sayest thou then, Shew us the Father?" (John 14:8-9.) Of his ministry after Jesus' ascension we know nothing.

6. *Bartholomew.*

Called also Nathanael, he is described by Jesus as an Israelite without guile; his witness from the beginning, as first spoken to Jesus, was: "Rabbi, thou art the Son of God; thou art the King of Israel." (John 1:49.) He received from Jesus the promise that he would see the heavens open and angels ascending and descending upon the Son of Man. We know little else of him but doubt not that the divine promise found fulfillment at the appointed time.

7. *Matthew.*

In his capacity as a special witness, Matthew took it upon himself to write of the generation, birth, ministry, passion, resurrection, and exaltation of the Lord Jesus. His spiritual talents and literary craftsmanship enabled him to record—more particularly for Jewish readers, who believed the prophets and pondered their Messianic utterances—many of the words and deeds of the one he knew to be the Son of God. Also known as Levi the son of Alpheus, he was a publican, one of that hated and despised group of Roman tax collectors; apparently he was well-to-do, as he gave a great feast in his own home to introduce many publicans and sinners to Jesus. The numerous quotations in his Gospel from the Old Testament identify him as a scriptural scholar and a trained theologian. His collecting and collating of the numerous events preserved for us in his Gospel establish him as a historian and preserver of that knowledge which Christ came to deliver to men. Aside from the obvious diligence manifest and the labors involved in preparing his written testimony, we know nothing of his ministry after the ascension of the Lord.

8. *Thomas.*

Clearly this holy man, known also as Didymus, was one of the most valiant and courageous of the Twelve, one whose sure witness of the divine Sonship is recorded in fervent and worshipful words. When others of the Twelve counseled Jesus not to go into Judea, where the Jews then sought his life and where Lazarus lay in need of divine help, it was Thomas who said, "Let us also go, that we may die with him." (John 11:16.) When Jesus told the Twelve that he was going to prepare a heavenly place for them and that they knew the way to obtain such a high status, it was Thomas who dared to say: "Lord, we know not whither thou goest; and how can we know the way?" (John 14:5), which brought forth the great pronouncement that Jesus was the way, the truth, and the life. And it was Thomas—absent when the others, in the upper room, felt the prints of the nails, thrust their hands into the riven side, and saw the resurrected Lord eat before them—it was Thomas, not understanding the corporeal nature of the resurrection, who expressed disbelief, only to have Jesus appear eight days later and say: "Thomas, Reach hither thy finger, and behold my hands; and reach hither thy hand, and thrust it into my side: and be not faithless, but believing." Then came from Thomas the inspired witness: "My Lord and my God" (John 20:27-28), which we may be assured he continued to bear as long as mortal breath was his.

9. *James.*

Of this James we know only that he was the son of Alpheus, and that he was ordained to the holy apostleship. That he was of apostolic stature, bore true witness, and taught sound doctrine is implicit in the known system governing the apostolate. Our lack of knowledge about him shows only the inadequacy of the accounts that have been preserved for us.

10. *Judas.*

Luke calls him "Judas the brother of James," and Matthew names him as "Lebbeus, whose surname was Thaddeus." As to his works and ministry we are not advised, and conclude only that he was of like spiritual stature with his brethren of the Twelve.

11. *Simon Zelotes.*

Of this member of the Twelve we know only that he was at one time one of the party of Zealots, but this fact of itself speaks volumes. The Zealots were a Jewish sect whose avowed purpose was to uphold the Mosaic ritual and stand as guardians of the law. Simon must have been a valiant leader in this politico-nationalistic movement, for Matthew, Mark, and Luke, all three, in identifying him append the name of the sect to his personal name. Luke calls him Simon Zelotes; Matthew and Mark call him Simon the Canaanite. In the original records the term Canaanite, in this instance, is the Syro-Chaldaic equivalent of the Greek word that has been translated into English as Zelotes.[3]

12. *Judas Iscariot.*

Eleven of the Twelve were Galileans; Judas only was from Judea, his name signifying, as it is supposed, that he came from Kerioth, a small town of the tribe of Judah. Ish Kerioth (Iscariot) signifies "a man of Kerioth." He was the steward and almoner for Jesus and the other disciples, receiving and dispensing, to the poor and otherwise, such monies as came into their hands. We suppose he had a testimony and followed Jesus willingly, although he well could have done so with ulterior motives—for money and power—and with evil intent. Certainly Satan was his chief master; greed and avarice dwelt in his heart; he was dishonest in caring for the monies placed in his hands; and for thirty pieces of silver he planted the traitor's kiss. Thereafter he hanged himself at Aceldama, the field of blood, which is on the southern slope of the valley of Hinnom outside Jerusalem. In the process he fell headlong, burst asunder, his bowels gushed out, and his spirit went to associate with Lucifer in that realm where traitors to the truth suffer the agonies of the damned.

These, then, are the Lord's Twelve—all save one are holy

and righteous men—the ministers called to bear witness of his holy name and build up his earthly kingdom, first among the Jews, and then among the Gentiles.[4] They were called of God by prophecy; power from on high was imparted by the laying on of hands; they all held the holy Melchizedek Priesthood; and each was ordained to the office of an apostle therein. "Ye have not chosen me"—men do not call themselves to the ministry!—"but I have chosen you, and ordained you," Jesus said. (John 15:16.) Of their call Mark, reflecting Peter's teaching, said: "He ordained twelve, that they should be with him, and that he might send them forth to preach, And to have power to heal sicknesses, and to cast out devils."

In due course Jesus will give, first to Peter, James and John, and then to all of the Twelve, the keys of the kingdom of heaven; these keys will enable them to preside over the earthly kingdom and direct all its affairs, to say nothing of that divine and eternal power which transcends the bounds of earth and endures beyond this mortal vale—the power to bind and seal on earth and in heaven. These keys enable the Lord's servants on earth to seal men up unto eternal life, on the one hand, and, on the other, "to seal them up unto the day when the wrath of God shall be poured out upon the wicked without measure." (D&C 1:9.)

For the meridian dispensation, vacancies in the Twelve were filled as they occurred. By the spirit of revelation, the Eleven chose Matthias—one who had companied with them all the time that the Lord Jesus went in and out among them—to serve in the place of Judas. This thirteenth apostle was "ordained" to be a witness with the others of the resurrection and to bear with them the burdens of the kingdom. The pattern being thus set, vacancies in the Quorum of the Twelve were filled until that day when the man-child "was caught up unto God and his throne," and the long night of apostate darkness descended upon the earth. (*Commentary* 3:513-19.)[5]

NOTES

1. These words are part of the heavensent pronouncement that these very Twelve shall "judge the whole house of Israel," so glorious, so high, and so exalted is their station.

2. There are reasons to believe that others of the original Twelve than Peter and Andrew, James and John, were related, and that some of them were cousins of Jesus, but of these things we cannot be sure. With our present source material only, it remains a fascinating but somewhat fruitless field of inquiry. Perhaps these two quotations, one from Farrar, the other from Edersheim, which do not themselves agree, will help those readers whose inclinations lie in this genealogical field to envision something of what is involved.

"Simon and Andrew the sons of Jonas, James and John the sons of Zabdia, and Philip, were of the village of Bethsaida. [As we have heretofore seen, Philip was *at* Bethsaida, not *of* Bethsaida, when Jesus first called him.] If Matthew be the same as Levi [and of this there is almost complete agreement], he was a son of Alpheus, and therefore a brother of James the Less and of Jude, the brother of James, who is generally regarded as identical with Lebbeus and Thaddeus. They belonged in all probability to Cana or Capernaum, and if there were any ground for believing the tradition which says that Mary, the wife of Alpheus or Klopas, was a younger sister of the Virgin, then we should have to consider these three brothers as first-cousins of our Lord. Nathanael or Bartholomew was of Cana in Galilee. Thomas and Simon Zelotes were also Galileans. Judas Iscariot was the son of a Simon Iscariot, but whether this Simon is identical with the Zealot cannot be determined." (Farrar, pp. 190-91.) This analysis makes Matthew, James the Son of Alpheus, and Jude brothers, and possible cousins of Jesus.

"The difficulties connected with tracing the family descent or possible relationship between the Apostles are so great, that we must forego all hope of arriving at any certain conclusion. . . . Some points at least seem clear. First, it appears that only the calling of those to the Apostolate is related, which in some sense is typical, viz. that of Peter and Andrew, of James and John, of Philip and Bartholomew (or Bar Telamyon, or Temalyon, generally supposed the same as Nathanael), and of Matthew the publican. Yet, secondly, there is something which attaches to each of the others. Thomas, who is called Didymus (which means 'twin'), is closely connected with Matthew, both in St. Luke's Gospel and in that of St. Matthew himself. James is expressly named as the son of Alpheus or Clopas. This we know to have been also the name of Matthew-Levi's father. But, as the name was a common one, no inference can be drawn from it, and it does not seem likely that the father of Matthew was also that of James, Judas, and Simon, for these three seem to have been brothers. Judas is designated by St. Matthew as Lebbeus, from the Hebrew *lebh,* a heart, and is also named, both by him and by St. Mark, Thaddeus. . . . St. Luke simply designates him Judas of James, which means that he was the brother (less probably, the son) of James. Thus his real name would have been Judas Lebbeus, and his surname Thaddeus. Closely connected with these two we have in all the Gospels, Simon, surnamed Zelotes or Cananean (not Canaanite), both terms indicating his original connection with the Galilean Zealot party, the 'Zealots for the Law.' His position in the Apostolic Catalogue, and the testimony of Hegesippus, seem to point him out as the son of Clopas, and brother of James, and of Judas Lebbeus. These three were, in a sense, cousins of Christ, since, according to Hegesippus, Clopas was the brother of Joseph, while the sons of Zebedee were real cousins, their mother Salome being a sister of the Virgin. Lastly, we have Judas Iscariot, or *Ish Kerioth,* 'a man of Kerioth,' a town in Judah. Thus the betrayer alone would be of Judean origin, the others all of Galilean." (Edersheim 1:521-22.) This analysis makes James the Less, Judas, and Simon Zelotes brothers and cousins of Christ through Joseph. James and John are listed as blood-cousins through Mary.

It is worthy of note that among the Nephite Twelve, Nephi and Timothy were brothers, as also were Mathoni and Mathonihah, and that Jonas was a son of Nephi. (3 Ne. 19:4.)

In the first Twelve called in this dispensation, Parley P. and Orson Pratt were brothers, as were Luke S. and Lyman E. Johnson. Joseph Smith, the Prophet, and Hyrum Smith, the Patriarch, were brothers; their brother William served in the Twelve, and their father, Joseph Smith, Sr., was the first Patriarch to the Church. Brigham Young, Jr., a son of President Brigham Young, was one of the Twelve. George A. Smith, John Henry Smith, and George Albert Smith constitute three generations of apostles, as do Franklin D. Richards, George F. Richards, and LeGrand Richards, and Amasa, Francis M., and Richard R. Lyman. President Joseph F. Smith and two of his sons, Hyrum Mack and Joseph Fielding, served in the Twelve. Lorenzo and Erastus Snow were related. John Taylor and his son John W., Wilford Woodruff and his son Abraham O., Matthias F. Cowley and his son Matthew, and George Q. Cannon and his son Sylvester were all apostles. Joseph F. Merrill was a son of Marriner W. Merrill, Ezra Taft Benson a great-grandson of the original Ezra T. Benson, and Stephen L Richards a grandson of Willard Richards. President Spencer W. Kimball is a grandson of Heber C. Kimball, and Gordon B. Hinckley a nephew of Alonzo A. Hinckley—plus the fact that there are many instances of cousins and more distantly related family members, all called to positions of apostolic power. Truly, faith runs in families, in all dispensations.

3. Referring to a work by Bruce, *Training of the Twelve,* Farrar, in a footnote, comments: "Bruce happily remarks that the choice of an ex-Zealot as an Apostle, giving grounds for political suspicion, is another sign of Christ's disregard of mere prudential wisdom. Christ wished the apostles to be the type and germ of the Church; and therefore we find in it a union of opposites—the tax-gatherer Matthew, and the tax-hater Simon—the unpatriotic Jew who served the alien, and the patriot who strove for emancipation." (Farrar, p. 192.)

4. In our dispensation, the Twelve Apostles are also called to be "special witnesses of the name of Christ in all the world," and "to build up the church, and regulate all the affairs of the same in all nations," but the order of priority where Jews and Gentiles are concerned is reversed. For our day, the gospel goes "first unto the Gentiles and secondly unto the Jews." (D&C 107:23, 33.)

5. "All of the brethren in the Church who knew by personal revelation that Jesus was the Christ, meaning all who had testimonies given by the Holy Ghost of his divine Sonship, were witnesses of the Lord. Such were Stephen, Philip, Prochorus, Nicanor, Timon, Parmenas, Nicolas, Ananias, John Mark, Simeon, Lucius, Manaen, Judas Barsabas, Silas, Timotheus, Apollos, Sopater, Aristarchus, Secundus, Gaius, Tychicus, Trophimus, Agabus, Mnason—all of whom are mentioned in Acts and are variously referred to as prophets, teachers, and disciples, but none of whom are called apostles. Only Barnabas, Paul, Matthias, James the Lord's brother, and the original Twelve are singled out to carry the apostolic appelation. The clear inference thus is that the name is being reserved for those who were ordained to the office of apostle in the Melchizedek Priesthood and therefore that Paul and Barnabas were members of the Council of the Twelve, having filled vacancies in the normal course of events. President Joseph Fielding Smith has written: 'Paul was an ordained apostle, and without question he took the place of one of the other brethren in that Council.' (Joseph Fielding Smith, *Doctrines of Salvation* 3:153.)" (*Commentary* 2:131.)

Chapter 41

THE SERMON ON THE MOUNT

His name shall endure for ever:
his name shall be continued as long as the sun:
and men shall be blessed in him:
all nations shall call him blessed.
Blessed be the Lord God,
the God of Israel,
who only doeth wondrous things.
And blessed be his glorious name for ever:
and let the whole earth be filled
with his glory. (Ps. 72:17-19.)

Come, ye blessed of my Father,
inherit the kingdom prepared for you
from the foundation of the world.
(Matt. 25:34.)

The Sermon on the Mount—Its Nature and Delivery

It is now our privilege to hear anew the Sermon on the Mount, the Sermon on the Plain, the Sermon in Bountiful—for they are all one; all contain the same truths; all fell from the same lips; all were spoken by the power of the same Spirit. We shall not hear the whole sermon, for no man, of whom we know, has been so privileged since the holy words fell from the lips of Him who chose in his own right, rather than by the mouths of his servants the prophets, to present such a wondrous compilation of the divine truth in a single sermon. But we shall both hear the words and feel the spirit of the portion that has come down to us in Holy Writ.

There may have been greater sermons preached to selected congregations of spiritual giants—as, for instance, at Adam-ondi-Ahman when the first man assembled together the high priests and patriarchs of his dispensation, along with other righteous saints of like spiritual capacity—there may have been other sermons preached to spiritual giants who could comprehend more of the truths of eternity than the general run of mankind. The Sermon on the Mount, however, was preached to instruct and counsel the newly ordained apostles; to open the door of spiritual progress for all newly called members of the Church and kingdom of God on earth; and to stand as a beacon inviting men of good will of every doctrinal persuasion to come to the Fount of Wisdom and learn those things which will assure them of peace in this world and eternal glory in the world to come.

This sermon is a recapitulation, a summary, and a digest of what men must do to gain salvation; and the eternal concepts in it are so stated that hearers (and readers) will get out of it as much as their personal spiritual capacity permits. To some it will point the way to further investigation; to others it will confirm and reconfirm eternal truths already learned from the scriptures and from the preachers of righteousness of their day; and to those few whose souls burn with the fires of testimony, devotion, and valiance, it will be as the rending of the heavens: light and knowledge beyond carnal comprehension will flow into their souls in quantities that cannot be measured. Every man must judge and determine for himself the effect the Sermon on the Mount will have upon him.

As the words of the sermon are spoken, anew, as it were, in our ears, there are some basic and simple realities of which we must be aware. The Sermon on the Mount has never been recorded in its entirety as far as we know; at least no such scriptural account is available to us. What has come to us is a digest; the words in each account that are attributed to Jesus are, in fact, verbatim recordings of what he said, but they are not all that he said by any means. He may have expounded on each point at extended length, with the Gospel historians who preserved his sayings being guided by the Spirit to write only those words which, in the infinite wisdom of Him who knoweth all things, should have been incorporated into their scriptural accounts. It may well be that the most perfect and elaborate sermon was delivered to the Nephites, for their congregation was composed only of spiritually attuned souls. Without question, when Matthew records a thought in one set of words and Luke does so in different language, both are preserving the verbatim utterances of the Lord. He said what both of them attribute to him as part of the whole sermon. The recording witnesses of his words simply chose to preserve different spoken sentences to present the eternal concepts involved.

And, finally, in this connection: The Sermon on the Mount is not an assemblage of disjointed sayings, spoken on diverse occasions, that have been combined in one place for convenience in presentation, as some uninspired commentators have speculated. It is rather selected sayings, all spoken by Jesus on one day, following the ordination of the Twelve; it is that portion of his words, spoken on that occasion, which the Spirit knew should be preserved for us and for all men who seek truth. It may well be that the sealed portion of the Book of Mormon contains more of the sermon than is now found in Third Nephi, and it may well be that future revelations—accounts of others of the apostles, for instance—will bring to light more that was said on the mountainous plain near Capernaum where Jesus spoke the Spirit-guided words to his Jewish friends.

No doubt what we receive in the future—as to this and all other scriptural expansions—will depend upon our spiritual maturity. When we exercise faith like unto the brother of Jared, we will learn by revelation what he knew, and feel by the power of the Spirit what he felt. Until then let us start with what we have, the glorious truths recorded in Matthew 5, 6, and 7; in Luke 6; and in 3 Nephi 12, 13, and 14; and let us lay the foundation for that knowledge and that perfection of life which it is ours to receive because we have what we have—the glorious Sermon on the Mount as now constituted.

Jesus Speaks the Beatitudes

(*3 Nephi 12:1-12; Matthew 5:1-12; JST, Matthew 5:3-5, 8, 10-12, 14; Luke 6:17-26; JST, Luke 6:20-21, 23*)

Jesus came in resurrected glory to a great multitude of the Nephites who were assembled round about the temple in the land Bountiful. At his invitation they all thrust their hands into his side and felt the print of the nails in his hands and in his feet, and all cried out with one accord: "Hosanna! Blessed be the name of the Most High God!" From among them Jesus chose Twelve, whom he ordained apostles, and to whom he gave power to proclaim his gospel, to baptize, to confer the gift of the Holy Ghost, and to do all things needful for the salvation of that remnant of the house of Israel.

To these Twelve and to the whole congregation Jesus taught his gospel, including faith, repentance, baptism of water and of the Spirit, and the keeping of the commandments of God. (3 Ne. 11.) Then, stretching forth his hand to the multitude, he began to deliver the Sermon in Bountiful, which was the Sermon on the Mount, as we conclude from Matthew's account, or the Sermon on the Plain, as we reason from Luke's recording of the same persuasive words.[1] His initial declarations in this sermon have been appropriately called the Beatitudes. To beatify is to make supremely happy or to announce that a person has attained the blessedness of heaven. Beatitude is a state of utmost bliss, and the Beatitudes are our Lord's declarations of the blessedness and eventual eternal glory of those who obey the various principles recited in them. May we now, with beatific vision, as it were, seek to envision the meaning of Jesus' blessed pronouncements on blessedness.

> *Blessed are ye if ye shall give heed unto the words of these twelve whom I have chosen from among you to minister unto you, and to be your servants; and unto them I have given power that they may baptize you with water; and after that ye are baptized with water, behold, I will baptize you with fire and with the Holy Ghost; therefore blessed are ye if ye shall believe in me and be baptized, after that ye have seen me and know that I am.*
>
> *And again, more blessed are they who shall believe in your words because that ye shall testify that ye have seen me, and that ye know that I am. Yea, blessed are they who shall believe in your words, and come down into the depths of humility and be baptized, for they shall be visited with fire and with the Holy Ghost, and shall receive a remission of their sins.*

These are the basic Beatitudes; these are the initial words of blessing; these are the beatific promises that precede all others; out of them all other blessings come. Before the blessedness of heaven; before the beatific state of supreme happiness; before the glory of utmost bliss can be gained; before we progress on the strait and narrow path leading to eternal life—before nearly all else, we must believe in the Lord Jesus Christ; we must give heed to the apostles and prophets who minister in his name; we must come down in the depths of humility and be baptized in his holy name; we must be visited with fire and with the Holy Ghost and receive a remission of our sins; and we must then walk in the light of the Spirit. It is only after the blessings promised in these beginning Beatitudes have been received that we can obtain the things promised in the Beatitudes that follow.

Jesus' beginning beatific statements in the Sermon on the Mount, as delivered on the mountainous plain near Capernaum, were similar to those made to the Nephites. Having spent the night on the mountain in prayer, Jesus chose the

Twelve, ordained them, and gave them the same powers and commission received by their Nephite fellow laborers. Then, Luke says, "he came down with them, and stood in the plain," meaning a high plateau area near where he, alone, had communed during the night with his Father.

Assembled before him were a host of disciples and a great multitude of people. Disciples and investigators had come together "out of all Judea and Jerusalem, and from the sea coast of Tyre and Sidon." They came to hear and heed, to be healed of their diseases, to bask in the divine Presence, to be fed spiritually. It was a day of miracles. Those vexed with unclean spirits were healed; multitudes thronged near seeking merely to touch him; faith was in every heart; he responded to their pleas; and "virtue went out of him, and healed them all." The account seems to indicate that thousands were present. He healed them all! All were given health of body and enlightenment of soul. The kinds and severities of their afflictions are not named, simply that he healed them all.

On other occasions, the healing of lepers, the opening of blind eyes, the restoring of withered legs and arms, the raising of dead bodies from their biers and graves—all are recounted in detail. But the great event of this day was not the miracles, but the sermon; and so, in the setting of faith where all present were healed, in a setting where the Spirit of the Lord was present, Jesus began the Sermon on the Plain. These beginning Beatitudes then fell from his lips:

> *Blessed are they who shall believe on me; and again, more blessed are they who shall believe on your words, when ye shall testify that ye have seen me and that I am.*
>
> *Yea, blessed are they who shall believe on your words, and come down into the depth of humility, and be baptized in my name; for they shall be visited with a fire and the Holy Ghost, and shall receive a remission of their sins.*

Believe in Christ; believe in the words of the apostles; come down in the depths of humility; be baptized; receive the gift of the Holy Ghost; gain a remission of sins—all of which must happen if men are to be led into all truth—and then comes an understanding of all the Beatitudes. It was in such a setting—a setting of faith, of belief in the Son of God; a setting of miracles and healings and worship—that Jesus spoke the Sermon on the Mount both in Galilee and in the land Bountiful.

> *And he lifted up his eyes on his disciples, and said, Blessed are the poor; for theirs is the kingdom of God.*
>
> *Yea, blessed are the poor in spirit, who come unto me; for theirs is the kingdom of heaven.*

We'll go to the poor, like our Captain of old,
And visit the weary, the hungry, and cold;
We'll cheer up their hearts with the news that he bore,
And point them to Zion and life evermore.[2]

"To the poor the gospel is preached." (Luke 7:22.) "Hath not God chosen the poor of this world rich in faith, and heirs of the kingdom which he hath promised to them that love him?" (James 2:5.) The poor in spirit! If they come unto Christ, salvation is theirs; and it is so often easier for those who are not encumbered with the cares and burdens and riches of the world to cast off worldliness and set their hearts on the riches of eternity than it is for those who have an abundance of this world's goods.

> *Blessed are they who weep now; for they shall laugh.*
>
> *And again, blessed are all they that mourn, for they shall be comforted.*

Those who are bereft of loved ones, having learned the purposes of the Lord in the brief separation called death, shall be comforted. The peace that passeth understanding shall rest upon all those who have a knowledge of the plan of salvation. What greater comfort is there than to know that lost loved ones shall be returned to the family unit, and that all the saints shall reign in joy and peace forever? And further: When He comes again whose right it is to rule, he "shall wipe away all tears from their eyes; and there shall be no more death, neither sorrow, nor crying, neither shall there be any more pain." (Rev. 21:4.) They that mourn shall be comforted!

Blessed are the meek: for they shall inherit the earth.

As things are now constituted, the meek do not inherit the earth; even He who said of himself, "I am meek and lowly in heart" (Matt. 11:29) had in fact no place of his own to lay his head. This world's goods were of little moment to him, and he had neither gold nor silver nor houses nor lands nor kingdoms. Peter was even directed to catch a fish in whose mouth a coin was lodged, that a levied tax might be paid for the two of them. The meek—those who are the God-fearing and the righteous—seldom hold title to much of that which appertains to this present world. But there will be a day when the Lord shall come to make up his jewels; there will be a day when Abraham, Isaac, and Jacob, and the faithful of ancient Israel shall dwell again in old Canaan; and there will be also an eventual celestial day when "the poor and the meek of the earth shall inherit it." (D&C 88:17.)

Blessed are they who hunger now; for they shall be filled.

And blessed are all they that do hunger and thirst after righteousness; for they shall be filled with the Holy Ghost.

Filled with the Holy Ghost! As starving men crave a crust of bread, as choking men thirst for water, so do the righteous yearn for the Holy Ghost. The Holy Ghost is a Revelator; he is a Sanctifier; he reveals truth, and he cleanses human souls. He is the Spirit of Truth, and his baptism is one of fire; he burns dross and evil out of repentant souls as though by fire. The gift of the Holy Ghost is the greatest of all the gifts of God, as pertaining to this life; and those who enjoy that gift here and now, will inherit eternal life hereafter, which is the greatest of all the gifts of God in eternity.

Blessed are the merciful: for they shall obtain mercy.

Mercy is for the merciful. In that great day of restoration

and judgment, when every man is rewarded according to the deeds done in the flesh, those who have manifest mercy to their fellowmen here will be treated mercifully by the Merciful One. Those who have acquired the godly attribute of mercy here shall have mercy restored unto them again in that bright day.[3]

> *And blessed are all the pure in heart; for they shall see God.*

How glorious is the voice we hear from him! Man may see his Maker! Did not Abraham, Isaac, and Jacob see the Lord? Did not Moses and Aaron, Nadab and Abihu, and seventy of the elders of Israel see the God of Israel, under whose feet was a paved work of a sapphire stone? Was it not thus with Isaiah and Nephi, with Jacob and Moroni, and with mighty prophets without number in all ages? Is God a respecter of persons who will appear to one righteous person and withhold his face from another person of like spiritual stature? Is he not the same yesterday, today, and forever, dealing the same with all people, considering that all souls are equally precious in his sight? Did not Moses seek diligently to sanctify his people, while they were yet in the wilderness, that they might see the face of God and live? Does not the scripture say that the brother of Jared had such a perfect knowledge of God that he could not be kept from seeing within the veil? Why then should not the Lord Jesus invite all men to be as the prophets, to purify themselves so as to see the face of the Lord?

It is written: "Verily, thus saith the Lord: It shall come to pass that every soul who forsaketh his sins and cometh unto me, and calleth on my name, and obeyeth my voice, and keepeth my commandments, shall see my face and know that I am." (D&C 93:1.) How glorious the concept is! What a wondrous reality! The pure in heart—all the pure in heart—shall see God!

> *And blessed are all the peacemakers; for they shall be called the children of God.*

The gospel of peace makes men children of God! Christ

came to bring peace—peace on earth and good will to men. His gospel gives peace in this world and eternal life in the world to come. He is the Prince of peace. How beautiful upon the mountains are the feet of them who preach the gospel of peace, who say unto Zion: Thy God reigneth! Let there be peace on earth, and let it begin with his saints. By this shall all men know the Lord's disciples: They are peacemakers; they seek to compose difficulties; they hate war and love peace; they invite all men to forsake evil, overcome the world, flee from avarice and greed, stand in holy places, and receive for themselves that peace which passeth understanding, that peace which comes only by the power of the Spirit.

And these are they who are adopted into the family of God. They become the sons and daughters of him whose we are. They are born again. They take upon themselves a new name, the name of their new Father, the name of Christ. Those who believe in him have power to become his sons and his daughters. Truly the peacemakers shall be called the children of God!

> *Blessed are ye, when men shall hate you, and when they shall separate you from their company, and shall reproach you, and cast out your name as evil, for the Son of man's sake. Rejoice ye in that day, and leap for joy; for behold your reward shall be great in heaven; for in the like manner did their fathers unto the prophets.*
>
> *Blessed are all they that are persecuted for my name's sake; for theirs is the kingdom of heaven. And blessed are ye, when men shall revile you, and persecute you, and shall say all manner of evil against you falsely, for my sake. For ye shall have great joy, and be exceeding glad; for great shall be your reward in heaven; for so persecuted they the prophets which were before you.*

How could it be said better? Jesus is speaking to the members of his earthly kingdom. In our day that kingdom is The Church of Jesus Christ of Latter-day Saints. It is composed of those who have taken upon them the name of Christ—covenanting in the waters of baptism to honor that name and to do nothing that will hold it up to contempt or ridicule. It is composed of those who have forsaken the world; who have crucified the old man of sin; who have become humble, meek, submissive, willing to conform to all that the Lord requires of them.

And, of course, the world loves its own and hates the saints. The world is the carnal society created by evil men; it is made up of those who are carnal and sensual and devilish. Of course the world persecutes the saints; the very thing that makes them saints is their enmity toward the things of the world. Let the ungodly and the evildoers reproach the Lord's people; let them cry transgression against his saints; let persecution rage against those who bear the Lord's name; let true believers be reviled and evilly spoken of—all for his name's sake. So be it!

Do they face trials of cruel mockings and scourgings? Are they stoned, sawn asunder, slain with the sword? Are they destitute, afflicted, tormented? Are they cast into dens of lions and furnaces of fire? Are they slain in gladiatorial arenas, lighted as torches on the walls of Rome, crucified head downward? Are they driven from Ohio to Missouri, and from Missouri to Illinois, and from Illinois to a desert wilderness—leaving their Prophet and Patriarch in martyrs' graves? No matter! They do not live for this life alone, and great shall be their reward in heaven.

Such are the Beatitudes—insofar as they have been preserved for us—those blessed statements about blessedness. As with all our Lord's sayings, they were unlike and superior to the Rabbinical beatitudes of the day.[4] No doubt Jesus made many more beatific declarations either in this sermon or on other occasions. Such of his statements as "It is more blessed to give than to receive" would take on the nature of a true beatitude if it were phrased thus: "Blessed are all they who give all they have for the building up of the Lord's kingdom on earth, for they shall receive the riches of eternity in the world to come."

Quite properly we glory in the Beatitudes, as Jesus

himself gloried in them. Edersheim says they are the New Testament counterpart of the Ten Commandments, and that they "present to us, not the observance of the Law written on stone, but the realization of that Law which, by the Spirit, is written on the fleshly tables of the heart." (Edersheim 1:529.) But as we glory in their greatness—and all the blessings thereunto appertaining—we must not overlook the fact that Jesus appended to them certain curses, curses for those who continue to live after the manner of the world and who do not walk in that course which leads to blessedness.

But woe unto you that are rich! for ye have received your consolation.

Woe unto you that are full! for ye shall hunger.

Woe unto you that laugh now! for ye shall mourn and weep.

Woe unto you, when all men shall speak well of you! for so did their fathers to the false prophets.

If there is a blessing, there must needs be a cursing. There can be no light without darkness, no good without evil, no blessed heights of glory and honor unless there are also cursed depths of despair and damnation.

If the pure in heart shall see God, those whose hearts are impure shall be shut out of his presence. If the peacemakers shall be called the children of God, those who foment war shall be the children of Lucifer their father. If those who hunger and thirst after righteousness shall be filled with the Holy Ghost, those whose appetites are fed on carnal and evil food shall be filled with a worldly spirit that breeds evil deeds. And so on with reference to all of the Beatitudes. All things have their opposites, and there must needs be an opposition in all things.

Woe, then, unto the rich, Jesus says, the rich whose hearts are set on the things of this world; on the gold in the mountains and the cattle on the hills; on the merchant's goods and the spices coming in on a thousand ships—for they have already received their consolation, the consolation and rewards of this life, rather than the riches of eternity.

Woe unto those whose bellies are full; who have laid up provisions in granaries and storehouses; who have been concerned only with feeding the body—for their spirits, being unfed, shall hunger.

Woe unto those who laugh now, as they rejoice in the things of this world—for they shall mourn and weep in the day of judgment.

Woe unto those who are held in high esteem by worldly and evil people; who revel in the praise of ungodly men; who gain the plaudits of carnal people—for in such manner were the false prophets treated in days of old.

"Ye Are the Light of the World"

(*Matthew 5:13-16; JST, Matthew 5:15-18; 3 Nephi 12:13-16*)

We repeat: The Sermon on the Mount, including the Beatitudes, was delivered to true believers; to the Twelve Apostles of the Lamb (it was their ordination sermon); to the saints of the Most High God; to members of the Church of Jesus Christ; to people who had been baptized and who were in process of seeking the riches of eternity. To them—after holding out the blessed and sanctified wonders of gospel obedience, as these are stated in the Beatitudes—Jesus now says: "Ye are the salt of the earth. . . . Ye are the light of the world." That is to say: 'Ye are the choicest and best people on earth; and ye must now be an example to all men, that others, seeing your good works, shall come unto me and glorify your Father who is in heaven.' Our Lord's words, insofar as they have been preserved for us, are:

> *Verily, verily, I say unto you, I give unto you to be the salt of the earth; but if the salt shall lose its savor, wherewith shall the earth be salted? the salt shall thenceforth be good for nothing, but to be cast out, and to be trodden under foot of men.*
>
> *Verily, verily, I say unto you, I give unto you to be the light of the world; a city that is set on a hill cannot be hid.*
>
> *Behold, do men light a candle and put it under a*

bushel? Nay, but on a candlestick; and it giveth light to all that are in the house.

Therefore, let your light so shine before this world, that they may see your good works, and glorify your Father who is in heaven.

Salt and light, symbols of the saints: salt because it has a seasoning, purifying, preserving power; light because it manifests the good works and wise words of the true believers! The saints, as the salt of the earth, are set forth to season their fellowmen, to keep society free from corruption, to help their fellow beings become wholesome, pure, and acceptable before the Lord.[5] The saints, as the light of the world, are to set an example of good works and charitable deeds, so they may say to all men, as does their Master, 'Follow thou me; and I will lead you in sure paths here and to heights above the clouds hereafter.'[6]

That Christ is the Light of the World, no Christian doubts; what Jesus is now saying is that all his disciples should be even as he is. That upright people who keep the commandments are the salt of the earth, none question; but we might add that the Lord Jesus himself is the Salt of the Earth. The seasoning, sanctifying, edifying, preserving, uplifting influence of his gospel keeps all the obedient from corruption and decay and sorrow.

If the saints lose their seasoning power and no longer set examples of good works, they are thenceforth as other worldly people to whom salvation is denied. The saints are as a city set on a hill that is open to the view of all. Their good works lead others to the truth and to glorify their Creator, their Redeemer, and the Holy Spirit who testifies of the truth of all things.

NOTES

1. "The plain" of Luke 6:17 is better rendered "level spot," which translation brings the account into complete harmony with Matthew's statement that the sermon was delivered in a mountain, meaning on a level plateau in a mountainous area.

2. "Ye Elders of Israel," *Hymns*, no. 44.

3. This principle applies to mercy and every godly attribute, as also to carnality and devilishness and every evil thing, as Alma has so well said: "The meaning of the word restoration is to bring back again evil for evil, or carnal for carnal, or devilish for devilish—good for that which is good; righteous for that which is righteous; just for that which is just; merciful for that which is merciful. Therefore, my son, see that you are merciful unto your brethren; deal justly, judge righteously, and do good continually; and if ye do all these things then shall ye receive your reward; yea, ye shall have mercy restored unto you again; ye shall have justice restored unto you again; ye shall have a righteous judgment restored unto you again; and ye shall have good rewarded unto you again. For that which ye do send out shall return unto you again, and be restored; therefore, the word restoration more fully condemneth the sinner, and justifieth him not at all." (Alma 41:13-15.)

4. This applies to all that Jesus did and said—it was unlike and superior to the prevailing preachments and performances in the same fields. For instance, there are in the Talmud many graphic statements and wise sayings that, quoted out of context, have been interpreted by some to mean that the Talmud is an inspired work comparable to the New Testament. But, as Edersheim expresses it: "Take these in their connection and real meaning, and what a terrible awakening! Who, that has read half-a-dozen pages successively of any part of the Talmud, can feel otherwise than by turns shocked, pained, amused, or astounded? There is here wit and logic, quickness and readiness, earnestness and zeal, but by the side of it terrible profanity, uncleanness, superstition, and folly. Taken as a whole, it is not only utterly unspiritual, but anti-spiritual. . . . Taken not in abrupt sentences and quotations, but as a whole, it is so utterly and immeasurably unlike the New Testament, that it is not easy to determine which, as the case may be, is greater, the ignorance or the presumption of those who put them side by side. . . . He who has thirsted and quenched his thirst at the living fount of Christ's Teaching, can never again stoop to seek drink at the broken cisterns of Rabbinism." (Edersheim 1:525-26.)

5. "When men are called unto mine everlasting gospel, and covenant with an everlasting covenant," the Lord says, "they are accounted as the salt of the earth and the savor of men; They are called to be the savor of men; therefore, if that salt of the earth lose its savor, behold, it is thenceforth good for nothing only to be cast out and trodden under the feet of men." (D&C 101:38-40. See also D&C 103:9-10.)

6. "Behold I am the light; I have set an example for you," Jesus said to the Nephites. Then of their obligation, he added: "Hold up your light that it may shine unto the world. Behold I am the light which ye shall hold up—that which ye have seen me do." (3 Ne. 18:16, 24.)

JESUS DISCOURSES ON THE LAW OF MOSES

The law is fulfilled
that was given unto Moses.
Behold, I am he that gave the law,
and I am he who covenanted with my people Israel;
therefore, the law in me is fulfilled,
for I have come to fulfil the law;
therefore it hath an end.
Behold, I do not destroy the prophets,
for as many as have not been fulfilled in me,
verily I say unto you,
shall all be fulfilled.
And because I said unto you
that old things have passed away,
I do not destroy that which hath been spoken
concerning things which are to come.
For behold, the covenant
which I have made with my people
is not all fulfilled;
but the law which was given unto Moses
hath an end in me.
Behold, I am the law, and the light.
Look unto me, and endure to the end,

and ye shall live; for unto him
that endureth to the end
will I give eternal life.
Behold, I have given unto you the commandments;
therefore keep my commandments.
And this is the law and the prophets,
for they truly testified of me.
(3 Ne. 15:4-10.)[1]

Jesus Fulfills and Honors the Law
(*Matthew 5:17-20; JST, Matthew 5:19-21; 3 Nephi 12:18-20, 46-47*)

Jesus has now spoken the Beatitudes; he is about to go forward in his glorious mountain sermon with some very plain statements about the law of Moses. A sweet spirit has filled our souls as we have heard and felt the sublime truths given in the Beatitudes. We cannot, however, avoid contrasting that which occurred on the Mount of Beatitudes with the heavenly manifestations displayed on Mount Sinai when the law itself was given.

Jesus as Jehovah spoke to Moses amid the fires and thunders and quakings of Sinai; smoke ascended as from a furnace; all Israel trembled at the display; and the Lord, in majesty, with a finger of fire, wrote his holy law for that man whom he had chosen to lead his people. Below were the camps of Israel, with their lowing cattle and bleating sheep, and with all the confusion of moving multitudes.

The law then given was a law of eternal verities—first, the gospel itself, which the people rejected, and, later, the lesser law; a law, however, that changed the course of history forever; a law that revealed Jehovah to his people and commanded them—at sword's point, as it were—to worship him or be damned. The crescendo of sounding trumpets proclaimed: 'Thou shalt not worship false gods, or violate the Sabbath, or commit adultery, or kill, or do any wickedness.' It set forth, as illustrated in Exodus 21 and 22, the minutia and detail and strictness and severity of the divine will where his slave-like people were concerned. For instance: "He that curseth his father, or his mother, shall surely be put to death. . . . Thou shalt give life for life, Eye for eye, tooth for tooth, hand for hand, foot for foot, Burning for burning, wound for wound, stripe for stripe. . . . If an ox gore a man or a woman, that they die: then the ox shall be surely stoned, and his flesh shall not be eaten; but the owner of the ox shall be quit. But if the ox were wont to push with his horn in time past, and it hath been testified to his owner, and he hath not kept him in, but that he hath killed a man or a woman; the ox shall be stoned, and his owner also shall be put to death." And so on and so on and so on.

Jehovah as Jesus spoke to the Twelve and to the multitude in the calm serenity of a summer morning, on a grassy plateau on the Mount of Beatitudes. Below them, in silver splendor, lay the rippling waters of the Sea of Galilee; all was calm; a spirit of peace and quietude overshadowed the worshipful throng. That which Jesus then spoke was not written with burnished swords of steel, but came forth as the gentle breeze of a cool and pleasant evening. There was no thunderous "Thou shalt not," only a soft spoken plea, "Here is the way; walk ye in it." It was a new day, a new order, a new way, a new gospel; the patterns of the future were being formed; from henceforth, through all generations, the Messiah and his disciples would teach correct principles and let all who heard govern themselves. Such is the perfect gospel standard.

And so now—as the Sermon on the Mount continues—Jesus, leaving the sweet bliss and serene blessedness of the Beatitudes, turns their thoughts to the harsh realities of the law of Moses; to the yoke that hung heavily on their bowed heads and aching shoulders; to these scrupulosities and performances by which they were bound. This yoke, with all its burdensome rituals and restrictions, was about to be removed by their Redeemer and Deliverer. The set time for him to fulfill the law and make an end to all its curtailing provisions was not far distant. His chosen Twelve in particular, and all his newly won disciples in general, must condition their minds to reject the old and receive the new, to turn their hearts from Moses, who bore record of the Messiah, to Jesus, who was the Messiah.

"Think not that I am come to destroy the law, or the prophets," Jesus said. For nearly fifteen hundred years all the faithful in Israel—and all the souls they had won from their Gentile neighbors and oftimes overlords—had bowed their backs and harnessed their strength as they struggled to keep the law of Moses the man of God. For all these years the law and the prophets had testified of a coming Messiah; the performances of the law were types and shadows of his ministry and mission; the words of the prophets were inspired utterances that bore the same witness. Now the Messiah had come, and soon he would—according to the promises—atone for the sins of the world and thus fulfill the law.

Nothing was to be lost; no act of the past would be shunted aside or deemed useless. The law had been the most glorious system of worship on earth during the period of its ascendancy. But now it was to be replaced; the schoolmaster's work was done, and the students of righteousness, yet in the elementary grades, were about to enter the gospel university where the fulness of revealed truth awaited their study.

"I am not come to destroy, but to fulfill," Jesus continued. "For verily I say unto you, Heaven and earth must pass away, but one jot or one tittle shall in no wise pass from the law, until all be fulfilled."

Even his disciples must continue to keep the law for the present. Sacrifices were still the order of the day. And he, with his disciples, would yet keep that final Passover feast when the sacrament of the Lord's Supper would be instituted; together they would then eat the paschal lamb, in similitude of the sacrifice of the Lamb of God; and they would do it during the last moments of the law's legal continuance; they would do it while the true Lamb of God was en route to Golgotha to be sacrificed. But for now, though true believers were beginning to receive the higher principles of the higher law, the law itself was still in force.

"Whosoever, therefore, shall break one of these least commandments, and shall teach men so to do, he shall in no wise be saved in the kingdom of heaven; but whosoever shall do and teach these commandments of the law until it be fulfilled, the same shall be called great, and shall be saved in the kingdom of heaven."

Then came this sobering indictment against their Jewish leaders: "For I say unto you, That except your righteousness shall exceed the righteousness of the scribes and Pharisees, ye shall in no case enter into the kingdom of heaven." What an awesome responsibility is assumed by self-styled ministers who teach the traditions of their fathers rather than the pure principles of revealed religion, and who thereby teach people to break "one of these least commandments," as it were!

When Jesus gave the Sermon in Bountiful to the Nephites, the law had been fulfilled. Gethsemane and the cross were past; the blood of the last authorized paschal lamb had been spilt in similitude of his eternal sacrifice; sacrifices by the shedding of blood were no longer required or accepted. "For verily I say unto you, one jot nor one tittle hath not passed away from the law," Jesus then said, "but in me it hath all been fulfilled."

> *And behold, I have given you the law and the commandments of my Father, that ye shall believe in me, and that ye shall repent of your sins, and come unto me with a broken heart and a contrite spirit. Behold, ye have the commandments before you, and the law is fulfilled.*
>
> *Therefore come unto me and be ye saved; for verily I say unto you, that except ye shall keep my commandments, which I have commanded you at this time, ye shall in no case enter into the kingdom of heaven. . . .*

Therefore those things which were of old time, which were under the law, in me are all fulfilled.

Old things are done away, and all things have become new.[2]

He Contrasts the Law of Moses and the Law of Christ

(*Matthew 5:21-47; JST, Matthew 5:23-26, 29, 31-34, 42-43, 50; 3 Nephi 12:21-37, 48; Luke 6:27-30, 32-35; 12:58-59; JST, Luke 6:27-30, 33*)

Jesus now sets a pattern for all other preachers of righteousness. He illustrates his profound and sobering concept relative to the law of Moses, and he states additional gospel concepts that grow out of his illustrations. These all are twelve in number.

1. *Murder and anger.*

Moses' law—more properly Jehovah's law given through Moses—forbade murder. "Thou shalt not kill; and whosoever shall kill, shall be in danger of the judgment of God." The same prohibition applies under the gospel law, but this higher law, in addition, raises a higher standard. It strikes at the cause of murder, which is anger. The man whose fired bullet misses its human target is as guilty as the marksman whose bullet brings death to the intended victim. It is the feeling one has in his heart that counts, not the eventuality that occurs. "Whosoever hateth his brother is a murderer: and ye know that no murderer hath eternal life abiding in him." (1 Jn. 3:15.) And so Jesus says: "But I say unto you that whosoever is angry with his brother, shall be in danger of his judgment."

Let us envision at this point, if we may, what Jesus is doing here and in all the illustrations that follow. He is saying: 'Jehovah of old—through Moses—said such and such; but now I say unto you something more or something different.' He is placing himself on a par with the God of Israel; he is saying: 'God Almighty did or said thus and so, but I, Jesus, add to, amend, alter, delete from, and change the word of God.' It is blasphemy, pure and simple, for a mortal so to speak; but, no, in this case it is an affirmation of Messiahship, and Jesus is guiltless in his affirmations, for he is Jehovah; and if Jehovah edits Jehovah, so be it—who has a better right!

2. *Profanity.*

Further: "Whosoever shall say to his brother, Raca, or Rabcah, shall be in danger of the council; and whosoever shall say to his brother, Thou fool, shall be in danger of hellfire." That is, profane and vulgar epithets and expressions—for such, in the Jewish culture, were the nature of the words here recited—when hurled at our fellowmen lead to damnation. The fires of Gehenna burn in the hearts of those whose minds think and speak evilly against their brethren. Among the abominations that the Lord hates is listed "an heart that deviseth wicked imaginations." (Prov. 6:16-19.) Men curse themselves when they think and speak ill of their brethren. Profane, vulgar, contemptuous, and unholy expressions degrade their author more than they taint the soul of the hearer.

3. *Reconciliation between brethren.*

We must do all in our power to assuage the hurt feelings of our brethren if we ourselves are to stand blameless before the Lord. "If ye shall come unto me, or shall desire to come unto me," Jesus says, "or if thou bring thy gift to the altar, and there rememberest that thy brother hath aught against thee, Leave thou thy gift before the altar, and go thy way unto thy brother, and first be reconciled to thy brother, and then come and offer thy gift." That is, if we choose to come unto Christ and to be one with him in his fold; if we bring our gifts to his holy altar, that our wealth and means may be used to further his work on earth; and if we then remember that others have aught against us, our obligation, more important than the gifts we bestow, is to heal the wounded feelings of our brethren. Jesus speaks here not of our anger or ill feeling toward others, but of their ill feelings, for whatever cause, against us. No matter that we are the one who has been wronged. The gospel standard calls for us to search out those whose anger is kindled against us and to do all in our power to douse the fires of hate and animosity. "Go thy way unto thy brother, and first be reconciled to thy brother," he said to the Nephites, "and then come unto me with full purpose of heart, and I will receive you."

4. *Avoiding legal entanglements.*

With particular reference to the Twelve and others engaged in missionary work, in ministerial service, and in building up the kingdom, Jesus said: "Agree with thine adversary quickly, whiles thou art in the way with him; lest at any time the adversary deliver thee to the judge, and the judge deliver thee to the officer, and thou be cast into prison. Verily I say unto thee, Thou shalt by no means come out thence, till thou hast paid the uttermost farthing." It was more important, in the social and political circumstances then prevailing, for the Lord's servants to suffer legal wrongs than that their ministries be hindered or halted by legal processes.

5. *Adultery.*

Mosaic fiat decreed: "Thou shalt not commit adultery." Jesus, who himself had given the decree to "them of old time," now says: "But I say unto you, That whosoever looketh on a woman to lust after her hath committed adultery with her already in his heart." His is now a higher law; it is not the immoral act alone that the gospel condemns—it is also the lewd and lustful desires that lead to its commission. "He that looketh on a woman to lust after her, or if any shall commit adultery in their hearts, they shall not have the Spirit, but shall deny the faith and shall fear." (D&C 63:16.)

6. *Casting sins away.*

Jesus has spoken of sins of the heart and of the mind and of the mouth. Anger is as murder; profanity leads to hell; ill feelings against our brethren canker the soul; lewdness, evil thoughts—adultery committed in the heart—are as the very act itself. Gospel standards govern what is in the hearts of men as well as the deeds they do. In this setting, he then says:

> *Behold, I give unto you a commandment, that ye suffer none of these things to enter into your heart;*
>
> *For it is better that ye should deny yourselves of these things, wherein ye will take up your cross, than that ye should be cast into hell.*

Based on this principle, the Master Teacher uses two parabolic illustrations that dramatize the severity—even harshness—of action that should be taken to rid ourselves of the sins involved and of all sin. "Wherefore," that is, in the light of the principles just enunciated, "if thy right eye offend thee, pluck it out and cast it from thee; for it is profitable for thee that one of thy members should perish, and not that thy whole body should be cast into hell. Or if thy right hand offend thee, cut it off and cast it from thee; for it is profitable for thee that one of thy members should perish, and not that thy whole body should be cast into hell." These statements about the eye and the hand were not included in the recorded account of the Sermon in Bountiful.

The severity of such a course—plucking out an eye or severing a hand—staggers reality. Scarcely is there an affliction calling for such a drastic operation. No suffering invalid parts with an eye or a hand unless life itself is at stake. And so, having selected with care the most drastic of all remedies, Jesus reveals his true meaning:

> *And now this I speak, a parable concerning your sins; wherefore, cast them from you, that ye may not be hewn down and cast into the fire.*

Have there ever been such teachings as this to show the need to cast away our sins, to cast them away lest we die spiritually, to cast them away lest our eternal souls be themselves cast into fire?

7. *Divorce.*

Under the law of Moses, divorce came easily; but recently freed from Egyptian slavery, the chosen race had yet to attain the social, cultural, and spiritual stability that exalts marriage to its proper place in the eternal scheme of things. Men were empowered to divorce their wives for any unseemly thing. "It hath been said, Whosoever shall put away his wife, let him give her a writing of divorcement."

No such low and base standard is acceptable under gospel law. Thus Jesus summarized his perfect marriage order by saying: "But I say unto you, That whosoever shall put away his wife, saving for the cause of fornication, causeth her to commit adultery: and whosoever shall marry her that is divorced committeth adultery." Divorce is totally foreign to celestial standards, a verity that Jesus will one day expound in more detail to the people of Jewry. For now, as far as the record reveals, he merely specifies the high law that his people should live, but that is beyond our capability even today. If husbands and wives lived the law as the Lord would have them live it, they would neither do nor say the things that would even permit the fleeting thought of divorce to enter the mind of their eternal companions. Though we today have the gospel, we have yet to grow into that high state of marital association where marrying a divorced person constitutes adultery. The Lord has not yet given us the high standard he here named as that which ultimately will replace the Mosaic practice of writing a bill of divorcement.

8. *Gospel oaths.*

Here again we come to a standard of conduct that—geared to the needs of various cultures and conditions—has varied, with divine approval, from one age to the next. Abraham and the ancients, who lived by gospel standards, were permitted to take oaths—to swear in the Lord's name, thus certifying that they would act or speak in a named way. Such a certification guaranteed their words because the oath made God their partner, and God cannot lie or fail. The words they then spoke became the Lord's words and were accepted as true; and the deeds they vowed by an oath to do became the Lord's performances, and they must be done at the peril of one's life, for God has all power and he cannot fail in any particular to do that which he is bound to do.

Today it is the practice among Christian people to swear with an oath to tell the truth, the whole truth, and nothing but the truth in certain judicial proceedings. Under the Mosaic law the taking of oaths was so common and covered such a variety of circumstances that, in practice, little verity attended statements that were not made with an oath. "If a man vow a vow unto the Lord, or swear an oath to bind his soul with a bond; he shall not break his word, he shall do according to all that proceedeth out of his mouth." (Num. 30:2.) And so Jesus, rejecting the old and proclaiming the new, said: "And again it is written, thou shalt not forswear thyself, but shalt perform unto the Lord thine oaths; But I say unto you, Swear not at all; neither by heaven; for it is God's throne: Nor by the earth; for it is his footstool: neither by Jerusalem; for it is the city of the great King. Neither shalt thou swear by thy head, because thou canst not make one hair white or black. But let your communication be Yea, yea; Nay, nay; for whatsoever cometh of more than these is evil."

Under the perfect law of Christ every man's word is his bond, and all spoken statements are as true as though an oath attended each spoken word.

9. *Retaliation.*

Retaliation—with the inevitable bitterness and smallness of soul that attends it—cannot do other than keep hatred alive in the souls of men. If a man gouge out the eye of his neighbor, what benefit accrues to the wounded person if he retaliate by gouging out the eye of the offender? Has he enlarged his own soul, or has he permitted it to shrivel to the same smallness as the soul of his attacker? "Ye have heard that it hath been said, An eye for an eye, and a tooth for a tooth," Jesus said, using words, found in the law of Moses, that summarized both the letter and the spirit of those ancient rules. "But I say unto you, That ye resist not evil," he continued, "but whosoever shall smite thee on thy right cheek, turn to him the other also." Luke preserves for us the more complete account and meaning of Jesus' saying on this point: "And unto him who smiteth thee on the cheek, offer also the other; or, in other words, it is better to offer the other, than to revile again. And him who taketh away thy cloak, forbid not to take thy coat also. For it is better that thou suffer thine enemy to take these things, than to contend with him. Verily I say unto you, Your heavenly Father who seeth in secret, shall bring that wicked one into judgment."

"Contention leads to bitterness and smallness of soul; persons who contend with each other shrivel up spiritually and are in danger of losing their salvation. So important is it to avoid this evil that Jesus expects his saints to suffer oppression and wrong rather than lose their inner peace and serenity through contention. 'He that hath the spirit of contention is not of me,' he told the Nephites, 'but is of the devil, who is the father of contention, and he stirreth up the hearts of men to contend with anger, one with another. (3 Ne. 11:29.)' " (*Commentary* 1:228.)

10. *Persecution by legal process.*

To his apostles and ministers—those whose talents and strength must be devoted, without hindrance, to the preaching of the gospel and the building up of the kingdom—Jesus had this special counsel: "And if any man will sue thee at the law, and take away thy coat, let him have it; and if he sue thee again, let him have thy cloak also. And whosoever shall compel thee to go a mile, go with him a mile; and whosoever shall compel thee to go with him twain, thou shalt go with him twain. Give to him that asketh of thee, and from him that would borrow of thee turn not thou away."

Nothing is so important as the spread of truth and the establishment of the cause of righteousness. The petty legal processes of that day must not be permitted to impede the setting up of the new kingdom.

11. *The law of love.*

Ye have heard that it hath been said, Thou shalt love thy neighbour, and hate thine enemy.

> *But I say unto you, Love your enemies, bless them that curse you, do good to them that hate you, and pray for them which despitefully use you, and persecute you;*
>
> *That ye may be the children of your Father which is in heaven: for he maketh his sun to rise on the evil and on the good, and sendeth rain on the just and on the unjust.*
>
> *For if ye love them which love you, what reward have ye? do not even the publicans the same?*
>
> *And if ye salute your brethren only, what do ye more than others? do not even the publicans so?*

Of olden time, and in ages past, Israel's enemies had been God's enemies, and the Gentile nations were kept away at sword's point; had it not been so, the chosen people would have been swallowed up by the world. Their world was one of force and violence in which whole nations were forced to believe what their rulers decreed or be destroyed from off the face of the earth. This tight grip on the minds of men has now been loosened, and now the gospel is to go to the world—all men everywhere are to hear the word. Israel must love the Gentiles, for they are to be adopted into the family of Jehovah.

All men will be judged by what is in their own hearts. If their souls are full of hatred and cursings, such characteristics shall be restored to them in the resurrection. Loving one's enemies and blessing one's cursers perfects the soul. Such perfection is the object of the gospel, and of it Jesus now chooses to speak.

12. *Perfection.*

As a climax to all his sayings contrasting the old Mosaic order with the new gospel law, and by way of commandment to all those who would forsake the old and cleave unto the new, Jesus proclaimed to the Jews:

> *Ye are therefore commanded to be perfect, even as your Father who is in heaven is perfect.*

To his Nephite brethren—to whom he spoke after his resurrection, after he had risen in immortal glory with a celestial body, after he had received all power in heaven and on earth—his proclamation was couched in these words:

Therefore I would that ye should be perfect even as I, or your Father who is in heaven is perfect.

Perfection—a relative degree of perfection in this life, and eternal perfection, the kind possessed by the Father, in the life to come—these are gained by full obedience to the fulness of gospel law. This is the doctrine of exaltation, the doctrine that as God now is, man may become; this is the doctrine that mortals have power to become like Deity in power, might, and dominion; in wisdom, knowledge, and truth; in love, charity, mercy, integrity, and in all holy attributes. "Ye shall be even as I am, and I am even as the Father; and the Father and I are one," Jesus said to certain faithful Nephite disciples. (3 Ne. 28:10.)

If the newly called saints overcome anger; if they are reconciled with their brethren; if they rise above lewd and lascivious thoughts and commit no adultery in their hearts; if they cast away their sins, as though severing an offending hand; if their every spoken word is true as though sworn with an oath; if they do not retaliate when others offend them; if they turn the other cheek and resist not evil impositions; if they love their enemies, bless those who curse them, and pray for those who despitefully use them and persecute them—if they do all these things, they will become perfect even as their Eternal Father is perfect. And perfection comes not by the law of Moses, but by the gospel. "If therefore perfection were by the Levitical priesthood, (for under it the people received the law,) what further need was there that another priest should rise after the order of Melchisedec, and not be called after the order of Aaron?" (Heb. 7:11), Paul asks. But—thanks be to God— "another priest," Jesus the Son of God, arose; and ministering in all the glory of the gospel, he is now fulfilling the old law and inviting men to believe and obey the new law.

At this point he is somewhat less than halfway through the Sermon on the Mount. Now he turns from contrasting the old and the new to an out-and-out proclamation of new and glorious standards.

NOTES

1. These words were spoken by the Lord to the Nephites after his resurrection, and hence after the law of Moses was fulfilled, a situation that did not prevail when he discoursed on the same subject near Capernaum in his Jewish Sermon on the Mount.

2. As it was with the Nephites, so it is with all who have received the word of truth in the same measure to which it came to them: 'Except all such keep the gospel commandments, which are thus offered to them, they shall in no case enter into the kingdom of heaven.' Salvation for the dead is for those only who would have received and lived the gospel with all their hearts had the principles been offered to them while they dwelt in mortality.

JESUS DISCOURSES ON GOSPEL STANDARDS

Good and upright is the Lord:
therefore will he teach sinners in the way.
The meek will he guide in judgment:
and the meek will he teach his way.
And all the paths of the Lord
are mercy and truth
unto such as keep his covenant
and his testimonies. (Ps. 25:8-10.)

Jesus Saith: 'Care for the Poor'

(*3 Nephi 13:1-4; Matthew 6:1-4; JST, Matthew 6:1, 3*)

A mighty sermon is in progress; Jesus is speaking by the power of the Holy Ghost; we are hearing wondrous words—words of light and truth and revelation. Our minds are open, our hearts are receptive, and our souls are afire with the spirit of everlasting life that attends each spoken thought. He is now counseling us to walk as becometh saints and to do the things that his disciples in all ages have always done. His next subsermon is: 'Care for the worthy poor; give alms in righteousness; impart of your substance to those in need; give generously because you love the Lord and your fellowmen.'

"Verily, verily, I say that I would that ye should do alms

unto the poor," he says. It is right; it is good; it is the will of the Master—we should care for the worthy poor among us. As long as greed and selfishness find place among us mortals, there will also be poor among us. And it is the will of the Lord that the poor among his people receive their just wants and needs. "It is my purpose to provide for my saints," he says, "for all things are mine. But it must needs be done in mine own way; and behold this is the way that I, the Lord, have decreed to provide for my saints, that the poor shall be exalted, in that the rich are made low. For the earth is full, and there is enough and to spare. . . . Therefore, if any man shall take of the abundance which I have made, and impart not his portion, according to the law of my gospel, unto the poor and the needy, he shall, with the wicked, lift up his eyes in hell, being in torment." (D&C 104:15-18.)[1]

"But take heed that ye do not your alms before men to be seen of them; otherwise ye have no reward of your Father who is in heaven." Poverty or wealth are too often the happenstance of climate or geography or war. Some men are born to wealth, others to slavery. Today's rich may be tomorrow's paupers. And alms should not be given to exalt the giver, but to save the recipient. "Therefore when thou doest thine alms, do not sound a trumpet before thee, as the hypocrites do in the synagogues and in the streets, that they may have glory of men. Verily I say unto you, They have their reward. But when thou doest alms, let it be unto thee as thy left hand not knowing what thy right hand doeth; That thine alms may be in secret: and thy Father which seeth in secret himself shall reward thee openly."

Jesus Teaches Men How to Pray

(*Matthew 6:5-15; JST, Matthew 6:7, 10-14, 16; 3 Nephi 13:5-15; Mark 11:25-26; Luke 11:1-8; JST, Luke 11:4-5*)

Prayer and works of charity go hand in hand. Amulek, in a moving sermon, calls upon men to pray unto the Lord for temporal and spiritual blessings; to pray in secret and in public; to pray vocally and in their hearts. Then he says: "After ye have done all these things, if ye turn away the needy, and the naked, and visit not the sick and afflicted, and impart of your substance, if ye have, to those who stand in need—I say unto you, if ye do not any of these things, behold, your prayer is vain, and availeth you nothing, and ye are as hypocrites who do deny the faith. Therefore, if ye do not remember to be charitable, ye are as dross, which the refiners do cast out." (Alma 34:17-29.)

Jesus, in his Sermon on the Mount, turns from almsgiving to prayer. Again, it is the will of the Lord that his people should pray. They are to pray to the Father, in the name of the Son, by the power of the Spirit; they are to thank the Lord for all they have received and to importune before his throne for all that in wisdom should be theirs. Jesus does not now give them the whole law of prayer, but he does chart for them a course which, if pursued, will save them from the prayer failures of the Pharisees and lead them to an eventual full understanding of the true order of prayer.

"And when thou prayest, thou shalt not be as the hypocrites are: for they love to pray standing in the synagogues and in the corners of the streets, that they may be seen of men. Verily I say unto you, They have their reward." Devout Jews, at set times, faced Jerusalem, covered their heads, cast their eyes downward, and ostentatiously went through the ritual of prayer. If the hour of prayer found them in the streets, so much the better, for all men would see their devoutness! To attract attention by saying one's own prayers aloud in the synagogue was not uncommon. Such were among the practices of the day.

"But thou"—who hast come into the fold of Christ, and who thereby know better than to follow these mocking imitations of true prayer—"when thou prayest, enter into thy closet, and when thou hast shut thy door, pray to thy Father which is in secret; and thy Father which seeth in secret shall reward thee openly." And further: "When ye pray, use not vain repetitions, as the hypocrites do; for they think that they shall be heard for their much speaking." The repetitious chants, the thoughtless "Hail Mary's," and the memorized "Our Father's" of modern Catholicism, the repeated mouthings of the poetic phrases of the prayer book—vain repetitions!—these are included in what Jesus here condemns. Prayers that ascend beyond the ceiling, to be heard before the Throne in the sidereal heavens, must be uttered "with all the energy of heart," as Mormon's colloquial expression puts it. (Moro. 7:48.)

"Be not ye therefore like unto them: for your Father knoweth what things ye have need of, before ye ask him." How then shall the saints pray? "After this manner therefore pray ye," Jesus says:

Our Father who art in heaven, Hallowed be thy name.

Thy kingdom come. Thy will be done on earth, as it is done in heaven.

Give us this day, our daily bread.

And forgive us our trespasses, as we forgive those who trespass against us.

And suffer us not to be led into temptation, but deliver us from evil.

For thine is the kingdom, and the power, and the glory, forever and ever, Amen.

Jesus did not say: 'This is the prayer to use; memorize it; say it by rote,' but he gave a pattern, a model, a type. 'Pray after this manner; in such simple words as these; in this general way; without ostentation. Call upon your Eternal Father, and ask him for your needs, both great and small.' And how wondrous are the words he used!

Our Father who art in heaven. God is our Father, the father of our spirits; we are his children, his offspring, literally. We lived in his presence, dwelt in his courts, and have seen his face. We were as well acquainted with him then as we are with our mortal fathers now. He is a holy man, has a body of flesh and bones, and dwells in a heavenly abode. When we approach his throne in prayer, we think—not alone that he is the Almighty, by whose word the earth, the sidereal heavens, and the universe came into being, but that he is a gracious and loving Father whose chief interest and concern is his family, and that he wants all his children to love and serve him and to become like him. Perfect prayer manifests our personal relationship to him who hears and answers the petitions of the faithful.

Hallowed be thy name. 'We approach thee in awe—reverentially—in the spirit of worship and thanksgiving, and we praise thy holy name. Thou art glorious beyond anything we can envision; all that is good we ascribe unto thee, and we desire to consecrate our life and being unto thee, for thou hast made us, and we are thine.'

Thy kingdom come. Thy will be done on earth, as it is in heaven. Thy kingdom: the earthly kingdom of God which is the Church. *Thy kingdom:* the millennial kingdom, the kingdom of heaven, which shall be when there is a new heaven and a new earth whereon dwelleth righteousness. These are the kingdoms for which we pray. After Jesus' resurrection and before his ascension, the newly ordained apostles, who by that time will be seasoned and tempered as few men have ever been, will ask him: "Lord, wilt thou at this time restore again the kingdom to Israel?" (Acts 1:6.) And even in our day, the faithful continue to pray: "May the kingdom of God go forth, that the kingdom of heaven may come, that thou, O God, mayest be glorified in heaven so on earth, that thine enemies may be subdued; for thine is the honor, power and glory, forever and ever." (D&C 65:6.)

'Thy kingdom come! Let it be, O Lord, for in that glorious millennial day; in that day when Zion shall cover the earth, when all Israel shall be gathered home from their long dispersion, when every corruptible thing shall have been consumed, when the vineyard shall have been burned and few men left—then shall thy will be done on earth as it is in heaven. May we, O Lord, prepare for that day by living as though it were here.'

Give us this day our daily bread. 'But our concerns are not alone for the promised day of triumph and glory when thy people shall prevail in all the earth. We need food, clothing, and shelter, health of body, and strength of mind.' Our daily wants must be supplied, and he who notes the sparrow's fall will also provide manna for his people from day to day. He calls upon us to sow and reap and harvest and bake and eat. The concerns of daily life, however trivial, are the concerns of Omnipotence, and we are to rely upon him in faith for all things.

And forgive us our trespasses, as we forgive those who trespass against us. Or, as it is otherwise rendered—less perfectly, we feel—"Forgive us our debts, as we forgive our debtors"; or, yet again: "Forgive us our sins; for we also forgive every one that is indebted to us." "For if ye forgive men their trespasses, who trespass against you, your heavenly Father will also forgive you; but if ye forgive not men their trespasses, neither will your heavenly Father forgive you your trespasses." When he judges whose judgment is just, he will, as it is written, "recompense unto every man according to his work, and measure to every man according to the measure which he has measured to his fellow man." (D&C 1:10.) We judge ourselves; forgive and be forgiven; sow mercy and reap the same, for every seed brings forth after his own kind. "Ye ought to forgive one another; for he that forgiveth not his brother his trespasses standeth condemned before the Lord; for there remaineth in him the greater sin." (D&C 64:1-14.)[2]

And suffer us not to be led into temptation, but deliver us from evil. "Lead us not into temptation." The Lord does not lead us into temptation, except in the sense that he has placed us here in a probationary estate where temptation is the order of the day. We are here in mortality to be tried and tested; to see if we will keep the commandments; to overcome the world. We are here to learn how to bridle our passions and control every lustful and evil desire. None of us want to be tested beyond our capacity to resist; we want to be delivered from evil, to flee from the presence of sin, and to go where goodness and righteousness are. The trials of life are difficult enough without any of us placing ourselves in a position where sin and evil are made attractive. Foolish indeed is that man who, intending to remain morally clean, yet exposes his mind to pornographic things that in their nature invite lustful thoughts and deeds into his life.

For thine is the kingdom, and the power, and the glory, forever and ever. All things are the Lord's. His is the kingdom—both the earthly kingdom, which is the Church, and that glorious realm of celestial rest prepared for his saints. His is the power—nothing is too hard for the Lord; he is omnipotent; he it is who will change this earth into a heaven, and he it is who will raise lowly mortals to that eternal exaltation which makes of man a god. His is the glory—that is, the dominion, the exaltation, and the endless kingdoms; and also, the light and truth and infinite wisdom and knowledge he possesses.

How glorious it is to address such a holy and exalted person by the greatest of all titles, Father, and to be privileged to have audience with him on our own invitation, anytime we pray in faith with all the strength and energy of our souls!

The Lord's Prayer, as we have come to call these expressive words, spoken by Jesus as part of the Sermon on the Mount (as we are aware from Matthew and 3 Nephi) was also recorded by Luke—apparently, however, as given by Jesus on a different occasion. To his account, Luke appends these instructive words of Jesus: "And he said unto them, Your heavenly Father will not fail to give unto you whatsoever ye ask of him. And he spake a parable, saying, Which of you shall have a friend, and shall go unto him at midnight, and say unto him, Friend, lend me three loaves; For a friend of mine has come to me in his journey, and I have nothing to set before him; And he from within shall answer and say, Trouble me not: the door is now shut, and my children are with me in bed; I cannot rise and give thee. I say unto you, Though he will not rise and give him because he is his friend, yet because of his importunity, he will rise and give him as many as he needeth."

"Lay Up for Yourselves Treasures in Heaven"

(*Matthew 6:16-24; JST, Matthew 6:22; Luke 11:33-36; 12:33-34; JST, Luke 11:37; 12:36; 3 Nephi 13:16-24*)

Jesus now says a few well-chosen words about fasting, about laying up treasures in heaven, and about seeking spiritual light.

In all ages the Lord has called upon his people to fast and pray and seek him with all their strength and power. Fasting—the abstaining from food and drink for a designated period—gives a man a sense of his utter dependence upon the Lord so that he is in a better frame of mind to get in tune with the Spirit. Moses and Jesus both fasted for forty days as they sought that oneness with the Father out of which great spiritual strength comes. As with almost all else, however, fasting among the Jews no longer served its true purpose; it had become degenerate, self-serving, and ostentatious. Jesus expected his new followers to fast—not as the Pharisees, but in a true spirit of worship and self-effacement.

"When ye fast," he said, thus endorsing fasting as such, and thus counseling his disciples that they should so do, "be not, as the hypocrites, of a sad countenance: for they disfigure their faces, that they may appear unto men to fast. Verily I say unto you, They have their reward." Their fathers—rebellious in spirit, reproachful of prophetic counsel—had fasted "for strife and debate, and to smite with the fist of wickedness," and to make—ostentatiously—their voice "heard on high." (Isa. 58:1-4.) "But thou, when thou fastest," Jesus instructed, "anoint thine head, and wash thy face; That thou appear not unto men to fast, but unto the Father which is in secret: and thy Father, which seeth in secret, shall reward thee openly."

"While yet on earth men may lay up treasures in heaven.

These treasures, earned here and now in mortality, are in effect deposited to our eternal bank account in heaven where eventually they will be reinherited again in immortality. Treasures in heaven are the character, perfections, and attributes which men acquire by obedience to law. Thus, those who gain such attributes of godliness as knowledge, faith, justice, judgment, mercy, and truth, will find these same attributes restored to them again in immortality. 'Whatever principle of intelligence we attain unto in this life, it will rise with us in the resurrection.' (D&C 130:18.) The greatest treasure it is possible to inherit in heaven consists in gaining the continuation of the family unit in the highest heaven of the celestial world." (*Commentary* 1:239-40; Alma 41:13-15; D&C 130:18.)

> *Lay not up for yourselves treasures upon earth, where moth and rust doth corrupt, and where thieves break through and steal:*
>
> *But lay up for yourselves treasures in heaven, where neither moth nor rust doth corrupt, and where thieves do not break through and steal:*
>
> *For where your treasure is, there will your heart be also.*

Christ is the light; the gospel is the light; the plan of salvation is the light; "that which is of God is light; and he that receiveth light, and continueth in God, receiveth more light; and that light groweth brighter and brighter until the perfect day." As the light of the sun enters the body through our natural eyes, so the light of heaven—the light of the Spirit which illuminates our souls—enters through our spiritual eyes. "The light of the body is the eye," Jesus says; "if therefore thine eye be single to the glory of God, thy whole body shall be full of light."

"But if thine eye be evil"—if we choose darkness rather than light—"And that which doth not edify is not of God, and is darkness" (D&C 50:23-24)—"thy whole body shall be full of darkness. If therefore the light that is in thee be darkness, how great is that darkness!"

"How great is that darkness!" If the saints of God cease to serve with an eye single to the glory of God; if their spiritual eyes are dimmed by sin; if their eyes, being evil, admit carnality and heresy and false doctrine into their souls; if the light that once was theirs turns to darkness, "how great is that darkness!"

Later, in Judea, teaching there what the Galileans have already heard, Jesus will express kindred concepts in these words:

> *No man, when he hath lighted a candle, putteth it in a secret place, neither under a bushel, but on a candlestick, that they which come in may see the light.*

"A light that is hidden, whose guiding rays are covered by a bushel, is of no value to one stumbling in darkness. Similarly, the true saints must let the gospel light shine forth from them to all men, lest the saints, [like] the hidden candle, fail to fulfill their purpose in life. Jesus in effect is saying: 'No man accepts the gospel and then buries its light by continuing to walk in darkness; rather, he holds the light up before men so that they, emulating his good works, may also come to the Father.' " (*Commentary* 1:240.)

> *The light of the body is the eye: therefore when thine eye is single, thy whole body also is full of light; but when thine eye is evil, thy body also is full of darkness. Take heed therefore that the light which is in thee be not darkness. If thy whole body therefore be full of light, having no part dark, the whole shall be full of light, as when the bright shining of a candle doth give thee light.*

"Through the natural eyes men see the light which guides them in their physical existence, through their spiritual eyes, the spiritual light which leads to eternal life. As long as the natural eyes are unimpaired, men can see and be guided by the light of day; and as long as the spiritual eyes are single to the glory of God—that is, as long as they are undimmed by sin and are focused solely on righteousness—men can view and understand the things of the Spirit. But if apostasy enters and the spiritual light turns to darkness, 'how great is that darkness!'" (*Commentary* 1:240.)

Also in Judea, in connection with one's treasure being where his heart is, Jesus will say:

> *Sell that ye have and give alms; provide not for yourselves bags which wax old, but rather provide a treasure in the heavens, that faileth not; where no thief approacheth, neither moth corrupteth.*

Truly treasures in heaven are to be preferred to those stored in purses that wear out and from which earthly treasures will be lost!

> *No man can serve two masters: for either he will hate the one, and love the other; or else he will hold to the one, and despise the other. Ye cannot serve God and Mammon.*

Light and darkness cannot dwell together. It cannot be both day and night at the same time; water cannot be both sweet and salty at the same hour. No man can serve God, who is the author of light and righteousness, while he is in the employ of Lucifer, who is the author of darkness and sin. Mammon is an Aramaic word for riches. 'Ye cannot serve God and love riches and worldliness at the same time.'

The Lord Supplies the Needs of His Twelve Ministers

(*3 Nephi 13:25-34; Matthew 6:25-34; JST, Matthew 6:25-30, 34, 36-39; Luke 12:22-32; JST, Luke 12:26, 30-34*)

Now Jesus turns to the Twelve. He has something to say specifically to them about their ministerial labors. They are to forsake worldly pursuits—their fishing boats, the customs house, their fields and vineyards, all temporal enterprises—and use all of their time, talents, and means for the building up of the earthly kingdom and the establishment of the cause of Christianity. Others also, the seventies among them, will tread a like path in due course. The Lord's missionaries and ministers engage in such important labors that no worldly pursuit can be permitted to interfere; nothing pertaining to this world can be allowed to dilute and divide the energy and strength of the Lord's servants.

Other members of the Church are expected—nay, obligated; it is a command; they must do it—to provide for their own. Work, industry, frugality—sowing, reaping, and eating our bread by the sweat of our faces—such is the royal order of life. From the beginning men have been commanded to labor in seed time and harvest and to lay up in store against times of winter and famine. Cain reaped in the fields and Abel tended his flocks; Abraham, Isaac, and Jacob had their flocks and herds, their fields and gardens and vineyards. This is a temporal world, and men who dwell thereon are appointed to deal with temporal concerns. The gospel law requires men to care for their own needs and those of their families. And, "if any provide not for his own, and specially for those of his own house, he hath denied the faith, and is worse than an infidel." (1 Tim. 5:8.)

But for selected ones who are called to spread the truth and minister for the salvation of their fellows, it is otherwise; they may be called to go forth without purse or scrip, to forsake houses and lands and orchards, to do whatever circumstances require, and to rely upon the Lord for food and drink and raiment and a place to lay their head—all to the end that the Lord's work may spread and be established among all men.

In the Nephite account we read that "Jesus . . . looked upon the twelve whom he had chosen, and said unto them: Remember the words which I have spoken. For behold, ye are they whom I have chosen to minister unto this people. Therefore I say unto you"—the command was to them, not to the whole congregation—"take no thought for your life, what ye shall eat, or what ye shall drink; nor yet for your body, what ye shall put on."

In Matthew's account the instructions are more extended and express. To the Twelve who were with him in his personal ministry, Jesus said: "I say unto you, Go ye into the world, and care not for the world; for the world will hate you, and will persecute you, and will turn you out of their synagogues. Nevertheless, ye shall go forth from house to house, teaching the people; and I will go before you. And your heavenly Father will provide for you, whatsoever things ye need for food, what ye shall eat; and for raiment, what ye shall wear or put on. Therefore I say unto you, Take no thought for your life," and so on.

We hear now the eloquent reasoning of the Master Teacher. "Is not the life more than meat, and the body than raiment?" he asks. Shall we concern ourselves with life itself—the life of the body and the life of the soul—or merely with the food we eat and the rags or robes we chance to use as covering raiment? Then, using words that are eloquent in their simplicity, and drawing his illustrations from the beauties of nature that surround them, Jesus continues:

> *Behold the fowls of the air, for they sow not, neither do they reap, nor gather into barns; yet your heavenly Father feedeth them. Are ye not much better than they? How much more will he not feed you?*
>
> *Wherefore take no thought for these things, but keep my commandments wherewith I have commanded you.*
>
> *For which of you by taking thought can add one cubit unto his stature?*
>
> *And why take ye thought for raiment? Consider the lilies of the field, how they grow; they toil not, neither do they spin.*
>
> *And yet I say unto you, that even Solomon, in all his glory, was not arrayed like one of these.*
>
> *Therefore, if God so clothe the grass of the field, which today is, and tomorrow is cast into the oven, how much more will he not provide for you, if ye are not of little faith?*
>
> *Therefore take no thought, saying, What shall we eat? or, What shall we drink? or, Wherewithal shall we be clothed?*

The leading servants and chief underlings of the kings of the earth dwell in palaces, command fortresses, and are waited upon by lesser servants. Robes and rich food and soft beds and lewd entertainment abound for them. Herod Antipas and his courtiers lived such a life. But not so with the great King. His disciples, dressed often in rags, eating the rough food of the poor, sleeping in guest chambers, or even with the beasts of burden when there was no room in the inn—his chief disciples, his apostles, were to travel and live as he himself did.

None but the Lord would dare call upon chosen followers to live such a life and pursue such a course, and none but he could assure them that their essential needs would be met. The contrast between the courtiers of earthly kings and the disciples of the Eternal King is dramatic. The gospel standard is high and soul developing. It is no wonder that the newly called and as yet untested apostles were troubled at the prospects of the future. For their comfort and assurance, Jesus said: "Why is it that ye murmur among yourselves, saying, We cannot obey thy words because ye have not all these things, and seek to excuse yourselves, saying that, After all these things do the Gentiles seek. Behold, I say unto you that your heavenly Father knoweth that ye have need of all these things." Then came that great and wondrous declaration:

> *Wherefore, seek not the things of this world but seek ye first to build up the kingdom of God, and to establish his righteousness, and all these things shall be added unto you.*

It is common among us to quote the less perfect translation of this statement, which says, "Seek ye first the kingdom of God, and his righteousness," rather than the inspired rendition, "Seek ye first to build up the kingdom of God, and to establish his righteousness." Both statements are true; both are profound; both present a standard and a concept around which the saints should rally; and the Nephite account does in fact preserve the first of the two, which is, of course, the ultimate objective of true believers. To seek the kingdom of God and his righteousness, in the ultimate and eternal sense, is to seek the celestial kingdom and the state of righteousness in which God dwells. The process by which this ultimate goal is attained is to devote oneself to building up the earthly kingdom, which is the Church, and to establish the Cause of Righteousness on earth. Having so taught, and as a summary for this mid-portion of the Sermon on the Mount, our Lord said: "Take, therefore, no thought for the morrow; for the morrow shall take thought for the things of itself. Sufficient unto the day shall be the evil thereof."

NOTES

1. "Blessed are the poor who are pure in heart, whose hearts are broken, and whose spirits are contrite, for they shall see the kingdom of God coming in power and great glory unto their deliverance; for the fatness of the earth shall be theirs. For behold, the Lord shall come, and his recompense shall be with him, and he shall reward every man, and the poor shall rejoice; And their generations shall inherit the earth from generation to generation, forever and ever." (D&C 56:18-20.)

2. This revelation also says: "I, the Lord, will forgive whom I will forgive, but of you it is required to forgive all men. And ye ought to say in your hearts—let God judge between me and thee, and reward thee according to thy deeds."

JESUS TEACHES DOCTRINE TO HIS SAINTS

The Lord hath anointed me to preach
good tidings unto the meek.
(Isa. 61:1.)

The Lord . . . hath anointed me to preach
the gospel to the poor. (Luke 4:18.)

He Saith: 'Judge Righteous Judgments'

(*Matthew 7:1-5; JST, Matthew 7:1-8; Luke 6:37-38, 41-42; 3 Nephi 14:1-5*)

In sweet and sublime simplicity, with an eloquence and power possessed by none other, the One sent to preach good tidings to the meek, to preach the gospel to the poor, continues to pour forth the inspired wisdom of his Sermon on the Mount. He has just finished the special counsel applicable only to those special witnesses and their associates whose commission it is to preach to the world and to build up the kingdom—the instruction relative to forsaking all earthly interests and devoting themselves exclusively to the service of the ministry. Now he has a message for all his people, apostles and disciples alike. All must live the law to gain the blessing; all must do good and work righteousness; all must acquire for themselves, here and now, the attributes of godliness, if they are to possess them in eternity; all must keep the commandments to be saved in his Father's kingdom.

Matthew introduces his account of this portion of the Sermon on the Mount by saying, "Now these are the words which Jesus taught his disciples that they should say unto the people. Judge not unrighteously, that ye be not judged; but judge righteous judgment. For with what judgment ye shall judge, ye shall be judged; and with what measure ye mete, it shall be measured to you again." The Nephite record says that when Jesus had spoken to the Twelve the message on missionary service, "he turned again to the multitude," to whom he said: "Verily, verily, I say unto you, Judge not, that ye be not judged," and so on. Luke's account includes this provision: "Condemn not, and ye shall not be condemned: forgive, and ye shall be forgiven: Give, and it shall be given unto you; good measure, pressed down, and shaken together, and running over, shall men give into your bosom."

These words, thus, are a message for his saints, for all the people, for those who choose him as the way, the truth, and the life. The sense and meaning of each rendition is expressive of the divine will: 'Condemn not, that ye be not condemned; judge wisely and righteously, so that ye shall be judged in like manner;[1] and the Lord shall recompense to every man according to his work, and measure to him "according to the measure which he has measured to his fellow man." (D&C 1:10.)'

Our Lord continues to speak: "And again, ye shall say unto them"—that is, Ye, my disciples, shall "say unto the people"—"Why is it that thou beholdest the mote that is in thy brother's eye, but considerest not the beam that is in thine own eye? Or how wilt thou say to thy brother, Let me pull out the mote out of thine eye; and canst not behold a beam in thine own eye?"

It was ever thus. Even the members of the kingdom, striving as they are to perfect their lives; even those who know the truth and who are seeking to live by the high standards of the gospel; even these chosen ones can see the motes—the small splinters, the tiny dry twigs or stalks, the lesser faults—in the doings of their brethren in the Church; but they cannot see the beams—the great roof-beams, the large pieces of timber that hold up the house—which are part of their own doings.

Once I said unto another,
In thine eye there is a mote,
If thou art a friend, a brother,
Hold, and let me pull it out.
But I could not see it fairly,
For my sight was very dim,
When I came to search more clearly
In mine eye there was a beam.

If I love my brother dearer,
And his mote I would erase,
Then the light should shine the clearer,
For the eye's a tender place.
Others I have oft reproved,
For an object like a mote,
Now I wish this beam removed,
Oh, that tears would wash it out![2]

At this point in the Jewish sermon, but not in the one delivered to the Nephites, Jesus rebukes in scathing terms the false ministers who then led the people astray. "And Jesus said unto his disciples," Matthew records, "Beholdest thou the scribes, and the Pharisees, and the priests, and the Levites? They teach in their synagogues, but do not observe the law, nor the commandments; and all have gone out of the way, and are under sin. Go thou and say unto them, Why teach ye men the law and the commandments, when ye yourselves are the children of corruption? Say unto them, Ye hypocrites,"—and here he extends the law of the mote and the beam to all men— "first cast out the beam out of thine own eye; and then shalt thou see clearly to cast out the mote out of thy brother's eye."

'Ye teach that Moses forbade adultery, but ye yourselves are adulterers. Ye teach that men should honor their parents, but ye have dishonored your own fathers by your disobedience. Ye teach that men must repent and gain a remission of their sins, and yet ye yourselves are full of corruption. Ye teach that the Messiah shall come to redeem his people, and yet the one who now ministers among you with Messianic power ye reject.'

He Saith: 'Seek to Know the Truth'

(*Matthew 7:6-14; JST, Matthew 7:9-12, 14-17, 22; 3 Nephi 14:6-14; Luke 6:31*)

Jesus personally is not destined to do all the teaching that must be done; he alone will not take the message of salvation to every person; he can be in only one place at one time; while he speaks to this congregation, assembled above Capernaum on the Mount of Beatitudes, there are other congregations—throughout Palestine, Asia, the realm of the Roman Caesars, and the whole world—that could be assembled to hear the word of truth. Others must be called and trained and sent forth to proclaim the everlasting word. And so Jesus continues to tell his disciples what they shall say as they carry his message to the hosts who shall never see his mortal face or hear his blessed voice.

"Go ye into the world," he directs, "saying unto all, Repent, for the kingdom of heaven has come nigh unto you."

'Go! No longer sit at ease in your homes and in your synagogues! Arise; gird up your loins, and go! The gospel must be preached everywhere; the whole earth must hear the message; the voice of truth must echo and re-echo in every ear; every heart must be penetrated; there are none to escape. The voice of the Lord is unto all men. Say: The kingdom of heaven is at hand; the gospel of salvation is here; the Church of Jesus Christ is now on earth; it is the kingdom of God on earth; and we are legal administrators who teach by the power of the Holy Ghost, and who perform the ordinances of salvation so they will be binding on earth and sealed everlastingly in the heavens. Repent, and believe the gospel. Live its laws and be saved.'

> *And the mysteries of the kingdom ye shall keep within yourselves; for it is not meet to give that which is holy unto the dogs; neither cast ye your pearls unto swine, lest they trample them under their feet.*
>
> *For the world cannot receive that which ye, yourselves, are not able to bear; wherefore ye shall not give your pearls unto them, lest they turn again and rend you.*

Any gospel truth, however easy and simple, that is not understood, or that is beyond the present spiritual capacity of a given person to understand, is to him a mystery. Faith, repentance, and baptism are mysteries to the unbelieving Gentiles. But the mysteries of the kingdom, of which Jesus here speaks, are quite another thing. This phrase has a special meaning; it refers to the deep and hidden things of the gospel—to the calculus, as it were, which can only be comprehended after the student has become proficient in arithmetic, algebra, and geometry; it refers to the temple ordinances; to the gifts of the Spirit; to those things which can be known only by the power of the Holy Ghost.

The saints are to keep the deep and more mysterious doctrines to themselves and not offer to the world more than people are able to bear. Until the newborn babe in Christ is weaned, he cannot eat meat; the milk of the world must suffice. Gospel pearls in the hands of Gentile swine enable those hoofed and snouted beasts, wallowing in the filth and swill of their rebellion and disbelief, to rend the saints with their evil fangs. Thus: "It is given unto many to know the mysteries of God; nevertheless they are laid under a strict command that they shall not impart only according to the portion of his word which he doth grant unto the children of men, according to the heed and diligence which they give unto him." (Alma 12:9.)[3]

How will the world know of the truth and divinity of the gospel message when it is taught by the disciples? When the command comes to 'repent and believe the gospel,' how can the hearers come to know they must believe and obey at the peril of their salvation? Jesus continues to counsel:

> *Say unto them, Ask of God; ask, and it shall be given you; seek, and ye shall find; knock, and it shall be opened unto you. For every one that asketh, receiveth; and he that seeketh, findeth; and unto him that knocketh, it shall be opened.*

It is the Lord's work that is involved; it is his gospel; he will bear record of its truth and divinity. He is no respecter of persons; he will give the Holy Ghost to those who hunger and thirst after righteousness, for, as Nephi said, "the Holy Ghost . . . is the gift of God unto all those who diligently seek him, as well in times of old as in the time that he should manifest himself unto the children of men."[4] Truth seekers must turn to the Lord for a final and conclusive answer on religious matters. Every person who hears the gospel preached by a legal administrator sent from God; every person who desires to know which of all the churches is right and which he should join; every person who is really concerned with the well-being of his eternal soul—every such person stands exactly where Joseph Smith stood at the beginning of this dispensation: He must ask of God, who giveth to all men liberally and upbraideth not.[5]

The preaching of the gospel, however, to those already mired in their own theological mud—no matter when or to whom or under what circumstances—always brings the same response; the reaction to the new message is as predictable as is the rising of the morning sun. Those who already think they possess the light of heaven; those who believe they are engaged in the Lord's service; those who have a form of godliness that satisfies their instinctive desires to worship—such will always say: 'We already have the truths of salvation; why should we give heed to this new nonsense which you preach?' Aware—partly by instinct and partly, no doubt, by the experiences already gained in discussing Jesus and his doctrines with others—that such a reaction would be forthcoming, "his disciples said unto him: They will say unto us, We ourselves are righteous, and need not that any man should teach us. God, we know, heard Moses and some of the prophets; but us he will not hear. And they will say, We have the law for our salvation, and that is sufficient for us."[6]

Jesus has already identified the door through which men must enter to gain a testimony of the new order that is now replacing the old Mosaic system. It is: Ask of God in faith and he will reveal the truth of it unto you by the power of the Holy Ghost. And so to answer the expressed anxieties of his disciples, he simply brings them back again to the basic reality involved: There is only one way to know the truth about God and his laws, and that is to receive personal revelation. "Then Jesus answered, and said unto his disciples, Thus shall ye say unto them:

> *What man among you, having a son, and he shall be standing out, and shall say, Father, open thy house that I may come in and sup with thee, will not say, Come in, my son; for mine is thine, and thine is mine?*
>
> *Or what man is there among you, who, if his son ask bread, will give him a stone?*
>
> *Or if he ask a fish, will he give him a serpent?*
>
> *If ye then, being evil, know how to give good gifts unto your children, how much more shall your Father who is in heaven give good things to them that ask him?*

To all this there is a conclusion to be reached, a grand climax to hear, a summit of inspired logic yet to shine forth. None but the one whose sermon we are hearing anew could have said it so well:

> *Therefore* [that is, in the light of all that he has just said] *all things whatsoever ye would that men should do to*

you, do ye even so to them: for this is the law and the prophets.

The Golden Rule, as we have come to call it; the law of Moses and the teachings of the prophets—all summarized in one sentence! Truly, never man spake as this Man!

And all this being so—the gospel being taught; the kingdom being once again established; the door being open for all who will to enter; the disciples being instructed in the part they are to play—Jesus now proclaims:

> *Repent, therefore, and enter ye in at the strait gate; for wide is the gate, and broad is the way that leadeth to destruction, and many there be who go in thereat. Because strait is the gate, and narrow is the way, which leadeth unto life, and few there be that find it.*

Enter in at the strait gate of baptism; find yourself on the strait and narrow path leading to the celestial kingdom. Enter in at the strait gate of celestial marriage; find yourself on the strait and narrow path leading to eternal life in the highest heaven of the celestial world. The broad gate is always open, and all the influences of the world urge and entice men to enter and go downward to darkness; the narrow gate is open only to those who desire righteousness and who seek the Lord and his goodness. It is written:

> Behold, the way for man is narrow,
> But it lieth in a straight course before him,
> And the keeper of the gate is the Holy One of Israel;
> And he employeth no servant there;
> And there is none other way save it be by the gate;
> For he cannot be deceived,
> For the Lord God is his name.
>
> And whoso knocketh, to him will he open;
> And the wise, and the learned, and they that are rich,
> Who are puffed up because of their learning, and their
> wisdom, and their riches—
> Yea, they are they whom he despiseth;

And save they shall cast these things away,
And consider themselves fools before God,
And come down in the depths of humility,
He will not open unto them.

But the things of the wise and the prudent
Shall be hid from them forever—
Yea, that happiness which is prepared for the saints.[7]

Jesus Speaks of Prophets, Good Works, and Salvation

(Matthew 7:15-29; 8:1; JST, Matthew 7:30-31, 33, 36-37; 3 Nephi 14:15-27; Luke 6:43-44, 46-49)

Now Jesus speaks some sharp and cutting words about the false prophets who are everywhere to be found in his day. But moments ago he pointed to the scribes, the Pharisees, the priests, and the Levites and said: "Ye yourselves are the children of corruption." They are apostate; they have all "gone out of the way"; they all are "under sin"; and neither do they "observe the law, nor the commandments." And the disciples, also but moments ago, have quoted these same blind guides of an erring race as saying: "God, we know, heard Moses and some of the prophets; but us he will not hear." Now Jesus excoriates these same teachers as, with reference to them—and in principle, also, to all future blind guides and erring religious teachers—he tells the people: "Beware of false prophets, which come to you in sheep's clothing, but inwardly they are ravening wolves."

False prophets—the curse and scourge of the world! How awful and awesome and evil it is when one pretends and professes to speak for God in leading men to salvation, but in fact has a message that is false, a doctrine that is not true, and a prophecy that will not come to pass. And how little do the Jewish people of Jesus' day know—or does the world today know—who among them are the false prophets. But then, false prophets are of the world; they follow the practices of the world; they teach what the carnal mind desires to hear; they are loved by the world.

Moses, in whom the Jews trusted, and whose name was reverenced in all their synagogues, was the one who said: "Would God that all the Lord's people were prophets, and that the Lord would put his spirit upon them!" (Num. 11:29.) Paul would soon say: "Ye may all prophesy," and, "covet to prophesy." (1 Cor. 14:31, 39.) And John the Beloved would in a not-distant day hear from angelic lips the gracious words: "The testimony of Jesus is the spirit of prophecy." (Rev. 19:10.)

A true prophet is one who has the testimony of Jesus; one who knows by personal revelation that Jesus Christ is the Son of the living God, and that he was to be—or has been—crucified for the sins of the world; one to whom God speaks and who recognizes the still small voice of the Spirit. A true prophet is one who holds the holy priesthood; who is a legal administrator; who has power and authority from God to represent him on earth. A true prophet is a teacher of righteousness to whom the truths of the gospel have been revealed and who presents them to his fellowmen so they can become heirs of salvation in the highest heaven. A true prophet is a witness, a living witness, one who knows, and one who testifies. Such a one, if need be, foretells the future and reveals to men what the Lord reveals to him.

A false prophet is the opposite of all this. He does not know by personal revelation of the divine Sonship of the Prophet who was like unto Moses. He does not enjoy the gift of the Holy Ghost or hold the holy priesthood, and he is not a legal administrator who has power to bind and seal on earth and in heaven. He is not a teacher of true doctrine; he may believe any of an infinite variety of false doctrines, but he does not teach, in purity and perfection, the fulness of the everlasting gospel. Because he does not receive revelation or enjoy the gifts of the Spirit, he believes these things have ceased. He thinks: 'God, I know, heard Moses and some of the prophets; but me he will not hear.' Because he teaches false doctrines, he does not lead men to salvation, and in cases not a few he becomes a ravening wolf in sheep's clothing.[8]

To denounce these ravening wolves among the scribes and Pharisees who, parading before the people as prophets, yet tore and gashed and mutilated the souls of men with their false teachings; to excoriate the hypocritical practices of the priests and Levites, as they performed their sacrificial rites in similitude of a future Messiah who had in fact come and been rejected by them; to acclaim as false that which is evil—to do all this is not to denounce or reject that which is true and good. All Israel knew there had been true prophets in days of old. All Israel knew that some then living were claiming prophetic stature. All Israel knew—this above all—that the Lord God of their fathers had, by the mouth of Moses, the man of God, promised to raise up a prophet like unto Israel's great lawgiver, and that the prophet so called forth would be the Messiah.

The Jews themselves had sent priests and Levites to John to ask, "Art thou that prophet?" (John 1:21.) And many people, among them the man who was blind from birth, said of Jesus, "He is a prophet." (John 9:17.) None among them questioned that there had been and were and would be true prophets. They knew that God always had spoken and always would speak by the mouths of men called by him to the prophetic office. The issue then was—and now is—how to identify the true prophets; how to know who among the professing prophets represent the Lord and who have no such divine commission; how to tell the true from the false.

"Ye shall know them by their fruits," Jesus said. By their fruits—their words, their acts, the wonders that they do—these things shall separate true prophets and teachers from false ones. Do they receive revelations and see visions? Does the Holy Ghost speak by their mouth? Are they legal administrators who have power to bind and seal on earth and in heaven? Is their doctine true and sound and in harmony with all that is found in Holy Writ? Do they enjoy the gifts of the Spirit, so that the sick are healed under their hands? And does the Lord God give his Holy Spirit to attest the truth of their words and to approve the acts that they do? Without true prophets there is no salvation; false prophets lead people astray; men choose, at the peril of their salvation, the prophets whom they follow.

"Do men gather grapes of thorns, or figs of thistles?" Jesus asks. Matthew records no answer to the query, only the application: "Even so every good tree bringeth forth good fruit; but a corrupt tree bringeth forth evil fruit. A good tree cannot bring forth evil fruit, neither can a corrupt tree bring forth good fruit." Luke's account, however, quotes Jesus as saying:

> *For a good tree bringeth not forth corrupt fruit; neither doth a corrupt tree bring forth good fruit. For every tree is known by his own fruit. For of thorns men do not gather figs, nor of a bramble bush gather they grapes.*

Or, in other words, as Moroni wrote, quoting the words of his father, Mormon:

> *A man being evil cannot do that which is good; neither will he give a good gift.*
>
> *For behold, a bitter fountain cannot bring forth good water; neither can a good fountain bring forth bitter water; wherefore, a man being a servant of the devil cannot follow Christ; and if he follow Christ he cannot be a servant of the devil.* (*Moro. 7:10-11.*)

By way of conclusion to this part of his sermon, Jesus continued: "Every tree that bringeth not forth good fruit is hewn down, and cast into the fire. *Wherefore by their fruits ye shall know them.*"

Our Lord's mighty sermon is drawing to its close. He is about to lay the capstone on the structure of doctrine and counsel and exhortation which his gracious words have built, and that capstone is: Keep the commandments so as to be able to withstand the trials and tests that are ahead.

"Verily I say unto you, it is not every one that saith unto me, Lord, Lord, that shall enter into the kingdom of heaven," he says, "but he that doeth the will of my Father who is in heaven." Lip service alone does not save; it is not confessing that Jesus is the Lord, without more, that opens heaven's door; belief without works has no saving power. Keep the commandments; do the will of the Father; work and labor and struggle and strive—then expect salvation. Baptism alone does not save; celestial marriage alone does not exalt; church membership without more does not assure an inheritance in celestial glory. "After ye have gotten into this straight and narrow path, I would ask if all is done?" Nephi queries, and his answer is, "Nay." Rather: "Ye must press forward with a steadfastness in Christ, having a perfect brightness of hope, and a love of God and of all men. Wherefore, if ye shall press forward, feasting upon the word of Christ, and endure to the end, behold, thus saith the Father: Ye shall have eternal life." (2 Ne. 31:19-20.)

"For the day soon cometh, that men shall come before me to judgment, to be judged according to their works." 'I am the Judge; I am the Messiah; look unto me and live; I shall sit in judgment upon the world.' And, "Many will say to me in that day, Lord, Lord, have we not prophesied in thy name? and in thy name have cast out devils? and in thy name done many wonderful works?" To whom is he speaking? Is it not to those who have been baptized; those who have gained the testimony of Jesus, which is the spirit of prophecy; those who have received the holy priesthood and have cast out devils and worked miracles?

Two answers of equivalent meaning are recorded to his question; both are answers that will be given to those saints who have not endured to the end, who have not kept the commandments, and who have not pressed forward with a steadfastness in Christ after baptism. In one, the account says: "And then will I profess unto them, I never knew you: depart from me, ye that work iniquity." In the other account the words are: "And then will I say, Ye never knew me; depart from me ye that work iniquity."

'I never knew you, and you never knew me! Your discipleship was limited; you were not perfect members of my kingdom. Your heart was not so centered in me as to cause you to endure to the end; and so for a time and a season you were faithful; you even worked miracles in my name; but in the end it shall be as though I never knew you.'

> *And why call ye me, Lord, Lord, and do not the things which I say?*

'If ye believe that I am he of whom the prophets testified; if ye accept me as the Promised Messiah; if I am the Son of God and ye call me Lord, then keep my commandments; endure to the end; worship the Father in my name, and ye shall be saved.' "Whosoever cometh to me, and heareth my sayings, and doeth them"—that is, he who is my disciple, he who believes my gospel and joins my church—"I will shew you to whom he is like:

> *He is like a man which built an house, and digged deep, and laid the foundation on a rock: and when the flood arose, the stream beat vehemently upon that house, and could not shake it: for it was founded upon a rock.*
>
> *But he that heareth, and doeth not, is like a man that without a foundation built an house upon the earth; against which the stream did beat vehemently, and immediately it fell; and the ruin of that house was great.*

Blessed are all they who receive the word with joy; who build their house of salvation upon him who is the Eternal Rock; and who then endure to the end—for they shall be saved with an everlasting salvation.

Blessed are all they who call Jesus, Lord, Lord; who have in their hearts the prophetic insight that men call the testimony of Jesus; and who are valiant in testimony all their days—for they shall wear the victor's crown.

Blessed are all they who keep the commandments; who are true and faithful to every trust; and who do ever those things which please Him whose we are—for they shall dwell everlastingly with him in celestial rest.

And so endeth the Sermon on the Mount, the Sermon on the Plain, the Sermon in Bountiful—the sermon like none other ever delivered. As for the people who heard him, they "were astonished at his doctrine; For he taught them as one having authority from God, and not as having authority from the scribes."

And so Jesus, as "great multitudes followed him," "was come down from the mountain," to be elsewhere and otherwise about his Father's business. The Lord be praised that we know as much as we do about what he said and did in his day!

NOTES

1. Mormon, who had the Nephite Sermon in Bountiful before him when he wrote, leaves us this analysis of properly judging all things: "Take heed, my beloved brethren, that ye do not judge that which is evil to be of God, or that which is good and of God to be of the devil. For behold, my brethren, it is given unto you to judge, that ye may know good from evil; and the way to judge is as plain, that ye may know with a perfect knowledge, as the daylight is from the dark night. For behold, the Spirit of Christ is given to every man, that he may know good from evil; wherefore, I show unto you the way to judge; for every thing which inviteth to do good, and to persuade to believe in Christ, is sent forth by the power and gift of Christ; wherefore ye may know with a perfect knowledge it is of God. . . . And now, my brethren, seeing that ye know the light by which ye may judge, which light is the light of Christ, see that ye do not judge wrongfully; for with that same judgment which ye judge ye shall also be judged." (Moro. 7:14-18.)

2. These are two of the verses of Eliza R. Snow's great Mormon hymn, "Truth Reflects Upon Our Senses," *Hymns,* no. 188.

3. This same truth, in principle, is found in latter-day revelation in these words: "Thou shalt declare glad tidings"—that is, present the message of the restoration to the world—"yea, publish it upon the mountains, and upon every high place, and among every people that thou shalt be permitted to see. . . . And of tenets [those doctrines which are over and above and deeper than the ones contained in the basic message itself] thou shalt not talk, but thou shalt declare repentance and faith on the Savior, and remission of sins by baptism, and by fire, yea, even the Holy Ghost." (D&C 19:29-31.)

4. In addition to the words quoted, Nephi also says: "For he that diligently seeketh shall find; and the mysteries of God shall be unfolded unto them, by the power of the Holy Ghost, as well in these times as in times of old, and as well in times of old as in times to come; wherefore, the course of the Lord is one eternal round." (1 Ne. 10:17-19.)

5. It was of James's words—"If any of you lack wisdom, let him ask of God, that giveth to all men liberally, and upbraideth not; and it shall be given"—that Joseph Smith said: "Never did any passage of scripture come with more power to the heart of man than this did at this time to mine." He pondered upon it again and again, until, guided by the Spirit, he was led to offer the prayer which rent the heavens and opened the dispensation of the fulness of times. (JS-H 1:10-20.)

6. "How similarly the spiritually closed mind operates in all ages! These Jewish attempts, to justify adherence to a false religion, sound as though they had been made by the ministers of modern Christendom. 'We ourselves are righteous, and what can these Mormon Elders teach us. True it is that God spoke to prophets of old, but revelation has ceased; there is no modern communion with heaven. We have the Bible and are Christians, and that is sufficient for us.' But Jesus' counsel is: 'Tell them to humble themselves, repent of their sins, and pray to the Father in mighty prayer so they may learn where the truth really lies.' " (*Commentary* 1:249.)

7. 2 Ne. 9:41-43.

8. Two statements from the Prophet Joseph Smith give prophetic sanction to the views on prophets here presented. First: "When a man goes about prophesying, and commands men to obey his teachings, he must either be a true or false prophet. False prophets always arise to oppose the true prophets and they will prophesy so very near the truth that they will deceive almost the very chosen ones." (*Teachings*, p. 365.) Second: "If any person should ask me if I were a prophet, I should not deny it, as that would give me the lie; for, according to John, the testimony of Jesus is the spirit of prophecy; therefore, if I profess to be a witness or teacher, and have not the spirit of prophecy, which is the testimony of Jesus, I must be a false witness; but if I be a true teacher and witness, I must possess the spirit of prophecy, and that constitutes a prophet; and any man who says he is a teacher or a preacher of righteousness, and denies the spirit of prophecy, is a liar, and the truth is not in him; and by this key false teachers and imposters may be detected." (*Teachings*, p. 269.)

JESUS MINISTERS AS ONE HAVING AUTHORITY

Across the sea, along the shore,
In numbers ever more and more,
From lonely hut and busy town,
The valley through, the mountain down,
What was it ye went out to see,
Ye silly folk of Galilee?
The reed that in the wind doth shake?
The weed that washes in the lake? . . .

A Teacher? Rather seek the feet
Of those who sit in Moses' seat.
Go, humbly seek, and bow to them
Far off in great Jerusalem. . . .
What is it came ye here to note?
A young Man preaching in a boat.

A Prophet! Boys and women weak!
    Declare—and cease to rave—
Whence is it He hath learnt to speak?
    Say, who His doctrine gave?
A Prophet? Prophet wherefore He
    Of all in Israel's tribes?—

He teacheth with authority
And not as do the scribes.[1]

He Speaks as One Having Authority
(*Matthew 7:28-29; JST, Matthew 7:36-37*)

We are now in a high state of spiritual exhilaration, even exultation. Gracious and God-given words echo and re-echo through every fiber of our being. We walk down the gentle slopes, covered with grass and flowers and shrubs, as we go from the high plateau on the Mount of Beatitudes to the busy getting and giving of Capernaum and its lake-near environs. We are basking in the light and love and beauty of the Sermon on the Mount. We ponder every spoken word; each phrase sinks into our heart as though by fire, and our bosom burns with the truth and reality of it all. Our souls could not be more stirred had we stood with Moses on Sinai as the smoke and fire ascended, as the thunders rolled, and as the Holy Mount quaked with Jehovah's presence.

Never man spake as we have just heard the Lord Jesus speak. "The people were astonished at his doctrine," Matthew says, "For he taught them as one having authority, and not as the scribes." Or, rather, as we have already seen, "He taught them as one having authority from God, and not as having authority from the scribes." His voice was the voice of the Incarnate Jehovah; his words, spoken by the power of the Holy Ghost, were the words of his Father. Others were authorized to preach and teach by the scribes; he had his "authority from God." He came in his Father's name, used his Father's voice, and exercised his Father's power. This we have seen him do in the Sermon on the Mount, which itself was the ordination sermon and charge for the Twelve special witnesses, whom he had chosen to testify of him in all the world.

It is better, no doubt, to have a false religion and to worship false gods than to have no religion and no worship at all. Neutrality is as nothing, and indifference is denigrating and damning. Those who are lukewarm—who are neither hot nor cold; who take no affirmative stand; who do not seek the blessings available through worship—will one day be spewed out of the divine mouth, as it were, and find their place in one of the lesser eternal realms. And this much we can say for the scribes: they were anything but lukewarm. They had a zeal for religion, a zeal for worship, a zeal for God, but it was a misplaced, a twisted, and a perverted zeal. But those who are zealous, even in false causes, are at least prospective zealots—as witness Saul of Tarsus—in true causes. Our concern here is the comparison between the teachings of the scribes, who spoke without divine approval, and the teachings of him who was the Divine Voice.

"The teaching of their Scribes was narrow, dogmatic, material; it was cold in manner, frivolous in matter, second-hand and iterative in its very essence; with no freshness in it, no force, no fire; servile to all authority, opposed to all independence; at once erudite and foolish, at once contemptuous and mean; never passing a hair's breadth beyond the carefully-watched boundary line of commentary and precedent; full of balanced inference and orthodox hesitancy, and impossible literalism; intricate with legal pettiness and labyrinthine system; elevating mere memory above genius, and repetition above originality; concerned only about Priests and Pharisees, in Temple and synagogue, or school, or Sanhedrin, and mostly occupied with things infinitely little. It was not indeed wholly devoid of moral significance, nor is it impossible to find here and there, among the *débris* of it, a worthy thought; but it was occupied a thousandfold more with Levitical minutia about mint, and anise, and cummin, and the length of fringes, and the breadth of phylacteries, and the washing of cups and platters, and the particular quarter of a second when new moons and Sabbath-days began." (Farrar, pp. 201-2.) Such are the well-chosen words that depict the teachings—to say nothing of the inner feelings and twisted religious instincts—of the scribes. Teachers—call them false prophets, if you will, for

Jesus so designated them in the great sermon just delivered—who are without authority, who are devoid of inspiration, and who do not and cannot in fact speak for the Almighty—such teachers turn, in the very nature of things, to learned commentary about what inspired teachers of other ages have spoken and which is preserved in the form of scripture.

Now, in contrast, let us summarize how the Master Teacher approached his podium. "This teaching of Jesus was wholly different in its character, and as much grander as the temple of the morning sky under which it was uttered was grander than stifling synagogues or crowded school. It was preached, as each occasion rose, on the hill-side, or by the lake, or on the roads, or in the house of the Pharisee, or at the banquet of the Publican; nor was it any sweeter or loftier when it was addressed in the Royal Portico to the Masters of Israel, than when its only hearers were the ignorant people whom the haughty Pharisees held to be accursed.

"And there was no reserve in its administration. It flowed forth as sweetly and as lavishly to single listeners as to enraptured crowds; and some of its very richest revelations were vouchsafed, neither to rulers nor to multitudes, but to the persecuted outcast of the Jewish synagogue, to the timid inquirer in the lonely midnight, and the frail woman by the noon-day well. And it dealt, not with scrupulous rites and ceremonial cleansings, but with the human soul, and human destiny, and human life—with Hope and Charity, and Faith. There were no definitions in it, or explanations, or 'scholastic systems,' or philosophic theorising, or implicated mazes of difficult and dubious discussion, but a swift intuitive insight into the very depths of the human heart—even a supreme and daring paradox that, without being fenced round with exceptions or limitations, appealed to the conscience with its irresistible simplicity, and with an absolute mastery stirred and dominated over the heart. Springing from the depths of holy emotions, it thrilled the being of every listener as with an electric flame. In a word, its authority was the authority of the Divine Incarnate; it was the Voice of God, speaking in the utterance of man; its austere purity was yet pervaded with tenderest sympathy, and its awful severity with an unutterable love. It is, to borrow the image of the wisest of the Latin Fathers, a great sea whose smiling surface breaks into refreshing ripples at the feet of our little ones, but into whose unfathomable depths the wisest may gaze with the shudder of amazement and the thrill of love. . . .

"How exquisitely and freshly simple is the actual language of Christ compared with all other teaching that has ever gained the ear of the world! There is no science in it, no art, no pomp of demonstration, no carefulness of toil, no trick of rhetoricians, no wisdom of the schools. Straight as an arrow to the mark His precepts pierce to the very depths of the soul and spirit. All is short, clear, precise, full of holiness, full of the common images of daily life.

"There is scarcely a scene or object familiar to the Galilee of that day, which Jesus did not use as a moral illustration of some glorious promise or moral law. He spoke of green fields, and springing flowers, and the budding of the vernal trees; of the red or lowering sky; of sunrise and sunset; of wind and rain; of night and storm; of clouds and lightning; of stream and river; of stars and lamps; of fire and salt; of quivering bulrushes and burning weeds; of rent garments and bursting wine-skins; of eggs and serpents; of pearls and pieces of money; of nets and fish. Wine and wheat, corn and oil, stewards and gardeners, labourers and employers, kings and shepherds, travellers and fathers of families, courtiers in soft clothing and brides in nuptial robes—all these are found in His discourses. He knew all life, and had gazed on it with a kindly as well as a kingly glance. He could sympathize with its joys no less than He could heal its sorrows, and the eyes that were so often suffused with tears as they saw the sufferings of earth's mourners beside the bed of death, had shone also with a kindlier glow as they watched the games of earth's happy little ones in the green fields and busy streets." (Farrar, pp. 202-5.)

Jesus Heals the Servant of a Gentile Centurion
(*Luke 7:1-10; Matthew 8:5-13; JST, Matthew 8:9-10, 12*)

This Man, who spake as none else before or since—whose words exceed in wisdom those even of Enoch, and Moses, and Isaiah, all of whom received their inspiration from him, but who expressed the thoughts after the manner of their language, and according to their own talents and abilities—this Man now goes forth to do deeds that no others, before or since, have ever assayed to do. His authority was not only to use the voice and speak the words of Him whose servant he was, but to use the power given him to heal the sick and raise the dead. His miracles will stand as an attesting seal, written in the souls of men, to the words that he spoke.

We are with him now in Capernaum, his own city. A Roman garrison is located here. One of its officers, a centurion of heathen-Gentile birth, who commands between fifty and a hundred men, has an esteemed servant who is "ready to die" of a paralytic seizure. This centurion, a soldier in the service of Herod Antipas, is no ordinary Gentile upon whom the curse of disbelief rests, or who revels in the carnal lusts by which soldiers sometimes entertain themselves. He may have been a "proselyte of righteousness," one adopted into the family of Abraham, one who chose to live as an Israelite and worship the Lord Jehovah. At least he was a friend of the Jews and had, out of his own munificence, built for them a synagogue in Capernaum. Hearing that Jesus was coming into their city, he besought the elders of the Jews to intercede on his behalf. "My servant lieth at home sick of the palsy, grievously tormented," he said. And the importuning Jews told Jesus "that he was worthy for whom he should do this: For he loveth our nation, and he hath built us a synagogue." Jesus said, "I will come and heal him."

Jesus and the Jewish elders—plus the select group upon whom his countenance shone—started their journey to the home of the centurion. We may suppose that this military commander knew of the nobleman, who also served Herod Antipas, and whose son in Capernaum had been healed by Jesus' word, spoken twenty miles away in Cana. In any event, when Jesus was "not far from the house, the centurion sent friends to him" who said: "Lord, trouble not thyself: for I am not worthy that thou shouldest enter under my roof: Wherefore neither thought I myself worthy to come unto thee: but say in a word, and my servant shall be healed. For I also am a man set under authority, having under me soldiers, and I say unto one, Go, and he goeth; and to another, Come, and he cometh; and to my servant, Do this, and he doeth it."

"The centurion's reasoning—profound in logic, perfect in showing forth faith—was to this effect: If I, a mere officer in the Roman army, must obey my superiors, and also have power myself to send others forth at my command, then surely the Lord of all needs but speak and his will shall be done." (*Commentary* 1:258.)

Those who were with Jesus marveled at the message from the centurion, and Jesus said: "I have not found so great faith, no, not in Israel." Such a teaching moment as this seldom arises, and of it the Master Teacher makes the most.

> *Many shall come from the east and west, and shall sit down with Abraham, and Isaac, and Jacob, in the kingdom of heaven. But the children of the wicked one shall be cast out into outer darkness; there shall be weeping and gnashing of teeth.*

In just a moment, he who was not sent but to the lost sheep of the house of Israel; he who came to his kindred, that the word of truth might go first to the Jews and at a later date to the Gentiles; he who was the God of Israel—in just a moment he was going to heal the servant of a Gentile whose faith exceeded the faith of the members of the chosen race.

But before doing so he chose to shake the theological foundations upon which Israel's preferential status rested. Many—not a few; Gentile hosts; members of the hated, alien nations—many would find glory in heaven with the ancient patriarchs, while the literal seed, being the children of Satan, Jews who should have been the children of the kingdom, would be cast out. How little his Jewish hearers understood the meaning of that which Jehovah had of old time said to Abraham: "As many as receive this Gospel shall be called after thy name, and shall be accounted thy seed, and shall rise up and bless thee, as their father." (Abr. 2:10.)

Then came the miracle, which attested to the truth of his doctrine. The message for the centurion was: "Go thy way; and as thou hast believed, so be it done unto thee. And his servant was healed in the selfsame hour."

Jesus Raises a Widow's Son from Death

(*Luke 7:11-17*)

It is now the day after the healing of the centurion's servant in Capernaum. Jesus, his disciples, and a great multitude have traversed their weary way—a distance of twenty-five miles—to a little Galilean village of no particular note, a place called Nain. It is, as we have seen, Jesus' wont to visit the towns and villages of Galilee, of Judea, and of all Palestine to preach the gospel and offer salvation to his people. Aside from the fact there was a funeral in Nain today, the day has been no different from the ceaseless caravan of days that pass endlessly along in hundreds of the sleepy villages of Israel. But ere the sun sets this day, such a miracle will be wrought in Nain as no man on earth has before seen. A dead youth, one prepared for consignment to the tomb, shall live again; one word from the Lord of life and the dried blood will flow again through a newly enlivened heart, and the breath of life will inflate anew the collapsed lungs of a dead corpse. Where there was death, with all its decay and sorrow, there will be life, with all its growth and joy. This is the day when the Prince of life will smite the angel of death with the breath of his lips, and that which was cold and stiff and lifeless will rise in warmth and vigor and all the strength and beauty of youth.

Two multitudes are about to meet: one sorrowing because the only son of his mother, a widow, has passed to the great beyond—sorrowing because such a promising Israelite, whose help was so much needed by a weeping mother, was about to be laid in a lifeless tomb; the other a joyful multitude—a group of believing, rejoicing disciples in whose bosoms the fires ignited on the Mount of Beatitudes still burned; a group who, but yesterday, had heard their Prophet-Leader command a centurion's servant to arise from his paralytic bed, and it was so.

In one group, where sorrow and sadness reign, the central figure is a weeping widow, trudging beside a funeral bier, as the cortege approaches the final corpse-prepared resting place for her only and beloved son. Her thoughts are filled with death and all its dreads. In her is fulfilled the ancient proverb: "Make thee mourning, as for an only son, most bitter lamentation." (Jer. 6:26.) The central figure in the other group—where joy abounds and words of life and light flow freely—is the one who has life in himself because God is his Father, and to whom what men call death is but the transfer of an eternal soul to another realm of life.

The sorrowing mother has suffered through the siege of sickness; every mortal means has been used to stay the grim reaper's hand. We cannot but think that she importuned in faith, before the Eternal Throne, for the life of her son, her only son; but death, in the end, has come off victorious. "The well-known blast of the horn has carried tidings, that once more the Angel of Death has done his dire behest. In passionate grief the mother has rent her upper garment. The last sad offices have been rendered to the dead. The body has been laid on the ground; hair and nails have been cut, and the body washed, anointed, and wrapped in the best the widow could procure." (Edersheim 1:554.) The funeral itself has now been held; its sermons are over; mourning women have been employed to chant "in weird strains the lament: 'Alas, the lion! alas, the hero!' or similar words," and "the funeral orator, if one was employed," is preceding "the bier, proclaiming the good deeds of the dead." The youth lies on the open bier; friends and neighbors take turns, as pallbearers, in carrying the mortal remains, and behind the bier come the mourning and sympathizing townspeople. "Up from the city close by came this 'great multitude' that followed the dead, with lamentations, wild chants of mourning women, accompanied by flutes and the melancholy tinkle of cymbals, perhaps by trumpets, amidst expressions of general sympathy. Along the road from Endor streamed the great multitude which followed the 'Prince of Life.' Here they met: Life and Death." (Edersheim 1:555-57.)

"And when the Lord saw her, he had compassion on her, and said unto her, Weep not." He who came to bear the sorrows of many was himself sorrowful. He "touched the bier: and they that bare him stood still." No doubt the pallbearers recognized the Prophet of Nazareth of Galilee whose fame was everywhere; at least his commanding presence and saintly demeanor stayed the funereal march. His words were simple; his command could not be gainsaid. There was no struggle, no stretching of "himself upon the child three times," no pleading with the Lord, as when Elijah raised the son of the widow of Zarephath from death. (1 Kgs. 17.) There was no shutting of the door, no praying to the Lord, no lying upon the child, so as to "put his mouth upon his mouth, and his eyes upon his eyes, and his hands upon his hands," as when Elisha raised from death the son of the great woman of Shunem. (2 Kgs. 4.)

With Jesus it was not so. He said simply: "Young man, I say unto thee, Arise. And he that was dead sat up, and began to speak." Then Jesus graciously, in tender solicitude, "delivered him to his mother."

The living die and the dead live again—because He wills it. There was no importuning of God, nor was there need for such. Jesus did it. Jehovah was there. His words were "I say unto thee, Arise." He was claiming divinity, Messiahship, eternal godhood—and proving his claim (there was no blasphemy here!) by raising the dead!

And is not this first known instance of calling mortals from death to life by Jesus but a type and a shadow—a heaven-sent similitude—of what this same Jesus shall do for all his people at an appointed time? Will he not say to all, 'Come forth from your graves; step out of your tombs; arise from your biers. Live again—this time in glorious immortality, never to suffer the pangs of death again'? And will he not then deliver the righteous into the arms of their mothers and fathers and loved ones?

As the marvel of what had this day happened in Nain dawned upon the throngs in whose presence the miracle was wrought, is it any wonder, as Luke recounts, that "there came a fear on all: and they glorified God, saying, That a great prophet is risen up among us; and, That God hath visited his people. And this rumour of him went forth throughout all Judea, and throughout all the region round about."

Yes, it went even into the dungeon at Machaerus, where John the Baptist suffered in imprisoned silence for the testimony of Jesus that was his. And of this imprisonment and the part it played in the teachings of Jesus we shall soon see.

NOTE

1. These sweet words are taken from a footnote in Farrar, p. 205, and are attributed by him to Arthur Hugh Clough.

JESUS AND JOHN TESTIFY OF EACH OTHER

John: "Behold the Lamb of God,
which taketh away the sin of the world. . . .
He must increase, but I must decrease. . . .
He that believeth on the Son
hath everlasting life."
(John 1:29; 3:30, 36.)

Jesus: "Among those that are born
of women
there is not a greater prophet
than John the Baptist." (Luke 7:28.)

John Sends His Disciples to Jesus

(*Luke 7:18-23; Matthew 11:2-6; JST, Matthew 11:3, 6*)

Our last report on the life and ministry of the one sent to prepare the way for Him by whom salvation comes; our last account relative to the blessed Baptist, who immersed the Son of God in Jordan's waters; our last record told of his imprisonment by Herod Antipas in a dungeon at the impregnable fortress at Machaerus. That word was that Jesus—compassionate, concerned, sorrowful because of the suffering of his beloved associate—sent angels to console and minister to his kinsman. John is still in his dungeon cell suffering manfully, as did so many of his fellow prophets, for the sure knowledge that is his that salvation is in the mighty Messiah whose witness he is.

We know little of what went on in the walled and barred place where the Baptist languished, only that the prisons of that day were places of unbearable torture and evil and heartless imposition. John did have visitors, however; there were times and circumstances when news from the outside could be spoken in his ears. His disciples were yet solicitous for his well-being, and they told him of the teachings and miracles of the Messiah. Word came to him of the eyes that were opened, the ears that were unstopped, and the lepers that were cleansed. He was told that the only son of a widow from Nain—dead, prepared for burial, en route to the cemetery—had responded to a gentle command, "Young man, I say unto thee, Arise," and was now secure in the arms of a rejoicing mother.

Apparently some of the Baptist's disciples desired not only to minister to his needs in the prison, not only to bring him news of the religious movement that was sweeping the land, but also to look to him, rather than to Jesus, as the prophet whom they should follow. Conversion is a process that seldom occurs in an instant suddenly. Gospel grace dawns gradually upon most believers. These disciples knew that John, whom they revered, had seen the heavens open and the Spirit of God descend upon Jesus, and they knew that he had heard the heavenly voice acclaim, "This is my beloved Son, in whom I am well pleased." (Matt. 3:17.) They knew that the son of Zacharias had sent others of his disciples, John the Beloved and Andrew among them, into the fold of Jesus by testifying: "Behold the Lamb of God!" (John 1:36) as Jesus walked among them. They knew that John claimed to be an Elias only, and that from the beginning he had taught that one who came after would baptize them with fire and with the Holy Ghost. All of the Baptist's teachings, every word that he spoke, and every act he performed pointed men toward the Messiah in whom they must believe to gain salvation. Yet there were some who still had not as yet followed his counsel to forsake the lesser light and cleave unto the Light of the world.

What can John do more than he has done? What more can he say than to them he hath said? Clearly there is only one remaining hope. John's disciples must come under the spell of Jesus' voice; they must feel the sweet spirit that comes forth from him; they must see his works, hear him teach the gospel, hear his voice testify of his own divine Sonship. They have heard John; let them now hear Jesus. Is this Prophet of Galilee, noble and renowned as he is, the very one of whom Moses taught? Is he the Messiah who was promised? Let them see and hear and learn for themselves; and so, at John's direction, they go from Machaerus, which is in the south of Perea, near the Dead Sea, to an unnamed location in Galilee.

Finding Jesus and the throngs who hear his words and whose sick he heals, they identify themselves; "John Baptist hath sent us unto thee," they say. Then comes the great question, the question upon which their salvation rests, the question that all investigators must answer for themselves: "Art thou he of whom it is written in the prophets that he should come, or do we look for another?" 'Art thou the Son of God who shall atone for the sins of the world, as promised by all the holy prophets since the world began—including John who sent us—or is our Messiah yet to come in another day to another people? We have heard John's witness. We know he said of you, "He is God's own Son, the Beloved One, the very Lamb of God who shall be sacrificed for the sins of the world," but we would hear the witness from your lips. Art thou the Deliverer, the Savior, the Redeemer, as John says you are?'

The question has been asked; it is a fair and proper inquiry; the issue is before the whole multitude; and Jesus will answer it—answer it in a way that no mortal imposter could. He will show in word and in deed that he is indeed the One of whom they speak.

Jesus Testifies of Himself and of John

(*Luke 7:21-35; JST, Luke 7:24; Matthew 11:6-19; JST, Matthew 11:7, 13-16, 21*)

John's disciples have zeroed in to the heart and core of revealed religion. They have asked: 'Art thou the Son of God, as John says, or is salvation to be found elsewhere and to come through another?' If Jesus answers 'I am he,' to what extent will he enhance the belief of John's followers, who already have heard their own teacher testify, in like words, to the divine Sonship of the one whom he baptized at Bethabara? It is not a spoken answer that is needed here; it is, rather, an answer written in fire, an answer that causes Sinai to quake and smoke to ascend like a furnace; it is an answer written in the flesh and blood and sinews of diseased bodies now made whole. Such an answer the Son of God is prepared to give. The abrupt query of John's disciples is left unanswered for the time being as far as spoken words are concerned. Jesus lets them listen to his sermons and see his miracles. "And in that same hour he cured many of their infirmities and plagues, and of evil spirits; and unto many that were blind he gave sight."

What must they think of one who John says is the Messiah, who does such wonders? Was it ever so in Israel of old? Did even Moses and the greatest of the prophets heal whole multitudes? Who before has ever opened the eyes of a legion of blind persons, or cured the infirmities and plagues of a whole nation of people? Jesus has answered their question, not in words but in works. Now he confirms with his lips the things his hands have done; he confirms the conclusion they must already have reached in their hearts. "Go your way," he says, "and tell John what things ye have seen and heard; how that the blind see, the lame walk, the lepers are cleansed, the deaf hear, the dead are raised, to the poor the gospel is preached." 'Tell John that his witness is true; know also within yourselves that I am he of whom the prophets spoke. These miracles attest to the truth of my words and of John's testimony. Ye have heard me preach the gospel to the poor, as Isaiah promised. What think ye, am I not he? Return and tell John what you have seen, and buoy up his spirit, in the prison of his depression, with the assurance that you now believe him because ye have seen the works I do.'

And further: Blessed is John—who has been faithful and true all his days, and who has been, and now is, valiant in the testimony of Jesus—and blessed also are "whosoever shall not be offended in me." That is, 'You yourselves also will be blessed with the saints if ye believe my words and are not offended by the strong doctrine that I teach.'

With this, the two disciples—who we must believe were now fully converted—left to make their wearisome way back to the south of Perea where an evil Antipas held John as a prisoner in the cause of righteousness. And we cannot but feel that their return southward was attended with a spirit of rejoicing that had not manifested itself in the long journey to see Him of whom the meridian Elias so fervently testified.

After their departure, Jesus said to the multitude concerning John: "What went ye out into the wilderness to see? Was it a reed shaken with the wind?" 'Why did you assemble by the thousands in the deserts around Bethabara, and in the waste places near Aenon? Was it to hear an uncertain sound blown on a muted trumpet? Did John ever waver in his testimony? Did the winds of false doctrine, and the hurricanes of disbelief of your rulers, cause him to so much as sway like a reed before them?' "And they answered him, No."

"But what went ye out for to see? A man clothed in soft raiment? Behold, they which are gorgeously apparelled, and live delicately, are in kings' courts." 'Was John clothed in the princely garments of Antipas, and Philip, and Archelaus, the royal sons of the wretched man who sat on the throne of Israel in the day I made flesh my tabernacle, which sons thereafter reigned in their father's stead? Or did he come in the rough and prophetic garb of an Elijah, from the peasant home of poor Judean folk, to whom all the graces of a kingly court were foreign?'

"But what went ye out for to see? A prophet? Yea, I say unto you, and much more than a prophet." How they had flocked to John to learn his doctrine and hear his testimony! By the thousands and the tens of thousands they had left their homes and traveled to Bethabara and to Aenon, journeys that meant camping overnight in the crude caravanserais of the day, on which occasions there was ample time to ponder and discuss the thunderous challenges of the fiery Judean preacher from Hebron. All Jerusalem, as the hyperbolic account expresses it, had gone out to hear a voice crying in the wilderness, a voice that commanded them to repent, to be baptized for the remission of sins, and to await the day when one coming after should baptize them with fire and the Holy Ghost; a voice that introduced, with testimony, the Lamb of God of whom Moses and all the prophets had spoken. Why had they gone forth to hear a voice that smote their consciences and called for a complete revolution in their way of life? What power swept over a whole people, impelling them to seek out the rugged, Elijah-like prophet of the deserts? And if they all esteemed John as a prophet, how could they escape believing his prophetic witness of the One who now ministered among them?

And he was more than a prophet—"much more than a prophet." It is as though Jesus said: 'Ye yourselves know John was a prophet. Ye went out to hear his voice because it was a prophetic voice, one that spoke the mind and will of the Lord, and now I say unto you that John was a prophet and much more than a prophet!'

How can a man be more than a prophet? What is there that is greater than to be a personal representative on earth of the Lord and to speak his mind and will to all men? Jesus gives a partial answer by now saying of John: "This is he, of whom it is written, Behold, I send my messenger before thy face, which shall prepare thy way before thee."

We learned from Jesus as he sat on the Mount of Beatitudes, delivering his incomparable Sermon on the Mount, that we should beware of false prophets—of the scribes and Pharisees, of the priests and Levites, who professed to be teachers and leaders and prophets but who were in fact ravening wolves in sheep's clothing. Though they wore the mantle of religious leadership, their false teachings tore apart the spiritual well-being of their flocks. Implicit in Jesus' denunciation of false prophets was the standing counsel to cleave unto true prophets. Now he is acclaiming John as a true prophet, "Yea . . . much more than a prophet." John, as a witness of his living Lord, was indeed a prophet, and, in addition, he prepared the way before that very Lord, so that the greatest prophetic ministry ever to grace the earth would be manifest. He served as the Lord's messenger, carrying the message that the Lord himself—the Great Immanuel, the God-with-us of whom Isaiah spoke—was indeed with them.

> *For I say unto you, Among those that are born of women there is not a greater prophet than John the Baptist: but he that is least in the kingdom of God is greater than he.*[1]

There is more than a touch of irony here. As to John, the people honored him as a prophet; but as to Jesus, there was no such unreserved acceptance, even though John testified of him. "Whom did Jesus have reference to as being the least?" Joseph Smith asked. "Jesus was looked upon as having the least claim in God's kingdom, and [seemingly, or at least in the minds of the unbelieving among them] was least entitled to their credulity as a prophet; as though He had said, 'He that is considered [by many of you, as] the least among you is greater than John—that is I myself.' " (*Teachings,* p. 276.) For that matter, if John is the equal or superior of all the prophets, how could anyone be greater than he, except that Prophet of whom Moses and the inspired witnesses of all the ages had spoken?

> *And from the days of John the Baptist until now the kingdom of heaven suffereth violence, and the violent take it by force.*
>
> *But the days will come, when the violent shall have no*

power; for all the prophets and the law prophesied that it should be thus until John. Yea as many as have prophesied have foretold of these days.

And if ye will receive it, verily, he was the Elias, who was for to come and prepare all things. He that hath ears to hear, let him hear.

From the hour John finished the days of his preparation in the wilderness; from the time he first cried repentance to a spiritually sick generation; from the moment he first baptized believing souls in the mighty Jordan—from then "until now," everywhere and in all parts of Palestine, "the kingdom of heaven suffereth violence." Mark it well: the kingdom of heaven set up by John, the kingdom of God on earth, the Church of Jesus Christ, "suffereth violence." And further: "The violent take it by force." There is persecution; there is bitterness. The hosts of hell oppose every investigator who comes near to the truth; the scribes and Pharisees, the priests and Levites—they being the false prophets of the day—marshal their forces. Violence is the result, violence that will mount in intensity until the Elias of preparation is beheaded in Machaerus and the Prophet whose way he prepared is crucified on Calvary. And even then it shall not cease. Violence, born of Beelzebub, ever was and ever will be manifest against the saints until the millennial day, "when the violent shall have no power."[2]

Jesus continues his witness about John: "And all the people that heard him [meaning John], and the publicans, justified God, being baptized with the baptism of John." What a mighty tide of conversion and baptism attended the ministry of the Baptist! The baptism of John—immersion in water by a legal administrator for the remission of sins, the ordinance that prepares men for the baptism of fire and of the Holy Ghost that comes after—this baptism, of which even the hated publicans partook, was ordained of God. All men must be baptized to gain salvation.

"But the Pharisees and lawyers rejected the counsel of God against themselves, being not baptized of him." The counsel of God! God counsels baptism, baptism in water, John's baptism. Some professors of religion do not; they say it is only an outward sign of an inward grace, and that all that matters is how one feels in his heart, or if not that, all that counts is the baptism of desire, or the baptism of the Spirit. But Jesus says that all men—the Pharisees and the lawyers of his day, the false ministers of religion of our day—all must choose whose counsel to take, the counsel that comes from God or that which comes from man.

Then, as a conclusion to this part of his teaching, Jesus asks: "Whereunto then shall I liken the men of this generation? and to what are they like?" He answers: "They are like unto children sitting in the marketplace, and calling one to another, and saying, We have piped unto you, and ye have not danced; we have mourned to you, and ye have not wept. For John the Baptist came neither eating bread nor drinking wine; and ye say, He hath a devil. The Son of man is come eating and drinking; and ye say, Behold a gluttonous man, and a winebibber, a friend of publicans and sinners! But wisdom is justified of all her children."

'What illustration can I choose to show how petty, peevish, and insincere are you unbelieving Jews? You are like fickle children playing games: when you hold a mock wedding, your playmates refuse to dance; when you change the game to a funeral procession, your playmates refuse to mourn. In like manner you are only playing at religion. As cross and capricious children you reject John because he came with the strictness of the Nazarites, and ye reject me because I display the warm human demeanor that makes for pleasant social intercourse.' (*Commentary* 1:263.)

We have now heard John, as an Elias of preparation, bear testimony of the Elias of restoration; and have heard Jesus, in turn, testify of the divine mission of his forerunner. Shortly we shall see John, now languishing in a vile prison, seal his testimony with his blood, preparatory to the receipt of that eternal life of which he is already assured.

NOTES

1. Joseph Smith gave three reasons why John was considered one of the greatest prophets: "First. He was entrusted with a divine mission of preparing the way before the face of the Lord. Whoever had such a trust committed to him before or since? No man.

"Secondly. He was entrusted with the important mission, and it was required at his hands, to baptize the Son of Man. Whoever had the honor of doing that? Whoever had so great a privilege and glory? Whoever led the Son of God into the waters of baptism, and had the privilege of beholding the Holy Ghost descend in the form of a dove, or rather in the *sign* of the dove, in witness of that administration? . . .

"Thirdly. John, at that time, was the only legal administrator in the affairs of the kingdom there was then on earth, and holding the keys of power. The Jews had to obey his instructions or be damned, by their own law; and Christ Himself fulfilled all righteousness in becoming obedient to the law which he had given to Moses on the mount, and thereby magnified it and made it honorable, instead of destroying it. The son of Zacharias wrested the keys, the kingdom, the power, the glory from the Jews, by the holy anointing and decree of heaven, and these three reasons constitute him the greatest prophet born of woman." (*Teachings,* pp. 275-76.)

2. In this connection, as I have written elsewhere: "Under the law of Moses a lower standard of personal conduct was required of members of the kingdom than became the case when the gospel fulness was restored. In the old kingdom violent and carnal men exercised undue influence, but in the new kingdom their power was diminished. But the millennium itself must arrive before 'the violent shall have no power.' " (*Commentary* 1:263.)

Chapter 47

JESUS FACES HIS PHARISAIC FOES

She sat and wept beside his feet; the weight
Of sin oppressed her heart; for all the blame,
And the poor malice of the worldly shame,
To her were past, extinct, and out of date;
Only the sin remained—the leprous *state*.
She would be melted by the heat of love,
By fires far fiercer than are blown to prove
And purge the silver ore adulterate.
She sat and wept, and with her untressed hair,
Still wiped the feet she was so blessed to touch;
And He wiped off the soiling of despair
From her sweet soul, because she loved so much.[1]

His Feet Anointed in Simon's House

(*Luke 7:36-50*)

It is now autumn, A.D. 28. Jesus has been traveling, teaching, testifying, and healing for nearly two years. Timewise most of his mortal ministry is accomplished, and in another year and a half, by April of A.D. 30, he will be lifted up upon the cross by sinful men—sinful scribes and Pharisees, sinful priests and Levites, who will use a Roman arm and a Roman cross, a Roman nail and a Roman spear, to do what they cannot do personally.

And we are now seeing a gradually rising tide of Pharisaic opposition that will roll forward, on waves of hatred and bitterness, until it becomes a mighty crescendo of tumult and thunderous denunciation, punctuated with shrill cries of, "Crucify him; crucify him; his blood be upon us and our children." Already we have seen him rejected by his own in Nazareth; we have heard the murmuring charges of blasphemy when he forgave and then healed the paralytic in Peter's home in Capernaum; we have gone with him to the second Passover in Jerusalem, seen him heal on the Sabbath the man who for thirty-eight years had taken no step on his own; and we have felt pity for those who thereafter sought to slay him because he worked a miracle on their holy day. Back in Galilee, again because he healed on the Sabbath, we have seen the Rabbis, scribes, and Sanhedrinists conspire with the Herodians as to how they might put him to death.

And through it all we have heard Jesus speak loving words to the penitent—as illustrated in the Beatitudes—and send forth harsh denunciations toward his foes and oppressors, as witness his declarations, just made, against those who had called the Son of Man a glutton and a winebibber because of his friendly social intercourse with the people, and a friend of publicans and sinners because his arms and heart were open to all who would hear his voice.

We cannot doubt that this rising tide of opposition was part of the divine plan. It was the preaching of the gospel and the performance of his miracles, strange as this latter may seem, that caused it to spring forth. There will even be Jewish opponents who will seek to slay Lazarus, after he rises from the dead, lest people seeing him alive believe in Christ.

Jesus may not have courted persecution and opposition as such, but the proclamation of a new gospel dispensation, proclaimed to those who fear for their craft, can have no other effect. Indeed, it would appear that "in the unfolding of His Mission to Man, the Christ progressively placed Himself in antagonism to the Jewish religious thought of his time, from out of which He had historically sprung. . . . From the first this antagonism was there in what He taught and did; and it appeared with increasing distinctness in proportion as He taught. We find it in the whole spirit and bearing of what he did and said—in the house at Capernaum, in the Synagogues, with the Gentile Centurion, at the gate of Nain, and especially here, in the history of the much forgiven woman who had much sinned." (Edersheim 1:562.)

And so now we join Jesus in the home of Simon the Pharisee to see what happens when the "much sinned" woman anoints his feet with her tears and with costly ointment brought in an alabaster box. We do not know the name of the city, who Simon was, or who the woman was; only that the banquet, the anointing, and the blessed words spoken by Jesus, all took place somewhere in Galilee. In Holy Writ a fragmentary account only is preserved for us. From it, in Luke's language, we learn that "one of the Pharisees desired him that he would eat with him. And he went into the Pharisee's house, and sat down to meat."

Jesus has often eaten with publicans and known sinners, for which he has, by sinning Pharisees, been condemned. Now he accepts the invitation of one who wears the mantle of religion, but who has not received a remission of his sins in the waters of baptism, and in whose presence a woman of ill repute will come to render to Jesus the obeisance and respect that his host chose not to bestow. It was the social custom of the day for leading Pharisees of a village or city to invite visiting Rabbis to break bread with them in their abodes. Some of Jesus' disciples would have been included by Simon in his invitation. Hospitality was a way of life among them, and it was honorable and proper to feed and shelter visiting teachers and travelers.

Guests entering Palestinian homes often removed their sandals, lest the pollutions of the street contaminate the mats and rugs on which family prayers were offered. At the dining table they reclined on couches with their feet outward from the table, and the dining hall was accessible to others than those bidden to partake of its appetite-satisfying bounties. All of this enabled "a woman in the city, which was a sinner," carrying "an alabaster box of ointment," to enter uninvited and to stand behind Jesus. According to the social customs of the day she could even speak to the guests without being bidden to depart by the master of the house. This, however, she did not do; rather, she "stood at his feet behind him weeping, and began to wash his feet with her tears, and did wipe them with the hairs of her head, and kissed his feet, and anointed them with the ointment."

All of the usual amenities of the day had been ignored by the day's host, as Jesus will soon remind him. But what the host should have done, however reluctantly, the unbidden spectator—and she a woman—had now done with a full heart and in a spirit of penitence and thanksgiving. Why did she do it? What would impel a woman whose life had been stained with sin—stained? perhaps drenched and buried in sin, for her past life could not have been other than one of gross immorality—what would impel such a person to come uninvited, face the Sinless One, and, as her tears bedewed his feet, wipe them with her tresses and seal the washing thus made with an anointing of costly ointment? She first washed the feet of Jesus with her tears, then anointed them with oil. Why? And was all this done by an evil sinner? No!—not by any means. All this was the work and worship of a devout and faithful woman who had been a sinner but who was now cleansed; who was now free from the crushing burden of many offenses; who now walked in a newness of life because of him whose feet she now kissed and upon whom she now bestowed all the reverent and awe-inspired love that her whole soul had power to possess.

This we must know if we are to envision what really transpired on this inspiring occasion in the home of Simon the Pharisee. Here is a woman who once was a sinner but now is clean. Jesus is not going to forgive her sins—he has already done so; it happened when she believed and was baptized in his name; it happened when she repented with full purpose of heart and pledged her life and every breath she thereafter drew to the Cause of Righteousness. We are dealing with a convert who has come to pour out, in the spirit of thanksgiving and rejoicing, the gratitude of her soul to him who has freed her, freed her in times past, from the chains of bondage and hell.

None of this is known to Simon. He is in his sins, being unbaptized; and like Nicodemus, the master in Israel who knew not that men can be born again, Simon is, in his present state, spiritually incapable of conceiving that a woman whose soul once was scarlet is now as white as snow.

Simon thus "spake within himself"; that is, he thought to himself—and as the ancient proverb says: "Guard well thy thoughts, for thoughts are heard in heaven"—Simon thought to himself: "This man, if he were a prophet, would have known who and what manner of woman this is that toucheth him: for she is a sinner." There is no sprouting faith here. Jesus is only "this man," not, as so many are saying, a mighty prophet and even the Messiah, who is called Christ, who is God's Son. Simon's thoughts toward his guest are no more respectful than were his deeds.[2]

"Jesus answering"—he is answering the unspoken thoughts—"said unto him, Simon, I have somewhat to say unto thee. And he saith, Master, say on." Jesus then said:

> *There was a certain creditor which had two debtors: the one owed five hundred pence, and the other fifty.*
>
> *And when they had nothing to pay, he frankly forgave them both. Tell me therefore, which of them will love him most?*

In this illustration, which can scarcely be classed as a parable, "Jesus entered into the Pharisees' own modes of reasoning. Of two debtors, one of whom owed ten times as much as the other, who would best love the creditor who had freely forgiven them? Though to both the debt might have been equally impossible of discharge, and both might love equally, yet a *Rabbi* would, according to his Jewish notions, say, that he would love most to whom most had been forgiven. If this was the undoubted outcome of Jewish theology—the so much for so much—let it be applied to the present case. If there were much benefit, there would be much love; if little benefit, little love. And conversely: in such case much love would argue much benefit; little love, small benefit." (Edersheim 1:567-68.) As anticipated, Simon answered, "I suppose," and in this beginning there seems to be a touch of supercilious aloofness, an indication that Simon had no idea of whom Jesus had spoken, "I suppose," he replies, "that he, to whom he forgave most."

Jesus said, "Thou hast rightly judged." The answer had been given; the scene was set. All at the dinner table were attentive; all were acutely aware of Simon's host-imposed failures, of the woman's worshipful act, and of the Divine Presence, whose gracious words always presented a heavenly message in the best way. And so, turning to the woman, but speaking to Simon, Jesus said:

> *Simon, Seest thou this woman? I entered into thine house, thou gavest me no water for my feet: but she hath washed my feet with tears, and wiped them with the hairs of her head.*
>
> *Thou gavest me no kiss: but this woman since the time I came in hath not ceased to kiss my feet.*
>
> *My head with oil thou didst not anoint: but this woman hath anointed my feet with ointment.*

How beautifully painted is the picture; how expertly chosen are the words. Simon—a Pharisee, a leader of the people and man of note, a pillar in the synagogue, who gloried in his supposed righteousness—Simon proffered none of the usual civilities and courtesies, however ritualistic and meaningless they often were; but this woman, unnamed and otherwise unknown, reputed to be a sinner to whom the services in the synagogue held no allure, who scarcely deserved any attention in such an august gathering, had poured out, from the depths of her soul, such gratitude and thanksgiving and worship as is seldom seen. Then came the crowning pronouncement:

Wherefore I say unto thee, Her sins, which are many, are forgiven, for she loved much: but to whom little is forgiven, the same loveth little.

Thus Simon received the word; he stood instructed and rebuked, but it was the woman to whom the blessing must come. To her Jesus said, "Thy sins are forgiven." Properly rendered, the two phrases, the first to Simon and the second to the woman, should read: "Forgiven have been her sins, the many," and "Thy sins have been forgiven, the many." (Edersheim 1:568-69.) That is to say, her sins were forgiven in times past, which Jesus now confirms, not her sins are now being forgiven by some special dispensation.[3]

To conclude the whole matter—while "they that sat at meat with him began to say within themselves, Who is this that forgiveth sins also?" for they, like Simon, knew not what was involved in the law of repentance and baptism and forgiveness—Jesus "said to the woman, Thy faith hath saved thee; go in peace," or, again, as it is more properly rendered, "Go into peace" (Edersheim 1:569), meaning continue in the peace that is yours because you have believed and obeyed the gospel law.

Jesus Continues to Travel and Preach with His Friends

(*Luke 8:1-3; JST, Luke 8:1*)

Throughout his whole ministry, Jesus traveled, preached, and healed. We are now with him in the autumn of A.D. 28 when he is making another tour of Galilee. An unnamed woman has but recently washed his feet with her tears, dried them with her tresses, and then anointed them with ointment—as she worshipped at his feet—while he sat, or rather reclined, at meat in the home of Simon the Pharisee. Now, in Galilee, he is visiting "every city and village, preaching and showing the glad tidings of the kingdom of God."

We repeat—and the concept must be ever before us, lest we slip into the sectarian concept that Jesus' ministry was one of teaching ethical verities only, that he was not, as a teacher, first and foremost one who taught doctrine, or that he was not a theologian of superlative capacity—we repeat that his teaching was "the glad tidings of the kingdom of God." In other words, he preached the gospel, as all the prophets preached it. He proclaimed the fatherhood of God, his own divine Sonship, the fall of Adam, and the resultant atoning sacrifice of a Savior of the world. His message was: 'Come unto Christ and be perfected in him; accept him as the Son of God; believe his words and live his law; repent of your sins and be baptized with the baptism of John, that, in due course, you may receive the baptism of fire and of the Holy Ghost.' Jesus taught the gospel; let us never forget it. Should we do so, we shall build on a foundation of sand, and when the rains of uncertainty fall and the winds of skepticism blow and the floods of persecution beat vehemently upon us, our house of partial faith, of partial knowledge, of partial understanding will fall.

With reference to this missionary journey, Luke specifies that Jesus took with him a large entourage. Apostles, disciples, and loyal followers were almost always with him as he taught and traveled. His work was not done in a corner, and always, by precept and by example, he was training others to do and be as he did and was. This time they included "the twelve who were ordained of him"—those chosen and foreordained witnesses who were now beginning to bear with him the burdens of the earthly kingdom, and who would carry a witness of his name to nations afar off, before their mortal ministries ended; he took with him the Twelve; also "certain women, which had been healed of evil spirits and infirmities"; also "Mary called Magdalene, out of whom went seven devils"; also "Joanna the wife of Chuza Herod's steward"; also Susanna; and also "many others." And all of these "ministered unto him of their substance," which is to say, he traveled without purse or scrip, as it were, relying on the goodness of God and the sustaining help of his believing friends for food and for clothing and for shelter. Jesus obeyed his own law that the laborer is worthy of his hire and that "they which preach the gospel should live of the gospel." (1 Cor. 9:14.)

And who shall say that it is anything less than a glorious privilege to feed and aid the Holy One of Israel in his mortal labors? Could those who had substance do other than rejoice at the privilege of sharing it—be it only a crust or a crumb—with him whose all things are, but who made himself subject to all of earth's ills and needs, that in due course he might rise above all things? And wherein is this different in principle from what the faithful always do when they share their substance with the servants of the Lord, or with their fellowmen, always knowing that whatsoever they do unto the least of the Lord's ministers, or to the least of his earthly brethren, they do unto him?

Would that we knew more—someday we will!—of the faithful ones who trod in the tracks of Jesus; who heard the truths of heaven from his divine lips; who saw the miracles he wrought; who learned from him how they, in turn, should carry the same message of salvation—the gospel message; "the glad tidings of the kingdom of God"—to yet others of earth's inhabitants. We have slivers of knowledge about each of the Twelve, which we have noted or will yet mention in other connections. Of Susanna we know nothing; of Joanna, the wife of Chuza Herod's steward, the record also is bare, although we speculate that she may have been the mother of the young man, the nobleman's son, who was healed by Jesus' word spoken in Cana while the youth was in Capernaum.

Of Mary, called Magdalene, we must make special mention. Her life was interwoven intimately with that of the Lord Jesus himself. She apparently came from Magdala, as the identifying appendage to her name signifies. At some unrecorded time she was healed by Jesus from severe physical and mental maladies, and from her body the Master—of the seen and the unseen—cast out seven devils. Hers was no ordinary illness, and we cannot do other than suppose that she underwent some great spiritual test—a personal Gethsemane, a personal temptation in the wilderness for forty days, as it were—which she overcame and rose above—all preparatory to the great mission and work she was destined to perform.

How often it is that the chosen and elect of God wrestle with physical, mental, and devilish infirmities as they cleanse and perfect their souls preparatory to the ministerial service they are called upon to render. A Moses with his stammering tongue, and a Paul with his thorn in the flesh, are called upon to rise above their flesh-born ills and be the teachers and witnesses they were destined to be. That Mary Magdalene passed whatever test a divine providence imposed upon her, we cannot doubt. And so we find her here, traveling with and ministering to the needs of the One who chose his intimates with perfect insight.

Hereafter we shall see her at the cross, a sword piercing her soul as it pierced that of another Mary, the Blessed Virgin, as they both witness the death struggles of the One who had life in himself. Then we shall find her at Joseph's tomb where Jesus' body is laid; and again, bringing spices and ointments to embalm his body; and again in the bare and open tomb whence his resurrected body has risen; and again, seeing the angelic shape and hearing the angelic words, "Why seek ye the living among the dead? He is not here, but is risen" (Luke 24:5-6); and yet again in the Garden, as the first mortal to see a resurrected personage, we shall see her with the Risen Lord, anxious to embrace him, and being restrained by his gentle command and explanation that he had not yet ascended to his Father. We suppose also that she was in the upper room with the other sorrowing worshippers when the Lord, whose body was one of flesh and bones, now appeared to his saints, that they might feel the nail marks in his hands and in his feet and thrust their hands into the gaping wound in his riven side. Can we do other than rank Mary Magdalene with the Blessed Virgin, with Mother Eve, and with Sarah, the wife of Abraham?[4]

As to the other "women, which had been healed of evil spirits and infirmities," and as to the "many others," even their names, for the present, are unknown. Those today who are kindred in spirit to them, who have like faith and like good works, may, of course, see their ancient counterparts in visions. And in that glorious day when all the faithful sit down in the kingdom of God, with Abraham, Isaac, and Jacob, and all the holy prophets, to go no more out, then all shall know and love each other, and, indeed, shall even remember the long association they had in preexistence—all in preparation for the probations of mortality, for the day when each, according to his assignment, would play his role in the eternal gospel drama, in the unfolding plan of the Almighty for the salvation of his children.

But for now let us continue our journey through Galilee with the Blessed Party, headed by the Blessed Personality, as the Blessed Teachings fall from his lips and the Blessed Acts of providence and goodness are wrought by his hands. Soon, with this select group of favored friends of our Friend, the Lord Jesus, we shall see him heal one whose affliction was imposed by an evil spirit inhabiting his body—because of which healing the tide of rising opposition will swell to new heights, and Jesus will come forth with new and strong doctrine.

NOTES

1. Hartley Coleridge, quoted, Farrar, p. 231.

2. "If 'this Man,' this strange, wandering, popular idol, with His strange, novel ways and words, Whom in politeness he must call 'Teacher,' Rabbi, *were* a Prophet, He would have known who the woman was, and, if He had known who she was, then would He never have allowed such approach." (Edersheim 1:567.)

3. "In effect Jesus is saying: 'Her sins were many, but she believed in me, has repented of her sins, was baptized by my disciples, and her sins were washed away in the waters of baptism. Now she has sought me out to exhibit the unbounded gratitude of one who was filthy, but is now clean. Her gratitude knows no bounds and her love is beyond measure, for she was forgiven of much. Had she been forgiven of but few sins, she would not have loved me so intensely.' " (*Commentary* 1:265.)

4. "She is not to be confused with the unnamed though repentant sinner who anointed Jesus' feet in the home of Simon. (Luke 7:36-50.) It is one of the basest slanders of all history to suppose that Mary of Magdala was a fallen woman and therefore to use the term *Magdalene* as an appellation descriptive of reformed prostitutes." (*Commentary* 1:266.)

THE FAMILY OF JESUS AND THE FAMILY OF LUCIFER

If ye were Abraham's children,
ye would do the works of Abraham. . . .
If God were your Father,
ye would love me. . . .
Ye are of your father the devil.
(John 8:39, 42, 44.)

"He Casteth out Devils through Beelzebub"

(*Matthew 12:22-30; JST, Matthew 12:20-23; Mark 3:22-27; JST, Mark 3:18-19; Luke 11:14-15; 17:23; JST, Luke 11:15, 18-19, 23*)

Our group of penitent believers—the Twelve, Mary Magdalene, Joanna, Susanna, and many others, both men and women—are traveling, preaching, healing, basking in the light of the Lord, through every city and village of Galilee. We say that they, all of them, were engaged in ministerial service, for we cannot doubt that Jesus called on others to express themselves, and delegated power and authority to worthy associates, as rapidly as they were able to perform the assigned labors. He was building men and sanctifying women, and though the records speak only of what he did and said—as they should, he being the Son of God—yet others were in process of growing in the things of the Spirit so that after his departure they would be prepared to step forth in dignity and with honor and carry on the work the Master had commenced.

They—our missionary group—come into Capernaum, the site of so many of Jesus' wondrous doings. Here there is brought to him "one possessed with a devil, blind, and dumb." This poor suffering soul, what manifold miseries weighed him down. He neither saw nor heard, and to top it all—an ill much greater than the physical imperfections—he was possessed by a devil, by one of the evil spirits who craved a body, even such a one as this, and even for such a moment of ill-gotten tenancy as was here allowed. Jesus healed him. He saw; he spoke; the devil departed. It was no ordinary miracle, for the affliction was of no common kind; it was of such magnitude as to deserve special recitation in Holy Writ. We cannot doubt that the man somehow had gained faith to make possible and bring to pass the marvelous deed; and we know that immediately thereafter, "all the people were amazed"—as well they might be—and that hosts said, as though in unison, "Is not this the son of David?" 'Is not this the Messiah who was to come? Is he not that Prophet of whom Moses spoke? Is he not the Son of God who is to redeem his people? And shall we not, therefore, follow him, and live his law?'[1]

Such a fame and a name has now fastened itself to this famous Galilean, that his steps are everywhere dogged with spies and enemies sent by the Sanhedrin to gain evidence against him. The rising tide of opposition is beating with increasing fury upon the Eternal Rock. And so, Mark says, "the scribes which came down from Jerusalem said, He hath Beelzebub, and by the prince of the devils casteth he out devils."

His miracle was a known reality. Blind eyes now saw; deaf ears now heard; the demon from hell had given up his stolen home. Jesus' act of mercy and healing was known to all. They were even hailing him as David's Son! Unless this and like miracles are explained away, the priestcrafts of the priests will be replaced by a new order; the scribes and

Pharisees must disabuse the public mind or lose their positions of power and influence over the people.

He casteth out devils by Beelzebub! That is the solution to their problem, and from their standpoint it is a good one. Since the miracle cannot be denied, the alternative is to say it was wrought by Satanic power, that Satan cast out Satan, that the prince of devils said to an underling in his kingdom, Depart hence. This would even explain the opened eyes and the unstopped ears, for if Jesus operated by evil power, then all that he did was morally wrong.

This Pharisaic approach to Jesus and his ministry; this Rabbinic way of turning light into darkness; this priest-ridden denial and denunciation not of the miracle itself, but of the power by which it was wrought—all this is a perfect illustration of how Lucifer, in all ages, fights the truth. The latter-day miracle of Mormonism—Oh, it is nothing, say the ministers, because there is a flaw, so they assume falsely, in the doctrine. Pay no attention to the fruits of the prophetically planted tree, say the divines of the day; what if the fruit is good, for we have found (as they falsely suppose) a theological flaw in their beliefs. And since anyone can debate doctrine, let's get the spirit of contention in every heart; let's get an argument going about dotted I's and crossed T's; then people will forget the great and eternal blessings that flow from the restored gospel.

And so with the Pharisees. How helpful, they reason, if we can get the people arguing about the source rather than the fact of Jesus' power. If we can make people think he works by Satan's power, then no matter whether he raises the dead or calls down manna from heaven, it will all be part of demoniac delusion from which men must flee.

So perfectly does this Satan-born, Lucifer-inspired, devil-directed attack of the Pharisees illustrate how the enemy of all righteousness fights the truth, so cunning and evil is the approach, that it is worth our while to dwell upon it with some particularity. "To *us* a single well-ascertained miracle would form irrefragable evidence of the claims of Christ; to *them* it would not," as Edersheim so persuasively reasons. "They could believe in the 'miracles,' and yet not in the Christ. To them the question would not be, as to us, whether they were miracles—but, By what power, or in what Name, He did these deeds? From our standpoint, their opposition to the Christ would—in view of His Miracles—seem not only wicked, but rationally inexplicable. But ours was not their point of view.

"And here, again, we perceive that it was enmity to the *Person* and *Teaching* of Jesus which led to the denial of His claims. The inquiry: By what power Jesus did these works? they met by the assertion, that it was through that of Satan, or the Chief of the Demons. They regarded Jesus, as not only temporarily, but permanently, possessed by a demon, that is, as the constant vehicle of Satanic influence. And this demon was, according to them, none other than Beelzebub, the prince of the devils. Thus, in their view, it was really Satan who acted in and through Him; and Jesus, instead of being recognised as the Son of God, was regarded as an incarnation of Satan; instead of being owned as the Messiah, was denounced and treated as the representative of the Kingdom of Darkness. All this, because the Kingdom which He came to open, and which He preached, was precisely the opposite of what they regarded as the Kingdom of God. Thus it was the essential contrariety of Rabbinism to the Gospel of Christ that lay at the foundation of their conduct towards the Person of Christ. We venture to assert, that this accounts for the whole after-history up to the Cross.

"Thus viewed, the history of Pharisaic opposition appears not only consistent, but is, so to speak, morally accounted for. Their guilt lay in treating that as Satanic agency which was of the Holy Ghost; and this, because they were of their father the Devil, and knew not, nor understood, nor yet loved the Light, their deeds being evil. They were not children of the light, but of that darkness which comprehended Him not Who was the Light. And now we can also understand the growth of active opposition to

Christ. Once arrived at the conclusion, that the miracles which Christ did were due to the power of Satan, and that He was the representative of the Evil One, their course was rationally and morally chosen. To regard every fresh manifestation of Christ's Power as only a fuller development of the power of Satan, and to oppose it with increasing determination and hostility, even to the Cross: such was henceforth the natural progress of this history." (Edersheim 1:574-75.)

Much as this reasoning may salve or sear the consciences of the Pharisaic practicers of priestcraft; much as it may make the ministers of our day feel that Mormonism is a monumental fraud; much as it may lay to rest, in the public mind, the rising dawn of a new day—yet it is weak, futile, and doomed to ultimate failure. The real issues are: What is the truth, where is the truth, and who has the truth. In Jesus' day, the true answers lay with him; in our day, they rest with those of us who are his latter-day servants. Jesus has heretofore taught that to find the truth about religion, men must gain personal revelation from God by the power of the Holy Ghost. Now he contents himself by saying that he cast out devils by the power of God and not the power of the devil, and his declaratory reasoning is irrefutable. "How can Satan cast out Satan?" he asks, and he says in answer:

> *Every kingdom divided against itself is brought to desolation; and every city or house divided against itself shall not stand.*

With this reasoning none can contend; even the scribes and Pharisees must agree—it is a simple summation of all secular history. Divided kingdoms fall, and the day comes when they are left desolate. And so, he continues:

> *If Satan cast out Satan, he is divided against himself; how then shall his kingdom stand?*

His conclusion is irrefutable. Such strength as Satan has is in the united power of his evil ways; if he divides his strength, what is left?

> *And if I by Beelzebub cast out devils, by whom do your*

children cast them out? therefore they shall be your judges.

This would be a sore point. Jesus was not alone in casting out devils. Others, by faith, had the same power: others of the house of Israel then ministered among them with power to control the demons in hell. What power did they use? This was no longer a personal matter, a matter dealing with him alone. He had made converts, and whole congregations had come into the kingdom. If so many others found the truth, why shouldn't these bickering scribes?

> *But if I cast out devils by the Spirit of God, then the kingdom of God is come unto you. For they also cast out devils by the Spirit of God, for unto them is given power over devils, that they may cast them out.*

Jesus cast out devils. He did it by the power of God, for Satan cannot cast out Satan, and, therefore, he is divine; the kingdom has been set up; the true Church has been established among them. And—mark it well—the others who cast out devils had the same power. They too were members of the Church; they too held the holy priesthood; they were followers of the One who then spoke to them.

> *Or else how can one enter into a strong man's house, and spoil his goods, except he first bind the strong man? and then he will spoil his house.*

The reasoning is good; the conclusion is true; the lesson is well taught. Christ has entered the worldly realm of Lucifer, has bound the strong man who reigns therein, has cast out his minions from their ill-gotten abodes, and will in due course spoil the whole house and send away into outer darkness those whose dwelling it is.

> *He that is not with me is against me: and he that gathereth not with me scattereth abroad.*

'I am Christ; I cast out devils in my Father's name; I heal the sick by his power; salvation comes by me. Let none of you longer stand neutral. Either ye are with me, or ye are against me. Unless you come unto me, and espouse my cause, and keep my commandments, ye are against me. There is no middle ground.'

Jesus Speaks of Forgiveness and the Unpardonable Sin

(*Matthew 12:31-37, 43-45; JST, Matthew 12:26, 37-39; Mark 3:28-30; JST, Mark 3:21-25; Luke 6:45; 11:24-26; 12:8-10; JST, Luke 11:25-27; 12:10-12*)

Our Theologian-Friend—for such he is: the Chief Theologian, among all the professors of religion ever to dwell on planet earth—our Theologian-Friend is now about to preach some strong, even harsh doctrine. He stands accused—by scribal scripturalists and Pharisaic preachers—of being in league with Lucifer; of casting out devils and working miracles by the power of Beelzebub, the prince of devils. They have said he is not an incarnate God but an incarnate devil. In his response he has shown that a house divided against itself cannot stand and that Satan cannot cast out Satan lest he destroy himself.

To understand the doctrine Jesus is about to preach, we must let our eyes rest, first, upon the scene of spiritual anarchy created by his miracles, by the resultant charges laid against him, and by his response thereto. Some of his hearers believe his teachings to the full; among them are the Twelve, Mary Magdalene, and the others who traveled and consorted with him. Some of his hearers are defiant, rebellious, hateful; in their hearts is the spirit of murder, and they would fain destroy him if they could. This group is headed and guided and influenced by the scribal spies of the Great Sanhedrin which sits in Jerusalem itself. Yet others of his hearers choose to stand neutral; their spiritual strength does not align them with the ensign of righteousness that he has raised. They fear the Pharisees and have postponed a decision as to where and with whom they will pledge their allegiance. It is of them that Jesus has just said that those who are not for him are against him—there is no such thing as neutrality in the cause of truth and righteousness, either on earth or in heaven—and they who do not gather with him, by their indifference and indecision, scatter abroad. But further, amid the religious contention aroused by Jesus' ministry, there were some of his disciples who had begun to fear and who, under the pressure of public opinion, had spoken against him.

As Luke records, Jesus said: "Whosoever shall confess me before men, him shall the Son of man also confess before the angels of God: But he that denieth me before men shall be denied before the angels of God." Then comes this explanation as to why these words had been forthcoming: "Now his disciples knew that he said this, because they had spoken evil against him before the people; for they were afraid to confess him before men. And they reasoned among themselves, saying, He knoweth our hearts, and he speaketh to our condemnation, and we shall not be forgiven."

We can envision somewhat the anxiety and anguish that engulfed their souls. They had known and still knew of his divine Sonship, and yet—fearing men, unable to withstand the social and religious pressures of the day—they had joined with the dominant religious groups and spoken evilly of this Man of whom Moses wrote. Can traitors be forgiven? Could they again find grace in his sight? His answer to their thoughts of anguish and sorrow was Christ-like. "Whosoever shall speak a word against the Son of man, and repenteth, it shall be forgiven him," he said, "But unto him who blasphemeth against the Holy Ghost, it shall not be forgiven him." The scene is thus set; we are now ready to hear Jesus' profound doctrine. In Matthew's account it follows the proclamation that those who are not for him are against him. Jesus now says:

> *Wherefore I say unto you, All manner of sin and blasphemy shall be forgiven unto men who receive me and repent; but the blasphemy against the Holy Ghost, it shall not be forgiven unto men.*
>
> *And whosoever speaketh a word against the Son of man, it shall be forgiven him: but whosoever speaketh against the Holy Ghost, it shall not be forgiven him, neither in this world, neither in the world to come.*

There is an unpardonable sin, a sin for which there is no

forgiveness, neither in time nor in eternity. It is blasphemy against the Holy Ghost; it is to deny Christ, to come out in open rebellion, to make open war against the Son of Man—after gaining, by the power of the Holy Ghost, a sure and perfect knowledge of the truth and divinity of the Lord's work. It is to shed innocent blood, meaning to assent unto the death of Christ—to crucify him afresh, Paul says[2]—with a full and absolute knowledge that he is the Son of God. It is to wage open warfare, as does Lucifer, against the Lord and his Anointed, knowing that the course so pursued is evil. It is to deny—to say the sun does not shine while seeing its blazing light—it is to deny Christ after a sure and irrevocable testimony has been received by the power of the Holy Ghost. Hence, it is a scurrilous and evil declaration against the Holy Ghost, against the sole and only source of absolute and sure knowledge. It is blasphemy against the Holy Ghost.[3]

Let men without this sure knowledge speak even against Christ himself; let them commit all manner of sins and blasphemies, even murder, and yet when the penalties have been paid and a proper repentance granted, men shall come forth in immortality and gain an inheritance in whatever kingdom of glory they merit. Only the sons of perdition shall be cast out eternally to live and reign with Lucifer in hell forever. Such is the mercy and wonder of that eternal plan—the gospel of God, now named after Christ his Son—which a gracious God has provided for all his children.[4]

We cannot reconstruct the sequential order in which each spoken sentence fell from the lips of Jesus. Our synoptic friends, in recounting the same episodes, select different portions of the same discourse to emphasize the doctrine or teaching that seemed to them to be of greatest import. And as Jesus so often taught in the midst of surging and moving throngs, it is natural to assume that he repeated, summarized, paraphrased, and expanded his expressions as the needs of the moment required. We can only use our best judgment in lacing the varying comments of Matthew,

Mark, and Luke into one consecutive narrative. Apparently at this point, as Mark records it, the following colloquy occurred:

> *And then came certain men unto him, accusing him, saying, Why do ye receive sinners, seeing thou makest thyself the Son of God.*

Need we remind ourselves at this late date, as we study and ponder the sayings and doings of the Master, that he always and everywhere, without hesitancy, fear, or the slightest degree of self-effacement, has acclaimed and taught that he was God's Almighty Son. This is one point upon which there has been and is to be no question, no doubt, no secrecy. If he sometimes speaks in figures, or similitudes, or parables, so be it; but the message is always the same. 'I am the Son of God; I am the Messiah. Believe and obey my words. I am he; I am the Great Jehovah.' The Jews of that day heard what he said and knew what the words meant; for them it was a matter of believing or disbelieving, as it is also today when the message of salvation is proclaimed to a wicked world.

> *But he answered them and said, Verily I say unto you, All sins which men have committed, when they repent, shall be forgiven them; for I came to preach repentance unto the sons of men.*

Thus, again we hear him phrase a profound proclamation. He came to cry repentance; there is no other course leading to salvation. Repent and believe the gospel; such ever has been and ever will be the divine will. Of course he received sinners. Who else is it that needs repentance? How else can he fulfill his divine commission to present the message of salvation to his mortal brethren?

> *And blasphemies, wherewith soever they shall blaspheme, shall be forgiven them that come unto me, and do the works which they see me do.*

Was it any different now than it had always been? Had not this same Jesus said to them of old, "As often as my people repent will I forgive them their trespasses against me." (Mosiah 26:30.) Did the very disciples themselves falter in their devotion and speak evilly of him? Let them repent. Were there those among men whose hearts were touched by the heavenly light and who desired salvation? Let them repent. Were there rebels, ungodly wretches, and scribes and Pharisees who thirsted for his blood? Let them repent. Repentance is for all accountable persons. There is no other gate through which men may walk to place their feet on the strait and narrow path leading to eternal life.

> *But there is a sin which shall not be forgiven. He that shall blaspheme against the Holy Ghost, hath never forgiveness; but is in danger of being cut down out of the world. And they shall inherit eternal damnation.*
>
> *And this he said unto them because they said, He hath an unclean spirit.*

Again the message is given that forgiveness is for all except those who shall be damned eternally, those who blaspheme against the Holy Ghost, those who crucify Christ afresh, as it were, having a perfect knowledge, born of the Spirit, that he is the Son of God. And even those who said he had an unclean spirit and cast out devils by Beelzebub, the prince of devils, could repent and be forgiven, if they would.

Now we come to that portion of our Lord's discourse in which he excoriates his Pharisaic foes and in which he tells those who oppose him why they shall be judged and found wanting.

> *Either make the tree good, and his fruit good; or else make the tree corrupt, and his fruit corrupt: for the tree is known by his fruit.*

'Be consistent, you Pharisees; make the tree good or bad. If it is good to cast out devils, and I cast them out, then my work is good, for a tree is known by its fruits; but if I am evil, as you say, then it must be a wicked thing to heal those possessed of evil spirits, for a corrupt tree bringeth forth evil fruit.' (*Commentary* 1:275.)

> *O generation of vipers, how can ye, being evil, speak*

good things? for out of the abundance of the heart the mouth speaketh.

A good man out of the good treasure of the heart bringeth forth good things: and an evil man out of the evil treasure bringeth forth evil things.

A parallel passage in Luke, spoken in another setting, that of the Sermon on the Plain, preserves for us these similarly oriented words: "A good man out of the good treasure of his heart bringeth forth that which is good; and an evil man out of the evil treasure of his heart bringeth forth that which is evil: for of the abundance of the heart his mouth speaketh." Such words need no exposition, only the spoken or unspoken reaffirmation, 'Never man spake as this Man.' He continues:

But I say unto you, That every idle word that men shall speak, they shall give account thereof in the day of judgment. For by thy words thou shalt be justified, and by thy words thou shalt be condemned.

Must men work the works of wickedness to be damned? Are overt and evil acts a requisite? Are they needed to warrant one's being cast down to hell? Jesus is here preaching strong doctrine: Something less than evil acts will pull down curses upon the heads of the children of men. It suffices to think evil thoughts and to speak evil words; these alone identify what is in the heart of man and, without more, show the nature and kind of being he is.[5]

Then came some of the scribes and said unto him, Master, it is written that, Every sin shall be forgiven; but ye say, Whosoever speaketh against the Holy Ghost shall not be forgiven. And they asked him, saying, How can these things be?

He has already taught the doctrine involved; he has already explained how forgiveness and pardoning grace operate. They have heard him say he came to preach repentance so that all sins might be forgiven; the question they ask has already been answered. And yet there is an exception to the law of forgiveness: it is that those who blaspheme against the Holy Ghost shall be damned eternally; for them there shall be no remission of sins—they cannot repent and they cannot be forgiven. But this condemnation is reserved for those only who have walked in the light and who now choose to say the sun does not shine while they see it. By raising the question again the scribes are going to great lengths to find fault with Jesus and raise questions in the public mind about his teachings.

And he said unto them, When the unclean spirit is gone out of a man, he walketh through dry places, seeking rest and findeth none; but when a man speaketh against the Holy Ghost, then he saith, I will return into my house from whence I came out; and when he is come, he findeth him empty, swept and garnished; for the good spirit leaveth him unto himself.

When a man is baptized for the remission of sins; when evil and iniquity are burned out of him as though by fire, by the power of the Holy Ghost; when he becomes clean, and pure, and spotless before the Lord; when he has thus sanctified his soul—if he then sins against the Holy Ghost and loses the Spirit of the Lord as his companion, he is left in a fit condition to be swallowed up in every form of evil and iniquity. The house that was once swept and garnished, that was once a fit habitation for the Holy Spirit of God—that house is now vacant. The Spirit of the Lord will not dwell there longer, and the spirit of evil returns—returns to a vacant house, with a force and vigor exceeding anything of the past. As Jesus further says:

Then goeth the evil spirit, and taketh with him seven other spirits more wicked than himself; and they enter in and dwell there; and the last end of that man is worse than the first. Even so shall it be also unto this wicked generation.

There were those among them, obviously, who, having chosen to follow the Son of Righteousness, were now turning back, turning to worldly things, turning to follow Lucifer, their father, because their deeds were evil.[6]

"An Evil Generation: They Seek a Sign"
(*Matthew 12:38-42; Luke 11:16, 29-32; JST, Luke 11:32-33*)

Our Lord has just wrought a wondrous miracle: one who was deaf and dumb and possessed with an evil spirit has been blessed with a threefold miracle. Now he sees and speaks and is free from the shackling bondage of the demon who controlled his every thought and word and movement. How glorious it is to see such a wonder in Israel; but oh, what a mixed reaction it receives! To all those who believe in him who did the deed, it is an added sign and witness that he is the Messiah, their Deliverer, Savior, Redeemer, and King. But to those whose craft is in danger; who have sealed their hearts and minds against the new gospel dispensation; who say, God heard Moses and some of the prophets, but us he will not hear—to these scribal sectarians, as it were, the mighty miracle shows only that Jesus himself is possessed with a devil, and that all he does is by the power of the prince of devils. This view they have expressed, poisoning the minds of all whom they can influence. And their view has been refuted—in power, logically and conclusively—by the one at whose door the charge was laid.

What course is now open to them, and how shall they react? How shall they divert attention from their present discomfiture and rouse further animosity against this Nazarene who has taken upon himself the blasphemous assumption that he is divine? They must raise a new issue, or at least what will seem to be a new point of controversy. And so, "certain of the scribes and of the Pharisees," "tempting him," say: "Master, we would seek a sign from thee." Or, as Luke records it, they "sought of him a sign from heaven."

A sign from heaven! What, in heaven's name, had they just received? "They had already seen signs in such number and variety as had never before in all history been poured out upon a people. In their streets, houses, and synagogues, the lame leaped, the blind saw, the dumb spoke, paralytics walked and carried their beds, all manner of diseases were cured, devils were cast out, the dead raised—all by the command of him whom they now tempted. Yet, in the face of all this, they now demanded something new and different, some heavenly portent which would prove that what they had already seen was from above and not from beneath." (*Commentary* 1:277.)

Were they looking for a cloud by day and a pillar of fire by night to surround the Twelve? Was Jesus to divide the waters of the Sea of Galilee—congealing them with a wall of water on the right hand and on the left—so they all could walk from Capernaum to the land of the Gadarenes on dry ground? Did they expect to see Mount Zion or Mount Moriah quake, while smoke ascended up on high as from a furnace? Were they expecting this new Teacher to call down fire from heaven and consume six hundred Roman centurions with the sixty legions in which they served? How little they knew about how the Lord of heaven operates among men! True signs they had seen; signs of the sort they sought cannot be given without interfering with the divine law of agency under which all men must live.

"But he answered and said unto them," as Matthew records, "An evil and adulterous generation seeketh after a sign," and as Luke has it, "This is an evil generation: they seek a sign." Then as both synoptists say, "There shall no sign be given to it, but the sign of the prophet Jonas: For as Jonas was three days and three nights in the whale's belly; so shall the Son of man be three days and three nights in the heart of the earth."

A sign from heaven! What part do signs play in the eternal scheme of things? Why do these scripturally wise detractors of the Holy One feel they can rouse further ill feelings against him by demanding a sign? Should he give some sign that he has not yet given? Is there some great heavenly portent that will prove he is the Son of God?

Jesus came, it is true, to give signs and to work miracles. It was part of his ministerial assignment, and in so doing he was acting in the power and authority of his Father. Signs are for the saints, not the world. Signs follow those that believe; they are not designed to convert the wicked and ungodly. Faith precedes the miracle. "I will show miracles, signs, and wonders, unto all those who believe on my name," the Lord says. "And whoso shall ask it in my name in faith, they shall cast out devils; they shall heal the sick; they shall cause the blind to receive their sight, and the deaf to hear, and the dumb to speak, and the lame to walk. . . . But without faith shall not anything be shown forth except desolations upon Babylon." (D&C 35:8-11.)

There shall also be other signs, signs in the heavens above and in the earth beneath, wondrous portents that identify and bear record of things that are happening among men that affect their eternal salvation. But these also are understood only by those who have the gift and power of the Holy Ghost; they are understood by the saints only. The sign of the star was given to announce the birth of the Star of Israel, but only those who had faith, those who were waiting for the Consolation of Israel—the wise men from the East and a cluster of faithful souls in Palestine and in the Americas—only these few knew what it meant.

Those who seek signs—either to create faith or to feed their egos—whether in or out of the Church, shall fail in their search for divine approval. "He that seeketh signs shall see signs, but not unto salvation. . . . Faith cometh not by signs, but signs follow those that believe. Yea, signs come by faith, not by the will of men, nor as they please, but by the will of God. Yea, signs come by faith, unto mighty works, for without faith no man pleaseth God; and with whom God is angry he is not well pleased; wherefore, unto such he showeth no signs, only in wrath unto their condemnation." (D&C 63:7-11.)

For the scribes and Pharisees of all generations; for the wicked and ungodly in every age; for those without faith, who walk in worldly paths, there is only one sign, one alone, to prove Christ's divinity, and that is the sign of the prophet Jonas. That sign is that Jesus was crucified, died, and rose again the third day in glorious immortality. It is that as

Jonah of old spent three days and three nights in the belly of a whale, so shall the Son of Man spend a like period in an earthly tomb. It is that as the whale vomited Jonah from the blackness of a living tomb, so Jesus comes forth in a newness of life from a grave that cannot hold him. It is that the Son of Man—the Son of God—burst the bands of death, became the firstfruits of them that sleep, and ever liveth in immortal glory. The resurrection proves that Jesus is the Messiah; it is the sign, given of God, to all men of the truth and divinity of his work.

What sign does Deity give that there is a God? To the saints there are many, but to the wicked and ungodly there is only one—the fact of creation. God is the Creator, and all things denote there is a God. How could there be a creation without a Creator? Truly, the creation bears witness of the Creator.

What sign does he give that Christ is the Son of God? Again, to the saints there are many, but to the scribes and Pharisees of the world there is only one—the fact of resurrection. Christ is the Redeemer, and his redemption from death establishes his divinity. How could there be a resurrection without a Redeemer? Truly, the resurrection bears witness of the Redeemer.

What sign does he give that the Holy Ghost is the witness and testator, the revealer of saving truth in all ages? Once again, where the saints are concerned the signs are many, but to worldly people—and the world cannot, without repentance, receive the Holy Ghost—there is only one sign. It is the gift of prophecy; it is the reality of prophetic insight; it is the fact that God reveals, beforehand, by the mouths of his holy prophets, all things that concern and affect the salvation of men on earth. The Holy Ghost is a revelator, and the fact of revelation and of prophecy and of spiritual gifts identifies him as the power and source whence they come. How could there be revelation without a revelator? The presence of the gifts of the Spirit bears witness of the third member of the Godhead.

Such are the signs—and there are none others—that God gives to the wicked and ungodly. If they believe and repent, if they are baptized and receive the Holy Ghost, if they walk uprightly before the Lord—then signs without end, miracles unceasing, wonders beyond mortal comprehension, all these flow unto them forever and ever. Such is the law that governs signs.

And so, heaping condemnation upon those then present, and speaking by way both of doctrine and of testimony, Jesus says:

> *For as Jonas was a sign unto the Ninevites, so shall also the Son of man be to this generation.*
>
> *The queen of the south* [*the Queen of Sheba*] *shall rise up in the day of judgment with the men of this generation, and condemn them; for she came from the utmost parts of the earth, to hear the wisdom of Solomon; and, behold, a greater than Solomon is here.*
>
> *The men of Nineve shall rise up in the day of judgment with this generation; and shall condemn it; for they repented at the preaching of Jonas; and, behold, a greater than Jonas is here.*

We must not leave these stern and prophetic declarations of the Prophet of Nazareth—given to sinners about signs—without an acute awareness of the effect of adultery upon spirituality. Adultery so dulls the spiritual sensitivities of men that it becomes exceedingly hard for them to believe the truth when they hear it. Sexual immorality is second only to murder in the category of personal crimes. For those guilty of so gross an offense against God and his laws, the road back to cleanliness and purity is a steep and a rocky course. It can be traversed but the way is not easy.

Further: "Some sins cannot be separated; they are inseparably welded together. There never was a sign seeker who was not an adulterer, just as there never was an adulterer who was not also a liar. Once Lucifer gets a firm hold over one human weakness, he also applies his power to kindred weaknesses." (*Commentary* 1:277.)[7]

Who Belongs to the Family of Jesus?

(*Matthew 12:46-50; JST, Matthew 12:44; Mark 3:31-35; JST, Mark 3:26; Luke 8:19-21; 11:27-28; JST, Luke 8:19-20; 11:29*)

Our attention now turns to the Blessed Virgin and her other sons and daughters, the offspring of Mary and Joseph. Mary and some of Jesus' half-brothers seek to converse with him, but are unable to do so because of the throngs. He is told: "Thy mother and thy brethren stand without, desiring to speak with thee."

It seems to us, from the inspired records now extant among us, that the Master Teacher always used each successive event in his life as an occasion to teach doctrine and testify of his own divinity. So commonplace an event as the presence of his mother and some of her children—with whom he grew to maturity in Nazareth; with whom he played and worked and associated in the Galilean hills of yesteryear—became an occasion for a formal and profound pronouncement. Jesus said:

> *Who is my mother? and who are my brethren?*
>
> *And he stretched forth his hand toward his disciples, and said, Behold my mother and my brethren!*
>
> *And he gave them charge concerning her, saying, I go my way, for my Father hath sent me. And whosoever shall do the will of my Father which is in heaven, the same is my brother, and sister, and mother.*

Either at this point or at another time—how can we ever be sure?—"a certain woman of the company lifted up her voice, and said unto him, Blessed is the womb which bare thee, and the paps which thou hast sucked. And he said, Yea, and blessed are all they who hear the word of God, and keep it."

There are some things more important than familial inheritances. True, Mary was blessed because she bare God's Son, but all women can be blessed with blessed Mary if they keep the commandments of the blessed God. True, these children of Mary were Jesus' brothers and sisters, the fruit of the same womb in which his mortal body was created from the dust of the same earth, but all the disciples were also his brothers and sisters if they did the will of his Father who is in heaven.

The blessings of heaven are available—freely, without money and without price—to all men. All men cannot be born into this world as the sons of God, after the manner of the flesh, but all, through righteousness, can be adopted into the family of the Eternal God and become joint-heirs with Christ of the fulness of the glory and power of the Father. All people cannot be the literal seed of Mary, but all, through righteousness, can be adopted into the family of her Firstborn Son and become his brothers and sisters. Indeed, the very plan of salvation itself calls for a new birth, a birth to righteousness, by which all disciples, all saints, become the sons and daughters of Jesus Christ. They are born again; they become members of his family.

And all these blessings are available because Jesus was the Son of God. Even in announcing them, lest Mary or any of his blood-kindred feel too great an intimacy, or feel they should exercise control over the Firstborn of Mary, he speaks of his own Father as being in heaven, and pointedly says: "I go my way, for my Father hath sent me."

Who, then, are members of the family of Lucifer, and who of the family of the Lord Jesus? Are we not all the children of him whom we list to obey? Is it not, as Alma said: "If a man bringeth forth good works he hearkeneth unto the voice of the good shepherd, and he doth follow him; but whosoever bringeth forth evil works, the same becometh a child of the devil, for he hearkeneth unto his voice, and doth follow him." (Alma 5:41.)

NOTES

1. Our account here given is from Matthew and accords with Mark. Another almost identical miracle, out of which grew the same counsel and analysis as Matthew and Mark append to this healing, is found in Luke in a different setting. Whether they are the same or different miracles cannot be determined by us or by anyone. There are as many views as there are scholars. It may well be that almost identical miracles brought forth like reactions from different people and resulted in a repetition by Jesus of substantially the same instruction. Or it may be, as so many exegetes conclude, that the Gospel authors de-

liberately grouped certain happenings together because of their content and without reference to their chronological evolvement. As Edersheim expresses it, "The Gospels present not a 'Life of Christ,' but the history of the Kingdom of God in its progressive manifestation." (Edersheim 1:570.) Each author must choose for himself how to handle the endless problems of this sort, problems that are left to us because of the fragmentary nature of the biblical accounts. In this instance, we are considering all of the related sayings and doings as though they composed one episode. Such at least makes for a cohesive, rounded presentation of the whole matter.

2. "It is impossible for those who were once enlightened, and have tasted of the heavenly gift, and were made partakers of the Holy Ghost, And have tasted the good word of God, and the powers of the world to come, If they shall fall away, to renew them again unto repentance; seeing they crucify to themselves the Son of God afresh, and put him to an open shame." (Heb. 6:4-6.)

3. "The blasphemy against the Holy Ghost, which shall not be forgiven in the world nor out of the world, is in that ye commit murder wherein ye shed innocent blood, and assent unto my death, after ye have received my new and everlasting covenant, saith the Lord God; and he that abideth not this law can in nowise enter into my glory, but shall be damned, saith the Lord." (D&C 132:27.)

4. "There is a difference between gaining forgiveness of sins and gaining salvation in the celestial kingdom. All men who do not commit the unpardonable sin will gain eventual pardon; that is, they will be forgiven of their sins; but those so forgiven, having been judged according to their works, will then be sent either to a telestial, terrestrial, or celestial kingdom, as the case may be. As a matter of fact, those destined to inherit kingdoms of glory will not be resurrected until they have repented and gained forgiveness of their sins. The telestial kingdom will be inhabited by those who have been tormented and buffeted in hell until they have gained forgiveness and become worthy to attain a resurrection." (*Commentary* 1:274-75.)

5. "If our hearts have been hardened"—and what more accurately describes the hearts of the scribes and Pharisees with whom we are here dealing?—"yea, if we have hardened our hearts against the word, insomuch that it has not been found in us, then will our state be awful, for then we shall be condemned. For our words will condemn us, yea, all our works will condemn us; we shall not be found spotless; and our thoughts will also condemn us." (Alma 12:13-14.)

6. In answering the question of these captious scribes, Jesus is saying in effect: 'If you gain a perfect knowledge of me and my mission, it must come by revelation from the Holy Ghost; that Holy Spirit must speak to the spirit within you; and then you shall know, nothing doubting. But to receive this knowledge and revelation, you must cleanse and perfect your own soul; that is, your house must be clean, swept, and garnished. Then if you deny me by speaking against the Holy Ghost who gave you your revelation of the truth, that is if you come out in open rebellion against the perfect light you have received, the Holy Ghost will depart, leaving you to yourself. Your house will now be available for other tenancy, and so the evil spirits and influences you had once conquered will return to plague you. Having completely lost the preserving power of the Spirit, you will then be worse off than if you had never received the truth; and many in this generation shall be so condemned.' (*Commentary* 1:276.)

7. In this connection, also, the Prophet Joseph Smith said: "When I was preaching in Philadelphia, a Quaker called out for a sign. I told him to be still. After the sermon, he again asked for a sign. I told the congregation the man was an adulterer; that a wicked and adulterous generation seeketh after a sign; and that the Lord had said to me in a revelation, that any man who wanted a sign was an adulterous person. 'It is true,' cried one, 'for I caught him in the very act,' which the man afterwards confessed when he was baptized." (*Teachings,* p. 278.)

SECTION VI

THE CONTINUING GALILEAN MINISTRY

THE CONTINUING GALILEAN MINISTRY

The Lord hath anointed me to preach
good tidings unto the meek;
. . . to comfort all that mourn;
To appoint unto them that mourn in Zion,
to give unto them beauty for ashes,
the oil of joy for mourning,
the garment of praise for the spirit of heaviness;
that they might be called trees of righteousness,
the planting of the Lord,
that he might be glorified.
(Isa. 61:1-3.)

We now see Jesus going forth in the majesty and glory of his eternal Godhood—preaching, healing, and testifying.

We see him among his Galilean neighbors and friends, some of whom have great faith; others have souls darkened by sin and unbelief.

He speaks in parables, particularly to those who are not prepared to receive the word in plainness. They hear of a sower, of seed that grows by itself, of wheat and tares, of mustard seed and of leaven, of hidden treasure and a pearl of great price, and of the gospel net.

He stills a storm on the Sea of Galilee, heals a demoniac

among the Gadarenes, raises the daughter of Jairus from death, heals the woman with the issue of blood, and causes the blind to see and the dumb to speak.

And in spite of it all, he is again rejected at Nazareth.

Then he instructs the Twelve and sends them forth, endowed with power from on high.

In sorrow we see the beloved Baptist beheaded by order of evil Antipas.

Then Jesus feeds the five thousand in a solitary place near Bethsaida-Julias, walks on the sea, and continues his miracles in the land of Gennesaret.

And finally, as the crowning event of this part of his ministry, we hear the sermon on the bread of life and the discourse on cleanliness.

How truly—according to the promises—did he replace mourning with the oil of joy, ashes with beauty, and the spirit of heaviness with the garment of praise!

O that all who saw and heard and felt what he then did might have believed in him—"that they might be called trees of righteousness" and "the planting of the Lord"!

JESUS TEACHES IN PARABLES

Give ear, O my people, to my law:
incline your ears to the words of my mouth.
I will open my mouth in a parable:
I will utter dark sayings of old:
Which we have heard and known,
and our fathers have told us.
(Ps. 78:1-3.)

Why Jesus Taught in Parables

(*Matthew 13:1-3, 9-17, 34-35; JST, Matthew 13:10-11, 13, 15-16; Mark 4:1-2, 9-12, 21-25, 33-34; JST, Mark 4:9, 18-20, 26; Luke 8:4, 8, 16-18; JST, Luke 8:18*)

Every schoolboy knows Jesus taught in parables, but there is scarcely a learned theologian or an educated divine in all the universities of academia who knows why he chose this unique form of pedagogy. There are, of course, a great many scripturists who are aware of why he *said* he used parables, but their approach, almost without exception, is to explain that he could not possibly have meant what he said in the literal and true sense of the word, and therefore that he used parables for such and such a reason of their own devising.

It is only fair to say that the scriptural exegetes who have speculated and pontificated, in the religious literature of the day, as to why our Lord used parables, and as to what those parables mean, have not had the advantages of what latter-day revelation says on the matters at hand. Nonetheless, for whatever reason, the shimmering fantasies of the learned men, as they pertain to our Lord's use of parables, are of little worth to us.

In our continuing struggle to learn of him by whom salvation comes, we are about to encounter the beginning of the parables. We do not know if these are the first parables related by Jesus—it is, in fact, a little unreasonable to assume that no others have been related in the twenty months or so since his baptism—but at least these are the first major parables preserved for us in the scriptural record. And it was their use at this time that caused his disciples to ask: "Why speakest thou unto them in parables?"

As a necessary prelude to our analysis of the parables as they fall from the divine lips, we shall do well to have before us the social and historical circumstances that brought them forth, and also an understanding of their nature, use, and purpose in the gospel plan. The following items of history and principle will help us gain the perspective we need.

1. *Nature of parables.*

"Parables are short stories which point up and illustrate spiritual truths. Those spoken by Jesus deal with real events, or, if fictitious, are so consistent and probable that they may be viewed as the commonplace experiences of many people." (*Commentary* 1:283.)

"The essential feature of a parable is that of comparison or similitude, by which some ordinary, well-understood incident is used to illustrate a fact or principle not directly expressed in the story. . . . The narrative or incident upon which a parable is constructed may be an actual occurrence or fiction; but, if fictitious, the story must be consistent and probable, with no admixture of the unusual or miraculous. In this respect the parable differs from the fable, the latter being imaginative, exaggerated and improbable as to fact; moreover, the intent is unlike in the two, since the parable is designed to convey some great spiritual truth, while the so-called moral of the fable is at best suggestive only of worldly achievement and personal advantage. Stories of trees, animals and inanimate things talking together or with men are wholly fanciful; they are fables or apologues whether the outcome be depicted as good or bad; to the parable these show contrast, not similarity. The avowed purpose of the fable is rather to amuse than to teach. The parable may embody a narrative as in the instances of the sower and the tares, or merely an isolated incident, as in those of the mustard seed and the leaven.

"Allegories are distinguished from parables by greater length and detail of the story, and by the intimate admixture of the narrative with the lesson it is designed to teach; these are kept distinctly separate in the parable. Myths are fictitious stories, sometimes with historic basis of fact, but without symbolism of spiritual worth. A proverb is a short, sententious saying, in the nature of a maxim, connoting a definite truth or suggestion by comparison. Proverbs and parables are closely related, and in the Bible the terms are sometimes used interchangeably." (Talmage, pp. 298-99.)

2. *Many doctrines are reserved for the faithful.*

Every gospel teacher—from the Chief Elder, who is Christ, to the least and lowest of his servants—must determine, in all teaching situations, what portion of eternal truth he will offer to his hearers of the moment. The gospel and its eternal truths are always the same: what was true two thousand years ago is true today; the truths that enabled Abraham to serve Jehovah and gain salvation are the same as those which enable us to serve Christ and gain a like reward. But not all people in all ages and under all circumstances are prepared to receive the fulness of all gospel truths. The Lord gives his word to men line upon line, precept upon precept, here a little and there a little, confirming their hope, building each new revelation upon the foundations of the past, giving his children only that portion of his word which they are able to bear.

When the elders of Israel go forth to proclaim the gospel

to the world, they are subject to two commandments that the spiritually untutored might assume are contradictory. In one of them the Lord says, "Teach the principles of my gospel, which are in the Bible and the Book of Mormon." (D&C 42:12.) Does this mean they are free to teach all they know about all of the doctrines found in the standard works? In another revelation, the Lord says: "Declare glad tidings, . . . And of tenets thou shalt not talk, but thou shalt declare repentance and faith on the Savior, and remission of sins by baptism and by fire, yea, even the Holy Ghost." (D&C 19:29-31.) The clear meaning, of course, is that the servants of the Lord go forth to teach what people are prepared to receive, nothing more. They are to declare glad tidings, to proclaim the message of the restoration, to teach the simple and easy doctrines, and to leave the mysteries alone. They are not to present lessons in calculus to students who must first learn arithmetic; they are not to reveal the mysteries of the kingdom until people believe the first principles; they are to give milk before meat.

Alma summarized the restrictions under which preachers of righteousness serve by saying: "It is given unto many to know the mysteries of God; nevertheless they are laid under a strict command that they shall not impart only according to the portion of his word which he doth grant unto the children of men, according to the heed and diligence which they give unto him." Such is the universal principle; it is not how much the teacher knows, but how much the student is prepared to receive. Strong and deep doctrine, spoken to rebellious people, drives them further away and widens the gulf between them and the saints of God.

Then Alma, in pointed and express language, describes, as it were, the scribes and Pharisees, on the one hand, and the faithful disciples who surrounded Jesus, on the other: "And therefore," he continues, "he that will harden his heart, the same receiveth the lesser portion of the word; and he that will not harden his heart, to him is given the greater portion of the word, until it is given unto him to know the mysteries of God until he know them in full. And they that will harden their hearts, to them is given the lesser portion of the word until they know nothing concerning his mysteries; and then they are taken captive by the devil, and led by his will down to destruction. Now this is what is meant by the chains of hell." (Alma 12:9-11.)

Even the true saints—the believing disciples, those who have accepted the gospel and received the gift of the Holy Ghost—are not prepared to receive all things. We have the fulness of the everlasting gospel, meaning we have every truth, power, priesthood, and key needed to enable us to gain the fulness of salvation in our Father's kingdom. But we do not have, and are not yet prepared to receive, the fulness of gospel truth.

This is perfectly illustrated by the fact that we do not have the sealed portion of the Book of Mormon. That treasurehouse of Holy Writ contains an account of the creation of the world, of the dealings of God with men in all ages, of the Second Coming of the Son of Man, and of the millennial era when the earth shall rest and Zion prosper to the full—all of which we are not prepared to receive. The doctrines revealed to the brother of Jared, and which are recorded in the sealed portion of the Book of Mormon, were had among the Jaredites; they were known to the Nephites during their Golden Era; certainly they were known and taught in Enoch's Zion; but when the Lehite people "dwindled in unbelief," Moroni was commanded to "hide them up." "They shall not go forth unto the Gentiles until the day that they shall repent of their iniquity, and become clean before the Lord," Moroni says.

We live in a preparatory day, a day in which we are preparing, it is hoped, to receive the further light and knowledge that a gracious God has in store for us. As Moroni records: "And in that day that they shall exercise faith in me, saith the Lord, even as the brother of Jared did, that they may become sanctified in me, then will I manifest unto them the things which the brother of Jared saw, even to the unfolding unto them all my revelations, saith Jesus Christ, the Son of God, the Father of the heavens and of the earth, and all things that in them are." (Ether 4:1-7.)

3. *Parables hide gospel doctrines from those whose hearts are hardened.*

By speaking in parables, Jesus is simply practicing what he has been preaching. In the Sermon on the Mount he told the Twelve they were to go forth into the world, preach the gospel, call upon men to repent, and invite them to join the Church. They were instructed, however, to keep the mysteries of the kingdom within themselves, and not to give that which was holy unto the dogs, or to cast their pearls before swine. Jesus told them that the world could not receive that which they themselves were scarcely able to bear, and that if they gave gospel pearls to the wicked and ungodly, such unbelieving and rebellious people would first reject the message, and then use the very truths they had heard to rend and destroy and wreak havoc among those whose faith was weak.

Now we find Jesus on the Galilean shore in the midst of a great congregation, gathered out of every city. Among them are the Twelve, many disciples who know he is the Messiah, and many others, influenced by the scribes and Pharisees, who reject him as an imposter and believe his miracles are wrought by an evil power. So great is the press of the people that he enters a ship, seats himself, and addresses the multitude standing on the shore. Many truths and much exhortation—as his custom is—fall from his lips, in addition to which, the record says, "He spake many things unto them in parables."

Later, being alone with the Twelve and certain other favored disciples, he is asked why he speaks in parables and what the parables mean. As to the choice of parables as a means of teaching, be it noted, the disciples did not ask, 'Why speakest thou unto *us* in parables?' but, "Why speakest thou unto *them*"—unto the scribes and Pharisees; unto the spies sent by the Sanhedrin to find fault with his every word;

unto those whose hearts were hardened against the word—"Why speakest thou unto *them* in parables?" Jesus answered:

> *Because it is given unto you to know the mysteries of the kingdom of heaven, but to them it is not given.*

These words are from Matthew. But, better still, as Mark preserves the account, Jesus said:

> *Unto you it is given to know the mystery of the kingdom of God: but unto them that are without, all these things are done in parables.*

That is to say, parables are for nonmembers of the Church, for those outside the kingdom, or, at best, as we shall see, for those who are weak in the faith; who are not prepared to receive the truth involved in plain words; from whom the full truth must, as yet, remain hidden. To the Twelve, Mary Magdalene, and the other faithful disciples, both male and female, who traveled and ministered with him, to all of the believing saints of his day—to them it was given to know the doctrine; for them it need not be hidden in a parable.

> *For whosoever receiveth, to him shall be given, and he shall have more abundance; But whosoever continueth not to receive, from him shall be taken away even that he hath.*
>
> *Therefore speak I to them in parables: because they seeing see not; and hearing they hear not, neither do they understand.*
>
> *And in them is fulfilled the prophecy of Esaias concerning them, which saith, By hearing, ye shall hear and shall not understand; and seeing, ye shall see and shall not perceive.*

4. *Parables reveal truths to those whose hearts are open and receptive.*

With it all, parables are majestic teaching devices, and they do reveal truth, and they do add light and understanding to those who already have the gift of understanding, as well as to those who are sincerely seeking truth.[1] The doctrines of salvation are presented in their most compelling and convincing form when they are phrased in aptly chosen words, as when the Risen Lord ministered among the Nephites. Be it noted that he spake not unto them in parables; they were a people prepared for their King. The wicked and ungodly among them had been destroyed by the quakings and fires and whirlwinds and desolations in the Americas that attended the crucifixion, and those among the Nephites who remained were ready to receive the word of truth as it came in simplicity and plainness.

Yet parables, planted in the minds of truth seekers, help them remember the issues involved until such time as the full and plain knowledge parts the parabolic veil and stands revealed for all to see. And parables form a reservoir of knowledge about which even the saints can ponder and inquire as they seek to perfect and expand their limited views of gospel themes.

Continuing his denunciation of those to whom he must speak in parables because they are neither worthy nor qualified to hear the word in plainness, Jesus says:

> *For this people's heart is waxed gross, and their ears are dull of hearing, and their eyes they have closed; lest at any time they should see with their eyes, and hear with their ears, and should understand with their heart, and should be converted, and I should heal them.*

Then Jesus makes the contrast and shows wherein his plain teachings and his parables, because these latter are also understood by his disciples, are of great worth unto those whose hearts are open.

> *But blessed are your eyes, for they see; and your ears, for they hear. And blessed are you because these things are come unto you, that you might understand them.*
>
> *And verily, I say unto you, many righteous prophets have desired to see these days which you see, and have not seen them; and to hear that which you hear, and have not heard.*

How blessed they were in that day to hear both the parables and the plain teachings! And yet how blessed are we to live in this day, a day when the word of God is again in the mouths of legal administrators, servants who now minister in the place and stead of him who filled his mission in Galilee and Judea and Perea and all Palestine!

5. *Parables are types and shadows of heavenly things.*

Pure doctrine is of heavenly origin. When it is revealed in plainness and simplicity, it lights the way to eternal life, as for instance the clear statement that men must repent and be baptized to gain salvation. But when for one reason or another it is unwise to set forth this or that truth in all its blazing grandeur, it may yet be appropriate to reveal a type or a shadow, a similitude, a dim and dawning light, something that points toward the doctrine in all its revealed splendor. So often such types and shadows and similitudes are parables. They bear record of eternal truths and point the attention of gospel students to the doctrines involved without specifying what the doctrines are or how they operate.

Thus parables are not sources to search to learn doctrine. They may serve as illustrations of gospel principles; they may dramatize, graphically and persuasively, some gospel truths; but it is not their purpose to reveal doctrine, or, standing alone, to guide men along the course leading to eternal life. Parables can only be understood, in their full and complete meaning, after one knows the doctrines about which they speak. For instance, in the course of revealing some things relative to unity, the Lord, in latter-day revelation, gives a very simple parable:

> *And let every man esteem his brother as himself, and practise virtue and holiness before me.*
>
> *And again I say unto you, let every man esteem his brother as himself.*
>
> *For what man among you having twelve sons, and is no respecter of them, and they serve him obediently, and he saith unto the one: Be thou clothed in robes and sit thou here; and to the other: Be thou clothed in rags and sit thou there—and looketh upon his sons and saith I am just?*

Behold, this I have given unto you as a parable, and it is even as I am. I say unto you, be one; and if ye are not one ye are not mine. (*D&C 38:24-27.*)

Here, then, is a parable that illustrates something about the Lord. What does it mean? Is he speaking of time or eternity? Is it dealing with temporal or spiritual equality, or both? Do all men enter this life, or the next, with equal endowments? Does it have any reference to the twelve apostles, or the twelve tribes or Israel? In what sense must the Lord's people be one? And so on and so on. Parables are types and shadows—something to ponder and analyze and pray about. Indeed, this is one of their allures. They are a sort of religious puzzle awaiting solution, a sacred mystery waiting to be uncovered.

"Perhaps no other mode of teaching was so common among the Jews as that by Parables," Edersheim says. Their parables, however, "were almost entirely illustrations of what had been said or taught." Our Lord's parables were also illustrations, but they were much more. They shed a light of their own, or perhaps they shed the light of heaven abroad. "All Parables bear reference to well-known scenes, such as those of daily life; or to events, either real, or such as every one would expect in given circumstances, or as would be in accordance with prevailing notions.

"Such pictures, familiar to the popular mind"—especially in the case of Jesus' parables—"are in the Parable [itself] connected with corresponding spiritual realities. . . . There is that which distinguishes the Parable from the mere illustration. The latter conveys no more than—perhaps not so much as—that which was to be illustrated; while the Parable conveys this and a great deal beyond it to those, who can follow up its shadows to the light by which they have been cast. In truth, Parables are the outlined shadows—large, perhaps, and dim—as the light of heavenly things falls on well-known scenes, which correspond to, and have their higher counterpart in spiritual realities. . . . Things in earth and heaven are kindred, and the one may become to us Parables of the other." (Edersheim 1:580-82.)

6. *Parabolic teaching is often an act of mercy.*

We are now aware that parables present only that portion of the Lord's word which he in his wisdom feels to convey to us at any given time. In many cases this very act of limiting the amount of truth offered to men is itself an act of mercy. "For of him unto whom much is given much is required; and he who sins against the greater light shall receive the greater condemnation." (D&C 82:3.) To offer truths to wicked and ungodly creatures, which they will most assuredly reject, is to do more than cast pearls before swine. It is to make possible a greater condemnation upon those who reject the greater light.

"There is plainly shown an element of mercy in the parabolic mode of instruction adopted by our Lord under the conditions prevailing at the time. Had He always taught in explicit declaration, such as required no interpretation, many among His hearers would have come under condemnation, inasmuch as they were too weak in faith and unprepared in heart to break the bonds of traditionalism and the prejudice engendered by sin, so as to accept and obey the saving word. Their inability to comprehend the requirements of the gospel would in righteous measure give Mercy some claim upon them, while had they rejected the truth with full understanding, stern Justice would surely demand their condemnation." (Talmage, pp. 296-97.)

7. *Parables open the door to added light and knowledge.*

We now, as a prelude to our study of the parables as such, have considered their nature and character. We have reminded ourselves that the Lord gives to men only that portion of his word which they are prepared, spiritually, to receive, and we have seen how parables hide the doctrines of salvation from those whose eyes are not open to spiritual realities. We have also set forth how these wondrously phrased and perfectly presented parabolic utterances of

Jesus do in fact reveal great spiritual truths to those whose hearts are open and whose souls hunger and thirst for the things of the Spirit, and we have even come to know that inspired parables are types and shadows of heavenly things, and that by them the light of heaven is cast earthward for the eternal betterment and blessing of all those upon whom its rays shine. And we have noted that it is an act of divine mercy to withhold from shriveled and spiritually sick souls the full light of heaven, lest its assured rejection further condemn the unreceptive and disbelieving among men.

There remains for us one added verity to consider, and it is, perhaps, the greatest and most important use to which parables are put. Jesus came to preach the gospel and bear the sins of all those who would believe his words and live his laws. He came to proclaim the acceptable year of the Lord, to bring good tidings to the meek, to open the prison doors of darkness and unbelief, and to let the light of heaven dwell in the hearts of men on earth. He came to give every man as much of the truth of heaven as each man's earthbound soul would permit him to receive.

If the righteousness that Jesus thus rained upon men fell on seams of rock and dunes of sand, it was sloughed off as of no worth; if it fell in the pleasant valley of the Jordan or within the gates of Eden, then it caused grain to grow and fruit to ripen and cattle to drink and live. Peter, James, and John were prepared—spiritually, intellectually, morally—to drink the downpouring of divine light in the form of pure doctrine, for they walked in the valley of the Jordan and sought for the gate of Eden. But when the heaven-sent and life-giving truths fell upon the scribal spies from the Sanhedrin, they brought forth no more fruit than would a desert cloudburst in a weary wasteland of rock and sand and sulphur.

And yet, perchance, there would be a day when even the desert would blossom as the rose; when springs of living water would burst forth in the rocky and sandy souls of those who now disbelieve the truth and reject the Purveyor.

To them parables are a reminder of half-seen truths yet to be learned; they contain a few rays of spiritual light, hidden by the clouds of unbelief, which rays at any moment might burst through the misty veil to let light into human souls. They contain drops of truth, trickling down from eternal springs, from which eternal sources all are invited to come and drink and never thirst more.

Parables are a call to investigate the truth; to learn more; to inquire into the spiritual realities, which, through them, are but dimly viewed. Parables start truth seekers out in the direction of further light and knowledge and understanding; they invite men to ponder such truths as they are able to bear in the hope of learning more. Parables are a call to come unto Christ, to believe his doctrines, to live his laws, and to be saved in his kingdom. They teach arithmetic to those who have the capacity to learn calculus in due course. They are the mild milk of the word that prepares our spiritual digestive processes to feast upon the doctrinal meat of the kingdom.

And so, Jesus, having delivered the parable of the sower, without more ado says: "He that hath ears to hear, let him hear." That is to say: 'If you are capable of understanding this parable, then do so. Study, pray, ponder; seek enlightenment; atune yourself to the whisperings of the Spirit, until its full meaning and significance dawns upon you. In this way you will learn more of me and my gospel.'

Even the Twelve, however, felt the need for further guidance, which they then asked for and received. And after Jesus himself had interpreted—partially, at least—the parable of the sower, he said:

> *No man, when he hath lighted a candle, covereth it with a vessel, or putteth it under a bed; but setteth it on a candlestick, that they which enter in may see the light.*

'I have given you this parable so that you may learn its meaning. It is as a candle set to give light in a house. I gave it so that you might learn more of my gospel; otherwise I would have hidden the candle under a vessel or a bed.' Or:

'No man who is a true minister, when he brings gospel light, covereth it with mystery and confusion (as is the case, for instance, with the sectarian creeds describing God), but he holds forth as much light before men as they are able to bear.' (*Commentary* 1:291.)

For there is nothing hid which shall not be manifested; neither was anything kept secret, but that it should in due time come abroad.

'For no parable, no teaching, no mystery, no hidden thing, is to be kept from the knowledge of the faithful; eventually all things shall be revealed, and the righteous shall know them.' (*Commentary* 1:291.)[2] Then again, Jesus repeated: "If any man have ears to hear, let him hear," which is his plea to all to learn the meaning of his parables. But there is yet more to come. Jesus continues:

Take heed what ye hear; for with what measure ye mete, it shall be measured to you; and unto you that continue to receive, shall more be given; for he that receiveth, to him shall be given; but he that continueth not to receive, from him shall be taken even that which he hath.

'But take heed how ye hear and accept gospel truth, for you shall be rewarded with new revelation only if you are prepared to receive it. The measure of attention you give to the truths already revealed will dictate how much new truth shall be meted to you. If you continue to receive light and truth, and abide in them, eventually you shall be perfected in the truth and know all things. But if you do not continue to receive gospel light, and to walk in that light, from you shall be taken even that light which you once had, and you shall walk in darkness.' (*Commentary* 1:291-92.)

And so, with all these principles and this exhortation before us, we are now ready to taste the sweetness of the first series of major parables recorded by our New Testament friends.

NOTES

1. Farrar, completely carried away in the witchery—the charm and fascination—of his

own words, calls our Lord's parabolic teaching "a method of instruction so rare, so stimulating, so full of interest—a method which, in its unapproachable beauty and finish, stands unrivalled in the annals of human speech." (Farrar, p. 246.) Doubtless our friend Farrar, being a devout man and a true believer, according to the limits of knowledge then available to him, has now, in the realms ahead, been privileged to read 3 Nephi in the Book of Mormon and discover the true "unapproachable beauty . . . of human speech," as it is there found in the plain words, devoid of parabolic covering, of the One who excelled all others in all things.

2. In this same connection, Nephi said: "There is nothing which is secret save it shall be revealed; there is no work of darkness save it shall be made manifest in the light; and there is nothing which is sealed upon the earth save it shall be loosed." (2 Ne. 30:17.)

PARABLES SPOKEN BY JESUS

Hear this, all ye people;
give ear, all ye inhabitants of the world:
Both low and high, rich and poor, together.
My mouth shall speak of wisdom;
and the meditation of my heart shall be
of understanding. I will incline mine ear
to a parable. (Ps. 49:1-4.)

Parable of the Sower

(*Matthew 13:3-9, 18-23; JST, Matthew 13:5, 19, 21; Mark 4:3-9, 13-20; JST, Mark 4:15-17; Luke 8:5-8, 11-15; JST, Luke 8:12-13, 15*)

"Behold, a sower went forth to sow"—to sow seeds of eternal truth in the souls of men; to sow the wonder-working word of Him whose name is Wonderful; to sow the seeds of eternal life in the hearts of men. And how beautiful upon the mountains are the feet of them who preach the gospel of peace, who say unto Zion: Thy God reigneth!

"A sower went out to sow his seed," and the seed he sows is "the word of the kingdom." Even now the Divine Sower, the Messenger of Salvation, is scattering his Father's word among them in soil of all sorts.

"The word of the kingdom"!—again we declare it: He is preaching the gospel; the plan of salvation; faith, repentance, and baptism; the receipt of the Holy Ghost; the everlasting word. He is speaking of a kingdom; a kingdom of God on earth; a church to be presided over by apostles and prophets; an organized body—surely the Lord's house is a house of order—that administers salvation to all who enter its strait door and mingle with its saintly citizens, the citizens of the kingdom. And how beautiful upon the mountains are the feet of the Lord who is the Author of Salvation, who himself preaches the gospel of peace, and who says unto Zion: I am thy God; come unto me.

But let the sower be Christ—who it is in this instance—or let it be any of the lesser sowers whom he calls to labor in his fields, the principle is the same. The seed is the word of God, the gospel of salvation. Jesus preaches it and he directs his servants so to do. And the seed is the same whether sown by the owner of the field or by the servants whom he employs. And as to whether the seed sprouts and grows and ripens and is harvested, such depends not upon the seed, but upon the soil. The seed is good, all the seed, whether sown by the Divine Sower or by those whom he sends to spread "the word of the kingdom."[1]

Thus, this parable of the sower, as we are wont to call it, might more aptly be considered as the parable of the four kinds of soil. The growth of the seed depends upon the nature of the soil; it depends upon the hearts and minds and souls of the hearers of the word. "The imagery of it was derived, as usual, from the objects immediately before His eyes—the sown fields of Gennesareth; the springing corn in them; the hard-trodden paths which ran through them, on which no corn could grow; the innumerable birds which fluttered over them ready to feed upon the grain; the weak and withering struggle for life on the stony places; the tangling growth of luxuriant thistles in neglected corners; the deep loam of the general soil, on which already the golden ears stood thick and strong, giving promise of a sixty and hundred-fold return as they rippled under the balmy wind." (Farrar, pp. 244-45.) We know the seed is good; let us then look to the soil in which it is sown.

1. *The soil by the wayside.*

"And as he sowed, some fell by the way side; and it was trodden down, and the fowls of the air devoured it." Such was the parabolic story; the interpretation, given later by Jesus to the disciples only, was: "Those by the way side are they that hear; then cometh the devil, and taketh away the word out of their hearts, lest they should believe and be saved."

How sad are the prospects for those by the wayside; those whose souls are so hardened by false doctrines and evil deeds that the seed of the word cannot even sprout and begin to grow in their hearts. These are the scribes and Pharisees of society, the ministers of false religions, and the wicked and ungodly who love darkness rather than light because their deeds are evil. They were the ones in Jesus' day who bound themselves with the formalisms of Mosaic worship and refused to let the light of a new dispensation enter their hearts. They are the religionists in our day who close their ears to new revelation and choose to believe such doctrines as that men are saved by grace alone, without more, thus leaving them free to walk in worldliness and still, as they suppose, gain salvation. They are the wicked and ungodly in general, the liars and sorcerers and adulterers, the people who feed their souls on pornographic words and pictures. They are worldly people who are carnal, sensual, and devilish by nature, and who choose so to remain. Repentance is always open to all men, but those by the wayside choose to retain their hardened and rebellious natures.[2]

2. *The soil in stony places.*

The parable: "Some fell upon stony places, where they had not much earth; and forthwith they sprung up; and when the sun was up, they were scorched, because they had no deepness of earth; and because they had no root, they withered away."

The interpretation: "But he that received the seed into stony places, the same is he that heareth the word and readily with joy receiveth it, yet he hath not root in himself, and endureth but for a while; for when tribulation or persecution ariseth because of the word, by and by he is offended." Luke's account includes the expression that "they . . . for a while believe, and in a time of temptation fall away."

These are they who believe the word; they know the Book of Mormon is true, as it were; there is no question in their minds that Joseph Smith is a prophet; they have the testimony of Jesus in their souls; and they rejoice in the light from heaven that has come into their lives. But they do not press forward with a steadfastness in Christ; they do not continue to learn the doctrines of salvation; they do not pay their tithes and offerings and serve in the Church. They do not endure to the end. Persecution arises; trials and tribulations block their path; their temptations are greater than they can bear. Because their roots are not deeply embedded in gospel soil, the new plant withers. It cannot stand the scorching rays of the sun.

Luke says "it lacked moisture." The sacrifices required of the saints were too great. Though the word, at the first, seemed as a pearl of great price, other considerations waylaid the gospel pilgrims, and the labors expected of them no longer seemed worth the effort. They withered and died spiritually, and the fruit of eternal life never ripened in their lives.

3. *The soil where thorns grow.*

The parable: "And some fell among thorns, and the thorns grew up, and choked it, and it yielded no fruit."

The interpretation: "And these are they who receive the word among thorns; such as hear the word, and the cares of this world, and the deceitfulness of riches, and the lusts of other things entering in, choke the word, and it becometh unfruitful." Luke's account adds the "pleasures of this life" as one of the things that choke the seeds so they "bring no fruit to perfection."

They hear and receive the word among thorns! The seed is good and the soil is good, but they choose to let thorns and thistles continue to grow along with the seeds of righteousness. They seek to serve both God and mammon at one and the same time. The plan of salvation calls for men to overcome this world and prepare for a better one which is to be, but the cares of this world lead them astray. The gospel calls for men to seek the riches of eternity and to let the wealth of this world take a place of secondary importance, but the deceitfulness of riches—the false sense of superiority they give—leads men in worldly rather than godly paths. The good word of God calls for men to bridle their passions, forsake all that is evil, and cleave unto all that is good, but the lusts of the flesh remaining in the hearts of believing men cannot do other than lead them on a downward course.

True saints seek, not the pleasures of this life—the things that money and power and learning confer—but the eternal joys born of the Spirit. The Lord wants no part-time saints. His people cannot have one foot in the kingdom and the other in the world and expect to survive spiritually. The Church and its interests must always take precedence in their lives; otherwise the thorns will choke the precious gospel plant; it will die and in due course be burned with the thorns.

4. *The good soil.*

The parable: "And other fell on good ground, and did yield fruit that sprang up and increased; and brought forth, some thirty, and some sixty, and some an hundred."

The interpretation: "But he that received seed into the good ground, is he that heareth the word and understandeth and endureth; which also beareth fruit, and bringeth forth, some an hundredfold, some sixty, and some thirty." In the Joseph Smith Translation, Luke has a variant reading: "But that which fell on the good ground are they, who receive the word in an honest and good heart, having heard the word, keep what they hear, and bring forth fruit with patience."

Hear, understand, endure, bring forth fruit; receive the word in an honest and good heart, keep the commandments, and bring forth fruit with patience. Such is the will of the

Lord. "If the seed falls on productive, fertile soil, and if it is thereafter nurtured and cared for, it bringeth forth a harvest. But even here crops of equal value are not harvested by all the saints. There are many degrees of receptive belief; there are many gradations of effective cultivation. All men, the saints included, shall be judged according to their works; those who keep the whole gospel law shall bring forth an hundred fold and inherit the fulness of the Father's kingdom. Others shall gain lesser rewards in the mansions which are prepared." (*Commentary* 1:289.)

Parable of the Seed Growing by Itself

(*Mark 4:26-29*)

In his first recorded parable, that of the sower, we heard Jesus speak of sowing the seed of the gospel kingdom in all sorts of soil. Seed sown on hard and beaten paths was trodden under foot, or eaten by the fowls of heaven; it was seed that neither sprouted nor took root nor grew. Seed sown on stony ground found growth for a moment in the scanty covering of soil, but the sprouting plants withered and died when persecutions and tribulations and temptations beset the new converts. Seed sown amid the thorns and thistles of worldliness, after an initial growth, was smothered and choked by the cares and riches and lusts of the world so that it brought forth no fruit unto perfection. Only the seed sown in good soil, and which was nurtured and dunged and cultivated, brought forth abundantly the fruit of eternal life. In this parable of the sower, Jesus himself, in particular, and all of his servants, in general, were the sowers of the seed.

Now he speaks a second parable that grows out of the first. It is concerned with the seed sown in good soil, the seed that brings forth fruit, the seed that is reaped and gathered unto eternal life. And it is addressed to his servants, those sent forth by him to sow his seeds; in it he counsels them as to how they should act when they sow their seeds of salvation in the hearts of men.

"And he said, So is the kingdom of God, as if a man

should cast seed into the ground; And should sleep, and rise night and day, and the seed should spring and grow up, he knoweth not how."

'My earthly kingdom; the church that I have established among men; that organization which is the church and kingdom of God on earth; the very organization among men which administers the gospel and offers salvation to all who believe and obey—this very kingdom of God—grows in this manner: My servants first cast seed into good soil; they preach the gospel to the honest in heart. Then they leave the event in the hands of that Lord whose seed it is; they go about their other business, or go elsewhere to preach the word. It is as though night and day pass; the sun sends forth his rays by day and the mists of the night water the seed; then it sprouts and grows. My servants know not how the conversion is brought to pass, only that the seed sown in good soil somehow brings souls into the kingdom.'

"For the earth bringeth forth fruit of herself; first the blade, then the ear, after that the full corn in the ear. But when the fruit is brought forth, immediately he putteth in the sickle, because the harvest is come."

Seeds sown in the soil of the earth and seeds sown in the souls of men, both spring forth by a power greater than that of the sower. Paul may plant and Apollos water, but it is God who giveth the increase. The life is in the seed, be it the corn sown in the soil or the word sown in the soul. As the earth brings forth, first the blade, then the ear, and finally the corn fully ripened for the harvest, so the good seed grows in the good soil of goodly souls, preparing them for the day when the servants of the Lord shall thrust in their sickles and reap, thus laying up in store saved souls for the Lord of the harvest.

Parable of the Wheat and the Tares

(*Matthew 13:24-30, 36-43; JST, Matthew 13:29, 39-44; D&C 86:1-7*)

Jesus has now put forth one parable concerning the sower who sowed the seeds of eternal truth in diverse kinds of soil, and another concerning the seed of truth itself as it grows, miraculously and unaided by human hands, in the souls of the honest in heart. In each instance, we at least, and certainly even his Jewish hearers to some extent, can discern his meaning and intent. It is not as though he had told us in plain words, as his wont was among the Nephites, what profound truths he was then dispensing. But he has left us, in language of unexcelled excellence, parabolic illustrations upon which we can ponder and about which we can pray, until their full and glorious meanings burst through the storm clouds of darkness that hold back the radiance of the sun.

Having given us this much experience in the manner of presentation, in the use, and in the interpretation of his parables, Jesus now presents us with one of his more complex and difficult parabolic utterances. It is the parable of the wheat and the tares, one that required a special interpretation for the apostles of old, and one that required a latter-day revelation to enable us to bring its deep and hidden meanings to light. And mayhap, even yet, we await further spiritual enlightenment before its full significance is spread before us.

In this literary gem, preserved for us by our friend Matthew only, we learn how the Son of Man and his servants sowed good seed throughout the world; how Lucifer and his servants over-sowed the wheat fields with tares; how and why the wheat and the tares were permitted to grow together until the day of burning; and how the wicked will then be thrust into a furnace of fire, while the righteous shall shine forth in celestial splendor in the kingdom of the Father. The parable ends with the challenge: "Who hath ears to hear, let him hear." Let us then attune our ears to the wondrous words now spoken by Him at whose feet we rejoice to sit and whose teachings we so desire to savor. We shall view the parable and its interpretation point by point.

The parable: "The kingdom of heaven is likened unto a man which sowed good seed in his field."

The interpretation: "He that soweth the good seed is the Son of man; The field is the world; the good seed are the children of the kingdom."

The latter-day interpretation: "Verily, thus saith the Lord unto you my servants, concerning the parable of the wheat and of the tares: Behold, verily I say, the field was the world, and the apostles were the sowers of the seed."

The Church of Jesus Christ, the earthly organization through which salvation is offered to men; the kingdom of God on earth that prepares men for an inheritance in the kingdom of God in heaven; the organization that is in effect the kingdom of heaven on earth; this blessed and holy congregation of true believers—it is likened unto the Son of Man, and his holy apostles, and all his righteous servants who went forth into the world, preached the gospel, and made converts.

The whole world—not just Galilee and Judea and all of Canaan—the whole world is the field in which converts are made. The gospel and the Church and the kingdom and the blessings and the glory of it all, these are offered to all men. The seeds that are sown in all the world are the children of the kingdom. The sowers are not planting truths in human soil as in the parable of the sower; they are not dropping doctrinal gems in the hearts of men and then awaiting that Divine Providence which brings forth the blade and the ear and the ripened corn as in the parable of the seed growing by itself. Here the seeds sown are people; they are converts to the truth; they are members of the Church; they are the children of the earthly and heirs of the heavenly kingdom; and they are scattered upon all the face of the earth. They are here and there and everywhere, for the whole world is the field, and the apostles and they who ministered at their direction were commanded to go into all the world and preach the gospel to every creature. The words used are the same as in the other parables, but the symbolism and meaning and message are different.

The parable: "But while men slept, his enemy came and sowed tares among the wheat, and went his way."

The interpretation: "The tares are the children of the wicked one; The enemy that sowed them is the devil."

The latter-day interpretation: "And after they [the apostles and their fellow ministers of old] have fallen asleep the great persecutor of the church, the apostate, the whore, even Babylon, that maketh all nations to drink of her cup, in whose hearts the enemy, even Satan, sitteth to reign—behold he soweth the tares; wherefore, the tares choke the wheat and drive the church into the wilderness."

Satan sows tares in the field of the Lord; or, rather, he over-sows or sows on top of the wheat. And as the seeds sown by the Son of Man and his servants are the children of the kingdom, the true saints of God, so the seeds sown by Satan—the tares—are the children of the devil. They are followers of that wicked one; they are carnal and sensual people who choose a false system of religion because it permits them to gratify their passions and live after the manner of the world.

Be it noted that the tares—as far as this parable is concerned—are sown after the day of Jesus and his meridian ministers. The great apostasy came after the apostles had "fallen asleep." When there were no longer apostles and prophets to guide the Church, the saints were tossed to and fro and carried about with every wind of doctrine. The tares choked the wheat; the children of the kingdom were led astray; and the Church was driven into the wilderness.[3]

The parable: "But when the blade was sprung up, and brought forth fruit, then appeared the tares also. So the servants of the householder came and said unto him, Sir, didst not thou sow good seed in thy field? from whence then hath it tares? He said unto them, An enemy hath done this. The servants said unto him, Wilt thou then that we go and gather them up?"

The latter-day interpretation: "But behold, in the last

days, even now while the Lord is beginning to bring forth the word, and the blade is springing up and is yet tender—Behold, verily I say unto you, the angels are crying unto the Lord day and night, who are ready and waiting to be sent forth to reap down the fields."

This is a multi-dispensation parable. It had its beginning when Jesus and the apostles sowed the children of the kingdom in the nations of the earth. In and after their day tares—the children of Satan—were planted in the earthly field, and the tares choked out the wheat. Then the seed was sown again; the children of the kingdom again were found in the field; the blade sprang up amid the tares; and the servants of the Lord, as in former days, would have destroyed the tares, and even the angels cried out for the hastening of the harvest.[4]

The parable: "But he said, Nay; lest while ye gather up the tares, ye root up also the wheat with them. Let both grow together until the harvest: and in the time of harvest I will say to the reapers, Gather ye together first the wheat into my barn; and the tares are bound in bundles to be burned."

The interpretation: "The harvest is the end of the world, or the destruction of the wicked. The reapers are the angels, or the messengers sent of heaven. As, therefore, the tares are gathered and burned in the fire, so shall it be in the end of this world, or the destruction of the wicked. For in that day, before the Son of man shall come, he shall send forth his angels and messengers of heaven. And they shall gather out of his kingdom all things which offend, and them which do iniquity, and shall cast them out among the wicked; and there shall be wailing and gnashing of teeth. For the world shall be burned with fire. Then shall the righteous shine forth as the sun, in the kingdom of their Father."

The latter-day interpretation: "But the Lord saith unto them, pluck not up the tares while the blade is yet tender (for verily your faith is weak), lest you destroy the wheat also. Therefore let the wheat and the tares grow together until the harvest is fully ripe; then ye shall first gather out the wheat from among the tares, and after the gathering of the wheat, behold and lo, the tares are bound in bundles, and the field remaineth to be burned."

The scope and sweep of the message here revealed is as broad as the earth and as enduring as the ages. The wheat is now being gathered out from among the tares. Israel is being gathered into the sheepfold of the Good Shepherd. Messengers from heaven—Peter, James, and John; Moses, Elijah, and Elias; and all the angelic host who have restored priesthoods, conferred keys, and given powers to men—have joined hands with mortals on earth to gather the elect and to seal up the law and bind up the testimony against those who are to be burned when the Son of Man comes. Soon the harvest will be fully ripe; the wheat will be stored in the Lord's barns; the tares will be bound in bundles; and the burning will commence.[5]

Parable of the Mustard Seed

(*Matthew 13:31-32; Mark 4:30-32; Luke 13:18-19*)

Though each of the parables stands by itself to teach a designated portion of eternal truth, it takes them all together to place in perspective those truths with which they deal. In the parable of the sower, the good word of God was sown in divers soils and only a portion of the seed grew and brought forth fruit. In the parable of the wheat and the tares even that portion which grew was choked by thorns; the kingdom was destroyed for a time; and only the latter-day sowing anew of the saving seeds enabled the growth of that wheat which would be gathered into barns before the burning of the bundles of tares. In each of these parables there is an element of sorrow and sadness; evil triumphs in many hearts; multitudes reject the gospel seed; and other multitudes who had the truth changed themselves from the wheat of the kingdom to the tares of the devil, and the field was burned. But now, in the parable of the mustard seed, we shall see how the kingdom of God on earth shall grow and increase, how it shall be displayed for all to see, and how success shall attend its labors.

"The kingdom of heaven," Jesus said, "is like to a grain of mustard seed, which a man took, and sowed in his field: Which indeed is the least of all seeds: but when it is grown, it is the greatest among herbs, and becometh a tree, so that the birds of the air come and lodge in the branches thereof."

One of the great beauties of parables is that they may have many meanings and applications all of which are true and proper. Their full significance is and can be known only to those who have an over-all knowledge of the dealings of Deity with men, and who also are enlightened by the power of the same Spirit that guided the one who gave the parables. "Parables must have been utterly unintelligible to all who did not see in the humble, despised, Nazarene, and in His teachings, the Kingdom. But to those whose eyes, ears and hearts had been opened, they would carry most needed instruction and most precious comfort and assurance." (Edersheim 1:592.)

To the more enlightened among his Jewish hearers, Jesus' words in this parable would have given some concept at least of the great truths he sought to convey. Two of his expressions—that of "mustard seed" and, as Luke expresses it, "a great tree"—were well known and had clear meaning. Their use and application in the case at hand is, of course, quite another matter.

As to the first: "The expression, 'small as a mustard-seed,' had become proverbial, and was used, not only by our Lord, but frequently by the Rabbis, to indicate the smallest amount, such as the least drop of blood, the least defilement, or the smallest remnant of sun-glow in the sky. 'But when it is grown, it is greater than the garden-herbs.' Indeed, it looks no longer like a garden-herb or shrub, but 'becomes,' or rather, appears like, 'a tree'—as St. Luke puts it, 'a great tree,' of course, not in comparison with other trees, but with garden-shrubs."

As to the second: "A tree, whose wide-spreading branches afforded lodgment to the birds of heaven, was a familiar Old Testament figure for a mighty kingdom that gave shelter to the nations. [Ezek. 31; Dan. 4.] Indeed, it is specifically used as an illustration of the Messianic Kingdom. [Ezek. 17:23.]" (Edersheim 1:592-93.)

To those in sectarian Christendom who have sufficient interest in scriptural study to seek for an interpretation of this parable, some such conclusion as this is generally reached: It contrasts the small and rising beginning of Christianity in Jesus' day with the worldwide dominion now enjoyed by those who suppose they are followers of the Nazarene. They assume, falsely, "that the Kingdom of Heaven, planted in the field of the world as the smallest seed, in the most humble and unpromising manner, would grow till it far outstripped all other similar plants, and gave shelter to all nations under heaven." (Edersheim 1:593.)[6]

The most complete and best application and meaning, however, is preserved for us in the language of Joseph Smith. After quoting the words of the parable, he says: "Now we can discover plainly that this figure is given to represent the Church as it shall come forth in the last days. Behold, the Kingdom of Heaven is likened unto it. Now, what is like unto it?

"Let us take the Book of Mormon, which a man took and hid in his field, securing it by his faith, to spring up in the last days, or in due time; let us behold it coming forth out of the ground, which is indeed accounted the least of all seeds, but behold it branching forth, yea, even towering, with lofty branches, and God-like majesty, until it, like the mustard seed, becomes the greatest of all herbs. And it is truth, and it has sprouted and come forth out of the earth, and righteousness begins to look down from heaven, and God is sending down His powers, gifts and angels, to lodge in the branches thereof.

"The Kingdom of Heaven is like unto a mustard seed.

Behold, then is not this the Kingdom of Heaven that is raising its head in the last days in the majesty of God, even the Church of the Latter-day Saints." (*Teachings,* pp. 98-99.)

Parable of the Leaven

(*Matthew 13:33; Luke 13:20-21*)

Yet another portion of the eternal picture portrayed in parables is seen in the parable of the leaven. The mustard seed became a tree that displayed the kingdom of heaven on earth before the world, but the leaven worked silently, without observation, unknown to many among men, to establish the plans and purposes of Divine Providence. Jesus said simply: "The kingdom of heaven is like unto leaven, which a woman took, and hid in three measures of meal, till the whole was leavened."

In this parable of the leaven we see the glory and triumph of the kingdom in the hearts of men. The Messianic kingdom comes not in martial splendor; there are no rolling drums and tramping feet; the Son of David does not march before his armies; trumpets do not herald his coming, and standard bearers raise no visible ensign to the nations. The new kingdom, like leaven, is hidden in the hearts of men. The leaven of life, the leaven of righteousness, the leaven of the word of God—the yeast of eternal truth—is "kneaded" into the souls of men. Then its spreading, penetrating, life-giving effect enlarges the soul and "raises" sinners into saints.

Legal administrators teach the gospel and testify of its divinity; their testimonies, hidden in the hearts and minds of men, begin the soul-enlarging process of conversion. Lumps of lifeless dough live, and after being baked in the ovens of life become as desirable to the taste as the manna once rained from heaven upon the Lord's people.[7]

Parable of the Hidden Treasure

(*Matthew 13:44; JST, Matthew 13:46*)

After giving the parable of the leaven, Jesus sent the

multitude away, went with his disciples into a house in Capernaum, and at the request of the disciples interpreted the parable of the wheat and the tares.[8] Then he gave three more parables to the disciples alone. The first of these is the parable of the hidden treasure. "Again, the kingdom of heaven is like unto a treasure hid in a field," Jesus said. "And when a man hath found a treasure which is hid, he secureth it, and, straightway, for joy thereof, goeth and selleth all that he hath, and buyeth that field."

"By seeming accident a man sometimes discovers the gospel treasure. Unaware of the saving grace of our Lord, devoid of true religious understanding, overburdened with the cares of the world, hardened by sin, walking in an ungodly and carnal course—he suddenly stumbles onto Christ and the pure Christianity found in his true Church. Immediately all else seems as dross. Temporal wealth becomes but glittering tinsel as compared to the eternal riches of Christ. Then worldly things are forsaken; then no sacrifice is too great for the new convert, as he seeks a valid title to the treasures of the kingdom." (*Commentary* 1:300.)[9]

A woman comes out of Sychar to draw water from Jacob's well and finds one there who gives her living water. Gentile nations, composed of people who have never heard of Christ and are devoid of any desire to gain the cleansing power of his blood, meet Paul and Silas and find a great treasure. Hosts of earth's pilgrims, traveling and wandering they know not where, with no knowledge of Joseph Smith and the restoration, chance to meet a Mormon missionary or move into a Mormon community, and suddenly the riches of eternity are opened to their view.

And so it is with the kingdom of heaven, with the only true and living church upon the face of the whole earth: Though it operates openly among men, though its gospel gifts and goodly fruits are seen on every hand, yet it is hidden from those whose hearts are not yet attuned to the Infinite; it is hidden until, of a sudden, the finder, scarcely having supposed that so great a treasure would be hidden in so unlikely a spot, makes a great discovery. The treasure is recognized for what it is, and it is available for the taking. Immediately the finder sells all that he hath—he cannot buy it for a lesser price; there is no fixed amount on a price tag; he cannot haggle and offer anything less than all he has; it is not for sale on a bargain counter; its purchase calls for the sacrifice of all things—and so the finder, be he rich or poor, sells all that he hath; he forsakes the world and its wealth; he turns from the worldliness of the past and walks in paths of righteousness; and he buyeth the field and possesseth the treasure. It is his. He found it.

Parable of the Pearl of Great Price

(*Matthew 13:45-46*)

"Again, the kingdom of heaven is like unto a merchant man, seeking goodly pearls: Who, when he had found one pearl of great price, went and sold all that he had, and bought it."

Now Jesus has somewhat more to say about how the struggling pilgrims of earth, far removed from their heavenly home, come to find the gospel, the most precious possession of life. The treasure hidden in the field is found by chance. Honest-hearted souls find themselves in contact with true ministers and the truths that from them flow, and they sell all that they have to purchase the newly discovered gospel of salvation.

But here Jesus speaks of earnest and devout investigators; of truth seekers who desire to better their circumstances; of people who consciously follow the dictates of their consciences; of those who follow the promptings and heed the whisperings of that Spirit, the light of Christ, which enlighteneth every man born into the world. These are those who know there is more to life than to eat, drink, and be merry. They are trying to cast off carnality and live by godly standards. They may be philanthropists or artists; they may serve on committees and join groups who work for freedom, social betterment, and the preservation of human rights; they study the Bible, seek truth, and join uplifting organizations, including various of the churches of the day. They are seeking goodly pearls.

After long and diligent search; after going from one level of light to heights of greater illumination; perhaps after joining one church or another in search of the peace that passeth understanding; after seeking truth with an open heart—after, shall we not say it, after reading and pondering and praying about the Book of Mormon; after investigating the prophetic claims of Joseph Smith and his successors—at the end of a long search, lo, the pearl of great price is found. It is the everlasting gospel. It is the Church and kingdom of God on earth. It is all that men can desire; its blessings are peace in this life and eternal life in the world to come.

Do investigators then sell all that they have to buy such a pearl? They can do nothing less. And the Lord, whose pearl it is, asks their all. As with those who find the hidden treasure, there is no haggling, no bargaining, no agreeing to come into the Church with this or that reservation, no offering of less than one's whole soul and all that the truth seekers have and are. What matters it if all the pearls of the past are sold, if all the causes and organizations, however "goodly," go by the board? The newly found pearl, the kingdom of heaven, will use all the talents and strength and abilities of those who give their all to gain it.[10]

Parable of the Gospel Net

(*Matthew 13:47-53; JST, Matthew 13:50-51, 53*)

The parable: "Again, the kingdom of heaven is like unto a net, that was cast into the sea, and gathered of every kind: Which, when it was full, they drew to shore, and sat down, and gathered the good into vessels, but cast the bad away."

The interpretation: "So shall it be at the end of the world. And the world is the children of the wicked. The angels shall come forth, and sever the wicked from the just, and shall cast them out into the world to be burned. There shall be wailing and gnashing of teeth."

What an awesome and ominous picture this is! The gospel net is cast into the sea; the fishers of men seek to draw all men into the kingdom. The catch is great, but it includes fish of all kinds, some of which are gathered in vessels to be saved, and others are cast away to be burned along with the wicked who were never caught in the gospel net. The net here meant is a draw net or a seine, which may be as much as half a mile in length; it is leaded below so it will sweep the bottom of the sea, while corks keep the top floating near the surface. As it is swept along the beach it gathers in fish of every sort without reference to their ultimate use or worth.

So it is with those who join the Church—they are oftimes as diverse and varied as men can be. "Rich and poor, bond and free, Jew and Gentile, learned and ignorant, sincere and hypocritical, stable and wavering—men of all races, cultures, and backgrounds accept the gospel and seek its blessings." (*Commentary* 1:302.) Some are repentant and worthy and will be put in vessels; others are swept along by the tides of social pressure. Some are drawn in by the tight net of business necessity and economic advantage; yet others join with the saints to inherit property, marry selected persons, or gain political preferment. And all such shall be cast away with the wicked to be burned. There are many reasons for coming into the earthly kingdom of heaven; salvation is a personal matter, and only those who meet the divine standards will find eternal place and lot with the saints.

> Though in the outward Church below
> Both wheat and tares together grow,
> Ere long will Jesus weed the crop
> And pluck the tares in anger up.[11]

The wheat and the tares together grow! Such, we have seen, was the parable telling of the present intermixture of the righteous and the wicked in the earthly kingdom, meaning more particularly the world. Now, in the parable of the draw net, we see that same condition within the Church and kingdom itself. And try as we may—men being weak and mortal and fallible; sins being hidden and devious and unknown—until the Son of Man comes, the kingdom will not be wholly cleansed.

Those in the Church are not perfect, and more than church membership is needed to save and exalt. Baptism alone is not enough: thereafter the newly born babes in Christ must grow to a spiritual maturity; they "must press forward with a steadfastness in Christ, having a perfect brightness of hope, and a love of God and of all men"; they must feast "upon the word of Christ, and endure to the end." (2 Ne. 31:20.) Those caught in the gospel net have power to become the sons of God; after baptism they must "work out" their "salvation with fear and trembling" before the Lord. (Philip. 2:12.)[12]

As of this moment, there are tares among the wheat. "In a great house"—and God's house is his church, his earthly kingdom—"there are not only vessels of gold and of silver, but also of wood and of earth; and some to honour, and some to dishonour." (2 Tim. 2:20.) For truly, "they are not all Israel, which are of Israel." (Rom. 9:6.) "If a man therefore purge himself from these"—his sins, the sins committed after baptism, the burdens of iniquity that rest upon him, though he was drawn in by the great gospel net—"he shall be a vessel unto honour, sanctified, and meet for the master's use, and prepared unto every good work." (2 Tim. 2:21.) This, then, is the conclusion—and also the moral—of the parable: "Let every one that nameth the name of Christ depart from iniquity." (2 Tim. 2:19.)

Such is the parable of the gospel net.[13] Following its recitation, and as he ended, for the moment, his preachments by parables, Jesus asked his disciples, "Have ye understood all these things? They say unto him, Yea, Lord." It is a mark of true discipleship to understand all scripture, the parables included; indeed, only those enlightened by the power of the Holy Ghost gain the full meaning and intent of the written word, for scripture is both given and understood by the same holy power, the power that comes from the Lord through his Spirit.[14]

Then Jesus said unto them: "Every scribe well instructed in the things of the kingdom of heaven, is like unto a householder; a man, therefore, which bringeth forth out of his treasure that which is new and old."

They—the Twelve, all the disciples, both male and female—knew the meanings of the parables, the deep, hidden, glorious meanings of these gems of literary elucidation and of gospel knowledge. Ergo: They must teach and testify of these very things. As a householder who displays his treasures—both the old and the new; that which hath value because of its antiquity, and that which is of great worth because it is new and can be used—as a householder displays his treasures, so the disciples must bring forth out of the storehouses of their souls the eternal truths of the gospel and teach them to their fellowmen. "It becometh every man who hath been warned to warn his neighbor." (D&C 88:81.)[15]

Truly, this Man, who spake as none other had ever done, fulfilled that "which was spoken by the prophet, saying, I will open my mouth in parables; I will utter things which have been kept secret from the foundation of the world." (Matt. 13:35.)

NOTES

1. "According to Jewish authorities there was twofold sowing, as the seed was either cast by the hand or by means of cattle. In the latter case, a sack with holes was filled with corn and laid on the back of the animal, so that, as it moved onwards, the seed was thickly scattered. Thus it might well be, that it would fall indiscriminately on beaten roadway, on stony places but thinly covered with soil, or where the thorns had not been cleared away, or undergrowth from the thorn-hedge crept into the field, as well as on good ground." (Edersheim 1:586-87.)

2. In commenting about this parable, Joseph Smith said: "Men who have no principle of righteousness in themselves, and whose hearts are full of iniquity, and [who] have no desire for the principles of truth, do not understand the word of truth when they hear it. The devil taketh away the word of truth out of their hearts, because there is no desire for righteousness in them." (*Teachings,* p. 96.)

3. "According to the common view, these tares represent what is botanically known as the 'bearded Darnel,' a poisonous rye-grass, very common in the East, 'entirely like wheat until the ear appears,' or else (according to some), the 'creeping wheat' or 'couch-grass,' of which the roots creep underground and become intertwined with those of the wheat. But

the Parable gains in meaning if we bear in mind that, according to ancient Jewish (and, indeed, modern Eastern) ideas, the Tares were *not* of different seed, but only a degenerate kind of wheat. Whether in legend or symbol, Rabbinism has it that even the ground had been guilty of fornication before the judgment of the flood, so that when wheat was sown tares sprang up. The Jewish hearers of Jesus would, therefore, think of these tares as [a] degenerate kind of wheat, originally sprung at the time of the Flood, through the corruptness of the earth, but now, alas! so common in their fields; wholly undistinguishable from the wheat, till the fruit appeared: noxious, poisonous, and requiring to be separated from the wheat, if the latter was not to become useless." (Edersheim 1:589.)

This view that the tares were a "degenerate kind of wheat" symbolically accords with the revealed interpretation of the parable that the tares are children of the wicked one who arose to replace the children of the kingdom. All men are of the same race; those who do good and work righteousness become children of the kingdom, and those who choose to do the works of him who is evil become the children of the devil.

4. "We learn by this parable," Joseph Smith wrote, "not only the setting up of the Kingdom in the days of the Savior, which is represented by the good seed, which produced fruit, but also the corruptions of the Church, which are represented by the tares, which were sown by the enemy, which His disciples would fain have plucked up, or cleansed the Church of, if their views had been favored by the Savior. But He, knowing all things, says, Not so. As much as to say, your views are not correct, the Church is in its infancy, and if you take this rash step, you will destroy the wheat, or the Church, with the tares; therefore it is better to let them grow together until the harvest, or the end of the world, which means the destruction of the wicked, which is not yet fulfilled." (*Teachings,* pp. 97-98.)

5. "The harvest and the end of the world have an allusion directly to the human family in the last days. . . . As, therefore, the tares are gathered and burned in the fire, so shall it be in the end of the world; that is, as the servants of God go forth warning the nations, both priests and people, and as they harden their hearts and reject the light of truth, these first being delivered over to the buffetings of Satan, and the law and the testimony being closed up, as it was in the case of the Jews, they are left in darkness, and delivered over unto the day of burning; thus being bound up by their creeds, and their bands being made strong by their priests, [they] are prepared for the fulfilment of the saying of the Savior—'The Son of Man shall send forth His angels, and they shall gather out of His Kingdom all things that offend, and them which do iniquity; and shall cast them into a furnace of fire, there shall be wailing and gnashing of teeth.' We understand that the work of gathering together of the wheat into barns, or garners, is to take place while the tares are being bound over, and [incident to] preparing for the day of burning: [and] that after the day of burnings, the righteous shall shine forth like the sun, in the Kingdom of their Father." (*Teachings,* p. 101.)

It should be clear that "in giving the parable of the wheat and the tares, Jesus was actually summarizing the doctrines of the apostasy, the restoration of the gospel in the latter-days, the growth and development of the latter-day kingdom, the millennial cleansing of the earth, the glorious advent of the Son of Man, and the ultimate celestial exaltation of the faithful." (*Commentary* 1:297.)

6. "The evident falsity of this interpretation is seen from the fact that the original, pure Christianity practiced by the primitive saints never did more than sprout its head above ground; within a relatively short time the original plant was trodden down, destroyed, and replaced by those noxious and thorny plants which make up the present churches of so-called Christendom. It is only in the dispensation of the fulness of times that the true Christian tree is to grow until it becomes 'a great tree'; it is only in this final age that the true gospel message is to roll forth until the knowledge of God covers the earth as the waters cover the sea. (D&C 65; Isa. 11.)" (*Commentary* 1:298.)

7. An application of this parable to the latter-day kingdom is given by the Prophet in these words: "It may be understood that the Church of the Latter-day Saints has taken its rise from a little leaven that was put into three witnesses. Behold, how much this is like the parable! It is fast leavening the lump, and will soon leaven the whole." (*Teachings,* p. 100.)

8. Whether our Lord gave all of the parables in the thirteenth chapter of Matthew in immediate consecutive order is a matter of some uncertainty. Two of them, the parable of

the mustard seed and the parable of the leaven, are recorded by Luke in a different setting. It may be that Matthew grouped them all together for convenience in presentation, or, what is yet more probable, that Jesus repeated the same parables on numerous occasions to different congregations. There is no reason to suppose that a parable once given should never be spoken again; if the message was worth the attention of one congregation, so it would be of another. We should, however, no matter what view we take of the time and circumstances of their delivery, know assuredly that the message they contain and the doctrines they allude to are what is important to us.

9. This parable has also an allusion to the gathering of Israel in the last days. "The Saints work after this pattern," the Prophet said, after quoting the parable. "See the Church of the Latter-day Saints, selling all that they have, and gathering themselves together unto a place that they may purchase for an inheritance, that they may be together and bear each other's afflictions in the day of calamity." (*Teachings,* p. 101.)

10. "Seekers after truth may acquire much that is good and desirable, and not find the greatest truth of all, the truth that shall save them. Yet, if they seek persistently and with right intent, if they are really in quest of pearls and not of imitations, they shall find. Men who by search and research discover the truths of the kingdom of heaven may have to abandon many of their cherished traditions, and even their theories of imperfect philosophy and 'science falsely so called,' if they would possess themselves of the pearl of great price." (Talmage, pp. 293-94.)

11. *Hymns,* no. 102.

12. "All who are caught in the gospel net are not saved in the celestial kingdom; church membership alone gives no unconditional assurance of eternal life. (2 Ne. 31:16-21.) Rather, there will be a day of judgment, a day of sorting and dividing, a day when the wicked shall be cast out of the Church, 'out into the world to be burned.' For those then living the Second Coming will be an initial day of burning, sorting, and judgment (Matt. 25:31-46; D&C 63:54); for all men of all ages the ultimate day of sorting and dividing will occur, after all men have been raised from the dead, at the final great day of judgment. (2 Ne. 9:15-16.)" (*Commentary* 1:302.)

13. Joseph Smith in applying this parable to latter-day conditions wrote: "Behold the seed of Joseph, spreading forth the Gospel net upon the face of the earth, gathering of every kind, that the good may be saved in vessels prepared for that purpose, and the angels will take care of the bad. So shall it be at the end of the world—the angels shall come forth and sever the wicked from among the just, and cast them into the furnace of fire, and there shall be wailing and gnashing of teeth." (*Teachings,* p. 102.)

14. With reference to the parables considered in this chapter, Joseph Smith said: "These things are so plain and so glorious, that every Saint in the last days must respond with a hearty Amen to them." (*Teachings,* p. 102.)

15. These treasures of truth, old yet ever new, are exemplified by "the Book of Mormon coming forth out of the treasure of the heart. Also the covenants given to the Latter-day Saints, also the translation of the Bible—thus bringing forth out of the heart things new and old." (*Teachings,* p. 102.)

JESUS MINISTERS AMONG THE GADARENES

Master, the tempest is raging!
The billows are tossing high!
The sky is o'er shadowed with blackness.
No shelter or help is nigh.

Carest thou not that we perish?
How canst thou lie asleep
When each moment so madly is threatening
A grave in the angry deep?[1]

He Stills a Storm on the Sea of Galilee

(*Mark 4:35-41; JST, Mark 4:30; Matthew 8:18-27; Luke 8:22-25; 9:57-62; JST, Luke 8:23*)

Some six miles south and east of the shore of the ofttimes turbulent Galilean sea lay the prosperous city of Gadara where dwelt the Gadarenes (Gergesenes). Straight across the lake from Capernaum was Gergesa. Those who lived in these and other eastern areas must see the face and hear the voice of the Son of God. His work must not be done in a corner; every ear must hear his words, every eye must see his glory; all must have the privilege to believe, to follow, to obey, to be saved. We have no record of any visit by the Man from Nazareth to this area of the Decapolis except that which he now plans to make, but the miracle and wonder of his brief ministry among the rebellious of that area is such that neither they nor any who hear of it will ever be able to erase the memory.

It has been a long day. Jesus is weary. Great multitudes have pressed upon him, so much so that he delivered his public parables from a ship while the thronged congregation stood on the shore. Thereafter in a house in Capernaum he continued to preach in parables and otherwise to his disciples. Again on the seashore the multitude throngs about, hanging on every word, their souls crying out for the divine message.

It is now evening, and he says to his disciples, "Let us go over unto the other side of the lake." This decision apparently takes them by surprise, for it is only then that they "sent away the multitude." Then, as Mark says, "they took him even as he was in the ship," which seems to mean they departed without preparation in the way of food or clothing or traveling necessities. Whether their departure was a change in plans or the continuation of a course already foreknown in the mind of the Master we do not know; of this only we cannot doubt: Jesus, following the dictates of the Spirit, was continuing his foreordained ministry, and the coming events—the stilling that night of the Galilean storm, and the confrontation the next day with the legion of evil spirits—were among the most dramatic events of his ministry.

As Jesus and the elect few—certainly all or part of the Twelve among them; perhaps only the Twelve, because of space limitations—as these few hastened to push off from shore into the beckoning seclusion of the waters of Gennesaret, a sudden interruption halted their progress. Three men, apparently men of note and prominence, came forward to pledge their allegiance to the Master's cause and to offer their services in his behalf. Their individual offers and the divine responses invoked to each were so instructive as to warrant their inclusion in the writings of the synoptists. The proffers of service and our Lord's rejoinders were:

1. *The case of the vainglorious scribe.*

Swept along by the tide of popular acclaim, feeling the exhilaration that always attends a new and great and achieving movement, a certain scribe—a recognized religious leader, a prominent minister of the day, as it were—stepped forward to offer his services in the newly established church. "Master, I will follow thee whithersoever thou goest," he said.

From Jesus' response it seems clear that the offer was a self-serving plea for a position of preferment—a minister of the old dispensation seeking an equivalent rank in the new. "But in spite of the man's high position, in spite of his glowing promises, He who cared less than nothing for lip-service, and who preferred 'the modesty of fearful duty' to the 'rattling tongue of audacious eloquence,' coldly checked His would-be follower. He who had called the hated publican gave no encouragement to the reputable scribe. He did not reject the proffered service, but neither did He accept it. Perhaps 'in the man's flaring enthusiasm, He saw the smoke of egotistical self deceit.' He pointed out that His service was not one of wealth, or honour, or delight; not one in which any could hope for earthly gain." (Farrar, p. 248.)

In short, the Lord Jesus chooses his own ministers. All men who repent may enter his earthly kingdom and become heirs of the universal blessings thereby offered to all. Only those prepared by foreordination, chosen, as it were, from before the foundations of the world, are selected to lead and guide the destinies of the holy kingdom. And so, without denying church membership, but while withholding approval of the proffered ministerial assistance, Jesus said:

> *The foxes have holes, and the birds of the air have nests; but the Son of man hath not where to lay his head.*

When and while men serve on full-time missions—as Jesus himself did for the more than three years here involved—all worldly matters slip away into relative insignificance. The Lord's ministers deny themselves of houses and lands and families and friends—of whatsoever need be—to carry on that work which excels in importance all other. There is no record that the scribe who sought to call himself to the ministry took any further steps to achieve his initially sought purpose.

2. *The case of the reluctant disciple.*

In contrast to the scribe who sought for himself an ecclesiastical appointment in the new kingdom, we see now a disciple who was, in fact, called by Jesus to serve on a mission. "Follow me," came the divine word; 'teach my gospel; testify of me; build up my kingdom; forsake all for my name's sake.' This disciple—whose heart was known to Him who calls His own—had faith; he knew the worth of the pearl of great price; but he also had worldly interests that seemed important to him. "Lord, suffer me first to go and bury my father," he implored. Back came the divine word:

> *Let the dead bury their dead: but go thou and preach the kingdom of God.*

'I have called you; forsake the things of this world and seek for those of a better. What is the life or death of family or friends to those who are taking life and salvation to a dying world? Let those who are spiritually dead bury those in whose bodies the breath of life no longer dwells. Go thou; preach the gospel of the kingdom; proclaim faith, repentance, baptism, and the gift of the Holy Ghost. Bring souls unto me, and you shall have rest with them in the kingdom of my Father.'

3. *The case of the delaying disciple.*

Yet another disciple—willing to serve, but concerned with the time and place of his call; willing to go on a mission and preach the gospel, but questioning the field of his present assignment—said: "Lord, I will follow thee; but let me first go bid them farewell, which are at home at my house." 'I will go, but let it be on my terms and conditions, not those of the Church.' To him Jesus gave the reply that has become proverbial for all time:

> *No man, having put his hand to the plough, and looking back, is fit for the kingdom of God.*[2]

But now, at last, they set sail, traveling eastward across those blessed waters which are so much a part of the lives of the Holy One and his holy apostles. Yet even now, they are not alone; so great is his fame, so popular his appeal, and so compelling his presence, that many seek to follow him onto the turbulent waters and into the descending dusk. "There were also with him other little ships," Mark says. What happened to them as the events of the evening rose to their fearsome yet triumphant climax we know not. Perhaps they returned to a safe harbor and a secure anchor as the impending storm rose in violence over the surging waters; perhaps they too were buffeted by the violent winds, as their fearsome passengers dreaded the seeming death that lay ahead in the angry deep; and perhaps those who sailed in these lesser crafts also marveled and worshipped when the awesome decree went forth, "Peace, be still," and the violent waters of Gennesaret became calm.

In Galilee, of great and wondrous fame, is found the Sea of Galilee—the lake of Gennesaret, the sea of Tiberias—an inland mere of fresh, fish-filled water. Into it on the north flows the newborn Jordan; out of it on the south drains the mature and mighty river in which both John and Jesus baptized, and which meanders downward through a rich and fertile valley to the Dead Sea. This lake of Galilee, which Jesus so much loved and from whose life-giving waters the sons of Jonas and the sons of Zebedee, and many others of the disciples, made their living, is some thirteen miles long and seven miles wide. It is 695 feet below sea level and lies at the base, on the east and west, of rugged hills and mountains cut by canyons and gorges down which tempestuous winds and atmospheric downdraughts blow, making the otherwise calm waters subject to sudden and violent storms.

Such an atmospheric assault came forth in the lowering dusk of this memorable evening as Jesus and his intimates set forth toward Perea and the eastern shore. Whether the storm arose wholly without warning or the experienced sailors who governed the craft saw signs of the tempest ahead and yet launched their ship forth because the passenger whose will they sought to do had so commanded, we cannot tell. Nor does it matter, though we prefer to believe they set forth knowing that peril lay ahead because He willed it.

In any event, it is clear that the storm itself was unusually fierce. "There arose a great tempest in the sea," Matthew says, "insomuch that the ship was covered with the waves." Mark says: "There arose a great storm of wind, and the waves beat into the ship, so that it was now full"; and Luke adds that "they were filled with fear, and were in danger."

Through it all, we see the Mortal Messiah seeking the physical refreshment his tired body so much needs at the moment. "Jesus is asleep, for very weariness and hunger, in the stern of the ship, His head on that low wooden bench, while the heavens darken, the wild wind swoops down those mountain-gorges, howling with hungry rage over the trembling sea; the waves rise and toss, and lash and break over the ship, and beat into it, and the white foam washes at His feet. His Humanity here appears as true as when He lay cradled in the manger; His Divinity, as when the sages from the East laid their offerings at His Feet." (Edersheim 1:600.)

None fear floods and storm-lashed seas more than those who work with water and know its onrushing power and the utter helplessness of mortal strength before its overpowering waves. Is it any wonder that Jesus was awakened from what must have been a deep sleep with cries of, "Master, carest thou not that we perish?" as Mark records; "Master, master, we perish," as Luke has it; and, "Lord, save us: we perish," as Matthew records—all of which expressions must have been part of the earnest and fear-filled importunings of that dread moment.

Jesus, now awake, before he arises from the wooden bench whereon he lay, says to those who sought his help: "Why are ye fearful, O ye of little faith?" After the storm is quelled, he will say to them again: "Where is your faith?" From this we need not suppose they were without faith. Their very importunings bore witness of their assurance that this man, whom they followed as the Messiah, could do whatever must be done to prevent disaster. Their lack of faith—as with all of us—was one of degree; had they believed with that fervor that might have been the case, they of themselves could have stilled the storm, without arousing their weary Lord from his needed rest.

But after this, "he arose, and rebuked the winds and the sea; and there was a great calm." The raging waters and the roaring winds ceased; the mighty waves became calm ripples. "Peace, be still," he said, and all was calm and serene. "When 'He was awakened' by the voice of His disciples, 'He rebuked the wind and the sea,' as Jehovah had of old ["He rebuked the Red sea also, and it was dried up"—Ps. 109]—just as He had 'rebuked' the fever, and the paroxysm of the demonised. For, all are His creatures, even when lashed to frenzy of the 'hostile power.' And the sea He commanded as if it were a sentient being: 'Be silent! Be silenced!' And immediately the wind was bound, the panting waves throbbed into stillness, and a great calm of rest fell upon the Lake. For, when Christ sleepeth, there is storm; when He waketh, great peace." (Edersheim 1:602.)

And they being afraid wondered, saying one to another, What manner of man is this! for he commandeth even the winds and water, and they obey him.

What manner of man, indeed! Heretofore he has cleansed lepers, cast out devils, and even given life to a cold corpse. Now the very elements obey his word. And yet it is not the miracles of themselves that cause the world to wonder; rather, it is the miracles coupled with the repeated personal witness that he is the Son of God, their Savior and Redeemer.

Others have performed miracles, always, however, in his name and by his authority; others have even controlled the elements, as he through them has willed it. Moses stretched forth his rod and the waters of the Red Sea parted. Whatever turbulence throbbed through their restless waves ceased at his word; the laws of gravity ceased to triumph and the very waters congealed, forming a wall on the right hand and on the left, between which the chosen seed then trod on dry ground. Enoch moved mountains and changed rivers from their courses. Elijah and Elisha smote the waters of Jordan with a holy mantle, and they divided hither and thither, leaving dry ground for their path. Unto the servants of the Lord "is given power to command the waters." (D&C 61:27.) It is not the miracle per se; it is the fact that Jesus, who performed the miracle, said he was God's Son—leaving the *deed* as proof of his *words.*[3]

We cannot leave our brief consideration of this stupendous miracle, however, without at least opening the door to the symbolic uses to which it may be put. For instance, manifestly it teaches that the Lord Jesus is ever near his friends and will preserve them in perilous circumstances, even if their safety calls for control of the elements.

Also, the sea—a raging, restless sea—is a symbol of a sinful and wicked world. The beasts seen by Daniel in vision and used as types of worldly kingdoms came up out of the sea, a sea upon which the four winds of heaven strove. (Dan. 7.) And the Lord said to Isaiah: "The wicked are like the troubled sea, when it cannot rest, whose waters cast up mire and dirt. There is no peace, saith my God, to the wicked" (Isa. 57:20-21)—leaving us to conclude that when Christ calms the seas of life, peace enters the hearts of men.

Further, there are those also who have likened the Church itself to a ship, steered and sailed by apostles and prophets through the waves of the world, which rage and toss, violently and with force, against the tempested bark, and yet never prevail. The divine ship never sinks; its faithful passengers never drown in the angry deep, because Christ sails his own ship. He may seem to be asleep on a bench with a pillow under his head, but he is there. And when in times of great peril he is aroused by the pleas of his servants, once again he rebukes the winds and the waters; he delivers those who have faith in his name; he speaks peace to troubled souls; his voice is heard again, "Peace, be still."

Jesus Heals a Demoniac among the Gadarenes

(*Mark 5:1-20; JST, Mark 5:6, 11, 13-15, 17; Luke 8:26-39; JST, Luke 8:27, 31-33, 35, 37; Matthew 8:28-34; JST, Matthew 8:29-30*)

Scarcely a ripple marred the calm surface of the lake of Gennesaret as the Jewish ship anchored near Gerasa (Gergesa) on the Perean side of the sea. Striving winds and raging billows and crashing waves—all part of the now-stilled storm—no longer beat upon the ship and the rock-strewn shore. He whose voice had spoken to matter unorganized and caused the earth to come rolling into existence; he who had gathered the waters into one place, calling the dry land *earth* and the gathering together of the waters *sea*—had spoken peace to the Galilean tempest, and all was calm. The elements were at rest.

Whether it was a late hour of the day of parables or an early hour of the day after, we do not know—only that the storm of the journey had been stilled and earth's elements were at peace. Jesus and his fellow preachers set foot on Perean soil and almost immediately they were confronted with a spiritual storm, a tempest of devilish opposition and human torment, that far overshadowed the recently silenced winds and quelled waves of their inland mere. They were met by a man out of the tombs who for a long time had been possessed by devils. He dwelt in no house, wore no clothing, and was "exceeding fierce," so much so "that no man might pass by that way." In his maddened and raging state "no man could bind him, no, not with chains: Because that he had been often bound with fetters and chains, and the chains had been plucked asunder by him, and the fetters broken in pieces: neither could any man tame him. And always, night and day, he was in the mountains, and in the tombs, crying, and cutting himself with stones."[4]

This poor, shrieking, tormented creature—his body bruised and gashed and naked—impelled by some power or instinct beyond human ken, seeing Jesus afar off, ran to meet him. There they stood—the Prince of Peace who had spoken peace to the winds and the waves, and the maddened maniac whose every act was subject to the will of the demons from hell—there they stood, good and evil facing each other, the one about to act, the other to be acted upon. Then, on his own motion, Jesus spoke the word that would restore lost harmony to the suffering demoniac, that would quell and allay the strife within him, a strife more perilous than the pounding waves of the sea. "Come out of the man, thou unclean spirit," he said.

But there was no immediate obedience. Other purposes were yet to unfold. Rather, the suffering Gadarene fell down, worshipped Jesus, and, his voice framing the words placed on the tongue by the evil power, acclaimed: "What have I to do with thee, Jesus, thou Son of the most high God?" There was no divine knowledge in the demented man; he neither knew nor in his present state cared whether Jesus was the Messiah. But the devils from the deep knew—and do know—that he is God's Son. Their memory of preexistence remains; they remember the day when, at his word, they fell as lightning from heaven. "The devils also believe, and tremble." (James 2:19.) Then from the mouth of the man came the blasphemous words of many devils, spoken as though there was but one: "I adjure thee by God, that thou torment me not." And also, this time speaking in the plural: "Art thou come hither to torment us before the time?" The devils, who know Jesus is the Lord, know also that their destiny is one of eternal torment, one in which they are cast out forever from the divine presence and from every ray of hope and light and betterment.

Jesus asked the man: "What is thy name?" or rather, "he commanded him saying, Declare thy name," and demons within him answered by his mouth: "My name is Legion: for we are many." Or: "He said, Legion: because many devils were entered into him." The poor soul was in complete subjection to the demoniac will; their words were his words, and his voice was their voice.

Knowing they had no choice but to come out of the man—for Jesus had so commanded—the devils "besought him much that he would not send them away out of the country." Apparently they were assigned to tempt those in that area and feared the wrath of Lucifer if they failed to bend to his will. Also, "they besought him that he would not command them to go out into the deep," meaning the eternal abyss, the abysmal pit of eternal torment, which shall be their eventual everlasting inheritance. "And he said unto them, Come out of the man."

Now there was, "a good way off," a great herd of swine, about two thousand in number, "feeding on the mountain." As Matthew records it, the demons said: "If thou cast us out, suffer us to go away into the herd of swine," and Jesus said, "Go." In Mark's account, the devils besought him, saying: "Send us into the swine, that we may enter into them. And forthwith Jesus gave them leave." Luke's conclusion is that "he suffered them" so to do.

Some cavilers exhibit a mocking concern as to whether Jesus commanded or merely permitted the devils to enter the swine, as though it made the slightest difference. They pretend to find in his act, whatever it was, an unwarranted destruction of the property of others. Surely it was an unethical if not an immoral act, they contend. If such it is assumed to be, so be it. But, realistically, who is to say that He who sends hail to beat down the ears of ripened corn, or storms to sink fish-filled boats, may not also send devils into swine to sweep them in a maddened surge to a watery grave?

But be that as it may be. "Then went the devils out of the man, and entered into the swine: and the herd ran violently down a steep place into the lake, and were choked." As to the locale, Edersheim tells us: "About a quarter of an hour to the south of Gersa [Gerasa] is a steep bluff, which descends abruptly on a narrow ledge of shore. A terrified herd running down this cliff could not have recovered its foothold, and must inevitably have been hurled into the

Lake beneath. Again, the whole country around is burrowed with limestone caverns and rock-chambers for the dead, such as those which were the dwelling of the demonised." (Edersheim 1:607.)

Why did the demons desire to enter the bodies of the swine? Or, for that matter, how came they to take up tenancy in the body of the man? We cannot tell and do not know how it is that evil spirits—few or many—gain entrance into the bodies of mortal men. We do know that all things are governed by law, and that Satan is precluded from taking possession of the bodies of the prophets and other righteous people. Were it not so, the work of God would be thwarted—always and in all instances—for Lucifer leads the armies of hell against all men, and more especially against those who are instrumental in furthering the Lord's work.

There must be circumstances of depression and sin and physical weakness that, within the restrictions of divine control, permit evil spirits to enter human bodies. We do know their curse is to be denied tabernacles, and we surmise that the desire for such tenancy is so great that they, when permitted, even enter the bodies of beasts.

And it may be, in this instance, that the devils, ejected from their ill-gotten home by a power they could not resist, sought to thwart His work by the next-best expedient available to them—that of destroying the livelihood of many people, so they would rise up in anger against Him who destroyed their craft. And, in fact, this is what happened.

When they who fed the swine saw what was done, " they fled, and went and told it in the city and in the country." The word was noised about in Gerasa and Gadara and the whole countryside. All the people were stirred up to a high point of wonder and amazement. The owners of the swine, those who knew the healed demoniac, and all who heard of the wondrous happenings hastened "to see what was done." They "came to Jesus, and found the man, out of whom the devils were departed, sitting at the feet of Jesus, clothed, and in his right mind: and they were afraid."

Our evangelist friends tell us only what happened and the few spoken words that tie the whole miraculous series of events together. Hours must have elapsed before the word reached the inhabitants of the area, and yet other hours before the multitudes assembled near the sea to hear and see for themselves. It may even be that more than one day was involved. No doubt the assembling hosts came in groups, both large and small, and arrived at different times.

Jesus and those who were with him would not have done other than teach them the gospel of the kingdom. Such was the message they were proclaiming in every city and place where a single listening ear would hearken to their words. The accounts do tell us that after the people assembled to the place where Jesus and the healed man sat, the feeders and keepers of the swine recited again, for all to hear, how he that was possessed of the devils was healed and also concerning the swine. Nor can we suppose that Jesus and the disciples remained silent. Never was there a time when Jesus was not the center of all eyes, when his words did not ring with clarity in nearby ears. Never was there a teaching situation that he did not utilize to proclaim his gospel to every creature. We cannot doubt that the Gadarenes, on that day or those days, as the case may be, heard the word of truth from him who is the Truth.

But when all had been done that he came to do, when those who walked in darkness had seen a great light, when the doctrine had been taught and the testimony borne—with the healed demoniac there as a living witness of the truth of it all—then was Jesus rejected by the Gadarenes. "Then the whole multitude of the country of the Gadarenes round about besought him to depart from them; for they were taken with great fear."

"'And they were afraid'—more afraid of that Holy Presence than of the previous furies of the possessed. The man indeed was saved; but what of that, considering that some of their two thousand unclean beasts had perished! Their precious swine were evidently in danger; the greed and gluttony of every apostate Jew and low-bred Gentile in the place were clearly imperilled by receiving such a one as they saw that Jesus was. With disgraceful and urgent unanimity they entreated and implored Him to leave their coasts. Both heathens and Jews had recognised already the great truth that God sometimes answers bad prayers in His deepest anger. Jesus Himself had taught His disciples not to give that which was holy to the dogs, neither to cast their pearls before swine, 'lest they trample them under their feet, and then turn again and rend you.' He had gone across the lake for quiet and rest, desiring, though among lesser multitudes, to extend to these semi-heathens also the blessings of the kingdom of God. But they loved their sins and their swine, and with a perfect energy of deliberate preference for all that was base and mean, rejected such blessings, and entreated Him to go away. Sadly, but at once, He turned and left them. Gergesa was no place for Him; better the lonely hill-tops to the north of it; better the crowded strand on the other side." (Farrar, p. 259.)

But Jesus and his associates did not depart without leaving a witness. The healed man desired to attach himself to the missionary group and go over the lake to Capernaum. To him, however, Jesus said: "Go home to thy friends, and tell them how great things the Lord hath done for thee, and hath had compassion on thee." Of his subsequent missionary service we know only that "he departed, and began to publish in Decapolis, how great things Jesus had done for him; and all that heard him did marvel."

We cannot doubt that the purposes of the Gadarene ministry were fulfilled—in the stilling of the storm as they journeyed thitherward; in the healing of the possessed demoniac near Gerasa; in the teaching and testifying that grew out of the miracle; and in the continuing witness of the one by whose mouth Satan once spoke but out of which now came a witness of Christ that no man could refute.[5]

NOTES

1. *Hymns,* no. 106.

2. " 'No man having joined the Church of Jesus Christ is fit for salvation in the celestial kingdom unless he endures to the end in keeping the commandments.' " (*Commentary* 1:305.)

3. In answer to those who argue that no miracle was involved during this darksome night on Gennesaret, Canon Farrar records these choicely chosen words: "If we believe that God rules; if we believe that Christ rose; if we have reason to hold, among the deepest convictions of our being, the certainty that God has not delegated His sovereignty or His providence to the final, unintelligent, pitiless, inevitable working of material forces; if we see on every page of the Evangelists the quiet simplicity of truthful and faithful witnesses; if we see in every year of succeeding history, and in every experience of individual life, a confirmation of the testimony which they delivered—then we shall neither clutch at rationalistic interpretations, nor be much troubled if others adopt them. He who believes, he who *knows,* the efficacy of prayer, in what other men may regard as the inevitable certainties or blindly-directed accidents of life—he who has felt how the voice of a Saviour, heard across the long generations, can calm wilder storms than ever buffeted into fury the bosom of the inland Lake—he who sees in the person of his Redeemer a fact more stupendous and more majestic than all those observed sequences which men endow with an imaginary omnipotence, and worship under the name of Law—to him, at least, there will be neither difficulty nor hesitation in supposing that Christ, on board that half-wrecked fishing boat, did utter His mandate, and that the wind and the sea obeyed; that His word was indeed more potent among the cosmic forces than miles of agitated water, or leagues of rushing wind." (Farrar, pp. 252-53.)

4. Matthew speaks of two demoniacs; Mark and Luke mention only one. Elder Talmage presents the usual sectarian explanation of this discrepancy by saying: "It is possible that one of the afflicted pair was in a condition so much worse than that of his companion that to him is accorded greater prominence in the narrative; or, one may have run away while the other remained." (Talmage, p. 310.) From the Inspired Version, however, we know there was only one; Matthew's account is corrected to conform to the accounts of Mark and Luke. If Elder Talmage had had access to this more perfect biblical account, his expressions relative to this and a number of other matters would have been different.

5. Taken as a whole, as I have written elsewhere, our accounts of the healing of the Gadarene demoniac teach the following truths:

"(1) That evil spirits, actual beings from Lucifer's realm, gain literal entrance into mortal bodies;

"(2) That they then have such power over those bodies as to control the physical acts performed, even to the framing of the very words spoken by the mouth of those so possessed;

"(3) That persons possessed by evil spirits are subjected to the severest mental and physical sufferings and to the basest sort of degradation—all symbolical of the eternal torment to be imposed upon those who fall under Satan's control in the world to come;

"(4) That devils remember Jesus from pre-existence, recognize him as the One who was then foreordained to be the Redeemer, and know that he came into mortality as the Son of God;

"(5) That the desire to gain bodies is so great among Lucifer's minions as to cause them, not only to steal the mortal tabernacles of men, but to enter the bodies of animals;

"(6) That the devils know their eventual destiny is to be cast out into an eternal hell from whence there is no return;

"(7) That rebellious and worldly people are not converted to the truth by observing miracles; and

"(8) That those cleansed from evil spirits can then be used on the Lord's errand to testify of his grace and goodness so that receptive persons may be led to believe in him." (*Commentary* 1:311.)

A CONTINUING MINISTRY OF MIRACLES

Jesus is the Christ, the Eternal God; . . .
he manifesteth himself unto all those
who believe in him,
. . . working mighty miracles, signs, and
wonders,
among the children of men according to
their faith.
(2 Ne. 26:12-13.)

Faith Precedes the Miracle

"It is by faith that miracles are wrought; . . . if these things have ceased, then has faith ceased also." (Moro. 7:37-38.) "If there be no faith among the children of men God can do no miracle among them." (Ether 12:12.)

"And who shall say that Jesus Christ did not many mighty miracles? . . . And the reason why he ceaseth to do miracles among the children of men is because that they dwindle in unbelief, and depart from the right way, and know not the God in whom they should trust." (Morm. 9:18-20.)

Miracles are the fruit of faith. Signs follow those who believe. If there is faith, there will be miracles; if there are no miracles, there is no faith. The two are inseparably intertwined with each other; they cannot be separated, and there cannot be one without the other. Faith and miracles go together, always and everlastingly. And faith precedes the miracle.

Faith is power, the power of God, the power by which the worlds were made. Where there is faith there is power, and where a people do not have power to heal the sick and perform miracles, they have no faith.

Faith is an eternal principle, an eternal law; it is built into the universe itself as a governing, controlling force; it is ordained of God and shall endure forever. It takes no special divine decree to cause the effects of the law of gravity to be manifest everywhere on earth at all times. The law has been established and the effects that flow from it are everlastingly the same. So it is with faith. He who has given a law unto all things has established faith as the power and force by which he and his shall operate in righteousness forever. No special divine decree is needed to utilize the power of faith; it is like gravity: anytime any person in any age conforms to the law involved, the ordained results will attend.

In this connection, be it also noted that among the gifts of the Spirit—where healings are involved—there are two gifts: one is faith to heal, the other, faith to be healed. Manifestly Jesus had faith to perform miracles under any and all circumstances and for whomsoever he chose; that his acts always conformed to holy and just principles is implicit in the very nature of things. We are aware that at times he performed miracles on his own motion and for his own purposes, as in the casting out of the legion of devils from the Gadarene demoniac and in the stilling of the storm on the lake of Gennesaret. But as we are about to see, except in special and unusual circumstances—and these were numerous in the life of Jesus—healing miracles are and should be performed as a result of the faith of the one receiving the divine blessing.

It is, of course, beyond our present purview to speak in

extenso about faith and the signs and miracles that are its companions; such would be a volume by itself.[1] But to envision why and how Jesus operated as he is about to do in his Galilean ministry, we must be reminded of at least the foregoing basic concepts.

Jesus Raises the Daughter of Jairus from Death

(*Mark 5:21-24, 35-43; JST, Mark 5:27-28; Luke 8:40-42, 49-56; JST, Luke 8:51; Matthew 9:1, 18-19, 23-26; JST, Matthew 9:24-25*)

After his Gadarene ministry, Jesus sailed some seven miles westward across the now calm Galilean waters to Capernaum and its environs. Great throngs awaited him on the shore—reverential, respectful, worshipful—hungering for more of the heavenly manna that he dispensed so freely. Perhaps those who set sail in the many small ships that followed him into the storm-darkened night had been with him near Gerasa—seeing what was done to the demoniac and hearing what was said to the Gadarenes—so that they now, returning ahead of him, had alerted the Galileans of his coming. But however the people learned of his return, as the isles shall wait for his law, so they upon whom his countenance now shone also waited for his word.

Among those on the shore—all hungering and thirsting after righteousness; all anxious to feed their souls with more of the heavenly bread that fell from his lips; all rejoicing in the parables of the past and the miracles that had been wrought among them—among these were two who needed special help, two upon whom his countenance was about to shine as it did on but few people in Palestine. One was Jairus, a ruler of the synagogue in Capernaum, whose twelve-year-old daughter lay even then at death's door; the other, an unnamed woman suffering from an incurable feminine malady, an issue of blood that none could heal.

Jesus' miracles varied according to the needs and circumstances of those on whose behalf they were wrought. He performed the same gracious acts in one way on one occasion, in other ways at subsequent times—all to the end that those involved might be led along the path to eternal life in his Father's kingdom. He has just spoken peace to a Galilean tempest and called a legion of devils out of a wracked and tormented body, acting in each case on his own authority, taking no steps to build up the faith of the beneficiaries of his goodness. Each of these miracles manifest the absolute power inherent in him; sometimes Jesus healed the sick because he had faith to heal and not because they had faith to be healed.

But now in the case of Jairus's daughter and the woman with the issue of blood, we are about to see healings because those who sought the blessing had faith to be healed. And in each instance we shall see the Blessed One—bearing in himself, as it were, the sicknesses and infirmities of his brethren—we shall see him, with tender solicitude, encourage and increase the faith of those who seek his goodness; we shall see him strengthen their faith lest by any chance they fail to obtain the blessings they seek.

One of the first to meet Jesus as he came ashore was Jairus, "a ruler of the synagogue" in Capernaum. We know Jesus had preached often and wrought miracles in that very house of worship, and we know that such preaching was done at the solicitation of the Jewish elders who held local synagogue rule. Thus Jesus and Jairus knew and respected each other; this devout Jew had heard Jesus preach, had believed his words, and had rejoiced in the knowledge of other miracles. Is it too much to suppose he was present on that glorious Capernaum Sabbath when Jesus cast the evil spirit from the man in the synagogue of that city?

But whatever their prior association, Jairus had faith in Christ, and coming this day, "he fell down at Jesus' feet" "and worshipped him." "My little daughter lieth at the point of death," he said. "I pray thee, come and lay thy hands on her, that she may be healed; and she shall live."

Can anyone doubt the faith of Jairus? Or that he knew and understood the ordinance of administration to the sick?

"Come and lay thy hands on her," he pled, "and she shall live"! "Is any sick among you? let him call for the elders of the church; and let them pray over him, anointing him with oil in the name of the Lord: And the prayer of faith shall save the sick, and the Lord shall raise him up." (James 5:14-15.) "And the elders of the church, two or more, shall be called, and shall pray for and lay their hands upon them in my name." (D&C 42:44.)

Jesus' miracles were wrought in divers ways, with or without oil, with or without the laying on of hands, always as occasion required; but the request of Jairus that he come and conform to the ritual he had ordained in his Church, and which he had followed on selected occasions in the past, was the logical and proper request for him to make. The ordinance of laying on of hands, in divers spiritual connections, was common among the Jews, as it had been in all dispensations that went before.

Jesus' heart was touched, and he purposed within himself that Jairus's faith should not go unrewarded. "And Jesus went with him; and much people followed him, and thronged him." And it was in the midst of this pressing, surging multitude that the woman with the issue of blood slipped forward in secret to but touch the hem of his garment, an episode that delayed their progress toward the home of Jairus and of which we shall speak more particularly hereafter.

As Jesus ceased speaking to the woman and the reason for their delay vanished, "there came from the ruler of the synagogue's house certain which said, Thy daughter is dead: why troublest thou the Master any further?" Receiving this word, what would be more natural than for Jairus to thank Jesus for coming thus far, and excuse himself to return home to comfort his wife and arrange for the funeral.

Jesus, however, overheard the message. Immediately, before any thought of doubt or fear or resignation to the will of a seeming divine providence could arise, he said: "Be not afraid, only believe." "Fear not: believe only, and she shall be made whole." 'She is dead; no matter, I am the Lord also of the dead; if thou canst but believe, she shall live again.' This miracle is to be wrought, as healings generally are, because of the faith of the family members, not because Jesus had absolute power within himself and could, if he chose, speak to the winds or the devils and have them obey.

That Jairus's faith remained firm, perhaps even increased, we cannot doubt, for Jesus—taking only Peter, James, and John with him—continued to Jairus's home, to do that which only one having the power of God can do. Indeed, it is not too much to suppose that Jairus knew of the raising of the widow's son from death at Nain. Word of such wondrous deeds spread like wildfire through the whole country; such deeds of mercy were not done in a corner, and each one fed the faith of others who needed and desired like blessings.

Arriving at the place where the dead daughter now lay, Jesus with her parents and the three chief apostles entered the home "and found it occupied by the hired mourners and flute-players, who, as they beat their breasts, with mercenary clamour, insulted the dumbness of sincere sorrow, and the patient majesty of death." (Farrar, p. 272.) To this wailing chorus of mourners—some bowed in true grief, others chanting and shrieking their false sorrows as the actors they were paid to be—Jesus said: "Why make ye this ado, and weep? the damsel is not dead, but sleepeth."

"Not dead, but sleepeth"! That she was dead they well knew, "and they laughed him to scorn." Yet how much more refined and consoling it is to say "Lazarus sleepeth," though for days the processes of decomposition have been at work in the former home of his spirit. "True, she was dead as men view death, for her spirit had left her body. Yet in the kindly perspective of eternity, the dead are merely as those who are asleep; for a moment the body, without life, is unconscious to its surroundings; but soon—as when the sleeping soul, following a night of repose, gains consciousness with the rising sun—the body will awaken to a new life of resurrected immortality. How comforting to know that the dead are only sleeping and that those who rest in the Lord shall awake to everlasting life." (*Commentary* 1:316.)

Then Jesus put forth the shrieking wailers with their mourning minstrelsy, "took the damsel by the hand"—she was a maid of about twelve years of age—"and said unto her, *Talitha cumi.*" "Damsel, I say unto thee, arise." 'Little maid, arise!' Then "her spirit came again"; the living, intelligent, sentient part of the human personality received a new mortal life; the spirit daughter of the Eternal Father entered again the body created from the dust of the earth. The maid arose; she walked; and Jesus "commanded to give her meat."

After the miracle, Jesus gave the parents certain instructions that are difficult for us to understand. "And her parents were astonished," Luke says, as well they should have been, "but he charged them that they should tell no man." Mark's account says "he charged them straitly that no man should know it." Matthew makes no mention of the restrictive counsel, but says only: "And the fame hereof went abroad into all that land."

We cannot suppose for a moment that Jesus was trying to keep this miracle secret. This wondrous deed that turned death into life; that bore record of the divinity of the One who even now was forecasting his own future victory over the grave; that could be performed only in righteousness and only by the power of God—this mighty miracle should, as Matthew says, send his fame into all the land.

Indeed, the parents could not enshroud in secrecy that which was already public knowledge; everyone in the whole area would soon know, because of the way Jesus himself had handled the successive events, that the little maid who once was dead now lived. Her death had been announced openly to the multitude as Jesus ended his conversation with the woman whom he healed of the issue of blood. Jesus himself had replied, openly and before the multitude, that notwithstanding her death she would "be made whole." All the people would soon know that she now lived, and would be expected to wonder how and by what means life had come to her again. The hired mourners, whose earnings had been aborted by the act of divine mercy, all knew of her death and would soon know that she now lived. The thing was not done in the dark; multitudes did and would know what the Master had wrought. Why then this charge of secrecy?

Perhaps, as is so often the case, the fragmentary accounts of our evangelist friends do not convey the full tenor and purport of the charge given by Jesus to the parents. We know, for instance, as a matter of standard gospel counsel, that those who enjoy the gifts of the Spirit and who possess the signs which always follow those who believe are commanded not to boast of these spiritual blessings. In our day, after naming the miraculous signs that always attend those who have faith, those who believe the very truths taught by Jesus anciently, the Lord says: "But a commandment I give unto them, that they shall not boast themselves of these things, neither speak them before the world; for these things are given unto you for your profit and for salvation." (D&C 84:73.) On another occasion the Lord in our day directed, "Talk not of judgments, neither boast of faith nor of mighty works." (D&C 105:24.)

Perhaps the charge to "tell no man" meant they were not to tell the account in a boastful way, lest a spirit of pride—a spirit of self-adopted superiority—should come into their souls. There were times when Jesus told the recipients of his healing power to go forth and testify of the goodness of God unto them, and other times when he limited the extent and detail of their witness. Without knowing the people and all the attendant circumstances, we cannot sit in judgment and determine why he gave differing directions to different people.

Jesus Heals the Woman with an Issue of Blood

(*Mark 5:25-34; Luke 8:43-48; Matthew 9:20-22*)

We come now to the staunching of the flow of feminine

blood of an unnamed woman to whom legend has given the name Veronica. Of her we know only that she was a woman of great faith—probably already a baptized member of the Church—who "had an issue of blood twelve years, And had suffered many things of many physicians, and had spent all that she had, and was nothing bettered, but rather grew worse."

Too ashamed even to mention the nature of her affliction, yet knowing Jesus had power to heal, she pressed near him as he and Jairus walked together and said within herself: "If I may but touch his garment, I shall be whole." Too timid, too shy to claim audience before him or to ask him to center his divine attention on such a lowly one as she esteemed herself to be, yet she sought just to be near him, just to feel his presence, just to touch the hem of the sacred garments he wore. Then she would be healed, and he need not so much as slacken his stride as he went with the ruler of the synagogue to raise to life the maid whose whole span of life measured the same as the years of her disease.

That there was no healing power in the hem of Jesus' garment, nor in any of the physical things he possessed, nor in any relic from any source, however saintly, goes without saying. It is axiomatic. But on the other hand, anything that enables a person to draw near unto the Lord and to center his affection and trust in him may properly be used to increase faith and to gain the blessings that come in no other way. Even the Urim and Thummim itself, carried in the breastplate of the ancient high priests in Israel, was but an instrument that enabled them to center their faith in Jehovah and receive, by revelation, his mind and will. And so it was, to a lesser extent, with the fringes and tassels on the borders of the garments of the Rabbis in Jesus' day.

From the beginning the garments of the saints have enjoyed a special and sacred place in true worship. They cover that nakedness which when exposed leads to lewd and lascivious conduct. They stand as a symbol of modesty and decency and are a constant reminder to true believers of the restraints and controls placed by a divine providence upon their acts. Adam and Eve made for themselves aprons of fig leaves to cover their nakedness and preserve their modesty. The Lord himself made coats of skins to cover the bodies of our first parents, that they, being clothed and wholesome before him, might attain those feelings which foster reverence and worship.

And the Lord Jehovah commanded Moses to direct the children of Israel, through all their generations, to "make them fringes [tassels] in the borders [corners] of their garments, . . . and that they put upon the fringe of the borders a ribband of blue." Why and of what moment was such a dress code? We can see how the dress standards given to Adam and Eve taught modesty and placed the new mortals in a frame of mind to live and worship by proper standards. Immodest, ornate, and worldly dress is an invitation to unclean thoughts and immoral acts, which are foreign to that conduct and worship desired by Him whose we are. But why such minutely prescribed dress requirements as these given to ancient Israel? Jehovah gives the answer: "It shall be unto you for a fringe, that ye may look upon it, and remember all the commandments of the Lord, and do them; and that ye seek not after your own heart and your own eyes, after which ye use to go a whoring." That is: 'Your garments, your clothing, shall be a shield and a protection to you. They shall cover your nakedness and keep from you the lusts of the eyes and the lusts of the flesh, and the special adornments on them shall remind you continually to walk as becometh saints.' All this is to be, Jehovah decreed, "That ye may remember, and do all my commandments, and be holy unto your God." (Num. 15:37-41.)

Now we see Jehovah, as Jesus, ministering personally among the people, and—we cannot doubt—dressed in the manner in which he himself had of olden times decreed that faithful Israelites should dress.[2] And now we see Veronica—if so she may be called—looking upon the fringes of his garments; remembering the ancient covenant that by so doing she was agreeing to keep the commandments; and feeling within herself that if she but touched the sacred fringes on the garments of him whom she accepted as God's Son, surely she would be healed. That such a desire should enter her heart was, under all the circumstances, both natural and proper. It was a sign—not of belief in magic or relics or any special power in the clothing itself, but of faith in him who wore the garments and who had designed them in such a way as to remind his people of their covenant to keep his commandments.

And so, she "came behind him, and touched the border of his garment: and immediately her issue of blood stanched." She was healed; she felt it in her body; her organs began to function according to the original plan and purposes of the great Creator; the hemorrhaging fountain of affliction no longer flowed. Overcome with emotion and gratitude she slipped back into the throng without a word.

"And Jesus, immediately knowing in himself that virtue had gone out of him, turned him about in the press, and said, Who touched my clothes?" There were immediate denials on the part of the disciples. Peter said, "Master, the multitude throng thee and press thee, and sayest thou, Who touched me?"[3]

This question—"Who touched me?"—was asked not to gain information, but to encourage the timid suppliant to identify herself and to bear testimony of the healing power that had come into her life. And she, seeing her act was not hidden from him by whose power she was now made whole, came forward—trembling, fearful, grateful—fell at his feet, and declared to him and to all "for what cause she had touched him, and how she was healed immediately." Jesus confirmed how and in what manner and by what means she had been blessed. "Daughter, thy faith hath made thee whole," he said, "go in peace, and be whole of thy plague."[4]

And so it is in the surging throngs of life. Many who are spiritually sick; who have had an issue of sorrow and sin, lo these many years; who spend their substance on the things of this world—many such are within arm's length of the Lord and need only to reach out and take hold of his church to find his healing power.

Jesus Causes the Blind to See and the Dumb to Speak

(*Matthew 9:27-34; JST, Matthew 9:36*)

Jesus now journeys from Jairus's home to the house in Capernaum where he abides when in that part of Galilee. He is followed by two blind men who plead for sight. "Thou son of David, have mercy on us" is the plea of the sightless ones. Jesus makes no response; he has no apparent intention of causing the light of the sun to break through the seal that physical imperfection has placed upon eyes that see nothing but everlasting night. At least any act on his part must result from a clear and firm faith in the hearts of those who seek his healing goodness.

Up to this point in his mortal ministry, there is no recorded instance of Jesus opening blind eyes. Lame men have leaped, lepers have been cleansed, and dead bodies have been reanimated as mortal houses for eternal spirits, but there is not as yet a specific account of sightless eyes seeing. We suppose the fault is with the scriptural accounts that have come down to us, for the opening of blind eyes is singled out in the Messianic prophecies as among the great wonders he shall work. The Book of Mormon Messianic assurance is that Jesus would work mighty miracles, heal the sick, raise the dead, cause the lame to walk, "the blind to receive their sight," and the deaf to hear, and that he would cure all manner of diseases. (Mosiah 3:5.) The biblical promise, as given by Isaiah in a passage of wondrous beauty, and which applies to his coming as a mortal and in millennial glory, is found in these words: "Your God will come. . . . Then the eyes of the blind shall be opened, and the ears of the deaf shall be unstopped. Then shall the lame man leap as an hart, and the tongue of the dumb sing." (Isa. 35:4-6.)

In the cases now before us, the two blind persons, having within themselves faith to be healed, follow Jesus into the house, continuing to importune for his healing power. "Believe ye that I am able to do this?" he asks them. Their answer is "Yea." "Then touched he their eyes, saying, According to your faith be it unto you. And their eyes were opened."[5]

"And straitly he charged them, saying, Keep my commandments, and see ye tell no man in this place, that no man know it." "Healed persons are obligated to repay Deity for his beneficent goodness to them, insofar as they can, by devoted service in his cause. They have no right to turn again to evil practices or former false beliefs. Such would make a mockery of the sacred power exercised in their behalf. Jesus was not going about healing people and leaving them free to continue in the ungodly practices and beliefs of the Jews. After being made whole by the Master Physician, the healed persons were obligated to keep the commandments, to join the Church of Jesus Christ, if they had not already done so, and to endure in righteousness to the end so that an eventual celestial inheritance would be assured." (*Commentary* 1:321.)

The command of secrecy was of a limited nature. They were told to "tell no man in this place," which we assume means in Capernaum. Matthew tells us that they "spread abroad his fame in all that country," which apparently means a much larger area than Capernaum. How strictly the healed persons kept the charge of secrecy we do not know. Nor can we tell why it was imposed. Perhaps Capernaum proper was such a wicked city that to testify of more miracles in that place would have been casting pearls before swine, giving the unbelievers among them occasion to turn again and rend the Great Healer.

Apparently, however, the two healed persons did not keep the charge of secrecy as fully at least as Jesus desired. Of this somewhat human reaction Farrar phrases these words of rebuke and condemnation: "There are some who have admired their disobedience, and have attributed it to the enthusiasm of gratitude and admiration," he says. Those to whom he here refers are Catholic apologists who applaud rather than condemn the men for their breach of confidence. "But was it not rather the enthusiasm of a blatant wonder, the vulgarity of a chattering boast?" he asks. Then he sets forth this reasoning: "Did not the holy fire of devotion which a hallowed silence must have kept alive upon the altar of their hearts die away in the mere blaze of empty rumour? Did not He know best? Would not obedience have been better than sacrifice, and to hearken than the fat of rams? Yes. It is possible to deceive ourselves; it is possible to offer to Christ a *seeming* service which disobeys His inmost precepts—to *grieve* Him, under the guise of honouring Him, by vain repetitions, and empty genuflexions, and bitter intolerance, and irreverent familiarity, and the hollow simulacrum of a dead devotion. Better, far better, to serve Him by doing the things He said than by a seeming zeal, often false in exact proportion to its obtrusiveness, for the glory of His name. These disobedient babblers, who talked so much of Him, did but offer Him the dishonouring service of a double heart; their violation of His commandment served only to hinder His usefulness, to trouble His spirit, and to precipitate His death." (Farrar, p. 273.)

As these two men left the house, glorying in their newly found sight, others "brought to him a dumb man possessed with a devil." He cast out the devil; the dumb spake; the multitudes marveled, saying, "It was never so seen in Israel." But the Pharisees continued their chant of hatred and evil by renewing the charge, "He casteth out devils through the prince of devils."

We read of no restriction being placed on this man as far as telling about his healing was concerned. But the Pharisaic reaction to it shows how knowledge of his miracles could interfere with Jesus' continuing ministry.

Jesus Is Again Rejected at Nazareth
(*Mark 6:1-6; Matthew 13:54-58*)

A year has passed since Jesus, preaching in the synagogue in Nazareth, announced that he came to fulfill Isaiah's great Messianic prophecies. Then it was that those of his own town "wondered at the gracious words which proceeded out of his mouth"; asked, "Is not this Joseph's son?"; were told, "No prophet is accepted in his own country"; and, being condemned for their unbelief, rose in anger, thrust him from their city, and attempted to cast him headlong from the brow of a hill. (See chapter 34, herein.)

Now, in part at least, and with even less excuse for such a rebellious course, the Nazarenes are about to reject again the one person who could save and redeem them. Leaving Capernaum with his disciples, he returns to Nazareth and on the Sabbath day once more teaches in their synagogue. What he said we do not know, but as with the previous preachment, the people were astonished; they marveled at his gracious words, so much so that they began to ask: "From whence hath this man these things."

Further, they now knew of his miracles and the wonders that his hands had done throughout all the land. Word had reached them of the blind eyes that now saw; of the lepers whose flesh was made whole; of the Gadarene demoniac out of whom a legion of devils had been cast; of the stilling of the storm on the lake of Galilee; of the raising of the widow's son in Nain and Jairus's daughter in Capernaum, both of whose spirits had gone on to another sphere while their bodies lay cold and dead and decomposing. His fame was everywhere, and the reason for it was known to all. And so his Nazarene neighbors asked: "And what wisdom is this which is given unto him, that even such mighty works are wrought by his hands?" And further: "Is not this the carpenter, the son of Mary, the brother of James, and Joses, and of Juda, and Simon? and are not his sisters here with us?"

"And they were offended at him." Why? Why should

anyone take offense because someone else goes about doing good? Why should men seek to slay a man because he raises the dead or stills a storm? Why should their spirits be stirred up within them because he preaches the Sermon on the Mount or gives forth with an endless flow of gracious words? These Nazarenes were witnesses against themselves. They heard his words and knew of his works, and yet they rejected him. It was not reason but emotion that motivated them. They were offended because their deeds were evil.

And so Jesus, who "marveled because of their unbelief," said unto them: "A prophet is not without honour, but in his own country, and among his own kin, and in his own house." His sisters still lived in Nazareth, married, we suppose, to Nazarenes; his mother and brothers had moved to Capernaum after the wedding feast at Cana; and of this whole body of kinfolk, only the Virgin Mother, as of this time, believed and knew of his divine mission.

And so, "he did not many mighty works there because of their unbelief," Matthew tells us. Mark is even more express: "He could there do no mighty work, save that he laid his hands upon a few sick folk, and healed them."

Truly, he who came with healing in his wings, to bear the sorrows and sickness of the people, limited his wonder-working miracles to those who by faith merited the inestimable blessings involved. And now Jesus—we cannot believe that it is other than in sadness—is leaving Nazareth for the last time. His own received him not. There is to be a brief moment for other ears to hear, and other eyes to see, and other hearts to be touched. He must continue to preach elsewhere, and he must send others forth to represent him, as he is now about to do.

NOTES

1. For a brief, initial analysis of the law of faith, reference may be made to *Mormon Doctrine*, 2nd ed., pp. 261-67.

2. The mode and manner of dress among the Jews of Jesus' day was itself a symbol of their religion and their way of life. Rabbis and leaders in particular took great pains to dress properly. We cannot doubt that Jesus and the apostles followed the standards of ex-

cellence in dress that then prevailed. This means that each of them—Jesus included—wore five standard articles of clothing. These were: (1) *Headgear,* which consisted either of a *Sudar,* or turban, or a *Maaphoreth,* "which seems to have served as a covering for the head, and to have descended over the back of the neck and shoulders, somewhat like the Indian pugaree." (2) *Sandals.* (3) *An inner garment.* Of that worn by Jesus, Edersheim says: "The *Chaluq,* or more probably the *Kittuna,* which formed his inner garment, must have been close-fitting, and descended to His feet, since it was not only so worn by teachers, but was regarded as absolutely necessary for any one who would publicly read or 'Targum' the Scriptures, or exercise any function in the Synagogue. As we know, it 'was without seam, woven from the top throughout;' and this closely accords with the texture of these garments." (4) *A girdle.* This was used to fasten the inner garment around the middle. (5) *An outer garment.* The square outer garment, or *Tallith,* was the one that carried "the customary fringes of four long white threads with one of hyacinth knotted together on each of the four corners." As we are aware, "the quaternion of soldiers who crucified Christ made division of the riches of His poverty, taking each one part of His dress, while for the fifth, which, if divided, would have been rent to pieces, they cast lots." (Edersheim 1:624-25.)

3. "Giving blessings and performing priesthood ordinances is often the most physically taxing labor which the Lord's true ministers ever perform. There is nothing perfunctory or casual about the performance of these holy ordinances; great physical exertion and intense mental concentration are part of the struggle to get that spirit of revelation so essential in an inspired blessing or other performance." (*Commentary* 1:319.)

Joseph Smith, under date of March 14, 1843, wrote in his journal: "Elder Jedediah M. Grant enquired of me the cause of my turning pale and losing strength last night while blessing children. I told him that I saw that Lucifer would exert his influence to destroy the children that I was blessing, and I strove with all the faith and spirit that I had to seal upon them a blessing that would secure their lives upon the earth; and so much virtue went out of me into the children, that I became weak, from which I have not yet recovered; and I referred to the case of the woman touching the hem of the garment of Jesus. The virtue referred to is the spirit of life; and a man who exercises great faith in administering to the sick, blessing little children, or confirming, is liable to become weakened." (*Teachings,* pp. 280-81.)

4. "Doubtless she dreaded His anger, for the law expressly ordained that the touch of one afflicted as she was, caused ceremonial uncleanness till the evening. But His touch had cleansed her, not hers polluted Him." (Farrar, p. 271.)

5. "Frequently in opening the eyes of the blind, Jesus, as here, coupled his spoken command with some physical act. On this and other occasions he touched the sightless eyes. (Matt. 20:30-34.) In healing the man in Jerusalem who was blind from birth, he anointed the man's eyes with clay made with spittle and then had the man wash in the pool of Siloam. (John 9:6-7.) The blind man of Bethsaida was healed by application of saliva to his eyes. (Mark 8:22-26.) Similarly, in healing a deaf man with a speech impediment, Jesus both touched the man's tongue and put his own fingers into the man's ears. (Mark 7:32-37.)

"None of these unusual and dissimilar acts are essential to the exercise of healing power. Healing miracles are performed by the power of faith and in the authority of the priesthood. By doing these physical acts, however, the Master's apparent purpose was to strengthen the faith of the blind or deaf person, persons who were denied the ability to gain increased assurance and resultant faith by seeing his countenance or hearing his words." (*Commentary* 1:320.)

JESUS SENDETH FORTH THE TWELVE

The twelve traveling councilors
are called to be the Twelve Apostles,
or special witnesses of the name
of Christ in all the world, . . .
to officiate in the name of the Lord,
. . . to build up the church,
and regulate all the affairs of the same
in all nations. (D&C 107:23, 33.)

Jesus Reaps a Plenteous Harvest

(*Matthew 9:35-38; Mark 6:6*)

Again as always; now as afore; in season and out of season; from the rising of the sun until men slumber in the darkness of the night—everlastingly—Jesus is found, in one city and village after another, "preaching the gospel of the kingdom."

He has just left Nazareth—for the last time, as we suppose—having there been rejected again by his own. The light of his countenance shall not again shine upon those among whom he grew to maturity. To them he is Joseph's son and Mary's son; he is the brother of James and Joses and Simon and Judas, none of whom believe he is the Prophet of whom Moses spoke. To the Nazarenes he is a carpenter, the son of a carpenter, whose sisters yet dwell among them, and who themselves—his own flesh, those conceived in the same womb that bare him—think no differently of him than they do of their other brothers.

And so Jesus, accompanied by his disciples, is touring and preaching again in "all the cities and villages" of Galilee. He teaches in their synagogues and preaches on their streets. His message: the gospel—the gospel of his Father; the eternal plan of salvation ordained in the heavens above before the foundations of the world; the gospel that he has made his own and that now bears his name. He is telling men what they must do to be saved in his Father's kingdom. His message: 'Come unto me and be perfected in me; accept me as the Son of God and live my law; repent; be baptized in my name for the remission of your sins; receive the promise of the companionship of the Holy Spirit; and press forward all your days in doing good and working righteousness.'

His is "the gospel of the kingdom"—none other—the gospel that admits men, here and now, into the kingdom of God on earth, which is the Church, and which prepares them for an inheritance in the celestial kingdom of heaven hereafter. And as he preaches, he heals "every sickness and every disease among the people," meaning that those who accept him and believe his gospel are healed, and those who—as in Nazareth—reject him, among them he can do no mighty works. Signs follow those who believe. Jesus is making converts, and the sick and the decrepit and the diseased among them are being healed of their afflictions.

Success attends his labors; multitudes hang on his every word; there is more ministerial service to be performed than one man can do. He can preach in only one village at a time; there are others who need to be healed, others who cry out for the cleansing of their spirits and the healing of their bodies, others than those to whom he can minister personally. "When he saw the multitudes, he was moved with compassion on them, because they fainted, and were scattered abroad, as sheep having no shepherd."

This, in part at least, is the day seen by the prophets of old. Had not Jehovah said by the mouth of Ezekiel: "Woe be to the shepherds of Israel"—to the priests and Levites, to the scribes and Pharisees, to those who should have been guides and lights and teachers of the people—"Woe be to the shepherds of Israel that do feed themselves! should not the shepherds feed the flocks?" Had not Jehovah said of those who should have cared for his flock: "The diseased have ye not strengthened, neither have ye healed that which was sick, neither have ye bound up that which was broken, neither have ye brought again that which was driven away, neither have ye sought that which was lost."

Did not Jehovah promise by the mouth of Ezekiel: "Behold, I, even I, will both search my sheep, and seek them out. . . . I will feed my flock, and I will cause them to lie down, saith the Lord God. I will seek that which was lost, and bring again that which was driven away, and will bind up that which was broken, and will strengthen that which was sick. . . . And I will make with them a covenant of peace. . . . And ye my flock, the flock of my pasture, are men, and I am your God, saith the Lord God." (Ezek. 34:2, 4, 11, 15-16, 25, 31.)

Had not Jehovah said by the mouth of Jeremiah: "Woe be unto the pastors that destroy and scatter the sheep of my pasture! saith the Lord. . . . Ye have scattered my flock, and driven them away, and have not visited them. . . . And I will gather the remnant of my flock. . . . And I will set up shepherds over them which shall feed them: and they shall fear no more, nor be dismayed, neither shall they be lacking, saith the Lord. Behold, the days come, saith the Lord, that I will raise unto David a righteous Branch." (Jer. 23:1-6.)

True, these divine prophecies shall see their most glorious fulfillment when Jehovah returns, continuing ever as the Branch of David, to bring again Israel into his fold in the last days, but even now he whom Jeremiah called "The Lord Our Righteousness," as he dwells in mortality among them, is reaching forth his arm to gather in his lost sheep. He is, for their day and generation, offering them the blessings of his earthly kingdom, to say nothing of the blessings of his Father's heavenly kingdom. He is setting up shepherds over them, that tender and loving care may be extended to all.

And so, viewing with compassion his fainting, scattered, diseased, and afflicted sheep, the Chief Shepherd—changing the figure from one of sheep and shepherds to one of fields and harvests—the Lord of the earthly harvest says: "The harvest truly is plenteous, but the labourers are few; Pray ye therefore the Lord of the harvest, that he will send forth labourers into his harvest."

Others than he must now labor in the vineyards of the Lord that more souls may be prepared for the eternal harvest that lies ahead. More converts must be made, and they must be fellowshipped with the earthly saints. Others than he must nourish the newborn babes in Christ who have joined his church and become members of his kingdom; others than he must keep them "continually watchful unto prayer, relying alone upon the merits of Christ," as Moroni expresses it. (Moro. 6:4.) Others than he must counsel those who are now numbered among the Church of God to add to their faith virtue, "and to virtue knowledge; And to knowledge temperance; and to temperance patience; and to patience godliness; And to godliness brotherly kindness; and to brotherly kindness charity"—all to the end that an entrance might be "ministered" unto them "abundantly into the everlasting kingdom" in heaven, as Peter expresses it. (2 Pet. 1:1-11.) Others than he must counsel them to build on the foundation of faith and repentance and baptism and "go on unto perfection," as Paul expresses it. (Heb. 6:1-3.) And the first to be so chosen are the Twelve Apostles of the Lamb.

Apostles Sent Forth to Labor in the Vineyard
(*Matthew 10:1, 5-15; JST, Matthew 10:12; Mark 6:7-13; Luke 9:1-6*)

Those chosen ones, the holy apostles—foreordained from before the foundations of the earth to be with Jesus in his mortal ministry; called anew by him as he traveled and taught in the land of their inheritance; ordained to the holy apostleship on a mountain near Capernaum—these special witnesses of the goodness and grace of the Son of God are now to be sent forth on missions.

That these chosen ones are prepared for the labors and sacrifices and persecutions that lie ahead we cannot doubt. Indeed we cannot conceive how any of the shepherds of Israel, any of the laborers in the vineyard of the Lord, could have been better prepared. Aside from their spiritual talents, acquired in ages past in the presence of God, they had all been the intimate associates—the students and disciples—of the Son of God for months or years, as the case may be. It may be that all of them walked and talked, and ate, slept and lived with him from the earliest days of his mortal ministry. It is logical so to assume. From the scanty snatches of historical data preserved for us from that day, however, we know at least the following:

John the Beloved, Andrew, Simon, Philip, and Nathanael—five of the Twelve—in February of A.D. 27, two years before, came to know, and so testified, that he was the Messiah. They, at that time, gladly put on the mantle of discipleship and began to walk in his paths, learn his ways, and minister on his errands. They were with him when he turned water into wine in Cana; when he attended the first Passover of his ministry, cleansed the temple, and wrought many miracles; when, for nine months, he traveled and preached and healed in Judea; when he ministered and taught in Samaria and then in Galilee. They were with him when he healed the nobleman's son and they heard his great

Messianic sermon in the synagogue in Nazareth when his own people sought to kill him. They received the priesthood, performed baptisms, and were themselves preachers of righteousness. And although they are not identified by name, the other seven of the Twelve may have been participants in all or most of these earthly acts of the Divine One.

During January or February of A.D. 28, Jesus called Peter and Andrew, and James and John to special ministerial service. He made them fishers of men; they were with him on that glorious Sabbath in Capernaum when he healed multitudes (including Peter's mother-in-law) and preached much; they accompanied him as he traveled and preached throughout Galilee, as others of the future Twelve may have done also. Jesus healed lepers, forgave sins, raised paralytic persons to health—all in their presence.

In March of A.D. 28, Matthew was called to forsake his post as a publican tax collector and to follow Jesus. Miracles and teachings continued. And in the early summer of that year the Twelve were chosen and ordained. They all may have been with him all along—mingling among the reverent and worshipful disciples who rejoiced in his doctrines and gloried in his deeds—but certainly they were all with him henceforth. They saw the centurion's servant healed and the widow's son raised from death. They saw the blind and the dumb healed, heard his parables, and wondered and feared when he spoke peace to the tempestuous waves on Galilee. They knew of the Gadarene out of whom went a legion of devils, of the woman with the issue of blood, and of Jairus's daughter. Miracles seen by their eyes, doctrines heard by their ears, spiritual experiences felt in their souls—these were a way of life with the Twelve. They themselves had taught and ministered and prayed and labored. They were now prepared to go forth, two by two, and magnify their callings as apostles of the Lord Jesus Christ.

True ministers—those whose words and deeds have divine approval—are always endowed with power from on high. They always hold the holy priesthood, which is the power and authority of God, delegated to man on earth, to act in all things for the salvation of men. They never call themselves; they do not and cannot endow themselves with divine authority. They must be called of God. Even Christ "glorified not himself to be made an high priest" (Heb. 5:5); even he was called and given power and sent forth by his Father.[1] Those who are called of God thus become his servants, his agents, his ambassadors. They are sent forth to do what he wants done and to represent him. Their words are his words and their acts his acts; when they serve within the field and scope of their authorization, it is as though the Lord himself had said or done whatever is involved.

And so Jesus "called his twelve disciples together, and gave them power and authority"—power and authority to preach the everlasting gospel; to proclaim the saving truths; to perform the ordinances of salvation—all so that men might be saved in his Father's kingdom. And in the very nature of things—it could not be otherwise—he "gave them power and authority over all devils, and to cure diseases." They had this power "to heal all manner of sickness and all manner of disease" because signs always follow faith; miracles always attend the preaching of the gospel; no man since the world was has had faith without having something along with it; and so, if any believed their words—and they taught the same gospel that He himself preached—there must be signs following. The sick must be healed; the dead must be raised; devils must be cast out; otherwise the power of God unto salvation, which is the gospel, would not be present. And so Jesus said to them, "Heal the sick, cleanse the lepers, raise the dead, cast out devils: freely ye have received, freely give."[2]

To whom shall they preach? To all men? No. There will be a day when they will be sent to all men everywhere, for the message of salvation shall go to every nation, and kindred, and tongue, and people. All are the children of the Father; he loves them all, and he seeks to save them all. But there is an order of priority. Every man is to hear the gospel in his time and in his own season; some are entitled to hear it first, others at a later date. "Go," then, "to the lost sheep of the house of Israel." It is their right and privilege, as the seed of Abraham, to step ahead of the aliens who know not God. "Go not into the way of the Gentiles, and into any city of the Samaritans enter ye not." Their day lies ahead; in due course the blessings of salvation shall be offered to them, but first, let the chosen seed open their hearts, if they will.[3]

What shall they preach? "Preach the kingdom of God." Say: "The kingdom of heaven is at hand." That is: 'Preach the gospel of the kingdom; proclaim that salvation comes by me; command all Israel to repent and be baptized; exhort them to keep the commandments and perfect their lives; say what ye have heard me say. I am the light; do that which ye have seen me do.'[4]

How are they to be sustained in their ministries? And how will their temporal needs be supplied? Those to whom they are sent will care for them, providing food, clothing, and shelter as their circumstances warrant. They are to rely on the Father; he will not let them go hungry or naked or without a place to lay their heads. They are to take neither gold nor silver nor brass in their purses. They are to carry no baskets of provisions—scrip, as such were called—nor bread to eat, nor "two coats apiece." The workman, they were told, was "worthy of his meat."[5] They were denied the luxury of leather shoes and were not to carry staves; rather, their feet were to be shod with sandals, and they might carry a single staff. Their dress was to be simple and their needs few, leaving them free to devote all their time and strength to the preaching of the word.

Do all of the Jews, all of those who are of Israel, have an equal right to hear the gospel? Are the Twelve to divide their time equally among the people? No. Even among the lost sheep of the house of Israel some have preference over others. "And into whatsoever city or town ye shall enter, inquire who in it is worthy; and there abide till ye go thence."

Just as Israel is to hear the message before it goes to the Gentiles, so those in Israel who are worthy, who desire righteousness, who are living according to the best light and knowledge they have—these are favored above their fellows; the gospel is to be taught to them first. Jesus is not sending his disciples out to find harlots and whoremongers and thieves and robbers—although any of these may repent and be saved—but he is sending them to find the honest in heart, the upright among men, those whose prior living has made them worthy to hear an apostolic voice. Such are the ones in whose homes the Twelve shall abide and where they shall leave their blessings.

"And when ye come into a house, salute it." Greet those who dwell therein with good will; honor them in all they have done that is good; offer to teach them the doctrines of salvation; account them worthy to receive the glad tidings that salvation can be theirs if they will believe and obey. Salute them in love and with an open heart, and seek to bring them into the kingdom of God on earth.[6]

"And if the house be worthy, let your peace come upon it: but if it be not worthy, let your peace return to you." 'If those in the house are worthy; if they are seeking light and truth and knowledge; if they desire righteousness and are willing to repent and forsake the world—then make with them a covenant of peace (as Jehovah promised through Ezekiel); make with them the gospel covenant, which is the covenant of peace. Assure them that through the glad tidings of great joy—the tidings of peace on earth, good will to men—they shall gain peace in this life and eternal life in the world to come. Let thy peace, which is my peace, which is gospel peace—the peace that passeth understanding—rest upon them. But if they are not worthy, if they do not believe and obey, the offer of eternal peace will have no efficacy; your peace will return to you, and you shall go hence and seek other houses where perchance your peace may rest forever.'

"And whosoever shall not receive you, nor hear your

words, when ye depart out of that house, or city, shake off the dust of your feet. Verily I say unto you, It shall be more tolerable for the land of Sodom and Gomorrha in the day of judgment, than for that city."

It is an awesome and a fearful thing to reject the word of truth. When Jesus speaks and men receive not his gracious words, they are damned for their disbelief. When his servants speak and men reject the same truths, they also are damned. When legal administrators preach the gospel by the power of the Holy Ghost, their teachings are binding on earth and in heaven. Those who believe and obey are saved; those who believe not and who keep not the commandments are damned. Believers are sealed up unto eternal salvation; unbelievers are sealed up unto eternal damnation. As we hear Jesus instruct the Twelve, it is as though we are hearing again the fiery words of that John who came before to prepare the way: "He that believeth on the Son hath everlasting life: and he that believeth not the Son shall not see life; but the wrath of God abideth on him." (John 3:36.)

In our day, as the Lord again sends laborers into his vineyards, as he again sends his servants to speak peace to the worthy and to condemn the ungodly, we hear him say: "They who go forth, bearing these tidings unto the inhabitants of the earth, to them is power given to seal both on earth and in heaven, the unbelieving and rebellious; Yea, verily, to seal them up unto the day when the wrath of God shall be poured out upon the wicked without measure—Unto the day when the Lord shall come to recompense unto every man according to his work, and measure to every man according to the measure which he has measured to his fellow man." (D&C 1:8-10.)

It is today as it was anciently. We preach the same gospel, we hold the same priesthood, and we are subject to the same divine direction. "In whatsoever place ye shall enter," the Lord tells us, "and they receive you not in my name, ye shall leave a cursing instead of a blessing, by casting off the dust of your feet against them as a testimony, and cleansing your feet by the wayside." (D&C 24:15.) It is as though those who reject the message are not worthy to receive even the dust that cleaves to an apostolic sandal.

And again: "Let all those take their journey, as I have commanded them," the Lord says, "going from house to house, and from village to village, and from city to city. And in whatsoever house ye enter, and they receive you, leave your blessing upon that house. And in whatsoever house ye enter, and they receive you not, ye shall depart speedily from that house, and shake off the dust of your feet as a testimony against them. And you shall be filled with joy and gladness; and know this, that in the day of judgment you shall be judges of that house, and condemn them; And it shall be more tolerable for the heathen in the day of judgment, than for that house; therefore, gird up your loins and be faithful, and ye shall overcome all things, and be lifted up at the last day." (D&C 75:18-22.)[7]

Having been properly instructed, the apostles, as Luke tells us, "went through the towns, preaching the gospel, and healing everywhere." Mark tells us "they went out, and preached that men should repent. And they cast out many devils, and anointed with oil many that were sick, and healed them."

As it had been and was with their Master, so it was and would be with those whom he had chosen. They preached the gospel; they cried repentance; they anointed with oil; they healed the sick. Then as now the gospel was true, and among true believers signs followed. The Lord be praised.

NOTES

1. "We believe that a man must be called of God, by prophecy, and by the laying on of hands, by those who are in authority, to preach the Gospel and administer in the ordinances thereof." (A of F 5.)

2. "Salvation is free." (2 Ne. 2:4.) "Come, my brethren, every one that thirsteth, come ye to the waters; and he that hath no money, come buy and eat; yea, come buy wine and milk without money and without price." (2 Ne. 9:50; Isa. 55:1.)

3. "In the providences of the Lord, the gospel, in the meridian of time, was offered first to the house of Israel and thereafter to the Gentiles. Jesus himself ministered primarily among his own kindred of the chosen seed. 'I am not sent but unto the lost sheep of the house of Israel,' he said. (Matt. 15:24.) Missionaries sent forth during Jesus' mortal

ministry were commanded to confine their labors to their wayward kindred of Jacob's lineage. Later, after our Lord's resurrection, they were to receive the commandment to carry the message of salvation to all men. (Mark 16:14-20.)" (*Commentary* 1:325.)

4. What does it mean to say "The kingdom of heaven is at hand?" It means: "The Church of Jesus Christ is here; it has been organized and established; it is the kingdom of God on earth; enter into it through the waters of baptism, and be ye saved." (*Commentary* 1:325.) Identically the same message is carried by the elders in this day: "Ye shall go forth baptizing with water, saying: Repent ye, repent ye, for the kingdom of heaven is at hand." (D&C 42:7; 33:9-11; 39:19-20.)

5. Hospitality was a way of life among the Jews. By way of modern analogy it is reported: "When travelling in the East no one need ever scruple to go into the best house of any Arab village to which he comes, and he will always be received with profuse and gratuitous hospitality. From the moment we entered any house, it was regarded as our own. There is not an Arab you meet who will not empty for you the last drop in his water-skin, or share with you his last piece of black bread. The Rabbis said that Paradise was the reward of willing hospitality." (Farrar, n. 3, p. 276.)

Similar but not wholly identical divine direction was given to missionaries in the early days of this dispensation. "Thou shalt take no purse nor scrip, neither staves, neither two coats," the Lord said, "for the church shall give unto thee in the very hour what thou needest for food and for raiment, and for shoes and for money, and for scrip." (D&C 24:18.) Also: "It is expedient that I give unto you this commandment, that ye become even as my friends in days when I was with them, traveling to preach the gospel in my power; For I suffered them not to have purse or scrip, neither two coats. Therefore, let no man among you, for this commandment is unto all the faithful who are called of God in the church unto the ministry, from this hour take purse or scrip, that goeth forth to proclaim this gospel of the kingdom." (D&C 84:77-78, 86.)

6. Gospel salutations not only lead people to receive the gospel, but they also cement the fellowship and good will that does and should exist among the Lord's saints. For those who have come into the kingdom and who are worthy of the blessings of the gospel, the revealed salutation is: "I salute you in the name of the Lord Jesus Christ, in token or remembrance of the everlasting covenant, in which covenant I receive you to fellowship, in a determination that is fixed, immovable, and unchangeable, to be your friend and brother through the grace of God in the bonds of love, to walk in all the commandments of God blameless, in thanksgiving, forever and ever. Amen. And he that is found unworthy of this salutation shall not have any place among you; for ye shall not suffer that mine house shall be polluted by him." (D&C 88:133-134.)

7. Related concepts are revealed in these words: "He that receiveth you not, go away from him alone by yourselves, and cleanse your feet even with water, pure water, whether in heat or in cold, and bear testimony of it unto your Father which is in heaven, and return not again unto that man. And in whatsoever village or city ye enter, do likewise. Nevertheless, search diligently and spare not; and wo unto that house, or that village or city that rejecteth you, or your words, or your testimony concerning me. Wo, I say again, unto that house, or that village or city that rejecteth you, or your words, or your testimony of me; For I, the Almighty, have laid my hands upon the nations, to scourge them for their wickedness." (D&C 84:92-96.)

JESUS INSTRUCTS THE TWELVE

He is a chosen vessel unto me,
to bear my name before the Gentiles,
and kings, and the children of Israel:
For I will shew him how great things he must suffer
for my name's sake. (Acts 9:15-16.)[1]

I think that God hath set forth
us the apostles last, as it were appointed to death:
for we are made a spectacle unto the world,
and to angels, and to men. . . .
Even unto this present hour we both hunger,
and thirst, and are naked,
and are buffeted, and have no certain
dwellingplace;
And labour, working with our own hands:
being reviled, we bless; being
persecuted, we suffer it:
Being defamed, we intreat: we are made
as the filth of the world,
and are the offscouring of all things
unto this day. (1 Cor. 4:9-13.)[2]

Apostles and Saints Face Persecutions and Trials
(*Matthew 10:16-23; JST, Matthew 10:14, 19-20; Luke 12:11-12; JST, Luke 12:13*)

Most of what Jesus said by way of commandment and instruction to the apostles, as he sent them forth on missions, was prophetic and eternal in nature. It applied not to the brief period—probably not more than three months—during which they traveled, two by two, through the cities and villages of Palestine, but to their lifelong ministries and to their successors in the apostolic office, including those who hold the same keys and powers today. Matthew preserves the most extended account of our Lord's words on this occasion, though some of what he recounts is recorded by Mark and Luke in other connections. That Jesus may have said some of the same things in different settings is of no moment one way or the other. For clarity and ease of presentation we shall consider the same expressions, wherever made, as though they were part of Matthew's one continuing account.

> *Behold, I send you forth as sheep in the midst of wolves: be ye therefore wise as serpents* [*be ye therefore wise servants*], *and harmless as doves.*

Jesus is not saying, 'Wolves shall come among you; wolves shall enter the flock; wolves shall rend the sheep; therefore, be wise in all you do.' What he does say is: 'Without are wolves—ravening, murderous, hunger-maddened wolves—and I send the sheep and the lambs of my flock out among them; ye are to leave the safety of the sheepcote and go out into the world where, except for my preserving care, ye shall be rent and destroyed. Therefore, be wise servants; give no unneeded offense; be to all to whom ye are sent as harmless as doves.' Neither the saints nor the apostles court persecution or martyrdom; rather, they do all they can, in honor, to avoid these Satan-spawned evils. Ordinarily the work progresses more rapidly and ascends to greater heights when peace and fair-mindedness prevail than when all the vomit and bitterness of hell are gushing forth upon the helpless sheep.[3]

But beware of men: for they will deliver you up to the councils, and they will scourge you in their synagogues; And ye shall be brought before governors and kings for my sake, for a testimony against them and the Gentiles.

Queries: Persecution—the heritage of the faithful—whence does it come? Who wields the sword that slays the saints, and who hurls the spear that pierces the side of Him who hangs on the cross?

Answers: It is a joint undertaking; a confederacy of evil powers unite to do the deeds; all participants play their parts as actors on an evil stage. Satan is the ultimate author; priests and ministers of false religions stir up the basest of men, who in turn wield the sword, and the legal processes of both church and state combine to justify, approve, and authorize the insane madness that fights the truth.

Persecution is an essential part of the creeds of all false religions. There is an eternal law—a law as eternal as heaven and earth and the universe—that truth will prevail. Left to itself true religion—though it may be delayed or hindered in its progress—must and will prevail. The only effective weapon of false religions—and it yields only momentary success—is to persecute true believers.

'Hence, ye apostles, ye missionaries, ye ambassadors of Christ, beware of evil men. They will deliver you to the council, to the local Sanhedrins, to the Jewish elders and priests, who will sit in judgment on your new wine, which cannot be contained in old bottles. They will scourge you in the synagogues to the chanting accompaniment of a psalm. And further, ye shall be brought before Felix and Festus and Herod, and even before Caesar himself; ye shall be hailed before the judgment bars of men, and then shall ye bear a testimony which shall stand as a witness against them before the eternal bar of the Great Jehovah.'

Yes, strange as it may seem, persecution is a religious rite; and whereas the Jews scourged their heretics in their synagogues, to the accompaniment of psalmic music, today's ministers of false religions heap revilings and persecutions upon the saints to the accompaniment of chants that say: "Delusion, false prophets, wife-stealers, non-Christians," or whatever else Satan puts in their minds. Such was the mad mania that confronted the apostles anciently, and such is the reborn dementia which opposes them today.

> *But when they deliver you up, take no thought how or what ye shall speak: for it shall be given you in that same hour what ye shall speak. For it is not ye that speak, but the Spirit of your Father which speaketh in you.*

Or, as Luke has it: "The Holy Ghost shall teach you in the same hour what ye ought to say." This is a power that none but the saints of God possess. They alone have the gift of the Holy Ghost, which is the right to the constant companionship of that member of the Godhead based on faithfulness. No man of himself could possibly know what to say, either by way of doctrine or of testimony, when hailed before earthly tribunals or when standing in the congregations of the wicked, for no man knows the hearts of men. But God, who knows all things, promises, by the power of his Spirit, to put words into the mouths of his servants. "Neither take ye thought beforehand what ye shall say," is his word, "but treasure up in your minds continually the words of life, and it shall be given you in the very hour that portion that shall be meted unto every man." (D&C 84:85.) Peter and John before the Sanhedrin, after the healing of the man lame from his mother's womb, and Paul before Agrippa, testifying that Jesus rose from the dead, are but illustrations of the power of speech given to the Lord's servants when the need for divine help requires it.

> *And the brother shall deliver up the brother to death, and the father the child: and the children shall rise up against their parents, and cause them to be put to death.*

O the depravity and wickedness and moral degeneracy that is practiced in the name of religion! Lucifer would slay, if he could, every righteous person—none of the true saints would be left in mortality—and when depraved fanatics submit themselves to the will of the devil, they willingly deliver up unto death even their own family members.

> *And ye shall be hated of all the world for my name's sake; but he that endureth to the end shall be saved.*

Though hated by all men; though the whole world oppose them; though every power of earth and hell combine to do them ill[4]—yet the apostles (and all the saints) must endure in righteousness all their days to merit celestial salvation. They must "press forward with a steadfastness in Christ, having a perfect brightness of hope, and a love of God and of all men, . . . feasting upon the word of Christ" (2 Ne. 31:20-21), doing good and working righteousness, if they are to gain eternal life. "I will prove you in all things," the Lord says to his saints, "whether you will abide in my covenant, even unto death, that you may be found worthy. For if ye will not abide in my covenant ye are not worthy of me." (D&C 98:14-15.)

> *But when they persecute you in one city, flee ye into another; for verily, I say unto you, Ye shall not have gone over the cities of Israel, till the Son of man be come.*

'Flee from persecution; do not court martyrdom; seek to live and spread the gospel; it is better to live for me than to die for me. There is work to be done; there are souls to be saved; you cannot carry forward my work on earth if you are dead. And so great is the labor, my servants will not have gone over the cities where scattered Israel is to be found till I come in my glory to gather the remainder of mine elect from the four winds, from one end of heaven to the other.'

Teach the Gospel Boldly and in Plainness

(*Matthew 10:24-33; JST, Matthew 10:26; Luke 6:40; 12:1-7*)

How will the people react to the teachings of the apostles? They are going forth to preach the gospel of the kingdom even as Jesus preaches it. They are going forth to heal the sick, cleanse the lepers, raise the dead, and cast out devils, even as Jesus does. They are to be his alter egos, to stand in his place and stead, to say what he would say and to do what he would do. How, then, will the people react to their words and deeds? Obviously they will respond as though Jesus himself were there. Already many have rejected Jesus; these same persons, and others of like mind and similar spiritual depravity, will now reject those who speak and heal in Jesus' stead. And so he counsels the Twelve, and, in principle, all of his followers:

> *The disciple is not above his master, nor the servant above his lord. It is enough for the disciple that he be as his master, and the servant as his lord. If they have called the master of the house Beelzebub, how much more shall they call them of his household?*

'Ye know how I have been received. The scribes and Pharisees reject my doctrine and disallow my testimony; they say I cast out devils and perform miracles by the power of the prince of devils; they have even called me Satan himself; and as it is with me, so shall it be with my disciples.' But that those who bear the ignominy shall also wear the crown, he affirmed by saying, as Luke has it: "The disciple is not above his master: but every one that is perfect shall be as his master." 'I am perfect; suffer and do as I suffer and do, and ye shall be perfect.' "And ye shall be even as I am, and I am even as the Father; and the Father and I are one." (3 Ne. 28:10.)

How then shall the disciples feel about the persecutions and evil speaking of those who serve another master? "Fear them not," Jesus says. Also: "Beware ye of the leaven of the Pharisees, which is hypocrisy," as Luke records in introducing the same thoughts, apparently repeated in a different setting, but having essentially the same meaning as when first spoken to the Twelve. 'Fear them not; go about your business; preach the gospel; do the things I sent you to do; let not opposition impede the work. Proclaim the gospel for all to hear.'[5]

> *For there is nothing covered, that shall not be revealed;*

neither hid, that shall not be known. Therefore whatsoever ye have spoken in darkness shall be heard in the light; and that which ye have spoken in the ear in closets shall be proclaimed upon the housetops.

'You have learned the doctrines of salvation from me as we have walked alone between the villages of Galilee; we have conversed together in the deserts and on the mountains. What you have heard in darkness, you must now speak in the light; that which was hidden from the world is now to go to them. Go forth; proclaim my word in every ear.' "For verily the voice of the Lord is unto all men, and there is none to escape; and there is no eye that shall not see, neither ear that shall not hear; neither heart that shall not be penetrated." (D&C 1:2.)

And I say unto you my friends, Be not afraid of them that kill the body, and after that have no more that they can do.

"And whoso layeth down his life in my cause, for my name's sake, shall find it again, even life eternal." (D&C 98:13.) Why then should the disciples fear death?

But I will forewarn you whom ye shall fear: Fear him, which after he hath killed hath power to cast into hell: yea, I say unto you, Fear him.

'Fear the Lord; fear him who holds the keys of death and hell; fear to do evil, lest you lose your souls.' "Fear him which is able to destroy both soul and body in hell." [6]

Are not five sparrows sold for two farthings, and not one of them is forgotten before God? But even the very hairs of your head are all numbered. Fear not therefore: ye are of more value than many sparrows.

Based on all this—on the prophetic counsel that persecution awaits his ministers; on the pronouncement that the disciples shall be treated even as their Master; on the solemn exhortation to preach the gospel, and the yet more solemn warning to be faithful in life and in death—based on these teachings, Jesus now says:

Whosoever therefore shall confess me before men, him

will I confess also before my Father which is in heaven. But whosoever shall deny me before men, him will I also deny before my Father which is in heaven.

God is his Father! Again and again he says it, and our salvation depends upon gaining for ourselves a sure testimony that such is the case. "Whosoever shall confess that Jesus is the Son of God, God dwelleth in him, and he in God." (1 Jn. 4:15.) "If thou shalt confess with thy mouth the Lord Jesus, and shalt believe in thine heart that God hath raised him from the dead, thou shalt be saved." (Rom. 10:9.)

What Happens When the Gospel Is Preached?

(*Matthew 10:34-42; 11:1; JST, Matthew 10:34; Mark 9:41; Luke 12:49-53; JST, Luke 12:58*)

Does the gospel bring peace on earth and good will among men? Such is its design and intent; such was the assurance in the anthem of praise sung by the angelic choir to acclaim the birth of the Prince of Peace; and such is the inborn longing and hope of the saints of all the ages. But the reality is far removed from the ideal. The gospel both saves and damns; it brings peace to the penitent and sorrow to sinners. And when the righteous and the wicked all mingle together in one social milieu, the preaching of the gospel spawns anarchy and contention and warfare. The enemies of God and the opponents of true doctrine do not take kindly to the gospel of the kingdom, to the building up of the kingdom of God on earth. When the apostles preach the gospel, what will the effect be on a weary and wicked world? Jesus answers:

Think not that I am come to send peace on earth: I came not to send peace, but a sword.

Suppose ye that I am come to give peace on earth? I tell you, Nay; but rather division.

The gospel divides men. Those who believe and obey go in one direction; the unbelieving and rebellious choose an opposite course. From among the unbelievers come the persecutors, and the persecutors wield the sword against the saints. They have wielded it against our Lord; they will yet thrust its cutting edge into the flesh of the apostles; and many of the saints shall seal their testimonies with their own blood. Such is the effect, among the wicked and ungodly, of the preaching of the gospel.

> *For they are not well pleased with the Lord's doings; therefore I am come to send fire on the earth; and what is it to you, if I will that it be already kindled?*
>
> *But I have a baptism to be baptized with; and how am I straitened till it be accomplished!*

'I am come to send the flames of turmoil and persecution, the burning agony of family discord, wherever my gospel is preached in the world; and, lo, this fire is already kindled on every hand. But do not be perturbed, for even I have a baptism of blood and death to be baptized with, for my own familiar friend shall lift up his hand against me, one of my own official church family shall betray me; and what a burdensome pressure and responsibility rests upon me until I have accomplished this very mission and ordeal for which I came into the world.'[7] As to the effect, even in the intimacy of the family circle, of the preaching of the gospel, Jesus says:

> *For I am come to set a man at variance against his father, and the daughter against her mother, and the daughter in law against her mother in law.*
>
> *And a man's foes shall be they of his own household.*
>
> *He that loveth father or mother more than me is not worthy of me: and he that loveth son or daughter more than me is not worthy of me.*

How severe the tests of life sometimes are! Mortals come here to be tried and tested, "to see if they will do all things whatsoever the Lord their God shall command them." (Abr. 3:25.) And if such necessitates a choice between father and mother, or son and daughter, and the saving power of the gospel of the Lord Jesus Christ, then so be it. But one thing is needful, and that is, to save our souls. No one is justified in maintaining family peace and unity if by so doing he must forsake the gospel and its saving truths.

> *And he that taketh not his cross, and followeth after me, is not worthy of me.*

'I shall carry my cross to the place of crucifixion, where I shall die in pain and agony, die as earth's Chief Martyr. He that is not willing to take his own cross and, following me, carry it to a martyr's death on Calvary, is not worthy of me and of that eternal life which my Father has prepared for all the faithful.'

> *He who seeketh to save his life shall lose it: and he who loseth his life for my sake shall find it.*

'He that saves himself from persecution and death by denying me and my gospel shall lose eternal life, while he who lays down his life for me and my gospel shall have eternal life.'

> *He that receiveth you receiveth me, and he that receiveth me receiveth him that sent me.*

How great the importance to rivet these eternal truths in the hearts of men! No one ever receives and accepts the Lord Jesus Christ without also receiving and accepting the apostles and prophets who bear witness of him. Christ and his prophets are one; they rise or fall together. No one in Jesus' day could believe he was the Son of the Father without also believing in the Father of the Son; no one could believe he was the Messiah without also believing Peter, James, and John were his apostles, his friends, his witnesses. Jesus and his apostolic witnesses can no more be separated than can the Father and the Son. To believe in one is to believe in the other. This is the law of agency, every agent of the Lord standing in His place and stead, representing Him, saying and doing what He wants said and done.

In a passage of transcendent beauty, the Lord Jesus, in modern times, says to his servants, his agents, those whom he has chosen and called to minister in his name and for and on his behalf in this dispensation: "Behold, I send you out to reprove the world of all their unrighteous deeds, and to teach them of a judgment which is to come. And whoso receiveth you, there I will be also, for I will go before your face. I will be on your right hand and on your left, and my Spirit shall be in your hearts, and mine angels round about you, to bear you up. Whoso receiveth you receiveth me; and the same will feed you, and clothe you, and give you money. And he who feeds you, or clothes you, or gives you money, shall in nowise lose his reward. And he that doeth not these things is not my disciple; by this you may know my disciples." (D&C 84:87-91.)

> *He that receiveth a prophet in the name of a prophet shall receive a prophet's reward; and he that receiveth a righteous man in the name of a righteous man shall receive a righteous man's reward.*
>
> *And whosoever shall give to drink unto one of these little ones a cup of cold water only in the name of a disciple, verily I say unto you, he shall in no wise lose his reward.*

How sound and glorious this is! Receive a prophet for what he is and gain a prophet's reward. What is the reward received by prophets? That it is eternal life, the greatest of all the gifts of God, none will doubt. Thus, by accepting a true prophet men gain eternal life. Full acceptance presupposes obedience to whatever prophetic counsel and direction is forthcoming. The same reasoning applies to receiving a righteous man and gaining a righteous man's reward, which reward is exaltation in the highest heaven of the celestial world. And even those who perform but the slightest service for the Lord's anointed, or for the little ones of his earthly kingdom—doing so because those served are the chosen of Jehovah—shall be rewarded for their goodness.

And so endeth the instructions to the Twelve. Having so spoken, Jesus "departed thence to teach and to preach in their cities," and the traveling witnesses of his name went forth to teach and testify in the way he had commanded them.

NOTES

1. These are the words of the Risen Lord, spoken with reference to Paul.

2. These words were written by Paul and are descriptive of himself and the others of the Twelve in his day.

3. There is an old tradition, dating back almost to apostolic times, that Peter, at this point, asked: "But how then if the wolves should tear the lambs?" To this Jesus is said to have answered: "Let not the lambs fear the wolves when the lambs are once dead, and do you fear not those who can kill you and do nothing to you, but fear Him who after you are dead hath power over soul and body to cast them into the Gehenna of fire." (Farrar, p. 277.)

4. As to the hatred of the world for the saints, the Roman historian Tacitus says that Nero "inflicted the most cruel punishments upon a sect of people who were holden in abhorrence for their crimes, and called by the vulgar 'Christians.' The founder of that name was Christ, who suffered death in the reign of Tiberius, under his procurator Pontius Pilate. . . This pernicious superstition, thus checked for a while, broke out again; and spread not only over Judea where the evil originated, but through Rome also, whither everything bad upon earth finds its way and is practised. . . . A vast multitude were apprehended who were convicted, not so much of the crime of burning Rome, as of hatred to mankind. . . . They were criminals, deserving the severest punishments." (Cited. *Dummelow,* p. 662.)

5. "Those who preach the gospel are to do so boldly, without timidity or trepidation, not fearing the face of man, but with the courage of their convictions and in the fervor of their testimonies. 'Use boldness, but not overbearance,' Alma said. (Alma 38:10-12.) Truths learned in the day of preparation and schooling are to be broadcast from the housetops." (*Commentary* 1:333.)

6. The destruction of the soul in hell is a figurative expression. It is a spiritual death; it is to die as pertaining to the things of the Spirit and to be cast into outer darkness until the full penalty has been paid for sin. See *Mormon Doctrine,* 2nd ed., pp. 756-59, and related passages.

7. This interpreting paraphrasing of Jesus' words is my own, taken from *Commentary* 1:335-36.

HEROD BEHEADS THE BLESSED JOHN

It is great sin to swear unto a sin;
But greater sin to keep a sinful oath.
Who can be bound by any solemn vow
To do a murderous deed?[1]

This Man Called John

We must now turn our attention to the ministry, mission, and martyrdom of the blessed Baptist—to him who prepared the way before the Blessed One; who served as an excelling Elias in time's meridian; and who is about to seal his testimony with his own blood. And when Jesus hears of the death of his kinsman—they were second cousins—and learns that a martyr's blood now stains a dungeon cell at Machaerus, it will have a marked effect on his own ministry.

Many things might be said of John Ben Zacharias—of this son of Zacharias and Elisabeth; of this man whose birthright it was to sit in Aaron's seat, the priestly ruler in Israel; of this man who did in fact seal up the old dispensation and usher in the new.

John Ben Zacharias—here is a man who sat in council with the Gods before ever the foundations of this earth were laid; who was a friend of Michael and Gabriel and Raphael; who made covenant with Abraham, and was an associate of

Isaiah and Nephi and Joseph Smith in that seraphic sphere where the sons of God awaited their mortal probations.

John Ben Zacharias—here is a man who was seen in vision by Lehi and Nephi and Isaiah, each of whom foresaw his ministry, and even foretold the very words he would speak: as the voice of one crying in the wilderness; as the baptizer of the One upon whom the Holy Spirit would descend bodily, in calmness and serenity, like a dove; as the witness of the divine sonship of the Lamb of God who taketh away the sins of the world.

John Ben Zacharias—here is a man whose birth was announced by that angelic ministrant who stands next to Michael in the holy hierarchy of the eternal worlds; whose mother was the aged Elisabeth, who, like Sarah, was past the childbearing years; and whose father, a pure Levite, would also suffer a martyr's death.

John Ben Zacharias—here is a man who was born in the hill country of Judea; who grew up in the desert areas of Hebron; who came from the deserts and wildernesses of Palestine, wearing the prophetic garb made of camel's hair, to proclaim repentance and to prepare the way before One who should come after.

This man called John; this holy and valiant Levite; this Elias; this forerunner; this voice crying in the wilderness; this one than whom there has not been a greater prophet—this man called John came to prepare the way before the Son of God.

He was filled with the Holy Ghost from his mother's womb and, in fact, bore his first mortal testimony of Jesus the Lord while he was yet in the womb of an aged mother.

He was ordained by an angel of God—Gabriel, we presume—when but eight days old, and given power to overthrow the kingdom of the Jews, and to make straight the way before the Lord.

He was himself baptized while yet in his childhood—it could not have been other than at eight years of age—and when he ministered and taught at Bethabara and Aenon and elsewhere, he in turn baptized many for the remission of their sins.

He held the Aaronic Priesthood—receiving it no doubt from his father—and was the last legal administrator of the Mosaic dispensation and the first divinely called and legally recognized agent of Jehovah in the newly-set-up Christian era.

He assembled great congregations of true believers—all Jerusalem came out to hear his prophetic words, and many heeded his call to repentance—but all who came to him were encouraged and invited—nay, commanded—to follow the One who came after who would baptize with fire and with the Holy Ghost.

His great cry—"Behold the Lamb of God, which taketh away the sin of the world" (John 1:29)—and his doctrinal testimony—"He that believeth on the Son hath everlasting life: and he that believeth not the Son shall not see life; but the wrath of God abideth on him" (John 3:36)—these were his crowning and oft-repeated declarations. There is no preaching to compare with sound doctrine mingled with pure testimony.

When this chosen and beloved prophet—John Ben Zacharias of the seed of Aaron—was imprisoned by that evil miscreant Antipas, then Jesus sent angels to his dungeon-bound kinsman to minister comfort and hope and eternal assurance. And we cannot doubt that this strait and severe prophet—who is akin to Adam and Abraham and Moses in faith and prophetic power—that this desert Elias not only entertained angels, as it is the right of one holding the Aaronic Priesthood so to do, but that he also beheld the visions of eternity and knew the things of God in a measure and to a degree seldom vouchsafed to mortal men.

This man called John stood, as no other has ever done, at the crossroads of history. He closed the door on the past and opened the door of the future. He proclaimed Jehovah's *amen*—the divine *so-be-it*; the heaven-sent *it is over and done*, as it were—as pertaining to the rituals and performances and ordinances of Moses, the greatest of Israel's prophets; and he opened the door to the simplicity and beauty of the fulness of the everlasting gospel.

How great is that prophet who can say to Moses: 'Thou man of God—thou mighty one like unto whom there was not again among the ancients such a prophet—Moses, thou man of God, be silent. No longer does thy law apply; no longer are your ordinances valid; sacrifices shall now cease; no longer shall those who sit in Aaron's seat make an atonement for the sins of repentant Israel. The law of Moses is now swallowed up by the law of Christ.'

How great is that prophet who can say to the Son of God: 'I am thy forerunner, thy Elias; my voice announces you to all who shall come after. By my priesthood I shall immerse you in baptism, and my act in so doing shall be binding on earth and in heaven. I am the friend of the Bridegroom. Great congregations shall come unto thee and be saved because of me.'

Praise be to God for the life and ministry of the blessed Baptist, of John the son of Zacharias—a ministry that is about to be ended with Herod's axe, so that John, dying before Christ, may serve as his forerunner among the departed dead and then rise with him in glorious immortality in the first resurrection to reign everlastingly in that heavenly kingdom where Gods and angels dwell.

Antipas Holds an Evil Feast

(*Mark 6:21-29; JST, Mark 6:22; Matthew 14:6-12*)

Herod the Great, a polygamist having ten wives and numerous progeny—many of whom he murdered, and all of whose descendants inherited his evil, voluptuous, and ruthless ways—left one son whose deeds of infamy have attained a fame and a name of almost as great ill-repute as that of his dissolute father. This was Herod Antipas, the sycophant who, under Rome, ruled in Galilee. Herod the Great sought the life of Christ and ended up, in mad dementia, slaughtering the Innocents of Bethlehem, a crime so unspeakably evil and so unutterably irresponsible as to send eternal shudders through all Christendom; and yet so numerous were his murders and so great was the river of blood shed by him that the slaughter of Rachel's children in the coasts of Bethlehem scarcely merits a mention in secular sources. Herod Antipas took the life of Christ's forerunner under circumstances showing forth such weakness of character and such submission to lecherous passion that once again all Christendom is repelled at the horror and evil of it all.

"Herod Antipas, to whom, on the death of Herod the Great, had fallen the tetrarchy of Galilee, was about as weak and miserable a prince as ever disgraced the throne of an afflicted country. Cruel, crafty, voluptuous, like his father, he was also, unlike him, weak in war and vacillating in peace. In him, as in so many characters which stand conspicuous on the stage of history, infidelity and superstition went hand in hand. But the morbid terrors of a guilty conscience did not save him from the criminal extravagances of a violent will. He was a man in whom were mingled the worst features of the Roman, the Oriental, and the Greek." (Farrar, p. 295.)

Our present concern is with Herod Antipas and two other sons of Herod the Great: Aristobulus and Herod Philip, not the tetrarch, but one of the royal family who lived as a private citizen in Rome. Aristobulus had a daughter, Herodias, who married her uncle, Herod Philip, and they in turn had a grown daughter name Salome. Herod Antipas was married to a daughter of Aretas, Emir of Arabia.

On a visit to Rome, Herod Antipas became entangled with Herodias, his brother Philip's wife, and she left Philip to marry Antipas, taking Salome with her. Thus Herod Antipas married his sister-in-law, who was also his niece; and as a result, the daughter of Aretas left Antipas and returned to her father, who later waged a victorious war against his quondam son-in-law.

It was this incestuous and illegal marriage that caused John the Baptist to say to Herod Antipas: "It is not lawful for thee to have her." It was this firm pronouncement that caused the Baptist to gain the undying enmity of Herodias and of Salome, and it was this same declaration that caused Herod to arrest John and imprison him in the dungeons of Machaerus. "And when he would have put him to death, he feared the multitude, because they counted him as a prophet." (Matt. 14:4-5.)

Among the wicked and ungodly, riotous living is the norm; their aim in life is to eat, drink, and be merry, and that which sates one's appetite and gratifies one's passions is to be desired above all. "All that is in the world, the lust of the flesh, and the lust of the eyes, and the pride of life" (1 Jn. 2:16)—these are the things their souls desire. It is one of the signs of the times that those who know not God and seek not his face will be eating and drinking—eating as gluttons and drinking as drunkards—until the Son of Man comes.

And nowhere are the gluttons more greedy nor the drunkards more sottish than among the degraded royalty of imperial courts. The Caesars in Rome hold great banquets for the great and mighty among them. They swill up delicacies with swinish gluttony, take an emetic, vomit up their guzzlings, and commence to gorge themselves anew. Belshazzar appoints a great feast for a thousand of his lords. They and their wives and concubines drink wine from the golden vessels taken from the holy Temple of Jerusalem, and in the midst of it all, the handwriting on the wall spells out the doom of their kingdom. Herod Antipas, aping the debauchery of Rome—a debauchery that will soon revel in orgies of immorality and in gladiatorial combats between human combatants—Herod Antipas appoints a feast day to honor himself. The scriptural account says simply:

> *But when Herod's birthday was come, he made a supper for his lords, high captains, and the chief priest of Galilee.*

And therein is set forth one of the signs of those times. The topers and gluttons who came together to eat and drink at Herod's board and to do honor to the tetrarch were his own rulers, the captains of his Roman mercenaries, and—mark it well—"the chief priest of Galilee." The leading Levites—Aaron's sons—were linking arms with their alien overlords. It was as when the Pharisees took counsel with the Herodians as to how they might destroy Jesus, because he healed a man with a withered hand on the Sabbath. And it is a far cry from the day of divine vengeance when fire came down from heaven and devoured Nadab and Abihu, Aaron's sons, because they offered strange fires, upon the altar, before the Lord. But perhaps even this which is to occur at Herod's feast is as handwriting on the wall foretelling his destruction, or as fire from heaven that will ultimately consume him, and his house, and Herodias, and Salome, and all who ally themselves with such as these.

Such feasts as this were not complete without entertainment, without something to feed the lusts and arouse the passions of those now gorged with food and half drunken with wine. Dancers, especially dancing women, were in great demand. Taking into account the sensuous nature of the Herods, the mean and vulgar demeanor of the military men, the adultery-centered proclivities of the chief priests; having in mind the depraved and vulgar displays Herod would have seen at Caesar's banquets; knowing of the perversions and sexual excesses found in all Oriental courts, and the loose and low moral standard of all the Gentiles and many of the Jews; being aware of all this, and more—over which a decent propriety must draw a curtain of silence—we have no difficulty envisioning the type of banquet entertainment that was presented at these kingly feasts.

As to how, in this instance, Salome became the featured dancer before Herod and his lords, we know not, but suppose that an evil Herodian craftily planned the sensuous spectacle, with an evil Salome both agreeing and taking delight in the prospect of exposing her body to the gawking eyes of her stepfather and his voluptuous friends. In any event, "when the banquet was over, when the guests were full of meat and flushed with wine, Salome herself, the daughter of Herodias, then in the prime of her lustrous beauty," danced—lewdly, lasciviously, seductively—before "those dissolute and half-intoxicated revellers." Then Herod, "in the delirium of his drunken approval, swore to this degraded girl, in the presence of his guests, that he would give her anything for which she asked, even to the half of his kingdom." (Farrar, p. 300.)[2]

Hearing this, the lewd daughter of an adulterous mother hastened to her maternal parent for further instructions. "What shall I ask?" she queried. The crafty and conniving Herodias, to whom adultery and murder were but the normal accompaniments of her depraved and godless course, replied: "The head of John the Baptist."

Then went Salome "straightway with haste unto the king." Immediately with haste! "What a touch is that! and how apt a pupil did the wicked mother find in her wicked daughter!" Then stood Salome before Antipas and all his lords, and said: "I will that thou give me by and by in a charger the head of John the Baptist." "Her indecent haste, her hideous petition, show that she shared the furies of her race." They show also how those enmeshed in immoral and lascivious living find it easy, perhaps natural, to make murder and every debasing crime a part of their way of life. 'Bring me here, now, as soon as the headsman's axe can fall, upon one of the golden dishes that grace thy table, the gory head of that Jew who dares to say it is not lawful for thee to have my mother as thy wife.'

Herod is stunned; he is plunged into sudden grief; his fawning friends are appalled. "It was a bitter termination of his birthday feast. Fear, policy, remorse, superstition, even whatever poor spark of better feeling remained unquenched under the dense white ashes of a heart consumed by evil passions, all made him shrink in disgust from this sudden execution. He must have felt that he had been duped out of his own will by the cunning stratagem of his unrelenting paramour."

Yet sin begets sin; pride builds upon pride; and he who

is guilty of one offense cannot escape the commission of another, lest he be punished or held up to disrepute for the first. As with Pilate, who gave the order to crucify One whom he knew to be innocent, lest it be reported in Rome that the procurator was not Caesar's friend, so with Antipas, who feared to lose face with his nobles should he break his intemperate oath.

"If a single touch of manliness had been left in him he would have repudiated the request as one which did not fall either under the letter or spirit of his oath, since the life of one cannot be made the gift to another; or he would have boldly declared that if such was her choice, his oath was more honoured by being broken than by being kept. But a despicable pride and fear of man prevailed over his better impulses. More afraid of the criticisms of his guests than of the future torment of such conscience as was left him, he immediately sent an executioner to the prison, and so at the bidding of a dissolute coward, and to please the loathly fancies of a shameless girl, the axe fell, and the head of the noblest of the prophets was shorn away."

Thus came the murder, for how else can it be named? And then was brought the head of one who had now sealed his testimony with his own blood, one whose earth-sealed lips would now cry out in a better realm for that vengeance which a just God lays upon those who make martyrs of his prophets. Placed "on one of the golden dishes which graced the board," the marred visage of the man of God would forever haunt the souls of his murderers.

According to tradition, Herodias celebrated her victory by ordering "the headless trunk to be flung out over the battlements for dogs and vultures to devour." "And his disciples came, and took up the body, and buried it, and went and told Jesus."

The forerunner's work on earth was done. What rejoicing there must have been that day in paradise as he mingled with the spirits of just men made perfect, proclaiming to them that He by whom salvation comes would soon minister among them, would open their prison doors—for the separation of their spirits from their bodies seemed as a prison to them—and would bring forth his saints in glorious immortality.

"Precious in the sight of the Lord is the death of his saints." (Ps. 116:15.) Jehovah reigneth, and all things are going forward according to his plans and purposes.

Jesus Hears of John's Death

(*Luke 9:7-9; Mark 6:14-16; Matthew 14:1-2, 13*)

As a mortal among mortals, Jesus learned of John's death from the Baptist's disciples who, with loving care, had taken up "his corpse, and laid it in a tomb." Had necessity required, he would have learned the sad fate—a fate both sad and glorious, for he that layeth down his life for Christ and his cause shall gain eternal life—had necessity required, Jesus would have known by the power of the Spirit that his forerunner had died a martyr's death. We know of no reason, in this instance, however, why he should have received by revelation that knowledge which other mortals would learn from their fellow mortals.

As our friend Farrar has it, there was at this time "an atmosphere already darkened by the storm-clouds of gathering opposition," and in this atmosphere, "like the first note of a death-knell tolling ruin, there broke the intelligence of a dreadful martyrdom. The heaven-enkindled and shining lamp has suddenly been quenched in blood. The great Forerunner—he who was greatest of those born of women—the Prophet, and more than a prophet, had been foully murdered."

After noting that it was at about this time that the apostles reported their missions, Farrar says: "Another piece of intelligence reached Jesus; it was that the murderous tetrarch was inquiring about Him; wished to see Him; perhaps would send and demand His presence when he returned to his new palace, the Golden House of his new capital at Tiberias. For the mission of the Twelve had tended more than ever to spread a rumour of Him among the people, and speculation respecting Him was rife. All admitted that He had some high claim to attention. Some thought that He was Elijah, some Jeremiah, others one of the Prophets; but Herod had the most singular solution to the problem.

"It is said that when Theodoric had ordered the murder of Symmachus, he was haunted and finally maddened by the phantom of the old man's distorted features glaring at him from a dish on the table; nor can it have been otherwise with Herod Antipas. Into his banquet hall had been brought the head of one whom, in the depth of his inmost being, he felt to have been holy and just; and he had seen, with the solemn agony of death still resting on them, the stern features on which he had often gazed with awe. Did no reproach issue from those dead lips yet louder and more terrible than they had spoken in life? Were the accents which had uttered, 'It is not lawful for thee to have her,' frozen into silence, or did they seem to issue with supernatural energy from the bloodless lips?

"If we mistake not, that dissevered head was rarely thenceforth absent from Herod's haunted imagination from that day forward till he lay upon his dying bed. And now, when but a brief time afterwards, he heard of the fame of another Prophet—of a Prophet transcendently mightier, and one who wrought miracles, which John had *never* done—his guilty conscience shivered with superstitious dread, and to his intimates he began to whisper with horror, '*This is John the Baptist whom I beheaded: he is risen from the dead,* and therefore these mighty works are wrought by him.' Had John sprung thus suddenly to life again to inflict a signal vengeance? Would he come to the strong towers of Machærus at the head of a multitude in wild revolt? or glide through the gilded halls of Tiberias, terrible, at midnight, with ghostly tread? 'Hast thou found me, O mine enemy?' "

And so it was that Jesus, aware of Herod's hallucinations and not at this time courting persecution or premature arrest, "departed thence by ship into a desert place apart," where the feeding of the five thousand took place.

And as to John, his body returned to the dust whence it came; his spirit continued to speak among the spirits of the dead—awaiting the day when body and spirit, inseparably connected, would rise with Christ in immortal glory, even then to continue his labors in the work of the Holy One whose eternal witness he is.

And, further, as to John: acting under the direction of Peter, James, and John, his apostolic superiors, he came to Joseph Smith and Oliver Cowdery, on the fifteenth day of May, 1829, on the banks of the Susquehanna River in western New York, and there conferred upon them the ancient Levitical order in which he had ministered while in mortality.

Upon you my fellow servants,
In the name of Messiah
I confer the Priesthood of Aaron,
Which holds the keys of the ministering of angels,
And of the gospel of repentance,
And of baptism by immersion for the remission of sins;
And this shall never be taken again from the earth,
Until the sons of Levi do offer again
An offering unto the Lord in righteousness. (*D&C 13.*)

And so once again there are those on earth who can sit in Aaron's seat; who, being subject to those who sit in Moses' seat, can prepare the way for that which—in the eternal providences of Him in whose hand is all power—is about to come to pass.

And again we say: Jehovah reigneth; blessed be his great and holy name, both now and forever. Amen.

NOTES

1. Shakespeare, *Henry VI,* Part II, act 5, sc. 1.
2. These words, and those hereafter quoted in this chapter, aside from the scriptural quotations themselves, are taken from chapter 28 of Farrar, pp. 294-305. Though containing the usual speculative conclusions, from the standpoint of literary craftsmanship, this is

one of Farrar's best essays. I have not hesitated to quote selected literary gems and to paraphrase others, as is also the case, occasionally, throughout this work, with particular reference to the writings of Edersheim and Farrar, two of the best sectarian authors. Short of receiving personal revelation on all points, no one author can think of all the meanings or set forth every nuance of thought on all points. Further, it seems a waste of literary talent not to preserve some of the thoughts and modes of expression that those of old, who wrote on the same subjects, were led by the spirit of truth to record. Those who are acquainted with the original sources—be they the two authors mentioned, or Josephus, Tacitus, or whosoever—will know that all authors have followed this practice. Elder Talmage does so in his scholarly work. It is also the course followed by the authors of the scriptures themselves, as when John the Apostle quotes and paraphrases, without identifying his original source, a prior account of John the Baptist, as is set forth in the first chapter of the Gospel of John.

JESUS FEEDS THE FIVE THOUSAND

And it came to pass that he brake bread again
and blessed it, and gave
to the disciples to eat.
And when they had eaten
he commanded them
that they should break bread,
and give unto the multitude.
And when they had given unto the multitude
he also gave them wine to drink,
and commanded them that they should give
unto the multitude.
Now, there had been no bread,
neither wine, brought by the disciples,
neither by the multitude;
But he truly gave unto them bread to eat,
and also wine to drink.
And he said unto them:
He that eateth this bread eateth of my body
to his soul; and he that drinketh of this wine
drinketh of my blood to his soul;
and his soul shall never hunger nor thirst,
but shall be filled. (3 Ne. 20:3-8.)

He Prepares a Table in the Wilderness

(*Luke 9:10-11; JST, Luke 9:10; Matthew 14:13; Mark 6:30-32; JST, Mark 6:32-33*)

Jesus now plans to feed five thousand men, "beside women and children," with five small barley loaves and two sardine-like fish. The spartan banquet—if such it may be called when contrasted with the gluttonous feasts at Machaerus—is to be held in a solitary meadow near Bethsaida-Julias to the north and east of the Sea of Galilee. As to the multiplying of the loaves and fishes, John tells us that Jesus "himself knew what he would do" beforehand (John 6:6), and that this foreknowledge applied also to the preparation for the desert feast we cannot doubt.

And so, before the miraculous banquet can be served, the table in the desert must be prepared. The question, "Can God furnish a table in the wilderness?" must be answered anew, as it was in the day of Moses when Jehovah served quail to all Israel. (Ps. 78:13-20.) Before the multiplying of the loaves and fishes, Jesus and his disciples must go to the expanse of "green grass" where the companies of fifty and of a hundred will sit; the guests must be invited; they must be famishing for want of food, with none available to them; the pressing need for divine intervention must be present; there must be a young lad there with five loaves and two fishes; Jesus must have taught and healed so that the miracle will bear witness of his doctrine and of his divinity; and then—all being in readiness—the wonder will occur.

It should not be thought a thing unreasonable among them that the Son of God would exercise his creative power to give meat to hungering men. Indeed, their tradition was that when the Messiah came he would—as Moses had done—give them bread from heaven, provide them water to drink, feed them flesh according to their needs. Others before had fed Israel miraculously when their needs were great. Should it not happen again?

Had not Moses, the servant of Jehovah—when they, lusting for the fleshpots of Egypt, said, "Why came we forth out of Egypt?"—had not he given all Israel, some three million of them, flesh for thirty days, until it came out of their nostrils and became loathsome unto them? (Num. 11:18-23, 31-33.) Had not Jehovah rained bread from heaven upon them, six days a week, for forty years, as they dwelt in the wilderness? (Ex. 16.)

Was not Elijah fed by the ravens as he hid himself by the brook Cherith? Did not the fowls of heaven bring him "bread and flesh in the morning, and bread and flesh in the evening," lest he die of the famine? And did he not say to the widow of Zarephath, "The barrel of meal shall not waste, neither shall the cruse of oil fail, until the day that the Lord sendeth rain upon the earth," and it was so? (1 Kgs. 17:1-16.)

And Elisha, upon whom the mantle of Elijah fell, did he not bring oil and bread and corn into being from the very elements, as it were? What of the widow whose husband had been a prophet and whose two sons were to be taken as bondmen by a creditor? Did not Elisha cause them to pour oil from one small vessel until many great vessels were full, so they might sell the great store of oil thus created and have sufficient means to meet their needs? And does not the scripture say of Elisha:

> *And there came a man from Baalshalisha, and brought the man of God bread of the firstfruits, twenty loaves of barley, and full ears of corn in the husk thereof. And he said, Give unto the people, that they may eat.*
>
> *And his servitor said, What, should I set this before an hundred men? He said again, Give the people, that they may eat: for thus saith the Lord, They shall eat, and shall leave thereof.*
>
> *So he set it before them, and they did eat, and left thereof, according to the word of the Lord.* (*2 Kgs. 4:1-7, 42-44.*)

Why, then, should it be thought a thing unreasonable among them that the Son of God himself should give them a simple peasant-type meal of barley loaves and fish? Had he not, for that matter, as they all knew, turned water into wine at Cana? Others acting in Jehovah's name had fed Jehovah's people in days of old. Why not Jehovah himself do now what his servants of old had done? Was not that which was done by the Messianic messengers of old but a type and a shadow of what would be when the Messiah, whose witnesses they were, came among men in power and glory, to save and redeem, both temporally and spiritually?

And so now, Jesus and his disciples leave Capernaum to go to Bethsaida-Julias; the preparations for the desert feeding of the hungry multitudes are going forward in a normal and natural way. There are, it would seem, at least five good and sufficient reasons why Jesus and his fellow itinerant preachers should make this journey. They are:

1. *Both he and the Twelve are greatly in need of physical rest.* They have all been teaching and healing and traveling, almost with greater zeal than their strength permits. The Twelve have just returned from their missions and have told Jesus "all things, both what they had done, and what they had taught." They too had been preaching the gospel of the kingdom, casting out devils, healing the sick, perhaps even raising the dead, for such was included in the promises made to them. And so Jesus said unto them: "Come ye yourselves apart into a solitary place, and rest a while; for there were many coming and going, and they had no leisure, not so much as to eat. And they departed into a solitary place by ship, privately."

2. *Their departure will have a much-needed quieting effect upon the people.* Galilee is in turmoil because of the murder of the Baptist, whom the people revered as a prophet. It is not expedient for great multitudes to assemble around Jesus and the Twelve, lest the Herodians esteem these teachers and witnesses to be political agitators deserving the same arrest and imprisonment suffered by John. Josephus tells us that the seeming political agitations of John were the excuse used for his arrest. This must not now happen to Jesus or any of the Twelve. And at this time there might be a political

uprising among the people if Jesus and his associates longer remain with them. They are considered as leaders by many, and the people are seeking a standard round which to rally.

3. *It seemed wise for Jesus and the Twelve to withdraw from the domains and power of Herod.* Capernaum in Galilee was part of the tetrarchy of Antipas. Bethsaida-Julias, though near the eastern border of Galilee, was subject to the more peaceful Philip. As we have seen, Herod Antipas, demented and maddened by the weight of sin, hearing of Jesus' miracles and fame, assumed he was John the Baptist risen from the dead and had sent forth word that "he desired to see him." The climate was ripe for further political persecution, and Jesus and his followers would do well to go away for a slight season while things cooled down.

4. *The feeding of the hungering thousands could only take place in a solitary place,* in the deserts and hills where no food was available; otherwise the need for divine intervention would not be compelling. *And Jesus must work this miracle, not alone to fulfill the Messianic tradition had among them, but to bear witness in a way none others can that he is indeed the One of whom Moses and the prophets spoke.* Those of old who had fed the hungering by divine power had all done it in Jehovah's name. Jesus must go forth and say he is the Son of God, the Promised Messiah, and then work the miracle; then exercise divine power; then multiply the loaves and fishes—a thing he could not do if he were a deceiver.

5. And, finally, as we shall hereafter see in some detail, *the multitude must be fed, at the appointed place, so that Jesus, back again in Capernaum, can preach his incomparable sermon on the bread of life.* The feeding of the multitude is but prelude to the doctrine he is about to teach. Men are not saved because miracles are wrought in their presence; salvation comes only to those who believe the doctrines of salvation and who then act in harmony with them. The teaching that is to grow out of the miracle is greater than the miracle itself, and the teaching cannot come, with anywhere near the desired effect, without the miracle.

Jesus Teaches, Heals, and Feeds the Multitude

(*John 6:1-15; JST, John 6:12-13; Mark 6:33-46; JST, Mark 6:36, 39; Matthew 14:14-23; Luke 9:11-17; JST, Luke 9:10-13*)

This miracle, with its attendant circumstances, is recounted by all four of the Evangelists. Each preserves his own views as to what transpired on this never-to-be-forgotten day, and all of the accounts taken together enable us to paint a vivid picture of the only scenes of this kind ever to transpire among men. The Man whose words we love and whose deeds we revere first taught his scattered sheep; then he healed those who were lame and maimed among them; after this, he fed them all with earthly manna; then he went off by himself to commune alone with his Father; and finally, he walked on the ridges of the waves as a tempestuous wind whipped the Galilean sea into a frothy and frenzied maelstrom.

John tells us the Feast of the Passover "was nigh," and Mark specifies that the multitudes sat on "green grass." It was spring—early April of A.D. 29—and great throngs of Galileans had left their fields and shops to travel to Jerusalem to worship the Lord and covenant anew to follow the God of their fathers. Thousands of pilgrims were free to dally in Capernaum or hasten to a solitary site near Bethsaida-Julias, where the voice of their own Galilean Prophet might be heard. Perhaps he would heal their sick as he had done elsewhere. Was he, in fact, the Messiah as both he and his confederates so often said? Public interest ran high, and the Eternal Paschal Lamb meant to teach the traveling throngs who were en route to sacrifice their own paschal offerings in Jerusalem.

Jesus and the Twelve took ship. From Capernaum to their east coast destination was six miles by water; it would be somewhat farther on land. "And he took them, and went aside privately into a solitary place belonging to the city called Bethsaida," Luke says. After disembarking, "Jesus went up into a mountain, and there he sat with his disciples," John adds.

Their departure was seen by the people, who followed on foot, out of all the cities; word of his destination went from mouth to mouth; a great congregation awaited him across from the Jordan and on the east of the lake. These all assembled in a green valley. John says that "a great multitude followed him, because they saw his miracles which he did on them that were diseased."

Perhaps Jesus and his party gained some rest, at least some respite from the crowds, as they crossed the sea and as they sat on the mountain. But when Jesus saw the multitudes, he "was moved with compassion toward them, because they were as sheep not having a shepherd; and he began to teach them many things." So says Mark. Luke says he "spake unto them of the kingdom of God."

Jesus was doing what he had done before. It was his age-old pattern; as he always did, he preached the gospel, summarized the plan of salvation, told the people in whom they must believe and what they must do to be saved. He told them who he was and who the Twelve were. How important it is to know this, and how often it is repeated by the inspired authors!

As he said at the first Passover of his ministry, 'Though men destroy this body, I shall rise again the third day'; as he said to Nicodemus, 'I am the Son of Man who came down from heaven; whosoever believeth in me shall not perish but have eternal life; I am the Only Begotten Son; through me all men may be saved'; as he said to the woman of Samaria at Jacob's Well, 'I that speak unto thee am the Messias'; as he said in the synagogue in Nazareth, 'I am he of whom Isaiah spake; in me are the Messianic prophecies fulfilled; I am the Messiah'; as he said in healing one sick of the palsy, 'I Jesus, who am God, forgive you of your sins'; as he said at the second Passover, after healing the impotent man at the pool of Bethesda, 'I am the Son of God; my Father and I are equal; the Father hath committed all judgment into my hands; he that believeth on me hath everlasting life; even the dead shall hear my voice; all men must honor me even as they honor the Father'—as he said day in and day out, everywhere and everlastingly, always, in season and out of season, early and late, to men, women, and children, to every living soul, so he said again to the multitude near Bethsaida-Julias: 'I am the Son of God; salvation comes by me; believe my words and live my law, and I will give you a place in my Father's kingdom.'

Again we say: How important it is to know this! Jesus preached the gospel first and healed afterwards; the healings came to those who believed his words and accepted him as God's Son. However much this runs counter to the speculative views of the divines, it yet remains as a basic reality that must be understood if we are to come anywhere near a true view of him who, though mortal for a season, is Lord of all everlastingly.

And so Jesus first preached the gospel to the multitudes who came to hear his word. Then, as Luke says, he "healed them that had need of healing," or as Matthew recounts, he "was moved with compassion toward them, and he healed their sick."

Sometime during the day, Jesus said to Philip, one of the Twelve: "Whence shall we buy bread, that these may eat?" That Jesus had no intention of buying bread but was simply testing Philip—and through him all of the Twelve—is clear from John's comment: "And this he said to prove him: for he himself knew what he would do." Philip answered: "Two hundred pennyworth of bread is not sufficient for them, that every one of them may take a little." That sum, obviously, was more than the disciples had in their common purse.

His conversation with Philip caused the apostles to discuss the matter among themselves, and to wonder what should be done. At some point in time, "One of his disciples, Andrew, Simon Peter's brother, saith unto him, There is a lad here, which hath five barley loaves, and two small fishes; but what are they among so many?" And Philip's words are but a far-off echo of a servitor in another day who said: "What, should I set this"—this meal of twenty barley loaves and a few ears of corn in the husk—"before an hundred men?" And Jesus' coming response was but an echo of Elisha's word: "Give the people, that they may eat: for thus saith the Lord, They shall eat, and shall leave thereof." (2 Kgs. 4:43-44.)

Finally, following full discussion among themselves, and after their faith had been tested—and found wanting—"when the day began to wear away, then came the twelve, and said unto him, Send the multitude away, that they may go into the towns and country round about, and lodge, and get victuals; for we are here in a solitary place."

This, then, was their answer; and this was the perfect teaching moment, the time for divine intervention. Jesus said: "They need not depart; give ye them to eat." They said: "Shall we go and buy two hundred penny-worth of bread, and give them to eat?" Jesus said: "How many loaves have ye? go and see." The answer came: "We have but five loaves and two fishes; and except we should go and buy meat, we can provide no more food for all this multitude."

"And he commanded them to make all sit down by companies upon the green grass. And they sat down in ranks, by hundreds, and by fifties. And when he had taken the five loaves and the two fishes, he looked up to heaven, and blessed, and brake the loaves, and gave them to his disciples to set before them; and the two fishes divided he among them all. And they did all eat, and were filled."

"When they had eaten and were satisfied, he said unto his disciples, Gather up the fragments that remain, that nothing be lost. Therefore they gathered them together, and filled twelve baskets with the fragments of the five barley loaves, which remained over and above unto them that had eaten."

Thus was the miracle wrought; so was the deed done; and such are the attendant circumstances. The concordant testimony of four independent witnesses appends a solemn certitude to the wonder that has happened. Needless to say, the creative power thus exercised by him who for the moment is as a mortal is in fact the power of God.

As the reality of what was done this day in a green lowland place not far from Bethsaida-Julias (literally, the *house of fishing,* or, as we might say, *Fisher-town*) dawns upon us; as we ponder the wonder of it all, bread and fish springing instantly into being, from the very elements, because he willed it—as we marvel at such a miracle, we ask: Why and for what purpose was it done? What message are we to receive from this miracle of two millenniums ago? To all of this, these thoughts readily occur:

1. *He did it*—and such an ordinary and prosaic reason it is!—*because men were hungry and there was no food available to them.* Unless men eat, they die; mortal meat is part of mortal life.

2. *He acted out of love and compassion for his fellowmen.* Though he would not turn stones into bread to appease his own hunger—a famishing, gnawing hunger born of forty days of fasting—yet for others, whose needs were less and whose hunger was but one day old, he would exercise his own divine power. As his Father makes the rains fall and the sun shine upon all his children, be they good or evil, so will the Son provide bread for those who have come to hear his words.

3. *But he will not glut their souls with the delicacies that grace Herod's board, nor will he sate their appetites with rich food.* They shall have barley bread, the foodstuff of the peasant and the poor. They shall spread upon this coarse product of the baker's oven a savory made of fish. John's account uses "a peculiar word for 'fish,' *opsarion,* which properly means what was eaten along with the bread, and specially refers to the small, and generally dried or pickled fish eaten with bread, like our 'sardines' or the 'caviar' of Russia, the pickled herrings of Holland and Germany, or a peculiar kind of small dried fish, eaten with the bones, in the North of Scotland." (Edersheim 1:682.)

4. In the course of the day, as various conversations led up to the climactic miracle, *he tested the faith of his disciples*—as he tests all of us hour by hour in the most ordinary affairs of our lives—and as we have seen, his chosen ones, in this case, failed to pass the test.

5. He dramatized his own saying, given in the Sermon on the Mount, that his missionaries, his servants, *those who go forth on his errand to teach his word, need take no thought for their temporal wants.* Such will be supplied by the Father. He who feeds the fowls of the air and clothes the lilies of the field will care for the needs of his own.

6. *The miracle came as a sign*—nay, not a sign only, but as a crowning proof—*of his Messiahship.* He first claimed to be the Son of God and then performed miracles, which he could not have done if he were a deceiver.

7. Would it be amiss, as some have done, to say *the miracle acclaimed him as the bread of the world;* as the source—unexhausted and inexhaustible—of all that sustains life; as the one in whom there is always enough and to spare; as the one who, now and always, will care for all the spiritual needs of all the hungering souls of all the ages?

8. *Does it not also testify that all that he does is organized and regulated?* His house is a house of order and not of confusion. The recipients of his goodness sat down in companies and in ranks; they were counted and numbered; there was no disorder, no commotion, no disturbance. None sought to come afore, and none resisted the command to be seated systematically. There was peace and serenity, and the Spirit of the Lord was present.

9. *Here also divine economy was in operation.* Though he could supply loaves and fishes that the world itself could not contain, yet the uneaten fragments, the crusts and crumbs, the slivers of uneaten fish—all these were picked up in baskets and saved, for waste is sin.

10. *Jesus offered a blessing on the food;* he gave thanks to a gracious God, who is the source of all good things, for that which was then supplied. And as he himself offered the

prayer, it means, according to the Jewish custom, that he himself also ate of the food.

11. *He manifest his own creative powers.* He did not call upon the Lord as did Elisha; he did not act in the name of another as had Elijah and Moses; but acting himself, in his own name, because he was God, he created loaves and fishes. If worlds come rolling into being at his word and by his creative power, then why not a few barley loaves and sufficient fish savory to go with them?

12. And, finally, *the supplying of bread from heaven, as it were, formed the basis for the not-far-distant sermon on the bread of life*—one of the greatest and most powerful sermons of his ministry, as we shall see.

No doubt other points could be made, and the attentive student can search out his own types and shadows and applications, as he should; but what is here given illustrates, at least, what can be learned from any of the glorious teaching situations concerning Jesus our Lord.

"The miracle produced a profound impression. It was exactly in accordance with the current expectation, and the multitude began to whisper to each other that this must undoubtedly be 'that Prophet which should come into the world'; the Shiloh of Jacob's blessing; the Star and the Sceptre of Balaam's vision; the Prophet like unto Moses to whom they were to hearken; perhaps the Elijah promised by the dying breath of ancient prophecy; perhaps the Jeremiah of their tradition, come back to reveal the hiding-place of the Ark, and the Urim, and the sacred fire." (Farrar, pp. 310-11.)

And since he was "that Prophet"—the very Messiah; their Deliverer; the one through whom all Israel might be saved—what then? To the expectant throng—had they not heard his wondrous words, seen his miracles, and been fed to the full?—to them it seemed as if the hour of Jewish triumph had come at long last. They must "make him a king"; nay, he was king already; rather, they must "take him by force" and require that he act in his kingly capacity. Let the Roman yoke fall; here at last was one who could defeat the armies of Antipas and more. Here was one who could strike the death blow against that wretched man, Caesar, who reveled in his orgies and lusts in his Gentile city.

That such misdirected zeal must not go unchecked was perfectly clear to the one around whom the swell of zealotry surged. His disciples must withdraw lest they partake of this false spirit, and the people must disperse to ponder, in less excitable circumstances, the true meaning and significance of the doings of that day. "And straightway Jesus constrained his disciples to get into a ship, and to go before him unto the other side." He was insistent that they depart immediately. They must leave the environs of Bethsaida-Julias and go to that Bethsaida which is the companion city to Capernaum, the two cities, but four miles apart, sharing a common Galilean harbor. With his disciples en route back it was easier for Jesus to send the multitude away.

Then "he went up into a mountain apart to pray." He must thank his Father for the marvels of that day, for he of himself did only that which his Father commanded. He must counsel again with the great God whose Son he was, lest he overstep any of the bounds or vary so much as a hair's breadth from the course decreed by the Father. He must receive that spiritual refreshment and guidance which even he needed to bear the growing burden that rested upon his divine shoulders. From the hallowed spot where he communed with the Eternal he soon returned—perhaps having been so directed by him to whom he prayed—to walk on the surging waves of that lake which was so much a part of his life.

JESUS WALKS ON THE SEA OF GALILEE

The waters saw thee, O God,
the waters saw thee;
they were afraid: the depths also were troubled.
Thy way is in the sea,
and thy path in the great waters. (Ps. 77:16, 19.)

The waters were gathered together,
the floods stood upright as an heap,
and the depths were congealed in the heart
of the sea. (Ex. 15:8.)

Jehovah Rules the Waters

Working with waters has always been part of the prophetic way. By faith the worlds were made; by faith the elements are controlled; by faith the mountains move and the seas divide. And the waters of the world are always used to subserve the purposes of faithful men.

From that creative day when Jehovah, by his word, divided the waters above the firmament from those beneath the broad expanse of heaven; from that primeval day when he gathered the waters into one place, calling the dry land earth and the great waters seas; from that antediluvian day when he caused the rains to fall and water the parched land, to give life to plants and herbs, to give drink for man and beast—from that day water has always been used for the benefit and blessing of created things.

Water, the liquid that falls from the clouds as rain; the unstable substance that flows in great rivers and small streams; the moisture that accumulates in ponds and lakes and seas; the element without which there cannot be life—the birth of man itself being brought to pass by water and blood and the spirit—water, wondrous water, was made for man. It was made to supply his needed fluids and to cleanse his body; to give life to animals and fowls and plants; to serve as a home for fish; to form vapors of steam, storms of snow, and glaciers of ice; to be handled and used and governed—all in the interests of God's crowning creation, the being whom he made in his own image.

Truly, water was made for man, made for him to use for his own purposes. His is the power to control and govern it. With it he irrigates his gardens and gives drink to his flocks and herds. From it he catches fish, and over it he sails. He freezes it into ice to refrigerate his products; he vaporizes it into steam to drive great locomotives; he uses its power to generate electricity. He swims in it, skis on its frozen crystals, and skates on its congealed surface. Its uses are as varied and broad as the earth itself.

And water is subject not alone to the natural laws that man must learn and to which he must conform, but it is subject also to the eternal law of faith, a law that in the eternal sense is also a natural law. And further, water is used by the Lord to further his own purposes—to give life to men; to cleanse them from their sins; to drown them in death when his judgments are poured out.

"I, the Lord, in the beginning blessed the waters"—so our revelations record in a passage whose full meaning has not yet been given—"but in the last days, by the mouth of my servant John, I cursed the waters." (D&C 61:14.)

Perhaps the cursing here involved will attain its dooming

destiny when the visions of the future that John saw become a reality. In one of these he saw that "a great mountain burning with fire was cast into the sea; and the third part of the sea became blood; And the third part of the creatures which were in the sea, and had life, died; and the third part of the ships were destroyed." (Rev. 8:8-9.) In another he saw that one of the angels who carry "the vials of the wrath of God, . . . poured out his vial upon the sea; and it became as the blood of a dead man; and every living soul died in the sea. And the third angel poured out his vial upon the rivers and fountains of waters; and they became blood." (Rev. 16:1-4.) And perhaps we are seeing even now a little trickling prelude of what John foretold as we struggle to maintain the natural purity of our rivers and seas into which great floods of contaminating chemicals and stinking refuse are poured as men seek to rid themselves of the rubbish and garbage of our so-called civilization.

"And, as I, the Lord, in the beginning cursed the land," our revelation continues, "even so in the last days have I blessed it, in its time, for the use of my saints, that they may partake the fatness thereof." (D&C 61:17.) That this blessing upon the land will attain its glorious fulfillment in the nearing millennial era is, of course, perfectly clear. In the meantime the first sprouting forth of the blessings that can grow from the soil are beginning to burst upon us as we learn better how to use the good earth from which we are fed.

But our concern, with reference to the miracle we are about to witness, is to know that Jehovah rules the waters, and that what he does to and with them—whether it be by his own voice or by the voice of his servants, it is the same.

Thus we see Jesus arranging for the immersion of Adam and his seed in water, that they may all come forth, born again, born anew from a second watery womb. We see baptism in water established as an eternal ordinance, with the waters in which it was performed in ancient Israel being called "the waters of Judah." (1 Ne. 20:1.) We see the saints, in all dispensations, in holy and sacred ordinances, sprinkled with water that they become clean from the carnality and evil of the world. We see men drink the sacramental wine and water in witness of the new covenant that God hath made with his people. And we hear a divine voice assure all men that whosoever so much as gives a cup of cold water to a prophet or righteous man—because he wears the prophetic mantle or walks in the paths of righteousness—shall in nowise lose his reward.

We see Enoch go forth and say to the mountains, 'Be thou removed,' and to the rivers, 'Turn thou into another course,' and it is so. We see a great land come up out of the depth of the sea to which the enemies of the people of God flee in the days of Enoch.

We see Jehovah, by the mouth of his servant Noah, sending in the floods until the valleys and hills and every high mountain are immersed in the surging torrents. It is the baptism of the earth. We see the earth divided in the days of Peleg—was it perchance by his mouth as he spoke Jehovah's word?—so that the dry lands that once were in one place become continents and islands surrounded by seas of water.

We see Moses, the man of God—by his own voice, which was the voice of Jehovah—stretch out his hand upon the waters of Egypt so they all turn to blood, including the waters that are in the Nile and in all the streams and rivers and ponds, and in all the pots and vessels. We see the fish die, smell the stench of the rivers, and know there is nothing for the Egyptians to drink.

We see Moses stretch forth his hand over the Red Sea and divide it so that all Israel, numbering in the millions, "went into the midst of the sea upon the dry ground: and the waters were a wall unto them on the right hand, and on their left." We learn that "the floods stood upright as an heap, and the depths were congealed in the heart of the sea." (Ex. 14:19-31; 15:8.) And we see the pursuing armies of Pharaoh drowned in the depths of the sea as the congealing power is withdrawn and the floods surge forth in all their unchecked fury.

When Israel thirsts for water in their desert wilderness, we see Moses, at Meribah, smite the rock with his rod, so that rivers of fresh water gush forth, that all Israel and their beasts die not for want of water.

When Israel, under Joshua, march to the flooding banks of Jordan, as soon as the soles of the feet of them that bare the ark are dipped in the brim of the water, lo—as Joshua by his own mouth decreed—we see the waters stand up as a heap and all Israel pass over on dry ground.

When the Lord sent a famine in Israel, it was by the mouth of Elijah that he sealed the heavens for three years and six months, that it rained not; and it was by his word that the dews of heaven and the moisture of the clouds came again.

At the time of the translation of Elijah, when he was taken up into heaven in a chariot of fire without tasting death, we see, first, Elijah, and then Elisha—by their own mouths—smite the waters of Jordan with a mantle, so that they divide hither and thither, permitting the prophetic feet to go over on dry ground.

We see a faithful man in Israel felling a beam with a borrowed axe; the head comes off and falls into the water. Then at the word of the prophet Elisha—mark it well—"the iron did swim," and the axe head is recovered. (2 Kgs. 6:1-7.) Solid iron swims in water as though it were a cork because Jehovah and his prophets, by faith, have power over the waters.

And we shall yet see, for these things are in the future, the Son of Man at his coming—perhaps by the mouths of his servants the prophets—"command the great deep, and it shall be driven back into the north countries, and the islands shall become one land; . . . and the earth shall be like as it was in the days before it was divided." (D&C 133:23-24.) And then, after his coming, upon those nations that go not up year after year to Jerusalem to keep the Feast of Tabernacles, "even upon them shall be no rain." (Zech. 14:16-19.) The Lord will use the elements to punish the people in the millennial day even as he speaks in this day by "the voice of thunderings, and the voice of lightnings, and the voice of tempests, and the voice of the waves of the sea heaving themselves beyond their bounds." (D&C 88:90.)

We have spoken thus about the waters of the world—and there is much more that could be acclaimed—to show how the Lord uses them at will to bless and to curse, that it might not seem a thing incredible to now see two men walk upon the waters of Gennesaret. Jesus and Peter are about to defy the gravitational forces of nature and make the rolling waves and surging foam their footpath. Few miracles seem to excite such wonder and interest as does this one. And it is indeed such a miracle as is not elsewhere inscribed in the hearts of the saints, nor found in the records of the Lord's people, but it is one that accords with the manner and way in which Jesus—whether as Jehovah, or as a mortal, or as the Risen God—deals with the faithful. And it is one that we might expect of him who turns water into wine, who stills storms, and who has power over the elements.

"Be of Good Cheer; It Is I; Be Not Afraid"

(*Matthew 14:24-33; Mark 6:47-52; JST, Mark 6:50; John 6:16-21*)

From the mountaintop where he prayed—shall we not rather say, communed and conversed—with his Father, Jesus saw the peril and strugglings of his beloved friends as they sought the safety of the western shore of the Galilean lake. They were seabound because he had "constrained" them so to travel. Their preference had been to remain with him and bask in the glory of that wondrous multiplying of five barley loaves and two small fish into a banquet that fed five thousand men, plus women and children, and yet left twelve baskets of uneaten food. His awareness of their plight must have come by the power of the Spirit rather than the natural eye, for they were more than four—perhaps were five or six—miles away. It was still night, and a tempestuous wind, blowing out of a darkened sky, was whipping the waves into a surging fury.

These noble souls who stood at Jesus' side, who believed his words and loved his law, who wrought miracles in his name, and who one day would bear witness of that blessed name before kings and rulers and before nations scarce then known to them—these chosen ones had embarked for Bethsaida and Capernaum, twin cities on the western shore of Galilee that shared a common harbor. Their seaborn journey, though not wholly a willing one, was at least one of obedient conformity to the Master's word. They had sailed in the calm of deepening dusk, only to encounter a storm of the night as the wild winds blew down the canyons and ravines and across the inland sea. Matthew says their "ship was . . . tossed with waves: for the wind was contrary." Mark says Jesus "saw them toiling in rowing," doing all in their power to avoid a disastrous shipwreck. And John says it was "dark, . . . And the sea arose by reason of a great wind that blew." In some eight or ten hours they traveled less than four miles from the shore.

Their peril was great. Even strong men cannot resist indefinitely the battering waves and the rolling power of a storm at sea. It was now the fourth watch of the night, sometime between three and six A.M. Jesus had left them to struggle and toil till their strength was spent. Now he came to the rescue. He came to them "walking on the sea"; his feet pressed on the crests of the waves; his weight was borne by the foaming liquid beneath his feet; it was as though the watery waves were a stone-set street. The iron swam when Elisha spoke; the waters of the Red Sea congealed at a word from Moses; the storm-tossed Sea of Galilee was as a dusty Galilean lane because Jesus willed it. He walked on the water—literally, actually, and in reality.

But even now he yet tests their faith by walking "as if he would have passed by them." "They all saw him, and were troubled." "It is a spirit," they said—and well might they so suppose, for since the world began there was no account of a mortal man, weighted down with flesh and bones and apparel, treading lightly on the waves of the sea. "They cried out for fear," as might be expected, for an added and unknown peril—a spirit from the unseen world—a peril beyond the winds and the waves with which they were acquainted, seemed more than they could then bear.

In answer to their cries Jesus spoke: "Be of good cheer," he said; "it is I; be not afraid."

Peter answered: "Lord, if it be thou"—or, better, 'Since it be thou'—"bid me come unto thee on the water." A single word of response, spoken above the whistling wind and the noise of the boisterous waves beating against the ship, pierced the darkness and din of the storm: "Come." And come Peter did. He too walked on the water. Jesus and Peter were both supported by the liquid highway beneath them, a highway that surged and rolled as the wind-driven waves responded to the tempestuous forces that disturbed their calm.

"Over the vessel's side into the troubled waves he sprang, and while his eye was fixed on his Lord, the wind might toss his hair, and the spray might drench his robes, but all was well; but when, with wavering faith, he glanced from Him to the furious waves, and to the gulfy blackness underneath, then he began to sink, and in an accent of despair—how unlike his former confidence!—he faintly cried, 'Lord, save me!' Nor did Jesus fail. Instantly, with a smile of pity, He stretched out His hand, and grasped the hand of His drowning disciple, with the gentle rebuke, 'O thou of little faith, why didst thou doubt?' And so, his love satisfied, but His over-confidence rebuked, they climb—the Lord and His abashed Apostle—into the boat; and the wind lulled, and amid the ripple of the waves upon a moonlit shore, they were at the haven where they would be; and all—the crew as well as His disciples—were filled with deeper and deeper amazement, and some of them, addressing Him by a title which Nathanael alone [as far as the written record shows] had applied to Him before, exclaimed, 'Truly Thou art the Son of God.' " (Farrar, p. 313.)

Our synoptist authors tell us that when Jesus and Peter

entered the ship, "the wind ceased," leaving us to believe that once again he stilled a Galilean storm with a word. At this point Matthew says: "Then they that were in the ship came and worshipped him, saying, Of a truth thou art the Son of God." We are left to conclude that those so doing were the sailors or other passengers, for the apostles had long since had such a witness in their souls. To the extent the chosen disciples joined in this worship, it was but a reaffirmation of that which they already knew, even as it is common among us to affirm and reaffirm our knowledge of the divine sonship of this same Holy Being.

Mark, however, says "they were sore amazed in themselves beyond measure, and wondered. For they considered not the miracle of the loaves: for their heart was hardened." It would appear that this amazement and wonder may have been the feelings of the disciples as well as the others who sailed in the battered bark. Why, in the light of all that has transpired in their lives, would there be a lingering strain of doubt and uncertainty in any disciple's mind? "The answer is found in the fact that the chosen disciples had not yet received the gift of the Holy Ghost. Though they were all pillars of spiritual strength and righteousness, save Judas only, yet 'the things of God knoweth no man, but the Spirit of God.' (1 Cor. 2:11.) Until the natural man becomes a new creature of the Holy Ghost, until man is born again, until his stony heart is touched by the Spirit of the living God, he cannot, by any power of his own, stand sure and steadfast in the cause of truth." (*Commentary* 1:348-49.)

It is no more difficult to believe that Jesus or Peter or any faithful person could walk on a tempestuous sea than it is to believe in any other miracle. "If, believing in God," as Farrar puts it, "we believe in a Divine Providence over the lives of men—and, believing in that Divine Providence, believe in the miraculous—and, believing in the miraculous, accept as truth the resurrection of our Lord Jesus Christ—and, believing that resurrection, believe that He was indeed the Son of God—then, however deeply we may realise the beauty and the wonder and the power of natural laws, we realize yet more deeply the power of Him who holds those laws, and all which they have evolved, in the hollow of His hand; and to us the miraculous, when thus attested, will be in no way more stupendous than the natural, nor shall we find it an impossible conception that He who sent His Son to earth to die for us should have put all authority into His hand."

Continuing, Farrar gives this aptly expressed application of the miracle here recounted: "So then if, like Peter, we fix our eyes on Jesus, we too may walk triumphantly over the swelling waves of disbelief, and unterrified amid the rising winds of doubt; but if we turn away our eyes from Him in whom we have believed—if, as it is so easy to do, and as we are so much tempted to do, we look rather at the power and fury of those terrible and destructive elements than at Him who can help and save—then we too shall inevitably sink. Oh, if we feel, often and often, that the water-floods threaten to drown us, and the deep to swallow up the tossed vessel of our Church and Faith, may it again and again be granted us to hear amid the storm and the darkness, the voices prophesying war, those two sweetest of the Savior's utterances—

'Fear not. Only believe.'
'It is I. Be not afraid.' "[1]

Jesus Heals in the Land of Gennesaret
(*Matthew 14:34-36; Mark 6:53-56*)

Gennesaret, meaning garden of riches, was a small region in Galilee, located on the western shore of the lake near Capernaum. It was also a city, perhaps Tiberias, south of Capernaum and Magdala. Rich soil and plenteous harvests supported a large population scattered in many villages and cities. It was here, apparently because the storm had driven them southward from their intended landing in the Capernaum-Bethsaida area, that Jesus and his disciples disembarked after the miracle of the walking on the sea.[2]

Jesus and his party were well known, and almost immediately they were surrounded by believing and worshipful souls who sought to hear his words and feel his power. Messengers "ran through that whole region round about"; people everywhere heard of his presence; and believing multitudes hastened to him, carrying on pallets "those that were sick," and bringing to him "all that were diseased." It was a day of rejoicing and miracles. Those who were diseased and sick, so great was their faith, "besought him that they might only touch the hem of his garment," that their maladies might be cured.[3] And they were blessed according to their desires, for "as many as touched were made perfectly whole."

Through all their villages and cities and country it was the same; the sick were placed in the streets where they needed but to touch the border of his garment to have health and vigor and cleanliness and strength surge anew through their diseased bodies.[4] This day was a pleasing and blessed interlude between the storm of the night and the coming confrontation in the synagogue of Capernaum when hatred and opposition would spring forth even among many of those who had eaten the loaves and feasted on the fishes. And it is to the deep and profound teachings of that contentious scene that we shall next turn our attention—teachings that marked the turning point in the mortal ministry of the Mortal Messiah.

NOTES

1. Farrar, p. 314. "Why did Jesus walk on the water and then quell the storm?

"(1) To reach the boat, keep a planned rendevous with the apostles, and save them in their hour of despair and physical exhaustion.

"(2) To teach again by concrete means, under circumstances where no natural explanation could spiritualize the miracle away, that faith is a principle of power by which natural forces are controlled. (*Mormon Doctrine,* 2nd ed., pp. 261-267.)

"(3) To bear testimony that he was indeed the promised Messiah, the Son of God, the Incarnate Word, who though made flesh to fulfil the Father's purposes, yet had resident in him the powers of divinity. Here in the boat with weak mortals was he 'who hath gathered the wind in his fists, who hath bound the waters in a garment' (Prov. 30:4), he who 'spreadeth out the heavens, and treadeth upon the waves of the sea.' (Job 9:8.) And that the disciples knew him for what he was, and saw in this renewed manifestation of his power the proof of his eternal godhood, is evident from the fact that they then worshiped him and acclaimed, 'Of a truth thou art the Son of God.' (Matt. 14:33.)" (*Commentary* 1:347.)

2. "The boat which bore the disciples had drifted out of its course—probably owing to the wind—and touched land, not where they had intended, but at Gennesaret, where they moored it. There can be no question, that by this term is meant 'the plain of Gennesaret,' the richness and beauty of which *Josephus* and the Rabbis describe in such glowing language. To this day it bears marks of having been the most favoured spot in this favoured region." (Edersheim 2:5.)

3. "Perhaps they had knowledge of the woman who, plagued for twelve years with an issue of blood, had been healed by touching the hem of his garment (Mark 5:25-34); perhaps they considered the garment fringe as holy because of the divine command that garments be bordered in blue so that all Israel might 'look upon it, and remember all the commandments of the Lord, and do them' (Num. 15:37-41); or perhaps, overpowered in the divine presence, they sought even the slightest and least physical contact with him. But in any event, so great was their faith that all partook of his infinite goodness and were healed." (*Commentary* 1:350-51.)

4. Comparable scenes and events drawn from the subsequent apostolic ministries include these: *As to Peter,* "And by the hands of the apostles were many signs and wonders wrought among the people, . . . Insomuch that they brought forth the sick into the streets, and laid them on beds and couches, that at the least the shadow of Peter passing by might overshadow some of them." (Acts 5:12-15.) *As to Paul,* "And God wrought special miracles by the hands of Paul: So that from his body were brought unto the sick handkerchiefs or aprons, and the diseases departed from them, and the evil spirits went out of them." (Acts 19:11-12.)

THE SERMON ON THE BREAD OF LIFE

And thou shalt remember all the way
which the Lord thy God led thee these forty years
in the wilderness, to humble thee,
and to prove thee, to know what was in thine heart,
whether thou wouldest keep
his commandments, or no.
And he humbled thee, and suffered thee to hunger,
and fed thee with manna,
which thou knewest not, neither did
thy fathers know; that he might make thee
know that man doth not live by bread only,
but by every word that proceedeth
out of the mouth of the Lord doth man live.
(Deut. 8:2-3.)

To him that overcometh will I give to eat
of the hidden manna. (Rev. 2:17.)

Manna Is for All Men

Jesus is about to speak of "the hidden manna" which none but those who believe and obey shall ever taste. For forty years Israel ate manna—bread from heaven—which all men saw. This "manna was as coriander seed, and the colour thereof as the colour of bdellium." It fell as dew upon the camp of Israel, each night except the one preceding the Sabbath. The people gathered it in containers, ground it in mills, beat it in mortars, baked it in pans, and made cakes of bread. It tasted like fresh oil, was the staple diet of the people, and preserved them from famine and death. For twelve thousand days—six days a week, fifty-two weeks a year, for forty years—Israel ate manna to their hearts' content. "I will rain bread from heaven for you," Jehovah said; and rain it, he did, a rain of temporal food suited for the digestive processes of mortal people who must eat or die. (Ex. 16:4-36; Num. 11:4-9.)

And so Israel ate and lived—temporally. Among them, from time to time, were those who understood that their diet of heavensent bread came in similitude of a greater food, a "hidden manna," an unseen heavenly bread, of which men must eat if they are to be fed spiritually. As men die temporally for want of temporal bread, so they die spiritually for want of spiritual food.

Israel's daily diet of manna—and they collected enough on the sixth day to satisfy their needs on the Sabbath—was given not alone to feed their bellies, but to test them spiritually. It came to the people, to all of them, from the Lord—to prove them, to signify what was in their hearts, to establish whether they would keep the commandments or continue to walk after the manner of the Egyptians whose fleshpots they had forsaken to eat the manna of the wilderness. "Man does not live by bread only," Moses proclaimed. Let there be temporal bread lest there be temporal death. But man lives—spiritually and eternally—only when he feasts upon "hidden manna," when he lives "by every word that proceedeth out of the mouth of the Lord." (Deut. 8:2-3.)[1]

Jesus, not for twelve thousand consecutive days as did Jehovah to their fathers, but for one glorious meal, rained bread from heaven. He fed, not the millions in all the camps of ancient Israel, but a few, a mere five thousand men plus women and children, in an isolated place near Bethsaida-Julias. Yet in the miracle of the loaves and fishes was manifest the same gracious goodness shown forth upon all Israel anciently: (1) Food came to hungry mouths to satisfy their temporal needs; and (2) it was done to bear record of that heavenly bread, that hidden manna, that spiritual food, of which all men must eat if they are to gain eternal life. This meaning of the miracle is what Jesus is about to expound in a synagogue, in a wicked city, to Israelites whose rebellion and unbelief ranks with that of their fathers in Moses' day.

And as the Lord tested Israel by means of the ancient manna, so Jesus is about to test Jewish Israel by expounding the meaning of the miracle in which they had gained such a great initial feeling of rejoicing. He is going to see whether they will "keep his commandments, or no"; and as it was anciently, so shall it now be. A few will believe and obey; most of the people will seek only to glut their souls with the bread of the world, which sustains life among those who are carnal, sensual, and devilish. The things of the Spirit—spiritual food—is not for them, as they will soon attest.

Only yesterday on the green fields near Bethsaida-Julias, on the eastern side of the Lake of Gennesaret, Jesus the Messiah, doing what no mortal of himself had power to do, fed the multitude with temporal food. From the beginning of his ministry to that day his popular appeal had swept over the land as a flood. His doctrine and his deeds testified of his divinity. All men, save those whose hearts were bound by the chains of priestcraft, flocked to his standard and desired his help and blessings.

There was a tradition, taught by the Rabbis and firmly entrenched in the public mind, that when Messiah came, he would feed them with bread from heaven. "The miracle of the manna had become a subject of the proudest remembrances and the fondest legends of the nation. 'God,' says the Talmud, 'made manna to descend for them, in which were all manner of tastes. Every Israelite found in it what best pleased him. The young tasted bread, the old honey, and the children oil.' It had even become a fixed belief that the Messiah, when He came, would signalize His advent by a repetition of this stupendous miracle. 'As the first Saviour—the deliverer from Egyptian bondage,' said the Rabbis, 'caused manna to fall for Israel from heaven, so the second Saviour—the Messiah—will also cause manna to descend for them once more.'" (Geikie, pp. 516-17.)

Thus, when Jesus multiplied the five barley loaves and the two small fishes, it was as though the traditional sign had been given. The peak of his popular appeal had come. In their eyes he stood on the summit. He was the Messiah, they reasoned, and must reign as their king. They must take him by force, if need be, and install him as the Deliverer who would break the Gentile yoke, to say nothing of providing them with bread from heaven as it had been in the day of Moses. No doubt many of them had doubts and anxious moments as they reflected during the night on his utter refusal to receive the Messianic mantle proffered by them.

And so now in the synagogue in Capernaum—the synagogue built by the good centurion whose son was healed; the synagogue ruled by Jairus, whose daughter was raised from death; the synagogue upon whose "lintel has been discovered . . . the device of a pot of manna, ornamented with a flowing pattern of vine leaves and clusters of grapes" (Edersheim 2:29)—in this setting Jesus will teach them of the hidden manna of which the loaves and fishes were but a symbol. And here his popularity will plummet. This sermon will mark the parting of the ways between him and the people generally. Previous opposition centered primarily in the scribes and Pharisees, the Rabbis and rulers, the Sadducees and Herodians; now the generality of the people will harden their hearts against Him who refused to conform to their concept of a temporal ruler.

It is a day of sorrow and a day of crises. Indeed: "The dawn of that day broke on one of the saddest episodes of our Saviour's life. It was a day in the synagogue at Capernaum on which He deliberately scattered the mists and exhalations of such spurious popularity as the Miracle of the Loaves had gathered about His person and His work, and put not only His idle followers, but some even of His nearer disciples, to a test under which their love for Him entirely failed. That discourse in the synagogue forms a marked crisis in His career. It was followed by manifestations of surprised dislike which were as the first mutterings [among the people generally] of that storm of hatred and persecution which was henceforth to burst over His head." (Farrar, p. 315.)

Jesus Brings the Hidden Manna

(*John 6:22-47; JST, John 6:26-27, 40, 44*)

By preparing a table in the wilderness where a hungering host was fed as though manna had again been rained from heaven, Jesus did two things:

1. He set the stage, prepared the way, and provided the symbolism that would enable him to teach, under circumstances in which none could ever forget his words, that there was an eternal bread, a spiritual food, a hidden manna, which men must eat to gain eternal life; and

2. He fanned the flames of Messianic expectancy into a raging fire—here at last was the Coming One who would feed them as Moses (so they supposed) had fed their fathers. "A few, doubtless, had worthier thoughts, but, to the mass, the Messiah's kingdom was as gross as Mahomet's paradise. They were to be gathered together into the garden of Eden, to eat, and drink, and satisfy themselves all their days, with houses of precious stones, beds of silk, and rivers flowing with wine, and spicy oil for all. It was that He might gain all this for them that they had wished to set Him up as king." (Geikie, pp. 516-17.)

Thus, as we have seen, they had, in the swelling emotion of the moment, sought to place a kingly crown upon that head whose only earthly crown was to be one of thorns. Their failure so to do sowed the seeds of doubt and dismay in many minds. Following this failure to start the rebellion against Rome that in their view would have led to the triumph of the Jews over all others, they had seen the disciples depart for the western shore in the only available boat. With some reluctance the excited multitude, at Jesus' behest, had themselves dispersed to seek lodging in the nearby cities and villages. Jesus, as they knew, had remained with them on the eastern side of the then placid waters, waters that would soon be whipped into a storm-tossed fury by the tempestuous winds of the night. When the morning came Jesus was gone. Later other boats came from Tiberias, and in them many of the people found passage back to Capernaum; others, no doubt, walked back to their home locales or continued as pilgrims, bound toward Jerusalem and their annual Passover.

Those who returned by the other boats must have numbered among them the Galileans who were more particularly offended by Jesus' refusal to accept a crown from their self-seeking hands. When they found him—apparently already in the synagogue—with an abruptness bordering on discourtesy, certainly with a demeanor lacking in civility, they asked: "Rabbi, when camest thou hither?"

That Jesus had spent the night communing with his Father; that he had walked on the fearful waves which all but sank the boat wherein the disciples rowed and struggled to stay afloat; that a sudden calm attended his entrance into the storm-tossed ship; that the blessed party had landed in the area of Gennesaret where multitudes flocked together to hear his words and feel his love; that messengers had run through all the region round about so their sick and diseased might be carried and brought to his presence; that he had healed them all, even those who but touched the hem of his garment—none of these things were as yet known to the harsh interrogators who had followed him in small boats from the fields where the table in the wilderness had been set, and where he had told them plainly that he would not be a judge and a divider over them in the temporal sense. Nor did Jesus feel any need to account to them for his goings and comings and his words and deeds. Waving their impertinent query aside, he answered:

> *Verily, verily, I say unto you, Ye seek me, not because ye desire to keep my sayings, neither because ye saw the miracles, but because ye did eat of the loaves and were filled.*
>
> *Labor not for the meat which perisheth, but for that meat which endureth unto everlasting life, which the Son of Man hath power to give unto you; for him hath God the Father sealed.*

As jackals devour their prey and are no longer ravished by the pangs of hunger; as wolves drink in the blood and gulp down the torn flesh of sheep to sate their ravenous appetites; and as oxen in their stalls are satisfied by the fodder put before them, so those who now confront Jesus had filled their bellies at his table and now desired to repeat the process.

'Give us corn without sowing, harvests without reaping, bread without baking. No longer need we labor at our oars and struggle with our nets when two small fish, at the Messiah's touch, will feed thousands. The Deliverer is here; he will feed us as Moses fed our fathers. Give us loaves and fishes forever, and in thy beneficent goodness add raisins and oil and wine to our diet. Surely we shall now feast more sumptuously than Herod himself.'

For them the whole point of the miracle of the loaves was lost. Their need was to keep his sayings, to feast upon the words of Christ, to drink from the Eternal Fountain. Loaves and fishes perish, but there is a food which is eternal, "which endureth unto everlasting life." This is the food he is prepared to give them; it is the everlasting word, the word of truth, the gospel of salvation. As the woman of Samaria was invited to drink living water and never thirst more; so they were invited to eat living bread and never hunger more. This bread was available, without money and without price, from the Son of Man, "for him hath God the Father sealed." Or in other words: "Him hath God the Father marked out or authenticated as his only Son; that is, he is the One, chosen, appointed, and *openly approved* (by unnumbered signs and evidences) to give the spiritual meat which endureth to everlasting life, for he is the Son of that holy Man who is the Father." (*Commentary* 1:351.)[2]

That Jesus' words—profound and deep as we might at first blush assume them to be—were understood by his Jewish hearers is perfectly clear from their response. It was the practice of all the Rabbis to speak in metaphors, and all the people were extensively schooled in understanding their hidden sayings.[3] Jesus' words meant, to them, that there was some added "labor" to be performed, something more than all the rituals and performances of their Mosaic system, if they were to gain eternal blessings. "What shall we do, that we might work the works of God?" they asked. 'What do you require of us more than we are already doing?'

His answer came back with all the authority and finality of Jehovah, speaking amid the fires and thunder of Sinai; his answering words were driven into their hearts with all the power of logic and divine wisdom. They were at the heart and core and center of true worship. There was indeed something more they must do; God their Father required it of them; it was, in fact, the very foundation upon which all else rested. He said:

> *This is the work of God, that ye believe on him whom he hath sent.*

"Believe on the Lord Jesus Christ, and thou shalt be saved." (Acts 16:31.)

"If thou shalt confess with thy mouth the Lord Jesus, and shalt believe in thine heart that God hath raised him from the dead, thou shalt be saved." (Rom. 10:9.)

This is the work of God! "This is my work and my glory—to bring to pass the immortality and eternal life of man." (Moses 1:39.)

"Jesus Christ . . . hath abolished death, and hath brought

life and immortality to light through the gospel." (2 Tim. 1:10.)

'Believe in Christ; believe that I am he; believe my gospel; give heed to the doctrines I have taught from Dan to Beersheba; this is the will of God concerning you.'

They knew the meaning of his words, but, in spite of all that had happened, they did not believe in their hearts that he was the one who would break the bands of death and bring life and immortality to all men. If he were what he claimed to be, let him prove his divinity. "What sign shewest thou then, that we may see, and believe thee? what dost thou work?"[4] Let him expand the miracle of the loaves until it fulfilled their tradition of what the Messiah would do. What was one meal as compared to a continual diet of heavenly food? Their tradition was that their Messiah would bring again manna from heaven. "For, all that the first deliverer Moses had done, the second—Messiah—would also do. And here, over their Synagogue, was the pot of manna—symbol of what God had done, earnest of what the Messiah would do: that pot of manna, which was now among the things hidden, but which Elijah, when he came, would restore again!

"Here, then, was a real sign. In their view the events of yesterday must lead up to some such sign, if they had any real meaning. They had been told to believe on Him, as the One authenticated by God with the seal of truth, and Who would give them meat to eternal life. By what sign would Christ corroborate His assertion, that they might see and believe? What work would He do to vindicate His claim?" (Edersheim 2:29-30.)

"Our fathers did eat manna in the desert; as it is written, He gave them bread from heaven to eat," they said. (John 6:31.) "To understand the reasoning of the Jews, implied but not fully expressed, as also the answer of Jesus, it is necessary to bear in mind . . . that it was the oft and most anciently expressed opinion that, although God had given them this bread out of heaven, yet it was given through the merits of Moses, and ceased with his death." (Edersheim 2:30.)

Up to this point in this discussion, the name of Moses has not been used either by Jesus or the Jews—only a reference to the manna that came from God that all concerned knew to have been in the days of Moses. Jesus, however, aware of their tradition that the manna had come "through the merits of Moses," now affirms:

> *Verily, verily, I say unto you, Moses gave you not that bread from heaven; but my Father giveth you the true bread from heaven.*

'Think not that Moses, through any merit of his own, gave manna to Israel; it was I, Jehovah, who so blessed my people. But now the Father himself, who is Lord above all, gives you the Eternal Bread.'

> *For the bread of God is he which cometh down from heaven, and giveth life unto the world.*

Again we must be aware of the Jewish tradition. It was that though their fathers had eaten manna, such was a figure of something greater. In their view: "The real bread from heaven was the Law." (Edersheim 2:30.) And so again those in conversation with Jesus could not have done other than suppose he was offering them something in addition to what they already had, something in addition to the law of Moses with all its rituals and performances. If such newly offered bread was to give "life unto the world"—and be it remembered that he is the life and the light of men, and that it is his gospel which brings life and immortality to light—if the offered bread was to bring life, surely they wanted such a reward. And so they said: "Lord, evermore give us this bread." Then came the great pronouncement:

> *I am the bread of life: he that cometh to me shall never hunger; and he that believeth on me shall never thirst.*

Salvation is in Christ; in one way or another the message goes forth. He is the bread that men must eat. They must feast upon his word. Those who do so shall be filled with the Holy Ghost.

But I said unto you, That ye also have seen me, and believe not.

O that they had believed in him! O that all men today might believe in him—believe in him as he is revealed and made known by the apostles and prophets whom he has sent forth to testify of his goodness and grace for this present day! And all who do believe shall receive the rewards of which he now speaks:

All that the Father giveth me shall come to me; and him that cometh to me I will in no wise cast out.

For I came down from heaven, not to do mine own will, but the will of him that sent me.

And this is the Father's will which hath sent me, that of all which he hath given me I should lose nothing, but should raise it up again at the last day.

And this is the will of him that sent me, that every one which seeth the Son, and believeth on him, may have everlasting life: and I will raise him up in the resurrection of the just.

Thus does Jesus bear testimony of his own divine Sonship and of that salvation which comes because of his atoning sacrifice. He is the Son of God. He came to do the will of the Father. All those who are given him by the Father shall be saved. All who believe in him shall have eternal life. He will raise them up in the resurrection of the just.

The testimony he bears is true; the witness he gives cannot be denied; the doctrine he teaches shall stand forever. How truth is flowing forth this day, direct from the great Fountain Head.

He looks! and ten thousands of angels rejoice,
And myriads wait for his word;
He speaks! and eternity, filled with his voice,
Re-echoes the praise of the Lord.[5]

But there are those who will not eat though the banquet tables are heaped high with the bounties of life; there are those who will not drink though the streams of living water overflow their banks; there are those who will not believe though God himself, by his own voice, teaches and testifies. Many of them are in Jairus's synagogue this day. They murmur; they complain; they find fault. They are offended because he said, "I am the bread which came down from heaven."

Above all, they are galled and embittered over his claim of divine Sonship. This always is the chief rock of offense and the main stone of stumbling for rebellious people. "Is not this Jesus, the son of Joseph, whose father and mother we know? how is it then that he saith, I come down from heaven?"

"Jesus never met these murmurs about His supposed parentage and place of birth by revealing to the common crowds the high mystery of His earthly origin." It sufficed for them to hear the witness borne that he was the Son of the Highest; let the details of his coming be reserved for those whose spiritual stature would enable them to receive the mysteries of godliness. These murmurings, as with all those that are forthcoming from rebellious people, were met "by a stronger, fuller, clearer declaration of the very truth which they rejected." (Farrar, p. 318.) To their seething sayings Jesus responded:

> *Murmur not among yourselves. No man can come unto me, except he doeth the will of my Father who hath sent me. And this is the will of him who hath sent me, that ye receive the Son; for the Father beareth record of him; and he who receiveth the testimony, and doeth the will of him who sent me, I will raise up in the resurrection of the just.*

Again the witness borne is plain, clear, and without ambiguity. He is the Son of God, and he so certifies, both in metaphors that their Jewish training permits them to understand, and in plain words that their Jewish disbelief will not let them misunderstand. He continues:

> *It is written in the prophets, And they shall be all taught of God. Every man therefore that hath heard, and hath learned of the Father, cometh unto me.*

'But ye receive not my Father, and shall not be found in his kingdom, for no man can receive the Father except he first receive the Son whom the Father hath sent. And ye shall be condemned by your own prophets, for they have written of the righteous, And they shall all be taught by God. Now ye are not taught by God, neither do ye know him, nor his truths, nor his laws, for ye receive not him whom the Father hath sent into the world. Every man therefore that heareth and believeth the words of the Son shall thereby come unto the Father also, and such shall be taught by the Holy Spirit sent forth from God to bear record of the Father and the Son.'

Not that any man hath seen the Father, save he which is of God, he hath seen the Father.

'Think not because the prophets have written of the righteous, And they shall all be taught of God, that ye shall see him or be taught by him, except ye repent and believe in the Son. For no man shall see the Father except the Son and he to whom the Son shall reveal him; yea, only those who are born of God shall see the Father, for no others can enter his presence.'

Verily, verily, I say unto you, He that believeth on me hath everlasting life.

'Solemnly and soberly I say unto you, He that believeth in me as the very Son of God, and who receiveth my gospel, obeying all the laws and ordinances thereof, and who endureth in righteousness and truth unto the end, behold, he shall have everlasting life, which is exaltation in my Father's kingdom.' (*Commentary* 1:356.)

Eating His Flesh and Drinking His Blood

(*John 6:48-59; JST, John 6:48-50, 54-55*)

We come now to the crowning teaching of the sermon on the bread of life, which is, that men are saved by eating the flesh and drinking the blood of the Son of God. With this proclamation, Jesus pushes back the walls of the synagogue so that his words go forth to all men on all the earth in all ages. His teachings are not alone for a handful of Galileans, not alone for the few million Jews who knew the meaning of the imagery used, but for all men of all nations no matter when or where they live. Eating the flesh and drinking the blood of Him who came down from heaven to shed his blood and mar his flesh is a mystery that can only be understood by the saints as they are enlightened by the power of the Spirit.

At this point in the sermon, Jesus raises the metaphors he is using—those figures of speech which suggest a resemblance of one thing to another—raises them into a gospel similitude. Our Jewish friends of old understood fully the metaphors—"the metaphors which Jesus used had not, to an educated Jew, one-hundredth part of the strangeness which they have to us" (Farrar, p. 319)—but these same Jewish religionists rejected outright the similitude which he offered them. We, on the other hand, with a little training can understand the imagery he uses, and we must accept and apply the similitude if we are to be saved. If we may be permitted to paraphrase the words of Paul relative to the eternal nature of the gospel, we might say: "For unto us was the gospel preached, as well as unto them: but the word preached did not profit them, not being mixed with faith in them that heard it." (Heb. 4:2.) And so Jesus continues:

> *I am that bread of life. This is the bread which cometh down from heaven, that a man may eat thereof; and not die. Your fathers did eat manna in the wilderness, and are dead.*
>
> *I am the living bread which came down from heaven: if any man eat of this bread, he shall live for ever: and the bread that I will give is my flesh, which I will give for the life of the world.*

The bread of life, of life eternal, living bread, the bread which came down from heaven—such is the language he uses to describe himself; and since his body is one of flesh and blood, to eat the heavensent bread, men must eat his flesh, the flesh he "will give for the life of the world," the flesh to be broken in his infinite and eternal atoning sacrifice. Knowing what Jesus' words meant but being wholly unable to understand how they applied to salvation and to the works they must do to gain eternal life, the Jews "strove among themselves, saying, How can this man give us his flesh to eat?" Then Jesus said:

> *Verily, verily, I say unto you, Except ye eat the flesh of the Son of man, and drink his blood, ye have no life in you.*
>
> *Whoso eateth my flesh, and drinketh my blood, hath eternal life; and I will raise him up in the resurrection of the just at the last day. For my flesh is meat indeed, and my blood is drink indeed.*

"To eat the flesh and drink the blood of the Son of God is, first, to accept him in the most literal and full sense, with no reservation whatever, as the personal offspring in the flesh of the Eternal Father; and, secondly, it is to keep the commandments of the Son by accepting his gospel, joining his Church, and enduring in obedience and righteousness unto the end. Those who by this course eat his flesh and drink his blood shall have eternal life, meaning exaltation in the highest heaven of the celestial world. Speaking of ancient Israel, for instance, Paul says: *They 'did all eat the same spiritual meat; And did all drink the same spiritual drink: for they drank of that spiritual Rock that followed them: and that Rock was Christ.'* (1 Cor. 10:3-4.)

"In the waters of baptism the saints take upon themselves the name of Christ (that is, they accept him fully and completely as the Son of God and the Savior of men), and they then covenant to keep his commandments and obey his laws. (Mosiah 18:7-10.) To keep his saints in constant remembrance of their obligation to accept and obey him—or in other words, to eat his flesh and drink his blood—the Lord has given them the sacramental ordinance. This ordinance, performed in remembrance of his broken flesh and spilled blood, is the means provided for men, formally and repeatedly, to assert their belief in the divinity of

Christ, and to affirm their determination to serve him and keep his commandments; or, in other words, in this ordinance—in a spiritual, but not a literal sense—men eat his flesh and drink his blood. Hence, after instituting the sacramental ordinance among the Nephites, Jesus commanded: 'Ye shall not suffer any one knowingly to partake of my flesh and blood unworthily, when ye shall minister it; For whoso eateth and drinketh my flesh and blood unworthily eateth and drinketh damnation to his soul; therefore if ye know that a man is unworthy to eat and drink of my flesh and blood ye shall forbid him.' (3 Ne. 18:28-29.)" (*Commentary* 1:358-59.)

And then finally:

He that eateth my flesh, and drinketh my blood, dwelleth in me, and I in him.

As the living Father hath sent me, and I live by the Father: so he that eateth me, even he shall live by me.

This is the bread which came down from heaven: not as your fathers did eat manna, and are dead: he that eateth of this bread shall live for ever.

The message is now delivered to the Jews and to us. The meaning is clear; the doctrine is strong; the effects of the teaching—either belief or disbelief; obedience or disobedience; eternal life or eternal death—such are now in the hands of those who have heard the message. And that the message may live anew in our hearts, we are commanded to go to the house of prayer on the Lord's day and there partake of the sacramental emblems, offered to us in similitude of the spilt blood and broken flesh of Him whose blood we must drink and whose flesh we must eat, if we are to be his and have life with him as he has life with his Father.

Jesus Winnows the Grain

(*John 6:60-71; JST, John 6:65*)

"One mightier than I cometh," proclaimed the blessed Baptist. 'He comes to baptize with fire and confer the unspeakable gift of the Holy Ghost; to take away the sins of the world; to save and exalt the sons of men! He comes to preach the gospel to the poor; to proclaim liberty to the captives, and the opening of the prison doors to them that are bound! He comes to be lifted up upon the cross, and, even as he has been lifted up of men, to draw all men to him on conditions of repentance! He comes to seek that which is lost and to save all those who will believe his words and live his law.'

"One mightier than I cometh," is the divine word of our Lord's Elias. 'He comes not to condemn the world, but that the world through him might be saved. His reward is with him and his work before him. He is the Savior of all men, especially of those who believe; and all who believe in him, who feast upon his words, who keep his commandments—who eat his flesh and drink his blood—shall have eternal life.'

But he cannot save those who believe and obey without also damning those who disbelieve and disobey. If men are freed from sin and saved from eternal torment by obedience to his word, on the one hand, they are also left in the bondage of sin—bound by the chains of hell—by disobedience to his law, on the other. If they put off the natural man and become clean by the power of the Holy Ghost, they also remain carnal, sensual, and devilish if that sanctifying power never enters their souls. And so, though he came to save, with all the righteous being rewarded, the effect of his coming is that the wicked shall be damned because they are not saved.

And so: "One mightier than I cometh," saith the Baptist, "Whose fan is in his hand, and he will throughly purge his floor, and will gather the wheat into his garner; but the chaff he will burn with fire unquenchable." (Luke 3:16-17.)

The Coming One—Jesus, our Blessed Lord—has now come; and in this sermon on the bread of life, as never before in his ministry, he has taken the winnowing fan of judgment in his hand to blow the chaff from the wheat. He is sifting out the hearts of men before his judgment seat. The eternal harvest has begun and shall not cease until the threshing floor of the world is thoroughly purged, with every straw of chaff blown away, leaving only the wheat to be garnered into a heavenly granary. And the chaff he will burn with fire unquenchable! So prophesied the Baptist, and the fulfillment is a matter of record this day in Capernaum.

"The Baptist had spoken of the fan in the hand of his great successor: this discourse was the realization of the figure. Those who had hoped to find a popular political leader in Him saw their dreams melt away: those who had no true sympathy for His life and words had an excuse for leaving Him. None who were not bound to Him by sincere loyalty and devotion had any longer a motive for following Him. Fierce patriotism burning for insurrection, mean self-interest seeking worldly advantage, and vulgar curiosity craving excitement, were equally disappointed. It was the first vivid instance of 'the offence of the Cross'—henceforth to become the special stumbling-block of the nation.

"The wishes and hopes of the crowds who had called themselves disciples had proved self-deceptions. They expected from the Messiah quite other favors than the identity of spiritual nature symbolized by the eating of His flesh and drinking His blood. The bloody death implied in the metaphor was in direct contradiction to all their ideas. A lowly and suffering Messiah thus unmistakably set before them was revolting to their national pride and gross material tastes. 'We have heard out of the law,' said some, a little later, 'that the Christ abideth for ever, and how sayest thou the Son of man must be "lifted up"—that is, crucified?' 'That be far from Thee, Lord: this shall not be unto Thee,' said even Peter almost at the last, when he heard from his Master's lips of the Cross, so near at hand.

"The Messiah of popular conception would use force to establish His kingdom, but Jesus, while claiming the Messiahship, spoke only of self-sacrifice. Outward glory and material wealth were the national dream: he spoke only of inward purity. If He would not head them with Almighty power, to get Judea for the Jews, they would not have Him. Their idea of the kingdom of God was the exact opposite of His." (Geikie, p. 520.)

"There is a teaching which is, and is intended to be, not only instructive but probationary; of which the immediate purpose is not only to *teach*, but to *test*. Such had been the object of this memorable discourse. To comprehend it rightly required an effort not only of the understanding, but also of the will. It was *meant* to put an end to the merely selfish hopes of that 'rabble of obtrusive chiliasts' whose irreverent devotion was a mere cloak for worldliness; it was *meant* also to place before the Jewish authorities words which they were too full of hatred and materialism to understand. But its sifting power went deeper than this. Some even of the disciples found the saying harsh and repulsive." (Farrar, p. 321.)

"This is an hard saying; who can hear it?" said the disciples. 'Must we indeed forsake the law of Moses—which the Rabbis say is the bread which came down from heaven—and center all our hope of salvation in this One Man? Is he alone to replace all of the teachings and ordinances of our fathers? Must we forsake the whole past, feast upon his words, eat his flesh and drink his blood to gain eternal life? Is there no other way?'

Knowing "in himself that his disciples murmured" at his teachings, Jesus said: "Doth this offend you?" And offend them it did, for even they—even those who believed he was more than a man; who believed he was sent of the Father to teach truth and perform miracles; who believed that he was the One of whom Moses and the prophets had spoken—even they had not yet purged themselves of all their old Jewish notions about a temporal Messiah. Even they—receiving truth line upon line, precept upon precept, here a little and there a little, as all men must—even they were not prepared to turn away from Moses and the law and believe that salvation came in the person of the one who now invited them to eat his flesh and drink his blood.

Jesus' reaction to their unbelief—their lack of full conversion—was normal and what we have come to expect of him. He reaffirmed the truth of his sayings—there must be no wavering or doubt in any believer's mind—and spoke of even greater witnesses that were yet to come.

What and if ye shall see the Son of man ascend up where he was before?

'If ye cannot believe my sayings that I am the living Bread which came down from heaven to give life to men, what will ye think when ye see me ascend up into heaven to sit on the right hand of my Father and reign with almighty power forever?'

It is the spirit that quickeneth; the flesh profiteth nothing: the words that I speak unto you, they are spirit, and they are life. But there are some of you that believe not.

'All these things which I have spoken unto you are spiritual and lead to eternal life, and they can only be understood by those who are spiritually enlightened. The Spirit must quicken your understanding if you are to comprehend the things of God. No man by his own intellect and reason can understand the things of the Spirit; the wisdom of the world, standing alone, profiteth nothing in comprehending the things of God. And there are some among you who rely on your own wisdom rather than the whisperings of the Spirit, and as a consequence some of you believe not my words.' (*Commentary* 1:362.)

At this point John, in whose writings alone are all these deep and wondrous sayings preserved, says by way of explanation: "For Jesus knew from the beginning who they were that believed not, and who should betray him." Jesus continues:

Therefore said I unto you, that no man can come unto me, except he doeth the will of my Father who hath sent me.

'And he said, It was for this reason that I said unto you, that no man can come unto me, except he doeth the will of my Father who hath sent me, for only those who do the will of my Father by keeping the commandments can receive the Spirit which shall bear record to them that all things which I have said about myself are true.' (*Commentary* 1:362.)

"From that time many of his disciples went back, and walked no more with him." The teaching which was intended to be not only instructive but also probationary had served its purpose. "By the simple expedient of teaching strong doctrine to the hosts who followed him, Jesus was able to separate the chaff from the wheat and choose out those who were worthy of membership in his earthly kingdom. . . . Unable to believe and accept his strong and plain assertions about eating his flesh and drinking his blood, even many classified as disciples fell away. And this process of sifting, trial, and testing was to continue with increasing intensity for the final climactic year of his mortal ministry." (*Commentary* 1:361.)

No doubt among the disciples who fell away were both believing investigators and those who had committed themselves by covenant, made in the waters of baptism, to love and serve him all their days. The test of strong doctrine is given to truth seekers both before and after they enter the Church. "This testing and sifting process has ever been part of the Lord's system. Men have been placed on earth to be tried and tested, 'to see if they will do all things whatsoever the Lord their God shall command them.' (Abr. 3:25.) After they accept the gospel and join the Church, this testing process continues, indeed, is often intensified. 'I have decreed in my heart, saith the Lord, that I will prove you in all things, whether you will abide in my covenant, even unto death, that you may be found worthy. For if ye will not abide in my covenant ye are not worthy of me.' (D&C 98:14-15.)" (*Commentary* 1:361.)[6]

"And so this was the great crisis in the History of the Christ. We have traced the gradual growth and development of the popular movement, till the murder of the Baptist stirred popular feeling to its inmost depth. With his death it seemed as if the Messianic hope, awakened by his preaching and testimony to Christ, were fading from view. It was a terrible disappointment, not easily borne. Now must it be decided, whether Jesus was really the Messiah. His Works, notwithstanding what the Pharisees said, seemed to prove it. Then let it appear; let it come, stroke upon stroke—each louder and more effective than the other—till the land rang with the shout of victory and the world itself re-echoed it. And so it seemed. That miraculous feeding—that wilderness cry of Hosanna to the Galilean King-Messiah from the thousands of Galilean voices—what were they but its beginning?

"All the greater was the disappointment: first, in the repression of the movement—so to speak, the retreat of the Messiah, His voluntary abdication, rather, His defeat; then, next day [or shortly thereafter, as we shall set forth in chapter 59], the incongruousness of a King, Whose few unlearned followers, in their ignorance and un-Jewish neglect of most sacred ordinances, outraged every Jewish feeling, and whose conduct was even vindicated by their Master in a general attack on all traditionalism, that basis of Judaism—as it might be represented, to the contempt of religion and even of common truthfulness in the denunciation of solemn vows! This was not the Messiah Whom the many—nay, Whom almost any—would own.

"Here, then, we are at the parting of the two ways; and, just because it was the hour of decision, did Christ so clearly set forth the highest truths concerning Himself, in opposition to the views which the multitude entertained about the Messiah." (Edersheim 2:35-36.)

"Then said Jesus unto the twelve, Will ye also go away? Then Simon Peter answered him, Lord, to whom shall we go? thou hast the words of eternal life. And we believe and are sure that thou art that Christ, the Son of the living God."

Peter knew; the Twelve knew (Judas only, perhaps, excepted); Mary Magdalene, who is identified by name as a traveling companion of Jesus and the Twelve, knew; many other disciples, both men and women, knew—and their knowledge came by revelation from the Holy Spirit of God. Only those who have the testimony of Jesus, which is the spirit of prophecy; only those who are in tune with the Infinite by the power of the Spirit; only those whose souls are alive with the light and truth of heaven, who hunger and thirst after righteousness, who love the Lord and keep his commandments—these only can withstand the buffetings and trials of life and drink in the strong doctrine that saves souls.

"*Thou hast the words of eternal life.*" The words of light and truth which chart the course and mark the way—these come from Christ. These words, and these only, lead to eternal life in his Father's kingdom. Only those—having opportunity so to do—who believe the words of eternal life in this world shall gain eternal glory in the world to come.

"*We believe and are sure.*" 'Our testimony comes by the power of the Spirit. Doubt and uncertainty are as foreign to us as the gibberish of alien tongues. The voice of the Spirit has spoken to our spirits. We are sure. There is absolute certainty in our souls.'

"*Thou art that Christ, the Son of the living God.*" 'Whatever notions the dissembling multitude may have about a Messiah and Deliverer who wears a coat of armor and wields a sword of vengeance; whatever the hungering hosts may believe as to a Messiah who will feed us daily from heaven as our fathers were fed; however others may choose to follow the traditions of the past and adhere to the letter of a dead law, rather than believe that salvation comes by you—no matter what others say or do, to us thou art "that Christ" who of old was promised, who is "the Son of the living God." '

"*Lord, to whom shall we go?*" How well Peter spoke! Where else can true disciples ever go to find peace in this life and a hope of eternal life in the world to come? The truth is with the saints; the gospel saves; light and revelation are shed forth upon the Lord's people. Where can a dissembling disciple go but to darkness and death and damnation?

"It is thus, also, that many of us, whose thoughts may have been sorely tossed, and whose foundations terribly assailed, may have found our first resting-place in the assured, unassailable spiritual experience of the past. Whither can we go for Words of Eternal Life, if not to Christ? If He fails us, then all hope of the Eternal is gone. But He *has* the Words of Eternal life—and we believed when they first came to us; nay, we know that He is the Holy One of God. And this conveys all that faith needs for further learning. The rest will He show, when He is transfigured in our sight." (Edersheim 2:36.)

Then, as a sad denouement to a sermon that had severed the sunshine disciples and the fair-weather friends from those who were steeled to withstand the storms of life, Jesus said: "Have not I chosen you twelve, and one of you is a devil?" And then our apostolic author adds: "He spake of Judas Iscariot the son of Simon: for he it was that should betray him, being one of the twelve."

From this hour our Lord's life was charted in the course leading to the cross. Heretofore the common people had heard him gladly, however much their teachers and rulers had assailed his teachings and ridiculed his miracles. Now he was sifting out the hearts of men—believers and unbelievers alike—and most were failing the test. "The greater the popular expectancy and disappointment had been, the greater the reaction and the enmity that followed. The hour of decision was past, and the hand on the dial pointed to the hour of His Death." (Edersheim 2:36.)

NOTES

1. Nephi's related statement is, "feasting upon the word of Christ," such being the bread from heaven of which all men must eat if they are to hear the heavenly voice acclaim: "Ye shall have eternal life." (2 Ne. 31:20.)

2. These words—"him hath God the Father sealed"—"which seem almost inexplicable in this connection," as Edersheim notes, "become clear when we remember that this was a well-known Jewish expression. According to the Rabbis, 'the seal of God was *Truth*.' . . . Thus the words of Christ would convey to His hearers that for the real meat, which would

endure to eternal life—for the better Messianic banquet—they must come to Him, because God had impressed upon Him His own seal of truth, and so authenticated His Teaching and Mission." (Edersheim 2:28-29.)

3. "The idea of eating, as a metaphor for receiving spiritual benefit, was familiar to Christ's hearers, and was as readily understood as our expressions of 'devouring a book,' or 'drinking in' instruction. In Isaiah 3:1, the words 'the whole stay of bread,' were explained by the Rabbis as referring to their own teaching, and they laid it down as a rule, that wherever, in Ecclesiastes, allusion was made to food or drink, it meant study of the Law, and the practice of good works. It was a saying among them—'In the time of the Messiah the Israelites will be fed by Him.' Nothing was more common in the schools and synagogues than the phrases of eating and drinking, in a metaphorical sense. 'Messiah is not likely to come to Israel,' said Hillel, 'for they have already eaten Him'—that is, greedily received His words—'in the days of Hezekiah.' A current conventionalism in the synagogues was that the just would 'eat the Shekinah.' It was peculiar to the Jews to be taught in such metaphorical language. Their Rabbis never spoke in plain words." (Geikie, p. 519.)

4. "Moses had given them manna from heaven; Jesus as yet—they hinted—had only given them barley-loaves of earth. But if He were the true Messiah, was He not, according to all the legends of their nation, to enrich and crown them, and to banquet them on pomegranates from Eden, and 'a vineyard of red wine,' and upon the flesh of Behemoth and Leviathan, and the great bird Bar Juchne?" (Farrar, p. 317.)

5. "Redeemer of Israel," *Hymns*, no. 195.

6. "In this dispensation, the promulgation of the law of plural marriage had an effect similar to the presentation of the doctrine of the Bread of Life in the meridian dispensation. Opposition from without the Church increased, while some unstable members of the kingdom itself found themselves unable to accept the fulness of the revealed program of the Lord. There were many important reasons why the Lord revealed the doctrine of plurality of wives. But if plural marriage had served no other purpose than to sift the chaff from the wheat, than to keep the unstable and semi-faithful people from the fulness of gospel blessings, it would have been more than justified." (*Commentary* 1:361-62.)

THE DISCOURSE UPON CLEANLINESS

The Jews were a stiffnecked people; . . .
because of their blindness, which blindness came
by looking beyond the mark, they must needs fall.
(Jacob 4:14.)

Because of priestcrafts and iniquities,
they at Jerusalem will stiffen their necks
against him, that he be crucified.
(2 Ne. 10:5.)

Priestcrafts are that men preach
and set themselves up
for a light unto the world,
that they may get gain and praise of the world;
but they seek not the welfare of Zion.
(2 Ne. 26:29.)

"What Concord Hath Christ with Belial?"[1]

It is the hour of the third Passover—the third Passover time during the ministry of the Mortal Messiah when all the sons of the law are commanded to go up to Jerusalem and appear before the Lord in his holy house.

It is the set time for all Israel to eat a paschal lamb, every family by itself apart—in remembrance of their deliverance from the bondage of Egypt; as a token that they have forsaken the world and chosen to live apart from other nations, as a people dedicated to the service of Jehovah; and in similitude of the promised sacrifice of the Lamb of God who cometh to take away the sins of the world.

It is the appointed time for the chosen people to renew their covenants with Jehovah, to pledge anew their allegiance to the God of their fathers, and to step forth in a newness of life. Out of these eight days—the days of the Feast of the Passover and of the Feast of Unleavened Bread—will come a renewed determination to honor Moses and keep his law; and with this refurbishing of the Israelite way of life will come also a reborn determination to oppose every force or person that challenges their law and threatens their traditions.

There is no indication that Jesus went from Capernaum to Jerusalem with the zealous throngs of Galilean pilgrims. Apparently he did not because it was a time when the Jews sought to kill him. Nor can we tell whether the Twelve took leave of the Master or not, whether they went to the City of the Great King to keep the not-yet-fulfilled law of Moses. But this much seems clear: After this Passover the rulers from Jerusalem—who heretofore had appointed spies and informers to dog his every footstep and overhear his every word—these priest-ridden rulers now sent new delegations to spy and to confront and to contend. Their zeal to oppose that which threatened their craft had been reborn in the emotion and worship at the Passover.

And so it is also an hour of sorrow and darkness—an hour in which the sifting process begun with the sermon on the bread of life will continue, will, indeed, rise in a mighty crescendo until, a year hence, a chorus of cries will chant "Crucify him, crucify him," and will contaminate forever the land and the people.

It is also an hour of crises, of the parting of the ways, of the division of a people. Heretofore virulence and hatred have been somewhat limited; only the rulers of the people have thirsted for his blood. Now the spirit of darkness and death is beginning to brood over whole cities and areas; whole multitudes are infected with the virus of apostasy and persecution and destruction. It is an hour when we shall see tribes and congregations, blinded by priestcrafts and looking beyond the mark, join with their rulers to oppose the Cause of truth and righteousness.

"*Looking beyond the mark*!" Such was the sin of the whole nation. Preserved from Egyptian bondage by the miracle at the Red Sea; born as a people during forty years of wilderness wanderings; entering their promised land when Joshua led them over Jordan; serving Jehovah as directed by their judges and prophets, Israel, the chosen seed, had been bathed in the light and revelation of heaven. They once knew the will of Jehovah; they once had the law of Moses in all its beauty and perfection; they once walked as pleased their Maker. But now—after the Babylonian captivity; after the long night of alien domination; after a long period without revelation; after an apostate era in which traditions and legends had become more important than the eternal word recorded in their scriptures—now, after such a period, they were looking beyond the mark. They had added to the ancient law a maze of tradition and legend. They had created ordinances and performances and rituals that had no foundation in revealed writ. They were doing more than need be done in the way of rituals and performances. Like Nadab and Abihu they were offering strange fires upon their altars. They were looking beyond the mark; salvation did not come in the way they supposed; it was not the outgrowth of their ritualistic absurdities; it came in a much easier and simpler way.

"I press toward the mark," Paul says, "for the prize of the high calling of God in Christ Jesus." (Philip. 3:14.) That too was all that the Jews needed to do; they must center their affection on the Messiah who ministered among them, not on the myriad ordinances and performances that had been added to what Moses gave them.

"Priestcrafts and iniquities!" These were at the root of their problem. Their rulers had developed an oral law that surpassed in importance the word of Jehovah given on Sinai; traditions became more important than truth; and personal righteousness faded away. It was an hour when men loved darkness rather than light because their deeds were evil. Priestcrafts and iniquities! It was an hour of persecution and rebellion, of darkness and dire days ahead.

Persecution is one of the chief weapons in the hands of false priests; they use it to preserve their false religions. Truth stands on its own; error must be defended by the sword. False ministers fear the truth because by it their crafts are in danger. They practice priestcrafts to get gain and the praise of the world, neither of which will be theirs if true religion sweeps them into a deserved oblivion. It is with them as it was with Demetrius, the silversmith, who made silver shrines for the worship of Diana. When Paul preached the gospel in Ephesus, "saying that they be no gods, which are made with hands," Demetrius responded by proclaiming that by such teaching, "not only this our craft is in danger to be set at nought; but also that the temple of the great goddess Diana should be despised, and her magnificence should be destroyed, whom all Asia and the world worshippeth." (Acts 19:21-41.) Similarly, if Jesus' new and revolutionary doctrines prevail, what would become of the priests and Levites? If publicans and fishermen become the new preachers, what of the scribes and Rabbis?

Persecutors can always justify—in their own minds—their own destructive courses. Those who raised their voices against Jesus; who testified falsely of his teachings; who sought to destroy his influence with the people—all such were doing what seemed right to them in their own minds. Nearly all propositions can be sustained to some extent or other, with arguments and reasons, when intellectuality and not spirituality is the governing standard.

With reference to Jesus the question, then, is not simply "Why was he persecuted?"—for the basic answer to that is the evil that dwelt in the hearts of the people—but, "How did they rationalize their conduct? What intellectual reasons did they give to make it seem that what they were doing was the will of him whom they supposed they worshipped?" From the Jewish standpoint, Jesus was persecuted—and finally slain—for what were, to them, three perfectly valid reasons:

1. *They said, falsely, that he was a sinner.*

This is, in fact, a perfectly valid premise, not for persecution but at least for rejection. Nothing justifies persecution; but if he were a sinner, he could not be the Messiah, the Holy One of Israel, the one sent of God to deliver his people. The Messianic prophecies foretold of a Messiah in whose mouth there would be no deceit; who would bring truth and light and gospel knowledge to his people; who would qualify as a light and a guide to all men.[2] If Jesus was a deceiver; if he was misleading the people; if his doctrine would damn rather than save—then he must be unmasked; his lies must be revealed; his iniquities must be made manifest. And it was then the duty of the Sanhedrin to bring his hidden evils and his false doctrines to light.

There is no question about the concept that the Messiah would rise above carnal things and not wallow in the mire of iniquity. The issue at hand was whether Jesus himself was a sinner or not. One day soon, facing this problem squarely, and aware of his own sinless life, he will issue the challenge, "Which of you convinceth me of sin?" (John 8:46.) At this point we need only recount why they contended he was a sinner, and the mere recitation of their reasons will suffice for us—though, in fairness, we must admit, not for them—to show the shallow and baseless nature of their reasoning.

There were some minor complaints that he was a glutton and a winebibber, because he ate and drank as others did; there was the charge that he and his disciples did not abide by the Pharisaic law of the fast; and there was considerable murmuring because he consorted with publicans and sinners, eating with them in their banquets, calling a prominent publican as one of the Twelve, and permitting a fallen woman to anoint his feet with oil. But all of this was of no great moment, and certainly would not suffice to raise a public hue and cry against him.

There were, however, two major activities that incensed and enraged the rulers of the people and the molders of public opinion. Both of these were violations of their traditions—not of any basic laws imposed by Deity, but the traditions of the elders—and both, in the eyes of the people, warranted the death penalty. One was his repeated Sabbath violations, as they supposed, and the other was the matter of eating with unwashen hands and the many formalities related thereto.

As to his Sabbath violations, and those of the disciples, we have already noted some of the traditions involved and have seen the discomfiture of his detractors when they challenged his conduct and that of his disciples. While passing through a field of corn on the Sabbath, the disciples plucked some ripened ears, rubbed them in their hands, and blew away the chaff. These acts—considered to be both reaping and threshing—were so criminally offensive and of such a magnitude in Jewish eyes as to call for the death penalty. Jesus defended his disciples by citing the case of David eating the shewbread and announcing that "the sabbath was made for man, and not man for the sabbath," and that the "Son of man is Lord even of the sabbath." (Mark 2:27-28.)

Many times Jesus himself sought occasion to perform miraculous healings on their holy day, as when, at the second Passover, he healed the impotent man at the pool of Bethesda, an act that so enraged the Jews that they sought to kill him; or, as on the occasion in the Galilean synagogue when the question was asked: "Is it lawful to heal on the sabbath days?" and he responded by asking, "Is it lawful to do good on the sabbath days, or to do evil? to save life, or to kill?" and by then saying to a man with a withered hand, "Stretch forth thine hand. And he stretched it out: and his hand was restored whole as the other." (Mark 3:2, 4-5.) And again the Pharisees sought how they might destroy him. In these and other like incidents, as we have seen, it was the violation of the Rabbi-imposed traditions relative to the Sabbath that brought down the wrath of Jewry upon the head of Jesus.

As to the matters of eating with unwashen hands and of avoiding responsibility for parental care by saying, "It is corban," we are about to see the depths to which ritualistic religion can sink. And this time we shall also see an open, almost defiant, break with the whole body of ritualistic absurdities imposed in the name of tradition.

2. *They said, falsely, that he performed his miracles by the power of Beelzebub—nay, more, that he was the Incarnation of Satan.*

"They accounted for the miracles of Christ as wrought by the power of Satan, whose special representative—almost incarnation—they declared Jesus to be. This would not only turn the evidential force of these signs into an argument against Christ, but vindicate the resistance of the Pharisees to His claims." (Edersheim 2:8.) But, as we have also seen, Satan cannot cast out Satan, for a house divided against itself will fall, and the imputation of satanic power still leaves all men with the need to decide whether the Holy Ghost or Satan spake by Jesus' mouth. That each person must determine this for himself is what life is all about; such is the very nature of this probationary estate.

3. *They said, falsely, that he was guilty of blasphemy in claiming equality with God; in testifying that he was the Son of the living God; in teaching that he was God.*

As to this crowning charge we shall have more, much more, to say hereafter. It lies at the heart and core of revealed religion. If our witness is true that he is God's Almighty Son, then salvation is in Christ and his is the only name given under heaven whereby salvation comes. If our witness—and his—is false, and thus blasphemous, then Christianity is a monstrous fraud and fallen man remains unredeemed. If our witness is false, man is still in his sins; there is no reconciliation with God; and the man sick of the palsy to whom he said, "Son, be of good cheer; thy sins be forgiven thee" (Matt. 9:2), remains as sin-stained as he ever was; and, for that matter, if our witness is false, this paralytic did not arise, take up his bed, and go to his own house.

For the present we need only observe that this "last charge against Jesus, which finally decided the action of the Council, could only be fully made at the close of His career. It might be formulated so as to meet the views of either the Pharisees or Sadducees. To the former it might be presented as a blasphemous claim to equality with God—the Very Son of the Living God. To the Sadducees it would appear as a movement on the part of a most dangerous enthusiast—if honest and self-deceived, all the more dangerous; one of those pseudo-Messiahs who led away the ignorant, superstitious, and excitable people; and which, if unchecked, would result in persecutions and terrible vengeance by the Romans, and in loss of the last remnants of their national independence." (Edersheim 2:8-9.)

And so, as we attune our ears to hear the discourse on cleanliness, we are reminded that Jesus has already begun the harvesting process. It started with the sermon on the bread of life. He is winnowing the grain, sifting the chaff from the wheat, garnering the wheat into the granaries of the Lord, and preparing the chaff for fire unquenchable. In the discourse on cleanliness he will identify the chaff, and, sorrowfully, it will consist of the generality of the people. But, joyfully, the harvested wheat, now free from husks and chaff, shall soon go on to the safety and security of the eternal granaries.

Will not Jesus on this day say to the faithful, as it were: "Be ye not unequally yoked together with unbelievers: for what fellowship hath righteousness with unrighteousness? and what communion hath light with darkness? And what concord hath Christ with Belial? or what part hath he that believeth with an infidel? And what agreement hath the temple of God with idols?" (2 Cor. 6:14-16.) The saints of the living God must come out of Babylon, separate themselves from the world, and be saints indeed. The foundations have long since been laid and it no longer suffices for believing disciples to stand with one foot on the sands of tradition and the other on the rock of revealed truth. The house of the Lord, if it is to stand forever, must be built on the rock of eternal truth and upon no other foundation.

The Ceremonial Washings of Rabbinism

(*Mark 7:1-8; JST, Mark 7:4, 7; Matthew 15:1-2, 7-9; JST, Matthew 15:8*)

Heretofore—with some inward revulsion—we have seen what the ritualistic robots of Rabbinism did to the Sabbath day. We have seen how they turned a day of freedom and worship and rejoicing into one of Rabbinical rules and restrictions. No longer were the Jews free to worship the Lord their God with a clear conscience on this holy day. Rather, the restrictions were so rigid, the controls so complete, the prohibitions so profuse, that it was as though man had been made for the Sabbath. Their failures on that day—for no man could keep all of the restrictions involved—created a great guilt complex over the whole nation. In some respects—for them—it was providential that the Sabbath came only one day in seven.

Now—again with some inward revulsion—we turn our attention to the ceremonial washings of Rabbinism; to the daily, almost hourly, ritualistic ablutions which alone, as they supposed, kept uncleanness from their doors. Man cannot eat with unwashen hands and be saved; judgment, mercy, and truth are as nothing compared to the Levitical lavings of the body; ceremonial washings are more important than keeping the commandments! So said the Rabbis, and such were the traditions of the elders, as we shall now see.

It is the time of the third Passover—April of A. D. 29—the time when the people are being refreshed spiritually and built up anew in religious zeal. There is not the slightest intimation that Jesus himself went to Jerusalem to appear before the Lord in his holy house, as he had done twice before during his ministry, and as he will do a year hence when he is to be sacrificed as the eternal Paschal Lamb. Whether the Twelve and the inner circle of disciples went by themselves is questionable. The Passover season was one of three festive occasions during the year when every adult male was expected to worship the Lord in the Holy City, but Jesus and his disciples are now openly breaking with the traditions of the past. It is logical to assume they chose not to face the mob spirit that would have confronted them within the hallowed walls of Herod's Temple.

That the Galileans attending the Passover gave firsthand accounts of our Lord's recent teachings and miracles we cannot doubt. His earlier teachings and miracles would have been well known. But now among all the millions of Passover pilgrims word would have soon spread of the feeding of the five thousand, the walking on the water, the healings in the land of Gennesaret, and the sermon on the bread of life. On previous occasions the chief priests and religious leaders had sent deputations to spy and harass. They must do so again. The prior assaults had been based on claims of Sabbath violations and had carried the charge that he cast out devils and performed miracles by the power of Satan. These assaults had failed. Now they would charge those of the New Order with eating when ceremonially unclean.

As to this ceremonial uncleanness, Mark says simply: "For the Pharisees, and all the Jews, except they wash their hands oft, eat not, holding the tradition of the elders. And when they come from the market, except they wash their bodies, they eat not. And many other things there be, which they have received to hold, as the washing of cups, and pots, brasen vessels, and of tables."

As with the restrictions relative to the Sabbath, so with

their ceremonial washings, volumes could be written reciting the policies, procedures, and absurdities involved. We shall, however, simply sample the source material. It will suffice for our purposes to know that failure to comply with these ceremonial washings ranked with apostasy and murder in criminality. Those so offending were deserving of death in the Rabbinical view, and to openly defy and challenge such sacred ceremonies created an impasse and raised an issue that was not subject to mediation. People either kept the traditions of the elders and retained their Jewish standing, or, failing so to do, they joined the degenerate Gentiles and traveled an irreversible course to a heathen hell.

"The law of Moses required purifications in certain cases, but the Rabbis had perverted the spirit of Leviticus in this, as in other things, for they taught that food and drink could not be taken with a good conscience when there was the possibility of ceremonial defilement. If every conceivable precaution had not been taken, the person or the vessel used might have contracted impurity, which would thus be conveyed to the food, and through the food to the body, and by it to the soul. Hence it had been long a custom, and latterly a strict law, that before every meal not only the hands but even the dishes, couches, and tables should be scrupulously washed.

"The legal washing of the hands before eating was especially sacred to the Rabbinist; not to do so was a crime as great as to eat the flesh of swine. 'He who neglects hand-washing,' says the book Sohar, 'deserves to be punished here and hereafter.' 'He is to be destroyed out of the world, for in hand-washing is contained the secret of the ten commandments.' 'He is guilty of death.' 'Three sins bring poverty after them,' says the Mishnah, 'and to slight hand-washing is one.' 'He who eats bread without hand-washing,' says Rabbi Jose, 'is as if he went in to a harlot.' The later Schulchan Aruch, enumerates twenty-six rules for this rite in the morning alone. 'It is better to go four miles to water than to incur guilt by neglecting hand-washing,' says the Talmud. 'He who does not wash his hands after eating,' it says, 'is as bad as a murderer.' The devil Schibta sits on unwashed hands and on the bread. It was a special mark of the Pharisees that 'they ate their daily bread with due purification,' and to neglect doing so was to be despised as unclean. . . .

"The Talmud maintains that 'any one living in the land of Israel, eating his daily food in purification, speaking the Hebrew of the day, and [engaging in] morning and evening praying duly with the phylacteries, is certain that he will eat bread in the kingdom of God.'

"It was laid down that the hands were first to be washed clean. The tips of the ten fingers were then joined and lifted up so that the water ran down to the elbows, then turned down so that it might run off to the ground. Fresh water was poured on them as they were lifted up, and twice again as they hung down. The washing itself was to be done by rubbing the fist of one hand in the hollow of the other. When the hands were washed before eating they must be held upwards; when after it, downwards, but so that the water should not run beyond the knuckles. The vessel used must be held first in the right, then in the left hand; the water was to be poured first on the right, then on the left hand, and at every third time the words repeated, 'Blessed art Thou who hast given us the command to wash the hands.' It was keenly disputed whether the cup of blessing or the hand-washing should come first; whether the towel used should be laid on the table or on the couch; and whether the table was to be cleared before the final washing or after it.

"This anxious trifling over the infinitely little was, however, only part of a system. If a Pharisee proposed to eat common food, it was enough that the hands were washed by water poured on them. Before eating *Terumah*—the holy tithes and the shew-bread—they must be dipped completely in the water, and before the portions of the holy offerings could be tasted, a bath must be taken. Hand-washing before prayer, or touching anything in the morning, was as rigidly observed, for evil spirits might have defiled the hands in the night. To touch the mouth, nose, ear, eyes, or the one hand with the other, before the rite, was to incur the risk of disease in the part touched. The occasions that demanded the observance were countless: it must be done even after cutting the nails, or killing a flea. The more water used, the more piety. 'He who uses abundant water for hand-washing,' says R. Chasda, 'will have abundant riches.' If one had not been out it was enough to pour water on the hands; but one coming in from without needed to plunge his hands into the water, for he knew not what uncleanness might have been near him while in the streets, and this plunging could not be done except in a spot where there were not less than sixty gallons of water.

"The same scrupulous, superstitious minuteness extended to possible defilements of all the household details of daily life. Dishes, hollow or flat, of whatever material, knives, tables, and couches, were constantly subjected to purifications, lest they should have contracted any Levitical defilement by being used by some one unclean." (Geikie, pp. 524-26.)

This digest of a portion of the rules governing ceremonial washings sets the scene and enables us to understand the significance of Mark's account of the confrontation on cleanliness. Scribes and Pharisees came to Jesus from Jerusalem. They had heard how he fed five thousand men with five barley loaves and two small fish, how the whole multitude was filled, how there were twelve baskets of fragments remaining, and how—O horrible thought!—the people had not washed their hands both before and after the miraculously supplied repast. How can this miracle be of God, they reasoned, when He who performed it did not also require the proper ceremonial washings!

And further, as these Judeans now "saw some of his disciples eat bread with defiled, that is to say, with unwashen, hands," as Mark says, "they found fault" yet again. "Why walk not thy disciples according to the tradition of the elders, but eat bread with unwashen hands?" they asked.

Here was an issue on which they were prepared to do battle. Their craft was in danger, and all men knew that ceremonial washings were essential to salvation, and that without them there was naught but sorrow and damnation!

"The traditions of the elders!" Scarcely does Satan have a more persuasive means of leading men from the glorious gospel truths set forth in the scriptures than to supplant and override these eternal verities with oral traditions. It is worthy of note that these scribes and Pharisees knew full well that their rituals and ceremonies grew out of the traditions of their fathers and were not taken from the written word given to Moses, whom they so greatly revered.

"The authority for this endless, mechanical religionism was the commands or 'traditions' of the Fathers, handed down from the days of the Great Synagogue, but ascribed with pious exaggeration to the Almighty, who, it was said, had delivered them orally to Moses on Mount Sinai. Interpretations, expositions, and discussions of all kinds were based, not only on every separate word, or on every letter, but even on every comma and semicolon, to create new laws and observances, and where these were not enough, oral traditions, said to have been delivered by God to Moses on Sinai, were invented to justify new refinements. These 'traditions' were constantly increased, and formed a New Law, which passed from mouth to mouth, and from generation to generation, till, at last, public schools rose for its study and development, of which the most famous were those of Hillel and Schammai, in the generation before Jesus, and even, perhaps, in His early childhood. In His lifetime it was still a fundamental rule that they should not be committed to writing. It was left to Rabbi Judah, the Holy, to commence the collection and formal engrossing of the almost countless fragments of which it consisted, and from his weary labour ultimately rose the huge folios of the Talmud.

"As in the case of the Brahminical theocracy of India, that of Judea attached more importance to the ceremonial precepts of its schools than to the sacred text on which they were based. Wherever Scripture and Tradition seemed opposed, the latter was treated as the higher authority. Pharisaism openly proclaimed this, and set itself, as the Gospel expresses it, in the chair of Moses, displacing the great lawgiver. 'It is a greater offence,' says the Mischnah, 'to teach anything contrary to the voice of the Rabbis, than to contradict Scripture itself. He who says [i.e. speaks] contrary to Scripture, "Is not lawful to wear the Tephillin" '—the little leather boxes containing texts of Scripture, bound, during prayer, on the forehead and on the arm—'is not to be punished as a troubler. But he who says there should be five divisions in the Totaphoth'—another name for the Tephillin, or phylacteries—'and thus teaches differently from the Rabbis, is guilty.' 'He who expounds the Scriptures in opposition to the Tradition,' says R. Eleazar, 'has no share in the world to come.' The mass of Rabbinical prescriptions—not the Scripture—was regarded as the basis of religion, 'for the Covenant of God was declared to have been made with Israel on account of the oral Law, as it is written, "After the tenor of these words I have made a covenant with thee and with Israel." [Ex. 34:27.] For God knew that, in after ages, Israel would be carried away among strange people, who would copy off the written Law, and therefore, he gave them the oral Law, that his will might be kept secret among themselves.' Those who gave themselves to the knowledge of the Traditions 'saw a great light,' for God enlightened their eyes, and showed them how they ought to act in relation to lawful and unlawful things, clean and unclean, which are not told thus fully and clearly in Scripture. It was, perhaps, good to give one's self to the reading of the Scripture, but he who reads diligently the Traditions receives a reward from God, and he who gives himself to the Commentaries on these traditions has the greatest reward of all. 'The Bible was like water, the Traditions like wine, the Commentaries on them like spiced wine.' 'My son,' says the Talmud, 'give more heed to the words of the Rabbis than to the words of the Law.' So exactly alike is Ultramontanism in every age, and in all religions!" (Geikie, pp. 526-27.)[3]

There is and can be only one answer to the charge that he and his disciples keep not "the tradition of the elders" because they "eat bread with unwashen hands." It is: 'The tradition is false; it is not of God; it leads men to destruction. I and my disciples are guiltless in this thing, but your religion is man made, and your worship is in vain. Repent or be damned.' Taking the offensive, Jesus, accordingly, says:

> *Well hath Esaias prophesied of you hypocrites, as it is written, This people honoureth me with their lips, but their heart is far from me.*
>
> *Howbeit, in vain do they worship me, teaching the doctrines and commandments of men.*
>
> *For laying aside the commandment of God, ye hold the tradition of men, as the washing of pots and cups: and many other such like things ye do.*

"It Is Corban"

(*Mark 7:9-13, 19; JST, Mark 7:9-13; Matthew 15:3-6; JST, Matthew 15:4-5*)

Our Lord's younger brother—James, a son of Joseph and Mary; a devout Jew during Jesus' lifetime; later a converted Christian and an apostle of Him whose brother he was—this wise and good man, not many years hence, will write these words: "Pure religion and undefiled before God and the Father is this, To visit the fatherless and widows in their affliction, and to keep himself unspotted from the world." (James 1:27.)

Pure religion! It is to put into living operation all the principles of eternal truth that dwell in the heart of the Great Jehovah. As an abstract principle faith is nothing; it is of no more worth than an abstract principle of mathematics. But faith in the heart of a man—a living, vibrant faith—can raise the dead, create worlds, and save souls. Love is nothing until it operates in the lives of men. Religion has saving power only when it dwells in a human heart, when it changes a human soul. Pure religion is to operate and use the eternal truths that flow from the Author of truth.

Pure religion revolves around, centers in, and operates primarily through the family unit. The whole purpose of revealed religion is to enable men to create for themselves eternal family units patterned after the family of God the Eternal Father. This life is the time appointed during which we learn how to live in the family unit with all the love and affection that must exist in an eternal family unit. And so Jehovah says to his people: "Honour thy father and thy mother: that thy days may be long upon the land which the Lord thy God giveth thee." (Ex. 20:12.)[5] And as though this were not enough, the further decree comes: "And he that curseth [revileth] his father, or his mother, shall surely be put to death." (Ex. 21:17; Lev. 20:9.)

How do we honor our parents? By emulating their righteous lives; by walking in the light as they are in the light; by keeping the faith and being true and steadfast as they are. And further, by caring for their temporal and physical needs in their aging years. We have no better illustration of the operation of this principle than is shown forth by the dying words of One on a cross who said to a sorrowing mother, "Woman, behold thy son," and to an intimate friend, "Behold thy mother," with the result that "from that hour that disciple took her unto his own home." (John 19:26-27.)

All these principles pertaining to parental honor and care were known to the Jews; all these things were written in their law; and all these things they chose, by their traditions, not to do. Pure religion was far from them; eternal principles found little good soil in the hearts of those in that day. Thus we hear Jesus say to his scribal antagonists and his Pharisaic enemies:

> *Yea, altogether ye reject the commandment of God, that ye may keep your own tradition. Full well is it written of you, by the prophets whom ye have rejected. They*

testified these things of a truth, and their blood shall be upon you.

"By professing to believe in the prophets, while in practice rejecting their teachings, the Jews were in reality rejecting the prophets. Thus, those Jews were placing themselves in the same position which their fathers occupied when those fathers slew the prophets; and so the blood of the prophets would be required at the hands of the Jews and their fathers, for both rejected them. Similarly, some today, by rejecting the teachings of the ancient apostles and prophets, are classifying themselves as people who would have slain the holy men of old, and so the blood of the true martyrs of religion shall be upon them." (*Commentary* 1:368.)

Ye have kept not the ordinances of God; for Moses said, Honor thy father and thy mother; and whoso curseth father or mother, let him die the death of the transgressor, as it is written in your law; but ye keep not the law.

Ye say, If a man shall say to his father or mother, Corban, that is to say, a gift, by whatsoever thou mightest be profited by me, he is of age. And ye suffer him no more to do aught for his father or his mother; making the word of God of none effect through your tradition, which ye have delivered; and many such like things do ye.

This is the picture Jesus is painting: Parents, perhaps aged and decrepit, are hungry, naked, and homeless. They cry out for a crust of bread; they need a homespun robe to cover their nakedness; they have not where to lay their heads during the long cold nights. But they have children—children who are prosperous and well to do; whose fields are fruitful; whose granaries are full; whose flocks graze on a thousand hills. Surely there is enough for all and to spare. But no, the children say: "It is corban." That is: 'We have vowed it to sacred purposes. You, our parents, may go cold and hungry and homeless; our property is not available to help you. We have a great zeal toward the Lord, and our property is vowed to him; and we cannot break our vows.'

Or: 'It is corban; I have vowed that my property shall be as if it were dedicated to sacred purposes, and though I may continue to use it all my life, you shall have none of it because of my vow.'

Or: 'It is corban; I have vowed that "whatsoever thou mightest be profited by" cannot be used for your benefit; that is, I have vowed that my property shall not be used for your support; and it is more important that I keep my vow than that I fulfill my obligation to support my parents. The oral traditions of the elders take precedence over the divine law written by Moses.'

It seems difficult to believe that religion could sink to such depths, and that a people who professed to serve the Jehovah of their fathers could so easily clear their consciences and feel themselves free from keeping his law. Already Jesus has called them hypocrites and said their worship is in vain, and these are only the beginning of the harsh invectives he will hurl upon their sin-ridden souls.

What Defiles a Man?

(*Mark 7:14-23; JST, Mark 7:15; Matthew 15:10-20; Luke 6:39*)

How and in what manner are men defiled—and thus damned? According to the Rabbinic way of worship, defilement came by violating the Levitical law; by treading upon the traditions of the elders; by eating with unwashed hands; by failing to conform to the ritualistic formalisms of the day.

What must men do to remain undefiled—and thus be saved? Again the answer is found in the field of tradition and superstition. Wash all pots and vessels before eating; scrub the tables whereon food is placed; cleanse the couches on which the diners recline. Carry no burden on the Sabbath; speak the approved Hebrew. These—and such like—are the laws by obedience to which salvation comes. It is not what is in a man's heart that counts, but how well he conforms to all of the minutia and trivia of their religious formalism.

Jesus, however, is now prepared to reject and denounce

the traditions of the elders and all of the evils that grow out of them. The scribal spies from Jerusalem have raised the issue of ceremonial washings; they say that those who eat with unwashed hands—"and many other such like things"—are defiled. Jesus meets the issue squarely. He calls the multitude unto him. "Hearken unto me every one of you, and understand," he says. "Not that which goeth into the mouth defileth a man; but that which cometh out of the mouth, this defileth a man." "If any man have ears to hear, let him hear."

These cutting words, along with others of like severity, incensed and outraged the Rabbinic religionists. If these words were true, their system of worship was false. "Knowest thou that the Pharisees were offended, after they heard this saying?" the disciples said to Jesus. His answer:

> *Every plant, which my heavenly Father hath not planted, shall be rooted up.*
>
> *Let them alone: they be blind leaders of the blind. And if the blind lead the blind, both shall fall into the ditch.*

Well might these words be written in the hearts of all false ministers with a pen of steel. False religions shall be rooted up; they shall wither and die and be as the chaff of a summer threshing floor. And those blind ministers whose eyes have not been opened by the light from on high, together with all others who close their eyes to the truth, shall fall in the ditch of that evil master whom they choose to serve.

Thus Jesus declares open war upon the scribes, upon the Pharisees, and upon all who hearken to the preachments and follow the counsel of these self-appointed interpreters and dispensers of the law. The assault is not alone upon the ceremonial sin of eating with unwashed hands; it is a frontal attack upon all their rituals and performances. The scribes set aside the sayings of Moses. Their traditions make the word of God of no effect! Hillel and Shammai overrule the Lord Jehovah!

Thus Jesus "arraigned Pharisaism, the dominant orthodoxy, as a whole. The system, so famous, so arrogant, so intensely Jewish, was only an invention of man; a subversion of the law it claimed to represent, an antagonism to the prophets as well as to Moses, the spiritual ruin of the nation! . . . It was vital that the people who followed the Rabbis and priests should know what the religion and morals thus taught by them were worth. The truth could not find open ears while men's hearts were misled and prejudiced by such instructors. No one would seek inward renewal who had been taught to care only for externals, and to ignore the sin and corruption within. Pharisaism was a creed of moral cosmetics and religious masks, as all ritual systems must ever be." (Geikie, p. 530.)

Jesus and his disciples are now in a house apart from the multitude. Peter speaks: "Declare unto us this parable." Jesus responds:

> *Are ye also yet without understanding? Do not ye yet understand, that whatsoever entereth in at the mouth goeth into the belly, and is cast out into the draught?*
>
> *But those things which proceed out of the mouth come forth from the heart; and they defile the man.*
>
> *For out of the heart proceed evil thoughts, murders, adulteries, fornications, thefts, false witness, blasphemies: These are the things which defile a man: but to eat with unwashen hands defileth not a man.*

Such is Matthew's account; Mark adds to the list of inner evils covetousness, wickedness, deceit, lasciviousness, an evil eye, pride, and foolishness. The meaning is clear, and Jesus has preached a sermon that no believing saint shall ever forget. Out of the abundance of the heart the mouth speaketh, and "as he thinketh in his heart, so is he." (Prov. 23:7.)

Mark also inserts in his account an inspired interpreting phrase that shows how fully and completely the sayings of this day are intended to overthrow even the true Mosaic system, to say nothing of the traditions that were added by the Rabbinists. Jesus speaks of that which "entereth . . . into the belly, and goeth out into the draught," and Mark adds that He does so "purging all meats," or in other words, as a better translation of the original manuscript has it, *"making all meats clean."*

In other words, though Moses of old had divided meats into clean and unclean—those which might be eaten and those which were forbidden—Jesus made all meats clean; all might be eaten. "It is nothing less than the plainest teaching ever given by Christ on the final abrogation of the Levitic Law," as Farrar so well says. "In the Levitic Law the distinction between clean and unclean meats was fundamental. Since the days of Ezra it had been insisted on with ever greater scrupulosity and everdeepening fanaticism.

"This, then, He said, sweeping aside Levitical ordinances as things which had no eternal validity, and 'making all meats clean.' St. Paul had to fight out to the bitter end the battle against the Judaism which attached importance to meats and drinks, and carnal ordinances which affect things which perish in the using, rather than to righteousness, temperance, justice, and the weightier matters of the Law; but Christ had already laid down the principles on which the battle was to be decided, and had uttered His fiat as to its eternal issue." (Farrar, p. 346.)

And we might add that Luke, who set forth the meaning and intent of our Lord's words here given, was also privileged to record in the Acts of the Apostles the vision of Peter affirming the same truth. Peter, as a prelude to the preaching of the gospel to the Gentiles, saw a great sheet descend from heaven whereon were "all manner of four-footed beasts of the earth, and wild beasts, and creeping things, and fowls of the air." A heavenly voice commanded: "Rise, Peter; kill, and eat." He replied: "Not so, Lord; for I have never eaten any thing that is common or unclean." Then came the divine fiat: *"What God hath cleansed, that call not thou common."* (Acts. 10:9-15. Italics added.)

And so, "purging all meats," Jesus not only repealed all the Mosaic restrictions of a bygone dispensation, but also foreshadowed the carrying of the gospel to the Gentile hosts of the new dispensation.

NOTES

1. 2 Cor. 6:15.

2. See the companion volume to this work: *The Promised Messiah—The First Coming of Christ.*

3. This concept that the traditions of the elders supersede, are greater than, and take precedence over the word of God is, in my judgment, the devil's substitute for the true doctrine that the inspired utterances of living oracles are binding upon the Lord's people and have equal standing with the written word. This true doctrine is predicated upon the fact that inspired men speak as moved upon by the Holy Ghost, which, of course, is precisely and exactly what happens when prophets give forth that which we call scripture. The traditions of the elders—as is also the case with the traditions of an apostate Christendom—are wholly devoid of the least scintilla of inspiration. They are, as Jesus said, "the commandments of men."

As I have written elsewhere: "This same process of transforming truth into traditions—of changing the law of God into 'the doctrines and commandments of men,' by the interpretations and additions of uninspired teachers—is precisely what took place in the great apostasy of the Christian Era. To the pure and simple doctrines of Christ, the scribes and priests of early Christendom added such things as: selling indulgences, which freed the wicked from past sins and authorized them to commit future crimes without divine penalty; forgiving sins (supposedly) through repeated and perfunctory confessions; praying departed persons out of purgatory; burning candles for the dead; praying to Mary or other so-called saints, rather than to the Lord; worshiping of images; turning of sacramental emblems into the literal flesh and blood of Jesus (transubstantiation); laying up a reservoir of good works in heaven which the so-called Church can sell to those who need them (supererogation); sacrificing Jesus over again in the mass; forbidding priests and other church officials to marry; doing penance to gain forgiveness of sins; adorning houses of worship with costly materials; wearing of expensive robes and costumes by priests and other church officers; using elaborate ministerial titles; augmenting the Church treasury by gambling; and so forth.

"All these, and many other like traditions, are counted of more importance by some than the law of God as originally given by the Master. Indeed, the so-called Christian Church today is founded in large part on the traditions of the 'elders' rather than on the revelations of heaven." (*Commentary* 1:366-67.)

4. Isaiah's words as found in our Old Testament read: "Forasmuch as this people draw near me with their mouth, and with their lips do honour me, but have removed their heart far from me, and their fear toward me is taught by the precept of men: Therefore, behold, I will proceed to do a marvellous work among this people, even a marvellous work and a wonder." (Isa. 29:13-14.) In his confrontation on cleanliness Jesus obviously targumed a portion of Isaiah's words and applied them to the scribes and Pharisees and their followers. The intended glorious fulfillment of the words of Israel's ancient seer was, of course, reserved for the latter days when the gospel would be restored for the final time. Jesus' use of the passage here illustrates perfectly the principle that many prophetic utterances have dual or multiple instances of fulfillment. When he appeared with his Father to usher in the dispensation of the fulness of times, the Lord Jesus said to his latter-day prophet that the modern "professors" of religion—the modern scribes and Pharisees, as it were—"were all corrupt," and that "they draw near to me with their lips, but their hearts are far from me, they teach for doctrines the commandments of men, having a form of godliness, but they deny the power thereof." (JS-H 1:219.)

"There is no salvation in worship as such, even though it be directed to the true God; worship based on false principles is in vain. Men may worship Deity their whole life long, according to their traditions and rituals, and never gain true faith, forgiveness of sin, or sanctifying grace. Worship leads to salvation only when it conforms to the revealed, divine pattern, only when it is based on the rock foundation of eternal truth. 'Not every one that saith unto me, Lord, Lord, shall enter into the kingdom of heaven; but he that doeth the will of my Father which is in heaven.' (Matt. 7:21.) There is no salvation in false worship." (*Commentary* 1:368.)

5. Those who truly honor their parents, in the full gospel sense, shall in fact dwell forever upon their promised land, for the meek shall inherit the earth forever in the celestial day. (D&C 88:17.)

INDEX

Peter's mother, 37-38; of afflicted at Capernaum, 38; of multitudes throughout Galilee, 39-40, 43; of man with leprosy, 45-46; of man sick of palsy, 48-52; of paralytic on Sabbath, 65-67; on Sabbath, lawfulness of, 89-90; of man with withered hand, 90; of Gentile centurion's servant, 181-83; due to faith of person seeking blessing, 289; of daughter of Jairus, 289-92; of woman with issue of blood, 294-96; of blind men, 297-98; those blessed by, are obligated to serve God, 298; physical acts accompanying, on many occasions, 302 n. 5; of people of Gennesaret, 363. *See also* Jesus Christ, miracles performed by; Miracles
Heaven, laying up treasures in, 152-53
Hebrew targumed into Aramaic, 20
Hem of Jesus' garment, woman touched, 294-96
Herod Antipas, 331; birthday feast of, 332-33; delivers John the Baptist's head to Salome, 335; hallucinations of, 337; Jesus withdrew from domain of, 344
Herod Philip, 331
Herod the Great, 330-31
Herodians, 91
Herodias, 331
Hidden treasure, parable of, 263-64
Holy Ghost, 122; manifests God's truths, 165; blasphemy against, 215-16, 218-20, 228 n. 2-3; gift of prophecy bears witness of, 224; necessity of, in understanding scriptures, 267-68; speaking with power of, before earthly tribunals, 318; without gift of, man's testimony cannot remain unshaken, 361
Honor: Christ received not, from men, 78-79; of men vs. that of God, 79; afforded to parents, 406-7
Hosea, 15
Hospitality, custom of, 199-200, 314 n. 5
Humility, 168
Hypocrisy, 162-63

Ignorance, man cannot be saved in, 81 n. 7
Illustrations, parables are, rather than revelations, 241-42
Immortality, Jesus inherited power of, 74
Isaiah: Messianic prophecies of, 15; Jesus interprets prophecies of, 21-24
Israel: Jesus was sent specifically to, 91, 313 n. 3; shepherds of, woe be to, 305; apostles were sent only to, 309-10; worthy people of, 311; Jesus tested, with miracle of loaves and fishes, 367; apostasy of, 392; traditions of, 403-5. *See also* Jews

Jairus, raising of daughter of, 289-92
James, son of Alpheus, 110
James, son of Zebedee, 33, 107
Jeremiah, 15
Jerusalem, 30; spies from, followed Jesus, 88, 391; Jesus came not to, for Passover, 399
Jesus Christ: proclaims his divine Sonship, 3, 70-73, 75, 375-76; Judean ministry of, 6-7; role of, in plan of salvation, 8, 72-73; fame of, began to precede him, 11, 18, 39-40; preaches in Nazarene synagogue, 20-24; Spirit of Lord was upon, 21; applies Messianic prophecies to himself, 23; Nazarenes sought to murder, 27; dignity of, 27-28; dwelt in Capernaum, 31; private prayers of, 38-39; empathy of, 41; judgment rests with, 72, 74-75; works of, bear witness of him, 77-78; visited spirits in prison, 80 n. 4; is Lord of Sabbath, 88; plans laid for destroying of, 91; prayed before calling apostles, 104; visited Nephites after his resurrection, 118; performing miracles in name of, is insufficient for salvation, 172-73; taught as one having authority, 174, 177; teachings of, 179-80; John the Baptist sends his disciples to, 188-89; repentant sinner washes feet of, 197, 200; preached the gospel, 204, 244; disciples of, supported him temporally, 204-5; is accused of working miracles through Beelzebub, 209-11, 396; family of, all disciples may belong to, 226-27; preaches in Galilee's cities and

Kingdom of God on earth, 9; administrators in, must be called of God, 103-4; keys of, were bestowed on the Twelve, 112; praying for, 149; seek first to build up, 158; suffered violence, 193-94; growth of, 254; tares sown in field of, 257; is likened to mustard seed, 260-61; Jews' idea of, was opposite from that of Jesus, 383. *See also* Church of Christ; Gospel

Laborers called to vineyards, 306
Last days, 258-59, 269 n. 5, 270 n. 13, 357-58
Law of Moses: Pharisees kept not, 60-61; putting away of, 61, 130; Jesus came to fulfill, 130-31, 133-34; giving of, on Mount Sinai, 131-32; contrasted with gospel, 132, 135-43; prepared men for fulness of gospel, 133; perfection comes not by, 143; difficulty in forsaking, for Christ, 383
Laying on of hands, 290
Leaven, parable of, 262, 269 n. 7
Legal entanglements, saints were to avoid, 137
Lehi, 101
Leprosy, 44-45, 53 n. 3; man with, Jesus heals, 45-46
Levitical cleanness, 46-47, 302 n. 4, 395, 398-402
Liberty, Christ proclaimed, to captives, 22
Life, losing, for Christ's sake, 324
Light: of the world, saints are, 127-28; filling whole body with, 153; should not be hidden, 154
Line upon line, God's word is revealed, 235
Loaves: friend in need of, 151-52; and fishes, dividing of, 347-48. *See also* Five thousand, feeding of
Looking beyond the mark, 392
Lord's Prayer, 148-51
Love for enemies, 141-42
Lukewarmness, 178
Lust, condemning of, 137

Mammon, man cannot serve God and, 155, 252
Manna, 365-68, 373-74
Mary Magdalene, 205-6, 207 n. 4
Mary, mother of Jesus, 226-27, 406
"Master, the Tempest Is Raging," 271
Matthew, 55-57, 109
Matthias, 112
Meats, clean and unclean, 411
Meek to inherit earth, 122
Mercy: is greater than sacrifice, 86-87; merciful shall obtain, 122-23; sowing and reaping, 150; Jesus showed, by teaching in parables, 243
Messiah, temporal: Jews viewed Jesus as, 351-52, 368, 371; Jesus' refusal to become, offended disciples, 382-83
Messianic prophecies, 14, 28 n. 3; fulfillment of, 15-16; definition of, 17; Jesus applies, to himself, 23; concerning miracles, 297; using imagery of sheep, 305-6. *See also* Prophets
Metaphors, Jewish understanding of, 378
Micah, 15, 86-87
Millennium, praying for, 149
Ministers, true, authority of, 308-9
Miracles: are part of gospel, 10, 42; Nazarenes wanted to see, 24-25; performed by Elijah and Elisha, 25-26; require faith, 26, 223, 286-87; wrought throughout Galilee, 39-40; identified Jesus' ministry, 41-43, 190; selective recording of, 43; performing, in Jesus' name, is insufficient for salvation, 172-73; Jesus is accused of working, through Beelzebub, 209-11, 396; mixed reactions to, 221; others have performed, in Jesus' name, 277-78; difficulty believing in, 285 n. 3; Jesus did not perform, in Nazareth, 301; were viewed by the apostles, 307-8; power to perform, Jesus bestowed, on apostles, 309; believing in, 361-62. *See also* Healing; Jesus Christ, miracles performed by
Missionaries: temporal needs of, 310, 314 n. 5; he who receives, receives Christ, 324
Missionary work: Jesus enjoins, 163; performed by healed demoniac, 284; sending of apostles to do, 307; in latter

37-38; home of, Jesus preaches in, 48; description of, 106-7; walks on water, 360; testimony of, 386-87; vision of, concerning cleanliness of meats, 411
Pharisaism, Jesus declares open war on, 409-10
Pharisees: ritual of fasting among, 58-59, 63 n. 2; Sabbath observance among, 65-66; righteousness of, was insufficient, 134; hypocrisy of, 162-63; opposition from, 198; Jesus breaks bread with, 199; opposition of, morally accounting for, 211-12; Jesus' disciples begin to fear, 214-15; sought a sign from heaven, 221-22; feared for their craft, 393; labeled by Jesus as blind leaders of blind, 409
Philip, Jesus' apostle, 108-9, 347
Philip, Herod's brother, 331
Physician, the whole need no, 57-58
Plan of salvation, 8-9
Plough, putting hand to, and looking back, 274
Plural marriage, 389 n. 6
Political leader, Jesus was not, 382
Political uprising, Jesus wished to avoid, 343-44
Pool of Bethesda, 66
Poor: in spirit, kingdom of heaven is promised to, 121; giving alms to, 145-46
Possession by evil spirits, 36-37, 282, 285 n. 5
Prayer: of Jesus in solitary place, 38-39; goes hand in hand with charity, 146-47; correct order of, 147-48; the Lord's, 148-51
Preachers in synagogues, 29
Priestcrafts, 390, 393
Priesthood, true ministers always hold, 309
Priests of temple, Sabbath labor of, 85-86
Profanity, gospel law forbids, 136
Prophecy: gift of, bears witness of Holy Ghost, 224; spirit of, 287. *See also* Messianic prophecies; Prophets
Prophets: those who believe, believe in Christ, 79, 81 n. 10; saw the Lord's face, 123; true, vs. false, 168-70, 175 n. 8; true, recognizing, by their fruits, 170-71; receiving reward of, 325; power of, over waters, 356-57; rejecting, while professing belief in, 406-7
Proverbs, 235
Publicans, 55-57
Pure in heart shall see God, 123
Pure religion and undefiled, 405-6

Rabbis, words of, took precedence over scripture, 404, 412 n. 3
Reconciliation, gospel law governing, 136-37
Rejection of Jesus: by Nazárenes, 24, 27; because he violated Sabbath laws, 83-84; by Gadarenes, 283-84; for second time by Nazarenes, 300-301; brings damnation, 312; because he claimed divine Sonship, 376; rationalizations for, 394-98
Religion, pure, and undefiled, 405-6
Repentance, gospel of, 9, 13 n. 1; Jesus came to preach, 217
Repetitions, vain, 147-48
Restoration of all things, 120 n. 3
Resurrection: Jesus alludes to, 72; to appropriate degree of glory, 80 n. 5; sign of, 223-24; Jesus promises, to faithful, 375-76
Retaliation, gospel law governing, 140-41
Revelation, new, 62, 63 n. 1; necessity of, in choosing apostles, 103-4; personal, 165-66; is necessary in discovering truth, 212; bears witness of Holy Ghost, 224; parables are not sources of, 241; must be obeyed before more is received, 246
Righteousness: hungering and thirsting after, 122; lack of desire for, 268 n. 2; reward of, 325
Rituals, Israel's, did not bring salvation, 392
Rock, foundation built upon, 173
Roots, gospel, lack of, 250-52

Sabbath day: in Capernaum, 34-35; true purposes of, 65, 87-88; perversion of, by scribes and Pharisees, 65-66, 93 n. 1-2, 398; paralytic carries his bed on, 67-69; Jesus is accused of breaking,

Targums, 20
Tax collectors, 55-56
Teaching methods, various types of, 234-35
Temporal needs: apostles were not to worry over, 156-59, 310, 314 n. 5; God will provide for, 350
Temporal savior: Jews mistook Jesus for, 351-52, 368, 371; Jesus' refusal to become, offended disciples, 382-83
Temptations, praying to avoid, 150-51
Testimony depends on Holy Ghost, 387
Testing of disciples, 383, 385
Thomas, 110
Thorns, seeds fallen among, 251-52
Traditions: of Israel, 403-5, 412 n. 3; transforming truth into, 412 n. 3
Treasure: in heaven, laying up, 152-53; hidden, parable of, 263-64
Truth: discovering and recognizing, 212; receiving fulness of, 237; seekers after parable pertaining to, 264-65, 270 n. 10; lack of desire for, 268 n. 2; will prevail, 317; seal of, 388-89 n. 2; Pharisaism kept people from, 410; transforming, into traditions, 412 n. 3
Twelve apostles: Jesus prepares to call, 99; role of, 102-3, 303; calling of, by Jesus, 104-5, 307-8; individual descriptions of, 105-11; ordination of, 112; Jesus bestowed keys upon, 112; filling vacancies in, 112; role of, in judgment, 113 n. 1; family relationships within, 113 n. 2; calling of, in America, 118; were not to worry over temporal needs, 156-59; sending of, on missions, 307; Jesus bestowed authority on, 309; were to preach only to Israel, 309-10; were as sheep in midst of wolves, 316; would be treated as was Jesus, 320; are counseled not to fear death, 321; Jesus approached, walking on sea, 359-60; healing of people by, 364 n. 4; did not forsake Jesus, 386-88

Unclean spirit, Jesus cast out, from possessed man, 35-36, 209
Uncleanness, Levitical, 398-402; Jesus is accused of, 395-96
Unpardonable sin, 215-16, 218, 228 n. 2-3

Vain repetitions, 147-48
Vineyards, laborers called to, 306
Violence, kingdom of heaven suffereth, 193-94
Vowing without using oaths, 139-40

Washings, ceremonial, 398-402
Water, 353-54; cursing of, in last days, 354-55; significance of, in history of gospel, 355-58; Jesus walks on, 359-61; reasons for Jesus' walking on, 363-64 n. 1
Wayside, seeds fallen by, 250
Weak things of the world to confound strong, 101
Wheat, separating chaff from, 381-82
Wheat and tares: parable of, 255-59, 269 n. 4; harvesting of, in last days, 258-59, 269 n. 5; grow together, 266
Wicked: were left without excuse, 43-44; murmurings of, 376; damnation of, 381
Widow: of Zarephath, 25; of Nain, 183-86; visiting, in affliction, 405
Wine, new, in old bottles, 61
Winnowing fan, Jesus wields, 381-82
Wisdom: those who lack, may ask of God, 174 n. 5; worldly, cannot impart spiritual understanding, 384
Witnesses: divine law of, Jesus obeyed, 76-77; of Jesus, 81 n. 8; difference between apostles and, 114 n. 5; of Jesus, he who receives, receives the Lord, 324
Women following Jesus, 205-7
Word of God: likened to seed, 248-49; manna was similitude of, 366
Words, condemnation because of, 219, 228 n. 5
Work: on Sabbath, 70; is order of life, 156
Works of Christ bear witness of him, 77-78
Worldly pleasures: allowing, to take precedence, 251-52; insignificance of, in missionary work, 273-74; Rome's preoccupation with, 332-33

Worship: true, depends on belief in
Christ, 372-73; false, 412-13 n. 4
Worthy, apostles were to bless, 311

Zarephath, widow of, 25
Zealots, 111

The Mortal Messiah

From Bethlehem to Calvary

Book III

The Mortal Messiah

From Bethlehem to Calvary
Book III

Bruce R. McConkie

Deseret Book Company
Salt Lake City, Utah

Vol. 3 ISBN 0-87747-825-2 (hardbound)
ISBN 0-87579-405-X (softbound)

Library of Congress Cataloging-in-Publication Data

McConkie, Bruce R.
The mortal Messiah.

Includes index.
1. Jesus Christ—Biography. 2. Christian biography—Palestine.
3. Judaism—History—Post-exilic period, 586 B.C.–210 A.D.
I. Title.
BT301.2.M16 232.9'01 79-19606

Printed in the United States of America

10 9 8 7 6 5 4 3 2

THE MESSIANIC TRILOGY

The forerunner of this work is *The Promised Messiah: The First Coming of Christ*, which deals with the Messianic Prophecies. This work, *The Mortal Messiah: From Bethlehem to Calvary*, is a Life of Christ published in four books. This is Book III.

BOOK III

Section VII The Galilean Ministry Reaches Its Peak
Section VIII The Later Judean Ministry
Section IX The Perean Ministry
Section X From the Anointing to the Royal Reign

The other books on the Life of Christ are published separately as follows:

BOOK I

Section I A Root Out of Dry Ground
Section II Jesus' Years of Preparation
Section III Jesus' Early Judean Ministry

BOOK II

Section IV Jesus Begins the Great Galilean Ministry
Section V The Twelve, The Sermon on the Mount, and Rising Pharisaic Opposition
Section VI The Continuing Galilean Ministry

BOOK IV

Section XI The Paschal Feast, The Private Prayers and Sermons, and Gethsemane
Section XII The Trials, The Cross, and The Tomb
Section XIII He Riseth; He Ministereth; He Ascendeth

The concluding work in this whole series will be *The Millennial Messiah: The Second Coming of the Son of Man.*

ABBREVIATIONS

Scriptural references are abbreviated in a standard and self-identifying way. Other books are cited by author and title except for the following:

Commentary I	Bruce R. McConkie, *Doctrinal New Testament Commentary.* Vol. 1, *The Gospels.* Bookcraft, 1965.
Edersheim	Alfred Edersheim, *The Life and Times of Jesus the Messiah.* 1883.
Farrar	F. W. Farrar, *The Life of Christ.* London: Cassell & Co., Ltd., 1874.
Geikie	Cunningham Geikie, *The Life and Words of Christ.* 1886.
Hymns	*Hymns, The Church of Jesus Christ of Latter-day Saints.* 1948.
JST	Joseph Smith Translation (Inspired Version) of the Bible.
Mormon Doctrine	Bruce R. McConkie, *Mormon Doctrine,* 2nd ed. Bookcraft, 1966.
Sketches	Alfred Edersheim, *Sketches of Jewish Social Life in the Days of Christ.* 1876.
Talmage	James E. Talmage, *Jesus the Christ.* 1915.
Teachings	Joseph Fielding Smith, comp., *Teachings of the Prophet Joseph Smith.* 1938.
Temple	Alfred Edersheim, *The Temple: Its Ministry and Services As They Were at the Time of Jesus Christ.*

CONTENTS

SECTION VII

THE GALILEAN MINISTRY REACHES ITS PEAK

Chapter 68

SECTION VIII

THE LATER JUDEAN MINISTRY

Chapter 69

Chapter 70

Chapter 71

Chapter 72

Chapter 73

Chapter 74

Chapter 75

Chapter 76

SECTION IX

THE PEREAN MINISTRY

Chapter 77

Chapter 78

Chapter 79

Chapter 80

Chapter 85

Chapter 86

Chapter 87

Chapter 88

Chapter 89

Chapter 93

SECTION VII

THE GALILEAN MINISTRY REACHES ITS PEAK

THE GALILEAN MINISTRY REACHES ITS PEAK

Thou art the Christ,
the Son of the living God.
(Matt. 16:16.)
This is my beloved Son,
in whom I am well pleased;
hear ye him.
(Matt. 17:5.)

Jesus our Lord, in whose mortal life we so much rejoice, now comes to a day of deepening opposition, even in Galilee.

He departs thence to visit the lost sheep among the heathen. In the coasts of Tyre and Sidon and throughout Decapolis his voice is heard, his miracles abound, and he feeds the four thousand.

He is challenged to show a sign from heaven, a sign of the sort the Messiah of Jewish expectation should show.

He warns his disciples of the leaven of the Pharisees and Sadducees.

Then in the coasts of Caesarea Philippi, Peter makes the great confession, with which all the disciples accord.

Jesus promises to give Peter the keys of the kingdom of heaven. Then upon Mount Hermon those keys are conferred upon Peter, James, and John. Shortly thereafter all of the

Twelve receive them and have power, thus, to bind and loose both on earth and in heaven.

Over and over again he who came to die speaks of being delivered into the hands of evil men, and of his death in Jerusalem, and of his rising again the third day.

On the Holy Mount, Jesus and the chosen three are transfigured. Moses and Elias minister unto them.

There on the heights of Hermon, Peter, James, and John see the wonders of eternity, including the transfiguration of the earth.

The Shekinah returns to Israel. Even the Father visits the Son and testifies: "*This is my beloved Son, in whom I am well pleased; hear ye him.*"

Jesus foretells the coming of Elias of the Restoration.

He begins the descent from the Mountain of Glory to the Valley of Humiliation and Death.

In the valley, he heals the demoniac youth, and he provides, miraculously, the temple-tax for himself and for Peter.

He discourses on meekness, on humility, on the salvation of children, on forgiveness, and on the sealing power. And he gives the parable of the unmerciful servant.

Then, from among his Galilean friends, he chooses the Seventy to stand with the Twelve, in bearing witness of his holy name in all the world.

And so closes his Galilean ministry—a ministry of preaching and healings and miracles and keys and powers and authorities and visions and heavenly confirmation of his divine Sonship.

As God's Son he goes to Jerusalem to do the thing for which he came into the world.

THE LOST SHEEP AMONG THE HEATHEN

From the rising of the sun
even unto the going down of the same
my name shall be great
among the Gentiles;
and in every place incense shall be offered
unto my name, and a pure offering:
for my name shall be great
among the heathen,
saith the Lord of hosts.
(Mal. 1:11.)

A Day of Deepening Opposition

(Matthew 15:21; John 7:1)

Lucifer is now loosing his legions to fight the Lord of Life. Heretofore opposition to him has centered mainly in the scribal-sectarian ministers, in the rabid Rabbinists, in the Sanhedrists, in the religious rulers and leaders of the people—all of whose crafts are endangered by the New Order. Among the peasant people, among the Galilean multitudes, among the common folk—whose thoughts, however, are greatly influenced by their leaders—there has been a division of opinion. Some have followed him gladly. He has been rejected twice by his own at Nazareth. There are those who believe he is the Messiah, and others who accept the Pharisaic sophistry that he is Satan Incarnate and casteth out devils and worketh miracles by the power of Beelzebub.

The foul murder by Antipas of the blessed Baptist has left the people in an excitable state. Herod was seeking Jesus to do to him what he did to John.[1] It was in the midst of this popular excitement that Jesus and the Twelve sought refuge from persecution and surcease from toil by sailing to the area of Bethsaida-Julias. In the green and solitary fields near that city—now famed forever for what took place there—Jesus fed the five thousand, and there was a brief, dazzling tide of popular acclaim that sought to force an earthly crown upon that head destined only, while on earth, to wear a crown of thorns.

Then came the sermon on the bread of life, which winnowed the chaff from the wheat and cleared the threshing floor of those who sought only the loaves and fishes and who chose not to eat the Bread that came down from heaven.

Next came the spies and scribes from the Sanhedrin—renewed in their persecuting zeal by the enthusiasm and emotion of their Passover worship—to confront him on the issue of the traditions of the elders.

And at this point Jesus himself declared war. His acts and those of his disciples in eating with unwashen hands—and many such like things—had no defense except that the traditions were evil, false, and base, and would lead men to hell. And he said so, plainly, clearly, emphatically.

"But the craft and violence of the half-heathen Antipas, was a slight evil compared with the hatred which glowed ever more intensely in the breasts of the Rabbis and priests of Jerusalem, and in those of the Pharisees, and other disciples of the schools, scattered over the country. The demands of Jesus were far beyond the mere summons of the Baptist, to prepare for a new and better time. He required immediate submission to a new Theocracy. He excited the fury of the dominant party, not like the Baptist, by isolated bursts of denunciation, but by working quietly, as a King in His own kingdom, which, while in the world, was something far higher. Hence, the feeling against Him was very different from the partial, cautious, and intermittent hatred of the Baptist. The hierarchy and the Rabbis, as the centre of that which, with all its corruptions, was the only true religion on earth as yet, felt themselves compromised directly and fatally by Him, and could not maintain themselves as they were, if He were tolerated. The whole spiritual power of Israel was thus arrayed against Him; a force slowly created by the possession, for ages, of the grandest religious truths known to the ancient world, and by the pride of a long and incomparably sublime national history. It had been assailed in the past, at long intervals, from without, but in recent years it had been for the first time attacked from within, by the Baptist, and now felt itself still more dangerously assaulted by this Galilean. To crush such an apparently insignificant opponent—a peasant of Nazareth, rising, singly and unsupported, against a power so colossal—seemed easy; nor could it be fancied more difficult to scatter and destroy His small band of followers, as yet, mostly, despised peasants." (Geikie, pp. 532-33.)

Now the war is open and fierce; opposition against him has spread out among the Galilean and Judean multitudes; and it is the people and the nation, not alone their religious leaders, who wield the sword. Lucifer's legions are fighting the saints on all fronts, and the warfare will not cease until the cross of crucifixion becomes the weapon of death; or, rather, until the great dragon himself, along with the false prophets who carry his banner, are cast into the bottomless pit.

Jesus is still in need of the rest he sought when he and his disciples set sail from Capernaum to the site where the five thousand Passover pilgrims were fed. The fires of political unrest, fanned by the Herodians, and the fires of religious hatred, fanned by the scribes and rulers from Jerusalem, are everywhere ablaze. Lest the fiery holocaust burn the scarcely built house of faith that he is building in the hearts of men, he must withdraw from Galilee and go far to the north, into Phoenicia. As to the opposition in Judea, which has been intense for a long time, John says: "After these things Jesus walked in Galilee: for he would not walk in Jewry, because the Jews sought to kill him." And as to the opposition now burning even in Galilee, Matthew says: "Then Jesus went thence, and departed into the coasts of Tyre and Sidon."

Tyre and Sidon! Cities of abominations, cities of wickedness, cities like Sodom and Gomorrah! They were Canaanitish, heathen, pagan cities, the home of the worship of Baal and Ashtoreth. Ashtoreth, whose worship Jezebel had imposed on Israel, was the goddess of sensual love; she was worshipped as a sacred prostitute and a divine courtesan, if such words may be used without committing blasphemy. For millenniums the Canaanitish worship had been lewd, lascivious, and immoral. Prostitute goddesses were the order of the age, and their devotees sought to be like those upon whose altars they offered their sacrifices. Such was the area into which the holy party now traveled to continue those labors which collectively are known as the Father's business.

Ministering Among the Heathen

(*Mark 7:24-30; JST, Mark 7:22-23, 26-27; Matthew 15:22-28*)

Whether Jesus entered Tyre and Sidon proper we do not know, only that he was in the area or region. It was not his practice to seek out Gentiles as such to hear his voice, though there would have been many Jews in the cities themselves. In Jesus' day Tyre, the larger of the two cities, was probably more populous than Jerusalem, and it would appear that he remained two or three months in the area before going on to Decapolis and his ministry in the cities there.

We have heretofore shown that the Gospels contain only selected sayings and doings of Jesus. Of the months he spent in the borders of Tyre and Sidon, like the period he spent visiting all of the cities and towns of Judea in the early Judean ministry, we know very little. It is inherent in the very nature of things that he taught the gospel, testified of his own divine Sonship, and worked miracles. Such words and deeds as have come down to us of any parts of his mortal ministry have been recorded by the Gospel authors, as guided by the Holy Spirit, to preserve the specific teachings intended for us by an all-wise Providence.

Once we have learned how and under what circumstances certain miracles are wrought, for instance, there is no compelling need to record numerous similar illustrations. Generally speaking our evangelist friends have selected matters to record that we need to know about and that, taken as a whole, give us the knowledge and understanding we need in order to follow him whose words and deeds should guide our lives.

As pertaining to the ministerial service here involved, this selection concerns a Syro-Phoenician woman. Mark, who gained his knowledge from Peter, begins the account by saying that when Jesus came "into the borders of Tyre and Sidon," he "entered into a house, and would that no man should come unto him. But he could not deny them; for he had compassion upon all men." Two things are apparent from this: first, that even here the Lord Jesus failed to find the rest he sought; and second, that the disciples, being present and aware of all that transpired, saw in our Lord's acts a reaffirmation of his compassion for all men, not for the house of Israel only.

Phoenicia, or Syria, lies to the north of Galilee and extends from the Mediterranean Sea to the river Jordan. It is ruled by Rome. Tyre and Sidon, about twenty miles apart, are on the seashore. Between them is Zarephath (Sarepta), where dwelt the widow whose son Elijah raised from death. Somewhere in this region now dwelt a Gentile woman of faith who believed that Jesus was the Messiah, the one by whom salvation comes. How she gained her testimony and how many other true believers, either Jews or Gentiles, there were in the area we do not know; perhaps there were whole congregations, and Jesus was visiting them as he ministered among those who were surrounded by pagans and heathens.

This we do know, the "woman of Canaan" came out of "the coasts of Tyre and Sidon" and, finding Jesus, cried out: "Have mercy on me, O Lord, thou son of David; my daughter is grievously vexed with a devil." Matthew says: "But he answered her not a word."

Mark says she was a Greek and a Syro-Phoenician by nation. She would thus be a subject of Rome. Accordingly, she was a Canaanite by birth, a Greek by ancestry, a Syro-Phoenician by political allegiance, and thus also a subject of the empire ruled by Rome. In other words, she was a Gentile of the Gentiles, a pure Gentile, who could claim no descent whatever from Abraham; in whose veins flowed none of the believing blood of Jacob; and who was outside the royal lineage and could not be classed, in any sense, as one of the chosen people. This we must know to envision what here transpired.

Her pleas fell on deaf ears. Jesus, compassionate and merciful as none other has ever been, would not even speak to her, let alone reward her faith and heal her daughter, as he had been doing in like cases in all Israel for more than two years. Her importunings must have been extended and repetitious, both to Jesus and to the Twelve, for the disciples, knowing that on occasions *he* had healed Gentiles, though he had instructed *them* to go only to the lost sheep of Israel in their ministries, "came and besought him, saying, Send her away; for she crieth after us." Implicit in this request is the plea, 'Grant her petition, let her daughter be healed,' as is evident from Jesus' reply, not to the woman but to the Twelve: "I am not sent but unto the lost sheep of the house of Israel."

Jesus is declining not only to heal, but even to give a courteous response, to a Gentile woman who has faith, for no other reason than the fact that she is a Gentile and not an Israelite. Sectarian commentators—not knowing the plans and purposes of the Lord; having no knowledge of preexistence and foreordination; incapable of explaining why and how a just God can show mercy and compassion to one person and deny it to another, and how he can "make one vessel unto honour, and another unto dishonour" (Rom. 9)—sectarian commentators almost go wild devising reasons and explanations to justify the course here pursued by the Compassionate One.

In reality he is doing only what he has always done. In all the earth he chose only Noah and his family to enter the ark; upon all the rest of mankind—men, women, and children—he sent the flood to sweep them into a watery grave. In all of Chaldea he chose only Abraham of Ur to be his friend; upon the others he poured out wrath. In all of Sodom and the cities of the plains he chose only Lot and his wife and two daughters to be saved; upon the masses of people he rained fire and brimstone, destruction and death. Out of Egypt he called only the seed of Jacob, leaving millions of Pharaoh's minions to temporal and spiritual ruin. And so it has always been: the Canaanites and Hittites and Philistines he destroyed, to make room for his people. Assyria and Babylon and Greece were all denied the blessings of his law. The word was sent to Israel, and to Israel only.

Why? Because the house of Israel is composed of the spirits from preexistence who there developed a talent for spirituality, and who are therefore entitled to the blessings of heaven in this life on a preferential basis. All men, in due course, either in this life or in the spirit world, will be offered the blessings of salvation. But there is an eternal system of priorities; there is a law of election, a doctrine of foreordination; and Israel is entitled to the blessings of the holy word ahead of their Gentile fellows. During his lifetime Jesus took the gospel and its blessings, with isolated exceptions, to his kinsmen in Israel; after his resurrection he will send his apostolic witnesses to all men, irrespective of creed or race or ancestry. The Lord Jehovah—Jesus in the flesh—is simply conforming to the eternal law of gospel priorities that he and his Father ordained from before the foundations of the world, and such a limited exception to the eternal provisions of the eternal law as may properly be made is about to be shown forth.

By combining the accounts of Matthew and Mark we are led to believe that the importunings of our Gentile friend began before Jesus entered the house, that they were made both to him and to his disciples, and that his refusal even to converse with her was in the open for all men to see. Then, after he sought seclusion in the house, she yet entered—we can suppose she insisted upon so doing—and fell at his feet importuning and worshipping. "Lord, help me," she pled, as "she besought him that he would cast forth the devil out of her daughter." It was as though she had made the suffering of her daughter her own sorrow, even as He would do who came to bear the griefs and carry the sorrows of all men on conditions of repentance.

No longer could Jesus remain silent, but even now his spoken words carried little hope to the sorrowing mother. "Let the children of the kingdom first be filled," he said—'Let the gospel and its blessings go in this day to the Jews; it is the right and privilege of the chosen seed first to hear the message'—"for it is not meet to take the children's bread, and to cast it unto the dogs."

"But not all the snows of her native Lebanon could quench the fire of love that was burning on the altar of her heart, and prompt as an echo came forth the glorious answer" (Farrar, p. 367): "Yes, Lord; thou sayest truly, yet the dogs under the table eat of the children's crumbs."

How common it was among the Jews to refer to those without—to the Gentiles—as dogs. The Jews were the children of the kingdom, as they supposed; the heathen, none of whom were more accursed than the Canaanites, were the dogs who growled and sniveled and snapped at those within. But here the reference is more particularly to the little dogs, the household pets, who, though still Gentile dogs, yet fed themselves with such cast-off food as fell from the Jewish table.

"O woman, great is thy faith: be it unto thee even as thou wilt," Jesus said. "And her daughter was made whole from that very hour." The woman of Canaan triumphed; hers were not only the crumbs, but she ate of the children's bread; by faith she was adopted into the house of Israel. At Jesus' invitation she now came from without and joined those within. She was no longer a Gentile; she was now a daughter of Abraham.[2]

"For this saying go thy way," Jesus said, "the devil is gone out of thy daughter. And when she was come to her house, she found the devil gone out, and her daughter laid upon the bed."

The Miraculous Healings in Decapolis

(*Mark 7:31-37; Matthew 15:29-31*)

From the heathen lands of Tyre and Sidon to the semi-pagan lands of Decapolis is a long, wearisome route. His work finished among the pagans of the Syro-Phoenician area, Jesus and his loyal friends now travel by an unnamed ministerial circuit to that area of ten cities located south and east of the Sea of Galilee. The Decapolis, or confederacy of ten cities, whose identities are only partially known,[3] was wedged between the tetrarchies of Philip and Antipas. These were free Greek cities subject only to the governor of Syria. Anciently this part of the promised land fell primarily to Gad and Manasseh, but since the Babylonian exile it had been the habitat primarily of Gentile peoples who worshipped idols and devils.[4]

As the holy party made their way to their new fields of labor, we cannot doubt that they preached and healed and baptized in the cities and villages en route. Divine voices, fired with a zeal borne of the Spirit, are wont to speak forth on every available occasion; the worth of souls is great, and the holy word must be sounded in every ear. Our next recorded miracle of wonder and healing, however, is the giving of speech and hearing to a deaf and speech-impeded man. Jesus and his power were not unknown among the pagans and Jewish people of Decapolis. Nor would the accounts of his miracles in Gennesaret and Capernaum and all Galilee be unknown to them. News of this sort traveled rapidly by word of mouth; it was spoken everywhere by the tongues of believers and belittlers alike.

It comes as no surprise, then, to see them bring to Jesus "one that was deaf, and had an impediment in his speech." Their plea is that our Lord will heal him by the laying on of hands, a request showing that they knew both of his power to heal and of the procedure he used in healing.

Whether Jesus did in fact bless this afflicted man by the laying on of hands is not recorded; he was at liberty to follow such formalities as he chose, as also are his servants who perform miracles in his name and by his power. Elijah stretched himself three times upon the dead body of the widow's son as he pled with the Lord that the child's soul might return, which it then did. When Elisha raised a child from death, he lay upon the child so that their eyes and mouths and hands touched, and after much struggling in the Spirit, life came again into the dead body. Naaman was required to immerse himself seven times in Jordan before his leprous flesh became again as the flesh of a child. And so it goes; such formalities and rituals are followed as will increase the faith of the person, or even of the prophet in whose hands is found the power of God. The Urim and Thummim itself is an instrument that increases the faith of the seer who is privileged to use it for holy purposes.

Mark, who alone preserves the account of this miracle, records these four things that Jesus did, and for each of them we can see a valid reason and an intelligent purpose:

1. He took him aside, away from the multitude. This was not to be a public but a private healing, and after it was performed, those privy to the miraculous happening were charged to keep the knowledge within themselves. For some

special and unspecified reason this miracle should not have been published to the world.[5] Our Lord's counsel, however, went unheeded, and the event was published abroad, to the astonishment of the people, who acclaimed: "He hath done all things well: he maketh both the deaf to hear, and the dumb to speak."

2. He put his own fingers into the deaf ears. Since the man could not hear, this act substituted for a vocal exhortation. It testified to ears unable to hear the spoken word that by faith the hearing obstruction would be pierced.

3. He spit and placed his own saliva on the man's tongue. Such was a practice commonly believed by the Rabbis and the Jews to have healing virtue; it thus encouraged the man to believe—or, rather, increased his faith—that his tongue would be loosed and his fluency restored.

4. Jesus looked up to heaven, signifying that the healing would come by the power of the Father; then "he sighed," and he said: "Ephphatha, that is, Be opened." From this we know that he was speaking the Aramaic of the day.

"St. Mark preserves for us the sigh, and the uplifted glance, as He spoke the one word, 'Ephphatha! Be opened!' Here again it is not revealed to us what were the immediate influences which saddened His spirit. He may have sighed in pity for the man; He may have sighed in pity for the race; He may have sighed for all the sins that degrade and all the sufferings which torture; but certainly He sighed in a spirit of deep tenderness and compassion, and certainly that sigh ascended like an infinite intercession into the ears of the Lord God of Hosts." (Farrar, p. 371.)[6]

Jesus, Matthew tells us, "went up into a mountain, and sat down there." Hearing of this miracle, knowing of other wondrous things attributed to him, and, no doubt, having heard him speak words of infinite wisdom in their hearing, "great multitudes came unto him, having with them those that were lame, blind, dumb, maimed, and many others, and cast them down at Jesus' feet; and he healed them."

Were there Gentiles as well as Jews among those restored

to health and vigor? The people of the area were made up of both cultures; and, as we have seen, in the case of the Syro-Phoenician woman who pled for the crumbs that fall from Israel's table, the compassion of the Great Healer, following great faith, extends beyond the children of the kingdom and takes in the Gentiles who are without. Matthew says simply: "The multitude wondered, when they saw the dumb to speak, the maimed to be whole, the lame to walk, and the blind to see: and they glorified the God of Israel." It is, thus, the same thing we have seen before in Galilee where Israel dwelt. The new dimension here is not *what* was done, but *those* upon whom the blessings were showered.

"Let us try to realize the scene. They have heard of Him as the wonder-worker, these heathens in the land so near to, and yet so far from, Israel; and they have brought to Him 'the lame, blind, dumb, maimed, and many others,' and laid them at His feet. Oh, what wonder! All disease vanishes in [the] presence of Heaven's Own Life Incarnate. Tongues long weighted are loosed, limbs maimed or bent by disease are restored to health, the lame are stretched straight; the film of disease and the paralysis of nerve-impotence pass from eyes long insensible to the light. It is a new era—Israel conquers the heathen world, not by force, but by love; not by outward means, but by the manifestation of life-power from above. Truly, this is the Messianic conquest and reign: 'and they glorified the God of Israel.' " (Edersheim 2:46.)

Jesus Feeds the Four Thousand

(*Mark 8:1-10; JST, Mark 8:3, 6-7; Matthew 15:32-39; JST, Matthew 15:34*)

Jesus has now been in the Decapolis area for some time, preaching, healing, declaring his own divine Sonship, giving his apostolic witnesses time to mingle among the people and do in their own right the same things the Chief Apostle is doing. As to the actual time period involved, we can only speculate; certainly it involved weeks and may have been a month or even two. It is the summer of A.D. 29. We know the places he went and certain of the things he said and did, but not how long he stayed in each place. During this season, from spring through autumn, he was in the region of Tyre and Sidon, the area of the Decapolis, back again in Galilee, in the region of Caesarea Philippi (where Peter bore his witness), and at Mount Hermon (where the transfiguration occurred). Now he is about to climax his ministry in the Decapolis area and return to Galilee.

We are about to see the Giver of Manna spread another table in the wilderness—not for all Israel as they dwelt in the deserts, awaiting the trumpet call to cross the famous river and enter their promised land; not for the Passover pilgrims, symbolical of all Israel, as they wended their way to the Paschal feast in the Holy City, but a table in the wilderness where Jews and Gentiles, as brethren in the new kingdom, will first feast upon his word and then eat the multiplying loaves and fishes together. Jesus is about to feed four thousand men, besides women and children, with seven loaves and a few small fishes.

This miracle and the prior one near Bethsaida-Julias have much in common, but also some major and vital differences. Who knows, for that matter, whether the Giver of Manna may not have fed many multitudes during his mortal ministry, multitudes who had faith to be fed and for whom he multiplied such provisions as were available. It may be that the inspired authors preserved only these two accounts so that we may know the basic foundation on which all such miracles rest, as well as the distinctive message proclaimed by each of these.

Here in Decapolis we are nearing the climax of our Lord's ministry among a semi-heathen people. He has now done what he did at Bethsaida-Julias: he has taught the plan of salvation; testified of his own divinity; invited all men to come unto him and be saved; performed many mighty miracles; and been accepted and glorified as the God of Israel. There is a spirit of faith and devotion and true worship among the people. Those about to partake of his bounty have been with him for three days in a wilderness area; many of them have traveled great distances from their home cities, and such provisions as they may have brought with them have long since been exhausted.

"I have compassion on the multitude, because they have now been with me three days, and have nothing to eat: And if I send them away fasting to their own houses, they will faint by the way: for divers of them came from far," Jesus said. "From whence can a man satisfy these men with bread here in the wilderness?" his disciples responded.

"They knew that there was in Him no prodigality of the supernatural, no lavish and needless exercise of miraculous power. Many and many a time had they been with multitudes before, and yet on one occasion only [of which we know] had he fed them; and moreover, after He had done so, He had most sternly rebuked those who came to Him in expectation of a repeated offer of such gifts, and had uttered a discourse so searching and strange that it alienated from Him many even of His friends. For them to suggest to Him a repetition of the feeding of the five thousand would be a presumption which their ever-deepening reverence forbade, and forbade more than ever as they recalled how persistently He had refused to work a sign, such as this was, at the bidding of others.

"But no sooner had He given them the signal of His intention, than with perfect faith they became His ready ministers. They seated the multitude on the ground, and distributed to them the miraculous multiplication of the seven loaves and the few small fishes; and, this time unbidden, they gathered the fragments that remained, and with them filled a large basket of rope seven times, after the multitude—four thousand in number, besides women and children—had eaten and were filled. And then kindly, and with no exhibition on the part of the populace of that spurious excitement which had marked the former miracle, the Lord and His Apostles joined in sending away the rejoicing and grateful throng." (Farrar, pp. 371-73.)[7]

When Jesus fed the five thousand, he was dealing with Jews and Jews alone; with those who kept the law of Moses; with a people who expected their Messiah to feed them temporal bread in the deserts of mortality; with brethren en route to Jerusalem to participate in those sacrifices which testified of the atoning sacrifice of the Lamb of God. Thereafter they sought to make him king, and he preached to them the sermon on the bread of life, with the deliberate intention of winnowing the chaff from the wheat.

Here in Decapolis the symbolism is quite different. Both Jews and Gentiles surround the sacred board; the table set in the wilderness is not for Israel only, but for all mankind. Here is the prefiguring of the Gentile harvest, the harvest scheduled to begin when he sends the apostles into all the world to preach the gospel to every creature. Here is the prefiguring of that day when the gospel will go to all mankind and there will truly be one God and one Shepherd over all the earth.

After this miracle and the witness it bore, the Decapolis ministry ended. Jesus and his associates returned by ship to Magdala, or as Mark says, "the parts of Dalmanutha," which must have been an area on the western side of the lake, there to continue his light-giving ministry among those who sat in darkness. Our next view of him, however, will be in Capernaum, when he again discourses about signs.

All things, as we would expect, are going forward as foreordained and designed; the work is being done as decreed by Him who governeth all things by his own omnipotent power. Jesus, the Son, is representing his Father, as that Holy Being designed, intended, and expected. The Father's business is well managed by the Son. And blessed be his holy name forever.

NOTES

1. "Rumours of possible action against Him by Antipas increased the difficulty of the situation. Every one knew that He and many of His followers had come from the school of the Baptist, whom Antipas had just murdered, and it was evident that His aim was more or

less similiar to John's, though His acts were more wonderful. Hence speculation was rife respecting Him. Was He the promised Elias? or, at least, Jeremiah, risen from the dead? or was He some special prophet sent from God? Many, indeed, were questioning if He might not even be the Messiah, and were willing to accept Him as such, if He would only head a national revolt, in alliance with the Rabbis and priests, against the Romans. To Antipas His appearance was doubly alarming, for it seemed as if the fancied revolutionary movement of John had broken out afresh more fiercely than ever, and superstition, working in an uneasy conscience, easily saw in Him a resurrection of the murdered Baptist, endowed, now, with the awful power of the eternal world from which He had returned. A second murder seemed needed to make the first effective, and to avoid this additional danger Jesus for a time sought concealment." (Geikie, p. 532.)

2. "As many as receive this Gospel shall be called after thy name," Jehovah said to Abraham, "and shall be accounted thy seed, and shall rise up and bless thee, as their father." (Abr. 2:10.)

3. It is not known whether the cities of the Decapolis either actually or always numbered ten. Names that have come down to us include Gerasa, Gadara, Hippos, Pella, Gergesa, Scythopolis (the ancient Bethshean), and Philadelphia.

4. "This extensive 'Ten Cities' district was essentially heathen territory. Their ancient monuments show, in which of them Zeus, Astarte, and Athene, or else Artemis, Hercules, Dionysos, Demeter, or other Grecian divinities, were worshipped." (Edersheim 2:44-45.)

5. "On some occasions a knowledge of healing miracles may engender faith, on others it fosters unbelief and persecution. Accordingly, Jesus sought either to advertise or keep secret his miraculous healings, depending upon the needs of the ministry at the particular time and place. On a previous occasion, when he was leaving this very region, he had commanded the man out of whom a legion of devils was cast to publish the miracle through all Decapolis. But now, sojourning, for a season in the area, the Master Healer sought to keep secret the dramatic nature of this particular miracle." (*Commentary* 1:373.)

6. Farrar's footnote to this passage reads: "It [the sigh] was not drawn from Him," says Luther, "on account of the single tongue and ears of this poor man; but it is a common sigh over all tongues and ears, yea, over all hearts, bodies, and souls, and over all men, from Adam to his last descendant." (Farrar, p. 371.)

7. "They knew full well the miraculous creative powers of the Master whom they followed. The question as here put is rather an expression of their own inability to feed such a multitude with the scanty provisions at hand. We may suppose also that in their subservient position as followers of him who exceeds all men in power and might, they modestly and properly left to their Lord the decision as to what should be done. It is evident that Jesus did not deem it necessary to test their faith, as he had done before, by saying, 'They need not depart; give ye them to eat'; this time he simply asked what provisions were at hand and gave directions as to their distribution." (*Commentary* 1:376.)

THE LEAVEN OF THE PHARISEES AND SADDUCEES

If there arise among you a prophet,
or a dreamer of dreams,
and giveth thee a sign or a wonder,
And the sign or the wonder come to pass,
whereof he spake unto thee,
saying, Let us go after other gods,
which thou hast not known,
and let us serve them;
Thou shalt not hearken unto the words
of that prophet, or that dreamer of dreams:
for the Lord your God proveth you,
to know whether ye love the Lord your God
with all your heart and with all your soul.
Ye shall walk after the Lord your God,
and fear him, and keep his commandments,
and obey his voice, and ye shall serve him,
and cleave unto him.
And that prophet, or that dreamer of dreams,
shall be put to death;
because he hath spoken to turn you away
from the Lord your God,

which brought you out of the land of Egypt,
and redeemed you out of the house of bondage,
to thrust thee out of the way
which the Lord thy God commanded thee
to walk in. So shalt thou put
the evil away from the midst of thee.
(Deut. 13:1-5.)

False Ministers Seek Signs

(*Matthew 16:1-4; JST, Matthew 16:2-3; Mark 8:11-12; JST, Mark 8:12*)

We have somewhat more to say about signs, sign-seekers, and the state of the souls of those whose hearts are centered on such portents. We have heretofore heard Jesus—it was in Capernaum, his own city—utterly defeat and discomfit certain of the scribes and of the Pharisees who demanded that he show them a sign from heaven. (Book 2, chap. 48.) The only sign for them, he then testified, was the sign of Jonah, the sign of his own resurrection, the sign of the glory and triumph of that kingdom which is not of this world.

That former dialogue created a division among the people. Those who believed and understood the truth from heaven as it fell from the lips of Jesus knew full well that signs of the sort sought by the scribes would do nothing but demean the One called upon to give them. True prophets—least of all earth's Chief Prophet—do not go about calling down fire from heaven, turning rivers upstream, or drying up seas, to prove their prophetic powers. Those whose hearts were hardened remained darkened in mind and spirit and continued to whine that he did his miracles by the power of Beelzebub—the lord of idolatrous worship—because he did not produce the heavenly display of fire and power that they said they would accept as a sign. They had learned by experience that however contrary to the true order their demand for a supernatural display might be, it would have the effect of prejudicing many people against him.[1]

This time the challenge is hurled not only by certain scribes and Pharisees, but by the Pharisees and the Sadducees combined, by the united power of all the rulers of the people. "Every section of the ruling classes—the Pharisees, formidable from their religious weight among the people; the Sadducees, few in number, but powerful from wealth and position; the Herodians, representing the influence of the Romans, and of their nominees the tetrarchs; the scribes and lawyers, bringing to bear the authority of their orthodoxy and their learning—were all united against Him in one firm phalanx of conspiracy and opposition, and were determined above all things to hinder His preaching, and to alienate from Him, as far as was practicable, the affections of the people among whom most of His mighty works were done." (Farrar, p. 375.)[2]

Their reasoning was persuasive; however false their premises, their arguments had the effect of destroying the influence of Jesus. If he gave no sign from heaven—which it was generally believed the Messiah would do—then he could not be the Messiah, and it must be true that his miracles were wrought by Satan's power. If, on the other hand, he did give a sign from heaven, of the sort Rabbi Eliezer would have given,[3] he was still a false prophet and worthy of death because his teachings did not conform to the Rabbinical standards. Had not Jehovah said by the mouth of Moses that if a prophet gave a sign or wonder that came to pass, the prophet nevertheless should be put to death, if his teachings controverted their system of revealed religion? (Deut. 13:1-5.) And surely everyone knew—it was common knowledge, and no proof need be offered—that the teachings of the Man of Nazareth were false because they contradicted what Moses said as interpreted by the scribes and Rabbis. This matter of demanding a sign from heaven, they reasoned, was truly the way to destroy this Galilean peasant who had attended none of their schools and certainly was not learned in Rabbinic lore.

But suppose, just suppose, he had given them a sign?

What then? Would it have proved the truth and divinity of his work? "If He had granted their request, what purpose would have been furthered? It is not the influence of external forces, but it is the germinal principle of life within, which makes the good seed to grow; nor can the hard heart be converted, or the stubborn unbelief removed, by portents and prodigies, but by inward humility, and the grace of God stealing downward like the dew of heaven, in silence and unseen. What would have ensued had the sign been vouchsafed? By its actual eye-witnesses it would have been attributed to demoniac agency; by those to whom it was reported it would have been explained away; by those of the next generation it would have been denied as an invention, or evaporated into a myth." (Farrar, pp. 375-76.)[4]

The demand that their Messiah prove his claim to divine Sonship by showing a sign from heaven has now been made again. His answer: The signs of the times are everywhere to be seen; they abound on every hand; all men are bound to interpret them correctly and to prepare for the storms ahead. "When it is evening ye say, The weather is fair, for the sky is red; and in the morning ye say The weather is foul today; for the sky is red and lowering." 'Ye hear me speak words of eternal truth whose verity is attested by the power of the Spirit. Ye hear my witnesses that God is my Father. Ye see me cast out devils, cleanse lepers, and raise the dead. Ye know that I have stilled storms, walked on water, and multiplied a few loaves and fishes to feed thousands. If I say I am the Son of God, and I then do all these wondrous works, can my words be other than true? What more do you want in the way of a sign?' "O hypocrites! ye can discern the face of the sky; but ye cannot tell the signs of the times."[5] Then came the biting denunciation:

> *A wicked and adulterous generation seeketh after a sign; and there shall no sign be given unto it, but the sign of the prophet Jonas.*

"The only sign to Nineveh was Jonah's solemn warning of near judgment, and his call to repentance—and the only sign now . . . was the warning cry of judgment and the loving call to repentance." (Edersheim 2:70.)

With this Jesus left his detractors, going by boat from Magdala toward the coast of Bethsaida-Julias, en route to the coasts of Caesarea Philippi where Peter will make his great confession.

Beware of the Leaven of Evil Men

(*Matthew 16:5-12; JST, Matthew 16:8-9; Mark 8:13-21; JST, Mark 8:16*)

Jesus came from the semiheathen region of the Decapolis to the Israelite area of Magdala. "For some time He had been absent from home. He had been sought out with trustful faith in the regions of Tyre and Sidon. He had been welcomed with ready gratitude in heathen Decapolis; here, at home, He was met with the flaunt of triumphant opposition, under the guise of hypocritical zeal." In Decapolis the multitudes believed his words, rejoiced in his miracles, ate of the loaves and fishes provided by his providence, and glorified him as the God of Israel. Back among his own he found "all the self-satisfied hypocrisies of a decadent religion drawn up in array to stop His path!" (Farrar, p. 376.) There among his own he was assailed by the rulers of the people, who, under the guise of demanding a sign from heaven, proclaimed their utter disbelief in and complete rejection of his Messianic claims.

Thus the issue was squarely set. It is the doctrine of the Almighty that Jesus Christ is the Son of the living God; that salvation comes by him and him alone; that he has abolished death and brought life and immortality to light through the gospel; and that all men everywhere must believe in him, repent of their sins, be baptized in water, receive the gift of the Holy Ghost, and work the works of righteousness, or they can in nowise enter into the kingdom of God.

It was the doctrine of the Pharisees—and all who joined

with them in opposing Jesus[6]—that salvation came by the law of Moses alone; that the man Jesus was a deluded fanatic without divine power; that he was a rabble-rouser, an anarchist, a subverter of all that was great and good in their traditions; that he was a blasphemer worthy of death; that he performed miracles by the power of the prince of devils, yea, that he was even Beelzebub Incarnate; and that he should be rejected, cast out, and stoned to death as one who prophesied falsely and led the people away from their ancient moorings.

And so Jesus, after deriding the sign-seekers as wicked and adulterous, chose to leave them and minister and heal among other people. Thanks to their darkened minds, their perverted consciences, and their stony hearts, he would go elsewhere to preach. "He did not press His mercies on those who rejected them. As in after days His nation were suffered to prefer their robber and their murderer to the Lord of Life, so now the Galileans were suffered to keep their Pharisees and lose their Christ." (Farrar, pp. 376-77.) He and his disciples set sail, leaving Magdala for the area of Bethsaida-Julias on the north and east of the sacred sea.

Their departure was made in haste, and the disciples failed to take food for their sustenance. Apparently after they landed at their destination, Jesus—ever anxious to strengthen them spiritually; concerned lest any of them be tainted in any degree by the damning doctrine of his enemies; and using their failure to bring bread as a teaching aid—took occasion to raise a warning voice. "Take heed and beware of the leaven of the Pharisees and of the Sadducees," he said. Mark tells us that he also warned them against "the leaven of Herod."

Those same disciples, at Jacob's Well, had missed the true meaning of his statement that he had meat to eat that they knew not of. But a short time back the metaphors about eating the bread which came down from heaven had failed to find quick and easy lodgment in their souls; and yet in the future they would miss the deep meaning of the expression about Lazarus sleeping and needing to be awakened. At this stage of their spiritual development, metaphors seemed to give them some trouble. They therefore "reasoned among themselves, saying, He said this because we have taken no bread."

Jesus, perceiving how foolish and spiritually immature they were, responded with a severe and stern rebuke. "O ye of little faith, why reason ye among yourselves, because ye have brought no bread?" he said. "Perceive ye not yet, neither understand? have ye your heart yet hardened? Having eyes, see ye not? and having ears, hear ye not? and do ye not remember? When I brake the five loaves among five thousand, how many baskets full of fragments took ye up? They say unto him, Twelve. And when the seven among four thousand, how many baskets full of fragments took ye up? And they said, Seven. And he said unto them, How is it that ye do not understand?" "How is it that ye do not understand that I spake it not to you concerning bread, that ye should beware of the leaven of the Pharisees and of the Sadducees?"

Only then, after such a rebuke, was Matthew able to conclude: "Then understood they how that he bade them not beware of the leaven of bread, but of the doctrine of the Pharisees and of the Sadducees." And, of course, of the Herodians and every other sect, party, cult, or denomination, for all such are not of God, and have not the fulness of the gospel, which alone sets forth the doctrine of God.

"Leaven was one of the very commonest types of sin, and especially of insidious and subterranean sin." (Farrar, p. 379.) Leaven—the fermenting, defiling, contaminating influence of those who opposed him! Leaven—the debasing, damning doctrines of those who would one day cause his death! Leaven—the views and feelings of those who were anti-Christ and who sought to keep others from accepting him as their Messiah and Deliverer! The leaven of the Pharisees, Sadducees, Herodians, scribes—of all who believed and preached false doctrine—such leaven was evil.

They must beware lest they be tainted in the slightest degree.[7]

Jesus Restores Sight by Stages
(*Mark 8:22-26*)

Every miracle is unique; no two are alike. Two blind men have their eyes opened by divine power, and each wondrous deed is as different from the other as are the two recipients of the heavensent goodness. Those few of Jesus' miracles which are recorded in any sort of detail were selected from the many by the spirit of inspiration; such accounts preserve for us patterns and types of miraculous acts, with a view to encouraging us—whatever our disabled or diseased condition may be—to ourselves rely on Him by whose power miracles are wrought, and to seek to gain an outpouring of his goodness and grace in our own lives.

Further, all healings do not happen instantaneously; the prophetic fingers do not always snap and cause a prostrate sufferer to leap from his pallet as though by magic. A sightless one may be sent to wash the spittle and clay from his eyes in the pool of Siloam; a leper may be required to immerse seven times in Jordan; a suffering soul may be tested to the full before hearing the blessed words: "Be it unto thee according to thy faith." It is no less a miracle when shattered bones weld themselves together gradually than when they reform in an instant. A withered arm that attains its proper and perfect frame through a growth process may be an exhibition of as great a miracle as one that bursts suddenly into being. And so we come to the miracle at hand, the only New Testament instance of a person being healed by stages.

Jesus is in Bethsaida-Julias. A blind man is brought to him. For reasons that are not recited, Jesus chooses not to perform a miracle in the city; perhaps the idolatrous infidels of this Gentile city are not even worthy to see a wonder wrought on one whose faith and works warrant such divine intervention in his behalf. "All that we can dimly see is

Christ's dislike and avoidance of these heathenish Herodian towns, with their spurious and tainted Hellenism, their tampering with idolatry, and even their very names commemorating, as was the case with Bethsaida-Julias, some of the most contemptible of the human race." (Farrar, pp. 380-81.)[8]

Rather, Jesus began a series of acts, each of which was designed to increase faith in the heart of the sightless one. First he led the blind man by the hand out of town; then he spat in his eyes, an act that was a well-known Jewish remedy for diseases of the eye; and then he performed the gospel ordinance of the laying on of hands. We cannot doubt that words of encouragement and exhortation and healing were spoken as he performed the ministerial service that is usually incident to the laying on of hands.

After this Jesus asked the man "if he saw ought." His reply: "I see men as trees, walking." Then the initial miracle was added upon. "He put his hands again upon his eyes, and made him look up: and he was restored, and saw every man clearly." Then Jesus sent the man away—not back into Bethsaida-Julias, but to his own house. "Neither go into the town, nor tell it to any in the town," Jesus said.

"Certainly the manner in which this healing took place teaches that men should seek the Lord's healing grace with all their strength and faith, though such is sufficient for a partial cure only, following the receipt of which, however, they may then gain the added assurance and faith to be made whole and well every whit. Men also are often healed of their spiritual maladies by degrees, step by step as they get their lives in harmony with the plans and purposes of Diety." (*Commentary* 1:379-80.)

NOTES

1. "They had already found by experience that the one most effectual weapon to discredit His mission and undermine His influence was the demand of a sign—above all, a sign from heaven. If He were indeed the Messiah, why should He not give them bread from heaven as Moses, they said, had done? where were Samuel's thunder and Elijah's

flame? why should not the sun be darkened, and the moon turned into blood, and the stars of heaven be shaken? why should not some fiery pillar glide before them to victory, or the burst of some stormy *Bath Kol* ratify His words?" (Farrar, p. 375.)

As to the meaning of the *Bath Kol* here named, and also as illustrative of the kind of signs sought, we take these words from Edersheim: "As regards 'a sign from heaven,' it is said that Rabbi Eliezer, when his teaching was challenged, successively appealed to certain 'signs.' First, a locust-tree moved at his bidding one hundred, or, according to some, four hundred cubits. Next, the channels of water were made to flow backwards; then the walls of the Academy leaned forward, and were only arrested at the bidding of another Rabbi. Lastly, Eliezer exclaimed: 'If the Law is as I teach, let it be proved from heaven!' when a voice fell from the sky (the *Bath Qol*): 'What have ye to do with Rabbi Eliezer, for the Halakhah is as he teaches?' " (Edersheim 2:69.)

2. In a footnote to this passage, Farrar notes a comparison of "the sects of the Jews to modern schools of thought." It is: Pharisees as pietists; Essenes as mystics; Sadducees as rationalists; Herodians as political clubs and the like; Zealots as radicals; and Samaritans as schismatics—all of this points up to the truism that Lucifer repeats himself, generation after generation, as he seeks to destroy the souls of men.

3. See footnote 1 above.

4. There is a striking parallel between the demands of the ancient Pharisees that Jesus show them a sign, and the demands of modern Pharisees that the Latter-day Saints produce the gold plates from which the Book of Mormon was translated, and the Urim and Thummim used in the translation process. Such, of course, is not the Lord's way of proving the truth and divinity of his work. With reference to this latter-day demand, the Lord said to Joseph Smith: "If they will not believe my words, they would not believe you, my servant Joseph, if it were possible that you should show them all these things which I have committed unto you. Oh, this unbelieving and stiffnecked generation—mine anger is kindled against them. . . . But this generation shall have my word through you." (D&C 5:7-8, 10.)

5. In like manner, worldly people today fail to discern the signs of our times; fail to see that the coming forth of the Book of Mormon and the restoration of the gospel, for instance, are signs certifying that the coming of the Son of Man is near; fail to understand that the wars and plagues and wickedness of our day are preparatory to that great confrontation between good and evil which will usher in the Second Coming. And much, much more. See *Mormon Doctrine,* 2nd ed., pp. 715-34.

6. "Strange bedfellows these—Sadducees and Pharisees, bitter religious enemies of each other, now uniting in an unholy alliance to fight Jesus and his doctrines. But such is ever the case with the various branches of the devil's Church. One thing always unites warring sects of religionists—their common fear and hatred of the pure truths of salvation. Sects of modern Christendom fight each other on nearly all fronts save one—on that they unite to oppose Joseph Smith and the gospel restored through his instrumentality." (*Commentary* 1:378.)

7. Similarly: Beware the leaven of the modern sects of Christendom—sects so near in one sense to salvation, and yet so far away in the eternal sense—sects that believe false doctrines. Beware of the leaven of the Baptists, that belief in Christ without more brings a spiritual rebirth. Beware of the leaven of the Lutherans, that men are justified by faith alone, without works of righteousness. Beware the leaven of all the sects and cults, for among them the fulness of the everlasting gospel is not found.

8. In his footnote to this passage, Farrar says: "Herod Philip had named his renovated capital in honor of Julia, the abandoned daughter of the Emperor Augustus."

THE TESTIMONY OF OUR LORD

Ye are blessed,
for the testimony which ye have borne
is recorded in heaven for the angels
to look upon; and they rejoice over you,
and your sins are forgiven you.
(D&C 62:3.)[1]

'I Am the Son of Man'

(*Matthew 16:13; Mark 8:27; Luke 9:18; JST, Luke 9:18*)

Jesus is now constrained to hold a testimony meeting with the disciples. He himself opens with prayer, names the subject for discussion, and invites any of those present who so desire to bear witness of what God, by the power of the Holy Ghost, has revealed to them. Whether others than the Twelve were present is not stated. On previous missionary journeys mention has been made of the presence of Mary Magdalene and other women, possibly wives of some of the apostles. Whatever the attendance on this occasion, we are sure it was only a select and favored few who were present to hear the witnesses borne and to feel the Spirit about to be poured out upon them.

The need for this meeting was real. The intimate friends

of the Master had been subject to severe trials of their faith in the days just past, and Jesus now planned for them some sacred moments of spiritual uplift. There had been disaffection and falling away when, though urged by thousands of his Israelite kin, he refused to step forth as King-Messiah and wear their proffered crown.

The winnowing effect of his bread of life sermon had blown Israelitish chaff to the four winds. His confrontation with the united leaders of the people, when they challenged him to show a sign from heaven—a sign of the sort the Jewish-Messiah was expected to show—had weakened his influence with many people. Multitudes who once basked in the light of his presence had now gone back to their wallowing in the mire of ritualistic Judaism. Jesus was now virtually an outcast and an escapee from Galilee, from Antipas, who had slain John, and from the people who no longer savored his sermons and believed his doctrines. Was it not true, they reasoned, that his miracles, as the Rabbis said, were done by the power of the devil? Indeed, so severe were the circumstances and so widespread the falling away that he had even felt constrained to warn his closest friends against the leaven of the Jewish leaders. In these dark and dire days, what was more natural than to assemble his friends around him for a period of spiritual refreshment?

Jesus himself bore the first testimony of his own divinity on this memorable occasion. Luke introduces his account by saying: "As he went alone with his disciples to pray, he asked them, saying, Who say the people that I am?" Matthew records the query as "Whom do men say that I the Son of man am?" What other things he may have said by way of introduction we do not know; perhaps it suffices to understand what he meant by saying, 'I am the Son of Man,' a designation he so frequently applied to himself.

To his Jewish disciples—who knew that the Almighty was their Father in heaven; who knew that God was a personal being in whose image man is created; who knew that Deity was a holy man—to his Jewish disciples, to say 'I am the Son of Man' meant 'I am the Son of God.' The two name-titles are and were totally synonymous. The Son of Man and the Son of God are one and the same because the *Man* involved is *God;* they are simply two designations of the same exalted person. From earliest times, speaking of the Father of us all, holy writ has testified: "In the language of Adam, Man of Holiness is his name, and the name of his Only Begotten is the Son of Man, even Jesus Christ, a righteous Judge, who shall come in the meridian of time." (Moses 6:57.)[2]

As we ponder the profound and deep import of Jesus' declaration that he is the Son of Man and therefore the Son of God, we must remind ourselves anew of the single most important truth in all eternity. It is that God himself, the Supreme Being, the maker, upholder, and preserver of all things, the creator of the universe, our Eternal Father, is a glorified and perfected man.[3] A knowledge of this truth is the beginning of all spiritual progression. This truth is the foundation upon which the whole plan of salvation rests. God himself, the Father of us all, ordained and established the plan of salvation to enable us, his children, to advance and progress and become like him. Salvation consists in becoming as God is. He is a holy man—Man of Holiness is his name—and his beloved Son is the Son of Man of Holiness, or, as Jesus now expresses it, *The Son of Man.*

"Thou Art the Christ"

(*Matthew 16:14-16; Mark 8:28-29; JST, Mark 8:31; Luke 9:19-20; JST, Luke 9:19-20*)

Our Lord has now testified to these favored few that he is the Son of God—a witness he has borne to many people in many places on many occasions. It is, as it were, a new and an everlasting testimony—*new* each time its burning fire sinks into a human heart; *everlasting* because it is always borne by Gods, angels, and men, whenever receptive hearers can be assembled to hear an inspired voice.

To Joseph and Mary the *Lad of Twelve* spoke of being about his Father's business; to the Passover throngs the *Cleanser of the Temple* spoke of his Messiahship and the death and resurrection that would attend it; to Nicodemus the *Teacher sent from God* spoke of his coming crucifixion and identified himself as the Only Begotten Son of God; to the woman of Samaria the *Weary Traveler* testified, "I who speak unto thee am the Messias"; to his own in Nazareth the *Promised Messiah* acclaimed that in him were the Messianic prophecies fulfilled; to the messengers who came from John, *Jesus* said his miracles and his teachings bore record that he was the promised one who should come; to the throngs in Capernaum the *Bread from Heaven* taught that men must eat his flesh and drink his blood to be saved; to thousands upon thousands of the house of Israel, in all the cities of Judea and Galilee and beyond, the *Preacher*, the *Healer*, the *Witness of Truth* preached the gospel of the kingdom, which is that men are saved through his atoning sacrifice; on occasions without number, the *son of Mary*, in plain words and in clear similitudes, taught that he was the *Son of God.*

It comes as no surprise, then, here in the coast of Caesarea Philippi, for his disciples to hear him say what they have heard him say before: *'I am the Son of that Holy Man who is God!'* It is the same witness he has always borne; it is a testimony that burns with heavenly fire in their hearts; it is a simple truth that they believe in their souls. As we shall see shortly, they did not as yet envision in full how and in what manner their holy Messiah would accomplish his work and bring life and immortality to light through his gospel. But they knew who he said he was, and they believed the witness he bore of himself.

What then of the question he now asked: "Whom do men say that I am?" It is as though he said: 'My words and my works bear testimony of my divine commission. If men do not accept me as the Son of God, how do they explain these things? Who do they suppose that I am? Am I a devil, as the Pharisees say? How do they explain me and my words if I am not the Son of Man?' Such ever is the dilemma facing unbelievers. How can the work prosper so gloriously if it be not true!

That these same questions tormented the minds of many people is clear from the response of the disciples. The human mind cries out for an explanation of the divine wonders everywhere to be seen. "Some say that thou art John the Baptist; some, Elias; and others, Jeremias, or one of the prophets" is the response; and it is a reply that shows how false and foolish Jewish traditions were, and how far those who believed them would go to avoid accepting revealed truth.

Antipas, who slew John—fearful, superstitious, with a sin-laden conscience, and exhibiting a touch of the madness and mental derangement that tortured the body and tormented the soul of his evil father—Antipas saw in Jesus the slain Baptist risen from death. Others, also darkened in mind and spirit, adopted the overcredulous superstitions of their depraved ruler, and this in spite of the fact Jesus and John were contemporaries. Such a way to account for Jesus and his works seems wholly incredible to us.

Some said he was Elias, who was to come and restore all things, according to one of their scriptures, which we no longer have; or he was Elijah, who was to return before the great and dreadful day of the Lord. Some also had thought that John the Baptist was one or the other of these prophets.

Others thought Jesus was Jeremiah, around whom Jewish tradition had spun a wondrous web of supernatural foolishness. They believed that this ancient prophet—he was ministering in Israel when Lehi left Jerusalem—had hidden the ark in a cave on Mount Nebo when their capital city was overrun by Nebuchadnezzar; that he had called Abraham, Isaac, Jacob, and Moses from their tombs to wail with him over the destruction of the temple; and that he and Elijah would prepare the way before the Messiah by returning the ark and the Urim and Thummim to the Holy of Holies.

And yet others supposed our Lord was this or that

ancient prophet returned again. There is never agreement among those who believe false doctrine; it matters not to their master what they believe so long as they do not believe the truth. And we can suppose there was a reservoir of rumors and a mountain of explanations relative to Jesus and his works.

"But whom say ye that I am?" he asks. It matters not what carnal men may think. The things of God are known only by the power of the Spirit. Where Christ and his gospel are concerned, the only witness of worth comes from his disciples. Thus Peter—for himself, for the Twelve, for the little group there assembled, for all truth believers in all ages—gives answer: "*Thou art the Christ, the Son of the living God.*" 'As thou hast said, Lord, thou art the Son of Man; thou art the Messiah; thou art the One of whom Moses and the prophets spoke; thou art the Son of God.'

Peter thus speaks that which they all believe and of which they all are sure. He confesses the Lord Jesus with his lips. No doubt he then said more than is recorded, and no doubt others bore like witness on this same occasion. But as for Peter, he is only repeating what he has said before. It is not a new testimony, simply a reaffirmation of that which has long been in his heart and which has often fallen from his lips. One of the most fluent and fervent of these prior testimonies of Peter was the one we heard following the sermon on the bread of life. As others dissembled, as the loaves-and-fishes disciples departed from the Living Bread, Peter testified—and it is the equal of his great Messianic confession here beyond the borders of Israel—

> *Lord . . . thou hast the words of eternal life. And we believe and are sure that thou art that Christ, the Son of the living God.* (John 6:68-69.)

"The Keys of the Kingdom of Heaven"

(*Matthew 16:17-20; Mark 8:30*)

"*The Son of the living God.*" An awesome thought; in itself a solemn sermon; wonder of wonders, miracle of miracles: that God should have a son! The Almighty, the First Great Cause, the Supreme Being, the Creator of all things from the beginning—God the Eternal Father begets a son! That holy Man, who is omnipotent and omniscient, who sits enthroned in eternal glory—the maker, preserver, and upholder of all things, before whom all things bow in humble reverence—that holy being, who is immortal and eternal, the Supreme God, fathers a son after the manner of the flesh. An immortal Man—glorified and exalted, having a body of flesh and bones—sires a son in mortality, a son who has a body of flesh and blood.

"The Son of the living God." Such a thing transcends human comprehension. How can it be, and if it is, how can such a truth be known? We are not dealing here with physical facts or chemical formulas; we are not solving geometric theorems or learning the principles of astronomy. That which pertains to God is in the realm of the Spirit. God stands revealed or he remains forever unknown. And if he has a son, such an awesome reality can only be known in the same way—by revelation.

"No man can say [know] that Jesus is the Lord, but by the Holy Ghost," Paul says. (1 Cor. 12:3.) "The testimony of our Lord"—of which Paul says we ought not be "ashamed" (2 Tim. 1:8)—what is it? It is to know by revelation that the man Jesus is the Son of Man. The Holy Ghost is a revelator whose mission is to bear witness of the Father and the Son. "To some it is given by the Holy Ghost to know that Jesus Christ is the Son of God." (D&C 46:13.) "I am thy fellowservant, and of thy brethren that have the testimony of Jesus," was the angelic word to John, "for the testimony of Jesus is the spirit of prophecy." (Rev. 19:10.) And so Peter, who is one of the prophets, proclaims his testimony: "Thou art the Christ, the Son of the living God." To this Jesus can give but one answer:

> *Blessed art thou, Simon Bar-jona: for flesh and blood hath not revealed it unto thee, but my Father which is in heaven.*

All who bear testimony by the power of the Holy Ghost are blessed; their inspired utterances are recorded in heaven for the angels—their fellowservants—to look upon. Peter is thus blessed. In contrast to Christ, who is the Son of God, Peter is the son of Jonah. Though he is blessed, he is as other men, born of a mortal father. There is only one whose Father was immortal, and Jesus maintains that distinction in dealing even with his intimate friends whom he is training to be his apostolic witnesses.

Mortal though Peter is, his testimony has come to him by revelation—not from reason, not by logic, not from man, but by revelation from the Father by the power of the Holy Ghost. It is a true testimony.

> *And I say also unto thee, That thou art Peter, and upon this rock I will build my church; and the gates of hell shall not prevail against it.*

Yet again Jesus reaffirms the difference between himself and his disciples. He calls Peter, Simon Bar-jona, Simon the son—not of God as He was, but of Jonah; Simon, who is called Peter, is distinguished from Jesus, who is called Christ.[4]

And having thus testified again of his divine Sonship, Jesus promises that upon the rock of revealed truth, the rock of revelation, the rock of personal testimony received by the power of the Holy Ghost—upon this rock he will build his church.[5] And thus it has ever been. Whenever God speaks and men hear; whenever there is revelation by the power of the Holy Ghost; whenever men enjoy the gift of the Holy Ghost—then they have the true church. And where any of these things are not, there the true church is not. And further, as long as the true saints walk in this light of heaven, the gates of hell do not and cannot prevail against them. Thus, in thought content, Jesus acclaims:

'Blessed art thou Peter, for thy unwearying devotion to my cause and for the testimony which thou hast borne of my divine Sonship; and this testimony was not revealed to thee by mortal man, but it came by revelation from my Father, by the power of the Holy Ghost. And now Peter, my chief apostle, know this: It is upon this very rock of revelation that I have built up my Church in all ages past, and upon which I will build and perfect it in this your day; for after I have ascended to my Father, ye and your brethren and all the worthy saints shall receive the gift of the Holy Ghost, so that you may receive revelation from me and learn all things that are expedient for you to know concerning the building up and rolling forth of my kingdom.' (*Commentary* 1:386.)[6]

> *And I will give unto thee the keys of the kingdom of heaven: and whatsoever thou shalt bind on earth shall be bound in heaven: and whatsoever thou shalt loose on earth shall be loosed in heaven.*

"The kingdom of heaven": the kingdom of God on earth; the Church of Jesus Christ organized among men; the earthly kingdom designed to prepare men for the heavenly kingdom of the Father—such is the meaning of the language of our Lord.

"The keys of the kingdom": the governing, controlling, regulating power over the Church or kingdom; the instrumentality that opens the door to the receipt of peace in this life and eternal life in the world to come—such is what Jesus meant by keys.

Since the earthly church, which is a kingdom, prepares men for the heavenly kingdom, which is in the celestial world, it follows that what is bound on earth is bound in heaven, and what is loosed on earth is loosed in heaven. If the Lord's legal administrators baptize repentant and worthy souls on earth, that baptism is binding in heaven and admits the faithful to celestial rest. If those legal administrators seal a worthy and faithful man to a worthy and faithful woman in the everlasting covenant of marriage, that marriage is binding in heaven and the blessed recipients of so great a bounty come forth in the resurrection as husband and wife and enter into eternal glory. And if the Lord's lawfully empowered servants, acting in his name and with his authorization, sever sinners from among the saints and turn them over to the buffetings of Satan on earth, all that might have been theirs is loosed in heaven, and they shall fail to gain what might have been theirs. It matters not whether the binding or loosing is done by the mouth of the Lord himself or by his servants who do and say what he directs. "Whether by mine own voice or by the voice of my servants, it is the same," he says. (D&C 1:38.)

Strange as these expressions about binding and loosing may seem to an apostate Christendom, they were understood by the Jewish disciples to whom Jesus then spoke. "No other terms were in more constant use in Rabbinic Canon-Law than those of 'binding' and 'loosing.' . . . In regard to some of their earthly decrees, they were wont to say that 'the Sanhedrin above' confirmed what 'the Sanhedrin beneath' had done. But the words of Christ, as they avoided the foolish conceit of His contemporaries, left it not doubtful, but conveyed the assurance that, under the guidance of the Holy Ghost, whatsoever they bound or loosed on earth would be bound or loosed in heaven." (Edersheim 2:85.)[7]

That Jesus, after hearing the witness of Peter and perhaps of others, charged them all "that they should tell no man that he was Jesus, the Christ" is not strange in the light of the historical circumstances. This very witness of his divine Sonship had been borne in congregations without number by him and his disciples for some two and a half years. Now, however, the opposition was so great, the hatred so intense, the desire to hinder the work so well organized, that it seemed the course of wisdom, for the moment, not to hold him forth as the Messiah. He had many things yet to accomplish before Jewish Sanhedrists turned him over to Roman soldiers to drive nails in his hands and feet and hurl a spear into his side.

NOTES

1. The relationship between the bearing of testimony by the power of the Holy Ghost and the forgiveness of sins illustrates a glorious gospel truth. It is that whenever faithful saints gain the companionship of the Holy Spirit, they are clean and pure before the Lord,

for the Spirit will not dwell in an unclean tabernacle. Hence, they thereby receive a remission of those sins committed after baptism.

This same eternal verity is illustrated in the ordinance of administering to the sick. A faithful saint who is anointed with oil has the promise that "the prayer of faith shall save the sick, and the Lord shall raise him up; and if he have committed sins, they shall be forgiven him." (James 5:14-15.) The reasoning of the ancient apostle James, in this instance, is that since the miracle of healing comes by the power of the Holy Ghost, the sick person is healed not only physically but spiritually, for the Spirit who comes to heal will not dwell in a spiritually unclean tabernacle.

2. "Behold, I am God; Man of Holiness is my name; Man of Counsel is my name; and Endless and Eternal is my name, also." (Moses 7:35.)

3. These words from the King Follett Sermon, delivered by the Prophet Joseph Smith, are the high point of Latter-day Saint doctrine on the points here involved: "God himself was once as we are now, and is an exalted man, and sits enthroned in yonder heavens! That is the great secret. If the veil were rent today, and the great God who holds this world in its orbit, and who upholds all worlds and all things by his power, was to make himself visible,—I say, if you were to see him today, you would see him like a man in form—like yourselves in all the person, image, and very form as a man; for Adam was created in the very fashion, image and likeness of God, and received instruction from, and walked, talked and conversed with him, as one man talks and communes with another.

"In order to understand the subject of the dead, for [the] consolation of those who mourn for the loss of their friends, it is necessary we should understand the character and being of God and how he came to be so; for I am going to tell you how God came to be God. We have imagined and supposed that God was God from all eternity. I will refute that idea, and take away the veil, so that you may see.

"These are incomprehensible ideas to some, but they are simple. It is the first principle of the Gospel to know for a certainty the Character of God, and to know that we may converse with him as one man converses with another, and that he was once a man like us; yea, that God himself, the Father of us all, dwelt on an earth, the same as Jesus Christ himself did." (*Teachings*, pp. 345-46.)

4. This same distinction between the Almighty and his servants was also carefully set forth by the spirit Jesus, before his mortal birth, when he gave the keys of the kingdom to Nephi the son of Helaman. "Blessed art thou, Nephi, for those things which thou hast done," the Lord said. "Behold, thou art Nephi, and I am God. . . . ye shall have power over this people. . . . Whatsoever ye shall seal on earth shall be sealed in heaven; and whatsoever ye shall loose on earth shall be loosed in heaven." (Hel. 10:4, 6-7.) The same heavensent power is, of course, in the true Church today. (D&C 132:46-47.)

5. "What rock? Revelation." (*Teachings*, p. 274.) So said the inspired seer of latter days. Edersheim, without the light of latter-day revelation, reached a somewhat similar conclusion. "Perhaps it might be expressed in this somewhat clumsy paraphrase," he said: " 'Thou art Peter (Petros)—a Stone or Rock—and upon this Petra—the Rock, the Petrine—will I found My Church.' " Thus, he reasons, the Church is to be built on "the Petrine in Peter: the heaven-given faith which manifested itself in his confession." That is, Christ "would build His Church on the Petrine in Peter—on his faith and confession." This is akin to saying that the rock is revelation; it is the heavensent faith, the Spirit-borne testimony, the revealed truth—the fact that God speaks by the power of the Spirit to mortal man.

"Nor would the term 'Church' sound strange in Jewish ears," our learned friend continues. "The same Greek word, as the equivalent of the Hebrew *Qahal*, 'convocation,' 'the called,' occurs in the LXX rendering of the Old Testament, and in 'the Wisdom of the Son of Sirach' and was apparently in familiar use at the time. In Hebrew use it referred to Israel, not in their national but in their religious unity. As here employed, it would convey the prophecy, that His disciples would in the future be joined together in a religious unity; that this religious unity or 'Church' would be a building of which Christ was the Builder; that it would be founded on 'the Petrine' of heaven-taught faith and confession; and that this religious unity, this Church, was not only intended for a time, like a school of thought, but would last beyond death and the disembodied state: that, alike as regarded Christ and

His Church—'the gates of Hades shall not prevail against it.' " (Edersheim 2:83-84.)

Farrar, also without the benefit of latter-day revelation, reaches the same general conclusion, which he climaxes by quoting these words of Origen: "If *any one* thus confess, when flesh and blood have not revealed it unto him, but our Father in heaven, *he,* too, shall obtain the promised blessings; as the letter of the Gospel saith indeed to the great St. Peter, but as its spirit teacheth to every man who hath become like what that great Peter was." (Farrar, p. 386.)

6. "The gates of hell are the entrances to the benighted realms of the damned where the wicked go to await the day when they shall come forth in the resurrection of damnation. Those beckoning gates prevail against all who pass through them. But those who obey the laws and ordinances of the gospel have the promise that the gates of hell shall not prevail against them. In this instance, Jesus is telling Peter that the gates of hell shall never prevail against the rock of revelation; that is, as long as the saints are living in righteousness so as to receive revelation from heaven, they will avoid the gates of hell and the Church itself will remain pure, undefiled, and secure against every evil. But when, because of iniquity, revelation ceases, then the gates of hell prevail against the people and also against the organization of which they are members.

"Similarly, the Lord, by revelation, has said in our day: 'Open your mouths and they shall be filled, saying: Repent, repent, and prepare ye the way of the Lord, and make his paths straight; for the kingdom of heaven is at hand; Yea, repent and be baptized, every one of you, for a remission of your sins; yea, be baptized even by water, and then cometh the baptism of fire and of the Holy Ghost. Behold, verily, verily, I say unto you, this is my gospel; and remember that they shall have faith in me or they can in nowise be saved; And upon this rock I will build my church; yea, upon this rock ye are built, and if ye continue, the gates of hell shall not prevail against you.' " (*Commentary* 1:388-89.)

7. Of the Catholic view of the text in question, Farrar uses these aptly chosen words: "Were it not a matter of history, it would have been deemed incredible that on so imaginary a foundation should have been rested the fantastic claim that abnormal power should be conceded to the bishops of a Church which almost certainly St. Peter did not found, and in a city in which there is no indisputable proof that he ever set foot. The immense arrogancies of sacerdotalism; the disgraceful abuses of the confessional; the imaginary power of absolving from oaths; the ambitious assumption of a right to crush and control the civil power; the extravagant usurpation of infallibility in wielding the dangerous weapons of anathema and excommunication; the colossal tyrannies of the Popedom, and the detestable cruelties of the Inquisition—all these abominations are, we may hope, henceforth and for ever, things of the past." (Farrar, p. 385.)

GOD'S SON—A SUFFERING SERVANT

Surely he hath borne our griefs,
and carried our sorrows:
yet we did esteem him stricken,
smitten of God, and afflicted.
But he was wounded for our transgressions,
he was bruised for our iniquities. . . .
He was oppressed, and he was afflicted. . . .
For the transgression of my people
was he stricken. . . .
Yet it pleased the Lord to bruise him:
he hath put him to grief. . . .
He shall see of the travail of his soul,
. . . for he shall bear their iniquities.
(Isa. 53:4-11.)

The Messiah Shall Die and Rise Again

(*Matthew 16:21-23; Mark 8:31-33; Luke 9:21-22; JST, Luke 9:21*)

We have seen Peter—like a giant redwood in the forest of the world—standing on the mountain height; receiving revelation from the Revelator; testifying of the divine Sonship; gaining a blessed benediction from the lips of Him whom he loved.

The revelation: 'Thou art the Messiah; thou art the Son of Man; thou art the Son of the living God.'

The divine benediction: 'Blessed art thou, Simon. Thy testimony has come to thee from the Father by the power of the Spirit; it is recorded in heaven, and the angels rejoice over it.'

The yet future promise of power and dominion and glory: 'Thine are the keys. Thou shalt preside over the earthly kingdom, and the true Sanhedrin in heaven shall be bound by thy decisions on earth.'

Peter and the favored few who surround the person of Him whom they all now know to be the Messiah have received the testimony of Jesus. They know, in a way and by means beyond their mortal powers to explain, that Mary's son had God for his Father. Jesus now plans to build on this foundation of revealed truth and to expound to them in plainness some of the mysteries of that new kingdom to which their testimonies bind them. New converts, having testimonies, are soon tested with new and deep doctrines that often do not accord with their preconceived notions about religion and salvation. From the mesas of exultation, where testimonies flourish, they are often led through the lowlands of despair, where deep doctrines test their allegiance. Having gained glory on the mountains of praise, they must prove their worthiness in the valleys of rebuke.

The witness has been borne as to *who* Jesus is; now he must teach them *what* he is destined to do to fulfill his life's mission. First, "he must go unto Jerusalem." His great Galilean ministry is drawing to a close; he has visited and preached and healed in every village and city, time and again. He has proclaimed in Galilee, from one end to the other, the everlasting word; his voice has been heard in all of the adjacent coasts, in Phoenicia (the Roman province of Syria), and in Decapolis, and through the tetrarchy of Herod Philip. And his own, if so they may be called, have rejected him. The gladsome acceptance with which his ministry began in his homeland has turned into a Satan-guided rejection. The leaven of the scribes and Pharisees has turned the populace against him. He will live in Galilee for another month or six weeks, two months at the most, and will then go to Jerusalem.

Jerusalem, the Holy City! There "the Son of man must suffer many things, and be rejected of the elders, and of the chief priests, and scribes, and be killed, and after three days rise again." Such now became the burden of his teachings. Galilee was the land of his miracles and preaching for most of his ministry; Judea, the land of his sorrow and suffering; in it was found the valley of the shadow of death. He had ministered among the rude peasants of Galilee, whose dialect and dress were ridiculed by the conceited and self-righteous in Judea, but he must now go up to the religious capital of the world to confront the leaders; to rebuke the rulers; to cleanse the temple again; to finish his work; and, finally, to die where so many of the prophets had been slain.

This announcement of his destined death and his assured resurrection was no new doctrine. Among the Jews there were some who waited for a Messiah who would be a suffering servant. Isaiah's words about One who would be smitten and afflicted, wounded and slain, were part of their prophetic library. And Jesus himself had, during his whole ministry, made frequent allusion to his future demise and his coming forth in a newness of resurrected life. He had spoken openly of the bridegroom being taken from the children of the bridechamber; of the Son of Man spending three days in the earth, as Jonah spent a like period in the whale's belly; of the raising up of the temple of his body after three days; of the Son of Man being lifted up, even as Moses lifted up the serpent in the wilderness; and of the need to eat his flesh as the living bread in order to inherit eternal life—all referring to his atoning sacrifice, death, burial, and resurrection.[1]

The doctrine is not new nor the concept strange. But now, coupled with the testimonies of Peter and the others of the divine Sonship, which give it a new dimension, and because of its apparent nearness—he "must go unto Jerusalem" *for that very purpose*—Jesus' teaching causes a tide of fear to rise up in the hearts of the disciples. It is one thing to have a general awareness that death will overtake us at some future time, and quite another to come face to face, suddenly and unexpectedly, with the destroyer's sword.

"Then Peter took him"—apparently aside from the others—"and began to rebuke him, saying, Be it far from thee, Lord: this shall not be unto thee." Or better: 'God forbid; this shall certainly not happen to thee.' Or: 'God forbid it; God be merciful to thee and keep this evil far from thee.' Peter is appealing, as had Lucifer before, to the human element in Christ's nature. 'Lord, this cannot be; you must prevent it by thy divine power. Thy kingdom cannot prosper if evil men afflict and slay its King. Such indignities must not fall upon thee, of all men.'

Temptation from the lips of a faithful friend and confidant is even worse than from the mouth of the arch-tempter himself. Are not a man's worst foes they of his own household when they seek to dissuade him from the course of duty and right? Do not his friends, who love him best, become his worst enemies, when they seek to drag him down from heights of self-sacrifice to the vulgar, the conventional, the comfortable?[2] To Lucifer Jesus had said, "Get thee behind me, Satan"; can he say less to the same allurement when it is proposed by the one whom he has just praised for the verity of his testimony? The answer comes like lightning, in a blazing flash of indignant fire:

> *Get thee behind me, Satan: thou art an offence unto me: for thou savourest not the things that be of God, but those that be of men.*

"This thy mere carnal and human view—this attempt to dissuade me from my 'baptism of death'—is a sin against the purposes of God. Peter was to learn—would that the Church which professes to have inherited from him its exclusive and superhuman claims had also learnt in time!—that he was far indeed from being infallible—that he was capable of falling, aye, and with scarcely a moment's intermission, from heights of divine insight into depths of most earthly folly." (Farrar, p. 388.)

Losing One's Life to Save It

(Matthew 16:24-26; JST, Matthew 16:26-29; Mark 8:34-37; JST, Mark 8:37-38; Luke 9:23-25; JST, Luke 9:24-25)

Jesus, whom they acclaim as King-Messiah, shall die. He shall lose his life to save it. He shall suffer many things of the Rabbinic rulers, and finally be slain, that he may rise again the third day. He shall lay down his life in his Father's cause that he may take it up in eternal glory and then receive an everlasting inheritance in the kingdom that is prepared.

Horrible thought? So Peter presumed, for he saw only the cross and not the crown; he looked only upon the loss of the Lord to the earthly kingdom and not upon the eternal blessings that would flow to all men through the atonement. Accordingly, to his sorrow—with the piercing sword of righteous indignation—he was rebuked by the Lord. And then, before the thunder of Christ's words ceased to roll in his tingling ears, the Master Teacher "called the people unto him with his disciples," that all might hear his further words on the death, the demise, yet to descend—not on the Lord Jesus only, but also on Peter and those who accepted the burdens of full discipleship.

The servants shall be as their Lord. If they suffer with him, they shall also be with him when men shall sorrow no more and all tears shall cease. If they lay down their lives in his cause, they shall take them up again in immortal glory and receive that eternal life which he came to prepare. Jesus has now taught his disciples—and angelic ministrants before an open tomb shall remind them that he did so—Jesus has now taught those who believe on his name that he, the mighty Messiah, shall, after suffering many things, be slain in Jerusalem. But such is only the beginning of sorrow, if sorrow it is. True disciples also must be prepared and willing to lay down their own lives in his cause, for his name's sake. He shall come forth, the firstfruits of them that sleep, to receive all power in heaven and on earth; and if his disciples expect to come forth and inherit eternal life, they must be prepared to suffer and die with him. His death is but the beginning; Peter, who dreaded to see Jesus suffer and die, must himself also step forward and be martyred.

> *Whosoever will come after me, let him deny himself, and take up his cross, and follow me.*
>
> *And now for a man to take up his cross, is to deny himself all ungodliness, and every worldly lust, and keep my commandments.*
>
> *Break not my commandments for to save your lives; for whosoever will save his life in this world, shall lose it in the world to come.*

'Come Peter; come James; come John; come all ye saints who seek salvation—come. Take up your cross; take it up daily and follow me. Your cross is to overcome the lusts of the flesh—all ungodliness—and to keep my commandments. Your cross is to bear the burdens placed on the backs of the saints. Your cross is to keep my commandments, and, if I will it, to lay down your lives even as I shall permit evil men to slay me. I shall carry my cross; if you are to be with me, you must carry yours. And whosoever will lose his life in this world, for my sake, shall find it in the world to come. Therefore, forsake the world, and save your souls.'

> *For whosoever will save his life, shall lose it; or whosoever will save his life, shall be willing to lay it down for my sake; and if he is not willing to lay it down for my sake, he shall lose it.*
>
> *But whosoever shall be willing to lose his life for my sake, and the gospel's, the same shall save it.*

Here indeed is strong doctrine. Jesus the Lord shall suffer before he enters into his glory. "Ought not Christ to have suffered these things, and to enter into his glory?" he shall ask two disciples on the Emmaus road. (Luke 24:26.) Truly, he shall do the will of the Father and withhold nothing, not even his own life. And so it must be with all who are his.

Though they do not court martyrdom, some shall be so honored, and all must be willing, if need be, so to die. "For he who is not able to abide the law of a celestial kingdom cannot abide a celestial glory." (D&C 88:22.) It is the law of heaven and the royal road to eternal life.[3]

> *Therefore, forsake the world, and save your souls; for what is a man profited, if he shall gain the whole world, and lose his own soul? Or what shall a man give in exchange for his soul?*
>
> *For what doth it profit a man if he gain the whole world, and yet he receive him not whom God hath ordained, and he lose his own soul, and he himself be a castaway?*

"What value is to be placed on a human soul? How can we determine its worth? Two things will give some indication of the priceless value of the souls of men: (1) What these souls have cost up to this point—the labor, material, and struggle that has gone into their creation and development; and (2) The effective use to which they can be put—the benefits that result when souls fill the full measure of their creation and take their rightful place in the eternal scheme of things.

"To use these standards of judgment it is necessary to view human souls in their relationship to the eternal plan of creation, progression, and salvation. Souls had their beginning, as conscious identities, when they were born as the spirit offspring of Deity. There then followed an infinitely long period of training, schooling, and preparation, so that these spirits might go on and attain their exaltation. 'God himself,' as the Prophet Joseph Smith expressed it, 'finding he was in the midst of spirits and glory, because he was more intelligent, saw proper to institute laws whereby the rest could have a privilege to advance like himself.'

"As part of this schooling process this earth was created; spirits were given temporal bodies; gospel dispensations were vouchsafed to men; prophets were sent forth to labor and preach; oftentimes they were persecuted, tormented, and slain; and even the Son of God taught and served among mortals, climaxing his ministry by suffering beyond mortal endurance in working out the infinite and eternal atonement. All this is included in the price already paid toward the purchase of human souls.

"Such of these souls as keep all the commandments shall attain eternal life. They shall go on to exaltation and glory in all things, becoming like the Father, begetting spirit offspring, creating worlds without number, and forever and endlessly rolling forth the eternal purposes of the Infinite God.

"How much is a human soul worth? No man can say, no tongue can tell, no mind can comprehend it. How apt, then, is Jesus' illustration. If a man—even if such a thing were possible—should gain the whole world, and lose his soul in the process, the acquired wealth would be slight indeed as compared to the value of his own soul.

"It is because of their understanding of this doctrine of the worth of souls that our Lord's ministers go forth with all the energy and capacity they have to labor in the vineyard, pleading with men to repent and save their souls, that they may have eventual eternal joy in the Father's kingdom." (*Commentary* 1:393-94.)

The Second Coming—A Day of Rewards

(*Matthew 16:27-28; Mark 8:38; 9:1; JST, Mark 8:40-44; Luke 9:26-27; JST, Luke 9:26-27*)

If ever there was a sermon showing that men do not live for this life only; if ever the saints were taught that the rewards for righteous works are reserved for a life to come; if ever the scant worth of worldliness was weighed in the balance and found wanting—such is found in Jesus' counsel that his disciples, his saints, must take up their cross, forsake the world, keep the commandments, and be willing to die martyrs' deaths, if they are to gain eternal life.

Eternal life: what is it and when shall its glories and

blessing rest upon the saints? It is full salvation; it is an inheritance in the highest heaven; it is exaltation. It is to sit down with Abraham, Isaac, and Jacob in the kingdom of God, to go no more out. It is the greatest of all the gifts of God, for it is to be like God, to inherit, receive, and possess as he does. It is to be a joint-heir with Christ of all the glory of his Father's kingdom. And it shall come to the faithful in that day when the Son of Man comes to make up his jewels. It is gained when those who so inherit come forth in the resurrection of the just.

> *For the Son of Man shall come in the glory of his Father with his angels; and then he shall reward every man according to his works.*

The Second Coming is a day of judgment, a day of rewards, a day of vengeance for the wicked, a day of glory and honor for the righteous. It is a day for which all men prepare by the lives that they live. Those who live as becometh saints shall be as their Lord; those who walk in carnal paths shall be cast out. (*Commentary* 1:396.)

> *Therefore deny yourselves of these, and be not ashamed of me. Whosoever shall be ashamed of me, and of my words, in this adulterous and sinful generation, of him also shall the Son of Man be ashamed, when he cometh in the glory of his Father with the holy angels.*
>
> *And they shall not have part in that resurrection when he cometh. For verily I say unto you, That he shall come; and he that layeth down his life for my sake and the gospel's, shall come with him, and shall be clothed with his glory in the cloud, on the right hand of the Son of Man.*

This, then, is the promised day. The martyrs, who lost their lives here, shall find their lives there. With Him they shall reign in eternal glory. What matter our momentary sorrows and sufferings—even though they be unto death—if we gain eternal life in the coming day? In that day "he shall come in his own kingdom, clothed in the glory of his Father, with the holy angels," and those on his right hand shall be in glory even as he is.

> *There be some standing here, which shall not taste of death, till they see the Son of Man coming in his kingdom.*

Enoch and his whole city were translated, taken up bodily into heaven without tasting death. There they served and labored with bodies of flesh and bones, bodies quickened by the power of the Spirit, until that blessed day when they were with Christ in his resurrection. Then, in the twinkling of an eye, they were changed and became immortal in the full sense of the word. So it was also with Moses and Elijah, who were taken up bodily into heaven for reasons that will be manifest on the Mount of Transfiguration. They too were with the Lord Jesus in his resurrection. (D&C 133:54-55.)

Of those here promised that they should "not taste of death" until the Second Coming, we have no knowledge except that the Beloved John was one of them, as shall hereafter be noted. The others are not named, nor has the Lord revealed their whereabouts or ministries to us in this dispensation.[4] Manifestly, there are many things that we do not know; but those things of which we have knowledge are sufficient to enable us to gain eternal life with the ancients if we, in our day, will live as they did in theirs.

NOTES

1. This summary is taken from *Commentary* 1:391.
2. These questions are framed from expressions made by Farrar in footnote 5, p. 388, who also quotes Stier as saying: "Those whose intentions towards us are the best, are the most dangerous to us when their intentions are merely human."
3. "And whoso layeth down his life in my cause, for my name's sake, shall find it again, even life eternal. Therefore, be not afraid of your enemies, for I have decreed in my heart, saith the Lord, that I will prove you in all things, whether you will abide in my covenant, even unto death, that you may be found worthy. For if ye will not abide in my covenant ye are not worthy of me." (D&C 98:13-15.)
4. It may be that they are the ones of whom our revelation says: "I will that all men shall repent, for all are under sin, except those which I have reserved unto myself, holy men that ye know not of." (D&C 49:8.)

THE TRANSFIGURATION

For we have not followed cunningly devised fables,
when we made known unto you the power
and coming of our Lord Jesus Christ,
but were eyewitnesses of his majesty.
For he received from God the Father
honour and glory, when there came
such a voice to him from the excellent glory,
This is my beloved Son,
in whom I am well pleased.
And this voice which came from heaven we heard,
when we were with him in the holy mount.
(2 Pet. 1:16-18.)
And the Word was made flesh,
and dwelt among us,
(and we beheld his glory,
the glory as of the only begotten of the Father,)
full of grace and truth. (John 1:14.)

Peter, James, and John Receive the Keys of the Kingdom

(*Matthew 17:1-3; Mark 9:2-4; JST, Mark 9:1-3; Luke 9:28-32; JST, Luke 9:28-32*)

Our Synoptic authors make brief mention of—in reality it is scarcely more than an allusion to—what happened on the heights of Hermon when they and Jesus spent a sacred night enwrapped in the visions of eternity. This blessed night was one of those seeric periods when the mysteries of the kingdom, "which surpass all understanding," are shown forth to souls who are in tune with the Infinite. So marvelous are such revealed truths that it is "not lawful for man to utter" them, "Neither is man capable to make them known, for they are only to be seen and understood by the power of the Holy Spirit." They are reserved by the Lord for those prophets and seers who, "while in the flesh," are yet able "to bear his presence in the world of glory." (D&C 76:114-118.)

In the providences of the Lord the saints know some things that the world does not know about the spiritual outpouring of divine grace that fell on the Mount of Transfiguration. But even latter-day revelation does not set forth the full account, and until men attain a higher state of spiritual understanding than they now enjoy, they will continue to see through a glass darkly and to know only in part the visionary experiences of the presiding officers of the meridian Church. That which is known, however, singles out this night as one of the most important and glorious in the lives of those who saw within the veil and who heard the voices of the heavenly participants.

Near Caesarea Philippi, Peter—a mortal man: impetuous, bold, highly spiritual—had borne a heavensent testimony, one revealed by the power of the Holy Ghost, of the divine Sonship of Christ. Then Jesus, of whom Simon testified, promised to give his chief apostle the keys of the kingdom, including the power to bind and loose on earth and in heaven. After this, Jesus taught them of his coming death and resurrection.

Now on the Mount of Transfiguration, a heavenly voice—that of the Almighty Father who is visiting his Son on planet earth—bears holy witness of the same divine Sonship. And now Jesus and angelic visitants, who do his bidding, join in conferring upon Peter, James, and John the promised keys of the kingdom with their sealing powers.

And these angelic ministrants—fellowservants of the apostles, who like their mortal friends need the blessings of the coming atonement—also speak with Jesus of his coming death and resurrection. The bearing of testimony, the use of the keys of the kingdom, the reality of the atonement—all these are operative on both sides of the veil. Both men on earth and the angels of God in heaven are saved and blessed by the same eternal laws.

From the great confession until Jesus took Peter, James, and John "into a high mountain apart by themselves" was either six or eight days, depending upon whether the day of the confession and the day of travel up the mountain slopes are counted. There is no record of the teachings of that week, but they must have centered around the sad and shocking announcement of the nearness of the death of their Messiah. We do know that the three apostles "asked him many questions concerning his sayings," as they journeyed up what Peter later called "the holy mount."[1] No doubt Jesus, by his answers, prepared them for the spiritual experiences ahead.

After they arrived at a proper and solitary place where they would be undisturbed in their worship and prayer, Luke tells us that Jesus prayed and that the apostles "were heavy with sleep." We are left to conclude that while they slept, even as it would be in Gethsemane, Jesus' prayers ascended to his Father, and—we say it reverently—he received such comfort and reassurance as he needed. Though he were a Son yet learned he obedience by the things which he suffered; and in Gethsemane itself he was strengthened by angelic assistance.

At the proper time the three chief apostles—the First Presidency of the Church—awoke; the time for their participation in the two-realm wonders of that night was at hand. They beheld their beloved Lord in prayer. We can suppose his petitions ascended up on high for himself and for the three spiritual giants who were about to receive the keys of the kingdom and view the wonders of eternity.

From the slivers of knowledge preserved for us in the New Testament of what then transpired, and from the allusions to the spiritual experiences then vouchsafed to those mortals, we can reconstruct the hallowed happenings somewhat along this line: "It was the evening hour when He ascended, and as He climbed the hill-slope with those three chosen witnesses—'The Sons of Thunder and the Man of Rock'—doubtless a solemn gladness dilated His soul; a sense not only of the heavenly calm which that solitary communion with His Heavenly Father would breathe upon the spirit, but still more than this, a sense that He would be supported for the coming hour by ministrations not of earth, and illuminated with a light which needed no aid from sun or moon or stars. He went up to be prepared for death, and He took His three Apostles with Him that, haply, having seen His glory—the glory of the only Begotten of the Father, full of grace and truth—their hearts might be fortified, their faith strengthened, to gaze unshaken on the shameful insults and unspeakable humiliation of the cross.

"There, then, He knelt and prayed, and as He prayed He was elevated far above the toil and misery of the world which had rejected Him. He was transfigured before them, and His countenance shone as the sun, and His garments became white as the dazzling snow-fields above them. He was enwrapped in such an aureole of glistering brilliance—His whole presence breathed so divine a radiance—that the light, the snow, the lightning are the only things to which the Evangelist can compare that celestial lustre." (Farrar, pp. 394-95.)

The apostles "were eyewitnesses of his majesty." (2 Pet. 1:16.) "And his raiment became shining, exceeding white, as snow; so white as no fuller on earth could whiten them." He himself "was transfigured before them."[2] Nor is this all. Peter, James, and John, as the powers of heaven fell upon them, were also transfigured and tasted themselves of the heavenly gifts.[3]

Then our apostolic friends, quickened by the power of

the Spirit—their souls attuned to the infinite; their spirit eyes wide open; their spirit ears unstopped—saw two men, Moses and Elijah, "who appeared in glory, and spake of his death, and also his resurrection, which he should accomplish in Jerusalem." *Moses,* whose very name is the personification of the law, the law of Jehovah, the law by which all Israel lived; *Elijah,* the prophetic defender of that law, the one whose name personified all the prophets; these two, both of whom were translated and taken up into heaven without tasting death, now discussed with their Lord that infinite and eternal atoning sacrifice by which their translated bodies would gain full immortality and yet shine forth with celestial glory. John the Baptist, a spirit personage whose mortal ministry completed what Moses had begun, was also present, rejoicing with his fellow laborers over the atonement about to be wrought.

Hear, O ye heavens, and give ear, O earth; let mortal men and angelic ministrants join hands; let all who belong to the family of the Father, whether on earth or in heaven, rejoice in the great atonement. By it redemption comes; by it the dead are raised; by it eternal life is gained. Truly, there is nothing of greater concern to men and angels than the "decease which he should accomplish at Jerusalem."

At this point, the angelic witness of the atoning sacrifice having been borne by Moses and Elijah, and no doubt by John the Baptist also—the two men from ancient Israel, having retained their physical bodies so they might confer priestly authority upon mortals—these two joined with Jesus in conferring upon Peter, James, and John the keys of the kingdom.[4] Moses conferred the keys of the gathering of Israel, Elijah the keys of the sealing power, so that whatever they bound or loosed on earth would be bound or loosed in heaven. Jesus himself gave them all else that they needed to preside over his earthly kingdom; to lead all men to eternal salvation in the mansions on high; to send the gospel to the ends of the earth; and to seal men up unto eternal life in the kingdom of his Father.[5] Truly Peter, James, and John, while on this holy mount, received their endowments and were empowered from on high to do all things for the building up and rolling forward of the Lord's work in their day and dispensation. (*Commentary* 1:399-404.) "Peter says that while there, they 'received from God the Father honour and glory,' seemingly bearing out this conclusion. It also appears that it was while on the mount that they received the more sure word of prophecy, it then being revealed to them that they were sealed up unto eternal life." (*Commentary* 1:400; 2 Pet. 1:16-19; D&C 131:5.)

Next came the great vision of the transfiguration of the earth; at least we cannot suppose it came earlier in the great spiritual outpourings of this night of nights. How many prophets have been blessed with such seeric foresight of the millennial state of this lowly orb we do not know. Perhaps Enoch, who saw the day when the earth should rest, when the New Jerusalem should come down from God out of heaven to men on earth, and who saw the Son of Man dwell a second time among men. (Moses 7:58-65.) Perhaps Isaiah, who spoke so much of the great age of restoration, and who wrote so plainly about the new heaven and the new earth, when "the wolf and the lamb shall feed together, and the lion shall eat straw like the bullock," and when "there shall be no more thence an infant of days, nor an old man that hath not filled his days: for the child shall die an hundred years old." (Isa. 65:17-25.)

But however much others may have known, the Lord himself, there on Mount Hermon, as part of the wonders of eternity then opened to the view of mortal men, showed unto the Three the transfiguration of the earth. We ourselves are not prepared to see or understand what then transpired. As of now we know only that those who come forth in the resurrection of the just "shall receive an inheritance upon the earth when the day of transfiguration shall come; When the earth shall be transfigured, even according to the pattern which was shown unto mine apostles upon the mount"—the Lord who was on the mount is speaking these words to Joseph Smith in August of 1831—"of which account the fulness ye have not yet received." (D&C 63:20-21.) How many things there are that we have not yet received because we have not attained the spiritual stature of the ancients to whom they were once revealed!

Elohim, the Shekinah, and the Son

(Matthew 17:4-9; JST, Matthew 17:5; Mark 9:5-10; JST, Mark 9:6; Luke 9:33-36; JST, Luke 9:33, 36)

At some time that night on the holy mount something happened—we know not what—that caused Peter to make an inappropriate statement about the practice followed by Israel at the Feast of Tabernacles, the practice of dwelling and worshipping in booths or tabernacles made of wattled boughs. Perhaps amid all the glory and wonder of that night shouts of hosanna and praise, like those that came from worshipful lips at Tabernacle Time, came from the united voices of Christ's servants on both sides of the veil. How could they have contained their joy as they came to understand the infinite scope of the infinite atonement soon to be made by the Infinite One, or as the visions of eternity, including the millennial destiny of the earth, rolled before their spiritually opened eyes? Or perhaps, amid the glory and wonder of it all, Peter sought simply to restrain the departure of those ancient ones whom all the faithful revered so highly. What is more natural than for spiritually endowed mortals, having gained the fellowship of heavenly beings, to desire to prolong that divine association? Whatever the cause, Peter, speaking impetuously, as was his nature, said: "Lord, it is good for us to be here"—and truly it was—"if thou wilt, let us make here three tabernacles; one for thee, and one for Moses, and one for Elias."

"As the splendid vision began to fade—as the majestic visitants were about to be separated from their Lord, as their Lord Himself passed with them into the overshadowing brightness—Peter, anxious to delay their presence, amazed, startled, transported, not knowing what he said—not knowing that Calvary would be a spectacle infinitely more transcendent than Hermon—not knowing that the Law and the Prophets were now [that is, soon would be] fulfilled—not fully knowing that his Lord was unspeakably greater than the Prophet of Sinai and the Avenger of Carmel," made the quoted statement which we, for want of full knowledge, cannot understand. "But it was not for Peter to construct the universe for his personal satisfaction. He had to learn the meaning of Golgotha no less than that of Hermon. Not in cloud of glory or chariot of fire was Jesus to pass away from them, but with arms outstretched in agony upon the accursed tree; not between Moses and Elias, but between two thieves, who 'were crucified with Him, on either side one.'" (Farrar, p. 396.)

All else of that night's wonders was but preliminary to what now was destined to be. Had they seen their Lord transfigured before them, his face and clothes shining as the sun in his strength? Had the Personifier of the Law and the Symbol of the Prophets—both holy men who were taken up into heaven without tasting death—conferred keys and powers upon their fellow servants? Had they seen in vision the transfigured earth in its millennial glory? Had their eyes and ears and souls been opened to understand the infinite and eternal import of the death and resurrection soon to be in Jerusalem? Had there been other spiritual outpourings of like magnitude and import? Truly all this was so. And yet now, on this foundation, the Father himself, the Almighty Elohim, that Holy Being who is the source of all things and all men, the Father himself is about to manifest himself to mortals.

The ancient Shekinah, the luminous cloud, the visible manifestation of the Divine Presence; the bright and flashing glory that rested upon Sinai when Jehovah conversed face to face with the man Moses; the divine brilliance out of which anciently a voice spoke from between the cherubim in the Holy of Holies—the Shekinah came down from heaven to shield the face and form of God from his earthbound creations.

Elohim was there in the cloud. That he was seen by the Son we cannot doubt. Whether our Lord's three companions saw within the veil we do not say. We do know that even now those who have been sealed up unto eternal life, whose calling and election has been made sure, have the privilege of receiving the Second Comforter; and that this Comforter "is no more nor less than the Lord Jesus Christ Himself," who then appears to them "from time to time"; and that "He will manifest the Father," and "they will take up their abode" with him, and the visions of heaven will be opened unto them. (*Teachings,* pp. 150-51.) Let each man determine for himself what happened there on the slopes of Mount Hermon in the summer or autumn of A.D. 29. All that is preserved for us in the New Testament account is that while Peter yet spake of making the three tabernacles for Moses, Elias, and Jesus, "behold, a bright cloud overshadowed them: and behold a voice out of the cloud, which said,

> *This is my beloved Son, in whom I am well pleased; hear ye him.*

Thus, once again the Divine Voice—the Father of us all; the one above all others whose right it is to command obedience and invite worship of himself—affirmed the eternal truth that Christ is the Son; that salvation comes by the Son; that all men must honor the Son and believe his words; that the only approved course for all men of all races in all ages is: "Hear ye him!" To say more about this, at this point, would but detract from the glorious simplicity of this great truth upon which salvation rests.

Hearing the Divine Voice, the three disciples fell on their faces "and were sore afraid." Thereupon Jesus touched them and in tender solicitude said simply, "Arise, and be not afraid." They did so, and "when they had looked round about with great astonishment, they saw no man any more, save Jesus only, with themselves. And immediately they departed."

As they came down the mountain, Jesus said, "Tell the vision to no man, until the Son of man be risen again from the dead." The wonders they had seen could not then lawfully be uttered even to the others of the Twelve, nor could they be understood by any without the enlightening power of the Holy Ghost. After the resurrection of their Lord, after the day of Pentecost when the promised enlightening gift would be given, it would be time enough to tell even those spiritual giants with whom they and Jesus associated on such intimate terms.

Mark, at this point, says they questioned "one with another what the rising from the dead should mean." Their questions could not have been about the reality of the resurrection; nor about its universal nature; nor about the fact Jesus would die and rise again the third day. All this Jesus has already taught them in plainness. In recent weeks his own decease, and his own rising as the firstfruits of them that sleep, has been the burden of his teachings. He has spoken openly and plainly about his own death and resurrection. They know what the resurrection as such is, and in fact have just seen in vision the resurrection that will usher in the millennial day, when the earth itself shall be transfigured. And they know what Jesus said at the Feast of the Passover: that all who are in their graves shall hear the voice of the Son of God and come forth, either in the resurrection of the just or that of the unjust.

It is true that there were many false doctrines taught by the Rabbis about the resurrection. "Current Jewish theology" abounded in conflicting views and unresolved problems in this field. There was no basic agreement among the Rabbis on any major points. "They had heard from some of the preachers in the synagogues, that Israel alone would rise; from others, that the resurrection would include godly heathen also, who had kept the seven commands given to the sons of Noah; from some, that all the heathen outside the holy land would be raised, but only to shame and everlasting contempt before Israel; while still others maintained, that neither the Samaritans, nor the great mass of their own nation, who did not observe the precepts of the Rabbis, would have part in the resurrection. But if there was confusion as to who should rise again, there was still more contradiction between what they had always heard before, of the occasion and time of the resurrection. . . . They had been trained to believe that all Israel would be gathered from the four quarters of the earth at the coming of the Messiah, and that the dead would be raised immediately after. . . . They had always, moreover, heard the synagogue preachers say that the holy dead, when thus raised, were to take part in the kingdom of the Messiah, at Jerusalem, and once more become fellowcitizens with the living." (Geikie, pp. 561-62.) For that matter, the Sadducees did not believe in any resurrection at all.

But none of this could have had any bearing on the questioning discussions the three disciples had among themselves. Their questions must have been the kind any believing disciples would have asked in similar circumstances: When will the resurrection be? How will it be brought to pass? With what body will we arise? Where do resurrected beings dwell? Does the family unit continue among them? And so forth. And like questions can be heard to this day in the congregations of the saints.

We know of one other subject discussed by Jesus and the Chosen Three as they descended the slopes of Hermon—that of Elias and the Restoration—and of this we shall now make more particular mention as we see the Son of Man begin the journey from sunshine into shadow, from the Mount of Transfiguration to the Valley of Humiliation and Death.

Elias of the Restoration

(*Matthew 17:10-13; JST, Matthew 17:10-14; Mark 9:11-13; JST, Mark 9:10-11*)

Elias—that figure of ancient renown about whom the world knows so little; whose mission is to bring to pass the restoration of all things before the great and dreadful day of the Lord—who is he and when shall he minister among men?

The Chosen Three, but hours before, had seen and conversed with translated Elias, who is Elijah, and with translated Moses, and from them and from Christ received the keys of the kingdom of heaven. These two ancient worthies had now departed to realms unknown without revealing themselves to the people generally. Further, they had come *after*—nearly three years after—the Messiah had commenced his ministry, not *before* as the scribes taught and as their scriptures testified. How could this be?

Nor had this vanishing and evanescent Elias, who had ministered in glory on Hermon's slopes, done any of the things he was expected to do. According to Jewish legend and scribal teaching, Elias was to come "three days before the coming of the Messiah." Then, they taught, "he will stand and weep and lament on the hills of Israel, over the desolate and forsaken land, till his voice is heard through the world." Further, "he will then cry to the mountains, 'Peace and blessing come into the world, peace and blessing come into the world!'—'Salvation cometh, salvation cometh!'" Then, he will "gather all the scattered sons of Jacob, and restore all things in Israel as in ancient times." He will "turn the hearts of all Israel to receive the Messiah gladly." (Geikie, p. 562.) Further, "the Jewish expectation" of the coming of Elias was so "well known" that "a thing of unknown ownership" might "be kept by the finder 'till the coming of Elias.' He was to restore to the Jews the pot of manna, the rod of Aaron," and so forth, and his coming generally was to be "a time of restoration." (Farrar, p. 397, footnote 2.) Indeed, at the Feast of the Passover it was customary to set an extra place at the table for Elias should he then choose to come and commence his legendary labors.

There had been no hint of any of this on the part of the now invisible being who had talked not of the life and temporal triumph of their Messiah, but of his sorrows and sufferings and death. Were all of the Rabbinic traditions and all of the scribal teachings wrong? To Jesus they said, "Why then say the scribes that Elias must first come?"

Jesus' companions knew that John the Baptist—whose spirit body they had seen on the holy mount—as Gabriel promised, had come before the Lord "in the spirit and power of Elias, to turn the hearts of the fathers to the children, and the disobedient to the wisdom of the just; to make ready a people prepared for the Lord." (Luke 1:17.) They knew that when the Jews sent priests and Levites from Jerusalem to ask John, "Who art thou? . . . Art thou Elias?" the Son of Zacharias had said "he was Elias," but that he was "not that Elias who was to restore all things." They knew that John, speaking of Christ, had then testified: "He is that prophet, even Elias, who, coming after me, is preferred before me, whose shoe's latchet I am not worthy to unloose, or whose place I am not able to fill." (JST, John 1:20-28.) They also knew that when John, imprisoned by Antipas in Machaerus, had sent messengers to Jesus, that they might learn for themselves of his divine Sonship, Jesus had said of John: "If ye will receive it, this is Elias, which was for to come." (Matt. 11:14.)

Clearly, they knew of John's mission as an Elias, as a forerunner, as one appointed to prepare the way, as the one who would prepare a people for the Lord. Yet, learning line upon line and precept upon precept, as the Lord's servants always do, there were still unanswered questions about that Elias who was to restore all things. And well might this have been, for the great restoration was not for their day, as they would learn on the Mount of Olives, after Christ's resurrection, when, still not fully advised in the premises, they will ask: "Lord, wilt thou at this time restore again the kingdom to Israel?" Then they will be told that the great restoration is not for their time; the return of Elias to restore all things is destined to occur in the last days, before the Second Coming of the Son of Man. (Acts 1:6-8.)

For their present edification, Jesus chose to teach them

that Elias the Forerunner was one thing, Elias of the Restoration another. The one had already come; the ministry of the other lay ahead. "Elias truly shall first come, and restore all things, as the prophets have written," Jesus said. Peter, learning his doctrine from the Lord, will later testify to all Israel that all the holy prophets "since the world began" have spoken of the latter-day "times of restitution." (Acts 3:19-21.) But now, Jesus continues:

> *And again I say unto you that Elias has come already, concerning whom it is written, Behold, I will send my messenger, and he shall prepare the way before me; and they knew him not, and have done unto him, whatsoever they listed. Likewise shall the Son of Man suffer of them.*
>
> *But I say unto you, Who is Elias? Behold, this is Elias, whom I sent to prepare the way before me.*

Such is the Lord's own testimony of the one whose voice, crying in the wilderness of sin and evil, called out to fallen Israel: 'Prepare ye the way of the Lord; make his paths straight; come unto him; repent; be baptized for the remission of your sins; live righteously and be ready to be numbered among his people, for the time is at hand.'

As we are aware, each Gospel author recorded fragments only of much longer conversations. In this instance Mark gives us this account:

> *Elias verily cometh first, and prepareth all things; and teacheth you of the prophets; how it is written of the Son of Man, that he must suffer many things, and be set at naught.*
>
> *Again I say unto you, That Elias is indeed come, but they have done unto him whatsoever they listed; and even as it is written of him; and he bore record of me, and they received him not. Verily this was Elias.*

John's work was well done; his mortal ministry was over; the way had been prepared for the Coming One. Elias had first come; he had come before the face of Him in whose hand is all power. But Elias also would yet come to restore all things; and so the inspired account attests: "Then the disciples understood that he spake unto them of John the Baptist, and also of another who should come and restore all things, as it is written by the prophets."[6]

NOTES

1. There can be little doubt that the Mount of Transfiguration is Mount Hermon, north of Caesarea Philippi, though Mount Tabor in the south of Galilee has been so considered by many. In the sixth century three churches were erected on Mount Tabor to commemorate Peter's desire to erect three tabernacles on "the holy mount." Jesus and his party are known to have been near Caesarea Philippi the week before, and Mark expressly says they did not return to Galilee until after the Transfiguration. (Mark 9:30.)

2. Something akin to this, though lesser in degree, happened to Moses. After spending forty days and nights with the Lord in the mountain, "the skin of his face shone," and he had to wear a veil when he talked with the children of Israel. (Ex. 34:28-35.)

3. Such also has been the case with many prophets in many ages when they have seen the wonders of eternity. "I was transfigured before him," Moses says as he recounts how he beheld God with his "spiritual eyes." (Moses 1:11.) "They were caught up into heaven, and saw and heard unspeakable things," the Nephite record says of the three Nephite disciples, the three who were comparable in the New World to Peter, James, and John in the Old World. "And it was forbidden them that they should utter; neither was it given unto them power that they could utter the things which they saw and heard; And whether they were in the body or out of the body, they could not tell; for it did seem unto them like a transfiguration of them, that they were changed from this body of flesh into an immortal state, that they could behold the things of God." (3 Ne. 28:13-15.) As to the transfiguration of Peter, James, and John, the Prophet Joseph Smith says: "The Savior, Moses, and Elias, gave the keys to Peter, James, and John, on the mount, when they were transfigured before him." (*Teachings*, p. 158.)

4. Moses and Elijah were translated—taken into heaven with physical bodies—so they could return, with their bodies, to confer keys upon Peter, James, and John on the Mount of Transfiguration. Of these two ancient prophets, President Joseph Fielding Smith says: "They had a mission to perform, and it had to be performed before the crucifixion of the Son of God, and it could not be done in the spirit. They had to have tangible bodies. Christ is the first fruits of the resurrection; therefore if any former prophets had a work to perform preparatory to the mission of the Son of God, or to the dispensation of the meridian of times, it was essential that they be preserved to fulfill that mission in the flesh. For that reason Moses disappeared from among the people and was taken up into the mountain, and the people thought he was buried by the Lord. The Lord preserved him, so that he could come at the proper time and restore his keys, on the heads of Peter, James, and John, who stood at the head of the dispensation of the meridian of time. (Deut. 34:5-6; Alma 45:18-19.) He reserved Elijah from death that he might also come and bestow his keys upon the heads of Peter, James, and John and prepare them for their ministry.

"But, one says, the Lord could have waited until after his resurrection, and then they could have done it. It is quite evident, due to the fact that it did so occur, that it had to be done before; and there was a reason. There may have been other reasons, but that is one reason why Moses and Elijah did not suffer death in the flesh, like other men do.

"After the resurrection of Christ, of course, they passed through death and the resurrection, and then as resurrected beings came to fulfill a mission of like import in the dispensation of the fulness of time. (D&C 110:11-16; 133:54-55.)" (*Doctrines of Salvation* 2:110-111.)

The concept here presented ties in with and is related to the pronouncements in section 129 of the Doctrine and Covenants about mortals being able to feel the bodies of resurrected persons but not the bodies of spirit beings.

5. When Peter, James, and John came to Joseph Smith and Oliver Cowdery in May or June of 1829, they conferred upon their mortal fellow laborers the Melchizedek Priesthood, including the holy apostleship, and "the keys of [the] kingdom, and a dispensation of the gospel for the last times." (D&C 27:12-13.) Of this divine conferral of power, the Prophet Joseph Smith said: "The voice of Peter, James, and John in the wilderness between Harmony, Susquehanna county, and Colesville, Broome county, on the Susquehanna river, declaring themselves as possessing the keys of the kingdom, and of the dispensation of the fulness of times!" (D&C 128:20.) That mortal men might receive again all that was possessed by their ancient counterparts, Moses and Elias and Elijah—and what others we do not know—came to Joseph Smith and Oliver Cowdery on April 3, 1836, and perhaps at other times, each conferring their "keys, and powers, and glories." (D&C 110; 128:18-21.) There may have been other messengers besides Moses and Elijah who also came to the Mount of Transfiguration, as for instance a translated person from Enoch's day, who also gave keys and authorities to the chosen heads of the dispensation of the meridian of time. We know so little—for want of spiritual preparation on our part—of what transpired on the holy mount.

6. For an analysis of the various usages of the name-title *Elias,* with particular reference to the coming of Elias of the Restoration in modern times, see *Mormon Doctrine,* 2nd ed., pp. 219-22.

FROM SUNSHINE TO SHADOW[1]

And whatsoever ye shall ask the Father
in my name, which is right,
believing that ye shall receive,
behold it shall be given unto you.
(3 Ne. 18:20.)

The Healing of the Demoniac Youth

(*Matthew 17:14-21; Mark 9:14-29; JST, Mark 9:15, 17-20, 23; Luke 9:37-43*)

Edersheim, in concluding his account of the Transfiguration, says: "To all ages it is like the vision of the bush burning, in which was the Presence of God. And it points us forward to that transformation, of which that of Christ was the pledge, when 'this corruptible shall put on incorruption.' As of old the beacon-fires, lighted from hill to hill, announced to them far away from Jerusalem the advent of solemn feast, so does the glory kindled on the Mount of Transfiguration shine through the darkness of the world, and tell of the Resurrection-Day.

"On Hermon the Lord and His disciples had reached the highest point in this history. Henceforth it is a descent into the Valley of Humiliation and Death! " (Edersheim 2:101.)

Elder James E. Talmage, at this same point in his analysis of the same transcendent happenings, makes this explanation: "Our Lord's descent from the holy heights of the Mount of Transfiguration was more than a physical return from greater to lesser altitudes; it was a passing from sunshine into shadow, from the effulgent glory of heaven to the mists of worldly passions and human unbelief; it was the beginning of His rapid descent into the valley of humiliation. From lofty converse with divinely-appointed ministers, from supreme communion with His Father and God, Jesus came down to a scene of disheartening confusion and a spectacle of demonized dominion before which even His apostles stood in impotent despair. To His sensitive and sinless soul the contrast must have brought superhuman anguish; even to us who read the brief account thereof it is appalling." (Talmage, p. 378.)

Farrar speaks in similar tones: "The imagination of all readers of the Gospels has been struck by the contrast—a contrast seized and immortalized forever in the great picture of Raphael—between the peace, the glory, the heavenly communion on the mountain heights, and the confusion, the rage, the unbelief, the agony which marked the first scene that met the eyes of Jesus and His Apostles on their descent to the low levels of human life." (Farrar, p. 398.)

At the foot of the holy mount, amid "the low levels of human life," Jesus and his three intimate apostles found the other members of the Quorum of the Twelve surrounded by a great multitude in the midst of an unseemly contention. His disciples were being accused, maligned, and ridiculed by the scribes, those self-exalting interpreters of the law who kept alive the traditions and legends of the past.

In their ministries the Twelve had gone forth on missions, preaching, healing, casting out devils, perhaps even raising the dead. They had done, in Jesus' name and by his will, what none others had power to achieve. But this day, though they had tried, they had failed to call down the powers of heaven to heal a poor, suffering soul. And their failure was the source of great satisfaction to the scribes. Had not multitudes forsaken the Galilean when he failed to place manna in their mouths that their bellies might bulge? Had he not failed the Messianic test when he did not show them a sign from heaven, not just a healing that could be done by Satan's power, but one of the great expected Messianic signs? How could he be their Messiah and Deliverer if he was going to die in Jerusalem? And now his disciples could work no miracles! Surely his influence was declining and soon they would be rid of this imposter who made such self-serving claims for himself!

Jesus' sudden appearance "greatly amazed" the people, though for what reason we do not know. Some have supposed that his face still shone to some extent as had Moses' when he came down from his holy mount. They all ran to him and saluted him, and he immediately assumed the part of his disciples in the contentious affray then in progress. "What question ye with them? " he asked the scribes.

There was no answer. His bearing, his dignity, their knowledge of what he had theretofore done, perhaps their fear of what he might yet do—for sinners always fear the righteous indignation that may burst forth at any time from godly souls—all these combined to lay a blanket of silence over the scribes. Nor did the disciples have opportunity to state their case. Rather, from the multitude came a certain man who said: "Master, I have brought unto thee my son, who hath a dumb spirit that is a devil; and when he seizeth him he teareth him; and he foameth, and gnasheth with his teeth, and pineth away: and I spake to thy disciples that they might cast him out; and they could not."

How sad a case is this! The boy is possessed with a devil—not an ordinary devil, though they all are evil and vicious beyond mortal comprehension, but a particularly violent and offensive follower of the father of lies. This evil spirit has imposed upon the lad all the misfortunes of lunacy, epilepsy, dumbness, atrophy, and suicidal mania. Though alive, the youth suffers a thousand deaths daily. "And I brought him to thy disciples, and they could not cure him," the father said.

Then Jesus, addressing himself to the disciples—whom he loved and to whom he had given power over diseases and evil spirits—and also to the multitudes in general, said: "O faithless and perverse generation, how long shall I be with you? how long shall I suffer you? bring him hither to me."

Heeding Jesus' command, they brought forth the lad. Luke says he was the man's "only child," though he must by now have been more than twelve years of age, for the account says: "And when the man saw him, immediately he was torn by the spirit; and he fell on the ground and wallowed, foaming."

Jesus seemed to be in no hurry to ease the burden and remove the sufferings imposed by the evil spirit. Perhaps, in part at least, he was letting the multitude assemble and giving them opportunity to envision how serious the affliction was. "How long a time is it since this came upon him?" Jesus inquired of the father. "When a child," came the response. "And ofttimes it hath cast him into the fire and into the water, to destroy him, but if thou canst, I ask thee to have compassion on us, and help us."

"If thou canst"—so importuned the father who had made the agony of his son the suffering of himself. *"If thou canst"*—there is little or no faith in such a plea, and to it Jesus does not even respond. He feels no need to tell anyone what he can or cannot do; his deeds speak for themselves.

"If thou wilt believe all things I shall say unto you, this is possible to him that believeth," he says. *"If thou wilt believe"*—that is the issue. The issue is not what Jesus can do—he is God and has all power—but what the *man* will do. All things are possible to those who have faith. This man has yet to learn the truths that will enable him to have faith. He is just beginning to believe. But no man has all faith and all assurance to begin with, and if anyone covenant in his heart to believe all that is spoken to him by the Lord or his servants, then the desired blessing will flow unto him.

In tears, the man who but moments before had knelt before Jesus pleading for mercy now cries out the twofold feelings of his heart. "I believe," and "help thou mine unbelief." And so it is with all of the Lord's suffering saints. They believe—nay, they know—that Jesus is their Lord and has all power and can do all things to bless and help them, and yet their need is for that divine assurance which will enable them to know that the divine help will be forthcoming in their case.

Having allowed time for the people to come running together, for this healing must not be done in secret, Jesus now speaks directly to the evil spirit within the man: "Thou dumb and deaf spirit, I charge thee, come out of him, and enter no more into him." There is a piercing scream; the spirit cries out; agony envelops the man; the spirit rends him; he falls to the earth as though dead; the evil spirit leaves; and many say, "He is dead." Jesus, however, takes him by the hand and lifts him up, and he arises and is delivered to his father. "And the child was cured from that very hour." That which could not be done by the disciples, to the joy of the scribes, has now been done by the Master, to their sorrow and discomfiture.

Jesus' triumph—as always—is complete. And yet his disciples are ill at ease; a feeling of failure fills their breasts. Alone in the house, they ask: "Why could not we cast him out?" The reply is clear, incisive, instructive:

> *Because of your unbelief: for verily I say unto you, If ye have faith as a grain of mustard seed, ye shall say unto this mountain, Remove hence to yonder place; and it shall be removed; and nothing shall be impossible unto you.*

Faith is power; by faith the worlds were made; nothing is impossible to those who have faith. If the earth itself came rolling into existence by faith, surely a mere mountain can be removed by that same power. 'Let Mount Hermon be cast into the Great Sea.' Such would not be one whit different than the brother of Jared saying "unto the mountain Zerin, Remove—and it was removed." (Ether 12:30.)[2]

However, in a less severe tone, Jesus gives this further

explanation as to the failure of the disciples. "Howbeit this kind goeth not out but by fasting and prayer," he says. Clearly there are degrees of malignity and evil powers among the demons in hell. Just as there is a heavenly hierarchy, so is there a satanic government that puts one evil spirit in charge of another; and just as there are degrees of righteousness and glory, so are there levels of lewdness and evil. And it takes greater faith to overcome greater evils. "If a man has not faith enough to do one thing," the Prophet Joseph Smith says, "he may have faith to do another: if he cannot remove a mountain, he may heal the sick." (*History of the Church* 5:355.)

And on this occasion of which we now speak, so great was the faith and so wondrous the miracle that Luke concludes: "They were all amazed at the mighty power of God."

Jesus Foretells His Death and Resurrection

(*Matthew 17:22-23; Mark 9:30-32; JST, Mark 9:27; Luke 9:43-45; JST, Luke 9:44*)

Our Lord, who but a few weeks ago left his Galilean homeland, seeking peace and rest in the coasts of Caesarea Philippi, is now about to return again to Capernaum, his own city. He came with a few of his intimate disciples to these northern reaches of the Holy Land to escape the scribal scrutiny and Rabbinic wrath that is now sweeping like a flood through all Galilee. He came to find rest from the throngs who scarcely allow him time to eat or sleep. Here he desired to be alone with and to teach his apostolic associates and the limited few of like spiritual stature who hold constant converse with him. And he came to be at the appointed place, on the heights of Hermon, there to meet with Moses and Elias, and there to confer upon Peter, James, and John the keys of the kingdom of heaven.

While in this half-Gentile area he has also received with approbation the testimony of Peter; has taught his intimates plainly concerning his death and resurrection; and he has cast out a particularly vicious and malignant devil from a suffering lad.

Now, however, the scribes and Rabbis have found his party and are again tempting, tormenting, and harassing them; the multitudes, aware of his presence, are again thronging about; and the day for his decease in Jerusalem is drawing near. There is time only for a brief visit in Capernaum and then he must go to the Holy City to keep the Feast of Tabernacles and do a certain few appointed and remaining deeds, there and in Judea and Perea, before the day of his demise. Thus we see him leaving the area around Caesarea Philippi and Dan, leaving the majestic mountain masses called Hermon and Lebanon, and traveling by an unusual and little-used route back to Capernaum. Mark says the blessed party "departed thence, and passed through Galilee privately." The reason: "He would not that any man should know it." The day of his public ministry in Galilee is past. His desire now is to instruct the favored few and prepare them for the coming ordeal and the burdens they must bear when it falls their lot to stand in his place and stead in taking salvation to a weary world of spiritually illiterate souls who prefer worldliness to godliness.

As they traveled, "and while they abode in Galilee," Jesus came back again to the matter that weighed most heavily upon him, the chief reason he came into the world—to die and be resurrected. "Let these sayings sink down into your hearts," he counseled as he spoke of his coming betrayal and death. As though the agonies of that hour were passing before his view, he said: "The Son of man is delivered into the hands of men, and they shall kill him; and after that he is killed, he shall rise the third day."

It was not intended that the full significance of this teaching should dawn upon all of them at this time. Such a full view of the eternal plan that centered in Him whose friends they were was reserved for a future day—a day when the women who then heard his words would weep before an open tomb and hear an angelic voice say: "He is not here, but is risen: remember how he spake unto you when he was yet in Galilee, Saying, The Son of man must be delivered into the hands of sinful men, and be crucified, and the third day rise again." (Luke 24:6-7.) But for the present, as Luke expresses it, "they understood not this saying, and it was hid from them, that they perceived it not: and they feared to ask him of that saying."

The Miraculous Payment of the Temple Tribute

(*Matthew 17:24-27*)

Jesus and his disciples are now back in Capernaum, and a situation is about to arise that will enable him to reaffirm his divine Sonship to Peter in a miraculous way. He is about to perform an unusual and unique miracle, one like none other ever wrought by his hands. He will pay a tax he does not owe, with money he has not earned, to appease those whom he prefers not to offend. He will use his gift of seership to find the needed coin, and Peter, in the process, will have another rough edge ground off from that impetuous nature which one day, smoothed and refined to perfection, will guide the destinies of the earthly kingdom.

Those who collect the tax for the temple in Jerusalem come to Peter and ask: "Doth not your master pay tribute?" Or better: "Doth not your master pay the half-shekel?" for, properly speaking, no tribute was involved. Tribute is payable to foreign powers; this was a tax, the "half a shekel after the shekel of the sanctuary," which every Jew, who had reached the age of twenty years, paid to the Lord as a "ransom for his soul." (Ex. 30:11-16.) This was money due Jehovah; it was comparable to the tithes imposed by the Lord upon his people. Its use: the repair and upkeep of the Lord's House; payment for the public sacrifices, the scapegoats and red heifers, and the incense and the shewbread; and the payment of the Rabbis, bakers, judges, and others connected with the temple services.

To the query of the tax collectors, which apparently was

asked in good faith—for the annual tax was nearly six months in arrears, and it was the custom of the collectors to compel compliance—Peter said, "Yes." "If he had thought a moment longer—if he had known a little more—if he had even recalled his own great confession so recently given—his answer might not have come so glibly. This money was, at any rate, in its original significance, a redemption-money for the soul of each man; and how could the Redeemer, who redeemed all souls by the ransom of His life, pay this money-ransom for His own? And it was a tax for the Temple services. How, then, could it be due from Him whose own mortal body was the new spiritual Temple of the Living God? He was to enter the veil of the Holiest with the ransom of His own blood. But He paid what He did not owe, to save us from that which we owed, but could never pay." (Farrar, p. 406.)

Deservedly, when Peter entered the house—no doubt his own, for this is Capernaum—"Jesus rebukes him." "What thinkest thou Simon?" he asked, "of whom do the kings of the earth take custom or tribute? of their own children, or of strangers?" To this there is only one reply: "Of strangers." Jesus' answer: "Then are the children free."

How inconsistent for the Messiah, who is the Son of God, to pay tribute for the upkeep of his Father's House, which is also the Son's House. If even earthly princes are exempt from capitation taxes, will not the Highest free his Son from such a burden? He who came to give his own soul a ransom for all surely should not pay a ransom for his own. Should he do so, he would be withdrawing his claim to Messiahship and attesting that he was a man like other men.

Notwithstanding all this, Jesus says, "Lest we should offend them, go thou to the sea, and cast an hook, and take up the fish that first cometh up; and when thou hast opened his mouth, thou shalt find a piece of money: that take, and give unto them for me and thee."

Jesus will not raise the issue of his divine Sonship with the tax collectors. Let them consider him as a man only if they choose, though it is of note that they addressed their query not to him, but to Peter. All men, believers and nonbelievers alike, held the Master in awe. Thus he pays the tax but does it in such a manner that distinctive and divine powers are reaffirmed, not alone to Peter but to all who learn of the miracle. How could any but divine wisdom devise such a teaching situation, and how could any but divine power place the coin in the mouth of the first fish to take the hook of an impetuous Peter? Again wisdom is justified of her children.

NOTES

1. This chapter title is also the one used by Elder James E. Talmage as he begins his description of what befell our Lord after the glorious happenings on the Mount of Transfiguration.

2. "And so great was the faith of Enoch, that he led the people of God, and their enemies came to battle against them; and he spake the word of the Lord, and the earth trembled, and the mountains fled, even according to his command; and the rivers of water were turned out of their course." (Moses 7:13.)

THE DISCOURSE ON MEEKNESS AND HUMILITY

Little children are whole,
for they are not capable of committing sin. . . .
Teach parents that they must repent
and be baptized, and humble themselves
as their little children,
and they shall all be saved
with their little children. . . .
I love little children with a perfect love;
and they are all alike and partakers of
salvation. . . . All little children are
alive in Christ. (See Moro. 8:5-26.)
And little children also have
eternal life. (Mosiah 15:25.)

On Becoming as a Little Child

(*Matthew 18:1-5; Mark 9:33-40; JST, Mark 9:31, 34-35; Luke 9:46-50; JST, Luke 9:49-50*)

During the wearisome hours of walking between the area of Caesarea Philippi and Capernaum, the disciples, no doubt out of earshot of Jesus, contended among themselves over the issue of precedence and position in the coming kingdom. Perhaps the fires of jealousy blazed forth because Jesus took only three of the Twelve with him on special occasions—into the home of Jairus when the maiden was raised from death, alone on the slopes of Hermon for what purpose the others did not even then know. Perhaps they still envisioned, to some degree, that their Messiah would be the Messiah of Jewish expectation with a court of courtiers, a cabinet of ministers, and an army of captains and generals. Who among them would serve as his prime minister, his secretary of state, the chief justice in his judiciary? Will Matthew collect the taxes, Judas keep the treasury, and the Sons of Thunder—who one day soon will speak of calling down fire from heaven upon their enemies—will they command the armies? Through it all Jesus is either not aware or takes no apparent note of the bickerings of the brethren.

But now, back in Peter's home in Capernaum, away from prying eyes and surrounded only by those whom he loves, Jesus chooses to disabuse their minds on this matter of position and rank and preferment. Even the slightest leaning toward that Pharisaic practice of seeking the highest seats in the synagogue must be corrected. The eyes of the disciples must be opened so as to see wherein true greatness lies and what manner of men they must be even to gain an inheritance in the kingdom of the saints.

"What was it that ye disputed among yourselves by the way?" he asked. There was silence, the silence of shame; none dared to answer him. As Mark says, "They held their peace, being afraid, for by the way they had disputed among themselves who was the greatest among them." Further, as they traveled by the way, there had arisen "a reasoning among them, which of them should be greatest." 'Who is the greatest among us now, and who shall reign supreme in the heavenly kingdom ahead? Who shall sit on his right hand and who on his left?' Such had been their thoughts and such their words as they had given vent to the jealousies of their hearts. "It must have been part of His humiliation and self-exinanition to bear with them," Edersheim says as he contrasts "this constant self-obtrusion, self-assertion, and low, carnal self-seeking, this Judaistic trifling," with the "utter self-abnegation and self-sacrifice of the Son of Man." (Edersheim 2:116.)[1]

Jesus then said, "If any man desire to be first, the same shall be last of all, and servant of all." Men should not seek to assign themselves to positions of preferment, in which one outranks the other, either in this world or in the world to come. True greatness consists in doing best those things which are the common lot of all mankind. Service to one's family and to his fellowmen in general—in such a course lies true greatness. It is greater to be a loving and wise father than a commanding general or a corporate executive.

At this point the disciples asked: "Who is the greatest in the kingdom of heaven?" In answer, "Jesus called a little child unto him," no doubt one of Peter's children, "and set him in the midst of them." Mark says he took the child "in his arms." With the scene thus set, Jesus said:

> *Verily I say unto you, Except ye be converted, and become as little children, ye shall not enter into the kingdom of heaven.*
>
> *Whosoever therefore shall humble himself as this little child, the same is greatest in the kingdom of heaven.*

Little children—holy and pure infants, scarcely out of the presence of their Eternal Father—come into this world free from any taint of sin. They are alive in Christ through the atonement, and of them, thus saith the Father: "Little children are redeemed from the foundation of the world through mine Only Begotten; Wherefore, they cannot sin, for power is not given unto Satan to tempt little children, until they begin to become accountable before me." (D&C 29:46-47.) Should they die before they partake of the sins and evils of this wicked world—being still pure and spotless; being yet qualified to dwell in that Celestial Presence whence they just came—they are thus saved in the kingdom of God.

Accountable men, to gain salvation, must become as

their little children. The refining powers of the gospel must operate in their lives. Sin and evil must be burned out of them as though by fire; they must receive the baptism of fire. They must be converted—changed from their carnal and fallen state to a state of righteousness, becoming again pure and spotless as they were in their infancy. Such is the state of those who become heirs of salvation. Then they will be "greatest in the kingdom of heaven." That is to say, all who gain salvation, which is eternal life, shall be greatest in the kingdom of heaven, "for there is no gift greater than the gift of salvation." (D&C 6:13.) All shall inherit alike in that eternal kingdom; all shall be greatest, for they shall possess, inherit, and receive all that the Father hath. Thus, Jesus continues:

> *Whosoever shall humble himself like one of these children, and receiveth me, ye shall receive in my name. And whosoever shall receive me, receiveth not me only, but him that sent me, even the Father.*

Recently we saw Peter rebuked for his rash and intemperate views. Jesus said Peter was an offense unto him and that his doctrine was satanic, when the chief apostle tried to dissuade the Lord from following the course to crucifixion. Now the beloved John comes in for censure. Having heard the instruction that they must receive in Christ's name all who humble themselves as little children, John confesses what he and the others had done. "Master, we saw one casting out devils in thy name, and he followeth not us: and we forbad him, because he followeth not us."

"He followeth not us," or, better, as Luke has it, "He followeth not *with* us"—he was not one of the Twelve, not one of the intimate group of disciples who traveled with Jesus and his party. They were contending over precedence and rank, debating who was the greatest among them and who would be the greatest in the kingdom of heaven! And, lo, they found another member of the Church, another faithful saint of the Most High—for "there was not any man who could do a miracle in the name of Jesus save he were cleansed every whit from his iniquity" (3 Ne. 8:1)—they found another priesthood holder casting out devils as they themselves had done. Him they rebuked lest he be greater than they.

Jesus' response—harmonious with his counsel that they must receive "in his name" all who humbled themselves and came unto him, for all men are equal in his kingdom: the apostles are to be as the seventies, and the seventies as the elders—Jesus' response was: "Forbid him not: for there is no man which shall do a miracle in my name, that can lightly speak evil of me. For he that is not against us is on our part." And further, again as Luke has it, "Forbid not any" who cast out devils or do good works in the name of Jesus, for he had many faithful followers, and the more of them who exercised their priesthood and worked righteousness the better.

On Casting Sinners Out of the Church

(*Matthew 18:6-11; JST, Matthew 18:9, 11; Mark 9:41-50; JST, Mark 9:40-50*)

All things have their opposites. Having spoken of the blessings awaiting those who receive his little ones in his name, Jesus now sets forth the curses that shall befall those who lead these guileless ones astray. If, as he said, "Whosoever shall give you a cup of water to drink in my name, because ye belong to Christ, verily I say unto you, he shall not lose his reward," then those who withhold water, or who give wine and vinegar to drink, as it were, shall be condemned.

"Every spirit of man was innocent in the beginning." We all started out in preexistence on an equal footing, though in due course Lucifer and one-third of the hosts of heaven rebelled. "And God having redeemed man from the fall, men became again, in their infant state, innocent before God." We all commence mortal life on an equal footing. No sin or taint attaches to any newborn infant: all are alike unto God; all leave his presence to come to earth; all are prepared to return to his presence if death overtakes them before they become subject to sin. But once again, in due course, sin and evil enter their lives. "And that wicked one cometh and taketh away light and truth, through disobedience, from the children of men, because of the tradition of their fathers." Hence the Lord's command to his saints "to bring up" their "children in light and truth." (D&C 93:38-40.)

When Judas of Galilee led an insurrection, the Romans in Galilee captured some of the leaders, tied millstones around their necks, and drowned them in the sea. Such was a Roman manner of execution in the days of Augustus. To show how serious it is to bring up children in a house of iniquity—to lead them into unbelief and wickedness "because of the tradition of their fathers"—Jesus says:

> *But whoso shall offend one of these little ones which believe in me, it were better for him that a millstone were hanged about his neck, and that he were drowned in the depth of the sea.*

Then Jesus reaches out with his words to include all his saints of whatever age: "Woe unto the world because of offences! for it must needs be that offences come, but woe to that man by whom the offence cometh!" Though the plan of salvation calls for a tempter; though man cannot be saved unless he overcomes opposition; though the Son of God must be betrayed by a traitor's kiss—yet the tempter, the opposer, the Judas, shall all suffer the wrath of God. Wo unto them.

> *Therefore, if thy hand offend thee, cut it off; or if thy brother offend thee and confess not and forsake not, he shall be cut off. It is better for thee to enter into life maimed, than having two hands, to go into hell.*
>
> *For it is better for thee to enter into life without thy brother, than for thee and thy brother to be cast into hell; into the fire that never shall be quenched, where their worm dieth not, and the fire is not quenched.*

Horrible as the prospect may be, it is better to saw off a gangrenous leg and walk through life on a wooden stump than to keep the mortified flesh and die an agonizing death. And so it is with church members who teach false doctrines and foster evil and lewd practices. "All those who preach false doctrines, and all those who commit whoredoms, and pervert the right way of the Lord, wo, wo, wo be unto them, saith the Lord God Almighty, for they shall be thrust down to hell!" (2 Ne. 28:15.)

In the course of this sermon, Jesus says: "And a man's hand is his friend, and his foot, also; and a man's eye, are they of his own household." It is better to sever evil people from the family of Christ, which is the Church, than, by retaining them in fellowship, to destroy those who otherwise would have been saved. It is better that one evil and wicked soul burn in the everlasting fires of Gehenna—where rats and worms and crawling things feast upon the garbage—which is his assured destiny in any event, than to permit him to poison the souls of others and lead them to a like damnation.

> *And again, if thy foot offend thee, cut it off; for he that is thy standard, by whom thou walkest, if he become a transgressor, he shall be cut off. It is better for thee, to enter halt into life, than having two feet to be cast into hell; into the fire that never shall be quenched.*

Men must not pin their faith on others. Faith centers in the Lord Jesus Christ, who alone was perfect. All others fall short to one degree or another. It is the doctrine and the principles of the gospel that are true. If men—weak, struggling, sinning mortals—fail and lose their souls, so be it. Let not others in the kingdom go down to hell with them.

> *Therefore, let every man stand or fall, by himself, and not for another; or not trusting another.*
>
> *Seek unto my Father, and it shall be done in that very moment what ye shall ask, if ye ask in faith, believing that ye shall receive.*
>
> *And if thine eye which seeth for thee, him that is appointed to watch over thee to show thee light, become a transgressor and offend thee, pluck him out.*

It is better for thee to enter into the kingdom of God, with one eye, than having two eyes to be cast into hell fire.

For it is better that thyself should be saved, than to be cast into hell with thy brother, where their worm dieth not, and where the fire is not quenched.

Jesus now—after teaching his disciples that salvation comes only to those who are converted and become as a little child; after showing them that true greatness, here and hereafter, is reserved for those who serve their fellowmen; after rebuking the false zeal that had forbidden others of his saints than the Twelve from casting out devils; after discoursing on the offenses that would come upon church members; and after dramatizing the need to cut off even leaders in the family and leaders in the Church who draw men astray, lest the pupil and the teacher both go down to hell—after all this (and certainly it is but a brief summary of what Jesus taught), Jesus now climaxes these teachings with a powerful illustration. It is one that only those then living in their Jewish social order could understand fully. We, however, can put ourselves in their position and view much of the brilliance and beauty of the words of the Master Teacher.

"For every one shall be salted with fire," he said. That is, "Just as salt is sprinkled over every sacrifice for its purification, so must every soul be purged by fire; by the fire, if need be, of the severest and most terrible self-sacrifice. Let this refining, purging, purifying fire of searching self-judgment and self-severity be theirs." (Farrar, p. 403.) Or, "Every member of the Church shall be tested and tried in all things, to see whether he will abide in the covenant 'even unto death,' regardless of the course taken by the other members of his family or of the Church. To gain salvation men must stand on their own feet in the gospel cause and be independent of the spiritual support of others. If some of the saints, who are themselves the salt of the earth, shall fall away, still all who inherit eternal life must remain true, having salt in themselves and enjoying peace one with another." (*Commentary* 1:421.)

"And every sacrifice shall be salted with salt," Jesus continues. That is, "No one is fit for the sacrificial fire, no one can himself be, nor offer anything as a sacrifice, unless it have been first, according to the Levitical Law, covered with salt, symbolic of the incorruptible." (Edersheim 2:121.)

> *But the salt must be good. For if the salt have lost his saltness, wherewith will ye season it?* (*the sacrifice;*) *therefore it must needs be that ye have salt in yourselves, and have peace one with another.*

"If the salt, with which the spiritual sacrifice is to be salted for the fire, 'have lost its savour, wherewith will ye season it?' " That is, 'If ye yourselves are not purified and clean; if ye have not risen above worldly things, including your bickerings about greatness; if ye have lost the spirit of the gospel, how shall your spiritual sacrifices be purified?' "Hence, 'have salt in yourselves,' but do not let that salt be corrupted by making it an occasion of offence to others, or among yourselves, as in the dispute by the way, or in the disposition of mind that led to it, or in forbidding others to work who follow not with you, but 'be at peace among yourselves.' " (Edersheim 1:121.)[2]

To understand Jesus' next pronouncement, we yet again must turn to the Jewish theological context in which it was made; we must know "the Rabbinic teaching about the Angels." It was: "In the Jewish view, only the chiefest of the Angels were before the Face of God within the curtained Veil, or *Pargod,* while the others, ranged in different classes, stood outside and awaited his behest. The distinction which the former enjoyed was always to behold His Face, and to hear and know directly the Divine counsels and commands." (Edersheim 2:122.) Thus, we suppose with Peter's son still enfolded in his arms, Jesus said:

> *Take heed that ye despise not one of these little ones; for I say unto you, That in heaven their angels do always behold the face of my Father which is in heaven*

To the disciples this was more than a refutation of the Jewish concept that in the hierarchy of the angelic world only Michael and Raphael and Gabriel and the great and mighty stood in the divine presence. The words "my Father" were, of course, a renewed witness of Jesus' divine Sonship, but the whole statement was an allusion to preexistence; perhaps it was an outright teaching of that doctrine, for the words recorded may be only a small part of what Jesus then said. Truly, the spirits of all children, prior to entering the mortal body, dwell in the presence of the Father. They see his face, hear his voice, and know his teachings. What a monstrous evil it is to lead little children—born with angelic purity—into the pit of false doctrine and the mire of worldly living!

> *For the Son of Man is come to save that which was lost, and to call sinners to repentance; but these little ones have no need of repentance, and I will save them.*

At this point Jesus gave the parable of the lost sheep with the emphasis "on keeping the sheep from getting lost, on showing how precious the sheep are, and on how reluctant the Shepherd is to lose even one." (*Commentary* 1:508.) Later, in Perea, he will give the same parable again in an expanded form and with an entirely different application. At that time he will make the scribes and Pharisees the shepherds, and it will be more appropriate for us to consider both versions together in the latter setting.

NOTES

1. When Edersheim speaks of Jesus' self-exinanition, he means that our Lord voluntarily abased himself, or, rather, emptied himself of all his divine power, or enfeebled himself by relying upon his humanity and not his Godhood, so as to be as other men and thus be tested to the full by all the trials and torments of the flesh.

2. "It is a well-known law, that every sacrifice burned on the Altar must be salted with salt. Indeed, according to the Talmud, not only every such offering, but even the wood with which the sacrificial fire was kindled, was sprinkled with salt. Salt symbolised to the Jews of that time the incorruptible and the higher. Thus, the soul was compared to the salt, and it was said concerning the dead:'Shake off the salt, and throw the flesh to the dogs.' The Bible was compared to salt; so was acuteness of intellect. Lastly, the question: 'If the salt have lost its savour, wherewith will ye season it?' seems to have been proverbial, and occurs in exactly the same words in the Talmud." (*Edersheim* 2:121-22.)

DISCOURSES ON FORGIVENESS AND THE SEALING POWER

My disciples, in days of old,
sought occasion against one another
and forgave not one another in their hearts;
and for this evil they were afflicted
and sorely chastened.
Wherefore, I say unto you,
that ye ought to forgive one another;
for he that forgiveth not his brother his trespasses
standeth condemned before the Lord;
for there remaineth in him the greater sin.
(D&C 64:8-9.)

On Forgiving One Another
(Matthew 18:15-17, 21-22)

We are still with Jesus, in the blessed home of Peter, in the evil city of Capernaum, upon which dire woes rest. The Master continues to counsel our souls and to enlighten our minds. Some of us have been offended by the words and deeds of our fellow disciples, and we have not forgiven them. Our brethren in the Church—the very people with whom we should be joined together as though we were one flesh—these our brethren have trespassed against us. We hear Jesus say:

Moreover if thy brother shall trespass against thee, go and tell him his fault between thee and him alone: if he shall hear thee, thou hast gained thy brother.

The burden is not on the guilty but upon the innocent. It is the one whose hands are clean and whose conscience is clear, not the culprit, who is to start the processes of reconciliation. "It is not the sinner, the trespasser, the offender, who is to take the initiative in restoring peace and unity among brethren. If perchance he should do so, well and good. But the Lord commands the innocent person, the one without fault, the one who has been offended, to search out his brother and seek to repair the breach. Thus: If thy brother trespass against thee, wait not for him to repent and make restitution; he is already somewhat hardened in spirit because of the trespass itself; rather, go to him, extend the hand of fellowship, shower him with love, and perchance 'thou hast gained thy brother.' " (*Commentary* 1:422-23.)

"I, the Lord, will forgive whom I will forgive, but of you it is required to forgive all men; And ye ought to say in your hearts—let God judge between me and thee, and reward thee according to thy deeds." (D&C 64:10-11.)

But if he will not hear thee, then take with thee one or two more, that in the mouth of two or three witnesses every word may be established.

How much better it is if brethren settle their differences in private, apart from the courts of the land, apart even from the judicial system of the Church. If an offense is known by others they may themselves take offense also. The mere knowledge of the existence of sin may be an invitation to commit sin.

And if he shall neglect to hear them, tell it unto the church: but if he neglect to hear the church, let him be unto thee as an heathen man and a publican.

Even if a matter must be brought before the Church itself, even if it must come before the organized body of believers who comprise the earthly kingdom, it is not to come before the congregation generally. "If thy brother or sister offend thee" is the divine decree, "thou shalt take him or her between him or her and thee alone; and if he or she confess thou shalt be reconciled. And if he or she confess not thou shalt deliver him or her up unto the church, not to the members, but to the elders. And it shall be done in a meeting, and that not before the world." (D&C 42:88-89.) Thus, if all else fails, and the offense is sufficiently serious, there remains no alternative but to withdraw from the offending brother the blessings of fellowship with the saints and membership in the earthly kingdom. He must be excommunicated and dropped from the brotherhood of Christ, becoming thus as the heathen and the publican.

Peter's reaction to all this was typically Jewish. Rabbinism called upon the offender to initiate a course of reconciliation with his brother and specified that forgiveness should not be extended more than three times to any offender. His soul as yet not afire with the Holy Spirit, Peter asked a question that, as he must have then supposed, assumed a far more liberal rule than that imposed by the Rabbis. "Lord, how oft shall my brother sin against me, and I forgive him? till seven times?" Jesus answered: "I say not unto thee, Until seven times: but, Until seventy times seven," meaning there is no limit to the number of times men should forgive their brethren. Forgiveness is qualitative, not quantitative. Forgive and be forgiven, for there will be a day when the Lord shall "measure to every man according to the measure which he has measured to his fellow man." (D&C 1:10.)

On the Sealing Power

(*Matthew 18:18*)

Verily I say unto you, Whatsoever ye shall bind on earth shall be bound in heaven; and whatsoever ye shall loose on earth shall be loosed in heaven.

Sometime after Jesus and the Three came down from

Hermon's slopes; sometime before these words were spoken in Capernaum; on some sacred, holy, and unnamed occasion, the remainder of the Twelve, all nine of them, received the keys of the kingdom of heaven. These keys, in their nature, were the right and power of full presidency, the right and power to preside over and direct all of the affairs of the kingdom of God on earth, and the right and power to bind and loose on earth and in heaven.

How wondrous are the ways of Him of whom Isaiah said, "His name shall be called Wonderful." (Isa. 9:6.) He, on the holy mount, assisted by Moses, Elias, and possibly by others, conferred upon the First Presidency of his earthly church all of the keys and powers they needed to govern the earthly kingdom and to seal men up unto eternal life in the heavenly kingdom.

Then he and the Three—acting, we may suppose, in concert—conferred those same keys and powers upon the others, all of whom (save Judas) used them for the salvation and exaltation of their fellowmen.

How glorious is the voice we hear from heaven! Keys and sealing powers are vested in mortal hands. Mortal men can now say to their fellow mortals: "We seal thee up to come forth in the morning of the first resurrection, clothed with glory, immortality, and eternal lives; we seal thee up to pass by the angels and the gods which guard the way, so that you may enter into the fulness of the glory of Him who is in all things, and through all things, and round about all things, even God, who sitteth upon his eternal throne; we seal thee up to be a Joint-Heir with the Natural Heir, to inherit, receive and possess as he does, and to sit with him in his throne even as he sits with his Father on the Great White Throne."

The sealing power! The apostolic power possessed by Adam and all the ancients; the heavenly endowment enjoyed by Enoch and Abraham and Elijah; the power of the Great God without which man cannot ascend to heights beyond the stars! Such now is resident with *all* of the

Twelve—not with Peter only, to whom it was promised; not with the Chosen Three, who received it by angelic and divine conferral on the mount of Transfiguration, but with *all* of the Twelve.

True, keys are the right of presidency, and only one man on earth can exercise them in their eternal fulness at any one time; but all other possessors of these powers can exercise them at any time under the direction of the senior apostle of God on earth.

And so Jesus now has his Twelve—holy men who hold the keys and have the sealing power; holy men, any one of whom has power to preside over and direct all of the affairs of the Church; holy men who shall now bind and seal on both sides of the veil, and who shall retain and remit sins as seemeth good to them and to the Holy Ghost.

Be it known that now, with the conferral of these keys and powers, the Church of Jesus Christ for the Meridian of Time is duly organized and officered, and all things can now go forward as seemeth good to Him whose kingdom it is.

On Faith and Unity

(*Matthew 18:19-20; JST, Matthew 18:19*)

Again, I say unto you, that if two of you shall agree on earth as touching any thing that they shall ask, that they may not ask amiss, it shall be done for them, of my Father which is in heaven.

For where two or three are gathered together in my name, there am I in the midst of them.

We have almost no way of knowing the wonders and marvels that would attend the Lord's work on earth if all of those who are engaged in it were perfectly united together in the same mind and in the same judgment. "Be one; and if ye are not one ye are not mine," he says. (D&C 50:29.) Our souls can scarcely conceive of the gifts and blessings that would be showered upon each of us individually if we possessed that faith which it is within our power to receive.

"By faith all of the righteous desires of the saints can be gained. There are no limits to the power of faith; nothing is too hard for the Lord. Prayer is the mode of communication by which the petitions of the saints are presented to their Eternal Father. 'Ye must always pray unto the Father in my name,' Jesus said to the Nephites, 'And whatsoever ye shall ask the Father in my name, which is right, believing that ye shall receive, behold it shall be given unto you.' " (*Commentary* 1:427.)

Now Jesus tells the Twelve that if any two of them are united—"that they may not ask amiss"—the Father will grant their petition. And as with the Twelve so with all the saints; there is no spiritual gift or heavenly endowment available to the Twelve that will not flow, following obedience to the same law, to the least and last of the saints. Jesus, by the power of his Spirit, will always be with even two or three of his true believers.

If the saints desire to be led, guided, and preserved by the power of the Holy Ghost, let them importune the Lord in unity and faith, and their petition shall be granted. If they desire eternal life in the kingdom of God, let them ask in faith, nothing doubting, and it shall be granted. If they desire new revelations from the Lord, by the voice of his prophet, let them make their united wants known, and the Lord will loose the tongue and open the spiritual eyes of the one who presides over his earthly kingdom. Deity gives unto his people according to their desires, and his promise to the Twelve and to all his people is: "If ye are purified and cleansed from all sin, ye shall ask whatsoever you will in the name of Jesus and it shall be done." (D&C 50:29.)

Parable of the Unmerciful Servant

(*Matthew 18:23-35; JST, Matthew 18:26-27*)

After teaching his disciples the gospel standard that requires men to forgive one another their trespasses, and after telling Peter that, contrary to Rabbinic standards, there was no limit to the number of times brethren should forgive each other, Jesus gave the parable of the unmerciful servant. It illustrates the glorious truth that "as Deity forgives men the immeasurable debt they owe to him, so men should forgive their fellowmen the relatively slight debts incurred when brethren sin against each other." (*Commentary* 1:428.) Part of a petition to the Lord for forgiveness is the spoken or unspoken pledge to forgive, in turn, one's fellowmen.

"Therefore," that is, in the light of all I have told you about forgiveness, "is the kingdom of heaven likened unto a certain king," Jesus said, "which would take account of his servants." The kingdom of heaven here named is the Church, the Church of Jesus Christ; it is the kingdom of God on earth, the earthly kingdom that prepares men to inherit the heavenly kingdom. The King is the Lord himself—the heavenly King and the earthly King—the One who reigns supreme over all the creatures of his creating, but to whom the members of his earthly kingdom have sworn an especial and a particular allegiance. And his servants are the members of his church, perhaps more especially those members who have been called to positions of trust and responsibility. Though all his saints will be called to account for their stewardships, those who are appointed to lead and guide others have a fiduciary relationship with the King, a relationship that calls for the exercise of special trust.

"And when he had begun to reckon, one was brought unto him, which owed him ten thousand talents." Clearly this servant was a high and trusted officer in the kingdom, one of the king's ministers perhaps, one who collected revenue and cared for treasures. An attic silver talent is worth about twelve hundred dollars, a Hebrew talent nearly twice that sum, and a gold talent about twenty-five times as much. The servant's debt is thus some twelve or twenty-four or three hundred million dollars, as the case may be—a sum indicative of the infinite debt the Lord's people have, and his servants in particular owe to him.

"But forasmuch as he had not to pay, his lord commanded him to be sold, and his wife, and children, and all that he had, and payment to be made." His infinite debt, admitted and acknowledged by him, was to be paid by his own suffering, as provided in the law of Moses. (Ex. 22:3; Lev. 25:39, 47.) No endorsement of slavery is intended; the procedure for payment is simply the established order found universally in the codes of antiquity.

"And the servant besought him, saying, Lord, have patience with me, and I will pay thee all. Then the lord of that servant was moved with compassion, and loosed him, and forgave him the debt. The servant, therefore, fell down and worshipped him."

"A more accurate representation of our relation to God could not be made. We are the debtors of our heavenly King, Who has entrusted to us the administration of what is His, and which we have purloined or misused, incurring an unspeakable debt, which we can never discharge, and of which, in the course of justice, unending bondage, misery, and utter ruin would be the proper sequence. But, if in humble repentance we cast ourselves at His Feet, He is ready, in infinite compassion, not only to release us from meet punishment, but—O blessed revelation of the Gospel!—to forgive us the debt.

"It is this new relationship to God which must be the foundation and the rule for our new relationship towards our fellow-servants." (Edersheim 2:295.) "But the same servant went out," forgetting the infinite forgiveness that was his, "and found one of his fellowservants, which owed him an hundred pence"—an almost inconsequential sum, a mere pittance as it were, a thin dime as compared to millions of dollars—"and he laid hands on him, and took him by the throat, saying, Pay me that thou owest." There is no mercy here, no feeling for the sorrows and sufferings of another, just a harsh, avaricious grasping to receive the uttermost farthing that is due.

"And his fellowservant fell down at his feet, and besought him, saying, Have patience with me, and I will pay thee all"—the very words the unmerciful servant had used in his own importuning before the king. "And he would not: but went and cast him into prison, till he should pay the debt." It is always sinners who seek to imprison those who sin against them. Men whose hearts are attuned to the gospel follow instead the counsel of Paul: "Brethren, if a man be overtaken in a fault, ye which are spiritual, restore such an one in the spirit of meekness; considering thyself, lest thou also be tempted." (Gal. 6:1.)

"So when his fellowservants saw what was done, they were very sorry, and came and told unto their lord all that was done." How meet and proper it is for the saints to importune at the throne of grace for the well-being of their fellowservants!

"Then his lord, after that he had called him, said unto him, O thou wicked servant, I forgave thee all that debt, because thou desiredst me: Shouldest not thou also have had compassion on thy fellowservant, even as I had pity on thee? And his lord was wroth, and delivered him to the tormentors, till he should pay all that was due unto him." "And so it is in the dealings of the Eternal King with his servants. Sooner or later all face an enforced rendering of accounts, all are subjected to temptation, trials, and impending death, and all are rewarded with mercy or justice as their situations merit. Mercy is for the merciful; justice, retribution, and punishment fall upon those who have dealt harshly with their fellow servants. 'With what measure ye mete, it shall be measured to you again.' 'Forgive us our debts, as we forgive our debtors.' " (*Commentary* 1:429.)

"So likewise shall my heavenly Father do also unto you, if ye from your hearts forgive not every one his brother their trespasses."

"Men are indebted to God for all that they have and are—for life itself, for the probationary experiences of mortality (including some measure of food, clothing, and shelter), for redemption from death, and for the hope of eternal life in his presence. These and all other debts owed to

Deity are listed on an account that shall never be marked paid. As King Benjamin expressed it, 'In the first place, he hath created you, and granted unto you your lives, for which ye are indebted unto him. And secondly, he doth require that ye should do as he hath commanded you; for which if ye do, he doth immediately bless you; and therefore he hath paid you. And ye are still indebted unto him, and are, and will be, forever and ever.' " (Ibid.)

JESUS SENDS FORTH THE SEVENTY

And the Lord said unto Moses,
Gather unto me seventy men
of the elders of Israel,
whom thou knowest to be the elders of the people,
and officers over them; . . .
And I will take of the spirit which is upon thee,
and will put it upon them;
and they shall bear the burden of the people
with thee, that thou bear it not
thyself alone. (Num. 11:16-17.)

Seventies: Their Position and Power

What of seventies? Who are they, and how do they fit into the eternal scheme of things? That their mission and ministry is unknown among the cults of Christendom is one of the great evidences of the apostate darkness that engulfs those who call themselves by the name of Him who called seventies to stand as especial witnesses of that very name. As it is with apostles, so it is with seventies: where they serve and minister, there is the Church and kingdom of God on earth; and where they are not, there is no earthly kingdom of that King who is preparing subjects to dwell with him in a heavenly realm.

As it was with Moses anciently, so it was with the Prophet like unto Moses in the meridian of time. Both had their Twelve and both had their Seventy, and if we had the full scriptural accounts, it is assumed we would know that in both dispensations these officers had like powers and ministered in a like manner. We do know that the Twelve in Moses' day were chosen, one from each tribe, to rule over their brethren; that they were "the princes of Israel, heads of the house of their fathers, . . . the princes of the tribes," who in Joshua's day were called "the princes of the congregation." It was their offerings that were used to dedicate the altar in the tabernacle of the congregation, and their names are given in the Holy Record as Nahshon, Nethaneel, Eliab, Elizur, Shelumiel, Eliasaph, Elishama, Gamaliel, Abidan, Ahiezer, Pagiel, and Ahira. (Num. 7; Josh. 9:15.)

We also know that when, thereafter, Moses needed added help to bear the burdens of the ministry, he was commanded to choose from among the elders of Israel seventy men, wise men, men of renown, men whom he knew to be leaders, so that they might "bear the burden of the people" with him. We do know that this was an occasion of such moment that Jehovah himself came down, met with the Seventy, and poured out his Spirit upon them so that "they prophesied, and did not cease." This is the occasion when Eldad and Medad, the only two of the Seventy who are named, prophesied in the camp, and when Moses made his great proclamation: "Would God that all the Lord's people were prophets, and that the Lord would put his spirit upon them!" (Num. 11.) These Seventy are the ones who, with Moses, Aaron, Nadab, and Abihu, "saw the God of Israel" when he appeared in his glory and majesty, all of them becoming thereby especial witnesses of his holy name. (Ex. 24:9-11.) We suppose that the Great Sanhedrin of Jesus' day, with its seventy members and judicial powers, was but a continuation or outgrowth of this ancient administrative body.

In our dispensation the first Twelve and the first Seventy were chosen from among those tested and tried souls who had laid their all on the altar in the march of Zion's camp. Of these two great councils, both of which operate as did their ancient counterparts, our revelations say: "The twelve traveling councilors are called to be the Twelve Apostles, or special witnesses of the name of Christ in all the world. . . . The Seventy are also called to preach the gospel, and to be especial witnesses unto the Gentiles and in all the world. . . . The Twelve are a Traveling Presiding High Council, to officiate in the name of the Lord, under the direction of the Presidency of the Church, agreeable to the institution of heaven; to build up the church, and regulate all the affairs of the same in all nations, first unto the Gentiles and secondly unto the Jews. The Seventy are to act in the name of the Lord, under the direction of the Twelve or the traveling high council, in building up the church and regulating all the affairs of the same in all nations, first unto the Gentiles and then to the Jews. . . . It is the duty of the traveling high council to call upon the Seventy, when they need assistance, to fill the several calls for preaching and administering the gospel, instead of any others." (D&C 107:23-38.)

Jesus Appoints Other Seventy

(Luke 9:57-62; 10:1; Matthew 8:19-22)

Jesus now—still in Galilee, but soon to depart for Judea—is about to appoint "other seventy" and send them "two and two before his face into every city and place, whither he himself would come." They are to be heralds of salvation, chosen witnesses who step forth to prepare a people for the coming of the Lord. As John the Baptist raised his voice in doctrine and testimony to prepare all Israel for the Coming One, so the apostles and seventies, called by the one who came, now go forth to teach and testify that he has come and now ministers among them.

What say the seventies? 'Forsake your vineyards and fields; leave your nets and plows; lay down your tools. Come to the synagogue; join the congregations in the streets and at the market place. He is here; give heed to his voice; he is the Messiah of whom John testified. Salvation is in Him. You must believe his words and live his law to gain eternal life. We join our testimony with that of Peter and the Twelve. Come and hear; believe the gospel message; this is he of whom Moses and the prophets spoke. The hour is at hand. He is the Son of God.'

When Jesus chose "the first seventy" we do not know, but suppose it must have been at the time he called the Twelve or soon thereafter.[1] In our dispensation the Twelve and "the first seventy" were called in February 1835. In the Mosaic age the Twelve Princes in Israel were regulating the affairs of their tribes before the seventy elders were chosen to bear with them and with Moses the burdens of the kingdom. We are left to assume that seventies have been serving in the meridian dispensation for almost as long as have the apostles, but that only now, as the final great witness of Christ is borne in Galilee, does the account call for an announcement of their ministry. Heretofore the emphasis, properly, has been upon the Twelve, as they ministered and taught and received the keys of the kingdom. Now as the kingdom expands, the Seventy are identified, instructed, and endowed with apostolic power.

Luke tells us that before the selection of these "other seventy," Jesus spoke pointedly and plainly to three different persons about service in the kingdom. These were: the scribe who offered to follow the Master wherever he went, and who was told, "The foxes have holes, and the birds of the air have nests; but the Son of man hath not where to lay his head." Also, the reluctant disciple who, having been called to the ministry, asked if he might first go and bury his father, and who was told, "Let the dead bury their dead: but go thou and preach the kingdom of God." And finally, the delaying disciple who sought to bid farewell to loved ones at home, and who was told, "No man, having put his hand to the plough, and looking back, is fit for the kingdom of God."

We have considered these or almost identical incidents in connection with the stilling of the storm on the sea of Galilee, which is the setting in which Matthew places them. (Chapter 51, Book 2.) If, however, they were an immediate prelude to the calling of additional seventies, then the persons involved may have been among those called to this apostolate, and the events mentioned were part of the testing that prepared them for their high ministerial responsibilities. Thus, with reference to the disciple who sought to bury his father before engaging in the ministry to which he had been called, Edersheim says: "We feel morally certain, that, when Christ called this disciple to follow Him, He was fully aware that at that very moment his father lay dead. Thus, He called him not only to homelessness—for this he might have been prepared—but to set aside what alike natural feeling and the Jewish Law seemed to impose on him as the most sacred duty. . . . There are higher duties than either those of the Jewish Law, or even of natural reverence, and a higher call than that of man. No doubt Christ had here in view the near call to the Seventy—of whom this disciple was to be one—to 'go and preach the kingdom of God.' When the direct call of Christ to any work comes, . . . then every other call must give way. For, duties can never be in conflict—and this duty about the living and life must take precedence of that about death and the dead. . . . There are critical moments in our inner history, when to postpone the immediate call, is really to reject it; when to go and bury the dead—even though it were a dead father—were to die ourselves!" (Edersheim 2:133.)

The Seventy: Their Charge and Commission
(Luke 10:2-11, 16; JST, Luke 10:2, 7, 17)

These seventies—having been called of God, as was Aaron; having been ordained and set apart to their high and holy callings either by Jesus personally or by members of the Twelve, at his direction; having thus received a divine commission to stand as especial witnesses of the Holy Name—these seventies are now sent forth into the missionary service. They go forth as representatives of the Lord Jesus Christ. They stand in his place and stead in administering salvation to the children of men. Their words are his words; their acts are his acts; the heed men give to them is the heed they would have given to the Messiah himself.

> *He that heareth you heareth me; and he that despiseth you despiseth me; and he that despiseth me despiseth him that sent me.*

What an awesome thing it is when the servants of the Lord stand before the people and teach the word of truth! It is as though the Lord himself were there, for their words, spoken by the power of the Holy Ghost, are his words. And so we now see these seventies go forth, with apostolic power, to preach Jesus Christ and him crucified. And as it had been with the Twelve, under whose direction they now served, so would it be with them.

Thus Jesus said: "The harvest truly is great, but the labourers are few: pray ye therefore the Lord of the harvest, that he would send forth labourers into his harvest." O that there were laborers enough to preach to all who will give ear. Always—except in the days of Noah, when all flesh had become corrupt before the Lord—there have been more receptive souls who would heed the message of salvation than there have been ministers to teach its truths. Those who have desires to serve God are always called into his ministry, and every missionary strives to bring souls into the kingdom so the newly found converts may in turn take the glad tidings of salvation to others of our Father's children.

"Go your ways: behold, I send you forth as lambs among wolves." 'Ye are the sheep of my fold. I, the Good Shepherd, have called you out of the deserts of the world into the sheepfold of Zion; now I send you forth among the wolves of wickedness to lead other sheep into my fold.'

"Carry neither purse, nor scrip, nor shoes."[2] 'Have faith. Rely upon your Father which is in heaven; he will care for your needs. Do not be encumbered by worldly possessions; your mission is more important than any temporal concerns.' "And salute no man by the way." 'Your mission is urgent. Be about your Father's business; do not stop by the way to make or renew personal friendships.'

"And into whatsoever house ye enter, first say, Peace be to this house. And if the son of peace be there, your peace shall rest upon it: if not, it shall turn to you again." 'You are sent forth to preach the gospel of peace; your message assures men of peace in this world and eternal life in the world to come. If those to whom you preach are worthy to hear your words, they shall find peace and rest to their souls; otherwise, the peace gained through the gospel will be yours only and will not come into their lives.'

"And into whatsoever house they receive you, remain, eating and drinking such things as they give: for the labourer is worthy of his hire. Go not from house to house. And into whatsoever city ye enter, and they receive you, eat such things as are set before you." 'Those who believe will account it a privilege to care for your needs. Their compensation is to hear my words from your lips. Seek not to be feasted and banqueted in the houses of the rich; eat the common fare of the people. Preach and receive sustenance in the homes of those who are receptive.'[3]

"And heal the sick that are therein, and say unto them, The kingdom of God is come nigh unto you." Heal the sick! These signs shall follow them that believe. Among the true saints healing miracles are always found. True ministers, endowed with power from on high, always walk in Jesus' path and do the things he did. Say to the faithful: 'You are citizens of the earthly kingdom, which is the Church, and heirs of the heavenly kingdom, which is found in celestial realms.'

"But into whatsoever city ye enter, and they receive you not, go your ways out into the streets of the same, and say,

Even the very dust of your city, which cleaveth on us, we do wipe off against you: notwithstanding be ye sure of this, that the kingdom of God is come nigh unto you."[4] Cursings as well as blessings attend the preaching of the gospel. Those who believe and obey are blessed eternally; those who harden their hearts, reject the truth, and continue to walk in worldly ways shall be damned.

The Damning Doom of Disbelief

(*Luke 10:12-15; JST, Luke 10:12-16; Matthew 11:20-24*)

How awful it is—how fearful and damning; how fraught with the most disastrous consequences—for men to reject the revealed truth that would save them. It is bad enough to live in spiritual darkness when the gospel sun does not shine, and to be denied the privilege of walking in the light; but it is far worse to see the sun shine, to turn away from the gospel light, and to walk willfully in the dark abyss of sin.

The seventies are now to go forth and carry the gospel light to a people who sit in darkness. The effect of their preaching will be as it is with their modern ministerial counterparts to whom the Lord says: "Verily, verily, I say unto you, they who believe not on your words, and are not baptized in water in my name, for the remission of their sins, that they may receive the Holy Ghost, shall be damned, and shall not come into my Father's kingdom where my Father and I am. And this revelation unto you, and commandment, is in force from this very hour upon all the world, and the gospel is unto all who have not received it." (D&C 84:74-75.)

And so, with reference to any city that rejected the seventies and their witness of revealed truth, Jesus said: "I say unto you, That it shall be more tolerable in the day of judgment for Sodom, than for that city. Then began he to upbraid the people in every city wherein his mighty works were done, who received him not, saying, Woe unto thee, Chorazin! Woe unto thee, Bethsaida! For if the mighty works had been done in Tyre and Sidon, which have been done in you, they would have repented, sitting in sackcloth and ashes. But it shall be more tolerable for Tyre and Sidon at the day of judgment, than for you." As to his own city, the place where he abode in the home of Peter, he acclaimed: "And thou, Capernaum, which art exalted unto heaven, shalt be brought down to hell: for if the mighty works, which have been done in thee, had been done in Sodom, it would have remained unto this day."

Matthew says these upbraiding words were spoken of "the cities wherein most of his mighty works were done, because they repented not." *Most of his mighty works!* How little we know of the mortal ministry of Jesus! We know of a blind man who was healed in Bethsaida and of a number of miracles wrought in Capernaum, but Chorazin is not so much as mentioned elsewhere in the scriptures, and if it were not for the statement here quoted we would not even know that such a city ever existed.

Tyre and Sidon were famous Gentile-Phoenician seaports, renowned for their moral decadence and spiritual degeneracy. Sodom sank to such degenerate depths in Abraham's day that the Lord rained fire and brimstone upon it and destroyed every living creature within its walls. Its very name was and is the symbol of all that is base and evil and lewd and lascivious in the world. Yet the judgment eternally destined for the inhabitants of these Gentile strongholds will be more tolerable than that of the cities of Israel that rejected their King. Truly, "it shall be more tolerable for the heathen in the day of judgment" than for houses and cities which reject the servants of the Lord. (D&C 75:18-22.) Why? Because of the eternal law that says: "For of him unto whom much is given much is required; and he who sins against the greater light shall receive the greater condemnation." (D&C 82:3.)[5]

We thus come, in our prayerful and Spirit-guided study of the one life that brought hope and life to a despairing and dying world, to the point where that One has been fully rejected by his own in Galilee. He has been rejected in Galilee of the Gentiles; in Galilee where Israelite blood had partaken of Gentile disbelief, "For they are not all Israel, which are of Israel" (Rom 9:6); in Galilee where stony hearts refused to receive his message—a message presented with such power that had it come in like manner to those centers of iniquity and immorality among the ancient heathen, the people would have believed and repented.

"Galilee had rejected Him, as Judea had rejected Him. On one side of the lake which He loved, a whole populace in unanimous deputation had besought Him to depart out of their coasts; on the other, they had vainly tried to vex His last days among them by a miserable conspiracy to frighten him into flight.

"At Nazareth, the sweet mountain village of His childish days—at Nazareth, with all its happy memories of His beloved boyhood and His mother's home—they had treated Him with such violence and outrage, that He could not visit it again. And even at Chorazin, and Capernaum, and Bethsaida—on those Edenshores of the silver lake—in the green delicious plain, whose every field He had traversed with His apostles, performing deeds of mercy, and uttering words of love—even there they loved the whited sepulchres of a Pharisaic sanctity, and the shallow traditions of a Levitical ceremonial, better than the light and the life which had been offered them by the Son of God.

"They were feeding on ashes; a deceived heart had turned them aside. On many a great city of antiquity, on Nineveh and Babylon, on Tyre and Sidon, on Sodom and Gomorrah, had fallen the wrath of God; yet even Nineveh and Babylon would have humbled their gorgeous idolatries, even Tyre and Sidon have turned from their greedy vanities, yea, even Sodom and Gomorrah would have repented from their filthy lusts, had they seen the mighty works which had been done in these little cities and villages of the Galilean sea." (Farrar, pp. 450-53.)

We must not leave this part of our account without re counting how desolation and death, in a few short years, overtook the cursed cities of Galilee. And was not this temporal doom but a type and a shadow of the spiritual fate that awaits those rebels in Israel when they shall stand before the bar of Him whose judgments are just to be judged according to the deeds done in the flesh?

'Woe unto thee Chorazin, Bethsaida, and Capernaum—cities in Israel who rejected their King! Wo unto thee!' As the Divine Voice decreed, so it was; as the heavenly judgment went forth, so the woes fell. "On all this land, and most of all on the region of it, the woe has fallen. Exquisite still in its loveliness, it is now desolate and dangerous. The birds still sing in countless myriads; the water-fowl still play on the crystal mere; the brooks flow into it from the neighbouring hills, 'filling their bosoms with pearl, and scattering their path with emeralds;' the aromatic herbs are still fragrant when the foot crushes them, and the tall oleanders fill the air with their delicate perfume as of old; but the vineyards and fruit-gardens have disappeared; the fleets and fishing-boats cease to traverse the lake; the hum of men is silent; the stream of prosperous commerce has ceased to flow.

"The very names and sites of the towns and cities are forgotten; and where they once shone bright and populous, flinging their shadows across the sunlit waters, there are now grey mounds where even the ruins are too ruinous to be distinguishable. A solitary palm-tree by one squalid street of huts, degraded and frightful beyond any, even in Palestine, still marks the site, and recalls the name of the one little town where lived that sinful penitent woman who once washed Christ's feet with her tears and wiped them with the hairs of her head.

"And the very generation which rejected Him was doomed to recall in bitter and fruitless agony these peaceful happy days of the Son of Man Thirty years had barely elapsed when the storm of Roman invasion burst furiously over that smiling land He who will, may read in the Jewish War of Josephus the hideous details of the slaughter which decimated the cities of Galilee, and wrung from the historian the repeated confession that 'it was certainly God who brought the Romans to punish the Galileans,' and exposed the people of city after city 'to be destroyed by their bloody enemies.'

"Immediately after the celebrated passage in which he describes the lake and plain of Gennesareth as 'the ambition of nature,' follows a description of that terrible sea-fight on these bright waters, in which the number of the slain, including those killed in the city, was six thousand five hundred. Hundreds were stabbed by the Romans or run through with poles; others tried to save their lives by diving, but if once they raised their heads were slain by darts; or if they swam to the Roman vessels had their heads or hands lopped off; while others were chased to the land and there massacred. 'One might then,' the historian continues, 'see the lake all bloody, and full of dead bodies, for not one of them escaped. And a terrible stink, and a very sad sight there was, on the following days over that country; for, as for the shores, they were full of shipwrecks and of dead bodies all swelled; and as the dead bodies were inflamed by the sun, and putrefied, they corrupted the air, insomuch that the misery was not only an object of commiseration to the Jews, but even to those that hated them, and had been the authors of the misery.'

"Of those that died amid this butchery; of those whom Vespasian immediately afterwards abandoned to brutal and treacherous massacre between Tarichea and Tiberias; of those twelve hundred 'old and useless' whom he afterwards caused to be slain in the stadium; of the six thousand whom he sent to aid Nero in his attempt to dig through the Isthmus of Athos; of the thirty thousand four hundred whom he sold as slaves—may there not have been many who in their agony and exile, in their hour of death and day of judgment, recalled Him whom they had repudiated, and remembered that the sequel of all those gracious words which had proceeded out of His lips had been the 'woe' which their obduracy called forth!" (Farrar, pp. 453-55.)[6]

The Mortal Messiah Leaves Galilee

(*John 7:1-10; Luke 9:51-56*)

Our Blessed Lord is now going to leave his homeland forever. He will not again in mortality gaze upon those rugged Galilean hills nor sail securely over the fish-filled waters of Gennesareth. Nazareth and Nain, Capernaum and Chorazin, Bethsaida and Magdala—cities of sin in which he has converted a few righteous souls—will not again see his face or hear his voice. Their lepers will be left to suffer and die in caves and tombs; their blind and deaf and lame shall neither see nor hear nor walk; their dead bodies shall rot and decompose in their graves, awaiting such a resurrection as they merit. But what is worse, sin-sick souls, who might have gained spiritual health and life by heeding the words of Him who came with healing in his wings, shall remain in their sins. It is a dark and dreary day. The Son of God is leaving Galilee.

Yes, the Son of God is leaving Galilee to go to Jerusalem. He will have a short ministry in Judea and Perea. Then, as the Paschal Lamb, he will be slain for the sins of the world. This will occur at the time of Passover. Now, however, it is the Feast of Tabernacles that approaches. And it is incumbent upon all the males in Palestinian Israel to appear before the Lord in his temple at Tabernacles Times. Jesus' "brethren," the other sons of Mary, say to him: "Depart hence, and go into Judea"—not as their intent should have been, that he keep the Feast of Tabernacles as required of faithful Israelites—but, "that thy disciples also may see the works that thou doest. For there is no man that doeth any thing in secret, and he himself seeketh to be known openly. If thou do these things, shew thyself to the world."

This is an ironical statement, a chiding challenge. John appends to it the explanation that "his brethren" did not "believe in him." John also tells us that Jesus was in Galilee and not in Judea "because the Jews sought to kill him." His brothers, then, those in whose veins flows the same blood bequeathed by Mary to him, are making this argument: 'If you are what you claim to be, then all men should see your miracles and hear your message. We know you are one of us; we had the same parents; we grew up with you in Nazareth. But if you are really what you claim, why do you hide out here in Galilee, when you could go to Jerusalem where all Israel will be assembled to keep the Feast of Tabernacles? There before all the people and before the rulers whose position it is to judge these matters, your claims can be adjudicated. If you are the Messiah, now is the time to show it in the Temple in the Holy City.'

Jesus replies: "My time is not yet come: but your time is alway ready. The world cannot hate you; but me it hateth, because I testify of it, that the works thereof are evil. Go ye up unto this feast: I go not up yet unto this feast; for my time is not yet full come."[7]

Jesus' response means that he will determine when to go to Jerusalem. He and his party will not go with the great caravans that parade openly and ostentatiously to the festive celebration. Such a journey befits Mary's other sons; they are of the world, and they can mingle with evil men without fear; the world loves its own. But the Son of Man is hated by worldly people because he testifies of their iniquities. Let his kinsmen travel as they choose, he will yet abide in Galilee and travel to Jerusalem at a time of his own choosing and with his own associates.

But even then he will walk in a troublesome way. When the time of his own choosing came to make the journey, he "sent messengers," possibly some of the seventies, "before his face: and they went, and entered into a village of the Samaritans, to make ready for him." Apparently all he sought was the normal hospitality—food, shelter, and a place to lay his head—which by oriental standards was offered freely to all who journeyed through any part of Palestine, Samaria included. That he also would have preached to the people, teaching gospel truths and proclaiming his own divine Sonship, is implicit in the proposal of his messengers. All itinerant Rabbis preached and taught as they traveled, and all Palestinians now knew that this rare and unusual Rabbi from Nazareth preached and taught everlastingly and accompanied his words with wondrous deeds.

But, Luke tells us, the Samaritans would "not receive him, because his face was as though he would go to Jerusalem." Their hatred of all things Jewish—including this Jewish Messiah, as he was acclaimed—was so great that they withheld from him and his associates even the normal civilities of life. And we cannot but think that in this instance they were joining with the Galileans in rejecting his Messianic pronouncements. In an earlier day, as he traveled away from Jerusalem, many Samaritans received him gladly, rejoiced at his teachings, and hailed him as the Promised Messiah. Since then the wonders of his word and the might of his miracles have been made known to them; apostles and seventies have taught and testified in their streets. But now this one who many say is the Messiah is going up to Jerusalem to minister and to worship. He cannot, therefore, be the Messiah; if he were, they reasoned, he would go to Mount Gerizim, not to Jerusalem, there to worship the Father in spirit and in truth. All of this dramatizes how false beliefs, false doctrines, false forms of worship—used as they so often are, as a standard to measure the truth—cause men to reject even God himself.[8]

"And when his disciples, James and John"—two of the favored Three; two whose valiance knew no bounds; two who were called the Sons of Thunder—saw that they would not receive him, they said, "Lord, wilt thou that we command fire to come down from heaven and consume them, even as Elias did?"

That James and John should propose such a penalty for Samaritans who worshipped false gods—"Ye worship ye know not what," Jesus had once said to them (John 4:22)—is far from strange. Harsh and pitiless as it may sound in Christian ears, it was akin to much that prevailed in the Mosaic system. When King Ahaziah lay at death's door, he sent messengers to "enquire of Baal-zebub the god of Ekron" whether he should recover of his disease. The angel of the Lord, however, sent Elijah "to meet the messengers of the king of Samaria, and say unto them, Is it not because there is not a God in Israel, that ye go to enquire of Baal-zebub the god of Ekron?" Further, Elijah pronounced the divine judgment that the king should surely die. When the king, hearing this message, sought to bring Elijah before him, that prophet twice called down fire from heaven to destroy a total of 102 armed men who would have taken him. (2 Kgs. 1.)

We can suppose that James and John reasoned that these Samaritans who now rejected the true King of Israel, because they worshipped Baalzebub the god of Ekron, as it were, were guilty of as gross a crime as the Samaritans of old whose lives were taken by the fiery flames from heaven. Further, they knew that the Messiah in whose presence they then stood would, in fact, destroy all the wicked by fire at his second coming. If the God of Israel destroyed his enemies by fire in days of old, and will do so again in days to come, why not execute a like judgment upon them now? The logic, though Mosaic and rational, was contrary to the new spirit of the new age with its new gospel. Jesus' rebuke came enveloped in a fire of righteous indignation:

> *Ye know not what manner of spirit ye are of. For the Son of man is not come to destroy men's lives, but to save them.*

How often the Lord's servants in all ages—as they are pressed by prejudices, anxieties, rebuffs, and persecutions, to curse rather than to bless—how often they must remind themselves of this eternal truth: The gospel is given to save and not to damn, "For God sent not his Son into the world to condemn the world; but that the world through him might be saved." (John 3:17.)

"And they went to another village." Had he not but recently said to the seventies that when rejected in one village or city they should go to another? And so shall it ever be until that day when the judgment is set, and the books are opened, and the wicked become as stubble, and the vineyard is cleansed by fire, and the lowly Messiah comes again to reign in might, power, and dominion on earth for a thousand years.

NOTES

1. After the Seventy were called in our dispensation, the Lord empowered their presidents, who are seven in number, "to choose other seventy besides the first seventy" until there were "seven times seventy, if the labor in the vineyard of necessity requires it." (D&C 107:95-96.) The meaning of this is that there can be as many seventies as are needed to administer the affairs of the earthly kingdom and to take the message of salvation to all men.

2. "And thou shalt take no purse nor scrip, neither staves, neither two coats, for the church shall give unto thee in the very hour what thou needest for food and for raiment, and for shoes and for money, and for scrip." (D&C 24:18.)

3. "Whoso receiveth you receiveth me; and the same will feed you, and clothe you, and give you money. And he who feeds you, or clothes you, or gives you money, shall in nowise lose his reward. And he that doeth not these things is not my disciple; by this you may know my disciples." (D&C 84:89-91.)

4. "And in whatsoever place ye shall enter, and they receive you not in my name, ye shall leave a cursing instead of a blessing, by casting off the dust of your feet against them as a testimony, and cleansing your feet by the wayside." (D&C 24:15.)

5. It was on this same basis that Jehovah said to rebellious Israel: "You only have I known of all the families of the earth: therefore I will punish you for all your iniquities." (Amos 3:2.)

6. Similar judgments of God—also rained forth in the providences of Him who does all things well—rested upon that Missouri area which persecuted and ravaged and slaughtered the Latter-day Saints in the early days of this dispensation. The punishment fell upon those persecutors of the saints and rejectors of the revealed word when the Civil War battles raged in their area. God will not be mocked.

7. That these blood brothers of God's Son were later converted and numbered with the saints is a matter of consolation for them and rejoicing for us all. One of them was "James the Lord's brother" (Gal. 1:19), who ministered in the holy apostleship; another Judas, who called himself "Jude, the . . . brother of James" (Jude 1), who wrote the epistle of Jude. Two others were named Joses (Joseph) and Simon. (Matt. 13:55.)

8. In like manner, how often it is that modern Samaritans, as it were, reject the living words of the latter-day witnesses of gospel truth, because the witness borne does not conform to the false creeds of an apostate Christendom. How can the words of those Mormon elders be true when they do not even believe the Nicene Creed?

SECTION VIII

THE LATER JUDEAN MINISTRY

THE LATER JUDEAN MINISTRY

The right way is to believe in Christ,
and deny him not;
and Christ is the Holy One of Israel;
wherefore ye must bow down before him, and
worship him with all your might, mind,
and strength, and your whole soul;
and if ye do this ye shall in nowise
be cast out. (2 Ne. 25:29.)

Our Galilean Friend—the Man from Nazareth—now returns to Judea, to minister again among those who are thirsting for his blood and devising his death.

He appears suddenly in the midst of the Feast of Tabernacles, mingles with the millions then in the Holy City, and speaks as never man spake before.

His message, then and throughout this whole Judean ministry: He is the Son of God who came into the world to do the will of the Father; all who believe in him shall be saved.

As the priests pour water from Siloam on the Great Altar, he invites all men to come to him and he will give them living water.

The woman taken in adultery is commanded: "Go, and sin no more."

Before those gigantic candelabra, fifty cubits in height, from which light goes forth from the temple, he acclaims: "I am the light of the world."

'Believe in me, or die in your sins,' he says.

To Abraham's seed comes the message: "The truth shall make you free," and 'Before Abraham, was I Jehovah.'

We hear the Seventies report on their apostleship; learn how Christ is the Father and the Son; are edified by the parable of the good Samaritan; and sit in on a familial scene in Bethany as Martha and Mary minister to the Master.

Other parables—the friend at midnight, the rich fool, the barren fig tree—salute our ears with joy.

Then we see how a man born blind is healed; how Pharisaic opposition mounts with satanic zeal; how the man is wiser than the Pharisees in council; and how Jesus says plainly he is the Son of God.

And finally—wonder of wonders—there is the matter of the Good Shepherd who giveth his life for the sheep; the Good Shepherd who has power over death; who says, again, "I am the Son of God"; and who teaches that all who believe and obey shall be gods themselves.

Truly, this later Judean ministry—with its Pharisaic opposition, its strong doctrine, its plain testimony—gives us a view of God's Son that will dwell in our hearts forever.

JESUS MINISTERS AT THE FEAST OF TABERNACLES

And it shall come to pass,
that every one that is left of all the nations
which came against Jerusalem
shall even go up from year to year
to worship the King, the Lord of hosts,
and to keep the feast of tabernacles.
And it shall be, that whoso will not come up
of all the families of the earth
unto Jerusalem to worship the King,
the Lord of hosts,
even upon them shall be no rain.
(Zech. 14:16-17.)[1]

He Preaches the Gospel at the Feast

(John 7:11-17)

Never from that day, a millennium and a half before, when Moses, the man of God, speaking for Jehovah, ordained and established the Feast of Tabernacles; never during their long and wearisome wanderings in the wilderness, nor during the years of their joy when Jerusalem was indeed a Zion unto them; never before, not even during the earlier life of our Lord, when he himself worshipped before the great altar and renewed his covenants to do the will of him whose Son he was—never was there such an outpouring of divine truth as we shall hear at this Feast of Tabernacles.

It is October 11, A.D. 29; four days ago, on the great day of atonement, "solemn expiation was made for the sins of all the people." (Farrar, p. 410.) It is now the Sabbath day, and seven and eight days hence—on October 17 and 18, on the great day of the feast and then on the next Sabbath or the Octave of the feast—the climax will be reached as the Hosanna Shout rends the air and as repeated eternal witness of the divine Sonship is borne. Then the Feast of Tabernacles will cease as a legally approved season of worship; then it will cease until its millennial restoration, when not only the Jews but all nations will go up to Jerusalem to worship the King, the Lord of Hosts, according to the new rituals and performances that are part of that eternal fulness which supersedes the lesser Mosaic system.

Under normal circumstances the Feast of Tabernacles is the most cosmopolitan of all the Jewish feasts. Linked with the day of atonement and coming at the time when the temple contributions are received and counted, it attracts more devout pilgrims from distant places than even the Passover or Pentecost. It also comes in the autumn, after the harvests are gathered, and when in a spirit of thanksgiving and rejoicing those who recognize the divine hand in all things are wont to praise and worship him for all he has given them.

How they love to assemble in the Holy Sanctuary "of marble, cedarwood, and gold, up there on high Moriah, symbol of the infinitely more glorious overshadowing Presence of Him, Who was the Holy One in the midst of Israel." How they rejoice in the multitude of sacrifices, including the seventy bullocks, symbolical of "the seventy nations of heathendom." How their souls are stirred by the chants of the Levites, the solemn responses of the *Hallel,* and the piercing blasts from the silver trumpets of the priests. And at night, when "the great Candelabras" are lighted in "the

Court of the Women," when the glare of the torches lights up the temple buildings, and when the "strange sound of mystic hymns and dances" rings in their ears, how their souls light up anew as they contemplate the future glory of the chosen race. Truly, "the Temple-illumination" is the light which shall "shine from out the Temple into the dark night of heathendom."

How they exult within themselves when the priests draw water from the spring of Siloam and pour it out in the holy place, "symbolical of the outpouring of the Holy Spirit," and giving to "the whole festival the name of House of Outpouring." How their voices rise in great crescendos of praise as they wave their *lulavs* and cry Hosanna, Hosanna, to God and the Lamb. And how they covenant anew to stand forever as Jews of the Jews when the solemn proclamation is made, "We are Jehovah's—our eyes are towards Jehovah." (Edersheim 2:149-50.)

Glorious as is each festive season at Tabernacle Times, this one is destined to surpass all the rest. This time the Son of God himself will come; he will announce who he is, what power he possesses, and whom he represents; and by his own voice he will tell his people and all men what they must believe and how they must live to gain celestial rest.

But he will not come at the beginning of the feast; and whether he will dwell in a booth, as the law requires, and present himself in the temple and bow to the ritualistic rules of the Rabbis, our inspired author does not tell us. We suppose that at this point in our Lord's ministry the practices of the priests and the laws of the Levites are of little concern to him. He has already declined to travel with his blood-brothers in the great Galilean caravan of pilgrims, choosing rather to journey with his disciples somewhat in secrecy.

This late arrival has the desired effect upon the people. The Galileans who preceded him have now recited in detail the wondrous works done in all their cities and villages. All Jerusalem hears again of the blind eyes that now see, the deaf ears that now hear, the lame legs that now leap, and of the lepers whose flesh has returned again to its clean and healthy state. All Jerusalem is reminded anew that storms have ceased, devils have departed, and dead corpses have walked again—all at his word. And all Jerusalem is left to ponder anew the words he has spoken and the sermons he has preached in Galilee, as these are now recited by the reputable witnesses who heard his voice.

Never in all her long history, reaching back at least to the days of Melchizedek, has Jerusalem seen such a ferment of opinion, felt such an anxiety about a doctrine, and had such a concern about a man. All people sought him. 'Where is he; when will he come; are the reports about him true; will he continue his ministry among us; is he the promised Messiah; will he deliver us from Roman bondage; is he the Son of God?'

None, however, went into the temple to preach sermons about him and his saving power; none gathered groups together in the bazaars or on the street corners to acclaim his doctrine publicly, or to trumpet his wondrous works in the ears of all men; none raised a Messianic standard and called others to enlist in the new cause—"for fear of the Jews," meaning the leaders of the people. No apostle or seventy was present to speak "openly of him." But among the people "there was much murmuring." In private conversations some were saying, "He is a good man"; others, "Nay; but he deceiveth the people." He who came not to bring peace on earth but a sword; who came to set members of the same household against each other; who came to divide families and sift the wheat from the tares—he whose gospel proclamation always divides mankind was accomplishing his purpose.

The good news of gospel grace was believed by some, rejected by others. The sifting processes were at work; the great Harvester was sifting out the hearts of men before his judgment seat. The sheep were getting ready to enter the sheepfold of the Good Shepherd, the goats to be driven out into the wilderness of spiritual darkness. The time for the arrival of the Man was at hand.

John says: "Now about the midst of the feast"—perhaps about the fourth or fifth day—"Jesus went up into the temple, and taught." Without warning he was there; his arrival was then as the Second Coming will be; to the wicked and ungodly and to all who are not waiting with anxious expectation for the promised day, it will come suddenly. On this day, the Lord whom they sought had come suddenly to his temple. Surely John and the other disciples were with him to hear his words and record his doings. As to the initial events surrounding his appearance, John, who alone records any of the happenings at the Feast of Tabernacles, tells us only that he came among them and "taught."

What did he teach? As to his spoken word, there is no record presently available where it can be read. Based on the responses that were forthcoming, and upon the questions raised by virtue of his sayings, and upon our prior knowledge of the general course he customarily pursued, however, there is little doubt as to the substance and purport of what he then said. He who is the same yesterday, today, and forever had preached, did then preach, and everlastingly will preach the gospel—the gospel of the kingdom; the gospel of salvation; the fulness of the everlasting gospel. In Galilee, in Judea, in Perea, in Phoenicia, in the Decapolis; among the Jews and to the Gentiles—everywhere and always—Jesus preached the gospel. This gospel is that he came into the world to work out the infinite and eternal atonement; that he is God's Son, the Promised Messiah; and that if men will believe in him and live his law they will be raised not alone in immortality but unto everlasting life in the Everlasting Presence.

How he couched the message on this occasion we know not. He may have used parables or dramatic illustrations, or recited eternal verities as he had done in the Sermon on the Mount. Perhaps he drew his illustrations from the sacrificial victims whose shed blood and burnt flesh adorned the great altar; or from the golden table whereon lay the holy bread, the bread of the Presence; or from the veil that shrouded the Holy of Holies, wherein the Shekinah, in olden times, had rested on the mercy seat between the cherubim. Whatever the words used, the thoughts expressed, and the doctrine taught, his preachments were not like those of the scribes. He spoke in his own right, with authority, and not by reciting a long concatenation of Rabbinical lore and tradition.

Consequently: "The Jews marvelled" at his teachings. Their natural queries were: "How knoweth this man letters, having never learned?" "He is no authorised Rabbi; He belongs to no recognised school; neither the followers of Hillel nor those of Shammai claim Him; He is a Nazarene; He was trained in the shop of the Galilean carpenter; how knoweth this man letters, having never learned? . . . In all ages there is a tendency to mistake erudition for learning, knowledge for wisdom; in all ages there has been a slowness to comprehend that true learning of the deepest and noblest character may co-exist with complete and utter ignorance of everything which absorbs and constitutes the learning of the schools." (Farrar, p. 413.) And so, to their misplaced queries, Jesus responds:

> *My doctrine is not mine, but his that sent me. If any man will do his will, he shall know of the doctrine, whether it be of God, or whether I speak of myself.*

Never man spake as this Man. The Lord Jesus Christ, supreme above all, ministers among men; he who made heaven and earth and the sea and the fountains of waters; he who is the Teacher of teachers, the Preacher to preachers, the One whose very word is perfect—this Man has no doctrine of his own! He speaks only those things which are in the bosom of the Father. It is the Father's plan; it is the gospel of the Father; those who do the will of the Father—and it is the will of God that men should believe in his Son—shall know by the power of the Holy Ghost of the truth and divinity of the gospel word.[2]

The Sinless One Acclaims His Divine Sonship
(*John 7:18-36; JST, John 7:24*)

Jesus now speaks of himself. Having announced that he was sent of God, having said that he did not speak of himself, he now adds: "He that speaketh of himself seeketh his own glory." Why else do the orators of the world, be they ministers or politicians, pour forth their mouthings except to gain prominence and position and power for themselves? "But he that seeketh his glory that sent him," that servant who glorifies the lord who sent him, even I myself who glorify my Father, "the same is true, and no unrighteousness is in him."

There is no unrighteousness in him! He is the Sinless One! All that he has done and said is perfect, which he here states in plainness—he is defending himself—because there are those then present who are plotting his death. The supposed sin: On his last visit to Jerusalem, some eighteen months ago, at the time of the Second Passover, he healed the blind man at the pool of Bethesda on the Sabbath day. "Did not Moses give you the law"—the law that says "Thou shalt not kill"—"and yet none of you keepeth the law" because ye go "about to kill me."

Those whose guilt has thus been revealed have no recourse but to plunge wildly on in their maddened course. "Thou hast a devil: who goeth about to kill thee?" they respond. Both their blasphemous charge against him and their own self-serving attestation of false innocence, he waves aside, as he continues his own defense: "I have done one work, and ye all marvel," he says. Even now, after a year and a half, the contention still raged among them: Was he the Messiah because he opened blind eyes, or was he possessed of a devil because he violated their self-imposed Sabbath restrictions?

"Moses therefore gave unto you circumcision," he continued, "(not because it is of Moses, but of the fathers;) and ye on the sabbath day circumcise a man." Such was a factual recitation of what they all knew to be true. "If a man on the sabbath day receive circumcision, that the law of Moses should not be broken; are ye angry at me, because I have made a man every whit whole on the sabbath day?"

This logic cannot be gainsaid. "On their own purely ritual and Levitical principle, . . . His word of healing had in no respect violated the Sabbath at all. . . . Moses had established, or rather re-established, the ordinance of circumcision on the eighth day, and if that eighth day happened to be a Sabbath, they without scruple sacrificed the one ordinance to the other, and in spite of the labour which it involved, performed the rite of circumcision on the Sabbath day. If the law of circumcision superseded that of the Sabbath, did not the law of Mercy? If it was right by a series of actions to inflict that wound, was it wrong by a single word to effect a total cure? If that, which was at the best but a *sign* of deliverance, could not, even on account of the Sabbath, be postponed for a single day, why was it criminal not to have postponed for the sake of the Sabbath a perfect deliverance?" (Farrar, pp. 414-15.)

Our Lord then concluded this line of reasoning with the bold counsel, nay, with the command, a command falling from divine lips: "Judge not according to your traditions, but judge righteous judgment."

Jesus spent many hours in the temple teaching; occasional sentences—those necessary to preserve the moving majesty of his life, as he went relentlessly to a martyr's doom on a Roman cross—occasional statements only have come down to us. As he spoke he was interrupted, heckled, and harassed; attempts were made to arrest him; many of his sayings were in response to the sophistries of the scribes, the ruses of the Rabbis, and the armed assaults of the temple guards. The open classroom, in which multitudes milled about and talked among themselves, was totally devoid of decorum; angry mobs mingled in the courts with believing souls; and his disciples participated in the affrays and were part of the great proselyting work then being done by earth's Chief Missionary.

Thus we now read in John's account that "some of them of Jerusalem," whose opinions had been molded by their scribes and Rabbis, asked: "Is not this he, whom they seek to kill?" It seemed incomprehensible to them that if he were Satan incarnate, as the rulers said, they would stand idly by and let him speak freely to the people. "Lo, he speaketh boldly, and they say nothing unto him. Do the rulers know indeed that this is the very Christ?"

Then, lest any think their zeal for Moses and the law had lessened, and lest any accuse them of departing from their ancient moorings, they aligned themselves against their Deliverer by saying, "Howbeit we know this man whence he is: but when Christ cometh, no man knoweth whence he is." Again their traditions led them astray; these included the teaching that the Messiah's coming would be sudden and unexpected, a view that may have arisen from Messianic utterances about the Second Coming. "Do not the Rabbis tell us," said some, "that the Messiah will be born in Bethlehem, but that He will be snatched away by spirits and tempests soon after His birth, and that when He returns the second time no one will know from whence He has come? But we know that this man comes from Nazareth. Our chief men, if they choose, may accept Him as the Messiah; we will not." (Geikie, p. 587.)

'He is a good man!' 'He is a deceiver!' The tension mounts and the division widens. Thereupon Jesus, in a loud voice that all the disputants might hear, cries out: "Ye both know me, and ye know whence I am." Our Lord—and blessed be his name—was making himself an active participant in their disputes. 'In a worldly sense you know me. You know I was born in Bethlehem; you know I am the Son who was called out of Egypt; you know I grew up in Nazareth, that I might be called a Nazarene. But in the true and eternal sense you neither know me nor from whence I came.'

And I am not come of myself, but he that sent me is true, whom ye know not. But I know him: for I am from him, and he hath sent me.

'I alone of myself do not claim to be the Messiah; I am sent by my Father. He is God, and I am his Son. His witness of me is true. Ye do not know that he is God, that he sent me, and that I came forth from him. But I know him and testify that I am the Messiah.'

At the pool of Bethesda, on the Sabbath when the impotent man, at his word, took up his bed and walked, Jesus said: "My Father worketh hitherto, and I work." On that occasion, for Sabbath violation and for blasphemy, as they supposed, the rulers sought his life. "The hostile part of the crowd rightly saw a similar claim repeated now, and with the wild fanaticism of their race in that age, proposed to lay hold of Him, and hurry Him outside the city on the instant, to stone Him, as the Law against blasphemy enjoined. But His hour had not yet come, and whether from fear of the Galileans at the feast, or from other reasons, their rage died away in words." (Geikie, p. 588.)

The long hours of teaching in the temple began to bear fruit. His words, his bearing, the spirit that attended him, the testimonies of disciples who mingled among them—perhaps also there were miracles—all softened the hearts of those who were spiritually receptive. "Many of the people believed on him," John says. "When Christ cometh," they asked, "will he do more miracles than these which this man hath done?"

With this turn of events, "the Pharisees and the chief priests sent officers to take him." He must be arrested before the spell of his presence caused the rabble to acclaim him King-Messiah as it was reported they had done near Bethsaida-Julias when he fed the five thousand. 'Unless he is silenced our craft is in danger. He defames our Sabbath; our traditions are set at naught. What will happen to our washings before we eat, our sacrifices on the great altar, the temple contributions that flow in from our people everywhere? He must be silenced!'

These temple police, warrant in hand, singled out by their distinctive dress, mingled with the multitudes, seeking opportunity to make the arrest without raising a tumult. To them in the hearing of all, Jesus said: "Yet a little while am I with you, and then I go unto him that sent me. Ye shall seek me, and shall not find me: and where I am, thither ye cannot come." The Master simply declines to be arrested; such does not accord with his needs and plan. "Your desire to take me is premature; I am to remain with you until the appointed time. Then I shall return to my Father, and we shall part company forever." 'In the troubles of the coming day ye shall seek your Deliverer, your Messiah.' But "ye shall not find me, for no unclean thing can come into my Father's kingdom. Later he will tell his repentant and faithful disciples that where he went they can come also. (John 14:1-6.)" (*Commentary* 1:444-45.)

Jesus' words—testifying that God is his Father, that he shall die and return to him whose Son he is, and that the unbelieving and rebellious shall not find place in the Divine Presence—these words refresh the hearts of the faithful and pour light into their souls. To the unbelieving among his hearers, their effect is the reverse. "Whither will he go, that we shall not find him?" they ask. The things of the Spirit are understood only by the power of the Spirit; these Jews know nothing of the Eternal Kingdom and the Father who reigns there, nor of the identity of the Son who is now on earth. "Will he go unto the dispersed among the Gentiles, and teach the Gentiles?" "What! Will he leave us to go to the scattered remnant of Israel among the Greeks? Will he leave us, the assembled and chosen people, to preach to Gentiles?" (*Commentary* 1:445.) "What manner of saying is this that he said, Ye shall seek me, and shall not find me: and where I am, thither ye cannot come?" Truly, there is no darkness as deep as spiritual darkness, and no mind as closed as one bound by the chains of a false religion.

Thus endeth, as far as the record goes, Jesus' ministry during the initial days of the Feast of Tabernacles. But all this is but the foundation for the proclamation he will make "in the last day, the great day of the feast," and for what he will say and do on the octave of the same festal season, as we are about to see.

NOTES

1. These prophetic words of Zechariah are found in a millennial setting. Their fulfillment will come after all nations have assembled at Armageddon; after "the day of the Lord cometh"; after his feet stand again "upon the mount of Olives"; after "the Lord my God shall come, and all the saints with thee"; after the Lord has become "king over all the earth," and is thus reigning in millennial splendor. Then not only the Jews but all nations shall worship him in the latter-day temple, in Jerusalem, the Holy City. (See Zech. 12 through 14.)

2. The Father, not the Son, is the author of the plan of salvation. The Father did not—as some have falsely supposed—ask for suggestions as to what he should do to save his children. Rather, the Father announced his own plan, explained its terms and provisions, including the need for a Redeemer, and then asked whom he should send to be his Son and the Redeemer. Then it was that the Lord Jesus and Lucifer made their offers, with the first being accepted and the second rejected. Thus Paul speaks of "the gospel of God . . . Concerning his Son Jesus Christ our Lord, which was made of the seed of David according to the flesh." (Rom. 1:1-3.) The gospel of the Father was adopted by the Son and is called by us the gospel of Jesus Christ, because our Lord is the one who, through his atoning sacrifice, put its terms and conditions into full operation.

Chapter 70

LIVING WATER FOR ALL MEN

I will pour water upon him that is thirsty,
and floods upon the dry ground:
I will pour my spirit upon thy seed,
and my blessing upon thine offspring.
(Isa. 44:3.)[1]

"Come Ye to the Waters"

(*John 7:37-39; JST, John 7:39*)

How men long for water in a dry and thirsty land! Moses smites the rock with his rod that Israel may drink and live. Elijah abides by the brook Cherith when the heavens are sealed for three and a half years. Without water, men die.

No metaphor is more intense than that offered by the longing for water among the dwellers in the desert. As the Lord laveth the desert soil, so he rains down righteousness upon his people. As he sendeth the early and latter rains, so pools of living water spring up in the parched soil; and where there are living prophets, there streams of living water flow, streams from which men may drink and never thirst more.

When Isaiah invites men to come unto Christ and believe his gospel, his cry is: "Ho, every one that thirsteth, come ye to the waters." (Isa. 55:1.) And in the echoing call recorded by the Beloved Revelator we hear: "Come. And let him that is athirst come. And whosoever will, let him take the water of life freely." (Rev. 22:17.) For our day, the day of restoration, the prophetic assurance promises: "And in the barren deserts there shall come forth pools of living water; and the parched ground shall no longer be a thirsty land." (D&C 133:29.)[2]

And when the ceremonial performances of the Feast of Tabernacles were perfected, they too were designed to depict an outpouring of divine grace upon all men of all nations, using water as the symbol of life. As Edersheim observes, this feast "points forward to that great, yet unfulfilled hope of the Church: the ingathering of Earth's nations to the Christ," including the nations of heathendom, for whom sacrifices were then offered. "This eventuality can, of course, only be realized through the outpouring of the Holy Spirit upon the Gentile nations. As we have already seen, the daily and ritualistic pouring out of the water, which gave the whole festival the name *House of Outpouring,* was understood by the Rabbis to be symbolical of the outpouring of the Holy Spirit." (Edersheim 2:156.)

Now we must describe this performance, hear the cries of Hosanna that attend it, and show how all this prepared the way for Jesus to testify that he was the source of that living water of which all men must drink to gain salvation. We must not pass over this or any of the local settings in which Jesus chose to proclaim his eternal truths, and none of them is more dramatic than that which we shall now recount.

It has been calculated that it took "not fewer than 446 priests," and an equal number of Levites, to carry out the sacrificial worship at the Feast of Tabernacles. On each of the seven days, and possibly also on the octave day, one of these sons of Aaron, after the morning sacrifice was laid on the altar, drew three *logs* of water—somewhat more than two pints—from the Pool of Siloam. Attended by throngs of worshippers who carried their palm branches, to be waved in the Hosanna Shout, this priest brought the water from the pool in a golden ewer. A solemn procession carried the "living water" to the temple; joyous blasts on the sacred trumpets heralded its arrival; and while one priest poured it into a silver basin on the western side of the altar, another poured the wine for the drink-offering into another silver basin on the eastern side.

Then came the chanting by the Levites, with responses from the people, of the Hallel, which consists of Psalms 113 through 118. At designated places the people responded with the following cries:

"*Hallelu Yah*" (Praise ye the Lord, from which Hebraic expression comes the designation, *Hallel*); "O then, work now salvation, Jehovah"; "O Lord, send now prosperity"; and "O give thanks to the Lord." As these expressions were made—similarly, we suppose, as is the case in the latter-day Hosanna Shout—they waved their palm branches toward the great altar.

Then followed the special sacrificial offerings for the day and the chanting, to instrumental accompaniment, of the appointed psalm. On "the last day, that great day of the feast," this was Psalm 82:5, which—perhaps not without divine irony—read: "They know not, neither will they understand; they walk on in darkness: all the foundations of the earth are out of course." This reading was attended by three threefold blasts from the priestly trumpets while all the people bowed in worship.

"In further symbolism of this Feast, as pointing to the ingathering of the heathen nations, the public services closed with a procession round the Altar by the Priests, who chanted 'O then, work now salvation, Jehovah! O Jehovah, send now prosperity.' But on 'the last, the Great Day of the Feast,' this procession of Priests made the circuit of the altar, not only once, but seven times, as if they were again compassing, but now with prayer, the Gentile Jericho which barred their possession of the promised land. Hence the seventh or last day of the Feast was also called that of 'the Great Hosannah.' As the people left the Temple, they saluted the altar with words of thanks, and on the last day of the Feast they shook off the leaves on the willow-branches round the altar, and beat their palm-branches to pieces." (Edersheim 2:159-60.)

In the light of all this, there can be little doubt as to when Jesus stood and cried: "If any man thirst, let him come unto me, and drink." "It must have been with special reference to the ceremony of the outpouring of the water, which, as we have seen, was considered the central part of the service. Moreover, all would understand that His words must refer to the Holy Spirit, since the rite was universally regarded as symbolical of His outpouring." (Edersheim 2:160.) Thus we hear Jesus say:

He that believeth on me, as the scripture hath said, out of his belly shall flow rivers of living water.[3]

To this John appends an explanation: "But this spake he of the Spirit, which they that believe on him should receive; for the Holy Ghost was promised unto them who believe, after that Jesus was glorified."

Further, in setting the scene for the great proclamation, Edersheim continues: "The forthpouring of the water was immediately followed by the chanting of the *Hallel.* But after that there must have been a short pause to prepare for the festive sacrifices. It was then, immediately after the symbolic rite of water-pouring, immediately after the people had responded by repeating those lines from Psalm 118—given thanks, and prayed that Jehovah would send salvation and prosperity, and had shaken their *Lulavs* towards the altar, thus praising 'with heart, and mouth, and hands,' and then silence had fallen upon them—that there rose, so loud as to be heard throughout the Temple, the Voice of Jesus. He interrupted not the services, for they had for the moment ceased: He interpreted, and He fulfilled them." (Edersheim 2:160.)

"Never Man Spake Like This Man"

(*John 7:40-50; 8:1*)

This great Man, on this great day, at this great feast—this Man, the mightiest of all the prophets of Israel—has now discharged the preacher's responsibility to this mob-multitude who mill about in the court of the temple, a court that can contain two hundred and ten thousand souls. He has preached the doctrine given him by his Father; he has reaffirmed his own divine Sonship; he has invited all men to come unto him and to drink that living water which quenches thirst forever. Now the event rests with the hearers. At the peril of their salvation they must make their choice. 'Is he the Christ, or wait we for another?' Multitudes, multitudes, in the Valley of Decision! For them the day of the Lord has come. He has thrust in his sickle to reap among a multitude whose wickedness is great. For some, the light of heaven blazes in their hearts; as to others, even the stars withdraw their shining.

Many said, "Of a truth this is the Prophet." The Prophet, the one like unto Moses, is the Messiah, their Deliverer, though as used here it may have meant to some, not the Anointed One himself, but his forerunner. Others said, "This is the Christ," a plain, straightforward declaration that partook of part of that spirit which attended the great confession of Peter.

Yet others queried: "Shall Christ come out of Galilee? Hath not our scripture said, That Christ cometh of the seed of David, and out of the town of Bethlehem, where David was?" How marvelously adept Lucifer is at quoting scripture for his own purposes! He did it to the Master himself, when after forty days of fasting Jesus was tempted in a face-to-face confrontation with Beelzebub. At that time he was totally discomfited by Him who gave the scripture. Now the evil one quotes holy writ by the mouths of his ministers, as it were, by the mouths of those who hearken to his enticements. And, as far as the record shows, there was none to refute their false assertions. Of course the Seed of David was to come from the City of David, from Bethlehem, as their scriptures said; but their scriptures also said that he was to come not only from Galilee, but from Nazareth in Galilee, that he, as the prophets foretold, would be called a Nazarene.[4]

"So there was a division among the people because of him," just as there is division in so-called Christendom today, *because of him,* because some—again at the peril of their salvation—choose to worship a Christ of one sort, some of another. And again, in the temple court, some sought to arrest him for blasphemy, that he might be stoned, as Moses in the law commanded. "But no man laid hands on him," he declining again to be arrested. And we are left to wonder, to ponder in our hearts, how many in the religious climate of today would deny his doctrines and use the processes of the law to impede his work if he again ministered personally among men. Would they do other to Christ than they do to his servants?

After this, "the chief priests and Pharisees"—members, no doubt of the Great Sanhedrin itself—demanded of the temple police, "Why have ye not brought him?" Why indeed? Could any man arrest the Son of God before his time? If no man can take his life from him so that he must lay it down of himself, can any arrest him and hail him before the council unless he wills it? He at whose word ten legions of angels wield fiery flaming swords had work yet to do. Though their orders were strict, the officers dared not make the arrest. Some of his divine words had pricked their hearts; they were words that sapped their strength and paralyzed their wills. To their military superiors they could only respond: "Never man spake like this man."

"Are ye also deceived?" asked the rulers. 'Ye sons of Levi who serve in the temple itself, have you no more sense and judgment than this rabble to whom he preaches?' "Have any of the rulers or of the Pharisees believed on him?" 'If his claims were true, would not the rulers in the Great Sanhedrin—those who sit in judgment on the people and the law—be the first to know it? Surely the wise and the learned—the scribes who interpret the law and the Pharisees who live it to the very letter—these are the ones who should judge his claims.' "But this people who knoweth not the law are cursed." 'This ignorant rabble who have not been taught in the schools of Hillel and Shammai, who have never attended a divinity school to learn how to interpret the scriptures, are led by their superstitions to ruin.'

One voice on the council, one member of the Great Sanhedrin, was raised in Jesus' defense. Nicodemus, with whom Jesus conversed by night at the time of the First Passover, asked: "Doth our law judge any man, before it hear him, and know what he doeth?" What else Nicodemus said, we do not know; it is idle to suppose his defense was limited to one sentence only. But this single sentence sufficed to cut his colleagues to the core. They knew Jehovah's charge to the judges: "Hear the causes between your brethren, and judge righteously between every man and his brother, and the stranger that is with him. Ye shall not respect persons in judgment; but ye shall hear the small as well as the great; ye shall not be afraid of the face of man, for the judgment is God's." (Deut. 1:16-17.)

There is no way to refute a right reply; the rulers fell back on their only recourse—taunts and derision. "Art thou also of Galilee?" they demanded of Nicodemus. "Search, and look: for out of Galilee ariseth no prophet." No? "Where then . . . was Gath-hepher, whence Jonah came? where Thisbe, whence Elijah came? where Elkosh, whence Nahum came? where the northern town whence Hosea came? . . . But there is no ignorance so deep as the ignorance that will not know; no blindness so incurable as the blindness which will not see. And the dogmatism of a narrow and stolid prejudice which believes itself to be theological learning is, of all others, the most ignorant and the most blind. Such was the spirit in which, ignoring the mild justice of Nicodemus, and the marvellous impression made by Jesus even on their own hostile apparitors, the majority of the Sanhedrin broke up, and went each to his own home." (Farrar, p. 421.)

"Jesus," however, "went unto the mount of Olives," and

perhaps beyond to Bethany where dwelt his friends Mary and Martha and Lazarus, whence, on the morrow, he will return to continue his teaching in the temple.

The Woman Taken in Adultery
(*John 8:2-11; JST, John 8:9-11*)

Early the next morning—October 18, A.D. 29, the day following "the Great Hosanna," when he had offered living water to all men—Jesus came early to the temple. Back from the quiet and peace and sweetness of the Mount of Olives, he was once again, at duty's call, amid the stench and smells and human filth of the city. When he was seated, probably in the Court of the Women, "all the people came unto him," to hear those words of eternal life which prepare men for immortal glory.

As his wondrous words flow forth, weaving themselves into the very fibers and sinews of believing souls, the scribes and Pharisees are about to confront him with one of the most devilish plots yet devised in their scheming minds. During the night a woman has been caught in the very act of adultery; they will ask him to judge her, thus forcing him to side, as they suppose, either with Moses or with Rome, where her heinous sin is involved. "The repeated instances in which, without a moment's hesitation, He foiled the crafty designs of His enemies, and in foiling them taught for ever some eternal principle of thought and action, are among the most unique and decisive proofs of His more than human wisdom; and yet not one of those gleams of sacred light which were struck from Him by collision with the malice or hate of man was brighter or more beautiful than this."[5]

"It is probable that the hilarity and abandonment of the Feast of Tabernacles, which had grown to be a kind of vintage festival, would often degenerate into acts of licence and immorality, and these would find more numerous opportunities in general disturbance of ordinary life caused by the dwelling of the whole people in their leafy booths."

"Master, this woman was taken in adultery, in the very act," taunted the scribal rulers and Pharisaic hypocrites as they, with physical persuasion, placed her in the midst of those whom Jesus was teaching. "Now Moses in the law commanded us, that such should be stoned," they said, "but what sayest thou?" This cunningly devised interrogatory was in no sense a search for guidance, nor did it raise any point with reference to an infamous act of adultery that needed a decision. Though it was the custom to consult distinguished Rabbis in cases of doubt or difficulty, this was not such a case. They knew, and everyone knew, that Moses decreed death for adulterers, both of them, the man and the woman, and that the accuser's hand should cast the first stone. This was not such a case. The guilty man was absent; the aggrieved husband was lodging no charge; and no witnesses had been summoned, that in the mouth of two or three witnesses every word might be established. Their purpose, rather, as John expresses it, was to tempt him, "that they might have to accuse him."

The character of the conniving religionists is seen perfectly in their callous use of the woman. "To subject her to the superfluous horror of this odious publicity—to drag her, fresh from the agony of detection, into the sacred precincts of the Temple—to subject this unveiled, dishevelled, terror-stricken woman to the cold and sensual curiosity of a malignant mob—to make her, with total disregard to her own sufferings, the mere passive instrument of their hatred against Jesus—and to do all this, not under the pressure of moral indignation, but in order to gratify a calculating malice—showed on their parts a cold, hard cynicism, a graceless, pitiless, barbarous brutality of heart and conscience, which could not but prove, in every particular, revolting and hateful to One who alone was infinitely tender, because He alone was infinitely pure."

These wily scribes and crafty Pharisees have done their work well. 'Master, what sayest thou of this adulteress and the penalty she should receive?' "They thought that now they had caught Him in a dilemma. They knew the divine trembling pity which had loved where others hated, and praised where others scorned, and encouraged where others crushed; and they knew how that pity had won for Him the admiration of many, the passionate devotion of not a few. They knew that a publican was among His chosen, that sinners had sat with Him at the banquet, and harlots unreproved had bathed His feet, and listened to His words. Would He then acquit this woman, and so make Himself liable to an accusation of heresy, by placing Himself in open disaccord with the sacred and fiery Law? or, on the other hand, would He belie His own compassion, and be ruthless, and condemn? And, if He did, would He not at once shock the multitude, who were touched by His tenderness, and offend the civil magistrates by making Himself liable to a charge of sedition? How could He possibly get out of the difficulty? Either alternative—heresy or treason—accusation before the Sanhedrin or delation to the Procurator—opposition to the orthodox or alienation from the many—would serve equally well their unscrupulous intentions. And one of these, they thought, *must* follow. What a happy chance this weak, guilty woman had given them! "

Thus their trap was baited; but Jesus—not deigning to respond, scarce considering their stratagem worthy of a fleeting notice—"stooped down, and with his finger wrote on the ground, as though he heard them not." Perhaps what he wrote were the words he was about to speak; perhaps the act was symbolical—a symbol of forgiveness, "a symbol that the memory of things thus written in the dust might be obliterated and forgotten." But his detractors, inattentive to what they might learn, insensitive to anything but the scheme they had so cunningly devised, continue to attack him with their repetitious question: 'What sayest thou?'

Jesus stood up. He spoke. "He that is without sin among you, let him first cast a stone at her." Those words alone sufficed. He spoke, and they knew he spoke, not of sins in general, but of the same sin—adultery—of which the woman was guilty. 'He among you that is not an adulterer, let him cast the first stone.' What saith the law of Moses? "The hands of the witnesses shall be first upon him to put him to death, and afterward the hands of all the people." (Deut. 17:7.) Jesus had read their hearts and discerned their sins. There were none fit to accuse her according to the law. "And again he stooped down, and wrote on the ground."

"The spirit which actuated these Scribes and Pharisees was not by any means the spirit of a sincere and outraged purity. In the decadence of national life, in the daily familiarity with heathen degradations, in the gradual substitution of a Levitical scrupulosity for a heartfelt religion, the morals of the nation had grown utterly corrupt. . . . Not even the Scribes and Pharisees—for all their external religiosity—had any genuine horror of an impurity with which their own lives were often stained. They saw in the accident which had put this guilty woman into their power nothing but a chance of annoying, entrapping, possibly even endangering this Prophet of Galilee, whom they already regarded as their deadliest enemy."

As Jesus pointedly ignored the evil and sinful leaders of the people, they slunk guiltily away. "Convicted by their own conscience," they went out of the temple "one by one, beginning at the eldest, even unto the last." "He had but calmly spoken a few simple words, but those words like the still small voice to Elijah at Horeb, had been more terrible than wind or earthquake. They had fallen like a spark of fire upon slumbering hearts, and lay burning there till 'the blushing, shame-faced spirit' mutinied within them. The Scribes and Pharisees stood silent and fearful; they loosed their hold upon the woman; their insolent glances, so full of guile and malice, fell guiltily to the ground. They who had unjustly inflicted, now justly felt the overwhelming anguish of an intolerable shame, while over their guilty consciences there rolled, in crash on crash of thunder, such thoughts as these:—'Therefore thou art inexcusable, O man, whosoever thou art that judgest: for wherein thou judgest another, thou condemnest thyself: for thou that judgest doest the same things. But we are sure that the judgment of God is according to truth against them which commit such things. And thinkest thou this, O man, that judgest them which do such things and doest the same, that thou shalt escape the judgment of God? Or despisest thou the riches of His goodness and forbearance, and long-suffering; not knowing that the goodness of God leadeth thee to repentance? but after thy hardness and impenitent heart treasurest up to thyself wrath against the day of wrath and revelation of the righteous judgment of God, who will render to every man according to his deeds.' (Rom. 2:1-6.) They were '*such*' as the woman they had condemned, and they dared not stay."

Permitting the sin-smitten scribes and the impure Pharisees to depart without so much as a glance, Jesus then stood up again. "Woman, where are those thine accusers? hath no man condemned thee? " he asked.

"No man, Lord," she replied. "Neither do I condemn thee; go, and sin no more. And the woman glorified God from that hour, and believed on his name." And, we cannot doubt, she repented of her sins, was washed clean in the waters of baptism, and joined herself to the true believers who through righteousness have their garments washed clean by the blood of the Lamb.

We cannot, at this point, refrain from expressing these words of sound doctrine: Jesus did not condone an adulterous act; rather, he did and does condemn those who commit any immoral act. Those guilty of sexual sins, including adultery and homosexual perversions, may repent and be saved in the kingdom of the Father. When he says here that he does not condemn this woman, his words carry two connotations: (1) He does not condemn her within the meaning of the Mosaic law where her accuser is obligated to sit in judgment and cast the first stone, and (2) he does not condemn her because she repented and became clean before him.

NOTES

1. The Targum that paraphrases this verse reads: "Behold, as the waters are poured on arid ground and spread over the dry soil, so will I give the Spirit of My Holiness on thy sons, and My blessing on thy children's children." (Edersheim 2:161.)

2. Other relevant passages say: "With joy shall ye draw water out of the wells of salvation." (Isa. 12:3.) "Thou shalt be like a watered garden, and like a spring of water, whose waters fail not." (Isa. 58:11.) "I will even make a way in the wilderness, and rivers in the desert. . . . Because I give waters in the wilderness, and rivers in the desert, to give drink to my people, my chosen." (Isa. 43:19-20.) Heretofore also we have heard Jesus speak of giving "living water" to the Samaritan woman, and of the fact that those who believe in him shall never thirst more. (John 4:10-14; 6:35.)

3. "There is no single Old Testament passage which promises that living waters shall flow from the disciples to others. Jesus is either quoting a prophecy which has not been preserved for us or he is combining such statements as those found in Isaiah 44:3, 55:1, and 58:11, in such a way as to give an interpretive rendition of them." (*Commentary* 1:446.) There is also a possibility he was adapting the prophecy in Ezekiel 47:1 through a play on the Hebrew word translated "threshold" and speaking of the living water coming therefrom. Compare Zechariah 14:8 and Revelation 22:1.

4. An interesting sidelight on Matthew's quotation that Jesus would be called a Nazarene because he dwelt in Nazareth (Matt. 2:23) is that Nazarene (*Netzer* in Hebrew) has the same root word as Branch. The Nazarene was the promised Branch. (Isa. 11:1; Jer. 23:5; 33:15; Zech. 3:8.)

5. This quotation and the balance of those in this subsection, "The Woman Taken in Adultery," are found in Farrar, chapter 40, pages 422-31. In this chapter, as Edersheim comments, Archdeacon Farrar has written "some of his most pictorial pages." (Edersheim 2:163, footnote 1.)

Chapter 71

MESSIAH—THE LIGHT OF THE WORLD

In me shall all mankind have light,
and that eternally, even they who shall believe
on my name. (Ether 3:14.)[1]
Behold I am the light;
I have set an example for you. . . .
Behold I am the light which ye shall hold up—
that which ye have seen me do.
(3 Ne. 18:16, 24.)[2]

"I Am the Light of the World"
(*John 8:12*)

Few of our Lord's bold utterances had such an effect on his Jewish hearers as did his claim to Messiahship by saying he was the Light of the World. Heretofore he has named himself as the Bread of Life, which if men eat they shall never hunger more. Only yesterday he offered living water to all who thirst for spiritual drink. His present claim to be the Light—the Example, Guide, Archetype, Model—the Perfect Pattern for all men, this claim surpasses in some respects all of the other Messianic symbolisms he has applied to himself.

To envision its meaning and effect upon his Jewish hearers, we must realize two things that they knew: (1) their

Messianic prophecies spoke plainly of a Deliverer who would bring light to Israel and—note it well—to all nations; and (2) those fonts of Jewish wisdom, the scribes and Rabbis, taught that the Messiah would be the Light of men.

What Jesus will now do is apply the Messianic prophecies and the Rabbinic teachings to himself. It is not the doctrinal principle that is at stake—there is universal agreement on that; it is the application of what the prophets and the Rabbis have said to the person of this Man from Galilee who has now come into Judea to say to the Jews what he has been saying all along to his Galilean compatriots.

Indeed, how could the Promised Messiah come to declare glad tidings to the meek, to preach the gospel to the poor, to free men from the bondage of sin, without bringing light into the world? How could the Holy One of Israel—who is sinless and perfect, and who is the same everlastingly—come into mortality without remaining as the Sinless One and therefore being a light and an example to all men? If the Great Jehovah—the Lord Omnipotent, who was and is from all eternity—was destined to make flesh his tabernacle, how could he do other than bring with him the effulgent light and glory which dwelt in his person?

With reference to his eternal status as the Lord Jehovah, the prophetic word abounds in such statements as: "The Lord is my light and my salvation." (Ps. 27:1.) "O send out thy light and thy truth: let them lead me." (Ps. 43:3.) "God is the Lord, which hath shewed us light." (Ps. 118:27.) "Thy word is a lamp unto my feet, and a light unto my path." (Ps. 119:105.) None can doubt that the Jewish Jehovah who led their fathers was himself the source of light and truth for all.

With reference to his future Messianic ministry, his ministry among mortals as the Son of God, it is written: "I will also give thee for a light to the Gentiles, that thou mayest be my salvation unto the end of the earth." (Isa. 49:6.) Of the kingdom he shall set up the prophetic word is: "And the Gentiles shall come to thy light, and kings to the brightness of thy rising." (Isa. 60:3.) And of his personal ministry among men, a ministry in the Gentile-infested lands of Zebulun and Naphtali, Isaiah says: "The people that walked in darkness have seen a great light: they that dwell in the land of the shadow of death, upon them hath the light shined." (Isa. 9:2.) And so the saintly Simeon, having long waited for the Consolation of Israel to come—while holding the Child in his arms in Jehovah's house, and while speaking as the Holy Ghost gave him utterance—this devout and righteous man acclaimed Mary's Son as "a light to lighten the Gentiles, and the glory of thy people Israel." (Luke 2:32.)

The teachings of the Rabbis, naming their Messiah as the great light-bearer to the world, are summarized in these words: In the Midrash we are told that, "while commonly windows were made wide within and narrow without, it was the opposite in the Temple of Solomon, because the light, issuing from the Sanctuary was to lighten that which was without." Further, "That, if the light in the Sanctuary was to be always burning before Jehovah, the reason was, not that He needed such light, but that He honoured Israel with this as a symbolic command. In Messianic times God would, in fulfilment of the prophetic meaning of this rite, 'kindle for them a Great Light,' and the nations of the world would point to them, who had lit the light for Him Who lightened the whole world." Still further, "The Rabbis speak of the original light in which God had wrapped Himself as in a garment, and which could not shine by day, because it would have dimmed the light of the sun. From this light that of the sun, moon, and stars had been kindled. It was now reserved under the throne of God for the Messiah, in Whose days it would shine forth once more." And finally, the Midrash designates "the Messiah . . . as the Enlightener." Of him it says: "The light dwelleth with Him." (Edersheim 2:166.)

Thus, he, the Jewish Messiah, according to their own prophetic recitations and according to their Rabbinic teachings, was destined to be a light, not alone to the scattered remnants of Jewish Israel, but to the heathens, the Gentile nations, those always supposed by the devout among them to be outside the pale of saving grace. Their Messiah was to be the Light of the World.

Jesus is now about to proclaim himself as the Light of the World. He is choosing Tabernacles Times as the setting for such a proclamation for two very good reasons: (1) This is the feast, as we have seen, when sacrifices are offered for the nations of heathendom, the season when the chosen seed turn their thoughts to sending forth light and truth to those who sit in darkness; and (2) this is the festal season when each night the great candelabra are lighted in the temple to symbolize the sending forth of light to the inhabitants of the city and the world. Perhaps some circumstance arose to point the attention of the multitudes to these gigantic candelabra, fifty cubits in height, whereon were the lamps from which the light went forth. In any event Jesus took occasion, in this setting and at this feast, to announce:

> *I am the light of the world: he that followeth me shall not walk in darkness, but shall have the light of life.*

The Light of the World! Jew and Gentile alike—all persons—must look to him. How well Jesus has applied the symbolisms of the feast to himself. 'I, Jesus, am the Source; light and truth shine forth from me. My word is light; it is truth. Follow me; I am the Exemplar. Believe my gospel and ye shall no longer walk in darkness; do as I do, and ye shall be as I am. Ye shall have the light which giveth life, the light leading to eternal life.'

The Pharisees Reject the Light

(*John 8:13-20*)

We now see something that makes us weep, weep for the spiritual blindness and depravity of a whole race of religionists. It is not as though the prophecies and Messianic concepts are foreign to them. They know, and have been taught for thousands of years, that one will come and announce himself as the Light of the World. They and their fathers have looked forward to this day for four millennia, a day when they that sit in darkness shall see a great light, a day when the Deliverer shall come to Israel to pierce the darkness of the night with the light of life, with the light of eternal life.

Here in the midst of the chosen race is a man like none other they have ever seen; here sitting in the treasury in the holy temple is one who says: 'I am the Light of the World; I am your promised Messiah; I am the Son of God. Come unto me and ye shall be saved.' He is the same man who is known by all the people as the one who opens blind eyes, unstops deaf ears, and commands the spirits of men to enter embalmed corpses so that dead men live again. He is the one who is known by all of them to cleanse lepers, cast out evil spirits, and to say to raging storms, 'Cease,' and it is so. He is the one who speaks—and this none of them can deny—as never man spake. His simple eloquence surpasses that of their greatest orators and their most profound preachers.

And yet they do not believe; they choose to reject him and his message. In direct response to his personal witness that he is the Light of the World, the Pharisees say: "Thou bearest record of thyself; thy record is not true." There are none so blind as they who will not see, none so deaf as those who will not hear. Why this utter disbelief? Why do they say the sun does not shine while they see it? The answer has been given before. It was at the First Passover. It is that men love darkness rather than light because their deeds are evil, and they come not to the light lest their evil deeds should be reproved. (See chapter 30, Book 1.)

But no man, least of all these pious Pharisees, says, 'I choose to walk in darkness because I am a sinner.' What, then, is the excuse they give for rejecting the Light? It is that his words do not comply with the requisites of their divine law of witnesses because he alone is attesting to their verity. This also is a matter that he has answered before, at the

Second Passover, when he acclaimed his divine Sonship in pointed and precise words and showed that the same witness had also been borne by John the Baptist, by his Father, by inspired witnesses as they were moved upon by the Holy Spirit, and by their whole body of scriptural writ. (See chapter 38, Book 2.) Now his response is:

> *Though I bear record of myself, yet my record is true: for I know whence I came, and whither I go; but ye cannot tell whence I come, and whither I go.*

By claiming Jesus could not bear a true witness of his own divinity, the Pharisees were attempting to use a rule of judicial procedure that rejected uncorroborated personal testimony. In court procedures all things were established in the mouths of two or three witnesses. They were thus presuming to sit in judgment on him. In a moment he will name another, his Father, who is also his witness; but first he rejects their assertion that even his unsupported testimony is not true, and in doing so makes himself the judge rather than the one on trial.

He knows his origin, whence he came, and whither he will soon go; they do not. He can testify of these things. He knows; they are without knowledge and can give only negative testimony, as it were. Witnesses can testify only to what they know, not what they do not know. Jehovah tells his people, "Ye are my witnesses, saith the Lord, that I am God." (Isa. 43:12.) Thus, those saints who know of the existence of God by revelation from the Holy Ghost can testify "I know God lives," but someone else who does not know this cannot testify "There is no God." The fact that someone does not know something is not evidence that the thing is not true. In this case Jesus can testify as to who he is because he knows; the Pharisees cannot deny this because it is something they do not know. Their only valid testimony would be that they did not know one way or the other. And so Jesus continues:

> *Ye judge after the flesh; I judge no man. And yet if I*

judge, my judgment is true: for I am not alone, but I and the Father that sent me.

'Ye seek to judge me by the law, which requires added witnesses. I do not involve myself in such contentions. When I sit in judgment on any matter, my decisions are true and righteous, for I do not judge by myself alone, but give the decision of him who sent me, who is the Father.' This assertion determined the matter from the eternal standpoint; such were the realities where the everlasting truths of salvation were concerned. He was Christ, and Christ is God, and his testimony alone sufficed on that point. But there was, in fact, more; even if they chose to sit in judgment on him according to their legal system, he nonetheless met their requirements.

It is also written in your law, that the testimony of two men is true. I am one that bear witness of myself, and the Father that sent me beareth witness of me.

This, as we have heretofore seen, is the divine law of witnesses. It operated in Jesus' case. Two "men" bore witness of him; he was one man, the Father was the other. God himself is a Holy Man.

Thereupon the Pharisees asked, not *who* is the Father—Jesus had made that abundantly clear on this and numerous occasions—but "Where is thy Father?" Perhaps in their spiritually benighted state they assumed the Father should come personally to bear witness of the Son, rather than doing it, as his eternal law provides, by the power of the Holy Ghost.

Ye neither know me, nor my Father: if ye had known me, ye should have known my Father also.

This is the sum and substance of the whole matter. Because they did not believe in the Son, they were unable to believe in the Father. How can anyone believe that the Son is the offspring of the Father without believing that the Father is the progenitor of the Son? To know one is to know the other; and to disbelieve in one is to disbelieve in the other. Having so spoken, having thus uttered words that had the ring of blasphemy in Pharisaic ears, the expected reaction should have been 'Let him be stoned as our law requires, for he maketh himself God.' But as John concludes, "No man laid hands on him; for his hour was not yet come."

'Believe in Me, or Die in Your Sins'

(*John 8:21-30*)

I go my way, and ye shall seek me, and shall die in your sins: whither I go, ye cannot come.

These words, spoken later, perhaps in one of the porches of the temple, are obviously the conclusion of some more extended teaching on Jesus' part. He is saying that the Son will go his own way back to the Father. He will not serve as the temporal Messiah whom they desire, though they will continue to seek for such a worldly ruler. But because they believe neither in him nor in his Father, they shall die in their sins. All men have sinned, and those only who believe, repent, are baptized, and receive the Holy Ghost become clean and qualify for a celestial inheritance. None others can go where he is.[3]

This doctrine is strong; the meaning is clear to Jewish ears; even these rebellious Jerusalemites know he is speaking of his atoning sacrifice and death, and of his heavenly abiding place with his Father. They know too that they have been plotting that very death. He must not, from their standpoint, be permitted to leave any implication that they, the Jews, will be guilty of his death. Alert to their own defense, they say—it is not a question to him but an assertion to the multitude—"Will he kill himself? because he saith, Whither I go, ye cannot come." 'See, he is going to commit suicide and go down to Sheol, where none of us Jews will go.'

Jesus knows their designs and intents. They shall not escape responsibility for their evil plans by such self-serving statements. He says:

Ye are from beneath; I am from above: ye are of this world; I am not of this world.

'Ye yourselves are from the nether realms; I am from

heaven. Ye are carnal, sensual, and devilish, and ye pursue a worldly course, a course that thirsts for my blood; I am righteous and live by a higher standard.'

> *I said therefore unto you, that ye shall die in your sins: for if ye believe not that I am he, ye shall die in your sins.*

'I repeat; your deeds are evil; you are sinners; ye seek that which is evil; and ye shall die in your sins. I alone can save you; remission of sins comes by faith, repentance, and baptism. If you do not believe in me, ye shall die in your sins and be damned in eternity.'

Again the meaning is clear; again Jewish ears know he is hurling anathemas upon them for rejecting him; again they know he is damning them for their contempt toward him. What is their defense? Perhaps they can trap him into saying something that is clearly blasphemous and that will further their death-devising schemes. "Who art thou? " they ask. His reply:

> *Even the same that I said unto you from the beginning.*

'Why try and trap me now? From the beginning of my ministry—throughout Judea and Galilee and among those who are aliens, always and everywhere—I have borne the same witness. My identity is of record. All who have heard me speak know what I have said about me and my Father.' And further:

> *I have many things to say and to judge of you: but he that sent me is true; and I speak to the world those things which I have heard of him.*

Sadly, as John records, there were among them those who "understood not that he spake to them of the Father." In spite of all that he had said and now said, a veil of disbelief covered their hearts. Wicked and carnal men cannot comprehend the things of the Spirit; only those who hearken to the promptings of that light—the light of conscience, the Light of Christ, that light with which all men are endowed—only those are led to the truth.

When ye have lifted up the Son of man, then shall ye know that I am he, and that I do nothing of myself; but as my Father hath taught me, I speak these things.

And he that sent me is with me: the Father hath not left me alone; for I do always those things that please him.

'I shall be crucified. Ye shall, by Roman hands, lift me up upon the cross; ye shall, by a Roman spear, pierce my side; and finally, in a distant day, ye shall look on me whom ye have pierced, and know that I am he who came to bring salvation. And yet, even I can do nothing of myself. I serve at my Father's behest; he taught me all I know, and I speak his words. He sent me. I am his Son, and he is ever with me, for I keep his commandments.'

"As he spake these words," John says, "many believed on him." Or better, as we are about to see, many began to believe on him, for their faith was not yet perfect, and they had much yet to do to become his disciples indeed.

NOTES

1. Such was the proclamation of the Promised Messiah, spoken to the brother of Jared more than two millennia before his mortal birth.

2. Such were the words of the Risen Lord, spoken to the Nephites after he had tabernacled in the flesh.

3. "Remission of sins before death (and the consequent status of cleanliness and purity which assures the sin-free person of eventual salvation) comes to accountable men in one way and one way only. By conformity to the following eternal principles sins are remitted: (1) Men must believe in Christ as the very Son of God, the actual Redeemer and Savior through whose atoning sacrifice the whole plan of redemption and salvation is made operative; (2) Then being moved upon by a godly sorrow for sin they must forsake evil, turn to righteousness, and repent of their wrongdoings with all their hearts; (3) Thereafter they must be baptized in water for the remission of sins, under the hands of a legal administrator; and (4) Following this, also under the hands of a legal administrator, they must receive the gift of the Holy Ghost.

"Those who take these steps and who endure in righteousness thereafter are saved; all others are damned. Thus by rejecting their King-Messiah these Jews would inevitably and surely die in their sins and be precluded from going to that eternal kingdom where the Eternal King reigns forever. And what was true for them applies in principle to men of all ages." (*Commentary* 1:454-55.)

ABRAHAM'S SEED

We be Abraham's children, the Jews said to Jove;
We shall follow our Father; inherit his trove.
But from Jesus our Lord came the stinging rebuke:
Ye are children of him whom ye list to obey;
Were ye Abraham's seed ye would walk in his path,
And escape the strong chains of the father of wrath.

We have Moses the seer, and the prophets of old;
All their words we shall treasure as silver and gold.
But from Jesus our Lord came the sobering voice:
If to Moses ye turn, then give heed to his word;
Only then can ye hope for rewards of great worth,
For he spake of my coming and labors on earth.

We have Peter and Paul; in their steps let us trod;
So religionists say, as they worship their God.
But speaks he who is Lord of the living and dead:
In the hands of those prophets, those teachers and
seers,
Who abide in your day have I given the keys;
Unto them ye must turn, the Eternal to please.

"The Truth Shall Make You Free"

(*John 8:31-36*)

As the festal fellowship and sociality of the Feast of Tabernacles comes to a close, the temple courts present a disconcerting scene of confusion and contention. A motley multitude assembles in groups in the various porches to hear the words of prominent Rabbis. In the courts are lowing cattle and bleating sheep destined to die in the sacrificial rites. The autumn breezes carry the smell of dung and the stench of urine. Moneychangers ply their trade; the temple bazaars do a thriving business; and the sons of Annas gather extortionate sums into their rapacious pockets.

Large crowds gather around Jesus in one of the porches as he seats himself to continue the day-long doctrinal dialogues that have now been going on for four or five days. Some of the multitude are friendly, some unfriendly; some are meek and lowly in heart, others are conniving and mendacious. Sanhedrinists are present, those sanctimonious souls who delight to bear the religious burdens of the nation. There are pious priests and supercilious scribes. The Pharisees, who make broad their phylacteries and from whose garments hang the holy tassels in token of their covenant to be a people set apart, mingle among them. We see rude Galileans, haughty Judeans, worldly-wise Gentiles. There are pilgrims from afar, from Egypt and Greece and Rome, even, perhaps, from so distant a land as Spain, for the Jews in this day are everywhere. Herodians, ever alert to the interest of Rome, are infiltrated among them, and Roman soldiers are not far off, awaiting the call, if needed, to keep the peace. Mingling also with the group are the disciples, Peter and John and the others, hearing the words of the Master and participating in numerous gospel discussions.

At one time Jesus converses with one group, at another with a different one. Certain among the multitude have just heard him testify—with power beyond compare—of his coming atonement and that God is his Father. They believe his doctrine and their hearts are pricked by the power of his testimony, but they are not yet as those who have borne with him the heat of the day and who have worked miracles in his name. To these newly gained partial believers he says:

> *If ye continue in my word, then are ye my disciples indeed; And ye shall know the truth, and the truth shall make you free.*

'You have begun to believe; you are exercising a particle of faith. My words, as a good seed, are beginning to sprout in your souls; and in this you have done well. But, if you are to be my true disciples—my intimate friends; those who are ever with me; those who sit with me in the kingdom of my Father—you must feast upon my words and keep my commandments. Then shall ye be my disciples. Then shall ye know the truth. Your minds shall be quick and active; ye shall receive revelation by the power of the Spirit; and the gifts of the Spirit shall be poured out upon you. Then ye shall know the truths of salvation; ye shall understand the gospel; ye shall know the things you must do to gain peace in this life and eternal life in the world to come. The truth will make you free—free from darkness, free from all the soul-shackling traditions that keep you from salvation.'

The truth shall make you free!—"Free from the damning power of false doctrine; free from the bondage of appetite and lust; free from the shackles of sin; free from every evil and corrupt influence and from every restraining and curtailing power; free to go on to the unlimited freedom enjoyed in its fulness only by exalted beings." (*Commentary* 1:456-57.)

With Jesus' statement—affirming that a knowledge of the truth as he revealed it would lead them to salvation—their faith died aborning. No, they would not continue in his word to gain the truth. Rather, "We be Abraham's seed," they said, "and were never in bondage to any man: how sayest thou, Ye shall be made free? "

'We are the chosen seed. God called Abraham, our father, and gave the truths of salvation to him and to his seed forever. None but the chosen seed have the truth; none but they shall be saved. All who are alien to Israel shall be damned. We are already free, free from all damning restraints of the heathens around us. We do not need you to make us free. You need not bring us another system of religion. We already have the Abrahamic covenant of salvation.'[1]

And all this has such a familiar spirit. These same Jews, when John the Baptist sought to introduce a new order of truth and salvation, said within themselves, "We have Abraham to our father." 'We do not need a new covenant. We are free from Gentile delusions; we shall be saved.' And such, sadly, is ever and always the cry of apostate peoples. Their wont is to rely on the promises made to prophets of old, rather than to accept the new revelation sent from heaven in their day. But to all this Jesus has a reply.

> *Verily, verily, I say unto you, Whosoever committeth sin is the servant of sin. And the servant abideth not in the house for ever: but the Son abideth ever. If the Son therefore shall make you free, ye shall be free indeed.*

'True, you are Abraham's seed in the literal and temporal sense; you are descended from him; and his blood flows in your veins. As such you abide in his house here in this life and suppose you shall so abide forever.' "Temporally speaking, only members of the family abide permanently in the house; servants come and go in their menial ministrations; they cannot abide forever in the house unless freed from their station as bondsmen; they remain outside the inner circle unless adopted as members of the family, thus being made legal heirs of all its privileges."

'But you are not Abraham's seed in the spiritual and eternal sense, because you commit sin and are therefore the servants of sin. Said I not unto you, If ye believe not that I am the Messiah, ye shall die in your sins?' "Only the family members, the freemen, the sons and daughters of God, shall abide forever in his kingdom; the servants, those bound by the chains of sin, shall minister in their assigned spheres; they cannot abide in the Father's house unless freed from sin through the cleansing power of the Son. To gain an inheritance in the spiritual kingdom, they must be spiritually begotten of the Father, adopted into his family as joint-heirs with the Son."

Thus: 'You may belong to the household of Abraham now in mortality, but it may not be so always. Only those who believe in me as the Son of God shall abide in the household of faithful Abraham in the eternal worlds. If ye forsake sin, and believe in the Son, he shall make you free from spiritual bondage, and only the free shall be Abraham's seed hereafter.' (*Commentary* 1:457.)

Who Are the Children of Abraham?

(*John 8:37-50; JST, John 8:43, 47*)

"Ye are the children of the prophets; and ye are of the house of Israel; and ye are of the covenant which the Father made with your fathers, saying unto Abraham: And in thy seed shall all the kindreds of the earth be blessed." So spoke the Risen Lord to the Nephite remnant of Israel; so might the Mortal Lord have spoken to those Jews who stood in his presence on this 18th day of October, A.D. 29, on the octave of the Feast of Tabernacles in that year; and so might he speak to that remnant of his ancient people who have been gathered into the true fold and kingdom in our day.

Children of the prophets! The literal seed of Abraham, the seed of his body, his posterity who are natural heirs of the blessings of their father! And those blessings are the blessings of celestial marriage, of an enduring family unit, of posterity both in the world and out of the world, as numerous as the sands upon the seashore or as the stars in the heavens. They are the blessings of eternal increase, of eternal life in the Everlasting Presence.

"The Father having raised me up unto you first, and sent me to bless you in turning away every one of you from his iniquities; and this because ye are the children of the covenant—And after that ye were blessed then fulfilleth the

Father the covenant which he made with Abraham, saying: In thy seed shall all the kindreds of the earth be blessed—unto the pouring out of the Holy Ghost through me upon the Gentiles." (3 Ne. 20:25-27.)

Children of the covenant! God covenanted with Abraham to save and exalt him, and his literal seed, and also all the Gentiles who would join his family by adoption—all on condition that those to be honored thus in eternity would accept the Messiah and keep his commandments. Even the Gentiles who were adopted into the family of Abraham would receive the Holy Ghost, the greatest gift that can be conferred upon men in mortality.

With reference to the dialogue digested in John 8:37-50, which we are here considering, I have written elsewhere: "For nearly 2,000 years all Israel had clung tenaciously to God's promise to Abraham: 'I will establish my covenant between me and thee and thy seed after thee in their generations for an everlasting covenant, to be a God unto thee, and to thy seed after thee.' Also: 'And in thy seed shall all the nations of the earth be blessed.' Now these unbelieving Jews, a remnant of the seed of faithful Abraham, glorying in their Abrahamic descent, contended with Jesus about their assumed preferential status as the 'seed' of that ancient patriarch.

"To understand this discussion between Jesus and his Jewish detractors, it must be remembered that men are born in various families, nations, and races as a direct result of their preexistent life. Many choice spirits from preexistence are sent in selected families. This enables them to undergo their mortal probations under circumstances where the gospel and its blessings will be more readily available to them.

"Abraham gained the promise from the Lord that his descendants, his 'literal seed, . . . the seed of the body,' would be natural heirs to all of 'the blessings of the Gospel.' His seed were to be 'lawful heirs, according to the flesh,' because of their 'lineage.' Accordingly, since Abraham's day, the Lord has sent a host of righteous spirits through that favored lineage.

"Further, Abraham also gained the divine assurance that all those who thereafter received the gospel, no matter what their literal lineage, should be 'accounted' his seed and should rise up and bless him as their father. By adoption such converts would 'become . . . the seed of Abraham.' Conversely, and in this spiritual sense, such of the literal seed of Abraham as rejected the gospel light would be cut off from the house of their fathers and be denied an eternal inheritance with Israel and Abraham. 'For they are not all Israel, which are of Israel,' as Paul explained it. 'Neither, because they are the seed of Abraham, are they all children: . . . That is, They which are the children of the flesh, these are not the children of God: but the children of the promise are counted for the seed.'

"Thus there are two distinct meanings of the expression, 'seed of Abraham': (1) There are his literal descendants who have sprung from his loins and who by virtue of their favored family status are natural heirs of the same blessings which Abraham himself enjoyed; and (2) There are those (including adopted members of the family) who become the 'seed of Abraham' in the full spiritual sense by conformity to the same gospel principles which Abraham obeyed. In this spiritual sense, the disobedient literal descendants of Abraham, being 'children of the flesh,' are not 'accounted' as Abraham's seed, but are cut off from the blessings of the gospel." (*Commentary* 1:458-60.)

Now we are ready for the conversation itself. Jesus said: "I know that ye are Abraham's seed; but ye seek to kill me, because my word hath no place in you. I speak that which I have seen with my Father: and ye do that which ye have seen with your father." 'Ye are Abraham's seed in this life, but you are not his children spiritually, because ye reject Him in whom Abraham believed and whose gospel he lived. Nay, more, ye even seek to kill me in whom Abraham believed. Ye seek to kill me because I speak that which I have received from my Father for your good. But in seeking to kill me, you do that which your father desires.' To this, without thought or reason, they chant back: "Abraham is our father." Jesus replies:

> *If ye were Abraham's children, ye would do the works of Abraham. But now ye seek to kill me, a man that hath told you the truth, which I have heard of God: this did not Abraham. Ye do the deeds of your father.*

The works of Abraham! The works of righteousness—for "Abraham believed God, and it was counted unto him for righteousness" (Rom. 4:3)—Abraham's works of righteousness were these: He had faith in the Lord Jehovah, whose gospel he believed and in whose paths he walked; he repented of his sins, was baptized, after the manner of his fathers, and received the gift of the Holy Ghost. Thereafter he endured in good works all his days—honoring the priesthood, living in the patriarchal order of matrimony, receiving visions and revelations and the gifts of the Spirit, and worshipping the Father in the name of the Son, as did Adam and all of the ancients. As to that celestial marriage practiced by Abraham and that eternal life which grows out of it, the revealed word to latter-day Israel is: "This promise is yours also, because ye are of Abraham, and the promise was made unto Abraham; and by this law is the continuation of the works of my Father, wherein he glorifieth himself. Go ye, therefore, and do the works of Abraham; enter ye into my law and ye shall be saved." (D&C 132:31-32.)

But these rebellious sons—sons physically but not spiritually—seek to slay the very Jehovah whom Abraham their father revered. And they do it because he tells them some of the same truths he revealed to Abraham, truths that he learned from his Father, Elohim. Such a course was counter to all that the ancient patriarch stood for, and these Jews, therefore, were doing the deeds not of righteous Abraham, but of an evil father. 'Ye are apostates who walk in the way of wickedness, being led by the devil whom ye have adopted as your father.'

"We be not born of fornication," they reply; "we have one Father, even God." 'The devil is not our father; we are not spiritually illegitimate. We are the children of Abraham and have the true religion, and hence God is our Father.'

> *If God were your Father, ye would love me: for I proceeded forth and came from God; neither came I of myself, but he sent me.*

'If ye had the true religion, thus making God your Father, ye would accept me, for God sent me to lead men to him. How can you believe in the Father and reject the Son, who is in the express image of the Father and who came forth from him, and who speaks his words and does his works?'

> *Why do ye not understand my speech? even because ye cannot bear my word. Ye are of your father the devil, and the lusts of your father ye will do.*

The wicked and ungodly cannot bear the word of God; it is a burden that crushes their souls and leaves them lifeless in the dust of despair. And further, "Just as surely as the obedient 'receive the adoption of sons,' becoming 'children of God,' so the disobedient are adopted into the Church or kingdom of the devil, thus becoming children of the devil." (*Commentary* 1:461.)[2] As to the satanic father of these satanic sons, Jesus now says:

> *He was a murderer from the beginning, and abode not in the truth, because there is no truth in him. When he speaketh a lie, he speaketh of his own: for he is a liar, and the father of it.*

Satan is real; he is personal; he is an entity, a personage, a spirit being. He is as personal and real as any of the spirit offspring of the Father—for such he is: "Lucifer, a son of the morning"; "Perdition," over whom "the heavens wept" (D&C 76:26); the devil, who rebelled and defied God and all the hosts of Michael; the old dragon, whose tail drew a third of the stars of heaven, in the day when there was war in heaven. He was a murderer from the beginning in that he sought to destroy light and truth and whispers to every evil Cain to choose and slay a righteous Abel. As the enemy of truth he is the friend of falsehood. He was a liar in preexistence and is so now. Any truths spoken by him or his servants are interlaced with lies in an effort to make his own "gospel" more palatable to the minds of men. He is the one who "stirreth up the children of men"—as in the case of these Jews—"unto secret combinations of murder and all manner of secret works of darkness." (2 Ne. 9:9.)

> *And because I tell you the truth, ye believe me not. Which of you convinceth me of sin? And if I say the truth, why do ye not believe me? He that is of God receiveth God's words; ye therefore receive them not, because ye are not of God.*

'I am without sin; my course of life is perfect. Since none of you can find any sin in me, it should be apparent that my life and teachings are in perfect harmony with the truth, and consequently what I tell you is true. Why then do ye not believe me? If ye had the truths of salvation so as to be the children of God, ye would accept the word of God which I now deliver unto you. But the very fact you do not accept my words shows you are not of God and do not have the true religion which is of God.'

Unable to answer him, and in a pitch of hatred and fury, the Jews ask—though it is more of a proclamation than a question—"Say we not well that thou art a Samaritan, and hast a devil? " How often they resort to the cry, 'Thou hast a devil,' to justify in their own minds their violent opposition. The demeaning slur that he is a Samaritan, however, is not an accusation that he came from Samaria or was one of that hated race. At this very feast they have attempted to belittle him as a Galilean, not a Samaritan. Edersheim tells us that the word meaning *Samaritan* "is almost as often used in the sense of heretic," and that it is "sometimes used as the equivalent of . . . the Prince of the demons." (Edersheim 2:174.) These evil men, steeped in iniquity and trained in priestcraft, are thus saying that he has a devil and is a heretic, or, worse, the very prince of demons himself. Our Lord's reply is simply to say:

> *I have not a devil; but I honour my Father, and ye do dishonour me. And I seek not mine own glory: there is one that seeketh and judgeth.*

'I am not possessed of a devil. If I were, my teachings and works would not honor and glorify my Father as they do. But ye dishonor me because I am of God and ye are not. I seek not mine own glory, as do those who are of the devil; but there is one, even God, who seeketh it for me, and he will judge those who dishonor me.'

'Before Abraham Was I Jehovah'

(*John 8:51-59*)

This period of preaching is rising toward its glorious climax. Soon, in a perfectly orchestrated crescendo of divine music, the Sinless One will acclaim his divine Sonship in words we have never before heard him use; his witness will be as when a bush burned and was not consumed, or when smoke and fire and quaking spread themselves over Sinai as the Lord Jehovah wrote the law on tablets of stone with his own finger. This time, however, the Man Jesus will write the witness in the broken hearts of believing disciples, while the stony hearts of the sons of Satan will maintain their granitic hardness. As the tempo and tone of the great orchestration takes on new power, Jesus says:

> *Verily, verily, I say unto you, If a man keep my saying, he shall never see death.*

Again he speaks of "my word," of "my saying," as well he might, for he is God; and the word comes from him even as it comes from his Father. "My word . . . is my law." (D&C 132:12.) Prophets speak of the word of the Lord; Jesus speaks of his own word and that of his Father. Those who keep his commandments shall never see death; they shall not die spiritually. It is the same doctrine he has taught before; it is a thoroughly Jewish way of speaking. According to their own traditions, the Messiah would come bringing salvation, having life in himself, ransoming and redeeming his people both temporally and spiritually. That is to say: "They knew he would come bringing those truths by which men are born again, enjoy spiritual life and avoid spiritual death. . . . These Jews knew that those who believed and obeyed the words of the true Messiah would never see spiritual death." (*Commentary* 1:463.)

Their disbelief on this occasion did not stem from any misunderstanding of his spoken word. Rather, it was an affirmative denial of his Messiahship. "Now we know that thou hast a devil," they said. Such is the only explanation that can justify their course in their own eyes. "Abraham is dead, and the prophets; and thou sayest, If a man keep my saying, he shall never taste of death. Art thou greater than our father Abraham, which is dead? and the prophets are dead: whom makest thou thyself? "

It may be they were baiting him. Would he make a plain Messianic claim for which he could be stoned? Was he on the verge of such a blasphemous claim to divinity—as they would interpret it—that a mob, in a panic-borne burst of zeal for their law, would strike him with death-inflicting stones? In their hearts they sought his death by whatever means might arise. His answer ignored the repeated charade of false pretense that insinuated demoniac possession. He said instead:

> *If I honour myself, my honour is nothing: it is my Father that honoureth me; of whom ye say, that he is your God: Yet ye have not known him; but I know him: and if I should say, I know him not, I should be a liar like unto you: but I know him, and keep his saying.*

'If I make myself the Messiah, my claim to divinity is of no validity; it is God my Father who honors me with divine Sonship. My honor comes from him who ye say is your God, but whom in truth ye have not known. Nevertheless, I know him for I am his Son, and if I should say that I know him not and am therefore not the Messiah, I would be a liar like unto you. But that I do know him and am the Messiah is shown by the fact that I keep his sayings perfectly, as only his Son could.' Then came the penultimate climax. After this there was but one blinding flash of eternal light, one thunderous roll of eternal truth, one supreme witness to bear. Its prelude came in these words:

Your father Abraham rejoiced to see my day: and he saw it, and was glad.

Abraham saw the day of Christ. Nearly two millennia before the Son of God made flesh his tabernacle, Abraham, the friend of God, the father of the faithful, saw in vision what would be in time's meridian. Abraham had the gospel. (Gal. 3:8.) Jehovah came personally to our great progenitor to tell him of the gospel, the priesthood, and eternal life. (Abr. 2:6-11.) To him the Almighty said: "The day cometh, that the Son of Man shall live." And he "looked forth and saw the days of the Son of Man, and was glad, and his soul found rest, and he believed in the Lord; and the Lord counted it unto him for righteousness." (JST, Gen. 15:11-12.)[3]

"Thou art not yet fifty years old," was the Jewish response, "and hast thou seen Abraham?" Either this question was a deliberate reversal and twisting of Jesus' statement—he had said Abraham saw his day, not that he had seen Abraham's day—or there is something left out of the account to which it is responsive. We may well suppose that the Jews did not want so much as to admit that Abraham saw the day of Jesus, lest it be concluded that this man was greater than their foremost patriarch. In any event, their assertion completed the foundation for the divine proclamation now to fall from Jesus' lips:

Verily, verily, I say unto you, Before Abraham was, I am.

Jesus-Jehovah has spoken, and so it is. "This is as blunt and pointed an affirmation of divinity as any person has or could make. 'Before Abraham was I Jehovah.' That is, 'I am God Almighty, the Great I AM. I am the self-existent,

Eternal One. I am the God of your fathers. My name is: I AM THAT I AM.'

"To Moses the Lord Jehovah had appeared, identified himself as the God of Abraham, Isaac, and Jacob, and said: 'I AM THAT I AM: . . . Thus shalt thou say unto the children of Israel, I AM hath sent me unto you. . . . This is my name for ever, and this is my memorial unto all generations.'

"Of a later manifestation, the King James Version has Deity say: 'I am the Lord: And I appeared unto Abraham, unto Isaac, and unto Jacob, by the name of God Almighty, but by my name JEHOVAH was I not known to them.' From latter-day revelation we know that one of our Lord's great pronouncements to Abraham was: 'I am the Lord thy God; . . . My name is Jehovah,' and accordingly we find the Inspired Version account reading: 'I appeared unto Abraham, unto Isaac, and unto Jacob. I am the Lord God Almighty; the Lord JEHOVAH. And was not my name known unto them?' " (*Commentary* 1:464.)

"Then took they up stones to cast at him," John says—for nothing could have been more blasphemous in their eyes than what they had just heard—"but Jesus hid himself, and went out of the temple, going through the midst of them, and so passed by."

He had preached his doctrine and borne his witness, and his crowning words were:

BEFORE ABRAHAM WAS I, JEHOVAH.

NOTES

1. It is unthinkable to me, as the weight of opinion assumes, that these Jews had any reference whatever to political freedom in their response to Jesus. They knew full well that their fathers had been slaves in Egypt for four hundred years; that ten of their tribes had been taken into Assyrian bondage and were lost to the knowledge of men; that their fathers had suffered a Babylonian exile, with only a remnant returning; and that even then a Roman yoke weighed heavily upon their bowed shoulders. In my mind the dialogue here involved is, in the mind of both Jesus and his opponents, one dealing with spiritual freedom, with the gospel freedom that leads to eternal life.

2. Some of the paraphrasing quotes involved in the dialogue here involved are also taken from this portion of my *Commentary*, vol. 1.

3. These words are not, of course, in the King James Version of the Bible. It is of con-

siderable interest and import, therefore, to note Edersheim's comment that "even Jewish tradition" asserted that "Abraham had, in vision, been shown not only this [that is, our Lord's day], but the coming world—and not only all events in the present 'age,' but also those in Messianic times." And further: "In the Targum Jerusalem on Gen. 15 also it seems implied that Abraham saw in vision all that would befall his children in the future, and also Gehenna and its torments." (Edersheim 2:176, including footnote 1.)

JESUS SPEAKS OF SPIRITUAL THINGS

I will hear what God the Lord will speak:
for he will speak peace unto his people,
and to his saints: . . .
Surely his salvation is nigh them that fear
him. (Ps. 85:8-9.)

The Seventies Report on Their Apostleship

(Luke 10:17-20; JST, Luke 10:19-20)

Shortly after the Feast of Tabernacles—at which all Israel worshipped for themselves; at which they offered sacrifices on behalf of the nations of heathendom; at which their rites symbolized the outpouring of the Holy Spirit upon the Gentiles—shortly after this great festal season, the seventies returned from their missions to report to that Lord whose witnesses they were. He had sent them—not as he soon would into all the world to declare his word to every creature, but to the cities and towns of Israel—to prepare the way for him, that receptive congregations might be assembled to hear the gospel, that attentive ears might be attuned to the Messianic voice.

All save one of the Twelve were Galileans. We suppose a like ratio was found among the Seventy. The Galilean chose his Galilean friends and kinsmen to echo his words of blessing and hope to Jew and Gentile alike. The Seventy were, like their brethren of the Twelve, rugged, forthright, and faithful souls who were scholastically untainted. The damning curse of scribal theology and the unbearable yoke of Rabbinic ritual weighed less heavily upon them than upon their Judean kinsmen. They had less of the doctrine of Hillel and fewer of the sayings of Shammai to forsake when they accepted the gospel than did the theologically contentious Judeans. Their present mission had commenced in the summer or autumn and now, three or four months later, they came together in a spirit of thanksgiving and rejoicing to report their labors. They had been successful. "Lord, even the devils are subject unto us through thy name," they said.

To cast out the spirit followers of Lucifer from their ill-gotten abodes, thus freeing suffering souls from physical maladies and spiritual suffering, could be accomplished only by the power of God. The Goliath of evil can only be slain by the David of righteousness. But Jesus had given them power—power to preach and heal and save. The gospel is power—the power of God by which salvation comes. The holy priesthood is power—the power and authority of God to act in all things for the salvation of men. The Holy Ghost comes with power—power to cleanse and perfect a human soul. Ministers without the power of the gospel, the power of the priesthood, the power of eternal truth, can never lead a soul to salvation. Satan is as naught only when he faces true ministers, and these seventies had subjected the evil one to their will through their Master's will. Rejoicing with them, Jesus said:

As lightning falleth from heaven, I beheld Satan also falling.

'When there was war in heaven, the rebel spirits were cast out. The same power that sent them as lightning from the realms of light to their benighted state on earth still controls them.' These seventies have ministered well, and they are now prepared for a greater ministry and a higher spiritual endowment.

> *Behold, I will give unto you power over serpents and scorpions, and over all the power of the enemy; and nothing shall by any means hurt you.*

How glorious is the Cause that makes every warrior a general, every soldier in the ranks a hero, every servant of the Lord the master of all things! What are the combined powers of earth and hell when arrayed against the servants of the Lord? "Nothing shall by any means hurt you." In the eternal sense there is nothing but glory and triumph for faithful ministers.

> *Notwithstanding in this rejoice not, that the spirits are subject unto you; but rather rejoice, because your names are written in heaven.*[1]

Christ Is the Father and the Son

(*Matthew 11:25-30; JST, Matthew 11:27-29; Luke 10:21-24; JST, Luke 10:22-23*)

Would that we knew all that the seventies said and could feel anew the fierce fervor and be warmed by the flaming faith that attended the testimonies they then bore. This must have been an occasion of spiritual refreshment comparable to that other day in Caesarea Philippi when the apostles themselves were bearing their testimonies. On this later occasion, as Matthew says, "there came a voice out of heaven," and as Luke says, in this hour "Jesus rejoiced in spirit." We cannot doubt that the words then spoken by the Father of us all placed a seal of divine approval upon the work and words of the seventies, which, naturally, would cause his Son, Jesus, to rejoice. Our Lord then said:

> *I thank thee, O Father, Lord of heaven and earth, that thou hast hid these things from them who think they are wise and prudent, and hast revealed them unto babes; even so, Father; for so it seemed good in thy sight.*

What things are hidden from the worldly wise but are revealed unto babes and sucklings, as it were? The truths just spoken by the Father; the testimonies just borne by the seventies; the revealed witness in the hearts of the faithful of the truth and divinity of the Lord's work; everything that pertains to God and godliness, to faith and faithfulness, to the Spirit and spirituality—all these things being of heavenly origin can only be understood by heavenly power. Among them are the great truths upon which Jesus now discourses. From Matthew's account we read:

> *All things are delivered unto me of my Father; and no man knoweth the Son, but the Father; neither knoweth any man the Father, save the Son, and they to whom the Son will reveal himself; they shall see the Father also.*

As with almost all of Jesus' recorded words, our Gospel authors are selecting for preservation the portions that they feel most completely summarize the great truths then presented. In this case, Luke's account preserves these blessed words:

> *All things are delivered to me of my Father; and no man knoweth that the Son is the Father, and the Father is the Son, but him to whom the Son will reveal it.*

It is evident that much more was said, but from these brief quotations from the transcripts of eternity, we receive a sunburst of truth seldom expressed in words so few. 'My Father, who is God, has placed all things in my hands because I am his Son and Heir, and I do ever those things which please him. And no man can know that I am the Son except by revelation from the Father; and no man can know my Father unless he comes unto me, for I am sent to bear record of the Father. And those who know by the power of the Holy Ghost that I am the Son of God, if they abide in me and keep my commandments, they shall see the Father also.

'And further, I, the Son, will reveal to the faithful that the Son is the Father, and the Father is the Son. We are one;

the Father is in me and I am in the Father. I am the manifestation of God in the flesh. God is in me revealing himself to the world, so much so that if you have seen me, you have seen the Father. The Father is as I am, for I am in his image and live and am as he is. I, the Son, am to you as the Father; and the Father, in whose image I am, is as the Son.'[2]

At this point, as Luke expresses it, "he turned him unto his disciples"—the seventies and others—"and said privately, Blessed are the eyes which see the things that ye see: For I tell you, that many prophets and kings have desired to see those things which ye see, and have not seen them; and to hear those things which ye hear, and have not heard them." And with this we concur completely, for we are among the number in question.

Thus, to his disciples he has spoken of the mysteries of the kingdom, telling them of his own divinity and how he is the incarnation of God so that it is as though he were the Father. In these disciples, already converted to the truth, he rejoices in spirit. But the message must not stop with them; what he has said to the seventies must go to all who will qualify to receive it. New disciples must be won; the kingdom is for all men. Downtrodden, burdened, suffering mankind; men staggering under the weight of their sins; children of a common Father, all with the potential of advancing and progressing and becoming like him—these may find rest in Christ. To them the cry goes forth:

Come unto me, all ye that labour and are heavy laden, and I will give you rest.

Those who then heard these words wore the yoke of Rabbinism. Around their necks and weighted upon their shoulders hung the yoke of the law, the yoke of the kingdom. This yoke—and it was so named by the Rabbis—was "one of laborious performances and of impossible self-righteousness. . . . Indeed, this voluntary making of the yoke as heavy as possible, the taking on themselves as many obligations as possible, was the ideal of Rabbinic piety."

(Edersheim 2:143-44.)[3] It is in this Rabbinic setting that we hear Jesus say:

> *Take my yoke upon you, and learn of me; for I am meek and lowly in heart: and ye shall find rest unto your souls. For my yoke is easy, and my burden is light.*

'Rid yourselves of the yoke of Rabbinism; cease from all your self-righteous washings and ordinances and performances; forsake the insane Sabbath restrictions which say ye cannot even heal the sick or care for the suffering on that day. Remove the yoke placed upon you by the scribes and Pharisees; they are the degenerate defenders of the dead days of old. Come unto me; learn of me; believe that I am the Messiah by whom salvation comes. I am meek and lowly in heart, not proud and pompous and austere as are those whom you now serve. Wear my yoke—the yoke of the gospel; compared to your religious restrictions my yoke is easy and my burden is light. In me ye shall find rest. No longer will ye be wafted about by every word of Rabbinic doctrine; no longer will you have to judge between Hillel and Shammai, or this Rabbinic school or that. I will give you rest.'

Parable of the Good Samaritan

(*Luke 10:25-37; JST, Luke 10:32-33, 36*)

Jesus now encounters one of those intellectual religionists who thrive on contention and delight in dissension. Found in every sect and cult, particularly in Jewish Israel, their self-appointed mission is to ask questions for question's sake. Their interests are primarily academic and theoretical, and they deal with hypothetical rather than real situations. They are the lawyers whose interest are in the dicta rather than the decision; the medical students who ask how to treat nonexistent diseases; the religionists who solve problems that may never arise in the lives of people. If they can ask questions that—to the embarrassment of their opponents—cannot be answered, so much the better.

Jesus must have been teaching something about eternal life, that glorious state of exaltation reserved for the faithful for whom the family unit continues in the realms ahead. As he did so, "a certain lawyer stood up, and tempted him," or, better, stood up to *test* him, to see how he as a Rabbi would answer one of the points of debate in the Rabbinical schools. The question: "Master, what shall I do to inherit eternal life?"

Jesus parried the question. He declined to stoop to the level of the debating Rabbis; let them revel in polemics—he would not do so. "What is written in the law? how readest thou?" he asked. 'It is your problem, not mine. You have the law before you; answer your own question.'

And the answer that was forthcoming from the learned lawyer was perfect; it was the very answer Jesus himself gave on at least two other occasions. Combining the statement in Deuteronomy 6:5, which is part of the *Shema* itself, with that in Leviticus 19:18—these two passages being the heart and core of the Mosaic law—the lawyer answered: "Thou shalt love the Lord thy God with all thy heart, and with all thy soul, and with all thy strength, and with all thy mind; and thy neighbour as thyself." Moses, who spoke for Jehovah, had phrased perfectly the two commandments by conformity to which eternal life is won, and the lawyer had quoted correctly that which he had read in the law.

But the question had been asked not to gain information, but rather, in the hope that Jesus might not give the proper answer—an answer already known to his interrogator and preserved for all to read in the law—and therefore that he would be embarrassed at his own lack of Rabbinical understanding. Do we not, then, detect a touch of irony in our Lord's response: "Thou hast answered right: this do, and thou shalt live." 'You knew the answer all along; if you would do the things you already know, you shall gain eternal life.'

Hoping to salvage such reputation as he could in a confrontation that had gone against him; desiring to justify his own hatred rather than love for many of his fellowmen; and knowing, by instinct or from some previous statement of Jesus, that our Lord and the other Rabbis differed widely as to who fell in the category of a neighbor, the lawyer asked: "And who is my neighbour? "

Had Jesus, this time, asked, "What says the law on this point? " he would have called forth all the old expressions of approved hatred toward all those of other nations. He himself had summarized the Mosaic standard by saying, "Ye have heard that it hath been said, Thou shalt love thy neighbour, and hate thine enemy," but 'I give unto you a higher standard.' To the Jews their neighbors were the members of the congregation of Israel; the Gentiles and all who opposed the Jewish people not only failed to qualify as neighbors, but were, in fact, enemies. "Whatever modern Judaism may say to the contrary, there is a foundation of truth to the ancient heathen charge against the Jews of *odium generis humani* (hatred of mankind)." (Edersheim 2:237.) And so Jesus himself gave the answer, his answer, the gospel answer, to the query "Who is my neighbour," and the divine definition shines forth in that wondrous parable of the good Samaritan.

> *A certain man went down from Jerusalem to Jericho, and fell among thieves, which stripped him of his raiment, and wounded him, and departed, leaving him half dead.*

A Jew, one of the elect, a member of the chosen people, traveling alone through the rocky gorges and rough terrain along the twenty-two-mile road from Jerusalem to Jericho, falls among Bedouin thieves. It is an evil area where men like Gadianton lurk. The thoroughfare itself was known as the Red Path or Bloody Way. On it our present victim is robbed, wounded, and left naked and half dead. The merciless thieves, perhaps frightened away by other itinerants, leave him to die while they hide nearby to await other victims.

And by chance, there came down a certain priest that way; and when he saw him, he passed by on the other side of the way.

By chance, or, rather, in the providences of the Almighty—for the seeming chances of life provide the testing experiences for men in this mortal probation—by chance a priest, a son of Aaron, one ordained to a holy calling, one whose divine appointment was to minister for the temporal well-being of his fellowmen, came, saw, recognized a Jewish brother, and chose to pass by. A priest, without compassion, left his brother, whom he could have saved, to die of wounds and thirst in a Bedouin desert.

And likewise a Levite, when he was at the place, came and looked upon him, and passed by on the other side of the way; for they desired in their hearts that it might not be known that they had seen him.

As with the priest, so with the Levite: both dishonored their priesthood; both brought disgrace upon their nation; both failed one of the great tests of mortality, choosing, rather, to say within themselves, "Am I my brother's keeper?" And they thought: "No man knows that I have seen this wounded and dying man, and who can condemn me?" And yet, there was a man who did know, and he is Judge of all.

But a certain Samaritan, as he journeyed, came where he was: and when he saw him, he had compassion on him, And went to him, and bound up his wounds, pouring in oil and wine, and set him on his own beast, and brought him to an inn, and took care of him.

A Samaritan, a hated Samaritan, a half-heathen and apostate worshipper of Jehovah, one through whose land the pilgrims from Galilee en route to Jerusalem would not even travel! A Samaritan, who could not be saved, and who some Rabbis said would not even be resurrected! A

Samaritan, who was an enemy and not a neighbor, chose to make this half-dead Jew his brother. Wine cleanses the wounds; oil salves the pain and removes the smart; bandages—perhaps torn from the benefactor's own clothing—protect the torn flesh; the ass of the one from the despised race carries the wounded Jew; and the owner of the beast walks. They go to the *khan* or hostelry by the road, where lodging is free but victuals for men and beasts can be had for a price. The Samaritan took care of the Jew, watched over him, and saved his life.

> *And on the morrow when he departed, he took out two pence, and gave them to the host, and said unto him, Take care of him; and whatsoever thou spendest more, when I come again, I will repay thee.*

Two pence, or, better, two dinars, the sum a laborer earned in two days—this, and an assurance of more if need be, was left with the host. "Which now of these three, thinkest thou, was neighbour unto him that fell among the thieves? " Jesus asked. The lawyer, even now not daring to commend a hated Samaritan by national designation, responded, "He that shewed mercy on him." Jesus said, "Go, and do thou likewise."

A Familial Scene

(*Luke 10:38-42*)

He who had not where to lay his head—not so much as the foxes who have holes and the birds of the air who have nests—yet during the whole of his mortality among us partook of the culture and sociality of many Jewish abiding places. A sliver of knowledge here, a ray of light there, an incidental comment somewhere else, all let us catch fleeting glimpses of the life he lived and the sociality that was his among those with whom he shared the intimacies incident to the days of his flesh.

We attuned our voices to those of the seraphic hosts in the heavenly choir when he made flesh his tabernacle in a roadside caravanserai in Bethlehem of Judea. We saw him draw his first mortal breath amid the tethered beasts of burden because there was no room in the inns for a woman big with child and whose travail was upon her. We watched as loving hands cared for his needs in the homes of Jewish friends and relatives in Bethlehem and Egypt and Nazareth. It was pleasant to see him learn to crawl and walk and speak in the Jewish home of Jewish Joseph there in the hill country of Galilee. There it was that he learned to pray, where he memorized the *Shema* and reverenced the *Mezuzah* attached to the doorpost as a symbol of Jehovah's protecting care over the homes of Israel.

We have seen his wants cared for in many homes by many people; have feasted with him at many banquets; have slept with him under the stars and in the little booths into which all Israel moved at Tabernacle Times. In the home of Peter in Capernaum of Galilee we saw him hold a child in his arms as he taught who was greatest in the kingdom of heaven. And in the guest chamber of the home of John, in Jerusalem, at the time of the First Passover, we listened attentively as he conversed with Nicodemus, a ruler of the Jews, one who sat on the Great Sanhedrin.

But at no other time and in no other place have we seen such a sweet and tender scene as now opens before us in the home of Martha in Bethany. Blessed Bethany, hidden from Jerusalem by a spur of the Mount of Olives, yet only two miles away, was the retreat to which Jesus so often went to rid himself of the influence and contentions of those who knew not God and who, because of priestcrafts, chose to reject his Son.

It seems clear that the two sisters, Martha and Mary, and their brother Lazarus, all dwelt in the house owned by Martha, who therefore must have been the oldest of the three. It seems apparent that they were well-to-do and had the means and facilities to care for their blessed guest. Because of the reverent curtain of silence drawn by the inspired authors over the family relationship and social intercourse of

Jesus and his friends, we know only that the three who dwelt in Bethany were loved by Jesus. It is of interest to note that the name *Martha* was truly Jewish and meant "lady" or "mistress," that *Mary* was the Greek equivalent of the ancient Hebrew "Miriam," and that *Lazarus* was the Greek form of "Eleazer." The inference is that the three children had been so named by parents who rejoiced in the present and looked forward to the future, including the coming of the Messiah, and the new kingdom, rather than looking back to the old glory of the old kingdom.

That Jesus came to Bethany for the express purpose of being with the sisters we cannot doubt; his disciples apparently had found lodging in other homes. Nor can we doubt there was an open, congenial, and friendly respect and association between them and our Lord. There must have been considerable prior association so that the parties knew each other well and were not restrained in their association by feelings of awe.

On this occasion Mary, whom Jesus loved, sat at his feet to hear his words. No doubt she asked questions and was fed spiritually as few of her sex have ever been. We feel to rank her, in spiritual stature, along with the other Marys—the Blessed Virgin who gave birth to God's Son, and the Mary called Magdalene, whom we have seen as one of the traveling missionary companions of Jesus, and whom we shall yet see as the first mortal to behold the Resurrected Person. Shall we not also rank her with Eve and Sarah and the widow of Zarephath, and the faithful ones of old who ministered to the prophets in their days?

Would that we knew what conversations passed between them, what questions Mary asked, what answers Jesus gave. Did they discuss the atonement through which all men are raised in immortality, while those who believe and obey ascend unto eternal life? Was eternal life defined as that state of glory and peace reserved for those who live everlastingly in the family unit? Were the glories of the celestial realm unfolded to the view of this true believer who had prepared herself by baptism and otherwise to receive the mysteries of the kingdom? Perhaps it is not amiss to say—and we so express ourselves reverently—that in that day when all things are revealed we shall learn of even these sacred and now secret hours in the life of the Divine Person and those whom he chose as his intimates.

Also on this occasion Martha, whom also Jesus loved, "was cumbered about much serving"; as the official hostess, so to speak, it was incumbent upon her to attend to the physical needs of her guest. Perhaps she was envious of the attention given her younger sister and wished herself to be seated at the feet of the Master and to hear those things which then fell from his lips. We cannot suppose she was one whit less spiritual than Mary; indeed, it will be Martha, a short while hence, on the occasion of the raising of their brother Lazarus from death, who will bear a witness of the divine Sonship that would do credit to a Peter, or a Moses, or an Abraham. Nor can we rank her a hair's breadth behind Mary in personal righteousness and in the desire to hear the words of eternal life here and now and be an inheritor of immortal glory hereafter. It just happens that on this occasion the burdens of hospitality had fallen primarily upon the older sister. It is not unnatural to think that Martha may have asked Mary for help that up to that moment had not been forthcoming.

In any event Martha says: "Lord, dost thou not care that my sister hath left me to serve alone? bid her therefore that she help me." Such a statement spoken to Jesus under these circumstances carries a wealth of meaning. It is as though Jesus had some obligation to see that Martha had help. It is not the plea of a person who is so awed by the presence of the Lord Jesus that she fears to speak up on a relatively trivial matter. It is not a statement in which a hostess is careful to avoid any seeming annoyance in the presence of a guest because of a family problem. Geikie even says her "complaint to Jesus" was "not free from irreverence," and that it was as though she had said, " 'Lord, do you not care that my sister has left me to do all the work alone? If *you* speak to her, she will help me.' " (Geikie, p. 601.)

Thereupon Jesus, as was his invarying wont, turned the circumstances at hand into a teaching situation. "Martha, Martha," he said in words of endearing tenderness, "thou art careful and troubled about many things: But one thing is needful: and Mary hath chosen that good part, which shall not be taken away from her."

"From Martha's housewifely complaint and Jesus' mild reproof, we learn the principle that, though temporal food is essential to life, once a reasonable amount has been acquired, then spiritual matters should take precedence. Bread is essential to life, but man is not to live by bread alone. Food, clothing, and shelter are essential to mortal existence, but once these have been gained in reasonable degree, there is only 'one thing' needful—and that is to partake of the spiritual food spread on the gospel table." (*Commentary* 1:473.)

That there is no mention on this occasion of Lazarus, whom also Jesus loved, neither adds to nor detracts from the domestic scene. He may well have been present, as an observer rather than a participant. We shall shortly meet Martha, and then Mary, and then Lazarus, under the most unusual circumstances ever to confront humankind in all the four millennia since mortality began.

NOTES

1. "Records are kept in heaven as well as on earth, and the faithful saints who have gained the promise of eternal life have their names recorded in the Lamb's Book of Life." (*Commentary* 1:465.)

2. This whole glorious concept of how Christ is both the Father and the Son is dealt with at length in *The Promised Messiah.* See particularly chapter 20.

3. In this connection, the Midrash says of Isaiah: "He had been privileged to prophesy of so many blessings, 'because he had taken upon himself the yoke of the Kingdom of Heaven with joy.' " (Edersheim 2:143.)

THE WONDROUS WORD POURS FORTH

Lo, I come: in the volume of the book
it is written of me, I delight to do thy will,
O my God: yea, thy law is within my heart.
I have preached righteousness. . . .
I have declared thy faithfulness and thy salvation:
I have not concealed thy lovingkindness
and thy truth from the great congregation.
(Ps. 40:7-10.)

Parable of the Friend at Midnight

(*Luke 11:1-13; JST, Luke 11:4-5, 14*)

The Galilean ministry has come to Judea; Jesus is now doing among the Judeans what he did in Galilee insofar as the people will receive it. The time period is from the Feast of Tabernacles (October 11-18, A.D. 29) through the Feast of Dedication (December 20-27, of the same year), and on into January of A.D. 30, a period of about three months.

His message is what it has always been—that he is the Messiah; that the gospel he brings from God, who is his Father, will save them; that he will work out the infinite and eternal atoning sacrifice and bring all men unto him on conditions of repentance. He speaks in plain words, by symbolic representations, and in parables. His deeds are now as they always have been: he heals the sick, speaks peace to sorrowing souls, and frees the penitent from the bondage of sin. The reaction to his words—it also is the same: a few believe, and the leaders and most of the Jews reject his sayings, claim he casts out devils by Beelzebub, and seek to slay him lest his new religion destroy their craft.

We have now seen his doings and heard his words at the Feast of Tabernacles; we have heard the report of the seventies and felt the impact of the deep and hidden things he then revealed to them. We heard the lawyer test his Rabbinic knowledge, and rejoiced in the spirit and meaning of the parable of the good Samaritan. Then for a few brief moments we sat with him in the home of the beloved sisters in Bethany.

Now we shall drink a few draughts of the living water that flow from the Eternal Fountain—and they are so few in comparison to the endless streams then sent forth to water men's arid hearts. We shall hear him repeat some things he has said before, climaxing it all with the grand pronouncement that he is the Good Shepherd and the stirring testimony: "*I am the Son of God.*" Then we shall go with him to Perea, as he testifies there before returning to Jerusalem for the week of his passion.

But first we encounter the situation that brought forth the parable of the friend at midnight. Jesus himself "was praying in a certain place." Prayers may be offered in all places and at all times, but we are dealing here with a particular prayer of the Divine Son to the Divine Father. Clearly it was a prayer in marked contrast to those customarily offered by the Jews in general. "When he ceased, one of his disciples said unto him, Lord, teach us to pray, as John also taught his disciples."

Not all prayers are the same; some are thoughtless chants filled with ritualistic mockery; others are the repetitious and meaningless cries of the heathen. Some consist of memorized phrases learned in youth or of scriptures learned in days past; others—albeit they are few in number—are the heart-stirring pleas of the righteous, poured forth with all the energy and power and faith that their whole souls can possess. John had led his followers away from the ostentatious and mechanical recitations of Rabbinic delight; would Jesus now teach the true order of prayer as found in the new religion that he was restoring? He had done so in Galilee; it was part of the Sermon on the Mount. Now he will do so in Judea for other ears to hear. For that matter, we suppose that he gave over again, perhaps then, perhaps frequently, the whole Sermon on the Mount. Gospel truths are not forever restricted to those who happen to be present when a legal administrator first utters the eternal words. And so now, as a sample and a pattern—with no intent to specify the exact words to be repetitiously chanted, with a religious mien, as some suppose—Jesus said:

> *Our Father which art in heaven, Hallowed be thy name. Thy kingdom come. Thy will be done, as in heaven, so in earth. Give us day by day our daily bread. And forgive us our sins; for we also forgive every one who is indebted to us. And let us not be led unto temptation; but deliver us from evil; for thine is the kingdom and power. Amen.*

These are not—probably advisedly so—the exact words used previously in Galilee, nor should they be. The Lord's Prayer for the Galileans need not be the Lord's Prayer for the Judeans or Pereans or anyone else. And the Lord's Prayer in Judea on one day may not be what it would be on any other. Prayers are to fit the needs of the moment; the models and patterns proffered by Jesus simply channel the thoughts and desires of mortal suppliants in the proper course. There is, however, a universal principle that Jesus then enunciated: "Your heavenly Father will not fail to give unto you whatsoever ye ask of him." Following this came the parable.

> *Which of you shall have a friend, and shall go unto him at midnight, and say unto him, Friend, lend me*

three loaves; For a friend of mind in his journey is come to me, and I have nothing to set before him?

This is a realistic setting. Eastern hospitality required that the host provide food and shelter. Having no bread in his own house, the host naturally turns, notwithstanding the hour, to his neighbor and friend.

And he from within shall answer and say, Trouble me not: the door is now shut, and my children are with me in bed; I cannot rise and give thee.

I say unto you, Though he will not rise and give him, because he is his friend, yet because of his importunity he will rise and give him as many as he needeth.

We need not seek for elaborate explanations nor varying applications. The meaning is clear. If a churlish, selfish man—annoyed and resentful because of a seemingly inopportune petition—will yet discommode himself and come to the aid of a friend, how much more will a gracious Father, who seeks to bless his children, grant petitions offered to him in faith. If there are special difficulties and great obstacles standing in the way, seemingly to prevent an answer to our prayers, yet our heavenly Friend will give heed to our petitions when they ascend to him in faith and righteousness.

And I say unto you, Ask, and it shall be given you; seek, and ye shall find; knock, and it shall be opened unto you. For every one that asketh receiveth; and he that seeketh findeth; and to him that knocketh it shall be opened.

To ask is one thing; to seek is a greater thing; and to knock at the very doors of heaven assures that those holy portals will be opened and that the desired blessings will be forthcoming. Those who take no thought save it be to ask are denied the blessing. "Let him ask of God, . . . But let him ask in faith" is the divine decree. (James 1:5-6; D&C 9:7-9.) Nothing is withheld from those who seek the Lord with all their heart. Those whose search falls short of the utmost bounds to which it should extend shall not find the desired treasure.

If a son shall ask bread of any of you that is a father, will he give him a stone? or if he ask a fish, will he for a fish give him a serpent? Or if he shall ask an egg, will he offer him a scorpion?

If ye then, being evil, know how to give good gifts unto your children, how much more shall your heavenly Father give good gifts, through the Holy Spirit, to them who ask him.

He Ministers in Judea as in Galilee

(*Luke 11:14-54; JST, Luke 11:15, 18-19, 23, 25-27, 29, 32-33, 37; Luke 12:13-21; JST, Luke 12:23*)

Jesus now continues to do in Judea what he did before in Galilee, and, predictably, is faced with the same reactions, to which he gives the same responses. He casts out a devil from one who is dumb, who then speaks, and the old familiar charge is hurled: "He casteth out devils through Beelzebub the chief of devils." His detractors also demand a sign from heaven, as those with a kindred evil spirit had done in the land to the north. There then follows the same discussion about a kingdom divided against itself; of Satan casting out Satan; of how their children can cast out devils; and of an evil generation of sign seekers who shall receive only the sign of the prophet Jonas. All this we have discussed in its Galilean setting in chapter 48 (Book 2).

Here also in Judea, Jesus is invited to eat in the home of a Pharisee, who marvels when our Lord refrains from the ritualistic washings imposed with such rigor upon the people. These burdensome washings we have considered at some length in their Galilean setting in chapter 59 (Book 2). Using the absurdities of these traditions of the elders as a basis, Jesus launches forth in a severe and merciless castigation of the Pharisees, scribes, and lawyers for their hypocrisy and evil deeds. He will repeat all this again on Tuesday, April 4, A.D. 30, the third day of the week of his atoning sacrifice, at which time we shall consider it in extenso.

It was also at this time that Jesus set forth the great and

wondrous concepts recorded in Luke 12. Those dealing with blasphemy and the unpardonable sin are considered in chapter 48 (Book 2); those pertaining to the preaching of the gospel boldly and in plainness, to the persecution and trials of the saints, and to the divisions among men that are created by the spread of the gospel are set forth in chapter 54 (Book 2). We shall hereafter come to grips with the portion of this chapter dealing with the second coming of the Son of Man, when Jesus delivers his great sermon on the Mount of Olivet on the third day of the week of the atoning sacrifice. We shall now, however, consider Luke's account of the parable of the rich fool.

Parable of the Rich Fool

(*Luke 12:13-21; JST, Luke 12:23*)

Jesus is speaking; words of wisdom are flowing forth from the Son of God; he who speaks as none other before or since is telling "an innumerable multitude of people," as Luke describes them, the very truths that will prepare the penitent for the riches of eternity. "Behold, he that hath eternal life is rich." (D&C 6:7.) He is speaking of spiritual things and telling the disciples that the Holy Ghost will guide them in the very hour in meting that measure of gospel truth which should go to every man

At this point he is interrupted. There is one present whose thoughts are not on the riches of eternity that it is Jesus' good pleasure to give his disciples, but on the things of this world. The preached words are finding no lodgment in his soul; he is concerned about some petty baubles of mortal pelf that shall fade away with the setting sun. Who but a fool interrupts the Son of God—and shortly Jesus will so designate him. "Master," he says, "speak to my brother, that he divide the inheritance with me."

Perhaps he reasoned that the majesty and persuasiveness of this man, this Rabbi of such excelling wisdom, would force his brother to give him an equal share of their inherited wealth. Under Jewish law the eldest son always inherited a double portion. Clearly, this man sought to use Jesus for worldly gain, even as some in all ages seek to use the Church and the gospel to further their financial interests.

"Man, who made me a judge or a divider over you?" Jesus responds. He will neither intervene in nor override their earthly judicial system. No more did he when they brought before him the woman taken in adultery and demanded of him whether she should be put to death, nor when the tax collectors demanded of Peter why his Master, the Messiah, had not paid the temple assessment due for Messiah's house.[1] But Jesus will and does take occasion to teach the people the perils of selfishness and trusting in uncertain riches.

Take heed, and beware of covetousness: for a man's life consisteth not in the abundance of the things which he possesseth.

"How often, in one dramatic way after another, do we find Him who had not where to lay his head, teaching that worldly wealth is of little eternal worth; that men should lay up for themselves treasures, not on earth, but in heaven; that they should seek first the kingdom of God and let the things of this world take a position of secondary importance; that one thing above all others is needful—to love and serve God and the Son whom he hath sent!

"In this conversation with a covetous, worldly-minded man, and in the resultant parable of the rich fool which grew out of it, our Lord teaches that those whose hearts are set on the things of this world shall lose their souls. The parable itself condemns worldly-mindedness, reminds men that death and judgment are inevitable, and teaches that they should seek eternal riches rather than those things which moth and rust corrupt and which thieves break through and steal." (*Commentary* 1:474.) This, then, is the parable:

The ground of a certain rich man brought forth plen-

tifully: And he thought within himself, saying, What shall I do, because I have no room where to bestow my fruits?

There is no hint of ill-gotten gain here. A gracious Father has given the rich man the means of acquiring great wealth, and through his industry he has done so. But he supposes he has no place to bestow the fruits of his labors. What? Are there no hungry mouths to feed, no naked bodies to clothe, no derelict souls who long for a roof over their heads? Are not the poor always with us? Are there none to whom a crust of bread and a sip of wine would make the difference between life and death? And for what purpose does the Lord bestow the bounties of earth except to care for the just needs and wants of all his children? Truly the law of riches is summed up in these prophetic words: "Think of your brethren like unto yourselves, and be familiar with all and free with your substance, that they may be rich like unto you. But before ye seek for riches, seek ye for the kingdom of God. And after ye have obtained a hope in Christ ye shall obtain riches, if ye seek them; and ye will seek them for the intent to do good—to clothe the naked, and to feed the hungry, and to liberate the captive, and administer relief to the sick and the afflicted." (Jacob 2:17-19.) But back to the parable and the feelings of the rich man:

And he said, This will I do: I will pull down my barns, and build greater; and there will I bestow all my fruits and my goods. And I will say to my soul, Soul, thou hast much goods laid up for many years; take thine ease, eat, drink, and be merry.

'*My* barns, *my* fruits, *my* goods, and *my* soul—I, a rich man, revel in the delicacies and power which *my* riches bring. I will rejoice in worldliness and ease; I will make "provision for the flesh, to fulfil the lusts thereof."' (Rom. 13:14.)

But God said unto him, Thou fool, this night thy soul shall be required of thee: then whose shall those things be, which thou hast provided? So is he that layeth up treasure for himself, and is not rich toward God.

Truly, the prosperity of fools shall destroy them! O that all men might be rich toward God—"Rich in the currency negotiable in the courts above; rich in eternal things; rich in the knowledge of the truth, in the possession of intelligence, in obedience to gospel law, in the possession of the characteristics and attributes of Deity, in all of the things which will continue to be enjoyed in eternity." (*Commentary* 1:474.)

"And then our Lord expanded the thought. He told them that the life was more than food, and the body than raiment. Again He reminded them how God clothes, in more than Solomon's glory, the untoiling lilies, and feeds the careless ravens that neither sow nor reap. Food and raiment, and the multitude of possessions, were not life: *they* had better things to seek after and to look for; let them not be tossed on this troubled sea of faithless care; be theirs the life of fearless hope, of freest charity, the life of the girded loin and the burning lamp—as servants watching and waiting for the unknown moment of their lord's return." (Farrar, p. 362.)

Parable of the Barren Fig Tree
(*Luke 13:1-9; JST, Luke 13:1, 6, 9*)

Jesus has just spoken of the signs of the times and of the desolations and sorrows that are ahead. These matters, as before noted, will be considered later in connection with other parallel pronouncements relative to the perils and destructions that shall come upon the Jewish nation because of their rebellion and rejection of their Redeemer. They are mentioned here only to show the setting in which the parable of the barren fig tree was given.

As though to illustrate the punishments they supposed were sent of God upon sinners, some of those then present told Jesus "of the Galileans, whose blood Pilate had mingled with their sacrifices." Overlooking the temple grounds was the fortress of Antonia, from which Roman soldiers had ready access to the sacred grounds. Apparently they had been called upon to quell some nationalistic uprising or other disturbance, slaying the Galileans involved as they offered sacrifices on the great altar.

A not-uncommon Jewish belief was that special punishments were meted out for special sins. It may be that in telling Jesus of this bloody turmoil in the temple itself, these Jews were saying: "Yes, signs of the times and of the coming storm! These Galileans of yours, your own countrymen, involved in a kind of Psuedo-Messianic movement, a kind of 'signs of the times' rising, something like that towards which you want us to look—was not their death a condign punishment?" (Edersheim 2:222.)

To such a charge Jesus had no intention of acceding. "Suppose ye that these Galileans were sinners above all the Galileans, because they suffered such things?" he asked. "I tell you, Nay: but, except ye repent, ye shall all likewise perish." Then our Lord chose a like illustration of his own. "Or those eighteen, upon whom the tower of Siloam fell, and slew them," he asks, "think ye that they were sinners above all men that dwelt in Jerusalem?" His answer: "I tell you, Nay: but, except ye repent, ye shall all likewise perish."

Jesus' illustration was even more persuasive than that concerning the Galileans. Pilate had taken the sacred temple monies—the *Qorban*—and used them to build an aqueduct into Jerusalem. As a result there was a terrible uprising, vengefully quelled with Roman steel. Surely if a tower at the Siloam pool fell and killed eighteen persons engaged in this hated Gentile building project, this was just retribution. But Jesus says, 'Not so. Their sins were as the sins of all Jerusalem, and all of you will perish spiritually as they perished temporally, except ye believe in me, repent of your sins, and work the works of righteousness.'

"True it is, as a general principle, that God sends disasters, calamities, plagues, and suffering upon the rebellious, and that he preserves and protects those who love and serve him. Such indeed were the very promises given to

Israel—obedience would net them the preserving and protecting care of the Lord, disobedience would bring death, destruction, desolation, disaster, war, and a host of evils upon them.

"But to say that particular individuals slain in war, killed in accidents, smitten with disease, stricken with plagues, or shorn of their property by natural calamities, have been singled out from among their fellows as especially deserving of such supposed retribution is wholly unwarranted. It is not man's prerogative to conclude in individual cases of suffering or accident that such has befallen a person as a just retribution for an ungodly course." (*Commentary* 1:475.)

These principles Jesus now illustrates with the parable of the barren fig tree. With reference to the choice of the fig tree as his illustration, we should be aware of the following: "Fig-trees, as well as palm and olive trees, were regarded as so valuable, that to cut them down if they yielded even a small measure of fruit, was popularly deemed to deserve death at the Hand of God. . . . The fig-tree was regarded as the most fruitful of all trees." However, "as trees were regarded as by their roots undermining and deteriorating the land, a barren tree would be of threefold disadvantage: it would yield no fruit; it would fill valuable space, which a fruit-bearer might occupy; and it would needlessly deteriorate the land. Accordingly, while it was forbidden to destroy fruit-bearing trees, it would, on the grounds above stated, be duty to cut down a 'barren' or 'empty' tree." (Edersheim 2:246-47.) And so now to the parable itself:

A certain man had a fig tree planted in his vineyard; and he came and sought fruit thereon, and found none. Then said he unto the dresser of his vineyard, Behold, these three years I come seeking fruit on this fig tree, and find none: cut it down; why cumbereth it the ground?

And he answering said unto him, Lord, let it alone this year also, till I shall dig about it and dung it: And if it bear fruit, the tree is saved, and if not, after that thou shalt cut it down. And many other parables spake he unto the people.

"A certain husbandman (God) had a fig tree (the Jewish remnant of Israel) planted in his vineyard (the world); and he came (in the meridian of time) and sought fruit thereon (faith, righteousness, good works, gifts of the Spirit), and found none. Then said he unto the dresser of his vineyard, (the Son of God), Behold, these three years (the period of Jesus' ministry) I come seeking fruit on this fig tree, and find none: cut it down (destroy the Jewish nation as an organized kingdom); why cumbereth it the ground (why should it prevent the conversion of the world by occupying the ground and preempting the time of my servants)? And he (the Son of God) answering said unto him (God, the husbandman), Lord, let it alone this year also till I shall dig about it, and dung it (preach the gospel, raise the warning voice, show forth signs and wonders, organize the Church, and offer every opportunity for the conversion of the Jewish nation). And if it bear fruit, the tree is saved (the Jewish nation shall be preserved as such and its members gain salvation), and if not, after that thou shalt cut it down (destroy the Jews as a nation, make them a hiss and a byword, and scatter them among all nations)." (*Commentary* 1:477.)[2]

NOTES

1. "Christ had not only no legal authority for interfering, but the Jewish law of inheritance was so clearly defined, and, we may add, so just, that if this person had any just or good cause, there could have been no need for appealing to Jesus. Hence it must have been 'covetousness,' in the strictest sense, which prompted it—perhaps, a wish to have, besides his own share as a younger brother, half of that additional portion which, by law, came to the eldest son of the family." (Edersheim 2:243.)

2. "God called Israel as a nation, and planted it in the most favored spot: as a fig-tree in the vineyard of His own Kingdom. 'And he came seeking,' as He had every right to do, 'fruit thereon, and found none.' It was the third year that He had vainly looked for fruit, when He turned to His Vinedresser—the Messiah, to Whom the vineyard is committed as its King—with this direction: 'Cut it down—why doth it also deteriorate the soil?' It is barren, though in the best position; as a fig-tree it ought to bear figs, and here the best; it fills the place which a good tree might occupy; and besides, it deteriorates the soil. And its three years' barrenness has established its utterly hopeless character. Then it is that the Divine Vinedresser, in His infinite compassion, pleads, and with far deeper reality than either Abraham or Moses could have entreated, for the fig-tree which Himself had planted

and tended, that it should be spared 'this year also,' 'until then that I shall dig about it, and dung it'—till He labour otherwise than before, even by His Own Presence and Words, nay, by laying to its roots His most precious Blood. 'And if then it bear fruit'—here the text abruptly breaks off, as implying that in such case it would, of course, be allowed to remain; 'but if not, *then* against the future (coming) *year* shalt thou cut it down.'" (Edersheim 2:247-48.)

THE MAN BORN BLIND

The Lord openeth the eyes
of the blind. (Ps. 146:8.)

The Miracle—One Born Blind Is Healed

(*John 9:1-12; JST, John 9:4*)

It is the joyous Sabbath—a day of rest, a day of peace, a day of worship. It is also the burdensome Sabbath—a day on which Rabbinism goes wild in enforcing petty, Satan-inspired restrictions that defy all sense and reason, restrictions that serve no purpose except to stand as a witness of the dire apostasy then prevailing among a once-chosen and a once-enlightened people.

Jesus and his disciples pass by one of the gates of the temple, as we suppose. It is a place where beggars ask alms, perhaps the same sacred site where a man lame from his mother's womb will one day entreat Peter and John for a few pence and receive instead full strength in his feet and ankles. But on this autumn day, a beggar is present who has been blind from birth. He cannot ask alms, for it is the Sabbath, though it would be legal for kindly disposed persons to make voluntary contributions to his welfare. The man and his state are well known to the disciples and, as we shall see, to great hosts of Jerusalemites. No doubt he is sitting in the place where he commonly plied his unhappy trade.

"Master, who did sin, this man, or his parents, that he was born blind?" the disciples ask. This question, propounded by spiritually enlightened disciples—men who, like Peter, James, and John, had seen within the veil and heard the voice of God—presupposes two verities: (1) that the sins of the fathers may be visited upon the children in the form of physical impairment, and (2) that mortal souls are capable of committing sin before they ever breathe the breath of life. Both of these concepts are true.

As we have seen—with reference to the slaughter of the Galileans, whose blood Pilate mingled with their sacrifices, and with reference to the eighteen upon whom the tower of Siloam fell—the Jews believed that calamities and accidents came as punishment for sin. Jesus denounced this heresy; those so slain, though sinners, were not unlike all of their fellows; their misfortunes were not the result of any evil in their lives that was greater than that of their neighbors.

On the other hand, God sent calamities and plagues upon Israel, as a people and as a nation, because they forsook him and kept not his commandments. And there may be specific parental sins that impose penalties upon children; immoral parents may contract a venereal disease that causes blindness in unborn children. And personal sins may bring physical punishment to individuals, as when illness is caused by disobedience to the Lord's law of health.

The question asked is not one that can be answered by glib generalities. Birth deformities may or may not result from parental disobedience, but we have no reason to believe that children are so afflicted because of acts done in the premortal life. All children are born free from the taint of sin because of the great plan of redemption ordained for them by a gracious God. And yet, again on the other hand, children, though starting life in innocence, are born in one race or another, at one time or another, with one talent or another—all as a direct result of the life lived before mortal birth. The question asked by the disciples is, in fact, a good one that presupposes a knowledge of the plan of salvation.

They are asking about *this case,* to gain a better understanding of how the eternal laws operate in all cases.

Jesus answers: "Neither hath this man sinned, nor his parents: but that the works of God should be made manifest in him." 'This is a special case, set apart from all others. This man has never seen; no ray of light has ever entered his eyes; he has seen no sunrise or sunset, no birds of the air, no lilies of the field. He is born thus for a purpose—so that I may heal him and he may stand forever as a witness that I am the Son of God. Through him the works of God shall be manifest forever to all those to whom my gospel comes.'

> *I must work the works of him that sent me, while I am with you; the time cometh when I shall have finished my work, then I go unto the Father. As long as I am in the world, I am the light of the world.*

'Let there be no misunderstanding with reference to what I shall now do. My Father sent me to do this work, and do it I shall as long as I am with you. When I have finished my work—all my work, this act of healing, my preaching, and finally my atoning sacrifice—then I shall return to the Father. And know this: I am the light of the world. Whenever, from this time forth, you remember that I opened these blind eyes, physically, remember also that I came to bring light to eyes, spiritually.'

Now comes the miracle. Jesus himself has set the stage; he has told the people *what* he is going to do and *why.* It but remains for them to see *how* it is done, and in this instance the how is of surpassing import. Their Messiah stoops down; he spits on the ground, he makes clay with the spittle; and he anoints the eyes of the blind man with the saliva-filled lump of the dust of the earth. Sick persons are healed by faith through the laying on of hands, not by rubbing them with daubs of spittle-made mud. Why, then, does Jesus so act? There can be little doubt that he is deliberately violating the law of the Sabbath in two major respects: (1) he made clay, and (2) he applied a healing remedy to an impaired person, which of itself was forbidden, and in addition there was a specific prohibition against the application of saliva to the eyes on the Sabbath. This strange restriction came into being because of a common belief that saliva was a remedy for diseases of the eye.

Thus Jesus is putting the people in the position of choosing between him as one sent of God to do the work of the Father, as one who can open blind eyes, and the traditions of the elders about Sabbath observance. They must make their choice at the peril of their salvation. Once again it will be a day in Israel when the trumpet sounds: "Choose ye this day whom ye will serve."

So far, be it noted, Jesus has said nothing to the man. He has made no effort to plant even the seeds of faith in the man's heart; the blind one does not even know who Jesus is, or that he is believed by some to be the Messiah. This miracle is being done at Jesus' initiative, by his own power, for his own purposes. He now says, "Go, wash in the pool of Siloam"—just that and nothing more. John here inserts the comment that Siloam means *sent*, thus signifying, as we suppose, that as the Father sent the Son, so the Son sent the man—all to the end that what was done might be for the glory of God. In any event, the man went, washed as directed, gained sight, and returned seeing. The miracle has been wrought.

The blind eyes that now see create a sensation everywhere; word of the event is on every tongue; neighbors, friends, kinsmen, those who merely knew him by sight—all marvel at what has happened. "Is not this he that sat and begged?" they ask. Some say, "This is he"; others, "He is like him." But he says, "I am he." "How then were thine eyes opened?" they demand. Having now learned Jesus' name, he responds: "A man that is called Jesus made clay, and anointed mine eyes, and said unto me, Go to the pool of Siloam, and wash: and I went and washed, and I received sight." Such a beautiful and straightforward account, glorious in its simplicity! "Where is he?" they ask, and he says, "I know not."

The Testing of the Miracle—Pharisaic Contention

(*John 9:13-29; JST, John 9:13, 27*)

It is the Sabbath. There are both believers and skeptics among those who know of the miracle. Some who are rigid formalists—zealous for the strict observance of the day—take him that was blind to the Pharisees in council and report: 'Jesus made clay and opened this man's eyes on the Sabbath.'

"The Rabbis had forbidden any man to smear even one of his eyes with spittle on the Sabbath, except in cases of mortal danger. Jesus had not only smeared *both* the man's eyes, but had actually mingled the saliva with clay! This, an act of mercy, was in the deepest and most inward accordance with the very causes for which the Sabbath had been ordained, and the very lessons of which it was meant to be a perpetual witness. But the spirit of narrow literalism and slavish minuteness and quantitative obedience—the spirit that hoped to be saved by the algebraical sum of good and bad actions—had long degraded the Sabbath from the true idea of its institution into a pernicious superstition. The Sabbath of Rabbinism, with all its petty servility, was in no respect the Sabbath of God's loving and holy law. It had degenerated into that which St. Paul calls it, a 'beggarly element.' And these Jews were so imbued with this utter littleness, that a unique miracle of mercy awoke in them less of astonishment and gratitude than the horror kindled by a neglect of their Sabbatical superstition." (Farrar, p. 439. Gal. 4:9.)

Those in the Pharisaic council inquired how the man had received sight. He told his story again. "He put clay upon mine eyes, and I washed, and do see." Clearly, this miracle was either of God or of Satan. Some among the Pharisees said of Jesus: "This man is not of God, because he keepeth not the sabbath day." Others replied: "How can a man that is a sinner do such miracles? " Faced with this division in their own ranks, the inquisitors asked further of the healed man: "What sayest thou of him, that he hath opened thine eyes?" The answer came in majestic simplicity: "He is a prophet."[1]

There was yet one ray of Pharisaic hope that might explain all this away. Perhaps the man had not been blind at all. 'How could blind eyes be opened?' they argued. With this in mind they called the parents and questioned them. "Is this your son, who ye say was born blind? how then doth he now see?" they asked.

To us the obvious answer should have been: 'He is our son. He was born blind. The man Jesus anointed his eyes with clay made of his own spittle; our son, at his direction, washed in the pool of Siloam, and now his eyes are open.' All this the parents knew to be true; and next to the healed one himself, who should have rejoiced more in the miracle than his parents? But in the Jewish setting, and because they were faced with the social and religious pressures of Rabbinism, their answer was lacking in full integrity of expression and failed to manifest the same moral courage found in the words of their son. "We know that this is our son, and that he was born blind," they said, for this none could deny; "But by what means he now seeth, we know not; or who hath opened his eyes, we know not: he is of age; ask him: he shall speak for himself."

A great miracle has been wrought; a man who was blind from birth now sees; it should be a time to rejoice and thank God for his goodness and grace. But the issue is not that a blind man sees; he is but a pawn, an infinitesimal nothing, in a great warfare that is raging in the souls of rebellious Israel. The issue is that the miracle was wrought by Jesus, by a sinner who breaks the Sabbath, by one who casts out devils by Beelzebub, by one who opens blind eyes by Satan's power; yes, by one who is Satan Incarnate. Thus John, in explaining the parental response, says: "These words spake his parents, because they feared the Jews: for the Jews had agreed already, that if any man did confess that he was Christ, he should be put out of the synagogue. Therefore said his parents, He is of age; ask him."

Lucifer, our common enemy, using as his agents those on earth who heed the whisperings of his voice, is here exerting on these parents, and upon all who do or may believe that Jesus is the Christ, such pressure as we can scarcely envision. They are to be "put out of the synagogue." Had the Judaic-Mosaic worshippers, who chose to reject their Messiah, simply excommunicated all who did believe in him, we would have little fault to find with their decision. Certainly a religious society is entitled to drop from membership those who depart from its beliefs and standards.

Excommunication among them, however, came successively and by degrees, until it built up to a terrible climax of hate and vengeance. Certain temporary restrictions might be imposed to begin with; these might be increased in extent and intensity; finally, the penalties included curses and anathemas, unbearable social and economic pressures, and all of the fears and torments of an eternal hell. One of the incomplete excommunications, when thrust upon a prominent person, included these restrictions: "Henceforth he would sit on the ground, and bear himself like one in deep mourning. He would allow his beard and hair to grow wild and shaggy; he would not bathe, nor anoint himself; he would not be admitted into an assembly of ten men, neither to public prayer, nor to the Academy; though he might either teach, or be taught, by single individuals. Nay, as if he were a leper, people would keep at a distance of four cubits from him. If he died, stones were cast on his coffin, nor was he allowed the honor of the ordinary funeral, nor were they to mourn for him."

This was only the beginning of what might be. "Still more terrible was the final excommunication, or *Cherem* [by which is meant being put out of the synagogue], when a ban of indefinite duration was laid on a man. Henceforth he was like one dead. He was not allowed to study with others, no intercourse was to be held with him, he was not even to be shown the road. He might, indeed, buy the necessaries of life, but it was forbidden to eat or drink with such an one."

There were twenty-four grounds for imposing this final type of excommunication, including resisting "the authority of the Scribes, or any of their decrees," and leading others "either away from 'the commandments,' or to what was regarded as profanation of the Divine Name." (Edersheim 2:184.) Those who confessed that Jesus was the Messiah would, of course, be guilty of these violations.

To be put out of the synagogue was more than excommunication; it was persecution, which led Jesus to say to the disciples: "They shall put you out of the synagogues: yea, the time cometh, that whosoever killeth you will think that he doeth God service." (John 16:2.) The dreadful burden of such a penalty was more than these parents—already so poor that their son begged for a living—dared to assume.

An evil spirit of bitterness and contention now blazes forth anew. Having failed utterly in their assault upon the parents; being unable to deny or explain the miracle; feeling a sense of sheer and utter perplexity—the Pharisaic council again calls in the man that once was blind. They will try another approach. "Give God the praise: we know that this man is a sinner," they say. In effect they are asking the man to recant. 'We now admit you have been healed; your parents make that clear; but give God the credit. Confess that Jesus had nothing to do with it; he is a sinner—one who has desecrated the Sabbath by molding a ball of clay and by rubbing saliva on your eyes—and, therefore, he could not perform a miracle.' They were asking the man to side completely with them, to deny Christ and to glorify—even deify—traditionalism. They sought the condemnation of Christ and the apotheosis of Rabbinism.

But our once blind friend is fearless. He may not know all the intricacies and nuances of Rabbinic reasoning; he may not know whether it is a sin to rub a glob of mud together on your fingers on the Sabbath or not; but one thing he does know: whereas once he was blind, now he sees. His response is his testimony: "Whether he be a sinner or no, I know not: one thing I know, that, whereas I was blind, now I see."

Shamed and discomfited, the Pharisees make one more attack. Perhaps a renewed recitation of the details will reveal some undotted "I" or an uncrossed "T" that they can twist into proof the miracle was wrought by demoniac power. If their questions cease now, it is an admission of defeat at the hands of an unlearned beggar. "What did he to thee? how opened he thine eyes?" they demand. Their star witness is wearied with the repeated wanderings over the same course. He has told his story; it stands; there is nothing to add. "I have told you already, and ye did not believe," he says. Then in a master stroke, filled with inspired irony, the man asks: "Wherefore would ye hear it again? will ye also be his disciples?" 'Why are you asking me again? Is it because I have converted you? Do you now believe? Are you ready to become his disciples?'

Reviling and bitterness pour forth in the Pharisaic response: "Thou art his disciple," they say, "but we are Moses' disciples. We know that God spake unto Moses: as for this fellow, we know not from whence he is." And with these words they rejected their King, cast their lot with Lucifer, and sealed their own doom.

The Purpose of the Miracle: Jesus Acclaims His Divinity

(*John 9:30-41; JST, John 9:32*)

The Pharisaic witness has been given: 'This fellow, this Nazarene of Galilee, this friend of publicans and sinners, we do not know whether he is of God or not.'

Now comes the true witness, contained in words of irrefutable logic, spoken—we cannot doubt—by the power of the Spirit. The man says: "Why herein is a marvellous thing, that ye know not from whence he is, and yet he hath opened mine eyes. Now we know that God heareth not sinners: but if any man be a worshipper of God, and doeth his will, him he heareth. Since the world began was it not heard that any man opened the eyes of one that was born blind, except he be of God. If this man were not of God, he could do nothing."

To this there is no answer; it cannot be gainsaid; the words carry within themselves the evidence of their own verity. There is nothing left for the Pharisees to do but to revile and to persecute. "Thou wast altogether born in sins" is their screeching cry—as though that had any bearing on the issue one way or the other—"and dost thou teach us? " Truly out of the mouths of babes and sucklings fall gems of eternal truth; the weak and the simple confound the wise and the learned, and the purposes of the Lord prevail. He had taught them, and they knew it, and he knew it. As a consequence, "they cast him out," and he was subjected to the dire penalties of excommunication and persecution. And so ever is it with those who forsake the world and cleave unto Christ. The world loves its own and hates those who are Christ's.

But the Lord loveth and careth for those who are his own, and when he who came to minister to his fellowmen learned of the excommunication, he sought out the man to teach him the truths of his everlasting gospel. No doubt he told him many things about a loving Father, the fall of man, and the atonement yet to be wrought by God's own Son. We know he asked this question:

Dost thou believe on the Son of God?

There is nothing figurative, nothing hidden, nothing left for interpretation, about the query. It is as plain as language can be; it strikes, as an arrow, into the very heart and core of revealed religion. "Who is he, Lord, that I might believe on him? " Jesus answers:

Thou hast both seen him, and it is he that talketh with thee.

And the man said, "Lord, I believe." And he worshipped

Jesus. That is, he who was born blind, whose eyes Jesus opened, received now a greater gift than sight itself. His lifelong spiritual blindness ceased also; his spirit eyes were opened; he knew Jesus was the Son of God through whom salvation comes, and he was prepared to follow him, worship him, and keep his commandments. Because of his belief in the Son, he was ready to enter in at the gate of repentance and baptism and to plant his feet firmly on the path leading to eternal life.

Here is a man who was born blind so that he might one day be a sign and a witness of the One who should open his eyes. And such came to pass according to that divine providence which cares for all things so that even a sparrow's fall merits divine notice. Here also is a man who was spiritually blind, upon whose soul the rays of gospel light had never shone, until one came who opened his spiritual eyes so that he saw in Jesus the Son of God. Can there be any doubt as to which is the greater miracle—to see with the eyes of mortality the things of this benighted sphere which shall pass away, or to see with the eyes of the spirit the things of a better world that shall endure forever? And does not the fact that Jesus opened the eyes that were blind physically testify that he also has power to open men's spiritual eyes so they can see the things of the Spirit and walk in the strait and narrow path leading to eternal life? And so Jesus said:

> *For judgment I am come into this world, that they which see not might see; and that they which see might be made blind.*

'I am come into the world to sit in judgment upon all men, to divide them into two camps by their acceptance or rejection of my word. Those who are spiritually blind have their eyes opened through obedience to my gospel and shall see the things of the Spirit. Those who think they can see in the spiritual realm, but who do not accept me and my gospel shall remain in darkness and be made blind to the true spiritual realities.' (*Commentary* 1:482.)

Knowing full well the meaning and import of Jesus'

words, some of the Pharisees asked, "Are we blind also?" The reply: "If ye were blind, ye should have no sin: but now ye say, We see; therefore your sin remaineth." 'If you did not have the law of Moses and the words of the prophets; if you did not profess to worship the God of Israel in your synagogues and to sacrifice to him in your temple; if you were not the chosen people to whom the word of truth once came, you would not be condemned as severely as you are. But because you have the greater light, and rebel against it, you commit sin.'[2]

NOTES

1. Farrar's footnote relative to this proclamation, "He is a prophet," is instructive: "And the Jews themselves went so far as to say [and what he now quotes is from Maimonides] that 'if a prophet of undoubted credentials should command all persons to light fires on the Sabbath day, arm themselves for war, kill the inhabitants &c., it would behove all to rise up without delay and execute all that he should direct without scruple or hesitation.'" (Farrar, p. 439, footnote 2.)

2. "'He who sins against the greater light shall receive the greater condemnation.' (D&C 82:3.) 'Where there is no law . . . there is no condemnation.' (2 Ne. 9:25.) Modern sectarians, to whom the message of the restoration is presented, are in this same state of blindness and sin. They have the scriptures before them; they study the gospel doctrines contained in them; they are concerned about religion in general; and then they hear the latter-day elders, speaking as those having authority, present the message of salvation—and yet they choose to remain in the churches of the day rather than accept the fulness of revealed truth. If they were blind, knowing none of these things, they would be under no condemnation for rejecting the light; but when the truth is offered to them and they reject it, claiming to have the light already, they are under condemnation, for their sin remaineth." (*Commentary* 1:482.)

THE GOOD SHEPHERD

The Lord is my Shepherd. (Ps. 23:1.)
The Lord God will come. . . .
He shall feed his flock like a shepherd:
he shall gather the lambs with his arm,
and carry them in his bosom,
and shall gently lead those that are with young.
(Isa. 40:10-11.)

Jesus Is the Good Shepherd

(*John 10:1-15; JST, John 10:7-8, 12-14*)

No figures of speech, no similitudes, no parables or allegories brought greater joy to Israelite hearts than those which led to the glorious pronouncement: *Jehovah is our Shepherd.*

Israel's very lives depended upon the safety and procreant powers of their sheep. Physically and spiritually their interests centered in their flocks and herds. From them came food for their tables, clothes for their bodies, sacrifices for their altars. In the lonely deserts, on the mountain slopes, in the valleys of the shadow of death, a strong bond of love and mutual reliance grew up between the sheep and their pastor. Those who cared for the flocks were not sheepherders but shepherds; sheep were not driven, but led; they hearkened to him whose voice they came to know. At night the flocks were commingled in one safe sheepfold where a single shepherd stood guard against the wolves and terrors of the night. In the morning each shepherd called his own sheep out and they followed him to green pastures and still waters.

Thus in their hymns of praise Israel sang: "Know ye that the Lord he is God: it is he that hath made us, and not we ourselves; we are his people, and the sheep of his pasture." (Ps. 100:3.) When Jehovah rebuked his recreant priests and teachers, his cry was: "Woe be to the shepherds of Israel that do feed themselves! should not the shepherds feed the flocks? . . . And ye my flock, the flock of my pasture, are men, and I am your God, saith the Lord God." (Ezek. 34:2, 31.) And when the people were called to repentance, the cry was: "O ye workers of iniquity; ye that are puffed up in the vain things of the world, ye that have professed to have known the ways of righteousness nevertheless have gone astray, as sheep having no shepherd, notwithstanding a shepherd hath called after you and is still calling after you, but ye will not hearken unto his voice! Behold, I say unto you, that the good shepherd doth call you; yea, and in his own name he doth call you, which is the name of Christ; and if ye will not hearken unto the voice of the good shepherd, to the name by which ye are called, behold, ye are not the sheep of the good shepherd. And now if ye are not the sheep of the good shepherd, of what fold are ye? Behold, I say unto you, that the devil is your shepherd, and ye are of his fold; and now, who can deny this?" (Alma 5:37-39.) And many of their Messianic prophecies spoke of the Shepherd of Israel, and of the day when the Son of David, sitting on the throne of David, should be King over them, when "they all shall have one shepherd." (Ezek. 37:24.)

It is in this setting, then, among a people who understand the similitudes and figures from days of old, that Jesus now bears testimony of himself as the Shepherd of Israel. In what has come down to us as an allegory—John calls it a parable, and such it may have been in the fuller versions extant in his day—the Lord Jesus now says:

Verily, verily, I say unto you, He that entereth not by the door into the sheepfold, but climbeth up some other way, the same is a thief and a robber.

He is addressing himself to the priests and scribes, to the Pharisees and Rabbis in particular—to those who have made themselves guides and lights and teachers to the people. These ministers, these pastors, these shepherds, like their fathers, were those of whom Ezekiel said: "Ye eat the fat, and ye clothe you with the wool, ye kill them that are fed: but ye feed not the flock. The diseased have ye not strengthened, neither have ye healed that which was sick, neither have ye bound up that which was broken, neither have ye brought again that which was driven away, neither have ye sought that which was lost; but with force and with cruelty have ye ruled them." (Ezek. 34:3-4.)

These false ministers ruled over such of Israel as was then known, over congregations assembled in Palestine and other lands, upon whom, as thieves and robbers, they imposed the burdens of a dead law and forbade the sheep to find pasture in Christ and to drink of the waters of life that he brought. Of them Elder James E. Talmage says that they "sought by avoiding the portal and climbing over the fence to reach the folded flock; but these were robbers, trying to get at the sheep as prey; their selfish and malignant purpose was to kill and carry off. . . . Never has been written or spoken a stronger arraignment of false pastors, unauthorized teachers, self-seeking hirelings who teach for pelf and divine for dollars, deceivers who pose as shepherds yet avoid the door and climb over 'some other way,' prophets in the devil's employ, who to achieve their master's purpose, hesitate not to robe themselves in the garments of assumed sanctity, and appear in sheep's clothing, while inwardly they are ravening wolves." (Talmage, pp. 417-18.)

But he that entereth in by the door is the shepherd of

the sheep. To him the porter openeth; and the sheep hear his voice: and he calleth his own sheep by name, and leadeth them out.

Jesus himself—a true Minister, the Shepherd of the Sheep—comes openly, boldly, visibly to the door. To him the one—his Father—who has preserved Israel in one place for this very day opens the sheepfold. The Son preaches his gospel; those who are his sheep, who came from pre-existence with the special talent to recognize the truth, heed his voice, and he leads them out of the Rabbinical past into the revelation of the present.

And when he putteth forth his own sheep, he goeth before them, and the sheep follow him: for they know his voice. And a stranger will they not follow, but will flee from him: for they know not the voice of strangers.

Christ goeth before his sheep; he is the pattern. They follow him and seek to do what he has done, because they know his voice—the voice of testimony, the voice of true doctrine, the voice of righteousness, the voice of the Lord. True disciples will not follow the false shepherds of the world. Should they do so, they will be eaten by the wolves of wickedness and lose their souls.

It is not strange that the spiritually untuned ears of the Rabbinists failed to receive into their souls the deep and awesome portent of Jesus' divine words. Accordingly, by way of doctrine and of testimony, he continues:

Verily, verily, I say unto you, I am the door of the sheepfold. All that ever came before me who testified not of me are thieves and robbers; but the sheep did not hear them.

'I am the door by which men must enter to be saved. All the ministers of the past, of the present, and of the future, who do not testify of me and teach my gospel—including you priests, scribes, Pharisees, and Rabbis—are thieves and robbers; you are teachers in the employ of Satan and are seeking to steal the souls of men. But the true sheep will not follow you.'

> *I am the door: by me if any man enter in, he shall be saved, and shall go in and out, and find pasture.*

'Salvation comes by me; it is not in the law of Moses, neither in the dead churches of Christendom, neither in the non-Christian religions. Come unto me; I am the Savior. Those in my sheepfold shall go forth to the pastures of salvation and drink the waters of eternal life.'

> *The thief cometh not, but for to steal, and to kill, and to destroy: I am come that they might have life, and that they might have it more abundantly.*

We are hearing Ezekiel all over again. False ministers feed and clothe themselves. Let the sheep be slain; let them lose their souls; it matters not what happens to the flock so long as the purposes of priestcraft are served. "Woe be to the shepherds of Israel." But Jesus came to bring life. His atoning sacrifice will cause all to live again in immortality, and those who believe and obey shall have an abundant life. They shall be added upon. All that the Father hath shall be theirs, for they shall inherit eternal life which is the kind of life that God lives.

> *I am the good shepherd: the good shepherd giveth his life for the sheep.*

What more can he say? How better can it be said? 'I am Jehovah, your Shepherd; because of me ye shall not want. I shall cause you to lie down in green pastures and shall lead you beside the still waters. I shall restore your souls and lead you in the paths of righteousness for my name's sake. Though you walk through the valley of the shadow of death, ye need fear no evil: for I will be with you; my rod and my staff shall comfort you. I shall prepare a table for you in the presence of your enemies; I shall anoint your head with oil; your cup runneth over. Surely goodness and mercy shall follow you all the days of your life; and you shall dwell in the house of the Lord forever in the eternities that are ahead—all because I am the Good Shepherd; I am the Lord

Jehovah, and I shall give my life for the sheep in the infinite and eternal atonement which is ahead.'

And the shepherd is not as a hireling, whose own the sheep are not, who seeth the wolf coming, and leaveth the sheep, and fleeth; and the wolf catcheth the sheep and scattereth them. For I am the good shepherd, and know my sheep, and am known of mine. But he who is a hireling fleeth, because he is a hireling, and careth not for the sheep. As the Father knoweth me, even so know I the Father.

'Now I shall tell you the difference between me and false ministers and teachers, between me and the scribes and Pharisees. I am the Shepherd, not a hireling. Those who practice priestcrafts—who preach for hire and divine for money, who seek the praise of the world—whose own the sheep are not, they forsake the sheep when trouble comes. But I am the Good Shepherd, the Lord Jehovah. The sheep are mine; I will care for them, even though it costs me my life. This is ordained by my Father, who is God, and who knoweth me, even as I know him.'

The Good Shepherd Has Power over Death

(*John 10:15-21*)

Jesus, as the Good Shepherd, came into the world to lay down his life for the sheep. He will save the sheep though he be slain; or, better, he will save the sheep because he is slain.

And I lay down my life for the sheep.

Then, before enlarging upon this theme—almost in a parenthetical pronouncement—he extends the Good Shepherd concept out beyond the borders of Palestine, beyond Egypt and Greece and Rome, beyond the Old World, to the utmost bounds of the everlasting hills, as Father Jacob described the place of the inheritance of the seed of his son Joseph. Jesus speaks thus of his Nephite sheep:

And other sheep I have, which are not of this fold: them also I must bring, and they shall hear my voice; and there shall be one fold, and one shepherd.

All Israel, all the promised seed, all the chosen race—all shall enter one sheepfold. All Israel, all of the seed of Abraham, all of the children of the prophets—all shall have one Shepherd. The flock of the Lord's pasture are men, the men of Israel. They shall hear his voice and see his face; theirs is the privilege, first and ahead of all others, to hear his voice. The time of the Gentiles is yet future. And so when the Risen Lord ministers among Nephite-Israel, he will say: "Ye are they of whom I said: Other sheep I have which are not of this fold; them also I must bring, and they shall hear my voice; and there shall be one fold, and one shepherd. And they understood me not, for they supposed it had been the Gentiles; for they understood not that the Gentiles should be converted through their preaching. And they understood me not that I said they shall hear my voice; and they understood me not that the Gentiles should not at any time hear my voice—that I should not manifest myself unto them save it were by the Holy Ghost. But behold, ye have both heard my voice, and seen me; and ye are my sheep, and ye are numbered among those whom the Father hath given me." (3 Ne. 15:21-24.)

Then the Lord told his Nephite sheep that he had yet "other sheep," the lost tribes of Israel, whom he would visit. (3 Ne. 16:1-5.) And finally, all who believe his gospel, Jew and Gentile alike, shall be gathered into his fold, "for there is one God and one Shepherd over all the earth." (1 Ne. 13:41.) But having digressed from his central theme, or, at least, having illustrated the magnitude and extent of his sheepfold, Jesus returns to the matter of his laying down his life for the sheep.

> *Therefore doth my Father love me, because I lay down my life, that I might take it again. No man taketh it from me, but I lay it down of myself. I have power to lay it down, and I have power to take it again. This commandment have I received of my Father.*

Thus Jesus proclaims the doctrine of the divine Sonship. From God who is his Father he inherited the power of immortality, the power to live forever. An immortal Being cannot die. No man can take his life from him. From Mary, who is his mother, he inherited the power of mortality, the power to separate body and spirit, the power to die. All mortal beings die; all lay down their lives in death. Jesus only of all mankind—Jesus, the Son of the living God; Jesus, the Son of the mortal Virgin—this One Man of all men had power to live or to die; and having chosen to die, he had power to live again in glorious immortality, never again to see death. All this is according to the commandment of the Father.

What possible response can his hearers—then or now—make to this divine doctrine? The response—then as now—can be but one of two things: belief or disbelief. There is no middle ground, no gray area, no room for compromise. Either he is the Atoning One or he is not. If he is not, the natural Jewish excuse for rejecting him, as it then came from those then present; is: "He hath a devil, and is mad; why hear ye him?" Of course he is mad, insane, totally devoid of reason or sense, unless these claims to divinity are true. Yet others who chose to believe did so on the basis of his words and his works. His words flowed forth with such a divine fluency and conviction that no Spirit-enlightened person could reject them. His works were those which none but one approved of God could perform. "These are not the words of him that hath a devil. Can a devil open the eyes of the blind?" And so, if one approved of God—as his works testify—says, in words, 'God is my Father,' how can his testimony be other than true?

Jesus Says: "I Am the Son of God"
(*John 10:22-42*)

"How long dost thou make us to doubt? If thou be the Christ, tell us plainly." So said the Jews to Jesus as he walked in the temple in Solomon's Porch at the Feast of Dedication.[1] It is December 20-27, A.D. 29; in just over three months, he will be lifted up upon the cross because he is the

Christ. Can it be that he has not as yet told the people plainly that he is their Messiah?

The fact is, for three years, of which we know, this man from Nazareth in Galilee has testified that he is the Christ, thousands upon thousands of times, always so couching his words as to avoid claiming the kind of political Messiahship of which so many of the Jews dreamed. He has said: 'I am the Christ; I am the Messiah; I am the Lord Jehovah; I am the Good Shepherd; God is my Father; in me and in me alone are the Messianic prophecies fulfilled.' During this same period he has accepted, freely and graciously, a like testimony from his disciples: 'Thou art he of whom Moses and the prophets spoke; thou art the Messiah; thou art the Christ, the Son of the living God. We worship thee.' And yet he has not let himself be hailed or crowned as the King-Messiah who would raise an army, throw off the Roman yoke, and lead a disconsolate people to national triumph and worldly renown.

The words of inquiry now spoken to him must have partaken of some of the nationalistic feeling that he should acclaim himself as an earthly king. His answer—that of one whose kingdom is not of this world—brings the matter of Messiahship back into the place and perspective where he intends it to be.

> *I told you, and ye believed not: the works that I do in my Father's name, they bear witness of me.*

'I have told you over and over again, and you have not believed me. I have wrought wondrous miracles in my Father's name, which I could not do without his approval—an approval that includes the words I speak. My words and my works bear witness that I am the Christ.'

> *But ye believe not, because ye are not of my sheep, as I said unto you. My sheep hear my voice, and I know them, and they follow me.*

'I am the Good Shepherd, the Lord Jehovah, who is the Shepherd of those who truly are of Israel. Ye are not my sheep; ye are not truly Abraham's seed. Ye are of your father, the devil, as I said unto you. My sheep hear my voice; they developed the talent for spirituality, the talent to recognize the truth, while yet in preexistence. It is easy for them to believe in me; and I know them; and they follow me, believe my gospel, join my church, and keep my commandments.'

And I give unto them eternal life; and they shall never perish, neither shall any man pluck them out of my hand.

My Father, which gave them me, is greater than all; and no man is able to pluck them out of my Father's hand.

I AND MY FATHER ARE ONE.

They asked to be told plainly that he was the Christ. He is answering their petition again, not in the language calling for a temporal Deliverer who will wield a worldly sword, but in language quoted from the registers of eternity. He, the Christ, will give his disciples eternal life; salvation is in him; and none can steal his sheep. The flocks of this world perish from hunger and cold and thirst. The Lord's sheep will never perish. The Father who gave the sheep to the Son and Shepherd has all power, and he, the Son, acts in the power of the Father. They are one.

Again there are two alternatives and two only. Either what he says is true or it is blasphemy. Either he is the Son of God, one with his Father, or he deserves to die for the most awesomely irreverent of all crimes. These Jews, who had been told many times that Jesus was the Christ but perhaps never so plainly and forcibly as on this occasion, and who always and ever rejected the divine witness, now took up stones again to stone him.

"Many good works have I shewed you from my Father," he says, "for which of those works do ye stone me?" 'Am I to die at your hands because I opened the eyes of a man born blind, or cleansed a leper, or fed thousands of hungry souls with a few barley loaves and a savory made of fish, or is it because I raised a widow's son from death?' The question is unanswerable. It is as though men would slay God because he created the earth, gave them life and being, and sends seedtime and harvest. Their answer: "For a good work we stone thee not: but for blasphemy; and because that thou, being a man, makest thyself God." Clearly they understood the meaning of the words Jesus had spoken. Now he says:

> *Is it not written in your law, I said, Ye are gods? If he called them gods, unto whom the word of God came, and the scripture cannot be broken; Say ye of him, whom the Father hath sanctified, and sent into the world, Thou blasphemest; because I said, I am the Son of God?*

'Do you not understand the plan of salvation that was revealed to your fathers? Do you not know that all of the children of the Father have power to advance and progress and become like him? Have you never read that those who received your law in olden times had the promise that they could attain godhood and be gods themselves? Why accuse me of blasphemy for testifying that I was sanctified and sent into the world by the Father? Does it offend you to hear me say that I am the Son of God? Do you not know that every righteous person to whom the word of God comes, and who then obeys the fullness of that law, shall become like the Father and be a god himself?'[2]

> *If I do not the works of my Father, believe me not. But if I do, though ye believe not me, believe the works: that ye may know, and believe, that the Father is in me, and I in him.*

'Ye say ye do not believe in me; very well, then believe in the works which I do, for ye cannot deny they have come by divine power; and if ye accept the works, then ye shall believe in me also, for I could not do the works alone; they came by the power of the Father. Then ye shall know and believe that the Father is in me and I in him; we are one; we have the same powers, perfections, and attributes.'

Then again they sought to take him, "but he escaped out of their hand." We suppose he overawed them with his presence, and that while they devised in their hearts some way to put him to death, he passed through the throng, out of the temple, and out of Judea, into Perea, to the place beyond Jordan "where John at first baptized." There he abode for a season, and "many resorted unto him" to be taught. "John did no miracle," they said, "but all things that John spake of this man were true."

"And many believed on him there."

NOTES

1. At this point we face, as we have on several previous occasions, a problem of chronology that cannot be resolved on the basis of the Gospel accounts as we now have them. Almost every scholar who pays for himself the full price of analytical and in-depth research comes up with a different conclusion. Our friend Farrar, for instance, at this point in his writings says: "Almost every inquirer seems to differ to a greater or less degree as to the exact sequence and chronology of the events which follow. Without entering into minute and tedious disquisitions where absolute certainty is impossible, I will narrate this period of our Lord's life in the order which, after repeated study of the gospels, appears to me to be the most probable, and in the separate details of which I have found myself again and again confirmed by the conclusions of other independent inquirers." (Farrar, p. 444.)

Other equally competent analysts find themselves at odds with Farrar and are able to call upon yet others to sustain their views. Contention in the field is needless; and in view of the present state of things, we are not inclined to feel harshly toward any sincere student, regardless of the conclusions he reaches. The issues are such that reasonable men can differ without in any way demeaning or questioning the grand design of the Grand Life. Our own President J. Reuben Clark, Jr., and our own Elder James E. Talmage, for instance, are in complete disagreement as to when various things happened on this and other occasions. It is only important for us to know there are problems in the field of chronology and to confess that we, as well as others of greater insight and capacity, can err on the points involved. And yet this is of no great import, for the over-all witness will be the same, and someday the true eventualities will be unraveled and set forth for all to know.

Regardless of the chronology conclusions reached, it is logical, for our purposes, to consider Jesus' statements about the Good Shepherd who gives his life for the sheep as though they were part of the same sermon given at the Feast of Dedication. Such may, in fact, have been the case; there are so many similar threads that it seems as though Jesus is weaving one grand tapestry by all that is recorded in John 10.

2. "Though 'there is none other God but one' for men on this earth to worship, yet 'there be gods many, and lords many' throughout the infinite expanse of eternity. (1 Cor. 8:4-7.) That is, there are many exalted, perfected, glorified personages who reign as gods over their own dominions. John saw 144,000 of them standing with Christ upon Mount Zion, all 'having his Father's name written in their foreheads' (Rev. 14:1), which is to say that they were gods and were so identified by wearing crowns so stating. Indeed, to each person who overcomes and gains exaltation, Christ has promised: 'I will write upon him the name of my God,' and he shall 'sit with me in my throne, even as I also overcame, and am set down with my Father in his throne.' (Rev. 3:12, 21.)

"Joseph Smith said: 'Every man who reigns in celestial glory is a god to his dominions.' (*Teachings*, p. 374.) All exalted persons 'are gods, even the sons of God.' (D&C 76:58.) Through obedience to the whole gospel law, including celestial marriage, they attain the 'fulness of the glory of the Father' (D&C 93:6-28) and 'a continuation of the seeds forever and ever. Then shall they be gods, because they have no end; therefore shall they be from everlasting to everlasting, because they continue; then shall they be above all, because all things are subject unto them. Then shall they be gods, because they have all power, and the angels are subject unto them.' (D&C 132:19-20.)

"But to us there is but one God, who is Elohim, and one Lord, who is the Lord Jehovah; the Holy Ghost acts as their minister; and these three are one Godhead, or as it is more graphically expressed, one God. Thus we find the Psalmist, whom Jesus quoted, saying: 'God standeth in the congregation of the mighty; he judgeth among the gods. . . . I have said, Ye are gods; and all of you are children of the most High.' (Ps. 82:1, 6.)" (*Commentary* 1:491.)

SECTION IX

THE PEREAN MINISTRY

THE PEREAN MINISTRY

But as it is written,
Eye hath not seen, nor ear heard,
neither have entered into the heart of man,
the things which God hath prepared for them that love him.
But God hath revealed them unto us by his Spirit:
for the Spirit searcheth all things,
yea, the deep things of God.
(1 Cor. 2:9-10.)

Jesus speaks; his words are wondrous; salvation is his theme.

Jesus ministers; his deeds are divine; blind men see and dead men live.

Jesus journeys; Jerusalem is his bourn; a cross awaits him there.

"Lord, are there few only that be saved?" he is asked. We hear his answer.

We learn that little children have eternal life; that men must be willing to lay their all on the altar—their possessions and families, even their very lives—to gain salvation.

We are told plainly: To gain eternal life, we must keep the commandments.

We stand before a sealed tomb and see the greatest

miracle of his mortal ministry: Lazarus after four days of decomposing death steps forth in vibrant life.

And we hear from his own lips the soul-filling testimony: "I AM THE RESURRECTION, AND THE LIFE: HE THAT BELIEVETH IN ME, THOUGH HE WERE DEAD, YET SHALL HE LIVE."

We see ten lepers healed; rejoice with blind Bartimeus as he sees again; and are grateful that the man with dropsy and the woman with an eighteen-year infirmity are now well and whole.

We hear sermons—his discourse on the kingdom of God; his discourse on marriage and divorce; his pronouncement that the law and the prophets testify of him.

What is this we hear? Peter asks what reward shall the Twelve receive. Jesus places them on twelve thrones, judging the twelve tribes of Israel. James and John seek a place on his right hand and on his left in the eternal worlds, and are rebuked for their presumption.

And there are parables, not a few: the prodigal son, that sweet story of infinite mercy and tenderness; Lazarus and Dives, which sets forth the divisions in the spirit world; the laborers in the vineyard, all of whom are paid alike; the parable of the pounds, of the lost sheep, of the great supper, and many others.

As we hear and see and feel of the miracle that he is, there comes also the satanic voice, heard in the Sanhedrin, as that spiritually dead quorum plots his death.

Truly, the one perfect ministry of the one perfect man is proceeding on its foreordained course—to a cross and to a crown!

SACRIFICE AND SALVATION

How can ye be saved,
except ye inherit the kingdom of heaven? . . .
Ye cannot be saved in your sins. . . .
Those who believe on his name . . .
these are they that shall have eternal life,
and salvation cometh to none else.
(Alma 11:37-40.)

More Sabbath Healings

(*Luke 13:10-17; 14:1-6; JST, Luke 13:11, 14, 17*)

As the day approaches for the final great conflict that will bring death to God's Son and doom to a once-chosen people, it seems as though Jesus is deliberately widening the gulf between him and them. Their sad perversion of true Sabbath worship creates an arena in which the conflict can be waged. On that holy day he openly chooses to defy their traditions and to place them in a position where they must choose between him as a Divine Healer sent of God and the burdensome traditions of Rabbinism.

Luke tells us of two such healings that took place on different Sabbaths in different cities in Perea. In one of these, while Jesus taught on the Sabbath in a synagogue, he healed a woman who had suffered for eighteen long years with a sickly, serious malady; in the other, while eating in the home of a leading Pharisee, he chose to heal a man afflicted with dropsy. Both healings comforted the afflicted, enraged the rebellious, and bore irrefutable witness of the divine power of the one who made his acts of healing of more import than all the inane Sabbatarianism that seemed so important to the Jews.

Jesus is teaching in a synagogue in Perea on the Sabbath. And we say again—though the repetition may seem monotonous—he is teaching the gospel. He is teaching the plan of salvation, the tender mercies of a loving Father, the Messianic mission of Israel's Deliverer, the salvation that God's Son is offering to the chosen people. Such is his message; he has none other.

There is present a devout and deserving woman—one of the regular worshippers in this synagogue—who for eighteen years has been bound by Satan with a malady having deep spiritual roots. Hers is both a moody and melancholic state and one in which her sickly and crooked frame is bound and crippled. She is unable to straighten up and use her muscles. Jesus sees her, calls her to him, and says: "Woman, thou art loosed from thine infirmity." As is his not uncommon practice, he lays his hands upon her, and, as is always the case when he speaks, she is healed. Jesus thus acts on his own initiative, without supplication, because he desires to bless mankind. And she glorifies God. After eighteen years of sorrow and suffering, bowed in grief and crippled in body, she arises whole, clean, mentally and spiritually renewed and refreshed. Jesus speaks and so it is.

Jesus is now interrupted. The ruler of the synagogue—a pitiful, petty scrub of a man—arises in his Satan-spawned wrath and pours out his venom, not directly upon Jesus, not directly upon the woman, but upon the people who were silent witnesses of the power of God. "There are six days in which men ought to work," he says; "in them therefore come and be healed, and not on the sabbath day."

What a scene we have just beheld! One of God's

daughters has been healed, and one of Satan's ministers has risen in wrath to condemn the Healer and warn his congregation against the sin of permitting such a thing to happen to them on the Sabbath. The healed woman broke forth into utterances of gratitude to God. "But her strain of thanksgiving was interrupted by the narrow and ignorant indignation of the ruler of the synagogue. Here, under his very eyes, and without any reference to the 'little brief authority' which gave him a sense of dignity on each recurring Sabbath, a woman—a member of *his* congregation—had actually had the presumption to be healed! Armed with his favorite 'texts,' and in all the fussiness of official hypocrisy, he gets up and rebukes the perfectly innocent multitude, telling them it was a gross instance of Sabbath-breaking for them to be healed on that sacred day, when they might just as well be healed on any of the other six days of the week. . . .

"Now, as the poor woman does not seem to have spoken one word of entreaty to Jesus, or even to have called His attention to her case, the utterly senseless address of this man could only by any possibility mean either, 'You *sick* people must not come to the synagogue at all on the Sabbath under present circumstances, for fear you should be led into Sabbath-breaking by having a miraculous cure performed upon you;' or 'If any one wants to heal you on a Sabbath, you must decline.' And these remarks he has neither the courage to address to Jesus Himself, nor the candour to address to the poor healed woman, but preaches *at* them both by rebuking the multitude, who had no concern in the action at all, beyond the fact that they had been passive spectators of it! The whole range of the Gospels does not supply any other instance of an interference so illogical, or a stupidity so hopeless." (Farrar, pp. 466-67.)

Jesus' response contains a stinging rebuke and an irrefutable argument. "Thou hypocrite," he acclaims, "doth not each one of you on the sabbath loose his ox or his ass from the stall, and lead him away to watering?" Such was their practice. No penalty attached to the labor of leading an animal, which had been without water for a few hours, to the place of watering. Animals must be cared for; their well-being was important. "And ought not this woman, being a daughter of Abraham"—surely, as such, she was as important as an ox or an ass—"whom Satan hath bound, lo, these eighteen years, be loosed from this bond on the sabbath day?"

It is no wonder that "when he had said these things, all his adversaries were ashamed; and all his disciples rejoiced for all the glorious things which were done by him." In this setting Jesus continued to teach and gave over again the parables of the mustard seed and of the leaven.

On yet another Sabbath, in yet another Perean city, we find Jesus in the house of "one of the chief Pharisees," perhaps one who is a member of the Great Sanhedrin itself. A great company is present, including many who are prominent and influential; it is a festal-Sabbath meal. There are also unbidden guests present, as custom allows; these are welcome to enter and observe, as did the woman who washed Jesus' feet with her tears and anointed them with ointment in the home of another Pharisee, but these observers are not among the banqueters themselves. One of these unofficial guests has dropsy. He and his condition are visible to all; the chief Pharisee, planning to taunt or test Jesus, may even have arranged for the prominent display of the afflicted man. In any event, all present watch Jesus to see what he will do, and he does not hesitate to use the occasion for his own purposes.

To the lawyers and Pharisees, he asks, "Is it lawful to heal on the sabbath day?" For an answer there is silence only, no spoken word. "They *would* not say, 'Yes;' but, on the other hand, they dared not say, 'No!' Had it been unlawful, it was their positive function and duty to say so then and there, and without any subterfuge to deprive the poor sufferer, so far as in them lay, of the miraculous mercy which was prepared for him. If they dared not say so—either for fear of the people, or for fear of instant refutation, or because the spell of Christ's awful ascendency was upon them, or out of a mere splenetic pride, or—to imagine better motives—because in their inmost hearts, if any spot remained in them uncrusted by idle and irreligious prejudices, they felt that it *was* lawful, and more than lawful, RIGHT—then, by their own judgment, they left Jesus free to heal without the possibility of censure. Their silence, therefore, was, even on their own showing, and on their own principles, His entire justification. His mere simple question, and their inability to answer it, was an absolute decision of the controversy in His favour. He therefore took the man, healed him, and let him go." (Farrar, pp. 470-71.)

"Which of you shall have an ass or an ox fallen into a pit," Jesus then asks, "and will not straightway pull him out on the sabbath day?" He has cited their own custom and practice; to care for their beasts was lawful and right on the Sabbath. This being established—and even they knowing that a man is more important than a beast—there is nothing more to be said. And so they said nothing.

Before leaving the arena where this Sabbath-warfare is being waged—an arena in which we see Jesus contend for the real meaning and purpose of the Lord's holy day, while the Pharisees seek rather to follow the base traditions of their fathers—before leaving this field of contest, we should note these instructive words of Farrar, which show why a whole people will submit to such a system of inanity, of scribal scrupulosity, and of Pharisaic perversion. "Again and again was our Lord thus obliged to redeem this great primeval institution of God's love from these narrow, formal, pernicious restrictions of an otiose and unintelligent tradition," he says. "But it is evident that He attached as much importance to the noble and loving freedom of the day of rest as they did to the stupefying inaction to which they had reduced the normal character of its observance.

Their absorbing attachment to it, the frenzy which filled them when He set at naught their Sabbatarian uncharities, rose from many circumstances."

It is these circumstances and this religious climate that illustrate why people will follow false and strict systems of religion to their doom. "They were wedded to the religious system which had long prevailed among them," our analyst says, "because it is easy to be a slave to the letter, and difficult to enter into the spirit; easy to obey a number of outward rules, difficult to enter intelligently and self-sacrificingly into the will of God; easy to entangle the soul in a network of petty observances, difficult to yield the obedience of an enlightened heart; easy to be haughtily exclusive, difficult to be humbly spiritual; easy to be an ascetic or a formalist, difficult to be pure, and loving, and wise, and free; easy to be a Pharisee, difficult to be a disciple; very easy to embrace a self-satisfying and sanctimonious system of rabbinical observances, very difficult to love God with all the heart, and all the might, and all the soul, and all the strength. In laying His axe at the root of their proud and ignorant Sabbatarianism, He was laying His axe at the root of all that 'miserable micrology' which they had been accustomed to take for their religious life." (Farrar, p. 469.)

Parable of the Wedding Guests

(*Luke 14:7-11; JST, Luke 14:7, 9-10*)

After the Sabbath-healing of the dropsical man, and while yet at the festal table of the chief Pharisee, Jesus gave two parables—the parable of the wedding guests and the parable of the great supper. Many persons of great eminence were then present—noted scribes, renowned scholars, respected Rabbis, prominent Pharisees, rich merchants. All had assembled to partake of the rich delicacies heaped high on the banquet board. As the setting for the parable of the wedding guests, there must have been some struggles for seating precedence among the ego-inflated guests. Their protocol placed prominent people in preferred positions. This raised the question of comparative prominence and of ruling on the problems raised by their own self-esteem and self-exaltation. And so, Luke says, Jesus "put forth a parable unto them concerning those who were bidden to a wedding; for he knew how they chose out the chief rooms, and exalted themselves one above another."

> *When thou art bidden of any man to a wedding, sit not down in the highest room; lest a more honourable man than thou be bidden of him; And he who bade thee, with him who is more honorable, come, and say to thee; Give this man place; and thou begin with shame to take the lowest room.*

To their shame, some of their chief concerns centered around rank and precedence, which, if it did nothing more, attested to the essential hollowness of their Rabbinical religion.

> *But when thou art bidden, go and sit down in the lowest room; that when he who bade thee, cometh, he may say unto thee, Friend, go up higher; then shalt thou have honor of God, in the presence of them who sit at meat with thee.*

Those who bridle their Pharisaic self-esteem and control their inflated self-satisfaction prepare themselves to receive honor from God. What matter the petty preferences of this probation as compared to the eternal honors that are his to confer?

> *For whosoever exalteth himself shall be abased; and he that humbleth himself shall be exalted.*

Parable of the Great Supper

(*Luke 14:12-24; JST, Luke 14:12*)

As a setting for this parable we have an assemblage of renowned persons. They are the friends of "one of the chief Pharisees." Also, Jesus has just given the parable of the wedding guests. Now, "concerning him who bade to the wedding," and speaking to a host whose assembled guests are the noble and great among men, he says: "When thou makest a dinner, or a supper, call not thy friends [an Oriental idiom meaning call not *only* thy friends], nor thy brethren, neither thy kinsmen, nor rich neighbors; lest they also bid thee again, and a recompense be made thee. But when thou makest a feast, call the poor, the maimed, the lame, and the blind"—the man healed of dropsy might well have been asked to stay and partake of the banquet delicacies—"And thou shalt be blessed; for they cannot recompense thee: for thou shalt be recompensed at the resurrection of the just."

Clearly these words were a reproof and a rebuke to a self-exalted host who esteemed highly those of his own ilk, but who looked with disdain and ill-will toward those in a lower caste. Perhaps to break the tension thus created, one of the self-esteeming, self-ennobling, self-exalting persons among the banqueters—one of those who in his own self-righteous frame of mind could, religiously, do no wrong—said: "Blessed is he that shall eat bread in the kingdom of God." In this reply there was more than meets the eye. Having in mind the Jewish tradition that the resurrection of the just and the setting up of the kingdom of God would be ushered in by a great festival of which all the members of the kingdom would partake, it was as though the speaker had acclaimed: 'Yea, Lord, we know that men will be rewarded for their good deeds in the resurrection of the just; and since we as members of the chosen people will be there at that time to partake of the feast of God, surely we shall be fully rewarded.'

In this setting, then, the Master Parabolist gave the parable of the great supper. "A certain man made a great supper, and bade many," he said. 'The Lord of all prepared for his people a great feast of fat kine, of wine on the lees well refined, of corn and cakes and honey. He offered to feed them with food celestial; theirs would be the privilege of eating at his table and never hungering more, of drinking at his board and never again wanting for water. He made ready a great gospel banquet that they might feast on the rich delicacies of eternity.'

He then "sent his servant at supper time to say to them that were bidden, Come; for all things are now ready." 'He sent his Servant, the Suffering Servant of whom Isaiah spoke; he sent his Son, sent him to the chosen people. Come, the Servant would say; Come, feast upon the words of Christ. The banquet table is set; there is meat and drink here for the soul. After fifteen hundred years of Mosaic preparation all things are now ready. The fulness of the everlasting gospel is now yours for the taking.'

"And they all with one consent began to make excuse." The whole nation sought to excuse themselves from attendance. The banquet was not to their liking; the food was seasoned with a new salt, the salt of humility and lowliness of heart. The fatted calf, now roasted before them, smelled not of the smoke of Mosaic fires, but was prepared more delicately for those of more refined sensitivities. This was no feast for them; they preferred rather to fatten themselves on the traditions of the elders and the teachings of the Rabbis.

"The first said unto him, I have bought a piece of ground, and I must needs go and see it: I pray thee have me excused." 'I am lawfully and properly engaged in tilling the soil of the past. My heart rejoices in the worldly possessions I have acquired. Why should I forsake all and believe in this new religion?' "And another said, I have bought five yoke of oxen, and I go to prove them: I pray thee have me excused." 'I am engaged in business enterprises of my own. If I spend the time required in this new religion, my business will suffer.' "And another said, I have married a wife, and therefore I cannot come." 'Mine are the pleasures of this present world; let me rejoice in my wife. Am I expected to give up the pleasant things of this world simply because a new religion promises me greater joys in the life to come?'

"So that servant came, and shewed his lord these things. Then the master of the house being angry said to his servant,

Go out quickly into the streets and lanes of the city, and bring in hither the poor, and the maimed, and the halt, and the blind." 'Turn from the scribes and Pharisees, from the rich and the noble in Israel; turn from those who are self-ennobling and self-exalting. Go to the publicans and sinners in your streets; go to the poor, to those who are considered to be spiritually maimed and halt and blind. Go to the common people, to the man born blind who in Pharisaic eyes knew not anything.' And it was done.

And then—because the gospel is for all men, because all are alike unto God, whether Jew or Gentile, bond or free, black or white—"Go out into the highways and hedges, and compel them to come in, that my house may be filled." 'Go outside the Holy City; go beyond the chosen people; go out upon the highways of the world; go to the heathen and the pagan. They have never heard of the gospel; they must be taught and commanded and compelled. Bring them in that my house may be filled.' "For I say unto you, That none of those men which were bidden shall taste of my supper."

"The application to all present was obvious. The worldly heart—whether absorbed in the management of property, or the acquisition of riches, or the mere sensualisms of domestic comfort—was incompatible with any desire for the true banquet of the kingdom of heaven. The Gentile and the Pariah, the harlot and the publican, the labourer of the roadside and the beggar of the streets, these might be [nay, would be] there in greater multitudes than the Scribe with his boasted learning, and the Pharisee with his broad phylactery." (Farrar, p. 474.) But the application to the whole nation and the manifestation of the eternal purposes of him who prepared the table and who issued the invitations are even more important. The gospel supper was spread, first, before the Jews as a nation and as a people. When the delicacies remained untouched—nay, when they were spurned and ignored and left to be carried as garbage to Gehenna—then the Gentiles and the ends of the earth were invited to come, to drink of the waters of life, to eat of the manna from heaven, to gain all of the blessings of the gospel.

Will Many or Few Be Saved?
(*Luke 13:22-33; JST, Luke 13:23-25, 27-34*)

Jesus, somewhere in Perea, is journeying toward Jerusalem. It is a missionary journey "through the cities and villages." Everywhere, as his custom is, he is telling people what they must do to be saved; his gospel, which he everlastingly preaches, is a gospel of salvation. He is asked: "Lord, are there few only that be saved?"

Few or many in comparison to what? Few as compared to the general masses of worldly men, or many when the billions of millennial men—almost all of whom will be saved—are thrown into the scales? The total number of saved souls is of academic interest only; it is of no especial concern in the real world of applied truth. A far better question is: What must we do to be saved? And so Jesus answers not the question that was asked, but the question that should have been asked.

> *Strive to enter in at the strait gate; for I say unto you, Many shall seek to enter in, and shall not be able; for the Lord shall not always strive with man.*

Men must seek salvation. They must labor and strive and struggle. The gate is both strait and straight. Even among those who seek to enter, many shall fail. The Lord wants people to be saved and he will strive with them—personally while he dwells among them, and by his Spirit, the Light of Christ, at all times. But his Spirit will not always strive with men. When they harden their hearts and sear their consciences, his Spirit ceases to plead, to enlighten, to guide. Men are then left unto themselves, to pursue the inevitable and unfailing course which dooms them to outer darkness. Now we hear Jesus say:

> *Therefore, when once the Lord of the kingdom is*

> *risen up, and hath shut the door of the kingdom, then ye shall stand without, and knock at the door, saying, Lord, Lord, open unto us. But the Lord shall answer and say unto you, I will not receive you, for ye know not from whence ye are.*

There comes a time when the judgment is set, when the books are opened, when the eternal decrees are issued. There is a day when the door to the kingdom closes with eternal finality. Thereafter no new citizens are admitted to the Celestial Presence.

> *Then shall ye begin to say, We have eaten and drunk in thy presence, and thou hast taught in our streets. But he shall say, I tell you, ye know not from whence ye are; depart from me, all ye workers of iniquity.*

The Lord Jesus who then walked among them is the Eternal King. He it is from whom the workers of iniquity shall hear their dread doom: Depart from me. He invites men to repent here and now; if they do not do so, theirs is an everlasting sorrow hereafter.

> *There shall be weeping and gnashing of teeth among you, when ye shall see Abraham, and Isaac, and Jacob, and all the prophets, in the kingdom of God, and you are thrust out.*

This is literal. Those who reject the testimony of the legal administrators who are sent to preach to them; those who fail to heed the witness of the elders of Israel who come preaching the gospel of peace; those who reject the living oracles of God in their day—those shall see, as it were, these very rejected ones with crowns on their heads, reigning in immortal glory, in the presence of the Great King. And O what weeping and howling there will be among those in whose streets these very witnesses once walked!

> *And verily I say unto you, They shall come from the east, and the west; and from the north, and the south, and shall sit down in the kingdom of God.*

All the ends of the earth shall hear the message of salvation—Jew and Gentile alike—and the righteous among them shall come out of Babylon into Zion, there to prepare themselves for celestial rest.

> *And, behold, there are last which shall be first, and there are first which shall be last, and shall be saved therein.*

" 'There are those Gentiles in all nations to whom the gospel is offered *last* who shall be saved ahead of you Jews to whom the word of God came *first,* and there are those among you who *first* had opportunity to hear the truth, who shall be *last* as to honor, preference, and salvation hereafter.' (1 Ne. 13:42.)" (*Commentary* 1:497.)

As Jesus thus spoke—of the Jews who would be cast out for rejecting Him who had taught in their streets, and of the Gentiles who would come from the ends of the earth to sit down with Abraham, Isaac, and Jacob, and all the prophets, in the kingdom of God—at this point, "certain of the Pharisees" came and said: "Get thee out, and depart hence: for Herod will kill thee."

That Jesus believed this Pharisaic report, and also that it was a matter of complete indifference to him whether Antipas sought his life or not, is evident from his reply: "Go ye and tell Herod," he said, "Behold, I cast out devils, and do cures to-day and to-morrow, and the third day I shall be perfected." For the present and for the immediate future he would continue his ministry; the day of his death, resurrection, and eternal perfection was a few months away. He would, in due course, be slain, not in Perea but in Jerusalem. "I must walk to-day and to-morrow, and the third day; for it cannot be that a prophet perish out of Jerusalem," he said. And Luke added, "This he spake, signifying of his death."

Sacrifice Prepares Disciples for Salvation

(*Luke 14:25-35; JST, Luke 14:25-26, 28-31, 35-38*)

After giving the parable of the wedding guests and the parable of the great supper—both in the house of one of the chief Pharisees—Jesus "departed thence, and there went great multitudes with him." To these he taught the law of sacrifice required of all disciples. Better for these throngs if they turned back now unless they were ready to pay the full price of discipleship. Better for them to remain with such light as they had in the dead law of the dead past, unless they were prepared to lay their all, including their very lives, upon the altar of sacrifice.

> *If any man come to me, and hate not his father, and mother, and wife, and children, and brethren, and sisters, or husband, yea and his own life also; or in other words, is afraid to lay down his life for my sake, cannot be my disciple.*

"A true disciple, if called upon to do so, forsakes all—riches, home, friends, family, even his own life—in the Master's Cause." (*Commentary* 1:503.) "And whoso is not willing to lay down his life for my sake is not my disciple." (D&C 103:28.) Are they even to hate their family members? "Not hate in the sense of intense aversion or abhorrence; such is contrary to the whole spirit and tenor of the gospel. Men are to love their enemies, to say nothing of their own flesh and blood. Rather, the sense and meaning of Jesus' present instruction is that true disciples have a duty toward God which takes precedence over any family or personal obligation." (*Commentary* 1:503.)

> *And whosoever doth not bear his cross, and come after me, cannot be my disciple. Wherefore, settle this in your hearts, that ye will do the things which I shall teach, and command you.*

Only those who make up their minds to do so—come what may come—have power to keep the commandments in times of trial and tribulation. To dramatize his teaching "that converts should count the cost *before* joining the Church; that they should come into the kingdom only if they are prepared to make the sacrifices required; that they should go the whole way in the gospel cause, or stay out entirely; that they 'not . . . follow him, unless' they are 'able to continue' in his word, to 'do the things' which he teaches and commands" (*Commentary* 1:504)—Jesus now gives two parables, the parable of the rash builder and the parable of the rash king.

> *For which of you intending to build a tower, sitteth not down first, and counteth the cost, whether he have money to finish his work? Lest, unhappily, after he has laid the foundation and is not able to finish his work, all who behold, begin to mock him, Saying, This man began to build, and was not able to finish.*

"And this he said," Luke tells us, "signifying there should not any man follow him, unless he was able to continue."

> *Or what king, going to make war against another king, sitteth not down first, and consulteth whether he be able with ten thousand to meet him that cometh against him with twenty thousand? Or else, while the other is yet a great way off, he sendeth an ambassage, and desireth conditions of peace.*

Then, by way of conclusion to the whole matter, Jesus said:

> *So likewise, whosoever he be of you that forsaketh not all that he hath, he cannot be my disciple.*

All that he hath! Possessions, family, life itself—all things—must be forsaken, if to retain them means losing the gospel and eternal life.[1]

These teachings that men must forsake all and follow Christ raise again the issue of Moses and his law. They crystallize in the Jewish mind the essential contrariety of their whole system of worship and the new doctrine proclaimed by this man who is neither a priest, nor a Levite, nor a scribe, nor a Pharisee, nor even, as they suppose, a follower of Moses, the man of God. It is time, as his antagonists reason, to ask again the question that will remind the people, as they also suppose, that there is no need for this Nazarene because they already have Moses and the plan of salvation set forth in the law that he gave. Accordingly, "certain of them came to him, saying, Good Master, we have Moses and the prophets, and whosoever shall live by them, shall he not have life?"

Salvation is available through Moses and his law! What need is there for you and your teachings? We have the sayings of all the seers, the prophecies of all the prophets, the ordinances and sacrifices ordained by Jehovah; what more do we need? Our fathers were saved because of Moses and the prophets; surely we also shall gain eternal life in the same way. Such was their reasoning. To it Jesus could make but one reply.

> *Ye know not Moses, neither the prophets; for if ye had known them, ye would have believed on me; for to this intent they were written. For I am sent that ye might have life.*

It is the age-old answer to the age-old heresy. Apostate peoples always look back to their fathers; always suppose they are treading where the saints have trod; always reject new prophets who seem to them to teach a new doctrine that differs from their traditions. And the answer always is: The old prophets foretold the coming of the new ones, and if men believed the ancient scriptures they would accept the new revelations that come in their day. And, in the case of Jesus, not only did Moses and all the prophets foretell his ministry and mission, but also, in his case he, and he alone, had come to make eternal life available for all men because he was the Son of God.

"Therefore I will liken it unto salt which is good," he continues; "But if the salt has lost its savor, wherewith shall it be seasoned? It is neither fit for the land, nor yet for the dung hill; men cast it out. He who hath ears to hear, let him hear." Luke adds: "These things he said, signifying that which was written, verily must all be fulfilled."

Thus we have Jesus saying in effect:

"1. 'Ye do err, for ye neither know nor understand the teachings of Moses or the prophets. If ye understood their teachings, ye would believe in me, for all their teachings were given to prepare men for my coming and the salvation which I would bring.'

"2. 'Further, even assuming that ye believe Moses and the prophets, yet ye must turn to me, for "salvation doth not come by the law alone," for it is only in and through my atoning sacrifice that life and salvation come.'

"3. 'And now that I have come, the law of Moses has lost such saving power as it had; it has become as salt that has lost its savor and it cannot be seasoned again; yea, the law is dead in me, and from henceforth it is not fit for anything except to be cast out. He who hath ears to hear, let him hear.' " (*Commentary* 1:506.)

NOTE

1. Nowhere do we find a better statement of this, the law of sacrifice, than that set forth by the Prophet Joseph Smith in these words: "For a man to lay down his all, his character and reputation, his honor, and applause, his good name among men, his houses, his lands, his brothers and sisters, his wife and children, and even his own life also—counting all things but filth and dross for the excellency of the knowledge of Jesus Christ—requires more than mere belief or supposition that he is doing the will of God; but actual knowledge, realizing that, when these sufferings are ended, he will enter into eternal rest, and be a partaker of the glory of God. . . .

"A religion that does not require the sacrifice of all things never has power sufficient to produce the faith necessary [to lead] unto life and salvation; for, from the first existence of man, the faith necessary unto the enjoyment of life and salvation never could be obtained without the sacrifice of all earthly things. It was through this sacrifice, and this only, that God has ordained that men should enjoy eternal life; and it is through the medium of the sacrifice of all earthly things that men do actually know that they are doing the things that are well pleasing in the sight of God. When a man has offered in sacrifice all that he has for the truth's sake, not even withholding his life, and believing before God that he has been called to make this sacrifice because he seeks to do his will, he does know, most assuredly, that God does and will accept his sacrifice and offering, and that he has not, or will not seek his face in vain. Under these circumstances, then, he can obtain the faith necessary for him to lay hold on eternal life.

"It is vain for persons to fancy to themselves that they are heirs with those, or can be heirs with them, who have offered their all in sacrifice, and by this means obtained faith in God and favor with him so as to obtain eternal life, unless they, in like manner, offer unto him the same sacrifice, and through that offering obtain the knowledge that they are accepted of him. . . .

"From the days of righteous Abel to the present time, the knowledge that men have that they are accepted in the sight of God is obtained by offering sacrifice. . . .

"Those, then, who make the sacrifice, will have the testimony that their course is pleasing in the sight of God; and those who have this testimony will have faith to lay hold on eternal life; and will be enabled, through faith, to endure unto the end, and receive the crown that is laid up for them that love the appearing of our Lord Jesus Christ. But those who do not make the sacrifice cannot enjoy this faith, because men are dependent upon this sacrifice in order to obtain this faith: therefore, they cannot lay hold upon eternal life, because the revelations of God do not guarantee unto them the authority so to do, and without this guarantee faith could not exist." (*Lectures on Faith,* pp. 58-60.)

THE LOST SHEEP, COIN, AND SON

Ye feed not the flock.
The diseased have ye not strengthened,
neither have ye healed that which was sick,
neither have ye bound up that which was broken,
neither have ye brought again
that which was driven away,
neither have ye sought that which was lost.
(Ezek. 34:3-4.)

Parable of the Lost Sheep

(*Matthew 18:11-14; JST, Matthew 18:11; Luke 15:1-7; JST, Luke 15:1, 4*)

We have no doubt that Jesus gave all of the parables many times. It strains the bands of sense and reason to suppose that each of his wise sayings was spoken only once. He came to preach the gospel and to save sinners, and the same message saves all men in all situations. If there were Galileans near Capernaum who were entitled to hear the Sermon on the Mount, surely there were Judeans near Jerusalem to whom the same words should be spoken. The Gospel authors repeatedly mention that Jesus was teaching and healing, but only occasionally do they record what he said or describe the cures he performed.

As to the parable of the lost sheep, we know he gave it twice, once in Galilee in response to claims of preeminence by those who wanted to be first in the kingdom of God, and later in Perea in response to murmurings that he ate with publicans and sinners. On that occasion in Capernaum he placed a little child in the midst of the disciples and taught them that they must become as little children in order to enter into the kingdom of heaven. "For the Son of Man is come to save that which was lost, and to call sinners to repentance; but these little ones have no need of repentance, and I will save them," he said. Then, with reference to those who are accountable for their sins, he asked:

> *How think ye? if a man have an hundred sheep, and one of them be gone astray, doth he not leave the ninety and nine, and goeth into the mountains, and seeketh that which is gone astray?*

He is speaking as the Good Shepherd; he is making himself the pattern. He has come to save the "little ones" who otherwise would be lost. "The emphasis is on keeping the sheep from getting lost, on showing how precious the sheep are, and on how reluctant the Shepherd is to lose even one." (*Commentary* 1:508.) And as he, the Chief Shepherd, does, so also should we do who are his servant-shepherds.

> *And if so be that he find it, verily I say unto you he rejoiceth more of that sheep, than of the ninety and nine which went not astray.*
>
> *Even so it is not the will of your Father which is in heaven, that one of these little ones should perish.*

In Perea the setting and tone are different. Jesus is consorting with publicans and sinners—eating at their tables, teaching in their homes, offering to such despised and lowly ones the same truths he made available to the noble and the great. Such is contrary to Rabbinical standards; these social outcasts are to be shunned, not received as equals. "And the Pharisees and scribes murmured, saying, This man receiveth sinners, and eateth with them."

To these complaining, self-esteeming ones, Jesus asked

which of them would not search for his one lost sheep and, finding it, place it on his shoulders with rejoicing.[1]

> *And when he cometh home, he calleth together his friends and neighbours, saying unto them, Rejoice with me; for I have found my sheep which was lost.*
>
> *I say unto you, that likewise joy shall be in heaven over one sinner that repenteth, more than over ninety and nine just persons, which need no repentance.*

"This time the Master Teacher places the emphasis on finding that which is lost; he shows the length the Shepherd will go to find the sheep and the rejoicing that takes place when the lost is found. This time, in applying the parable, the complaining religious leaders, who considered themselves as just men needing no repentance, become the shepherds who should have been doing what the Chief Shepherd was doing—seeking to find and save that which was lost." (*Commentary* 1:508.)

Jesus is speaking to Jews—to scribes and Pharisees in particular—and they and their friends and neighbors all rejoice when a lost sheep is found. Such was the practice. But what about the saving of a lost soul? Are there any like feelings when such occurs? We cannot, of course, answer as to the feelings of rejoicing that may have been in the hearts of individual Jews when Gentiles were converted, but we can quote the Rabbinic word that has come down to us. It is: "There is joy before God when those who provoke Him perish from the world." (Edersheim 2:256.) What a contrast this is to the gospel view of joy in heaven when a sinner repents!

It is not unlikely that Jesus, in the Perean rendition of this parable, was contrasting their rejoicing over their sheep with their almost total indifference toward human souls, even as he had recently contrasted their concern for thirsty cattle with the physical well-being of diseased and crippled humans.

Parable of the Lost Coin
(*Luke 15:8-10*)

As a second illustration of the joy in the heavenly kingdom that results from the reclaiming of a lost member of the earthly kingdom, Jesus gave the parable of the lost coin:

> *Either what woman having ten pieces of silver, if she lose one piece, doth not light a candle, and sweep the house, and seek diligently till she find it? And when she hath found it, she calleth her friends and her neighbours together, saying, Rejoice with me; for I have found the piece which I had lost.*[2]
>
> *Likewise, I say unto you, there is joy in the presence of the angels of God over one sinner that repenteth.*

The lost sheep strayed from the fold by choice, seeking green pastures and still waters out in the deserts of the world. But the lost coin, a silver drachma, was lost through the inattention of the officers of the kingdom. The Lord's servants neglected their responsibility to care for the needs of the saints, and one of the saintly coins slipped to the floor and rolled into the dust in a dark corner where, except for diligent search, it would remain lost until swept out with the refuse.

"The woman who by lack of care lost the precious piece may be taken to represent the theocracy of the time, and the Church as an institution in any dispensational period; then the pieces of silver, every one a genuine coin of the realm, bearing the image of the great King, are the souls committed to the care of the Church; and the lost piece symbolizes the souls that are neglected and, for a time at least, lost sight of, by the authorized ministers of the gospel of Christ." (Talmage, p. 456.)

The angels rejoice! And why not? Are they not our brethren, children of the same Eternal Father? Who should have greater interest in the spiritual well-being of mortals than their immortal kin beyond the veil who are themselves also seeking that eternal life which consists in the perfecting of the eternal family unit?

Parable of the Prodigal Son
(*Luke 15:11-32*)

As a gem in a crown of gold, so is the parable of the prodigal son among the parables. Even Jesus' words are not all of equal splendor, and the Son of God in this parable climbs the mountain height. In wonder and reverence we view his terse eloquence.

> *A certain man had two sons: And the younger of them said to his father, Father, give me the portion of goods that falleth to me. And he divided unto them his living.*
>
> *And not many days after the younger son gathered all together, and took his journey into a far country, and there wasted his substance with riotous living.*

Each son received his portion; each was entitled, according to the Jewish law of inheritance, to a specified share of his father's possessions, though neither could claim it while the father lived. The eldest son received a double portion; the younger gained one-third of the movable property, which apparently is all that was bequeathed at this time. "The demand of the younger son for a portion of the patrimony, even during his father's lifetime, is an instance of deliberate and unfilial desertion; the duties of family cooperation had grown distasteful to him, and the wholesome discipline of the home had become irksome. He was determined to break away from all home ties, forgetful of what home had done for him and the debt of gratitude and duty by which he was morally bound. He went into a far country, and, as he thought, beyond the reach of his father's directing influence. He had his season of riotous living, of unrestrained indulgence and evil pleasure, through it all wasting his strength of body and mind, and squandering his father's substance; for what he had received had been given as a concession and not as the granting of any legal or just demand." (Talmage, p. 458.)

And when he had spent all, there arose a mighty famine in that land; and he began to be in want. And he went and joined himself to a citizen of that country; and he sent him into his fields to feed swine. And he would fain have filled his belly with the husks that the swine did eat: and no man gave unto him.

Divine Providence uses the forces of nature to humble the children of men and to lead them to repentance. Deity speaks to earth's inhabitants by "the voice of thunderings, and the voice of lightnings, and the voice of tempests, and the voice of the waves of the sea heaving themselves beyond their bounds." (D&C 88:90.) Here his voice is heard in "a mighty famine," which forces the hunger-driven younger son into the most degrading of all occupations—herding swine. Jews who kept swine were cursed, and the husks that these particular swine ate were totally unfit for human consumption. "The Jews detested swine so much, that they would only speak of a pig euphemistically as *dabhar acheer,* 'another thing.' The husks are the long bean-like pods of the carob-tree, or Egyptian fig. . . . They are stringy, sweetish, coarse, and utterly unfit for human sustenance. . . . The tree was called the 'locust-tree,' from the mistaken notion that its pods are the 'locusts' on which St. John fed." (Farrar, p. 328, footnote 1.)

And when he came to himself, he said, How many hired servants of my father's have bread enough and to spare, and I perish with hunger! I will arise and go to my father, and will say unto him, Father, I have sinned against heaven, and before thee, And am no more worthy to be called thy son: make me as one of thy hired servants.

"Where, in the entire range of human literature, sacred or profane, can anything be found so terse, so luminous, so full of infinite tenderness—so faithful in the picture which it furnishes of the consequences of sin, yet so merciful in the hope which it affords to amendment and penitence—as this little story? How does it summarise the consolations of religion and the sufferings of life! All sin and punishment, all penitence and forgiveness, find their best delineation in these few brief words. The radical differences of temperament and impulse which separate different classes of men—the spurious independence of a restless free-will—the preference of the enjoyments of the present to all hopes of the future—the wandering far away from that pure and peaceful region which is indeed our home, in order to let loose every lower passion in the riotous indulgence which dissipates the rarest gifts of life—the brief continuance of those fierce spasms of forbidden pleasure—the consuming hunger, the scorching thirst, the helpless slavery, the unutterable and uncompassionated degradation that must inevitably ensue—where have these myriad-times-repeated experiences of sin and sorrow been ever painted—though here painted in a few touches only—by a hand more tender and more true than in the picture of that foolish boy demanding prematurely the share which he claims of his father's goods; journeying into a far country, wasting his substance with riotous living; suffering from want in the mighty famine; forced to submit to the foul infamy of feeding swine, and fain to fill his belly with the swine-husks which no man gave? And then the coming to himself, the memory of his father's meanest servants who had enough and to spare, the return homewards, the agonised confession, the humble, contrite, heart-broken entreaty, and that never-to-be-equalled climax which, like the sweet voice from heaven, has touched so many million hearts to penitence and tears." (Farrar, pp. 327-28.)

And he arose, and came to his father. But when he was yet a great way off, his father saw him, and had compassion, and ran, and fell on his neck, and kissed him. And the son said unto him, Father, I have sinned against heaven, and in thy sight, and am no more worthy to be called thy son.[3]

The father, who yet loved his wayward son, was waiting, hoping, praying for his return. He has a fatted calf in the stall for a planned feast; now he sees the erring one a great way off, hastens to him, and greets him with tender compassion. The son confesses his sins—without which forgiveness cannot come—and because he has been so graciously received as a son, he does not make the contemplated offer to serve in a menial capacity as a hired servant. The two of them return to the home.

But the father said to his servants, Bring forth the best robe, and put it on him; and put a ring on his hand, and shoes on his feet: And bring hither the fatted calf, and kill it; and let us eat, and be merry: For this my son was dead, and is alive again; he was lost, and is found. And they began to be merry.

Back came the prodigal, into the household, as a member of the family; back he came to a position of honor and dignity, where his wants and needs would be cared for by the servants; back came the repentant son—not to inherit all that his father had, for such was reserved for the faithful son who had served during the heat of the day, but back he came from reveling with harlots, eating husks, and wallowing in a pigsty to his place with the family in the ancestral home. From his back the servants took the ragged, tattered, and coarse garb of the swineherd and replaced it with a choice *stola,* the upper garment of the higher classes. On his finger went the ring of a ruler, and his bare and mire-encrusted feet were cleansed and shod with sandals. Thus crowned with the three symbols of wealth and position—the robe, the ring, and the shoes—he joined in eating the fatted calf and making merry with the family. A lost sheep had returned to the sheepcote.

Now his elder son was in the field: and as he came and drew nigh to the house, he heard musick and dancing. And he called one of the servants, and asked what these things meant. And he said unto him, Thy brother is come; and thy father hath killed the fatted calf, because he hath received him safe and sound.

And he was angry, and would not go in: therefore came his father out, and intreated him. And he answering said to his father, Lo, these many years do I serve thee, neither transgressed I at any time thy commandment: and yet thou never gavest me a kid, that I might make merry with my friends: But as soon as this thy son was come, which hath devoured thy living with harlots, thou hast killed for him the fatted calf.

"Never certainly in human language was so much—such a world of love and wisdom and tenderness—compressed into such few immortal words. Every line, every touch of the picture is full of beautiful eternal significance. The poor boy's presumptuous claim for all that life could give him—the leaving of the old home—the journey to a far country—the brief spasm of 'enjoyment' there—the mighty famine in that land—the premature exhaustion of all that could make life noble and endurable—the abysmal degradation and unutterable misery that followed—the coming to himself, and recollection of all that he had left behind—the return in heart-broken penitence and deep humility—the father's far-off sight of him, and the gush of compassion and tenderness over this poor returning prodigal—the ringing joy of the whole household over him who had been loved and lost, and had now come home—the unjust jealousy and mean complaint of the elder brother—and then that close of the parable in a strain of music—"

And he said unto him, Son, thou art ever with me, and all that I have is thine. It was meet that we should make merry, and be glad: for this thy brother was dead, and is alive again; and was lost, and is found.

"All this is indeed a divine epitome of the wandering of man and the love of God such as no literature has ever equalled, such as no ear of man has ever heard elsewhere. Put in the one scale all that Confucius, or Sakaya Mouni, or

Zoroaster, or Socrates ever wrote or said—and they wrote and said many beautiful and holy words—and put in the other the Parable of the Prodigal Son alone, with all that this single parable connotes and means, and can any candid spirit doubt which scale would outweigh the other in eternal preciousness—in divine adaptation to the wants of man?" (Farrar, p. 483.)

"*All that I have is thine!*" The elder and younger sons no longer stand on a plane of equality. Though received back to honor and dignity, the erstwhile wayward one does not receive all that his father hath; though he wears the *stola*, has a ring on his finger, and is shod with sandals, he does not reign on the throne, nor exercise control, rulership, and dominion in the place and stead of the father. Such an inheritance is reserved for the one whose service and devotion merit that inestimably great inheritance.[4]

NOTES

1. "The Midrash relates how, when Moses fed the sheep of Jethro in the wilderness, and a kid had gone astray, he went after it, and found it drinking at a spring. As he thought it might be weary, he laid it on his shoulder and brought it back, when God said that, because he had shown pity on the sheep of a man, He would give Him his own sheep, Israel, to feed." (Edersheim 2:257-58.)

2. From the Midrash we learn, as "a Rabbi notes, that, if a man had lost a *Sela* (drachm) or anything else of value in his house, he would light ever so many lights till he had found what provides for only one hour in this world. How much more, then, should he search, as for hidden treasures, for the words of the Law, on which depends the life of this and of the world to come!" (Edersheim 2:258.)

3. "As marking the absolute contrast between the teaching of Christ and of Rabbinism, . . . we have in one of the oldest Rabbinic works a Parable exactly the reverse of this, when the son of a friend is redeemed from bondage, not as a son, but to be a slave, that so obedience might be demanded of him. The inference drawn is, that the obedience of the redeemed is not that of filial love of the pardoned, but the enforcement of the claim of a master. How otherwise in the Parable and teaching of Christ!" (Edersheim 2:262.)

4. Speaking of those who magnify their callings in the Holy Priesthood and who are thereby true and faithful in all things, fulfilling all the terms and conditions of their priesthood covenant, the Lord promises: "All that my Father hath shall be given unto" them. (D&C 84:33-40.) All that the Father hath is eternal life or exaltation; it is to inherit, receive, and possess that which the Father now has and to be like him. Such was the promise to the elder son in this parable of parables.

THE TWO PECULIAR PARABLES

Give ear, O my people, to my law:
incline your ears to the words of my mouth.
I will open my mouth in a parable:
I will utter dark sayings. (Ps. 78:1-2.)

Parable of the Unjust Steward
(*Luke 16:1-13*)

This parable and that of Lazarus and the rich man are difficult to understand, sow seeds of confusion and uncertainty among sectarian scripturalists, and in fact can only be understood by the saints as they are enlightened by the power of the Holy Spirit. In them Jesus opens his mouth to "utter dark sayings," as far as the scriptural exegetes of the world are concerned. But both of them, when received and understood for what they are, shed wondrous light on glorious gospel verities.

The parable of the unjust steward was spoken to the disciples, to members of the Church—to the publicans and sinners who now followed Jesus, to the extreme annoyance and displeasure of the Pharisees—and was intended not to countenance their prior evil deeds, but to show what they could learn from their previous life of sin.

There was a certain rich man, which had a steward;

and the same was accused unto him that he had wasted his goods. And he called him, and said unto him,

How is it that I hear this of thee? give an account of thy stewardship; for thou mayest be no longer steward.

As Eliezer of Damascus ruled over all that Abraham possessed, so was this steward the overseer of all his master's property. But unlike Eliezer, to whom Abraham entrusted the high duty of getting Rebekah as a wife for Isaac, our unnamed steward was untrue to his trust. He squandered his master's money and wasted his goods, perhaps in riotous living. Summoned before his employer, he made no defense, was discharged, and was given time to get his accounts in order for his successor.

Then the steward said within himself, What shall I do? for my lord taketh away from me the stewardship: I cannot dig; to beg I am ashamed. I am resolved what to do, that, when I am put out of the stewardship, they may receive me into their houses.

So he called every one of his lord's debtors unto him, and said unto the first, How much owest thou unto my lord? And he said, An hundred measures of oil. And he said unto him, Take thy bill, and sit down quickly, and write fifty. Then said he to another, And how much owest thou? And he said, An hundred measures of wheat. And he said unto him, Take thy bill, and write fourscore.

And the lord commended the unjust steward, because he had done wisely: for the children of this world are in their generation wiser than the children of light.

Here we see an unjust servant, an unrighteous steward—an evil Eliezer—violating every standard of honesty and integrity. His acts are within the letter of the law, for his power of attorney is still in force, and he can still buy and sell and contract at will. But he defrauds his employer and enriches the debtors, who he is confident will feel an obligation to favor him in future business arrangements. For such conduct we would anticipate, at the least, a severe rebuke, and, more likely, an attempt at legal prosecution. Instead we hear praise for his wise and prudent acts, with which conclusion Jesus concurs as he gives this moral: "For the children of this world are in their generation wiser than the children of light."

Having spiritual insight, the disciples to whom the dissertation has come could not have failed to see in this parable an endorsement, not of dishonesty and perfidy, but of worldly sagacity and wisdom in caring for one's own interests. To claim it, as some have done, as a parable that commends and sanctions cheating simply shows how far afield uninspired commentators can go. But now we hear how Jesus himself interpreted and applied the account.

> *And I say unto you, Make to yourself friends of the mammon of unrighteousness; that, when ye fail, they may receive you into everlasting habitations.*

"Our Lord's purpose was to show the contrast between the care, thoughtfulness, and devotion of men engaged in the money-making affairs of earth, and the half-hearted ways of many who are professedly striving after spiritual riches. Worldly-minded men do not neglect provision for their future years, and often are sinfully eager to amass plenty; while the 'children of light,' or those who believe spiritual wealth to be above all earthly possessions, are less energetic, prudent, or wise. By 'mammon of unrighteousness' we may understand material wealth or worldly things. . . .

"If the wicked steward, when cast out from his master's house because of unworthiness, might hope to be received into the homes of those whom he had favored, how much more confidently may they who are genuinely devoted to the right hope to be received into the everlasting mansions of God!"

> *He that is faithful in that which is least is faithful also in much: and he that is unjust in the least is unjust also in much. If therefore ye have not been faithful in*

the unrighteous mammon, who will commit to your trust the true riches? And if ye have not been faithful in that which is another man's, who shall give you that which is your own?

No servant can serve two masters: for either he will hate the one, and love the other; or else he will hold to the one, and despise the other. Ye cannot serve God and mammon.

"Make such use of your wealth as shall insure you friends hereafter. Be diligent; for the day in which you can use earthly riches will soon pass. Take a lesson from even the dishonest and the evil; if they are so prudent as to provide for the only future they think of, how much more should you, who believe in an eternal future, provide therefor! If you have not learned wisdom and prudence in the use of 'unrighteous mammon,' how can you be trusted with the more enduring riches? If you have not learned how to use properly the wealth of another, which has been committed to you as a steward, how can you expect to be successful in the handling of great wealth should such be given you as your own? Emulate the unjust steward and the lovers of mammon, not in their dishonesty, cupidity, and miserly hoarding of the wealth that is at best but transitory, but in their zeal, forethought, and provision for the future. Moreover, let not wealth become your master; keep it to its place as a servant." (Talmage, pp. 463-64.)

The Law and the Prophets Testify of Christ

(*Luke 16:14-18; JST, Luke 16:16-18, 20-23*)

Never in all history was there a people unto whom God sent his word, by the mouths of his servants the prophets, who were left so completely without excuse for their disbelief as were these Jews. They had the law and the prophets; the scriptures lay open before them; the mind and will of the Lord was recorded for all to read. And the man of whom the ancient records taught stood among them, spake as never man spake, performed miracles as none other had ever done, and lived and was as only God's Son could live and be. And yet their sins led them to reject him.

He has just taught his disciples, among whom are repentant publicans—and sinners—a group detested by the Pharisees—that to gain a heavenly reward they must use their earthly wealth in accordance with gospel standards. If men cannot be faithful in handling the unrighteous mammon—the things of this world—why should they think their heavenly Father will place in their hands the true riches of eternity?

Mingling with the disciples, and also hearing the parable of the unjust steward, were pious Pharisees who loved money and had their hearts set on the mammon of unrighteousness. They were covetous, grasping, avaricious. To cheat in business was a way of life with them.[1] And their reaction to Jesus' instruction on the proper use of wealth was to scoff and sneer and deride. In response Jesus said: "Ye are they which justify yourselves before men; for that which is highly esteemed among men is abomination in the sight of God."

These words, coming with a voice of authority, from one having authority, stand as a divine rejection of them and their way of life. Either they must be refuted or these Pharisees stand condemned before their race; and the sole means of overthrowing a divinely inspired prophetic utterance is to attack the prophet. If the word came from God, it is true; if the prophet can be rejected, his words fall with him. And so, "they said unto him, We have the law, and the prophets; but as for this man we will not receive him to be our ruler; for he maketh himself to be a judge over us."

How often they have taken this approach: 'What need have we for Jesus and his new doctrine? His gospel is a needless appendage to our system of religion; we already have the plan of salvation as given by Moses and all the prophets. As for this man Jesus, he and his doctrine are nothing to us.'

To such rebellious feelings, testimony mingled with doctrine is the only perfect answer. Thus Jesus says:

> *The law and the prophets testify of me; yea, and all the prophets who have written, even until John, have foretold of these days. Since that time, the kingdom of God is preached, and every man who seeketh truth presseth into it.*

By definition and in its very nature, a prophet is one to whom the Holy Ghost reveals that Jesus Christ is the Son of God. The testimony of Jesus is the spirit of prophecy. Every prophet from Adam to John foretold the coming of him who then preached in their streets and ate at their tables. Had they not done so, they would not have been prophets. But now the new kingdom is being proclaimed, and every man who seeketh truth, who desires righteousness, who yearns for salvation—all such come and join the Church.

> *And why teach ye the law, and deny that which is written; and condemn him whom the Father hath sent to fulfill the law, that you might all be redeemed?*
>
> *O fools! for you have said in your hearts, There is no God. And you pervert the right way; and the kingdom of heaven suffereth violence of you; and you persecute the meek; and in your violence you seek to destroy the kingdom; and ye take the children of the kingdom by force. Woe unto you, ye adulterers!*

To all this—their condemning of the One who came to fulfill the law; the announcement that he had come to redeem them; the assertion that in their hearts they did not even believe in God; the charges of perverting the truth, of persecuting the Church, of using violence against the kingdom, of physically assaulting his disciples—to all this they gave no heed. Passing over their whole Satan-guided rejection of him, his laws, and his new kingdom—let these things be as they were—they came to the one thing that gave them supreme offense. He said they were adulterers. All else for which they were arraigned was openly known and could not be denied. Their immoral acts, however, were done in secret; and because Jesus lifted this veil and charged them openly with sex immorality, they reviled him. His response was to single out certain acts of adultery that were public knowledge, and that we shall consider later in connection with his teachings on marriage and divorce. He said:

> *Whosoever putteth away his wife, and marrieth another, committeth adultery; and whosoever marrieth her who is put away from her husband, committeth adultery.*

Such, then, were the words and feelings that called forth the parable of Lazarus and the rich man.

Parable of Lazarus and the Rich Man

(*Luke 16:19-31; JST, Luke 16:23-24*)

Jesus is facing his Pharisaic foes. Because of their love of money, their obdurate refusal to accept him, and their vicious persecution of his disciples, he is speaking sharp and stinging words. He calls them fools and adulterers. Then to climax his acrid and harsh sayings against these imperious self-exaltants who worship the mammon of unrighteousness, he says:

> *Verily I say unto you, I will liken you unto the rich man. For there was a certain rich man, who was clothed in purple, and fine linen, and fared sumptuously every day.*
>
> *And there was a certain beggar named Lazarus, which was laid at his gate, full of sores, And desiring to be fed with the crumbs which fell from the rich man's table: moreover the dogs came and licked his sores.*

Two more extreme opposites could scarcely have been chosen. A rich Pharisee, not so much as dignified by name, revels in wealth and luxury. His linen apparel and his upper garment, dyed a royal and costly violet-purple, are his constant dress. He banquets daily on all the delicacies money can buy. He is rich, powerful, and selfish, using his wealth to gratify his love of luxury. There is here none of that wise use of the mammon of unrighteousness which will prepare his soul for an everlasting inheritance.

On the other hand we see a poor, diseased beggar—one Lazarus by name, a name that means "God help him," and from which we derive the word *lazar*, meaning leper. He is laid at the gate of the opulent Pharisee, to beg, to plead, to cry out—along with the whining dogs—for crumbs that fall from the banquet board. Dressed in rags, burdened with disease, famished for want of food, he is seen by the lordly Pharisee, who worships before the great altar and makes broad his phylactery, but who has no dried crust of barley bread for his suffering fellow mortal. He is too immersed in the weighty things of wealth and in the intricacies of Mosaic performances to concern himself with a diseased and starving son of Abraham. And the dogs lick Lazarus's sores, which neither alleviates the pain nor softens the suffering; the uninvited canines merely aggravate the ache.

Such, then, is the temporal and physical state of Lazarus, who, however, from what follows, we know to have been a morally upright and righteous person. And such also is the earthly state of the rich man, whom we have come to call Dives, such being the Latin designation for his state of riches. But one's earthly state, be he Lazarus or Dives, is transitory; and so Jesus continues:

> *And it came to pass, that the beggar died, and was carried by the angels into Abraham's bosom: the rich man also died, and was buried; And in hell he lift up his eyes, being in torments, and seeth Abraham afar off, and Lazarus in his bosom.*[2]

Then death came—as come it must to all—first to Lazarus, hastened by hunger and assured by disease; then to Dives, who lived out his days of wealth and worship and high self-esteem. But how different were their deaths. For Dives there was earthly pomp and ceremony, an embalmed corpse, a costly funeral with paid mourners, a carved tomb in a choice cave where marble statuary was placed. Lazarus, his body uncared for, unwrapped, without ointment or spices or embalming service, was hauled on a wooden cart to a pauper's grave in a potter's field.

So much for their mortal remains. As to their immortal spirits things were quite different. One went to paradise, the other to hell. Lazarus was carried by the angels to Abraham's bosom, there to mingle with prophets and patriarchs; there to find rest and peace from all care and sorrow; there to enjoy the companionship of the righteous of all past ages until the day of resurrection. Dives descended to hell, to Hades, to Sheol, to the spirit prison, to outer darkness, to a place of weeping and wailing and gnashing of teeth, a place where sinners sorrow and howl because of the torments that have come upon them. Nor can we refrain from reciting that revelation in which the Lord says: "If any man shall take of the abundance which I have made, and impart not his portion, according to the law of my gospel, unto the poor and the needy, he shall, with the wicked, lift up his eyes in hell, being in torment." (D&C 104:18.) Then Dives speaks:

> *And he cried and said, Father Abraham, have mercy on me, and send Lazarus, that he may dip the tip of his finger in water, and cool my tongue; for I am tormented in this flame.*
>
> *But Abraham said, Son, remember that thou in thy lifetime receivedst thy good things, and likewise Lazarus evil things: but now he is comforted, and thou art tormented.*
>
> *And beside all this, between us and you there is a great gulf fixed: so that they which would pass from hence to you cannot; neither can they pass to us, that would come from thence.*

How things have changed. The beggar on earth—whose body was pained with sores, whose belly cried out for food—now, well and whole, clothed in robes of righteousness, feasts on eternal bread in paradisiacal palaces. The rich man on earth—who rejoiced in the multitude of things that his soul possessed—now begs for a drop of water to cool the flame of tormented conscience that burns unchecked in his miserably small soul. Lazarus's mask of pain and poverty has been stripped away to reveal a healthy soul prepared to receive and manage the riches of eternity, while Dives's removed mask reveals the shriveled soul of a moral weakling who, now stripped of wealth and influence, suffers eternal pain in an eternal hell.[3]

And as they knew each other in mortality, so they remember their former acquaintanceship. But no longer are they accessible to each other so that one might minister to the needs of the other. Christ has not yet bridged the gulf between the prison and the palace, and there is as yet no communion between the righteous in paradise and the wicked in hell.

> *Then he said, I pray thee therefore, father, that thou wouldest send him to my father's house: For I have five brethren; that he may testify unto them, lest they also come into this place of torment.*
>
> *Abraham saith unto him, They have Moses and the prophets; let them hear them. And he said, Nay, father Abraham: but if one went unto them from the dead, they will repent.*
>
> *And he said unto him, If they hear not Moses and the prophets, neither will they be persuaded, though one rose from the dead.*

To pass from this life to the next, to die, as we are wont to say, simply means that the eternal spirit—wherein the mind of man is found, and which is the believing, knowing, sentient, intelligent part of the human personality—steps out of the mortal body and continues to live in another sphere. Beliefs do not change; prejudices remain; faith or its absence is still the order of the day. Those who believe the truth in this life believe it in the next; those who reject God's eternal laws here reflect that same rebellion hereafter. There may and will be repentance and changes in process of time, but there is no immediate change. Dives's five brethren—were they the five sons of Annas, the high priest, as some have speculated?—knew Jesus had raised the dead, and they did not believe in him. Why would they be converted if a ghostly apparition—which could be rationalized away as a misty nothingness—should appear to them? Faith does not come in that way. Only those who accept Moses and the prophets would have the spiritual insight to recognize what was involved should one rise from the dead. There is indeed a certain eternal finality connected with death. It is this day of life that is given to men to prepare for eternity, and the day of death is one of rejoicing for all the Lazaruses of life and a day of sorrow for all the Diveses of death.

Parable of the Unprofitable Servant
(Luke 17:1-10; JST, Luke 17:5-6, 9-10)

Jesus now has somewhat to say to his disciples about those who bring offenses, saying that it were better for them if a millstone were hanged about their necks and they drowned in the sea than that they should offend one of his little ones. This is a repetition of similar expressions made earlier in Capernaum that we have considered in chapter 66. He also repeats some counsel about rebuking and forgiving our erring brethren—"And if he trespass against thee seven times in a day, and seven times in a day turn again to thee, saying, I repent; thou shalt forgive him"—all of which we also considered in the Capernaum setting in chapter 67. Now the apostles say unto him: "Increase our faith." Only a brief sentence of what must have been an extended exposition is preserved for us by Luke, and then Jesus gives the parable of the unprofitable servant. As to faith he says:

> *If you had faith as a grain of mustard seed, you might say unto this sycamore tree, Be thou plucked up by the roots, and be thou planted in the sea; and it should obey you.*

We cannot doubt that Jesus on this and many occasions discoursed to the apostles, to all of his disciples, and to Jew and Gentile alike, that faith was the first principle of the gospel and that it came by obedience to those laws upon which its receipt is predicated.

Faith, the moving cause of all action in intelligent beings; faith, the hope in that which is not seen which is true; faith, the assurance of things hoped for, the evidence of things not seen; faith, the mighty, moving power by which the worlds were made and by which all things are upheld and sustained in their ordained spheres; faith, the power by which miracles are wrought, by which God's work goes forth, by which the gospel is preached and souls are saved; faith, the very power of the Lord Almighty himself—faith is power.

Faith is borne of knowledge and matures through righteousness. To gain faith unto life and salvation, men must first adopt the concept that God actually exists; they must have a correct idea of his character, perfections, and attributes; and they must obtain an actual knowledge that the course of life they are pursuing is according to his omnipotent will. These and many like things we know about faith; would that we knew all that Jesus said to the apostles on this occasion, for who can know too much about faith and righteousness? But now for the parable:

> *But which of you, having a servant plowing or feeding cattle, will say unto him by and by, when he is come from the field, Go and sit down to meat? And will not rather say unto him, Make ready wherewith I may sup, and gird thyself, and serve me, till I have eaten and drunken; and afterwards thou shalt eat and drink?*
>
> *Doth he thank that servant because he doeth the things which were commanded him? I say unto you, Nay. So likewise ye, when ye shall have done all those things which are commanded you, say, We are unprofitable servants. We have done that which was no more than our duty to do.*

Jesus thus teaches that his saints grow in faith by obedience and service in the kingdom; also, "that Deity has a claim upon the services of his saints, and that even though they serve him with all their hearts, mights, mind, and strength, yet they are unprofitable servants." (*Commentary* 1:527.) As to faith growing in the hearts of men, first the seed sprouts; then, as it is cared for, the plant grows and the fruit ripens; and finally the faithful saints pluck and eat the fruit of eternal life. As to faithful service that yet leaves the servant as unprofitable, how can it be expressed better than King Benjamin did it: "If ye should serve him who has created you from the beginning, and is preserving you from day to day, by lending you breath, that ye may live and move and do according to your own will, and even supporting you from one moment to another—I say, if ye should serve him with all your whole souls yet ye would be unprofitable servants. And behold, all that he requires of you is to keep his commandments; and he has promised you that if ye would keep his commandments ye should prosper in the land; and he never doth vary from that which he hath said; therefore, if ye do keep his commandments he doth bless you and prosper you. And now, in the first place, he hath created you, and granted unto you your lives, for which ye are indebted unto him. And secondly, he doth require that ye should do as he hath commanded you; for which if ye do, he doth immediately bless you; and therefore he hath paid you. And ye are still indebted unto him, and are, and will be, forever and ever; therefore, of what have ye to boast?" (Mosiah 2:21-24.)

NOTES

1. In an instructive footnote dealing with Pharisaic covetousness, Farrar says: "The vice of avarice seems inherent in the Jewish race. To this day, says Dr. Thomson, speaking of the Jews in Palestine, 'Everybody trades, speculates, cheats. The shepherd-boy on the mountain talks of *piastres* from morning till night; so does the muleteer on the road, the farmer in the field, the artisan in the shop, the merchant in his magazine, the pacha in his palace, the kadi in the hall of judgment, the mullah in the mosque, the monk, the priest, the bishop—money, money, money! the desire of every heart, the theme of every tongue, the end of every aim. Everything is bought and sold—each prayer has its price, each sin its tariff.' Quarrels about the money, complaints of the greed and embezzlement of the Rabbis, wrong distribution of the *chaluka,* or alms, and the *kadima,* or honorary pay, form the main history of the Jews in modern Jerusalem. It is a profoundly melancholy tale, and no

one who knows the facts will deny it—least of all pious and worthy Jews." (Farrar, p. 475, footnote 1.)

2. "Now, concerning the state of the soul between death and the resurrection—Behold, it has been made known unto me by an angel, that the spirits of all men, as soon as they are departed from this mortal body, yea, the spirits of all men, whether they be good or evil, are taken home to that God who gave them life. And then shall it come to pass, that the spirits of those who are righteous are received into a state of happiness, which is called paradise, a state of rest, a state of peace, where they shall rest from all their troubles and from all care, and sorrow. And then shall it come to pass, that the spirits of the wicked, yea, who are evil—for behold, they have no part nor portion of the Spirit of the Lord; for behold, they chose evil works rather than good; therefore the spirit of the devil did enter into them, and take possession of their house—and these shall be cast out into outer darkness; there shall be weeping, and wailing, and gnashing of teeth, and this because of their own iniquity, being led captive by the will of the devil. Now this is the state of the souls of the wicked, yea, in darkness, and a state of awful, fearful looking for the fiery indignation of the wrath of God upon them; thus they remain in this state, as well as the righteous in paradise, until the time of their resurrection." (Alma 40:11-14.)

3. In this connection, these words of *Chrysostom* are worthy of preservation: "For as on the stage some enter, assuming the masks of kings and captains, physicians and orators, philosophers and soldiers, being in truth nothing of the kind; so also in the present life, wealth and poverty are only masks. As then, when thou sittest in the theatre, and beholdest one playing below who sustains the part of a king, thou dost not count him happy, nor esteemest him a king, nor desirest to be such as he; but knowing him to be one of the common people, a ropemaker or a blacksmith, or some such a one as this, thou dost not esteem him happy for his mask, and his robe's sake, nor judgest of his condition from these, but holdest him cheap for the meanness of his true condition: so also, here sitting in the world as in a theatre, and beholding men playing as on a stage, when thou seest many rich, count them not to be truly rich, but to be wearing the masks of rich. For as he, who in the stage plays the king or captain, is often a slave, or one who sells figs or grapes in the market, so also this rich man is often in reality poorest of all. For if thou strip him of his mask, and unfold his conscience, and scrutinize his inward parts, thou wilt there find a great penury of virtue; thou wilt find him to be indeed the most abject of men. And as in the theatre, when evening is come and the spectators are departed, and the players are gone forth thence, having laid aside their masks and their dresses, then they who before showed as kings and captains to all, appear now as they truly are; so now, when death approaches and the audience is dismissed, all, laying aside the masks of wealth and poverty, depart from hence, and, being judged only by their works, appear some indeed truly rich, but some poor; and some glorious, but others without honor."

THE RAISING OF LAZARUS

For behold, this is my work and my glory—
to bring to pass the immortality
and eternal life of man.
(Moses 1:39.)

The Message That Lazarus Is Sick

(*John 11:1-6; JST, John 11:1-2, 6, 16*)

Who shall say what was the greatest miracle performed by the Man of Miracles during the years of his ministry? Clearly the most wondrous event of the ages was to bring to pass the immortality and eternal life of man. This he alone could do because God was his Father; and this he did do—commencing in Gethsemane when he sweat great drops of blood from every pore; continuing on the cross when he voluntarily gave up his life; and crowned in the Arimathean's tomb when his spirit entered again that body which never would see corruption.

What greater miracle did he perform than to come forth from the tomb; than to rise in glorious immortality; than to unite his body and spirit inseparably in the resurrected state? What miracle compares with that of passing on to all men the effects of his resurrection, so that all shall rise from death to life; so that all shall put off this corruption and put on incorruption; so that all shall rise from mortality to immortality? And what greater joy and attainment is there—miraculous joy and attainment—than to be raised in immortality and unto eternal life in the everlasting kingdom of the Everlasting Father?

But as to the miracles that mortals can perform—and how he labored and lived and loved in the full bloom and beauty of that mortality which is the happy lot of all the worthy offspring of the Father—as to these miracles, which was the greatest? Was it to open blind eyes, cast out devils, or cleanse lepers? Was it to calm storms, walk on water, or feed thousands with a few barley loaves and a little savory of fish? Or was it to raise from death the daughter of Jairus in Capernaum or the widow's son near Nain, thus giving life to cold corpses and calling back spirits from the realms of the departed?

Perhaps the greatest miracle is none of these; perhaps it is the healing of sin-sick souls so that those who are spiritually blind and deaf and diseased become again pure and clean and heirs of salvation. Perhaps the greatest miracle of all is that which happens in the life of each person who is born again; who receives the sanctifying power of the Holy Spirit of God in his life; who has sin and evil burned out of his soul as though by fire; who lives again spiritually, and, perchance, if need be, is also healed physically.

With these words of introduction we now turn to the raising of Lazarus from death. We shall hear and see and feel what the Lord of Life—and blessed be his name—chose to do near Bethany of Judea a short while before he also chose to lay down his own life and take it up again at Jerusalem. We shall seek to tune our spirits to his as he performs what has become known as the miracle of miracles—this raising of Lazarus—the miracle that he singled out as the chief one to bear witness that he is the resurrection and the life; that by him immortality and eternal life come; and that he would in due course perform the infinitely and miraculously great atoning sacrifice. And as we weep with the mourners, including Jesus himself, and rejoice with the faithful when a decomposing body again becomes the tenement of an eternal spirit, perhaps we shall envision why this miracle stands preeminent over them all.

Now Lazarus lived in the town of Bethany some two miles east of Jerusalem, but hidden from the Holy City by a spur of the mount of Olives. There also dwelt in this Judean village of blessed memory the beloved sisters Mary and Martha, in whose family circle the Lord Jesus so often found surcease from toil and rest from his labors. They and their brother Lazarus were three of the most intimate friends Jesus had on earth. Of this intimacy we shall speak more particularly when we see Mary, just before the Fourth Passover, anoint Jesus' feet with very costly spikenard. At this time Mary "lived with her sister Martha, in whose house her brother Lazarus was sick." Whether Lazarus at this time was married and had a family of his own, we know not, only that in connection with this illness the industrious and compassionate Martha was caring for him in her home. If he was about the age of Jesus, the custom of the day would have required him long since to assume the normal familial responsibilities.

Jesus is in Perea at least a score of miles away, perhaps more, but his whereabouts are known to the two sisters in Bethany. We cannot escape the conclusion that they kept in touch with each other as friends and intimates normally do. From the two sisters came this message: "Lord, behold, he whom thou lovest is sick." Perhaps the messenger also said, 'It is urgent that you come immediately, for Lazarus lieth at the door of death. He cannot last much longer; only you can heal him.' The fact is, by that time Lazarus was dead and his body lay in a tomb, which thing Jesus must have known by the power of inspiration. It would take one day for the messenger to travel from Bethany to Perea and find Jesus. Our Lord then remained two days, teaching and ministering among the people, without apparent concern for his beloved friend; it took him another day to reach the Judean town, and when he finally arrived Lazarus had lain four days in the grave.

"This sickness is not unto death," Jesus said, "but for the glory of God, that the Son of God might be glorified thereby." No doubt the messenger returned bearing this somewhat enigmatic reply, which meant, as the subsequent events witness, 'Lazarus shall die—nay, has already passed from life to death—but he shall not remain long in the tomb. His passing was for the glory of God. At my command he shall return to mortality to stand as a witness to all generations that I am the Son of God and have power over life and death. He shall live again as a sign that he and all men shall rise in the resurrection because of me, for I am the resurrection and the life.'

Lazarus's sickness was "for the glory of God"! Shall we not set it forth plainly? Lazarus was foreordained to die; it was part of the eternal plan. His spirit must separate from its mortal tenement; it must remain in paradise until the tabernacle of clay began to decay, until corruption and decomposition were well under way. Then his destiny was to live again; to take up a physically renewed mortal body; to dwell again in mortality, from which temporal state he could escape only by dying again.

One wonders why this beloved friend of Jesus was not chosen as one of the Twelve. One answer is that he may have been at a later time, filling a vacancy caused by the martyrdom of one of the original special witnesses. Or Lazarus may have been one of the Seventy; or his may have been a special work that would heap upon him respect and renown in all ages, as is the case with many of the Lord's valiant servants today who serve neither in the Twelve nor among the Seventy.

When Jesus' work in Perea was finished; when sufficient time had elapsed for the purposes of the Father to be fulfilled in Lazarus's death; when he had "tarried two days, after he heard that Lazarus was sick"—then our Lord said: "Let us go into Judea again." Such a course was fraught with peril. His disciples remonstrated with him: "Master, the Jews of late sought to stone thee; and goest thou thither again?" Jesus, using figurative language, attempted to calm their fears:

> *Are there not twelve hours in the day? If any man walk in the day, he stumbleth not, because he seeth the light of the world. But if a man walk in the night, he stumbleth, because there is no light in him.*

"During the twelve hours of His day of work He could walk in safety, for the light of His duty, which was the will of His Heavenly Father, would keep Him from danger." (Farrar, p. 506.) 'Though it be the eleventh hour of my life, yet there are twelve hours in the day, and during that designated period, I shall do the work appointed me without stumbling or faltering. This is the time given me to do my work. During the appointed day I shall walk in safety; my Father will preserve me. I cannot wait for the night when perchance the opposition will die down. He that shirks his responsibilities and puts off his labors until the night shall stumble in darkness and his work shall fail.'

Then, that they might more fully understand, he said: "Our friend Lazarus sleepeth; but I go, that I may awake him out of sleep." Though it was as common a figure among the Jews as it is among us to speak of those who have passed away as being asleep; though this was the obvious meaning of Jesus' statement, otherwise anyone could have awakened him and Jesus' presence would not have been needed; and though they knew he had raised the sleeping dead on at least two previous occasions—yet the disciples failed to grasp his meaning. "Lord, if he sleep, he shall do well," they said.

"Then said Jesus unto them plainly, Lazarus is dead. And I am glad for your sakes that I was not there, to the intent ye may believe; nevertheless let us go unto him." What Jesus will soon do will be a witness of his own divine Sonship that none, either in that day or this, can reject without losing his soul. It will be done in such a way that none can fail to envision the event or avoid discerning its meaning. None but a God can do what he is about to do.

Seeing, then, that he is determined to go, Thomas, who was willing to lay down his life in the gospel cause, but who had failed to understand Jesus' statement that he would be preserved during the appointed twelve hours of his mortal ministry, said to the group: "Let us also go, that we may die with him." As soon would be evident, however, Jesus' death must await the time of the coming Passover, and the martyrdom of Thomas and the others must not take place until after the apostolic witness of a resurrection has been borne to the nations of the world.

And so the holy party went to the Judean town of Bethany, there to become witnesses of the miracle of miracles, the raising of Lazarus after four days of death.

"Lazarus, Come Forth"

(*John 11:17-46; JST, John 11:17, 29*)

"And when Jesus came to Bethany, to Martha's house, Lazarus had already been in the grave four days." Such was part of the divine program. After four days, according to Jewish tradition, the spirit no longer remained near his erstwhile tenement, and the uninhabited corpse was considered as the dust of the earth. Decay and decomposition were in full swing; the finality of death was a reality; mourning and weeping would continue for thirty days, as the lives of the living adjusted to an existence without the presence of the dead one.

From all that is written about them, it is clear that the two sisters and their brother were part of a prominent family that was amply endowed with this world's goods. Lazarus, therefore, his body having been anointed with myrtle, aloes, and many spices, was laid in a cave or rock-hewn tomb, probably in a garden, as befitted his station in life. Even those of moderate means had their own private burial places, which were passed on to their heirs as was the case with all realty.

Many friends of the family had come out from Jerusalem to comfort the bereaved sisters. Though all the family members were disciples, whose belief in Christ was openly avowed, they had not as yet been put out of the synagogue and made subject to the penalties and persecutions of excommunication. Had Lazarus been esteemed as an apostate of Judaism, his death would have called for demonstrations, not of mourning but of rejoicing, from his Jewish neighbors and associates. But here we find hosts of people participating in the overly ostentatious weepings and howlings that substituted for genuine mourning in that day. We may assume, since the refining fires of the gospel had long burned in the hearts of Martha and Mary, that the pretentious and pompous wailings so common among them were somewhat modified.

Word of Jesus' coming was brought first to Martha, who immediately went forth to meet him, while Mary, apparently unaware of the Master's return, remained in the house mourning with her friends. And from Martha's lips, when she met Jesus, fell some of the sweetest words ever uttered, words of faith and surety that were Petrine in caliber:

> *Lord, if thou hadst been here, my brother had not died. But I know, that even now, whatsoever thou wilt ask of God, God will give it thee.*

Martha, who served in the household; Martha, who was cumbered about with many things; Martha, whose younger sister had chosen the better part, as she sat at Jesus' feet, and who would yet again do so when she anointed them with oil; Martha of blessed memory, this day both spoke herself and heard from him such divine words as seldom have saluted the ears of mortal. Her words so far spoken can have but one meaning: 'I know thou wouldst have healed him hadst thou been here. But even now—as it was with the daughter of Jairus; as it was with the widow's son—I know thou canst call him forth from the death of the tomb to the life of mortals. God will hear thee.' The full import of these words, spoken by the power of the Holy Ghost, may not, as we shall soon see, have dawned fully upon this faithful and sweet sister, but she was in tune with the Spirit, and her faith enabled her to speak them, and glorious is her name for so doing.

Jesus said to her, "Thy brother shall rise"—meaning, 'I shall call him back to mortal life.' To this Martha, relying on that faith and knowledge which long had been hers, replied: "I know that he shall rise again in the resurrection at the last day." Then Jesus, in all the awesome majesty of his eternal godhood, spoke to his beloved Martha, in the presence of his Father, of the holy angels, and of his mortal apostolic witnesses; then Jesus, speaking as the Great Jehovah, speaking as God's Almighty Son, gave this divine testimony of his own divine Sonship:

> *I am the resurrection, and the life: he that believeth in me, though he were dead, yet shall he live: and whosoever liveth and believeth in me shall never die. Believest thou this?*

Thus saith the Lord. He has spoken and so it is. He is the resurrection; it comes by him; without him there would be no immortality; he is the personification of that power which molds the dust of the grave into an immortal man. He it was who asked: "Can these bones live?" And he it was who answered: "Thus saith the Lord God unto these bones; Behold, I will cause breath to enter into you, and ye shall live: And I will lay sinews upon you, and will bring up flesh upon you, and cover you with skin, and put breath in you, and ye shall live; and ye shall know that I am the Lord." (Ezek. 37:3, 5-6.)

He also is the life; eternal life comes by him. Without him there would be no salvation in the highest heaven, no exaltation, no continuation of the family unit in eternity, no fulness of joy in the realms ahead. He is the personification of that power which gives eternal life to all those who are born again, who are alive in Christ. Those who believe and obey, though they die the natural death, yet shall they gain eternal life in the resurrection. Yea, those who believe in Christ shall never die spiritually; they shall be alive to the things of the Spirit in this life, and they shall have eternal life in the world to come. Death, as men view it, is nothing to sorrow about where the faithful saints are concerned; what if they, as do all men, lose their lives here—they shall yet gain the far more glorious reward of eternal life hereafter.

To Jesus' question, "Believest thou this?" Martha—still guided by the power of the Spirit, still speaking with certainty from the depths of her soul, still uttering words that are Petrine in caliber, but now building on the foundation Jesus has just laid, that immortality and eternal life come by him—the blessed Martha, in this setting, replies:

> *Yea, Lord: I believe that thou art the Christ, the Son of God, which should come into the world.*

In spiritual things there is no difference between men and women. Adam and Eve both teach their children by the power of the Spirit. Peter and Martha both bear witness that Jesus is the Christ, the Son of the Living God. Mary Magdalene, even ahead of the apostles, bows before the Risen Lord and hails him yet with the affectionate *Rabboni.* Martha has now borne her testimony, and that she might do so is one of the reasons all things relative to Lazarus's death and raising were arranged as they are now unfolding. Martha is on record; her testimony is recorded by the angels; and as Jesus said aforetime, with reference to such cases, her sins are forgiven. Now he must give Mary the same opportunity.

Martha came to Jesus while he was yet outside the town. Now she returned and spoke to Mary in secret. "The Master is come, and calleth for thee," she said. Mary arose quickly and, without even excusing herself from those who were comforting her in the house, hastened to Jesus, all of which indicates there were dangers in Jesus' coming and that his friends felt the need to take precautions. Those who were with Mary followed. "She goeth unto the grave to weep there," they said.

Coming to Jesus, Mary fell at his feet and said the same words Martha had first spoken: "Lord, if thou hadst been here, my brother had not died," indicating that this was something the beloved sisters probably had discussed between themselves. Perhaps also she added the same sure witness of Christ's eternal power that had fallen from the lips of her older sister; and the Lord Jesus may have said to her what he had already said to Martha about being the resurrection and the life, even receiving back from the younger sister the same inspired testimony of his own divinity. We have no reason to believe that Jesus would do other than treat his two friends with equal tenderness and solicitude, and that he would try the faith of each of them to the full in the same way.

When Jesus saw Mary weeping, "and the Jews also weeping which came with her, he groaned in the spirit, and was troubled, And said, Where have ye laid him? They said unto him, Lord, come and see." Perhaps there were other events, not recorded, that brought forth this display of divine emotion. It may be that John is telling us that Jesus was troubled in spirit because of the artificial wailings of the paid mourners, or the rebellion that he saw in the hearts of many who were present, or that his reaction was one of pure love and tenderness toward the two sisters and their now seemingly lost Lazarus.

Or perhaps it may be, as Farrar speculates, with reference to the sorrow of Mary and her friends, something along this line: "The sight of all that love and misery, the pitiable spectacle of human bereavement, the utter futility at such a moment of human consolation, the shrill commingling of a hired and simulated lamentation with all this genuine anguish, the unspoken reproach, 'Oh, why didst Thou not come at once and snatch the victim from the enemy, and spare Thy friend from the sting of death, and us from the more bitter sting of such a parting?'—all these influences touched the tender compassion of Jesus with deep emotion. A strong effort of self-repression was needed—an effort which shook His whole frame with a powerful shudder—before He could find words to speak, and then He could only ask, 'Where have ye laid him?' " (Farrar, pp. 507-8.)

We now see Jesus himself weeping, his eyes streaming with silent tears. Among the observing Jews are both friends and enemies. Those who are kindly disposed say: "Behold how he loved him!" Others whose hearts are hardened and who seek to discount his powers say: "Could not this man, which opened the eyes of the blind, have caused that even this man should not have died?" It was as though they said: 'True, this man opened the eyes of a blind man, whom he did not know, but he could not save his own friend from death. Perhaps after all his powers are of a limited, uncertain, and capricious nature.' And so again, confronted with such a malignant outpouring of unbelief, Jesus groaned in himself. Or perhaps, as Farrar says, "Jesus knew and heard their comments, and once more the whole scene—its genuine sorrows, its hired mourners, its uncalmed hatreds, all concentrated around the ghastly work of death—came so powerfully over His spirit, that, though He knew that He was going to wake the dead, once more His whole being was swept by a storm of emotion." (Farrar, p. 508.)

Jesus is now at the grave; it is a cave; a stone lies upon it, sealing the entrance. "Take ye away the stone," he says. He who can raise the dead can surely find a grave site, and yet he asked to be shown where Lazarus lay. He who can call forth a dead corpse can surely cause a stone to roll aside, and yet he called for human hands to move the obstacle that barred the way. Each step was taken with deliberation, to test and purify the faith of those who believed. And so Martha, who had before spoken of Jesus' power to raise the dead, now, fearful for the moment, struggling to believe that which almost no mortal could believe, said, "Lord, by this time he stinketh: for he hath been dead four days." And Jesus, strengthening, encouraging, desiring to see her faith increase, asks: "Said I not unto thee, that, if thou wouldest believe, thou shouldest see the glory of God?" Then Martha, strengthened and reassured, reminded of the assurances that had already come to her by the power of the Spirit, nodded the legal approval needed to unseal the tomb, and strong arms pushed aside the great stone that covered the place where Lazarus lay.

Before the great miracle, one thing yet remained. "And Jesus lifted up his eyes, and said, Father, I thank thee that thou hast heard me. And I knew that thou hearest me always: but because of the people which stand by I said it, that they may believe that thou hast sent me." This miracle is going to prove that Jesus is the Christ, the Messiah, the Promised One. None but the Son of God could do what he is about to do. He had prayed and struggled and prepared for this moment, and the Father, whose power he held, had granted his pleas.

Thus, at this moment—with the hearts of Martha and Mary perfectly united with that of their beloved Lord; with the body of Lazarus lying in the dust, eaten by worms, every vital organ in process of rotting away; with the spirit of this man of divine destiny, in paradise, awaiting the Promised Voice—at this moment the Lord of Life spoke: "LAZARUS, COME FORTH."

"Those words thrilled once more through that region of impenetrable darkness which separates us from the world to come; and scarcely were they spoken when, like a spectre, from the rocky tomb issued a figure, swathed indeed in its white and ghastly cerements—with the napkin round the head which had upheld the jaw that four days previously had dropped in death, bound hand and foot and face, but not livid, not horrible—the figure of a youth with the healthy blood of a restored life flowing through his veins; of a life restored—so tradition tells us—for thirty more long years to life, and light, and love." (Farrar, p. 510.)

"Loose him, and let him go," Jesus said. And there the inspired account ends. A reverent curtain of silence drops over the sayings and doings of Lazarus—from his youth to the day he fell asleep in the arms of death; during the four days his spirit visited with friends in paradise, as he awaited the call to come back to the turmoils of life; and from the time he again breathed the breath of life until he laid down again his mortal tabernacle, this time to await that glorious day of resurrection of which Martha spoke. Lazarus lived and Lazarus died and Lazarus rose again—that he might continue his mortal probation; that he might die again; that he might be, for his day and for all days, a living witness of the power of him who ministered in Bethany as the Son of God. We cannot doubt that he bore many fervent testimonies to many Jewish brethren relative to the life and death and life that was his.

We have now heard Jesus claim divine Sonship and accept the concurring witness of his beloved Martha. Then we have seen him prove the truth of his own testimony by creating a living Lazarus where only a dead one lay. What effect did this miracle have on the Jews? John says: "Then many of the Jews which came to Mary, and had seen the things which Jesus did, believed on him." And well they might, for which glory be to God. "But some of them went their ways to the Pharisees, and told them what things Jesus had done," and they as a result plotted his death.

Truly we are hearing an echo here in Bethany and in Jerusalem of a Perean Voice acclaiming: "If they hear not Moses and the prophets, neither will they be persuaded, though one rose from the dead." Or is it an echo? Perhaps what we hear are rolling claps of thunder, roaring and crashing from one end of heaven to the other, as part of the dooming storm that shall destroy all those who willfully close their eyes and ears to eternal truth.

The Sanhedrin Plots Jesus' Death
(*John 11:47-54; JST, John 11:47*)

There is no language to describe the religious idiocy and the Pharisaic fanaticism that swept through Jerusalem and Judea because Jesus raised Lazarus from death. Lazarus lives and therefore Jesus must die; indeed, it would be well if Lazarus's own testifying lips could be sealed in death also. Let us slay them both and be done with this menace that subverts our Mosaic religion and runs counter to the traditions of the elders.

Within an hour of the time Lazarus walked from his tomb in or near Bethany, Jewish zealots were in the temple in Jerusalem reporting to the Pharisees and rulers on all that they had seen and heard in that Judean town. The prayers of thanksgiving and the hymns of praise that were then ascending in the home of Martha found their counterpart in the curses and revilings being poured forth in the now desecrated house of Jewish worship. The great Sanhedrin convened immediately to hear the witnesses.

Their detailed investigation of the opening of the eyes of the man born blind and their complete discomfiture in the presence of an unlearned beggar who testified that Jesus was a mighty prophet were fresh in their minds. And now this—a man whose decaying body had rotted and spewed out stench for four days—was alive and well and vibrant. What kind of a man was it who opened blind eyes and reanimated cold corpses? This thing must be stopped even if it requires the death of a god. "If we let him thus alone," they reasoned, "all men will believe on him"—and what a sad thing that would be—"and the Romans shall come and take away both our place and nation." Their dilemma was both religious and political. 'If this man's gospel is true, the day of Moses and the law is past, and we shall lose our prominence and power as rulers in Israel. The people will rally round him as their Messiah and Deliverer, and Rome will then destroy us with the sword.'

As hatred and perplexity dominated the Sanhedrinists, the high priest, Joseph Caiaphas, a civil appointee of Rome who had gained his position by bribery, rose to address them. Apparently his intention was to advocate Jesus' death on the theory that it was better for this one man to die than that the whole nation should perish at the hands of Rome. His was to be a political speech of expediency. The problem before them was not a matter of right or wrong; they must forget whether Jesus was the Messiah or not. Regardless of anything, he must be destroyed lest their nation be brought to ruin.

But whatever Caiaphas's intention was, Deity ordained otherwise. And however evil and wicked he was, yet he held the office of high priest, and as such he had a commission to speak for God to the people, which he then, unwittingly, did. The words that came out were these: "Ye know nothing at all, Nor consider that it is expedient for us, that one man should die for the people, and that the whole nation perish not." John says: "This spake he not of himself: but being high priest that year, he prophesied that Jesus should die for that nation; And not for that nation only, but that also he should gather together in one the children of God that were scattered abroad."

Caiaphas's intent had been evil but his words had been prophetic; however, the Sanhedrin was no more inclined to believe prophetic words than they were to accept the divinity of one who raised the dead. Their decision was that Jesus must die for political reasons. "Then from that day forth they took counsel together for to put him to death."

Thereupon Jesus and his disciples slipped quietly away to a small village called Ephraim, whose locale is no longer known, and there they remained some weeks in seclusion, awaiting the appointed time for his return to Jerusalem and for the crowning events of the life of earth's only Divine Being. The time in Ephraim was spent preparing the disciples for the ministerial teachings and trials that lay ahead.

MORE HEALINGS, PARABLES, AND SERMONS

To day if ye will hear his voice,
Harden not your heart, as in
the provocation,
and as in the day of temptation
in the wilderness:
When your fathers tempted me,
proved me, and saw my work.
(Ps. 95:7-9.)

Jesus Cleanses Ten Lepers

(*Luke 17:11-19*)

As Jesus, after a few weeks of seclusion in Ephraim, begins his last journey to Jerusalem, no doubt by a leisurely and circuitous route, he continues to warn and teach and heal. He continues to work wonders in Israel as he did among their fathers in generations past, and Jacob's seed, as always, seeks to tempt and prove and provoke him. His words and his works are as they have ever been; he preaches the gospel and takes upon himself the infirmities of his suffering kinsmen.

Just two years ago in Galilee we saw him heal a leper; we then marveled as he freed a faithful soul from leprosy—that dread and evil plague which makes of life a living death. (See chapter 36, Book 2.) No doubt since then there have been scores or hundreds of lepers cleansed, for what affliction would create in the heart of the Healing One such compassion as this stench-spreading sickness, which rotted away the organs of the body piecemeal? Our inspired authors, however, as we are aware, sift out selected samples of his healing power to teach such general principles and illustrate such special virtues as the needs of their respective narratives warrant.

Now, as Jesus passes through the midst of Samaria and Galilee, he enters an unnamed village where he meets, standing afar off, ten men who are lepers. Either this is a place where lepers are segregated to keep their putrefying plague from spreading, or, which accords with the sense and feeling of the whole episode, these ten, alerted to the coming of the Lord, had assembled that perchance his shadow, as it were, might touch them as he passed by. As is the requisite for those who seek healing blessings, they believed in him and had faith in his name and power. Their call to him, no doubt uttered with repetitious urgency, is a plea for healing from their deathlike doom: "Jesus, Master, have mercy on us."

"There was something in that living death of leprosy—recalling as it did the most frightful images of suffering and degradation—corrupting as it did the very fountains of the life-blood of man, distorting his countenance, rendering loathsome his touch, slowly encrusting and infecting him with a plague-spot of disease far more horrible than death itself—which always seems to have thrilled the Lord's heart with a keen and instantaneous compassion." (Farrar, p. 462.) Jesus calls out: "Go shew yourselves unto the priests." His meaning is clear: they must show themselves to the priests and be pronounced clean, free from leprosy, before they can again mingle with their fellowmen. True, it is a test of their faith to start their journey before they are healed, but so be it. He has spoken, and they are assured of that blessed physical relief that none but the leprous can desire so devoutly. There is none of the spirit of Naaman the Syrian in their souls. And so, as they journey, they are healed, we suppose, degree by degree, as health and vigor and strength return.

Ten lepers are now clean and whole; ten men whose fate was worse than death now glory in a new life of health and vigor; ten of the discards of society are now returned to the mainstream of life. It is with them as when Lazarus came forth from his tomb; where once there was death, now there is life. When a leper lives again, what does he do? Nine of the group—apparently all Jews—rushed home to embrace their loved ones; to weep with joy on the necks of their friends; to show themselves to the priests, lest any scrupulosity of the law be forgotten. One of the ten—and he a Samaritan—hastened back to Jesus, fell at his feet, gave thanks, "and with a loud voice glorified God." His loved ones and the priests could wait; first, let God be praised and his Healing Son be thanked.

"Were there not ten cleansed?" Jesus asked, "but where are the nine?" Surely there is sorrow in his voice as he continues: "There are not found that returned to give glory to God, save this stranger." And then, to the Samaritan he said: "Arise, go thy way: thy faith hath made thee whole"—which can only be interpreted to mean that this one Samaritan, singled out of the group, received added spiritual blessings that were withheld from the nine.

The sin of ingratitude, how common it is! As Jesus cleansed ten lepers physically, so he cleanses all his saints spiritually from the leprosy of sin. Are we more grateful for our blessings than were the healed lepers who hastened on their ways, heedless of the beneficent goodness of the One whose words had made them new creatures?

Well might we remember that he, who in his life healed men physically, is the one who, in his death, made it possible for all men to be healed spiritually. Well might we rejoice because he who cleansed the lepers, when he dwelt on earth, is the one who, through his atoning sacrifice, enables all men to cast off their leprous bodies of corruption, exchanging them for those glorious bodies which are refreshed and renewed in immortality.

And well ought we—lest the sin of ingratitude overtake us—praise his holy name forever.

The Discourse on the Kingdom of God

(Luke 17:20-37; JST, Luke 17:21)

This is a day of Pharisaic confrontation, one in which Jesus is repeatedly harassed, harried, and heckled by these pious preservers of the Mosaic status quo. After the healing of the ten lepers and while the holy party is still in Galilee, traveling with Jerusalem as their destination, these learned Rabbinists decide to put our Lord's Messianic claims to the test. He has testified everywhere that he is the Promised One, the Deliverer sent of God to Israel; he speaks everlastingly of the gospel of the kingdom of God. And yet he utterly refuses to wear a Messianic crown, rally the people round him, and lead the assault on their Romish-Gentile overlords that will free the chosen people from an alien yoke. Has not the time come to wring from him a declaration as to when the kingdom will be restored to Israel? If his answers are found wanting, perhaps his followers can be weaned away. Haughtily, imperiously, the Pharisees "demanded" to know "when the kingdom of God should come." 'Once and for all answer this question,' they say.

But they are not equal to him whose kingdom is not of this world, and who came not to lead a revolt against Rome, nor to place swords and shields in the hands of his followers, but to wage a revolution in the hearts of men. Their imperious demands are deftly swept aside as he restates the simple gospel verity that equates his earthly church with the kingdom of God on earth:

> *The kingdom of God cometh not with observation: Neither shall they say, Lo, here! or, Lo, there! For, behold, the kingdom of God has already come unto you.*

'My kingdom is already here; there will be no martial displays of military might; no bands will play, no legions march. My soldiers will not capture the fortress of Antonia, nor overrun Machaerus, where John was slain. Heralds will not go forth crying, Assemble here, or, Go there, for my kingdom, which is not of this world, has already come. It is the Church which I have set up, which Church administers the gospel, which gospel is the power of God unto salvation. And these Twelve hold the keys; they shall direct the destiny of my kingdom.' Nothing more is recorded of this confrontation, leaving us to suppose the Pharisees had no more to say on the subject.

But the issue of the future glorious millennial reign having thus been raised, Jesus turned from the Pharisees to his disciples and delivered a great discourse relative to that kingdom which shall sweep away the decadent kingdoms of men and hold sway over all the earth. In substance and thought content he will repeat these same truths in the Olivet discourse, during the last week of his mortal life, and we will there consider them.

Parable of the Unjust Judge

(*Luke 18:1-8; JST, Luke 18:8; D&C 101:81-92*)

Having spoken *to the Pharisees* about the kingdom of God then set up among men, meaning the Church, and having spoken *to the disciples* about that great millennial kingdom which will be established when he comes again, Jesus now teaches, in a parable, how the preserving prayers *of the saints* will finally prevail in the day of his coming. He is not here speaking of the simplistic principle that earnest and repetitious importunings will eventually be heard and answered, though this may be true in some cases. It is not a matter of an importunate widow gaining redress from an unjust judge because of her insistent pleadings, and that therefore those who pray to Him who is just will have their petitions granted if they earnestly and everlastingly importune at the throne of grace. Prayers are answered when there is faith; faith is founded on truth and can only be exercised in harmony with the plan of heaven. Only those petitions which are just and right are granted. Rather, this parable, as we shall see, teaches that if the saints will continue to importune in faith for that which is right, and because their cause is just, though the answers to their prayers may be long delayed, yet, finally in the day of vengeance when he judges whose judgment is just, when he comes again to rule and reign, the faithful shall be rewarded.

"Men ought always to pray, and not to faint," Luke says in introducing the parable, meaning that the disciples, the saints of God, the children of Zion, the members of that kingdom which is the Church, ought to importune everlastingly for the success and triumph of their cause because their cause is just and right.

> *There was in a city a judge, which feared not God, neither regarded man.*

These introductory words have a ring of reality to his hearers, for such all too frequently was the case with those non-Jewish judges in Palestine. Appointed by Herod or the Romans, many of these magistrates were amenable to bribery; cared nothing for public opinion; were openly contemptuous of principles of equity and justice; flouted the divine law in their decisions; and issued decrees that were grossly unjust.

> *And there was a widow in that city; and she came unto him, saying, Avenge me of mine adversary. And he would not for a while: but afterward he said within himself, Though I fear not God, nor regard man; Yet because this widow troubleth me, I will avenge her, lest by her continual coming she weary me.*

The widow's plea is for the magistrate to make legal inquiry; to call in him who has wronged her; to set things right and let justice be done. The judge's sole concern is expediency: what is the political thing to do; how can he benefit most from the case; why not grant the petition and be free of the annoyance of repetitious importunings.

And the Lord said, Hear what the unjust judge saith. And shall not God avenge his own elect, which cry day and night unto him, though he bear long with them?

This parable is one of contrasts. If an evil magistrate, caring nothing for a poor widow, will finally adjudge her case, how much more shall the Judge of all the earth, who loves his saints, finally, in the day of vengeance at his coming, avenge his elect upon all their enemies.

I tell you that he will come, and when he does come, he will avenge his saints speedily. Nevertheless, when the Son of Man cometh, shall he find faith on the earth?

In his own providences, and for their own development—that they may be tested to the full—it will seem to the Lord's praying saints as if the Just Judge delayeth his coming so that he will scarcely find any left who have faith.[1]

We must not overlook the fact that the Church itself, in Christ's absence, is a widow. And in the latter-day version of this parable, we find the Lord directing "the children of Zion" to importune for redress of grievances at the feet of the judge, the governor, and the president, each in turn; and if none of these heed their pleas,

Then will the Lord arise and come forth out of his hiding place, and in his fury vex the nation; And in his hot displeasure, and in his fierce anger, in his time, will cut off those wicked, unfaithful, and unjust stewards, and appoint them their portion among hypocrites, and unbelievers; Even in outer darkness, where there is weeping, and wailing, and gnashing of teeth.

Pray ye, therefore, that their ears may be opened unto your cries, that I may be merciful unto them, that these things may not come upon them.

Parable of the Pharisee and the Publican

(*Luke 18:9-14*)

In every major sect, party, and denomination there are both Pharisees and publicans. Among the Jews the Pharisees were the pious, proud, pompous self-appreciators who boasted of their charities and extolled their own good works. They esteemed themselves as far superior to the common, garden-variety of mankind, and they rejoiced in their separate, superior status. The publicans, on the other hand, were the tax collectors who made their living by extorting from the people more than they turned in to the Roman treasury. Almost without exception they were sinners whose hearts were so hardened that they could appropriate—with greed and avarice—the last sheep of the shepherd and the last mite of the widow. The nature of their employment, by an alien power, dulled their sensitivities and left them to ponder and plan how to exact by force a poor man's last farthing. In this parable Jesus speaks of the haughty pride of all Pharisees and of a welcome display of humility of a certain publican whose soul was wracked because of the sorrows of his avaricious life. It is addressed to "certain which trusted in themselves that they were righteous, and despised others."

> *Two men went up into the temple to pray; the one a Pharisee, and the other a publican. The Pharisee stood and prayed thus with himself, God, I thank thee, that I am not as other men are, extortioners, unjust, adulterers, or even as this publican. I fast twice in the week, I give tithes of all that I possess.*
>
> *And the publican, standing afar off, would not lift up so much as his eyes unto heaven, but smote upon his breast, saying, God be merciful to me a sinner.*
>
> *I tell you, this man went down to his house justified rather than the other: for every one that exalteth himself shall be abased; and he that humbleth himself shall be exalted.*

"By the parable of the haughty, respectable, fasting, alms-giving, self-satisfied Pharisee—who, going to make his boast to God in the Temple, went home less justified than the poor Publican, who could only reiterate one single cry for God's mercy as he stood there beating his breast, and with downcast eyes—He taught them that God loves better a penitent humility than a merely external service, and that a broken heart and a contrite spirit were sacrifices which He would not despise." (Farrar, p. 482.)

It is clear that the prayer of the Pharisee portrayed the life he lived—a separatist life full of holier-than-thou conduct that was offensive to God and man. As for the publican, he had come to himself, as did the prodigal son, and we may safely assume he then was or soon would become a disciple of the One through whose blood mercy is dispensed to the penitent.

The Discourse on Marriage and Divorce

(*Matthew 19:1-12; JST, Matthew 19:2, 11; Mark 10:1-12; JST, Mark 10:1-2; Luke 16:18; JST, Luke 16:23*)

Still en route to Jerusalem, traveling from Galilee into Perea, Jesus and the holy party come to that Perean area where a few weeks ago he encountered violent Pharisaic opposition. On that occasion he called these Pharisees adulterers and lashed out at their loose marriage and divorce practices with the bold assertion: "Whosoever putteth away his wife, and marrieth another, committeth adultery: and whosoever marrieth her that is put away from her husband committeth adultery." (Luke 16:18.) We then reserved consideration of this pronouncement until the discourse on marriage and divorce he is now about to deliver.

Great multitudes now follow him; he teaches the gospel; many believe on him, and he heals them. Into this setting where there is peace and righteousness, and where the grace of God is being poured out in abundant measure upon penitent souls, there now comes an evil, divisive, hateful influence. Those Pharisees whom he had condemned as adulterers come to mingle with the multitudes. With the help of Satan, their master, these malignant and evil devils, clothed in human form, have built a trap from which, as they suppose, Jesus can find no escape. It may be that even their hellish cunning has never devised a question fraught with so many difficulties and so much emotion as that which they now use to tempt him. No matter what answer he gives, he will surely alienate, they reason, a large portion of the people; and if he takes the same view thundered forth by his forerunner, the Blessed Baptist, then they hope Herod Antipas will send forth his soldiers and carry off Jesus, as he did John, to the dungeons of Machaerus, there to await a convenient time for the headsman's ax to fall. Their question, which calls for a religious decision in a sensitive field, and which may pull down political wrath upon Him to whom it is asked, is couched thus: "Is it lawful for a man to put away his wife for every cause?"

Marriage and divorce, the one a blessing, the other a curse; how long a family unit endures; how to salvage all that may be saved in the case of divorce—these matters are of more concern in the society of men than are any others. It is the divine design that men create for themselves eternal family units patterned after the family of God the Eternal Father. In such a process there can be no divorce; if all men and all women lived in complete harmony with the law of the gospel, there would be no divorces. It is the purpose of the Almighty to create eternal family units; under his system, when it operates perfectly, families are never divided by divorce.

But just as God exalts and glorifies the family, so Satan seeks to weaken and destroy this most basic of all units of society. If Lucifer had his way, no men would ever marry; they would live like animals and breed like cattle; or, being married, they would live without sexual restraint and as if there were no moral law; or divorces would be so easy to obtain, and the dissolution of the family unit so common, that men would interchange wives freely; or divorces would be so hard to obtain that marriage partners would leave each other and live in open sin with others because no realistic system of divorce prevailed; or whatever circumstances or situations might be devised to increase immorality and demean the family as such.

Manifestly, the marriage discipline and the divorce requirements among various cultures and peoples depend upon that portion of the Lord's law which they are able to live. The Lord may allow divorces in one day among a certain people and deny them in another day among a more enlightened populace. Marriage and divorce may be regulated one way among the heathen, another in the Gentile nations, and yet another according to Mosaic discipline. Even in the church and kingdom of God on earth—where men have the gospel itself—the divinely approved laws of marriage and divorce may vary from time to time. Plural marriage is practiced under certain circumstances and at designated times; divorce is allowed—with consequent remarriage of divorced persons—when such laws are in the best interest of the people; and in the highest type gospel situation, there is no divorce and all families become eternal.

In the Jewish culture of Jesus' day there were many discordant and divisive voices crying out in defense of divergent divorce standards and advocating differing marriage disciplines. Plural marriage, handed down from their fathers, was still practiced, though it does not seem to have been the dominant order of matrimony. Their main difficulties, however, seem to have grown out of the meaning of this Mosaic statement: "When a man hath taken a wife, and married her, and it come to pass that she find no favour in his eyes, because he hath found some uncleanness in her: then let him write her a bill of divorcement, and give it in her hand, and send her out of his house. And when she is departed out of his house, she may go and be another man's wife." (Deut. 24:1-2.)

The Pharisaic question assumes the propriety of divorce; the issue, as they express it, is, may it be granted "for every cause"; and, in theory at least, this depends upon the meaning of the Mosaic phrase "some uncleanness," which may also be translated "some unseemly thing," or "some matter of shame," or, literally, "some matter of nakedness." On this point the School of Shammai interpreted the Mosaic standard so as to allow divorce only for unchastity, while the School of Hillel allowed almost any trivial act to sever a marriage. Among these the Mishnah recites such things as: seeing another woman who pleased him more; feeling any disgust toward the wife; spoiling her husband's dinner; breaking the law of tithing, or other Mosaic requirement; going in public with an uncovered head; spinning in the public streets; brawling or being troublesome, or quarrelsome, or of ill repute; being childless for ten years; and on and on and on. These differences between the two major schools led, it is said, to the Jewish proverb: "Hillel loosed what Shammai bound." In practice there were many divorces for minor reasons. But Jesus, in his reply, as his wont was, rose above the battleground of the Rabbinists and went back to first principles.

Have ye not read, that he which made them at the beginning made them male and female, And said, For this cause shall a man leave father and mother, and shall cleave to his wife: and they twain shall be one flesh?

Wherefore they are no more twain, but one flesh. What therefore God hath joined together, let not man put asunder.

This is the very heart and core of the whole matter. God made man, male and female created he them, so they could marry; so they could provide bodies for his spirit children; so they could create for themselves eternal family units. God brought the woman unto the man and gave her to him to be his wife. He did it in Eden, before the fall; all things were then immortal; death had not entered the world. The first marriage—performed by the Lord God himself—was a celestial marriage, an eternal marriage, a union of Adam and Eve that was destined to last forever. There was no death; there was to be no divorce; the man and his wife were to be one flesh forever. Such was the pattern. All men thereafter should be as their first parents. Men and women should marry as did Adam and Eve—in celestial marriage—and should cleave unto each other as the divine pattern required.

What God does is forever. And what he hath joined in eternal union, let not man put asunder. Divorce is no part of the eternal plan. That these caviling, querulous, quarrelsome Pharisees understood these words and knew exactly what Jesus was saying, there can be no doubt. When we consider the conversation with the Sadducees about marriage in heaven, we shall see that the concept of eternal marriage was part of Jewish theology. And so the Pharisees now ask, "Why did Moses then command to give a writing of divorcement, and to put her away?"

Needless to say, Moses never gave any such command. What he did was to permit the recalcitrant and rebellious rebels who went by the name of Israel, but who were unable to live the full law as the Lord gave it to them—for they had the Melchizedek Priesthood, the sealing power, and celestial marriage—to divorce each other in proper cases. Hence Jesus replies:

> *Moses because of the hardness of your hearts suffered you to put away your wives: but from the beginning it was not so.*
>
> *And I say unto you, Whosoever shall put away his wife, except it be for fornication, and shall marry another, committeth adultery: and whoso marrieth her which is put away doth commit adultery.*

Moses permitted divorce because Israel was unable to live the perfect law. His teachings were a schoolmaster to prepare men for the fulness of the gospel. That gospel is now among them, and under this perfect law, marriage once again is eternal. Once again it is performed by the Lord or by his word; and once again it has no end. Such marriages can only be put asunder as a result of unchastity. If the man and his wife sever their union for lesser reasons and marry others, all concerned commit adultery, for in the eyes of the Lord his eternal marriage compact has never been broken. All of its terms and conditions are in force and have full efficacy and divine standing.

Thus Jesus recited the full and perfect law to the

Pharisees. Its provisions were only binding upon those who received his gospel, but he had declared unto them that very gospel, and they must accept it—including its law of marriage and divorce—at the peril of their salvation. Later, in a house away from the multitudes, the disciples, themselves troubled at the severity and strictness of the doctrine, "asked him again of the same matter." Later they said: "If the case of the man be so with his wife, it is not good to marry."

Jesus repeated to the disciples the basic law of marriage and divorce, applying its principles to both men and women—for women can gain divorces as well as men—and then added:

> *All cannot receive this saying; it is not for them save to whom it is given. For there are some eunuchs, which were so born from their mother's womb: and there are some eunuchs, which were made eunuchs of men: and there be eunuchs, which have made themselves eunuchs for the kingdom of heaven's sake.*
>
> *He that is able to receive it, let him receive it.*

From these words it is clear that the high standards of marriage and divorce of which Jesus speaks were for those only to whom they were given by revelation. Needless to say they have not been given to us in our day in their eternal fulness, and marriages to divorced persons do not of themselves constitute adultery. That this high state of marriage discipline will prevail again during the millennium also goes without saying. It is difficult for us, however, to envision fully the illustration here used about eunuchs. The record must be incomplete, for these words cannot, as is sometimes assumed, have reference to a celibate ministry. Perhaps they simply mean that even as special provision must be made for those who for physical reasons cannot marry, so the Lord makes special provision in his marriage discipline, so that all things required will meet the needs and circumstances of people in whatever society and culture they live.

NOTE

1. "Yet ere the Son of man comes to redress the wrongs of His Church, so low will the hope of relief sink, through the length of the delay, that one will be fain to ask, 'Will He find any faith of a coming avenger left on the earth?' From this we learn, (1.) That the *primary* and *historical* reference of this parable is to the Church in its *widowed,* desolate, oppressed, defenceless condition during the present absence of her Lord in the heavens; (2.) That in these circumstances importunate, persevering prayer for deliverance is the Church's fitting exercise; (3.) That notwithstanding every encouragement to this, so long will the answer be delayed, while the need of relief continues the same, and all hope of deliverance will have nearly died out, and 'faith' of Christ's coming scarcely to be found." (Robert Jamieson, A. R. Fausset, and David Brown, *Commentary on the Whole Bible,* Grand Rapids, Mich.: Zondervan Publishing House, 2:118.)

GAINING ETERNAL LIFE

If thou wilt do good,
yea, and hold out faithful to the end,
thou shalt be saved in the kingdom of God,
which is the greatest of all the gifts of God;
for there is no gift greater
than the gift of salvation.
(D&C 6:13.)
Salvation consists in the glory, authority,
majesty, power and dominion
which Jehovah possesses and in nothing else;
and no being can possess it
but himself or one like him.
(*Lectures on Faith*, p. 64.)
And, if you keep my commandments and endure
to the end you shall have eternal life,
which gift is the greatest
of all the gifts of God. (D&C 14:7.)

Little Children Shall Be Saved

(*Matthew 19:13-15; JST, Matthew 19:13-14; Mark 10:13-16; JST, Mark 10:12; Luke 18:15-17*)

A scene of surpassing sweetness now unfolds before our eyes. Little children, still retaining the sinless purity of the sacred seraphs who surround the throne of God, are brought to Jesus to be blessed. He enfolds them in his arms, lays his hands upon them, and speaks wondrous words about them. Then he commands all men to be as they are.

We are still with our Blessed Lord and his select group of disciples in a Perean house. He has just proclaimed the sacred and holy nature of the marital union. It is ordained of God for the benefit of man; the Lord God made man, male and female, that they might marry and provide bodies for his spirit children. "And they twain shall be one flesh, and all this that the earth might answer the end of its creation; And that it might be filled with the measure of man, according to his creation before the world was made," and "Whoso forbiddeth to marry is not ordained of God." (D&C 49:15-17.) As the Pauline word has it: "Marriage is honourable in all, and the bed undefiled." (Heb. 13:4.) Such is our Lord's doctrine. And so it is that we see Jesus take "part in a scene that has charmed the imagination of poet and painter in every age. For as though to destroy all false and unnatural notions of the exceptional glory of religious virginity, He, among whose earliest acts it had been to bless a marriage festival, made it one of His latest acts to fondle infants in His arms." We see "fathers and mothers and friends" bring "to Him the fruits of holy wedlock—young children and even babes—that He might touch them and pray over them." (Farrar, pp. 500-501.)

They are rebuked by the disciples, who say, "There is no need, for Jesus hath said, Such shall be saved." It is evident that the adult male followers of Jesus feel they should not be disturbed in the deep doctrinal discussions then in progress. To them women and children, in keeping with Jewish practice and tradition, should remain in the background. "But when Jesus saw and heard them, he was much displeased," and he rebuked his disciples. Then he uttered those words of wonder and beauty and glory that shall stand forever among the great doctrinal verities of pure Christianity:

> *Suffer little children to come unto me, and forbid them not; for of such is the kingdom of heaven.*

For of such is the kingdom of heaven! Little children, blessed spirits, pure and holy children of the Father, scarce removed from the Celestial Presence—such, in their innocence and perfection, are heirs of full salvation. "And little children also have eternal life," Abinadi said (Mosiah 15:25); and Joseph Smith, in recording a vision of the celestial kingdom, tells us: "And I also beheld that all children who die before they arrive at the years of accountability are saved in the celestial kingdom of heaven" (D&C 137:10). Such being the law that Jesus had theretofore taught his meridian disciples, we can almost anticipate his next words:

> *Verily I say unto you, Whosoever shall not receive the kingdom of God as a little child shall in no wise enter therein.*

Riches and Eternal Life

(*Matthew 19:16-26; JST, Matthew 19:18, 26; Mark 10:17-27; JST, Mark 10:16, 22, 26; Luke 18:18-27; JST, Luke 18:27*)

Jewish Rabbis in Jesus' day were often asked by their disciples what course they should pursue to gain an inheritance with Abraham, Isaac, and Jacob in the kingdom of God. Rabbinists discussed, freely and at length, what the chosen people must do to gain eternal life. It was a dominant theme of discussion in all the Rabbinical schools. And always the course leading to salvation was lighted by their varying views and interpretations of the Mosaic and prophetic writings. It is said, for instance, that "when the Angel of Death came to fetch the R. Chanina, he said, 'Go and fetch me the Book of the Law, and *see whether there is anything in it which I have not kept.*' " (Farrar, p. 502, footnote 2.) Jesus himself, but recently, encountered a lawyer who sought to test his Rabbinical knowledge, hoping to find a flaw or a fault, by asking: "Master, what shall I do to inherit eternal life?" And it was out of the resultant colloquy that the parable of the good Samaritan came.

We are now about to witness a scene that so impressed the Synoptists that all three preserved its essential details. With the same question weighing heavily upon him, a rich young ruler, probably the ruler of the local synagogue, came running to Jesus. He knelt, affirmatively doing obeisance. Evidently he was sincere, but his words were so phrased as to specify that Jesus was only a great and good Rabbi and not the Divine One, not the Messiah, not the one whose answer would be the *ipse dixit* that would settle the matter forever. His words, coupled with Jesus' reply, have always been somewhat troublesome and difficult to understand; but by placing them—and particularly Jesus' answer—in their Jewish setting, we get a radically different meaning than otherwise would be the case. The devout young man said: "Good Master, what good thing shall I do, that I may have eternal life?"

Now, in all Jewish literature there is no such thing as addressing a Rabbi as *good.* It is said that the whole Talmud contains no single instance of such an accolade. It simply was not done in that day. He might be called Rab, Rabbi, or Rabboni, as when Mary Magdalene knelt before the Risen Lord in the garden, but not Good Rabbi, or Good Master. We have seen his disciples and those made whole by his healing power kneel before him, worship his person, and call him the Messiah, the God of Israel, and the Son of God. This our rich young ruler does not do—he has some reservations about the claims of this Rabbi; and yet it is clear to him that here is one who is more than other Rabbis; and so he seeks a middle ground, one that will honor Jesus more than the mere title Rabbi, and yet one that will avoid ascribing to him divine Messianic status. He says, "Good Master." It is as though he said, 'I salute you as a great Rabbi, one whose wisdom is greater than these others, but I refrain from calling you the Messiah, as do your disciples.'

In reply, Jesus said: "Why callest thou me good? there is none good but one, that is, God." 'Do not address me by the title *good* unless you acknowledge me as God, for none but

God is good, none but he is sinless, none but he is perfect. I am indeed the Sinless One, and therefore I am good. As I have heretofore taught, no one convicts me of sin; and so unless you are ready to accede this, do not call me good.' By this answer, which carries a touch of irony, Jesus affirms by inference his divinity and makes it plain to the young ruler that his halfhearted attempt to laud the one who needs no honor from men does not suffice. "He would as little accept the title 'Good,' as He would accept the title, 'Messiah,' when given in a false sense. He would not be regarded as that mere 'good Rabbi,' to which, in these days, more than ever, men would reduce Him. So far, Jesus would show the youth that when he came to Him as to one who was more than man, his address, as well as his question, was a mistake. No mere man can lay any other foundation than that which is laid, and if the ruler committed the error of simply admiring Jesus as a Rabbi of preeminent sanctity, yet no Rabbi, however saintly, was accustomed to receive the title of 'good,' or prescribe any amulet for the preservation of a virtuous life." (Farrar, p. 502.) In this setting, then, Jesus turns to the issue at hand, and makes a pronouncement of wondrous import:

If thou wilt enter into life, keep the commandments.

This is the sum and substance of the whole matter. Salvation, eternal life, rewards in all their degrees and varieties—all come by obedience to the laws and ordinances of the gospel. Salvation must be won; it is not a free gift. "Let us hear the conclusion of the whole matter: Fear God, and keep his commandments: for this is the whole duty of man." (Eccl. 12:13.) But what of grace? Grace is the love, mercy, and condescension of God in making salvation available to men. "It is by grace that we are saved, after all we can do." (2 Ne. 25:23.) Eternal life is freely available; salvation is free in that all may drink of the waters of life; all may come and partake; but none gains so high a reward as eternal life until he is tried and tested and found worthy, as were the ancients.

This is the answer the rich young man should have expected to hear. Any reputable Rabbi would have said the same thing. The differences arose as to what the commandments were and what one must do to keep them. The law of marriage and divorce, but recently expounded by Jesus, is an illustration of the divergent views of recognized Rabbinical schools on some of the most important of all human conduct. And so in answer to Jesus' pronouncement calling upon men to keep the commandments, the young ruler of the local synagogue asks: "Which?" 'Do I follow the School of Shammai or the School of Hillel? Must I observe the Sabbath and fast twice a week as do the Pharisees? Must I eat the paschal lamb with my loins girded and my feet shod, as did our fathers? Everyone says, Keep the commandments; I need to know the particulars.' Jesus, as always, goes back to basics:

Thou shalt not kill. Thou shalt not commit adultery. Thou shalt not steal. Thou shalt not bear false witness. Honour thy father and thy mother: and, Thou shalt love thy neighbour as thyself.

To this recitation, the answer came: "All these things have I kept from my youth up: what lack I yet?" Clearly our young friend was a man of devotion, decency, and integrity. From his youth he had walked in the available light, as millions in modern Christendom do before they ever hear of the restoration of the fulness of the gospel. That he knew little of the real meaning of some of those commandments we are about to see when he declines to do more than give lip service to loving his neighbors. But at this point, "Jesus beholding him loved him," and said to him:

One thing thou lackest: go thy way, sell whatsoever thou hast, and give to the poor, and thou shalt have treasure in heaven: and come, take up the cross, and follow me.

Eternal life can come to those only who put first in their lives the things of God's kingdom; who love the riches of eternity more than a handful of mortal pelf; who are willing to forsake all and follow Christ. Where a man's treasure is, there will his heart be also. For this man, the needful thing was to overcome the love of money and the power of riches; for others of us, the testing process calls upon us to forsake some other prized possession or ardent desire; every man has his own Gethsemane.[1] Having heard Jesus' counsel, the young man was sad and went away grieving, for he was richly endowed with this world's goods. Jesus then said to the disciples:

> *How hardly shall they that have riches enter into the kingdom of God!*

Heretofore Jesus has said many things about laying up treasures in heaven. He has taught that a man's life consisteth not in the abundance of the things that his soul possesses; he has spoken of those who lay up treasures for themselves and are not rich toward God; he has repeatedly called upon men to forsake all and follow him, and many such like things; but now he makes it almost seem as though rich men cannot be saved. His disciples are astonished. This is a straiter gate and a narrower path than they had supposed was the case. Jesus, in words of tenderness, responds to their feelings by amplifying his words:

> *Children, how hard is it for them that trust in riches to enter into the kingdom of God! It is easier for a camel to go through the eye of a needle, than for a rich man to enter into the kingdom of God.*

Their astonishment increases. It is a common Jewish proverb that even in a man's dreams he will not see an elephant pass through the eye of a needle. It is a proverb that points to that which cannot be. As with an elephant, so with a camel; a bloated beast of gargantuan size cannot pass through an opening made only large enough for a silken thread. As Mark expresses it, "they were astonished out of measure," and asked among themselves, "Who then can be saved?" Jesus gives answer:

> *With men that trust in riches, it is impossible; but not impossible with men who trust in God and leave all for my sake, for with such all these things are possible.*

How better could it be said? Truly, never man spake as this man. And as to the rich young ruler whose questions and conduct brought forth these gems of eternal truth, no further mention is made. Our last view of him is one of a man who prefers the comforts and ease of great wealth to the riches of eternity; it is of a sincere and devout man who is nonetheless deceived by the deceitfulness of riches; it is of one who dares not pay out a *temporal-all* in the cause of truth and righteousness here, so as to purchase an *eternal-all* in the realms ahead. We cannot but hope that he—being one upon whom Jesus looked with affection—came to himself, returned and accepted our Lord as the Messiah, and made his means available to feed the hungry, clothe the naked, shelter the homeless, and further the eternal gospel cause.

Riches and Rewards in the Day of Regeneration

(*Matthew 19:27-30; JST, Matthew 19:28; Mark 10:28-31; JST, Mark 10:30-31; Luke 18:28-30*)

As the rich young ruler, clinging to his wealth as a miser grasps his pennies, departs in sorrow, choosing to revel in ease and comfort rather than to use his possessions to bless mankind; as Jesus ends his terse and piercing words about forsaking all to gain eternal life; and as the full significance of his sayings begins to dawn upon the disciples, showing them that those who trust in riches and will not forsake all to follow Christ and further his gospel cause cannot be saved—in this setting, in a boastful way, claiming an apostolic preference and preeminence, Peter says: "Behold, we have forsaken all, and followed thee; what shall we have therefore?" In answer Jesus speaks first to the Twelve:

> *Verily I say unto you, that ye who have followed me, shall, in the resurrection* [in the regeneration, as the King James Version has it], *when the Son of Man shall come sitting on the throne of his glory, ye shall also sit upon twelve thrones, judging the twelve tribes of Israel.*

Not only shall the Twelve have eternal life, but these noble souls also shall continue to serve in their high and holy administrative roles in the eternal worlds. Neither Peter nor any of his fellow apostles could ever have dreamt of so high and exalted a station as is here named. Jacob begat Israel and sired them as a nation; Moses led the chosen people out of Egyptian bondage and gave them their law; Elijah and Isaiah and the prophets guided them in the hours of their despair; Jesus, the Son of God, had come to redeem them—but now it is revealed that the Twelve shall, at Christ's behest, sit in judgment on Abraham's seed. Thus saith the Lord: "It hath gone forth in a firm decree, by the will of the Father, that mine apostles, the Twelve which were with me in my ministry at Jerusalem, shall stand at my right hand at the day of my coming in a pillar of fire, being clothed with robes of righteousness, with crowns upon their heads, in glory even as I am, to judge the whole house of Israel, even as many as have loved me and kept my commandments, and none else." (D&C 29:12.)[2]

All this was to be in the day of regeneration, the day when the earth would be refreshed and renewed and receive again its paradisiacal glory. This is the day that Peter, James, and John had seen in vision in the holy mount when Christ and they were transfigured, and when the Father bore witness that Jesus was his Son. But the blessings of the gospel are not for the Twelve only. Jesus continues:

> *Verily I say unto you, There is no man that hath left house, or brethren, or sisters, or father, or mother, or wife, or children, or lands, for my sake, and the gospel's, But he shall receive an hundredfold now in this time, houses, and brethren, and sisters, and mothers, and children, and lands, with persecutions; and in the world to come eternal life.*

Of what does sacrifice consist? In the eternal perspective it is giving up a handful of clay—held and owned but tremulously and for a moment on this lowly earth—in exchange for a universe in the eternal ages that are to be. And yet, from our mortal view, it may mean giving up that which is of great worth unto us for the moment. Do we forsake family and friends and possessions and receive persecutions instead? If so, the gospel cause provides us with kinfolk who become closer than blood relatives; we are welcome to use the lands of others; and the possessions of all the saints become ours as we need them—all of which is only the beginning. There are rewards—with persecutions—in this life; and, finally, there is eternal life in the world ahead, which eternal life is all that the Father hath.[3]

Having set forth these wondrous truths, Jesus turned to Peter, who, with some pride of self-accomplishment, had posed the question. "But there are many who make themselves first," Jesus said, "that shall be last, and the last first." To this Mark adds: "This he said, rebuking Peter." And this, we might also add, formed an introduction to the parable of the laborers in the vineyard, which was immediately forthcoming.

Parable of the Laborers in the Vineyard
(*Matthew 20:1-16*)

Peter's statement, "we have forsaken all, and followed thee," said after the rich young ruler made his great refusal, declining as he did to follow Christ, was followed by the question: "What shall we have therefore?" Jesus' answer—glorious beyond belief—we have heard, together with his rebuke of Peter relative to some who made themselves first and who would, in fact, be last. Such is the setting for the present parable. "To impress upon them still more fully and deeply that the kingdom of heaven is not a matter of mercenary calculation or exact equivalent—that there could be no bargaining with the Heavenly Householder—that before the eye of God's clearer and more penetrating judgment Gentiles might be admitted before Jews, and Publicans before Pharisees, and young converts before aged Apostles—He told them the memorable Parable of the Labourers in the Vineyard. That parable, amid its other lessons, involved the truth that, while all who serve God should not be defrauded of their just and full and rich reward, there could be in heaven no murmuring, no envyings, no jealous comparison of respective merits, no base strugglings for precedency, no miserable disputings as to who had performed the maximum of service, or who had received the minimum of grace." (Farrar, p. 504.)

For the kingdom of heaven is like unto a man that is an householder, which went out early in the morning to hire labourers into his vineyard. And when he had agreed with the labourers for a penny a day, he sent them into his vineyard.

The kingdom of heaven on earth is the Church of Jesus Christ, which prepares men for an inheritance in the kingdom of heaven hereafter, which is the celestial kingdom. The householder is God; the hired laborers are his servants; the vineyard is his kingdom; it is also the house of Israel and all the inhabitants of the earth to whom his servants are sent. It was the practice of the day to employ daily laborers in the marketplace. The agreed compensation, a penny or denarius, was the normal wage for a single day's service. The great importance of the work is shown by the fact that the householder himself employed the laborers, not trusting it to a steward.

And he went out about the third hour, and saw others standing idle in the marketplace. And said unto them; Go ye also into the vineyard, and whatsoever is right I will give you. And they went their way. Again he went out about the sixth and ninth hour, and did likewise.

The work day lasted from sunup to sunset. The others were employed for a just but unspecified wage; the Lord's servants do not always know what rewards he has in store for them, nor, in reality, could they conceive of them if they were named and identified.

And about the eleventh hour he went out, and found others standing idle, and saith unto them, Why stand ye here all the day idle? They say unto him, Because no

> *man hath hired us. He saith unto them, Go ye also into the vineyard; and whatsoever is right, that shall ye receive.*

Laborers called throughout the day are assumed to have been available at any time, but were called only as indicated. Deity calls his own servants according to his own will and on his own schedule. A new and grander vision of those called into the Master's service at the eleventh hour is seen in the revelation, received June 8, 1978, offering the full blessings of the gospel, including the priesthood and the blessings of the temple, to those of every race and color. All such, called at the eleventh hour, have the same obligation of priesthood service that the divine Householder has given to any of his servants, and they shall be rewarded on an equal basis.

> *So when even was come, the lord of the vineyard saith unto his steward, Call the labourers, and give them their hire, beginning from the last unto the first. And when they came that were hired about the eleventh hour, they received every man a penny. But when the first came, they supposed that they should have received more; and they likewise received every man a penny.*
>
> *And when they had received it, they murmured against the goodman of the house, Saying, These last have wrought but one hour, and thou hast made them equal unto us, which have borne the burden and heat of the day.*
>
> *But he answered one of them, and said, Friend, I do thee no wrong: didst not thou agree with me for a penny? Take that thine is, and go thy way: I will give unto this last, even as unto thee. Is it not lawful for me to do what I will with mine own? Is thine eye evil, because I am good?*

In its initial application, the parable applied to Peter and the apostles; they bore the burdens of the kingdom during the heat of the day and came off marvelously well. But there were others—Gentiles, heathen, the seed of Cain—all of whom in due course would be called to service in the vineyard of the world. What if some of them, laboring but for an hour, should receive equal or even greater rewards than the first laborers—all of which brings us back to the introductory statement, made to Peter, which Jesus now restates by way of summary.

> *So the last shall be first, and the first last: for many be called, but few chosen.*

These concluding words—"many be called, but few chosen"—stand forth as the warning-climax of the parable, not alone to Peter and the other first laborers, but to all who are called to service in the vineyard of the Lord. Many are called into the earthly kingdom, but few shall gain full salvation in the heavenly kingdom; many are called to serve missions, but few shall reap the reward that might have been theirs; many are called to the holy priesthood—covenanting thereby to love and serve God and their fellowmen with all their hearts, might, mind, and strength—but few shall be chosen for eternal life in the kingdom of Him whose we are. As he who gave the parable anciently has said to us in our day: "There are many who have been ordained among you, whom I have called but few of them are chosen. They who are not chosen have sinned a very grievous sin, in that they are walking in darkness at noon-day. . . . If you keep not my commandments, the love of the Father shall not continue with you, therefore you shall walk in darkness." (D&C 95:5-6, 12; 121:34-40.)

Many are called but few are chosen. It is an awesome warning.

NOTES

1. "Keep my commandments, and seek to bring forth and establish the cause of Zion; Seek not for riches but for wisdom, and behold, the mysteries of God shall be unfolded unto you, and then shall you be made rich. Behold, he that hath eternal life is rich." (D&C 6:6-7.)

2. For a brief summary of how men are judged by a great hierarchy of judges—with Judge Jesus at the head—see *Commentary* 1:558-59.

3. Because the Prophet Joseph Smith laid his all on the altar, the Lord by revelation said of him: "I will bless him and multiply him and give unto him an hundred-fold in this world, of fathers and mothers, brothers and sisters, houses and lands, wives and children, and crowns of eternal lives in the eternal worlds." (D&C 132:55.)

Chapter 83

JOURNEYING TOWARD THE CROSS

Suffer it to be so now:
for thus it becometh us to fulfil
all righteousness. (Matt. 3:15.)

The Coming Baptism of Blood

(*Matthew 20:17-28; JST, Matthew 20:23; Mark 10:32-45; JST, Mark 10:40, 42; Luke 18:31-34; JST, Luke 18:34*)

Two scenes now come into view that dramatize the agony and the glory that lie ahead for Him who came to ransom fallen man from the bottomless abyss. They are (1) the announcing anew of his coming death and resurrection, and (2) the strivings of two of the Twelve for precedence and dominion in the kingdom of heaven.

We are traveling with Jesus, en route to "the great city, which spiritually is called Sodom and Egypt," where also he will be "crucified." (Rev. 11:8.) He must needs go to Jerusalem; he left Ephraim with that fixed design. He has ministered and taught, somewhat leisurely along the way, but now the time of the Fourth Passover draws nigh. It must needs be that he arrive on schedule, enter the Holy City amid shouts of Hosanna, perform his final ministry there, and then submit to the Roman scourge and the crucifier's nails.

Jesus' feet have trod the dusty lanes of Palestine for some thirty-three years; he has been in and out of the gates of Jerusalem hundreds of times; but there has never been such a journey as this one. In the past his steps have taken him to scenes of joy and healing and friendly intercourse with beloved associates; now they are traversing a steady descent into the valley of the shadow of death. And there is a solemnity, an awe—yes, a reverence—about the journey itself. Mark tell us Jesus went before the Twelve, and that they were amazed and afraid as they followed him. As he went forth on "the journey which was to end at Jerusalem," Farrar—whose way with words is wondrous—tells us, "A prophetic solemnity and elevation of soul struggling with the natural anguish of the flesh, which shrank from that great sacrifice, pervaded His whole being, and gave a new and strange grandeur to every gesture and every look. It was the Transfiguration of Self-sacrifice; and, like that previous Transfiguration of Glory, it filled those who beheld it with an amazement and terror which they could not explain. There are few pictures in the gospels more pathetic than this of Jesus going forth to His death, and walking alone along the path into the deep valley, while behind Him, in awful reverence, and mingled anticipations of dread and hope—their eyes fixed on Him, as with bowed head He preceded them in all the majesty of sorrow—the disciples followed, and dared not disturb His meditations." (Farrar, pp. 516-17.) But as they journeyed, Jesus said:

Behold, we go up to Jerusalem, and all things that are written by the prophets concerning the Son of man shall be accomplished.

He was following a foreordained course; he came to preach and heal and die; his death lay just ahead. Of him all the prophets had testified, and every jot and tittle spoken by them must be fulfilled.

Behold, we go up to Jerusalem; and the Son of man shall be betrayed unto the chief priests and unto the scribes, and they shall condemn him to death, And shall deliver him to the Gentiles to mock, and to scourge, and to crucify him: and the third day he shall rise again.

This is now the third time, of which we know, when this same Jesus has spoken in plainness of his betrayal, trial, scourging, death, and resurrection. It was said just before he and the Three went up the Mount of Transfiguration and, thereafter, when the apostolic party—including the women who were with them—returned to Galilee. But this is the first time the word *crucify* is recorded. Of what he has now said, Luke editorializes: "And they understood none of these things; and this saying was hid from them; neither remembered they the things which were spoken." As the apostles were to be observers, witnesses, and to some extent participants in the atoning events that lay ahead, and as those events were to be tests for them as well as for the Lord Jesus, their full meaning was kept from them and they were not permitted to remember them again until after the testing period was past.

Now the scene changes, though the holy party is still traveling their fateful course toward Jerusalem. Life with Jesus was like a refiner's fire. Day after day and conversation after conversation, his incisive words burned dross and imperfections out of the souls of his apostles and out of all others who could bear the heat of the fiery furnace. Now Salome—the wife of Zebedee, the sister of the Blessed Virgin, the mother of James and John, the aunt of the Lord Jesus—with her two sons, the sons of thunder, who one day sought to call down fire from heaven upon certain persons in Samaria who rejected Jesus—these three, a mother and her two sons, came to Jesus in secret. They fell before him in reverential worship; theirs was the sure knowledge, born of the Spirit, that the Man of Nazareth was the Holy Messiah who should reign on the throne of David forever.

Knowing they desired something of him, Jesus asked: "What wilt thou?" Salome answered: "Grant that these my two sons may sit, the one on thy right hand, the other on the left, in thy kingdom." James and John uttered the same petition. "Master, we would that thou shouldest do for us whatsoever we shall desire," they said. And when he responded, "What would ye that I should do for you," they repeated the plea of their mother: "Grant unto us that we may sit, one on thy right hand, and the other on thy left hand, in thy glory."

The echo of Jesus' voice, rebuking Peter when the Chief Apostle sought to make himself first in the kingdom of God, has scarcely stopped ringing in their ears. The message of the parable of the laborers in the vineyard—that all servants worthy of exaltation would be rewarded alike—is still part of their ponderings. And yet, filled with holy zeal and boundless ambition—as true saints should be, within proper limits—these intimates of the Lord asked for that which exceeded the bounds of propriety. "Jesus bore gently with their selfishness and error. They had asked in their blindness for that position which, but a few days afterwards, they were to see occupied in shame and anguish by the two crucified robbers. Their imaginations were haunted by twelve thrones; His thoughts were of three crosses. They dreamt of earthly crowns; He told them of a cup of bitterness and a baptism of blood." (Farrar, pp. 517-18.) "Ye know not what ye ask," he said. "Are ye able to drink of the cup that I shall drink of, and to be baptized with the baptism that I am baptized with?" Their answer, "We are able."

Then said Jesus: "Ye shall drink indeed of my cup, and be baptized with the baptism that I am baptized with: but to sit on my right hand, and on my left, is not mine to give, but it shall be given to them for whom it is prepared of my Father."[1] As Jesus was baptized by John in Jordan to fulfill all righteousness, so for the same reason would all of the Twelve be baptized in blood, as it were, when the severity of the scourge, and the cruelties of the cross, and the sharpness of the spear fell upon them. James would be slain at Herod's order and John would be banished to Patmos. The baptism of blood was indeed at their door.

When the rest of the Twelve heard what Zebedee's family sought, they were "much displeased with James and

John," and Jesus, calling them all together, used the occasion to teach them how true greatness in God's kingdom is gained:

> *Ye know that they who are appointed to rule over the Gentiles exercise lordship over them; and their great ones exercise authority upon them. But so shall it not be among you: but whosoever will be great among you, shall be your minister: And whosoever of you will be the chiefest, shall be servant of all.*
>
> *For even the Son of man came not to be ministered unto, but to minister, and to give his life a ransom for many.*

If Jesus came to be the servant of all; if he came to minister to the eternal well-being of all men; if he came to pay the ransom, by the shedding of his own blood, for the captive souls of men—then how ought his greater stewards and lesser servants labor in his vineyard?

The Healing of Zaccheus and of Bartimeus

(*Luke 18:35-43; 19:1-10; JST, Luke 18:43; 19:7-8; Mark 10:46-52; Matthew 20:29-34*)

In Jericho of ancient fame there dwelt two men, Zaccheus and Bartimeus, whose lives are about to be changed forever by the touch of the Master's hand. Zaccheus, the Jew, is a hated and despised publican; nay, more, he is "the chief among the publicans," of whom there is a large colony in this prosperous city. He is a rich man and a sinner who lives a life of extortion and fraud. How evil it is for a tax collector to take more than the law allows and to keep it for himself! Zaccheus has a sin-sick soul. Bartimeus, the Jew, is poor and blind and makes his living by begging on the streets. He is a social nonentity for whom none care, and whose life is tolerated only because blindness and begging go together in this culture, a culture that leaves its invalids to suffer alone and to gain such crumbs and crusts as chance to fall their way.

Jericho, a verdant tropical city filled with flowers and

palm trees, located on a watered plain, is called the paradise of God. It is truly the Eden of Palestine, the most fruitful area of the whole land, and to it masses of people flock as desert denizens to a flowery oasis. Through its streets pass many of the Perean and Galilean pilgrims en route to keep the Passover in Jerusalem. Among them this time are Jesus, the Twelve, and others of the disciples, including women, one of whom, Salome, has but recently interceded with him for her sons.

Jesus' fame is such that the whole city turns out to see him. This is he who sent one born blind to wash in the pool of Siloam and he came seeing. This is he who said to Lazarus of Bethany, whose decomposing body had lain in the tomb for four days, "Come forth," and it was so. This is he whom the scribes hate and the Sanhedrin seek that they may put him to death. Is he the Messiah, as we have heard, or does he do all these miracles by the power of Satan? Will he do any of his marvelous works in our streets? Is he the Messiah or the antichrist? Perhaps we will be able to tell as we see what happens to Zaccheus and to Bartimeus.

Jesus, now in Jericho, is surrounded by throngs of people; there are multitudes on every side. Zaccheus, who is small of stature, cannot so much as glimpse the Messianic face; he runs ahead and climbs a sycamore tree. Jesus stops under the tree, looks up, and says, "Zaccheus, make haste, and come down; for to day I must abide at thy house."

"And he made haste, and came down, and received him joyfully." He who ever stands at the door and knocks; he who is ever ready to come in and sup with all who will open unto him; he who seeks to be an unseen guest in every home at every meal—he this day chose a rich and hated publican to be his host. Why? No reasons are given, nor need they be. We cannot doubt that Zaccheus by study and prayer and pondering had made himself ready to receive the Guest of guests, and that Jesus came—as a Laborer worthy of his hire—to impart to a repenting publican that spiritual health which he alone can give. "And when the disciples saw it, they all murmured, saying, That he was gone to be a guest with a man who is a sinner."

Once there was no room for him in the inns; now he chooses to spend the night with a sinner who is hated by all, and that not without cause. Often he has slept with his disciples under the Palestinian stars to be rid of the conniving and evil influences of the day; now he elects to associate with a sinner of ill repute. In this self-selected abode there is time to relax and eat, to rest and to teach. Much is said by Jesus about the gospel and repentance and salvation and the glories of the eternal world. At a point of climax, Zaccheus's heart is pricked. He stands and says: "Behold, Lord, the half of my goods I give to the poor; and if I have taken any thing from any man by unjust means, I restore him fourfold."

Jesus has gained a convert. This man will be baptized and become a disciple. Jesus says: "This day is salvation come to this house, forsomuch as he also is a son of Abraham." And to all of this, then comes the grand climax:

> *For the Son of man is come to seek and to save that which was lost.*

Such is the story of Zaccheus, as far as it has been preserved for us. His soul is healed and he is a new man. Jesus has wrought one of his greatest miracles. As to Bartimeus, the beggar, the blessing prepared for him is reserved until the next morning as Jesus and his party leave Jericho, and it becomes in effect a divine seal on the preaching and spiritual healing of which we have already spoken.

Luke tells us that as Jesus and his party approached Jericho, they met "a certain blind man" who sat begging by the way. Hearing the multitude, he asked what it meant, and was told, "Jesus of Nazareth passeth by." Immediately the sightless one cried out, "Jesus, thou son of David, have mercy on me." He was rebuked by those who accompanied Jesus and was told to hold his peace, which he did not do, but continued to cry out, "Thou son of David, have mercy on me." Jesus stopped, commanded the blind one to be brought, and asked, "What wilt thou that I shall do unto thee?" He said, "Lord, that I may receive my sight." Jesus said, "Receive thy sight: thy faith hath saved thee." Immediately his sight came, and he followed Jesus and glorified God. "And all the disciples when they saw this, gave praise unto God." Then, as Luke has it, "Jesus entered and passed through Jericho."

Mark tells us that this healing took place when Jesus "went out of Jericho with his disciples," and adds to Luke's account that the beggar was named Bartimeus, the son of Timeus; that when the beggar was called to come to Jesus, he was told, "Be of good comfort, rise; he calleth thee"; and that the beggar cast away his garment as he came. Matthew agrees with Mark as to when the blind eyes were opened, but says there were two beggars, not one, and that Jesus "touched their eyes." There is no question, of course, that if we had the full recitations, as originally written, there would be no contradictions. We are left, therefore, to draw our own conclusions as to the details here involved. We know Jesus normally taught the gospel first and then stretched forth his hands to work miracles so that the healing acts would place a seal of divinity upon his teachings. We suppose that is what he did in this instance also. In any event, as pertaining to Bartimeus, his repeated designation of Jesus as the Son of David, who had power to open blind eyes, shows that he had prior faith and qualified as one entitled to receive the divine blessing that came to him.

Parable of the Pounds

(*Luke 19:11-28; JST, Luke 19:11, 14, 17, 23-25*)

Jesus has set his face like flint to go to Jerusalem, where the cruel cross of crucifixion awaits his outstretched arms and nailed hands. He has many things yet to say in the few remaining days of his flesh, but, with it all, Jehovah must die so that together with his dead body many that sleep in the dust shall come forth. He as a nobleman sent of God must now travel to a far country, there, in the presence of his Father, to be crowned with glory and power everlasting.

Before he departs he will leave his earthly affairs in the hands of his servants to whom, in due course, he will return and call for an accounting of their stewardships.

This, however, is not what all Israel suppose. They are yet seeking a temporal deliverer upon whose head a kingly crown may be placed; they have yet to learn that the way to the crown is by the cross. Even some of the disciples—not, we suppose, those of the Twelve or of the Seventy—yet feel that this man should be crowned, not crucified, when he arrives in the Holy City.

And so now we find Jesus and his party, and a great host of Passover pilgrims, plodding onward from Jericho to Jerusalem. Mingled among them are many who could be drawn into the scribal stream of hostility and evil where the enemies of God will raise a sword against his Son. As a warning to them, and so that his disciples may understand more perfectly his purposes, and because they are "nigh to Jerusalem," "and because the Jews taught that the kingdom of God should immediately appear"—the scene being thus set—Jesus delivers the parable of the pounds.

> *A certain nobleman went into a far country to receive for himself a kingdom, and to return. And he called his ten servants, and delivered them ten pounds, and said unto them, Occupy till I come. But his citizens hated him, and sent a messenger after him, saying, We will not have this man to reign over us.*

This is a story that friends and foes alike will ponder in their hearts. Hearing it, they will recall the numerous "noblemen" who left Palestine and went to far-off Rome to receive suzerainty from Caesar, that they might return and reign with blood and horror over the citizens of their assigned kingdoms. They will remember in particular that some thirty years before, Archelaus went to Augustus in Rome to gain confirmation of the provisions of the will of his father, Herod the Great, so that the Idumean's offspring could reign in his appointed kingdom. They will recall how the Jews sent to Augustus a deputation of fifty to recount the cruelties and oppose the claims of Herod's son; how "Philippus defended the property of Archelaus during his absence from the encroachments of the Proconsul Sabinus"; and how Archelaus, upon his return, avenged this Jewish act of rebellion with the blood of his enemies. (Farrar, p. 524, footnote 1; Edersheim 2:466.) They will also realize that Jesus is speaking of himself as the nobleman who goes to a far country; that his servants have a period of labor before his return; and that the Messianic kingdom for which they yearn will not be established until a future day.

> *And it came to pass, that when he was returned, having received the kingdom, then he commanded these servants to be called unto him, to whom he had given the money, that he might know how much every man had gained by trading.*
>
> *Then came the first, saying, Lord, thy pound hath gained ten pounds. And he said unto him, Well done, thou good servant; because thou hast been faithful in a very little, have thou authority over ten cities. And the second came, saying, Lord, thy pound hath gained five pounds. And he said likewise to him, Be thou also over five cities.*
>
> *And another came, saying, Lord, behold, here is thy pound, which I have kept laid up in a napkin: For I feared thee, because thou art an austere man: thou takest up that thou layedst not down, and reapest that thou didst not sow.*
>
> *And he saith unto him, Out of thine own mouth will I judge thee, thou wicked servant. Thou knewest that I was an austere man, taking up that I laid not down, and reaping that I did not sow: Wherefore then gavest not thou my money into the bank, that at my coming I might have received mine own with usury?*
>
> *And he said unto them who stood by, Take from him the pound, and give it to him who hath ten pounds.*

Each servant has a like endowment and a like responsibility. It is with the elders and seventies as it is with the apostles. Each receives the Holy Priesthood; each is called to minister for the salvation of men; each takes upon himself the covenant and rejoices in the oath of the priesthood; and each has power to work out his own salvation and gain eternal reward if true and faithful in all things. As it turns out, the respective labors of each determine his kingdom and dominion in the day of his Lord's return. The power to work in the kingdom here becomes the power to rule in the kingdom hereafter. As to the slothful servant, who did no labor here, he enjoys no dominion hereafter. His pound is given to the one who can make the best use of it—it shall go "to him that hath ten pounds." Such is the surprise of his hearers at this decision that they interrupt Jesus to say, "Lord, he hath ten pounds." Our Lord's response is:

> *For I say unto you, That unto every one who occupieth, shall be given; and from him who occupieth not, even that he hath received shall be taken away from him.*

Service is essential to salvation! Labor in the vineyard or be damned. Those who receive the Holy Priesthood must magnify their callings; they must use the priesthood to teach the gospel, to perform ordinances, and to work miracles, as Jesus did; otherwise they have no reward.

> *But those mine enemies, which would not that I should reign over them, bring hither, and slay them before me.*

Jesus' enemies—worldly people; those who do not heed the voice of his servants; those who reject him and his gospel; those who will not have him to rule over them—they shall be slain at his coming. "And the day cometh that they who will not hear the voice of the Lord, neither the voice of his servants, neither give heed to the words of the prophets and apostles, shall be cut off from among the people." (D&C 1:14.) It shall be "when the Lord Jesus shall be revealed from heaven with his mighty angels, In flaming fire taking vengeance on them that know not God, and that obey not the gospel of our Lord Jesus Christ: Who shall be punished with everlasting destruction from the presence of the Lord, and from the glory of his power." (2 Thes. 1:7-9.)

Such is the eternal intent; such is the long-term meaning of the parable. But for that generation of Jews there was to be an immediate application of the curse pronounced upon those who would not have him to rule over them; who proclaimed, "We have no king but Caesar"; who said, "Write not, The King of the Jews; but that he said, I am King of the Jews"; who after he ascended into heaven continued to exhibit violent hostility against the infant Church—upon that generation of Jews the curse was to fall with unslaked fury. True, "The parable was one of many-sided application; it indicated His near departure from the world; the hatred which should reject Him; the duty of faithfulness in the use of all that He entrusted to them; the uncertainty of His return; the certainty that, when He did return, there would be a solemn account; the condemnation of the slothful; the splendid reward of all who should serve Him well; the utter destruction of those who endeavoured to reject His power." (Farrar, p. 525.)

"But as regards His 'enemies,' that would not have Him reign over them—manifestly, Jerusalem and the people of Israel—who, even after he had gone to receive the Kingdom, continued the personal hostility of their 'We will not that this One shall reign over us'—the ashes of the Temple, the ruins of the City, the blood of the fathers, and the homeless wanderings of their children, with the Cain-curse branded on their brow and visible to all men, attest, that the King has many ministers to execute that judgment which obstinate rebellion must surely bring, if His authority is to be vindicated, and His Rule to secure submission." (Edersheim 2:467.)

"And when he"—the Nobleman who will reign as King in a future day—"had thus spoken," Luke tells us, "he went before, ascending up to Jerusalem," allowing his hearers to ponder and marvel at the gracious words they had heard.

NOTE

1. As I have written elsewhere with reference to the statement that a position on his right hand or on his left was not his to give: "Certainly it is Christ's to give, for he has all power (Matt. 28:18) and all judgment is committed to the Son. (John 5:22.) Rather: 'It is not mine to give as a matter of favoritism; it can be given only in accordance with justice. To sit on my right hand or on my left is not mine to give, except to them for whom it is prepared according to the Father's will, and the Father and I are one.' " (*Commentary* 1:566.)

SECTION X

FROM THE ANOINTING TO THE ROYAL REIGN

FROM THE ANOINTING TO THE ROYAL REIGN

THIS IS JESUS
THE KING OF THE JEWS.
(Matt. 27:37.)
Blessed be the King that cometh
in the name of the Lord:
peace in heaven,
and glory in the highest.
(Luke 19:38.)

As Samuel poured oil on the head of Saul and anointed him to be captain over the Lord's inheritance, and all Israel then marched at their king's word;

As he also poured oil on David and anointed him in the midst of his brethren, so that the Spirit of the Lord came upon him from that day forward;

And as Zadok took an horn of oil and anointed Solomon, and all the people said, "God save king Solomon"—

So Mary of Bethany, in the home of Simon the leper, as guided by the Spirit, poured costly spikenard from her alabaster box upon the head of Jesus, and also anointed his feet, so that, the next day, the ten thousands of Israel might acclaim him King and shout Hosanna to his name.

We see Jesus thus anointed and acclaimed, heading a triumphal procession into the Holy City. So commences the first day of the week of the atoning sacrifice.

On the second day he curses the barren fig tree and cleanses the temple a second time.

On the third day he discourses on faith; confounds the Jews on the question of authority, and delivers the three parables to the Jews—the parable of the two sons, the parable of the wicked husbandmen, and the parable of the marriage of the king's son.

That same day the Jews provoke, tempt, and reject him; they seek to ensnare him on the question of tribute and are confounded; he proclaims the law of eternal marriage; and then he gives his great pronouncement about the first and great commandment.

Then he propounds the question: "What think ye of Christ?"

After all this comes the great denunciation. Such woes—eight in number—as seldom come from divine lips are heaped, with a vengeance, upon the rebellious scribes and Pharisees.

Thereupon he laments over doomed Jerusalem, speaks of the widow's mite, offers salvation to the Gentiles, and testifies boldly that he is the Son of Man. Thus endeth his public ministry.

During the closing hours of that day, he gives the incomparable Olivet Discourse.

In it his voice is raised, first, against Jerusalem and the Holy House soon to be left desolate.

He speaks of the persecutions and martyrdom that await his disciples.

He tells of the universal apostasy that will precede the Second Coming; then of the glorious era of Restoration; of the desolations of the latter days; and of the coming in of the Gentile fulness.

His disciples learn that the abomination of desolation shall again sweep Jerusalem; that signs and wonders shall fill the heavens and the earth; and that he shall come as a thief in the night.

Those who shall abide the day are identified, and all men are commanded to watch, pray, take heed, and be ready.

He then speaks the parable of the ten virgins and the parable of the talents, and, finally, gives the great decree that he and the Twelve shall sit on thrones in judgment upon the world.

And in that day all his saints who have served their fellow men shall learn that their good deeds were in fact done unto him, and they shall have eternal life.

Chapter 84

"HOSANNA TO THE SON OF DAVID"

Rejoice greatly, O daughter of Zion;
shout, O daughter of Jerusalem:
behold, thy King cometh unto thee:
he is just, and having salvation;
lowly, and riding upon an ass,
and upon a colt the foal of an ass. . . .
He shall speak peace unto the heathen:
and his dominion shall be from sea even to sea,
and from the river even to the ends of the earth.
(Zech. 9:9-10.)

Mary Anoints Jesus at Simon's Supper

(*John 11:55-57; 12:1-11; JST, John 11:56; 12:7; Matthew 26:6-13; JST, Matthew 26:5-10; Mark 14:3-9; JST, Mark 14:4-8*)

As the time of the Fourth Passover draws near, fanatical tides of religious anarchy sweep through Jerusalem—through the Holy City, the City of David, through the religious capital of the world. Never in the whole history of the world have religious feelings and fanaticism built themselves up to such a crises as now impends—not when the Lord confounded the tongues at Babel; not when he slew the firstborn in every Egyptian home; not when an evil and militant spirit swept the Crusades across Europe; not at any time.

There is a veritable maelstrom of divergent opinion about Him who is everywhere proclaiming his own divine Sonship and then working miracles to attest the divinity of his word. For three and a half years Jesus has taught and preached and worked miracles in every city and village throughout the land. Apostles and seventies, and disciples without number, both male and female, have echoed his words and testified of his goodness and grace to them. His gospel message has been proclaimed from the mountaintops; nothing has been done in a corner. Just as all Israel knew that Moses led them through the Red Sea and that six days of each week Jehovah rained manna from heaven upon them, so these Jews all know that there is one among them who claims to be the Son of God. It is as though each day the press, radio, and television carry new banner headlines and relay extensive broadcasts telling his doings of that day. There are press releases quoting his words; accounts of eyewitnesses who saw his miracles; the testimonies of those who were healed; the views of his enemies that he works by the power of Beelzebub and is even Satan incarnate; and the analytical columns setting forth the marvels of his ministry, or the evils of forsaking Moses to follow him, as each author expounds the views he espouses. Every Sabbath in the synagogues his doings and sayings are discussed by friends and foes. Every marketplace is ablaze with gossip and rumor about him. On every street corner men congregate to exchange opinions and gain new views. The raising of Lazarus is discussed in every home; the name of Jesus is on every tongue.

Passover pilgrims from the country areas are arriving in Jerusalem ahead of the feast itself so they can "purify themselves" in the temple. Their conversations are about the one thing uppermost in all minds. "What think ye of Jesus?" they ask one another. His disciples, whose views are fixed, move among them and bear testimony of the knowledge of salvation that has come into their hearts. Many rustic Galileans speak of him in reverent tones. "Will he not come to the feast?" they ask, and none seem to know. Influenced by their Rabbis and swayed by their scribes, most of the sophisticated Judeans have gained an undying hatred of this man of Galilee—out of which country, as they pretend to believe, cometh no prophet. And the chief priests and the Pharisees have given a commandment that if anyone knows where Jesus is, "he should shew it, that they might take him."[1]

Before placing his person in the midst of this war of words and tumult of opinions; before showing himself to the people, that all things shall be fulfilled which have been spoken of him in the law and in the prophets; before carrying his cross for the week of his passion, Jesus chose to spend a quiet Sabbath, his last on earth, in his beloved Bethany. There in the home of Simon the leper, enjoying sociality with Mary and Martha and Lazarus and those of his intimate circle, he will receive the holy anointing preparatory to his kingly burial; there he will take into his lungs the last peaceful breaths of Judean air before the tumultuous hours and days of his passion. It is Friday, Nisan 8, A.U.C. 780—March 31, A.D. 30, according to our calendar—and Jesus and his select friends are just arriving from Jericho. As we learned in the passing and raising of Lazarus there was communication between our Lord and his associates in Bethany, and it would not surprise us if the beloved sisters and others came out to meet and greet him and his party as they neared the place where they designed to spend the approaching Sabbath.

But before recounting the circumstances surrounding the sacred ordinance, which will transpire in this Judean village of blessed memory, on the Sabbath which will dawn, as it were, with the setting sun, we must note the intimate and felicitous friendships that prevailed between Jesus and the beloved sisters and their brother Lazarus. We have reason to believe this relationship was like none other enjoyed by him who came to do all things well and gain all the experiences of mortality. All scripturalists and authors of insight and renown are aware of the unique and unusual familial scenes portrayed by the Gospel authors with reference to the various happenings in this secluded and peaceful village. Let us note, for instance, how Farrar speaks of Jesus' friends in Bethany.

"We seem to trace in the Synoptists a special reticence about the family at Bethany," he says. "The house in which they take a prominent position is called 'the house of Simon the leper'; Mary is called simply 'a woman' by St. Matthew and St. Mark; and St. Luke contents himself with calling Bethany 'a certain village,' although he was perfectly aware of the name. There are, therefore, good grounds for the conjecture that when the earliest form of the Gospel of St. Matthew appeared, and when the memorials were collected which were used by the other two Synoptists, there may have been special reasons for not recording a miracle [the raising of Lazarus] which would have brought into dangerous prominence a man who was still living, but of whom the Jews had distinctly sought to get rid as a witness of Christ's wonder-working power. Even if this danger had ceased, it would have been painful to the quiet family of Bethany to have been made the focus of an intense and irreverent curiosity, and to be questioned about those hidden things none have ever revealed. Something, then, seems to have 'sealed the lips' of those Evangelists—an obstacle which had been long removed when St. John's Gospel first saw the light." (Farrar, p. 511.)[2]

As to our Lord's last Sabbath on earth, we assume he preached in the local synagogue or counseled in quiet seclusion with the Twelve and other intimates. When the hour came for the festive Sabbath meal, they held it in his honor. John says, "they made him a supper," as though it were a community expression of goodwill toward their Guest of renown. Matthew and Mark placed the banquet "in the house of Simon the leper." Martha served—indeed, she seems to have been in charge of the serving and arrangements; Lazarus sat at the table with Jesus; the Twelve and others of the disciples partook of the feast; and—as the custom was—others milled about as observers.

Bethany that evening was the focal point of Jewish interest. Many people, learning that Jesus was there, came from Jerusalem to see him and to see Lazarus, "whom he had raised from the dead." Among them were those whose souls were penitent and who sought that righteousness which this Galilean brought; and among them also were those whose hearts were hardened and who were devising ways to slay both Lazarus and Jesus. Lazarus alive was a living witness of the power of Him whose new doctrine meant the death of the Mosaic system, and of all the religious formalities so dear to the hearts of those whose means of livelihood it was. And so, "the chief priests"—the very rulers of the nation—"consulted that they might put Lazarus also to death," John tells us, "Because that by reason of him many of the Jews went away, and believed on Jesus." Scarcely is there a lower depth than this to which malice and hatred and depravity can sink.

Emotions ran high this memorable evening in Bethany, not only among those who came to view and wonder, or to plot and connive, as their desires might be, but also among those in whose house the feast was held. And in the souls of none did the fires of love, and devotion, and worship, burn more brightly than in the soul of the beloved Mary. She who loved to sit at Jesus' feet and hear his words; she whose soul drank in truth as the parched desert absorbs the heavensent rain; she who had seen her brother Lazarus come forth from the tomb after four days of decomposing death—this beloved one now sought some means of expressing her love and worship of the Master before he went to his death. She took from her treasures an alabaster box containing "a pound of ointment of spikenard, very costly," and poured it on his head, and anointed his feet, and wiped them with her hair, "and the house was filled with the odour of the ointment." Truly the sweet smell of incense, symbolical of the prayers of the heart, ascended up on high this night.

"To understand this solemn scene one must both know and feel the religious significance of Mary's act. Here sat the Lord of Heaven, in the house of his friends, as the hour of his greatest trials approached, with those who loved him knowing he was soon to face betrayal and crucifixion. What act of love, of devotion, of adoration, of worship, could a mere mortal perform for him who is eternal? Could a loved one do more than David had said the Good Shepherd himself would do in conferring honor and blessing upon another, that is: 'Thou anointest my head with oil'?" (*Commentary* 1:700.)[3]

"But there was one present to whom on every ground the act was odious and repulsive. There is no vice at once so absorbing, so unreasonable, and so degrading as the vice of avarice, and avarice was the besetting sin in the dark soul of the traitor Judas. The failure to struggle with his own temptations; the disappointment of every expectation which had first drawn him to Jesus; the intolerable rebuke conveyed to his whole being by the daily communion with a sinless purity; the darker shadow which he could not but feel that his guilt flung athwart his footsteps because of the burning sunlight in which for many months he now had walked; the sense too that the eye of his Master, possibly even the eyes of some of his fellow-apostles, had read or were beginning to read the hidden secrets of his heart;—all these things had gradually deepened from an incipient alienation into an insatiable repugnancy and hate. And the sight of Mary's lavish sacrifice, the consciousness that it was now too late to save that large sum for the bag—the mere possession of which, apart from the sums which he could pilfer out of it, gratified his greed for gold—filled him with disgust and madness. He had a devil. He felt as if he had been personally cheated; as if the money were by right *his,* and he had been, in a senseless manner, defrauded of it. 'To what purpose is this waste?' he indignantly said; and, alas! how often have his words been echoed, for wherever there is an act of splendid self-forgetfulness there is always a Judas to sneer and murmur at it. 'This ointment might have been sold for three hundred pence and given to the poor!' *Three hundred pence*—ten pounds or more! There was perfect frenzy in the thought of such utter perdition of good money; why, for barely a third of such a sum, this son of perdition was ready to sell his Lord. Mary thought it not good enough to anele Christ's sacred feet: Judas thought a third part of it sufficient reward for selling His very life." (Farrar, 527- 28.)

Mary loved much and was rewarded infinitely. Her act of adoring worship—born, we cannot doubt, from the promptings of the Spirit—gained for her a name and a fame that shall endure everlastingly. How sweet the words we now hear Jesus speak:

> *Why trouble ye the woman? For she hath wrought a good work upon me.*
>
> *Ye have the poor with you always, and whensoever ye will, ye may do them good; but me ye have not always.*
>
> *Let her alone; for she hath preserved this ointment until now, that she might anoint me in token of my burial.*
>
> *She has done what she could, and this which she has done unto me, shall be had in remembrance in generations to come, wheresoever my gospel shall be preached; for verily she has come beforehand to anoint my body to the burying.*
>
> *And in this thing that she hath done, she shall be blessed; for verily I say unto you, Wheresoever this gospel shall be preached in the whole world, this thing that this woman hath done, shall also be told for a memorial of her.*
>
> He that hath ears to hear, let him hear!

Jesus Enters Jerusalem as King Messiah

(*Matthew 21:1-11; JST, Matthew 21:2, 4-5, 9; Mark 11:1-11; JST, Mark 11:10-13; Luke 19:29-44; John 12:12-19; JST, John 12:14*)

"Rejoice greatly, O daughter of Zion; shout, O daughter of Jerusalem"; let all who dwell in David's City cry

Hosanna. Come, all ye Judeans and Galileans and Pereans and Samaritans; come, ye Gentiles whose lives are touched by Israel and her divine destiny; come, ye three million souls who are celebrating the Passover in your capital city—for this day ye shall see the seeric words of Zechariah fulfilled.

"Behold," O Jerusalem, the Holy City, for "thy King cometh unto thee." He cometh from Bethany on the east, where but yesterday he sat at meat with Lazarus, whom he raised from death; where in the house of Simon the leper, his beloved Mary anointed his royal head and poured costly spikenard on his kingly feet—all in token of his burial, which is to be later this week.

Hail him as your King; heed his words, for "he is just, and having salvation." Accept him as the Just One, your Deliverer—from death, hell, the devil, and endless torment. Know that all who believe in him shall be saved; he is your Savior; salvation comes by him; he is the resurrection and the life, as he said.

How shall he come? As the prophetic word foretells, ye shall see him "lowly, and riding upon an ass," the symbol of Jewish royalty. He shall be "upon a colt the foal of an ass." Messianic shouts shall rend the air; his disciples shall wave palm branches of peace; and the Roman soldiers in Antonia will smile and say, "What manner of King is this," not knowing that his kingdom is not of this world.

Come, join in the celebration, for this is he of whom it is written: "He shall speak peace unto the heathen: and his dominion shall be from sea even to sea, and from the river even to the ends of the earth." And those who accept him now will reign with him then in that great millennial day.

It is Sunday, April 2, A.D. 30, and Jesus with his disciples—that all things shall be fulfilled which are written of him—departs from Bethany, going toward Jerusalem. Multitudes from the Judean village follow along. When he arrives at the mount of Olives, near Bethphage, a suburb of Jerusalem, he says, as we suppose, to Peter and John: "Go your way into the village over against you: and as soon as ye be entered into it, ye shall find a colt tied, whereon never man sat; loose him, and bring him. And if any man say unto you, Why do ye this? say ye that the Lord hath need of him; and straightway he will send him hither."

They went. All things happened as Jesus' seeric foresight had specified, and they "brought the colt, and put on it their clothes; and Jesus took the colt and sat thereon; and they followed him." Then many, "a very great multitude"—those who came out from Jerusalem to meet the Messianic party, and those who followed from Bethany—spread their garments, and the branches they cut from the trees, to make a path before him. His disciples—both Judeans and Galileans coming out from the City of the Great King, and those from Bethany who were with him "when he called Lazarus out of his grave, and raised him from the dead"—they all "took branches of palm trees" and waved them as they gave the Hosanna Shout. It was a spontaneous, Spirit-guided acclamation of holy praise and divine testimony, patterned after the acclamations of adulation and glory given to Jehovah at the Feast of Tabernacles. Their King—meek and lowly in heart, riding in their midst on a lowly ass—heard thousands of voices cry out in perfect praise:

Hosanna: Blessed is the King of Israel that cometh in the name of the Lord.

Blessed be the King that cometh in the name of the Lord: peace in heaven, and glory in the highest.

Hosanna to the son of David: Blessed is he that cometh in the name of the Lord; Hosanna in the highest.

Hosanna! Blessed is he that cometh in the name of the Lord; That bringeth the kingdom of our father David; Blessed is he that cometh in the name of the Lord; Hosanna in the highest.

Such blasphemy as this could not go unchallenged. This mob of unlearned followers of this discredited Galilean were ascribing to *him* the very cries of praise reserved for Jehovah alone. Here were men crying Hosanna—meaning *save now,* or *save we pray,* or *save we beseech thee*—to *him,* as though *he* were God and could save them. Here the very words of the Hallel—"Save now, I beseech thee, O Lord: O Lord, I beseech thee, send now prosperity. Blessed be he that cometh in the name of the Lord"—were being sung in praise to One whose works were from beneath. To the Pharisees among them this was as gall and wormwood; it was blasphemy. "Master, rebuke thy disciples," they said. But Jesus, knowing the full significance of what was then in process, replied: "I tell you that, if these should hold their peace, the stones would immediately cry out." These cries were destined to be made. He was the King of Israel and was to be acclaimed as such by believing people before Pilate wrote over his cross: "THIS IS JESUS THE KING OF THE JEWS."

Drawing near to Jerusalem, and beholding the city, Jesus wept. "He had dropped *silent* tears at the grave of Lazarus; here He wept aloud. All the shame of His mockery, all the anguish of His torture, was powerless, five days afterwards, to extort from Him a single groan, or to wet His eyelids with one trickling tear; but here, all the pity that was within Him overmastered His human spirit, and He not only wept, but broke into a passion of lamentation, in which the choked voice seemed to struggle for its utterance. A strange Messianic triumph! a strange interruption of the festal cries! The Deliverer weeps over the city which it is now too late to save; the King prophesies the total ruin of the nation which He came to rule!" (Farrar, pp. 534-35.) His lamenting words:

> *If thou hadst known, even thou, at least in this thy day, the things which belong unto thy peace! but now they are hid from thine eyes.*

'O that thou hadst known me and believed my gospel and gained that peace which I came to bring. O that thou hadst exchanged thy heart of flint for a heart of flesh and had hearkened unto the Son of Man who has taught in thy streets. But now all these things are hidden from thine eyes.'

For the days shall come upon thee, that thine enemies shall cast a trench about thee, and compass thee round, and keep thee in on every side, And shall lay thee even with the ground, and thy children within thee; and they shall not leave in thee one stone upon another; because thou knewest not the time of thy visitation.

"Sternly, literally, terribly, within fifty years was that prophecy fulfilled. Four years before the war began, while as yet the city was in the greatest peace and prosperity, a melancholy maniac traversed its streets with the repeated cry, 'A voice from the east, a voice from the west, a voice from the four winds, a voice against Jerusalem and the holy house, a voice against the bridegrooms and the brides, and a voice against this whole people.' No scourgings or tortures could wring from him any other words except, 'Woe! Woe! to Jerusalem; woe to the city; woe to the people; woe to the holy house!' until seven years afterwards, during the siege, he was killed by a stone from a catapult. His voice was but the renewed echo of the voice of prophecy.

"Titus had not originally wished to encompass the city, but he was forced, by the despair and obstinacy of the Jews, to surround it, first with a palisaded mound, and then, when this *vallum* and *agger* were destroyed, with a wall of masonry. He did not wish to sacrifice the Temple—nay, he made every possible effort to save it—but he was forced to leave it in ashes. He did not intend to be cruel to the inhabitants, but the deadly fanaticism of their opposition so extinguished all desire to spare them, that he undertook the task of well-nigh exterminating the race—of crucifying them by hundreds, of exposing them in the amphitheatre by thousands, of selling them into slavery by myriads. Josephus tells us that, even immediately after the siege of Titus, no one, in the desert waste around him, would have recognised the beauty of Judea; and that if any Jew had come upon the city of a sudden, however well he had known it before, he would have asked 'what place it was?' And he who, in modern

Jerusalem, would look for relics of the ten-times-captured city of the days of Christ, must look for them twenty feet beneath the soil, and will scarcely find them. In one spot alone remain a few massive substructions, as though to show how vast is the ruin they represent; and here, on every Friday, assemble a few poverty-stricken Jews, to stand each in the shroud in which he will be buried and wail over the shattered glories of their fallen and desecrated home." (Farrar, pp. 535-37.)

Then Jesus, continuing with the triumphal procession, entered Jerusalem, and, Matthew tells us, "all the city was moved, saying, Who is this?" It was never intended that the events of this day be hidden from view; for nearly six hundred years all Israel had awaited the fulfillment of Zechariah's prophecy, and now the divine Hosannas rent the air. The answer to their question came from the multitude who hailed him as the Son of David. "This is Jesus of Nazareth, the prophet of Galilee," they said.

Continuing into the courts of the temple, where two hundred and ten thousand can assemble at one time, Jesus "looked round about upon all things, and blessed the disciples." What a sweet and tender touch this is! The Son of David, whose Father is God, and who has this day been hailed by believing souls as the Blessed One who was to come, has in his heart a feeling of gratitude. However deserving he knows himself to be—of all the glory and honor and worship that this day has been heaped upon him—yet he now blesses his disciples for the spirit of adoration they have manifest. He blesses them for fulfilling the Messianic word, for crying out: "Blessed is he who cometh in the name of the Lord."

Meanwhile the Pharisees—oppressed, hateful, vengeful—unable to stay the surging tide of divine acclaim that is this day hailing Jesus as Israel's King, say among themselves: "Perceive ye how ye prevail nothing? behold, the world is gone after him." And Jesus, when "the eventide was come," the work of this day being accomplished, "went out unto Bethany with the twelve."

NOTES

1. Something akin to this state of affairs in Palestine was also going on among the Israelite Nephites in the New World at this same time. The people were looking with great earnestness for the sign of the Messiah's death, as such had been given by Samuel the Lamanite. "And there began to be great doubtings and disputations among the people, notwithstanding so many signs had been given." (3 Ne. 8:1-4.)

2. Later, in discussing the supper in the home of Simon the leper, Farrar says: "We are again driven to the conclusion that there must have been some good reason, a reason which we can but uncertainly conjecture, for their marked reticence on this subject; and we find another trace of this reticence in their calling Mary 'a certain woman,' in their omission of all allusion to Martha and Lazarus, and in their telling us that this memorable banquet was served in the house of 'Simon the leper.' " (Farrar, p. 526.)

3. "To anoint the head of a guest with ordinary oil was to do him honor; to anoint his feet also was to show unusual and signal regard; but the anointing of head and feet with spikenard, and in such abundance, was an act of reverential homage rarely rendered even to kings. Mary's act was an expression of adoration; it was the fragrant outwelling of a heart overflowing with worship and affection." (Talmage, p. 512.)

JESUS—ONE HAVING AUTHORITY

And no man taketh this honour unto himself,
but he that is called of God,
as was Aaron. So also Christ glorified
not himself to be made an high priest;
but he that said unto him,
Thou art my Son, to day have I begotten thee.
As he saith also in another place,
Thou art a priest for ever
after the order of Melchisedec. . . .
Called of God an high priest
after the order of Melchisedec.
(Heb. 5:4-6, 10.)

He Curseth a Barren Fig Tree

(*Mark 11:12-14, 20-26; JST, Mark 11:14-16, 24-26; Matthew 21:18-22; JST, Matthew 21:17, 20*)

Here is a man who says he is the Son of God; who preaches a gospel that he says is the plan of salvation; who works miracles as a witness that his words are true and that God is his Father. Whence comes his authority, and in what power does he act?

Our Gospel authors do not preserve for us his sermons on priesthood and priestly offices; they do not speak of his ordinations, or even have a great deal to say of the divine commissions conferred upon him by his Father. He is simply described as going forward doing what could not be done without authority. Our inspired writers do not tell how he received the same priesthood and power that was before held by Melchizedek, or how he was called by his Father to rule and reign in that priestly power forever. And yet, implicit in every word that he spoke and every deed that he did is the issue of divine authority. Never man spake as this man; he spake as one having authority and not as the scribes. Never man wrought as this man did; his works required power—the power of God. And priesthood is the power and authority of God delegated to man on earth to act in all things for the salvation of men. It is also the power and authority by which worlds come rolling into existence, by which mountains are moved and seas divided, and by which fig trees are cursed. And if ever there was a people who knew their prophets must have authority from on high, it was Jewish Israel. We are about to see Jesus curse a fig tree and cleanse again his Father's house, and then the chief priests will confront him on the very issue of authority itself. But first the matter of the fig tree.

Bethany of blessed memory—the beautiful and beloved village—has once again been the bivouac of the Bridegroom and of the twelve special friends who ever attend him. It is now early Monday. How the holy party spent the night we do not know—perhaps in communion with each other; perhaps in sacred and solitary prayer; perhaps resting in the home of Simon the leper. Now they are en route to the city and the temple. Jesus is hungry. Afar off he sees a solitary fig tree having leaves. Such trees are planted by the way, and their fruit is common property of all. It is not the season for newly ripened figs, but it is common to find autumn figs still clinging to the trees; and since the new crop develops before the leaves, there should have been a sweet and edible though unripened crop of spring figs.

"But when He came up to it, He was disappointed. The

sap was circulating; the leaves made a fair show; but of fruit there was none. Fit emblem of a hypocrite, whose external semblance is a delusion and sham—fit emblem of the nation in whom the ostentatious profession of religion brought forth no 'fruit of good living'—the tree was barren. And it was *hopelessly* barren; for had it been fruitful the previous year, there would still have been some of the *kermouses* hidden under those broad leaves; and had it been fruitful *this* year, the *bakkooroth* would have set into green and delicious fragrance before the leaves appeared; but on this fruitless tree there was neither any promise for the future, nor any gleanings from the past.

"And therefore, since it was but deceptive and useless, a barren cumberer of the ground, He made it the eternal warning against a life of hypocrisy continued until it is too late, and, in the hearing of His disciples, uttered upon it the solemn fiat, 'Never fruit grow upon thee more!' Even at the word, such infructuous life as it possessed was arrested, and it began to wither away." (Farrar, pp. 546-47.)

Matthew tells us that Jesus having so spoken, "Presently the fig tree withered away. And when the disciples saw it, they marvelled, saying, How soon is the fig tree withered away!" Mark says that the next morning as the little group passed by on the same route, "they saw the fig tree dried up from the roots." That this miracle is unique is apparent to all; it seems at first glance, from the standpoint of the fig tree, to be a miracle that curses instead of blesses. But miracles are for the benefit and blessing of men, not for trees and shrubs. All things are and were created for man, to whom dominion over them has been given. Man is the prince of creation. If created things do not serve him and his purposes, should they not be replaced with others that will? That it is also a manifestation of the power of faith resident in him who creates and destroys as seemeth good to him is also apparent. And who are we to question divine wisdom when destructions come?

To cavilers whose aim is to find fault, this miracle becomes an excuse to upbraid and question the justice of the One who does all things well. To all such it is perhaps sufficient answer to say: "When the hail beats down the tendrils of the vineyard—when the lightning scathes the olive, or 'splits the unwedgeable and gnarled oak'—do any but the utterly ignorant and brutal begin at once to blaspheme against God? Is it a crime under *any* circumstances to destroy a *useless* tree? If not, is it *more* a crime to do so by miracle? Why, then, is the Savior of the world—to whom Lebanon would be too little for a burnt-offering—to be blamed by petulant critics because He hastened the withering of one barren tree, and founded, on the destruction of its uselessness, three eternal lessons—a symbol of the destruction of impenitence, a warning of the peril of hypocrisy, an illustration of the power of faith?" (Farrar, p. 548.)

Did Jesus ever miss an opportunity to teach the principles of the gospel? It almost seems that everything he or his asssociates either saw or heard or did became a text for preaching a new and an everlasting doctrine. When Peter said to him on Tuesday, "Master, behold, the fig tree which thou cursedst is withered away," Jesus answered:

> *Have faith in God. For verily I say unto you, That whosoever shall say unto this mountain, Be thou removed, and be thou cast into the sea; and shall not doubt in his heart, but shall believe that those things which he saith shall come to pass; he shall have whatsoever he saith fulfilled.*
>
> *Therefore I say unto you, Whatsoever things ye desire, when ye pray, believe that ye receive, and ye shall have whatsoever ye ask.*

This is familiar doctrine, but by tying it now to a miracle of such a dramatic nature, who among his hearers will ever forget it? And if trees wither, will not mountains move? Clearly, faith is a power over both animate and inanimate objects. And all are governed for the benefit and blessing of Adam's seed. "But, since in this one instance the power had been put forth to destroy, He added a very important warning. They were not to suppose that this emblematic act gave them any licence to wield the sacred forces which faith and prayer would bestow on them, for purposes of anger or vengeance; nay, *no* power was possible to the heart that knew not how to forgive, and the *unforgiving* heart could never be forgiven. The sword, and the famine, and the pestilence were to be no instruments for *them* to wield, nor were they even to dream of evoking against their enemies the fire of heaven or the 'icy wind of death.' The secret of successful prayer was faith; the road to faith in God lay through pardon of transgression; pardon was possible to them alone who were ready to pardon others." (Farrar, p. 555.)

And when ye stand praying, forgive, if ye have ought against any: that your Father also which is in heaven may forgive you your trespasses. But if ye do not forgive, neither will your Father which is in heaven forgive your trespasses.

Jesus Cleanseth the Temple the Second Time

(*Matthew 21:12-17; JST, Matthew 21:13-14; Mark 11:15-19; Luke 19:45-48; 21:37*)

When we went with Jesus into the temple three years ago, at the time of the First Passover, and saw him drive out, with force and violence, the moneychangers and the wicked men who made merchandise of his Father's house, we took occasion to describe the desecrating filth and the evilness of spirit that there prevailed. (See chapter 29, Book 1.) We need not describe anew the physical filth, nor the spiritual degeneracy that then overspread those sacred courts. Suffice it to say that the cleansing of the past was but for a moment. Once again the changers of coins ply their dishonest course; the keepers of doves and the sellers of sheep still haggle over prices and shortchange the Passover pilgrims; the lowing of cattle and the bleating of sheep still add to the confusion and bespeak the spirit of religious anarchy that rages through the city; and the piles of dung and the stench of urine still foul the air. The House of the Lord at Passover time is still as filthy as a pig sty, and many who commune with each other in its courts are still breathing the spirit of hate and vengeance and murder.

Once again, in a spirit of righteous indignation, Jesus drives them out, we suppose with a scourge of cords, as in the first instance; once again he overturns the money tables, frees the doves, and refuses entrance to those who seek to carry vessels through the holy courts, as though they were streets of commerce. But this time he does not say "Make not my Father's house an house of merchandise," but, rather, "My house shall be called the house of prayer; but ye have made it a den of thieves." Three years have passed. Everywhere he has now testified that he and his Father are one; that he speaks the word of his Father; that whatsoever is the Father's is his also; and so now, it is Jesus' house. Let him be charged with blasphemy, if they will. It is his house. It is the house of the Lord Jehovah. He is Jehovah. And it must meet such standards of cleanliness as he can impose for these final hours and days of his teachings therein.

As peace and serenity fell over the sacred courts, Jesus resumed his teachings. The Gospel Voice was heard again; disciples crowded around him to drink deeply from the Everlasting Fountain; faith welled up in the hearts of men; "And the blind and the lame came to him in the temple; and he healed them." The same spirit of worship and adoration that fell mightily upon the multitudes the day before, in the triumphal entry into the city, came again. Shouts of hosanna rent the air; from the children of the kingdom came the cries, "Hosanna to the son of David," and believing souls knew in their hearts that this prophet of Galilee was the Promised Messiah.

But "when the chief priests and scribes saw the wonderful things that he did" and heard the shouts of hosanna and the pleas for salvation that came from the disciples, "they were sore displeased." "Hearest thou what these say?" they demanded. And Jesus said: "Yea; have ye never read the scriptures which saith, Out of the mouth of babes and sucklings, O Lord, thou hast perfected praise?" Then they sought how they might destroy him, and he returned to Bethany for the night.

Jesus Confoundeth the Jews on the Question of Authority

(*Matthew 21:23-27; Mark 11:27-33; JST, Mark 11:34; Luke 20:1-8*)

On Saturday, April 1, the holy Sabbath, the Lord Jesus—having but recently accomplished his glorious Perean ministry, with all its miracles and wonders—was honored by the people of Bethany with a banquet in the house of Simon the leper. There, while Lazarus whom he raised from the dead looked on, Mary anointed Jesus' head and feet; anointed him—shall we not say it?—as King in Israel; anointed him for his burial, for their King was to die and rise again, that glory and triumph might come to them all, if they would receive it. Though these deeds were done in comparative privacy, in an obscure village, this was a crowning day in the life of Him who would, first, be lifted up upon an earthly cross, and then, have placed on his head an eternal crown.

On Sunday, April 2, Jesus rode on an ass, in triumph, into Jerusalem, amid cries of Hosanna and bold acclamations that he was the Blessed One who came to establish the kingdom of his Father. That evening he returned to Bethany.

On Monday, April 3, he returned; cursed the barren fig tree en route; cleansed the temple a second time; and taught and healed, with great power, in the newly cleansed courts. Again he returned to Bethany for the night.

These were days of glory and honor and triumph. He was being received by believing souls, and they were pledging a Spirit-borne allegiance to him who came to fulfill the old and establish the new. Those in Bethany rejoiced in his presence; many from Jerusalem and multitudes of Passover pilgrims who were there for the feast hailed him as King and Lord; and the common people found pleasure in the cleansing of the temple and the overturning of the money-gouging bazaars of the sons of Annas.

But days of glory and honor and triumph are also days of enmity and opposition and hatred. Mingling with the friendly folk in Bethany were those—taking their cues from the chief priests—who sought the death of Lazarus, that he might no longer stand as a witness of the power of Him who is the resurrection and the life. Infiltrating the hosannic chorus were Pharisaic voices that demanded, "Master, rebuke thy disciples," and that lamented among themselves, "Perceive ye how ye prevail nothing? behold, the world is gone after him."

And so, on Monday night, some of these voices—made up of the chief priests and the scribes and the elders—consulted together as to how they might halt the tide of popular acclaim now attending the ministry of this Galilean rebel, this disturber of the Mosaic order, this Rabbi from Nazareth who would destroy their craft. What arraignment can they bring against him? They have heretofore charged him with casting out devils by Beelzebub; they have demanded Messianic signs from heaven; they have raised questions of marriage and divorce and of doctrines without number; they have sought in every way for more than three years to silence his voice and void his message—all to no avail. Nay, more, all his replies and every rejoinder he has made have left them silent, embarrassed, beaten. What issue can they now raise? With that cunning which has guided them in the past, they devise a new trap. Perhaps they can show he is not an approved Rabbi and has no right even to speak, let alone work miracles. If only the people can be brought to see that he has no Rabbinical authority to utter a word of doctrine or lift a finger to perform a ministerial act, perhaps they will no longer give him glory and honor and cry out: "Lord, save us, we pray; O bring us salvation, we beseech thee; for, blessed is he that cometh in the name of the Lord; hosanna to the Son of David."

Thus, on Tuesday, April 4, Jesus comes again from Bethany; he discourses en route on faith, as the disciples view the smitten fig tree; he enters the temple, where—as always!—he "preached the gospel." The word of everlasting salvation is again going forth; he must be stopped; soon he will be causing the blind to see and the lame to leap, as he has done before. Now is the time for the chief priests and the scribes and the elders to make their confrontation. It is to be a formal and planned challenge. Thus, as Jesus taught the gospel to a receptive congregation, his enemies made their assault. "A formidable deputation approached them, imposing alike in its numbers and its stateliness. The chief priests—heads of the twenty-four courses—the learned scribes, the leading rabbis, representatives of all the constituent classes of the Sanhedrin were there, to overawe Him—whom they despised as the poor contemptible Prophet of Nazareth—with all that was venerable in age, eminent in wisdom, or imposing in authority in the great Council of the nation. The people whom He was engaged in teaching made reverent way for them, lest they should pollute those floating robes and ample fringes with a touch; and when they had arranged themselves around Jesus, they sternly asked Him, 'By what kind of authority doest thou these things, and who gave thee this authority?' They demanded of Him His warrant for thus publicly assuming the functions of Rabbi and Prophet, for riding into Jerusalem amid the hosannas of attendant crowds, for purging the Temple of the traffickers, at whose presence they connived." (Farrar, pp. 548-49.)

To envision the cunning import of these scribal demands—"By what authority doest thou these things? and who gave thee this authority?"—we must know the Jewish setting in which they were made. In Jesus' day, approved Rabbinical ministries must meet two standards:

1. *All formal teaching must be both authoritative and authorized.*

"There was no principle more firmly established by universal consent than that *authoritative* teaching required previous authorization," Edersheim tells us. "Indeed, this logically followed from the principle of Rabbinism. All teaching must be authoritative, since it was traditional—approved by authority, and handed down from teacher to disciple. The highest honour of a scholar was, that he was like a well-plastered cistern, from which not a drop had leaked of what had been poured into it. The ultimate appeal in cases of discussion was always to some great authority, whether an individual Teacher or a Decree by the Sanhedrin. In this manner had the great Hillel first vindicated his claim to be the Teacher of his time and to decide the disputes then pending. And, to decide differently from authority, was either the mark of ignorant assumption or the outcome of daring rebellion, in either case to be visited with 'the ban' [excommunication]."

2. *Authorization for Rabbinical teaching came by ordination.*

"No one would have thought of interfering with a mere Haggadist—a popular expositor, preacher, or teller of legends. But authoritatively to teach, required warrant. In fact there was regular ordination (*Semikhah*) to the office of Rabbi, Elder, and Judge, for the three functions were combined in one. . . . Although we have not any description of the earliest mode of ordination, the very name—*Semikhah*—implies the imposition of hands. Again, in the oldest record, reaching up, no doubt, to the time of Christ, the presence of at least three ordained persons was required for the ordination. . . . In the course of time certain formalities were added. The person to be ordained had to deliver a Discourse; hymns and poems were recited; the title 'Rabbi' was formally bestowed on the candidate, and authority given him to teach and to act as Judge [to bind and loose, to declare guilty or free]."

Thus, "at the time of our Lord, no one would have ventured authoritatively to teach without proper Rabbinic authorisation. The question, therefore, with which the Jewish authorities met Christ, while teaching, was one which had a very real meaning, and appealed to the habits and feelings of the people who listened to Jesus. Otherwise, also, it was cunningly framed. For, it did not merely challenge Him for teaching, but also asked for His authority in what He *did;* referring not only to His work generally, but, perhaps especially to what had happened on the previous day. They were not there to oppose Him; but, when a man did as He had done in the Temple, it was their duty to verify his credentials. Finally, the alternative question reported by St. Mark: 'or'—if thou has not proper Rabbinic commission—'who gave Thee this authority to do these things?' seems clearly to point to their contention, that the power which Jesus wielded was delegated to Him by none other than Beelzebub." (Edersheim 2:381-83.)

Then Jesus answered their question. He did not, as some have supposed, avoid the necessity of answering by asking a question of his own; rather, his question was so framed as to constitute a complete, though partially unspoken, answer. "I also will ask you one thing, which if ye tell me," Jesus said, "I in like wise will tell you by what authority I do these things." This, then, was his question: "The baptism of John, whence was it? from heaven, or of men?"

'The baptism of John—meaning, his whole work and ministry, the doctrines he taught, the testimonies he bore, the ordinances he performed—were they of God?' As to John—than whom there was not a greater prophet—we are reminded that "all the people that heard him, and the publicans, justified God, being baptized with the baptism of John. But the Pharisees and lawyers rejected the counsel of God against themselves, being not baptized of him." (Luke 7:29-30.) His baptism—the sign of his ministry; the witness that all that he taught was true—if they believed in John they must believe in Christ, for John's whole ministry was one of preparation for the One who came after. Here then was their answer. Jesus is saying *'John has already answered your questions. My authority comes from higher than Rabbinic sources; it comes from my Father, as John testified when he said: "Behold the Lamb of God!" If ye believed John, ye would believe in me, for he testified of me.'*

But they had not believed in John. How then could they respond? "If we shall say, From heaven," they reasoned, "he will say, Why then believed ye him not?" Their rebellion of the past bore witness of their sins of the present. "But and if we say, Of men," they continued, "all the people will stone us: for they be persuaded that John was a prophet." How then could they answer? "We cannot tell," they said.

"There is an admirable Hebrew proverb which says, 'Teach thy tongue to say, "I do not know."' But to say, 'We do not know,' in this instance, was a thing utterly alien to their habits, disgraceful to their discernment, a deathblow to their pretensions. It was ignorance in a sphere wherein ignorance was for them inexcusable. They, the appointed explainers of the Law—they, the accepted teachers of the people—they, the acknowledged monopolisers of Scriptural learning and oral tradition—and yet to be compelled, against their real convictions, to say, and that before the multitude, that they *could not tell* whether a man of immense and sacred influence—a man who acknowledged the Scriptures which they explained, and carried into practice the customs which they reverenced—was a divinely inspired messenger or a deluding imposter! Were the lines of demarcation, then, between the inspired Prophet and the wicked seducer so dubious and indistinct? It was indeed a fearful humiliation, and one which they never either forgot or forgave. And yet how just was the retribution which they had thus brought on their own heads! The curses which they had intended for another had recoiled upon themselves; the pompous question which was to be an engine wherewith another should be crushed, had sprung with sudden rebound, to their own confusion and shame." (Farrar, p. 550.)

"Neither tell I you by what authority I do these things," Jesus said. 'Why try to involve me in your petty Rabbinical squabbles? What is this dead Rabbinical school or that? Of what concern is it whether some blind guide had ordained me to speak authoritatively or not? You have your answer; John gave it to you at Bethabara, and my Father confirmed it by his own voice out of heaven when he said at my baptism: "This is my Beloved Son, in whom I am well pleased. Hear ye him." '

THREE PARABLES TO THE JEWS

Utter a parable
unto the rebellious house.
(Ezek. 24:3.)

Parable of the Two Sons

(*Matthew 21:23, 25, 28-32; JST, Matthew 21:31-34*)

All Israel, as it were—through their legally designated agents, the chief priests and the scribes and the elders, as these arrayed themselves for combat in the courts of Jehovah's House—all Israel confronted Israel's Incarnate God with the demand, made relative to all that he did and all that he said, "By what authority doest thou these things? and who gave thee this authority?"

The Incarnate One, by the way of reply, asked of them: "The baptism of John, whence was it? from heaven, or of men?" To this, as they knew in their hearts, there was only one reply: 'John was sent of God; he bore testimony that you are the Lamb of God, the Son of the Eternal Father; his baptism was to prepare men to receive you; and therefore you have divine authority that came to you from God who is your Father. We heard John say of you, "The Father loveth the Son, and hath given all things into his hand. He that believeth on the Son hath everlasting life: and he that believeth not the Son shall not see life; but the wrath of God abideth on him." (John 3:35-36.) We have answered our own question. Yours is the authority of God, and he gave it to you.' To their shame they could not and did not respond in this way because they were among those who "rejected the counsel of God against themselves, being not baptized of him." (Luke 7:30.)

Their silence being an answer that all present understood, Jesus, nonetheless, means now to tell them vocally the answer to his question as to whether John's baptism was of God, and hence, also to tell them the source of his own authority and to do it by a parable.

> *But what think ye? A certain man had two sons; and he came to the first, and said, Son, go work to day in my vineyard. He answered and said, I will not: but afterward he repented, and went. And he came to the second, and said likewise. And he answered and said, I go, sir: and he went not. Whether of them twain did the will of his father?*

It is a plain and simple story. So far there can be no misunderstanding, and there is only one answer to his question. They are compelled to say, "The first." And thereupon Jesus applies his teaching:

> *Verily I say unto you, That the publicans and harlots shall go into the kingdom of God before you. For John came unto you in the way of righteousness, and bore record of me, and ye believed him not; but the publicans and the harlots believed him; and ye, afterward, when ye had seen me, repented not, that ye might believe him.*
>
> *For he that believed not John concerning me, cannot believe me, except he first repent. And except ye repent, the preaching of John shall condemn you in the day of judgment.*

The Father of us all, the Great God, whose arm is not shortened that he cannot save, and who desires to save all his children, calls both of his sons to labor in his vineyard. The first son is wicked, rebellious, ungodly, unclean, having no interest in spiritual things. He refuses the call. Religion is not for him. He is, symbolically, as the harlots and the publicans. And what is more evil than the immoral degeneracy of a prostitute or the avaricious greed of an extortionate and dishonest tax collector? The second son—wearing a veneer of spirituality; fasting two days in each week; making broad his phylacteries and lengthening the fringes on his garments; praying on the street corners to be seen of men; keeping the traditions of the fathers with a scrupulosity beyond sense and reason; separating himself from the lesser breed of men—the second son, symbolically, is the chief priests and the scribes and the elders. He is the Pharisees and the Rabbinists, the leaders of Jewry. They are the ones who, professing to be about their Father's business, have let his vineyard degenerate into a fruitless wilderness. Tares grow where wheat was sown; vines shed their fruit untimely; fig trees are barren; olives rot on the ground; and swine forage in the fields.

John comes; he bears witness of Christ; his message is one of righteousness and salvation; the publicans and harlots repent; they join the people who are preparing themselves to receive the Coming One. The lawyers and the leaders believe not, no, not even after Christ himself ministers among them. Nor, having rejected John, can they believe in Christ, unless they repent. Jesus and John are one; they testify of each other; to believe in John is to believe in Jesus; each bears witness of the authority of the other, and the words of each shall condemn the rebellious and unbelieving in the day of judgment. Such is the message of the parable of the two sons.

Parable of the Wicked Husbandmen

(*Matthew 21:33-46; JST, Matthew 21:34-35, 42-43, 48-56; Mark 12:1-12; JST, Mark 12:12; Luke 20:9-19; JST, Luke 20:10*)

We are in the midst of a mighty confrontation. A religious war is in progress, reminiscent of—or better, a continuation of—the war in heaven when Michael led the armies of the just in their verbal conflict with Lucifer and his evil ones. We are in the temple, which but yesterday was cleansed again. Jesus is here to teach. His disciples rejoice in each spoken word; arrayed against them are the chief priests, scribes, Pharisees, and elders. It is a formal setting; the lawyers and leaders of the people have set themselves forth in their official capacity to defend and uphold the established order and to overthrow and destroy this new order being set up by this upstart Galilean who violates the traditions of their fathers. Our Lord's antagonists have just been defeated and humiliated on the issue of authority, and their souls have been cut to the quick by the parable of the two sons. Many hearers are assembled, some friendly and receptive, others vengeful and rebellious. Jesus says: "Unto you that believe not, I speak in parables; that your unrighteousness may be rewarded unto you." The spirit of rebellion that fills their souls denies them the right to hear the word of truth in plainness; it is their fate, as a rebellious house, to be told of their rebellion in story form. Both now and hereafter they will ponder these parables, see their application to themselves, and always wonder whether they have learned their full significance.

> *Hear another parable: There was a certain householder, which planted a vineyard, and hedged it round about, and digged a wine press in it, and built a tower, and let it out to husbandmen, and went into a far country:*
>
> *And when the time of the fruit drew near, he sent his servants to the husbandmen, that they might receive the fruits of it. And the husbandmen took his servants, and beat one, and killed another, and stoned another. Again, he sent other servants more than the first: and they did unto them likewise.*

All this was familiar business procedure. Householders commonly leased their lands or placed them in the custody of husbandmen who had full control over their management. Owners then traveled or attended to other business, and the fruits in due season were divided between them and the lessees or husbandmen.

Here the Eternal Householder—one Jehovah by name—had planted his people on earth, beginning with Adam, the first husbandman, and had then returned to a distant heaven, leaving the first man of all men to till and farm the garden. Or, more specifically, the Great Jehovah had planted his people Israel in their promised land; had entered into a covenant with them amid the smoke and fire and thunder of Sinai; had given direction in the Mosaic law for the care and keeping of his vineyard; had traveled back to his eternal abode; and had sent his servants the prophets from time to time to serve in the vineyard and receive an accounting with reference to the fruits thereof.

That Israel's prophets were tortured, mocked, scourged, imprisoned, stoned, sawn asunder, and slain was axiomatic. All who heard Jesus speak of the ill treatment received by the Householder's servants would remember how their own scriptures said of their fathers: "All the chief of the priests, and the people, transgressed very much . . . And the Lord God of their fathers sent to them by his messengers, rising up betimes, and sending; because he had compassion on his people, and on his dwelling place: But they mocked the messengers of God, and despised his words, and misused his prophets, until the wrath of the Lord arose against his people, till there was no remedy." (2 Chr. 36:14-16.) All who heard Jesus' words would know that even in their day "another servant," as both Mark and Luke call him—one John by name—had come and been rejected by the chief priests, arrested by Antipas, imprisoned in Machaerus, and slain to appease Salome.

And further: Jesus' words would seem but a distant echo of Isaiah's parabolic utterance: "Now will I sing to my well beloved a song of my beloved touching his vineyard. My well beloved hath a vineyard in a very fruitful hill: And he fenced it, and gathered out the stones thereof, and planted it with the choicest vine, and built a tower in the midst of it, and also made a winepress therein: and he looked that it should bring forth grapes, and it brought forth wild grapes. And now, O inhabitants of Jerusalem, and men of Judah, judge, I pray you, betwixt me and my vineyard. What could have been done more to my vineyard, that I have not done in it? wherefore, when I looked that it should bring forth grapes, brought it forth wild grapes?" (Isa. 5:1-4.) In this setting, with a full understanding on the part of all concerned, Jesus continues the parable:

But last of all he sent unto them his son, saying, They will reverence my son. But when the husbandmen saw the son, they said among themselves, This is the heir; come, let us kill him, and let us seize on his inheritance. And they caught him, and cast him out of the vineyard, and slew him.

When the lord therefore of the vineyard cometh, what will he do unto those husbandmen?

"I will send my beloved son" are the words of the householder as Luke records them. 'This Is My Beloved Son' is the eternal testimony of the Father himself. "I am the Son of God" is the witness Jesus has everywhere been bearing of himself. And now be it noted, according to the words of the parable, the husbandmen—the chief priests, scribes, Pharisees, elders, Rabbinists, lawyers, and rulers of the people—the husbandmen appointed in that day to labor in the vineyard and raise fruit for the Lord knew who the Heir was and chose willfully to cast him out and slay him lest he disturb them in their petty Mosaic ministrations. And so now, for the third time in a row—the other two were in connection with the matter of authority and in the parable of the two sons—they are forced by their own lips to judge themselves. In answer to Jesus' question, they say: "He will destroy those miserable, wicked men, and will let out the vineyard unto other husbandmen, who shall render him the fruits in their season."

Such is the parable proper, together with the self-condemnation it heaped upon the wicked husbandmen against whom the forces of righteousness were then arrayed. And we cannot doubt that those so responding to Jesus knew they were echoing Isaiah's words: "And now go to," he says with reference to the song of the well-beloved and the vineyard, "I will tell you what I will do to my vineyard," because it brought forth wild grapes. "I will take away the hedge thereof, and it shall be eaten up; and break down the wall thereof, and it shall be trodden down: and I will lay it waste: it shall not be pruned, nor digged; but there shall come up briers and thorns: I will also command the clouds that they rain no rain upon it. For the vineyard of the Lord of hosts is the house of Israel, and the men of Judah his pleasant plant: and he looked for judgment, but behold oppression; for righteousness, but behold a cry." (Isa. 5:5-7.) But lest there be any question, Jesus then drew his own conclusions and said unto them:

Did ye never read in the scriptures, The stone which the builders rejected, the same is become the head of the corner: this is the Lord's doing, and it is marvellous in our eyes?

Therefore say I unto you, The kingdom of God shall be taken from you, and given to a nation bringing forth the fruits thereof.

And whosoever shall fall on this stone shall be broken: but on whomsoever it shall fall, it will grind him to powder.

In thus applying to himself the Messianic words of the Psalmist (Ps. 118:22-26),[1] Jesus is saying he is the one whom the wicked husbandmen will cast out and slay. When the chief priests, scribes, Pharisees, and others heard this parable, "they perceived that he spake of them, And they said among themselves, Shall this man think that he alone can spoil this great kingdom? And they were angry with him. But when they sought to lay hands on him, they feared the multitude, because they learned that the multitude took him for a prophet." Later, we suppose in answer to their questions, Jesus said to his disciples:

> *Marvel ye at the words of the parable which I spake unto them? Verily, I say unto you, I am the stone, and those wicked ones reject me.*
>
> *I am the head of the corner. These Jews shall fall upon me, and shall be broken. And the kingdom of God shall be taken from them, and shall be given to a nation bringing forth the fruits thereof;* (*meaning the Gentiles.*)
>
> *Wherefore, on whomsoever this stone shall fall, it shall grind him to powder. And when the Lord therefore of the vineyard cometh, he will destroy those miserable, wicked men, and will let again his vineyard unto other husbandmen, even in the last days, who shall render him the fruits in their season.*

Following this, as Matthew so aptly concludes: "And then understood they the parable which he spake unto them, that the Gentiles should be destroyed also, when the Lord should descend out of heaven to reign in his vineyard, which is the earth and the inhabitants thereof."

Parable of the Marriage of the King's Son

(*Matthew 22:1-14; JST, Matthew 22:3-4, 7, 14*)

Jewish theology, Jewish tradition, and Jewish hope all united to fix in the minds of the Jews one great Messianic expectancy: the kingdom of their Messianic Deliverer would be ushered in by a great feast, a marriage feast, a feast to celebrate the marriage, symbolically, of the Promised Messiah and his covenant people. That this Messianic hope—though misunderstood, misinterpreted, and misapplied by the Rabbinic expounders of their law and tradition—is a true one, we shall see in the ensuing parable, as Jesus continues and, for the moment, climaxes his confrontation with the enemies of all righteousness who are arrayed before him in the temple court.

True it is, as we shall see, that there shall be a "supper of the Lord" to usher in his millennial reign, a great feast to which "all nations shall be invited"—a banquet held in honor of the Bridegroom, the Son of the Great King, whose bride is the Church. It will not be a closed and restricted feast attended only by the Jews, as the Rabbinists suppose, and it will not take place in full until the King's Son comes a second time to rule and reign on earth a thousand years. All this will now appear as the Master Parabolist gives the parable of the marriage of the king's son.

> *The kingdom of heaven is like unto a certain king, which made a marriage for his son, And when the marriage was ready, he sent forth his servants to call them that were bidden to the wedding; and they would not come.*
>
> *Again he sent forth other servants, saying, Tell them that are bidden, Behold, I have prepared my oxen, and my fatlings have been killed, and my dinner is ready, and all things are prepared; therefore come unto the marriage.*

The Church of Jesus Christ—which is the kingdom of God on earth; which organization administers the gospel of the kingdom; which gospel is the bread of life, upon which men may feast and never hunger more—this church, with all its saving power, is like unto a king who makes a marriage for his son. So begins the parable. Deity is the King; Jesus (Jehovah) is the Son; and those first invited to "the marriage of the Lamb"—those invited to come unto Christ and feast upon the good word of God—are the chosen and favored hosts of ancient Israel, to whom the saving truths were offered in days of old. The servants who heaped the banquet tables high with heavenly manna were Moses and Isaiah and all the prophets; they were all the messengers of old who testified of the Son of God and pled with Abraham's seed to feast upon the word of Christ and partake of that eternal bread which he alone can give. "Thy Maker is thine husband," Isaiah proclaimed to Israel, "the Lord of hosts is his name." (Isa. 54:5.)

Oriental custom called for two invitations to marriage feasts—the first, an invitation of preparation, the second, to announce that the seven- or fourteen-day feasting period, as the case may be, had arrived. With the advent of the Son, the second invitation went forth; the Old Testament proclamations prepared the way for the renewed proclamation of the same message in New Testament times. And so, "other servants" again bid the covenant people to come and eat. Again the dinner is ready. Again the Bridegroom will be the Husband of all who believe. Again the invitation goes forth to Israel: "The Lord hath called thee as a woman forsaken and grieved in spirit, and a wife of youth." (Isa. 54:6.) "Come unto the marriage" is the call.

> *But they made light of it, and went their ways, one to his farm, another to his merchandise: And the remnant took his servants, and entreated them spitefully, and slew them.*
>
> *But when the king heard that his servants were dead, he was wroth; and he sent forth his armies, and destroyed those murderers, and burned up their city.*

Jewish Israel is composed of murderous rebels. They have a form of godliness that cloaks their avaricious interest in farms and merchandise and the things of this world. They slay the apostles and prophets who invite them to the gospel table, and they defy and rebel against Him who sent them. He in turn, using Roman steel and the vengeance of fire, in A.D. 70 destroys the murderers and burns Jerusalem. The words of the parable are the voice of prophecy.

> *Then saith he to his servants, The wedding is ready, but they which were bidden were not worthy. Go ye therefore into the highways, and as many as ye shall find, bid to the marriage.*
>
> *So those servants went out into the highways, and gathered together all as many as they found, both bad and good: and the wedding was furnished with guests.*

Thus Israel's day of preferential treatment ends; having rejected their King and his Son, they are no longer worthy to receive the blessings of Abraham. Now the gospel goes to all men, Jew and Gentile alike. From Jerusalem to the highways of the world; from the seed of Abraham to all the seed of Adam; from the favored few to the whole body of mankind—thus is the new order prefigured in the parable.

And so it is today, as "those servants" appointed in this age perform their labors. Their voices cry out: "Prepare ye the way of the Lord, prepare ye the supper of the Lamb, make ready for the Bridegroom." (D&C 65:3.) They go forth "that a feast of fat things might be prepared for the poor; yea, a feast of fat things, of wine on the lees well refined, that the earth may know that the mouths of the prophets shall not fail; Yea, a supper of the house of the Lord, well prepared, unto which all nations shall be invited. First, the rich and the learned, the wise and the noble; And after that cometh the day of my power," saith the Lord. "Then shall the poor, the lame, and the blind, and the deaf, come in unto the marriage of the Lamb, and partake of the supper of the Lord, prepared for the great day to come." (D&C 58:8-11.)

> *And when the king came in to see the guests, he saw there a man which had not on a wedding garment: And he saith unto him, Friend, how camest thou in hither not having a wedding garment? And he was speechless.*
>
> *Then said the king to the servants, Bind him hand and foot, and take him away, and cast him into outer darkness; there shall be weeping and gnashing of teeth.*
>
> *For many are called, but few chosen; wherefore all do not have on the wedding garment.*

Those gathered in are both bad and good; the gospel net catches fish of all kinds. Only those who make themselves worthy are saved. All who come into the Church must forsake the world, repent of their sins, and keep the commandments; otherwise they will be cast out with the wicked and rebellious and suffer the sorrows of the damned.

Salvation is a personal matter; it comes to individuals, not congregations. Church membership alone does not save; obedience after baptism is required. Each person called to the marriage feast will be examined separately, and of the many called to partake of the bounties of the gospel, few only will wear the robes of righteousness which must clothe every citizen in the celestial heaven. True it is that the Lord "hath bid his guests," as Zephaniah said, but "all such as are clothed with strange apparel" shall be cast out. (Zeph. 1:7-8.)

"Let us be glad and rejoice, and give honour to him: for the marriage of the Lamb is come, and his wife hath made herself ready. And to her was granted that she should be arrayed in fine linen, clean and white: for the fine linen is the righteousness of saints. And he saith unto me, Write, Blessed are they which are called unto the marriage supper of the Lamb." (Rev. 19:7-9.)

NOTE

1. These words are, of course, part of the *Hallel*, which all Jewry chanted in their ceremonies.

Chapter 87

THE JEWS PROVOKE, TEMPT, AND REJECT JESUS

He shall be . . . for a gin
and for a snare to the inhabitants
of Jerusalem. And many among them shall stumble,
and fall, and be broken,
and be snared, and be taken.
(Isa. 8:14-15.)
Him whom man despiseth, . . .
him whom the nation abhorreth, . . .
a servant of rulers (Isa. 49:7),
He is despised and rejected of men (Isa. 53:3).
For they that dwell at Jerusalem,
and their rulers, because they knew him not,
nor yet the voices of the prophets
which are read every sabbath day,
they have fulfilled them in condemning him.
(Acts 13:27.)

Render unto God and Caesar Their Own

(*Matthew 22:15-22; Mark 12:13-17; Luke 20:20-26; JST, Luke 20:21*)

If ever a plot was conceived in hell, born in hate, and acted out with satanic cunning, it was the jointly concocted stratagem of the Pharisees and Herodians on the matter of paying tribute to Caesar. When these two parties—the Pharisees whose extreme and intemperate devotion to Jehovah rejected the mere thought of Roman rule, and the Herodians whose fawning sycophancy toward Roman rule made them the open enemies of the Pharisees—when these political foes came forward to ask Jesus to rule in favor of one or the other of them (supposing that a pro-Pharisaic answer would cause his arrest by Roman authority, and a pro-Herodian answer his rejection by the people); when the hierarchical scrupulosity of the Pharisees and the political expediency of the Herodians united their voices, surely their questions must have been framed in the council rooms of Satan himself.

The Pharisees, Rabbinists, priests, elders, and leaders of the people, "foiled in their endeavor to involve Him with the ecclesiastical"—that is, having devised the questions, "By what authority doest thou these things? and who gave thee this authority?" in their attempt to show he had no Rabbinical right either to teach or perform miracles; having been humiliated by his answer and by their inability to account for John's testimony of his divine Sonship; and having been condemned, rebuked, and left bruised and bleeding, as it were, by the cutting words of the three parables that he directed against them—thus, "foiled in their endeavor to involve Him with the ecclesiastical, they next attempted the much more dangerous device of bringing Him in collision with the civil authorities," as Edersheim expresses it.

"Remembering the ever watchful jealousy of Rome, the reckless tyranny of Pilate, and the low artifices of Herod, who was at that time in Jerusalem, we instinctively feel, how even the slightest compromise on the part of Jesus in regard to the authority of Caesar would have been absolutely fatal. If it could have been proved, on undeniable testimony, that Jesus had declared Himself on the side of, or even encouraged, the so-called 'Nationalist' party, He would have quickly perished, like Judas of Galilee. The Jewish leaders would thus have readily accomplished their object, and its unpopularity have recoiled only on the hated Roman power. How great the danger was which threatened Jesus, may be gathered from this, that, despite His clear answer, the charge that He perverted the nation, forbidding to give tribute to Caesar, was actually among those brought against Him before Pilate." (Edersheim 2:383-84; Luke 23:2.)

Our dealings with the Pharisees, in many places and at numerous times, have left us wary of these religious extremists—these fanatics who fast twice in a week; who make broad their phylacteries and lengthen the sacred fringes on their garments; who pray on the streets to be seen of men; and who turn simple living into a morbid hell by their Sabbath restrictions, ceremonial washings, and baseless traditions. But who are the Herodians, and how do they fit into the social milieu of Jewry? They "occur but seldom in the Gospel narrative. Their very designation—a Latinised adjective applied to the Greek-speaking courtiers of an Edomite prince who, by Roman intervention, had become a Judean king—showed at once their hybrid origin. Their existence had mainly a *political* significance, and they stood outside the current of religious life, except so far as their Hellenising tendencies and worldly interests led them to show an ostentatious disregard for the Mosaic law.

"They were, in fact, nothing better than provincial courtiers; men who basked in the sunshine of a petty tyranny which, for their own personal ends, they were anxious to uphold. To strengthen the family of Herod by keeping it on good terms with Roman imperialism, and to effect this good understanding by repressing every national aspiration—this was their highest aim. And in order to do this they Grecised their Semitic names, adopted ethnic habits, frequented amphitheatres, familiarly accepted the symbols of heathen supremacy, even went so far as to obliterate, by such artificial means as they could, the distinctive and covenant symbol of Hebrew nationality.

"That the Pharisees should tolerate even the most temporary partnership with such men as these, whose very existence was a violent outrage on their most cherished prejudices, enables us to gauge more accurately the extreme virulence of hatred with which Jesus had inspired them. And that hatred was destined to become deadlier still. It was already at red-heat; the words and deeds of this day were to raise it to its whitest intensity of wrath." (Farrar, pp. 555-56.)

And so we find the Pharisees and Herodians counseling together, in secret, as to "how they might entangle him in his talk." Their plot: Certain disciples of the Pharisees—some of their young scholars who had not as yet openly confronted Jesus and who would be unknown to him—would join with the Herodians in asking him to decide the great political issue which divided them. These men—Luke calls them "spies"—"should feign themselves just men." They would raise the issue of paying tribute to Rome. If he sided with the Herodians and endorsed the Roman taxing power, he would antagonize the people, perhaps be rejected by them. If, by so much as an intimation, he questioned Romish rule and Romish taxes, their intent was to "deliver him unto the power and authority of the governor."

"If one, whom they take to be the Messiah, should openly adhere to a heathen tyranny, and sanction its most galling burdens, such a decision will at once explode and evaporate any regard which the people may feel for Him. If, on the other hand, as is all but certain, 'He should adopt the views of His countryman Judas the Gaulonite, and answer, '*No, it is not lawful,*' then, in that case too, we are equally rid of Him; for then He is in open rebellion against the Roman power, and these new Herodian friends of ours can at once hand Him over to the jurisdiction of the Procurator. Pontius Pilate will deal very roughly with His pretentions, and will, if need be, without the slightest hesitation, mingle His blood, as he has done the blood of other Galileans, with the blood of the sacrifices." (Farrar, p. 558.)

Their approach was respectful, deferential, courteous. Who but one so wise as he could guide their course in this matter upon which they were so widely divided? But their respect was feigned, their deference a sham, and their courtesy a thin veneer hiding an implacable hatred. "Master, we know that thou art true, and teachest the way of God in truth, neither carest thou for any man," came the sycophantic praise designed to catch him off guard, "for thou regardest not the person of men." 'Thou alone art true; thou alone speakest what God wants said; thou only can rise above the petty politics of the day; at long last thy divine wisdom will chart our course.' The problem: "Is it lawful to give tribute to Caesar, or not? Shall we give, or shall we not give?"

Matthew says that Jesus "perceived their wickedness"; Luke comments that "he perceived their craftiness"; and Mark says he knew "their hypocrisy." The time has long since passed when even these evil conspirators should presume to deceive him who has repeatedly said: 'I am the Son of God; all things are given me of my Father.' His reply was curt and pointed: "Why tempt ye me, ye hypocrites? Shew me the tribute money." They produced a penny, a Roman denarius, bearing the image of Tiberius Caesar, emperor of Rome. "Whose is this image and superscription?" Jesus asked. The answer: "Caesar's." His reply—nay, his decision, his decree—answered for then and for now the question of Church versus state:

> *Render therefore unto Caesar the things which are Caesar's; and unto God the things that are God's.*

For their day and for ours, King-Messiah's kingdom is not of this world; it is a spiritual kingdom, an ecclesiastical kingdom, a church and congregation into which true believers may come to find peace in this world and gain a hope of eternal life in the world that is to be. For their day and for ours, men render unto Caesar that which is his own and in the process subject themselves to the powers that be. Having been so instructed, the conspirators marveled at his doctrine, "and left him, and went their way."

If there is a further lesson to be learned from this

confrontation, perhaps it is aptly summarized in these words of Elder James E. Talmage: "Every human soul is stamped with the image and superscription of God, however blurred and indistinct the line may have become through the corrosion or attrition of sin; and as unto Caesar should be rendered the coins upon which his effigy appeared, so unto God should be given the souls that bear His image. Render unto the world the stamped pieces that are made legally current by the insignia of worldly powers, and give unto God and His service, yourselves—the divine mintage of His eternal realm." (Talmage, pp. 546-47.)

Jesus Teaches the Law of Eternal Marriage

(*Matthew 22:23-33; Mark 12:18-27; JST, Mark 12:23, 28, 32; Luke 20:27-40; JST, Luke 20:35*)

This very day—Tuesday, April 4, A.D. 30, the third day of the week of the atoning sacrifice—in the temple courts, Jesus has overcome the evil assaults and triumphed over the satanic plots of the Sanhedrinists, the chief priests, the scribes, the elders, the rulers and leaders of the people, the Rabbinists and teachers, the Pharisees and their disciples, and the hated Herodians. Now the Sadducees join the chorus of reviling rebels whose goal it is to goad, provoke, and belittle the Son of God, all with the hope that he will be rejected by the common people and condemned to death by the Roman Procurator.

Their devilish devisings take the form of a scoffing, sneering, deriding attack on the doctrine of the resurrection. Theirs is to be the weapon of ridicule. They already know the answer to the question they will ask; it is one commonly debated in the Rabbinical schools and for which the Pharisees and people generally have an accepted and prevailing view. They come with "an old stale piece of casuistry, conceived in the same spirit of self-complacent ignorance as are many of the objections urged by modern Sadducees against the resurrection of the body, but still sufficiently puzzling to furnish them with an argument in favour of their disbeliefs, and with a 'difficulty' to throw in the way of their opponents." (Farrar, p. 561.) In this case their opponents are both Jesus, by whom the resurrection comes, and the Pharisees, who, with all their faults, do believe that the bodies of dead men will rise from their graves and live in glorious immortality.

Thus, from their malignant hearts of disbelief—for the Sadducees say "there is no resurrection"—and from spiteful Sadducean lips, in tones of scorn and derision, these agnostic worshippers, if such they may be called, began their colloquy with Jesus by saying: "Master, Moses said, If a man die, having no children, his brother shall marry his wife, and raise up seed unto his brother."

Such, as far as it went, was a true summary of the levirate law.[1] Moses had indeed given such a commandment to Israel when they were subject to all of the terms and conditions of the new and everlasting covenant of marriage—including plurality of wives. Moses had indeed included such a requirement in the revealed marriage discipline of his day, so that worthy men who died without seed might yet have them in eternity where they would live forever in the family unit. Moses had made such a provision for faithful holders of the Melchizedek Priesthood whose chief aim and goal in life was to create for themselves eternal family units patterned after the family of God their Heavenly Father. The Sadducean use of the Mosaic principle as a basis for their caviling query indicates that some remnant of levirate marriage—we assume a twisted and perverted one—still prevailed in Jewry.

Having given lip service to Moses' levirate declaration, the Sadducees now mention a certain woman who, seeking seed, married seven brothers in turn, each of whom predeceased her. "In the resurrection whose wife shall she be of the seven?" they ask, "for they all had her." It is difficult to understand why they would ask such a foolish question, even in ridicule, for every informed person already knew the answer. The matter had been fully analyzed and debated in the Rabbinical schools. "The Pharisees," for instance, as Farrar points out, "had already settled the question in a very obvious way, and quite to their own satisfaction, by saying that she should in the resurrection be the wife of the first husband." (Farrar, p. 561.) From our vantage point, we say she would be the wife of the one to whom she was married for time and for all eternity. Any other marriage, being only until death parted the covenanting parties, would end when the mortal life of one or the other of them ceased.

But underlying this seemingly innocent query is the unspoken ridicule of the doctrine of the resurrection. 'How foolish to believe in a literal resurrection in which the family unity continues—as the Pharisees believed and the Rabbis teach!—when everyone knows a sevenfold widow cannot have seven husbands at one time.' Such an approach, in its historical setting, seems to us to present a petty and a poor argument. But we suppose it was the best one the Sadducees—who, whatever else they may have been, were neither scripturalists nor theologians—could devise at the moment.

Jesus answered, as a tolerant teacher might, without the biting sarcasm and stinging invective that at this late date so often attended answers given to the scribes and Pharisees. "Ye do err," he said, "not knowing the scriptures, nor the power of God."

Not knowing the scriptures! How little they knew of the intent and meaning of that which was written. Had they "not read, that he which made them at the beginning"—*the beginning,* note it well; it is the time before death entered the world—"made them male and female"? Did they not know that the Eternal Creator who married Adam and Eve in an eternal union, there then being no death in the world, had said, "For this cause"—that they might live together forever—"shall a man leave father and mother, and shall cleave to his wife: and they twain shall be one flesh?" Had it escaped them that such married partners "are no more twain, but one flesh," and "what therefore God hath joined together"—again mark it well, what *God,* not *man*—"let not man put asunder"? (Matt. 19:4-6.) Was the scripture entirely new to them that "whatsoever God doeth, it shall be for ever"? (Eccl. 3:14.) Were they unaware of the scriptural teachings that only those who believe the gospel; only those who hold the Holy Priesthood; only those who believe in Christ and keep his commandments—that these alone are the ones to whom Moses' levirate law applies? There neither is nor can be a continuation of the family unit in eternity for any others. Celestial marriage and the resultant eternal relation as husband and wife have no application whatever to ungodly people who live after the manner of the world.

Not knowing . . . the power of God! As with all carnal men, they were incapable of knowing how he who created man from primal element could also call his dead body back from dust to life. The power of God—the power that creates, the power that snuffs out mortal breath, the power that gives life again to the dead elements of a hopeless corpse! If God creates, can he not also resurrect? And if he causes men to live again in glorious immortality, can he not solve such a petty little problem as whose wife she shall be of the seven? How narrow, inglorious, and grudging are the views of those who know neither the scriptures nor the power of God!

Three accounts follow as to what Jesus then said. Matthew gives his teaching thus:

> *For in the resurrection THEY neither marry, nor are given in marriage, but are as the angels of God in heaven.*

Mark gives the same teaching in substantially equivalent words:

> *For when THEY shall rise from the dead, THEY neither marry, nor are given in marriage; but are as the angels which are in heaven.*

In view of the common sectarian heresy, based on substantially the same scriptural ignorance as that which enveloped the Sadducees, that there is no marrying nor giving in marriage in the world of resurrected glory, we cannot stress too strongly the imperative need to identify who are *they* to whom Jesus here refers. It is, accordingly, to Luke that we turn for the most extended, complete, and enlightening account of the inspired words of him who, as Jehovah—before death had entered the world—sealed the first man, Adam, and the first woman, Eve, in an eternal marriage union:

> *THE CHILDREN OF THIS WORLD marry, and are given in marriage: But they which shall be accounted worthy to obtain that world, and the resurrection from the dead, neither marry, nor are given in marriage: Neither can they die any more: for THEY are equal unto the angels; and are the children of God, being the children of the resurrection.*

Now, these words were spoken to Jesus' detractors who did not believe in a resurrection; they were spoken about a question on marriage that had been asked as a ploy only, and not because information was being sought about how marriage and the family unit operated in the realms ahead; and they were spoken to people who knew perfectly well that the Pharisees and the Rabbis and the people believed not only in a resurrection, but in the kind of a resurrection in which the same sociality—including marriage and the family unit—that exists among mortals would continue among immortals. It is true that some believed, as a certain "Rabbi Raf is reported to have often said, 'In the world to come they shall neither eat, nor drink, nor beget children, nor trade. There is neither envy nor strife, but the just shall sit with crowns on their heads, and shall enjoy the splendor of the Divine Majesty.'" This, however, was a minority view—shall we not say, as far as they were concerned, a heretical view. "The majority inclined to a materialistic view of the resurrection. The pre-Christian book of Enoch [from which Jude quotes in the New Testament] says that the righteous after the resurrection shall live so long that they shall beget thousands. The received doctrine is laid down by Rabbi

Saadia, who says, 'As the son of the widow of Sarepton, and the son of the Shunamite, ate and drank, and doubtless married wives, so shall it be in the resurrection'; and by Maimonides, who says, 'Men after the resurrection will use meat and drink, and will beget children, because since the Wise Architect makes nothing in vain, it follows of necessity that the members of the body are not useless, but fulfil their functions.' The point raised by the Sadducees was often debated by the Jewish doctors, who decided that 'a woman who married two husbands in this world is restored to the first in the next.' "[2]

Who then are *they* to whom Jesus refers when he says *they* neither marry nor are given in marriage in the resurrection? They are the children of this world; they are worldly and carnal and rebellious people; they are those who live after the manner of the world. They are the wicked and ungodly who "know not God, and that obey not the gospel of our Lord Jesus Christ: Who shall be punished with everlasting destruction from the presence of the Lord, and from the glory of his power; When he shall come to be glorified in his saints." (2 Thes. 1:8-10.) They are the Sadducees and their ilk who do not even believe in a resurrection, to say nothing of the eternal joy of eternal familyhood.

Of such persons the Lord says: "If a man marry him a wife in the world, and he marry her not by me nor by my word, and he covenant with her so long as he is in the world and she with him, their covenant and marriage are not of force when they are dead, and when they are out of the world; therefore, they are not bound by any law when they are out of the world. Therefore, when they are out of the world they neither marry nor are given in marriage; but are appointed angels in heaven, which angels are ministering servants, to minister for those who are worthy of a far more, and an exceeding, and an eternal weight of glory. For these angels did not abide my law; therefore, they cannot be enlarged, but remain separately and singly, without exaltation, in their saved condition, to all eternity; and from henceforth are not gods, but are angels of God forever and ever." (D&C 132:15-17.)

> *And as touching the dead, that they rise: have ye not read in the book of Moses, how in the bush God spake unto him, saying, I am the God of Abraham, and the God of Isaac, and the God of Jacob? He is not therefore the God of the dead, but the God of the living; for he raiseth them up out of their graves. Ye therefore do greatly err.*

Addressing Sadducees—who believed neither the prophets, nor in preexistence, nor in angels, nor in spirits, nor in life after death, nor in a resurrection, nor in kingdoms of eternal glory where family felicities are perfected—addressing these Jewish agnostics, Jesus did not call up the words recorded by Isaiah that say to Israel: "Thy dead men shall live, together with my dead body shall they arise. . . . and the earth shall cast out the dead." (Isa. 26:19.) He did not hark back to the words of Daniel, which say that "many of them that sleep in the dust of the earth shall awake, some to everlasting life, and some to shame and everlasting contempt." (Dan. 12:2.) Nor did he remind them of Ezekiel's vision of the valley of dry bones—the bones of all Israel—which came forth with sinews and flesh and skin to live again; nor of the promise of the God of Israel to his people: "I will open your graves, . . . and bring you into the land of Israel." (Ezek. 37:1-14.) Nor did he call attention to anything that the prophets of old had spoken relative to that life and immortality which is brought to pass through the atonement of God's Son.

Rather, our Lord, turning to the Pentateuch, brought forth an irrefutable proof of the resurrection that is nobler and grander even than prophetic words or seeric visions. He equated the resurrection with the very existence of God and man. The Eternal One is not the God of the dead but of the living! How unworthy, how impotent, how lowly and base is God if all things are created for naught; if his mortal children vanish away and their bodies become "grey handfuls of crumbling dust." Unless Abraham, Isaac, and Jacob live; unless their spirits dwell with the just, as they await their resurrection; unless they shall rise again to become like Him whose children they are; unless there is victory over the grave—the purposes of creation vanish away, God is dethroned, and his plans and purposes fail.

But he is not the God of the dead. Indeed, there are no dead. All live unto him. To what, if there is no resurrection, had the trust of Abraham, Isaac, and Jacob come? "To death, and nothingness, and an everlasting silence, and 'a land of darkness, as darkness itself,' after a life so full of trials that the last of these patriarchs had described it as a pilgrimage of few and evil years! But God meant more than this. He meant—and so the Son of God interpreted it—that He who helps them who trust in Him here, will be their help and stay for ever and for ever, nor shall the future world become for them 'a land where all things are forgotten.'" (Farrar, pp. 562-63.)

It is no wonder that "when the multitude heard this [all that he had said both about marriage and about the resurrection], they were astonished at his doctrine," and that "certain of the scribes answering said, Master, thou hast well said."

"The First and Great Commandment"

(*Matthew 22:34-40; Mark 12:28-34*)

Those who believed in a literal resurrection and in the continuation of the family unit in eternity found themselves with ambivalent feelings when Jesus routed the Sadducees. They gloried in his answer, but remained repulsed by his person. They took satisfaction in seeing the false Sadducean doctrines exposed, and yet this Galilean must be shown up as a false prophet and a fraud in some other way. Some of the scribes had the good grace to say, "Master, thou hast well said," as they saw the total discomfiture of the high and mighty Sadducees. But one of their number—one who was also designated as a lawyer, one who was an expert on their law, and who was held out as an expounder of the law and a teacher of the people—one held in high esteem among them, resorted to an observing group of Pharisees to consult as to what assault could be made on Him who always came off triumphant in the forays against him. Though these agnostic Sadducees, these nonscholars, these nontheologians, who made little pretense of scriptural knowledge, were no match for the Master, yet the learned scribes and Pharisees—they would yet devise a problem to which any answer he gave would cause division and opposition against him.

After consulting with the Pharisees, one of the scribes presented this problem: "Master, which is the greatest commandment in the law?" To us this may seem to be a perfectly normal and reasonable inquiry; in its Jewish setting, however, we soon see why Matthew says it was asked as a means of "tempting him." It was, in fact, a matter around which considerable contention centered. "The Rabbinical schools, in their meddling, carnal, superficial spirit of word-weaving and letter-worship, had spun large accumulations of worthless subtlety all over the Mosaic code. Among other things they had wasted their idleness in fantastic attempts to count, and classify, and weigh, and measure all the separate commandments of the ceremonial and moral law. They had come to the sapient conclusion that there were 248 affirmative precepts, being as many as the members in the human body, and 365 negative precepts, being as many as the arteries and veins, or the days of the year: the total being 613, which was also the number of letters in the Decalogue.

"They arrived at the same result from the fact that the Jews were commanded to wear fringes (*tsitsith*) on the corners of their *tallith,* bound with thread of blue; and as each fringe had eight threads and five knots, and the letters of the word *tsitsith* make 600, the total number of commandments was, as before, 613. Now surely, out of such a large number of precepts and prohibitions, *all* could not be of quite the same value; and some were 'light' (*kal*), and some were 'heavy' (*kobhed*). But which? and what was the greatest commandment of all? According to some Rabbis, the most important of all is that about the *tephillin* and the *tsitsith,* the fringes and phylacteries; and 'he who diligently observes it is regarded in the same light as if he had kept the whole Law.'

"Some thought the omission of ablutions as bad as homicide; some that the precepts of the Mishna were all 'heavy'; those of the Law were some heavy and some light. Others considered the *third* to be the greatest commandment. None of them had realised the great principle, that the wilful violation of one commandment is the transgression of all (James 2:10) because the object of the entire Law is the spirit of *obedience to God.* On the question proposed by the lawyer the Shammaites and Hillelites were in disaccord and, as usual, both schools were wrong: the Shammaites, in thinking that mere trivial external observances were valuable, apart from the spirit in which they were performed, and the principle which they exemplified; the Hillelites, in thinking that *any* positive command could in itself be unimportant, and in not seeing that great principles are essential to the due performance of even the slightest duties." (Farrar, pp. 565-66.)

Faced with these variant, petty, and uninspired views, these interpretations of the law that came from blind guides whose spiritual perceptions were almost nil, Jesus followed his usual course. He simply swept aside the minutia and haggling of the schools and turned their attention back to the foundation upon which the whole law rested. He may even have pointed to the *tephillin* (phylactery) worn by the inquiring scribe as he answered, for in it was the *Shema,* which all the faithful recited twice daily and which was itself a recitation of the first and great commandment.

> *The first of all the commandments is, Hear, O Israel; The Lord our God is one Lord: And thou shalt love the Lord thy God with all thy heart, and with all thy soul, and with all thy mind, and with all thy strength: this is the first commandment.*

And the second is like, namely this, Thou shalt love thy neighbour as thyself. There is none other commandment greater than these.

This answer, thus given, was not new. It contained none of the "contentions, and strivings about the law" that Paul acclaimed as "unprofitable and vain." (Titus 3:9.) And there were among the Rabbis those with the sense and discernment to single it out for themselves. We have, in fact, heretofore heard a lawyer tempt Jesus with the question, "Master, what shall I do to inherit eternal life?" and he himself be asked in turn, "What is written in the law? how readest thou?" This learned Jew gave the same answer here repeated by Jesus, and then, "willing to justify himself," asked, "Who is my neighbour?" which brought forth from our Lord the wondrous parable of the good Samaritan. Jesus, however, to the two commandments, recorded as they are in the law,[3] expanded their meaning by saying:

On these two commandments hang all the law and the prophets.

To his everlasting credit, the scribal lawyer responded: "Well, Master, thou hast said the truth: for there is one God; and there is none other but he: And to love him with all the heart, and with all the understanding, and with all the soul, and with all the strength, and to love his neighbour as himself, is more than all whole burnt offerings and sacrifices."

Jesus then said, "Thou art not far from the kingdom of God." We can only hope that the light of truth grew brighter in the lawyer's heart until its full blaze and glory guided him into the earthly kingdom where alone is found the course leading to eternal life.

With this colloquy, the day of Rabbinic-Pharisaic-scribal questioning ceased. "And no man after that durst ask him any question." He had answered all things well, and aside from some things that he would yet say and do on his own motion, he had delivered his Father's message in full.

"What Think Ye of Christ?"

(*Matthew 22:41-46; Mark 12:35-37; JST, Mark 12:40, 44; Luke 20:41-44*)

Salvation is in Christ! He is the Son of the living God. No man cometh unto the Father but by him. He is the Savior of the world and the Redeemer of men. He came into the world to do the will of the Father. His Father sent him to ransom all men from the grave and to raise those who believe and obey unto eternal life in the eternal kingdom. To gain salvation, men must come unto him, believe his gospel, and live his laws. This is the doctrine he has taught and the witness he has borne from that day in the temple when he, but twelve years of age, asked Mary if she knew not that he must be about his Father's business, to this, his last day in the temple, when all but the climactic events of his ministry are passed. But as one of these crowning events he must once again let all who will hear know that he is God's Son.

He has defeated his enemies—God's enemies!—at every turn and on every hand. That is evident to all; but none must be left to assume, nor must there be the slightest intimation, that his triumphs have come simply because he is a great prophet, or a wise philosopher, or a learned Rabbi. He must be identified for what he is—the Son of the Highest. Thus, to the Pharisees assembled there in great numbers and dressed in regal splendor, while yet in the court of his Father's house, he says:

What think ye of Christ? whose son is he?

Their answer—he could have expected none other—crystallized the whole Jewish concept of a Temporal Deliverer who would once again wield the sword of David, wear the crown of that great king, and sit on a throne from which laws would go forth to the Gentile aliens whose yoke they now wore. Their answer presupposed that the downtrodden of Israel would, under their Messiah, tread on the necks of their enemies as they rejoiced in their new Messianic kingdom. They said: "The son of David." They said: 'A mighty king, a great deliverer, a supreme ruler.' In reply Jesus said:

> *How then doth David in spirit call him Lord, saying, The Lord said unto my Lord, Sit thou on my right hand, till I make thine enemies thy footstool? If David then call him Lord, how is he his son?*

Psalm 110, given to David by the power of the Holy Ghost—that glorious Messianic psalm in which the Eternal Father swore with an oath that his Son would be a priest forever after the order of Melchizedek—such is the scriptural source to which Jesus refers as a means of raising the issue of his own divinity. As interpreted by the Son of God—and here we may discard all the vagaries of men on the passage involved; we may ignore the higher critics who say David never wrote the psalm; we may throw aside the "learned" assumptions that someone other than Elohim was testifying of his Son—David's Messianic utterance speaks of one Lord saying to another—of one God saying to another, of Elohim saying to Jehovah, of the Eternal Father saying to his Beloved Son—sit thou on my right hand. Lo, that God who then spoke unto men by his Son; that Son whom he "hath appointed heir of all things"; that Son who is "the brightness of his glory, and the express image of his [Father's] person"; the very Son who now, having ascended into heaven, sits "on the right hand of the Majesty on high"—this Son and this Father, they are the Gods mentioned in the Messianic prophecy. (Heb. 1:1-3.) These are the ones of whom the inspired utterance speaks.

Jesus' logic was unassailable. "How say the scribes that Christ is the Son of David?" he asked. If "David . . . himself calleth him Lord," he continued, "whence is he then his son?" How could he be David's Son—as he was—if David also called him Lord? "How then could the Messiah be David's son? Could Abraham have called Isaac or Jacob or Joseph, or any of his own descendants near or remote, his *lord?* If not, how came David to do so? There could be but one answer—because that Son would be divine, not human—David's son by human birth, but David's Lord by divine subsistence. But they could not find this simple explanation, nor, indeed, any other; they could not find it, because Jesus was their Messiah, and they had rejected Him. They chose to ignore the fact that He was, in the flesh, the son of David; and when, as their Messiah, He had called Himself the Son of God, they had raised their hands in pious horror, and had taken up stones to stone Him." (Farrar, p. 567.)

Jesus' testimony of himself, implicit in the divine logic that he used, left the Pharisees without hope or answer, but brought rejoicing to those whose minds had not been poisoned by the theological seminaries of the day. Thus it is written: "And no man after that durst ask him, saying, Who art thou?" And also: "The common people heard him gladly; but the high priest and the elders were offended at him." So be it.

NOTES

1. Levirate marriage is so named from the Latin word *levir*, "a brother-in-law." Some of its original provisions are set forth in Deuteronomy 25:5-10.

2. J. R. Dummelow, *The One Volume Bible Commentary*, p. 698. In this connection it is worthy of note that Jesus, after his resurrection, ate fish and an honeycomb in the presence of his disciples. (Luke 24:41-43.) Peter says the disciples "did eat and drink with him after he rose from the dead." (Acts 10:41.)

3. Leviticus 19:18 speaks of loving one's neighbor as himself, and Deuteronomy 6:4-5 contains the great commandment to love the Lord above all. The passages contained in the four compartments of the *tephillin* were Exodus 13:1-10, 11-16; Deuteronomy 6:4-9 and 11:13-21. As set forth in the latter-day revelation, the two greatest of the commandments are given in these more perfected words: "Thou shalt love the Lord thy God with all thy heart, with all thy might, mind, and strength; and in the name of Jesus Christ thou shalt serve him. Thou shalt love thy neighbor as thyself." (D&C 59:5-6.)

THE GREAT DENUNCIATION

Prophesy against the shepherds of Israel,
prophesy, and say unto them,
Thus saith the Lord God unto the
shepherds;
Woe be to the shepherds of Israel
that do feed themselves! should not the
shepherds feed the flocks? . . .
Behold, I am against the shepherds;
and I will require my flock at their hand,
and cause them to cease
from feeding the flock.
(Ezek. 34:2, 10.)
O the wise, and the learned, and the rich,
that are puffed up in the pride of their
hearts,
and all those who preach false doctrines,
and all those who commit whoredoms,
and pervert the right way of the Lord,
wo, wo, wo be unto them,
saith the Lord God Almighty,
for they shall be thrust down to hell!
(2 Ne. 28:15.)

Jesus Speaks with the Voice of Vengeance
(*Matthew 23:1-12; JST, Matthew 23:2, 4-7, 9; Luke 11:43*)

"Vengeance is mine; I will repay, saith the Lord" (Rom. 12:19), the Lord who is both Jehovah and Jesus. "Is God unrighteous who taketh vengeance?" Paul asks. He answers: "God forbid: for then [that is, if otherwise] how shall God judge the world?" (Rom. 3:5-6.) And be it remembered that the Father judgeth no man, but hath committed all judgment unto the Son. And so, as we now hear the meek and lowly One—who came to teach, and bless, and heal—raise his voice in cutting invective, we must be mindful that he is also a God of vengeance, and that the power to bless is also the power to curse. He who came, according to the Messianic word, "to preach good tidings unto the meek" and "to bind up the broken-hearted" came also "to proclaim the acceptable year of the Lord, and the day of vengeance of our God." (Isa. 61:1-2.) He it is whose destiny was to "bring forth judgment unto truth." He is the one concerning whom Isaiah promised: "He shall not fail nor be discouraged, till he have set judgment in the earth: and the isles shall wait for his law." (Isa. 42:1-7.)

When the Holy Messiah comes again—suddenly, as the promise is—to his temple, which is the earth, those whom he finds in its courts will fall into two categories. For some he calls it "the day of vengeance which was in my heart," and he says he will trample them in his fury and tread upon them in his anger. For others he names it "the year of my redeemed," those who "shall mention the loving kindness of their Lord, and all that he has bestowed upon them according to his goodness, and according to his loving kindness, forever and ever." (D&C 133:50-52.)

Even so now, here in his earthly temple, where tens of thousands of Passover pilgrims mill about, surrounded by faithful disciples who rejoice in his goodness and loving kindness, and in the midst of scribes and Pharisees, who hate his person and whose every faculty is bent on shedding his blood—here in a scene prefiguring the day of his later coming, he sits in judgment on his fellowmen. It is a present day in which he is revealing what shall be in the future day of judgment and burning. For his disciples it is a day of added doctrinal enlightenment and the consequent courage to hold fast to that iron rod which is the word of God. For the scribes and Pharisees it is a day of vengeance in which they shall hear about the fires of hell that await them.

In what has already taken place the priests and Rabbis and Pharisees and leaders of the people have been identified as blind leaders of the blind. "And they"—how sad it is to say—"loved their blindness," because, as we are so well aware, their deeds were evil. Further: "They would not acknowledge their ignorance," so fully demonstrated in all that has just transpired. And "they did not repent them of their faults; the bitter venom of their hatred to Him was not driven forth by His forbearance; the dense midnight of their perversity was not dispelled by His wisdom. Their purpose to destroy Him was fixed, obstinate, irreversible. If one plot failed, they were but driven with more stubborn sullenness into another. And, therefore, since Love had played her part in vain, 'vengeance leaped upon the stage;' since the Light of the World shone for them with no illumination, the lightning flash should at last warn them of their danger. There could now be no hope of their becoming reconciled to Him; they were but being stereotyped in unrepentant malice against Him. Turning, therefore, to His disciples, but in the audience of all the people, He rolled over their guilty heads, with crash on crash of moral anger, the thunder of His utter condemnation." (Farrar, p. 569.)

The scribes and the Pharisees sit in Moses' seat: All, therefore, whatsoever they bid you observe, they will make you observe and do; for they are ministers of the law, and they make themselves your judges. But do not ye after their works; for they say, and do not. For they bind heavy burdens and grievous to be borne, and lay them on men's shoulders; but they themselves will not move them with one of their fingers.

Moses' seat, the seat of judgment and power! For the few brief remaining hours until, at this very Passover, the Paschal Lamb is slain, the scribes and Pharisees continue as legal administrators of the Mosaic order. They are still the ministers of the law; none others on earth can offer up sacrifices on the great altar so as to make atonement for the sins of repentant souls. Theirs is still the obligation to teach, not their traditions, but the true principles set forth by Moses and the prophets. But O how men must be warned against their false teachings, their evil examples, their works of wickedness!

No man, before the judgment bar, will be excused for believing false doctrines or doing evil acts on the excuse that he followed a minister, who he supposed taught true principles and gave good counsel, but who in fact declared false doctrine and wrought evil works. No matter that, in showy piety, we bear grievous burdens in the name of religion (as all the Jews did), or win great theological conflicts (as the Rabbis and scribes were wont to do), or display a superabundance of supposed good works (as some modern religionists suppose they do); no matter what else we may do in a false hope of gaining salvation—all that will matter in the day of judgment will be whether we have kept, truly and faithfully, the commandments of God. Let false ministers be damned, if such is the judgment they deserve; the members of their congregations must nonetheless work out their salvation by conforming to true principles of religion.

> *And all their works they do to be seen of men. They make broad their phylacteries, and enlarge the borders of their garments, and love the uppermost rooms at feasts, and the chief seats in the synagogues, and greetings in the markets, and to be called of men, Rabbi, Rabbi* (*which is master.*)

True ministers labor with an eye single to the glory of God. Their interests and concerns are in the welfare of the sheep and the salvation of the souls of men. False ministers supplant priesthood service with the self-exaltation of priestcraft. Their interests and concerns are in their own self-ennoblement, not in the welfare of the sheep. They have not strengthened the diseased, nor healed the sick, nor bound up the broken, nor brought again that which was driven away, nor sought that which was lost, as true shepherds must, "but with force and with cruelty" have they "ruled them." (Ezek. 34:4.)

Indeed, "priestcrafts are that men preach and set themselves up for a light unto the world, that they may get gain and praise of the world; but they seek not the welfare of Zion." (2 Ne. 26:29.) Scarlet robes and jeweled gowns, golden crowns and costly scepters, girdles of fine-twined linen, gold and silver and silks, and all manner of precious clothing—these become the desires of those who seek to serve God through personal exaltation. Did all the Jews wear their phylacteries—those leather straps placed on the foreheads and left arms, near the heart, and containing parchments reciting the *Shema* and other scriptures—when praying? Those of the scribes and Pharisees must be broader and bear witness of a showy display of supposed piety. Is it the practice of all to wear garments whereon dangle sacred blue tassels in remembrance of covenants made with Jehovah? Those plying their trade of priestcraft must have gaudy and distinguishable adornments, lest any fail to see the sign of their religious devotion. Are people seated by rank and greeted in public with laudatory titles? How the ministers of men must vie for preferential status in all situations! What a difference there is between true and false religion—even in outward symbols! Without true doctrines to ponder and teach, false ministers turn to the trappings of ritualistic formalism to satisfy man's innate leanings toward things in the spiritual realm. Of all this the disciples must beware.

But be not ye called Rabbi; for one is your master, which is Christ; and all ye are brethren.

And call no one your creator upon the earth, or your

heavenly Father; for one is your creator and heavenly Father, even he who is in heaven.

Neither be ye called masters; for one is your master, even he whom your heavenly Father sent, which is Christ; for he hath sent him among you that ye might have life.

But he that is greatest among you shall be your servant. And whosoever shall exalt himself shall be abased of him; and he that shall humble himself shall be exalted of him.

This counsel to the disciples seems of obvious and self-evident value to us. In its Jewish setting, however, it took on an even deeper import and meaning, a meaning that grew out of the unbelievable—sometimes even blasphemous—honor sought by and bestowed upon Rabbis. For instance: The heathen Governor of Caesarea was said to have seen Rabbis in vision with the faces of angels. The Governor of Antioch was supposed to have "seen their faces and by them conquered," which is not far different from the Catholic legend about Constantine the Great. Rabbis ranked higher than kings, their curses (though unjustified) always, as they supposed, came to pass, and one of them chose to "be buried in white garments, to show that he was worthy of appearing before his Maker." (Edersheim 2:409.) But perhaps the greatest illustration of pretentious self-assertion is seen in this Talmudic account: "They represent heaven itself as a Rabbinic school, of which God is the Head Rabbi. On one occasion God differs from all the angels on a question as to a leper being clean or unclean. They refer the decision to R. Ben Nachman, who is accordingly slain by Azrael, and brought to the heavenly Academy. He decides with God, who is much pleased." (Farrar, footnote 4, p. 569.) In the light of such monstrous and blasphemous absurdities, it is no wonder that Jesus commanded the disciples to designate no one on earth as their heavenly Father, which in effect is what this Rabbinic account does. No doubt there were numerous other local legends on this and related points that have not been preserved to our day.

The Eight Woes against the Scribes and Pharisees

(*Matthew 23:13-33; JST, Matthew 23:11-13, 17, 21, 28-29; Mark 12:38-40; Luke 11:37-42, 44-48; 20:45-47; JST, Luke 11:42-43*)

Jesus now bursts forth with eight denunciations of woe upon the scribes and Pharisees.[1] He arraigns them "with a veritable torrent of righteous indignation, through which flashed the lightning of scorching invective, accompanied by thunder peals of divine anathema." (Talmage, p. 554.) For three and a half years he has offered them blessings—the Sermon on the Mount itself contains eight beatitudes, eight eternal blessings for all who will believe and obey—all of which blessings they have repeatedly rejected. The sun has now set on the day for blessings, and the darkness of night with its woeful cursings is upon them. Both blessings and curses grow out of a way of life; the righteous are blessed, the wicked are cursed. Upon them comes a deep and inconsolable grief and misery. So it is now with the scribes and Pharisees; divine wrath, holy wrath, the wrath of a Divine Being is now poured out upon them, almost without measure. We shall consider each woe in turn.

1. *The Woe for Rejecting Christ and Salvation:*

> *But woe unto you, scribes and Pharisees, hypocrites! for ye shut up the kingdom of heaven against men: for ye neither go in yourselves, neither suffer ye them that are entering to go in.*

"Woe unto them, for the ignorant erudition which closed the gates of heaven, and the injurious jealousy which would suffer no others to enter in!"[2]

What false minister is ever content to damn himself alone, to lose his own soul only, to go without companions on his head-strong course to hell? It is inherent in the ministerial role to get others to believe and live as the preacher proclaims. Christ—whom the scribes and Pharisees rejected—is the door to salvation. Not only did they thus lose their own souls, but with all their power they sought to deny the gospel blessings to others.

2. *The Woe against Avarice and Hypocrisy:*

Woe unto you, scribes and Pharisees! for ye are hypocrites! Ye devour widows' houses, and for a pretence make long prayers; therefore ye shall receive the greater punishment.

"Woe unto them for their oppressive hypocrisy and greedy cant!"

Thou shalt not covet; the love of money is the root of all evil; how hardly can a rich man enter into the kingdom of heaven; where a man's treasure is, there will his heart be also—these and a host of scriptural truisms, taught by Jesus, accepted instinctively by the spiritually inclined, and known to the scribes and Pharisees—all these bore testimony against them. Avarice, greed, covetousness, the amassing of great wealth by questionable means—all such was a way of life among the leaders in Israel. Under cover of religious duty, they extorted enormous sums from the ever-present widows and orphans, salving their consciences with pretentious prayers. To gain salvation, they must not only repent of their rapacious and grasping ways, but they must also affirmatively make their riches available to the poor and the needy—sell all that they have and go and follow Christ, as he himself said to the rich young ruler. How truly and well it is written: "Wo unto you rich men, that will not give your substance to the poor, for your riches will canker your souls; and this shall be your lamentation in the day of visitation, and of judgment, and of indignation: The harvest is past, the summer is ended, and my soul is not saved!" (D&C 56:16.) Add to this the deliberate and designed vice of hypocrisy, and we have a scribal-Pharisaic person whose heart is fixed on the things of this world and who will inherit accordingly in the world to come.

3. *The Woe for Converting Souls to a False Church:*

Woe unto you, scribes and Pharisees, hypocrites! For

ye compass sea and land to make one proselyte; and when he is made, ye make him two-fold more the child of hell than he was before, like unto yourselves.

"Woe for the proselytising fanaticism which did but produce a more perilous corruption!"

O the wickedness of converting a soul, a human soul, a child of God to a false system of religion, be it Judaism or Pharisaism or one of the sects of Christendom! If a mortal child of the Eternal God is seeking truth and willing to forsake an undesirable past, how dire and calamitous it is to lead him into greater darkness! There may be times when truth seekers improve their lot by going from a sect that is more abominable to one that is less evil, but when the True Light is present, there can be only one acceptable course—turn to Him. It is said of Jewish proselytizing of that day: "Out of a bad heathen they made a worse Jew." As with the other woes, this one befell them because they rejected Him who came to bring them light and truth and salvation.

4. *The Woe against Moral Blindness Shown in the Breaking of Oaths:*

Woe unto you, blind guides, who say, Whosoever shall swear by the temple, it is nothing; but whosoever shall swear by the gold of the temple, he committeth sin, and is a debtor. Ye fools and blind: for whether is greater, the gold, or the temple that sanctifieth the gold?

And, Whosoever shall swear by the altar, it is nothing; but whosoever sweareth by the gift that is upon it, he is guilty. Ye fools and blind: for whether is greater, the gift, or the altar that sanctifieth the gift? Verily I say unto you, Whoso, therefore, sweareth by it, sweareth by the altar, and by all things thereon.

"Woe for the blind hair-splitting folly which so confused the sanctity of oaths as to tempt their followers into gross profanity!"

In few things did the moral depravity of Pharisaism rear

its ugly head with such studied wickedness as in their profane perversion of the divine law relative to oaths. From the beginning, down through the patriarchal dispensations, and through the whole Mosaic era, Jehovah had allowed his people the privilege of swearing with an oath—of making a divine affirmation, of asserting an assured verity in a sacred way—so as to guarantee the immutable verity of the spoken word. An oath made God a partner in the matter to which solemn attestation was being made. It could not, therefore, fail; for God does not fail, and the Cause of Righteousness is as prevailing and eternal as Deity himself.

But these Jews—in their apostate debauchery—had so perverted the true order of vows and oaths that they had become a sword of evil instead of a shield of good. Technical, trifling rules by which oaths could be annulled and avoided came forth from the Great Sanhedrin. An indulgence here, some special privilege there, as the Rabbinists taught, enabled men to ignore their solemn vows made in Jehovah's name. Causistry of the most complicated kind guided the Pharisees in their avoidance of their moral and sworn obligations. Thus: "If a man swore by the temple, the House of Jehovah, he could obtain an indulgence for breaking his oath; but if he vowed by the gold and treasure of the Holy House, he was bound by the unbreakable bonds of priestly dictum. Though one should swear by the altar of God, his oath could be annulled; but if he vowed by the corban gift or by the gold upon the altar, his obligation was imperative. To what depths of unreason and hopeless depravity had men fallen, how sinfully foolish and how wilfully blind were they, who saw not that the Temple was greater than its gold, and the altar than the gift that lay upon it! In the Sermon on the Mount the Lord had said 'Swear not at all'; but upon such as would not live according to that higher law, upon those who persisted in the use of oaths and vows, the lesser and evidently just requirement of strict fidelity to the terms of self-assumed obligations was to be enforced, without unrighteous quibble or inequitable discrimination." (Talmage, p. 556.)

5. *The Woe against Supplanting Eternal Principles with Religious Trifles:*

> *Woe unto you, scribes and Pharisees, hypocrites! for ye pay tithe of mint and anise and cummin, and have omitted the weightier matters of the law, judgment, mercy, and faith: these ought ye to have done, and not to leave the other undone. Ye blind guides, who strain at a gnat, and swallow a camel; who make yourselves appear unto men that ye would not commit the least sin, and yet ye yourselves, transgress the whole law.*

"Woe for the petty paltry sham scrupulosity which paid tithes of potherbs, and thought nothing of justice, mercy, and faith—which strained out animalculae from the goblet, and swallowed camels into the heart!"

One of the marks of personal or universal apostasy is to center on religious trifles to the exclusion of eternal principles. Abstain from the use of tea, coffee, and tobacco, but indulge in lustful acts or forsake standards of business integrity; refrain from picking an olive or shucking an ear of maize on the Sabbath, but ignore the command to worship the Father in spirit and in truth on his holy day; pay tithing on the leaves and stalks of herbs grown in pots on the windowsill, but give no heed to judgment, mercy, and faith—such are the marks of apostate fanaticism. By such a course it is easy to have a form of godliness and a zeal for religion without doing the basic things that require the whole heart and the whole soul. Those so doing filter their drinking water through a linen cloth to avoid swallowing an unclean insect while, figuratively, gulping down a camel.

6. *The Woe against Hiding Wickedness Under a Religious Cloak:*

> *Woe unto you, scribes and Pharisees, hypocrites! for ye make clean the outside of the cup and of the platter, but within they are full of extortion and excess. Thou blind Pharisee, cleanse first that which is within the cup and platter, that the outside of them may be clean also.*

"Woe for the external cleanliness of cup and platter contrasted with the gluttony and drunkenness to which they ministered!"

Again the woe pronounced by Jesus has application to the apostate scribes and Pharisees of all ages and among all peoples. Under a religious cloak, with unbounded zeal, they perform some ritualistic minutae, as though such solved all the problems of life and attuned them forever to the Infinite One. Cups and platters must be polished to perfection; they must be ceremonially clean; what does it matter that the contents are purchased with the gold of extortion, or that the meat will pander to gluttony, or that the wine will assure drunkenness. It is the form, not the substance, with which Rabbinism is concerned.

Earlier in Perea, while dining in the home of a Pharisee, Jesus abstained from the ritualistic washings that played such a vital role in their lives. On that occasion he denounced the same hypocritical pettiness with even greater exacerbation.

> *Now do ye Pharisees make clean the outside of the cup and the platter; but your inward part is full of ravening and wickedness. Ye fools, did not he that made that which is without make that which is within also?*
>
> *But if ye would rather give alms of such things as ye have; and observe to do all things which I have commanded you, then would your inward parts be clean also.*

7. *The Woe against a False Outward Appearance of Righteousness:*

> *Woe unto you, scribes and Pharisees, hypocrites! for ye are like unto whited sepulchres, which indeed appear beautiful outward, but are within full of dead men's bones, and of all uncleanness. Even so ye also outwardly appear righteous unto men, but within ye are full of hypocrisy and iniquity.*

"Woe to the tombs that simulated the sanctity of temples—to the glistening outward plaster of hypocrisy which did but render more ghastly by contrast the reeking pollutions of the sepulchre within!"

"It was an awful figure, that of likening them to whitewashed tombs, full of dead bones and rotting flesh. As the dogmas of the rabbis made even the slightest contact with a corpse or its cerements, or with the bier upon which it was borne, or the grave in which it has been lain, a cause of personal defilement, which only ceremonial washing and the offering of sacrifices could remove, care was taken to make tombs conspicuously white, so that no person need be defiled through ignorance or proximity to such unclean places; and, moreover, the periodical whitening of sepulchres was regarded as a memorial act of honor to the dead. But even as no amount of care or degree of diligence in keeping bright the outside of a tomb could stay the putrescence going on within, so no externals of pretended righteousness could mitigate the revolving corruption of a heart reeking with iniquity." (Talmage, p. 558.)

On that previous occasion in Perea, while sitting at meat in a Pharisaic home, Jesus had likened the scribes and Pharisees to "graves which appear not, and the men that walk over them are not aware of them." This woe he has now perfected and expanded. Clearly, his gift of plain and incisive speech is without parallel in all history.

8. *The Woe against Rejecting Living Prophets:*

Woe unto you, scribes and Pharisees, hypocrites! because ye build tombs of the prophets, and garnish the sepulchres of the righteous, And say, If we had been in the day of our fathers, we would not have been partakers with them in the blood of the prophets.

Wherefore, we are witnesses unto yourselves of your own wickedness, and ye are the children of them who killed the prophets; And will fill up the measure then of your fathers; for ye, yourselves, kill the prophets like unto your fathers.

"Woe for the mock repentance which condemned their

fathers for the murder of the prophets, and yet reflected the murderous spirit of those fathers—nay, filled up and exceeded the measure of their guilt by a yet deadlier and more dreadful sacrifice!"

Of all the woes, this is the chief and crowning one. To reject living prophets, under the pretext of honoring the seers of old, is to deny all the prophets and forfeit any hope of eternal reward. We have long since learned that to believe in Abraham, or Moses, or any of the prophets, or John the Baptist, meant to believe in Christ, for they all testified of him. All the prophets of all the ages bear the same testimony; all preach the same saving truths; all bear witness of the same Atoning One. Salvation is in Christ, and the prophets are his messengers who announce his saving truths to the mortals of their day.

And to reject the prophets of any age is to reject those of all ages, for they all teach the same truths; they all bear the same witness; they all possess the same spirit. The spirit of murderous rebellion that thirsts for the blood of Christ is the same spirit that caused Jeremiah to be cast into a dungeon, Isaiah to be sawn asunder, and prophets without number to seal their testimonies with their own blood. The great test for all men is whether they will believe and obey the living oracles sent to them, not what they suppose they think about the prophets of old.

If these scribes and Pharisees, these priests and Rabbis, these Jewish elders and Israelite guides—if they and all the people would but believe in Christ, no woes would befall them. When any people believe the word which Deity sends to them—let it come from earth's Chief Prophet or the Lord's lowest elder—then past cursings slink away like a jackal before a lion, to be replaced by the blessed glories of the gospel. But always the religious pretext for rejecting living prophets, the conscience-salving excuse for turning away from living oracles, is a supposed belief in dead prophets and is an assumed reverence for buried seers. By professing to believe the prophetic word of old—which brought salvation to them of old—the door of salvation seems open and the need for new revelation to be done away. Come, then, let us slay the living prophets lest they muddy the prophetic message of the past.

On that previous occasion in Perea, our Lord's similarly phrased invective, against others equally evil, came forth in these words:

> *Woe unto you also, ye lawyers! for ye lade men with burdens grievous to be borne, and ye yourselves touch not the burdens with one of your fingers.*
>
> *Woe unto you! for ye build the sepulchres of the prophets, and your fathers killed them. Truly ye bear witness that ye allow the deeds of your fathers: for they indeed killed them, and ye build their sepulchres.*

Truly, the woe for rejecting living prophets is the woe of woes—the woe that thrusts men into the eternal woes of an eternal hell with its eternal damnation where their worm dieth not and the fire is not quenched!

> *Fill ye up then the measure of your fathers. Ye serpents, ye generation of vipers, how can ye escape the damnation of hell?*

Jewish Accountability for the Sins of Their Ancestors

(*Matthew 23:34-36; JST, Matthew 23:33-35; Luke 11:49-54; JST, Luke 11:53-54*)

What other woes Jesus may have thundered forth on this ominous day—"with crash on crash of moral anger"—we do not know. Matthew records only the eight we have considered, and we cannot believe that he has preserved for us all that was said with reference to any of them. Inspired authors often write only in headlines and follow the practice of digesting and abridging much that falls from prophetic lips. We do know that on that prior Perean occasion when Jesus rebuked others whose hearts were black and whose deeds were evil, he had some cutting things to say about those who had not cared properly for the scriptural records entrusted to them.

Woe unto you, lawyers! For ye have taken away the key of knowledge, the fulness of the scriptures; ye enter not in yourselves into the kingdom; and those who were entering in, ye hindered.

"The holy scriptures"—the mind and will and word and voice of the Lord—how can their worth be weighed? Who can tell what wonders have been wrought because the pure word of the Perfect God lay open before men? And who can envision what evils have befallen the sons of men when the pure word has been tainted and twisted and made to say that which is not true?

"The holy scriptures," Paul said to Timothy, which "from a child thou hast known . . . are able to make thee wise unto salvation through faith which is in Christ Jesus." (2 Tim. 3:15.) Did not Jesus say, "They are they which testify of me"? (John 5:39.) Sad though it be, few are the men who hear the audible voice, thundering from Sinai, revealing in prophetic ears the mind and will of Jehovah; few are they who hear the still small voice, whispering in prophetic ears, revealing the principles and ordinances of the gospel; but millions comprise the hosts of earth's inhabitants who have before them the recorded words of holy men who wrote as they were prompted from on high. And all those who read these words—words preserved in the holy scriptures—and who do so by the power of the Holy Ghost can testify that they have heard the Lord's voice and know his words. (D&C 18:33-36.) And so, Paul continues, "All scripture is given by inspiration of God"—or, better, every scripture inspired of God—"is profitable for doctrine, for reproof, for correction, for instruction in righteousness: That the man of God may be perfect, throughly furnished unto all good works." (2 Tim. 3:16-17.)

And yet these evil leaders of an erring people had taken away the fulness of the scriptures. The word no longer lay open before the chosen seed. We have no reason to believe they had the writings of Abraham, the complete Book of Enoch, the portions of Genesis revealed anew through Joseph Smith, or the words of Zenos or Zenock or Neum or, perhaps, hosts of prophets whose very names are buried with their lost writings.

But let us return to the woes pronounced this day in the temple. In spite of all the evils of the scribes and Pharisees, Jesus yet offered his saving truths to the people. Though these blind spiritual guides comprised a generation of serpents and vipers whose assured destination was hell, the Blessed One said:

> *Behold, I send unto you prophets, and wise men, and scribes: and some of them ye shall kill and crucify; and some of them shall ye scourge in your synagogues, and persecute them from city to city: That upon you may come all the righteous blood shed upon the earth, from the blood of righteous Abel unto the blood of Zacharias son of Barachias, whom ye slew between the temple and the altar. Verily I say unto you, All these things shall come upon this generation.*
>
> *Ye bear testimony against your fathers, when ye, yourselves, are partakers of the same wickedness. Behold your fathers did it through ignorance, but ye do not; wherefore, their sins shall be upon your heads.*

This is strong doctrine. In it is a great principle of eternal truth that none but the true saints can comprehend; from it we learn, with an impact scarcely found elsewhere, how all generations of men tie together and how all of us are truly our brother's keeper.

Jesus sends apostles and prophets among the Jews of his day. He is Jehovah; he calls the prophets and wise men; the true scribes bear a true witness of him by the power of his Spirit. Even he himself ministers among them, testifying with words such as no other man ever spake, and in deeds such as no other man ever did, that he is truly God's Son. All this they reject, and they are damned; no man can reject the light of heaven and be saved—of course they are damned; they are a generation of vipers who cannot escape the damnation of hell. They shall die in their sins. Thus saith Jesus.

But this is not all. They are accountable for the sins of their fathers who through ignorance rejected the message of salvation. Such is the worst of woes, the crowning curse—to be accountable, not alone for their own sins, but for the sins of those who might have been saved had these spiritual leaders done their duty. From the day of Abel the son of Adam, whom Cain slew, to the day of Zacharias the father of John, who "was slain by Herod's order, between the porch and the altar" (*Teachings,* p. 261)—between these two days, which covered the whole span of earth history, many good men lived and died without a knowledge of the gospel. All these could have been freed from their spirit prison by the men of Jesus' day, if those to whom Jesus then preached had believed his words.

Joseph Smith, in the course of a sermon on salvation for the dead, and after quoting the denunciation of these scribes and Pharisees by Jesus, said: "Hence as they possessed greater privileges than any other generation, not only pertaining to themselves, but to their dead, their sin was greater, as they not only neglected their own salvation but that of their progenitors, and hence their blood [that of the progenitors] was required at their hands." (*Teachings,* pp. 222-23.)

"Am I my brother's keeper?" Cain responded when the Lord asked him about Abel (Gen. 4:9), whom he had slain, who was indeed slain for the love of God and the testimony of Jesus, as also was Zacharias. "My brother's keeper!" Truly it is so. All men, Jesus included, are brothers, children of the same Father. And as Christ laid down his life to save all men, his ministers are called to do all things necessary, even unto death, to save such portion of their brethren as they can.

NOTES

1. "The Talmud itself, with unwonted keenness and severity of sarcasm, has pictured to us the seven classes of Pharisees, out of which *six* are characterized by a mixture of haughtiness and imposture. There is the 'Shechemite' Pharisee, who obeys the law from self-interest (Gen. 34:19); the *Tumbling* Pharisee, who is so humble that he is always

stumbling because he will not lift his feet from the ground: the *Bleeding* Pharisee, who is always hurting himself against walls, because he is so modest as to be unable to walk about with his eyes open lest he should see a woman: the *Mortar* Pharisee, who covers his eyes as with a mortar, for the same reason: the *Tell-me-another-duty-and-I-will-do-it* Pharisee—several of whom occur in our Lord's ministry: and the *Timid* Pharisee, who is actuated by motives of fear alone. The seventh class only is the class of *Pharisees from love*, who obey God because they love Him from the heart." (Farrar, pp. 571-72.)

2. This statement, as well as each of the first-sentence quotations set forth in the discussion of the eight woes, is taken from Farrar, p. 570.

Chapter 89

JESUS' FINAL TEACHING IN THE TEMPLE

He that believeth on me,
believeth . . . on him that sent me.
I am come a light into the world.
I came . . . to save the world.
I have not spoken of myself.
. . . even as the Father said unto me, so I speak.
(John 12:44-50.)

He Laments over Doomed Jerusalem

(*Matthew 23:37-39; JST, Matthew 23:36-41; Luke 13:34-35; JST, Luke 13:34-36*)

As the great denunciation of the evil guides of a blinded people ended, the rupture between Jesus and the Jews was complete. Virtue and vice can only be reconciled when vice becomes virtue, and those whom Jesus has just arraigned before Jehovah's bar have neither the desire nor the will to repent. Their hearts of stone will retain their flinty hardness until they are melted in the fires of Gehenna.

As the woes ceased, our Lord's lamentation began. As the rolling thunders of his moral indignation no longer echoed within the walls of Jehovah's House, Jesus was heavy of heart. These blind guides, these scribes and Pharisees whom he has just called serpents and vipers and for whom he has decreed the damnation of hell, have also led thousands of their fellow Israelites in the paths of destruction. The people are following the false teachings and supporting the dark deeds of their rulers even though the Light of Life in all its brilliance now shines in their streets, and in their synagogues, and is even, at this very moment, teaching in the temple courts. Can we imagine the sorrow that filled the Divine Being as he "began to weep over Jerusalem," saying:

> *O Jerusalem! Jerusalem! Ye who will kill the prophets, and will stone them who are sent unto you; how often would I have gathered your children together, even as a hen gathers her chickens under her wings, and ye would not. Behold, your house is left unto you desolate!*[1]

But yesterday when he cleansed the temple for the second time, he called it "my house," for such it was, and such it had been through the ages. Their fathers had built it at his behest. His ordinances were performed therein. Now, however, he is withdrawing his divine approval from that splendid and magnificent structure, which is no longer needed in his dealings with men on earth. The House of the Lord, constructed to meet Mosaic needs, is no longer needed in the eternal scheme of things. Jesus is establishing new ordinances—sacramental emblems instead of sacrificial offerings, among others—and the need for the old temple is over. He is now giving it back to men; it is no longer "my house," but "your house."

Nor was the temple to be the only desolate house. Jesus is also turning Jerusalem itself back into the hands of men. From the days of Melchizedek who was king in Salem, and with reference to Israel, from the days of David, who took Jerusalem from the Jebusites, it had been the Lord's own city, the Zion of God, the religious capital of the world. Soon it would be left to evil men and the new Zion would be the congregations of the pure in heart as they assembled to worship the Father in the name of Jesus in all the nations of the earth. It was as though "my city" was now to be "your city."

And so it became as we shall see in our consideration of the Olivet Discourse. (Chapter 90.) And all this came upon them because they rejected him whose temple it was, and him whose city it was. And so Jesus continued:

> *For I say unto you, that ye shall not see me henceforth, and know that I am he of whom it is written by the prophets, until ye shall say, Blessed is he who cometh in the name of the Lord, in the clouds of heaven, and all the holy angels with him.*

Matthew says: "Then understood his disciples that he should come again on the earth, after that he was glorified and crowned on the right hand of God." And Luke, recording what was said in Perea, when our Lord said he must go up to Jerusalem, for—and what biting irony this is—"it cannot be that a prophet perish out of Jerusalem," Luke tells us that Jesus then said:

> *And verily I say unto you, Ye shall not know me, until ye have received from the hand of the Lord a just recompense for all your sins; until the time come when ye shall say, Blessed is he who cometh in the name of the Lord.*

Jesus is withdrawing his face from the Jews until they pay the penalty for their sins and until they learn that he is their Messiah, the one of whom all the prophets have written! And in the providences of the Lord that is a not far distant day.

The Widow's Mite

(*Mark 12:41-44; JST, Mark 12:50; Luke 21:1-4*)

We pass now from the thunderous woes that consigned the scribes and Pharisees to hell, and from the tears of sorrow that wet the divine cheeks as Jesus withdrew his approval from the temple and the city, and turn rather to a sweet and hallowed scene. Jesus has left the porches and the wrangling, and the contentious mobs of men who are there debating his words and defaming his person. He seats himself "over against the treasury," apparently upon the steps that gave him a view of the Court of the Women. Under the colonnades that surround this court are thirteen trumpet-shaped boxes into which various religious and charitable contributions may be placed. Each of the trumpets bears an inscription that identifies the object of the contributions placed therein.

Jesus' heart is brimful with sorrow as he reflects on the sins of the people and their rejection of him. His tears of a few moments before have dried on his cheeks. The hour of the daily sacrifice is past, and those now in the court are engaged in private devotions, private sacrifices, and the paying of their various offerings. He watches as rich and affluent people, desiring to be seen of men and with that ostentation so common among them, drop great treasures of silver and gold into the receptacles. Among the worshippers is a poor widow, identified by her garb of mourning. She comes quietly, meekly, hoping perhaps that others will not see the smallness of her offering; she drops two mites—the smallest legal amount that can be given—into one of the chests.

Two mites! Together they are less than a farthing. Her total contribution is about half a cent in American money. But it is all she has. She has lived the law of sacrifice to the full. Jesus calls his disciples and says:

> *Verily I say unto you, That this poor widow hath cast more in, than all they which have cast into the treasury: For all the rich did cast in of their abundance; but she, notwithstanding her want, did cast in all that she had; yea, even all her living.*

No word was spoken to the sorrowing widow who in her penury had sacrificed her all, nor did she then so much as know that the Judge of all had weighed her gift in the eternal scales and found it of more worth than the wealth of kings. It is pleasant to suppose, however, that she now knows that her deed, done in secret and with no thought of reward, was not far removed from that of Mary of Bethany, who poured the anointing oil on the feet of the Master. Both acts have been memorialized forever among those whose hearts are centered upon sacred things.

Nor should we miss the message—that on the records kept by the angels of God in heaven, the meager gifts of faithful people far outweigh the ostentatiously bestowed largess of the rich who bestow their bounties to be seen of men; and that those who expend the Lord's money to build up his kingdom and further his interests should do so as though it all came from the mites of sorrowing widows.

Jesus Offers Salvation to the Gentiles

(*John 12:20-33*)

We are now nearing the end and the climax of Jesus' public ministry. He is yet in the temple on this the third day of the week of his passion. What is about to transpire, and which has been preserved for us by the Beloved John only, is Jesus' crowning demonstration that his saving truths are for all men, Jew and Gentile alike. After his resurrection he will tell his apostolic witnesses to go into all the world and preach the gospel to every creature, Jew and Gentile alike. Now he will foreshadow that glorious change of direction—a change from his previous command that they should go only to the lost sheep of the house of Israel—by himself proclaiming the message of salvation to certain Greeks. True they were proselytes of Judaism, but they were not Abraham's seed, and the blood of the ancient patriarch did not flow in their veins; they were not part of the chosen people in the true and full sense of the word.

These Greeks had come up to Jerusalem to the Passover "to worship at the feast." They were Jews by adoption and had submitted to circumcision so as to be allowed fellowship in the regular worship. As devout men they were now feeling the exhilaration of the first three days of Passover worship and more particularly the impact of Jesus on the festive celebration.

They may well have been caught up in the outpouring of

the Spirit that accompanied the triumphal entry into Jerusalem, amid shouts of Hosanna to the Son of David, on the first day; in any event they would have been fully apprised of that prophetically wondrous day. They must have been present when Jesus cleansed the temple on the second day, and manifestly on this third day they had heard and seen and felt such glorious things as have seldom fallen to the lot of men on earth to experience.

No doubt they were present when our Lord discomfited the chief priests and rulers on the question of authority, and then heard the parables of the two sons, the wicked husbandman, and the king's son. Jesus' discussion with the Pharisees on the tribute money and his pronouncements to the Sadducees about eternal marriage were still ringing in their ears. They had heard the discussion with the lawyer relative to the first and great commandment; had heard him ask the Pharisees, "What think ye of Christ? whose son is he?"; and had heard him heap woes upon the scribes and Pharisees, and seen him weep over doomed Jerusalem.

They were devout men in whose hearts a spirit of faith now welled up. Unlike those Jews who had in their veins the blood of Abraham naturally, these Greeks had not been led far astray by the blind guides of the day. They had come to the Passover as "Proselytes of Righteousness," as the Jews called their converts, but after hearing, and seeing, and feeling the message of Jesus, they had become in their hearts disciples of "the Lord our Righteousness," as Jesus was Messianically called.

But with it all they were timid, hesitant to approach Jesus directly. Perhaps they were overawed by his personal majesty; perhaps their cultural background called for a personal introduction; perhaps they felt that as Jewish non-Jews they might not receive the welcome reserved for Israel proper. The separation of the Jew from the Gentile was well fixed in every mind in that day. In any event they came to Philip and said, "Sir, we would see Jesus." Aware of the reasons for their timidity, and accepting them as proper,

Philip himself hesitated to approach Jesus with the Greek entourage. Instead he went to Andrew; then these two apostles, obviously after consultation together, took the matter to Jesus.

It is evident that these Gentile converts were then taught by our Lord, but only a few fragmentary portions of what was said have been preserved for us by John. We suppose the Greeks acclaimed him as Lord and testified of his Messiahship, perhaps in words that meant he was soon to rule and reign on an earthly throne, as some Jews had affirmed in the past. Our Lord's first recorded words to them were:

> *The hour is come, that the Son of man should be glorified. Verily, verily, I say unto you, Except a corn of wheat fall into the ground and die, it abideth alone: but if it die, it bringeth forth much fruit.*

"The simile is an apt one, and at once impressively simple and beautiful. A farmer who neglects or refuses to cast his wheat into the earth, because he wants to keep it, can have no increase; but if he sow the wheat in good rich soil, each living grain may multiply itself many fold, though of necessity the seed must be sacrificed in the process." (Talmage, pp. 518-19.) To this Jesus then added:

> *He that loveth his life shall lose it; and he that hateth his life in this world shall keep it unto eternal life.*

"The Master's meaning is clear; he that loves his life so well that he will not imperil it, or, if need be, give it up, in the service of God, shall forfeit his opportunity to win the bounteous increase of eternal life; while he who esteems the call of God as so greatly superior to life that his love of life is as hatred in comparison, shall find the life he freely yields or is willing to yield, though for the time being it disappear like the grain buried in the soil; and he shall rejoice in the bounty of eternal development. If such be true of every man's existence, how transcendently so was it of the life of Him who came to die that men may live? Therefore was it necessary that He die, as He had said He was about to do;

but His death, far from being life lost, was to be life glorified." (Talmage, p. 519.)

We suppose also that they said something about their Grecian ancestry and pleaded for the blessings of the gospel for those not of the chosen race. In any event Jesus said:

> *If any man serve me, let him follow me; and where I am, there shall also my servant be: if any man serve me, him will my Father honour.*

Jesus' death was to be for *all men,* Jew and Gentile alike. *Any man*—let him be of whatever nation or kindred or tongue or people, black or white, bond or free, male or female, Jew or Gentile—*any man* may come unto Christ and be saved. There is no aristocracy except the aristocracy of personal righteousness, no nobility except the nobility of worthiness, no salvation except the salvation that comes by obedience to the laws and ordinances of the gospel. All are to be saved on the same terms and conditions, and the salvation involved is exaltation: it is to be where he is; it is to be like him: it is to sit down on his throne, even as he sits on the throne of his Father.

As thoughts of his coming suffering and death pressed in upon Jesus; as the awesome reality and nearness of it all hung heavily upon him; as he seemed to feel in advance some of the agonizing pains of Gethsemane and the cross, he exclaimed:

> *Now is my soul troubled; and what shall I say? Father, save me from this hour: but for this cause came I unto this hour. Father, glorify thy name.*

Thus a God speaks to a God. Overwhelming as the coming agony might be, crushing as the weight of his burden might be, yet this was the very purpose for which he had come to earth; yet he would glorify the Father's name by drinking the dregs of the bitter cup. "Then came there a voice from heaven," the voice of the Father, saying:

> *I have both glorified it, and will glorify it again.*

Twice has the Gentile world, prefiguring that which is to be, come to the Mortal Messiah to testify and worship—once at his birth in Bethlehem and now at his death in Jerusalem. Wise men from the East bowed before his cradle, and Gentiles from Greece now kneel before his cross. And thrice has the Father spoken from heaven to testify and strengthen his Son—once at Bethabara when the Holy Ghost descended bodily in calm serenity like a dove; then on Mount Hermon when Jesus was transfigured before the Three; and now in the temple as the message is given that the gospel is for all men. And on none of these occasions was it clear to the wicked and ungodly what wondrous realities were then being portrayed. This time, perhaps at all times, it was an audible voice that all present heard. This time, as also on the previous occasions, some besides Jesus understood the spoken words; others now said, "It thundered"; and yet others, "An angel spake to him." Then Jesus said:

> *This voice came not because of me, but for your sakes. Now is the judgment of this world: now shall the prince of this world be cast out. And I, if I be lifted up from the earth, will draw all men unto me.*[2]

There is glory and triumph in these words. Jesus is comforted by his Father's voice; the people, having heard the sound from heaven, have a witness from on high of his divine Sonship, and Jesus, speaking of things to come as though they were already accomplished, announces that Satan, "the prince of this world," is doomed. Righteousness will eventually triumph. As to our Lord's being "lifted up," John says: "This he said, signifying what death he should die." After Gethsemane he would suffer the agony of the cross.

"Who Is This Son of Man?"
(*John 12:34-50*)

Jesus is to be lifted up and slain for all men, not for the Jews only. This message he has given to the Gentile Greeks. We cannot doubt that they understood his words and rejoiced in his goodness. But the captious, caviling critics among his own people chose to ignore this concept of a universal religion, brought by the Savior of all men, and to take issue with him instead on the matter of whether he could be the Savior of any people, let alone all men of all races.

"We have heard out of the law that Christ abideth for ever," the people then said, having reference to their Messianic traditions and the teachings of the Rabbis that Messiah's reign would be followed by the resurrection. How, then, could the Messiah be lifted up and slain as Jesus now said? "How sayest thou, The Son of man must be lifted up? who is this Son of man?" they asked. How can the Son of Man be the Messiah if he is to lose his life?[3]

Jesus will answer their question, with power and authority, in words of doctrine and of testimony. It is the very question he has been answering for nearly three and a half years from one end of Palestine to the other—to the Jews of Judea, the Galileans of Galilee, the Samaritans of Samaria, and the Pereans of Perea, and to the Gentiles in Phoenicia and the mixed races around Decapolis. There has not been, there is not now, and there never shall be any doubt in the minds of spiritually enlightened persons as to who this Son of Man is.

The Father is a Holy Man. "In the language of Adam, Man of Holiness is his name, and the name of his Only Begotten is the Son of Man, even Jesus Christ, a righteous Judge." (Moses 6:57.) Jesus will now make such a proclamation. He will not quibble about their interpretation of their law. What he has heretofore said about their false traditions, their legends and fantasies, their wicked wresting of holy writ—all such is well known to them. Rather he will deliver his last public sermon, and he will make it a fitting testimony of himself and his Father. He begins with these words:

> *Yet a little while is the light with you. Walk while ye have the light, lest darkness come upon you: for he that walketh in darkness knoweth not whither he goeth. While ye have the light, believe in the light, that ye may be the children of light.*

He who is the Light of the World, whose spirit enlighteneth every man born into the world, who invites all men to believe in him and come unto the Father by him—the Blessed Christ again issues his new and everlasting plea. 'Come, believe in me. I am the Light; believe in the Light. Become my sons and daughters, the children of Light. If ye do not this, darkness will come upon you, and those who walk in darkness trudge an undeviating course to everlasting doom.'

At this point, before the full sermon is preached, John makes some parenthetical comments about the disbelief of the Jews and includes this statement: "These things spake Jesus, and departed, and did hide himself from them." This statement clearly should have been made at the end, not in the middle of the sermon.

As is always the case when the gospel is preached, some believe, many disbelieve, and even among believers there are those who will not make an open confession. Of the Jews generally John says: "Though he had done so many miracles before them, yet they believed not on him."

Let there be no misunderstanding on this point: Some few accepted Jesus as the Messiah, but the generality of the people rejected him with a vengeance. This rejection was not the isolated act of their leaders or of a few rabble rousers. It had the sustaining support of the generality of the people and was the outgrowth of their whole religious system. As evidence that such would be the case, John quotes Isaiah's Messianic word: "Lord, who hath believed our report? and to whom hath the arm of the Lord been revealed?" Further, John says, "they could not believe," because as Isaiah prophesied: "He hath blinded their eyes, and hardened their heart; that they should not see with their eyes, nor understand with their heart, and be converted, and I should heal them."

A further sad note, interjected into John's account at this point, says: "Nevertheless among the chief rulers also many believed on him; but because of the Pharisees they did not confess him, lest they should be put out of the synagogue: For they loved the praise of men more than the praise of God." Truly it was an onerous burden—religiously, socially, economically—to be cast out of the synagogue by the judges of men, but how much greater is it to be cast out eternally from the society of the saved by the Eternal Judge.

Now we return to the sermon about the Son of Man. In it Jesus probably said many things that are not preserved for us. This we do know, however, that the rest of his recorded words were proclaimed in a loud voice, and we cannot do other than believe they were the climax of his sayings in this his last public sermon.

> *He that believeth on me, believeth not on me, but on him that sent me. And he that seeth me seeth him that sent me.*

"*Who is this Son of Man?*" He is the Son of Man of Holiness. There is a Father and a Son. Those who believe in the Son must of necessity believe in the Father. It is not possible to believe a man is a son without believing he has a father, nor to believe a man is a father unless he has offspring. God the Eternal Father is a father because he has children. The Son of God is God because God is his Father. And in this case, to see one is to see the other, as it were, because they are in the express image of each other.

> *I am come a light into the world, that whosoever believeth on me should not abide in darkness.*

"*Who is this Son of Man?*" He is the Light of the World, the perfect pattern for all men, the great Exemplar, the only one who can say, without any limitation whatever: "What manner of men ought ye to be? Verily I say unto you, even as I am." (3 Ne. 27:27.) Those who believe in him leave the darkness of the world and come into the marvelous light of Christ.

> *And if any man hear my words, and believe not, I judge him not: for I came not to judge the world, but to save the world.*
>
> *He that rejecteth me, and receiveth not my words,*

hath one that judgeth him: the word that I have spoken, the same shall judge him in the last day.

"*Who is this Son of Man?*" He is a preacher of righteousness whose words have saving power. He came to save the world through the gospel. If men do not believe his words, they reject him; and if they reject him, his words will condemn them in the day of judgment when he standeth to judge the world.

For I have not spoken of myself; but the Father which sent me, he gave me a commandment, what I should say, and what I should speak.

"*Who is this Son of Man?*" He is the Son of God, his servant, his agent, his ambassador, his representative. The Father sent him into the world, and he speaks the word of the Father.

And I know that his commandment is life everlasting: whatsoever I speak therefore, even as the Father said unto me, so I speak.

"*Who is this Son of Man?*" He is the Son of God who speaks the word of the Father, and the Father's commandments lead men to eternal life, which is the greatest of all the gifts of God.

Thus Jesus ended his public teaching: ended it with a testimony of his own divine Sonship; ended it with a call to all men to believe in him and live his laws; ended it with the promise that all the obedient shall have eternal life in his Father's kingdom.

With this he left the temple forever.

NOTES

1. Be it noted that these are the words of the Lord Jesus; he is the One who shall gather his children. Implicit in the context is another affirmation of his divine Sonship. A similar lament has come from his lips in modern times: "O, ye nations of the earth," his solemn voice intones, "how often would I have gathered you together as a hen gathereth her chickens under her wings, but ye would not!" (D&C 43:24.)

2. To the Nephites, Jesus gave utterance to this same thought in these words: "My Father sent me that I might be lifted up upon the cross; and after that I had been lifted up upon the cross, that I might draw all men unto me, that as I have been lifted up by men even so should men be lifted up by the Father, to stand before me, to be judged of their works, whether they be good or whether they be evil—And for this cause have I been lifted

up; therefore, according to the power of the Father I will draw all men unto me, that they may be judged according to their works." (3 Ne. 27:14-15.)

3. "Of course the scriptures said Christ and his kingdom should abide forever (Isa. 9:7; Ezek. 37:25; and Dan. 7:14, among many others); and so shall it be commencing in the millennial day when 'the kingdoms of this world are become the kingdoms of our Lord, and of his Christ; and he shall reign for ever and ever.' (Rev. 11:15.)

"But the scriptures also said that King-Messiah 'was wounded for our transgressions, . . . bruised for our iniquities,' 'brought as a lamb to the slaughter,' and *'cut off out of the land of the living.'* They said, *'he made his grave with the wicked, and with the rich in his death'* (Isa. 53); that he, 'the Lord Jehovah' would 'swallow up death in victory,' and bring to pass the resurrection of all men. Indeed, it was the great Jehovah himself who had said to their fathers: 'Thy dead men shall live, *together with my dead body shall they arise.'* (Isa. 25:8; 26:4, 19.)

"There was no occasion for Jesus' captious critics either to have or to feign ignorance of the true mortal ministry of their Messiah." (*Commentary* 1:631.)

THE OLIVET DISCOURSE: JERUSALEM AND THE TEMPLE

The end is come upon my people of Israel. . . .
And the songs of the temple
shall be howlings in that day,
saith the Lord God:
there shall be many dead bodies
in every place; they shall
cast them forth with silence.
(Amos 8:2-3.)
Messiah [shall] be cut off, . . .
and the people of the prince that shall come
shall destroy the city and the sanctuary;
and . . . he shall cause the sacrifice
and the oblation to cease,
and for the overspreading of abominations
he shall make it desolate,
even until the consummation,
and that determined shall be poured upon the
desolate. (Dan. 9:26-27.)

"Your House Is Left unto You Desolate"

(*Matthew 24:1-2; JST, Matthew 24:1-2; Mark 13:1-2; JST, Mark 13:1-6; Luke 21:5-6*)

To mortal eyes it seemed as though all the wealth and glory and grandeur of the world was centered in the Temple of Jehovah, which crowned the Holy City. We know of no other buildings either before or since that have shown forth such splendid architectural perfection and such surpassing beauty. And yet he who had blessed it with his presence now cursed it with his mouth: "Your house is left unto you desolate," he said as tears of sorrow streamed down his cheeks.

And now Jesus was leaving the temple forever. Henceforth the House of God could be a den of thieves; no matter, it had served its purpose, and its end had come. It was a sad moment; tears might well flow again on every cheek. Was all this glory and beauty to be as Sodom and Gomorrah? How could such grandeur turn to dust? Luke tells us that then "some spake of the temple, how it was adorned with goodly stones and gifts." But Jesus said:

> *As for these things which ye behold, the days will come, in the which there shall not be left one stone upon another, that shall not be thrown down.*

We can understand how the feelings of the disciples were engulfed in despair as the divine decree was uttered. "The feelings of the Apostles still clung with the loving pride of their nationality to that sacred and memorable spot. They stopped to cast upon it one last lingering gaze, and one of them was eager to call His attention to its goodly stones and priceless offerings—those nine gates overlaid with gold and silver, and the one of solid Corinthian brass yet more precious; those graceful and towering porches; those polished and bevelled blocks forty cubits long and ten cubits high, testifying to the toil and munificence of so many generations; those double cloisters and stately pillars; that lavish adornment of sculpture and arabesque; those alternate blocks of red and white marble, recalling the crest and hollow of the sea-waves; those vast clusters of golden grapes, each cluster as large as a man, which twined their splendid luxuriance over the golden doors.

"They would have Him gaze with them on the rising terraces of courts—the Court of the Gentiles with its monolithic columns and rich mosaic; above this the flight of fourteen steps which led to the Court of the Women; then the flight of fifteen steps which led up to the Court of the Priests; then, once more, the twelve steps which led to the final platform crowned by the actual Holy, and Holy of Holies, which the Rabbis fondly compared for its shape to a couchant lion, and which, with its marble whiteness and golden roofs, looked like a glorious mountain whose snowy summit was gilded by the sun.

"It is as though they thought that the loveliness and magnificence of this scene would intercede with Him, touching His heart with mute appeal. But the heart of Jesus was sad. To Him the sole beauty of a Temple was the sincerity of its worshippers, and no gold or marble, no brilliant vermilion, or curiously-carven cedar-wood, no delicate sculpturing or votive gems, could change for Him a den of robbers into a House of Prayer. The builders were still busily at work, as they had been for nearly fifty years, but their work, unblessed of God, was destined—like the earthquake-shaken forum of guilty Pompeii—to be destroyed before it was finished." (Farrar, pp. 577-78.)

Thus we find the disciples, as "Jesus went out, and departed from the temple," coming to him and saying: "Master, show us concerning the buildings of the temple; as thou hast said; They shall be thrown down, and left unto you desolate." His answer:

Behold ye these stones of the temple, and all this great work, and buildings of the temple? Verily I say unto you, they shall be thrown down and left unto the Jews desolate.

See ye not all these things, and do ye not understand them? Verily I say unto you, There shall not be left here upon this temple, one stone upon another, that shall not be thrown down.

Literal fulfillment of this dire prophecy came in 70 A.D. when Titus and his legions turned Jerusalem into a ghastly ruin and wrenched each temple stone from its place and foundation as the heathen forces searched out every carat of gold and every gem of worth, and the temple treasures were carried to Rome. What had once adorned the House of God found its way to the synagogue of Satan.

And Jesus, having so spoken, "left them and went upon the mount of Olives."

The Dispensation of Persecution and Martyrdom

(*Matthew 24:3-5, 9-13; JST, Matthew 24:3-4, 8, 11; Mark 13:3-6, 9, 11-13; JST, Mark 13:7-13; Luke 21:7-8, 12-19; JST, Luke 21:7-8, 11-14, 16; D&C 45:15-21*)

Upon that holy mount, east of Jerusalem—from which the Risen Lord shall soon ascend unto his Father, and where at the day of his glorious return he shall again place his feet—there Jesus and the Twelve rested quietly after an arduous day in the wicked city below them. Alone there, apart from the maddening throngs of Passover pilgrims and separated from the cursed leaders of a damned people, Jesus was prepared to teach and the Twelve to receive the mysteries of the kingdom. Thoughts of the doomed temple and of the Lord's return to receive the glad acclaim, "Blessed is he who cometh in the name of the Lord, in the clouds of heaven, and all the holy angels with him," are uppermost in the minds of the spiritual giants there seated. They propose to the Lord two questions:

1. "Tell us, when shall these things be which thou hast said concerning the destruction of the temple, and the Jews?"

2. "And what is the sign of thy coming, and of the end of the world? (or the destruction of the wicked, which is the end of the world.)"

Portions of our Lord's reply are found in Matthew, in

Mark, and in Luke, and a revealed account of other parts was given to the Prophet Joseph Smith. Each account lays emphasis upon one part or another of his reply. As nearly as we can piece his sermon together, the doctrine came forth as we shall now recite in this and the next three chapters.

> *As ye have asked of me concerning the signs of my coming, in the day when I shall come in my glory in the clouds of heaven, to fulfil the promises that I have made unto your fathers, For as ye have looked upon the long absence of your spirits from your bodies to be a bondage, I will show unto you how the day of redemption shall come, and also the restoration of the scattered Israel.*

As is his wont, he will answer their questions by a recital of basic principles, and he will tell them additional things that even they had not been led to ask.

> *And now ye behold this temple which is in Jerusalem, which ye call the house of God, and your enemies say that this house shall never fall.*
>
> *But, verily I say unto you, that desolation shall come upon this generation as a thief in the night, and this people shall be destroyed and scattered among all nations. And this temple which ye now see shall be thrown down that there shall not be left one stone upon another.*
>
> *And it shall come to pass, that this generation of Jews shall not pass away until every desolation which I have told you concerning them shall come to pass.*

Such is his introduction, given in general terms and reaffirming what had just fallen from his lips relative to the magnificent buildings comprising the holy temple, which the scribes and leaders boasted should never fall. And yet this very generation of proud and haughty ones shall see and feel and sorrow as desolations come upon them as a thief in the night. As pertaining to these desolations about to be poured out upon their generation, Jesus said:

> *The time draweth near, and therefore take heed that*

ye be not deceived; for many shall come in my name, saying, I am Christ; go ye not therefore after them.

False prophets always arise to oppose those who are truly sent of God. False Christs will always be proclaimed when the truth from heaven is being set forth by true ministers. False religions will forever arise to fight the Lord's saints. And because error cannot long stand against truth, evil men will turn to persecution and begin to wield those satanic forces of hatred and evil which have ever been hurled at the faithful.

But take heed to yourselves: for they shall deliver you up to councils; and in the synagogues ye shall be beaten: and ye shall be brought before rulers and kings for my sake, for a testimony against them.

'All the civil and religious power of the world will combine against you. The councils (the Sanhedrins, both local and general) with their civil power; the synagogues, which exercise the power of the church; kings and rulers, who wield the sword and command armies—all these shall combine to fight against God.' Nor is it any different today. Many governments in many lands, influenced by the religions of men and of devils, proscribe the preaching of true religion and provide legal penalities for those sent to bear witness of the truth.

But when they shall lead you, and deliver you up, take no thought beforehand what ye shall speak, neither do ye premeditate: but whatsoever shall be given you in that hour, that speak ye: for it is not ye that speak, but the Holy Ghost.

Though they are persecuted; though prison walls house their bodies; though priests deride and rulers mock; though all the forces of earth and hell combine to close the mouths of the living witnesses of the Lord Jesus Christ, yet their voices must and shall be heard; yet the words will be his, for the Holy Ghost will speak by their mouths.

Now the brother shall betray the brother to death, and the father the son; and children shall rise up against their parents, and shall cause them to be put to death.

Then shall they deliver you up to be afflicted, and shall kill you, and ye shall be hated of all nations for my name's sake.

And then shall many be offended, and shall betray one another; and many false prophets shall arise, and shall deceive many;

And because iniquity shall abound, the love of many shall wax cold; but he that shall endure unto the end, the same shall be saved.

With two millennia to separate us from the early Christians, the agony of their sufferings, the burden of their pains, and the horrors of the persecutions heaped upon them seem to fade away. But if ever there was a dispensation of martyrdom it was in the day of Jesus and Peter and Paul. In that day to join the Church was to prepare to die. Lest we forget, let us note a few lines from the history of the past; let us view a small part of the persecutions of the saints in time's meridian.

Rome went up in flames, it is supposed by the hand of a mad tyrant, Nero. He immediately "endeavoured to fix the odious crime of having destroyed the capital of the world upon the most innocent and faithful of his subjects—upon the only subjects who offered heartfelt prayers on his behalf—the Roman Christians. They were the defenceless victims of this horrible charge; for though they were the most harmless, they were also the most hated and the most slandered of living men. . . .

"Nero sought popularity and partly averted the deep rage which was rankling in many hearts against himself, by torturing men and women, on whose agonies he thought that the populace would gaze not only with a stolid indifference, but even with fierce satisfaction. . . .

"It is clear that a shedding of blood—in fact, some form or other of human sacrifice—was imperatively demanded by popular feeling as an expiation of the ruinous crime which had plunged so many thousands into the depths of misery . . . Blood cried for blood, before the sullen suspicion against Nero could be averted, or the indignation of Heaven appeased. . . .

"No man is more systematically heartless than a corrupted debauchee. Like people, like prince. In the then condition of Rome, Nero well knew that a nation 'cruel, by their sports to blood inured,' would be most likely to forget their miseries, and condone their suspicions, by mixing games and gaiety with spectacles of refined and atrocious cruelty, of which, for eighteen centuries, the most passing record has sufficed to make men's blood run cold. . . .

"Tacitus tells us that '. . . *a huge multitude* were convicted, not so much on the charge of incendiarism as for their hatred to mankind.' " Then he adds: " 'And various forms of mockery were added to enhance their dying agonies. Covered with the skins of wild beasts, they were doomed to die by the mangling of dogs, or by being nailed to crosses; or to be set on fire and burnt after twilight by way of nightly illumination. Nero offered his own gardens for this show, and gave a chariot race, mingling with the mob in the dress of a charioteer, or actually driving about among them."

The gardens of Nero "were thronged with gay crowds, among whom the Emperor moved in his frivolous degradation—and on every side were men dying slowly on their crosses of shame. Along the paths of those gardens on the autumn nights were ghastly torches, blackening the ground beneath them with streams of sulphurous pitch, and each of those living torches was a martyr in his shirt of fire. And in the amphitheatre hard by, in sight of twenty thousand spectators, famished dogs were tearing to pieces some of the best and purest of men and women, hideously disguised in the skins of bears or wolves. Thus did Nero baptize in the blood of martyrs the city which was to be for ages the capital of the world!"[1]

A compassionate providence impels us to draw the curtain over a further recitation of such scenes. It suffices for us to know that the saints in that day—in the dispensation of death, in the era of martyrdom—became followers of the lowly Nazarene, only to have their blood mingled with the blood of all the martyrs of the past, that together that great river of blood might cry unto the Lord of Hosts till he, in his own good time, chose to avenge it.

Jerusalem and the Abomination of Desolation

(*Matthew 24:15-22; JST, Matthew 24:12-21; Mark 13:14-20; JST, Mark 13:14-23; Luke 17:31-33; 21:20-24; JST, Luke 17:31; 21:20*)

Whatever may be said of the sufferings and sorrows and death of the Lord's saints in the age of martyrdom, it was but a type and a shadow of the vengeance and slaughter destined to be poured out upon the Jews of that generation. The synagogues in which apostles were scourged would soon be drenched in the blood of those who wielded the lash. The currents of hatred that swept many of Jesus' disciples to untimely deaths would soon become a great tidal wave of anger and animosity against the Jewish people that would destroy their city, overrun their nation, and scatter their people. Those who with Roman hands crucified their King at Jerusalem would soon themselves be hanging by the thousands upon Roman crosses in that same benighted area. The sensitivities of refined persons will overflow with revulsion as we now hear the dire predictions of Jesus against his own people and then see the beginning of their fulfillment in the very day of those then living.

> *When ye therefore shall see the abomination of desolation, spoken of by Daniel the prophet concerning the destruction of Jerusalem, then ye shall stand in the holy place.*

At this point in Jesus' discourse, Matthew and Luke insert the statement, "Whoso readeth let him understand." We know that Daniel foretold that desolation, born of abomination and wickedness, would sweep Jerusalem as with a flood in the day that the Messiah was cut off from among the living. (Dan. 9:27; 11:31; 12:11.) According to Luke's account, Jesus said: "And when ye shall see Jerusalem compassed with armies, then know that the desolation thereof is nigh." The sorrows and evils of this dread day we shall relate shortly. The counsel that the saints should then "stand in the holy place" means that they should assemble together where they could receive prophetic guidance that would preserve them from the desolations of the day. The place of their assembly became holy because of the righteousness of the holy ones who comprised the Lord's congregation.[2] As Matthew recorded:

> *Then let them who are in Judea, flee into the mountains. Let him who is on the housetop, flee, and not return to take anything out of his house: Neither let him who is in the field, return back to take his clothes.*

Luke's account speaks similarly: "Then let them who are in Judea flee to the mountains; and let them who are in the midst of it, depart out; and let not them who are in the countries, return to enter into the city." "Remember Lot's wife."

> *And woe unto them that are with child, and unto them that give suck in those days! Therefore, pray ye the Lord, that your flight be not in the winter, neither on the Sabbath day.*

In all this, speedy flight is enjoined. 'Flee to the mountains. Let him who is on the housetop take the outside staircase, or go over the roofs of the houses. Let him who is in the field go in his work clothes. Abandon your property. Those who are in country areas must not return into the city. The time for escape will be short. Look not back to Sodom and the wealth and luxury you are leaving. Stay not in the burning house, in the hope of salvaging your treasures, lest the flame destroy you. Pray that your flight will not be impeded by the cold of winter or the shut gates and travel restrictions of the Sabbath. Flee, flee to the mountains.' (And when the day came, the true saints, guided as true saints always are by the spirit of revelation, fled to Pella in Perea and were spared.)

For then, in those days, shall be great tribulation on the Jews, and upon the inhabitants of Jerusalem; such as was not before sent upon Israel, of God, since the beginning of their kingdom, (for it is written their enemies shall scatter them,) until this time; no, nor ever shall be sent again upon Israel.

All things which have befallen them, are only the beginning of the sorrows which shall come upon them; and except those days should be shortened, there should none of their flesh be saved. But for the elect's sake, according to the covenant, those days shall be shortened.

Behold, these things I have spoken unto you concerning the Jews.

To this we must add those words of Jesus which Luke preserved: "For these be the days of vengeance, that all things which are written may be fulfilled. . . . For there shall be great distress in the land, and wrath upon this people. . . . And they shall fall by the edge of the sword, and shall be led away captive into all nations."

Before viewing the desolation that came upon them—lest we think the historical account be overdrawn—we must remind ourselves of the prophetic word that foresaw the awful horrors of that day. Jesus has just said: "For it is written their enemies shall scatter them," and "These be the days of vengeance, that all things which are written may be fulfilled." Though many prophets spoke of these days, none did so with such force and power as Moses, the man of God in whom they trusted. He it was who placed before their forebears the blessings of obedience and the cursings of disobedience.

Israel, the favored and chosen of Jehovah, in the very day of their birth as a nation, heard from the mouth of Moses such an array of curses as no other people has ever faced. In more than fifty consecutive verses of Holy Writ, Jehovah proclaimed the calamities, desolations, diseases, plagues, and evils that would befall his people if they forsook him and his law.

And now fourteen hundred years later that remnant of the chosen seed which resided in old Canaan had waged open war against Jehovah as he walked in their streets, taught in their synagogues, and worked wonders in the holy house that bore his name and that they viewed as the glory of the whole earth. And so the ax was laid at the root of the rotted tree; Jerusalem was about to suffer all that the prophets had foretold.

The specific word and the exact portion of the ancient curses about to be fulfilled were these: Thou shalt "serve thine enemies which the Lord shall send against thee, in hunger, and in thirst, and in nakedness, and in want of all things: and he shall put a yoke of iron upon thy neck, until he have destroyed thee.

"The Lord shall bring a nation against thee from far, from the end of the earth, as swift as the eagle flieth; a nation whose tongue thou shalt not understand; A nation of fierce countenance, which shall not regard the person of the old, nor shew favour to the young. . . .

"And he shall besiege thee in all thy gates, until thy high and fenced walls come down, wherein thou trustedst, throughout all thy land. . . .

"*And thou shalt eat the fruit of thine own body, the flesh of thy sons and of thy daughters,* which the Lord thy God hath given thee, in the siege, and in the straitness, wherewith thine enemies shall distress thee. . . .

"The tender and delicate woman among you, which would not adventure to set the sole of her foot upon the ground for delicateness and tenderness, her eye shall be evil toward the husband of her bosom, and toward her son, and toward her daughter, And toward her young one that cometh out from between her feet, and toward her children which she shall bear: for *she shall eat them for want of all things* secretly in the siege and straitness, wherewith thine enemy shall distress thee in thy gates. . . .

"And the Lord shall scatter thee among all people, from the one end of the earth even unto the other; . . . And among these nations shalt thou find no ease, neither shall the sole of thy foot have rest: but the Lord shall give thee there a trembling heart, and failing eyes, and sorrow of mind: And thy life shall hang in doubt before thee; and thou shalt fear day and night, and shalt have none assurance of life: In the morning thou shalt say, Would God it were even! and at even thou shalt say, Would God it were morning!" (Deut. 28:15-68.)

Thus saith Jehovah; such is the prophetic word, and his word shall not return unto him void. Summarizing the details given by Josephus of the siege of Jerusalem, our friend Farrar, with his usual literary craftsmanship, says: "Never was a narrative more full of horrors, frenzies, unspeakable degradations, and overwhelming miseries than is the history of the siege of Jerusalem. Never was any prophecy more closely, more terribly, more overwhelmingly fulfilled than this of Christ.

"The men going about in the disguise of women with swords concealed under their gay robes; the rival outrages and infamies of John and Simon; the priests struck by darts from the upper court of the Temple, and falling slain by their own sacrifices; 'the blood of all sorts of dead carcases—priests, strangers, profane—standing in lakes in the holy courts'; the corpses themselves lying in piles and mounds on the very altar slopes; the fires feeding luxuriously on cedar-work overlaid with gold; friend and foe trampled to death on the gleaming mosaics in promiscuous carnage; priests, swollen with hunger, leaping madly into the devouring flames, till at last those flames had done their work, and what had been the Temple of Jerusalem, the beautiful and holy House of God, was a heap of ghastly ruin, where the burning embers were half-slaked in pools of gore.

"And did not all the righteous blood shed upon the earth since the days of Abel come upon that generation? Did not many of that generation survive to witness and feel the unutterable horrors which Josephus tells?—to see their fellows crucified in jest, 'some one way, and some another,' till 'room was wanting for the crosses, and crosses for the carcases?'—to experience the 'deep silence' and the kind of deadly night which seized upon the city in the intervals of rage?—to see 600,000 dead bodies carried out of the gates?—to see friends fighting madly for grass and nettles, and the refuse of the drains?—to see the bloody zealots 'gaping for want, and stumbling and staggering along like mad dogs?'—to hear the horrid tale of the miserable mother who, in the pangs of famine, had devoured her own child?—to be sold for slaves in such multitudes that at last none would buy them?—to see the streets running with blood, and the 'fire of burning houses quenched in the blood of their defenders?'—to have their young sons sold in hundreds, or exposed in the amphitheatres to the sword of the gladiator or the fury of the lion, until at last, 'since the people were now slain, the Holy House burnt down, and the city in flames, there was nothing farther left for the enemy to do?'

"In that awful siege it is believed that there perished 1,100,000 men, besides the 97,000 who were carried captive, and most of whom perished subsequently in the arena or the mine; and it was an awful thing to feel, as some of the survivors and eyewitnesses—and they not Christians—*did* feel, that 'the city had deserved its overthrow by producing a generation of men who were the causes of its misfortunes;' and that 'neither did any other city ever suffer such miseries, nor *did any age ever breed a generation more fruitful in wickedness than this was, since the beginning of the world.*' " (Farrar, pp. 573-74.)[3]

Thus saith the Lord: "Vengeance is mine; I will repay." (Rom. 12:19.)

NOTES

1. F. W. Farrar, *The Early Days of Christianity* (London, 1882), 1:58-69.

2. Similarly the saints of latter days are to stand in holy places and be not moved when the scourges and desolations preceding the Second Coming sweep over the earth. (D&C 45:31-32.)

3. As an introduction to the quoted passage, Farrar says: "Speaking of the murder of

the younger Hanan, and other eminent nobles and hierarchs, Josephus says, 'I cannot but think that *it was because God had doomed this city to destruction as a polluted city, and was resolved to purge His sanctuary by fire,* that He cut off these their great defenders and well-wishers; while those that a little before had worn the sacred garments and presided over the public worship, and had been esteemed venerable by those that dwelt in the whole habitable earth, were cast out naked, and seen to be the food of dogs and wild beasts.' " (Farrar, *The Life of Christ*, pp. 572-73.)

THE OLIVET DISCOURSE: THE LAST DAYS

He shall send Jesus Christ,
which before was preached unto you:
Whom the heaven must receive
until the times of restitution of all things,
which God hath spoken by the mouth
of all his holy prophets
since the world began.
(Acts 3:20-21.)

Universal Apostasy Before the Second Coming

(*Matthew 24:23-27; JST, Matthew 24:22-24, 27; Mark 13:21-23; JST, Mark 13:24-26, 28-29; Luke 17:22-25; JST, Luke 17:22-24*)

How sad and dire it is to hear the babble of discordant voices saying, "Lo, here is Christ, and lo, there," each voice supposing that his philosophy of religion is the one that will save men in the everlasting realms ahead!

How far from the truth it is for men to suppose that what Jesus taught would remain in its pure and perfect form, with all its saving power, so that men in the latter days would, through it, have the same blessings as their forebears!

Has no one read the promises made of old that the Lord Jesus cannot return "except there come a falling away first"

(2 Thes. 2:1-12); that before that day, "darkness shall cover the earth, and gross darkness the people" (Isa. 60:2; D&C 112:23-24); that the whole earth "is defiled under the inhabitants thereof; because they have transgressed the laws, changed the ordinance, broken the everlasting covenant" (Isa. 24:5)?

Does anyone really suppose that the sects of modern Christendom—with their silks and robes and rituals; with their notions of a salvation without works and by grace alone; with neither signs, nor miracles, nor apostles, nor prophets, nor revelation—does anyone really believe such a Christianity is the same as that of Jesus and Peter and Paul?

Truly, before the Lord returns, the divine decree is: Lucifer shall have his day; Satan shall reign in the hearts of men; the man of sin—who is the master of sin and the father of lies—shall hold dominion over all the earth. The Lord, according to the promises, will make the earth empty; his saving truths shall be taken away, and universal apostasy shall prevail.

Thus, Jesus—having spoken to the disciples of what shall be in their generation; having told of the destruction of Jerusalem and the scattering of the Jews; having warned those then living of what impends in their day—Jesus now raises his warning voice to us relative to what is to be in the latter days.

> *And again, after the tribulation of those days which shall come upon Jerusalem, if any man shall say unto you, Lo! here is Christ, or there; believe him not; For in those days, there shall also arise false Christs, and false prophets, and shall show great signs and wonders; insomuch that, if possible, they shall deceive the very elect, who are the elect according to the covenant.*

In the day preceding our Lord's return, false religions will cover the earth. Each will be, as it were, a false Christ, inviting men to this or that system of salvation; each will have its own ministers and evangelists who, as false prophets, will propound its doctrines and extol its wonders.[1]

So great and wondrous will be these false systems that men will think, How could a church be false that builds such cathedrals as these? How could a church be false that crowns kings and emperors; that sends forth armies into battle; that commands the services of artists and sculptors; that has, as it seems, all the gold and power of earth? With such "signs" and "wonders" as these, will not all but the very elect be deceived?

> *Behold, I speak these things unto you, for the elect's sake. Behold, I have told you before. Wherefore if they shall say unto you, Behold, he is in the desert; go not forth: behold, he is in the secret chambers; believe it not.*
>
> *For as the light of the morning cometh out of the east, and shineth even unto the west, and covereth the whole earth; so shall also the coming of the Son of Man be.*

Let the elect know of the great apostasy of latter days; let them shun false teachers who would reveal Christ, as they suppose, in a life of asceticism in the deserts, or in the seclusion of secret monastic chambers; let them know that when the restored truths of everlasting life come again among men, they shall be as the rising sun which gradually sheds its wholesome rays over all the earth. Let them know that the Son of Man will not come to reign personally on earth until this light, in millennial brilliance, shall have cast out all the darkness of long ages of apostasy.

An Era of Restoration Before the Second Coming

(*Matthew 24:14, 28; JST, Matthew 24:28, 32; Mark 13:10; JST, Mark 13:30-31, 36*)

As set forth in our scriptural text that heads this chapter, Christ cannot come again—he must be retained in heaven—until the great era of restoration, "until the times of restitution" in which the Lord will restore all things which he hath spoken "by the mouth of all his holy prophets since the world began." Jesus now names two of these things—things that must be given again before his Second Advent. They are: the fulness of the everlasting gospel and the gathering together again of the house of Israel.

> *And now I show unto you a parable. Behold, wheresoever the carcass is, there will the eagles be gathered together; so likewise shall mine elect be gathered from the four quarters of the earth. . . .*
>
> *And again, this gospel of the kingdom shall be preached in all the world, for a witness unto all nations, and then shall the end come, or the destruction of the wicked.*

Nothing so touched the hearts of Jewish-Israel as the many prophetic assurances that the dispersed and scattered remnants of that once favored nation would someday come together to worship the Lord their God as in former days. Nothing instilled in them a greater hope of ultimate glory and triumph than the divine word that some day the kingdom would be restored to Israel and that the Gentiles would then bow beneath their rod. It is this very hope in the hearts of the Twelve that will cause them a little more than forty days hence, on this very Mount, to ask the then-risen Lord, ere he ascends to his Father, when it is that such a restoration shall take place. They will then be reminded of its deferral to a later day. But here Jesus tells them that the gathering of Israel will commence before he comes again. It is one of the signs of the times.

And in this connection the very gospel he has given them, the same saving truths, the same plan of salvation that they have received, will, in that future day, come forth to be preached in all the world for a witness unto all nations. Until this has been done the Lord Jesus will not return.

How aptly do these words of the Lord Jesus lay a foundation for those yet to be written by the Beloved John, who will tell of the angelic ministrant flying through the midst of heaven to restore, in a day subsequent to New Testament times, the fulness of the everlasting gospel. (Rev. 14:6-7.)[2]

Sad it is that there will be universal apostasy for a long

period before the great and dreadful day of the Lord. But, praise be to him, there shall also be a day of restoration when the ancient blessed truths shall come again, and when Israel shall be gathered to the ancient standard, a standard that shall again be set up on earth.

Desolations Precede the Second Coming

(*Matthew 24:6-8; JST, Matthew 24:25, 29-31; Mark 13:7-8; JST, Mark 13:27, 32-35; Luke 21:9-11; JST, Luke 21:9*)

In the latter-day age of restoration, when once again the glorious wonders of the gospel are available to men, and when Israel is gathering again round the ancient standard, the powers of evil will be unleashed as never before in all history. Satan will then fight the truth and stir up the hearts of men to do evil and work wickedness to an extent and with an intensity never before known.

> *And ye also shall hear of wars, and rumors of wars; see that ye be not troubled; for all I have told you must come to pass. But the end is not yet.*
>
> *And they shall hear of wars, and rumors of wars. Behold I speak unto you for mine elect's sake. For nation shall rise against nation, and kingdom against kingdom; there shall be famine and pestilences, and earthquakes in divers places.*
>
> *And again, because iniquity shall abound, the love of men shall wax cold; but he that shall not be overcome, the same shall be saved.*

There will be wars and rumors of wars in the day of the Twelve to whom Jesus then spoke, but they are not to be troubled thereby; many things must yet transpire before the day of Jesus' return, and the end of all things is not for their day.

But when those of us who live in the day of restoration hear of wars; when voices of contention and conspiracy among us threaten to use the sword in this eventuality or that; when we hear reports and rumors about the use of atomic bombs, poisonous gases, and other weapons of unbelievable power and cruelty; when these things happen in our day, it is quite another thing. Such things are among the signs of the times, and the wars and desolations of our day will make the hostilities of the past seem like feeble skirmishes among childish combatants.

Ours is the dispensation of desolation and war that will be climaxed by a worldwide Armageddon of butchery and blood at the very hour of the coming of the Son of Man. Jesus speaks thus for the elect's sake; none others can read the signs of the times. Carnal men will consider war as a way of life and a norm of society, not as a scourge sent of God to cleanse the earth preparatory to the return of his Son.

Nor is war all we face; as the crusades of carnage increase, so will the plagues and pestilence. Famine and disease will stalk the earth. And for some reason, as yet undiscovered by modern geologists, earthquakes will increase in number and intensity. These are the last days, and the judgments of God are at hand.

All this shall be because iniquity abounds. Sin is the father of all the ills poured out upon mankind.

Gentile Fulness Ends Before the Second Coming
(*Luke 21:24-28; JST, Luke 21:23-28; D&C 45:22-35*)

As we have seen, Jerusalem, the Holy City, was to become a ghastly ruin; the pleasant home of the prophets was to be turned into a field of blood; its strong walls and magnificent Temple were to be as ashes and dust. And as we know, all that was promised came speedily to pass. Then, on the ancient site, there arose a Gentile Jerusalem, which remains unto this day. Of it Jesus now says:

> *And Jerusalem shall be trodden down of the Gentiles, until the times of the Gentiles be fulfilled.*

He is here classifying all men as Jews or Gentiles. There are no others. Jews are the Israelites, no matter what their tribal ancestry (Paul, for instance, was of Benjamin), who in the meridian of time comprised the Israelite inhabitants of Palestine plus their kindred who had spread forth from them into Egypt and Greece and Rome and other nations where they dwelt as distinct groups. All other people are Gentiles, including Israelites who were not Jewish nationals as herein defined. In this sense Joseph Smith, a pure Ephraimite, was a Gentile, and the Book of Mormon came forth as promised by way of the Gentile. In this sense those of us of Ephraim and Manasseh and other tribes who are already gathered with latter-day Israel are Gentiles. The Gentiles are the non-Jews within the meaning of words as here used.

The times of the Gentiles is the period during which the gospel will be preached to the Gentiles in preference to the Jews, and the times of the Jews is the similar period when the Jewish nationals, so to speak, will again receive the message of salvation that is in Christ. We are living in the times of the Gentiles, but that era is drawing to its close, and the gospel will soon go to the Jews.

> *In the generation in which the times of the Gentiles shall be fulfilled, there shall be signs in the sun, and in the moon, and in the stars; and upon the earth distress of nations with perplexity, like the sea and the waves roaring. The earth also shall be troubled, and the waters of the great deep; Men's hearts failing them for fear, and for looking after those things which are coming on the earth: for the powers of heaven shall be shaken.*

We see here, again, the perplexities and problems of nations and kingdoms, as wars and evil abound; we see men, subject to disease and pestilence, as their hearts fail them; and we see the geological changes out of which come earthquakes, tidal waves, and changes in the sea. In this respect, from the more amplified account of what Jesus said, we learn:

> *Ye say that ye know that the end of the world cometh; ye say also that ye know that the heavens and the earth shall pass away; And in this ye say truly, for so it is; but these things which I have told you shall not pass away until all shall be fulfilled.*

Though there will be a new heaven and a new earth whereon dwelleth righteousness, such a millennial condition will not come into being until all the things of which Jesus is now speaking have been fulfilled.

And this I have told you concerning Jerusalem; and when that day shall come, shall a remnant be scattered among all nations; But they shall be gathered again; but they shall remain until the times of the Gentiles be fulfilled.

The scattered remnants of the ancient Jews are even now in all nations, where, in the main, they will remain until they accept their Messiah and believe in the true gospel. That stirrings within them are preparing the way for this day of conversion is seen from the religious-political movement that already has assembled some—still in their unbelief—back to the land of their ancestors. The identifying characteristics of the day when the Jews will begin to believe and come again into the true fold are described in these words:

And in that day shall be heard of wars and rumors of wars, and the whole earth shall be in commotion, and men's hearts shall fail them, and they shall say that Christ delayeth his coming until the end of the earth. And the love of men shall wax cold, and iniquity shall abound.

This is the description of the world in which we now live. Of this there can be no doubt. The signs of the times are being fulfilled, and the elect can discern their true meaning by the power of the Spirit.

And when these things begin to come to pass, then look up and lift up your heads, for the day of your redemption draweth nigh.

Such are our Lord's words as Luke has preserved them. The revealed account given in our day says:

And when the times of the Gentiles is come in, a light shall break forth among them that sit in darkness, and it shall be the fulness of my gospel; But they receive it not; for they perceive not the light, and they turn their hearts from me because of the precepts of men. And in that generation shall the times of the Gentiles be fulfilled.

The time is at hand; the light has broken forth; it is the fulness of the everlasting gospel. So far the Jews have not received it, with isolated exceptions, because of the precepts of men. But soon the times of the Gentiles will be fulfilled, and the day of the Jews will commence.

And there shall be men standing in that generation, that shall not pass until they shall see an overflowing scourge; for a desolating sickness shall cover the land.

But my disciples shall stand in holy places, and shall not be moved; but among the wicked, men shall lift up their voices and curse God and die.

And there shall be earthquakes also in divers places, and many desolations; yet men will harden their hearts against me, and they will take up the sword, one against another, and they will kill one another.

That the disciples of old should have been sorely troubled by these words is almost self-evident. Hence Jesus said:

Be not troubled, for, when all these things shall come to pass, ye may know that the promises which have been made unto you shall be fulfilled.

That as modern disciples we should feel as our Lord counseled his ancient disciples is also self-evident. As the glorious conclusion of it all, Jesus said:

And then shall they see the Son of man coming in a cloud, with power and great glory.

NOTES

1. A perfect illustration of this religious turmoil is found in the religious revival that swept the frontier areas of America in the day of Joseph Smith. "It commenced with the Methodists," he said, "but soon became general among all the sects in that region of country. Indeed, the whole district of country seemed affected by it, and great multitudes united themselves to the different religious parties, which created no small stir and division amongst the people, some crying, 'Lo, here!' and others, 'Lo, there!' Some were contending for the Methodist faith, some for the Presbyterian, and some for the Baptist." (Joseph Smith—History 1:5.)

2. How glorious is the voice we hear, announcing the fulfillment of that which

John wrote. "I have sent forth mine angel flying through the midst of heaven," the voice says. "having the everlasting gospel. who hath appeared unto some and hath committed it unto man. who shall appear unto many that dwell on the earth. And this gospel shall be preached unto every nation. and kindred. and tongue. and people. And the servants of God shall go forth. saying with a loud voice: Fear God and give glory to him. for the hour of his judgment is come: And worship him that made heaven. and earth. and the sea. and the fountains of waters." (D&C 133:36-39.)

Chapter 92

THE OLIVET DISCOURSE: THE SECOND COMING

Prepare ye for the coming
of the Bridegroom;
go ye, go ye out to meet him.
(D&C 133:19-20.)
Behold, the day of the Lord cometh. . . .
And his feet shall stand in that day
upon the mount of Olives,
which is before Jerusalem on the east.
(Zech. 14:1, 4.)

The Abomination of Desolation at the Second Coming

(*Matthew 24:29; 34-35; JST, Matthew 24:33-36; Mark 13:24-25, 30-31; JST, Mark 13:37-40; Luke 21:32-33; JST, Luke 23:32*)

Titus crucified Jerusalem on a cross of Roman steel; desolation and death swept down the streets where apostles and prophets once taught; the spiritual capital of the world became the synagogue of Satan; the Holy City sank to the depths of Sodom and Egypt; and Jehovah's House was torn to bits—to rise no more. The Jewish Jerusalem made way for a Gentile Jerusalem that would continue until the day when the abomination of desolation would again pour its fury upon the place and the people.

In "the generation when the times of the Gentiles be fulfilled," this awesome scene will be reenacted. Jerusalem, this time besieged by the armies of the earth, shall be direly desolated. But this time there will be a different destiny. The Lord himself will come to fight her battles; a remnant of the people will be saved; and the Gentile Jerusalem will become again a Jewish Jerusalem. Sodomic influences will be consumed with devouring fire, and the New Jerusalem will become, in all her glory and magnificence, the spiritual capital of the world. Jehovah himself will come to the new temple, there to be constructed after the order of his new kingdom, and the saints shall worship in those sacred halls for a thousand years. And so, as Jesus continues the Olivet Discourse, we hear him say:

> *And again shall the abomination of desolation, spoken of by Daniel the prophet, be fulfilled. And immediately after the tribulation of those days, the sun shall be darkened, and the moon shall not give her light, and the stars shall fall from heaven, and the powers of heaven shall be shaken.*
>
> *Verily I say unto you, this generation, in which these things shall be shown forth, shall not pass away until all I have told you shall be fulfilled. Although the days will come that heaven and earth shall pass away, yet my word shall not pass away; but all shall be fulfilled.*

"I will gather all nations against Jerusalem to battle," the Lord says of this coming day, "and the city shall be taken, and the houses rifled, and the women ravished; and half of the city shall go forth into captivity, and the residue of the people shall not be cut off from the city." This is the dread day of Armageddon, the day when Satan shall be arrayed against freedom and light, the day when the armies of men shall number two hundred million men of arms. "Then shall the Lord go forth," the prophetic record says, "and fight against those nations, as when he fought in the day of battle. And his feet shall stand in that day upon the mount of Olives, which is before Jerusalem on the east. . . . And the

Lord my God shall come, and all the saints with thee. . . . And the Lord shall be king over all the earth: in that day shall there be one Lord, and his name one." (Zech. 14:2-5, 9.)

Be it noted that the Lord—who is the lowly Nazarene, and who is also a man of war—will come in his glory when war and desolation are sweeping the earth; when all nations are engaged in mortal combat; when the powers of earth are arrayed, ready for the burning destruction he will bring.

And be it also noted that it is "immediately after the tribulation of those days" that the heavenly manifestations incident to the Second Coming will shower their display before men, and that all this shall surely come to pass in the generation when the times of the Gentiles is fulfilled.

The Glories Attending Our Lord's Return

(*Matthew 24:30-31; JST, Matthew 24:37-40; Mark 13:26-27; JST, Mark 13:41-44; D&C 45:39-55*)

And as I said before, after the tribulation of those days, and the powers of the heavens shall be shaken, then shall appear the sign of the Son of Man in heaven; and then shall all the tribes of the earth mourn.

After the abomination of desolation sweeps Jerusalem in the last days; after the city is taken, its houses rifled, its women ravished, and half its inhabitants taken into captivity; after the sun and the moon refuse to give light and the stars fall from heaven—then will appear one grand sign of the Son of Man in heaven. At this time, the Lord in his wisdom has not seen fit to reveal the nature of this sign, though from what follows it is clear that the elect will recognize it as the heavenly portent given to announce the coming of their King.[1]

When the sign appears, there will be such mourning throughout the earth as has not before been known. As to the mourning in Israel, the prophetic word acclaims: "They shall mourn for him, as one mourneth for his only son, and shall be in bitterness for him, as one that is in bitterness for his firstborn. In that day shall there be a great mourning in Jerusalem, . . . And the land shall mourn, every family apart." (Zech. 12:10-12.)

And they shall see the Son of Man coming in the clouds of heaven, with power and great glory;

And whoso treasureth up my word shall not be deceived.

For the Son of Man shall come; and he shall send his angels before him with the great sound of a trumpet, and they shall gather together the remainder of his elect from the four winds, from one end of heaven to the other.

Lo, he cometh; none can stay his hand, and all who remain on earth shall see him and know who he is. Once as the Suffering Servant he sat with his weary disciples on the Mount of Olives; now as Lord and Master that same mountain will cleave at his touch, and he shall be King over all the earth. And whereas the gathering of his people has heretofore been directed by fallible mortals, now the angels will direct the work, and none who deserve to be saved with chosen Israel shall be overlooked.

In the revealed account of the Olivet Discourse, the Lord gives us more of the words spoken on that sacred spot than have been preserved by the three Synoptists. From this latter-day record we take these additions and amplifications of the biblical accounts:

1. *Signs and Wonders Shall Precede the Second Coming.*

And it shall come to pass that he that feareth me shall be looking forth for the great day of the Lord to come, even for the signs of the coming of the Son of Man.

And they shall see signs and wonders, for they shall be shown forth in the heavens above, and in the earth beneath. And they shall behold blood, and fire, and vapors of smoke. And before the day of the Lord shall come, the sun shall be darkened, and the moon be turned into blood, and the stars fall from heaven.

Signs follow those who believe; signs are for people who have faith; signs reveal the handdealings of the Lord to those who treasure up his word. From the standpoint of the disciples, sitting with Jesus on Olivet, surely railroads and airplanes, radio and television, and satellites orbiting the earth would be signs and wonders on earth and in heaven. Vapors of smoke spray forth when atomic bombs are exploded; blood and fire are descriptive of modern warfare; and the sun, moon, and stars will yet speak forth their messages. When "the earth shall tremble and reel to and fro as a drunken man" (D&C 88:87) and "shall remove out of her place" (Isa. 13:10-13); when "the islands shall become one land" (D&C 133:23) and the whole face of the earth be changed, as a new heaven and a new earth is born, it will seem as though the very stars in the sidereal heavens are hurling themselves out of their places. These are signs that have been, signs that are, and signs that will yet herald the coming of the Promised One.

2. *The Jews Shall Gather at Jerusalem Before the Second Coming.*

> *And the remnant shall be gathered unto this place; And then they shall look for me, and, behold, I will come; and they shall see me in the clouds of heaven, clothed with power and great glory; with all the holy angels; and he that watches not for me shall be cut off.*

These Jews, gathered at Jerusalem—pursuant to the command: "Let them who be of Judah flee unto Jerusalem, unto the mountains of the Lord's house" (D&C 133:13)—shall be members of The Church of Jesus Christ of Latter-day Saints. They will be Christians; they will believe in Christ; they will accept him as their Messiah; and they will be looking forward to his return. As Ezekiel prophesied, the Lord will make with them "a covenant of peace," they will receive his "everlasting covenant," and he will set his "sanctuary in the midst of them for evermore." (Ezek. 37:26-28.)[2]

3. *The Saints Shall Be Resurrected When the Lord Comes.*

All the faithful—their bodies in the grave, their spirits in paradise—shall come forth in glorious immortality; they shall rise in celestial splendor; they shall meet their gracious Lord and then return with him as part of his triumphal entourage. And the mortal saints, though they be scattered to the four quarters of the earth, shall be caught up to meet him and shall return to live and reign with him a thousand years. (D&C 88:95-98.)

> *But before the arm of the Lord shall fall, an angel shall sound his trump, and the saints that have slept shall come forth to meet me in the cloud.*
>
> *Wherefore, if ye have slept in peace blessed are you; for as you now behold me and know that I am, even so shall ye come unto me and your souls shall live, and your redemption shall be perfected; and the saints shall come forth from the four quarters of the earth.*

4. *Calamity and Mourning Shall Attend the Second Coming.*

> *Then shall the arm of the Lord fall upon the nations.*
>
> *And then shall the Lord set his foot upon this mount, and it shall cleave in twain, and the earth shall tremble, and reel to and fro, and the heavens also shall shake.*
>
> *And the Lord shall utter his voice, and all the ends of the earth shall hear it; and the nations of the earth shall mourn, and they that have laughed shall see their folly.*
>
> *And calamity shall cover the mocker, and the scorner shall be consumed; and they that have watched for iniquity shall be hewn down and cast into the fire.*

This is the day of vengeance which was in the heart of the Lord. It is the day when mourning and sorrow shall be universal; it is the day when all the nations of the earth shall weep because of the calamities that have befallen them; it is the day when rivers of blood shed in battle shall leave every family in deep anguish.

What of those who laughed at the upright and the godly, at those who would not stoop to live after the manner of the world? They shall see their folly, a folly that leaves them bound with the hellish chains of sin.

What of those who mocked the saints and derided the humble followers of Christ? The judgments of God will rest upon them; the calamities of nature will fall as hail and lightning from heaven.

What of the scorners, wise in their own worldly conceits, who belittle true believers for their creeds and doctrine? They shall be consumed by the glory of His presence.

And what of those who watched for iniquity? Would God they had watched and waited instead for the Lord, for they shall be hewn down, cast into the fire, and consigned to a burning endless hell.

5. *The Jewish Remnant Shall View Jesus' Wounds When He Returns.*

> *And then shall the Jews look upon me and say: What are these wounds in thine hands and in thy feet? Then shall they know that I am the Lord; for I will say unto them: These wounds are the wounds with which I was wounded in the house of my friends. I am he who was lifted up. I am Jesus that was crucified. I am the Son of God.*
>
> *And then shall they weep because of their iniquities; then shall they lament because they persecuted their king.*

The nail marks in his hands and in his feet, the gaping spear wound in his side—these are the signs of the cross; the signs of his crucifixion; the signs that he is the One who was lifted up that he might draw all men unto him on conditions of repentance. He manifests them in his resurrected flesh as and when occasion requires.

"And one shall say unto him," Zechariah prophesied, "What are these wounds in thine hands? Then shall he answer, Those with which I was wounded in the house of my friends." (Zech. 13:6.) Hearing the answer, the Jews will lament and mourn for their own iniquities—and on behalf of their fathers—because they persecuted and slew their King. Then shall the great conversion of the Jews take place; then shall be fulfilled that which the Lord spake by the mouth of Zechariah: "I will pour upon the house of David, and upon the inhabitants of Jerusalem, the spirit of grace and of supplications: and they shall look upon me whom they have pierced." (Zech. 12:10.)

6. *The Heathen Shall Be Redeemed and Satan Bound at the Second Coming.*

> *And then shall the heathen nations be redeemed, and they that knew no law shall have part in the first resurrection; and it shall be tolerable for them. And Satan shall be bound, that he shall have no place in the hearts of the children of men.*

A gracious Lord offers to all men all that they are capable of receiving. Even the heathen who are without the law shall come forth in the afternoon of the first resurrection and be blessed with a terrestrial inheritance that shall be tolerable for them. And, finally, O glorious millennial reality, Satan shall be bound for a thousand years by "the righteousness" of men, and he shall have "no power over the hearts of the people, for they dwell in righteousness, and the Holy One of Israel reigneth." (1 Ne. 22:26.)

When Will the Son of Man Come?

(*Matthew 24:32-33, 36-39; JST, Matthew 24:41-45; Mark 13:28-29, 32; JST, Mark 13:45-49; Luke 17:26-30; 21:29-31; D&C 45:34-38*)

"What is the sign of thy coming, and of the end of the world, or the destruction of the wicked, which is the end of the world?" Such was the question propounded by the Twelve as they sat with their Lord on the pleasant slopes of the Mount of Olives. He has answered by naming the signs that will take place in the "generation" of his return. He will not particularize beyond this; indeed, he is about to decline to name the day and the hour. But first he will give the parable of the fig tree. The disciples are troubled, as well they might be, at the desolations and sorrows that will yet befall men; at the bloodshed and wickedness that shall reign until the end comes; and over the many souls who shall be lost because men harden their hearts against the Holy One. Jesus says:

Be not troubled, for, when all these things shall come to pass, ye may know that the promises which have been made unto you shall be fulfilled.

And when the light shall begin to break forth, it shall be with them like unto a parable which I will show you—

Ye look and behold the fig-trees, and ye see them with your eyes, and ye say when they begin to shoot forth, and their leaves are yet tender, that summer is now nigh at hand; Even so it shall be in that day when they shall see all these things, then shall they know that the hour is nigh.

As Matthew records it, Jesus said: "Mine elect, when they shall see all these things, they shall know that he is near, even at the doors."

Thus: "Jesus both reveals and keeps hidden the time of his coming. The parable is perfect for his purposes. It announces that he will most assuredly return in the 'season' when the promised signs are shown. But it refrains from specifying the day or the hour when the figs will be harvested, thus leaving men in a state of expectant hope, ever keeping themselves ready for the coming harvest. . . .

"This parable pertains to the latter days. The restoration of the gospel, with the light that thereby breaks forth in darkness, is the beginning of the shooting forth of the leaves of the fig tree." (*Commentary* 1:664.)

But of that day and hour no one knoweth; no, not the angels of God in heaven, but my Father only.

But as it was in the days of Noah, so it shall be also at the coming of the Son of Man. For it shall be with them as it was in the days which were before the flood; for until the day that Noah entered into the ark, they were eating and drinking, marrying and giving in marriage, and knew not until the flood came and took them all away; so shall also the coming of the Son of Man be.

Likewise also as it was in the days of Lot; they did eat, they drank, they bought, they sold, they planted, they builded; But the same day that Lot went out of Sodom it rained fire and brimstone from heaven, and destroyed them all. Even thus shall it be in the day when the Son of man is revealed.

The flood of Noah and the destruction of Sodom and Gomorrah are types of the Second Coming. In Noah's day the normal affairs of life continued until the flood came to destroy the world that then was; in Lot's day, all went on, as was common among men, until the Lord rained fire and brimstone from heaven upon those wicked cities and destroyed their world. So shall it be with the destruction of the wicked, which is the end of the world. Such shall come without warning, as a thief in the night, where the wicked and ungodly are concerned. But with the elect of God, it is quite another matter. Though even they do not know the day or the hour, yet the season and the generation are clearly revealed. It shall be the season and the generation in which the signs of the times are manifest.

"Who May Abide the Day of His Coming?"

(*Matthew 24:40-41; JST, Matthew 24:46-48; JST, Mark 13:50-51; Luke 17:34-37; JST, Luke 17:34-40*)

When the Lord comes—

Then shall be fulfilled that which is written, That in the last days, two shall be in the field, one shall be taken and the other left. Two shall be grinding at the mill: the one taken, and the other left.

We have no present source for the scripture here quoted by Jesus relative to the last days. Malachi, however, in a Messianic passage of superlative power, says of the Second Coming: "The Lord, whom ye seek, shall suddenly come to his temple, . . . But who may abide the day of his coming? and who shall stand when he appeareth? for he is like a refiner's fire, and like fullers' soap. . . . For, behold, the day cometh, that shall burn as an oven; and all the proud, yea, and all that do wickedly, shall be stubble: and the day that cometh shall burn them up, saith the Lord of hosts, that it shall leave them neither root nor branch." In addition to "the proud, yea, and all that do wickedly," this passage also names sorcerers, adulterers, false swearers, those who oppress the hireling, the widow, and the fatherless in their wages, those who lead men away from the truth, and members of the true Church who do not pay an honest tithing—all these are named as among those who will not abide the day. (Mal. 3, 4.) Paul speaks of "them that know not God, and that obey not the gospel," as among those "who shall be punished with everlasting destruction from the presence of the Lord" at his Second Coming. (2 Thes. 1:7-9.) And our revelation proclaims that when he comes, "Every corruptible thing, both of man, or of the beasts of the field, or of the fowls of the heavens, or of the fish of the sea, that dwells upon all the face of the earth, shall be consumed." (D&C 101:24.)

Thus, when the Lord Jesus returns, he will destroy the wicked by the breath of his lips, the ungodly shall be burned as stubble, and the vineyard shall be cleansed of corruption. Though two, seemingly alike, work or walk or sleep or live together, one shall be destroyed by the brightness of his coming and the other preserved to enjoy the fruits of the millennial earth.

In an earlier day, in Galilee, after proclaiming this same doctrine, Jesus was asked: "Where, Lord, shall they be taken?" His answer:

> *Wheresoever the body is gathered; or, in other words, whithersoever the saints are gathered, thither will the eagles be gathered together.*

Luke, our recorder of this prior teaching, writing by way of prophecy and revelation, then said: "This he spake, signifying the gathering of his saints; and of angels descending and gathering the remainder unto them; the one from the bed, the other from the grinding, and the other from the field, whithersoever he listeth. For verily there shall be new heavens, and a new earth, wherein dwelleth righteousness." Truly the angels shall complete the gathering of the elect. And as to those who are consumed and who abide not the day, Luke continues: "And there shall be no unclean thing; for the earth becoming old, even as a garment, having waxed in corruption, wherefore it vanisheth away, and the footstool remaineth sanctified, cleansed from all sin." Such is the new heaven and the new earth which shall come into being at the end of the world, which is the destruction of the wicked.

Watch, Pray, Take Heed, Be Ready!

(*Matthew 24:42-51; JST, Matthew 24:49-50, 56; Mark 13:33-37; JST, Mark 13:52-61; Luke 12:35-48; 21:34-36; JST, Luke 12:38-57; 21:34, 36*)

Prophetic preachments have a purpose; doctrines are not taught simply to entertain, or even to edify without more. Jesus has now taught the doctrine of the Second Coming of the Son of Man so that his disciples—and all future followers into whose hands the teachings come—may use them to prepare their own souls for salvation.

If there is to be a universal apostasy before the Lord returns, the elect must know this, lest they espouse false religions and lose their souls. If the gospel is to be restored and Israel gathered, let the chosen seed find the new gospel and learn where they should gather, lest they fail to gain the promised blessings. If the Gentile fulness is at hand and Jewish Israel is soon to be favored again, let this be known to the Jews, lest they remain in darkness and be rejected with their fathers. If there are to be wars and calamities, desolations and signs, let the elect view these things in their eternal perspective, lest they remain as other men and reap the curses that shall be poured out without measure. If at our Lord's return the wicked will be as stubble and every corruptible thing shall be consumed by the brightness of his coming, how important it is to know how to escape the flames!

Thus, Jesus calls upon his disciples and all men to watch, pray, take heed, and be ready!

> *And what I say unto one, I say unto all men; Watch, therefore, for ye know not at what hour your Lord doth come. But know this, if the good man of the house had known in what watch the thief would come, he would have watched, and would not have suffered his house to have been broken up; but would have been ready.*
>
> *Therefore be ye also ready: for in such an hour as ye think not, the Son of Man cometh.*

The illustration is perfect; the application can never be forgotten. He will come as a thief in the night, unexpectedly and without warning, where the wicked and ungodly are concerned. And even as pertaining to his saints, it shall be at such an hour—though the generation is known!—which they think not.

> *Who then is a faithful and wise servant, whom his Lord hath made ruler over his household, to give them meat in due season? Blessed is that servant, whom his lord when he cometh shall find so doing. Verily I say unto you, That he shall make him ruler over all his goods.*
>
> *But and if that evil servant shall say in his heart, My lord delayeth his coming; And shall begin to smite his fellowservants, and to eat and drink with the drunken; The lord of that servant shall come in a day when he looketh not for him, and in an hour that he is not aware*

of, And shall cut him asunder, and appoint him his portion with the hypocrites: there shall be weeping and gnashing of teeth.

So the Lord purposes with reference to his own! His holy apostles, all his disciples, the army of servants who hold his holy priesthood—let them care for his earthly church. Their reward? Rulership over all his house everlastingly. But those servants who are overcome by the world, though they retain their church title and power, shall be as the stubble of the world. The blessed hour of his return overtaking them unawares, they shall be cast out to be damned with their ilk.

Both Mark and Luke, in recording the Olivet Discourse, preserve for us some expressive verities not contained in the Matthew version and not revealed anew in Doctrine and Covenants, section 45. Mark tells us that Jesus said:

Take ye heed, watch and pray: for ye know not when the time is. For the Son of man is as a man taking a far journey, who left his house, and gave authority to his servants, and to every man his work, and commanded the porter to watch.

Watch ye therefore: for ye know not when the master of the house cometh, at even, or at midnight, or at the cockcrowing, or in the morning: Lest coming suddenly he find you sleeping.

And what I say unto you I say unto all, Watch.

That is: Jesus leaves his church and journeys to his Father; he gives his disciples authority to regulate his earthly kingdom in his absence. They know not the time of his return, whether in the darkness of the night or the dawning of the day. They and all men must watch and be ready, lest when he comes he find them indifferent to their Lord's business. Similar counsel, couched in different words, has been preserved for us by Luke:

Let my disciples therefore take heed to themselves, lest at any time their hearts be overcharged with surfeiting, and drunkenness, and cares of this life, and that day come upon them unawares. For as a snare shall it come on all them that dwell on the face of the whole earth.

And what I say unto one, I say unto all, Watch ye therefore, and pray always, and keep my commandments, that ye may be counted worthy to escape all these things which shall come to pass, and to stand before the Son of Man when he shall come clothed in the glory of his Father.

Three sins, common everywhere and among all peoples; three sins, which are scarcely deemed by men to be transgressions of the divine will; three sins, which are part of the common walk of almost all men—such are here named by Jesus; and the disciples are counseled to avoid them. They are:

1. *The sin of surfeiting*—the intemperate indulgence in food and drink, symbolical of setting one's heart and interests on carnal rather than spiritual things.

2. *The sin of drunkenness*—literally, the dulling of one's mental and spiritual faculties by alcohol; figuratively, the dulling of one's spiritual senses by imbibing the false doctrines and views of the world.

3. *The sin of being overcome by the cares of this life*—temporal pursuits, business dealings, civic and political positions, educational attainments, everything that detracts from putting first in one's life the things of God's kingdom.

These sins are a snare that entraps the whole earth. Only those who avoid them and who keep the commandments will be prepared to stand before the Son of Man when he comes again in glory.

Between four and six months before, at an unnamed place in Judea, perhaps in Jerusalem, Jesus taught some similar things that it is opportune for us to consider here:

Let your loins be girded about and have your lights burning; That ye yourselves may be like unto men who wait for their Lord, when he will return from the wed-

ding; that, when he cometh and knocketh, they may open unto him immediately.

Verily I say unto you, Blessed are those servants, whom the Lord when he cometh shall find watching; for he shall gird himself, and make them sit down to meat, and will come forth and serve them.

This is a sweet and lovely illustration, one that warns the Twelve (and all disciples) to be ready for the Second Coming, which will come suddenly. The Lord leaves his servants to care for his church while he ascends into heaven. Their loins are girded for labor, for there is work to be done; there are souls to be saved. Their lamps are lighted, for they must enlighten a dark and sinful world; their words must shine forth in celestial splendor, and their deeds must be beacons of brightness to be seen by all men. The Lord's return from the marriage feast is either his Second Advent or, as we shall see, the judgment of each individual soul at death.

What blessed joy shall fill the hearts of those who watch for his return! They will be in his presence and eat at his table, where he himself will serve them. Having so taught, Jesus then shows how the blessings of the Second Coming will attend all faithful watchers, even though they do not live at the day and the hour of his glorious return.

For, behold, he cometh in the first watch of the night, and he shall also come in the second watch, and again he shall come in the third watch.

And verily I say unto you, He hath already come, as it is written of him; and again when he shall come in the second watch, or come in the third watch, blessed are those servants when he cometh, that he shall find so doing; For the Lord of those servants shall gird himself, and make them to sit down to meat, and will come forth and serve them.

And now, verily I say these things unto you, that ye may know this, that the coming of the Lord is as a thief in the night. And it is like unto a man who is an

> *householder, who, if he watcheth not his goods, the thief cometh in an hour of which he is not aware, and taketh his goods, and divideth them among his fellows.*

All men shall not be alive at the day of his coming, but whenever they live, it will be as though the great and dreadful day of the Lord had come in their day. If his servants have served faithfully in his earthly house—the Church and kingdom of God on earth—his coming (to them) will be the year of his redeemed. If they have eaten and drunken with the wicked; if their lives have been overcharged with surfeiting and the cares of this life; if they have been proud and evil and prone to wickedness—his coming (to them) will be the day of vengeance which was in his heart.

And not only that—he hath come already! For those then living, the Second Coming, as it were, was passed. The Lord was there—at least their day of judgment had come—and those who watched for righteousness were saved while those who watched for iniquity were ready for the fire. He was about to gird himself, wash the feet of the Twelve, and serve them as they partook of the Passover meal. To them he had already come as thief in the night. If they had watched, their goods would not now be ready for the flames, for "the fire shall try every man's work of what sort it is." (1 Cor. 3:12-15.)

Hearing and understanding all these things, the disciples "said among themselves, If the good man of the house had known what hour the thief would come, he would have watched, and not have suffered his house to be broken through and the loss of his goods." To this Jesus said:

> *Verily I say unto you, be ye therefore ready also; for the Son of Man cometh at an hour when ye think not.*

Peter, even then acting as a spokesman for the group, asked: "Lord, speakest thou this parable unto us, or unto all?" To this Jesus said: "I speak unto those whom the Lord shall make rulers over his household, to give his children their portion of meat in due season." The word is addressed to the servants of the Lord! They are accountable for the welfare of their brethren. Anxious to know their own state in this respect, they asked, "Who then is that faithful and wise servant?" Jesus replied:

It is that servant who watcheth, to impart his portion of meat in due season. Blessed be that servant whom his Lord shall find, when he cometh, so doing. Of a truth I say unto you, that he will make him ruler over all that he hath.

But the evil servant is he who is not found watching. And if that servant is not found watching, he will say in his heart, My Lord delayeth his coming; and shall begin to beat the menservants, and the maidens, and to eat, and drink, and to be drunken.

The Lord of that servant will come in a day he looketh not for, and at an hour when he is not aware, and will cut him down, and will appoint him his portion with the unbelievers.

And that servant who knew his Lord's will, and prepared not for his Lord's coming, neither did according to his will, shall be beaten with many stripes.

But he that knew not his Lord's will, and did commit things worthy of stripes, shall be beaten with few. For unto whomsoever much is given, of him shall much be required; and to whom the Lord has committed much, of him will men ask the more.[3]

NOTES

1. "But what will the world do," the Prophet Joseph Smith asked, when they see the sign of the Coming of the Son of Man? "They will say it is a planet, a comet, etc. But the Son of man will come as the sign of the coming of the Son of Man, which will be as the light of the morning cometh out of the east." (*Teachings,* p. 287.)

2. Joseph Smith said: "Judah must return, Jerusalem must be rebuilt, and the temple. . . . It will take some time to rebuild the walls of the city and the temple, etc.; and all this must be done before the Son of Man will make His appearance." (*Teachings,* p. 286.)

3. "For of him unto whom much is given much is required; and he who sins against the greater light shall receive the greater condemnation." (D&C 82:3.)

THE OLIVET DISCOURSE: PARABLES AND THE JUDGMENT

In prison I saw him next, condemned
To meet a traitor's doom at morn;
The tide of lying tongues I stemmed,
And honored him 'mid shame and scorn.
My friendship's utmost zeal to try,
He asked if I for him would die;
The flesh was weak; my blood ran chill;
But the free spirit cried, "I will!"

Then in a moment to my view
The stranger started from disguise;
The tokens in his hands I knew;
The Savior stood before mine eyes.
He spake, and my poor name he named,
"Of me thou hast not been ashamed;
These deeds shall thy memorial be,
Fear not, thou didst them unto me."
(*Hymns,* no. 153.)

Parable of the Ten Virgins

(*Matthew 25:1-13; JST, Matthew 25:1, 8, 11*)

If the disciples of old, seated with Jesus on the gentle slopes of Olivet, desired to know when he would return, in all the glory of his Father's kingdom, how much more ought we who live in the generation when the promised signs, one by one, are making their appearance, how much more ought we to desire to know when the glorious day will be.

If those who, in that day, were destined to die for the name of Jesus and the testimony that was theirs, sought to read the signs of the times, how much more ought we, in this day, who are privileged to live to honor his name and testify of his goodness, how much more ought we to see and read the signs heralding his coming.

If the saints of former days who knew his coming would not be in their generation, were yet counseled to watch, pray, take heed, and be ready, how much more ought the saints of latter days, who know his coming will be in their generation (for the signs have now been given!), how much more ought they to make themselves ready.

"To impress yet more indelibly upon their minds the lessons of watchfulness and faithfulness, and to warn them yet more emphatically against the peril of the ungirdled loin and the smouldering lamp,[1] He told them the exquisite Parables—so beautiful, so simple, yet so rich in instruction—of the Ten Virgins and of the Talents; and drew for them a picture of that Great Day of Judgment on which the King should separate all nations from one another as the shepherd divideth his sheep from the goats." (Farrar, p. 584.)

All these things shall find fulfillment in this, the dispensation of the fulness of times, for the other signs have now been given and the time is at hand. He standeth at the door! In this setting, then, let us consider each of these events. First we must view this precious parable about the Bridegroom, the wedding feast, the virgins who attended the bride, and the lamps that lighted their way and gave a festive spirit to the marriage celebration.

> *And then, at that day, before the Son of Man comes, the kingdom of heaven shall be likened unto ten virgins, who took their lamps, and went forth to meet the bridegroom.*

The Bridegroom, as he has before designated himself, is the Lord Jesus, returning from a far country, to attend the marriage feast when he will take the Church as his bride.[2] The ten virgins are the members of the Church; they are in the house of the Lord (which is the Church) awaiting his return and the great feast of good things of which the faithful will then partake. "The 'lamps'—not 'torches'—which the Ten Virgins carried, were of well-known construction. They bear in Talmudic writings commonly the name *Lappid,* but the Aramaised form of the Greek word in the New Testament also occurs as *Lampad* and *Lampadas.* The lamps consisted of a round receptacle for pitch or oil for the wick. This was placed in a hollow cup or deep saucer—the *Beth Shiqqua*—which was fastened by a pointed end into a long wooden pole, on which it was borne aloft. According to Jewish authorities, it was the custom in the East to carry in a bridal procession about ten such lamps. We have the less reason to doubt that such was also the case in Palestine, since, according to rubric, ten was the number required to be present at any office or ceremony, such as at the benedictions accompanying the marriage-ceremonies. And, in the peculiar circumstances supposed in the Parable, Ten Virgins are represented as going forth to meet the Bridegroom, each bearing her lamp." (Edersheim 2:455.)

And five of them were wise, and five were foolish. They that were foolish took their lamps, and took no oil with them: But the wise took oil in their vessels with their lamps.[3]

"And at that day, when I shall come in my glory," the Lord tells us in latter-day revelation, "shall the parable be fulfilled which I spake concerning the ten virgins. For they that are wise and have received the truth, and have taken the Holy Spirit for their guide, and have not been deceived—verily I say unto you, they shall not be hewn down and cast into the fire, but shall abide the day." As to their reward, the Great Judge continues: "And the earth shall be given unto them for an inheritance; and they shall multiply and wax strong, and their children shall grow up without sin unto salvation. For the Lord shall be in their midst, and his glory shall be upon them, and he will be their king and their lawgiver." (D&C 45:56-59.)

> *While the bridegroom tarried, they all slumbered and slept. And at midnight there was a cry made, Behold, the bridegroom cometh; go ye out to meet him.*

The call is to the Church, to those who have forsaken the world, to those who are under covenant to wait for their Lord and to prepare themselves for his return. And now, almost two thousand years after he gave the parable, the call has gone forth. "O my people," saith the Lord, "sanctify yourselves; gather ye together, O ye people of my church. . . . Go ye out from Babylon. Be ye clean that bear the vessels of the Lord. Call your solemn assemblies, and speak often one to another. And let every man call upon the name of the Lord." Be ready; prepare yourselves; cleanse your souls; take the Holy Spirit as a guide; seek the Lord; keep his commandments. "Yea, let the cry go forth among all people: Awake and arise and go forth to meet the Bridegroom; behold and lo, the Bridegroom cometh; go ye out to meet him. Prepare yourselves for the great day of the Lord. Watch, therefore, for ye know neither the day nor the hour." (D&C 133:4-11.)

These are the last days—church members sleep; they are not watching on the towers of Zion; it is so long since the ascension; so many have waited in vain for his return; surely he will not come in our day. And then, at midnight, while the world sleeps—a most unlikely hour for a bridegroom to come and claim his bride—behold he cometh and his reward is with him.

> *Then all those virgins arose, and trimmed their lamps. And the foolish said unto the wise, Give us of your oil; for our lamps are gone out. But the wise answered, saying, Lest there be not enough for us and you, go ye rather to them that sell, and buy for yourselves.*

And while they went to buy, the bridegroom came; and they that were ready went in with him to the marriage: and the door was shut.

Afterward came also the other virgins, saying, Lord, Lord, open to us. But he answered and said, Verily I say unto you, ye know me not.

Watch therefore, for ye know neither the day nor the hour wherein the Son of man cometh.

Salvation is a personal matter. It comes only to those who keep the commandments and whose souls are filled with the Holy Spirit of God. No man can keep the commandments for and on behalf of another; no one can gain the sanctifying power of the Holy Spirit in his life and give or sell that holy oil to another. Every man must light his own lamp with the oil of righteousness which he buys at the market of obedience. Few doctrines are more evil and wicked than the false doctrine of supererogation, which is, that the saints, by doing more than is necessary for their own salvation, build up an immense treasure of merit in heaven, which can be dispensed and assigned to others so they too can be saved.

All that one person can do for the salvation of another is to preach, teach, expound, and exhort; all that one man can do for his fellows is to teach them the truth and guide their feet into paths of virtue and rectitude. All that the five wise virgins can do for the foolish is to tell them how to gain oil for themselves.

And the foolish virgins who do not come to know the Bridegroom by the power of the Spirit will not qualify to sit down with him at the marriage feast and there partake of the blessings reserved for the wise.

Parable of the Talents

(*Matthew 25:14-30; JST, Matthew 25:13-14, 24-31*)

There is an eternal principle that states: *Service is essential to salvation.* In the parable of the ten virgins, Jesus dramatized the truth that to gain salvation men must keep the commandments and be guided by the Holy Spirit. Thus, *Obedience is essential to salvation.* By now giving the parable of the talents, he completes the picture. Not only must mortals keep the commandments to gain an inheritance in the Father's kingdom, but they must also get outside themselves in service to their fellowmen. It is one thing to be virtuous and pay tithing; it is another to persuade others to walk in paths of purity and to make their means available for the building up of the Lord's earthly kingdom. The Lord will not be satisfied with the salvation of Moses alone; he expects that great lawgiver to guide all Israel to the summit of Sinai. Both obedience and service are essential to salvation.[4] And so Jesus says:

> *Now I will liken these things unto a parable. For it is like as a man travelling into a far country, who called his own servants, and delivered unto them his goods.*
>
> *And unto one he gave five talents, to another two, and to another one; to every man according to his several ability; and straightway took his journey.*

Jesus is speaking to the Twelve, who, in this as in all things, are made a pattern and a type of all disciples. In principle, thus, he is speaking to all of his servants and to all the members of his kingdom; and, for that matter, the same principle can be applied to all men in their varied walks, for all have talents and all will be accountable before the judgment bar for the use to which their talents are put. But the specific intent of the parable is to teach how the servants of the Lord must use their native endowments to further the work of Him who is now going on a long journey to a far-off heaven, there to be with his Father until that day when he shall return to live and reign on earth a thousand years.

Members of the Church in general and those called to ministerial service in particular are endowed with "spiritual gifts." All do not receive the same gift, and all are not endowed with the same talents. "There are diversities of gifts," Paul says, all of which come from "the same Spirit."

To one is given the gift of prophecy, to another the working of miracles, to yet another the gift of knowledge, or of wisdom, or of scriptural understanding, or any of the thousands of things that edify and uplift the souls of men. (1 Cor. 12.)

Further, all men, and the servants of the Lord in particular, acquired, in preexistence, by obedience to law, the specific talents and capacities with which they are endowed in this life. Men are not born equal; they come into mortality endowed with the abilities earned and developed in a long period of premortal schooling. And a just and equitable Being, who deals fairly and impartially with all his children, expects each of them to use the talents and abilities with which they are endowed and the gifts that are given them by a divine Providence.

> *Then he that had received the five talents went and traded with the same, and made them other five talents. And likewise he that had received two, he also gained other two. But he that had received one went and digged in the earth, and hid his lord's money.*

Those who "embark in the service of God" are commanded to serve him with all their "heart, might, mind and strength." (D&C 4:2.) It is the will of Him who created us that "men should be anxiously engaged in a good cause, and do many things of their own free will, and bring to pass much righteousness." (D&C 58:27.) All those who are sent forth to preach the gospel are subject to the divine decree: "Thou shalt not idle away thy time, neither shalt thou bury thy talent that it may not be known." (D&C 60:13.) "Be not weary in well-doing," is the counsel to all, for "the Lord requireth the heart and a willing mind." (D&C 64:33-34.) The Lord expects his servants to be diligent; to be occupied till he comes; to labor on his errand with all the strength and power they possess.

> *After a long time the lord of those servants cometh, and reckoneth with them. And so he that had received five talents came and brought other five talents, saying,*

Lord, thou deliveredst unto me five talents: behold, I have gained beside them five talents more.

His lord said unto him, Well done, thou good and faithful servant: thou hast been faithful over a few things, I will make thee ruler over many things: enter thou into the joy of thy lord.

The reward for faithful service is twofold:

1. *To be made ruler over many things.* This life is the probationary estate in which the Lord's servants learn how to rule their own houses—"For if a man know not how to rule his own house, how shall he take care of the church of God?" Paul asks (1 Tim. 3:5)—and how to rule some small part of the Lord's earthly kingdom. Men are called to rule a deacons quorum, an auxiliary organization, a Sunday School class, a ward or a stake, or whatever, all to gain experience for future eternal administration. Those who operate on true principles and succeed in this life will have power and ability to rule greater and larger kingdoms hereafter.

2. *To enter into the joy of the Lord.* Eternal life itself is to dwell in the presence of God, to receive, inherit, and possess as he does. The fulness of the joy of the Lord is to be like him, to be one with him, to have glory and exaltation forever as he does.

He also that had received two talents came and said, Lord, thou deliveredst unto me two talents: behold, I have gained two other talents beside them.

His lord said unto him, Well done, good and faithful servant; thou hast been faithful over a few things, I will make thee ruler over many things: enter thou into the joy of thy lord.

Again the reward is the same—to be ruler over many things and to enter into the joy of the Lord. No matter that one man serve with apostolic fervor in administering the worldwide kingdom of Him whose witness he is, while the other labor in a bishopric where the boundaries are scarcely a stone's throw in length—both gain the same reward. Truly, of those who reign in celestial splendor, it is written: "And he makes them equal in power, and in might, and in dominion." (D&C 76:95.) And also: "And the saints shall be filled with his glory, and receive their inheritance and be made equal with him." (D&C 88:107.)

Then he who had received the one talent came, and said, Lord, I knew thee that thou art a hard man, reaping where thou hast not sown, and gathering where thou hast not scattered. And I was afraid, and went and hid thy talent in the earth; and lo, here is thy talent; take it from me as thou hast from thine other servants, for it is thine.

This is idleness and indifference and more. It is also disobedience and dereliction; it is even defiance of him who is Master and Lord. The Lord's servants are under covenant, made in the waters of baptism, to love and serve him all their days. They have agreed to mourn with those that mourn, to weep with those that weep, and to bear the burdens of their brethren. Having put their hands to the plough, they must not look back lest they certify thereby that they are not fit for the kingdom of God. Hence:

His lord answered and said unto him, O wicked and slothful servant, thou knewest that I reap where I sowed not, and gather where I have not scattered. Having known this, therefore, thou oughtest to have put my money to the exchangers, and at my coming I should have received mine own with usury.

When the Lord's servants neglect and fail to do their Master's work, they are wicked!

I will take, therefore, the talent from you, and give it unto him who hath ten talents. For unto every one who hath obtained other talents, shall be given, and he shall have in abundance.

But from him that hath not obtained other talents, shall be taken away even that which he hath received.

And his lord shall say unto his servants, Cast ye the unprofitable servant into outer darkness; there shall be weeping and gnashing of teeth.

As arms that are never used wither; as legs that never walk shrivel; as eyes that are never opened become dull and blind—so the gifts of God that are unexercised soon fall away. As those who never walk lose the power of mobility, so those who bury their talents soon become as though they were never endowed with goodly gifts and glorious graces. The lot of the one is to be lame forever, of the other to die as pertaining to goodness and righteousness.

Christ Shall Sit in Judgment at His Coming
(*Matthew 25:31-46; JST, Matthew 25:33-34*)

As a crown of pure gold, signaling kingship and victory, so are these concluding words of the Olivet Discourse. Seldom—nay, never—has such a sweet and tender presentation been made relative to the coming of the Son of Man. Nothing shows more clearly the basis on which the disciples will then be judged.

Jesus has told the Twelve the things that will precede his coming; he has testified of the desolations and sorrows that will attend his return; his apostolic friends now know that the wicked will be as stubble and the vineyard will be cleansed by the brightness of his Presence.[5] Now he speaks of sitting with them in judgment on his saints, saints who in that day will be scattered—a few here and a small congregation there—in all the nations of the earth.

> *When the Son of man shall come in his glory, and all the holy angels with him, then shall he sit upon the throne of his glory: And before him shall be gathered all nations: and he shall separate them one from another, as a shepherd divideth his sheep from the goats: And he shall set the sheep on his right hand, but the goats on his left.*
>
> *And he shall sit upon his throne, and the twelve apostles with him.*

This is the day of judgment for the saints of the Most High. For them the judgment is set and the books are opened. Their eternal destiny is to be determined on the basis of their earthly works. This is the great day of division in the Church, the sheep being divided from the goats, the one group going to the right hand of honor, the other to the left hand of disgrace. It is the story of the ten virgins all over again—five wise, five foolish—half of whom entered the house and sat at the marriage feast and half of whom were locked out because they never knew the Bridegroom.

What feelings of wonderment and exultation must have filled the breasts of these humble Galileans—who served as his witnesses—to learn that they too would sit on thrones with their Lord and play a part in this glorious day of judgment.[6]

> *Then shall the King say unto them on his right hand, Come, ye blessed of my Father, inherit the kingdom prepared for you from the foundation of the world: For I was an hungred, and ye gave me meat: I was thirsty, and ye gave me drink: I was a stranger, and ye took me in: Naked, and ye clothed me: I was sick, and ye visited me: I was in prison, and ye came unto me.*

"From the foundation of the world," from the beginning, from all eternity—for such a length of time that no man can measure it—for just such a time has "the kingdom" been prepared for the faithful. And their inheritance therein is dependent upon their charitable works in mortality, upon how they give of themselves to serve their Lord and King.

> *Then shall the righteous answer him, saying, Lord, when saw we thee an hungred, and fed thee? or thirsty, and gave thee drink? When saw we thee a stranger, and took thee in? or naked, and clothed thee? Or when saw we thee sick, or in prison, and came unto thee?*
>
> *And the King shall answer and say unto them, Verily I say unto you, Inasmuch as ye have done it unto one of the least of these my brethren, ye have done it unto me.*

Such is the law of life. All men cannot feed and clothe and heal the Son of God; his mortal life was but for a moment in an appointed day; and his personal contacts were limited to the thousands who dwelt in the lands of his dwelling. But the billions of earth's inhabitants, everywhere and in all ages, are also the children of the Father of us all. And "when ye are in the service of your fellow beings ye are only in the service of your God." (Mosiah 2:17.) Or, as it is similarly expressed: "He that loveth not his brother whom he hath seen, how can he love God whom he hath not seen?" (1 Jn. 4:20.) Or, as he said it in our day, "He that receiveth my servants receiveth me." (D&C 84:36.)

> *Then shall he say also unto them on the left hand, Depart from me, ye cursed, into everlasting fire, prepared for the devil and his angels: For I was an hungred, and ye gave me no meat: I was thirsty, and ye gave me no drink: I was a stranger, and ye took me not in: naked, and ye clothed me not: sick, and in prison, and ye visited me not.*
>
> *Then shall they also answer him, saying, Lord, when saw we thee an hungred, or athirst, or a stranger, or naked, or sick, or in prison, and did not minister unto thee?*
>
> *Then shall he answer them, saying, Verily I say unto you, Inasmuch as ye did it not to one of the least of these, ye did it not to me.*
>
> *And these shall go away into everlasting punishment: but the righteous into life eternal.*

And thus, on this high note, ended the Olivet Discourse, as far as the written word attests; other things Jesus may have said on this memorable day—Tuesday, April 4, A.D. 30, the third day of the week of the atoning sacrifice—were for the ears of the disciples only. And so we leave them, for the moment, as the dusk of day spreads over the holy mount and as the setting sun of his life drops low in the western sky. The crucifixion is only three days away.

NOTES

1. Farrar gives as a translation of the phrase "our lamps *are gone out,*" as found in Matt. 25:8, "are smouldering," or, "are *being* quenched," which he, quite aptly, interprets

to mean that the light of God's Holy Spirit is dying away in the "earthen vessels" of their lives. (Farrar, p. 584, footnote 1.)

2. Of the millennial day, ushered in by the Second Coming, when there shall be "a new heaven and a new earth," the Beloved John says: "I . . . saw the holy city, new Jerusalem, coming down from God out of heaven, prepared as a bride adorned for her husband." (Rev. 21:1-2.) Thereafter an angelic ministrant said to him, "Come hither, I will shew thee the bride, the Lamb's wife." What he saw was "that great city, the holy Jerusalem, descending out of heaven from God." (Rev. 21:9-10.) Both the New Jerusalem, which will be set up on earth during the Millennium, and the Holy Jerusalem, which shall abide on this sphere when it becomes a celestial orb, are inhabited by the saints, the faithful members of the Lord's Church and kingdom. Hence the well-known expression in the text that the Church is the Lamb's bride.

3. "Not good and bad, not righteous and wicked, but *wise* and *foolish.* That is, all of them have accepted the invitation to meet the Bridegroom; all are members of the Church; the contrast is not between the wicked and the worthy. Instead, five are zealous and devoted, while five are inactive and lukewarm; ten have the testimony of Jesus, but only five are valiant therein. Hence, five shall enter into the house where Jesus is and five shall remain without—all of which raises the question: What portion of the Church shall be saved? Surely this parable is not intended to divide half the saints into one group and half into another. But it does teach, pointedly and plainly, that there are foolish saints who shall fail to gain the promised rewards." (*Commentary* 1:685.)

4. "The Parable of the Talents—their use and misuse—follows closely on the admonition to watch, in view of the sudden and certain Return of Christ, and the reward or punishment which will then be meted out. Only that, whereas in the Parable of the Ten Virgins the reference was to the *personal state,* in that of 'the Talents' it is to the *personal work* of the Disciples. In the former instance, they are portrayed as the bridal maidens who are to welcome His Return; in the latter, as the servants who are to give an account of their stewardship." (Edersheim 2:459.)

5. Of these same events, the Lord has told us in latter-day revelation: "For the hour is nigh and the day soon at hand when the earth is ripe; and all the proud and they that do wickedly shall be as stubble; and I will burn them up, saith the Lord of Hosts, that wickedness shall not be upon the earth; For the hour is nigh, and that which was spoken by mine apostles must be fulfilled; for as they spoke so shall it come to pass; For I will reveal myself from heaven with power and great glory, with all the hosts thereof, and dwell in righteousness with men on earth a thousand years, and the wicked shall not stand." (D&C 29:9-11.)

6. "Mine apostles, the Twelve which were with me in my ministry at Jerusalem, shall stand at my right hand at the day of my coming in a pillar of fire, being clothed with robes of righteousness, with crowns upon their heads, in glory even as I am, to judge the whole house of Israel, even as many as have loved me and kept my commandments, and none else." (D&C 29:12.)

INDEX

Healing: of Gentile woman's daughter, 9-13; formalities involved in, 14, 28-29; of deaf and dumb man, 14-15; of multitudes in Decapolis, 15-16; may inspire faith or persecution, 20 n. 5; of blind man, by stages, 28-29; of demoniac boy, disciples fail in, 70-71; Jesus succeeds in, where disciples had failed, 72-74; is sign of true church, 105; on Sabbath day, 127-28; of blind man on Sabbath, 198-201; of woman on Sabbath, 228-29; at Sabbath banquet of Pharisees, 230-31; spiritual, 269; of ten lepers, 284-85; spiritual, of Zaccheus, 317; of blind Bartimeus, 317-18

Heathen nations, redemption of, 453

Heaven, new, and new earth, 457

Hell, gates of, 42 n. 6

Hermon, Mount. *See* Mount of Transfiguration

Herod Antipas, 19-20, 35, 239

Herodians, 370-72

Holy Ghost: is a revelator, 37; comes with power, 172; apostles are to rely on, 426

Hosanna Shout, 339

Humility: salvation depends on, 82; greatness requires, 393

Husbandmen, wicked, parable of, 360-64

Husks fed to swine, 249

Hypocrisy: barren fig tree as symbol of, 346; Jesus condemns Pharisees for, 395

I Am, Jesus as the great, 168-69

Ignorance of Pharisees, 390

Immortality, Jesus inherited power of, from his Father, 216-17

Ingratitude, sin of, 285-86

Inheritance, Jewish law of, 191, 196 n. 1, 248

Innocent: all men are, when born, 83; should seek out guilty to restore peace, 90

Isaiah, 58, 184 n. 3

Israel: Jesus was sent only to, 10; house of, is comprised of faithful from preexistence, 11-12, 161; adoption into house of, 13; gathering of, keys for, 57; punishment of, 115 n. 5; failure of, to bear fruit, 196 n. 2; Nephites were of, 216; gathering of, 216, 439; received gospel first, 365. *See also* Jews

James, 55-58, 113-14, 313-14

Jealousy among disciples, 79-80

Jeremiah, some thought Jesus was, 35

Jericho, 315-16

Jerusalem: Jesus was destined to return to, 45, 311; Peter counseled Jesus to avoid, 46; Jesus' journey to, 111-13, 312; triumphal entry into, 338-40; Jesus wept over, 340-41, 408; destruction of, by Titus, 341; siege of, 433-34; Josephus' comments on, 435 n. 3; to be trodden down of Gentiles, 441; Jews to flee unto, in last days, 450; rebuilding of, 463 n. 2; the New, 476 n. 2

Jesus Christ: continuing Galilean ministry of, 3-4; increasing opposition to, 5-7; departed into Tyre and Sidon, 8; compassionate sighing of, 15, 20 n. 6; viewed by some as resurrected John the Baptist, 19-20 n. 1, 35; salvation comes through, 25, 214, 385; Pharisaic view of, 26; as Son of Man, 32-33, 416; bears testimony of himself, 33-34; various men's views of, 34-36; as Son of living God, 36-37, 174; sufferings of, 43; had to lose his life, 45, 47; prayer of, on Mount of Transfiguration, 55-56; God the Father bore witness of, 61; prophesies of his death and resurrection, 75-76, 155, 312-13; performing miracles in name of, 82-83; voluntarily abased himself, 88 n. 1; rejection of, in Galilee, 107-8; leaves Galilee for Jerusalem, 111; brethren of, challenge him, 111-12; later Judean ministry of, 119-20; rumors of, preceded him into Jerusalem, 123-24; taught in temple at Tabernacle Time, 125-26; is accused of having a devil, 127, 165-66; men plot death of, 127, 153, 281-82; controversy surrounding, 128-29, 137-38, 332-33; Pharisees order arrest of, 130-31, 138; adulteress brought before, 140-44; proclaims himself as light of the world, 146, 149, 200,

New Jerusalem, 476 n. 2
Nicodemus, 139
Noah, days of, 454-55

Oaths, swearing with, 396-97
Obedience is essential to salvation, 469
Offenders: fate of, 84; aggrieved should seek out, to make peace, 90-91
Ointment, Mary anoints Jesus with 335-37
Olives, Mount of, 424
Oneness of God and Christ, 174-75, 219
Opposition to Jesus: increasing, 5-7; uniting of factions in, 23, 30 n. 6, 370-72; intensity of, 40; by deputation of religious leaders, 352
Ordination, authority bestowed by, 353
Other sheep, Jesus speaks of, 215-16

Parable: of unmerciful servant, 95-98; of good Samaritan, 178-80; of friend at midnight, 187-89; of rich fool, 191-93; of barren fig tree, 195-96; of wedding guests, 232-33; of great supper, 233-36; of lost sheep, 245-46; of lost coin, 247; of prodigal son, 248-53; of unjust steward, 254-57; of Lazarus and rich man, 260-63; of unprofitable servants, 265; of unjust judge, 287-89; of Pharisee and publican, 290-91; of laborers in vineyard,307-10; of the pounds, 319-22; of two sons, 358-59; of wicked husbandmen, 360-64; of marriage of king's son, 364-68; of fig trees, 454; of ten virgins, 465-68; of talents, 469-73
Passover, 331-32
Peace, missionaries preach gospel of, 105
Perean ministry of Jesus, 225-26
Persecution, Jesus warns apostles of, 426
Peter: bears testimony of Christ, 36; as son of Jonah, 38; testimony of, came through revelation, 38; blessings promised to, 44; counsels Jesus to avoid Jerusalem, 46; experiences of, on Mount of Transfiguration, 55-58; desired to build tabernacles for Moses and Elias, 59-60; pays temple tax with coin from fish's mouth, 77-78
Pharisee and publican, parable of, 290-91
Pharisees: demand arrest of Jesus, 130-31, 138; reject light of the world, 150; refuse to acknowledge Jesus' hand in miracle, 205-6; as robbers of sheepfold, 212; Sabbath banquet of, Jesus heals man at, 230-31; concern of, with rank, 233; covetousness of, 258; Jesus condemns, 259, 390-91; attempt to trap Jesus with question about divorce, 290-91; challenge Jesus' authority, 351-52; Jesus confounds, with question about baptism of John, 354-55; attempted to trap Jesus politically, 370-73; called Jesus the son of David, 385-86; ignorance of, 390; eight denunciations of woe upon, 394-402; parents' sins will fall upon, 404-5; seven classes of, 405-6 n. 1
Plough, putting hand to, and looking back, 103
Politics, Pharisees turned to, to trap Jesus, 370-73
Pounds, parable of, 319-22
Power: of faith, 72, 73-74, 93-94, 347; of gospel, 172
Prayer: of Jesus on Mount of Transfiguration, 55-56; in faith, 94; different types of, 186-87; the Lord's, 187; parables concerning, 287-91
Preexistence: faithful from, comprise house of Israel, 11-12, 161; allusion to, by Jesus, 88
Priesthood is power and authority from God, 345
Priests, craft of, was endangered by Jesus, 130-31. *See also* Pharisees
Prodigal son, parable of, 248-53
Prophets: false, 21-22, 212, 437; obedience to, Jewish views on, 209 n. 1; rejecting testimony of, 238, 400-402; persecution of, 361
Publican: and Pharisee, parable of, 290-91; chief, Jesus resides with, 316-17
Punishment, sufferings seen as, 194-95, 199
Purification, salt as symbol of, 87
Purse and scrip, traveling without, 105, 115 n. 2

Questioning: for questioning's sake, 176; of Pharisees, cessation of, 384

Rabbi Eliezer, signs given by, 30 n. 1
Rabbis, stature of, in Israel, 393
Rank, Pharisaic concern with, 233
Records kept in heaven, 184 n. 1
Regeneration, day of, 306
Rejection: of gospel, condemnation accompanying, 106-7; of living prophets, 400-402; of Jesus by majority of Jews, 417
Religion: letter vs. spirit in, 232; importance of sacrifice in, 243 n. 1; true, vs. false, 392; focusing on trifles of, 398; false, shall abound in last days, 437-38, 444 n. 1
Religious anarchy, 331-32
Remission of sins, 155 n. 3
Repentance: little children have no need of, 88, 245; leading men to, 249; belief in Jesus depends on, 358
Restoration: of all things, 65-66; era of, 438-39
Resurrection: of the just, 51, 234; conflicting views concerning, 62-63; miracle of, 268-69; and life, Jesus is, 275; day of, reward of apostles in, 305-6; Sadducees did not believe in, 374-75; Rabbis' statements on, 378-79; prophecies concerning, 380; at time of Second Coming, 451
Revelation: necessity of, in understanding God, 37, 174; Jesus' church is built on rock of, 38-39, 41-42 n. 5
Rich fool, parable of, 191-93
Riches: sharing, with others, 192; young man could not forsake, for gospel, 303-4
Righteous: state of, after death, 267 n. 2; rewards of, in resurrection, 306
Righteousness: of Abraham, 163; outward appearance of, 399-400
Roman invasion of Galilee, 109-10
Ruler over many things, becoming, 471

Sabbath: restrictions of, Jesus broke, 127-28, 198-202, 227-28; Jesus heals blind man on, 198-201; Rabbinical, 202; Jesus heals Perean woman on, 227-29; banquet of Pharisees on, Jesus heals man at, 230-31; Jesus spends his last, in Bethany, 333-37
Sacrifice: importance of, to religion, 243 n. 1; definition of, 306-7
Sadducees, 374-80
Saints: must be tried in all things, 86; duty of, to God, 265-66; persecution of, in meridian of time, 427-29; resurrection of, at Second Coming, 451; responsibilities of, in Christ's absence, 461
Salome, mother of James and John, 313-14
Salt: symbolism of, 87, 88 n. 2; with lost savor, 242
Salvation: comes through Christ, 25, 214, 385; Pharisaic view of, 26; becoming as children to gain, 82; is individual affair, 86, 367, 468; plan of, was created by God the Father, 132 n. 2; truth leads to, 158; plan of, Jews failed to understand, 220; gate of, is strait, 237; law of Moses is insufficient for, 242-43; greatness of gift of, 298; keeping commandments leads to, 302; closing door to, Pharisees condemned for, 394-95; obedience is essential to, 469
Samaritan: the good, parable of, 178-80; leprous, gave thanks for healing blessing, 285
Samaritans: refused to receive Jesus, 112-13; name of, as epithet, 165
Sanhedrin plot death of Jesus, 281-82
Satan: repeats his tactics throughout generations, 30 n. 2; Jesus' miracles attributed to, 32; quotes scripture for his own purposes, 137; children of, 163-64; was a liar from the beginning, 164-65; fall of, 172; seeks to destroy family unit, 292; shall have his day, 437; binding of, 453
Scriptures: Satan quotes, for his own purposes, 137; not knowing, the Sadducees erred in, 376; taking away fulness of, 403
Sealing power, 91-93; keys of, bestowed on Peter, James, and John, 57
Second Coming of Christ, 51, 436-63; signs of, 425, 449-50; restoration of gospel must precede, 438-49; grand sign of, 448, 463 n. 1; day of, who may abide, 455-56; saints are to watch for, 458; hour of, is nigh, 476 n. 5

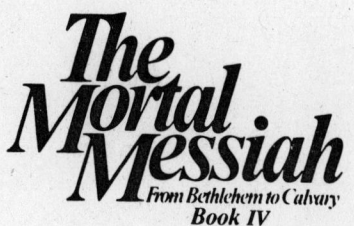

The Mortal Messiah

From Bethlehem to Calvary

Book IV

The Mortal Messiah

From Bethlehem to Calvary

Book IV

Bruce R. McConkie

Deseret Book Company
Salt Lake City, Utah

Vol. 4 ISBN 0-87747-856-2 (hardbound)
ISBN 0-87579-406-8 (softbound)

Library of Congress Cataloging-in-Publication Data

McConkie, Bruce R.
The mortal Messiah.

Includes index.
1. Jesus Christ—Biography. 2. Christian biography—Palestine.
3. Judaism—History—Post-exilic period, 586 B.C.–210 A.D.
I. Title.
BT301.2.M16 232.9'01 79-19606

Printed in the United States of America

10 9 8 7 6 5 4 3 2

THE MESSIANIC TRILOGY

The forerunner of this work is *The Promised Messiah: The First Coming of Christ,* which deals with the Messianic Prophecies. This work, *The Mortal Messiah: From Bethlehem to Calvary,* is a Life of Christ published in four books. This is Book IV.

BOOK IV

Section XI *The Paschal Feast, The Private Prayers and Sermons, and Gethsemane*
Section XII *The Trials, The Cross, and The Tomb*
Section XIII *He Riseth; He Ministereth; He Ascendeth*

The other books on the Life of Christ are published separately as follows:

BOOK I

Section I *A Root Out of Dry Ground*
Section II *Jesus' Years of Preparation*
Section III *Jesus' Early Judean Ministry*

BOOK II

Section IV *Jesus Begins the Great Galilean Ministry*
Section V *The Twelve, The Sermon on the Mount, and Rising Pharisaic Opposition*
Section VI *The Continuing Galilean Ministry*

BOOK III

Section VII *The Galilean Ministry Reaches Its Peak*
Section VIII *The Later Judean Ministry*
Section IX *The Perean Ministry*
Section X *From the Anointing to the Royal Reign*

The concluding work in this whole series will be *The Millennial Messiah: The Second Coming of the Son of Man.*

ABBREVIATIONS

Scriptural references are abbreviated in a standard and self-identifying way. Other books are cited by author and title except for the following:

Commentary I	Bruce R. McConkie, *Doctrinal New Testament Commentary.* Vol. 1, *The Gospels.* Bookcraft, 1965.
Edersheim	Alfred Edersheim, *The Life and Times of Jesus the Messiah.* 1883.
Farrar	F. W. Farrar, *The Life of Christ.* London: Cassell & Co., Ltd., 1874.
Geikie	Cunningham Geikie, *The Life and Words of Christ.* 1886.
Hymns	*Hymns, The Church of Jesus Christ of Latter-day Saints.* 1948.
JST	Joseph Smith Translation (Inspired Version) of the Bible.
Mormon Doctrine	Bruce R. McConkie, *Mormon Doctrine,* 2nd ed. Bookcraft, 1966.
Sketches	Alfred Edersheim, *Sketches of Jewish Social Life in the Days of Christ.* 1876.
Talmage	James E. Talmage, *Jesus the Christ.* 1915.
Teachings	Joseph Fielding Smith, comp., *Teachings of the Prophet Joseph Smith.* 1938.
Temple	Alfred Edersheim, *The Temple: Its Ministry and Services As They Were at the Time of Jesus Christ.*

CONTENTS

SECTION XI

THE PASCHAL FEAST, THE PRIVATE PRAYERS AND SERMONS, AND GETHSEMANE

Chapter 98

Chapter 99

Chapter 100

Chapter 101

Chapter 102

SECTION XII

THE TRIALS, THE CROSS, AND THE TOMB

Chapter 103

Chapter 104

Chapter 105

Chapter 106

Chapter 111

Chapter 112

Chapter 113

Chapter 114

Chapter 115

Chapter 121

Chapter 122

SECTION XI

THE PASCHAL FEAST, THE PRIVATE PRAYERS AND SERMONS, AND GETHSEMANE

THE PASCHAL FEAST, THE PRIVATE PRAYERS AND SERMONS, AND GETHSEMANE

Salvation was, and is,
and is to come,
in and through the atoning blood
of Christ, the Lord Omnipotent.
(Mosiah 3:18.)
If we walk in the light,
as he is in the light,
we have fellowship one with another,
and the blood of Jesus Christ
his Son
cleanseth us from all sin.
(1 Jn. 1:7.)

Jesus who is called Christ—and blessed be his name!—is preparing himself to die, and his disciples to accept that divine destiny which is his.

He takes the Twelve apart by themselves and tells them in plain words what is about to be—his betrayal and crucifixion.

Then Judas leaves their presence to conspire, plot, and bargain; he sells his soul for the price of a slave.

Peter and John make ready the Passover, which with Jesus and the rest they eat in an upper chamber in the house of a disciple.

At the Paschal table Jesus washes the feet of the disciples and names Judas as his betrayer; after that unworthy one has gone out into the night, the Master institutes the sacrament of the Lord's Supper in remembrance of his own death.

That blessed night he commands the disciples to love one another; discourses on the Two Comforters—one the Holy Ghost, the other he himself; and proclaims himself as the Way, the Truth, and the Life.

"If ye love me, keep my commandments," he says, and gives the grandest of all the allegories: that of the Vine, the Husbandman, and the Branches.

He speaks at length of love, of the persecutions ahead, and of the Holy Ghost who will guide his saints into all truth.

Then comes the greatest of all the recorded prayers—the Intercessory Prayer in which he defines eternal life and pleads for the Twelve and all of the saints, that they may be one as he and the Father are one.

Then it is Gethsemane! Alone, in the greatest ordeal ever borne by man or God, in agony beyond compare, sweating great drops of blood from every pore, in a way beyond mortal comprehension, he takes upon himself the sins of all men on condition of repentance.

The infinite and eternal atonement, in large measure, is accomplished. Jesus has done what none but he could do.

After that, the betrayal and the arrest. Judas earns his thirty pieces of silver and loses his own soul. The Son of God chooses to bow to the will of wicked men—and the cross is just ahead.

Chapter 94

PREPARING FOR THE CRUCIFIXION

They shall consider him a man,
and say that he hath a devil,
and shall scourge him,
and shall crucify him.
(Mosiah 3:9.)
He came into the world, even Jesus,
to be crucified for the world,
and to bear the sins of the world,
and to sanctify the world,
and to cleanse it
from all unrighteousness.
(D&C 76:41.)
I came into the world
to do the will of my Father,
because my Father sent me.
And my Father sent me
that I might be lifted up
upon the cross.
(3 Ne. 27:13-14.)

Preparing the Disciples for His Death

(Matthew 26:1-2)

Steadily, ominously, borne by a tide that no man can stop—that neither God nor his Son in their infinite wisdom will stop—Jesus is going to his death. He came into the world to die upon the cross for the sins of the world, to die that men might live; and die he will and die he must. And in death he will gain his greatest victory.

Two days of life remain. He is with the Twelve and perhaps others who are beloved by him. We suppose he is in Bethany; if not, he is in that immediate vicinity. The last words we heard him speak came forth on the Mount of Olives as a lowering dusk ended the same day on which he bore the final public witness of his own divine Sonship. He and his friends rested somewhere that night near the Mount of Ascension. We like to think that he, at least, found peace and companionship within those hallowed walls in Bethany where the beloved sisters dwelt.

But now it is Wednesday, April 5, 13th Nisan, A.D. 30, and tomorrow is the day for the slaying of thousands of Paschal lambs. It must be early in the day, a day that Jesus is devoting to his intimate friends. Of all that transpired on this day only one sentence has come down to us, but oh, what a significant declaration it is:

> *Ye know that after two days is the feast of the passover, and the Son of man is betrayed to be crucified.*

Specifying that it is two days before the Passover preserves for us the chronology and continuity of the events of the week of his passion; the statement about his betrayal and crucifixion reveals the subject that was uppermost in the minds of all of them as the climax of the one perfect ministry approached.

As to the day on which Jesus spoke these words, Edersheim says: "The day before that on which the Paschal Lamb [that is, he himself] was to be slain, with all that was to follow, would be one of rest, a Sabbath to His Soul before its Great Agony. He would refresh Himself, gather Himself up for the terrible conflict before Him. . . . Only two days more, as the Jews reckoned them—that Wednesday and Thursday—and at its Even the Paschal supper! And Jesus knew it well, and He passed that day of rest and preparation in quiet retirement with His disciples—perhaps in some hollow of the Mount of Olives, near the home of Bethany—speaking to them of His Crucifixion on the near Passover." (Edersheim 2:468-69.)[1]

As to his betrayal and crucifixion, we have somewhat more to say. We are speaking of the death of a God. God himself—the Great Creator, "the Lord Omnipotent who reigneth, who was, and is from all eternity to all eternity," who had "come down from heaven among the children of men" (Mosiah 3:5)—God himself, subjecting himself to the will of the Father in all things, was appointed to die. He who was born in a lowly stable is about to die upon a cruel cross.

Yea, he is to do more than die in the manner and way common to all mankind. As he came into mortality in the lowliest circumstances—born in a stable, cradled in a manger, crooned to by braying asses and lowing cattle—so he is to depart this life in the most ignominious way then known in a cruel and merciless world. Roman nails driven by Jewish hands will tear his flesh. As he hangs, like a common criminal, between two thieves, a Roman spear, hurled with pharisaic zeal, will rend his side; then his marred body will be placed in a borrowed grave, and the seal of death and failure will be placed, by unbelieving zealots, upon his life and mission.

Though the Twelve and others have been with him through his whole ministry, even they must be further conditioned to accept that which is about to be. Any remaining slivers of false Jewish tradition must be swept from their minds. Their Deliverer is to die; their God is to be crucified; their Messiah is to fail—as far as the Jewish concept is concerned. Everything that is about to happen in his life will run counter to all that the scribes and Pharisees have supposed and believed and taught. Jesus, as we assume, has set apart this day to counsel and strengthen his chosen ones with reference to his coming demise and the glorious resurrection that will result therefrom.

That the Promised Messiah was appointed unto death, unto an agonizing death on a crucifier's cross, was something of which the prophets of old had spoken freely. They had said in plain words, and in many similitudes, that death and crucifixion awaited the mortal Son of the immortal Father. Of all this, fervent and extended witness is elsewhere borne. (*The Promised Messiah*, pp. 527–36.) For our present purposes we need only recount some of the numerous occasions of which we know, and there must have been many others, when the Mortal Messiah spoke of his coming crucifixion—all preparatory to this day on which, we cannot doubt, he taught and explained the coming reality in fulness.

1. *At the first Passover.*

Three years before, at the Passover, as he began his early Judean ministry, Jesus made the first such declaration of which we know. After the first cleansing of the temple, and in answer to the Jewish demands as to his authority for so doing, he said: "Destroy this temple"—as John says, "he spake of the temple of his body"—"and in three days I will raise it up." It was not, however, until after "he was risen from the dead" that the full significance of this pronouncement dawned upon his disciples. (John 2:13-22.) Yet it was the beginning; he was commencing the process of indoctrination that one day would leave them with a perfect knowledge of his death and resurrection.

2. *To Nicodemus.*

In the great Born-Again Sermon, delivered, as we suppose, in the home of John in Jerusalem, Jesus told

Nicodemus, a friendly Sanhedrist: "As Moses lifted up the serpent in the wilderness, even so must the Son of man be lifted up." (John 3:14.) How apt are the figures and how plain the similitudes that bear record of Him!

3. *To the disciples of John.*

When these worthies asked Jesus why his disciples did not fast often, as was the case with them and the Pharisees, our Lord replied: "Can the children of the bride-chamber mourn, as long as the bridegroom is with them? but the days will come, when the bridegroom shall be taken from them, and then shall they fast." (Matt. 9:14-15.) In keeping with the Jewish custom of pondering and discussing religious questions morning, noon, and night, seven days a week, how often thereafter must the disciples of John have thought and spoken of this reply.

4. *To the sign-seeking scribes and Pharisees.*

"For as Jonas was three days and three nights in the whale's belly; so shall the Son of man be three days and three nights in the heart of the earth," he said as he excoriated them for their evil and adulterous lives. (Matt. 12:38-40.) Again, we are left to suppose that many people thereafter saw in the miraculous experience of Jonah a sign and a type of their Messiah.

5. *To the Twelve.*

At the time of the sending forth of the Twelve, and as a part of a statement about losing one's life for Jesus' sake, our Lord said: "And he that taketh not his cross, and followeth after me, is not worthy of me." (Matt. 10:38-39.) The allusion is clear and the portent ominous.

6. *In the sermon on the bread of life.*

All those whose hearts were open, familiar as they were with the usage of Jewish figures and symbolism, saw in his declarations that he was the Bread of Life who came down from heaven, a reaffirmation of his divine Sonship. When he said, "And the bread that I will give is my flesh, which I will give for the life of the world," they knew he meant he would be slain, so that, figuratively, all men might eat his flesh and drink his blood. (John 6:48-56.)

7. *Following Peter's testimony near Caesarea Philippi.*

After Peter's solemn and Spirit-born confession, Matthew says: "From that time forth began Jesus to shew unto his disciples, how that he must go unto Jerusalem, and suffer many things of the elders and chief priests and scribes, and be killed, and be raised again the third day." (Matt. 16:21.) From this it appears that both then and on many subsequent occasions Jesus spoke in plainness to his chosen and favored ones of his death and resurrection.

8. *On the Mount of Transfiguration.*

Though at the time the knowledge of such was reserved for Peter, James, and John only, Jesus discussed "his decease which he should accomplish at Jerusalem" with Moses and Elias, when those translated beings ministered to him on the Mount of Transfiguration. (Luke 9:28-31.)

9. *To the disciples in Galilee.*

After they came down from the Holy Mount—hallowed forever because of the Transfiguration—and returned to Galilee, the scripture says: "And while they abode in Galilee, Jesus said unto them, The Son of man shall be betrayed into the hands of men: And they shall kill him, and the third day he shall be raised again. And they were exceeding sorry." (Matt. 17:22-23.)

10. *En route to Jerusalem.*

Again we but need to quote the scripture: "And Jesus going up to Jerusalem took the twelve disciples apart in the way, and said unto them, Behold, we go up to Jerusalem; and the Son of man shall be betrayed unto the chief priests and unto the scribes, and they shall condemn him to death, And shall deliver him to the Gentiles to mock, and to scourge, and to crucify him: and the third day he shall rise again." (Matt. 20:17-19.)

11. *In the teachings about the good shepherd.*

How could he have spoken more plainly or with greater

clarity than when he said: "I am the good shepherd: the good shepherd giveth his life for the sheep. . . . As the Father knoweth me, even so know I the Father: and I lay down my life for the sheep. . . . Therefore doth my Father love me, because I lay down my life, that I might take it again. No man taketh it from me, but I lay it down of myself. I have power to lay it down, and I have power to take it again. This commandment have I received of my Father." (John 10:11-18.)

12. *In the parable of the wicked husbandmen.*

"They will reverence my son," said the householder whose servants had been beaten, stoned, and killed. But instead, when the wicked "husbandmen saw the son, they said among themselves, This is the heir; come, let us kill him, and let us seize on his inheritance. And they caught him, and cast him out of the vineyard, and slew him." Jesus then announced himself as the Stone which the builders rejected, and the chief priests and Pharisees knew that "he spake of them" as the slayers of the Son. (Matt. 21:33-46.)

We cannot believe that all these sayings—given as allusions, as similitudes, and in plain words—constituted a tithe, or a hundredth, or a thousandth part of what the Blessed One said of his coming death and crucifixion and of his resurrection on the third day. Nor can we think that the people generally were unaware of his teachings; friends and foes alike had fixed in their minds that such was his announced course. That few truly envisioned the import and glory of it all, there is no doubt. Even the Twelve needed yet added teachings about his atoning sacrifice. And we conclude that on this day, alone with them and others of like spiritual stature, he taught them all that they were then able to receive about his coming ordeal and the glory and exaltation—for himself and for the faithful—which would result therefrom.

Judas and the Jews Plot His Death

(Matthew 26:3-5, 14-16; Mark 14:1-2, 10-11; JST, Mark 14:1-3, 31-32; Luke 22:1-6)

If a God is to die, what circumstances shall attend his demise? If the Great Deliverer is to be destroyed, how can the deed be done? If the Jewish Messiah is to be murdered—in cold blood, with malice aforethought, by evil men—how shall it be brought to pass?

As with all else that unto this mortal probation doth appertain, the awful act will come about by seemingly normal means. It will grow out of the social, political, and religious milieu of the moment. And those who do the evil deed will justify themselves in their own sinful and knavish minds. Satan always has an explanation for wickedness—even the murder of a God!—which will suffice for those who love darkness rather than light because their deeds are evil.

And so it was on this dark day. "It was inevitable that the burning words of indignation which Jesus had uttered on this last great day of His ministry should exasperate beyond all control the hatred and fury of the priestly party among the Jews. Not only had they been defeated and abashed in open encounter in the very scene of their highest dignity, and in the presence of their most devoted adherents; not only had they been forced to confess their ignorance of that very Scripture exegesis which was their recognised domain, and their incapacity to pronounce an opinion on a subject respecting which it was their professed duty to decide; but, after all this humiliation, He whom they despised as the young and ignorant Rabbi of Nazareth—He who neglected their customs and discountenanced their traditions—He on whose words, to them so pernicious, the people hung in rapt attention—had suddenly turned upon them, within hearing of the very Hall of Meeting, and had pronounced upon them—upon *them* in the odour of their sanctity—upon *them* who were accustomed to breathe all their lives the incense of unbounded adulation—a woe so searching, so scathing, so memorably intense, that none who heard it could forget it forevermore.

"It was time that this should end. Pharisees, Sadducees, Herodians, Priests, Scribes, Elders, Annas the astute and tyrannous, Caiphas the abject and servile, were all now aroused; and, dreading they knew not what outburst of religious anarchy, which would shake the very foundations of their system, they met together"—probably while Jesus was in quiet seclusion with his loved ones at or near Bethany—"in the Palace of Caiaphas, sinking all their differences in a common inspiration of hatred against that long-promised Messiah in whom they only recognised a common enemy. It was an alliance for His destruction, of fanaticism, unbelief, and worldliness; the rage of the bigoted, the contempt of the atheist, and the dislike of the utilitarian; and it seemed but too clear that from the revengeful hate of such a combination no earthly power was adequate to save.

"Of the particulars of the meeting we know nothing; but the Evangelists record the two conclusions at which the high conspirators arrived—the one a yet more decisive and emphatic renewal of the vote that He must, at all hazards, be put to death without delay; the other, that it must be done by subtilty, and not by violence, for fear of the multitude; and that, for the same reason—*not* because of the sacredness of the Feast—the murder must be postponed, until the conclusion of the Passover had caused the dispersion of the countless pilgrims to their own homes." (Farrar, pp. 588–89.)

Their plan was to slay their Savior after the Passover; after the Galilean patriots had returned to their rugged homeland; after any sympathetic souls from outlying areas had departed for their dwelling places. But Jesus had named the Passover as the time when the Lamb of God should pour out his soul unto death in the supreme atoning sacrifice. And as he had spoken, so must it be.

Accordingly, Judas, one of the Twelve, believed to be

the only Judean among them, left the Holy Party and aligned himself with the unholy alliance of wicked men whose hearts were hardened by priestcrafts and iniquities; and he—a traitor—then "promised" to betray Jesus and deliver him up "in the absence of the multitude." If he could be arrested, tried, sentenced, and slain without such a tumult as to arouse their Roman overlords or permit him to be rescued by a mob, then let his death come soon; he could not die too soon to please his implacable foes.

Judas, be it realized, took the initiative in the betrayal; his was a willful act; he went to the evil-hearted Sanhedrists—to the sin-hardened Satanists—to tell them how he would place his Master into their hands. But he would do it for a price. The price of a slave? Nay, the price of his soul! Yet the words spoken by the mouth of Zechariah must not fail; not one jot or tittle must fall short of the prophetic mark. They must weigh for the price of their King "thirty pieces of silver"! (Zech. 11:12.) "What greedy chafferings took place we are not told, nor whether the counter-avarices of these united hatreds had a struggle before they decided on the paltry blood-money. If so, the astute Jewish priests beat down the poor ignorant Jewish Apostle. For all that they offered and all they weighed to him was thirty pieces of silver—about three pounds, sixteen shillings—the ransom-money of the meanest slave. For this price he was to sell his Master, and in selling his Master to sell his own life, and to gain in return the execration of the world for all generations yet to come." (Farrar, p. 529.)

Thirty pieces of silver! (Ex. 21:28-32.) "They 'weighed out' to him from the very Temple-treasury those thirty pieces of silver. . . . It was surely as much in contempt of the seller as of Him Whom he sold, that they paid the legal price of a slave. Or did they mean some kind of legal fiction, such as to buy the Person of Jesus at the legal price of a slave, so as to hand it afterwards over to the secular authorities? Such fictions, to save the conscience by a logical quibble, are not so uncommon—and the case of the Inquisitors handing over the condemned heretic to the secular authorities will recur to the mind. But, in truth, Judas could not now have escaped their toils. They might have offered him ten or five pieces of silver, and he must still have stuck to his bargain. Yet none the less do we mark the deep symbolic significance of it all, in that the Lord was, so to speak, paid for out of the Temple-money which was destined for the purchase of sacrifices, and that He, Who took on Him the form of a servant, was sold and bought at the legal price of a slave." (Edersheim 2:477.)

Why did Judas become a traitor and seek to betray Jesus? Mark says, "He turned away from him, and was offended because of his words." Luke says simply: "Then entered Satan into Judas." And Matthew preserves for us the words spoken by this evil apostle to the chief priests: "What will ye give me, and I will deliver him unto you?" John said of him: "He was a thief." (John 12:1-6.) In all of this Judas displays disbelief, a rejection of the gospel, personal offense against the word—all because of the gospel truism: "The guilty taketh the truth to be hard, for it cutteth them to the very center." (1 Ne. 16:2.) In all this there is selfishness, avarice, dishonesty, and a grasping after worldly things that resulted in a satanic domination of his soul. Satan can have no power over human souls unless it is given to him by them. People are subject to him only when they hearken to his enticements. In other words, Judas was an evil traitor because of personal wickedness, because he preferred to live after the manner of the world, because he "loved Satan more than God." He truly had become "carnal, sensual, and devilish" by choice.[2]

It is common, almost classical, to ask: What were the motives of this man? Who can attempt to fathom the unutterable abyss, to find his way amid the weltering chaos, of a heart agitated by unresisted and besetting sins?

From such a launching pad, every self-appointed theologian and every pseudo-doctrinaire who writes about the life of Christ seems to feel an obligation—almost a compulsion—to explain Judas and to tell why he planted the traitor's kiss on the cheek of Him who did no sin. The act in itself is so revolting and is looked upon with such abhorrence that writers and expounders seek for some explanation other than the obvious one. They point to avarice, of course, but then seek to probe what must have been in the mind of one who would turn the Son of God over to his enemies. They speculate as to what all-consuming passion must have burned in the soul of one who would betray the Sinless One into the hands of sinful men.

Having named avarice as the ruling passion in the life of Judas, Farrar speculates in this way: "Doubtless other motives mingled with, strengthened—perhaps to the self-deceiving and blinded soul substituted themselves for—the predominant one. 'Will not this measure,' he may have thought, 'force Him to declare His Messianic kingdom? At the worst, can He not easily save Himself by miracle? If not, has He not told us repeatedly that He will die; and if so, why may I not reap a little advantage from that which is in any case inevitable? Or will it not, perhaps, be meritorious to do that of which all the chief priests approve?' A thousand such devilish suggestions may have formulated themselves in the traitor's heart, and mingled with them was the revulsion of feeling which he suffered from finding that his self-denial in following Jesus would, after all, be apparently in vain; that he would gain from it not rank and wealth, but only poverty and persecution. Perhaps, too, there was something of rancour at being rebuked [this in regard to his views relative to selling Mary's ointment for three hundred pence]; perhaps something of bitter jealousy at being less loved by Jesus than his fellows; perhaps something of frenzied disappointment at the prospect of failure; perhaps something of despairing hatred at the consciousness that he was suspected.

"Alas! sins grow and multiply with fatal fertility, and

blend insensibly with hosts of their evil kindred. 'The whole moral nature is clouded by them; the intellect darkened, the spirit stained.' Probably by this time a turbid confused chaos of sins was weltering in the soul of Judas—malice, worldly ambition, theft, hatred of all that was good and pure, base ingratitude, frantic anger, all culminating in this foul and frightful act of treachery—all rushing with blind, bewildering fury through this gloomy soul."

But Farrar, whose gift is to wield the witchery of words, also points to the basic and obvious reason for Judas's act. It was sin—evil, wicked, soul-blackening sin. In this—and let there be no mistake on this point—Judas was no different from the thousands and millions of sinners who preceded him and the billions who have come after. Why does any traitor betray his friends? Why are there crimes and murders and wars? "From whence come wars and fightings among you?" James asks. His declarative answer, though given in the form of a question, is: "Come they not hence, even of your lusts that war in your members?" (James 4:1.) The world has been cursed with Judases without number, and one is no different from any of the others; yet one does stand out above them all because he happened to betray *the Greatest of All.* Similarly, the world has suffered from Pilates without end at whose word innocent men have gone to their graves, and one is no different from any of the others; yet one stands out above them all because he chanced to stand at the crossroads of history and authorized the legal murder of the one who was *the Innocent above All.*

And so, with proper insight, Farrar says, in answer to his question about the motive of Judas: "The commonest observance of daily facts which come before our notice in the moral world, might serve to show that the commission of crime results as frequently from a motive that seems miserably inadequate, as from some vast temptation. . . . The sudden crisis of temptation might seem frightful, but its issue was decided by the entire tenor of the traitor's previous life; the sudden blaze of lurid light was but the outcome of that which had long burnt and smouldered deep within his heart." (Farrar, pp. 592–94.)

Thus Judas—traitorous, evil, wicked, as he was—was in reality no different from his Jewish forebears of whom Jehovah said: "They sold the righteous for silver, and the poor for a pair of shoes." (Amos 2:6; 8:6.) Nor was he any different from those anciently who, "for handfuls of barley and for pieces of bread," slew "the souls that should not die." (Ezek. 13:19.) Judas betrayed the Son of Man himself, but is it not written: "Inasmuch as ye have done it unto one of the least of these my brethren, ye have done it unto me"? (Matt. 25:40.) It is sad to contemplate how many Judases there really are among the hosts of men.

And on this note ends the day of conspiracy; the day on which Jesus taught the eleven who were righteous about the glory and wonder of his death and resurrection; the day on which the one of the Twelve who was evil became an incarnate devil to plan the very death out of which life for all men would come—and in that act Judas sold his soul to another master whose disciple and follower he thus became.

This night the Son of Man will lay down his head in sleep "for the last time on earth." On the Thursday morning he will awake "never to sleep again." (Farrar, p. 595.)

NOTES

1. As to the way the Jews reckoned days, "the day always belonged to the previous night. . . . The day lasted till three stars became visible. . . . In regard to the Passover, it is distinctly stated that it began with the darkness on the 14th Nisan." (Edersheim 2:468-69, footnote 2.)

2. The quoted words are taken from earliest days. After Adam and Eve had "made all things" that God had revealed to them "known unto their sons and their daughters," the scripture says: "And Satan came among them, saying: I am also a son of God; and he commanded them, saying: Believe it not; and they believed it not, and they loved Satan more than God. And men began from that time forth to be carnal, sensual, and devilish." (Moses 5:12-13.)

THE PASCHAL SUPPER

In the fourteenth day
of the first month
at even [between the two evenings]
is the Lord's passover. (Lev. 23:5.)
Your lamb shall be without blemish, . . .
And ye shall keep it up
until the fourteenth day of the same month:
and . . . shall kill it
in the evening [between the two evenings].
. . . And they shall eat the flesh in that night,
roast with fire, and unleavened bread;
and with bitter herbs they shall eat it. . . .
It is the Lord's passover.
(Ex. 12:5-11.)

Peter and John Make Ready the Passover[1]

(Matthew 26:17-19; Mark 14:12-16; Luke 22:7-13)

It is the time of the Lord's Passover!

Nay, more, it is the Passover of Passovers. In Jehovah's House, in Jerusalem the Holy City, on this very day—April 6, A.D. 30—calculating on the basis of one yearling lamb for each ten persons, some two hundred and sixty thousand lambs will be slain. And then on the Passover morrow the Lamb of God himself will be sacrificed; he in whose name and honor countless lambs have had their blood sprinkled on the holy altar will himself have his blood shed that its saving power may be sprinkled upon believing souls forever.

From that dark Egyptian night a millennium and a half before, when two million of their fathers were prepared to march out of bondage, to this bright Palestinian day, when, though still subject to a Gentile yoke, they were free to worship and rejoice in a long and glorious history—from then until now, there had never been such a Passover as this. This was to be the climax and the end. Never again would any Passover meet with divine approval; and, indeed, a few years hence, with the destruction of the temple, the sacrificial parts of the feast would cease. But now, "Everyone was going to Jerusalem, or had those near and dear to them there, or at least watched the festive processions to the Metropolis of Judaism. It was a gathering of universal Israel, that of the memorial of the birth-night of the nation, and of its Exodus, when friends from afar would meet, and new friends be made; when offerings long due would be brought, and purification long needed be obtained—and all [would] worship in that grand and glorious Temple, with its gorgeous ritual. National and religious feelings were alike stirred in what reached far back to the first, and pointed far forward to the final Deliverance. On that day a Jew might well glory in being a Jew." (Edersheim 2:479-80.)

Jesus' disciples felt the fervor of the festive season. They knew that on Nisan 14, *between the two evenings*—for so the revealed rubric reads in Hebrew—their Paschal lamb must be slain. And Nisan 14 had begun on the *evening* before, on Wednesday the 13th, when the first of three stars appeared; and it will end the *evening* of this Thursday when the same three heavenly luminaries make their reappearance. Then before the midnight that will follow, their Paschal lamb, properly roasted, with the bitter herbs and all else appertaining to the Paschal supper must be eaten. Any of the lamb that remains until morning must be burned in the fire.

And so, on Thursday morning, knowing that the preparations must be made to eat the Passover meal, the disciples ask Jesus: "Where wilt thou that we go and prepare that thou mayest eat the passover?" Will it be in blessed Bethany, which was designated by Rabbinical authority as part of Jerusalem for the purposes of the feast, or back in the city proper? Only a few hours remain in which the needed lamb could be slain in the temple; what arrangements, therefore, shall they make?

Then Jesus, using seeric power—the power to see beforehand the happenings that shall be—calls Peter and John and says: "Go and prepare us the passover, that we may eat." They ask: "Where wilt thou that we prepare?" Jesus answers: "Behold, when ye are entered into the city, there shall a man meet you, bearing a pitcher of water; follow him into the house where he entereth in. And ye shall say unto the goodman of the house, The Master saith unto thee, Where is the guestchamber, where I shall eat the passover with my disciples? And he shall shew you a large upper room furnished: there make ready."

From this we can draw no conclusion except that a favored disciple had foreknowledge that Jesus and the Twelve desired to eat the Passover in his house. Whether this knowledge came by the spirit of inspiration or in some other way, we are not told. This we know: A man bearing a pitcher of water did in fact go out to meet them; he led them to the house; obviously they conversed en route; upon arrival they told the homeowner that the Master—thus identifying Jesus—asked for a guestchamber in which he and his disciples could eat the Passover; he then took them to an upper room that was already "furnished and prepared." The table was set; the couches were arranged; the dinnerware was in place; the cups and herbs and bowls and wine were there; cakes of unleavened bread were at hand; food was available; the goodman of the house had prepared for thirteen guests. It was his blessed privilege to host Him who should make an end to the Passover and in its place institute the sacrament of the Lord's Supper; and his house—clearly it was a large and commodious one—was the chosen place. What loving care must have attended the preparation that preceded the arrival of Peter and John!

Drawing on our learned friend Edersheim, we now note a most remarkable coincidence; or, rather, we discover a marvelous example of that divine attention to detail which ever delights the souls of those who ponder the words of holy writ. By combining the accounts of the three Synoptists, the message spoken by Peter and John to the goodman of the house comes out thus: 'The Master saith, My time is at hand—with thee [that is, in thy house: the emphasis is on this] I hold the Passover with my disciples. Where is my hostelry [or hall], where I shall eat the Passover with my disciples?'

The Hebrew word used here for hostelry or hall is *Katalyma;* and it is used only one other place in the whole New Testament. It is the word used to designate the inn or hostelry in Bethlehem where the Lord Jesus was born of Mary; where he drew his first mortal breath; where he began the mortal life that was destined to end at this very Passover time. As we are aware, Jesus was born in an open *Khan,* among the beasts, because there was no room in any of the inns or guestchambers that surrounded and opened upon the open courtyard. And this day in Jerusalem, the disciples did not ask for the upper chamber, but for a hostelry or hall that opened upon the *Khan* of the house. This Khan was the place in the house where, as in the open Khan, the beasts of burden were unloaded, and where shoes and staff, and dusty garments and burdens were put down. Apartments or guestchambers opened upon it. "He Who was born in a 'hostelry'—*Katalyma*—was content to ask for His last meal in a *Katalyma*." Born in the humblest of circumstances, he was prepared to remain in them all his days.

But now at this Passover, he made one provision with reference to the guest chamber; it was to be "my Katalyma." His purpose was to eat his last meal alone with his apostles. None of his other followers were to be present—not even his Blessed Mother, nor Mary Magdalene, who had so often traveled with the Twelve in their missionary journeys, nor Mary who worshipped at his feet in Bethany. He and the Twelve were more than the minimum of ten needed for the Passover meal, and he and they had sacred ordinances to perform before he went to Gethsemane to take upon himself the combined weight of all the sins of all men.

But as we have seen—and as Jesus foreknew—the goodman of the house took Peter and John to "a large upper room," "perhaps the very room where three days afterwards [as we shall note shortly] the sorrow-stricken Apostles first saw their risen Saviour—perhaps the very room where, amid the sound of a rushing mighty wind, each meek brow was first mitred with Pentecostal flame." (Farrar, p. 598.)

Who was the homeowner whose gracious preparations so well served the needs of Jesus on this memorable occasion? He is not named, and we do not know. No doubt Jesus withheld his name for two reasons: so that Peter and John, following his instructions, would learn anew of his seeric powers, and also to keep the knowledge from Judas. That unworthy one, who by now had returned from conspiring with the chief priests, must not be able to lead them to Jesus until after all things had been accomplished at the Passover meal and in the Garden of Gethsemane. The traitor must first go with the others to eat the Paschal meal, and then he must be told to leave and carry out his evil work.

As to the identity of the disciple who hosted the Lord Jesus in his last meal in mortality, many have speculated that it was the father of John Mark. The reasoning involved is to this effect: From the account in Acts relative to the freeing of Peter from prison we know that the family home of John Mark was a large one where the saints were wont to gather. (Acts 12:1-17.) From the fact that Mark alone tells about the young man who was accompanying Christ as he was led away captive, and who himself escaped arrest by fleeing naked as his captors tore from him his sole article of apparel, a loose linen garment—this has led to the universal assumption that Mark himself was the young man. (Mark 14:51-52.) What, then, is more natural than to conclude that Judas returned to the Passover-home with the arresting soldiers, only to find that Jesus and the other apostles had departed for Gethsemane; that in the commotion at the home young John Mark was aroused from sleep and hastily put on a loose tunic and followed the soldiers to the garden; that there he was a witness and an unwilling observer of the betrayal and arrest; and that he lost his own garment in fleeing from those who held captive his Lord? Someday it will be gratifying to know all things relative to these memorable days and to acclaim those disciples who then laid their all on the altar as they confessed before men Him who has since confessed them before his Heavenly Father.

But back to the Passover preparations. Certain ritualistic performances were an essential part thereof. One of these, the solemn search for leaven—for this also was the Feast of Unleavened Bread—had already occurred under the direction of the homeowner. On the evening of Nisan 13, as Nisan 14 commenced, this search was made in each house. Any leaven that had been hidden or lost must be found, put in a safe place, and later destroyed. From mid-day on the 14th nothing leavened might be eaten, and it was, in fact, the custom to fast on that day preparatory to eating the Paschal supper.

Further: The ordinary evening service and sacrifice in the temple must precede the supper. On this feast day this service began an hour early, or at about 1:30 P.M., with the evening sacrifice itself being offered at about 2:30 P.M. This was the time for the slaying of the Paschal lambs by their owners and the sprinkling of their blood upon the altar by the priests. Both Mark and Luke say that Peter and John were to "make ready" the Passover meal, and they both record that "they made ready the passover." Of necessity this means that the two apostles, rather than the home-owner or some other person, were required to and did attend the temple services for the formal slaying and preparation of the lamb; and to this assumption there is a certain fitness and propriety: two of the chief apostles, for themselves and on behalf of their Lord and their brethren, were complying to the full to the letter of the law on the last day on which its provisions were in force. When, on the morrow, the true Paschal Lamb was slain, the old order would be over and the new covenant only would have binding efficacy and force.

And so we can envision Peter and John in the temple courts, amid the massive throngs of worshippers, submitting for the last time in this respect to the law of Moses, and there witnessing and participating in the ceremonial performances so familiar to them. We cannot leave this scene without singling out certain of the scriptural words chanted that day by the Levites. The language is recorded in Psalm 81, and as there and then given—"broken three times by the threefold blast from the silver trumpets of the priests"—it included a promise and a call to Israel to serve their God and also a prophecy of their fate if they did not do so. This is the call and the promise:

Hear, O my people, and I will testify unto thee: O

Israel, if thou wilt hearken unto me; There shall no strange god be in thee; neither shalt thou worship any strange god. I am the Lord thy God, which brought thee out of the land of Egypt: open thy mouth wide, and I will fill it.

Then came the seeric and prophetic pronouncement—and what sad and mournful significance it must have had to apostolic ears on this day:

But my people would not hearken to my voice; and Israel would [have] none of me. So I gave them up unto their own hearts' lust: and they walked in their own counsels. Oh that my people had hearkened unto me, and Israel had walked in my ways!

And further, as the blood of thousands of lambs was sprinkled on the altar, the Levites chanted the *Hallel* (Psalms 113 to 118), with the people responding with cries of Hallelujah (praise Jehovah) at the proper places, and with the people, also at the proper place, saying:

Save now, I beseech thee, O Lord: O Lord, I beseech thee, send now prosperity. Blessed be he that cometh in the name of the Lord.

This chant—the same one shouted amid cries of Hosanna by the exultant throngs, as Jesus rode triumphantly into the Holy City—was thus here given for the last authorized time by the legal administrators of the Mosaic order. Its recitation here could not have done other than relight in the breasts of Peter and John those fires of testimony and rejoicing which burned so brightly on that triumphal day.

After attending to all that was incumbent upon them, Peter and John—with their lamb flayed and cleansed, and with the required parts left on the altar for burning—returned to the appointed home to meet Jesus and the others, there to partake of the crowning Paschal supper of the ages. The two appointed apostles had done their work well; the Paschal supper was made ready; all things had happened as Jesus foretold—such being in itself a witness that all things he had said of his coming betrayal, crucifixion, and resurrection would also come to pass.

Jesus and the Twelve Recline at the Paschal Table
(Matthew 26:20; Mark 14:17; Luke 22:14)

Peter and John have now done their work; they and the homeowner have made ready the guest chamber. The lamb has been roasted on a pomegranate spit; the unleavened cakes, the bitter herbs, the dish with vinegar—all are in place. Such items of food as needed are on the movable table; the festive lamps are lit; it is eventime, and the meal is ready.

"It was probably as the sun was beginning to decline in the horizon that Jesus and the other ten disciples descended once more over the Mount of Olives into the Holy City. Before them lay Jerusalem in her festive attire. All around pilgrims were hastening towards it. White tents dotted the sward, gay with the bright flowers of early spring, or peered out from the gardens or the darker foliage of the olive plantations. From the gorgeous Temple buildings, dazzling in their snow-white marble and gold, on which the slanting rays of the sun were reflected, rose the smoke of the altar of burnt-offering. These courts were now crowded with eager worshippers, offering for the last time, in the real sense, their Paschal lambs.

"The streets must have been thronged with strangers, and the flat roofs covered with eager gazers, who either feasted their eyes with a first sight of the Sacred City for which they had so often longed, or else once more rejoiced in view of the well-remembered localities. It was the last day-view which the Lord had [free and unhindered] of the Holy City—till His resurrection! Only once more in the approaching night of His betrayal was he to look upon it in the pale light of the full moon. He was going forward to 'accomplish His death' in Jerusalem; to fulfil the type and prophecy, and to offer Himself up as the true Passover

Lamb—'the Lamb of God, which taketh away the sin of the world.'

"They who followed Him were busy with many thoughts. They knew that terrible events awaited them, and they had only a few days before been told that these glorious Temple-buildings, to which, with a national pride not unnatural, they had directed the attention of their Master, were to become desolate, not one stone being left upon the other. Among them, revolving his dark plans, and goaded on by the great Enemy, moved the betrayer. And now they were within the city. Its Temple, its royal bridge, its splendid palaces, its busy marts, its streets filled with festive pilgrims, were well known to them, as they made their way to the house where the guestchamber had been prepared for them. Meanwhile the crowd came down from the Temple-mount, each bearing on his shoulders the sacrificial lamb, to make ready for the Paschal Supper." (*Temple,* pp. 226–28.)

The Holy Party (one of whom was unholy) entered the chosen house and ascended the stairs to the appointed upper chamber. Assuming it to be the house of Mark, Edersheim asks: "Was this [the] place of Christ's last, also that of the Church's first, entertainment; that, where the Holy Supper was instituted with the Apostles, also that, where it was afterwards first partaken of by the Church; the Chamber where He last tarried with them before His death, that in which He first appeared to them after His resurrection; that, also, in which the Holy Ghost was poured out, even as (if the Last Supper was in the house of Mark) it undoubtedly was that in which the Church was at first wont to gather for common prayer?" His answer (and ours): "We know not, and can only venture to suggest, deeply soul-stirring as such thoughts and associations are." (Edersheim 2:490.)

We do feel, however, that we can with measurable certainty reach some conclusions relative to the Paschal supper and all that it means in the eternal scheme of things.

The Lord Jesus, in the more than a dozen years of his mature life, may have presided over other Paschal suppers, thus being the One who offered the slain lamb in similitude of his own coming sacrifice. The likelihood, however, is that such was not the case. At any prior Passover spent in Jerusalem, where alone the sacrificial lambs could be offered, he would have been a guest at someone else's table. At each table a minimum of ten diners was required, and the host was the one who made the offering.

It is pleasant to suppose that this is the one Paschal supper over which Jesus presided, and that, therefore, he offered *the last symbolic sacrifice* preparatory to his offering of *the only real sacrifice* which would free men from their sins. If this is the case, the only sacrifices in which he involved himself (and there is a certain reverential fitness about such being the case) would be the symbolical one on Thursday whose emblems betokened the infinite and eternal one on Friday. Thus he would endorse and approve all of the similitudes of the past and announce their fulfillment in him. Thus also would the past, the present, and the future all be tied together in him, with the assurance held out to all the faithful of all ages, that all who look to him and his atoning sacrifice shall be saved.

Two of the ordinances given of God to his people, without which accountable men cannot be saved, are baptism and the sacrament of the Lord's Supper; and with one Jesus commenced, and with the other he concluded his ministry. Both ordinances bear record of his death, burial, and resurrection. The faithful, buried with him in baptism and thereby dying unto sin, then come forth from the watery grave in a newness of life and in the likeness of his resurrection. Similarly when they partake of his Holy Supper—made efficacious because the Lamb of God shed his own blood in an eternal Passover—they remember anew that death out of which comes life.

On this Passover night, in the home of Mark, the Lord of Life is prefiguring his own death, even as he had done at

Bethabara when he was baptized of John. And he is now testifying that all the righteous sacrifices and baptisms of the past have his approval, even as all the righteous sacramental ordinances of the future shall find eternal efficacy in him. The old and the new—all things—center in him.

Thus there is, in reality, only one sacrifice—the sacrifice of the Lord Jesus Christ. All of the symbolisms are swallowed up in him. As Paul said, "Christ our passover is sacrificed for us: Therefore let us keep the feast"—and in this sense we shall keep the Feast of the Passover forever—"not with old leaven, neither with the leaven of malice and wickedness; but with the unleavened bread of sincerity and truth." (1 Cor. 5:7-8.)

The Passover is not the child of the Mosaic law. As part of the gospel, which the Lord first gave to Israel's ancient lawgiver, it was administered under the Mosaic system until the coming of Christ. It was given before the law, and its truths remain after the law. "It was not of the Law, for it was instituted before the Law had been given or the Covenant ratified by blood; nay, in a sense it was the cause and foundation of all the Levitical Sacrifices and of the Covenant itself. And it could not be classed with either one or the other of the various kinds of sacrifices, but rather combined them all, and yet differed from them all. Just as the Priesthood of Christ was real, yet not after the order of Aaron, so was the Sacrifice of Christ real, yet not after the order of Levitical sacrifices but after that of the Passover. And as in the Paschal supper all Israel were gathered around the Paschal Lamb in commemoration of the past, in celebration of the present, in anticipation of the future, and in fellowship in the Lamb, so has the Church been ever since [when it has been on earth] gathered together around its better fulfilment in the Kingdom of God." (Edersheim 2:492.)

One other matter of considerable interest is the seating arrangement at the Paschal table, or, rather, the reclining positions assumed by the partakers of the meal. With reference to that first Passover night in Egypt, the divine word was: "And thus shall ye eat it; with your loins girded, your shoes on your feet, and your staff in your hand; and ye shall eat it in haste." (Ex. 12:11.) But in Jesus' day it was different; the Rabbinic decree then was that all who ate should recline at a table, to indicate rest, safety, and liberty. Low, moveable tables were used—sometimes they even hung from the ceiling so as not to touch the floor and be defiled—and it was the custom for each person to occupy a separate divan or pillow, to lie on his left side and lean on his left hand, the feet stretching back towards the ground. The couches upon which the diners reclined were set on two sides and one end of the table so as to leave about a third of the table free for serving trays and dishes. Needless to say, the reality had no resemblance to the paintings of Leonardo da Vinci and others whose genius has memorialized this event through the ages.

It is interesting, based on the scriptural allusions and inferences, to place Jesus and at least three of the Twelve in the positions they may have occupied at the table. This we shall now do, reserving for more extended recitation the specific matters that bear upon our suggestive conclusions.

As the Twelve began to take selected positions at the table, a contention arose, evidently over precedence in seating. By instinct we feel Judas—who was out of harmony with his brethren, and who at this late date was manifesting none of the Christian attributes of tolerance, charity, or concern for the comfort and well-being of his associates—we feel instinctively that Judas was at the root of the trouble. Various inferences and allusions found in the general setting and set forth in the scriptural accounts bear this out.

Among the Pharisees this matter of rank and precedence, of what place each person occupied at the table, was a matter of great concern; and Judas—influenced, nay, dominated by the prince of this world, who is Lucifer—was more of a Pharisee than a Christian. He, by training and inclination, would follow the Pharisaic custom and seek for himself the seat of honor. John speaks, in connection with the supper, of the devil having entered into Judas; and as Jesus said, in another connection, "He that hath the spirit of contention is not of me, but is of the devil, who is the father of contention, and he stirreth up the hearts of men to contend with anger, one with another." (3 Ne. 11:29.)

We reason, thus, that Judas's acts caused the contention in which he gladly participated. With whom would he contend? Obviously with Peter, who was in fact the chief apostle and who knew his place was at the Lord's side in the position of honor and precedence. When Jesus rebuked the contention, a very natural thing would happen: impetuous Peter would go and take the lowest seat, while spiritually hardened Judas, immune to feelings of conscience and decency, would maintain his claim and take the seat of honor at the side of Jesus. This suggests the position of two of the Twelve.

As to the Beloved John, he leaned on the Master's bosom, which could only be done if he were on Jesus' right side. It was the custom for the chief personage at a feast to have someone on either side. Thus, starting on one side of the table, we would have John, then Jesus, and then Judas; the others would place themselves where they chose, but Peter would go across from John at the foot of the semicircle. Thus when Christ told John the sign by which the traitor would be known, none of the others would hear him. Thus Jesus, as part of the Paschal ceremony, could give the sop first to Judas, who sat in the seat of honor at his left hand. Thus when Judas asked if his treachery was known, and received an affirmative answer, none of the others knew what was involved. And thus Peter, having placed himself at the foot, would have to beckon to John to ask who it was who should betray the Lord. At least that is the reasoning involved; and, once again, we say this is something that someday we shall know with certainty. All that will be required is for the Lord to show one of his servants, in a vision or a dream, what happened that Passover night two millennia ago.

NOTE

1. The Jewish customs, practices, and traditions relative to Paschal matters are digested and summarized from Edersheim, whose life's work it was to search them out from the abundant and voluminous original sources.

THE LAST SUPPER

We'll wash and be washed,
    and with oil be anointed,
Withal not omitting the washing of feet;
For he that receiveth his penny appointed
Must surely be clean at the harvest of wheat.[1]

Strife Erupts at the Passover Table
(Luke 22:24-30; JST, Luke 22:26-27, 30)

As the Holy Party prepare to recline on the couches around the Passover table, the flaring fires of strife are ignited, as we suppose, by Judas, whose spirit is evil and whose judgment is warped. It is over the age-old question, raised anew, that has caused strife and contention from the beginning of time. Who among them shall be accounted the greatest? Who shall have the place of honor at the table? For all such things do the Pharisees seek; and does not Judas have the same spirit as those with whom he is conspiring to shed innocent blood?

But a short time before, when James and John and their mother sought to have Zebedee's two sons chosen—to the indignation of the other disciples—to sit on Jesus' right and left hand in his kingdom, our Lord had severely rebuked such strivings. It seems sad that at this solemn hour, when the precedence of the cross, if so it may be called, is coming into view, such a contention should arise again. Well might their feelings have been: Who will take precedence in suffering for His name now, that they may be named by him before his Father hereafter? Yet, where there is an evil spirit, contention is ever found; and so Jesus patiently rehearses the old gospel verities over again:

> *The kings of the Gentiles exercise lordship over them, and they that exercise authority upon them are called benefactors. But it ought not to be so with you; but he who is greatest among you, let him be as the younger; and he who is chief, as he who doth serve.*
>
> *For whether is he greater, who sitteth at meat, or he who serveth? I am not as he who sitteth at meat, but I am among you as he who serveth.*

The servants of the Lord in all ages, even as with Him whom they serve, are to forget the honors of men and the glories of the world. Where now is the grandeur that was Greece and the glory that was Rome? Are those who held sway in any of the ancient empires anything more than handfuls of dead dust? What will it matter a few years hence what earthly honors were conferred by mortals on their fellows? Who will even remember tomorrow who sat where at what table? With the Lord's servants, all strife over precedence must cease; theirs is a ministry of service and not of rulership. To this Jesus' whole life and ministry attested. And yet even those who serve tables in his earthly kingdom shall not go unrewarded. As also he has said aforetime, he now repeats:

> *Ye are they who have continued with me in my temptations. And I appoint unto you a kingdom, as my Father hath appointed unto me; That ye may eat and drink at my table in my kingdom; and sit on twelve thrones, judging the twelve tribes of Israel.*

What more can they ask than to have eternal association with their Lord, even to eating and drinking at his table forever? And how few will hold greater positions in eternity than those Twelve who return in glory with the Son of Man, and who are then appointed to sit on twelve thrones judging the whole house of Israel?

Jesus Washes the Feet of His Disciples
(John 13:1-17; JST, John 13:8, 10)

After reclining at the Passover table, Jesus and his apostolic friends ate the Passover meal with such portion of its rites and ceremonies as then suited their purposes. Then he introduced the gospel ordinance of the washing of feet, identified Judas as the one who would betray him, sent the traitor out into the night, and gave the ordinance of the sacrament. Since the sacramental rites grew out of the Passover procedures, we shall reserve our consideration of the Passover meal itself until we take up the sacrament of the Lord's Supper. To keep things in proper perspective, however, it is important to emphasize that the washing of feet came in the course of the meal, not at the beginning, and it was not simply an illustration of Godly humility, devised by Jesus to demonstrate his teachings about precedence, but was in fact the introduction of a new gospel ordinance.

John alone records such portions of what transpired relative to the foot-washing ordinance as have come down to us from biblical sources; our more extended knowledge relative thereto comes from latter-day revelation. The Beloved Disciple begins his Passover recitations by saying that "before the feast of the passover"—and what he is about to say is something of which we too are aware—"when Jesus knew that his hour was come that he should depart out of this world unto the Father," there yet remained something of great concern to him. "Having loved his own which were in the world," he must yet, incident to the Passover meal, manifest to them how "he loved them unto the end." And the two ordinances about to be revealed—those of the washing of feet and of the partaking of the emblems of his flesh and blood—these two become an eternal manifestation of the grace and goodness and love of the Lord for the Twelve and for all who believe and obey his gospel, thereby making themselves worthy to receive each of these ordinances.

And so, John says, "supper being ended," or, rather 'during supper,' "the devil having now put into the heart of Judas Iscariot, Simon's son, to betray him" (these words read like a formal indictment) and "Jesus knowing that the Father had given all things into his hands, and that he was come from God, and went to God; He riseth from supper, and laid aside his garments; and took a towel, and girded himself. After that he poureth water into a basin, and began to wash the disciples' feet, and to wipe them with the towel wherewith he was girded."

This appears to be a general summary of all that transpired. What then follows are some of the particulars. As to these particulars, John says: "Then cometh he to Simon Peter: and Peter saith unto him, Lord, dost thou wash my feet?" Jesus replied: "What I do thou knowest not now; but thou shalt know hereafter." That is: 'You assume that I am acting only as any slave or host might, which is far from the case. I am about to perform a sacred ordinance, the meaning of which I will explain, and in due course you will know its true meaning.' Still impulsive and reticent, the Chief Apostle said: "*Thou*"—our Master and Lord!—"*Thou,*" of all people, "needest not to wash my feet." 'Even though it be a sacred ordinance, let someone else do it instead!'

If we judge aright, Peter was the first one to have his feet washed, as he should have been, he being the senior apostle and the future president of the Church. John's phrase, "Then cometh he to Simon Peter," means, not that he came to him after the others, but either that he came to him from across the table or from the place where the basin and water for purification had stood. It would have been quite inappropriate, a self-serving assertion of excessive humility on his part, if Peter had first seen Jesus wash the feet of others and had then objected to the performance of the same act on his behalf. Since it was common for slaves and servants to wash the feet of guests, Peter's objection was to the Lord of heaven, as though he were merely a slave, washing the feet of one so unworthy as he deemed himself to be. It compares with previous like reactions on the part of the man Simon. "Depart from me; for I am a sinful man, O Lord" was his cry when, though he had toiled all night and caught nothing, yet, casting once again at Jesus' command, in one sweep the net became so full that it brake. (Luke 5:1-11.) "Be it far from thee, Lord: this shall not be unto thee," was his reaction when Jesus told the disciples that he must suffer many things of the elders and chief priests and scribes, and be killed, and be raised again the third day. (Matt. 16:21-23.) After hearing the conversation with Peter, and learning somewhat the meaning and import of the ordinance, none of the others would have objected.

Jesus then said: "If I wash thee not, thou hast no part with me." Catching a partial glimpse of the cleansing power of the new ordinance, Peter, ever impetuous, ever desiring to do all and more than need be, exclaimed: "Lord, not my feet only, but also my hands and my head." Jesus replied: "He that has washed his hands and his head, needeth not save to wash his feet, but is clean every whit; and ye are clean, but not all."

At this point, with reference to the ordinance itself, John explains: "Now this was the custom of the Jews under their law; wherefore, Jesus did this that the law might be fulfilled." The full significance of this is not apparent to the casual reader, nor should it be, for the washing of feet is a sacred ordinance reserved to be done in holy places for those who make themselves worthy. It is evident, however, that the Jews also had sacred ordinances performed in their temple, a knowledge of which has not been preserved, nor could it be, in any literature that has come down to us.

As to Jesus' statement that the Twelve were "clean, but not all," John explains: "For he knew who should betray him; therefore said he, Ye are not all clean. So after he had washed their feet, and had taken his garments, and was set down again, he said unto them, Know ye what I have done to you?"

What had he done? He had instituted—nay, reinstituted, for "the order of the house of God has been, and ever will be, the same"[2]—he had reinstituted one of the holy ordinances of the everlasting gospel. Those who have been washed in the waters of baptism, who have been freed from sin and evil through the waters of regeneration, who have come forth thereby in a newness of life, and who then press forward with a steadfastness in Christ, keeping the commandments and walking in paths of truth and righteousness, qualify to have an eternal seal placed on their godly conduct. They are thus ready to be endowed with power from on high. Then, in holy places, they cleanse their hands and their feet, as the scripture saith, and become "clean from the blood of this wicked generation." (D&C 88:74-75, 137-141.) Then, as the scripture also saith, they receive anointings and washings and conversations and statutes and judgments. (D&C 124:37-40.) Then they receive what Jesus here gave the Twelve, for as the Prophet said: "The house of the Lord must be prepared, . . . and in it we must attend to the ordinance of washing of feet. It was never intended for any but official members. It is calculated to unite our hearts, that we may be one in feeling and sentiment, and that our faith may be strong, so that Satan cannot overthrow us, nor have any power over us here." (*Commentary* 1:709.)

Did the Twelve then know what Jesus had done in their behalf? Perhaps in part, with the full significance to come to them after receiving that pentecostal endowment from on high which is the Holy Ghost. No doubt, also, Jesus then said more to them than John chose to record, for many things relative to these holy things are too sacred to publish to the world. It should be clear to all, however, that just as the act of immersion in water only hints at the true significance and power of baptism, so the act of the washing of feet is far more than the cleansing and refreshing of dusty and tired pedal extremities. It is an eternal ordinance, with eternal import, understood only by enlightened saints. That it might be continued by those having divine authorization to perform it, Jesus said:

> *Ye call me Master and Lord: and ye say well; for so I am. If I then, your Lord and Master, have washed your feet; ye also ought to wash one another's feet. For I have given you an example, that ye should do as I have done to you.*
>
> *Verily, verily, I say unto you, The servant is not greater than his lord; neither he that is sent greater than he that sent him. If ye know these things, happy are ye if ye do them.*

Jewish proverbial expressions that give added depth and meaning to Jesus' words are set forth for us by Edersheim. "He, Who really was Lord and Master, had rendered this lowest service to them as an example that, as He had done, so should they do. No principle [was] better known, almost proverbial in Israel, than that a servant was not to claim greater honour than his master, nor yet he that was sent than he who had sent him. . . .

"The Greek word for 'the towel,' with which our Lord girded Himself, occurs also in Rabbinic writings, to denote the towel used in washing and at baths (*Luntith* and *Aluntith*). Such girding was the common mark of a slave, by whom the service of footwashing was ordinarily performed. And, in a very interesting passage, the Midrash contrasts what, in this respect, is the way of man with what God had done for Israel. For, He [God] had been described by the prophet as performing for them [Israel] the service of washing, and others usually rendered by slaves." It scarcely needs to be here interjected that such a Jewish concept is purely Messianic in nature.

"The idea, that if a man knows (for example, the Law) and does not do it, it were better for him not to have been created, is not unfrequently expressed. But the most interesting reference is in regard to the relation between the sender and the sent, and a servant and his master. In regard to the former, it is proverbially said, that while he that is sent stands on the same footing as he who sent him, yet he must expect less honour. And as regards Christ's statement that 'the servant is not greater than his Master,' there is a passage in which we read this, *in connection with the sufferings of the Messiah:* 'It is enough for the servant that he be like his Master.' " (Edersheim 2:501-2.)

And in conclusion, well might we ask: If true disciples are to wash each other's feet, where among the sects of Christendom is this done? And how could it be done except by revelation? Who would know all that is involved unless God revealed it? Is not this holy ordinance one of the many signs of the true Church?

Jesus Names Judas as His Betrayer

(John 13:18-30; JST, John 13:19; Matthew 26:21-25; Mark 14:18-21; JST, Mark 14:30; Luke 22:21-23)

The blessed Twelve, their feet washed in an holy ordinance, their whole bodies being thereby cleansed from the blood and sins of that evil and adulterous generation in which they lived—the blessed Twelve were clean, "clean every whit"—"but not all." Judas yet sat in their circle; his deed of shame and infamy lay ahead; he must yet raise the standard of betrayal and sin round which all the traitors of all the ages might rally. "The hands of the Lord of Life had just washed the traitor's feet. Oh, strange unfathomable depth of human infatuation and ingratitude! that traitor, with all the black and accursed treachery in his false heart, had seen, had known, had suffered it; had felt the touch of those kind and gentle hands, had been refreshed by the cleansing water, had seen that sacred head bent over his feet, stained as they yet were with that hurried secret walk which had taken him into the throng of sanctimonious murderers over the shoulder of Olivet. But for him there had been no purification in that lustral water; neither was the devil within him exorcised by that gentle voice, nor the leprosy of his heart healed by that miracle-producing touch." (Farrar, p. 602.) Truly all ordinances must be sealed by the Holy Spirit of Promise, else they are not binding on earth and sealed everlastingly in the heavens! And none are so sealed and ratified except for those who are just and true.

> *I speak not of you all: I know whom I have chosen: but that the scripture may be fulfilled, He that eateth bread with me hath lifted up his heel against me. Now I tell you before it come, that, when it is come to pass, ye may believe that I am the Christ.*

King David—whose son, now reclining at the Passover table, has inherited the ancient throne—using his own experiences as a base, wrote these Messianic words: "All that hate me whisper together against me: against me do they devise my hurt. . . . Yea, mine own familiar friend, in whom I trusted, which did eat of my bread, hath lifted up his heel against me. But . . . as for me, thou upholdest me in mine integrity, and settest me before thy face for ever." (Ps. 41:7-12.) [3] In these words, David declaimed both his own betrayal by his counselor, Ahithopel, and the betrayal of his Lord by Judas in the coming day. Both Judas and Ahithopel, their conspiracies not unfolding as they had supposed, went and hanged themselves, that the ancient promise might be a perfect type of the evil deed to be done in the Messianic day. (2 Sam. 15:10-12; 17.) At this point Jesus said:

> *Verily, verily, I say unto you, He that receiveth whomsoever I send receiveth me; and he that re-*

ceiveth me receiveth him that sent me.

"Soon should they know with what full foreknowledge He had gone to all that awaited Him; soon should they be able to judge that, just as the man who receives in Christ's name His humblest servant receiveth Him, so the rejection of Him is the rejection of His Father, and that this rejection of the Living God was the crime which at this moment was being committed in their very midst." (Farrar, p. 603.) Having so spoken, Jesus "was troubled in spirit"—not, as we suppose, because of what lay ahead for him, but for the evil deed spawned in the heart of his "own familiar friend." He said:

> *Verily, verily, I say unto you, that one of you shall betray me.*
>
> *One of you which eateth with me shall betray me.*
>
> *But, behold, the hand of him that betrayeth me is with me on the table.*

"And they were exceeding sorrowful," Matthew says. Indeed, "a deep unspeakable sadness had fallen over the sacred meal. Like the sombre and threatening crimson that intermingles with the colours of sunset, a dark omen seemed to be overshadowing them—a shapeless presentiment of evil—an unspoken sense of dread. If all their hopes were to be thus blighted—if at this very Passover, He for whom they had given up all, and who had been to them all in all, was indeed to be betrayed by one of themselves to an unpitied and ignominious end—if *this* were possible, *anything* seemed possible. Their hearts were troubled." (Farrar, p. 604.)

One by one, eleven of the Twelve, "doubting of whom he spake," each asked in turn, "Is it I?" Their consciences were clear, and yet none dared ask, "Is it he?" "Better the penitent watchfulness of a self-condemning humility than the haughty Pharisaism of censorious pride. The very horror that breathed through their question, the very trustfulness which prompted it, involved their acquittal." (Farrar, p. 604.)

John, at this point, was leaning on Jesus' bosom. Peter beckoned to him to ask Jesus who it was; he asked, and Jesus answered:

> *He it is, to whom I shall give a sop, when I have dipped it.*
>
> *It is one of the twelve, that dippeth with me in the dish.*
>
> *The Son of man goeth as it is written of him: but woe unto that man by whom the Son of man is betrayed! it had been good for that man if he had not been born.*

Better for Judas if he had never been born! Yea, and better for all those who knowingly and willfully reject the truth and defy the Christ, better for them also if they had never been born! Their position in preexistence—in the presence of God—limited though their progression could be in the spirit state, was better than to be consigned to that state of which it is written: "Where God and Christ dwell they cannot come, worlds without end." (D&C 76:112.) Judas is not alone as an inheritor of the awesome wo here pronounced, as this Book of Mormon language reveals: "And wo be unto him that will not hearken unto the words of Jesus, and also to them whom he hath chosen and sent among them; for whoso receiveth not the words of Jesus and the words of those whom he hath sent receiveth not him; and therefore he will not receive them at the last day; And it would be better for them if they had not been born. For do ye suppose that ye can get rid of the justice of an offended God, who hath been trampled under feet of men, that thereby salvation might come?" (3 Ne. 28:34-35.)

As to the sign by which the traitor might be known—dipping with Jesus in the common bowl and the taking of the sop from his hand—such was neither designed nor intended to identify Judas with clarity and certainty, and it did not have such an effect. All who sat at the table dipped their hands in the bowl, and all received a sop from Jesus' hand as part of the Passover rituals, as we shall see shortly, though it would appear that Judas was the first so served, or, perhaps, that he received an additional sop. In any event Jesus then "dipped the sop" and gave it to Judas, and then, and then only, did Judas ask, "Master, is it I?" Jesus answered: "Thou hast said," apparently whispering the reply only to Judas, without making the others aware in words who the traitor was.

Of Judas John tells us that after the sop, "Satan entered into him." Thus—"As all the winds, on some night of storm, riot and howl through the rent walls of some desecrated shrine, so through the ruined life of Judas envy and avarice, and hatred and ingratitude, were rushing all at once. In that bewildering chaos of a soul spotted with mortal guilt, the Satanic had triumphed over the human; in that dark heart earth and hell were thenceforth at one; in that lost soul sin had conceived and brought forth death." (Farrar, p. 605.)

Jesus then said: "What thou doest, do quickly; but beware of innocent blood." John notes that none of them at the table "knew for what intent he spake this unto him." Some thought the keeper of the bag was being sent to buy provisions for the continuing period of the feast, others that he was being sent to give alms to the poor who even then, this being a day of festivity, were still mingling in the courts of the temple. But Judas, "having received the sop went immediately out." "And so from the lighted room, from the holy banquet, from the blessed company, from the presence of his Lord, he went immediately out, and—as the beloved disciple adds, with a shudder, letting the curtain of darkness fall for ever on that appalling figure—'*and it was night*.' " (Farrar, pp. 605–6.)

NOTES

1. This is a verse from the hymn "The Spirit of God Like a Fire Is Burning," by W.W. Phelps, as that glorious hymn of praise and exultation was sung at the dedication of the Kirtland Temple, March 27, 1836.

2. The quoted phrase is from the Prophet Joseph Smith and was spoken in connection with the holy endowment and the ordinance of the washing of feet. For a full discussion, including the Prophet's explanations, see *Commentary* 1:707-10.

3. There is "a terrible literality about this prophetic reference to one who ate his bread," as is seen from the fact that "Judas, like the rest, lived of what was supplied to Christ, and at that very moment sat at His table." (Edersheim 2:503, footnote 1.)

Chapter 97

THE SACRAMENT OF THE LORD'S SUPPER

He that eateth this bread
eateth of my body to his soul;
and he that drinketh of this wine
drinketh of my blood to his soul;
and his soul shall never
hunger nor thirst,
but shall be filled.
(3 Ne. 20:8.)

Jesus Saith: 'Love One Another'
(John 13:31-35)

Jesus has more to say—much, much more—about his love for his disciples, about their love for him, and about their love for each other. He will say it this night in this upper room in the home of John Mark. And his own beloved John will preserve for us a digest of his sayings in which we shall rejoice forever.

Already we have pondered John's own summary of Jesus' feelings as he reclined with his friends to partake of the Passover. "Now before the feast of the passover," our apostolic colleague wrote, "when Jesus knew that his hour was come that he should depart out of this world unto the Father, having loved his own which were in the world, he loved them unto the end." (John 13:1.) As death approached, love was uppermost in the divine mind. O if they could but love him as he loved them; O if they would but love each other as his law required; O if they would but love the Lord their God with all their heart, might, mind, and strength—then all would be well with them in time and in eternity!

And, as we have seen, the ordinance of the washing of feet was a manifestation of Jesus' eternal love for his own, a love that impelled the Loving One to do all in his power to seal his friends up unto eternal life in his Father's kingdom. Now we shall see how the sacrament of the Lord's Supper, for the same reason, is also a message of love to all mankind. And so, with Judas out groping in the boundless night that enveloped his sin-blackened soul, Jesus can turn to the law of love as a prelude to instituting the sacrament of love.

"No sooner had Judas left the room, than, as though they had been relieved of some ghastly incubus, the spirits of the little company revived. The presence of that haunted soul lay with a weight of horror on the heart of his Master, and no sooner had he departed than the sadness of the feast seems to have been sensibly relieved. The solemn exultation which dilated the soul of their Lord—that joy like the sense of a boundless sunlight behind the earth-born mists—communicated itself to the spirits of His followers. The dull clouds caught the sunset colouring. . . . Now it was that, conscious of the impending separation and fixed unalterably in His sublime resolve, He opened His heart to the little band of those who loved Him, and spoke among them those farewell discourses." (Farrar, pp. 609–10.)

> *Now is the Son of man glorified, and God is glorified in him. If God be glorified in him, God shall also glorify him in himself, and shall straightway glorify him.*

Let the Twelve be reassured—no matter that Judas has left to play his ill and evil part; let that be as it may—what truly matters is that the Son of Man is true and faithful in all things. Shortly he shall be glorified; he shall "receive power, and riches, and wisdom, and strength, and honour, and glory, and blessing." (Rev. 5:12.) And even God is glorified in him, for the glory and honor and dominion and kingdoms gained by the Son are added to those of the Father, thus glorifying him.[1] Indeed, the Father "glorifieth himself" whenever any of his children gain exaltation, and the added kingdoms thereby brought into being constitute "the continuation" of his works. (D&C 132:29-31.) And— " 'If the Father is glorified and exalted to a higher station because of the works and triumphs of the Son, then the Father will further reward the Son with the Father—and the hour for all this is at hand; it shall straightway take place.' " (*Commentary* 1:726.)

Little children, yet a little while I am with you. Ye shall seek me: and as I said unto the Jews, Whither I go, ye cannot come; so now I say to you.

"The time which remained for Him to be with them was short; as He had said to the Jews, so now he said to them, that whither He was going they could not come. And in telling them this, for the first and last time, he calls them 'little children.' In that company were Peter and John, men whose words and deeds should thenceforth influence the whole world of man until the end—men who should become the patron saints of nations—in whose honour cathedrals should be built, and from whom cities should be named; yet their greatness was but a dim, faint reflection from His risen glory, and a gleam caught from that Spirit which He would send. Apart from Him they were nothing, and less than nothing—ignorant Galilean fishermen, unknown and unheard of beyond their native village—having no intellect and no knowledge save that He had thus regarded them as his 'little children.' And though they could not follow Him whither he went, yet he did not say to them, as He had said to the Jews, that they should seek Him and not find Him. [John 7:34; 8:21.] Nay, more, He gave them a new commandment, by which, walking in His steps, and being known by all men as His disciples, they should find Him soon." (Farrar, p. 610.)[2]

> *A new commandment I give unto you, That ye love one another; as I have loved you, that ye also love one another. By this shall all men know that ye are my disciples, if ye have love one for another.*

A new commandment! Love one another! Yea, and an old commandment, one in force from the beginning, one that dwelt with God in eternity before ever the foundations of the earth were laid! Indeed, it was a new and an everlasting commandment—new each time it fell from divine lips; everlasting because it had lain at the root of all saving fellowship from the beginning, from the day when Adam first gloried in the name of Christ, to that present moment. Thus saith Jehovah to Moses: "Thou shalt love thy neighbour as thyself: I am the Lord." (Lev. 19:18.) "For this is the message that ye heard from the beginning, that we should love one another," John said. (1 Jn. 3:11.) But it came then to the Twelve, as it always comes, with a new emphasis, a new prominence, a new influence. They were true disciples and had become such in the waters of baptism. If now they would manifest, one toward another, that love upon which the everlasting gospel is founded, then all men would recognize them for what they were: apostles of the Lord Jesus Christ.

They Eat the Passover Meal

(Luke 22:15-20; JST, Luke 22:16)

This night in the Passover meal and in the sacrament of the Lord's Supper all of the sacrificial similitudes of all the ages combined to bear testimony of the infinite and eternal atoning sacrifice—the sacrifice of the Lamb of God who taketh away the sins of the world. The heart and center and core of revealed religion is that the Son of God will shed his blood, in a garden and on a cross; that he will take upon himself the sins of all men on conditions of repentance; that he will ransom men from the temporal and spiritual death brought into the world by the fall of Adam; that he will abolish death and bring life and immortality to light through his gospel; that through him all men will be raised in immortality, while those who believe and obey will ascend unto eternal life—all because of his atoning sacrifice.

From the day of the first Adam (the first man, the first flesh, the first mortal) to the day of the Second Adam (who will be the first to rise in immortality, the first to gain eternal life)—for all these four thousand years, the Lord's people have offered the firstlings of their flocks in sacrifice in similitude of the coming sacrifice of the Son of God.[3] From the Exodus to this hour the annual Feast of the Passover has been one of the chief occasions on which these sacrifices, with all that they typify, have been performed. A few hours hence and Jesus will be lifted up upon the cross; sacrifices by the shedding of blood will cease among the faithful;[4] and in their place the saints of the Most High will pay their devotions by partaking of the sacramental emblems in remembrance of the torn flesh and spilt blood of the Atoning One. Jesus and the Twelve are about to end the old similitudes of the past and institute the new symbolisms of the future. This very night they shall perform the ordinance which *looks forward* to the sacrifice of God's Son, and also the ordinance performed *in remembrance* of his death. In this setting—portentous, momentous, of eternal importance—it is no wonder, then, that we hear Jesus say to the Twelve:

> *With desire I have desired to eat this passover with you before I suffer; For I say unto you, I will not any more eat thereof, until it be fulfilled which is written in the prophets concerning me. Then I will partake with you, in the kingdom of God.*

This night in Gethsemane, and tomorrow before the rulers of this world and on Calvary, he will suffer, suffer as none other has ever done, either before or since. But first—the Passover! They must eat it together, for they will not do so again—note it well!—until the Messianic prophecies concerning his death are fulfilled; until, in resurrected glory, they keep the feast in the kingdom of God. Jesus and the Twelve are going to eat the Passover meal again incident to his glorious return, a return when the kingdom of God, in all its glorious perfection, will be set up on the millennial earth! But first, in the course of this Passover in the upper room this night, "he took the cup, and gave thanks," as the Passover ritual required, and said:

> *Take this, and divide it among yourselves: For I say unto you, I will not drink of the fruit of the vine, until the kingdom of God shall come.*

Again it is the Passover of which he speaks. He will not drink again of the wine of the feast until the latter-day kingdom comes, until He rules whose right it is. At this point, as Luke recounts, he breaks and blesses the bread and blesses the wine, identifies them as the sacramental emblems, and gives them to the Twelve. Then, as we shall see, he repeats—this time with reference to the sacramental wine—that he will not drink it again until that same blessed day when he shall also eat and drink the Passover meal again.

In summary, then, the sacrificial performances pointed men's minds forward to the future death of their Savior, and the sacramental emblems are partaken in remembrance of a death that is past. Sacrifices were performed until he came; the sacrament is the new order that serves the same purpose since he came—except that there was at least one sacramental ordinance before he came, and there shall be certain sacrificial performances after his coming.

In an ordinance prefiguring the sacrament, as Abraham returned from the slaughter of the kings, he was met by that great high priest from whom the Father of the Faithful himself had received the priesthood. At this time "Melchizedek, king of Salem"—the same to whom Abraham paid tithes—"brought forth bread and wine; and he break bread and blest it; and he blest the wine, he being the priest of the most high God, And he gave to Abram." (JST, Gen. 14:17-18.) Such was the prefiguring of the sacramental ordinance. And in a yet future day, to complete the restitution of all things, the sacrifices that were part of the gospel, and that antedated the law of Moses, will again be performed.[5] Since Jesus says he will eat of the Passover again with the Twelve, as well as partake of the sacrament with them, we can well suppose he may do both things again, at the same time, even as he did them this night in the upper room. As to his partaking of the sacrament at his coming, we will have more to say as we consider the institution of the sacramental ordinance itself. First, however, it will profit us to recount the Passover performances so as to see how easily and naturally the sacrament grew out of them.

The Passover procedures have varied through the ages. It is common to speak of the Egyptian Passover that Israel kept in her early years as a nation, and of the permanent Passover kept in later generations. In each the symbolisms and performances were geared to the assumed needs of the respective days. In spite of extensive source material, we cannot with absolute certainty define each rite and step as it prevailed in Jesus' day, and it may be that some of these varied and changed even in the short span of his life. From reliable sources we suggest something to the following effect took place in thousands of Jewish homes in Jerusalem on this April 6, A.D. 30. We will concern ourselves particularly with what took place in the upper room.

1. The head of the company—in this case Jesus—took the first of four cups of wine, said two benedictions over it, and then all present drank of the cup. It will help us feel the spirit of the solemn occasion to quote the two benedictions customarily spoken, both of which are accepted as having been in use in Jesus' day. One was in these words: "Blessed art Thou, Jehovah our God, who hast created the fruit of the vine!" The other was more extended and self-exulting: "Blessed art Thou, Jehovah our God, King of the Universe, who hast chosen us from among all people, and

exalted us from among all languages, and sanctified us with Thy commandments! And Thou hast given us, O Jehovah our God, in love, the solemn days for joy, and the festivals and appointed seasons for gladness; and this the day of the feast of unleavened bread, the season of our freedom, a holy convocation, the memorial of our departure from Egypt. For us hast Thou chosen; and us hast Thou sanctified from among all nations, and Thy holy festivals with joy and with gladness hast Thou caused us to inherit. Blessed art Thou, O Jehovah, who sanctifiest Israel and the appointed seasons! Blessed art Thou, Jehovah, King of the Universe, who hast preserved us alive and sustained us and brought us to this season!"

As we have seen, Luke tells us Jesus took the first cup, "gave thanks," and passed it to the Twelve. In so stating Luke is speaking of the Passover cup, not the sacramental cup, which he mentions later. We cannot, however, believe that Jesus used the words of these prayers. It probably was common for individuals to exercise freedom in what they said, and certainly the Giver of the feast would not have been bound by the Rabbinic rituals. All we know is that he did offer a blessing of some sort over the cup, and that he and the Twelve drank therefrom.

2. Next came the washing of his own hands by the head of the company, as he recited these words: "Blessed art Thou, Jehovah our God, who hast sanctified us with thy commandments, and hast enjoined us concerning the washing of our hands." Later, after the meal proper, all present would wash their hands. We cannot believe that Jesus performed this act of washing; we have heretofore heard him excoriate the Jewish formalists for their adherence to the washing traditions of the elders. It is probable that at this point he did wash the feet of the disciples; and we know that he said to Peter, "He that has washed his hands and his head, needeth not save to wash his feet, but is clean every whit." John's comment on this was that Jesus so acted because it "was the custom of the Jews under their

law,'' and that he did it ''that the law might be fulfilled.'' Of this we have already taken note.

3. A table was then brought in upon which were placed the bitter herbs, the unleavened bread, the *charoseth* (a dish made of dates, raisins, and vinegar), the Paschal lamb, and the flesh of the *chagigah* (a festive sacrifice in addition to the Paschal lamb). The head of the company, usually the father, dipped a piece of herb in the *charoseth,* ate it, offered a benediction, and distributed a similar morsel to all. Then the second cup was filled but not drunk.

4. Then came the inquiries from a son or the youngest person present. 'Why is this night different from all others? Why do we eat only unleavened bread, bitter herbs and roasted lamb? Why are the herbs dipped twice rather than only once?' Then the officiating head recounted the history of Israel, beginning with Abraham and with particular emphasis on the deliverance from Egypt and the giving of the law.

5. Next the items used in the feast were explained and the head of the company offered a prayer that included these words: ''We are bound to thank, praise, laud, glorify, extol, honour, bless, exalt, and reverence Him, because He hath wrought for our fathers, and for us all these miracles. He brought us forth from bondage into freedom, from sorrow into joy, from mourning to a festival, from darkness to a great light, and from slavery to redemption. Therefore let us sing before Him: Hallelujah!'' Thereupon they sang the first part of the Hallel (Psalms 113 and 114) and offered this benediction: ''Blessed art Thou, Jehovah our God, King of the Universe, who hast redeemed us and redeemed our fathers from Egypt.''

6. Then the second cup was drunk, hands were washed a second time, with the same prayer as before, one of the unleavened cakes was broken, and a thanks was given. The thanksgiving followed the breaking of the bread, rather than preceded it, as was the case with the sacrament soon to be instituted.

7. "Pieces of the broken cake with bitter herbs between them, and dipped in the *Charoseth,* were next handed to each in the company. This, in all probability, was 'the sop' which, in answer to John's inquiry about the betrayer, the Lord 'gave' to Judas. The unleavened bread with bitter herbs constituted, in reality, the beginning of the Paschal Supper, to which the first part of the service had only served as a kind of introduction. But as Judas, after 'having received the sop, went immediately out,' he could not even have partaken of the Paschal lamb, far less of the Lord's Supper." It was the practice in the day of Jesus for this sop to consist of flesh from the Paschal lamb, a piece of unleavened bread, and bitter herbs.

8. At this point the Paschal supper itself was eaten.

9. "Immediately afterwards the third cup was drunk, a special blessing having been spoken over it. There cannot be any reasonable doubt that this was the cup which our Lord connected with His own Supper. It is called in Jewish writings, just as by St. Paul, 'the cup of blessing,' partly because it and the first cup required a special 'blessing,' and partly because it followed on the 'grace after meat.' "

10. The service ended with the drinking of the fourth cup, the singing of the second part of the Hallel (Psalms 115, 116, 117, and 118), and the giving of two more prayers of the same general type as already quoted.

Thus was the Paschal supper conducted in the day of the Lord Jesus. Since he was, in fact, celebrating the supper and fulfilling the law, we must conclude that he followed, insofar as they did not violate true principles, the successive steps in the general format set forth. And building on this foundation he then brought into being the sacramental ordinance itself.

Whether the cups drunk at the Paschal supper were also in similitude of the coming decree that men must drink his blood, we cannot say. Certain it is, however, that the sacrificial lamb, and all that appertained to its offering, was in similitude of the sacrifice of the Only Begotten of the Father.

An interesting Messianic sidelight to this whole procedure is the fact that "to this day, in every Jewish home, at a certain part of the Paschal service—just after the third cup, or the cup of blessing, has been drunk—the door is opened to admit Elijah the prophet as forerunner of the Messiah, while appropriate passages are at the same time read which foretell the destruction of all heathen nations."[6]

But now let us turn to the Lord's Supper itself.

Jesus Giveth Them the Sacrament

(3 Nephi 18:1-14, 27-33; 20:1-9; Moroni 4:1-3; 5:1-2; Matthew 26:26-29; JST, Matthew 26:22-25; Mark 14:22-25; JST, Mark 14:20-25; Luke 22:15-20; JST, Luke 22:16; 1 Corinthians 11:20-34; D&C 20:75-79; 27:1-14)

No single account of the institution of the sacrament of the Lord's Supper, standing alone, contains enough to let us know the reality and the glory and the wonder of what happened in that upper room as the Paschal supper died and the sacramental supper was born. Nor for that matter do all the biblical accounts taken together reveal the glorious mystery of it all.

John does not preserve a single word on the subject, though he is the one who recorded the great sermon on the bread of life, which includes the statements about eating the flesh and drinking the blood of the One who came down from heaven. Luke confines his account to two sentences, which scarcely do more than announce that the new ordinance came into being; Matthew and Mark each give a partial account, from which, however, the full significance of what then transpired cannot be discerned; and Paul, who learned either by revelation or from the testimonies of the participants of what then occurred, does not shed any great additional flood of light upon the blessed events. Providentially the Nephite accounts do contain portions of what

Jesus said to the American Hebrews as he instituted the same sacramental services among them. Even they, however, do not record the words of blessing spoken by the Lord over the bread and over the wine, though we know such words were preserved at the time, for, nearly four hundred years later, Moroni copied them into his inspired writings. We also have received them by revelation, as well as an account of the drinking of the sacramental wine in the millennial day. It is our privilege now to weave all these accounts into one unified whole and catch for ourselves a vision of what Jesus did that April night and what it has meant ever since to the saints of the Most High.

"And as they were eating"—no doubt as they neared the end of the Paschal supper—"Jesus took bread and brake it, and blessed it, and gave to his disciples, and said":

> *Take, eat; this is in remembrance of my body which I give a ransom for you.* (Matthew.)
>
> *Take it, and eat. Behold, this is for you to do in remembrance of my body; for as oft as ye do this ye will remember this hour that I was with you.* (Mark.)
>
> *This is my body which is given for you: this do in remembrance of me.* (Luke.)
>
> *Take, eat: this is my body, which is broken for you: this do in remembrance of me.* (Paul.)

In the Nephite setting, "Jesus commanded his disciples," the Nephite Twelve, whom he had called and chosen for a like apostolic ministry to that of the Jerusalem Twelve, "that they should bring forth some bread and wine unto him. And while they were gone for bread and wine, he commanded the multitude that they should sit themselves down upon the earth. And when the disciples had come with bread and wine, he took of the bread and broke and blessed it; and he gave unto the disciples and commanded that they should eat. And when they had eaten and were filled, he commanded that they should give unto the multitude. And when the multitude had eaten and were filled, he said unto the disciples":

Behold there shall one be ordained among you, and to him will I give power that he shall break bread and bless it and give it unto the people of my church, unto all those who shall believe and be baptized in my name.

And this shall ye always observe to do, even as I have done, even as I have broken bread and blessed it and given it unto you.

And this shall ye do in remembrance of my body, which I have shown unto you. And it shall be a testimony unto the Father that ye do always remember me. And if ye do always remember me ye shall have my Spirit to be with you. (Nephi the Disciple.)

To this account we need only append the words of thanks and blessing spoken by Jesus and the picture will be complete. And we cannot doubt that the words spoken—thereby becoming the pattern for use among the Lord's people in all places and in all ages—conformed, at least in substance and thought content, to the following:

O God, the Eternal Father, we ask thee in the name of thy Son, Jesus Christ, to bless and sanctify this bread to the souls of all those who partake of it; that they may eat in remembrance of the body of thy Son, and witness unto thee, O God, the Eternal Father, that they are willing to take upon them the name of thy Son, and always remember him, and keep his commandments which he hath given them, that they may always have his Spirit to be with them. Amen. (Moroni.)

All these accounts, woven into one majestic tapestry to hang in the halls of the heart of every true saint, enable us to understand what the Master does for his saints in the sacrament. From them we learn: (1) He gave himself, his body, the very flesh of which he was composed, to ransom men. His was a supreme sacrifice—that of his own life, his own body. The ransom paid delivers his brethren from the temporal and spiritual death brought into the world by the fall of Adam. (2) "In memory of the broken flesh, We eat the broken bread; And witness with the cup, afresh, Our faith in Christ, our Head."[7] We eat in remembrance—in remembrance of that Paschal hour, in remembrance of Gethsemane, of Calvary, of an open tomb. (3) The sacrament must be administered by legal administrators; it is a holy ordinance; those who break and bless the bread must be ordained unto that very power; it is not a prerogative men can assume without divine approval. (4) It is administered only to those who believe and have been baptized (except in the case of little children, who need no baptism); indeed, it is the very ordinance whereby the saints renew the covenants made in the waters of baptism. (5) It is a perpetual, continuing, everlasting ordinance; the faithful always observe its rites and provisions. (6) Those who partake testify to the Father that they will always remember his Son. (7) They also repeatedly renew their covenant to take upon them the name of the Son, to be the Lord's own peculiar people, to set themselves apart from the world, to live as becometh saints, to hold his name in everlasting reverence. (8) In this ordinance the solemn promise is made to keep the commandments of God. (9) In consequence of all this the worthy partakers of this blessed and sanctified emblem receive the promise that they will always have the Lord's Spirit to be with them. (10) And as we shall hereafter note, if any partake unworthily, they thereby eat and drink damnation to their souls.

"And he took the cup, and when he had given thanks, he gave it to them; and they all drank of it. And he said unto them":

> *This is in remembrance of my blood which is shed for many, and the new testament which I give unto you; for of me ye shall bear record unto all the world.* (Mark.)

Drink ye all of it. For this is in remembrance of my blood of the new testament, which is shed for as many as shall believe on my name, for the remission of their sins. (Matthew.)

This cup is the new testament in my blood which is shed for you. (Luke.)

This cup is the new testament in my blood: this do ye, as oft as ye drink it, in remembrance of me. For as often as ye eat this bread, and drink this cup, ye do shew the Lord's death till he come. (Paul.)

Among the Nephites, "he commanded his disciples that they should take of the wine of the cup and drink of it, and that they should also give unto the multitude that they might drink of it. And it came to pass that they did so, and did drink of it and were filled; and they gave unto the multitude, and they did drink, and they were filled. And when the disciples had done this, Jesus said unto them":

Blessed are ye for this thing which ye have done, for this is fulfilling my commandments, and this doth witness unto the Father that ye are willing to do that which I have commanded.

And this shall ye always do to those who repent and are baptized in my name; and ye shall do it in remembrance of my blood, which I have shed for you, that ye may witness unto the Father that ye do always remember me. And if ye do always remember me ye shall have my Spirit to be with you. (Nephi the Disciple.)

Again to complete the beauteous tapestry, we append the words of blessing and thanks similar to those that must have fallen from Jesus' lips on these sacred occasions:

O God, the Eternal Father, we ask thee, in the name of thy Son, Jesus Christ, to bless and sanctify this wine to the souls of all those who drink of it, that they may do it in remembrance of the blood of thy Son, which was shed for them; that they may witness unto thee, O God, the Eternal Father, that they do always remember him, that they may have his Spirit to be with them. Amen. (Moroni.)

Again, all these accounts, becoming part of our tapestry of love and faith and triumph, enable us to understand what Jesus has done for us. Again we learn of a ransom that was paid—paid in blood, paid in the spilt blood of the Lamb. This blood is a new testament—a new covenant!—a testament that replaces the old covenant of Moses. Of it—the new covenant, the gospel covenant—the saints bear record to the world. They drink in remembrance of the blood of the new covenant, the blood shed by Jesus the Mediator of the new covenant, which is shed for those who believe. They gain "the remission of their sins"—through baptism and through the renewal of the baptismal covenant as they partake worthily of the sacrament. And again, as often as the saints do these things, they show the Lord's death till he come. Their acts are the fulfilling of the commandment and a witness before the Father that they will keep the commandments of his Son. The same covenant of obedience that appertains to the broken bread is made anew with the wine, and the glorious promise comes again to the saints—for only those who have repented and been baptized are involved—that they shall always have his Spirit to be with them.

And as oft as ye do this ordinance, ye will remember me in this hour that I was with you, and drank with you of this cup, even the last time in my ministry. (Mark.)

And I give unto you a commandment, that ye shall observe to do the things which ye have seen me do, and bear record of me even unto the end. (Matthew.)

And I give unto you a commandment that ye shall do these things. And if ye shall always do these things blessed are ye, for ye are built upon my rock. But whoso among you shall do more or less than these are not built upon my rock, but are built upon a sandy foundation; and when the rain descends,

> *and the floods come, and the winds blow, and beat upon them, they shall fall, and the gates of hell are ready open to receive them.*
>
> *Therefore blessed are ye if ye shall keep my commandments, which the Father hath commanded me that I should give unto you.* (Nephi the Disciple.)

The true saints, remembering the Lord Jesus—and to most of us the remembrance is rooted in what we have read in holy writ—are commanded to do all the things he has done and to bear record of him all their days. Those who so act, being thus built upon the gospel rock, are blessed. Those who do either more or less than he has commanded, either with reference to the sacramental ordinance itself or to any other gospel verity, are built on a sandy foundation; their house shall fall, and they shall be welcomed in the gates of hell. And oh, how many there are in so-called Christendom, where the sacramental ordinance itself is concerned, who even now do either more or less than the Lord Jesus ordained.[8] And oh, how many there are even among the saints who have partaken unworthily of the sacred emblems when the ordinance was administered according to the divine standard.[9] And so, continuing his instruction to the Nephites, Jesus said:

> *Behold verily, verily, I say unto you, I give unto you another commandment. . . . And now behold, this is the commandment which I give unto you, that ye shall not suffer any one knowingly to partake of my flesh and blood unworthily, when ye shall minister it;*
>
> *For whoso eateth and drinketh my flesh and blood unworthily eateth and drinketh damnation to his soul; therefore if ye know that a man is unworthy to eat and drink of my flesh and blood ye shall forbid him.*
>
> *Nevertheless, ye shall not cast him out from among you, but ye shall minister unto him and shall pray for him unto the Father, in my name; and if it*

so be that he repenteth and is baptized in my name, then shall ye receive him, and shall minister unto him of my flesh and blood.

But if he repent not he shall not be numbered among my people, that he may not destroy my people, for behold I know my sheep, and they are numbered.

Nevertheless, ye shall not cast him out of your synagogues, or your places of worship, for unto such shall ye continue to minister; for ye know not but what they will return and repent, and come unto me with full purpose of heart, and I shall heal them; and ye shall be the means of bringing salvation unto them.

Therefore, keep these sayings which I have commanded you that ye come not under condemnation; for wo unto him whom the Father condemneth. (Nephi the Disciple.)

Gross perversions of the true meaning and intent of the sacrament of the Lord's Supper crept into the Church itself even in Paul's day. Apparently, patterning their actions too literally after what Jesus and the Twelve did at the Paschal supper, the Corinthian saints were assembling together and banqueting themselves before partaking of the blessed emblems. The apostle directed them to cease this practice, to eat at home, and when they came together, to partake only of the emblems of the body and blood of their Lord. This they must do in worthiness.

Wherefore whosoever shall eat this bread, and drink this cup of the Lord, unworthily, shall be guilty of the body and blood of the Lord.

But let him examine himself, and so let him eat of that bread, and drink of that cup. For he that eateth and drinketh unworthily, eateth and drinketh damnation to himself, not discerning the Lord's body. (Paul.)

But to return to the upper room, the concluding sacramental expressions of which we have record were these:

But I say unto you, I will not drink henceforth of this fruit of the vine, until that day when I drink it new with you in my Father's kingdom. (Matthew.)

Verily I say unto you, Of this ye shall bear record; for I will no more drink of the fruit of the vine with you, until that day that I drink it new in the kingdom of God. (Mark.)

Were it not for latter-day revelation, no one would know the significance of this promise. In the revelation authorizing the use of water or other liquids besides wine, the word of the Lord Jesus Christ to his prophet, Joseph Smith, was: "It mattereth not what ye shall eat or what ye shall drink when ye partake of the sacrament, if it so be that ye do it with an eye single to my glory—remembering unto the Father my body which was laid down for you, and my blood which was shed for the remission of your sins." Then, with reference to the use of wine, the direction was: "You shall partake of none except it is made new among you; yea, in this my Father's kingdom which shall be built up on the earth."

With reference to the very words spoken in the upper room, the same voice, heard again in latter days, promised: "Marvel not, for the hour cometh that I will drink of the fruit of the vine with you on the earth." Having so announced, the Lord named others who would be present to partake of the blessed emblems in the great assemblage that is to come together at Adam-ondi-Ahman incident to the return of the Son of Man to rule and reign in righteousness among men on earth. Those named were: Moroni, Elias of the restoration, who is also identified as being Gabriel or Noah; John the Baptist, Elijah, Joseph who was sold into Egypt, Jacob, Isaac, Abraham, Michael who is Adam, and Peter, James, and John. The New Testament promise was that Jesus would partake of the sacrament with the eleven who first ate the bread and drank the wine in the upper room. To all of this the latter-day word adds: "And also with all those whom my Father hath given me out of the world,'' which is to say that the righteous saints of all ages, from Adam down to that hour, will all assemble with the Lord Jesus in that great congregation just before the great and dreadful day of the Lord arrives.

Such, then, is the law of the sacrament—the system ordained in the infinite wisdom of God to aid in the cleansing and perfecting of human souls, the system that manifests the infinite love of an infinite being to all us finite creatures here below. And so we conclude our consideration of this part of our Lord's ministry with these words, spoken by him when, for a second time, he administered the sacrament to the Nephites:

> *He that eateth this bread eateth of my body to his soul; and he that drinketh of this wine drinketh of my blood to his soul; and his soul shall never hunger nor thirst, but shall be filled.*

NOTES

1. In this connection, Joseph Smith said: "What did Jesus do? Why; I do the things I saw my Father do when worlds came rolling into existence. My Father worked out his kingdom with fear and trembling, and I must do the same; and when I get my kingdom, I shall present it to my Father, so that he may obtain kingdom upon kingdom, and *it will exalt him in glory.* He will then take a higher exaltation, and I will take his place, and thereby become exalted myself. So that Jesus treads in the tracks of his Father, and inherits what God did before; and *God is thus glorified and exalted in the salvation and exaltation of all his children.*" (*Teachings*, pp. 347–48. Italics added.)

2. Using a similar tender approach, the Lord addressed his latter-day servants in like manner. "Fear not, little children," he said, "for you are mine, and I have overcome the world, and you are of them that my Father hath given me." (D&C 50:40-41; 78:17-18.)

3. Of the sacrifices offered by Adam, who had been commanded so to do, the angelic ministrant said: "This thing is a similitude of the sacrifice of the Only Begotten of the Father, which is full of grace and truth." (Moses 5:5-8.)

4. "It is expedient that there should be a great and last sacrifice," Amulek taught, "and then shall there be, or it is expedient there should be, a stop to the shedding of blood; then shall the law of Moses be fulfilled; yea, it shall be all fulfilled, every jot and tittle, and none shall have passed away. And behold, this is the whole meaning of the law, every whit pointing to that great and last sacrifice; and that great and last sacrifice will be the Son of God, yea, infinite and eternal." (Alma 34:13-14.) The Risen Lord himself said to the Nephites: "Ye shall offer up unto me no more the shedding of blood; yea, your sacrifices and your burnt offerings shall be done away, for I will accept none of your sacrifices and your burnt offerings. And ye shall offer for a sacrifice unto me a broken heart and a contrite spirit." (3 Ne. 9:19-20.)

5. From Joseph Smith we quote: "It is generally supposed that sacrifice was entirely done away when the Great Sacrifice, the sacrifice of the Lord Jesus was offered up. . . . [But] the offering of sacrifices has ever been connected and forms a part of the duties of

the Priesthood. It began with the Priesthood, and will be continued until after the coming of Christ, from generation to generation. We frequently have mention made of the offering of sacrifice by the servants of the Most High in ancient days, prior to the law of Moses; which ordinances will be continued when the Priesthood is restored with all its authority, power and blessings. . . .

"These sacrifices, as well as every ordinance belonging to the Priesthood, will, when the Temple of the Lord shall be built, and the sons of Levi be purified, be fully restored and attended to in all their powers, ramifications, and blessings. This ever did and ever will exist when the powers of the Melchizedek Priesthood are sufficiently manifest; else how can the restitution of all things spoken of by the Holy Prophets be brought to pass. It is not to be understood that the law of Moses will be established again with all its rites and variety of ceremonies; this has never been spoken of by the Prophets; but those things which existed prior to Moses' day, namely, sacrifice, will be continued." (*Teachings*, pp. 172–73.)

6. The data summarized and the quotations given are from Edersheim, Farrar, and Dummelow, who are in agreement on the basics but disagree on some details. Edersheim may be taken as the most authoritative in cases where views are divergent. (*Temple*, pp. 229–48; Edersheim 2:490-512; Farrar, pp. 596–608; Dummelow, pp. 710–12.) Extensive other literature is also available for those desiring to pursue the matter further.

7. Eliza R. Snow, "How Great the Wisdom and the Love," *Hymns*, no. 68.

8. Speaking of those who have done "more" than Jesus commanded, Farrar comments: "The 'transubstantiation' and 'sacramental' controversies which have raged for centuries round the Feast of Communion and Christian love are as heart-saddening as they are strange and needless. They would never have arisen if it had been sufficiently observed that it was a characteristic of Christ's teaching to adopt the language of picture and of emotion. But to turn metaphor into fact, poetry into prose, rhetoric into logic, parable into systematic theology, is at once fatal and absurd. It was to warn us against such error that Jesus said so emphatically, '*It is the spirit that quickeneth; the flesh profiteth nothing: the words that I speak unto you, they are spirit and they are life*.' (John 6:63.)" (Farrar, p. 608, footnote 2.)

9. "See that ye are not baptized unworthily; see that ye partake not of the sacrament of Christ unworthily; but see that ye do all things in worthiness, and do it in the name of Jesus Christ, the Son of the living God; and if ye do this, and endure to the end, ye will in nowise be cast out." (Morm. 9:29.)

Chapter 98

THE DISCOURSE ON THE TWO COMFORTERS

I now send upon you another Comforter,
even upon you my friends,
that it may abide in your hearts,
even the Holy Spirit of promise;
which other Comforter is the same
that I promised unto my disciples,
as is recorded in the testimony of John.
This Comforter is the promise
which I give unto you of eternal life,
even the glory of the celestial kingdom;
Which glory is that
of the church of the Firstborn,
even of God, the holiest of all,
through Jesus Christ his Son.
(D&C 88:3-5.)

"In My Father's House Are Many Mansions"

(John 13:36-38; 14:1-6; JST, John 14:3)

Jesus and the Twelve (minus Judas) have now finished the Paschal feast with its Jewish rituals and performances, except that they must yet drink the fourth cup and sing the remaining part of the Hallel. Both of these they shall do shortly. The holy party has also partaken, for the first time, of the sacramental emblems, in remembrance of spilt blood and broken flesh of the One who then instituted this new ordinance in his earthly kingdom. The appointed hour for the Atoning One to walk the short distance to Gethsemane, there to take upon himself the sins of the world, is almost at hand. There remain only the private sermons, the Intercessory Prayer, and some conversations with Peter (and the others) about the testing to which they also are being subjected. Then the dread hour of infinite agony will begin.

It is out of Peter's solemn assertion—"I will lay down my life for thy sake"—that the private sermons come. We have already heard Jesus tell the apostles that he will soon be glorified and that where he is going they cannot come. It is this that causes Peter to ask, "Lord, whither goest thou?" Jesus replies: "Whither I go, thou canst not follow me now; but thou shalt follow me afterwards." To this Peter asks, "Lord, why cannot I follow thee now?" and makes the rash promise that he is prepared to lay down his life for Jesus' sake. "Wilt thou lay down thy life for my sake?" Jesus asks, and then says: "Verily, verily, I say unto thee, The cock shall not crow, till thou hast denied me thrice." We shall consider the import of this conversation—here placed by John (and Luke) in the upper room—when we come to similar and more extended statements made, as recorded by Matthew and Mark, when Jesus and the apostles were en route to Gethsemane. For the present we refer to them simply as the basis for the discourse and discussion that followed. Jesus then said:

> *Let not your heart be troubled: ye believe in God, believe also in me.*

Truly, the Son of Man will soon depart; he will be separated from them for a season; they shall follow him at a later time. But why should this worry them? They believe in God and know of his overruling providences in the lives of men; they must continue to believe in Jesus. He is the

Son, and it is as easy to believe that the Father has a son as to believe in the Father alone. Indeed, how can God be a father unless he has a son? How can there be a son of God unless God is the father? It is as easy to believe in one as in the other.

In my Father's house are many mansions: if it were not so, I would have told you. I go to prepare a place for you.

Jesus endorses the Jewish concept that there are degrees of reward in eternity; that those who enter the kingdoms of glory shall have different abodes; that they will be rewarded as they merit. It is true that in his Father's house there are many kingdoms. Such is implicit in the eternal scheme of things. If mortality is a testing and probationary estate, if men are to be judged according to the deeds done in the flesh, and if there are as many degrees of righteousness here on earth as there are men, then a just God could not do other than have an infinite number of kingdoms and rewards in the realms ahead. "If it were not so, I would have told you." That is: All men should by instinct know there are different degrees of glory and many levels of reward in the hereafter. If such were not the case, Jesus would have so stated. And he was going to prepare a place in the highest heaven for the faithful saints.

And if I go and prepare a place for you, I will come again, and receive you unto myself; that where I am, there ye may be also.

Theirs is to be a place in the presence of their Lord; the disciple shall be as his Master, and the servant as his Lord; they shall be even as he is, and he is even as the Father. Though it would not be their privilege to follow him immediately, yet he gave them this assurance: "And whither I go ye know, and the way ye know." Thomas responded: "Lord, we know not whither thou goest; and how can we know the way?" This brought forth from Jesus one of the greatest divine proclamations of his entire ministry:

I am the way, the truth, and the life: no man cometh unto the Father, but by me.

Salvation is in Christ! The plan of salvation is the gospel of God; it is the system ordained by the Father to enable his spirit children, Christ included, to advance and progress and become like him. But Christ is the Redeemer of men, the Savior of the world, the one by whom all men are raised in immortality, and by whom those who believe and obey may gain eternal life. He has abolished death, as the scriptures say, and brought life and immortality to light through the gospel. He is the Resurrection and the Life. He is the way: he charts the course; he invites all men to follow him. He is the truth, the embodiment and personification of this holy attribute: his word is truth, and truth alone saves. He is the life: life exists because of him; he is the Creator. No man cometh unto the Father but by him. He redeemeth from the fall; he raiseth men from death; he maketh eternal life possible. He is our Advocate with the Father: without him we are nothing; because of him we can attain all things. Truly, salvation was, and is, and is to come, in and through his holy name, and in no other way.

"He That Hath Seen Me Hath Seen the Father"

(John 14:7-14)

God was in Christ manifesting himself to the world. The Great God, the Almighty Father, the Creator, Upholder, and Preserver of all things, revealed himself to all men by sending his Son who is in the express image of his Father's person. Both holy beings now have tangible bodies of flesh and bones; both eat and digest food; both occupy space, travel from place to place, and possess the fulness of all good things. Both are exalted and perfected Men, Holy Men, Men in whose image mortals are made. While he was on earth, Jesus was in the image and likeness of the Father. He came to reveal the Father. By knowing the Son men thereby knew the Father.

If ye had known me, ye should have known my Father also: and from henceforth ye know him, and have seen him.

But Philip, not satisfied to see Christ only, and in that way to envision who and what the Father is, asked: "Lord, shew us the Father, and it sufficeth us." 'Let us see him as well as his Prototype and it will suffice us.' But Jesus said:

Have I been so long time with you, and yet hast thou not known me, Philip? he that hath seen me hath seen the Father; and how sayest thou then, Shew us the Father?

" 'Philip, after all your association with me, have you not come to know that I am the Son of God, and that the Father is manifesting himself to the world through me? Surely by this time you should know that he who hath seen me hath seen the Father, as it were, for I am so fully and completely like him. Why, then, do you ask for that which you are not now ready to receive, by saying, Show us the Father also?' " (*Commentary* 1:731.)

Believest thou not that I am in the Father, and the Father in me? the words that I speak unto you I speak not of myself: but the Father that dwelleth in me, he doeth the works. Believe me that I am in the Father, and the Father in me: or else believe me for the very works' sake.

The Father and the Son dwell in each other in that they both think the same thoughts, say the same words, and do the same acts. The words that fall from the lips of the Son, and the works that his arm performs, are the very words the Father would speak and the identical works the Father would perform, if he personally were present. They are thus one and dwell in each other. If men cannot believe and know that Christ is in the Father, and the Father in him, then they should believe in Christ because of his works, works that none but God could do.

Verily, verily, I say unto you, He that believeth on me, the works that I do shall he do also; and greater works than these shall he do; because I go unto my Father.

This night Jesus designs to reveal to his disciples some of the mysteries of his kingdom, some of the deep and hidden doctrines, some things that can be understood only by the power of the Spirit. His answer to Peter about the many mansions, his explanation to Philip about the indwelling of the Father and the Son in each other, and now this pronouncement that believing disciples will do not only the same works he has done, but even greater works "because" he went unto the Father—all of these are numbered with the mysteries of the kingdom.

That the disciples by faith—for by faith all things are possible and nothing is too hard for the Lord—can do among men what their Master had done is self-evident. The same measure of faith always has borne and always will bear the same fruit. But what of the greater works? Are the disciples to surpass the mighty miracles of their Lord? Yes—in eternity! No ministry shall ever equal his on earth, but that ministry was only a small foretaste of the miraculous powers to be wielded by all the faithful in the oncoming ages yet to be. "The greater works which those that believed on his name were to do were to be done in eternity, where he was going and where they should behold his glory."[1]

And whatsoever ye shall ask in my name, that will I do, that the Father may be glorified in the Son. If ye shall ask any thing in my name, I will do it.

Ask in my name! Ask and ye shall receive; ask in faith and receive an answer; but ask in the name of Christ. Pray unto the Father; pray in faith and God will grant the petition; but pray in the name of Christ. His is the name that the saints take upon them in the waters of baptism; his is the name by which the faithful are called; in his name are miracles wrought, prophecies made, and salvation gained. "Thou shalt do all that thou doest in the name of the Son." (Moses 5:8.) "And whatsoever ye shall ask the Father in my name, which is right, believing that ye shall receive, behold it shall be given unto you." (3 Ne. 18:20.)

I will do it! Prayers are made to the Father; answers come from the Son, who is the Mediator between God and man. All things are committed into his hands, and God the Father "hath highly exalted him, and given him a name which is above every name." (Philip. 2:9-11.)

Jesus Speaks of the Two Comforters

(John 14:15-26)

"If ye love me, keep my commandments."

Through this whole night—a night of blessing and of agony—the Blessed Lord, whose coming agony will redeem his brethren, repeatedly centers the hearts of his disciples on the rock foundation of love. Nowhere is this more evident than in the forthcoming words about the two Comforters. The disciples must love one another or they are not his; his Father so loved the world that he sent his Only Begotten Son to work out, this night, the infinite and eternal atoning sacrifice; he himself came to do the will of the Father because of his infinite love for mankind; and the disciples must love him and signify the same by obedience and service. Nay, more: unless they kept his commandments and do his will and serve their fellowmen, they do not in fact love him to the degree and in the way they must to gain an everlasting inheritance with him in that kingdom which he is about to prepare.[2]

> *And I will pray the Father, and he shall give you another Comforter, that he may abide with you for ever; Even the Spirit of truth; whom the world cannot receive, because it seeth him not, neither knoweth him: but ye know him; for he dwelleth with you, and shall be in you.*

As long as Jesus has been with them, he has been their Comforter; he has spoken peace to their souls; those who were heavy laden with the sorrows and sufferings and struggles of the world came to him and found rest for their souls. He comforted the widow and was a father to the fatherless. His words lifted believing souls to new heights of serenity and peace. Now he is leaving, but he will send another Comforter—the Holy Ghost—to abide with the faithful forever.

For all men except those few who heard his voice in mortality, the Holy Ghost is the first Comforter. This member of the Godhead speaks peace to the souls of the righteous in all ages. The Holy Ghost "is the gift of God unto all those who diligently seek him, as well in times of old as in the time that he should manifest himself unto the children of men" (1 Ne. 10:17), and, as well also, in times to come. He is the Spirit of truth—as also is Christ—but the world cannot receive the Holy Ghost because the Spirit will not dwell in unclean tabernacles.

Further, the Spirit cannot be seen by mortal eyes. "The wind bloweth where it listeth, and thou hearest the sound thereof, but canst not tell whence it cometh, and whither it goeth," as Jesus said to Nicodemus, "so is every one that is born of the Spirit." (John 3:8.) But the disciples know the Spirit; they hear the whisperings of the still small voice; they feel the sanctifying influence he sends forth; they receive the revelations of truth that he broadcasts out into all immensity—all because he dwells in them. They have the gift of the Holy Ghost, which is the right to the constant companionship of that member of the Godhead based on faithfulness.[3]

I will not leave you comfortless: I will come unto you.

For the faithful saints who receive the Holy Ghost, which is the first Comforter, there is more—much, much more—ahead. The Lord Jesus himself will come to them. Though he has ascended to his Father, yet will he return to show himself to each individual who abides the law which enables men to rend the heavens and see the visions of eternity.

Yet a little while, and the world seeth me no more; but ye see me: because I live, ye shall live also.

The disciples shall see their resurrected Lord, and because he lives—has both immortality and eternal life—so shall they also inherit that fulness of life which is both immortality and eternal life.

At that day ye shall know I am in my Father, and ye in me, and I in you. He that hath my commandments, and keepeth them, he it is that loveth me: and he that loveth me shall be loved of my Father, and I will love him, and will manifest myself to him.

Even as the Father and the Son dwell in each other, so do the faithful saints, by the power of the Holy Ghost, dwell in both the Father and the Son, and so also do the Gods of heaven dwell in men. It is figurative, symbolic language. All those who think the same thoughts, speak the same words, and do the same deeds dwell in each other; and all who are as Christ is shall surely, while dwelling as mortals, see his face and converse with him as one friend speaketh with another.[4]

Such wondrous doctrine, comprehensible only to those whose souls are afire with the enlightening power of the Spirit, was too much for the disciples at that point in time. Judas Thaddeus, otherwise known as Lebbeus, asked: "Lord, how is it that thou wilt manifest thyself unto us, and not unto the world?" Jesus replied:

If a man love me, he will keep my words: and my Father will love him, and we will come unto him, and make our abode with him.

With reference to these words our revelations recite: "The appearing of the Father and the Son, in that verse, is a personal appearance; and the idea that the father and the Son dwell in a man's heart is an old sectarian notion, and is false." (D&C 130:3.)

And with reference to the whole concept of the Second Comforter, we have these words of divine and eternal truth given to us by the Prophet Joseph Smith: "There are two

Comforters spoken of. One is the Holy Ghost, the same as given on the day of Pentecost, and that all saints receive after faith, repentance, and baptism. This first Comforter or Holy Ghost has no other effect than pure intelligence. . . .

"After a person has faith in Christ, repents of his sins, and is baptized for the remission of his sins and receives the Holy Ghost (by the laying on of hands), which is the first Comforter, then let him continue to humble himself before God, hungering and thirsting after righteousness, and living by every word of God, and the Lord will soon say unto him, Son, thou shalt be exalted. When the Lord has thoroughly proved him, and finds that the man is determined to serve Him at all hazards, then the man will find his calling and his election made sure, then it will be his privilege to receive the other Comforter, which the Lord hath promised the Saints, as is recorded in the testimony of St. John. . . .

"Now what is this other Comforter. It is no more nor less than the Lord Jesus Christ Himself; and this is the sum and substance of the whole matter; that when any man obtains this last Comforter, he will have the personage of Jesus Christ to attend him, or appear unto him from time to time, and even He will manifest the Father unto him, and they will take up their abode with him, and the visions of the heavens will be opened unto him, and the Lord will teach him face to face, and he may have a perfect knowledge of the mysteries of the Kingdom of God; and this is the state and place the ancient Saints arrived at when they had such glorious visions—Isaiah, Ezekiel, John upon the Isle of Patmos, St. Paul in the three heavens, and all the Saints who held communion with the general assembly and Church of the Firstborn." (*Teachings*, pp. 149–51.)

He that loveth me not keepeth not my sayings: and the word which ye hear is not mine, but the Father's which sent me. These things have I spoken unto you, being yet present with you.

But the Comforter, which is the Holy Ghost, whom the Father will send in my name, he shall teach you all things, and bring all things to your remembrance, whatsoever I have said unto you.

Though Thaddeus and the others could not then envision in full the import of the divine words, yet there would be a day, after Pentecost, when, as the fire of the Spirit burned in their souls, they would know for themselves of the marvels here taught. The Holy Spirit of God would bring the words back into their minds and would impress upon their hearts and souls the true meanings and significance of the language used. The Holy Ghost would teach them all things.[5]

"My Father Is Greater than I"

(John 14:27-31; JST, John 14:29-31; Matthew 26:30; Mark 14:26; JST, Mark 14:26-27; Luke 22:39)

Their time together in the upper room—a sacred, blessed period, of infinite worth to them and to us—is drawing to its close. The deep doctrine of the Second Comforter has saluted their ears, and some fifty days hence, after Pentecost, it will begin to burn in their hearts. Now Jesus says:

Peace I leave with you, my peace I give unto you: not as the world giveth, give I unto you. Let not your heart be troubled, neither let it be afraid.

Gospel peace! The peace possessed by the saints! What a marvelous blessing this is! "He who doeth the works of righteousness shall receive his reward, even peace in this world, and eternal life in the world to come." (D&C 59:23.) Christ is the Prince of Peace, the revealer and dispenser of that inner serenity known only to those who have received the gift of the Holy Ghost. Peace is one of the gifts of the Spirit. Thus, Jesus speaks not of the worldly salutation, "Peace be with you," which was commonly spoken among the Jews, but of that inner serenity reserved for those who have entered into the rest of the Lord and who know of the truth and divinity of the Lord's earthly kingdom.

Ye have heard how I said unto you, I go away, and come again unto you. If ye loved me, ye would rejoice, because I said, I go unto the Father: for my Father is greater than I.

If all faithful saints envisioned the glories that lie ahead for them, they would rejoice at the prospects of going where God and Christ and holy beings are. And as to Jesus himself, he is going to eternal glory with his Father who—and again we catch a glimpse of one of the mysteries of the kingdom—is greater than he is.

Jesus' Father is greater than he! "Are they not one? Do they not both possess all power, all wisdom, all knowledge, all truth? Have they not both gained all godly attributes in their fulness and perfection? Verily, yes, for the revelations so announce and the Prophet so taught. And yet our Lord's Father is greater than he, greater in kingdoms and dominions, greater in principalities and exaltations. One does and shall rule over the other everlastingly. Though Jesus is himself God, he is also the Son of God, and as such the Father is his God as he is ours. 'I ascend unto my Father, and your Father; and to my God, and your God,' he is soon to say.

"Joseph Smith, with inspired insight, tells how Jesus is God's heir; how he receives and possesses all that the Father hath, and is therefore (as Paul said) 'equal with God' and yet at the same time is subject to and less than the Father. These are his words: 'What did Jesus do? Why; I do the things I saw my Father do when worlds came rolling into existence. My Father worked out his kingdom with fear and trembling, and I must do the same; and when I get my kingdom, I shall present it to my Father, so that he may obtain kingdom upon kingdom, and it will exalt him in glory. He will then take a higher exaltation, and I will take his place, and thereby become exalted myself. So that Jesus treads in the tracks of his Father, and inherits what God did before; and God is thus glorified and exalted in the salvation and exaltation of all his children.' "[6]

And now I have told you before it come to pass, that, when it is come to pass, ye might believe. Hereafter I will not talk much with you; for the prince of darkness, who is of this world, cometh, but hath no power over me, but he hath power over you. And I tell you these things, that ye may know that I love the Father; and as the Father gave me commandment, even so do I. Arise, let us go hence.

Jesus has overcome the world. The prince of darkness, who opposes the Prince of peace and of light, has no power over him. The disciples, however, are still subject to the world and all its evils and darkness. But Jesus—blessed be his name—is fulfilling the Father's will. He is prepared to go to Gethsemane. And so, having first "sung a hymn," undoubtedly the latter part of the Hallel, as Mark says, the disciples "were grieved, and wept over him." Then they arose from the Paschal table to go forth to "the mount of Olives."

It will help us better to gain for ourselves a feeling of what then was in the hearts of the Twelve if we ponder some of the words of the hymn then sung. Included, as we suppose, for they were following the Passover format, were these Davidic expressions, which must have enveloped the disciples like a gloomy mist:

I love the Lord, because he hath heard my voice and my supplications. . . .

The sorrows of death compassed me, and the pains of hell gat hold upon me: I found trouble and sorrow. Then called I upon the name of the Lord; O Lord, I beseech thee, deliver my soul. . . .

What shall I render unto the Lord for all his benefits toward me? I will take of the cup of salvation, and call upon the name of the Lord. . . .

Precious in the sight of the Lord is the death of his saints. . . .

The Lord is on my side; I will not fear: what can man do unto me? . . .

Thou hast thrust sore at me that I might fall: but the Lord helped me. The Lord is my strength and song, and is become my salvation. . . .

The stone which the builders refused is become the head stone of the corner. This is the Lord's doing; it is marvellous in our eyes. . . .

Blessed be he that cometh in the name of the Lord. . . .

God is the Lord. . . .

Thou art my God, and I will praise thee: thou art my God, I will exalt thee. O give thanks unto the Lord; for he is good: for his mercy endureth for ever. (Psalms 116-118.)

With these thoughts and upon this tone the Paschal feast ends. Jesus will now speak a few more words to the chosen Twelve and then go to Gethsemane and the cross.

NOTES

1. The words are those of Joseph Smith as recorded in the *Lectures on Faith*, pp. 64–66. Additional explanations on the point involved are found in *Commentary* 1:732-33.

2. "If thou lovest me thou shalt serve me and keep all my commandments." (D&C 42:29.) For more extended commentary on this point and the other matters forming part of this discourse on the two Comforters, see *Commentary* 1:734-41.

3. "The Holy Ghost has not a body of flesh and bones, but is a personage of Spirit. Were it not so, the Holy Ghost could not dwell in us. A man may receive the Holy Ghost, and it may descend upon him and not tarry with him." (D&C 130:22-23.) "Therefore it is given to abide in you; the record of heaven; the Comforter; the peaceable things of immortal glory; the truth of all things; that which quickeneth all things, which maketh alive all things; that which knoweth all things, and hath all power according to wisdom, mercy, truth, justice, and judgment." (Moses 6:61.)

4. "Verily, thus saith the Lord: It shall come to pass that every soul who forsaketh his sins and cometh unto me, and calleth on my name, and obeyeth my voice, and keepeth my commandments, shall see my face and know that I am." (D&C 93:1.) "Because of the knowledge of this man," the Book of Mormon says with reference to the brother of Jared, "he could not be kept from beholding within the veil; and he saw the finger of Jesus, which, when he saw, he fell with fear; for he knew that it was the finger of the Lord; and he had faith no longer, for he knew, nothing doubting. Wherefore, having this perfect knowledge of God, he could not be kept from within the veil; therefore he saw Jesus; and he did minister unto him." (Ether 3:19-20.)

5. "And by the power of the Holy Ghost ye may know the truth of all things." (Moro. 10:5.)

6. *Commentary* 1:743; *Mormon Doctrine*, pp. 492–93; John 20:17; *Teachings*, pp. 347–48.

THE DISCOURSE ON THE LAW OF LOVE

Beloved, let us love one another;
for love is of God;
and every one that loveth
is born of God, and knoweth God.
He that loveth not, knoweth not God;
for God is love.
In this was manifested
the love of God toward us,
because that God sent his only begotten Son
into the world, that we might live
through him. Herein is love,
not that we loved God, but that he loved us,
and sent his Son to be the propitiation
for our sins.
Beloved, if God so loved us,
we ought also to love one another.
No man hath seen God at any time,
except them who believe. If we love one another,
God dwelleth in us, and his love
is perfected in us. . . .
And we have known and believed the love
that God hath to us. God is love;

and he that dwelleth in love
dwelleth in God, and God in him.
Herein is our love made perfect,
that we may have boldness
in the day of judgment; because as he is,
so are we in this world.
There is no fear in love;
but perfect love casteth out fear;
because fear hath torment.
He that feareth is not made perfect in love.
We love him, because he first loved us.
If a man say, I love God,
and hateth his brother,
he is a liar;
for he that loveth not his brother
whom he hath seen, how can he love God
whom he hath not seen?
And this commandment have we from him,
That he who loveth God love his brother also.
(JST, 1 Jn. 4:7-21.)[1]

"I Am the Vine, Ye Are the Branches"

(John 15:1-8)

Jesus and eleven of the Twelve—the holy party—have now finished the Paschal meal; the last legal performances of the law, given by Jehovah to Moses, have been performed by Him who gave the law; new emblems, symbolical of the sacrifice of God's Son, have been introduced into the New Order; the washing of feet has been attended to; the disciples have risen from their couches; and the musical chanting of the Hallel is over. But "before they started for their moonlight walk to the Garden of Gethsemane, perhaps while yet they stood around their Lord when the Hallel was over, He once more spoke to them." (Farrar, p. 116.)[2]

I am the true vine, and my Father is the husbandman.

Every branch in me that beareth not fruit he taketh away: and every branch that beareth fruit, he purgeth it, that it may bring forth more fruit. Now ye are clean through the word which I have spoken unto you.

The allegory of the vine, the husbandman, and the branches! "A grander analogy is not to be found in the world's literature. Those ordained servants of the Lord were as helpless and useless without Him as is a bough severed from the tree. As the branch is made fruitful only by virtue of the nourishing sap it receives from the rooted trunk, and if cut away or broken off withers, dries, and becomes utterly worthless except as fuel for the burning, so those men, though ordained to the Holy Apostleship, would find themselves strong and fruitful in good works, only as they remained in steadfast communion with the Lord. Without Christ what were they, but unschooled Galileans, some of them fishermen, one a publican, the rest of undistinguished attainments, and all of them weak mortals? As branches of the Vine they were at that hour clean and healthful, through the instructions and authoritative ordinances with which they had been blessed, and by the reverent obedience they had manifested." (Talmage, pp. 604–5.)

Abide in me, and I in you. As the branch cannot bear fruit of itself, except it abide in the vine; no more can ye, except ye abide in me.

I am the vine, ye are the branches: He that abideth in me, and I in him, the same bringeth forth much fruit: for without me ye can do nothing.

If a man abide not in me, he is cast forth as a branch, and is withered; and men gather them, and cast them into the fire, and they are burned.

"By their fruits ye shall know them." (Matt. 7:20.) And whatever else—as a foul fungus, or some spongy excrescence, or other parasitic or morbid growth—whatever else may grow on a dead vine, it is not the fruit of eternal life. Only those living branches, into whose vascular tissues flow revelation from the Vine and heavenly power from on high—only such living branches can bear fruit unto eternal life. And any man, be he the highest apostolic minister or the lowest branch in the living Church—any man who does not abide in Christ shall wither away and be cast into eternal fire in the dread day of burning that is to be.

If ye abide in me, and my words abide in you, ye shall ask what ye will, and it shall be done unto you.

There are no limits to the power of faith. By it the worlds were made; by it all things are; by it the heavens and the earth shall pass away. Faith is the supreme, ruling power in the universe; it is the power of God; it is infinite and eternal. If the earth itself, the universe, the sidereal heavens—all things—were created and are preserved and upheld by faith, who is to say that the little things of this life shall not be governed by that same infinite power? There is nothing the Twelve shall seek—in faith—that shall not be granted! "But no man is possessor of all things except he be purified and cleansed from all sin. And if ye are purified and cleansed from all sin, ye shall ask whatsoever you will in the name of Jesus and it shall be done. But know this, it shall be given you what you shall ask." (D&C 50:28-30.)

Herein is my Father glorified, that ye bear much fruit; so shall ye be my disciples.

God is glorified, as we have seen, when his children gain exaltation, with resultant kingdoms of their own, for all such are added to his dominions.

Such, then, is the grandest allegory of them all. How better could Jesus have taught that he and his prophets are one; that the life-giving power comes from the Vine; but that the branches must bear the fruit? How better could he have shown that true ministers must receive their power from him? Or that " 'every apostle, prophet, and legal administrator whom I have commissioned to offer the fruit of eternal life to men shall be cut off by my Father unless he carries forward my work; and every minister who is faithful in my service shall be pruned of dead foliage (divested of worldly distractions) and given power to bring forth more fruit.' " (*Commentary* 1:745.)

Truly—and how often have we said it—never man spake as this Man!

"The Royal Law: Love Thy Neighbour"[3]

(John 15:9-17)

"Which is greater and more to be desired, to love God or be loved by him? In his providences the one grows out of the other, for Deity reciprocates in full and abundant measure the love his children confer upon him. And Jesus here speaks, not of the divine decree that men should love God, but of the special and preferential love bestowed by the Lord upon those who love and serve him. Such are singled out by Deity to receive special grace and goodness because they are in process of becoming one with him." (*Commentary* 1:747.)

> *As the Father hath loved me, so have I loved you: continue ye in my love. If ye keep my commandments, ye shall abide in my love; even as I have kept my Father's commandments, and abide in his love.*

Love is the child of obedience, and the greater the obedience the greater the love. As Jesus follows the Father, so must we follow the Son; as the Father loves the Son, so the Son loves us. As the Father's love for the Son comes because of the obedience of the Son, so Jesus' love for us comes because we keep his commandments.

> *These things have I spoken unto you, that my joy might remain in you, and that your joy might be full.*

As a father has joy and rejoicing in his righteous children, so Jesus finds—and here expresses—his joy in the obedient Twelve. To them he holds out the hope that they may have a fulness of joy, for "Men are, that they might have joy" (2 Ne. 2:25), and both he and his Father, being no respecters of persons, desire to reward all men with the choicest blessings of time and eternity. To others of his apostolic witnesses, three of the Twelve on the American continent, he will soon give an even greater promise. "Ye have desired that ye might bring the souls of men unto me, while the earth shall stand," he will say. "And for this cause ye shall have fulness of joy; and ye shall sit down in the kingdom of my Father; yea, your joy shall be full, even as the Father hath given me fulness of joy; and ye shall be even as I am, and I am even as the Father; and the Father and I are one." (3 Ne. 28:9-10.) This is a promise of exaltation, and to gain exaltation is to have a fulness of joy.

> *This is my commandment, That ye love one another, as I have loved you. Greater love hath no man than this, that a man lay down his life for his friends.*

Love is a commandment! Thou shalt love the Lord thy God; thou shalt love thy neighbor as thyself; thou shalt love thy wife and family; thou shalt love one another. Christ is the Prototype; as he loved us, so we must love one another. And he will soon lay down his life in the atonement of love, the supreme manifestation of his love for his brethren.

> *Ye are my friends, if ye do whatsoever I command you. Henceforth I call you not servants; for the servant knoweth not what his lord doeth: but I have called you friends; for all things that I have heard of my Father I have made known unto you.*

As Abraham was the Friend of God, so the Twelve are the friends of Jesus; and as it was with those worthies, so shall it be with all who are on intimate terms with their Maker. Friends hold each other in high regard and associate on terms of intimacy and love. Their aims and goals are similar; they walk arm in arm; and, if need be, they are prepared to die for each other.[4]

Friends confide in each other, and Jesus has told his

intimates among the Twelve all things they are able to understand. Peter, James, and John are the only ones, for instance, who know what transpired on the Mount of Transfiguration, though the eternal verities there revealed will in due course be given to all of them. And shortly, this very night, Jesus will say to them that there are many things they cannot yet bear that will be manifest to them when they receive the gift of the Holy Ghost.

> *Ye have not chosen me, but I have chosen you, and ordained you, that ye should go and bring forth fruit, and that your fruit should remain: that whatsoever ye shall ask of the Father in my name, he may give it you.*
>
> *These things I command you, that ye love one another.*

Jesus, the Lord, chooses his own friends; he calls his own servants; he names whom he will to stand as his agents. True ministers do not call themselves to apostolic positions, nor to serve as elders or in any ministerial capacity. Jesus came in his Father's name, bearing his Father's power and authority, doing and saying what his Father commanded. The servants of the Son act similarly. They are called by Christ; he endows them with power from on high; they go forth, duly commissioned, in his name; and they do and say what he commands. They are ordained; they hold Aaronic or Melchizedek authority; they have the gift of the Holy Ghost so they can receive direction from their Lord and Master and Friend.

All other would-be servants are false ministers, false apostles, false prophets. Such do not preach the fulness of the everlasting gospel in all its glory, beauty, and perfection; such cannot perform the ordinances of salvation so they are binding on earth and in heaven. Whatever they may do, so be it; whatever ethical principles they may teach, let them stand; whatever improvements their exhortations may make in the lives of ungodly men, it is all to the good—but theirs can never be more than a preparatory work. Only those called of God, by his own voice, or by angelic ministrations, or by the gift of the Holy Ghost—such only are true apostles and true ministers. Theirs only is the prerogative to seal men up unto eternal life. They are the ones whose fruit will endure. They are the ones who shall ask the Father in the name of Christ for whatsoever they will, and it shall be given them. They are the ones who love one another, thereby testifying before the world that they are true disciples.

God's Enemies Hate Christ and His Work

(John 15:18-27; 16:1-4)

According to the eternal law of opposites—the law which recites: "It must needs be, that there is an opposition in all things" (2 Ne. 2:11)—according to this law, if there is love, there must be hate. Neither of these attributes can exist without the other. Unless there is darkness, there can be no light; unless there is vice, there can be no virtue; unless there is hate, there can be no love. Love is of God and is manifest in the lives of the friends of God; hate is of the world and is manifest in the lives of the enemies of God. And so, having spoken of love and the blessings that flow therefrom, the Lord of love now speaks of hate and the cursings that attend this evil-given attribute.

> *If the world hate you, ye know that it hated me before it hated you. If ye were of the world, the world would love his own: but because ye are not of the world, but I have chosen you out of the world, therefore the world hateth you.*

The world—what is it? It is the state of carnality and evil that dwells in the hearts of those who live on the earth and who have become, since the fall of Adam, "carnal, sensual, and devilish, by nature." (Alma 42:10.) It is the sum total of the social conditions created by carnal men, on a fallen earth, which conditions will continue to prevail until "the end of the world, or the destruction of the wicked, which is the end of the world." (JS-H 1:4.) Of course the world loves its own and hates the saints. How could it be otherwise? The worldly forces, the forces of worldliness, are but the armies of Lucifer, who first fought against God in preexistence and who now continue, here on earth, that primeval war. "Know ye not that the friendship of the world is enmity with God?" James asks. His answer: "Whosoever therefore will be a friend of the world is the enemy of God." (James 4:4.)

> *Remember the word that I said unto you, The servant is not greater than his lord. If they have persecuted me, they will also persecute you; if they have kept my saying, they will keep yours also.*

As with the Master, so with his servants. If persecution is the heritage of the Son of God, will not those who have taken upon them the name of Christ, those who are thus members of his family, will not they also be persecuted? If Christ be scourged, will not his servants feel the biting lash? If Christ be crucified, what if his disciples lay down their lives for the testimony of Jesus and the joy reserved for the saints? And the few among the many who would give heed to the words of Jesus, should he personally minister among them—such are the ones who will receive his servants and give heed to their words.

> *But all these things will they do unto you for my name's sake, because they know not him that sent me.*

Everywhere—on every hand, among all sects, parties, and denominations; everywhere—among every nation, and kindred, and tongue, and people; everywhere—from one end of the earth to the other—everywhere those who hate and persecute the saints do it because they reject Christ. No matter that they may give lip service to his holy name; no matter that they think he is their God; no matter that they follow what they falsely suppose is his plan of salvation—they in fact are rejecting the living Christ when they reject and persecute those whom he hath called and sent forth to preach his word. And all of this is because, regardless of what false assumptions they may make as to their own forms of worship, they know not the One who sent Christ into the world.

If I had not come and spoken unto them, they had not had sin: but now they have no cloke for their sin.

He that hateth me hateth my Father also.

If I had not done among them the works which none other man did, they had not had sin: but now have they both seen and hated both me and my Father.

But this cometh to pass, that the word might be fulfilled that is written in their law, They hated me without a cause.

How awful and fearful it is to reject light and truth! "For of him unto whom much is given much is required; and he who sins against the greater light shall receive the greater condemnation." Men "become transgressors," when otherwise they would have been blameless, because they receive added light and knowledge from on high and do not walk in its blazing glory. (D&C 82:3-4.) The Son of God walks among men, speaks as never man spake, and performs miracles that none else have ever done. Those who reject him thereby become sinners; they can no longer cloak their sins, and they are damned for choosing to walk in darkness at noonday. In Christ they have seen and heard both him and his Father. They have hated both of them without a cause.

But when the Comforter is come, whom I will send unto you from the Father, even the Spirit of truth, which proceedeth from the Father, he shall testify of me: And ye also shall bear witness, because ye have been with me from the beginning.

However much the world may hate and deny and reject both the Father and the Son; however much carnality may reign in the hearts of the enemies of God; however much the saints may be persecuted and slain—yet Jesus will send the Comforter, from the Father, to the faithful. Then this testator will testify to those whose hearts are contrite; he will proclaim to them the divinity of God's Son and bear record of the saving truths that are in Christ. The faithful then shall raise their voices in the congregations of the wicked, for all who receive the Holy Ghost become living witnesses of the truth and divinity of the Lord's person and work.

> *These things have I spoken unto you, that ye should not be offended. They shall put you out of the synagogues: yea, the time cometh, that whosoever killeth you will think that he doeth God service.*
>
> *And these things will they do unto you, because they have not known the Father, nor me. But these things have I told you, that when the time shall come, ye may remember that I told you of them. And these things I said not unto you at the beginning, because I was with you.*

Saul of Tarsus thought he did God's service when, assenting to the death of Stephen, he held the cloaks of those who hurled the stones. "Indeed, according to Jewish Law, 'a zealot' might have slain without formal trial those caught in flagrant rebellion against God—or in what might be regarded as such, and the Synagogue would have deemed the deed as meritorious as that of Phinehas." (Edersheim 2:524.)

And in this connection, well might it be said: "Sincerity has almost nothing to do with gaining salvation. Men who slay the saints can be just as sincere as those who thus become martyrs. Men can believe so devoutly in falsehood that they will even lay down their own lives for it. What does it matter that those who killed the prophets, either ancient or modern, thought they did God service? The thing that counts is truth, pure God-given truth." (*Commentary* 1:752.)

NOTES

1. The disciple whom Jesus loved, called by us John the Beloved, and who alone has

preserved for us Jesus' words about love as spoken on this Passover day, is also the author of these transcendentally beautiful words.

2. "The Discourse of Christ recorded in St. John 16, and His prayer [recorded in John 17], were certainly uttered *after* they had risen from the Supper, and *before* they crossed the brook Kidron [en route to Gethsemane]. In all probability they were, however, spoken before the Saviour left the house. We can scarcely imagine such a Discourse, and still less such a Prayer, to have been uttered while traversing the narrow streets of Jerusalem on the way to Kidron." (Edersheim 2:513. Italics added.)

3. James 2:8.

4. Similar divine affirmations have been made by the same Lord to his latter-day disciples. "As I said unto mine apostles, even so I say unto you, for you are mine apostles, even God's high priests; ye are they whom my Father hath given me; ye are my friends; . . . for from henceforth I shall call you friends." (D&C 84:63, 77.) Also: "Verily, I say unto my servant Joseph Smith, Jun., or in other words, I will call you friends, for you are my friends, and ye shall have an inheritance with me—I called you servants for the world's sake, and ye are their servants for my sake." (D&C 93:45-46.)

THE DISCOURSE ON THE HOLY GHOST

And the twelve did teach the multitude;
and behold, they did cause
that the multitude should kneel down
upon the face of the earth,
and should pray unto the Father
in the name of Jesus.
And the disciples did pray unto the Father
also in the name of Jesus. . . .
And they did pray
for that which they most desired;
and they desired that the Holy Ghost
should be given unto them.
And when they had thus prayed
they went down unto the water's edge,
and the multitude followed them.
And it came to pass that
Nephi went down into the water
and was baptized.
And he came up out of the water
and began to baptize. And he baptized
all those whom Jesus had chosen.
And it came to pass

when they were all baptized and had come up
out of the water,
the Holy Ghost did fall upon them,
and they were filled with the Holy Ghost
and with fire. (3 Ne. 19:6-13.)

"The Comforter Knoweth All Things"[1]

(John 16:5-15)

There is a certain fitness of things—or, better, a divine, controlling providence—about what lies ahead for Jesus. Our Blessed Lord has climbed one majestic peak after another; his mortal life is coming not simply to an end, but to an awesome climax of triumph and glory. His miracles, save only the crowning miracle of the atonement and the resurrection, are part of the tapestry of the past. His teachings have been shown forth upon one mountain crest after another. After such sermons as the one on the Second Comforter and on love, what is there left to say? There remains only—and this is the divine fitness of which we speak—the discourse on the Holy Ghost, a few remaining words about his coming death and resurrection, the great Intercessory Prayer with its assurance of eternal life for the faithful, and then Gethsemane, Calvary, an open tomb, a resurrected ministry, and the ascension on Olivet.

After all that he has said, through three and a half years of ministerial service, what can he now do better than to speak of the gift of the Holy Ghost and of the atonement which assures the saints that they may receive that divine and heavenly gift? Eternal life itself is the greatest of all the gifts of God, for it consists of receiving, inheriting, and possessing the same glorious exaltation enjoyed by the Father himself. It is to be like God, to be one with the Father and the Son. But eternal life is gained only in eternity.

The greatest gift known to and enjoyed by mortals is the gift of the Holy Ghost, which is the right to the constant companionship of that member of the Godhead based on righteousness. This gift, given by the laying on of hands, is enjoyed by those who love God with all their hearts. Into their lives flow revelations of eternal truth; they see the visions of eternity and entertain the angels of heaven; they are in tune with the Infinite, as were their kindred spirits of old who held apostolic offices and served in the majesty of their prophetic callings. The Holy Ghost is a revelator. And into their lives comes the sanctifying and cleansing power that perfects the lives of men, so they become fit friends and companions of Gods and angels. The Holy Ghost is a sanctifier. And so, what is more natural at this point—with all that has been said and all that has been done during the greatest ministry ever performed—what is more natural than to hear Jesus say:

> *But now I go my way to him that sent me; and none of you asketh me, Whither goest thou? But because I have said these things unto you, sorrow hath filled your heart.*

Their Lord and Friend is about to return to his Father. Sorrow fills their hearts; the prospects of his death and their separation from him are not pleasant. He chides them gently: " 'Instead of being sorrowful and silent because I said I am going to the Father, why don't you ask me more about it and learn the great gospel truths which are involved.' " (*Commentary* 1:753.)

> *Nevertheless I tell you the truth; It is expedient for you that I go away: for if I go not away, the Comforter will not come unto you; but if I depart, I will send him unto you.*

'Though I am the Son of God and have been with you this long time—teaching, admonishing, guiding, giving to you all that you have been able to receive—yet there is something even more wondrous which awaits you. I will send the Comforter. As long as I have been with you, this right to the constant companionship of the Holy Spirit of God has not been yours. My word has sufficed on all matters. Now I shall work out the atoning sacrifice—for which purpose I came into the world—and you shall receive, from the Holy Ghost, the cleansing power that will prepare your souls for celestial rest.'

And when he is come, he will reprove the world of sin, and of righteousness, and of judgment:

Of sin, because they believe not on me;

Of righteousness, because I go to my Father, and ye see me no more;

Of judgment, because the prince of this world is judged.

" 'When you receive the companionship of the Spirit, so that you speak forth what he reveals to you, then your teachings will convict the world of sin, and of righteousness, and of judgment. The world will be convicted of *sin* for rejecting me, for not believing your Spirit-inspired testimony that I am the Son of God through whom salvation comes. They will be convicted for rejecting your testimony of my *righteousness*—for supposing I am a blasphemer, a deceiver, and an imposter—when in fact I have gone to my Father, a thing I could not do unless my works were true and righteous altogether. They will be convicted of false *judgment* for rejecting your testimony against the religions of the day, and for choosing instead to follow Satan, the prince of this world, who himself, with all his religious philosophies, will be judged and found wanting.' " (*Commentary* 1:754.)

I have yet many things to say unto you, but ye cannot bear them now.

Howbeit when he, the Spirit of truth is come, he will guide you into all truth: for he shall not speak of himself; but whatsoever he shall hear, that he shall speak; and he will shew you things to come.

Though they had been with him during his whole ministry; though they had heard unnumbered sermons and seen more healing miracles than any mortals from the beginning; though they knew more than all the scribes and Pharisees combined, ten thousand times over—yet it was but the beginning. After the receipt of the gift of the Holy Ghost, then their days of learning would really begin.

"*He will guide you into all truth.*" First comes a testimony of the truth and divinity of the Lord's earthly work, of the fact that he gives to men the power to keep his commandments and gain eternal life; then the doctrines of salvation are revealed in plainness; then all things pertaining to God and man and the universe will be shown forth. Whence came God? How was creation possible? What of man, and all forms of life upon the earth, to say nothing of the sidereal heavens and the endless creations of the Endless One? How can we learn redemption's mystery? Or how the resurrection is brought to pass? Or how the great God in heaven speaks to his lowly creatures on earth by the power of his Spirit? The questions are endless; the answers are eternal; and the power of the Holy Ghost, which makes them manifest, is infinite.

As Jesus said a few moments before, the world cannot receive the Comforter; this blessed gift is reserved for the saints, and he will abide in the faithful forever. True it is that honest truth seekers come to know of the truth and divinity of the Lord's work by the power of the Holy Ghost: they receive a flash of revelation telling them that Jesus is the Lord, that Joseph Smith is his prophet, that the Book of Mormon is the mind and will and voice of the Lord, that The Church of Jesus Christ of Latter-day Saints is the only true and living Church upon the face of the whole earth. They gain a testimony before baptism. But it is only after they pledge their all in the cause of Christ that they receive the gift of the Holy Ghost, which is the heavenly endowment of which Jesus spoke. Then they receive a fulfillment of the promise: "By the power of the Holy Ghost ye may know the truth of all things." (Moro. 10:5.) Then they receive "the spirit of revelation," and the Lord tells them in their heart and in their mind whatsoever he will. (D&C 8:1-3.)[2]

"He shall not speak of himself." Rather, he is Christ's minister; his commission is to bear record of the Father and the Son; he is appointed to reveal the truths of eternity to receptive souls. Jesus is going away, and the Holy Ghost is coming to act in the place and stead of the Lord, to say what Jesus wants said, to say what Jesus would say if he were personally present. The Holy Ghost speaks what he has heard from the Father and the Son for he is one with them and knows all things. And thus it is that the Lord's mortal agents have this promise: "And as ye shall lift up your voices by the Comforter, ye shall speak and prophesy as seemeth me good; For, behold, the Comforter knoweth all things, and beareth record of the Father and the Son." (D&C 42:16-17.)

"He will shew you things to come." He is a revelator. That which is past, that which is present, that which is future—all are known to him. "God shall give unto you knowledge by his Holy Spirit, yea, by the unspeakable gift of the Holy Ghost"—is the voice of the Lord to his saints—knowledge "that has not been revealed since the world was until now." (D&C 121:26-32.)[3] To all those who serve him in righteousness and in truth, the Lord Jesus says:

> *To them will I reveal all mysteries, yea, all the hidden mysteries of my kingdom from days of old, and for ages to come, will I make known unto them the good pleasure of my will concerning all things pertaining to my kingdom.*
>
> *Yea, even the wonders of eternity shall they know, and things to come will I show them, even the things of many generations.*
>
> *And their wisdom shall be great, and their understanding reach to heaven; and before them the wisdom of the wise shall perish, and the understanding of the prudent shall come to naught.*

> *For by my Spirit will I enlighten them, and by my power will I make known unto them the secrets of my will—yea, even those things which eye has not seen, nor ear heard, nor yet entered into the heart of man.* (D&C 76:1-10.)

Knowing, as we do, that the New Testament accounts are wont to digest the words of Jesus and to set forth only selected gems from the rich treasure house of his sayings, we may not be far off in suggesting that these very words—those afore quoted—or their equivalent may have been spoken to the ancient Twelve. But back to John's account of what Jesus then said:

> *He shall glorify me: for he shall receive of mine, and shall shew it unto you.*

In the same sense in which the Father is glorified when his children gain eternal life, thus adding to his kingdoms and dominions, so it is with the Son. He is glorified because souls are saved, because his brethren enlist in his cause, because great numbers sit down with him and with his Father in the kingdom of God to go no more out. And the Holy Ghost receives from Christ that which will lead souls to salvation and gives it to men.

> *All things that the Father hath are mine: therefore said I, that he shall take of mine, and shall shew it unto you.*

It is the Father's kingdom, but he has given it to the Son, and therefore the Son, who is exalted with the Father, can give these things, by the power of the Spirit, to the disciples.[4]

Jesus Shall Die and Rise Again

(John 16:16-33; JST, John 16:23)

His discourse on the Holy Ghost being ended—and how grateful we are for that portion which has been preserved for us—Jesus then, somewhat enigmatically, said: "A little while, and ye shall not see me: and again, a little while, and ye shall see me, because I go to the Father.'' To us, in retrospect, the message is clear. He was about to leave them in death; they would not then see him in mortality. But he would rise from the grave, that he might return in glorious immortality to his Father; then, after the resurrection, they would see him again. To the disciples, however, the statement was not immediately clear. They said among themselves: ''What is this that he saith unto us, A little while, and ye shall not see me: and again, a little while, and ye shall see me: and, Because I go to the Father?'' They also said: ''What is this that he saith, A little while? we cannot tell what he saith.'' It is evident that Jesus gave them time to ponder and wonder so that when he revealed the full import of his saying, it would sink with greater force into their hearts.

Knowing they desired to ask him the meaning of his statement, Jesus said: ''Do ye inquire among yourselves of that I said, A little while, and ye shall not see me: and again, a little while, and ye shall see me?'' The teaching moment had arrived; their minds were ready to receive the message. Jesus said:

> *Verily, Verily, I say unto you, That ye shall weep and lament, but the world shall rejoice: and ye shall be sorrowful, but your sorrow shall be turned into joy.*
>
> *A woman when she is in travail hath sorrow, because her hour is come: but as soon as she is delivered of the child, she remembereth no more the anguish, for joy that a man is born into the world.*
>
> *And ye now therefore have sorrow: but I will see you again, and your heart shall rejoice, and your joy no man taketh from you.*

How better could he have stated it? For a brief moment he will go away to visit the spirits in prison. Because they live together in love, they shall weep at his death. But when he appears again—resurrected, glorified, perfected—their joy will be unbounded. Death is but the birth pang of life; as a man child is born through travail, so immortality is the child of death. Sorrow is for a moment; joy is eternal.

> *And in that day ye shall ask me nothing but it shall be done unto you. Verily, verily, I say unto you, Whatsoever ye shall ask the Father in my name, he will give it you.*
>
> *Hitherto have ye asked nothing in my name: ask, and ye shall receive, that your joy may be full.*

"*In my name.*" 'Let your prayers now be perfected. As long as I have been with you—teaching, guiding, leading—you have not received the gift of the Holy Ghost; my presence and words sufficed. As long as I have been with you, your petitions have come to me or you have prayed to the Father according to the traditions of your fathers. Now as I leave you, having worked out my own salvation by doing all that my Father sent me to do, now your prayers are always to be in my name. I am the Savior, the Redeemer; salvation comes by me. I am the Way, the Truth, and the Life; no man cometh unto the Father but by me. Ye shall always use my name in your prayers. Pray always to the Father, and to none other; pray always in my name, and in none other. My name is the only name given under heaven whereby salvation cometh. "Ye must pray always, and not faint; . . . ye must not perform any thing unto the Lord save in the first place ye shall pray unto the Father in the name of Christ, that he will consecrate thy performance unto thee, that thy performance may be for the welfare of thy soul." ' (2 Ne. 32:9.)

> *These things have I spoken unto you in proverbs: but the time cometh, when I shall no more speak unto you in proverbs, but I shall shew you plainly of the Father.*

Proverbs were used to hide the truth, or, at least, they limited the extent of the understanding of the disciples. However, after they received the companionship and enlightenment of the Holy Spirit of God, then—and then only—could they receive the mysteries of the kingdom in plainness. Then—and then only—could Jesus manifest to them the Father.

At that day ye shall ask in my name: and I say not unto you, that I will pray the Father for you: For the Father himself loveth you, because ye have loved me, and have believed that I came out from God.

Their prayers in Jesus' name are to begin after his resurrection. Then they will no longer need to rely upon him to pray to the Father for them. The Father loves them and they have direct access to him. Having the Holy Ghost, they then will be able to formulate their own Spirit-guided petitions; then they will feel secure in coming boldly "unto the throne of grace," that they "may obtain mercy, and find grace to help in time of need." (Heb. 4:16.)

I came forth from the Father, and am come into the world: again, I leave the world, and go to the Father.

To all this the disciples responded: "Lo, now speakest thou plainly, and speakest no proverb. Now are we sure that thou knowest all things, and needest not that any man should ask thee: by this we believe that thou camest forth from God." That is, their faith had been strengthened; they believed Jesus came from God, and they were willing to direct their petitions to the Father, as he directed. To their response, Jesus asked, "Do ye now believe?" It is as though he were saying: 'I am glad you believe, for there are hard times ahead for you.'

Behold, the hour cometh, yea, is now come, that ye shall be scattered, every man to his own, and shall leave me alone: and yet I am not alone, because the Father is with me.

Until, at Pentecost, they receive the gift of the Holy Ghost, they will remain weak and wayward and will be scattered before the persecutor's sword. After Pentecost, when the Holy Spirit will burn in their hearts like fire, they will be gathered again, never to depart from the truth, never to do aught save that which He commands them.

These things I have spoken unto you, that in me ye might have peace. In the world ye shall have tribulation: but be of good cheer; I have overcome the world.

Jesus' words bring peace; the preaching of the word to believing souls brings peace; the gospel is a message of peace, of peace on earth and good will to men. Peace is one of the gifts of the Spirit. No matter that there is tribulation in the world; no matter that there is persecution and sorrow and evil; the war cry of the saints is, "Be of good cheer," for Jesus has overcome the world. And because he overcame the world—overcame carnality and evil to the full—he is now ready to be offered. There remains, then, only the Intercessory Prayer, and then he and the disciples will depart for Gethsemane and the atoning ordeal.

NOTES

1. D&C 42:17.

2. "A person may profit by noticing the first intimation of the spirit of revelation; for instance, when you feel pure intelligence flowing into you, it may give you sudden strokes of ideas, so that by noticing it, you may find it fulfilled the same day or soon; that is, those things that were presented unto your minds by the Spirit of God, will come to pass; and thus by learning [to recognize] the Spirit of God and understanding it, you may grow into the principle of revelation, until you become perfect in Christ Jesus." (*Teachings*, p. 151.)

3. This passage names with particularity some of the marvels to be revealed in the dispensation of the fulness of times.

4. In this connection, the Lord Jesus has promised "all that my Father hath" to all of his brethren who keep the terms and conditions of the covenant of the Holy Priesthood. (D&C 84:33-44.)

THE INTERCESSORY PRAYER

Listen to him who is the advocate
with the Father,
who is pleading your cause before him—
Saying: Father, behold the sufferings and death
of him who did no sin,
in whom thou wast well pleased;
behold the blood of thy Son which was shed,
the blood of him whom thou gavest
that thyself might be glorified;
Wherefore, Father, spare these my brethren
that believe on my name,
that they may come unto me
and have everlasting life. (D&C 45:3-5.)

The Prayer for Eternal Life

(John 17:1-5)

If holy writ contains—and Jehovah be praised, it does!—a prayer that truly merits the designation "The Lord's Prayer," that divine litany of praise and communion is in the 17th chapter of the Gospel of the Beloved John. At least therein we have a digest of what Jesus then said to his Father, what he said as he was about to go to Gethsemane to pray again as the burdens of all the sins of all the ages fell upon him. We know that on other occasions—two, at least, of which we have knowledge—he offered greater prayers than the one preserved for us by John; and even on this occasion he may have uttered words too sacred and holy to be recorded for the spiritually untutored to read. What pleases us beyond any measure of expression is that we have what we have. If his sermons—filled with eternal truths—reached their peak in his pronouncements about the Comforter, who would lead the faithful into all truth, surely his recorded prayers attained the summit of summits when he interceded with the Father for the Twelve and for the faithful of all ages in the Intercessory Prayer.[1]

The only two prayers of which we are aware that were intended to be heard by mortal ears, and that were greater than the Intercessory Prayer, were given among the Nephites. When he prayed alone the night before the calling of the Twelve or in Gethsemane on the night of his agony, the prayers were his own, as they were, no doubt, on many occasions during his prayer-filled life. Of such prayers we cannot speak; no doubt they were like or greater than his expressions made in the presence of the Nephite multitude.

As to the Nephite prayers, the scripture saith: "He himself also knelt upon the earth; and behold he prayed unto the Father, and the things which he prayed cannot be written, and the multitude did bear record who heard him. And after this manner do they bear record: The eye hath never seen, neither hath the ear heard, before, so great and marvelous things as we saw and heard Jesus speak unto the Father; And no tongue can speak, neither can there be written by any man, neither can the hearts of men conceive so great and marvelous things as we both saw and heard Jesus speak; and no one can conceive of the joy which filled our souls at the time we heard him pray for us unto the Father. And it came to pass that when Jesus had made an end of praying unto the Father, he arose; but so great was the joy of the multitude that they were overcome." (3 Ne. 17:15-18.)

Also: "And it came to pass that he went again a little way off and prayed unto the Father; And tongue cannot speak the words which he prayed, neither can be written by man the words which he prayed. And the multitude did hear and do bear record; and their hearts were open and they did understand in their hearts the words which he prayed. Nevertheless, so great and marvelous were the words which he prayed that they cannot be written, neither can they be uttered by man. And it came to pass that when Jesus had made an end of praying he came again to the disciples, and said unto them: So great faith have I never seen among all the Jews; wherefore I could not show unto them so great miracles, because of their unbelief. Verily I say unto you, there are none of them that have seen so great things as ye have seen; neither have they heard so great things as ye have heard." (3 Ne. 19:31-36.)

But now, still in the home of John Mark, as we have supposed, Jesus "lifted up his eyes to heaven, and said":

> *Father, the hour is come; glorify thy Son, that thy Son also may glorify thee: As thou hast given him power over all flesh, that he should give eternal life to as many as thou hast given him.*

This was Jesus' appointed hour—the hour for which he came into the world; the hour when he would take upon himself the sins of the world. For this purpose was he born; for this purpose had he lived. And because he would accomplish the appointed purpose, he would soon rise in immortal glory—for which glory he now prayed. 'Glorify me, Father, and I will glorify thy name.' Jesus is asking for eternal life. Prayers should fit the needs of the hour; the petitions they contain should be expressive of present needs; but there are two things that may, with propriety, be included in all prayers and on all occasions. They are (1) that God will give us his Spirit here and now in this mortal sphere, and (2) that he will save us in his kingdom in the world to come. Salvation is eternal life, and—we repeat—Jesus now prays that he may have eternal life. He is God's Son, God's Almighty Son. His mortal probation is drawing to its close; he has done all things well, and with him the Father is well pleased. All this he knows, and yet his prayer, for himself, is: 'O Father, grant me eternal life with thee in thy kingdom.' Can there be a more perfect pattern in prayer than this?

Jesus has power over all flesh; all things are subject to him. He is the Creator and Redeemer; he judges all men. He is "the Lord Omnipotent who reigneth, who was, and is from all eternity to all eternity." (Mosiah 3:5.) He can give, in his Father's name, eternal life to all who believe and obey; he rewards all men. The Father has placed all things in his hands; salvation and eternal life come because of him. "There is no flesh that can dwell in the presence of God, save it be through the merits, and mercy, and grace of the Holy Messiah." (2 Ne. 2:8.) And since there is no greater gift than eternal life, no greater gift that can be gained by men or Gods, it is the very reward that he himself seeks. Of what does such a high reward consist that it is even the desire of the heart of a God? Jesus continues:

> *And this is life eternal, that they might know thee the only true God, and Jesus Christ, whom thou hast sent.*

Eternal life is God's life; it is the name of the kind of life he lives. The Father has eternal life for two reasons: (1) He has all power in heaven and on earth; he is omnipotent, omniscient, and, by the power of his Spirit, omnipresent; all things are subject to him; he possesses what, in summary, is called the fulness of the Father, or the fulness of the glory of the Father. (2) He lives in the family unit; he has eternal increase; he has a continuation of the seeds and of the lives forever and ever.

Eternal life thus comes only to those who know the Father and the Son, and who know them in the sense of doing and experiencing what it is their eternal lot to do and experience. In this sense, no one can know God without possessing the knowledge and exercising the power vested in Deity, without creating as he creates, without fathering spirit children as he fathers his eternal progeny, without doing all that he does. Since eternal life is the name of the kind of life God lives, no man can possess it unless and until he becomes like his Eternal Father and has the same eternal powers that are resident in the Eternal One. Of those so obtaining it is written: "Then shall they be gods, because they have no end; therefore shall they be from everlasting to everlasting, because they continue; then shall they be above all, because all things are subject unto them. Then shall they be gods, because they have all power, and the angels are subject unto them." (D&C 132:20.)[2]

> *I have glorified thee on the earth: I have finished the work which thou gavest me to do. And now, O Father, glorify thou me with thine own self with the glory which I had with thee before the world was.*

Speaking of things to come as though they already were, Jesus announces the completion of his work on earth and asks for a return of that glory which was his in preexistence. In his spirit state, he was the Firstborn of the Father, the Beloved and Chosen from the beginning, the Creator of all things, the Lord Jehovah, the God of Israel, the Lord God Almighty. Now that his mortal work is over he seeks—and is assured of—all that once was his. And is not this a pattern of what shall be with all of the noble and great? Will not Adam and Enoch and Abraham and all the rest return to receive that glory which was theirs before the world was? And will not they, as with Jesus after the resurrection, receive all power in heaven and on earth, which is eternal life?

The Prayer for the Apostles

(John 17:6-19; 3 Nephi 19:19-36)

Having laid the foundation by holding out the hope of eternal life to all who come unto him and his Father, Jesus now begins to plead the cause of the faithful ones who have been with him in the days of his ministry.

> *I have manifested thy name unto the men which thou gavest me out of the world: thine they were, and thou gavest them me; and they have kept thy word.*

What a tribute this is! The Twelve are Jesus' special friends! They marched under his banner before the world was; they were foreordained as he himself was; they were noble and great sons of the Father whom he gave to Christ to be his mortal companions. To them Jesus has manifest the Father's doctrine, and they have kept his word.

> *Now they have known that all things whatsoever thou hast given me are of thee. For I have given them the words which thou gavest me; and they have received them, and have known surely that I came out from thee, and they have believed that thou didst send me.*

These apostles—all of them—believed in Christ; they knew he came from the Father; they accepted the Father as the source of that pure religion which was theirs. It is neither fitting nor proper to belittle or demean them in any way; their mortal shortcomings, which they freely announced, existed because they had not yet received the Comforter. If ever there were spiritual giants among men, such were these friends of Jesus.

In the comparable prayer, given among the Nephites after the Nephite Twelve had received the Holy Ghost, Jesus said:

> *Father, I thank thee that thou hast given the Holy Ghost unto these whom I have chosen; and it is because of their belief in me that I have chosen them out of the world.*

Father, I pray thee that thou wilt give the Holy Ghost unto all them that shall believe in their words.

Father, thou hast given them the Holy Ghost because they believe in me; and thou seest that they believe in me because thou hearest them, and they pray unto me; and they pray unto me because I am with them.

The Nephite Twelve, the Jewish Twelve—all men—are blessed and favored on the same basis. The Gods of heaven are no respecters of persons, and the gifts of the Spirit are available for the faithful on all continents and in all worlds. Let us return to the Twelve in Jerusalem. Jesus continues his prayer:

I pray for them: I pray not for the world, but for them which thou hast given me; for they are thine. And all mine are thine, and thine are mine; and I am glorified in them.

Jesus pleads the cause of the Twelve—and all the saints—in the courts above. He is their Mediator, Advocate, and Intercessor. He makes intercession for them, because they have forsaken the world and come unto him; he advocates their cause, for their cause is his cause and they have received his gospel; he performs a divine service of mediation, reconciling fallen man to his Maker, because the fallen ones choose now to associate with those who are not of this world. Jesus prays, thus, not for the world, but for those who have kept his commandments; who have reconciled themselves to God through faith and repentance; who are preparing themselves for an abode with him and his Father. And his interceding petitions are always available for all men, if they will but believe his word and obey his law.[3]

And now I am no more in the world, but these are in the world, and I come to thee. Holy Father, keep through thine own name those whom thou hast given me, that they may be one, as we are.

Among the Nephite Hebrews—they having received

the gift of the Holy Ghost, which did not come to the Twelve in Jerusalem until Pentecost—among the Nephite Hebrews, Jesus' words of intercession and his prayer for unity were even more express.

> *Father, I thank thee that thou hast purified those whom I have chosen, because of their faith, and I pray for them, and also for them who shall believe on their words, that they may be purified in me, through faith on their words, even as they are purified in me.*
>
> *Father, I pray not for the world, but for those whom thou hast given me out of the world, because of their faith, that they may be purified in me, that I may be in them as thou, Father, art in me, that we may be one, that I may be glorified in them.*

Jesus here introduces into his Jewish prayer—and in this instance the prayer is also a sermon—the theme of unity; he speaks of the perfect oneness that should prevail among the saints and between them and those divine beings whose they are. We shall hear more on this shortly. For the moment we note only the great need for the Twelve to be one while they are yet in the world, where they are subject to all the tuggings and temptations that might drive a wedge among them, and between them and their Lord, who is departing to his Father. In the Nephite account the Twelve, having received the Holy Ghost, are already purified, and Jesus' petitions are that all who believe may attain a like purity of person and become, like the Twelve, one with him and his Father. With reference to the Jewish Twelve he continues:

> *While I was with them in the world, I kept them in thy name: those that thou gavest me I have kept, and none of them is lost, but the son of perdition; that the scripture might be fulfilled.*

Jesus' ministry where the Twelve are concerned has succeeded. He has cared for the spiritual well-being of the souls entrusted to him. Only Judas has been lost; and even he, though a son or follower of Satan, who is perdition, as we have heretofore seen, is probably not a son of perdition in the sense of eternal damnation. Judas, of course, is not with them as these words are spoken. He departed from the upper room some time ago that he might conspire with the chief priests and bargain for the life of his Lord.

> *And now come I to thee; and these things I speak in the world, that they might have my joy fulfilled in themselves.*

Jesus' words—spoken to the Father, heard by the Twelve—are designed to give them the joy he himself possesses. Those who are "sanctified from all sin," as the scripture saith, "enjoy the words of eternal life in this world, and eternal life in the world to come, even immortal glory." (Moses 6:59.)

> *I have given them thy word; and the world hath hated them, because they are not of the world, even as I am not of the world.*

Why does the world hate and persecute the saints? With what insight Jesus goes to the heart of the matter! Sinners hate righteous people because they are righteous. Sinners love sinners and hate the obedient. Misery loves company. Lucifer was cast out of heaven and became "miserable forever"; accordingly, he now seeks to make "all mankind" miserable like unto himself. (2 Ne. 2:18.) So also do all those who are of the world; they follow their exemplar, who is the prince of this world, and seek to pull all men down to their low and carnal state.

> *I pray not that thou shouldst take them out of the world, but that thou shouldst keep them from the evil. They are not of the world, even as I am not of the world.*

Jesus and his disciples are in the world, but are not of the world. They live in the midst of carnality and evil, but do not partake of the ever-present wickedness. Such is the divine purpose and intent: this life is a probationary estate, and all men must be subject to the lusts and enticements of the flesh; if they shun that which is evil and cleave unto that which is good, they thereby overcome the world and gain salvation.

> *Sanctify them through thy truth: thy word is truth.*
>
> *As thou hast sent me into the world, even so have I also sent them into the world. And for their sakes I sanctify myself, that they also might be sanctified through the truth.*

To be sanctified is to be cleansed from all sin; it is to stand pure and spotless before the Lord; it is to overcome the world and be a fit candidate for a celestial inheritance. The "sanctified" are "them of the celestial world." (D&C 88:2.) The Holy Ghost is a sanctifier. His baptism of fire burns dross and evil out of repentant souls as though by fire. Sanctification comes only to the obedient; it is the truth of heaven—the very word of God, his everlasting gospel—which sanctifies the souls of men. As the Father sent Jesus to proclaim his gospel, so Jesus sent the Twelve to proclaim the same word of truth; and as Jesus sanctified himself by obedience to the words of the Father, so the Twelve may sanctify themselves through the truth Jesus has given them.

The Prayer for the Saints

(John 17:20-26)

Deity, in his infinite wisdom, presents the truths of salvation to his children on earth in the most graphic and plain manner they are able to bear. One of his standard approaches is to hold up his prophets and apostles as examples before their fellows, and then to say to other men: 'Go and be thou as these are.' He has the practice of rewarding the noble and great for their spiritual achievements, and then of saying: 'All men can achieve as these favored ones have done.' "Take, my brethren, the prophets, who have spoken in the name of the Lord," James says, "for an example of suffering affliction, and of patience." They are your patterns. "Ye have heard of the patience of Job, and have seen the end of the Lord; that the Lord is very pitiful, and of tender mercy." (James 5:10-11.) And nowhere is this divine practice of selecting certain patterns, and inviting all men to be as they are, set forth in a better way than in the Intercessory Prayer. Jesus has extolled and honored the Twelve. He has spoken of their mission and sanctification; now he is going to extend out to every faithful person all that he has given or promised the Twelve.

> *Neither pray I for these alone, but for them also which shall believe on me through their word; That they all may be one; as thou, Father, art in me, and I in thee, that they also may be one in us: that the world may believe that thou hast sent me.*

Such were Jesus' words in Jerusalem. In the land Bountiful, among a kindred people, for whom another Twelve had been ordained, he said:

> *And now Father, I pray unto thee for them, and also for all those who shall believe on their words, that they may believe in me, that I may be in them as thou, Father, art in me, that we may be one.* (3 Ne. 19:23.)

Jesus prays for all the saints; he is their Intercessor, Mediator, and Advocate, as well as he is for the Twelve. And all who believe are to be one—one in belief, one in godly attributes, one in good works, one in righteousness. He is as his Father, and he and the Father are one; the Twelve are as he is, and he and the Twelve are one; all the saints are as the Twelve, and they are all one. And Jesus dwells in the Father, because they are one; the Twelve dwell in Jesus, because they are one; and all the saints dwell in the Twelve, because the same perfect unity prevails in their hearts. "The Lord our God is one Lord" (Deut. 6:4), and his command to all his disciples is: "Be one; and if ye are not one ye are not mine" (D&C 38:27).

And the glory which thou gavest me I have given them; that they may be one, even as we are one: I in them, and thou in me, that they may be made perfect in one; and that the world may know that thou hast sent me, and hast loved them, as thou hast loved me.

God gave his glory to the Son; Jesus gave that same glory to the Twelve; and the Twelve, in turn, make the same eternal fulness, the same glory, the same eternal life, available to all the saints. All of the Lord's people may thus become one with the Gods of heaven. To Adam the Lord said: "Behold, thou art one in me, a son of God; and thus may all become my sons." (Moses 6:68.) And as with Adam—for he is but the pattern and the type—all who live the perfect law of unity "become the sons of God, even one in me as I am one in the Father, as the Father is one in me, that we may be one." (D&C 35:2.) The unity and oneness of the saints is one of the great evidences of the truth and divinity of the Lord's work on earth.

Father, I will that they also, whom thou hast given me, be with me where I am; that they may behold my glory, which thou hast given me: for thou lovedst me before the foundation of the world.

The intercessory pleadings continue: 'Father, wilt thou give these my brethren eternal life; may they reign in everlasting glory with me in my kingdom, for they are as I am, and I am as thou art. Thou lovedst me and them before the foundation of the world, and as it was in the beginning so shall it be everlastingly.'

O righteous Father, the world hath not known thee: but I have known thee, and these have known that thou hast sent me. And I have declared unto them thy name, and will declare it: that the love wherewith thou hast loved me may be in them, and I in them.

Again Jesus bears witness that the Twelve know he was sent by his Father; they know he is the Son of God. Jesus has taught them of the Father, and the Father loveth them as he loves his own Son, for they are in the Son and he is in them. And as with the Twelve, so with all the saints, of whom the scripture saith: "Know ye not your own selves, how that Jesus Christ is in you, except ye be reprobates?" (2 Cor. 13:5.)

And so ends the Intercessory Prayer, or in other words these are the last words of the prayer preserved for us by the Beloved John. And so Jesus and the Twelve leave the Holy City to find a hallowed spot in the Garden of Sorrow and Anguish where the miracle of the atonement will take place.

NOTES

1. The Intercessory Prayer is also called the High-Priestly Prayer because, as commentators have chosen to conclude, it was offered by Jesus in his capacity as the Great High Priest, whatever that may be deemed to mean. Of this prayer, Farrar summarized: "He lifted up His eyes to heaven, and uttered His great High-Priestly prayer; first, that His Father would invest His voluntary humanity with the eternal glory of which He had emptied Himself when He took the form of a servant; next, that He would keep through His own name these His loved ones who had walked with Him in the world; and then that He would sanctify and make perfect not these alone, but all the myriads, all the long generations, which should hereafter believe through their word." (Farrar, p. 617.)

2. Two other passages have a significant bearing on the matters here considered. "If you keep my commandments and endure to the end you shall have eternal life, which gift is the greatest of all the gifts of God." (D&C 14:7.) And: "This is eternal lives—to know the only wise and true God, and Jesus Christ, whom he hath sent." (D&C 132:24.)

3. Any concept that others than Jesus can mediate between man and his Maker is not of God. Paul says: "There is one God, and one mediator between God and men, the man Christ Jesus." (1 Tim. 2:5.) And the Nephite Jacob testifies: "He shall make intercession for all the children of men; and they that believe in him shall be saved. And because of the intercession for all, all men come unto God; wherefore, they stand in the presence of him to be judged of him according to the truth and holiness which is in him." (2 Ne. 2:9-10.)

IN GETHSEMANE

I command you to repent—
repent, lest I smite you by the rod
of my mouth, and by my wrath,
and by my anger,
and your sufferings be sore—
how sore you know not,
how exquisite you know not,
yea, how hard to bear you know not.
For behold, I, God, have suffered these things
for all, that they might not suffer
if they would repent;
But if they would not repent
they must suffer even as I;
Which suffering caused myself, even God,
the greatest of all, to tremble
because of pain, and to bleed
at every pore, and to suffer
both body and spirit—
and would that I might not drink
the bitter cup, and shrink—
Nevertheless, glory be to the Father,
and I partook and finished my preparations
unto the children of men.
(D&C 19:15-19.)

The Trial of Peter's Faith

(Luke 22:31-38; JST, Luke 22:21-36; John 13:36-38; Matthew 26:31-35; Mark 14:27-31; JST, Mark 14:33)

As nearly as we can determine from the sacred accounts, while Jesus and his friends were yet in the upper room, finishing their Paschal ceremonies and partaking of the sacrament of the Lord's Supper, some conversations began about the tests that lay ahead for all of them, and of the allegiance they would manifest to their Lord. The colloquy then commenced was interrupted by the discourse on the two comforters, by that on the law of love, and then by that on the Holy Ghost, and also by the offering of the Intercessory Prayer. Then as the holy party left the city, crossed the wadi called Kidron, and came near the Mount of Olives, the same theme was picked up again.

Through it all it is evident that the tests now facing his apostolic associates were of deep concern to Jesus, and that he desired to encourage and strengthen them so they would come off triumphant. It was not his purpose to stay the tempter's power nor to shelter his chosen ones from the onslaught of evil. They must overcome the world even as he had done, if they were to be with him and partake of his glory. He would, however, do all in his power to strengthen their faith that they might be victorious in the warfare with Satan. How true it is that the Lord "scourgeth every son whom he receiveth." (Heb. 12: 6.) Let the lash fall; let their flesh be cut; let their faith be tested—but let them bear up under it all.

If Abraham must be willing to offer Isaac, if Isaac and Jacob and all the holy prophets must lay their all on the altar, not even withholding their lives in many cases—then those who would dwell everlastingly with faithful Abraham, those who would sit down in the kingdom of God with Abraham, Isaac, and Jacob, and all the holy prophets, must also pass the same tests of faith and devotion as did their faithful forebears. And next to the agonies about to engulf Jesus himself, the greatest tests ahead were for Peter. What they were we are not told, nor does it matter, for every man's tests—in the wisdom of Him who ordained all things well—are those which are suited to him and him alone. But we do know that in principle the higher one of the Lord's servants stands in the hierarchy of righteousness, the more severe are the tests to which his faith will be subjected. Jesus is about to carry the greatest burdens ever placed upon a mortal soul. Shall the Twelve, who stand next to him—with Peter at their head—escape their share of the tests and burdens ahead?

And so, Jesus, while they were yet in the upper room, said to Peter: "Simon, Simon, behold, Satan hath desired you, that he may sift the children of the kingdom as wheat." Satan sought the soul of Simon. Every lost soul adds to the revelry and rebellion in the lower realms. Satan seeks to harvest all the souls of men, to sift the saints as wheat is harvested on the threshing floor, so that both the wheat and the tares may be garnered into his granary. And oh, if he can only topple Peter from his high place; if only the chief apostle can be destroyed spiritually; if only the defenders of Zion can be destroyed—how much easier it will be to harvest the then unprotected fields.

"But I have prayed for you," Jesus says to Peter, "that your faith fail not; and when you are converted strengthen your brethren." Peter has a testimony; he knows that Jesus is the Christ, the Son of the living God; he has preached and baptized other believing souls; he has wrought many mighty miracles in the name of Christ; he has been valiant, true, and obedient. But he is not as yet converted. He has not yet become a new creature by the power of the Holy Ghost; he has not as yet put off the natural man, and put on Christ, and become "as a child, submissive, meek, humble, patient, full of love, willing to submit to all things which the Lord seeth fit to inflict upon him, even as a child doth submit to his father." (Mosiah 3:19.) All this can be his only after Pentecost; only after the descent of the Holy Spirit; only after he receives the gift of the Holy Ghost.

But Peter, "being aggrieved" at Jesus' words to him, said: "Lord, I am ready to go with you, both into prison, and unto death." 'Surely I am converted and will stand by thee in all things, though it cost me my life.' Jesus replied: "I tell you, Peter, that the cock shall not crow this day, before that you will thrice deny that you know me."

Then, by way of reassurance, to remind them all that a Divine Providence would preserve them in the tests ahead, Jesus asked: "When I sent you without purse and scrip, or shoes, lacked ye any thing?" Their answer: "Nothing." Jesus continued: "I say unto you again, He who hath a purse, let him take it, and likewise his scrip; and he who hath no sword, let him sell his garment and buy one." In the troublesome times ahead, when the hands of all men would be against them, they would need to provide their own food, clothing, and shelter, and for their own protection.[1]

Whatever lay ahead for the disciples, however—whether they were to be preserved by Divine Providence or by means of their own wise planning and defense, as the varying situations might require—they must not overlook the great reality that their Lord was about to leave them in death. They must not take his passing upon the cross as a sign of defeat. Lest they do so, he reminds them of the Messianic prophecies which speak of his death, and, indeed, he quotes one of them. "For I say unto you," Jesus continues, "This that is written must yet be accomplished in me, And he was reckoned among the transgressors; for the things concerning me have an end." The reference, of course, is to Isaiah's Messianic pronouncement that he should "pour out his soul unto death" and in that hour be "numbered with the transgressors." (Isa. 53:12.) To this the disciples respond, "Lord, behold, here are two swords," falsely assuming that he is asking for a means of defense for himself, rather than telling them they may defend themselves in the treacherous days ahead. Their offer is waved aside by the Lord: "It is enough," he says, meaning, 'Enough of this kind of talk; it is not my purpose to be defended by the arm of flesh.'

For the continuation of this theme—and how heavily it must have weighed on the mind of Jesus—we go now with him and the Twelve toward the Mount of Olives. In "that night" when "the fierce wind of hell was allowed to sweep unbroken over the Saviour, and even to expend its fury upon those that stood behind in His Shelter" (Edersheim 2:535), we hear him say to his friends, "All ye shall be offended because of me this night: for it is written, I will smite the shepherd, and the sheep of the flock shall be scattered." "What a dreadful thing it is to call for a sword against God; and yet it is part of the plan. Jesus is to die; the Shepherd is to be slain; the sheep are to be scattered." (*Commentary* 1:769.) Did not Jehovah by the mouth of Zechariah foretell what was to be in this dark hour? "Awake, O sword, against my shepherd, and against the man that is my fellow, saith the Lord of hosts," is the prophetic word; and "smite the shepherd, and the sheep shall be scattered: and I will turn mine hand upon the little ones." (Zech. 13:7.) But through it all—and this they must never forget—the Lord Jesus, risen in glorious immortality, shall go before them into Galilee; there they will meet again and their joy will be full.

Once again Peter, still brooding over what he esteems to be his total devotion to his Lord, says: "Though all men shall be offended because of thee, yet will I never be offended." Again the prophetic word falls from the lips of the Chief Prophet: "Verily I say unto thee, That this day, even in this night, before the cock crow twice, thou shalt deny me thrice." And still Peter persists: "Though I should die with thee, yet will I not deny thee." And Matthew adds: "Likewise also said all the disciples," for all, in one degree or another, were also being tested.

Jesus Prays and Suffers in Gethsemane

(Matthew 26:36-46; JST, Matthew 26:43; Mark 14:32-42;

JST, Mark 14:36-38, 40, 42-43, 47; Luke 22:40-46; JST, Luke 22:45; John 18:1-2)

Outside Jerusalem's walls, across the wadi Kidron, part-way up the slopes of Olivet, in (as we suppose) a secluded vale, was the Garden of the Oil Press—the Garden of Gethsemane. Thither "Jesus ofttimes resorted . . . with his disciples." Surely the site, known to Judas, was the possession of some worthy believer who rejoiced that the Lord often chose his spot of earth as a place to pray and ponder and teach and rest. Though often dry, the wadi, with its precipitous sides, was in April the host of a surging stream. The gentle slopes of Olivet were familiar land to the little party of spiritual giants who were now pondering the truths they had been taught and sorrowing over the separation of which they had been told.

Mark says: "They came to a place which was named Gethsemane, which was a garden; and the disciples began to be sore amazed, and to be very heavy, and to complain in their hearts, wondering if this be the Messiah." Though they all knew, as Jesus himself attested in the private sermons and prayer just delivered, that he was the Son of God, yet he did not fit the popular pattern for the Jewish Messiah, and the disciples, of course, had not yet received the gift of the Holy Ghost, which means they did not have the constant companionship of that member of the Godhead. "And Jesus knowing their thoughts, said to his disciples"—that is, to eight of them—"Sit you here, while I shall pray." Also: "Pray that ye enter not into temptation."

Then he took Peter, James, and John with him on into the Garden. As they went he "rebuked them"—apparently for the doubt that arose in their hearts that he was the Messiah—and said: "My soul is exceeding sorrowful, even unto death; tarry ye here and watch." Then he withdrew from them "about a stone's cast, and kneeled down, and prayed." The statement that he "kneeled" is Luke's; Mark says he "fell on the ground [that is, prostrated himself], and prayed." Matthew says he "fell on his face." No doubt he did all of these things, over a long period and in the course of repeated prayers.

We cannot recount with surety the order in which each thing happened, nor reconstruct with certainty the sequence of Jesus' spoken words, this night in this garden—in this "other Eden, in which the Second Adam, the Lord from heaven, bore the penalty of the first, and in obeying gained life." (Edersheim 2:534.) What has been preserved for us is only a sliver from a great tree, only a few sentences of what was said, only a brief glimpse of what transpired. It would appear that Jesus and the disciples spent some hours there in Gethsemane; that one (or many!) angels were present; and that Jesus poured out his soul in agony as he interceded for the faithful and felt the weight of the world's sins upon his own sinless soul. There is no mystery to compare with the mystery of redemption, not even the mystery of creation. Finite minds can no more comprehend how and in what manner Jesus performed his redeeming labors than they can comprehend how matter came into being, or how Gods began to be. Perhaps the very reason Peter, James, and John slept was to enable a divine providence to withhold from their ears, and seal up from their eyes, those things which only Gods can comprehend. We do know, however, that these words were included in Jesus' prayer:

> *O my Father, if it be possible, let this cup pass from me: nevertheless not as I will, but as thou wilt.* (Matthew.)
>
> *Abba, Father, all things are possible unto thee; take away this cup from me; nevertheless, not my will, but thine be done.* (Mark.)
>
> *Father, if thou be willing, remove this cup from me: nevertheless not my will, but thine, be done.* (Luke.)

Then, as nearly as we can determine, and as Luke records: "There appeared an angel unto him from heaven, strengthening him." The angelic ministrant is not named. We know that on the Mount of Transfiguration "Moses and Elias . . . appeared in glory, and spake of his decease which he should accomplish at Jerusalem" (Luke 9:30-31); and if we might indulge in speculation, we would suggest that the angel who came into this second Eden was the same person who dwelt in the first Eden. At least Adam, who is Michael, the archangel—the head of the whole heavenly hierarchy of angelic ministrants—seems the logical one to give aid and comfort to his Lord on such a solemn occasion. Adam fell, and Christ redeemed men from the fall; theirs was a joint enterprise, both parts of which were essential for the salvation of the Father's children.

But back to Luke. "And being in an agony he prayed more earnestly: and his sweat was as it were great drops of blood falling down to the ground." The Son of God who did all things well—whose every thought and act and deed was perfect; whose every prayer pierced the firmament and ascended to his Father—the Son of God himself (note it well) "prayed more earnestly." Even he reached a pinnacle of perfection in prayer that had not always been his. And as to the blood that oozed from his pores, we cannot do better than recall the words of the angelic ministrant, spoken to the Nephite Hebrew, Benjamin: "And lo, he shall suffer temptations, and pain of body, . . . even more than man can suffer, except it be unto death; for behold, blood cometh from every pore, so great shall be his anguish for the wickedness and the abominations of his people." (Mosiah 3:7.)

"And when he rose up from prayer," Luke continues, "and was come to his disciples"—meaning Peter, James, and John—"he found them sleeping; for they were filled with sorrow; And he said unto them, Why sleep ye? rise and pray, lest ye enter into temptation." This same occurrence as recorded by Mark happened this way: "Simon, sleepest thou? Couldest not thou watch one hour? Watch ye and pray, lest ye enter into temptation." At this point, they—the three of them—answered: "The spirit truly is ready, but the flesh is weak."

Jesus then left the chosen three and prayed again: "O my Father, if this cup may not pass away from me, except I drink it, thy will be done." Returning, Jesus found them sleeping again, which presupposes he had been away some time and had offered many petitions to his Father. This time they knew not how to answer him. Jesus went away and prayed the third time, "saying the same words." Returning this last time, he said, "Sleep on now, and take your rest." Then, as Mark has it, "After they had finished their sleep, he said, Rise up, let us go; lo, he who betrayeth me is at hand."

Thus ends such accounts as we have of Jesus' suffering in Gethsemane. It is now over and he has won the victory; the atonement, in large measure, has been worked out, and he is now ready for the shame and humiliation and pain of the cross. Then will come the resurrection and the crown.

As he went into Gethsemane, it was with a total awareness of what lay ahead. "Jesus knew that the awful hour of His deepest humiliation had arrived—that from this moment till the utterance of that great cry with which He expired, nothing remained for Him on earth but the torture of physical pain and the poignancy of mental anguish. All that the human frame can tolerate of suffering was to be heaped upon His shrinking body; every misery that cruel and crushing insult can inflict was to weigh heavy on His soul; and in this torment of body and agony of soul even the high and radiant serenity of His divine spirit was to suffer a short but terrible eclipse. Pain in its acutest sting, shame in its most overwhelming brutality, all the burden of the sin and mystery of man's existence in its apostasy and fall—this was what He must now face in all its most inexplicable accumulation." (Farrar, pp. 622–23.)

There is no language known to mortals that can tell what agony and suffering was his while in the Garden. Of it Farrar says: "A grief beyond utterance, a struggle beyond endurance, a horror of great darkness, a giddiness and stupefaction of soul overmastered Him, as with the sinking swoon of an anticipated death. . . . How dreadful was that paroxysm of prayer and suffering through which He passed." (Farrar, p. 624.)

And as to the prayer in the Garden—repeating, as it did, his divine promise made in the councils of eternity when he was chosen for the labors and sufferings of this very hour; the divine prayer in which he said, "Father, thy will be done, and the glory be thine forever" (Moses 4:2)—as to the prayer in the Garden, "That prayer in all its infinite reverence and awe was heard; that strong crying and those tears were not rejected. We may not intrude too closely into this scene. It is shrouded in a halo and a mystery into which no footstep may penetrate. We, as we contemplate it, are like those disciples—our senses are confused, our perceptions are not clear. We can but enter into their amazement and sore distress. Half waking, half oppressed with an irresistible weight of troubled slumber, they only felt that they were dim witnesses of an unutterable agony, far deeper than anything which they could fathom, as it far transcended all that, even in our purest moments, we can pretend to understand. The place seems haunted by presences of good and evil, struggling in mighty but silent contest for the eternal victory. They see Him, before whom the demons had fled in howling terror, lying on His face upon the ground. They hear that voice wailing in murmurs of broken agony, which had commanded the wind and the sea, and they obeyed Him. The great drops of anguish which fall from Him in the deathful struggle, look to them like heavy gouts of blood." (Farrar, p. 624.) And so they were.

And as he came out of the Garden, delivering himself voluntarily into the hands of wicked men, the victory had been won. There remained yet the shame and the pain of his arrest, his trials, and his cross. But all these were overshadowed by the agonies and sufferings in Gethsemane. It was on the cross that he "suffered death in the flesh," even as many have suffered agonizing deaths, but it was in Gethsemane that "he suffered the pain of all men, that all men might repent and come unto him." (D&C 18:11.)

The first Adam brought death, both temporal and spiritual, into the world and was cast out of the first Eden. The second Adam (Paul says he is the Lord from heaven) brought life—spiritual life, eternal life—into the world when he bore the sins of all men on that awesome night in a second Eden. Let God be praised that Adam fell; let Gods and angels rejoice that the Messiah came in the meridian of time to ransom men from the effects of the fall! In part the ransom was paid on a cross—having particular reference to the immortality that passes upon all men because Jesus rose from the dead. But primarily the ransom was paid in a garden—for there eternal life was won for the obedient—in the Garden of the Oil Press, where Judas now stands, strengthened by the arm of flesh, ready to betray the Atoning One.

The Betrayal and the Arrest

(Matthew 26:47-56; JST, Matthew 26:47-48; Mark 14:43-52; JST, Mark 14:52-53, 56-57; Luke 22:47-53; John 18:3-12)

That which Jesus himself had foretold—"how . . . he must go unto Jerusalem, and suffer many things of the elders and chief priests and scribes, and be killed, and be raised again the third day" (Matt. 16:21)—is now coming to pass. Every detail is taking place; every jot and tittle is being fulfilled; the cruel deeds of a cruel week are unfolding—all with a power and vengeance that no human hand can stay; all with a hatred and malignity that should have made even the demons of the deep shudder in their hellish home. The agonies of Gethsemane have seen the blood of a God fall in oozing drops from every pore to hallow forever that sacred spot, where, among the olive trees, apart even from his intimate friends, he took upon himself that weight which none other could bear. His blood, the choicest blood on earth, the atoning blood of God's Son, is now dried on the rocks and mingled with the soil of the Garden where the greatest miracle of the ages has been wrought.

Even now Judas—"mine own familiar friend, in whom I trusted, which did eat of my bread, hath lifted up his heel against me" (Ps. 41:9), as the Psalmist described him—has arrived to plant the traitor's kiss and supervise the arrest. Judas, into whom Satan has entered, is the one to whom the world—the Gentile world, of which Rome is the symbol, and the ecclesiastical world, of which the Jewish hierarchy are the leaders—Judas is the one upon whom the god of this world now depends to bring to pass his nefarious purposes.

Judas, standing in Satan's stead, is at the head of a motley band composed of the servants of the chief priests and many elders and Pharisees, of the temple guards with their officers, and of a contingent of Roman soldiers from the tower of Antonia, under the command of a tribune. They are armed with swords and staves—with swords to slay their opponents, if need be; with staves to quiet any tumult or disperse any bellicose rabble. They are carrying lanterns and torches, lest he whom they seek slip away from their iron grasp into the darkness of the night. Probably there are six hundred armed men in the arresting force, for this is no small thing they are undertaking; at last their Galilean enemy, who subverts their religion and rebels against their traditions, is to be done away with. A great multitude of the curious and of those whose sympathies are with the arresting cohort also dog the steps of the fierce Romans and the vengeful Jews sent to arrest the Son of Man. That such an army—at Passover time, when the watchful eye of Rome kept her soldiers on alert to quell disturbances—could not have moved without the prior approval of the Roman procurator, one Pontius Pilate, is perfectly clear. Indeed, a prior authorization of the arrest by Pilate accounts for his subsequent readiness to participate in the events of this dread night.

Having conspired beforehand with the chief priests and Pharisees—"Whomsoever I shall kiss, that same is he: hold him fast," was his promise—Judas must first have led the evil band to the house in Jerusalem where the holy party celebrated the Feast of the Passover. Finding them gone, and, as we suppose, rousing John Mark in the process, Judas then led those under his command to Gethsemane which he knew was the place to which they commonly resorted. Finding Jesus and the Eleven, Judas called out "Hail master"—'Hail Rabbi'—and kissed him; or, better, as the Greek text conveys, "not only kissed but covered Him with kisses, kissed Him repeatedly, loudly, effusively." (Edersheim 2:543.) There must be no mistake made as to the identity of Jesus; the promised sign must be clear and certain. It was the custom to greet friends and guests with a kiss; Jesus himself had condemned his host, Simon the Pharisee, by saying, "Thou gavest me no kiss." (Luke 7:45.) There must be absolute certainty in the kiss of betrayal, and so Judas showered Jesus with kisses, which but makes the traitorous act all the more repulsive. Jesus then said: "Judas, betrayest thou the Son of man with a kiss?" And then: 'Friend'—for so Judas is identified in the Messianic prophecy—'do that for which thou art come.'

Judas had made the identification. But the armed cohort—whose daily business it was to quell riots, subdue disturbers of the peace, and arrest malefactors—stood in awe. The Presence was more than they were ready to face. Jesus stepped forward, voluntarily and without hesitation, and asked: "Whom seek ye?" They answered, "Jesus of Nazareth," to which Jesus rejoined, "I am he." At this the arresting soldiers, who many times before had arrested criminals and faced armed foes without fear, "went backward, and fell to the ground." No more could Jesus be arrested without his consent than could his life be taken unless he willed it. Even though all the armies of all the nations of men had come to take him—no matter—he was master of all things. But as he would soon choose to die, so now he chose to be arrested. Again he asked the powers of this world: "Whom seek ye?" and again they answered, "Jesus of Nazareth." Then Jesus said: "I have told you that I am he: if therefore ye seek me, let these go their way."

This "last remark had reference to the apostles, who were in danger of arrest; and in this evidence of Christ's solicitude for their personal safety, John saw a fulfilment of the Lord's then recent utterance in prayer, 'Of them which thou gavest me have I lost none.' It is possible that had any of the Eleven been apprehended with Jesus and made to share the cruel abuse and torturing humiliation of the next few hours, their faith might have failed them, relatively immature and untried as it then was; even as in succeeding years many who took upon themselves the name of Christ yielded to persecution and went into apostasy." (Talmage, pp. 615-16.)

"Then came they, and laid hands on Jesus, and took him." He consented to the arrest; he permitted himself to be taken; the Son of God was then bound as a common criminal by men. "The Great Prophet had voluntarily resigned Himself; He was their helpless captive. No thunder had rolled; no angel flashed down from heaven for His deliverance; no miraculous fire devoured amongst them. They saw before them nothing but a weary unarmed man, whom one of His own most intimate followers had betrayed, and whose arrest was simply watched in helpless agony by a few terrified Galileans." (Farrar, p. 634.)

Seeing this turn of events, the disciples asked: "Lord, shall we smite with the sword?" Not waiting for an answer, Peter drew his sword and slashed off the right ear of Malchus, the servant of the high priest.

Then, turning to Peter, Jesus said: "Put up thy sword into the sheath: the cup which my Father hath given me, shall I not drink it?" And also: "He who taketh the sword shall perish with the sword." And yet further: "Thinkest thou that I cannot now pray to my Father, and he shall presently give me more than twelve legions of angels? But how then shall the scriptures be fulfilled, that thus it must be?" Eleven weak mortals—as mortals—were as nothing before this assembled army; and he who could command twelve legions of angels, and more, would make no move to stay the course he must pursue to fulfill all of the Messianic prophecies about his death and resurrection. Having so spoken—and shall we not say he was planning another evidence of his own divinity, of which the high priest shall soon hear?—Jesus asked for the sufferance of the arresting soldiers, while "he put forth his finger and healed the servant of the high priest."

Then Jesus, bound securely and subject to them, spoke to "the chief priests, and captains of the temple, and the elders"—that is, to the leaders of the Jews, through whose evil machinations he had been taken—and asked: "Are ye come out, as against a thief, with swords and with staves to take me? I was daily with you in the temple teaching, and ye took me not: but the scriptures must be fulfilled." And as Luke adds, he also said: "But this is your hour"—your hour of trial and evil—when for the moment "the power of darkness" shall seem to prevail.

"And the disciples, when they heard this saying, all forsook him and fled," thus fulfilling his word that the sheep should be scattered. That their danger was real is seen from the fact that there was then present "a certain young man, a disciple, having a linen cloth cast about his naked body," whom the soldiers attempted to arrest. But he—and we assume he was John Mark—"left the linen cloth and fled from them naked, and saved himself out of their hands."

NOTE

1. "When faced with persecution, do the Lord's ministers turn the other cheek or raise the sword in their own defense? Do they go forth supplying their own needs or do they rely for their daily wants upon the generosity of those among whom they minister? Who but God can answer such questions, for the answers depend on a full knowledge both of present conditions and of the future. Jesus counseled one course at one time and the opposite at another. There is, thus, no sure guide for the Lord's people except present day revelation." (*Commentary* 1:771.)

SECTION XII

THE TRIALS,
THE CROSS,
AND THE TOMB

Section XII

THE TRIALS, THE CROSS, AND THE TOMB

Let him be crucified. . . .
Let him be crucified.
(Matt. 27:22-23.)
Crucify him. . . . Crucify him.
(Mark 15:13-14.)
Crucify him, crucify him.
(Luke 23:21.)
Away with him, away with him,
crucify him. (John 19:15.)
Jesus of Nazareth,
a man approved of God among you
by miracles and wonders and signs,
which God did by him
in the midst of you, . . .
Him, being delivered by
the determinate counsel and foreknowledge
of God, ye have taken,
and by wicked hands
have crucified and slain.
(Acts 2:22-23.)

From Gethsemane they take Him to evil Annas—an adulterous Jew; a one-time high priest; the father-in-law of Caiaphas—and there He is examined and smitten. This is their hour—the hour of darkness.

In all Israel there is not a more wicked or influential man than Annas, who commits himself to see that Jesus is put to death.

They take him before Caiaphas and the Sanhedrin. They plot a judicial murder, seek false witnesses, find him guilty of blasphemy, and say: "He is worthy of death."

He is maltreated by the guards as they await the morning trial. Peter, before the cock crows twice, thrice denies that he knows him.

Then he is hailed before the Sanhedrin in formal session, where he testifies that he is the Son of God, and "the whole council condemned him" and sent him bound to Pilate.

Pilate, whose hands reek with blood, yet seeks to free him. Jesus testifies that he is a king, but that his kingdom is not of this world.

As a Galilean he is sent to Herod to be examined and derided. There he remains silent.

Before Pilate again he is charged with sedition and treason. Pilate seeks to release him, but the people demand Bar-Abbas instead and shriek, "Crucify him, crucify him."

He is scourged, mocked, derided, and sentenced to be crucified.

Iscariot commits suicide.

Jesus carries his cross for a ways, and then Simon of Cyrene is impressed into service.

They crucify their King.

Pilate places a superscription over his head in Latin, and in Greek, and in Aramaic, reading: "JESUS OF NAZARETH, THE KING OF THE JEWS."

The soldiers cast lots for his garments. The Sanhedrists incite mockery and derision against him.

He ministers from the cross, promising the penitent thief, "This day shalt thou be with me in paradise," and committing the care of the Blessed Virgin to the Beloved Disciple.

He hangs on the cross for six hours, during the last three of which darkness covers the land, and he suffers again the pains of Gethsemane. The atonement is complete. His work is finished. He voluntarily lays down his life.

A Roman spear pierces his side, but no bone of his body is broken.

Pilate permits Joseph of Arimathea to have the body, and he and Nicodemus prepare it for burial. They place it in the Arimathean's tomb.

Jesus meanwhile enters paradise, preaches to the righteous dead there assembled, organizes the work, and declares liberty to the captives and the opening of the prison doors to them that are bound.

Chapter 103

THE JEWISH PRE-TRIALS

There is save one Messiah
spoken of by the prophets,
and that Messiah is he who should be rejected
of the Jews. (2 Ne. 25:18.)
The Jews at Jerusalem sought to kill Jesus,
according to his word. (4 Ne. 1:31.)
Believe in Jesus Christ,
that he is the Son of God,
and that he was slain by the Jews.
(Morm. 7:5.)

Jesus Is Examined and Smitten before Annas

(John 18:12-14, 19-23)

"This is your hour," saith the Lord Jesus, the hour of "the power of darkness"! And if it was true in Gethsemane, how much more does the message tingle in every ear with reference to the unjudicial court procedures of the night and the day that followed.

From Gethsemane—a sacred place, hallowed by the blood of Jesus, sweat in agonizing drops from every pore—to the palace of Annas—an evil, wicked, adulterous Jew—Jesus was taken, bound and subservient, by the Roman soldiers and the temple guards. The alien power and the Jewish rulers were placing the Judge of all the earth into the custody of wicked men to be judged by an evil and apostate court system.

The account of the false and blasphemous travesty that swept him from Annas to Caiaphas to Pilate to Herod and back to Pilate is preserved for us by all four of the Evangelists. Each Gospel recitation is fragmentary; each supplements the others; and from them all we gain such a vision of the sad happenings of that doleful night and day as a divine providence has seen fit to preserve for us. That there are gaps and discrepancies in the account, which cause reputable scholars to disagree on the details of the trials, is of no moment. There is no divine *ipse dixit,* no voice from an archangel, and as yet no revealed latter-day account of all that transpired when God's own Son suffered himself to be judged by men so that he could voluntarily give up his life upon the cross. Needless to say, however, the overall picture that we shall paint—allowing for divergence of views as to details—is true, eternally true. Jesus was judged of men that the scriptures might be fulfilled, that the atonement might be completed, that immortality might pass upon all men, and that the saints of the Most High might be inheritors of eternal life in the Everlasting Presence.[1] We shall draw freely upon the words and phrases of some of Christianity's ablest apologists as we recite what happened, and—what is equally important—seek to *feel* the ignominy and the victory interlaced with the balance of the life of Him of whom we testify.

Jesus was subjected to three Jewish trials. The first, before Annas, though unofficial in the strict sense, was the one that assured the ultimate Roman-imposed penalty of death. It was the crowning act of conspiratorial evil; the authoritative prejudging of him who, according to their law, should have been presumed to be innocent. It was the practical trial; the one before the *de facto* high priest; before the recognized source of Jewish power; before the one who wielded the real power of the Jewish people.

The second trial, before Caiaphas, though involved primarily with preliminary questioning, was the occasion when the real or formal determination was made that the Guiltless One, the Sinless One, was worthy of death. And the third trial, before the Sanhedrin, constituted a ratification of the illegal procedures before Annas and Caiaphas; in it the formal decision was pronounced; strictly speaking it was the only real and legal trial, though, as we shall see, it too violated almost every basic and established rule, order, and law set down for Sanhedrinic operation.

As to the trial before Annas, a brief comment about him and his influence in the Jewish social structure will show why the cunning conspirators would choose first to take Jesus before his bar. Under his guidance Caiaphas and the whole Sanhedrin would nod, almost as a reflex action, a firm approval of the plot that would only succeed when Jesus' body lay in the grave.

Who was Annas, as he is called by the Evangelists? He was the best known, one of the wealthiest, and certainly the most influential Jew of his day; and if wickedness be measured by evil opposition to the truth and by a desire to shed innocent blood, he ranks with Judas among the abominable of the earth. He was Hanan, the son of Seth, the Ananus of Josephus. He had been the actual high priest for some seven years, and since being deposed by the Procurator Valerius Gratus, he had been the power behind the priestly throne. In his degenerate day, when the high priests were appointed and deposed by Gentile overlords; when the office was more of a political than a religious one; when, in spite of the general moral decay, the office did require "a certain amount of external dignity and self-denial which some men would only tolerate for a time" (Farrar, p. 639)—under these circumstances, to appoint and control a high priest was greater and more to be desired than to be one.

"The Jewish historian calls this Hanan the happiest man of his time, because he died at an advanced old age, and because both he and five of his sons in succession—not to mention his son-in-law [and a grandson]—had enjoyed the shadow of the High Priesthood; so that, in fact, for nearly half a century he had practically wielded the sacerdotal power. But to be admired by such a renegade as Josephus is a questionable advantage. In spite of his prosperity Hanan seems to have left behind him but an evil name, and we know enough of his character, even from the most unsuspected sources, to recognize in him nothing better than an astute, tyrannous, worldly Sadducee, unvenerable for all his seventy years, full of a serpentine malice and meanness which utterly belied the meaning of his name [Clement or merciful], and engaged at this very moment in a dark, disorderly conspiracy, for which even a worse man would have had cause to blush. It was before this alien and intriguing hierarch that there began, at midnight, the first stage of that long and terrible inquisition. . . .

"*If there were one man who was more guilty than any other of the death of Jesus, that man was Hanan.* His advanced age, his preponderant dignity, his worldly position and influence, as one who stood on the best terms with the Herods and the Procurators, gave an exceptional weight to his prerogative decision. . . . If we may believe not a few of the indications of the Talmud, that Sanhedrin was little better than a close, irreligious, unpatriotic confederacy of monopolizing and time-serving priests—the Boethusim, the Kamhits, the Phabis, the family of Hanan, mostly of non-Palestinian origin—who were supported by the government, but detested by the people, and of whom this bad conspirator was the very life and soul." (Farrar, pp. 639–41. Italics added.)[2]

We can see on every hand reasons why the scribes and Pharisees would seek the death of Jesus. From the beginning of his ministry, day in and day out, in one setting after another, it had been his unvarying practice to deride and defame their cherished Mosaic traditions and to hurl bolts of divine wrath upon them for their ignorance and selfish self-exultation. We can scarcely count the times he has called them hypocrites, liars, adulterers, a generation of vipers, a people fit only for the burning fires of Gehenna. In much of this anathema the Sadducees took secret delight, for they too ignored the strict formalities of the law, and could not have been other than gratified to see both their scribal and their Pharisaic foes repeatedly routed by this rustic Galilean and his Rabbinically unschooled friends.

But why the Sadducean rage against him? Why did Judas and the temple guards make sure Jesus was delivered into Sadducean hands to be tried by a Sadducean Sanhedrin? Why would anyone who felt the pulse of the people know that Annas would lead out in opposition to Jesus?

We cannot doubt that the underlying reason for the rebellion of all sects, parties, and groups—the Sadducees included—was religious. Though as sects they fought among themselves, their one common point of agreement was opposition to Jesus. But there was something more. To the Sadducees, Jesus was an economic threat. Their crafts were in danger. He was destroying the thriving business enterprises that poured the wealth of the world into their rapacious pockets. We cannot escape the conclusion that "the rage of these priests was mainly [or, at least, in large measure] due to our Lord's words and acts concerning that House of God which they regarded as their exclusive domain, and, above all, to His second public cleansing of the Temple. . . . The first cleansing might have been passed over as an isolated act of zeal, to which little importance need be attached, while the teaching of Jesus was mainly confined to despised and far-off Galilee; but the second had been more public, and more vehement, and had apparently kindled a more general indignation against the gross abuse which called it forth. Accordingly, in all three Evangelists we find that those who complained of the act are not distinctively Pharisees, but 'Chief Priests and Scribes,' who seem at once to have derived from it a fresh stimulus to seek His destruction.

"But, again, it may be asked, Is there any reason beyond this bold infraction of their authority, this indignant repudiation of an arrangement which *they* had sanctioned, which would have stirred up the rage of these priestly families? Yes—for we may assume from the Talmud that it tended *to wound their avarice, to interfere with their illicit and greedy gains*. Avarice—the besetting sin of Judas—the besetting sin of the Jewish race—seems also to have been the besetting sin of the family of Hanan. It was they who had founded the *chanujoth*—the famous four shops under the twin cedars of Olivet—in which were sold things legally pure, and which they had manipulated with such commercial cunning as artificially to raise the price of doves to a gold coin apiece, until the people were delivered from this gross imposition by the indignant interference of a grandson of Hillel. There is every reason to believe that the shops which had intruded even under the Temple porticoes were not only sanctioned by their authority, but even managed for their profit. To interfere with these was to rob them of one important source of that wealth and worldly comfort to which they attached such extravagant importance. There was good reason why Hanan, the head representative of 'the viper brood,' as a Talmudic writer calls them, should strain to the utmost his cruel prerogative of power to crush a Prophet whose actions tended to make him and his powerful family at once wholly contemptible and comparatively poor." (Farrar, pp. 641–42.)

Thus Jesus is hailed before a gold-bloated usurper, who exercises the power of an office he does not hold, and who has already determined what judgment should be rendered. Jesus had been arrested at night and on the testimony of an accomplice, both of which acts were illegal under Jewish law. Now he is before Annas—who is sitting as a sole judge, and it is still night, both of which conditions make the hearing itself illegal. Though he has been arrested, there is as yet no charge lodged against him. Annas, therefore, questions him about two things: his disciples and his doctrine. Perhaps some charge of sedition can be lodged against his followers; perhaps there is some doctrinal statement that can be construed as false or blasphemous. As far as the record goes, Jesus ignored the attempt to involve his followers; he, not they, was to suffer and die at this time; their day of martyrdom lay ahead. As to the doctrinal inquisition, he said: "I spake openly to the world; I ever taught in the synagogue, and in the temple, whither the Jews always resort; and in secret have I said nothing. Why askest thou me? ask them which heard me, what I have said unto them: behold, they know what I said." Such a reply by the Prisoner was proper; he was entitled to be confronted by his accusers; there was nothing for him to confess; if they wanted to try him, let them present their case. "Even the minions of Annas felt the false position of their master under this calm rebuke; they felt that before the transparent innocence of this youthful Rabbi of Nazareth the hypocrisy of the hoary Sadducee was abashed. 'Answerest thou the High Priest so?' said one of them with a burst of illegal insolence; and then, unreproved by this priestly violator of justice, he profaned with the first infamous blow the sacred face of Christ. Then first that face which, as the poet-preacher says, 'the angels stare upon with wonder as infants at a bright sunbeam,' was smitten by a contemptible slave." (Farrar, p. 643.) Jesus answered simply: "If I have spoken evil, bear witness of the evil: but if well, why smitest thou me?"[3]

Jesus before Caiaphas and the Council

(Matthew 26:57-66; JST, Matthew 26:59-61, 67; Mark 14:53-64; JST, Mark 14:65; Luke 22:54; John 18:24)

Joseph Caiaphas, the legal high priest—the son-in-law of that evil and avaricious Annas, and himself also of like nature and disposition—was the next Jewish ruler to hurl his anathematizing curse upon the Son of God. He was, John says, "the high priest that same year," which we cannot do other than accept as an ironical slur against the apostate system under which the life-long office of high priest was passed around among the family of Annas, as though they were designating which steward should care for their interests for the year.

"Now Caiaphas was he"—as John is also careful to mention at this point—"which gave counsel to the Jews, that it was expedient that one man should die for the people." (John 18:14.) As we are aware, this counsel of Caiaphas was a prophetic utterance. God had used him as he used Baalam's ass to proclaim a message to his people, and that message did not carry the meaning and intent that was in the evil heart of the wicked man whose tongue was then guided in what he said. With reference to Jesus' work and miracles, other members of the Supreme Council had then said: "If we let him thus alone, all men will believe on him: and the Romans shall come and take away both our place and nation." Intending to concur with this view and seeking to incite bitterness against Jesus, Caiaphas had then said: "Ye know nothing at all, Nor consider that it is expedient for us, that one man should die for the people, and that the whole nation perish not." Thus he "had been the first to enunciate in plain words what seemed to him *the political necessity for the judicial murder of Christ*. There had been no pretense on his part of religious motives or zeal for God; he had cynically put it in a way to override the scruples of those old Sanhedrists by raising their fears. What was the use of discussing about forms of Law or about that Man? it must in any case be done; even the friends of Jesus in the Council, as well as the punctilious observers of [the] Law, *must regard His Death as the less of two evils*. He spoke as the bold, unscrupulous, determined man that he was; Sadducee in heart rather than by conviction: a worthy son-in-law of Annas." (Edersheim 2:546. Italics added.) But a divine power decreed otherwise, and his words—John says "he prophesied"—became an announcement that Jesus would die as the Deliverer of the Jews, "And not for that nation only, but that also he should gather together in one the children of God that were scattered abroad." (John 11:49-52.) That, like Baalam's ass, Caiaphas knew no more after the divine word fell from his lips than he did before is evident from the course he is now pursuing. He is still bent on finding a way to bring death to Him by whom life comes.

Having failed to elicit any incriminating evidence against Jesus, Annas "sent him"—not "had sent," as a poor biblical translation has it, but "sent him bound unto Caiaphas the high priest."[4] And it stretches the bounds of credulity to suppose that Annas himself remained aloof from the continuing inquisition; certain it is that he went with the guards and their prisoner, that he might add his influence and prestige and be a personal witness of the hoped-for triumph over his enemy. The leading elders, scribes, and chief priests—alerted as they were that Jesus would be arrested that night—were already assembled; and Peter and John, having overcome the first flush of panic that swept over them in Gethsemane, were also present as sorrowing observers.

There, in the palace of Caiaphas, then "took place the second private and irregular stage of the trial. There—for though the poor Apostles could not watch for one hour in sympathetic prayer, these nefarious plotters could watch all night in their deadly malice—a few of the most desperate enemies of Jesus among the Priests and Sadducees were met." (Farrar, pp. 643–44.) At least twenty-three members of the Great Sanhedrin were present, the number required for a quorum, for both Matthew and Mark call the meeting one of the council which is the Sanhedrin.

They had before them a prisoner charged with no crime. Innocent of all crimes, as he was, even these conspiring Satanists had not been able to come up with an offense for which he could be arraigned. Annas had failed in his attempt to charge the disciples with sedition and Jesus with teaching false and apostate doctrines. Their dilemma was real, for they themselves were sharply divided on all major issues save one—that the man Jesus must die. "If they dwelt on any supposed opposition to civil authority, *that* would rather enlist the sympathies of the Pharisees in His favour; if they dwelt on supposed Sabbath violations or the neglect of traditional observances, that would accord with the views of the Sadducees. The Sadducees dared not complain of His cleansing of the Temple: the Pharisees, or those who represented them, found it useless to advert to His denunciations of tradition. But Jesus, infinitely nobler than His own noblest Apostle, would not foment these latent animosities, or evoke for His own deliverance a contest of these slumbering prejudices. He did not disturb the temporary compromise which united them in a common hatred against Himself." (Farrar, pp. 645–46.)

Since a charge must be lodged to justify Jesus' arrest, since they themselves were not sufficiently united to bring up any of their old doctrinal objections, and since the charge must be one that the Romans would consider to be a capital offense, "the chief priests, and elders, and all the council" (after counseling with Satan whose servants they were) chose the most evil of all possible courses. They "sought false witness"!

Read it again, for it is forever inscribed in the records of eternity—they sought not witnesses, but *false witnesses*. Let none come forward but those who will perjure their souls; who will condemn the Holy One and the Just; who will cry, 'Away with him. Crucify him, crucify him.' No voice must be raised in his defense; no lie must be refuted; no falsehood shall be denied. This is God's Son (oh, the shame of it all!) and the leaders of his own people—acting for their constituents; reflecting the feelings that smoldered like the fires of hell in the breasts of all recalcitrant Jewry of the time—these leaders "sought false witness against Jesus, to put him to death." He must not live; let him die the death, and whatever perjured word is needed to nail him to a Roman cross, so be it!

Nor was it difficult to find those to whom Jehovah's word spoken to Moses the man of God, amid the fires and thunders of Sinai—"Thou shalt not bear false witness against thy neighbour" (Ex. 20:16)—was as alien gibberish. Search was made only among the rabble who followed the arresting party, who followed in the hopes of seeing one whom they hated suffer an ignominious death. And "though many false witnesses came," Matthew says, "they found none that could accuse him." None could devise a charge that would stand up before the Roman law. "For many bare false witness against him," as Mark records it, "but their witness agreed not together." "Though the agents of these priests were eager to lie, yet their testimony was *so* false, so shadowy, so self-contradictory, that it all melted to nothing, and even those unjust and bitter judges could not with any decency accept it." (Farrar, p. 646.)

Finally, "there arose certain"—meaning, apparently, that there arose some from among their own number; from among the priests themselves; from among those who were present when Jesus first cleansed the temple—"there arose certain" to "bear false witness against him" that would cause Roman ears to listen. It will be remembered that on the occasion of the first Passover, Jesus drove from the temple the moneychangers and those who sold oxen and sheep and doves; that he thus made a shamble of the bazaars of the sons of Annas; and that when asked for a sign as to his authority for so doing, he told them that if they would destroy the temple of his body, he would raise it up again in three days. There was to be no sign given to that wicked and adulterous generation except the sign of the prophet Jonas, the sign of his resurrection. Now, three years later, his words are to be twisted and perverted by false witnesses. We suppose Annas and Caiaphas, who suffered financially on the first purgation of Jehovah's house, were the ones who now saw the possibility of using what Jesus then said as a basis for a criminal charge against him.

The perjured words of the false priests included such statements as, "We heard him say, I will destroy this temple that is made with hands, and within three days I will build another made without hands." That there were other perversions of his word is clear from Mark's conclusion, "But neither so did their witness agree together." This charge that Jesus would first destroy and then rebuild, in three days, the most magnificent building of their age; that stone for stone he would put back together, in three days, what had been under construction for forty-six years, and was far from finished; that in a moment of time, as it were, he would bring into being what thousands of workers had spent scores of years to build—this fantastic claim (which he had never made) would indicate to the Romans that he was a dangerous seducer of the people with magical pretensions. He thus would be one who would rally the people around him in a revolt that would destroy the peace of the land. And, be it remembered, "The purpose of the High-Priest was not to formulate a capital charge in *Jewish* Law, since the assembled Sanhedrists had no intention so to try Jesus, but to formulate a charge which would tell before the Roman Procurator. And here none other could be so effective as that of being a fanatical seducer of the ignorant populace, who might lead them on to wild tumultuous acts." (Edersheim 2:559.)

Through all this "Jesus listened in silence while His disunited enemies hopelessly confuted each other's testimony. . . . But that majestic silence troubled, thwarted, confounded, maddened them. It weighed them down for the moment with an incubus of intolerable self-condemnation. They felt, before that silence, as if *they* were the culprits, He the judge. And as every poisoned arrow of their carefully-provided perjuries fell harmless at His feet, as though blunted on the diamond shield of His white innocence, they began to fear lest, after all, their thirst for His blood would go unslaked, and their whole plot fail. Were they thus to be conquered by the feebleness of their own weapons, without His stirring a finger, or uttering a word? Was this Prophet of Nazareth to prevail against *them,* merely for lack of a few consistent lies? Was His life charmed even against calumny confirmed by oaths? It was intolerable.

"Then Caiaphas was overcome with a paroxysm of fear and anger. Starting up from his judgment-seat, and striding into the midst—with what a voice, with what an attitude we may well imagine!"—he would set this court proceeding on its proper course. Their own false witnesses—carefully selected, screened, and coached, that their every word would be dipped in the poison of death—their own appointed perjurers, though they skirted the truth and gave a devilish twist to what Jesus had said—they, nonetheless, could arouse no response from Him who had spoken only the truth; the lips of innocence were closed against their calumnies. But Caiaphas himself would hurl the question: "Answerest thou nothing?" How can a man be silent when, knowing his life is at stake, he hears others lie about him? "Knowest thou what these witness against thee?" 'Their false words will cost thee thy life, and yet thou sayest nothing.' "Had not Jesus been aware that these His judges were wilfully feeding on ashes and seeking lies, He might have answered; but now His awful silence remained unbroken.

"Then, reduced to utter despair and fury, this false High Priest—with marvellous inconsistency, with disgraceful illegality—still standing as it were with a threatening attitude over his prisoner, exclaimed, 'I adjure Thee by the living God to tell us'—what? whether Thou art a malefactor? whether Thou *hast* secretly taught sedition? whether Thou hast openly uttered blasphemy?—no, but (and surely the question showed the dread misgiving which lay under all their deadly conspiracy against Him)—'WHETHER THOU

ART THE CHRIST, THE SON OF GOD?' " (Farrar, pp. 646–47.)

How intense was the hatred of that hour! How many unseen demons must have laughed in the background as the legal high priest in Israel, speaking in Jehovah's name, adjured Jehovah himself to proclaim his own divine Sonship! No doubt the prince of devils himself was there; what is more natural than to expect the master of all evil to come face to face with Him that is the embodiment of all that is good? "Tell us whether thou be the Christ, the Son of God!" Suppose, just suppose he was, what then of Caiaphas, and the Sanhedrin, and the Jewish nation? Would they be buffeted and scattered and scourged and hated of all men until the times of restitution?

"Strange question to a bound, defenceless, condemned criminal; and strange question from such a questioner—a High Priest of His people! Strange question from the judge who was hounding on his false witnesses against the prisoner! Yet so adjured, and to such a question, Jesus could not be silent; on such a point He could not leave Himself open to misinterpretation. In the days of His happier ministry, when they would have taken Him by force to make Him a King—in the days when to claim the Messiahship in *their* sense would have been to meet all their passionate prejudices half way, and to place himself upon the topmost pinnacle of their adoring homage—in *those* days He had kept His title of Messiah utterly in the background: but now, at this awful decisive moment, when death was near—when, humanly speaking, nothing could be gained, everything *must* be lost, by the avowal—there thrilled through all the ages—thrilled through that Eternity, which is the synchronism of all the future, and all the present, and all the past—the solemn answer, 'I AM: *and ye shall see the Son of Man sitting on the right hand of power, and coming in the clouds of heaven.*' " (Farrar, pp. 647–48.)

'Art thou the Messiah? Art thou the Son of God?' 'I AM; I AM THAT I AM: I am the Eternal One; I am the Lord Jehovah; I am Jesus Christ the Son of the living God; I am the Son of that Holy Man who is your Father in heaven. Ye shall reject me now and do with me as ye will; but I shall come again, in all the glory of my Father's kingdom. Then shall ye see me sitting on the right hand of power, and coming in the clouds of heaven; then shall ye know that I am he of whom Moses and all the prophets spake. I am the Christ. I am the Son of God.'

"In that answer the thunder rolled—a thunder louder than at Sinai, though the ears of the cynic and the Sadducee heard it not then, nor hear it now. In overacted and ill-omened horror, the unjust judge who had thus supplemented the failure of the perjuries which he had vainly sought—the false High Priest rending his linen robes before the True [High Priest]—demanded of the assembly His instant condemnation.

" 'BLASPHEMY!' he exclaimed; 'what further need have we of witnesses? See, *now* ye *heard* his blasphemy! What is your decision?' And with the confused tumultuous cry, 'He is *ish maveth,*' 'A man of death,' 'Guilty of death,' the dark conclave was broken up, and the second stage of the trial of Jesus was over." (Farrar, p. 648.)

"He is guilty of death." Thus saith the Sanhedrin.

"And they all condemned him to be guilty of death." Thus saith the Sanhedrin.

We do not say this was a sentence of death, for the Sanhedrin had no such power in that day. Rather, it was their heartfelt, devil-inspired pronouncement: 'He is *worthy* of death; he *ought* to die, according to our law, for he is a blasphemer.' "And yet is it not after all true—that He was either the Christ, the Son of God, or a blasphemer? This Man, alone so calm and majestic among those impassioned false judges and false witnesses; majestic in His silence, majestic in His speech; unmoved by threats to speak, undaunted by threats when He spoke; Who saw it all—the end from the beginning; the Judge among His judges, the Witness before His witnesses: which was He—the Christ or a blaspheming imposter? Let history decide; let the heart and conscience of mankind give answer. If He had been what Israel said, He deserved the death of the Cross; if He is what the Christmas-bells of the Church, and the chimes of the Resurrection-morning ring out, then do we rightly worship Him as the Son of the Living God, the Christ, the Saviour of men." (Edersheim 2:561–62.)

Yea, and let more than history record; let more than the heart and conscience of mankind speak out—for though history turn into myth and legend, and though the conscience of mankind be seared with a hot iron, yet He remains true and faithful. Let the answer then come from the lips of those to whom he has revealed himself anew in the latter days. We are they, and we say: He is God's Son, the true Messiah; he spake no blasphemy; and all who would live and reign with him and his Father must believe the witness he bore of himself. He is the Son of God.

NOTES

1. Along this line Farrar testifies: "After repeated study, I declare, quite fearlessly, that though the slight variations are numerous—though the lesser particulars cannot in every instance be rigidly and minutely accurate—though no one of the narratives taken singly would give us an adequate impression—yet, so far from their being, in this part of the Gospel story, any irreconcilable contradiction, we can see how one Evangelist supplements the details furnished by another, and can understand the true sequence of the incidents by combining into one whole the separate indications which they furnish. It is easy to call such combinations arbitrary and baseless; but they are only arbitrary in so far as we cannot always be absolutely *certain* that the succession of facts was exactly such as we suppose; and so far are they from being baseless, that, to the careful reader of the Gospels, they carry with them a conviction little short of certainty. If we treat the Gospels as we should treat any other authentic documents recording all that the authors know, or all that they felt themselves commissioned to record, of the crowded incidents in one terrible and tumultuous day and night, we shall, with care and study, see how all that they tell us falls accurately into its proper position in the general narrative, and shows us a sixfold trial, a quadruple derision, a triple acquittal, a twice-repeated condemnation of Christ our Lord." (Farrar, p. 637.)

2. "No figure is better known in contemporary Jewish history than that of Annas; no person deemed more fortunate or successful, but none also more generally execrated than the late High-Priest. He had held the Pontificate for only six or seven years; but it was filled by not fewer than five of his sons, by his son-in-law Caiaphas, and by a grandson. And in those days it was, at least for one of Annas' disposition, much better to have been than to be the High-Priest. He enjoyed all the dignity of the office, and all of its influence also, since he was able to promote to it those most closely connected with him. And, while they acted publicly, he really directed affairs, without either the responsibility or the restraints which the office imposed. His influence with the Romans he owed to the religious views which he professed, to his open partisanship of the foreigner, and to his

enormous wealth. The Sadducean Annas was an eminently safe Churchman, not troubled with any special convictions nor with Jewish fanaticism, a pleasant and a useful man also, who was able to furnish his friends in the Praetorium with large sums of money. We have seen what immense revenues the family of Annas must have derived from the Temple-booths, and how nefarious and unpopular was the traffic. The names of those bold, licentious, unscrupulous, degenerate sons of Aaron were spoken with whispered curses. Without referring to Christ's interference with that Temple-traffic, which, if His authority had prevailed, would, of course, have been fatal to it, we can understand how antithetic in every respect a Messiah, and such a Messiah as Jesus, must have been to Annas. He was as resolutely bent on His death as his son-in-law, though with his characteristic cunning and coolness, not in the hasty, bluff manner of Caiaphas. It was probably from a desire that Annas might have the conduct of the business, or from the active, leading part which Annas took in the matter, . . . [and] that it was desirable to dismiss the Roman soldiery as quickly as possible—that Christ was first brought to Annas, and not to the actual High-Priest." (Edersheim 2:547.)

3. Our King James Version says the officer struck Jesus "with the palm of his hand." The Revised Version says "with a rod." Edersheim comments and speculates: "We are almost thankful that the text leaves it in doubt, whether it was with the palm of the hand, or the lesser indignity—with a rod. Humanity itself seems to reel and stagger under this blow. In pursuance of His Human submission, the Divine Sufferer, without murmuring or complaining, or without asserting His Divine Power, only answered in such tone of patient expostulation as must have convicted the man of his wrong, or at least have left him speechless. May it have been that these words and the look of Christ had gone to his heart, and that the now strangely-silenced malefactor became the confessing narrator of this scene to the Apostle John?" (Edersheim 2:550.)

4. This change in a verb tense in John 18:24 is one of the reasons we know there was a separate examination before Annas, the high priest in fact, before Jesus was taken to Caiaphas, the titular high priest.

THE FORMAL JEWISH TRIAL

I gave my back to the smiters,
and my cheeks to them
that plucked off the hair:
I hid not my face from shame and spitting.
(Isa. 50:6.)
It pleased the Lord to bruise him;
he hath put him to grief.
(Isa. 53:10.)

They Maltreat Jesus

(Matthew 26:67-68; Mark 14:65; Luke 22:63-65)

Annas and Caiaphas had done their work well. As the high priests in Israel—one the real, the other the titular high priest—they had guided the Sadducean-dominated Sanhedrin, representative of the hosts of the people, to find Jesus guilty of blasphemy because he said he was the Son of God. And the garments of Caiaphas had been rent in everlasting witness that the blasphemer before them was worthy of death. They had spoken; the council had spoken; and through them, as the representative leaders of all Jewry, the whole nation had spoken; the collective judgment of the Jews (though yet to be formally ratified) had nonetheless been given. "And this was how the Jews at last received their promised Messiah—longed for with passionate hopes during two thousand years; since then regretted in bitter agony for well-nigh two thousand more! From this moment He was regarded by all the apparitors of the Jewish Court as a heretic, liable to death by stoning; and was only remanded into custody to be kept till break of day, because by daylight only, and in the *Lishcat Haggazzith,* or Hall of Judgment, and only by a full session of the entire Sanhedrin, could He be legally condemned. And since now they looked upon Him as a fit person to be insulted with impunity, He was haled through the court-yard to the guard-room with blows and curses, in which it may be that not only the attendant menials, but even the cold but now infuriated Sadducees took their share."[1]

Then, "in the guard-room to which He was remanded to await the break of day"—or in whatever place his captors kept their prisoner—"all the ignorant malice of religious hatred, all the narrow vulgarity of brutal spite, all the cold innate cruelty which lurks under the abjectness of Oriental servility, was let loose against Him. His very meekness, His very silence, His very majesty—the very stainlessness of His innocence, the very grandeur of His fame—every divine circumstance and quality which raised Him to a height so infinitely immeasurable above His persecutors—all these made Him an all the more welcome victim for their low and devilish ferocity. They spat in His face; they smote Him with rods; they struck Him with their closed fists and with their open palms. In the fertility of their furious and hateful insolence, they invented against Him a sort of game. Covering His eyes, they hit Him again and again, with the repeated question, 'Prophesy to us, O Messiah, who it is that smote thee.' So they wiled away the dark cold hours till the morning, revenging themselves upon His impassive innocence for their own present vileness and previous terror; and there, in the midst of that savage and wanton varletry, the Son of God, bound and blindfold, stood in His long and silent agony, defenceless and alone. It was His first derision—His derision as the

Christ, the Judge attainted, the Holy One a criminal, the Deliverer in bonds." (Farrar, p. 654.)

This night, as time seemed to stand still, the prince of devils worked his will through those mortal devils who submitted their wills to his. It seems clear enough that among those degenerate humans who so reveled in their base and evil sport were members of the Sanhedrin itself. Matthew records that the members of that council said, "He is guilty of death," and his very next words are: "Then did *they* spit in his face, and buffeted him; and *others* smote him with the palms of their hands." That is, the members of the Great Council, the legal lights and leaders of the people, spurted their foul spittle into the face of their Messiah, while others, their servants and menials, struck him with physical force. Mark also seems to differentiate between those who did the spitting and the buffeting and "the servants" who did the striking. Luke speaks as though the soldiers—"the men that held Jesus"—were the ones who mocked and smote him. This truly was their hour, and they were enveloped in darkness!

Peter Denies Knowing Who Jesus Is

(Matthew 26:69-75; Mark 14:66-72; JST, Mark 14:81-82; Luke 22:55-62; John 18:15-18, 25-27)

Peter and John—blessed brethren of infinite valor and faith—recovering quickly (sooner than any of the other apostles) from that panic which swept over them in Gethsemane, set out to follow Jesus and the soldiers who held him bound. One or both of them may have been present when Annas began the Jewish inquisition that was designed to find a legal reason to slay the man whose death was already a foregone conclusion in their minds. We know that both were present at the palace of Caiaphas. John was known to the high priest, and apparently to his servants; he gained ready admittance. "Peter stood at the door without," unable to gain entrance; strict security measures were in force on this evil night, for one of the followers of

Jesus, with a flashing sword, had, in Gethsemane, already slashed off the ear of Malchus; there must be no further dissension or uproar. But John, apparently not without some influence in high places, went out and persuaded the portress who kept the gate, and who also must have known him, to admit his fellow apostle.

John hastened into the palace where Jesus stood arraigned before the Sanhedrin, or such portion of it as was assembled at this dread hour; Peter, discreetly or of necessity, remained in the hall or courtyard where he mingled with the servants and court followers and warmed himself over a coal fire. As Peter sat among these rowdies and malcontents, listening to the accounts of the arrest and hearing the predictions of what lay ahead for his Master, the damsel who had admitted him realized who he was. "Art not thou also one of this man's disciples?" she first asked. He replied, "I am not." She persisted: "Thou also wast with Jesus of Nazareth." To the others present she said, "This man was also with him." But Peter continued to disassociate himself from his Lord. "I know not, neither understand I what thou sayest," he affirmed. And also: "Woman, I know him not." Disconcerted by this challenge to his presence, Peter left the fire, "And he went out into the porch; and the cock crew."

While Peter was out on the porch, another maid—perhaps a replacement for the portress who had admitted him—said to those there assembled: "This fellow was also with Jesus of Nazareth." Again Peter denied, this time with an oath, saying, "I do not know the man." A man standing by agreed with the maid and said, "Thou art also of them." Peter said, "Man, I am not." All of this, as nearly as we can tell, may be counted the second denial.

About an hour then elapsed—such quite likely being the time during which Caiaphas held his hearing and issued his blasphemous adjuration—and it appears that Peter was back, standing beside the fire, warming himself with the others, for it was cold. One of those who stood by them said, "Surely thou also art one of them; for thy speech bewrayeth thee," as Matthew has it; or: "Surely thou art one of them: for thou art a Galilean, and thy speech agreeth thereto," as Mark has it; or: "Of a truth this fellow also was with him: for he is a Galilean," as Luke has it. Or, as John's account says, "Art not thou also one of his disciples?" to which he said, "I am not." At this point a kinsman of Malchus recognized Peter and said, "Did not I see thee in the garden with him?" To all of this came firm denials. Peter cursed and swore with an oath, "I know not the man." Also: "I know not this man of whom ye speak." And: "Man, I know not what thou sayest." All this may be accounted the third denial. And immediately, for the second time, the cock crew.

At this point, "the Lord turned, and looked upon Peter." Peter then remembered the prophecy, "Before the cock crow twice, thou shalt deny me thrice." Then he went out and wept bitterly.

Such is the sparsely worded account of Peter's so-called denial of his Lord, a denial that was rather a failure to stand up and testify of the divine Sonship when an occasion afforded than a denial of any divinity resident in the Son of Man.[2]

Two eloquent passages deserve preservation in our present record, for both help us to *feel* as well as to *know* what happened in Peter's life this night.

"The Lord in the agony of His humiliation, in the majesty of His silence—'*the Lord turned and looked upon Peter.*' Blessed are those on whom, when He looks in sorrow, the Lord also looks with love! It was enough. Like an arrow through his inmost soul, shot the mute eloquent anguish of that reproachful glance. As the sunbeam smites the last hold of snow upon the rock, ere it rushes in avalanche down the tormented hill, so the false self of the fallen Apostle slipped away. It was enough: 'he saw no more enemies, he knew no more danger, he feared no more death.' Flinging the fold of his mantle over his head, he too, like Judas, rushed forth into the night. Into the night, but not as Judas; into the unsunned outer darkness of miserable self-condemnation, but not into the midnight of remorse and of despair; into the night, but, as has been beautifully said, it was 'to meet the morning dawn.' If the angel of Innocence had left him, the angel of Repentance took him gently by the hand. Sternly, yet tenderly, the spirit of grace led up this broken-hearted penitent before the tribunal of his own conscience, and there his old life, his old shame, his old weakness, his old self was doomed to that death of godly sorrow which was to issue in a new and spiritual birth." (Farrar, pp. 653–54.)

"The Lord turned round and looked upon him—yes, in all that assembly, upon Peter! His eyes spake His Words; nay, much more; they searched down to the innermost depths of Peter's heart, and broke them open. They had pierced through all self-delusion, false shame, and fear: they had reached the man, the disciple, the lover of Jesus. Forth they burst, the waters of conviction, of true shame, of heart-sorrow, of the agonies of self-condemnation; and, bitterly weeping, he rushed from under those suns that had melted the ice of death and burnt into his heart—out from that cursed place of betrayal by Israel, by its High Priest—and even by the representative Disciple.

"Out he rushed into the night. Yet a night lit up by the stars of promise—chiefest among them this, that the Christ up there—the conquering Sufferer—had prayed for him. God grant us in the night of our conscious self-condemnation the same star-light of His Promises, the same assurance of the intercession of the Christ, that so, as Luther puts it, the particularness of the account of Peter's denial, as compared with the briefness of that of Christ's Passion, may carry to our hearts this lesson: 'The fruit and use of the sufferings of Christ is this, that in them we have the forgiveness of our sins.' " (Edersheim 2:564.)

Jesus before the Sanhedrin
(Luke 22:66-71; 23:1; Matthew 27:1-2; Mark 15:1; JST, Mark 15:1-2)

"Gather unto me seventy men of the elders of Israel, whom thou knowest to be the elders of the people, and officers over them," the Lord commanded Moses, "and they shall bear the burden of the people with thee, that thou bear it not thyself alone." (Num. 11:16-17.) Thus was the Lord's system of government perfected in ancient Israel. Moses served as the prophet, seer, and revelator; at his side were "the princes of Israel," twelve in number, comparable to the Twelve Apostles, one of whom presided over each of the tribes (Num. 7); then came the Seventy—holy and noble men who also sat in judgment and regulated the affairs of the people. And a millennium and a half later, the Jews still maintained the form of their ancient order; the Great Sanhedrin—either patterned after or descended from the Quorum of Seventy called by Moses—still attempted to rule over the people. Albeit, to their sorrow, those of whom it was composed in time's meridian were no longer the spiritual giants who were qualified to go up into the Holy Mount and see "the God of Israel," as had been their predecessors in office. (Ex. 24:9-11.)

At the time the Great Sanhedrin, in its apostate and fallen state, chose to seek out and sit in judgment on that God who himself had called their predecessors, the tribunal was composed of seventy-one persons. Their traditional meeting place had been in one of the temple chambers—the *Lishkath haGazith* (*Lishcat Haggazzith*) or Chamber of Hewn Stones—but now it was common for them to meet in the merchandising booths of the sons of Annas. Their members were ordained and set apart by the laying on of hands, and twenty-three of their number constituted a quorum for the transaction of business. There is some confusion and uncertainty as to the powers and place of the Sanhedrin in that day; probably these varied from year to year depending upon the political climate. The council, as a stabilizing influence, operated with Roman approval and the Procurator appointed the high priests. Its authority was limited to religious matters, and it did not have the power to inflict the death penalty, though in fact the Roman authorities seemed to overlook some judicial murders made on religious grounds. Stephen was convicted before the Sanhedrin on suborned testimony and suffered death by stoning. (Acts 6-7.) Paul would have been killed by act of the Council had he not been rescued by Roman soldiers. (Acts 23.) And the Jews, without reference to Rome, had sought on previous occasions to kill Jesus. (John 5:18; 7:25.)

But let us return to the Jewish trials of Jesus. Caiaphas and the Sanhedrin had "condemned him to be guilty of death." (Mark 14:64.) But—"The law and the practice of the time required that any person found guilty of a capital offense, after due trial before a Jewish tribunal, should be given a second trial on the following day; and at this later hearing any or all of the judges who had before voted for conviction could reverse themselves; but no one who had once voted for acquittal could change his ballot. A bare majority was sufficient for acquittal, but more than a majority [two more, in fact] was required for conviction. By a provision that must appear to us most unusual, if all the judges voted for conviction on a capital charge the verdict was not to stand and the accused had to be set at liberty; for, it was argued, a unanimous vote against a prisoner indicated that he had had no friend or defender in court, and that the judges might have been in conspiracy against Him. Under this rule in Hebrew jurisprudence the verdict against Jesus, rendered at the illegal night session of the Sanhedrists, was void, for we are specifically told that 'they all condemned him to be guilty of death.'

"Apparently for the purpose of establishing a shadowy pretext of legality in their procedure, the Sanhedrists adjourned to meet again in early daylight. Thus they technically complied with the requirement—that on every case in which the death sentence had been decreed the court should hear and judge a second time in a later session—but they completely ignored the equally mandatory provision that the second trial must be conducted on the day following that of the first hearing. Between the two sittings on consecutive days the judges were required to fast and pray, and to give the case on trial calm and earnest consideration." (Talmage, pp. 627–28.)[3]

And so the continued happenings of that doleful night were these: "At last the miserable lingering hours were over"—the hours before Annas and Caiaphas, during which he was derided, mocked, slapped, cursed, and showered with spittle—"and the grey dawn shuddered, and the morning blushed upon that memorable day. And with the earliest dawn, . . . the Sanhedrin had been summoned, for His third actual, but His first formal and legal trial. It was now probably about six o'clock in the morning, and a full session met. Well-nigh all—for there were the noble exceptions at least of Nicodemus and of Joseph of Arimathea, and we may hope also of Gamaliel, the grandson of Hillel—were inexorably bent upon His death. The Priests were there, whose greed and selfishness He had reproved; the Elders, whose hypocrisy He had branded; the Scribes, whose ignorance He had exposed; the worse than all, the worldly, skeptical, would-be philosophic Sadducees, always the most cruel and dangerous of opponents, whose empty sapience He had so grievously confuted. All these were bent upon His death; all filled with repulsion at that infinite goodness; all burning with hatred against a purer nature than any which they could even conceive in their loftiest dreams. And yet their task in trying to achieve his destruction was not easy. . . . The fact was that the Sanhedrists had not the power of inflicting death, and even if the Pharisees might have ventured to usurp it in a tumultuary sedition, as they afterwards did in the case of

Stephen, the less fanatic and more cosmopolitan Sadducees would be less likely to do so.

"Not content, therefore, with the *cherem,* or ban of greater excommunication, their only way to compass His death was to hand Him over to the secular arm. At present they had only against Him a charge of constructive blasphemy, founded on an admission forced from Him by the High Priest, when even their own suborned witnesses had failed to perjure themselves to their satisfaction. There were many old accusations against Him, on which they could not rely. His violations of the Sabbath, as they called them, were all connected with miracles, and brought them, therefore, upon dangerous ground. His rejection of oral tradition involved a question on which Sadducees and Pharisees were at deadly feud. His authoritative cleansing of the Temple might be regarded with favour both by the Rabbis and the people. The charge of esoteric evil doctrines had been refuted by the utter publicity of His life. The charge of open heresies had broken down, from the total absence of supporting testimony. The problem before them was to convert the ecclesiastical charge of constructive blasphemy into a civil charge of constructive treason. But how could this be done? Not half the members of the Sanhedrin had been present at the hurried, nocturnal, and therefore illegal, session in the house of Caiaphas; yet if they were all to condemn him by a formal sentence, they must all hear something on which to found their vote. In answer to the adjuration of Caiaphas, He had solemnly admitted that He was the Messiah and the Son of God. The latter declaration would have been meaningless as a charge against Him before the tribunal of the Romans; but if He would repeat the former, they might twist it into something politically seditious. But He would not repeat it, in spite of their insistence, because He knew that it was open to their wilful misinterpretation, and because they were evidently acting in flagrant violation of their own express rules and traditions, which demanded that every arraigned criminal should be regarded and treated as innocent until his guilt was actually proved." (Farrar, pp. 654–56.)

Thus Caiaphas, now before the whole council, demanded: "Art thou the Christ? tell us." Perhaps he would say something that the Romans would interpret as being seditious. After all, the Jewish concept of a Messiah was one of a Deliverer, a Deliverer from all alien yokes, Rome included. But Jesus: "If I tell you, ye will not believe." "How sad and how true! Gospel truth is taught by testimony: the spiritually alive, believe; the spiritually sick, question; the spiritually dead, deny and reject. And here stands the Lord Omnipotent, the being by whose hands all things are, the being through whom salvation comes, ready to testify again of his divine Sonship with full knowledge that his testimony will avail his hearers nothing." (*Commentary* 1:796.)

Jesus continued: "And if I also ask you, ye will not answer me, nor let me go. Hereafter shall the Son of man sit on the right hand of the power of God." Thus was the foundation laid for the question of the whole council: "Art thou then the Son of God?" To this Jesus replied: "Ye say that I am," which they all understood to mean: 'It is as ye have said, I am.' Then as Caiaphas had done earlier, they all cried out, "What need we any further witnesses? for we ourselves have heard of his own mouth." This man was a blasphemer worthy of death!

"And the whole council condemned him, and bound him," Mark said, "and carried him away, and delivered him to Pilate."

NOTES

1. Farrar, pp. 649–50. It is, of course, the speculative license of an author to say Jesus was taken from the place where he had been judged to a guardroom. There is nothing in the inspired account to indicate where or in what place the maltreatment took place. All we know for certain is that, from whatever place he was kept, Jesus was able to look upon Peter when that apostle made his third denial. Further, as shall be seen hereafter, the so-called formal trial of Jesus in all probability took place in the palace of

Caiaphas and not in the Hall of Judgment, though, as Farrar indicates, that is the only place it could have been held legally.

2. "Peter failed on this occasion to testify as becometh one who is a special witness of the Lord, but so in effect had all the disciples, for they all forsook him and fled. But Peter was not yet the man he was to be, for about fifty days hence, at Pentecost, he and all the saints were to receive the gift of the Holy Ghost. Perhaps, then, the great lesson to be learned from this experience of the chief apostle is this: if men are to resist and overcome the world; if they are to stand valiantly in the Cause of Christ; if they are to be faithful and true in all things—they must have the gift of the Holy Ghost." (*Commentary* 1:794.)

3. Edersheim argues—falsely, we are confident to assert—that Jesus was never formally tried by the Sanhedrin. In so doing he gives an instructive recitation of the illegalities that would have existed had the procedures of the night been a trial. That they were, in fact, a trial Talmage and many others assert with confidence, and so it seems to us. "Alike Jewish and Christian evidence establish the fact, that Jesus was not formally tried and condemned by the Sanhedrin," Edersheim contends. "It is admitted on all hands, that forty years before the destruction of the Temple the Sanhedrin ceased to pronounce capital sentences. This alone would be sufficient. But, besides, the trial and sentence of Jesus in the Palace of Caiaphas would (as already stated) have outraged every principle of Jewish criminal law and procedure." (And so it did!) "Such causes could only be tried, and capital sentence pronounced, in the regular meeting-place of the Sanhedrin, not, as here, in the High-Priest's Palace; no process, least of all such an one, might be begun in the night, not even in the afternoon, although if the discussion had gone on all day, sentence might be pronounced at night. Again, no process could take place on Sabbaths or Feastdays, or even on the eves of them, although this would not have nullified [the] proceedings, and it might be argued on the other side, that a process against one who had seduced the people should preferably be carried on, and sentence executed, at the great public Feasts, for the warning of all. Lastly, in capital causes there was a very elaborate system of warning and cautioning witnesses, while it may safely be affirmed, that at a regular trial Jewish judges, however prejudiced, would *not* have acted as the Sanhedrists and Caiaphas did on this occasion." (This, as we view it, is exactly what these prejudiced and hate-filled judicial officers did.)

"But as we examine it more closely, we perceive that the Gospel-narratives do not speak of a formal trial and sentence by the Sanhedrin. . . . The four Gospels equally indicate that the whole proceedings of that night were carried on in the Palace of Caiaphas, and that during that night no formal sentence of death was pronounced. . . . And when in the morning, in consequence of a fresh consultation, also in the Palace of Caiaphas, they led Jesus to the Praetorium, it was not as a prisoner condemned to death of whom they asked the execution, but as one against whom they laid certain accusations worthy of death, while, when Pilate bade them judge Jesus according to Jewish Law, they replied, not: that they had done so already, but, that they had no competence to try capital causes." (All of this ignores the condemnation of guilt imposed for blasphemy, the penalty for which, under Jewish law, was death by stoning. For Jesus to have died by stoning, as in the case of Stephen, would have nullified the Messianic word about the cross. Hence the divine providence that guided his foes to seek a Roman death sentence for a Roman offense, such as for sedition or treason. Jesus must die, not by Jewish stoning, but by Roman crucifixion. Thus it was written, and thus it must be.)

"But although Christ was not tried and sentenced in a formal meeting of the Sanhedrin, there can, alas! be no question that His Condemnation and Death were the work, if not of the Sanhedrin, yet of the Sanhedrists—of the whole body of them ('all the council'), in the sense of expressing what was the judgment and purpose of all the Supreme Council and Leaders of Israel, with only very few exceptions. We bear in mind, that the resolution to sacrifice Christ had for some time been taken. Terrible as the proceedings of that night were, they even seem a sort of concession—as if the Sanhedrists would fain have found some legal and moral justification for what they had determined to do." (Edersheim 2:556–58.)

Chapter 105

THE FIRST TWO ROMAN TRIALS

He is despised and rejected of men;
a man of sorrows, and acquainted with grief:
and we hid as it were our faces from him;
he was despised, and we esteemed him not. . . .
We did esteem him stricken,
smitten of God, and afflicted. . . .
He was oppressed, and he was afflicted,
yet he opened not his mouth:
he is brought as a lamb to the slaughter,
and as a sheep before her shearers is dumb,
so he openeth not his mouth. . . .
Yet it pleased the Lord to bruise him;
he hath put him to grief.
(Isa. 53:3-10.)

Jesus before Pilate

(John 18:28-38; Matthew 27: 2, 11-14; JST, Matthew 27:12, 15; Mark 15:2-5; JST, Mark 15:4; Luke 23:2-5; JST, Luke 23:3)

Jesus who is called Christ—the same whom all Israel had for ages worshipped as the Lord Jehovah, the one Holy Being who was incapable of falsely ascribing divinity to himself—has now been convicted by the Great Sanhedrin of that very blasphemous offense, and by them condemned, according to Jewish law, to pay the supreme penalty; this Man of Galilee, bound and with a cord around his neck (Matthew says: "When they had bound him, they led him away"), is led, like a common criminal, to Pontius Pilate, the Roman Procurator. It would surprise us if Annas and Caiaphas and the Sanhedrin did not lead the tumultuous Jewish mob as the temple guards delivered their Jewish prisoner to the Gentile ruler. By these Jewish leaders the prisoner was taken to the magnificent palace of Herod, occupied at Passover time by Pilate, whose normal residence was Caesarea Palestina.

Pontius Pilate—into whose hands the Lord of Life is being delivered, that the penalty of death decreed by the Sanhedrin may be ratified—this ignoble Roman governor was, as were all the Gentile overlords of the day, a murderous, evil despot who ruled with the sword and was a master at political intrigue. He was neither better nor worse than others of his ilk, but his name is engraved forever in Christian memory because he sent the Son of God to the cross. This act of infamy on his part required preparation. No ruler—however supreme and autocratic; however subject to the political pressures and passions of the populace; however prejudiced toward a race and a people—no ruler knowingly and willfully sends an innocent man to death unless prior sins have seared his conscience, tied his hands, and buried his instinct to deal justly. Through all his length of days, Pilate had been and then was an evil man, inured to blood and hardened against violence.

"What manner of man was this in whose hands were placed, by power from above, the final destinies of the Saviour's life? . . . In Judea he had acted with all the haughty violence and insolent cruelty of a typical Roman governor. Scarcely had he been installed as Procurator, when, allowing his soldiers to bring with them by night the silver eagles and other insignia of the legions from Caesarea to the Holy City, he excited a furious outburst of Jewish feeling against an act which they regarded as idolatrous profanation. For five days and nights—often lying prostrate on the bare ground—they surrounded and almost stormed his residence at Caesarea with tumultuous and threatening entreaties, and could not be made to desist on the sixth, even by the peril of immediate and indiscriminate massacre at the hands of soldiers whom he sent to surround them. He had then sullenly given way, and this foretaste of the undaunted and fanatical resolution of the people with whom he had to deal, went far to embitter his whole administration with a sense of overpowering disgust."[1]

On another occasion, to build an aqueduct to bring water from the Pools of Solomon, Pilate confiscated money from their sacred treasury. "The people rose in furious myriads to resent this secular appropriation of their sacred fund. Stung by their insults and reproaches, Pilate disguised a number of his soldiers in Jewish costume, and sent them among the mob, with staves and daggers concealed under their garments, to punish the ringleaders. Upon the refusal of the Jews to separate quietly, a signal was given, and the soldiers carried out their instructions with such hearty good-will, that they wounded and beat to death not a few both of the guilty and the innocent, and created so violent a tumult that many perished by being trodden to death under the feet of the terrified and surging mob."

And on yet another occasion, a "seditious tumult" arose which "must still more have embittered the disgust of the Roman Governor for his subjects, by showing him how impossible it was to live among such a people—even in a conciliatory spirit—without outraging some of their sensitive prejudices. In the Herodian palace at Jerusalem, which he occupied during the festivals, he had hung some gilt shields dedicated to Tiberius." Whether this was done out of wanton malice or as part of a harmless work or ornamentation is not clear. But he felt he could not remove them "without some danger of offending the gloomy and suspicious Emperor to whose honour they were dedicated. Since he would not give way, the chief men of the nation wrote a letter of complaint to Tiberius himself. It was a part of Tiberius's policy to keep the provinces contented, and his masculine intellect despised the obstinacy which would risk an insurrection rather than sacrifice a whim. He therefore reprimanded Pilate, and ordered the obnoxious shields to be transferred from Jerusalem to the Temple of Augustus at Caesarea. . . .

"Besides these three outbreaks, we hear in the Gospels of some wild sedition in which Pilate had mingled the blood of the Galileans with their sacrifices. [Luke 13:1.] . . . Such was Pontius Pilate, whom the pomps and perils of the great yearly festival had summoned from his usual residence at Caesarea Phillipi to the capital of the nation which he detested, and the head-quarters of a fanaticism which he despised."

And yet—be it noted—"of all the civil and ecclesiastical rulers before whom Jesus was brought to judgment, Pilate was the least guilty of malice and hatred, the most anxious, if not to spare His agony, at least to save His life." It is to the conspiratorial evils of this day of judgment and of crucifixion to which we now turn our attention.

After a dread and evil night—whenever was there such a night as this, a night when God himself was spit upon and cursed and smitten?—Jesus is led by his captors into the Hall of Judgment of the palace of Herod. It is a Gentile house where there might be some crust of unleavened bread. Hence: "The great Jewish hierarchs, shrinking from ceremonial pollution, though not from moral guilt—afraid of leaven, though not afraid of innocent blood—refused to enter the Gentile's hall, lest they should be polluted, and should consequently be unable that night" to continue their Paschal celebration. Pilate, no doubt annoyed and condescending, but willing for the moment to placate their superstitions, thus went out to them. An experienced ruler, and probably having personally authorized Jesus' arrest the night before, the Roman Procurator asked, abruptly: "What accusation bring ye against this man?"

Taken by surprise—they had come to receive a ratifying approval of their already imposed death penalty; they had come to gain Roman approval for Jesus' death, so that none of his friends could raise a tumult; they had come to arrange a Roman crucifixion, which was more demeaning than a Jewish stoning; they had come to gain a license to kill, an approval to perform a judicial murder—thus, taken by surprise at Pilate's apparent intent to assume original jurisdiction and hold a Roman trial, they responded: "If he were not a malefactor, we would not have delivered him up unto thee." 'We have found him guilty; he has broken our law; he should be punished.'

"But Pilate's Roman knowledge of law, his Roman instinct of justice, his Roman contempt for their murderous fanaticism, made him not choose to act upon a charge so entirely vague, nor give the sanction of his tribunal to their dark disorderly decrees. He would not deign to be an executioner where he had not been a judge." Accordingly, Pilate said: "Take ye him, and judge him according to your law."[2] Their response: "It is not lawful for us to put any man to death." This reply, John says, was given, "That the saying of Jesus might be fulfilled, which he spake, signifying what death he should die." And thus, "they are forced to the humiliating confession that, having been deprived of the 'right of the sword,' they cannot inflict the death which alone will satisfy them; for indeed it stood written in the eternal councils that Christ was to die, not by Jewish stoning or strangulation, but by that Roman form of execution which inspired the Jews with a nameless horror, even by crucifixion; that He was to reign from His cross—to die by that most fearfully significant and typical of deaths—public, slow, conscious, accursed, agonising—worse even than burning—the worst type of all possible deaths, and the worst result of that curse which He was to remove for ever."

Caiaphas and his conspiring confederates—though they had hoped it might be otherwise—dropped the charge of blasphemy and raised the cry of sedition and treason. Under Roman law all the gods of all the nations of all the earth were revered and accepted; even the emperors deified themselves that they might be worshipped; any charge of blasphemy against this Jewish Jehovah would have been as empty nothingness, to Pilate. And so new charges were hurled. They said—Caiaphas, as we suppose, being voice—"We found this fellow perverting the nation, and forbidding to give tribute to Caesar, saying that he himself is Christ a King."

As to any perverting of the nation, Pilate could not care less; the Jews were already a benighted mob of religious fanatics in his view—let them be what they were. As to giving tribute to Caesar, that charge was idle rhetoric; grasping publicans and Roman steel saw to the taxes of the day. But a would-be king, that was another matter. Thereupon Pilate went into the Judgment Hall, called Jesus, and asked: "Art thou the King of the Jews?" "Thou poor, friendless, wasted man, in thy poor peasant garments, with thy tied hands, and the foul traces of the insults of thine enemies on thy face, and on thy robes—thou, so unlike the fierce magnificent Herod, whom this multitude which thirsts for thy blood acknowledged as their sovereign—art *thou* the King of the Jews?"

Jesus' answer will depend on what Pilate means. Is he speaking temporally or spiritually? Yes, this Suffering Servant is the king of the Universe; before him every knee shall one day bow, while every tongue acclaims him Lord of all. No, he is not the temporal Messiah, the Deliverer of Jewish expectation, the kind of a king who would lead an armed assault against a Roman fortress. "Sayest thou this thing of thyself," Jesus asks, "or did others tell it thee of me?"

Pilate's response is disdainful. "Am I a Jew?" he says. "Thine own nation and the chief priests have delivered thee unto me." As with the priests, so with the people; the derision, declaiming, and denunciation of Christ is not an isolated act of a few rabid partisans; the nation and its leaders have delivered him up to their Gentile overlord. Even without hearing Jesus' answer, it is hard for Pilate to envision him as a temporal ruler, and so he asks: "What hast thou done?" What indeed! 'I have preached the gospel to the poor, proclaimed liberty to the captives, and opened the prison door to those who were bound. I have opened blind eyes, unstopped deaf ears, and given strength to lame legs; I have cast out devils and called back rotting corpses from their graves; I have fed multitudes, stilled storms, walked on raging waves; I have been and am the manifestation among men of the Father who is in heaven. I am his Son.'

> *My kingdom is not of this world: if my kingdom were of this world, then would my servants fight, that I should not be delivered to the Jews: but now is my kingdom not from hence.*

His was no Jewish Messianic kingdom; no political dominion ruled from palaces with floors of agate and lazuli; no kingdom that wages war with its neighbors and makes slaves of the conquered. His kingdom was not of this world; not one comprised of carnal, sensual, and devilish souls; not a kingdom of revelry and lust and wickedness. Rather, his kingdom on earth was made up of the saints of the Most High; and his kingdom in heaven was the everlasting kingdom of his Eternal Father. His royalty was the royalty of holiness, of righteousness, of eternal life. "Art thou a king then?" Pilate marvels. 'Can one who speaks of ruling in spiritual realms, as you do, really be a king!' Jesus answered:

> *Thou sayest that I am a king. To this end was I born, and for this cause came I into the world, that I should bear witness unto the truth. Every one that is of the truth heareth my voice.*

Or, as Matthew has it, "Thou sayest truly; for thus it is written of me." 'And not only am I an eternal king, but my kingly mission is to proclaim the truth—the truth that makes men free; the truth that saves and exalts eternally; the truth which brings peace to the souls of men in my earthly kingdom, and then assures them of eternal life in my eternal kingdom. Everyone who seeks truth and loves righteousness believes my words.'

"Yes!" Jesus was a king, "but a king not in this region of falsities and shadows, but one born to bear witness unto the truth, and one whom all who were of the truth should hear. 'Truth,' said Pilate impatiently, 'what is *truth*?'[3] What had he—a busy, practical Roman governor—to do with such dim abstractions? what bearing had they on the question of life and death? what unpractical hallucination, what fairyland of dreaming phantasy was this? Yet, though he contemptuously put the discussion aside, he was touched and moved. A judicial mind, a forensic training, familiarity with human nature which had given him some insight into the characters of men, showed him that Jesus was not only wholly innocent, but infinitely nobler and better than His raving sanctimonious accusers. He wholly set aside the floating idea of an unearthly royalty; he saw in the prisoner before his tribunal an innocent and high-souled dreamer, nothing more. And so, leaving Jesus there, he went out again to the Jews, and pronounced his first emphatic and unhesitating acquittal: 'I FIND IN HIM NO FAULT AT ALL.'

"But this public decided acquittal only kindled the fury of His enemies into yet fiercer flame. After all that they had hazarded, after all that they had inflicted, after the sleepless night of their plots, adjurations, insults, was their purpose to be foiled after all by the intervention of the very Gentiles on whom they had relied for its bitter consummation? Should this victim, whom they had thus clutched in their deadly grasp, be rescued from High Priests and rulers by the contempt or the pity of an insolent heathen? It was too intolerable! Their voices rose in wilder tumult."

Unable to raise the cry of blasphemy, and their charges of sedition and treason having failed, they now burst forth in a panic of pathetic charges. Mark says "the chief priests accused him of many things." But Jesus "answered nothing." Having been "brought as a lamb to the slaughter, and as a sheep before her shearers is dumb, so he openeth not his mouth." (Isa. 53:7.) So fierce were the charges, so vile the things named against him, that, to Pilate, it was unbelievable that Jesus would not respond. "Answerest thou nothing?" he said, "behold how many things they witness against thee." And even to the procurator's words, Jesus remained silent, "so that Pilate marvelled."

Then, amid the babble and tumult, a loud voice acclaimed: "He stirreth up the people, teaching throughout all Jewry, beginning from Galilee to this place." Pilate heard these words; he knew that Galilee had been the scene of most of Jesus' works, and instantaneously a plan was formulated in his mind. "Eager for a chance of dismissing a business of which he was best pleased to be free, he proposed, by a master-stroke of astute policy, to get rid of an embarrassing prisoner, to save himself from a disagreeable decision, and to do an unexpected complaisance to the unfriendly Galilean tetrarch, who, as usual, had come to Jerusalem—nominally to keep the Passover, really to please his subjects, and to enjoy the sensations and festivities offered at that season by the densely-crowded capital. Accordingly Pilate, secretly glad to wash his hands of a detestable responsibility, sent Jesus to Herod Antipas, who was probably occupying the old Asmonean palace, which had been the royal residence at Jerusalem until it had been surpassed by the more splendid one which the prodigal tyrant, his father, had built. And so, through the thronged and narrow streets, amid the jeering, raging, multitudes, the weary Sufferer was dragged once more."

Jesus before Herod
(Luke 23:6-12)

"Herod will kill thee." (Luke 13:31-33.) Such were the

words of warning spoken to Jesus in an earlier day with reference to the designs and intentions of Herod Antipas; and now, with Jesus before him in bonds, and with the chief priests and the people all crying for his blood, what an opportunity to decree a judicial murder! This same Antipas, the tetrarch of Galilee and Perea, is the one who ordered the head of John the Baptist brought in before his reveling courtiers on a charger. He is the one who flaunted both incest and adultery before the nation and to whom one or many murders meant no more than did the slaughter of the Innocents in Bethlehem to his evil father, Herod the Great. And yet even he, after a mocking and deriding trial, found in Jesus "nothing worthy of death" (Luke 23:14-15), and acquitted him publicly for the second time.

Words almost fail us in setting forth the dire and despicable and degenerate state of Herod Antipas, whom the people in fawning flattery called king, though Rome had conferred no such title upon him. "If ever there was a man who richly deserved contempt, it was the paltry, perjured princeling—false to his religion, false to his nation, false to his friends, false to his brethren, false to his wife—to whom Jesus gave the name of 'this fox.' The inhuman vices which the Caesars displayed on the vast theatre of their absolutism—the lust, the cruelty, the autocratic insolence, the ruinous extravagance—all these were seen in pale reflex in these little Neros and Caligulas of the provinces—these local tyrants, half Idumean, half Samaritan, who aped the worst degradations of the Imperialism to which they owed their very existence. Judea might well groan under the odious and petty despotism of these hybrid Herodians—jackals who fawned about the feet of the Caesarean lions. Respect for 'the powers that be' can hardly, as has well been said, involve respect for all the impotences and imbecilities." (Farrar, pp. 449–50.)

"We have caught glimpses of this Herod Antipas before, and I do not know that all History, in its gallery of portraits, contains a much more despicable figure than this wretched, dissolute Idumean Sadducee—this petty princeling drowned in debauchery and blood."

At one time Herod had feared that Jesus was John the Baptist risen from the dead to plague him. The mental madness that stirred his soul after the Baptist's murder, however, seems to have subsided; now his interest in Jesus is that of a superstitious simpleton who wants to see some great miracle performed in his kingly presence. Thus we find him questioning Jesus "in many words," taunting, deriding, challenging, all to no avail. Jesus remained silent. "As far as we know, Herod is further distinguished as the only being who saw Christ face to face and spoke to Him, yet never heard his voice. For penitent sinners, weeping women, prattling children, for the scribes, the Pharisees, the Sadducees, the rabbis, for the perjured high priest and his obsequious and insolent underling, and for Pilate the pagan, Christ had words—of comfort or instruction, of warning or rebuke, of protest or denunciation—yet for Herod the fox He had but disdainful and kingly silence." (Talmage, p. 636.)

In his trial before Herod, Jesus was vehemently accused by the chief priests and scribes. In this court, before a Jewish king with Roman power, the accusations made would have included both blasphemy and treason, none of which Herod deigned to consider seriously. Then "Herod with his men of war set him at nought, and mocked him, and arrayed him in a gorgeous robe, and sent him again to Pilate." Thus Antipas, though finding no fault in Jesus, and though a just judge is morally obligated to release an innocent man from his bonds, yet sent him back to another court, can it be other than with the hope that another judge will find reason to have this friend of the Baptist put to death as the chief priests and scribes so devoutly desire?

NOTES

1. No man of whom I know has written so consistently and so well—in such shining English prose—about the dramatic and miraculous happenings in the life of our Lord as

has Canon Farrar, whose words I have freely quoted from time to time in this work. It is my observation that when either I, or Elder Talmage, or Edersheim, or other authors—and all of us have done it—when any of us put the thoughts of Farrar in our own words, however excellent our expression may be, it loses much of the incisive and pungent appeal found in the language of our British friend from the Church of England. With this realization in mind, and because it seems a shame not to preserve the best literary craftsmanship available, to portray the greatest events in the most wondrous life ever lived, I shall feel free in this and the remaining chapters of this work to draw more heavily than otherwise upon the genius of Farrar. In the instant chapter, unless otherwise indicated by footnotes, all of the quoted material is from pages 661 to 672 of his work. By way of addendum may I express the hope—nay, offer the prayer—that both Farrar and Edersheim, and others who had faith and believed in the Messiah, according to the best light and knowledge they had, now that they are in the world of spirits where Elder Talmage continues his apostolic ministry, may have received added light and knowledge and will have pursued that strait and narrow course that will make them inheritors of the fulness of our Father's kingdom. Truly they were Eliases of a greater day and harbingers of a greater light.

2. Pilate's reaction was like that of Gallio when the Jews haled Paul before him with the charge: "This fellow persuadeth men to worship God contrary to the law." Gallio responded: "If it were a matter of wrong or wicked lewdness, O ye Jews, reason would that I should bear with you: but if it be a question of words and names, and of your law, look ye to it; for I will be no judge of such matters." (Acts 18:12-16.)

3. "And truth is knowledge of things as they are, and as they were, and as they are to come." (D&C 93:24.)

Chapter 106

THE FINAL ROMAN TRIAL

The Jews . . . shall crucify him, . . .
and there is none other nation on earth
that would crucify their God.
For should the mighty miracles be wrought
among other nations they would repent,
and know that he be their God.
But because of priestcrafts and iniquities,
they at Jerusalem will stiffen their necks
against him, that he be crucified.
(2 Ne. 10:3-5.)

Jesus Again before Pilate

(Matthew 27:15-23; JST, Matthew 27:20; Mark 15:6-14; JST, Mark 15:8-10, 13, 15; Luke 23:13-23; John 18:39-40)

Bound, mocked, derided, smitten, spat upon, wearing the gorgeous white robe in which he had been scornfully draped by Herod's men of war, the Judge of all the earth is now back in the Hall of Judgment to be judged and condemned by wicked men. Pilate has "called together the chief priests and the rulers and the people," those by whose mouths the charges of sedition and treason had been hurled with such vile venom and hatred. Assembling with them are great hosts from all parts of Jerusalem. Word of

Jesus' arrest has swept like a tidal wave through the streets and into the homes of the people; and, also, this is the day when the idle and the curious come to see the Governor make the Passover release of an infamous prisoner. Will it be this foul felon Bar-Abbas who, under the shallow cover of political aspirations, led an insurrection and committed murder, but for whose revolutionary zeal there was great public sympathy?

Pilate speaks: "Ye have brought this man unto me, as one that perverteth the people," and who forbids the paying of tribute to Caesar, and who claims that he himself is a king, "and, behold, I, having examined him before you, have found no fault in this man touching those things whereof ye accuse him"—'He is innocent; as I said unto you before, I find in him no fault at all'—"No, nor yet Herod: for I sent you to him; and, lo, *nothing worthy of death is done unto Him.*" So spoke Pilate the Procurator; so spoke Herod the king. There was, then, only one just thing to do: Release the Innocent Man; and further, if need be, protect him from the anger and hatred of the wailing mobs.

Thus "came the golden opportunity for him to vindicate the grandeur of his country's imperial justice, and, as he had pronounced Him absolutely innocent, to set Him absolutely free. But exactly at that point he wavered and temporised. The dread of another insurrection haunted him like a nightmare. He was willing to go half-way to please these dangerous sectaries. To justify them, as it were, in their accusation, he would chastise Jesus—scourge Him publicly, as though to render His pretensions ridiculous—disgrace and ruin Him—'make Him seem vile in their eyes'—and *then* set Him free."[1] These were Pilate's words: "I will therefore chastise him, and release him."

This attempt at compromise and appeasement failed; the hunger-maddened pack of ravening wolves would be satisfied with nothing but the blood of the Lamb; their cry was for blood, and blood it must be. Knowing and sensing their refusal—perhaps also it was spoken to him—Pilate felt unable to temporize. But there was another possibility. Because "it was common at the feast, for Pilate to release unto them one prisoner, whomsoever they desired," the Procurator then said: "Ye have a custom, that I should release unto you one at the passover: will ye therefore that I release unto you the King of the Jews?" That is: 'Though he is innocent, I will find him guilty and then release him as a convicted criminal.' He offered, therefore, to make the release of Jesus, not an act of "imperious justice, but of artificial grace."

There were those in the multitude who wanted Jesus freed. He had healed their sick, raised their dead, and spoken sweet words of comfort to their sorrowing souls. "And the multitude, crying aloud," Mark tells us, "began to desire him to deliver Jesus unto them." Heartened by this vocal sentiment, Pilate asked: "Will ye that I release unto you the King of the Jews?" Others, however, cried out for the release of Bar-Abbas, and Pilate yet asked: "Whom will ye that I release unto you? Barabbas, or Jesus which is called Christ?" Though the people might be divided on the issue, the chief priests were not, and, as Pilate knew, they "had delivered him for envy."

The issue was thus squarely put; the choice lay with the people; it was theirs, not Pilate's; such was their custom; and if any prisoner was to be freed, it must be by their voice. Nor could two more divergent extremes than Jesus and Bar-Abbas have been offered to them. One was guilty, the other innocent; one was a murderer, the other brought life where there had been death; one led an insurrection, the other had proclaimed peace; one was guilty of sedition and treason, the other had commanded the people to render unto Caesar the things that were his; one was named Jesus Bar-Abbas, which means Jesus the Son of the Father, the other was the Son of the living God. Do we state it too strongly when we say one was Christ, the other antichrist? The Jewish choice that day was to be made between their

Messiah and a murderer; rejecting their King, they would be denied entrance into his kingdom, and accepting Bar-Abbas (an antichrist), they would themselves be murdered and cursed for generations yet to come.

But before the choice was made, and while "the chief priests and elders" moved among the mob and "persuaded the multitude that they should ask Barabbas, and destroy Jesus," the trial was interrupted. Claudia Procula, the wife of Pilate, who either then or later may have been a proselyte to the true faith, sent a dire warning to her husband. "Have thou nothing to do with that just man," she said, "for I have suffered many things this day in a vision because of him."

There are times—not a few in the course of a life—when men would do well to give heed to the wise counsel of their wives. If ever there was such a time in the life of Pilate, this was it. The Lord in his goodness to her—and also, for his own purposes, that another witness might be borne of his Son—had revealed to this woman that Jesus was Lord of all and that calamity and sorrow awaited those who opposed him. Nor was Pilate unsympathetic to her message; in reality it but confirmed his own feelings and desires.

"Gladly, most gladly, would Pilate have yielded to his own presentiments—have gratified his pity and his justice—have obeyed the prohibition conveyed by this mysterious omen. Gladly even would he have yielded to the worse and baser instinct of asserting his power, and thwarting these envious and hated fanatics, whom he knew to be ravening for innocent blood. That they—to many of whom sedition was as the breath of life—should be sincere in charging Jesus with sedition was, as he well knew, absurd. Their utterly transparent hypocrisy in this matter only added to his undisguised contempt. If he could have dared to show his real feelings, he would have driven them from his tribunal with all the haughty insouciance of a Gallio. But Pilate was guilty, and guilt is cowardice, and cowardice is weakness. His own past cruelties, recoiling in kind on his own head, forced him to crush the impulse of pity, and to add to his many cruelties another more heinous still.

"He knew that serious complaints hung over him. Those Samaritans whom he had insulted and attacked—those Jews whom he had stabbed promiscuously in the crowd by the hand of his disguised and secret emissaries—those Galileans whose blood he had mingled with their sacrifices—was not their blood crying for vengeance? Was not an embassy of complaint against him imminent even now? Would it not be dangerously precipitated if, in so dubious a matter as a charge of claiming a kingdom, he raised a tumult among a people in whose case it was the best interest of the Romans that they should hug their chains? Dare he stand the chance of stirring up a new and apparently terrible rebellion rather than condescend to a simple concession, which was rapidly assuming the aspect of a politic, and even necessary compromise? His tortuous policy sprang back upon himself, and rendered impossible his own wishes. The Nemesis of his past wrong-doing was that he could no longer do right."

"Willing to release Jesus," Pilate asked: "Whether of the twain will ye that I release unto you?" The chief priests and elders had done their work well; sentiment among the people had crystallized. "Not this man, but Barabbas," they said. "What shall I do then with Jesus which is called Christ?" To this the cry came back—from them all—"Let him be crucified." Pilate said: "Why, what evil hath he done? *I have found no cause of death in Him:* I will therefore chastise him, and let him go." But they cried out the more, "Deliver him unto us to be crucified. Away with him. Crucify him." "And the voices of them and of the chief priests prevailed."

"Hounded on by the Priests and Sanhedrists, the people impetuously claimed the Paschal boon of which he had reminded them; but in doing so they unmasked still more decidedly the sinister nature of their hatred against their Redeemer. For while they were professing to rage against the asserted seditiousness of One who was wholly obedient and peaceful, they shouted for the liberation of a man whose notorious revolt had been also stained by brigandage and murder. Loathing the innocent, they loved the guilty, and claimed the Procurator's grace on behalf, not of Jesus of Nazareth, but of a man who, in the fearful irony of circumstance, was also called Jesus—Jesus Bar-Abbas—who not only *was* what they falsely said of Christ, a leader of sedition, but also a robber and an assassin. It was fitting that *they,* who had preferred an abject Sadducee to their True Priest, and an incestuous Idumean to their Lord and King, should deliberately prefer a murderer to their Messiah.

"It may be that Bar-Abbas had been brought forth, and that thus Jesus the scowling murderer and Jesus the innocent Redeemer stood together on that high tribunal side by side. The people, persuaded by their priests, clamoured for the liberation of the rebel and the robber. To him every hand was pointed; for him every voice was raised. For the Holy, the Harmless, the Undefiled—for Him whom a thousand Hosannas had greeted but five days before—no word of pity or of pleading found an utterance. 'He was despised and rejected of men.' "

Jesus Is Scourged and Prepared for the Crucifiers

(Matthew 27:24-30; JST, Matthew 27:26-27; Mark 15:15-19; John 19:1-3)

Pilate next did that which has made all the more terrible the guilt of these blathering, frustrated fiends whose cries, "Crucify him, crucify him," pierced his ears and scourged his soul. He performed in their presence the two symbolical acts which certified to the innocence of the accused—one a Gentile witness, the other a Jewish. First, having declared the innocence of Jesus in plain words, he rose from the judgment seat, signifying he would impose no sentence; that there would be no judicial murder and no shedding of innocent blood; that he would free himself from the blood of the Innocent One. Having in mind the judicial tendency among all peoples, to preserve the rights of the accused, such an act—a Gentile symbol of innocence, if you will—should have freed Jesus without more. But it was not to be so. The legal court was Gentile; the real court was Jewish. The Roman sentence had already been imposed in the Jewish mind, and nothing must hinder the onrolling momentum of that evil cause which was taking their Christ to his cross.

Knowing and sensing all this, Pilate, with a keen and intuitive insight into the Jewish mind, performed before them their own rite, the Jewish rite that symbolized innocence and freed the soul from innocent blood. According to their law, for instance, if an unsolved murder had been committed, the elders of the city were required to slay a heifer, "wash their hands over the heifer," and say: "Our hands have not shed this blood, neither have our eyes seen it. Be merciful, O Lord, unto thy people Israel, whom thou hast redeemed, and lay not innocent blood unto thy people." Thus they were "forgiven," and thus they "put away the guilt of innocent blood" from among them, provided they did that which was "right in the sight of the Lord." (Deut. 21:1-9; Ps. 26:6; 73:13.)

Accordingly, on this dread morning, "When Pilate saw that he could prevail nothing, but that rather a tumult was made, he took water, and washed his hands before the multitude, saying, I am innocent of the blood of this just person; see that ye do nothing unto him." No longer is he saying, "Take ye him, and judge him according to your law," as it was at the first; now Pilate has stood in the Divine Presence; now he knows Jesus is innocent of both Jewish and Roman offenses; in justice the prisoner must be freed; neither the Jew nor the Gentile must do anything to him.

No one will contend that by these acts Pilate freed himself from the awful guilt of sending a God to the cross. Every man is accountable for his own sins, and those of Pilate were deep and red and evil. But we must credit the Procurator with trying to free his prisoner; his instinctive allegiance to justice was right; the spirit was willing but the flesh was weak. Further, this symbolic washing came *before* the decree to scourge and to crucify, and was, in fact, an attempt to free the man so that both Pilate and the Jews might "put away the guilt of innocent blood" because they did the thing—in releasing Jesus—which was "right in the sight of the Lord."

But whatever his intent and whatever his purpose—no matter whether his course was right or wrong—he was no longer an agent unto himself. The truth had not made him free; he was in bondage to the sins of his past. Whatever his purpose, it "was instantly drowned in a yell, the most awful, the most hideous, the most memorable that History records." *"His blood come upon us" and —God help us!—upon "our children."*

"And now mark, for one moment, the revenges of History.[2] Has not His blood been on them, and on their children?[3] Has it not fallen most of all on those most nearly concerned in that deep tragedy? Before the dread sacrifice was consummated, Judas died in the horrors of a loathsome suicide. Caiaphas was deposed the year following. Herod died in infamy and exile. Stripped of his Procuratorship very shortly afterwards, on the very charges he had tried by a wicked concession to avoid, Pilate, wearied out with misfortunes, died in suicide and banishment, leaving behind him an execrated name.[4] The house of Annas was destroyed a generation later by an infuriated mob, and his son was dragged through the streets, and scourged and beaten to his place of murder. Some of those who shared in and witnessed the scenes of that day—and thousands of their children—also shared in and witnessed the long horrors of that siege of Jerusalem which stands unparalleled in history for its unutterable fearfulness. 'It seems,' says Renan, 'as though the whole race had appointed a rendezvous for extermination.'

"They had shouted, 'We have no king but Caesar!' and they *had* no king but Caesar; and leaving only for a time the fantastic shadow of a local and contemptible royalty, Caesar after Caesar outraged, and tyrannised, and pillaged, and oppressed them, till at last they rose in wild revolt against the Caesar whom they had claimed, and a Caesar slaked in the blood of its best defenders the red ashes of their burnt and desecrated Temple. They had forced the Romans to crucify their Christ, and though they regarded this punishment with especial horror, they and their children were themselves crucified in myriads by the Romans outside their own walls, till room was wanting and wood failed, and the soldiers had to ransack a fertile inventiveness of cruelty for fresh methods of inflicting this insulting form of death.[5]

"They had given thirty pieces of silver for their Saviour's blood, and they were themselves sold in thousands for yet smaller sums. They had chosen Bar-Abbas in preference to their Messiah, and for them there has been no Messiah more, while a murderer's dagger swayed the last counsels of their dying nationality. They had accepted the guilt of blood, and the last pages of their history were glued together with the rivers of their blood, and that blood continued to be shed in wanton cruelties from age to age.

"They who will, may see in incidents like these the mere unmeaning *chances* of History; but there is in History nothing unmeaning to one who regards it as the Voice of God speaking among the destinies of men; and whether a man sees any significance or not in events like these, he must be blind indeed who does not see that when the murder of Christ was consummated, the axe was laid at the root of the barren tree of Jewish nationality. Since that day Jerusalem and its environs, with their 'ever-extending miles of grave-stones and ever-lengthening pavement of tombs and sepulchres,' have become little more than one vast cemetery—an Aceldama, a field of blood, a potter's field to bury strangers in. Like the mark of Cain, which clung to the murderer, the guilt of that blood seemed to cling to them—as it ever must until that same blood effaceth it. For, by God's mercy, that blood was shed for them also who made it flow; the voice which they strove to quench in death was uplifted in its last prayer for pity on His murderers. May that blood be efficacious! may that prayer be heard!"[6]

Pilate, having thus announced Jesus' innocence; having risen from the judgment seat; having washed his hands—for himself and for all Israel, that all might remain free from innocent blood—yet, in weakness, unable to withstand the pressures of the Jewish mob, freed Bar-Abbas and had Jesus scourged. "This scourging was the ordinary preliminary to crucifixion and other forms of capital punishment. It was a punishment so truly fearful, that the mind revolts at it; and it has long been abolished by that compassion of mankind which has been so greatly intensified, and in some degree even created, by the gradual comprehension of Christian truth. The unhappy sufferer was publicly stripped, was tied by the hands in a bent position to a pillar, and then, on the tense quivering nerves of the naked back, the blows were inflicted with leathern thongs, weighted with jagged edges of bone and lead; sometimes even the blows fell by accident—sometimes, with terrible barbarity, were purposely struck—on the face and eyes. It was a punishment so hideous that, under its lacerating agony, the victim generally fainted, often died; still more frequently a man was sent away to perish under the mortification and nervous exhaustion which ensued."

After the scourging came the derision. After he had borne so great a burden—in Gethsemane, before Pilate and Herod, by means of the lead and leather of the flagellum—Pilate placed him in the hands of those coarse and brutal warriors whose mission it was to wound and kill, and whose chief delight was to gloat over the agonies and pains of their foes. These men of war took the Man of Peace; these scarred and war-trained veterans of many a tumultuous fray took the Prince of Heaven; these cursing, jeering foes of all that is decent in the world took the Son of God—they took him, in bonds, with the approval of Pilate, to do with him according to their evil desires. "The low vile soldiery of the Praetorium—not Romans, who might have had more sense of the inborn dignity of the silent sufferer, but mostly the mere mercenary scum and dregs of the provinces—led Him into their barrack-room, and there mocked, in their savage hatred, the King whom they had tortured. It added keenness to their enjoyment to have in their power One who was of Jewish birth, of innocent life, of majestic bearing. The opportunity broke so agreeably the coarse monotony of their life, that they summoned all of the cohort who were disengaged to witness their brutal sport. In sight of those hardened ruffians"—and Pilate himself may well have been among the observers—"they went through the whole ceremony of mock coronation, a mock investiture, a mock homage. Around the brows of Jesus, in wanton mimicry of the Emperor's laurel, they twisted a green wreath of thorny leaves; in His tied and trembling hands they placed a reed for a sceptre; from His torn and bleeding shoulders they stripped the white robe with which Herod had mocked Him—which must now have been all soaked with blood—and flung on Him an old scarlot paludament—some cast-off war cloak, with its purple laticlave, from the Praetorian wardrobe. This, with feigned solemnity, they buckled over His right shoulder, with its glittering fibula; and then—each with his derisive homage of bended knee—each with his infamous spitting—each with the blow over the head from the reed-sceptre, which His bound hands could not hold—they kept passing before Him with their mock salutation of 'Hail, King of the Jews!' "

Pilate Sends Jesus to the Cross

(John 19:4-16; Luke 23:24-25)

After the great derision, Pilate went forth from the Praetorium where the soldiers had made sport of the King of kings and said to the Jewish multitude: "Behold, I bring him forth to you, that ye may know that I FIND NO FAULT IN HIM." "Even now, even yet, Pilate wished, hoped, even strove to save Him. He might represent this frightful scourging, not as the preliminary to crucifixion, but as an inquiry by torture, which had failed to elicit any further confession. And as Jesus came forth—as He stood beside him, with that martyr-form on the beautiful mosaic of the tribunal—the spots of blood upon His green wreath of torture, the mark of blows and spitting on His countenance, the weariness of His deathful agony upon the sleepless eyes, the *sagum* of faded scarlet, darkened by the weals of His lacerated back, and dropping, it may be, its stains of crimson upon the tessellated floor—even then, even so, in that hour of His extremest humiliation—yet, as He stood in the grandeur of His holy calm on that lofty tribunal above the yelling crowd, there shone all over Him so Godlike a pre-eminence, so divine a nobleness, that Pilate broke forth with that involuntary exclamation which has thrilled with emotion so many million hearts—

" 'BEHOLD THE MAN!'

"But his appeal only woke a fierce outbreak of the scream, 'Crucify! crucify!' The mere sight of Him, even in this His unspeakable shame and sorrow, seemed to add fresh fuel to their hate. In vain the heathen soldier appeals for humanity to the Jewish priest; no heart throbbed with responsive pity; no voice of compassion broke that monotonous yell of 'Crucify!'—the howling refrain of their wild 'liturgy of death.' The Roman who had shed blood like water, on the field of battle, in open massacre, in secret assassination, might well be supposed to have an icy and a stony heart; but yet icier and stonier was the heart of those scrupulous hypocrites and worldly priests."

With roll on roll of thunderous hate the storm of Sadducean evil has reached its peak; priestcraft is in control; Pilate can no longer delay the dread sentence: "Take ye him, and crucify him: FOR I FIND NO FAULT IN HIM." 'Let him die; let it be by your hand; he has committed no crime worthy of death; there is no sedition or treason here; Rome faces no peril; he is innocent; but if this wild tumult, this insensate hate, this vile outpouring of vengeance, if all this cannot be stayed in any other way, I will bend to your will. Let him be crucified!' Roman law bows to Jewish priestcraft, and the Jewish Jesus is sent to his death by Roman hands.

Has the issue now at last been decided? Not so; far from it. "What the Jews want—what the Jews *will have*—is *not* tacit connivance, but absolute sanction. They see their power. They see that this blood-stained Governor dares not hold out against them; they know that the Roman statecraft is tolerant of concessions to local superstition. Boldly, therefore, they fling to the winds all question of a political offense, and with all their hypocritical pretenses calcined by the heat of their passion, they shout, '*We have a law, and by our law He ought to die, because He made Himself a Son of God.*' "

Was there any question in their minds as to the teachings of this Galilean? He said he was the Son of God! Was there any doubt as to the charge they hurled against him, as to the reason they thirsted for his blood? It was his claim to Messianic divinity! They had kept it from Pilate until death by crucifixion was approved; now let the world know; let them and their children be in opposition to Christ forever. They have succeeded in their conspiracy; he is to die; and how little they know that his death and resurrection will prove forever his divine Sonship. His death will be but the seed from which his message will sprout; and that seed, growing into his glorious resurrection, will soon become a great vine which covers the whole earth. Yes, let him die, but through death he shall live again; and because he lives, all men shall rise again in mortality.

At this new declaration, Pilate was startled, fearful. Heathen and pagan superstition surpasses that of any other people. The Son of God! What there was about this man that pulled at his heart strings, he did not know. Were his long felt presentiments bringing him a message that he had not yet understood? And the vision and warning of his wife—what of them? Pilate, accordingly, went again into the Judgment Hall and asked Jesus: "Whence art thou?"

Jesus did not deign to answer. Pilate, in anger, demanded: "Speakest thou not unto me? knowest thou not that I have power to crucify thee, and have power to release thee?" To kill or to let live? To scourge and to crucify? Can Pilate save a soul, speak peace to an aching heart, or raise a worthy man in immortal glory? Eternal power rests with the Man of Sorrows, and even such profane power as a worldly despot may exercise is only by the grace of Him in whom all things center. And Pilate—does he dare affront Annas or offend Tiberius by freeing this innocent man? "And Jesus pitied the hopeless bewilderment of this man, whom guilt had changed from a ruler into a slave." Then he who could not look upon any sin with the least degree of allowance spoke first of the sins of Pilate and then of those of Judas and Annas and Caiaphas and the Sanhedrin and the Jewish nation. "Thou couldest have no power at all against me, except it were given thee from above"—'My Father is permitting all this that I may now be lifted up upon the cross, as the Messianic word requires'—"therefore he that delivered me unto thee hath the greater sin."

"In the very depths of his inmost soul Pilate felt the truth of the words—silently acknowledged the superiority of his bound and lacerated victim. . . . All of his soul that was not eaten away by pride and cruelty thrilled back an unwonted echo to these few calm words of the Son of God.

Jesus had condemned his sin, and so far from being offended, the judgment only deepened his awe of this mysterious Being, whose utter impotence seemed grander and more awful than the loftiest power. From that time Pilate was even yet more anxious to save him." But his attempts were futile. Back from the satanic mob came the cry: "If thou let this man go, thou art not Caesar's friend: whosoever maketh himself a king speaketh against Caesar."

Then Pilate, the sin-bound ruler of Judea, led Jesus, the thong-bound ruler of the earth, forth into "a place that is called the Pavement, but in the Hebrew, Gabbatha." Pilate "sat down in the judgment seat." It was Friday, April 7, A.D. 30. The Roman trials had begun about 6 A.M. and it was now some three hours later. To the Jews Pilate said: "BEHOLD YOUR KING!"

Their cries increased; their shrieking wails pierced the Judean air; their faces were as flint, their hearts as stone. There was no mercy here—only hate and envy and a lust for vengeance. Lucifer was their Lord. "Away with him, away with him," they screamed, "crucify him." To this Pilate said: "SHALL I CRUCIFY YOUR KING?" Their answer: "We have no king but Caesar."[7] "At that dark terrible name of Caesar, Pilate trembled. It was a name to conjure with. It mastered him. He thought of that terrible implement of tyranny, the accusation of *laesa majestas,* into which all other charges merged, which had made confiscation and torture so common, and had caused blood to flow like water in the streets of Rome. He thought of Tiberius, the aged gloomy Emperor, then hiding at Caprea his ulcerous features, his poisonous suspicions, his sick infamies, his desperate revenge. At this very time he had been maddened into a yet more sanguinary and misanthropic ferocity by the detected falsity and treason of his only friend and minister, Sejanus, and it was to Sejanus himself that Pilate is said to have owed his position. There might be secret delators in that very mob. Panic-stricken, the unjust judge, in obedience to his own terrors, consciously betrayed the innocent victim to the anguish of death. He who had so often prostituted justice, was now unable to achieve the one act of justice which he desired. He who had so often murdered pity, was now forbidden to taste the sweetness of a pity for which he longed. He who had so often abused authority, was now rendered impotent to exercise it, for once, on the side of right. Truly for him, sin had become its own Erinnys, and his pleasant vices had been converted into the instrument of his punishment!"

"And Pilate gave sentence that it should be as they required."

"He delivered Jesus to their will."

"Then delivered he him therefore unto them to be crucified."

Judas Iscariot Commits Suicide

(Matthew 27:3-10; JST, Matthew 27:5-6, 10; Acts 1:15-21)

As an addendum to this night's evil deeds, we inscribe in our record the death of a devil—not a demon from hell, for such never die; they are doomed to Gnolom, to dwell in hell worlds without end—but a mortal devil, one into whom Satan had entered; one who conspired to put his Lord to death; one who sold his soul for thirty pieces of silver; one who led a cohort of armed men into the seclusion of Gethsemane; one who betrayed the Son of Man with an effusive outpouring of seeming love and respect that was, in fact, jealousy and hate. He was Judas of Kerioth—Judas Iscariot—the only Judean among the Twelve.

We do not know when Judas took his own life—only that he seems to have preceded his Lord in death. As the full impact of his traitorous deed began to dawn upon his sin-sick soul, it ignited within him the fires of Gehenna; a near madness possessed his being. "Terribly soon did the Nemesis fall on the main actor in the lower stages of this [night's] iniquity. Doubtless through all those hours Judas had been a secure spectator of all that had occurred, and when the morning dawned upon that chilly night, and he knew the decision of the Priests and of the Sanhedrin, and saw that Jesus was now given over for crucifixion to the Roman Governor, then he began fully to realize all that he had done. There is in a great crime an awfully illuminating power. It lights up the theatre of the conscience with an unnatural glare, and, expelling the twilight glamour of self-interest, shows the actions and motives in their full and true aspect. In Judas, as in so many thousands before and since, this opening of the eyes which follows the consummation of an awful sin to which many other sins have led, drove him from remorse to despair, from despair to madness, from madness to suicide." (Farrar, p. 659.)

Matthew says that when Judas saw that Jesus "was condemned"—probably by Pilate to be crucified—he "repented himself, and brought again the thirty pieces of silver to the chief priests and elders." Repented? Only in the sense that he had remorse of conscience and wished that he had not lifted up his heel against his own familar Friend, whose bread he ate—not repentance in the true Godly sense. True repentance is a gift of God that grows out of faith in Christ and carries with it a firm determination to love and serve the Lord. Judas regretted what he had done, but he was still a thief at heart, still a traitor, and still destined to suffer the wrath of God in Sheol until death and hell deliver up the dead which are in them. And yet he had the good grace to say: "I have betrayed the innocent blood."

That much at least he knew. The sorrows of the damned were already welling up within him. "The road, the streets, the people's faces—all seemed now to bear witness against him and for Jesus. He read it everywhere; he felt it always; he imagined it, till his whole being was on flame. What had been; what was; what would be! Heaven and earth receded from him; there were voices in the air, and pangs in the soul—and no escape, help, counsel, or hope anywhere." (Edersheim 2:574.) And yet this much he knew: "I have betrayed the innocent blood." 'This Man is innocent; he ought to go free.'

Their reply, like a dagger thrust into the heart of a fleeing man, both stunned and cursed him: "What is that to us?" they said. "See thou to it; thy sins be upon thee." And thus it ever is: conspirators and traitors forsake each other, and the devil sustaineth not his own. Judas "must get rid of these thirty pieces of silver, which, like thirty serpents, coiled round his soul with [the] terrible hissing of death." (Edersheim 2:574.) His infamy was his own. "He felt that he was of no importance any longer; that in guilt there is no possibility of mutual respect, no basis for any feeling but mutual abhorrence. His paltry thirty pieces of silver were all that he would get. For these he had sold his soul; and these he should no more enjoy than Achan enjoyed the gold he buried, or Ahab the garden he had seized. Flinging them wildly down upon the pavement into the holy place where the priests sat, and into which he might not enter, he hurried out into the despairing solitude from which he was not destined to emerge alive." (Farrar, p. 659.)

Judas is about to die by his own hand and become not only the father of traitors but the father of suicides from henceforth. But he is going to die in a particular manner, at an appointed place, to fulfill the divine word—a word uttered more than a thousand years before by David, more than six hundred years before by Jeremiah, and nearly six hundred years before by Zechariah. It was David who, as Peter expressed it, said of Judas: "Let his habitation be desolate, and let no man dwell therein: and his bishoprick let another take."[8] It was Jeremiah who was commanded to take a potter's vessel out into the potter's field—into the Valley of Hinnom; the Valley of Slaughter; the place called Tophet; the place called Gehenna in Jesus' day; the place where apostate Israel had burned their children to Baal; the place which was filled with the blood of innocents. There, in that vile and evil setting, while the leaders of the people listened, Jeremiah was commanded to break the potter's vessel and to prophesy that even so would it be with Judah and Jerusalem. "Thus saith the Lord of hosts; Even so will I break this people and this city, as one breaketh a potter's vessel, that cannot be made whole again: and they shall bury them in Tophet, till there be no place to bury." (Jer. 19.) And then it was Zechariah who prophesied that the chief priests and rulers would weigh, for the price of the Lord, thirty pieces of silver and that they would then be cast "to the potter in the house of the Lord." (Zech. 11:12-13.)

And so, now, in fulfillment of all this, Judas is to do his evil deed. "And he cast down the pieces of silver in the temple," Matthew says, "and departed, and went, and hanged himself on a tree. And straightway he fell down, and his bowels gushed out, and he died." "Out he rushed from the Temple, out of Jerusalem, into solitude. Whither shall it be? Down into the horrible solitude of the Valley of Hinnom, the 'Tophet' of old, with its ghastly memories, the Gehenna of the future, with its ghostly associations. But it was not solitude, for it seemed now peopled with figures, faces, sounds. Across the Valley, and up the steep sides of the mountain! We are now on 'the potter's field' of Jeremiah—somewhat to the west above where the Kidron and Hinnom valleys merge. It is cold, soft clayey soil, where the footsteps slip, or are held in clammy bonds. Here jagged rocks rise perpendicularly: perhaps there was some gnarled, bent, stunted tree. Up there he climbed to the top of that rock. Now slowly and deliberately he unwound the long girdle that held his garment. It was the girdle in which he had carried those thirty pieces of silver. He was now quite calm and collected. With that girdle he will hang himself on that tree close by, and when he has fastened it, he will throw himself off from that jagged rock.

"It is done; but as, unconscious, not yet dead perhaps,

he swung heavily on that branch, under the unwonted burden the girdle gave way, or perhaps the knot, which his trembling hands had made, unloosed, and he fell heavily forward among the jagged rock beneath, and perished in the manner of which St. Peter reminded his fellow disciples in the days before Pentecost.'' (Edersheim 2:575.)

Then ''the chief priests took the silver pieces'' and said: ''It is not lawful for to put them into the treasury, because it is the price of blood.'' After counseling together, they—the chief priests!—''bought with them the potter's field, to bury strangers in.'' Peter says that Judas ''purchased a field with the reward of iniquity,'' and that it was called ''Aceldama, . . . The field of blood.'' Of this whole episode, Edersheim says: ''It was not lawful to take into the Temple-treasury, for the purchase of sacred things, money that had been unlawfully gained. In such cases the Jewish Law provided that the money was to be restored to the donor, and, if he insisted on giving it, that he should be induced to spend it for something for the public weal. This explains the apparent discrepancy between the accounts in the Book of Acts and by St. Matthew. By a fiction of law the money was still considered to be Judas', and to have been applied by him in the purchase of the well-known 'potter's field,' for the charitable purpose of burying in it strangers.

''But from henceforth the old name of 'potter's field' became popularly changed into that of 'field of blood.' And yet it was the act of Israel through its leaders: 'they took the thirty pieces of silver—the price of him that was valued, whom they of the children of Israel did value, and gave them for the potter's field!' It was all theirs, though they would have fain made it all Judas': the valuing, the selling, and the purchasing. And the 'potter's field'—the very spot on which Jeremiah had been Divinely directed to prophesy against Jerusalem and against Israel: how was it now all fulfilled in the light of the completed sin and apostasy of the people, as prophetically described by Zechariah! This Tophet of Jeremiah, now that they had valued and sold at thirty shekel Israel's Messiah-Shepherd—truly a Tophet, and become a field of blood! Surely, not an accidental coincidence this, that it should be the place of Jeremy's announcement of judgment: not accidental, but veritably a fulfilment of his prophecy! And so St. Matthew, targuming this prophecy in form as in its spirit, and in true Jewish manner stringing to it the prophetic description furnished by Zechariah, sets the event before us as the fulfilment of Jeremy's prophecy." (Edersheim 2:575-76.)

Judas, guilty, thus paid the first installment on the punishment decreed; Judas, guilty, yet added to his guilt by taking that which only God can give; Judas, guilty, thus carried his guilt to hell, where it will remain until he, having paid the uttermost farthing and been beaten with many stripes, bows the knee to Him whom he betrayed, truly repents, and comes forth to receive his place in the realms of Him who is merciful and gracious to all men.

NOTES

1. As explained in note 1 of the previous chapter, we are continuing our practice of quoting Farrar; the quotations in this chapter are from pages 673–87.

2. These same "revenges of history" are summarized by Edersheim in these words: "Some thirty years later, and on that very spot, was judgment pronounced against some of the best in Jerusalem; and among the 3,600 victims of the Governor's fury, of whom not a few were scourged and crucified right over against the Praetorium, were many of the noblest of the citizens of Jerusalem. A few years more, and hundreds of crosses bore Jewish mangled bodies within sight of Jerusalem. And still have these wanderers seemed to bear, from century to century, and from land to land, that burden of blood; and still does it seem to weigh 'on us and our children.' " (Edersheim 2:578.)

3. The student of history will be reminded of the persecutions and slaughter of the Jews, since the day of Farrar, as these have been seen in Russia, Germany, and other nations, particularly those decreed by the evil hand of Hitler during World War II, to say nothing of the Islamic ill will toward their fellow descendants of Abraham. That these national and racial hatreds will yet play a great part in the wars and turmoil leading up to the Second Coming of the Son of Man is known to all students of the scriptures.

4. In this connection, Jeremy Taylor, in his *Life of Christ,* as quoted in a footnote by Farrar, says: "Upon all murderers God hath not thrown a thunderbolt, nor broken all sacrilegious persons upon the wheel of an inconstant and ebbing estate, nor spoken to every oppressor from heaven in a voice of thunder, nor cut off all rebels in the first attempts of insurrection; but because He hath done so to some, we are to look upon those judgments as divine accents and voices of God, threatening all the same crimes with the like events, and with the ruins of eternity." And we may add: In the providences of Him whose judgments are just, all men, be they Jew or Gentile, will be accountable for their own sins when they stand before the bar of the Great Jehovah. Others who have

scourged and crucified and persecuted lesser persons—those who are the least of these his brethren—shall be rewarded along with Judas and Annas and Caiaphas and the Jews of that day for the evil deeds that are theirs.

5. Farrar at this point, in a footnote, quotes these apt words of Jeremy Taylor: "The blood of Jesus shed for the salvation of the world became to them a curse. . . . So manna turns to worms, and the wine of angels to vinegar and lees, when it is received into impure vessels or tasted by wanton palates, and the sun himself produces rats and serpents when it reflects upon the slime of Nilus."

6. Lest the words in the text be deemed harsh or intemperate or unfair, Farrar, in a footnote at this point, says: "It is in the deepest sincerity that I add these last words. Any one who traces a spirit of vindictiveness in the last paragraph wholly misjudges the spirit in which it is written. This book may perhaps fall into the hands of Jewish readers. They, of all others, if true to the deepest lessons of the faith in which they have been trained, will acknowledge the hand of God in History. And the events spoken of here are not imaginative; they are indisputable facts. The Jew at least will believe that in external consequences God visits the sins of the fathers upon the children. Often and often in History have the crimes of the guilty *seemed* to be visited even on their *innocent* posterity. The apparent injustice of this is but on the surface. There is a fire that purifies, no less than a fire that scathes; and who shall say that the very afflictions of Israel—afflictions, alas! so largely caused by the sins of Christendom—may not have been meant for a refining of the pure gold? God's judgments—it may be the very sternest and most irremediable of them—come, many a time, in the guise, not of affliction, but of immense earthly prosperity and ease."

We would be remiss if we did not append to these recitations, and to those in the text, all of which are true and must be said, at least this reminder of the more glorious day that lies ahead for the Jewish people: In the wisdom and providences of Him who knoweth all things and who doeth all things well, there shall yet be a day of rejoicing and restoration for the Jewish nation. We do not speak of the political gathering of a remnant of their number back to Palestine, but of that glorious future day when they accept their true King and return to their true Messiah. The full blessings of peace in this life and eternal life in the world to come are received by all men—Jew and Gentile alike—only when they accept Christ as their King and worship the Father in his holy name.

7. "*We have no king but Caesar.*" "With this cry Judaism was, in the person of its representatives, guilty of denial of God, of blasphemy, of apostasy. It committed suicide; and, ever since, has its dead body been carried in show from land to land, and from century to century: to be dead, and to remain dead, till He come a second time, Who is the Resurrection and the Life!" (Edersheim 2:581.)

8. Psalms 69 and 109, which are the source of Peter's declaration, abound in Messianic phrases that speak both of Jesus and of Judas.

Chapter 107

THE CRUCIFIXION

He was lifted up upon the cross
and slain for the sins of the world.
(1 Ne. 11:33.)
They shall consider him a man, . . .
and shall crucify him. (Mosiah 3:9.)

From Gabbatha to Golgotha

(Matthew 27:31-33; JST, Matthew 27:35; Mark 15:20-22; JST, Mark 15:25; Luke 23:26-32; JST, Luke 23:31-32; John 19:16-17; JST, John 19:17)

As we come now to that awful hour when a Roman mallet drives rough nails into sinless hands—the hour when a God dies—we are faced with the awesome task of setting forth how he died and by whom he was crucified. True it is that a Roman hammer drove the sharp ferrous spikes into his quivering and aching hands; true, that a Roman arm hurled the steel-headed spear into his suffering side; true, that a Roman Procurator profaned the Holy One by turning the Sanhedrist shriek, "Crucify him," into a Roman decree. But how can the life of a God be taken? How can the Great Jehovah, who made heaven and earth and the sea and the fountains of waters—and all things that in them are—how can the Lord Omnipotent, the Creator of all things from the beginning, how can he die? And at whose door is the demonish deed laid?

The Messianic word identifies his murderers as "the Jews"—as a people and as a "nation"—and ascribes their heinous course to "priestcrafts and iniquities." (2 Ne. 10:3-5.) And around his cross, mingling with the gaping crowds who gained vicarious pleasure from his agonies, we find the Sanhedrists and chief priests inciting the people to mock and revile and defy the one who had been lifted up and whose blood then watered the dusty soil of Calvary. As to the dire deeds of this dread day, they happened on this wise:

While seated on the Roman judgment seat in Gabbatha, the sinful and proud Procurator asked if he, Pilate, should crucify their Jewish King Jesus. Cursing themselves with their own words, and dooming their own race out of their own mouths, the chief priests and Sanhedrists said they had no king but Caesar. Then Pilate delivered Jesus to them, the Jews, to be crucified. So it is written by John. Matthew and Mark tell us that before the death procession started for Golgotha, Jesus was taken by the soldiers into the Praetorium where—clothed in purple, pained with a crown of thorns, mocked and smitten by the rude soldiery—he was hailed as the demeaned king of a damned race. After these degrading acts of demonish sport, the men of war and of the world took off the purple robe, reclothed him in his own raiment, and led him away to crucify him. Caesar, their adopted king, would that day do for the Jews what they could not do for themselves—crucify their true King. Among the seed of Jacob the death penalty could only be imposed by strangulation, beheading, burning, or stoning. So it is written in the Mishnah. But Jesus, according to the eternal providences, must suffer the opprobium of a non-Jewish crucifixion. The Romans must do the deed for the Jews. And this is the day; the appointed hour is upon them.

Now it was the custom among them for a condemned man to carry his cross. We do not know the kind and type of cross upon which Jesus was lifted up. Three types were in common usage, one shaped like an "X," another like a "T," and the third in the traditional Latin form. Probably this latter was used as it would have provided a place for the superscription. It consisted of two parts, an eight- or nine-foot pole and a movable crosspiece or patibulum. Ordinarily the patibulum consisted of two parallel beams fastened together between which, as he carried his heavy burden, the neck of the criminal was placed. "The cross was not, and could not have been, the massive and lofty structure with which such hundreds of pictures have made us familiar. Crucifixion was among the Romans a very common punishment, and it is clear that they would not waste any trouble in constructing the instrument of shame and torture. It would undoubtedly be made of the very commonest wood that came to hand, perhaps olive or sycamore, and knocked together in the very rudest fashion."[1]

And so Jesus, bearing his cross, was led along the dolorous way to a place of burial, of skulls, of death. Four Roman soldiers went beside him. It was the purpose and intent to attract attention, to demean the criminal, and to frighten others so they would not themselves come to a like end. A sign, either hanging around his neck or carried by one of the soldiers, announced the crimes of the crucifee. Two condemned criminals, each bearing his cross and each attended by four soldiers, followed Jesus to the place of agony and death.

"To support the body of a man, a cross would require to be of a certain size and weight; and to one enfeebled by the horrible severity of the previous scourging, the carrying of such a burden would be an additional misery. But Jesus was enfeebled not only by this cruelty, but by previous days of violent struggle and agitation, by an evening of deep and overwhelming emotion, by a night of sleepless anxiety and suffering, by the mental agony of the garden"—and this suffering in Gethsemane, when great drops of blood oozed from every pore, bore in more heavily upon him than all else combined—"by three trials and three sentences of death before the Jews, by the long and exhausting scenes in the Praetorium, by the examination before Herod, and by the brutal and painful derisions which He had undergone, first at the hands of the Sanhedrin and their servants, then from Herod's body-guard, and lastly from the Roman cohort. All these, superadded to the sickening lacerations of the scourging, had utterly broken down His bodily powers. His tottering footsteps, if not His actual falls under that fearful load, made it evident that He lacked the physical strength to carry it from the Praetorium to Golgotha."

Shortly after the parade of death began, certainly by the time the melancholy marchers reached the gates of the city, Jesus was no longer able to bear the burden of the cross. Thereupon the soldiers laid hold upon Simon of Cyrene, who chanced—or was it an instance of an intervening providence—to be coming in from the country; him they compelled to bear the cross of Jesus. Mark identifies him as "the father of Alexander and Rufus," showing that at a later date at least the members of his family were disciples of renown whose names were familiar to the saints. It is pleasant to suppose that even as Jesus kept the Feast of the Passover in the home of a devout disciple, so a Divine Providence provided for him at this hour another believing soul who would rejoice in days to come that he had been privileged to lift some of the fatiguing burden from him whose burdens were greater than mortal man can bear.

It is clear that the Roman-Jewish design to herald the crucifixion of Jesus from the housetops surpassed their wildest dreams. Such crowds as had listened to him in the temple were present. A marvelous moving multitude marched with the death party. These were the ten thousands of Judea and the thousands of Galilee, both men and women. As far as the record recites, none of the men in that mighty mass came to his defense, but with the women it was otherwise. "From the *men* in that moving crowd He does not appear to have received one word of pity or of sympathy. *Some* there must surely have been who had seen His miracles, who had heard His words; some of those who had been almost, if not utterly, convinced of His Messiahship, as they hung upon His lips while He uttered His great discourses in the Temple; some of the eager crowd who had accompanied Him from Bethany five days before with shouted hosannas and waving palms. Yet if so, a faithless timidity or a deep misgiving—perhaps even a boundless sorrow—kept them dumb. But these women, more quick to pity, less susceptible to controlling influences, could not and would not conceal the grief and amazement with which this spectacle filled them. They beat upon their breasts and rent the air with their lamentations, till Jesus Himself hushed their shrill cries with words of solemn warning. Turning to them—which He could not have done had He still been staggering under the burden of His cross—He said to them":

> *Daughters of Jerusalem, weep not for me, but weep for yourselves, and for your children.*
>
> *For, behold, the days are coming, in the which they shall say, Blessed are the barren, and the wombs that never bare, and the paps which never gave suck. . . .*
>
> *For if they do these things in a green tree, what shall be done in the dry?*[2]

To this expression relative to the green tree and the dry tree, Luke says: "This he spake, signifying the scattering of Israel, and the desolation of the heathen, or in other words, the Gentiles," meaning the Israelitish scattering that took place at the destruction of Jerusalem, and meaning the desolations that would fall upon all men in the latter days, the days of wickedness and vengeance that should precede his Second Coming.

"Many of them, and the majority of their children,

would live to see such rivers of bloodshed, such complications of agony, as the world had never known before—days which would seem to overpass the capacities of human suffering, and would make men seek to hide themselves, if it might be, under the very roots of the hill on which their city stood. The fig-tree of their nation's life was still green: if such deeds of darkness were possible *now,* what should be done when that tree was withered and blasted, and ready for the burning?—if in the days of hope and decency they could execrate their blameless Deliverer, what would happen in the days of blasphemy and madness and despair? If, under the full light of day, Priests and Scribes could crucify the Innocent, what would be done in the midnight orgies and blood-stained bacchanalia of Zealots and Murderers? This was a day of crime; that would be a day when Crime had become her own avenging fury.

"The solemn warning, the last sermon of Christ on earth"—unless he made some unrecorded statements from the cross—"was meant primarily for those who heard it; but, like all the words of Christ, it has deeper and wider meaning for all mankind. These words warn every child of man that the day of careless pleasure and blasphemous disbelief will be followed by the crack of doom; they warn each human being who lives in pleasure on the earth, and eats, and drinks, and is drunken, that though the patience of God waits, and His silence is unbroken, yet the days shall come when He shall speak in thunder, and His wrath shall burn like fire."

They Crucify Their King

(Matthew 27:34-38; JST, Matthew 27:39-42; Mark 15:23-28; JST, Mark 15:26, 28-31; Luke 23:33-34, 38; JST, Luke 23:35; John 19:18-24)

At about 9 A.M. the dread procession arrived at Golgotha, which is Calvary—"a place of burial." There the final preparations for crucifixion were performed. So horrible was death on the cross that custom permitted an act that lessened the pain and agony. "Utterly brutal and revolting as was the punishment of crucifixion, which has now for fifteen hundred years been abolished by the common pity and abhorrence of mankind, there was one custom in Judea, and [also] one occasionally practised by the Romans, which reveal some touch of passing humanity. The latter consisted in giving to the sufferer a blow under the arm-pit, which, without causing death, yet hastened its approach. Of this I need not speak, because, for whatever reason, it was not practised on this occasion." We cannot believe other than that a Divine Providence—which guided in the minutest detail all that this day transpired—so controlled events as to prevent its happening, and that for the very reasons involved in the other proffered act of mercy that Jesus himself voluntarily prevented.

"The former [act of mercy], which seems to have been due to the milder nature of Judaism, and which was derived from a happy piece of Rabbinic exegesis on Proverbs 31:6, consisted in giving to the condemned, immediately before his execution, a draught of wine medicated with some powerful opiate.[3] It had been the custom of wealthy ladies in Jerusalem to provide this stupefying potion at their own expense, and they did so quite irrespectively of their sympathy for any individual criminal. It was probably taken freely by the two malefactors, but when they offered it to Jesus He would not drink it. The refusal was an act of sublimest heroism. The effect of the draught was to dull the nerves, to cloud the intellect, to provide an anesthetic against some part, at least, of the lingering agonies of that dreadful death. But He, whom some modern skeptics have been base enough to accuse of feminine feebleness and cowardly despair, preferred rather 'to look Death in the face'—to meet the king of terrors without striving to deaden the force of one agonising anticipation, or to still the throbbing of one lacerated nerve."

This, then, is the awful hour. They crucify him. The

scene probably was acted out somewhat along this line: "The three crosses were laid on the ground—that of Jesus, which was doubtless taller than the other two, being placed in bitter scorn in the midst. Perhaps the cross-beam was now nailed to the upright, and certainly the title, which had either been borne by Jesus fastened round His neck, or carried by one of the soldiers in front of Him, was now nailed to the summit of His cross. Then He was stripped of His clothes, and then followed the most awful moment of all. He was laid down upon the implement of torture. His arms were stretched along the cross-beams; and at the centre of the open palms, the point of a huge iron nail was placed, which, by the blow of a mallet, was driven home into the wood. Then through either foot separately, or possibly through both together as they were placed one over the other, another huge nail tore its way through the quivering flesh. Whether the sufferer was *also* bound to the cross we do not know; but, to prevent the hands and feet being torn away by the weight of the body, which could not 'rest upon nothing but four great wounds,' there was, about the centre of the cross, a wooden projection strong enough to support, at least in part, a human body which soon became a mass of agony."[4]

We are wont to speak of seven words or utterances made by Jesus from the cross. It was probably at this point that he made the first of these: "Father, forgive them; for they know not what they do." The reference, of course, is to "the soldiers who crucified him," not to Judas or Annas or Caiaphas or the chief priests or the Sanhedrin or Pilate or Herod or Lucifer or any who have rebelled against him and chosen to walk in darkness at noonday. All these are left in the hands of Divine Justice, and mercy cannot rob justice, else God would cease to be God.[5]

Jesus is speaking, rather, of the Roman soldiers who have no choice but to do the will of Pilate and those whose minions they are. And he is not asking the Father to forgive them of their sins and to prepare them, thus, to dwell with clean and pure persons in celestial rest. He is simply asking that the deed of crucifixion be not laid at their door; let the responsibility rest with the Jews and with the Procurator of Rome, not with these who are doing—albeit in a gross and cruel manner—no more than they have been commanded to do. Had his concern been the remission of their sins, he could have acted on his own, for, as his ministry amply attests, the Son of Man had power to forgive sins on earth. And, further, if these Roman robots are to receive forgiveness of sins and the salvation that flows therefrom, it must be on the same basis as with all others who cleanse themselves from sin. The course is one of faith, repentance, baptism, and the receipt of that baptism of fire which burns dross and evil out of a human soul as though by fire. Yet the mercy and majesty and might of Him who conquered all is manifest in his petition. As pains beyond compare wrack his tortured body, his concern and interest centers in the spiritual well-being of these ruffians of the baser sort who are the creators of much of the agony.

But back now to the modus operandi of the crucifixion. As the cross lay on the ground, Jesus was nailed thereto. "And then the accursed tree—with its living human burden hanging upon it in helpless torment, and suffering fresh tortures as every movement irritated the fresh rents in hands and feet—was slowly heaved up by strong arms, and the end of it fixed firmly in a hole dug deep in the ground for that purpose. The feet were but a little raised above the earth. The victim was in full reach of every hand that might choose to strike, in close proximity to every gesture of rage and hatred. He might hang for hours to be abused, insulted, even struck, by the ever-moving multitude who, with that desire to see what is horrible which always characterises the coarsest hearts, had thronged to gaze upon a sight which should rather have made them weep tears of blood.

"And there, in tortures which grew ever more insupportable, ever more maddening as time flowed on, the unhappy victims might linger in pain so cruelly intolerable, that often they were driven to entreat and implore the spectators, or the executioners, for dear pity's sake, to put an end to anguish too awful for man to bear—conscious to the last, and often, with tears of abject misery, beseeching from their enemies the priceless boon of death.[6]

"For indeed a death by crucifixion seems to include all that pain and death *can* have of [the] horrible and [the] ghastly—dizziness, cramp, thirst, starvation, sleeplessness, traumatic fever, tetanus, publicity of shame, long continuance of torment, horror of anticipation, mortification of untended wounds—all intensified just up to the point at which they can be endured at all, but all stopping just short of the point which would give to the sufferer the relief of unconsciousness. The unnatural position made every movement painful; the lacerated veins and crushed tendons throbbed with incessant anguish; the wounds, inflamed by exposure, gradually gangrened; the arteries—especially of the head—became swollen and oppressed with surcharged blood; and while each variety of misery went on gradually increasing, there was added to them the intolerable pang of a burning and raging thirst; and all these physical complications caused an internal excitement and anxiety, which made the prospect of death itself—of death, the awful unknown enemy, at whose approach man usually shudders most—bear the aspect of a delicious and exquisite release."

Lest there be any question in any mind as to the identity of the one on the chief of the three crosses—for Jerusalem was full of Passover pilgrims, assembled from all Palestine and from Jewish settlements in distant lands—Pilate wrote "a title," "a superscription," "his accusation," and put it upon the cross. The words were recorded in the official Latin, in the current Greek, and in the vernacular Aramaic. The message read: "JESUS OF NAZARETH, THE KING OF THE JEWS."

"When the cross was uplifted, the leading Jews, for the first time, prominently noticed the deadly insult in which

Pilate had vented his indignation. Before, in their blind rage, they had imagined that the manner of His crucifixion was an insult aimed at *Jesus;* but now that they saw Him hanging between the two robbers, on a cross yet loftier, it suddenly flashed upon them that it was a public scorn inflicted upon *them*. . . . With the passionate ill-humour of the Roman governor there probably blended a vein of seriousness. While he was delighted to revenge himself on his detested subjects by an act of public insolence, he probably meant, or half meant, to imply that this *was,* in one sense, the King of the Jews—the greatest, the noblest, the truest of His race, whom therefore His race had crucified. The King was not unworthy of His kingdom, but the kingdom of the King. There was something loftier even than royalty in the glazing eyes which never ceased to look with sorrow on the City of Righteousness, which had now become a city of murderers. The Jews felt the intensity of the scorn with which Pilate had treated them. It so completely poisoned their hour of triumph, that they sent their chief priests in deputation, begging the Governor to alter the obnoxious title."

"It should be written and set up over his head," they said to Pilate, "his [own] accusation, This is he that said he was Jesus, the King of the Jews." To their importuning plea, Pilate answered curtly: "What I have written, I have written; let it alone." And the superscription remained to testify to them and to all men that here indeed was he of whom Moses and the prophets spake—the one who came to deliver, to redeem, and to save: their Messiah, their King, their Lord and their God.

Strange as it may seem to the carnal mind, the hidden hand of Him who governs in the affairs of men did not let so much as a jot or a tittle of the Messianic word fall. Mark testifies that with him were crucified two thieves, "the one on his right hand, and the other on his left," that Isaiah's word might be fulfilled, "And he was numbered with the transgressors." (Isa. 53:12.) And when he was crucified, the four soldiers ordered to guard the cross—lest a half-dead person be taken down by his friends and revived—both divided and cast lots for his garments. His headgear, the outer cloaklike garment, the girdle, and the sandals, differing little in value, were easily divided among them. But for the seamless woven inner garment, an article of appreciable worth, they cast lots, "that the scripture might be fulfilled, which saith, They parted my raiment among them, and for my vesture they did cast lots." (Ps. 22:18.)

NOTES

1. Quotations in this chapter that are not otherwise footnoted are from pages 688–99 of Farrar.

2. "If Israel's oppressors could do what was then in process to the 'Green Tree,' who bore the leafage of freedom and truth and offered the priceless fruit of life eternal, what would the powers of evil not do to the withered branches and dried trunk of apostate Judaism?" (Talmage, p. 654.) Farrar gives the traditional interpretation of Jesus' statement thus: "If, in the fulfillment of God's purposes, I the Holy and the Innocent must suffer thus—if the green tree be thus blasted—how shall the dry tree of a wicked life, with its abominable branches, be consumed to the uttermost burning?" With reference to the martyrdom of the Prophet and the Patriarch of this dispensation, the inspired account contains this expression: "If the fire can scathe a green tree for the glory of God, how easy it will burn up the dry trees to purify the vineyard of corruption." (D&C 135:6.)

3. "Give strong drink unto him that is ready to perish, and wine unto those that be of heavy hearts." (Prov. 31:6.)

4. The spiritually enlightened will envision, in this connection, the fulfillment of Isaiah's Messianic word concerning "the nail that is fastened in the sure place." (Isa. 22:21-25.)

5. Near the close of a long sermon on mercy and justice, Alma says: "Justice exerciseth all his demands, and also mercy claimeth all which is her own; and thus, none but the truly penitent are saved. What, do ye suppose that mercy can rob justice? I say unto you, Nay; not one whit. If so, God would cease to be God." (Alma 42:24-25.) Alma's reasoning, thus, is that unless God conformed to his eternal laws he would not be God, for it is his total and complete conformity to law that makes him God. Jesus, thus, could not abandon the whole system of law and forgive and save the thieves who were far from being penitent and obedient as of the time they hung with him on their crosses.

6. Edersheim suggests a somewhat different modus operandi with reference to the crucifixion of Jesus. "Avowedly, the punishment was invented to make death as painful and as lingering as the power of human endurance. First, the upright wood was planted in the ground. It was not high, and probably the Feet of the Sufferer were not above one or two feet from the ground. Thus could the communication described in the Gospels take place between Him and others; thus, also, might His Sacred Lips be moistened with the sponge attached to a short stalk of hyssop. Next, the transverse wood was placed on the ground, and the Sufferer laid on it, when His Arms were extended, drawn up, and bound to it. Then (this not in Egypt, but in Carthage and Rome) a strong, sharp nail was driven, first into the Right, then into the Left Hand. Next, the Sufferer was drawn up by means of ropes, perhaps ladders; the transverse either bound or nailed to the upright, and a rest or support for the Body fastened on it. Lastly, the Feet were extended, and either one nail hammered into each, or a larger piece of iron through the two. We have already expressed our belief that the indignity of exposure was not offered at such a Jewish execution. And so might the crucified hang for hours, even days, in the unutterable anguish of suffering, till consciousness at last failed." (Edersheim 2:589.)

ON THE CROSS OF CALVARY

My Father sent me
that I might be lifted up upon the cross;
and after that I had been lifted up
upon the cross, that I might draw
all men unto me,
that as I have been lifted up
by men even so should men be lifted up
by the Father, to stand before me,
to be judged of their works,
whether they be good
or whether they be evil—
And for this cause have I been lifted up;
therefore, according to the power
of the Father I will draw
all men unto me, that they may be judged
according to their works.
(3 Ne. 27:14-15.)

The Sanhedrists Incite Mockery and Derision against Him

(Matthew 27:39-43; JST, Matthew 27:46; Mark 15:29-32; Luke 23:35-37)

With Jesus nailed to the cross, with the nails driven in a sure place, with an agonizing death assured, the floodgates of derision and hatred and venom are opened upon him. All of the vile passions and evil powers that framed the cry, "Crucify him, for we have no king but Caesar," are now hurled at him in the base challenge to prove his claimed divinity by saving himself and ascending an earthly throne.

The Roman soldiers have done their cruel deed and done it well. While Jesus hangs in agony they have naught to do but keep the peace and protect the cross, lest any of his friends steal the body of the Suffering One. They seat themselves before the instrument of death which they have raised; they begin to eat and drink and make merry. They quaff the cheap wine of the countryside and drink pledges to the Jewish King, and even offer him some of their vinegar-like liquor so that he can toast them. Theirs, we should note, is no special hatred toward him as a person; to them he is just another Jew, another member of a hated and despised race, another religious fanatic whose zeal has brought him to a deserved death. Their derision comes forth against him in his representative capacity, against him as a symbol of the benighted people who are so repulsive to them, against him as a supposed king. "If thou be the king of the Jews, save thyself," they say.

But it was not of a quarterion of coarse and brutal Gentile warriors that the Messianic word spake. The Jewish Messiah, whose hands and feet had been pierced, whose garments had been parted among them, and for whose vesture they had cast lots, said of himself, by the mouth of David: "All they that see me laugh me to scorn: . . . They gaped upon me with their mouths, as a ravening and a roaring lion." (Ps. 22:7, 13.) It was a nation and a people and their priestly rulers who crucified their King, not simply a few alien men of war; and it was a nation and a people and their priestly rulers who mocked and scoffed before his cross. We have seen how incensed the chief priests were over the mocking superscription nailed to the summit of the cross; this wound was deepened by the raillery of the soldiers that ascribed Jewish kingship to their mortal enemy. To turn these Roman taunts away from the Jews and to this Jesus of Galilee, we see the rulers and the chief priests and the scribes and the elders both mocking him and inciting the people to go and do likewise. The same satanic souls who had orchestrated the calls for crucifixion now led the same chorus of voices in chanting a derisive hymn of hate and vengeance against the one who had been crucified.

Their taunting cries assailed the whole ministry and work of Jesus among them. If they had planned and labored for long hours in their secret chambers to formulate their derisive charges, they could not have done better than they did in reciting those which Lucifer put into their minds almost without forethought. Their jeers cast contempt upon him in these respects:

He had announced that the Mosaic law was no longer binding upon them; that their temple-centered sacrificial system of salvation was now to cease; that they would be saved through the temple of his body; and that the destruction of that bodily temple and its resurrection in three days would be the only sign given them of his divine Sonship. Now, as they passed by and reviled and wagged their heads, they taunted him with the cry: "Ah, thou that destroyest the temple, and buildest it in three days, Save thyself, and come down from the cross." 'If salvation centers in thee, and not in Moses' law, come down now from thy cross and save thyself first and us later.'

He had testified that God was his Father; that he and the Father were one; that no man came unto the Father but by the Son; and that he was the Son of God. Now they taunt: "If thou be the Son of God, come down from the cross." What are these words but an echo, by the mouths of the Jews, of those spoken in the wilderness by the devil: "If thou be the Son of God, command that these stones be made bread," or 'Cast thyself down from the pinnacle of the Temple' (Matt. 4:1-11), to prove it. Whether by his own voice or by the voice of his servants, Lucifer's word is the same!

Jesus had saved others from all manner of disease and perils; he had calmed storms and fed multitudes; he had even raised rotting corpses from stench-filled tombs—all in similitude of the spiritual healings and salvation found in his words. Miracles were a way of life with him. Now they challenge him to save himself. "He saved others; himself he cannot save." "He saved others; let him save himself, if he be Christ, the chosen of God." Such were their words.

He had proclaimed himself as their King, their Deliverer, their Messiah. He came to reign in the hearts of the righteous. His kingdom, though not of this world, was as real as any realm ever inhabited by any people. Now they tempted him with these words: "If he be the King of Israel, let him now come down from the cross, and we will believe him." "Let Christ the King of Israel descend now from the cross, that we may see and believe." Believe? Yes, as they did when he opened the eyes of one who was blind from birth, or when he cast evil spirits from a Gadarene demoniac, or when he raised a man from Bethany from death!

As though to put an eternal seal on Him whom they derided, the Sanhedrists said—quoting, wittingly or otherwise, the Messianic word: "He trusted on the Lord that he would deliver him: let him deliver him, seeing he delighted in him" (Ps. 22:8)—the Sanhedrists said: "He trusted in God; let him deliver him now; if he will save him, let him save him; for he said, I am the Son of God." Thus bore they testimony against themselves. He trusted in God! They knew he had lived a righteous life!

Jesus Ministers from His Cross

(Matthew 27:44; JST, Matthew 27:47-48; Mark 15:32; JST, Mark 15:37; Luke 23:39-43; JST, Luke 23:40; John 19:25-27)

Our Lord's earthly mission to the wicked and ungodly among men ceased when he implored his Father to forgive the Roman soldiers who drove the sharp nails into his quivering flesh. Thereafter, through all the taunts and insults, as the heads of the wicked wagged and the jeering of the ungodly bespoke its satanic source, he maintained a kingly silence. The blasphemous bleatings of the black sheep of Israel no longer concerned him. He had delivered his Father's word to them in days past; he had raised the warning voice with power and conviction; now their sins were upon their own heads; his garments were clean. But to those who sought him, and those who yet relied on the strength of his eternal arm, he still had words of comfort and counsel. One of these was the so-called penitent thief; another was his mother, the Blessed Virgin.

One of the malefactors who was crucified with him joined the general chorus of hate and satanism; he cast into Jesus' teeth the same blasphemous cries as did those beneath the cross. "If thou art the Christ, save thyself and us," he taunted, *knowing* within himself that Jesus was *not* the Christ and that there was no hope of salvation. But the other one rebuked his fellow criminal. "Dost not thou fear God, seeing thou art in the same condemnation? And we indeed justly; for we receive the due reward of our deeds: but this man hath done nothing amiss." It is pleasant to suppose that this partially penitent prisoner-on-his-cross may have had some prior contact with the Chief Prisoner on the Cross of Calvary. Perhaps it was on a mountain in Galilee when Jesus said, "Blessed are they that mourn: for they shall be comforted" (Matt. 5:4), or near Bethany when the brother of the beloved sisters came forth from his tomb, still enwrapped in the clothes of death—but no matter, there was in any event some spark of spirituality in his darkened soul. "As a flame sometimes leaps up among dying embers, so amid the white ashes of a sinful life which lay so thick upon his heart, the flame of love towards his God and his Saviour was not quite quenched." He was not yet prepared to join such voices as still felt to sing songs of redeeming love to Him who had been lifted up, but at least he would not curse and defame the Innocent One.

"Under the hellish outcries which had broken loose around the cross of Jesus, there had lain a deep misgiving. Half of them seemed to have been instigated by doubt and fear. Even in the self-congratulations of the priests we catch an undertone of dread. Suppose that even now some imposing miracle should be wrought? Suppose that even now that martyr-form should burst indeed into Messianic splendour, and the King, who seemed to be in the slow misery of death, should suddenly with a great choice summon His legions of angels, and springing from His cross upon the rolling clouds of heaven, come in flaming fire to take vengeance upon His enemies? And the air seemed to be full of signs. There was a gloom of gathering darkness in the sky, a thrill and tremor in the solid earth, a haunting presence as of ghostly visitants who chilled the heart and hovered in awful witness above that scene." (Farrar, p. 702.)

Whatever the feelings of the more wicked of the malefactors, the other's heart was touched with remorse and pity—remorse that he had led a life of sin, pity for the suffering of one who had done no sin. "This man is just, and hath not sinned," he said. Then, "he cried unto the Lord that he would save him." "Lord, remember me when thou comest into thy kingdom," he pleaded. If this plea came from a Jewish heart, which envisioned only that temporal Messianic kingdom for which they all so fervently prayed, the penitent thief must have thought that Jesus was the Messiah—in spite of the cross—and that he would yet reign in the promised kingdom. But we would rather hope that the one in whose heart the fires of remorse and repentance were beginning to burn knew something of another kingdom, a kingdom that is not of this world, a kingdom into which the righteous will go, and where they will serve their Eternal King forever. Pleased that here was one, even in death, who would seek him and desire blessings, Jesus uttered the marvelous, though hidden and enigmatic statement, "THIS DAY THOU SHALT BE WITH ME IN PARADISE." This is the second utterance from the cross.

Paradise—the abode of righteous spirits, as they await the day of their resurrection; paradise—a place of peace and rest where the sorrows and trials of his life have been shuffled off, and where the saints continue to prepare for a celestial heaven; paradise—not the Lord's eternal kingdom, but a way station along the course leading to eternal life, a place where the final preparation is made for that fulness of joy which comes only when body and spirit are inseparably connected in immortal glory! Thither Jesus this day is going. And in that general realm—the realm of departed spirits—so also will the so-called penitent thief find himself. He will not this day sit down on a throne on the right side of the Lord; even James and John were denied an assurance of such a reward. He will not stand in the congregation of the righteous when Jesus meets with Adam and Noah and Abraham and all the righteous dead; but he will be in the realm of the departed where he can learn from the Lord's legal administrators all that he must do to work out his salvation. If we had the most accurate possible translation, one that conveyed Jesus' real intent, his words to his fellow crucifee would convey this thought: 'This day shalt thou be with me in the world of spirits. There you can learn of me and my gospel; there you can begin to work out your salvation with fear and trembling before me.'

The issue is not deathbed repentance, as it were, under which a dying soul by simply saying, "I believe," or, "I repent," is immediately, without more, ready for the same eternal reward reserved for Peter and Paul, who fought good fights and laid their all upon the altar of service and sacrifice. The issue is that there is a possibility of repentance and conversion and progress after death and in the realm of the departed. There Jesus went when he left his life; there he met the righteous of all ages who had preceded him in death; there he taught the gospel; there he organized his work so that penitent thieves and repentant sinners—those who would have believed and obeyed had the fulness of truth been offered to them in this life—may yet become heirs of eternal salvation.[1] Thus it is written: "For this cause was the gospel preached also to them that are dead, that they might be judged according to men in the flesh, but live according to God in the spirit." (1 Pet. 4:6.)

And in all this the Messianic word is fulfilled. Isaiah foretold: "When thou shalt make his soul an offering for sin, he shall see his seed." (Isa. 53:10.) And in his death our Lord visited his seed in the spirit world. He visited those who had taken upon themselves his name; those who had been adopted into his family; those who had become his sons and his daughters by faith. (D&C 138.)

Jesus' attention is now turned to a scene of sorrow and despair. By the cross stands his mother, the Virgin of Galilee, the one chosen of God to bear his Son, the one who had suckled and cradled and reared Israel's Messiah. With her are three other faithful women—her sister, Salome, the wife of Zebedee and the mother of James and John (who thus were cousins of Jesus); Mary the wife of Cleophas; and Mary Magdalene. On the resurrection morn Jesus will pay to Mary Magdalene one of the greatest compliments ever given a mortal being: he will appear to her first, even ahead of Peter and the Twelve. But now his concern is his mother. A sword is piercing her soul as the saintly Simeon had prophesied that day in the temple. How the mother must have suffered to see her Son bear the infinite burden placed upon him!

With these four sisters was the Beloved John, the one who leaned on Jesus' breast and for whom the Master had greater love than for any other. It is clear that Joseph, the husband of Mary, had passed on; it appears also that Mary's other sons had not yet joined the household of faith and accepted Jesus, their brother, as the Son of God; and we are led to believe that the apostle John had a home in Jerusalem. Clearly, Mary's future lot must be cast with the Twelve and the Church and the apostolic witnesses whom Jesus will soon command to carry his message to all the world. Thus to his mother he says: "Woman, behold thy son!" And to John the word is given: "Behold thy mother!" These words comprise the third utterance from the cross. "And from that hour that disciple took her unto his own home."

Atonement Completed on the Cross

(Matthew 27:45-51; JST, Matthew 27:54; Mark 15:33-38; JST, Mark 15:41; Luke 23:44-46; John 19:28-30; JST, John 19:29; 3 Ne. 8:5-25)

That which began in Gethsemane was finished on the cross and crowned in the resurrection. Jesus took upon himself the sins of all men when he suffered and sweat great drops of blood from every pore in Gethsemane. It was then that his suffering caused himself, even God, to suffer both body and spirit in a way which is totally beyond mortal comprehension. Then again on the cross—in addition to all the physical pain of that horrifying ordeal—he felt the spiritual agonies of the sins of others, as we shall see. How the resurrection ties in to the atonement, we do not know and cannot tell, only that the scriptures testify that the effects of the resurrection of Christ passed upon all men so that, because he rose from death, all are raised in immortality. In some way, incomprehensible to us, Gethsemane, the cross, and the empty tomb join into one grand and eternal drama, in the course of which Jesus abolishes death, and out of which comes immortality for all and eternal life for the righteous.

Jesus has now been hanging in agony on the accursed tree for about three hours, from somewhere near 9 A.M. to noon. He will continue to suffer the curses of crucifixion for another three hours, until around 3 P.M. when he voluntarily gives up the ghost. Of these coming hours, Matthew and Mark say only that it was a period when there was darkness over all the land; Luke extends this turning of day into night to cover a greater area. "There was a darkness over all the earth," he says, "and the sun was darkened." The fact of the darkness, for which there is no known scientific explanation, is known to us, but its purpose and what happened during those three seemingly endless hours remain outside the bounds of our understanding. Could it be that this was the period of his greatest trial, or that during it the agonies of Gethsemane recurred and even intensified?

That this darkness did cover the whole earth we surmise from the Book of Mormon account. The Nephite prophets had spoken, Messianically, of three days of darkness that would be a sign unto them of the crucifixion of Christ. At that time the rocks would rend and there would be such upheavals in nature that those on the isles of the sea would say, "The God of nature suffers." (1 Ne. 19:10-12; Hel. 14:20-24.) The Nephite record tells of the fulfillment of these prophecies; of the darkness and storms and destructions that then occurred; of cities sinking into the seas; of mountains and valleys being created; of the rocks rending and the whole face of the earth being deformed. It is of more than passing import that the storms and tempests and earthquakes lasted "for about the space of three hours," and then "there was darkness upon the face of the land." It was a "thick darkness," and the people could "feel the vapor of darkness. And there could be no light, because of the darkness, neither candles, neither torches; neither could there be fire kindled with their fine and exceedingly dry wood, so that there could not be any light at all; And there was not any light seen, neither fire, nor glimmer, neither the sun, nor the moon, nor the stars, for so great were the mists of darkness which were upon the face of the land."

Among the Nephites, where the darkness was accompanied with destructions, "there was great mourning and howling and weeping among all the people." If the darkness in the Old World was like that in the Americas, we can suppose that the hearts of those around the cross were filled with deep misgivings. Emotions of dread and horror must have filled the hearts of the guilty and the innocent. "Of the incidents of those last three hours we are told nothing, and that awful obscuration of the noonday sun may well have overawed every heart into an inaction respecting which there was nothing to relate. What Jesus suffered *then* for us men and our salvation we cannot know, for during those hours He hung upon His cross in silence and darkness; or, if He spoke, there were none there to record His words. But towards the close of that time His anguish culminated, and—emptied to the very uttermost of that glory which He had since the world began—drinking to the very deepest dregs the cup of humiliation and bitterness—enduring, not only to have taken upon Him the form of a servant, but also to suffer the last infamy which human hatred could impose on perfect helplessness—He uttered that mysterious cry, of which the full significance will never be fathomed by man."[2]

"Eli, Eli, lama sabachthani?" That is: *"My God, My God, why hast thou forsaken me?"*

Spoken with a loud voice, these words, quoted from David's Messianic prophecies, are the fourth utterance from the cross. "What mind of man can fathom the significance of that awful cry? It seems, that in addition to the fearful suffering incident to crucifixion, the agony of Gethsemane had recurred, intensified beyond human power to endure. In that bitterest hour the dying Christ was alone, alone in most terrible reality. That the supreme sacrifice of the Son might be consummated in all its fulness, the Father seems to have withdrawn the support of His immediate Presence, leaving to the Savior of men the glory of complete victory over the forces of sin and death." (Talmage, p. 661.)

Some of those who stood by said, "Behold, he calleth

for Elias," whose name was associated in their legends with the coming and work and ministry of the Messiah. "The readiness with which they seized this false impression is another proof of the wild state of excitement and terror—the involuntary dread of something great, and unforeseen, and terrible—to which they had been reduced from their former savage insolence. For Elijah, the great prophet of the Old Covenant, was inextricably mingled with all the Jewish expectations of a Messiah, and these expectations were full of wrath. The coming of Elijah would be the coming of a day of fire, in which the sun should be turned into blackness and the moon into blood, and the powers of heaven should be shaken. Already the noonday sun was shrouded in unnatural eclipse: might not some awful form at any moment rend the heavens and come down, touch the mountains and they should smoke? The vague anticipation of conscious guilt was unfulfilled." (Farrar, p. 705.)

The infinite and eternal atonement has now been wrought. Jesus has gained the victory; he has done all that his Father sent him to do; now he faces only the physical agonies of the cross, and he can think of his own bodily needs. He calls out, "I thirst," and these are the fifth words from the cross. "It is probable that a few hours before, the cry would have only provoked a roar of frantic mockery; but now the lookers-on were reduced by awe to a readier humanity. Near the cross there lay on the ground the large earthen vessel containing the *posca,* which was the ordinary drink of the Roman soldiers. The mouth of it was filled with a piece of sponge, which served as a cork. Instantly some one—we know not whether he was friend or enemy, or merely one who was there out of idle curiosity—took out the sponge and dipped it in the *posca* to give it to Jesus. But low as was the elevation of the cross, the head of the Sufferer, as it rested on the horizontal beam of the accursed tree, was just beyond the man's reach: and therefore he put the sponge at the end of a stalk of hyssop—about a foot long—and held it up to the parched and dying lips." (Farrar, pp. 706–7.) Jesus drank what was offered, thus fulfilling the Messianic prophecy: "They gave me also gall for my meat; and in my thirst they gave me vinegar to drink." (Ps. 69:21.)

As he drank, the heartless among them called out: "Let him alone; let us see whether Elias will come to take him down." At Jesus' behest Elijah and twelve legions of angels would have attended the cross at any time; at his word heaven and earth would pass away; by his voice nothing was impossible—and yet there was no divine intervention. Our Pattern, our Prototype, our Exemplar marked the path for all men. He endured to the end.[3] Would God that it may be so for all of us!

Thereupon Jesus made his final earthly report to the one who had sent him. 'Father, it is finished, thy will is done,' he said; and this is the sixth utterance from the cross. How, then, does a God die? It is a voluntary act; no man taketh his life from him; he lays it down of himself; he has power to lay it down and power to take it again. Jesus makes his seventh utterance from the cross. He says simply: "Father, into thy hands I commend my spirit," quoting thus, as was his wont, the Messianic word concerning himself. (Ps. 31:5.) "And having said thus, he gave up the ghost." He did not taste of death, for it was sweet unto him. As he, with the Eleven, had sung in the Hallel the night before: "Precious in the sight of the Lord is the death of his saints." (Ps. 116:15.)

As Jesus passed through the door from mortality to the spirit world; as his eternal spirit divested itself of its tenement of clay; as he left his mortal remains to be cared for by the loving persons whose friend he was—two portentous events marked his glorious victory. For one, "the earth did quake, and the rocks rent"; and, for another, "the veil of the temple was rent in twain from the top to the bottom."

As to the earthquake, it came in fulfillment of Enoch's word. He, among others of the ancients, had seen "the Son of Man lifted up on the cross, after the manner of men; And he heard a loud voice; and the heavens were veiled; and all the creations of God mourned; and the earth groaned; and the rocks were rent." (Moses 7:55-56.) Had the earthquake among the Jews been as it was among the Nephites, Jerusalem itself would have scarcely survived.

As to the rending of the veil of the temple, it was the one thing that would symbolize, in power, the end of the old Jewish dispensation and the beginning of the new Christian day. The veil itself—shielding the Holy of Holies from the gaze of any but the high priest, and from him except once a year, on the day of atonement, when he entered the sacred portal to atone for the sins of the people—the veil is said to have been sixty feet long, thirty feet wide, "of the thickness of the palm of the hand, and wrought in 72 squares, which were joined together." It was so heavy that it took hundreds of priests to manipulate it. "If the Veil was at all such as is described in the Talmud, it could not have been rent in twain by a mere earthquake or the fall of the lintel, although its composition in squares fastened together might explain, how the rent might be as described in the Gospel.

"Indeed, everything seems to indicate that, although the earthquake might furnish the physical basis, the rent of the Temple-Veil was—with reverence be it said—really made by the Hand of God. As we compute, it may just have been the time when, at the Evening-Sacrifice, the officiating Priesthood entered the Holy Place, either to burn the incense or to do other sacred service there. To see before them, not as the aged Zacharias at the beginning of this history the Angel Gabriel, but the Veil of the Holy Place rent from top to bottom—that beyond it they could scarcely have seen—and hanging in two parts from its fastenings above and at the side, was, indeed, a terrible portent, which would soon become generally known, and must, in some form or other, have been preserved in tradition. And they all must have understood, that it meant that God's Own Hand had rent the Veil, and for ever deserted and thrown open that Most Holy Place where He had so long dwelt in the mysterious gloom, only lit up once a year by the glow of the censer of him, who made atonement for the sins of the people." (Edersheim 2:611-12.)

Thus did Jesus, the Atoning One, through whose blood all men may freely pass through the veil into the presence of the Lord, thus did he, by the rending of the veil of the old temple, signify that its ordinances of atonement and forgiveness were done away in him. Thus did he, making his own body a new temple, as it were, signify that his atonement, and the forgiveness of sins made possible thereby, shall admit all true believers into his eternal Holy of Holies. "For Christ is not entered into the holy places made with hands, which are the figures of the true; but into heaven itself, now to appear in the presence of God for us." (Heb. 9:24.)

And as every true believer ponders upon the wonder and glory of it all—as he contemplates the atonement wrought in the garden and on the cross; as he meditates about the immortality and eternal life that come through Christ—he marvels at what God has done for him. "He sees in the cross of Christ"—and the cross is used in the prophetic word as a symbol for the atonement—"He sees in the cross of Christ something which far transcends its historical significance. He sees in it the fulfillment of all prophecy as well as the consummation of all history; he sees in it the explanation of the mystery of birth, and the conquest over the mystery of the grave. In that life he finds a perfect example; in that death an infinite redemption. As he contemplates the Incarnation and the Crucifixion, he no longer feels that God is far away, and that this earth is but a disregarded speck in the infinite azure, and he himself but an insignificant atom chance-thrown amid the thousand million living souls of an innumerable race, but he exclaims in faith and hope and love, 'Behold, the tabernacle of God is with men; yea, He will be their God, and they shall be His people.' 'Ye are the temple of the living God; as God hath said, I will dwell in them, and walk in them.' " (Farrar, p. 711; Ezek. 37:27; 2 Cor. 6:16.)

NOTES

1. The common sectarian heresy that Jesus went to Hades while his body lay in the tomb has at least a grain of truth in it. He did go to a world of departed spirits, where he "preached unto the spirits in prison" (1 Pet. 3:18-20), to those who considered the long separation of their bodies from their spirits as a prison. (D&C 138.)

2. Farrar, p. 704.

3. Our friend Farrar gives us his summary of the sufferings of the Lord Jesus in these words:

"It is difficult adequately to realise the multitude and variety of the forms of spiritual distress and mental anguish, of scorn, and torture, to which the sinless Son of Man was continuously subjected from the time that He left the mount of Olives to enter Jerusalem for the Last Supper.

"1. At the Last Supper He had the heavy sorrow of reading the heart of the traitor, and of uttering His last farewells—mingled with prophecies of persecution as the path to final triumph—to those whom He loved best on earth.

"2. Then came the agony in the garden, which filled Him with speechless amazement and shuddering, until He had to fling Himself with His face to the earth in the tense absorption of prayer, and His sweat was like great gouts of blood streaming to the ground."

This was the hour of his greatest agony. It was here that he took upon himself, in a way incomprehensible to us, the sins of all men on conditions of repentance. It was here that he suffered in body and in spirit more than it is possible for other mortals to suffer. Those hours in the Garden of Gethsemane have no parallel among mortals in any age. Only a God could suffer or endure the lot that then and there was his.

"3. Then the horror of Judas's over-acted traitor-kiss, the seizure, the binding, the leading away, the desertion of Him by all His disciples in His hour of need.

"4. Then the long trials which, only broken by insult, lasted the whole night through; the sense of utter injustice; the proof that all those hierophants who should have been the very first to welcome Him with humble yet triumphant gladness, were fiercely bent on destroying Him by any means, however foul.

"5. Then the insolent blow in the face from one of the servants.

"6. Then the hearing His chief Apostle deny Him with oaths and curses.

"7. Then the night trial before Caiaphas and his most confidential adherents, with all its agitating incidents, its tumult of sneering voices, its dreadful adjuration, and the sentence on Him as 'a Man of Death' by the 'spiritual' court.

"8. Then the accumulations of brutal insult as the crowd of vile underlings mocked Him, and slapped and beat Him, and spat into His face, and, bandaging His eyes, bade Him name the wretches who had smitten Him.

"9. Then the early morning trial before the whole Sanhedrin, with its continuance of agitating appeals, and the final proof that 'He had come unto His own possessions, and His people received Him not.'

"10. Then, if we read the record rightly, another derision by the Priests and Sanhedrists.

"11. Then the long and thrilling scenes of the trial before Pilate, as He stood in the centre of a crowd thirsting for His blood, yelling for His crucifixion; heaping lies and insults upon Him; preferring to Him the robber and the murderer; defeating, by their ferocious pertinacity, the obvious desire of the Roman Governor to set Him free.

"12. Then the leading through the city to Herod, and the vain attempt of that despicable prince to wring some answer or some sign from Him.

"13. Then the coarse derision of Herod's myrmidons as, in mock homage, they stripped Him of His own garments and arrayed Him in a shining robe, with every accumulation of disdainful insolence and cruelty.

"14. Then the final sentence of crucifixion, pronounced by Pilate after vain appeals and efforts to overcome the furious animosity of His accusers.

"15. Then the brutal mockery by the whole band of Roman soldiers as He stood helpless among them. These coarse legionaries were only too much rejoiced to pour on Him the contempt and detestation which they felt for all Jews, and seized the opportunity to vent their callous savagery on One who, as they were taught to believe, had claimed to be a King. This King should have the insignia of royalty—a cast-off military *sagum* of scarlet; a crown—only twisted of torturing thorns; a sceptre—a reed which they could every now and then snatch out of His tied hands, and beat Him with it as well as with rods; the mock homage of bended knees varied by execrable spitting, and blows on the head, and slaps on the face with the open palm, and words of uttermost contempt.

"16. Then He was mangled and lacerated almost to death by the horrible and excruciating *flagellum,* inflicted by executioners who had no sense of pity, with scourges loaded with balls of lead and sharp-pointed bones.

"17. Then came the stripping bare of the robes, and the bending under the load of the cross—or, rather, of its *patibulum*—the transverse beam of the cross, which He was too much exhausted to carry, while the herald went before Him proclaiming the supposed crime for which He was condemned.

"18. Then the sight of the weeping and wailing daughters of Jerusalem.

"19. Then the driving of the lacerating, crushing nails through His feet, and through either hand, and the uplifting on the cross. . . .

"20. Then the sight of all the world's worst vileness flowing beneath His eyes in its noisy stream, as the Elders, in their heartlessness, wagged their heads at Him, and jeered, and blasphemed; and the soldiers mocked, and the crowd howled their insults, and the two wretched robbers who shared with Him that hour of shame—though *they* were guilty and He was innocent—joined in the continuous pitiless reviling.

"21. Then the sight of His mother in her unspeakable desolation.

"22. Then the darkening by anguish of His human soul, which wrung from Him the cry, 'My God, My God, why hast Thou forsaken Me?'

"Yet, amid all these accumulations of anguish, only one word of physical pain was wrung from Him—the cry, '*I thirst*':—and so deep was the impression caused by His majestic patience, as well as by the portents which followed, that the whole crowd was overawed and hushed, and returned to Jerusalem beating their breasts, and saying, 'Truly, this was a righteous man;' and the penitent robber implored Him to receive him into His Kingdom; and even the Pagan Roman centurion spoke of Him as 'a Son of God.'

"The uttermost depth of superhuman woe seems to be revealed by His cry, 'My God, My God, why hast Thou forsaken Me?' " (F. W. Farrar, *The Life of Lives,* pp. 506–11.)

To this we add, if we interpret the holy word aright, that all of the anguish, all of the sorrow, and all of the suffering of Gethsemane recurred during the final three hours on the cross, the hours when darkness covered the land. Truly there was no sorrow like unto his sorrow, and no anguish and pain like unto that which bore in with such intensity upon him.

Chapter 109

IN THE ARIMATHEAN'S TOMB

Verily, verily, I say unto you,
The hour is coming, and now is,
when the dead shall hear the voice
of the Son of God:
and they that hear shall live. . . .
Marvel not at this:
for the hour is coming,
in the which all that are in the graves
shall hear his voice.
(John 5:25-29.)

The Roman Spear Pierces His Side

(John 19:31-37; Matthew 27:54-56; JST, Matthew 27:59; Mark 15:39-41; JST, Mark 15:45; Luke 23:47-49)

Never was there such a crucifixion as this one. Scourging was always or often a prelude to the cross. Nails had been pounded into hands and feet by the thousands. To insult and demean dying sufferers was the common sport of the coarse ruffians who gaped on the mangled bodies. Perhaps others had been crowned with plaited thorns. But whenever did the rocks rend, and the earth shake, and a dire and deep darkness envelop the whole land for three long hours? And when else did the dying one, yet having strength and vigor in his whipped and beaten body, shout with a loud voice and seem to end his mortality of his own will and in full control of his faculties?

To all this the centurion and his soldiers were witnesses, and when they saw it all, they greatly feared and said: "Truly this was the Son of God." And the centurion himself glorified God—perhaps in praise and prayer—and said: "Certainly this was a righteous man."[1]

Nor were the centurion and his soldiers alone in their fearful and awe-filled feelings. A congregation of the friends and acquaintances and disciples of Jesus had now gathered at the cross, many of them being Galileans. They "smote their breasts," and were sorrowful. Particular mention is made of "the women that followed from Galilee." They had come to minister unto him "for his burial," and among them were Mary Magdalene, Mary the mother of James the younger and Joses, and Salome the wife of Zebedee and the mother of James and John. The Blessed Virgin is not mentioned, leaving us to suppose that John has by now taken her to his home so she will no longer be a personal witness of the agonies of her Son. Since Jesus' friends were there, we take the liberty of assuming this included the Eleven; surely all of them, scattered at Gethsemane, would have long since rallied again round his side.

But now, "the sun was westering as the darkness rolled away from the completed sacrifice. They who had not thought it a pollution to inaugurate their feast by the murder of their Messiah, were seriously alarmed lest the sanctity of the following day—which began at sunset—should be compromised by the hanging of the corpses on the cross. And, horrible to relate, the crucified often lived for many hours—nay, even for two or three days—in their torture." (Farrar, pp. 711–12.) According to their law the body of an executed criminal could not be left hanging overnight lest the land be defiled. (Deut. 21:22-23.) And, further, in this instance the coming day was doubly sacred; it was both a Sabbath and the second Paschal day, the one on which the wavesheaf was offered to the Lord. Hence the Jews besought Pilate to have the legs of the three crucified persons broken. "Sometimes there was added to the punishment of crucifixion that of breaking the bones (*crurifragium*) by means of a club or hammer. This would not itself bring death, but the breaking of the bones was always followed by a *coup de grace,* by sword, lance, or stroke, which immediately put an end to what remained of life. Thus the 'breaking of the bones' was a sort of increase of punishment, by way of compensation for its shortening by the final stroke that followed." (Edersheim 2:613.)

Pilate acceded to their pleas; the soldiers broke the legs and then killed the two malefactors with the sword. Finding Jesus already dead, "they brake not his legs," that it might be fulfilled which was written concerning him as the Paschal Lamb ("Neither shall ye break a bone thereof"), and concerning him as the Suffering Servant ("He keepeth all his bones: not one of them is broken"). (Ex. 12:46; Num. 9:12; Ps. 34:20.) However, one of the soldiers, perhaps to make sure that Jesus was dead, hurled his spear into his side, in the region of the heart, this, again, happening that the prophetic word might come to pass. Zechariah, speaking of the millennial day when "the spirit of grace and of supplication" shall be poured out upon the Jews "and upon the inhabitants of Jerusalem," foretold that their Messiah would then say: "They shall look upon me whom they have pierced." This, our inspired New Testament author tells us, shall come to pass because of the wound then gashed into Jesus' side. And we might add, as Zechariah promises, that in that future day the Jews will say to Jesus: "What are these wounds in thine hands?" and he will answer: "Those with which I was wounded in the house of my friends." (Zech. 12:10; 13:6.) Or, more perfectly, as the account is found in latter-day revelation: "What are these wounds in thine hands and in thy feet?" Of this question the Wounded One says: "Then shall they know that I am the Lord; for I will say unto them: These wounds are the wounds with which I was wounded in the house of my friends. I am he who was lifted up. I am Jesus that was crucified. I am the Son of God. And then shall they weep because of their iniquities; then shall they lament because they persecuted their king." (D&C 45:51-53.)

But there is more. From the spear wound—and it was of major proportion, as witness Jesus' statement to the Nephites, "Thrust your hands into my side" (3 Ne. 11:14)—from the spear wound, "forthwith came there out blood and water." Of this unusual occurrence, John testifies: "And he that saw it bare record, and his record is true: and he knoweth that he saith true, that ye might believe."

"Why does John, as though he were recording some great miracle, tell us that both blood and water flowed from Christ's pierced side, and then add his solemn certification that he spoke the truth in so stating? It appears that the Beloved Disciple was showing how one of the great doctrines of revealed religion, that of being born again, rests upon and is efficacious because of the atonement. As the inspired record recites, men are 'born into the world by water, and blood, and the spirit' thereby becoming mortal souls. To gain salvation they must thereafter 'be born again into the kingdom of heaven, of water, and of the Spirit, and be cleansed by blood,' meaning the blood of Christ. Thus when men see birth into this world, they are reminded of what is required for birth into the kingdom of heaven.

"Since this spiritual rebirth and consequent salvation in the kingdom of heaven are available because of the atonement, how fitting it is that the elements present in that infinite sacrifice are also water, blood, and spirit. Accordingly, when men think of the crucifixion of Christ, they are reminded of what they must do to be born again and gain that full salvation which comes because of his atonement.

"John, who was eye witness to the water and blood gushing from Jesus' side after his spirit had left his body, later wrote of being 'born of God' through the atonement in these words: 'Whatsoever is born of God overcometh the world. . . . Who is he that overcometh the world, but he that believeth that Jesus is the Son of God? This is he that came by water and blood, even Jesus Christ; not by water only, but by water and blood. And it is the Spirit that beareth witness, because the Spirit is truth. . . . And there are three that bear witness in earth, the spirit, and the water, and the blood.' (1 John 5:1-8.)" (*Commentary* 1:834-35.)

Jesus' Body Is Claimed, Buried, Guarded

(Matthew 27:57-66; JST, Matthew 27:65; Mark 15:42-47; JST, Mark 15:47-48; Luke 23:50-56; JST, Luke 23:51-52; John 19:38-42)

Those three corpses, hanging on their accursed crosses, must be disposed of before the setting sun ushers in the Sabbath. "The Jews had taken every precaution to prevent the ceremonial pollution of a day so sacred, and were anxious that immediately after the death of the victims had been secured, their bodies should be taken from the cross. About the sepulture they did not trouble themselves, leaving it to the chance good offices of friends and relatives to huddle the malefactors into their nameless graves. The dead body of Jesus was left hanging till the last, because a person who could not easily be slighted had gone to obtain leave from Pilate to dispose of it as he wished." (Farrar, p. 716.) Without this aid—shall we not say there was a divine hand in it?—and as far as the chief priests were concerned, the body of Jesus might have been dumped with the refuse in the Valley of Hinnom, there to rot and decay and be burned by the everlasting fires of Gehenna. Perhaps this is what happened to the bodies of the two thieves.

All four of the Gospel authors speak in laudatory tones of Joseph of Arimathea. They identify him as a rich man, an honorable counselor, one who waited for the kingdom of God, a good man and a just one, and a disciple (although John says he kept his discipleship secret, "for fear of the

Jews"). So they speak of the man in whose new tomb the body of the Lord Jesus was to lie for a few brief hours. "This was Joseph of Arimathea, a rich man, of high character and blameless life, and a distinguished member of the Sanhedrin. Although timidity of disposition, or weakness of faith, had hitherto prevented him from openly declaring his belief in Jesus, yet he had abstained from sharing in the vote of the Sanhedrin, or countenancing their crime. And now sorrow and indignation inspired him with courage. Since it was too late to declare his sympathy for Jesus as a living Prophet, he would at least give a sign of his devotion to Him as the martyred victim of a wicked conspiracy. Flinging secrecy and caution to the winds, he no sooner saw that the cross on Golgotha now bore a lifeless burden, than he went to Pilate on the very evening of the crucifixion, and begged that the dead body might be given him. Although the Romans left their crucified slaves to be devoured by dogs and ravens, Pilate had no difficulty in sanctioning the more humane and reverent custom of the Jews, which required, even in extreme cases, the burial of the dead." (Farrar, pp. 716–17.)

Pilate marveled at the report of such an early death, apparently not yet knowing that in the case of the two thieves death had been hastened by the *crurifragium*. First, Pilate asked the Arimathean if Jesus "were already dead," and then, "calling the centurion, he asked him, If he had been any while dead." Receiving the sure witness of his own military commander—and with what severity and finality divine providence is *proving* His death, as a prelude to *proving* his resurrection—receiving this assurance, Pilate gave the body to Joseph.

Then the cross was lowered and laid upon the ground; from the mangled hands and bloody feet the Roman nails were drawn out; and the body was washed and cleaned and taken to a new tomb, hewn but recently from the rock. "At the entrance to the tomb—and within the rock—there was a court, nine feet square, where ordinarily the bier was deposited, and its bearers gathered to do the last offices for the Dead. Thither we suppose Joseph to have carried the Sacred Body." (Edersheim 2:617.) At some time, probably when the cross was lowered or else in the court of the tomb, Joseph was joined by Nicodemus, who had come to Jesus by night three years before at the First Passover. "If, as seems extremely probable, he be identical with the Nakdimon Ben Gorion of the Talmud, he was a man of enormous wealth; and however much he had held back during the life of Jesus, now, on the evening of His death, his heart was filled with a gush of compassion and remorse, and he hurried to His cross and burial with an offering of truly royal munificence. The faith which had once required the curtain of darkness can now venture at least into the light of sunset, and [be] brightened finally into noonday confidence. Thanks to this glow of kindling sorrow and compassion in the hearts of these two noble and wealthy disciples, He who died as a malefactor was buried as a king. 'He made His grave with the wicked, and with the rich in His death.' The fine linen which Joseph had purchased was richly spread with the hundred *litras* of myrrh and perfumed aloe-wood which Nicodemus had brought, and the lacerated body—whose divinely-human spirit was now in the calm of its Sabbath rest in the Paradise of God—was thus carried to its loved and peaceful grave. . . .

"The preparations had to be hurried, because when the sun had set the Sabbath would have begun. All that they could do, therefore, was to wash the corpse, to lay it amid the spices, to wrap the head in a white napkin, to roll the fine linen round and round the wounded limbs, and to lay the body reverently in the rocky niche. Then they rolled a *golal,* or great stone, to the horizontal aperture; and scarcely had they accomplished this when, as the sun sank behind the hills of Jerusalem, the new Sabbath dawned.

"Mary of Magdala, and Mary the mother of James and Joses, had seated themselves in the garden to mark well the place of sepulture, and other Galilean women had also noticed the spot, and hurried home to prepare fresh spices and ointments before the Sabbath began, that they might hasten back early on the morning of Sunday, and complete that embalming of the body which Joseph and Nicodemus had only hastily begun. They spent in quiet that miserable Sabbath, which, for the broken hearts of all who loved Jesus, was a Sabbath of anguish and despair.

"But the enemies of Christ were not so inactive. The awful misgiving of guilty consciences was not removed even by His death upon the cross. They recalled, with dreadful reminiscence, the rumored prophecies of His resurrection—the sign of the prophet Jonah, which He had said would alone be given them—the great utterance about the destroyed Temple, which He would in three days raise up; and these intimations, which were but dim to a crushed and wavering faith, were read, like fiery letters upon the wall, by the illuminating glare of an uneasy guilt. Pretending, therefore, to be afraid lest His body should be stolen by His disciples for the purposes of imposture, they begged that, until the third day, the tomb might be securely guarded. Pilate gave them a brief and haughty permission to do anything they liked; for—apparently in the evening, when the great Paschal Sabbath was over—they sent their guard to seal the *golal,* and to watch the sepulchre." (Farrar, pp. 717–19.)

In the Realm of Disembodied Spirits
(D&C 138)

"And he bowed his head, and gave up the ghost." (John 19:30.) Between life and death there is only the twinkling of an eye, only a breath of air in the lungs of a man, only an eternal spirit in its tenement of clay. The spirit steps out of the body, to live in another realm, and we call it death. Jesus died—voluntarily, for he had the power of immortality, and no man could take his life from him—he died of his own will and choice; his spirit laid down its temporal body of flesh and blood and chose to live in an unembodied state in the realm of the departed. Jesus gave up the ghost and entered the paradise of God. He was as other men in that his spirit went to live in a spirit world to await the day of his resurrection, the day when the eternal spirit would be reunited with its body, thereafter to live eternally in immortal glory, having a body of flesh and bones.

When Jesus died—that very moment—his mortal ministry ended and his ministry among the spirits in prison began. Then it was, according to the Messianic word, that he began to "proclaim liberty to the captives, and the opening of the prison to them that are bound" (Isa. 61:1); then the work commenced "to bring out the prisoners from the prison, and them that sit in darkness out of the prison house" (Isa. 42:7); then it was that he who had now suffered for our sins, the Just for the unjust, having been put to death in the flesh but continuing to live in the spirit, "went and preached unto the spirits in prison" (1 Pet. 3:18-20).

How marvelous are the dealings of God with man! How infinite is his mercy, how glorious his grace! He provideth a way whereby all his children—either in mortality or in the spirit world, awaiting their resurrection—may hear the gospel of salvation. All shall stand before his eternal bar to be judged according to their works. All "shall give account to him that is ready to judge the quick and the dead." And "for this cause"—that the living and the dead shall all be judged by the same gospel standard—is "the gospel preached also to them that are dead, that they might be judged according to men in the flesh, but live according to God in the spirit." (1 Pet. 4:5-6.)

From Adam to Christ, through four thousand years of births and deaths, unnumbered millions died without a knowledge of Christ and the salvation which is in him. And yet his is the only name given under heaven—now or ever, in time or in eternity—whereby men can be saved. His gospel is the one plan of salvation; it charts the one course to celestial rest; no man cometh unto the Father but by him and his law. From righteous Abel to Zacharias the son of Barachias who was slain for the testimony of the truth, all the righteous dead had gone to the paradise of peace and beauty, there to await the day of their coming forth in the resurrection of the just. Even they considered the long separation of their bodies and spirits as a prison. During the same long millenniums of rebellion and war and disease and death, millions died without a knowledge of the truth and went to hell, an abode of darkness and suffering and sorrow, there to await the resurrection of the unjust. In their benighted state they were without hope, not even knowing whether there would be a resurrection and an eventual reward for them in one of the kingdoms of their Father. Truly, if ever spirits were in prison, these were they. And so the Messianic word proclaims: "And they shall be gathered together, as prisoners are gathered in the pit, and shall be shut up in the prison, and after many days shall they be visited." (Isa. 24:22.)

With the death of Jesus, the day of their visitation is at hand. He goes to the spirit world to preach the gospel, which is the plan of salvation; if they believe its laws and desire to obey its ordinances, they may be heirs of salvation. For them, the living will perform the vicarious ordinances needed for their salvation. And when the day comes for "death and hell" to deliver up the dead which are in them, then all shall be judged by gospel standards. (Rev. 20:12-15.) Even David's soul will not always be left "in hell." (Ps. 16:10.) Those who lived in the days of Noah shall again hear the truth, for they, too, are among "the spirits of men kept in prison, whom the Son visited, and preached the gospel unto them, that they might be judged according to men in the flesh; Who received not the testimony of Jesus in the flesh, but afterwards received it." (D&C 76:71-80.) Theirs, however, shall be a terrestrial inheritance, and not a celestial, because they rejected the gospel in this life and then received it in the spirit world.

As the body of Jesus lies in its borrowed grave, what,

then, do we see in the spirit world? We see a great host assembled to greet the Son of God. We see Joseph the husband of Mary; we see some of the shepherds who heard the angelic choir sing glory to God in the highest and peace and goodwill to men on earth; we see the saintly Simeon and the blessed Anna, who testified of Him in the temple; we see Zacharias and Elisabeth and John the Baptist; we see the faithful of all the ages—all assembled to hear the voice of Him in whom they trusted.

And there were gathered together in one place an innumerable company of the spirits of the just, who had been faithful in the testimony of Jesus while they lived in mortality; And who had offered sacrifice in the similitude of the great sacrifice of the Son of God, and had suffered tribulation in their Redeemer's name. . . .

I beheld that they were filled with joy and gladness, and were rejoicing together because the day of their deliverance was at hand. They were assembled awaiting the advent of the Son of God into the spirit world, to declare their redemption from the bands of death. . . .

While this vast multitude waited and conversed, rejoicing in the hour of their deliverance from the chains of death, the Son of God appeared, declaring liberty to the captives who had been faithful; And there he preached to them the everlasting gospel, the doctrine of the resurrection and the redemption of mankind from the fall, and from individual sins on conditions of repentance. . . .

And the saints rejoiced in their redemption, and bowed the knee and acknowledged the Son of God as their Redeemer and Deliverer from death and the chains of hell. Their countenances shone, and the radiance from the presence of the Lord rested upon them, and they sang praises unto his holy name.

Then, as he ministered in the world of spirits, Jesus

"organized his forces and appointed messengers, clothed with power and authority, and commissioned them to go forth and carry the light of the gospel to them that were in darkness, even to all the spirits of men; and thus was the gospel preached to the dead." And what a glorious day it was! Adam, Seth, and Enos; Abel, Noah, and Shem; Abraham, Isaac, and Jacob; Isaiah, Ezekiel, and Daniel; Nephi, Alma, and Abinadi; Helaman, Mormon, and Moroni—all the prophets! all the saints! all the righteous! of all past ages!—all assembled to bow the knee, and hear the voice, and cry hosanna.

In his mortal ministry, Jesus the King, as a mortal, had spoken such words as never before man spake; yet they were addressed to weak and faltering and oftentimes rebellious mortals, none of whose hearts had yet begun to burn with the fires of the Spirit. Now in the paradise of God, among the righteous, who already knew the doctrines of salvation; who already had a hope of eternal life; and, above all, whose souls were already afire with the Holy Spirit of God—what wonders of divine truth he must have spoken as he prepared them for their not-distant resurrection! We assume he ministered and spoke almost continuously from the hour of his death to the hour of his resurrection, for, among them, there was no need to rest; none would grow weary or become inattentive. The weaknesses of the flesh were no longer theirs. Perhaps, also, he opened their minds and quickened their understandings so that they saw in vision the wonders of eternity. That we have not yet learned by revelation what was said and done there simply means that our weak and fragile spiritual stature does not as yet qualify us to know and understand what others more worthy and more qualified have received.

These righteous dead "had looked upon the long absence of their spirits from their bodies as a bondage." And all "these the Lord taught"—there in the quiet peace and perfect serenity of a paradisiacal Eden—"and gave them power to come forth, after his resurrection from the dead, to enter into his Father's kingdom, there to be crowned with immortality and eternal life, And continue thenceforth their labor as had been promised by the Lord, and be partakers of all blessings which were held in reserve for them that love him."

Jesus, As a Spirit, Speaks to the Nephites

(3 Nephi 9:1-22; 10:1-8)

After the great destructions in the Americas that took place during the three hours of darkness, and while Jesus' body lay in the Arimathean's tomb, his voice was raised among the Nephites. He did not then appear and his face was not seen among them. But "there was a voice heard among all the inhabitants of the earth, upon all the face of this land." The first spoken words were:

> *Wo, wo, wo unto this people; wo unto the inhabitants of the whole earth except they shall repent; for the devil laugheth, and his angels rejoice, because of the slain of the fair sons and daughters of my people.*

A day of destruction and desolation shall surely come upon all the wicked and rebellious. When their cup of iniquity is full, they are always swept from the face of the earth. Fire and brimstone consumed those in Sodom and Gomorrah and the cities of the plains; the floods swept those in Noah's day to a watery grave; the Jaredite and Nephite nations fell by the sword; Titus turned Jerusalem into a dung heap; and at the Second Coming the wicked and ungodly shall be as stubble. During the three hours of darkness, sixteen cities in the Americas, together with their inhabitants, were utterly destroyed. All this the voice announced, saying repetitiously that it was done "to hide their wickedness and abominations from before my face, that the blood of the prophets and the saints should not come up any more unto me against them." Those who had been spared were identified as the more righteous and were called upon to repent and be converted that Jesus might heal them.

Yea, verily I say unto you, if ye will come unto me ye shall have eternal life. Behold, mine arm of mercy is extended towards you, and whosoever will come, him will I receive; and blessed are those who come unto me.

Behold, I am Jesus Christ the Son of God. I created the heavens and the earth, and all things that in them are. I was with the Father from the beginning. I am in the Father, and the Father in me; and in me hath the Father glorified his name.

I came unto my own, and my own received me not. And the scriptures concerning my coming are fulfilled.

And as many as have received me, to them have I given to become the sons of God; and even so will I to as many as shall believe on my name, for behold, by me redemption cometh, and in me is the law of Moses fulfilled.

I am the light and the life of the world. I am Alpha and Omega, the beginning and the end.

And ye shall offer up unto me no more the shedding of blood; yea, your sacrifices and your burnt offerings shall be done away, for I will accept none of your sacrifices and your burnt offerings.

And ye shall offer for a sacrifice unto me a broken heart and a contrite spirit. And whoso cometh unto me with a broken heart and a contrite spirit, him will I baptize with fire and with the Holy Ghost. . . .

Behold, I have come unto the world to bring redemption unto the world, to save the world from sin.

Therefore, whoso repenteth and cometh unto me as a little child, him will I receive, for of such is the kingdom of God. Behold, for such I have laid down

> *my life, and have taken it up again; therefore repent, and come unto me ye ends of the earth, and be saved.*

So the voice spoke to the Nephites; and nowhere in the whole New Testament account, where the same doctrines are taught, is there such a plain and sweet and simple summary of the glorious mission of Jesus the Messiah as these words contain. They stand by themselves, scarcely needing further exposition, though in fact the shining truths they set forth have been explained in this work in their various New Testament contexts. For clarity's sake we need only add that the climax of this sermon, which speaks of Jesus having laid down his life and having taken it up again, is merely reciting what is to be as though it were already accomplished; just so surely would his almost-then resurrection come to pass.

The voice ceased, and "there was silence in the land for the space of many hours." And the people "did cease lamenting and howling for the loss of their kindred which had been slain." Then the voice came again, uttering words applicable to them, and to the Jews in Jerusalem, and to all the house of Israel, no matter when or where they lived.

> *O ye people of these great cities which have fallen, who are descendants of Jacob, yea, who are of the house of Israel, how oft have I gathered you as a hen gathereth her chickens under her wings, and have nourished you.*
>
> *And again, how oft would I have gathered you as a hen gathereth her chickens under her wings, yea, O ye people of the house of Israel, who have fallen; yea, O ye people of the house of Israel, ye that dwell at Jerusalem, as ye that have fallen; yea, how oft would I have gathered you as a hen gathereth her chickens, and ye would not.*
>
> *O ye house of Israel whom I have spared, how oft*

will I gather you as a hen gathereth her chickens under her wings, if ye will repent and return unto me with full purpose of heart.

But if not, O house of Israel, the places of your dwellings shall become desolate until the time of the fulfilling of the covenant to your fathers.

With these words our knowledge of the disembodied ministry of Jesus ends. The next time we hear the voice it will be housed in its celestial body, and the words will let us know that the redemption has been brought to pass and that though a man dies, yet shall he live again.

NOTE

1. Edersheim indulges in the interesting speculation that the centurion may thereafter have been converted to Christianity and been the source of some of the details of the crucifixion which Luke alone records. (Edersheim 2:612.)

SECTION XIII

HE RISETH;
HE MINISTERETH;
HE ASCENDETH

HE RISETH; HE MINISTERETH; HE ASCENDETH

I know that ye seek Jesus,
which was crucified. He is not here:
for he is risen, as he said.
(Matt. 28:5-6.)
Ye seek Jesus of Nazareth,
which was crucified: he is risen;
he is not here.
(Mark 16:6.)
Why seek ye the living among the dead?
He is not here, but is risen.
(Luke 24:5-6.)
Behold my hands and my feet,
that it is I myself:
handle me, and see;
for a spirit hath not flesh and bones,
as ye see me have.
(Luke 24:39.)

Death is swallowed up in victory; Jesus comes forth from the tomb; he is the firstfruits of them that slept. Though a man dies, yet shall he live again.

He appears to Mary Magdalene, of eternal fame and renown, and she is the first mortal to see a resurrected soul. She is restrained from embracing him.

He appears to the other women, who hold him by the feet.

Next, as we suppose, he appears to Simon Peter, and then to Cleopas and Luke on the Emmaus road, to whom he expounds the Messianic prophecies.

Then in the upper room, to a group of disciples, including ten of the Twelve, he appears, invites them to feel the prints of the nails in his hands and in his feet, and before them he eats a piece of broiled fish and of an honeycomb.

One week later he appears to Thomas and the others of the Twelve, again in the upper room, and invites his doubting friend to reach forth his finger and feel the prints of the nails and to thrust his hand into the spear wound.

Next he appears at the Sea of Tiberias to seven of the Twelve, who had fished all night and caught nothing. He fills their net with fish and they eat fish and bread which he has prepared. Peter is commanded, thrice, to feed the flock of God.

Then on a mountain in Galilee to more than five hundred brethren at once (and, as we suppose, to women and children also) he comes, ministers, and sends his messengers forth to proclaim his gospel in all the world.

At some unspecified time he appears to his own blood brother James, and then upon the Mount of Olives he ascends up to his Father with the promise that he shall come again to reign personally upon the earth.

Thereafter came the Nephite ministry during which thousands upon thousands (we suppose tens and scores of thousands) heard his voice, felt the nail marks in his hands and feet, thrust their hands into his side, and (many of them) wet his feet with their tears.

Among the Nephites he preached the gospel, wrought miracles, called Twelve Disciples, perfected his work among the seed of Joseph, and left a witness of his holy name that exceeds that which is preserved in the Bible itself.

He also visited the Lost Tribes of the house of Israel and did for them, as we suppose, what he had done for others.

Among the Nephites his doctrine, his miracles, and the outpouring of the Holy Ghost exceeded anything manifest among the Jews. Among them he expounded all the scriptures from the beginning and taught that the coming forth of the Book of Mormon would be the sign whereby all men might know that the work of the Father had commenced in the latter days unto the fulfilling of the covenant made with the house of Israel.

CHRIST IS RISEN

He will swallow up death in victory;
and the Lord God will wipe away tears
from off all faces; . . .
And it shall be said in that day,
Lo, this is our God.
(Isa. 25:8-9.)
Trust ye in the Lord for ever:
for in the Lord Jehovah is everlasting strength. . . .
Thy dead men shall live,
together with my dead body shall they arise.
Awake and sing, ye that dwell in dust:
for thy dew is as the dew of herbs,
and the earth shall cast out the dead. . . .
The earth also shall disclose her blood,
and shall no more cover her slain.
(Isa. 26:4, 19, 21.)
There is no saviour beside me. . . .
I will be thy king. . . .
I will ransom them from the power of the grave;
I will redeem them from death:
O death, I will be thy plagues;
O grave, I will be thy destruction.
(Hosea 13:4, 10, 14.)

"Death Is Swallowed Up in Victory"

And now the dawn!

After the midnight of starlit darkness comes the rising of the morning sun. After the sorrow and scourging of mortality come the joy and peace of immortality. After the darkness of death comes the light of a new day of life. After the pain and blood and burden of Gethsemane and Golgotha come the joy and peace and glory of the resurrection.

Once there was mangled flesh and spilt blood; now there is glorious immortality in a state where sorrow and pain fade away into nothingness. Once the creature was earth-bound, limited, an inhabitant of a few dusty feet of earth-soil; now the Creature comes forth with power to traverse the sidereal heavens and to receive, inherit, and possess worlds without number.

There is a death and there is a resurrection; there is an earth-bound body and a heaven-healed body; there is flesh and blood and there is flesh and bones; there is a temporary tenement for the spirit man, and there is an eternal and perfected palace in which the Son of the Father shall dwell everlastingly. "It is sown in corruption; it is raised in incorruption: It is sown in dishonour; it is raised in glory; it is sown in weakness; it is raised in power: It is sown a natural body; it is raised a spiritual body."

And, be it known, "The first man Adam"—Adam in the generic sense, Adam as the name for all mankind—"The first man Adam was made a living soul." We are all mortal; we all live in an earthy sphere; we are all living souls, mortal souls. But, "the last Adam was made a quickening spirit. . . . The first man is of the earth, earthy: the second man is the Lord from heaven. As is the earthy, such are they also that are earthy: and as is the heavenly, such are they also that are heavenly. And as we have borne the image of the earthy, we shall also bear the image of the heavenly. Now this I say, brethren, that flesh and blood cannot inherit the kingdom of God; neither doth corruption inherit incorruption."

But glory be to God who is the Father, and praise be to God who is the Son, the earthy shall become heavenly, and the mortal shall live again in immortality. "And the dead shall be raised incorruptible, . . . For this corruptible must put on incorruption, and this mortal must put on immortality. So when this corruptible shall have put on incorruption, and this mortal shall have put on immortality, then shall be brought to pass the saying that is written, Death is swallowed up in victory. O death, where is thy sting? O grave, where is thy victory?" (1 Cor. 15:42-55.)

And so the dawn. This is resurrection morn. Christ the firstfruits rises from the tomb; his is the first immortal flesh; his body is now like that of his Father's. "The Father has a body of flesh and bones as tangible as man's; the Son also." (D&C 130:22.) And as Jesus rose from the dead, as he burst the bands of death, as he came forth in immortal glory, so shall it be with all men; all shall come forth from the prison of the grave; all shall live again; all shall become immortal. Death and hell shall deliver up the dead which are in them, "For as in Adam all die, even so in Christ shall all be made alive." (1 Cor. 15:22.) We know not how it is done any more than we know how creation commenced or how Gods began to be. Suffice it to say, man is; and suffice it to say, he shall live again. "For as death hath passed upon all men, to fulfill the merciful plan of the great Creator, there must needs be a power of resurrection." (2 Ne. 9:6.) And Christ is the resurrection and the life; immortality and eternal life come by him. He "hath abolished death, and hath brought life and immortality to light through the gospel." (2 Tim. 1:10.)

We speak thus as a prelude to proclaiming the rising from the grave of the Son of God; as a prelude to hearing the testimonies of those who saw and felt and handled his immortal body; as a prelude to gaining a renewed witness from the Holy Spirit of God that the Risen Lord is our Lord, our God, and our King. For, be it known, the resurrection proves the divine Sonship. If Jesus rose from the dead, he is God's Son; if he is divine, his gospel and his alone can save men. Thus Paul speaks of "the gospel of God, (Which he had promised afore by his prophets in the holy scriptures,) Concerning his Son Jesus Christ our Lord, which was made of the seed of David according to the flesh." And how shall we know that Jesus is the Son of God? Paul gives answer: He is "declared to be the Son of God with power, according to the spirit of holiness, *by the resurrection from the dead.*" (Rom. 1:1-4. Italics added.) The resurrection proves the divine Sonship.

Thus also, Peter, in meeting with Cornelius and his friends, told them "how God anointed Jesus of Nazareth with the Holy Ghost and with power," and how this same Jesus "went about doing good, and healing all that were oppressed of the devil; for God was with him." Then came this mighty testimony—the testimony which contains the sure knowledge of the divinity of the Son and, therefore, of the saving power of his gospel. "And we are witnesses of all things which he did," Peter says, "both in the land of the Jews, and in Jerusalem; whom they slew and hanged on a tree: Him God raised up the third day, and shewed him openly; Not to all the people, but unto witnesses chosen before of God, even to us, who did eat and drink with him after he rose from the dead. And he commanded us to preach unto the people, and to testify that it is he which was ordained of God to be the Judge of quick and dead. To him give all the prophets witness, that through his name whosoever believeth in him shall receive remission of sins." (Acts 10:34-43.)

We repeat: The resurrection proves the divinity of the gospel cause. And so, with Paul, we say: "If there be no resurrection of the dead, then is Christ not risen: And if Christ be not risen, then is our preaching vain, and your faith is also vain. Yea, and we are found false witnesses of God; because we have testified of God that he raised up Christ: whom he raised not up, if so be that the dead rise not. For if the dead rise not, then is not Christ raised: And if Christ be not raised, your faith is vain; ye are yet in your sins. Then they also which are fallen asleep in Christ are perished. If in this life only we have hope in Christ, we are of all men most miserable. But now is Christ risen from the dead, and become the firstfruits of them that slept." (1 Cor. 15:13-20.)

"At the moment when Christ died, nothing could have seemed more abjectly weak, more pitifully hopeless, more absolutely doomed to scorn, and extinction, and despair, than the Church which He had founded. It numbered but a handful of weak followers, of whom the boldest had denied his Lord with blasphemy, and the most devoted had forsaken Him and fled. They were poor, they were ignorant, they were helpless. They could not claim a single synagogue or a single sword. If they spoke their own language, it bewrayed them by its mongrel dialect; if they spoke the current Greek, it was despised as a miserable *patois*. So feeble were they and insignificant, that it would have looked like foolish partiality to prophesy for them the limited existence of a Galilean sect. How was it that these dull and ignorant men, with their cross of wood, triumphed over the deadly fascinations of sensual mythologies, conquered kings and their armies, and overcame the world? What was it that thus caused strength to be made perfect out of abject weakness? There is one, and one only *possible* answer—the resurrection from the dead. All this vast revolution was due to the power of Christ's resurrection." (Farrar, pp. 715–16.)

Jesus Appears to Mary Magdalene

(John 20:1-18; JST, John 20:1, 17; Matthew 28:2-4; JST, Matthew 28:2-3; Mark 16:9-11; Luke 24:12; JST, Luke 24:11; 3 Ne. 10:9-17)

Jesus appeared first to Mary Magdalene and then to certain other women, speaking peace to their troubled souls. Then he came to the Brethren, at various times and places, giving them counsel and direction concerning their own salvation and the administration of the affairs of his earthly kingdom. The sequence of events, insofar as they can be determined, and the transcendent wonders attending these appearances of the First Immortal One to various of his friends and loved ones, we shall attempt, reverentially, to recount. There is a certain awe and an infinite spiritual depth where visitations from the unseen world are concerned that few can plumb. Let us, then, rely on such accounts as have been preserved for us; let us ponder them in our hearts; and let us seek the Spirit as we strive to know and to feel what is here involved. Perhaps our hearts, too, shall burn with living fire as did the hearts of those of old who saw and felt and knew and testified.

It is now the first Easter day. In the Americas the darkness has dispersed from off the face of the land, the rocks have ceased to rend, and the earth is cleaving together again. The mourning and lamentations of the people have ended, and they are now united in songs of praise and hymns of thanksgiving "unto the Lord Jesus Christ, their Redeemer. . . . And it was the more righteous part of the people who were saved, and it was they who received the prophets and stoned them not; and it was they who had not shed the blood of the saints, who were spared"—spared from all the natural desolations that swept from one end of the land to the other. They, in their isolated land, are coming to know that he who is their Messiah also has worked out the infinite and eternal atonement. Later in the year he will minister personally among them, and their joy will be full. Then they will see him and feel the nail marks in his hands and in his feet; then they will thrust their hands into the great gaping wound in his side; and then will they become personal witnesses of his resurrection.

But the setting of our present story is laid in Palestine. There the body of Jesus, anointed and wrapped in choice linen, but only partially cared for—for he was buried in haste—lies in Joseph's tomb; his Spirit is nearby in Paradise where he has now finished his ministrations among the just. How and in what way it was done we know not, but at the appointed moment, the infinitely great Spirit Being entered again into the body which was his—the body conceived in the womb of Mary; the body which was begotten of the Father; the body from which that Spirit had departed when his mortal work was finished—and that Spirit, now housed in its eternal home, now inseparably connected with its body in immortal glory, that Spirit, together with the reanimated dust of the earth, became the first immortal soul. Christ is risen; immortality is assured; the victory has been won; death is abolished.

Thereupon, or at least in immediate connection therewith, perhaps after the resurrection itself, "two angels of the Lord descended from heaven, and came and rolled back the stone from the door, and sat upon it." Their heaven-created power caused "a great earthquake, . . . And their countenance was like lightning, and their raiment white as snow; and for fear of them the keepers did shake, and became as though they were dead." So much for the guards set by the chief priests, lest, as they pretended to suppose, Jesus' disciples might steal the dead body and fabricate a story that he has risen on the third day as he said. But now, as the angelic visitants stood by, the open tomb itself testified of the Risen Lord; its solid rocks wept for joy, and all eternity joined the great Hallelujah chorus: He is risen; he is risen; Christ the Lord is risen today!

It is now Sunday, April 9, A.D. 30—the 17th of Nisan—the day of the resurrection. It is the first day of the week—"according to Jewish reckoning the third day from His Death." According to Jewish tradition, "the soul hovered round the body till the third day, when it finally parted from its earthly tabernacle," and it was on that day that "corruption was supposed to begin." Up to that time relatives and friends were in the habit of "going to the grave, . . . so as to make sure that those laid there were really dead." (Edersheim 2:630-31.) These Rabbinical concepts grew out of Hosea's statement, "in the third day he will raise us up, and we shall live in his sight." (Hosea 6:2.)

We cannot suppose that Mary Magdalene had any of this in mind when very early—"when it was yet dark," John says—she went to the sepulchre. Hers was a mission of pure love and proper honor to Him who had healed her and with whom, along with the Twelve, she had traveled on many missionary journeys. Indeed, no female name plays a more prominent part in the gospel accounts than that of the convert from Magdala, save only the Blessed Virgin herself. Arriving at the garden tomb, the Magdalene found "the stone taken away from the sepulchre, and two angels sitting thereon." Without question she looked in and found an empty tomb. Immediately she ran to Peter and to John—the inference is that they abode at separate places—and announced to them: "They have taken away the Lord out of the sepulchre, and we know not where they have laid him."

"What a picture John has left us of this unique moment in history. Fear fills the hearts of Peter and John; wicked men must have stolen the body of their Lord. They race to the tomb. John, younger and more fleet, arrives first, stoops down, looks in, but does not enter, hesitating as it were to desecrate the sacred spot even by his presence. But Peter, impetuous, bold, a dynamic leader, an apostle who wielded the sword against Malchus and stood as mouthpiece for them all in bearing testimony, rushes in. John follows. Together they view the grave-clothes-linen strips that have not been unwrapped, but through which a resurrected body has passed. And then, upon John, reflective and mystic by nature, the reality dawns first. It is true! They had not known before; now they do. It is the third day! Christ is risen! 'Death is swallowed up in victory.' " (*Commentary* 1:841–42.)

Then the two apostles went again to their homes. But Mary Magdalene, having returned, "stood without at the sepulchre weeping." She stooped down and looked in and saw "two angels in white sitting, the one at the head, and the other at the feet, where the body of Jesus had lain." Presumably they are the same two whom she had already seen sitting on the stone that had blocked the door. If they were present when Peter and John entered the tomb—and certainly they would have been—the spiritual eyes of these apostles were not opened so as to see them.

"Woman, why weepest thou?" the angelic visitants asked. "Because they have taken away my Lord," she replied, "and I know not where they have laid him." As much as she knew about the doctrine of the resurrection; as frequently as she had heard Jesus tell that he would be crucified and rise again the third day; as great as was her faith in him and in his word—yet in the dawning light of this Easter day, the full import of the open tomb had not yet dawned within her soul.

It was then that she turned away from the tomb and "saw Jesus standing, and knew not that it was Jesus." He asked: "Woman, why weepest thou? whom seekest thou?" In her anxiety, concerned only with her own sorrow, having neither interest in nor concern about others at that moment, she supposed the speaker was the gardener. The garden tomb was empty; who but the gardener would have carried away the body of her Lord? "Sir, if thou have borne him hence," she pleaded, "tell me where thou hast laid him, and I will take him away." Though none others were available to help, yet she would do all that a mortal can to reverence a departed loved one.

Jesus said simply: "Mary." Mary, his beloved; he spoke her name, nothing more. It was as when the still small voice sank into the soul of Elijah; it was as though the heavens had been rent and the very throne of God set forth before men; it was as though angelic choirs had sung her name—MARY! The recognition was instantaneous. Her river of tears became a sea of joy. It is He; he has risen; he lives; I love him as of old. With soul-filled exuberance she cried, "Rabboni"—'Oh, my Master!'—and would have embraced him as she had done so many times before in earlier days. His gentle word:

> *Hold me not; for I am not yet ascended to my Father; but go to my brethren, and say unto them, I ascend unto my Father, and your Father; and to my God, and your God.*

We cannot believe that the caution which withheld from Jesus the embrace of Mary was anything more than the building of a proper wall of reserve between intimates who are now on two sides of the veil. If a resurrected brother appeared to a mortal brother, or if a resurrected husband appeared to a mortal wife, would they be free to embrace each other on the same terms of intimacy as had prevailed when both were mortals? But perhaps there was more in Jesus' statement than Mary related or than John recorded, for in a very short time we shall see a group of faithful women hold Jesus by his feet as they worship him.[1] The seeming refusal of Jesus to permit Mary to touch him, followed almost immediately by the appearance in which the other women were permitted to hold his feet, has always been the source of some interpretative concern. The King James Version quotes Jesus as saying "Touch me not." The Joseph Smith Translation reads "Hold me not." Various translations from the Greek render the passage as "Do not cling to me" or "Do not hold me." Some give the meaning as "Do not cling to me any longer," or "Do not hold me any longer." Some speak of ceasing to hold him or cling to him, leaving the inference that Mary was already holding him. There is valid reason for supposing that the thought conveyed to Mary by the Risen Lord was to this effect: "You cannot hold me here, for I am going to ascend to my Father." But the great message that was preserved for us is Jesus' eternal relationship to his Father. "My" Father and "your" Father—Elohim is the Father of all men in the spirit, and of the Lord Jesus in an added and special sense. He is the Father of both Jesus' spirit and his body. "My" God and "your" God—and again Elohim is the God of all men, but in Jesus' case, though he himself is a God and has all power, though he is a member of the very Godhead itself, yet is he everlastingly in subjection to the same God who is our Father.

After these things Mary Magdalene, as he had directed, went to the Twelve, told them all that happened, and bore to them this testimony: 'I have seen the Lord!'

Jesus Appears to the Other Women

(Matthew 28:1, 5-10; JST, Matthew 28:1, 4; Mark 16:1-8; JST, Mark 16:3-6; Luke 24:1-11; JST, Luke 24:1-4)

For reasons of his own, the Risen Lord singled out Mary Magdalene to be the first witness, in point of time, of his resurrection. She was the first mortal of all mortals ever to see a resurrected person. She saw his face and heard his voice, and she was commanded to tell the Twelve of the appearance and of the coming ascension when he would report to Him whose he was.[2] Then, still in his own infinite wisdom, Jesus chose to appear to and be handled by a group of other women—all before he came even to Peter and the rest of the Twelve, all before his appearances to the hundreds of brethren who were privileged to see him before that day on the Mount of Olives when he ascended to reign on the right hand of Everlasting Power forever.

These other women included Mary the mother of Joses; Joanna, evidently the wife of Chuza, Herod's steward (Luke 8:3); and Salome, the mother of James and John. Among them were women who had been with Jesus in Galilee. Certainly the beloved sisters from Bethany were there; and, in general, the group would have been made up of the same ones who had hovered in sorrow around the cross. Their total number may well have been in the dozens or scores. We know that women in general are more spiritual than men, and certainly their instincts and desires to render compassionate service exceed those of their male counterparts. And these sisters came "bringing the spices which they had prepared'' to anoint the body of their Lord.

It was very early, just as the Sunday dawn began to pierce the darkness of the night. They said among themselves: ''Who shall roll us away the stone from the door of the sepulchre?'' But when they came to the sepulchre, they found the stone already rolled away, though it was very great, ''and two angels sitting thereon, clothed in long white garments; and they were affrighted.'' When they entered the tomb, they ''found not the body of the Lord Jesus,'' and ''they were much perplexed.'' At this point the angels delivered their message, but the accounts vary as to what was said, quite possibly because more than one group of devout sisters was involved, or because they could only crowd into or around the sepulchre in small groups. It seems evident that each account, though partial, is true and accurate as far as it goes. As recorded by Matthew the angels said:

> *Fear not ye; for we know that ye seek Jesus who was crucified.*
>
> *He is not here: for he is risen, as he said. Come, see the place where the Lord lay.*
>
> *And go quickly, and tell his disciples that he is risen from the dead; and, behold, he goeth before you into Galilee; there shall ye see him: lo, I* [or, rather, we] *have told you.*

The message is one of peace for themselves; of crucifixion; of resurrection; of linen death-cloths lying unwound with the head-napkin by itself; of the sisters announcing the glorious message to the brethren; and of Jesus preceding them into Galilee, where the Twelve and the other brethren shall see him. The women ''departed quickly from the sepulchre with fear and great joy; and did run to bring his disciples word.''

Jesus met them with a cry of ''All hail.'' The recognition was immediate; they knew their Lord; in awe and reverence ''they came and held him by the feet, and worshipped him.'' What tears of joy they must have shed as they kissed his feet, felt the nail marks therein, and bathed them with their tears. We do not know what words of comfort and assurance he spoke to the group, or to individuals among them; the inspired authors pass over the holy words and holy feelings of the holy occasion in reverent silence. This only of what he said has come down to us:

> *Be not afraid: go tell my brethren that they go into Galilee, and there shall they see me.*

He thus confirms the angelic word and sends the women to give the word to the Brethren. Certainly among those faithful sisters there were some or all of the wives of the apostles; perhaps also there were sisters or even daughters. But whoever they were, Jesus is using them and the fact of his resurrection to show the unity and oneness and equality of the man and the woman. "Neither is the man without the woman, neither the woman without the man, in the Lord." (1 Cor. 11:11.) Together they form an eternal family unit; together they serve in the earthly kingdom; together they gain the spiritual stature to see visions and converse with those who abide beyond the veil. To such of the women as heard what Mark records, the angelic word was:

> *Be not affrighted: Ye seek Jesus of Nazareth, which was crucified: he is risen; he is not here: behold the place where they laid him.*
>
> *But go your way, tell his disciples and Peter that he goeth before you into Galilee: there shall ye see him, as he said unto you.*

Again there is the calm counsel to banish fear; the reminder of the crucifixion; the divine pronouncement that he has risen; and the invitation to see where he had lain and how the burial clothes were placed. But this time the instruction is to tell both Peter and the disciples that He goeth before them into Galilee where they shall see him. This use of Peter's name leaves an added witness that he was called to preside over the Twelve and the church and was expected to lead out in governing the affairs of the earthly kingdom; it also leaves us to assume that some woman with a special relationship to Peter was in the group hearing these particular angelic words. And this time the meeting in Galilee is described as one of which the Brethren already know; on the night of his betrayal and arrest, he had said unto them: "After I am risen again, I will go before you into Galilee." (Matt. 26:32.) The meeting itself took place when Jesus manifested himself to more than five hundred brethren at once on a mountain in Galilee and there gave his great and eternal commission to the Twelve.

To his account Mark adds that the women, "entering into the sepulchre, saw the place where they laid Jesus," thus becoming eye witnesses that his body was gone and that the burial clothes were left in such a way as to show that his resurrected body had passed through their folds and strands without the need of unwinding the strips or untying the napkin. Then the account says "they went out quickly, and fled from the sepulchre; for they trembled and were amazed: neither said they any thing to any man; for they were afraid"—this latter meaning that they did not, at that time, speak to any except those to whom they had been sent.

And now as to Luke's account, it gives us yet another view and some added understanding of the glorious drama that was then unfolding. He tells us how the women, arriving very early with their spices, "found the stone rolled away from the sepulchre, and two angels standing by it in shining garments. And they entered into the sepulchre, and not finding the body of the Lord Jesus, they were much perplexed thereabout; And were affrighted, and bowed down their faces to the earth. But behold the angels said unto them":

> *Why seek ye the living among the dead? He is not here, but is risen: remember how he spake unto you when he was yet in Galilee, Saying, The Son of man must be delivered into the hands of sinful men, and be crucified, and the third day rise again.*

These are women who were with Jesus in Galilee. There they heard him say: "The Son of man shall be betrayed into the hands of men: And they shall kill him, and the third day he shall be raised again." (Matt. 17:22-23; Mark 9:30-32; Luke 9:44-45.) Matthew tells us that from the time of Peter's confession in the coasts of Caesarea Philippi, Jesus had begun to reveal these things to his disciples; and it seems clear that he must have done so *in extenso*. (Matt. 16:21.) Now the angelic voices bring these teachings to their remembrance, lest they think the death-dealing deeds of Annas and the Jews, and of Pilate and his soldiers, had thwarted the designs and purposes of Divine Providence. Again, it is worthy of note that among those who heard the word in Galilee were these very women who now in faith and sorrow sought their Lord in a sepulchre. It is just as important to preach the gospel to a woman as to a man, for the souls of all are equally precious in the sight of Him whose we all are.

Then these women returned from the sepulchre, told what they had seen and heard to the apostles and all the rest, "and their words seemed to them as idle tales, and they believed them not." But soon they shall believe, for they too shall hear and see and feel and know. The Risen Lord has manifest himself to the faithful women of his kingdom, for their spiritual insight warranted such precedence; soon the same witness shall be given to the Brethren.

NOTES

1. "One may wonder why Jesus had forbidden Mary Magdalene to touch Him, and then, so soon after, had permitted other women to hold Him by the feet as they bowed in reverence. We may assume that Mary's emotional approach had been prompted more by a feeling of personal yet holy affection than by an impulse of devotional worship such as the other women evinced. Though the resurrected Christ manifested the same friendly and intimate regard as He had shown in the mortal state toward those with whom He had been closely associated, He was no longer one of them in the literal sense. There was about Him a divine dignity that forbade close personal familiarity. To Mary Magdalene Christ had said: 'Touch me not; for I am not yet ascended to my Father.' If the second clause was spoken in explanation of the first, we have to infer that no human hand was to be permitted to touch the Lord's resurrected and immortalized body until after He had

presented Himself to the Father. It appears reasonable and probable that between Mary's impulsive attempt to touch the Lord, and the action of the other women who held Him by the feet as they bowed in worshipful reverence, Christ did ascend to the Father, and that later He returned to earth to continue His ministry in the resurrected state." (Talmage, p. 682.)

2. Of her Edersheim says: "Mary Magdalene—as prominent among the pious women as Peter was among the Apostles." (Edersheim 2:631.)

Chapter 111

JESUS' RESURRECTED MINISTRY

Jesus began both to do and teach,
Until the day in which he was taken up,
after that he through the Holy Ghost
had given commandments unto the apostles
whom he had chosen:
To whom also he shewed himself alive
after his passion by many infallible proofs,
being seen of them forty days,
and speaking of the things
pertaining to the kingdom of God.
(Acts 1:1-3.)

Peter and Others Learn of His Resurrection

(Matthew 27:52-53; 28:11-15; JST, Matthew 27:56; Luke 24:34)

He is risen; he has gained the victory over the grave; he hath abolished death; life and immortality are available to all; these glad tidings of great joy have commenced to go forth; already faithful women are bearing witness that he lives again; and he now has begun his resurrected ministry among mortals. Let God be praised for the wonder of it all!

Now his work must be organized, and his apostles must be sent forth to bear witness of his holy name and to build up and regulate all the affairs of his kingdom in all the world, first unto the Jews and then unto the Gentiles. What then is his next step? It must needs be that he appear to Peter—to Peter the rock; to Peter the seer; to Peter the chief apostle; to Peter to whom he has already given the keys of his earthly kingdom. Peter must now step forward and preside and govern during the absence of his Lord. He is the senior apostle of God on earth. As long as he lives—and he too, according to Jesus' word, will suffer death upon the cross—he will teach and preach and govern, and the gospel net will begin to gather in fish of all kinds.

That Jesus did appear to Peter we know; that this appearance came after that to Mary Magdala, and after that to the other women, we also know—thus making it, as we suppose, his third appearance. But we do not know where or under what circumstances he came, or what words of comfort and counsel and direction he gave. In the upper room, with Peter present, the apostolic witness was borne: "The Lord is risen indeed, and hath appeared to Simon"; and Paul says, "he was seen of Cephas, then of the twelve." (1 Cor. 15:5.)

No longer are the words of the women "as idle tales"; the chief apostle has himself seen and heard and, we suppose, felt the nail marks in the mangled hands and in the bruised feet. Neither Peter nor any of the inspired authors, except Luke and Paul, make mention of this appearance, but we feel free to suppose it was one in which the tears of Peter's denial in the court of Caiaphas were dried; one in which he was assured that though Satan desired to sift him as wheat, yet because Jesus had prayed for him, the noble Peter would yet come off triumphant; one in which a blessed bond of unity, of love, and of peace was established between the Master and his servant. As we have indicated with so many other things, there will surely be a day—when we are worthy to receive the enlightenment involved—when we, by revelation, shall learn in full of that holy appearance of the Lord to his chief apostle on the very day he came forth from the grave.

In this connection, and in this time frame, some events transpired involving great numbers of people, all of which stand as an everlasting witness of the raising of Jesus from death. Be it remembered that when Jesus ministered in the spirit world, he preached to "an innumerable company of the spirits of the just." With reference to all of these the holy word says: "Their sleeping dust was to be restored unto its perfect frame, bone to his bone, and the sinews and the flesh upon them, the spirit and the body to be united never again to be divided, that they might receive a fulness of joy." And also: "These the Lord taught, and gave them power to come forth, after his resurrection from the dead, to enter into his Father's kingdom, there to be crowned with immortality and eternal life." (D&C 138:12, 17, 51.)

Matthew tells us that these righteous spirits exercised the power given them. "And the graves were opened," he says, "and the bodies of the saints which slept, arose, who were many, And came out of the graves after his resurrection, and went into the holy city, and appeared unto many." Similar manifestations were poured out among the Nephites in the New World at this same time. Samuel the Lamanite had prophesied that in the day when the Father glorified his own name by raising his Son Jesus from the grave, then "there were many saints who should arise from the dead, and should appear unto many, and should minister unto them"—all of which came to pass. (3 Ne. 23:9-13.) And all of this—on both continents—bore record that Jesus had risen from the dead, thereby making possible the resurrection of all men, each in his own order.

And we cannot doubt that the chief witness borne by each resurrected saint, as he ministered to a mortal friend or relative, would be to testify that the Son of God had himself come forth from the grave, and that the effects of his resurrection were now passing upon others. Our knowledge of the resurrection is such that we can envision these righteous dead coming forth, each in his own order, each at the appointed moment, each prepared to enter into that eternal glory which is prepared for those who love and serve their Lord. Indeed, it was to be with them as it was with their Lord. They were to sit down with Abraham, Isaac, and Jacob, and all the prophets, in the kingdom of God, to go no more out.

Thus did the proclamation of the resurrection go forth among the righteous, to be carried by them to all men. But among the wicked and ungodly it was an entirely different thing. The chief priests learned of it from the guards whose mission it had been to keep the tomb sealed. "It was useless for the guards to stay beside an empty grave. With fear for the consequences, and horror at all that they had seen, they fled to the members of the Sanhedrin who had given them their secret commission. To these hardened hearts belief and investigation were alike out of the question. Their only refuge seemed to be in lies. They instantly tried to hush up the whole matter. They suggested to the soldiers that they must have slept, and that while they did so the disciples had stolen the body of Jesus. But such a tale was too infamous for credence, and too ridiculous for publicity. If it became known, nothing could have saved these soldiers, supposing them to have been Romans, from disgrace and execution. The Sadducees therefore bribed the men to consult their common interests by burying the whole matter in secrecy and silence. It was only gradually and later, and to the initiated, that the base calumny was uttered. Within six weeks of the resurrection, that great event was the unshaken faith of every Christian; within a few years of the event the palpable historic proofs of it and the numerous testimonies of its reality—strengthened by a memorable vision vouchsafed to himself—had won assent from the acute and noble intellect of a young Pharisaic zealot and persecutor whose name was Saul. But it was only in posthumous and subterranean whispers that the dark falsehood was disseminated which was intended to counteract this overwhelming evidence. St. Matthew says that when he wrote his Gospel it was still commonly bruited among the Jews. It continued to be received among them for centuries, and is one of the blaspheming follies repeated and amplified twelve centuries afterwards in the *Toldoth Jeshu.*" (Farrar, pp. 722–23.)

Jesus Appears on the Emmaus Road

(Luke 24:13-32; Mark 16:12-13)

Jesus now chooses to appear, first, on the Emmaus road, and then in the upper room, under circumstances that prove he has risen from the grave and that also teach the literal and corporeal nature of a resurrected body. During all his mortal ministry he had chosen the perfect teaching moments and brought forth the ideal illustrations to teach his doctrines and present his message in a way none other had ever done. Nor will he depart from that practice now. None but he could have done what he is now commencing. The two appearances, which are part of the same sermon in stone, as it were, comprise the only way in which both the fact and the nature of the resurrection could be taught in perfection.

It is the afternoon of the day of his resurrection. Two disciples not of the Twelve, one called Cleopas, the other undoubtedly Luke,[1] who recorded the events, are walking the some eight miles from Jerusalem to Emmaus. They can think and ponder and speak of only one thing—the Lord Jesus and his death and the reports relative to his resurrection. There is a sense of anxiety and perplexity and wonder in their words as they commune and reason together. There has never been such a Passover as this one, never such a trial and crucifixion as Jesus suffered, never such a day of wonder and rumor as this day, no, not from the beginning of time until now. Their minds are not at rest, and their spirits are stirred and anxious within them.

A stranger, Jesus himself, seemingly but another Passover pilgrim, draws nigh and walks with them. They feel some irritation, perhaps are a little peevish, that this unknown one should intrude himself on a conversation that is both personal and sacred. It suits his purpose not to be recognized, and so their eyes are covered with a veil, as it were, and the stranger is an unknown one. He asks: "What manner of communications are these that ye have one to another, as ye walk, and are sad?"

There is surprise and skepticism in the voice of Cleopas as he turns to speak to the uninvited intruder. How could anyone have been in Jerusalem this week and been unaware of the tumult and trials and crucifixion of the most renowned person in all Palestine? He asks: "Art thou only a stranger in Jerusalem, and hast not known the things which are come to pass there in these days?" Jesus said: "What things?"

Both of the disciples responded with a fluent outpouring of words that stir the soul. Luke digests their response: "Concerning Jesus of Nazareth," they said, "which was a prophet mighty in deed and word before God and all the people." There is no doubt here, no equivocation; they knew the wonder of his words, the depth of his deeds, the might of his ministry. "And how the chief priests and our rulers delivered him to be condemned to death," they continued, "and have crucified him." Herein lay their sorrow; their Friend had suffered, died, and was buried. All his promises and teachings seemed vague and uncertain in their minds.

"But we trusted that it had been he which should have redeemed Israel: and beside all this, to day is the third day since these things were done." The third day! Had he not promised to rise again the third day? But where was he? Had their Redeemer's work failed? "Yea, and certain women also of our company made us astonished, which were early at the sepulchre," they continued, "And when they found not his body, they came, saying, that they had also seen a vision of angels, which said that he was alive." This we cannot understand, they say, "And certain of them which were with us went to the sepulchre, and found it even so as the women had said: but him they saw not."

Peter and John had checked the "idle tales" of the women, but Jesus was not to be found. (Apparently Cleopas and Luke had not yet heard the clear witness of Mary Magdalene and of the other women that they had seen the Lord.) Having let them lay the foundation for his words, Jesus then said:

O fools, and slow of heart to believe all that the prophets have spoken:

Ought not Christ to have suffered these things, and to enter into his glory?

Having so spoken, Jesus quoted from Moses and all the prophets and expounded to them from all of the scriptures "the things concerning himself." How marvelous it would be if we knew what he said. They may have walked together for as long a time as two hours. And all the while to have the Son of God interpret for them the Messianic word! Are there meanings in the Messianic words of Moses and David and Isaiah, and "all the prophets," that so far have escaped us? Perhaps some day the conversations of this Emmaus walk will be revealed. But our Lord had a purpose over and above that of interpreting the Messianic word—he could leave that to Peter and Paul and the others, as they were enlightened by the power of the Holy Spirit; his mission was to show them what a resurrected person is like, and so far he has seemed so much like any mortal that his identity has remained hidden.

Nearing Emmaus, Jesus acted as though he would travel on. They constrained him to stay with them. "Abide with us: for it is toward evening, and the day is far spent," they said. Having heard his scriptural explanations, all feelings of anxiety and resentment vanished; now they sought his continuing company. He consented. And as they sat at meat, "he took bread, and blessed it, and brake, and gave to them." It was as though he removed the veil from their eyes; the sweet words of blessing, the passing of the bread, the loving demeanor of their Lord—it was all familiar to them. He was doing what he had done before, a rite that identified him in their minds. The covering—first imposed, but now removed, all by divine power—was no more. "They knew him; and he was taken up out of their sight."

Then they said—and the feelings thus described are the conclusive witness of the divine Sonship—they said: "Did not our heart burn within us, while he talked with us by the way, and while he opened to us the scriptures?" Cleopas and Luke now knew for themselves that He had risen. They must tell the others, and so they returned immediately to Jerusalem.

Jesus Appears in the Upper Room

(Luke 24:33-49; JST, Luke 24:34, 40; Mark 16:14; John 20:19-23)

As "it becometh every man who hath been warned to warn his neighbor" (D&C 88:81); as every person who has received the gospel is duty-bound to carry the same glad tidings to our Father's other children; as living witnesses of the truth and divinity of the Lord's work have become such, among other reasons, so they can bear their witness to their fellowmen—so Cleopas and Luke hastened to Jerusalem to testify to their fellow disciples that they had seen the Lord. They knew the trysting place and went directly there. We believe it was an upper room—perhaps the same room, in the home of John Mark, where Jesus and the Twelve celebrated the Feast of the Passover. A large group of disciples was present, including all of the eleven except Thomas. Certainly it was not a meeting for men only. Many faithful women were there and possibly even children. The whole group was eating an evening meal and, in effect, holding a testimony meeting as they ate. What each had seen and heard and knew of that day's happenings was recited and particularly the account of the appearance of the Lord to Peter. No doubt the Chief Apostle told them freely all that had transpired on that holy occasion.

Into this dinner meeting—this assemblage where both temporal and spiritual food was being freely dispensed—

came the two who had walked and conversed with Jesus on the Emmaus road. They heard the account of Jesus' appearance to Peter—"The Lord is risen indeed, and hath appeared to Simon," someone said—and as one testimony builds upon another, they were thus encouraged to testify on their own. "And they told what things they saw and heard in the way, and how he was known to them, in breaking of bread." How the believing souls there assembled must have rejoiced in the description of the stranger; in the Messianic interpretations he gave of the words of Moses and David and all the prophets; in the reminder they heard of his known practice of blessing and breaking bread; in the hearing about the flaming fires of testimonial surety that burned in the hearts of Cleopas and Luke as the Master Teacher had interpreted for them the scriptures!

Just at this moment, as the ones from Emmaus concluded their testimony, as though materializing from the midst of eternity, "Jesus himself stood in the midst of them." The doors were closed and locked; there was no window through which a man could enter; these friends of Jesus were guarding themselves "for fear of the Jews." His first words were the familiar "Peace be unto you." Mark tells us he "upbraided them with their unbelief and hardness of heart, because they believed not them"—Mary Magdalene and the other women—"which had seen him after he was risen." The inference is that they have believed the witness of Peter, but that they felt that the sisters had seen not a resurrected person, but some ghostly spectre, some spirit, some ethereal impression of wispy nothingness from another sphere. And even now, Luke records, "they were terrified and affrighted, and supposed that they had seen a spirit." How else, they thought, could this seeming man have entered the room? Jesus spoke:

> *Why are ye troubled? and why do thoughts arise in your hearts? Behold my hands and my feet, that it is I myself: handle me, and see; for a spirit hath not flesh and bones, as ye see me have.*

He stood there as a man; a spirit is a man; this they knew. He had been a spirit before his birth. "This body, which ye now behold, is the body of my spirit; . . . and even as I appear unto thee to be in the spirit will I appear unto my people in the flesh" (Ether 3:16), he had said to the brother of Jared in days gone by. He had been a spirit when he preached to the other spirits in paradise. But now he had a body—not of flesh and blood as do mortals, but of flesh and bones as do those whose bodies and spirits are inseparably joined in immortality. Flesh and bones is tangible; it can be felt and handled. He is continuing his "living sermon"; he is teaching them the reality and corporeity of the resurrection; though he had come through the enclosed room, yet he was a tangible being.

Then "he shewed them his hands and his feet." They felt the nail marks therein. What a marvel it is for mortal flesh to handle immortal flesh. "And while they yet wondered and believed not for joy, he said unto them, Have ye here any meat?" Their meal included broiled fish and honeycomb. These were handed to Jesus, and—marvel of marvels—he took them and ate them. A resurrected person eats and digests food; the body, though immortal, is tangible and real. If ever there was a "living sermon," such is being seen and believed and understood by the favored faithful in the upper room this night! Then he said:

> *These are the words which I spake unto you, while I was yet with you, that all things must be fulfilled, which were written in the law of Moses, and in the prophets, and in the psalms, concerning me.*

The Messianic prophecies! Every jot, every tittle have been fulfilled; not one word in the Psalms, not a single prophetic utterance, not one sacrificial similitude has been overlooked—all things have been fulfilled in Christ. He gave the word, he fulfilled the word, and the work is now accomplished. "Then opened he their understanding, that they might understand the scriptures." The miraculous nature of this gift should not be overlooked. They had not yet received the companionship of the Holy Ghost, but, nonetheless, their understandings are being quickened, though the total fulfillment of this will not be theirs until after Pentecost. Jesus continued:

> *Thus it is written, and thus it behoved Christ to suffer, and to rise from the dead the third day:*
>
> *And that repentance and remission of sins should be preached in his name among all nations, beginning at Jerusalem.*
>
> *And ye are witnesses of these things.*

Christ came; he was crucified, died, and rose again the third day; he worked out the infinite and eternal atonement, all with but one end in view: to bring to pass the immortality and eternal life of man, to enable men to repent and be baptized and gain eternal life. That message is now to go to "all nations," not to the Jews only, but to every nation and kindred and tongue and people. And it is to be carried by testimony. The disciples are to teach the gospel and seal their teachings with the witness that God has revealed to them that Jesus rose from the dead, that as a consequence his gospel is true, and that to gain salvation men must believe and obey.

> *And, behold, I send the promise of my Father upon you: but tarry ye in the city of Jerusalem, until ye be endued with power from on high.*

Herein we see a dual promise: one, that the disciples shall receive that sacred endowment which is given in holy places,[2] and the other, that they shall receive the gift of the Holy Ghost, which is itself an endowment from on high. They are already under instructions to go to Galilee and there meet the Lord on a mountain. This they will do shortly, and they will then return to Jerusalem, where they will tarry until Pentecost, when they will receive the Holy Ghost. We suppose they tarried in Jerusalem for the other sacred endowment and received it before they went to Galilee; otherwise Jesus' instruction loses its plain meaning.

> *Peace be unto you: as my Father hath sent me, even so send I you.*

Those to whom Jesus thus spoke had been called, ordained, given priesthood and keys and authority, and promised the companionship of the Holy Ghost, and now they are being sent forth to do among men as they have seen their Master do. They are to preach, ordain, and work miracles. They are legal administrators who represent the Lord Jesus, saying and doing what he wants said and done, even as he acted in a like capacity for his Father.

Then, as John expressed it, Jesus "breathed on them"—which in the very nature of things must be taken as a figure of speech—and said:

> *Receive ye the Holy Ghost:*
>
> *Whose soever sins ye remit, they are remitted unto them; and whose soever sins ye retain, they are retained.*

As to the receipt of the Holy Ghost, we know from many revelations exactly what is involved. The Holy Ghost is a personage of spirit, a spirit man, a member of the Godhead. Because he is a spirit person he has power to reveal truth to our spirits, to sanctify our souls, and to dwell in us in a figurative sense. We do not know how the eternal laws involved operate, only that they do. The gift of the Holy Ghost is the right to the constant companionship of this member of the Godhead based on faithfulness. This gift is given by the laying on of hands after baptism. It is reserved for members of the Church. These members may or may not actually receive the companionship of the Spirit; those who are clean and pure and worthy do; others do not. Jesus here tells his disciples to receive the Holy Ghost, meaning the gift of the Holy Ghost. In the very nature of things this means that he either conferred the gift upon them by the laying on of hands, or he confirmed verbally that he had theretofore given them that gift by the laying on of hands. The gift itself came on the day of Pentecost.

As to remitting and retaining sins, this is something that is implicit in the gospel system. The gospel is the plan of salvation; by obedience to its laws and ordinances men have power to free themselves from sin; their sins are washed away in the waters of baptism; and sin and evil are burned out of their souls as though by fire when they are baptized by the Holy Spirit. Thus the legal administrators who preach the gospel have power to remit the sins of men in the waters of baptism, and they have power to retain the sins of those who do not repent and are not baptized for the remission of sins.

And further: Those to whom power is given to bind on earth and seal in heaven have power to remit the sins of the saints on conditions of repentance or to retain them if they do not repent. In the ultimate sense, God alone forgives sins; but he can and does use his servants to speak for him in this as in many things, and whether by his own voice or by the voice of his servants, the result is the same. Needless to say, this, the Lord's system of forgiveness, operates only in the Church and kingdom of God on earth; only legal administrators who have been endowed with power from on high can either remit or retain sins; and they must be guided by the power of the Holy Ghost in all that they do, or their acts will not be binding on earth and sealed everlastingly in the heavens.[3]

Jesus Appears to Thomas and the Disciples

(John 20:24-29)

Once again it is Sunday,[4] the first weekly anniversary of the first resurrection. The disciples, beginning the practice of worshipping on Sunday rather than on the Jewish Sabbath, and coming together to commemorate the rising of Jesus from death, are again in the upper room. The doors are shut, probably guarded. No mention is made of food, but the worshipful group may have been eating, and certainly they were conversing about the resurrection and reciting the accounts of His appearances. So far there have been five of which we know—to Mary Magdalene, to the other women, to Peter, to Cleopas and Luke on the Emmaus road, and to a small congregation of saints in the upper room.

During the week the disciples had said to Thomas, "We have seen the Lord," and, 'We felt the nail marks in his hands and in his feet: we gave him a piece of a broiled fish and of a honeycomb, both of which he ate before us. And he told us such and such things about himself and about our commission to testify of him in all nations.' Thomas had believed in the resurrection, but not in the literal corporeity of His body, not in the fact that Jesus now ate food, not in the fact that the nail marks remained in his flesh and bones. He had said: "Except I shall see in his hands the print of the nails, and put my finger into the print of the nails, and thrust my hand into his side, I will not believe."

Thomas is now present with the others, and of a sudden, as on the week afore, Jesus "stood in the midst." Again he utters the familiar greeting: "Peace be unto you." Then to Thomas came the command:

> *Reach hither thy finger, and behold my hands; and reach hither thy hand, and thrust it into my side: and be not faithless, but believing.*

Thomas complied; he would not have dared to do otherwise. He now felt and handled as the others had done; he was a living, personal witness of the corporeity of the body of the Lord Jesus. Whether Jesus called for food and ate again is not recorded. Such would not have been necessary, because Thomas, feeling the nail prints and the spear wound, could not do other than believe the account about the broiled fish and the honeycomb. From the lips of the now believing apostle, we suppose as he knelt to touch the marks in Jesus' feet, came the worshipful cry: "My Lord and my God." Thereupon Jesus said:

> *Thomas, because thou hast seen me, thou hast*

believed: blessed are they that have not seen, and yet have believed.

Thomas, who once offered to go with Jesus to Bethany, there to die with him, saw and believed—believed in the literal nature of the resurrection and that Jesus after death lived again as a man. Ever since he has been called, somewhat unkindly, Doubting Thomas. Whatever they may have been, his doubts were of a passing and transitory nature. He became and remained a believer in the full sense. Rather than point the finger of scorn at his supposed disbelief, would it not be better to be fearful of the fate of the ten thousand times ten thousand, plus unnumbered more, of the Doubting Thomases in a doubting Christendom where none believe that the Lord Jesus now reigns with his Father in eternal glory—both of them glorying in their exalted bodies of flesh and bones?

Thus we know that resurrected beings, containing their glory within themselves, can walk as mortals do on earth; that they can converse and reason and teach as they once did in mortality; that they can both withhold and manifest their true identities; that they can pass with corporeal bodies through solid walls; that they have bodies of flesh and bones that can be felt and handled; that, if need be, and at special times, they can retain the scars and wounds of the flesh; that they can eat and digest food; that they can vanish from mortal eyes and transport themselves by means unknown to us.

How glorious it has been to hear the living sermon preached by the greatest Preacher of all time as he ministered on the Emmaus road and in the upper room!

NOTES

1. If, as is generally believed, the unnamed disciple was our Gospel author Luke, then, interestingly, "each of the Gospels would, like a picture, bear in some dim corner the indication of its author: the first, that of the publican; that by St. Mark, that of the young man, who, in the night of the Betrayal, had fled from his captors; that of St. Luke in the companion of Cleopas; and that of St. John, in the disciple whom Jesus loved." (Edersheim 2:638.)

2. "I gave unto you a commandment that you should build a house," the Lord said to his Latter-day Saints, "in the which house I design to endow those whom I have chosen with power from on high; For this is the promise of the Father unto you; therefore I command you to tarry, even as mine apostles at Jerusalem." (D&C 95:8-9; 105:11-12, 18, 33.)

3. "I have conferred upon you the keys and power of the priesthood," the Lord said to Joseph Smith, "and whosesoever sins you remit on earth shall be remitted eternally in the heavens; and whosesoever sins you retain on earth shall be retained in heaven." (D&C 132:45-46.)

4. John, speaking after the Jewish pattern, says "after eight days," meaning, to us, seven days later. Their measurement of Jesus' tenure in the tomb is also counted this same way.

Chapter 112

THE GALILEAN APPEARANCES

Arise and come forth unto me,
that ye may thrust your hands into my side,
and also that ye may feel
the prints of the nails
in my hands and in my feet,
that ye may know that I am the God of Israel,
and the God of the whole earth,
and have been slain
for the sins of the world.
And it came to pass that the multitude went forth,
and thrust their hands into his side,
and did feel the prints of the nails
in his hands and in his feet;
and this they did do,
going forth one by one
until they had all gone forth,
and did see with their eyes
and did feel with their hands,
and did know of a surety and did bear record,
that it was he, of whom it was written
by the prophets, that should come.
And when they had all gone forth

and had witnessed for themselves,
they did cry out with one accord, saying:
Hosanna! Blessed be the name
of the Most High God!
And they did fall down at the feet of Jesus,
and did worship him.
(3 Ne. 11:14-17.)

Jesus Appears at the Sea of Tiberias
(John 21:1-24)

After Jesus rose from the dead, our apostolic friends received two commands—one, to go to Galilee and meet Jesus on a mountain according to a prior appointment; the other, to tarry in Jerusalem until he sent the promise of the Father upon them and they were endowed with power from on high. Apparently they have been endowed in the initial sense of the word—though an additional heavenly endowment of divine power will come, in Jerusalem, on the day of Pentecost—for they have now left the Holy City and traveled to their native Galilee. It will be remembered that all of the Twelve, save Judas, were Galileans, and that most of their apostolic training, as well as their ministerial service, had been in their beloved homeland. Their appointment to meet the Lord was a definite one to which more than five hundred brethren had been invited. As they awaited the day, and having need to supply their families with this world's goods, Peter said: "I go a fishing." Six of the eleven were with him—James, John, Thomas, Nathanael, and two who are not named but probably were Andrew and Philip, since those two had been engaged with Peter and the others in like ventures in earlier days. This group said to Peter: "We also go with thee."

They all went forth into a ship and spent the whole night fishing in the Sea of Galilee, also known as the Sea of Tiberias and as the Lake of Gennesaret. They caught nothing. In the morning Jesus stood on the shore, "but the disciples knew not that it was Jesus." Apparently he withheld his identity as he had done to the two who walked with him on the Emmaus road. He called out: "Children, have ye any meat?" They answered, "No." He said, "Cast the net on the right side of the ship, and ye shall find." They did so, and immediately the net was so full "they were not able to draw it for the multitude of fishes." Perhaps the three—Peter, James, and John—remembered that other occasion when they had toiled all night on the same lake, had caught nothing, and then, casting again at His word, had filled their net until it brake. In any event, John, who seems to have been more spiritually sensitive than the rest, said to Peter: "It is the Lord." Peter, who was naked, "girt his fisher's coat unto him," jumped from the ship, and swam to shore to meet the Master. The others changed into a small ship and dragged the net and the fish about a hundred yards to the shore.

When they came to shore they found a fire of coals with fish broiling and a supply of bread. Jesus said: "Bring of the fish which ye have now caught." Peter waded into the shallow water, pulled the net to shore, and the fish were counted—a hundred and fifty-three in all, so many that the record marvels that the net was not broken. Jesus said: "Come and dine." John says none of the disciples dared ask him, "Who art thou?" because they knew "it was the Lord." Jesus then gave them bread and fish to eat, and although the account does not so state, he himself must also have eaten, for, as in the upper room, such would have been one of the main purposes of providing the food. John says this was "the third time that Jesus shewed himself to his disciples"—meaning to them as a group—"after that he was risen from the dead."

"So when they"—meaning, as we suppose, both Jesus and the apostles—"had dined," Jesus said to Simon Peter: "Simon, son of Jonas, lovest thou me more than these?" More than these fish, more than the things of this world, more than all else, even life itself! 'Lovest thou me above all? If so, Keep my commandments.' To Peter—who but a short while before had said, "Lord, I am ready to go with thee, both into prison, and to death," and who, as Jesus foretold, had then thrice denied that he even knew Christ, and that before the cock crew twice (Luke 22:32-34)—to Peter, the Chief Apostle, Jesus was asking for a new and unshakable avowal of allegiance. Peter said: "Yea, Lord; thou knowest that I love thee." Jesus said: "Feed my lambs." Once near this spot Jesus had said to Peter and Andrew, "Follow me, and I will make you fishers of men." (Matt. 4:18-22.) That call was still in force, but to it now was added the commission to feed the flock of God.

Jesus asked a second time: "Simon, son of Jonas, lovest thou me?" Again came the answer: "Yea, Lord; thou knowest that I love thee." To this Jesus said: "Feed my sheep." Then again, for the third time, came the question: "Simon, son of Jonas, lovest thou me?" Peter, grieved at the repetition, responded: "Lord, thou knowest all things; thou knowest that I love thee." Again came the test of love and of true discipleship: "Feed my sheep." He who had thrice denied, now thrice affirmed; he who with an oath had said, "I know not this man of whom ye speak" (Mark 14:66-72), now pledged, in the presence of his brethren, to love his Lord with all his heart; he who had said he would die for Christ, now is committed to live for him.

Lovest thou me! Jesus had asked and Peter had answered; thrice was the question put and thrice the answer came. Lovest thou me! Ah, Peter, truly hast thou testified of thy love for thy Lord. And how shall that love be measured? In service to thy fellowmen ("Feed my sheep") and in obedience to the holy law ("If ye love me, keep my commandments" [John 14:15])—in these two ways while thou livest. But there is more. Thy love for me shall be perfected and sanctified by thy death. ("Greater love hath no man than this, that a man lay down his life for his friends." [John 15:13.]) And so Jesus, still singling out the leader among the apostolic witnesses, said to his servant: "When thou wast young, thou girdedst thyself, and walkedst whither thou wouldest: but when thou shalt be old, thou shalt stretch forth thy hands, and another shall gird thee, and carry thee whither thou wouldest not." Of this John said: "This spake he, signifying by what death he should glorify God," meaning that Peter would lay down his life for his Chief Friend, lay it down upon a cruel cross, lay it down even as that Friend had laid down his life for his friends. "I will lay down my life for thy sake," Peter had said. "Thou shalt follow me" in death, was Jesus' assurance to him. (John 13:36-38.) "How literally the Master then spoke, and how fully Peter is to do as he offered, he now learns. He is to be crucified, a thing which John in this passage assumes to be known to his readers. Peter's arms are to be stretched forth upon the cross, the executioner shall gird him with the loin-cloth which criminals wear when crucified, and he shall be carried where he would not, that is to his execution." (*Commentary* 1:863-64.)

Having so spoken, Jesus said to Peter, "Follow me"—follow me apart from the others; follow me in ministerial service; follow me in faith and obedience and righteousness; follow me in all things. And as they walked, Peter, "turning about," saw John, his closest colleague and most intimate mortal friend, and asked Jesus: "Lord, and what shall this man do?" Shall he also have his arms stretched forth upon the cross? Will he too be girded and bound upon the inhuman instrument of torture? Shall it be with him, as thou hast said of me? Jesus said: "If I will that he tarry till I come, what is that to thee? follow thou me."

Perhaps it was at this time that John, joining Jesus and Peter as they walked, was asked by the Lord: "John, my beloved, what desirest thou? For if you shall ask what you will, it shall be granted unto you." In John's reply we see the measure of the man; the apostolic witness he desired to bear; the works he desired to do; the souls he desired to save: "Lord, give unto me power over death," he asked, "that I may live and bring souls unto thee." Such a request, aside from the perfect faith that knows that such a plea can be granted, is a manifestation of missionary zeal scarce known among men. To preach the gospel and save souls until the Son of Man comes in his glory—what a wondrous work! And Jesus replied:

> *Verily, verily I say unto thee, because thou desirest this thou shalt tarry until I come in my glory, and shalt prophesy before nations, kindreds, tongues and people.*

In writing of this promise John gives a more amplified account of the conversation there on the shores of Gennesaret. Not only did Jesus say to Peter, "If I will that he tarry till I come, what is that to thee?" but also: "He desired of me that he might bring souls unto me, but thou desiredst that thou mightest speedily come unto me in my kingdom. I say unto thee, Peter, this was a good desire; but my beloved has desired that he might do more, or a greater work yet among men than what he has before done. Yea, he has undertaken a greater work; therefore I will make him as a flaming fire and a ministering angel; he shall minister for those who shall be heirs of salvation who dwell on the earth. And I will make thee to minister for him and for thy brother James; and unto you three I will give this power and the keys of this ministry until I come. Verily I say unto you, ye shall both have according to your desires, for ye both joy in that which ye have desired." (D&C 7:1-8.)

And thus endeth such knowledge as we have of the words of him who is Lord of all as he spoke them this wondrous morning in the calm setting of a Galilean lake where he and his hearers had spent so many pleasant hours together. Without doubt he then told them many other things. Oh, how little we know of all that he said! How little we have seen of all that he did! And how seldom do we get in tune with the Infinite so that we can both know and feel even that which has been preserved for us! We suppose, however, that he confirmed with them the time and the place of their coming meeting on a Galilean mountain; for it is there we shall see them next.

Jesus Appears on a Mountain in Galilee
(Matthew 28:16-20; Mark 16:15-18; 3 Nephi 11)

We come now to the greatest of all the appearances of the Risen Lord to and among his disciples in Palestine—to his appearance on a mountain in Galilee. What happened at this appearance is not even mentioned by John or Luke; and Matthew uses only five verses to recount its wonders, and Mark only four. But in all of this there was a divine purpose; in it all there was a reason of surpassing import why more was not preserved in the New Testament—which purpose and reason we shall hereafter set forth.

First, however, we must give to this Galilean appearance such a setting and such a New Testament background as the sacred record does provide. Jesus himself was a Galilean; he lived as a child in Nazareth, and his boyish feet trod the Galilean hills. The eleven were all Galileans; most of his ministry and most of theirs had been in the cities and villages of that rustic, rugged, rural part of Palestine. There was more believing blood and less priestcraft, more pure worship and less rebellion, more of the love of the Lord and less of the worship of worldliness, in Galilee than in Judea. The spies that dogged his footsteps came from Jerusalem; the scribes and Rabbinical schools were centered in the Holy City. The proud Sadducees and the haughty Sanhedrists made the temple their headquarters. Pharisaic sophistry and priestly ritualism centered in Judea, not in Galilee. What would have been more natural than that the thoughts and hearts of the apostles would have turned to their beloved homeland in the trials of these days? And how compassionate and tender was their Friend in choosing to take them back to their own land to manifest himself to them and to renew with them in glory the experiences they had once had with him there in the days of their trials? Would their thoughts have been as the words of our hymn?

Each cooing dove and sighing bough
That makes the eve so blest to me
Has something far diviner now
It bears me back to Galilee.

Each flow'ry glen and mossy dell
Where happy birds in song agree
Thro' sunny morn the praises tell
Of sights and sounds in Galilee.

And when I read the thrilling lore
Of Him who walked upon the sea
I long, oh, how I long once more
To follow Him in Galilee.

O Galilee! sweet Galilee!
Where Jesus loved so much to be;
O Galilee! blue Galilee!
Come, sing thy song again to me.
—*Hymns,* no. 38

And so that night in the upper room, at the Paschal feast, having quoted the Messianic word that the Shepherd will be smitten and the sheep scattered, Jesus said: "But after I am risen again, I will go before you into Galilee." (Matt. 26:32.) And so, lest they forget, at the open tomb the angelic ministrants told the faithful women: "Go your way, tell his disciples and Peter that he goeth before you into Galilee: there shall ye see him, as he said unto you." (Mark 16:7.) And even the Risen Lord himself said to these same women: "Go tell my brethren that they go into Galilee, and there shall they see me." (Matt. 28:10.) The import, glory, and grandeur of this Galilean meeting could not have been impressed more strongly upon them. Nor can we doubt that the word went out—repetitiously—to all who were invited and that elaborate preparations were made. This was to be no small and insignificant thing; many of them had already seen the Risen Lord, but all that had gone before was but a shadow and a foretaste of what was to be.

Paul recounted some of the resurrected appearances. He reminded the Corinthians that he had preached to them the gospel by which salvation comes. "For I delivered unto you first of all," he said, "that which I also received, how that Christ died for our sins according to the scriptures; And that he was buried, and that he rose again the third day according to the scriptures"—and these things are what comprise the gospel—"And that he was seen of Cephas." Peter saw him, as was announced that night in the upper room. Then he was seen "of the twelve," meaning in the upper room when Cleopas and Luke made their report, and again a week later in that same place by the same group with Thomas also being present. "After that, he was seen of above five hundred brethren at once; of whom the greater part remain unto this present, but some are fallen asleep." This is the appearance on the Galilean mountain of which we are about to speak. "After that, he was seen of James." This is understood to be an appearance to James the brother of the Lord, who became one of the Twelve and a mighty pillar of strength and righteousness in due course. Of it the scriptures say nothing except the words here quoted from Paul.[1] Then he was seen, Paul continues, "of all the apostles," having reference to the time of his ascension on the Mount of Olivet. "And last of all he was seen of me also, as of one born out of due time," our apostolic friend records, identifying himself as one abortively added to the apostolic family. (1 Cor. 15:1-8.)

Paul's recitation is not intended in any sense to be complete. He says nothing about the appearance—the first of all others—to Mary Magdalene; nor to the other women; nor to the two disciples on the Emmaus road; nor to seven of the Twelve on the shore of the sea of Tiberias; nor does he mention, as Luke does, that when Jesus first came to the upper room there were others present in addition to the apostles. Indeed, all of the inspired authors record only fragments and slivers of the full story. Matthew mentions the "eleven disciples" only as being present on the mountain in Galilee, and Mark strings together the appearance in the upper room and the commission, given in Galilee, to go into all the world, as though they both occurred at the same time and place. Providentially we can take a sliver from here and a sliver from there and construct a large board. And having thus learned how the accounts must be interpreted, we can reach reasonable conclusions as to what happened. Thus when Paul speaks of more than five hundred brethren being present on one occasion, we have every reason to believe there may have been five hundred or a thousand women in the same congregation and perhaps an unnumbered host of children. We know how and under what circumstances the Lord ministered among the Nephites and have every reason to believe that he followed the same pattern in Palestine. The Nephites were a select group of saints because the wicked among them had been destroyed during the period of darkness at the crucifixion, and the group that assembled on the mountain in Galilee was one called from the midst of the wicked in the land so that they might receive on a mountain sanctuary the mysteries of the kingdom.

We must not leave this part of our discussion without recording that, without question, there were many unmentioned appearances. We know He was with them, from time to time, for forty days; and it is unthinkable to assume that he did not appear to the Blessed Virgin whose Son he was, to Lazarus whom he called forth from four days of death, to Mary and Martha whom he loved, and to hosts of others whose names were written in the Lamb's Book of Life, never to be blotted out. It is true that various of these may have been with the "other women" at the tomb, with the apostles in the upper room, or with the great congregation on the Galilean mountain. But it is not the time or the place that matters; rather, it is the reality of the appearances and the fact that it was clearly his purpose to manifest himself to all who had prepared themselves to stand in the Divine Presence. It is written of Jared's brother that "because of the knowledge of this man, . . . he could not be kept from within the veil; therefore he saw Jesus; and he did minister unto him." (Ether 3:19-20.) And so it was with the faithful among whom Jesus had ministered before his death. They too had a perfect knowledge that he was the Son of God; they knew he had fulfilled his promise and risen from the dead; they knew he had appeared to Peter and to others; and they knew he would appear to them also if they sought him with all their hearts. Further: He desired to appear to them, to give comfort and consolation in their sorrow, and to wipe away all tears from their crying eyes; he wanted them to grow in faith and to bear witness to the world of his resurrection and of the resurrection of all men; and, we may rest assured, by obedience to the laws involved the veil was rent and they saw and felt and handled and worshipped.

But now, as to the appearance on the mountain Galilee, it is pleasant to suppose it happened at the same site on which he preached the Sermon on the Mount, for that was the ordination sermon of the Twelve, and he now designs to give those same apostolic witnesses their great commission to carry the gospel into all the world. What would be more fitting than to have the great commission to take the gospel to all the world come forth at the same sacred spot whence they received their first apostolic commission, from the mountain which had become to them a holy temple? It is also pleasant to suppose that after the invited disciples were all assembled, awaiting his appearance in reverential awe, perhaps seated, at the direction of Peter and the Twelve, on the greening slopes in prayer and meditation, at such a moment he appeared, and that his first words to them paralleled those to be spoken later to his Nephite disciples:

Behold, I am Jesus Christ, whom the prophets testified shall come into the world.

And behold, I am the light and the life of the world; and I have drunk out of that bitter cup which the Father hath given me, and have glorified the Father in taking upon me the sins of the world, in the which I have suffered the will of the Father in all things from the beginning.

When Jesus spoke these words among the Nephites, "the whole multitude," in a spontaneous act of reverential worship, "fell to the earth," even as Thomas had done when he was invited to feel the nail prints and thrust his hand into the side of the Risen One. Then Jesus invited these New World Hebrews—these Nephite Jews whose fathers had come forth from Jerusalem—to themselves come forth and thrust their hands into his side and feel the prints of the nails in his hands and in his feet, and learn for themselves that he was the God of Israel, and the God of the whole earth, and that he had been slain for the sins of the world. This they did, worshipping Jesus and rending the air with cries of Hosanna. And we do not suppose that the divine scene was much different on the Galilean mountain. Of it Matthew says, "when they saw him, they worshipped him," adding, sadly we suppose, "but some doubted," meaning that among the multitude there were those who had not yet come to know—as all of the apostles then knew—of the tangible nature of his body of flesh and bones. That this doubt, as with Thomas, blossomed into glorious faith we cannot doubt as soon as they—as it had been with Thomas and all of the Twelve—had felt and handled the once mangled and now glorified body of their Lord. How marvelous it is that Jesus welcomes those of all lands and nations, and that, from his standpoint, there cannot be too many who are worthy to see and touch and handle and know for themselves that he is the Redeemer of the world and the Savior of all who come unto him with full purpose of heart.

In this setting of worship and adoration, Jesus bore to his Galilean friends this testimony of himself: "ALL POWER IS GIVEN UNTO ME IN HEAVEN AND IN EARTH." Even for a

God, this is a new day of power and might and dominion! A resurrected body adds eternal blessings that cannot be gained in any other way. Even a God must be resurrected to inherit, possess, and receive all things. Thus saith Jehovah: "My dead body shall . . . arise." (Isa. 26:19.) Jesus, who is Jehovah, was God before the world was. Speaking to good king Benjamin, the angelic ministrant called him "the Lord Omnipotent who reigneth, who was, and is from all eternity to all eternity." (Mosiah 3:5.) To Isaiah he was "The mighty God, The everlasting Father" (Isa. 9:6), and to Abinadi he was "God himself" who should "come down among the children of men" and "redeem his people" (Mosiah 15:1). He was the Lord God Almighty before he was ever born, because he was "like unto God" (Abr. 3:24), and he was, under the Father, the Creator of worlds without number. There are no words to describe, no language to convey, no tongue which can tell, his greatness and glory as it was even before the foundations of the world were laid. And yet, even he came to earth to be "added upon" (Abr. 3:26), to undergo the trials and tests of mortality, and to come forth in the resurrection with a body of flesh and bones like that of his Father. The Spirit Jehovah, thus clothed in immortal glory, became an inheritor of eternal life in the full and unlimited sense. In the resurrection "he received a fulness of the glory of the Father; And he received all power, both in heaven and on earth, and the glory of the Father was with him, for he dwelt in him." (D&C 93:16-17.)

Jesus has thus finished his mortal labors; now he is eternal; from henceforth he shall reign on the right hand of the Majesty on High; others, who are yet mortal, must carry forward the work of salvation among men on earth. And so he says to his apostles:

Go ye therefore, and teach all nations, baptizing them in the name of the Father, and of the Son, and of the Holy Ghost:

Teaching them to observe all things whatsoever I have commanded you: and, lo, I am with you alway, even unto the end of the world.

Thus the Twelve are commissioned anew. Apostolic power came to them on the Mount of Beatitudes when they were ordained to the holy apostleship; they received the keys of the kingdom of God on earth after Jesus was transfigured on the heights of Holy Hermon; they were recalled to ministerial service when he appeared to them in the upper room and again at the sea of Tiberias; now they are to go to all nations and take the message of salvation to all men. Once they were sent only to the lost sheep of the house of Israel; now all our Father's children, of all nations and kindreds, are to hear the divine word. The gospel must be taught; baptism is for all; salvation is available to all on conditions of obedience. All that Jesus has taught them is to be taught to all men as rapidly as they are able to bear it, and he will be with the faithful in all nations always.

Go ye into all the world, and preach the gospel to every creature. He that believeth and is baptized shall be saved; but he that believeth not shall be damned.

Thus saith thy God. The gospel is for all; baptism is for all; salvation is for all—for all who will believe and obey. The residue of men, and they are many, shall be damned. Men must first be baptized, then they must "observe all things"—meaning, keep the commandments—and thus, having endured to the end, they shall be saved with an everlasting salvation.

Nor were these eternal truths taught in Galilee any different from those presented among the Nephites. After that branch of the house of Israel had gained their witness of the divine Sonship of Jesus and had felt and handled the flesh and bones he then possessed, he called Nephi the Disciple to come forth. Nephi "bowed himself before the Lord and did kiss his feet," and Jesus said to him: "I give unto you power that ye shall baptize this people when I am again ascended into heaven." Others were called forth and given like power. That these disciples were already performing authoritative baptisms we know; but it was now to be with them as with their Old World counterparts. They were receiving a new commission as part of a new dispensation. What we have come to call—somewhat inaccurately—the Christian era was beginning among them. Their commission, however, was to administer salvation to the Nephites in the Americas as contrasted with that of the Old World Twelve who were sent to all nations. To his Nephite disciples Jesus then said, as in all likelihood he did to his Galilean followers:

> *On this wise shall ye baptize; and there shall be no disputations among you. Verily I say unto you, that whoso repenteth of his sins through your words and desireth to be baptized in my name, on this wise shall ye baptize them—Behold, ye shall go down and stand in the water, and in my name shall ye baptize them.*
>
> *And now behold, these are the words which ye shall say, calling them by name, saying: Having authority given me of Jesus Christ, I baptize you in the name of the Father, and of the Son, and of the Holy Ghost. Amen.*
>
> *And then shall ye immerse them in the water, and come forth again out of the water. And after this manner shall ye baptize in my name; for behold, verily I say unto you, that the Father, and the Son, and the Holy Ghost are one; and I am in the Father, and the Father in me, and the Father and I are one.*

That all of this had been taught to and was in operation among the Twelve of Jerusalem is not open to question; but so also was it the case among the Nephites. They too had been taught true principles and were practicing true ordinances. And yet Jesus now renews and clarifies these policies and procedures among them, as we suppose he did also in Galilee. There must be no divergence of belief or practice on matters of such eternal import.

> *And according as I have commanded you thus shall ye baptize. And there shall be no disputations among you, as there have hitherto been; neither shall there be disputations among you concerning the points of my doctrine, as there have hitherto been.*
>
> *For verily, verily I say unto you, he that hath the spirit of contention is not of me, but is of the devil, who is the father of contention, and he stirreth up the hearts of men to contend with anger, one with another.*
>
> *Behold, this is not my doctrine, to stir up the hearts of men with anger, one against another; but this is my doctrine, that such things should be done away.*

O that the blaspheming self-exulters of Christendom, who contend from their pulpits and before the microphones of their so-called radio ministries, O that they knew what the Lord thinks of contention!

O that those who say, Lo here is Christ and lo there, who say, Believe this or believe that in order to be saved, O that they knew he reveals himself, not in the midst of debate, but in the sanctuary of peace!

O that those in the Church who are more concerned with defending their prejudices and upholding their private interpretations than they are in seeking the truth, O that they would shun contention and seek for unity with the Lord's earthly standard bearers and with those whom he hath appointed to interpret and define his doctrines for the children of men!

> *Behold, verily, verily, I say unto you, I will declare unto you my doctrine. And this is my doctrine, and it is the doctrine which the Father hath given unto me; and I bear record of the Father, and the Father*

beareth record of me, and the Holy Ghost beareth record of the Father and me; and I bear record that the Father commandeth all men, everywhere, to repent and believe in me.

Even Jesus has no doctrine of his own; even he receives his doctrine from the Father; and it is the doctrine of the Father, and of the Son, and of the Holy Ghost, that all men must believe in Christ, repent of their sins, and live his laws to be saved. Men choose what they believe and what they do at the peril of their own salvation. Ought we not to learn and know what Deity thinks about a doctrine, rather than what seems, for one reason or another, to be desirable to us?

And whoso believeth in me, and is baptized, the same shall be saved; and they are they who shall inherit the kingdom of God.

And whoso believeth not in me, and is not baptized, shall be damned.

Verily, verily, I say unto you, that this is my doctrine, and I bear record of it from the Father; and whoso believeth in me believeth in the Father also; and unto him will the Father bear record of me, for he will visit him with fire and with the Holy Ghost.

And thus will the Father bear record of me, and the Holy Ghost will bear record unto him of the Father and me; for the Father, and I, and the Holy Ghost are one.

Jesus' words, thus spoken, are so plain, so easy, so simple, that none need err with reference to them. The course is clearly marked. And if any, reading what he here says, do not have their bosoms burn as did those of Cleopas and Luke on the Emmaus road, they may know thereby that they are not the Lord's sheep, and that they need to repent and get in tune with the Holy Spirit so they can believe and understand the witness of the Father and of the Son and of the Holy Ghost, which is one God everlastingly.

And again I say unto you, ye must repent, and

> *become as a little child, and be baptized in my name, or ye can in nowise receive these things.*
>
> *And again I say unto you, ye must repent, and be baptized in my name, and become as a little child, or ye can in nowise inherit the kingdom of God.*
>
> *Verily, verily, I say unto you, that this is my doctrine, and whoso buildeth upon this buildeth upon my rock, and the gates of hell shall not prevail against them.*
>
> *And whoso shall declare more or less than this, and establish it for my doctrine, the same cometh of evil, and is not built upon my rock; but he buildeth upon a sandy foundation, and the gates of hell stand open to receive such when the floods come and the winds beat upon them.*
>
> *Therefore, go forth unto this people, and declare the words which I have spoken, unto the ends of the earth.*

None who are enlightened by the power of the Spirit need further commentary on these glorious words—words that testify of the goodness and grace of Jesus and of the divine mission of the Prophet Joseph Smith, because they have come forth in our day through his instrumentality. Let us, rather, turn to the remainder of the New Testament account of the greatest of all the appearances of the Risen Lord:

> *And these signs shall follow them that believe; In my name shall they cast out devils; they shall speak with new tongues; They shall take up serpents; and if they drink any deadly thing, it shall not hurt them; they shall lay hands on the sick, and they shall recover.*

These words were spoken almost verbatim by Jesus to the Nephite disciples, and to them he then added: "And whosoever shall believe in my name, doubting nothing, unto him will I confirm all my words, even unto the ends of the earth." (Morm. 9:22-25.) And thus it is in all ages and at all times and among all people: signs and miracles abound where faith is found. As gravity pulls down the raindrops from the sky, so faith brings forth signs and miracles; as law operates in the natural field, so it does in the spiritual; and so when faith is exercised, miracles are wrought. As God is our witness, we testify that whenever and wherever there is faith, there the gifts of the Spirit will be manifest. Signs always have, do now, and always will follow those who believe. If there are none of the gifts, there is no faith, men have not believed the true gospel, and they do not have a hope of salvation. Faith is power; and if a people do not have power to open blind eyes, and unstop deaf ears, and loose dumb tongues, and raise dead corpses, how can they have power to save a soul? So it has always been, so it is now, and so it will ever be. Signs follow those who believe.

NOTE

1. "Respecting this appearance to James we know nothing further, unless there be any basis of true tradition in the story preserved to us in the Gospel of the Hebrews. We are there told that James, the first Bishop of Jerusalem, and the Lord's brother, had, after the Last Supper, taken a solemn vow that he would neither eat nor drink until he had seen Jesus risen from the dead. Early, therefore, after His resurrection, Jesus, when He had given the *sindon* to the servant of the priest, had a table with bread brought out, blessed the bread, and gave it to James, with the words, 'Eat thy bread now, my brother, since the Son of Man has risen from the dead.' " (Farrar, p. 731.)

Chapter 113

THE NEPHITE MINISTRY

I lay down my life for the sheep.
And other sheep I have, which are not
of this fold: them also I must bring,
and they shall hear my voice;
and there shall be one fold, and one shepherd.
(John 10:15-16.)
Ye are they of whom I said:
Other sheep I have which are not of this fold;
them also I must bring,
and they shall hear my voice;
and there shall be one fold, and one shepherd.
(3 Ne. 15:21.)
There is one God and one Shepherd
over all the earth.
(1 Ne. 13:41.)

Appearances to the Other Sheep

(3 Nephi 11–15; 16:1-3)

The Nephites adjusted their calendar so as to begin a new dating era with the birth of Jesus; and according to their chronology, the storms and the darkness and the crucifixion came to pass on the fourth day of the first month of the thirty-fourth year. (3 Ne. 8.) Then "in the ending" of that year (3 Ne. 10:18-19), several months after the Ascension on Olivet, Jesus ministered personally among the Nephites for many hours on many days. He came as "a Man descending out of heaven"; introduced himself as the God of Israel; permitted the multitude to feel the prints of the nails in his hands and feet and to thrust their hands into his side; called a quorum of twelve; gave them keys and powers and authorities; healed the Nephite sick and introduced the sacramental ordinance in the Western Hemisphere; taught the people in plainness and with an excellence surpassing much that was done in his Palestinian ministry; gave them the gift of the Holy Ghost; and ascended to his Father.

Third Nephi is often called the fifth Gospel because it preserves for us so much that was said and so much that was done among the Nephites that parallels what he said and did among the Jews. Many of these teachings and ministerial acts we have considered in their "Jewish-Nephite" contexts. There remain, however, some matters of transcendent glory and wonder to which we must now refer for these reasons:

1. The words he spoke and the deeds he did among the Nephites are a crowning capstone to his earthly ministry. Many of the passages far excel anything in the biblical accounts; they reveal his grandeur and greatness in a way not otherwise known, and they round out our knowledge of the nature and kind of life that he lived among men.

2. The literary excellence and the doctrinal clarity of his teachings in the Americas is so great as to place the Book of Mormon as the equal or superior of the Bible. Shakespeare could not have coined better phrases than Jesus used among the Nephites, and Peter and Paul could not have propounded such glorious doctrines.

3. These Book of Mormon recitations, coming as they did through the instrumentality of Joseph Smith, prove to

the honest in heart everywhere that this seer of latter days was called of God; that he translated the Nephite record by the gift and power of God; and that he was and is the Lord's prophet, revealer, and witness for this generation.

4. And, finally, the glorious restoration of latter days; the promised marvelous work and a wonder that was destined to come forth in our day; the restitution of all things which God hath spoken by the mouth of all his holy prophets since the world began; the setting up anew of the Church and kingdom of God on earth; the gathering of scattered Israel from the ends of the earth into the fold of their True Shepherd; the position of The Church of Jesus Christ of Latter-day Saints as the only true and living Church upon the face of the whole earth—all these things are established, proved if you will, because the Book of Mormon and the ministry of the Risen Lord, as therein recorded, are eternal verities.

And so, as the account attests, after Jesus came and was known to the Nephites; after he preached the sermon on baptism, which we have equated with his similar teachings in Galilee; and after he had called the Nephite Twelve, then he delivered the Sermon on the Mount, as it were. And, may we say, it is found in a more excellent form in Third Nephi, chapters 12, 13, and 14, than it is in Matthew, chapters 5, 6, and 7. We have already considered in their contexts the many teachings of this sermon. Having respoken its wondrous truths for his Nephite sheep, Jesus said:

> *Behold, ye have heard the things which I taught before I ascended to my Father; therefore, whoso remembereth these sayings of mine and doeth them, him will I raise up at the last day.*

Salvation comes by living the doctrines proclaimed in the Sermon on the Mount! That sermon—properly understood—is far more than a recitation of ethical principles; rather, it summarizes the Christian way of life, and it charts the course true saints must pursue to become even as He is.

In the Nephite version of the Sermon on the Mount, as he had done among the Jews, Jesus made the contrasts between the law of Moses and the gospel standard, saying that various things which Moses had approved were done away and that now men should live by a higher law. These included the commandments about murder, adultery, divorce, the taking of oaths, the requirement of an eye for an eye and a tooth for a tooth, and the like. But having so spoken to the Nephites, he added these words, which could not, properly, have been said to the Jews at the *beginning* of his ministry:

> *Therefore those things which were of old time, which were under the law, in me are all fulfilled. Old things are done away, and all things have become new.*

When he spoke on the Mount of Beatitudes, the law was not yet fulfilled; now that he had eaten the Last Supper and introduced the sacrament; now that he had suffered in the garden and on the cross; now that he had come forth in immortality—the law was fulfilled. It would appear, however, that many among the Nephites, during these transitional months, had not fully envisioned that the lesser law of Moses had been supplanted by the higher law of Christ. And so now Jesus "perceived that there were some among them who marveled, and wondered what he would concerning the law of Moses; for they understood not the saying that old things had passed away, and that all things had become new." He said:

> *Marvel not that I said unto you that old things had passed away, and that all things had become new. Behold, I say unto you that the law is fulfilled that was given unto Moses.*
>
> *Behold, I am he that gave the law, and I am he who covenanted with my people Israel; therefore, the law in me is fulfilled, for I have come to fulfil the law; therefore it hath an end.*

'I am the Lord Jehovah. Moses spake my word; at my

command he gave the law. And the whole purpose of the law was to prepare men for my coming; its ordinances and performances prefigured my atoning sacrifice. Now I have come; the atonement hath been wrought; that which the sacrifices of your fathers prefigured has been accomplished; and the law in me is fulfilled.'

Behold, I do not destroy the prophets, for as many as have not been fulfilled in me, verily I say unto you, shall all be fulfilled.

And because I said unto you that old things have passed away, I do not destroy that which hath been spoken concerning things which are to come.

For behold, the covenant which I have made with my people is not all fulfilled; but the law which was given unto Moses hath an end in me.

O if only all the saints among the Jews had known and understood these things! As Paul said, "The law was our schoolmaster to bring us unto Christ, that we might be justified by faith. But after that faith is come, we are no longer under a schoolmaster." (Gal. 3:24-25.) The law was fulfilled, but the prophetic promises pertaining to the future remained! Also: The covenant Jehovah made with Abraham and all the righteous saints in all dispensations remained! The gospel promises and the gospel covenants—which were before the law—were still in force, and all the prophetic recounting of what was yet to be would surely come to pass.

Behold, I am the law, and the light. Look unto me, and endure to the end, and ye shall live; for unto him that endureth to the end will I give eternal life.

Behold, I have given unto you the commandments; therefore keep my commandments. And this is the law and the prophets, for they truly testified of me.

'Look no more to Moses, except insofar as he testified of me. I am the light; salvation comes by my law; turn ye to my everlasting gospel; I am the law. Believe in me; keep my commandments; endure to the end; and I will give you eternal life, for I am God and the atonement comes by me. In this way you shall honor Moses, for he was my witness. If ye keep my commandments ye thereby fulfill both the law and the prophets, for they testify of me.'

Then to the Nephite Twelve Jesus spake these words, which affirmed the place and status of the Nephites in the house of Israel:

> *Ye are my disciples; and ye are a light unto this people, who are a remnant of the house of Joseph. And behold, this is the land of your inheritance; and the Father hath given it unto you.*

As Jesus is the Light of the world, so his ministers, reflecting his light, are lights to those to whom they are sent. The Americas are the land of Joseph—the land of Ephraim and Manasseh, the land of the Nephites, the land of the Ephraimites who are gathering in the latter days.

> *And not at any time hath the Father given me commandment that I should tell it unto your brethren at Jerusalem. Neither at any time hath the Father given me commandment that I should tell unto them concerning the other tribes of the house of Israel, whom the Father hath led away out of the land.*
>
> *This much did the Father command me, that I should tell unto them: That other sheep I have which are not of this fold; them also I must bring, and they shall hear my voice; and there shall be one fold, and one shepherd.*
>
> *And now, because of stiff-neckedness and unbelief they understood not my word; therefore I was commanded to say no more of the Father concerning this thing unto them.*
>
> *But, verily, I say unto you that the Father hath commanded me, and I tell it unto you, that ye were*

separated from among them because of their iniquity; therefore it is because of their iniquity that they know not of you.

And verily, I say unto you again that the other tribes hath the Father separated from them; and it is because of their iniquity that they know not of them.

And where, we might even now ask, are the lost tribes of Israel? And why is it that we do not know about them? Is it because of our stiffneckedness and unbelief? And how many other things might we know if we were faithful and true in all things?

And verily I say unto you, that ye are they of whom I said: Other sheep I have which are not of this fold; them also I must bring, and they shall hear my voice; and there shall be one fold, and one shepherd.

And they understood me not, for they supposed it had been the Gentiles; for they understood not that the Gentiles should be converted through their preaching.

And they understood me not that I said they shall hear my voice; and they understood me not that the Gentiles should not at any time hear my voice—that I should not manifest myself unto them save it were by the Holy Ghost.

But behold, ye have both heard my voice, and seen me; and ye are my sheep, and ye are numbered among those whom the Father hath given me.

Is not the soul of a Jew in the Americas as precious in the sight of the Lord as the soul of a Jew in Jerusalem? Or the soul of any of the lost tribes of the house of Israel? Will not the Lord Jehovah treat all Israel on the same basis, if their erring members repent and come unto him? And if one branch of the house of Jacob is entitled to hear his voice and see his face, does not every other branch have the same right? Let the message go by the power of the Holy Ghost to the Gentiles; but Israel—the Israel of God—they are the chosen seed; and Jesus will fulfill in them the covenants made with Abraham, Isaac, and Jacob, that in them and in their seed—the literal seed of the body—should all the nations of the earth be blessed.

> *And verily, verily, I say unto you that I have other sheep which are not of this land, neither of the land of Jerusalem, neither in any parts of that land round about whither I have been to minister.*
>
> *For they of whom I speak are they who have not as yet heard my voice; neither have I at any time manifested myself unto them.*
>
> *But I have received a commandment of the Father that I shall go unto them, and that they shall hear my voice, and shall be numbered among my sheep, that there may be one fold and one shepherd; therefore I go to show myself unto them.*

Jesus Promises the Gospel to the Gentiles

(3 Nephi 16:4-20)

Even as on the mountain in Galilee, when Jesus commanded his Jewish apostles to go into all the world and preach the gospel to every creature—to go beyond the borders of Israel, out among the Gentiles—so now among the Nephites he teaches the same doctrine, the doctrine of a Gentile harvest of souls. And the Book of Mormon—a volume of holy scripture, a new witness for Christ, an inspired account containing the fulness of the everlasting gospel—the Book of Mormon will be the means of gathering in the remnants of scattered Israel and of proclaiming the gospel of salvation among the Gentiles in the last days. After announcing that he would visit the lost tribes of Israel, even as he was then visiting the "other sheep" who were Nephites, he said:

> *And I command you that ye shall write these sayings after I am gone, that if it so be that my people at Jerusalem, they who have seen me and*

been with me in my ministry, do not ask the Father in my name, that they may receive a knowledge of you by the Holy Ghost, and also of the other tribes whom they know not of, that these sayings which ye shall write shall be kept and shall be manifested unto the Gentiles, that through the fulness of the Gentiles, the remnant of their seed, who shall be scattered forth upon the face of the earth because of their unbelief, may be brought in, or may be brought to a knowledge of me, their Redeemer.

This matter of identifying the Jews, Gentiles, and those who are of Israel is an extremely complex and difficult problem, primarily because the words are used in varying and even contradictory senses. They are used by the prophets and in holy writ to mean one thing in one age and another at a different time. To the Nephites, the Jews were the nationals of the kingdom of Judah whence they came, and all other peoples and nations were aliens or Gentiles, including those among them who were remnants of the various tribes of Israel. Gentiles were aliens, citizens of other nations, nations who served other gods than the Lord Jehovah.

To the Nephites, the Jews were the Jewish nationals in Jerusalem and elsewhere who rejected their Deliverer and crucified their King when he ministered among them as the Mortal Messiah. Tribal descent was not the issue; among them were those of Judah and Gad and Benjamin and other tribes, but all these were Jews and Jewish and all others were Gentiles, including the members of the lost tribes who were scattered among them. To the Nephites, they themselves were Jews because they came out from the nation of the Jews, brought with them the worship of the Jewish Jehovah, and kept the law of Moses as had their fathers. (2 Ne. 33:8.)

Thus the fulness of the gospel as restored to and through Joseph Smith was given by the Lord "unto the Gentiles." (1 Ne. 15:13.) Joseph Smith and his associates were considered by the Nephites to be Gentiles—for they were not Jewish nationals—even though they were of the pure blood of Israel. Thus the Book of Mormon came forth by way of the Gentiles though it is the Stick of Joseph in the hands of Ephraim. Thus the United States is a nation of the Gentiles; and thus all the nations of the earth are Gentile nations, even though the people in them who accept the gospel are blood descendants of Father Jacob.

Having this perspective, then, we can envision what Jesus here said to the Nephites. His words have been fulfilled in that (1) the Jews at Jerusalem did not ask the Father in his name for a knowledge of their Nephite kinsmen; (2) nor did they learn of the lost tribes of Israel; (3) hence, the sayings of Jesus, recorded and preserved in the Book of Mormon, were manifest to the Gentiles (meaning to us); (4) and, when the fulness of the Gentiles comes in (meaning the appointed period or times when the gospel goes preferentially to us Gentiles), (5) then it will go to the remnant of the seed of the Jews who lived at Jerusalem, which remnant will then be scattered "upon all the face of the earth because of their unbelief"; (6) and then shall the Jews (as here defined and as now generally known in the world) "be brought to a knowledge of me, their Redeemer."

> *And then will I gather them in from the four quarters of the earth; and then will I fulfill the covenant which the Father hath made unto all the people of the house of Israel.*

Two things are here promised: (1) When the fulness of the Gentiles is come in, then the remnant of the Jews will be gathered in from the ends of the earth—gathered into the true fold and be numbered with their Shepherd's sheep, gathered to the land of their fathers; and (2) the covenant to save all the tribes of Israel, though they be lost and unknown and scattered, will be fulfilled.

> *And blessed are the Gentiles, because of their belief in me, in and of the Holy Ghost, which wit-*

> *nesses unto them of me and of the Father.*

Those of us Israelites who are here deemed to be Gentiles shall in the last days be blessed because we believe in Christ, as he is manifest by the power of the Holy Ghost, in contrast to his personal appearances among the Jews of Jerusalem and the Jews in the Americas.

> *Behold, because of their belief in me, saith the Father, and because of the unbelief of you, O house of Israel, in the latter day shall the truth come unto the Gentiles, that the fulness of these things shall be made known unto them.*

Israel of old forsook the Lord Jehovah, and their nation and kingdom went into oblivion. Because they rejected Christ they were scattered and persecuted. But—O glorious promise!—in the latter days those among the Gentiles who believe shall receive the fulness of the gospel and the fulness of the blessings that flow therefrom.

> *But wo, saith the Father, unto the unbelieving of the Gentiles—for notwithstanding they have come forth upon the face of this land, and have scattered my people who are of the house of Israel; and my people who are of the house of Israel have been cast out from among them, and have been trodden under feet by them;*
>
> *And because of the mercies of the Father unto the Gentiles, and also the judgments of the Father upon my people who are of the house of Israel, verily, verily, I say unto you, that after all this, and I have caused my people who are of the house of Israel to be smitten, and to be afflicted, and to be slain, and to be cast out from among them, and to become hated by them, and to become a hiss and a byword among them—*
>
> *And thus commandeth the Father that I should say unto you: At that day when the Gentiles shall sin against my gospel, and shall be lifted up in the pride of their hearts above all nations, and above all the*

people of the whole earth, and shall be filled with all manner of lyings, and of deceits, and of mischiefs, and all manner of hypocrisy, and murders, and priestcrafts, and whoredoms, and of secret abominations; and if they shall do all those things, and shall reject the fulness of my gospel, behold, saith the Father, I will bring the fulness of my gospel from among them.

How plainly Jesus foretells what is to be in the day of restoration: (1) The unbelieving among the Gentiles who are assembled in the Americas shall scatter the house of Israel; (2) Lehi's seed, in both North and South America, shall be cast out and trodden under foot by the Gentiles; (3) these things shall come to pass because of the mercies of the Father upon the Gentiles and because of his judgments upon his Israelitish people; (4) but then, the Gentiles in the New World—meaning the generality of them—shall reject the gospel and pursue an evil and ungodly course; (5) so that the gospel will be taken from among them.

And then will I remember my covenant which I have made unto my people, O house of Israel, and I will bring my gospel unto them.

And I will show unto thee, O house of Israel, that the Gentiles shall not have power over you; but I will remember my covenant unto you, O house of Israel, and ye shall come unto the knowledge of the fulness of my gospel.

Jehovah's covenant with his people is that through Abraham and his seed shall all the nations of the earth be blessed; it is that the seed of Abraham, Isaac, and Jacob shall have a right to the gospel and the priesthood; it is that they shall bear his priesthood and be his ministers to take his gospel to all people; it is that the house of Israel shall be saved with an everlasting salvation in the kingdom of the Father. (Abr. 2:8-11.) And after the gospel has been restored in a Gentile nation, those of scattered Israel in all nations shall begin to believe, and they shall come into the latter-day kingdom and be blessed according to the promises.

> *But if the Gentiles will repent and return unto me, saith the Father, behold they shall be numbered among my people, O house of Israel.*

This shall come to pass according to the promise made by Jehovah to his friend Abraham: "As many as receive this Gospel shall be called after thy name, and shall be accounted thy seed, and shall rise up and bless thee, as their father." (Abr. 2:10.) For, as Nephi said: "All are alike unto God, both Jew and Gentile." (2 Ne. 26:33.)

> *And I will not suffer my people, who are of the house of Israel, to go through among them, and tread them down, saith the Father.*
>
> *But if they will not turn unto me, and hearken unto my voice, I will suffer them, yea, I will suffer my people, O house of Israel, that they shall go through among them, and shall tread them down, and they shall be as salt that hath lost its savor, which is thenceforth good for nothing but to be cast out, and to be trodden under foot of my people, O house of Israel.*

These things lie ahead; they are pre-millennial; as the great destructions and wars unfold that shall usher in that reign of peace, then we shall learn how and in what manner they shall be fulfilled. Our feelings are that the Gentiles will not repent and that there will be a day when Israel shall triumph over her ancient enemies according to the promises.

> *Verily, verily, I say unto you, thus hath the Father commanded me—that I should give unto this people this land for their inheritance.*
>
> *And then the words of the prophet Isaiah shall be fulfilled, which say: Thy watchmen shall lift up the voice; with the voice together shall they sing, for*

they shall see eye to eye when the Lord shall bring again Zion.

Break forth into joy, sing together, ye waste places of Jerusalem; for the Lord hath comforted his people, he hath redeemed Jerusalem.

The Lord hath made bare his holy arm in the eye of all the nations; and all the ends of the earth shall see the salvation of God.

These words are millennial. They exult in the final glory and triumph of Israel—after her warfare with the Gentiles, after the days of her sorrows and suffering, after she has been a hiss and a byword among all people. Israel—Jacob's seed!—shall come off triumphant, and those Gentiles who join with her shall be as she is, and be accounted the seed of him who fathered Israel in the flesh, and Him also whose house it is.

Chapter 114

STILL AMONG THE AMERICAN JEWS

We are made alive in Christ because
of our faith. . . .
And we talk of Christ, we rejoice in Christ,
we preach of Christ, we prophesy of Christ,
and we write according to our prophecies,
that our chidren may know
to what source they may look
for a remission of their sins. . . .
The right way is to believe in Christ
and deny him not; for by denying him
ye also deny the prophets and the law. . . .
Christ is the Holy One of Israel;
wherefore ye must bow down before him,
and worship him with all your might, mind,
and strength, and your whole soul;
and if ye do this ye shall in nowise
be cast out.
(2 Ne. 25:25-29.)

A Ministry of Miracles and Angelic Ministrations
(3 Nephi 17:1-25)

What a blessed day this is, a day when the Blessed One—resurrected and glorified—ministers among his people!

They have now heard the announcement of the atonement; felt the prints of the nails in his hands and in his feet; been instructed as to baptism and the witness that both the Father and the Holy Ghost bear of him; heard the calling of his American apostolic witnesses; rejoiced in the wondrous words of the Sermon on the Mount; learned of the fulfillment of the law of Moses; been identified as the Lord's "other sheep"; and heard the glad tidings of the restoration of the gospel, of its proclamation among the Gentiles, of the latter-day gathering of Israel and the final triumph of the chosen seed. Hours have elapsed. How can any congregation absorb more of the Lord's word at one time than this? And so we hear him say:

> *Behold, my time is at hand. I perceive that ye are weak, that ye cannot understand all my words which I am commanded of the Father to speak unto you at this time.*
>
> *Therefore, go ye unto your homes, and ponder upon the things which I have said, and ask of the Father, in my name, that ye may understand, and prepare your minds for the morrow, and I come unto you again.*
>
> *But now I go unto the Father, and also to show myself unto the lost tribes of Israel, for they are not lost unto the Father, for he knoweth whither he hath taken them.*

Such is the perfect pattern for hearing the word of the Lord. Let the speaker speak by the power of the Holy Ghost; let the hearers hear by that same power; then let the hearers ponder and pray and seek to know—by revelation—the full meaning of the spoken word; and then let them join again in the assembly of the saints to hear more of the eternal saving word. But in this instance the multitude is in tears; the unspoken pleas of their heart are that Jesus will tarry longer and teach more, and their faith prevails.

> *Behold, my bowels are filled with compassion towards you. Have ye any that are sick among you? Bring them hither. Have ye any that are lame, or blind, or halt, or maimed, or leprous, or that are withered, or that are deaf, or that are afflicted in any manner? Bring them hither and I will heal them, for I have compassion upon you; my bowels are filled with mercy.*
>
> *For I perceive that ye desire that I should show unto you what I have done unto your brethren at Jerusalem, for I see that your faith is sufficient that I should heal you.*

All those who were sick—their lame, their blind, and their dumb, and those with any manner of affliction—all were brought, and one by one he healed them. Then they who were whole and they who were healed bowed down at his feet and worshipped him, and "they did bathe his feet with their tears." Jesus then asked them to bring their little children, which they did, and "he commanded the multitude that they should kneel down upon the ground." Then Jesus, standing in the midst of them, said: "Father, I am troubled because of the wickedness of the people of the house of Israel." At this point "he himself also knelt upon the earth; and behold he prayed unto the Father, and the things which he prayed cannot be written."

There are things that it is "not lawful for man to utter; Neither is man capable to make them known, for they are only to be seen and understood by the power of the Holy Spirit, which God bestows on those who love him, and purify themselves before him." (D&C 76:115-116.) Such was it on this occasion. As to what Jesus said in his prayer we know not, only that the multitude testified: "The eye hath never seen, neither hath the ear heard, before, so great and marvelous things as we saw and heard Jesus speak unto the Father; And no tongue can speak, neither can there be written by any man, neither can the hearts of men conceive so great and marvelous things as we both saw and heard Jesus speak; and no one can conceive of the joy which filled our souls at the time we heard him pray for us unto the Father." Indeed, "so great was the joy of the multitude that they were overcome," and they could not arise until Jesus bade them to do so. "Blessed are ye because of your faith," he said unto them. "And now behold, my joy is full."

Then he wept, and "took their little children, one by one, and blessed them, and prayed unto the Father for them." Then he wept again and said: "Behold your little ones." Then came the miracle that testifies of the purity and perfection of innocent children, children who have but recently left the presence of the Father, children whose lives are not yet tainted with sin, children who, should they die in their innocence, shall return in purity to the Father and there inherit eternal life. And so, as the multitude "looked to behold they cast their eyes towards heaven, and they saw the heavens open, and they saw angels descending out of heaven as it were in the midst of fire; and they came down and encircled those little ones about, and they were encircled about with fire; and the angels did minister unto them." And of this the multitude—all twenty-five hundred of them—did bear record.

The Nephites Receive the Gift of the Holy Ghost

(3 Nephi 18:1-39; 19:1-36; 20:8-9)

Our Blessed Lord then had bread and wine brought, which he gave to them to eat and drink in remembrance of his broken flesh and spilt blood. Of these Nephite ministrations we have written in connection with the same ordinance as administered among those in Jerusalem. As the sacramental ordinance was concluded Jesus said to the Twelve:

> *Blessed are ye if ye shall keep my commandments, which the Father hath commanded me that I should give unto you.*
>
> *Verily, verily, I say unto you, ye must watch and pray always, lest ye be tempted by the devil, and ye be led away captive by him.*
>
> *And as I have prayed among you even so shall ye pray in my church, among my people who do repent and are baptized in my name. Behold I am the light; I have set an example for you.*

Above all others Satan seeks to ensnare the shepherds of the Lord's flock, thereby preparing the way for the scattering of the sheep. Church officers are to live and pray as Jesus lived and prayed, that they may be lights to the saints. Then to the multitude Jesus said:

> *Behold, verily, verily, I say unto you, ye must watch and pray always lest ye enter into temptation; for Satan desireth to have you, that he may sift you as wheat.*
>
> *Therefore ye must always pray unto the Father in my name; And whatsoever ye shall ask the Father in my name, which is right, believing that ye shall receive, behold it shall be given unto you.*
>
> *Pray in your families unto the Father, always in my name, that your wives and your children may be blessed.*

Never has it been stated better. Unless the saints watch their conduct and keep it in harmony with the divine will, and unless they pray to the Father in the name of Christ, with all the energy of their souls, Satan—not the Lord—will harvest their souls. The grim reaper of death and destruction will cut them down, and they will be stored with the wicked in the granaries of despair. But—O glorious promise!—all of the righteous desires of the faithful saints shall be granted. Anything they ask for that is right shall be given them! And for whom shall they pray with more fervor and faith than for themselves and their wives and their children? God be praised for the power of prayer!

> *And behold, ye shall meet together oft; and ye shall not forbid any man from coming unto you when ye shall meet together, but suffer them that they may come unto you and forbid them not;*
>
> *But ye shall pray for them, and shall not cast them out; and if it so be that they come unto you oft ye shall pray for them unto the Father, in my name.*

As the body needs bread, so also must the soul be fed. Man does not live by bread alone; unless the soul is fed, man dies spiritually. There must be frequent gospel banquets; the soul of man must be offered every word that proceedeth forth from the mouth of God. And we must pray for those who come to our meetings desiring to feast upon the good word of God, but whose souls as yet can only digest the milk and not the meat of the word.

> *Therefore, hold up your light that it may shine unto the world. Behold I am the light which ye shall hold up—that which ye have seen me do. Behold ye see that I have prayed unto the Father, and ye all have witnessed.*
>
> *And ye see that I have commanded that none of you should go away, but rather have commanded that ye should come unto me, that ye might feel and see; even so shall ye do unto the world; and whosoever breaketh this commandment suffereth himself to be led into temptation.*

Jesus is the light; his example is perfect; all who do as he did shall be as he is; and such places them on the course leading to eternal life. And having so taught them, Jesus said to the Twelve: "Behold verily, verily, I say unto you, I give unto you another commandment, and then I must go unto my Father that I may fulfil other commandments which he hath given me." The other commandment was that they, as his administrators and representatives on earth, should not suffer anyone knowingly to partake of his flesh and blood in unworthiness. All such, he said, would eat and drink damnation to their own souls. All this we have considered in its Jewish context in the Jerusalem account. To it Jesus appended the commandment that they should not cast such persons out of their synagogues, but should pray for them, plead with them to repent, offer them the blessings of baptism, and guide them in all things toward that salvation which the gospel promises. If they pursued such a course they would not be condemned by the Father. This counsel was given to them, he said, because of prior disputations among them. "And blessed are ye if ye have no disputations among you," he said. Then he announced he must go to the Father, and he touched each of the Twelve and "gave them power to give the Holy Ghost," after which a cloud overshadowed the multitude so they could not see Jesus, but the Twelve saw and bore record that "he ascended again into heaven."

For the rest of that day, and for all the night long, messengers carried forth the word of Jesus' ministry among them and of his promise to return on the morrow; and "an exceeding great number, did labor exceedingly all that night" so as to be at the appointed place on the next day. Their number was so great—surely there must have been scores of thousands—that the Twelve divided them into twelve bodies so as to teach them. They all—the disciples and the multitude—knelt and prayed to the Father in the name of Jesus. Then the Twelve—and the pattern thus set is perfect—"ministered those same words which Jesus had spoken—nothing varying from the words which Jesus had spoken." All the multitude thus received a verbatim account of all that was said and done by the Lord of Life to the smaller congregation of twenty-five hundred on the previous day. Then the disciples knelt and prayed again. "And they did pray for that which they most desired; and they desired that the Holy Ghost should be given unto them."

Then they went down to the water's edge; Nephi and the rest of the Twelve were baptized, and "the Holy Ghost did fall upon them, and they were filled with the Holy Ghost and with fire." It was the New World Pentecost! Cloven tongues of fire, and more, rested upon them! "And behold, they were encircled about as if it were by fire; and it came down from heaven, and the multitude did witness it, and did bear record; and angels did come down out of heaven and did minister unto them."

While the heavens were thus open; while angels ministered and holy fire cleansed their souls from sin; while righteousness was falling as the gentle dew from heaven—"Jesus came and stood in the midst and ministered unto them." He commanded them all, both the disciples and the multitude, to kneel and pray, "and they did pray unto Jesus, calling him their Lord and their God." Jesus separated himself from the group, bowed himself to the earth, and prayed:

> *Father, I thank thee that thou hast given the Holy Ghost unto these whom I have chosen; and it is because of their belief in me that I have chosen them out of the world.*
>
> *Father, I pray thee that thou wilt give the Holy Ghost unto all them that shall believe in their words.*
>
> *Father, thou hast given them the Holy Ghost because they believe in me; and thou seest that they believe in me because thou hearest them, and they pray unto me; and they pray unto me because I am with them.*
>
> *And now Father, I pray unto thee for them, and also for all those who shall believe on their words, that they may believe in me, that I may be in them as thou, Father, art in me, that we may be one.*

By the power of the Holy Ghost the saints are one—they in Christ, and he in them; the Father in them, and they in him; and all the saints in each other—for they are one. This we have already seen in our consideration of the Intercessory Prayer. Having so spoken, Jesus came to the disciples who continued to pray, "and they did not multiply many words, for it was given unto them what they should pray, and they were filled with desire." Thereupon, "Jesus blessed them as they did pray unto him; and his countenance did smile upon them, and the light of his countenance did shine upon them, and behold they were as white as the countenance and also the garments of Jesus; and behold the whiteness thereof did exceed all the whiteness, yea, even there could be nothing upon earth so white as the whiteness thereof." Jesus told them to continue to pray, and he went a little way off, bowed himself to the earth, and prayed again:

> *Father, I thank thee that thou hast purified those whom I have chosen, because of their faith, and I pray for them, and also for them who shall believe on their words, that they may be purified in me, through faith on their words, even as they are purified in me.*
>
> *Father, I pray not for the world, but for those whom thou hast given me out of the world, because of their faith, that they may be purified in me, that I may be in them as thou, Father, art in me, that we may be one, that I may be glorified in them.*

These concepts, though not expressed as well as in this Book of Mormon account, we heard in the Intercessory Prayer. Having here spoken them, Jesus returned to the Twelve, smiled upon them as they continued to pray—"and behold they were white, even as Jesus"—and then "went again a little way off and prayed unto the Father." Of what then transpired the inspired record recites: "And tongue cannot speak the words which he prayed, neither can be written by man the words which he prayed." But the multitude heard and bore record, "and their hearts were open and they did understand in their hearts the words which he prayed. Nevertheless, so great and marvelous were the words which he prayed that they cannot be written, neither can they be uttered by man." After his prayer, Jesus said:

> *So great faith have I never seen among all the Jews; wherefore I could not show unto them so great miracles, because of their unbelief.*
>
> *Verily I say unto you, there are none of them that have seen so great things as ye have seen; neither have they heard so great things as ye have heard.*

In our view, these marvelous happenings—when the Holy Ghost fell mightily upon the people; when the sanctifying power of the Holy Spirit of God cleansed their souls; when mortal men were quickened by the Spirit until their countenances shone (as did that of Moses after he was with the Lord for forty days in the holy mount); when Jesus spoke words that could not be written and could only be understood by the power of the Spirit—these marvelous events were the high point of Jesus' ministry among his "other sheep." Seldom, if ever, has there been such a scene on planet earth. Perhaps in the Zion of Enoch, when the Lord came and dwelt with his people; perhaps at Adam-ondi-Ahman, in the assembly of high priests, when the Lord appeared and ministered comfort unto Adam, and the Ancient of Days predicted whatsoever should befall his posterity unto the latest generation; perhaps on the Mount of Transfiguration, when only Peter, James, and John were present—perhaps there have been other like outpourings of God's goodness and grace, of which we have no knowledge, but nowhere do our scriptures preserve in such detail such wondrous events as are here recorded. Truly they are a sample and an illustration of what shall be in that great millennial day when He whose we are reigns personally among those who remain on earth after the wicked and ungodly have been burned as stubble.

After the events of this hour had been savored to the full, Jesus commanded the multitude to cease their vocal prayers but to continue to pray in their hearts. Then as a seal on the spiritual experience they had enjoyed, he provided bread and wine miraculously, blessed the sacred emblems, and distributed them to the Twelve. At his direction they in turn brake bread and passed it and the wine to the multitude. Then Jesus said, as we have heretofore quoted in connection with the Old World sacramental performances, what is probably the greatest one sentence pronouncement on the sacrament of the Lord's Supper which is found in all holy writ:

> *He that eateth this bread eateth of my body to his soul; and he that drinketh of this wine drinketh of my blood to his soul; and his soul shall never hunger nor thirst; but shall be filled.*

And as a perfect account of the blessings which are poured out upon those who partake worthily of the emblems representing the broken flesh and spilt blood, the Nephite scripture says: "Now, when the multitude had all eaten and drunk, behold, they were filled with the Spirit; and they did cry out with one voice, and gave glory to Jesus, whom they both saw and heard."

And thus are these glorious things recorded in that holy book, the Book of Mormon, which causes us to marvel greatly and wonder why it is that all who call themselves Christians do not accept and believe this volume of American scripture as readily as they suppose they believe the scriptural accounts originating in the Old World. Surely a tree is known by its fruits.

THE RESTORATION OF THE KINGDOM TO ISRAEL

For a small moment have I forsaken thee,
but with great mercies will I gather thee.
In a little wrath I hid my face
from thee for a moment,
but with everlasting kindness
will I have mercy on thee,
saith the Lord thy Redeemer. . . .
For the mountains shall depart
and the hills be removed,
but my kindness shall not depart from thee,
neither shall the covenant of my people
be removed, saith the Lord
that hath mercy on thee. . . .
And all thy children shall be taught
of the Lord; and great shall be the peace
of thy children. In righteousness
shalt thou be established;
thou shalt be far from oppression
for thou shalt not fear, and from terror
for it shall not come near thee.
(3 Ne. 22:7-8, 10, 13-14.)

Israel Shall Be Gathered

(3 Nephi 20:10-24)

Soon we shall hear the Twelve in Jerusalem ask the Resurrected One: "Lord, wilt thou at this time restore again the kingdom to Israel?" and we will observe with great interest the answer he gives them. But before we turn back to that scene on Olivet, just before he ascends to his Father, it is our privilege to learn about the restoration of the kingdom to Israel, as he expounded the glorious truths involved to his Nephite-Jews in the Americas.

Israel the chosen seed; Israel the Lord's people; Israel the only nation since Abraham that had worshipped Jehovah; Israel the children of the prophets; Israel who had been cursed and scattered for her sins; Israel in whose veins believing blood flows—the Israel of God shall be gathered, and fed, and nurtured, and saved, in the last days! Let there be no misunderstanding about this; salvation is of the Jews, and if there are believing Gentiles, they will be adopted into the believing family and inherit with the chosen seed. "And so all Israel shall be saved: as it is written, There shall come out of Sion the Deliverer, and shall turn away ungodliness from Jacob: For this is my covenant unto them, when I shall take away their sins." (Rom. 11:26-27.) But sadly: "They are not all Israel, which are of Israel" (Rom. 9:6), and only those who turn to their God and accept him as the Promised Messiah shall inherit with the chosen seed either in time or in eternity.

While his Nephite sheep were filled with the Spirit, and were singing praises to his holy name—and blessed be that glorious name forever!—Jesus said: "Behold now I finish the commandment which the Father hath commanded me concerning this people, who are a remnant of the house of Israel." He then began to preach unto them the doctrine that his Father—the Father of us all—desired them (and us!) to hear:

> *Ye remember that I spake unto you, and said that when the words of Isaiah should be fulfilled—behold*

> *they are written, ye have them before you, therefore search them—*
>
> *And verily, verily, I say unto you, that when they shall be fulfilled then is the fulfilling of the covenant which the Father hath made unto his people, O house of Israel.*

Be it recalled also that when we recorded what Jesus quoted from Isaiah—how the watchmen should see eye to eye when the Lord brought again Zion; how the Lord would comfort his people and redeem Jerusalem; how he would make bare his arm in the eyes of *all* nations, so that *all* the ends of the earth should see the salvation of God—when we recorded these words, we identified them as being millennial. That is, they shall come to pass when the Son of Man comes to dwell and reign on earth. To this we now add that certain initial fulfillment will commence before that dread yet glorious day of his coming. As we shall now see, when the gospel is restored, preparatory to the establishment of the Zion and the Jerusalem of old, men shall begin to see eye to eye, and the message of salvation shall begin to go forth to the nations of the earth. The gathering of Israel must needs begin before Zion is fully established so there will be a people to build the city and man the walls and serve in the watchtowers.

> *And then shall the remnants, which shall be scattered abroad upon the face of the earth, be gathered in from the east and from the west, and from the south and from the north; and they shall be brought to the knowledge of the Lord their God, who hath redeemed them.*

The gathering of Israel is twofold: it is both spiritual and temporal. It is (1) into the Church and kingdom of God on earth; into the true fold where the true faith is found; into The Church of Jesus Christ of Latter-day Saints, which is the kingdom of God on earth, and which administers the gospel, which is the plan of salvation; and (2) unto those portions of the earth's surface which are appointed by revelation as places of gathering, so there may be congregations that can worship together, whose members can strengthen each other, and where all the blessings of the house of the Lord may be gained. In our day the gathering of Israel is in all the nations of the earth; in all the places where stakes of Zion are being established; in the lands where houses of the Lord are being built; in "all the nations," so that "all the ends of the earth shall see the salvation of God." To these Nephites, however, Jesus said:

> *And the Father hath commanded me that I should give unto you this land, for your inheritance.*

America is the land of Joseph. The Nephites are of the house of Joseph; and they, along with us, who also have that tribal ancestry, are destined to inherit these lands which are choice above all other lands.

> *And I say unto you, that if the Gentiles do not repent after the blessing which they shall receive, after they have scattered my people—*
>
> *Then shall ye, who are a remnant of the house of Jacob, go forth among them; and ye shall be in the midst of them who shall be many; and ye shall be among them as a lion among the beasts of the forest, and as a young lion among the flocks of sheep, who, if he goeth through both treadeth down and teareth in pieces, and none can deliver.*
>
> *Thy hand shall be lifted up upon thine adversaries, and all thine enemies shall be cut off.*

This is millennial; it refers to the Second Coming of Christ. It is not a war that a few Lamanites or any remnant of Israel shall wage against Gentile oppressors; the Lord does not operate in that manner. When he comes the wicked shall be destroyed and the righteous preserved; those who have not hearkened to the prophets shall be cut off from among the people; thus, the "enemies" of Israel "shall be cut off." And it shall be with power, as though a young lion went forth rending and tearing in pieces a helpless flock of sheep. And so, if the Gentiles do not repent and believe in Christ after the gospel is restored among them, then, when the Lord comes, they will be destroyed and the triumph of Israel—because they kept the commandments and did receive the gospel—that triumph will be complete.

> *And I will gather my people together as a man gathereth his sheaves into the floor.*

In all this Jesus is but quoting and paraphrasing what the Lord revealed to Micah concerning the *whole* house of Israel. After that ancient prophet foretold the establishment of the house of the Lord in the tops of the mountains in the last days, and spoke of all nations flowing unto it; after he prophesied about the Second Coming and the day when men would beat their swords into plowshares and their spears into pruning hooks; after he spoke of the whole earth being at peace and of the Lord reigning in Mount Zion forever, then he told about the destruction of the Gentile nations in that day. "Now also many nations are gathered against thee"—meaning against Israel—"that say, Let her be defiled, and let our eye look upon Zion." To this there is an answer; it comes from the Lord; he says: "But they know not the thoughts of the Lord, neither understand they his counsel: for he shall gather them as the sheaves into the floor." Israel shall be gathered out of the Babylonish nations; she shall return to the true fold. "Arise and thresh, O daughter of Zion: for I will make thine horn iron, and I will make thy hoofs brass: and thou shalt beat in pieces many people: and I will consecrate their gain unto the Lord, and their substance unto the Lord of the whole earth." (Micah 4:1-13.) Or, as Jesus now says it to the Nephites:

> *For I will make my people with whom the Father hath covenanted, yea, I will make thy horn iron, and I will make thy hoofs brass. And thou shalt beat in pieces many people; and I will consecrate their gain unto the Lord, and their substance unto the Lord of the whole earth. And behold, I am he who doeth it.*

And it shall come to pass, saith the Father, that the sword of my justice shall hang over them at that day; and except they repent it shall fall upon them, saith the Father, yea, even upon all the nations of the Gentiles.

Again the message is the triumph of his people in the day of his coming. It is the destruction of all the wicked in all nations among all the Gentiles in that great and dreadful day. Here the reference is broader than to the Nephite remnants of Israel; it is to all those of Israel with whom the covenant has been made; it is to all the house of Israel. It is speaking of the sword of justice falling "upon all the nations of the Gentiles," not alone on those Gentile nations which scattered and persecuted the seed of Lehi.

And it shall come to pass that I will establish my people, O house of Israel.

The Lord's people—Israel—scattered in all the nations of the earth shall, wherever they are, be gathered into the true fold of Christ in their nations; then the Lord will come and destroy the wicked, who are their enemies, and then they will triumph to the full. But as to the Nephites, Jesus continued:

And behold, this people will I establish in this land, unto the fulfilling of the covenant which I made with your father Jacob; and it shall be a New Jerusalem. And the powers of heaven shall be in the midst of this people; yea, even I will be in the midst of you.

As to the house of Joseph, their inheritance is in the Americas, even as Father Jacob promised in the blessing given to Joseph, that he should be "a fruitful bough, even a fruitful bough by a well; whose branches run over the wall," and that the blessings of Joseph should prevail above those of all the other tribes and extend "unto the utmost bound of the everlasting hills." (Gen. 49:22, 26.) All this shall find total fulfillment only in that day when the Lord reigns in the midst of men. Then, still having in mind the destruction of the Gentile nations who have opposed his people, and who are their enemies and his enemies, Jesus reminded the Nephites of the words of Moses concerning their Messiah:

> *Behold, I am he of whom Moses spake, saying: A prophet shall the Lord your God raise up unto you of your brethren, like unto me; him shall ye hear in all things whatsoever he shall say unto you. And it shall come to pass that every soul who will not hear that prophet shall be cut off from among the people.*
>
> *Verily I say unto you, yea, and all the prophets from Samuel and those that follow after, as many as have spoken, have testified of me.*

Those who will not hear the voice of the Lord, as proclaimed by his servants the prophets, shall be cut off from among the people when he comes again, comes, as Paul expresses it, "in flaming fire taking vengeance on them that know not God, and that obey not the gospel of our Lord Jesus Christ." (2 Thes. 1:8.) This is the promise that "all thine enemies shall be cut off." There ought not be any confusion or misunderstanding on these points.

"Ye Are the Children of the Covenant"
(3 Nephi 20:25-46)

Why is the Lord gathering Israel in these last days? It is to fulfill the covenant made with Abraham and renewed with Isaac and Jacob and others. What is that covenant? It is not the gathering of Israel *per se,* but something far more important than the mere assembling of a people in Jerusalem or on Mount Zion or at any designated place. It is not the allocation of Palestine for the seed of Abraham, or the designation of the Americas as the inheritance of Joseph, though each of these arrangements has a bearing on the fulfillment of the covenant. The gathering of Israel, at whatever place Deity specifies, is a necessary condition precedent, something that makes possible the fulfilling of the ancient covenant. What, then, is the covenant itself?

Jehovah promised—covenanted with—his friend Abraham that in him and in his seed, meaning the literal seed of his body, should "all the families of the earth be blessed, even with the blessings of the Gospel, which are the blessings of salvation, even of life eternal." (Abr. 2:8-11.)

Jehovah promised—covenanted with—his friend Abraham that his seed after him, again meaning the literal seed of his body, should have the right to the priesthood and the gospel, and should be the Lord's ministers to carry these blessings to all nations and kindreds.

Jehovah promised—covenanted with—his friend Abraham that he and his seed after him should have the ordinance of celestial marriage, which opens the door to a continuation of the family unit in eternity, which is what constitutes eternal life in our Father's kingdom.

Jehovah promised—covenanted with—his friend Abraham that his seed, the fruit of his loins, should continue eternally, "both in the world and out of the world should they continue as innumerable as the stars; or, if ye were to count the sand upon the seashore ye could not number them." (D&C 132:29-32.)

These same promises were made to Isaac and to Jacob and to their posterity after him. They are "the promises made to the fathers," which, by the hand of Elijah the prophet, have been planted in "the hearts of the children." (D&C 2:1-3.) These are the promises that make us "the children of the covenant," the covenant made with our fathers, the covenant into which we are privileged to enter, the covenant of eternal life, of eternal lives, of a continuation of the seeds forever and ever. And in order to fulfill this covenant, Jehovah promised to gather Israel; he promised to bring them into the fold of Christ, so they could strengthen each other in the holy faith; he promised to prepare them for the ordinances of his holy house, through which the blessings of eternal life come. And so now Jesus says to the remnant of Jacob that he has gathered around him in the land of the Nephites in the meridian of time:

> *And behold, ye are the children of the prophets; and ye are of the house of Israel; and ye are of the covenant which the Father made with your fathers, saying unto Abraham: And in thy seed shall all the kindreds of the earth be blessed.*
>
> *The Father having raised me up unto you first, and sent me to bless you in turning away every one of you from his iniquities; and this because ye are the children of the covenant.*

These American Israelites were natural heirs according to the flesh of all the blessings of Abraham, Isaac, and Jacob. It was their right to receive, inherit, and possess the fulness of the Father's kingdom through the continuation of the family unit in eternity. It was their privilege to have a continuation of the seeds forever and ever, to have posterity in eternity as numerous as the stars in the heavens or as the sand upon the seashore. And all of this shall have efficacy, virtue, and force because Jesus atoned for the sins of the world, because he took upon himself the sins of all men on conditions of repentance, because he turned away every obedient man "from his iniquities."

> *And after that ye were blessed then fulfilleth the Father the covenant which he made with Abraham, saying: In thy seed shall all the kindreds of the earth be blessed—unto the pouring out of the Holy Ghost through me upon the Gentiles, which blessing upon the Gentiles shall make them mighty above all, unto the scattering of my people, O house of Israel.*

Not only shall the seed of Abraham be blessed through the covenant made with their father, but all the kindreds of the earth, even the Gentile nations, may be blessed in like manner, if they will believe in Christ and receive the Holy Ghost and keep the commandments, for, as Jehovah said to Abraham, "as many as receive this Gospel shall be called after thy name, and shall be accounted thy seed, and shall rise up and bless thee, as their father." (Abr. 2:10.) Then, speaking of the American Gentiles and their dealings with the seed of Lehi, Jesus said:

> *And they shall be a scourge unto the people of this land. Nevertheless, when they shall have received the fulness of my gospel, then if they shall harden their hearts against me I will return their iniquities upon their own heads, saith the Father.*

Neither Jew nor Gentile shall be cleansed from sin through the gospel, by the Holy Ghost, except on conditions of repentance and obedience. The iniquities of the rebellious shall return upon their own heads. Having thus spoken of the American-Israelites and the American-Gentiles, Jesus turns to his ancient covenant people, the Jews, who are scattered in all nations.

> *And I will remember the covenant which I have made with my people; and I have covenanted with them that I would gather them together in mine own due time, that I would give unto them again the land of their fathers for their inheritance, which is the land of Jerusalem, which is the promised land unto them forever, saith the Father.*

The covenants are for all the house of Israel; all are entitled to the blessings of the priesthood and the gospel and that eternal life which consists of the continuation of the family unit in the celestial kingdom. But all shall not gather to the same lands; all shall not be taught in the same synagogues; all shall not receive their blessings in the same temples. The Jews of Palestine shall return to the land of Jerusalem, there to be blessed from on high.

> *And it shall come to pass that the time cometh, when the fulness of my gospel shall be preached unto them; And they shall believe in me, that I am Jesus Christ, the Son of God, and shall pray unto the Father in my name.*

When the times of the Gentiles are fulfilled, the times of the Jews will commence. The gospel will then go to the

Jewish seed of Abraham, and they shall believe; and, except for a limited few, the great day of Jewish conversion will be in the millennial day, after they have seen him whom they crucified and have heard him attest that the wounds in his hands and in his feet are those with which he was wounded in the house of his friends. Of that millennial day, Jesus continues:

Then shall their watchmen lift up their voice, and with the voice together shall they sing; for they shall see eye to eye. Then will the Father gather them together again, and give unto them Jerusalem for the land of their inheritance.

Then shall they break forth into joy—Sing together, ye waste places of Jerusalem; for the Father hath comforted his people, he hath redeemed Jerusalem.

The Father hath made bare his holy arm in the eyes of all the nations; and all the ends of the earth shall see the salvation of the Father; and the Father and I are one.

Such is Jesus' interpreting paraphrase of the words of Isaiah—a Nephite targum, if you will—that he had before quoted to them. It is the setting forth of the millennial glory of the Jews, the glory that will be theirs when they accept their Messiah and become heirs of all the promises made to Abraham their father. "And then," Jesus continues—meaning in the day when the kingdom has been restored in all its fulness to Israel; in the day when Zion has been redeemed; in the day when He rules whose right it is—"then shall be brought to pass that which is written" (and what he quotes is an improved version of Isaiah):

Awake, awake again, and put on thy strength, O Zion; put on thy beautiful garments, O Jerusalem, the holy city, for henceforth there shall no more come into thee the uncircumcised and the unclean.

Shake thyself from the dust; arise, sit down, O Jerusalem; loose thyself from the bands of thy neck,

O captive daughter of Zion. For thus saith the Lord: Ye have sold yourselves for naught, and ye shall be redeemed without money.

Verily, verily, I say unto you, that my people shall know my name; yea, in that day they shall know that I am he that doth speak.[1]

Jerusalem—Jerusalem of the Jews—David's ancient city shall become holy; no more shall Gentile dogs defile its holy streets with their uncircumcised hearts. No longer will the Jews boast that salvation is theirs simply because of the Abrahamic token cut in their flesh, for then it will come to pass, as the apostle has written: "He is not a Jew, which is one outwardly; neither is that circumcision, which is outward in the flesh: But he is a Jew, which is one inwardly; and circumcision is that of the heart, in the spirit, and not in the letter; whose praise is not of men, but of God." (Rom. 2:25-29.) In that blessed day, those who walk the streets of the Holy City shall be clean, clean because they have "come forth out of the waters of Judah, or out of the waters of baptism." (1 Ne. 20:1.)

Jerusalem—Jerusalem of the Jews—she who sold herself for naught and went into captivity for her sins, she shall arise from the dust and sit down with the mighty. Her captive daughters will loose the bands of darkness with which they have been bound and return unto the Lord who will reveal himself to them. In that day they shall know their King, their Messiah, their Lord. And he is Christ. He it is that shall then speak to them.

And then shall they say: How beautiful upon the mountains are the feet of him that bringeth good tidings unto them, that publisheth peace; that bringeth good tidings unto them of good, that publisheth salvation; that saith unto Zion: Thy God reigneth![2]

Surely in this day, as never before, shall the hearts of the Jews—for the Lord will give them a new heart and a new spirit—surely in this day shall the Jews, having a new heart, acclaim the beauty of the feet of those who brought them the gospel. How glorious are the messengers who bring us the gospel of peace! Who has expressed it better than Abinadi? "And these are they who have published peace," he said, "who have brought good tidings of good, who have published salvation; and said unto Zion: Thy God reigneth! And O how beautiful upon the mountains were their feet! And again, how beautiful upon the mountains are the feet of those that are still publishing peace! And again, how beautiful upon the mountains are the feet of those who shall hereafter publish peace, yea, from this time henceforth and forever! And behold, I say unto you, this is not all. For O how beautiful upon the mountains are the feet of him that bringeth good tidings, that is the founder of peace, yea, even the Lord, who has redeemed his people; yea, him who has granted salvation unto his people; For were it not for the redemption which he hath made for his people, which was prepared from the foundation of the world, I say unto you, were it not for this, all mankind must have perished." (Mosiah 15:14-19.)

It is here that Isaiah, in his discourse, speaks of the watchmen who shall see eye to eye when the Lord brings again Zion, of Jerusalem being redeemed, and of all the ends of the earth seeing the salvation of God. As Jesus has twice already quoted these words to the Nephites, he now passes them by and picks up Isaiah's account by saying: "And then shall a cry go forth":

> *Depart ye, depart ye, go ye out from thence, touch not that which is unclean; go ye out of the midst of her; be ye clean that bear the vessels of the Lord.*
>
> *For you shall not go out with haste nor go by flight; for the Lord will go before you, and the God of Israel shall be your rearward.*[3]

When the kingdom is restored to Israel and the redemption of Zion begins, then the Jews who are scattered in all nations must flee from their Babylonish habitats and return unto their God. That this should now commence is our witness, for already the ecclesiastical kingdom has been set up; already the pure in heart—who are Zion—are beginning to build up again the Zion of God, and the millennial day is not far off. Then the political kingdom will be restored to Israel and Jerusalem will become a world capital whence the word of the Lord shall go to all nations.

At this point the subject seems to change, and what Jesus continues to quote is Messianic. The words are Isaiah's introduction to his great prophecy about the Suffering Servant:

> *Behold, my servant shall deal prudently; he shall be exalted and extolled and be very high.*
>
> *As many were astonished at thee—his visage was so marred, more than any man, and his form more than the sons of men—*
>
> *So shall he sprinkle many nations; the kings shall shut their mouths at him, for that which had not been told them shall they see; and that which they had not heard shall they consider.*

In these words we see a triumphant millennial Christ—one whose visage was marred and whose form was mangled when he dwelt among men—we see him in glory and dominion, in whose presence kings remain silent and before whom their mouths are shut. We see his cleansing blood sprinkle all nations, with devout men everywhere turning to the saving truths that they have not before heard and to the words of truth that they have not theretofore considered. And having finished, for the moment, his quotations, Jesus said:

> *Verily, verily, I say unto you, all these things shall surely come, even as the Father hath commanded me. Then shall this covenant which the Father hath covenanted with his people be fulfilled; and then shall Jerusalem be inhabited again with my people, and it shall be the land of their inheritance.*

Then shall the children of the covenant inherit, receive,

and possess—equally and fully—with their fathers of old! Then shall the Lamanites flourish in the Americas; then shall the Jews prosper in Jerusalem; then shall Ephraim—the Lord's firstborn!—confer on all the tribes their eternal blessings; and then shall all the promises relative to Israel and Zion be fulfilled.

The Lord be praised for what lies ahead for his people!

NOTES

1. Compare Isaiah 52:1-3, 6. In this connection, and by way of question and answer, the inspired word says: "What is meant by the command in Isaiah, 52d chapter, 1st verse, which saith: Put on thy strength, O Zion—and what people had Isaiah reference to? He had reference to those whom God should call in the last days, who should hold the power of priesthood to bring again Zion, and the redemption of Israel; and to put on her strength is to put on the authority of the priesthood, which she, Zion, has a right to by lineage; also to return to that power which she had lost. What are we to understand by Zion loosing herself from the bands of her neck; 2d verse? We are to understand that the scattered remnants are exhorted to return to the Lord from whence they have fallen; which if they do, the promise of the Lord is that he will speak to them, or give them revelation. See the 6th, 7th, and 8th verses. The bands of her neck are the curses of God upon her, or the remnants of Israel in their scattered condition among the Gentiles." (D&C 113:7-10.)

2. Compare Isaiah 52:7.

3. These words and those that follow have their root in Isa. 52:11-15, though as the astute student will observe, Jesus here gives them in a more perfect form.

THE BUILDING UP OF ZION

The Lord loveth the gates of Zion
more than all the dwellings of Jacob.
Glorious things are spoken of thee,
O city of God. . . .
And of Zion it shall be said,
This and that man was born in her:
and the highest himself shall
establish her.
(Ps. 87:2-5.)
Thou shalt arise, and have mercy upon Zion:
for the time to favour her,
yea, the set time, is come.
For thy servants take pleasure in her stones,
and favour the dust thereof.
So the heathen shall fear the name of the Lord,
and all the kings of the earth thy glory.
When the Lord shall build up Zion,
he shall appear in his glory.
He will regard the prayer of the destitute,
and not despise their prayer.
This shall be written for the generation to come:
and the people which shall be created
shall praise the Lord.
(Ps. 102:13-18.)

Reading the Signs of the Times
(3 Nephi 21:1-13)

When, O when, will all these things come to pass? When will the Lord restore again the kingdom to Israel? When will Jerusalem become holy and Zion be redeemed? The promises are so wondrous, the glories so grand, the triumph so splendid, that every believing heart cries out—When, O Lord, will it be? And every prayerful voice pleads that it may be in his day. In a great chorus of worship and desire, the prayers of the saints ascend to the Great God: "Thy kingdom come. Thy will be done in earth, as it is in heaven," they say. (Matt. 6:10.) 'Even so come Lord Jesus that we, the children of the covenant, may receive that which was promised to Abraham and his seed; that in us and in our seed all generations may be blessed; that we may have a continuation of the seeds forever and ever; that our posterity also may be as numerous as the sands upon the seashore or the stars in the broad expanse of heaven. Let the gospel be restored; let Israel be gathered; let Jerusalem be redeemed; let Zion be established; let the Lord Jesus reign in peace and glory on earth for a thousand years.'

That the times and the seasons might be known; that his ancient covenant people might know when and under what circumstances the glorious promises would be fulfilled; but, more particularly, that his covenant people in the last days might know and believe and prepare for the wonders that are to be, Jesus said to his Nephite saints:

> *And verily I say unto you, I give unto you a sign, that ye may know the time when these things shall be about to take place—that I shall gather in, from their long dispersion, my people, O house of Israel, and shall establish again among them my Zion.*

The restoration of the gospel, the gathering of Israel, and the establishment of Zion are one and the same thing; or, at least, they are so inseparably intertwined as one that they cannot be separated—for it is the Lord who gives the gospel, and it is the gospel that gathers Israel, and it is

Israel that builds Zion. Now it is not the Lord's plan to hide his purposes from those who seek him. True, the day and the hour of his Second Coming is between him and his Father. It is wisdom in them to let the saints in successive ages look forward with expectancy, in the spirit of watchfulness and prayer, for that great day. But the times and the seasons in which the great events associated with that coming are to transpire—wherein the gospel is to be restored, Israel gathered, and Zion established—these are to be known, so that men in those days will be more watchful and more prayerful as they await the wonders that are to be.

> *And behold, this is the thing which I will give unto you for a sign—for verily I say unto you that when these things which I declare unto you, and which I shall declare unto you hereafter of myself, and by the power of the Holy Ghost which shall be given unto you of the Father, shall be made known unto the Gentiles that they may know concerning this people who are a remnant of the house of Jacob, and concerning this my people who shall be scattered by them.*

(For clarity's sake we must interject our commentary into Jesus' sermon, even before he finishes his thoughts, for his presentation is so complex and his expressions are so broad that we might otherwise fail to envision their full meaning.) Thus, the promised sign is to include (1) the things Jesus now speaks, (2) those he shall thereafter speak to them, and (3) those he shall later reveal by the power of the Holy Ghost—when all these things shall be made known to the Gentiles in the latter days (through the coming forth of the Book of Mormon), so that the Gentiles learn of the ancient Nephites, and also of the latter-day Lamanites whom they have scattered.

> *Verily, verily, I say unto you, when these things shall be made known unto them of the Father, and*

shall come forth of the Father, from them unto you;

That is, when all the doctrine and all the witness of truth found in the Book of Mormon shall come forth by the power of God, and shall go from the Gentiles to the seed of Lehi.

For it is wisdom in the Father that they should be established in this land, and be set up as a free people by the power of the Father, that these things might come forth from them unto a remnant of your seed, that the covenant of the Father may be fulfilled which he hath covenanted with his people, O house of Israel;

That is, in the eternal providences of Him who governs in the affairs of men; who raises up nations and casts down thrones; who gives one nation, and then another, a rulership for a season—according to his eternal purposes a great nation (the United States of America) shall be set up, with constitutional guarantees of freedom, by the power of God, so that the gospel may be restored, the Book of Mormon come forth, its message go to the American remnant of Jacob, all to the end that the eternal covenants of the Lord with his people might be fulfilled.

Therefore, when these works and the works which shall be wrought among you hereafter shall come forth from the Gentiles, unto your seed which shall dwindle in unbelief because of iniquity;

That is, when all that was then done and that should thereafter be done among the Nephites, should come forth in the Book of Mormon and go from the Gentiles unto Father Lehi's children, who by then would have dwindled in unbelief because of their sins.

For thus it behooveth the Father that it should come forth from the Gentiles, that he may show forth his power unto the Gentiles, for this cause that the Gentiles, if they will not harden their hearts, that they may repent and come unto me and be baptized in my name and know of the true points of my doctrine, that they may be numbered among my people, O house of Israel;

That is: It is the Father's good pleasure that the Book of Mormon shall come forth by way of the Gentiles, that they too may know his power, receive revelation, and learn the wonders of eternity, all to the end that the Gentiles, if they will, may repent and come unto Christ, and be baptized, and learn the doctrines of salvation, and be numbered with the house of Israel.

And when these things come to pass that thy seed shall begin to know these things—it shall be a sign unto them, that they may know that the work of the Father hath already commenced unto the fulfilling of the covenant which he hath made unto the people who are of the house of Israel.

What wonders the Lord has in store for his people! How glorious is his plan; how marvelous are his purposes; what great things he has reserved for the latter days! Israel—his chosen ones—shall be gathered in from their long dispersion; though they have been scattered in all the nations of the earth, yet they shall come out of darkness into the marvelous light of Christ when the Lord raises an ensign to the nations. "Ye shall be gathered one by one, O ye children of Israel . . . and shall worship the Lord in the holy mount at Jerusalem." (Isa. 27:12-13.)

Zion—the Holy City, the pure in heart, the people of the Most High—Zion shall be established "on the mountains of Adam-ondi-Ahman, and on the plains of Olaha Shinehah, or the land where Adam dwelt." (D&C 117:8.) A New Jerusalem shall arise in the tops of the mountains and in the land of Missouri; Jerusalem of old shall shine forth in the waste places long trodden down of the Gentiles; and the Lord's people shall be redeemed in all the nations of the earth. The Lord Jehovah "shall cause them that come of Jacob to take root: Israel shall blossom and bud, and fill the face of the world with fruit." (Isa. 27:6.)

The longings and desires, the prayers and the pleadings of all the prophets have been that Israel would come off triumphant; that she would tread on the necks of her foes; that a remnant would be among the Gentiles as a young lion among the flocks of sheep; that the Lord would make the horn of his people iron and their hoofs brass; that they would shine forth as a nation, "fair as the moon, clear as the sun, and terrible as an army with banners" (Song. 6:10); and, in fine, that all Israel would be saved. All the prophets looked forward to the day when the ancient covenant would be renewed with the seed of Abraham; when the Lord would make anew the old covenant; when men again would know that in them and in their seed all generations should be blessed; when they would rejoice again in the prophetic promise that their seed—"out of the world"—would be as the stars and the sands. Or in other words: All of the prophets and all of the saints of olden times looked forward to the restitution of all things, to the restoration of the fulness of the everlasting gospel. All of them looked forward to the day when those who did not give heed to the words of the apostles and prophets then sent among them would, as Moses said, be cut off from among the people.

The great issue was not *what* the Lord designed to do in the latter days, but *when* it should come to pass. What was the sign and when should it be given? And now Jesus has given the answer, an answer that is plain and clear to us. The promised sign is the Book of Mormon. When that volume of holy scripture comes forth, then all men may know that the Lord has already commenced his work.

It is the Book of Mormon that gathers Israel. When the Stick of Judah and the Stick of Joseph, in the hands of Ephraim, become one in the hands of his people, then the Lord God will gather them; then will they come forth from among the heathen and receive the gospel; then shall they come into their own land according to the covenant. And "Thus saith the Lord God: . . . Neither shall they defile themselves any more with their idols, nor with their detestable things, nor with any of their transgressions: but I will save them out of all their dwellingplaces, wherein they have sinned, and will cleanse them: so shall they be my people, and I will be their God." (Ezek. 37:20-23.)

We cannot state it too plainly; we cannot affirm it too positively; we cannot proclaim it with too great a fervor—the Book of Mormon is the sign given of God to herald the fulfillment of the covenants made of old. And now that holy volume is going forth to Lehi's seed and to all men, that all may know that the work of the Lord has commenced anew and that all that was promised will soon come to pass. That holy book has come forth, "Proving to the world that the holy scriptures are true, and that God does inspire men and call them to his holy work in this age and generation, as well as in generations of old; Thereby showing that he is the same God yesterday, today, and forever." (D&C 20:11-12.) It has come forth "to the convincing of the Jew and Gentile that Jesus is the Christ, the Eternal God, manifesting himself unto all nations." (Title Page, Book of Mormon.) It has come forth as a new witness of Christ; as a witness that the everlasting gospel has been restored; as a witness that Joseph Smith and his successors wear the prophetic mantle; as a witness that The Church of Jesus Christ of Latter-day Saints is the only true and living church upon the face of the whole earth; as a witness that the Lord has raised his latter-day ensign to the nations; as a witness that the covenant made with Abraham of old is now being fulfilled.

> *And when that day shall come, it shall come to pass that kings shall shut their mouths; for that which had not been told them shall they see; and that which they had not heard shall they consider.*

Jesus now begins to speak of the things that shall come to pass after the coming forth of the Book of Mormon, after the restoration of the gospel. What he says is not a chronological listing of successive events, but simply an announcement of and a commentary on various things that are to be. We are left—as wisdom dictates should be the case—to interpret and apply his inspired utterances, the first being that the great and mighty shall be so amazed at the Lord's latter-day work that they shall not know what to say and shall feel impelled to consider the wondrous work which rolls before their eyes. So far there has been a small amount of this; what the future holds is limitless.

> *For in that day, for my sake shall the Father work a work, which shall be a great and a marvelous work among them; and there shall be among them those who will not believe it, although a man shall declare it unto them.*

The restoration of the gospel, including all that appertains to it, is a marvelous work and a wonder. How men ought to marvel at the wonders that have already come in these the latter days! What can compare with the appearance of the Father and the Son to a young lad in his fifteenth year; or to the coming forth of the Book of Mormon, which contains a record of God's dealings with a people who had the fulness of the everlasting gospel; or to the ministry of Moroni, and John the Baptist, and Peter and James and other resurrected beings again on earth; or to the setting up of the true church and kingdom of God again on earth; or to the gathering of millions of our Father's children out of Babylon into the True Fold? And all of this is but the beginning; the marvels and wonders that lie ahead are beyond the capacities of us mortals to comprehend or conceive.

"I will proceed to do a marvellous work among this people," the Lord said by the mouth of Isaiah, "even a marvellous work and a wonder: for the wisdom of their wise men shall perish, and the understanding of their prudent men shall be hid." (Isa. 29:14.) Then, as our dispensation dawned, the Lord repeatedly said such things as: "A great and marvelous work is about to come forth unto the children of men," and that "the field is white already to harvest; therefore, whoso desireth to reap, let him thrust in his sickle with his might, and reap while the day lasts, that he may treasure up for his soul everlasting salvation in the kingdom of God.'' (D&C 6:1-4.) And also: "By your hands I will work a marvelous work among the children of men, unto the convincing of many of their sins, that they may come unto repentance, and that they may come unto the kingdom of my Father.'' (D&C 18:44.)

Implicit in all this, as Jesus has just stated to the Nephites, is the fact that many will not believe the latter-day message of salvation, though it be declared unto them by the man whom God hath sent to reveal his word. It shall be among us as it was when He whose gospel it is ministered personally on earth, of which ministry the Messianic word asks: "Who hath believed our report? and to whom is the arm of the Lord revealed?'' (Isa. 53:1.)

> *But behold, the life of my servant shall be in my hand; therefore they shall not hurt him, although he shall be marred because of them. Yet I will heal him, for I will show unto them that my wisdom is greater than the cunning of the devil.*

Isaiah's prophecy about the marred servant is clearly Messianic and applies to Jesus who was crucified and rose from the dead to sprinkle the saving power of his blood in all nations. It is of him that kings shall shut their mouths as they ponder the marvel of his resurrection and all that he did. (Isa. 52:13-15.) But in this whole discourse Jesus is applying the prophetic word to the latter days, meaning that, as with many prophecies, the divine word has a dual fulfillment. In this setting we may properly say that Joseph Smith—whose voice declared the word for this dispensation—was marred, as his Lord had been, and yet should be healed, in the eternal sense, as was his Lord. And it may yet well be that there will be other latter-day servants to whom also it will apply. All of the Lord's servants who are marred or hurt or persecuted in this life—and who remain faithful—shall have all their sorrows made up to them in manifold measure in the resurrection.

Therefore it shall come to pass that whosoever will not believe in my words, who am Jesus Christ, which the Father shall cause him to bring forth unto the Gentiles, and shall give unto him power that he shall bring them forth unto the Gentiles, (it shall be done even as Moses said) they shall be cut off from among my people who are of the covenant.

Those who do not believe the restored gospel; who reject the messengers of salvation who are sent to them; and who continue to live after the manner of the world—they shall be cut off from among the people who are of the covenant. This we have already noted. It refers to the return of the Son of Man; to the day when every corruptible thing shall be destroyed; to the day when the wicked shall be burned as stubble; to the day when the vineyard shall be burned and none shall remain except those who are able to abide the day. It is then, and in this way, that the Lord's people will triumph over their enemies.

And my people who are a remnant of Jacob shall be among the Gentiles, yea, in the midst of them as a lion among the beasts of the forest, as a young lion among the flocks of sheep, who, if he go through both treadeth down and teareth in pieces, and none can deliver.

Their hand shall be lifted up upon their adversaries, and all their enemies shall be cut off.

Building the New Jerusalem

(3 Nephi 21:14-29)

Having spoken of the coming forth of the Book of Mormon; having announced the restoration of the gospel in the latter days; having promised that Israel would be gathered again into the fold of the True Shepherd; having assured his people that the Great Jehovah would renew with their seed the covenant made with their fathers—Jesus now turns to building a New Jerusalem. Zion, as a place and as a city, is to be established, so that Zion, as a people and as the pure in heart, may have a capital whence the law may go forth. The building of the New Jerusalem grows out of these other things that he has taught them, and we must take care to study his words in the setting he gave them.

Jesus has made repeated references—both quoting and paraphrasing, as best suited his purposes—to the words of Micah. That ancient prophet said: "And the remnant of Jacob shall be in the midst of many people as a dew from the Lord, as the showers upon the grass, that tarrieth not for man, nor waiteth for the sons of men." That is, the Lord's people will be everywhere, scattered in all nations, and their presence will seem as natural as the settling of the dew and the falling of the rains; their influence will be to give life and strength to the nations, even as the moisture from heaven gives life and growth to the crops of the earth.

"And the remnant of Jacob shall be among the Gentiles in the midst of many people as a lion among the beasts of the forest, as a young lion among the flocks of sheep: who, if he go through, both treadeth down, and teareth in pieces, and none can deliver. Thine hand shall be lifted up upon thine adversaries, and all thine enemies shall be cut off." These concepts, including most of the very words themselves, Jesus has quoted, and he has explained that their fulfillment will be in the day when the wicked are cut off as Moses promised. After Micah gave them, he said: "And it shall come to pass in that day, saith the Lord, that I will" do such and such, referring to certain conditions that will prevail during the Millennium and after the destruction of the wicked at the Second Coming of the Son of Man. (Micah 5:7-15.) After Jesus said the same things, he also, using most of the very words of Micah, spoke of these millennial events:

Yea, wo be unto the Gentiles except they repent; for it shall come to pass in that day, saith the Father, that I will cut off thy horses out of the midst of thee, and I will destroy thy chariots; And I will cut off the cities of thy land, and throw down all thy strongholds.

When the Lord comes and Israel triumphs, the armies of the Gentile nations will be destroyed, their fortifications thrown down, and their cities cease to be. Every corruptible thing—including the wicked Jew and the evil Gentile—shall be destroyed.

And I will cut off witchcrafts out of thy land, and thou shalt have no more soothsayers; Thy graven images I will also cut off, and thy standing images out of the midst of thee, and thou shalt no more worship the works of thy hands; And I will pluck up thy groves out of the midst of thee; so will I destroy thy cities.

False doctrine, false ordinances, false worship, false religion—all shall cease. The images and idols, in their churches and in their hearts, shall be as when God overthrew Sodom and Gomorrah. The groves where Baal of old was worshipped, and the cathedrals where Baal of the latter days was adored, shall be as when the walls and buildings of Jericho fell.

And it shall come to pass that all lyings, and deceivings, and envyings, and strifes, and priestcrafts, and whoredoms, shall be done away.

For it shall come to pass, saith the Father, that at that day whosoever will not repent and come unto my Beloved Son, them will I cut off from among my people, O house of Israel.

These words are not in Micah's account; Jesus here inserts them to give depth and understanding to the Old Testament account from which he is quoting. They tell of that day when wickedness, as we know it, ceases, the day when men have beaten their swords into plowshares and their spears into pruning hooks, the day when peace prevails and the Prince of Peace is Lord over all the earth. And in that day wo unto those who do not repent and believe in the Beloved Son. Of them the divine word is:

> *And I will execute vengeance and fury upon them, even as upon the heathen, such as they have not heard.*

With these words the quotations from Micah cease, at least as far as our Bible preserves his words for us. The meaning is, of course, self-evident and accords with Zechariah's word that those families and nations—after the Second Coming—who go not up to Jerusalem to keep the Feast of Tabernacles, upon them no rain shall fall and they shall be smitten with a plague. (Zech. 14:16-19.)

> *But if they will repent and hearken unto my words, and harden not their hearts, I will establish my church among them, and they shall come in unto the covenant and be numbered among this the remnant of Jacob, unto whom I have given this land for their inheritance;*
>
> *And they shall assist my people, the remnant of Jacob, and also as many of the house of Israel as shall come, that they may build a city, which shall be called the New Jerusalem.*

Both Jew and Gentile shall build the New Jerusalem. The remnant of Jacob in the Americas (meaning the Lamanites), and the gathered remnants of the whole house of Israel—indeed, all people from all nations who are righteous and pure and believing, all who keep the commandments—all shall join in building the Holy City. And the Jews (other than the Lamanite Jews) who believe and repent and purify themselves shall build up anew the Jerusalem of old. All this is set forth by Moroni, as he wrote of Ether, in these words: "Behold, Ether saw the days of Christ, and he spake concerning a New Jerusalem upon this land. And he spake also concerning the house of Israel, and the Jerusalem from whence Lehi should come—after it should be destroyed it should be built up again, a holy city unto the Lord; wherefore, it could not be a new Jerusalem for it had been in a time of old; but it should be built up again, and become a holy city of the Lord; and it should be built unto the house of Israel. And that a New Jerusalem should be built upon this land, unto the remnant of the seed of Joseph, for which things there has been a type. For as Joseph brought his father down into the land of Egypt, even so he died there; wherefore, the Lord brought a remnant of the seed of Joseph out of the land of Jerusalem, that he might be merciful unto the seed of Joseph that they should perish not, even as he was merciful unto the father of Joseph that he should perish not. Wherefore, the remnant of the house of Joseph shall be built upon this land; and it shall be a land of their inheritance; and they shall build up a holy city unto the Lord, like unto the Jerusalem of old; and they shall no more be confounded, until the end come when the earth shall pass away.

"And there shall be a new heaven and a new earth; and they shall be like unto the old save the old have passed away, and all things have become new. And then cometh the New Jerusalem; and blessed are they who dwell therein, for it is they whose garments are white through the blood of the Lamb; and they are they who are numbered among the remnant of the seed of Joseph, who were of the house of Israel. And then also cometh the Jerusalem of old; and the inhabitants thereof, blessed are they, for they have been washed in the blood of the Lamb; and they are they who were scattered and gathered in from the four quarters of the earth, and from the north countries, and are partakers of the fulfilling of the covenant which God made with their father, Abraham." (Ether 13:4-11.) And of this day when Zion, the New Jerusalem, is established on the American continent, Jesus said:

> *And then shall they assist my people that they may be gathered in, who are scattered upon all the face of the land, in unto the New Jerusalem. And*

then shall the power of heaven come down among them; and I also will be in the midst.

The prophecies relative to the gathering of Israel will be fulfilled both before and after the Second Coming. The remnants shall first assemble, set up the ecclesiastical kingdom, and build up Zion. Then the Lord will come and the final glorious gathering and triumph of Israel will come to pass. It will be in the day when the Lord is in the midst of men. Having so taught, Jesus returns to general commentary about the sign whereby men may know that his strange and wondrous work—the marvelous work and a wonder of latter days—has commenced again on earth.

And then shall the work of the Father commence at that day, even when this gospel shall be preached among the remnant of this people. Verily I say unto you, at that day shall the work of the Father commence among all the dispersed of my people, yea, even the tribes which have been lost, which the Father hath led away out of Jerusalem.

Yea, the work shall commence among all the dispersed of my people, with the Father, to prepare the way whereby they may come unto me, that they may call on the Father in my name.

Yea, and then shall the work commence, with the Father, among all nations, in preparing the way whereby his people may be gathered home to the land of their inheritance.

And they shall go out from all nations; and they shall not go out in haste, nor go by flight, for I will go before them, saith the Father, and I will be their rearward.

In this summary we are reminded: (1) that when the gospel goes to the Lamanites, it will be a sign that the great latter-day work has begun; (2) that in that day the gospel will go to all the dispersed of Israel, including the lost tribes; (3) that its purpose will be to bring Israel unto Christ so they can call upon the Father in his name; (4) that the work will go forward in all nations so that the chosen seed may be gathered to the lands of their inheritances; and (5) that they shall go out, not as escapees from oppression or for political reasons, but in glory and beauty and truth—the Lord himself going before and preparing the way and being also their rearward.

Let God be praised for the wonders that now are and for the even greater wonders that are to be!

EXPOUNDING THE SCRIPTURES

Search the scriptures;
for . . . they are they which testify of me.
(John 5:39.)
The holy scriptures . . . are able
to make thee wise unto salvation
through faith which is in Christ Jesus.
And all scripture given by inspiration of God,
is profitable for doctrine,
for reproof, for correction,
for instruction in righteousness;
That the man of God may be perfect,
thoroughly furnished unto all good works.
(JST, 2 Tim. 3:15-17.)
And whoso treasureth up my word,
shall not be deceived. (JS-M 1:37.)

Searching the Scriptures

(3 Nephi 22:1-17; 23:1-5)

Jesus' teachings among the Nephite Jews rose to far greater heights than did his teachings among the Palestinian Jews. At least the biblical accounts do not compare in doctrinal beauty and scriptural exposition with those in the

Book of Mormon. Jesus gave no parables to the Nephites, for he had no occasion to hide his doctrines or conceal his concepts as far as they were concerned. He spent no time contending with them about their traditions and false beliefs, and he was not at any time faced with a spirit of disbelief or rebellion among them. Such things as the Sermon on the Mount, the Intercessory Prayer, and the doctrine relative to the sacrament were given in plainness on both continents. But many doctrinal concepts were given to the Nephites of which there is no New Testament account. It is true, of course, that on the mountain in Galilee or in other private gatherings Jesus gave the Jews more than is recorded in the New Testament. But in the very nature of things—the wicked and ungodly among the Nephites having been destroyed—there is a higher tone and a more pleasing feel to what he told the Nephites than to what he gave the people in the Old World. And one of the things he did among his New World saints was to quote extensively from the prophets, and to do it in such a way as to endorse and to show the true meaning and intent of the prophetic word.

And so, having presented his doctrine relative to the restoration of the gospel, the gathering of Israel, and the establishment of Zion—all in the latter days—Jesus said: "And then shall that which is written come to pass," at which point he quoted, with minor improvements, the whole fifty-fourth chapter of Isaiah. In poetic language, using figures of speech common in his day, Isaiah proclaimed that Israel—scattered, barren, without seed born under the covenant—would again break forth into singing; that Zion would enlarge her borders, strengthen her stakes, break forth on the right hand and on the left, and build up the ancient and desolate cities; and that the saints of latter days would no longer be ashamed, nor remember the reproach of their scattered days nor the sorrows of their widowhood.

He announced that Jehovah was their Bridegroom, their

Husband, their Maker, their Redeemer, and that he was the God of Israel and of the whole earth. He told how Israel had been forsaken for a small moment but would be gathered with great mercies; and how in a little wrath the Lord had hidden his face from her, but with everlasting kindness would shower mercy upon her children. He gave the Lord's promise (1) that as the flood of Noah was assuaged, never to return, so Jehovah's wrath against Israel would cease, and (2) that though the mountains and hills should depart, yet the Lord would not break his covenant to show mercy upon Israel. Her children—"afflicted, tossed with tempest, and not comforted"—would be gathered in peace into Zion.

The Holy City would be built with riches and jewels, and all her children would be taught of the Lord who reigned among them. The saints would then dwell in peace, and righteousness would prevail; oppression would cease, terror flee away, and all who opposed them would fall. No weapon formed against the Lord's people should prosper, and every tongue that spoke against them should be condemned. Such, said Isaiah, "is the heritage of the servants of the Lord," for their righteousness is of him. And when Jesus had quoted all these words, he said:

> *And now, behold, I say unto you, that ye ought to search these things. Yea, a commandment I give unto you that ye search these things diligently; for great are the words of Isaiah.*
>
> *For surely he spake as touching all things concerning my people which are of the house of Israel; therefore it must needs be that he must speak also to the Gentiles.*

Scripturalists are wont to refer to Isaiah as the Messianic prophet because of his many prophecies about the birth and ministry and death and resurrection of the Lord Jehovah. And truly he was; no Old Testament seer has left us a greater wealth of words about the Eternal Word than this son of Amoz, who prophesied in the days of Uzziah,

Jotham, Ahaz, and Hezekiah, all kings of Judah, and who, according to tradition, was sawn asunder for the counsel he gave and the testimony of Jesus he bore. But what is of equal or even greater import is that Isaiah's Messianic word shines forth far beyond time's meridian; he is the great prophet of the restoration. It is his voice that speaks of the restoration of the gospel in the last days, of the coming forth of the Book of Mormon, of the raising of an ensign to the nations, of the gathering of Israel, of the building of the house of the Lord in the tops of the mountains, of the conversion of many Gentiles, of the building of Zion, of the Second Coming of the Son of Man, and of the millennial era of peace and righteousness. Truly, "great are the words of Isaiah."

> *And all things that he spake have been and shall be, even according to the words which he spake.*
>
> *Therefore give heed to my words; write the things which I have told you; and according to the time and the will of the Father they shall go forth unto the Gentiles.*
>
> *And whosoever will hearken unto my words and repenteth and is baptized, the same shall be saved. Search the prophets, for many there be that testify of these things.*

When the words of Isaiah go forth unto the Gentiles—and are understood by them—they will believe in Christ, repent of their sins, be baptized by the legal administrators sent of God in this day, and become members of The Church of Jesus Christ of Latter-day Saints. And with this all the prophetic word accords.

Adding to the Scriptures
(3 Nephi 23:6-14; 24:1-18; 25:1-6; 26:1-2)

Jesus now did something among the Nephites that he had never done, as far as we know, among the Jews. He "expounded all the scriptures unto them which they had received." What a wondrous thing this must have been! On the Emmaus road he expounded to Cleopas and Luke "in all the scriptures the things concerning himself." (Luke 24:27.) But here to thousands upon thousands of saints who had received the gift of the Holy Ghost and were prepared to receive the mysteries of the kingdom, he expounded all that was written in their holy books. They had the brass plates, which contain the five books of Moses, and the prophecies of the prophets down to the reign of Zedekiah, king of Judah, including many prophecies and covenants of the Lord that have been lost from our Old Testament. They had the plates of Nephi and other records telling what the Lord had revealed to their fathers during the 634 years since Lehi left Jerusalem. And, above all, they had the Jaredite scriptures, those inspired accounts which are in the sealed portion of the Book of Mormon. When we think that all these things were expounded unto them by Him who gave the holy word and whose scriptures they were, it makes us feel somewhat insignificant spiritually. When we compare the small stream of revelation we have received with the mighty rivers of revealed truth that flowed to those of old, we long for the day when the Lord will come and reveal all things to us so that we will know what our counterparts of old knew in their days.

Then Jesus said to the people, "Behold, other scriptures I would that ye should write, that ye have not." To Nephi he commanded: "Bring forth the record which ye have kept," which they did. Finding it did not contain the prophecy of Samuel the Lamanite, that many saints would come forth from their graves after the resurrection of Christ, he said: "How be it that ye have not written this thing, that many saints did arise and appear unto many and did minister unto them?" Samuel's prophetic words were then duly recorded, and Jesus "expounded all the scriptures in one," and "commanded them that they should teach the things which he had expounded unto them."

After the Jews returned from Babylon, and after the days of Ezra and Nehemiah and the building of the walls of

Jerusalem, the Lord sent the great prophet Malachi to give his word to the chosen seed. That the seed of those who had escaped from the Holy City before Nebuchadnezzar took their fathers into captivity, that the seed of Joseph that had been separated from their brethren might rejoice in the words of so great a one as Malachi, whose words close our Old Testament, Jesus first gave many of them to his American saints, and then expounded to them their deep and wondrous meanings. All we know of what then happened is that he gave them chapters 3 and 4 in almost the verbatim language of our Bible.

Malachi's prophetic words here involved speak of the messenger who should prepare the way before the face of the Lord, in a sense for his mortal ministry, but primarily in that great millennial day when the wicked will be destroyed and the sons of Levi serve again in their priestly roles. They tell us that Judah and Jerusalem shall be restored to their ancient glory, and that their Lord—who is Jehovah—coming to reign on earth will destroy the wicked: the sorcerers, adulterers, false swearers, those who oppress their fellowmen and who do not fear the Lord.

They speak of robbing God and being cursed therefor, through failure to pay tithes and offerings, and of the temporal and spiritual blessings reserved for tithe payers. Those who walk mournfully before the Lord are promised great reward in due time, though the proud and the wicked seem to enjoy greater rewards in this life. Those who serve the Lord shall be his when he comes to make up his jewels; he will spare them in that day, and then shall all discern between the righteous and the wicked.

Malachi foretells the day of the Second Coming when the proud and the wicked shall be burned as stubble; when the Son of Righteousness shall arise with healing in his wings; when Israel shall grow up as calves in the stall with all their needs cared for; and when they shall tread down the wicked—their enemies—as ashes under the soles of their feet. And then, as a fitting climax, Malachi speaks of the return of Elijah the prophet to reveal the priesthood before the great and dreadful day of the Lord and to plant in the hearts of the children the promises made to the fathers, lest the whole earth be utterly wasted in that day. Then Jesus said:

> *These scriptures, which ye had not with you, the Father commanded that I should give unto you; for it was wisdom in him that they should be given unto future generations.*

They are primarily for our benefit. We live in the day of which they speak; we are the children in whose hearts the promises have been planted; we are the ones who are striving so to live that we will abide the day of His coming. And it is in our day that Elijah has come, according to the promises, bringing again the sealing power so that legal administrators may bind on earth and have it sealed eternally in the heavens—for all of which the Lord be praised.

Seeking More Scriptures
(3 Nephi 26:3-21; Ether 4:1-19)

Who has seen such marvelous things as Jesus did among the Nephites? And who has heard such wondrous words of divine wisdom as fell from his lips on the American continent? To our shame we know only the hundredth part. Our friend Mormon—the prophet-historian who has given us such as we do have—at this point in his inspired writing said of the teachings of the Blessed One, which he so freely gave to the spiritually attuned ears in the New World: Jesus "did expound all things, even from the beginning until the time that he should come in his glory—yea, even all things which should come upon the face of the earth, even until the elements should melt with fervent heat, and the earth should be wrapt together as a scroll, and the heavens and the earth should pass away; And even unto the great and last day, when all people, and all kindreds, and all nations and tongues shall stand before God, to be judged of their works, whether they be good or whether they be evil—If they be good, to the resurrection of everlasting life; and if they be evil, to the resurrection of damnation; being on a parallel, the one on the one hand and the other on the other hand, according to the mercy, and the justice, and the holiness which is in Christ, who was before the world began."

In the providences of the Lord, we have slivers and fragments of what Jesus gave the Nephites. Sections 29, 45, 63, 76, 77, 88, 93, 101, 107, 132, 133, and 138 in the Doctrine and Covenants, and the books of Moses and Abraham in the Pearl of Great Price, all contain truths of transcendent worth about the doings of Deity from the beginning to the end. But what we have is only the milk of the present, which prepares us for the meat of the future. We do not have what he told the Nephites, and we do not have what he revealed to the brother of Jared, nor will we until the sealed portion of the Book of Mormon comes forth. "There cannot be written in this book even a hundredth part of the things which Jesus did truly teach unto the people," Mormon says. The plates of Nephi do contain the more part of his teachings, but with reference to the lesser part that has come to us, Mormon says: "I have written them to the intent that they may be brought again unto this people, from the Gentiles, according to the words which Jesus hath spoken." Then Mormon gives us this concept of infinite worth:

> *And when they shall have received this, which is expedient that they should have first, to try their faith, and if it shall so be that they shall believe these things then shall the greater things be made manifest unto them.*
>
> *And if it so be that they will not believe these things, then shall the greater things be withheld from them, unto their condemnation.*
>
> *Behold, I was about to write them, all which were engraven upon the plates of Nephi, but the Lord*

forbade it, saying: I will try the faith of my people.

Along with the teachings given by Jesus in that day, the Nephites had also the inspired writings of the brother of Jared. These accounts had been sealed up for some two millenniums, so they would not "come unto the children of men until after" Jesus had been "lifted up upon the cross." During the golden era of Nephite worship they were opened before all the people. But when these Israelites, after some two centuries of true worship, again dwindled in unbelief, these sacred words were again sealed up and their glories withheld from men. They are now found in the sealed portion of the Book of Mormon, and of them Moroni said: "There never were greater things made manifest than those which were made manifest unto the brother of Jared." And with respect to them, the Lord said:

> *They shall not go forth unto the Gentiles until the day that they shall repent of their iniquity, and become clean before the Lord.*
>
> *And in that day that they shall exercise faith in me, saith the Lord, even as the brother of Jared did, that they may become sanctified in me, then will I manifest unto them the things which the brother of Jared saw, even to the unfolding unto them all my revelations, saith Jesus Christ, the Son of God, the Father of the heavens and of the earth, and all things that in them are.*

It is with the writings of Jareditish Moriancumer even as it is with most of the Nephite teachings of Jesus. They are reserved for the faithful, they can be understood only by the power of the Spirit, and they have not been revealed as yet to us. Though the milk of the word, as found in the translated portion of the Book of Mormon, has been given to prepare us for the meat of the word, as found in the sealed portion of that holy book, it is clear that our faith is not yet great enough to enable us to receive the hidden mysteries of the kingdom.

And he that will contend against the word of the Lord, let him be accursed; and he that shall deny these things, let him be accursed; for unto them will I show no greater things, saith Jesus Christ; for I am he who speaketh.

And at my command the heavens are opened and are shut; and at my word the earth shall shake; and at my command the inhabitants thereof shall pass away, even so as by fire.

How can those who do not believe and obey the law already given ever expect to receive more revelation from on high? If men will not believe the Book of Mormon, they shut out of their lives the other revelations that have come in this dispensation. And if they do not believe all that God has now revealed, what justification would there be for him to reveal other great and important things pertaining to his earthly affairs and his heavenly kingdom?

And he that believeth not my words believeth not my disciples; and if it so be that I do not speak, judge ye; for ye shall know that it is I that speaketh, at the last day.

But he that believeth these things which I have spoken, him will I visit with the manifestations of my Spirit, and he shall know and bear record. For because of my Spirit he shall know that these things are true; for it persuadeth men to do good.

And whatsoever thing persuadeth men to do good is of me; for good cometh of none save it be of me. I am the same that leadeth men to all good; he that will not believe my words will not believe me—that I am; and he that will not believe me will not believe the Father who sent me. For behold, I am the Father, I am the light, and the life, and the truth of the world.

How wondrous are the words of Christ! Their plainness, the reasoning and logic they set forth, the self-evident witness they bear of their divine origin—where else in all that is written are there words like these? Truly he that does not believe these words and others like them does not believe in Christ, and he that does believe shall receive the manifestations of the Holy Spirit and shall prepare himelf for ever greater revelations. And so the cry goes forth among us:

> *Come unto me, O ye Gentiles, and I will show unto you the greater things, the knowledge which is hid up because of unbelief.*
>
> *Come unto me, O ye house of Israel, and it shall be made manifest unto you how great things the Father hath laid up for you, from the foundation of the world; and it hath not come unto you, because of unbelief.*

The call is unto us; the call is unto the Jews; the call is unto the Gentiles; the call is unto all men: Come, believe, obey, and prepare for the greater revelation that is promised!

> *Behold, when ye shall rend that veil of unbelief which doth cause you to remain in your awful state of wickedness, and hardness of heart, and blindness of mind, then shall the great and marvelous things which have been hid up from the foundation of the world from you—yea, when ye shall call upon the Father in my name, with a broken heart and a contrite spirit, then shall ye know that the Father hath remembered the covenant which he made unto your fathers, O house of Israel.*

O that we might rend the heavens and know all that the ancients knew! O that we might pierce the veil and see all that our forebears saw! O that we might see and know and feel what the elect among the Jaredites and among the Nephites saw and heard and felt! He who is no respecter of persons calls us with his own voice; if we will but attune our ears we shall hear his words!

> *And then shall my revelations which I have caused to be written by my servant John be unfolded in the eyes of all the people. Remember, when ye see these things, ye shall know that the time is at hand that they shall be made manifest in very deed.*
>
> *Therefore, when ye shall receive this record ye may know that the work of the Father has commenced upon all the face of the land.*

Soon the apocalypse of John shall appear before men in plainness, for the same truths are found on the sealed plates. And we know that the work of the Father has already commenced among men.

> *Therefore, repent all ye ends of the earth, and come unto me, and believe in my gospel, and be baptized in my name; for he that believeth and is baptized shall be saved; but he that believeth not shall be damned; and signs shall follow them that believe in my name.*
>
> *And blessed is he that is found faithful unto my name at the last day, for he shall be lifted up to dwell in the kingdom prepared for him from the foundation of the world. And behold it is I that hath spoken it. Amen.*

As we recount these Nephite teachings, and as we learn thereby why Jesus has withheld from the generality of men those great and wondrous things given to an elect few in days gone by, we know exactly why our New Testament friends did not record more of what happened on the mountain in Galilee. What there transpired was for those then present. Such truths as found their way into the biblical accounts were to prepare the way for the greater truths yet to come. The Lord is testing our faith. When we believe the Bible and the Book of Mormon and the other things he has revealed in our day, then will the greater things be manifest unto us.

For the moment, however, we can at least rejoice that

Jesus did minister so gloriously among our Nephite brethren. As Mormon sets forth, the Lord taught the people for three days and thereafter showed himself to them often, "and did break bread oft, and bless it, and give it unto them." We know that he performed healings of every sort among them and that he raised a man from the dead. We know that he taught their children and loosed their tongues so that "they did speak unto their fathers great and marvelous things, even greater than he had revealed unto the people," and that "even babes did open their mouths and utter marvelous things; and the things which they did utter were forbidden that there should not any man write them."

We know also that the disciples went forth preaching, baptizing, and conferring the Holy Ghost. "And many of them saw and heard unspeakable things, which are not lawful to be written." In that day "they had all things common among them, every man dealing justly, one with another." They were saints of God indeed and were worthy of their membership in Christ's Church.

THE HOLY GOSPEL

The gospel of God, . . .
Concerning his Son Jesus Christ our Lord,
which was made of the seed of David
according to the flesh;
And declared to be the Son of God with power,
according to the spirit of holiness,
by the resurrection from the dead:
By whom we have received grace
and apostleship. . . .
For it is the power of God unto salvation
to every one that believeth;
. . . For therein is the righteousness
of God revealed.
(Rom. 1:1-5, 16-17.)

What Is the Name of the True Church?

(3 Nephi 27:1-12)

Jesus, name of wondrous glory!

Jesus, blessed name, holy name, the name above all names!

Salvation is in Christ—how often have we said it! His is the only name given under heaven whereby man may be saved!

He "made himself of no reputation, and took upon him the form of a servant, and was made in the likeness of men: And being found in fashion as a man, he humbled himself, and became obedient unto death, even the death of the cross. Wherefore God also hath highly exalted him, and given him a name which is above every name: That at the name of Jesus every knee should bow, of things in heaven, and things in earth, and things under the earth; And that every tongue should confess that Jesus Christ is Lord, to the glory of God the Father." (Philip. 2:7-11.)

We are commanded to repent and call upon God in the name of the Son forevermore.

We take upon ourselves his name in the waters of baptism and again when we partake of the emblems of his suffering and death.

Whatsoever we ask the Father, in his name, that is right and good, in faith believing that we shall receive, it is granted.

In his name the lame walk, the blind see, the deaf hear. His name raises the dead, parts the Red Sea, quenches the violence of fire, closes the mouths of lions. His name rends the heavens, sends angels to earth, pours out revelation upon the faithful, sends visions to the seers.

In his name death is abolished and life and immortality reign. Through him the Father brings to pass the immortality and eternal life of man.

The gospel of God is also his gospel—his everlasting gospel—the plan of salvation revealed in all dispensations to all the holy prophets.

He is our King, our Lawgiver, our Lord, and our God.

How then and in what name shall his Church be called? Is there any name, other than his, that can identify the saving truths administered by the Church and kingdom of God on earth?

From our vantage point it is difficult to understand why there should have been any question about this either among the Nephites, among the early Christians in the Old

World, or among the early Latter-day Saints in this dispensation. It is *his* Church; all things are done in *his* name; and therefore the Church should bear *his* name. True, his names are many and his manners of manifesting himself to men are numerous; one name emphasizes one aspect of his mission and work, and another name singles out some other aspect of these. He is the Creator because he created, the Redeemer because he redeemed, the Savior because he saves, the Son of God because God is his Father. A knowledge of his many names helps us to envision the majesty and extent of his doings.

There might be a legitimate question as to which names to select, or as to what combination of them to use, but there can be no question as to whose name the Church should bear. There is no record that this question was resolved in perfection in the Old World—though we must assume it was; indeed, it could not have been otherwise—but the Nephite record does preserve both the reasoning and the inspiration underlying the name by which the Lord's people should be called.

Mormon's account tells us that "they who were baptized in the name of Jesus were called the church of Christ." (3 Ne. 26:21.) Then he recounts how their knowledge on this point came to them. The Twelve were out in their ministry, journeying, preaching, and baptizing in the name of Jesus. And as they "were gathered together and were united in mighty prayer and fasting," Jesus again appeared. "What will ye that I shall give unto you?" he asked. They said: "Lord, we will that thou wouldst tell us the name whereby we shall call this church; for there are disputations among the people concerning this matter." Jesus replied:

> *Verily, verily, I say unto you, why is it that the people should murmur and dispute because of this thing?*
>
> *Have they not read the scriptures, which say ye must take upon you the name of Christ, which is my*

name? For by this name shall ye be called at the last day; And whoso taketh upon him my name, and endureth to the end, the same shall be saved at the last day.

Men cannot be saved unless they take upon themselves the name of Christ. The saints are adopted into his family; they become his sons and his daughters; they are born again; they have a new Father; and they bear the name of their Father, who is Christ. "Take upon you the name of Christ," King Benjamin said to his people, "And it shall come to pass that whosoever doeth this shall be found at the right hand of God, for he shall know the name by which he is called; for he shall be called by the name of Christ."[1] And those who honor their new name and retain membership in their new family shall dwell with their Father in the heavenly home he has prepared for all those who bear his name. They shall be called by the name of Christ here and now and shall continue to bear that sacred name in eternity. And if all individuals who are baptized into his Church, and are thus born again, if they all bear the name of Christ, then the Church is the family of Christ, or in other words it is the Church of Christ.

Therefore, whatsoever ye shall do, ye shall do it in my name; therefore ye shall call the church in my name; and ye shall call upon the Father in my name that he will bless the church for my sake.

In every age from Adam to the present, and from this hour until time is no more, the family of Christ is the Church of Christ. We today—as with our fellow believers in days of old—are members of "the Church of Christ." (D&C 20:1.) And wherever the true Church is found, there also is revelation; and so the Lord reveals to his people the specific and formal words by which his Church shall be known at any given time. We were known as "the Church of Christ" from April 6, 1830, to April 26, 1838, when the Lord announced the formal title, "The Church of Jesus Christ of Latter-day Saints." (D&C 115:3-4.)

> *And how be it my church save it be called in my name? For if a church be called in Moses' name then it be Moses' church; or if it be called in the name of a man then it be the church of a man; but if it be called in my name then it is my church, if it so be that they are built upon my gospel.*

If a church is Moses' church, it can offer any rewards Moses is able to give; and salvation does not come by the law of Moses, but through the atonement of Him who was Moses' Lord. If a church is that of a man, it can offer any rewards that a man has power to create; and no man can resurrect himself or create a celestial realm where saved beings may dwell, for salvation is in Christ and in him only. If a church is the church of the devil, it can offer such rewards as Lucifer has prepared for those who walk in carnal paths and worship him, and his great reward is a place in the kingdom of the devil. And if a church pretends to be the Church of Christ and to bear that name, but is not so in reality and in fact, the name alone adds nothing. Thus it is written of those who shall go to a telestial kingdom: "For these are they who are of Paul, and of Apollos, and of Cephas. These are they who say they are some of one and some of another—some of Christ and some of John, and some of Moses, and some of Elias, and some of Esaias, and some of Isaiah, and some of Enoch; But [they] received not the gospel, neither the testimony of Jesus, neither the prophets, neither the everlasting covenant." (D&C 76:99-101.)

> *Verily I say unto you, that ye are built upon my gospel; therefore ye shall call whatsoever things ye do call, in my name; therefore if ye call upon the Father, for the church, if it be in my name the Father will hear you;*
>
> *And if it so be that the church is built upon my gospel then will the Father show forth his own works in it.*

The ultimate test of the truth and divinity of any church

is its fruits. Do men gather grapes of thorns or figs of thistles? Signs shall follow them that believe. Those who belong to the true Church—which is built upon the true gospel—increase in righteousness; they acquire the attributes of godliness; virtue and integrity and morality shine in their faces; they heal the sick and raise the dead, for they are the Lord's people.

> *But if it be not built upon my gospel, and is built upon the works of men, or upon the works of the devil, verily I say unto you they have joy in their works for a season, and by and by the end cometh, and they are hewn down and cast into the fire, from whence there is no return.*
>
> *For their works do follow them, for it is because of their works that they are hewn down; therefore remember the things that I have told you.*

Those portions of Jesus' words that Mormon was permitted to record, in the account destined to come forth in our day, contain the directions and counsel needed in today's world. Let the world, learning these things, take heed, lest those who are in the world cleave unto those churches which allow men to perform works of unrighteousness, which works lead not to heaven, but to hell.

What Is the Gospel of Salvation?

(3 Nephi 27:13-22)

How glorious is the gospel; how wondrous is the word; how marvelous are its messengers; how blessed is the Lord!

The gospel is the plan of salvation—the eternal plan of the Eternal Father. It is the laws and truths and powers by conformity to which the spirit children of the Father (Christ included) can advance and progress and become like him. It includes the creation and peopling of the earth, the testing processes of mortality, and death, the resurrection, and eternal judgment. It is founded and grounded upon the atoning sacrifice of Christ and is operative because he laid down his life for all men.

> *Behold I have given unto you my gospel, and this is the gospel which I have given unto you—that I came into the world to do the will of my Father, because my Father sent me.*

It is the gospel of God; the plan originated with the Father; it is his gospel. It concerns Jesus Christ our Lord because he was chosen to come into this world as the Son of God, to work out the infinite and eternal atonement, and to put into full force all of the terms and conditions of the Father's plan. The Son does the will of the Father; the Son did not devise a plan and suggest it to the Father; the Son obeyed and conformed and adopted. He espoused and championed the cause of his Father.

> *And my Father sent me that I might be lifted up upon the cross; and after that I had been lifted up upon the cross, that I might draw all men unto me, that as I have been lifted up by men even so should men be lifted up by the Father, to stand before me, to be judged of their works, whether they be good or whether they be evil—*
>
> *And for this cause have I been lifted up; therefore, according to the power of the Father I will draw all men unto me, that they may be judged according to their works.*

Jesus came to die—to die upon the cross. He came to ransom men from the temporal and spiritual death brought into the world by the fall of Adam; he came to abolish death, both temporal and spiritual; he came to bring immortality to all men and eternal life to all who believe and obey. Through his atoning sacrifice, begun in Gethsemane and completed on the cross, he has power to draw all men unto him, to bring them from the grave, to arraign them before his bar, to judge them according to their works. Annas engineered his death; Caiaphas issued the decree of the Sanhedrin that he was worthy of death; Pilate sent him to the cross; and the elders and chief priests rejoiced in his death. All these shall stand before his bar. He died for them and for all men; he died for the Jews and for the Gentiles; he is the Redeemer of the world.

> *And it shall come to pass, that whoso repenteth and is baptized in my name shall be filled; and if he endureth to the end, behold, him will I hold guiltless before my Father at that day when I shall stand to judge the world.*
>
> *And he that endureth not unto the end, the same is he that is also hewn down and cast into the fire, from whence they can no more return, because of the justice of the Father.*
>
> *And this is the word which he hath given unto the children of men. And for this cause he fulfilleth the words which he hath given, and he lieth not, but fulfilleth all his words.*

Repent, be baptized, be filled with the Holy Ghost, endure to the end, and be saved. Jesus shall judge the world. Those who have entered in at the gate of repentance and baptism, those who are members of the Church, those who have started out on the strait and narrow path leading to eternal life—all such who do not endure to the end shall be hewn down and cast into the fire. They shall be damned. Such is according to the justice of the Father; it is part of his eternal plan.

> *And no unclean thing can enter into his kingdom; therefore nothing entereth into his rest save it be those who have washed their garments in my blood, because of their faith, and the repentance of all their sins, and their faithfulness unto the end.*

Fallen men are carnal, sensual, and devilish by nature; they are unclean; they are worldly. To be saved they must become clean; God himself is clean and pure, and only those who become as he is can dwell in his presence. None others are saved. Of the saints John said: "If we walk in the light, as he is in the light, we have fellowship one with another, and the blood of Jesus Christ his Son cleanseth us from all sin." (1 Jn. 1:7.) This is the doctrine of blood atonement.

> *Now this is the commandment: Repent, all ye ends of the earth, and come unto me and be baptized in my name, that ye may be sanctified by the reception of the Holy Ghost, that ye may stand spotless before me at the last day.*

How can men become clean and pure? How can they be sanctified? What power can burn dross and evil out of a human soul as though by fire? To be saved men must be born again; they must be sanctified by the Spirit; they must receive the baptism of fire and of the Holy Ghost; they must become clean and spotless by obedience to law. The Holy Ghost is a sanctifier; no man can be saved unless he receives the gift of the Holy Ghost. Men humble themselves and are baptized by legal administrators sent of God so that, following the laying on of hands, they may receive the companionship of the Holy Spirit of God.

> *Verily, verily, I say unto you, this is my gospel; and ye know the things that ye must do in my church; for the works which ye have seen me do that shall ye also do; for that which ye have seen me do even that shall ye do; Therefore, if ye do these things blessed are ye, for ye shall be lifted up at the last day.*

This is my gospel! As Jesus began his ministry so he ended it: "preaching the gospel of the kingdom of God, And saying, The time is fulfilled, and the kingdom of God is at hand: repent ye, and believe the gospel." (Mark 1:14-15.) The gospel, the everlasting gospel, the gospel of God! Jesus calls it "my gospel," and so it is, for he has adopted it; and the Father—that all men might honor the Son even as they honor the Father—has called his own gospel after the name of his Son: *The Gospel of Jesus Christ.* His part in the eternal plan was to work out the infinite and eternal atonement. Man's part is to believe and obey; as far as any act on our part is concerned, the gospel is faith, repentance, baptism, the receipt of the Holy Ghost, and enduring in righteousness all our days. Such is the message Jesus gave to the Nephites; and such—we cannot doubt—is the same message, stated with the same clarity, that he gave to worthy persons in his own Galilee.

By Whom Shall Men Be Judged?
(3 Nephi 27:23-33)

How glorious is the Judge of all the earth! And—if we may paraphrase Isaiah's words about the messengers who preach us the gospel of peace—how beautiful upon the mountains are the feet of them who stand with Him to judge the nations of men. Yea, how glorious are the messengers who, first, preach the gospel, and who, then, sit in judgment at the Eternal Bar. And so Jesus continues:

> *Write the things which ye have seen and heard, save it be those which are forbidden. Write the works of this people, which shall be, even as hath been written, of that which hath been.*
>
> *For behold, out of the books which have been written, and which shall be written, shall this people be judged, for by them shall their works be known unto men.*
>
> *And behold, all things are written by the Father; therefore out of the books which shall be written shall the world be judged.*

When the judgment is set and the books are opened, all men will be judged out of that which is written in the books. They will be judged by the recitations there found of their own deeds. The tithing records will name the full tithe payers; the books on Sabbath observance will tell those who went to the house of prayer on the Lord's day to pay their devotions to the Most High. But, beyond this, the books will specify the standards that men should have met and tell the way they should have lived. Christians will be judged out of the Bible, for that holy book tells them how to live to please the Lord. People to whom the Book of Mormon comes will be judged out of it and will be accountable for rejecting the witness it bears of the Lord Jesus and of the prophet by whose instrumentality this latter-day witness of truth came forth. And, even beyond this, every man will be judged out of the book of his own life, out of the record of obedience or disobedience that is written in the flesh and sinews and soul of his own body. And however imperfect the records kept on earth may be, all things are written by the Father, into the very body and spirit of each person, so that none will be judged amiss or from an imperfect ledger.

> *And know ye that ye shall be judges of this people, according to the judgment which I shall give unto you, which shall be just. Therefore, what manner of men ought ye to be? Verily I say unto you, even as I am.*

Jesus is the Judge of all. The Father judgeth no man but hath committed all judgment unto the Son. But the Twelve in Jerusalem shall sit on twelve thrones judging the whole house of Israel; the Nephite Twelve, having been so judged, will in turn judge the Nephite nation; and we may well conclude that the hierarchy of judgment expands out to other legal administrators in the various dispensations. Just as the noble and great participated with the Great Creator in the creation, so those who are chosen and worthy shall participate with the Great Judge in the day of judgment. That the lesser judges must be as the Great Judge is self-evident.

> *And now I go unto the Father. And verily I say unto you, whatsoever things ye shall ask the Father in my name shall be given unto you.*
>
> *Therefore, ask, and ye shall receive; knock, and it shall be opened unto you; for he that asketh, receiveth; and unto him that knocketh, it shall be opened.*

How often it must be said: "Ask, and ye shall receive." How many things we might know if we would ask. How many doors might be opened if we would but knock. The Lord wants us to seek light and truth and revelation.

And now, behold, my joy is great, even unto fulness, because of you, and also this generation; yea, and even the Father rejoiceth, and also all the holy angels, because of you and this generation; for none of them are lost.

Behold, I would that ye should understand; for I mean them who are now alive of this generation; and none of them are lost; and in them I have fulness of joy.

When else was it ever thus? In Zion of Enoch, be it answered, for the saints of that day were translated and taken up into heaven; but there has been no other time of which we have knowledge when righteousness has prevailed among so many people to the degree here manifest. And what joy is found in heaven when the righteous so live as to merit eternal life.

But behold, it sorroweth me because of the fourth generation from this generation, for they are led away captive by him even as was the son of perdition; for they will sell me for silver and for gold, and for that which moth doth corrupt and which thieves can break through and steal. And in that day will I visit them, even in turning their works upon their own heads.

When men set their hearts upon the wealth of the world and the good things of the earth in preference to the things of the Spirit, they thereby sell Christ for silver and gold and lose their own souls. Hence Jesus said:

Enter ye in at the strait gate; for strait is the gate, and narrow is the way that leads to life, and few there be that find it; but wide is the gate, and broad the way which leads to death, and many there be that travel therein, until the night cometh, wherein no man can work.

Again the message is primarily for us. Life or death lies before us all; obedience brings life, rebellion, death; and for the rebellious, those who have rejected the gospel in this life, the night of darkness holds no hope of salvation.

NOTE

1. Mosiah 5:7-14. To us in this day the Lord has said: "Take upon you the name of Christ, and speak the truth in soberness. And as many as repent and are baptized in my name, which is Jesus Christ, and endure to the end, the same shall be saved. Behold, Jesus Christ is the name which is given of the Father, and there is none other name given whereby men can be saved; Wherefore, all men must take upon them the name which is given of the Father, for in that name shall they be called at the last day; Wherefore, if they know not the name by which they are called, they cannot have place in the kingdom of my Father." (D&C 18:21-25.)

THE THREE NEPHITES

If I will that he tarry till I come,
what is that to thee?
(John 21:22.)
Thou shalt tarry until I come in my glory,
and shalt prophesy before nations,
kindreds, tongues and people.
(D&C 7:3.)

They Shall Never Taste of Death

(3 Nephi 28:1-12)

It appearing that the allotted time of his Nephite ministry is over, Jesus prepares to return to his Father. Before doing so, he asks the Twelve: "What is it that ye desire of me, after that I am gone to the Father?" Nine of them reply: "We desire that after we have lived unto the age of man, that our ministry, wherein thou hast called us, may have an end, that we may speedily come unto thee in thy kingdom." We conclude from this that they desired to remain in paradise for but a short time, after which they would come forth in immortal glory and sit down with Abraham, Isaac, and Jacob in the kingdom of God, to go no more out. Jesus grants their request. "Blessed are ye because ye desired this thing of me," he said, "therefore, after that ye are seventy and two years old ye shall come unto me in my kingdom; and with me ye shall find rest."

Jesus then turns to the other three. "What will ye that I should do unto you, when I am gone unto the Father?" he asks. Though they are spiritual giants and feel themselves on intimate terms with the Lord, they sorrow in their hearts and dare not give vocal expression to their desires. "Behold, I know your thoughts," Jesus says, "and ye have desired the thing which John, my beloved, who was with me in my ministry, before that I was lifted up by the Jews, desired of me." These three Nephite disciples, because of their desires, had in store for themselves such blessings as we have no way of comprehending, nor has the Lord seen fit to do more than reveal a sliver of what was to be in their future lives.

> *Therefore, more blessed are ye, for ye shall never taste of death; but ye shall live to behold all the doings of the Father unto the children of men, even until all things shall be fulfilled according to the will of the Father, when I shall come in my glory with the powers of heaven.*

Eternal life—no, not that glorious immortality in which resurrected beings become like their God, but to live forever on earth, as mortals, without disease or sorrow, having health and vigor, preaching the gospel and being witnesses to and participants in all that was to be! What a tempting prospect. How many faithful souls would rejoice in such a ministerial assignment. And wonder of wonders, for them it was to be.

> *And ye shall never endure the pains of death; but when I shall come in my glory ye shall be changed in the twinkling of an eye from mortality to immortality; and then shall ye be blessed in the kingdom of my Father.*

Will translated beings ever die? Remember John's enigmatic words relative to his own translation: "Then went this saying abroad among the brethren, that that disciple should not die: yet Jesus said not unto him, He shall not die; but, If I will that he tarry till I come, what is that to thee?" (John 21:23.) Note the distinction between avoiding death as such and living till the Lord comes. Then note that Jesus promises the Three Nephites, not that they shall not die, but that they "shall never taste of death" and shall not "endure the pains of death." Again it is an enigmatic declaration with a hidden meaning. There is a distinction between death as we know it and tasting of death or enduring the pains of death. As a matter of doctrine, death is universal; every mortal thing, whether plant or animal or man, shall surely die. Jacob said: "Death hath passed upon all men, to fulfil the merciful plan of the great Creator." (2 Ne. 9:6.) There are no exceptions, not even among translated beings. Paul said: "As in Adam all die, even so in Christ shall all be made alive." (1 Cor. 15:22.) Again the dominion of death over all is acclaimed. But the Lord says of *all* his saints, not that they will not die, but that "those that die in me shall not taste of death, for it shall be sweet unto them; And they that die not in me, wo unto them, for their death is bitter." (D&C 42:46-47.) The distinction is between dying as such and tasting of death itself. Again the Lord says: "He that liveth when the Lord shall come, and hath kept the faith, blessed is he; nevertheless, it is appointed to him to die at the age of man. Wherefore, children shall grow up until they become old; old men shall die; but they shall not sleep in the dust, but they shall be changed in the twinkling of an eye." (D&C 63:50-51.) Thus, this change from mortality to immortality, though almost instantaneous, is both a death and a resurrection. Thus, translated beings do not suffer death as we normally define it, meaning the separation of body and spirit; nor do they receive a resurrection as we ordinarily describe it, meaning that the body rises from the dust and the spirit enters again into its fleshly home. But they do pass through death and are changed from mortality to immortality, in the eternal sense, and they thus both die and are resurrected in the eternal sense.

This, we might add, is why Paul wrote: "Behold, I shew you a mystery; We shall not all sleep, but we shall all be changed, In a moment, in the twinkling of an eye, at the last trump: for the trumpet shall sound, and the dead shall be raised incorruptible, and we shall be changed." (1 Cor. 15:51-52.)

> *And again, ye shall not have pain while ye shall dwell in the flesh, neither sorrow save it be for the sins of the world; and all this will I do because of the thing which ye have desired of me, for ye have desired that ye might bring the souls of men unto me, while the world shall stand.*

During the Millennium all men will be translated, as it were; in that day "there shall be no sorrow because there is no death. In that day an infant shall not die until he is old; and his life shall be as the age of a tree; And when he dies he shall not sleep, that is to say in the earth, but shall be changed in the twinkling of an eye, and shall be caught up, and his rest shall be glorious." (D&C 101:29-31.)

> *And for this cause ye shall have fulness of joy; and ye shall sit down in the kingdom of my Father; yea, your joy shall be full, even as the Father hath given me fulness of joy; and ye shall be even as I am, and I am even as the Father; and the Father and I are one;*
>
> *And the Holy Ghost beareth record of the Father and me; and the Father giveth the Holy Ghost unto the children of men, because of me.*

These words—the last recorded words spoken by Jesus in his Nephite ministry—contain the greatest doctrinal concept ever revealed. They are the Book of Mormon pronouncement that as God now is, man may become; they are the Book of Mormon proclamation that those who gain eternal life inherit, receive, and possess all that the Father hath; they are the Book of Mormon announcement that man—in glorious exaltation—becomes one with the Father, Son, and Holy Ghost.

And as we hear such words as these fall from the lips of the Son of God, there is no better place to insert our witness of the truth and divinity of that volume of holy scripture—the Book of Mormon—which contains the account of Jesus' Nephite ministry. In words of soberness we say: No man having the Spirit of the Lord as his guide can read the Book of Mormon account without knowing in the depths of his soul that it came from God and is verily true. No such man can read it and think that either Joseph Smith or any man wrote the account of himself. It came from God by the power of the Holy Ghost, and it is the mind and will and voice of the Lord to all men. And because it came forth through the instrumentality of Joseph Smith, it follows that the book itself, being true, is a witness, beyond any peradventure of doubt, that Joseph Smith was called of God.

But back to our Nephite setting. After Jesus had spoken the wondrous words which burn with eternal conviction in our heart, he touched the nine apostles, but not the three, with his finger, "and then he departed."

Their Transfiguration and Ministry

(3 Nephi 28:13-40)

Mortal man—shackled as it were in a tabernacle of clay; imprisoned on a single planet that is itself but a speck of dust in an endless universe; bound by time and space, and living for only a few brief moments—mortal man, a spirit son of God, dwells in the depths of ignorance, away from his Father, without a knowledge of eternal things. We are born, we live, we die, and in the process we are privileged—some of us—to receive a few little glimmerings of eternal truth by revelation. And there are few among us, even in sober moments, who ponder the wonders of eternity and seek to know what lies beyond the ken of humankind. What of creation itself, of worlds without number, all inhabited, all crowned with an infinite variety of life? How did Gods begin to be, and whence came the order and system in a universe whose outer limits we shall never see? How little we know of preexistence, both ours and that of all forms of life; or of death and the world of waiting spirits; or of the resurrection which raises sleeping dust to glorious life. What are Abraham, Isaac, and Jacob doing today? How can Moroni hie to Kolob in the twinkling of an eye? Where are Annas and Caiaphas and Pilate, and what kind of a life are they living? How little we know about creation, about redemption, about immortal glory.

And yet there are those—a favored few—who break the time-bound bands, who see beyond the veil, who come to know the things of eternity. Portions of what they learn they are permitted to reveal to the rest of us. Enoch, after his translation, was high and lifted up, even in the bosom of the Father and the Son, where he saw and heard things of infinite wonder and glory, some few of which are recorded in the Book of Moses. Moriancumer saw and beheld and knew and recorded such glorious things that they were withheld from the children of men until after the resurrection of Christ, and even then they were shown only to the Nephites, and that for a brief season. Since then they have been sealed up, and, as we suppose, they shall not be manifest again until after the Second Coming of the Son of Man. John the Revelator saw the wonders of eternity, some few of which he was permitted to record, in figures and types and shadows, in the Book of Revelation. Others of the prophets—and for aught we know their number may be many—have seen and heard and felt and known far more than has come to us in any of our scriptures. Among these are the Three Nephite Disciples.

We do not know the great things revealed to the chosen three, nor could we comprehend them if they were recorded in our holy books. Milk must precede meat, and those who have yet to learn the basics of arithmetic can scarcely comprehend the mysteries of calculus. Hence, as Alma said: "It is given unto many to know the mysteries of God; nevertheless they are laid under a strict command that they shall not impart only according to the portion of his word which he doth grant unto the children of men, according to the heed and diligence which they give unto him." (Alma 12:9.) Of the experience of the Three Nephites, Mormon wrote: "And behold, the heavens were opened, and they were caught up into heaven, and saw and heard unspeakable things. And it was forbidden them that they should utter; neither was it given unto them power that they could utter the things which they saw and heard; And whether they were in the body or out of the body, they could not tell; for it did seem unto them like a transfiguration of them, that they were changed from this body of flesh into an immortal state, that they could behold the things of God."

It was with them as with Paul and Joseph Smith and others of the prophets. There are no words that can convey the spiritual feelings or the truths learned by those who receive these greater manifestations of divine understanding. Speaking of himself, Paul says he was "caught up to the third heaven," which is the celestial kingdom—"whether in the body, or out of the body, I cannot tell: God knoweth," he says—and that he "heard unspeakable words, which it is not lawful for a man to utter." (2 Cor. 12:1-4.) After recording the vision of the degrees of glory, Joseph Smith spoke similarly of other things that he had seen and heard while enwrapped in the heavenly manifestation then vouchsafed to him.[1]

In recording that the Three Disciples were caught up into heaven, Mormon first wrote: "Whether they were mortal or immortal, from the day of their transfiguration, I know not." After pondering and praying about their status, however, he said: "Since I wrote, I have inquired of the Lord, and he hath made it manifest unto me that there must needs be a change wrought upon their bodies, or else it needs be that they must taste of death; Therefore, that they might not taste of death there was a change wrought upon their bodies, that they might not suffer pain nor sorrow save it were for the sins of the world. Now this change was not equal to that which shall take place at the last day; but there was a change wrought upon them, insomuch that Satan could have no power over them, that he could not tempt them; and they were sanctified in the flesh, that they were holy, and that the powers of the earth could not hold them. And in this state they were to remain until the judgment day of Christ; and at that day they were to receive a greater change, and to be received into the kingdom of the Father to go no more out, but to dwell with God eternally in the heavens." These words apply equally to John the Beloved, whose mission and ministry is the same as that of his Nephite brethren.

As to their ministry among those of that generation, they went forth preaching the gospel, baptizing, conferring the Holy Ghost, and building up the Church of Christ, until all of that generation were blessed as Jesus had promised.

As to their later ministry among the Nephites, though they continued to serve with unwearying diligence, opposition arose. They were cast into prisons, which were rent at their word, and they went forth free. They were cast into pits of the earth and freed by the power of God. "And thrice they were cast into a furnace and received no harm. And twice were they cast into a den of wild beasts; and behold they did play with the beasts as a child with a suckling lamb, and received no harm." Finally, in the days of Mormon, in about A.D. 322, the Lord took them from among the people (Morm. 1:13), and in the year A.D. 401, Moroni records that, though their whereabouts was unknown, they had ministered unto him and his father (Morm. 8:10-11).

As to their continuing mortal ministry, we know only that they shall be among the Jews, and among the Gentiles, and among "all the scattered tribes of Israel," and among "all nations, kindreds, tongues and people, and shall bring out of them unto Jesus many souls." And this also applies to John the Beloved. "And they are as the angels of God, and if they shall pray unto the Father in the name of Jesus they can show themselves unto whatsoever man it seemeth them good. Therefore, great and marvelous works shall be wrought by them, before the great and coming day when all people must surely stand before the judgment-seat of Christ; Yea even among the Gentiles shall there be a great and marvelous work wrought by them, before that judgment day."

At this point in his writing, Mormon, as moved upon by the Holy Ghost, gives us this word from the Lord:

> *And wo be unto him that will not hearken unto the words of Jesus, and also to them whom he hath chosen and sent among them; for whoso receiveth not the words of Jesus and the words of those whom he hath sent receiveth not him; and therefore he will not receive them at the last day;*
>
> *And it would be better for them if they had not been born. For do ye suppose that ye can get rid of the justice of an offended God, who hath been trampled under feet of men, that thereby salvation might come?*

Jesus and his servants are one; to believe in those whom he hath sent is to believe in him, and to reject his messengers is to reject him.

Nephite, Jewish, and Gentile Apostasy

(3 Nephi 29, 30; 4 Nephi; Mormon 1 to 9; Moroni 1 to 10)

We cannot leave our study of the life of him whose gospel is the power that saves without recording what happened to the saving truths he gave to men on both continents. Jesus restored the gospel in the Old World and set up his earthly kingdom among men. In the New World he added to the gospel truths they already had, perfected his kingdom, and shed forth upon them such rays of heavenly light as have seldom pierced the gloom and darkness of earth. In the Old World the true Church was set up in the midst of worldly forces, and after a century or so the world prevailed, the saints became sinners, and the churches of men and of devils replaced the true Church of Christ. Among the Nephites all the people were converted, and for 167 or so years, until A.D. 201, perfect peace and righteousness prevailed. Then apostasy began; false churches sprang up; wickedness prevailed; wars swept the land; and except for a few saints, the true Church was overcome by the world. By A.D. 421 Satan's triumph was complete and the whole Nephite civilization had been destroyed, with Moroni only remaining true to the faith.

We can scarcely imagine the gospel blessings that first prevailed among the Nephites. Contentions and disputations ceased; every man dealt justly with his brother; they had all things common among them; there were no rich nor poor; none were in bondage; all were free and partook of the heavenly gift. "And there were great and marvelous works wrought by the disciples of Jesus, insomuch that they did heal the sick, and raise the dead, and cause the lame to walk, and the blind to receive their sight, and the deaf to hear; and all manner of miracles did they work among the children of men." Of these American saints Mormon said: "There was no contention in the land, because of the love of God which did dwell in the hearts of the people. And there were no envyings, nor strifes, nor tumults, nor whoredoms, nor lyings, nor murders, nor any manner of lasciviousness; and surely there could not be a happier people among all the people who had been created by the hand of God. There were no robbers, nor murderers, neither were there Lamanites, nor any manner of -ites; but they were in one, the children of Christ, and heirs to the kingdom of God. And how blessed were they! For the Lord did bless them in all their doings."

But beginning in the 201st year some were lifted up in pride; they began to wear costly apparel; the people no longer had all things in common; society was divided into classes; and men "began to build up churches unto themselves to get gain, and began to deny the true church of Christ." Soon "there were many churches which professed to know the Christ, and yet they did deny the more parts of his gospel, insomuch that they did receive all manner of wickedness, and did administer that which was sacred unto him to whom it had been forbidden because of unworthiness." And "there was another church which denied the Christ; and they did persecute the true church of Christ, because of their humility and their belief in Christ; and they did despise them because of the many miracles which were wrought among them." These were the days when the Three Disciples were persecuted and imprisoned and cast into fiery furnaces.

By the day of Mormon, miracles and healings had ceased; "there were no gifts from the Lord, and the Holy Ghost did not come upon any, because of their wickedness and unbelief." Once again the Gadianton robbers infested the land, and "there were sorceries, and witchcrafts, and magics; and the power of the evil one was wrought upon all the face of the land." There was war, and blood, and carnage, and revolution everywhere; women and children were sacrificed to idols, and the judgments of God rested upon the land. "It is impossible for the tongue to describe," Mormon said, "or for man to write a perfect description of the horrible scene of the blood and carnage which was among the people, both of the Nephites and of the Lamanites; and every heart was hardened, so that they delighted in the shedding of blood continually. And there never had been so great wickedness among all the children of Lehi, nor even among all the house of Israel, according to the words of the Lord, as was among this people." Those whose fathers had been more righteous and who had received greater blessings than any in all Israel had now sunk to greater wickedness and were more severely cursed than any of the chosen seed had ever been.

Our inspired records let us speak thus—with accuracy

and verity—of what transpired in the Americas. In principle it was the same among the Jews and Gentiles of the Old World. Grievous wolves attacked the flock; lewd and evil men led them astray; pride welled up in the hearts of many; and shortly after the death of the apostles the apostasy was complete. As in the New World "there were many churches which professed to know the Christ, and yet they did deny the more parts of his gospel." All manner of wickedness prevailed, and sacred ordinances were administered to those who were unworthy. Gifts and miracles ceased, and darkness covered the earth. Wars and anarchy and desolation have been poured out upon all nations ever since, and it will continue so to be until the great and dreadful day of the Lord comes.

In this setting we return to the writings of Mormon. He refers to the coming forth of the Book of Mormon as a sign "that the covenant which the Father hath made with the children of Israel, concerning their restoration to the lands of their inheritance, is already beginning to be fulfilled." Mormon is directing his words to us in this day, to the scattered remnants of Israel, and to the Gentile nations. When the Book of Mormon comes forth, "Ye may know that the words of the Lord, which have been spoken by the holy prophets, shall all be fulfilled," he says, "and ye need not say that the Lord delays his coming unto the children of Israel."

And further: "Ye need not imagine in your hearts that the words which have been spoken are vain, for behold, the Lord will remember his covenant which he hath made unto his people of the house of Israel. And when ye shall see these sayings coming forth among you, then ye need not any longer spurn at the doings of the Lord, for the sword of his justice is in his right hand; and behold, at that day, if he shall spurn at his doings he will cause that it shall soon overtake you." Then come these superlative words of power and inspiration:

Wo unto him that spurneth at the doings of the Lord; yea, wo unto him that shall deny the Christ and his works!

Yea, wo unto him that shall deny the revelations of the Lord, and that shall say the Lord no longer worketh by revelation, or by prophecy, or by gifts, or by tongues, or by healings, or by the power of the Holy Ghost!

Yea, and wo unto him that shall say at that day, to get gain, that there can be no miracle wrought by Jesus Christ; for he that doeth this shall become like unto the son of perdition, for whom there was no mercy, according to the word of Christ!

Next he delivers a message as to what our attitude should be toward the Jews. "Yea, and ye need not any longer hiss, nor spurn, nor make game of the Jews, nor any of the remnant of the house of Israel; for behold, the Lord remembereth his covenant unto them, and he will do unto them according to that which he hath sworn. Therefore ye need not suppose that ye can turn the right hand of the Lord unto the left, that he may not execute judgment unto the fulfilling of the covenant which he hath made unto the house of Israel."

Our great and good friend, in fine, issues a mighty proclamation to the Gentiles: "Hearken, O ye Gentiles," he says, "and hear the words of Jesus Christ, the Son of the living God, which he hath commanded me that I should speak concerning you, for, behold he commandeth me that I should write, saying":

Turn, all ye Gentiles, from your wicked ways; and repent of your evil doings, of your lyings and deceivings, and of your whoredoms, and of your abominations, and your idolatries, and of your murders, and your priestcrafts, and your envyings, and your strifes, and from all your wickedness and abominations, and come unto me, and be baptized in my name, that ye may receive a remission of your sins, and be filled with the Holy Ghost, that ye may be numbered with my people who are of the house of Israel.

NOTE

1. D&C 76:114-119. In beginning the account of the vision of his brother Alvin in the celestial kingdom, the Prophet wrote: "The heavens were opened upon us, and I beheld the celestial kingdom of God, and the glory thereof, whether in the body or out I cannot tell." (D&C 137:1.)

Chapter 120

THE ASCENSION

It is finished. (John 19:30.)
I ascend unto my Father, and your Father;
and to my God, and your God.
(John 20:17.)
For I know that my redeemer liveth,
and that he shall stand at the latter day
upon the earth: And though
after my skin worms destroy this body,
yet in my flesh shall I see God:
Whom I shall see for myself,
and mine eyes shall behold, and not another;
though my reins be consumed within me.
(Job 19:25-27.)

Jesus Returns to His Father

(Acts 1:1-14; Mark 16:19-20; Luke 24:50-53)

The day has arrived; the hour is at hand; the Lord Jesus who descended from the courts of glory is about to return to the presence of the Father forever. He who "made himself of no reputation, and took upon him the form of a servant, and was made in the likeness of men" is about to be exalted above all thrones and principalities and to sit down "on the right hand of the Majesty on high." He who was "found in fashion as a man," who "humbled himself, and became obedient unto death, even the death of the cross," is about to ascend the throne of eternal power and wear a kingly crown. He who, "being in the form of God, thought it not robbery to be equal with God," is about to be given a name above all names. (Philip. 2:5-11; Heb. 1:3.)

"It is finished." His mortal work is done; the atonement hath been wrought; let all men praise his holy name forever. "Worthy is the Lamb that was slain to receive power, and riches, and wisdom, and strength, and honour, and glory, and blessing." (Rev. 5:12.)

"I have finished the work which thou gavest me to do!" He has glorified the name of the Father on earth. His High Priestly Prayer is about to be answered: "And now, O Father, glorify thou me with thine own self with the glory which I had with thee before the world was." (John 17:4-5.)

He is going to his Father; they are one; let both their holy names be in every worshipping heart and on every praising lip forever. "Blessing, and honour, and glory, and power, be unto him that sitteth upon the throne, and unto the Lamb for ever and ever." (Rev. 5:13.)

What work has he done; what wonders hath he wrought; what achievements now are his? By the grace of God—by the condescension, mercy, and love of the Father—he came to earth, because his Father sent him, to die upon the cross for the sins of the world. By his own goodness and grace—by the condescension, mercy, and love of the Son—he stepped down from the throne of eternal power, to be like man almost, to save men from their sins. He came as the Light of the World to lead all men to salvation.

> He marked the path and led the way,
> And every point defines
> To light and life and endless day
> Where God's full presence shines.
> —*Hymns,* no. 68

And by him salvation comes. He paid the price for Adam's fall; he ransomed men from death and hell; he gave his life that man might live.

For us the blood of Christ was shed,
For us on Calvary's cross he bled,
And thus dispelled the awful gloom
That else were this creation's doom.

The law was broken; Jesus died
That justice might be satisfied,
That man might not remain a slave
Of death, of hell, or of the grave,

But rise triumphant from the tomb,
And in eternal splendor bloom,
Freed from the power of death and pain,
With Christ, the Lord, to rule and reign.
—*Hymns,* no. 217

And now his work is done. A God has died; a God has risen; a God ascends to his Father.

The rising Lord forsook the tomb.
In vain the tomb forbade him rise;
Cherubic legions guard him home,
And shout him welcome to the skies.
—*Hymns,* no. 263

From the Sunday of his rising to the holy day of his ascension was forty days, and from the Friday of his crucifixion to the day of Pentecost was fifty days. Thus he died on a Friday; he rose on a Sunday (which was three days as the Jews counted time); he ministered among his disciples, from time to time, for forty days; he then ascended to his Father; and on the day of Pentecost they received the gift of the Holy Ghost. "They were all with one accord in one place," on the day of Pentecost. "And suddenly there came a sound from heaven as of a rushing mighty wind, and it filled all the house where they were sitting." They could have been in that same memorable upper room where so many of the wonders of eternity had been poured out upon them.[1] "And there appeared unto them cloven tongues like as of fire, and it sat upon each of them." We shall note shortly the names and identities of those who in all probability were present, and who received this divine outpouring of grace from on high. "And they were all filled with the Holy Ghost, and began to speak with other tongues, as the Spirit gave them utterance."

When word of this Pentecostal outpouring of heavenly fire was "noised abroad," a great "multitude came together." Among them were "Jews, devout men, out of every nation under heaven." And they "were confounded, because that every man heard them speak in his own language. And they were all amazed and marvelled, saying one to another, Behold, are not all these which speak Galileans? And how hear we every man in our own tongue, wherein we were born?" Then Peter, the chief disciple, preached a mighty sermon and bore a powerful testimony of Jesus his Lord. "Let all the house of Israel know assuredly," he said by way of climax, "that God hath made that same Jesus, whom ye have crucified, both Lord and Christ."

Having seen the miracle, having heard the sermon, and having felt the power of the Spirit, as Luke tells us, "they were pricked in their heart, and said unto Peter and to the rest of the apostles, Men and brethren, what shall we do?" Faith was beginning to sprout in their hearts. They were believers of the Eternal Word; the Holy Ghost changes the hearts of men. Peter said:

> *Repent, and be baptized every one of you in the name of Jesus Christ for the remission of sins, and ye shall receive the gift of the Holy Ghost. For the promise is unto you, and to your children, and to all that are afar off, even as many as the Lord our God shall call.*

"And with many other words did he testify and exhort, saying, Save yourselves from this untoward generation.

Then they that gladly received his word were baptized: and the same day there were added unto them about three thousand souls. And they continued stedfastly in the apostles' doctrine and fellowship, and in breaking of bread, and in prayers. And fear came upon every soul: and many wonders and signs were done by the apostles. And all that believed were together, and had all things common; And sold their possessions and goods, and parted them to all men, as every man had need. And they, continuing daily with one accord in the temple, and breaking bread from house to house, did eat their meat with gladness and singleness of heart, Praising God, and having favour with all the people. And the Lord added to the church daily such as should be saved." (Acts 2:1-47.) And thus, by the power of the Holy Ghost, the work went forth among the Jews, even as it would among the Nephites in due course.

But let us return to the Ascension. As Luke tells us, the Risen Lord "shewed himself alive after his passion by many infallible proofs, being seen of them forty days, and speaking of the things pertaining to the kingdom of God." We have considered such of these infallible proofs of the resurrection as are found in holy writ. And there is no more infallible proof than the testimony of one who has seen with his eyes and felt with his hands and known by the power of the Spirit that the Risen One now has a body of flesh and bones. How else can the resurrection be proved except by testimony?

Thus Jesus was with them "until the day in which he was taken up, after that he through the Holy Ghost had given commandments unto the apostles whom he had chosen." These commandments included one that they "should not depart from Jerusalem, but wait for the promise of the Father, which, saith he, ye have heard of me. For John truly baptized with water; but ye shall be baptized with the Holy Ghost not many days hence." And so, having kept their appointment on the mountain in Galilee, having been taught all that it was expedient for them to know at that time, and having been commanded and commissioned to go into all the world, to preach the gospel, and to build up the kingdom, they are now back in Jerusalem awaiting the receipt of the gift of the Holy Ghost.

They are assembled together. Jesus leads them out toward Bethany. It is their last walk with him, reminiscent of all the other times they have traversed this same course. They arrive at the Mount of Olives. He is about to ascend, but they are still troubled with one thing. They ask: "Lord, wilt thou at this time restore again the kingdom to Israel?"

What words are these? *Restore again the kingdom to Israel!* Are these the Nephite Twelve who are speaking? Reversing the chronology—that a more cohesive account of the life of our Lord might be given—we have already considered *in extenso* Jesus' discussion about the restoration of the kingdom to his people in the latter days. Surely the kingdom will be restored as of old, for so all the prophets have foretold. Indeed, the ponderings of their hearts, the desires of their souls, and their continuing petitions to the Majesty on High—all sought for the restoration of Israel. And further: All the prophets knew that the children of the prophets—the children of the covenant—should again receive the ancient promise of eternal life and the assurance that in them and in their seed all generations should be blessed. Jehovah's word to Abraham would not return unto him void. And so we have seen that the sign letting all men know when these things shall be is the coming forth of the Book of Mormon. How plainly and how repetitively it was said among the Nephites.

Now the apostles in Jerusalem desire to learn the same thing. But the Old World witnesses—whose lack of faith had kept them from knowing of their Nephite brethren—are not to learn the sign, at least not in its plainness and perfection. It is true that Peter and the others will hereafter speak of the restoration of all things (including the kingdom to Israel); that is, they will talk of a universal apostasy and of the setting up anew of God's kingdom on earth in the latter days—but they shall not, as mortals, learn the account with that fulness which was given to the "other sheep." And so Jesus said:

> *It is not for you to know the times or the seasons, which the Father hath put in his own power.*
>
> *But ye shall receive power, after that the Holy Ghost is come upon you: and ye shall be witnesses unto me both in Jerusalem, and in all Judea, and in Samaria, and unto the uttermost part of the earth.*

That is, in a day subsequent to New Testament times, the Lord will perform a mighty work with Israel. He will give them their kingdom as of old; they will have revelation and visions and prophets; the heavens will be opened again; the covenants and promises made to the ancients will be fulfilled; Israel will be gathered into all their lands of promise; Zion shall be built up again; a New Jerusalem shall rise; the waste places of the Old Jerusalem shall be reclaimed; the children of the prophets and the children of the covenant will glory in the ancient promises given anew in their times; and the Lord—the God of Israel—will reign gloriously among his saints. But this is not to be the work of the apostles of that day; other apostles must arise to do the work of latter days. Those who were with him then are to be witnesses of his name unto the uttermost parts of the earth. Let them preach to those then living; their successors in interest and in power and in faith shall carry on the work of latter days when the times and the seasons shall arrive.

"And when he had spoken these things, while they beheld"—and while with uplifted hands he blessed them—"he was taken up; and a cloud received him out of their sight. And while they looked stedfastly toward heaven as he went up, behold, two men stood by them in white apparel; Which also said,"

> *Ye men of Galilee, why stand ye gazing up into heaven? this same Jesus, which is taken up from you*

into heaven, shall so come in like manner as ye have seen him go into heaven.

These apostles, all of whom were Galileans (Judas only, the one traitor among them, was a Judean), were now left to do the work appointed for them. After Pentecost, with the Holy Spirit of God as their monitor, how gloriously they succeeded! But we cannot leave this scene on Olivet without testifying that Jesus' ascension was literal and personal and real. A Man having a body of flesh and bones—a Personal Being who walked and talked and ate with his disciples—ascended bodily into heaven. "The Father has a body of flesh and bones as tangible as man's; the Son also." (D&C 130:22.) And Jesus our Lord has just "ascended into heaven, to sit down on the right hand of the Father, to reign with almighty power according to the will of the Father." (D&C 20:24.) And as he went up, so is he now; and as he is now, so will he be when he comes again to reign on earth a thousand years; and as he will be during the Millennium, so will he remain to all eternity: a glorified, perfected, exalted Man—the Son of Man of Holiness, who is his Father. Praise ye the Lord.

After the Ascension, as Luke writes in his Gospel account, "They worshipped him, and returned to Jerusalem with great joy: And were continually in the temple, praising and blessing God." Quite naturally they would go to the temple, the holiest spot known to them, to continue their worship. The break with the past would come by degrees. In his account in Acts, Luke says: "Then returned they unto Jerusalem from the mount called Olivet, which is from Jerusalem a sabbath day's journey. And when they were come in, they went up into an upper room, where abode both Peter, and James, and John, and Andrew, Philip, and Thomas, Bartholomew, and Matthew, James the son of Alpheus, and Simon Zelotes, and Judas the brother of James. These all continued with one accord in prayer and supplication, with the women, and Mary the mother of Jesus, and with his brethren."

We have speculated, in connection with the Last Supper, that the upper room was in the home of the father of John Mark and have given our reasons therefor. All of the Eleven have come together and are living at the same place as they await the Pentecostal outpouring of the Spirit that will soon come upon them. What is more natural than that they should come to this same large and spacious building? We suppose that it was the same upper room where the saints were assembled at meat when Jesus, following the walk on the Emmaus Road, appeared and invited them to handle and feel and learn that he had a body of flesh and bones. Still further, on the day of Pentecost they—and we assume this means the apostles and others—were in a "house" when the Spirit first fell upon them. Again we suggest that this may have been the upper room of note and fame. And when Peter standing in the midst of a hundred and twenty of them arranged for the selection of a successor to Judas, we suppose it was in the same meeting place. We must keep in mind also that there were believers other than the apostles present on all these sacred occasions, including that Pentecostal day when cloven tongues of fire rested upon them. "Mary the mother of Jesus," and her other children, "his brethren," and those called only "the women," meaning Mary Magdalene and the others, are named as being among the saints on these memorable occasions. Thc new kingdom was starting out, not as a church for apostles only, but as the New Sheepfold for all believers, including the more than three thousand converts who were baptized on the day of Pentecost.

Jesus Is the Son of God

(John 20:30-31; 21:24-25)

Jesus hath ascended into heaven to sit down on the right hand of the Majesty on high. "When he ascended up on high," Paul says, "he led captivity captive," meaning that he broke the bands of death which up to then held all men captive, and he "gave gifts unto men." (Eph. 4:8-16.) Glorious doctrine this! The effects of Jesus' resurrection pass upon all men so that all shall rise from the dead, all shall become immortal, all shall live forever having bodies of flesh and bones. And also, he "gave gifts unto men." What gifts? Paul names apostles, prophets, evangelists, pastors, and teachers (those who teach the gospel). We add elders, seventies, and high priests, deacons, teachers (holders of the ordained office), priests, and bishops, and all the officers of the kingdom of God on earth. Apostles, prophets, and seventies, in particular, and all officers in general, are appointed to be witnesses of the name of Christ, to bear record of his divine Sonship, and to teach his gospel to the world.

Our revelations in naming the gifts of the Spirit list as the first the gift of prophecy, which gift, by definition, is to have the testimony of Jesus, "for the testimony of Jesus is the spirit of prophecy." (Rev. 19:10.) "To some it is given by the Holy Ghost," the revealed word says, "to know that Jesus Christ is the Son of God, and that he was crucified for the sins of the world." Then the inspired word adds: "To others it is given to believe on their words, that they also might have eternal life if they continue faithful." (D&C 46:13-14.)

We have, thus, two gifts named as coming from the Ascended One. The first is to know by personal revelation, given of God by the power of the Holy Ghost, that Jesus is the Lord, the Son of the Highest, whose atoning blood ransoms men from the spiritual and temporal death brought into the world by the fall of Adam. The second gift is to believe the testimony of those officers who are appointed to bear witness of his divine Sonship and of the salvation which he has made available. And those who believe the testimony of His witnesses, and continue faithful, shall have eternal life in his everlasting kingdom.

In this setting, then, we come to the words of the Beloved John, who says of his Gospel account (called by

Joseph Smith The Testimony of St. John), "These are written," meaning the things in his Gospel account, "that ye might believe that Jesus is the Christ, the Son of God; and that believing ye might have life through his name."

Thus, the heart and core of our message; the very purpose of all the scriptures ever given; the reason why there are legal administrators, sent of God, to preach the gospel—all that the Lord has given us is to bear testimony and to prove that Jesus, who is called Christ, is in literal reality the Son of the living God and that he was crucified for the sins of the world. And we have written this work—in agony and in ecstasy; in sweat and in tears; in depression and in elation; through seasons of sorrow and in times of unbounded joy—all to the end that men might believe and know that God's Almighty Son ministered as a Man among men, and that believing, perchance, they might be faithful and gain eternal life.

We know that "God is no respecter of persons," and that "in every nation he that feareth him, and worketh righteousness," is acceptable before him. And, with Peter, we testify that salvation is for "the children of Israel," and for the Gentiles, and for those of every nation and kindred and tongue and people; and that the word of God—"preaching peace by Jesus Christ: he is Lord of all"—that word is for all men everywhere. We know that "God anointed Jesus of Nazareth with the Holy Ghost and with power"; that he "went about doing good, and healing all that were oppressed of the devil, for God was with him"; that he was slain "and hanged on a tree"; that "Him God raised up the third day, and shewed him openly, Not to all the people, but unto witnesses chosen before of God"; and that they "did eat and drink with him after he rose from the dead." And we testify that he has commanded us, as he commanded them, "to preach unto the people, and to testify that it is he which was ordained of God to be the Judge of quick and dead." And further: "To him give all the prophets witness, that through his name whosoever believeth in him shall receive remission of sins." (Acts 10:34-43.)

We testify, with Paul, that "God was manifest in the flesh, justified in the Spirit, seen of angels, preached unto the Gentiles, believed on in the world, received up into glory." (1 Tim. 3:16.) We rejoice that "God hath not given us the spirit of fear; but of power, and of love, and of a sound mind"; that we, therefore, are "not . . . ashamed of the testimony of our lord," but account it, rather, a privilege to partake "of the afflictions of the gospel according to the power of God." We glory in the fact that he "hath saved us, and called us with an holy calling, not according to our works, but according to his own purpose and grace, which was given us in Christ Jesus before the world began"; and above all that "our Saviour Jesus Christ . . . hath abolished death, and hath brought life and immortality to light through the gospel." (2 Tim. 1:7-10.)

We say with Peter: "Thou art the Christ, the Son of the living God." (Matt. 16:16.) And with Martha: "I believe that thou art the Christ, the Son of God, which should come into the world." (John 11:27.) And with Mary Magdalene: "Rabboni." (John 20:16.) And with Thomas: "My Lord and my God." (John 20:28.) And with Joseph Smith: "I saw two Personages, whose brightness and glory defy all description, standing above me in the air. One of them spake unto me, calling me by name and said, pointing to the other—*This is My Beloved Son. Hear Him!*" (JS-H 1:17.) And again: "We saw the Lord standing upon the breastwork of the pulpit, before us; and under his feet was a paved work of pure gold, in color like amber. His eyes were as a flame of fire; the hair of his head was white like the pure snow; his countenance shone above the brightness of the sun; and his voice was as the sound of the rushing of great waters, even the voice of Jehovah, saying: I am the first and the last; I am he who liveth, I am he who was slain; I am your advocate with the Father." (D&C 110:2-4.) And yet again: "And now, after the many testimonies which have been given of him, this is the testimony, last of all, which we give of him: That he lives! For we saw him, even on the right hand of God; and we heard the voice bearing record that he is the Only Begotten of the Father—That by him, and through him, and of him, the worlds are and were created, and the inhabitants thereof are begotten sons and daughters unto God." (D&C 76:22-24.) And all of these witnesses are our witness also.

With John we have seen him, as it were, in heaven, upon a white horse, bearing the name "Faithful and True," and judging and making war "in righteousness." "His eyes were as a flame of fire, and on his head were many crowns. . . . He was clothed with a vesture dipped in blood: and his name is called The Word of God. And the armies which were in heaven followed him upon white horses, clothed in fine linen, white and clean. And out of his mouth goeth a sharp sword, that with it he should smite the nations: and he shall rule them with a rod of iron: and he treadeth the winepress of the fierceness and wrath of Almighty God. And he hath on his vesture and on his thigh a name written, KING OF KINGS, AND LORD OF LORDS." (Rev. 19:11-16.)

And, in fine, let Job's words be our words: "I know that my redeemer liveth, and that he shall stand at the latter day upon the earth." (Job 19:25.) We need not multiply witnesses. This work itself is our witness. It testifies that he was God before the worlds were; that he was born of Mary in a stable, God himself being his Father; that he ministered among men, preaching the gospel and working miracles; that he was delivered into the hands of wicked men, and by them hanged upon a tree; that he bore the sins of all who believe and obey; that he is the Resurrection and the Life; that immortality and eternal life come by him; that he hath risen from the dead; and that finally he ascended to his Father, there to reign with almighty power until he shall come again to reign on earth. The fact of the resurrection is the most certain surety in all history; a cloud of witnesses testify thereto, including those in our day who also have seen and felt and handled; and all who will, may receive the same sure witness from the Holy Spirit of God. The resurrection from the dead—above all else—proves he is the Son of God. This is our witness; there is no doubt whatever: Jesus Christ is the Son of the Living God who was crucified for the sins of the world.

NOTE

1. In chapter 9 we reasoned that the disciples were in fact in the temple itself when the Pentecostal fires of the Spirit fell so mightily upon them. This seems more likely than the suggestion here given that they could have been in the upper room.

Chapter 121

"THE BRIDEGROOM COMETH"

And, lo, I am with you alway,
even unto the end of the world.
(Matt. 28:20.)
Let the cry go forth among all people:
Awake and arise and go forth
to meet the Bridegroom;
behold and lo, the Bridegroom cometh;
go ye out to meet him.
Prepare yourselves
for the great day of the Lord.
(D&C 133:10.)

Jesus Is with Us Yet

Lo, he is with us—always!

Though he has returned to his Father, yet where two or three are gathered together in his name, having perfect faith and worshipping the Father in his name, he will be in their midst—by the power of his Spirit.

Some of the faithful and elect, on occasion, see his face and hear his voice. "It is your privilege, and a promise I give unto you," he says to all the faithful elders of his kingdom, "that inasmuch as you strip yourselves from jealousies and fears, and humble yourselves before me, . . .

the veil shall be rent and you shall see me and know that I am—not with the carnal neither natural mind, but with the spiritual." (D&C 67:10.) His command to his ministers is: "Sanctify yourselves that your minds become single to God, and the days will come that you shall see him; for he will unveil his face unto you, and it shall be in his own time, and in his own way, and according to his own will." (D&C 88:68.) And his promise to all is: "It shall come to pass that every soul who forsaketh his sins and cometh unto me, and calleth on my name, and obeyeth my voice, and keepeth my commandments, shall see my face and know that I am." (D&C 93:1.)

Such is his law, and he is no respecter of persons. The reason more people do not pierce the veil and see his face is simply that more do not live the law qualifying them for such a transcendent spiritual experience. "For no man has seen God at any time in the flesh, except quickened by the Spirit of God. Neither can any natural man abide the presence of God, neither after the carnal mind. Ye are not able to abide the presence of God, neither after the carnal mind. Ye are not able to abide the presence of God now"—he is speaking to some of the early elders of this dispensation, and conditions have not materially changed since then—"neither the minstering of angels; wherefore, continue in patience until ye are perfected."[1] For most of us a cloud has received him out of our sight, a cloud that can only be pierced by the eye of faith.

"Between us and His visible presence—between us and that glorified Redeemer who now sitteth at the right hand of God—that cloud still rolls. But the eye of Faith can pierce it; the incense of true prayer can rise above it; through it the dew of blessing can descend. And if He is gone away, yet He has given us in His Holy Spirit a nearer sense of His presence, a closer infolding in the arms of His tenderness, than we could have enjoyed even if we had lived with Him of old in the home of Nazareth, or sailed with Him in the little boat over the crystal waters of Gennesareth. We may be as near to Him at all times—and more than all when we kneel down to pray—as the beloved disciple was when he laid his head upon His breast. The word of God is very nigh us, even in our mouths and in our hearts. To ears that have been closed His voice may seem indeed to sound no longer. The loud noises of War may shake the world; the eager calls of Avarice and of Pleasure may drown the gentle utterance which bids us 'Follow Me.' . . .

"But the secret of the Lord is with them that fear Him, and He will show them His covenant. To all who will listen He still speaks. He promised to be with us always, even to the end of the world, and we have not found [that] His promise[s] fail. It was but for thirty-three years of a short lifetime that He lived on earth; it was but for three broken and troubled years that He preached the Gospel of the Kingdom; but for ever, even until all the Eons have been closed, and the earth itself, with the heavens that now are, have passed away, shall every one of His true and faithful children find peace and hope and forgiveness in His name, and that name shall be called Emmanuel, which is, being interpreted, 'GOD WITH US.' "[2]

Jesus Shall Come Again
(Acts 1:9-11)

There has been a First Coming of Christ, and there shall be a Second Coming of the Son of Man. He came once, born of Mary—to gain his own body, to minister among men, to work out the infinite and eternal atoning sacrifice. He shall come again in all the glory of his Father's kingdom—to live again on earth, to perfect the salvation of his fellows, to deliver the kingdom, in due course, spotless to his Father. After some thirty-three years of mortal life, while angels attended, he ascended up to sit on the right hand of Eternal Power. This same Jesus—living and being as he was, and is, and ever shall be—shall return, accompanied by ten thousands of his angelic saints, to live on earth a thousand years. Then, after a short season, cometh the end, and this earth will attain its celestial destiny.

> *Hear O Israel, thy King cometh unto thee; he is glorious in his attire and red in his apparel; he rideth upon the clouds and descendeth in his fury. He is just and having salvation; his word is law; and he shall reign forever and ever.*

He shall come in a day when many shall say: "There is no Christ, and such a person shall not come. We have no need of another to save us from our sins; God alone has all power, and we have no need for an Advocate or an Intercessor." They will say: "There is no God but Allah and Mohammed is his prophet; Allah has but to speak and a thing is done; he hath no need of a Son." They will say: "Our Messiah will yet come; he will save us; he is our King and our Deliverer; we will wait for him."

But so said they of Jesus when he came of old: "Is not this the carpenter's son; is not his father called Joseph and his mother, Mary; and are not his brothers and sisters with us? Why say ye that he is the Son of God? Does he claim to preach a gospel? His sayings cannot be true; they run counter to our traditions; we will follow Moses instead. Does he pretend to work miracles? What are they but deeds done by Beelzebub the prince of devils. Away with him; crucify him; we have no king but Caesar; his blood be upon us and—God help us!—on our children."

But, no matter, he was God's Son then, and he is God's Son now. He ministered in power and glory then; he proved his divine Sonship by rising from the dead; and he shall come again in a power and glory ten thousand times greater than before. He carried a cross in that day, and he shall wear a crown in this. And they who fight against him and his gospel shall be banished from his presence forever.

He shall come in a day when even those who call themselves Christians shall say: "The Lord delayeth his coming; let us eat, drink, and be merry. If we act amiss, he shall beat us with a few stripes, but eventually we shall be saved in the kingdom of God."

And so said they of old who bought delicacies and jeweled garments at the bazaars of the sons of Annas; so said they who made His Father's house a den of thieves; so said they who sowed, and reaped, and laid up their harvests in great barns, and who said within themselves, "Soul take thine ease, for we are rich; we live sumptuously; we have an abundance of this world's goods."

But, no matter, he came then at the appointed time, and he shall come again when his hour arrives. He came then to destroy their kingdom and leave their house desolate; he said then to those who trusted in riches, "This night shall thy soul be required of thee; then whose shall all these things be?" And he shall say when he comes again, "All those who have laid up treasures on earth and who are not rich unto God, their treasures shall be tried so as by fire, and they only shall abide the day who have laid up treasures in heaven."

He shall come in a day when many professors of religion shall say: "He has come already; he dwells in the hearts of his people. The promised era of peace will come when men learn to love one another; then they will beat their swords into plowshares and their spears into pruning hooks. Men will create and usher in their own Millennium by their good works. All these things which the prophets have said about a kingdom of God on earth are spiritual; they cannot be taken literally."

But, no matter, such men are no different from the Sadducees of old, who believed neither in preexistence, nor in angels, nor in marriage in heaven, nor in the resurrection, nor in eternal glory, nor that He who walked among them was the Son of the living God. What carnal men may think about spiritual things—however much they profess to be religious—is of so little consequence that it scarcely bears repeating. Jesus was the Son of God then, and he is the Son of God now. And to the modern Sadducees, who spiritualize away the prophetic word, we need only say: "Judge ye, for in that fearsome and dread day when he descends, with the trump of God and the shout of the archangel, to take vengeance on all those who know not God and who obey not his gospel—judge ye, for in that great and dreadful day it will be everlastingly too late to prepare for a Second Coming that has passed." When "this same Jesus," who was "taken up . . . into heaven," returns "in like manner" as he went up, then the judgment will be set and the books be opened, and all men shall stand before his bar to be judged according to the deeds done in the flesh.

When first he came—and after he rose from the dead—he walked and talked and ate and drank with his disciples, and he shall do so again in that great day which lies ahead. When—as a symbol of his nation—Thomas doubted and would not believe, except he feel the nail prints in Jesus' hands and in his feet and the spear wound in his side, the troubled apostle was invited to see and feel and know and be not faithless but believing. And so shall it be in the latter days when a troubled people, long in doubt, shall see him again, when they shall look on him whom they have pierced. Then shall these be his words:

> *Behold the prints of the nails in my hands and in my feet; look upon my riven side; stretch forth thine hands; feel and know; and be not faithless, but believing.*
>
> *Lo, these are the wounds with which I was wounded in the house of my friends; I am he who was lifted up; I am he who was crucified; I am Jesus of Nazareth of Galilee; I am the Son of God. Come unto me; I died for thee and for all men.*

But before the Lord Jesus comes again, all of the promised signs and wonders shall surely come to pass. Ours is the generation in which they are being poured forth. And our need is to learn to read the signs of the times, lest we fail to meet and accept our Promised Messiah as did so many when he came in the meridian of time. We must search the scriptures and heed the Messianic message. The children of light need not be deceived; that day need not come upon them unawares. "And whoso treasureth up my word," he says, "shall not be deceived." (JS-M 1:37.) That day will be one of vengeance for the wicked and of redemption and glory and salvation for the saints. And after he comes, all of the glorious things spoken concerning Israel and Zion and glory and eternal peace shall have their glorious fulfillment.

Arise, O Jerusalem; gather in, O ye dispersed of Judah; hear ye his voice, O scattered ones of Joseph. Let all Israel now rejoice in him who dwells between the cherubim.

Come forth, O Zion, upon the holy mount; let Israel now be gathered home. Come, all ye people; build the city of holiness; let the pure in heart assemble together.

Open thy gates, O Zion, for into thee shall come those of all nations; and the Gentiles shall come to thy light and kings to the brightness of thy rising; and unto thee shall be gathered all those who know the name of the Lord, and who worship the Father in spirit and in truth; and they shall dwell safely within thy walls.

And now what more need we say? We have spoken of him; our message is recorded; our witness is borne.[3] Christ the Lord is God's Almighty Son. He came that man might live, and living, find a place with him where he and his Father dwell eternally. And he shall come again to receive us unto himself.

Ring out ye bells in every belfry of all Christendom. Cry out, ye souls awaiting your redemption. Sing together, ye cherubic hosts; let heaven's dome be filled with anthems of eternal praise.

Ye saints of God, ye holy ones—rejoice. Ye noble souls, ye faithful ones—rejoice. Come now, ye cho-

sen ones—be lifted up: Inherit the kingdom prepared for you from the foundation of the world.

When Will He Come Again?

As we testify of his First Coming and bear record that he dwelt among men in the meridian of time; as we study the deeds he did as a mortal and marvel at how wondrous they were; as our heart burns within us, letting us know of a surety of his divine Sonship—our thoughts turn to the day of his return. We long to be with him then, even as the prophets of old longed to see the day of his mortal ministry.

As we ponder upon these things, it seems clear to us that we are in an even better position to read the signs of *our* times than the Jews were to read the signs of *their* times. They had the prophetic word telling of his promised birth; of the words he would speak and the works he would do; of the atoning sacrifice he would make; of his coming forth from the grave; and of the consequent resurrection of all men. Many were the signs and portents then testifying that the day for all those wondrous works was near even at their doors. We in like manner have the holy scriptures, which tell us of the events and describe to us the conditions that shall precede and attend his triumphal return. We know he is going to come in the clouds of glory in the midst of that great era of restoration in which we now live. Many are the evidences—yea, the infallible proofs—that the hour of his coming is nigh, even at our doors. Though we do not know the very day and the very hour of his coming, we do know the generation; it is our generation, the generation (dispensation, if you will) of the fulness of times.

Thus saith the Lord; for I am God, and have sent mine Only Begotten Son into the world for the redemption of the world, and have decreed that he that receiveth him shall be saved, and he that receiveth him not shall be damned—

And they have done unto the Son of Man even as they listed; and he has taken his power on the right hand of his glory, and now reigneth in the heavens, and will reign till he descends on the earth to put all enemies under his feet, which time is nigh at hand—

I, the Lord God, have spoken it; but the hour and the day no man knoweth, neither the angels in heaven, nor shall they know until he comes. . . .

And again, verily I say unto you, that the Son of Man cometh not in the form of a woman, neither of a man traveling on the earth.

Wherefore, be not deceived, but continue in steadfastness, looking forth for the heavens to be shaken, and the earth to tremble and to reel to and fro as a drunken man, and for the valleys to be exalted, and for the mountains to be made low, and for the rough places to become smooth—and all this when the angel shall sound his trumpet. (D&C 49:5-7, 22-23.)

But—be it repeated—we are in a better position to read the signs of the times today than our Jewish brethren were in their day. The reason: We have seen the fulfillment of the prophetic word relative to the First Coming and know of a surety that he who then came was the Son of God. We know that he rose from the dead and ascended into heaven. Accordingly, we are bound to believe that he will come again and that the prophetic word relative thereto will come to pass "in like manner" as did the word relative to his ancient ministry.

And yet, no man can know that Jesus is the Lord but by the Holy Ghost, and no man can read the signs of the times except by that same power. As we search the scriptures and seek to know what is destined to happen in our generation we must, above all else, be guided by the Holy Spirit of God. All those who have exercised the power to become, by faith, the sons of God have the right to the constant companionship of that member of the Godhead. Thus the Beloved Disciple said:

Behold, what manner of love the Father hath bestowed upon us, that we should be called the sons of God: therefore the world knoweth us not, because it knew him not.

Beloved, now are we the sons of God, and it doth not yet appear what we shall be: but we know that, when he shall appear, we shall be like him; for we shall see him as he is.

And every man that hath this hope in him purifieth himself, even as he is pure. (1 Jn. 3:1-3.)

NOTES

1. D&C 67:11-13. In this connection, note these words spoken by the Lord to Moses: "Thou canst not see my face at this time, lest mine anger be kindled against thee also, and I destroy thee, and thy people; for there shall no man among them see me at this time, and live, for they are exceeding sinful. And no sinful man hath at any time, neither shall there be any sinful man at any time, that shall see my face and live." (JST, Ex. 33:20.)

2. Farrar, pp. 732–33. These words are used by Farrar to end and climax his *Life of Christ*. Since I have quoted freely from this eminent biblical scholar and recognized literary genius, perhaps I should now append the following. After my first reading of Farrar, I wrote these words on the last page of his work: "In literary craftsmanship—Churchillian in concept and flow; a wondrous witchery of words; a delight to read. In scope and purpose—faith promoting and edifying; written by one who believed, as measured by sectarian standards; and yet much fancy fiction is set forth and much sectarian nonsense and delusion." Manifestly the portions quoted in this work are deemed to be sound and proper; they are, in general, quotations that express the sought-for thought in language seldom equaled and almost never surpassed.

At this point a word about almost all sectarian commentaries and biographies about Christ might not be amiss. It is my judgment that most of the modern publications are far from faith promoting. In most cases it is necessary to go back a hundred years or so to find authors who believed in the divine Sonship with sufficient fervor to accept the New Testament passages as meaning what they say. After all, every "Life of Christ"—this one included—is in large measure a reflection of the faith and knowledge of the author. Providentially, as Latter-day Saints, we have a wealth of sound doctrine available to guide us in all that we write about this or any subject that is not accepted as it should be by the scholars of the world.

3. Edersheim, who devoted seven years of arduous labor and intensive research to his magnum opus, *The Life and Times of Jesus the Messiah,* appended to his work these words of poignant faith and testimony: "*Easter Morning,* 1883.—Our task is ended—and we also worship and look up. And we go back from this sight into a hostile world, to love, and to live, and to work for the Risen Christ. But as earth's day is growing dim, and, with earth's gathering darkness, breaks over it heaven's storm, we ring out—as of old they were wont, from church-tower, to the mariners that hugged a rock-bound coast—our Easter-bells to guide them who are belated, over the storm-tossed sea, beyond the breakers, into the desired haven. Ring out, earth, all thy Easter-chimes; bring your offerings, all ye people; worship in faith, for—'This Jesus, Which was received up from you into heaven, shall so come, in like manner as ye beheld Him going into heaven.' 'Even so, Lord Jesus, come quickly!' " (Edersheim 2:652.)

"PREPARE YE THE WAY OF THE LORD"

The voice of him
that crieth in the wilderness,
Prepare ye the way of the Lord,
make straight in the desert
a highway for our God.
Every valley shall be exalted,
and every mountain and hill shall be made low:
and the crooked shall be made straight,
and the rough places plain:
And the glory of the Lord
shall be revealed,
and all flesh shall see it together:
for the mouth of the Lord hath spoken it.
(Isa. 40:3-5.)

"This Is My Beloved Son. Hear Him!"[1]

"Behold my Beloved Son, in whom I am well pleased, in whom I have glorified my name—hear ye him." (3 Ne. 11:7.)

On this note we began, on this note we shall end, and the clarion sweetness of this eternal truth shall ring forth forever in all worlds, among all the children of the Eternal Father. The Beloved Son ministered among mortals on planet earth. Jesus our Lord, beloved and chosen from the beginning, came from the Father to do his will, to glorify his name, to save "all the works of his hands, except those sons of perdition who deny the Son after the Father has revealed him." (D&C 76:43.) Then he returned to the glorious Majesty on high. And through the holy accounts we have seen his deeds, learned his law, and felt his Spirit. How glorious is the Word who came down from heaven! What wonders he has shown us, and what spiritual refreshment he has given us!

We saw him make flesh his tabernacle in a stable at Bethlehem of Judea and heard the heavenly choirs acclaim his divine Sonship.

Planted, thus, as a root in dry ground, we saw him grow up as a tender plant in a Jewish home in Nazareth; marveled when he, as a youth, both taught and confounded the wise men in the temple; and rejoiced that he had no need to be taught of men, for God was his Father.

We went with him to Bethabara, where his stern forerunner immersed him in the murky waters of the mighty Jordan; and then, lo, the heavens opened, the Holy Ghost came down in bodily form, serene and calm as a dove, and the Father spoke: "This is my beloved Son, in whom I am well pleased. Hear ye him."

Then we saw him overcome the world when tempted in the wilderness; heard him go forth preaching the gospel of the kingdom of God; gloried as he cleansed his Father's House at the First Passover and again at the Fourth; and heard him say, repeatedly, that he was the Promised Messiah.

We heard him call the Twelve and the Seventy; marveled at the wisdom of his Sermon on the Mount, his discourse on the law of Moses, and then on gospel standards. How we were fed spiritually when he gave the sermon on the bread of life, and the discourse on cleanliness, and on meekness and humility, and on forgiveness and the sealing power, and on the good shepherd, and, then, the sermon on Olivet, and, finally, those in the upper room (the discourse on the two Comforters, and on the law of love, and on the Holy Ghost)! And as to his parables, we need only say, "Never man spake as this Man."

And O the miracles we have seen him work! Before our eyes the lame walked, the blind saw, the deaf heard, paralytics carried their couches, lepers were cleansed, devils were cast out, and the dead were raised. The calm command, "Lazarus, come forth," still echoes in our soul as we remember how he who had been dead four days stood, yet enshrouded in his burial clothes, at the door of his tomb! And all these miracles were as nothing compared to his healing of sin-sick souls; of saying to the sin-encumbered, "Son, thy sins be forgiven thee"; of calling forth the spiritually dead to spiritual life.

We saw him still storms, walk on the tumultuous waves of tempestuous Gennesaret, feed thousands with a few small fishes and a few barley loaves, and walk unharmed through mobs that sought to stone him.

And O the testimonies we have heard! His own: "I am the Son of God"; Peter's: "Thou art the Christ, the Son of the living God"; Martha's: "Thou art the Christ, the Son of God, who should come into the world." Those of believing souls in all walks of life, uttered in unison, ascending as incense to the Father. Thou art the Promised Messiah, the king of Israel, our Deliverer, Savior, and Redeemer. Thou art our God!

And ought we not mention the Mount of Transfiguration, when his face shown with heavenly light and his clothes glistened with celestial brightness, when Moses and Elias came to him, and when Peter, James, and John saw the transfiguration of the earth and received the keys of the kingdom of God on earth?

And then there is Gethsemane, the garden of the olive press, where he sweat great drops of blood from every pore, so great was his suffering and so intense his anguish as he took upon himself the sins of all men on conditions of repentance.

But in nothing have we felt such shame and horror and revulsion as when he was led before Annas and Caiaphas and the Sanhedrin and Pilate and Herod and Pilate again; when the Innocent One was found guilty by the ecclesiastical and civil powers of the world; when he was mocked, derided, spit upon, cursed, smitten, scourged, and led away to be crucified.

There on Calvary we saw Gentile hands drive Roman nails into Jewish flesh; we saw him raised in agony upon the accursed tree; and we wept with his disciples as he drank the dregs of the bitter cup his Father had given him.

But glory be to the Father, he partook. The Beloved One finished his work, voluntarily laid down his life, and then, the third day, took it up again in glorious immortality.

We were with him at the tomb when Mary Magdalene worshipped before him, and when the other women held him by the feet. Then we wept with Peter as the Risen Lord stood gloriously before the Chief Apostle and commissioned him anew to head the earthly kingdom for that day.

And O how our hearts burned within us as we heard him expound the Messianic prophecies on the Emmaus road; as we saw and felt and handled (on two occasions) in the upper room; as we communed and ate on the shore of the Sea of Tiberias; and as we knelt and worshipped on the mountain in Galilee as part of the great congregation.

All these things we saw—and they are not a tithe of it all; nay, they are not a ten thousandth of all that we saw and felt and knew—as he ministered as a mortal among men. And we, therefore, do know and do testify that Jesus of Nazareth was the Son of the living God and that he was crucified for the sins of the world. That the generality of the Jews were not prepared, mentally and spiritually, to receive this knowledge and all that came to the faithful is a matter of sorrow and sadness for them and for their children. And as it was with them, so shall it be with those in all nations in the latter days, unless they prepare themselves to receive this same Jesus at his Second Coming.

As to all these things—and thousands more—what we have written, we have written. For good or for ill, with stumbling words and in halting speech—professing (with Paul) to know nothing among men, save Jesus Christ and him crucified; and yet (we say it humbly) with some inspiration and occasional flights of fluent expression—we have taught and testified of this Jewish Jesus in his Jewish setting. Our work in this respect—meaning with reference to this opus—is ended. And there remaineth but one thing more. We must, for so we have been commanded—it is our divine commission, our sober and sacred duty—we must say to all to whom these words may come: True it is that Jesus ministered among men in the meridian of time, and true it is also that he shall soon come to rule and reign in millennial splendor. And unless our words pertaining to his mortal life prepare and inspire men to make ready for his Second Coming, we have failed indeed.

"My Messenger: . . . He Shall Prepare the Way Before Me"[2]

Isaiah proclaims: "Prepare ye the way of the Lord." (Isa. 40:3.) Our revelations say: "Prepare yourselves for the great day of the Lord." (D&C 133:10.) To prepare the way before the Lord is to bring to pass those things which must be done before he comes. It is to gather Israel, to build Zion, to proclaim the gospel to every nation and people; it is to prepare a people for that dread and glorious day. To prepare ourselves for that great day is to join with the saints, to gather with Israel, to dwell in Zion, to so live that we shall abide the day of his coming. Those who prepare the way before the Lord, by that very process prepare themselves for that which lies ahead. And those who are prepared shall be saved; they shall abide the day;

their seed shall inherit the earth from generation to generation. Those who are not prepared have no such promises.

When Jesus dwelt among men, he chose his friends with care. He preached to all, invited all to believe and obey, called upon all to forsake the world and to join the kingdom. But he chose his friends and close associates from among those who sought to do the things he said. Those who leaned on his bosom, who ate and traveled and lived with him—his friends—were a select and chosen group. In the spirit world he did not even so much as go among the wicked and ungodly; those only who were worthy heard the words of life as they fell from his lips. And so shall it be when he comes again. His voice will be raised among the faithful; his countenance will shine upon the obedient; his friends—those who abide the day—will be the Godfearing and the righteous. Our preparation for that day is fourfold:

1. *We must believe what Jesus believed.*

Repent and believe the gospel. He that believeth shall be saved; he that believeth not shall be damned; signs shall follow those who believe. Believe on the Lord Jesus Christ and thou shalt be saved. Believe in him; believe in his prophets; believe the words of his apostles and elders. Believe and be blessed; disbelieve and be cursed. The first great test of mortality is whether men will believe the everlasting word when it is preached to them. Those who believe the truth can be saved; those who believe a lie shall be damned. At our peril we must choose to believe as Jesus believed, and unless and until we do, we shall never begin the preparation that will qualify us to be his friends. When we believe as he believes; when we gain the mind of Christ; when we think as he thinks; when our desires are harmonious with his—then we will have so much in common that we can be friends. He believed he was the Son of God, and we must believe the same. He believed his Father sent him, and we must have no reservations relative thereto. He believed all the truths of the everlasting gospel, and we must do likewise. No one ever applies eternal truth in his life until he believes and knows it to be what it everlastingly is—eternal truth.

2. *We must preach and teach and testify as Jesus did.* It becometh every man who hath been warned to warn his neighbor. Every friend of the Lord must tell others of his Eternal Friend. The gospel cause is to go forth from mouth to mouth and from heart to heart until the knowledge of God covers the earth as the waters cover the sea. All who join the Church are under covenant, made in the waters of baptism, to stand as witnesses of Christ at all times and in all places and to all people, even unto death. It does not suffice to believe and do nothing more; every believer is commanded to take every opportunity to give to others a reason for the hope which is his.

Thus, Jesus proclaimed the word of truth and salvation and we must do likewise, and in our day it is the glorious message of the restoration; of the gathering of Israel; of the redemption of Zion; of salvation for the dead; of the imminent return of "this same Jesus." We must proclaim—boldly and without fear—such things as these, for they are true as God is true:

There has been a famine in the land—not a famine of bread, nor a thirst for water, but of hearing the word of the Lord. Now all those who hunger and thirst after righteousness can drink of the waters of life and feast on the good word of God.

There has been a long night of gloom and darkness and apostasy. Now the glory of a new day is dawning; darkness flees; the gospel light shines brightly as before; and the millennial day is upon us.

The Lord's people have been scattered, spurned, cursed; they have been a hiss and a byword in all the nations whither he hath driven them. Now they hear his voice and heed his cry; now they gather round his gospel standard in every place where it is raised.

During the long night of darkness—the night when darkness covered the earth and gross darkness the minds of the people—who has heard the voice of heaven, or seen an angelic face, or gloried in the gifts of the Spirit? But now the ancient powers are restored—the voice of God is heard again: angels minister among us mortals; and signs, gifts, and miracles abound as in olden times.

Once again apostles and prophets mingle among us; they preach and prophesy. Once again the elders of Israel go forth to seek their scattered kin; they preach and minister in power and great glory. Once again the kingdom has been set up on earth in all its glory, beauty, and perfection; its ministers, both male and female, carry forward as did their counterparts among their forebears.

What then say we?

Our voice is one crying in the wilderness—in the wilderness of sin, of apostasy, of worldliness: Repent ye, repent ye, why will ye die O ye nations! Return unto the Lord, O ye people; forsake the world, flee from sin, turn unto the truth. Come unto Christ, and be ye saved.

Our voice is one calling out of the dark, dry deserts of death—out of the waterless waste places of the world: Come, drink of the waters of life; drink deep from the rivers that flow, direct from the great Fountain Head. Come unto him, and drink from the wells of salvation.

Our voice is a voice of joy and gladness—it is one of thanksgiving and the voice of melody: Hear, O ye heavens, and give ear, O earth, for the Lord hath spoken in our day; he hath given again the fulness of his everlasting gospel; every truth, doctrine, power, priesthood, key gift and grace, all things, needed to save and exalt men are now on earth again.

Our voice proclaims—in words of truth and soberness—that the Great God has called his servant, Joseph Smith, Jr., and spoken unto him from heaven, and given him commandments, pursuant to which The Church of Jesus Christ of Latter-day Saints has been set up among men, as the only true and living Church upon the face of the whole earth.

Our voice testifies—by the power and influence of the Holy Spirit of God—that this Church administers the gospel, and that all who come to this ensign, raised anew on the mountains of Israel, can gain peace in this world and eternal life in the world to come.

3. *We must live as Jesus lived.*

Jesus kept the commandments of his Father and thereby worked out his own salvation, and also set an example as to the way and the means whereby all men may be saved. Salvation is available because of his atoning sacrifice and comes by obedience to the laws and ordinances of the gospel. As to how and why and in what manner we must live to gain salvation, we need only quote the teachings of the Prophet Joseph Smith as they are given in the Lectures on Faith.

"Where shall we find a prototype into whose likeness we may be assimilated, in order that we may be made partakers of life and salvation?" the Prophet asked, "or, in other words, where shall we find a saved being? for if we can find a saved being, we may ascertain without much difficulty what all others must be in order to be saved. We think that it will not be a matter of dispute, that two beings who are unlike each other cannot be saved; for whatever constitutes the salvation of one will constitute the salvation of every creature which will be saved; and if we find one saved being in all existence, we may see what others must be, or else not be saved.

"We ask, then, where is the prototype? or where is the saved being? We conclude, as to the answer of this question, there will be no dispute among those who believe the Bible, that it is Christ: all will agree in this, that he is the prototype or standard of salvation; or, in other words, that he is a saved being. And if we should continue our interrogation and ask how it is that he is saved? the answer would be—because he is a just and holy being; and if he were anything different from what he is, he would not be saved; for his salvation depends on his being precisely what he is and nothing else; for if it were possible for him to change, in the least degree, so sure he would fail of salvation and lose all his dominion, power, authority and glory, which constitute salvation; for salvation consists in the glory, authority, majesty, power and dominion which Jehovah possesses and in nothing else; and no being can possess it but himself or one like him."

Then, after quoting various passages of scriptures, the Prophet continued: "These teachings of the Saviour most clearly show unto us the nature of salvation, and what he proposed unto the human family when he proposed to save them—that he proposed to make them like unto himself, and he was like the Father, the great prototype of all saved beings; and for any portion of the human family to be assimilated into their likeness is to be saved; and to be unlike them is to be destroyed; and on this hinge turns the door of salvation." (Lecture 7, cited in *Mormon Doctrine*, 2nd ed., pp. 257–58.)

4. *We must do the things that Jesus did.*

He preached the gospel, performed the ordinances of salvation, wrought miracles, and kept the commandments. So must it be with us. He carried his cross and laid his all upon the altar. So, if called upon, must we do. His promise to us is: "He that believeth on me, the works that I do shall he do also." (John 14:12.) Also: "Ye shall be even as I am, and I am even as the Father; and the Father and I are one." (3 Ne. 28:10.)

"Hosanna in the Highest"[3]

And so we say: He came once and he shall come again. If we have learned well the lessons of his First Coming, we also shall read the signs of the times and be ready for his Second Coming.

> Lo, the mighty God appearing;
> From on high Jehovah speaks!
> Eastern lands the summons hearing,

O'er the west his thunder breaks.
Earth behold him! Earth behold him!
Universal nature shakes.

Zion, all its light unfolding,
God in glory shall display.
Lo! he comes! nor silence holding,
Fire and clouds prepare his way,
Tempests round him! Tempests round him!
Hasten on the dreadful day.

To the heav'ns his voice ascending,
To the earth beneath he cries;
Souls immortal, now descending,
Let their sleeping dust arise!
Rise to judgment; Rise to judgment;
Let thy throne adorn the skies.

—*Hymns,* no. 264

And, now, one thing only remains—the recording of our witness of the divine Sonship of him of whom we have written. To all we have said we append this seal of testimony:

Of Mary's Son, we testify—as God is our witness!—that he is the Holy One of Israel, the Promised Messiah, the Son of God.

As to Jesus of Nazareth we say: He is the God of Israel, the Eternal One, the Great Jehovah, who made flesh his tabernacle and lived as mortals do in a world of sin and sorrow.

As to the Crucified One, him whom they took and by evil hands hanged on a tree, our witness is: He is risen; he came forth from the Arimathean's tomb; he lives; he ascended to his Father; and he reigns on the right hand of the Majesty on high.

Of him who is called Christ, we testify: He is the Redeemer of the world, the Savior of all who believe; he has abolished death and brought life and immortality to light through the gospel; he is the Resurrection and the Life; and in him shall all men have life and that eternally.

And this same Jewish Jesus, whom God hath made both Lord and Christ, shall soon return as the Second David, to rule and reign on the throne of his Father forever.

God grant that we may abide the day. And God grant, further, that our voice shall never cease to speak—in life and in death, in time and in eternity, now and forever—in bearing testimony of Him who has ransomed us from death, hell, the devil, and endless torment.

We write it here; let it also be inscribed in the eternal records; let it be written on earth and in heaven; and let all who read be enlightened by the power of the same Spirit which approves the written word—let all men know (and we so testify) that Jesus Christ is the Son of the living God; that he worked out the infinite and eternal atonement; that he was crucified for the sins of the world; that he rose from death the third day; that he ascended to his Father; that he has restored the fulness of his everlasting gospel in our day; and that he will soon come to reign in power and great glory among those who abide the day and who are not consumed by the brightness of his coming.

He is our King, our Lord, and our God!

Blessed be his great and holy name both now and forever!

Blessed be he that cometh in the name of the Lord. Hosanna in the highest!

NOTES

1. JS-H 1:17.
2. Mal. 3:1.
3. Matt. 21:9.

INDEX

Abraham, 52-53; God's covenant with, 337-39
Acquittal of Jesus: by Pilate, 177; by Herod, 179
Adam, first and second, 51, 124, 128
Adam-ondi-Ahman, 350
Advocate with Father, 105
Ahithopel, a type of Judas, 42
America: darkness and destruction in, at Jesus' death, 225-26; dispersal of darkness from, 260; is land of Joseph's inheritance, 311, 334, 336; establishment of free people in, 349
Anesthetic given before crucifixion, 210
Angels: appearance of, to strengthen Jesus in Gethsemane, 124-25; roll stone back from tomb, 261; encircle Nephite children, 323
Annas, 143-44, 156-57 n. 2; trial of Jesus before, 142, 146-67; failed to bring sufficient charges against Jesus, 149-50
Antipas, 179-80
Apostasy, 397-99
Apostles. *See* Twelve Apostles
Apostolic commission, 297, 299-304
Appearances of Jesus after resurrection, summary of, 295-97
Arimathea, Joseph of, 237-39
Arrest of Jesus, 131
Ascension of Jesus, 408-9
Ask and ye shall receive, 73-74, 85, 102, 385-86
Atonement: was made primarily in Gethsemane, 128; completion of, on cross, 224; was part of plan of salvation, 381. *See also* Death of Jesus; Gethsemane
Authority: ministers must have, 88; Jesus bestows, on Twelve, 282-83
Avarice, besetting sin of Sadducees was, 146

Baalam's ass, Caiaphas likened to, 148-49
Baptism, 29-30; of Nephites, 94-95; Nephites were instructed in ordinance of, 301; of three thousand souls on day of Pentecost, 406
Barabbas, 183-87
Belief in Christ: is gift of Spirit, 411; is step in preparing to meet him, 431
Betrayal of Jesus: Judas's motivation for, 15-18; Jesus predicts, 43; Judas performs, with kiss, 130
Blasphemy: Jesus is accused of, 155, 170-71; converting charge of, into charge of treason, 167
Blood: of Christ, new testament of, 62; Jesus sweat, from every pore, 125; Christ's, has come upon Jews, 189-90; and water issued forth from Jesus' side, 236-37
Body of Jesus reunites with his spirit, 261
Bones: breaking of, to end crucifixion, 235
Book of Mormon: special contribution of, 307-8, 313; coming forth of, is sign of times, 349, 351-52; to come forth from Gentiles, 349; sealed portion of, 370; testimony of, 392
Branches of true vine, disciples are, 84-85
Bread: of life, sermon on, 9-10; sacramental, 58
Brother of Jared, 81 n. 4, 296-97, 370
Burial clothes of Jesus, 262, 268

Caiaphas, 147-48; trial of Jesus before, 143, 149-56; orders Jesus to speak, 153-54
Calvary, 209
Celestial kingdom, Joseph Smith saw, in vision, 401 n. 1
Celestial marriage, ordinance of, promised to Abraham, 338
Childbirth, analogy of, 101
Children: Jesus addresses disciples as, 49; saints are called, 66 n. 2; of Nephites, Jesus blesses, 322-23
Church of Jesus Christ: sad state of, after Jesus' death, 259; must bear his name, 376-79; many joined, on day of Pentecost, 406; officers in, 411; of Latter-day Saints, 433
Cleopas, 275, 278
Commandment, new, to love one another, 50

James, 305 n. 1
Jared, brother of, 81 n. 4, 296-97, 370
Jeremiah, 200-202
Jerusalem: sunset over, 27-28; sanctifying of, 342; splendor of, in last days, 350
Jesus Christ: prepares for his death, 3-4, 6-7; infuriates Jewish leaders, 12-13; washes disciples' feet, 37-38; love of, for his disciples, 47-48; follows his Father's example, 66 n. 1, 79; prophesies of his separation from disciples, 69; goes to prepare place for disciples, 70; is the way, the truth, and the life, 71; God manifested himself in, 71-72; as Second Comforter, 75-77; was seen by brother of Jared, 81 n. 4, 296-97; is the true vine, 84-85; friends of, disciples are called, 87; rejection of, by world, 90-91; as our advocate with the Father, 105; is only accepted mediator, 117 n. 3; in Gethsemane, 124-28; pain suffered by, exquisiteness of, 126-27; betrayal of, by Judas, 130; arrest of, 131; posed economic threat to Sadducees, 145-46; trial of, before Annas, 146-47; false charges against, 150-52; answered nothing to refute accusations, 152-53; is found guilty of blasphemy, 155, 158; is smitten and spit upon, 259-60; looks upon Peter, after denial, 162-63; is taken before Pilate, 171; speaks of his kingdom, 176; Pilate finds no fault in, 177, 183; appears before Herod and remains silent, 180; contrasted with Barabbas, 184-85; scourging of, 191-92; Pilate delivers, to will of Jews, 197; stumbles under weight of cross, 206-7; promises place in paradise to penitent thief, 222; provides for his mother, 223-24; calls out for his Father, 226; gives up his life, 228; soldier pierces, with spear, 235; burial of, 238-40; ministers to spirits in prison, 241-45; speaks to Nephites as a spirit, 245-48; is risen, 251, 261; appears to Mary Magdalene, 263-65; appears to other women, 265-67; joins disciples on Emmaus road, 275-78; appears to disciples in upper room, 279-82; appears to Thomas, 284-85; on shore of Sea of Galilee, 289; instructs Peter to feed His sheep, 289-90; has all power, 298-99; did not destroy prophets, but fulfilled them, 309-10; is the law, 310-11; heals sick among Nephites, 322; blesses Nephite children, 322-23; spoke more plainly to Nephites than to Palestinians, 362-63; work of, is finished, 402-4; ascension of, 408-9; testimony of, is spirit of prophecy, 411; belief in, importance of, 412, 432; testimonies of, 412-15, 436-37; faithful shall see, 416-17; Second Coming of, 418-22; summary of work of, 426-30; prepare ye the way of, 430; example of, men must follow, 434-35
Jews: factions of, unite to destroy Jesus, 12-13; divisions among, make it difficult to accuse Jesus, 150; Pilate's encounters with, 172-73; could not inflict death penalty, 174; Pilate's fear of, 185-86; revenges of history upon, 189-90, 202 n. 2-3, 209; latter-day restoration of, 203 n. 6; taunts of, to Jesus on cross, 217-19; will look upon wounds of Jesus, 235-36, 341, 421; differentiating, from Gentiles, 314-15; conversion of, 340-43. *See also* Israel
John the Beloved, 32; gained admittance to Caiaphas's palace, 160-61; Jesus commits his mother to care of, 223-24; rushes to empty tomb, 262; is to tarry until Second Coming, 291-92
Jonah, sign of, 9
Joseph, son of Jacob, America is land of, 311, 334, 336
Joseph of Arimathea, 237-39
Joy, fulness of, 86-87, 386, 391
Judas: blood money paid to, 14-15; motives of, for betraying Jesus, 15-18; modern counterparts of, 17; contention stirred by, 31-32; sat by Jesus at Last Supper, 32-33; Jesus washed feet of, 41-42; would be better had he not been born, 44; receives sop and leaves, 44-45; departure of, lifts spirits of group, 48; betrays Jesus with kiss, 129-30; begins to recognize Jesus' innocence, 197-98; tries to return the silver, 198-99; death of, was prophesied, 199-200; hangs himself, 200
Judgment: inevitability of, 202-3 n. 4, 208-9; belongs to Christ, 216; all shall undergo,

241; out of records kept, 384-85; hierarchy of, 385
Justice, mercy cannot rob, 211, 215 n. 5

Katalyma, or hostelry, 22-23
King of the Jews, 175, 213-14
Kingdom: eternal, Jesus appoints, unto disciples, 35; of Christ is not of this world, 176
Kiss, Judas betrays Jesus with, 130

Lamb, slaying of, 25
Last Supper: seating arrangement at, 31-33; contention afflicts, 34-35; sadness falls over, 43. *See also* Passover
Law of Moses, Jesus fulfilled, 309-10
Leaven, search for, prior to Passover, 24
Life, laying down, is greatest manifestation of love, 87. *See also* Eternal life
Light, greater, sinning against, 91, 397-99
Lord's Supper. *See* Sacrament
Lots, soldiers cast, for Jesus' robe, 215
Love: of Jesus for the Twelve, 48; is new commandment, 50, 87; showing, by keeping commandments, 74; is of God, 82-83; casteth out fear, 83; of God, 86; manifesting, by laying down life, 87
"Lovest thou me," Jesus asks, of Peter, 289-91
Luke, 275, 278, 285 n. 1

Magdalene, Mary: Jesus appears to, 262-65; is forbidden to touch Jesus, 264, 269-70 n. 1; prominence of, 270 n. 2
Malachi, 367-68
Malchus, Peter wounds, and Jesus heals, 131-32
Mansions, many, Father's house has, 70
Mark, 24
Marred servants, 354
Mary, mother of Jesus, 223-24
Meetings, saints are to hold, 325
Melchizedek, 52-53
Mercy cannot rob justice, 211, 215 n. 5
Messianic prophecies, fulfillment of, 280-81
Micah, 335, 356
Michael, 125
Millennium, prayers of righteous for, 347. *See also* Second Coming
Missionary work: Twelve are called to do, 281-82, 299-300; of John the Beloved, 292
Mob, gathering of, to arrest Jesus, 129
Mockery: Jesus submitted to, 192; of Jesus on cross, 217-19
Mortality, man's limited knowledge in, 392-93
Mosaic law: Passover is not child of, 30; had been fulfilled when Jesus visited Nephites, 309
Moses, Lord commanded, to call Seventy, 164
Mount of Transfiguration, 10
Mountain in Galilee, Jesus' apparance on, 295-305
Mysteries of godliness: Holy Ghost reveals, 99-100; receiving, requires faith, 369-70; many receive, but cannot impart them, 393-94

Nail fastened in sure place, 215 n. 4
Name of Christ: prayers offered in, 73, 102-3; performing works in, 376; true Church must be called in, 376-79; men must take, upon themselves, 378, 387 n. 1
Nephi the Disciple, 300-301
Nephites: sacrament given to, 59, 323-24, 330; twelve disciples among, teach and baptize, 94-95, 326-27; Jesus' prayers among, 106-7, 110-12, 327-28; darkness and destruction among, at Jesus' death, 225-26; Jesus speaks to, as a spirit, 245; righteous among, are spared from destruction, 260; are Jesus' "other sheep," 306, 312; Jesus' work among, 307, 374; were not known to brethren at Jerusalem, 311; are sent home to ponder Jesus' words, 321; Jesus heals sick among, 322; Jesus blesses children of, 322-23; thousands of, gather to meet Jesus, 326; receive Holy Ghost, 327; great faith of, 329; are heirs of Abrahamic covenant, 339; Jesus spoke more plainly to, than to Palestinians, 362-63; Jesus expounds scriptures to, 363-68; the Three, 389-90, 394-96; gospel blessings prevailing among, 397; apostasy of, 397-99
New Jerusalem, 350, 358-59
Nicodemus, 8-9, 75, 239

Officers in Church organization, 411

Oneness: of God and Jesus, 72; of all believers, 115-16, 327-28
Opposition in all things, 89
Ordinances: of baptism and sacrament, 29-30; of washing of feet, 36-41; sacramental, Christ institutes, 57-63; to be done in worthiness, 67 n. 9; of celestial marriage, promised to Abraham, 338
"Other sheep," Nephites referred to as, 306, 312

Paradise, 222
Paschal supper: Jesus presides over, 29; partakers of, ate in reclining positions, 31; format of, 53-57. *See also* Passover
Passover, 19-21; Jesus instructs disciples to prepare, 21; rituals involved in, 24-25, 53-57; temple ceremony of, 25-26; is not child of Mosaic law, 30; is in similitude of Christ's sacrifice, 50-51; Jesus eats, for last time, 51-52; conclusion of, 68-69, 80-81
Paul, 258-59, 295
Peace: Jesus leaves, with disciples, 78; gospel brings, 104
Penitent thief on cross, 220-22
Pentecost, 103, 404-6
Perdition, son of, 113
Persecution of disciples, Jesus prophesies, 90
Peter: Jesus washes feet of, 37-38; Jesus prophesies denial of, 69, 120-21, 122; accompanies Jesus into Gethsemane, 123; falls asleep in Gethsemane, 125-26; slashes off ear of Malchus, 131; follows Jesus to Caiaphas's palace, 160; denies Jesus thrice, 161-62; Jesus looks upon, after denial, 162-63; failure of, to be valiant, 169 n. 2; testimony of, to Cornelius, 258; rushes to empty tomb, 262; Jesus appears to, 272; goes fishing, 288; swims to shore to meet Jesus, 289; Jesus instructs, "Feed my sheep," 289-91; crucifixion of, Jesus foretells, 291
Pharisees, hatred of, for Jesus, 144-45
Philip, 72
Pilate, Pontius: modern counterparts of, 17; Jesus is taken before, 171; character of, 171-73; asks Jesus if he is King of Jews, 175; asks, "What is truth," 177; finds no fault in Jesus, 177, 183; sends Jesus to Herod, 178; Jesus is returned to, 182; offers to scourge Jesus, 183; would release either Jesus or Barabbas, 184-87; wife of, urges Jesus' release, 185; feared to arouse Jews, 185-86; rises from judgment seat, 188; washes his hands before Jews to signify innocence, 188-89; has Jesus scourged, 191-92; bids Jews look upon scourged Christ, 193; could have no power except that given from above, 195; delivers Jesus to will of Jews, 197; orders superscription "King of the Jews" placed above cross, 213-14; allows Joseph of Arimathea to take Jesus' body, 238
Posca, drink given Jesus on cross, 227-28
Posterity, blessings of, promised to Abraham, 338
Potter's field, 199-202
Power, Jesus had all, 298-99
Prayer: offering, in Jesus' name, 73, 102-3; intercessory, of Jesus, 105-6, 107-17; of Jesus when among Nephites, 106-7, 110-12, 327-28; two elements universally appropriate in, 107-8; of Jesus in Gethsemane, 124, 127; to avoid temptation, 324
Preparing to meet the Lord, 430-35
Priesthood, bearers of, may receive all the Father hath, 104
Prints of nails in Jesus' hands and feet, Thomas feels, 284; Jesus invites Nephites to feel, 287-88; Nephites felt, 298
Prison, spirits in, Jesus ministers to, 241-45
Prophecy, testimony of Jesus is spirit of, 411
Prophets: act as examples of men, 114-15; those who will not hear, will be cut off, 337; all looked forward to last days, 357; cannot impart all that they see, 393-94
Proverbs, hiding truth in, 102
Purse and scrip, disciples were now to provide, for themselves, 121

Questions asked by child at Passover, 55

Rank, Judas's concern with, 32
Repentance: neglect of, brings exquisite suffering, 118; deathbed, 222; Jesus cries, to Nephites, 245; is step in preparing to meet the Lord, 431
Restoration: of gospel, prophecies

Sop: Jesus gives, to Judas, 44-45; of unleavened bread, 56
Sorrow of disciples will be short, 101
Spear thrust into Jesus' side, 235
Spirit: being born of, 75; of Jesus, reuniting with body, 261; gifts of, 411
Spirit world, gospel preached in, 222-23, 241-45
Spirits of the just: gathering of, 243; resurrection of, 273
Spitting, Jesus endured, 159-60
Suffering of Jesus: exquisiteness of, 118, 126-27; summary of, 231-32 n. 3
Sword, he who taketh, shall perish with, 132

Temple: of his body, Jesus was to raise up, 8, 151; Passover ceremony of, 25-26; cleansing of, affected Sadducees most directly, 145-46; plotting to destroy and rebuild, Jesus is accused of, 152; veil of, rent at Jesus' death, 229-30
Ten tribes, lost, 312-13
Testimonies of Jesus, 412-15, 436-47
Tests of faith: importance of, 119; to beset Peter, 119-21
Thieves, two: Jesus is crucified between, 214; conversation of, 220-22
Third day, Jewish tradition concerning, 261-62
Third Nephi, special contributions of, 307-8
Thirst of Jesus on cross, 227
Thirty pieces of silver, 14-15, 1?8-99
Thomas, 284-85
Three Nephites: desire to tarry as did John, 389; revelations given to, 393-94; transfiguration of, 394-95; ministry of, 395-96
Tomb: provided by Joseph of Arimathea, 238-39; guard is set over, 240; angels roll stone back from, 261
Tongues, gift of, on day of Pentecost, 405
Transfiguration: Mount of, 10; of Three Nephites, 394-95
Transgressors, Jesus to be numbered with, 121
Translation of men, 389-91
Transubstantiation, 67 n. 8
Treason: converting charge of blasphemy into one of, 167; Jews accuse Jesus of, before Pilate, 175
Trials of Jesus: by Jews, fragmentary accounts of, 142; before Annas, 142, 146-47; before Caiaphas, 149-56; reconciling accounts of, 156 n. 1; before the Sanhedrin, 165-68; before Pilate, 175-77; before Herod, 180
Truth: Spirit of, 74-75, 97; Holy Ghost shows, to men, 98; being sanctified through, 114; the sinful will reject, 168; those who seek, hear Jesus' voice, 176-77; Pilate asks concerning, 177; definition of, 181 n. 3
Twelve apostles: had to accept Jesus' death, 7-8; Jesus prepared, for his crucifixion, 10; will judge the twelve tribes of Israel, 35-36; each asked if he was traitor, 43; Jesus addresses, as "little children," 49; Jesus commands, to love one another, 50; are branches of the true vine, 84-85; Jesus names, as friends, 87; were ordained ministers, 88; world will hate, 89-92; are to see Jesus in "a little while," 100-101; Jesus prays for, 110-11; tests of, were important to their growth, 119; offer to defend Jesus by sword, 121, 131; fled when Jesus was taken, 132; Jesus sends women to, to testify of resurrection, 267; Jesus appears to, in upper room, 279-82; are called as witnesses, 281-82; receive gift of Holy Ghost, 282, 404-6; Jesus instructs, to remain in Jerusalem, 406-7; return to Jerusalem after ascension, 409

Unbelief, rending veil of, 372
Unity: need for, among the Twelve, 112; among saints, Jesus prays for, 115
Unleavened bread, 56
Upper room: Jesus and Twelve gather in, 28-29; Jesus appears to disciples in, 279-82, 410
Unworthy partaking of sacrament, 63-64, 326

Veil: of temple, rending of, 229-30; piercing of, 417
Victory, death is swallowed up in, 255-57
Vine, true, Jesus is, 84-85

Washing of feet: Jesus instituted ordinance

For behold, the time cometh,
and is not far distant, that with power the Lord Omnipotent
who reigneth, who was, and is from all eternity
to all eternity, shall come down from heaven among
the children of men, and shall dwell
in a tabernacle of clay, and shall go forth
amongst men, working mighty miracles, such as healing
the sick, raising the dead, causing the lame to walk,
the blind to receive their sight, and the deaf to hear,
and curing all manner of diseases.
And he shall cast out devils, or the evil spirits which
dwell in the hearts of the children of men.
And lo, he shall suffer temptations,
and pain of body, hunger, thirst, and fatigue,
even more than man can suffer,
except it be unto death; for behold, blood cometh
from every pore, so great shall be his anguish
for the wickedness and the abominations of his people.
And he shall be called Jesus Christ,
the Son of God, the Father of heaven and earth,
the Creator of all things from the beginning;
and his mother shall be called Mary.
And lo, he cometh unto his own, that salvation
might come unto the children of men
even through faith on his name; and even after all this
they shall consider him a man, and say that he
hath a devil, and shall scourge him, and shall crucify him.
And he shall rise the third day
from the dead; and behold, he standeth
to judge the world; and behold, all these things are done
that a righteous judgment might
come upon the children of men.
—Mosiah 3:5-10

The Promised Messiah

The first coming of Christ

Bruce R. McConkie

Deseret Book Company
Salt Lake City, Utah

ISBN 0-87747-702-7 (hardbound)
ISBN 0-87579-402-5 (softbound)

Library of Congress Cataloging-in-Publication Data

McConkie, Bruce R.
The promised Messiah.

Includes index.
1. Jesus Christ—Mormon interpretations. 2. Messiah—Prophecies.
3. Mormons and Mormonism—Doctrinal and controversial works.
I. Title.
BX8643.J4M32 232'.12 78-3478

Printed in the United States of America

10 9 8 7 6 5 4 3 2

CONTENTS

CHAPTER 9

CHAPTER 10

CHAPTER 11

CHAPTER 12

MESSIAH IS THE PERFECT ONE 197

CHAPTER 13

MESSIAH REDEEMS MANKIND 217

CHAPTER 14

MESSIAH ATONES AND RANSOMS 231

CHAPTER 15

CHAPTER 16

CHAPTER 17

CHAPTER 18

CHAPTER 19

CHAPTER 20

CHAPTER 27

CHAPTER 28

CHAPTER 29

CHAPTER 30

CHAPTER 31

CHAPTER 32

ABBREVIATIONS

Scriptural references are abbreviated in a standard and self-identifying way. Other books are cited by author and title except the following: *Mormon Doctrine* (Bruce R. McConkie, *Mormon Doctrine,* Bookcraft, 2nd ed.) and *Teachings* (Joseph Fielding Smith, comp., *Teachings of the Prophet Joseph Smith,* Deseret Book).

PREFACE

Since the Lord laid his hands upon me, on October 12, 1972, by the hands of his servant, President Harold B. Lee, and ordained me to the holy apostleship, I have had but one desire—to testify of our Lord's divine Sonship and to teach, in purity and perfection, the truths of his everlasting gospel.

I was born with a testimony, and from my earliest days have known with absolute certainty of the truth and divinity of his great latter-day work. Doubt and uncertainty have been as foreign to me as the gibberish of alien tongues. But even so, a gracious God has now given me a new heart and a renewed and increased determination to bear witness of spiritual things and to proclaim, insofar as I am able, the truths of salvation, in all their glory, beauty, and perfection.

And so now, with holy zeal—having no private views to expound, no personal doctrines to set forth, no ideas that originate with me alone—I desire to present those things which will cause men of good will everywhere to believe in Him by whom salvation comes.

This work is sent forth to persuade men to believe in Christ, to accept him as their Lawgiver, Savior, and King, and to guide them in that course of obedience and devotion which will prepare them to enjoy his companionship forever in eternal glory. It deals with revealed truth as such is found in the Holy Scriptures. My objective is to interpret those scriptures by the power of that same Spirit which inspired the apostles and prophets who first recorded the eternal truths which in them are. And it is devoutly to be hoped that all who read and study the teachings here declared will ponder their deep import and seek wisdom from the one Source from which spiritual things can be known with perfect surety.

Our Lord came once, in time's meridian, to reveal his Father, to teach his truths, and to work out the infinite and eternal atonement. All of the holy prophets, during the four long millenniums from Adam to the son of Zacharias, looked forward to that coming; all knew that the Promised Messiah would dwell as a mortal on earth; all taught that portion of his saving truth which their hearers were prepared to receive; and their message was that salvation, and all that appertains to it, is in Christ who was to come.

Our Lord shall come again, in the fulness of times, in all the glory of his Father's kingdom, to complete the salvation of men and to reign in glory on this earth after it has been renewed and has received again its paradisiacal glory. And no subject is of greater concern to men today than his return in power and glory to divide the sheep from the goats and to say to those who believe in him: "Come, ye blessed of my Father, inherit the kingdom prepared for you from the foundation of the world." (Matt. 25:34.)

At his First Coming he performed the most transcendent work ever wrought by man or God from creation's morn to eternity's endless duration. Standing as the Resurrection and the Life, at his Father's behest, he brought to pass the immortality and eternal life of man and ransomed all creation from its fallen doom.

While he dwelt on earth he lived a life like no other mortal who ever came forth from a mother's womb. His words and deeds, his teachings and miracles, his triumph over the tomb—all that he did and said—all things appertaining to him have neither equal nor parallel among all the billions of souls who have breathed or shall breathe the breath of life on planet earth.

At his Second Coming he shall reap the harvest, sown in Gethsemane, as all those who have washed their garments in his blood come forth to live and reign with him on earth a thousand years.

What wonders of redeeming grace were manifest when he dwelt among men as Mary's Son and took upon himself the sins of the world on conditions of repentance!

And what miracles of glory, triumph, and victory shall attend his return as God's Almighty Son to take vengeance on the wicked and usher in the year of his redeemed!

This work—*The Promised Messiah: The First Coming of Christ*—is my attempt to distill in one volume the teachings of the ancient prophets about his First Coming. And be it remembered that what is here considered was the heart and core of the teachings of all the preachers of righteousness who lived before he dwelt among men, which is to say that herein we shall view the gospel as it is seen through the eyes of Enoch and Elijah, Moses and Melchizedek, Abraham and Moriancumer, and all those whom God favored with a sure knowledge of his divine truth.

It is my desire and intent—the Lord willing, and building upon the foundation herein laid—to publish, hereafter, *The Mortal Messiah*, which will deal with the life he lived among men.

Then finally, to complete this triad, this trilogy, this trinity—again the Lord willing, and building upon the two preceding works—it is my desire and intent to set forth in summary form those things which we know about his near advent, under the title *The Millennial Messiah*.

As with my other published works, I am deeply indebted to a most efficient and able secretary, Velma Harvey, for her thoughtful suggestions and careful handling of the many details involved.

MESSIAH BRINGETH SALVATION TWICE

God Ministers Among Men Twice

Salvation is in Christ—now and forever!

He came once—born in a stable, cradled in a manger—to redeem his people; to restore his everlasting gospel; to work out the infinite and eternal atonement; *to bring salvation.*

He shall come again—with ten thousands of his saints, in all the glory of his Father's kingdom—to slay the wicked by the breath of his lips; to cleanse the vineyard of corruption; to ransom those who love his appearing; *to bring salvation.*

He is the Lord Omnipotent by whom all things are and through whose atoning blood redemption cometh.

He is the Father and the Son, the Lord Jehovah, the Almighty God.

He is our King.

He is our Lawgiver.

He is our Judge.

It is in his holy name, his name only, that we may gain eternal life.

It is he who has given a law unto all things, and no man cometh unto the Father but by him and by his law.

Without him there would be no creation; no mortal probation; no redemption from death, hell, the devil, and endless torment.

Without him there would be no life after death; no eternal life for those who believe and obey; no eternal felicity for all created things.

And the most transcendent event in his entire eternal existence, the most glorious single happening from creation's dawn to eternity's endless continuance, the crowning work of his infinite goodness—such took place in a garden called Gethsemane, outside a city called Jerusalem, when he, tabernacled in the flesh, bore the weight of the sins of all those who believe in his name and obey his gospel.

He came into the world in time's meridian to put into full operation all the terms and conditions of his Father's plan; to bring to pass immortality and to make eternal life available to man; to abolish death and bring life and immortality to light through his gospel.

And he shall come again—perhaps while some of us on earth yet live as mortals—first, to dwell and reign on earth a thousand years, and then, after a short season, to transform this earth into his own celestial home, where he shall dwell, from time to time, among exalted beings.

These are the most glorious events in the whole history of planet earth. From Adam to John, called the Baptist, all the prophets looked forward to both of these comings; and from Peter to the last apostle who shall rise up in this dispensation, all have and shall testify of his destined return in power, attended by the hosts of heaven, to bring surcease from all care and sorrow to those who have been valiant in the cause of truth and righteousness.

How to Read the Signs of the Times

Those who lived when he was born of Mary in Bethlehem of Judea needed the spirit of inspiration to discern the signs of the times, to know which of the prophetic utterances described his First Coming, which his Second. Theirs was the responsibility to search the scriptures and seek the Spirit so they could know and believe the truths revealed by him in their dispensation.

And those of us who now live as mortals—and more particularly those who are members of his latter-day kingdom—need and seek the spirit of revelation to read the signs of the times, to know when he will come again, to know which parts of the revealed word have reference to the millennial cleansing of the earth, and which have reference to the earth in its final celestial state.

We have the advantage of hindsight in pondering the Messianic prophecies and seeing their fulfillment in the mortal ministry of the Son of God among men. Their meanings are clear, and the understanding of them is certain, because the events forecast have transpired; because their application to these events has been confirmed by latter-day revelation; because of the spirit of interpretation shed forth upon the saints by the Holy Spirit of God.

Accordingly, as we rejoice in the efficacy and virtue of the infinite and eternal atonement, wrought by God himself in a dispensation past, we also search, ponder, and pray to know how to interpret and apply Holy Writ in the dispensation present. We desire to know how to read the signs of our times, as they read the signs of theirs.

We desire to know of our Lord's promised return to dwell among us; and next to the spirit of revelation and prophecy itself, there is probably no better guide than to know and understand those Messianic utterances whose fulfillment is now a matter of assured reality. To know how Deity has dealt with men is to forecast how he will continue to do so, for he is the same yesterday, today, and forever; his course is one eternal round; and as he offered goodness and grace to the ancients, so will he to us, if we walk as they did. The fact is, no one can comprehend the future Second Coming without first gaining a knowledge of the First Coming.

In this work we shall consider the testimony and teachings of the prophets of old relative to the Promised Messiah: the First Coming of Christ. This knowledge will lay the foundation for an understanding of the life that he lived among mortals and of his future return to reign among them during the Millennium.

Come unto Christ and Learn of Him

We shall, by the doctrine taught and the testimony borne in this work, invite men to come unto Christ, believe his word, live his law, and gain salvation in his Father's kingdom.

We know—with absolute certainty—that the teachings given and testimonies borne by the ancient prophets, concerning Him who is their Lord and our Lord, are true. And we shall attempt to interpret these Messianic utterances by the power of the same Spirit that rested upon those of old who taught that "salvation was, and is, and is to come, in and through the atoning blood of Christ, the Lord Omnipotent." (Mosiah 3:18.)

Our purpose, as we launch forth on the great ocean of truth relative to the Lord Jesus Christ and his eternal ministry, is to persuade men to believe that he is the Son of God by whom salvation comes.

We know that men are saved no faster than they gain a knowledge of God, of Christ, and of the laws which they have ordained. We cannot be saved in ignorance of the One who made salvation possible, nor of the everlasting gospel which bears his name.

We know that it is life eternal to know the Father, who is God above all, and the Son, who is in the image of the Father and through whom are transacted all the dealings of Deity with mortals.

We also know that the Father is revealed by the Son; that no man cometh unto the Father but through the Son; and that to know One is to know the Other.

We know that the plan of salvation is always and everlastingly the same; that obedience to the same laws always brings the same reward; that the gospel laws have not changed from the day of Adam to the present; and that always and everlastingly all things pertaining to salvation center in Christ.

We shall, therefore, learn of Christ and his laws as such knowledge is set forth in the Messianic preachings and prophecies of old, and we shall know that these same laws and doctrines will guide us, as they guided the saints of old, to that eternal life which we and they so devoutly desire.

We shall—reverently, with awe and adoration, in the true spirit of worship—turn our attention to the Lord Jesus Christ. We shall seek to learn who he is, what he has done for us, and what we must do to pay the debt.

The Messiah and "the Mystery of Godliness"

Our revelations speak of "the mystery of godliness" and say, "How great is it!" Then they explain that eternal punishment does not last forever, that endless punishment has an end, and that the scriptures which speak of them have an express and unique meaning that is not conveyed by a mere knowledge of the usual definition of terms. (D&C 19:10-13.)

We shall attempt in this work to uncover the *mystery of the Messiah,* as it were, so that he and his mission will be revealed clearly before us. All gospel mysteries become plain and simple and easy to understand once the light of heaven sheds its darkness-dispelling rays into the hearts and souls of sincere seekers of truth.

It is almost superfluous to suggest that those who seek the truth and desire understanding will, by instinct, reserve judgment on issues they may not understand (as, for instance, that Christ is both the Father and the Son; or that the Father, Son, and Holy Ghost are one God in a sense far greater than merely being one in purpose) until the mystery of godliness, on whatever point is involved, has been set forth in full. After full investigation and an analysis of all the scriptures involved, we are confident that all gospel students whose hearts are open will come with us to a unity of the faith with reference to the great concepts we are now to consider.

We shall study many things about the Son of the Highest, some of them plain and easy and simple; others, deep, hidden, and mysterious. We shall ponder, pray, and seek wisdom from on high as we weigh and evaluate the various Messianic utterances, for we know "that no prophecy of the scripture is of any private interpretation." Revealed truth came when "holy men of God spake as they were moved by the Holy Ghost." (2 Pet. 1:20-21.) That same Holy Spirit will interpret the sayings of the seers of old, and there is no other sure and certain means of receiving spiritual truth.

The Holy Scriptures—all of them, both ancient and modern—speak of many things that are hard to understand without an over-all knowledge of the plan of salvation and without the enlightening power of the Holy Ghost. For instance:

The Book of Mormon teaches that "Christ the Son, and God the Father, and the Holy Spirit . . . is one Eternal God." (Alma 11:44.) Is there one God or are there three Gods; and if there are three, how and in what manner are they one?

Abinadi says "that God himself shall come down among the children of men, and shall redeem his people. And because he dwelleth in flesh he shall be called the Son of God, and having subjected the flesh to the will of the Father, being the Father and the Son—The Father, because he was conceived by the power of God; and the Son, because of the flesh; thus becoming the Father and Son—And they are one God, yea, the very Eternal Father of heaven and of earth. And thus the flesh becoming subject to the Spirit, or the Son to the Father, being one God, suffereth temptation, and yieldeth not to the temptation, but suffereth himself to be mocked, and scourged, and cast out, and disowned by his people." (Mosiah 15:1-5.) What is Abinadi's message? He tells us that God comes down and is called the Son; he is the Father, and as the Son, he is subject to the Father. So it is recorded in the Book of Mormon; the translation is correct and the doctrine is true. Ought we not to understand these things and to come to a knowledge of what is meant by the inspired author? Are we not obligated to know the true meaning of all that is in the Book of Mormon and in all the scriptures?

Christ said to the brother of Jared, "I am Jesus Christ. I am the Father and the Son." (Ether 3:14.) If the Father and the Son are two Personages—as we know from their appearance to Joseph Smith in the Sacred Grove—why does Christ here say he is the Father and the Son?

He also said, "Man have I created after the body of my spirit." (Ether 3:16.) Why does Christ say he created man, when other scriptures affirm that the Father is our Creator?

Isaiah calls Christ "The mighty God, The everlasting Father." (Isa. 9:6.) Again, why this emphasis on Christ as the Father?

John says of Christ, "The worlds were made by him; men were made by him; all things were made by him, and through him, and of him." (D&C 93:10.) Isaiah says he is man's "Maker." (Isa. 17:7.) Again we are faced with our Lord's role in the creation of man. Shall we not seek to learn what these things mean and why they are so recorded in Holy Writ?

Paul tells the faithful saints that "Jesus Christ is in you." (2 Cor. 13:5.) Is God a spirit essence or is there some other meaning?

John says the saints have "power to become the sons of God" (John 1:12); King Benjamin says the true saints are "the children of Christ, his sons, and his daughters" (Mosiah 5:7); and when we are baptized and again when we partake of the sacrament, we take upon ourselves the name of Christ. What doctrine is this and why is it taught with such emphasis?

Isaiah prophesies that the Messiah, who is Christ, "shall see his seed." (Isa. 53:10.) Who are the seed of the Promised Messiah?

Many scriptures recite the laws relative to the infinite and eternal atonement; to a temporal and spiritual redemption; to a resurrection of life and of damnation; to reconciliation, intercession, advocacy, mediation, justification, sanctification, and salvation by grace. What doctrines are these, and how do they affect us?

Others tell how God is omnipotent, omnipresent, and omniscient—terms that are seldom mentioned in the Church but find common usage among sectarian theologians. Again, shall we not seek to learn the truth and to put each scriptural passage in its proper relationship to all else found in the Holy Word?

That scriptures dealing with all these and a host of other Messianic matters might easily be misconstrued, as they have been by the learned in an apostate Christendom, is perfectly clear. Our problem is to come to a proper understanding of their meaning. We cannot brush them aside as though they were an unnecessary part of revealed writ. The mere fact that the Lord has preserved them for us in the scriptures is a sufficient witness that he expects us to ponder their deep and hidden meanings so that we shall be as fully informed about his eternal laws as were the saints of old.

The mystery of godliness! How great it is! With the help of the Lord we shall turn the light of understanding upon many of the mysteries, glories, and wonders of his kingdom as we now pursue our study of the Messianic prophecies and doctrines.

MESSIAH'S FATHER IS GOD

Who Is the Father?

Before we can comprehend either of our Lord's ministries on earth, we must come to know his Father and the infinite and eternal plan of salvation which he ordained for the glory, honor, and exaltation of Christ and of all his spirit children.

That there never was a son without a father, nor a father without a son, is self-evident; and in the very nature of things both sire and son partake of the same nature and are members of the same house and lineage.

In the exalted family of the Gods, the Father and the Son are one. They have the same character, perfections, and attributes. They think the same thoughts, speak the same words, perform the same acts, have the same desires, and do the same works. They possess the same power, have the same mind, know the same truths, live in the same light and glory. To know one is to know the other; to see one is to see the other; to hear the voice of one is to hear the voice of the other. Their unity is perfect. The Son is in the express image of his Father's person; each has a body of flesh and bones as tangible as man's; and both reign in power, might, and dominion over all the creations of their hands.

Who, then, is the Father, by whom the Son came? Who is the Almighty God, by whom all things are? How can he (and his Son) be known by mortal man? Can man comprehend God? Can the finite envision the infinite, the worm comprehend the universe, and the dust of the earth conceive of the grandeur of the galaxies of heaven?

Two great truths chart our course as we seek to know God and to conform to his image:

1. He is a glorified and perfect Being, a Holy Man, an exalted Person, a Personage of tabernacle, who has a resurrected body of flesh and bones and who lives in the family unit.

2. He is "the one supreme and absolute Being; the ultimate source of the universe; the all-powerful, all-knowing, all-good Creator, Ruler, and Preserver of all things." (*Mormon Doctrine,* 2nd ed., p. 317.)

As to his personal nature, the revealed word says that "in the language of Adam, Man of Holiness is his name" (Moses 6:57); that he "has a body of flesh and bones as tangible as man's" (D&C 130:22); that he created man "in the image of his own body" (Moses 6:9); and that we are his offspring, his spirit children (Heb. 12:9; Moses 6:36; D&C 93:21-23).

As to his glory, might, and omnipotence, our revelations say simply: "There is a God in heaven, who is infinite and eternal, from everlasting to everlasting the same unchangeable God, the framer of heaven and earth, and all things which are in them," and that he "gave his Only Begotten Son" to redeem the world. (D&C 20:17, 21.)

Where Gods Began to Be

We do not now know, nor can the mortal mind discern, how all things came to be. We have the divine promise that if we are faithful in all things, the day will come when we shall know "all things" (D&C 93:28) and "comprehend even God" (D&C 88:49). But for the present our finite limitations shut out the view of the infinite. How element, matter, life, organized intelligence, and God himself first came into being, we can no more comprehend than we can suppose that life, the earth, and the universe shall vanish away. And so we sing:

If you could hie to Kolob
In the twinkling of an eye,
And then continue onward
With that same speed to fly,
D'ye think that you could ever,
Through all eternity,
Find out the generation
Where Gods began to be?

Or see the grand beginning,
Where space did not extend?
Or view the last creation,
Where Gods and matter end?
Methinks the Spirit whispers,
"No man has found 'pure space'."
Nor seen the outside curtains,
Where nothing has a place.

The works of God continue,
And worlds and lives abound;
Improvement and progression
Have one eternal round.
There is no end to matter;
There is no end to space;
There is no end to spirit;
There is no end to race.

—*Hymns*, no. 257

And yet these things we do know:

1. Life, matter, and time (continuance) have existed and do and shall exist, everlastingly and without end, as eternities roll.

2. There is a Supreme Organized Intelligence who governs, controls, organizes, and reorganizes in all things both temporal and spiritual.

3. This Supreme Intelligence—the Lord our God—has, from our perspective, existed from eternity; yet, in the language of the Prophet Joseph Smith, "God himself was once as we are now, and is an exalted man, and sits enthroned in yonder heavens! . . . I am going to tell you how God came to be God. We have imagined and supposed that God was God from all eternity. I will refute that idea, and take away the veil, so that you may see. . . . It is the first principle of the Gospel to know for a certainty the Character of God, and to know that we may converse with him as one man converses with another, and that he was once a man like us; yea, that God himself, the Father of us all, dwelt on an earth, the same as Jesus Christ himself did; and I will show it from the Bible. . . .

"Here, then, is eternal life—to know the only wise and true God; and you have got to learn how to be Gods yourselves, and to be kings and priests to God, the same as all Gods have done before you, namely, by going from one small degree to another, and from a small capacity to a great one; from grace to grace, from exaltation to exaltation, until you attain to the resurrection of the dead, and are able to dwell in everlasting burnings, and to sit in glory, as do those who sit enthroned in everlasting power. . . . [Such persons are] heirs of God and joint heirs with Jesus Christ. What is it? To inherit the same power, the same glory and the same exaltation, until you arrive at the station of a God, and ascend the throne of eternal power, the same as those who have gone before." (*Teachings,* pp. 345-47.)

Who Is the Lord Our God?

Having before us, then, these eternal verities: that there are Gods many and Lords many; that God himself was once as we are now and is an exalted Man; that we may become as he is in the same way he gained his exaltation; and that, in fact, as Joseph Smith said, "Every man who reigns in celestial glory is a God to his dominions" (*Teachings,* p. 374)—with this perspective and background before us, let us turn to those Gods with whom we have to do, to that Eternal Godhead which created and rules our universe, each member of which has all power, all might, and all dominion.

From Joseph Smith we learn: "Everlasting covenant was made between three personages before the organization of this earth, and relates to their dispensation of things to men on the earth; these personages, according to Abraham's record, are called God the first, the Creator; God the second, the Redeemer; and God the third, the witness or Testator." (*Teachings,* p. 190.)

From the pen of Paul we read: "There is none other God but one. For though there be . . . gods many, and lords many, . . . to us there is but one God, the Father, of whom are all things, and we in him; and one Lord Jesus Christ, by whom are all things, and we by him." (1 Cor. 8:4-6.)

And from God himself comes this word to his people: "Before me there was no God formed, neither shall there be after me. I, even I, am the Lord; and beside me there is no saviour." (Isa. 43:10-11.) "I am the Lord, and there is none else, there is no God beside me." (Isa. 45:5; 46:9.) "The Lord is God, and beside him there is no Savior." (D&C 76:1.)

Our Godhead consists of the Father, Son, and Holy Ghost. They are supreme over all, and though they administer their kingdoms through a hierarchy of appointed angels who also are exalted, one of whom is Adam or Michael, in the ultimate sense these members of the Eternal Godhead are the only Gods with whom we have to do. We worship the Father, in the name of the Son, by the power of the Holy Ghost. We follow the Son as he follows his Father. We labor and strive to be like the Son as he is like the Father, and the Father and Son and Holy Ghost are one. For these holy Beings we have unbounded love, reverence, and worship.

How to Find and Know God

How can man find and know his God?

However much philosophers may reason and reach this or that conclusion as to what God must be, or whence he came, or why things are as they are; however much scientists may assert that there must be an intelligent, directing force in this well-ordered universe; however much pagan or Christian man by instinct may choose to worship wood or stone, the sun, moon, or stars, or the forces and powers of nature; however much any mortal man by finite means seeks to find and know the Infinite, yet he has failed and shall fail for this one reason: God is known only by revelation. God stands revealed or he remains forever unknown.

The truth seeker asks, "Canst thou by searching find out God? canst thou find out the Almighty unto perfection?" (Job 11:7.)

The answer: Yes and no. Yes, if the search is in the realm of the Spirit so that the laws are learned and lived whereby revelation comes; no, if the search is in the laboratory, in the philosopher's classroom, or through the scientist's telescope. Yes, if the spiritual laws by which he may be found are obeyed; no, in all other circumstances. Truly did the Holy Ghost say, by the mouth of Paul: "For after that in the wisdom of God the world by wisdom knew not God, it pleased God by the foolishness of preaching to save them that believe." (1 Cor. 1:21.)

And so thanks be to God, revelation has come to many and is available to all, and the Eternal Father may be found and known by any or all of the following means:

1. *By personal appearance, or by the opening of the heavens so that he is seen in vision.*

Before the fall, the Father was with Adam in Eden's garden. In the spring of 1820, accompanied by his Beloved Son, he appeared to Joseph Smith to usher in this dispensation; and nearly sixteen years later, on January 21, 1836, that same prophet "beheld the celestial kingdom of God" and saw "the blazing throne of God, whereon was seated the Father and the Son." (JS-V 1, 3.) Just before he suffered death by stoning for the testimony of Jesus and the love of the Lord which was his, Stephen saw "the heavens opened, and the Son of man standing on the right hand of God" (Acts 7:56), and the Beloved Revelator, banished on Patmos, saw the Eternal Father, the "Lord God Almighty," seated on his throne in heaven (Rev. 4:1-4). "After that Zion was taken up into heaven, . . . Enoch was high and lifted up, even in the bosom of the Father, and the Son of Man," and he then saw glorious visions and had extended discussions with both of those exalted Beings. (Moses 7:23-69.)

And as with any of the prophets of any age who have seen God, either in vision or by personal appearance, so with any of his saints who perfect their faith—they too may come unto him and partake of his goodness in the actual, literal, and personal sense of the word, for he is no respecter of persons.

"If a man love me, he will keep my words," Jesus said, "and my Father will love him, and we will come unto him, and make our abode with him." (John 14:23.) This "appearing of the Father and the Son," the Prophet wrote by way of revelation, "is a personal appearance." (D&C 130:3.) Concerning those whose calling and election has been made sure and whose "privilege" it thereby is "to receive the other Comforter," the Prophet said: "When any man obtains this last Comforter, he will have the personage of Jesus Christ to attend him, or appear unto him from time to time, and even He will manifest the Father unto him, and they will take up their abode with him, and the visions of the heavens will be opened unto him, and the Lord will teach him face to face, and he may have a perfect knowledge of the mysteries of the Kingdom of God; and this is the state and place the ancient Saints arrived at when they had such glorious visions—Isaiah, Ezekiel, John upon the Isle of Patmos, St. Paul in the three heavens, and all the Saints who held communion with the general assembly and Church of the Firstborn." (*Teachings,* pp. 150-51.)

2. *By the power of the Holy Ghost.*

God the Witness or Testator has this divine commission: He "witnesses of the Father and the Son." (2 Ne. 31:18.) "The Holy Ghost is a Revelator." (*Teachings,* p. 328.) His appointed labor is to reveal God and Christ and the laws of salvation which they have ordained. "And by the power of the Holy Ghost ye may know the truth of all things." (Moro. 10:5.) He is broadcasting all eternal truth out into all immensity all of the time, and any person who attunes himself to those broadcasts learns by revelation that God our Father is an exalted and perfected Being in whom all fulness and perfection dwell.

3. *By the testimony of others.*

One of the gifts of the Spirit is to believe the testimony of others who have had direct and personal revelation relative to God and his goodness. Thus, speaking specifically of the divine Sonship of Christ, but in principle of all revealed truth, our revelation on spiritual gifts proclaims: "To some it is given by the Holy Ghost to know that Jesus Christ is the Son of God, and that he was crucified for the sins of the world. To others it is given to believe on their words, that they also might have eternal life if they continue faithful." (D&C 46:13-14.) It follows that God the Father may be found and known by hearkening to the teachings and testimony of the prophets and apostles and others who have received personal revelation and therefore know him for themselves, independent of others.

Thus, Paul is a witness whose testimony has convincing power in the hearts of receptive truth seekers. He testifies that the Son of God possesses the "brightness" of his Father's "glory," is in "the express image of his person," and sits on his "right hand." (Heb. 1:3.) That is, the resurrected Lord, whose immortal body of "flesh and bones" was seen and felt and handled by his disciples (Luke 24:36-43), is in all respects like his Father, who also "has a body of flesh and bones" (D&C 130:22).

For our day, Joseph Smith is the chief and greatest witness of both the Father and the Son. In recording the most transcendent theophany of which we have record, he said: "I saw two Personages, whose brightness and glory defy all description, standing above me in the air. One of them spake unto me, calling me by name and said, pointing to the other—This is My Beloved Son. Hear Him!" (JS-H 17.)

Then with reference to the "prejudice," "reviling," and "bitter persecution" heaped upon him by "professors of religion" and their followers, he said that his position was like Paul before Agrippa. Opposition and ridicule could not change the reality of his experience. "I had actually seen a light, and in the midst of that light I saw two Personages, and they did in reality speak to me," he testified, "and though I was hated and persecuted for saying that I had seen a vision, yet it was true; and while they were persecuting me, reviling me, and speaking all manner of evil against me falsely for so saying, I was led to say in my heart: Why persecute me for telling the truth? I have actually seen a vision; and who am I that I can withstand God, or why does the world think to make me deny what I have actually seen? For I had seen a vision; I knew it, and I knew that God knew it, and I could not deny it, neither dared I do it." (JS-H 17-25.)

And so it is with the faithful elders of latter-day Israel, to all of whom Deity says: "Ye are my witnesses, saith the Lord, that I am God." (Isa. 43:12.) Accordingly, this disciple, as one among many, adds his testimony that he has found the Father; that he knows by personal revelation, given by the power of the Holy Ghost, that God himself is an exalted and perfected Being, possessed of infinite power, wisdom, and goodness; that he is a Holy Man in whose image we are; and that if we are faithful in all things we shall dwell with him in immortal glory and be as he is.

4. *By accepting Christ as the Son of God.*

God was and is in Christ manifesting himself to the world. Christ came to reveal his Father to mankind. There is no better way to envision who and what the Father is than to come to know his Son. The Son is in all respects as the Father. They look alike; each is in the express image of the person of the other. Their thoughts are the same; they speak forth the same eternal truths; and every deed done by one is the same thing the other would do under the same circumstances. In their great doctrinal exposition on the Father and the Son, the First Presidency and the Twelve say: "In all his dealings with the human family Jesus the Son has represented and yet represents Elohim His Father in power and authority . . . so far as power, authority, and Godship are concerned His words and acts were and are those of the Father." (Cited in James E. Talmage, *Articles of Faith,* pp. 470-71.) Truly the Father and the Son are one in all things.

Jesus said: "He that believeth on me, believeth not on me, but on him that sent me. And he that seeth me seeth him that sent me." (John 12:44-45.)

Also: "No man cometh unto the Father, but by me. If ye had known me, ye should have known my Father also: and from henceforth ye know him, and have seen him. . . . He that hath seen me hath seen the Father." And as to how all this could be, he explained that he was in the Father and the Father in him, even as his disciples should be in him and he in them. (John 14:6-20.)

5. *By keeping the commandments of God.*

In the final and all-comprehensive sense, the sole and only way to find and know God is to keep his commandments. As a result of such a course, knowledge and revelation will come in one way or another until man knows his Maker. The more obedient a person is, the clearer his views become, the nearer he approaches his God, and the more he comes to know those holy Beings whom to know is eternal life. (John 17:3.)

"And hereby we do know that we know him, if we keep his commandments. He that saith, I know him, and keepeth not his commandments, is a liar, and the truth is not in him. But whoso keepeth his word, in him verily is the love of God perfected: hereby know we that we are in him." (1 Jn. 2:3-5.)

Those who keep the whole law of the whole gospel finally, in celestial exaltation, know God in full. They then think as he thinks, say what he says, do what he does, and experience what he experiences. They are Gods and they have eternal life, which is the name of the kind of life he lives.

God Is Omnipotent, Omnipresent, and Omniscient

Joseph Smith taught these seven things about God our Eternal Father:

1. He is "the only supreme governor and independent Being in whom all fulness and perfection dwell."
2. He is "omnipotent, omnipresent, and omniscient."
3. He is "without beginning of days or end of life."
4. "In him every good gift and every good principle dwell."
5. "He is the Father of lights."
6. "In him the principle of faith dwells independently."
7. "He is the object in whom the faith of all other rational and accountable beings center for life and salvation." (*Lectures on Faith,* p. 9, cited in *Mormon Doctrine,* 2nd ed., pp. 317-18.)

These are simple, basic, scriptural truths. The Prophet here summarizes them by the spirit of inspiration, and his statements are the doctrines of the Church; they are the mind and will of the Lord relative to himself and the powers he possesses. Unfortunately some have supposed that the Almighty is not almighty, that he has not attained the high ultimates of perfection and power here named, and that somehow he is still learning new truths and progressing in knowledge and wisdom. Such a view comes from a total misconception of what eternal progress really is. The simple, unadorned fact is that God is omnipotent and supreme. He has all power, all knowledge, all truth, and all wisdom, and is everywhere present by the power of his Spirit. In him every good and wholesome attribute dwells independently and in its eternal fulness and perfection. There is no charity, no love, no honesty, no integrity, no justice, mercy, or judgment, that he does not possess in the absolute and total and complete sense of the word. If there were some truth he did not know, some power that was denied him, some attribute of perfection still to be obtained, he would not be God; and if progression lay ahead for him where his character, perfections, or attributes are concerned, then retrogression would also be a possibility; and by falsely so assuming, we would soon find ourselves mired in such a morass of philosophical absurdities that we would be as far removed from saving truth as are the pagans and heathens.

Our mission is not to belittle but to exalt that Being "who is infinite and eternal" (D&C 20:17); who "made the world and all things therein," and is in fact "Lord of heaven and earth" (Acts 17:24); who is indeed the Creator of "worlds without number," and whose plan of redemption, salvation, and eternal life applies to all the creatures of his creating on all the creations of his hands (Moses 1:33-39).

How, then, can we envision the greatness and status of such a Being? As Isaiah asked relative to the Son-Jehovah, "To whom then will ye liken God? or what likeness will ye compare unto him?" (Isa. 40:18.) We know of no better way to show God's incomparable position than to point to the works of his hands and the results of his labors—to the earth, the universe, all living beings of whom man is chief, and to the assurance of immortality and the glory of eternal life. And so Isaiah himself, seeking to set forth the supreme station of Deity, asked: "Who hath measured the waters in the hollow of his hand, and meted out heaven with the span, and comprehended the dust of the earth in a measure, and weighed the mountains in scales, and the hills in a balance? Who hath directed the Spirit of the Lord, or being his counseller hath taught him? With whom took he counsel, and who instructed him, and taught him in the path of judgment, and taught him knowledge, and shewed to him the way of understanding?" (Isa. 40:12-14.)

Let us consider man and all forms of life; let us look upon the earth and all the laws which govern it; let us view the universe and the ordered expanse of unnumbered worlds; let us think of preexistence, of mortality, of an eternal resurrection for all things—and then let us ask why and how all these things are, and how anyone but an exalted Being who knows all things and has all power could have brought them into being.

Truly, "The heavens declare the glory of God; and the firmament sheweth his handywork." (Ps. 19:1.) And truly, as he said of all the orbs that move in the sidereal heavens, "any man who hath seen any or the least of these hath seen God moving in his majesty and power." (D&C 88:47.)

MESSIANIC PROPHECIES: THEIR NATURE AND USE

Who Is the Messiah?

No questions have greater impact—not alone for the Jews and for the rest of us who are of Israel (and whose Deliverer he is), but for all mankind—than these: Who is the Messiah? Who is the Anointed One who cometh to save his people from their sins? Who is the promised Christ?

"We have found the Messias, which is, being interpreted, the Christ." (John 1:41.) So spake Andrew to his brother Simon Peter, whose destiny was to become the chief witness of Him whom the Baptist had but recently immersed in Jordan to fulfill all righteousness.

"I know that Messias cometh, which is called Christ," said the Samaritan woman at Jacob's well.

"I that speak unto thee am he" (John 4:25-26) was the simple response of Him to whom Nathanael but shortly before had testified: "Thou art the Son of God; thou art the King of Israel." (John 1:49.)

To the spiritually benighted Jews of his day, the Messiah was deemed to be a temporal Deliverer, one who would free them from the yoke of Roman bondage and restore again the glory of David's throne. But to those who then did or yet would come to a true knowledge of the prophetic utterances concerning his coming and mission, he was the One who would ransom all mankind from the temporal and spiritual death brought upon them by the fall of Adam; he was the One by whom salvation comes.

And of this there is no doubt: The Lord Jesus—begotten by the Supreme God, conceived by Mary, born in Bethlehem, crucified on Calvary—the Lord Jesus, who is called Christ, is the Messiah. He is the Redeemer and Deliverer, the King of Israel, the Son of God, the Savior of the world.

What Is a Prophet?

To many of the spiritually illiterate in modern Christendom, prophets are strange, perhaps even freakish, characters from bygone ages to whom the Lord somehow revealed future events. In fact prophets are simply members of the true Church who have testimonies of the truth and divinity of the work. They are the saints of God who have learned by the power of the Holy Ghost that Jesus is the Christ, the Son of the living God.

A heavenly visitant, upon whom the Lord had placed his name, told the Beloved Revelator: "The testimony of Jesus is the spirit of prophecy." (Rev. 19:10.) That is, every person who receives revelation so that he knows, independent of any other source, of the divine Sonship of the Savior, has, by definition and in the very nature of things, the spirit of prophecy and is a prophet. Thus Moses exclaimed, "Would God that all the Lord's people were prophets, and that the Lord would put his spirit upon them!" (Num. 11:29.) And thus Paul counseled all the saints, "Covet to prophesy," and promised the faithful among them, "Ye may all prophesy." (1 Cor. 14:31-39.)

A testimony comes by revelation from the Holy Ghost, whose mission it is to bear "record of the Father and the Son." (Moses 1:24.) Of Christ, Moroni says: "Ye may know that he is, by the power of the Holy Ghost." (Moro. 10:7.) Prophecy comes from the same source and by the same power. In Peter's language, "Prophecy came not in old time by the will of man: but holy men of God spake as they were moved by the Holy Ghost." (2 Pet. 1:21.)

When a person abides the law which enables him to gain a revealed knowledge of the divine Sonship of our Lord, he thereby abides the law which empowers him, as occasion may require, to prophesy. In Nephite history we find an account of a people who gained testimonies and as a consequence had also the gift of prophecy. After expounding the plan of salvation, as such operates through the atoning blood of Christ, King Benjamin desired "to know of his people if they believed the words which he had spoken unto them." Their answer: "We believe all the words which thou hast spoken unto us; and also, we know of their surety and truth, because of the Spirit of the Lord Omnipotent." That is, they had gained testimonies. Then they said, "We, ourselves, also, through the infinite goodness of God, and the manifestations of his Spirit, have great views of that which is to come; and were it expedient, we could prophesy of all things." (Mosiah 5:1-3.) That is, the testimony of Jesus is the spirit of prophecy; both testimony and prophecy come by the power of the Holy Ghost; and any person who receives the revelation that Jesus is the Lord is a prophet and can, as occasion requires and when guided by the Spirit, "prophesy of all things."

What Is Scripture?

Prophetic utterances, both oral and written, are scripture. "To some it is given by the Holy Ghost to know that Jesus Christ is the Son of God, and that he was crucified for the sins of the world." (D&C 46:13.) Testimonies borne by such persons, when moved upon by the Spirit, are scripture. In fact, all the elders of the Church, by virtue of their ordination, are called "to proclaim the everlasting gospel, by the Spirit of the living God," with this promise: "Whatsoever they shall speak when moved upon by the Holy Ghost shall be scripture, shall be the will of the Lord, shall be the mind of the Lord, shall be the word of the Lord, shall be the voice of the Lord, and the power of God unto salvation." (D&C 68:1, 4.) And as it is with the elders on earth, so it is with their fellow servants beyond the veil. The words of the angels of God in heaven are scripture, for, "Angels speak by the power of the Holy Ghost; wherefore, they speak the words of Christ." (2 Ne. 32:3.)

Manifestly, all prophets are not equal, and all scripture is not of identical worth. Most persons with the spirit of testimony, of inspiration, and of prophecy are prophets to themselves only, or to their families. Some are called to preside over and give inspired guidance to one organization or another. In our day the First Presidency and the Twelve are sustained as prophets, seers, and revelators to the whole Church, with the revealed provision that the President of the Church, who is the senior apostle of God on earth at any given time, shall "preside over the whole church" and "be like unto Moses," being "a seer, a revelator, a translator, and a prophet, having all the gifts of God which he bestows upon the head of the church." (D&C 107:91-92.) To the Church, the Lord says: "Thou shalt give heed unto all his words and commandments which he shall give unto you as he receiveth them, walking in all holiness before me; For his word ye shall receive, as if from mine own mouth, in all patience and faith." (D&C 21:4-5.)

Such scripture as is canonized—meaning, at the present moment, the Bible, the Book of Mormon, the Doctrine and Covenants, and the Pearl of Great Price—comes from prophets who held positions of leadership and trust in the Lord's earthly kingdom. It is binding upon the Church and the world and is the standard by which all men shall be judged when they shall stand before the pleasing bar of the great Jehovah to receive according to their works.

What Are Messianic Prophecies?

Prophets reveal Christ to the world. "To him give all the

prophets witness, that through his name whosoever believeth in him shall receive remission of sins." (Acts 10:43.) All those who spake before his coming were looking forward to a future event, and their utterances were *Messianic prophecies.* Those who have spoken since he ministered in mortality have looked back to that time, and their utterances are *Messianic testimonies,* though they may, of course, also prophesy of the future.

Salvation is in Christ—eternally. It matters not what age of the earth is involved. Adam and all his seed, down to the last person who shall dwell upon the earth, all are subject to the same law. Every accountable person must live the same law to gain a celestial inheritance. There is no exception. All who gain eternal life must believe in Christ, accept his everlasting gospel, live in harmony with its laws, and devote their whole souls to the Cause of Righteousness. As Abinadi said: "There could not any man be saved except it were through the redemption of God." (Mosiah 13:32.)

When the Father speaks of Christ, when our Lord speaks of himself, when the Holy Ghost bears record of the Son, when angels testify of salvation, and when prophets, as struggling, persecuted mortals, bear their witness of eternal truth, all have one concordant testimony: Salvation is in Christ.

Thus, whenever there have been prophets, they have spoken of Christ; whenever the Lord has sent teachers, they have taught of Christ; whenever legal administrators have ministered among men, they have performed the ordinances of salvation which are ordained by Christ; whenever the Lord has performed signs and wonders, either by his own voice or by the voice of his servants, such have been witnesses of the goodness and greatness of Christ.

Moses prophesied "concerning the coming of the Messiah, and that God should redeem his people." And Abinadi asked: "Even all the prophets, who have prophesied ever since the world began—have they not spoken more or less concerning these things? Have they not said that God himself should come down among the children of men, and take upon him the form of man, and go forth in mighty power upon the face of the earth? Yea, and have they not said also that he should bring to pass the resurrection of the dead, and that he, himself, should be oppressed and afflicted?" (Mosiah 13:33-35.) And Peter, speaking of that salvation which is in Christ, said that the ancient prophets, to say nothing of "the angels" themselves, "inquired and searched diligently, . . . Searching what, or what manner of time the Spirit of Christ which was in them did signify, when it testified beforehand the sufferings of Christ, and the glory that should follow." (1 Pet. 1:10-12.)

How many Messianic prophecies have there been? In the real and true perspective of things, ten thousand times ten thousand is not a beginning to their number. They are in multitude like the sand upon the seashore. Obviously, all the prophetic utterances about Christ and the plan of salvation were Messianic in nature. But such teachings merely introduce the subject. For instance:

Every proper and perfect prayer uttered by a righteous man, woman, or child, from the day Adam stepped through Eden's portals into his lone and dreary habitation, to the day the angelic hosts acclaimed the birth of God's own Son, was in fact a Messianic prophecy. The mere saying, with sincerity and understanding, of the words of the prayer itself constituted a Messianic affirmation. Why? Because all the prophets, saints, and righteous hosts prayed to the Father in the name of Christ, thus witnessing that they knew that salvation came through him and his atoning blood. Similarly, every true prayer today is a reaffirmation that Jesus is the Lord and that through his blood the believing saints are redeemed.

Every shout of praise and exultation to the Lord Jehovah was Messianic in nature, for those who so acclaimed worshiped the Father in the name of Jehovah-Messiah who would come to redeem his people.

And so with every baptism, every priesthood ordination,

every patriarchal blessing, every act of administering to the sick, every divine ordinance or performance ordained of God, every sacrifice, symbolism, and similitude; all that God ever gave to his people—all was ordained and established in such a way as to testify of his Son and center the faith of believing people in him and in the redemption he was foreordained to make.

Why Have Messianic Prophecies?

In the economy of God there is a reason for all things, and the greater the event, the more important the reason. For four millenniums nothing ever said by men or angels was as important as their Messianic prophecies. From that day in Eden when the Lord said that Eve's Seed should crush the serpent's head, to a glorious night four thousand years later in the Judean hills, when angelic hosts sang praise to the Seed of Eve and Mary, the most important utterances made on earth were the Messianic prophecies. And from Messiah's birth as long as time endures, the most glorious language that has been or can be spoken contains the Messianic testimonies borne by the power of the Spirit for the edification, blessing, and salvation of the receptive part of earth's inhabitants.

There are three reasons why Messianic prophecies began with Adam and continued among all the righteous people on earth until the coming of the Son of God among men. These are:

1. *Messianic prophecies enabled those who lived from the beginning down to the time of his coming to have faith in Christ and thereby gain salvation.*

Salvation is administered on the same terms and conditions to all men in all ages. Whether it be in Adam's day or in ours it is the same. In every dispensation obedience to the same laws confers the same blessings. Everlastingly and always salvation is in Christ; his atoning sacrifice brings life and immortality to light through the same gospel in every era of the history of the earth. All men from the beginning to the end must have faith in him; repent of all their sins; be baptized for their remission in his holy name; receive the gift of the Holy Ghost, which the Father sends because of him; and then press forward in steadfastness and obedience to his laws, if they are to gain eternal life with him in his Father's kingdom. And so it is written, "That as many as would believe and be baptized in his holy name, and endure in faith to the end, should be saved—Not only those who believed after he came in the meridian of time, in the flesh, but all those from the beginning, even as many as were before he came, who believed in the words of the holy prophets, who spake as they were inspired by the gift of the Holy Ghost, who truly testified of him in all things, should have eternal life, As well as those who should come after, who should believe in the gifts and callings of God by the Holy Ghost, which beareth record of the Father and of the Son." (D&C 20:25-27.)

In this day we believe on the Lord Jesus Christ and gain salvation, and the prophets and apostles of our day reveal him to the world and serve as the legal administrators to perform the ordinances of salvation in his name so that such ordinances will be binding on earth and sealed everlastingly in the heavens. So likewise was it in days of old. Salvation was in Christ then as it is now, and the prophets of those days taught the same doctrines we teach today.

At the very beginning of his ministry, the prophet Nephi recorded his purpose and summarized his divine commission by saying, "For the fulness of mine intent is that I may persuade men to come unto the God of Abraham, and the God of Isaac, and the God of Jacob, and be saved." (1 Ne. 6:4.) King Benjamin (reciting the words spoken to him by an angel) affirmed and expanded the same concept in these words: "Salvation cometh . . . through repentance and faith on the Lord Jesus Christ. And the Lord God hath sent his holy prophets among all the children of men, to declare these things to every kindred, nation, and tongue, that thereby whosoever should believe that Christ should come, the same might receive remission of their sins, and rejoice with exceeding great joy, even as though he had already come among them." (Mosiah 3:12-13.)

Alma's son Corianton, rebellious and carnally inclined, was unable to understand "concerning the coming of Christ." His father said to him, "I will ease your mind somewhat on this subject. Behold, you marvel why these things should be known so long beforehand." And this was Alma's reasoning:

"Is not a soul at this time as precious unto God as a soul will be at the time of his coming?"

"Is it not as necessary that the plan of redemption should be made known unto this people as well as unto their children?"

"Is it not as easy at this time for the Lord to send his angel to declare these glad tidings unto us as unto our children, or as after the time of his coming?" (Alma 39:15-19.)

2. *Messianic prophecies enable those who lived at the time of and after the coming of Christ to believe that it was he of whom the prophets had spoken so that they too might be saved.*

"These glad tidings"—that salvation was in Christ and came by obedience to his holy gospel—were declared unto those in the so-called pre-Christian era so "that salvation might come unto them," and also "that they may prepare the minds of their children to hear the word at the time of his coming." (Alma 39:16.)

That relatively few who lived when he came, or who have thereafter dwelt on this benighted globe, were in fact prepared to receive him as Savior, Lord, and King is the saddest commentary found in all the history of his dealings with men. However, many of the prophecies (together with much of the doctrine interwoven as an essential part thereof) are still extant, and, the Lord guiding, many sincere souls will yet be brought to a knowledge of the truth through a Spirit-led study of them.

3. *Messianic prophecies reveal the manner and system of prophetic utterance and fulfillment so that the prophecies relative to the Second Coming may be understood, thus enabling men to prepare for that great day and the salvation that attends it.*

Prophetic utterances foretell the future. That God who knows the end from the beginning, before whose face all things are present, and who views the future as men recall the past, speaks to his prophets, and they, in his name, announce what is to be. Such proclamations are prophecies.

For the first four thousand years of this earth's temporal continuance, the Lord's prophets, though concerned with all things relative to their Master's hand dealings with men, yet knew of and sought foreknowledge about the two most glorious events destined to occur on earth. These were:

1. Our Lord's First Coming, his birth as God's Son, having life in himself so he could work out the infinite and eternal atoning sacrifice whereby immortality and eternal life come; and
2. His return in glory and might to cleanse his vineyard from corruption, to gather the remainder of his elect from the four quarters of the earth, and to reign in their midst for a thousand years of peace and perfection.

For the past two thousand years of our planet's existence, those with seeric vision, already knowing of the fulfillment of the Messianic utterances, have desired above all else to tell what shall precede, accompany, and prevail after our Lord's return in all the glory of his Father's kingdom.

Knowing that the God they worship is a being in whom there is no variableness, neither shadow of turning from that course which he has and shall pursue everlastingly, it is no surprise to spiritually literate souls to learn that the prophecies of the First Coming are but types and shadows of similar revelations relative to the Second Coming.

If the prophetic system embraced some plain and some hidden prophecies relative to our Lord's meridian ministry—so that all men, because of the plainness, would be left without excuse, while the more obedient souls, having as a consequence greater spiritual insight, would thereby know more about his coming—so we may expect it to be relative to his imminent millennial ministry.

If some of the ancient prophecies about his birth, death, and resurrection were hidden in historical recitations of little-known events, so may we anticipate it will be with some things concerning his future appearance.

If his ministers used similitudes and types and shadows to tell of one coming, such also will be their approach to his later appearing.

If it took the spirit of prophecy and revelation to know and understand what was said and written about his mortal ministry, so shall it be with reference to his immortal reign on earth.

And all of this means that a knowledge of what was foretold and fulfilled in his first ministry becomes the basis of comprehending what shall be before, at, and after his imminent ministry again among men, albeit this time he shall minister only among the righteous who abide the day of his coming.

Why Prophets Are Persecuted

Look and behold the righteous ones, the prophets of God:

Abel—slain because he worshiped the Lord, slain by the hand of one who glorified in wickedness, who loved Satan more than God (Moses 5:16-41);

Three virgins, daughters of Onitah—sacrificed on Potiphar's Hill because they "would not bow down to worship gods of wood or stone" (Abr. 1:5-11);

Abraham—taken by violence, bound upon an Egyptian altar, appointed unto death in the name of Pharaoh's god (Abr. 1:12-20);

Moses—rejoicing in "the reproach of Christ" and "choosing rather to suffer affliction with the people of God, than to enjoy the pleasures of sin for a season" (Heb. 11:25-26);

And others without number: Daniel, in a den of lions (Dan. 6); Shadrach, Meshach, and Abednego, walking unharmed in the fiery furnace (Dan. 3); Isaiah, sawn asunder, as we suppose (Heb. 11:37); Jeremiah, in a dungeon and a prison (Jer. 38:6; 1 Ne. 7:14); Zenos, slain (Hel. 8:19); Zenock, stoned (Alma 33:17); Nephi, smitten (1 Ne. 3:28-29); Alma and Amulek, delivered from cords and prison (Alma 14); Joseph and Hyrum, martyred in Carthage jail (D&C 135), and their people, the saints of the Most High, driven by godless fiends from Ohio to Missouri, from Missouri to Illinois, and from Illinois to the deserts of western America; and, finally, Christ our Lord—mocked, smitten, scourged, derided—now hanging in agony on a cross (Matt. 27:31-38; Mark 15:20-28; Luke 23:26-38; John 19:16-22).

As the horror of the vision spreads before us, we wonder: Why? Why should the best blood of earth be shed? Why are prophets smitten, spit upon, and stoned? Why are they cursed, criticized, crucified? Why does the world reject the very ones who light the path to the kingdom of heaven? In revealed writ we find these answers:

1. *Prophets are persecuted because they testify of Christ.*

"Which of the prophets have not your fathers persecuted?" was the stinging rebuke of Stephen to those who stoned him. "They have slain them which shewed before of the coming of the Just One," he said, "of whom ye have been now the betrayers and murderers." (Acts 7:52.) One of those killed because of the witness he bore of the promised Messiah was Zenock. Because he "testified of the Son of God," Alma said, "they stoned him to death." (Alma 33:17.)

The reason worldly and ungodly people so react to the witness of the truth is clear. Salvation is in Christ, and prophets preach Christ and his saving truths to the world. Where there are prophets, salvation is available; and where there are no prophets, there is no hope of salvation. It is no wonder that Lucifer hates prophets and seeks their destruction.

2. *Prophets are persecuted because there are false churches.*

Nephi saw in vision "a church which is most abominable above all other churches, which slayeth the saints of God, yea, and tortureth them and bindeth them down, and yoketh them with a yoke of iron, and bringeth them down into captivity." (1 Ne. 13:5.) From this vision we learn two of the saddest truths of all history: (1) prophets are persecuted by religiously inclined people, and (2) the fact that there are false churches is itself the very reason why the Lord's saints suffer at the hands of evil and ungodly men.

There are different churches because there are different doctrines. No two churches espouse and expound the same plan of salvation. If all men believed the same doctrines, all would belong to the same church. The mere existence of a false church of itself requires the support of false doctrines, false ordinances, false teachers, false prophets. In the very nature of things, a false church, in an attempt to survive, must oppose the truth as it is found in the true Church, and this includes opposition to true doctrine, true ordinances, true teachers, and true prophets. Accordingly, we find the Prophet Joseph Smith teaching that there always has been and always will be "opposition in the hearts of unbelievers and those that know not God, against the pure and unadulterated religion of heaven," and that such adherents to false systems of worship "will persecute, to the uttermost, all that worship God according to his revelations, receive the truth in the love of it, and submit themselves to be guided and directed by his will." (*Lectures on Faith,* p. 57.)

Thus it is that persecution comes from religious zealots. Those who are lukewarm or neutral in the realm of religion, those who have no interest in spiritual things, could not care less whether prophets succeed or fail. It is those who have strong religious convictions who rise up to oppose the truth and fight its exponents.

There have been no more zealous religionists on earth than the inhabitants of Jerusalem, nor has there been another locale where more of the blood of the prophets has flowed. Truly, there is more than irony and sorrow in our Lord's pronouncement: "It cannot be that a prophet perish out of Jerusalem. O Jerusalem, Jerusalem, which killest the prophets, and stonest them that are sent unto thee." (Luke 13:33-34.)

When the hosts of Israel forsook the Lord and his law, when they "transgressed very much after all the abominations of the heathen," when they "polluted the house of the Lord which he had hallowed in Jersualem," yet he in his mercy—"because he had compassion on his people, and on his dwelling place"—sent messengers to call them to repentance, to plead with them to return to the Lord their God and his law. The issue was thus squarely set. Those in Israel must either repent and forsake their evils or—to justify their apostate course—they must fight the prophets. And as worldly people are wont to do, "They mocked the messengers of God, and despised his words, and misused his prophets." (2 Chr. 36:14-16; 1 Kgs. 19:10-14; Rom. 11:1-3.)

When Paul preached with power in Ephesus and all Asia that salvation was in Christ and not their graven images, and when converts forsook the worship of Diana and no longer patronized the silversmiths who made the silver shrines in the worship of this pagan deity, what choice had the religionists of the day but to receive the truth or persecute Paul? And what better rallying cry for fighting against God than to exclaim, "Our craft is in danger"? (See Acts 19:21-41.)

When Joseph Smith "saw two Personages, whose brightness and glory defy all description," standing above him in the air; when the Beloved Son of Almighty God commanded him to join none of the churches then on earth, saying plainly that "they were all wrong; . . . that all their creeds were an abomination in his sight" and "that those professors were all corrupt"—what choice did these modern religionists have but to accept the newly revealed light from heaven or heap their opprobrium on its purveyor? "It seems as though the adversary was aware, at a very early period of my life," the Prophet said, "that I was destined to prove a disturber and an annoyer of his kingdom; else why should the powers of darkness combine against me? Why the opposition and persecution that arose against me, almost in my infancy?" (JS-H 17-20.)

Persecution is the child of Satan; it proceeds forth from perdition; it is used because no weapon that is formed can destroy truth. Persecution comes by and from false churches. If there were no religionists whose crafts were endangered by the onrush of truth, the Lord's prophets would be free to preach and guide men without let or hindrance.

3. *Prophets are persecuted as a form of false worship.*

"The time cometh," our Lord said to his ancient disciples, "that whosoever killeth you will think that he doeth God service." (John 16:2.) Serve God by killing his prophets! The very thought seems unbelievable, but such is the fact. In our dispensation most of the persecution poured out upon the Lord's people has been and is planned and led by ministers of other churches who, we may assume, were and are sincere in their belief that by destroying Mormonism they will free men from what they esteem to be its snares and delusions.

Like the Jews who rejected their Messiah when he ministered among them, such religious zealots suppose they believe in the ancient prophets and that they are only fighting against false prophets. But of them the Lord Jesus said: "Ye build the tombs of the prophets, and garnish the sepulchres of the righteous, And say, If we had been in the days of our fathers, we would not have been partakers with them in the blood of the prophets. Wherefore ye be witnesses unto yourselves, that ye are the children of them which killed the prophets. Fill ye up then the measure of your fathers. Ye serpents, ye generation of vipers, how can ye escape the damnation of hell?" (Matt. 23:29-33.)

Samuel the Lamanite raised the same cry against the Nephites of his day. "Ye do cast out the prophets," he said, "and do mock them, and cast stones at them, and do slay them, and do all manner of iniquity unto them, even as they did of old time. And now when ye talk, ye say: If our days had been in the days of our fathers of old, we would not have slain the prophets; we would not have stoned them, and cast them out. Behold ye are worse than they; for as the Lord liveth, if a prophet come among you and declareth unto you the word of the Lord, which testifieth of your sins and iniquities, ye are angry with him, and cast him out and seek all manner of ways to destroy him; yea, you will say that he is a false prophet, and that he is a sinner, and of the devil, because he testifieth that your deeds are evil." (Hel. 13:24-26.)

In the very nature of things, persecution of true prophets includes the acceptance of false prophets. It is a philosophical impossibility to reject truth without accepting error, to depart from true teachers without cleaving to false ones, to reject the Lord's ministers without giving allegiance to those who follow the other Master. How aptly these further words of Samuel, spoken of those of old, describe the popular teachers both of Christendom and pagandom: "If a man shall come among you and shall say: Do this, and there is no iniquity; do that and ye shall not suffer; yea, he will say: Walk after the pride of your own hearts; yea, walk after the pride of your eyes, and do whatsoever your heart desireth—and if a man shall come among you and say this, ye will receive him, and say that he is a prophet. Yea, ye will lift him up, and ye will give unto him of your substance; ye will give unto him of your gold, and of your silver, and ye will clothe him with costly apparel; and because he speaketh flattering words unto you, and he saith that all is well, then ye will not find fault with him." (Hel. 13:27-28.)

4. *Prophets are persecuted because they reveal the wickedness and abominations of the people.*

It is just as simple as that. Implicit in the proclamation that Christ comes to save sinners is the fact that men must repent and forsake their evil ways or they will lose their souls. "He that believeth not shall be damned." (Mark 16:16.) Tell a man he is a liar, a thief, a murderer who is destined to dwell in an endless hell, and he will hate and persecute you. Tell him he has forsaken the truth, that his beliefs are false, his practices carnal, and he will fight back with the only weapon at his command—persecution.

Lehi delivered the Lord's message to the Jews, and they "did mock him because of the things which he testified of them; for he truly testified of their wickedness and their abominations; and he testified that the things which he saw and heard, and also the things which he read in the book, manifested plainly of the coming of a Messiah, and also the redemption of the world. And when the Jews heard these things they were angry with him; yea, even as with the prophets of old, whom they had cast out, and stoned, and slain; and they also sought his life, that they might take it away." (1 Ne. 1:19-20.)

5. *Prophets are persecuted and slain as a witness against the wicked and ungodly.*

In a revelation to Brigham Young, the Lord said: "Thy brethren have rejected you and your testimony, even the nation that has driven you out; And now cometh the day of their calamity, even the days of sorrow, like a woman that is taken in travail; and their sorrow shall be great unless they speedily repent, yea, very speedily. For they killed the prophets, and them that were sent unto them; and they have shed innocent blood, which crieth from the ground against them." (D&C 136:34-36.)

That same Lord, in even more severe language, said to the Jews whose hearts were set on killing him and his ancient apostles: "I send unto you prophets, and wise men, and scribes: and some of them ye shall kill and crucify; and some of them shall ye scourge in your synagogues, and persecute them from city to city: That upon you may come all the righteous blood shed upon the earth, from the blood of righteous Abel unto the blood of Zacharias son of Barachias, whom ye slew between the temple and the altar." (Matt. 23:34-35.)

That is, the condemnation prepared for those who reject God and his ministers is justified because of the magnitude of their rebellion against him. Having shed the best blood in this fallen and benighted world, the judgments of a just God rest righteously upon them in time and eternity. These are they who are cast out with "the fearful, and unbelieving, and the abominable, and murderers, and whoremongers, and sorcerers, and idolaters, and all liars," and who "shall have their part in the lake which burneth with fire and brimstone: which is the second death." (Rev. 21:8.)

6. *Prophets are persecuted to test their integrity, to make sure of their allegiance to that Lord whose they are.*

Life never was intended to be easy, and when persecution is poured out upon the Lord's people, it is but part of the testing, probationary experiences which prepare them for celestial crowns. "I will try you and prove you," the Lord says to his saints. "And whoso layeth down his life in my cause, for my name's sake, shall find it again, even life eternal. . . . I will prove you in all things, whether you will abide in my covenant, even unto death, that you may be found worthy." (D&C 98:12-14.)

When Joseph Smith pled with the Lord for surcease from the wrongs and oppressions heaped upon him and his fellows, the answer that came was: "My son, peace be unto thy soul; thine adversity and thine afflictions shall be but a small moment; And then, if thou endure it well, God shall exalt thee on high; thou shalt triumph over all thy foes." (D&C 121:7-8.)

After this same prophet (together with his brother Hyrum) had met a martyr's death, the Lord said: "Many have marveled because of his death; but it was needful that he should seal his testimony with his blood, that he might be honored and the wicked might be condemned." (D&C 136:39.) "And their innocent blood on the floor of Carthage jail is a broad seal affixed to 'Mormonism' that cannot be rejected by any court on earth, and their innocent blood on the escutcheon of the State of Illinois, with the broken faith of the State as pledged by the governor, is a witness to the truth of the everlasting gospel that all the world cannot impeach; and their innocent blood on the banner of liberty, and on the magna charta of the United States, is an ambassador for the religion of Jesus Christ, that will touch the hearts of honest men among all nations; and their innocent blood, with the innocent blood of all the martyrs under the altar that John saw, will cry unto the Lord of Hosts till he avenges that blood on the earth." (D&C 135:7.)

How Prophets Are Rewarded

But look again! Let your vision extend without limit! This time behold beyond the bounds of mortality! View now within the veil! What do you see relative to the righteous ones now? In this brief life the prophets are persecuted. In this moment of mortality the apostles "are made a spectacle unto the world," are esteemed "as the filth of the world," and are deemed to be "the offscouring of all things." (1 Cor. 4:9, 13.) But what of the eternal days ahead?

One who viewed within the veil and saw the end of those who had overcome the world was the Beloved John. As he beheld, an angelic ministrant asked: "What are these which are arrayed in white robes? and whence came they?" Answering his own question, the heavenly being proclaimed: "These are they which came out of great tribulation, and have washed their robes, and made them white in the blood of the Lamb. Therefore are they before the throne of God, and serve him day and night in his temple: and he that sitteth on the throne shall dwell among them." (Rev. 7:13-15.)

These are they who have been faithful and true in this mortal probation. These are they who have eternal life. These are they of whom the Lord Jesus said: "And blessed are all they who are persecuted for my name's sake, for theirs is the kingdom of heaven. And blessed are ye when men shall revile you and persecute, and shall say all manner of evil against you falsely, for my sake; For ye shall have great joy and be exceeding glad, for great shall be your reward in heaven; for so persecuted they the prophets who were before you." (3 Ne. 12:10-12.)

Let us, then—and let all men who desire righteousness—accept the Lord and his prophets, hearken to their teachings, and strive to be like them, for it is written: "He that receiveth a prophet in the name of a prophet shall receive a prophet's reward." (Matt. 10:41.) And a prophet's reward is eternal life in the kingdom of God.

How Messianic Prophecies Came

There is one way and one way only in which Messianic prophecies came (or by which Messianic testimonies can be borne), and that is by the power of the Holy Ghost. "No man can say"—or know, as Joseph Smith says (*Teachings* p. 223), or reveal, or testify—"that Jesus is the Lord, but by the Holy Ghost." (1 Cor. 12:3.)

True, the prophecy itself may have been spoken by the Eternal Father, as when he said in Eden that the Seed of Eve should bruise the serpent's head (Gen. 3:15); or it may have been uttered by Jehovah himself, as when he said to Enoch, "I am Messiah, the King of Zion, the Rock of Heaven," who shall be "lifted up on the cross" (Moses 7:53, 55); or it may have come from the lips of an angel, as when such a heavenly ministrant said to King Benjamin: "The Lord Omnipotent . . . shall come down from heaven among the children of men, and shall dwell in a tabernacle of clay" (Mosiah 3:5). But always and without exception the Holy Spirit of God is present and rests upon the recipient so that the spoken words carry their Messianic meaning into the recipient's heart. The words themselves, without an accompanying and interpreting spirit, would be jangling jargon, without meaning, without sense, nothing more than the ravings of a deranged mind.

Most Messianic prophecies, however, were uttered by mortal men as they were moved upon by the power of the Holy Ghost. In some instances the Holy Spirit dictated the very words to be spoken, as when the Holy Ghost, "which beareth record of the Father and the Son," "fell upon Adam, . . . saying: I am the Only Begotten of the Father from the beginning, henceforth and forever, that as thou hast fallen thou mayest be redeemed, and all mankind, even as many as will." (Moses 5:9.) But in most cases, without question, the Holy Spirit simply planted the thought in the mind of that man who had, as it were, attuned his receiving set to the wave band upon which the Lord's eternal Revelator, who is the Holy Ghost, was broadcasting eternal truth; and that man was then left to phrase the thought in his own words, to speak revealed truth, "after the manner" of his language. (D&C 1:24.)

How to Understand Messianic Prophecies

There are numerous keys that open the door to a partial understanding of the Messianic prophecies, but there is only one way in which their full meaning can sink into a human heart with converting power.

It is helpful—indeed, almost imperative—that those of us who seek to know the deep and hidden things about Christ and his coming first gain an overall knowledge of the plan of salvation. Unless we believe in an Eternal Father who is God, we cannot conceive of a Son of God who is Christ. Unless we know that God created us in his own image, that he is our Father, that he ordained the laws whereby we may advance and progress and become like him, and that those laws are made operative through an infinite and eternal atonement; unless we believe and accept the eternal truths relative to the great plan of redemption, we are in no position to envision the meaning of the prophetic utterances concerning the birth, ministry, death, and resurrection of Christ.

It is also helpful—extremely so—to know that revelations and prophetic utterances given during and since our Lord's mortal ministry hark back to what was foretold about him anciently, and announce, plainly, that the former prophetic utterances about him are fulfilled. The Book of Mormon is by all odds the best source of this knowledge, as witness his own declaration to the Nephites: "Behold, I am Jesus Christ, whom the prophets testified shall come into the world." (3 Ne. 11:10.) "And the scriptures concerning my coming are fulfilled." (3 Ne. 9:16.) The New Testament also abounds in passages that quote or allude to the Messianic prophecies and then testify that these are fulfilled in the coming and ministry of Mary's Son. Revealed truths about his birth and ministry, with particular reference to those which tell of his atoning sacrifice and the salvation which comes by him, as these are found in the Doctrine and Covenants and other latter-day inspired writings, have this same effect. They affirm the verity and interpret the hidden meanings of those things which were foreknown, foreseen, and foreannounced by those who knew the mind and will of the Great Jehovah in olden times.

Help and understanding also comes—and this is a matter of no small moment—to those who acquaint themselves with "the manner of prophesying" among those who ministered in the name of Christ before he manifested himself among men. (2 Ne. 25:1-8.) Isaiah's prophecy of the virgin birth, for instance, is dropped into the midst of a recitation of local historical occurrences so that to the spiritually untutored it could be interpreted as some ancient and, to us, unknown happening that had no relationship to the mortal birth of the Lord Jehovah some seven hundred years later. (Isa. 7.)

Many of the prophets used types and shadows, figures and similitudes, their purpose ofttimes being, as it were, to hide that which is "holy" from the "dogs" and "swine" of their day (Matt. 7:6), while at the same time revealing it to those whose hearts were prepared for that light and knowledge which leads to salvation. Nephi, on the other hand, because of both the isolation and the spiritual development of his people, chose in the main to couch his prophetic utterances in plain and simple declarations. And so it is that, with propriety, we consider the context, the people involved, their social, cultural, and spiritual state, and the degree of understanding they already had of Messianic things.

But in the final analysis, there is no way—absolutely none (and this cannot be stated too strongly!)—to understand any Messianic prophecy, or any other scripture, except to have the same spirit of prophecy that rested upon the one who uttered the truth in its original form. Scripture comes from God by the power of the Holy Ghost. It does not originate with man. It means only what the Holy Ghost thinks it means. To interpret it, we must be enlightened by the power of the Holy Spirit. As Peter said, "No prophecy of the scripture is of any private interpretation. For the prophecy came not in old time by the will of man: but holy men of God spake as they were moved by the Holy Ghost." (2 Pet. 1:20-21.) Truly, it takes a prophet to understand a prophet, and every faithful member of the Church should have "the testimony of Jesus" which "is the spirit of prophecy." (Rev. 19:10.) Thus, as Nephi says, "The words of Isaiah"—and the principle applies to all scripture, all inspired writing, all Messianic prophecies—"are plain unto all those that are filled with the spirit of prophecy." (2 Ne. 25:4.) This is the sum and substance of the whole matter and an end to all controversy where discovering the mind and will of the Lord is concerned.

Seek Knowledge of Christ

It is now our purpose, prayerfully and perceptively, to

pore over the ponderous works of the prophets of the past, to find the Messianic prophecies proclaimed by our predecessors, and then to show their fulfillment in the birth, ministry, death, resurrection, and ascension into heaven of Him who is the source of saving truth, the Savior of those who believe in him and keep his word.

It is now our desire to know what the voice of God has spoken by the mouths of his servants the prophets in all ages concerning Jesus Christ our Lord, so that believing (and obeying!) we may become his friends and associates in the kingdom of his Father. We approach our most pleasant task with the realization that there are no unneeded scriptures, no prophecies without a purpose, no Messianic utterances devoid of worth, and that we—and all who read and ponder the recitations herein written—need above all the guidance and enlightenment which the Almighty sheds forth by the power of his Spirit. If we do not find and analyze to the full all that is now extant that tells of Christ and his coming, at least we shall build such a mountain of knowledge and truth on the various points involved that none who truly seek truth will be left without excuse or be unaware of the wealth of revealed truth about the Messiah that is available.

Can we do better than to guide our seeking steps with these words of Moroni: "Seek this Jesus of whom the prophets and apostles have written, that the grace of God the Father, and also the Lord Jesus Christ, and the Holy Ghost, which beareth record of them, may be and abide in you forever." (Ether 12:41.) And then, can we do better than to add to them these words of promise, written by that same Nephite prophet: "And by the power of the Holy Ghost ye may know the truth of all things." (Moro. 10:5.)

MESSIAH DWELT WITH GOD

Christ Is the Firstborn

The Lord Jesus, who is called Christ, was in the beginning with God. He was the "Only Begotten Son, who was in the bosom of the Father, even from the beginning." (D&C 76:13.) He was "prepared from before the foundation of the world." (Moses 5:57; 3 Ne. 26:5.) And his solemn prayer, uttered near the climax of his mortal ministry, was: "O Father, glorify thou me with thine own self with the glory which I had with thee before the world was." (John 17:5.)

Though he has now attained unto that exalted state in which he is described as being "from everlasting to everlasting" (D&C 61:1) and "from all eternity to all eternity" (D&C 39:1)—as will eventually be the description and state of all those who gain exaltation (D&C 132:20)—yet, as a conscious identity, he had a beginning. He was born, as were all the spirit children of the Father. God was his Father, as he is of all the rest. For him, as for all men—and he is the Prototype—the eternal spirit element that has neither beginning nor end, and is self-existent by nature, was organized into a spirit body. He was one of "the intelligences that were organized before the world was." (Abr. 3:22.) He was and is the Firstborn of the Father.

In a Messianic vein, in the midst of a number of prophecies about his coming, the Psalmist records the mind of the

Father in these words: "I will make him my firstborn, higher than the kings of the earth" (Ps. 89:27), and nearly three millenniums later our Lord said to Joseph Smith, "I was in the beginning with the Father, and am the Firstborn" (D&C 93:21). His servant Paul spoke of him as "the firstborn among many brethren" (Rom. 8:29) and as "the firstborn of every creature" (Col. 1:15). And as *The Church of Jesus Christ* is his earthly church, so *The Church of the Firstborn* is his heavenly church, albeit its members are limited to exalted beings, for whom the family unit continues and who gain an inheritance in the highest heaven of the celestial world. (Heb. 12:22-23; D&C 93:22.)

Messiah Was a Spirit Man

Spirits are eternal beings, men and women created in the image of the Eternal Father, whose offspring they are. Their bodies are made of a more pure and refined substance than that which composes the mortal body. "All spirit is matter," the Prophet said, "but it is more fine or pure, and can only be discerned by purer eyes." (D&C 131:7.)

And this was the nature and kind of body possessed by the Firstborn before it was clothed upon with clay through the mortal birth processes. Nowhere is this truth preserved to us as perfectly as in the extract we have of the writings of Moriancumer, the greatest of the Jaredite prophets. Some twenty-two hundred or more years before our Lord took upon himself flesh and blood, he permitted the brother of Jared to see his spirit finger and then his whole spirit body, withdrawing more completely the veil between him and mortals than had ever been done before. "This body, which ye now behold, is the body of my spirit," he said, "and even as I appear unto thee to be in the spirit will I appear unto my people in the flesh." (Ether 3:16.)

Moroni, who preserved for us this Jareditish vision, appended to it this comment: "Jesus showed himself unto this man in the spirit, even after the manner and in the likeness of the same body even as he showed himself unto the Nephites." (Ether 3:17.) In this connection, the ancient apostles, assembled in the upper room, recognized the Risen Lord as the same Being with whom they had been on familiar terms as a mortal (Luke 24:36-49), all of which taken together is as though the Eternal Messiah had said:

'As a Spirit Man, I had hands and feet and all the parts of a normal body, all patterned after my Father's glorified body of flesh and bones. In mortality I appeared as I appeared in the spirit. And then I came forth from Joseph's tomb, glorified and exalted, with a body of flesh and bones, which in appearance is like both my Spirit Body and my Mortal Body; and as it is with me, so shall it be with all men. I am the Prototype.'

Elohim Presents His Plan

God the Eternal Father, the Father of the Firstborn and of all the spirit hosts, as an exalted and glorified Being, having all power and dominion, possessing all knowledge and all truth, personifying and being the embodiment of all godly attributes, did, of his own will, ordain and establish the plan of salvation whereby Christ and all his other spirit children might have power to advance and progress and become like him.

God ordained the plan. He established it. It is his plan. It was not adopted by the Father following one suggestion coming from Christ and another originating with Lucifer. The Father is the author of the plan of salvation, a plan that he created so that Christ, his Firstborn, plus all the rest of his spirit children might be saved. As Joseph Smith expressed it: "God himself, finding he was in the midst of spirits and glory, because he was more intelligent, saw proper to institute laws whereby the rest could have a privilege to advance like himself." (*Teachings,* p. 354.)

The Father's plan, known first as the gospel of God, was taught to Christ, to Lucifer, and to all our Father's spirit children. Each person, endowed with the divine power of agency, was free to believe or disbelieve, to obey or disobey, to follow Elohim or reject his goodness and grace. The plan itself included the creation and peopling of an earth. God's children were to have the privilege of gaining mortal bodies and of being tried and tested in a probationary estate to see if they would keep their Father's commandments at all hazards. The plan called for one of Deity's spirit sons to be born into mortality as the Only Begotten in the flesh, who would thus inherit from the Father the power of immortality; it called for this Chosen One to work out an infinite and eternal atonement whereby fallen men would be raised in immortality, while those who believed and obeyed would also gain eternal life.

After this plan had been taught to all the hosts of heaven; after it was known and understood by all; after all its facets had been debated and evaluated—then the Father asked for a volunteer to put the full terms and all of the conditions of his plan into force. Then it was, after all else was in readiness, that the call went forth in the Grand Council, "Whom shall I send" to be the Savior and Redeemer? (Abr. 3:27.) That is: Who will work out the infinite and eternal atoning sacrifice? Who will champion my cause? Who will go forth and do my will? Who will put all the terms and conditions of my plan in operation? Who will be my Son? Who will be the Messiah?

And thus the scene was set; thus the appointed time had come; thus the choosing and foreordination of the Messiah was at hand!

Christ Adopts the Father's Plan

Two spirits of renown, two men of power and influence, two whose voices had been heard by all the hosts of heaven, stepped forth to answer the Father's call, "Whom shall I send?" (Abr. 3:27.) One was Christ, the other Lucifer.

Our Lord said: "Father, thy will be done, and the glory be thine forever." (Moses 4:2.) That is: 'Father, I accept all of the terms and conditions of thy plan. I will do thy will. I will go down as thy Son, the Only Begotten in the flesh. With thy help I will atone for the sins of the world, and will ascribe the honor and the glory unto thee in all things.'

Lucifer said: "Behold, here am I, send me, I will be thy son, and I will redeem all mankind, that one soul shall not be lost, and surely I will do it; wherefore give me thine honor." (Moses 4:1.) That is: 'I reject thy plan. I am willing to be thy Son and atone for the sins of the world, but in return let me take thy place and sit upon thy throne. Yea, "I will ascend into heaven, I will exalt my throne above the stars of God; . . . I will be like the most High." ' (Isa. 14:13-14.)

It was of the dramatic and transcendent events of that day that Elder Orson F. Whitney has written these words:

A stature mingling strength with grace
Of meek though Godlike mien,
The glory of whose countenance
Outshone the noonday sheen.
Whiter his hair than ocean spray,
Or frost of alpine hill.
He spake:—attention grew more grave,
The stillness e'en more still.

"Father!"—the voice like music fell,
Clear as the murmuring flow
Of mountain streamlet trickling down
From heights of virgin snow.
"Father," it said, "since one must die,
Thy children to redeem,
Whilst earth, as yet unformed and void,
With pulsing life shall teem;

"And mighty Michael foremost fall,
That mortal man may be,
And chosen Savior Thou must send,
Lo, here am I—send me!

I ask, I seek no recompense,
Save that which then were mine;
Mine be the willing sacrifice,
The endless glory Thine."

—In Joseph Fielding Smith, *Way to Perfection,* p. 52

Then came the decree. The issue was settled, except for the rebellion and war that was to follow. The voice of the Almighty said: "I will send the first." (Abr. 3:27.) The God of heaven said: "My Beloved Son, which was my Beloved and Chosen from the beginning," shall be the Savior and Redeemer, the Deliverer and Messiah. (Moses 4:2.)

Lucifer rebelled. He and one-third of the hosts of heaven, all being of one mind and one spirit, were cast down to earth, denied mortal bodies, and forever damned, damned to suffer the fulness of the wrath of Him whose plan they rejected. (Moses 4:3-4; Abr. 3:28; Rev. 12:7-9.)

From the beginning the destined Deliverer had adopted, advocated, and sponsored the Father's plan. Now with the decree issued that he should redeem and save mankind, that his atonement would enable men to become like their Father and God, and that the purposes of the Eternal Elohim should be brought to pass in full—now that all this was assured, two things transpired:

1. Messiah "verily was foreordained" (1 Pet. 1:20), and became "the Lamb slain from the foundation of the world" (Rev. 13:8).

2. The gospel of God became the gospel of Jesus Christ; or, as Paul was later to write, "The gospel of God, . . . Concerning his Son Jesus Christ our Lord." (Rom. 1:1, 3.) And so the very plan of salvation itself—to signify that salvation comes through Christ—was named after the One who was "Beloved and Chosen from the beginning." (Moses 4:2.) He thus, as Paul expressed it, "became the author," or as the better translation states, "the cause," "of eternal salvation unto all them that obey him." (Heb. 5:9.) He became "the

captain," meaning leader, of the salvation of the faithful. (Heb. 2:10.)

What Is the Gospel?

"The gospel of Jesus Christ is the plan of salvation. It embraces all of the laws, principles, doctrines, rites, ordinances, acts, powers, authorities, and keys necessary to save and exalt men in the highest heaven hereafter. It is the covenant of salvation which the Lord makes with men on earth." (*Mormon Doctrine,* 2nd ed., p. 331.)

From the perspective of the Eternal Elohim, the gospel is all that he has arranged and ordained to save his children. It is the laws given them in preexistence; it is the creation of the earth; it is the choosing of a Redeemer; it is this second estate wherein they are exposed to the lusts of the flesh; and it is the hope of everlasting life with him and his saints forever.

From the perspective of him who is our Redeemer, the gospel is the atoning sacrifice which puts into full operation and makes binding and efficacious all that the Father has prepared for them that love him. It is our Lord's birth in Bethlehem, his childhood in Nazareth, his ministry in Judea and Perea. It is the miracles he wrought, the works he did, the laws he made known. It is the Garden of Gethsemane and the hill of Calvary. It is great drops of blood dripping from every pore, as he took upon himself the sins of the world. It is a Roman spear piercing a sinless side. It is an open tomb outside a city wall. It is all power given him in heaven and on earth. It is immortality as a free gift for all and eternal life for the faithful.

From the perspective of man, the gospel is a better way of life. It is light bursting forth in a wilderness of darkness. It is faith, repentance, baptism, and the gift of the Holy Ghost. It is signs and gifts and miracles. It is the eyes of the blind being opened, the ears of the deaf unstopped, and the dead rising from their funeral biers. It is persecution and suffering and trials. It is learning to live as becometh a saint. It is overcoming the world until, eventually, in glorious immortality, the true saints dwell with Him who is their Friend and into whose image they have been molded.

The gospel is all this and ten thousand times ten thousand things more. But all that it is, all that it has ever been, all that it shall ever be, all that appertains to it centers in Him of whom the prophets testify and of which this work speaks. How can we say too often that salvation is in Christ and comes to the contrite souls who live his law!

Christ Became Like God

Abraham saw in vision all the spirit hosts of heaven. Among them were "the noble and great ones" who participated in the creation of this earth and who were foreordained to serve the Almighty in special capacities while they dwelt in mortality. Christ was there, the foremost spirit of the innumerable host. Of him the account says: "There stood one among them that was like unto God, and he said unto those who were with him: We will go down, for there is space there, and we will take of these materials, and we will make an earth whereon these may dwell." (Abr. 3:24.)

"Like unto God!" Like the Exalted Elohim who, in the ultimate sense, is the Creator, Upholder, and Preserver of the universe! Like unto God—how and in what way? Like him in length of days or the possession of progeny or the exalted nature of his tangible body? No, for the Son of the Father had yet to pass through a mortal probation, to overcome the world, to attain a resurrection, and to come back to his Father with his own glorious and tangible body. But like him in intelligence, in knowledge and understanding, in the possession of truth, in conformity to divine law, and therefore in power. Like him in plan and purpose, in desires for righteousness, in a willingness to serve his brethren, in all things that lead to that fulness of the glory of the Father which none can receive until they live in the eternal family unit as he does. Like him as a guide and a light to all others. Like him as a Creator of worlds and planets innumerable.

But mighty and glorious as the Spirit-Messiah then was—and the title "The Lord Omnipotent" (Mosiah 3:5) is descriptive of his already attained Eternal Godhood—he yet had to gain a mortal and then an immortal body before he could enter into the fulness of the glory of his Father and his God. He had to work out his own salvation by doing on earth the will of the Father in all things. "Though he were a Son," Paul says, "yet learned he obedience by the things which he suffered" (Heb. 5:8), meaning that "The Lord Omnipotent" himself had to overcome the world and stand against all opposition before he could (and again it is Paul's language) be "made perfect" (Heb. 5:9) in the ultimate and absolute sense of the term; that is, "perfect, even as your Father which is in heaven is perfect" (Matt. 5:48). After his resurrection, when he had so obtained, this Sermon-on-the-Mount statement, as given to the Nephites, was properly expanded to say: "Perfect even as I, or your Father who is in heaven is perfect." (3 Ne. 12:48.)

It was John, whom men call the Baptist, who saw the heavens open, the Holy Ghost descend, and heard the Father's voice proclaim, "This is my Beloved Son"—it was this John who left us the most perfect account known of the mortal progression and achievements of Him who was God before the world was. "And I, John," he wrote, "saw that he received not of the fulness at the first, but received grace for grace; And he received not of the fulness at first, but continued from grace to grace, until he received a fulness; And thus he was called the Son of God, because he received not of the fulness at the first." Then this ancient witness told of the baptism itself, and continued: "And I, John, bear record that he received a fulness of the glory of the Father; And he received all power, both in heaven and on earth, and the glory of the Father was with him, for he dwelt in him" (D&C 93:12-17)—which accords with our Lord's own pronouncement, made after his resurrection, to his ancient apostles: "All power is given unto me in heaven and in earth" (Matt. 28:18).

Christ Is the Creator

"We will go down, for there is space there, and we will take of these materials, and we will make an earth whereon these may dwell." So spake the One who was "like unto God." (Abr. 3:24.) And so they did—Christ, Michael, and all that great host of "noble and great ones," all laboring in their assigned spheres, all aiding the Great Creator who is Christ, and he and they all subject to the Father of them all, in whom all fulness and perfection dwells.

But where Christ himself was concerned, this small planet was but one speck of dust in a storm swirling over the Sahara. There is not one earth, but many; not one planet inhabited by our Father's children, but an infinite number. Moses, by the power of God, "beheld many lands; and each land was called earth, and there were inhabitants on the face thereof," and the Almighty said to him: "For mine own purpose have I made these things. . . . And by the word of my power, have I created them, which is mine Only Begotten Son, who is full of grace and truth. And worlds without number have I created; . . . and by the Son I created them, which is mine Only Begotten. . . . For behold, there are many worlds that have passed away by the word of my power. And there are many that now stand, and innumerable are they unto man; but all things are numbered unto me, for they are mine and I know them." (Moses 1:29-35.)

Worlds without number! Innumerable unto man! There is no finite way to envision the extent of the worlds created by Christ at the behest of his Father. Count the grains of sand on all the seashores and Saharas of the world, add the stars in the firmament for good measure, multiply the total by like sums from other worlds, and what do we have? Scarcely a dot in the broad expanse of an infinite universe—all created by Christ. Enoch, as guided by the Spirit, in conversation with the Lord expressed it this way: "Were it possible that man could number the particles of the earth, yea, millions of earths like this, it would not be a beginning to the number of thy creations; and thy curtains are stretched out still." (Moses 7:30.)

And Christ is the Creator of them all, a fact which, though not quite as dramatically expressed as by Enoch, has been known in all ages when spiritual enlightenment rested upon the people. Does not our revelation say, "By him, and through him, and of him, the worlds are and were created"? (D&C 76:24.) Did not John record, "All things were made by him; and without him was not anything made that was made"? (John 1:3.) And Paul, did he not say of the Father, "God . . . hath . . . spoken unto us by his Son, whom he hath appointed heir of all things, by whom also he made the worlds"? (Heb. 1:1-2.) And yet again, are not these his words concerning Christ: "There is but . . . one Lord Jesus Christ, by whom are all things, and we by him"? (1 Cor. 8:6.) And again, speaking of God's "dear Son," "By him were all things created, that are in heaven, and that are in earth, visible and invisible, whether they be thrones, or dominions, or principalities, or powers: all things were created by him, and for him: And he is before all things, and by him all things consist." (Col. 1:13-17.) Is it any wonder then that he was foreknown as "The Lord Omnipotent who reigneth, who was, and is from all eternity to all eternity, . . . the Father of heaven and earth, the Creator of all things from the beginning"? (Mosiah 3:5, 8.)

Messiah: Father of Heaven and Earth

"Thus saith the Lord your God, even Jesus Christ, . . . I am the same which spake, and the world was made, and all things came by me." (D&C 38:1, 3.) So spake the Great Creator, "the very Eternal Father of heaven and of earth" (Mosiah 15:4), to his servant and seer, Joseph the Prophet. "I am Jesus Christ the Son of God. I created the heavens and the earth, and all things that in them are. I was with the Father from the beginning." (3 Ne. 9:15.) So he spake to the preserved remnant of the Nephites when he descended from heaven to minister personally among them. And some four hundred years later, to Moroni, the last of the Nephite prophets, he identified himself as "Jesus Christ, the Son of God, the Father of the heavens and of the earth, and all things that in them are." (Ether 4:7.)

Accordingly, there neither is nor can be any question as to who created the earth and all things that are therein. And so we read in the Ten Commandments: "In six days the Lord made heaven and earth, the seas, and all that in them is" (Ex. 20:11), and ask: Who is speaking? Who is the Great Creator? Who made the heavens and the earth? The answer thunders back: The Great Jehovah who is the Lord Jesus Christ. And we thereby learn that all of the statements, of all of the prophets, of all of the ages, which speak of God the Creator are Messianic in nature. They are speaking of that Being who came in time's meridian to do the only work equal to that of creation, to do the work of redemption.

Our ancient scriptures are speaking of Christ when they say, "Our help is in the name of the Lord, who made heaven and earth." (Ps. 124:8.) "The Lord that made heaven and earth bless thee out of Zion." (Ps. 134:3.) "Happy is he that hath the God of Jacob for his help, whose hope is in the Lord his God: Which made heaven, and earth, the sea, and all that therein is." (Ps. 146:5-6.) "The Lord thy maker, . . . hath stretched forth the heavens, and laid the foundations of the earth." (Isa. 51:13.) After saying that Christ "made the worlds," Paul quotes this Old Testament scripture to prove it: "Thou, Lord, in the beginning hast laid the foundation of the earth; and the heavens are the works of thine hands: They shall perish; but thou remainest; and they all shall wax old as doth a garment; And as a vesture shalt thou fold them up, and they shall be changed: but thou art the same, and thy years shall not fail." (Heb. 1:2, 10-12; Ps. 102:25-27.) And it also follows that all the rest of the Old Testament scriptures which speak of this same Lord, though explicit words are not used identifying him as the Creator, are also Messianic in nature.

But it is to the Book of Mormon that we turn for the most perfect illustrations of Messianic prophecies that identify the Creator as the promised Deliverer. We find there that the Father of heaven and earth has ministered or will minister in the following ways:

1. *He is the God of Abraham and the prophets.*

He, "the Father of heaven," is the one, Nephi says, who covenanted "unto Abraham, saying: In thy seed shall all the kindreds of the earth be blessed," and these covenants shall be made known again in the last days. (1 Ne. 22:9.) We have already noted, in this connection, that the Psalmist called him "the God of Jacob." (Ps. 146:5.)

2. *He is the Only Begotten of the Father.*

"The day cometh," prophesied Nephi, "that the Only Begotten of the Father, yea, even the Father of heaven and of earth, shall manifest himself unto them in the flesh." (2 Ne. 25:12.)

3. *He shall dwell in Jerusalem and die for the sins of men.*

"In the body he shall show himself unto those at Jerusalem, . . . for it behooveth the great Creator that he suffereth himself to become subject unto man in the flesh, and die for all men, that all men might become subject unto him." (2 Ne. 9:5.)

4. *He shall atone for the sins of the world and bring to pass the resurrection.*

"For as death hath passed upon all men, to fulfil the merciful plan of the great Creator, there must needs be a power of resurrection. . . . It must needs be an infinite atonement—save it should be an infinite atonement this corruption could not put on incorruption." (2 Ne. 9:6-7.) "O have mercy, and apply the atoning blood of Christ that we may receive forgiveness of our sins, and our hearts may be purified; for we believe in Jesus Christ, the Son of God, who created heaven and earth, and all things; who shall come down among the children of men." (Mosiah 4:2.)

5. *He is the Lord Omnipotent.*

"I would that ye should be steadfast and immovable," King Benjamin exhorted his people, "always abounding in good works, that Christ, the Lord God Omnipotent, may seal you his, that you may be brought to heaven, that ye may have everlasting salvation and eternal life, through the wisdom, and power, and justice, and mercy of him who created all things, in heaven and in earth, who is God above all." (Mosiah 5:15.)

6. *He shall take upon him flesh and blood.*

Speaking of the death of Abinadi at the hands of King Noah and his wicked followers, Limhi said to his people: "A prophet of the Lord have they slain, . . . because he said unto them that Christ was the God, the Father of all things, and said that he should take upon him the image of man, and it should be the image after which man was created in the beginning; or in other words, he said that man was created after the image of God, and that God should come down among the children of men, and take upon him flesh and blood, and go forth upon the face of the earth—And now, because he said this, they did put him to death." (Mosiah 7:26-28.)

7. *He offers salvation through baptism and personal righteousness.*

"This is my church," he said to Alma, and "whosoever is baptized shall be baptized unto repentance. And whomsoever ye receive shall believe in my name; and him will I freely forgive. For it is I that taketh upon me the sins of the world; for it is I that hath created them; and it is I that granteth unto him that believeth unto the end a place at my right hand. For behold, in my name are they called; and if they know me they shall come forth, and shall have a place eternally at my right hand." (Mosiah 26:22-24.)

8. *He is the Redeemer.*

At the time of his conversion, Alma the younger confessed his past rebellion by saying: "I rejected my

Redeemer, and denied that which had been spoken of by our fathers; but now that they may foresee that he will come, and that he remembereth every creature of his creating, he will make himself manifest unto all." (Mosiah 27:30.)

9. *He is the Son of God who shall redeem his people.*

Zeezrom asked: "Is the Son of God the very Eternal Father?" Amulek replied: "Yea, he is the very Eternal Father of heaven and of earth, and all things which in them are; he is the beginning and the end, the first and the last; And he shall come into the world to redeem his people." (Alma 11:38-40.) Samuel the Lamanite prophesied of "the coming of Jesus Christ, the Son of God, the Father of heaven and of earth, the Creator of all things from the beginning." (Hel. 14:12.)

Did Christ Create Man?

We have now seen that Christ created all things—this earth and all that on it is. "By him were all things created, that are in heaven, and that are in earth." (Col. 1:16.) We have seen that he is "the very Eternal Father of heaven and of earth, and all things which in them are" (Alma 11:39)—that is, that he created all forms of life on the face of the earth. Are we to understand that this means he created man? So it might be reasoned from the blanket assertions made in these and other revelations, and as a matter of fact there are some scriptures which we shall now note which, according to the plain usage of words, some might interpret to mean that mortal man was in fact created not by the Father, but by the Son.

In a deep and difficult passage revealed to Joseph Smith, Christ says: "The Father and I are one—The Father because he gave me of his fulness, and the Son because I was in the world and made flesh my tabernacle, and dwelt among the sons of men. I was in the world and received of my Father, and the works of him were plainly manifest." Then this revelation quotes from an ancient record written first by

John the Baptist but paraphrased and preserved in part by John the Revelator in his gospel, which speaks of Christ in his creative capacity and includes these words: "The worlds were made by him; men were made by him; all things were made by him, and through him, and of him." Then the account explains that "he was called the Son of God, because he received not of the fulness at the first," but that in due course, after the resurrection, "he received a fulness of the glory of the Father." (D&C 93:3-16.) Now, bear in mind that this passage, among other things, is treating Christ in his capacity as both the Father and the Son. It is much the same thought as that expressed by Abinadi when he said of Christ: "Because he dwelleth in the flesh he shall be called the Son of God, and having subjected the flesh to the will of the Father, being the Father and the Son—The Father, because he was conceived by the power of God; and the Son, because of the flesh; thus becoming the Father and Son—And they are one God, yea, the very Eternal Father of heaven and of earth." (Mosiah 15:2-4.)

In the most complete revelation of himself ever given up to that time, our Lord said to the brother of Jared: "I am Jesus Christ. I am the Father and the Son. . . . Seest thou that ye are created after mine own image? Yea, even all men were created in the beginning after mine own image. Behold, this body, which ye now behold, is the body of my spirit." (Ether 3:14-16.) Bear in mind once more that this passage also is treating Christ in his capacity as both the Father and the Son.

In a passage already quoted by us in another connection, Limhi rehearses the teaching of Abinadi "that Christ was the God, the Father of all things, and said that he should take upon him the image of man, and it should be the image after which man was created in the beginning; or in other words, he said that man was created after the image of God, and that God should come down among the children of men, and take upon him flesh and blood, and go forth upon the face of the earth." (Mosiah 7:27.) Note that this passage is affirming in large measure the same truth relative to the creation of man which the Lord Jesus had afore given to the brother of Jared, and that therefore Christ's status as the Father and the Son is necessarily involved.

In a passage of great doctrinal worth and of surpassing literary beauty, Isaiah speaks of the Lord Jehovah, "the Holy One of Israel," who is Christ, as man's "Maker." "I have made the earth, and created man upon it," says he who is the Son of God. "I, even my hands, have stretched out the heavens, and all their host have I commanded." (Isa. 45:9-12.) And once again we have the creation of man ascribed, seemingly, to the Son of God.

However, from other sacred sources we know that Jehovah-Christ, assisted by "many of the noble and great ones" (Abr. 3:22), of whom Michael is but the illustration, did in fact create the earth and all forms of plant and animal life on the face thereof. But when it came to placing man on earth, there was a change in Creators. That is, the Father himself became personally involved. All things were created by the Son, using the power delegated by the Father, except man. In the spirit and again in the flesh, man was created by the Father. There was no delegation of authority where the crowning creature of creation was concerned.

"I am the Beginning and the End, the Almighty God," says the great Elohim. "By mine Only Begotten I created these things; yea, in the beginning I created the heaven, and the earth." (Moses 2:1.) That is, God did all these things by and through his Son. Then of the planned and proposed creation of mortal man, the inspired record says: "And I, God, said unto mine Only Begotten, which was with me from the beginning: Let us make man in our image, after our likeness; and it was so." (Moses 2:26.) But when the plan becomes a reality and the proposal an accomplished fact, then the record personalizes the occurrence and centers it in the Supreme Head. "And I, God, created man in mine own image, in the image of mine Only Begotten created I him; male and female created I them." (Moses 2:27.) That is, God himself, personally, created man, although he continued to honor the Son in that the creature of his creating came forth in the image of both the Father and the Son, as necessarily must have been the case because they were in the image of each other.

In this connection, we find it worthy of note that Joseph Smith said: "Everlasting covenant was made between three personages before the organization of this earth, and relates to their dispensation of things to men on the earth; these personages, according to Abraham's record, are called God the first, the Creator; God the second, the Redeemer; and God the third, the witness or Testator." (*Teachings,* p. 190.) From this we learn that the work of the Father is creation (though he uses the Son and others in the creation of all things except man); the work of the Son is redemption (though he performs this infinite work by the power of the Father); and the work of the Holy Ghost is to bear witness of the Father and the Son, whose minister he is.

In 1916, the duly constituted heads of the earthly Church, who have the ultimate responsibility, under Deity, to interpret and promulgate the mind and will of the Lord to mortals, issued a document entitled *The Father and The Son: A Doctrinal Exposition by The First Presidency and The Twelve.* Therein are set forth, among other things, three distinct senses in which Christ is also known as the Father. These are:

1. He is the Father as Creator, the Father of the heavens and the earth.

2. He is the Father of those who abide in his gospel, the Father of all those who take upon themselves his name and are adopted into his family.

3. He is the Father by divine investiture of authority, meaning that the Father-Elohim has placed his name upon the Son, has given him his own power and authority, and has authorized him to speak in the first person as though he were the original or primal Father.

"In all his dealings with the human family," the Brethren

set forth in their official exposition, "Jesus the Son has represented and yet represents Elohim his Father in power and authority. This is true of Christ in his pre-existent, antemortal, or unembodied state, in the which he was known as Jehovah; also during his embodiment in the flesh; and during his labors as a disembodied spirit in the realm of the dead; and since that period in his resurrected state. . . . The Father placed his name upon the Son; and Jesus Christ spoke and ministered in and through the Father's name; and so far as power, authority, and Godship are concerned his words and acts were and are those of the Father." (*The Father and The Son: A Doctrinal Exposition by The First Presidency and The Twelve,* cited in James E. Talmage, *Articles of Faith,* pp. 465-73.)

"His words and acts were and are those of the Father!"

He speaks in the first person as though he were the Father. They are so perfectly united in all things that, in like circumstances, they think the same thoughts, speak the same words, and do the same acts.

The Son may speak to man in his own name, and then, to dramatize and teach more effectively and powerfully whatever is involved, he may begin to speak in his Father's name, without so much as a break in thought presentation. He begins section 29 in the Doctrine and Covenants by saying, "Listen to the voice of Jesus Christ, your Redeemer, the Great I Am, whose arm of mercy hath atoned for your sins," and without hesitation or explanation he soon assumes the voice of the Father, saying, "I the Lord God" shall "send forth angels to declare unto them repentance and redemption, through faith on the name of mine Only Begotten Son." (D&C 29:1, 42-43.) In such a context the meaning is clear; Christ is choosing to speak in the first person as though he were the Father.

And so we read the various passages in which he says he created man, and although the meanings are not as plainly and clearly set forth as is his declaration in section 29, the principle is the same. He is once again teaching what the

Father did, although to the spiritually untutored it seems as though he is saying that he did it. His words are those of the Father. And upon us the obligation rests, in Paul's language, of "rightly dividing the word of truth" (2 Tim. 2:15)—which we have here done, as should be clear to all.

PROPHETS REVEAL THE COMING OF CHRIST

Man Comes to Dwell on Earth

From our premortal life as spirit beings, to this mortal vale of sorrow and tears, is one simple, easy step. Life on a celestial sphere, in the Eternal Presence, is but a breath removed from life on this fallen orb. The one step is birth, and the breath of difference that divides spirit men from mortal men is the breath of life. Our home here is but a temporary abiding place, one where we are separated, for the moment, from the home eternal.

And so, in his infinite wisdom, for his own purposes and for our advancement and progression, God our Father placed us here on earth. "God created man, in the likeness of God made he him; In the image of his own body, male and female, created he them, and blessed them, and called their name Adam, in the day when they were created and became living souls in the land upon the footstool of God." (Moses 6:8-9.) God is our Father, and "Adam . . . was the son of God, with whom God, himself, conversed." (Moses 6:22.)

After he had taken the step from preexistence to this newly created earth, after the breath of life filled his being, Adam our father, "the first man of all men" (Moses 1:34), chose to fall from his paradisiacal state to one in which the full woes of mortality would weigh upon him. His fall brought temporal and spiritual death into the world. In his mortal and fallen state the procreative powers promised in the Garden of Eden became his natural inheritance, and patterning his course after that of his Eternal Father, he begat sons and daughters "in his own likeness, after his own image." (Moses 6:10.) His posterity, in their fallen and lost state, became "carnal, sensual, and devilish, by nature." (Alma 42:10.)

What Is Messiah's Mission?

To save mankind from eternal temporal death (which is the grave) and from eternal spiritual death (which is everlasting banishment from the presence of God), a gracious Father provided a Savior, his Son, a promised Deliverer or Messiah. Deliverance was to come through his atoning sacrifice, coupled—in the case of salvation from spiritual death—with obedience on the part of man to the laws and ordinances of His everlasting gospel. In the wisdom of God, this infinite and eternal atonement would cause all men to come forth from the grave (thus ransoming them from temporal death) and would bring the believing and obedient saints back into the presence of God, which is eternal life (thus ransoming them from spiritual death). Immortality, which is resurrection, is a free gift for all men; eternal life, which is the kind of life God lives, is reserved for those who are true and faithful in all things. Thus the probationary nature of man's mortal estate is established.

The promised Messiah must thus be the Son of God, who inherits from his Father the power of immortality whereby he can bring to pass, through his redeeming death, the immortality and eternal life of man. He must be the resurrection and the life.

The Messiah thus becomes the One through whom salvation comes. The gospel of God, which is the plan of salvation, becomes his gospel.

The Messiah thus stands as the Mediator between God

and man, as man's Advocate with the Father, as the One who pleads the cause of his brethren in the courts above.

The Messiah thus steps forward as the God of his people, their Savior and Redeemer, the God of Israel, the Revealer of eternal truth, the Lord of Hosts.

The Messiah is Christ.

How far removed from these saving truths are the billions of non-Christians who dwell on earth! They know neither the Father nor the Son, and are without the knowledge leading to that pure and perfect worship which cleanses and sanctifies the souls of men.

How far removed from these saving truths are millions of professing Christians! They have yet to envision that Jesus who is called Christ is in fact the Lord Jehovah of old; that his truths of salvation have been shed forth in one gospel dispensation after another from the days of Adam to the present; and that an unchangeable God has prophets again on earth who minister in his name with binding and sealing power.

How far afield the once chosen race has gone from the knowledge of their Messiah is seen in this statement summarizing their concept of deliverance:

"The Messiah whom we expect is not to be a god, nor a part of the godhead, nor a Son of God in any sense of the word; but simply a man eminently endowed, like Moses and the prophets in the days of the Bible, to work out the will of God on earth in all that the prophets have predicted of him.

"His coming, we believe, will be the signal for universal peace, universal freedom, universal knowledge, universal worship of the One Eternal; objects all of high import, and well worthy to be attested by the visible display of the divine glory before the eyes of all flesh, just as was the presence of the Lord manifested at Sinai, when the Israelites stood assembled to receive the law which was surrendered to their keeping. In the days of this august ruler, the law, which was at first given as 'an inheritance of the congregation of Jacob,' will become the only standard of righteousness, of salvation, for all mankind, when will be fulfilled to its fullest extent the blessings conferred upon Abraham, Isaac, and Jacob, that 'in their seed all the families of the earth should be blessed.'

"We believe, further, that the time of this great event is hidden from our knowledge, and is only known to the Creator, who in his own good time will regenerate the earth, remove the worship of idols, banish all erroneous beliefs, and establish his kingdom firmly and immovably over the hearts of all the sons of man, when all will invoke Him in truth, and call him God, King, Redeemer, the One who was, is, and will be, for ever and ever.

"We believe that the time may be distant, thousands of years removed; but we confidently look forward to its coming, in the full confidence that He who has so miraculously preserved his people among so many trials and dangers, is able and willing to fulfil all he has promised, and that his power will surely accomplish what his goodness has foretold; and that he will not rest in the fulfilment of his word, till all the world shall acknowledge his power, and ceaseless incense ascend to his holy name from the rising of the sun even unto his setting; when the altars of falsehood shall crumble, and the dominion of unbelief be swept from the face of the earth." (Isaac Lesser, *History of the Jews and Their Religion,* p. 7.)

God Giveth His Gospel to Man

Christ is the promised Messiah by whom salvation comes, and so an angel of the Lord commanded Adam: "Thou shalt do all that thou doest in the name of the Son, and thou shalt repent and call upon God in the name of the Son forevermore." (Moses 5:8.) Then, by the power of the Holy Ghost, Adam, in his lost and fallen state, heard the voice of the Son, saying: "I am the Only Begotten of the Father from the beginning, henceforth and forever, that as thou hast fallen thou mayest be redeemed, and all mankind, even as many as will." (Moses 5:9.) And Eve, knowing what was being taught, acclaimed the blessings given them through the fall and redemption, saying: "Were it not for our transgression we never should have had seed, and never should have known good and evil, and the joy of our redemption, and the eternal life which God giveth unto all the obedient." (Moses 5:11.)

Beginning in this early day, that God who is no respecter of persons, and in whose sight the souls of those in all ages are equally precious, began to reveal the plan of salvation to his mortal children. The knowledge of a Deliverer was made known unto them. They were promised salvation by obedience to the laws and ordinances of Messiah's gospel, and the decree went forth: "Believe on his Only Begotten Son, even him whom he declared should come in the meridian of time, who was prepared from before the foundation of the world." Then the record says: "And thus the Gospel began to be preached, from the beginning, being declared by holy angels sent forth from the presence of God, and by his own voice, and by the gift of the Holy Ghost. And thus all things were confirmed unto Adam, by an holy ordinance, and the Gospel preached, and a decree sent forth, that it should be in the world, until the end thereof; and thus it was." (Moses 5:57-59.)

This same gospel was revealed to Enoch, Noah, and Abraham; to Melchizedek, Moses, and Moriancumer; to the Jaredites and the Nephites, and insofar as they would receive it, to the prophets and apostles of all ages and on all continents. It was restored from time to time in new and glorious dispensations, especially and particularly in time's meridian by the Son of God himself. The final dispensation of grace is that in which we now live—the dispensation of Joseph Smith, the dispensation which will prepare a people for the Second Coming of the Messiah.

In all these dispensations the plan of redemption and salvation has been the same, namely, that salvation comes through the atoning blood of Him whom Almighty God sent to atone for the sins of the world.

In all these dispensations the faithful have received the same gospel, known the same truths, rejoiced in the same knowledge, enjoyed the same gifts of the Spirit, and had the same hope of eternal life.

In all these dispensations, following the pattern set in Adam's day, those who have received the everlasting gospel have heard the voice of God, received the ministering of angels, and possessed the gift of the Holy Ghost.

In all of these dispensations salvation has been in Christ; those who have received the gospel have received him; and by faith they have gained peace in this life and a guarantee of eternal life in the mansions that are prepared.

Messiah Revealed to Men

Our sources of knowledge concerning King Messiah all stem back to God who is our Father. Every true and authorized witness borne of Christ has come by the power of the Holy Ghost; it has been planted and sealed in the hearts of men by the Holy Spirit. However, for convenience in study, we may properly classify Messianic utterances in the following categories:

1. Those spoken by the mouth of God, meaning by either the Father or the Son.
2. Revelations given by the Holy Ghost to all those who prepare themselves to receive the promptings of this divine Revelator.
3. Angelic proclamations delivered to righteous men, women, and children.
4. Utterances of prophets, men whose mission it is to reveal and bear record of their Messiah.
5. Testimonies of living witnesses, meaning all the saints, all of the members of the Church, all who hold the holy priesthood, all who have the testimony of Jesus. Properly speaking, all of these are prophets—prophets to themselves

and their families, as distinguished from those who wear the prophetic mantle which obligates them to proclaim and send the witness of truth to all the world.

6. That which is recorded in the Holy Scriptures and is thus preserved for all men to study and ponder.

Messianic Prophecies Borne by Gods and Angels

The greatest witness of the Son is the Father. "I bear witness of myself," the Lord Jesus said to the Jews. (JST, John 5:31.) Then of his Father—concerning whom he was later to say, "My Father is greater than I" (John 14:28)—our Lord said: "The Father himself, which hath sent me, hath borne witness of me. Ye have neither heard his voice at any time, nor seen his shape." (John 5:37.)

But other men in other days had both heard his voice and seen his shape. His voice had been the voice of One testifying of the divine Sonship of the promised Messiah, and his shape had been the express image of that of the Son. (Heb. 1:3.) Indeed, the Lord's eternal law is: "No man hath seen God at any time, except he hath borne record of the Son." (JST, John 1:19.) Nephi is one who heard the voice, and the record it bore to him was: "The words of my Beloved are true and faithful." (2 Ne. 31:15.) Six centuries later, hosts of his descendants were to hear the same voice acclaim: "Behold my Beloved Son, in whom I am well pleased, in whom I have glorified my name—hear ye him." (3 Ne. 11:7.)

Of Enoch's Zion, the record says: "The Lord came and dwelt with his people, and they dwelt in righteousness." (Moses 7:16.) That he bore testimony among them of his own divine status and redeeming power is self-evident. Then, after "Zion, in process of time, was taken up into heaven . . . Enoch beheld angels descending out of heaven, bearing testimony of the Father and Son; and the Holy Ghost fell on many, and they were caught up by the powers of heaven into Zion." (Moses 7:21, 27.) Then it was that the same Lord who had dwelt among them said to Enoch: "I am Messiah, the King of Zion, the Rock of Heaven, which is broad as eternity; whoso cometh in at the gate and climbeth up by me shall never fall." (Moses 7:53.)

As the time of Christ's coming drew near—the year was about 82 B.C.—the great prophet Alma said to his Nephite brethren: "Now is the time to repent, for the day of salvation draweth nigh." Then follows this profound and comprehensive explanation of how angels were foretelling the coming of Christ and how they would announce the fulfillment of their prophecies to other men in due course: "Yea, and the voice of the Lord, by the mouth of angels," Alma continues, "doth declare it unto all nations; yea, doth declare it, that they may have glad tidings of great joy; . . . For behold, angels are declaring it unto many at this time in our land; and this is for the purpose of preparing the hearts of the children of men to receive his word at the time of his coming in his glory. And now we only wait to hear the joyful news declared unto us by the mouth of angels, of his coming; for the time cometh, we know not how soon. . . . And it shall be made known unto just and holy men, by the mouth of angels, at the time of his coming, that the words of our fathers may be fulfilled, according to that which they have spoken concerning him, which was according to the spirit of prophecy which was in them." (Alma 13:21-26.) And the impartiality of God is shown from the fact these "glad tidings" and this "joyful news" were being imparted "by angels unto men, . . . women [and] . . . little children." (Alma 32:23.) Probably the most glorious angelic pronouncements about Christ, his coming and his atoning sacrifice, were made by the heavenly ministrant who visited King Benjamin, as is recorded in the third chapter of Mosiah. That chapter contains a sermon preached by an angel on the most important of all gospel subjects, the atonement of the Lord Jesus Christ.

But probably the best summary we have of how and why God spoke by his own voice and sent angels to confirm his word is given by Mormon in these words: "God knowing all things, being from everlasting to everlasting, behold, he sent angels to minister unto the children of men, to make manifest concerning the coming of Christ; and in Christ there should come every good thing. And God also declared unto prophets, by his own mouth, that Christ should come. And behold, there were divers ways that he did manifest things unto the children of men, which were good; and all things which are good cometh of Christ; otherwise men were fallen, and there could no good thing come unto them. Wherefore, by the ministering of angels, and by every word which proceeded forth out of the mouth of God, men began to exercise faith in Christ; and thus by faith, they did lay hold upon every good thing; and thus it was until the coming of Christ." (Moro. 7:22-25.)

Messianic Prophecies Borne by the Holy Ghost

As already set forth in that portion of Chapter 3 entitled "How Messianic Prophecies Came," all such prophecies have come by the power of the Holy Ghost, even though they were spoken by Gods, angels, or men. Let us here bring into focus how and under what circumstances this third member of the Godhead bears record of Christ, so that believing men may abide the law involved and gain for themselves the personal witness that Jesus is the Messiah.

In this connection, be it noted: "No man can receive the Holy Ghost without receiving revelations. The Holy Ghost is a Revelator." (*Teachings,* p. 328.) The question, then, is how to gain revelation from the Lord's Revelator, and the answer is easily found: Obey the law upon which the receipt of that revelation is predicated. That law is:

1. The Holy Ghost will not dwell in an unclean tabernacle. "The Lord hath said he dwelleth not in unholy temples, but in the hearts of the righteous doth he dwell." (Alma 34:36.)

2. Sins are remitted through faith, repentance, and bap-

tism. Thereby, and thereby only, is the contrite soul made clean so as to become a fit recipient of revelation from the Revelator.

An honest and sincere truth-seeker may receive a flash of revelation from the Holy Ghost telling him that Jesus is the Christ; that Joseph Smith is a prophet of God; that the Lord has restored the fulness of his everlasting gospel in this day; that the Book of Mormon is the mind and will and voice of God to the world today. That blaze of newly encountered light will be as lightning in a night storm; it will show the path leading to the pure light of day; but unless the one receiving the light walks therein, unless he follows the path, he will remain in darkness and lose the new knowledge he was once ready to receive.

In the full and complete sense required to receive enduring revelations of the divine Sonship of our Lord, the Comforter, "whom the world cannot receive" (John 14:17) and whose companionship is reserved for the saints of God, comes only to Church members. It is the faithful only who receive the gift of the Holy Ghost. This gift is the right to the constant companionship of that member of the Godhead. It is received by the laying on of hands following faith and repentance. It is only then that those who love the Lord receive a fulfillment of the promise: "By the power of the Holy Ghost ye may know the truth of all things." (Moro. 10:5.)

To prepare men to receive revelation from the Holy Ghost, the Lord sends forth his Spirit—meaning the Light of Christ, the omnipresent Spirit that quickens the mind and enlightens the intellect, that leads and guides into paths of righteousness, and that entices men to come to the covenant of baptism and receive the gift of the Holy Ghost. (D&C 84:45-58.) Thus the record says of the Nephites in about 78 B.C.: "The Lord did pour out his Spirit on all the face of the land to prepare the minds of the children of men, or to prepare their hearts to receive the word which should be taught among them at the time of his coming—That they might not be hardened against the word, that they might not be unbelieving, and go on to destruction, but that they might receive the word with joy, and as a branch be grafted into the true vine, that they might enter into the rest of the Lord their God." (Alma 16:16-17.) Those who followed the promptings of this Spirit received the gospel, were baptized, gained the gift of the Holy Ghost, and became the recipients of personal revelation concerning Christ and his coming.

When the servants of the Lord preach the gospel by the power of the Holy Ghost to those who have hearkened to the Light of Christ, the persons thus mellowed and prepared receive the truth, repent of their sins, and gain for themselves the gift of the Holy Ghost. When the scripture says, "The Lord God called upon men by the Holy Ghost everywhere and commanded them that they should repent" (Moses 5:14), it means that the Lord called upon them by the mouths of his servants who were inspired and guided by the Holy Ghost, not that unclean persons received the promptings of that Holy Being.

And thus it is that men come to know of "the Messiah who is the Lamb of God, of whom the Holy Ghost beareth record, from the beginning of the world until this time, and from this time henceforth and forever." (1 Ne. 12:18.)

All the Prophets Prophesied of Christ

Man is fallen; man is lost. There is no hope for Adam's seed. Death prevails and darkness reigns. God alone can loose the bands; he alone can break the chains. There must be a Deliverer, a Savior of the world. "How great the importance to make these things known unto the inhabitants of the earth, that they may know that there is no flesh that can dwell in the presence of God, save it be through the merits, and mercy, and grace of the Holy Messiah." (2 Ne. 2:8.) His coming and ministry, the atonement he was to make, the redemption provided through his blood, the resurrection that would pass upon all men because of him, eternal life with the Gods of heaven for all the faithful—these are the things that were the burden of the messages and ministries of all the holy prophets since the world began, even as they are of the prophets and apostles who have come since he ministered among mortal men.

Such sectarian scholars as happen to believe in Messianic prophecies suppose that these divine statements are few in number and came from a comparatively few seeric souls. The fact is, these prophecies are in number as the sands upon the seashore, and those who spoke them are sufficient in number to people cities, populate nations, and cover continents. All of the prophets, all of the ancient preachers of righteousness, all of the citizens of Zion, all of the saints of old, all of those from Adam to John who had the gift of the Holy Ghost—all of these bore testimonies in Messianic terms. They all had a Spirit-borne hope in Christ who was to come, and fortunately some few of them were called to be prophets to the people and have had portions of their words preserved for us.

Nephi speaks of the visions and prophecies of his father, Lehi, who taught that "a prophet would the Lord God raise up among the Jews—even a Messiah, or, in other words, a Savior of the world. And he also spake concerning the prophets, how great a number had testified of these things, concerning this Messiah, of whom he had spoken, or this Redeemer of the world." (1 Ne. 10:4-5.)

Nephi's brother Jacob says of the Nephite people: "We also had many revelations, and the spirit of much prophecy; wherefore, we knew of Christ and his kingdom, which should come." (Jacob 1:6.) "We knew of Christ, and we had a hope of his glory many hundred years before his coming; and not only we ourselves had a hope of his glory, but also all the holy prophets which were before us." (Jacob 4:4.) Then Jacob recites the great and eternal truths pertaining to the atonement, and says: "We are not witnesses alone in these things; for God also spake them unto prophets of old." (Jacob 4:13.) In his contention with the anti-Christ, Sherem, Jacob testified: "None of the prophets have written, nor prophesied, save they have spoken concerning this Christ." (Jacob 7:11.)

As part of one of the greatest sermons ever delivered on the atonement, the angelic preacher said to King Benjamin: "And the Lord God hath sent his holy prophets among all the children of men, to declare these things to every kindred, nation, and tongue, that thereby whosoever should believe that Christ should come, the same might receive remission of their sins, and rejoice with exceeding great joy, even as though he had already come among them." (Mosiah 3:13.)

Abinadi, who had a talent for speaking plainly and bluntly and leaving a testimony that could not be refuted, asked: "Did not Moses prophesy unto them concerning the coming of the Messiah, and that God should redeem his people? Yea, and even all the prophets who have prophesied ever since the world began—have they not spoken more or less concerning these things? Have they not said that God himself should come down among the children of men, and take upon him the form of man, and go forth in mighty power upon the face of the earth? Yea, and have they not said also that he should bring to pass the resurrection of the dead, and that he, himself, should be oppressed and afflicted?" (Mosiah 13:33-35.) "All the holy prophets," he said, "have prophesied concerning the coming of the Lord." (Mosiah 15:11.)

Nephi the son of Helaman comments on the extent of the prophetic witness of our Lord by citing the testimony of Moses and then saying: "Moses did not only testify of these things, but also all the holy prophets, from his days even to the days of Abraham. Yea, and behold, Abraham saw of his coming, and was filled with gladness and did rejoice. Yea, and behold I say unto you, that Abraham not only knew of these things, but there were many before the days of Abraham who were called by the order of God; yea, even after the order of his Son; and this that it should be shown unto the people, a great many thousand years before his coming, that even redemption should come unto them. And now I would that ye should know, that even since the days of Abraham there have been many prophets that have testified these things." He then names Zenos, Zenock, Ezias, Isaiah, and Jeremiah as among the group, and looking back on nearly six hundred years of Nephite history he says further: "Nephi also testified of these things, and also almost all of our fathers, even down to this time; yea, they have testified of the coming of Christ, and have looked forward, and have rejoiced in his day which is to come." (Hel. 8:16-22.)

Peter, our Lord's chief apostle of the last previous dispensation, quoted a Messianic utterance of Moses and then affirmed: "Yea, and all the prophets from Samuel and those that follow after, as many as have spoken, have likewise foretold of these days." (Acts 3:22-24.) On a later occasion, Peter said of his Lord: "To him give all the prophets witness." (Acts 10:43.) And Stephen, with biting irony, said to the murderous mob who made him a martyr: "Which of the prophets have not your fathers persecuted? and they have slain them which shewed before of the coming of the Just One; of whom ye have been now the betrayers and murderers." (Acts 7:52.)

King Messiah Shall Come

We shall now present, prophet by prophet, doctrine by doctrine, and testimony by testimony, a summary of the knowledge revealed to them of old about Him who was to come and redeem his people. By way of introduction, let us name a few of the inspired men of ancient days who knew of the coming of a Messiah and of the salvation that would come because of him. Other prophets will be named and their teachings and testimonies analyzed, as the whole Messianic message is set forth, line upon line and precept upon precept, in succeeding chapters.

Messianic truths were revealed to the first man, and he taught them to his children and wrote them in a Book of Remembrance. His righteous posterity read them in the recorded revelations and prevailed upon God to give them personal prophetic insight. After naming Adam, Seth, Enos, Cainan, Mahalaleel, Jared, and Enoch, the line of prophets through whom priesthood powers and gospel truths descended, the inspired historian Moses concludes: "And they were preachers of righteousness, and spake and prophesied, and called upon all men, everywhere, to repent; and faith was taught unto the children of men." (Moses 6:23.)

Then came the prophets Methuselah, Lamech, and Noah, each in turn, with the scripture saying that "Noah prophesied, and taught the things of God, even as it was in the beginning." (Moses 8:16.) From Noah the prophetic powers passed to Shem and his descendants, including Melchizedek. Up to this point the perfect patriarchal system had prevailed and the prophetic powers and patriarchal priesthood had passed from father to son. Melchizedek conferred the priesthood upon Abraham, and soon it was spread out among peoples and nations of whom we have no knowledge, spread out without apparent reference to the perfect system of patriarchal descent. By way of lineage, it went from Abraham to Isaac, Jacob, Joseph, Ephraim and Manasseh, and to the increasing hosts of Israel. But from Esaias, who lived in the days of Abraham and of whom we know nothing else, it went successively to Gad, Jeremy, Elihu, Caleb, and Jethro, who was the father-in-law of Moses and the one who conferred the priesthood upon Israel's greatest prophet. (D&C 84:5-16.)

All of these, and all of the prophets in Israel, sang the same song, the song of redeeming grace as found in God's own Son. Isaiah, known as the Messianic prophet because of the multitude of his inspired sayings concerning the coming and mission of Israel's God, gave of him, among a host of others, such declarations as these: "I will wait upon the Lord, . . . and I will look for him," he said, after prophesying that some among the Jews would accept him, while to others he would be a stumbling block. (Isa. 8:13-17.) "The Lord cometh," he proclaimed as part of a resurrection passage.

(Isa. 26:19-21.) "Your God will come. . . . He will come and save you," was his reassurance to disconsolate Israel. (Isa. 35:1-10.) "Prepare ye the way of the Lord," for "the Lord God will come with strong hand," was part of his oft-repeated message. (Isa. 40:1-11.) "I the Lord have called thee in righteousness," Isaiah quoted the Father as saying of Christ, "and will hold thine hand, and will keep thee, and give thee for a covenant of the people, for a light of the Gentiles." (Isa. 42:6.) As part of one of his longest and most wondrous prophecies, he affirmed: "Thy God Reigneth! . . . The Lord shall bring again Zion. . . . [He] shall deal prudently, he shall be exalted and extolled, and be very high." (Isa. 52 and 53.)

Other prophets also spoke of his coming. For instance, Haggai said, "The desire of all nations shall come." (Hag. 2:7.) And scattered through the Psalms are great numbers of Spirit-inspired statements such as these: "Blessed be he that cometh in the name of the Lord" (Ps. 118:26), and "Then said I, Lo, I come: in the volume of the book it is written of me, I delight to do thy will, O my God: yea, thy law is within my heart" (Ps. 40:7-8). And it was of this great body of prophetic utterances that he himself spoke when, after his resurrection, he said to his apostles: "All things must be fulfilled, which were written in the law of Moses, and in the prophets, and in the psalms concerning me." (Luke 24:44.)

But all of these Biblical passages are either hidden in difficult contexts, have other matters interwoven with them which open the door to uncertainty as to their real meaning, or have a dual application; that is, they apply both to our Lord's First Coming, when he was subject to mortal men, and to his Second Coming, his glorious appearing, when all men shall be subject unto him. That they might be understood following his mortal ministry among them, the scripture says of his ancient disciples: "Then opened he their understanding, that they might understand the scriptures." (Luke 24:45.)

Nephite Prophets Reveal Christ

It is to our Nephite brethren that we turn for our plain and perfect prophetic utterances about "the Apostle and High Priest of our profession, Christ Jesus." (Heb. 3:1.) By way of illustration only, let us note:

Lehi saw in vision the coming of Christ and the Twelve who ministered with him. He was given a book by a heavenly ministrant, and "the things which he read in the book, manifested plainly of the coming of a Messiah, and also the redemption of the world." (1 Ne. 1:19.)

Nephi had many visions and revelations, and from the knowledge thus gained, he was able to say authoritatively: "The Messiah cometh; . . . and according to the words of the prophets, and also the word of the angel of God, his name shall be Jesus Christ, the Son of God." (2 Ne. 25:19.)

"The great question," as Amulek termed it—and there neither is nor can be a more important one—"is whether the word be in the Son of God, or whether there shall be no Christ." His answer: "The word is in Christ unto salvation." His personal testimony: "These things are true. . . . I do know that Christ shall come among the children of men, to take upon him the transgressions of his people, and that he shall atone for the sins of the world; for the Lord God hath spoken it." (Alma 34:5-8.)

"Believest thou in Jesus Christ, who shall come?" (Alma 45:4.) Such was the question put by Alma to his son Helaman, less than a century before our Lord's birth. As he had borne it to Korihor, Alma's own testimony was: "I know there is a God, and also that Christ shall come." (Alma 30:39.) His similar testimony to his son Corianton was: "I say unto you, that it is he that surely shall come to take away the sins of the world; yea, he cometh to declare glad tidings of salvation unto his people." (Alma 39:15.)

Teaching that salvation was in Christ, and then bearing testimony that such teachings were true, was the perfect missionary approach then as it is now. When Ammon stood before King Lamoni, for instance, "he began at the creation of the world, and also the creation of Adam, and told him all things concerning the fall of man. . . . But this is not all; for he expounded unto them the plan of redemption, which was prepared from the foundation of the world; and he also made known unto them concerning the coming of Christ." (Alma 18:36, 39.) Similarly, when Aaron was doing missionary work among the Lamanites, he asked: "Believest thou that the Son of God shall come to redeem mankind from their sins?" After receiving a negative reply, he "began to open the scriptures unto them concerning the coming of Christ, and also concerning the resurrection of the dead, and that there could be no redemption for mankind save it were through the death and sufferings of Christ, and the atonement of his blood." (Alma 21:7-9.)

When prophets and missionaries bear record of Christ and his gospel, such has the effect of dividing the people. They either believe and obey, or disbelieve and disobey. This is true in and out of the Church. In Alma's day, many who belonged to the Church itself had a spirit of disbelief and rebellion, "and the wickedness of the church was a great stumbling-block to those who did not belong to the church; and thus the church began to fail in its progress." This spirit of iniquity encouraged nonmembers of the Church in courses of evil, until the whole Nephite nation was full of corruption. "Now this was a great cause for lamentations among the people, while others were abasing themselves, succoring those who stood in need of their succor, such as imparting their substance to the poor and the needy, feeding the hungry, and suffering all manner of afflictions, for Christ's sake, who should come according to the spirit of prophecy; Looking forward to that day, thus retaining a remission of their sins; being filled with great joy because of the resurrection of the dead, according to the will and power and deliverance of Jesus Christ from the bands of death." (Alma 4:10-14.) What an effect the preaching of the word has upon the righteous! And the unrighteous!

MESSIAH REVEALED IN ALL THE WORLD

Witnesses Testify of Christ

In this mortal probation it is the design and purpose of the Lord to test us: to see if we will believe in him and obey his laws now that we no longer dwell in his presence, hear his voice, and see his face. He already knows how we respond—what we believe and how we act—when we walk by sight. Now he is testing our devotion to him when we walk by faith: when his presence is veiled, his voice is afar off, and his face is seen by few men only.

Accordingly, he has ordained the law of witnesses, the law whereby he reveals himself to prophets and righteous men and sends them forth to teach his laws and bear testimony of their truth and divinity. "In the mouth of two or three witnesses shall every word be established." (2 Cor. 13:1.) "Whether by mine own voice or by the voice of my servants, it is the same." (D&C 1:38.)

This law of witnesses is described by Isaiah in a glorious prophecy about the gathering of Israel and the spread of truth in the last days. In so applying the law he is simply projecting to a future dispensation the principles that were in full operation in his own day, and for that matter had been binding upon his forebears back to the first man. "I am the Lord thy God, the Holy One of Israel, thy Saviour," was the voice of Israel's God to Isaiah. Then came the prophecy: "I will bring thy seed from the east, and gather thee from the west." I will "bring my sons from far, and my daughters from the ends of the earth; Even every one that is called by my name." That is, in the last days Israel shall be gathered again, and those who come to a knowledge of their true Messiah shall take upon them his name and become members of his family. To them, as Isaiah records it, comes this promise and directive: "Ye are my witnesses, saith the Lord, . . . ye may know and believe me, and understand that I am he. . . . I, even I, am the Lord; and beside me there is no saviour. . . . Ye are my witnesses, saith the Lord, that I am God." (Isa. 43:3-12.)

Christ and his laws are known to and taught by witnesses. Salvation was made available before his coming by those who testified that they knew he would come to redeem his people. Salvation has been made available since his coming by those who now testify that he has come and shed his blood in an infinite and eternal atoning sacrifice. The Israelites of old carried with them in the wilderness a portable tabernacle, the tabernacle of the congregation, a place of worship. To signify its use and purpose, it was named "the tent of testimony" (Num. 9:15), or "the tabernacle of witness" (Num. 17:7). Therein testimony was borne of the coming of the Messiah.

Those of us today in whose veins the blood of Father Jacob flows, who are of the blood lineage of those who moved with Moses from Egypt toward their promised land, have built our synagogues, as it were, our houses of worship, wherein we teach and testify of him who has now come and whose redeeming blood has been shed for all those who have faith in him. Our houses of worship are the tents of testimony and the tabernacle of witness of the last days. And our missionaries, who are witnesses, bear—on the streets, in the homes, at whatever place people are found—the same testimony of the divine Sonship that was borne by their counterparts of old.

Scriptures Testify of Christ

There is no way to overstate the importance of a written language and of having scriptural accounts that preserve the knowledge that God has revealed to prophets both past and present. Civilization could not exist without a written language. By the simple process of erasing all writing and of ceasing to teach people to write, civilization would end in one generation. All of earth's inhabitants would sink into that social and cultural limbo possessed by the pygmies in the African jungles.

As society is now constituted, and under the circumstances in which men now dwell on earth, salvation could not be made available without written scripture. If men could neither read nor write—and as a consequence God's holy word was not available to guide them—the hope of salvation would cease except to those prophets to whom God and angels appear, plus such as could personally hear their voices and be baptized by them. For all practical purposes the spread of saving truth would cease and Satan would come off triumphant in the warfare for the souls of men.

And so, from the beginning, the Lord provided a language and gave men the power to read and write. "It was given unto as many as called upon God to write by the spirit of inspiration. And by them their children were taught to read and write, having a language which was pure and undefiled." (Moses 6:5-6.) The thing which they first wrote, and which of all their writings was of the most worth unto them, was a Book of Remembrance, a book in which they recorded what the Lord had revealed about himself, about his coming, and about the plan of salvation, which plan would have force and validity because of his atonement. This was the beginning of the Holy Scriptures, than which inspired writing there is nothing that is more important.

"The law of the Lord is perfect, converting the soul: the testimony of the Lord is sure, making wise the simple. The statutes of the Lord are right, rejoicing the heart: the commandment of the Lord is pure, enlightening the eyes. The fear of the Lord is clean, enduring for ever: the judgments of the Lord are true and righteous altogether. More to be desired are they than gold, yea, than much fine gold: sweeter also than honey and the honeycomb. Moreover by them is thy servant warned: and in keeping of them there is great reward." (Ps. 19:7-11.)

Jesus said: "Search the scriptures; for . . . they are they which testify of me." (John 5:39.) What better use can language be put than to use it as a vehicle to gain a knowledge of Christ? Of certain devout and honest truth seekers of Paul's day, it is written: "They received the word with all readiness of mind, and searched the scriptures daily." (Acts 17:11.) Should our search for salvation be any less intensive than theirs?

After quoting extensively from Isaiah, Jesus also said: "Ye ought to search these things. Yea, a commandment I give unto you that ye search these things diligently; for great are the words of Isaiah." Then he said: "Write the things which I have told you; and according to the time and the will of the Father they shall go forth unto the Gentiles." At this point he expanded his counsel that his people should be gospel scholars: "Search the prophets, for many there be that testify of these things." And finally, making himself the Perfect Pattern, he "expounded all the scriptures unto them which they had received" and commanded them to write "other scriptures" which had not previously been preserved according to his mind and purpose.

"And now it came to pass that when Jesus had said these words he said unto them again, after he had expounded all the scriptures unto them which they had received, he said unto them: Behold, other scriptures I would that ye should write, that ye have not. And it came to pass that he said unto Nephi: Bring forth the record which ye have kept. And when Nephi had brought forth the records, and laid them before him, he cast his eyes upon them and said: Verily I say unto you, I commanded my servant Samuel, the Lamanite, that he should testify unto this people, that at the day that the Father should glorify his name in me that there were many saints who should arise from the dead, and should appear unto many, and should minister unto them. And he said unto them: Was it not so? And his disciples answered him and said: Yea, Lord, Samuel did prophesy according to thy words, and they were all fulfilled. And Jesus said unto them: How be it that ye have not written this thing, that many saints did arise and appear unto many and did minister unto them? And it came to pass that Nephi remembered that this thing had not been written. And it came to pass that Jesus commanded that it should be written; therefore it was written according as he commanded. And now it came to pass that when Jesus had expounded all the scriptures in one, which they had written, he commanded them that they should teach the things which he had expounded unto them." (3 Ne. 23:1-14.)

A perfect illustration of the blessings that flow to a nation and people who have the scriptures and search them is seen in the account of the Nephites, an account that tells of their problems, sorrows, triumphs, and final destruction. When Nephi and his brethren went back to Jerusalem to get the brass plates from Laban, Nephi said: "It is wisdom in God that we should obtain these records, that we may preserve unto our children the language of our fathers; And also that we may preserve unto them the words which have been spoken by the mouth of all the holy prophets, which have been delivered unto them by the Spirit and power of God, since the world began, even down unto this present time." (1 Ne. 3:19-20.)

Without question the revealed accounts on these plates of brass—and "they did contain the five books of Moses, which gave an account of the creation of the world, and also of Adam and Eve, who were our first parents; And also a record of the Jews from the beginning, even down to the commencement of the reign of Zedekiah, king of Judah; And also the prophecies of the holy prophets, from the beginning, even down to the commencement of the reign of Zedekiah; and also many prophecies which have been spoken by the mouth of Jeremiah," including a genealogy of Lehi's fathers (1 Ne. 5:10-14)—without question these accounts contained that guidance which led generation after generation of people to walk in paths of truth and righteousness. A part of their use and value was summarized by Alma as he spoke to his son Helaman: "It has hitherto been wisdom in God that these things should be preserved; for behold, they have enlarged the memory of this people, yea, and convinced many of the error of their ways, and brought them to the knowledge of their God unto the salvation of their souls. Yea, I say unto you, were it not for these things that these records do contain, which are on these plates, Ammon and his brethren could not have convinced so many thousands of the Lamanites of the incorrect tradition of their fathers; yea, these records and their words brought them unto repentance; that is, they brought them to the knowledge of the Lord their God, and to rejoice in Jesus Christ their Redeemer." (Alma 37:8-9).

Similarly, for nearly four hundred years the King James Version of the Bible has been one of the most stabilizing forces in all Christendom. It has been one of the chief means of preserving the English language as such; but more than this, it has kept right principles before millions of people who have been and are without personal contact with the prophets and witnesses who teach personally the Lord's message of salvation to his earthly children.

In contrast, the Lamanites and the Mulekites dwindled in unbelief and apostasy because they did not have the holy scriptures to guide them. King Benjamin, speaking of the brass plates, said to his sons: "Were it not for these plates, which contain these records and these commandments, we must have suffered in ignorance, even at this present time, not knowing the mysteries of God. For it were not possible that our father, Lehi, could have remembered all these things, to have taught them to his children, except it were for the help of these plates; for he having been taught in the language of the Egyptians therefore he could read these engravings, and teach them to his children, that thereby they could teach them to their children, and so fulfilling the commandments of God, even down to this present time. I say unto you, my sons, were it not for these things, which have been kept and preserved by the hand of God, that we might read and understand of his mysteries, and have his commandments always before our eyes, that even our fathers would have dwindled in unbelief, and we should have been like unto our brethren, the Lamanites, who know nothing concerning these things, or even do not believe them when they are taught them, because of the traditions of their fathers, which are not correct." (Mosiah 1:3-5.)

As to the Mulekites, they followed Mulek the son of King Zedekiah from Jerusalem to the Western Hemisphere; and when they were discovered by Mosiah and his people, "their language had become corrupted; and they had brought no records with them; and they denied the being of their Creator." (Omni 17.) What a contrast this is with the Nephite peoples whose forebears said: "We talk of Christ, we rejoice in Christ, we preach of Christ, we prophesy of Christ, and we write according to our prophecies, that our children may know to what source they may look for a remission of their sins." (2 Ne. 25:26.)

The Book of Mormon Testifies of Christ

For the first four thousand years of earth's temporal continuance the prophetic writings, of which the Old Testament is a fragmentary part, contained Deity's doctrine about the Messiah and the plan of salvation. During this period the Jaredite scriptures and much of the Nephite record were composed and used; also, many prophets kept sacred accounts of what the Lord revealed to them, of which accounts we have little or no knowledge.

During and after our Lord's ministry on earth the New

Testament record came into being, along with that portion of the Book of Mormon starting with Third Nephi. The Book of Mormon, however, does not contain "even a hundredth part of the things which Jesus did truly teach unto the people." (3 Ne. 26:6.) And the Beloved John gives us to understand that the New Testament preserves for us only a drop of the great ocean of our Lord's Old World teachings. (John 20:30-31; 21:25.)

Each part of the prophetic writings has come forth for the guidance of those then living and those who thereafter should be privileged to study and ponder its contents. But the amount of Holy Writ that the Lord makes available in any given day depends upon the spiritual status of the people then living. As Alma said: "It is given unto many to know the mysteries of God; nevertheless they are laid under a strict command that they shall not impart only according to the portion of his word which he doth grant unto the children of men, according to the heed and diligence which they give unto him. And therefore, he that will harden his heart, the same receiveth the lesser portion of the word; and he that will not harden his heart, to him is given the greater portion of the word, until it is given unto him to know the mysteries of God until he know them in full. And they that will harden their hearts, to them is given the lesser portion of the word until they know nothing concerning his mysteries; and then they are taken captive by the devil, and led by his will down to destruction." (Alma 12:9-11.)

Thus, for instance, we have that knowledge about the three degrees of glory which is written in section 76, but we do not have a full understanding of those kingdoms of eternal glory, "which surpass all understanding in glory, and in might, and in dominion." Such added knowledge was received by the Prophet and Sidney Rigdon, but they were forbidden to write it, and it is "not lawful for man to utter." (D&C 76:114-19.)

Although we do not have a fraction of the teachings of the Resurrected Lord to the Nephites, "the plates of Nephi do contain the more part of the things which he taught the people." (3 Ne. 26:7.) If and when we ever receive these added truths depends upon us. In making his abridgment of the ancient records, Mormon said of those living in our day: "When they shall have received this, which is expedient that they should have first, to try their faith, and if it shall so be that they shall believe these things then shall the greater things be made manifest unto them. And if it so be that they will not believe these things, then shall the greater things be withheld from them, unto their condemnation. Behold, I was about to write them, all which were engraven upon the plates of Nephi, but the Lord forbade it, saying: I will try the faith of my people." (3 Ne. 26:9-11.)

On this same basis the Lord withheld from the Nephites who lived before his birth the Messianic knowledge he had given the Jaredites. "Thou shalt not suffer these things which ye have seen and heard to go forth unto the world," he told the brother of Jared, "until the time cometh that I shall glorify my name in the flesh." (Ether 3:21.) When Moroni made his abridgment of the book of Ether, he kept these same things back so that they are not known unto us. "They shall not go forth unto the Gentiles," he wrote, "until the day that they shall repent of their iniquity, and become clean before the Lord. And in that day that they shall exercise faith in me, saith the Lord, even as the brother of Jared did, that they may become sanctified in me, then will I manifest unto them the things which the brother of Jared saw, even to the unfolding unto them all my revelations, saith Jesus Christ, the Son of God, the Father of the heavens and of the earth, and all things that in them are." (Ether 4:6-7.)

Now, these comments about the canon of scripture of the past and of the present bring us to this point of understanding, namely, that the Book of Mormon is that portion of the Lord's word which he has preserved for our day to introduce and establish his work. As a source for testimony about Christ, and as a source for an understanding of the plain and simple doctrines of salvation, the Book of Mormon surpasses any scripture now available to men. We have already seen, and shall yet hereafter see more fully, the purity, perfection, and beauty of the Messianic message found in these writings of Nephite origin.

As early as the day of Enoch, the Lord made this promise: "Righteousness will I send down out of heaven; and truth will I send forth out of the earth, to bear testimony of mine Only Begotten; his resurrection from the dead; yea, and also the resurrection of all men." (Moses 7:62.) The same thought, written by the Psalmist, with reference to the Book of Mormon, came forth as: "Truth shall spring out of the earth; and righteousness shall look down from heaven." (Ps. 85:11.) And on the title page of the book itself, in language coined by Moroni, the announcement is made that it shall come forth "to the convincing of the Jew and Gentile that Jesus is the Christ, the Eternal God, manifesting himself unto all nations."

Our course, then, is clear. It is incumbent upon us to believe the Book of Mormon, to rivet its truths in our souls, to accept them without reservation, to ponder their deep and hidden meanings, and to live in harmony with them. Then, and then only, shall we receive the added words spoken by Jesus to the Nephites, and the added teachings had by the Jaredites.

Messianic Knowledge Revealed in All Nations

Most Christians assume, falsely, that such slivers of Messianic knowledge as they suppose were known of old were reserved for and had by a few patriarchs, a few prophets, and a limited number of the so-called chosen race. But such is not the Lord's manner and way of dealing with the races of men. All men are precious in his sight; and in the providences of the Father of us all, and on his own timetable, salvation is made available to every living soul from the first to the last man. There is a destined day, either in this life or the next, either in mortality or in the world of spirits while awaiting a resurrection, when all men shall have borne to them the witness of the living Lord. "The voice of the Lord is unto all men, and there is none to escape; and there is no eye that shall not see, neither ear that shall not hear, neither heart that shall not be penetrated." (D&C 1:2.) "And he inviteth them all to come unto him and partake of his goodness; and he denieth none that come unto him, black and white, bond and free, male and female, and he remembereth the heathen; and all are alike unto God, both Jew and Gentile." (2 Ne. 26:33.)

Here and now, while in the flesh, the word of revealed truth is destined to go, in one form or another, to far more of our Father's children than some may have supposed. "The voice of warning shall be unto all people," the Lord says, "by the mouths of my disciples, whom I have chosen in these last days." (D&C 1:4.)

Moroni wrote on the title page of the Book of Mormon, "Jesus is the Christ, the Eternal God, manifesting himself unto all nations." That is, Christ manifests himself unto all nations, both unto the Jews and unto the Gentiles. Speaking of the fact that the Jews would reject and crucify the Messiah and would then be scattered by other nations, Nephi says: "And after they have been scattered, and the Lord God hath scourged them by other nations for the space of many generations, yea, even down from generation to generation until they shall be persuaded to believe in Christ, the Son of God, and the atonement, which is infinite for all mankind—and when that day shall come that they shall believe in Christ, and worship the Father in his name, with pure hearts and clean hands, and look not forward any more for another Messiah, then, at that time, the day will come that it must needs be expedient that they should believe these things." (2 Ne. 25:16.) As to the revelation of the knowledge of Christ to the Gentiles, Nephi says: "As I spake concerning the convincing of the Jews, that Jesus is the very Christ, it must needs be that the Gentiles be convinced also that Jesus is the Christ, the Eternal God; And that he manifesteth himself unto all those who believe in him, by the power of the Holy Ghost; yea, unto every nation, kindred, tongue, and people, working mighty miracles, signs, and wonders, among the children of men according to their faith." (2 Ne. 26:12-13.)

By revelation to Nephi, the Lord proclaimed the same truth. "I speak the same words unto one nation like unto another," he said. "For behold, I shall speak unto the Jews and they shall write it; and I shall also speak unto the Nephites and they shall write it; and I shall also speak unto the other tribes of the house of Israel, which I have led away, and they shall write it; and I shall also speak unto all nations of the earth and they shall write it." (2 Ne. 29:8-12.) Certainly the United States of America is a nation to which God hath spoken in our day through Joseph Smith, Jr., his prophet and seer. And certainly, for that matter, that same prophet has spoken to all the nations of the earth, inviting their inhabitants to repent and believe the restored gospel and thus become heirs of salvation in the kingdom of heaven.

As the day of our Lord's mortal birth drew nigh, and as it was requisite that men should repent and gain salvation, Alma was caused by the Spirit to say: "The voice of the Lord, by the mouth of angels, doth declare it unto all nations; yea, doth declare it, that they may have glad tidings of great joy; yea, and he doth sound these glad tidings among all his people, yea, even to them that are scattered abroad upon the face of the earth; wherefore they have come unto us. And they are made known unto us in plain terms, that we may understand, that we cannot err; and this because of our being wanderers in a strange land; therefore, we are thus highly favored, for we have these glad tidings declared unto us in all parts of our vineyard." (Alma 13:22-23.)

The issue is not whether the Lord manifests himself unto all nations, but how and to what extent he does so. It is clear that angels minister to the faithful, that the Holy Ghost is poured out upon all those who believe and obey, and that the visions of eternity are opened to those who abide the laws entitling them so to receive. But there are also some preparatory works done among and for those who are not yet prepared to receive the full message of salvation. Alma, whose desire was to cry repentance in plain language to every soul, came to know that some other things had to precede his pure testimony. "The Lord doth grant unto all nations," Alma said, "of their own nation and tongue, to teach his word, yea, in wisdom, all that he seeth fit that they should have; therefore we see that the Lord doth counsel in wisdom, according to that which is just and true." (Alma 29:8.)

For our day it seems clear that one of the ways in which the Lord sends his word forth in all nations is to make the Bible available to them. Of itself this volume of ancient scripture bears witness of Christ, teaches his doctrines, and leads good people everywhere to live by higher standards. But what is equally, perhaps even more, important in the long run is that the Bible prepares men for the Book of Mormon and therefore for belief in living prophets who have power both to teach the truth and to administer the ordinances of salvation. Truly we are coming nearer and nearer to that day spoken of by the angel to King Benjamin, "when the knowledge of the Savior shall spread throughout every nation, kindred, tongue, and people." (Mosiah 3:20.)

Messianic Prophecies Fulfilled in Christ

From what has already been set forth, from our overall knowledge of the plan of salvation, and from the expressions set forth in the Messianic prophecies themselves, it is self-evident that they all found fulfillment in our Lord's coming. Perhaps these plain statements of the Resurrected Lord to the Nephites will show the seal of divine approval that accompanies Messianic utterances:

"I came unto mine own, and my own received me not. And the scriptures concerning my coming are fulfilled. . . .

By me redemption cometh, and in me is the law of Moses fulfilled." (3 Ne. 9:16-17.)

"They saw a Man descending out of heaven; and he was clothed in a white robe; and he came down and stood in the midst of them; and the eyes of the whole multitude were turned upon him, and they durst not open their mouths, even one to another, and wist not what it meant, for they thought it was an angel that had appeared unto them. And it came to pass that he stretched forth his hand and spake unto the people, saying: Behold, I am Jesus Christ, whom the prophets testified shall come into the world." (3 Ne. 11:8-10.)

"Behold, I have given unto you the commandments; therefore keep my commandments. And this is the law and the prophets, for they truly testified of me." (3 Ne. 15:10.)

"I am he of whom Moses spake. . . . Yea, and all the prophets from Samuel and those that follow after, as many as have spoken, have testified of me." (3 Ne. 20:23-24.)

And so it is that all the prophets testify of Christ; and so it is that all their prophecies were fulfilled in Jesus of Nazareth; and so it is that "by denying him ye also deny the prophets and the law." (2 Ne. 25:28.)

MESSIAH IS GOD

Christ Is the Lord God Omnipotent

Christ-Messiah is God!

Such is the plain and pure pronouncement of all the prophets of all the ages. In our desire to avoid the false and absurd conclusions contained in the creeds of Christendom, we are wont to shy away from this pure and unadorned verity; we go to great lengths to use language that shows there is both a Father and a Son, that they are separate Persons and are not somehow mystically intertwined as an essence or spirit that is everywhere present. Such an approach is perhaps essential in reasoning with the Gentiles of sectarianism; it helps to overthrow the fallacies formulated in their creeds.

But having so done, if we are to envision our Lord's true status and glory, we must come back to the pronouncement of pronouncements, the doctrine of doctrines, the message of messages, which is that Christ is God. And if it were not so, he could not save us. Let all men, both in heaven and on earth, hear the proclamation and rejoice in its eternal verity: "The Lord is God, and beside him there is no Savior." (D&C 76:1.)

Without the need to explain away the vagaries found in the writings of uninspired men, those who knew by personal revelation what the fact is have left us such statements as these:

Both Nephi and Moroni testified: "Jesus is the Christ, the Eternal God." (2 Ne. 26:12; Title Page, Book of Mormon.)

Nephi also said: "There is a God, and he is Christ, and he cometh in the fulness of his own time." (2 Ne. 11:7.) "The Jews," he said, "shall crucify him—for thus it behooveth our God, and there is none other nation on earth that would crucify their God." (2 Ne. 10:3.) For truly, Nephi explains, "The Lord God . . . layeth down his own life that he may draw all men unto him." (2 Ne. 26:23-24.)

The angelic ministrant who taught King Benjamin the doctrine of the atonement called Christ "The Lord Omnipotent who reigneth, who was, and is from all eternity to all eternity" (Mosiah 3:5), and King Benjamin spoke of him as "Christ, the Lord God Omnipotent" (Mosiah 5:15).

Moses taught "concerning the coming of the Messiah, and that God should redeem his people," and Abinadi said that "God himself should come down among the children of men, and take upon him the form of man." (Mosiah 13:33-34.) Yea, "God himself shall come down among the children of men," Abinadi prophesied, "and shall redeem his people" (Mosiah 15:1; 17:8), and Nephi said this deliverance should be made by "the Mighty God" (2 Ne 6:17), which title was also used by Isaiah in prophesying of his birth into mortality (Isa. 9:6).

"God will redeem my soul from the power of the grave," said David. (Ps. 49:15.) "God himself atoneth for the sins of the world" is the inspired word given by Alma. (Alma 42:15.) Nephi the son of Helaman, just a score of years before the birth of Christ, said of the Nephite prophets who preceded him: They "have testified of the coming of Christ, and have looked forward, and have rejoiced in his day which is to come. And behold, he is God." (Hel. 8:22-23.) And when the Risen Lord did minister among the Nephites, he called himself "The Lord their God, who hath redeemed them." (3 Ne. 20:13.)

"Prepare ye the way of the Lord," proclaimed Isaiah. "Say unto the cities of Judah, Behold your God! Behold, the

Lord God will come with strong hand. . . . He shall feed his flock like a shepherd." (Isa. 40:3-11.)

And after his coming the prophets and seers were still acclaiming, "Alleluia: for the Lord God omnipotent reigneth." (Rev. 19:6.)

Truly, Christ is God. Thus it is written, and thus it is.

Christ Is the Lord Jehovah

Christ is Jehovah!

Among those whose source of religious knowledge is the intellect and not the spirit of revelation, it is falsely supposed that the designations *Father, Son*, and *Holy Ghost* are three terms identifying the same incomprehensible spirit essence, which is everywhere and nowhere in particular present, and which they assume is God. This is untrue. The fact is, and Holy Writ so avers, that the three members of the Godhead are separate and distinct Persons; that they have their own bodies, occupy identifiable space, and are in one place only at a given time.

Being thus aware of how far astray the religious intellectualists have gone in defining their three-in-one God, it comes as no surprise to learn that they thrash around in the same darkness in trying to identify Elohim and Jehovah and to show their relationship to the promised Messiah. Some sectarians even believe that Jehovah is the Supreme Deity whose Son came into mortality as the Only Begotten. As with their concept that God is a Spirit, this misinformation about the Gods of Heaven is untrue. The fact is, and it too is attested by Holy Writ, that Elohim is the Father, and that Jehovah is the Son who was born into mortality as the Lord Jesus Christ, the promised Messiah.

As Paul said of those in his day, that "in the wisdom of God the world by wisdom knew not God" (1 Cor. 1:21), so say we of all those in our day who seek God by study and research alone. He is not to be discovered by an archaeologist's pick, a translator's interpretation of an ancient text, nor a theologian's imagination about how he was named and known by them of old. God is and can be known only by revelation; the wisdom of the wise does not make him manifest, and all the conjecture and debate as to how this or that ancient name-title should be translated is as naught compared to one plain inspired utterance. These utterances we have, and because of them we know what was meant by the ancient prophets when they spoke of him under his name Jehovah. The Almighty has such names as he has, and these are known to man only when he reveals them. We shall now, by way of illustration only and without any attempt at comprehensive coverage, note some of the revealed truths showing that Jehovah and Christ are one and the same person, the Eternal Son of the Eternal Father.

Jehovah Sits on the Right Hand of God

Of whom spake David when his tongue was touched by the Holy Spirit and he testified, "The Lord said unto my Lord, Sit thou at my right hand, until I make thine enemies thy footstool"? (Ps. 110:1.) Two Lords are here involved: one is speaking to the other; one is greater than the other; one is making provision for the triumph and glory of the other. Who are they and what message is contained in this Messianic prophecy?

"What think ye of Christ?" our Lord asked certain of his detractors toward the end of his mortal ministry. "Whose son is he?" Is Christ the Son of God or of someone else? Is he to be born of a divine Parent or will he be as other men—a mortal son of a mortal father? That he was to be a descendant of David was a matter of great pride to all the Jews. And so they answered, "The Son of David."

David's son? Truly he was. But he was more, much more. And so our Lord, with irrefutable logic and to their complete discomfiture, asked, "How then doth David in spirit call him Lord, saying, The Lord said unto my Lord, Sit thou on my right hand, till I make thine enemies thy footstool? If David then call him Lord, how is he his son?" That is, if he is only the Son of David, how is it that the great King, acting under inspiration, calls him Lord and worships him as such? And we might add: Who is the other Lord, the one who spake unto David's Lord? Can there be any question as to how Jesus is interpreting the words of the Psalm? He is saying that it means: 'The Father said unto the Son, Elohim said unto Jehovah, sit thou on my right hand, until after your mortal ministry; then I will raise you up to eternal glory and exaltation with me, where you will continue to sit on my right hand forever.' Is it any wonder that the inspired account concludes the matter by saying, "And no man was able to answer him a word, neither durst any man from that day forth ask him any more questions." (Matt. 22:41-46.)

Peter gave precisely this same inspired interpretation of David's declaration. As to the Lord Jehovah being the Son of David, Peter said: "God had sworn with an oath to him, that of the fruit of his loins, according to the flesh, he would raise up Christ to sit on his throne." But as to this same Lord Jesus' status as the Son of God, Peter testified that Jesus had come forth from the tomb and that he had then been exalted "by the right hand of God," even as David had prophesied in the Psalm, which prophecy Peter then quoted, concluding with his own testimony: "Therefore let all the house of Israel know assuredly, that God hath made that same Jesus, whom ye have crucified, both Lord and Christ." (Acts 2:22-36.)

That this same Jesus, "when he had by himself purged our sins," did in fact sit "down on the right hand of the Majesty on high" (Heb. 1:3) is abundantly testified to by many prophets. Paul says he is the one of whom David spoke who should sit on the Lord's right hand. (Heb. 1:13; 8:1; 12:2.) Stephen, "being full of the Holy Ghost, looked up stedfastly into heaven, and saw the glory of God, and Jesus standing on the right hand of God." And then, dying a martyr's death, he passed to his reward with this testimony on his lips: "Behold, I see the heavens opened, and the Son of man standing on the right hand of God." (Acts 7:55-56.)

And that the same witness might be had in our day, Joseph Smith wrote by way of prophecy and revelation: "He was crucified, died, and rose again the third day; And ascended into heaven, to sit down on the right hand of the Father, to reign with almighty power according to the will of the Father." (D&C 20:23-24.)

Jehovah Is the Great I Am

Out of the bush that burned and was not consumed, God spoke unto Moses, identifying himself as "the God of thy father, the God of Abraham, the God of Isaac, and the God of Jacob," and commanded him to deliver Israel from her Egyptian bondage. "When I come unto the children of Israel," Moses said, "and shall say unto them, The God of your fathers hath sent me unto you; and they shall say to me, What is his name? what shall I say unto them?" Then the Eternal One, the Great Jehovah, he who has neither beginning of days nor end of years, replied: I AM THAT I AM. . . . Thus shalt thou say unto the children of Israel, I AM hath sent me unto you." Lest there be any misunderstanding, and to reassure Israel that the Everlasting God, whose course is one eternal round, who is "from everlasting to everlasting" (Ps. 90:2), was in fact the same God who had appeared to Abraham their father, he also said: "Thus shalt thou say unto the children of Israel, The Lord God of your fathers, the God of Abraham, the God of Isaac, and the God of Jacob, hath sent me unto you: this is my name for ever, and this is my memorial unto all generations." (Ex. 3:2-15.)

In his mortal ministry, our Lord announced to the Jews that he was the Great I AM. When they refused to countenance this claim, as we shall set forth more fully under the heading "Jehovah's Birth, Death, and Resurrection Revealed to Abraham," he responded, "Before Abraham was, I am." (John 8:57-58.) That is: 'Before Abraham, was I AM; before Abraham, was I Jehovah; before Abraham, was I the Eternal One, for I am the Everlasting God.' And in our day, to Joseph, his prophet, the same unchanging Being said: "Hearken and listen to the voice of him who is from all eternity to all eternity, the Great I AM, even Jesus Christ." (D&C 39:1.)

Jehovah Appeared to Abraham and the Prophets

When Satan's minions, in the guise of priests of Pharaoh, sought to sacrifice Abraham to their false gods, the Father of the Faithful pleaded with his God for deliverance. "I lifted up my voice unto the Lord my God," Abraham said, "and the Lord hearkened and heard, and he filled me with the vision of the Almighty. . . . And his voice was unto me: Abraham, Abraham, behold, my name is Jehovah, and I have heard thee, and have come down to deliver thee. . . . I will lead thee by my hand, and I will take thee, to put upon thee my name, even the Priesthood of thy father, and my power shall be over thee. As it was with Noah so shall it be with thee; but through thy ministry my name shall be known in the earth forever, for I am thy God." (Abr. 1:15-19.)

Referring back to this and other appearances to the ancient patriarchs, it is written: "And God spake unto Moses, and said unto him, I am the Lord; And I appeared unto Abraham, unto Isaac, and unto Jacob. I am the Lord God Almighty; the Lord JEHOVAH. And was not my name known unto them?" (JST, Ex. 6:2-3.)

Appearances of Jehovah to prophets and righteous men have been many. Three of them deserve special note because they contain descriptive detail of his person, and they tie together the fact that the spirit Jehovah who is Christ, and the resurrected Jehovah who is Christ, are one and the same person.

One account says: "Moses, and Aaron, Nadab, and Abihu, and seventy of the elders of Israel" went up into the mount. "And they saw the God of Israel: and there was under his feet as it were a paved work of a sapphire stone, and as it were the body of heaven in his clearness." (Ex. 24:9-10.)

The next account tells us what happened on Patmos, a bare island in the Aegean Sea, where the Beloved Revelator had been banished "for the word of God, and for the testimony of Jesus Christ." Being "in the Spirit on the Lord's day," John saw "one like unto the Son of man. . . . His head and his hairs were white like wool, as white as snow, and his eyes were as a flame of fire; And his feet like unto fine brass, as if they burned in a furnace; and his voice as the sound of many waters. . . . His countenance was as the sun shineth in his strength." Of this vision John says: "When I saw him, I fell at his feet as dead. And he laid his right hand upon me, saying unto me, Fear not; I am the first and the last: I am he that liveth, and was dead; and, behold, I am alive for evermore." (Rev. 1:9-18.)

And the final account, for us the most glorious of all, was vouchsafed to Joseph Smith and Oliver Cowdery in the Kirtland Temple on April 3, 1836. "The veil was taken from our minds, and the eyes of our understanding were opened," the scriptural record recites. "We saw the Lord standing upon the breastwork of the pulpit, before us; and under his feet was a paved work of pure gold, in color like amber. His eyes were as a flame of fire; the hair of his head was white like the pure snow; his countenance shone above the brightness of the sun; and his voice was as the sound of the rushing of great waters, even the voice of Jehovah, saying: I am the first and the last; I am he who liveth, I am he who was slain; I am your advocate with the Father." (D&C 110:1-4.)

Jehovah Gave His Gospel to Abraham

We speak of the gospel of the Lord Jesus Christ. We teach that it is the great plan of salvation which is made operative through the atoning sacrifice of the Son of God, and that salvation is in Christ.

We might with equal propriety speak of the gospel of the Lord Jehovah. We might appropriately teach, as they did anciently, that this very plan of salvation, this everlasting and unchanging gospel, centers in the atonement of the Son of Elohim, and that salvation is in Jehovah.

Abraham—and for that matter all the prophets and patriarchs from Adam to Moses, plus many thereafter—had the gospel. What gospel? The gospel of the Lord Jehovah who is Christ and in whose name alone salvation comes. "The Lord appeared unto me," Abraham records. "I am the Lord thy God," he said. "I dwell in heaven; the earth is my footstool; I stretch my hand over the sea, and it obeys my voice; I cause the wind and the fire to be my chariot; I say to the mountains—Depart hence—and behold, they are taken away by a whirlwind, in an instant, suddenly. My name is Jehovah, and I know the end from the beginning; therefore my hand shall be over thee."

Then came the promises that the Lord would make of Abraham a great nation, that in him and in his seed all generations would be blessed, and that his seed "shall bear this ministry and Priesthood unto all nations." Included in this Abrahamic covenant was the Lord's promise: "As many as receive this Gospel shall be called after thy name, and shall be accounted thy seed, and shall rise up and bless thee, as their father," and that through his seed "shall all the families of the earth be blessed, even with the blessings of the Gospel, which are the blessings of salvation, even of life eternal." (Abr. 2:6-11.)

Knowing of these promises given of old by the Lord Jehovah to Abraham, Paul, a special witness of the Lord Jesus Christ, said, "They which are of faith, the same are the children of Abraham," and "God . . . preached before the gospel unto Abraham. . . . They which be of faith are blessed with faithful Abraham." Paul's conclusion: "If ye be Christ's, then are ye Abraham's seed, and heirs according to the promise." (Gal. 3:7-29.)

Jehovah Gave His Gospel to Moses

As those who are spiritually literate well know, the plan of salvation, which is the gospel, has been revealed to man in successive ages or dispensations beginning with Adam and going down through Enoch, Noah, Abraham, Moses, and many others. We shall, under the next heading, "Jehovah Led Israel," quote Paul's Spirit-given declaration that it was Christ who went before Israel in a cloud by day and a pillar of fire by night. (1 Cor. 10:1-4.) But let us now, for the record, point to his Bible-located statement in which he taught that the saints of Moses' day had the same plan of salvation offered to them that Christ and the apostles had given to the saints in the meridian of time. "For unto us was the gospel preached, as well as unto them: but the word preached did not profit them, not being mixed with faith in them that heard it." (Heb. 4:2.) Let us also record his explanation that the I AM THAT I AM, the Great Jehovah who appeared to Moses in the burning bush, was named Christ. "Moses," he said, "when he was come of years," chose "rather to suffer affliction with the people of God, than to enjoy the pleasures of sin for a season; Esteeming the reproach of Christ greater riches than the treasures in Egypt: for he had respect unto the recompence of the reward." (Heb. 11:24-26.) Then Paul explains that it was by faith in this same Christ, whom they worshiped as Jehovah, that all of the prophets had that faith which worked miracles, wrought righteousness, raised the dead, and sealed men up unto eternal life. (Heb. 11.)

Jehovah Led Israel

Who delivered Israel from Egyptian bondage by the hand of Moses his servant? Who parted the Red Sea so that the waters congealed, forming a wall of water on the right hand and a wall of water on the left? Who revealed unto them his law amid the thunders and smoking of Sinai? Who gave them manna for forty years as they wandered in a desert wilderness, preparing themselves spiritually to enter their promised land? Who drove out before them the Hittites and the Amorites, the Canaanites and the Perizzites, the Hivites and the Jebusites, so that Israel ate of vineyards they did not plant and drank from wells they had not digged? Who was the Lord their God?

The Old Testament says it was Jehovah. The New Testament and the Book of Mormon reaffirm this, but call him by the name-title of Christ.

In Moses' account it is written: "And the Lord went before them by day in a pillar of a cloud, to lead them the way; and by night in a pillar of fire, to give them light; to go by day and night: He took not away the pillar of the cloud by day, nor the pillar of fire by night, from before the people." (Ex. 13:21-22.) The Psalmist wrote: "He spread a cloud for a covering; and fire to give light in the night." (Ps. 105:39.) That none in the Church should be confused as to what God did these mighty works, Paul wrote: "Brethren, I would not that ye should be ignorant, how that all our fathers were under the cloud, and all passed through the sea; And were all baptized unto Moses in the cloud and in the sea; And did all eat the same spiritual meat; And did all drink the same spiritual drink: for they drank of that spiritual Rock that followed them: and that Rock was Christ." (1 Cor. 10:1-4.) And in the Book of Mormon account, we read these words spoken by the Risen Lord to the Nephites: "I am the God of Israel, and the God of the whole earth, and have been slain for the sins of the world." (3 Ne. 11:14.)

Jehovah to Be Resurrected

Isaiah says plainly that Jehovah shall be resurrected, or rather, Jehovah says it through the mouth of Isaiah. First we read, "He will swallow up death in victory" (Isa. 25:8), and are counseled: "Trust ye in the Lord for ever: for in the Lord JEHOVAH is everlasting strength." Then comes the promise of the greatest triumph ever wrought by his "everlasting strength": "Thy dead men shall live, together with my dead body shall they arise. Awake and sing, ye that dwell in dust: . . . and the earth shall cast out the dead." (Isa. 26:4-21.)

How plainly it is stated! Jehovah comes forth from the tomb. Jehovah breaks the bands of death. Jehovah takes captivity captive. Jehovah is resurrected. And therefore Jehovah was born: "The mighty God" (Isa. 9:6) becomes mortal. And therefore Jehovah died: "he hath poured out his soul unto death," "he was cut off out of the land of the living, . . . he made his grave with the wicked, and with the rich in his death." (Isa. 53:8-12.) All this transpired that he and all men might be resurrected. And who is it other than Christ who hath done all these things?

Jehovah's Birth, Death, and Resurrection Revealed to Abraham

To believe in Abraham is to believe in Christ. No one can claim true kinship to that ancient patriarch without believing what he believed and accepting the testimony he bore. Jesus once said to the unbelieving Jews: "Had ye believed Moses, ye would have believed me: for he wrote of me. But if ye believe not his writings, how shall ye believe my words?" (John 5:46-47.) And so it is with Abraham. Had the Jews believed in their great patriarch—who of old worshiped Jehovah and looked forward to his mortal birth and atoning sacrifice—they would have accepted that same Jehovah when he ministered among them.

"Your father Abraham rejoiced to see my day," Jesus said to them, "and he saw it, and was glad." Refusing to give credence to the claim that Jesus was Jehovah by so much as responding to this bold assertion, our Lord's enemies replied with a complete *non sequitur;* they twisted Jesus' words so as to respond, with a question, to a statement he had not made.

"Thou art not yet fifty years old," they said, "and hast thou seen Abraham?" True it was that Jesus had in fact seen Abraham and in turn been seen by him; and so our Lord responded, "Before Abraham was, I am." That is, 'Before Abraham, was I AM; before Abraham, was I Jehovah.' That the Jews understood perfectly the claim of divinity which thus fell from the lips of the lowly Nazarene is evident from what followed. "Then took they up stones to cast at him," the record says—an almost instinctive reaction on their part to an utterance that they esteemed as blasphemy. (John 8:56-59.)

The specific scriptural account to which Jesus referred in this great proclamation of his own divine Sonship, which account in all probability was had among the Jews, was the ancient Patriarch's discussion with the Lord as to how he and his seed could inherit their promised Palestine. "Lord God, how wilt thou give me this land for an everlasting inheritance?" Abraham asked. "And the Lord said, Though thou wast dead, yet am I not able to give it thee? And if thou shalt die, yet thou shalt possess it, for the day cometh, that the Son of Man shall live; but how can he live if he be not dead? he must first be quickened." Having been so instructed relative to the birth and death and resurrection of the Son of Man, and of his own resurrection and that of his seed, Abraham then saw in vision the very thing our Lord had named. "And it came to pass, that Abram [his name had not yet been changed] looked forth and saw the days of the Son of Man, and was glad, and his soul found rest, and he believed in the Lord; and the Lord counted it unto him for righteousness." (JST, Gen. 15:9-12.)

Jehovah to Judge All Men

After all the testimonies borne by him and his Hebrew brethren, Moroni concludes his Nephite record with this crowning certification: "I soon go to rest in the paradise of God, until my spirit and body shall again reunite, and I am brought forth triumphant through the air, to meet you before the pleasing bar of the great Jehovah, the Eternal Judge of both quick and dead." (Moro. 10:34.)

Among the many testimonies which Jesus bore of himself, we find this forthright proclamation: "The Father judgeth no man, but hath committed all judgment unto the Son: That all men should honour the Son, even as they honour the Father." (John 5:22-23.)

The issue is thus squarely put. Jehovah is the Eternal Judge of all men. None are judged by the Father, for he is Elohim, not Jehovah. Christ only is appointed to sit in judgment on all men. Thus Jehovah is Christ, and Christ is Jehovah; they are one and the same person.

Praise Jehovah, Who Is Christ

One of the most interesting of all the prophetic pronouncements revealing that Jehovah and Christ are one and the same in person and identity is the great liturgical call of praise given to each of them by inspired authors. Let us note with particularity the words used and their meaning both in the original Hebrew and in the tongues into which they have been transliterated.

Yahweh is the name of the God of the Hebrews. The Anglicized or English rendition of this name is *Jehovah.* The shortened form of *Yahweh* is *Yah,* and the contracted form of *Jehovah* (*Jahveh* or *Yahweh*) is *Jah.* Thus David writes: "Sing unto God, sing praises to his name: extol him that rideth upon the heavens by his name JAH, and rejoice before him." (Ps. 68:4.) Most Old Testament passages containing the name *Jah* (for *Jehovah*) have been translated *Lord.*

Halleluyah is the Hebrew term meaning "Praise ye Yah," or as we would say, "praise ye the Lord." The transliterated form of *Halleluyah* is *Hallelujah* (*Hallelu-Jah*). It is thus clear how ancient Israel sang praises to her God who was the Lord Jehovah.

Alleluia is the New Testament rendition of *Hallelujah;* it is derived from the Greek form of *Halleluyah.* In other words, *Alleluia* means "Praise ye Jah," or "praise ye Jehovah," or "praise ye the Lord."

And so when the apostles of New Testament times desired to sing praises to Jehovah who had been born and resurrected, and whom they worshiped as the Lord Jesus Christ, they cried, "Alleluia." And when their fellow servants beyond the veil joined in the chorus of praise to Christ, the words of the eternal choir were: "Alleluia; Salvation, and glory, and honour, and power, unto the Lord our God: For true and righteous are his judgments. . . . Alleluia: for the Lord God omnipotent reigneth. . . . And his name is called The Word of God. . . . And he hath on his vesture and on his thigh a name written, KING OF KINGS, AND LORD OF LORDS." (Rev. 19:1-16.)

And should we not sing praises to his holy name forever? Hath he not redeemed us from death, hell, the devil, and endless torment? Are we not begotten sons and daughters unto God through his atoning sacrifice? Hath he not made us joint-heirs with him of all the glory of his Father's kingdom? Alleluia, for the Lord God Omnipotent reigneth, and through his atoning blood we shall have salvation and glory and honor forever!

Chapter 8

THERE IS ONE GOD

Are There Three Gods or One?

It is written that there is one God—not two Gods, not three Gods, not many Gods. And so it is: There is but one God, beside whom there are no others.

It is also written that there are two Gods, and three Gods, and many Gods—not one God only. And so also is it: We worship two Gods who are personages of tabernacle; there are three Gods in the Godhead; and there are Lords many and Gods many, all of whom are exalted beings having eternal dominion.

To those devoid of spiritual understanding, it is as though the inspired authors had set out, deliberately and with earnest intent, to sow the seeds of darkness and misunderstanding as to the God or Gods who live and abide and are. And again, in a manner of speaking, so it is, for "without controversy great is the mystery of godliness." (1 Tim. 3:16.) At least to the spiritually sick and to the spiritually dead, who seek God through reason and the intellect alone, the scriptures appear to be a compilation of confusion and contradiction. And it was not intended to be otherwise, for salvation is of the Spirit and comes only to those who are spiritually alive and well, those who come to know God, not by reason and the intellect alone, but through the spirit of prophecy and revelation.

God is revealed by preachers who speak by the power of the Holy Ghost, who "speak the wisdom of God in a mystery" (1 Cor. 2:7), who have the same Spirit resting upon them that inspired the prophets of old who wrote of the Lord and his ways. It is, as Paul says, "After that in the wisdom of God the world by wisdom knew not God, it pleased God by the foolishness of preaching to save them that believe." (1 Cor. 1:21.)

"The Lord Our God Is One Lord"

The Father and the Son are personages of tabernacle; they have bodies of flesh and bones and are in fact resurrected, glorified, and holy Men. The Holy Ghost is a personage of spirit, a spirit person, a spirit entity. These three individuals, each of whom is separate from the other, comprise the Godhead; each is God in his own right. They are three Gods as distinct from each other as are the man Peter, the man John, and the man James, who together comprised the First Presidency of the Church in time's meridian.

And yet, let there be no misunderstanding, the revelations teach that there is one God. In one of the most profound proclamations ever to fall from his lips, Moses proclaimed: "Hear, O Israel: The Lord our God is one Lord." (Deut. 6:4.) Paul picked up the same theme and said simply: "God is one" (Gal. 3:20), and "There is none other God but one" (1 Cor. 8:4). Jesus quoted Moses' teaching with approval (Mark 12:29), and Zechariah, speaking of the millennial day, confirmed the same eternal truth in these words: "The Lord shall be king over all the earth: in that day shall there be one Lord, and his name one" (Zech. 14:9). So speaks the Bible on the oneness of God.

The Book of Mormon is even more express and even more expansive. After setting forth the terms and conditions of the plan of salvation, Nephi says: "This is the doctrine of Christ, and the only and true doctrine of the Father, and of the Son, and of the Holy Ghost, which is one God, without end." (2 Ne. 31:21.) Amulek speaks plainly of salvation in the kingdom of heaven, of being raised from death to life through the atonement of Christ, of the wicked retaining a bright recollection of their guilt, and of the eternal judgment that awaits them, when they "shall be brought and be arraigned before the bar of Christ the Son, and God the Father, and the Holy Spirit, which is one Eternal God, to be judged according to their works, whether they be good or whether they be evil." (Alma 11:44.) Mormon records that the righteous shall be found guiltless in that great day and shall "dwell in the presence of God in his kingdom, to sing ceaseless praises with the choirs above, unto the Father, and unto the Son, and unto the Holy Ghost, which are one God, in a state of happiness which hath no end." (Morm. 7:7.)

Truly, there is one God, and one God only!

Men Make Their Own Gods

This one-God concept is preserved in the creeds of Christendom in such a way as to subvert and alter, completely and totally, the truth about those Holy Beings whom it is life eternal to know. These creeds are confessions of faith brought forth in councils of confusion and contention. They preserve the names of each member of the Godhead and attempt to show how these three are one.

These creedal confessions of faith are numerous. For instance, the first Article of Religion of the Church of England, entitled "Of Faith in the Holy Trinity," sets forth this view: "There is but one living and true God, everlasting, without body, parts, or passions; of infinite power, wisdom, and goodness; the Maker, and Preserver of all things both visible and invisible. And in unity of this Godhead there be three Persons, of one substance, power, and eternity; the Father, the Son, and the Holy Ghost." (*Book of Common Prayer.*)

But of all the creeds ever composed, the one named for Athanasius spreads more darkness and preserves more contradictions than any other. The portion of the

Athanasian creed dealing with the Godhead contributes this mass of confusion to what men call Christianity: " 'Whosoever will be saved, before all things it is necessary that he hold the Catholic Faith. Which Faith except everyone do keep whole and undefiled, without doubt he shall perish everlastingly. And the Catholic Faith is this, that we worship one God in Trinity and Trinity in Unity. Neither confounding the Persons, nor dividing the Substance. For there is one Person of the Father, another of the Son, and another of the Holy Ghost. But the Godhead of the Father, of the Son and of the Holy Ghost is all One, the Glory Equal, the Majesty Co-Eternal. Such as the Father is, such is the Son, and such is the Holy Ghost. The Father Uncreate, the Son Uncreate, the Holy Ghost Uncreate. The Father Incomprehensible, the Son Incomprehensible, and the Holy Ghost Incomprehensible. The Father Eternal, the Son Eternal, and the Holy Ghost Eternal and yet they are not Three Eternals but One Eternal. As also there are not Three Uncreated, nor Three Incomprehensibles, but One Uncreated, and One Incomprehensible. So likewise the Father is Almighty, the Son Almighty, and the Holy Ghost Almighty. And yet they are not Three Almighties but One Almighty.

" 'So the Father is God, the Son is God, and the Holy Ghost is God. And yet they are not Three Gods, but One God. So likewise the Father is Lord, the Son Lord, and the Holy Ghost Lord. And yet not Three Lords but One Lord. For, like as we are compelled by the Christian verity to acknowledge every Person by Himself to be God and Lord, so are we forbidden by the Catholic Religion to say, there be Three Gods or Three Lords. The Father is made of none, neither created, nor begotten. The Son is of the Father alone; not made, nor created, but begotten. The Holy Ghost is of the Father, and of the Son; neither made, nor created, nor begotten, but proceeding.

" 'So there is One Father, not Three Fathers; one Son, not Three Sons; One Holy Ghost, not Three Holy Ghosts.

And in this Trinity none is afore or after Other, None is greater or less than Another, but the whole Three Persons are Co-eternal together, and Co-equal. So that in all things, as is aforesaid, the Unity in Trinity, and the Trinity in Unity is to be worshipped. He therefore that will be saved, must thus think of the Trinity.' " (*Catholic Encyclopedia* 2:33-34.)

These creedal certifications, along with all the others devised during the long night of apostate darkness, came from uninspired men who had lost communion with those in the celestial realm who alone have power to reveal the truth about the Godhead. That such would be the case was foreknown and forerevealed by the prophets of old. It was Jeremiah, for one, who told how scattered Israel, in her dispersed state, would "serve other gods" than the Lord, but that in the day of restoration and gathering she would once more come to the knowledge of the Lord Jehovah. Of his gathered house, the Lord would then say: "I will this once cause them to know"—and the new knowledge commenced to come in the spring of 1820 with the appearance of the Father and the Son to Joseph Smith—"I will cause them to know mine hand and my might; and they shall know that my name is The Lord."

Of the false and apostate concepts theretofore had, gathered Israel, as Jeremiah expressed it, would come together from the ends of the earth and say: "Surely our fathers have inherited lies, vanity, and things wherein there is no profit. Shall a man make gods unto himself, and they are no gods?" (Jer. 16:10-21.)

Is it any wonder that the Lord of heaven, as he stood by his Father's side on that glorious day in 1820, speaking of all the churches in all Christendom, told young Joseph "that all their creeds were an abomination in his sight." (JS-H 19.)

How the Father and the Son Are One

To those who are bound to defend the mass of confusion in the creeds of Christendom, the concept that the Father,

Son, and Holy Ghost are one God is totally incomprehensible. They are baffled by their beliefs, confused by their creeds, unconverted by the incomprehensible. Their only recourse is to glory in the mystery of godliness and to suppose there is something wonderful in worshiping a spirit nothingness that is neither here nor there any more than he exists now or then. The total inability to know God becomes the most basic tenet of their religion and closes the door to that progress which leads to exaltation and Godhood.

To those who are free from creedal chains and who can and do turn to the teachings of the prophets and apostles to whom God revealed himself, there is no problem, no confusion, no uncertainty. To them the oneness of the Godhead is neither unknown nor mysterious. They know that God is their Father and that a father is a parent whose offspring bear the image, bodily and spiritually, of the progenitor. They know that Christ is the Son in the literal and full sense of the word, that he is in the express image of his Father's person, and that having come forth in the resurrection, he now has a glorified body of flesh and bones like that of the Father whose Child he is. Their ability to comprehend even God—as in due course they shall!—becomes the most important doctrine of their religion and opens the door to that eternal progress which enables them to become like him.

For reasons that we shall delineate hereafter—in language as plain, as simple, and as persuasive as in our power lies—Jesus taught, repetitiously, both while a mortal man and after being raised in glorious immortality, that he and his Father are one. And implicit in all of his utterances to this effect is found the nature of their oneness, the manner in which, though separate personages, they are one in a way of tremendous import to the children of men.

While a mortal he said to his Jewish brethren: "I and my Father are one," which they understood to mean that he "being a man" was making himself "God." (John 10:30-33.) Speaking of his Twelve Disciples he prayed: "Holy Father, keep through thine own name those whom thou hast given me, that they may be one, as we are." Then because every blessing bestowed upon or offered to those who hold the holy apostleship is also available for and offered to all of the faithful, he also said to his Father: "Neither pray I for these alone, but for them also which shall believe on me through their word; That they all may be one; as thou, Father, art in me, and I in thee, that they also may be one in us: that the world may believe that thou hast sent me." At this point in his great Intercessory Prayer, his petitions again centered on the Twelve, though in principle all that he said does or shall apply to all the saints. "And the glory which thou gavest me I have given them," he said, "that they may be one, even as we are one: I in them, and thou in me, that they may be made perfect in one. . . . And I have declared unto them thy name, and will declare it: that the love wherewith thou hast loved me may be in them, and I in them." (John 17:11-26.)

After the inseparable union of his body and spirit in immortal glory, he said to his Nephite brethren: "I am in the Father, and the Father in me; and in me hath the Father glorified his name." (3 Ne. 9:15.) Also: "Verily I say unto you, that the Father, and the Son, and the Holy Ghost are one; and I am in the Father, and the Father in me, and the Father and I are one. . . . I bear record of the Father and the Father beareth record of me, and the Holy Ghost beareth record of the Father and me; . . . Whoso believeth in me believeth in the Father also; and unto him will the Father bear record of me, for he will visit him with fire and with the Holy Ghost. And thus will the Father bear record of me, and the Holy Ghost will bear record unto him of the Father and me; for the Father, and I, and the Holy Ghost are one." (3 Ne. 11:27-36.)

Later, of the whole body of Nephite believers, in a prayer reminiscent of and greater than his mortal Intercessory Prayer, our Lord said: "And now Father, I pray unto thee for them, and also for all those who shall believe on their words, that they may believe in me, that I may be in them as thou, Father, art in me, that we may be one. . . . Father, I pray not for the world, but for those whom thou hast given me out of the world, because of their faith, that they may be purified in me, that I may be in them as thou, Father, art in me, that we may be one, that I may be glorified in them." (3 Ne. 19:23, 29.)

From these and related teachings found in revealed writ, and all such are declarations which cannot be gainsayed, we learn these truths relative to the Gods we worship:

1. They are three in number, three separate persons: the first is the Father; the second, the Son; and the third, the Holy Ghost. They are three individuals who meet together, counsel in concert, and as occasion requires travel separately through all immensity. They are three holy men, two having bodies of flesh and bones, the third being a personage of spirit.

2. They are one and dwell in each other, meaning: They have the same mind one with another; they think the same thoughts, speak the same words, and perform the same acts—so much so that any thought, word, or act of one is the thought, word, or act of the other.

3. They possess the same character, enjoy the same perfections, and manifest the same attributes, each one possessing all of these in their eternal and godly fulness.

4. Their unity in all things, their perfect oneness in mind, power, and perfections, marks the course and charts the way for faithful mortals, whose chief goal in life is to unite together and become one with them, thereby gaining eternal life for themselves.

5. Our Lord is the manifestation of the Father, meaning: God is in Christ revealing himself to men so that those who believe in the Son believe also in the Father, and unto such the Father gives the Holy Ghost, and they being thus purified in Christ are fit to dwell with him and his Father forever.

That this glorious unity of which these and other revelations speak is attainable for mortals is shown by the righteous works of certain ancient saints, of whom the record says: "The Lord came and dwelt with his people, and they dwelt in righteousness. . . . And the Lord called his people ZION, because they were of one heart and one mind, and dwelt in righteousness." These were they who dwelt in "the City of Holiness, even ZION," which "in process of time, was taken up into heaven," because they had made themselves one with their Lord. (Moses 7:16-21.)

That other faithful saints—being otherwise assigned to labor in the Lord's vineyard, and not being translated as were Enoch's people—have yet attained similar unity with each other and with him whose they are, is attested by Paul's pronouncement relative to certain ones in his day: "We have the mind of Christ." (1 Cor. 2:16.) That is, by obedience and righteousness there were those in his day who, guided by the power of the Holy Spirit, thought and spoke and acted as the Lord would have them do. To the extent that they were so inspired, they were one with their God.

Jehovah Speaks the Words of Elohim

In discussing how and in what sense Christ created man, we have already noted in Chapter 4 that "the Father placed his name upon the Son; and [that] so far as power, authority, and Godship are concerned his words and acts were and are those of the Father." (*The Father and the Son: A Doctrinal Exposition by the First Presidency and the Twelve,* cited in James E. Talmage, *Articles of Faith,* pp. 465-73.) As we now set forth the basic thesis that the Father and the Son are one, we come to the most extensive, perhaps the greatest illustration of how this unity of thought and word operates.

Our illustrations will show, not alone how the Father and the Son operate as one, but why uninspired scriptural exegetes have so much difficulty in seeking to learn spiritual truths by the power of the intellect alone. When Jesus (the Son) quotes Jehovah (the Son), in teaching the Nephites, he attributes the pronouncements so made to Elohim (the Father). Why? Because the words so revealed by Jehovah to the prophets of old are and were those of both the Father and the Son.

We shall hereafter set forth in some detail the fact that Jehovah-Christ is the God of Israel. For our present purposes we shall note only that when he, as a resurrected person, invited the Nephites to feel the prints of the nails in his hands and in his feet, he did it so that they may know that he was the God of Israel, and the God of the whole earth, and had been "slain for the sins of the world." (3 Ne. 11:14.) As Israel's God, it is clear that he and not the Father spoke to all the ancient prophets—to Moses, Isaiah, Malachi, to all who were called as guides and lights to the Lord's ancient peoples. He it was who gave the Law of Moses, and in him it was fulfilled. (3 Ne. 15:1-10.) In fact, the whole Old Testament is most explicit that the Deity in whose name the ancient prophets spoke was Jehovah, not Elohim. Of this there is no question.

But in the Book of Mormon, in one sentence he says he is the One who covenanted with the house of Israel and in another he attributes the ancient hand dealings of Deity to the Father. When the resurrected Lord quoted what he himself as the spirit Jehovah had told Micah, Isaiah, and Malachi, he attributed the words to the Father. (3 Ne. 20-22, 24-25; Isa. 52, 54; Mal. 3-4; Micah 4.) His quotations, standing alone and taken out of context, leave the impression that it was Elohim and not Jehovah who spoke to the ancient prophets when in fact it was Jehovah relaying the word of Elohim, for the Father and the Son, as one, both speak the same words.

Peter did precisely the same thing in principle. He applied one of Christ's chief titles to the Father: "The God of Abraham, and of Isaac, and of Jacob, the God of our fathers," who is in fact the Lord Jehovah, "hath glorified his Son Jesus," Peter says, thus applying the name of the Son to the Father. (Acts 3:13.)

How truly they are one! The name of the one is the name of the other. The words of the one are the words of the other.

The thoughts, acts, purposes, and perfections of the one are identical to those of the other.

He that hath seen one hath seen the other. He that hath heard the voice of one hath heard the voice of the other. He that hath felt the spirit of one has felt the spirit of the other. He that hath lived the laws of the one has lived the laws of the other.

"I and my Father are one." (John 10:30.)

Christ Dwelleth in His Saints

As we have seen, Paul taught that faithful saints "have the mind of Christ." (1 Cor. 2:16.) That is: They think what he thinks; they say what he says; they do what he does; and their souls are attuned to his—all because they live the way he lives and have acquired the same attributes and perfections that he possesses.

As we have also seen, our Lord prayed that he might be in his saints in the same sense that the Father was in him, so that Christ and his people would ever be one. (3 Ne. 19:23.) And this brings us to one of the most glorious of all gospel doctrines—that Jesus Christ dwelleth in his saints.

This wondrous concept is one about which the apostles of old had much to say. "I am crucified with Christ" (Gal. 2:20), Paul said, meaning that he had "crucified" the "old man, . . . the body of sin," that henceforth he "should not serve sin" (Rom. 6:6). As a result—that is, because he had forsaken the world to "walk in newness of life" (Rom. 6:4), and had "put on Christ" (Gal. 3:27)—he was able to say: "Christ liveth in me: and the life which I now live in the flesh I live by the faith of the Son of God" (Gal. 2:20).

As taught by the inspired men of old, this doctrine is that the true saints turn from all evil and cleave unto all good "until Christ be formed" in them. (Gal. 4:19.) They are then able to say: We shall triumph over all the trials of mortality because we go forth, "Always bearing about in the body the dying of the Lord Jesus, that the life also of Jesus might be made manifest in our body." Their pledge then is: We shall so live "that the life also of Jesus might be made manifest in our mortal flesh." (2 Cor. 4:10-11.)

Paul said to his Ephesian brethren: I pray to the Father that you shall "be strengthened with might by his Spirit in the inner man; That Christ may dwell in your hearts by faith," until through knowledge, obedience, and righteousness "ye might be filled with all the fulness of God." (Eph. 3:14-19.)

"The fulness of God"! What is it? It is to be one with the Father. Jesus spoke of gaining "all power . . . in heaven and in earth." (Matt. 28:18.) Such is the reward for all those who "pass by the angels, and the gods, . . . to their exaltation and glory in all things, . . . which glory shall be a fulness. . . . Then shall they be gods." (D&C 132:19-20.)

This doctrine that man crucifies his old, sinful self so that Christ can dwell in him, and that man as a consequence has power, through faith, to inherit all things, is truly a mystery to spiritually untutored souls. And Paul so designates it. If the saints "continue in the faith grounded and settled, and be not moved from the hope of the gospel," he says, they shall through this doctrine become "holy and unblameable and unreproveable" in the Lord's sight. They shall then understand this great mystery, "even the mystery which hath been hid from ages and from generations, but now is made manifest to his saints; To whom God would make known what is the riches of the glory of this mystery among the Gentiles; which is Christ in you, the hope of glory." (Col. 1:21-27.)

What is the mystery? It is that Christ dwells in the hearts of those who have crucified the old man of sin, and that as a consequence they have a hope of eternal glory! Such is what the Lord requires of his children in working out their "own salvation with fear and trembling" before him. (Phil. 2:12.) And it is in this connection that Paul says, somewhat caustically, "But if our gospel be hid, it is hid to them that are lost." (2 Cor. 4:3.)

Hidden from the world, but revealed in the hearts of those who are enlightened by the Spirit, this doctrine becomes the measuring rod by which the saints determine whether they are faithful and true. "Examine yourselves, whether ye be in the faith; prove your own selves," Paul directs. His standard for such self-judgment is: "Know ye not your own selves, how that Jesus Christ is in you, except ye be reprobates?" (2 Cor. 13:5.)

How to Cause Christ to Dwell in Us

Now let us set forth the New Testament formula whereby the Lord's saints can measure whether and to what extent Christ dwells in them. It is:

1. *Know the true God.*

It is life eternal to know the Father and the Son. It is the first principle of revealed religion to know the nature and kind of being that God is. There is no real progress in spiritual things until we know who God is and what his character, perfections, and attributes are. "We know that the Son of God is come, and hath given us an understanding," John says. Why? His answer: "That we may know him that is true." There is no substitute for a true knowledge of God, which truth having been taught, the beloved apostle drives home this point: "And we are in him that is true, even in his Son Jesus Christ." Then speaking of the Father and the Son as the one God that they are, he concludes: "This is the true God, and eternal life." (1 Jn. 5:20.) Thus those who know the Father and the Son, and are thereby inheritors of eternal life, so obtain because they are in God and he is in them and they twain are one.

2. *Believe in Christ.*

Believe in him in the literal and true sense of the word, not in some figurative and mystical way; believe that God was his Father, "after the manner of the flesh" (1 Ne. 11:18), as the angelic ministrant affirmed to Nephi; believe that the Father-Son relationship is as real and personal as that which exists between parent and child among us mortals—all of which presupposes that his Father is an immortal Man of Holiness. Believe that because of this holy relationship the Offspring had power to work out the infinite and eternal atonement.

"We have seen and do testify that the Father sent the Son to be the Saviour of the world," John certifies. Of all who have this same knowledge, he then proclaims: "Whosoever shall confess that Jesus is the Son of God, God dwelleth in him, and he in God." (1 John 4:14-15.)

3. *Keep the commandments; live righteously.*

Obedience is the first law of heaven. All progression, all perfection, all salvation, all godliness, all that is right and just and true, all good things come to those who live the laws of Him who is Eternal. There is nothing in all eternity more important than to keep the commandments of God.

Christ himself set the example. "I and my Father are one" because I keep the commandments and do "the works of my Father," and thereby you "may know, and believe, that the Father is in me, and I in him," was his teaching. (John 10:30-38.)

"Believest thou not that I am in the Father, and the Father in me?" he asked. To explain how this was and why it came to pass, he continued, "The words that I speak unto you I speak not of myself: but the Father that dwelleth in me, he doeth the works. Believe me that I am in the Father, and the Father in me." (John 14:10-11.)

If Christ was in the Father because he did the works of the Father (and the Father was thereby in him), it follows that if we do the works of Christ, we will be in him (and he in turn will dwell in us). And so it is, for the scripture saith: "He that keepeth his commandments dwelleth in him, and he in him." (1 Jn. 3:24.) And further: "He that saith he abideth in him ought himself also so to walk, even as he walked." Why? Because "whoso keepeth his word, in him is the love of God perfected: [and] hereby know we that we are in him." (1 Jn. 2:5-6.)

4. *Obtain the gift of the Holy Ghost.*

It is well known among the saints that our bodies are "the temple of the Holy Ghost," which is in us, "which we have of God." (1 Cor. 6:19.) Of us the scripture asks: "Know ye not that ye are the temple of God, and that the Spirit of God dwelleth in you?" (1 Cor. 3:16.)

When we are confirmed members of the only true and living church, we receive the gift of the Holy Ghost. This gives us the right to the constant companionship of that member of the Godhead based on faithfulness. The world cannot receive this priceless gift. It is to the faithful saints only that the promise is made: "He dwelleth with you, and shall be in you." (John 14:17.)

What did Paul mean when he said of the saints: "Ye are not in the flesh, but in the Spirit, if so be that the Spirit of God dwell in you. Now if any man have not the Spirit of Christ, he is none of his. And if Christ be in you, the body is dead because of sin; but the Spirit is life because of righteousness. But if the Spirit of him that raised up Jesus from the dead dwell in you, he that raised up Christ from the dead shall also quicken your mortal bodies by his Spirit that dwelleth in you." (Rom. 8:9-11.)

And what did John mean when he said, "And hereby we know that he abideth in us, by the Spirit which he hath given us"? (1 Jn. 3:24.) And also: "Hereby know we that we dwell in him, and he in us, because he hath given us of his Spirit"? (1 Jn. 4:13.)

Truly, Christ dwells in those who enjoy the gift of the Holy Ghost, and they in turn are in their Lord!

5. *Partake worthily of the sacrament.*

In his church we partake often of the sacrament, to renew our baptismal covenant, to assert anew that we will "always remember him and keep his commandments," and to plead that we "may have his Spirit" to be with us. (D&C 20:77.) When this is done in righteousness, by those who are just and true, the Spirit of the Lord comes to dwell in their hearts; and as we have seen, Christ himself thereby dwells in them and they in him. Thus we find our Lord teaching: "He that eateth my flesh, and drinketh my blood, dwelleth in me, and I in him." (John 6:56.)

6. *Acquire the attributes of godliness.*

The Father and the Son possess, in their fulness and perfection, all godly graces and all ennobling attributes. They have all charity, all love, and all mercy; they are the possessors of the fulness of judgment, the fulness of justice, and the fulness of truth; and so it is through every good thing. They are thus one, for if the Father has all charity and the Son likewise, they are thus alike where that attribute is concerned, and so it is with them where all uplifting and edifying attributes are concerned. And to the extent that we acquire charity or love or any godly attribute, we also dwell in God and he in us.

"God is love," John writes, "and he that dwelleth in love dwelleth in God, and God in him." (1 Jn. 4:16.) Also: "If we love one another, God dwelleth in us, and his love is perfected in us." (1 Jn. 4:12.) Similarly, God is charity (meaning he is the personification and embodiment of this attribute), and he that dwelleth in charity (that is, possesses it) dwelleth in God, and he in him; and if we have charity one for another, then God dwelleth in us, and his charity is perfected in us. The same reasoning applies to all of the attributes of his nature.

7. *Reward of those who dwell in God and he in them.*

Of Christ our Prototype it is written: "In him dwelleth all the fulness of the Godhead bodily." (Col. 2:9.) In other words, in Christ is found every godly attribute in its perfection, which means that the Father dwells in him and he in the Father. It follows that when men so attain, they become like God, or, as Joseph Smith expressed it:

"Those who keep his commandments shall grow up from grace to grace, and become heirs of the heavenly kingdom, and joint-heirs with Jesus Christ; possessing the same mind, being transformed into the same image or likeness, even the express image of him who fills all in all; being filled with the fulness of his glory, and become one in him, even as the Father, Son and Holy Spirit are one." (*Lectures on Faith,* cited in *Mormon Doctrine,* 2nd ed., pp. 320-21.)

What Is Salvation?

As a necessary prelude to a full comprehension of why the Lord and his prophets put such repeated and strong emphasis on the one-God concept, we must know what is meant by salvation in the true and ultimate sense of the word.

We are ofttimes prone to create artificial distinctions, to say that salvation means one thing and exaltation another, to suppose that salvation means to be resurrected, but that exaltation or eternal life is something in addition thereto. It is true that there are some passages of scripture that use salvation in a special and limited sense in order to give an overall perspective of the plan of salvation that we would not otherwise have. (2 Ne. 9:1-27; D&C 76:40-49; 132:15-17.) These passages show the difference between general or universal salvation that consists of coming forth from the grave in immortality, and specific or individual salvation that consists of an inheritance in the celestial kingdom. All men will be resurrected and all men (except the sons of perdition) will thus be saved from death, hell, the devil, and endless torment. But only those who keep the commandments will "be raised [both] in immortality [and] unto eternal life." (D&C 29:43.)

Since it is the prophetic purpose to lead men to full salvation in the highest heaven of the celestial world, when they speak and write about salvation, almost without exception, they mean eternal life or exaltation. They use the terms *salvation, exaltation,* and *eternal life* as synonyms, as words that mean exactly the same thing without any difference, distinction, or variance whatever. Thus Amulek says that "no unclean thing can inherit the kingdom of heaven," and then asks: "How can ye be saved, except ye inherit the kingdom of heaven?" He teaches that men "cannot be saved" in their sins; that Christ will come to "take upon him the transgression of those who believe on his name"; and that "these are they that shall have eternal life, and salvation cometh to none else." Having thus spoken of the salvation which the saints seek, he also says: "The wicked remain as though there had been no redemption made, except it be the loosing of the bands of death," meaning they shall come forth in immortality. (Alma 11:37-41.) Thus all men—except the sons of perdition who are cast out into an eternal hell—are saved, in that they become immortal and go to a telestial or terrestrial inheritance, but only those who believe and obey become inheritors of that celestial rest which the whole body of revealed writ speaks of as salvation.

Eternal life is the name of the kind of life which God lives and is therefore "the greatest of all the gifts of God" (D&C 14:7); and because those who gain it become like God, they are one with him.

Exaltation consists of an inheritance in the highest heaven of the celestial world, where alone the family unit continues and where each recipient gains for himself an eternal family unit, patterned after the family of God our Heavenly Father, so that every exalted person lives the kind of life which God lives and is therefore one with him.

Salvation consists in gaining—and this is Joseph Smith's language—"the glory, authority, majesty, power and dominion which Jehovah possesses and in nothing else; and no being can possess it but himself or one like him" (*Lectures on Faith,* cited in *Mormon Doctrine,* 2nd ed., p. 258), and since he is one with his Father, so also are all saved beings. Truly, "There is no gift greater than the gift of salvation." (D&C 6:13.)

Thus, to be saved, to gain exaltation, to inherit eternal life, all mean to be one with God, to live as he lives, to think as he thinks, to act as he acts, to possess the same glory, the same power, the same might and dominion that he possesses.

Thus also, the Father is the great Prototype of all saved beings, and he and his Son, who also has become a saved being, are the ones into whose "likeness" Joseph Smith said we should be "assimilated." (*Lectures on Faith,* cited in *Mormon Doctrine,* 2nd ed., p. 258.) And thus, all those who overcome by faith, who become joint-heirs with Christ, who become one in him, as he is one in the Father, become themselves saved beings.

Why the Gods Proclaim Themselves as One

Now let us turn to the immeasurably great and important reason why three Gods proclaim themselves to be One God. We find it in this concept:

The greatest teaching device ever devised by Deity, whether in heaven or on earth, whether in time or in eternity, is embraced within the simple statement: "Hear, O Israel: The Lord our God is one Lord," followed as it then is by the divine decree: "And thou shalt love the Lord thy God with all thine heart, and with all thy soul, and with all thy might." (Deut. 6:4-5.)

Why is this so, and wherein is this such a transcendent teaching device? Rightly understood, these seven words—"The Lord our God is one Lord"—point the way and mark the course to eternal life in our Father's kingdom. Every true believer, every person who worships the Father in spirit and in truth, knows because of this one-God concept that if he himself is to be saved, he must be one with his fellow saints and with the Gods of heaven, as they are one with each other.

Would it be amiss now to reason together on this matter, to reason together as to why men must know the nature and kind of being God is, if they are ever to become like him and go where he is?

Since salvation comes by worshiping the true God; since to be saved is to be one with Christ as he is one with the Father; since salvation and eternal life consist of living the kind of life that Deity lives—and the fact that man can be as God is, is the greatest concept that can enter the heart of man—it follows that any teaching, any doctrine, any dramatization that can keep the mind of man riveted on his goal and what he must do to gain it, any such device is the greatest of all teaching devices.

And so it is that now and always—past, present, and future—for all those who have accepted the Lord as their God, the rallying cry, the slogan of slogans, the divine statement which crystallizes in the minds of men what they must do to be saved is the great Mosaic proclamation: "The Lord our God is one Lord." (Deut. 6:4.)

The Lord speaks with one voice. He is the creator of one plan of salvation. There is only one way to become like him. That way is to come to a knowledge of him and to obey the laws which lead men to a like status of glory and exaltation. No one can pursue such a course until he knows of its existence. No one will ever make the sacrifice necessary to gain eternal life until he believes in his heart that the reward is worth the price. There can never be any true and saving worship without a knowledge of the nature and kind of being God is. Immortality is a free gift; eternal life is reserved for those who believe and obey, who keep the commandments, who are faithful and true in all things, who become one with their Lord.

Satan speaks with many voices and sponsors many plans of salvation. He says: There is no God; atheism and pure reason—these are all that count. Or: God is a spirit—an essence, force, or power—that fills immensity and is everywhere and nowhere in particular present. Or: He is the laws of nature, some great First Cause, some impersonal power in the universe—as all scientists and thinking men must agree! Or: He is made of wood or stone, is carved by man's device, and sits as Diana in her Parthenon atop her Athenian acropolis. Or: The Godhead is the Father, Son, and Holy Ghost, but this Holy Trinity compose one spirit nothingness that is really not three Gods but one God, which means they are not really one God but three Gods—incomprehensible, unknowable, incorporeal, and uncreated. Or: Whatever the mind of man can imagine or the machinations of devils devise, it matters not. As long as men believe in false Gods they are damned. What else need Lucifer do than to spawn and sponsor systems of false worship? There is no salvation in anything except truth—pure, diamond truth, the truth about God and his laws.

"As God Now Is, Man May Be"

No doctrine is more basic, no doctrine embraces a greater incentive to personal righteousness, and no doctrine so completely embraces the whole realm of revealed religion as does the wondrous concept that man can be as his Maker. It was revealed first to Adam, to whom—after his baptism, after he had received the holy priesthood, after he had walked in paths of righteousness—the Lord said: "Thou art one in me, a son of God; and thus may all become my sons." (Moses 6:68.) Thereafter, in all ages, whenever the Lord has had a people on earth, the same hope and the same promise have been renewed.

After this doctrine had been revealed to Enoch, in a declaration of wonder and exultation, he exclaimed to the Lord: "Thou hast made me, and given unto me a right to thy throne." (Moses 7:59.) In ancient Israel the repeated proclamation of their God was: "Ye shall be holy: for I the Lord your God am holy." (Lev. 19:2.) The Risen Lord, being holy and desiring that all his spirit brethren attain a like state of holiness and oneness with him, uttered these words: "To him that overcometh will I grant to sit with me in my throne, even as I also overcame, and am set down with my Father in his throne." (Rev. 3:21.) And to certain faithful disciples among the Nephites who had so qualified he said: "Ye shall sit down in the kingdom of my Father; yea, your joy shall be full, even as the Father hath given me fulness of joy; and ye shall be even as I am, and I am even as the Father; and the Father and I are one." (3 Ne. 28:10.)

"Let this mind be in you," writes our theological friend Paul, "which was also in Christ Jesus: Who, being in the form of God, thought it not robbery to be equal with God" (Phil. 2:5-6), thus showing how Christ, our Prototype, has attained oneness with his Father. Paul's associate apostle John takes the next step and applies the same principle to all who by faith become the sons of God. "Now are we the sons of God," he wrote, meaning that here and now while in mortality we have been adopted into the family of Deity and have become joint-heirs with his natural Son. "And it doth not yet appear what we shall be," he continues, meaning that no mortal man can conceive of the glory and dominion which shall be heaped upon those who reign on thrones in the exalted realms. "But we know that, when he shall appear [the Second Coming of our Lord], we shall be like him; for we shall see him as he is." As a natural conclusion to such a doctrine, John draws this obvious conclusion: "And every man that hath this hope in him purifieth himself, even as he is pure." (1 John 3:2-3.)

Pondering these words of the two ancient apostles, Paul and John, President Lorenzo Snow, a modern apostle—who also is the author of the couplet: "As man now is, God once was; As God now is, man may be"—addressed these poetically phrased truths to Paul:

Dear Brother:

Hast thou not been unwisely bold,
Man's destiny to thus unfold?
To raise, promote such high desire,
Such vast ambition thus inspire?

Still, 'tis no phantom that we trace
Man's ultimatum in life's race;

This royal path has long been trod
By righteous men, each now a God:

As Abra'm, Isaac, Jacob, too,
First babes, then men—to gods they grew.
As man now is, our God once was;
As now God is, so man may be,—
Which doth unfold man's destiny.

For John declares: When Christ we see
Like unto him we'll truly be.
And he who has this hope within,
Will purify himself from sin.

Who keep this object grand in view,
To folly, sin, will bid adieu,
Nor wallow in the mire anew;

Nor ever seek to carve his name
High on the shaft of worldly fame;
But here his ultimatum trace:
The head of all his spirit-race.

Ah, well: that taught by you, dear Paul,
'Though much amazed, we see it all;
Our Father God, has ope'd our eyes,
We cannot view it otherwise.

The boy, like to his father grown,
Has but attained unto his own;
To grow to sire from state of son,
Is not 'gainst Nature's course to run.

A son of God, like God to be,
Would not be robbing Deity;
And he who has this hope within,
Will purify himself from sin.

You're right, St. John, supremely right:
Whoe'er essays to climb this height,
Will cleanse himself of sin entire—
Or else 'twere needless to aspire.
—Cited in *Commentary* 2:532-33

In the light of all that in our revelations is written, is it any wonder that the same God who has offered salvation to his brethren in all dispensations should say, "*Be one; and if ye are not one ye are not mine.*" (D&C 38:27. Italics added.)

MESSIAH IS THE SON OF GOD

Son of God Chosen in Preexistence

As set forth in Chapter 4, the Father ordained and established the plan of salvation to enable his spirit children (Christ included) to advance and progress and become like him. According to the terms and conditions of this plan, the Father chose one of his spirit sons to be born among mortal men as the Son of God. This Chosen One was destined to inherit from his Father the power of immortality so that—in a way incomprehensible to us, but known to God—he could work out the infinite and eternal atonement. As a result of this atoning sacrifice all mortal men were destined to be raised in immortality while those who believed and obeyed the fulness of gospel law would also inherit eternal life.

The Firstborn of the Father, who was the Spirit-Jehovah, was the One, beloved and chosen of the Father, to be born among men as his Son. Salvation was to be made available to all men in and through the atonement of this promised Messiah, this Son of God who would be born in the meridian of time. To return to the presence of the Father, men would be required to believe in their Deliverer, to accept him as their Savior, and to live in harmony with the laws ordained by him and his Father.

It follows that whenever the Lord has had a people on earth, whenever the saving truths of his plan of salvation have been revealed to men, whenever there has been a dispensation of the gospel, the faithful saints have known that their Messiah and Deliverer would be the Son of God.

Son of God Revealed to Adam

As part of the first unfoldment of the plan of salvation to mortal man, Father Adam was told that redemption from the fall came through "the Only Begotten of the Father" and was available to him "and all mankind, even as many as will." An angel from the Eternal Presence relayed to him this command of Deity: "Thou shalt do all that thou doest in the name of the Son, and thou shalt repent and call upon God in the name of the Son forevermore." (Moses 5:8.) In that early day, "the Lord God called upon men by the Holy Ghost everywhere and commanded them that they should repent; And as many as believed in the Son, and repented of their sins, should be saved; and as many as believed not and repented not, should be damned." (Moses 5:14-15.) Thus, from the beginning, the great and eternal decree was: "Believe on his Only Begotten Son, even him whom he declared should come in the meridian of time, who was prepared from before the foundation of the world." As a result of this proclamation, the record says: "Thus the Gospel began to be preached, from the beginning." (Moses 5:57-58.)

This gospel, as revealed to Adam, was, "If thou wilt turn unto me, and hearken unto my voice, and believe, and repent of all thy transgressions, and be baptized, even in water, in the name of mine Only Begotten Son, who is full of grace and truth, which is Jesus Christ, the only name which shall be given under heaven, whereby salvation shall come unto the children of men, ye shall receive the gift of the Holy Ghost, asking all things in his name, and whatsoever ye shall ask, it shall be given you." (Moses 6:52.)

This gospel was, "That the Son of God hath atoned for original guilt." This gospel was "the plan of salvation unto all men." This gospel was "the record of the Father, and the

Son, from henceforth and forever." (Moses 6:54, 62, 66.)

Thus, beginning with Adam, "the first man of all men" (Moses 1:34), and with Eve, "the mother of all living" (Moses 4:26), and continuing to the day of the Lord's birth on earth, every man, woman, and child having prophetic insight knew that the Messiah would be the Son of God.

Christ Is the Son of Man

Our Lord assumed the prerogative, during his mortal ministry, of identifying himself as the Son of Man. For instance, to justify himself and his disciples in violating the restrictive Jewish rules relative to Sabbath observance he said, "The Son of man is Lord also of the Sabbath." (Mark 2:23-28.) And to Peter and the other apostles he put the incisive question, "Whom do men say that I the Son of man am?" and received the Spirit-revealed answer: "Thou art the Christ, the Son of the living God." (Matt. 16:13-17.) There are in fact some seventy New Testament passages in which he identifies himself as the Son of Man and speaks of such things as having power on earth to forgive sins; of his betrayal, crucifixion, death, and resurrection; of confessing fellowship with the righteous before his Father; and of returning in great power and glory, attended by the angelic hosts.

Why this designation? Did he have in mind the sectarian notion that he was the offspring of a mortal woman and that therefore he was born of man? Obviously the title could be so applied if we simply looked at the words used and had no spirit of scriptural interpretation and understanding. But the fact is that this exalted name-title has a deep and glorious connotation and is in many respects one of the most meaningful and self-identifying appellations applying to the divine Son. Its greatest significance lies in the fact that it identifies and reveals who the Father is.

In the early dispensations, the Father revealed many of his names. "Behold, I am God; Man of Holiness is my name; Man of Counsel is my name; and Endless and Eternal is my name, also," he said to Enoch. (Moses 7:35.) As we shall see shortly, another of his names is "Righteousness," or, perhaps better, "Man of Righteousness." In other words, to signify that he is the personification and embodiment of those godly attributes which men must obtain if they are to be one with him, he takes these attributes as his names. Thus we read that it was said to the first man: "In the language of Adam, Man of Holiness is his name, and the name of his Only Begotten is the Son of Man, even Jesus Christ, a righteous Judge, who shall come in the meridian of time." (Moses 6:57.)

That is, the Father is a Holy Man. Man of Holiness is his name, and the name of his Only Begotten is the Son of Man of Holiness, or in its abbreviated form, the Son of Man.

Joseph Smith received a revelation in which the question was put, "What is the name of God in the pure language," and the answer came, "Ahman." A second question was, "What is the name of the Son of God," and the answer came, "Son Ahman." (*Mormon Doctrine,* 2nd ed., p. 29.) In two of the revelations in the Doctrine and Covenants the Lord calls himself "Son Ahman." (D&C 78:20; 95:17.) As nearly as we can tell, Man of Holiness is the English rendition of Ahman, and Son of Man of Holiness, of Son Ahman.

Enoch received extensive visions in which the Only Begotten Son—then still a spirit being in the presence of God—was identified as the Son of Man. This ancient seer "was high and lifted up, even in the bosom of the Father, and of the Son of Man." One of the questions he asked was, "When the Son of Man cometh in the flesh, shall the earth rest?" By way of answer, "he looked and beheld the Son of Man lifted up on the cross, after the manner of men; And he heard a loud voice; and the heavens were veiled; and all the creations of God mourned; and the earth groaned; and the rocks were rent; and the saints arose, and were crowned at the right hand of the Son of Man, with crowns of glory." Enoch also "beheld the Son of Man ascend up unto the

Father" after his meridian ministry and learned that he would come again. "And it came to pass that Enoch saw the day of the coming of the Son of Man, in the last days, to dwell on the earth in righteousness for the space of a thousand years." (Moses 7:24, 54-56, 59, 65.)

Abraham saw in vision the Great Council in which the Son of Man volunteered to be born as the Son of God and work out the infinite and eternal atonement. (Abr. 3:23.) He also "saw the days of the Son of Man, and was glad, and his soul found rest, and he believed in the Lord; and the Lord counted it unto him for righteousness." He saw further that the Son of Man should die and be resurrected. (JST, Gen. 15:9-12.) It was of this vision of our Lord's mortal ministry that Jesus spoke when he said, "Abraham rejoiced to see my day: and he saw it, and was glad," and when he made the great proclamation, "Before Abraham was, I am." (John 8:56-58.)

While dying as a martyr, Stephen saw "the heavens opened, and the Son of man standing on the right hand of God." (Acts 7:56.) There are numerous revelations in the Doctrine and Covenants, mainly those dealing with his Second Coming, in which the Lord identifies himself in this same exalted way.

In the same sense that the Father's name is Man of Holiness and the Son's name is the Son of Man, so the Father's name is Righteousness and the Son's is the Son of Righteousness.

Our King James Version of the Bible records a prophecy of Malachi about the Second Coming of the Son of Man that specifies that "all the proud, yea, and all that do wickedly, shall be stubble" in that day. "But unto you that fear my name," the prophetic utterance continues, "shall the Sun of righteousness arise with healing in his wings." (Mal. 4:1-2.) That this is a prophecy relative to the Second Coming is clear from the context, and it was confirmed by Moroni as such when he appeared to Joseph Smith. (JS-H 36-39.) So that the account would be had among the Nephites, the resurrected Jesus quoted it to them in A.D. 34, but what he said was that "the Son of Righteousness" shall "arise with healing in his wings." (3 Ne. 25:2.) The book of Ether tells us that Emer, a righteous ruler among the Jaredites, "saw the Son of Righteousness, and did rejoice and glory in his day." (Ether 9:21-22.) Nephi the son of Lehi used the same thoughts expressed by Malachi, but applied them to the first coming of the Messiah. Speaking of the righteous Nephite people at the time of our Lord's resurrected ministry among them, he said: "But the Son of Righteousness shall appear unto them; and he shall heal them, and they shall have peace with him, until three generations shall have passed away, and many of the fourth generation shall have passed away in righteousness." (2 Ne. 26:9.)

Old Testament Prophets Speak of the Son of God

Statements by the seers of Old Testament times, which have been preserved for us, that God should have a Son are few and far between. There are a great many prophetic utterances that speak of his birth, ministry, death, and resurrection—in all of which it is implicit in the very nature of things that God was to be his Father—but there are only a few places where he is spoken of as a Son in so many words. This, however, is not overly strange. There is also very little in the Old Testament about baptism for the remission of sins or the laying on of hands for the receipt of the Holy Ghost. And yet these ordinances began with Adam and were performed ever thereafter among the faithful. Providentially, a knowledge of them and of our Lord's divine Sonship have been restored in that portion of the Old Testament now published in the Pearl of Great Price. It is apparent that these plain and precious truths are among those deleted from Holy Writ by evil and conspiring men, along the line indicated by Nephi. (1 Ne. 13.) But perhaps also that Old Testament had among the ancient Jews contained as much of the truth in as great plainness as that rebellious and spiritually benighted people were entitled to possess. The Lord gives only that portion of his word to any people which they are prepared spiritually to receive. (Alma 12:9-11.)

But we do have some utterances which, though not all that might be desired, are somewhat helpful. In the midst of a passage that is clearly Messianic, the Lord says of the Seed of David: "I will be his father, and he shall be my son." (2 Sam. 7:14.) In the second Psalm, the whole of which is also clearly Messianic, occurs this statement: "Thou art my Son; this day have I begotten thee." (Ps. 2:7.) Paul quotes both of these statements in Hebrews 1:5 and says they are prophecies that Christ would come as the Son of God. This second Psalm contains the instruction, "Kiss [or better, receive instruction from] the Son. . . . Blessed are all they that put their trust in him" (Ps. 2:12), which manifestly is a Messianic message.

Paul also quotes from Psalm 45, which again is Messianic in its entirety, these words: "Thy throne, O God, is for ever and ever: the sceptre of thy kingdom is a right sceptre. Thou lovest righteousness, and hatest wickedness: therefore God, thy God, hath anointed thee with the oil of gladness above thy fellows." (Ps. 45:6-7.) He says in Hebrews 1:8 that they were said "unto the Son," meaning that when words speak of one God who himself has a God, they are speaking of a Son who has a Father. A prophecy about the coming of the Son that is not found in our version of the Old Testament reads: "And let all the angels of God worship him." This Paul says finds fulfillment in the bringing of "the firstbegotten into the world." (Heb. 1:6.) The only Old Testament reference in which the plain words "the Son of God" are used is in the case of Shadrach, Meshach, and Abednego being cast into the fiery furnace. What Nebuchadnezzar sees is not three, but "four men loose, walking in the midst of the fire, and they have no hurt; and the form of the fourth is like the Son of God." (Dan. 3:25.)

Actually the Book of Mormon tells us more about the usage of the name *the Son of God* by Old Testament prophets than does that volume of Holy Writ itself. Nephi the son of Helaman, as he sought diligently to prepare his people for the coming of their Messiah, told them that both Moses and Abraham bore record "that the Son of God should come"; that "many before the days of Abraham" so certified; that "all the holy prophets" from Abraham to Moses did likewise; and that "since the days of Abraham there have been many prophets that have testified of these things," including Zenos, Zenock, Ezias, Isaiah, and Jeremiah, all of whom labored among Old Testament peoples. The same witness, he said, had been born by "almost all of our fathers" among the Nephites. (Hel. 8:13-23.)

Alma, with the brass plates of Laban as his source, quoted these words from a prayer of Zenos: "And thou didst hear me. And again, O God, when I did turn to my house thou didst hear me in my prayer. And when I did turn unto my closet, O Lord, and prayed unto thee, thou didst hear me. Yea, thou art merciful unto thy children when they cry unto thee, to be heard of thee and not of men, and thou wilt hear them. Yea, O God, thou hast been merciful unto me, and heard my cries in the midst of thy congregations. Yea, and thou hast also heard me when I have been cast out and have been despised by mine enemies; yea, thou didst hear my cries, and wast angry with mine enemies, and thou didst visit them in thine anger with speedy destruction. And thou didst hear me because of mine afflictions and my sincerity; and it is because of thy Son that thou hast been thus merciful unto me, therefore I will cry unto thee in all mine afflictions, for in thee is my joy; for thou hast turned thy judgments away from me, because of thy Son." Also: "Thou hast turned away thy judgments because of thy Son." And these expressions of Zenock: "Thou art angry, O Lord, with this people, because they will not understand thy mercies which thou hast bestowed upon them because of thy Son." (Alma 33:3-16.)

Fragmentary as our records are, it is nonetheless clear

that all of the prophets of Old Testament times knew and taught that the promised Messiah would be the Son of God.

The Book of Mormon Testifies of the Son of God

It is the will and purpose of the Lord to reveal to his children on earth as much about Christ and salvation as they are prepared to receive. Some, like the brother of Jared, gain a perfect knowledge of these things (Ether 3:6-26); others are taught in dark similitudes only, as was often the case with Israel from the time of Moses to our Lord's coming; and yet others, including portions at least of the Nephite nation, were taught the truth in relative perfection and fulness.

Nephi says that the limitations placed upon the Jews, whence he and his father came, were because "their works were works of darkness, and their doings were doings of abominations," but that his purpose was to prophesy in "plainness" unto his people. (2 Ne. 25:1-10.) Subsequent Book of Mormon prophets followed Nephi's pattern so that we now have in that volume of divine truth a great treasure house of light and knowledge about Him who came as God's Son to redeem his people. If ever there was a compilation of inspired writings that stand as a witness of the divine Sonship of the Lord Jesus Christ, that work is the Book of Mormon!

Of it, and the great restoration of eternal truth of which it is a part, the inspired Psalmist wrote: "I will hear what God the Lord will speak: for he will speak peace unto his people, and to his saints: but let them not turn again to folly. Surely his salvation is nigh them that fear him; that glory may dwell in our land. Mercy and truth are met together; righteousness and peace have kissed each other. Truth shall spring out of the earth; and righteousness shall look down from heaven." (Ps. 85:8-11.)

Of it, as he revealed his latter-day purposes to Enoch, that Lord who comprehended the end from the beginning said: "Righteousness will I send down out of heaven; and truth will I sent forth out of the earth, to bear testimony of mine Only Begotten; his resurrection from the dead; yea, and also the resurrection of all men." (Moses 7:62.)

Through it, as Isaiah so prophetically foresaw, "the eyes of the blind shall see out of obscurity, and out of darkness. The meek also shall increase their joy in the Lord, and the poor among men shall rejoice in the Holy One of Israel"; "They also that erred in spirit shall come to understanding, and they that murmured shall learn doctrine." (Isa. 29.)

Because it came forth, as the seeric insight of Ezekiel has so plainly set forth, latter-day Israel would be gathered, her people would become clean before the Lord, he would make with them again his everlasting gospel covenant, and his tabernacle and temple would be in their midst forevermore. (Ezek. 37:15-28.)

And to it we now turn to take samples only of that pure prophecy, of that plain and perfect utterance, which reveals the commission of the Holy Messiah to come to earth as the Son of God. Since the whole purpose of the Book of Mormon, a companion volume to the Bible, written as it was "by the spirit of prophecy and of revelation," is to convince "the Jew and Gentile that Jesus is the Christ, the Eternal God" (title page), it comes as no surprise to find the record abounding in such plain statements as these:

"The great question," Amulek taught, "is whether the word be in the Son of God, or whether there shall be no Christ." His testimony was: "The word is in Christ unto salvation." (Alma 34:5-6.)

In presenting the message of salvation to nonmembers of the Church, Aaron asked: "Believest thou that the Son of God shall come to redeem mankind from their sins?" He then testified: "There could be no redemption for mankind save it were through the death and sufferings of Christ, and the atonement of his blood." (Alma 21:7, 9.)

And the testimony of all the prophets of this branch of the house of Israel was: "The gate of heaven is open unto all, even to those who will believe on the name of Jesus Christ, who is the Son of God." (Hel. 3:28.)

Nephi, on whose shoulders so much of the future of his people rested, spoke of the faith of his father, Lehi, in the Son of God, and then said: "The Son of God was the Messiah who should come." (1 Ne. 10:17.) Nephi also identified this Savior as "the Son of the most high God" (1 Ne. 11:6), "the Son of the Eternal Father" (1 Ne. 11:21), and "the Son of the everlasting God" (1 Ne. 11:32). "The Messiah," Nephi said, "shall be Jesus Christ, the Son of God" (2 Ne. 25:19), and he is "the Holy One of Israel" (2 Ne. 30:2). The 31st chapter of Second Nephi contains several plain statements about the Father and the Son, as does also the 15th chapter of Mosiah.

The angel who taught the doctrine of the atonement to King Benjamin called our Lord "Jesus Christ, the Son of God, the Father of heaven and earth." (Mosiah 3:8.) Alma said: "Jesus Christ shall come, yea, the Son, the Only Begotten of the Father, full of grace, and mercy, and truth." Also: "The Son of God cometh in his glory, in his might, majesty, power, and dominion." (Alma 5:48, 50.) And so, in plainness, using language that cannot be misunderstood, one after another of the Nephite prophets testified of Him through whom salvation comes. Similar passages, all interwoven into the same general theme, are quoted by the score in other parts of this heaven-sent work.

Our Lord's Disciples Testify of Him

We have seen how the prophets who were before him bore record of the coming birth and ministry of their Messiah as the Son of God. For four thousand years all those with prophetic insight looked forward to his redemptive sacrifice and the salvation resulting therefrom. But those four millenniums of prophecy were but the beginning of what is to be. After he came, the same witness of his divine Sonship fell from the lips of his mortal disciples, and it continues now on the tongues of all who are like-minded with the ancients and who are endowed with the same power from on high which they possessed. A prophet is a prophet whether he lived before Christ came, during his mortal ministry, or since his ascension to sit on the right hand of the Majesty on high—and all prophets everlastingly are witnesses of their Lord.

Among those who saw him while he dwelt as a mortal on earth and to whom the Spirit bore record that he was the Lord's Christ we note the following:

Mary, his mother. She it was to whom Gabriel came with the message, "Thou shalt conceive in thy womb, and bring forth a son, and shalt call his name JESUS. He shall be great, and shall be called the Son of the Highest." (Luke 1:31-32.) She it was to whom the angel said: "The Holy Ghost shall come upon thee, and the power of the Highest shall overshadow thee: therefore also that holy thing which shall be born of thee shall be called the Son of God." (Luke 1:35.) She it was who "was carried away in the Spirit" and became "the mother of the Son of God, after the manner of the flesh." (1 Ne. 11:18-19.) Mary knew that the fruit of her womb was the Eternal One.

Joseph, the carpenter. It was to this quiet, self-effacing man that the angelic ministrant said: "Fear not to take unto thee Mary thy wife: for that which is conceived in her is of the Holy Ghost. And she shall bring forth a son, and thou shalt call his name JESUS: for he shall save his people from their sins." (Matt. 1:20-21.) It was to him that an angel of the Lord came, declaring: "Arise, and take the young child and his mother, and flee into Egypt, and be thou there until I bring thee word: for Herod will seek the young child to destroy him." (Matt. 2:13.) It was to him that Mary confided what great things had been done to her. Joseph knew who Jesus was.

Elisabeth, the mother of John. Dwelling in an unnamed city of Judah, her womb housing the unborn Baptist, she it was to whom Mary fled for consolation and comfort after

Gabriel gave forth his grave pronouncement. And she, Elisabeth, seeing Mary, "was filled with the Holy Ghost," and it was revealed to her that Mary was to be the "mother of my Lord." (Luke 1:36-45.)

John the Baptist. This is he who stands alone among all earth's inhabitants of whom we have knowledge. He was "filled with the Holy Ghost from his mother's womb." (D&C 84:27.) While still encased therein, Elisabeth his mother being in "the sixth month" of her pregnancy, the unborn John was filled with the Holy Ghost and "leaped in her womb," as he received the witness that the mother of his Lord was present. (Luke 1:36-45.) This is he who baptized Jesus, saw the heavens open and the Holy Ghost descend in calm serenity, and heard the voice of the Father say, "This is my beloved Son, in whom I am well pleased." (Matt. 3:13-17; Luke 3:21-22.) This is he whose enduring witness for all ages is: "Behold the Lamb of God, which taketh away the sin of the world." (John 1:29.)

Peter, the chief apostle. Speaking for all of the Twelve, he gave this witness: "Thou art the Christ, the Son of the living God." (Matt. 16:16.) And: "We believe and are sure that thou art that Christ, the Son of the living God." (John 6:69.)

Martha of Bethany. "I believe that thou art the Christ, the Son of God, which should come into the world." (John 11:27.)

John the apostle. "Jesus is the Christ, the Son of God." (John 20:31.)

Andrew, Simon Peter's brother. "We have found the Messias, which is, being interpreted, the Christ." (John 1:41.)

Philip of Bethsaida. "We have found him, of whom Moses in the law, and the prophets, did write, Jesus of Nazareth." (John 1:45.)

Nathaneal. "Rabbi, thou art the Son of God; thou art the King of Israel." (John 1:49.)

Simeon, a just and devout man. "It was revealed unto him by the Holy Ghost" that Jesus was "the Lord's Christ." (Luke 2:25-35.)

Anna, a prophetess. As with Simeon, she too knew of our Lord's divinity by the power of the Spirit, "and spake of him to all them that looked for redemption in Jerusalem." (Luke 2:36-38.)

Unnamed and Unnumbered Others. The ancient scriptures do not pretend to record all the testimonies of all the witnesses who knew by revelation from on high that Jesus was the Lord, any more than our modern scriptures attempt to name and record the witness of all who believe and know in our day. Did not Mary of Bethany believe with the same fervor found in the heart of her sister Martha? Were not Peter's words simply a sample of what all the apostles felt and knew in their souls? Surely Lazarus, whose spirit had spent four days in paradise and who was called back to mortal life by the voice of Him to whom all things are subject, surely he knew Jesus was Lord of all. And what of the man blind from birth who came seeing at Jesus' word; and the shepherds who saw the angelic ministrant and heard the heavenly choir; and the wise men who came from the east; and the many who believed because Lazarus arose and because of the other miracles; and what of all those who were converted by the Master's teachings and by the ministry of the apostles and seventies; and so we might go on and on. Truly, the testimony of Jesus was had by and borne among his fellow mortals. The record is not silent in letting it be known that faithful men, women, and children knew and testified that he was God's Holy Son.

Disciples Testify of the Resurrected Lord

Testimonies borne by inspired mortals gained a new dimension after our Lord rose from the dead. Now his witnesses could point to the fact of his resurrection as the conclusive proof that God was his Father. That our Lord appeared as a resurrected being many times to hosts of people is well known to the saints. Pages 839 to 876 of volume one of my *Doctrinal New Testament Commentary* contain a discussion of his various appearances in the Old World. Chapters 11 through 30 of Third Nephi in the Book of Mormon tell of his resurrected ministry among the Nephites, so that thousands of that noble race would become living witnesses of his status as the Savior and Redeemer of men. For our purposes here, let us but sample the post-resurrection witness borne by saints who knew whereof they spoke.

After Jesus rose from the dead, Peter and the congregation (probably composed of male and female believers) who saw him in the upper room were able to say: 'We felt the nail marks in his hands and in his feet; we thrust our hands into his wounded side; we felt the flesh and bones of which his body is composed; he ate before us; we heard his voice; we recognized him as the same Jesus with whom we walked and talked and lived for three and a half years; and we know he is the Son of God.' (See Luke 24.)

After he rose from the dead, Thomas knelt before him and exclaimed in worshipful awe: "My Lord and my God." (John 20:28.)

After he rose from the dead, he appeared to Paul on the Damascus road, and that newly found witness, being converted, straightway "preached Christ in the synagogues, that he is the Son of God." (Acts 9:20.)

After he rose from the dead, he stood before his beloved John, then banished on Patmos, placed his right hand upon that holy apostle, and said: "Fear not; I am the first and the last: I am he that liveth, and was dead; and, behold, I am alive for evermore, Amen; and have the keys of hell and of death." (Rev. 1:17-18.)

After he rose from the dead, he was introduced by his Father to the Nephites in these words: "Behold my Beloved Son, in whom I am well pleased, in whom I have glorified my name—hear ye him." (3 Ne. 11:7.) He thereupon ministered personally among that remnant of the house of Israel, set up his kingdom as he had done in Jerusalem, called Twelve to whom he gave apostolic keys and power, and prepared the way for other chosen vessels to bear record of his holy name. Such of their witness as we now have is in the Book of Mormon, of which record one of them, Mormon, says: It was written that men "may be persuaded that Jesus is the Christ, the Son of the living God." (Morm. 5:14.) This same Mormon, writing to his brethren the Lamanites, bore this testimony: "Know ye that ye must come to the knowledge of your fathers, and repent of all your sins and iniquities, and believe in Jesus Christ, that he is the Son of God, and that he was slain by the Jews, and by the power of the Father he hath risen again, whereby he hath gained the victory over the grave." (Morm. 7:5.)

But as pertaining to us, and to all who live in our day, the crowning and most important testimony of the risen Lord is that given by those called and sent so to testify at this time. Of these Joseph Smith is the chief. "I saw two Personages," he says of the great theophany which ushered in this dispensation, "whose brightness and glory defy all description, standing above me in the air. One of them spake unto me, calling me by name and said, pointing to the other—*This is My Beloved Son. Hear Him!*" (JS-H 17.) Later, he and Oliver Cowdery gave us this testimony: "We saw the Lord," whom they then described, and he said unto them: "I am the first and the last; I am he who liveth, I am he who was slain; I am your advocate with the Father." (D&C 110:1-4.) And it was Joseph Smith and Sidney Rigdon who left us this fervent witness: "And now, after the many testimonies which have been given of him, this is the testimony, last of all, which we give of him: That he lives! For we saw him, even on the right hand of God; and we heard the voice bearing record that he is the Only Begotten of the Father." (D&C 76:22-23.)

Who can doubt that believing disciples have seen Him whose Father is God and whose atoning sacrifice has given efficacy, virtue, and force to the Father's plans and purposes?

Our Lord Bears Testimony of Himself

If the Man Jesus, a Jewish Rabbi, who was born of Mary in Bethlehem of Judea, who grew to manhood in Nazareth of Galilee, who ministered among men for three and a half years in Palestine, and who was crucified outside Jerusalem's wall at a place called Golgotha; if this Man was the Son of God, if he came to fulfill all that was spoken from the beginning by all the holy prophets, we would expect him to know it and to say so. And that is precisely what happened. He knew God was his Father, and he so testified again and again and again, day in and day out, early and late, to every receptive person who would give heed to his voice. The four Gospels contain one continuous proclamation of his divine Sonship, with our Lord himself doing nearly all of the teaching. His personal testimony is everywhere to be found. For our purposes, although some of his testimonies fall into more categories than one, let us note six ways and means used by him to teach his divine Sonship:

1. *Pure testimony: that is, plain, categorical statements that he was the Messiah, the Son of God.*

The first of these, in point of time and of which we have record, is his famous reply to Mary and Joseph when he was but twelve years of age: "Wist ye not that I must be about my Father's business?" It is clear that he, even then, considered his teaching in the temple as the work of Him whose Son he was. (Luke 2:42-52.) How much more teaching and how many more testimonies he bore between then and the commencement of his formal ministry when he was about thirty years of age we can only guess.

During his formal ministry he found opportunity to say: "I and my Father are one," which his hearers considered blasphemy, at which point in their colloquy he said plainly, "I am the Son of God." (John 10:30-36.)

At Jacob's well, the Samaritan woman said, "I know that

Messias cometh, which is called Christ: when he is come, he will tell us all things." With that simplicity and plainness by which the greatest of all truths are conveyed, Jesus replied: "I that speak unto thee am he." (John 4:25-26.)

Because the Jews persecuted him for healing a man on the Sabbath, he said, "My Father worketh hitherto, and I work. Therefore the Jews sought the more to kill him, because he not only had broken the sabbath, but said also that God was his Father, making himself equal with God." Thereupon Jesus made an elaborate statement amplifying and explaining his relationship with his Father, including an announcement of these eternal verities about the Son: He worked by the power of the Father; he would bring to pass the resurrection; he was to be honored along with the Father; he would judge all men; he would preach to the spirits in prison and open the graves of earth's departed ones; he had life in himself, even as did the Father—all this and much, much more, ending with this stinging rebuke: "Do not think that I will accuse you to the Father: there is one that accuseth you, even Moses, in whom ye trust. For had ye believed Moses, ye would have believed me: for he wrote of me. But if ye believe not his writings, how shall ye believe my words?" (John 5:1-47.)

When Jesus made no response to the false witnesses who testified against him during the nighttime trial before Caiaphas, the high priest, that conspiring functionary said: "I adjure thee by the living God, that thou tell us whether thou be the Christ, the Son of God. Jesus saith unto him, Thou hast said: nevertheless I say unto you, Hereafter shall ye see the Son of man sitting on the right hand of power, and coming in the clouds of heaven." (Matt. 26:63-64.) Mark's account of this same blasphemously spoken query and its divinely inspired answer is: "Art thou the Christ, the Son of the Blessed? And Jesus said, I am: and ye shall see the Son of man sitting on the right hand of power, and coming in the clouds of heaven." (Mark 14:61-62.)

Then, when it was morning and he came formally before the Sanhedrin, he was asked: "Art thou the Christ? tell us. And he said unto them, If I tell you, ye will not believe: And if I also ask you, ye will not answer me, nor let me go. Hereafter shall the Son of man sit on the right hand of the power of God. Then said they all, Art thou then the Son of God? And he said unto them, Ye say that I am." (Luke 22:67-70.) The statement "Ye say that I am" is an idiomatic expression meaning 'You asked the question, and the answer is Yes,' and it was so understood by all who heard it.

Later, before Pilate, the Roman governor asked: "Art thou the King of the Jews? Jesus answered him, Sayest thou this thing of thyself, or did others tell it thee of me? Pilate answered, Am I a Jew? Thine own nation and the chief priests have delivered thee unto me: what hast thou done? Jesus answered, My kingdom is not of this world: if my kingdom were of this world, then would my servants fight, that I should not be delivered to the Jews: but now is my kingdom not from hence. Pilate therefore said unto him, Art thou a king then? Jesus answered, Thou sayest that I am a king. To this end was I born, and for this cause came I into the world, that I should bear witness unto the truth." (John 18:33-37.) And truly the greatest truths of which he bore record were that God was his Father and that he was the promised Son.

2. *Figurative statements understood by all who were acquainted with Jewish theology to mean that he was the Christ.*

These were numerous and for all practical purposes were as clearly understood by his hearers as any of his claims to divinity. To the extent we have learned the Jewish system of similitudes and imagery they are also envisioned by us. For instance:

Jesus said, "I am the good shepherd" (John 10:14), which was tantamount to saying, 'I am the Lord Jehovah,' because his Jewish hearers revered the Davidic declaration: "Jehovah is my shepherd; I shall not want," and so on through the 23rd Psalm. Our anglicized reading is "The Lord is my shepherd," but in the Hebrew the title *Lord* is the name *Jehovah.*

Speaking in a parable, Jesus said, "I am the door of the sheep. . . . I am the door: by me if any man enter in, he shall be saved, and shall go in and out, and find pasture." (John 10:7-9.) That is, 'I am the Messianic Deliverer who is to come. I am he of whom Isaiah wrote: "He shall feed his flock like a shepherd: he shall gather the lambs with his arm, and carry them in his bosom, and shall gently lead those that are with young." ' (Isa. 40:11.)

Jesus said: "I am the bread of life. . . . I am living bread which came down from heaven." (John 6:35, 51.) Their fathers had lived for forty years on manna, doing so, in the language of Moses, to certify that "man doth not live by bread only, but by every word that proceedeth out of the mouth of the Lord doth man live." (Deut. 8:3.) To those with this background and understanding, our Lord's declaration that he was the living bread meant that he was the Lord in whose memory their fathers had eaten manna in the wilderness and that he had now come down from heaven to give them that living bread.

Other of our Lord's statements—such as, "I am the way, the truth, and the life: no man cometh unto the Father, but by me" (John 14:6); "I am the light of the world" (John 8:12); "I am the true vine, and my Father is the husbandman" (John 15:1)—all had similar meanings and bore record that salvation was in him and that therefore he was the Messiah. His declaration "Before Abraham was, I am" (John 8:58) meant to his hearers: 'Before Abraham was I, the Great I AM,' or 'Before Abraham was I, Jehovah.' And his practice of quoting known and recognized Messianic prophecies and then saying, "This day is this scripture fulfilled in your ears" (Luke 4:16-21), had no effect except to identify the speaker as the One of whom the ancient prophet spoke.

3. *Doctrinal teachings which, spoken by Jesus and*

weighed in context, presuppose that the Speaker is more than a mortal.

These are interwoven in nearly all his preachments and are illustrated by the following:

"Not every one that saith unto me, Lord, Lord, shall enter into the kingdom of heaven; but he that doeth the will of my Father which is in heaven. Many will say to me in that day, Lord, Lord, have we not prophesied in thy name? and in thy name have cast out devils? and in thy name done many wonderful works? And then will I profess unto them, I never knew you: depart from me, ye that work iniquity." (Matt. 7:21-23.)

"All things are delivered unto me of my Father: and no man knoweth the Son, but the Father; neither knoweth any man the Father, save the Son, and he to whomsoever the Son will reveal him. Come unto me, all ye that labour and are heavy laden, and I will give you rest." (Matt. 11:27-28.)

"I will give unto thee the keys of the kingdom of heaven: and whatsoever thou shalt bind on earth shall be bound in heaven: and whatsoever thou shalt loose on earth shall be loosed in heaven." (Matt. 16:19.)

"He that heareth my word, and believeth on him that sent me, hath everlasting life, and shall not come into condemnation; but is passed from death unto life. Verily, verily, I say unto you, The hour is coming, and now is, when the dead shall hear the voice of the Son of God: and they that hear shall live. For as the Father hath life in himself; so hath he given to the Son to have life in himself." (John 5:24-26.)

"He that believeth on me hath everlasting life. . . . Whoso eateth my flesh, and drinketh my blood, hath eternal life; and I will raise him up at the last day." (John 6:47, 54.)

"If ye believe not that I am he, ye shall die in your sins." (John 8:24.)

"He that hath seen me hath seen the Father." (John 14:9.)

"All things that the Father hath are mine." (John 16:15.)

"And this is life eternal, that they might know thee the

only true God, and Jesus Christ, whom thou hast sent. I have glorified thee on the earth: I have finished the work which thou gavest me to do. And now, O Father, glorify thou me with thine own self with the glory which I had with thee before the world was." (John 17:3-5.)

Implicit in these and hundreds of other passages is the simple truth that he is the Son of God. Truly, never man spake as this man spake.

4. *Our Lord's repeated Son of Man pronouncements.*

These are so numerous, so persuasive, and yet so little understood in their status as testimony of his divine Sonship that, although they might be classified merely as testimony by him about himself, they deserve special consideration. Whenever he used the designation Son of Man, it was as though he said Son of God, for the Man to whom he referred was Man of Holiness, his Father.

"The Son of man came not to be ministered unto, but to minister," he said, "and to give his life a ransom for many." (Matt. 20:28.) In the day when that ransoming sacrifice is made, "The Son of man shall be betrayed into the hands of men: And they shall kill him, and the third day he shall be raised again." (Matt. 17:22-23.) "Ye know that after two days is the feast of the passover, and the Son of man is betrayed to be crucified." (Matt. 26:2.) "When ye have lifted up the Son of man, then shall ye know that I am he, and that I do nothing of myself; but as my Father hath taught me, I speak these things. And he that sent me is with me: the Father hath not left me alone; for I do always those things that please him." (John 8:28-29.) "Whosoever therefore shall be ashamed of me and of my words in his adulterous and sinful generation; of him also shall the Son of man be ashamed, when he cometh in the glory of his Father with the holy angels." (Mark 8:38.)

5. *The works he performed bear record of his divinity.*

It is not in word only that true testimony is borne. False ministers and the devils themselves can claim to represent the true Master and to present the true gospel. Satan himself came personally to Moses and commanded: "I am the Only Begotten, worship me." (Moses 1:19.) Good works must always accompany the testimony of true ministers. When true words are spoken by the power of the Spirit, all who hear are obligated to believe that which is said and to make it a part of their lives. Jesus' spoken testimony, standing alone, is binding. But it is also proper to view his works along with his words.

When his Jewish detractors doubted his testimony, the Man Jesus said: "The works which the Father hath given me to finish, the same works that I do, bear witness of me, that the Father hath sent me." (John 5:36.) Also: "If I do not the works of my Father, believe me not. But if I do, though ye believe not me, believe the works: that ye may know, and believe, that the Father is in me, and I in him." (John 10:37-38.)

It was this test of eternal verity that he used when two men came and said: "John Baptist hath sent us unto thee, saying, Art thou he that should come? or look we for another?" The scripture records no immediate answer to this interrogatory. Instead it says: "And in that same hour he cured many of their infirmities and plagues, and of evil spirits; and unto many that were blind he gave sight." After the miracles were wrought, "Then Jesus answering said unto them, Go your way, and tell John what things ye have seen and heard; how that the blind see, the lame walk, the lepers are cleansed, the deaf hear, the dead are raised, to the poor the gospel is preached. And blessed is he, whosoever shall not be offended in me." (Luke 7:20-23.)

6. *His works, coupled with the spoken word, combine to bear witness that he is God's Son.*

Such are the most irrefutable of all testimonies. The spoken word is there. Those who hear it are aware of the issue involved. A miracle, which cannot be denied or gainsaid, is performed. None but God or one approved by him could do the miracle. Sinners do not raise the dead. Blind eyes are not opened by impostors. "There was not any man who could do a miracle in the name of Jesus save he were cleansed every whit from his iniquity." (3 Ne. 8:1.) And so when Jesus both performed miracles and said he was the Son of God, who could deny the fact? Three illustrations will suffice for our purpose:

First, he forgave sins (which none but God can do), and then to prove he had the power so to act, he healed the same person from his palsy. "Son, be of good cheer; thy sins be forgiven thee," he said. (Matt. 9:2.) Those who heard this reasoned: "Why doth this man thus speak blasphemies? who can forgive sins but God only?" (Mark 2:7.) Thereupon Jesus said: "Wherefore think ye evil in your hearts? For whether is easier, to say, Thy sins be forgiven thee; or to say, Arise, and walk? But that ye may know that the Son of man hath power on earth to forgive sins, (then saith he to the sick of the palsy,) Arise, take up thy bed, and go unto thine house. And he arose, and departed to his house." (Matt. 9:4-7.)

Second, he sought out and opened the eyes of a man born blind. He let the word of the miracle spread throughout the city. There was a division among the people, some saying he was a sinner, others that he was of God. To the one whose eyes had been opened, Jesus said: "Dost thou believe on the Son of God? He answered and said, Who is he, Lord, that I might believe on him? And Jesus said unto him, Thou hast both seen him, and it is he that talketh with thee. And he said, Lord, I believe. And he worshipped him." (John 9:35-38.) Then to the multitude who had assembled because the fact of the miracle had been noised about, he preached his great sermon on the good shepherd, announcing himself as the Lord Jehovah and as the Son of God. "There was a division therefore again among the Jews for these sayings. And many of them said, He hath a devil, and is mad; why hear ye him? Other said, These are not the words of him that hath a devil. Can a devil open the eyes of the blind?" (John 10:1-41.) Thus, the issue was clearly put. He said he was the Son of God and he did what no one could do without God's approval. Truly his testimony is irrefutable.

Third, he received word of Lazarus' death, deliberately waited four days before arriving at the tomb, heard the importuning pleas of Martha, told her, "Thy brother shall rise again," and then said, "I am the resurrection, and the life: he that believeth in me, though he were dead, yet shall he live: And whosoever liveth and believeth in me shall never die." (John 11:25-26.) That is: 'Immortality and eternal life come by me. As thou hast said, I am the Son of God, and if ye believe in me, ye shall have eternal life.' She replied: "I believe that thou art the Christ, the Son of God, which should come into the world." (John 11:27.) Then it was that the Lord of Life called, "Lazarus, come forth," and he who had been dead four days, whose body stank, whose flesh and bones had started to decay and to return to mother earth, then it was that the dead and decomposing body came forth to live again. If he who does such things says he is the Son of God, surely it is so.

Was the Man Jesus the Promised Son of God?

Who can doubt that the Great Jehovah was chosen before the world was to be the Son of God? Who will question that he was revealed to Adam? That all of the prophets of all the ages—inspired men on both continents—foretold his birth and ministry? That he was to be the promised Messiah, the Great Deliverer, our Savior and Redeemer? So it is written, and so it is!

And similarly may we inquire: Was the Man Jesus the promised Son of God? Was he who dwelt on earth in time's meridian the One prepared from all eternity to work out the infinite and eternal atonement? He testified that he was, and the Jews understood his witness. Before Pilate, as calls of "Crucify him, crucify him" filled the air, they testified: "By our law he ought to die, because he made himself the Son of

God." (John 19:6-7.) While he hung in agony upon the cross these same voices mocked: "He saved others; himself he cannot save. If he be the King of Israel, let him now come down from the cross, and we will believe him. He trusted in God; let him deliver him now, if he will have him: for he said, I am the Son of God." (Matt. 27:42-43.)

There is no question that the mortal testimony of the Son of Man was known for what it was by those who heard it. Nor is there any question that he spoke the truth. The Son of Man came to be a ransom for many—to save all men from that everlasting prison, the grave, and to save those who believe and obey from that everlasting darkness which is spiritual death.

He is God's Son. This we know. And the Spirit beareth witness.

CHRIST IS THE GOD OF ISRAEL

Who Is the God of Our Fathers?

This is the word of the Lord to all Israel: "Hearken unto me, ye that follow after righteousness. Look unto the rock from whence ye are hewn, and to the hole of the pit from whence ye are digged. Look unto Abraham, your father, and unto Sarah, she that bare you." (2 Ne. 8:1-2.)

Why? What purpose is there in looking to Abraham, our father, and to Sarah, our mother? The answer is not hard to find. Abraham, as also Isaac and Jacob, worshiped the Father in spirit and in truth and thereby gained an inheritance in the kingdom of heaven; if we who are Israel can look to them and do the works they did, we can have a like inheritance of glory and honor with them. "Go ye, therefore, and do the works of Abraham" is the Lord's decree; "enter ye into my law and ye shall be saved." (D&C 132:32.)

Salvation comes only by worshiping the true God. Abraham and "all the holy prophets . . . believed in Christ and worshiped the Father in his name." (Jacob 4:4-5.) They have now entered into their exaltation and sit upon their thrones. (D&C 132:29-37.) To rivet our minds forever on the eternal truth that we must worship and live as they did, that Lord who saves us chose to call attention to their true form of worship by naming himself after Abraham, Isaac, and Jacob.

Abraham saw the Lord. "I am the Almighty God; walk before me, and be thou perfect," was the message given him. (Gen. 17:1.) Also: "I am the Lord thy God," came the word; "I dwell in heaven; the earth is my footstool. . . . My name is Jehovah, and I know the end from the beginning; therefore my hand shall be over thee. And I will make of thee a great nation." (Abr. 2:7-9.) Isaac and Jacob, each in turn, received similar visions and promises. (Gen. 26:1-5, 28:10-15.)

When this same God appeared to Moses in the burning bush, he announced himself as "The Lord God of your fathers, the God of Abraham, the God of Isaac, and the God of Jacob," and then proclaimed: "This is my name for ever, and this is my memorial unto all generations." (Ex. 3:15.)

Who, then, is the God of our Fathers, the God of Abraham, of Isaac, and of Jacob? He is the one who "yieldeth himself, . . . as a man, into the hands of wicked men, to be lifted up, . . . to be crucified, . . . and to be buried in a sepulchre" (1 Ne. 19:10), and to rise again in glory and triumph. He is Christ. It was Christ who appeared to Abraham. It was Christ who covenanted with him and then with Isaac and with Jacob. It was Christ of whom Nephi spoke when he said: "The fulness of mine intent is that I may persuade men to come unto the God of Abraham, and the God of Isaac, and the God of Jacob, and be saved." (1 Ne. 6:4.)

Who Is the God of Israel?

Before weighing and interpreting the numerous and expressive designations of Deity used by the prophets in Israel, we should have securely lodged in our hearts the everlasting verity that Christ is the God of Israel. Whatever the world may imagine, whatever any of the cultist sects of Christendom may attempt to expound relative to Jehovah, whatever the wisdom of men may suppose, the plain, unalterable fact is that the Lord Jehovah was the promised Savior, Redeemer, Deliverer, and Messiah, and that he is

Christ. This truth is recorded in the Old Testament so that all who will believe may do so. But it is set forth so specifically and plainly in the Book of Mormon that one either believes and accepts the witness or he rejects the book itself.

One of Nephi's great Messianic prophecies proclaimed that when "the very God of Israel" dwelt among men, they would "set him at naught, and hearken not to the voice of his counsels," and would themselves "be scourged by all people, because they crucify the God of Israel." (1 Ne. 19:7-14.) The most perfect witness that Israel's God and Mary's Son were one and the same person was borne by the resurrected Jesus to the Nephites in these words: "I am Jesus Christ. . . . Come forth unto me, that ye may thrust your hands into my side, and also that ye may feel the prints of the nails in my hands and in my feet, that ye may know that I am the God of Israel, and the God of the whole earth, and have been slain for the sins of the world." (3 Ne. 11:10-14.)

With this reality firmly established, we are now ready to analyze and interpret many of the Messianic utterances which are interwoven in the ancient scriptures.

Israel's God Is the Eternal One

Our Lord, who is the Firstborn spirit child of the Eternal Elohim, is himself also the Eternal One. Implicit in his spirit birth as the Firstborn is the fact that, as with all the spirit children of the Father, he had a beginning; there was a day when he came into being as a conscious identity, as a spirit entity, as an organized intelligence. How then is he the Eternal One? It might be said that he is eternal, as all men are, meaning that spirit element—the intelligence which was organized into intelligences—has always existed and is therefore eternal. But the full and complete meaning of the designation is that he has become eternal as an individual; he has joined the ranks of eternal beings; and he is thus described as being from eternity to eternity.

Eternity is the name of that infinite duration of existence when we lived as the spirit children of the Eternal Father. It contrasts with time, which is our temporal or mortal existence. Eternity is also that existence gained by exalted beings who gain eternal families of their own that are patterned after the family of God the Father. When our revelations say of Christ, "From eternity to eternity he is the same, and his years never fail" (D&C 76:4), they mean that from one preexistence to the next he does not vary, his course is one eternal round. They mean, for instance, that from our premortal or preexistent state to the day when the exalted among us provide a preexistence for our spirit children, he is the same.

Those who enter the order of celestial marriage have the potential of being "from everlasting to everlasting" (D&C 132:20), which means from one preexistence to the next. Theirs also is the state of exaltation, because they are married for time and *all* eternity, the designation *all eternity* being one which would be redundant were it not for the scriptural use of the word *eternity* as applying to the successive and recurring expanses of the creative periods.

Israel's prophets made it clear to that ancient people that their God was the Eternal One; our Lord's meridian ministers asserted the same verity in describing him in their day; and those of us in the sheepfold that is latter-day Israel have received the revealed word reasserting the same truth for our day.

"The eternal God is thy refuge," said Moses to those whom he led. (Deut. 33:27.) "I am the first, and I am the last," he himself said to Isaiah. (Isa. 44:6.) "Art thou not from everlasting, O Lord my God, mine Holy One?" intoned Habakkuk. (Hab. 1:12.) From Psalms resounds the answer: "Thou art from everlasting" (Ps. 93:2), "even from everlasting to everlasting, thou art God" (Ps. 90:2). "Thy years are throughout all generations." (Ps. 102:24.) "He is the beginning and the end, the first and the last" is Alma's testimony.

(Alma 11:39.) All these things were said of Israel's God anciently.

After his mortal probation, Paul said of him: "Jesus Christ the same yesterday, and to day, and for ever." (Heb. 13:8.)

As a resurrected being, he said to John: "I am Alpha and Omega, the first and the last. . . . Fear not; I am the first and the last: I am he that liveth, and was dead; and, behold, I am alive for evermore." (Rev. 1:11, 17-18.) This accords with his declaration to Joseph Smith and Oliver Cowdery, "I am the first and the last; I am he who liveth, I am he who was slain." (D&C 110:4.) "I am Alpha and Omega, the beginning and the end," was his affirmation to the Nephites. (3 Ne. 9:18.) It is clear that he—"the Holy One, who is without beginning of days or end of life" (D&C 78:16), who is "Alphus" and "Omegus; even Jesus Christ" (D&C 95:17)—wants a record kept, in all scripture both ancient and modern, that he is an everlasting and eternal being in whom all fulness and perfection dwell.

Christ Is the Holy One of Israel

The prophets and peoples of olden times paid homage to Jehovah under his names Holy (Isa. 57:15), Holy One (Hab. 1:12), Holy One of Jacob (Isa. 29:23), and Holy One of Israel (Isa. 45:11), thereby being constantly aware that he being holy, so should they be. (Lev. 11:45.)

Our Lord's friends and enemies acclaimed him as the Holy One when he dwelt on earth. Peter so designated him in speaking to his Jewish brethren of the great day of restoration that was to be. (Acts 3:14-21.) The better translation of one of Peter's earlier testimonies is: "We believe and are sure that thou art that Christ, the Holy One of God." (John 6:69.) Both Peter and John praised the Lord for sending his "holy child Jesus" to earth (Acts 4:23-30), and John designated him as the Holy One in his major epistle (1 Jn.

2:20). Even an unclean spirit, being cast from his ill-gotten human habitation by the Savior, cried out: "I know thee who thou art, the Holy One of God." (Mark 1:24; Luke 4:34.) And the resurrected Lord described himself to John as "He that is holy." (Rev. 3:7.)

Our Nephite brethren, both before and after our Lord's mortal sojourn, used these same terms with reference to him. Lehi called him the Holy Messiah and the Holy One. (2 Ne. 2:8-10.) Nephi (1 Ne. 22:5), Jacob (2 Ne. 9:11-51), and Amaleki (Omni 1:25-26) designated him as the Holy One of Israel. Alma (Alma 5:52) and Nephi the son of Helaman (Hel. 12:2) said simply the Holy One, as did Moroni after the bands of death had been broken (Morm. 9:14). In latter-day revelation he is called the Holy One and the Holy One of Zion. (D&C 78:15-16.)

Can anyone suppose other than that Israel's God, the mortal Master, and the risen Lord are one and the same, and that he is the Eternal Christ? So it is; and it comes, accordingly, as no surprise to find the plain-speaking Nephite prophets saying: "Christ is the Holy One of Israel" (2 Ne. 25:29), and of their setting forth the terms and conditions of the whole plan of salvation in terms of the Holy One of Israel working out the infinite and eternal atonement and of men having faith in his name to gain salvation (2 Ne. 9).

With the knowledge thus before us that the Holy One of Israel is Christ, the door is open to us to gain a new insight into the deeper and hidden meanings of many passages.

Isaiah expounds about the glory and praise to be heaped upon the Holy One of Israel in the day of restoration and of millennial peace. "In that day," he says—meaning when Israel is gathered the second time and millennial peace is settling over all the earth—Israel will be comforted and will say: "Behold, God is my salvation; I will trust, and not be afraid; for the Lord JEHOVAH is my strength and my song." In that day, Jehovah's atoning sacrifice being a thing of the past, they will say: "He also has become my salvation." To men in that day the promise is: "Therefore, with joy shall ye draw water out of the wells of salvation." In that day believing Israel shall say: "Praise the Lord, call upon his name, declare his doings among the people, make mention that his name is exalted." They shall "sing unto the Lord; for he hath done excellent things; this is known in all the earth." And then shall the righteous say: "Cry out and shout, thou inhabitant of Zion; for great is the Holy One of Israel in the midst of thee." (2 Ne. 22:1-5.)

The Holy One of Israel in the midst of thee! The Lord reigns personally upon the earth! He who came once has come again, and he is Christ the Holy One!

Christ Is the Rock of Heaven

"I am Messiah, the King of Zion, the Rock of Heaven, which is broad as eternity." (Moses 7:53.) So spake the Lord to Enoch. "I will publish the name of the Lord: ascribe ye greatness unto our God. He is the Rock, his work is perfect: for all his ways are judgment: a God of truth and without iniquity, just and right is he." (Deut. 32:3-4.) So proclaimed Moses the great lawgiver. "O thou Rock of our Salvation,/Jesus, Savior of the world" (*Hymns,* no. 130) and "Rock of Ages, cleft for me,/Let me hide myself in thee" (*Hymns,* no. 382)—so sing the modern saints. And all of this is to teach that the great Redeemer, who is Christ the Lord, is the secure foundation, a foundation "broad as eternity," upon which all men must build if they are to inherit, receive, and possess the full blessings of the infinite and eternal atonement.

Christ is the foundation upon which the house of salvation is built, and "other foundation can no man lay than that is laid, which is Jesus Christ." (1 Cor. 3:11.) He is the Rock; by him salvation comes; without him there would be neither immortality nor eternal life; and all those who build upon him, when the rains descend and the floods come and the winds blow, their houses shall stand, for they are founded upon the Rock.

"Fear not, little flock," is the voice of the Lord to his Latter-day Saints, "do good; let earth and hell combine against you, for if ye are built upon my rock, they cannot prevail." (D&C 6:34.) "Build upon my rock, which is my gospel," is his decree. (D&C 11:24.) In commanding his little flock to preach faith, repentance, baptism, and the receipt of the Holy Ghost, he says: "This is my gospel." Then of those to whom it is preached comes this word: "They shall have faith in me or they can in nowise be saved; And upon this rock I will build my church; yea, upon this rock ye are built, and if ye continue, the gates of hell shall not prevail against you." (D&C 33:12-13.) To his Nephite saints he taught that all who repent and are baptized, who remember him and keep his commandments, who partake worthily of the sacrament and have the companionship of the Holy Spirit, "are built upon my rock. But whoso among you shall do more or less than these are not built upon my rock, but are built upon a sandy foundation; and when the rain descends, and the floods come, and the winds blow, and beat upon them, they shall fall, and the gates of hell are ready open to receive them." (3 Ne. 18:12-13.)

Knowing all these things—and they have also been known by the faithful people in all ages—it comes as no surprise to find prophets in all ages speaking of the Lord as their Rock. Knowing all these things, we can also discern the inspired Messianic meanings of the many passages which extol the Rock.

David, exulting over the goodness of God, sang these words: "The Lord is my rock, and my fortress, and my deliverer; The God of my rock; in him will I trust: he is my shield, and the horn of my salvation, my high tower, and my refuge, my saviour." (2 Sam. 22:2-3.) The Psalms abound in such statements as: "Thou art my rock and my fortress." (Ps. 71:3.) "Thou art my father, my God, and the rock of my salvation." (Ps. 89:26.) "Let us make a joyful noise to the rock of our salvation." (Ps. 95:1.)

"Of the Rock that begat thee thou art unmindful," Moses

said in upbraiding rebellious Israel, "and hast forgotten God that formed thee." (Deut. 32:18.) Isaiah spoke of the desolation that should come upon them "because thou hast forgotten the God of thy salvation, and hast not been mindful of the rock of thy strength." (Isa. 17:10.)

Expounding the same truths—albeit more plainly, as it was their wont to do—Nephite prophets said such things as: "It is upon the rock of our Redeemer, who is Christ, the Son of God, that ye must build your foundation; that when the devil shall send forth his mighty winds, yea, his shafts in the whirlwind, yea, when all his hail and his mighty storm shall beat upon you, it shall have no power over you to drag you down to the gulf of misery and endless wo, because of the rock upon which ye are built, which is a sure foundation, a foundation whereon if men build they cannot fall." (Hel. 5:12.) Also: "Come unto that God who is the rock of your salvation." (2 Ne. 9:45.)

Paul, with a plainness rivaling in this instance that of his Nephite compatriots, endorsed the whole body of Old Testament terminology in which Israel's God is called the Rock. Theologian and scriptorian that he was, Paul referred to the ancient hand-dealings of Deity with Moses and those who followed him and the fact that "the Lord went before them by day in a pillar of a cloud, to lead them the way; and by night in a pillar of fire, to give them light." (Ex. 13:21.) He noted that being thus guided, the hosts of Israel passed through the Red Sea (Ex. 14), at which time they "did all eat the same spiritual meat; And did all drink the same spiritual drink: for they drank of that spiritual Rock that followed them: and that Rock was Christ." (1 Cor. 10:1-4.) This is one of the plainest and bluntest New Testament declarations that the God of Israel and Jesus who is called Christ are one and the same person.

The language of the Old Testament prophets describes God as their Rock, their fortress, their buckler and shield and the like. Our Christian Era hymn, written by Martin Luther, acclaims: "A mighty fortress is our God,/A tower of strength ne'er failing." (*Hymns,* no. 3.) In keeping with this view relative to the strength and power of Deity, we have the expressive declaration of Samuel: "The Strength of Israel will not lie nor repent: for he is not a man, that he should repent." (1 Sam. 15:29.) This name, the Strength of Israel, might also be translated the Victory of Israel or the Glory of Israel—all of which are designations appropriate for the Lord of Hosts, who is "a man of war" (Ex. 15:3), a God of Battles, who at his Second Coming shall "go forth, and fight against those nations [who oppose him], as when he fought in the day of battle." (Zech. 14:3.)

Christ Is the Stone of Israel

"The mighty God of Jacob . . . is the shepherd, the stone of Israel." (Gen. 49:24.) His role as a Shepherd we shall discuss shortly. His status as the Stone of Israel is akin to that of the Rock of Heaven; that is, he is the stone or foundation upon which all men must build to gain salvation in his Father's kingdom. "I am the good shepherd, the stone of Israel. He that buildeth upon this rock shall never fall" is his declaration in our day. (D&C 50:44.)

There are three great Messianic prophecies that deal with the blessings and curses to fall upon men through their acceptance or rejection of the Stone of Israel. These three prophetic utterances were generally accepted by the people of Jesus' day as being Messianic, though their full meaning and application were matters of extended study and debate.

In one of them, Isaiah's record says: "Thus said the Lord God, Behold, I lay in Zion for a foundation a stone, a tried stone, a precious corner stone, a sure foundation: he that believeth shall not make haste." (Isa. 28:16.) The emphasis here is clearly upon the blessings which shall flow from building a house of faith and salvation upon the only sure foundation, which is Christ.

In another of them, the Lord says by the mouth of Isaiah: "Sanctify the Lord of hosts himself; and let him be your fear, and let him be your dread." (Isa. 8:13.) Now, note it well, the prophecy is speaking of the God of Israel, of the Lord Jehovah. He is the one they are to fear. The dread of him is to rest upon the disobedient.

"And he shall be for a sanctuary; but for a stone of stumbling and for a rock of offence to both the houses of Israel." (Isa. 8:14.) Israel's God shall be—the tense is future—a blessing or a cursing to the whole house of Israel, to both the kingdom of Ephraim and the kingdom of Judah, and for that matter to the whole of mankind. Those who believe and obey shall find peace and rest and security in his arms; he is their sanctuary. Those who stumble at his doctrine, who are offended by his claims of divinity, shall be cast out and rejected for their disbelief.

"And he shall be . . . for a gin and for a snare to the inhabitants of Jerusalem." (Isa. 8:14.) Here the prophecy deals specifically with those among whom he ministers in mortality—"the inhabitants of Jerusalem." They lose their souls because they reject their Messiah. They are caught in the traps and snares of the adversary. "And many among them shall stumble, and fall, and be broken, and be snared, and be taken." (Isa. 8:15.)

"Bind up the testimony, seal the law among my disciples." (Isa. 8:16.) This refers to the fate of men who reject the Lord and his law. As set forth in latter-day revelation, the "disciples," those who are the Lord's servants, "go forth" with power given them "to seal both on earth and in heaven, the unbelieving and rebellious; Yea, verily, to seal them up unto the day when the wrath of God shall be poured out upon the wicked without measure." (D&C 1:8-9.) Of these wicked and unbelieving ones the revealed word says: "Behold, and lo, there are none to deliver you; for ye obeyed not my voice when I called to you out of the heavens; ye believed not my servants, and when they were sent unto you ye received them not. Wherefore, they sealed up the testimony and bound up the law, and ye were delivered over unto darkness. These shall go away into outer darkness, where there is weeping, and wailing, and gnashing of teeth." (D&C 133:71-73.)

The gospel brings blessings or curses. Both are administered to men by the Lord's agents. Those whom they bless are blessed, and those whom they curse are cursed. (D&C 124:93.) The Lord's servants go forth "to bind up the law and seal up the testimony, and to prepare the saints for the hour of judgment which is to come." (D&C 88:84.) The crowning blessing bestowed is: "And of as many as the Father shall bear record, to you shall be given power to seal them up unto eternal life." (D&C 68:12.)

As we ponder the deep and wondrous meaning of these Messianic words given through Isaiah, there comes to mind the kindred expression of another, one John Baptist, than whom there was no greater prophet. He said: "He that believeth on the Son hath everlasting life: and he that believeth not the Son shall not see life; but the wrath of God abideth on him." (John 3:36.)

In the third of these Old Testament utterances, which are all in effect linked together as one, we read: "The stone which the builders refused is become the head stone of the corner. This is the Lord's doing; it is marvellous in our eyes." (Ps. 118:22-23.) The meaning here is clear. The Jews reject their Messiah, but he nonetheless becomes and remains the Stone which holds the whole structure of salvation together, a thing that is marvelous in all eyes.

At this point we might well insert these words of Nephi's brother Jacob: "I perceive by the workings of the Spirit which is in me," he said, "that by the stumbling of the Jews they will reject the stone upon which they might build and have safe foundation." So he speaks of the rejection by the Jews of their King. "But behold, according to the scriptures," he says—speaking of a yet future day when the Jews, at the Second Coming, will be converted—"this stone shall become the great, and the last, and the only sure foundation, upon which the Jews can build." (Jacob 4:15-16.)

How were these prophecies about the Stone of Israel

used and interpreted by Jesus and his disciples in New Testament times? As it happens our Lord took special occasion to endorse and approve the concept that he was the Stone of Israel, and Peter and Paul, the two chief theologians among the ancient apostles, used the prophetic utterances to testify of Christ and to teach doctrines of deep import.

In the parable of the wicked husbandmen, Jesus taught that a householder (who is God) planted and prepared a vineyard; that he let it out to husbandmen; that he sent his servants (his prophets) to receive the fruit; and that one after another they were beaten, stoned, and killed. Finally he sent his son (Christ), who also was cast out of the vineyard and slain. With this recitation before them, the Jews admitted that the householder would destroy the wicked men and let out his vineyard to others who would render fruit in due season. (*Doctrinal New Testament Commentary,* 1:590-95.)

Then the record says: "Jesus saith unto them, Did ye never read in the scriptures, The stone which the builders rejected, the same is become the head of the corner: this is the Lord's doing, and it is marvellous in our eyes? Therefore say I unto you, The kingdom of God shall be taken from you, and given to a nation bringing forth the fruits thereof. And whosoever shall fall on this stone shall be broken: but on whomsoever it shall fall, it will grind him to powder. And when the chief priests and Pharisees had heard his parables, they perceived that he spake of them." (Matt. 21:42-45.)

Resentful that Jesus so spake of them, "They said among themselves, Shall the man think that he alone can spoil this great kingdom? And they were angry." And at this point in the account, the Prophet Joseph Smith, acting by the spirit of revelation, inserted the following:

"And now his disciples came to him, and Jesus said unto them, Marvel ye at the words of the parable which I spake unto them? Verily, I say unto you, I am the stone, and those wicked ones reject me. I am the head of the corner. These Jews shall fall upon me, and shall be broken. And the kingdom of God shall be taken from them, and shall be given to a nation bringing forth the fruits thereof; (meaning the Gentiles.) Wherefore, on whomsoever this stone shall fall, it shall grind him to powder. And when the Lord therefore of the vineyard cometh, he will destroy those miserable, wicked men, and will let again his vineyard unto other husbandmen, even in the last days, who shall render him the fruits in their seasons. And then understood they the parable which he spake unto them, that the Gentiles should be destroyed also, when the Lord should descend out of heaven to reign in his vineyard, which is the earth and the inhabitants thereof." (JST, Matt. 21:48-56.)

Paul's usage of the Stone of Israel prophecies is part of a long doctrinal presentation showing that the gospel was to go to the Gentiles, who through faith in Christ and personal righteousness would gain its blessings. "But Israel, which followed after the law of righteousness, hath not attained to the law of righteousness." That is, Israel sought righteousness and salvation through their system of worship, but had not in fact obtained it. "Wherefore? Because they sought it not by faith, but as it were by the works of the law"—meaning that they sought righteousness and salvation through the works of the Mosaic law alone rather than by faith in Christ. "For they stumbled at that stumblingstone; As it is written, Behold, I lay in Sion a stumblingstone and rock of offence: and whosoever believeth on him shall not be ashamed." (Rom. 9:31-33.)

To those, both Jew and Gentile, who did accept the saving truths of the gospel, Paul wrote: "Ye are no more strangers and foreigners, but fellowcitizens with the saints, and of the household of God; And are built upon the foundation of the apostles and prophets, Jesus Christ himself being the chief corner stone; In whom all the building fitly framed together groweth unto an holy temple in the Lord: In whom ye also are builded together for an habitation of God through the Spirit." (Eph. 2:19-22.)

Peter's usage of the prophecies is similar. When he and John were examined by the Jews as to the power and name used by them in healing the man lame from his mother's womb, Peter said with boldness: "Be it known unto you all, and to all the people of Israel, that by the name of Jesus Christ of Nazareth, whom ye crucified, whom God raised from the dead, even by him doth this man stand here before you whole. This is the stone which was set at nought of you builders, which is become the head of the corner. Neither is there salvation in any other; for there is none other name under heaven given among men, whereby we must be saved." (Acts 4:10-12.)

Later, Peter wrote that Christ was "a living stone, disallowed indeed of men, but chosen of God, and precious. . . . Wherefore also it is contained in the scripture, Behold, I lay in Sion a chief corner stone, elect, precious: and he that believeth on him shall not be confounded. Unto you therefore which believe he is precious: but unto them which be disobedient, the stone which the builders disallowed, the same is made the head of the corner, And a stone of stumbling, and a rock of offence, even to them which stumble at the word, being disobedient: whereunto also they were appointed."

Interwoven with this testimony about and these teachings concerning our Lord, Peter exhorts those who have accepted the "living stone" to be themselves "lively stones," to build up that "spiritual house" which is the Church, and to honor and use the "holy priesthood" which they possess. (1 Pet. 2:4-9.)

Christ Is the Good Shepherd

One of the sweetest and most tender terms by which the Lord was known anciently was that of the Shepherd of Israel. To a pastoral people who loved their sheep, who cared for them with tender solicitude, and whose very lives depended upon keeping them safe, this designation taught great truths about the relationship of the Lord to his people.

Father Jacob called him "the shepherd . . . of Israel"

(Gen. 49:24), and ever thereafter he was so identified by Israel's hosts. "He is our God; and we are the people of his pasture, and the sheep of his hand." (Ps. 95:7; 100:3.) "Give ear, O Shepherd of Israel, thou that leadest Joseph like a flock. . . . Come and save us. Turn us again, O God, and cause thy face to shine; and we shall be saved." (Ps. 80:1-3.) So sang the people in their Psalms.

Of his future ministry among mortals, Isaiah said: "The Lord God will come. . . . He shall feed his flock like a shepherd: he shall gather the lambs with his arm, and carry them in his bosom, and shall gently lead those that are with young." (Isa. 40:10-11.)

And his Nephite counterparts spoke the same truth, using words having a familiar spirit. "There is one God and one Shepherd over all the earth," Nephi said. "And the time cometh that he shall manifest himself unto all nations, both unto the Jews and also unto the Gentiles"—meaning that when he is born as a mortal on earth, his gospel will be offered first to his Jewish kin and later will go to the nations of the Gentiles.

"And after he has manifested himself unto the Jews and also unto the Gentiles, then he shall manifest himself unto the Gentiles and also unto the Jews, and the last shall be first, and the first shall be last" (1 Ne. 13:41-42)—meaning that in the last days his everlasting gospel will be revealed to the non-Jews (who are here called Gentiles) and from them will go in due course to his Jewish kinsmen. It is of this latter-day work that Nephi says: "The Holy One of Israel must reign in dominion, and might, and power, and great glory. And he gathereth his children from the four quarters of the earth; and he numbereth his sheep, and they know him; and there shall be one fold and one shepherd; and he shall feed his sheep, and in him they shall find pasture." (1 Ne. 22:24-25.)

Speaking as the Shepherd of Israel, the Lord said to Alma the elder, "He that will hear my voice shall be my sheep; and him shall ye receive into the church, and him will

I also receive." (Mosiah 26:21.) After his conversion Alma the younger taught, "The good shepherd doth call you; yea, and in his own name he doth call you, which is the name of Christ. . . . The good shepherd doth call after you; and if you will hearken unto his voice he will bring you into his fold, and ye are his sheep." (Alma 5:38, 60.) Describing the degenerate and apostate state of his people, Mormon wrote: "They are without Christ and God in the world. . . . They were once a delightsome people, and they had Christ for their shepherd." (Morm. 5:16-17.)

In Palestine sheep are led, not driven. The American practice is for sheepherders to drive sheep; the Palestinian custom is for the shepherds to go before their sheep, to call them by name, and to lead them to green pastures and beside still waters. At night the flocks of several shepherds are sheltered and protected together in one sheepfold. In the morning each shepherd calls his own sheep by name, out of the larger intermingled flock, and they follow him into the places of food and water.

Jesus reminded the Jews of this practice, equated himself with the porter who guarded the sheep during the night, and said: "I am the door of the sheep. . . . I am the door: by me if any man enter in, he shall be saved, and shall go in and out, and find pasture." In other words: 'Even as sheep are pastured and preserved by their shepherds, so are men, the people of the Lord's pasture, led and saved by me.' "I am come that they might have life, and that they might have it more abundantly," Jesus continued. "I am the good shepherd: the good shepherd giveth his life for the sheep. . . . I am the good shepherd, and know my sheep, and am known of mine. As the Father knoweth me, even so know I the Father: and I lay down my life for the sheep."

To all who heard his declaration "I am the good shepherd," with its accompanying assertions about his Father, the meaning was clear. To a people who studied the scriptures and knew the imagery and meaning of what the prophets had said, who themselves exulted in the Psalm,

"The Lord is my shepherd" (Psalm 23), Jesus' spoken words meant: 'I am the Lord Jehovah, and I shall work out the infinite and eternal atonement by laying down my life for the sheep.'

However, captious and conniving as they were, they still propounded to him the question: "If thou be the Christ, tell us plainly." In other words: 'We know you are claiming to be the Lord Jehovah in figurative language, but we hesitate to stone you for blasphemy until you say plainly that such is the case.' Jesus answered by saying, "I told you, and ye believed not." And truly he had. "But ye believe not," he continued, "because ye are not of my sheep, as I said unto you. My sheep hear my voice, and I know them, and they follow me." (John 10:1-28.)

It was during this discourse that the Master spoke of other sheep which were not of the Jewish fold, a group whom he subsequently identified by saying to the Nephites, "Ye are they of whom I said: Other sheep I have which are not of this fold; them also I must bring, and they shall hear my voice; and there shall be one fold, and one shepherd." (3 Ne. 15:21.)

Jesus' statements to Peter, "Feed my lambs" and "Feed my sheep," spoken after his resurrection, are a reaffirmation of his standing as the Shepherd of Israel. (John 21:15-17.) It was this same presiding apostle who wrote that our Lord was "the Shepherd and Bishop" of our souls (1 Pet. 2:25) and also the "chief Shepherd" who shall come again in glory in due course. (1 Pet. 5:4.) Paul, in testifying that the good Shepherd and Christ are one and the same, uttered this prayer: "Now the God of peace, that brought again from the dead our Lord Jesus, that great shepherd of the sheep, through the blood of the everlasting covenant, Make you perfect in every good work to do his will." (Heb. 13:20-21.)

Christ Is Known by Many Names

Our Lord is and has been known by many names. Some

have been revealed in one dispensation, some in another; some have been used in a single age, some in many; and no doubt there are many names yet to be revealed. To collect and analyze all those by which he is known to us would be a work of major proportions and constitute a large volume by itself. Our purpose in this work is to note the more important instances in which he was known both before and after his coming by the same names, thus showing that the mortal Christ and the promised Messiah are one and the same. In addition to the designations so far noted, and to those not scheduled for more elaborate consideration later in this work, we here note the following:

1. *He is the Servant of the Lord.*

Jesus came to do the will of his Father because his Father sent him. (3 Ne. 27:13-14.) He was the Servant, not the master, in his relationship with his Father. "I am among you as he that serveth," he said. (Luke 22:27.) Also: "The Son can do nothing of himself, but what he seeth the Father do: for what things soever he doeth, these also doeth the Son likewise." (John 5:19.) Submissive, willing, obedient, walking only in the path charted for him by his Father—such was the course pursued by the Son.

How natural it is to find Christ serving both the Father and his fellowmen, for so it had been predicted. The introductory sentence of the longest single Messianic prophecy in the Old Testament (and one of the greatest and most comprehensive of them all) says: "Behold, my servant shall deal prudently, he shall be exalted and extolled, and be very high." (Isa. 52:13.) Another of Isaiah's long and plain predictions about the coming of the Messiah begins: "Behold my servant, whom I uphold; mine elect, in whom my soul delighteth; I have put my spirit upon him: he shall bring forth judgment to the Gentiles." (Isa. 42:1.) "I will bring forth my servant" (Zech. 3:8) is the scriptural promise, as also: "O Lord, truly I am thy servant: I am thy servant, and the son of thine handmaid: thou hast loosed my bonds. I will offer to thee the sacrifice of thanksgiving, and will call upon the name of the Lord. I will pay my vows unto the Lord now in the presence of all his people, in the courts of the Lord's house, in the midst of thee, O Jerusalem." (Ps. 116:16-19.)

And so, truly, did our Lord act during his mortal ministry! Truly, this is he of whom it is written: "He shall stand and feed in the strength of the Lord, in the majesty of the name of the LORD his God; . . . for now shall he be great unto the ends of the earth." (Mic. 5:4.)

2. *He is the Star out of Jacob.*

Of him Balaam prophesied: "I shall see him, but not now: I shall behold him, but not nigh: there shall come a Star out of Jacob, and a Sceptre shall rise out of Israel. . . . Out of Jacob shall come he that shall have dominion." (Num. 24:17-19.) "In figurative language, the spirit hosts in pre-existence are referred to as the stars of heaven." (*Mormon Doctrine,* 2nd ed., pp. 765-66.) The morning stars who joined with all the sons of God when the foundations of the earth were laid were the noble and preeminent spirits. As the Star who came out of Jacob, Christ is thus the most outstanding one of all the hosts of that unnumbered house. And so he testified of himself: "I am . . . the bright and morning star." (Rev. 22:16.)

3. *He is the Beloved and Chosen One.*

Before, during, and after his mortal ministry he was and is known as the Beloved and Chosen One, terms that carry a connotation of election and selection, of choosing and foreordination. He is "My Beloved and Chosen from the beginning" (Moses 4:2); "My Chosen" (Moses 7:39); "My Beloved" (2 Ne. 31:15); "My Well Beloved" (Hel. 5:47); "His most Beloved" (Morm. 5:14); and "My Beloved Son" (3 Ne. 11:7; Matt. 3:17; JS-H 17).

4. *He is the Anointed One.*

A number of Messianic passages speak of "the Lord, and . . . his anointed" (Ps. 2:2), signifying that the Chosen One was consecrated and set apart for the ministry and mission that was his. Jesus applied these passages to himself by quoting Isaiah's prophecy, "The Lord hath anointed me to preach good tidings unto the meek" (Isa. 61:1), and then saying: "This day is this scripture fulfilled in your ears" (Luke 4:21). Peter made the same application by speaking of "thy holy child Jesus, whom thou hast anointed" (Acts 4:27), and by telling "how God anointed Jesus of Nazareth with the Holy Ghost and with power" (Acts 10:38). In a revealed prayer, given in our day, we find this petition: "Wilt thou turn away thy wrath when thou lookest upon the face of thine Anointed." (D&C 109:53.)

5. *He is the Bridegroom.*

"Thy Maker is thine husband; the Lord of hosts is his name; and thy Redeemer the Holy One of Israel; The God of the whole earth shall he be called. For the Lord hath called thee as a woman forsaken and grieved in spirit, and [as] a wife of youth." (Isa. 54:5-6.) "And as the bridegroom rejoiceth over the bride, so shall thy God rejoice over thee." (Isa. 62:5.) So spake the Eternal One to his chosen Israel. Speaking of his Second Coming, this same Jesus called himself the Bridegroom (Matt. 25:1-13), and the same terminology has been preserved in latter-day revelation (D&C 133:10, 19).

Paul makes quite a point of this concept. "The husband is the head of the wife," he says, "even as Christ is the head of the church." That is, it is as though Christ were married to the Church. "Therefore as the church is subject unto Christ, so let the wives be to their own husbands in every thing. Husbands, love your wives, even as Christ also loved the church, and gave himself for it." Then because of the figurative nature of the language used, he says: "This is a great mystery: but I speak concerning Christ and the church." (Eph. 5:23-32.)

6. *He is the Hope of Israel.*

In and through and by and because of him we and all men have a hope of peace in this life and eternal glory in the world to come. He is our Hope. Without him we would have no hope of immortality, no hope of eternal life, no hope of the continuation of the family unit, no hope of eternal progress, no hope of exaltation, no hope of any good thing. All the hopes of all the righteous of all the ages center in him. "O Lord, the hope of Israel, all that forsake thee shall be ashamed, and they that depart from me shall be written in the earth, because they have forsaken the Lord, the fountain of living waters." (Jer. 17:13; 14:8; 50:7.)

"We are saved by hope" (Rom. 8:24), and the "Lord Jesus Christ . . . is our hope," said Paul (1 Tim. 1:1). The lives of the righteous are spent "looking for that blessed hope," he also said, which hope is for "the glorious appearing of the great God and our Saviour Jesus Christ." (Titus 2:13.)

7. *He is the Nazarene.*

In a prophecy no longer found in any scripture now had among us, it is written: "He shall be called a Nazarene," which was fulfilled, Matthew tells us, because he dwelt "in a city called Nazareth." (Matt. 2:23.) Subsequent developments confirmed that he was to bear that designation during and after his mortal probation. While he yet dwelt in mortality, he was called Jesus of Nazareth by his disciples (John 1:45), and after he rose from the dead, he himself said to Paul, "I am Jesus of Nazareth whom thou persecutest" (Acts 22:8). Peter spoke of him similarly (Acts 2:22), although when he healed the lame man, he used the more formal words, "In the name of Jesus Christ of Nazareth rise up and walk" (Acts 3:6).

"THE LORD IS OUR KING"

Who Is Our Eternal King?

From the earliest days of the earth's existence righteous men have known that the Lord our God is its King. In one form or another this truth has been taught and preached among the saints of all dispensations. They envisioned him as being a King while he yet dwelt as a Spirit Son in his Father's court; while he lived on earth among mortals; and after he came forth from the grave to reign forever in glorious immortality. We shall now touch briefly upon some of the ways in which he was known to be and announced as King.

"I am Messiah, the King of Zion." (Moses 7:53.) So spoke the Son of Man to that Enoch who founded the City of Zion. Millenniums later, David, exulting that Mount Zion was "the joy of the whole earth," acclaimed it also as "the city of the great King, . . . the city of the Lord of hosts, . . . the city of our God." (Ps. 48:1-8.)

Speaking of the Lord Jehovah, the record says such things as: "God is my King." (Ps. 74:12.) "The Lord is a great God, and a great King above all gods." (Ps. 95:3.) "Let the children of Zion be joyful in their King." (Ps. 149:2.) That there are hosts of similar Psalmic declarations is well known.

He is also called "the King of glory" (Ps. 24), "the King

of Jacob" (Isa. 41:21), "the King of Israel, and his redeemer the Lord of hosts" (Isa. 44:6), "your Holy One, the creator of Israel, your King" (Isa. 43:15), and "the Holy One of Israel" (Ps. 89:18). Jeremiah said, "The Lord is the true God, he is the living God, and an everlasting king" (Jer. 10:10), and Isaiah testified: "Mine eyes have seen the King, the Lord of hosts" (Isa. 6:5). Declarations of this sort abound in Holy Writ. None can doubt that the God of ancients, the God of Israel, the great Jehovah of old was universally acclaimed as Lord and King.

Christ Is Our Eternal King

Interwoven with the repeated assertions that Jehovah was Lord and King are the declarations that this same King-Messiah shall come to save and redeem his people. Speaking Messianically, Isaiah said, "Behold, a king shall reign in righteousness" (Isa. 32:1), which no king could do, in the full sense of the word, except the Holy One. In prophesying that "the Son of God cometh in his glory, in his might, majesty, power, and dominion," Alma said: "Behold the glory of the King of all the earth; and also the King of heaven shall very soon shine forth among all the children of men." (Alma 5:50.) And Zechariah even spelled out in detail one of the events in the mortal life of the King of Zion. "Rejoice greatly, O daughter of Zion," he proclaimed; "shout, O daughter of Jerusalem: behold, thy King cometh unto thee: he is just, and having salvation; lowly, and riding upon an ass, and upon a colt the foal of an ass." (Zech. 9:9.)

That many people recognized Jesus as the promised King is clear from the New Testament account. Following his birth in Bethlehem, "there came wise men from the east to Jerusalem, Saying, Where is he that is born King of the Jews?" (Matt. 2:1-2.) Before Pilate, Jesus himself answered "Thou sayest," meaning "I am," when asked, "Art thou the King of the Jews?" and that Roman governor, over the objection of the Jews, placed this writing over the cross: "THIS

IS JESUS THE KING OF THE JEWS." (Matt. 27:11-37.)

And as to Zechariah's prophecy, it was fulfilled in detail. "Go into the village over against you," Jesus said to two of his disciples, when the time had arrived for his triumphal entry into Jerusalem, "and straightway ye shall find an ass tied, and a colt with her: loose them, and bring them unto me. And if any man say ought unto you, ye shall say, The Lord hath need of them; and straightway he will send them."

"All this was done," Matthew recites, "that it might be fulfilled which was spoken by the prophet, saying, Tell ye the daughter of Sion, Behold, thy King cometh unto thee, meek, and sitting upon an ass, and a colt the foal of an ass. And the disciples went, and did as Jesus commanded them, And brought the ass, and the colt, and put on them their clothes, and they set him thereon. And a very great multitude spread their garments in the way; others cut down branches from the trees, and strawed them in the way. And the multitudes that went before, and that followed, cried, saying, Hosanna to the Son of David: Blessed is he that cometh in the name of the Lord; Hosanna in the highest." (Matt. 21:1-9.) That the multitude spoke with the deliberate intent of testifying that our Lord was their promised King is seen from the fact that they mingled with their shouts of Hosanna and praise the Messianic prophecy taken from the Psalms, "Blessed be he that cometh in the name of the Lord." (Ps. 118:26.)

After Jesus rose from the dead he continued to bear his kingly title. Paul wrote of him that he "is the blessed and only Potentate, the King of kings, and the Lord of lords, to whom be honor and power everlasting." (JST, 1 Tim. 6:15.) John called him "the prince of the kings of the earth" (Rev. 1:5), the "King of saints" (Rev. 15:3), and the "Lord of lords, and King of kings" (Rev. 17:14; 19:16).

In due course this same Almighty King shall come again to reign on earth and to fulfill in their entirety all of the Messianic prophecies. "And the Lord shall be king over all the earth," Zechariah says, and "in that day shall there be one Lord, and his name one." This will be the day when men "shall even go up [to Jerusalem] from year to year to worship the King, the Lord of hosts, and to keep the feast of tabernacles." (Zech. 14:9, 16.)

Why David Is a Symbol of the Messiah

No single concept was more firmly lodged in the minds of the Jews in Jesus' day than the universal belief that their Messiah would be the Son of David. They expected him to come and reign on David's throne. They looked for a temporal deliverer who would throw off the yoke of Roman bondage and make Israel free again. They sought a ruler who would restore that glory and worldwide influence and prestige which was enjoyed when the Son of Jesse sat on Israel's throne. The true concepts of deliverance from spiritual darkness, of being freed from the bondage of sin, of a kingdom which is not of this world—all made possible through an infinite and eternal atonement—all this was lost and unknown doctrine to them.

It comes as no surprise, then, when Jesus asks, "What think ye of Christ? whose son is he?" to have them respond, "The son of David." (Matt. 22:42.) That their answer was true is of no particular moment. Of course Christ was the Son of David; who had any doubt about that? What really counted was that God was his Father, and hence that he had power to ransom and redeem. Their acceptance of him as David's Son—nothing more—still left them without salvation. It is as though we should ask today: "What think ye of Christ? Is he the Savior of the world?" and receive the response, "He is the greatest moral teacher that ever lived." True. But salvation comes to us not because we accept him as the greatest teacher of the ages, which he was, but because he is known to us to be the Son of God.

With these distinctions before us, we shall now consider our Lord's status as the Son of David, see why he was so designated, and learn from the Davidic-Messianic prophecies those truths which the prophetic mind intended to convey by using David, the great king, as a type and shadow of his infinitely greater Son.

First we must note David's place and stature in Israel and the high esteem in which he was held by all. Born in Bethlehem in 1085 B.C., the youngest of the eight sons of Jesse, he grew up as a shepherd; endowed with great physical strength and courage, he slew Goliath and became a national hero; anointed king by Samuel, he reigned over part of the people for seven years and over all of them for another thirty-three. His military conquests were legendary, his court comparable to those of the great Oriental sovereigns, and his influence in world affairs like that of the greatest kings and warriors in history.

He was a poet, a musician and sweet singer, a man of deep religious bent. Indeed he was a man after the Lord's own heart (1 Sam. 13:13-14), until the day he forsook the path of righteousness and lost his soul through sin. He "served his own generation by the will of God" (Acts 13:36), and there were none before and none after whose privilege it was to hold temporal rule in Israel, who so caught the imagination of the people and so dramatized the greatness that comes by following inspiring leadership.

As he was the destined ancestor of the Messiah, it was the most natural thing in the world for the prophets in Israel to use him and his kingly glory to crystallize in the minds of men the kingly state and everlasting dominion that would rest in due course upon the promised Seed of David.

Christ Is the Son of David

David himself was the first to receive the prophetic word that the Seed of Israel's temporal king would be her Eternal King. "I will set up thy seed after thee," was the Lord's word given by Nathan the prophet, "and I will establish his kingdom. . . . And I will stablish the throne of his kingdom for ever." In substance and thought content Gabriel reaffirmed this same truth to Mary when he said in Luke 1:33, "And he shall reign over the house of Jacob for ever; and of his kingdom there shall be no end."

"I will be his father, and he shall be my son," the word continued to David, thus formulating the Messianic statement which Paul used in Hebrews 1:5 to show that Christ was the Son of God. Then, by way of Nathan, came this assured promise: "And thine house and thy kingdom shall be established for ever before thee: thy throne shall be established for ever." (2 Sam. 7:12-16.)

Later we find David receiving direct and personal revelation relative to the perpetuity of his throne and the divinity of the Seed who should sit thereon. "The Lord hath sworn in truth unto David; he will not turn from it," came the word, that "of the fruit of thy body will I set upon thy throne. . . . I will make the horn of David to bud," and surely "shall his crown flourish." (Ps. 132:11-18.) And also: "I have made a covenant with my chosen, I have sworn unto David my servant, Thy seed will I establish for ever, and build up thy throne to all generations. . . . His seed shall endure for ever, and his throne as the sun before me." (Ps. 89:3-36.) Needless to say the inspired references are to the eternal throne of him who is Eternal and not to the temporal throne which tottered and swayed and fell, never to rise again after its original pattern.

In Hebrews 1:8-9, Paul applied these Davidic words about the eternal throne to the eternal Christ: "Thy throne, O God, is for ever and ever: the sceptre of thy kingdom is a right sceptre. Thou lovest righteousness, and hatest wickedness: therefore God, thy God, hath anointed thee with the oil of gladness above thy fellows." (Ps. 45:6-7.) And the same application should be made of these Psalmic syllables, said of "the glorious majesty of his kingdom": "Thy kingdom is an everlasting kingdom, and thy dominion endureth throughout all generations." (Ps. 145:12-13.)

Isaiah said of his future Savior: "The government shall

be upon his shoulder. . . . Of the increase of his government and peace there shall be no end, upon the throne of David, and upon his kingdom, to order it, and to establish it with judgment and with justice from henceforth even for ever." (Isa. 9:6-7.) Further: "And in mercy shall the throne be established: and he shall sit upon it in truth in the tabernacle of David, judging, and seeking judgment, and hasting righteousness." (Isa. 16:5.) Zechariah prophesied: "He shall speak peace unto the heathen: and his dominion shall be from sea even to sea, and from the river even to the ends of the earth." (Zech. 9:10.) And even Balaam, of questionable fame, proclaimed by the inspiration of the Almighty: "A Sceptre shall rise out of Israel. . . . Out of Jacob shall come he that shall have dominion." (Num. 24:17-19.)

As all the Jews knew and all the prophets from David's day onward have testified, the promised Messiah was to be the Son of David who should reign on the throne of Israel's greatest king. When Jesus performed miracles and testified of himself, an instinctive reaction among the common people was, "Is not this the son of David?" (Matt. 12:23.) Blind men sought sight at his hands with the plea: "Thou son of David, have mercy on us." (Matt. 9:27.) Even the non-Israelitish woman of Canaan claimed his attention with the cry: "O Lord, thou son of David; my daughter is grievously vexed with a devil." (Matt. 15:22.) Indeed, people on every hand so identified him and so addressed him, in all of which was the implicit realization that they were speaking to the mighty Messiah.

Truly, "Of this man's seed," the man called David, "hath God according to his promise raised unto Israel a Saviour, Jesus." (Acts 13:23.)

Christ Reigns on David's Throne

When shall the Son of David, within the full meaning of the Messianic messages, reign in power and might upon the throne of David his father?

It is true that as a mortal man he exercised justice and judgment and went forth in power and majesty among his fellowmen. But such was only a sample and a foretaste of what is to be at his Second Coming. Nearly all that is written of his power and dominion will find complete fulfillment only when he comes to dwell among men during the millennial era. Such, for instance, shall be the day when "he shall have dominion also from sea to sea, and from the river unto the ends of the earth," and when "all nations shall call him blessed." (Ps. 72:8, 17.)

Since it takes a first and a second coming to fulfill many Messianic prophecies, we of necessity must consider them here, and in the case of the Davidic-Messianic utterances show also how they apply to our Lord's Second Coming. Christ is the Son of David, the Seed of David, the inheritor, through Mary his mother, of the blood of the great king. He is also called the Stem of Jesse and the Branch, meaning Branch of David. Messianic prophecies under these headings deal with the power and dominion he shall wield as he sits on David's throne, and have reference almost exclusively to his second sojourn on planet earth.

Jesse was the father of David. Isaiah speaks of the Stem of Jesse, whom he also designates as a branch growing out of the root of that ancient worthy. He recites how the Spirit of the Lord shall rest upon him; how he shall be mighty in judgment; how he shall smite the earth and slay the wicked; and how the lamb and the lion shall lie down together in that day—all of which has reference to the Second Coming and the millennial era thereby ushered in. (Isa. 11.) As to the identity of the Stem of Jesse, the revealed word says: "Verily thus saith the Lord: It is Christ." (D&C 113:1-2.) This also means that the Branch is Christ, as we shall now see from other related scriptures.

By the mouth of Jeremiah, the Lord foretells the ancient scattering and the latter-day gathering of his chosen Israel. After they have been gathered "out of all countries whither I have driven them," after the kingdom has been restored to

Israel as desired by the ancient apostles in Acts 1:6, then this eventuality, yet future and millennial in nature, shall be fulfilled: "Behold, the days come, saith the Lord, that I will raise unto David a righteous Branch, and a King shall reign and prosper, and shall execute judgment and justice in the earth. In his days Judah shall be saved, and Israel shall dwell safely: and this is his name whereby he shall be called, THE LORD OUR RIGHTEOUSNESS." (Jer. 23:3-6.) That is to say, the King who shall reign personally upon the earth during the Millennium shall be the Branch who grew out of the house of David. He shall execute judgment and justice in all the earth because he is the Lord Jehovah, even him whom we call Christ.

Through Zechariah the Lord spoke similarly: "Thus saith the Lord of hosts: . . . I will bring forth my servant the BRANCH. . . . I will remove the iniquity of the land in one day [meaning that the wicked shall be destroyed and the millennial era of peace and righteousness commence]. In that day, saith the Lord of hosts, shall ye call every man his neighbour under the vine and under the fig tree." (Zech. 3:7-10.) Of that glorious millennial day the Lord says also: "Behold the man whose name is The BRANCH; and he shall grow up out of his place, and he shall build the temple of the Lord: Even he shall build the temple of the Lord; and he shall bear the glory, and shall sit and rule upon his throne." (Zech. 6:12-13.)

That the Branch of David is Christ is perfectly clear. We shall now see that he is also called David, that he is a new David, an Eternal David, who shall reign forever on the throne of his ancient ancestor. "It shall come to pass in that day, saith the Lord of hosts," that is, in the great millennial day of gathering, that "they shall serve the Lord their God, and David their king, whom I will raise up unto them." (Jer. 30:8-9.)

"In those days, and at that time, will I cause the Branch of righteousness to grow up unto David; and he shall execute judgment and righteousness in the land. In those days shall Judah be saved, and Jerusalem shall dwell safely: and this is the name wherewith she shall be called, The Lord our righteousness," which is to say that because the Great King himself reigns in her midst, even the city shall be called after him. "For thus saith the Lord; David shall never want a man to sit upon the throne of the house of Israel. . . . If ye can break my covenant of the day, and my covenant of the night, and that there should not be day and night in their season; Then may also my covenant be broken with David my servant, that he should not have a son to reign upon his throne." (Jer. 33:15-21.) David's temporal throne fell long centuries before our Lord was born, and that portion of Israel which had not been scattered to the ends of the earth was in bondage to the iron yoke of Rome. But the promises remain. The eternal throne shall be restored in due course with a new David sitting thereon, and he shall reign forever and ever.

In one of his great Messianic prophecies Nephi acclaimed: "There is one God and one Shepherd over all the earth." Of the Lord's First Coming and his Second Coming, this Hebrew prophet then said: "And the time cometh that he shall manifest himself unto all nations, both unto the Jews and also unto the Gentiles; and after he has manifested himself unto the Jews and also unto the Gentiles, then he shall manifest himself unto the Gentiles and also unto the Jews, and the last shall be first, and the first shall be last." (1 Ne. 13:41-42.)

Through Ezekiel, the Lord speaks of this One Shepherd in this way: "I will save my flock. . . . And I will set up one shepherd over them, and he shall feed them, even my servant David; he shall feed them, and he shall be their shepherd. And I the Lord will be their God, and my servant David a prince among them." When that day comes, "I will make with them a covenant of peace," the Lord says, meaning they shall have again the fulness of the everlasting gospel. Then "there shall be showers of blessing"; all Israel shall dwell safely and know that the Lord is their God. (Ezek. 34:22-31.)

Through Ezekiel, the Lord also tells of the coming forth of the Book of Mormon, which becomes the instrument in his hands to bring to pass the gathering of Israel. Of that day of gathering he says, "I will make them one nation in the land upon the mountains of Israel; and one king shall be king to them all." In that day he promises to "cleanse them," by baptism, "so shall they be my people, and I will be their God. And David my servant shall be king over them; and they all shall have one shepherd: they shall also walk in my judgments, and observe my statutes, and do them. And they shall dwell in the land that I have given unto Jacob my servant, wherein your fathers have dwelt; and they shall dwell therein, even they, and their children, and their children's children for ever: and my servant David shall be their prince for ever."

Then the Lord restates that his gathered people shall have his everlasting gospel with all its blessings; that he will set his sanctuary, meaning his temple, in their midst forevermore (as Zechariah recorded); and all Israel shall know that the Lord is their God. (Ezek. 37:15-28.)

How glorious shall be the coming day when the second David, who is Christ, reigns on the throne of the first David; when all men shall dwell safely; when the earth shall be dotted with temples; and when the gospel covenant shall have full force and validity in all the earth!

Christ the Lord Reigneth

"The Lord reigneth, he is clothed with majesty." (Ps. 93:1.) "The Lord is our King." (Isa. 33:22.) "He is a great King over all the earth." (Ps. 47:2.) He is that David whose throne shall be established forever. His "kingdom is an everlasting kingdom," and his "dominion endureth throughout all generations." (Ps. 145:13.)

He is "the Root of David" (Rev. 5:5), for David came by him. "I am the root and the offspring of David" (Rev. 22:16), he said, for David was his father. It was of him that the Lord said through Isaiah: "And I will clothe him with thy robe, and strengthen him with thy girdle, and I will commit thy government into his hand: and he shall be a father to the inhabitants of Jerusalem, and to the house of Judah. And the key of the house of David will I lay upon his shoulder; so he shall open, and none shall shut; and he shall shut, and none shall open. . . . And he shall be for a glorious throne to his father's house. And they shall hang upon him all the glory of his father's house." (Isa. 22:20-24.) And it was he himself who said: "These things saith he that is holy, he that is true, he that hath the key of David, he that openeth, and no man shutteth; and shutteth, and no man openeth." (Rev. 3:7.)

And the day soon cometh when that which is written shall be fulfilled: "The kingdoms of this world are become the kingdoms of our Lord, and of his Christ; and he shall reign for ever and ever." (Rev. 11:15.)

"Alleluia: for the Lord God omnipotent reigneth." (Rev. 19:6.)

MESSIAH IS THE PERFECT ONE

Messiah Is Always the Same

"From eternity to eternity he is the same." (D&C 76:4.) So it is written of that Lord who is both Jehovah and Jesus. And so it is. As the *Unembodied One,* while he dwelt in preexistence as the Firstborn spirit Son of the Eternal Elohim; as the *Embodied One,* while he dwelt among us, with his spirit shackled in a tabernacle of clay, a tabernacle created in the womb of Mary whose Son he was; as the *Disembodied One,* while he ministered for a moment among the spirits of the righteous dead; and finally as the *Reembodied One,* which he became when he rose from the dead, clothed with glory, immortality, and eternal life—in all of these states he was and is the same. He does not vary. His course is one eternal round. In every state of existence he was and is the possessor and personification of every godly attribute and characteristic in its fulness and perfection.

Among the *attributes* of God are knowledge, faith or power, justice, judgment, mercy, and truth. As the Supreme Being, as the Source of Righteousness, all such things dwell in him independently.

His *character* fits a like pattern. He was the same God before the earth was created that he now is. From everlasting to everlasting, he is merciful and gracious, slow to anger, and abundant in goodness. With him there is no variableness; he changes not; neither doth he walk in crooked paths; and his course is one eternal round. He is a God of truth; he cannot lie; his word endureth to all generations. He is no respecter of persons, and that man only is blessed who keeps his commandments. And he is love.

As to his *perfections,* they are the perfections which belong to all of the attributes of his nature, which is to say that he has all knowledge, all power, all truth, and the fulness of all good things. These statements about his character, perfections, and attributes are simply a digest and a paraphrase of the teachings of the Prophet Joseph Smith. (*Mormon Doctrine,* 2nd ed., pp. 262-63.)

And as with the Father, so with the Son. The attributes of one are the attributes of the other; the character of each is the same; and both are possessors of the same perfections in their eternal fulness. The Messiah is truly "like unto God." (Abr. 3:24.) He was such in preexistence; he is such now as he sits on the right hand of the Majesty on high; and what is of special concern to us in our Messianic studies, he was the possessor of the same character, perfections, and attributes while he dwelt as a mortal among men. Indeed, the very fact that Jesus of Nazareth enjoyed these godly graces and manifested them in the acts of his life—as he taught truth, as he wrought miracles, as he lived without sin, and as he atoned for the sins of others—the very fact that he pursued such a course is one of the great evidences that he was all that he claimed to be: the Son of God. It is to this portion of the Messianic message that we now turn our attention.

Christ Is the Word of God

Messiah is the Word of God. He speaks for the Father. His voice is the voice of the Father. He is the mouthpiece of and spokesman for the Most High. The message he delivers is one of glory and honor, of immortality and eternal life. He is thus the Messenger of Salvation.

These truths have been known and taught in all dispensations. To dramatize this high status of the Son, this peculiar prerogative he alone possessed, he bears the name-title "the Word of God." Generally this designation is associated with the creative enterprises of the Father as these are accomplished by the Son, the unique designation thus bearing witness that the Father used the Son to perform the creative acts.

Thus, in revealing to Moses the creation of "worlds without number," Deity says: "By the Son I created them, which is mine Only Begotten." Worlds come and worlds go, he said, "by the word of my power." (Moses 1:33, 35.) With reference to various creative steps taken in the organizing of this earth from existent matter, Deity said to Moses: "And this I did by the word of my power" (Moses 2:5, 16; 3:7), meaning "by the power of mine Only Begotten" (Moses 4:3). The Book of Mormon prophets also speak of "the power of his word" and point to the creation of the earth as the great manifestation of this omnipotence. (Jacob 4:9; Morm. 9:17.) Our modern revelations pick up the same theme. "All things," the Lord says, "I have created by the word of my power, which is the power of my Spirit. For by the power of my Spirit created I them." (D&C 29:30-31.)

John the Beloved began his gospel account by speaking of the then risen Lord in the same way. "In the beginning was the Word," he said, "and the Word was with God, and the Word was God. The same was in the beginning with God. All things were made by him; and without him was not anything made that was made. . . . And the Word was made flesh, and dwelt among us, (and we beheld his glory, the glory as of the only begotten of the Father,) full of grace and truth." (John 1:1-3, 14.) A more perfect rendition of John's writing was revealed to Joseph Smith in these words: "I saw his glory, that he was in the beginning, before the world was; Therefore, in the beginning the Word was, for he was the Word, even the messenger of salvation—The light and the Redeemer of the world; the Spirit of truth, who came into the world, because the world was made by him, and in him was the life of men and the light of men. The worlds were made by him; men were made by him; all things were made by him, and through him, and of him. And I, John, bear record that I beheld his glory, as the glory of the Only Begotten of the Father, full of grace and truth, even the Spirit of truth, which came and dwelt in the flesh, and dwelt among us." (D&C 93:6-11.) In this connection we should also note that his coming was announced by calling him "the messenger of the covenant." (Mal. 3:1.)

John it was also who saw the resurrected Christ in glory and was taught: "His name is called The Word of God" (Rev. 19:13), and who wrote of him as "the Word of life" (1 Jn. 1:1).

Closely associated with this concept that the Lord Jesus is the Word of God is the kindred verity that he is the Truth. "Thy word," O God, "is truth." (John 17:17.) "The word of the Lord is truth." (D&C 84:45.) Jehovah, says Isaiah, is "the God of truth" (Isa. 65:16), and when he dwells in mortality, "he shall bring forth judgment unto truth" (Isa. 42:3). That the living Word, dwelling among men as the Truth, should bring forth that truth which saves is implicit in many prophetic utterances, such as: "Thy law is the truth. . . . Thy word is true from the beginning." (Ps. 119:142, 160.) "The Lord, . . . Which made heaven, and earth, the sea, and all that therein is . . . keepeth truth for ever." (Ps. 146:5-6.) How aptly and conclusively the Lord Jesus tied all these pronouncements into himself when he said: "I am the way, the truth, and the life." (John 14:6.)

Messiah Is the Sinless One

Sin entered the world with Adam. Through his transgression man became mortal and was cast out from the presence of God. Temporal and spiritual death thus entered the world. And every accountable mortal who has lived on earth, from that day onward, has committed sin. This is inherent in the very nature of existence. It is part of the divine plan; it is a necessary requisite for all who undergo the probationary experiences of mortality.

Sin and death are absolutely universal among us mortals. There are no exceptions. "As by one man sin entered into the world, and death by sin; and so death passed upon all men, for that all have sinned." (Rom. 5:12.) "All have sinned, and come short of the glory of God." (Rom. 3:23.)

Knowing, then, that death and sin are the established, unvarying order of existence, suppose, among the teeming billions of earth's inhabitants, we found one person who did no sin and upon whom death had no power. What would we think of such a one? Truly might we exclaim: "He is God, the Son of God, the promised Messiah."

We shall speak hereafter of his power over death, noting for the present that it goes hand in hand with his sinless state. Reason alone should tell us that if there was or is or shall be one alone among all men who is sinless, he is more than a mortal and must be the One of whom the prophets spoke. Our analysis on this point might well follow this line:

First, God himself is holy and without sin. He is just and true and perfect. His ways are righteous and there is no iniquity in any of his doings.

Second, he shall come as the Mighty Messiah to save his people. When he comes he shall be without sin. No guile shall be found in his mouth. His judgments shall be just, for he is both God and God's Son.

And third, among all who have dwelt on earth, the Carpenter of Nazareth of Galilee, he only, has been without sin. He alone walked in perfect uprightness before the Father, and therefore he is the sole claimant to Messiahship. He alone is the sinless Son of God.

Having so reasoned, let us see if the revelations accord with our views.

Of the great Jehovah, they say: "He is the Rock, his work is perfect: for all his ways are judgment: a God of truth and without iniquity, just and right is he." (Deut. 32:4.) "There is no iniquity with the Lord our God, nor respect of persons, nor taking of gifts." (2 Chr. 19:7.) "Doth God pervert judgment? or doth the Almighty pervert justice?" (Job 8:3.) "Far be it from God, that he should do wickedness; and from the Almighty, that he should commit iniquity." (Job 34:10.) "The Lord our God is holy." (Ps. 99:9.) He is "the high and lofty One that inhabiteth eternity, whose name is Holy." (Isa. 57:15.) These are but samples from Holy Writ. There neither is nor can be any question whatever as to the righteousness and perfection of God.

Knowing that he is the same eternally, we would expect him to manifest the same character, perfections, and attributes as a mortal that possessed his being before his spirit entered its earthly tenement. The Messianic utterances say he will do so: "Enoch saw the day of the coming of the Son of Man, even in the flesh; and his soul rejoiced, saying: The Righteous is lifted up, and the Lamb is slain from the foundation of the world." (Moses 7:47.) The Righteous, seen by Enoch, said through Isaiah: "My righteousness shall not be abolished," and "My righteousness shall be for ever" (Isa. 51:6, 8), which of necessity means that even as he was righteous in preexistence, so shall that attribute attend him in mortality. And so Isaiah, speaking of the day of his mortal death, prophesied: "He had done no violence, neither was any deceit in his mouth." (Isa. 53:9.) Of him also the record says: "With righteousness shall he judge the poor, and reprove with equity for the meek of the earth. . . . And righteousness shall be the girdle of his loins, and faithfulness the girdle of his reins." (Isa. 11:4-5.) Also: "I the Lord have called thee in righteousness." (Isa. 42:6.) And there is, of course, much more.

Now as to his mortal life, what say the scriptures? He himself drove the point home with unerring accuracy when he asked: "Which of you convinceth me of sin?" (John 8:46), echoing, as it were, the ancient query: "Who can say," of God, "Thou hast wrought iniquity?" (Job 36:23.) Peter says, "Christ . . . did no sin, neither was guile found in his mouth." (1 Pet. 2:21-22.) Paul says, "He knew no sin" (2 Cor. 5:21);

that he "was in all points tempted like as we are, yet without sin" (Heb. 4:15); that he was "holy, harmless, undefiled, separate from sinners" (Heb. 7:26); and that he shall "appear the second time without sin unto salvation" (Heb. 9:28). John says his very name is "Faithful and True" and that "in righteousness he doth judge and make war." (Rev. 19:11.)

Truly he was and is righteous, sinless, and perfect forever, which course of conduct while in mortality identifies him beyond peradventure as the Messiah.

"The Lord Is Our Lawgiver"

Jehovah is our Lawgiver! Few eternal verities are more obvious, more axiomatic than this. The Lord God is the source of truth and light and law. He it is that ordains the way and says to men, 'Walk ye in it.' "I will give thee tables of stone, and a law, and commandments which I have written; that thou mayest teach them," he said to Moses. (Ex. 24:12.) "A law shall proceed from me" (Isa. 51:4), is his voice to Israel, and Isaiah echoes the call by proclaiming Messianically, "the isles shall wait for his law" (Isa. 42:4), and "the Lord is our lawgiver" (Isa. 33:22).

Unto what then can we liken his law, and with it what can compare? "O how love I thy law! it is my meditation all the day" (Ps. 119:97), for, "The law of the Lord is perfect" (Ps. 19:7). So sang the Psalmist. To us the Lord says: "I am the Lord thy God; and I give unto you this commandment—that no man shall come unto the Father but by me or by my word, which is my law, saith the Lord." (D&C 132:12.) And of him it is written: "He hath given a law unto all things, by which they move in their times and their seasons." (D&C 88:42.) And also: "Ye shall have no laws but my laws when I come, for I am your lawgiver, and what can stay my hand?" (D&C 38:22.) Is it any wonder that he said to the Nephites, "I am the law, and the light." (3 Ne. 15:9.)

Clearly our concern is not alone one of extolling his law,

or of identifying him as the Lawgiver, or of knowing that to him and his word all things must bow in submissive reverence. Our concern is to crystallize in the minds of men that the great Lawgiver walked among men and that his name was Jesus. "Judah is my lawgiver" (Ps. 108:8) is the Messianic proclamation that he who held the Scepter would come in that lineage. And when he came, it was still his prerogative to give the law. The prophets who went before had said: 'Thus saith the Lord: These are the words of my law; walk ye in them and live.' Our Lord followed no such pattern. Instead he assumed, as was his right, the stance of the Lawgiver himself. He altered, amended, and revoked the word of God as given by the prophets of old. "Ye have heard that it hath been said," relative to such and such, "but I say unto you," do thus and so instead. (Matt. 5.)

Truly, "There is one lawgiver, who is able to save and to destroy" (James 4:12), and he is Christ!

Messiah Giveth Living Water

Without water man dies—temporally and spiritually. Bread and breath and water, these three, they are the essentials of existence. If any one of them is withdrawn, life ceases—temporally and spiritually.

Our concern at this point is with water, with the strivings men undergo to gain it, and with the agony that engulfs the mortal soul when it is taken away. Even the Son of God—pierced, bleeding, in pain beyond recording, hanging at death's door on the cross of Calvary—had but one plea pertaining to his physical suffering, and that was the agonizing cry, "I thirst." (John 19:28.) How vital it is that men have water. A dearth of drink deals death to those so deprived. Those who dwell in deserts and pitch their tents on arid plains, as ancient Israel often did, have the need and desire for drink ever before them.

How natural it was, then, for the Lord and his prophets to use the search for water as a pattern for the search for salvation. Just as a man is spared temporally by drinking the life-giving liquids of mortality, so he is saved eternally by downing great draughts of living water. Moses at Meribah smote the rock and a great flood of water gushed forth to give drink to all Israel and their cattle, thus teaching them that if they would look to Jehovah, by whose power the miracle was wrought, they might drink forever from streams of living water. (Num. 20:1-13.) Jeremiah proclaimed that "the Lord" was "the fountain of living waters." (Jer. 17:13.) And the Lord himself, complaining about the rebellious nature of his people, said: "For my people have committed two evils; they have forsaken me the fountain of living waters, and hewed them out cisterns, broken cisterns, that can hold no water." (Jer. 2:13.) After his resurrection this same Jehovah, identifying himself as the Lord Jesus Christ, spoke similarly to Moroni in these words: "Faith, hope and charity bringeth unto me—the fountain of all righteousness." (Ether 12:28.)

Under the circumstances we might well expect to find Messianic prophecies saying that King-Messiah, during his mortal ministry, would be the source of living waters. And so it is. One of the greatest of these is Isaiah's proclamation that "a king shall reign in righteousness," and that among other things, he shall be "as rivers of water in a dry place." (Isa. 32:1-4.) Most of the Messianic utterances of this nature, however, were destined to have only partial fulfillment in the meridian of time and were to come to a glorious consummation in the dispensation of restoration when the promised King would reign personally upon the earth.

Speaking of the latter-day gathering of Israel, Jehovah's promise is: "I will open rivers in high places, and fountains in the midst of the valleys: I will make the wilderness a pool of water, and the dry land springs of water." (Isa. 41:18.) That this has reference to more than climatic changes which bring forth literal streams is shown by the latter-day revelation which speaks of the barren deserts bringing forth "pools of living water" (D&C 133:29), meaning among other things that when the desert blossoms as a rose in the literal sense of the word, it will be but a similitude of the living waters then being poured out upon the Lord's people.

Another great Messianic utterance says: "I will pour water upon him that is thirsty, and floods upon the dry ground: I will pour my spirit upon thy seed, and my blessing upon thine offspring." (Isa. 44:3.) Similar truths are found in Isaiah 41:10-20; 48:20-21; and 49:9-12. Isaiah 12 tells of a millennial day when men shall "draw water out of the wells of salvation"; and Zechariah, speaking of that same day of peace and righteousness, tells how "living waters shall go out from Jerusalem" (Zech. 14:8).

From all this it is perfectly clear that men must drink living water to be saved. As Moroni expressed it: "Come unto the fountain of all righteousness and be saved." (Ether 8:26.) And the same truths flow from the same fountain yesterday, today, and forever.

Before his mortal birth our Lord's call was: "Ho, every one that thirsteth, come ye to the waters, . . . and I will make an everlasting covenant with you." (Isa. 55:1-3; 2 Ne. 9:50.) To the Nephites he said: "Come unto me and ye shall partake of the fruit of the tree of life; yea, ye shall eat and drink of the bread and the waters of life freely." (Alma 5:34.) And Alma echoed his words by saying: "Whosoever will come may come and partake of the waters of life freely." (Alma 42:27.)

During his mortal sojourn it was the same. On the eighth day of the Feast of Tabernacles, while the priest poured water upon the altar and the words of Isaiah were sung, "With joy shall ye draw water out of the wells of salvation" (Isa. 12:3), our Lord stepped forth and proclaimed: "If any man thirst, let him come unto me, and drink." (John 7:37.) Earlier, at Jacob's Well, he had said to the woman of Samaria, "If thou knewest the gift of God, and who it is that saith to thee, Give me to drink; thou wouldest have asked of him, and he would have given thee living water. . . . Whosoever drinketh the water that I shall give him shall never thirst; but the water that I shall give him shall be in him a well of water springing up into everlasting life." (John 4:7-14.)

After his resurrection, the same proclamation was continued. The risen Lord still feeds his flock, still leads them "unto living fountains of waters" (Rev. 7:17), for, he says, "I will give unto him that is athirst of the fountain of the water of life freely" (Rev. 21:6). The message to all is: "Come. And let him that is athirst come. And whosoever will, let him take the water of life freely." (Rev. 22:17.) And the same promise has been renewed by revelation in our day. (D&C 10:66.)

Those who do come to quench their thirst, and who are true and faithful, shall drink forever from the pure fountain. As Isaiah expressed it, their "waters shall be sure" (Isa. 33:16), meaning they shall be as their Lord, enjoying and possessing the same eternal life which he lives. As he said in our day: "Unto him that keepeth my commandments I will give the mysteries of my kingdom, and the same shall be in him a well of living water, springing up unto everlasting life." (D&C 63:23.)

"I Am the Light and the Life of the World"

If there is a self-evident truth—one that needs no proof, one that must be accepted automatically by all men everywhere—it is that life and being and existence come from God. He is the Source of existence, the Creator of all things, the Originator and Organizer of the universe, the Father of Spirits. Without him there would be nothing; life comes by him; because of him all things are. He is the Life.

That this Supreme Being, who is the Author of Life, has appointed his Well-Beloved Son to stand in his place and stead, in administering salvation and giving life and light to the children of men, is the burden of the scriptures. The Lord Jesus, at his Father's behest, has become and is the Life of the World. Under the Father he is the Creator of all things. It is the Light of Christ, which "proceedeth forth from the presence of God to fill the immensity of space," that "giveth life to all things." (D&C 88:12-13.) And through him eternal life comes, so that in every sense he is the Life of the World.

Speaking Messianically, both Abinadi and Alma said, "He is the light and the life of the world." (Mosiah 16:9; Alma 38:9.) One of his meridian witnesses recorded: "In him was life; and the life was the light of men" (John 1:4); or, as translated so as to reveal how he is the life of men: "In him was the gospel, and the gospel was the life, and the life was the light of men" (JST, John 1:4). During his mortal ministry Jesus said: "As the Father hath life in himself; so hath he given to the Son to have life in himself." (John 5:26.) After his resurrection, he has continued to proclaim to the Nephites, to Moroni, and to Joseph Smith: "I am the light and the life of the world." (3 Ne. 9:18; 11:11; Ether 4:12; D&C 10:70.)

There are at least three ways, each intertwined with the others, in which our Lord is the Light of the World. These are:

1. Through the Light of Christ he governs and controls the universe and gives life to all that therein is.

2. By this same immensity-filling light—and also, to certain faithful ones, by the power of the Holy Ghost!—he enlightens the mind and quickens the understanding.

3. By his own upright, sinless, and perfect course, in preexistence, in mortality, and in resurrected glory, he sets a perfect example and is able to say to all men: "Follow thou me." (2 Ne. 31:10.)

Our understanding of the Light of Christ is limited. Finite powers and capacities cannot comprehend that which is infinite. But we do know certain basic principles, among which are these:

1. That it is the light which proceeds forth from the presence and person of Deity to fill immensity, and that it is therefore everywhere present;

2. That it is the agency of God's power, the law by which all things are governed;

3. That it is the divine power which gives life to all things, and that if it were completely withdrawn life would cease;

4. That it enlightens the mind and quickens the understanding of every person born into the world (all have a conscience!);

5. That it strives with all men (the Holy Ghost testifies but does not strive) unless and until they rebel against light and truth, at which time the striving ceases, and in that sense the Spirit is withdrawn;

6. That those who hearken to its voice come unto Christ, receive his gospel, are baptized, and gain the gift of the Holy Ghost. (Moro. 7:12-18; D&C 84:43-53; 88:7-13.)

In the light of all this, we find the ancient prophets ascribing to the Lord Jehovah all things connected with the Light of Christ, and we find the Lord Jesus and his apostles ascribing those same things to him who was Mary's Son.

Of Jehovah the scriptures say: "Thou wilt light my candle: the Lord my God will enlighten my darkness." (Ps. 18:28.) "The Lord is my light and my salvation." (Ps. 27:1.) "O send out thy light and thy truth: let them lead me." (Ps. 43:3.) "God is the Lord, which hath shewed us light." (Ps. 118:27.) "Thy word is a lamp unto my feet, and a light unto my path." (Ps. 119:105.) And much, much more.

As a means of applying all of this—and much, much more—to himself, Jesus said: "I am the light of the world." (John 9:5.)

Isaiah foretold that Israel's Messiah would come as "a light to the Gentiles" (Isa. 49:6) and that the light would pierce the darkness of error and unbelief (Isa. 60:1-3). Concerning those dwelling in "the land of Zebulun and the land of Naphtali," Israel's Messianic seer said: "The people that walked in darkness have seen a great light: they that dwell in the land of the shadow of death, upon them hath the light shined." (Isa. 9:1-2.) Matthew quoted this prophecy and pronounced its fulfillment on the occasion that Jesus, "leaving Nazareth, . . . came and dwelt in Capernaum, which is upon the sea coast, in the borders of Zabulon and Nephthalim." (Matt. 4:13-16.)

The spirit Jehovah, destined to be the mortal Jesus and the resurrected Christ, is the great Exemplar, our guide and leader, the one who everlastingly marked the way and charted the course for all of his brethren. "Be holy, for I am holy" (Lev. 11:45), was Jehovah's counsel to Israel. Peter applied these words to Christ and counseled the saints of his day that "as he which hath called you is holy, so be ye holy." (1 Pet. 1:13-16.)

When he came in resurrected glory to the Nephites he said: "Behold, I am the law, and the light. Look unto me." (3 Ne. 15:9.) Also: "Behold I am the light; I have set an example for you. . . . Therefore, hold up your light that it may shine unto the world. Behold I am the light which ye shall hold up—that which ye have seen me do." (3 Ne. 18:16, 24.)

In all dispensations the saints "rejoice" because of his "judgments. . . . For this God"—be he called Jehovah, or Jesus, or Christ—"is our God for ever and ever: he will be our guide." (Ps. 48:11-14.)

Truly, as he said to Moriancumer two thousand years before his mortal birth: "In me shall all mankind have light, and that eternally, even they who shall believe on my name." (Ether 3:14.)

Messiah Offereth Peace to All

If the scriptures teach that peace comes from the Lord Jehovah, that he is the source, author, and founder of this greatly to be desired state of mind and being, and that such a blessing and feeling comes from no other source; and if these same holy writings acclaim with equal fervor and finality that peace comes from the Lord Jesus, that he is the author and source thereof, and that none can so obtain except in and through him and by obedience to the laws of his everlasting gospel—if such are the pronouncements of all the prophets who have ever spoken on these matters, it is thereby irrefutably established that the Lord Jehovah and the Lord Jesus are one and the same. And none but those who willfully choose to reject the Spirit-borne witness, falling from the lips of Spirit-led teachers, can reach any other conclusion.

What, then, say the scriptures as to peace—whose it is, whence it comes, and how struggling, feeble, wayward man may gain it?

1. They say: *Peace comes from Jehovah.*

"Jehovah," or, as it has been Anglicized in the translation process, "the Lord," says the Psalmist, "will bless his people with peace." (Ps. 29:11.) "He will speak peace unto his people, and to his saints." (Ps. 85:8.) The great blessing, revealed through Moses and pronounced upon all Israel, contained the promise: "The Lord lift up his countenance upon thee, and give thee peace." (Num. 6:26.) And it was Jehovah himself who said, "If ye walk in my statutes, and keep my commandments, and do them, . . . I will give peace in the land." (Lev. 26:3-6.) He it is who promises to make, with the righteous of all ages, his "covenant of peace," which is the gospel covenant. (Ezek. 37:26; Isa. 54:10.)

2. They say: *The Messiah shall bring peace.*

Much that is Messianic centers around the theme of peace. As Isaiah set forth the sufferings of our Lord, when he was "wounded for our transgressions," he used this poetic and prophetic phrase: "The chastisement of our peace was upon him," meaning that through his atonement our Lord bore the chastisement for sins that, save for our faith and repentance, would justly rest upon us. (Isa. 53:5.) This same Messianic prophet, in exulting strains of joy, called our Lord "The Prince of Peace" and said, "Of the increase of his government and peace there shall be no end." (Isa. 9:6-7.)

Micah's seeric pronouncement that the Messiah would be born in "Bethlehem Ephratah" contains this graphic expression: "And this man shall be the peace," thus setting forth that the bringing forth of peace by the Messiah is so vital a part of his ministry that he is the very personification of that godly attribute. (Micah 5:2-5.) Zechariah's vision of the Man Jesus' triumphal entry into Jerusalem includes this promise: "He shall speak peace unto the heathen." (Zech. 9:9-10.) And Haggai's inspired declaration, that "the desire of all nations shall come" in the latter days to reign among restored Israel, includes this divine assurance: "In this place will I give peace, saith the Lord of hosts." (Hag. 2:5-9.)

When our Messianic friend Isaiah wrote, "How beautiful upon the mountains are the feet of him that bringeth good tidings, that publisheth peace; that bringeth good tidings of good, that publisheth salvation: that saith unto Zion, Thy God reigneth!" (Isa. 52:7), he afforded Paul the chance to identify the "good tidings" as "the gospel of peace" (Rom. 10:15), and he provided a text for Abinadi, whose sermon contained this Messianic doctrine: "O how beautiful upon the mountains are the feet of him that bringeth good tidings, that is the founder of peace, yea, even the Lord, who has redeemed his people; yea, him who has granted salvation unto his people" (Mosiah 15:18).

3. They say: *The Lord Jesus brought peace.*

It is clear that the Lord Jehovah is the source of peace for his people. It is also clear that the promised Messiah would bring peace to those same people. Fully aware of these verities, the Lord Jesus—whose very birth had been heralded by angelic choirs singing "Glory to God in the highest, and on earth peace, good will toward men" (Luke 2:14)—this same Jesus near the climax of his ministry said: "Peace I leave with you, my peace I give unto you" (John 14:27), and "in me ye might have peace" (John 16:33). That is to say: 'I am the Lord Jehovah who is the source of peace; I am the Messiah who is the founder of peace; look unto me and gain peace unto your souls.'

4. They say: *Peace comes through the gospel of him who is our Lord.*

Because he "established righteousness" among his people, Melchizedek (who is one of the prototypes of Christ) was called "the King of peace." (JST, Gen. 14:36.) Similarly, the Prince of Peace, through his gospel, establishes peace in the hearts of those who believe and obey. Peace in this life and eternal life in the world to come are the greatest of all blessings, and they are the reward reserved for those who do the works of righteousness. (D&C 59:23.)

This doctrine that the Founder of Peace brings to the faithful is interwoven through and implicit in all of the revelations. Peter counsels, "Eschew evil, . . . do good, . . . seek peace" (1 Pet. 3:11), and says that the very message of salvation which God sends to men is one of "preaching peace by Jesus Chirst" (Acts 10:36). Paul calls this same Jesus "the Lord of peace" (2 Thess. 3:16), speaks of that peace which "passeth all understanding" (Phil. 4:7), and says that "the kingdom of God" itself is "righteousness, and peace, and joy in the Holy Ghost" (Rom. 14:17). And so it goes throughout revealed writ. Peace is reserved for the faithful saints, for the meek and the upright (Ps. 37:11, 37), and for those who love the Lord's law (Ps. 119:165). On the other hand, "The wicked are like the troubled sea, when it cannot rest, whose waters cast up mire and dirt. There is no peace, saith my God, to the wicked." (Isa. 57:20-21.)

"The Lord Is Our Judge"

"Shall not the Judge of all the earth do right?" (Gen. 18:25.) So asked Abraham as he conversed with the Almighty—which raises the question: Who is the great Judge? Is it Elohim or Jehovah? Is it the Father, Son, and Holy Spirit, acting in unison as one Godhead? And what of delegated power to judge, as the ancient Twelve who shall sit with their Lord upon thrones judging certain specified ones?

By way of answer, we turn to these words of Jesus: "The Father judgeth no man, but hath committed all judgment unto the Son: That all men should honour the Son, even as they honour the Father." (John 5:22-23.) The Lord Jesus Christ is the Judge of all!

And so once again we discover that both reason and revelation testify that the Lord Jesus is the Lord Jehovah. Since the Old Testament word is that Jehovah only is the sole judge of both quick and dead, and Jesus proclaims that this power is his, it follows that Israel's Jehovah must be and is the Son of God.

To catch the vision of the Messianic message involved, let us note a few of the great prophetic utterances. Moroni speaks of the day when his spirit and body shall come forth in the resurrection and he shall come forth triumphant to meet us "before the pleasing bar of the great Jehovah, the Eternal Judge of both quick and dead." (Moro. 10:34.)

Speaking of Jehovah, various of the Old Testament prophets made such assertions as: "The Lord shall judge the people." (Ps. 7:8.) "He shall judge the world in righteousness." (Ps. 9:8.) "The Lord reigneth; . . . he shall judge the people righteously." (Ps. 96:10.) "The Lord is our judge." (Isa. 33:22.) And there are a great many more.

And speaking of Jehovah-Messiah, we find ancient prophecies of this sort: "He cometh to judge the earth: he shall judge the world with righteousness, and the people with his truth." (Ps. 96:13.) "He shall not judge after the sight of his eyes, neither reprove after the hearing of his ears: But with righteousness shall he judge the poor, and reprove with equity for the meek of the earth." (Isa. 11:3-4.) "In mercy shall the throne be established: and he shall sit upon it in truth in the tabernacle of David, judging, and seeking judgment, and hasting righteousness." (Isa. 16:5.) And again there are many more.

To Adam the Lord revealed that "the name of his Only Begotten is the Son of Man, even Jesus Christ, a righteous Judge, who shall come in the meridian of time." (Moses 6:57.) Peter, in his day, testified that "God anointed Jesus of Nazareth with the Holy Ghost and with power," that after his crucifixion the Father raised him up in glorious immortality, and that the ancient apostles were commanded to testify that "it is he which was ordained of God to be the Judge of quick and dead." (Acts 10:38-42.)

But as is not uncommon in our Messianic questing, it is to the Book of Mormon that we turn for the plainest and most perfect preannouncements of the eternal truth that judgment is the Lord's and that the Lord's name is Christ. Lehi said that all men shall stand in the presence of "the Holy Messiah, . . . to be judged of him according to the truth and holiness which is in him." (2 Ne. 2:8-10.) Jacob taught that after all men are resurrected, "they must appear before the judgment-seat of the Holy One of Israel; and then cometh the judgment," and that "he suffereth the pains of all men" and bringeth to pass the resurrection of all, so "that all might stand before him at the great and judgment day." (2 Ne. 9:15-22.) Alma was bold to say that to the Redeemer, "every knee shall bow, and every tongue confess, . . . even at the last day, when all men shall stand to be judged of him, [and] then shall they confess that he is God." (Mosiah 27:30-31.) And so the teachings go, prophet after prophet, throughout the whole history of the Nephite peoples, with the crowning statement of them all being the words of the risen Christ as he ministered personally among that favored remnant of Israel: "My Father sent me that I might be lifted up upon the cross; and after that I had been lifted up upon the cross, that I might draw all men unto me, that as I have been lifted up by men even so should men be lifted up by the Father, to stand before me, to be judged of their works, whether they be good or whether they be evil." (3 Ne. 27:14.)

The scriptural assertion that all men "shall be brought and be arraigned before the bar of Christ the Son, and God the Father, and the Holy Spirit, which is one Eternal God, to be judged according to their works, whether they be good or whether they be evil" (Alma 11:44) means simply that Christ's judicial decisions are those of the other two members of the Godhead because all three are perfectly united as one. The ancient Twelve and the Nephite Twelve, and no doubt others similarly empowered, will sit in judgment, under Christ, on selected portions of the house of Israel; but their decrees will be limited to those who love the Lord and have kept his commandments, "and none else." (D&C 29:12; 3 Ne. 27:27; Matt. 19:28.)

MESSIAH REDEEMS MANKIND

Fall and Atonement Foreordained

In Chapter 4 we set forth that Christ our Lord is the Firstborn of the Father; that the great Elohim ordained and established a gospel plan whereby the Firstborn and all his spirit kindred might advance and progress and become like their Eternal Father; that this same preeminent Spirit Son adopted the Father's plan and was chosen and foreordained to be the Savior and Redeemer therein; and that the Gospel of God thus became the gospel of Jesus Christ and was and is the plan of salvation for all men.

In Chapter 5 we saw man come to dwell on earth; we beheld the fall of Adam, which brought temporal and spiritual death into the world; and we learned thereby of the need for a Redeemer to ransom Adam and all men from the effects of the planned and foreordained fall. We saw that this mortal life became a probationary estate, and that a gracious God gave his gospel to men so they might believe on his Only Begotten and be raised, not alone in immortality, but unto eternal life; and that this gospel plan (destined to be on earth in a series of gospel dispensations) consisted of believing in Christ, accepting his atoning sacrifice, and living in harmony with his revealed laws.

Now we shall turn our attention to that infinite and eternal atonement, that redemption wrought for all mankind, which is the very heart and core and center of the gospel of our Lord. This atoning sacrifice; this redemption of the world; this most transcendent of all events from creation's dawn to the endless ages of eternity; this shedding of the blood of a God, which was to occur in Gethsemane and on Calvary; this ransom paid for man, for all forms of life, and for the very earth itself—all this rests on two foundations. Either these foundations are secure or there is no atonement of Christ, no plan of salvation, no immortality, no eternal life, and no purpose in creation. These foundations, whose importance cannot be overemphasized, are:

1. The fall of Adam whereby that greatest of all mortal men (save Jesus only) became mortal and began the process of providing bodies for those of our Father's children who kept their first estate; and

2. The divine Sonship of Him who gained power from the Father to ransom himself and all his fellow mortals from their fallen state.

We shall here show the relationship of the fall and the atonement; the matter of the divine Sonship will be developed in Chapter 25 when we consider our Lord's birth into mortality.

Lucifer Rebels and Falls

"It must needs be"—that is, it is inherent in the very nature of life and being, it is something without which there could be neither life nor being—"that there is an opposition in all things." So say the scriptures. Then they set forth that if there were no opposites—righteousness and wickedness; good and bad; life and death; corruption and incorruption; happiness and misery; sense and insensibility—there would be nothing, and "all things must have vanished away." (2 Ne. 2:10-13.) All this is self-evident. Unless there is light there can be no darkness; unless there is vice there can be no virtue; without love there is no hate; without damnation, no salvation, for all these are opposites; they are in opposition to each other.

As it happens, and we need not reason on the whys and wherefores, but simply accept the realities as they are, Lucifer (and his followers) are in opposition to the Lord and his eternal purposes. Agency means freedom of choice. With God and his goodness pulling in one direction and Satan and his evil forces pulling in the other, man is in a position to choose. Thus it is written: "Men are free according to the flesh; and all things are given them which are expedient unto man. **And they are free to choose liberty and eternal life, through the great Mediator of all men, or to choose captivity and death, according to the captivity and power of the devil;** for he seeketh that all men might be miserable like unto himself." (2 Ne. 2:27.)

Our revelations recite that Lucifer and his fellow rebels are, like us, the spirit children of the Father. Lucifer himself is a son of the morning. He and his like-minded associates comprised one-third of the hosts of heaven, and because of their open rebellion against light and truth, because they defied God and his government, knowing perfectly what the will of the Father was, they were cast out of heaven onto this earth. Their punishment: eternal damnation. Progression ceased for them. No mortal bodies would ever house their spirit forms. For them there was to be no second estate, no probationary experiences, no resurrection, no eternal life—nothing but darkness and defiance; nothing but wickedness and rebellion; nothing but hatred and evil to all eternity, because they came out in open rebellion and with a perfect knowledge of the course they then pursued and of the consequences that attended it; they fought against God. It is an awful thing to defy the Lord, to make open warfare against the Supreme Being.

"I beheld Satan as lightning fall from heaven," Jesus said. (Luke 10:18.) "And I, Lehi, according to the things which I have read, must needs suppose that an angel of God, according to that which is written, had fallen from heaven; wherefore, he became a devil, having sought that which was evil before God." (2 Ne. 2:17.) Certainly one of the scriptures Lehi had read, with spiritual insight and understanding, was Isaiah's great pronouncement setting forth how Lucifer was "fallen from heaven," which ends with the statement that he shall not "be joined" with mortals "in burial," meaning he shall have no mortal body to go down in due course to the grave. (Isa. 14:12-20.)

Truly Lucifer fell with an everlasting fall, a fall from which there is no redemption. No ransom will ever be paid for his soul. He is damned, as are those also who are his, meaning those who, with him, rebelled in the Eternal Presence. And being himself miserable, he seeks a like misery for all mankind.

Adam Obeys and Falls

To "the first man of all men" (Moses 1:34), who is called Adam, and to "the first of all women," who is Eve, "the mother of all living" (Moses 4:26)—while they were yet immortal and thus incapable of providing mortal bodies for the spirit children of the Father—the command came: "Be fruitful, and multiply, and replenish the earth." (Moses 2:28.)

Be fruitful! Multiply! Have children! The whole plan of salvation, including both immortality and eternal life for all the spirit hosts of heaven, hung on their compliance with this command. If they obeyed, the Lord's purposes would prevail.

If they disobeyed, they would remain childless and innocent in their paradisiacal Eden, and the spirit hosts would remain in their celestial heaven—denied the experiences of mortality, denied a resurrection, denied a hope of eternal life, denied the privilege to advance and progress and become like their Eternal Father. That is to say, the whole plan of salvation would have been frustrated, and the purposes of

God in begetting spirit children and in creating this earth as their habitat would have come to naught.

"Be fruitful, and multiply." 'Provide bodies for my spirit progeny.' Thus saith thy God. Eternity hangs in the balance. The plans of Deity are at the crossroads. There is only one course to follow: the course of conformity and obedience. Adam, who is Michael—the spirit next in intelligence, power, dominion, and righteousness to the great Jehovah himself—Adam, our father, and Eve, our mother, must obey. They must fall. They must become mortal. Death must enter the world. There is no other way. They must fall that man may be.

Such is the reality. Such is the rationale. Such is the divine will. Fall thou must, O mighty Michael. Fall? Yes, plunge down from thy immortal state of peace, perfection, and glory to a lower existence; leave the presence of thy God in the garden and enter the lone and dreary world; step forth from the garden to the wilderness; leave the flowers and fruits that grow spontaneously and begin the battle with thorns, thistles, briars, and noxious weeds; subject thyself to famine and pestilence; suffer with disease; know pain and sorrow; face death on every hand—but with it all bear children; provide bodies for all those who served with thee when thou led the hosts of heaven in casting out Lucifer, our common enemy.

Yes, Adam, fall; fall for thine own good; fall for the good of all mankind; fall that man may be; bring death into the world; do that which will cause an atonement to be made, with all the infinite and eternal blessings which flow therefrom.

And so Adam fell as fall he must. But he fell by breaking a lesser law—an infinitely lesser law—so that he too, having thereby transgressed, would become subject to sin and need a Redeemer and be privileged to work out his own salvation, even as would be the case with all those upon whom the effects of his fall would come.

Adam and Eve Bear Children

Death and mortality go together; they are inseparably intertwined; one cannot exist without the other. Mortality is the state in which men are subject to death, and the existence of death is what makes man or any living creature mortal. And with mortality comes child bearing; mortal creatures father mortal children; mortality is the state where bodies are made of the dust of the earth to provide temporary residences for spirit creations.

And so, Adam and Eve partook of the forbidden fruit, were driven out of the Garden of Eden, "And they have brought forth children; yea, even the family of all the earth." (2 Ne. 2:20.) Every member of the human race is a descendant of the first man. Adam is our common progenitor. There are no exceptions.

Lehi, whose inspired words are so pointed and clear as to the heaven-directed fall of our first primeval parents, tells us that "if Adam had not transgressed he would not have fallen, but he would have remained in the garden of Eden." (2 Ne. 2:22.) Had this been the case, the billions of mortals who have dwelt on this lowly planet during the past six thousand years would still be spirit beings in the presence of the Lord; they would still be waiting for their mortal probation.

Having so taught with reference to the human race, Lehi expands the principle to cover every form of life, animals, plants, the fowls of the air, and the fish of the watery world; for all of them there is neither mortality nor death until the results of the fall were forthcoming. "All things which were created must have remained in the same state in which they were after they were created," Lehi says, "and they must have remained forever, and had no end." (2 Ne. 2:22.) That is, Edenic immortality would have reigned forever in every department of creation, among all created things, and there would have been no death for any form of life. It must be remembered that this earth and all forms of life were created in a paradisiacal state, that its present mortal state commenced with the fall, and that it will be renewed and receive again its paradisiacal state when the Lord comes to usher in the millennial era.

Of this Edenic or paradisiacal state of our first parents, Lehi says: "And they would have had no children; wherefore they would have remained in a state of innocence, having no joy, for they knew no misery; doing no good, for they knew no sin." (2 Ne. 2:23.) Eve spoke similarly when she gave forth this inspired utterance: "Were it not for our transgression we never should have had seed, and never should have known good and evil, and the joy of our redemption, and the eternal life which God giveth unto all the obedient." (Moses 5:11.)

This doctrine of the fall, of mortality and death beginning on earth, of the consequent peopling of the world, and of the redemption thereby required to save man, the earth, and all things thereon from the effects of the fall, has been known and taught by prophets in all dispensations. And all teachings connected therewith that occurred before the coming of Christ were Messianic in the very nature of things.

It was Enoch who said: "Because that Adam fell, we are; and by this fall came death; and we are made partakers of misery and woe. . . . [But] the Son of God hath atoned for original guilt, wherein the sins of the parents cannot be answered upon the heads of the children, for they are whole from the foundation of the world." (Moses 6:48-54.) And it was Father Lehi who phrased one of the most noted of all statements about the fall in these words: "Adam fell that men might be; and men are, that they might have joy. And the Messiah cometh in the fulness of time, that he may redeem the children of men from the fall." (2 Ne. 2:25-26.)

Christ Atones and Redeems

"Of every tree of the garden thou mayest freely eat" were the words of the Lord God to Adam, "But of the tree of the knowledge of good and evil, thou shalt not eat of it, nevertheless, thou mayest choose for thyself, for it is given unto thee; but, remember that I forbid it, for in the day thou eatest thereof thou shalt surely die." (Moses 3:16-17.) Adam ate, as eat he must; and Adam died, as die he must; and the death thereby brought into the world passed upon all mankind. Having transgressed and become mortal, Adam was cast out of the garden, lest he then partake of the fruit of the tree of life and, "having no space for repentance," live forever in his sins. Thus, "our first parents were cut off both temporally and spiritually from the presence of the Lord." (Alma 42:5-7.) Death reigned through Adam.

The first death, in point of time, was spiritual. Spiritual death is to die as pertaining to the things of the Spirit; it is to die as pertaining to the things of righteousness; it is to be cast out of the presence of the Lord, in which presence spirituality and righteousness abound. Adam died this death when he left Eden, and he remained dead until he was born again by the power of the Spirit following his baptism.

Temporal death is the natural death. It consists of the separation of the body and the spirit, the one going to the grave, the other to a world of waiting spirits to await the day of resurrection. Adam died temporally within a thousand years, which is a day unto the Lord.

Thus the *temporal fall* is to die and lose the house prepared as an habitation for the eternal spirit, and the *spiritual fall* is to be denied the presence of God and the righteousness which there abounds.

"To atone is to ransom, reconcile, expiate, redeem, reclaim, absolve, propitiate, make amends, pay the penalty." (*Mormon Doctrine,* 2nd ed., p. 62.) Our Lord's atoning sacrifice was one in which he conquered both temporal and spiritual death. Since by one man, Adam, death entered the world, so by one man, Christ, death is abolished. It ceases; it is no more. Life alone remains. "As in Adam all die, even so in Christ shall all be made alive." (1 Cor. 15:22.) All men come forth from the grave in immortality; all are resurrected. Adam's fall enables body and spirit to separate in the natural death; Christ's atonement causes body and spirit to reunite, inseparably, in immortality, never again to see that corruption which returns a mortal body to the dust whence its elements came. "O grave, where is thy victory?" (1 Cor. 15:55.) Truly, it is swallowed up by Him who holds the keys of death.

But immortality alone does not suffice. Those who inherit realms where the faces of God and Christ are never seen shall have immortality. The full glory of the atoning sacrifice of the Holy Messiah causes man to return to the presence of his God and to enjoy that kind and quality and state of life which is the possession of him who is the Father of us all. Those who, through faith and repentance and righteousness, are redeemed from the spiritual fall are raised not alone in immortality but unto eternal life. Whereas they were once dead as pertaining to the things of the Spirit, now they are alive in Christ and enjoy the fulness of the blessings of the Holy Spirit. Whereas they were dead as pertaining to the things of righteousness, now they are clean and pure and holy, and their immortal souls radiate righteousness. Whereas, being unclean and unworthy, they had been cast out of the presence of their Lord, now they are welcomed into his bosom, the light of his countenance shines upon them, and they dwell in the presence of the Father and Son forever. They are reconciled to God spiritually. They are redeemed in the full sense of the word. They have attained at-onement through the atonement.

It is clear; it is plain; it is perfect—the fall is father to the atonement. As Moroni expressed it, God "created Adam, and by Adam came the fall of man. And because of the fall of man came Jesus Christ, . . . and because of Jesus Christ came the redemption of man." (Morm. 9:12.)

Thus, if there had been no Adam, there would be no need for Christ. Those who are redeemed by him who is God's Son are the descendants of Adam. "His blood atoneth for the sins of those who have fallen by the transgression of Adam." (Mosiah 3:11.) "The atonement . . . was prepared from the foundation of the world for all mankind, which ever were since the fall of Adam, or who are, or who ever shall be even unto the end of the world. And this is the means whereby salvation cometh. And there is none other salvation save this." (Mosiah 4:7-8.)

Implicit in the doctrine of the fall and the consequent atonement is the bitter reality—if such it must be to those whose spiritual understanding has not yet been opened to the full truth—that there were no pre-Adamites, for mortality, death, and procreation began with Adam. And there is no salvation provided for any except Adam's seed, for it is they for whom Christ died.

Salvation Comes by Obedience

Redemption from the temporal fall, from the natural death, is a free gift; immortality comes to all men. But redemption from the spiritual fall comes by obedience to the laws and ordinances of the gospel. Its receipt is conditional. All mankind may be saved if they will believe and obey. "They that believe not," though they have been "raised in immortality," shall remain forever separated from the Lord and his righteousness, "for they cannot be redeemed from their spiritual fall, because they repent not; For they love darkness rather than light, and their deeds are evil, and they receive their wages of whom they list to obey." (D&C 29:43-45.) The atonement of Christ—coupled with conformance to his laws!—leads to a celestial inheritance.

"Redemption cometh in and through the Holy Messiah, . . . unto all those who have a broken heart and a contrite spirit; and unto none else." (2 Ne. 2:6-7.) So spake Lehi. "And he cometh into the world that he may save all men if they will hearken unto his voice." (2 Ne. 9:21.) So spake Jacob. "Speak of the atonement of Christ, and attain to a perfect knowledge of him"; through faith gain "a good hope of glory in him"; and "be reconciled" to God that ye may "be presented as the first-fruits of Christ" unto him. (Jacob 4:11-12.) So Jacob continues to speak.

From King Benjamin, as he quoted the words of an angel, we learn: Christ "cometh unto his own, that salvation might come unto the children of men, even through faith on his name. . . . For salvation cometh to none . . . except it be through repentance and faith on the Lord Jesus Christ. . . . For the natural man is an enemy to God, and has been from the fall of Adam, and will be, forever and ever, unless he yields to the enticings of the Holy Spirit, and putteth off the natural man and becometh a saint through the atonement of Christ the Lord, and becometh as a child, submissive, meek, humble, patient, full of love, willing to submit to all things which the Lord seeth fit to inflict upon him, even as a child doth submit to his father." (Mosiah 3:8-19.) Again from King Benjamin: "The atonement . . . has been prepared from the foundation of the world, that thereby salvation might come to him that should put his trust in the Lord, and should be diligent in keeping his commandments, and continue in the faith even unto the end of his life." (Mosiah 4:6.)

And so, if need be, we might continue until we fill volumes. Everywhere and always when inspired men speak or write of being redeemed from the spiritual fall, of gaining salvation in the presence of Gods and angels, their voice is one of faith, repentance, baptism, and of receiving the Holy Ghost, and of thereafter pressing forward with steadfastness and devotion conforming to every principle of eternal truth.

What If There Were No Atonement?

If there were no creation, we would not be, neither the earth, nor any life thereon. All things, in effect, would vanish away. And if there were no atonement, the purposes of creation would be frustrated; man would remain lost and fallen forever; there would be no resurrection nor eternal life;

Adam and all his posterity would be as Lucifer, cast out, damned, without hope, lost forever.

The Book of Mormon prophets have made these things exceedingly clear. In plain words, as they proclaimed the infinite glories of the atonement, they have affirmed such things as: "Were it not for the atonement, which God himself shall make for the sins and iniquities of his people, . . they must unavoidably perish. . . . For . . . there could not any man be saved except it were through the redemption of God." (Mosiah 13:28, 32; 15:19; 16:4; Jacob 7:12.) "There could be no redemption for mankind save it were through the death and sufferings of Christ, and the atonement of his blood." (Alma 21:9.)

Indeed, it is Nephi's brother Jacob to whom we turn for what is probably the clearest explanation found in any scripture now extant for the doctrinal explanation as to why all men would be lost if there were no atonement. "Our flesh must waste away and die," he says, which fact is one of the truisms of life. Then he puts death in its true perspective in the eternal plan with this explanation: "For as death hath passed upon all men, to fulfil the merciful plan of the great Creator, there must needs be a power of resurrection, and the resurrection must needs come unto man by reason of the fall; and the fall came by reason of transgression; and because man became fallen they were cut off from the presence of the Lord." (2 Ne. 9:4-6.) Thus, Adam accomplished his mission to fall and create the need for a Redeemer.

What then of redemption, of the promised deliverance, of the expiatory sacrifice of Him who did no sin, "who layeth down his life according to the flesh, and taketh it again by the power of the Spirit, that he may bring to pass the resurrection of the dead"? (2 Ne. 2:8.) Of his sinless sacrifice Jacob said: "It must needs be an infinite atonement—save it should be an infinite atonement this corruption could not put on incorruption." (2 Ne. 9:7.) Save for the infinite power of this, the most selfless act ever performed, Paul would never have been able to write of man's body: "It is sown in corruption; it is raised in incorruption: It is sown in dishonour; it is raised in glory: it is sown in weakness; it is raised in power: It is sown a natural body; it is raised a spiritual body." (1 Cor. 15:42-44.)

Save for this atonement, Jacob continues, "the first judgment which came upon man"—his banishment from the presence of the Lord because he transgressed the law and partook of the forbidden fruit, and also the natural death that attends his newly found mortal state—"must needs have remained to an endless duration. And if so, this flesh must have laid down to rot and to crumble to its mother earth, to rise no more." (2 Ne. 9:7.) There would have been no resurrection, no immortality, no reunion of body and spirit, no victory over the grave—nothing but endless death.

"But behold, all things have been done in the wisdom of him who knoweth all things." (2 Ne. 2:24.) The purposes of the Almighty neither have been nor can be frustrated. The fall was part of his plan; he designed and decreed it from the beginning. Its gloom is to turn into joy and gladness as both temporal and spiritual death are abolished in Gethsemane and on Calvary. And so Jacob exclaims: "O the wisdom of God, his mercy and grace! For behold, if the flesh should rise no more our spirits must become subject to that angel who fell from before the presence of the Eternal God, and became the devil, to rise no more." (2 Ne. 9:8.) Subject to whom? To Lucifer, the traitor and rebel who defied Deity and spread the woes of war in the heavenly courts. Christ is now our King and we worship him because we will it so. Had there been no atonement Lucifer would have been our eternal head and we would have worshiped him because he willed it so. Agency and freedom would have ceased for all those whom God had sired.

But this is not all. Jacob continues: "And our spirits must have become like unto him, and we become devils, angels to a devil, to be shut out from the presence of our God, and to remain with the father of lies, in misery, like unto himself." (2 Ne. 9:9.) Devils! Angels to a devil! Damned souls, denied a grave, denied a resurrection, purposeless creatures in whose souls the light we once had would become darkness!

"God himself shall come down among the children of men, and shall redeem his people." (Mosiah 15:1.) He shall redeem them from that (otherwise) everlasting death which is the grave, and that (otherwise) everlasting death which is eternal, abysmal darkness where none of the light of heaven is found, and where they would have no choice but to grovel before the Angel of Darkness. Ought we not, then, as did our friend Jacob, extol our Redeemer and Savior in such words of doctrine and beauty as these:

"O how great the goodness of our God, who prepareth a way for our escape from the grasp of this awful monster; yea, that monster, death and hell, which I call the death of the body, and also the death of the spirit.

"And because of the way of deliverance of our God, the Holy One of Israel, this death, of which I have spoken, which is the temporal, shall deliver up its dead; which death is the grave.

"And this death of which I have spoken, which is the spiritual death, shall deliver up its dead; which spiritual death is hell; wherefore, death and hell must deliver up their dead, and hell must deliver up its captive spirits, and the grave must deliver up its captive bodies, and the bodies and the spirits of men will be restored one to the other; and it is by the power of the resurrection of the Holy One of Israel.

"O how great the plan of our God! For on the other hand, the paradise of God must deliver up the spirits of the righteous, and the grave deliver up the body of the righteous; and the spirit and the body is restored to itself again, and all men become incorruptible, and immortal, and they are living souls, having a perfect knowledge like unto us in the flesh, save it be that our knowledge shall be perfect.

"O the greatness of the mercy of our God, the Holy One of Israel! For he delivereth his saints from that awful monster the devil, and death, and hell, and that lake of fire and brimstone, which is endless torment." (2 Ne. 9:10-13, 19.)

Chapter 14

MESSIAH ATONES AND RANSOMS

Who Has Known of the Atonement?

How widespread has the knowledge been that salvation is in Christ because of his atoning sacrifice? Who has known that Adam our father—the great Michael, who led the hosts of heaven when Lucifer unwillingly left his heavenly home—that this noble personage who was "the first flesh upon the earth" (Moses 3:7) is he who laid the foundation for Messiah's ministry?

These are questions to which there are clear and positive answers; this is a field in which there need be no uncertainty, no misunderstanding, no speculation. All of the prophets, all of the saints, and all of the Lord's people in all dispensations have known of the fall, the atonement, and the salvation available to all men as a result thereof; for it is this very knowledge that makes a man a prophet, that sets a person apart as a saint, and that identifies an individual as one of the Lord's people.

This whole work—*The Promised Messiah: The First Coming of Christ*—contains one continuous recitation and analysis of how and under what circumstances and in what ways this knowledge was had and taught and foretold. For our present purposes let us sample some of the most explicit and plain of these prophetic utterances.

Lehi's Seed Testified of Atonement

Lehi, father of the Nephite and Lamanite nations, received from a heavenly visitant a book in which he read of the coming of a Messiah and the redemption of the world. (1 Ne. 1.) Later he taught plainly of the fall, with all its ills, and of the atonement, with all its blessings. (2 Ne. 2.) Nephi gloried in the redemption of his soul from hell (2 Ne. 1:15) and taught of the atonement, which is infinite for all mankind (2 Ne. 25:16). Jacob propounded some of the most fundamental concepts about the infinite and eternal atonement that are found in any scriptures. (2 Ne. 9.) An angel from heaven recited to King Benjamin what well may be the greatest sermon ever delivered on the atonement of Christ the Lord. (Mosiah 3.) Abinadi made it clear that God himself would redeem his people (Mosiah 13:32-33), that were it not for this redemption all mankind must have perished, and that the Lord redeemeth none of those who rebel against him and die in their sins (Mosiah 15).

Alma left us some of the most extensive utterances now known about the great plan of redemption. It is he who tells us, among other things, that "the time is not far distant [it was then about 83 B.C.] that the Redeemer liveth and cometh among his people," and that he would be the Son of God. (Alma 7:7-13.) "He cometh to redeem those who will be baptized unto repentance, through faith on his name," Alma says. (Alma 9:27.) Alma's explanations to Corianton about the fall and the great plan of redemption that it necessitated are superlative in every respect. (Alma 42.)

Amulek, who learned both from Alma and directly from the Spirit of the Lord, bore similar testimonies to those of his missionary companion. It was he who taught that the Son of God "shall come into the world to redeem his people; and he shall take upon him the transgressions of those who believe on his name; and these are they that shall have eternal life, and salvation cometh to none else." (Alma 11:37-45.) His explanations of the fall, the plan of redemption, and the atoning sacrifice of the Son of God, as these are recorded in the 12th and 34th chapters of Alma, show forth prophetic insight that is seldom equaled and never surpassed.

Nephi the son of Helaman spoke much of the atonement, including the fact that Abraham and the prophets who lived thousands of years before the coming of the Son of God in the flesh knew that their promised Redeemer would come and save them. (Hel. 8:14-23.) And Samuel the Lamanite was not one whit behind his Nephite brethren in proclaiming like eternal truths. (Hel. 14.)

Israel's Prophets Testified of Atonement

This partial summary of what the Hebrew prophets on the American continent knew about the fall of our first parents and about Him whose atoning and redeeming sacrifice brought to pass the purposes of the Father of us all—these plain and precious expositions of eternal truth found in the most correct of all books, the Book of Mormon, do not stand alone. Our Lehite brethren in America were one with their Israelitish kin in what men choose to call the Old World. The Biblical seers and revelators, inspired by the same spirit which spake peace to the hearts of their New World kindred, also knew and wrote of the same eternal truths.

As appears from the present Biblical accounts, Isaiah, the son of Amoz, commonly praised as the chief Messianic prophet, is the one who knew and taught more about redemption and atonement than any of Israel's seers. Let us now sample what his inspired pen has left us.

Abinadi preaches of "the coming of the Messiah"; states plainly "that God himself should come down among the children of men, and take upon him the form of a man, and go forth in mighty power upon the face of the earth"; and makes it clear that this doctrine, "that God himself should redeem his people," has been taught by "all the prophets who have prophesied since the world began," and that all have "spoken more or less concerning these things." (Mosiah 13:33-34.)

I will make a more affirmative declaration than did Abinadi, which is, that not only have all the prophets "spoken more or less concerning these things," but that prophetic utterances about Christ and his atonement have been the most prominent part of the preachments of all the prophets, and that the testimony of Jesus consisted in knowing by revelation from the Holy Ghost that our Lord's redemption was and is the greatest work ever wrought.

But as to Abinadi's witness, having made the Spirit-guided utterance that was his, he then chose to quote as his chief illustration the entire 53rd chapter of Isaiah. To have the picture before us, let us quote a few phrases from that chapter, all of which are clear and plain when read in the light of the Nephite explanations to which we have already alluded. Of the atoning sacrifice of the future Messiah, Isaiah said:

> Surely he has borne our griefs, and carried our sorrows.
> He was wounded for our transgressions.
> He was bruised for our iniquities.
> The chastisement of our peace was laid upon him.
> With his stripes we are healed.
> The Lord has laid on him the iniquities of us all.
> He is brought as a lamb to the slaughter.
> He was cut off out of the land of the living.
> For the transgression of my people was he stricken.
> It pleased the Lord to bruise him; he hath put him to grief.
> Thou shalt make his soul an offering for sin.
> He shall see the travail of his soul.
> By his knowledge shall my righteous servant justify many; for he shall bear their iniquities.
> He hath poured out his soul unto death.
> He bore the sins of many, and made intercession for the transgressors. (Mosiah 14; Isaiah 53.)

Chapter 15 of Mosiah contains Abinadi's prophetic interpretation of these and the other Messianic pronouncements of Isaiah 53. As our New Testament now stands, we find Matthew (Matt. 8:17), Philip (Acts 8:27-35), Paul (Rom. 4:25), and Peter (1 Pet. 2:24-25) all quoting, paraphrasing, enlarging upon, and applying to the Lord Jesus various of the verses in this great 53rd chapter of Isaiah. How many sermons have been preached, how many lessons have been taught, how many testimonies have been borne—both in ancient Israel and in the meridian of time—using the utterances of this chapter as the text, we can scarcely imagine.

Who Is the Redeemer?

The great question confronting all men of all ages of time is whether the word of salvation is in Christ or whether (if men are to be ransomed from their fallen state) we must look for another. Men are. They live and move and have a being. All are mortal; all are fallen; death reigns supreme over all the sons of Adam. The problem is one of finding a Redeemer, lest all mankind be lost eternally.

Lucifer, our common enemy, hearing the invitation of the Father which said in effect: 'Whom shall I send to be my Son, to redeem mankind, to work out the infinite and eternal atonement' (Abr. 3:27)—Lucifer who is Satan stepped forth and said: "Behold, here am I, send me, I will be thy son, and I will redeem all mankind, that one soul shall not be lost, and surely I will do it; wherefore give me thine honor." (Moses 4:1.) That his offer was declined with power all are aware; and then burst forth that war with unrighteousness which, starting in the very heavens themselves, continues now among us here on earth. (Rev. 12.)

That no man of himself, and no mass of men through any combined power that in them lies, can bring to pass a ransom, a redemption, a resurrection, is not open to question. "None of them can by any means redeem his brother, nor give to God a ransom for him: . . . That he should still live for ever, and not see corruption." (Ps. 49:7-9.) "There is not any man that can sacrifice his own blood which will atone for the sins of another." (Alma 34:11.) No, never! Man can no more redeem himself than he can create himself. It takes a God to create and to redeem. And so Abinadi says: "God himself shall come down among the children of men, and shall redeem his people." (Mosiah 15:1.)

The issue then is: Who, if anyone, is the God who has or will redeem mankind? Where, if anywhere, is there a Savior of the world? Is salvation in Christ, or look we for another? Who is the Redeemer of men?

By opening the scriptures, almost at random we find the answers pleading to be believed. "I am the Only Begotten of the Father," came the word to Adam, and "as thou hast fallen thou mayest be redeemed, and all mankind, even as many as will." (Moses 5:9.) "I am he who was prepared from the foundation of the world to redeem my people" are the words of our Spirit Lord, spoken to Moriancumer millenniums before His mortal birth. And then He ties redemption in to Him who will be born in Bethlehem, saying simply: "Behold, I am Jesus Christ." (Ether 3:14.) "Redeem Israel, O God" (Ps. 25:22) was the pleading prayer of the prophets, and the echoing answer of the Spirit was, "The Lord redeemeth the soul of his servants: and none of them that trust in him shall be desolate" (Ps. 34:22).

Among the Lord's ancient people, no knowledge was more precious, no doctrine more cherished, than that "God was their rock, and the high God their redeemer." (Ps. 78:35.) Isaiah delighted to designate his Deity by the exalted name-titles Redeemer and Savior, doing so in a score of passages. He identified him specifically as the Lord Jehovah and "the Holy One of Israel" (Isa. 41:14; 43:14), as "the Lord of hosts" (Isa. 47:4), as "the Redeemer of Israel" (Isa. 49:7), as "thy Saviour and thy Redeemer, the mighty One of Jacob" (Isa. 49:26), and as "The God of the whole earth" (Isa. 54:5). How plain and precious are the words of the Great Jehovah, announcing to all who will hear: "I am the

Lord thy God, the Holy One of Israel, thy Saviour." (Isa. 43:3.)

Similar usage of these ransoming titles is found in the Book of Mormon. In more than forty passages her prophets speak of the Redeemer, and in a dozen he is called the Savior. Among others, the Book of Mormon speaks of the Messiah, who is the "Lord," the "Savior of the world," and the "Redeemer of the world" (1 Ne. 10:4-5, 14; 2 Ne. 1:10), and of "the gospel" of the Redeemer (1 Ne. 15:14). It promises that gathered Israel will come to know "that the Lord is their Savior and their Redeemer, the Mighty One of Israel." (1 Ne. 22:12; 2 Ne. 10:2.) It states plainly that "Jesus Christ" is the "Redeemer" (Alma 37:9), and says in so many words "that the Lamb of God is the Son of the Eternal Father, and the Savior of the world; and that all men must come unto him, or they cannot be saved" (1 Ne. 13:40).

But with it all—and the scriptures are not remiss in recording revelations relative to the redemption wrought by the Redeemer—what is more tender and true than the testimony of Job, spoken out of the depths of a perfect knowledge: "I know that my redeemer liveth, and that he shall stand at the latter day upon the earth: And though after my skin worms destroy this body, yet in my flesh shall I see God: Whom I shall see for myself, and mine eyes shall behold, and not another; though my reins be consumed within me." (Job 19:25-27.)

All this, known and believed of old, was revealed anew in the day that Jesus came to dwell in the flesh, even as it has been given yet again in our day. Of himself, while ministering among his fellowmen, Jesus said: "The Son of man came . . . to give his life a ransom for many" (Matt. 20:28)—that is, to ransom men from the effects of the fall, to pay the penalty for a broken law, to purchase those who otherwise were lost, to redeem his fellowmen.

After paying the price, after effecting the redeeming sacrifice, after he had himself come forth in immortality, he said: "By me redemption cometh. . . . And whoso cometh unto me with a broken heart and a contrite spirit, him will I baptize with fire and with the Holy Ghost. . . . Behold, I have come unto the world to bring redemption unto the world, to save the world from sin." (3 Ne. 9:17-22; Morm. 7:7; 9:12-14.)

We might say more—ten or a hundred or a thousand times more—all of which would but echo and re-echo the rolling thunders of eternity as they forever acclaim and re-acclaim that Christ our Lord is the Redeemer and Savior of the world; that he paid the ransom; that redemption comes by him; and that we should therefore glorify and praise his name forever.

Christ Freeth the Prisoners

We have seen that if there were no atonement of Christ, all mankind would be lost eternally—none would be resurrected; the bodies of all would remain in their graves forever; the spirits of all would remain dead as to the things of righteousness; all would become devils, angels to a devil, subject to the father of lies forever; and the whole plan of salvation, and the very purposes of creation itself, would be frustrated and come to naught. We have also seen that through Christ none of this will happen, but men instead will be saved from death (which is the grave), from hell (which is spiritual death), from the devil (who is Lucifer the liar), and from endless torment (which is and would be the state of uncleansed souls).

Now let us review those Messianic prophecies which describe in a most graphic way how the Lord saves men from the direful fate that would be theirs if he had not atoned for their sins. It is known as freeing the hosts of men from prison—from the prison of death, of hell, of the devil, and of endless torment. And how apt and pointed the illustration is, for the prisons of ancient times were hell holes of death, disease, and despair. They were dungeons of filth, corruption, and creeping denizens. Sheol itself was known as the pit, the dungeon of despair, the nether realms of torment, the Hades of hell. To be in prison was worse than a living hell, and to be freed therefrom was to arise from death to life. It is no wonder that the prophetic mind seized upon this illustration to teach what the Redeemer would do to ransom men from the fate that would be theirs if there were no atonement.

Thus it is that the Messianic witnesses proclaimed: "The Lord [who is Jehovah!] looseth the prisoners." (Ps. 146:7.) The Lord looketh down "from the height of his sanctuary, from heaven"; he heareth "the groaning of the prisoner" and looseth "those that are appointed to death." (Ps. 102:19-20.) Even those that "sit in darkness and in the shadow of death," who are "bound in affliction and iron; Because they rebelled against the words of God, and contemned the counsel of the most High"—even these, "He brought down their heart with labour; they fell down, and there was none to help. Then they cried unto the Lord in their trouble, and he saved them out of their distresses. He brought them out of darkness and the shadow of death, and brake their bands in sunder. Oh that men would praise the Lord for his goodness, and for his wonderful works to the children of men!" (Ps. 107:10-15.)

The prisoners even in hell cry out and the Lord hears! "Bring my soul out of prison," each repentant one pleads, "that I may praise thy name." (Ps. 142:7.) Of the wicked in general, and of those who perished in the flood of Noah in particular, Deity decrees: "I will shut them up; a prison have I prepared for them. And That which I have chosen [who is Christ] shall return unto me, and until that day they shall be in torment." (Moses 7:36-39.)

Isaiah's voice is also heard in the prophetic chorus that tells of prisoners being freed from their chains of darkness and hell. In one of his long Messianic prophecies that tells many things relative to our Lord's mortal ministry, Isaiah includes the promise that the Messiah will come "to open the blind eyes, to bring out the prisoners from the prison, and them that sit in darkness out of the prison house." (Isa.

42:7.) In contrast, Isaiah says that Lucifer, who sought redeeming power and was rejected, shall himself "be brought down to hell, to . . . the pit," and it shall be said of him, "Is this the man . . . that opened not the house of his prisoners." (Isa. 14:12-17.) In another passage Isaiah foretells that the Messiah, "in a day of salvation," shall "say to the prisoners, Go forth." He shall command "them that are in darkness, Shew yourselves, . . . for he . . . hath mercy on them." (Isa. 49:8-10.)

And in yet another passage, dealing also with several subjects, Isaiah records the voice of the Lord, speaking in the first person, relative to his coming ministry as the Messiah. These words are included: "The Spirit of the Lord God is upon me; because the Lord hath anointed me . . . to proclaim liberty to the captives, and the opening of the prison to them that are bound." (Isa. 61:1.) Of this and the longer passage of which it is a part, the Man Jesus, in Nazareth of Galilee, speaking in the synagogue on the sabbath day, bore record of his own divine Sonship by saying, "This day is this scripture fulfilled in your ears." (Luke 4:16-21.)

Messiah Visits Spirits in Prison

This doctrine that the Lord will free the prisoners from their prison, that he will deliver them from the depths of their dungeon, and that they will come forth from the pit and be free—free from the sorrow of sin, free from the chains of hell, free from that spiritual death which is to be dead as pertaining to the things of righteousness—all this is part of the glorious doctrine of salvation for the dead, and it includes the fact that our Lord ministered personally to the spirits in prison.

The doctrine of salvation for the dead is that all who die without a knowledge of the gospel, without a knowledge of Christ and his atoning sacrifice, without having the opportunity to believe and obey in this life and thereby qualify for celestial salvation—the doctrine of salvation for the dead is that all such, if they would have received the gospel with all of their hearts, had it been available to them, all such shall hear and believe and obey in the spirit world and thereby become heirs of the celestial kingdom of heaven. Gospel ordinances—baptisms, endowments, marriages, sealings—will be performed for them vicariously by those yet in mortality.

It was of these that Zechariah prophesied when as part of a longer Messianic utterance, he spoke of "prisoners of hope"; it was of these that he gave assurance that "the Lord their God shall save them." He gives the Messianic message in these words: "By the blood of thy covenant"—that is, because of the gospel covenant, which is efficacious because of the shedding of the blood of Christ—"I have sent forth thy prisoners out of the pit wherein is no water." (Zech. 9:11-16.) "Wherein is no water"—how aptly and succinctly this crystallizes the thought that the saving water, which is baptism, is an earthly ordinance and cannot be performed by spirit beings while they dwell in the spirit world. Did not Paul say in this same connection, "What shall they do which are baptized for the dead, if the dead rise not at all? why are they then baptized for the dead?" (1 Cor. 15:29.)

"It shall come to pass," intones Isaiah, "that the Lord shall punish the host of the high ones that are on high, and the kings of the earth upon the earth. And they shall be gathered together, as prisoners are gathered in the pit, and shall be shut up in the prison, and after many days shall they be visited." (Isa. 24:21-22.)

Visited? By whom? When and why? Jesus answers: "Verily, verily, I say unto you, The hour is coming, and now is, when the dead shall hear the voice of the Son of God: and they that hear shall live." (John 5:25.) He that hath "the keys of hell and of death" (Rev. 1:18); "he that openeth, and no man shutteth" (Rev. 3:7); he who seeks his own in the depths of hell, shall speak peace to the prisoners. They shall hear his voice. The voice of the Son of God shall be heard in the realms of the dead. His gospel shall be preached to all men, either in the body or in the spirit, for he is no respecter of persons. Thus it is that Peter testified that Christ himself, as a spirit Being, while his body lay in Joseph's tomb, "went and preached unto the spirits in prison," including those who were swept into watery graves in the days of Noah. (1 Pet. 3:18-20.) Preached what? The same gospel which he and all the prophets had proclaimed to the living, all to the end that they "might be judged according to men in the flesh, but live according to God in the spirit." (1 Pet. 4:6.)

How is it that the prison doors swing open? What power unshackles the prisoners? Whence comes the newly found freedom that is theirs? Truly, it is with the dead as with the living. The spirit offspring of Deity, whether encased in clay or roaming free in the realms of the departed dead, are all subject to the same eternal laws. Our Lord's infinite and eternal atonement reaches out to all in every sphere of creation. Freedom from the bondage of sin, from the chains of hell, from the darkness of doubt and despair come to both the quick and the dead on the same terms and conditions, and these are made operative through his atoning sacrifice. All must repent to be free. All must obey to gain gospel blessings. All must keep the commandments to merit mercy. In the case of those who dwell in the realm "wherein is no water," we shall be baptized for them, and they with us will become heirs of salvation.

"Let your hearts rejoice, and be exceedingly glad," wrote the Prophet Joseph Smith as he pondered this glorious doctrine which opens the dungeons of death and lets the children of the Eternal Father flee from the pit. "Let the earth break forth into singing. Let the dead speak forth anthems of eternal praise to the King Immanuel, who hath ordained, before the world was, that which would enable us to redeem them out of their prison; for the prisoners shall go free. Let the mountains shout for joy, and all ye valleys cry aloud; and all ye seas and dry lands tell the wonders of your Eternal King! And ye rivers, and brooks, and rills, flow down with gladness. Let the woods and all the trees of the field praise the Lord; and ye solid rocks weep for joy! And let the sun, moon, and the morning stars sing together, and let all the sons of God shout for joy! And let the eternal creations declare his name forever and ever!" (D&C 128:22.)

"His Mercy Endureth Forever!"

Our revelations abound in prophetic utterances about the mercy of God, about his infinite goodness in claiming and saving that which is lost; about the hope that lost and fallen man will be reclaimed and saved because the Lord is merciful. There is scarcely a more compassionate and soul-satisfying doctrine than that crystallized in the oft-repeated declaration—"His mercy endureth forever!"

Unfortunately the professors of religion in an uninspired Christendom, along with masses of would-be Christians in general, including many in the true church itself, assume that somehow or other mercy will be poured out upon the generality of Christian mankind and that eventually they will be saved in the kingdom of heaven. How common it is to hear such things as: "Surely, if I confess the Lord Jesus with my lips and accept him as my personal Savior, a merciful God will save me in his kingdom." Or: "Surely a merciful God will not deny me my family in eternity just because I wasn't married in the temple in this mortal life." Or: "Surely, in the mercy of God, men will be able to progress from one kingdom of glory to another in the next life, so that if I don't gain the celestial kingdom in the first instance, eventually I will." Or: "Even if I don't keep the commandments and work out my salvation in this life, the Lord is merciful; he will give me another chance in the spirit world; and even those who reject it here will have a second chance there, and eventually they will be saved." Or any of a thousand other sophistries that Satan delights to whisper into the ears of the spiritually untutored.

But the doctrinal reality is that aside from the fact that a merciful and gracious Father created us and placed us here on earth to undergo a mortal probation; aside from the fact that "he maketh his sun to rise on the evil and on the good, and sendeth rain on the just and on the unjust" (Matt. 5:45); aside from certain mortal blessings which come to the righteous and the wicked as a necessary part of mortality—aside from the fact that a merciful God provides immortality for all his children as a free gift—aside from such things as these, there is no such thing as mercy except for those who love the Lord and signify such by keeping his commandments. In other words, mercy is reserved for the faithful members of the Church and kingdom of God on earth, and for none else, except little children or others who have not arrived at the years of accountability.

As is so abundantly set forth in this work, with that emphasis and repetition which is essential to an analysis of all parts of the doctrine, we know that in the infinite wisdom of Him who knoweth all things, who created man in his own image and after his own likeness, who ordained and established the laws whereby his children could advance and progress and become like him—in the infinite wisdom of this holy being, Adam fell. We know that this fall came because of transgression, and that Adam broke the law of God, became mortal, and was thus subject to sin and disease and all the ills of mortality. We know that the effects of his fall passed upon all his posterity; all inherited a fallen state, a state of mortality, a state in which temporal and spiritual death prevail. In this state all men sin. All are lost. All are fallen. All are cut off from the presence of God. All have become carnal, sensual, and devilish by nature. Such a way of life is inherent in this mortal existence. Thus all are in the grasp of justice, and because God is just, all must pay the penalty for their sins.

This, Alma tells us, is the rationale "concerning the justice of God in the punishment of the sinner." Lost and fallen and sinful and carnal man has been in this state of opposition to God since the fall of Adam; such is his present state, and he will so remain forever, unless provision is made whereby he can escape from the grasp of justice. The provisions of the law of justice are so basic and so unvarying that if they ceased to operate, "God would cease to be God."

As justice is the child of the fall, so mercy is the offspring of the atonement. "Mercy cometh because of the atonement," Alma says, "and mercy claimeth the penitent." If there were no atoning sacrifice there would be no mercy—only justice. Thus all of the scriptures acclaiming the mercy of God presuppose that there will be or has been an atonement. Thus all of the Old Testament teachings about mercy are in fact Messianic declarations.

To his son Corianton, Alma said: "The plan of mercy could not be brought about except an atonement should be made; therefore God himself atoneth for the sins of the world, to bring about the plan of mercy, to appease the demands of justice, that God might be a perfect, just God, and a merciful God also. Now, repentance could not come unto men except there were a punishment, which also was eternal as the life of the soul should be, affixed opposite to the plan of happiness, which was as eternal also as the life of the soul. Now, how could a man repent except he should sin? How could he sin if there was no law? How could there be a law save there was a punishment? Now, there was a punishment affixed, and a just law given, which brought remorse of conscience unto man. . . .

"And if there was no law given, if men sinned what could justice do, or mercy either, for they would have no claim upon the creature? But there is a law given, and a punishment affixed, and a repentance granted; which repentance mercy claimeth; otherwise, justice claimeth the creature and executeth the law, and the law inflicteth the punishment; if not so, the works of justice would be destroyed, and God would cease to be God." The end conclusion of all this is then given in these words: "Justice exerciseth all his demands, and also mercy claimeth all which is her own; and thus, none but the truly penitent are saved." (Alma 42.)

Of these same principles, Abinadi says that the Son of

God "breaketh the bands of death" and maketh "intercession for the children of men," and that having so done, he "ascended into heaven, having the bowels of mercy; being filled with compassion towards the children of men; standing betwixt them and justice; having broken the bands of death, taken upon himself their iniquity and their transgressions, having redeemed them, and satisfied the demands of justice." (Mosiah 15:8-9.)

Amulek's words on the same matter are these: "God did call on men, in the name of his Son, (this being the plan of redemption which was laid) saying: If ye will repent, and harden not your hearts, then will I have mercy upon you, through mine Only Begotten Son; Therefore, whosoever repenteth, and hardeneth not his heart, he shall have claim on mercy through mine Only Begotten Son, unto a remission of his sins; and these shall enter into my rest. And whosoever will harden his heart and will do iniquity, behold, I swear in my wrath that he shall not enter into my rest." (Alma 12:33-35.)

These Book of Mormon statements (and they are but samples of much more that might be quoted) are plain and explicit. Mercy is for the merciful; mercy is reserved for the righteous; mercy comes to those who keep the commandments. And the Old Testament prophets had similar insight. Hosea said: "Sow to yourselves in righteousness, reap in mercy; break up your fallow ground: for it is time to seek the Lord, till he come and rain righteousness upon you." (Hosea 10:12.)

The great Sinaitic proclamation, issued through Moses, is built on the same foundation: "The Lord, The Lord God, merciful and gracious, longsuffering, and abundant in goodness and truth, Keeping mercy for thousands, forgiving iniquity and transgression and sin, and that will by no means clear the guilty." (Ex. 34:6-7.)

David, whose sins swept him from the hallowed blessings of mercy back into the awful grasp of justice, yet set forth the true Messianic principle, when he wrote: "The Lord is merciful and gracious, slow to anger, and plenteous in mercy. . . . The mercy of the Lord is from everlasting to everlasting upon them that fear him, and his righteousness unto children's children; To such as keep his covenant, and to those that remember his commandments to do them." (Ps. 103:8, 17-18.)

What is this reconciling of the claims of justice and mercy, but a recitation of why men must suffer for their own sins unless they repent? Men are commanded to repent lest they be smitten by the Lord's wrath and their sufferings be both sore and exquisite. "I God, have suffered these things for all, that they might not suffer if they would repent; But if they would not repent they must suffer even as I." (D&C 19:16-17.) Truly, "mercy cometh because of the atonement" (Alma 42:23), and He "who was wounded for our transgressions" and who "bare the sins of many" (Isa. 53:5, 12) did so "on conditions of repentance" (D&C 18:12).

MESSIAH'S BLOOD ATONES AND RECONCILES

Blood Atonement Brings Salvation

There is no more basic doctrine in the gospel than that of the atonement. This doctrine is that in and through the blood of Christ we have power, in our lost and fallen state, to be reconciled to God and to return to his presence and there inherit that eternal life which he himself enjoys. This doctrine is that "salvation was, and is, and is to come, in and through the atoning blood of Christ, the Lord Omnipotent." (Mosiah 3:18.) This doctrine is that "if we walk in the light, as he [God] is in the light, we have fellowship one with another, and the blood of Jesus Christ his Son cleanseth us from all sin." (1 Jn. 1:7.) This doctrine is that "the righteous shall sit down in his kingdom, to go no more out," because their garments are "made white through the blood of the Lamb." (Alma 34:36.)

Formulated in the wisdom of the Father, the doctrine of blood atonement was taught first in preexistence; was then revealed to all the ancient prophets who foretold the coming of our Lord; has been the burden of the preaching of inspired men from the day he shed his blood to ransom fallen man to the present moment; and will be the subject of praise and adoration forever, as saints and angels sing the song of the redeemed.

In the courts on high, while we all dwelt in the presence

of our Eternal Father, Christ was chosen and foreordained as the one whose blood should be shed to redeem mankind. It was known to us there that he would be born into mortality as the Son of God so that he would have power to live or to die, power to lay down his life and to take it up again, power to shed his blood that eternal life might come to all those who would believe in him. Having this in mind, Peter exhorts us, "Pass the time of your sojourning here in fear," because we have been "redeemed . . . with the precious blood of Christ, as of a lamb without blemish and without spot: Who verily was foreordained before the foundation of the world." (1 Pet. 1:17-19.)

The first proclamation on earth relative to the blood of Him who died on Calvary, and the redeeming power that is available because that blood would be shed by evil and conspiring men, is as old as mortal man. Some six thousand years ago, in giving Adam knowledge about "his Only Begotten . . . even Jesus Christ, a righteous Judge, who shall come in the meridian of time," the Lord said to all men: "By reason of transgression cometh the fall, which fall bringeth death"—truths of which we are so abundantly and acutely aware!—"and inasmuch as ye were born into the world by water, and blood, and the spirit, which I have made, and so became of dust a living soul, even so ye must be born again into the kingdom of heaven, of water, and of the Spirit, and be cleansed by blood, even the blood of mine Only Begotten; that ye might be sanctified from all sin, and enjoy the words of eternal life in this world, and eternal life in the world to come, even immortal glory." Then came from the mouth of Deity that ponderous proclamation: "By the water ye keep the commandment; by the Spirit ye are justified, and by the blood ye are sanctified," and it was followed by this conclusion, which put the whole matter in perfect perspective: "This is the plan of salvation unto all men, through the blood of mine Only Begotten, who shall come in the meridian of time." (Moses 6:57-62.)

Aware of these teachings, Enoch, the seventh from

Adam, whose life, however, began while the first man of all men was yet among mortals, "cried unto the Lord, saying: When shall the day of the Lord come? When shall the blood of the Righteous be shed, that all they that mourn may be sanctified and have eternal life? And the Lord said: It shall be in the meridian of time, in the days of wickedness and vengeance." Then Enoch, in vision, "saw the day of the coming of the Son of Man." (Moses 7:45-47.)

As we have seen, Zechariah foretold that the King of Israel would free the prisoners out of the pit by the blood of the covenant (Zech. 9:11), meaning that through the shedding of his blood even the spirits in hell have power, through faith and repentance, to escape their direful dungeon and come forth to honor and reward in the kingdoms of resurrection and glory.

As we have seen and shall see, other Old Testament prophets spoke of his death by violence—a death in which he would be smitten, wounded, and bruised; in which he would be brought "as a lamb to the slaughter"; and in which he would pour out his soul (Isa. 53), in all of which the shedding of his blood is an unspoken and assumed eventuality.

And as we shall set forth in detail in Chapters 21, 22, and 23, animal sacrifices were performed from Adam's day onward until the Lamb of God himself would be sacrificed for the sins of the world, all in "similitude of the sacrifice of the Only Begotten of the Father." (Moses 5:7.) That these sacrifices involved the deliberate shedding of blood and its subsequent use in specified rituals we shall hereafter note.

Nephites Teach Doctrine of Blood Atonement

As with almost all Messianic matters, it is to the Book of Mormon prophets that we turn for the clearest and plainest inspired assertions. In speaking, some six centuries before their day, of the twelve apostolic ministers who should direct the affairs of the Lord's earthly kingdom on the American continent, Nephi said: "They are righteous forever; for because of their faith in the Lamb of God their garments are made white in his blood" (1 Ne. 12:10), a statement that presupposes an extensive if not a complete understanding of how our Lord's blood was a symbol of his atonement and the redemption that comes thereby. Some five hundred years after Nephi's day, Alma, in propounding the doctrine of that priesthood which is "after the order of the Son, the Only Begotten of the Father," expands this sanctifying effect of the blood of the Lamb out far beyond the Nephite Twelve. "There were many who were ordained and became high priests of God; and it was on account of their exceeding faith and repentance, and their righteousness before God, they choosing to repent and work righteousness rather than to perish; Therefore they were called after this holy order, and were sanctified, and their garments were washed white through the blood of the Lamb. Now they, after being sanctified by the Holy Ghost, having their garments made white, being pure and spotless before God, could not look upon sin save it were with abhorrence; and there were many, exceeding great many, who were made pure and entered into the rest of the Lord their God." (Alma 13:9-12.)

We clean our garments by washing them in water. Filth, dirt, germs, odors, and whatever is unclean and offensive is thus removed; our wearing apparel becomes clean and spotless. A saved person is one whose soul is clean and spotless, one who is free from the filth and corruption of sin; and the prophetic way of describing such a person is to say that his garments are clean. Since the only way a human soul can be cleansed and perfected is through the atonement of Christ, it follows that the symbolic way of describing this process is to say that such a one has washed his garments in the blood of the Lamb, as we have here learned Nephi and Alma did.

In what is without question the greatest sermon of which we have knowledge on the subject of being "born of God," our friend Alma reasons on this matter of being saved through the blood of Christ. To members of the Church he says: "Can ye look up to God at that day with a pure heart and clean hands? . . . Can ye think of being saved when you have yielded yourselves to become subjects to the devil? I say unto you, ye will know at that day that ye cannot be saved; for there can no man be saved except his garments are washed white; yea, his garments must be purified until they are cleansed from all stain, through the blood of him of whom it has been spoken by our fathers, who should come to redeem his people from their sins. And now I ask of you, my brethren, how will any of you feel, if ye shall stand before the bar of God, having your garments stained with blood and all manner of filthiness? Behold, what will these things testify against you? Behold will they not testify that ye are murderers, yea, and also that ye are guilty of all manner of wickedness? Behold, my brethren, do ye suppose that such an one can have a place to sit down in the kingdom of God, with Abraham, with Isaac, and with Jacob, and also all the holy prophets, whose garments are cleansed and are spotless, pure and white? . . . Could ye say, if ye were called to die at this time, . . . That your garments have been cleansed and made white through the blood of Christ, who will come to redeem his people from their sins?" (Alma 5:19-27.)

Blood atonement makes salvation available to every living soul. "Through the atonement of Christ, all mankind may be saved, by obedience to the laws and ordinances of the Gospel." (A of F 3.) Little children and those who do not have opportunity to receive the gospel in this life reap special benefits from it. As to its universal application, Mosiah's son Aaron says, "There could be no redemption for mankind save it were through the death and sufferings of Christ, and the atonement of his blood." (Alma 21:9.) With reference to those who die without a knowledge of the truth, the angel said to King Benjamin: "His blood atoneth for the sins of those who have fallen by the transgression of Adam, who have died not knowing the will of God concerning them, or who have ignorantly sinned." And as to little children, that same angelic ministrant affirmed: "As in

Adam, or by nature, they fall, even so the blood of Christ atoneth for their sins." (Mosiah 3:11, 16.)

Blood Atonement Revealed in Our Lord's Day

When the time came to take upon himself the sins of all men on conditions of repentance, our Lord, dwelling in mortality, retired to Gethsemane to undergo the greatest suffering ever borne by man or God. While Peter, James, and John slept, he pled with his Father, "If thou be willing, remove this cup from me: nevertheless not my will, but thine, be done." Then there appeared an angel from heaven, who strengthened him as he bore the infinite burden that only he could carry. "And being in agony he prayed more earnestly: and his sweat was as it were great drops of blood falling down to the ground." (Luke 22:42-44.) It was of this agony beyond compare that he said to Joseph Smith: "Which suffering caused myself, even God, the greatest of all, to tremble because of pain, and to bleed at every pore, and to suffer both body and spirit—and would that I might not drink the bitter cup, and shrink—Nevertheless, glory be to the Father, and I partook and finished my preparations unto the children of men." (D&C 19:18-19.)

Later, on the cross, his life blood dripped from the cruel wounds in his tortured hands and feet, and finally, when the Roman spear pierced his side, "forthwith came there out blood and water" (John 19:34), after which he voluntarily gave up his life, that there might be three to "bear witness in earth, the spirit, and the water, and the blood" (1 Jn. 5:8).

After his demise, and the glorious resurrection that came thereby, his prophetic witnesses continued to teach that salvation was a living reality because he shed that blood which had given him mortal life. We have quoted the words of the Beloved John as to those who are cleansed from sin through "the blood of Jesus Christ." (1 Jn. 1:7.) We have also noted the testimony of Peter as to those who are redeemed "with the precious blood of Christ, as of a lamb without blemish and without spot." (1 Pet. 1:18-19.) To these inspired declarations we now add the testimony of our beloved friend Paul.

As Paul journeyed to Jerusalem to face bonds and chains for the testimony of Jesus, he charged the Ephesian elders, whose faces he would not again see in mortality, "to feed the church of God, which he hath purchased with his own blood." (Acts 20:17-28.) To both the Colossians and the Ephesians he wrote that the saints have "redemption through his blood, even the forgiveness of sins." (Col. 1:14. See also Eph. 1:7.) To the Romans he testified that the law of justification itself is operative because of "his blood" (Rom. 5:9), and that we are thereby "justified freely by his grace through the redemption that is in Christ Jesus: Whom God hath set forth to be a propitiation through faith in his blood." That is to say, "remission of sins" comes to those who have "faith in his blood"; it is to them that the effects of his propitiatory sacrifice are given. (Rom. 3:24-25.) To the Hebrews, whose practice it then was to shed the blood of animals in blood sacrifices, Paul taught that all Mosaic sacrifices were in fact similitudes of the coming sacrifice of the Messiah. He showed them that under both the old and the new covenants sins are purged only "with blood," and that "without shedding of blood is no remission." His witness was that "the blood of Christ, who . . . offered himself without spot to God," was the only thing that would purge men from "dead works" and evil deeds and enable them "to serve the living God" and gain salvation in his kingdom. (Heb. 9.)

Also after our Lord's resurrection, we find John writing of him that he "loved us, and washed us from our sins in his own blood." (Rev. 1:5.) From John's writings we learn that the only way the saints can overcome the world and escape the wiles of Satan is "by the blood of the Lamb, and by the word of their testimony." (Rev. 12:11.) It was John also who saw the angelic hosts around the throne of God, worshiping him and the Lamb, and heard the angelic elder ask: "What are these which are arrayed in white robes? and whence come they?" He it was who then heard the heavenly pronouncement: "These are they which came out of great tribulation, and have washed their robes, and made them white in the blood of the Lamb." (Rev. 7:9-14.) And it was John who saw our Lord coming in power and great glory in the last days, and, lo, "he was clothed with a vesture dipped in blood." (Rev. 19:13.)

But certainly one of the greatest of all proclamations on the atoning blood of Christ the Lord is his own words, given to the Nephites as he ministered among them in resurrected glory. Speaking of the law which the Father of us all has given to mankind, the Risen Lord said: "And no unclean thing can enter into his kingdom; therefore nothing entereth into his rest save it be those who have washed their garments in my blood, because of their faith, and the repentance of all their sins, and their faithfulness unto the end. Now this is the commandment: Repent, all ye ends of the earth, and come unto me and be baptized in my name, that ye may be sanctified by the reception of the Holy Ghost, that ye may stand spotless before me at the last day." (3 Ne. 27:19-20.)

Man Perverts Doctrine of Blood Atonement

This doctrine that blessings come through the shedding of the blood of the Sinless One—as with all pure and perfect principles and practices—has been subject to gross and evil and wicked perversions among degenerate and apostate peoples in all ages. To Abraham, for instance, the Lord said: "My people have gone astray from my precepts, and have not kept mine ordinances, which I gave unto their fathers; And they have not observed mine anointing, and the burial, or baptism wherewith I commanded them; But have turned from the commandment, and taken unto themselves the washing of children, and the blood of sprinkling; And have said that the blood of the righteous Abel was shed for sins; and have not known wherein they are accountable before me." (JST, Gen. 17:4-7.)

That these words of Deity, spoken to his friend Abraham and revealed anew in our day to Joseph Smith, were also known to Paul is apparent from the ancient apostle's statement about the saints coming "to Jesus the mediator of the new covenant, and to the blood of sprinkling, that speaketh better things than that of Abel." (Heb. 12:24.) It was, of course, the approved practice for the Levitical priests in Israel to sprinkle blood from their sacrifices in prescribed ways (Heb. 9:19-21), but as here used, "the blood of sprinkling" has clear reference to the blood of Jesus, which is symbolically sprinkled upon all the faithful.

This twisting of the divine intent in Abraham's day, where blood atonement is concerned, is only a fraction of what has prevailed among those who have gone astray in many nations and among many peoples. For the first four thousand years of man's mortal continuance on earth, sacrifices of all sorts were common among pagan peoples and even among such "enlightened" worshipers as the citizens of ancient Rome. Being a form of false worship, "that which is offered in sacrifice to idols," and "the things which the Gentiles sacrifice, they sacrifice to devils, and not to God." Having so said, Paul counsels: "And I would not that ye should have fellowship with devils." (1 Cor. 10:19-20.)

But the most horrifying and revolting perversion of the divine sacrificial system has been human sacrifice, the shedding of mortal blood by mortal man on one religious pretext or another. As Amulek said, "There is not any man that can sacrifice his own blood which will atone for the sins of another." (Alma 34:11.) Nor is God appeased, nor are the forces of nature controlled, by the most sincere slaying of the purest virgins or others. Such acts are the basest form of false worship. Performed by those whose religions ape portions of what once was had in perfection among their ancestors, they are almost inconceivable desecrations of the true and holy system of forgiveness through sacrifice. Mortal man is not authorized, except in imposing the requisite death penalties for crimes, to take the blood of his fellow beings under any circumstances. From the beginning, the Lord's law has been: "And whoso sheddeth man's blood, by man shall his blood be shed; for man shall not shed the blood of man. For a commandment I give, that every man's brother shall preserve the life of man, for in mine own image have I made man." (JST, Gen. 9:12-13.)

And yet Satan has such great hold on the hearts of men that he has prevailed upon them to sacrifice each other by the thousands in the name of religion. Unnumbered hosts were sacrificed—or should we say murdered?—on the altars of the Aztecs. In the days of Moses, and for centuries thereafter, sacrifices of children were made to Molech, the god of the Ammonites. The penalty for any in Israel who so dealt with their offspring was death. (Lev. 20:1-5.) And so it has been among many peoples in many places, the souls of men have poured out their blood in gory rituals on the altars of idols, all in the name of religion, all pursuant to Lucifer's will, which is to destroy the souls of men.

Why Blood Is the Symbol of Life and Death

When the Lord gave Israel their system of animal sacrifices, all to be performed in similitude of the future sacrifice of their Messiah, he singled out the blood as the sacrificial element to which special attention should be given. It was not the flesh of the sacrificial animal, not the sacred altar on which the Lord's fires burned, not the manner in which the Levites of Israel should perform their ministerial labors (though all these had a bearing and bore a relative share of importance), but it was the blood of the animals that concerned the Lord. He gave, as we have seen, detailed instructions as to sprinkling the blood in the ransoming rituals, and the blood was singled out as the symbol of the whole atoning process.

Indeed, so sacred was the blood element in the sacrificial ordinance that Jehovah directed Moses to forbid the people to eat any blood at any time, lest they fail to reverence, as his law required, the particular blood chosen to make an atonement for them. The penalty for disobedience to what otherwise would have been an irrelevant and unreasonable dietary restriction was to be severed from one's inheritance in Israel. The penalty for any soul who ate blood was to be "cut off from among his people."

As to the sacrificial blood, the Lord said: "For the life of the flesh is in the blood," which is a truism that is both obvious and important to a proper understanding of the doctrine of blood atonement. Blood is the element and symbol of mortal life. When it courses in mortal veins, mortal life (meaning the temporary union of body and spirit) is present. When it is spilled or otherwise ceases to perform its life-giving function, death overtakes whatever form of mortal life is involved. Having so said, the Lord continues: "And I have given it to you upon the altar to make an atonement for your souls." That is, the element which assures mortal life will give eternal life. The blood by which men live on earth will be the blood which makes everlasting life available in heaven. "The life . . . is in the blood." The symbolism is perfect. And so the Lord concludes: "It is the blood that maketh an atonement for the soul." (Lev. 17:10-11.) From all of this it is apparent that those in Israel who were spiritually enlightened knew and understood that their sacrificial ordinances were in similitude of the coming death of Him whose name they used to worship the Father, and that it was not the blood on their altars that brought remission of sins, but the blood that would be shed in Gethsemane and on Calvary.

With all this in mind, no longer need men ask, "Why this emphasis on the shedding of blood? Why dwell with such emphasis, and so repetitively, on our Lord's death and the manner in which it came to pass?" The reasons are clear and compelling. Where salvation is concerned, we are dealing with life and death; we are born into mortality so that we may have the privilege of dying and coming forth in immortality. In our search for salvation, we are dealing with mortal life and the natural death; we are dealing with immortality and eternal life; we are seeking to learn how mortality becomes immortality, and how men, having bowed to the natural death, can yet come forth and gain eternal life. To crystallize in our minds and to dramatize before our eyes what is involved in all this, the Lord has chosen blood as the symbol of both life and death.

Death is ever before us. It is seen on every hand. All men must die, and all men are aware, daily or oftener, of the existence of death and the separations it entails. But it is not death, but life, upon which the mind of man should dwell. It is not the despair of the grave, but the joy of our redemption, that should fill our souls. How, then, can we make every death a reminder of life, every departure from this life a witness of an entrance into a better realm? How can we turn the sorrow of the grave into the joy of immortal glory? The shedding of man's blood brings death. The shedding of Christ's blood brings life. As death passes upon all men by Adam, so life comes to all by Christ. As in Adam, or by nature, all men fall and are subject to spiritual death, so in Christ and his atoning sacrifice all men have power to gain eternal life in the presence of their Creator. To every true believer every death becomes a reminder of life. That reminder is in the shedding of man's blood, which brings death, and the shedding of Christ's blood, which brings life. God be praised for the perfection of his similitudes!

"Be Ye Reconciled to God"

"The man Gabriel" came to Daniel and taught him that "Messiah the Prince" should come "to make reconciliation for iniquity, and to bring in everlasting righteousness." (Dan. 9:24-25.) That is to say, the Messiah would come to make possible a reconciliation between God and man.

In his lost and fallen condition, man is in a state of sin and spiritual darkness and is himself subject to and guilty of sin. "All have sinned, and come short of the glory of God." (Rom. 3:23.) "There is not a just man upon the earth, that doeth good, and sinneth not." (Eccl. 7:20.) Christ only was sinless. All accountable men having sinned are thereby unclean and unable to dwell with or be in the presence of their God. Accordingly, "all men, everywhere, must repent, or they can in nowise inherit the kingdom of God, for no unclean thing can dwell there, or dwell in his presence; for, in the language of Adam, Man of Holiness is his name." (Moses 6:57.) As Amulek expressed it, "No unclean thing can inherit the kingdom of heaven; therefore, how can ye be saved, except ye inherit the kingdom of heaven? Therefore, ye cannot be saved in your sins." (Alma 11:37.)

Thus, to restore man to a state of harmony and unity with Deity, man must repent, receive a remission of his sins, become clean, and be thereby ransomed from his lost and fallen state. To be saved, man must be reconciled to God through the atonement of his Son. "Be reconciled unto him through the atonement of Christ, his Only Begotten Son," Jacob preached, "and ye may obtain a resurrection, according to the power of the resurrection which is in Christ, and be presented as the first-fruits of Christ unto God, having faith, and [having] obtained a good hope of glory in him." (Jacob 4:11.)

Can there be any more glorious concept than this, that lowly and fallen and mortal and sinful man—that all of us—can forsake our evil and wicked ways and find harmony and unity with our Eternal Father? Ought we not to shout praises to the Holy One of Israel forever for his goodness to us? "Cheer up your hearts," Jacob says to all of us, "and remember that ye are free to act for yourselves—to choose the way of everlasting death or the way of eternal life. . . . Reconcile yourselves to the will of God, and not to the will of the devil and the flesh; and remember, after ye are reconciled unto God, that it is only in and through the grace of God that ye are saved." (2 Ne. 10:23-24.) "Believe in Christ," Nephi adds, and "be reconciled to God; for we know that it is by grace that we are saved, after all we can do." (2 Ne. 25:23.) Also: "Be reconciled unto Christ, and enter into the narrow gate, and walk in the straight path which leads to life, and continue in the path until the end of the day of probation." (2 Ne. 33:9.)

Paul says that Christ came "to make reconciliation for the sins of the people." (Heb. 2:17.) "He is the propitiation for our sins." (1 Jn. 2:2.) If we repent, are baptized, receive the gift of the Holy Ghost, and keep the commandments, we are in fact reconciled to Deity. The great propitiation operates in our lives. We are then, as Paul expressed it, "in Christ." We have become new creatures. It is of such that the ancient apostle says: "God . . . hath reconciled us to himself by Jesus Christ, and hath given to us the ministry of reconciliation." That is, being reconciled we have also certain obligations. We have received not only the fact of reconciliation, and how glorious that is, but also "the ministry of reconciliation."

This ministry of reconciliation, in Paul's language, consists of two things: (1) "That God was in Christ, reconciling the world unto himself, not imputing their trespasses unto them," provided, of course, that they pursued a course of truth and righteousness; and (2) that he "hath committed unto us the word of reconciliation," that is, that he hath given to his legal administrators the message which must be preached and believed if any of us are to gain the blessings of reconciliation with that Man of Holiness, from whom we have been separated because we are unholy.

Having so taught, our apostolic friend of olden times gives this exhortation to all those who have yet to commit themselves in full to the cause of Christ: "Now then we are ambassadors for Christ, as though God did beseech you by us: we pray you in Christ's stead, be ye reconciled to God." (2 Cor. 5:17-20.) That is to say: 'We represent the Lord Jesus Christ; he has commissioned us; we have his authority; and since we are legal administrators, when we speak it is as though the Father himself beseeched you to come and be reconciled to his Son, for the Son speaks the words of the Father, and we stand in the place and stead of Christ when we preach; we have his mind; we speak his words, and those words are: Be ye reconciled to God.'

Our mission is to preach "Jesus Christ, and him crucified." (1 Cor. 2:2.) Our mission is to proclaim the message of reconciliation to all men. Our mission also is to persuade men to forsake their sins, to "come unto Christ, and be perfected in him," and to deny themselves "of all ungodliness." (Moro. 10:32.)

"How great the importance to make these things known unto the inhabitants of the earth, that they may know that there is no flesh that can dwell in the presence of God, save it be through the merits, and mercy, and grace of the Holy Messiah," and then only when they believe and obey his laws. (2 Ne. 2:8.)

MESSIAH BRINGETH THE RESURRECTION

Resurrection Proves Christ Is the Messiah

We shall now turn our attention to the resurrection—not the doctrine of resurrection in all its parts and phases; not to how the dead are raised up or with what body they shall come; not to the fact there is a resurrection of the just and of the unjust; not to the whole basic concept of immortality, which makes the trials of life bearable (though all these have some bearing upon the problem at hand), but rather to these two simple facts: (1) There is a resurrection; and (2) the Messiah bringeth it to pass.

If, as is clearly set forth in the poetry and prose of the prophets, the Promised Messiah was to be himself resurrected, being the first-fruits thereof, and if the effects of that resurrection were to pass upon all mankind, then any scriptures so teaching, plus any that merely mention or refer to the fact of being raised from death to life, are Messianic in nature. And if, as is also clearly set forth in the wondrous words of the New Testament and of latter-day revelation, the one who in fact burst the bands of death and thereby gave assurance that all men would come forth from the grave in due course, if such a one was the Man Jesus who is called Christ, then he is the Messiah; they are one and the same and are to be worshiped as such.

Further, if the Man Jesus was resurrected; if he came

forth from the Arimathean's tomb in glorious immortality; if he ate and drank with his disciples after he rose from the dead, and was by them handled and felt; if he was the first-fruits of them that slept, then he is the Son of God. And if he is God's Son, then all his words are true; his gospel has saving and damning power; and we, weak mortals that we are, must turn to him for a hope of eternal life.

We are witnesses that all of these things are true, that there neither is nor can be any question as to their verity, and that all those who accept them with full purpose of heart are on the course leading to that immortal glory which comes from God by way of his Son. Accordingly, as we pursue our Messianic studies, we shall now turn to the revealed records to see what they say as to our Lord's resurrection and the resurrection of all men.

Jehovah Shall Rise from Death

Our beginning point is the fact that the Lord Jehovah—after being brought as a lamb to the slaughter; after pouring out his soul unto death; after making his grave with the wicked, and being with the rich in his death, all as saith the prophet (Isa. 53)—was destined to come forth from the tomb and live forever in resurrected glory.

This concept of a God being resurrected, of a Redeemer and Savior coming to ransom his people, is neither novel nor mysterious. It was not a hidden nor unknown doctrine in days of old. It was not only inherent in, but was in fact the great cornerstone upon which the whole gospel plan rested. All those who had the gospel in ancient times knew of the future redemption and rejoiced in the One who should come to bring it to pass. This is perfectly clear and is not our present concern. What we are now desirous of doing is to show that it was the Lord Jehovah, so named and so identified, who would himself be resurrected and would make the resurrection possible for all others.

Isaiah, speaking for himself and for faithful Israel, addressed himself to their God, the God of Israel. As he spoke, the words which came forth in Hebrew were: "O Jehovah, thou art my God; I will exalt thee, I will praise thy name," and so forth. As these words now read in our King James Version of the Bible, the Hebrew for *Jehovah* has been anglicized to read *Lord,* and so Isaiah's cry of praise is preserved to us as "O Lord, thou art my God," and so forth.

After numerous expressions of praise for all that the Lord has done for his people, Isaiah called him "the Lord of hosts," and said of him: "He will swallow up death in victory; and the Lord God will wipe away tears from off all faces." Our incomparable theologian, Paul, writing and interpreting by the power of the Holy Ghost, as part of his greatest essay on the resurrection of Christ, picks up a part of Isaiah's prophecy and says: "For this corruptible must put on incorruption, and this mortal must put on immortality. So when this corruptible shall have put on incorruption, and this mortal shall have put on immortality, then shall be brought to pass the saying that is written, Death is swallowed up in victory." Having so stated, our apostolic interpreter gives the true meaning of Isaiah's prophecy. Paul asks: "O grave, where is thy victory?" His own inspired answer is: "Thanks be to God, which giveth us the victory through our Lord Jesus Christ." (1 Cor. 15:53-57.)

Let there be no misunderstanding here. Isaiah (who was inspired!) said that Jehovah would swallow up death in victory, meaning bring to pass the resurrection of all men; and Paul (who also was inspired!) said that the Lord Jesus Christ had in fact swallowed up death in victory, because Isaiah's words about Jehovah were Messianic and applied to Jesus our Lord. As to the promise that "God shall wipe away all tears from their eyes," we find John reciting that this will be fulfilled when Christ reigns among men during the millennial era. (Rev. 21:3-4; D&C 101:23-31.)

But now back to Isaiah. Having told of Jehovah's swallowing up of death in victory and of the millennial joy that shall prevail, Israel's great prophet continues: "And it shall be said in that day, Lo, this is our God; we have waited for him, and he will save us: this is the Lord; we have waited for him, we will be glad and rejoice in his salvation." (Isa. 25:9.)

Then Isaiah records a song which shall be sung in the land of Judah, sung to Jehovah, in praise and thanksgiving and adoration for all that he has done for his people. Israel will say, among other things, "Trust ye in the Lord for ever: for in the Lord JEHOVAH is everlasting strength." Thereupon Jehovah will answer, "Thy dead men shall live, together with my dead body shall they arise." The Lord Jehovah will be resurrected! He that poured out his soul unto death shall live again! He that died upon the cross shall come forth from the grave! A God dies and a God lives! A mortal Messiah becomes an immortal being, like his Father, so that he may gain all power in heaven and on earth!

But it is not the great Jehovah only who shall live again. It is all men. "Thy dead men shall live," he says. "Awake and sing, ye that dwell in dust: for thy dew is as the dew of herbs, and the earth shall cast out the dead. . . . The earth also shall disclose her blood, and shall no more cover her slain." (Isa. 26.)

Perhaps one more prophetic passage as to Jehovah's resurrection will suffice for our present purposes. In a psalm of praise to Jehovah, David said: "Sing unto God, sing praises to his name: extol him that rideth upon the heavens by his name JAH, and rejoice before him." JAH is the familiar form of JEHOVAH. To this Jah, who is Jehovah, the song of praise extols: "Thou hast ascended on high, thou hast led captivity captive," and hast given gifts unto men. He is then identified as the God of our salvation, because "unto God the Lord belong the issues of death." (Ps. 68.) The issues of death? Our children are our issue; they come forth from us. The issues of death are those that come forth from the grave because Jah took captivity captive. That is, the captivity of the grave was swallowed up; it was overcome; it became the captive of Him who had power over death. Lest there be any doubt as to the identity of Jehovah who took captivity captive, we turn to Paul's writing. He says: It is Christ. (Eph. 4:7-10.)

Messiah Shall Rise from Death

What the prophets foretold of the resurrection of the Great Jehovah, they also said of him under his designation as the Messiah, as the Son of Man, as Jesus Christ, or whatever name they chose to apply to the Offspring of the Father. To list those prophets who so preannounced, and we do not have their full accounts, would be synonymous with listing those who were prophets. From the accounts that have come to us, we know, for instance:

Enoch saw that he was lifted up, meaning on the cross; that he was slain; that he arose from the dead and ascended to his Father; and that "the saints arose, and were crowned at the right hand of the Son of Man, with crowns of glory." (Moses 7:47-59.)

Abraham was told that though he should die, yet he should rise again to possess his Palestinian home as an "everlasting inheritance," and also that "the Son of Man" should live again in immortality. "But how can he live if he be not dead?" was the question put by Deity to the Father of the faithful. The heaven-sent answer was: "He must first be quickened." Then the record says: "And it came to pass, that Abram looked forth and saw the days of the Son of Man, and was glad, and his soul found rest, and he believed in the Lord; and the Lord counted it unto him for righteousness." (JST, Gen. 15:9-12.)

Lehi taught that after the Jews "had slain the Messiah, . . . he should rise from the dead, and should make himself manifest, by the Holy Ghost, unto the Gentiles." (1 Ne. 10:11.) Also: That "the Holy Messiah . . . layeth down his life according to the flesh, and taketh it again by the power of the Spirit, that he may bring to pass the resurrection of the dead, being the first that should rise." (2 Ne. 2:8.)

Nephi foretold that "they will crucify . . . the Messiah," who is "the Only Begotten of the Father, . . . and after he is laid in a sepulchre for the space of three days he shall rise from the dead, with healing in his wings; and all those who shall believe on his name shall be saved in the kingdom of God. Wherefore, my soul delighteth to prophesy concerning him, for I have seen his day, and my heart doth magnify his holy name." (2 Ne. 25:12-13; 26:3.)

King Benjamin said: "He shall be called Jesus Christ, the Son of God, . . . And he shall rise the third day from the dead." (Mosiah 3:8-10.)

Abinadi expressed it this way: "The bands of death shall be broken, and the Son reigneth, and hath power over the dead; therefore, he bringeth to pass the resurrection of the dead." Further: "All the prophets, and all those who have believed on their words, or all those that have kept the commandments of God, shall come forth in the first resurrection. . . . They are raised to dwell with God who has redeemed them; thus they have eternal life through Christ, who has broken the bands of death." (Mosiah 15:20-23.)

What need we say more? As to the prophetic word, particularly among the Nephite prophets, the record is clear and extensive. There is added testimony from Abinadi (Mosiah 16:7-15); the first Alma taught the doctrine of Abinadi at the waters of Mormon (Mosiah 18:1-9); the second Alma, who is the American Paul, as it were, was profound, prolific, and profuse in his prophetic utterances (Alma 4:14; 7:12-13; 16:19-20; 27:28; 33:22; 40:1-26; 41:1-15; 42:1-31). We have also the words of Amulek (Alma 11:37-45), of Aaron (Alma 22:14), and of Samuel the Lamanite (Hel. 14:15-17, 25; 3 Ne. 23:7-14). There was no want of inspired teaching, among the Americans of the house of Israel, relative to Christ and his coming, the redemption he alone would make, and the resurrection that would result therefrom, nor was there any among their Old World contemporaries and ancestors; but unfortunately the Old World accounts have not been preserved for us with the same clarity and perfection that appertains where Book of Mormon writings are concerned.

Old Testament Prophets Tell of Resurrection

Those prophecies about being raised from death to life which we have so far brought to the fore all speak of Christ, under one name-title or another, as the One through whom the resurrection is brought to pass. Their Messianic meaning is clear. Being thus fully indoctrinated with the eternal truth that he and he alone is the one by whom immortality comes, we are free—nay, we are bound and required—to read all revelations pertaining to the resurrection as being Messianic in nature, whether they mention our Lord by name, by necessary implication, or not at all. Since he brings to pass the resurrection, and without him there would be naught but dolorous death forever, it follows that the fact of resurrection is itself a witness of his wondrous works.

Let us be aware, then, of the true Messianic nature of what the Old Testament prophets were saying when they spoke of the resurrection, as they did, with greater force and factualness than some have supposed. What had the Psalmist in mind, for instance, but the resurrection when he sang to Jehovah, "I will behold thy face in righteousness: I shall be satisfied, when I wake, with thy likeness"? (Ps. 17:15.) Was it not the same assurance expressed by John when he wrote of Christ, "When he shall appear, we [meaning the faithful saints] shall be like him"? (1 Jn. 3:2.) And of what sang the Psalmist when he said to Jehovah, "My soul cleaveth unto dust: quicken thou me according to thy word"? (Ps. 119:25.) Was he not speaking of the same resurrection that Paul had in mind when he testified that all men would be quickened by the power of Christ when they were raised from mortality to immortality? (1 Cor. 15.)

"All the days of my appointed time will I wait, till my change come," are the words of Job. His Redeemer lived; he knew it; and therefore he knew he would be changed from mortality to immortality, from corruption to incorruption, and that the grave would have no victory over him. So it has always been with the faithful. With Job, each of them says to the Lord: "Thou shalt call, and I will answer thee: thou wilt have a desire to the work of thine hands." (Job 14:14-15.) Truly, the work of the Lord's hands shall answer his call and the bands of death shall be broken for each individual.

Daniel spoke plainly of the resurrection at the end of the world in these words: "And many of them that sleep in the dust of the earth shall awake, some to everlasting life, and some to shame and everlasting contempt" (Dan. 12:2), which brings to mind our Lord's like-worded promise: "The hour is coming, in the which all that are in the graves shall hear" the voice of the Son of God, "and shall come forth; they that have done good, unto the resurrection of life; and they that have done evil, unto the resurrection of damnation." (John 5:28-29.)

To and of Israel, by the mouth of Hosea, the Lord God said: "There is no saviour beside me. . . . I will be thy king. . . . I will ransom them from the power of the grave; I will redeem them from death; O death, I will be thy plagues; O grave, I will be thy destruction." (Hosea 13:4-14.) That is: 'I Jehovah will do it,' all of which brings us to Paul's like-expressed witness that Christ shall ransom and redeem and resurrect, so that it may truly be said: "O death, where is thy sting? O grave, where is thy victory?" (1 Cor. 15:55.)

Nowhere in the scriptures do we have as explicit and as detailed a description of the resurrection as in the writings of Ezekiel. The Lord Jehovah, by the power of his Spirit, carried that ancient prophet to a valley that was full of dry bones, which were identified as the bones of the whole house of Israel. They were the bones of those who had been promised an inheritance in Palestine, which they had never received in the full sense of the word. "Can these bones live?" the Lord asked. By way of answer, Jehovah said to the bones: "I will cause breath to enter into you, and ye shall live: And I will lay sinews upon you, and will bring flesh upon you, and cover you with skin, and put breath in you, and ye shall live."

There is nothing more real, more literal, more personal than the resurrection, as Ezekiel then beheld in vision. He saw the dead live again, live literally and personally, each one becoming in physical makeup as he had been in mortality. It was with each of them as it would be with their Lord, when he, having also come forth from his valley of dry bones, stood in the upper room with his disciples, ate before them, and permitted them to handle his physical body. To his people the Lord's voice came: "I will open your graves, and cause you to come up out of your graves, and bring you into the land of Israel." (Ezek. 37:1-14.) He who shall do all this, as we are now acutely aware, is the Lord Jesus Christ who is the God of Israel.

What Are the Sure Mercies of David?

King David's story is one of the saddest in all history. In his youth and in the forepart of his reign as king, he was faithful and true, a man after the Lord's own heart. (1 Sam. 13:13-14.) His throne and kingdom were established with power and became the symbol of the future throne and kingdom of the Son of David. But in the matter of Uriah and Bathsheba he fell; adultery stained his soul, and innocent blood dripped from his hands. In tears he sought forgiveness, which, because of Uriah's murder, was not forthcoming.

David knew he had forfeited his claim to eternal life and the continuation of the family unit in the realms ahead. Yet he importuned the Lord for such blessings as he still might receive. And though a just God could no longer confer upon his erring servant the fulness of that reward which might have been his, yet according to the great plan of mercy, which causes the resurrection to pass upon all men, he could bring him up eventually to a lesser inheritance. His soul need not be cast off eternally to dwell with Lucifer and those who are in open and continuing rebellion against righteousness. True, because of his sins, he had cast his lot with the wicked "who suffer the vengeance of eternal fire," and "who are cast down to hell and suffer the wrath of Almighty God, until the fulness of times, when Christ shall have subdued all enemies under his feet, and shall have perfected his work." (D&C 76:105-6.) But in that day when death and hell deliver up the dead which are in them (Rev. 20:13), David and his fellow sufferers shall come forth from the grave. Because he was a member of the Church and had entered into the new and everlasting covenant of marriage and then had fallen into sin, the revelation says of him: "He hath fallen from his exaltation, and received his portion." (D&C 132:39.)

Implicit in this historical recitation of what David did to lose his salvation, and in the doctrinal laws which nonetheless guaranteed him a resurrection and a lesser degree of eternal reward, are two great truths: (1) That the Holy One of Israel, the Holy One of God, the Son of David, would die and then be resurrected; and (2) that because he burst the bands of death and became the first-fruits of them that slept, all men also would be resurrected, both the righteous and the wicked, including saints who became sinners, as was the case with David their king.

These two truths became known as and were called "the sure mercies of David," meaning that David in his life and death and resurrection was singled out as the symbol to dramatize before the people that their Holy One would be resurrected and that all men would also come forth from the grave. David knew and understood this and wrote about it. So also did Isaiah, which means the principle was known and taught in ancient Israel; and both Peter and Paul made it the basis of persuasive New Testament sermons, in which they identified the Holy One of Israel as that Jesus whom they preached.

Speaking of his own resurrection and that of his Lord, David wrote: "My flesh also shall rest in hope," meaning,

'My body shall come forth from the grave,' "For thou wilt not leave my soul in hell," meaning, 'My spirit shall not remain in hell forever, but shall be joined with my body when I am resurrected.' Death and hell shall thus deliver up dead David who is in them. Then David came forth with the great Messianic pronouncement, "Neither wilt thou suffer thine Holy One to see corruption." (Ps. 16:7-11.) That is, 'The Holy One of Israel shall come forth in his resurrection before his dead body is permitted to decay and become dust.'

With accusing words, Peter charged his fellow Jews with taking "Jesus of Nazareth, a man approved of God among you by miracles and wonders and signs," and causing him to be "crucified and slain" by wicked hands. But God hath raised him up, Peter testified, "having loosed the pains of death." Then Peter quotes the whole of that Messianic message with which we are now dealing, doing so with some improvement over the way it is recorded in the Old Testament. Peter says: "For David speaketh concerning him, I foresaw the Lord always before my face, for he is on my right hand, that I should not be moved: Therefore did my heart rejoice, and my tongue was glad; moreover also my flesh shall rest in hope: Because thou wilt not leave my soul in hell, neither wilt thou suffer thine Holy One to see corruption. Thou hast made known to me the ways of life; thou shalt make me full of joy with thy countenance."

This prophecy means, Peter says, that David "spake of the resurrection of Christ, that his soul was not left in hell, neither did his flesh see corruption." Then the Chief Apostle bears testimony of the fulfillment of the prophecy. "This Jesus hath God raised up," he says, "whereof we all are witnesses. . . . Therefore let all the house of Israel know assuredly, that God hath made that same Jesus, whom ye crucified, both Lord and Christ." He is the Lord who was ever before David's face. He is the Holy One who should come forth from the grave. Thus Peter has used David's words to prove the Holy One would be resurrected, and he has used his own testimony and that of his fellow apostles to prove that he was resurrected.

Lest his hearers be left in doubt, however, as to David's personal state, the Chief Apostle says, "Let me freely speak unto you of the patriarch David, that he is both dead and buried, and his sepulchre is with us unto this day. . . . For David is not ascended into the heaven." (Acts 2:22-36.) Further, David has not yet been resurrected, for he is numbered with "the spirits of men who are to be judged, and are found under condemnation; And these are the rest of the dead; and they live not again until the thousand years are ended, neither again, until the end of the earth." (D&C 88:100-101.)

Isaiah recorded the Lord's invitation that men should come unto him, believe his word, live his law, and be saved. Part of the invitation was couched in these words of Deity: "Incline your ear, and come unto me: hear, and your soul shall live; and I will make an everlasting covenant with you, even the sure mercies of David. Behold, I have given him for a witness to the people." (Isa. 55:1-4.) That is to say: To all who will believe in him, the Lord of heaven will make the same covenant that he made with David, in that they too will know of their Messiah's resurrection, and that the souls of all men are thereby raised from the grave. David had the promise that he would be saved from death and hell, through Christ, and all the faithful could have that same assurance, though, as here expressed, David is made the illustration, the "witness," the symbol of these great truths.

Paul preached that of David's seed "hath God according to his promise raised unto Israel a Saviour, Jesus." He said that those at Jerusalem, "and their rulers, because they knew him not, nor yet the voices of the prophets" who had prophesied of him, caused that he be put to death. After he was slain, Paul says, "they took him down from the tree, and laid him in a sepulchre. But God raised him from the dead: And he was seen many days of them which came up with him from Galilee to Jerusalem, who are his witnesses unto the people."

Having so taught and testified, Paul followed the same course we have seen Peter pursue; he turned to David and his great Messianic utterance about the resurrection, but he wove in also Isaiah's statement about the sure mercies of David. "As concerning that he raised him up from the dead," Paul said, "now no more to return to corruption, he said on this wise, I will give you the sure mercies of David. Wherefore he said also in another psalm, Thou shalt not suffer thine Holy One to see corruption. For David, after he had served his own generation by the will of God, fell on sleep, and was laid unto his fathers, and saw corruption: But he, whom God raised again, saw no corruption." (Acts 13:22-37.)

"I Am the Resurrection and the Life"

Jesus our Lord, ministering as the mortal Messiah, on numerous occasions taught his apostolic witnesses, and his disciples generally, that he would die and rise again the third day. First he led them along the course of spiritual progression until they gained testimonies of his divine Sonship and were able to say, as Peter did, "Thou art the Christ, the Son of the living God." After they gained this witness, the record says: "From that time forth began Jesus to shew unto his disciples, how that he must go unto Jerusalem, and suffer many things of the elders and chief priests and scribes, and be killed, and be raised again the third day." (Matt. 16:13-21.) His enigmatic "Destroy this temple, and in three days I will raise it up," which "he spake of the temple of his body," had the same meaning. (John 2:19, 21.)

Though Jesus spoke often of his own resurrection and the resurrection of all men, in my judgment the most persuasive and convincing witness, both of his divine Sonship and of the reality of the resurrection, that ever came from mortal lips, his or any others, were the words he spoke at the tomb of Lazarus—Lazarus whom he loved; Lazarus the brother of Mary and Martha, whom also he loved. This blessed family lived in Bethany, on the outskirts of Jerusalem. Jesus and his disciples were in Perea. Lazarus was sick and the sisters sent word to Jesus. The Master deliberately remained away, letting Lazarus die and be buried. When our Lord finally chose to go to his friends, Martha said: "Lord, if thou hadst been here, my brother had not died. But I know, that even now, whatsoever thou wilt ask of God, God will give it thee." Where have we seen faith like unto this? 'Lord, if thou wilt, thou canst raise my brother from the grave; he will live again; once more we shall enjoy his association as a mortal man!'

"Jesus saith unto her, Thy brother shall rise again." 'Thy faith shall be rewarded; I will return the departed dead one to the intimacy of the family circle.'

Hearing but not understanding, "Martha saith unto him, I know that he shall rise again in the resurrection at the last day." Martha's faith was founded on knowledge, as true faith must always be. She knew the doctrine of the resurrection. She believed the gospel. The stage was now set for the momentous pronouncement that Jesus had come to make, a pronouncement Jesus would soon prove by doing that which never man has done before or since.

"Jesus saith unto her, I am the resurrection, and the life: he that believeth in me, though he were dead, yet shall he live: And whosoever liveth and believeth in me shall never die. Believest thou this?"

What wondrous words are these! The Carpenter of Galilee is making himself God. He is saying that he is the One who brings both immortality and eternal life; that he is the Messiah who has gained the power of immortality from his Immortal Father; that if men believe in him and obey his gospel laws, they shall be alive to the things of the Spirit in this life and gain eternal life in the realms ahead.

Does Martha believe? "Yea, Lord," she says, "I believe

that thou art the Christ, the Son of God, which should come into the world." Her faith is perfect.

Thereupon Mary is summoned. Jesus is taken to the cave where Lazarus is laid. At his direction the stone is rolled back so that he who has been dead four days—he who is rotting, decaying, stinking; he whose every vital organ has long since ceased to function; he whose spirit is in Abraham's bosom with the other Lazarus who ate the crumbs that fell from the rich man's table—at Jesus' direction the stone is rolled back, and the Son of God, in his own right and in his own name, says simply, "Lazarus, come forth." (John 11.) And it is so. The dead man rises. Life comes again. The corruption ceases; maggots no longer gnaw at his vital organs; the worms of death find other dust for their meal. Lazarus lives.

And so we ask: Is Jesus the Son of God or a blaspheming imposter? Can we deny or disbelieve the witness he bears of himself when he offers the living body of his friend Lazarus as living proof of his words?

To have before us the full import of the words "I am the resurrection, and the life," we should here note that in substance and thought content they are the same as the words spoken anciently by Deity: "This is my work and my glory—to bring to pass the immortality and eternal life of man." (Moses 1:39.) They have the same meaning as those written by Paul to Timothy: "Our Saviour Jesus Christ, . . . hath abolished death, and hath brought life and immortality to light through the gospel." (2 Tim. 1:10.) They contain the same message revealed to Joseph Smith that through the atonement of Christ, all men are "raised in immortality unto eternal life, even as many as would believe." (D&C 29:43.)

"Now Is Christ Risen"

Now is Christ risen! Or is he? How do we know? And whence comes our knowledge that the effects of his resurrection shall pass upon all mankind and that all shall gain the victory over the grave? As Job said: "If a man die, shall he live again?" (Job 14:14.) And when we speak of resurrection, what do we mean? As Paul noted, "Some man will say, How are the dead raised up? and with what body do they come?" (1 Cor. 15:35.) Does the resurrection mean that our dry bones shall live? That the Lord will lay sinews upon us, and restore flesh, and cover us again with skin? And how shall we know these things?

There are answers to all these queries, or better, there is an answer to them all. The answer is: God must reveal to prophets and apostles what the eternal verities relative to resurrection are, and then the recipients of the divine word must bear testimony to the residue of men. There is no other way to gain sure knowledge in the realm that here concerns us. We may hope or reason or speculate that there is or might be a resurrection and that it consists of this or that, but until the voice of God is heard on the matter, no man can know with certainty.

After he came forth from his borrowed tomb, the risen Lord appeared to various of his saints, among them both men and women, so that they might become witnesses, first, that he was in fact raised from death to life, and second, as to the nature and kind of being he had then become. And as to the resurrection of others than our Lord, it is written: "And the graves were opened; and many bodies of the saints which slept arose, And came out of the graves after his resurrection, and went into the holy city, and appeared unto many." (Matt. 27:52-53.) Each person to whom such a resurrected saint ministered became a witness both of the resurrection and of such revealed knowledge relative to resurrected beings as he then received. (Hel. 14:25; 3 Ne. 23:7-13.)

As to the coming forth of Jesus as the first-fruits of the resurrection, as to the fact that the great Jehovah took up his body again, we know at least the following:

1. There was a great earthquake and two angels descended from heaven and rolled back the stone from the

door of the tomb and sat upon it. Those guarding the grave became as though they were dead men. (Matt 28:2-4; JST, Matt. 28:2-3.)

2. Mary Magdalene came to the sepulchre, early in the morning while it was yet dark, found the stone taken away and the tomb empty, and saw two angels sitting thereon. (JST, John 20:1.)

3. She told Peter and John, who then came hastily, entered the tomb, and found the burial clothes wrapped together as when they enshrouded the body of him who was dead, but the body of their Lord they found not. Peter and John then returned to their home. (John 20:1-10.)

4. Mary remained at the garden tomb weeping, where, taking precedence even over the apostles, she became the first mortal of whom we have record to see the risen Lord. He came. She saw. But she was restrained from embracing him. (John 20:11-18; Mark 16:9-11.)

5. Other women, also early in the morning, came to the sepulchre to anoint Jesus' body with sweet spices. Mary the mother of Joses, Salome, the mother of James and John, Joanna, and others who are not named were present. They all saw the stone rolled away, the angels sitting thereon, and they too entered the sepulchre and found not the body. It was to them that the angels said, "He is risen," and they were told to tell the disciples that Jesus would meet them in Galilee as he had promised. As they went to deliver the message, Jesus met these faithful sisters, and they were permitted to hold him by the feet as they worshiped him. (Matt. 28:1, 5-10; JST, Matt. 28:1, 4; Mark 16:1-8; JST, Mark 16:3-6; Luke 24:1-11; JST, Luke 24:1-4.)

6. Two disciples, Cleopas and another (possibly Luke, as it is he who records the event), walked from Jerusalem to Emmaus, some six or seven miles. As they discussed the reports of those who had seen the open tomb and heard the words of the angels, Jesus himself joined them in their travels. They walked and talked. He seemed in all respects like any wayfaring man. His speech, demeanor, dress,

physical appearance were all deemed by them to be that of a fellow mortal. They invited him to spend the night with them, and his true identity was made known only as he brake bread. How better could he have taught them the literal and personal nature of resurrected beings.

7. Jesus appeared to Peter. When and where we do not know, nor do we have any knowledge of what was experienced, felt, or taught, but it accords with the proprieties and the proper order in church administration to find Him whose church it is appearing to the one he had chosen to be the earthly head of his kingdom for the time and season then involved. (Luke 24:33-35; 1 Cor. 15:5.)

8. In an upper room in a dwelling in Jerusalem, where a group of believing disciples were assembled, among them ten of the Twelve, Jesus came to teach the nature of the resurrection as only he could. The group was eating and hearing the report of Cleopas and the other with whom the Lord had communed on the Emmaus road. Suddenly Jesus was there. He had come through the wall or roof. He spake. He said his body was one of flesh and bones. He permitted them to feel the nail marks in his hands and feet and to thrust their hands into his side. He ate fish and honeycomb before them. Why? Clearly it was to teach the fact of resurrection and the nature and kind of bodies possessed by resurrected beings. (Mark 16:14; Luke 24:36-44.)

9. Thomas was not present in the upper room, and he apparently questioned, not the fact of resurrection, but its literal nature. He had not yet envisioned that the nail marks and spear wound remained, and that resurrected personages ate food. Again to the disciples, through the opaque building, Jesus came. Thomas saw and felt and handled and became like his brethren a special witness. (John 20:24-29.)

10. Seven of the disciples, having fished all night without success, were invited by Jesus to cast their nets on the other side, which doing, they were immediately filled, almost to the breaking point. Then they recognized their Lord. Peter

swam ashore to greet him. Fish was eaten and instruction given. (John 21:1-14.)

11. Sometime along the line, Jesus apparently appeared to his brother James, but his great and glorious appearance was on a mountain in Galilee, and of it we know almost nothing. That it was a planned meeting, made by prearrangement, is clear. It may well have been the occasion when "he was seen of above five hundred brethren at once" (1 Cor. 15:6), and we may assume that it was in many respects comparable to his resurrected ministry among the Nephites (Matt. 28:16-20).

12. Thereafter, for forty days he ministered from time to time to his disciples, teaching them all things which it was expedient for them to know concerning the building up and rolling forth of his great work. (Acts 1:3.)

13. On the mount of Olives east of Jerusalem, in the presence of his disciples, while angels attended, a cloud receiving him out of their sight, Jesus our Lord ascended to his Father, there to reign with Almighty power forever. (Mark 16:19-20; Luke 24: 50-53.)

14. Later he came to Paul on the Damascus road (Acts 9:1-9); he was seen by John as he suffered banishment on Patmos, and no doubt by hosts of others of whom we have no record.

15. Sometime following his resurrection he appeared and ministered on successive days and at appreciable length among the Nephites, who also saw and felt and handled and knew. His resurrected ministry among the lost tribes of Israel is also noted in the Nephite record. (3 Ne. 11 through 26.)

16. In our day, he has appeared to Joseph Smith and others, not a few. Of some of these appearances we have record; others are sealed in secrecy in the hearts of the recipients.

17. All this is scarcely the beginning of his resurrected ministry among men. Every faithful member of his church—The Church of Jesus Christ of Latter-day Saints—has power,

through righteousness, to see his face and become a special witness of his holy name in this personal sense, while he or she yet dwells in mortality. (D&C 67:10-14; 93:1; 107:18-19.) And in a not distant day, when he shall reign personally among men, all of earth's inhabitants shall see and know for themselves.

How, then, can it be proved that Christ gained the victory over the grave and came forth with the same body he laid down? That all men—"every man in his own order" (1 Cor. 15:23)—shall come forth in like manner? The Lord's system is to prove his word by witnesses. "Ye are my witnesses, saith the Lord, that I am God." (Isa. 43:12.) To illustrate: When Peter was sent to the house of Cornelius the centurion, the Lord's chief apostolic witness proved to the complete satisfaction of all there assembled that Jesus rose from the dead. It was done by the simple expedient of bearing a personal, Spirit-filled witness of that fact. "Him God raised up the third day," Peter testified, "and shewed him openly; Not to all the people, but unto witnesses chosen before of God, even to us, who did eat and drink with him after he rose from the dead." (Acts 10:34-43.)

What more need Peter say? What is more conclusive and binding than personal testimony? Peter knew. What is there to argue about, and who can contend successfully against him who says: 'I was in an upper room; the doors and windows were closed; there was no opening into the room. The Lord Jesus appeared. He was the same Person with whom I traveled and ministered in Palestine, the same who dwelt in my home in Capernaum. He spoke; I recognized his voice. He ate and drank; I saw him consume food. He said his body was one of flesh and bones; I felt the nail marks in his hands and in his feet. I know. I saw and felt and handled and heard. He is the Son of God. He rose from the dead.'

Peter does not stand alone; others were with him in the upper room, and they heard and saw and felt and knew. Thomas gained the same witness eight days later, in the same upper room, the doors again being shut, Jesus again standing in their midst and saying: "Thomas, Reach hither thy finger, and behold my hands; and reach hither thy hand, and thrust it into my side," to which Thomas responded, "My Lord and my God." (John 20:27-28.)

And all of this is but the beginning. The ever-enlarging ocean of true believers will continue to increase until the knowledge of God shall cover the earth "as the waters cover the sea" (Isa. 11:9), until all men know, as this disciple knows, that Jesus is Lord of all, and that he rose from the dead, as all men shall. There is no fact of revealed religion more surely established than the fact of resurrection. And there is no Messianic utterance more certainly known than that the great Jehovah, Israel's Deliverer and Savior, is the Messiah who came and who has now risen from the grave.

SALVATION IS IN CHRIST

How the Gospel Is Everlasting

We say, with justifiable pride and complete verity, that we have the everlasting gospel, God's eternal plan of salvation, the plan devised by the great Elohim to bring to pass the immortality and eternal life of all his spirit children, those on this little dot of a planet and those on all the infinite worlds that his hands have made. (Moses 1:29-39.) Our view and perspective and understanding of that which God hath wrought, both here among us and on the endless expanse of orbs and spheres which roll forth everlastingly at his word, our view of all this is as daylight compared to darkness, when we contrast it with what is known and believed in Christendom.

Those who have not yet had their souls illumined by the blazing light of the restored gospel assume that this earth only is inhabited and that only such portion of its inhabitants as have lived in the so-called Christian Era have had the gospel. By such persons it is naively imagined that Deity had some other system of salvation for all who lived before the coming of our Lord, some Mosaic law, or some patriarchal order that was less than and preparatory to the fulness that Christ brought. Let us now, however, open our hearts to that greater light and knowledge which a gracious God offers to all his children, and in doing so we shall crystallize in our minds what is meant by the everlasting gospel.

While banished on Patmos for the word of truth and the testimony of our Lord, the Beloved Revelator saw an angel flying in the midst of the latter-day heavens, "having the everlasting gospel to preach unto them that dwell on the earth." (Rev. 14:1-7.) Now, that which is everlasting, whether it be the gospel or anything else, has neither beginning nor ending; it is from all eternity to all eternity; it did not commence and it will not cease. It is everlasting.

The everlasting gospel was with God in the beginning; it was taught in the councils of eternity before the foundations of this world were laid; we have it now; and it will continue forever, being enjoyed in its eternal fulness in those realms of light and joy where celestial beings abide. The Holy Book records: "In the beginning was the gospel preached through the Son." That is, the Son of God, before he was ever born into mortality, preached the gospel, preached it in the presence of the Father to all the spirit hosts of heaven. "And the gospel was the word," meaning the word of salvation, "and the word was with the Son, and the Son was with God," for he was yet in preexistence, "and the Son was of God. . . . In him was the gospel, and the gospel was the life, and the life was the light of men; And the light shineth in the world, and the world perceiveth it not." (JST, John 1:1-5.) And as John so wrote, two millenniums ago, so it is today: "the world perceiveth it not." The gospel is reserved for those who forsake the world, who come out of darkness into the marvelous light of Christ.

The gospel was in preexistence; the gospel is now on earth among mortals; the gospel is found in the paradise of God among the righteous spirits; and the gospel is perfected in the lives of all those who have so far come forth from the grave. Those who were with Christ in his resurrection included "all of the prophets, and all those that have believed in their words, or all those that have kept the commandments of God." (Mosiah 15:22.)

Further, the gospel is in operation in all the worlds created by the Father and the Son. Their work and their glory, in all the infinite creations that their hands have made, is to bring to pass immortality and eternal life for the children of the Father. Through the atonement of Christ, the inhabitants of all these worlds have power to become his sons and his daughters, to become joint-heirs with him of all the glory of his Father's kingdom, to be adopted into the family of the Father, which is to say that the inhabitants of all worlds "are [thus] begotten sons and daughters unto God." (D&C 76:24.)

The Gospel Is for All Men

Did the Lord save Adam and Abraham by one set of laws and requirements and use a different standard for Peter, James, and John? Will Moses and Elijah pass by the angels and the gods to their exaltation and glory in all things by obedience to a lesser law than that imposed upon Paul and Matthew? The questions answer themselves. Either God treats all men the same or he is not God. If he respects persons and shows partiality, he does not possess those attributes of perfection which make him the exalted being that he is.

Anyone who, with James, knows that the Almighty is a being "with whom is no variableness, neither shadow of turning" (James 1:17) thereby knows also that the gospel is everlasting and that all men are saved by conforming to the same eternal standards.

Anyone who, with Paul, believes the statement "Jesus Christ the same yesterday, and to day, and for ever" (Heb. 13:8), knows that Adam and Abraham, Moses and Elijah were saved by faith in the same person in whom the New Testament saints believed.

Anyone who, with Moroni, knows "that God is the same yesterday, today, and forever, and in him there is no variableness neither shadow of changing" (Morm. 9:9), also knows, automatically and instinctively, that Adam had the gospel of Jesus Christ in the same literal sense that the same plan of salvation was enjoyed by Paul. Modern religionists, with the light before them, choose darkness rather than light if they elect to believe that an eternal and unchangeable God saves one soul on one set of standards and another soul in some other way.

In Chapter 4 we defined the gospel. In Chapter 7 we set forth that this gospel was revealed to Abraham and Moses and others in a series of dispensations. Our purpose here is to make it plain that everyone, from the beginning, who has received the gospel has known of Christ and has worshiped the Father in his name. This means Adam, Enoch, Noah, Abraham, and Moses. It includes the Jaredites and the Nephites, through all their tumultuous years. It includes the house of Israel whenever there were prophets among them who held the Melchizedek Priesthood. It includes the lost tribes whom the Savior visited after his resurrection, to say nothing of peoples and nations of whose identity and existence we know next to nothing. We do not know how many dispensations there have been, and we do not know all the peoples and nations who have been favored with prophetic leadership and teachings, but we do know that whenever and wherever the Lord has revealed his truths to any people or nation, those favored mortals have known that salvation was in Christ.

Preparatory to the setting up of the formal church organization in this dispensation, the Prophet Joseph Smith, writing by the spirit of prophecy and revelation, summarized the great truths of revealed religion. He said: "We know that there is a God in heaven, who is infinite and eternal, from everlasting to everlasting the same unchangeable God"; that he created man in his own image; that man was commanded to worship the Lord, but that he fell and became sensual and devilish; that, accordingly, the Only Begotten came to ransom fallen man and atone for the sins of the world—all to the end "that as many as would believe and be baptized in his holy name, and endure in faith to the end, should be saved." The plan of salvation, designed by the Father, was thus made operative through the atonement of his Son.

Having so summarized, the Prophet, with Spirit-guided insight, threw back the shroud of sectarian darkness that had so long covered Christendom. In keeping with the principles taught in the Book of Mormon, he announced that the saving truths of the gospel had been had in all ages when prophets guided the people. He said that the revealed truths of salvation applied to all men—"Not only those who believed after he came in the meridian of time, in the flesh, but all those from the beginning, even as many as were before he came, who believed in the words of the holy prophets, who spake as they were inspired by the gift of the Holy Ghost, who truly testified of him in all things, should have eternal life, As well as those who should come after, who should believe in the gifts and callings of God by the Holy Ghost, which beareth record of the Father and of the Son." (D&C 20:17-27.)

Salvation Is Always in Christ

After the fall, the Lord revealed himself to Adam and his posterity and sent selected preachers forth to call upon all men everywhere, by the power of the Holy Ghost, to repent and believe the gospel. "And as many as believed in the Son, and repented of their sins, should be saved; and as many as believed not and repented not, should be damned. . . . And thus the Gospel began to be preached, from the beginning, being declared by holy angels sent forth from the presence of God, and by his own voice, and by the gift of the Holy Ghost. And thus all things were confirmed unto Adam, by an holy ordinance, and the Gospel preached, and a decree sent forth, that it should be in the world [in a series of dispensations], until the end thereof." (Moses 5:15, 58-59.)

The gospel which was thus preached from the beginning was, in the Lord's language, as follows: "If thou wilt turn unto me, and hearken unto my voice, and believe, and repent of all thy transgressions, and be baptized, even in water, in the name of mine Only Begotten Son, who is full of grace and truth, which is Jesus Christ, the only name which shall be given under heaven, whereby salvation shall come unto the children of men, ye shall receive the gift of the Holy Ghost, asking all things in his name, and whatsoever ye shall ask, it shall be given you. . . . And now, behold, I say unto you: This is the plan of salvation unto all men, through the blood of mine Only Begotten, who shall come in the meridian of time." (Moses 6:52, 62.)

Man's course on earth is thus charted for him. An all-wise Father announces the provisions whereby mortals may return to his presence. Jesus Christ is the way. His gospel contains the laws which must be obeyed. In the beginning it was so; during all dispensations thereafter it was the same; it so remains to this hour; and it shall be so everlastingly. There is only one gospel, one plan of salvation, one Christ, one course back to our Father. God does not vary.

Let us sample the prophetic word which echoes and re-echoes the truths of which we now speak. Nephi says that "the Son of God was the Messiah who should come" and that the Holy Ghost "is the gift of God unto all those who diligently seek him, as well in times of old as in the time that he should manifest himself unto the children of men. For he is the same yesterday, to-day, and forever; and the way is prepared for all men from the foundation of the world, if it so be that they repent and come unto him. For he that diligently seeketh shall find; and the mysteries of God shall be unfolded unto them, by the power of the Holy Ghost, as well in these times as in times of old, and as well in times of old as in times to come; wherefore, the course of the Lord is one eternal round." (1 Ne. 10:17-19.)

Jacob says that "he cometh into the world that he may save all men if they will hearken unto his voice." (2 Ne. 9:21.) The plan of salvation is perfectly summarized in the 31st chapter of Second Nephi, at the conclusion of which is this assertion: "This is the way; and there is none other way nor name given under heaven whereby man can be saved in the kingdom of God. And now, behold, this is the doctrine of Christ, and the only and true doctrine of the Father, and of the Son, and of the Holy Ghost." (2 Ne. 31:21.)

To King Benjamin the angel said: "Salvation was, and is, and is to come"—which is past, present, and future—"in and through the atoning blood of Christ, the Lord Omnipotent." (Mosiah 3:18.) "Ought ye not to tremble and repent of your sins," Abinadi asked, "and remember that only in and through Christ ye can be saved?" (Mosiah 16:13.) Alma taught: "There is no other way or means whereby man can be saved, only in and through Christ. Behold, he is the life and the light of the world. Behold, he is the word of truth and righteousness." (Alma 38:9.)

Christ Bringeth Salvation

To a cult called Zoramites who had departed from the true faith, Amulek said: "The great question which is in your minds is whether the word be in the Son of God, or whether there shall be no Christ." By way of answer, he testified: "The word is in Christ unto salvation." (Alma 34:5-6.) To Zeezrom, burning with fever "caused by the great tribulations of his mind on account of his wickedness," and yet being repentant in his heart, Alma asked: "Believest thou in the power of Christ unto salvation?" Receiving an affirmative answer, Alma healed and baptized the zealot who had theretofore opposed the truth. (Alma 15:3-12.)

And so we now come to the basic premise that Christ came to bring salvation, a truth that is bountifully clear from all we have written in this work. We shall, at this point, simply note that the Messianic witnesses did so testify with clarity and emphasis. The Spirit Messiah said to Enoch: "Whoso cometh in at the gate and climbeth up by me shall never fall." (Moses 7:53.) The mortal Messiah said to his disciples: "I am the way, the truth, and the life: no man cometh unto the Father, but by me." (John 14:6.) Also: "All that ever came before me who testified not of me are thieves and robbers." (JST, John 10:8.)

To the first Alma, the Spirit Messiah said: "It is I that taketh upon me the sins of the world." (Mosiah 26:23.) Of him the second Alma said: "It is he that surely shall come to take away the sins of the world; yea, he cometh to declare glad tidings of salvation unto his people." (Alma 39:15.) "He bare the sin of many," said Isaiah. (Isa. 53:12.) Of the mortal Messiah, John the Baptist testified: "Behold the Lamb of God, which taketh away the sin of the world." (John 1:29.) Speaking as the resurrected Messiah, he himself said: "I have drunk out of that bitter cup which the Father hath given me, and have glorified the Father in taking upon me the sins of the world, in the which I have suffered the will of the Father in all things from the beginning." (3 Ne. 11:11.)

Amulek said: "He shall come into the world to redeem his people; and he shall take upon him the transgressions of those who believe on his name; and these are they that shall have eternal life, and salvation cometh to none else." (Alma 11:40.) Also: "He has all power to save every man that believeth on his name and bringeth forth fruit meet for repentance." (Alma 12:15.) Moroni called him "the author and the finisher" of our faith (Moro. 6:4), and Paul identified him as "the author [meaning *cause*] of eternal salvation unto all them that obey him" (Heb. 5:9).

Without Christ All Is Lost

Since Christ came to bring salvation, it follows that if he had not come, there would be no salvation. Since his atonement ransoms man from temporal and spiritual death, it follows that if there had been no atonement, there would be no ransom—all mankind would have been lost forever. "According to the great plan of the Eternal God there must be an atonement made, or else all mankind must unavoidably perish." (Alma 34:9; Mosiah 15:19.)

Since he came to save men from death, hell, the devil, and endless torment, it follows that if he had not come, the bodies of all men would have remained in the grave, their spirits would have stayed in hell, the devil would have been their ruler, and eternal torment would have been their way of life.

If Christ had not come, there would be no resurrection, no immortality, no hope of eternal glory, no eternal life, no exaltation in the kingdom of God. If he had not come, all men would be devils, angels to a devil, sons of perdition, suffering the torments of the damned forever. If Christ had not come, there would be no forgiveness of sins, no return to the presence of the Father, no spiritual rebirth, no continuation of the family unit in eternity—nothing of moment or merit. The purposes of creation would have vanished away, and all things would have come to naught. (2 Ne. 9.)

Is it any wonder that Nephi said: "My soul delighteth in proving unto my people that save Christ should come all men must perish." Indeed, the inexorable logic of the situation led that prophet to conclude and to testify: "If there be no Christ there be no God; and if there be no God we are not, for there could have been no creation. But there is a God, and he is Christ, and he cometh in the fulness of his own time." (2 Ne. 11:6-7.)

Believe in Christ

To gain salvation, men must believe in Christ. It matters not when or where they live. He is the Savior of all men, of all ages, and of all races. Let them dwell in darkest Africa or on the lost land of Atlantis; let them live four thousand years before his mortal birth or in our decadent day; let them be of Israel or Gentile lineage; let them be bond or free, black or white, pygmies or giants; let them be whosoever they are, live whensoever they do, dwell wheresoever they may, or be whatsoever it falls their lot to be—all must believe in Christ to be saved. Such is the law ordained by him and his Father before the world was.

Needless to say, the Lord wants men to be saved. Every soul who gains eternal life adds to Deity's kingdoms and glory. And so, in every dispensation, he reveals Christ and his laws. If men believe and obey, salvation will be their lot and eternal life their inheritance. In Adam's day the first proclamation of the gospel went forth in these words: "Believe on his Only Begotten Son, even him whom he declared should come in the meridian of time, who was prepared from before the foundation of the world." It is of this pronouncement that the record says: "And thus the Gospel began to be preached, from the beginning." (Moses 5:57-59.)

All the prophets taught this same doctrine. "To him give all the prophets witness," Peter said, "that through his name whosoever believeth in him shall receive remission of sins." (Acts 10:43.) One of the greatest Messianic utterances, relative to believing in Christ who should come, is contained in these words, spoken some five hundred and fifty years before his mortal birth: "The right way is to believe in Christ and deny him not; for by denying him ye also deny the prophets and the law. . . . The right way is to believe in Christ, and deny him not; and Christ is the Holy One of Israel; wherefore ye must bow down before him, and worship him with all your might, mind, and strength, and your whole soul; and if ye do this ye shall in nowise be cast out." (2 Ne. 25:28-29.)

After he came, the witness was the same. Always and everlastingly men are commanded to believe in him. "Whosoever believeth in him should not perish, but have everlasting life." (John 3:16.)

John the Baptist bore this witness: "He that believeth on the Son hath everlasting life: and he that believeth not the Son shall not see life; but the wrath of God abideth on him." (John 3:36.) And Jesus himself said: "Ye believe in God, believe also in me." (John 14:1.) "He that believeth on me hath everlasting life." (John 6:47.) "This is the work of God, that ye believe on him whom he hath sent." (John 6:29.)

How to Believe in Christ

We now have before us this basic verity: "He shall bring salvation to all those who shall believe on his name." (Alma 34:15.) So he shall. As an abstract principle, this concept presents no great problem. Our difficulties arise when we begin to define what is meant by believing in Christ and when we begin to segregate out the true believers from those whose ideas on the subject are false, but who nonetheless suppose that they believe in him.

What does it mean to believe in Christ? It means to accept him as the Son of God in the literal and full sense of the word. It means to believe that God is his Father in the same sense that all mortal men have fathers. It means to believe that the Spirit Jehovah was born as the Son of Mary; that the great Creator took upon himself a tabernacle of clay; that he came into the world to work out the infinite and eternal atonement. It presupposes that his Father is a personal being in whose image man is made. It presupposes that the Father is one person, the Son another. It presupposes a receptive, believing frame of mind, one that is willing and ready to hope for that which is not seen which is true.

It does not mean to believe that he is part of a spirit essence that fills the immensity of space, is everywhere and nowhere in particular present, and is in some indefinable and incomprehensible way three beings in one. It does not mean to believe that he is the same person as the Father, and that, as the Son, he is simply manifesting himself under a different name. It does not mean to believe that he finished his work in ages past and no longer works among men, in power, by revelation, performing signs and miracles by the hands of the faithful.

How do we identify true believers? Amid the cries "Lo, here is Christ; Lo, there," can we sift out those who truly believe from those who use gospel language without envisioning what the words really mean? It is one thing to believe Christ is the Son of God in some figurative way and another to believe that his Father has a body of flesh and bones as tangible as man's. Even in the Church itself, where the true doctrine is taught and should be known, there are those with limited and twisted ideas about their Lord, even as was the case in the meridian of time. "Some indeed preach Christ even of envy and strife," Paul said, "and some also of good will: The one preach Christ of contention," or of faction, "But the other of love." (Phil. 1:15-17.)

What are the signs by which true believers may be known? Do we believe in Christ if we reject revelation and signs and miracles? If we fail to accept the inspired utterances of living apostles and prophets? If we do not believe the Bible, or the Book of Mormon, or the Doctrine and Covenants? Belief is a serious and solemn thing. The issue is not sincerity of purpose, but one of fact and reality and truth. If we believe the truth, we can be saved; if we believe a lie, we shall surely be damned.

To identify true believers and to indicate how all may be numbered with that select and favored group, we should ponder and apply the following:

1. *Learn of Christ.*

Manifestly this is the beginning point. No man can believe in anything of which he is ignorant. Until we learn about our Lord we cannot exercise an intelligent judgment on the issue of belief or disbelief. A knowledge of Christ is found in the scriptures and is taught by his servants who are members of his church and who have already come to believe that he is Lord of all.

2. *Believe the words he has spoken.*

Some of our Lord's words are recorded in the Standard Works—that is, in the Bible, the Book of Mormon, the Doctrine and Covenants, and the Pearl of Great Price. Anyone who believes the words there written believes in Christ. Implicit in this statement is the fact that the words mean what they say. There are those who suppose they believe the Bible who do not believe in the true Christ because they choose to interpret the Biblical teachings to conform not to sense and reason, but to their preadopted and preconceived creeds. Words must be accepted according to their clear and obvious meaning and intent, and in the final analysis must be interpreted by the power of the Spirit.

Jesus said: "He that will not believe my words will not believe me—that I am," that is to say, that I exist, that I am the Christ, that I am he of whom the prophets testified, "and he that will not believe me will not believe the Father who sent me." He also said: "But he that believeth these things which I have spoken, him will I visit with the manifestations of my Spirit, and he shall know and bear record. For because of my Spirit he shall know that these things are true; for it persuadeth men to do good." (Ether 4:11-12.)

3. *Believe the testimonies of his disciples.*

Some of these are in the scriptures; others are found in various publications; many are never written down, except that they ofttimes sink into the hearts of receptive persons with such fixity that it is as though they were written in the souls of men. And our Lord's system for presenting truth to the world is to do it by the mouth of witnesses. He gives the Holy Ghost to his servants, and the words which they then speak are his own. They are his voice, his mind, and his will. They are scripture. (D&C 68:1-4.) They reveal Christ. Hence, to believe in him we must believe in his words as they fall from the lips of those who speak by the power of the Holy Ghost.

"He that receiveth whomsoever I send receiveth me," Jesus said, "and he that receiveth me receiveth him that sent me." (John 13:20.) Also: "And he that believeth not my words believeth not my disciples." (Ether 4:10.) And, of course, the reverse of that is also true, that he that believeth the words of the disciples believeth in him. "For whoso receiveth not the words of Jesus and the words of those whom he hath sent receiveth not him; and therefore he will not receive them at the last day." (3 Ne. 28:34.) We know of Christ today because he has been manifest through the teachings of his disciple Joseph Smith, to whom the Lord said: "This generation shall have my word through you." (D&C 5:10.) And, we might add, if they do not get it through Joseph Smith, they will not get it.

4. *Believe the Book of Mormon.*

This volume of holy scripture is sent forth "to the convincing of the Jew and Gentile that Jesus is the Christ, the Eternal God, manifesting himself unto all nations." (Title Page, Book of Mormon.) The book itself is a new witness for Christ. From first to last it bears record that he is the Son of God and teaches in plainness and perfection the truths of his everlasting gospel. Anyone who believes the Book of Mormon believes in Christ. And conversely, anyone who believes in Christ believes in the Book of Mormon.

"Believe in Christ," Nephi said, "And if ye shall believe in Christ ye will believe in these words [those written in the Book of Mormon], for they are the words of Christ, and he hath given them unto me." (2 Ne. 33:10.) In this connection, it is worthy of note that anyone who believes the Bible will also believe the Book of Mormon. (Morm. 7:8-9.) The great problem in the sectarian world is that people have the Bible but neither understand nor believe it, except in a casual and superficial way; and they know about Christ but neither accept nor believe in him in the full sense required to attain salvation with him and his Father.

5. *Receive the Holy Ghost.*

This is the perfect and conclusive way to know of the divine Sonship of our Lord. The Holy Ghost is a revelator; that is his commission as a member of the Godhead. He bears witness of the Father and the Son. (2 Ne. 31:18.) Anyone who receives the Holy Ghost thereby knows that Jesus is the Christ. Moroni said: "Ye may know that he is, by the power of the Holy Ghost." (Moro. 10:7.) The thing which the Lord requires of men is that they obey the law which entitles them to receive the Holy Ghost so they can thereby believe in Christ and chart for themselves a course leading to eternal life.

6. *Keep the commandments.*

Jesus said: "My doctrine is not mine, but his that sent me. If any man will do his will, he shall know of the doctrine, whether it be of God, or whether I speak of myself." (John 7:16-17.) It follows, unfailingly and absolutely, that any person who keeps the commandments of God, as he would have him do, shall gain the knowledge that Christ is the Lord. Among the commandments are these:

"Search the scriptures." (John 5:39.)

Treasure up "my word." (JS-H 37.)

Repent, be baptized, receive the Holy Ghost, and endure in righteousness to the end. (3 Ne. 27:20-21.)

Seek that salvation prepared for the faithful, for "he cometh into the world that he may save all men if they will hearken unto his voice." (2 Ne. 9:21.)

7. *Work miracles.*

If there is one thing that always attends and identifies those who believe in Christ it is this: they work miracles. Signs and gifts always attend their ministry. However much it may run counter to the course of Christendom, however severe the indictment may seem, speaking of the gifts of the Spirit, the word of the Lord is: "These signs shall follow them that believe." (Mark 16:17.) "And if it so be that the church is built upon my gospel then will the Father show forth his own works in it." (3 Ne. 27:10.)

Anyone who believes what the apostles believed will receive the same gifts they enjoyed, will perform the same miracles, and will do the same works. "He that believeth on me, the works that I do shall he do also." (John 14:12.)

8. *See his face.*

We repeat again what so few know in the full and true sense of the word, that those who believe and obey the whole law shall see the face of their Lord while they yet dwell as mortals on earth. He is no respecter of persons. If the brother of Jared, because of his perfect knowledge, "could not be kept from beholding within the veil," so shall it be with any of like spiritual perfection. (Ether 3:19-26.)

"Hallowed Be Thy Name"

As with the Father, so with the Son: "Hallowed be thy name." (Matt. 6:9.) To the Son hath God the Father given a name and a power that are above all names and powers whether in heaven or on earth. Only the Father is above him. Because the Son ransoms and redeems and saves, the hopes and the destinies of all men center in him. His name is above all names. His character and honorable reputation, his illustrious fame, his rank and position, all are above those of men and angels.

Of him it is written: He "made himself of no reputation, and took upon him the form of a servant, and was made in the likeness of men: And being found in fashion as a man, he humbled himself, and became obedient unto death, even the death of the cross." Such was the mortal life of the Eternal One. Hence, also, it is written: "Wherefore God also hath highly exalted him, and given him a name which is above every name: That at the name of Jesus every knee should bow, of things in heaven, and things in earth, and things under the earth; And that every tongue should confess that Jesus Christ is Lord, to the glory of God the Father." (Phil. 2:7-11.)

There is no language available to men or angels that can record with deserved emphasis the reality that salvation is in Christ and that his holy name is exalted above all others. Nephi said: "All those who believe on his name shall be saved in the kingdom of God. . . . And as the Lord God liveth, there is none other name given under heaven save it be this Jesus Christ, of which I have spoken, whereby man can be saved." (2 Ne. 25:13, 20.) The angel said to King Benjamin: "There shall be no other name given nor any other way nor means whereby salvation can come unto the children of men, only in and through the name of Christ, the

Lord Omnipotent." (Mosiah 3:17.) Peter echoed the same thought in his day in these words: "There is none other name under heaven given among men, whereby we must be saved." (Acts 4:12.) And now, for myself and all others who have like knowledge and feelings, I say:

The name of Jesus—wondrous name—the name in which the truths of salvation are taught; the name in which the ordinances of salvation are performed; the name in which miracles are wrought, in which the dead are raised and mountains moved;

The name of Jesus—wondrous name—the name by which worlds come rolling into existence; the name by which redemption comes; the name which brings victory over the grave and raises the faithful to eternal life;

The name of Jesus—wondrous name—the name by which revelation comes and angels minister; the name of him by whom all things are and into whose hands the Father hath committed all things; the name of him to whom every knee shall bow and every tongue confess in that great day when the God of Heaven makes this planet his celestial home.

Is it any wonder, then, that we preach that all men everywhere should live a Christ-centered life, and that those who have knowledge of these things, who are the Latter-day Saints, above all others, should let their thoughts dwell upon him unceasingly!

We are counseled: "Feast upon the words of Christ; for behold the words of Christ will tell you all things what ye should do." (2 Ne. 32:3.)

We are promised: "If ye shall press forward, feasting upon the word of Christ, and endure to the end, behold, thus saith the Father: Ye shall have eternal life." (2 Ne. 31:20.)

O that it might be said of us, as it was of them of old, "We talk of Christ, we rejoice in Christ, we preach of Christ, we prophesy of Christ, and we write according to our prophecies, that our children may know to what source they may look for a remission of their sins." (2 Ne. 25:26.)

"Come unto Christ"

We are approaching the day—it has not yet arrived, but soon shall—"when the knowledge of a Savior shall spread throughout every nation, kindred, tongue, and people." Even in this age of enlightenment, there are many yet upon the earth who know nothing of Christ and his laws or who have only a casual awareness that there is such a thing as Christianity. They do not know enough, as yet, to form an intelligent opinion that they should come unto Christ, live his laws, and prepare for a continuing life with him hereafter.

But when the knowledge of a Savior is taken to them—and I take it that such knowledge has already gone to all who have the Bible—then "none shall be found blameless before God, except it be little children, only through repentance and faith on the name of the Lord God Omnipotent." (Mosiah 3:20-21.) That is, all who know of Christ and all who should know because the opportunity is available have the responsibility to seek him out. Men have an obligation to seek the truth. The Spirit of Christ is given to every soul born into the world; its function is to guide them to that light and truth which saves, and all who follow its enticings and promptings come unto Christ and salvation. Those who die without this knowledge because it was not available to them shall have opportunity to believe and obey in the spirit world, and if they do so with all their hearts, they shall be heirs with the living of salvation in our Father's kingdom.

It is true that we have an obligation to preach the gospel to the world and invite them to receive that further light and knowledge that a gracious Father offers to all his children. But this does not diminish or abrogate their responsibility to follow the light they already have, to seek truth, and to come to the place and people where salvation is found. This applies to pagan and Christian alike—all are to come unto Him of whom we here teach and testify.

What we here say applies only to those who are accountable, meaning those who have arrived at the age of accountability, which is eight years, and those who have normal faculties and mentality. Little children are saved through the atonement of Christ without any act on their part. He does not bear their sins, for they have none. "Little children are redeemed from the foundation of the world through mine Only Begotten," the Lord says, "Wherefore, they cannot sin, for power is not given unto Satan to tempt little children, until they begin to become accountable before me." (D&C 29:46-47.) "Little children," Abinadi said, "have eternal life." (Mosiah 15:25.) "Little children are alive in Christ, even from the foundation of the world." (Moro. 8:12.)

As to those whose mental circumstances preclude them from getting a knowledge of Christ, those who do not therefore know right from wrong, the revelation says: "Whoso having knowledge, have I not commanded to repent? And he that hath no understanding, it remaineth in me to do according as it is written." (D&c 29:49-50.) All such, being as little children, are saved through the atonement of their Lord.

But as to accountable persons, the eternal decree is: Come unto Christ; come unto him with full purpose of heart and be saved. Hear the prophetic voices:

King Benjamin tells us who can be saved, in these thoughtful and Spirit-filled words: "If ye have come to a knowledge of the goodness of God, and his matchless power, and his wisdom, and his patience, and his long-suffering towards the children of men; and also, the atonement which has been prepared from the foundation of the world, that thereby salvation might come to him that should put his trust in the Lord, and should be diligent in keeping his commandments, and continue in the faith even unto the end of his life, I mean the life of the mortal body—I say, that this is the man who receiveth salvation, through the atonement which was prepared from the foundation of the world for all mankind, which ever were since the fall of Adam, or who are, or who ever shall be, even unto the end of the world. And this is the means whereby salvation cometh. And there is none other salvation save this which hath been spoken of; neither are there any conditions whereby man can be saved except the conditions which I have told you." (Mosiah 4:6-8.)

Amaleki, who kept the Nephite records in his day, issued this proclamation: "Come unto Christ, who is the Holy One of Israel, and partake of his salvation, and the power of his redemption. Yea, come unto him, and offer your whole souls as an offering unto him, and continue in fasting and praying, and endure to the end; and as the Lord liveth ye will be saved." (Omni 26.)

Moroni climaxed his writings with this plea: "Come unto Christ, and be perfected in him, and deny yourselves of all ungodliness; and if ye shall deny yourselves of all ungodliness and love God with all your might, mind and strength, then is his grace sufficient for you, that by his grace ye may be perfect in Christ." (Moro. 10:32.)

And the Lord Jesus, he who rose from the dead and who liveth still, issues this invitation to all his brethren, spirit children of the same Father: "I have come unto the world to bring redemption unto the world, to save the world from sin. Therefore, whoso repenteth and cometh unto me as a little child, him will I receive, for of such is the kingdom of God. Behold, for such I have laid down my life, and have taken it up again; therefore repent, and come unto me ye ends of the earth, and be saved." (3 Ne. 9:21-22.)

Who can question this call? What more need we say? Christ is God. Salvation is in him. Those who believe and obey shall gain peace in this life and eternal life in the world to come. So be it.

SALVATION IS IN JEHOVAH

Christ Has Many Names

Since salvation is in Christ and him only in all ages of the world; since his is the only name given under heaven whereby men can be saved, whether they lived before, during, or after his mortal ministry—why do we not find his name in the Old Testament? Several facts and circumstances should be noted in seeking an answer to this vital question:

1. His name was in the Old Testament when the books comprising that holy volume were first written. At least his name, as there recorded in Hebrew, should have been translated into the Greek as Christ. We know this because of the way the Prophet Joseph Smith has given us the Book of Moses in the Pearl of Great Price. It is there specified that all of the prophets and saints, from Adam to Noah and his sons, called him Jesus Christ, and we may rest assured that they taught their children after them the same nomenclature.

2. He was known by the name of Jesus Christ among the Jaredites, whose historical time span covered about two millenniums, commencing in the day of the tower of Babel (Ether 1:4-5) and going down to the day of Coriantumr and the city of Zarahemla (Omni 21).

3. Approximately 87 percent of the Book of Mormon deals with history and doctrine that preceded the personal ministry of our Lord among the Nephites. Through all of the

more than 450 pages of Holy Writ covering that ancient period, our Lord was known among the people as Jesus Christ. All of this is of course Old Testament times; Nephi and Jeremiah, for instance, were contemporaries.

4. By joining the foregoing with the practice of the Christian Era, it is clear that we can trace the usage of our Lord's most prevalent name during the entire six thousand years of time that has elapsed since Adam was cast out of Eden.

5. We should note here that many plain and precious parts of the Old Testament were torn from between its sacred covers by evil and designing men in days long past. (1 Ne. 13.) It is perfectly clear that their intent was to destroy the knowledge of Christ and of the plan of salvation, because many of the things restored by Joseph Smith, by the spirit of inspiration, deal specifically with these things. We have seen that the Book of Moses restores to the Old Testament the knowledge about the Son of God under his New Testament names. This restoration is made in the Book of Genesis down to the 13th verse of the 6th chapter; Genesis, chapter 14, in the Joseph Smith Translation contains additions that name our Lord as the Son of God.

6. Careless scribes and poor translators, not knowing that our Lord had revealed himself by the name of Christ from the beginning, failed to translate references to him by that designation. An example of making a translation conform to a prevailing doctrinal concept is found in the 8th Psalm where the original account says that God made man a little lower than Elohim. Not knowing that man is of the same race as Deity, that he dwelt with his Father in preexistence, and that his potential is to become as Elohim is, the translators made the passage read that God had made man a little lower than the angels.

7. "All the holy prophets which were before us," said the Nephite Jacob, "believed in Christ and worshiped the Father in his name, and also we worship the Father in his name." (Jacob 4:4-5.) This blanket assertion includes the

worship performed by Abraham, Isaac, and Jacob, by Moses, Elijah, and Samuel, by Isaiah, Hosea, and Micah, and by all the inspired saints from Adam's day on down. And what was said of those who went before applies also to all who came after. God does not change.

8. In our present Old Testament, Christ is called the Lord, which is the anglicized rendition of Jehovah. Thus, Christ is Jehovah. Our Messianic studies would fall far short of the mark if we were not keenly aware that these two great name-titles apply to one and the same person. Such is shown repetitiously throughout this work.

9. Names applied to our Lord are numerous. Each has a differing shade of meaning and teaches some special thing relative to him and his work. But each refers to the same individual. Old Testament prophets refer to him as the Savior, Redeemer, Deliverer, Messiah, God of Israel, Jehovah, and so forth, all being names that identify the Only Begotten of the Father. It follows that a prayer to the Father in any of these names is a prayer in the name of Christ. Indeed, the great command to Adam was, "Thou shalt do all that thou doest in the name of the Son, and thou shalt repent and call upon God in the name of the Son forevermore." (Moses 5:8.) Sometimes today we hear prayers in the name of the Son, or in the name of Israel's God, or in whatever title the sincere supplicant chooses to use, all of which is valid and proper and approved.

Salvation Is the Burden of the Scriptures

In Chapter 8 we set forth that, in the true and complete sense of the word, salvation is eternal life. It is exaltation in the highest heaven of the celestial kingdom. It is to be as God is. Chapter 17 is devoted to the thesis that salvation is in Christ, that it comes in and through his holy name and in no other way. Our present concern is to make it clear beyond controversy or question that salvation is in Jehovah and comes in and through and because of him, and therefore that Jehovah is Christ.

To gain salvation is and should be the chief concern of all men. Those who are spiritually inclined and enlightened make it the chief goal of their very existence. "If thou wilt do good, yea, and hold out faithful to the end," the Lord says, "thou shalt be saved in the kingdom of God, which is the greatest of all the gifts of God; for there is no gift greater than the gift of salvation." (D&C 6:13.) That the Lord wants men to be saved is axiomatic. Making immortality and eternal life available is his work, his business, the active enterprise to which he devotes all of his strength and power. And in those holy scriptures which come from him, he sets forth the terms and conditions whereby this greatest of all gifts may be won.

Salvation is mentioned by name 62 times in the Psalms, 28 times in Isaiah, and another 26 times in the balance of the Old Testament, for a total of 116 times in that ancient scripture. All of these references, plus two in the Book of Abraham, talk about salvation as it relates to, comes from, and is effected by the Lord Jehovah. All of them are in that sense Messianic, and many of them apply expressly and pointedly to the mortal ministry of that member of the Godhead.

By way of comparison, there are 44 references to salvation by name in the New Testament, 88 in the Book of Mormon, 50 in the Doctrine and Covenants, and four (besides the two in Abraham) in the Pearl of Great Price. All of these associate salvation with Christ. In all of the scriptures, but especially in those received by us during the so-called Christian Era, there are many passages dealing with salvation which do not use the word itself.

To catch the vision of how the ancient scriptures associate salvation with Jehovah, let us, in addition to the numerous illustrations quoted elsewhere in this work, note the following:

"My name is Jehovah," the Lord said to Abraham, "And I will make of thee a great nation, . . . for as many as receive this Gospel shall be called after thy name, . . . and in thy seed after thee . . . shall all the families of the earth be blessed, even with the blessings of the Gospel, which are the blessings of salvation, even of life eternal." (Abr. 2:8-11.) That is to say: The gospel of the Lord Jesus Christ—the everlasting gospel!—is the gospel of the Lord Jehovah.

After his resurrection, the Savior appeared to his disciples in an upper room, permitted them to touch and handle his glorified body, ate before them, and then said: "These are the words which I spake unto you, while I was yet with you, that all things must be fulfilled, which were written in the law of Moses, and in the prophets, and in the psalms, concerning me." (Luke 24:44.) They then received from him power to understand the scriptures.

The law of Moses, the prophets, and the psalms—these were the sources to which those in time's meridian could turn for Messianic knowledge. And now that our Lord had been raised from the dead, now that his mortal ministry and atoning sacrifice were accomplished fact, the disciples could look back to these sources and see wherein they foretold all that had happened in the life of him whom they accepted as Lord and Christ.

As to the Psalms, truly do they abound in declarations that Jehovah is the Savior. "Save me, O my God. . . . Salvation belongeth unto the Lord." (Ps. 3:7-8.) "We will rejoice in thy salvation, and in the name of our God." (Ps. 20:5.) "He only is my rock and my salvation. . . . In God is my salvation and my glory." (Ps. 62:6-7.) "Shew us thy mercy, O Lord, and grant us thy salvation." (Ps. 85:7.) "The Lord taketh pleasure in his people: he will beautify the meek with salvation." (Ps. 149:4.) And so the pleas for grace and the songs of praise continue through more than three score passages. In each of them the Lord mentioned is Jehovah. He will save. Salvation is in him.

As illustrations from Isaiah, let us quote these passages,

all having reference to Jehovah: "Behold, God is my salvation; I will trust, and not be afraid: for the Lord JEHOVAH is my strength and my song; he also is become my salvation." (Isa. 12:2.) After reciting how Jehovah will "swallow up death in victory" and "wipe away tears from off all faces," Isaiah says: "And it shall be said in that day, Lo, this is our God; we have waited for him, and he will save us: this is the Lord; we have waited for him, we will be glad and rejoice in his salvation." (Isa. 25:8-9.) One of the most noted of all Isaiah's utterances says: "The Lord is our judge, the Lord is our lawgiver, the Lord is our King; he will save us." (Isa. 33:22.) Truly, O Israel, "thy salvation cometh," and "his [Jehovah's] reward is with him, and his work before him." (Isa. 62:11.) There are, of course, many other such passages in the prophetic writings of Israel's Messianic seer.

Truly, "Salvation is of the Lord." (Jonah 2:9.) Such is the burden of the scriptures and the message of the Old Testament prophets. And our message is that all of their sayings tie into Christ through whose atoning power salvation has now come. Those who are his saints have put on "the breastplate of faith and love; and for an helmet, the hope of salvation." As Paul says: "God hath not appointed us to wrath, but to obtain salvation by our Lord Jesus Christ, Who died for us, that . . . we should live together with him." (1 Thes. 5:8-10.)

And so the heavenly choirs sing of Christ. "Alleluia [meaning, praise Jehovah]; Salvation, and glory, and honour, and power, unto the Lord our God. . . . Alleluia: for the Lord God omnipotent reigneth." (Rev. 19:1, 6.)

Jehovah Is the Savior

All believing Christians accept Jesus as the Savior of the world. This concept is set forth clearly in the New Testament, the Book of Mormon, and the Doctrine and Covenants. It is one of the plainest and most widely received truths of revealed religion. From the day the angelic ministrant hailed his birth by saying, "Unto you is born this day in the city of David a Saviour, which is Christ the Lord" (Luke 2:11), the apostles and prophets of the New Testament acclaimed and accepted him as their Savior. Beginning with Nephi, who spoke of "a Messiah, or, in other words, a Savior of the world" (1 Ne. 10:4), the inspired preachers on the American continent bore the same witness. Among many passages, the Doctrine and Covenants speaks of him as "the Savior of the world, even of as many as believe" on his name. (D&C 66:1.)

It is hoped that all those who accept Jesus as Lord and Savior know also that the Old Testament prophets and seers knew him as Jehovah, which is to say, Jehovah is the Savior of the world. The writings of Moses, as originally recorded by the great lawgiver, contained these words: "Mine Only Begotten is and shall be the Savior, for he is full of grace and truth." (Moses 1:6.) Isaiah and various of the prophets recorded the words of the Eternal Jehovah in such ways as: "I am the Lord thy God, the Holy One of Israel, thy Saviour. . . . I, even I, am the Lord; and beside me there is no saviour." (Isa. 43:3, 11.) "I am the Lord thy God. . . . There is no saviour beside me." (Hosea 13:4.) And there are many other such statements.

To show that the New Testament authors knew that Christ their Savior was Jehovah, the Savior of Israel, let us examine these words spoken by Jehovah to Isaiah. That holy being identifies himself as the "God of Israel, the Saviour"; announces that "Israel shall be saved in the Lord with an everlasting salvation"; says to "the seed of Jacob: . . . There is no God else beside me; a just God and a Saviour; there is none beside me." Having so spoken to Israel, his chosen, he then affirms: "Look unto me, and be ye saved, all the ends of the earth: for I am God, and there is none else." (Isa. 45:15-22.)

That is to say, Jehovah is the Savior; come unto him, all ye ends of the earth; he "is the Saviour of all men, specially of those that believe." (1 Tim. 4:10.) "The Lord is God and beside him there is no Savior." (D&C 76:1.) Let all men come to him.

Having so stated, having issued the great invitation to come to him, the Lord Jehovah then says: "I have sworn by myself, the word is gone out of my mouth in righteousness, and shall not return, That unto me every knee shall bow, every tongue shall swear." (Isa. 45:23.) Before Jehovah, Judge of all, shall all things bow in humble reverence; to him every tongue that speaks shall swear an allegiance that shall never end! Well and gloriously spoke the great God by the mouth of Isaiah.

Now, what says our friend Paul of this same day of coming judgment? With the same Spirit resting upon him that gave utterance to Isaiah, the theologically gifted apostle wrote: "Christ both died, and rose, and revived, that he might be Lord both of the dead and living, . . . for we shall all stand before the judgment seat of Christ. For it is written, As I live, saith the Lord, every knee shall bow to me, and every tongue shall confess to God." (Rom. 14:9-11.) It is thus from Christ's bar that judgment shall be rendered; it is he who is judge of all; it is to him that every knee shall bow; and it is to him that every tongue shall swear eternal allegiance. Blessed be his holy name!

Jehovah Is the Redeemer

Who is the Redeemer? That it is Christ, all sound theologians agree. But, surprisingly, the Lord Jesus is not so named in our present New Testament. What the New Testament does is teach that salvation comes "through the redemption that is in Christ Jesus" (Rom. 3:24), and that "we have redemption through his blood, the forgiveness of sins, according to the riches of his grace." (Eph. 1:7.) Such being the case, it is easy, in propriety and in truth, for Christians to pick up the name itself from Job's testimony—"I know that my redeemer liveth" (Job 19:25)—and from other Old Testament passages.

That it is Christ, we also know from numerous latter-day revelations and from a multitude of Messianic pronouncements found in the Book of Mormon. Nephi, for instance, speaks of Israel coming "to the knowledge of the true Messiah, their Lord and their Redeemer." (1 Ne. 10:14.) In about 83 B.C., Alma prophesied that "the time is not far distant that the Redeemer liveth and cometh among his people." (Alma 7:7.) Some ten years later that same prophet taught that "the Lord their God" was "Jesus Christ their Redeemer." (Alma 37:9.)

But our present purpose is to point out that the Old Testament prophets identified Jehovah as the Redeemer, and that the New Testament authors taught that the Holy One so identified was Christ. The Psalmist said, "God was their rock, and the high God their redeemer." (Ps. 78:35.) Jeremiah said of Israel: "Their Redeemer is strong; the Lord of hosts is his name." (Jer. 50:34.) And Isaiah recorded many statements from Jehovah himself to this effect: "Thy Maker is thine husband," he said to Israel; "the Lord of hosts is his name; and thy Redeemer the Holy One of Israel; The God of the whole earth shall he be called. . . . With everlasting kindness will I have mercy on thee, saith the Lord thy Redeemer." (Isa. 54:5-8.) "And the Redeemer shall come to Zion, and unto them that turn from transgression in Jacob, saith the Lord." (Isa. 59:20.)

An Old Testament passage that was spoken by Jehovah of himself, and which has clear and plain fulfillment in Christ, is preserved for us in these words: "Thus saith the Lord the King of Israel, and his redeemer the Lord of hosts; I am the first, and I am the last; and beside me there is no God. . . . For the Lord hath redeemed Jacob, and glorified himself in Israel." (Isa. 44:6, 23.) We are, of course, fully aware that Christ is the one who redeemed both Israel and all who would join with the chosen people in doing the deeds of true devotion. But it is more than mere chance to hear the voice of the risen and embodied Lord say to John the same thing the yet-unborn and unembodied Lord had said to Isaiah. "I am the first and the last," came the Voice, "I am he that liveth, and was dead; and, behold, I am alive for evermore." (Rev. 1:17-18.)

We need have no hesitancy, in view of all that is known and written, in both general and specific terms, to testify that Jehovah the Redeemer is he who was born of Mary and who is known in all Christendom as Christ the Redeemer.

Have Faith in the Lord Jesus Christ

Most Christians believe their salvation is based upon accepting Christ as their Savior; some feel it is also necessary to receive certain ordinances or sacraments or both; and a limited few even envision the eternal verity that it is necessary to keep the commandments and live godly and upright lives. What Christians in general do not know is that the same beliefs, the same ordinances, the same obedience and personal righteousness which now lead to salvation were also required of all men from the beginning. That is to say, salvation comes through faith in the Lord Jesus Christ no matter what age of the earth is involved. It was so with Adam and Enoch; it was so with Noah and Abraham; it was so with Moses and Elijah; it was so with Peter and Paul; and it is so today. Faith in the Lord Jesus Christ is the first principle of the gospel, the beginning of all righteousness, the open door to the path leading to eternal life in our Father's kingdom.

Mormon, whose name is forever enshrined in the hearts of true believers because he abridged the Nephite records, spoke plainly and powerfully of faith in Christ with words to this effect: "God knowing all things, being from everlasting to everlasting," he said, "sent angels to minister unto the children of men, to make manifest concerning the coming of Christ. . . . And God also declared unto prophets, by his own mouth, that Christ should come. . . . Wherefore, by the ministering of angels, and by every word which proceeded forth out of the mouth of God, men began to exercise faith in

Christ; . . . and thus it was until the coming of Christ." (Moro. 7:22-25.)

From the day of the first prophet, whose name was Adam, to the day of the messenger, whose name was John and who prepared the way before and introduced the Savior to his Israelitish kinsmen—during those four long millenniums of mortal existence, every prophet, every seer, every saint, all true believers, without exception and without deviation from the divine pattern, all had faith in the Lord Jesus Christ! He is eternal. His laws are eternal. The gospel is eternal. Truth never varies. Salvation always comes in the same way. And so our friend Mormon says: "And after that he came men also were saved by faith in his name." (Moro. 7:26.) We today but follow the pattern of the past. God does not vary.

With this concept in our minds, let us sample the sayings of our brethren of old who believed as we believe, and who rejoiced in Christ as we rejoice in him. In the days of Helaman the second, the Church among the Nephites prospered exceedingly. Tens of thousands of souls were converted and baptized. In abridging the events of that period, Mormon wrote: "Thus we see that the gate of heaven is open unto all, even to those who will believe on the name of Jesus Christ, who is the Son of God. Yea, we see that whosoever will may lay hold upon the word of God, which is quick and powerful, which shall divide asunder all the cunning and the snares and the wiles of the devil, and lead the man of Christ in a straight and narrow course across that everlasting gulf of misery which is prepared to engulf the wicked—And land their souls, yea, their immortal souls, at the right hand of God in the kingdom of heaven, to sit down with Abraham, and Isaac, and with Jacob, and with all our holy fathers, to go no more out." (Hel. 3:28-30.)

Be it known that Abraham, Isaac, and Jacob, and "all our holy fathers," were men of Christ, men who believed and obeyed, men who wrought righteousness, men who perfected their faith in that Lord for whose coming they looked and whose law they loved. They in their day were as the faithful in Helaman's day, of whom the record says: "They did fast and pray oft, and did wax stronger and stronger in their humility, and firmer and firmer in the faith of Christ, unto the filling their souls with joy and consolation, yea, even to the purifying and the sanctification of their hearts, which sanctification cometh because of their yielding their hearts unto God." (Hel. 3:35.)

We need not pursue this issue further. Any truth seeker, with the Book of Mormon in hand, can discover scores of passages from many prophets, all written in the so-called pre-Christian Era, which state plainly that faith in that Christ who shall come is essential to salvation. Manifestly this same truth is interwoven into all that the New Testament teaches about him whose name we so much revere and on whose arm we everlastingly rely.

Have Faith in the Lord Jehovah

It is by faith that miracles are wrought—not faith as an abstract, unembodied, vaporous nothingness, floating like a fog in the universe, but faith in the living Lord, faith centered in Christ our Head. The eternal law is: "Whoso believeth in Christ, doubting nothing, whatsoever he shall ask the Father in the name of Christ it shall be granted him; and this promise is unto all, even unto the ends of the earth." (Morm. 9:21.) Accordingly, any person who has ever performed a miracle, in any age, has done it by faith in Christ. For the past, at the present, and in the future, all miracles are wrought by faith in that Lord who is Christ.

Jesus our Lord said to his apostles: "These signs"—meaning gifts and miracles—"shall follow them that believe." (Mark 16:17.) The signs involved were the same as those which had followed true believers from the beginning. Faith is power. Where the Lord's power is poured out upon his people, there is faith, and where the power of God is not found, there is no faith. "When faith comes," the Prophet said, "it brings its train of attendants with it—apostles, prophets, evangelists, pastors, teachers, gifts, wisdom, knowledge, miracles, healings, tongues, interpretation of tongues, etc. All these appear when faith appears on the earth, and disappear when it disappears from the earth; for these are the effects of faith, and always have, and always will, attend it. For where faith is, there will the knowledge of God be also, with all things which pertain thereto—revelations, visions, and dreams, as well as every necessary thing, in order that the possessors of faith may be perfected, and obtain salvation; for God must change, otherwise faith will prevail with him. And he who possesses it will, through it, obtain all necessary knowledge and wisdom, until he shall know God, and the Lord Jesus Christ, whom he has sent—whom to know is eternal life." (*Lectures on Faith,* p. 69.)

With these principles before us, we come to a consideration of those Old Testament miracles performed by faith in Jehovah, and once again we hear the apostolic witness testify that Jehovah is Christ. In his great sermon on faith, Paul tells us it was by faith (power!) that the world was made. He says Abel, Enoch, Noah, Abraham, Isaac, Jacob, and Joseph wrought their mighty deeds by faith, meaning faith in that Jehovah whom they all served. Then he comes to Moses to whom the great I AM revealed himself, saying, "I appeared unto Abraham, unto Isaac, and unto Jacob. I am the Lord God Almighty; the Lord JEHOVAH. And was not my name known unto them?" (JST, Ex. 6:3.)

Who appeared to Moses, in whose ministry did he serve, and at whose behest did he labor? The Lord JEHOVAH! But what says Paul? Hear these words: "By faith Moses, when he was come to years, refused to be called the son of Pharaoh's daughter; Choosing rather to suffer affliction with the people of God, than to enjoy the pleasures of sin for a season; Esteeming the reproach of Christ greater riches than the treasures in Egypt: for he had respect unto the recompence of the reward." Having named Christ as the center of Moses' faith, our apostolic author recites various deeds done by Moses through faith. Faith in whom? Jehovah? Yes. Faith in Christ? Yes.

"And what shall I say more?" Paul asks, as he proceeds to name the Old Testament worthies, "Who through faith subdued kingdoms, wrought righteousness, obtained promises, stopped the mouths of lions, Quenched the violence of fire, escaped the edge of the sword, out of weakness were made strong, waxed valiant in fight, turned to flight the armies of the aliens." (Heb. 11.) The miracles of the Old Testament, performed as our Christian brethren suppose by faith in Jehovah, were in fact performed by faith in the Lord Jesus Christ, which makes every miracle, of itself, a Messianic performance.

Enter into the Rest of the Lord

One of the sweet and gracious doctrines of the gospel, a doctrine that brings comfort and serenity to the saints, is that those who are true and faithful in all things enter into the rest of the Lord their God.

Mortality is the state in which men are tried and tested; in which they are subject to temptation, disease, sorrow, and death; in which there is violent opposition to every true principle; in which the generality of mankind is wafted hither and yon by every wind of doctrine; in which Satan has great hold upon the hearts of most of mankind. It is not a state of peace and rest; in it there is work and turmoil and dissension. It is a probationary estate where choices must be made; where all men, the saints included, are being tried and tested, to see if they will choose liberty and eternal life through the atonement of Christ the Lord, or whether they will walk in subjection to that angel who fell from before the presence of the Eternal God and became the devil to rise no more.

Peace and rest, in the full and true sense, come only

through the gospel and are reserved for those who place themselves in harmony with those Holy Beings who are the embodiment of these godly attributes.

What does it mean to enter into the rest of the Lord? To this question there is a three-pronged answer: one aspect deals with the rest of the Lord here and now in mortality; the next is concerned with a more perfected rest that comes to those who, departing this sphere, find themselves in the paradise of God; and the final one applies to the saved saints who have risen in immortal glory ever to be with their Lord.

Mormon had some counsel for the saints, for those who believe the gospel and are seeking to live its laws. He addressed them in this way: "I would speak unto you that are of the church, that are the peaceable followers of Christ, and that have obtained a sufficient hope by which ye can enter into the rest of the Lord, from this time henceforth until ye shall rest with him in heaven." (Moro. 7:3.) To enter into the rest of the Lord in this life is to gain a sure knowledge of the truth and divinity of the Lord's work on earth. It is to have the testimony of Jesus and to know by personal revelation that The Church of Jesus Christ of Latter-day Saints is the kingdom of God on earth. It is to have such fixity of purpose that the calls, Lo, here is Christ, and Lo, there, seem like idle chatter. Those who have entered into the rest of the Lord here and now are not driven about by every wind of doctrine. They are not trying to find the truth. The Holy Spirit of God has already manifest to their souls where the truth is. They have charted a course leading to that eternal rest which is eternal life. They have received that peace which passeth all understanding and is known and felt only by the power of the Holy Ghost.

As to the rest of the Lord enjoyed by faithful saints when they depart this life, Alma says: "The spirits of those who are righteous are received into a state of happiness, which is called paradise, a state of rest, a state of peace, where they shall rest from all their troubles and from all care, and sorrow." (Alma 40:12.)

As to that rest which is enjoyed by those who dwell in immortal glory, Amulek says: "God did call on men, in the name of his Son, (this being the plan of redemption which was laid) saying: If ye will repent, and harden not your hearts, then will I have mercy upon you, through mine Only Begotten Son; Therefore, whosoever repenteth, and hardeneth not his heart, he shall have claim on mercy through mine Only Begotten Son, unto a remission of his sins; and these shall enter into my rest." (Alma 12:33-35.)

There are a number of other Book of Mormon exhortations that men should so live as to enter into the rest of the Lord. Christ, who is Jehovah, is of course the Lord who is meant, as he himself testified in this comforting invitation: "Come unto me, all ye that labour and are heavy laden, and I will give you rest. Take my yoke upon you, and learn of me; for I am meek and lowly in heart: and ye shall find rest unto your souls. For my yoke is easy, and my burden is light." (Matt. 11:28-30.)

Now let us see how the God of the Old Testament invites people to enter his rest and how the New Testament specifies that the God so speaking is Christ. Jehovah speaks, let earth give ear, "For the Lord is a great God, and a King above all gods. . . . For he is our God; and we are the people of his pasture, and the sheep of his hand. To day if ye will hear his voice, Harden not your heart, as in the provocation, and as in the day of temptation in the wilderness: When your fathers tempted me, proved me, and saw my work. Forty years long was I grieved with this generation, and said, It is a people that do err in their heart, and they have not known my ways: Unto whom I sware in my wrath that they should not enter into my rest." (Ps. 95:3-11.) It is of this same period of Israelitish rebellion and unbelief that our latter-day revelation says: "The Lord in his wrath, for his anger was kindled against them, swore that they should not enter into his rest while in the wilderness, which rest is the fulness of his glory." (D&C 84:24.)

We now turn to the use Paul made of these words from

the 95th Psalm, which he says were given to David by the Holy Ghost. Addressing himself to those who hold the holy priesthood, Paul says: "Brethren, . . . consider the Apostle and High Priest of our profession, Christ Jesus," who "was counted worthy of more glory than Moses." Why? Because he as God built the house in which Moses served. Moses was a faithful servant who bare testimony of Christ who should come, which Christ, Paul says, is the one who sware in his wrath that ancient Israel should not enter his rest because of unbelief. With this example of what happens to those who reject their Lord, as many in ancient Israel did, Paul exhorts the Hebrew saints of his day to be faithful lest they too fail, as did some of their fathers, to gain the promised blessings. "Let us therefore fear, lest, a promise being left us of entering into his rest, any of you should seem to come short of it. For unto us [the saints in Paul's day] was the gospel preached, as well as unto them [those in ancient Israel]: but the word preached did not profit them, not being mixed with faith in them that heard it. . . . There remaineth therefore a rest to the people of God." (Heb. 3 and 4.)

O that all men might come unto Christ and gain that rest and peace, both now and forever, that comes from him and him only!

Beware of False Gods

The worship of false gods and the following of false Christs lie at the root of all the ills and all the evils of all the world. There is no salvation in worshiping a false god, and a false Christ will never lift the burden of sin from fallen man nor lead him into realms of joy and light. Man was not created by idols of stone; he was not redeemed by the forces of nature; he will not come forth from the grave at the call of Baal; and an incomprehensible nothingness did not make ready a place for him in the mansions that are prepared. False gods have no power to create or redeem or enlighten or save or do any of the things which further the interests of men either in this world or in the world to come. And men must either worship the true God and follow the true Christ, or they shall with the wicked lift up their eyes in hell, being in torment.

That almost all men have and do worship false gods and follow false Christs is the saddest fact of all history. The divine decree is: "Thou shalt worship the Lord thy God, and him only shalt thou serve." (Luke 4:8.) But to name nations and peoples, with isolated exceptions, is to list those who have not had the true order and system of worship while in this life.

Few things are more offensive to the modern mind than to view the worship of past peoples. We have a justified feeling of revulsion toward Molech of the Ammonites and Chemosh of the Moabites, both hideous idols in whose worship children were sacrificed by fire; and yet Solomon himself, in his declining and apostate years, built places of worship for these and other gods of abomination on the Mount of Olives beside the Holy City. We shudder and stare in unbelief at the lascivious practices and child sacrifice, all in the name of religion, that were involved in the worship of Baal of the Canaanites; and yet this abomination of the heathens was the god of Ahab and Jezebel, and it took a confrontation on Mount Carmel, in which fire came down from heaven, for Elijah to dramatize before Israel that Jehovah and not Baal was the God of power. We find it difficult to believe that the Babylonians worshiped Bel, and yet their sincerity and devotion was such that they cast Shadrach, Meshach, and Abednego into the fiery furnace when these devout Hebrews refused to bow before his image. Nor can we look with any favor on the intellect that would worship Diana; and yet her temple at Ephesus was one of the seven wonders of the world. Athena, whose image was in the Greek Parthenon on the acropolis at Athens, and to whom Paul referred when he said, "God that made the world and all things therein, seeing that he is Lord of heaven and earth, dwelleth not in temples made with hands" (Acts 17:24), is in a like category.

Nor has the picture of false worship changed among the seemingly and supposedly more civilized peoples of the world. Rome accepted and honored all the gods of all the nations conquered by her sword, and for that matter deified some of her emperors. Buddha, symbolized by an obese idol, is worshiped in central and eastern Asia. Allah is the Supreme Being of the Mohammedans, and their scripture, the Koran, in its most meaningful and pointed passages denies the divinity of Christ and ridicules the concept that God had need of a Son. There are those today who suppose that the forces of nature or the laws of the universe, however they came to be, are the only god or gods.

There are others whose political and social philosophies supplant religious feelings. Communism is a way of life that becomes a religion in the hearts of those who espouse it to the full. If the creeds of Christendom may be believed—and they cannot be by anyone whose mind has been touched by sense and logic—the Christian God is incomprehensible, unknowable, and uncreated; he is a spirit essence that fills immensity and is everywhere and nowhere in particular present; he is incorporeal and has neither body, parts, nor passions; and in some mystical way he is three gods and yet one god.

Knowing the proclivity of wayward men to forsake the living God and go after gods of wood and stone and gold; knowing their tendency to revere the forces of nature, to worship mystical spirits and powers, to center their hearts on false philosophies; and knowing also that blessings here and hereafter flow from true worship only—is it any wonder that the Eternal Jehovah commanded his people Israel: "I am the Lord thy God. . . . Thou shalt have no other gods before me. Thou shalt not make unto thee any graven image, or any likeness of any thing that is in heaven above, or that is in the earth beneath, or that is in the water under the earth: Thou shalt not bow down thyself to them, nor serve them." (Ex. 20:2-5.) Is it any wonder that he forewarned them of false teachers who would come among them, saying, "Let us go after other gods, which thou hast not known, and let us serve them." In all such eventualities the decree of Jehovah was: "Thou shalt not hearken" unto any such, "for the Lord your God proveth you, to know whether ye love the Lord your God with all your heart and with all your soul. Ye shall walk after the Lord your God, and fear him, and keep his commandments, and obey his voice, and ye shall serve him, and cleave unto him." (Deut. 13:1-4.)

Beware of False Christs

Just as men have and do worship false gods, so they have and do follow false Christs. As Jesus and his disciples sat upon the Mount of Olives, our Lord told them that false prophets and false Christs would come in their day and again in the last days before his Second Coming. As to the day then involved, he said: "Many shall come in my name, saying—I am Christ—and shall deceive many. . . . And many false prophets shall arise, and shall deceive many." As to our day, the latter days, our Lord said: "In those days there shall also arise false Christs, and false prophets, and shall show great signs and wonders, insomuch, that, if possible, they shall deceive the very elect, who are the elect according to the covenant." (JS-H 1-22.)

In practical effect it is the same whether we are dealing with false gods (and their priests) who may lead ancient Israel away from the worship of the true Jehovah, or false Christs (and false teachers) who may lead us away from true religion. Since the Nephites used the name Christ with reference to Jehovah, we find Book of Mormon prophets inveighing against false Christs and false prophets. (W. of M. 15-16.) Korihor, for one, to whom the devil appeared as an angel of light, was anti-Christ. (Alma 30.) In one period of Nephite history, the record says: "There was another church which denied the Christ; and they did persecute the true church of Christ." (4 Ne. 29.) The saints in New Testament times faced the same problem. "Many false prophets are gone out into the world," John wrote, for "every spirit that confesseth not that Jesus Christ is come in the flesh is not of God: and this is that spirit of antichrist, whereof ye have heard that it should come; and even now already is it in the world." (1 Jn. 4:1-3.) "He is antichrist, that denieth the Father and the Son." (1 Jn. 2:22.)

It is not difficult to envision that there will be false prophets and false teachers in the last days. But what of the promise that there will be false Christs? In our age of enlightenment and sophistication, as we suppose, is it to be assumed that there will be those come who will profess to be Christ? As a prelude to finding answer to these questions, let us note these words of Jesus, spoken along with the others on the Mount of Olives: "If they shall say unto you: Behold, he is in the desert; go not forth; Behold, he is in the secret chambers; believe it not; For as the light of the morning cometh out of the east, and shineth even unto the west, and covereth the whole earth, so shall also the coming of the Son of Man be." (JS-H 25-26.)

There are, of course, those deluded souls who announce, from time to time, that they are Christ or God or the Holy Ghost, or one mighty and strong, or whatever Satan or the workings of a deranged mind places in their thoughts. But in a larger and more realistic sense, false Christs are false systems of religion that use his name and profess to present his teachings to the world. The cries, "Lo, here," and "Lo, there," which went forth in Joseph Smith's day, when "some were contending for the Methodist faith, some for the Presbyterian, and some for the Baptist" (JS-H 5), meant that each group of gospel expounders was saying, "Lo, here is Christ; we have his system of salvation; ours is the true church; we know the way; come, join with us."

Beware of false gods. The Lord is God and beside him there is no other. He alone is Creator, Redeemer, and Savior. Gods of wood and stone, or of spirit nothingness, or whatever, have no saving power.

Beware also of false Christs. There is one Christ, and he

is God and has but one true system of salvation. He is not found in a desert retreat of a monastic order. His doctrine is not hidden in secret chambers to be withheld from all those who are without. The great restoration of all things has begun, and like the light of the rising sun, it shall spread over all the earth until the darkness of Babylon shall be no more, and the Son of Man shall come to be seen and admired by those who wait for him.

"Salvation Is Free"

Come unto Christ; come unto Jehovah; salvation is free! The way is prepared from the foundation of the world, and all who will may walk therein and be saved. "Ho, every one that thirsteth, come ye to the waters," saith Jehovah, "and he that hath no money; come ye, buy, and eat; yea, come ye, buy wine and milk without money and without price. . . . Hearken diligently unto me, and eat ye that which is good, and let your soul delight itself in fatness." (Isa. 55:1-2.)

"The Spirit is the same yesterday, today, and forever"—in the day of Jehovah, in the day of Christ, in all days, both now and forever. "And the way is prepared from the fall of man, and salvation is free." (2 Ne. 2:4.)

"Hath he commanded any that they should not partake of his salvation?" Nephi asks. "Behold I say unto you, Nay," he replies, "but he hath given it free for all men; and he hath commanded his people that they should persuade all men to repentance. Behold, hath the Lord commanded any that they should not partake of his goodness? Behold I say unto you, Nay; but all men are privileged the one like unto the other, and none are forbidden. . . . And he inviteth them all to come unto him and partake of his goodness; and he denieth none that come unto him, black and white, bond and free, male and female; and he remembereth the heathen; and all are alike unto God, both Jew and Gentile." (2 Ne. 26:27-28, 33.)

MESSIAH—OUR ADVOCATE, INTERCESSOR, AND MEDIATOR

What Is the Law of Intercession?

We have heretofore seen that the Almighty God sent his Only Begotten Son into the world to work out the infinite and eternal atonement; that through this supreme sacrifice all men are ransomed from their temporal fall in that they shall be resurrected; and that those who believe and obey are ransomed from their spiritual fall in that they shall come forth, not only in immortality, but shall be raised unto eternal life. We have seen that mercy comes because of the atonement and is the gift of God to the penitent; that mercy is the gracious inheritance of those whose sins are borne by their loving Lord; and that it is through repentance and righteousness that men are freed from the grasp of that justice which otherwise would impose upon them the full penalty for their sins. (Chapter 14.) We are aware that intercession is made for the saints by their Friend and Advocate, the Lord Jesus. Now it is our purpose to inquire more particularly into the nature of that intercession and to catch the vision of the great Messianic utterances which have taken it as their theme.

As we take up this portion of our inquiry into the Messianic status of him who was both Jehovah and Jesus, we must first ask: What are the laws of intercession, of advocacy, and of mediation? Why must someone intercede on our behalf? What need is there for a Mediator? How do the divine laws operate with respect to these matters?

By way of answer we might raise such queries as these: Did man create himself? Did he cause to come into being the earth and all that thereon is? Is he the author of the plan of salvation? Can he choose to live or die at will? Is annihilation of the soul within his power? Can he resurrect himself? Or crown himself with eternal glory?

Whether we like it or not, whether we are pleased or displeased with the eternal realities involved, the fact is we are not creatures of our own creating. We are not masters of our fate. Within the limits assigned to us, we can live and move and have our being. We can eat and drink and breathe and sleep and think. We can use our agency within the sphere of our assignment. But we cannot waft ourselves from orb to orb or choose the planet upon which to plant our feet. We are subject to law, law ordained by Him who created us and to whom we are and were and everlastingly shall be in subjection.

And the eternal realities—which can be known only by revelation—are these: There is a God who is our Father. He is a glorified, perfected Man of Holiness with a body of flesh and bones as tangible as man's. He begat us as spirits, and we were born in his courts. He ordained the laws, and he prepared the plan whereby we might advance and progress and become like him.

To become like him, we needed tangible bodies, bodies which were first mortal and then immortal. To become like him, we needed the probationary experiences of earth life, experiences we could gain in no other way. To become like him, we needed to taste the bitter that we might know the sweet; we needed to be subject to sin and death and to gain the victory over them both. Such was his plan.

Accordingly, he placed the spirit Michael and his chosen consort in the Garden of Eden and gave them immortal bodies made from the dust of the earth. Known then as Adam and Eve, our first parents then dwelt in a state of innocence, "having no joy, for they knew no misery; doing no good, for they knew no sin." (2 Ne. 2:23.) Agreeable to the divine will, these first members of the human family chose to fall from their paradisiacal state and to bring mortality, disease, death, sin, and sorrow into the world. They chose to estrange themselves from God; they elected to depart from the divine presence; they sought the toils and trials and tests of mortality—all with a purpose—all to see if they could overcome the world and prove worthy of eternal blessings. They were cast out of the presence of God; they died spiritually; they lost the light which had guided them in Eden—all to enable them to be tried and tested to the full. Such was the divine plan.

The divine plan also called for a Savior, a Chosen Vessel: One endowed by the Father with the power of immortality; One who could thereby gain the victory over the grave and restore fallen mortals to their immortal state; One who could restore them to their sinless state, if they would cleanse themselves in the way he provided. That way was to be in and through his atoning sacrifice and by obedience to the laws and ordinances of his gospel.

All of this is the foundation for the doctrine of advocacy, of intercession, and of mediation. To be saved man must be reconciled with God. He must rise above the natural man and become a saint. He must be freed from the chains of sin. He must return again in harmony, love, and peace to the eternal family circle. The blessings of Eden—and more, yea, infinitely more—must be his again.

But how can it be? Who will ransom and atone? Who will pay the penalty for man's sins? Who will satisfy the demands of divine justice? Who will intercede for fallen man before the Father's throne? Who will advocate his cause in the courts above? Who will mediate the differences between him and his Maker, so that once again he can have peace and harmony with his God? Verily, it is Christ. He is our Advocate, Intercessor, Mediator. Such is the rationale underlying the laws of intercession, of advocacy, and of mediation. Such is the divine plan.

Messiah Maketh Intercession

Addressing himself to the Father, Zenos said: "Thou hast turned away thy judgments because of thy Son." Zenock prayed similarly: "Thou art angry, O Lord, with this people, because they will not understand thy mercies which thou hast bestowed upon them because of thy Son." (Alma 33:13, 16.) Why is it that judgments are withheld and mercies are poured out—because of the Son? The answer is clear: He intercedes on man's behalf, advocating his cause in the courts above. "He . . . made intercession for the transgressors." (Isa. 53:12.) In the atonement that he wrought, he paid the penalty for the sins of men, on conditions of repentance, so that all might escape the judgments decreed for disobedience. In the same way and for the same reason, mercy replaces the justice that otherwise would impose the decreed judgments. Such is the law of intercession, a law that is valid and operative because of the atonement.

As taught by Lehi, this law is that "the Holy Messiah . . . shall make intercession for all the children of men; and they that believe in him shall be saved. And because of the intercession for all, all men come unto God" (2 Ne. 2:8-10), meaning they come unto God and are reconciled to their Maker if they believe and obey.

As taught by Abinadi this law is that God gave "the Son power to make intercession for the children of men," and that he thereby "redeemed them, and satisfied the demands of justice." (Mosiah 15:8-9.) Those, on the other hand, for whom no intercession is made are said by Abinadi to be damned—"Having gone according to their own carnal wills and desires; having never called upon the Lord while the arms of mercy were extended towards them; for the arms of mercy were extended towards them, and they would not;

they being warned of their iniquities and yet they would not depart from them; and they were commanded to repent and yet they would not repent." (Mosiah 16:12.)

As taught by Paul, the pleasing reality is that Christ "is able to save them to the uttermost that come unto God by him, seeing he ever liveth to make intercession for them." (Heb. 7:25.) Mormon expressed it this way: "He advocateth the cause of the children of men; and he dwelleth eternally in the heavens." (Moro. 7:28.)

But the most perfect summary of this law found anywhere in Holy Writ is given to us in these words of latter-day revelation: "Listen to him who is the advocate with the Father, who is pleading your cause before him—Saying: Father, behold the sufferings and death of him who did no sin, in whom thou wast well pleased; behold the blood of thy Son which was shed, the blood of him whom thou gavest that thyself might be glorified; Wherefore, Father, spare these my brethren that believe on my name, that they may come unto me and have everlasting life." (D&C 45:3-5; 110:4.)

Jehovah Maketh Intercession

It is Jehovah—the promised Messiah!—who makes intercession for his people. From the foundations of the world, in anticipation of the atonement he would make in Gethsemane's gloomy garden, the Great Jehovah pled the cause of righteous men before the fiery throne of his Father.

Men in Noah's day rebelled, rejected the Lord and his gospel, and were buried in a watery grave. Their spirits then found themselves in that prison prepared for those who walk in darkness when light is before them. Are they lost forever? Who will plead their cause?

To Enoch, concerning them, came these words of the Father: "And That which I have chosen hath plead before my face. Wherefore, he suffereth for their sins; inasmuch as they will repent in the day that my Chosen shall return unto me, and until that day they shall be in torment." (Moses 7:39.)

Ancient Israel rebelled, rejected the Lord and his prophets, and were scattered to the ends of the earth. From then until now, they and their seed have been far removed from the wonders and miracles and truth that blessed their fathers. But are they lost forever, and who will plead their cause?

Through Isaiah, in a marvelous and moving passage, Jehovah calls to the scattered remnants of his ancient people. "Look unto the rock from whence ye are hewn," he pleads. Return unto me, "For the Lord shall comfort Zion. . . . He will make her wilderness like Eden, and her desert like the garden of the Lord. . . . Hearken unto me, my people; and give ear unto me, O my nation: for a law shall proceed from me, and I will make my judgment to rest for a light of the people." That is to say, 'The fulness of my everlasting gospel shall be restored, and it shall be as it was in days of old.' Those who believe and obey shall be blessed. And then "the redeemed of the Lord shall return, and come with singing unto Zion; and everlasting joy shall be upon their head." And how shall all this be? The answer: "Thus saith thy Lord the Lord, and thy God"—Jehovah!—"that pleadeth the cause of his people, Behold, I have taken out of thine hand the cup of trembling, even the dregs of the cup of my fury; thou shalt no more drink it." (Isa. 51.)

This same offer of forgiveness, of joy and comfort, and of salvation for gathered Israel is held out to them in the great Messianic prophecy which includes the declaration: "Comfort ye, comfort ye my people, saith your God. Speak ye comfortably to Jerusalem, and cry unto her, that her warfare is accomplished, that her iniquity is pardoned." (Isa. 40:1-2.) In another wondrous and scarcely known passage, Jehovah tells of his power to save, of Israel's apostasy, of the need for an intercessor, and of how he put on the breastplate of righteousness and the helmet of salvation in the warfare that finally turned transgression from Jacob and brought them again into his everlasting covenant. (Isa. 59.) Truly, when his people repent and return unto him, the importunings of the Great Jehovah are heeded by his Father and our Father and by his God and our God.

Christ-Jehovah Forgives Sins

Both Jehovah and Jesus forgive sins; or rather, Jehovah who is Jesus forgives sins; or even more particularly, sins are forgiven by the Lord, who is Jehovah, at all times, and they were forgiven by that same Lord, who is Jesus, during his mortal ministry, and at such times and among such peoples as he, Jehovah, was known and revered by the more familiar name, Jesus.

Anciently, in Palestine, Israel had failed to perform the sacrificial ordinances to Jehovah, by which forgiveness of sins came to them. "Thou has not . . . honoured me with thy sacrifices," the Lord said, "but thou hast made me to serve with thy sins, thou hast wearied me with thine iniquities." Israel had not made use of the saving processes whereby the Lord's people become clean and spotless before him. And so he issued anew the great proclamation: "I, even I, am he that blotteth out thy transgressions for mine own sake, and will not remember thy sins." 'I, Jehovah, am he who doeth it.' Therefore, "Put me in rememberance." 'Return to me; keep my law; forgiveness and salvation are available to you through me; I am your Intercessor with the Father.' "Let us plead together." That is, 'I, Jehovah, will join with you in a plea for forgiveness from our Father, if you will keep my commandments.' (Isa. 43:22-28.)

Glorious doctrine this—Jehovah pleads for his people. He is their Intercessor. He it is who forgives sins through his atoning sacrifice. "I have blotted out, as a thick cloud, thy transgressions, and, as a cloud, thy sins: return unto me; for I have redeemed thee. Sing, O ye heavens; for the Lord hath done it: shout, ye lower parts of the earth: break forth into singing, ye mountains, O forest, and every tree therein: for the Lord hath redeemed Jacob, and glorified himself in Israel." (Isa. 44:22-23.)

This matter of turning to Jehovah so that sins might be blotted out, so that the Lord's people might become spotless and clean before him, was in full operation on the American continent also, except that the name of Jehovah in common usage was Christ. "Concerning the coming of Christ," Alma said, "it is he that surely shall come to take away the sins of the world." (Alma 39:15.) His own proclamation, made to the Nephites after his resurrection, confirmed the prophetic promises. "I . . . have glorified the Father in taking upon me the sins of the world, in the which I have suffered the will of the Father in all things from the beginning," he said. (3 Ne. 11:11.)

One of the sweetest and most refreshing stories of repentance and conversion, of forgiveness and salvation, of turning to that Jesus who blots out sins, is that of Alma the younger. The time was about one hundred years before our Lord's birth among mortals. This American Paul, along with the equally rebellious sons of Mosiah, had been going about destroying the Church of God. An angelic visitant, exhibiting the power of God so that the earth shook, called him to repentance. For the space of three days and three nights, the future witness of the name of Christ lay unconscious to his mortal surroundings, while he suffered the agonies of the damned and was then blessed with marvelous spiritual manifestations. Here are his words, written in sweet sublimity and with convincing power:

"I was racked with eternal torment, for my soul was harrowed up to the greatest degree and racked with all my sins. Yea, I did remember all my sins and iniquities, for which I was tormented with the pains of hell; yea, I saw that I had rebelled against my God, and that I had not kept his holy commandments. Yea, and I had murdered many of his children, or rather led them away into destruction; yea, and in fine so great had been my iniquities, that the very thought of coming into the presence of my God did rack my soul with inexpressible horror. Oh, thought I, that I could be banished and become extinct both soul and body, that I might not be brought to stand in the presence of my God, to be judged of my deeds.

"And now, for three days and for three nights was I racked, even with the pains of a damned soul. And it came to pass that as I was thus racked with torment, while I was harrowed up by the memory of my many sins, behold, I remembered also to have heard my father prophesy unto the people concerning the coming of one Jesus Christ, a Son of God, to atone for the sins of the world. Now, as my mind caught hold upon this thought, I cried within my heart: O Jesus, thou Son of God, have mercy on me, who am in the gall of bitterness, and am encircled about by the everlasting chains of death. And now, behold, when I thought this, I could remember my pains no more; yea, I was harrowed up by the memory of my sins no more.

"And oh, what joy, and what marvelous light I did behold; yea, my soul was filled with joy as exceeding as was my pain! Yea, I say unto you, my son, that there could be nothing so exquisite and so bitter as were my pains. Yea, and again I say unto you, my son, that on the other hand, there can be nothing so exquisite and sweet as was my joy. Yea, methought I saw, even as our father Lehi saw, God sitting upon his throne, surrounded with numberless concourses of angels, in the attitude of singing and praising their God; yea, and my soul did long to be there. But behold, my limbs did receive their strength again, and I stood upon my feet, and did manifest unto the people that I had been born of God." (Alma 36:12-23; 38:8.)

This same power, vested in Jehovah and seen by Alma to reside in the yet unborn Jesus, was also exercised by our Lord as he dwelt among men. For instance, in Capernaum, his own city, probably in the home of Peter, our Lord taught a multitude through whom it was not possible to make a path because of their number and the crowded circumstances. Four men came bearing on a couch one sick of the palsy—a paralytic—whom they lowered down through the roof. Jesus said: "Son, be of good cheer; thy sins be forgiven thee." The scribes and Pharisees reasoned on the point, saying, "Who can forgive sins, but God alone?" Jesus, perceiving their reaction to his assumption of divine powers and with the clear intent of proving that he was that Jehovah who forgave sins, said: "Whether is easier, to say, Thy sins be forgiven thee; or to say, Rise up and walk? But that ye may know that the Son of man hath power upon earth to forgive sins, (he said unto the sick of the palsy,) I say unto thee, Arise, and take up thy couch, and go into thine house. And immediately he rose up before them, and took up that whereon he lay, and departed to his own house, glorifying God." (Matt. 9:1-8; Mark 2:1-12; Luke 5:18-26.)

Sing Praises to Jehovah

As is clear from the whole body of revealed writ, the eternal decree of the Eternal God is that men should worship the Father, in the name of the Son, by the power of the Holy Ghost. As it is written: "All the holy prophets . . . believed in Christ and worshiped the Father in his name." (Jacob 4:4-5.)

There is nothing clearer or plainer than this. We pray to the Father, not the Son; but according to the laws of intercession, advocacy, and mediation, our answers come from the Son. Reference to nearly every section in the Doctrine and Covenants bears this out. None, therefore, need to suppose, as is found in the prayer books of sectarianism, that it is proper to pray to either Christ or the Holy Ghost.

However, righteous persons do have a close, personal relationship with their Savior. It is through him that forgiveness comes. Because of his atonement we may be free from sin. Salvation is in Christ. He pleads our cause. He is our Mediator and Intercessor. And we do and should sing praises to his holy name, as do the angels of God in heaven also. Among their hymns of praise are such wondrous words as these: "Worthy is the Lamb that was slain to receive power, and riches, and wisdom, and strength, and honour, and glory, and blessing. . . . Blessing, and honour, and glory, and power, be unto him that sitteth upon the throne, and unto the Lamb for ever and ever." (Rev. 5:9-13.)

There is no language of worship and adoration that surpasses the language of prayer. What is more natural than to use the noblest and most perfect expressions utterable by mortal tongues in addressing Him who sits upon the great white throne? It is no wonder, then, that in praising the Lord Jehovah we often do so as though we were addressing him in prayer, even as though we were pleading with him for eternal blessings.

We have already seen that Alma, in wonder and amazement at the forgiving grace poured out upon him, addressed Jesus in words of praise and thanksgiving. The Old Testament prophets followed a similar course. Having the same understanding prevalent among the Nephites, they sought to extol and magnify that name by which these incalculably great blessings come. The words of the Psalmists, because they were writing hymns of praise, show forth the most numerous examples of this type of divine salutation. One Psalmic utterance says of "the Holy One of Israel," who of course is Jehovah, that "he, being full of compassion, forgave their iniquity, and destroyed them not" (Ps. 78:38-41), which by itself is simply a doctrinal and historical statement. But another Psalmic declaration, dwelling on the same concept, could be interpreted, if we did not know better, as a prayer to Jehovah in these words: "O remember not against us former iniquities: let thy tender mercies speedily prevent us: for we are brought very low. Help us, O God of our salvation, for the glory of thy name: and deliver us, and purge away our sins, for thy name's sake." (Ps. 79:8-9.) The 86th Psalm, though in the language of prayer, is in reality a hymn of praise: "I will praise thee, O Lord my God, with all my heart: and I will glorify thy name for evermore." (Verse 12.) Psalms of praise, in language akin to that of prayer, and dealing with the mercy of the Great Jehovah, are also found in such references as Psalm 89:1-2, 14; 103:11-22; 136:1-26; and 145:8-9.

For that matter, we even have in the Doctrine and Covenants, in a revealed prayer addressed to the "Father, in the name of Jesus Christ," such expressions as, "O Jehovah, have mercy upon this people, and as all men sin forgive the transgressions of thy people, and let them be blotted out forever" (D&C 109:4, 34)—all of which simply means that we pray to the Father, and because our answers come from Jehovah, we sometimes give forth accolades of praise to him, in the language of prayer, which those untutored in the things of the Spirit might mistakenly interpret to be prayers to the Son and not the Father.

How to Gain Forgiveness

The Messiah came to "bare the sin of many" (Isa 53:12); to suffer "the pain of all men . . . on conditions of repentance" (D&C 18:11-12); to redeem those who believe and obey; to give mercy to the repentant and justice to the unrepentant. The great problem facing all of us is how to gain a forgiveness of sins; it is how to be numbered with those whose sins are born by the Lord; it is how to become clean and spotless so we can go where God and Christ are and enjoy the fulness of light and glory in their presence.

Forgiveness is available because of the atoning sacrifice of the Great Jehovah. Forgiveness is available because Christ the Lord sweat great drops of blood in Gethsemane as he bore the incalculable weight of the sins of all who ever had or ever would repent. Forgiveness is available because "God suffereth according to the flesh that he might take upon him the sins of his people, that he might blot out their transgressions according to the power of his deliverance." (Alma 7:13.) Forgiveness comes because of the effectual and fervent pleadings of Him who is our Intercessor and Advocate. Forgiveness precedes salvation, and salvation comes after men are freed from their sins. Thus forgiveness is in Christ, even as salvation is in Christ. But he has done his work. The atonement is an accomplished fact. It is inscribed forever in the eternal records; it is written for all to read in the wracked body and the spilt blood of the one perfect man who bowed in agony, alone, in a garden outside Jerusalem's walls. The issue now is, What must each of us do to come within the pale of saving grace and thus gain forgiveness of our sins?

The divine formula is an easy one; the way and the path provided is clearly marked; none need stumble or be diverted onto bye and forbidden paths. The way to gain forgiveness is as follows:

1. *Come to a knowledge of the truth.*

In plain, simple language, as pertaining to all men now living, this means to accept the gospel as restored by Joseph Smith and to join The Church of Jesus Christ of Latter-day Saints. As it was in Paul's day, so it is today, there is "one Lord, one faith, one baptism, One God and Father of all." (Eph. 4:5-6.) Truth is not a conflicting mass of confusion; it is not divergent views that are diametrically opposed to each other; it is not the vagaries and nonsense of sectarianism. Truth is the everlasting gospel restored anew in our day. It is things as they are, and as they were, and as they shall be.

There is neither forgiveness nor salvation in worshiping false gods or following false systems of religion. However much some people may think that cows or crocodiles are god, neither the four-legged bovine nor the big lizard in the dismal swamp has power to forgive, or to resurrect, or to save. And as with cows and crocodiles, so with the spirit nothingness to which professors of religion ascribe the attributes of Deity. As Alma said, Ye must "worship the true and the living God," and through that worship "look forward for the remission of your sins, with an everlasting faith." (Alma 7:6.)

2. *Believe in the Lord Jesus Christ.*

Forgiveness of sins comes only to those who believe in

Christ. It never has, does not now, and never will come to anyone else. It is Christ "that cometh to take away the sins of the world, yea, the sins of every man who steadfastly believeth on his name." (Alma 5:48.) "Believe on the Lord Jesus Christ, and thou shalt be saved." (Acts 16:31.) That is, 'Believe on him and thou shalt be forgiven of thy sins, and being thus free from sin, salvation shall be thy natural inheritance.' To believe in Christ is to accept his gospel; it is to accept the prophets and apostles whom he has sent to reveal him to the world; in our day it is to accept without reservation the divine mission of the Prophet Joseph Smith and those who have since worn his prophetic mantle. To believe in Christ is to accept him as the promised Messiah, to worship him as the Great Jehovah, to know that he is the Son of God. Jesus said: "If ye believe not that I am he"—the Messiah, the Son of God—"ye shall die in your sins." (John 8:24.)

3. *Keep the commandments.*

Having chosen to worship the true and living God, him by whom all things are and who is our Eternal Father; having elected to believe in his Son, through whose atoning sacrifice salvation comes, there remains but one requisite to gain forgiveness, and it is: *to keep the commandments.*

What commandments? They are many, and they may be stated in many ways. In one manner of speaking they are all embraced within the divine decrees: (1) "Thou shalt love the Lord thy God with all thy heart, with all thy might, mind, and strength; and in the name of Jesus Christ thou shalt serve him," and (2) "Thou shalt love thy neighbor as thyself." (D&C 59:5-6.) "On these two commandments hang all the law and the prophets." (Matt. 22:40.)

But embraced within the plan of worship and service thus decreed are many things. All men everywhere are commanded to repent and believe the gospel and to be baptized in the name of Jesus Christ for the remission of their sins. (D&C 33:9-11.) "Now this is the commandment," so the risen Lord announced to the Nephites; "Repent, all ye ends of the earth, and come unto me and be baptized in my name, that ye may be sanctified by the reception of the Holy Ghost, that ye may stand spotless before me at the last day." (3 Ne. 27:20.) "Yea, blessed are they who shall believe in your words," that same Lord said to his Nephite apostles, "and come down into the depths of humility and be baptized, for they shall be visited with fire and with the Holy Ghost, and shall receive a remission of their sins." (3 Ne. 12:2.) Baptism for the remission of sins is a commandment! Those who do not repent and are not baptized thereby break the commandment of God, and for this disobedience they shall be damned. (3 Ne. 11:34.)

But baptism alone, baptism without more, baptism without subsequent obedience to all of the laws and ordinances of the gospel—that is, the mere rite of being authoritatively immersed in water—does not of itself save a soul. From the lips of the Lord Jesus we quote: "And no unclean thing can enter into his kingdom; therefore nothing entereth into his rest save it be those who have washed their garments in my blood, because of their faith, and the repentance of all their sins, and their faithfulness unto the end." (3 Ne. 27:19.) Obedience follows baptism. For those who have entered in at the gate of repentance and baptism, the command is: "Ye must press forward with a steadfastness in Christ, having a perfect brightness of hope, and a love of God and of all men. Wherefore, if ye shall press forward, feasting upon the word of Christ, and endure to the end, behold, thus saith the Father: Ye shall have eternal life." (2 Ne. 31:20.)

All of the saints are tried and tested after baptism. All commit sins. All must renew the covenant of obedience made in the waters of baptism. (Mosiah 18:8-14.) All must gain anew, time and time again, the assurance "that they may always have his Spirit to be with them." (D&C 20:77.) This occurs when the faithful partake worthily of the sacrament.

The first Alma, the one who baptized at the waters of Mormon, received a revelation that perfectly sets forth the law of forgiveness as it pertains both to those in and out of the Church. The occasion was one in which many Nephites were rebelling and refusing to believe in Christ and become members of the true church. These unbelievers persuaded many members of the Church to walk in the ways of wickedness and to commit grievous sins. Alma was the president of the Church, and he pleaded with the Lord for guidance as to what action should be taken against the erring saints. In answer the Lord set forth his law of forgiveness as it applies to member and nonmember alike.

"Whoso is baptized shall be baptized unto repentance," came the voice from heaven. "And whomsoever ye receive shall believe in my name; and him will I freely forgive. For it is I that taketh upon me the sins of the world." Such is the law as pertaining to nonmembers, with the added proviso, "that he that will not hear my voice, the same shall ye not receive into my church, for him I will not receive at the last day."

As to erring members of the Church, the Lord Jesus, more than a hundred years before his mortal birth, gave this direction: "Whosoever transgresseth against me, him shall ye judge according to the sins which he has committed; and if he confess his sins before thee and me, and repenteth in the sincerity of his heart, him shall ye forgive, and I will forgive him also. Yea, and as often as my people repent will I forgive them their trespasses against me. . . . And whosoever will not repent of his sins the same shall not be numbered among my people." (Mosiah 26:1-32.)

David, a member of the Church, sets forth in the 25th Psalm a classical plea for personal forgiveness. Daniel, also a member of the Church, speaking for all Israel, whose hosts constituted the Church in that day, preserves for us in the ninth chapter of his writings the classical pleas to the Lord for forgiveness for a whole people. These two Old Testament passages speak of mercy, of pardoning iniquity, of prayer, supplication, fasting, repenting in sackcloth and ashes, and of keeping the commandments. I have collated and analyzed the details of the law of forgiveness for members of the Church in *Mormon Doctrine,* 2nd ed., pages 292-98. For our purposes here, as part of this Messianic study, it suffices for us to know that belief in Christ is the sure foundation upon which the house of salvation is built; that those who believe—who believe in Spirit and in truth!—immediately, automatically, in the very nature of things, begin to build the walls, the roof, and all the parts of the house of their salvation.

"I do know that Christ shall come among the children of men," Amulek said, "to take upon him the transgressions of his people, and that he shall atone for the sins of the world." It is our Lord's divine Sonship, his status as God's Son; it is his atoning sacrifice; it is the burden he bore in Gethsemane; it is his death upon the cross; it is the fact that he voluntarily laid down his life that he might take it again—these are the things that enabled him to take upon himself the transgressions of his people. These are the things that enabled him to bear the sins of repentant persons. These are the things that enable men to gain a forgiveness of sins. Without the atonement, "all mankind must unavoidably perish."

"Thus"—that is, in the light of all these things—as Amulek taught, "he shall bring salvation to all those who shall believe on his name." Through his atonement, mercy overpowers justice so that men "may have faith unto repentance." That is to say, forgiveness comes to those who forsake their sins. Forgiveness and consequent salvation are for those only who have faith unto repentance. They alone gain mercy rather than justice. "And thus mercy can satisfy the demands of justice, and encircles them in the arms of safety, while he that exercises no faith unto repentance is exposed to the whole law of the demands of justice; therefore only unto him that has faith unto repentance is brought about the great and eternal plan of redemption." (Alma 34:8-16.)

To those who have made covenant in the waters of baptism to forsake the world and serve the Lord, and who have fallen short of the mark, his call is: "Seek ye the Lord while he may be found, call ye upon him while he is near: Let the wicked forsake his way, and the unrighteous man his thoughts: and let him return unto the Lord, and he will have mercy upon him; and to our God, for he will abundantly pardon." (Isa. 55:6-7.)

Christ Justifies the Righteous

Mediation is akin to and not divisible from intercession and advocacy. Christ the Lord is our Mediator, even as he is our Advocate and our Intercessor. In prophesying that the Messiah would come, Lehi said to his sons: "I would that ye should look to the great Mediator, and hearken unto his great commandments; and be faithful unto his words, and choose eternal life, according to the will of his Holy Spirit." (2 Ne. 2:28.) We shall hereafter consider, in Chapter 24, our Lord's status as the great Mediator, the Mediator of the new covenant, when we set forth how Moses, the mediator of the old covenant, was a prototype of that Lord whose witness he was.

With reference to our present analysis, that forgiveness of sins comes because of the advocacy, intercession, and mediation of the Messiah, we shall add to what we have here written only the concepts that remission of sins is reserved for those who are justified and that justification and salvation are free.

In the constitutional document of the restored Church we read: "And we know that justification through the grace of our Lord and Savior Jesus Christ is just and true." (D&C 20:30.) In summarizing the plan of salvation for Adam, the Lord said: "By the water ye keep the commandment; by the Spirit ye are justified, and by the blood ye are sanctified." (Moses 6:60.) Both Paul and James write extensively about how men are justified—by faith, by works, by the blood of Christ, by the power of the Spirit, and so forth. A large part of Paul's Epistle to the Romans deals with this subject.

What, then, is the doctrine of justification, and what are the Messianic implications? To be justified is to be made righteous and therefore to be saved. Men are justified in what they do when their deeds conform to divine standards. Righteous acts are approved of the Lord; they are ratified by the Holy Ghost; they are sealed by the Holy Spirit of Promise; or, in other words, they are justified by the Spirit. Such divine approval must be given to "all covenants, contracts, bonds, obligations, oaths, vows, performances, connections, associations, or expectations"—that is, to all things—if they are to have "efficacy, virtue, or force in and after the resurrection from the dead." (D&C 132:7.) Such a requirement is part of the terms and conditions of the gospel covenant.

It comes as no surprise, then, to read that the Messiah, as the Prototype of salvation, would be and was justified in all that he did, and that all those who believe in him must be justified, in like manner, if they are to go where he is and be like him. David speaks of Jehovah being justified (Ps. 51:4), and Paul quotes this truism with approval (Rom. 3:4). In one of Isaiah's most pointed Messianic prophecies—the one in which he has the Messiah say: "I gave my back to the smiters, and my cheeks to them that plucked off the hair: I hid not my face from shame and spitting"—he also has the Messiah say: "The Lord God will help me. . . . He is near that justifieth me." (Isa. 50:5-8.) And Paul, speaking of Jehovah, meaning Christ, says: "God was manifest in the flesh, justified in the Spirit, seen of angels, preached unto the Gentiles, believed on in the world, received up into glory." (1 Tim. 3:16.) It is thus perfectly clear that the Lord Jehovah, the Promised Messiah, and Jesus who is called Christ—all being one and the same Person—was justified, saved, and exalted, as a pattern for all those to whom he says: Follow thou me.

As Christ is not alone in baptism, nor in good works, nor in righteous deeds, nor in pursuing the course back to the presence of the Eternal Father, so he is not alone in the need to be justified. It is Jehovah who shall justify his people, as Isaiah says. "Look unto me, and be ye saved" is Jehovah's invitation to "all the ends of the earth," for he it is unto whom "every knee shall bow, every tongue shall swear." The faithful shall have "righteousness and strength" in him, "and all that are incensed against him shall be ashamed." Having thus set forth that salvation is in Christ, Isaiah proclaims: "In the Lord"—that is, in Jehovah who is the Messiah—"shall all the seed of Israel be justified, and shall glory." (Isa. 45:22-25.) Israel—the faithful!—shall be justified, which is to say, "All Israel shall be saved." (Rom. 11:26.)

All Israel shall be justified; all Israel shall be saved—meaning, all those who keep the commandments shall be saved and justified, and those so doing shall be called by the name *Israel.* As Paul expressed it: "They are not all Israel, which are of Israel: Neither, because they are the seed of Abraham, are they all children: . . . That is, They which are the children of the flesh, these are not children of God." (Rom. 9:6-8.) In the eternal sense, Israel consists of the members of the Church who keep the commandments and are thereby justified in this life and saved in the life to come. The wicked, of course, are not justified. (Alma 41:13-15.)

With the concept thus before us that Jehovah justifies the faithful, let us note this Messianic prophecy: "By his knowledge shall my righteous servant justify many; for he shall bear their iniquities." (Isa. 53:11.) Then let us note these words of Paul: "Be it known unto you therefore, men and brethren, that through this man is preached unto you the forgiveness of sins." What man? The Lord Jesus Christ. "And by him all that believe are justified from all things, from which ye could not be justified by the law of Moses." (Acts 13:38-39.) As to this matter of the law, Lehi said: "The law is given unto men. And by the law no flesh is justified; or, by the law men are cut off. Yea, by the temporal law they were cut off; and also, by the spiritual law they perish from that which is good, and become miserable forever. Wherefore, redemption cometh in and through the Holy

Messiah; for he is full of grace and truth." (2 Ne. 2:5-6.) And as to the matter of who it is that justifies the faithful, we have this revealed answer: Jehovah justifies; Messiah justifies; Christ justifies—all of which brings us again up against the stark reality that these three are one and the same Person.

Salvation and Justification Come by Grace

All that we have said about advocacy, intercession, and mediation; about the forgiveness of sins and the justification of the righteous; about the fact that it is Jehovah-Messiah-Christ who is our Advocate, Intercessor, and Mediator, the One by whose power we are forgiven, justified, and saved—all of this comes to us by the grace of God.

"Salvation is free." (2 Ne. 2:4.) Justification is free. Neither of them can be purchased; neither can be earned; neither comes by the law of Moses, or by good works, or by any power or ability that man has. Rather, the invitation of the Lord Jehovah is: "Ho, every one that thirsteth, come ye to the waters, and he that hath no money; come ye, buy, and eat; yea, come, buy wine and milk without money and without price." (Isa. 55:1.) Come and partake freely of the goodness and grace of the Lord. Come to him through whose goodness and grace all men are raised in immortality. Come to him through whose goodness and grace eternal salvation is available for all those who believe and obey. Salvation is free, freely available, freely to be found. It comes because of his goodness and grace, because of his love, mercy, and condescension toward the children of men.

When the prophets who were before Christ preached that salvation is free, they were announcing the same doctrine that would thereafter fall from apostolic lips in the pronouncement that we are saved by grace. Free salvation is salvation by grace. The questions then are: What salvation is free? What salvation comes by the grace of God? With all the emphasis of the rolling thunders of Sinai, we answer: All salvation is free; all comes by the merits and mercy and grace of the Holy Messiah; there is no salvation of any kind, nature, or degree that is not bound to Christ and his atonement. Specifically, our Lord's atoning sacrifice brings all men forth in the resurrection with immortal bodies, thus freeing them from death, hell, the devil, and endless torment; and our Lord's atoning grace raises those who believe and obey, not only in immortality, but unto eternal life; it raises them to sit down with Abraham, Isaac, and Jacob in God's everlasting kingdom forever.

"How great the importance to make these things known unto the inhabitants of the earth," Lehi says, "that they may know that there is no flesh that can dwell in the presence of God, save it be through the merits, and mercy, and grace of the Holy Messiah." That is to say, 'All men must partake of that salvation which is freely available, if they are to go to the celestial kingdom; all who gain eternal life do so because of the grace of God.' Then Lehi says that by this same power Christ shall "bring to pass the resurrection of the dead," meaning that all shall come forth from the grave because of his grace, but, Lehi adds, only "they that believe in him shall be saved." (2 Ne. 2:8-9.)

"O the wisdom of God, his mercy and grace!" Jacob exults. Why? Because if there were no atonement, there would be no resurrection; and if there were no resurrection, "our spirits must become subject to that angel who fell from before the presence of Eternal God, and became the devil, to rise no more. And our spirits must have become like unto him, and we become devils, angels to a devil, to be shut out from the presence of our God, and to remain with the Father of lies, in misery, like unto himself." (2 Ne. 9:8-9.) That is to say, if there were no resurrection, which comes by the grace of God, all men would be sons of perdition, the most horrible and awful punishment in all the eternities.

As to that salvation which consists of both immortality and eternal life, Jacob says that after men are reconciled to God by obedience to the laws of his gospel, it is still "only in and through the grace of God" that they are saved. We shall be raised "from death by the power of the resurrection," he says, and also, we "may be received into the eternal kingdom of God" because of that same atonement, all to the end that we "may praise him through grace divine." (2 Ne. 10:24-25.) "My soul delighteth in his grace," Jacob continues, "and in his justice, and power, and mercy in the great and eternal plan of deliverance from death. And my soul delighteth in proving unto my people that save Christ should come all men must perish." (2 Ne. 11:5-6.)

Jacob's brother Nephi preaches the same doctrine. "Believe in Christ, and . . . be reconciled to God," he says, "for we know that it is by grace that we are saved, after all we can do." (2 Ne. 25:23; 33:9.) And as he climaxes his writings on the plates of Mormon, the great Moroni relates the grace of God to an inheritance of eternal life in these pleading words: "Come unto Christ, and be perfected in him, and deny yourselves of all ungodliness; and if ye shall deny yourselves of all ungodliness and love God with all your might, mind and strength, then is his grace sufficient for you, that by his grace ye may be perfect in Christ." (Moro. 10:32.)

What more need we say than to praise God for his goodness and grace? What more need we do than to keep the commandments of Him who hath done all things for us?

CHRIST IS "THE EVERLASTING FATHER"

The Lord's People Are Born Again

We set forth in Chapter 4 how the blessed Christ, in his role as Creator, is the Father of heaven and earth. In Chapter 8 we considered how Christ is the Father by divine investiture of authority, in that the Father has placed his name upon the Son so that the words and acts of the Offspring become and are the sayings and deeds of the Parent. It is now our purpose to show how Christ, in and through and because of his atoning sacrifice, becomes the Father of all those who believe and obey his laws. To envision what is involved in this concept, we must first consider the matter of being born again.

We are the spirit children of the Eternal Elohim with whom we lived and dwelt in the premortal eternities. We entered mortality by birth. Each of us was sired by a mortal father, conceived in the womb of a mortal mother, and came forth by the birth processes to breathe the breath of mortal life. In this way the eternal spirit takes upon itself a tabernacle of clay, is born into mortality, and launches forth into the probationary experiences of this sphere of existence. This passing from preexistence to mortality is called birth; for our purposes now it is considered to be the first birth.

Death entered the world by means of Adam's fall—death of two kinds, temporal and spiritual. Temporal death passes upon all men when they depart this mortal life. It is then that the eternal spirit steps out of its earthly tenement, to take up an abode in a realm where spirits are assigned, to await the day of their resurrection. Spiritual death passes upon all men when they become accountable for their sins. Being thus subject to sin they die spiritually; they die as pertaining to the things of the Spirit; they die as pertaining to the things of righteousness; they are cast out of the presence of God. It is of such men that the scriptures speak when they say that the natural man is an enemy to God and has become carnal, sensual, and devilish by nature.

If a man "yields to the enticings of the Holy Spirit, and putteth off the natural man and becometh a saint through the atonement of Christ the Lord" (Mosiah 3:19), then he is born again. His spiritual death ceases. He becomes alive to the things of the Spirit; he returns to the presence of God because he receives the gift of the Holy Ghost; and he is alive to the things of righteousness. He crucifies the old man of sin, becomes a new creature of the Holy Ghost, and walks in a newness of life. This is what is meant by being born again.

We have no better scriptural account of what happens in the life of a repentant sinner when he is born again than the record of what Alma came to know and feel and be. Of the marvelous spiritual rebirth that came to him, he said: "I have repented of my sins, and have been redeemed of the Lord; behold I am born of the Spirit. And the Lord said unto me: Marvel not that all mankind, yea, men and women, all nations, kindreds, tongues and people, must be born again; yea, born of God, changed from their carnal and fallen state, to a state of righteousness, being redeemed of God, becoming his sons and daughters; And thus they become new creatures; and unless they do this, they can in nowise inherit the kingdom of God. I say unto you, unless this be the case, they must be cast off; and this I know, because I was like to be cast off. Nevertheless, after wandering through much tribulation, repenting nigh unto death, the Lord in mercy hath seen fit to snatch me out of an everlasting burning, and I am born of God. My soul hath been redeemed from the gall of bitterness and bonds of iniquity. I was in the darkest abyss; but now I behold the marvelous light of God. My soul was racked with eternal torment; but I am snatched, and my soul is pained no more." (Mosiah 27:24-29.)

As to the way in which men are born again, Jesus said they must "be born of water and of the Spirit" (John 3:5), meaning by baptism and by the laying on of hands for the gift of the Holy Ghost. The symbolism here involved is more fully set forth, in the Lord's language, as he commanded Adam to teach his children—"That by reason of transgression cometh the fall, which fall bringeth death, and inasmuch as ye were born into the world by water, and blood, and the spirit, which I have made, and so became of dust a living soul, even so ye must be born again into the kingdom of heaven, of water, and of the Spirit, and be cleansed by blood, even the blood of mine Only Begotten; that ye might be sanctified from all sin, and enjoy the words of eternal life in this world, and eternal life in the world to come, even immortal glory; For by the water ye keep the commandment; by the Spirit ye are justified; and by the blood ye are sanctified." (Moses 6:59-60.)

Sometimes men are born again miraculously and suddenly, as was Alma. They become alive to the things of the Spirit and completely reverse the whole course of their life almost in an instant. But for most members of the Church the spiritual rebirth is a process that goes on gradually. The faithful are sanctified degree by degree as they add to their faith and good works. The tests which set forth the extent to which the saints have been born again are set forth in the 5th chapter of Alma.

Saints Are the Children of Christ

Few doctrines are better known by members of the true church than the doctrine of preexistence. We are well aware that all men are the children of God, the offspring of the Father, his sons and his daughters. We know that we were all born in his courts as spirit beings, long before the foundations of this earth were laid, and that the Lord Jehovah was in fact the Firstborn Son. What is not so well known is that nearly all the passages of scripture, both ancient and modern, which speak of God as our Father and of men on earth being the sons of God, have no reference to our birth in preexistence as the children of Elohim, but teach rather that Jehovah is our Father and we are his children.

In setting forth that all men must be born again to gain salvation, we have seen that this means they must be "born of God, changed from their carnal and fallen state, to a state of righteousness, being redeemed of God, becoming his sons and daughters." (Mosiah 27:25.) Whose sons and whose daughters do we become when we are born again? Who is our new Father? The answer is, Christ is our Father; we become his children by adoption; he makes us members of his family. Nowhere is this set forth better than in the words of King Benjamin to his Nephite subjects. "Because of the covenant ye have made," he said (and it is the same covenant all of us make in the waters of baptism), "ye shall be called the children of Christ, his sons, and his daughters; for behold, this day he hath spiritually begotten you; for ye say that your hearts are changed through faith on his name; therefore, ye are born of him and have become his sons and his daughters." (Mosiah 5:7.) Something akin to this appears to have occurred in ancient Israel when "Jehoiada made a covenant between the Lord and the king and the people, that they should be the Lord's people." (2 Kgs. 11:17.)

Among the first words recorded by the Beloved John in the Gospel account that bears his name is the affirmation that "the Word" who "was made flesh, and dwelt among" men "came unto his own, and his own received him not. But as many as received him, to them gave he power to become the sons of God, even to them that believe on his name." (John 1:11-14.) When this same Lord came to the Nephites, resurrected and glorified as he then was, he confirmed the words of his Beloved Disciple. "I came unto my own, and my own received me not," he said, "And as many as have received me, to them have I given to become the sons of God; and even so will I to as many as shall believe on my name." (3 Ne. 9:16-17.) And he has reaffirmed these same truths again and again in our day (D&C 11:30; 34:2-3; 39:1-4; 42:52; 45:8), with this added exposition: "He that receiveth my gospel receiveth me; and he that receiveth not my gospel receiveth not me" (D&C 39:5).

What we are here saying is that "by faith" we may "become the sons of God." (Moro. 7:26.) First we must believe and be baptized. This puts us in a position to exercise the "power" referred to in the foregoing passages. As Mormon said, "If ye will lay hold upon every good thing, and condemn it not, ye certainly will be a child of Christ." (Moro. 7:19.) After Alma baptized at the waters of Mormon, he organized the people and taught them their duties—to dwell together in unity and love, to honor the sabbath day, to impart of their substance to the poor, to walk uprightly before the Lord—"and thus they became the children of God." (Mosiah 18.) That is to say, these Nephites, following baptism, exercised the power to become the sons of God and did in fact attain that blessed state.

Those who become the sons of God in this life gain exaltation in the life to come. They are sons of God here; they are Gods in eternity—because they are like Christ and are one in him as he is one in the Father. Thus we read: "I am Jesus Christ, the Son of God, who was crucified for the sins of the world, even as many as will believe on my name, that they may become the sons of God, even one in me as I am one in the Father, as the Father is one in me, that we may be one." (D&C 35:2.) Also: "Ye shall be even as I am, and I am even as the Father; and the Father and I are one." (3 Ne. 28:10.)

Addressing himself to the saints, and speaking of the high status reserved for those who become members of the family of their Lord, the apostle John wrote: "Behold, what manner of love the Father hath bestowed upon us, that we should be called the sons of God." It is with wonder and amazement that we even dare to think of such a thing. Sons of God! Members of the family of Christ, who shall see his face and abide in his presence! "Beloved," John continues, "now are we the sons of God"—that is, here and now, while yet weak, faltering mortals, we have been adopted—"and it doth not yet appear what we shall be: but we know that, when he shall appear, we shall be like him; for we shall see him as he is." Like Christ! One with him as he is one with the Father! Because Christ was "like unto God" (Abr. 3:24), he became the Creator of all things from the beginning. If we become like unto him, what shall we be? Is it any wonder that John concludes: "And every man that hath this hope in him purifieth himself, even as he is pure." (1 Jn. 3:1-3.) Or is it any wonder that Mormon acclaimed: "My beloved brethren, pray unto the Father with all the energy of heart, that ye may be filled with this love"—the same love of which John wrote—"which he hath bestowed upon all who are true followers of his Son, Jesus Christ; that ye may become the sons of God; that when he shall appear we shall be like him, for we shall see him as he is; that we may have this hope; that we may be purified even as he is pure." (Moro. 7:48.)

Saints Become the Sons of Elohim

It is perfectly clear that faithful saints become the sons and daughters of Jesus Christ by adoption. But there is more than this to the doctrine of becoming sons of God. Those who so obtain are adopted also into the family of Elohim. They become his adopted sons so that they can receive, inherit, and possess along with his natural Son.

To envision what is meant by being sons of God, meaning the Father, let us follow Paul's reasoning in two passages of superlative insight and inspiration. To the Romans our apostolic friend of old wrote: "For as many as are led by the

Spirit of God, they are the sons of God." Standing alone, this could be taken to mean that by faith the saints become the sons of the Lord Jesus. But the perspective begins to change when our apostolic colleague says: "Ye have received the Spirit of adoption, whereby we cry, Abba, Father." That is, we call upon our Eternal Father in a familiar and friendly way, as children here call to their fathers with whom they maintain a familiar intimacy. Having attained this state of friendship with the Eternal One, "The Spirit itself beareth witness with our spirit," Paul continues, "that we are the children of God." He has now laid the groundwork. A pronouncement of deep and wondrous import is immediately forthcoming. "And if children"—note it well—"then heirs; heirs of God, and joint-heirs with Christ." (Rom. 8:14-17.)

Now here is a wondrous presumption, one that neither Paul nor any sane man would dare make, unless its verity burst upon him by the spirit of revelation. It is a case of a man making himself a God. It is a plain statement that mortal man shall inherit equally with Christ. It is the promise: "All that my Father hath shall be given unto him." (D&C 84:38.) The reasoning is perfect. The Father had a Son, a natural Son, his own literal Seed, the Offspring of his body. This Son is his heir. As an heir he inherits all things from his Father—all power, all might, all dominion, the world, the universe, kingship, eternal exaltation, all things. But our revelations speak of men being exalted also and of their ascending the throne of eternal power. How is it done? Paul has explained it perfectly. They are adopted into the family of the Father. They become joint-heirs with his natural Son, "For it became him, for whom are all things, and by whom are all things, in bringing many sons unto glory, to make the captain of their salvation perfect." (Heb. 2:10.)

Analyzing the problem in a similar way for the saints in Galatia, and through them for all of us, the ancient apostle said: "Ye are all the children of God by faith in Christ Jesus.

For as many of you as have been baptized into Christ have put on Christ." Here again we have the concept of adoption for those who make the gospel live in their lives. "And if ye be Christ's, then are ye Abraham's seed, and heirs according to the promise." Heirs according to the promise? What promise? Heirs according to the promise which God gave to Abraham: the promise of exaltation, the promise that in him and in his seed all generations should be blessed. "Abraham received promises concerning his seed, and of the fruit of his loins . . . which were to continue so long as they were in the world; and as touching Abraham and his seed, out of the world should they continue; both in the world and out of the world should they continue as innumerable as the stars; or, if ye were to count the sand upon the seashore ye could not number them. This promise is yours also, because ye are of Abraham, and the promise was made unto Abraham." (D&C 132:30-31.) That is to say, the seed of Abraham, who through faith become the "children of God," shall inherit the same blessings of exaltation promised to their faithful father.

"Now I say," Paul continues, "That the heir, as long as he is a child, differeth nothing from a servant, though he be lord of all; But is under tutors and governors until the time appointed of the father." Thus, men are schooled, tested, trained, prepared, made ready for the day of adoption, the day in which they step out of their role as servants and receive the homage of sons. That this might come to pass, "God sent forth his Son, . . . that we might receive the adoption of sons. And because we are sons, God hath sent forth the Spirit of his Son into your hearts, crying, Abba, Father. Wherefore thou art no more a servant, but a son; and if a son, then an heir of God through Christ." (Gal. 3:26-29; 4:1-7.)

This time Paul calls us heirs rather than joint-heirs, but the meaning is the same. We are adopted into the family of the Father; we are adopted sons, appointed to inherit along with his natural Son.

The laws whereby faithful men may enter into their exaltation and become "gods, even the sons of God" (D&C 76:58) are infinite and eternal. They govern in all worlds and from one eternity to the next without end. They constitute the sole and only way the eternal increase of an Eternal Father can become like their great Progenitor. As pertaining to this earth, they were revealed first to father Adam. He was baptized, born again, received the priesthood, and kept the commandments. As a result thereof, "a voice out of heaven" proclaimed: "Thou art one in me, a son of God; and thus may all become my sons." (Moses 6:65-68.) "Our father Adam taught these things," the scripture says, "and many have believed and become the sons of God, and many have believed not, and have perished in their sins." (Moses 7:1.)

As to the infinite scope of the laws of adoption and sonship, the voice from heaven spoke also to Joseph Smith and Sidney Rigdon, bearing testimony that the Lamb of God is the Only Begotten of the Father, and saying: "That by him, and through him, and of him, the worlds are and were created, and the inhabitants thereof are begotten sons and daughters unto God." (D&C 76:21-24.) This means that through the infinite and eternal atonement, those who are true and faithful on all the endless creations of Christ are adopted into the family of the Father as heirs, as joint-heirs, who will with him receive, inherit, and possess all that the Father hath.

Saints Are the Children of Jehovah

Aware, as we are, that faithful mortals become the sons and daughters of Christ; knowing, as we do, that this system of adoption has been in force from the beginning; and realizing, as is the case, that the Lord Jesus and the Lord Jehovah are one and the same person—we would expect to find Old Testament passages that refer to Jehovah as the Father and to the saints as his sons and daughters. And this is precisely what we do find. As we now refer to some of these, we should do so with the realization that each one is a Messianic prophecy; each attributes to Jehovah what we have seen from the New Testament and latter-day revelation is in fact referring to the Lord Jesus.

"Ye are the children of the Lord your God," that is, of Jehovah your God, Moses proclaimed to Israel. Even if it were falsely supposed that Jehovah was the Father and not the Son, as some sectarian Christians do believe, still it would be apparent that this statement could not be a reference to the preexistence of spirits, which the sectarians do not believe in anyway, because it is not speaking of all men but of a chosen few. The context says: "For thou art an holy people unto the Lord thy God, and the Lord hath chosen thee to be a peculiar people unto himself, above all the nations that are upon the earth." Peculiar indeed! They had been adopted into the family of their God; they were his children, heirs of the promises made to Abraham their father.

Speaking of Jehovah, their "Rock," who had "spiritually begotten" (Mosiah 5:7) his people, Moses asked: "Is not he thy father that hath bought thee?" Then referring to Israel's oft-repeated acts of rebellion and wickedness, Moses said: "Of the Rock that begat thee thou art unmindful, and hast forgotten God that formed thee." (Deut. 32:4, 6, 18.) Speaking of Jehovah, the Psalmist in similar vein intoned: "Thou art my father, my God, and the rock of my salvation." (Ps. 89:26.) One of Isaiah's Messianic prophecies says: "He shall be a father to the inhabitants of Jerusalem, and to the house of Judah." (Isa. 22:21.) "Thou, O Lord, art our father," Isaiah also said, "our redeemer; thy name is from everlasting. . . . Our adversaries have trodden down thy sanctuary. We are thine: thou never barest rule over them; they were not called by thy name." (Isa. 63:16-19.) "But now, O Lord, thou art our father." (Isa. 64:8.)

Some of our best Old Testament pronouncements on the Fatherhood of Jehovah and the sonship of his people are found in prophecies telling of the gathering of scattered Israel in the day of restoration. "It shall come to pass," Hosea prophesied, "that in the place where it was said unto them, Ye are not my people, there it shall be said unto them, Ye are the sons of the living God. Then shall the children of Judah and the children of Israel be gathered together." (Hosea 1:10-11; Rom. 9:25-26.) During the darkness of their long dispersion, Israel shall not be known as the Lord's people, but when they accept the restored gospel, they shall once again be adopted into the same family in which their ancient forebears found peace and salvation.

"I have redeemed thee," Jehovah says to Israel, ". . . thou art mine. . . . I am the Lord thy God, the Holy One of Israel, thy Savior. . . . I will bring thy seed from the east, and gather thee from the west; I will say to the north, Give up; and to the south, Keep not back: bring my sons from far, and my daughters from the ends of the earth; Even every one that is called by my name." (Isa. 43:1-7.) Truly this is what has been and is transpiring in this day. The scattered remnants of Israel, hearing again the voice of their Shepherd, are believing his gospel, accepting baptism at the hands of his servants, coming into his sheepfold, taking upon themselves his name, and once again becoming his sons and his daughters.

Messiah Shall See His Seed

Of the Messiah who shall come, Isaiah says: "When thou shalt make his soul an offering for sin, he shall see his seed, he shall prolong his days, and the pleasure of the Lord shall prosper in his hand." (Isa. 53:10.)

He shall see his seed! How aptly, in poetic and prophetic language, this reminds all who believe that they are the children of their Messiah. Seed is the progeny of the species. Among us men it is our children. The children of the Lord Jesus Christ are those who believe in him and obey his gospel, those who exercise the power given them to become his sons and his daughters, and who as a consequence are adopted into his family.

It is to Abinadi that we turn for the inspired interpretation of Isaiah's prophecy about Christ's seed. Our Nephite friend has just quoted all of the 53rd chapter of Isaiah. He is now expounding on verse 10. "Behold, I say unto you," he says, "that when his soul has been made an offering for sin he shall see his seed. And now what say ye? And who shall be his seed?"

By way of definition and in language that cannot be misunderstood, Abinadi now identifies Messiah's seed. "Behold I say unto you," he continues, "that whosoever has heard the words of the prophets, yea, all the holy prophets who have prophesied concerning the coming of the Lord—I say unto you, that all those who have hearkened unto their words, and believed that the Lord would redeem his people, and have looked forward to that day for a remission of their sins, I say unto you, that these are his seed, or they are the heirs of the kingdom of God. For these are they whose sins he has borne; these are they for whom he has died, to redeem them from their transgressions. And now, are they not his seed? Yea, and are not the prophets, every one that has opened his mouth to prophesy, that has not fallen into transgression, I mean all the holy prophets ever since the world began? I say unto you that they are his seed. And these are they who have published peace, who have brought good tidings of good, who have published salvation; and said unto Zion: Thy God reigneth!" (Mosiah 15:10-14.)

Included in this group of whom Abinadi speaks are all those who have been faithful from the day of father Adam to that moment; all are members of their Messiah's family. They are his spiritual progeny, his seed, his children. In principle the same thing will apply to all the faithful yet to come, all who shall be spiritually born of him. But Isaiah's prophecy and Abinadi's interpretation speak only of those who have been and not of those who shall yet believe and who shall gain the adoption of sonship in a future day. A clear awareness of this fact is essential to a full understanding of what Isaiah and Abinadi really mean.

With our Lord's seed thus clearly identified, let us note the time and circumstances under which he will see them. Abinadi's rendition of Isaiah's inspired utterance says: "When his soul has been made an offering for sin he shall see his seed." In other words, he shall see his seed after he has worked out the infinite and eternal atonement. He shall see his seed after he has sweat great drops of blood in Gethsemane; after he has been crucified by wicked men; after he has said, "It is finished"; after he has voluntarily let his spirit leave its mortal tenement.

What was it that then occurred which enabled him to see his seed? His own declaration, made while on the cross itself, was that he would go that very day to paradise. (Luke 23:40-43.) Peter affirmed that he did in fact go to a world of waiting spirits, to those who were awaiting the day of their resurrection, to those who felt themselves imprisoned because of the long absence of their spirits from their bodies, and that there he preached the gospel. (1 Pet. 3:18-20; 4:6.) In his glorious vision of the redemption of the dead, President Joseph F. Smith saw what transpired when the Messiah visited the departed dead. "The eyes of my understanding were opened, and the Spirit of the Lord rested upon me," he said, "and I saw the hosts of the dead, both small and great. And there were gathered together in one place an innumerable company of the spirits of the just, who had been faithful in the testimony of Jesus while they lived in mortality. . . . All these had departed the mortal life, firm in the hope of a glorious resurrection, through the grace of God the Father and his Only Begotten Son, Jesus Christ." (JFS-V 11-14.) The promise was that when his soul should be made an offering for sin, then he would see his seed, which seed consisted of all the righteous persons who had departed this life up to that time. How wondrously this prophecy was fulfilled reminds us anew of the depth and glory of the Messianic utterances which deal with Him who has adopted us into his family.

This vision of what Isaiah meant by the Messiah seeing his seed gives sense and meaning to the balance of the prophetic statement: "When thou shalt make his soul an offering for sin, he shall see his seed, he shall prolong his days, and the pleasure of the Lord shall prosper in his hand." (Isa. 53:10.) If this prophecy was meant to be fulfilled during his mortal sojourn on earth, we would list it as having failed. He did not prolong his days; a voluntary death overtook him in the prime of life. Nor did the pleasure of the Lord find full fruition while he dwelt in a state where death lies in wait for the weary pilgrim. It is only in the resurrection that the pleasure of the Lord is perfected, for it is only when "spirit and element" are "inseparably connected" that either God or man can "receive a fulness of joy." (D&C 93:33.) Thus, having made his soul an offering for sin; having seen his seed—all the righteous dead from the days of Adam to that moment—as they assembled to greet and worship him in the paradise of their Lord; and having thereafter risen in glorious immortality to live and reign forever, our Messiah truly fulfilled the prophetic utterance, for then his days were prolonged forever and the pleasure in his hand was infinite.

There is one other Old Testament passage that speaks of Christ's seed, this time with a different emphasis. It is not a prophecy in which our Lord sees and rejoices in his righteous family members, but one in which they pledge allegiance to him as he is loved, served, and worshiped by them. As part of a great Messianic Psalm, David looks forward from the sorrow and seeming defeat of the cross to the millennial triumph of truth and righteousness. He speaks of the praise the Crucified One shall receive when "all the ends of the world shall remember and turn unto the Lord: and all the kindreds of the nations shall worship before" him; when "the kingdom is the Lord's: and he is the governor among the nations." In that day—"A seed shall serve him. . . . They shall come, and shall declare his righteousness." (Ps. 22.)

Needless to say, those who are now his seed look forward with rejoicing and fervently pray that his kingdom may come and that there will soon be ushered in that day in which all shall love and serve him without molestation or hindrance of any sort.

Saints Bear Their Lord's Name

Family members bear the family name; by it they are known and called and identified; it sets them apart from all those of a different lineage and ancestry. Adopted children take upon themselves the name of their newfound parents and become in all respects as though they had been born in the family. And so it is that the children of Christ, those who are born again, those who are spiritually begotten by their new Father, take upon themselves the name of Christ. By it they are known; in it they are called; it identifies and sets them apart from all others. They are now family members, Christians in the real and true sense of the word.

Do they themselves become Christs? Not in the sense that they are called upon to atone for the sins of others and make immortality and eternal life available for themselves or their fellowmen on this or any world. But they do carry his name and are obligated to bear it in decency and dignity. No taint of shame or disgrace, no sliver of dishonor must ever be permitted to attach itself to that name "which is above every name," for "at the name of Jesus every knee should bow" (Phil. 2:9-10) and pay homage to him who is above all save the Father only. The saints of God must remember who they are and act accordingly.

Thus, when King Benjamin desired to set his people apart from the world and plant their feet in that course leading to peace and joy here in mortality and to everlasting renown in the realms ahead, he said: "I shall give this people a name, that thereby they may be distinguished above all the people which the Lord God hath brought out of the land of Jerusalem; and this I do because they have been a diligent people in keeping the commandments of the Lord. And I give unto them a name that never shall be blotted out, except it be through transgression." (Mosiah 1:11-12.)

Later, in a tender and moving passage, addressing himself to those who had been born again, thereby becoming "the children of Christ, his sons, and his daughters," the beloved and upright King of the Nephites counseled his people: "Take upon you the name of Christ. . . . And it shall come to pass that whosoever doeth this shall be found at the right hand of God, for he shall know the name by which he is called; for he shall be called by the name of Christ. And now it shall come to pass, that whosoever shall not take upon him the name of Christ must be called by some other name; therefore, he findeth himself on the left hand of God. And I would that ye should remember also, that this is the name that I said I should give unto you that never should be blotted out, except it be through transgression; therefore, take heed that ye do not transgress, that the name be not blotted out of your hearts. I say unto you, I would that ye should remember to retain the name written always in your hearts, that ye are not found on the left hand of God, but that ye hear and know the voice by which ye shall be called, and also, the name by which he shall call you. For how knoweth a man the master whom he has not served, and who is a stranger unto him, and is far from the thoughts and intents of his heart?" (Mosiah 5:7-13.)

When the first Alma was struggling with the administrative burdens of the Church in his day, he pled with the Lord for direction relative to church members who transgressed the laws of their Sovereign. Included in the answer from the Lord were these words: "Blessed is this people who are willing to bear my name; for in my name shall they be called; and they are mine. . . . For it is I that taketh upon me the sins of the world; for it is I that hath created them; and it is I that granteth unto him that believeth unto the end a place at my right hand. For behold, in my name are they called; and if they know me they shall come forth, and shall have a place eternally at my right hand." (Mosiah 26:18, 23-24.)

Thus we learn that those who take upon themselves the name of Christ, who thereafter hearken and hear when he continues to call them in the name which is both his and theirs, and who keep the standards of the Christian family, having enjoyed the fellowship of hosts of brothers and sisters in the Church, go on to eternal joy and felicity as members of the family of God in the celestial kingdom! What a pleasing concept this is! (Alma 34:38; D&C 18:21-25.)

In the same sense in which faithful people become the sons and daughters of their Lord, thus inheriting from him the joys of salvation, so rebellious and unbelieving people become the sons and daughters of Satan, thus inheriting from him the sorrows of damnation. So we find the second Alma, as part of his great sermon on being born again, addressing himself to "workers of iniquity" in this way: "The good shepherd doth call you; yea, and in his own name he doth call you, which is the name of Christ; and if ye will not hearken unto the voice of the good shepherd, to the name by which ye are called, behold, ye are not the sheep of the good shepherd.

"And now if ye are not the sheep of the good shepherd, of what fold are ye? Behold, I say unto you, that the devil is your shepherd, and ye are of his fold; and now, who can deny this? Behold, I say unto you, whosoever denieth this is a liar and a child of the devil. For I say unto you that whatsoever is good cometh from God, and whatsoever is evil cometh from the devil. Therefore, if a man bringeth forth good works he hearkeneth unto the voice of the good shepherd, and he doth follow him; but whosoever bringeth forth evil works, the same becometh a child of the devil, for he hearkeneth unto his voice, and doth follow him. And whosoever doeth this must receive his wages of him; therefore, for his wages he receiveth death, as to things pertaining unto righteousness, being dead unto all good works." (Alma 5:38-42.)

These views of the American Paul accord perfectly with

those of the Lord Jesus, spoken to rebellious Jews, in these words: "Ye are of your father the devil, and the lusts of your father ye will do." (John 8:44.)

The way in which the name Christian is bestowed upon those who take upon themselves the name of Christ is set forth in that episode of Nephite history when General Moroni set up the title of liberty. On that occasion, the record says, "he prayed mightily unto his God for the blessings of liberty to rest upon his brethren, so long as there should a band of Christians remain to possess the land—For thus were all the true believers of Christ, who belonged to the church of God, called by those who did not belong to the church. And those who did belong to the church were faithful; yea, all those who were true believers in Christ took upon them, gladly, the name of Christ, or Christians as they were called, because of their belief in Christ who should come. And therefore, at this time, Moroni prayed that the cause of the Christians, and the freedom of the land might be favored." (Alma 46:13-16.)

This doctrine whereunder the true saints take upon themselves the name of their Lord so that ever thereafter they are called by the sacred name of Christ, or Christians, is also the basis for the proper choice of the name of the Church. "Lord, we will that thou wouldst tell us the name whereby we shall call this church; for there are disputations among the people concerning this matter," was the petition of the Nephite Twelve to the risen Lord Jesus. "Why is it that the people should murmur and dispute because of this thing?" he replied. "Have they not read the scriptures, which say ye must take upon you the name of Christ, which is my name? For by this name shall ye be called at the last day; And whoso taketh upon him my name, and endureth to the end, the same shall be saved at the last day.

"Therefore, whatsoever ye shall do, ye shall do it in my name; therefore ye shall call the church in my name; and ye shall call upon the Father in my name that he will bless the church for my sake. And how be it my church save it be called in my name? For if a church be called in Moses' name then it be Moses' church; or if it be called in the name of a man then it be the church of a man; but if it be called in my name then it is my church, if it so be that they are built upon my gospel." (3 Ne. 27:3-8.)

Saints Bear Jehovah's Name

As we are aware, the chief designation of Christ that has been preserved for us in the Old Testament, as that ancient work is now published, is the exalted name-title Jehovah. Since the saints must take upon themselves the name of Christ to gain salvation, it follows that they took upon themselves the name of Jehovah when that was the designation being applied to the Messiah. Accordingly, all Old Testament passages that show that the Lord's people either knew or had taken upon themselves or were called by the name of Jehovah are Messianic in nature. The whole system of Old Testament worship was one in which the Lord's people were to "fear this glorious and fearful name, THE LORD THY GOD" (Deut. 28:58), the Lord Jehovah. It will profit us to note some of the passages that apply the name itself to the Lord's people.

Our clearest recitation of the fact that the ancients took upon themselves Jehovah's name is found in the newly revealed writings of Old Testament Abraham. To the father of the faithful, the Lord appeared saying: "Abraham, Abraham, behold, my name is Jehovah. . . . Behold, I will lead thee by my hand, and I will take thee, to put upon thee my name. . . . As it was with Noah so shall it be with thee; but through thy ministry my name shall be known in the earth forever, for I am thy God." (Abr. 1:16-19.) Again: "I have purposed . . . to make of thee a minister to bear my name. . . . My name is Jehovah." (Abr. 2:6, 8.)

In the Old Testament record itself, Jehovah says: "Put my name upon the children of Israel; and I will bless them." (Num. 6:27.) Why put his name upon them? Because, as he said, "Thou art an holy people unto the Lord thy God: the Lord thy God hath chosen thee to be a special people unto himself, above all people that are upon the face of the earth." (Deut. 7:6.) With what result? "All people of the earth shall see that thou art called by the name of the Lord; and they shall be afraid of thee." (Deut. 28:10.)

Would it be amiss here to note that when the Lord places his name upon a people they become Christians? True, we are dealing with the so-called pre-Christian Era, but so were we also when we quoted the account about General Moroni. (Alma 46.) And for that matter, did not true Christianity begin with Adam, who had faith, repented of his sins, was baptized by immersion, received the gift of the Holy Ghost, and worked righteousness all his days?

These words were spoken by the Lord to one of his ancient servants: "If my people, which are called by my name, shall humble themselves, and pray, and seek my face, and turn from their wicked ways; then will I hear from heaven, and will forgive their sin, and will heal their land." To whom did this message come? Was it Alma or Moroni or Samuel the Lamanite? It sounds as though it came right out of the Book of Mormon and that the Lord Jesus was calling his people, those who had taken upon themselves his name, to repentance. And well might these words have come to these or others of the Hebrew prophets who dwelt on the American continent, but in fact they are the words of Jehovah to Solomon as recorded in Second Chronicles, chapter 7, verse 14. But what does it matter to whom the message came? Or by what name the Speaker was known? The words spoken are true. The name placed upon the Lord's people has the same saving power be it Jehovah or Jesus.

As we have already seen, in the day of Israel's gathering Jehovah promised to bring his sons from afar and his daughters from the ends of the earth. Now, however, let us note that those being thus gathered again into the sheepfold of the good Shepherd are identified as "Even every one that is called by my name" (Isa. 43:7), that is, by the name of Jehovah.

Speaking of this day when Israel shall be gathered in from her long dispersion, when Jerusalem shall become again a holy city, when the redeemed of the Lord shall once again know the God of their fathers, Jehovah says: "Therefore my people shall know my name: therefore they shall know in that day that I am he that doth speak: behold, it is I." (Isa. 52.) The risen Christ, ministering among the Nephites, quotes, paraphrases, and amplifies Isaiah's writings about the glorious latter-day work of restoration and gathering and then takes these words of Jehovah and specifically and expressly applies them to himself, saying: "Verily, verily, I say unto you, that my people shall know my name; yea, in that day they shall know that I am he that doth speak." (3 Ne. 20.) Jehovah who spoke to Isaiah of the day when Israel would receive again her ancient glory was this same Jesus who taught the same truths to the Nephites.

From all of the foregoing it is apparent that whenever Jehovah says, "Thou art my people" (Isa. 51:16); or whenever the people say of Jehovah, "We are his people, and the sheep of his pasture" (Ps. 100:3); or when they say, "Thou, O Lord, art in the midst of us, and we are called by thy name; leave us not" (Jer. 14:9); or "Our adversaries have trodden down thy sanctuary. We are thine: thou never barest rule over them; they were not called by thy name" (Isa. 63:18-19); or when Jehovah promises (of gathered Israel), "They shall know that my name is The Lord" (Jer. 16:21)—whenever these or any equivalent utterances are made, they mean that the name of the Lord Jehovah (who is Christ) has been placed upon his people, and they, knowing the name by which they are called, are heirs of salvation.

Christ Is the Father and the Son

As we are now aware, there are three senses in which Christ is the Father. He is the Father of heaven and earth, by which we mean he is the Creator. He is the Father by divine investiture of authority, meaning that the Father has placed his name and power upon the Son, so that the words and acts of the Son are and become those of the Father. He is the Father of all those who believe on his name, who are born again, who are adopted into his family.

Our clearest Messianic prophecy, equating the Fatherhood of Christ with his status as the newfound Father of every true believer, is contained in the conversations he had with Moriancumer when that seer ascended the summits of Shelem with the sixteen small stones which were soon to give light in the Jareditish barges. When the Lord withdrew the veil from the eyes and mind of Jared's brother, the eternal words then uttered by Deity were: "Ye are redeemed from the fall; therefore ye are brought back into my presence; therefore I show myself unto you." These words are being spoken more than two millenniums before what men choose to call the Christian Era. They continue: "Behold, I am he who was prepared from the foundation of the world to redeem my people. Behold, I am Jesus Christ. I am the Father and the Son. In me shall all mankind have light, and that eternally, even they who shall believe on my name; and they shall become my sons and my daughters." (Ether 3:13-14.)

"I am Jesus Christ. I am the Father and the Son." How so? 'I am the Only Begotten Son, the One chosen and foreordained from the beginning, the One destined to be born into mortality as the offspring of the Father. But I am also the Father, the Father of all who shall believe on my name, for they shall become my sons and my daughters, members of my family, chosen vessels to bear my name.' There was never any ambiguity or uncertainty about this pleasing doctrine so far as the saints of old were concerned. Nor was there any difficulty in the minds of the ancients where his Fatherhood as Creator or his Fatherhood as the voice and agent of the Father were concerned. The confusion and delusion relative to the status and relationship of the Father and the Son that now prevails is an outgrowth from the false creeds of an apostate Christendom.

Some passages that specify that Christ is the Father do not spell out the sense in which the designation is being used. In these cases there is no impropriety in interpreting the prophetic statements as applying to any or all of the senses in which our Lord carries his Father's name. In one of the most famous of all Messianic statements, Isaiah exults: "Unto us a child is born, unto us a son is given: and the government shall be upon his shoulder: and his name shall be called Wonderful, Counseller, The mighty God, The everlasting Father, The Prince of Peace." (Isa. 9:6.) The everlasting Father! In what sense? Perhaps in all of them, in every way and sense in which the Son carries that exalted name-title.

In the course of an exposition relative to the creation, the fall, and the redemption, Moroni says: God "created Adam, and by Adam came the fall of man. And because of the fall of man came Jesus Christ, even the Father and the Son; and because of Jesus Christ came the redemption of man." (Morm. 9:12.) How is our Lord the Father? It is because of the atonement, because he received power from his Father to do that which is infinite and eternal. This is a matter of his Eternal Parent investing him with power from on high so that he becomes the Father because he exercises the power of that Eternal Being.

Nephi the son of Nephi, on the night before our Lord's birth into mortality, received this message from that holy being: "Behold, I come unto my own, to fulfil all things which I have made known unto the children of men from the foundation of the world, and to do the will, both of the Father and of the Son—of the Father because of me, and of the Son because of my flesh." (3 Ne. 1:14.) It is clear that he is the Son because of the flesh, meaning that he was born into the world as other mortals are. He had a body that was conceived and nurtured in the womb of a mortal woman. It is more difficult to envision how he was the Father because of himself. This can only be taken to mean that he was the Father because he had the power of the Father; that his will was swallowed up in the will of the Father; that he could do all things because of his inheritance from that Supreme Being. The same thought is put forth in latter-day revelation in these words: "I am in the Father, and the Father in me, and the Father and I are one—The Father because he gave me of his fulness, and the Son because I was in the world and made flesh my tabernacle, and dwelt among the sons of men." (D&C 93:3-4.)

After Moroni, in abridging the writings of Ether, sets forth that Christ is the Father because those who believe in him become his sons and his daughters, he receives a revelation of his own which is identified as coming from "Jesus Christ, the Son of God, the Father of the heavens and of the earth, and all things that are in them." In this revelation the Son continues to speak and in due course gives forth this declaration: "He that will not believe my words will not believe me—that I am; and he that will not believe me will not believe the Father who sent me. For behold, I am the Father, I am the light, and the life, and the truth of the world." (Ether 4:7-12.) When he says "I am the Father," in what sense does he mean it? Perhaps this is another case where the name-title is of general and not specific application.

Abinadi's exposition relative to the Father and the Son and the great atoning sacrifice to be wrought by him in his capacity as the Son, as he acted in the power of the Father, is one of the deepest and most thought-filled Messianic passages we have. "God himself shall come down among the children of men, and shall redeem his people," Abinadi says. This is clear: Christ is God; he is the Lord Omnipotent; he is like unto the Father. "And because he dwelleth in flesh he shall be called the Son of God, and having subjected the flesh to the will of the Father, being the Father and the Son—The Father, because he was conceived by the power of God; and the Son, because of the flesh; thus becoming the

Father and Son—And they are one God, yea, the very Eternal Father of heaven and of earth. And thus the flesh becoming subject to the Spirit, or the Son to the Father, being one God, suffereth temptation, and yieldeth not to the temptation, but suffereth himself to be mocked, and scourged, and cast out, and disowned by his people." He shall be slain, Abinadi says, "the will of the Son being swallowed up in the will of the Father. And thus God breaketh the bands of death, having gained the victory over death; giving the son power to make intercession for the children of men." (Mosiah 15:1-9.)

In this powerful passage we have a wondrous summary of divine truth. Christ is God and he comes to redeem his people. He is the Son because he is born into mortality. He is the Father because he inherits from his Father all the might of omnipotence, and what he says and what he does become and are the words and works of him whose name he bears.

ALL THINGS BEAR RECORD OF CHRIST

"All Things Denote There Is a God"

An all-wise Creator has structured all the creations of his hands in such a way, not only to call attention to himself as the Maker, Preserver, and Upholder of all things, but to bear record of the nature and kind of Being he is. The mere fact that all things are, that fact standing alone, establishes that there is a Supreme Being; and the orderliness and system which prevails in the universe is a sufficient witness that the Creator is almighty, knows all things, and has made man, his crowning creature, as the natural heir of all his goodness.

Thus David acclaims, "The heavens declare the glory of God; and the firmament sheweth his handywork." In the sidereal heavens, in the broad expanse of the universe, in all the orbs that roll in their assigned spheres, in the heavens above and the earth beneath, is seen the hand of God. The sun rises in the morning; lilies bloom in the fields; wheat whitens for the harvest; birds soar in the firmament above and fish swim in the waters beneath—all nature operating in harmony with the laws of Nature's God—all things denote (nay, prove!) there is a God.

"Day unto day uttereth speech, and night unto night sheweth knowledge." Whose speech? Whose knowledge? Though the voice of the Creator be stilled, yet the voice of his creations declare his divinity. The heavens and the earth declare his glory. His voice is heard in the rolling thunder; his words are read in the vivid lightning; his speech is recorded in the lilac's bloom. "There is no speech nor language, where their voice"—the voice of all created things—"is not heard. Their line is gone out through all the earth, and their words to the ends of the world." (Ps. 19:1-4.) None but fools say, "We have not heard the voice of Deity," for that voice is everywhere. If men fail to live that law which enables them to see the divine face and converse with their Creator in plain words, at least they are obligated to hear the voice of Nature, which is also the voice of God.

This concept was taught to Joseph Smith by "him who sitteth upon the throne and governeth and executeth all things." Speaking of himself, the Divine Teacher averred: "He comprehendeth all things, and all things are before him, and all things are round about him; and he is above all things, and in all things, and is through all things, and is round about all things; and all things are by him, and of him, even God, forever and ever."

Continuing to speak of himself, Christ the Creator says: "He hath given a law unto all things, by which they move in their times and their seasons; And their courses are fixed, even the courses of the heavens and the earth, which comprehended the earth and all the planets. And they give light to each other in their times and in their seasons, in their minutes, in their hours, in their days, in their weeks, in their months, in their years—all these are one year with God, but not with man. The earth rolls upon her wings, and the sun giveth his light by day, and the moon giveth her light by night, and the stars also give their light, as they roll upon their wings in their glory, in the midst of the power of God."

Then comes the question: "Unto what shall I liken these kingdoms, that ye may understand?" There follows a parable which teaches that he will visit "every kingdom"—and the inhabitants thereof—"in its hour, and in its time, and in its season." But our immediate concern is the divine announcement: "All these are kingdoms, and any man who hath seen any or the least of these hath seen God moving in his majesty and power. I say unto you, he hath seen him; nevertheless, he who came unto his own was not comprehended." It is then said that in a future day the faithful shall "comprehend even God," as pertaining to which time it is written: "Then shall ye know that ye have seen me." (D&C 88:40-62.)

In these sayings we find reinforcement of two great verities: (1) All men have seen God, in preexistence, for they lived and dwelt with him before ever the foundations of this earth were laid, a fact which all will remember at a future time; and (2) God is seen in the heavens above and the earth beneath, whose voices combine to declare his glory and goodness.

In a dramatic confrontation, Korihor (an intellectual without faith!) defied Alma and derided what he called "the foolish ordinances and performances" of the gospel. He accused the church leaders of keeping the saints in bondage, "that ye may glut yourselves with the labors of their hands." His thesis was that no man could know there was a God, or a fall of man, or that Christ would come to redeem his people. In reply, Alma testified, "there is a God, and . . . Christ shall come." There is, of course, no way to argue with a testimony. Then Alma said: "And now what evidence have ye that there is no God, or that Christ cometh not? I say unto you that ye have none, save it be your word only. But, behold, I have all things as a testimony that these things are true; and ye also have all things as a testimony unto you that they are true. . . . The scriptures are laid before thee, yea, and all things denote there is a God; yea, even the earth, and all things that are upon the face of it, yea, and its motion, yea, and also all the planets which move in their regular form do witness that there is a Supreme Creator." Thereafter, because he demanded a sign, Korihor was struck dumb, confessed he had been deceived by the devil, and suffered an ignominious death. (Alma 30:23-60.)

Gospel Taught with Similitudes

To crystallize in our minds the eternal verities which we must accept and believe to be saved, to dramatize their true meaning and import with an impact never to be forgotten, to center our attention on these saving truths, again and again and again, the Lord uses similitudes. Abstract principles may easily be forgotten or their deep meaning overlooked, but visual performances and actual experiences are registered on the mind in such a way as never to be lost. It is one thing to talk of faith as an abstract principle, another to see the Red Sea parted by its power. It is one thing to talk of the word of God coming down from heaven, another to actually gather and taste the angelic manna. It is one thing to teach that God is our Father in an abstract and impersonal way, thus expecting all Christendom to envision that he is a personal being in whose image man is created. It is another thing to say: Here is his Son; he is in the express image of his Father's person; he is in the similitude of the Father; observe what he does and see how he acts and you will know what the Father is like, for God is in Christ manifesting himself to men.

"I . . . am the Lord thy God," is the introduction of Jehovah to his people. Such is the voice of him who knows all things, reveals what he will, and chooses what his children shall be taught. How, then, does he present his message? "I have also spoken by the prophets," he says, "and I have multiplied visions, and used similitudes, by the ministry of the prophets." (Hosea 12:9-10.) He uses ordinances, rites, acts, and performances; he uses similarities, resemblances, and similitudes so that whatever is done will remind all who are aware of it of a greater and more important reality. He uses similes; he uses parables; he uses allegories. If two things have the same semblance or form, if they are like each other in appearance, if they correspond in qualities, it may suit his purposes to compare them. To liken one thing to another is one of the best teaching procedures.

After setting forth that as men were born into the world of water, and blood, and the spirit, and so became of dust living souls, so they must be born again of water, and of the Spirit, and be cleansed by the blood of Christ to enter the kingdom of heaven—itself a perfect similitude—the Lord says: "Behold, all things have their likeness, and all things are created and made to bear record of me, both things which are temporal, and things which are spiritual; things which are in the heavens above, and things which are on the earth, and things which are in the earth, and things which are under the earth, both above and beneath: all things bear record of me." (Moses 6:59-63.) "All things" includes the heavens and the earth, as also all of the ordinances and performances of the gospel.

"My soul delighteth in proving unto my people the truth of the coming of Christ," says Jacob, the Nephite, "for, for this end hath the law of Moses been given; and all things which have been given of God from the beginning of the world, unto man, are the typifying of him." (2 Ne. 11:4.) It follows that if we had sufficient insight, we would see in every gospel ordinance, in every rite that is part of revealed religion, in every performance commanded of God, in all things Deity gives his people, something that typifies the eternal ministry of the Eternal Christ. The performance of all such ordinances or acts, from Adam to Christ, falls thereby into the category of Messianic acts and performances. We shall now consider samples of these matters and note some of their Messianic implications.

"Why Dost Thou Offer Sacrifices?"

In point of time one of the first great symbolic ordinances was that of sacrifice, animal sacrifice, the shedding of the blood of chosen beasts in similitude of that which was to be in time's meridian. After Adam and Eve were cast out of Eden to till the dust whence they came and to gain the experiences available only in a mortal probation, the Lord "gave unto them commandments, that they should worship the Lord their God, and should offer the firstlings of their flocks, for an offering unto the Lord. And Adam was obedient unto the commandments of the Lord." He complied with the heavenly commandments and worshiped the Lord, in manner and form, as that holy being had directed, including the offering of sacrifices.

We do not know the details and specifics of his worship, except that the gospel plan was given to him, line upon line and precept upon precept, until he was the possessor of its everlasting fulness. He must have been told how and in what manner to offer sacrifices; at least what he did gained the approval of his Lord. And so it was that "after many days," how long we can only surmise, but certainly long enough for him to prove his devotion and integrity, "an angel of the Lord appeared unto Adam, saying: Why dost thou offer sacrifices unto the Lord? And Adam said unto him: I know not, save the Lord commanded me."

Blind obedience? Perhaps, although probably not more so than is the case with much that the Lord directs us to do. Adam knew he was obligated to keep the commandments and that blessings would flow therefrom, just as we do, although we cannot see, nor could he, the treasures being laid up on earth and in heaven by obedience to the laws of the Lord. In any event, "the angel spake, saying: This thing is a similitude of the sacrifice of the Only Begotten of the Father, which is full of grace and truth. Wherefore, thou shalt do all that thou doest in the name of the Son, and thou shalt repent and call upon God in the name of the Son forevermore." (Moses 5:4-8.)

There we have it. Sacrifice is a similitude. It is performed to typify the coming sacrifice of the Son of God. For four thousand long years, from Adam to that bleak day when our Lord was lifted up by sinful men, all of his righteous followers sought remission of their sins through sacrifice. It was an ordinance of the Melchizedek Priesthood; it antedated the law of Moses by two and a half millenniums, although that lesser law did give rise to many sacrificial requirements not theretofore practiced. We shall consider the details of sacrifical symbolism in Chapter 23 as part of our consideration of the law of Moses. For our purposes now it suffices to know that there neither was nor could have been any ordinance or system devised that would have dramatized more perfectly the coming eternal sacrifice that was and is the heart and core of revealed religion. For our purposes now it suffices to say that such Messianic utterances as that of Isaiah, that the Messiah should "make his soul an offering for sin" (Isa. 53:10), or that of Lehi, that "he offereth himself a sacrifice for sin" (2 Ne. 2:7), were well and perfectly understood by all Israel and all others in whose hearts the light of truth dwelt, and that the righteous of all ages looked forward with hope to the day when the Lamb of God should be slain for the sins of the world.

After the final great sacrifice on the cross, the use for the similitude that looked forward to our Lord's death ceased. Blood sacrifices became a thing of the past. New symbolisms, found in the sacrament of the Lord's supper, were adopted so that the saints might look back with reverence and worship upon his atoning ordeal. "Ye shall offer up unto me no more the shedding of blood," the risen Lord said to the Nephites, "yea, your sacrifices and your burnt offerings shall be done away, for I will accept none of your sacrifices and your burnt offerings. And ye shall offer for a sacrifice unto me a broken heart and a contrite spirit." (3 Ne. 9:19-20; Ps. 51:17.)

"Behold the Lamb of God"

As the prophets sought for similitudes to use in teaching the great and eternal truths of salvation to the people, how natural it was for them to designate him who should sacrifice himself for the sins of the world as the Lamb of God. He was to be God's Son. He would "bare the sin of many." (Isa. 53:12.) He would lay down his life for his people. Through his atoning sacrifice the way would be open to gain a remission of sins. Sacrifices were performed in similitude of his infinite and eternal sacrifice. In large measure the firstlings of the flocks slain on the altars of sacrifice were lambs, lambs without spot or blemish. What could be more appropriate than to name Him who would make the supreme sacrifice, whose own shed blood would give efficacy and force to four thousand years of sacrificial ordinances, to designate him who came from God to sacrifice his soul as the Lamb of God.

And so it was. In point of time, the first Messianic designation of Christ as the Lamb of which we have record came from the lips of Enoch, who "saw the day of the coming of the Son of Man, even in the flesh; and his soul rejoiced, saying: The Righteous is lifted up, and the Lamb is slain from the foundation of the world." (Moses 7:47.) Our Nephite brethren, having the fulness of the gospel as Enoch had it, and also being Israelites and living in the Mosaic dispensation, offered sacrifices according to the order of heaven. It was, therefore, perfectly natural for them to use this same terminology. Thus when Lehi saw in vision the ministry of John, as the forerunner of the Lord and as the one who should immerse him in the murky waters of Jordan, we find the Nephite record saying of John: "And after he had baptized the Messiah with water, he should behold and bear record that he had baptized the Lamb of God, who should take away the sins of the world." (1 Ne. 10:10; 11:27.) Thus when Nephi saw in vision the Virgin of Nazareth who was to be "the mother of the Son of God, after the manner of the flesh," and when he saw her "bearing a child in her arms," he was also privileged to hear the angelic proclamation: "Behold the Lamb of God, yea, even the Son of the Eternal Father!" (1 Ne. 11:13-21.)

Knowing and rejoicing in this title of his Lord, Nephi called the church which should be set up by restoration in the last days "the church of the Lamb." (1 Ne. 14:12.) Thus also the Nephite Alma invited those of his nation to "come and be baptized unto repentance, that ye may be washed from your sins, that ye may have faith on the Lamb of God, who taketh away the sins of the world, who is mighty to save and to cleanse from all unrighteousness." (Alma 7:14.) Alma also spoke of the faithful having "their garments . . . washed white through the blood of the Lamb." (Alma 13:11; 34:36.) If we had the full and complete accounts of all the sayings of all the prophets, and especially those who lived when the law of Moses was imposed upon the Lord's people, we would undoubtedly find many references to the Messiah as the Lamb. Isaiah, for one, who also prophesied of the virgin birth, would have known in substance and thought content the same things that his fellow prophets Lehi and Nephi were privileged to know.

Our New Testament accounts pick up the same manner of identifying Him who laid down his life in sacrifice for the sins of the world. As Lehi had foreseen, John the Baptist testified: "Behold the Lamb of God, which taketh away the sin of the world." (John 1:29.) With the sacrificial system of his ancestors in mind, Peter, the chief apostle, said the saints were "redeemed . . . with the precious blood of Christ, as of a lamb without blemish and without spot." (1 Pet. 1:18-19.) And John, the beloved apostle, had much to record that adds perspective and luster to the proper use of the Lamb's name. As did Enoch, John spoke of "the Lamb slain from the foundation of the world." (Rev. 13:8.) He saw in vision "a Lamb as it had been slain"; he saw heavenly creatures fall "down before the Lamb" in worship; and he heard heavenly choirs, composed of one hundred million voices, sing praises to his holy name. "Thou wast slain, and hast redeemed us to God by thy blood out of every kindred, and tongue, and people, and nation," they sang. Also: "Worthy is the Lamb that was slain to receive power, and riches, and wisdom, and strength, and honour, and glory, and blessing." At this point the vision expanded, the numbers in the choirs increased, and the ancient apostle heard every living creature join in the grand amen, saying: "Blessing, and honour, and glory, and power, be unto him that sitteth upon the throne, and unto the Lamb for ever and ever." (Rev. 5:6-13.) Of the Lamb, John also says: "He is Lord of lords, and King of kings" (Rev. 17:14), to whose marriage supper the faithful shall be invited, on which occasion they will sing: "Alleluia"—praise Jehovah! (for Jehovah is the Lamb)—"for the Lord God omnipotent reigneth." (Rev. 19:5-7.)

"This Do in Remembrance of Me"

A long, wearisome road runs from Eden to Gethsemane, from the garden in which the promise of a Redeemer was first given to the garden in which the promised redemption was wrought. Long, wearisome centuries—forty periods of one hundred years each—separated the promise of a Redeemer from his destined crucifixion. During all these slow-passing years millions upon millions of faithful souls looked forward, with an eye of faith, to that day when Messiah's infinite and eternal atoning sacrifice would free them from their sins. Lest they forget, the Lord gave them the ordinance of sacrifice, an ordinance perfectly designed to keep them in remembrance of that which was to be. "This thing," the angelic voice proclaimed, "is a similitude of the sacrifice of the Only Begotten of the Father." (Moses 5:7.)

A long, wearisome road also runs from Calvary and the cross to us mortals who now seek the same blessings sought by the ancients—a forgiveness of sins through our Lord's atoning sacrifice. Two millenniums—twenty centuries—now separate us from the death of a God at Golgotha. Lest we forget, the Lord has given us a sacramental ordinance that points our attention back to his spilt blood and broken flesh. It is as though we heard the angelic voice proclaim: 'This thing also is a similitude; it is an ordinance designed to keep thee in remembrance of that which Messiah-God has done for thee.' As four thousand years of sacrifices kept the Lord's people in remembrance of what their Messiah would do for them in a garden and on a cross, so two thousand years of sacramental administrations have kept them in remembrance of what he did for them in time's meridian.

The sacrament of the Lord's supper is an ordinance of salvation in which all the faithful must participate if they are to live and reign with him. It may well have been prefigured, some two thousand years before its formal institution among men, when "Melchizedek, king of Salem, brought forth bread and wine; and he brake bread and blest it, and he blest the wine, he being the priest of the most high God. And he gave to Abram." (JST, Gen. 14:17-18.) It will be administered after the Lord comes again, to all the faithful of all ages, as they in resurrected glory assemble before him. (D&C 27.) It had its beginning as an authorized ordinance and as a required rite when Jesus and his apostolic witnesses celebrated the feast of the Passover during the week of our Lord's passion. In *Doctrinal New Testament Commentary,* volume 1, pages 716-25, I have set forth in detail how the blessing and eating and drinking of the bread and the wine grew naturally out of similar requisites that were then part of that Jewish feast. As to the symbolism of that which Jesus then instituted we read: "That the Lord Jesus the same night in which he was betrayed took bread: And when he had given thanks, he brake it, and said, Take, eat: this is my body, which is broken for you: this do in remembrance of me. After the same manner also he took the cup, when he had supped, saying, This cup is the new testament in my blood: this do ye, as oft as ye drink it, in remembrance of me. For as often as ye eat this bread, and drink this cup, ye do shew the Lord's death till he come." (1 Cor. 11:23-26.)

This sacred ordinance in which bread is eaten, in similitude and remembrance of our Lord's broken flesh, and in which water or wine is drunk, in similitude and remembrance of his spilt blood, will be found among the Lord's people so long as the earth shall stand. It was had, of course, among the Nephites, and it is from their sacred writings that we gain the most perfect recitation of its meaning and purpose. Jesus had his Nephite disciples bring bread and wine, which he brake and blessed and gave to them to eat. He then commanded that this should thereafter be done "unto the people of my church, unto all those who shall believe and be baptized in my name. . . . And this shall ye do in remembrance of my body, which I have shown unto you. And it shall be a testimony unto the Father that ye do always remember me. And if ye do always remember me ye shall have my Spirit to be with you." Then he caused them to drink of the wine, after which he gave this counsel and commandment: "Blessed are ye for this thing which ye have done, for this is fulfilling my commandments, and this doth witness unto the Father that ye are willing to do that which I have commanded you. And this shall ye always do to those who repent and are baptized in my name; and ye shall do it in remembrance of my blood, which I have shed for you, that ye may witness unto the Father that ye do always remember me. And if ye do always remember me ye shall have my Spirit to be with you." (3 Ne. 18:1-14.)

In the waters of baptism faithful people covenant to take upon themselves the name of Christ, to love and serve him all their days, and to keep his commandments. He in turn promises them that if they so do, he will "pour out his Spirit more abundantly" upon them, and they shall "be redeemed of God, and be numbered with those of the first resurrection," and "have eternal life." (Mosiah 18:8-10.) Having in mind this same conformity to his eternal law and speaking in beautiful symbolism, our Lord said to the Jews: "Whoso eateth my flesh, and drinketh my blood, hath eternal life; and I will raise him up at the last day." (John 6:54.)

From Paul's instruction to the Corinthians (1 Cor. 11:24-30), from the Nephites' account of the introduction of the sacrament among them (3 Ne. 18), and from the sacramental prayers as revealed both to the Nephites and to us (Moro. 4 and 5; D&C 20:75-79), it is clear that when we partake worthily of the sacramental ordinance we renew the covenant made in the waters of baptism. Once again we covenant to remember and rely upon the atoning sacrifice of

Christ, to take his name upon us, and to keep his commandments. He in turn promises us that we shall always have his Spirit to be with us and that we shall have eternal life in his Father's kingdom.

Baptism is for the remission of sins. Those who are baptized worthily have their sins remitted because of the shedding of the blood of Christ. Their garments are washed in the blood of the Lamb. When they thereafter partake worthily of the sacrament, they renew the covenant made in the waters of baptism. The two covenants are the same. In each the promise is given that the Lord's Spirit will be poured out upon the contrite soul, and since the Spirit will not dwell in an unclean tabernacle, this means, of necessity and in the very nature of things, that the recipient of this glorious indwelling power becomes free from sin. In Chapter 23 we shall analyze the Mosaic sacrificial system, with specific reference to the fact that sacrifices were performed to free the people from their sins—all of which leads to the inescapable conclusion that those who were participants in sacrifices anciently were in fact making covenants with the Lord to always remember him, to take his name upon them, and to keep his commandments, all in return for his promise to let his Spirit be with them and to give them the eventual inheritance of eternal life. Symbolisms change but the principles are always the same.

Baptism Bears Record of Christ

Every baptism—properly performed by a legal administrator!—from Adam to Christ was itself a Messianic prophecy. It bore record of Christ, who was to come, and was so understood by the saints of old. Similarly, every baptism—properly performed by a legal administrator!—from our Lord's day to the present moment (and it shall so continue forever) has been an act of testimony, an ordinance that bears record of Jesus the Messiah. It matters not what uninspired Christendom may think relative to the need for or the mode of performance of this sacred ordinance. In the hearts of all those to whom the Spirit has borne witness that Jesus is the Lord is found the desire to be immersed in water after the manner of his burial and to come forth out of the water in a newness of life after the manner of his resurrection. Baptism in all ages bears witness of Christ.

Baptism began with Adam. "He was caught away by the Spirit of the Lord, and was carried down into the water, and was laid under the water, and was brought forth out of the water." He was given to know, by revelation, that he was thus "born again into the kingdom of heaven." He was expressly told that this new birth—symbolic of mortal birth, which comes "by water, and blood, and the spirit"—was also one in which men must be born "of water, and of the Spirit, and be cleansed by blood, even the blood of mine Only Begotten." He was then taught that "by the blood ye are sanctified," meaning that the cleansing power of baptism rests upon and grows out of the atoning sacrifice of the Only Begotten. (Moses 6:59-68.) That is to say, without the atonement and without the shedding of the blood of God's Son, neither baptism nor any ordinance would have any efficacy, virtue, or force in and after the resurrection of the dead.

These three elements—water, blood, and spirit—are associated not only with birth into mortality and with birth into the kingdom of heaven, which second birth comes because of the blood of Christ, but they are also the three elements present in the death of Christ, thus pointing our attention to the fact that it is his atoning sacrifice that makes the blessing of salvation available through baptism.

Speaking of Jesus as the Son of God, John says: "This is he that came"—came to make his soul a ransom for sin; came as the Savior and Redeemer—"This is he that came by water and blood, even Jesus Christ; not by water only, but by water and blood. And it is the Spirit that beareth witness, because the Spirit is truth." (1 Jn. 5:5-6.) That is to say, water, blood, and spirit were all present and played their part in his atoning sacrifice. As to the presence of blood, the meaning is clear. Our Lord sweat great drops of blood from every pore as he bowed in agony in Gethsemane; then again, on the cross, his blood was shed as Roman steel pierced his flesh. As to the presence of spirit, the meaning also is clear. He voluntarily gave up his mortal life; he chose to let the eternal spirit, the Spirit which was the Great Jehovah, leave the tenement of clay and enter the paradise of peace. But what of the element of water? How was this present in his atoning sacrifice? The answer is given to us in the words of the same John who set forth that water, blood, and spirit were all present on that transcendent occasion. Of the last moments of our Lord's mortal life, the Beloved Apostle wrote: "One of the soldiers with a spear pierced his side, and forthwith came there out blood and water. And he that saw it bare record, and his record is true: and he knoweth that he saith true, that ye might believe." (John 19:34-35.)

With the vision of that cruel event still shining in his mind, John later wrote, "There are three that bear record in heaven, the Father, the Word, and the Holy Ghost: and these three are one." He is speaking of those that bear record that "Jesus is the Son of God," and having first identified those who bear this witness in heaven, he turns to a symbolical witness that is borne on earth. "And there are three that bear witness in earth," he says, "the spirit, and the water, and the blood: and these three agree in one." That is to say, the presence of these three elements in the death of Christ unite in testifying of his divine Sonship. "If we receive the witness of men, the witness of God is greater: for this is the witness of God which he hath testified of his Son"—meaning: 'We believe the testimony of men when they certify to what they know to be true; should we not more readily accept the testimony which God himself bears of his Son, whom he sent by water, and blood, and the spirit to atone for the sins of the world.' "He that believeth on the Son of God hath the witness in himself." (1 Jn. 5:5-10.) In other words, those with faith and understanding not only know of the Lord's divine mission by the power of the Spirit, but their minds are also riveted on the blessings which come from the cross of crucifixion as symbolized in the water, blood, and spirit, which were the elements of his death. How aptly the Lord uses similitudes to teach his everlasting truths.

It is common among us to say that baptisms are performed in similitude of the death, burial, and resurrection of Christ, and that they should therefore be performed by immersion. This is true, but it is an oversimplification and tells only part of the story. Baptism is a new birth; it is symbolical of our new life in the kingdom of God, which new birth is a living reality because of the shedding of the blood of Christ, or in other words because of his death, burial, and resurrection. The new birth grows out of the atonement wrought by our Lord; the newness of life comes to the repentant sinner because he has bowed to the will of the Lord and has been immersed in water by a legal administrator. Paul states it this way: "Know ye not, that so many of us as were baptized into Jesus Christ were baptized into his death?" That is, even as Christ died on the cross, so we die in baptism. "Therefore we are buried with him by baptism into death." Dead people are buried, Christ in the Arimathean's tomb, every baptized person in a watery grave. But death is not eternal, and "like as Christ was raised up from the dead by the glory of the Father, even so we also should walk in newness of life." That is to say: 'Glory be to the Father by whose almighty power our Lord rose from the dead; he took up his body again in glorious immortality; the resurrection became a reality; he lived again. And even so, every baptized person, coming forth from the water, lives again in a newness of life.' "For if we have been planted together in the likeness of his death, we shall be also in the likeness of his resurrection: Knowing this, that our old man is crucified with him, that the body of sin might be destroyed, that henceforth we should not serve sin." Sometimes the spiritual struggle to slay sin, that the new convert may be free therefrom, is as savage a warfare as death by crucifixion. But when sin is destroyed in our lives, it is no longer our master.

We are "dead indeed unto sin, but alive unto God through Jesus Christ our Lord." (Rom. 6:3-11.)

Why, then, must baptisms be performed by immersion? (3 Ne. 11:26; D&C 20:74; 128:12.) For the same reason that sacrifices required the shedding of blood, and the sacrament requires the eating of bread and the drinking of water or wine. All these things are performed in similitude of and center attention in the atoning sacrifice of the Messiah. We might as well perform sacrifices by chopping down trees or digging holes in the ground, or we might as well partake of the sacrament by eating a wafer while an officiator sips wine, as to baptize by pouring or sprinkling. Baptism is either in similitude of the death, burial, and resurrection of Christ or it is not. It either serves to dramatize the crucifixion of the old man of sin and the resurrection, as it were, of the man of God to a newness of life—all through the atonement of Him whose we are—or it does not. Any so-called baptisms, or for that matter any gospel ordinances of any kind or form, which do not center the attention of those for whom they are performed in the atoning sacrifice of Him whose blood makes all ordinances efficacious, any such ordinances fail to meet the requirements of the law of similitudes and therefore do not have divine approval.

The Sabbath Bears Witness of Christ

Sabbath worship, that system which singles out one day in seven to be used exclusively for spiritual things, is a sign which identifies the Lord's people. Whatever the world may do, day in and day out, without cessation, in the way of toil and revelry, the saints of God rest from their labors and pay their devotions to the Most High on his holy Sabbath. True religion always has and always will call for a Sabbath on which men rest from their temporal labors and work exclusively on spiritual matters. True religion requires—it is not optional; it is mandatory—that one day in seven be devoted exclusively to worshiping the Father in Spirit and in truth.

Without a Sabbath of rest and worship, men's hearts will never be centered on the things of the Spirit sufficiently to assure them of salvation.

The law of the Sabbath is so basic, so fundamental, that the Lord Jehovah named it as number four in the Ten Commandments themselves. The first three commandments call upon men to worship the Lord and reverence his great and holy name. The fourth gives us the Sabbath day as the weekly occasion on which we perfect our worship and put ourselves in tune to the full with Him by whom all things are. It is in no sense an exaggeration nor does it overstate the fact one whit to say that any person who keeps the Sabbath, according to the revealed pattern, will be saved in the celestial kingdom. The Sabbath is a day of worship; the requirement to rest from our labors, to do no servile work therein, is simply an incident to the real purpose of the day. Vital as it is to refrain from toil and to turn away from temporalities, these requirements are for the purpose of putting men in a position to do what should be done on the Sabbath, that is, to worship the Father in the name of the Son, to worship him in Spirit and in truth. True worship includes keeping the commandments, and those who devote their Sabbaths to true and proper worship obtain the encouragement that leads to full obedience.

From all this it follows that there are few things which bear a more pointed witness of the Holy Messiah and his mission than, first, the fact that there is a Sabbath, and secondly, the nature and kind of worship carried out on this holy day. The great thing about the Sabbath is that it is the day appointed for men to learn to know those Holy Beings whom it is life eternal to know. (John 17:3.) "I am the Lord your God," came the voice of Jehovah to Ezekiel as he spoke by way of commandment to all Israel; "walk in my statutes, and keep my judgments, and do them; And hallow my sabbaths; and they shall be a sign between me and you." Why were they to keep the commandments, why should they hallow the Lord's Sabbaths? The answer: "That ye may know that I am the Lord your God." (Ezek. 20:19-20; Ex. 31:12-17.) God is known by revelation; revelation comes to those who worship the Lord; and worship is perfected on the Sabbath day. It was neither chance nor happenstance that the Beloved Revelator wrote, "I was in the Spirit on the Lord's day," when he heard the voice of one saying, "I am Alpha and Omega, the first and the last," and when he saw "the Son of man" in power and glory, and heard him say, "I am the first and the last: I am he that liveth, and was dead; and, behold, I am alive for evermore." (Rev. 1:10-18.) This is Sabbath worship perfected to the point that mortal man not only knows of the reality of his Maker by the power of the Holy Ghost, but is also privileged to hear his voice and see his face.

Sabbath worship requires attendance at those meetings which are appointed as the times and places where the knowledge of God and his laws are taught. It is as much a law in our day as it was three thousand years ago. "The children of Israel shall keep the sabbath, to observe the sabbath throughout their generations, for a perpetual covenant." (Ex. 31:16.) Keeping the Sabbath includes worshiping in the congregation of the saints. "Six days shall work be done," saith the Lord, "but the seventh day is the sabbath of rest, an holy convocation; ye shall do no work therein: it is the sabbath of the Lord in all your dwellings. . . . In the seventh day it is an holy convocation: ye shall do no servile work therein." (Lev. 23:3, 8.) A holy convocation? A gathering together of the people for holy purposes, a sacrament meeting, as it were; an occasion when the saints gather to worship the Lord and partake of his Spirit; or, as he has said to us in our day: "That thou mayest more fully keep thyself unspotted from the world, thou shalt go to the house of prayer and offer up thy sacraments upon my holy day; For verily this is a day appointed unto you to rest from your labors, and to pay thy devotions unto the Most High; Nevertheless thy vows shall be offered up in righteousness on all days and at all times; But remember that on this, the Lord's day, thou shalt offer thine oblations and thy sacraments unto the Most High, confessing thy sins unto thy brethren, and before the Lord. And on this day thou shalt do none other thing, only let thy food be prepared with singleness of heart that thy fasting may be perfect, or, in other words, that thy joy may be full. Verily, this is fasting and prayer, or in other words, rejoicing and prayer." (D&C 59:9-14.)

When we begin to envision the true meaning of the Sabbath and the part it plays in preparing men to gain that salvation which is in Christ, we can see the eternal wisdom in such scriptural accounts as the following:

1. Rest from temporal pursuits is to be total and complete on the Sabbath. (Ex. 20:10; D&C 59:13.) Israel is to do no work, neither in the time of ploughing nor of harvest. (Ex. 34:21.) No fires are to be lit (Ex. 35:3), nor purchases to be made (Neh. 10:31).

2. Wrath and desolation come upon the Lord's people for "profaning the sabbath." (Neh. 13:18; Jer. 17:27.)

3. The penalties for Sabbath violation anciently are listed as both excommunication and death, probably depending on the severity of the offense. (Ex. 31:14; 35:2; Num. 15:32-36.)

4. There was even a Sabbath for the land itself, a year in which crops were not to be planted nor harvested. (Ex. 23:10-12.)

5. Temporal prosperity is promised those who keep the Sabbath. (D&C 59:16-17.)

6. Eunuchs and foreigners and strangers—those who according to ancient law were cut off from the blessing of Israel—should yet be saved if they would accept the Lord's covenant and keep his Sabbath. (Isa. 56:4-8.)

7. Israel was promised that if she kept the Sabbath she would remain a glorious and triumphant nation forever. "Hallow the sabbath day," the Lord said, giving this promise if such should eventuate: "Then shall there enter into the gates of this city kings and princes sitting upon the throne of David, riding in chariots and on horses, they, and their

princes, the men of Judah, and the inhabitants of Jerusalem: and this city shall remain for ever." (Jer. 17:25.)

In addition to all that is here written, as to how the Sabbath day is used as an occasion to learn of Christ and his laws and as a day on which to bear witness of him and his goodness, we shall now note how the day itself stands as a witness of our Lord's divinity. In this connection there are three related, yet differing, situations:

1. Christ is the Creator. "By him, and through him, and of him, the worlds are and were created." (D&C 76:24.) Specifically, at the direction of his Father, he created this earth in six days; and on the seventh day, as he viewed the finished work and saw that it was good, he rested from all his creative labors. "And I, God, blessed the seventh day, and sanctified it; because that in it I had rested from all my work which I, God, had created and made." (Moses 3:1-3.) Accordingly, he appointed the seventh day as a Sabbath in which man was commanded to commemorate and rejoice in the creative enterprises by which this earth came into being as a place where the spirit offspring of the Father might undergo their mortal probations. The Sabbath day thus bears witness that Christ is the Creator; it is a weekly reminder that he rested from his creative labors on the seventh day; it keeps us in remembrance of his grace and goodness in providing an earth whereon we might dwell for a time and a season. Thus when the Ten Commandments were first given to Moses, the reason for Sabbath observance was listed as being: "For in six days the Lord made heaven and earth, the sea, and all that in them is, and rested the seventh day: wherefore"—that is, for this very reason, to commemorate the creation—"the Lord blessed the sabbath day, and hallowed it." (Ex. 20:11.) This is the reason men kept the Sabbath day from Adam to Moses.

2. Christ is the God of Israel who delivered the children of Israel from Egyptian bondage. It was his voice that spoke to Moses in the burning bush: "Come now therefore, and I will send thee unto Pharaoh, that thou mayest bring forth

my people the children of Israel out of Egypt." (Ex. 3:10.) It was his mighty and outstretched arm that poured out the plagues on Pharaoh and his people. It was his power that parted the Red Sea so that the "waters were divided," forming "a wall unto them on their right hand, and on their left." (Ex. 14:21-22.) He brought the quails, sent the manna, gave the revelations, drove out the inhabitants of the land before them, and settled his people in a garden spot. How important it was for Israel to have in continuous remembrance all these and ten thousand other wonders that attended their deliverance from the merciless taskmasters of a wicked king! What better way to do this than to commemorate, each week, the day of this mighty and miraculous deliverance. What day was it? It was the day the Lord designated as their Sabbath.

Thus when Moses received the Ten Commandments the second time, as part of the Mosaic law rather than as part of the fulness of the gospel, the reason for keeping the Sabbath was changed. No longer was it to commemorate the creation (at least not that alone), but now it was to keep the children of Israel in remembrance of the glory of their deliverance from Egypt. Hence the Lord said, as part of the commandment itself, "And remember that thou wast a servant in the land of Egypt, and that the Lord thy God"—who is Christ—"brought thee out thence through a mighty hand and by a stretched out arm: therefore the Lord thy God commanded thee to keep the sabbath day." (Deut. 5:15.) Manifestly a Sabbath of this sort no longer falls on the seventh day, but is in fact on a different day each year. Samuel Walter Gamble, in his book *Sunday, the True Sabbath of God,* has analyzed this and a host of related and difficult Old Testament passages, all of which show that from Moses to Christ the Jewish Sabbath changed days of the week each year. And during all that period, for nearly fifteen hundred of the four thousand years that passed between Adam and Christ, the purpose of the Sabbath was to commemorate, not the creation (except incidentally), but those events of deliverance from Egyptian bondage that so exulted the feelings of all Israel.

3. Christ is also the resurrection and the life. He is the firstfruits of them that sleep. He burst the bands of death, and in a way incomprehensible to us the effects of his resurrection pass upon all men so that all are raised from the grave. His atonement is the crowning event of all history, and the resurrection is the triumphant climax of the atonement. How those of all ages should rejoice in the fact of our Lord's coming forth in glorious immortality to live and reign forever with his Father. How important it is for all men, if they are to follow in his footsteps, so that they also shall live and reign in celestial glory, how important it is for them to have always in remembrance the atonement and resurrection that makes this possible. How shall this be done? Again it is through Sabbath worship. And so the Lord appointed the day of the resurrection, the first day of the week, to be the new Sabbath, the day of remembrance and worship. It is still called the Sabbath, which means day of rest, but it is also now called the Lord's day, meaning the day on which he rose from the dead. This is the day on which the saints worshiped in the meridian of time. (Acts 20:7.) And it is the day on which the Lord has commanded us to pay our devotions to him in an especial manner, although we are to remember him on all days. (D&C 59:9-17.)

Our present needs call for us to mention but one other thing pertaining to the great system of Sabbath worship which the Lord our God has given us. It is that the millennial era of this earth, the period of one thousand years that is just ahead, is destined to be the earth's Sabbath, the day when the earth shall rest and peace and righteousness shall abide on its face. In that day the Lord himself will dwell personally among his brethren on earth and the worship of all who are privileged to live in such a glorious era will be perfect.

All Ordinances Bear Witness of Christ

We shall speak of the symbolisms commemorated in the Feast of the Passover when we consider the law of Moses and the great host of similitudes found therein. We shall not endeavor to point out the likenesses and figures found in temple ordinances, priesthood ordinations, the blessing of children, administrations for the sick, celestial marriage, and other matters. Suffice it to say that in "the ordinances" of the holy priesthood "the power of godliness is manifest" unto men (D&C 84:20), and that those whose interests lead them in that direction can find true and proper symbolisms in all things. For our present purposes we desire only to mention three special symbolical situations that existed anciently for limited periods only. That the Lord may give us special symbols and similitudes in the future is evident, but here are the three of special interest in this present study:

1. *Manna—the bread from heaven.*

For forty long, tiring years as Israel trudged wearily from one desert camp to another, awaiting the death of the rebels among them who must pass away before their promised inheritance could be gained, during all these years they sowed no crops, reaped no harvests, and built no granaries. Instead they ate manna from heaven. Six days each week this bread from heaven was spread before them as the morning dew; each day they gathered for that day only; any left over until the next day crawled with worms and stank with decay, except that on the sixth day they gathered for two days and the angelic food was preserved in purity for Sabbath use. This heaven-sent food was ground in mills, beaten in mortars, baked in pans, and eaten as cakes. It had the taste of fresh oil. Because of it, Israel lived; without it starvation and death would have been inevitable. There was no other food and no other way to gain food for all those years of desert wandering. (Ex. 16; Num. 11:6-9.) The manna ceased thc first day after Israel ate of the dry corn of their promised land. (Josh. 5:12.)

Why did the Lord choose to feed his people in this way? Why not send them rains so they could plant crops? Why not lead them to a land where they could grow their own food? Certainly the supplying of manna, without which they could not have survived, taught them to depend upon the Lord for their temporal sustenance. As Moses said to them with reference to this bread from heaven, "The Lord thy God led thee forty years in the wilderness, to humble thee, and to prove thee, to know what was in thine heart, whether thou wouldest keep his commandments, or no. And he humbled thee, and suffered thee to hunger, and fed thee with manna, which thou knewest not, neither did thy fathers know." Having so said, with Israel reminded of their need to rely daily on the Lord even for the food to maintain life, Moses gave this as the reason the Lord had chosen that particular way to feed his people: "That he might make thee know that man doth not live by bread only, but by every word that proceedeth out of the mouth of the Lord doth man live." (Deut. 8:2-3.) Thus, the fact of receiving daily manna to keep them alive temporally was a repeated witness that if they were to live spiritually and have that eternal life reserved for the faithful, they must live each day in harmony with the word of Jehovah their Savior. The symbolism is perfect. What better daily reminder could there be of their need for spiritual food?

Our Jewish brethren, even in Christ's day, understood what was involved in the manna showered upon their fathers. They knew it symbolized their need to rely continually upon Jehovah and to live by every word that proceeded forth from his mouth—all of which laid the foundation for some of the most powerful testimony born by Jesus during his mortal ministry. After he had fed the five thousand with loaves and fishes provided miraculously by his creative power, our Lord spoke of the manna that Jehovah had given their fathers and said that he himself was the living bread, the word of God by which they must live to gain salvation. It was the will of the Father, he said, that all men "believe on him whom he hath sent," who had come down from heaven, "and giveth life unto the world." That none might misunderstand he said: "I am the bread of life: he that cometh to me shall never hunger; and he that believeth on me shall never thirst. . . . He that believeth on me hath everlasting life. I am the bread of life. Your fathers did eat manna in the wilderness, and are dead. This is the bread which cometh down from heaven, that a man may eat thereof, and not die. I am the living bread which came down from heaven: if any man eat of this bread, he shall live for ever. . . . As the living Father hath sent me, and I live by the Father: so he that eateth me, even he shall live by me. This is the bread which came down from heaven: not as your fathers did eat manna, and are dead: he that eateth of this bread shall live for ever." (John 6:1-58.)

For their whole sojourn in the wilderness, nearly fifteen thousand consecutive days, their fathers had eaten manna, to preserve them temporally, in similitude of the fact that all men forever, both they and their fathers and all others, must eat of the Bread of Life if they are to gain eternal life. That their fathers understood this, even if it was hidden from some of them, is seen from these words of Paul: "Our fathers," he said, "did all eat the same spiritual meat; And did all drink the same spiritual drink: for they drank of that spiritual Rock that followed them: and that Rock was Christ." (1 Cor. 10:1-3.)

2. *The brazen serpent—a likeness of Christ.*

During one of the Israelites' more rebellious periods, as they dwelt in the wilderness awaiting the day when their feet should be planted on Canaan's sod, "the Lord sent fiery serpents among the people" to punish them, and the serpents "bit the people; and much people of Israel died." Thereupon "Moses prayed for the people. And the Lord said unto Moses, Make thee a fiery serpent, and set it upon a pole: and it shall come to pass, that every one that is bitten, when he looketh upon it, shall live." Moses did as he was bidden, made a serpent of brass, and placed it upon a pole. Then, "if a serpent had bitten any man, when he beheld the serpent of brass, he lived." (Num. 21:4-9.)

Knowing, as we do, that by faith all things are possible, we may conclude that the brazen serpent became a means of helping the people center their faith in the Lord so as to gain his healing power. One of the gifts of the Spirit that Christ promised his saints is that "they shall take up serpents" and yet be free from their poisonous bites. (Mark 16:18.) In any event, those anciently who were bitten had but to look, in the approved manner, and they lived, while those failing so to do died.

Our Old Testament simply preserves the story of the serpents and how life or death hung in the balance for those who were bitten. It makes no explanation of what the Lord was really doing for his people and why he chose this unique way to bring to pass his purposes. But from the New Testament and the Book of Mormon we learn why and in what manner the Lord was testing his people. Nephi confirms and amplifies the Old Testament account by saying the Lord "sent fiery flying serpents among them." We have no idea what kind of poisonous creatures were here used, but we do know that after men were bitten, the Lord "prepared a way that they might be healed; and the labor which they had to perform was to look; and because of the simpleness of the way, or the easiness of it, there were many who perished." (1 Ne. 17:41; 2 Ne. 25:20.)

Alma speaks of the brazen serpent as a type of something else. "A type was raised up in the wilderness," he says, "that whosoever would look upon it might live. And many did look and live. But few understood the meaning of those things, and this because of the hardness of their hearts." (Alma 33:19.) As to the full meaning of the type, we turn to the writings of Nephi the son of Helaman. "Moses . . . hath spoken concerning the coming of the Messiah," he writes. "Yea, did he not bear record that the Son of God should come? And as he lifted up the brazen serpent in the wilderness, even so shall he be lifted up who should come." The brazen serpent was lifted up upon the pole in similitude of the fact that the Redeemer of the world would be lifted up upon the cross. And as to the lesson thus taught, Nephi continues: "And as many as should look upon that serpent should live, even so as many as should look upon the Son of God with faith, having a contrite spirit, might live, even unto that life which is eternal." (Hel. 8:13-15.)

Now back to the words of Alma. "But there were many who were so hardened that they would not look" upon the serpent, "therefore they perished," he continues. "Now the reason they would not look is because they did not believe that it would heal them." And we might interject: 'And there are many whose hearts are so hardened that they will not look to Christ, and they shall perish.' And is it too much to add that the reason they do not look to Christ is because they do not believe that he will save them if they keep his commandments. "O my brethren, if ye could be healed by merely casting about your eyes that ye might be healed," Alma pleads, "would ye not behold quickly, or would ye rather harden your hearts in unbelief, and be slothful, that ye would not cast about your eyes, that ye might perish?" And our echoing cry is: 'If we can be saved by accepting Christ; if we can gain eternal life by living his laws, why should we harden our hearts and perish in unbelief? If there is joy and peace in this life and eternal reward in the life to come for all those who keep the commandments, why should we be slothful? Why should we hesitate to walk in paths of truth and righteousness?' (Alma 33:20-21.)

We have from the lips of the Lord Jesus his own witness of the doctrines here expounded. Said he: "As Moses lifted up the serpent in the wilderness, even so must the Son of man be lifted up: That whosoever believeth in him should not perish, but have eternal life." (John 3:14-15.) The New Testament does not amplify the teaching, but from this statement of our Lord it is clear that it was known and understood and taught by and among the true believers in Palestine in the meridian of time. Their teachings and their exhortations would have been no different from those of their Book of Mormon counterparts, which brings us again back to the words of Alma. The conclusion he draws from the fact that those who cast their eyes upon the brazen serpent were healed is that men should cast their eyes upon Christ and thereby be saved. "Cast about your eyes and begin to believe in the Son of God," he says, "that he will come to redeem his people, and that he shall suffer and die to atone for their sins; and that he shall rise again from the dead, which shall bring to pass the resurrection, that all men shall stand before him, to be judged at the last and judgment day, according to their works." (Alma 33:22.)

3. *The Liahona—a likeness of Christ.*

Our Nephite brethren were given a special type and shadow of Christ that was akin to the brazen serpent of Moses, but that was suited to the particular needs and circumstances in which Lehi and his family found themselves. Called the Liahona, it was a compass, "a round ball of curious workmanship." Like Moses' serpent, it was made of fine brass. "Within the ball were two spindles," which pointed out the course they should travel. Nephi says these pointers worked "according to the faith and diligence and heed which we did give unto them." From time to time messages of divine origin were written upon the Liahona, also "according to the heed and diligence which we gave unto it." (1 Ne. 16:10, 28-29.) This divine compass ceased to work whenever its Nephite owners acted in unrighteousness. (1 Ne. 18:12.)

Alma explained the use and purpose of the Liahona to his son Helaman in these words: "It did work for them according to their faith in God; therefore, if they had faith to believe that God could cause that those spindles should point the way they should go, behold, it was done." That this same requisite was present when people were healed by looking at the brazen serpent there can be no doubt. But it was with the Nephites as it had been with their Israelite ancestors; they were not always faithful. Alma says: "They were slothful, and forgot to exercise their faith and diligence and then those marvelous works ceased, and they did not progress in their journey; Therefore, they tarried in the wilderness, or did not travel a direct course, and were afflicted with hunger and thirst, because of their transgressions."

Of itself the Liahona was a great blessing. Food was found, courses were charted through perilous areas, and messages of incomparable worth were written on its face. But as with the brazen serpent, its greatest function was the witness of Christ that came because of its proper usage. "These things are not without a shadow," Alma said, "for as our fathers were slothful to give heed to this compass (now these things were temporal) they did not prosper; even so it is with things which are spiritual. For behold, it is as easy to give heed to the word of Christ, which will point to you a straight course to eternal bliss, as it was for our fathers to give heed to this compass, which would point unto them a straight course to the promised land. And now I say, is there not a type in this thing? For just as surely as this director did bring our fathers, by following its course, to the promised land, shall the words of Christ, if we follow their course, carry us beyond this vale of sorrow into a far better land of promise." (Alma 37:38-45.)

LAW OF MOSES BEARS WITNESS OF CHRIST

The Gospel of Christ and the Gospel of Moses

There are two gospels—the preparatory gospel and the fulness of the everlasting gospel. There are two proclamations, two pronouncements of glad tidings, two messages of light and truth and power, which God has given to his people at one time or another. What the people receive at any given moment in time depends upon them. The Lord gives them all of his word, or only a portion, depending on "the heed and diligence which they give unto him." If all men had open hearts and receptive minds; if they desired righteousness and sought truth in preference to all else; if they conformed to every true principle they received—all would accept the fulness of his gospel and join that church and kingdom which is always administered for the benefit and blessing of mankind. As it is written: "He that will harden his heart, the same receiveth the lesser portion of the word; and he that will not harden his heart, to him is given the greater portion of the word, until it is given unto him to know the mysteries of God until he know them in full." (Alma 12:9-10.)

As is evident from the pure meaning of the words themselves, the fulness of the everlasting gospel has always existed and will continue to endure forever; the preparatory gospel, on the other hand, is not eternal in nature, but is something that goes before and makes people ready for the receipt of the fulness of saving truth. The everlasting gospel existed before the world was; it is "the gospel of God . . . Concerning his Son Jesus Christ our Lord" (Rom. 1:1-3), and it now bears the name of the Son and is called the gospel of Christ. In contrast, the preparatory gospel is as an Elias who goes before to prepare the way for something greater; it is reserved for those who are not yet able to bear the eternal fulness. Our revelations speak of "the gospel of Abraham," meaning the divine commission given to the father of the faithful to bless himself and his seed after him. (D&C 110:12.) Since the preparatory gospel was a divine commission given to Israel through Moses, to bless and train them through all the generations when they were a distinct and separate people, it is with propriety that we call it the gospel of Moses, though in fact it came from the Lord Jehovah, as also did the divine commission or gospel given to Abraham.

Since salvation is in Christ, and not in Moses or any other man, the Lord always seeks to dispense from heaven his everlasting gospel to his children on earth. If they will receive the fulness of the message of salvation, it is theirs to enjoy, theirs for the taking, without money and without price. Adam, Enoch, Noah, Abraham, and many of the ancients had dispensations of the gospel and enjoyed its saving powers in their eternal fulness. The fulness of the everlasting gospel consists of all the truths, powers, priesthoods, keys, ordinances, laws, and covenants by conformity to which mortal men can obtain a fulness of eternal glory in the highest heaven of the celestial world.

In keeping with the pattern followed for twenty-five hundred years in his dealings with men, the Lord revealed the fulness of the everlasting gospel to Moses, and this mighty man of faith sought diligently to persuade his Israelitish brethren to believe its truths and live its laws. They refused. They hardened their hearts and chose to walk in carnal paths. The eternal fulness was more than they could bear. As a consequence, God in his mercy—lest they be damned for rejecting that which they could not live, and as a means of preparing them and their seed for the higher standards which all saved beings must eventually live—the Lord in his mercy gave them the law of Moses. It did not replace the gospel, which had been offered to them in the first instance; rather, it was added to the more perfect system, for as we shall see, there were times when the ancient and chosen seed had both the fulness of the gospel and the preparatory gospel, when they had all of the saving truths and yet kept the terms and conditions of the law of Moses.

Among our sectarian brethren it is falsely assumed that Deity dealt in one way with the patriarchs, in another with the Israel of Moses, and in yet another with mankind after he sent his Son to open the so-called Christian Era. Knowing, however, that the gospel is everlasting; that God is the same yesterday, today, and forever; and that all flesh, no matter when it is found in mortal guise, will be saved on the same principles—we are in a position to comprehend the true relationship between the gospel and the law of Moses and to understand Paul's statements with reference to them. To the Galatians he said plainly, "God . . . preached before the gospel unto Abraham." Then he spoke of the law of Moses and said, "No man is justified by the law," meaning that salvation does not come by the law alone. It is, rather, "Christ [that] hath redeemed us," so that "the blessing[s] of Abraham . . . through Jesus Christ" are still in effect. That is to say, the blessings of Abraham, which are the blessings of the gospel, because Abraham had the gospel, were in effect for him, and are in effect for us, because of Christ and his atonement. Then came this inspired utterance: "The covenant, that was confirmed before of God in Christ, the law, which was four hundred and thirty years after, cannot disannul, that it should make the promise of none effect." In other words, 'God gave the gospel of Jesus Christ to Abraham, and the law of Moses which came 430 years later cannot disannul or replace the gospel promises.' "Wherefore then serveth the law?" Paul asks, meaning, 'Why did the Lord give the law of Moses since the gospel itself had been given to the ancestors of Moses?' He answers: "It was added because of transgressions," but, he repeats, righteousness and salvation do not come by the law, but through faith in Christ and obedience to his gospel law. Hence: "The law was our schoolmaster to bring us unto Christ, that we might be justified by faith." We are thus saved because of faith in Christ, and "after that faith is come, we are no longer under a schoolmaster." (Gal. 3.)

"How long shall I bear with this evil congregation, which murmur against me?" So spake the Lord of his chosen yet rebelling people. "Your carcases shall fall in this wilderness," he said. All who were twenty years of age and older, except Joshua and Caleb, should die in the wilderness; only the younger generation should have an inheritance in their promised land. And so it was. (Num. 14:27-38.) And such was the historical situation Paul had in mind when he said that many, but not all, who came out of Egypt hardened their hearts and provoked the Lord. "With whom was he grieved forty years?" Paul asks. "Was it not with them that had sinned, whose carcases fell in the wilderness?" It is in that context that Paul explains to the Hebrews, in effect, how the law of Moses was "added because of transgressions." "For unto us was the gospel preached, as well as unto them: but the word preached did not profit them, not being mixed with faith in them that heard it." (Heb. 3:15-19; 4:1-2.) The saints in Paul's day had the gospel, the same gospel that had been offered in the Mosaic era. The meridian saints accepted its saving truths; ancient Israel, lacking faith, ended up with a schoolmaster to lead them until they could abide the higher law.

There were, of course, those in Israel, in the day of Moses and during the long years during which they awaited the advent of their Messiah, who had faith and were blessed with the fulness of the gospel, as we shall hereafter point out. Moses was one of these, in consequence of which the New

Testament testimony of him is that he chose "to suffer affliction with the people of God" because he esteemed "the reproach of Christ greater riches than the treasures of Egypt." (Heb. 11:25-26.)

The Law of Christ and the Law of Moses

There are two laws—the law of Christ and the law of Moses. The one is the gospel, the other is the preparatory gospel. There are two sets of commandments—the commandments which assure a celestial inheritance, and the law of carnal commandments, which, standing alone, carry no such assurance of eternal reward. The one is for those who are "anxiously engaged in a good cause," who "do many things of their own free will," who use their agency to "bring to pass much righteousness"; the other is for those who are slothful and rebellious by nature, who need to be commanded in all things, who neglect good works unless they are compelled to perform them. (D&C 58:26-27.) Of these two laws, John wrote: "The law was given through Moses, but life and truth came through Jesus Christ. For the law was after a carnal commandment, to the administration of death; but the gospel was after the power of an endless life, through Jesus Christ, the Only Begotten Son, who is in the bosom of the Father." (JST, John 1:17-18.)

Christ's law is his gospel. By obedience to its laws and by conformity to its ordinances, all mankind may gain a celestial inheritance. It is, in fact, the law of a celestial kingdom and has been given to us mortals to qualify us to go where God and Christ and holy beings are. "And they who are not sanctified through the law which I have give unto you," the Lord says, "even the law of Christ, must inherit another kingdom, even that of a terrestrial kingdom, or that of a telestial kingdom. For he who is not able to abide the law of a celestial kingdom cannot abide a celestial glory." (D&C 88:21-22.)

Moses' law is the law of carnal commandments, or in

other words the law which is concerned, in detail and specifically, with carnal and evil acts—warning, exhorting, encouraging, commanding, all to the end that men will be left without excuse and, hopefully, will avoid the snares of the evil one. Paul uses the name "the law of a carnal commandment" (Heb. 7:16) to describe it, and also calls it "the law of commandments contained in ordinances" (Eph. 2:15). Abinadi speaks of it as "a law of performances and of ordinances, a law which they were to observe strictly from day to day, to keep them in remembrance of God and their duty towards him." (Mosiah 13:30.) Our revelation, speaking of the preparatory gospel, says: "Which gospel is the gospel of repentance and of baptism, and the remission of sins, and the law of carnal commandments, which the Lord in his wrath caused to continue with the house of Aaron among the children of Israel until John." (D&C 84:27.)

Historically, this law first came into being when Israel rejected the gospel and failed to live as Jehovah, their Lord, commanded them to do. Moses, having destroyed the tablets of stone on which the law as first revealed was written, received this commandment from the Lord: "Hew thee two other tables of stone, like unto the first, and I will write upon them also, the words of the law, according as they were written at the first on the tables which thou brakest; but it shall not be according to the first, for I will take away the priesthood out of their midst; therefore my holy order, and the ordinances thereof, shall not go before them; for my presence shall not go up in their midst, lest I destroy them. But I will give unto them the law as at the first, but it shall be after the law of a carnal commandment; for I have sworn in my wrath, that they shall not enter into my presence, into my rest, in the days of their pilgrimage." (JST, Ex. 34:1-2.)

The Priesthood of Christ and the Priesthood of Israel

There are two priesthoods—the priesthood of Melchizedek and the priesthood of Aaron. The one is the highest and holiest order on earth or in heaven; it is "The Holy Priesthood, after the Order of the Son of God"; it has power, dominion, and authority over all things; "all other authorities or offices in the church are appendages" to it; and it holds "the keys of all the spiritual blessings of the church." The other—"the Aaronic or Levitical Priesthood"—is the lesser; "it was conferred upon Aaron and his seed, throughout all their generations"; it holds "the keys of the ministering of angels"; and it is empowered "to administer in outward ordinances, the letter of the gospel." (D&C 107:1-20.) Beginning in the meridian of time, since Israel was no longer to exist as a separate nation and the offering of Levitical sacrifices was discontinued, the Lord authorized others who were not of the tribe of Levi or the lineage of Aaron to hold this lesser priesthood.

For our purposes here, the great distinction between the Melchizedek Priesthood and the Aaronic or Levitical Priesthood is this: The Melchizedek Priesthood administers the gospel in its everlasting fulness, but the Aaronic Priesthood administers the preparatory gospel only, which preparatory gospel is the law of Moses and includes the law of carnal commandments.

All of the prophets from Adam to Moses held the higher or Melchizedek Priesthood. There was no Aaronic Priesthood during the two and a half millenniums there involved. The higher priesthood "continueth in the church of God in all generations, and is without beginning of days or end of years." It is an eternal priesthood and has existed with God from all eternity. "This greater priesthood administereth the gospel and holdeth the key of the mysteries of the kingdom, even the key of the knowledge of God." (D&C 84:17-19.) Those who hold it and are true and faithful in all things "have the privilege of receiving the mysteries of the kingdom of heaven, to have the heavens opened unto them, to commune with the general assembly and church of the Firstborn, and to enjoy the communion and presence of God the Father, and Jesus the mediator of the new covenant."

(D&C 107:19.) Worthy holders "can see the face of God, even the Father." Such were its powers anciently, such are they today, with reference to which our scriptures say: "Now this Moses plainly taught to the children of Israel in the wilderness, and sought diligently to sanctify his people that they might behold the face of God; But they hardened their hearts and could not endure his presence; therefore, the Lord in his wrath, for his anger was kindled against them, swore that they should not enter into his rest while in the wilderness, which rest is the fulness of his glory. Therefore, he took Moses out of their midst, and the Holy Priesthood also." (D&C 84:22-25.)

When the Lord took Moses and the holy priesthood from Israel, he thereby took from them the fulness of his everlasting gospel, because it takes the Melchizedek Priesthood to administer the gospel. For one thing it is only this higher priesthood that can lay on hands for the gift of the Holy Ghost. The Holy Ghost is a sanctifier, and unless men are sanctified they cannot see the face of God; as we have seen, it was their failure to use this power whereby sanctification comes that caused the Lord to withdraw it from them. But when the Lord left the Aaronic Priesthood in Israel he thereby left the power and authority to administer the law of Moses in all its parts and ramifications.

We should here observe that the Aaronic Priesthood was added to the Melchizedek. This is true even though the power of the lesser priesthood is automatically embraced within the greater power of the higher priesthood. The historical fact is that Aaron and his sons already held the Melchizedek Priesthood and were numbered with the elders of Israel when the Lord first conferred the lesser authority upon them. This is precisely what we do today when we take a holder of the Melchizedek Priesthood and ordain him a bishop in the Aaronic Priesthood. But our point is that in the day of the origin of the lesser order, it was with the lesser priesthood as it was with the law of Moses, both were "added because of transgressions." (Gal. 3:19.) A lesser law was added to a higher law, and a lesser priesthood was added to a greater priesthood.

We should here observe also that when the scripture says the Lord took Moses and the holy priesthood out of the midst of Israel, it means that he took from them the prophet who held the keys and who could authorize the priesthood to be conferred upon others. Any who thereafter held either the keys or the Melchizedek Priesthood gained them by special dispensation. The Aaronic Priesthood thus became the priesthood of administration; it was in effect the priesthood of Israel; it handled the affairs of the Church and officiated in the offering of sacrifices. However, there were at many times and may have been at all times prophets and worthy men who held the Melchizedek Priesthood. Joseph Smith said, "All the prophets had the Melchizedek Priesthood and were ordained by God himself." (*Teachings,* p. 181.) Elijah was the last prophet in Israel to hold the keys of the sealing power, and the Melchizedek Priesthood was the only priesthood held by the Nephites for the first 634 years of their separate existence. There were, of course, none of the tribe of Levi among them, and the Levites were the only ones anciently who held the lesser priesthood.

A New Priesthood Brings a New Law

Priesthood, without which the true church cannot exist, and without which the gospel cannot be administered, is always found among the Lord's people. Whenever men possess the fulness of the priesthood they have also the fulness of the gospel. The higher priesthood administers the whole gospel system; the lesser priesthood can go no further than to operate the performances and ordinances of the law of Moses. When Jesus came among the Jews they had Levitical power only. Zacharias was a priest of that order, and the priests and Levites, as legal administrators whose acts were recognized by Jehovah, were offering sacrifices, receiving tithes, and giving guidance to the people. Theirs was the power to baptize, but not to confer the Holy Ghost. Priestly administrations were limited to outward ordinances; the people were not blessed with the higher authority which deals with inward ordinances, as it were, that is, with spiritual things. John the Baptist was the last recognized legal administrator who held the keys and powers of the Aaronic Priesthood. As the Elias who prepared the way before the Lord, he said: "I indeed baptize you with water unto repentance: but he that cometh after me is mightier than I, whose shoes I am not worthy to bear: he shall baptize you with the Holy Ghost, and with fire." (Matt. 3:11.) John held the Aaronic Priesthood, Christ the Melchizedek. Ordinances and blessings denied the people by John were freely offered to them by Jesus.

Most of the Jews of that day, being darkened in their mind and apostate in their feelings, rejected their Messiah and chose to believe that their Levitical powers sufficed for salvation. What need had they, so they thought, for new revelation, new powers, a new priesthood, a new gospel. It was as though they said, 'We have Aaron and his sons who serve as priests; we have all these Levites to minister to our needs; we walk where Moses walked; what else could such a blessed people want?' But, so that the whole matter might be set at rest, once and for all, and that they might know that the Mosaic system laid the foundation for and introduced the new law of the Lord, Paul wrote his Epistle to the Hebrews. In it he reasoned thus:

'You Jews—meaning those who had gone before, for the kingdom had been taken from those then living—you Jews have the law of Moses with all its powers and prerogatives. Your priests are called of God to offer sacrifices and to direct all the performances of that divine system. They hold the Aaronic Priesthood. Aaron is their father, and they act in his name and use his priesthood. But come now, let us "consider the Apostle and High Priest of our profession, Christ Jesus." (Heb. 3:1.) He is "Jesus the Son of God," "a great high priest," who has "passed into the heavens." (Heb. 4:14.)

Your own scriptures testify of him, saying, "Thou art my Son, to day have I begotten thee," and also, "Thou art a priest for ever after the order of Melchisedec." (Heb. 5:5-6.) Even as your priests, who served after the order of Aaron, offered "sacrifices for sins" (Heb. 5:1), so did this "Jesus" whom God "made an high priest for ever after the order of Melchisedec" (Heb. 6:20), for he truly offered up himself as a sacrifice for sin. The sacrifices of your priests are made daily, "But this man, because he continueth ever, hath an unchangeable priesthood. Wherefore he is able also to save them to the uttermost that come unto God by him, seeing he ever liveth to make intercession for them. For such an high priest became us, who is holy, harmless, undefiled, separate from sinners, and made higher than the heavens; Who needeth not daily, as those high priests, to offer up sacrifice, first for his own sins, and then for the people's: for this he did once, when he offered up himself." (Heb. 7:24-27.) And that he was to come and change your law you know because David, your father, who was subject to the law of Moses as then administered by the priests of the Aaronic order, in prophesying of a day future to his own, said that a priest would arise after the order of Melchizedek, and this priest, who is Christ, would bring a new and higher law so that salvation might come to his people. "If therefore perfection were by the Levitical priesthood, (for under it the people received the law), what further need was there that another priest should arise after the order of Melchisedec, and not be called after the order of Aaron? For the priesthood being changed, there is made of necessity a change also of the law. For he of whom these things are spoken pertaineth to another tribe, of which no man gave attendance at the altar. For it is evident that our Lord sprang out of Juda; of which tribe Moses spake nothing concerning priesthood. And it is yet far more evident: for that after the similitude of Melchisedec there ariseth another priest, Who is made, not after the law of a carnal commandment, but after the power of an endless life. For he testifieth, Thou art a priest for ever after the order of Melchisedec." ' (Heb. 7:11-17.)

Why There Was a Law of Moses

Why was there a law of Moses? Two reasons are apparent:

1. It was a divine and uplifting system of goodness and right. Those who obeyed its precepts and kept its ordinances bettered themselves temporally and spiritually. They were in the line of their duty, received revelations, and came to know their God. While the world around them was in darkness, the morning rays of divine truth were opening their vision to the wonders and glories mortal man might obtain. It was not that eternal fulness which earth's pilgrims must receive if they are to return to that Presence whence they came, but it was an open door, an invitation to step forward and receive the fulness of the word. It was a preparatory gospel. And it is better to walk in godly paths for fear of the penalties of disobedience than not to walk in them at all. It is better to maintain marital fidelity for fear of the death penalty imposed on adulterers by the law of Moses than to walk in unclean paths and go to hell when earth's probation is over. We must not belittle or downgrade the law of Moses. It was the most perfect system of worship known to man, excepting only the fulness of the gospel. Out of it have come nearly all the principles of ethics and decency that have been incorporated into our whole system of modern jurisprudence. And lest there be any doubt in anyone's mind as to the excellence and beauty of the Mosaic system, let us ponder this conclusion: Even now, after two thousand years of exposure to the new covenant, there are but few of earth's inhabitants who conform to the standards of decency, excellence, and righteousness that even approach those which God imposed upon his ancient covenant people by the mouth of Moses the great lawgiver.

2. Just as our conformity to gospel standards, while dwelling as lowly mortals apart from our Maker, prepares us to return to his presence with an inheritance of immortal glory, so the Mosaic standards prepared the chosen of Israel to believe and obey that gospel by conformity to which eternal life is won. The law of Moses was an Elias; it prepared the way for something far greater. "Ye have heard that it was said by them of old time, Thou shalt not commit adultery," Jesus said of the Mosaic proscription, saying it as a prelude to giving them the gospel standard in these words: "But I say unto you, That whosoever looketh on a woman to lust after her hath committed adultery with her already in his heart." (Matt. 5:27-28.) The law of Moses urged, almost compelled, obedience; at least it put great pressures on Israel to keep ever before them the goodness of their Lord and to seek his face. The gospel says instead: 'Here is the way; walk ye in it; choose of your own free will to do good and work righteousness; and the Lord will bless you accordingly,' all of which makes for much greater development of character; it is, in fact, a greater test of personal integrity than were the provisions of the old covenant. Hence, everything connected with the lesser law pointed to the higher law, or in other words it pointed to Christ and his gospel. Each Mosaic performance was so arranged and so set up that it was a type and a shadow of what was to be. Their sacrifices were performed in similitude of the coming sacrifice of their Messiah; the rituals out of which they gained forgiveness of sins were tokens of what was to be in the life of Him whose atonement made forgiveness possible; their every act, every ordinance, every performance—all that they did—pointed the hearts and minds of believing worshipers forward to Jesus Christ and him crucified. All this was understood by those among them who were faithful and true; the rebellious and slothful were like their modern counterparts, unbelieving, nonconforming, unsaved.

It is the will of the Lord, and has been from the beginning, that all men everywhere should believe in Christ, accept the fulness of his everlasting gospel, and rely on the merits of his atoning sacrifice for salvation. Accordingly, as affirmed by an angel to King Benjamin, "the Lord God hath sent his holy prophets among all the children of men, to declare these things to every kindred, nation, and tongue, that thereby whosoever should believe that Christ should come, the same might receive remission of their sins, and rejoice with exceeding great joy, even as though he had already come among them. Yet the Lord God saw that his people were a stiffnecked people, and he appointed unto them a law, even the law of Moses. And many signs, and wonders, and types, and shadows showed he unto them, concerning his coming; and also holy prophets spake unto them concerning his coming; and yet they hardened their hearts, and understood not that the law of Moses availeth nothing except it were through the atonement of his blood." (Mosiah 3:13-15.)

With this same theme in mind, Abinadi said: "It was expedient that there should be a law given to the children of Israel, yea, even a very strict law; for they were a stiffnecked people, quick to do iniquity, and slow to remember the Lord their God; Therefore there was a law given them, yea, a law of performances and of ordinances, a law which they were to observe strictly from day to day, to keep them in remembrance of God and their duty towards him. But behold, I say unto you, that all these things were types of things to come." (Mosiah 13:29-31.)

Paul named various of the Mosaic ordinances and performances and said they were a "shadow of heavenly things." (Heb. 8:4-5.) The "meats and drinks, and divers washings, and carnal ordinances, imposed on them until the time of reformation," he said, were designed as "a figure for the time then present." He spoke of the various formalities involved in sprinkling blood as "patterns" of things of a much higher nature. "The law," he said, was "a shadow of good things to come." (Heb. 9:1-10, 19-23; 10:1.) But perhaps Amulek's statement is the clearest and best of them all. He said: "This is the whole meaning of the law, every whit pointing to that great and last sacrifice; and that great and last sacrifice will be the Son of God, yea, infinite and eternal." (Alma 34:14.)

Salvation Cannot Come by the Law of Moses

Israel had many wicked kings who led the chosen seed astray. Some adopted false religions and imposed false ordinances upon the people; others gave lip service to the law of Moses, but chose to walk in carnal paths and be guided by apostate priests who drew near to the Lord with their lips but whose hearts were far from him. To such kings and false priests the Lord sent his prophets, crying repentance, warning, exhorting, condemning, as the needs required. One such king was the American Hebrew, Noah, to whom Abinadi was sent, who, being so commanded, prophesied ill against the people and the kingdom. In a confrontation with the false priests who upheld King Noah's wicked course, Abinadi asked: "What teach ye this people?" They answered, "We teach the law of Moses." Abinadi's prophetic condemnation then fell upon them in these words: "If ye teach the law of Moses why do ye not keep it? Why do ye set your hearts upon riches? Why do ye commit whoredoms and spend your strength with harlots, yea, and cause this people to commit sin, that the Lord has cause to send me to prophesy against this people, yea, even a great evil against this people?"

Change the names and move to another day and location and we can see Samuel rejecting Saul, or Nathan condemning David, or Elijah cursing Ahab. Wickedness is the same in every day and at all times. Only the people and the historical settings change. And so Abinadi, reacting to the needs of his hour and giving the word of the Lord to those before whom he stood, said these prophetic words: "It shall come to pass that ye shall be smitten for your iniquities, for ye have said that ye teach the law of Moses. And what know ye concerning the law of Moses? Doth salvation come by the law of Moses? What say ye?" The question might have been asked by a long line of prophets of a long line of false priests who also had lost the meaning and import of the divine pronouncements made by mighty Moses. And so, sadly for their sake and that of their people, the record says that Noah's priests answered "that salvation did come by the law of Moses." (Mosiah 12.)

After some further doctrinal exposition, Abinadi said: "I say unto you that it is expedient that ye should keep the law of Moses as yet; but I say unto you, that the time shall come when it shall no more be expedient to keep the law of Moses. And moreover, I say unto you, that salvation doth not come by the law alone; and were it not for the atonement, which God himself shall make for the sins and iniquities of his people, that they must unavoidably perish, notwithstanding the law of Moses." Following this he spoke of the strict and straitened nature of the restrictions and performances imposed in the law, and of how others, in addition to these false priests of Noah, had not understood the law; he told how all the prophets had spoken of the coming of a Messiah; and with reference to their testimony, he asked: "Have they not said that God himself should come down among the children of men, and take upon him the form of a man, and go forth in mighty power upon the face of the earth? Yea, and have they not said also that he should bring to pass the resurrection of the dead, and that he, himself, should be oppressed and afflicted?" At this point he quoted the incomparable Messianic prophecies of Isaiah 53, expounded their meaning at some length, and concluded with these warning words: "And now, ought ye not to tremble and repent of your sins, and remember that only in and through Christ ye can be saved? Therefore, if ye teach the law of Moses, also teach that it is a shadow of those things which are to come—Teach them that redemption cometh through Christ the Lord, who is the very Eternal Father." (Mosiah 13, 14, 15, and 16.)

In his writings to the Hebrews, Paul bears a similar testimony. As we have already seen, he taught that "perfection" did not come "by the Levitical priesthood," but through "the order of Melchisedec," which Christ should restore. One obvious reason for this is that it is by the power of the Melchizedek Priesthood that men receive the gift of the Holy Ghost, and without the Holy Ghost they cannot be sanctified. Hence, says Paul, "the law made nothing perfect, but the bringing in of a better hope did; by the which we draw nigh unto God." (Heb. 7:11-19.) There are a number of other like assertions in Hebrews, and a good portion of Romans was written to show that salvation is not in the law of Moses but in Christ. I have written on this at some length on pages 221 to 248 of *Doctrinal New Testament Commentary,* volume 2. But to put the whole matter to rest forever, the Lord has said in our day: "All old covenants have I caused to be done away, . . . for you cannot enter in at the strait gate by the law of Moses, neither by your dead works." (D&C 22.)

Nephites Followed Both Moses and Christ

Those Israelites known as Nephites, though separated from their forebears and kindred by oceans of water, yet kept the law of Moses. (2 Ne. 5:10; Jarom 1:5; Hel. 15:5.) But they did so with a proper understanding, knowing that salvation was in Christ who should come and that "the law of Moses was a type of his coming." Accordingly, "They did not suppose that salvation came by the law of Moses; but the law of Moses did serve to strengthen their faith in Christ; and thus they did retain a hope through faith, unto eternal salvation, relying upon the spirit of prophecy, which spake of those things to come." (Alma 25:15-16.) The souls of their prophets delighted in proving unto the people "the truth of the coming of Christ; for, for this end hath the law of Moses been given." (2 Ne. 11:4.) Of the Nephite worship, Jacob says: "We knew of Christ, and we had a hope of his glory many hundred years before his coming; and not only we ourselves had a hope of his glory, but also all the holy prophets which were before us. Behold, they believed in Christ and worshiped the Father in his name, and also we worship the Father in his name. And for this intent we keep the law of Moses, it pointing our souls to him." (Jacob 4:4-5; Jarom 1:11.) To them the law was not an end in itself, but a means to an end. The blindness of their Jewish relatives in the Old World came "by looking beyond the mark" (Jacob 4:14), meaning they did not have a proper perspective of the law and know how it was designed to lead them to Christ and his gospel.

These Nephites, who were faithful and true in keeping the law of Moses, had the Melchizedek Priesthood, which means they had also the fulness of the gospel. In many respects, for instance, the greatest sermon we have on baptism and the receipt of the Holy Ghost is 2 Nephi 31; our best passages on being born again are in Mosiah 27 and Alma 5; our most explicit teachings on the atonement of Christ are in 2 Nephi 2 and 9 and Alma 34; and some of our best information about the Melchizedek Priesthood is found in Alma 13—all of which doctrines were set forth during what men falsely call the pre-Christian Era.

Of this remarkable situation, in which men lived under both the law and the gospel at one and the same time, Nephi says: "We labor diligently to write, to persuade our children, and also our brethren, to believe in Christ, and to be reconciled to God; for we know that it is by grace that we are saved, after all we can do. And, notwithstanding we believe in Christ, we keep the law of Moses, and look forward with steadfastness unto Christ, until the law shall be fulfilled. For, for this end was the law given; wherefore the law hath become dead unto us, and we are made alive in Christ because of our faith; yet we keep the law because of the commandments. And we talk of Christ, we rejoice in Christ, we preach of Christ, we prophesy of Christ, and we write according to our prophecies, that our children may know to what source they may look for a remission of their sins. Wherefore, we speak concerning the law that our children may know the deadness of the law; and they, by knowing the deadness of the law, may look forward unto that life which is in Christ, and know for what end the law was given. And after the law is fulfilled in Christ, that they need not harden their hearts against him when the law ought to be done away." (2 Ne. 25:23-27.)

That there were selected portions of Old World Israel to whom the law became dead and who rejoiced in their perfect knowledge of Christ and his gospel laws is perfectly clear. Such would have been the case with all of the prophets, for they all held the Melchizedek Priesthood. Elijah, for instance, had the fulness of the gospel—meaning all that was necessary to save and exalt him with a fulness of glory in the highest heaven—for he was the very one chosen of the Lord to restore this power and authority in modern times.

Law of Moses Fulfilled in Christ

If Jesus Christ was the promised Messiah, then the law of Moses was fulfilled in his coming. If he was not the Son of God, then the law of Moses is still in force, and we and all who seek religious truth should be engaged in a diligent performance of all its rites and ordinances. The fact is that Mary's Child was God's Son and that he did in fact work out the infinite and eternal atoning sacrifice. And since the whole purpose of the law is to prepare men to receive him and his gospel, it automatically follows that when he came and established that gospel, the purpose of the law was fulfilled. Since all the sacrifices and performances of the law looked forward to and were in similitude of his atoning sacrifice, it follows that once he had shed his blood for the sins of repentant men, sacrifices should cease. Since the preparatory priesthood of Aaron was to train and qualify men to take the covenant appertaining to the Melchizedek

Priesthood, it is instinctive to know that when that higher priesthood comes it swallows up the lesser order, and men are no longer governed by the system that the lesser order was authorized to administer.

True, our Lord's coming was in a day when Jewish Israel was blinded in mind and spirit. Like so many of their fathers, they had made the law of Moses an end in itself; its real purpose and import was lost to them; and they, looking beyond the mark, failed to recognize Him of whom the law testified. Hence we find repeated and emphatic declarations in Holy Writ that teach that the old order no longer prevailed because He of whose coming it testified had in fact made flesh his tabernacle and had performed all the works assigned him of his Father. For instance, Paul said that Christ "obtained a more excellent ministry" than Moses, and came to be "the mediator of a better covenant, which was established upon better promises" than was the case with the old covenant of Mosaic vintage. "For if that first covenant had been faultless," the apostle wrote, "then should no place have been sought for the second. But finding fault with them," the Lord promised to "make a new covenant with the house of Israel." With reference to this, Paul reaches this conclusion: "In that he [the Lord] saith, A new covenant, he hath made the first old. Now that which decayeth and waxeth old is ready to vanish." (Heb. 8:6-13.) Paul then launches forth into a detailed comparison of many of the features of the two covenants. (Heb. 9 and 10.) Amulek expresses the same principle in this way: "It is expedient that there should be a great and last sacrifice; and then shall there be, or it is expedient there should be, a stop to the shedding of blood; then shall the law of Moses be fulfilled; yea, it shall be all fulfilled, every jot and tittle, and none shall have passed away." (Alma 34:13.)

Our Lord, ministering among his beloved Nephites, explained when and how and why the law was fulfilled. "Believe on my name," he said, "for behold, by me redemption cometh, and in me is the law of Moses fulfilled. I am the light and the life of the world." (3 Ne. 9:17-18.) From that day forth men were to turn to him and his law; he was the light; no longer were they to perform Mosaic ordinances; redemption had now come unto all those who would believe.

Shortly thereafter, as part of what we have come to call the Nephite version of the Sermon on the Mount, he said: "Think not that I am come to destroy the law or the prophets. I am not come to destroy but to fulfil; For verily I say unto you, one jot nor one tittle hath not passed away from the law, but in me it hath all been fulfilled. And behold, I have given you the law and the commandments of my Father, that ye shall believe in me, and that ye shall repent of your sins, and come unto me with a broken heart and a contrite spirit. Behold, ye have the commandments before you, and the law is fulfilled. Therefore come unto me and be ye saved." (3 Ne. 12:17-20.) Again his people are commanded to look to him—not to Moses of old, but to him and the new covenant; he it is in whom salvation is found. "Those things which were of old time, which were under the law, in me are all fulfilled. Old things are done away, and all things have become new." (3 Ne. 12:46-47.)

In spite of these plain declarations, there were yet some among them who marveled and wondered concerning the law, and so our Lord climaxed his teachings to them by saying: "Marvel not that I said unto you that old things had passed away, and that all things had become new. Behold, I say unto you that the law is fulfilled that was given unto Moses. Behold, I am he that gave the law, and I am he who covenanted with my people Israel; therefore, the law in me is fulfilled, for I have come to fulfill the law; therefore it hath an end. Behold, I do not destroy the prophets, for as many as have not been fulfilled in me, verily I say unto you, shall all be fulfilled. And because I said unto you that old things have passed away, I do not destroy that which hath been spoken concerning things which are to come. For behold, the covenant which I have made with my people is not all fulfilled; but the law which was given unto Moses hath an end in me. Behold, I am the law, and the light. Look unto me, and endure to the end, and ye shall live; for unto him that endureth to the end will I give eternal life. Behold, I have given unto you the commandments; therefore keep my commandments. And this is the law and the prophets, for they truly testified of me." (3 Ne. 15:2-10.)

From all of this, can we do other than to conclude that if the law of Moses was divine, then Jesus Christ is the Messiah?

MOSAIC FEASTS AND SACRIFICES TESTIFY OF CHRIST

Sacrifice—A Form of Worship

Sacrifice was a way of worship in Israel. The divine decree, given to Adam, that men should repent and call upon God in the name of the Son forevermore, was still in force among them. Compliance with that decree still required them to "offer the firstlings of their flocks" as sacrifices in "similitude of the sacrifice of the Only Begotten of the Father." (Moses 5:5-8.) In addition, through Moses they had received an intricate, extensive, and detailed sacrificial system, a system of performances and ordinances that called upon them to pledge new allegiance to the Lord each day of their lives. They did not inherit their sacrificial rites from their pagan neighbors, nor did they perform them in imitation of what other peoples were doing in that day and age. What others did was, in fact, a degenerate imitation and perversion of what had come down by descent from the pure and perfect system revealed to Adam. But what Israel did, she did by direct revelation, just as what the Latter-day Saints do is performed by the command of Deity and is not patterned after the fallen forms of Christianity that surround them.

We need not weigh and evaluate all the performances and ordinances of the law of Moses, and for that matter, from the fragmentary recitations preserved in the Old Testament, it is not possible so to do. We cannot always tell, for instance, whether specific sacrificial rites performed in Israel were part of the Mosaic system or whether they were the same ordinances performed by Adam and Abraham as part of the gospel law itself. Further, it appears that some of the ritualistic performances varied from time to time, according to the special needs of the people and the changing circumstances in which they found themselves. Even the Book of Mormon does not help us in these respects. We know the Nephites offered sacrifices and kept the law of Moses. Since they held the Melchizedek Priesthood and there were no Levites among them, we suppose their sacrifices were those that antedated the ministry of Moses and that, since they had the fulness of the gospel itself, they kept the law of Moses in the sense that they conformed to its myriad moral principles and its endless ethical restrictions. We suppose this would be one of the reasons Nephi was able to say, "The law hath become dead unto us." (2 Ne. 25:25.) There is, at least, no intimation in the Book of Mormon that the Nephites offered the daily sacrifices required by the law or that they held the various feasts that were part of the religious life of their Old World kinsmen. For our purposes it will suffice to give an overview of the "law of performances and of ordinances" (Mosiah 13:30), and to select enough of the detailed procedures to show that all that was done was a figure, a type, a shadow, a similitude of Him of whom the rituals and performances bore record.

To have the proper understanding and perspective, however, of what went on ordinance-wise in Israel, we must keep in remembrance that their sacrifices were a mode and form of worship. This is our key to a proper understanding, whether we are speaking of the public sacrifices made for the whole nation or of the private sacrifices made for families or individuals or small groups of people having special needs at the time involved. Without launching forth on a treatise on sacrifices, suffice it to say that the Old Testament preserves for us accounts of sacrifices that were performed—as pure acts of worship and veneration, as covenant renewal ceremonies, as acts of atonement, on occasions of thanksgiving, when seeking forgiveness, in fulfillment of vows, in confirmation of a treaty, as acts of dedication and rededication to the Lord's work, as acts of consecration, in expiation for sins, to extend hospitality to a guest, at the cleansing of a leper, for purification after childbirth, at the consecration of a priest or Levite, upon the release of a Nazarite from his vows, at sanctuary dedications, at royal coronations, on days of national penitence, in preparation for battle, and no doubt on other occasions. A classical example of worship through sacrifice is found in the account of Father Lehi's family. So gratified were they when Nephi and his brethren returned with the plates of brass, which had been in the custody of Laban, that the whole family "did rejoice exceedingly, and did offer sacrifice and burnt offerings unto the Lord; and they gave thanks unto the God of Israel." (1 Ne. 5:9.)

Feast of the Passover—A Type of Christ

Three times each year all male Israelites were commanded to appear before the Lord, at a place appointed, to worship him and renew their covenants. The first of these was the Feast of the Passover (including the Feast of Unleavened Bread); the Passover portion of the feast lasted one day, with the Feast of Unleavened Bread continuing for an additional seven. It was to celebrate the Passover that Joseph and Mary took the boy Jesus when he, having attained the age of twelve, was considered to be "a son of the law," one upon whom its obligations then rested. It was there that he confounded the learned doctors of the law with his heaven-sent wisdom; it was there that he bore the first testimony, of which we have record, of his own divine Sonship. (Luke 2:41-50.) The other two feasts to which attendance was mandatory were the Feast of Weeks (also called the Feast of the Harvest, or the Feast of the Firstfruits, or—to us today—

simply, the day of Pentecost), and the Feast of Tabernacles, which was called also the Feast of Ingathering. Sacrifices were offered at all three of these great feasts, and the instructions to all who attended were: "They shall not appear before the Lord empty: Every man shall give as he is able." (Deut. 16:16-17.)

At the time appointed for their deliverance from Egyptian bondage, the Lord commanded each family in Israel to sacrifice a lamb, to sprinkle its blood on their doorposts, and then to eat unleavened bread for seven more days—all to symbolize the fact that the destroying angel would pass over the Israelites as he went forth slaying the firstborn in the families of all the Egyptians; and also to show that, in haste, Israel should go forth from slavery to freedom. As a pattern for all the Mosiac instructions yet to come, the details of the performances here involved were so arranged as to bear testimony both of Israel's deliverance and of her Deliverer. Among other procedures, the Lord commanded, as found in Exodus 12:

1. "Your lamb shall be without blemish, a male of the first year," signifying that the Lamb of God, pure and perfect, without spot or blemish, in the prime of his life, as the Paschal Lamb, would be slain for the sins of the world.

2. They were to take of the blood of the lamb and sprinkle it upon the doorposts of their houses, having this promise as a result: "And the blood shall be to you for a token upon the houses where ye are: and when I see the blood, I will pass over you, and the plague shall not be upon you to destroy you," signifying that the blood of Christ, which should fall as drops in Gethsemane and flow in a stream from a pierced side as he hung on the cross, would cleanse and save the faithful; and that, as those in Israel were saved temporally because the blood of a sacrificial lamb was sprinkled on the doorposts of their houses, so the faithful of all ages would wash their garments in the blood of the Eternal Lamb and from him receive an eternal salvation. And may we say that as the angel of death passed by the

families of Israel because of their faith—as Paul said of Moses, "through faith he kept the passover, and the sprinkling of blood, lest he that destroyed the firstborn should touch them" (Heb. 11:28)—even so shall the Angel of Life give eternal life to all those who rely on the blood of the Lamb.

3. As to the sacrifice of the lamb, the decree was, "Neither shall ye break a bone thereof," signifying that when the Lamb of God was sacrificed on the cross, though they broke the legs of the two thieves to induce death, yet they brake not the bones of the Crucified One "that the scripture should be fulfilled, A bone of him shall not be broken." (John 19:31-36.)

4. As to eating the flesh of the sacrificial lamb, the divine word was, "No uncircumcised person shall eat thereof," signifying that the blessings of the gospel are reserved for those who come into the fold of Israel, who join the Church, who carry their part of the burden in bearing off the kingdom; signifying also that those who eat his flesh and drink his blood, as he said, shall have eternal life and he will raise them up at the last day. (John 6:54.)

5. As "the Lord smote all the firstborn in the land of Egypt" because they believed not the word of the Lord delivered to them by Moses and Aaron, even so should the Firstborn of the Father, who brings life to all who believe in his holy name, destroy worldly people at the last day, destroy all those who are in the Egypt of darkness, whose hearts are hardened as were those of Pharaoh and his minions.

6. On the first and seventh days of the Feast of Unleavened Bread, the Israelites were commanded to hold holy convocations in which no work might be done except the preparation of their food. These were occasions for preaching and explaining and exhorting and testifying. We go to sacrament meetings to be built up in faith and in testimony. Ancient Israel attended holy convocations for the same purposes. Knowing that all things operate by faith, would it be

amiss to draw the conclusion that it is as easy for us to look to Christ and his spilt blood for eternal salvation as it was for them of old to look to the blood of a sacrificed lamb, sprinkled on doorposts, to give temporal salvation, when the angel of death swept through the land of Egypt?

It was, of course, while Jesus and the Twelve were keeping the Feast of the Passover that our Lord instituted the ordinance of the sacrament, to serve essentially the same purposes served by the sacrifices of the preceding four millenniums. After that final Passover day and its attendant lifting up upon the cross of the true Paschal Lamb, the day for the proper celebration of the ancient feast ceased. After that Paul was able to say: "Christ our passover is sacrificed for us," and to give the natural exhortation that flowed therefrom: "Therefore let us keep the feast, not with old leaven, neither with the leaven of malice and wickedness; but with the unleavened bread of sincerity and truth." (1 Cor. 5:7-8.)

Feast of Pentecost—A Type of Christ

One of the three great feasts to which all the males of Israel must go each year was the Feast of Weeks, the Feast of Firstfruits, the Feast of the Harvest, or, as we are wont to say, the Feast of Pentecost. It came fifty days after the beginning of the Feast of the Passover. The burnt offerings of Pentecost included a sin-offering and a peace-offering, indicating that the great purpose of the feast was to gain a remission of sins and obtain a reconciliation with God. The procedures also called for a holy convocation in which the truths of heaven would be taught and instruction given to the people. (Lev. 23:15-22.)

With the closing of the Old and the opening of the New Dispensation, the Feast of Pentecost ceased as an authorized time of religious worship. And it is not without significance that the Lord chose the Pentecost, which grew out of the final Passover, as the occasion to dramatize forever the fulfillment of all that was involved in the sacrificial fires of the past. Fire is a cleansing agent. Filth and disease die in its flames. The baptism of fire, which John promised Christ would bring, means that when men receive the actual companionship of the Holy Spirit, then evil and iniquity are burned out of their souls as though by fire. The sanctifying power of that member of the Godhead makes them clean. In similar imagery, all the fires on all the altars of the past, as they burned the flesh of animals, were signifying that spiritual purification would come by the Holy Ghost, whom the Father would send because of the Son. On that first Pentecost of the so-called Christian Era such fires would have performed their purifying symbolism if the old order had still prevailed. How fitting it was instead for the Lord to choose that very day to send living fire from heaven, as it were, fire that would dwell in the hearts of men and replace forever all the fires on all the altars of the past. And so it was that "when the day of Pentecost was fully come, they were all with one accord in one place. And suddenly there came a sound from heaven as of a rushing mighty wind, and it filled all the house where they were sitting. And there appeared unto them cloven tongues like as of fire, and it sat upon each of them. And they were all filled with the Holy Ghost." (Acts 2:1-4.)

Feast of Tabernacles—A Type of Christ

One of the three great feasts at which the attendance of all male Israelites was compulsory, the Feast of Tabernacles, was by all odds Israel's greatest feast. Coming five days after the Day of Atonement, it was thus celebrated when the sins of the chosen people had been removed and when their special covenant relation to Jehovah had been renewed and restored. Above all other occasions it was one for rejoicing, bearing testimony, and praising the Lord. In the full sense, it is the Feast of Jehovah, the one Mosaic celebration which, as part of the restitution of all things, shall be restored when Jehovah comes to reign personally upon the earth for a thousand years. Even now we perform one of its chief rituals in our solemn assemblies, the giving of the Hosanna Shout, and the worshipers of Jehovah shall yet be privileged to exult in other of its sacred rituals.

Also known as the Feast of Booths, because Israel dwelt in booths while in the wilderness, and as the Feast of Ingathering, because it came after the completion of the full harvest, it was a time of gladsome rejoicing and the extensive offering of sacrifices. More sacrifices were offered during the Feast of the Passover than at any other time because a lamb was slain for and eaten by each family or group, but at the Feast of Tabernacles more sacrifices of bullocks, rams, lambs, and goats were offered by the priests for the nation as a whole than at all the other Israelite feasts combined. The fact that it celebrated the completion of the full harvest symbolizes the gospel reality that it is the mission of the house of Israel to gather all nations to Jehovah, a process that is now going forward, but will not be completed until that millennial day when "the Lord shall be king over all the earth," and shall reign personally thereon. Then shall be fulfilled that which is written: "And it shall come to pass, that every one that is left of all the nations . . . shall even go up from year to year to worship the King, the Lord of hosts, and to keep the feast of tabernacles. And it shall be, that whoso will not come up of all the families of the earth unto Jerusalem to worship the King, the Lord of hosts, even upon them shall be no rain." (Zech. 14:9-21.) That will be the day when the law shall go forth from Zion and the word of the Lord from Jerusalem. Manifestly when the Feast of Tabernacles is kept in that day, its ritualistic performances will conform to the new gospel order and not include the Mosaic order of the past.

Included in the Feast of Tabernacles was a holy convocation, which in this instance was called also a solemn assembly. In our modern solemn assemblies we give the Hosanna Shout, which also was associated with the Feast of Tabernacles anciently, except that ancient Israel waved palm branches instead of white handkerchiefs as they exulted in such declarations as "Hosanna, Hosanna, Hosanna, to God and the Lamb." By the time of Jesus some added rituals were part of the feast, including the fact that a priest went to the Pool of Siloam, drew water in a golden pitcher, brought it to the temple, and poured it into a basin at the base of the altar. As this was done the choir sang the Hallel, consisting of Psalms 113 to 118. "When the choir came to these words, 'O give thanks to the Lord,' and again when they sang, 'O work then now salvation, Jehovah;' and once more at the close, 'O give thanks unto the Lord,' all the worshippers shook their lulavs [palm branches] towards the altar," which is closely akin to what we do in giving the Hosanna Shout today. "When, therefore, the multitudes from Jerusalem, on meeting Jesus, 'cut down branches from the trees, and strewed them in the way, and . . . cried, saying, O then, work now salvation to the Son of David!' they applied, in reference to Christ, what was regarded as one of the chief ceremonies of the Feast of Tabernacles, praying that God would now from 'the highest' heavens manifest and send that salvation in connection with the Son of David, which was symbolised by the pouring out of water." (Alfred Edersheim, *The Temple,* p. 279.)

Jesus and his disciples celebrated this and other Jewish feasts during the period of our Lord's active ministry. It was on "the last day, that great day of the feast," called in the Rabbinical writings the "Day of the Great Hosannah," as the priest was pouring out the water from the Pool of Siloam and the multitudes were waving their palm branches toward the altar, that "Jesus stood and cried, saying, If any man thirst, let him come unto me, and drink. He that believeth on me, as the scripture hath said, out of his belly shall flow rivers of living water." (John 7:37-38.) It was as though he said: 'This feast is designed to point your attention to me and the salvation which I bring. Now I have come; if ye will believe in me, ye shall be saved; and then from you, by the power of the Spirit, shall also go forth living water.'

There were also other feasts in Israel: the Feast of Trumpets, which came on the new moon of the seventh month; the Feast of Purim, which was instituted in the days of Esther; and the Feast of Dedication, a post-Old Testament feast, which, however, was kept in the days of Jesus and his disciples. It goes without saying that all of these feasts involved ordinances and worship that should have centered the hearts of the people on their Promised Messiah.

The Day of Atonement—A Type of Christ

Now we come to the heart and core and center of the whole Mosaic structure, namely, the atonement of the Lord Jesus Christ. This is what the law of Moses is all about. The law itself was given so that men might believe in Christ and know that salvation comes in and through his atoning sacrifice and in no other way. Every principle, every precept, every doctrinal teaching, every rite, ordinance, and performance, every word and act—all that appertained to, was revealed in, and grew out of the ministry of Moses, and all the prophets who followed him—all of it was designed and prepared to enable men to believe in Christ, to submit to his laws, and to gain the full blessings of that atonement which he alone could accomplish. And the chief symbolisms, the most perfect similitudes, the types and shadows without peer, were displayed before all the people once each year, on the Day of Atonement.

On one day each year—the tenth day of the seventh month—Israel's high priest of the Levitical order, the one who sat in Aaron's seat, was privileged to enter the Holy of Holies in the house of the Lord, to enter as it were the presence of Jehovah, and there make an atonement for the sins of the people. In the course of much sacrificial symbolism, he cleansed himself, the sanctuary itself, the priesthood bearers as a whole, and all of the people. Sacrificial animals were slain and their blood sprinkled on the mercy seat and before the altar; incense was burned, and all of the imagery and symbolism of the ransoming ordinances was carried out. One thing, applicable to this day only, is of great moment. Two goats were selected, lots were cast, and the name of Jehovah was placed upon one goat; the other was called Azazel, the scapegoat. The Lord's goat was then sacrificed as the Great Jehovah would be in due course, but upon the scapegoat were placed all of the sins of the people, which burden the scapegoat then carried away into the wilderness. The high priest, as the law required, "lay both his hands upon the head of the live goat" and confessed "over him all the iniquities of the children of Israel; and all their transgressions in all their sins, putting them upon the head of the goat." The goat then bore upon him "all their iniquities unto a land not inhabited," even as the Promised Messiah should bear the sins of many. "For on that day shall the priest make an atonement for you, to cleanse you," Moses said, "that ye may be clean from all your sins before the Lord." (Lev. 16.)

Knowing, as we do, that sins are remitted in the waters of baptism; that baptisms were the order of the day in Israel; and that provision must be made for repentant persons to free themselves from sins committed after baptism—we see in the annual performances of the Day of Atonement one of the Lord's provisions for renewing the covenant made in the waters of baptism and receiving anew the blessed purity that comes from full obedience to the law involved. In our day we gain a similar state of purity by partaking worthily of the sacrament of the Lord's supper.

The symbolism and meaning of the ordinances and ceremonies performed on the Day of Atonement are set forth by Paul in his Epistle to the Hebrews. He calls the tabernacle-temple "a worldly sanctuary," wherein sacrificial ordinances were performed each year by Levitical priests to atone for the sins of men and prepare them to enter the Holy of Holies. These ordinances were to remain "until the time of reformation," when Christ should come as a high priest of "a greater and more perfect tabernacle," to prepare himself and all men, by the shedding of his own blood, to obtain "eternal redemption" in the heavenly tabernacle. The old covenant was but "a shadow of good things to come, . . . For it is not possible that the blood of bulls and of goats should take away sins. . . . But this man, after he had offered one sacrifice for sins for ever, sat down on the right hand of God." (Heb. 9 and 10.) How perfectly the Mosaic ordinances testify of Him by whom salvation comes and in whose holy name all men are commanded to worship the Eternal Father forevermore!

Chapter 24

PROPHETIC TYPES OF CHRIST

Moses—Mediator of the Old Covenant

It has pleased God to make covenants with his people, from time to time, according to the heed and diligence that they give unto him. Those who devote themselves to righteousness receive more of his word and inherit greater rewards; those who harden their hearts and stiffen their necks are denied what otherwise would be theirs.

Covenants are contracts. Gospel covenants are made between God in heaven and men on earth. These covenants are the solemn promises of Deity to pour out specified blessings upon all those who keep the terms and conditions upon which their receipt is predicated. The new and everlasting covenant is the fulness of the gospel; it is new in every age and to every people to whom it comes; it is everlasting in that from eternity to eternity it is the same, and its laws and conditions never change. From Adam to Moses, righteous men received and rejoiced in the everlasting covenant. It was offered to and rejected by Israel as a nation, and in its stead came a lesser law, a law of ordinances and performances designed to prepare them for the eventual receipt of the fulness of the gospel. Thus when the original covenant of salvation was revealed anew by Christ in his day, it was called the new covenant or new testament, in contrast to the old covenant or old testament to which the people had been subject for the preceding fifteen hundred years.

For each covenant—the old covenant and the new—there is both a revelator and a mediator. The revelator makes known the mind and will of the Lord, which the people are then privileged to accept or reject. The mediator stands between the Giver of the covenant and the people to mediate their differences; he interposes himself between the two parties of the covenant when they are at variance; he seeks to reconcile them to each other, to bring them into agreement. Moses was the mediator of the old covenant; Jesus is the mediator of the new covenant.

Moses' struggles and sorrows as a revelator and a mediator are seen in the sad story of the golden calf. Because he was so long gone from them into the holy mountain, where he received the Ten Commandments and the law of the gospel, backsliding Israel prevailed upon Aaron to make a calf of gold, like unto the gods of Egypt. "These be thy gods, O Israel, which brought thee up out of the land of Egypt," they then said, and—unbelievably—they worshiped and offered sacrifices to this molten idol. While Moses was yet on the mount, the Lord told him of the idolatrous worship and revelry going on in the camp. "I have seen this people, and, behold, it is a stiffnecked people," the Lord said. "Now therefore let me alone, that my wrath may wax hot against them, and that I may consume them: and I will make of thee a great nation." (Ex. 32:1-10.)

Thereupon Moses pled for the people. Among other things he said to the Lord: "Wherefore should the Egyptians speak, and say, For mischief did he bring them out, to slay them in the mountains, and to consume them from the face of the earth? Turn from thy fierce wrath. Thy people will repent of this evil; therefore come thou not out against them." Then Moses reminded the Lord of the promises made to Abraham, Isaac, and Jacob concerning their seed, and the Lord, relenting, said to Moses: "If they will repent of the evil which they have done, I will spare them, and turn away my fierce wrath; but, behold, thou shalt execute my judgment upon all that will not repent of this evil this day.

Therefore, see thou do this thing that I have commanded thee, or I will execute all that which I had thought to do unto my people." (JST, Ex. 32:12-14.)

Returning to the camp, Moses in righteous anger brake the two tablets of stone on which the law was written; destroyed the calf; sent forth the cry, "Who is on the Lord's side"; accepted the offer of the Levites, and sent them forth to slay three thousand of the wicked in Israel. On the morrow, Moses said to Israel: "Ye have sinned a great sin: and now I will go up unto the Lord; peradventure I shall make an atonement for your sin. And Moses returned unto the Lord, and said, Oh, this people have sinned a great sin, and have made them gods of gold. Yet now, if thou wilt forgive their sins—; and if not, blot me, I pray thee, out of thy book which thou hast written. And the Lord said unto Moses, Whosoever hath sinned against me, him will I blot out of my book." (Ex. 32:15-35; 33:13; 34:9; Deut. 5:5; 9:24-29; 10:10; Ps. 106:23.)

Jesus—Mediator of the New Covenant

Knowing that Moses was the mediator of the old covenant gives meaning to the scriptural passages which speak of Jesus as the mediator of the new covenant. If Moses had not been the mediator of the old covenant, the inspired writers would have spoken of our Lord's mediatorial role as such, without the repeated scriptural stress on the fact that his mediation pertained to the new covenant. But it is in fact the contrast between the role of Moses and the infinitely greater role of Christ that enables us to comprehend what Jesus actually does in the way of intercession and mediation. Moses' status as a mediator thus becomes—as all things in the law of Moses were—a type and shadow of a greater mediatory labor that was to be when the Messiah of whom Moses testified came to work out the infinite and eternal atonement. Thus we find Paul writing, "The law was added because of transgressions, till the seed should come to whom the promise was made in the law given to Moses, who was ordained by the hand of angels to be a mediator of this first covenant, (the law). Now this mediator was not a mediator of the new covenant; but there is one mediator of the new covenant, who is Christ, as it is written in the law concerning the promises made to Abraham and his seed. Now Christ is the mediator of life; for this is the promise which God made unto Abraham." (JST, Gal. 3:19-20.) Also: "For this is good and acceptable in the sight of God our Saviour; Who is willing to have all men to be saved, and to come unto the knowledge of the truth which is in Christ Jesus, who is the Only Begotten Son of God, and ordained to be a Mediator between God and man; who is one God, and hath power over all men. For there is one God, and one mediator between God and men, the man Christ Jesus; Who gave himself a ransom for all, to be testified in due time." (JST, 1 Tim. 2:3-6.)

Salvation is in Christ, not in Moses. Israel's ancient lawgiver mediated the cause of his people to prepare them for the gospel. Israel's later Lawgiver mediated their cause to prepare them for eternal life. "It was by faith that they of old were called after the holy order of God," Moroni said. "Wherefore, by faith was the law of Moses given. But in the gift of his Son hath God prepared a more excellent way." (Ether 12:10-11.) Hence, as Lehi said: "Look to the great Mediator, and hearken unto his great commandments; and be faithful unto his words, and choose eternal life, according to the will of his Holy Spirit." (2 Ne. 2:28.)

We respect and reverence Moses, but we worship Christ. We admire and appreciate the lesser law, but we enjoy and rejoice in the higher. Moses went before to prepare the way; Christ came after to fulfill and to save. "Consider the Apostle and High Priest of our profession," Paul says, "Christ Jesus; Who was faithful to him that appointed him, as also Moses was faithful in all his house. For this man was counted worthy of more glory than Moses, inasmuch as he who hath builded the house hath more honour than the house. For every house is builded by some man; but he that built all things is God. And Moses verily was faithful in all his house, as a servant, for a testimony of those things which were to be spoken after; But Christ as a son over his own house; whose house are we, if we hold fast the confidence and the rejoicing of the hope firm unto the end." (Heb. 3:1-6.) Christ, thus, hath "obtained a more excellent ministry, by how much also he is the mediator of a better covenant, which was established upon better promises." (Heb. 8:6.)

And all those who receive this new covenant and conform to its terms and conditions shall be saved. They are the ones for whom Christ intercedes; they are reconciled to God because of his mediation. "These are they who are just men made perfect through Jesus the mediator of the new covenant, who wrought out this perfect atonement through the shedding of his own blood." (D&C 76:69; 107:19; Heb. 12:22-24.)

Moses—Like unto Christ

Moses was in the similitude of Christ, and Christ was like unto Moses. Of all the hosts of our Father's children, these two are singled out as being like each other. All men are created in the image of God, both spiritually and temporally. "In the day that God created man, in the likeness of God made he him; In the image of his own body, male and female, created he them, and blessed them, and called their name Adam." (Moses 6:8-9.) And all men are endowed with the characteristics and attributes which, in their eternal fulness, dwell in Deity. But it appears there is a special image, a special similitude, a special likeness where the man Moses and the man Jesus are concerned. It is reasonable to suppose that this similarity, this resemblance, is both physical and spiritual; it is a likeness where both qualities and appearance are concerned. Nor should this seem unreasonable or outside the realm of the probabilities. Christ stands preeminent among all the spirit children of the Father. While yet in preexistence he became "like unto God." (Abr. 3:24.) But surely some of the other spirit sons approached him in goodness and obedience, and hence in might, power, and dominion. It is clear that Michael (Adam) stood next to the Firstborn, and that Gabriel (Noah) ranks next to our first father. Where the priorities then fall we do not know, but surely the great dispensation heads are next, including Enoch, Abraham, and Moses. Specific orders of priority do not especially concern us, but on principle it is clear that Moses was one of the six or eight or ten or twenty, or at least one of a small and select group, of the greatest of all the spirit hosts. Is it unreasonable, then, that he should be in the similitude of the Only Begotten, who should in turn be like unto him? For that matter, all who gain exaltation—not just Adam, Enoch, Noah, Abraham, Moses and the mighty ones—shall become like Christ, joint-heirs with him, inheriting, receiving, and possessing as he does in glorious immortality in due course.

And so we find the Father, speaking by the mouth of the Son, upon whom he has placed his name, saying: "I have a work for thee, Moses, my son; and thou art in the similitude of mine Only Begotten; and mine Only Begotten is and shall be the Savior, for he is full of grace and truth." Thereafter, when Satan came to Moses and said "Worship me," that mighty prophet had the courage and confidence to reply: "Who art thou? For behold, I am a son of God, in the similitude of his Only Begotten. . . . For God said unto me: Thou art after the similitude of mine Only Begotten." (Moses 1:1-16.) That is to say, Moses bore the resemblance of his Lord. In appearance, guise, and semblance, they were the same. The qualities of the one were the qualities of the other. Any differences were in degree only.

As Moses summarized the law he had given to Israel, and left that counsel and direction which the Almighty desired them to receive, the great lawgiver gave forth this Messianic prophecy: "The Lord thy God will raise up unto thee a

Prophet from the midst of thee, of thy brethren, like unto me; unto him ye shall hearken." Then Moses said: "And the Lord said unto me, . . . I will raise them up a Prophet from among their brethren, like unto thee, and will put my words in his mouth; and he shall speak unto them all that I shall command him. And it shall come to pass, that whosoever will not hearken unto my words which he shall speak in my name, I will require it of him." (Deut. 18:15-19.)

This Mosaic-Messianic prophecy is quoted twice in the Book of Mormon, twice in the New Testament, and once in the Pearl of Great Price. In each of these five places, the latter part of the prophecy is quoted differently than it is now found in Deuteronomy. The words "I will require it of him" are quoted as meaning "Shall be cut off from among the people," which more accurately describes the fate of those who reject the Messiah. Thus the Risen Lord, appearing to the Nephites, says: "Behold, I am he of whom Moses spake, saying: A prophet shall the Lord your God raise up unto you of your brethren, like unto me; him shall ye hear in all things whatsoever he shall say unto you. And it shall come to pass that every soul who will not hear that prophet shall be cut off from among the people." (3 Ne. 20:23.) When Nephi quoted Moses' words, he did so substantially the same way that Jesus did, and then added, "This prophet of whom Moses spake was the Holy One of Israel; wherefore, he shall execute judgment in righteousness." (1 Ne. 22:20-21.) Peter and Stephen both quoted Moses' words and applied them to Christ. (Acts 3:22-23; 7:37.) And Moroni recited them to the Prophet Joseph Smith as he told him about the coming forth of the Book of Mormon and other great latter-day events. He said the prophet foretold was Christ and that the time would soon come when "they who would not hear his voice should be cut off from among the people," meaning that such would occur at his Second Coming. (JS-H 40.)

How Christ Was Like unto Moses

To set forth in full how our Lord's life and ministry was patterned after and like unto that of Moses is beyond the scope of this work. It would involve, among other things, a more extended analysis of the law of Moses than is of general value and interest now that the law itself has been fulfilled and replaced. The following partial outline will show sufficient of what is involved for our purposes and perhaps serve as an open door for further analysis by those whose interests fall in this field. Christ was like unto Moses in at least the following particulars:

1. Both were among the noble and great in the premortal life; both kept the commandments, followed the Father, and acquired the attributes of godliness before ever they were born into mortality; both participated in the creation of this earth and looked forward with rejoicing to that day when each should gain a mortal body, undergo earth's probationary experiences, and qualify for immortality and eternal life in the full and unlimited sense of the word.

2. Both were foreordained to perform the mortal labors chosen for them, and both were called by name, generations before their mortal births, with their specified labors being set forth in advance by the spirit of prophecy—the work of Christ being to redeem his people, that of Moses to "deliver my people out of Egypt in the days of thy bondage, . . . for a seer will I raise up to deliver my people out of the land of Egypt; and he shall be called Moses. And by his name he shall know that he is of thy house [the house of Joseph who was sold into Egypt]; for he shall be nursed by the king's daughter, and shall be called her son." (JST, Gen. 50:24-29.)

3. Moses delivered Israel from Egypt, from bondage, from the lash, from abject and hopeless slavery, from a state in which they were physically oppressed and spiritually sick;

and then for forty years he led them through a wasted wilderness, schooling and training the while, that they might finally be prepared for their promised land. Christ, the Great Deliverer, offers freedom to all who are under the bondage of sin and leads them through the wilderness of life to an Eternal Promised Land, where they will be free forever from the slavery of sin and the oppression of unrighteousness.

4. Moses was the lawgiver of Israel, the one who revealed to that favored nation the laws, in detail and with prolixity, that served them well for generations; Christ was the great Lawgiver who set forth for all peoples of all ages the system of heavenly rule by which they can qualify for a celestial inheritance.

5. As we have seen, Moses was the mediator of the old covenant, Christ of the new—Moses in his day pleading, interceding, reconciling, standing between the Lord and his people; Christ in all days and at all times intervening between God and man so that all who believe and obey may be reconciled to the Father.

6. Jesus and Moses were both born in perilous times, the One when the nation whence they both sprang was subject to the yoke of Rome, the other when Pharaoh's rule was imposed upon the people. Both were preserved in birth and childhood by divine providence. Jesus was born in a stable and was soon thereafter preserved from Herod's sword, at the time the other innocents were slain, because an angel warned Joseph to flee with the young child into Egypt. Moses was preserved in birth because the Hebrew midwives defied the king of Egypt and slew not the male children of their race, and soon thereafter he was preserved in an ark hidden in the bulrushes, lest he be found and slain by Pharaoh's executioners.

7. Moses performed many signs and wonders and miracles before Pharaoh and his court and in the presence of all Israel. Our Lord acted in like manner throughout his whole ministry as he opened blind eyes, loosed dumb tongues, strengthened lame legs, and raised dead bodies.

8. Both Moses and Jesus had control over mighty waters. The one stretched forth his hand over the Red Sea, the waters divided, and Israel went through on dry ground, with walls of water congealed on the right hand and on the left. The Other walked on the waters of the Galilean Sea and also commanded the wind and the waves to cease their tempestuous raging. Moses turned the water at Marah from bitter to sweet and smote the rock at the waters of Meribah, in both instances providing drink for thirsting Israel. Our Lord smites the rocks of unbelief and rebellion in the hearts of sinful men, so that all who will may drink living water and thirst no more forever.

9. Under Moses' ministry manna fell from heaven, that Israel, for forty years, perished not for want of food. Jesus came to bring that bread from heaven which if men eat they shall never hunger more.

10. Moses sat on the judgment seat, from morning to night, hearing the causes of the people and dispensing judgment, even as the great Judge shall dispense justice and judgment forever.

11. "Now the man Moses was very meek, above all the men which were upon the face of the earth." (Num. 12:3.) Jesus said: "I am meek and lowly in heart." (Matt. 11:29.) The meek are the godfearing and the righteous.

12. Moses and Christ were prophets, mighty prophets, the one foreshadowing the Other, but both acclaiming the divine Sonship of Him of whom all the prophets testify. "And there arose not a prophet since in Israel like unto Moses, whom the Lord knew face to face." (Deut. 34:10.) Nor has there been, nor shall there be, a greater prophet than Jesus, not in Israel only, but in all the world and among all peoples of all ages.

13. Those who defied Moses and rebelled against his law were destroyed, like Korah and his band, concerning whom it is written that the earth opened and they and their houses and all that appertained to them were swallowed up. At our Lord's Second Coming all those who are in rebellion against

Christ and his laws shall be cut off from among the people, for they that come shall burn them up, leaving neither root nor branch.

14. There are no doubt many other ways in which Christ was like unto Moses; and certainly there are other ways of summarizing the numerous realities involved. But whatever approach is made to the matter, all proper presentations lead to this one conclusion, here stated in the words of the Lord Jesus: "Do not think that I will accuse you to the Father: there is one that accuseth you, even Moses, in whom ye trust. For had ye believed Moses, ye would have believed me: for he wrote of me. But if ye believe not his writings, how shall ye believe my words?" (John 5:45-47.) Christ and Moses go together. If one was a prophet, sent of God, so was the other. If the words of one are true, so are those of the other. They are one, and their united voice is that Jesus Christ is the Son of the living God—the Promised Messiah.

All Prophets Are Types of Christ

With the foundation securely built that Christ was like unto Moses, we are prepared to build thereon and show that all the ancient prophets and all righteous men who preceded our Lord in birth were, in one sense or another, patterns for him. That is, to the degree they were true and faithful and acquired for themselves the attributes of godliness, their Elder Brother, the Lord Jesus, is like unto them. All the prophets testified of him, for it was the very fact of knowing and proclaiming his divinity that caused them to be prophets. A prophet is one who has the testimony of Jesus, who knows by the revelations of the Holy Ghost to his soul that Jesus Christ is the Son of God. In addition to this divine knowledge, many of them lived in special situations or did particular things that singled them out as types and patterns and shadows of that which was to be in the life of him who is our Lord. Let us illustrate this principle by naming some of those who are listed in the scriptures as types of Christ:

1. Paul names one of these as Adam. "Death reigned from Adam to Moses," he says, "even over them that had not sinned after the similitude of Adam's transgression, who is the figure of him that was to come." That is, Adam is a similitude of Christ. How and in what way? It is because Adam brought death and sin into the world, as the natural inheritance of all men, as a prelude to our Lord's bringing life and righteousness to all who will believe and obey. Death passes upon all through Adam; life comes to all through Christ. One man brought death for all; one man brought life for all. "Therefore as by the offence of one judgment came upon all men to condemnation; even so by the righteousness of one the free gift came upon all men unto justification of life. For as by one man's disobedience many were made sinners, so by the obedience of one shall many be made righteous." (Rom. 5:14-21.)

Writing of this personal relationship between Adam and Christ, a relationship in which one is a type of the other, Paul also said: "The first man Adam was made a living soul; the last Adam was made a quickening spirit." That is, the first Adam, the one who dwelt in Eden, was the first flesh upon the earth, the first mortal man; and the last Adam, who is Christ, was the first person resurrected, the first immortal man. Adam's mortality reaches perfection in Christ's immortality. "The first man is of the earth, earthy: the second man is the Lord from heaven." Adam was made of the dust of the earth, for mortality goes with this sphere of existence, but the Second Adam came down from heaven with the power of immortality so that death could be swallowed up in life through his atonement. "As is the earthy, such are they also that are earthy: and as is the heavenly, such are they also that are heavenly. And as we have borne the image of the earthy, we shall also bear the image of the heavenly." (1 Cor. 15:45-49.)

2. Melchizedek is named as a type of Christ. Our revelations tell us he was known as the Prince of Peace, the King of Peace, the King of Heaven, and the King of Righteous-

ness, all of which are the very name-titles that apply to our Lord. Further, the priesthood held by Melchizedek is the very priesthood promised the Son of God during his mortal sojourn, which is to say that Christ was to be like unto Melchizedek.

Our revelations say that "Melchizedek was a man of faith, who wrought righteousness," that he was "approved of God" and "ordained an high priest after the order of the covenant which God made with Enoch, It being after the order of the Son of God; which order came, not by man, nor the will of man; neither by father nor mother; neither by beginning of days nor end of years; but of God; And it was delivered unto men by the calling of his own voice, according to his own will, unto as many as believed on his name. . . . And now, Melchizedek was a priest of this order; therefore he obtained peace in Salem, and was called the Prince of peace. . . . And this Melchizedek, having thus established righteousness, was called the king of heaven by his people, or, in other words, the King of peace." (JST, Gen. 14:26-36.) In referring to these things, Paul adds to Melchizedek the title King of Righteousness. (JST, Heb. 7:1-3.)

One of the great Messianic prophecies, spoken by the mouth of David, says: "The Lord hath sworn, and will not repent, Thou art a priest for ever after the order of Melchizedek." (Ps. 110:4.) Paul names Christ as the "High Priest of our profession" (Heb. 3:1), who came in fulfillment of David's prophecy; shows that his coming involved the receipt of a different priesthood than that held by the Levites; and says that Christ came "after the similitude of Melchisedec" (Heb. 7:15). It appears that Paul's statement—"Who in the days of his flesh, when he had offered up prayers and supplications with strong crying and tears unto him that was able to save him from death, and was heard in that he feared; Though he were a Son, yet learned he obedience by the things which he suffered" (Heb. 5:7-8)—has reference both to Melchizedek and to Christ, which harmonizes with the concept that Christ was like unto Melchizedek.

3. Every holder of the Melchizedek Priesthood is or should be a type of Christ. Those who lived before he came were types and shadows and witnesses of his coming. Those who have lived since he came are witnesses of such coming and are types and shadows of what he was. Thus Paul says that Melchizedek was "King of righteousness, and after that also King of Salem, which is, King of peace; For this Melchizedek was ordained a priest after the order of the Son of God, which order was without father, without mother, without descent, having neither beginning of days, nor end of life. And all those who are ordained unto this priesthood are made like unto the Son of God, abiding a priest continually." (JST, Heb. 7:1-3.)

Alma, in about 82 B.C., discoursed at length on the Melchizedek Priesthood and on those who held it from the beginning. "Those priests," he said, meaning high priests of the Melchizedek Priesthood, "were ordained after the order of his Son, in a manner that thereby the people might know in what manner to look forward to his Son for redemption." That is to say, they were types and shadows of our Lord's coming; they were living, walking, breathing Messianic prophecies, even as we should be living witnesses that he has come.

They were "called with a holy calling, yea, with that holy calling which was prepared with, and according to a preparatory redemption." They could preach redemption; they could foretell its coming; but their work was preparatory only. Redemption itself would come through the ministry of Him of whom they were but types and shadows. Then, after setting forth many things connected with this priesthood, Alma says: "Now these ordinances were given after this manner, that thereby the people might look forward on the Son of God, it being a type of his order, or it being his order, and this that they might look forward to him for a remission of their sins, that they might enter into the rest of the Lord." (Alma 13:1-13.)

4. "Take now thy son, thine only son Isaac, whom thou lovest, and get thee into the land of Moriah; and offer him there for a burnt offering upon one of the mountains which I will tell thee of." (Gen. 22:2.) Of this Paul says: "By faith Abraham, when he was tried, offered up Isaac: and he that had received the promises offered up his only begotten son, Of whom it is said, That in Isaac shall thy seed be called: Accounting that God was able to raise him up, even from the dead; from whence also he received him in a figure." (Heb. 11:17-19.) What is the figure of which Paul speaks? Jacob answers in these plain words: "Abraham," he explains, was "obedient unto the commands of God in offering up his son Isaac, which is a similitude of God and his Only Begotten Son." (Jacob 4:5.) How many thousands of sermons have been preached since that day, preached among those with faith and understanding, all using this dramatic episode from the life of the father of the faithful!

5. King David was a type of Christ in two respects: First, his Seed, who is Christ, should reign on his throne forever, as we have heretofore set forth; and, second, through Christ would come the resurrection which, in spite of David's sins, would eventually redeem his soul from hell. "I will make an everlasting covenant with you," the Lord says to his people, "even the sure mercies of David," which mercies are that the resurrection will pass even upon the wicked. "Behold, I have given him for a witness to the people" is the promise. (Isa. 55:3-4.) In other words, if David, who committed adultery and on whose hands was found the blood of Uriah, will be resurrected, then all men should rest in the hope that they shall rise from the grave.

6. We must not overlook Jonah as one whose life and conduct became a type of Christ. His experiences with the great fish have ever since been known as "the sign of the prophet Jonas." It was Jesus who left us this symbolic meaning of the acts of Jonah: "For as Jonas was three days and

three nights in the whale's belly," he said, "so shall the Son of man be three days and three nights in the heart of the earth." (Matt. 12:39-40.)

7. No doubt there are many events in the lives of many prophets that set those righteous persons apart as types and shadows of their Messiah. It is wholesome and proper to look for similitudes of Christ everywhere and to use them repeatedly in keeping him and his laws uppermost in our minds. But let us conclude this part of our inquiry by noting that the whole house of Israel was a type and a shadow of their Messiah. An illustration of this is the use Matthew makes of one of Hosea's statements. "When Israel was a child, then I loved him, and called my son out of Egypt" (Hos. 11:1), Hosea said with apparent reference to the deliverance of Israel from Egyptian bondage. But Matthew, guided by the Holy Ghost, saw in this statement a prophetic foretelling that Joseph and Mary and the child Jesus would flee to Egypt to escape the sword of Herod and would there remain until the Lord called them forth to continue their habitation in Palestine. (Matt. 2:12-15.) In other words, the passage has a dual meaning and was intended as a type and a shadow of one of the important occurrences in the life of a Child who was God's Son.

JEHOVAH BECOMES THE MORTAL MESSIAH

Why Messiah Became Mortal

Two views and perspectives face us as we consider the gospel verity that God himself should be born among mortals, should grow to maturity, and should, himself a mortal, partake of the normal experiences incident to that state of existence. They are:

1. How almost unthinkable it is that a God should become a man; that the Creator of all things from the beginning should come down and be himself created from the dust of the earth; that he being infinite forever should become finite for a season; that the Maker of men should become subject to them; that he who has ascended above all things should now descend below them all; that he who knows all things and has all might, power, and dominion should begin anew, as it were, and go himself from grace to grace until the eternal fulness was his once again.

2. And yet how normal and right such a process is! How could it be otherwise? If the spirit Michael needed a body and the experiences of mortality to gain all power in heaven and on earth, why not the spirit Jehovah also? If the secondborn son of the Father, whoever he may have been, needed the probationary experiences of earth life, why not the Firstborn also? If the plan of salvation, ordained by the

Father, was to enable all of his spirit children to advance and progress and become like him, then Jehovah also was subject to its terms and conditions. And how better could he be favored above all others than to be born, not of mortality only but of Immortality, not of man only but of God, not of the earth only but of Heaven?

With these two perspectives before us—one, that it is wondrous beyond belief that a God becomes mortal; the other, that it is the most normal, natural, and needful course that could be devised—we are prepared to suggest why the Messiah became mortal. Let us, then, suggest three reasons why, in the wisdom of Him who knoweth all things, the Eternal One should take upon himself a mortal state; why the Lord Jehovah should become the Lord Jesus; why he was born among men as the Son of God. These are:

1. *Our Lord's mortality was a preparation for and a condition precedent to his atonement.*

The great plan of redemption, prepared from before the foundations of the world, contemplated that one should fall and Another redeem; that the first Adam should bring temporal and spiritual death into the world, with the Second Adam ransoming men from the otherwise eternal effects of these two deaths; and that as Adam, who was immortal, became mortal so that mortality would pass upon all men, even so Christ, who as the Seed of Adam had taken upon himself mortality, should become immortal so that immortality should become the unquestioned inheritance of all his brethren.

It must needs be, for so it was ordained of the Father, that One subject to death gain the victory over the grave; and One who was in all points tempted like his brethren should so live that he, being sinless, gained eternal life, thus showing that man could be ransomed from both the temporal and the spiritual fall. The atonement must needs come by power, not alone the power of the Father which opened the grave, but the power of the mortal Son that overcame the world. The plan called for a mortal Man, endowed with

God's power, to ransom men from the dual effects of Adam's fall.

2. *Our Lord's mortality was essential to his own salvation.*

The eternal exaltation of Christ himself—though he was a God and had power and intelligence like unto his Father—was dependent upon gaining a mortal body, overcoming the world by obedience, passing through the portals of death, and then coming forth in glorious immortality with a perfected celestial body. Christ came into the world to work out his own salvation with fear and trembling before the Father. There neither was, nor is, nor shall be any other way for anyone. To house a spirit body, even that of a God, in an eternal tabernacle like that of the Father, requires a mortal birth and a mortal death. Christ wrought his atonement, first for himself and his own salvation, then for the salvation of all those who believe on his name, and finally and in a lesser degree for all the sons of Adam.

3. *Our Lord's mortality shows man can be saved by obedience to the laws and ordinances of his everlasting gospel.*

While in mortality He, by whom all things are, lived a perfect life. He kept the whole law of the whole gospel. He was and is the Sinless One. He rose above temptation, overcame the world, and rebuked the devourer. His life set the perfect pattern in all things, and it is his voice we hear, saying: "What manner of men ought ye to be? Verily I say unto you, even as I am." (3 Ne. 27:27.) And also: "Follow thou me." (2 Ne. 31:10.)

Our Lord's perfect life shines as a beacon beckoning all those from Adam on down to choose to live as he lived and to merit the rewards he himself gained. Most of earth's total inhabitants shall dwell as mortals in the so-called Christian Era. All of these are invited to look back at his life, to see how he lived, and to go forth themselves and do likewise. Those who lived before his day, who were righteous, knew by the spirit of inspiration that his would be the perfect life, and they, therefore, buoyed up by this knowledge, sought beforehand to be even as he would be in the day of his mortal probation.

When Messiah Shall Come

In our day we look forward with hope and joy to the Second Coming of the Son of Man, and to the setting up of the millennial kingdom of peace and righteousness, over which he shall assume personal rule for the space of a thousand years. We do not know and shall not learn either the day or the hour of that dreadful yet blessed day. We are expected to read the signs of the times and know thereby the approximate time of our Lord's return and to be in constant readiness therefor.

There was an element of this same uncertainty associated with his first coming, although such appears to have arisen because of lack of faith on the part of the people and not from the deliberate design of the Lord to withhold such knowledge from them. The Nephites, whose faith was greater, did know the precise year in which he should be born. It was identified as six hundred years from the time Lehi left Jerusalem. (1 Ne. 10:4; 19:8; 2 Ne. 25:19.) As the time drew near, mention of this fact was made by various of the American prophets. (Alma 7:7; 9:26-27; 13:25-26.)

In a wondrous outburst of spiritual insight, Samuel the Lamanite was privileged to name the time and set forth the attendant signs to be shown forth incident to our Lord's mortal birth. "Behold, I give unto you a sign," he said, "for five years more cometh, and behold, then cometh the Son of God to redeem all those who shall believe on his name. And behold, this will I give unto you for a sign at the time of his coming; for behold, there shall be great lights in heaven, insomuch that in the night before he cometh there shall be no darkness, insomuch that it shall appear unto man as if it was day. Therefore, there shall be one day and a night and a day, as if it were one day and there were no night; and this shall be unto you for a sign; for ye shall know of the rising of the sun and also of its setting; therefore they shall know of a surety that there shall be two days and a night; nevertheless the night shall not be darkened; and it shall be the night before he is born. And behold, there shall a new star arise, such an one as ye never have beheld; and this also shall be a sign unto you. And behold this is not all, there shall be many signs and wonders in heaven. And it shall come to pass that ye shall all be amazed, and wonder, insomuch that ye shall fall to the earth. And it shall come to pass that whosoever shall believe on the Son of God, the same shall have everlasting life." (Hel. 14:2-8.) It does not appear that the Lord had any design or purpose for keeping secret the time of his mortal birth.

We do not know what revelations were extant among the Jews in Jerusalem that would lead them to know to some extent what the Nephites knew. Perhaps the Lord gave the American Hebrews more signs and wonders to identify the time because they were far removed from the scene of action. But it does appear that the Jews had some knowledge on the subject of which we are not aware.

We do know that all of the ancient prophets had looked forward with great anticipation to Messiah's mortal ministry and that some of them had sought to learn when it would be. Enoch asked: "When shall the day of the Lord come? When shall the blood of the Righteous be shed, that all they that mourn may be sanctified and have eternal life?" He was answered: "It shall be in the meridian of time, in the days of wickedness and vengeance." (Moses 7:45-46.) Father Jacob had prophesied: "The sceptre shall not depart from Judah, nor a lawgiver from between his feet, until Shiloh come; and unto him shall the gathering of the people be." (Gen. 49:10.) From the Joseph Smith Translation we learn that "the Messiah . . . is called Shilo." (JST, Gen. 50:24.) And from historical sources we know that Jewish kings still reigned and the Jewish Sanhedrin still functioned until the destruction of

Jerusalem in A.D. 70, when the temple was destroyed, the sacrificial system discontinued, and the Jews as a nation and as a people scattered among all nations.

Isaiah spoke of the Messiah coming "in an acceptable time" (Isa. 49:8), and Daniel named the very time, but he used imagery and figurative language that can only be understood by the spirit of revelation. He said that "from the going forth of the commandment to restore and to build Jerusalem unto the Messiah the Prince shall be seven weeks, and threescore and two weeks." He said that after that period "shall Messiah be cut off." Then he described the post-New Testament destruction of Jerusalem by the Roman legions. (Dan. 9:24-26.) And it was Jesus who said to some of his disciples: "Blessed are your eyes, for they see: and your ears, for they hear. For verily I say unto you, That many prophets and righteous men have desired to see those things which ye see, and have not seen them; and to hear those things which ye hear, and have not heard them." (Matt. 13:16-17.)

But none of this lets us know why the Jews were so anxiously expecting their Messiah in the very day in which he came. As is well known, their whole social structure was alive with the ferment of Messianic hope. False messiahs found followers; true prophets were queried to ascertain their claims, if any, to Messiahship. When John the Baptist cried repentance and immersed worthy souls in Jordan for the remission of their sins, it was an automatic thing for the Jews to send "priests and Levites from Jerusalem to ask him, Who art thou? . . . What sayest thou of thyself?" As to the main point at issue, his witness was: "I am not the Christ." (John 1:19-25.) And it did not seem to strike anyone as strange, neither Herod nor the masses of the people, that wise men should come from the east, asking: "Where is he that is born King of the Jews? for we have seen his star in the east, and are come to worship him." The account says "all Jerusalem" was troubled as to where he might be, out of which fearful anxiety, coupled with the evil jealousy of a wicked king, came the slaughter of the innocent children in Bethlehem. (Matt. 2.)

But however much the people knew or did not know, whatever their state of spirituality, it was the six-hundredth year since Lehi left the locale in which Messiah should come, and so come he did as come he must. Among the Nephites the unbelievers had appointed a day on which all who looked forward to his coming should be put to death unless the promised sign was seen. Nephi the son of Helaman cried mightily unto the Lord for the preservation of the faithful, and the answering voice acclaimed: "Lift up your head and be of good cheer; for behold, the time is at hand, and on this night shall the sign be given, and on the morrow come I into the world." (3 Ne. 1:13.)

In Jewry, as most of the people walked in their own willful ways, a few righteous souls came to know the purposes and acts of the Lord. To Zacharias, Elisabeth, Mary, and Joseph, each in turn, an angelic ministrant made known the conception and coming forth of the Lord and his forerunner. Sheltered in a stable, Mary brought forth that which had been conceived by the power of the Holy Ghost; a heavenly herald announced to the shepherds: "I bring you good tidings of great joy, which shall be to all people. For unto you is born this day in the city of David a Saviour, which is Christ the Lord"; and the celestial choirs sang: "Glory to God in the highest, and on earth peace, good will toward men." (Luke 2:1-14.)

Truly, a God now dwelt in mortality!

Where Messiah Became Mortal

Planet earth is of immense proportion from the standpoint of the people who tread its paths. In what corner of its great expanse would the Heavenly King be born? Would it be in the Holy City, in the palace of the king, perhaps even in the Temple of the Most High itself? How can you find a place good enough for a God to choose as his natal home? No doubt many of the prophets wondered and inquired about the place where the Messiah would begin his mortal life. Nephi was told by an angel that "Christ . . . should come among the Jews" (2 Ne. 10:3), and he saw in vision that Mary would dwell in Nazareth (1 Ne. 11:13). Alma said that our Lord would "be born of Mary, at Jerusalem which is the land of our forefathers" (Alma 7:10), meaning that he would be born in the land of Jerusalem. Bethlehem, being some six miles from Jerusalem's walls, is in effect in the metropolitan area of that great city.

But it was to Micah, as far as our present scriptures reveal, that the actual site of our Lord's birth was given. "Thou, Bethlehem Ephratah, though thou be little among the thousands of Judah, yet out of thee shall he come forth unto me that is to be ruler in Israel; whose goings forth have been from of old, from everlasting." The everlasting God shall be born in Bethlehem! "She which travaileth hath brought forth," Micah says of our Lord's mother. Then of her Son, he speaks these Messianic words: "And he shall stand and feed in the strength of the Lord, in the majesty of the name of the Lord his God; and they shall abide: for now shall he be great unto the ends of the earth." (Micah 5:2-4.) That this prophecy, spoken by Micah some seven hundred years before the promised event, was understood by the Jews of Jesus' day is seen from the fact that when Herod demanded of "the chief priests and scribes . . . where Christ should be born," they responded: "In Bethlehem of Judea: for thus it is written by the prophet, And thou Bethlehem, in the land of Juda, art not the least among the princes of Juda: for out of thee shall come a Governor, that shall rule my people Israel." This reply was the basis for the search and slaughter in Bethlehem and its environs. (Matt. 2.)

Accordingly, that our Lord might enter mortality at the proper place, Joseph and Mary left Nazareth, as part of the taxation requirements of their day, and went "unto the city of David, which is called Bethlehem." There, not in a palace, not in a temple, but in a stable, "because there was no room for them in the inn," Mary "brought forth her firstborn son, and wrapped him in swaddling clothes, and laid him in a manger." (Luke 2:1-7.)

No room in the inn—not an inn as we know such places today, but probably a caravansary, a kind of inn known among eastern peoples where caravans rest for the night; a covered place where travelers slept and prepared their food, while their animals, after being unharnessed, were tethered nearby. If such was the inn in Bethlehem, as seems probable, then the Jewish Messiah was symbolically rejected by his people even in birth, as they relegated his travailing mother to a bed of straw with the beasts of burden rather than make room for her among the camping members of the human race.

How Messiah Became Mortal

Messiah is the firstborn Spirit Son of Elohim. How came he into mortality that he then might be raised in immortality and become like his Father in the full and eternal sense? What was the process by which he traveled from his primeval spirit home to that state of resurrected glory which he now possesses, and in which he has received "all power . . . in heaven and in earth"? (Matt. 28:18.)

In most respects his coming was comparable to that of all mortals; in one respect—and oh, how vital this is!—his coming was singled out and set apart and different from that of any other person who ever has or ever will dwell on earth. That the true account of his coming might be had among the faithful, Matthew begins his recitation of how the Messiah became mortal; how he took upon himself flesh and blood; how he made clay his tabernacle; how our Elder Brother in the spirit took upon himself that mortality which we all undergo—that all this might be known, Matthew commences his account by saying: "Now the birth of Jesus Christ was on this wise," and then follows a recitation of what took place.

Thus, the Messiah was born! On the one hand, his birth was like that of all men; on the other it was unique, unlike that of any of the infinite hosts of our Father's children. And so Matthew says: "When as his mother Mary was espoused to Joseph, before they came together, she was found with child of the Holy Ghost." The marriage discipline of the day called, in effect, for two ceremonies. The participating parties were considered to be husband and wife after the first ceremony, comparable to a formal engagement in our culture, but they did not commence their association as husband and wife until the final marriage ceremony, which often was performed an appreciable period later. It was during this period that Mary "was found with child," a situation that would cause great embarrassment and sorrow among those who believed in and followed the divine laws of chastity and virtue.

Thus the record says: "Then Joseph her husband, being a just man, and not willing to make her a publick example, was minded to put her away privily"—a reaction that dramatizes the compassion and spiritual stature of the one destined to be the foster father of our Lord—"But while he thought on these things, behold, the angel of the Lord appeared unto him in a dream, saying, Joseph, thou son of David, fear not to take unto thee Mary thy wife: for that which is conceived in her is of the Holy Ghost. And she shall bring forth a son, and thou shalt call his name JESUS: for he shall save his people from their sins. . . . Then Joseph being raised from sleep did as the angel of the Lord had bidden him, and took unto him his wife: And knew her not till she had brought forth her firstborn son: and he called his name JESUS." (Matt. 1:18-25.)

Jesus was thus conceived in the womb of Mary. He took upon himself the nature of man in the same way that all men do. And yet the account is particular to say Mary "was found with child of the Holy Ghost," and "that which is conceived in her is of the Holy Ghost." If this is interpreted to mean that the Holy Ghost is the Father of our Lord, we can only say the record has come down to us in a corrupted form, for the Holy Spirit and the Father are two separate personages. But providentially there are parallel passages that clarify and expand upon the paternity of Him whom Mary bare.

The Messianic language of Abinadi, speaking of things to come as though they had already happened, says: "He was conceived by the power of God." (Mosiah 15:3.)

Gabriel's great proclamation to Mary was: "Behold, thou shalt conceive in thy womb, and bring forth a son, and shalt call his name JESUS. He shall be great, and shall be called the Son of the Highest: and the Lord God shall give unto him the throne of his father David: And he shall reign over the house of Jacob for ever; and of his kingdom there shall be no end." Mary asked how this could be, "seeing I know not a man?" Gabriel replied: "The Holy Ghost shall come upon thee, and the power of the Highest shall overshadow thee: therefore also that holy thing which shall be born of thee shall be called the Son of God." (Luke 1:31-35.)

All ambiguity and uncertainty of meaning, if there is any, is removed by Alma, whose Messianic utterance announced: "The Son of God cometh upon the face of the earth. And behold, he shall be born of Mary, . . . she being a virgin, a precious and chosen vessel, who shall be overshadowed and conceive by the power of the Holy Ghost, and bring forth a son, yea, even the Son of God." (Alma 7:9-10.) Jesus, thus, is the Son of God, not of the Holy Ghost, and properly speaking Mary was with child "by the power of the Holy Ghost," rather than "of the Holy Ghost," and she was, of course, "overshadowed" by the Holy Spirit, in a way incomprehensible to us, when the miraculous conception took place.

"A Virgin Shall Conceive"

An easy heresy to grow into would be that since the Messiah is a God; since he is the Eternal One, the Lord Jehovah, who created all things; since he has all power, all might, and all dominion—and yet must be born among men—surely he must have more than a mortal woman as a mother. High prelates and persons of note and influence in the Catholic fold have argued that Mary should be proclaimed co-redemptrix with Christ, making her bear equally with him the sins of the world. But lest there be any misconceptions in the minds of men, the Messianic messages are pointed and clear as to the person and status of the one chosen to be the mother of God's Son.

In extolling his maternal source, a certain woman said to Jesus, "Blessed is the womb that bare thee, and the paps which thou hast sucked." Our Lord's response admitted the blessed status of her to whom Gabriel had truly said, "Blessed art thou among women" (Luke 1:28), but adroitly turned the thinking of the conversationalist away from undue adoration and toward that which all men must do to be saved. He said: "Yea rather, blessed are they that hear the word of God, and keep it." (Luke 11:27-28.)

Mary's name and appointment to be the chief mother in Israel were known and discussed by them of old. Ammon testified: "I have seen my Redeemer; and he shall come forth, and be born of a woman, and he shall redeem all mankind who believe on his name." (Alma 19:13.) Jeremiah proclaimed: "The Lord hath created a new thing in the earth, A woman shall compass a man." (Jer. 31:22.) The angelic preacher who taught the doctrine of the atonement to King Benjamin said: "He shall be called Jesus Christ, the Son of God, . . . and his mother shall be called Mary." (Mosiah 3:8.) As we have already seen, Alma called her Mary and spoke of her as "a virgin, a precious and chosen vessel" (Alma 7:10); she herself told Gabriel she had never known a man (Luke 1:34), and Matthew left us the witness that she was with child before she and Joseph had associated together as man and wife (Matt. 1:18-25). The great Biblical pronouncement as to the virgin birth comes, of course, from Isaiah, who foretold: "A virgin shall conceive, and bear a son, and shall call his name Immanuel." (Isa. 7:14.) Matthew tells us this prophecy was fulfilled in the birth of Jesus. (Matt. 1:22-23.) And Nephi bears a like testimony, as we shall now see in discussing the condescension of God. (1 Ne. 11:13-19.) For our present purposes, suffice it to say that our Lord was born of a virgin, which is fitting and proper, and also natural, since the Father of the Child was an Immortal Being.

"Knowest Thou the Condescension of God?"

Nearly six hundred years before Mary was with child of God, by the power of the Holy Ghost, Nephi saw in vision what would transpire in time's meridian. "I beheld the city of Nazareth," he says, "and in the city of Nazareth I beheld a virgin, and she was exceedingly fair and white." Clearly the vision was intended to show the high and holy place of Mary. She was foreordained. There is only one Mary, even as there is only one Christ. We may suppose that she was more highly endowed spiritually than any of her mortal sisters, but with it all, she was a mortal, not a God. Her mission was to bring the Son of God into the world, not to redeem mankind, not to intercede for them. She was destined to be a mother, not a mediator; hers was the blessed privilege, being mortal, to bring into the world Him by whom immortality should come. And blessed is she forever!

Asked by an angel what he saw, Nephi said: "A virgin, most beautiful and fair above all other virgins." Then, from the lips of the heavenly being came this question of eternal import: "Knowest thou the condescension of God?" And since even the greatest of prophets do not know all things—their knowledge, as with the rest of us, coming line upon line and precept upon precept—Nephi responded: "I know that he loveth his children; nevertheless, I do not know the meaning of all things." Thereupon the angel answered his own question by saying: "Behold, the virgin whom thou seest is the mother of the Son of God, after the manner of the flesh."

The angelic answer is perfect. The great God, the Eternal Elohim, the Father of us all, the Supreme Being, the Maker and Upholder and Preserver of all things, the Creator of the sidereal heavens, the One whose might and omnipotence we can scarcely glimpse and cannot begin to comprehend, this Holy Being to whom we, by comparison, are as the dust of the earth, this Almighty Personage, in his love, mercy, and grace, condescended to step down from his Almighty throne, to step down to a lesser and benighted state, as it were, and become the Father of a Son "after the manner of the flesh."

"And it came to pass that I beheld," Nephi writes, "that she was carried away in the Spirit; and after she had been carried away in the Spirit for the space of a time the angel spake unto me, saying: Look! And I looked and beheld the virgin again, bearing a child in her arms. And the angel said unto me: Behold the Lamb of God, yea, even the Son of the Eternal Father!" This then is the condescension of God—that a God should beget a man; that an Immortal Parent should father a mortal Son; that the Creator of all things from the beginning should step down from his high state of exaltation and be, for a moment, like one of the creatures of his creating.

Later the angelic ministrant bade Nephi to look and behold the condescension of God, meaning this time that of the Son, and Nephi did so, seeing the persecutions and trials of the Redeemer of the world as he, in condescension, ministered among his fellow mortals. (1 Ne. 11:13-36.)

Messiah Is the Only Begotten

We have spoken plainly of our Lord's conception in the womb of Mary; in reality the plain assertions are found in the revealed word, and we have but certified that the words mean what they say and cannot be spiritualized away. And as it is with reference to our Lord's mother, so it is as pertaining to his Father. The scriptures say that Jesus Christ is the Only Begotten Son. The problem is that the intellectually led ministry and laity of the day assume, as Satan leads them to do, that a name-title of this sort is simply figurative and does not have the same literal meaning as when the words are spoken in ordinary conversation. Perhaps again the best service we can render, on the issue here involved, is somehow to get the message across that words mean what they say, and that if Christ is the Only Begotten of the Father, it means just that.

Some words scarcely need definition. They are on every tongue and are spoken by every voice. The very existence of intelligent beings presupposes and requires their constant use. Two such words are *father* and *son.* Their meaning is known to all, and to define them is but to repeat them. Thus: A son is a son is a son, and a father is a father is a father. I am the son of my father and the father of my sons. They are my sons because they were begotten by me, were conceived by their mother, and came forth from her womb to breathe the breath of mortal life, to dwell for a time and a season among other mortal men.

And so it is with the Eternal Father and the mortal birth of the Eternal Son. The Father is a Father is a Father; he is not a spirit essence or nothingness to which the name Father is figuratively applied. And the Son is a Son is a Son; he is not some transient emanation from a divine essence, but a literal, living offspring of an actual Father. God is the Father; Christ is the Son. The one begat the other. Mary provided the womb from which the Spirit Jehovah came forth, tabernacled in clay, as all men are, to dwell among his fellow spirits whose births were brought to pass in like manner. There is no need to spiritualize away the plain meaning of the scriptures. There is nothing figurative or hidden or beyond comprehension in our Lord's coming into mortality. He is the Son of God in the same sense and way that we are the sons of mortal fathers. It is just that simple. Christ was born of Mary. He is the Son of God—the Only Begotten of the Father.

These are points upon which we need not elaborate. The concordances to the Standard Works list the numerous references involved. Let us quote but one Messianic prophecy from the Old Testament and one from the Book of Mormon. We suppose this declaration in one of the Messianic Psalms is plain enough: "Thou art my Son," is the voice of the Father to the Messiah; "this day have I begotten thee." (Ps. 2:7.) And certainly there can be no gainsaying these words of Nephi: "When the day cometh that the Only Begotten of the Father, yea, even the Father of heaven and of earth, shall manifest himself unto them in the flesh, behold, they will reject him, because of their iniquities, and the hardness of their hearts, and the stiffness of their necks. Behold, they will crucify him; and after he is laid in a sepulchre for the space of three days he shall rise from the dead, with healing in his wings; and all those who shall believe on his name shall be saved in the kingdom of God." (2 Ne. 25:12-13.)

What Is the Doctrine of Divine Sonship?

When, on the mount, "the veil was taken from off the eyes of the brother of Jared," that worthy "saw the finger of the Lord; and it was as the finger of a man, like unto flesh and blood." In fear and wonder he exclaimed, "I knew not that the Lord had flesh and blood." In response Jehovah said, "I shall take upon me flesh and blood. . . . This body, which ye now behold, is the body of my spirit; . . . and even as I appear unto thee to be in the spirit will I appear unto my people in the flesh." To this account Moroni appends this comment: "Jesus showed himself unto this man in the spirit, even after the manner and in the likeness of the same body even as he showed himself unto the Nephites." (Ether 3:16-17.) That is to say, as a spirit being, as a mortal being, and as a resurrected being, our Lord appeared to be and was the same except for the putting on and taking off of the house provided for his spirit.

When this Jesus, seen thus by Moriancumer, came in the flesh, he was born as God's Son. His birth was the birth of a God. He came as the Offspring of the Father. The Messianic promise was: "God should come down among the children of men, and take upon him flesh and blood, and go forth upon the face of the earth." (Mosiah 7:27.) The fulfillment is recorded in these words: "And the Word was made flesh, and dwelt among us, (and we beheld his glory, the glory as of the only begotten of the Father,) full of grace and truth." (John 1:14.) Isaiah's prophecies that identify the Messiah as both God and the Son of God include these two: "For unto us a child is born, unto us a son is given: and the government shall be upon his shoulder: and his name shall be called Wonderful, Counseller, The Mighty God, The everlasting Father, The Prince of Peace. Of the increase of his government and peace there shall be no end, upon the throne of David, and upon his kingdom to order it, and to establish it with judgment and with justice from henceforth and for ever." (Isa. 9:6-7.) Also, Isaiah said that the name of the Child born to the virgin should be "Emmanuel," which means "God with us." (Matt. 1:23.)

"Thou, being a man, makest thyself God," was the charge hurled at Jesus by certain Jews who "took up stones again to stone him." The basis of this charge was our Lord's sermon, which included these assertions: "I am the good shepherd: the good shepherd giveth his life for the sheep. . . . As the Father knoweth me, even so know I the Father: and I lay down my life for the sheep. . . . Therefore doth my Father love me, because I lay down my life, that I might take it again. No man taketh it from me, but I lay it down of myself. I have power to lay it down, and I have power to take it again. This commandment have I received of my Father. . . . I and my Father are one." (John 10.)

What, then, is the doctrine of the divine Sonship? It is:

1. That God was his Father, from which Immortal Per-

sonage (who has a body of flesh and bones as tangible as man's) he inherited the power of immortality, which is the power to live forever; or, having chosen to die, it is the power to rise again in immortality, thereafter to live forever without again seeing corruption; and

2. That Mary was his mother, from which mortal woman (who was like all other women as pertaining to her mortality) he inherited the power of mortality, which is the power to die, the power to separate body and spirit, the one going back to the dust whence it came and the other going to a world of waiting spirits, there to remain until the trump of God calls both body and spirit forth.

It was because of this doctrinal reality, this intermixture of the divine and the mortal in one person, that our Lord was able to work out the infinite and eternal atonement. Because God was his Father and Mary was his mother, he had power to live or to die, as he chose, and having laid down his life, he had power to take it again, and then, in a way incomprehensible to us, to pass on the effects of that resurrection to all men so that all shall rise from the tomb.

"Who Shall Declare His Generation?"

Who shall give the genealogy of the Messiah? Who shall tell the Source whence he sprang? Who can name his ancestors and tell the progenitors who preceded him? What of his Father and mother, his grandparents? Who shall declare his beginning, his genesis, his generation?

Matthew begins his gospel by saying, "The book of the generation of Jesus Christ, the son of David." Thereupon he names an apparent genealogical line from Abraham to "Joseph the husband of Mary, of whom was born Jesus, who is called Christ." (Matt. 1:1-17.) Luke starts with Joseph and travels genealogically back to Adam without conforming to Matthew's account. (Luke 3:23-28.) Scholars are unable to unravel or bring into harmony the accounts here involved, and we have not been told by revelation the specifics of our Lord's ancestry. There is no way from a historical standpoint to search out the generation of Christ. One of the Biblical accounts may be the genealogy of Mary, the other of Joseph; one may assay to set forth kingly descent, the other give the lineal ancestry. We do not know. The only point upon which there is surety is the fact that Mary was his mother and God was his Father; other than that, his generation, his genesis, his beginnings are lost in antiquity except for a few obvious facts, as we shall now note.

"Blessed is he [Noah] through whose seed Messiah shall come," the Lord said to Enoch. We know in general terms and within a broad framework who some of his ancestors were. Manifestly he is a descendant of Adam, the first man. Indeed, the first Messianic prophecy of which we have record was spoken to Eve, "the mother of all living" (Gen. 3:20), while she and Adam were yet in Eden's garden. "I will put enmity between thee and the woman," the Lord said to Lucifer, "between thy seed and her seed; and he shall bruise thy head, and thou shalt bruise his heel." (Moses 4:21.) Ever since, the seed of Satan, those who follow him, have thwarted and plagued the Lord's work, as far as in them lay, with the ultimate triumph and success in the great warfare of life being reserved for Him as he crushes Satan and his followers under his heel.

Manifestly our Lord's descent, going downward, is Adam, Seth, Enos, Cainan, Mahalaleel, Jared, Enoch, Methuselah, Lamech, and Noah. It was to Noah that the Lord said, "With thee will I establish my covenant, even as I have sworn unto thy father Enoch, that of thy posterity shall come all nations." (JST, Gen. 8:23.) After Noah we go down through Shem to Abraham, Isaac, Jacob, and Judah. In that tribe we center in David, and then the problem of tracing descent is beyond our ability to solve.

But perhaps Isaiah's query "Who shall declare his generation?" has a greater Messianic meaning than is found in a mere attempt to trace genealogical ancestry. It is a true principle that "no man can say [or, rather, know] that Jesus is the Lord, but by the Holy Ghost." (1 Cor. 12:3.) The testimony of Jesus, which is also the spirit of prophecy, is to know by personal revelation that Jesus Christ is the Son of the living God. In the full and complete sense of the word no one ever knows that Jesus is Lord of all except by personal revelation; and all persons to whom that testimony or revelation comes are then able to declare His generation, to assert from a standpoint of personal knowledge that they know that Mary is his mother and God is his Father. And so, in the final analysis it is the faithful saints, those who have testimonies of the truth and divinity of this great latter-day work, who declare our Lord's generation to the world. Their testimony is that Mary's son is God's Son; that he was conceived and begotten in the normal way; that he took upon himself mortality by the natural birth processes; that he inherited the power of mortality from his mother and the power of immortality from his Father—in consequence of all of which he was able to work out the infinite and eternal atonement. This is their testimony as to his generation and mission.

Chapter 26

MESSIAH MINISTERS AS A MORTAL

Why Messiah Ministered Among Mortals

To minister is to act in the name and place and stead of another in teaching those truths and performing those acts which are necessary for the salvation of those on whose behalf the ministerial service is rendered. We are the Lord's agents and represent him in administering salvation by teaching his truths and performing his ordinances. We stand in his place and stead, and act in his name, in doing for others what they cannot do for themselves. He in like manner came to earth to minister in his Father's name, power, and authority for and on behalf of all mankind, all of whom are our Father's children. He came as the Father's agent and representative to do for all men one thing that no other man, and no group of men, could do for themselves, and to do many things that no one else could do as well as he did them. His earthly ministerial service may be summarized under these heads:

1. *He came to atone for the sins of the world.*

This is the chief and crowning purpose of his earthly sojourn, the one thing none other could do. It required a mortal man who possessed the power of immortality because God was his Father. No other person or power could take captivity captive, could raise all men in immortality, with those who believe and obey ascending to heights of glory and exaltation. The concepts here involved are spread throughout this whole work and are considered particularly in Chapters 13 and 25.

2. *He came to reveal his Father.*

To gain salvation, men must worship and serve the true God and him only. He is the Father, and he was in Christ manifesting himself to the world. Matthew, Mark, Luke, and John, the four New Testament Gospels, contain more revealed truth about the nature and kind of being that God is than all the rest of the scriptures combined, simply because they reveal the personality, powers, and perfections of the Son of God, who is in the express image and likeness of the Father. The mere fact of knowing the Son and those things which unto him do appertain is of itself sufficient to reveal and identify the Father, because they are like each other in personality and appearance and in character, perfections, and attributes. Hence, the saying of Jesus, "He that hath seen me hath seen the Father." (John 14:9.)

3. *He came to testify of himself.*

Faith in the Lord Jesus Christ, founded as it is on the fact that God is his Father, is the first principle of the gospel. It is the beginning point on the path to salvation. Salvation is in Christ and no other. He alone made it available according to the terms and conditions of the Father's plan. Hence, he came to testify of his own divine Sonship, as set forth, among other places, in Chapter 9 herein.

4. *He came to set a perfect example for all men.*

This we have set forth in Chapter 12. Christ is our Pattern, our Exemplar, the One we must imitate if we are to become one in him as he is one in his Father.

5. *He came to teach the gospel, set up the kingdom, bless those among whom he ministered, and perform the ordinances of salvation.*

It is now our purpose, as we shall set forth in this and the next two chapters, to inquire into those things in his teaching and ministry which were known to and foretold by those who testified of his coming. The foreknown details of his mortal ministry are more than a miracle. Their recitation in ancient Messianic writ makes us wonder if some of the ancient prophets did not then know as much about his future mortal life as we now know with the records of the past open before us. In any event, that Power which knows the end from the beginning and is pleased to let faithful men know in advance all things pertaining to their salvation which they are prepared to receive, that Omnipotent Power revealed to his prophets a great reservoir of detail about the daily life of the only perfect life ever lived. We shall now sample the sayings of the seers relative to the life of our Savior.

What Manner of Man Was the Messiah?

We know very little about the personality, form, visage, and general appearance of the Lord Jesus. Whether he had long or short hair, was tall or short of stature, and a thousand other personal details, are all a matter of speculation and uncertainty. We suppose he was similar in appearance to other Abrahamic Orientals of his day, and that he was recognized by those who knew him and went unheeded in the crowds by those unacquainted with him. A Judas was needed to identify him to the arresting officers; people spoke of him as though he were the carpenter's son; and he seemingly appeared as other men do. Perhaps the New Testament is silent on these points because it is more important to center attention on the principles poured forth than on the physical appearance of the Person who pronounced them. Perhaps also it makes it easier for us to dwell on his moral stature rather than any bodily perfection he may have had, and it certainly is a deterrent to the making of those graven images which apostate peoples so anxiously desire to venerate.

We suppose that a knowledge of these personal matters—his appearance, demeanor, and familial relationships—was also withheld from the ancients. Their

JOHN C. NELSON, M.D.

A PROFESSIONAL CORPORATION

Eye Physician and Surgeon

Mountain West Physician's Plaza

3465 South 4155 West
West Valley City, Utah 84120

Hours by Appointment
Phone (801)966-0081

NAME Joseph Porter DATE 12-20-89

℞

	SPH.	CYL.	AXIS	PRISM	BASE	VERTEX	VISION
O.D.	-3.25						
O.S.	-4.00						

ADD O.D.	
O.S.	

BIFOCAL STYLE ____________

TRI-FOCALS ☐

PLASTIC LENSES ☐

TINT ☐

.... M.D.

Messianic prophecies, at least, also draw a reverent veil of silence over many things in the realm of human interest. There are, however, two passages that do have a general bearing on his physical and human nature: one is in Isaiah, the other in the Psalms. These we should note, leaving in part at least to each person the problem of application and interpretation, for we too are bound to maintain the same curtain of dimness over those things upon which our ancient counterparts have not seen fit to dwell.

Of the Promised Messiah, Isaiah said: "He shall grow up before him as a tender plant, and as a root out of dry ground: he hath no form nor comeliness; and when we shall see him, there is no beauty that we should desire him." (Isa. 53:2.) Would it be amiss to interpret these words of our Messianic friend somewhat along these lines:

"He," the Messiah, "shall grow up before him," his Father; that is the growing, maturing, aging processes shall follow their normal course. We know he was born; we know he suckled at Mary's breasts; the record speaks of him as a "young child." (Matt. 2:11.) We know he "grew up with his brethren" (JST, Matt. 3:24), and that when he was about thirty years of age he began a strenuous full-time mission that would tax the strength of the most physically powerful of men. During that ministry we read of him eating and drinking; of his being hungry, tired, and thirsty; of his walking long distances, climbing high mountains, and sleeping soundly amid storms and terrors. We know he was smitten, scourged, and crucified, and that nails pierced his hands and feet and a spear was thrust into his side. There can be no doubt that he grew up and lived as other men live, subject to the ills and troubles of mortality.

"He shall grow up . . . as a tender plant, and as a root out of a dry ground"—"not like a stately tree, but like a lowly plant, struggling in arid soil. So the human life of the Messiah was one of obscurity and humility." (*Dummelow,* p. 446.) Or: "Messiah grew silently and insensibly, as a sucker from an ancient stock, seemingly dead (*viz.,* the house of

David, then in a decayed state)." (*Jamieson,* p. 490.) Or: Perhaps better still, he grew up as a choice and favored plant whose strength and achievement did not come because of the arid social culture in which he dwelt; it was not poured into him by the erudition of Rabbinical teachers; but it came from the divine Source whence he sprang, for as the Inspired Version has it, "He spake not as other men, neither could he be taught; for he needed not that any man should teach him." (JST, Matt. 3:25.)

"He hath no form nor comeliness; and when we shall see him, there is no beauty that we should desire him." There is no mystique, no dynamic appearance, no halo around his head, thunders do not roll and lightnings do not flash at his appearance. He is the Son of the Highest, but he walks and appears as the offspring of the lowest. He is a man among men, appearing, speaking, dressing, seeming in all outward respects as they are.

When he was a young child, not yet three years of age, Joseph being warned in a dream so to do, the Offspring of the Most High was taken into Egypt to escape Herod's executioners. Egypt was chosen as the place of temporary exile, so that upon his return, while he was still in his youth, the Messianic utterance might be fulfilled which says, "Out of Egypt have I called my son." (Hosea 11:1.) The slaughter of the innocent children of Bethlehem fulfilled Jeremiah's prophecy that Rachel should weep for her children and not be comforted (Jer. 31:15), and the fact that he was taken to Nazareth to live and grow and mature fulfilled the words of an unknown prophet, "He shall be called a Nazarene" (Matt. 2).

From one of the great Messianic Psalms we extract these references, spoken of the mortal life of the Messiah. "Thou art fairer than the children of men." This language, in the light of Isaiah's comments about our Lord's lack of comeliness, is not to be interpreted as meaning that Jesus was overly beautiful or handsome in appearance. Dictionary definitions of *fair* include the following: "Clean; pure; spotless; as, a fair name." Also: "Characterized by frankness, honesty impartiality, or candor; just." Any such usage has obvious meaning as applied to the Lord Jesus.

"Grace is poured into thy lips," the Psalmist continues, meaning the Messiah would have great powers of speech, and "therefore God hath blessed thee for ever." The kingship, "truth and meekness and righteousness," of the Messiah are then extolled, followed by these two verses: "Thy throne, O God, is for ever and ever: the sceptre of thy kingdom is a right sceptre. Thou lovest righteousness, and hatest wickedness: therefore God, thy God, hath anointed thee with the oil of gladness above thy fellows," which verses are quoted by Paul in Hebrews 1:8-9 and applied to Christ. The oil of gladness is a token of gladness, as used anciently in feast times or other times of solemn joy. The Psalm then continues in Messianic vein. (Ps. 45.)

"Prepare Ye the Way of the Lord"

Messiah's mortal ministry among men did not come unannounced. His was to be no secret mission; his message was not to be limited to a chosen few. His coming was no surprise to those who read the prophets and who rejoiced in the library of inspired literature in which the Messianic teachings were recorded.

For four thousand years all the holy prophets had foreseen, foreknown, and foretold what was to be in time's meridian. Each inspired witness of a coming Lord had told what people in his day and in all days should do to prepare for the divine advent. Alma, for instance, though a continent and a century removed from the Personal Presence who would dwell in the land of Canaan, said to his Nephite brethren such things as: "Repent ye, and prepare the way of the Lord, and walk in his paths, which are straight; for behold, the kingdom of heaven is at hand, and the Son of God cometh upon the face of the earth." (Alma 7:9) Also: "Not many days hence the Son of God shall come in his glory;

and his glory shall be the glory of the Only Begotten of the Father, full of grace, equity, and truth, full of patience, mercy, and long-suffering, quick to hear the cries of his people and to answer their prayers. And behold, he cometh to redeem those who will be baptized unto repentance, through faith on his name. Therefore, prepare ye the way of the Lord, for the time is at hand that all men shall reap a reward of their works, according to that which they have been, . . . and ye ought to bring forth works which are meet for repentance." (Alma 9:26-30.) That is to say, the way for men to prepare for the advent of their coming Lord, regardless of the day in which they lived, was to believe his gospel, repent of all their sins, be baptized for their remission, and then keep his commandments! And as it was with his first coming, so it is among us today as we prepare for his return: the voice of preparation has again been heard, and it is a voice of repentance and baptism and righteousness.

It is common, however, to speak of one prophet in particular as the forerunner of our Lord, because he is the one who proclaimed the message of preparation at the very hour when the Son of God came forth to commence his ministry. That prophet is John, John the Baptist—so named, not alone because he baptized repentant souls in great numbers, for many there were and many there are who have performed such sacred ordinances in great numbers, but because he alone baptized the Messiah himself.

Isaiah, speaking in measured tones of both the first and the second advents of our Lord, and with greater emphasis on the final glorious appearing, proclaimed a message of comfort and peace to the remnants of Israel. Among other things, he spoke of "the voice of him that crieth in the wilderness, Prepare ye the way of the Lord, make straight in the desert a highway for our God." (Isa. 40:1-11.) Malachi, speaking also of both comings but more particularly of the great and dreadful day yet ahead, gave forth the Lord's promise in these words: "Behold, I will send my messenger, and he shall prepare the way before me." (Mal. 3:1-6.)

Our Lord himself applied Malachi's prophecy to John by saying: "This is he, of whom it is written, Behold, I send my messenger before thy face, which shall prepare thy way before thee," to which pronouncement he added this testimony relative to his cousin and forerunner: "Among them that are born of women there hath not risen a greater than John the Baptist: notwithstanding, he that is [considered] least in the kingdom of heaven [that is, I myself] is greater than he." (Matt. 11:9-11.)

Matthew, writing of John's preparatory preaching and of the baptism of Jesus, said: "In those days came John the Baptist, preaching in the wilderness of Judea, And saying, Repent ye: for the kingdom of heaven is at hand. For this is he that was spoken of by the prophet Esaias, saying, The voice of one crying in the wilderness, Prepare ye the way of the Lord, make his paths straight." (Matt. 3:1-3.)

Hearing John's message, the people asked, "What shall we do then?" His answers were specific. Already they had been told to repent. Now the word came, "He that hath two coats, let him impart to him that hath none; and he that hath meat, let him do likewise." To the publicans he added, "Exact no more than that which is appointed you," and to the soldiers, "Do violence to no man, neither accuse any falsely; and be content with your wages"—that is to say, having repented and been baptized, now work the works of righteousness that you may be prepared for the fellowship of Him who is to follow. Thus Luke says, "And as the people were in expectation, and all men mused in their hearts of John, whether he were the Christ, or not; John answered, saying unto them all, I indeed baptize you with water; but one mightier than I cometh, the latchet of whose shoes I am not worthy to unloose: he shall baptize you with the Holy Ghost and with fire." (Luke 3:10-16.)

That these prophetic words of Isaiah and Malachi apply with force and vigor to John and his mission (though in their contexts they are oriented primarily toward the latter appearing of our Lord) is also borne out by Nephi, who recorded that his father Lehi "spake also concerning a prophet who should come before the Messiah, to prepare the way of the Lord—Yea, even he should go forth and cry in the wilderness: Prepare ye the way of the Lord, and make his paths straight; for there standeth one among you whom ye know not; and he is mightier than I, whose shoe's latchet I am not worthy to unloose." (1 Ne. 10:7-8.)

Why Jesus Was Baptized

Since baptism always has been and always will be singled out as the symbol and token of conversion to the gospel; since those who believe and are baptized shall be saved, while those who do not believe and are not baptized shall be damned; since baptism is the way earth's inhabitants receive the sanctifying power of the Holy Ghost and gain the constant companionship of that Holy Spirit; and since the Messiah came to earth to work out his own salvation, as well as to make salvation available to all men—we are justified in concluding that he himself needed baptism, and that the ancient prophets foreknew such would be the case. Indeed, the fact that baptism would apply to him as well as to all others is inherent in the whole scheme of things.

If we had the teachings of all the prophets, there is no question we would find our Lord's mortal baptism referred to by many of them. The Book of Mormon gives us our direction in this regard. In recording his father's teaching that a prophet should prepare the way before the Messiah, Nephi included these words: "My father said he [our Lord's forerunner] should baptize in Bethabara, beyond Jordan; and he also said he should baptize with water; even that he should baptize the Messiah with water. And after he had baptized the Messiah with water, he should behold and bear record that he had baptized the Lamb of God, who should take away the sins of the world." (1 Ne. 10:9-10.) Since Isaiah foreknew and wrote of this same prophetic preparation for the mortal labors of the Messiah, we may suppose that he also knew that Jesus would be baptized by the one sent to prepare the way before him.

Indeed, baptism is the very thing that prepares men for ministerial service, and why should anyone think that the Chief Minister of all other ministers would forgo the blessings which attend the performance of such a sacred and holy ordinance?

As we have seen, baptism, with its purifying power, prepared men for the coming of their Lord in the meridian of time. As we are also aware, this same ordinance purifies and prepares men for the Second Coming of the Son of Man. And as we also know, baptism has prepared and does prepare all of the Lord's agents for their ministerial service. Does it come then as a surprise to find Jesus undergoing that same ordinance to prepare him for his formal ministry?

When the time for his ministry had arrived, Jesus came "from Galilee to Jordan"—"in Bethabara beyond Jordan," John says (John 1:28)—"unto John, to be baptized of him. But John forbad him, saying, I have need to be baptized of thee, and comest thou to me? And Jesus answering said unto him, Suffer it to be so now: for thus it becometh us to fulfil all righteousness. Then he suffered him. And Jesus, when he was baptized, went up straightway out of the water: and, lo, the heavens were opened to him, and he [John the Baptist] saw the Spirit of God descending like a dove, and lighting upon him: And lo a voice from heaven, saying, This is my beloved Son, in whom I am well pleased." (Matt. 3:13-17.)

So speaks the sacred script. Our Lord is baptized! In a miraculous manner the forerunner who performed the ordinance sees the heavens open and the personage of the Holy Ghost come down: "I saw the Spirit descending from heaven like a dove, and it abode upon him." (John 1:32.) How closely these solemn occurrences conform to what Lehi and Nephi had seen in vision more than six centuries before! "And I looked and beheld the Redeemer of the world, of whom my father had spoken," Nephi said, "and I also beheld the prophet who should prepare the way before him. And the Lamb of God went forth and was baptized of him; and after he was baptized, I beheld the heavens open, and the Holy Ghost come down out of heaven and abide upon him in the form of a dove." (1 Ne. 11:27.)

In a passage of surpassing literary and doctrinal excellence, Nephi sets forth the rationale underlying the baptism of a sinless and perfect Being, one who had no need to be baptized for the remission of sins, for he had none. "If the Lamb of God, he being holy, should have need to be baptized by water, to fulfil all righteousness, O then, how much more need have we, being unholy, to be baptized, yea, even by water!" he reasons.

Then comes the query: "And now, I would ask of you, my beloved brethren, wherein the Lamb of God did fulfil all righteousness in being baptized by water?" That is, why be baptized for the remission of sins that do not exist? What divine providence is fulfilled, what righteous purpose is served under such circumstances? "Know ye not that he was holy?" Nephi continues. "But notwithstanding he being holy, he showeth unto the children of men that, according to the flesh he humbleth himself before the Father, and witnesseth unto the Father that he would be obedient unto him in keeping his commandments."

Our Lord was baptized as a token of humility. Can the proud and the mighty of the earth expect to do less in subjecting themselves to the divine will? By baptism Jesus entered into a covenant to keep the commandments; he bore record that he would conform to the will of the Father. Who among us can do less?

"Wherefore, after he was baptized with water the Holy Ghost descended upon him in the form of a dove." Such is the way and the means provided of the Father for mortals to receive the constant companionship of his Holy Spirit, and the law applies to his Only Begotten Son and to all his other children.

"And again, it showeth unto the children of men the

straightness of the path, and the narrowness of the gate, by which they should enter, he having set the example before them." The Great I Am, the Almighty Jehovah, the Messiah, the very Son of God, the King of the kingdom, he who presides supreme in his own celestial realm, even he cannot return from mortality to his state of eternal glory without entering in at the gate, the gate of baptism. "Except a man be born of water and of the Spirit, he cannot enter into the kingdom of God." (John 3:5.) The Lord Jesus, being a man, required baptism, even as other men. There is no other way.

"And he said unto the children of men: Follow thou me. Wherefore, my beloved brethren, can we follow Jesus save we shall be willing to keep the commandments of the Father? And the Father said: Repent ye, repent ye, and be baptized in the name of my Beloved Son. And also, the voice of the Son came unto me, saying: He that is baptized in my name, to him will the Father give the Holy Ghost, like unto me; wherefore, follow me, and do the things which ye have seen me do." (2 Ne. 31:5-12.) The great Exemplar has acted; he has marked the way. Let all men follow in his footsteps. The Holy Ghost descended upon him, and so shall it come upon all those who do as he did.

Elias Both Precedes and Attends Messiah

As I have written elsewhere (*Mormon Doctrine,* 2nd ed., pp. 219-22; *Doctrinal New Testament Commentary,* 1:128-30) the designation *Elias* is, among other things, the name of a number of different persons, a title conferred upon any prophet who performs a specified preparatory work, and a spirit and calling that attended John the Baptist. This whole matter, though complex and confusing to those who are not fully advised in the premises, is nonetheless one of considerable import to us and one that was of great concern among the Jews of Jesus' day. It is evident that they knew of some Messianic utterances that are lost to us, but which associated the ministries of Elias and Messiah. They knew that Elias would come and prepare the way before the Messiah, and also that Elias would come to restore all the might and glory and doctrine and power that their fathers in days past had possessed.

From inspired statements now available to us, we can piece together this much of the Elias picture. Gabriel came to Zacharias with the word that Elisabeth should bear a son, John the Baptist, whose ministry and work would be great in the sight of the Lord. "Many of the children of Israel shall he turn to the Lord their God," Gabriel said. "And he shall go before him"—that is, before the Lord—"in the spirit and power of Elias, to turn the hearts of the fathers to the children, and the disobedient to the wisdom of the just; to make ready a people prepared for the Lord." (Luke 1:13-17.)

This is perfectly clear. John was foreordained to go before his Lord and prepare the way. He was to prepare a people, by baptism, for their King. This he did, and it was the same thing that had been done by others before him as they sought also to prepare their people to see the face of that same Lord. "The spirit of Elias is to prepare the way for a greater revelation of God," Joseph Smith said. It "is the Priesthood of Elias, or the Priesthood that Aaron was ordained unto. And when God sends a man into the world to prepare for a greater work, holding the keys of the power of Elias, it was called the doctrine of Elias, even from the early ages of the world." (*Teachings,* pp. 335-41.)

Jewish knowledge of Messianic prophecies dealing with Elias as a forerunner and with Elias as a restorer is shown in the account of the conversation of John the Baptist with the priests and Levites who asked, "Who art thou?" The record says: "And he confessed, and denied not that he was Elias; but confessed, saying; I am not the Christ. And they asked him, saying; How then art thou Elias? And he said, I am not that Elias who was to restore all things. And they asked him, saying, Art thou that prophet? And he answered, No. Then said they unto him, Who art thou? that we may give an answer to them that sent us. What sayest thou of thyself? He said, I am the voice of one crying in the wilderness, Make straight the way of the Lord, as saith the prophet Esaias. And they who were sent were the Pharisees. And they asked him, and said unto him; Why baptizest thou then, if thou be not the Christ, nor Elias who was to restore all things, neither that prophet? John answered them, saying; I baptize with water, but there standeth one among you, whom ye know not; He it is of whom I bear record. He is that prophet, even Elias, who, coming after me, is preferred before me, whose shoe's latchet I am not worthy to unloose, or whose place I am not able to fill; for he shall baptize, not only with water, but with fire, and with the Holy Ghost." (JST, John 1:21-28.) Thus, for that day and dispensation, John is the Elias who was to prepare the way, and Jesus is the Elias who was to restore those things which had been had aforetimes.

Peter, James, and John were with Jesus in the holy mount when our Lord was transfigured before them and when Moses and Elijah, Israelite prophets who were taken into heaven without tasting death, ministered to him and to them. It was then that the Lord's apostles received from him and from Moses and Elijah (Elias) the keys of the priesthood. (*Teachings,* p. 158.) As they came down from the mountain, the three disciples asked Jesus: "Why say the scribes that Elias must first come?" That is, why do the scribes teach that Elias will precede the coming of the Lord, when in fact the Lord came first and then Elias (Elijah) came and gave the keys on this very mountain? "And Jesus answered and said unto them, Elias truly shall first come, and restore all things, as the prophets have written." This is a clear reference to some ancient prophetic utterance, known to the scribes, known to Jesus, and known to his disciples, but unknown to us. "And again I say unto you," Jesus continued, "that Elias has come already, concerning whom it is written, Behold, I will send my messenger, and he shall prepare the way before me; and they knew him not, and have done unto him, whatsoever they listed. Likewise shall also the Son of Man suffer of them. But I say unto you, Who is Elias? Behold, this is Elias, whom I sent to prepare the way before me. Then the disciples understood that he spake unto them of John the Baptist, and also of another who should come and restore all things, as it is written by the prophets." (JST, Matt. 17:1-14.)

MESSIAH MINISTERS AS A MAN OF SORROWS

Messiah Wrought Miracles

Jesus wrought miracles, as the Messiah was destined to do. If there is any one thing all Christendom knows about him, it is that he healed the sick, caused the lame to leap, unstopped deaf ears, gave sight to blind eyes, and raised the dead. The trademark of his ministry is that he made the sick and the decrepit, the lame and the palsied, the diseased and the leper to be new again. Health and sight and hearing and life returned to those whom he blessed and who in faith sought his goodness and grace. Miracles were a way of life with him. And the perfecting of the diseased, the disabled, and the decrepit was but a type of that greater healing—the making whole of sin-sick souls, the destroying of diseases of the mind, and the spiritual rebirth of those who were dead to the things of righteousness.

We need not quote or cite the inspired record to remind ourselves of such things as a certain beggar, blind from his mother's womb, who saw again because he had faith to go at Jesus' behest and wash in the pool of Siloam; or of ten lepers who shed their leprous plague because he spoke; or of Lazarus, dead four days, his body rotting and stinking in a sealed tomb, coming forth because the divine Son so decreed; or of any of the almost endless stream of health-creating acts that attended his way of life. Everyone knows that health and healings, sight and hearing, life and vigor, were everywhere because he willed it so.

Let us instead alert ourselves to the fact that the prophets of old foretold that their Messiah would perform a ministry of healing and of health-giving such as had never before been known. Healing and miracles have been common among the Lord's people from the beginning. Jehovah himself is in fact the Great Healer. "I am the Lord that healeth thee," he said to his people Israel as he promised to remove from them the diseases of Egypt. (Ex. 15:26.)

It is but natural that the prophets, feeling and knowing their Lord's healing powers, would speak of his using them when he came to earth as a mortal. Thus, in speaking of our Lord's humiliation and suffering, Isaiah says, "Surely he hath borne our griefs, and carried our sorrows." (Isa. 53:4.) Alma and Matthew both paraphrase Isaiah's words and apply them to Christ's mortal labors. Alma says, as he also speaks Messianically, "He shall go forth, suffering pains and afflictions and temptations of every kind; and this is that the word might be fulfilled which saith he will take upon him the pains and sicknesses of his people. . . . And he will take upon him their infirmities, that his bowels may be filled with mercy, according to the flesh, that he may know according to the flesh how to succor his people according to their infirmities." (Alma 7:11-12.) Matthew speaks of the fulfillment of these Messianic utterances when he says, "They brought unto him many that were possessed with devils: and he cast out the spirits with his word, and healed all that were sick: That it might be fulfilled which was spoken by Esaias the prophet, saying, Himself took our infirmities, and bare our sicknesses." (Matt. 8:16-17.)

Nephi saw in vision what Isaiah and others must also have seen. "I beheld the Lamb of God going forth among the children of men," he said. "And I beheld multitudes of people who were sick, and who were afflicted with all manner of diseases, and with devils and unclean spirits. . . . And they were healed by the power of the Lamb of God; and the devils and the unclean spirits were cast out." (1 Ne. 11:31.) The angelic ministrant who came to King Benjamin foretold that the Lord "shall come down from heaven among the children of men, and shall dwell in a tabernacle of clay, and shall go forth amongst men, working mighty miracles, such as healing the sick, raising the dead, causing the lame to walk, the blind to receive their sight, and the deaf to hear, and curing all manner of diseases. And he shall cast out devils, or the evil spirits that dwell in the hearts of the children of men." (Mosiah 3:5-6.)

What he had done as the Lord Jehovah for ancient Israel, what he did among the Jews as their mortal Messiah, he continued to do among the Nephites after he rose from the dead. "Have ye any that are sick among you?" he asked. "Bring them hither. Have ye any that are lame, or blind, or halt, or maimed, or leprous, or that are withered, or that are deaf, or that are afflicted in any manner? Bring them hither and I will heal them, for I have compassion upon you; my bowels are filled with mercy. . . . And it came to pass that when he had thus spoken, all the multitude, with one accord, did go forth with their sick and their afflicted, and their lame, and with their blind, and with their dumb, and with all them that were afflicted in any manner; and he did heal them every one as they were brought unto him." (3 Ne. 17:7-9.)

And again we say that all of our Lord's healings—dramatic and wondrous as they were—are but similitudes and types that point to the even greater reality, that through him the spiritually sick, the spiritually diseased, the sin crippled of the world, may come forth in a newness of life if they have faith in his holy name. He it is, according to the promises made to his people, who "healeth the broken heart, and bindeth up their wounds." (Ps. 147:3.) And he it is who has arisen "with healing in his wings" (Mal. 4:2; 2 Ne. 26:9), with the spiritual healing that qualifies his brethren for an inheritance with him and his Father. "The Lord openeth the eyes of the blind"—temporally and spiritually. (Ps.146:8.)

Messiah Rejected by the Jews

"I am become a stranger unto my brethren, and an alien unto my mother's children." (Ps. 69:8.) Such was the Messianic prophecy. "He came unto his own, and his own received him not." (John 1:11.) Such was the Messianic fulfillment.

What an indictment! God himself ministers among men and they reject him! His own people, his own kindred, his own house, his own nation—the very people who knew the Messianic prophecies, who read the scriptures in their synagogues each Sabbath, who offered sacrifices in similitude of his infinite sacrifice—these are the ones who closed their minds and sealed their hearts, and whose voices acclaimed: Him we will not receive, away with him, crucify him. And this, in spite of all that he did among them. He healed the sick, blind eyes saw, deaf ears heard, lame men leaped, dead men breathed anew the breath of life, stinking corpses partook again of the sweet smell of life—and yet he was rejected! A God was rejected! The one perfect man, the only member of Adam's race who did all things well, whose every act and thought was for the benefit and blessing of his fellowmen—he it was who was rejected by the bigots, the fanatics, the insanely jealous, the mad religionists, and (note it well!) the generality of those among whom he ministered.

We need not refer to the New Testament account nor to the historical recitations of uncounted authors to remind ourselves that the Jews rejected their Messiah. As with the miracles he wrought, so with the fact of his rejection—it is an established and universally known verity. It is something of which the court of world opinion takes judicial knowledge, and therefore no evidence is required to prove it. Let us, then, simply follow our established pattern of pointing out that the prophets who went before knew by the spirit of revelation that their promised Messiah would be rejected, reviled, cursed, and (as we shall note more particularly hereafter) persecuted, scourged, and finally crucified.

Let us start with our friend Isaiah, a noble soul whose preserved Messianic teachings exceed those of any of the Old Testament seers, at least when we speak of direct teachings in words and do not take into account the Messianic performances revealed through Moses. Thus saith Isaiah, or better, thus saith the Lord by the mouth of Isaiah: The Promised Messiah shall—and these words we extract from the midst of more extended Messianic pronouncements—the Promised Messiah shall be one "whom man despiseth, . . . whom the nation abhoreth, . . . a servant of rulers." (Isa. 49:7.) Also: "When I came, was there no man? when I called, was there none to answer? Is my hand shortened at all, that it cannot redeem?" (Isa. 50:2.) And further (and we are but sampling): "He is despised and rejected of men; a man of sorrows, and acquainted with grief: and we hid as it were our faces from him; he was despised, and we esteemed him not." (Isa. 53:3.)

The second Psalm is Messianic. The first two verses speak of the rejection of Jesus by the Jews in these words: "Why do the heathen rage, and the people imagine a vain thing? The kings of the earth set themselves, and the rulers take counsel together, against the Lord, and against his anointed." Habakkuk, in a passage having no immediately apparent Messianic association, records, "Behold ye among the heathen, and regard, and wonder marvellously: for I will work a work in your days, which ye will not believe, though it be told you." (Hab. 1:5.) That these words are Messianic is certified by Paul, who, in speaking of Christ, says that "through this man is preached unto you the forgiveness of sins: And by him all that believe are justified from all things, from which ye could not be justified by the law of Moses. Beware therefore, lest that come upon you, which is spoken of in the prophets; Behold, ye despisers, and wonder, and perish: for I work a work in your days, a work which ye shall in no wise believe, though a man declare it unto you." (Acts 13:38-41.) It was in this same sermon that the ancient apostle said: "They that dwell at Jerusalem, and their rulers, because they knew him not, nor yet the voices of the prophets which are read every sabbath day, they have fulfilled them in condemning him." (Acts 13:27.)

Our Nephite brethren had similar views as to how their Jewish kinsmen in Jerusalem would treat the Lord of Life who would come among them. That they expressed themselves more pointedly and clearly than did those Old Testament prophets whose words have come down to us goes almost without saying. Nephi tells us: "Even the very God of Israel do men trample under their feet; I say, trample under their feet but I would speak in other words—they set him at naught, and hearken not to the voice of his counsels. . . . And the world, because of their iniquity, shall judge him to be a thing of naught." (1 Ne. 19:7-9; 2 Ne. 25:12.) His brother Jacob said "that Christ . . . should come among the Jews, among those who are the more wicked part of the world; and they shall crucify him, . . . and there is none other nation on earth that would crucify their God. For should the mighty miracles be wrought among other nations they would repent, and know that he be their God." (2 Ne. 10:3-4; Jacob 4:15.)

How Men Reject the Messiah

We speak with wonder and horror, and properly we should, of the fact that the Jews, with the scriptures, the miracles, and the mighty works before them, yet rejected their God, and did it so violently and with such a fixed determination that they brought about his death by Roman hands. To enable us to keep our perspective, however, we need to view with fairness and dispassion how and in what manner he was rejected and ask whether he would be so treated today. As Jacob said, only the Jews, among all the then existing nations, seeing the miracles he did and being aware of the wonders he performed, would have crucified him. (1 Ne. 19:7-9.) But would others among men have rejected him, and how and in what manner do men reject so great a thing as the ministry of a God among them?

In our day, that Lord who of old was rejected by his own, in speaking of that very rejection, said: "He that receiveth my gospel receiveth me; and he that receiveth not my gospel receiveth not me." (D&C 39:1-6.) Therein is the key. When men reject a man they reject a message; when they reject a message they reject the bearer thereof. To reject Christ is to reject his gospel, and to reject his gospel is to turn one's back on him and, if the animus attending the rejection is of sufficient proportion, to trample him underfoot and cause him to be crucified.

Speaking Messianically, Isaiah asked: "Who hath believed our report? and to whom is the arm of the Lord revealed?" (Isa. 53:1.) That is to say: Who among mortals has accepted the Messiah and his message? That it was not those among whom he ministered, we read in the words of John, who said: "Though he had done so many miracles before them, yet they believed not on him: That the saying of Esaias the prophet might be fulfilled, which he spake, Lord, who hath believed our report? and to whom hath the arm of the Lord been revealed? Therefore they could not believe, because that Esaias said again"—and this itself is another Messianic utterance (Isa. 6:10)—"He hath blinded their eyes, and hardened their heart; that they should not see with their eyes, nor understand with their heart, and be converted, and I should heal them. These things said Esaias, when he saw his glory, and spake of him." (John 12:37-41.)

Paul also made the acceptance of the gospel the deciding factor in whether men accepted their Lord. Inviting men to confess the Lord Jesus with their lips and believe in their hearts that God had raised him from the dead, he said: "But they have not all obeyed the gospel. For Esaias saith, Lord, who hath believed our report?" (Rom. 10:9-17.)

It was, of course, of both the message and the Man that the Lord spoke (through Isaiah) when he said: "This people draw near me with their mouth, and with their lips do honour me, but have removed their heart far from me, and their fear toward me is taught by the precept of men." (Isa. 29:13.) Or, as the latter portion might better be translated, "And their fear toward me is a commandment of men which hath been taught them." Having in mind the many rituals, traditions, and formalities followed by the Jews in their form of worship, which imitated but did not conform to the Mosaic standard, they asked our Lord: "Why walk not thy disciples according to the tradition of the elders, but eat bread with unwashen hands?" His excoriating reply contains the perfect rendition of Isaiah's prophetic words. Jesus said: "Well hath Esaias prophesied of you hypocrites, as it is written, This people honoureth me with their lips, but their heart is far from me. Howbeit in vain do they worship me, teaching for doctrines the commandments of men." (Mark 7:1-9.)

In vain do we worship him, unless we accept him and his gospel!

We would be remiss if we did not at this point bear record that the Lord Jesus has in these last days revealed himself anew from heaven and given again the fulness of his everlasting gospel, which, if men accept, they accept him, and which, if they reject, they reject him. And the reason for rejection is the same today as it was then: "Men loved darkness rather than light, because their deeds were evil." (John 3:19.)

Messiah Oppressed, Persecuted, Mocked, Scourged

Arrested, bound, on trial for his life, our Lord was questioned by the high priest about his disciples and his doctrine. Jesus responded that his teachings had been in public, and therefore his interrogator should ask those who heard him. "When he had thus spoken, one of the officers which stood by struck Jesus with the palm of his hand, saying, Answerest thou the high priest so? Jesus answered him, If I have spoken evil, bear witness of the evil: but if well, why smitest thou me?" (John 18:12-14, 19-23.)

Later, before Caiaphas, having been mistreated and accused of blasphemy, it was said, "He is guilty of death. Then did they spit in his face, and buffeted him; and others smote him with the palms of their hands, Saying, Prophesy unto us, thou Christ, Who is he that smote thee?" (Matt. 26:57-68.)

Before Pilate for the second time, he, "willing to content the people, released Barabbas unto them, and delivered Jesus, when he had scourged him, to be crucified." (Mark 15:15-19.) "This brutal practice [of scourging], a preliminary to crucifixion, consisted of stripping the victim of clothes, strapping him to a pillar or frame, and beating him with a scourge made of leather straps weighted with sharp pieces of lead and bone. It left the tortured sufferer bleeding, weak, and sometimes dead." (*Doctrinal New Testament Commentary,* 1:807.) After the scourging, "they clothed him with purple, and platted a crown of thorns, and put it about his head, And began to salute him, Hail, King of the Jews! And they smote him on the head with a reed, and did spit on him, and bowing their knees worshipped him." (Mark 15:17-19.)

Decent men in all ages shudder at the vile and demeaning indignities heaped upon the Sinless Soul who came to save and redeem even the most degenerate of men on conditions of repentance. It shocks the souls of refined persons everywhere simply to think of the Satanic mockery, of the foul and blasphemous language, of the filthy spittle spewed in his face, of the pain wrought by piercing thorns and bloody scourge. And yet it was all part of the plan; it was all foreknown and foretold. The advance account is found in the Messianic prophecies.

"They shall smite the judge of Israel with a rod upon the cheek," Micah prophesies. (Micah 5:1.) "They gather themselves together against the soul of the righteous, and condemn the innocent blood," intones the Psalmist. (Ps. 94:21.) "We did esteem him stricken, smitten of God, and afflicted. . . . He was oppressed, and he was afflicted," Isaiah says. (Isa. 53:4, 7.) He "suffereth himself to be mocked, and scourged, and cast out, and disowned by his people," Abinadi testifies. (Mosiah 15:5.) And Nephi gives these details: "They scourge him, and he suffereth it; and they smite him, and he suffereth it. Yea, they spit upon him, and he suffereth it, because of his loving kindness and his long-suffering towards the children of men." (1 Ne. 19:9.) Through David, the Lord speaks in the first person, saying, "All that hate me whisper together against me: against me do they devise my hurt." (Ps. 41:7.) Through Isaiah, also given in the first person, the Messianic promise is: "I was not rebellious, neither turned away back. I gave my back to the smiters, and my cheeks to them that plucked off the hair: I hid not my face from shame and spitting." (Isa. 50:5-6.) And Jesus himself, speaking before the events, said to the Twelve: "Behold, we go up to Jerusalem; and the Son of Man shall be betrayed unto the chief priests and unto the scribes, and they shall condemn him to death, And shall deliver him to the Gentiles to mock, and to scourge, and to crucify him: and the third day he shall rise again." (Matt. 20:17-19.)

Messiah Suffers and Is Tempted

We take up now the philosophical question of whether a God can suffer and be tempted. We shall speak of suffering as undergoing pain of body and mind, and of being tempted as being enticed and induced to do that which is wrong with an accompanying promise of pleasure or gain. And we shall approach our problem with a full awareness that the scripture says: "God cannot be tempted with evil." (James 1:13.)

But we are not now dealing with God in his glorified and exalted state, a state in which he has overcome all things and become like all the Gods who so attained before him. We are speaking of the Lord our God as he dwelt among men; as he ate and drank and slept; as he was thirsty, hungry, and tired; as he dwelt as an earthbound mortal—not as he wafts himself in immortal glory from universe to universe.

As a mortal, Jesus our Lord was like all other mortals. He too was here to gain the experiences of earth life, to choose good rather than evil, to overcome the world, that he might rise in immortal glory and be like his Father. Pain, suffering, and temptation are an essential part of every adult probation. Without opposition we cannot overcome; and unless we overcome we cannot progress; and unless we advance and progress we cannot become like Him whose we are. Only little children who die before they arrive at the years of accountability are relieved from facing the temptations of this evil, wicked world.

It follows that the Mortal Messiah was destined to suffer pain and anguish and sorrow—"a man of sorrows, and acquainted with grief," Isaiah says (Isa. 53:3)—and that he would be tempted as all men are. That he did so is fully attested in the inspired records.

As to our Lord being tempted, Matthew tells us that Jesus was "led up of the spirit into the wilderness to be tempted of the devil." There, after a forty-day fast, weakened physically but strengthened spiritually, he met Lucifer the arch-tempter and was invited to turn stones into bread that he might feed his hunger and prove his divine Sonship. Passing this test, he was enticed to prove his divine status by casting himself from a high pinnacle and letting the angels save him from death. Then came the enticement to worship Satan in return for all the kingdoms and glory of the world. (Matt. 4:1-11.) That these temptations were real, poignant, actual tests, given to prove his devotion to the Father, we cannot doubt. Our latter-day revelation says simply: "He suffered temptations but gave no heed unto them." (D&C 20:22.)

As to our Lord suffering pain and sorrow and anguish, this is inherent in the whole account of his mortal life. He wept over doomed Jerusalem (Luke 19:41-44), the Holy City, "which spiritually is called Sodom and Egypt" (Rev. 11:8). We are aware of his physical and mental sufferings in many situations, climaxed in the agonies of Gethsemane and the cruelties of the cross—"Which suffering caused myself, even God, the greatest of all, to tremble because of pain, and to bleed at every pore, and to suffer both body and spirit," he says. (D&C 19:18.) Indeed, so much was he subject to suffering that even after his resurrection he prayed: "Father, I am troubled because of the wickedness of the people of the house of Israel" (3 Ne. 17:14), and he also said to the Nephites, "It sorroweth me because of the fourth generation from this generation, for they are led away captive" by sin and lust (3 Ne. 27:32).

Paul's Spirit-guided reasoning on the matter of the temptations and sufferings to which our Lord was subject brought forth these gospel conclusions: "Jesus," he said, came to suffer "death," and to "taste death for every man." Accordingly, Paul continues, "It became him, for whom are all things, and by whom are all things, in bringing many sons unto glory, to make the captain [leader] of their salvation perfect through sufferings." Jesus attained perfection, eternal perfection, through sufferings! And all others who so obtain must do likewise. "Wherefore in all things it behoved him [Christ] to be made like unto his brethren, that he might be a merciful and faithful high priest in things pertaining to God, to make reconciliation for the sins of the people. For in that he himself hath suffered being tempted, he is able to succour them that are tempted." (Heb. 2:10, 17-18.) "Jesus the Son of God," Paul says, is "touched with the feeling of our infirmities," because he "was in all points tempted like as we are, yet without sin." (Heb. 4:14-15.)

Peter held up our Lord's incomparably great sufferings and the manner in which he bore them as a standard for all the saints. In effect the Chief Apostle says: 'Be thou as he was, suffering all things for righteousness' sake.' "Christ also suffered for us, leaving us an example, that ye should follow his steps." It was Christ our Lord, he said, "who did no sin, neither was guile found in his mouth." It was he "who, when he was reviled, reviled not again; when he suffered, he threatened not; but committed himself to him that judgeth righteously." It was he "who his own self bare our sins in his own body on the tree, that we, being dead to sins, should live unto righteousness: by whose stripes ye were healed." (1 Pet. 2:21-24.) "Forasmuch then as Christ hath suffered for us in the flesh," Peter continues with the voice of exhortation, "arm yourselves likewise with the same mind: for he that hath suffered in the flesh hath ceased from sin; That he no longer should live the rest of his time in the flesh to the lusts of men, but to the will of God." (1 Pet. 4:1-2.) Peter concludes this part of his sayings with these words of prayer: "The God of all grace, who hath called us unto his eternal glory by Christ Jesus, after that ye have suffered a while, make you perfect, stablish, strengthen, settle you." (1 Pet. 5:10.)

It was in this same spirit that James wrote that the Immortal and Eternal God cannot be tempted. The context of his words is: "Blessed is the man that endureth temptation: for when he is tried, he shall receive the crown of life, which the Lord hath promised to them that love him. Let no man say when he is tempted, I am tempted of God: for God cannot be tempted with evil, neither tempteth he any man: But every man is tempted, when he is drawn away of his own lust, and enticed." (James 1:12-14.)

Having set forth the fact of our Lord's temptations and sufferings, and having seen the inspired doctrinal teachings based on these realities, let us now sample the Messianic utterances which spoke of them in advance. We have already used in various contexts Isaiah's pronouncements that he was a man of sorrows and acquainted with grief; that he hath borne our griefs, and carried our sorrows; that he was stricken, smitten of God, and afflicted; that he was wounded for our transgressions, and bruised for our iniquities; that with his stripes we are healed; that the Lord hath laid upon him the iniquity of us all; that he was oppressed and afflicted; that he was cut off out of the land of the living; that he was stricken for the transgression of his people; that he made his soul an offering for sin; that he bare the iniquities of many; that he poured out his soul unto death; and that he bare the sins of many—implicit in all of which is the fact of temptation, of anguish, of sorrow, of suffering. (Isa. 53.)

To these Biblical prophecies let us add the agreeing and concurring witness of the Nephite prophets. King Benjamin, quoting the angelic sermon, gives us this Messianic word: "And lo, he shall suffer temptations, and pain of body, hunger, thirst, and fatigue, even more than man can suffer, except it be unto death; for behold, blood cometh from every pore, so great shall be his anguish for the wickedness and the abominations of his people." (Mosiah 3:7.) Abinadi says, "He suffereth temptation, and yieldeth not to the temptation." (Mosiah 15:5.) Alma says, "He shall go forth, suffering pains and afflictions and temptations of every kind; and this that the word [spoken by Isaiah] might be fulfilled which saith he will take upon him the pains and the sicknesses of his people." (Alma 7:11; 16:19; 22:14.) And Samuel the Lamanite said that He "shall suffer many things and shall be slain for his people." (Hel. 13:6.)

Shall Messiah Save the Gentiles?

Those of Israel who, by the time Jesus began his ministry, had not been scattered among all people and on the isles of the sea; those who then dwelt in their promised Canaan and in Jerusalem, the city of the Great King; those who then looked for the coming of a Messiah, to save and deliver and redeem; those who considered themselves to be the chosen people and who looked upon all others as outside the pale of saving grace; those to whom the Messiah did in fact come and by whom he was summarily rejected—this race and assemblage of people believed, with a fixity and determination that could not be shaken, that their Messiah would come to save them, and them alone, and that for the Gentiles there was no hope. In their darkened state they failed utterly to understand the Messianic utterances relative to salvation going to the Gentiles, and of the Messiah being the God of the whole earth and not of them only. It is to this concept and to these scriptures that we will now give attention.

To read Isaiah (with understanding!) is to know that the Messianic gospel was for all men; that none were to be denied its blessings; that this included the Gentiles, however hated and opposed they had been theretofore; and that King-Messiah would surely say to his loyal followers: "Go ye into all the world, and preach the gospel to every creature." (Mark 16:15.) The God of the whole earth would offer salvation to the inhabitants of the whole earth. None were excepted.

The Stem of Jesse, that is, the Branch growing out of the root of David's father, is Christ. (D&C 113:1-2.) After naming him, Isaiah delineates the manner in which he will minister among men at both his first and second comings. With particular reference to the Second Coming, Israel's Messianic prophet says that an ensign shall be raised around which the outcasts of Israel shall rally. Part of the promise is: "To it shall the Gentiles seek." (Isa. 11.) Paul takes this whole passage, destined to have complete fulfillment only in our day, and uses it to justify his course of taking the gospel to Gentiles in his day. "Esaias saith," he records, in his paraphrasing quotation of the great prophet's words, "There shall be a root of Jesse, and he that shall rise to reign over the Gentiles; in him shall the Gentiles trust." (Rom. 15:12.) For Paul's immediate purpose, the quotation he selected established, at least, that the gospel was to go to the Gentiles, and that it was an ensign to which "the nations," who are the Gentiles, should look. He might, however, have chosen other Isaiah passages better suited to his purposes, some of which passages we shall now note.

Included in a long Messianic prophecy, other parts of which are quoted Messianically in the New Testament, we find these promises: "He shall bring forth judgment to the Gentiles," and the Lord calls him "for a light of the Gentiles." (Isa. 42:1-7.) In another passage, which Paul says specifically has reference to "Christ" (Rom. 14:10-11), Isaiah has "Christ" say: "Look unto me, and be ye saved, all the ends of the earth: for I am God, and there is none else." (Isa. 45:22-23.) That is to say, that salvation which is in Israel's Messiah is for all men, for all the ends of the earth. A parallel passage in the Psalms says: "All the ends of the earth have seen the salvation of our God." (Ps. 98:3.)

When Paul and Barnabas ceased to give Israel preferential treatment in hearing the gospel message and turned their attention to the Gentiles, Paul quoted Isaiah's Messianic words: "I have set thee to be a light of the Gentiles, that thou shouldest be for salvation unto the ends of the earth." (Acts 13:44-52.) This inspired interpretation is one of several reasons we know that this particular chapter of Isaiah's writings is Messianic. In it, in addition to the words quoted by Paul, we find the Messianic assurances that "Kings shall see and arise, princes also shall worship, because of the Lord that is faithful, and the Holy One of Israel." He it is that shall say "to the prisoners, Go forth." Of the way in which these kings and princes, these who are not of the house of Israel, shall help that chosen people, Isaiah says: "Thus saith the Lord God, Behold, I will lift up mine hand to the Gentiles, and set up my standard to the people: and they shall bring thy sons in their arms, and thy daughters shall be carried upon their shoulders. And kings shall be thy nursing fathers, and their queens thy nursing mothers. . . . And all flesh shall know that I the Lord am thy Saviour and thy Redeemer, the mighty One of Jacob." (Isa. 49.)

It is also Isaiah who preserves for us this promise: "Behold, my servant [the Messiah] shall deal prudently, he shall be exalted and extolled, and be very high. . . . So shall he sprinkle [startle] many nations; the kings shall shut their mouths at him: for that which had not been told them shall they see; and that which they had not heard shall they consider." (Isa. 52:13-15.) These, incidentally, are the words which introduce the great Messianic message of Isaiah 53, and the things which shall be startling and new are summarized in the Messianic message there recorded.

Lest their thinking remain forever provincial and limited, Isaiah tells Israel, "Thy Redeemer the Holy One of Israel," whom we have long since shown to be the Lord Jesus Christ, is "The God of the whole earth." So "shall he be called," says the prophet. (Isa. 54:5.) Further, the promise is that the Lord will gather strangers, the sons of strangers, eunuchs, and "others," along with Israel, and they shall all be saved together. (Isa. 56:1-8.)

As to the glory of Zion and of Israel, the record says: "Arise, shine; for thy light is come, and the glory of the Lord is risen upon thee." What wondrous blessings await faithful Israel! But then the record adds: "And the Gentiles shall come to thy light, and kings to the brightness of thy rising. . . . Thou shalt also suck the milk of the Gentiles, and shalt suck the breast of kings: and thou shalt know that I the Lord am thy Saviour and thy Redeemer, the mighty One of Jacob." (Isa. 60.) Further: "They shall declare my glory among the Gentiles." (Isa. 66:19.)

Other prophets add their testimony to that of Isaiah. Through Malachi the Lord said: "From the rising of the sun even unto the going down of the same my name shall be great among the Gentiles; . . . for my name shall be great among the heathen, saith the Lord of hosts." (Mal. 1:11.) Even Moses said, "Rejoice, O ye nations, with his people" (Deut. 32:43), which Paul interpreted to mean "Rejoice, ye Gentiles, with his people" (Rom. 15:10). The Psalmist wrote: "O praise the Lord, all ye nations: praise him, all ye people" (Ps. 117:1), which Paul recorded as "Praise the Lord, all ye Gentiles; and laud him, all ye people" (Rom. 15:11).

From all this, and there is more that could be presented, it should be perfectly clear that there is no justification whatever for the provincial views found in Jerusalem and her environs, and in all of Canaan, that there was no hope or salvation for the Gentiles; and it is also clear beyond question that Paul knew what he was about when he said: "Lo, we turn to the Gentiles." (Acts 13:46.)

How the Gospel Is for Both Jew and Gentile

If the Messiah meant to bring salvation and honor and truth to the Gentiles as well as the Jews; if his name was to be adored among them as well as in the house of Israel; if the heathen were to be blessed along with the chosen and royal seed; if the God of Israel was also the God of the whole earth—what of the doctrine of a chosen people? How is it that the great Redeemer had dealt only with Abraham's seed for some two thousand years? If for two millenniums all other nations had been cursed by the Lord of hosts, as his armies smote and drove and destroyed all who opposed his chosen Israel, why should things change with the personal coming of the Messiah?

Based on the revealed word, and as a matter of sense and reason, we know that a just and impartial Deity has offered and will offer his blessings to all of his children, whether Jew or Gentile, on the same terms and conditions. The issue is not whether the Messiah and his gospel will bless all mankind; that assurance is given in the scriptures and is itself so just and right that we would be bound, in sense and wisdom, to assume it to be so even if it had not been revealed. The sole issue is, When will the Messiah come; when will he minister to Israel; when will his truth go to the Gentiles; and why does it not go to all men at the same time?

To set forth how and when the gospel goes to Jew and Gentile is simply to specify the system of priorities prepared and provided by Him who made salvation possible. As a result of preexistent faithfulness, certain of the Father's children earned the right to receive preferential treatment during their mortal sojourn. Some who were noble and great were foreordained, as the Messiah himself was to his mission, to minister as apostles and prophets on earth. Others merited birth into the house of Jacob, so they would be in a position to hear the word of truth and begin the processes of repentance, and of working out their salvation, before that same gift was given to others.

Abraham's mortal seed, because of long ages of preparation and devotion, while they yet dwelt as spirits in the presence of their Eternal Father earned the "right" to the gospel and the priesthood and an eventual inheritance of eternal life. (Abr. 2:10-12.) That is, they were foreordained to be the children of the father of the faithful and to work the works of righteousness as did faithful Abraham. Though the gospel is for all men, in due course—"For verily the voice of the Lord is unto all men, and there is none to escape; and there is no eye that shall not see, neither ear that shall not hear, neither heart that shall not be penetrated" (D&C 1:2)—yet some are entitled to receive it before it is presented to others. The Lord sends forth his word on a priority basis. It goes to all men eventually, but some are entitled to hear the voice before others.

When the Messiah ministered among men, he said, "I am not sent but unto the lost sheep of the house of Israel." (Matt. 15:24.) When he sent the Twelve forth, while he was yet among them, he commanded: "Go not into the way of the Gentiles. . . . But go rather to the lost sheep of the house of Israel." (Matt. 10:5-6.) For the time and season that then was, the gospel was for the Jews and not for the Gentiles. But after the Messiah rose from the dead, the apostolic commission to proclaim the word of truth was expanded to include all men. "Go ye into all the world, and preach the gospel to every creature," our Lord then said. (Mark 16:15.) That the import of this new commandment did not register fully in the minds of his apostolic witnesses is shown by the fact that Peter thereafter was given a vision and a renewed command to take the gospel to others than those of the chosen seed. (Acts 10.) And much of Paul's preaching and writing was designed to show that at long last the day of the Gentile had fully come.

For our present purposes it suffices to say that in the meridian of time the gospel went first to the Jews and then to the Gentiles, but that in our day it goes first to the Gentiles (meaning those who are not Jews, but who are in fact a remnant of scattered Israel) and then to the Jews. Thus Nephi wrote: "There is one God and one Shepherd over all the earth. And the time cometh that he shall manifest himself unto all nations, both unto the Jews and also unto the Gentiles; and after he has manifested himself unto the Jews and also unto the Gentiles, then he shall manifest himself unto the Gentiles and also unto the Jews, and the last shall be first, and the first shall be last." (1 Ne. 13:41-42.)

As to how and by what means the gospel should go to Israel and to the Gentiles, the arrangement was that during his earthly ministry—including his mortal labors among the Jews in Jerusalem and his immortal labors among the Jews on the American continent, for the Nephites also were Jews (2 Ne. 33:8)—the Messiah would present his message in person, with the Holy Ghost bearing record that he spoke the truth. But for the Gentiles to whom the word of salvation would come after the resurrection, there was to be no personal manifestation of the Son of God. Rather, the gospel would be preached by the Lord's ministers, with the Holy Ghost attesting to the truth and verity of their inspired utterances. Lehi spoke of "the gospel which should be preached among the Jews, and also concerning the dwindling of the Jews in unbelief." He told also that "after they had slain the Messiah, who should come, and after he should rise from the dead," then he "should make himself manifest, by the Holy Ghost, unto the Gentiles." (1 Ne. 10:11.) Continuing his personal ministry in time's meridian, our Lord said to the Nephites: "Ye are they of whom I said: Other sheep I have which are not of this fold; them also I must bring, and they shall hear my voice; and there shall be one fold, and one shepherd. . . . And they [the disciples in Jerusalem] understood me not that I said they shall hear my voice; and they understood me not that the Gentiles should not at any time hear my voice—that I should not manifest myself unto them save it were by the Holy Ghost." (3 Ne. 15:21-23.)

MESSIAH CAME TO PREACH AND TEACH

Why the Messiah Came as a Teacher

Gospel teaching is one of the most desirable of all talents, and gospel preaching the most needed of all gifts. The world needs now, as it needed in Jesus' day, teachers and preachers to present the word of truth and righteousness so that salvation will be available to the children of men. "It pleased God by the foolishness of preaching," the holy record says, "to save them that believe." (1 Cor. 1:21.) Men are saved if they believe, damned if they do not. Salvation comes to those who believe in the Lord, who call upon his holy name, who receive by revelation his laws and ordinances, and who keep the commandments. "How then shall they call on him in whom they have not believed? and how shall they believe in him of whom they have not heard? and how shall they hear without a preacher?" True it is that "faith cometh by hearing" the word of God taught by a legal administrator who has power and authority from his Maker to present the words of eternal life to his fellow beings. (Rom. 10:12-17.) What more important thing can any man do than present the message of salvation to his fellowmen so that they, if they believe and obey, can merit eternal life in the eternal kingdom of the Eternal God?

In the eternal perspective, and where the Lord's work among men is concerned, teachers stand next in importance to apostles and prophets, who themselves also are teachers and who could not perform their apostolic and prophetic labors unless they were. In listing the gifts given of God to those who believe and obey, Paul places them in this order: "God hath set some in the church," he said, "first apostles, secondarily prophets, thirdly teachers." After these three come "miracles, then gifts of healings, helps, governments, [and] diversities of tongues." (1 Cor. 12:28.)

From Adam down, whenever the Lord has had a people on earth who would receive his word and hearken to his voice, he has had among them "preachers of righteousness" who have spoken, prophesied, taught faith, and called upon men to repent. (Moses 6:23.) These preachers, these teachers, these personal representatives of the Lord in heaven have made known to the residue of men the things which must be done to return to the Eternal Presence. That the Son of God, ministering as a mortal, should be the preeminent Preacher of Righteousness, the greatest Teacher ever to grace the earth, is an obvious and self-evident reality. As the Chief Prophet and the Presiding Apostle, as the Pattern and Exemplar in all things, it follows that he was destined to be the Master Teacher whose message and methods would set the perfect standard for all apostles, all prophets, all preachers of righteousness, all teachers, of all ages. And so, as we would expect, we find prophetic pronouncements in profuse abundance telling of the teaching ministry of the Messiah, and we find in the life of our Lord a flow of spoken words and performed deeds that woven together comprise the greatest teaching labor ever performed among men on this or any of the endless creations of Him whose we are.

Messiah Shall Come to Teach

Messiah came to save man. No one can be saved in ignorance of God, of Christ, and of the truths of that everlasting gospel which comes from them. It follows that the Messiah came to teach the gospel, the Father's gospel and his gospel, the Father's plan of salvation and his plan of salvation. He came to chart the course and mark the way, the way to perfection. He came to teach, preach, exhort, command, and plead with fallen man to be reconciled with the Father.

When the time came to choose and foreordain a Savior and Redeemer, who would be born as the Son of God and who would make operative the Father's eternal plan, this call went forth from the Father: "Whom shall I send?" (Abr. 3:27.) Christ volunteered, and he was chosen and foreordained to work out the infinite and eternal atonement on planet earth in time's meridian. When the time came to designate and foreordain the One, above all others, who would take the Father's message of salvation to the earth, a similar call was made: "Whom shall I send, and who will go for us?" The answer came from the same preeminent Spirit Son: "Here am I; send me." Then came this instruction to the One so chosen: "Go, and tell this people, Hear ye indeed, but understand not; and see ye indeed, but perceive not. Make the heart of this people fat, and make their ears heavy, and shut their eyes; lest they see with their eyes, and hear with their ears, and understand with their heart, and convert, and be healed." (Isa. 6:8-10.) That these words, preserved for us by Isaiah, are Messianic, and that they applied to the ministry of the Lord Jesus among men, is amply attested in the New Testament record. Jesus quotes them as applying to himself (Matt. 13:14-15; Mark 4:12; Luke 8:10), and both John and Paul use them to describe our Lord's teachings (John 12:39-41; Acts 28:23-31; Rom. 11:8). They have obvious reference to the fact that the Messiah's message would be rejected by the generality of those who heard it.

Many passages recite that the Lord Jehovah will teach his people. "He will teach us of his ways," Isaiah records. (Isa. 2:3.) Also: "I am the Lord thy God which teacheth thee, . . . which leadeth thee by the way that thou shouldst go." (Isa. 48:17.) Such scriptures have immediate reference to the Lord's teachings before and after he dwelt as a mortal, but since he is eternal and unvarying, they apply also to the stream of sayings that fell from his lips while he dwelt in his tabernacle of clay.

Many other passages speak with specific reference to the teachings he would give as the Mortal Messiah. Speaking Messianically, Isaiah gives him the very name "Counseller" (Isa. 9:6), thereby dramatizing the directions that he would give. "The spirit of the Lord shall rest upon him," Isaiah foretold, "the spirit of wisdom and understanding, the spirit of counsel and might, the spirit of knowledge and of the fear of the Lord." (Isa. 11:2.) Also: "I have raised up one, . . . and he shall come: from the rising of the sun shall he call upon my name. . . . He is righteous. . . . I will give to Jerusalem one that bringeth good tidings." (Isa. 41:25-29.) Of this One, Isaiah continues: "Behold my servant, whom I uphold; mine elect, in whom my soul delighteth; I have put my spirit upon him: he shall bring forth judgment to the Gentiles." Then come these words, which apply to those occasions when he spoke only to his disciples and did not proclaim his message, for one reason or another, to the people generally: "He shall not cry, nor lift up, nor cause his voice to be heard in the street."

Despite all that happened to him, and in the face of the almost total rejection of his teachings, we find Isaiah giving forth these remarkable words: "He shall not fail nor be discouraged, till he have set judgment in the earth: and the isles shall wait for his law." Part of his ministry was "to open the blind eyes, to bring out the prisoners from the prison, and them that sit in darkness out of the prison house. . . . I will bring the blind by a way that they knew not; I will lead them in paths that they have not known: I will make darkness light before them, and crooked things straight." (Isa. 42:1-16.) All of this, the promised Messiah would do in and through the teachings he gave.

Nor is this all. Isaiah records these words spoken by the Messiah: "The Lord God hath given me the tongue of the learned, that I should know how to speak a word in season; . . . he wakeneth mine ear to hear as the learned. . . . For the Lord God will help me; therefore shall I not be confounded; . . . I know that I shall not be ashamed." (Isa. 50:4-7.) But among all the sayings of the seers relative to our Lord's teaching ministry, perhaps nothing is so sweet and expressive, to a pastoral people, as the declaration: "The Lord God will come. . . . He shall feed his flock like a shepherd: he shall gather the lambs with his arm, and carry them in his bosom, and shall gently lead those that are with young." (Isa. 40:10-11.)

There are various passages in the Psalms that bear agreeing witness with the words of Isaiah. (Ps. 25:8-10; 32:8-9; 45:2; 119:12, 26, 29, 33; 143:10.) One of these deserves particular note: "Lo, I come: in the volume of the book it is written of me, I delight to do thy will, O my God: yea, thy law is within my heart. I have preached righteousness. . . . I have declared thy faithfulness and thy salvation. I have not concealed thy lovingkindness and thy truth from the great congregation." (Ps. 40:7-10.)

Our Nephite friends had similar foreknowledge of what the Master Teacher would do among his brethren. Lehi said he would preach "the gospel . . . among the Jews" (1 Ne. 10:11), and Nephi saw in vision that he would go "forth ministering unto the people, in power and great glory; and the multitudes were gathered together to hear him" (1 Ne. 11:28). Alma said simply: "He cometh to declare glad tidings of salvation unto his people." (Alma 39:15.)

The fulfillment of the many Messianic prophecies relative to our Lord's teaching ministry is found in the New Testament. Mark records, for instance, that "Jesus came into Galilee, preaching the gospel of the kingdom of God, And saying, The time is fulfilled, and the kingdom of God is at hand: repent ye, and believe the gospel." (Mark 1:14-15.) To his account of the Sermon on the Mount, Matthew appends these words: "When Jesus had ended these sayings, the people were astonished at his doctrine: For he taught them as one having authority, and not as the scribes." (Matt. 7:28-29.) Even his enemies testified: "Never man spake like this man." (John 7:46.)

How the Gospel Should Be Taught

Teaching the gospel is a unique and peculiar process, unlike any other teaching, distinct and different from any other forms of pedagogy. Special powers are available to those so engaged, and they are also subject to some very limiting restrictions. We have what may be termed "The Teacher's Divine Commission," which is the only approved way to present those truths which come from God in heaven and are sent to man on earth for his benefit and blessing and salvation.

Those who are properly authorized to teach the gospel are agents and representatives of the Lord. He authorizes them to present his truths in the way he wants them presented and in no other way. The Lord is the Author of the plan of salvation, and it is his right and prerogative to say what portion of his truth shall be taught at any given time and to prescribe the manner and way in which it goes from the heart and lips of the teacher to the ears and souls of the hearers. Jesus our Lord taught in strict conformity to this divine commission, he being the agent and representative of his Father. Indeed, the pattern he set perfectly shows how all others should teach. The provisions of the teacher's divine commission are:

1. *Teach the gospel.*

This means teach the plan of salvation. Stay with gospel truths. Personal views and speculation are unwelcome. The Lord's agents are authorized to tell others what they must do to be saved. Men are entitled to hear the word of God taught so that faith will dwell in their hearts. It is gospel truths and gospel truths only which beget faith. "Teach the principles of my gospel," the Lord says. (D&C 42:12.) "The law of the Lord is perfect, converting the soul: the testimony of the

Lord is sure, making wise the simple. The statutes of the Lord are right, rejoicing the heart: the commandment of the Lord is pure, enlightening the eyes." (Ps. 19:7-8.)

2. *Teach from the scriptures.*

Use the Standard Works of the Church as the basic source of gospel knowledge. Therein is found the approved summary of the plan of salvation. Search the scriptures is the unvarying counsel of Him whose Spirit inspired those who wrote the holy records. It is the scriptures which testify of Christ. In them is found the basic and approved foundation upon which the Lord's house of doctrine is built. In our day the scriptures mean the Bible, the Book of Mormon, the Doctrine and Covenants, and the Pearl of Great Price.

3. *Teach by the power of the Holy Ghost.*

This is the great overriding consideration, the chief and greatest requisite for all gospel teachers. Gospel teachers have the gift of the Holy Ghost, meaning they have the right to the constant companionship of that member of the Godhead based on faithfulness. The Holy Ghost is a Revelator. He is the agent the Lord uses to reveal to his earthly representatives those things they should say and do at any given moment. So basic is this concept that the revelation decrees: "The Spirit shall be given unto you by the prayer of faith; and if ye receive not the Spirit ye shall not teach." When an earthly agent teaches without the Spirit, he is on his own. Only when he is moved upon by the Holy Ghost do his words become the mind and voice and word of the Lord. "As ye shall lift up your voices by the Comforter," the Lord promises, "ye shall speak and prophesy as seemeth me good; For, behold, the Comforter knoweth all things, and beareth record of the Father and of the Son." (D&C 42:14-17.)

Those who preach by the power of the Holy Ghost use the scriptures as their basic source of knowledge and doctrine. They begin with what the Lord has before revealed to other inspired men. But it is the practice of the Lord to give added knowledge to those upon whose hearts the true meanings and intents of the scriptures have been impressed. Many great doctrinal revelations come to those who preach from the scriptures. When they are in tune with the Infinite, the Lord lets them know, first, the full and complete meaning of the scriptures they are expounding, and then he ofttimes expands their views so that new truths flood in upon them, and they learn added things that those who do not follow such a course can never know. Hence, as to "preaching the word," the Lord commands his servants to go forth "saying none other things than that which the prophets and apostles have written, and that which is taught them by the Comforter through the prayer of faith." (D&C 52:9.) In a living, growing, divine church, new truths will come from time to time and old truths will be applied with new vigor to new situations, all under the guidance of the Holy Spirit of God.

4. *Apply the principles taught to the needs of the hearers.*

It does not suffice to present gospel truths in an abstract and impersonal way. True principles benefit mankind only when they live in the souls of men. Testimony as an abstract principle has no saving power, but a testimony in the heart of a living person opens the door to a course leading to eternal life. Gospel principles are always the same; they never vary. But the circumstances in which men find themselves are as varied as the number of living persons. The inspired teacher always applies the eternal truths to the circumstances of his hearers. Thus Nephi, in quoting the truths taught by Isaiah, says: "Hear ye the words of the prophet, which were written unto all the house of Israel, and liken them unto yourselves." (1 Ne. 19:24.) That is, Isaiah wrote concerning the whole house of Israel, and Nephi is now applying his words to the Nephites and the peculiar situation in which they found themselves.

5. *Teach with the seal of personal testimony.*

The crowning, convincing, converting power of gospel teaching is manifest when an inspired teacher says, "I know by the power of the Holy Ghost, by the revelations of the Holy Spirit to my soul, that the doctrines I have taught are true." This divine seal of approval makes the spoken word binding upon the hearers. Alma preached a powerful sermon about the spiritual rebirth that should come into the life of every true saint. He quoted the sayings of the fathers and expounded his doctrinal views with clarity and certainty. Then he said: "And this is not all. Do ye not suppose that I know of these things myself? Behold, I testify unto you that I do know that these things whereof I have spoken are true." It should be noted that Alma is not bearing testimony that the work in which he is engaged is true; he is certifying that the doctrinal principles he is expounding are themselves the mind and will of the Lord. "And how do ye suppose that I know of their surety?" he asks. "Behold, I say unto you they are made known unto me by the Holy Spirit of God," he replies. "Behold, I have fasted and prayed many days that I might know these things of myself," he continues. "And now I do know of myself that they are true; for the Lord God hath made them manifest unto me by his Holy Spirit; and this is the spirit of revelation which is in me." (Alma 5:45-46.) It should be added that when the Lord's servants preach in power, by the promptings of the Holy Spirit, the Lord adds his own witness to the truth of their words. That witness comes in the form of signs and gifts and miracles. Such are always found when the preached word, given in power, is believed by hearers with open hearts. And we shall now take particular note of how the Lord Jesus interwove his spoken words and his healing powers to leave a witness of his own divine calling that could not have been given in any other way. We shall see, by way of sample only, how and in what manner he taught gospel truths.

How Jesus Taught the Greatest Truths

Let us name the greatest truths known to Gods, angels, or men; known in time or in eternity; known on this or any earth; known either here among us or among any intelligent beings in all the wide expanse of immensity. Then let us note how Jesus our Lord, the Master Teacher, chose to teach and reveal these truths to his fellowmen.

We believe it to be self-evident that the greatest truth in all eternity is: That there is a God in heaven who created all things—the universe, man, and all forms of life; that there is existence, creation, and being—all controlled and governed by an intelligent Head; that God is, and we are, and all things exist. As to the facts of existence and creation, such need no proof. As to the wisdom and omnipotence of the Creator, such is shown by the extent, complexity, and organized nature of created things.

But as to the fact that the Most High God is a Holy Man, an Eternal Father, an Exalted Personage in whose image man is created, this is something that must be revealed. It is something that men must learn from sources other than reason. And the greatest revelation ever given of the Father is the revelation of the Son. It is that the Father had a Son who in the very nature of things was a manifestation of his Parent. As set forth in Chapter 2, God was in Christ manifesting himself to the world. Christ is the revelation of the Father; by learning about the Son we automatically know what kind of Being his Father is. Thus the accounts about our Lord, as recorded by Matthew, Mark, Luke, and John, become the most extended and perfect recitations about thc Father himself. Jesus taught the greatest of all truths—the facts about his Father—by the life he lived, the deeds he did, and the words he spoke.

We also believe it to be self-evident that the second greatest truth in all eternity is that Christ our Lord is the Son of God who came into the world to manifest his Father and to bring to pass the immortality and eternal life of man. In Chapter 9 we gave three illustrations of how he both taught and proved that he was the Son of God. One was the instance in which he forgave the sins of a paralytic, which none but God can do, and then when the Jews murmured at his seeming blasphemy, in order to show that he himself was

God, he commanded the sick of palsy to arise, take up his bed, and walk. Another case was that of healing the man born blind. This he did in order to gain a congregation of hearers so that he could declare unto them in plain words that he was the Good Shepherd and that he and his Father were one. And the third instance was that of raising Lazarus from his four-day sleep of death, after he first declared to Martha and Mary and the Jewish mourners that he himself was in fact the resurrection and the life. The reasoning in each of these case studies is that when he said "I am the Son of God" (John 10:36), either in plain words or by necessary implication, his teaching must be true because he was also causing the lame to walk, the blind to see, and the dead to rise. To these three illustrations might be added such other instances as his feeding of the five thousand, on which occasion he taught that he was the Bread of Life who came down from heaven. (John 6.)

It may well be that the third greatest truth in the eternal scheme of things is that man can commune with his Maker and gain a knowledge of the plan of salvation by the power of the Holy Ghost. Such an order of priorities centers the greatest of all truths in the Father, the next greatest in the Son, and the third in the Holy Ghost. In any event, there is little in life as important to man as coming to a knowledge of those things he must believe and do to gain eternal life.

This matter of gaining knowledge from the Holy Spirit was taught by the Master Teacher primarily in plain words. "Ask, and it shall be given you," he said. (Matt. 7:7.) Also: "Blessed are all they that do hunger and thirst after righteousness; for they shall be filled with the Holy Ghost." (JST, Matt. 5:8.) And: "When he, the Spirit of truth, is come, he will guide you into all truth: for he shall not speak of himself; but whatsoever he shall hear, that shall he speak: and he will shew you things to come." (John 16:13.)

It may not be amiss to insert at this point what so many of those who become bewitched with teaching methodology so often overlook, which is that one of the best ways to teach a doctrine is just to state it in plain and simple and persuasive language. Teaching aids and symbolisms play their part in proper situations and for special reasons, but nothing can overshadow the simple pedagogical approach of saying what is involved in a pleasing and compelling way. Such was the course pursued in large measure by the resurrected Lord when he taught the Nephites, and such also was the course pursued by the Nephite prophets in general as they preached the various doctrines of peace and salvation.

How Jesus Taught the Doctrine of Resurrection

May we suggest that the fourth greatest truth centers around that immortality and eternal life which our Lord came to bring. In this connection, what teaching on the matter of the resurrection equals that given by Jesus on the Emmaus road and in the upper room? Jesus, being resurrected, walked for perhaps eight miles along a dusty Judean lane with Cleopas and another disciple, probably Luke. He talked and appeared as any mortal would. He took special occasion to expound the scriptures concerning Christ as they are found in Moses and in the Psalms. In dress, demeanor, and physical appearance, he was like any wayfaring teacher of the day. And the disciples knew him not until he chose to make his identity known when at eventide he brake bread with them. How better could he have taught that immortality is but a continuation of mortality, and that when men rise from the dead, they go on living in tangible bodies like those they had before death and the resurrection?

Cleopas and his fellow disciple immediately returned to Jerusalem, found the apostles and a congregation of saints who were eating in a closed upper room, and recited what had transpired. As they recounted their experiences with a Resurrected Being, that same Jesus, whose body was tangible and real, came through the wall of the room. He spoke, teaching doctrine, reciting that he had a body of flesh and bones which those present were invited to handle and feel.

He was recognized; the congregation knew him. He asked for food, which he ate before them. The apostles felt the nail marks in his hands and feet and thrust their hands into the spear wound in his side, all to the end that this congregation of saints, this group of living witnesses, might know that a resurrected person has power over physical objects and yet is a personal being, having a body of flesh and bones which can eat and digest food as though mortal. Surely the Master Teacher here crowns his and all other teaching about the nature of resurrected bodies! (Luke 24.)

And what teaching about eternal life compares with the doctrine of John 17:3: "And this is life eternal, that they might know thee, the only true God, and Jesus Christ, whom thou hast sent," which means that to gain eternal life we must become like the Gods of heaven, knowing and experiencing as they do, and living in the family unit as does our own Eternal Father. Could a teacher couch an eternal truth in words more graphically than Jesus did here in his great Intercessory Prayer?

Jesus' Teachings Fulfill Messianic Promises

Volumes have been written about the methods and approaches and techniques of the Master Teacher. Authors generally have been more concerned with his use of parables and of the common things of Jewish culture and geography to drive home his points than they have been with the infinitely important truths he taught. They analyze his use of illustrations involving flowers and birds and animals, his references to seed time and harvest, and the like; they speak primarily of the how and the manner of his teaching, rather than the nature and import of the message. These procedures and techniques are simply the garments used to clothe the eternal truths set forth. Important as they are, the great glory and beauty and perfection of the teaching of the Mortal Messiah are found in the doctrine he taught, the truths he expounded, as he set an example of how all other teachers should operate within the terms and conditions of the teacher's divine commission.

It is not our purpose to dwell upon the excellence and transcendent nature of his manner of teaching. We are simply showing that as a teacher he excelled all others, and that his teaching ministry was foreknown to the ancients and foretold by them in their Messianic utterances. We need not here evaluate our Lord's Sermon on the Mount, which presented gospel truths for the benefit of all men, nor his discourse on the Second Coming, which presented doctrines that only his spiritually enlightened disciples could understand. It is not our purpose to show how the parable of Lazarus and the rich man reveals great truths relative to salvation for the dead, and how the parable of the wheat and the tares hides from all but the enlightened saints the doctrine our Lord was then teaching. (D&C 86.)

For our purposes, it suffices to gain an acute awareness that when Jesus taught, he was fulfilling his foreordained destiny. When he dwelt and taught in Capernaum, for instance, he was doing so "in the borders of Zabulon and Nephthalim: That it might be fulfilled which was spoken by Esaias the prophet, saying, The land of Zabulon, and the land of Nephthalim, by the way of the sea, beyond Jordan, Galilee of the Gentiles; The people which sat in darkness saw great light; and to them which sat in the region and shadow of death light is sprung up." (Matt. 4:12-16; Isa. 9:1-2.) When he blessed little children, he was but carrying the lambs of his flock in his arms as Isaiah foretold. (Isa. 40:11.) When he chose Twelve to carry his message, he was but fulfilling the Nephite prophecies. (1 Ne. 1:9-11; 11:29-36; 12:7-10; 13:26.)

Truly, as spake the Psalmist of him: "Grace is poured into thy lips: therefore God hath blessed thee for ever." (Ps. 45:2.)

MESSIAH CRUCIFIED AND SLAIN

A God Dies!

Interwoven into every concept presented throughout this whole work is the great reality that God himself must die for man; that the Almighty Jehovah, the Creator of all things from the beginning, the Mighty Messiah, Israel's Deliverer, must lay down his life; that the Lord Jesus Christ, the very Son of God, came into the world—above all other reasons—to die, to die upon the cross, to die as he suffered more than man can suffer.

The death of a God! The great Creator dies! Not only does he die—he is slain, crucified, pierced. Nails are driven through his hands and feet. A Roman spear is hurled into his side. He hangs in agony upon a cross, feeling again the weight of the sorrow he bore in Gethsemane.

A God dies and the rocks rend; a God dies and all creation shudders; a God dies and all the hosts of heaven both sorrow and rejoice. A God dies that he may live again; that he may come forth from the tomb as the firstfruits of them that sleep; that he may bring immortality to all and eternal life to those who believe and obey. A God dies that all the terms and conditions of the Father's plan may be fulfilled. A God descends below all things that he may rise to heights above the stars; he lives again, as all men shall; and the infinite and eternal atonement is complete. The will of the

Son is swallowed up in the will of the Father. The will of the Father in all things from the beginning is done!

All these things have been known in greater or lesser degree by prophets and saints in all dispensations. The nature of this work is such that we have referred to many things concerning the Lord Messiah's death as we have dealt with the various Messianic concepts. It is now, however, our privilege to collate and comment upon the Messianic utterances relative to his death as such, so that we may have before us the wondrous things known by the ancients about Him who is our Deliverer.

Jehovah, Israel's God, Shall Die

We are aware that the ancient prophets and saints knew that their Messiah must die. He is spoken of as "the Lamb slain from the foundation of the world" (Rev. 13:8), meaning his sacrificial death was planned and foreordained from the beginning as part of the Father's plan. And the revelatory processes making the fact and reasons for his death known to mortal man commenced in the day of the first man. Each time the Lord revealed his atoning truths, the death of the Atoner was set forth, either in plain words or by necessary implication. The angelic pronouncement to Adam that his sacrificial performances were in "similitude of the sacrifice of the Only Begotten of the Father" (Moses 5:7) carries with it the verity that the Only Begotten will lay down his life in sacrifice. Throughout this work we have considered those passages and doctrines which presuppose and assume Messiah's death. Now we shall show some of the revelations which deal specifically with matters connected with his passing from mortality.

First, let us make it clear that the ancient prophets had in mind that it was the Lord Jehovah, their Creator, the Lord God of Israel, who should die. Nephi says that "even the very God of Israel do men trample under their feet," and that "the God of Abraham, and of Isaac, and the God of Jacob, yieldeth himself" into the hands of men to be slain. (1 Ne. 19:7, 10.) Jacob says, "It behooveth the great Creator that he suffereth himself to become subject unto man in the flesh, and to die for all men." (2 Ne. 9:5.) Also, "The Lord God . . . loveth the world, even that he layeth down his own life that he may draw all men unto him." (2 Ne. 26:23-24.) And our angelic co-laborer told King Benjamin that it was "the Lord Omnipotent who reigneth, who was, and is, from all eternity to all eternity" who should suffer death for his people. (Mosiah 3:5-7.) These passages illustrate the plainness with which Book of Mormon prophets spoke in identifying the Person who should come to redeem mankind.

The numerous statements in Isaiah to the effect that Jehovah is the Redeemer and Savior have the same meaning. One particularly expressive Old Testament passage counsels: "Trust ye in the Lord for ever: for in the Lord JEHOVAH is everlasting strength." In that setting the voice of Jehovah then says to his people: "Thy dead men shall live, together with my dead body shall they arise. Awake and sing, ye that dwell in the dust: . . . and the earth shall cast out the dead." (Isa. 26:4, 19.) Jehovah, having first died, shall rise in immortality and thereby bring to pass the resurrection of all men.

Messiah Shall Be Slain

Most of what the prophets foretold relative to the death of the Infinite One speaks of him under the name-title of *Messiah,* which is the Hebrew designation, or of *Christ,* which is the Greek rendition of the same word. By way of illustration, the Messiah passages say that the Jews shall slay "the Messiah, who should come," and that "the Son of God was the Messiah who should come." (1 Ne. 10:11, 17.) They say that "the Holy Messiah . . . layeth down his life according to the flesh, and taketh it again by the power of the

Spirit" (2 Ne. 2:8), and that "after the Messiah shall come there shall be signs given unto my people [the Nephites] of his birth, and also of his death and resurrection" (2 Ne. 26:3). Daniel speaks of the fact that the "Messiah shall be cut off." (Dan. 9:26.) And we shall note other Messianic passages when we speak of the mode and manner of his death, that of crucifixion.

Also by way of illustration, the even more numerous passages using the name *Christ* say such things as: "We would to God that we could persuade all men not to rebel against God, to provoke him to anger, but that all men would believe in Christ, and view his death, and suffer his cross and bear the shame of the world." (Jacob 1:8.) "The resurrection of the dead, and the redemption of the people . . . was to be brought to pass through the power, and sufferings, and death of Christ, and his resurrection and ascension into heaven." (Mosiah 18:2.) "Now Aaron began to open the scriptures unto them concerning the coming of Christ, and also concerning the resurrection of the dead, and that there could be no redemption for mankind save it were through the death and sufferings of Christ, and the atonement of his blood." (Alma 21:9.) "Nothing can save this people save it be repentance and faith on the Lord Jesus Christ, who surely shall come into the world, and shall suffer many things and shall be slain for his people." (Hel. 13:6.) "Jesus Christ, the Son of God, . . . the Creator of all things from the beginning, . . . surely must die that salvation may come; yea, it behooveth him and becometh expedient that he dieth, to bring to pass the resurrection of the dead, that thereby men may be brought into the presence of the Lord." (Hel. 14:12, 15.) Indeed, so profuse are these prophecies and so commonly were they taught among the saints that Nephi the son of Helaman said, "Almost all of our fathers, even down to this time . . . have testified of the coming of Christ, and have rejoiced in his day which is to come. And behold, he is God, and he is with them, and he did manifest himself unto them, that they were redeemed by him; and they gave unto him glory, because of that which is to come." (Hel. 8:22-23.)

These prophetic declarations of the appointed slaying of earth's Chief Citizen continued right up to the hour of our Lord's betrayal and crucifixion. Even he kept the concept alive in the hearts of his disciples by saying such things as: "The Son of man shall be betrayed into the hands of men: And they shall kill him, and the third day he shall be raised again." (Matt. 17:22-23.) Of his statements along this line, Matthew says: "From that time forth began Jesus to shew unto his disciples, how that he must go unto Jerusalem, and suffer many things of the elders and chief priests and scribes, and be killed, and be raised again the third day." (Matt. 16:21.)

Messiah Shall Be Crucified

It did not suffice for the Messianic prophecies to set forth that Christ should die to redeem his people. It pleased God to show beforehand the way and manner of his death, a death on a cross, a death by cruel crucifixion. The very manner in which his redeeming blood was shed was itself a means of teaching great truths connected with the atonement. For instance, it enabled him, after the event, to say: "My Father sent me that I might be lifted up upon the cross; and after that I had been lifted up upon the cross, that I might draw all men unto me, that as I have been lifted up by men even so should men be lifted up by the Father, to stand before me, to be judged of their works, whether they be good or whether they be evil—And for this cause have I been lifted up; therefore, according to the power of the Father I will draw all men unto me, that they may be judged according to their works." (3 Ne. 27:14-15.)

And so we now turn to the Messianic prophecies that tell the fact of crucifixion and that go into remarkable detail as to the words and acts that become part of that humiliating and agonizing indignity. "Enoch saw the day of the coming of the Son of Man," which caused him to give forth this exulting statement: "The Righteous is lifted up, and the Lamb is slain from the foundation of the world. . . . And the Lord said unto Enoch: Look, and he looked and beheld the Son of Man lifted up on the cross, after the manner of men." (Moses 7:47, 55.) Obviously this doctrine that Christ would be crucified was taught among all the ancient saints.

From the Nephite record we learn that Nephi "saw that he was lifted up upon the cross and slain for the sins of the world." (1 Ne. 11:33.) An angel also told Nephi that Christ would yield himself "into the hands of wicked men, to be lifted up, according to the words of Zenock, and to be crucified, according to the words of Neum. . . . And as for those who are at Jerusalem," Nephi said, "they shall be scourged by all people, because they crucify the God of Israel." (1 Ne. 19:10, 13.) Nephi's brother Jacob left the witness that "the Lord God, the Holy One of Israel, should manifest himself unto them in the flesh [who were at Jerusalem]; and after he should manifest himself they should scourge him and crucify him." (2 Ne. 6:9.) Nephi said of the Jews that "there is none other nation on earth that would crucify their God." (2 Ne. 10:3; 25:12-13.) After all the marvels of his ministry, in the angelic language received by King Benjamin, "they shall consider him a man, and say that he hath a devil, and shall scourge him, and shall crucify him." (Mosiah 3:9.) "Yea, even so he shall be led, crucified, and slain," Abinadi prophesied, "the flesh becoming subject even unto death, the will of the Son being swallowed up in the will of the Father." (Mosiah 15:7.)

Jesus' own Messianic declarations concerning his coming demise, and the manner in which it would be accomplished, are thus recorded: "And Jesus going up to Jerusalem took the twelve disciples apart in the way, and said unto them, Behold, we go up to Jerusalem; and the Son of man shall be betrayed unto the chief priests and unto the scribes, and they shall condemn him to death, And shall deliver him to the Gentiles to mock, and to scourge, and to crucify him: and the third day he shall rise again." (Matt. 20:17-19.) And also: "Ye know that after two days is the feast of the passover, and the Son of man is betrayed to be crucified." (Matt. 26:2.)

Old World Prophets Tell of the Crucifixion

Old Testament prophecies about the crucifixion, as that volume of Holy Writ now stands, do not use the word crucify, but notwithstanding this, in some respects they are even more pointed and express than their Book of Mormon counterparts. Isaiah says the Messianic Servant, who came to do his Father's will, would suffer intense pain and disfigurement. "His visage"—his aspect and appearance, his countenance and the way he looked—"was so marred more than any man"—this because of the anguish and pain which writhed through his soul both in Gethsemane and on the cross—"and his form more than the sons of men"—having reference among other things to the gashing holes made by the nails and the gaping wound left by the spear. (Isa. 52:14-15.) Ezra even speaks of "a nail in his holy place" (Ezra 9:8), and Isaiah of "the nail that is fastened in the sure place." having reference to the nails driven in the Crucified One. "And I will fasten him as a nail in a sure place; and he shall be for a glorious throne to his father's house. And they shall hang upon him all the glory of his father's house." (Isa. 22:21-25.) As to these prophecies, whoso readeth let him understand.

Isaiah says further that he was despised, rejected, stricken, smitten, afflicted, wounded, bruised, beaten with stripes, and oppressed, and that he went as a lamb to the slaughter. He opened not his mouth, meaning he did not defend himself when hailed before wicked earthly tyrants. He was cut off out of the land of the living, made his soul an offering for sin, and poured out his soul unto death (Isa. 53), meaning that he was slain, that he was sacrificed by Satanic priests as it were, and that even so he voluntarily gave up his life. "No man taketh it from me," he said, "but I lay it down of myself. I have power to lay it down, and I have power to take it again. This commandment have I received of my Father." (John 10:18.)

"All things must be fulfilled, which were written in the law of Moses, and in the prophets, and in the psalms, concerning me," the risen Lord said to the assembled saints in the upper room. (Luke 24:44.) To Cleopas and another disciple, on the Emmaus road, the resurrected Jesus said: "O fools, and slow of heart to believe all that the prophets have spoken: Ought not Christ to have suffered these things, and to enter into his glory? And beginning at Moses and all the prophets, he expounded unto them in all the scriptures the things concerning himself." (Luke 24:25-27.) Surely those things we shall now quote from the Psalms—pointed, express, detailed utterances about his sufferings, death, and atoning sacrifice—were included in those things which he expounded unto them.

The Holy Ghost, through David, said: "My God, my God, why hast thou forsaken me?" (Ps. 22:1)—thus revealing aforetime the very words Jesus would speak on the cross in that moment when, left alone that he might drink the dregs of the bitter cup to the full, the Father would entirely withdraw his sustaining power. And so Matthew records: "And about the ninth hour Jesus cried with a loud voice, saying, Eli, Eli, la ma sabach tha ni? that is to say, My God, my God, why hast thou forsaken me?" (Matt. 27:46.)

The same Psalm says: "All they that see me laugh me to scorn: they shoot out the lip, they shake the head, saying, He trusted on the Lord that he would deliver him: let him deliver him, seeing he delighted in him." (Ps. 22:7-8.) The fulfillment, as Jesus hung on the cross, is found in these words: "The chief priests mocking him, with the scribes and elders, said, He saved others; himself he cannot save. If he be the King of Israel, let him now come down from the cross, and we will believe him. He trusted in God; let him deliver him now, if he will have him: for he said, I am the

Son of God. The thieves also, which were crucified with him, cast the same in his teeth." (Matt. 27:41-44.)

Next the Psalmist speaks of our Lord's birth, of his reliance on God, of his troubles, and then coming back to the mob at the foot of the cross, he says: "They gaped upon me with their mouths, as a ravening and a roaring lion." Then the record says: "I am poured out like water" (Ps. 22:9-14), an expression akin to Isaiah's that "he hath poured out his soul unto death" (Isa. 53:12).

"Thou hast brought me into the dust of death," the Psalmist continues, "For dogs have compassed me, the assembly of the wicked have inclosed me: they pierced my hands and my feet," which is exactly what transpired on the gloomy day of crucifixion. Then this: "They part my garments among them, and cast lots upon my vesture" (Ps. 22:15-18), of which prediction Matthew says, "And they crucified him, and parted his garments, casting lots: that it might be fulfilled which was spoken by the prophet, They parted my garments among them, and upon my vesture did they cast lots" (Matt. 27:35). John gives this more extended account of the fulfillment of this promise: "Then the soldiers, when they had crucified Jesus, took his garments, and made four parts, to every soldier a part; and also his coat: now the coat was without seam, woven from the top throughout. They said therefore among themselves, Let us not rend it, but cast lots for it, whose it shall be: that the scripture might be fulfilled, which saith, They parted my raiment among them, and for my vesture they did cast lots. These things therefore the soldiers did." (John 19:23-24.)

After this the Psalmist has the Messiah say, in words applicable to his Father, "I will declare thy name unto my brethren: in the midst of the congregation will I praise thee," a course that our Lord pursued with diligence during his whole ministry. And then this counsel: "Ye that fear the Lord, praise him; all ye the seed of Jacob, glorify him; and fear him, all ye the seed of Israel." Following this is the promise that the Lord shall be praised "in the great congregation," and that "all the ends of the world shall remember and turn unto the Lord: and all the kindreds of the nations shall worship before thee. For the kingdom is the Lord's: and he is the governor of the nations." Clearly this has reference to the final millennial triumph of truth, a triumph that is to be when the gospel brought by the Messiah is restored again and carried according to his will to all men. Finally, in this Psalm, it is of the Messiah that the account speaks in these words: "A seed shall serve him; it shall be accounted to the Lord for a generation"; that is, the Seed of David, generated by the Father, shall serve in righteousness, with this result: "They shall come, and shall declare his righteousness unto a people that shall be born, that he hath done this." (Ps. 22:22-31.) And in harmony with this prophetic assurance, we now declare unto all people born after Messiah's day, the righteousness of the Father in sending his Son and the righteousness of the Son in doing all things for men that needed to be done to bring to them both immortality and eternal life.

Other Psalms also revealed, before the events, additional specifics that would attend or be associated with the cross of Christ and the agonizing death he would suffer thereon. With reference to the conniving and conspiring plots incident to our Lord's arrest and judicial trials the prophecy was: "They took counsel together against me, they devised to take away my life." (Ps. 31:13.) As to the role of Judas in those conspiracies, the Psalmist says: "Mine own familiar friend, in whom I trusted, which did eat of my bread, hath lifted up his heel against me." (Ps. 41:9.) On that occasion when he washed their feet, Jesus spoke in laudatory terms of the twelve, but, said he, "I speak not of you all," for a moment later he was to say, "one of you shall betray me." "I know whom I have chosen," he continued, "but that the scripture may be fulfilled, He that eateth bread with me hath lifted up his heel against me. Now I tell you before it come, that, when it is come to pass, ye may believe that I am he." After a few more words, he dipped the sop and gave it to

Judas, thus identifying the traitor in their midst. (John 13:18-30.)

"The zeal of thine house hath eaten me up," is the Messianic word which foretold the driving of the money changers from the temple and caused Jesus to say, "Make not my Father's house an house of merchandise," and which caused his disciples to remember the words of the Psalm. (John 2:13-17.) But the full Messianic statement, which forecasts more than the cleansing of the then-polluted temple, says: "The zeal of thine house hath eaten me up; and the reproaches of them that reproached thee are fallen upon me. . . . Reproach hath broken my heart; and I am full of heaviness: and I looked for some to take pity, and there was none; and for comforters, but I found none." (Ps. 69:9, 20.) Who can fail to see in these words our Lord's piteous state as, hailed before the rulers of this world, he found none to comfort him, but instead was reproached for testifying of that Father whom his Jewish persecutors had rejected?

After these words comes the Psalmic declaration: "They gave me also gall for my meat; and in my thirst they gave me vinegar to drink." (Ps. 69:21.) Their fulfillment is noted by Matthew in these words: "They gave him vinegar to drink mingled with gall: and when he had tasted thereof, he would not drink. And they crucified him." Also: After Jesus had, as they supposed, called for Elias, the account says: "And straightway one of them ran, and took a spunge, and filled it with vinegar, and put it on a reed, and gave him to drink." (Matt. 27:34-35, 47-48.) John's account of this same occurrence ties the act at the crucifixion in with David's prediction by recounting: "Jesus knowing that all things were now accomplished, that the scripture might be fulfilled, saith, I thirst." It is as though advisedly and with deliberation, though he was in agony beyond compare, yet he consciously continued to the last moment of mortal life, with the avowed purpose of fulfilling all of the Messianic utterances concerning his mortal Messiahship. "Now there was set a vessel full of vinegar," John's account continues, "and they filled a spunge with vinegar, and put it upon hyssop, and put it to his mouth. When Jesus therefore had received the vinegar, he said, It is finished: and he bowed his head, and gave up the ghost." (John 19:28-30.)

Viewing in advance, as it were, this last awesome moment of the Messiah's mortal life, David wrote: "Into thine hand I commit my spirit." (Ps. 31:5.) Recording after the fact what took place as the last breath of mortal air filled the lungs of the Man on the cross, Luke said: "And when Jesus had cried with a loud voice, he said, Father, into thy hands I commend my spirit: and having said thus, he gave up the ghost." (Luke 23:46.)

With our Lord's last breath, all things were fulfilled which pertained to that period when the breath of life sustained his life and being. But other predicted acts were to occur while his body yet hung on the cross, and still others pertaining to his burial and resurrection, after that body was taken down. Of the events on the cross, John says: "The Jews therefore, because it was the preparation, that the bodies should not remain upon the cross on the sabbath day, (for that sabbath day was an high day,) besought Pilate that their legs might be broken, and that they might be taken away. Then came the soldiers, and brake the legs of the first, and of the other which was crucified with him. But when they came to Jesus, and saw that he was dead already, they brake not his legs: But one of the soldiers with a spear pierced his side, and forthwith came there out blood and water. And he that saw it bare record, and his record is true: and he knoweth that he saith true, that ye might believe. For these things were done, that the scripture should be fulfilled, A bone of him shall not be broken. And again another scripture saith, They shall look on him whom they pierced." (John 19:31-37.)

Three scriptures were thus fulfilled. In the account of the original passover, it was expressly provided with reference to the lamb slain in similitude of the coming sacrificial offering of the Lamb of God, "neither shall ye break a bone thereof."

(Ex. 12:46.) These words are the actual source of John's quotation, but their thought content and meaning were restated by David in this way: "He keepeth all his bones; not one of them is broken." (Ps. 34:20.) The scripture "They shall look upon me whom they have pierced" (Zech. 12:10) is part of a long passage in Zechariah that deals with the Second Coming of Christ and the conversion of the Jewish people at that time. Manifestly those around the cross did look upon the Pierced One, for the wound was then gashed into his unprotected side. But the great fulfillment of Zechariah's prophecy is yet ahead. As a people, those Jews who remain after the destructions incident to our Lord's return shall look on him whom they pierced and shall be converted. It is then, as Zechariah also records, that they shall say: "What are these wounds in thine hands? Then he shall answer, Those with which I was wounded in the house of my friends." (Zech. 13:6.) These conversationally expressed statements, uttered by Zechariah, preserved to us in the Old Testament and confirmed as part of the divine plan by the New Testament reference to them, these words in their more complete and perfect rendition are: "Then shall the Jews look upon me and say: What are these wounds in thine hands and in thy feet? Then shall they know that I am the Lord; for I will say unto them: These wounds are the wounds with which I was wounded in the house of my friends. I am he who was lifted up. I am Jesus that was crucified. I am the Son of God." (D&C 45:51-52.)

It was also Zechariah who said in the course of this same Messianic recitation: "Smite the shepherd, and the sheep shall be scattered: and I will turn mine hand upon the little ones." (Zech. 13:7.) After instituting the sacrament and as he turned his face to Gethsemane, Jesus said to the Twelve: "All ye shall be offended because of me this night: for it is written, I will smite the shepherd, and the sheep of the flock shall be scattered abroad." (Matt. 26:31.)

Then Jesus went to Gethsemane for his atoning ordeal. Returning therefrom he met the traitor to whom the chief priests had given thirty pieces of silver to betray his Master. "What will ye give me, and I will deliver him unto you?" he asked. "And they covenanted with him for thirty pieces of silver. And from that time he sought opportunity to betray him." (Matt. 26:14-16.) And this was to fulfill that which Zechariah had said: "If ye think good, give me my price; and if not, forbear. So they weighed for my price thirty pieces of silver. And the Lord said unto me, Cast it unto the potter: a goodly price that I was prised at of them. And I took the thirty pieces of silver, and cast them to the potter in the house of the Lord." (Zech. 11:12-13.) "Then Judas, which had betrayed him, when he saw that he was condemned, repented himself, and brought again the thirty pieces of silver to the chief priests and elders, Saying, I have sinned in that I have betrayed the innocent blood. And they said, What is that to us? see thou to that. And he cast down the pieces of silver in the temple, and departed, and went and hanged himself. And the chief priests took the silver pieces, and said, It is not lawful for to put them into the treasury, because it is the price of blood. And they took counsel, and bought with them the potter's field, to bury strangers in. Wherefore that field was called, The field of blood, unto this day. Then was fulfilled that which was spoken by Jeremy the prophet, saying, And they took the thirty pieces of silver, the price of him that was valued, whom they of the children of Israel did value; And gave them for the potter's field, as the Lord appointed me." (Matt. 27:3-10.)

Prophets Reveal Signs of Messiah's Death

Matthew alone of the Gospel authors tells of the physical upheaval in Jerusalem that came as Jesus died. "Jesus, when he had cried again with a loud voice, yielded up the ghost," the account says. "And, behold, the veil of the temple was rent in twain from the top to the bottom; and the earth did quake, and the rocks rent. . . . Now when the centurion, and they that were with him, watching Jesus, saw the earthquake, and those things that were done, they feared greatly, saying, Truly this was the Son of God." (Matt. 27:50-54.)

That the very elements themselves were revolted at the death of a God we cannot doubt. Certainly the earthquake, of such magnitude that it rent the rocks, was felt throughout the whole area where the evil crucifixion was wrought. But compared to the other events there and then crying for the attention of those who recorded the events connected with the life and death of their Lord, the physical changes in the earth were of lesser importance. Earthquakes of the sort there shown forth had occurred in great numbers, in many places, and at many times. But only at this one time and place had a God been lifted up upon a cross under circumstances that fulfilled the ancient prophecies in detail. For those in the Old World who were privy to all the circumstances surrounding the crucifixion, or who might learn them from witnesses who saw and heard and knew for themselves, these circumstances were a sufficient witness that the Messiah had been slain. The earthquake was only incidental to other and more important matters. Hence, neither Mark, Luke, nor John thought it of sufficient import to include in their recitation of the transcendent events of that gloomy day.

For that matter, our Old Testament, as it now stands, does not preserve for us any pointed prophecies foretelling the destructions and physical upheavals destined to attend the death of the One by whom life would come. The Messianic prophecies in that volume of ancient scripture were for the especial guidance of those in the Old World and dealt with things that would identify as the Messiah the One who ministered personally among them. We do have one prophecy recorded in Moses that would have been had among the Jews if the ancient record had been preserved in its perfection. In that passage Enoch, seeing the crucifixion in vision, also "heard a loud voice; and the heavens were veiled; and all the creations of God mourned; and the earth groaned; and the rocks were rent; and the saints arose, and were crowned at the right hand of the Son of Man, with crowns of glory." (Moses 7:56.)

One of Israel's prophets, Zenos, whose writings have been lost to us, but which were on the brass plates of Laban and were thus preserved for Nephite usage, did speak of the destructions that would attend our Lord's death. "He spake concerning the three days of darkness," we are told, "which should be a sign given of his death unto those who should inhabit the isles of the sea," and which should be "more especially given unto those who are of the house of Israel." That is to say, the portions of Israel far removed from Jerusalem and Canaan and who would not see the Messiah personally, or hear the testimony of those who did, were destined to receive special signs of his death and the atoning ransom that came thereby.

"The Lord God surely shall visit all the house of Israel at that day," Zenos prophesied, "some with his voice, because of their righteousness, unto their great joy and salvation," and this would include those Nephites who were righteous and were not slain in the destructions; "and others [would be visited] with the thunderings and lightnings of his power, by tempest, by fire, and by smoke, and vapor of darkness, and by the opening of the earth, and by mountains which shall be carried up"; these would include all those among the Nephites who were slain because they were the more wicked part of the people. "And all these things must surely come, saith the prophet Zenos. And the rocks of the earth must rend; and because of the groanings of the earth, many of the kings of the isles of the sea shall be wrought upon by the Spirit of God, to exclaim: The God of nature suffers."

Then come these words pertaining to those in Canaan: "And as for those who are at Jerusalem, saith the prophet, they shall be scourged by all people, because they crucify the God of Israel, and turn their hearts aside, rejecting signs and wonders, and the power and glory of the God of Israel. And because they turn their hearts aside, saith the prophet, and have despised the Holy One of Israel, they shall wander in the flesh, and perish, and become a hiss and a byword, and be hated among all nations." (1 Ne. 19:10-14.) That is to say, the scattering and treatment of the Jews as a people during the past two thousand years is itself a sign and a witness that they crucified their God.

Because the Nephites were on the opposite side of the world from where the actual events would occur, and would have no way except by prophetic pronouncement to know what there transpired, the Lord set up signs to signify when their Deliverer's death had occurred. Nephi saw that very meridian day in vision and described what he saw in these words: "And it came to pass that I saw a mist of darkness on the face of the land of promise; and I saw lightnings, and I heard thunderings, and earthquakes, and all manner of tumultuous noises; and I saw the earth and the rocks, that they rent; and I saw mountains tumbling into pieces; and I saw the plains of the earth, that they were broken up; and I saw many cities that they were sunk; and I saw many that they were burned with fire; and I saw many that did tumble to the earth, because of the quaking thereof. And it came to pass after I saw these things, I saw the vapor of darkness, that it passed from off the face of the earth; and behold, I saw multitudes who had fallen because of the great and terrible judgments of the Lord. And I saw the heavens open, and the Lamb of God descending out of heaven; and he came down and showed himself unto them." (1 Ne. 12:4-6.)

Also: "And after the Messiah shall come there shall be signs given unto my people of his birth, and also of his death and resurrection; and great and terrible shall that day be unto the wicked, for they shall perish; and they perish because they cast out the prophets, and the saints, and stone them, and slay them; wherefore the cry of the blood of the saints shall ascend up to God from the ground against them. Wherefore, all those who are proud, and that do wickedly, the day that cometh shall burn them up, saith the Lord of Hosts, for they shall be as stubble. And they that kill the prophets, and the saints, the depths of the earth shall swallow them up, saith the Lord of Hosts; and mountains shall cover them, and whirlwinds shall carry them away, and buildings shall fall upon them and crush them to pieces and grind them to powder. And they shall be visited with thunderings, and lightnings, and earthquakes, and all manner of destructions, for the fire of the anger of the Lord shall be kindled against them, and they shall be as stubble, and the day that cometh shall consume them, saith the Lord of Hosts. O the pain, and the anguish of my soul for the loss of the slain of my people! For I, Nephi, have seen it, and it well nigh consumeth me before the presence of the Lord; but I must cry unto my God: Thy ways are just. But behold, the righteous that hearken unto the words of the prophets, and destroy them not, but look forward unto Christ with steadfastness for the signs which are given, notwithstanding all persecution—behold, they are they which shall not perish. But the Son of righteousness shall appear unto them; and he shall heal them, and they shall have peace with him, until three generations shall have passed away, and many of the fourth generation shall have passed away in righteousness." (2 Ne. 26:3-9.)

Samuel the Lamanite, centuries later and a bare forty years before the crucifixion, rehearsed in detail to the Nephites the destructions and desolations that would attend that event. "In that day that he shall suffer death," the Lamanite prophet said, "the sun shall be darkened and refuse to give his light unto you; and also the moon and the stars; and there shall be no light upon the face of this land, even from the time that he shall suffer death, for the space of three days, to the time that he shall rise again from the dead." While our Lord's body lay in the tomb, while his eternal Spirit preached among the righteous dead, darkness enshrouded the Americas. Far removed though they were from the criminal events, no Nephite and no Lamanite would be unaware that their prophets had foretold the death of their Messiah and said that it would be known by three days of dooming darkness. Where else in all the history of the earth have continents been enveloped in darkness for three days? How could such an event do aught but witness the truth of the promised event?

"Yea, at the time that he shall yield up the ghost," Samuel continued, "there shall be thunderings and lightnings for the space of many hours, and the earth shall shake and tremble; and the rocks which are upon the face of this earth, which are both above the earth and beneath, which ye know at this time are solid, or the more part of it is one solid mass, shall be broken up; Yea, they shall be rent in twain, and shall ever after be found in seams and in cracks, and in broken fragments upon the face of the whole earth, yea, both above the earth and beneath. And behold, there shall be great tempests, and there shall be many mountains laid low, like unto a valley, and there shall be many places which are now called valleys which shall become mountains, whose height is great. And many highways shall be broken up, and many cities shall become desolate. And many graves shall be opened, and shall yield up many of their dead; and many saints shall appear unto many. And behold, thus hath the angel spoken unto me; for he said unto me that there should be thunderings and lightnings for the space of many hours. And he said unto me that while the thunder and the lightning lasted, and the tempest, that these things should be, and that darkness should cover the face of the whole earth for the space of three days."

It is perfectly clear that these destructions came as a just judgment upon the wicked, and that they are in similitude of the outpourings of wrath that shall come upon the whole world at the Second Coming, but they also came as a sign and a witness to the righteous who remained and who were not destroyed. "And the angel said unto me," Samuel went on to say, "that many shall see greater things than these, to the intent that they might believe that these signs and these wonders should come to pass upon all the face of this land, to the intent that there should be no cause for unbelief among the children of men—And this to the intent that whosoever will believe might be saved, and that whosoever will not believe, a righteous judgment might come upon them; and also if they are condemned they bring upon themselves their own condemnation." (Hel. 14:20-29.)

No single historical event in the whole Book of Mormon account is recorded in so great detail or at such extended length as the fulfillment of the signs signifying that Jesus had been lifted up upon the cross and had voluntarily laid down his life for the world. Here is part of the account: "And the people began to look with great earnestness for the sign which had been given by the prophet Samuel, the Lamanite, yea, for the time that there should be darkness for the space of three days over the face of the land. And there began to be great doubtings and disputations among the people, notwithstanding so many signs had been given. And it came to pass in the thirty and fourth year, in the first month, on the fourth day of the month, there arose a great storm, such an one as never had been known in all the land. And there was also a great and terrible tempest; and there was terrible thunder, insomuch that it did shake the whole earth as if it was about to divide asunder. And there were exceeding sharp lightnings, such as never had been known in all the land. And the city of Zarahemla did take fire. And the city of Moroni did sink into the depths of the sea, and the inhabitants thereof were drowned. And the earth was carried up upon the city of Moronihah that in the place of the city there became a great mountain. And there was a great and terrible destruction in the land southward.

"But behold, there was a more great and terrible destruction in the land northward; for behold, the whole face of the land was changed, because of the tempest and the whirlwinds and the thunderings and the lightnings, and the exceeding great quaking of the whole earth; And the highways were broken up, and the level roads were spoiled, and many smooth places became rough. And many great and notable cities were sunk, and many were burned, and many were shaken till the buildings thereof had fallen to the earth, and the inhabitants thereof were slain, and the places were left desolate. And there were some cities which remained; but the damage thereof was exceeding great, and there were many of them who were slain. And there were some who were carried away in the whirlwind; and whither they went no man knoweth, save they know that they were carried away. And thus the face of the whole earth became deformed, because of the tempests, and the thunderings, and the lightnings, and the quaking of the earth. And behold, the rocks were rent in twain; they were broken up upon the face of the whole earth, insomuch that they were found in broken fragments, and in seams and in cracks, upon all the face of the land. And it came to pass that when the thunderings, and the lightnings, and the storm, and the tempest, and the quakings of the earth did cease—for behold, they did last for about the space of three hours; and it was said by some that the time was greater; nevertheless, all these great and terrible things were done in about the space of three hours—and then behold, there was darkness upon the face of the land. And it came to pass that there was thick darkness upon all the face of the land, insomuch that the inhabitants thereof who had not fallen could feel the vapor of darkness; And there could be no light, because of the darkness, neither candles, neither torches; neither could there be fire kindled with their fine and exceedingly dry wood, so that there could not be any light at all; And there was not any light seen, neither fire, nor glimmer, neither the sun, nor the moon, nor the stars, for so great were the mists of darkness which were upon the face of the land.

"And it came to pass that it did last for the space of three days that there was no light seen; and there was great mourning and howling and weeping among all the people continually; yea, great were the groanings of the people, because of the darkness and the great destruction which had come upon them. And in one place they were heard to cry, saying: O that we had repented before this great and terrible day, and then would our brethren have been spared, and they would not have been burned in that great city Zarahemla. And in another place they were heard to cry and mourn, saying: O that we had repented before this great and terrible day, and had not killed and stoned the prophets, and cast them out; then would our mothers and our fair daughters, and our children have been spared, and not have been buried up in that great city Moronihah. And thus were the howlings of the people great and terrible." (3 Ne. 8:3-25.)

Then it was that the people who were yet alive heard the voice of the Lord as he spoke in the first person and announced that he had wrought all these destructions, adding more details to the account. (3 Ne. 9; 10:1-8.) "And now it came to pass that after the people had heard these words, behold, they began to weep and howl again because of the loss of their kindred and friends. And it came to pass that thus did the three days pass away. And it was in the morning, and the darkness dispersed from off the face of the land, and the earth did cease to tremble, and the rocks did cease to rend, and the dreadful groanings did cease, and all the tumultuous noises did pass away. And the earth did cleave together again, that it stood; and the mourning, and the weeping, and the wailing of the people who were spared alive did cease; and their mourning was turned into joy, and their lamentations into the praise and thanksgiving unto the Lord Jesus Christ, their Redeemer. And thus far were the scriptures fulfilled which had been spoken by the prophets.

"And it was the more righteous part of the people who were saved, and it was they who received the prophets and stoned them not; and it was they who had not shed the blood of the saints, who were spared—And they were spared and were not sunk and buried up in the earth; and they were not drowned in the depths of the sea; and they were not burned by fire, neither were they fallen upon and crushed to death; and they were not carried away in the whirlwind; neither were they overpowered by the vapor of smoke and of darkness.

"And now, whoso readeth, let him understand; he that hath the scriptures, let him search them, and see and behold if all these deaths and destructions by fire, and by smoke, and by tempests, and by whirlwinds, and by the opening of the earth to receive them, and all these things are not unto the fulfilling of the prophecies of many of the holy prophets. Behold, I say unto you, Yea, many have testified of these things at the coming of Christ, and were slain because they testified of these things. Yea, the prophet Zenos did testify of these things, and also Zenock spake concerning these things, because they testified particularly concerning us, who are the remnant of their seed." (3 Ne. 10:8-16.)

Messiah Shall Be Buried in a Sepulchre

Crucified criminals and other victims of Roman vengeance were often left on their crosses to rot away as signs and warnings to others. Blasphemers and others who were stoned to death among the Jews often had their bodies dumped unceremoniously in the Valley of Hinnom outside Jerusalem where the fires of Gehenna burned everlastingly. Decent burial was a mark of honor and respect. Reverence for those who passed on was unbounded. Abraham purchased the cave of Machpelah from the sons of Heth as a resting place for his beloved Sarah. Joseph required Israel to covenant that they would take his bones out of Egypt when they returned to their promised Canaan so that he could be buried with his fathers. It would have been the most natural and expected thing for the ingrates and rebels who instigated the death of their King to expect to add the ignominy and disgrace of a tombless disposal of his remains. And yet things were not intended to and did not eventuate in this way.

Joseph of Arimathea, a rich man who had an expensive tomb hewn from the rock, a tomb in which no man had lain, entreated Pilate that he might have the body of the deceased

Christ. Pilate, after receiving the assurance of the centurion that Jesus was in fact dead, and because it was contrary to the Jewish custom for one of their people to hang on the cross on the Sabbath, granted the Arimathean's request. Nicodemus, another rich and influential Jew, brought myrrh and aloes in large amounts for the embalming. The faithful women embalmed and clothed the body that soon was to rise from death, wrapping it carefully in linen clothes as was the custom among the Jews. Then it was placed in the tomb, which was sealed with a large stone, and a guard was placed, lest Jesus' followers steal the body and claim he had risen on the third day as he had promised to do. But on resurrection morn, angelic power rolled back the stone; he arose, went forth from the tomb, and began a series of appearances to faithful followers. Peter and John, entering the tomb, found the linen wrappings placed in such a manner as to show that they had not been unwrapped, but rather that the immortal body of their Lord had risen through the mortal cloth as a resurrected body would naturally do.

Why all this detail where his death and burial and coming forth were concerned? Would it not have sufficed, he having been slain, for him simply to rise from the dead no matter where his body was and without regard to the manner in which it had been cared for after his demise? Perhaps; but how much more persuasive it was for a cloud of witnesses to know the intimate details of his burial and coming forth and to be able to certify from personal knowledge to the reality of all the events incident thereto. Obviously it was so intended because the prophets of old had made special mention of the burial and the sepulchre and the wealth of those who would lay the body away, and so in this as in all things it was needful that the scriptures be fulfilled.

Isaiah said, "He made his grave with the wicked, and with the rich in his death" (Isa. 53:9), both of which promises were fulfilled. Zenos said he would "be buried in a sepulchre." (1 Ne. 19:10.) Nephi gave this promise: "They will crucify him; and after he is laid in a sepulchre for the space of three days he shall rise from the dead." (2 Ne. 25:13.) The prophet Jonah's unparalleled experience in being swallowed and then vomited up by a great fish was all done in similitude of and to teach the fact of our Lord's burial and resurrection. When the Jews sought from Jesus a sign, he condemned them as "an evil and adulterous generation," and said, "There shall no sign be given to it, but the sign of the prophet Jonas: For as Jonas was three days and three nights in the whale's belly; so shall the Son of man be three days and three nights in the heart of the earth." (Matt. 12:38-40.)

Truly, "though they found no cause of death in him," yet they caused "that he should be slain. And when they had fulfilled all that was written of him, they took him down from the tree, and laid him in a sepulchre. But God raised him from the dead: And he was seen many days of them which came up with him from Galilee to Jerusalem, who are his witnesses unto the people. And we declare unto you glad tidings, how that the promise which was made unto the fathers, God hath fulfilled the same unto us their children, in that he hath raised up Jesus again." (Acts 13:28-33.)

Truly, "He was crucified, died, and rose again the third day." (D&C 20:23.)

Chapter 30

BLESSED BE THE LORD

What Think Ye of Christ?

The Promised Messiah—what think ye of him? Who is he, and has he come? What is his work, and what has he done for that innumerable host of spirits, all children of the Eternal Father?

We shall set forth in Chapter 31 the crowning mortal blessing bestowed upon all those who turn to their Messiah with full purpose of heart and who gain a perfect knowledge of him and his mission. That blessing is to see his face, to stand in his presence, and to have intimate and personal communion with him as did many of those of old.

Before taking up the holy and sacred matters there summarized, however, we must be sure the house of faith and knowledge has been built with no part missing. And so we ask: What think ye of Christ, of his Father, of their plan of salvation, of the infinite and eternal atonement wrought by the Son of God, of the holy gospel through which life and immortality come? What think ye of the Promised Messiah?

We need not restate our conclusions in extenso, nor quote again the inspired word upon which they are based, but we should at least summarize the great and eternal truths concerning Christ and his ministry that have come to us from him who is the Author of our being and who is the Maker, Upholder, and Preserver of all things. This we now do both by way of doctrine and of testimony.

There is a God in heaven who is infinite and eternal. He has all power, all might, and all dominion. He knows all things, and there is nothing which he takes into his heart to do that he cannot accomplish. He is the Creator of all things—this earth and all forms of life and the very universe itself. He is omnipotent, omniscient, and omnipresent.

This Eternal God is a Holy Man in whose image mortal men are made. He has a body of flesh and bones as tangible as man's. He is a resurrected, glorified, exalted Personage of tabernacle. And he lives in the family unit.

We are the spirit children of God the Eternal Father, as also are all those yet unborn and all those who have and do and will dwell on any of the infinite number of earths he has created, in an ever-expanding universe, already composed of worlds without number. All of us lived in his presence, saw his face, heard his voice, knew him as our Father, and were taught eternal truths by him. He endowed us with agency and ordained and established those laws, by obedience to which we could advance and progress and become like him, those laws whereby we could gain eternal life, which is the name of the kind of life he lives. The plan of salvation which he established and offered to all his spirit offspring is named *The Gospel of God.*

The Lord Jesus Christ was the Firstborn Spirit Son of the Father. He was born as a spirit man, as were all his spirit brethren; he was the Offspring of the Almighty, as all of us were. In that spirit state he was true and faithful, obedient to every trust. His advancement was such that he became like the Father in power and intelligence. He became, under the Father, the Creator of worlds without number. His name was Jehovah, the Great I AM, the Eternal One. He was the Lord Omnipotent who was and is from all eternity to all eternity.

After The Gospel of God had been taught to all the hosts of heaven; after it was known that the course of progression leading to eternal life required a mortal probation; after we all knew that to become like our Father we must gain mortal bodies, pass through death, and rise again in immortality; after we knew that mortality was to be a probationary estate, a time of testing, a period when we would walk by faith and not by sight; after it was known that Adam must fall and bring temporal and spiritual death into the world; after the need for a Redeemer had been explained; after we knew that the Father would beget a mortal Son, an Only Begotten in the flesh, who would have power to work out the infinite and eternal atonement—after all this and much more, the Father asked for volunteers to be the Redeemer. 'Whom shall I send? Who will be my Son? To whom shall I give the power of immortality so that he can come forth in the resurrection himself and also bring to pass the resurrection of all men? Who will ransom men from the effects of Adam's fall?'

Then it was that the One, the Lord's Beloved and Chosen from the beginning, said, 'Father, here am I, send me; I will be thy Son and do thy will; thy gospel shall be my gospel; and the glory be thine forever.'

Then it was that the Father said: 'Thou art the man; thou shalt be my Son; thou shalt go down, the noblest of great Michael's race. A virgin shall thy mother be, and thou shalt redeem all mankind, even as many as will. My gospel shall be thy gospel.'

Then it was that the Promised Messiah was foreordained, became the Lamb slain from the foundation of the world, became the Word of God, the Messenger of Salvation for all men. His message was The Gospel of God, now named after the Son and known as *The Gospel of Jesus Christ.*

Thus it is that salvation is in Christ. He abolished death and brought life and immortality to light through the gospel. Through his atoning sacrifice all men are raised in immortality, while those who believe and obey inherit also the glories of eternal life and become as he and his Father are.

If there had been no atonement of Christ, there would be no salvation, no immortality, no eternal life, and the whole purpose and plan of the Father would have been frustrated. The very purposes of creation itself would have come to naught. All men would have mouldered forever in the grave, their bodies being sleeping dust forever and their spirits becoming devils, angels to a devil. If there had been no atonement of Christ, all men would be sons of perdition, cast out and cast off, doomed to suffer the wrath of God to all eternity.

From the beginning, from the day of the first mortal man, who is Adam our father, salvation became available because of the shedding of the blood of Christ. It was won by those who had faith in him, repented of all their sins, received the sanctifying power of the Holy Ghost in their lives, and then continued, all their mortal days, to do the works of righteousness.

Our Lord thus became the Mediator and Intercessor between fallen man and his Maker. His mission was one of reconciliation, of bringing his mortal brethren into full fellowship with the Infinite.

That all men might know of the great plan of redemption, our Lord revealed himself and his laws to Adam and to those among his posterity who obeyed the laws which permitted that revelation to come. By definition a prophet is one to whom the Lord gives revelation relative to some phase of his divine Sonship. All of the prophets from Adam to Christ foretold one thing or another about that redeeming day. All of the prophets and apostles who have lived since he came have testified by the power of the Holy Ghost of those same eternal gospel truths.

In ancient Israel, the Promised Messiah was known as the God of Abraham, Isaac, and Jacob, the God of Israel, the Holy One of Israel. He revealed himself as their Redeemer and Savior, their friend Jah, the Great Jehovah. He was the Shepherd of Israel, the Stone of Israel, the Branch, the Stem of Jesse, the Son of David, and a host of other things. Each name taught some special thing concerning his mission and ministry.

All of the ancient prophets and saints worshiped and served the Father in his holy name. Upon those in all ages who had faith, he poured out the gifts of the Spirit. Miracles abounded among them. Their sick were healed, their dead raised, seas parted, rivers turned out of their course, the sun stopped in the firmament, and the armies of opposing nations were destroyed.

All things given the saints in all ages were so ordained as to bear record of the Messiah. Sacrifices were performed in similitude of the future sacrifice of the Only Begotten. Baptisms were in similitude of his death, burial, and resurrection. The Sabbath day testified of his creative powers. All the ordinances and feasts and performances of the Mosaic law centered the attention of the people in their Messiah.

At the appointed time he came, born of Mary, in Bethlehem of Judea. He worked out his own salvation, revealed his Father, preached the gospel, wrought miracles, organized anew the earthly kingdom, was rejected by his own, and died a voluntary death on a cross at Calvary.

In a garden called Gethsemane, outside Jerusalem's walls, in agony beyond compare, he took upon himself the sins of all men on conditions of repentance. Then he yielded himself into the hands of traitors and wicked men to have his flesh gashed and pierced and his body hung on a tree. He came into the world to die, and die he did, die as only a God could.

Then on a Sunday morning, on the Lord's day, angelic power rolled back the stone from the Arimathean's tomb, and the only Perfect Man who ever lived arose from the dead in both physical and spiritual perfection. For forty days his ministry continued among selected mortals, and finally on Olivet, not far from Gethsemane, while his disciples looked on and angels attended, he ascended to his Father.

These are some of the things which we think of Christ, and they are but a small part of his doings. "There are also many other things which Jesus did, the which, if they should be written every one," the Beloved Disciple says, "even the world itself could not contain the books that should be written." (John 21:25.) But what we have written suffices for our purposes because it enables us to know that salvation is in Christ, and that all blessings flow to us because of him. Into his hands the Father hath committed all things. He has become the Author and Finisher of our faith, and in him do we trust and glory.

Sing unto the Lord

Music is part of the language of the Gods. It has been given to man so he can sing praises to the Lord. It is a means of expressing, with poetic words and in melodious tunes, the deep feelings of rejoicing and thanksgiving found in the hearts of those who have testimonies of the divine Sonship and who know of the wonders and glories wrought for them by the Father, Son, and Holy Spirit. Music is both in the voice and in the heart. Every true saint finds his heart full of songs of praise to his Maker. Those whose voices can sing forth the praises found in their hearts are twice blest. "Be filled with the Spirit," Paul counseled, "Speaking to yourselves in psalms and hymns and spiritual songs, singing and making melody in your heart to the Lord." (Eph. 5:18-19.) Also: "Let the word of Christ dwell in you richly in all wisdom; teaching and admonishing one another in psalms and hymns and spiritual songs, singing with grace in your hearts to the Lord." (Col. 3:16.)

Unfortunately not all music is good and edifying. Lucifer uses much that goes by the name of music to lead people to that which does not edify and is not of God. Just as language can be used to bless or curse, so music is a means of singing praises to the Lord or of planting evil thoughts and desires in the minds of men. Of that music which meets the divine standard and has the Lord's approval, he says: "My soul delighteth in the song of the heart; yea, the song of the righteous is a prayer unto me, and it shall be answered with a blessing upon their heads." (D&C 25:12.)

In view of all that the Lord Jesus Christ has done for us,

ought we not to sing praises to his holy name forever? "I will sing unto the Lord; I will sing praise to the Lord God of Israel," said Deborah and Barak. (Judg. 5:3.) King Benjamin so lived that he would go down to the grave in peace, so that his "immortal spirit may join the choirs above in singing the praises of a just God." (Mosiah 2:28.) Mormon preached that men should "believe in Jesus Christ" and all that he has done for them; that "he hath brought to pass the redemption of the world, whereby he that is found guiltless before him at the judgment day hath it given unto him to dwell in the presence of God in his kingdom, to sing ceaseless praises with the choirs above, unto the Father, and unto the Son, and unto the Holy Ghost, which are one God, in a state of happiness which hath no end." (Morm. 7:5-7.)

The Lord's inspired counsel on singing praises to his name is found in such passages as: "I will be glad and rejoice in thee: I will sing praise to thy name, O thou most High. . . . Sing praises to the Lord, which dwelleth in Zion: declare among the people his doings." (Ps. 9:2, 11.) "Sing unto the Lord, O ye saints of his, and give thanks at the remembrance of his holiness." (Ps. 30:4.) "Make a joyful noise unto God, all ye lands: Sing forth the honour of his name: make his praise glorious." (Ps. 66:1-2.) "Sing unto God, sing praises to his name: extol him that rideth upon the heavens by his name JAH, and rejoice before him." (Ps. 68:4.) "O sing unto the Lord a new song: for he hath done marvellous things: . . . the Lord hath made known his salvation. . . . All the ends of the earth shall see the salvation of our God. Make a joyful noise unto the Lord, all the earth: make a loud noise, and rejoice, and sing praise. Sing unto the Lord with the harp; with the harp, and the voice of a psalm. With trumpets and sound of cornet make a joyful noise before the Lord, the King." (Ps. 98:1-6; 96:1-7.) There is of course much more; and from all of it we learn that the true saints praise the Lord in song, both here and hereafter, both now and forever, for all that he has done for them and for all men.

"Praise Ye the Lord"

Among the true saints, cries of praise and blessing and thanksgiving to the Lord Jehovah are spoken from every lip. So great is their gratitude to him for his redeeming power that, from the rising of the sun to its going down, in every heart is found one grand Hallelujah, one great cry, praise ye the Lord, praise Jah, praise Jehovah. There are three obvious ways in which the saints praise their Messiah:

1. They sing the songs of Zion and the great Christian anthems, which musical presentations teach and testify of our Lord's wondrous works. Cries of "We thank thee, O God, for a prophet" are heard in every congregation. Great choirs acclaim: "We'll sing and we'll shout with the armies of heaven, Hosanna, hosanna to God and the Lamb! Let glory to them in the highest be given, Henceforth and forever; Amen and amen!" And the sound of worshipful voices sings: "Jesus, our Lord and God, Bore sin's tremendous load; Praise ye his name! Tell what his arm has done, What spoils from death he won; Sing his great name alone, Worthy the Lamb!"

2. They preach mighty sermons, pray in faith to the Father in the name of the Son, shout praises, speak forth the thoughts, intents, and desires of their hearts—all as guided by the Comforter, who "knoweth all things, and beareth record of the Father and of the Son." (D&C 42:17.)

3. They live as their Lord lived, keep his commandments, do as he did, and thus become living witnesses of the truth and divinity of his work. They become living epistles in whose hearts and lives the gospel is seen and is available to be "known and read of all men." (2 Cor. 3:2.) Others, seeing their good works, are thus led to glorify Those whose work it is. "Be holy, for I am holy" (Lev. 11:45) was Jehovah's word to Israel. There neither is nor can be any greater or more perfect way to praise the Lord than to keep his commandments, to become like him, and to let him thereby live in and through his obedient follower.

It is the divine will that the saints praise their God. Hence such scriptural injunctions as these: Be baptized and receive the Holy Ghost, and "then cometh the baptism of fire and of the Holy Ghost; and then can ye speak with the tongue of angels, and shout praises unto the Holy One of Israel." (2 Ne. 31:13.) "Fear this glorious and fearful name, THE LORD THY GOD," spake Moses to Israel. (Deut. 28:58.) "Bless ye the Lord," said Deborah and Barak. (Judg. 5:9.) "Let the Lord be glorified," as it is written in Isaiah. (Isa. 66:5.) Speaking Messianically, Isaiah said: "He shall be exalted and extolled, and be very high" (Isa. 52:13), and, "I will divide him a portion with the great, and he shall divide the spoil with the strong" (Isa. 53:12).

In the course of a longer Messianic recitation, the Psalmist says: "Blessed be he that cometh in the name of the Lord." (Ps. 118:26.) The believing multitude, on the occasion of our Lord's triumphal entry into Jerusalem, gave their witness on this point by acclaiming: "Hosanna to the son of David: Blessed is he that cometh in the name of the Lord; Hosanna in the highest." (Matt. 21:9.) And Jesus himself certified that the rebellious of Jerusalem "shall not see me henceforth, till ye shall say [at my Second Coming], Blessed is he that cometh in the name of the Lord." (Matt. 23:39.)

From the Psalms we extract these samples of the divine counsel that men should praise Jehovah: "I will praise the Lord according to his righteousness: and will sing praise to the name of the Lord most high." (Ps. 7:17.) "O Lord our Lord, how excellent is thy name in all the earth!" (Ps. 8:1.) "Let my mouth be filled with thy praise and with thy honour all the day. . . . My mouth shall shew forth thy righteousness and thy salvation all the day." (Ps. 71:8, 15.) "Bless the Lord, O my soul: and all that is within me, bless his holy name. Bless the Lord, O my soul, and forget not all his benefits. . . . Bless the Lord, ye his angels, that excel in strength, that do his commandments, hearkening unto the voice of his word. Bless ye the Lord, all ye his hosts; ye ministers of his, that do his pleasure. Bless the Lord, all his works in all places of his dominion: bless the Lord, O my soul." (Ps. 103:1-2, 20-22.) "Bless the Lord, O my soul. O Lord my God, thou art very great; thou art clothed with honour and majesty." (Ps. 104:1.) "Oh that men would praise the Lord for his goodness, and for his wonderful works to the children of men!" (Ps. 107:8.) Psalms 148, 149, and 150 recite who should praise the Lord and tell why. They end with these exulting words: "Let every thing that hath breath praise the Lord. Praise ye the Lord."

Pray unto the Lord

Brief reference was made in Chapter 19 to the fact that prayers are always made to the Father, but that the language and form of prayer are also used in praising and extolling the Son, and also, that when we pray to the Father, because of the laws of mediation and intercession, answers come from the Son. These concepts are basic to our whole system of worship and must be understood by those who come to know the only true God and Jesus Christ whom he hath sent, both of whom must be known if we are to gain eternal life. (John 17:3.) Accordingly, let us now set forth with some particularity the true form of prayer and show how and in what manner both the Father and the Son are involved.

Proper prayers are made to the Father, in the name of the Son, by the power of the Holy Ghost. The Father answers prayers, but he does it through the Son, into whose hands he has committed all things. For instance, Joseph Smith prayed to the Father in the name of Christ—seeking guidance, direction, doctrine—and the answers included such language as: "Thus saith the Lord your God, even Jesus Christ, the Great I AM, Alpha and Omega, the beginning and the end." (D&C 38:1.)

The Nephite Twelve "were united in mighty prayer and fasting. . . . They were praying unto the Father in the name of Jesus." This is the perfect pattern for gaining revelation or whatever is needed. In this setting, the record says: "And Jesus came and stood in the midst of them, and said unto them: What will ye that I shall give unto you?" (3 Ne. 27:1-2.) The prayer was addressed to the Father; the answer came by way of the Son.

As we are also aware, whenever the Son speaks, he assumes the prerogative of speaking in the first person as though he were the Father. "Listen to the voice of Jesus Christ, your Redeemer, the Great I AM, whose arm of mercy hath atoned for your sins; . . . Behold, I say unto you, that little children are redeemed from the foundation of the world through mine Only Begotten." (D&C 29:1, 46.) Christ speaks, but when occasion requires, he speaks by divine investiture of authority as though he were the Father.

The patterns of prayer were set in the earliest days of man's mortal probation. In revealing to Adam that sacrifices were offered in "similitude of the [future] sacrifice of the Only Begotten of the Father," an angelic ministrant said: "Wherefore"—that is, because the Only Begotten will sacrifice himself for mankind, and because he "is full of grace and truth"—"thou shalt do all that thou doest in the name of the Son, and thou shalt repent and call upon God in the name of the Son forevermore." (Moses 5:7-8.)

Proper prayers are not addressed to the Blessed Virgin, though we may suppose she was the greatest mortal of her sex. They are not addressed to Eve, the mother of all living, nor to Sarah, who with Abraham has entered into her exaltation and sits at her husband's side on the throne of eternal power. They are not made to any of the saints of either sex, whether they became such by Catholic fiat, as they suppose, or whether they gained that blessed state by faith and righteousness. They are not made to Moses, the mediator of the Old Covenant, nor to Jesus, the Mediator of the New Covenant, nor to the Holy Spirit of God, who knows all things and has all power. Proper prayers are offered to the Father, and to him only, but they are always offered in the name of his Only Begotten Son, or any of its synonyms. If this truth were known and believed, men would stand at the starting point and be in a position to get in tune with the Infinite and receive personal revelation from him.

All of the ancient prophets and all of the ancient saints followed the pattern given to Adam by the angel. They prayed to the Father in the name of his Only Begotten. Enoch prayed: "I ask thee, O Lord, in the name of thine Only Begotten, even Jesus Christ, that thou wilt have mercy upon Noah and his seed, that the earth might never more be covered by the floods." (Moses 7:50.) To Moses the Lord said: "Call upon God in the name of mine Only Begotten." (Moses 1:17.) "We knew of Christ, and we had a hope of his glory many hundred years before his coming," wrote the Nephite Jacob, "and not only we ourselves had a hope of his glory, but also all the holy prophets which were before us. Behold, they believed in Christ and worshiped the Father in his name, and also we worship the Father in his name." (Jacob 4:4-5.) All of the holy prophets worshiped the Father in the name of the Son! There is no other way. The first and great commandment, revealed anew in our day but given to the Lord's people in all dispensations, is: "Thou shalt love the Lord thy God with all thy heart, with all thy might, mind, and strength; and in the name of Jesus Christ thou shalt serve him." (D&C 59:5.)

Prayer and faith are perfectly united in the instructions of Jesus to the Nephites. "Ye must always pray unto the Father in my name," he told them, "And whatsoever ye shall ask the Father in my name, which is right, believing that ye shall receive, behold it shall be given unto you. Pray in your families unto the Father, always in my name, that your wives and your children may be blessed." (3 Ne. 18:20-21.) Explicit instruction to this effect abounds in the Nephite record. (2 Ne. 32:8-9; 33:12; 3 Ne. 18:30; Moro. 2:2; 3:2; 4:2; 7:48; 8:3.) Indeed, Jesus himself, as a mortal among the Jews (John 17) and as an immortal among the Nephites (3 Ne. 17), prayed in persuasive power to his Father. And for that matter the angels of God in heaven both speak and pray by the power of the Holy Ghost and in the name of that same Savior who is also our Savior.

There is one other great and eternal truth about prayer that cannot be emphasized too strongly. It is that if there had been no atonement of Christ; if the Son of God, in whose name we pray, had not ransomed man from the fall; if he had not put the great plan of redemption into operation by the shedding of his blood—except for these things, prayer in his name or any name, offered to the Father or any other person or thing, would be of no avail. Prayer is efficacious because of the atonement. As we have repeatedly pointed out in other connections, if there had been no atonement, the Father's plan would have been frustrated and all his purposes, including the reason for creation itself, would have become void. Thus, with reference to prayer, Amulek is able to say: "May God grant unto you, my brethren, that ye may begin to exercise your faith unto repentance, that ye begin to call upon his holy name, that he would have mercy upon you." (Alma 34:17.) That is to say, exercise faith, repent, and call upon God in the name of the Son for that mercy which comes because of the atonement to those who believe and obey. Truly, the atonement is the rock foundation of revealed religion.

We are being very express and pointed in setting forth the one and only true doctrine of prayer and worship in order to avoid any uncertainty or misapprehension in now noting that there are three exceptions, or seeming exceptions, to the order that prayers are to be offered to the Father in the name of the Son and in no other way. These are:

1. On that Pentecostal occasion when the Nephites received the gift of the Holy Ghost, they offered approved prayers directly to Jesus and not to the Father. But there was a special reason why this was done in this instance and on a onetime basis. Jesus had already taught them to pray in his name to the Father, which they first did. "They knelt again and prayed to the Father in the name of Jesus," the record says. "And they did pray for that which they most desired;

and they desired that the Holy Ghost should be given unto them." Thereupon the heavens opened, they were circled about with fire, angels ministered unto them, and Jesus commanded them to pray again. They did so. But this time "they did pray unto Jesus, calling him their Lord and their God." Jesus was present before them as the symbol of the Father. Seeing him, it was as though they saw the Father; praying to him, it was as though they prayed to the Father. It was a special and unique situation that as far as we know has taken place only once on earth during all the long ages of the Lord's hand-dealings with his children. It is analogous to the fact that the true believers in Jerusalem did not receive and enjoy the gift of the Holy Ghost as long as Christ personally ministered among them, although the receipt of that member of the Godhead as a gift, and the enjoyment of the companionship of the Holy Spirit, is essential to salvation.

At this point in the Nephite experience, Jesus prayed to the Father, thanking him for all that was then transpiring, and saying: "Thou seest that they believe in me because thou hearest them, and they pray unto me; and they pray unto me because I am with them." (3 Ne. 19:8-22.) When the special circumstances here involved no longer prevailed; when the circling flames of fire no longer blazed around them; and when the angels had returned to their heavenly abodes, the Nephites reverted to the established order and prayed again to the Father in the name of the Son. (3 Ne. 27:2.)

2. It is part of the divine program to use the form and language of prayer in crying Hallelujah, which means praise Jehovah, or praise the Lord, or praise Christ who is Jehovah. These ejaculations of joy are uttered in the spirit of prayer and of thanksgiving. They arise from every believing heart because of all that Christ the Lord has done in bringing to pass the immortality and eternal life of man. Such cries or shouts or expressions of praise to Jehovah, and also a formal prayer to the Father, given in the true and proper sense of the word, are perfectly linked together in the revealed dedi-

catory prayer of the Kirtland Temple. With joy and in the spirit of exultation the revelation begins: "Thanks be to thy name, O Lord God of Israel, who keepest covenant and showest mercy unto thy servants who walk uprightly before thee, with all their hearts"—that is, thanks be to Christ whose arm of mercy is over his saints—"Thou who hast commanded thy servants to build a house to thy name in this place [Kirtland]. And now thou beholdest, O Lord, that thy servants have done according to thy commandment." The command to build the house came from the Lord Jesus. He conveyed the Father's will and gave the direction. It was his voice that spoke to Joseph Smith.

"And now we ask thee, Holy Father, in the name of Jesus Christ, the Son of thy bosom, in whose name alone salvation can be administered to the children of men, we ask thee, O Lord, to accept of this house, the workmanship of the hands of us, thy servants, which thou didst command us to build." (D&C 109:1-4.) The dedicatory prayer is addressed to the Father, as all prayers should be; it is addressed to the One whose original command it was that the house be built, which direction had been revealed to the builders by the Son through whom all revelation comes. The only occasions when the Father gives personal direction and revelation are when he introduces and bears testimony of the Son, as in the case of Joseph's First Vision. Having made the introduction and given the testimony, the instruction then is, "Hear Him!" (JS-H 17.) Man then receives his instruction from the Son.

3. We also worship Christ in the true and proper sense of the word, which concept we shall now set forth.

Worship the Lord Jesus Christ

Nephi sets the stage for an understanding of the doctrine that true believers worship Christ, as well as the Father, in these words: "We talk of Christ, we rejoice in Christ, we preach of Christ, we prophesy of Christ, and we write according to our prophecies, that our children may know to what source they may look for a remission of their sins." (2 Ne. 25:26.) Remission of sins and consequent salvation come because of Christ! Hence, our worship of him: "Worthy is the Lamb that was slain to receive power, and riches, and wisdom, and strength, and honour, and glory, and blessing." (Rev. 5:13.) And worship! "[My words] are sufficient to teach any man the right way," Nephi continues, "for the right way is to believe in Christ and deny him not. . . . And Christ is the Holy One of Israel; wherefore ye must bow down before him, and worship him with all your might, mind, and strength, and your whole soul; and if ye do this ye shall in nowise be cast out." (2 Ne. 25:28-29.)

Perhaps the most dramatic and detailed account of perfect worship being given to Jesus is in connection with his immortal ministry among the Nephites. He appeared and testified of himself. He invited the multitude, all twenty-five hundred of them, to come forth one by one and thrust their hands into his side and to feel the prints of the nails in his hands and in his feet. They did so. "And when they had all gone forth and had witnessed for themselves, they did cry out with one accord, saying: Hosanna! Blessed be the name of the Most High God! And they did fall down at the feet of Jesus, and did worship him. . . . And Nephi . . . went forth, and bowed himself before the Lord and did kiss his feet." (3 Ne. 11:1-19.) Later, after Jesus taught them and healed their sick, "they did all, both they who had been healed and they who were whole, bow down at his feet, and did worship him; and as many as could come for the multitude did kiss his feet, insomuch that they did bathe his feet with their tears." (3 Ne. 17:10.)

In small part and to a lesser degree some of these same feelings of gratitude, adoration, and worship had welled up in the hearts of Jewish believers in Jerusalem, when "a very great multitude spread their garments in the way" and strewed branches before him as they acclaimed: "Hosanna to the son of David: Blessed is he that cometh in the name of the Lord; Hosanna in the highest." (Matt. 21:8-9.) And it was Jesus, quoting the Messianic message of Jehovah and applying it to himself, who said: "In vain they do worship me, teaching for doctrines the commandments of men." (Matt. 15:9.)

Throughout our Lord's mortal ministry there were in fact numerous instances when certain believers worshiped him. The wise men from the east, guided by the star and finding "the young child with Mary his mother, . . . fell down, and worshipped him." (Matt. 2:11.) As he came down from the mountain, having just preached that incomparable sermon, the Sermon on the Mount, "there came a leper and worshipped him, saying, Lord, if thou wilt, thou canst make me clean. And Jesus put forth his hand, and touched him, saying, I will; be thou clean. And immediately his leprosy was cleansed." (Matt. 8:1-3.)

Jesus raised the daughter of Jairus from the dead because that ruler "came . . . and worshipped him, saying, My daughter is even now dead: but come and lay thy hand upon her, and she shall live." (Matt. 9:18-25.) After Jesus walked on the water, bade Peter so to do, and calmed the boisterous waves with his word, the record says: "Then they that were in the ship came and worshipped him, saying, Of a truth thou art the Son of God." (Matt. 14:22-33.) A Gentile woman of Canaan, whose daughter was "grievously vexed with a devil," besought Jesus for help, which he declined to give, saying, "I am not sent but unto the lost sheep of the house of Israel." But the earnest supplicant was not to be denied. She yet came "and worshipped him, saying, Lord, help me." After further importuning, because of her faith and worship, Jesus commended her for her faith and healed her daughter. (Matt. 15:21-28.)

Jesus cast a legion of unclean spirits out of a man, fettered and bound in the tombs, when "he ran and worshipped him," and when one of the spirits by the mouth of the man called out, "thou Son of the most high God." These were the evil spirits which our Lord permitted to enter the herd of swine, causing their consequent destruction. (Mark 5:1-20.) The man born blind, whose eyes were opened as a prelude to Jesus' great sermon on the Good Shepherd, testified to the Great Healer: "Lord, I believe. And he worshipped him." (John 9 and 10.) At the open tomb, the seal of death having been broken, the angelic word was given to certain women, commanding them to tell the disciples that Jesus had risen. "And as they went to tell his disciples, behold, Jesus met them, saying, All hail. And they came and held him by the feet, and worshipped him." Later when the disciples "saw him," they also "worshipped him." (Matt. 28:1-17.)

With both the Nephite and the Jewish accounts before us, each of them showing that Jesus our Lord accepted the reverential worship of his fellow beings, and indeed expected it of them, we are led to ask: What kind of a Man was he? That he considered himself to be and was in fact the Son of God, who can doubt? But our present inquiry, dealing as it does with Messianic utterances, should lead us also to answer that all of the worship here and everywhere bestowed upon God's Almighty Son came in direct fulfillment of the Messianic promises. Some of these we shall now note. Quoting a passage from the Septuagint, which is not in our King James Bible, Paul preserves for us a Messianic utterance relative to bringing "the firstbegotten into the world," which says: "And let all the angels of God worship him." (Heb. 1:6.) Christ is worshiped by men and angels! In their great vision of the degrees of glory, Joseph Smith and Sidney Rigdon "saw the holy angels, and them who are sanctified before his throne, worshiping God, and the Lamb, who worship him forever and ever." (D&C 76:21.)

From the Psalms—those wondrous poetical recitations which so abundantly speak of our Lord's great ministries: that is, of his work in preexistence, of his mortal deeds, and of his eternal continuance in glorious exaltation—we take these sample statements: "Kiss the Son. . . . Blessed are all they that put their trust in him." (Ps. 2:12.) "Give unto the Lord the glory due unto his name; worship the Lord in the beauty of holiness." (Ps. 29:2; 96:1-13.) "He is thy Lord; and worship thou him." (Ps. 45:11.) "All the earth shall worship thee, and shall sing unto thee; they shall sing to thy name." (Ps. 66:4.) "Worship him, all ye gods." (Ps. 97:7.)

How to Worship the Father and the Son

Jesus said: "It is written, Thou shalt worship the Lord thy God, and him only shalt thou serve." (Luke 4:8.) The great Creator gave unto Adam and Eve, and through them to all of their posterity, "commandments that they should love and serve him, the only living and true God, and that he should be the only being whom they should worship." (D&C 20:19.) The plan of salvation for all men, the plan of worship for all men, is that they should worship the Father in the name of the Son. This is our whole approach to true and revealed religion. It is the pattern that has been followed in all dispensations. To the Samaritan woman with whom he conversed at Jacob's well, Jesus said: "The hour cometh, and now is, when the true worshippers shall worship the Father in spirit and in truth; for the Father seeketh such to worship him. For unto such hath God promised his Spirit. And they who worship him, must worship in spirit and in truth." (JST, John 4:25-26.)

We have also learned that in addition to worshiping the Father, our great and eternal Head, by whose word men are, there is a sense in which we worship the Son. We pay divine honor, reverence, and homage to him because of his atoning sacrifice, because immortality and eternal life come through him. He does not replace the Father in receiving reverence, honor, and respect, but he is worthy to receive all the praise and glory that our whole souls have power to possess.

It is our purpose now to ask how we worship the Lord, be he the Father or the Son or both. The forms of worship are many. Prayers, sermons, testimonies, gospel ordinances, attendance at church meetings, doing missionary service, visiting the fatherless and the widows in their afflictions, and a great many other things are all part of pure religion and true worship. But there is a way of worship that includes all these and yet is more than any one of them alone or all of them together. That way is made known to us in one of our deepest and most profound revelations.

We have in the first chapter of the Gospel of John an account of our Lord's status as the Word of God, as the Creator of all things, and as the life of the world. This account leads into the ministry and experience of John the Baptist in preparing the way before the Lord. In section 93 in the Doctrine and Covenants, we have a partial revelation of what is called "John's record," which deals with and adds to this same account and which includes what the Baptist saw after he immersed the Lord Jesus in Jordan. Clearly the original account of these doings was written by John the Baptist, portions of it were quoted by John the Beloved in his gospel, and added portions (with more yet to come) were revealed to Joseph Smith in modern times. Our present chief interest is in some of the things revealed anew in our day.

Our revelation says: "And I, John," meaning John the Baptist, "bear record that I beheld his glory, as the glory of the Only Begotten of the Father, full of grace and truth, even the Spirit of truth, which came and dwelt in the flesh, and dwelt among us." To our Lord's cousin and kinsman the heavens had been opened. He had seen and knew of the glory and greatness of the One whose forerunner he was and of whom he testified: "Behold the Lamb of God, which taketh away the sin of the world." (John 1:29.) "And I, John, saw that he received not of the fulness at the first, but received grace for grace," the newly revealed data continues, "And he received not of the fulness at first, but continued from grace to grace, until he received a fulness; And thus he was called the Son of God, because he received not of the fulness at the first." At this point John tells of seeing the heavens opened and the Holy Ghost descending upon Jesus, and tells of hearing the voice out of heaven say: "This is my beloved Son."

Then comes the climax of John's account, a climax that is in large measure the reason why the whole recitation was revealed. It says: "And I, John, bear record that he received a fulness of the glory of the Father. And he received all power, both in heaven and on earth, and the glory of the Father was with him, for he dwelt in him." This ends the renewed setting forth of what was known anciently.

Then the Lord says to Joseph Smith: "I give unto you these sayings that you may understand and know how to worship, and know what you worship, that you may come unto the Father in my name, and in due time receive of his fulness." Receive of his fulness, the fulness of the glory of the Father! Receive all power in heaven and on earth! Of those who so obtain it is written: "They shall pass by the angels, and the gods, which are set there, to their exaltation and glory in all things, . . . which glory shall be a fulness and a continuation of the seeds forever and ever. Then shall they be gods. . . . Then shall they be above all, because all things are subject unto them." (D&C 132:19-20.) Eternal life is to receive the fulness of the Father; it is to be like him; it is to live as he lives; it is the greatest of all the gifts of God; it is the object and end of our existence. Then the revelation sets forth this promise: "For if you keep my commandments you shall receive of his fulness, and be glorified in me as I am in the Father; therefore, I say unto you, you shall receive grace for grace." (D&C 93:6-20.)

Come worship the Lord! How is it done? Perfect worship is emulation. We honor those whom we imitate. The most perfect way of worship is to be holy as Jehovah is holy. It is to be pure as Christ is pure. It is to do the things that enable us to become like the Father. The course is one of obedience, of living by every word that proceedeth forth from the mouth of God, of keeping the commandments.

How do we worship the Lord? We do it by going from grace to grace, until we receive the fulness of the Father and are glorified in light and truth as is the case with our Pattern and Prototype, the Promised Messiah.

"SEEK THE FACE OF THE LORD ALWAYS"

Seek the Spirit

Our divine commission—the teacher's divine commission, whose terms and conditions are binding upon all legal administrators, upon all who are authorized to teach the Lord's gospel—our divine commission calls for us:

To teach the principles of the everlasting gospel, to teach them unmixed with personal opinions and the philosophies of the world;

To teach them out of the scriptures, and as they are revealed by the Comforter;

To do it by the power of the Holy Ghost;

To apply the teachings to our present needs; and

To do it all with the seal of personal testimony.

We have followed this pattern, and conformed to the best of our ability to this divine commission, in our consideration of all things relative to *The Promised Messiah—The First Coming of Christ.* We have dealt with the life and mission and ministry of the Lord Jesus Christ, showing that all the holy prophets since the world began have prophesied of him and his wondrous works; showing that they and all the saints of all ages have known and do now know that salvation is in Christ; and showing that his atoning sacrifice is the rock foundation upon which revealed religion rests.

Our source material has come almost exclusively from

the Standard Works; we have searched the scriptures diligently to learn all that the prophets have said about Him in whom our faith centers. We have sought to interpret the prophetic utterances by the spirit of inspiration, knowing that "no prophecy of the scripture is of any private interpretation" and that if "holy men of God spake as they were moved by the Holy Ghost" (2 Pet. 1:20-21), we must be moved upon by that same Spirit if we are to catch the full vision and meaning of the prophecies. In the very nature of things we have shown, and it also has been stated in plain words over and over again, that if the truths presented are believed and lived, they will assure us of peace in this life and eternal life in the world to come. The seal of personal testimony has been interwoven throughout the whole work as occasion has required and propriety has permitted. The work itself is what it is, and stands or falls on its own merits.

There are, however, two additional applications to be made of these great and eternal truths concerning the Promised Messiah. As believing saints it is our privilege:

1. To enjoy the gift of the Holy Ghost; to receive personal revelation; to possess the signs that always follow true believers; to work miracles; and to have the gifts of the Spirit; and

2. To see the Lord face to face; to talk with him as a man speaketh with his friend; to have his Person attend us from time to time; and to have him manifest to us the Father.

Members of the true church receive the gift of the Holy Ghost by the laying on of hands. This gift is the right to the constant companionship of this member of the Godhead based on faithfulness. It is well known among us that the Holy Ghost is a Revelator and a Sanctifier; that if we ask of God in faith, we shall receive revelation upon revelation, until the mysteries of the kingdom are unfolded in full; that faith precedes the miracle; and that signs always follow those who believe. Our obligation is to seek and obtain the Spirit so that all of these things will flow to us as they did to the ancients.

As to the possession of signs and the working of miracles, we have this assurance from the Lord Jesus: "Whatsoever ye shall ask the Father in my name, which is right, believing that ye shall receive, behold it shall be given unto you." (3 Ne. 18:20.) Four centuries later, the prophet Mormon rendered Jesus' promise in these words: "Whatsoever thing ye shall ask the Father in my name, which is good, in faith believing that ye shall receive, behold, it shall be done unto you." (Moro. 7:26.) If it be right, if it be good, faith will bring it to pass. Moroni affirmed the same truth by saying: "Whoso believeth in Christ, doubting nothing, whatsoever he shall ask the Father in the name of Christ it shall be granted him; and this promise is unto all, even unto the ends of the earth." (Morm. 9:21.) Moroni then quotes Jesus' promise that miracles and signs shall follow them that believe.

With specific reference to the fact that miracles are always found among faithful people, our Book of Mormon prophets leave us these testimonies: "Who shall say that Jesus Christ did not many mighty miracles? And there were many mighty miracles wrought by the hands of the apostles. And if there were miracles wrought then, why has God ceased to be a God of miracles and yet be an unchangeable Being? And behold, I say unto you he changeth not; if so he would cease to be God; and he ceaseth not to be God, and is a God of miracles. And the reason why he ceaseth to do miracles among the children of men is because that they dwindle in unbelief, and depart from the right way, and know not the God in whom they should trust." (Morm. 9:18-20.) "Have miracles ceased?" Mormon asked. "I say unto you, Nay," he answers, "for it is by faith that miracles are wrought; and it is by faith that angels appear and minister unto men; wherefore, if these things have ceased wo be unto the children of men, for it is because of unbelief, and all is vain. For no man can be saved, according to the words of Christ, save they shall have faith in his name; wherefore, if these things have ceased, then has faith ceased also; and awful is the state of man, for they are as though there had been no redemption made." (Moro. 7:27, 37-38.)

As to personal revelation—not revelation to apostles and prophets for the guidance and direction of the Lord's earthly affairs, but personal revelation for the perfecting of each individual saint—we have some wondrous words of counsel and direction that the Lord gave to Joseph Smith. They are appropriately prefaced with these expressions of praise and glory to Him from whom revelation comes: "Hear, O ye heavens, and give ear, O earth, and rejoice ye inhabitants thereof, for the Lord is God, and beside him there is no Savior. Great is his wisdom, marvelous are his ways, and the extent of his doings none can find out. His purposes fail not, neither are there any who can stay his hand. From eternity to eternity he is the same, and his years never fail." In this setting the inspired record continues: "For thus saith the Lord—I, the Lord, am merciful and gracious unto those who fear me, and delight to honor those who serve me in righteousness and in truth unto the end. Great shall be their reward and eternal shall be their glory. And to them will I reveal all mysteries, yea, all the hidden mysteries of my kingdom from days of old, and for ages to come, will I make known unto them the good pleasure of my will concerning all things pertaining to my kingdom. Yea, even the wonders of eternity shall they know, and things to come will I show them, even the things of many generations. And their wisdom shall be great, and their understanding reach to heaven; and before them the wisdom of the wise shall perish, and the understanding of the prudent shall come to naught. For by my Spirit will I enlighten them, and by my power will I make known unto them the secrets of my will—yea, even those things which eye has not seen, nor ear heard, nor yet entered into the heart of man." (D&C 76:1-10.)

God is no respecter of persons. His invitation to all men is: "If any of you lack wisdom, let him ask of God, that giveth to all men liberally, and upbraideth not; and it shall be given him." (James 1:5.) All who ask in faith receive an answer, and the greater the faith the more wondrous are the forthcoming revelations. After receiving and recording the Vision of the Degrees of Glory, Joseph Smith, still writing by way of revelation, said: "This is the end of the vision which we saw, which we were commanded to write while we were yet in the Spirit. But great and marvelous are the works of the Lord, and the mysteries of his kingdom which he showed unto us, which surpass all understanding in glory, and in might, and in dominion; Which he commanded us we should not write while we were yet in the Spirit, and are not lawful for man to utter; Neither is man capable to make them known, for they are only to be seen and understood by the power of the Holy Spirit, which God bestows on those who love him, and purify themselves before him; To whom he grants this privilege of seeing and knowing for themselves; That through the power and manifestation of the Spirit, while in the flesh, they may be able to bear his presence in the world of glory. And to God and the Lamb be glory, and honor, and dominion forever and ever." (D&C 76:113-19.)

A great congregation of Nephites had one of the experiences here described on that sacred occasion when Jesus prayed to the Father for them. "The eye hath never seen, neither hath the ear heard, before, so great and marvelous things as we saw and heard Jesus speak unto the Father," the account says. "And no tongue can speak, neither can there be written by any man, neither can the hearts of men conceive so great and marvelous things as we both saw and heard Jesus speak; and no one can conceive of the joy which filled our souls at the time we heard him pray for us unto the Father." (3 Ne. 17:16-17.)

We need not pursue further the concept that all saints, all true believers, all who have faith in the Lord Jesus Christ, all who love and serve him with all their hearts, receive revelations and spiritual gifts, enjoy signs, and work miracles. Suffice it to say that true greatness, from an eternal standpoint, is measured not in worldly station nor in ecclesiastical office, but in the possession of the gifts of the Spirit and in the enjoyment of the things of God. If an application is needed for all the Messianic messages with which we are dealing, it is surely found in the fact that those with true Messianic insight will be led to seek and obtain the Holy Spirit of God and all the consequent gifts that attend the receipt of this incomparable gift.

The Pure in Heart Shall See God

After the true saints receive and enjoy the gift of the Holy Ghost; after they know how to attune themselves to the voice of the Spirit; after they mature spiritually so that they see visions, work miracles, and entertain angels; after they make their calling and election sure and prove themselves worthy of every trust—after all this and more—it becomes their right and privilege to see the Lord and commune with him face to face. Revelations, visions, angelic visitations, the rending of the heavens, and appearances among men of the Lord himself—all these things are for all of the faithful. They are not reserved for apostles and prophets only. God is no respecter of persons. They are not reserved for one age only, or for a select lineage or people. We are all our Father's children. All men are welcome. "And he inviteth them all to come unto him and partake of his goodness; and he denieth none that come unto him, black and white, bond and free, male and female; and he remembereth the heathen; and all are alike unto God, both Jew and Gentile." (2 Ne. 26:33.)

Seeing the Lord is not a matter of lineage or rank or position or place of precedence. Joseph Smith said: "God hath not revealed anything to Joseph, but what he will make known unto the Twelve, and even the least saint may know all things as fast as he is able to bear them, for the day must come when no man need say to his neighbor, Know ye the Lord; for all shall know him . . . from the least to the greatest." (*Teachings*, p. 149.) The fact is that the day of personal visitations from the Lord to faithful men on earth has no more ceased than has the day of miracles. God is an unchangeable Being; otherwise he would not be God. The sole issue is finding people who have faith and who work righteousness. "For if there be no faith among the children of men God can do no miracle among them; wherefore, he showeth not himself until after their faith." (Ether 12:12.)

In the Sermon on the Mount, Jesus said: "Blessed are the pure in heart: for they shall see God." (Matt. 5:8.) The Book of Mormon rendition is even more express. It says: "And blessed are all the pure in heart, for they shall see God." (3 Ne. 12:8.) Ten days after the laying of the cornerstones for the Kirtland Temple, the Lord said to his little flock: "Inasmuch as my people build a house unto me in the name of the Lord, and do not suffer any unclean thing to come into it, that it be not defiled, my glory shall rest upon it; Yea, and my presence shall be there, for I will come into it, and all the pure in heart that shall come into it shall see God. But if it be defiled I will not come into it, and my glory shall not be there; for I will not come into unholy temples." (D&C 97:15-17.)

When the Lord has a house on earth, it is the natural and normal place for him to use in visiting his earthly friends. In the spring of 1820 the Father and the Son came to a grove of trees in western New York, because there was no temple on earth dedicated to serve as their abode. In May of 1829 John the Baptist came to Joseph Smith and Oliver Cowdery on the banks of the Susquehanna River; shortly thereafter Peter, James, and John came to them in a wilderness area. But once the saints had built a holy house for the Lord to use, he and his messengers visited that house to give instruction and confer keys. It was to the Kirtland Temple, the first holy temple of this dispensation, that Jehovah came on April 3, 1836, to be followed by Elias, Elijah, and Moses, each of which angelic ministrants conferred keys and powers upon their earthly fellow laborers. And so we turn to the Kirtland

Temple to see the literal nature of these promises that the pure in heart shall see God, and what happened in the Kirtland Temple is but illustrative of what can be in any of the Lord's houses whenever his worshiping saints generate the faith to pull down from heaven these same heavenly manifestations.

By January of 1836 the saints were getting ready to dedicate the Kirtland Temple. Because of their faith and as an expression of the divine approval that attended their labors, the Lord poured out upon them great Pentecostal manifestations. On January 21, the Prophet Joseph Smith; his father, Joseph Smith, Sr.; Oliver Cowdery; and the two counselors in the First Presidency, Sidney Rigdon and Frederick G. Williams, were participating in sacred ordinances in an upper room in the Kirtland Temple. "The heavens were opened upon us," the Prophet said, "and I beheld the celestial kingdom of God, and the glory thereof, whether in the body or out I cannot tell. I saw the transcendent beauty of the gate through which the heirs of that kingdom will enter, which was like unto circling flames of fire; Also the blazing throne of God, whereon was seated the Father and the Son." (JS-V 1-3.)

That same day, and on others that followed, the Prophet and many others saw vision upon vision. Included among them were these: "The visions of heaven were open to them also," the Prophet said with reference to the First Presidency and the members of bishoprics and high councils from both Zion and Kirtland. "Some of them saw the face of the Savior, and others were ministered unto by holy angels, and the spirit of prophecy and revelation was poured out in mighty power; and loud hosannas, and glory to God in the highest, saluted the heavens, for we all communed with the heavenly host." (*History of the Church,* 2:382.)

On January 28, 1836, "president Zebedee Coltrin, one of the seven presidents of the Seventy, saw the Savior extended before him, as upon the cross, and a little after, crowned with glory upon his head above the brightness of the sun."

(*Ibid.,* p. 387.) Of a meeting attended by about three hundred members, on March 30, 1836, in the Kirtland Temple, the Prophet wrote: "The brethren continued exhorting, prophesying, and speaking in tongues until five o'clock in the morning. The Savior made his appearance to some, while angels ministered to others, and it was a Pentecost and an endowment indeed, long to be remembered." (*Ibid.,* pp. 432-33.) The crowning appearance of the Lord during that special period of grace occurred, of course, on April 3, when the Great Jehovah appeared in his glory and majesty to Joseph Smith and Oliver Cowdery. (D&C 110.) These appearances of the Lord to his saints are but samples taken from a fragmentary account and covering a brief period of spiritual rejoicing, but they suffice for our purposes. There is no question but that the pure in heart do see God.

Associated with the promise that the pure in heart shall see God is the decree that those who are not pure in heart shall not see their Lord. Even Moses, with whom it was the practice of God to converse on a face-to-face basis, was denied that privilege on one occasion, as these words of scripture attest: "And he said unto Moses, Thou canst not see my face at this time, lest mine anger is kindled against thee also, and I destroy thee and thy people; for there shall no man among them see me at this time, and live, for they are exceeding sinful. And no sinful man hath at any time, neither shall there be any sinful man at any time, that shall see my face and live." (JST, Ex. 33:20.)

How to Seek and See the Lord

If we keep the commandments and are true and faithful in all things, we shall inherit eternal life in our Father's kingdom. Those who attain this high state of glory and exaltation shall dwell in the presence of God. They shall see his face and converse with him mouth to mouth. They shall know him in the full sense of the word because they have become like him. And all who are now living those laws to the full which will enable them to go where God and Christ are, and there enjoy eternal association with them—that is, all those who are now living in its entirety the law of the celestial kingdom—are already qualified to see the Lord. The attainment of such a state of righteousness and perfection is the object and end toward which all of the Lord's people are striving. We seek to see the face of the Lord while we yet dwell in mortality, and we seek to dwell with him everlastingly in the eternal kingdoms that are prepared.

Our scriptures contain such counsel as: "Seek ye the Lord while he may be found, call ye upon him while he is near: Let the wicked forsake his way, and the unrighteous man his thoughts: and let him return unto the Lord, and he will have mercy upon him; and to our God, for he will abundantly pardon." (Isa. 55:6-7.) "Seek the Lord, and ye shall live. . . . Seek him that maketh the seven stars and Orion. . . . The Lord is his name." (Amos 5:6, 8.) "Seek ye the Lord, all ye meek of the earth, which have wrought his judgment; seek righteousness, seek meekness." (Zeph. 2:3.) "Seek the face of the Lord always, that in patience ye may possess your souls, and ye shall have eternal life." (D&C 101:38.)

We know that all things are governed by law, and that "when we obtain any blessing from God, it is by obedience to that law upon which it is predicated." (D&C 130:20-21.) "For all who will have a blessing at my hands shall abide the law which was appointed for that blessing," the Lord says, "and the conditions thereof, as were instituted from before the foundation of the world." (D&C 132:5.) This means that if we obey the law that enables us to see the Lord, so shall it be, but if we do not meet the divine standard, our eyes shall not behold him. There is no secret as to what laws are involved. They are everywhere recited in the scriptures. That which must be done is described in various ways in different passages. But the general meaning is the same. It all comes down to one basic conclusion—that of keeping the commandments. Let us now consider some of the specific things the scriptures say we must do if we are to see the face of God while we yet dwell as mortals.

The pure in heart shall see God. This we have already seen, but we restate it again because the process of becoming pure in heart is the process that prepares us to see the face of Deity. In an early revelation, the Lord spoke of the members of his newly set up earthly kingdom as "mine own elect." Of them he said: "They will hear my voice, and shall see me, and shall not be asleep, and shall abide the day of my coming; for they shall be purified, even as I am pure." (D&C 35:21.) John spoke similarly when he described what is now our Lord's imminent appearance: "When he shall appear, we shall be like him," he said, "for we shall see him as he is. And every man that hath this hope in him purified himself, even as he is pure." (1 Jn. 3:2-3.) Knowing that Christ is pure, and that if we are to see him now, or be with him hereafter, we must be pure as he is pure, this becomes a great incentive to the purifying of our lives.

A perfectly stated and marvelously comprehensive formula that shows us what we must do to see the Lord is given us in these words: "Verily, thus saith the Lord: It shall come to pass that every soul who forsaketh his sins and cometh unto me, and calleth on my name, and obeyeth my voice, and keepeth my commandments, shall see my face and know that I am." (D&C 93:1.) Who made the promise? The Lord Jesus Christ. To whom is it given? To every living soul. What must we do to see his face? Five specifics are named: (1) Forsake our sins, for no unclean or impure person, no sinful man, can abide in his presence. (2) Come unto him; accept him as our Savior; receive his gospel, as it has been restored in our day. (3) Call on his name in mighty prayer as did the brother of Jared. (4) Obey his voice; do what he directs; put first in our lives the things of his kingdom; close our ears to the evil voices of the world. (5) Keep the commandments; endure in righteousness; be true to the faith. Those who do these things, being pure in heart, shall see God.

Faith and knowledge unite together to pave the way for the appearance of the Lord to an individual or to a whole people. The brother of Jared saw the Lord because he had a perfect knowledge that the Lord could and would show himself. His faith on the point of seeing within the veil was perfect; it had become knowledge. Because he knew, nothing doubting, he saw. Moroni, who had the plates of Ether and who summarized the account of Moriancumer's great vision, tells us why that prophet saw his God: "Because of the knowledge of this man he could not be kept from beholding within the veil," Moroni says, "and he saw the finger of Jesus, which, when he saw, he fell with fear; for he knew that it was the finger of the Lord; and he had faith no longer, for he knew, nothing doubting. Wherefore, having this perfect knowledge of God, he could not be kept from within the veil; therefore he saw Jesus; and he did minister unto him." (Ether 3:19-20.)

It was on this same basis that Jared's brother saw all the inhabitants of the earth and many other things that he wrote, but that "shall not go forth unto the Gentiles until the day that they shall repent of their iniquity, and become clean before the Lord. And in that day that they shall exercise faith in me, saith the Lord, even as the brother of Jared did, that they may become sanctified in me, then will I manifest unto them the things which the brother of Jared saw, even to the unfolding unto them all my revelations, saith Jesus Christ, the Son of God, the Father of the heavens and of the earth, and all things that in them are. And he that will contend against the word of the Lord, let him be accursed; and he that shall deny these things, let him be accursed; for unto them will I show no greater things, saith Jesus Christ; for I am he who speaketh." (Ether 4:6-8.) The message here is so clear that it cannot be clarified by commentary. The brother of Jared saw the Lord because of his faith and knowledge and because he sanctified himself before the Lord. Other men do not receive the same blessings because they have not built the same foundation of righteousness. If and when we obtain the spiritual stature of this man Moriancumer, then we shall see what he saw and know what he knew.

Commenting upon the appearance of Christ to the thousands of Nephites in the land Bountiful, Moroni says: "Faith is things which are hoped for and not seen; wherefore, dispute not because ye see not, for ye receive no witness until after the trial of your faith. For it was by faith that Christ showed himself unto our fathers, after he had risen from the dead; and he showed not himself unto them until after they had faith in him; wherefore, it must needs be that some had faith in him, for he showed himself not unto the world." (Ether 12:6-8.)

In a revelation addressed to those among the saints whom he considered to be his "friends," the Lord gave this commandment: "Call upon me while I am near—Draw near unto me and I will draw near unto you; seek me diligently and ye shall find me; ask, and ye shall receive; knock, and it shall be opened unto you." Surely, this is what we must do if we ever expect to see his face. He is there waiting our call, anxious to have us seek his face, awaiting our importuning pleas to rend the veil so that we can see the things of the Spirit.

"Whatsoever ye ask the Father in my name," he continues, "it shall be given unto you, that is expedient for you." Would it be expedient for us to see and know what the brother of Jared saw and knew? Are there blessings others have received that should be withheld from us? "And if your eye be single to my glory, your whole bodies shall be filled with light, and there shall be no darkness in you; and that body which is filled with light comprehendeth all things." Clearly this is the state attained by Moriancumer when he saw and understood all things and when the Lord could not withhold anything from him.

"Therefore, sanctify yourselves that your minds become single to God"—and now we come to the crowning promise of the gospel—"and the days will come that you shall see him; for he will unveil his face unto you, and it shall be in his own time, and in his own way, and according to his own will." That is the Lord's promise, his great promise, his crowning promise, his last promise. What is there that can excel in importance the obtaining of that spiritual stature which enables one to see the Lord? And so the next words spoken by the Lord to his friends were: "Remember the great and last promise which I have made unto you."

Then follows some counsel relative to right living, which is climaxed with these words, the full import of which is known only by those who are endowed with power from on high in holy places: "Sanctify yourselves; yea, purify your hearts, and cleanse your hands and your feet before me, that I may make you clean; That I may testify unto your Father, and your God, and my God, that you are clean from the blood of this wicked generation." Why? "That I may fulfil this promise, this great and last promise," this promise that you shall see me and that I will unveil my face, that I may fulfill this promise "which I have made unto you, when I will." (D&C 88:62-75.) To those of understanding we say: The purpose of the endowment in the house of the Lord is to prepare and sanctify his saints so they will be able to see his face, here and now, as well as to bear the glory of his presence in the eternal worlds.

In a poetic passage, which can only be understood, as is the case with most of the book of Isaiah, by those with a background knowledge of the gospel, Isaiah says of the righteous in Israel: "Thine eyes shall see the king in his beauty." That is: You shall see the face of the Lord. Any who so obtain are identified with this language: "He that walketh righteously, and speaketh uprightly; he that despiseth the gain of oppressions, that shaketh his hands from holding of bribes, that stoppeth his ears from hearing of blood, and shutteth his eyes from seeing evil." (Isa. 33:15.) These are the ones who shall see the Lord in this life and dwell with him in the life to come.

"How do men obtain a knowledge of the glory of God,

his perfections and attributes?" asked the Prophet Joseph Smith. His answer: "By devoting themselves to his service, through prayer and supplication incessantly strengthening their faith in him, until, like Enoch, the Brother of Jared, and Moses, they obtain a manifestation of God to themselves." (*Lectures on Faith,* p. 32.)

Those Whose Calling and Election Is Sure May See the Lord

It is the privilege of all those who have made their calling and election sure to see God; to talk with him face to face; to commune with him on a personal basis from time to time. These are the ones upon whom the Lord sends the Second Comforter. Their inheritance of exaltation and eternal life is assured, and so it becomes with them here and now in this life as it will be with all exalted beings in the life to come. They become the friends of God and converse with him on a friendly basis as one man speaks to another.

It is not our present purpose to discuss what it means to have one's calling and election made sure nor to recite the things that must be done so to obtain. A full discussion of these matters is found in my *Doctrinal New Testament Commentary,* volume 3, pages 323 to 355. For our present needs we shall simply quote this one sentence found on pages 330 and 331: "To have one's calling and election made sure is to be sealed up unto eternal life; it is to have the unconditional guarantee of exaltation in the highest heaven of the celestial world; it is to receive the assurance of godhood; it is, in effect, to have the day of judgment advanced, so that an inheritance of all the glory and honor of the Father's kingdom is assured prior to the day when the faithful actually enter into the divine presence to sit with Christ in his throne, even as he is 'set down' with his 'Father in his throne.' (Rev. 3:21.)"

In one of his greatest doctrinal expositions, the Prophet Joseph Smith equated the making of one's calling and election sure, spoken of by Peter, with "the sealing power spoken of by Paul." He said that those who were sealed up unto eternal life were the ones of whom Jeremiah spoke when he said that the Lord "will make a new covenant with the house of Israel, and with the house of Judah." In the day of this new covenant the Lord promised: "I will put my law in their inward parts, and write it in their hearts; and will be their God, and they shall be my people." Then comes the glorious promise that those who receive the covenant and keep its terms and conditions shall see the Lord. "And they shall teach no more every man his neighbour, and every man his brother, saying, Know the Lord: for they shall all know me, from the least of them unto the greatest of them, saith the Lord: for I will forgive their iniquity, and I will remember their sin no more." (Jer. 31:31-34.)

Having referred to this promise, the Prophet Joseph Smith asked: "How is this to be done?" How will it come to pass that every man shall know the Lord? Why will it not be necessary for men to continue to teach one another the doctrines of the kingdom? The Prophet answers: "It is to be done by this sealing power, and the other Comforter spoken of, which will be manifest by revelation."

Building on that foundation, he then proceeds to give forth his discourse on the Two Comforters. He tells how converted persons receive the Holy Ghost, are born again, become new creatures, and, if they are of Gentile lineage, how they are adopted into the house of Israel. "The other Comforter spoken of is a subject of great interest, and perhaps understood by few of this generation. After a person has faith in Christ, repents of his sins, and is baptized for the remission of his sins and receives the Holy Ghost, (by the laying on of hands), which is the first Comforter, then let him continue to humble himself before God, hungering and thirsting after righteousness, and living by every word of God, and the Lord will soon say unto him, Son, thou shalt be exalted. When the Lord has thoroughly proved him, and finds that the man is determined to serve Him at all hazards, then the man will find his calling and his election made sure, then it will be his privilege to receive the other Comforter, which the Lord hath promised the saints. . . .

"Now what is this other Comforter? It is no more nor less than the Lord Jesus Christ Himself; and this is the sum and substance of the whole matter; that when any man obtains this last Comforter, he will have the personage of Jesus Christ to attend him, or appear unto him from time to time, and even he will manifest the Father unto him, and they will take up their abode with him, and the visions of the heavens will be opened unto him, and the Lord will teach him face to face, and he may have a perfect knowledge of the mysteries of the Kingdom of God; and this is the state and place the ancient saints arrived at when they had such glorious visions—Isaiah, Ezekiel, John upon the Isle of Patmos, St. Paul in the three heavens, and all the saints who held communion with the general assembly and Church of the Firstborn." (*Teachings,* pp. 149-51.)

There are, of course, those whose callings and election have been made sure who have never exercised the faith nor exhibited the righteousness which would enable them to commune with the Lord on the promised basis. There are even those who neither believe nor know that it is possible to see the Lord in this day, and they therefore are without the personal incentive that would urge them onward in the pursuit of this consummation so devoutly desired by those with spiritual insight.

Priesthood Prepares Men to See God

When we speak of seeing the Lord and of talking to him face to face, we have reference to the Lord Jesus Christ, to our Messiah, to the Son of the Father who comes to represent his Father, to minister for and on his behalf and to act in his place and stead. But as we are aware, those who receive the Second Comforter not only have the personage of Jesus Christ to attend them from time to time, but the Son manifests the Father unto them, and the two of them take up their abode, as it were, with mortal men, men who also hold "communion with the general assembly and Church of the Firstborn." (*Teachings,* p. 151.)

It follows that both the Father and the Son may be and often are involved in the appearances of Deity to man. In his own discourse on the Second Comforter, and after having said that he himself would come to his disciples, the Lord Jesus said: "If a man love me, he will keep my words: and my Father will love him, and we will come unto him, and make our abode with him." (John 14:23.) With reference to this, speaking by the spirit of revelation, the Prophet Joseph Smith said: "John 14:23—The appearing of the Father and the Son, in that verse, is a personal appearance; and the idea that the Father and the Son dwell in a man's heart is an old sectarian notion, and is false." (D&C 130:3.) In point of practical reality, it is fair to say that there have been, as we shall note shortly, "many, exceeding great many" appearances of the Lord, meaning Christ, and a more limited number of appearances of the Lord, meaning the Father. And we shall also hereafter note the limitations that the Father imposes upon himself with reference to his own personal appearances.

Brethren whose calling and election is made sure always hold the holy Melchizedek Priesthood. Without this delegation of power and authority they cannot be sealed up unto eternal life. Our revelation itself says: "The more sure word of prophecy means a man's knowing that he is sealed up unto eternal life, by revelation and the spirit of prophecy, through the power of the Holy Priesthood." (D&C 131:5.)

It follows that the priesthood is the power, authority, and means that prepares men to see their Lord; also, that in the priesthood is found everything that is needed to bring this consummation to pass. Accordingly, it is written: "The power and authority of the higher, or Melchizedek Priesthood, is to hold the keys of all the spiritual blessings of the church—To have the privilege of receiving the mysteries of the kingdom of heaven, to have the heavens opened unto them, to commune with the general assembly and church of the Firstborn, and to enjoy the communion and presence of God the Father, and Jesus the mediator of the new covenant." (D&C 107:18-19.)

"The keys of all the spiritual blessings of the church"! Clearly no spiritual blessing is available to mortal man on earth that can compare with personal communion and converse with the Gods of heaven. Such attainments on the part of the prophets of old are the very things that set them apart above all their fellows. Keys open doors; keys are the directing and controlling power where priestly things are concerned. Thus, through the priesthood the door may be opened and the way provided for men to see the Father and the Son. From all of this it follows, automatically and axiomatically, that if and when the holy priesthood operates to the full in the life of any man, he will receive its great and full blessings, which are that rending of the heavens and that parting of the veil of which we now speak.

Truly, as Paul said of holders of the Melchizedek Priesthood who magnified their callings, thus qualifying to receive all of the blessings held in store for such faithful persons: "Ye are come unto mount Sion, and unto the city of the living God, the heavenly Jerusalem, and to an innumerable company of angels"; that is, the heavens are opened unto you, and as with Enoch and Moses and the brother of Jared, nothing is withheld from your view and understanding. "Ye are come . . . To the general assembly and church of the firstborn, which are written in heaven, and to God the Judge of all, and to the spirits of just men made perfect"; that is, you are in communion with the faithful of all ages past who now mingle together in a state of exaltation, you see God who is the Judge of all, and you commune with the departed spirits of the just. "Ye are come . . . To Jesus the mediator of the new covenant, and to the blood of sprinkling, that speaketh better things than that of Abel"; that is, you see Jesus, by the sprinkling of whose blood, as it were, salvation comes. Having so taught, Paul issues this warning: "See that ye refuse not him [the Lord] that speaketh." (Heb. 12:22-25.) Rather, accept the priesthood and let it operate in your life to the full until all these blessings flow to you as they flowed to those of old who magnified their callings.

All of the holy prophets and righteous men of old held the holy Melchizedek Priesthood. This "priesthood continueth in the church of God in all generations, and is without beginning of days or end of years. . . . And this greater priesthood administereth the gospel and holdeth the key of the mysteries of the kingdom, even the key of the knowledge of God." God is known in and through and because of the priesthood; without it he would remain unknown. Through the priesthood the Holy Ghost is given to men, which Comforter is sent forth to bear record of the Father and the Son; also, through the priesthood men are able to progress in spiritual things until they gain personal communion with Deity. "Therefore, in the ordinances thereof," the revelation continues, "the power of godliness is manifest. And without the ordinances thereof, and the authority of the priesthood, the power of godliness is not manifest unto men in the flesh; For without this no man can see the face of God, even the Father, and live." That is to say, in and through the holy priesthood, including all the laws and rites that go with it, the power of godliness, or in other words the power of righteousness, is brought to pass in the lives of men. Without these priesthood laws and powers, God's power and glory would not be revealed to man on earth. Without them they would not see the face of God, for if they did, his glory would destroy them. Sinful men cannot see the face of God and live. (JST, Ex. 33:20.)

"Now this Moses plainly taught to the children of Israel in the wilderness, and sought diligently to sanctify his people that they might behold the face of God; But they hardened their hearts and could not endure his presence; therefore, the Lord in his wrath, for his anger was kindled against them, swore that they should not enter into his rest while in the wilderness, which rest is the fulness of his glory. Therefore, he took Moses out of their midst, and the Holy Priesthood also." (D&C 84:17-26.) What a calamity! Because they did not use the priesthood for the purpose for which it was given—and it was given that they might sanctify themselves so as to "behold the face of God"—the Lord withdrew the very priesthood itself. Israel, as a people, was left with the preparatory gospel only, with the law of Moses. Her people were denied what they might have had because they did not magnify their callings in the priesthood. A little thoughtful reflection will cause us to conclude that there are those in latter-day Israel who are not striving to use the Melchizedek Priesthood for the purpose for which it was given any more than did our ancient ancestors. Again—what a calamity!

However sad it is that Israel (except for isolated groups and occasional instances) failed to use the holy priesthood to sanctify themselves so as to be able to see the face of God and live, it is refreshing to know that there were other peoples in other places who did take advantage of these blessings when they were offered to them. From Alma's great discourse on the higher priesthood we learn: "There were many who were ordained and became high priests of God; and it was on account of their exceeding faith and repentance, and their righteousness before God, they choosing to repent and work righteousness rather than to perish; Therefore they were called after this holy order, and were sanctified, and their garments were washed white through the blood of the Lamb. Now they, after being sanctified by the Holy Ghost, having their garments made white, being pure and spotless before God, could not look upon sin save it were with abhorrence; and there were many, exceeding great many, who were made pure and entered into the rest of the Lord their God." Though Israel failed to sanctify themselves and enter into the rest of the Lord, others did; others by faith and righteousness attained the fulness of the glory of God. And note how many were so involved: "There were many, exceeding great many."

After having recited what others had obtained through righteousness, Alma exhorted his own people in these words: "My brethren, I would that ye should humble yourselves before God, and bring forth fruit meet for repentance, that ye may also enter into that rest." (Alma 13:10-13.) Along this same line, the Prophet Joseph Smith said to his brethren, the elders of latter-day Israel: "It is the privilege of every elder to speak of the things of God; and could we all come together with one heart and one mind in perfect faith the veil might as well be rent today as next week, or any other time, and if we will but cleanse ourselves and covenant before God, to serve him, it is our privilege to have an assurance that God will protect us." (*Teachings,* p. 9.)

In November 1831, the Lord said to the little flock of elders so far ordained in his newly established latter-day kingdom: "It is your privilege, and a promise I give unto you that have been ordained unto this ministry, that inasmuch as you strip yourselves from jealousies and fears, and humble yourselves before me, for ye are not sufficiently humble, the veil shall be rent and you shall see me and know that I am—not with the carnal neither natural mind, but with the spiritual. For no man has seen God at any time in the flesh, except quickened by the Spirit of God. Neither can any natural man abide the presence of God, neither after the carnal mind. Ye are not able to abide the presence of God now, neither the ministering of angels; wherefore, continue in patience until ye are perfected. Let not your minds turn back; and when ye are worthy in mine own due time, ye shall see and know that which is conferred upon you by the hands of my servant Joseph Smith, Jun." (D&C 67:10-14.) That which had been conferred upon them by the Prophet was the power to see the Lord. The name of that power is the Melchizedek Priesthood. Many of these first elders in the kingdom did qualify in due course, while they yet dwelt in the flesh, to see the face of their King. How much spiritual progress we have made in the Church since the day of this revelation may be measured in terms of the number of the elders of Israel for whom the veil has been rent and who have seen the face of Him whose we are.

Apostles and Elders Should See God

All Christendom knows, or should know, that the ancient apostles were special witnesses of the Lord's name; that they saw him after he rose from the dead; that he spent forty days with them as a resurrected being, teaching them all things that it was expedient for them to know pertaining to his kingdom. Those who believe the Book of Mormon are aware that, as with the Twelve in Jerusalem, so with the Twelve on the American continent: they were all witnesses of the Lord—they all felt the nail marks in his hands and feet; they all thrust their hands into his side. There is general awareness in the Church that the latter-day Twelve hold the same office, possess the same priesthood and keys, and bear the same witness of the divine Sonship of him who redeemed us as did their predecessors in days of old. It is true that the witness of the Holy Ghost is sure and absolute and that a man can know with a perfect knowledge, by the power of the Holy Ghost, that Jesus Christ is the Son of the living God who was crucified for the sins of the world. This unshakeable certainty can rest in his soul even though he has not seen the face of his Lord. But it is also true that those who have this witness of the Spirit are expected, like their counterparts of old, to see and hear and touch and converse with the Heavenly Person, as did those of old.

Oliver Cowdery, the Associate President of the Church, who held the keys of the kingdom jointly with the Prophet Joseph Smith, having received them from holy angels sent to earth for that very purpose, was appointed to give the apostolic charge to the first quorum of apostles called in this dispensation. Speaking by the spirit of inspiration and by virtue of visions he had received, Elder Cowdery set forth, in the spirit of pure inspiration, the nature of the apostolic office and what is expected of those who hold it. We shall quote those portions of his charge which deal with the obligation that rests upon all members of the Council of the Twelve to see the face of Him whose witnesses they are.

In a special charge to Elder Parley P. Pratt, we find these words: "The ancients . . . had this testimony—that they had seen the Savior after he rose from the dead. You must bear the same testimony; or your mission, your labor, your toil, will be in vain. You must bear the same testimony, that there is but one God, one Mediator; he that hath seen him, will know him, and testify of him."

In the general charge to all of the Twelve, Elder Cowdery said: "It is necessary that you receive a testimony from heaven to yourselves; so that you can bear testimony to the truth of the Book of Mormon, and that you have seen the face of God. That is more than the testimony of an angel. When the proper time arrives, you shall be able to bear this testimony to the world. When you bear testimony that you have seen God, this testimony God will never suffer to fall, but will bear you out; although many will not give heed, yet others will. You will therefore see the necessity of getting this testimony from heaven.

"Never cease striving until you have seen God face to face. Strengthen your faith; cast off your doubts, your sins, and all your unbelief; and nothing can prevent you from coming to God. Your ordination is not full and complete till God has laid his hand upon you. We require as much to qualify us as did those who have gone before us; God is the same. If the Savior in former days laid his hands upon his disciples, why not in latter days? . . .

"The time is coming when you will be perfectly familiar with the things of God. . . . You have our best wishes, you have our most fervent prayers, that you may be able to bear this testimony, that you have seen the face of God. Therefore call upon him in faith in mighty prayer till you prevail, for it is your duty and your privilege to bear such a testimony for yourselves." (*History of the Church* 2:192-98.)

Few faithful people will stumble or feel disbelief at the doctrine here presented that the Lord's apostolic witnesses are entitled and expected to see his face, and that each one individually is obligated to "call upon him in faith in mighty prayer" until he prevails. But the Twelve are only a dozen in number. There are seldom more than fifteen men on earth at a time who have been ordained to the holy apostleship, which brings us to another statement made by Elder Cowdery in his apostolic charge: "God does not love you better or more than others." That is, apostles and prophets do not gain precedence with the Lord unless they earn it by personal righteousness. The Lord loves people, not office holders. Every elder is entitled to the same blessings and privileges offered the apostles. Indeed, an apostle is an elder; such is the title by which he is proud to be addressed. The priesthood is greater than any of its offices. No office adds any power, dignity, or authority to the priesthood. All offices derive their rights, virtues, authorities, and prerogatives from the priesthood. It is greater to hold the Melchizedek Priesthood than it is to hold the office of an elder or of an apostle in that priesthood. The Lord loves his priesthood holders, all of whom are given the same opportunity to do good and work righteousness and keep the commandments. All of the elders in the kingdom are expected to live the law as strictly as do the members of the Council of the Twelve, and if they do so live, the same blessings will come to them that flow to apostles and prophets.

Apostles and prophets are named as examples and patterns of what others should be. The Quorum of the Twelve should be a model quorum after which every elders quorum in the Church might pattern its course. For instance, before long there will be a great sacrament meeting at which the Lord Jesus himself will partake of the sacrament. Others who will be in attendance and who will partake of the sacrament also will be Moroni, Elias, John the Baptist, Elijah,

Abraham, Isaac, and Jacob, Joseph the son of Jacob, Peter, James, and John, and Michael the archangel who is Adam. These are the ones who are listed by name in the revelation. They shall all be there. The immediate impression arises—what a marvelous meeting this will be, to have the Lord Jesus and all these holy prophets in attendance. Such an impression is of course proper.

But those named are listed merely to illustrate and dramatize what is to be. After naming them as the ones with whom the Lord will partake of the sacrament, the revelation says, "And also with all those whom my Father hath given me out of the world." (D&C 27:5-14.) In other words, every faithful person in the whole history of the world, every person who has so lived as to merit eternal life in the kingdom of the Father will be in attendance and will partake, with the Lord, of the sacrament.

I repeat: apostles and prophets simply serve as patterns and examples to show all men what they may receive if they are true and faithful. There is nothing an apostle can receive that is not available to every elder in the kingdom. As we have heretofore quoted, from the Prophet's sermon on the Second Comforter: "God hath not revealed anything to Joseph, but what he will make known unto the Twelve, and even the least saint may know all things as fast as he is able to bear them." (*Teachings,* p. 149.) It follows that everything stated by Elder Oliver Cowdery in his charge to the apostles could also be given as a charge to all elders. Every elder is entitled and expected to seek and obtain all the spiritual blessings of the gospel, including the crowning blessing of seeing the Lord face to face.

WHO HAS SEEN THE LORD?

Many Prophets See the Lord

We have in Holy Writ numerous accounts of prophets and holy men who have seen the Lord—some face to face, others in dreams and visions; some in his glory, others when that glory was withheld from mortal view. These accounts have been preserved for us as examples and patterns of what has been, what is, and what yet shall be. They let us know the manner in which the Lord works, and they show us that other men, with passions and faults like ours, have yet overcome the world and gained surpassing outpourings of spiritual enlightenment.

When we speak of seeing the Lord, we have the Lord Jesus Christ in mind, although there are instances when the Father appears. Those who receive the Second Comforter have not only the personage of Jesus Christ to appear to them from time to time, but he also manifests unto them the Father. But the Father's appearances are for the purpose of introducing and bearing testimony of the Son.

Our King James Bible says: "For the law was given by Moses, but grace and truth came by Jesus Christ. No man hath seen God at any time; the only Begotten Son, which is in the bosom of the Father, he hath declared him." (John 1:17-18.) This passage should read: "For the law was given through Moses, but life and truth came through Jesus Christ.

For the law was after a carnal commandment, to the administration of death; but the gospel was after the power of an endless life, through Jesus Christ, the only Begotten Son, who is in the bosom of the Father. And no man hath seen God at any time, except he hath borne record of the Son; for except it is through him no man can be saved." (JST, John 1 17-19.) That is to say, the Father appears for the sole purpose of attesting the divine Sonship of him through whom the word of truth and salvation does and must come to the children of men. This is what is involved in the law of intercession and of mediation. Christ is the Mediator between God and man, and he reveals the Father; and unless men accept the Son, they cannot receive the Father. "No man cometh unto the Father, but by me," Jesus said. (John 14:6.) The Father dealt directly with Adam before the fall, and he apparently (as we shall note shortly) dealt directly with Enoch after that prophet was translated. Otherwise, all the dealings of Deity with men on earth have been through the Son.

We shall now collate and comment upon some of the more important manifestations of Deity to man so as to have before us what we may expect if we have faith like the ancients.

1. *Adam sees the Lord.*

Adam, our father, the first man, was the first of earth's inhabitants to see the Lord. He and his wife, Eve, had intimate and extended association with both the Father and the Son before the fall and while they dwelt in Eden's hallowed vales. (Moses 3 and 4.) They then knew, before mortality entered the world, that they were the offspring of Exalted Parents in whose image they were made. It was as automatic and instinctive for them to know their ancestry, their family relationship, and the exalted destiny they might obtain, as it is for mortal children to grow and assume they will be like their parents.

Then came the fall. Adam and Eve, his wife, were cast out of the Garden. Theirs was no longer a life of peace and serenity in Eden. Thorns and thistles, briars and noxious weeds sprang up unwanted in their earthly dwelling place. Deserts and drouths, disease and death now entered their lives. They and their posterity were shut out from the presence of God. We know that after the fall Adam was visited by angels, that he heard the voice of God, received revelations, and was in tune with the spiritual realm. How often he saw the Lord personally we do not know. It has been revealed to us, however, that after mortal life had gone on for nearly a thousand years, the ancient saints held a great conference to which the Lord came personally. "Three years previous to the death of Adam," the scripture says, "he called Seth, Enos, Cainan, Mahalaleel, Jared, Enoch, and Methuselah, who were all high priests, with the residue of his posterity who were righteous, into the valley of Adam-ondi-Ahman, and there bestowed upon them his last blessing. And the Lord appeared unto them, and they rose up and blessed Adam, and called him Michael, the prince, the archangel. And the Lord administered comfort unto Adam, and said unto him: I have set thee to be at the head; a multitude of nations shall come of thee, and thou art a prince over them forever. And Adam stood up in the midst of the congregation; and, notwithstanding he was bowed down with age, being full of the Holy Ghost, predicted whatsoever should befall his posterity unto the latest generation." (D&C 107:53-56.)

2. *Enoch sees the Lord.*

Those who saw the Lord, and who understood his gospel, taught the saving truths to their fellow mortals so that others might believe and gain spiritual experiences of their own. Enoch, who was present in the great Adam-ondi-Ahman congregation when the Lord appeared, also had continual personal communion with him. "He saw the Lord, and he walked with him, and was before his face continually; and he walked with God three hundred and sixty-five years," before he was translated. (D&C 107:49; Moses 6:39.)

It may well be that more people saw the Lord in Enoch's

day than at any other time in the entire history of the earth, or that more people saw him than at all other times combined. "I beheld the heavens open, and I was clothed upon with glory," Enoch said, "And I saw the Lord; and he stood before my face, and he talked with me, even as a man talketh one with another, face to face; and he said unto me: Look, and I will show unto thee the world for the space of many generations." Enoch was commanded to preach and baptize, and the resultant faith among his converts was so great that the record says: "The Lord came and dwelt with his people, and they dwelt in righteousness." The Lord called his people Zion; they built the City of Holiness, even Zion, which in process of time was taken up into heaven. Then Enoch "was high and lifted up, even in the bosom of the Father, and of the Son of Man," which is to say that he saw both the Father and the Son and conversed with them. There are then recorded some three and a half pages of these conversations, some statements being made by the Father, others by the Son. (Moses 7.)

3. *The brother of Jared sees the Lord.*

Moriancumer, Jared's brother, took sixteen small stones, which were "white and clear, even as transparent glass," to the top of a mountain where he asked the Lord to touch them that they might give light in the seagoing vessels that the Jaredites had built. "And the veil was taken from off the eyes of the brother of Jared, and he saw the finger of the Lord; and it was as the finger of a man, like unto flesh and blood." He said: "I knew not that the Lord had flesh and blood." The Lord responded: "I shall take upon me flesh and blood; and never has man come before me with such exceeding faith as thou hast."

Then the Lord said: "I am he who was prepared from the foundation of the world to redeem my people. Behold, I am Jesus Christ. . . . And never have I showed myself unto man whom I have created, for never has man believed in me as thou hast." That is to say: 'Never have I showed myself in the manner and form now involved; never has there been such a complete revelation of the nature and kind of being I am; never before has the veil been lifted completely so that a mortal man has been able to see my spirit body in the full and complete sense of the word.'

As the brother of Jared beheld the spirit body of the Firstborn of the Father, he was told: "Behold, this body which ye now behold, is the body of my spirit; . . . and even as I appear unto thee to be in the spirit will I appear unto my people in the flesh." In commenting upon this Moroni said, "Jesus showed himself unto this man in the spirit, even after the manner and in the likeness of the same body even as he showed himself unto the Nephites. And he ministered unto him even as he ministered unto the Nephites." (Ether 3:1-18.)

4. *Abraham sees the Lord.*

Abraham saw the Lord many times; and he saw him because he sought him in faith. When Pharaoh's priests tried to sacrifice Abraham upon an altar, the father of the faithful lifted up his voice unto the Lord his God and pleaded for deliverance. In answer he was "filled with the vision of the Almighty. . . . And his voice was unto me: Abraham, Abraham, behold, my name is Jehovah, and I have heard thee, and have come down to deliver thee." (Abr. 1:15-16.) After Abraham left Ur, of the Chaldees, and went to Haran to dwell, his account says: "The Lord appeared unto me, and said unto me: . . . I am the Lord thy God. . . . My name is Jehovah, and I know the end from the beginning; therefore my hand shall be over thee. And I will make of thee a great nation." (Abr. 2:6-9.) Again upon the plains of Moreh, Abraham says, "The Lord appeared unto me in answer to my prayers, and said unto me: Unto thy seed will I give this land." (Abr. 2:18-19.)

Of another appearance the record says: "I, Abraham, talked with the Lord, face to face, as one man talketh with another; and he told me of the works which his hands had made; And he said unto me: My son, my son (and his hand was stretched out), behold I will show you all these. And he put his hand upon mine eyes, and I saw those things which his hands had made, which were many; and they multiplied before mine eyes, and I could not see the end thereof." (Abr. 3:11-12.) Genesis also preserves for us accounts of some of the appearances of Deity to his friend Abraham. (Gen. 12:1-7; 13:14-18; 15:1-21; 17:1-21; 18:1-33; 22:15-18.)

5. *Moses sees the Lord.*

Moses stands preeminent above all Israel's prophets. "With him will I speak mouth to mouth, even apparently, and not in dark speeches," the Lord said, "and the similitude of the Lord shall he behold." (Num. 12:8.) Hence we read: "And the Lord spake unto Moses face to face, as a man speaketh unto his friend." (Ex. 33:11.) And: "Moses stood in the presence of God, and talked with him face to face." (Moses 1:31.) After he was taken from the midst of Israel, the account attests: "And there arose not a prophet since in Israel like unto Moses, whom the Lord knew face to face." (Deut. 34:10.)

Two of the Lord's appearances to Moses deserve special mention. In one of them the record says: "Then went up Moses, and Aaron, Nadab, and Abihu, and seventy of the elders of Israel: And they saw the God of Israel: and there was under his feet as it were a paved work of sapphire stone, and as it were the body of heaven in his clearness. . . . They saw God, and did eat and drink." (Ex. 24:9-11.) It was following this that Moses went up into the mount to receive the tables of stone and the commandments.

In the other account "Moses was caught up into an exceedingly high mountain, And he saw God face to face, and he talked with him, and the glory of God was upon Moses; therefore Moses could endure his presence." The God here involved was the Lord Jehovah, though his words were those of the Father; he was, of course, speaking by divine investiture of authority. After Moses had seen "the world and the ends thereof," and had come to know many things, he said: "Now mine own eyes have beheld God; but not my natural, but my spiritual eyes, for my natural eyes could not have beheld; for I should have withered and died in his presence; but his glory was upon me; and I beheld his face, for I was transfigured before him." (Moses 1:1-11.) Moses' experience accords with the reality revealed to Joseph Smith that "no man has seen God at any time in the flesh, except quickened by the Spirit of God," and that "neither can any natural man abide the presence of God, neither after the carnal mind." (D&C 67:11-12.)

6. *Joseph Smith sees the Lord.*

Joseph Smith saw the Father and the Son, as we assume was also the case with all dispensation heads. "I saw two Personages," he testified, "whose brightness and glory defy all description, standing above me in the air. One of them spake unto me, calling me by name, and said, pointing to the other —*This is My Beloved Son. Hear Him!*" (JS-H 17.) The Son, who is the Mediator, then delivered the message. The Father's part was to introduce the One into whose hands he had committed all things.

Jehovah came to Joseph Smith and Oliver Cowdery on the third day of April in 1836 in the Kirtland Temple. "The veil was taken from our minds, and the eyes of our understanding were opened," the scripture says. "We saw the Lord standing upon the breastwork of the pulpit, before us; and under his feet was a paved work of pure gold, in color like amber. His eyes were as a flame of fire; the hair of his head was white like the pure snow; his countenance shone above the brightness of the sun; and his voice was as the sound of the rushing of great waters, even the voice of Jehovah, saying: I am the first and the last; I am he who liveth, I am he who was slain; I am your advocate with the Father." (D&C 110:1-4.)

7. *Many other prophets have seen the Lord.*

We have singled out Adam, Enoch, the brother of Jared, Abraham, Moses, and Joseph Smith because the various accounts of what they saw, taken together, are sufficiently detailed to give us a general concept of what is involved. Great hosts of other prophets have also seen and heard and felt and known. Some of their writings have been preserved for our study and use, and here and there in these prophetic writings we find language which means that the authors had seen within the veil.

We have every reason to believe that the Father himself was present on the mount of transfiguration and that his Son communed with him face to face. Peter, James, and John, however, were only aware that a bright cloud overshadowed the transfigured persons and that a voice from the cloud said, "This is my beloved Son, in whom I am well pleased; hear ye him." (Matt. 17:1-9.) Isaac and Jacob, each in turn, saw and learned what had previously been manifest to their father Abraham. (Gen. 26:1-25; 28:10-22; 32:24-30; 35:9-15.) "And God revealed himself unto Seth." (Moses 6:3.) Emer "saw the Son of Righteousness, and did rejoice and glory in his day." (Ether 9:22.) Nephi, Isaiah, and Jacob all saw their Redeemer. (2 Ne. 11:2-3.)

"In the year that king Uzziah died I saw also the Lord sitting upon a throne, high and lifted up, and his train filled the temple. Above it stood the seraphims," Isaiah said, "And one cried unto another, and said, Holy, holy, holy, is the Lord of hosts: the whole earth is full of his glory." Then Isaiah testified: "Mine eyes have seen the King, the Lord of hosts." (Isa. 6:1-5.)

Joshua (Josh. 5:12-15), Manoah and his wife (Judg. 13:22), Ezekiel (Ezek. 1:1; 10:1), and Daniel (Dan. 10:5-6) were all similarly visited. Solomon saw him twice in a vision. (1 Kgs. 3:5-14; 9:2-9.) Joseph Smith and Sidney Rigdon also saw him in vision in the eternal worlds. (D&C 76:11-24.) Lehi and Nephi both saw him born of Mary and growing up in Nazareth. (1 Ne. 11.) Lehi, being "overcome with the Spirit, . . . was carried away in a vision, even that he saw the heavens open, and he thought he saw God sitting upon his throne, surrounded with numberless concourses of angels in the attitude of singing and praising their God." Thereafter "he saw one descending out of the midst of heaven, and he beheld that his luster was above that of the sun at noon-day.

And he also saw twelve others following him." (1 Ne. 1:7-12.) Alma was privileged to see what his father Lehi had seen. (Alma 36:22.) Stephen saw the heavens open "and Jesus standing on the right hand of God." (Acts 7:51-60.) The beloved John saw our Lord in his transcendent glory, even as he was seen by our modern prophet in the Kirtland Temple. (Rev. 1:13-18.)

One of the sweetest and most appealing accounts of all is that of Moroni, who said: "And now I, Moroni, bid farewell unto the Gentiles, yea, and also unto my brethren whom I love, until we shall meet before the judgment-seat of Christ, where all men shall know that my garments are not spotted with your blood. And then shall ye know that I have seen Jesus, and that he hath talked with me face to face, and that he told me in plain humility, even as a man telleth another in mine own language, concerning these things; And only a few have I written, because of my weakness in writing. And now, I would commend you to seek this Jesus of whom the prophets and apostles have written, that the grace of God the Father, and also the Lord Jesus Christ, and the Holy Ghost, which beareth record of them, may be and abide in you forever." (Ether 12:38-41.)

How Many People Have Seen or Will See the Lord?

We all saw the Lord (meaning the Father) in preexistence. Every living soul, every spirit offspring of the Eternal Father saw him and dwelt in his presence. We saw his face, heard his voice, felt his power and influence, and knew he was our God. Even the very devils now in hell enjoyed an intimate familiarity with him in that day. They were acquainted with his person and his teachings; indeed, the very reason they became devils was that they rebelled against him and his laws with the full and perfect knowledge that he was their Omnipotent Father and had himself established the rules of conduct for his spirit offspring.

We all saw the Lord (meaning the Son) in preexistence.

We lived in the Father's presence for millions of years and knew that his Firstborn Son was next to him in power and might and dominion. We were present in the Grand Council when Christ was chosen and foreordained to be the Savior and Redeemer. We knew him; he was our brother. We associated with him in the family unit. We saw his face, heard his voice, and felt his power and influence. Our knowledge of him was like our knowledge of the Father.

Speaking of the planets and orbs that spin in the sidereal heavens, the Lord says: "Any man who hath seen any or the least of these hath seen God moving in his majesty and power." That is, the heavens themselves declare the glory of God. The existence of the sun, moon, and stars, and of all things, is a witness that he lives and has all power. But the Lord says this simply to introduce a much greater truth, which is, that all of us who see these things have also seen him personally. "I say unto you, he hath seen him," the Lord continues, "nevertheless, he who came unto his own was not comprehended. The light shineth in darkness, and the darkness comprehendeth it not." All this has reference to the coming of our Lord into mortality and his rejection by his own, they preferring darkness rather than light because their deeds were evil. "Nevertheless, the day shall come when you shall comprehend even God, being quickened in him and by him. Then shall ye know that ye have seen me, that I am, and that I am the true light that is in you, and that you are in me; otherwise ye could not abound." (D&C 88:47-50.) We have seen God; true, it was in that day when we walked by sight; and now, walking by faith, we no longer remember our association with him; nonetheless, we have in fact seen him.

We have no way of knowing how many mortal persons have seen the Lord. Individual saints and prophets have seen him in all dispensations, and sometimes he has appeared to large congregations. We know that "many, exceeding great many" (Alma 13:12), as Alma expressed it, have enjoyed this privilege. We are left to assume that there are far more occasions—thousands or tens of thousands of times over—that we do not know of than those of which we do have knowledge. Let us look at the rays of light that have come through to us and reason a little as to how many people were of necessity involved.

We know categorically that from the fall of Adam to the Second Coming of Christ is a period of some six thousand years, and that the millennial era will then continue for another thousand years. Such is the chronology recited in the Bible, which has been confirmed by revelation to the Prophet Joseph Smith. Our revelation speaks of "this earth during the seven thousand years of its continuance, or its temporal existence," and also specifies that Christ will come "in the beginning of the seventh thousand years." (D&C 77.) This in no way names the day nor the hour of our Lord's return, and it does not put a stamp of divine approval upon our calendars as they now exist. It simply lets us know that the Biblical account of the chronology relative to Adam and his posterity is either correct or substantially so. The number of years there recited is either accurate or so nearly so that it does not make any real difference for our purposes.

According to the Biblical chronology, Adam fell in 4004 B.C. and died 930 years later, in 3074 B.C.. By latter-day revelation we know that the meeting at Adam-ondi-Ahman, which was attended by all of his righteous posterity and to which the Lord himself came, was three years previous to Adam's death, that is, in 3077 B.C. (D&C 107:53-56.) Also according to Biblical chronology, Enoch was translated in 3017 B.C., his city having existed for the preceding 365 years, which means that it was founded in 3382 B.C. "And all the days of Zion, in the days of Enoch, were three hundred and sixty-five years. And Enoch and all his people walked with God, and he dwelt in the midst of Zion; and it came to pass that Zion was not, for God received it up into his own bosom; and from thence went forth the saying, ZION IS FLED." (Moses 7:68-69.)

The chronology with which we are dealing is thus as follows:

4004 B.C.—Adam and Eve fall and become mortal.

3382 B.C.—Enoch founds "the city of Holiness, even Zion."

3077 B.C.—The Lord appears at the meeting in Adam-ondi-Ahman.

3074 B.C.—Adam dies.

3017 B.C.—Enoch and his city are translated and taken up into heaven.

3382 B.C. to 3017 B.C.—A duration of 365 years, a period of one year for each day of our years, during which the Lord Jesus Christ personally dwelt on earth and was seen by his people. We assume, of course, that he came and went during this period, as he will during that millennial age when he is destined, again, to dwell personally upon the earth.

Our present interest in this chronology is to call attention to the great number of people who, in the very nature of things, saw their Lord in the early days of this earth's temporal existence. We do not know how many there were, and we do not say how many there were. But it is perfectly obvious there were "many, exceeding great many." (Alma 13:12.) We do not know the population of the earth in the days before the flood. We do know that the childbearing years of women continued to great ages and that sufficient time was involved for great populations to arise. If the population of the earth had doubled every thirty-three years, from the day of Adam to the appearing of the Lord at Adam-ondi-Ahman, there would have been four and a half billion people on earth. We do not suppose for a moment that such was the case, but we cannot escape the conclusion that many people were then alive, and we do know that all the righteous among them saw the Lord.

If Enoch founded his city with a mere one thousand people, and they doubled in population every third of a century, there would have been more than a million saints resident therein when the Lord took them to his abodes. Our sole point in drawing these numbers out of the ethereal blue, as it were, is to show that great hosts of people saw the Lord in days gone by even as great hosts will see him in the coming millennial day.

As to the millennial era itself, once again we have no way of knowing how many people will dwell on earth, but whatever their number, all will see the Lord. Certainly the totals will be billions upon billions. We cannot escape the conclusion that more people will dwell on the earth, many times over, when it becomes again an Edenic garden, than have dwelt thereon during the long years of its fallen state.

As to the number of people assembled in paradise to wait upon the Lord, while his body lay in the tomb, again we can only speculate. We know that all the righteous dead from Adam to that time, plus those who had dwelt in Enoch's Zion, were there to hear him proclaim the glad tidings of redemption. And we also know that he did not go among the wicked and ungodly who were then in their spirit prison. (Joseph F. Smith—Vision.)

We do have some reasonable judgments to make relative to various of his other appearances. During his mortal ministry, those who believed in him saw the divinity that set him apart from all men. "The Word was made flesh, and dwelt among us, (and we beheld his glory, the glory as of the only begotten of the Father,) full of grace and truth," John says. (John 1:14.) Though his glory was clothed in mortal flesh, those with true spiritual insight recognized him for what he was. And for that matter, it is only those with great spiritual insight who see him as God's Son whether on this or the other side of the veil. Comparatively, those who saw, in his Mortal Person, the divinity that was his were few in number, and yet in their aggregate they totaled many souls.

Before his birth he appeared to Moses, Aaron, Nadab, Abihu, and seventy of the elders of Israel, seventy-four souls at once. (Ex. 24:9-11.) After his resurrection he walked on the Emmaus road with two disciples and then appeared in the upper room to ten of the Twelve, "and them that were with them," possibly a small congregation. (Luke 24.) He made a series of visits to various disciples, including one on a mountain in Galilee, which probably was the time when "he was seen of above five hundred brethren at once." (1 Cor. 15:6.) He of course continued with the apostles for forty days after his resurrection, "speaking of the things pertaining to the kingdom of God." (Acts 1:2-3.)

Our most detailed account of his resurrected appearances is of those appearances he made to the Nephites. What then transpired is recounted in chapters 11 to 26 inclusive in Third Nephi. Those who first heard his words in the land Bountiful "were in number about two thousand and five hundred souls; and they did consist of men, women, and children." (3 Ne. 17:25.) This, however, was only the beginning of what was to be. After Jesus ascended into heaven that first day, "it was noised abroad among the people immediately, before it was yet dark, that the multitude had seen Jesus, and he had ministered unto them, and that he would also show himself on the morrow unto the multitude." On the next day, among the increased throngs, the record says of the Twelve: "They went forth and stood in the midst of the multitude. And behold, the multitude was so great that they did cause that they should be separated into twelve bodies." Soon thereafter, "Jesus came and stood in the midst and ministered unto them." (3 Ne. 19:1-15.)

How many Nephites were then and there assembled to hear the teachings of the risen Lord? The inference is that there were twelve times as many as on the first day. That would be a total of thirty thousand, which is not unreasonable to suppose. In any event great numbers of righteous persons were involved. And it was not just a happenstance of coming to a group who chanced to be there at the moment. Those involved were qualified by personal righteousness to see the face of their God. As Moroni says, "it was by faith that Christ showed himself unto our fathers, after he had risen from the dead; and he showed not himself unto them until after they had faith in him." (Ether 12:7.)

Leaving his Nephite kinsmen, our Lord, risen and glorified, went to minister unto the lost tribes of Israel. (3 Ne. 16:1-5; 17:4.) Where he went and what he did we do not know. Did he visit one group or many? Did twenty-five hundred or thirty thousand more Israelites see his face? Someday we shall know. As of now we know in principle that these other Israelites were prepared and worthy, as all men must be who stand in the divine presence.

The tribes of Israel also have the promise that they shall again see their God in the days of redemption and gathering. "I will plead with you face to face. Like as I pleaded with your fathers in the wilderness of the land of Egypt, so will I plead with you, saith the Lord God. And I will cause you to pass under the rod, and I will bring you into the bond of the covenant. . . . And ye shall know that I am the Lord." (Ezek. 20:33-38.) To some extent this has already been fulfilled through the restoration of the gospel covenant and the appearance of the Lord to certain of his prophets. A yet more glorious fulfillment lies ahead and will be found when Israel's God appears personally to each worthy member of that chosen race.

Some appearances of the Lord, glorious and awesome ones, shall yet be made to infinitely large numbers of people. "Wo unto all those who die in their sins," Jacob says, "for they shall return to God, and behold his face, and remain in their sins." (2 Ne. 9:38.) On the other hand, it is said of the righteous, "When he shall appear, we shall be like him; for we shall see him as he is." (1 Jn. 3:2.) And finally, in celestial exaltation, all who gain eternal life shall forever behold the face of him who redeemed them. John saw a group of these singing praises to the Lamb and said that they numbered one hundred million, plus thousands of thousands. (Rev. 5:9-13.)

There will be another great gathering of saints at Adam-ondi-Ahman. Once again the Lord will be there, this time to receive from Adam, the Ancient of days, an accounting of his stewardship. This gathering, at which the Lord will be given "dominion, and glory, and a kingdom, that all people, nations, and languages, should serve him," will usher in the millennial reign. Those in attendance will be the righteous of all ages, each of whom in turn will give an accounting of his own stewardship. We suppose it will be those of all ages who shall partake of the sacrament with their risen Lord. (D&C 27:4-14.) As to their number, Daniel's account speaks of ten thousand times ten thousand and of thousands of thousands, which is to say an innumerable host. All these, being present, shall see and worship the Lord. (Dan. 7:9-14.)

Now this Lord, whose face has been seen by hosts of the righteous and whose face will yet be seen by multitudes that cannot be numbered, is in our midst from time to time, and we as a people do not see him nearly as often as we should. We are not speaking of him being in our midst in the spiritual sense that he is here by the power of his Spirit. We are speaking of his personal literal presence. "Lift up your hearts and be glad, for I am in your midst, and am your advocate with the Father; and it is his good will to give you the kingdom." (D&C 29:5.) "Verily, verily, I say unto you that mine eyes are upon you. I am in your midst and ye cannot see me; But the day soon cometh that ye shall see me, and know that I am; for the veil of darkness shall soon be rent, and he that is not purified shall not abide the day." (D&C 38:7-8.)

In this connection let us note one of the visions shown forth to the Prophet Joseph Smith during that Pentecostal period which preceded and attended the dedication of the Kirtland Temple. "I saw the Twelve Apostles of the Lamb, who are now upon the earth," he said, "who hold the keys of this last ministry, in foreign lands, standing together in a circle, much fatigued, with their clothes tattered and feet swollen, with their eyes downward, and Jesus standing in their midst, and they did not behold him. The Savior looked upon them and wept." (*History of the Church,* 2:381.) "I am in your midst, and I am the good shepherd, and the stone of Israel. He that buildeth upon this rock shall never fall. And the day cometh that you shall hear my voice and see me, and know that I am." (D&C 50:44-45.) It is worthy of note that the Lord uses the same kind of language to describe his personal presence on earth during the millennial era as he uses with reference to his unseen visits from time to time among the Latter-day Saints. "For the Lord shall be in their midst," he says of his coming millennial sojourn on earth, "and his glory shall be upon them, and he will be their king and their lawgiver." (D&C 45:59.)

The Promised Messiah Is the Lord

We have now made our presentation. We have searched the scriptures diligently, choosing the most important Messianic prophecies for our study and exposition. We have set forth in simple language how and in what manner the prophetic word has found fulfillment in Christ. Through it all we have interwoven our personal witness of the divinity of Him of whom all the prophets testify.

From the first Alpha on the first page to the last Omega on the last page, the message of this work is:

God is our Father, by whom all things are;

Jesus Christ is the Son of the living God, by whom redemption cometh;

Salvation is in Christ, whose atoning blood ransoms men from the temporal and spiritual death brought into the world by the fall of Adam; and

All the prophets, from first to last—from father Adam, who dwelt in Eden's vale, to John the Baptist, who abode in the deserts of Judea; from the first man, who partook of the forbidden fruit that man might be, and who was given a coat of skins to cover his nakedness, to the man John, our Lord's forerunner, who ate locusts and honey and wore raiment made of camel's hair; from Moses, who worshiped in the holy mount, and with whom God spake face to face and not in dark similitudes, to Peter, James, and John, who, also on a holy mount, saw Christ transfigured before them and heard the voice of the Father attest our Lord's divinity—from the beginning to the end, be they whosoever they were, all of the prophets were witnesses of Christ. All proclaimed him as the Son of God. All taught the principles of eternal truth by conformity to which the faithful have power to ascend the throne of eternal power and sit with God on his throne.

And as we bring our own Messianic writings to a close we rejoice in spirit with all the prophets of the past. Their words sink deep into our hearts. Our bosoms burn within us. We feel in our souls the truth and divinity of the testimonies they have borne and the doctrines they have preached.

As with Lehi and Alma—both of whom, being enlightened by the power of the Spirit, thought they "saw God sitting upon his throne, surrounded by numberless concourses of angels in the attitude of singing and praising their God" (1 Ne. 1:8; Alma 36:22)—so we seem to hear and seem to see again what our fellowservants heard and saw in times past.

We seem to hear their voices anew as they acclaim, by the power of the Holy Ghost, that Jesus, who is called Christ, is Lord of all. We seem to see anew the vision of "the Lord sitting upon a throne, high and lifted up," and hear the cries: "Holy, holy, holy, is the Lord of hosts: the whole earth is full of his glory." (Isa. 6:1, 3.)

We hear a modern voice, addressed to all men, to the living and the dead, saying: "Hear, O ye heavens, and give ear, O earth, and rejoice ye inhabitants thereof, for the Lord is God, and beside him there is no Savior. Great is his wisdom, marvelous are his ways, and the extent of his doings none can find out. His purposes fail not, neither are there any who can stay his hand. From eternity to eternity he is the same, and his years never fail." (D&C 76:1-4.)

We see an angel before an open tomb. "I know that ye seek Jesus, which was crucified," he says. Then comes the portentous proclamation from angelic lips: "He is not here:

for he is risen, as he said. . . . He is risen from the dead." (Matt. 28:5-7.) Christ, the Lord, is risen! "Death is swallowed up in victory. . . . O grave, where is thy victory?" (1 Cor. 15:54-55.)

We hear a great choir—"ten thousand times ten thousand, and thousands of thousands" in number—saying: "Worthy is the Lamb that was slain to receive power, and riches, and wisdom, and strength, and honour, and glory, and blessing."

An echoing chorus fills heaven's dome as all created things acclaim: "Blessing, and honour, and glory, and power, be unto him that sitteth upon the throne, and unto the Lamb for ever and ever." (Rev. 5:9-13.)

"Great voices" from out the wide expanse of eternity add their testimony: "The kingdoms of this world are become the kingdoms of our Lord, and of his Christ; and he shall reign for ever and ever." (Rev. 11:15.)

From others comes the cry: "Alleluia; Salvation, and glory, and honour, and power, unto the Lord our God: . . . [He is] KING OF KINGS, AND LORD OF LORDS." (Rev. 19:1, 16.)

To the voices of the past is added one of latter days. "Let the mountains shout for joy," cries Joseph Smith, the American witness of Christ, "and all ye valleys cry aloud; and all ye seas and dry lands tell the wonders of your Eternal King! And ye rivers, and brooks, and rills, flow down with gladness. Let the woods and all the trees of the field praise the Lord; and ye solid rocks weep for joy! And let the sun, moon, and the morning stars sing together, and let all the sons of God shout for joy! And let the eternal creations declare his name forever and ever! And again I say, how glorious is the voice we hear from heaven, proclaiming in our ears, glory, and salvation, and honor, and immortality, and eternal life; kingdoms, principalities, and powers!" (D&C 128:23.)

How fitting is the oft-repeated Psalmic word: "Praise ye the Lord . . . Let everything that hath breath praise the Lord. Praise ye the Lord." (Ps. 150:1-6.) Hallelujah!

"And now, after the many testimonies which have been given of him, this is the testimony, last of all, which we give of him: That he lives! For we saw him, even on the right hand of God; and we heard the voice bearing record that he is the Only Begotten of the Father—That by him, and through him, and of him, the worlds are and were created, and the inhabitants thereof are begotten sons and daughters unto God." (D&C 76:22-24.)

And now it but remains for this disciple, in plain words, to testify that he also, independent of all others, does, by the power of the Holy Ghost, know of the truth and verity of that which is written concerning God's Son.

Jesus Christ is the Son of the living God; he was crucified for the sins of the world; he is our Lord, our King, our God—the Promised Messiah!

He came in the meridian of time to work out the infinite and eternal atonement.

He has set up his kingdom again on earth in these last days to prepare a people for his Second Coming.

He shall soon come again to live and reign on earth with faithful men for the space of a thousand years.

Blessed be his holy name both now and forever.

"Praise ye the Lord."

INDEX

Aaron: teachings of, to Lamanites, 83; on atonement, 146
Aaronic or Levitical Priesthood: administers preparatory gospel only, 410; ordaining a bishop in, 411; power of, is limited to performing outward ordinances, 412-13
Abel, slaying of, 32
Abinadi: prophesied of Christ, 26-27, 61; explanation of, about Christ as Father and Son, 61, 372-73; on prophets, 78; on Christ's Godhood, 99; knew of atonement, 232, 233-34; quotes Isaiah, 234; on atonement, 245-46; on resurrection, 268; on salvation, 290; on the wicked who receive not mercy, 329-30; identifies seed of Messiah, 360; on law of Moses, 409, 417, 419; preaching of, to King Noah, 418-19
Abraham: capture of, 32, 104, 600; saw the hosts of heaven, 53; Christ is God of, 103, 163-64, 551; Jehovah's covenant with, 106, 110, 164, 308; belief in, is belief in Christ, 109-10; saw the days of the "Son of Man," 141; look unto, 163; on resurrection, 267; men become heirs of God according to promise made to, 356; was called by Jehovah's name, 367; was to sacrifice Isaac in similitude of God's offering of Christ, 452; seed of, were foreordained, 507; saw the Lord many times, 600-601
Accountability, age of, 302
Adam, 79, 328; fall of, 66-67, 217, 244; was commanded to perform works in Christ's name, 69, 138, 306, 558; was commanded to be fruitful, 220; was commanded to fall, 221; and Eve brought forth children, 222; knew doctrine of blood atonement, 249; preaching of gospel in time of, 288, 293; offered up sacrifices, 379; is a similitude of Christ, 449; dwelt with God, 597; bestows his last blessing, 598. *See also* Fall
Adam-ondi-Ahman: Lord visits Adam at, 598; latter-day gathering at, 610-11
Adoption: into Christ's family, 352, 354; into Elohim's family, 354, 356-67
Agency: men possess, 219; atonement preserves, 229
Ahman and Son Ahman, 140
Allah, 322
Alleluia: translation of, 111-12; heavenly choirs sing, 309
Alma the elder, teachings of, on law of forgiveness, 340-41
Alma the younger: speaks to

Corianton about Messianic prophecies, 30, 82; prepares Nephites to receive Christ, 73, 232, 479-80; on sacred records, 89; on understanding scriptures, 91; on glad tidings, 95; on Christ's Godhood, 99; quotes Old Testament prophets, 144; testifies of Christ, 147; on Christ as shepherd, 179, 365; on justice and mercy, 245; on those sanctified by Christ's blood, 251, 590-91; on becoming clean, 251-52; on salvation, 290; heals Zeezrom, 290; on paradise, 318; story of conversion of, 333-34; on being born again, 350-51; bears testimony to Korihor, 376; called Christ the Lamb, 381-82; on the brazen serpent raised up by Moses, 400, 401; on the Liahona, 402-3; on Melchizedek Priesthood, 451-52; on birth of Christ, 464; on Christ's healing ministry, 490; bore testimony to the truth of his own words, 517

Alpha and Omega, Christ is, 167

Amaleki admonishes men to come unto Christ, 303

Ammon, teachings of, to King Lamoni, 82-83

Amulek: testified of Christ, 82, 146; on oneness of God, 115; on salvation, 129-30, 291, 342; knew of fall and atonement, 232-33; on repentance, 246; preaches to Zoramites of Christ, 290; on the rest of the Lord, 319; on law of Moses, 417-18, 423

Andrew, 149

Angels: testify of Christ, 73-74; rolled back stone from Christ's tomb, 278-79; ministered unto men, 313

Anna, 150

Anointed One, Christ is, 182-83

Antichrist, definition of, 324

Apostles: ancient, appearance of Christ to, 48; and prophets are examples, 594-95; latter-day, Christ stood among, and they beheld him not, 611. *See also* Prophets; Twelve Apostles

"As man now is, God once was," 134-36

"Ask, and ye shall receive," 582

Athanasian creed, 115-17

Atonement: definition of, 224; Day of, 435-37. *See also* Jesus Christ, atonement of

Attributes: God possesses all, in perfection, 19-20; acquiring of Godlike, 128; of God, 197

Baal, worship of, 321

Baptism: is commanded of God, 339-40, 485; for remission of sins, 340; is not enough by itself, 340; partaking of sacrament renews covenants of, 385-86; is a similitude of Christ's death, burial, and resurrection, 389; is a new birth, 389; must be performed by immersion, 390; of fire, 432; is the key to sanctification, 482; Christ needed, 482; prepares men for Second Coming, 483; prepares men for ministerial service, 483; story of Christ's, 483-84

Belief in Christ: is necessary to salvation, 125-26, 292-93; definition of, 294; presuppositions contained in, 294; is not constituted of certain things, 294; identification of those possessing, 294-99; implies belief in his words, 295-96; comes through the Holy Ghost, 297-98, 473; forgiveness of sins through, 338-39; men may become sons of God through, 352-53

Beloved and Chosen One, Christ is, 182

Benjamin, King: on prophets, 29-30, 78; on importance of scriptures, 89-90; on Christ's Godhood, 99; on the natural man, 227; on atonement, 227, 252; knew of fall and atonement, 232; on resurrection, 268; on salvation, 290, 299, 302; on becoming the

children of Christ, 352; gave his followers a name to be called by, 363-64; on law of Moses, 417; on Christ's healing ministry, 491
Bethlehem: was to be birthplace of Christ, 461; Joseph and Mary went unto, 461; Christ was born in, 462
Bible: prepares men for the Book of Mormon, 96; belief in, implies belief in the Book of Mormon, 297; many truths are lost from, 305; chronology of, 606-7
Birth, 66, 349; of water, blood, and spirit, 249, 351, 387; of Christ was like all others and yet unique, 462-63
Blessings, gospel brings, 174
Blind man healed by Christ, 160, 489, 519
Blood: of Christ, garments are made white in, 248, 251, 340; was symbol of atonement, 251, 258; Christ sweat great drops of, 253; of sprinkling, 255, 256; no man shall shed another man's, 257; was the vital element in sacrifice, 257; is symbol of mortal life, 258
Blood atonement: is basic to the gospel, 248; was taught in preexistence, 248-49; was taught to Adam, 249; Paul's testimony of, 254; perversion of doctrine of, 255-57
Body, Christ's, 47-48, 371; stages of, 197
Bones of Christ were not broken, 534-35
Book of Mormon: testifies of fulfillment of Messianic prophecies, 43; as a source for understanding doctrines, 92-93; witnesses of Christ's divine Sonship, 145; purpose of, 146; teachings in, concerning judgment, 215; teachings in, concerning need for atonement, 228-30; teachings in, about resurrection, 267-68; belief in, implies belief in Christ, 297; calls the Lord by the name of Jesus Christ, 304-5; prophecies in, concerning Christ's death, 526-27, 528; account in, of physical destructions attending Christ's death, 542-44
Book of Remembrance, 86
Born of God, man must be, 351-52
Branch of David, Christ is, 192-93
Brass plates of Laban, 88-89
Bread of life, Christ is, 156, 399
Bridegroom, Christ is the, 183
Brother of Jared, 298; saw Christ, 47, 61, 370, 469, 599-600; faith of, made him worthy to see the Lord, 581
Buddha, 322
Burial: decent, is a sign of respect, 545; of Christ in a sepulchre, 545-47; prophecies concerning Christ's, 546-47

Caiaphas, 154, 497
Calling and election made sure: those who have had their, see God, 584; definition of, 584; brethren must hold the Melchizedek Priesthood to have their, 587
Calvary, Christ atones on, 253
Canonization of scripture, 25
"Carnal, sensual, and devilish," man became, 67, 350
Catholics, conception of Trinity among, 116-17
Character of God, 197-98
Children: effects of atonement upon, 252, 253; little, are not accountable, 302; of God, becoming, 352-53; of Christ bear his name, 363; of the devil, 365
Christ. *See* Jesus Christ
Christendom, theories of, 284, 322
Christians, 366
Chronology, biblical, 606-7
Church of Jesus Christ, 47
Church of the Firstborn, 47
Churches, false: Nephi's vision of, 34; most oppose the true Church, 34
Cleanliness: of soul depends on atonement, 251; need for, 251-52;

Christ teaches of, 255
Cleopas, 279
Comforter, the last, 15, 584, 585-86; the first, 585
Commandments: obedience to, strengthens testimony, 18-19, 298; forgiveness comes through keeping the, 339-40; two great, 339; to repent and be baptized, 339-40; celestial vs. carnal, 408
Condescension of God, 466-67
Corianton, Alma speaks to, 30, 82
Council in heaven, 48-52; poem about, 50-51
Covenant: Christ maketh a new, 423, 424, 438; definition of, 438; Moses was mediator of the old, 439-40; Christ is Mediator of the new, 440-42; all who receive the new, shall be saved, 442
Cowdery, Oliver: vision of, in Kirtland Temple, 105, 152, 602; gives the apostolic charge to first quorum of latter-day apostles, 592-94
Creations of God bear witness of him, 20-21, 374-76, 605
Creator: Christ as, 7, 55-65; Sabbath bears witness of, 394
Creeds of Christendom, 115-17, 322
Crucifixion: of the "old man," 123, 389; of Christ, 523; symbolism of, 527; Enoch beheld, 527-28; Messianic prophecies of, 527-36

Daniel: on resurrection, 270; plea of, for forgiveness, 341
Darkness: was to cover the earth for three days and nights, 538, 540, 541; fulfillment of prophecies concerning, 543-44
David: on Christ's Godhood, 99; Christ is son of, 101-2, 188-91, 196; on restoration of truth, 145; on Christ as rock of salvation, 170; was a type and shadow of Christ, 189, 452; life of, 189; God's promise to, 190; Christ is Branch of, 192-93; Christ will sit upon throne of, 192-95; on God's mercy, 246-47; on resurrection, 266, 269, 272-73; fall of, 271-72; sure mercies of, 271-75, 452; was symbol of universal resurrection, 272; plea of, for forgiveness, 341; on Christ's seed serving him, 362. *See also* Psalms
Day of Atonement: was Israel's most important similitude, 435; sacrificial procedure on, 435-36; selection of goats on, to bear sins away, 436; symbolism of ordinances on, 436
Dead: salvation for the, 240-42; baptism for the, 241
Death: temporal and spiritual, 67, 200, 204, 224; Christ's power over, 200; is inseparably connected with mortality, 222, 259; reign of, through Adam, 224, 349-50; atonement delivers man from, 224, 230; is a reminder of life, 259; of a God to raise mankind, 523
Destructions, physical, at Christ's death: Bible tells little of, 536-37; Zenos speaks of, 538-39; Nephi prophesies of, 539-40; Samuel the Lamanite prophesies of, 540-41; were a judgment upon the wicked, 541; Book of Mormon account of, 542-44
Devils: men would all become, except for atonement, 229-30, 292; knew God in preexistence, 604
Diana, temple of, 321
Disciples of Christ: bore witness of him, 147; Christ appeared to, in upper room, 280, 308, 520-21, 609; testimony of, is scripture, 296; ancient, worshiped Christ, 564-65
Dispensations, all, have received the same gospel, 70-71
Divine investiture of authority, 63-65, 370, 558
Divine Sonship, doctrine of, 470-71
Doctrines: questions concerning, 6-8; testifying of Christ's divine Sonship, 156-58
Dove, Holy Ghost descended upon Jesus in form of, 483, 484

Earth: creation of, 55; Christ is the creator of, 59
Earthquake at time of resurrection, 278, 536-37
Eden, state of living creatures in, 222-23
Egypt, Christ was called out of, 478
Elders: seventy, of Israel, saw the Lord, 104-5, 601, 608; apostles are addressed as, 594; are entitled to same blessings as apostles and prophets, 594; are entitled to all spiritual blessings of the gospel, 595
Elias: definition of, 485; John the Baptist was, 485, 486-87; any preparatory ministry is doctrine of, 486; Jesus was, 486, 487; precedes the coming of the Lord, 487-88
Elijah, 422; overcometh Baal, 321; was the last prophet in Israel to hold the Melchizedek Priesthood, 412
Elisabeth, mother of John the Baptist, 148-49
Elohim: is the Father, 100; man is made a little lower than, 305. *See also* God the Father
Emmaus, Christ appears to disciples on road to, 279-80, 520, 609
Emulation, perfect worship is, 568
Endowment, purpose of, 583
Endure to the end, 340
Enoch: saw the Lord, 15, 72-73, 598-99; on creation, 55-56; beheld the "Son of Man," 140-41, 202, 250; Christ's words to, on restoration of truth, 146; on Adam's fall, 223; on resurrection, 267; on physical destruction at Christ's death, 537
Eternal life: is to know God, 12, 521; assurance of, 20; steps to obtaining, 29; definition of, 130, 225; depends on unity, 131-32; is reserved for the faithful, 132; differentiation of, from immortality, 225; is to receive the fulness of God, 568
Eternal One, Christ is the, 165
Eternity, definition of, 166
Eve: rejoices in redemption, 70, 223; brought forth children, 222
Exaltation, 129; definition of, 130; sons of God will gain, 353; laws governing, 357; those who attain, will see the Lord, 610
Ezekiel: on Book of Mormon, 146; vision of, concerning resurrection, 270-71

Faith: is necessary to salvation, 313; is the first principle of the gospel, 313, 475; men began to exercise, 313-14; miracles are wrought by, 315, 576; is power, 315-16, 572; unto repentance, 342; is a prerequisite to seeing the Lord, 581; men walk by, rather than by sight, 605
Fall: of Adam, 66-67, 217; was a foundation for atonement, 218, 225; purpose for, 220-21, 222; temporal, 224; spiritual, 224; redemption from spiritual, depends on obedience, 226-27; made man subject to sin and death, 244. *See also* Adam
False Christs: in the last days, 323; recognition of, 324; are false religious systems, 324
False gods: have no power, 320-21; widespread worship of, 321, 322; God forbids worship of, 322; there is no salvation in worshiping, 338. *See also* Idols
Father: Christ as, 6-7, 61, 63-64; of heaven and earth, 57, 369; of righteous men, 352, 370; and the Son, Christ is, 370-73; definition of, 468; God is Christ's, 468
Feasts, Mosaic, were types of Christ, 429-35
Fire, baptism of, 432
First and the last, Jehovah is, 312-13
First Coming of Christ. *See* Jesus Christ, First Coming of
Firstborn, Christ is the, 46, 137, 165, 549
Fish, Christ ate, after his resurrection, 280-81
Five thousand, feeding of the, 519

Grace, salvation comes by, 346-48
Graves, opening of, 278

Hallelujah: translation of, 111; is uttered in spirit of prayer, 561
Healings: Christ performed many, 489-91; among Nephites, 491; physical, are similitudes of spiritual healings, 491
Heart of man is far from Christ, 496
Heirs of God: men can become, 355; according to the promise made to Abraham, 356
Herod, 459-60
Holy Ghost: aid of, in interpreting scripture, 6; is a revelator, 16, 23, 71, 74-76; prophecy comes by power of, 24, 41-42, 44; dwells only in clean tabernacles, 74-75; gift of, 571; importance of obtaining, 127; is the gift of God to those who seek him, 289; belief in Christ comes through, 297-98, 473; role of, in helping to obtain peace, 318; only Melchizedek Priesthood holders can lay on hands to bestow, 411; apostles filled with, on day of Pentecost, 432; descended as a dove at Christ's baptism, 483, 484; teachers should teach by power of, 515; third greatest eternal truth centers in, 519; gaining knowledge through, 519; is the First Comforter, 585; bears sure witness of Christ, 592
Holy One, Christ is the, 167-69
Holy Spirit of Promise, sealing by, 344
Hope of Israel, Christ is, 183-84
Hosanna Shout, 433-34
Hosea, teachings of, on mercy, 246
Human sacrifice, 256-57
Husbandmen, parable of the, 175-76

I AM, Christ is the Great, 103-4
Idols: sacrifice to, 256, 321; God expressly forbids worship of, 332. *See also* False gods
"If You Could Hie to Kolob," 11
Ignorance, man cannot be saved in, 4, 510
Imagery used by Christ: the good shepherd, 155-56, 177-80; the bread of life, 156, 399; the true vine, 156; light of the world, 156. *See also* Similitude, Types
Immortality: Messiah must possess, 67; all will receive, 132, 224; alone is not enough, 225; Christ's work is to bring to pass, 277, 307
Infinity, comprehension of, 10-11
Inspiration, necessity of, in reading signs of the times, 2-3
Intelligence, Supreme, 11-12
Intercession: questions concerning, 326-27; Christ made, 329, 551; law of, is valid because of atonement, 329; hath no effect for some, 329; scriptural summary of law of, 330; Jehovah maketh, 330
Isaac, sacrifice of, was in similitude of Christ, 452
Isaiah: Messianic prophecies of, 80-81; on gathering of Israel and witnesses of God, 84-85; on Christ's Godhood, 99-100, 470; on resurrection, 108-9; on restoration of truth, 146; on millennial praise of God, 168-69; on Christ as stumbling block to wicked, 173; on Christ as shepherd, 178; on Christ's righteousness, 202; on the atoning sacrifice, 234; on Lucifer's imprisonment, 240; on resurrection, 265; on the sure mercies of David, 274; on salvation through Jehovah, 308-9; on Christ as Father, 371; on Christ's physical appearance, 477; on Jews' rejection of Christ, 493; on Christ's blessings extending to Gentiles, 503-5; on Christ's role as teacher, 512-13; on crucifixion of Christ, 529; on seeing the Lord, 583
Israel: persecution of prophets by, 35; gathering of, 85, 359; seventy of the elders of, saw God, 104-5, 601, 608; Christ is God of,

men knew, in preexistence, 604-5; many mortals have seen, 605, 607-12. *See also* Jehovah; Messiah

——atonement of: salvation comes through, 1, 4, 26, 105, 290; in Gethsemane, 2, 253, 552; was part of God's plan of salvation, 49, 52, 137; saves man from death, 67, 224, 230; is the core of the gospel, 218; Adam's fall is foundation of, 218; is dependent on Christ's divine Sonship, 218, 471; causes body and spirit to reunite, 225; was foreordained, 225-26, 249; absence of, would frustrate purposes of creation, 227-30, 238, 292, 550-51; must be infinite, 228; mercy cometh because of, 245; on Calvary, 253; made possible reconciliation between God and man, 260; mankind would be lost but for, 291; makes valid the law of intercession, 329; forgiveness of sins is available because of, 337, 343; Messiah shall see his seed after, 361; water, blood, and spirit were part of, 387-88; Sabbath observance keeps us in memory of, 396; required him to be mortal, 455; was the chief purpose of Christ's life, 474; prayer becomes effective because of, 560. *See also* Atonement

——First Coming of: purpose for, 2; prophets looked forward to, 2, 31, 458-59; knowledge of, is important to understanding of Second Coming, 31-32; is a prophetic type of Second Coming, 32; Nephites knew precise year of, 457-58; Jews looked anxiously forward to, 459-60

——mortality of: man's difficulty in comprehending, 454; need for, 454-55; was preparation for and condition of his atonement, 455-56; was essential to his own salvation, 456, 552; gave man an example to follow, 456-57, 475; began in Bethlehem, 461-62; coming about of, 462-64; came by the power of God, 464; chief purpose for, was to atone for man's sins, 474; prophetic foreknowledge of details of, 475-76; Christ's physical appearance during, little is known about, 476-77; made him subject to ills and troubles of all men, 477; Christ's disciples recognized his glory during, 608

——prophecies concerning. *See* Messianic prophecies

——relationship of, to God, 13; unity in, 9, 18, 119-20; eternal nature of, 46; as his Son, 53-54, 118, 468-69, 549; in creating man, 62; oneness of words and acts in, 64, 121-22; similarities in, 198; allowed Christ to inherit immortality, 471; as his minister and agent, 474

——role of: in plan of salvation, 1-2, 49-52, 550-51, 612; in revealing the Father, 4, 17, 475, 518; mysteries concerning, 6-8; in creation, 7, 55-65, 199; as last Comforter, 15, 584, 585-86; was foreordained, 49, 161; as Father of heaven and earth, 57, 369; as Savior from temporal and spiritual death, 67, 309-10; as God, 98, 122; in judgment, 111, 213, 311; explained by Christ, 154; in forgiving sins, 160, 332-35; in working miracles, 160-61, 489; as foundation upon which men must build, 169; in sitting upon David's throne, 192-95; in offering living water, 205-7; in redemption, 236-38; in reconciliation, 259-62; in answering prayers, 335, 557-58; in justifying mankind, 345-46; as Father of the righteous, 352, 370; as the Father and the Son, 370; in fulfilling the law of Moses, 422-25, 441-42; as Mediator of the new covenant, 440-42, 551; as Elias, 486, 487; in healing the

sick, 489-91; in teaching the gospel, 510-14
——Second Coming of: purpose for, 2; all prophets have looked forward to, 2, 31; Malachi's prophecy concerning, 141-42; battle at time of, 172; Christ's dominion at, 192; Davidic-Messianic utterances concerning, 192-93; living water to flow at time of, 205-6; Christ will reign personally on earth during, 281-82; false Christs to appear shortly before, 323; wicked will be cut off at, 447-48; baptism prepares men for, 483; Christ will partake of sacrament with saints at, 594-95, 611. *See also* Millennium
——teachings of: on coming to God, 18; on religious persecutors, 36-37, 38-39; on martyrdom, 39-40; on searching the scriptures, 87; to Nephites concerning their scriptures, 87-88; on fulfillment of Messianic prophecies, 96-97; on his oneness with God, 118-20; on man becoming as God, 133-34; on being one, 136; on his divine Sonship, 153-58; on the wicked husbandmen, 175; on his status as Good Shepherd, 179; on his role as Redeemer, 236, 237-38; on becoming clean through his blood, 255; on resurrection, 270, 275, 520-21; on plan of salvation, 288-89; on believing in him, 293-94; invites men to repent and come unto him, 303; to the heavy laden, 319; on graven images, 322; on forgiveness, 341; on bearing his name, 364-65; on naming his church, 366-67; on creations bearing witness of him, 375-76; on partaking of sacrament, 384, 385; to Nephites on fulfillment of the law of Moses, 423-25; on prayer, 559; on his covenant people, 585
——titles of: Messiah, 22-23, 68; Firstborn of the Father, 46, 137, 165, 549; Jehovah, 100, 164-65; Son of David, 101-2, 189-91, 196, 551; the Great I AM, 103-4; God of Abraham, Isaac, and Jacob, 103, 163-64, 551; the Rock, 108, 169-72, 201; Son of Man, 139-41, 158; Good Shepherd, 155-56, 177-80, 194, 470; Bread of Life, 156; God of Israel, 164-65, 551; Eternal One, 165; Alpha and Omega, 167; Holy One, 167-69, 202, 236; Strength of Israel, 172; Stone of Israel, 172-77, 551; Servant of the Lord, 181-82; Star out of Jacob, 182; Beloved and Chosen One, 182; Anointed One, 182-83; Bridegroom, 183; Hope of Israel, 183-84; Nazarene, 184, 478; King, 185-88; Branch of David, 192-93, 551; Stem of Jesse, 192, 551; Word of God, 198-200; Lawgiver, 203-4; Life of the World, 207; Light of the World, 208-10; Redeemer, 236-37; Savior, 236-37; in Old Testament, as compared with Book of Mormon, 304-5; are numerous, 306; Lamb of God, 380-83; Only Begotten, 468
Jews: conception of Messiah among, 68-69; rejection of Christ by, 94, 99, 173-75, 492-94; scattering of, 94; writings of, 95; God shall manifest himself unto, 178; thought Aaronic Priesthood was enough, 413; knowledge among, of Christ's First Coming, 457-60
Job: on redeemer, 237; on resurrection, 269-70
John the Baptist: on Christ's progression in grace, 54, 567-68; leaped in his mother's womb, 149; baptized Jesus, 149, 482; held the Aaronic Priesthood, 413; prepared people for Christ's coming, 480-82, 486; prophets spoke of, 480-82; as Elias, 485-86; was foreordained, 486
John the Beloved: saw God, 15, 104; saw the prophets, 40; knew Jesus was the Christ, 149; saw the

resurrected Christ, 151, 500; on Christ as the Word of God, 199-200; on blood atonement, 254-55; on the beginning of the world, 285; on becoming sons of God, 354; called Christ the Lamb, 382-83; on the three that bear witness, 388
Jonah was a type of Christ, 452-53, 547
Joseph of Arimathea, 545-46
Joseph Smith. *See* Smith, Joseph
Joseph Smith Translation of the Bible restores many plain and precious truths, 305
Joseph the carpenter: knew Jesus was the Christ, 148; angel appeared to, 463
Judas: identified by Christ as traitor, 532-33; covenanted with chief priests for thirty pieces of silver, 536; hanged himself, 536
Judgment: Jehovah to sit in, 111, 311; God committed all, to Christ, 111, 213; day of, 214-16
Justice: man became subject to law of, 244-45; exerciseth all his demands, 245; mercy can satisfy demands of, 342
Justification, 343; definition of, 344

Keys to spiritual blessings, Melchizedek Priesthood encompasses all, 587-88
King, Christ is, 185-88
King Noah, Abinadi preached to, 418
Kings, wicked, 418
Kirtland Temple: visions of God in, 105, 576-78; dedicatory prayer of, 562
Knowledge: of God and Christ is necessary to salvation, 4, 125, 132; of Christ precedes belief, 295; none shall be found blameless who could possess, 301; accompanies faith, 316; the rest of the Lord is found in, 318; of God comes through priesthood, 589
Koran, 322
Korihor, the anti-Christ, 323, 376

Lamb: of God, 380-83; sacrifice of, during Feast of Passover, 429-30; slain from the foundation of the world, 524
Language, God provided, 86
Law: all are subject to the same, 26, 28, 242, 286; of the Lord is perfect, 86-87, 203, 514-15; Christ giveth, 203-4; necessity of, 245; of creation, men are subject to, 327; of Christ vs. law of Moses, 408
Law of Moses, 308; was added because of transgressions, 407; 411; acted as schoolmaster, 407; is law of carnal commandments, 408-9; improved people temporally and spiritually, 415; begat principles of ethics and decency, 415; was an Elias, 416; was a type and shadow of Christ's law, 416, 417-18; Nephites kept, with proper understanding, 420; was fulfilled in Christ, 422-25. *See also* Preparatory gospel
Laying on of hands, 75
Lazarus, raising of, 150, 161, 276-77, 489
Lehi: persecution of, 38; taught of Christ, 77, 82; on Lucifer, 220; on fall of Adam, 222, 223; taught of the fall and atonement, 232; on resurrection, 267; on justification, 345-46; on salvation through grace, 347; offered sacrifice upon Nephi's return with brass plates, 428
Lepers, ten, cleansing of, 489
Liahona was a likeness of Christ, 402-3
Life eternal. *See* Eternal life
Light of Christ, 75, 76; giveth life to all things, 208; definition and power of, 208-9
Light of the World, Christ is, 208
Limitations: of mortal mind, 10; because of wickedness, 145; in understanding light of Christ, 208
"Lord" is anglicized rendition of Jehovah, 306

Christ's sufferings, 497-98, 501-2; of Christ's teaching ministry, 522. *See also* Prophets
Micah prophesies of Christ's birth in Bethlehem, 461
Michael: Adam is, 221; led the hosts of heaven against Lucifer, 231
Millennium: is the earth's Sabbath, 396; many will see the Lord during, 608. *See also* Jesus Christ, Second Coming of
Miracles: gospel of Christ is, 52; bear witness of Christ, 159-61; identify true believers in Christ, 298, 315, 552, 572; are wrought by faith, 315; trademark of Christ's ministry is, 489; cease only when faith ceases, 572-73
Mission of saints is to preach of Christ, 262
Molech, sacrifices to, 257
Mormon: on oneness of God, 115; testifies to Lamanites of Christ, 152; on how men began to exercise faith, 313-14; on salvation through faith, 314; on entering into the rest of the Lord, 318; on becoming sons of God, 354; on ceasing of miracles, 572-73
Moroni: on seeking Christ, 45; on judgment, 110-11; admonishes men to come unto Christ, 303; on grace, 348; on Christ as Father and Son, 371, 372; on faith, 582; hath seen Christ, 604
Moroni, General, prayed for Christians, 366
Mortality: is a probationary state, 84, 217, 317; definition of, 222. *See also* Jesus Christ, mortality of
Moses: prophesied of Christ, 26; esteemed the "reproach of Christ," 32, 107, 316, 408; on prophets, 80; on Christ's Godhood, 99; God appeared to, in burning bush, 164; on Christ as Rock, 170-71; smote the rock for water, 205; on mercy, 246; was told to forbid people to eat blood, 258; gospel of, 405; received a lower set of commandments for Israel, 409; was mediator of the old covenant, 439, 446; mediation of, was a type of Christ's mediation, 440; hath not Christ's glory, 441-42; was in the similitude of Christ, 442-44; similarities between Christ and, 445-48; premortal works of, 445; foreordination of, 445; spoke with the Lord face to face, 601-2
Mount of transfiguration, 603
Mulekites, corruption of language among, 90
Multiply and replenish the earth, Adam and Eve were commanded to, 220-21
Music: edifying, is a divine means of expressing praise to God, 553; can be corrupt, 553
Mystery of Godliness: uncovering of, 5; examples of, 6-8; great is, 113; understanding of, 124
Name of Christ: taking of, upon ourselves, 7, 364; is above all others, 299; bringeth salvation, 299-300; Christ's children are called by, 363
Nathaneal, 149
Nation: God speaks to every, 94-96; kindred, tongue, and people, knowledge of God will spread to every, 301
Natural man, putting off of, 350
Nazarene, Christ is called a, 184, 478
Nephi: intent of, to bring men to God, 29; couched prophecies in plain language, 44; heard God's voice, 72; prophesied of Christ, 82, 147, 469; on obtaining the records, 88; on Christ's Godhood, 99; on oneness of God, 114-15; on righteous Nephites at time of Christ, 142; on God of Israel, 165; on Christ's First and Second Comings, 194; taught of fall and atonement, 232; on the twelve apostles, 250-51; on being reconciled to God, 261; on resurrection, 268; on salvation through Christ's name, 299; on

salvation by grace, 348; on Christ as Lamb, 381; on the brazen serpent raised up by Moses, 400; on the law of Moses and the hope of Christ, 421-22; saw Mary in vision, 466-67; on John the Baptist, 482; on Christ's baptism, 482, 483-84; on Christ's healing power, 490-91; on Jews' rejection of Christ, 494; on the gospel being offered to both Jews and Gentiles, 508; on death of God, 524-25; on physical upheavals at Christ's death, 539-40; on worshiping Christ, 563
Nephi, Helaman's son: on prophets, 78-79, 144; on Christ's Godhood, 99; knew of atonement, 233; on the brazen serpent raised up by Moses, 400-401
Nephites: gift of prophecy among 24; heard God's voice, 72; received God's Spirit, 75-76; corruption among, 83; Christ views scriptures of, 87-88; Christ's resurrected ministry among, 151-52, 281, 609; on Christ as rock, 171; many, came to Christ, 314, 315; became children of God, 353; were called Christians, 366; Christ instituted sacramental ordinances among, 384-85; held the Melchizedek Priesthood, 412, 421; kept law of Moses with proper understanding, 420, 427; offered sacrifices, 427; knew the precise year Christ was to come, 457-58; Christ healed sick among, 491; Christ identifies, as "other sheep," 508; prayed directly to Christ when he was in their midst, 560-61; worshiped Christ, 563
Noah, wicked men in days of, 330
Noah, King, Abinadi preached to, 418

Obedience: gaining testimony through, 18-19, 298; salvation comes through, 67, 126, 226; is necessary in receiving Holy Ghost, 297-98; forgiveness comes through, 339-40; follows baptism, 340; is a form of praise and worship, 555, 568; blessings are predicated upon, 579
Obligation: of saints to preach of Christ, 262, 301; of men to seek the truth, 301
Old Testament: deletion of truths from, 142, 305; "Son of God" mentioned in, 143; Christ called Rock in, 171-72; name of Christ in, 304; prophecies of Christ's crucifixion in, 529-35
Omnipotent, omnipresent, and omniscient, God is, 8, 19-21
One God, existence of only, 114-15
Oneness of God and Christ: misconceptions concerning, 117-18; Christ's teachings concerning, 118-20
Onitah, daughters of, were sacrificed, 32
Opposition in all things, need for, 218-19, 499
Ordinances of the gospel: are Messianic in nature, 27-28, 378, vicarious performance of, 241; perversion of, 255; are similitudes of Christ's ministry, 378, 390, 552; outward, Aaronic Priesthood is limited to, 412-13; inward or spiritual, require Melchizedek Priesthood, 413
Organizer of universe, 11

Palestine, sheepherding in, 179
Parables: Christ's use of, is not as important as the truths he taught, 521; hid doctrines from all but the spiritually enlightened, 522
Paradise, 318, 361; hosts of, saw Christ, 608
Passover, Feast of, 428; sacrificial procedure of, 429-30; was a type of Christ, 429-30; Christ instituted sacrament during, 431
Patmos, Isle of, 105, 151, 289
Paul: testimony of, 16; persecution of, 35; on being "crucified with Christ," 123; Lorenzo Snow's letter to, 136; interpretation of

Old Testament prophecies by, 143; conversion of, 151; on Christ as Rock of Israel, 171; on those who accept gospel, 176; testifies of blood atonement, 254; on reconciliation, 261-62; on resurrection, 265, 274; on sure mercies of David, 275; on faith of early prophets, 316-17; on the rest of the Lord, 320; on being children and heirs of God, 354-56; on baptism, 389; reasons with Jews about priesthood, 413-14; on the new covenant, 423; on Christ as mediator, 440-41; on Christ suffering temptations, 500; took gospel to Gentiles, 504-5; on Melchizedek Priesthood holders, 588-89
Peace: comes from Jehovah, 211; Messiah was to bring, 211-12; Christ offers, 212; comes through the Lord's gospel, 212-13, 317; Melchizedek was called King of, 213
Pentecost, Feast of, 428-29; purpose of, 431; baptism of fire during, 432
Perfection, God possesses all attributes in, 19-20, 198
Persecution of prophets: because they testify of Christ, 33-34; because of false churches, 34-36; by religious people, 34; by Israel, 35; as form of false worship, 36; condemned in scriptures, 36-37; because they reveal sin, 38; as a witness against the wicked, 38-39; to test their integrity, 39-40
Peter: on prophets, 79; on Christ, 102; knew Jesus was the Christ, 149; saw the resurrected Christ, 151; on Christ as Stone, 176-77; admonished by Christ to feed his sheep, 180; quotes David to prove resurrection, 273-74; bears testimony of Christ's resurrection, 282; on salvation through Christ's name, 300; on Christ's suffering, 500-501
Philip of Bethsaida, 149
Pilate, Christ before, 155, 186-87, 497
Pillar of fire, 108
Plan of salvation: is always the same, 4, 107, 138-39, 284; necessity of understanding, 42-43; is God's plan, 48-49, 137; gospel of Jesus Christ is, 52, 105; God revealed, to man, 70; depended on fall of Adam, 220-21; summary of, 327-28; is foundation for advocacy, intercession, and mediation, 328; teachers should teach only, 514
Plant, Christ as a tender, 477-78
Pool of Siloam, 434
Praise: language of, 336, 561; music is a form of, 553; to the Lord, men ought to sing, 554, 556-57; methods of giving, 555; is linked with prayer, 561-62; to the Lord forever, 613-15
Prayer: is Messianic prophecy or testimony, 27; is addressed to God in Christ's name, 335, 557; answers to, come through Christ, 335, 557-58; language of, 336; is not addressed to anyone but God, 558; effectiveness of, depends on atonement, 560; praise is linked with, 561-62; dedicatory, of Kirtland Temple, 562
Preexistence, 351-52
Preparatory gospel, 404-5. *See also* Law of Moses
Priesthood: system of bestowing of, 80; comparison of Melchizedek and Aaronic, 409-12; prepares men to see God, 587. *See also* Aaronic Priesthood; Melchizedek Priesthood
Prison: Christ frees men from, 238-40, 512; description of ancient, 238; Messianic prophecies of release from, 239-40; Christ visits spirits in, 241
Probation, mortality is time of, 84, 217
Procreation, 67
Progression: of man, 12, 133-36; is denied to Lucifer, 219

Promise: Holy Spirit of, 344; the Lord's last and great, 583. *See also* Covenant
Prophecies. *See* Messianic prophecies
Prophecy: gift of, 23-24; among Nephites, 24; spirit of, 44, 113; testimony of Christ is, 123
Prophets: looked forward to both comings of Christ, 2, 31; definition of, 23; spheres of authority of, 25; all who bear testimony are, 25, 72; have always taught the same doctrines, 29, 77, 293, 551, 613; reasons for persecution of, 32-40; Lucifer hates, 34; false, 37; rewards of, 40-41; Christ's Godhood affirmed by, 99-100; bore record of Christ's coming birth, 147; are witnesses of the Lord, 148; have taught of the fall of Adam, 223, 231; have all known of the atonement, 231, 233-34; Nephite, all taught of resurrection, 268; all worshiped God in Christ's name, 305-6, 335, 559; all had faith in Christ, 314; all held the Melchizedek Priesthood, 410, 412, 589; knew their Messiah must die, 524; many, have seen the Lord, 602-4. *See also* Apostles; Messianic prophecies; Twelve apostles
Propitiation, Christ is, 201
Psalms: on Christ as rock of salvation, 170; on the Lord as King, 185-86; on salvation through Jehovah, 308; praising God, 336-37, 554, 614; on the fairness of Christ, 478-79; on Christ's role as teacher, 513; on the events surrounding Christ's death, 530-35; contain fulfillment of prophecies on Christ's death, 530-35; on worshiping Christ, 565-66. *See also* David
Punishment, 245
Pure: sons of God become, 354; in heart shall see God, 576, 580

Realities, eternal, 327
Reason, insufficiency of, in knowing God, 113
Rebirth: of water, blood, and spirit, 249, 351; spiritual, 350
Reconciliation: between God and man, made possible by Christ, 260; through the atonement, 260; ministry of, 261
Redeemer: Christ is, 237-38, 311-12; Jehovah is, 312
Redemption: comes through Christ, 226-27, 237-38, 311-12; from spiritual fall, 226; Jehovah bringeth, 312
Rejection of Christ: by Jews, 94, 99, 173-75, 492-94; through rejection of his message, 495
Repentance: mercy claimeth, 245, 247, 319; is prerequisite to reconciliation, 260; is commanded of God, 339-40
Rest of the Lord: the faithful enter into, 317; three stages of, 318; definitions of, 318-19; Israel was denied, 319-20, 407, 411, 589-90
Resurrection: Christ's ministry after his, 150-52, 278-81, 552; proves Christ's divinity, 263-64; of Jehovah foretold, 264-66; all will have part in, 266; all prophets taught of, 267; questions concerning, 277-78; of Christ, events following, 278; Messiah saw his seed after his, 362; Christ teaches of, 520-21
Revelation: God is known only by, 14, 101; through visions, 14-15; by the power of the Holy Ghost, 16, 75; through testimony of others, 16-17; through accepting Christ, 17-18; through obedience, 18-19; comes as quickly as men prepare themselves, 145, 575; is necessary to understand resurrection, 278; personal, 573
Rigdon, Sidney, testifies of Christ, 152
Right hand of God, Christ sits on, 102-3, 152
Righteousness: God is called, 141; Son of, 141-42; of Christ, 202; is

ratified by the Holy Ghost, 344
Rock: of Israel, Christ is, 108; build upon the Lord's, 169-71; many prophets speak of Christ as their, 169, 170-72; Jehovah is, 358
Rome, false worship in, 322

Sabbath observance: identifies the Lord's people, 390; is a commandment, 391; puts man in tune with God, 391, 392; bears witness of Christ, 391; requires attendance at meetings, 392; rules and penalties governing, 393; symbolizes the day Christ rose from the dead, 393; witnesses of Christ as Creator, 394; reason for, 394; to keep Israel in remembrance of her God, 394-95
Sacrament: worthy partaking of, 127-28, 340; replaced sacrifice, 380; is a similitude, 383; was officially instituted at Feast of the Passover, 384, 431; Christ introduced ordinance of, to Nephites, 384-85; partaking of, renews baptismal covenants, 385-86; Christ will partake of, with saints, 594-95, 611
Sacrifices: of animals, in similitude of Christ's sacrifice, 250, 257, 379; Mosaic, were similitudes, 254, 258, 427; to idols and devils, 256, 321; human, 256-57; blood was the vital element in, 257; failure of Israel to perform, 332; ceased with the crucifixion, 380; lambs offered as, 381; were a form of worship in Israel, 426, 427-28; occasions for, 428; ritual for, during Passover, 429-30
Salvation: is in Christ, 1, 26, 290, 612; is available to all, 93, 325; is of the Spirit, 113; universal vs. individual, 129; definition of, 130, depends on unity, 131-32; depends on obedience, 226; for the dead, 240-42; men must believe in Christ to gain, 292; is in Jehovah, 306; should be man's chief concern, 307; number of references to, in Holy Writ, 307; has always come through faith in Christ, 313, 551; is free, 325, 346-47; forgiveness of sins precedes, 337-38; house of, 342
Samaritan woman at Jacob's well, 153-54, 206, 566
Samuel the Lamanite: on persecution of prophets, 37; on false prophets, 37; Christ commands Nephites to write of, 87-88; knew of atonement, 233; on the sign of Christ's birth, 457-58; on signs of Christ's death, 540-41
Sanctification comes through blood of Christ, 249
Sanhedrin, Christ before the, 155
Satan: whisperings of, about God's nature, 132-33; fall of, as lightning, 219; incites men to sacrifice each other, 256; children of, 365. *See also* Lucifer
Savior: Christ as, 67, 309; man's need for, 76; Jehovah is, 310
Scapegoat, purpose for, in Israel, 436
Scourging, 497
Scripture: modern application of, 3; definition of, 24-25; canonization of, 25; importance of studying, 45; is Messianic utterance, 72; necessity of, to salvation, 86, 88-90; withholding of, 91-92; points to Christ as Redeemer, 236; belief in, implies belief in Christ, 295; mention of salvation in, 307; teachers should utilize, 515
Sealing: of the wicked unto judgment, 173; of the righteous unto eternal life, 174
Second Comforter, 15, 584, 585-86
Second Coming. *See* Jesus Christ, Second Coming of
Seed: of Abraham, promises concerning, 106, 110, 164, 308, 356; definition of, 359; Messiah shall see his, 359; of Messiah identified, 360; of Abraham were foreordained, 507
Seeing the Lord: all pure men may

gospel truths, 514-15; should teach from the scriptures, 515; should teach by power of the Holy Ghost, 515-16; should apply principles to needs of hearers, 516; should bear testimony of truths taught, 516-17; can most effectively use plain and simple language, 520
Temples: the Lord will not come into unholy, 576; God will visit men in his, 576. *See also* Kirtland Temple
Temptations: are an important part of mortality, 498-99; of Christ in wilderness, 499
Test, earth life is a, 84
Testimony: of others, belief in, 16-17, 296; of author, 17, 615; of Jesus is spirit of prophecy, 23, 71-72; Messianic, 26, 71; of Christ was borne by his associates, 148-50; pure, borne by Christ of his divine Sonship, 153-56; teachers should teach with the seal of personal, 516-17; Oliver Cowdery admonishes Twelve to gain, 593
Thomas saw the resurrected Christ, 151, 280, 282-83
Throne of David, Christ will sit upon, 192-95
Tomb of Christ, 546; stone rolled back from, 278-79, 552; women came to, 279
Translation of Bible left out many truths, 305
Trinity: Church of England's conception of, 115; Catholics' conception of, 116-17
Truth: men are obligated to seek, 301; definition of, 338; naming of greatest, 517-18; second greatest, 518-19; third greatest, 519; fourth greatest, 520
Twelve apostles, ancient and Nephite: to sit in judgment, 216; were special witnesses of the Lord, 592; of latter day bear the same witness as, 592. *See also* Apostles; Prophets
Types, prophetic: of Second Coming, 31; reasons for using, 43-44; David, 189, 452; manna, 398-99; brazen serpent, 400-401; the Liahona, 402-3; law of Moses, 416; Feast of the Passover, 429-30; Feast of Pentecost, 431-32; Feast of Tabernacles, 432-35; Day of Atonement, 435-37; Moses, 442-48; Adam, 449; Melchizedek, 449-51; Melchizedek Priesthood holders, 451; Abraham's sacrifice of Isaac, 442; Jonah, 452-53; house of Israel, 453. *See also* Imagery; Similitude

Unity: mortal attainment of, 120-21, 260, 353; of saints with Christ, 123-24; salvation is, 130-32
Uriah, murder of, 271

Variableness, there is none in God, 286
Vinegar, Christ was given, 533-34
Virgin birth, 464, 465-66
Visions, God reveals himself in, 14-15

Water: need for, 204; imagery of, 204-5; living, Christ offers, 205-7, 434
Water, blood, and spirit: birth of, 249, 351, 387; were all a part of the atonement, 387-88; bear witness on earth, 388
War in heaven, 51, 231, 235
Weeks, Feast of, 428-29, 431-32
Whitney, Orson F., poem by, 50-51
Wicked, curses to fall upon, 173-77
Wickedness, prophets reveal, 38
Will of the Son swallowed up in the Father's, 524
Wisdom, God is not known by, 100-101, 114
Wise men: came in search of the King, 186; worshiped Christ, 564
Witnesses: law of, 84; salvation made available through, 85; of the resurrection, 278; Christ works through, 282, 296; three, in

heaven and on earth, 388; manna, 398-99; brazen serpent, 400-401; Liahona, 402-3; men become living, of Christ's truth, 555; Twelve Apostles were and are special, 592
Word of God, Christ is, 198-200
Words of Christ, feasting upon, 300
Works of Christ bear witness of him, 158-61
Worlds without number, 55
Worship: of Christ, 562-66; of God, 566; forms of, are many, 566-67; perfect, is emulation, 568
Written language, importance of, 86

Yesterday, today, and forever, Christ is the same, 167, 286, 289
Yoke of Christ is easy, 319

Zechariah: prophecy of, on Christ's entry into Jerusalem, 186, 187; on crucifixion, 535; on the thirty pieces of silver, 536
Zeezrom, 290
Zenock: Alma quotes, 144; on mercies through Christ, 329
Zenos: Alma quotes a prayer of, 144; on judgment, 329; on physical signs attending Christ's death, 538
Zion, 15, 72, 120, 599; as city of the King, 185
Zoramites, 290

The Lord shall come to recompense
unto every man according to his work,
and measure to every man according to the measure
which he has measured to his fellow man.
Wherefore the voice of the Lord is unto the ends
of the earth, that all that will hear may hear:
Prepare ye, prepare ye for that
which is to come, for the Lord is nigh;
And the anger of the Lord is kindled,
and his sword is bathed in heaven,
and it shall fall upon the inhabitants of the earth.
And the arm of the Lord shall be revealed;
and the day cometh that they
who will not hear the voice of the Lord,
neither the voice of his servants,
neither give heed to the words
of the prophets and apostles,
shall be cut off from among the people.
—D&C 1:10-14

For the hour is nigh and the day soon at hand
when the earth is ripe;
and all the proud and they that do wickedly
shall be as stubble;
and I will burn them up, saith the Lord of Hosts,
that wickedness shall not be upon the earth. . . .
For I will reveal myself from heaven
with power and great glory, with all the hosts thereof,
and dwell in righteousness with men on earth
a thousand years, and the wicked shall not stand.
—D&C 29:9, 11

Wherefore, prepare ye, prepare ye, O my people;
sanctify yourselves. . . . Yea, let the cry go forth
among all people: Awake and arise
and go forth to meet the Bridegroom;
behold and lo, the Bridegroom cometh;
go ye out to meet him. Prepare yourselves
for the great day of the Lord. Watch, therefore,
for ye know neither the day nor the hour.
—D&C 133:4, 10-11

The Millennial Messiah

The Second Coming of the Son of Man

Bruce R. McConkie

Deseret Book Company
Salt Lake City, Utah

ISBN 0-87747-896-1 (hardbound)
ISBN 0-87579-407-6 (softbound)

Library of Congress Cataloging-in-Publication Data

McConkie, Bruce R.
The millennial Messiah.

Includes index.
1. Second Advent. 2. Mormon Church—Doctrinal and controversial works. I. Title
BT886.M42 236'.3 81-19599
AACR2

Printed in the United States of America

10 9 8 7 6 5 4 3 2

THE MESSIANIC TRILOGY

The forerunners of this work are *The Promised Messiah: The First Coming of Christ*, which deals with the Messianic prophecies, and *The Mortal Messiah: From Bethlehem to Calvary*, a life of Christ published in four books as follows:

BOOK I

Section I *A Root Out of Dry Ground*
Section II *Jesus' Years of Preparation*
Section III *Jesus' Early Judean Ministry*

BOOK II

Section IV *Jesus Begins the Great Galilean Ministry*
Section V *The Twelve, The Sermon on The Mount, and Rising Pharisaic Opposition*
Section VI *The Continuing Galilean Ministry*

BOOK III

Section VII *The Galilean Ministry Reaches Its Peak*
Section VIII *The Later Judean Ministry*
Section IX *The Perean Ministry*
Section X *From the Anointing to the Royal Reign*

BOOK IV

Section XI *The Paschal Feast, The Private Prayers and Sermons, and Gethsemane*
Section XII *The Trials, The Cross, and The Tomb*
Section XIII *He Riseth; He Ministereth; He Ascendeth*

ABBREVIATIONS

Scriptural references are abbreviated in a standard and self-identifying way. Other books are cited by author and title except for the following:

Commentary	Bruce R. McConkie, *Doctrinal New Testament Commentary,* vol. 3. Bookcraft, 1965.
JST	Joseph Smith Translation (Inspired Version) of the Bible.
Mormon Doctrine	Bruce R. McConkie, *Mormon Doctrine*, 2nd ed. Bookcraft, 1966.
Teachings	Joseph Fielding Smith, comp., *Teachings of the Prophet Joseph Smith*. 1938.

CONTENTS

Chapter 10

Chapter 11

Chapter 12

Chapter 13

Chapter 27

Chapter 28

Chapter 29

Chapter 30

Chapter 31

Chapter 32

Chapter 33

Chapter 34

Chapter 35

Chapter 36

Chapter 42

Chapter 43

Chapter 44

Chapter 45

Chapter 46

Chapter 47

Chapter 48

Chapter 49

Chapter 50

Chapter 51

Chapter 52

Chapter 53

Chapter 54

Chapter 55

Chapter 56

PREFACE

Our Blessed Lord, who came once as the *Promised Messiah,* shall soon come again in all the glory of his Father's kingdom.

The King of Israel, who dwelt among men as the *Mortal Messiah*, shall soon rule and reign over his chosen Israel and over all others who abide the day of his coming.

God's own Son shall soon come as the *Millennial Messiah*. It is of that millennial coming—*The Second Coming of the Son of Man*—that this work testifies.

There is not a more important course to pursue, for any of us who now live on earth, than to prepare for the Second Coming. The gospel has been restored and the great latter-day kingdom established in order to prepare a people for that dreadful yet glorious day.

There is also probably no doctrine and no event that is less understood than our Lord's personal return to live and be once more with men. Many strange and peculiar and false opinions are afloat. The Second Coming is totally unknown among non-Christians, totally misunderstood among Christians generally, and even some of the very elect need more enlightenment than they now have relative to what lies ahead.

In this work we attempt to set forth what the scriptures themselves, as properly interpreted, have to say about the great and coming day. We speak of the events precedent, the events concurrent, and the events subsequent. We speak of what must occur between his first and second advents, of the plagues and wars attending his return, and of the peace and glories that shall prevail during his millennial reign.

In the spirit of gratitude and appreciation I record here the name of Velma Harvey, a most able and efficient secretary. She has made many thoughtful suggestions, given much wise counsel. and handled a host of matters requiring care and insight.

The Millennial Messiah

The Second Coming of the Son of Man

THE SUPPER OF THE LORD

Come: Learn of the Second Coming

Come feast on the good word of God; come learn of the Second Coming of the Son of Man!

Come feast on the word of Christ that he has given to prepare us for the great and dreadful day that even now is at the door—the day when every corruptible thing will be consumed as the elements melt with fervent heat, the day when the righteous shall be caught up to meet their Lord in the air.

Come and partake of "the supper of the Lord" that is now prepared at his "house" and "unto which all nations" are invited.

It is "a feast of fat things, of wine on the lees well refined." (D&C 58:8-11.) Heaped high on the table is that meat of which man may eat and never hunger more and that water of which he may drink and never thirst again.

Let all men forsake the tables of carnality and of false doctrine, where the scoffers of the world, "walking after their own lusts," are eating and drinking with gluttonous abandon as men did in the days of Noah. Let them no longer say: "Where is the promise of his coming?" (2 Pet. 3:3-4.) And let them no longer suppose that the promised hope of a millennial era of peace is something that must be brought to pass by the good deeds of men, rather than by the shaking of the heavens and with power from on high.

But be it known—whatever the ungodly may suppose, whatever views the spiritually untutored may espouse, whatever foods may be eaten at the evil tables of the world—that here at the Lord's table is found living bread; here is the fountain from which streams of living water flow.

By his own voice the Lord has commanded his latter-day servants: "Prepare ye the way of the Lord, prepare ye the supper of the Lamb, make ready for the Bridegroom."

The marvelous work of restoration, reserved for the last days, has now commenced among the children of men; and to all who believe the restored gospel the Voice commands: "Pray unto the Lord, call upon his holy name, make known his wonderful works among the people."

The Church of Jesus Christ of Latter-day Saints, which is the kingdom of God on earth—the kingdom designed to prepare men to sit down with Abraham, Isaac, and Jacob, and all the holy prophets in the eternal kingdom—has been set up among men; and to all the citizens of the kingdom, the Voice commands: "Call upon the Lord, that his kingdom may go forth upon the earth, that the inhabitants thereof may receive it, and be prepared for the days to come, in the which the Son of Man shall come down in heaven, clothed in the brightness of his glory, to meet the kingdom of God which is set up on the earth." (D&C 65:3-5.)

And so it is that the servants of the Lord have prepared the supper. The banquet tables are heaped high with heavenly manna. The food and drink consists of "none other things than that which the prophets and apostles have written," and "that which is taught them by the Comforter through the prayer of faith." (D&C 52:9.)

We have invited "the rich and the learned, the wise and the noble," to come and bask in the light of the Lord and find nourishment for their souls. They have declined the invitation and continue to gorge themselves with the delicacies of Babylon. And so now, in the providences of Him who gives bread in the wilderness and who rains manna from heaven upon his people, cometh the day of his power. Now "shall the poor, the lame, and the blind, and the deaf, come in unto the marriage of the Lamb, and partake of the supper of the Lord, prepared for the great day to come." (D&C 58:10-11.)

As we begin to eat at the Lord's tables, we are both humbled and exhilarated by the glory and wonder of it all. Many prophets and righteous men saw this day, in dreams when the moon ruled the night and in visions when the sun ruled the day. Many of the ancient saints—saints from all the dispensations of the past—longed for the day of triumph and glory that was promised to the saints of latter days. Many would fain have changed places with us, that their eyes might see what we behold and their hands be put to the plough with which we labor in the fields of the Lord. Ours is the glorious privilege to lay the foundations of Zion with the full assurance that we, or our children, or their descendants after them, will live to see the face of Him who shall come to dwell with his saints and to reign among the righteous.

At the tables prepared in the Lord's house, we shall speak of the coming of the Son of Man, of the return of God's Almighty Son to take vengeance upon the wicked and to usher in the year of his redeemed. We shall talk of the signs of the times; of those things which the apostles and prophets say must precede his glorious advent; of the circumstances that shall attend his return; and of the paradisiacal glory that shall cover the earth when the wicked are destroyed and all things become new.

We shall also record in this work in plain words, often using the very words of holy writ, what has been revealed relative to the coming of the millennial King. Our words will take on life and breath as we interweave with them parables and similitudes and add the inspired imagery that unveils hidden and mysterious things.

We shall write living words, words that flow from the pen of prophecy, dipped in the ink of inspiration. Our message shall be one of joy and rejoicing for those who treasure up revealed truth, who desire righteousness, who seek the face of the Lord. It will be one of weeping and mourning for those who "know not God, and that obey not the gospel of our Lord Jesus Christ." (2 Thes. 1:8.)

We shall now turn the key, open the door, and enter the holy realm where the knowledge of God is poured out without measure upon the faithful. We shall seek the face of him who shall suddenly come to his temple; it is our desire to know all things relative to the Second Coming of the Son of Man. "Prepare to meet thy God, O Israel." (Amos 4:12.)

Come: Believe in the Millennial Messiah

Our words are written to those who believe, those who have the testimony of Jesus burning in their souls, those who look forward with joy to that day when "the saints of the most High shall take the kingdom, and possess the kingdom for ever." (Dan. 7:18.) The feast that the Lord's servants have prepared in the last days is the fulness of the everlasting gospel. Only those who have oil in their lamps and who have taken the Holy Spirit for their guide will be seated at the banquet tables.

To set a proper tone and have a right spirit at our banquet—we are feasting in the house of the Lord, on the good word of God, as guided by the Comforter!—and to maintain that high spirituality which must shine forth from any work that speaks of our Lord's return to reign personally on earth, we shall make a brief introductory statement by way of testimony and of doctrine. This is our witness:

We know when Christ will come in the clouds of glory, attended by angelic hosts, to be with men on earth again—not the day or the hour, or even the month or the year, but we do know the generation.

We know where he will appear and the places on which the soles of his feet will once again walk. These are identifiable roads and known mountains whose descriptions and names are given in the prophetic word.

We know, if not all, at least the major things that must transpire before he comes again, those events that will attend his triumphal return, and those events that will result because his personal presence once more graces his earthly vineyard.

We shall name the time, identify the places, and set forth the attendant circumstances in due course. It is the privilege of the saints of the Most High to read the signs of the times, to stand in holy places, to escape (partially at least) the plagues and pestilences of the last days, and to abide the day of his coming. Those who treasure up his word are promised that they will not be deceived with respect to all these things.

We know that Christ is the Firstborn of the Father; that long eternities before the foundations of this earth were laid, he became like unto God; and that by him and through him and of him the worlds—worlds without number, all the worlds in all immensity—are and were created. He, under the Father, is the Creator, Upholder, and Preserver of all things.

We know that he was and is the God of our fathers, the God of the ancients, the God of Abraham, Isaac, and Jacob; that he is the Great Jehovah, the Eternal One, the Lord Omnipotent, who revealed himself and his gospel to Adam and the holy prophets; and that he is the same yesterday, today, and forever.

We know that he is the God of Israel who chose the house of Jacob as his own peculiar people; that he is the Promised Messiah of whom all the prophets testified; and that he is a God of miracles who delights to bless and honor those who love and serve him in righteousness and truth all their days.

We know that he came as the Seed of David and the Son of the Highest; that Mary was his mother and God was his Father; and that he was born, after the manner of the flesh, inheriting from his mother the power of mortality and from his Father the power of immortality.

We rejoice in his mortal ministry and know that when he dwelt as a man on earth he fulfilled all that was written of him for that day. In him the Messianic prophecies were all fulfilled, the law of Moses was both fulfilled and replaced, and the glorious gospel was again restored and preached to the world. Our knowledge of how and in what manner the Messianic word was honored and accomplished in time's meridian will guide us in learning how the prophetic word pertaining to his Second Coming will find a full consummation.

We know he worked out the infinite and eternal atonement, which was the crowning act of a glorious and perfect ministry; that he was crucified, died, and rose again the third day; and that he has ascended into heaven, there to reign with almighty power on the right hand of the Father whose son he is.

We know that when he comes again, he will take vengeance on the wicked and ungodly and usher in the year of his redeemed. He will establish Zion and build up the New Jerusalem, and he will reign on the throne of David, in peace and with equity and justice over all the earth, for the space of a thousand years. And his chosen Israel shall then walk in the light of his love—as the beloved and chosen people that they are—for the whole Millennium.

We know that when he comes the vineyard shall be burned; the wicked shall be as stubble, for they that come shall burn them up; and every corruptible thing, both of men and of beasts and of fowls, shall be consumed.

We know that all those who have overcome the world by the word of his power, who have kept the faith, who have been true and faithful in all things, shall live and reign with him on earth a thousand years.

We seek also to worship the Father, in the name of the Son, by the power of the Holy Spirit, and hope to be with them all on this earth when it becomes a celestial heaven, when the meek, who are the God-fearing and the righteous, inherit it forever and ever.

Having this testimony and knowing these doctrines, relying with a perfect surety on all of the promises made to the faithful, and rejoicing in such measure of the Holy Spirit as has been poured out upon us—in this setting, we the saints sit down at the supper of the Lamb and feast upon that of which only the God-fearing and the righteous can eat and drink.

Come: See Him Ascend into Heaven

To those living in his day and dispensation, Jesus asked: "What and if ye shall see the Son of man ascend up where he was before?" (John 6:62.) To all those who live in our day and dispensation, we ask: What and if you "shall see the Son of Man coming in the clouds of heaven, with power and great glory"? (JS-M 1:36.) And these two questions—his pertaining to his ascension to eternal glory, and ours as to his return in that glory which is his—are inseparably interwoven into one. There can be no Second Coming of the Son of Man unless there was a first coming, and he cannot descend from heaven above unless he first ascended to those heights beyond the skies. Indeed, the foundation we are laying for our study of his return, and all that is incident thereto, must include a sure knowledge of these four eternal verities:

1. That there is a God in heaven who is infinite and eternal; that he is a Holy Man, having a body of flesh and bones; and that he sent his Only Begotten Son to redeem fallen man and put into full operation all of the terms and conditions of the gospel of God.

2. That the Lord Jesus, born of Mary in Bethlehem of Judea, was the Son of God in the literal and full sense of the word, and that he inherited from God his Father the power of immortality and from Mary his mother the power of mortality.

3. That this same Jesus, having worked out the infinite and eternal atonement in Gethsemane and on the cross, and having laid down his life to bring to pass the immortality and eternal life of man—this same Jesus rose from the dead in glorious immortality, having a resurrected body of flesh and bones like that of his Father.

4. That he ascended into heaven to sit down on the right hand of the Majesty on high, there to reign with almighty power until the day and hour appointed by the Father for his return to live and reign on earth a thousand years.

Of all these eternal verities we, with the ancients, bear witness. As to the doctrine of his ascension, we say with Peter: He "is gone into heaven, and is on the right hand of God; angels and authorities and powers being made subject unto him." (1 Pet. 3:22.) With Paul we say: "God was manifest in the flesh, justified in the Spirit, seen of angels, preached unto the Gentiles, believed on in the world, received up into glory." (1 Tim. 3:16.) Also: "Jesus the Son of God," our "great high priest," hath "passed into the heavens" (Heb. 4:14) where he is "holy, harmless, undefiled, separate from sinners, and made higher than the heavens" (Heb. 7:26). Again with Paul we testify that "God . . . hath in these last days spoken unto us by his Son, whom he hath appointed heir of all things, by whom also he made the worlds; Who being the brightness of his glory, and the express image of his person, and upholding all things by the word of his power, when he had by himself purged our sins, sat down on the right hand of the Majesty on high." (Heb. 1:1-3.) We also testify, yet again in Paul's words, that "when he ascended up on high, he led captivity captive, and gave gifts unto men," meaning that when he "ascended up far above all heavens," he freed men from the captivity of sin and of the grave and gave them, as gifts, apostles, prophets, and true ministers. (Eph. 4:8-16.)

Knowing that the Lord Jesus was destined to ascend to his Father, there to reign until the day of his Second Coming, we are ready to view the events of that day of ascension. It is Thursday, May 18, A.D. 30, just forty days after he rose from the grave. The inhabitants of Jerusalem are ripening in iniquity. Having shed the blood of their King, they now seek to slay his apostles and friends. Some forty years hence, when their cup of iniquity is full, they shall be slain and scattered in such a blood bath as has seldom been known among men. Jerusalem will then die by the sword of Titus, and her temple will become a dung heap, every stone being wrenched from its foundation.

But now the new dispensation of Christians are walking in the marvelous light that quickens their souls. Many are yet glorying in the appearances of the resurrected saints to them. It is the day when Jesus is to be "taken up." And he has come to "the apostles whom he had chosen: To whom also he shewed himself alive after his passion by many infallible proofs, being seen of them forty days, and speaking of the things pertaining to the kingdom of God: And, being assembled together with them, commanded them that they should not depart from Jerusalem, but wait for the promise of the Father, which, saith he, ye have heard of me. For John truly baptized with water; but ye shall be baptized with the Holy Ghost not many days hence." (Acts 1:2-5.)

Luke in his Gospel tells us that on this occasion, after giving the promise that they would "be endued with power from on high," "he led them out as far as to Bethany, and he lifted up his hands, and blessed them. And it came to pass, while he blessed them, he was parted from them, and carried up into heaven." (Luke 24:49-51.) Mark says simply that "he was received up into heaven, and sat on the right hand of God." (Mark 16:19.)

But it is in the book of Acts, also written by Luke, that the details are given that set the stage for the Second Coming. Our inspired author identifies the place as "the mount called Olivet," records the conversation about the restoration of the kingdom to Israel, and then says: "And when he had spoken these things, while they beheld, he was taken up; and a cloud received him out of their sight. And while they looked stedfastly toward heaven as he went up, behold, two men stood by them in white apparel; Which also said, Ye men of Galilee, why stand ye gazing up into heaven? this same Jesus, which is taken up from you into heaven, shall so come in like manner as ye have seen him go into heaven." (Acts 1:6-12.)

What then is the promise of his coming? It is that the same Holy Being who burst the bands of death and gained the victory over the grave shall come again. He shall return, as he went up; he shall return to the Mount of Olives, having the same body of flesh and bones that was seen and felt and handled by the disciples of old. He shall again eat and drink with the faithful as of old. And as a few spiritually enlightened souls in ancient days awaited the coming of the Consolation of Israel, so a few believing souls today await his triumphant return.

What a glorious day that will be! For all of us, when we dwelt as spirits in the Eternal Presence, the most transcendent of all the events of preexistence—that which was of greatest concern and most worth unto us—was the selection of God's Beloved and Chosen One to be the Savior and Redeemer, to be born into the world as the Son of God, to come, thus, with power to work out the atoning sacrifice, which brings immortality to all men and eternal life to those who believe and obey.

For Adam and Eve and their children—those spirit children of the Father, at long last housed in tabernacles of clay—the great concern, which weighed so heavily upon them, was to pattern the earthly kingdom after the heavenly one whence they came. It was to set in order the system that would enable the hosts of heaven to come here, gain mortal bodies, and work out their salvation with fear and trembling before the Lord. It was to learn for themselves, and to teach their children after them, what all men must do as mortals to be born again into the kingdom of heaven so as to merit eternal life in the presence of Him who is Eternal.

For the wicked and rebellious who lived in the days of Noah, when all flesh was corrupt before the Lord, there was nothing of greater import than to cease from gluttony and sin and return unto the Lord, lest he send in the floods upon them, sweep their bodies to a watery grave, and send their spirits to that prison whence there was no escape until they were visited by the Chosen One and had the privilege of hearing again the truths of his everlasting gospel.

For Abraham—in Ur with his idol-worshipping father; in Egypt reasoning on astronomy in Pharaoh's court; in Palestine caring for his cattle on a thousand hills—that which was of greatest concern and worth to him was to enter that order of celestial marriage which would give him an eternal posterity, both in the world and out of the world, a posterity as numerous as the sand upon the seashore or the stars in the heavens.

For Moses and the house of Jacob, then enslaved by Pharaoh, that which concerned them above all else was to travel between the watery walls of the Red Sea, through a forty-year habitat in the wilderness and then into a land flowing with milk and honey where they would build the City of Zion.

For Jewish Israel—and all men—the great and burning questions were: Is this Jesus the one of whom Moses and the prophets spoke? Is he our Deliverer and Messiah, or does he do these works by the power of Beelzebub? Is he the Son of God, as he says, or look we for another?

And for the saints of God today—indeed, for all of earth's inhabitants, for every living soul in this day of preparation—the burning questions are: Will he come again, and if so, when? What will attend and precede the great and dreadful day of the Lord? Who will prepare the way? Will a people be prepared on earth to receive him, and if so, who? And who will abide the day of his coming and who shall stand when he appeareth?

It is to these and like matters that we shall now turn our attention.

Chapter 2

ETERNITY AND THE SEVEN AGES

Come: View His Return in Perspective

The Second Coming of the Son of Man is not an isolated comet blazing its way through the sidereal heavens without reference to the cosmos of which it is a part. It is not a single star whose rays pierce the darkness of heaven's dome, nor is it some shining sun that stands apart from the other luminaries of the skies, nor is it even the center of the universe around which all else revolves. But it is one bright and shining sun in a celestial galaxy composed of many suns, all moving in their orbits, all giving light and life according to the divine plan. It is one clear and brilliant star around which lesser stars revolve and which itself rolls forth in endless orbit around yet greater and more central rulers of the skies. It is part of an infinite universe, part of the eternal scheme of things, part of those great events which are all tied together into one eternal system. And in order to understand the Second Coming, we must view it in perspective, in its relation to other eternal verities, in its connection to all things. We shall approach our problem by naming the seven ages of eternity and noting the transcendent events transpiring or destined to transpire in each of them.

1. *Our Creation and Life as Spirits.*

It is the dawn of the first day. The great Elohim—he who dwells on high, whose throne is in the heavens above, whose kingdoms are governed from Kolob—that glorious and perfected being who is our Father in heaven has a Son, a spirit Son, a Son who is the Firstborn. The Father of us all takes of the self-existing spirit element and creates spirit children, or in other words, he organizes spirits or souls from the intelligence that exists; and such spirit beings become "the intelligences that were organized before the world was." (Abr. 3:22.) They are the sons and daughters of God; creation has commenced; the eternal family of the Eternal God has its beginning.

As eternity rolls everlastingly onward, endless billions of spirit children are born. They become conscious entities in a sphere governed by laws, laws ordained by the Father to enable them to advance and progress and become like him. These laws are called the gospel of God. With their spirit birth they are endowed with agency; they may obey or disobey—the choice is theirs.

All are taught the gospel. In due course they develop talents of all kinds. Some acquire spirituality; others are rebellious and defiant. The noble and great among them are foreordained to be prophets and seers in the coming mortality. Christ, the Firstborn, is chosen to be born into mortality as the Son of God so that he can work out the infinite and eternal atonement. Lucifer and one-third of the spirits destined to come to this earth rebel; there is war in heaven; and the rebels are cast out, denied bodies, damned everlastingly.

Such was our creation and life as the spirit children of the Holy Man whose name, in the Adamic language, is Man of Holiness. Such was the establishment of the plan of salvation and the choosing of a Savior who would come to earth as the Only Begotten in the flesh to make salvation possible.

How glorious is creation! How wondrous the eternal plan of the Father! If there had been no creation, we would not be, and all things would vanish away into a primordial nothingness, having neither sense nor insensibility. If there were no plan of progression and advancement, none of the spirit children of the Father would be able to attain the exalted state he possesses and receive the eternal life he gives to all the obedient. Can we extol too highly the fact of creation and the ordaining of the great and eternal plan of salvation?

2. *The Temporal Creation and Our Life as Mortals.*

It is the age of the creation and peopling of planet earth. It is the day when those who have kept their first estate shall go down to receive the schooling and probation of mortality. It is the day when mighty Michael shall fall that mortal man may be. It is the age that shall set the stage and prepare the way for the redemption of man, for his immortality, for eternal life itself.

We are present in a grand council convened in the midst of eternity; we hear the voices of the Gods of Heaven speak. One who is like unto God, who was beloved and chosen from the beginning, says to the noble and great spirits who are his friends and with whom he serves: 'We will go down to yonder place; there is space there; and we will take of these materials and make an earth whereon we and all our fellows may dwell.'

We see the powers of heaven manifest as a new earth rolls forth in its ordained orbit. The temporal elements are organized and divided from the firmament of heaven; light and darkness divide the day from the night; dry land appears; seeds bring forth after their kind; and fowl and fish and animals are created and commanded to multiply, each in his sphere and after his own kind. The events of each creative day roll before our eyes, and on the sixth day man—a Son of God, his spirit housed in a tabernacle of clay—begins his life on earth.

Then we see the fall of man. Adam and Eve choose to step down from their immortal state to one of mortality; they forsake the paradisiacal glory of Eden for a world of wickedness and sorrow; and death—temporal death and spiritual death—enter the world. The first man and the first woman can now have children; they can begin the process of providing bodies for the eternal spirit children of the Eternal Father.

The effect of the fall passes upon the earth and all forms of life on its face. All things become mortal; death reigns supreme in every department of creation; and the probationary nature of man's second estate is in full operation. Thorns, thistles, briers, and noxious weeds afflict man. He is subject to disease, sorrow, and death. Plagues, pestilence, famines, and ills of every sort pour in upon him. And the great command comes forth that he must work; he must earn and eat his bread in the sweat of his face.

We see a gracious God reveal his gospel truths. The need for a Redeemer to ransom man from the temporal and spiritual death brought into the world by the fall of Adam is clearly set forth. If man will believe and obey, he will be redeemed and return to the presence of the Father. But Lucifer, the common enemy of all mankind, comes among the children of men; he teaches false doctrines and entices man to walk in carnal paths.

Thus we see the commencement of the long history of God's dealings with his earthly children. Prophets and seers teach and testify of that salvation which is in Christ. False prophets and Satanic powers spread hate and evil and war everywhere. The war begun in heaven is being fought anew on earth. And so it is that man gains experience that could come in no other way; thus he is privileged to pass through an existence that prepares him for eternal glory; thus it is possible for him to gain immortality and eternal life.

If there had been no temporal creation, this earth would not exist as an abiding place for man and all forms of life. If Adam had not fallen, there would have been no mortality either for man or for any form of life. Rather, "All things which were created must have remained in the same state in which they were after they were created; and they must have remained forever, and had no end." (2 Ne. 2:22.) And if there were no mortality, there could have been no immortality, no eternal life. Birth and death are as essential to the plan of holiness of the Father as is the very wonder of resurrection. Can we glory too much in the wonder of temporal creation, in the marvel of the peopling of our planet with mortal men, and in the heaven-sent revelation, to all who will receive it, of the plan of salvation?

3. *Redemption and the Age of the Atoning One.*

It is the meridian of time, the high point in the history of humankind, the day when a God will die to redeem those who otherwise would be doomed to eternal death. The Son of Righteousness is about to take upon himself the form of a man, to suffer as a servant, to lay down his life for the sheep, and to rise triumphant from the tomb. The Lord Omnipotent, the Eternal God, the Son of that living God who is our Father, is coming to perform the most transcendent act that ever has occurred or ever will occur among the children of the Father. He will work out the infinite and eternal atonement. It is the age of incarnation and the age of redemption.

Again we are present in spirit and see and hear the wonders of his life and the works that he wrought. We, with Nephi, see a virgin most beautiful and fair above all the daughters of Eve. She dwells in Nazareth of Galilee. An angelic ministrant attests that the God of all gods has chosen her to be the mother of his Son after the manner of the flesh. And therein we are told is the condescension of God.

We are present in a humble peasant home in Nazareth when Gabriel, next in the heavenly hierarchy to Michael himself, comes down and delivers the divine word. Mary, for such is her blessed name, shall conceive by the power of the Holy Ghost, and the Fruit of her Womb shall be the Lamb of God, the Son of the Highest. He will thus inherit from her the power of mortality and from his Eternal Father the power of immortality. Being thus endowed, he will have power to lay down his life and to take it again as required of the Atoning One.

It is sometime in 4 B.C. (or earlier). Herod the Great reigns with Roman power as king of the Jews. He will die a demeaning and loathsome death—as befits one whose life has reeked with cruelties, blood, and a stream of murders—a few weeks after a lunar eclipse that is astronomically calculated to occur in early March of 4 B.C. But now, by decree of imperial Augustus, the evil Caesar of the moment, the world of Rome is to be counted so that capitation taxes may be imposed. And hated Herod, seeking to humor the prejudices of the people of Palestine, has decreed that this enrollment shall take place in their ancestral homelands. Hence Joseph and Mary, each a descendant of David, must go from Nazareth in the north to the Judean city of Bethlehem where David once reigned. There they will be numbered according to the decree of Rome.

We see the caravan of which they are a part, weary from long travel, arrive at the caravanserai where they desire to camp for the night. Their travel has been slow because Mary is big with child.

When they arrive all the inns or rooms surrounding the open courtyard where animals are tethered are full. Joseph and Mary and their party must bed down with the animals or go elsewhere. It is late. There is little time to cook a meager meal over an open fire and prepare for the needed rest that a well-earned sleep will bring. They stop and arrange to camp with the animals.

In all this there is a divine providence. Where must the Atoning One be born? Not in that glorious temple, the spiritual center of the world, whose very stones are covered with gold; not in the palace of the high priest, who once each year enters the holy of holies to make an atonement for the sins of the people; not in the courts of Caesar in the capital of the world, nor even in Herod's palace in Jerusalem, as might befit the king of the Jews; not in any place of worldly power, renown, or wealth. Rather, the Almighty must descend below all things; he must breathe his first breath in Bethlehem; he must lie in a manger among the beasts as he begins his mortal life. The prophetic word must be fulfilled. He whose goings forth have been from of old, from everlasting, must be born in Bethlehem of Judea according to the Messianic word.

And lo, he is born! A God becomes a man! It is what we call the incarnation. The Incarnate One dwells on earth. That body created in Mary's womb houses the Lord Jehovah. The Atoning One has come to work out the infinite and eternal atonement.

We see it all. He grows to a majestic maturity. When the hour of his ministry is come, he is baptized of John in Jordan; he goes forth speaking wondrous words and working mighty miracles; and after more than three years of crying in the wilderness of wickedness, he bows before the Father in Gethsemane to do that for which he came into the world—to suffer both body and spirit, bleeding from every pore, as he takes upon himself the sins of all men on conditions of repentance. We see him there, in agony beyond compare, an angel strengthening him, as the greatest miracle of the ages is wrought—the miracle of redemption.

And finally on the cross, climaxing and completing what commenced in Gethsemane, we see him suffer until the cry goes forth, "It is finished." His work is done; he voluntarily gives up the ghost. The ransom is paid; the redemption is a reality; the atonement is accomplished. The work and glory of God—to bring to pass the immortality and eternal life of man—is now made glorious in the voluntary sacrifice of his Son. Let heaven and earth acclaim the deed, than which there has been no greater.

What need we say more? The miracle of incarnation! The mystery of redemption! The purposes of God prevail. Can we do aught but sing praises to Him who has done these things for us that we might live? Is there any language known to man that will portray the wonder and glory of it all?

4. *The Age of Immortality.*

It is very early in the morning of Sunday, April 9, A.D. 30. It is 784 A.U.C. in the calculations of the imperial Romans; and it is the seventeenth day of the Jewish month of Nisan. It is the day of the first resurrection of the first mortal, the day when the bands of death shall be broken, when the Victorious One shall take up the body with the riven side and use again the hands and feet wherein are the jagged gashes made by Roman nails.

Somewhere in Jerusalem a Jewish father is adjusting the Mezuzah on his doorpost and reminding himself that the Lord his God is one Lord, and his name one. He is also telling himself that the death, three days before, of the Prophet of Nazareth of Galilee removed from their midst an impostor whose miracles were wrought by the power of Beelzebub.

In a Galilean village—yes, in Nazareth itself—another Jew is reciting the Shema and telling his children they are to love the Lord their God with all their heart, might, mind, and strength. He is unmindful that scarcely forty-eight hours have elapsed since his friends and relatives in Jerusalem, urged on by the priestly spokesmen of their nation, had chanted, before Pilate and with reference to the very Lord of whom the Shema speaks, "Crucify him, crucify him." But his spirit is one with theirs, and he also recalls that Sabbath day three years ago when he and others drove the Son of Joseph from their synagogue because he claimed—oh, blasphemous thing!—that the Messianic prophecies were fulfilled in him.

A devout Jew in Bethany, a neighbor of Simon the leper and an acquaintance of Lazarus whom Jesus called back to mortal life, is at this very moment at that point in the Hallel where it is said:

"Save now, I beseech thee, O Lord. . . . Blessed be he that cometh in the name of the Lord." (Ps. 118:25-26.) But as he chants these words of praise to the God of Israel, his soul is filled with hate toward that Nazarene who accepted from the multitude, just one week ago, the blasphemous acclaim: "Hosanna to the Son of David: Blessed is he that cometh in the name of the Lord; Hosanna in the highest." (Matt. 21:9.) And in the same spirit of hate and murder, he recalls in his mind that scene at the nearby tomb of Lazarus, where his body, dead and decaying for four days, had come forth live and vibrant, filled with power and vigor. And the devout Jew is glad that he and others had reported this devil-born miracle to the chief priests and had conspired with them to slay Lazarus lest the ignorant multitude believe that this Galilean, whose voice had power over death, was indeed their Messiah.

Like scenes are unfolding on every side through all Jewry. The priests and Levites and Rabbis and elders and lawyers and leaders, together with the multitudes who heed their counsel, are all rejoicing in the death of this false prophet—was he not Beelzebub incarnate?—this false Messiah, this blasphemer who made himself God. They have returned from Golgotha to their homes and synagogues and street corners to thank God that they are not as these alien Gentiles around them, and to remind Jehovah that they keep the Sabbath, fast twice a week between the Paschal week and Pentecost, and between the Feast of Tabernacles and that of the Dedication of the Temple, and that they can read his law in the pure Hebrew of their fathers. Once more they can devote themselves to calculating their tithes on mint and anise and cummin, as the weightier matters of the law go unheeded. Thank God, they say, for the law of Moses and the traditions of their fathers to which they can now give full attention without the caustic denunciations of this Jesus Ben Joseph who lies in the Arimathean's tomb.

The Roman soldiers are still quenching a drunken thirst. Pilate, hardened in soul and resolute in demeanor, has cast off his fears. He is pleased that no deputation carried word of Jesus' claim to kingship to that half-mad wretch Tiberias. Now that this strange Galilean is dead, the Roman Procurator can occupy himself with more important matters. Herod Antipas, insulted because Jesus would not even speak to him, has visions by day and dreams by night of a gory head on a charger as Salome's lust-inspiring body dances in the background. He too rejoices in the death of one who defied him, one who reminded him of that stern and unrequiting man from the deserts of Hebron who had called him an adulterer and accused him of incest.

It is also a day when a select and favored few, the elect of God, are preparing themselves spiritually to become living witnesses that the age of immortality has arrived. Among them we see Peter and John and their apostolic fellows; among them we find those valiant souls who serve as seventies; among them also are choice disciples in all the villages and cities of Palestine. Could the deaf who hear, the blind who see, the lame who walk, the lepers who are cleansed, the dead who live—all because He willed it to be so—could any of them do other than believe him when he said he would rise again?

Favored among them all, early this Easter morning, we see Mary Magdalene; Mary, the mother of Joses; Salome, the sister of the Blessed Virgin and the mother of James and John; Joanna, the wife of Chuza, who is Herod's steward; and other women. We suppose the beloved sisters from Bethany, Mary and Martha, are among them, though we have no reason to believe the Virgin Mother herself was there. They are bringing spices and costly ointments to anoint and embalm the body of their Lord.

They arrive at the tomb, and lo, it is as though the earth stopped spinning on her axis; it is as though the sun ceased to shine and the stars hurled themselves from the firmament of heaven; it is as though time stood still and space ceased to be—for He is not there! He is risen! One that was dead lives. A cold corpse has escaped corruption. The linen strips wrapped around him by Joseph and Nicodemus and the napkin that covered his head lie as though wound still around his body. But he is risen; he is not here; he lives. Why seek they the living among the dead? Christ the Lord is risen this day. Alleluia!

Angelic voices testify that he who came to Jerusalem to die upon the cross of Calvary has risen on the third day as he promised. Then he himself appears to many. They walk and talk and commune and eat with him as though he were yet mortal. They feel the nail marks in his hands and feet and thrust their hands into his riven side as thousands of Nephites shall thereafter do. They eat and drink with him after he has risen from the dead. They are becoming witnesses, special witnesses, living witnesses, that he is the firstfruits of them that sleep.

First he spends a few sacred and precious moments with Mary Magdalene in the garden; then he appears to all of the women and they hold him by the feet. Next he appears to Simon; then he walks and talks with Luke and Cleopas on the Emmaus road; then he stands before a large group of disciples in an upper room. They see him with their eyes, feel him with their hands, and watch as he eats a piece of broiled fish and of honeycomb. All this happens the very day of his resurrection.

A week later a like visual witness is borne over again to the disciples and also to Thomas, who was not present on the first Easter evening. Still later, at the sea of Tiberias, the Risen Lord and six of the Twelve eat together. Then on a mountain in Galilee comes the grand appearance. More than five hundred brethren are present and many things transpire. Still later he appears to James, the son of Joseph and Mary, and finally to the eleven apostles at the time of his ascension. And not only does he appear, but many graves also are opened and saints long dead arise and appear to many in the Holy City. Each risen saint becomes a living witness that he who is Lord of all has himself first risen. It is the dawn of the age of immortality.

Christ is risen and all shall rise. The power of his resurrection passes upon all mankind. Immortality is as real as mortality, and indeed it applies not only to man but to all created things. It is no more difficult to believe in resurrection than in creation; one is not a greater mystery than the other. And so, as we see the eternal verities in perspective, shall we not praise the Lord for immortality and all that appertains to it, even as we praise him for life and being and for the atonement that makes all things operative?

5. *The Age of Triumph, Glory, and Millennial Splendor.*

This is the age whose dawning rays are now breaking through the mists and darkness that cover a weary and wicked world. It is the age of which we shall write in this work. It is the day sought by all the prophets and saints from the time of Adam to the present moment. It is the day when the earth shall rest and the saints find peace. And it shall be ushered in by the Second Coming of the Son of Man, to "sanctify the earth, and complete the salvation of man, and judge all things." (D&C 77:12.)

As we go forward in our study, we shall see apostasy, war, pestilence, and plagues; nations shall be drunken with their own blood; and the blood of the saints shall cry unto the Lord for vengeance. We shall see the fulfillment of every jot and tittle that has been promised.

We shall see a marvelous work and a wonder come forth; the gospel shall be restored; Israel shall gather; temples shall rise in many nations; the elect shall be gathered out of Babylon into the marvelous light of Christ; and all of the signs of the times shall be fulfilled.

Then, at the time appointed by the Father, the Son of Man will come in the clouds of heaven. It is an unknown day in the beginning of the seventh thousand years of the earth's temporal continuance. War, such as has not been known from the beginning of time, is in progress. All nations are assembled at Armageddon.

All things are in commotion. Never has there been such a day as this. The newspapers of the world, as well as radio and television, speak only of war and calamity and the dread that hangs like a millstone around every neck. False ministers speak seductive words into hired microphones, giving their twisted views of the signs of the times. Their private interpretations of the prophetic word are at odds with world events. The priests and preachers of every doctrine are confused and uncertain. Has God forsaken the world, or is it true, as millions now acclaim, that there is no God?

Cabinets are in session planning death and destruction. Kings and presidents make unholy alliances as they conspire to spread death and carnage in the assembled armies. A general is calling for atomic bombs on the plain of Esdraelon. All hell rages as the unseen demons join hands with men to spread sin and sickness, death and desolation, and every evil thing in all parts of the earth.

And the signs in heaven above are like nothing man has ever

seen. Blood is everywhere; fire and vapors of smoke fill the atmospheric heavens. No man has seen a rainbow this year. And that great sign in the eastern sky—does it portend an invasion from outer space? Or is a collision with another planet imminent?

And above all are the vexing words of those Mormon Elders! They are everywhere preaching their strange doctrine, saying that the coming of the Lord is near, and that unless men repent and believe the gospel they will be destroyed by the brightness of his coming.

In this setting, as these and ten thousand like things are in progress, suddenly, quickly, as from the midst of eternity, He comes! Fire burns before him; tempests spread destruction; the earth trembles and reels to and fro as a drunken man. Every corruptible thing is consumed. He sets his foot on the Mount called Olivet; it cleaves in twain. The Lord has returned and the great millennium is here! The year of his redeemed has arrived!

Now we see the salvation of our God. Israel is gathered; the waste places of Zion are built up. The law goes forth from Zion and the word of the Lord from Jerusalem. Those men who remain have beaten their swords into plowshares and their spears into pruning hooks. It is the day of the Prince of Peace; the Lord himself reigns gloriously among his people. It is the age of triumph, glory, and millennial splendor.

6. *The Day of Celestial Exaltation and Eternal Rewards.*

After the Millennium plus a little season—perhaps itself another thousand years—during which men turn again to wickedness, then cometh the end, not of the world, which occurred at the Second Coming, but the end of earth. Then the final battle against Gog and Magog, the battle of the Great God, will be fought. Michael will lead the armies of heaven and Lucifer the legions of hell. Again there will be a new heaven and a new earth, but this time it will be a celestial earth. This earth will then be an eternal heaven, and the meek, who are the God-fearing and the righteous, shall inherit it forever and ever.

In their state of glorious exaltation, earth's inhabitants will then be as their God. They will have eternal life, which consists of life in the family unit and the possession of the fulness of the power of the Almighty. This is the final day toward which all things point.

7. *The Seventh Age—Eternity Begins Anew.*

When the elect are exalted, when the family unit continues in the highest heaven of the celestial kingdom, when the saints have spirit children in the resurrection, then the cycle begins again. It is, as it were, the age of the Sabbath, an eternal Sabbath in which there is rest from the toil and sorrow that went before.

Exalted parents are to their children as our Eternal Parents are to us. Eternal increase, a continuation of the seeds forever and ever, eternal lives—these comprise the eternal family of those who gain eternal life. For them new earths are created, and thus the on-rolling purposes of the Gods of Heaven go forward from eternity to eternity.

And thus we place the Second Coming of the Son of Man in its proper eternal perspective. Our foundation is laid. Let us feast at the table of the Lord and drink deeply of the sweet wine served at his banquet.

THE TIME OF HIS COMING

Let Us Pray: "Thy Kingdom Come"

Jesus our Lord—and blessed be his name—shall soon come down from heaven in all the glory of his Father's kingdom to be with men again on earth!

Weeping over doomed Jerusalem, testifying to the Jews that their temple and their city would be left unto them desolate, he said: "Ye shall not see me henceforth and know that I am he of whom it is written by the prophets, until ye shall say: Blessed is he who cometh in the name of the Lord, in the clouds of heaven, and all the holy angels with him."

Of this prophetic utterance the scripture says: "Then understood his disciples that he should come again on the earth, after that he was glorified and crowned on the right hand of God." (JS-M 1:1.)

How glorious is this word of truth! He shall come again. All glory to his holy name. He shall come to complete the salvation of men and give glory and dominion to his saints. Let saints and angels sing. Let those on both sides of the veil look forward with anxious expectation for that great and gracious day. "Thy kingdom come. Thy will be done in earth, as it is in heaven." (Matt. 6:10.)

In every devout and believing heart the burning questions are: When will he come? Will it be in my day, or the day of my children, or in some distant age? And will I be worthy to abide the day and to stand with him in glory when he appeareth? And so we find the disciples, alone with him on the Mount of Olives, pondering his pronouncement about the Second Coming. They ask: "What is the sign of thy coming, and of the end of the world?" (JS-M 1:4.) His answer is the majestic Olivet Discourse, each portion of which we shall study hereafter in its proper place and setting.

It is our privilege and our duty to learn the signs of his coming and to seek his face. Each of us would do well to take the prophetic pledge: "I will wait upon the Lord, that hideth his face from the house of Jacob, and I will look for him." (Isa. 8:17.) Indeed, "he that feareth me shall be looking forth for the great day of the Lord to come," he says, "even for the signs of the coming of the Son of Man. . . . And, behold, I will come. . . . And he that watches not for me shall be cut off." (D&C 45:39-44.) To his saints the command is: "Prepare for the revelation which is to come, when . . . all flesh shall see me together. . . . And seek the face of the Lord always." (D&C 101:23, 38.)

Those who seek his face and who long for his coming shall be rewarded with everlasting glory in that day. "For behold, the Lord God hath sent forth the angel crying through the midst of heaven, saying: Prepare ye the way of the Lord, and make his paths straight, for the hour of his coming is nigh." (D&C 133:17.) Their preparation consists in believing and obeying all the laws and ordinances of the gospel.

And for their blessing and use, the Lord revealed this prayer: "Hearken, and lo, a voice as of one sent down from on high, who is mighty and powerful, whose going forth is unto the ends of the earth, yea, whose voice is unto men—Prepare ye the way of the Lord, make his paths straight. . . . Pray unto the Lord, call upon his holy name, make known his wonderful works among the people. Call upon the Lord, that his kingdom may go forth upon the earth, that the inhabitants thereof may receive it, and be prepared for the days to come, in the which the Son of Man shall come down in heaven, clothed in the brightness of his glory, to meet the kingdom of God which is set up on the earth. Wherefore, may the kingdom of God go forth, that the kingdom of heaven may come, that thou, O God, mayest be glorified in heaven so on earth, that thine enemies may be subdued; for thine is the honor, power and glory, forever and ever. Amen." (D&C 65:1, 4-6.)

In seeking all these things, not only is it our privilege to learn from holy writ, but if we are true and faithful in all things we can also see and feel the very things that came to those whose words we have canonized. Thus the Prophet Joseph Smith teaches and testifies: "Search the revelations of God; study the prophecies, and rejoice that God grants unto the world Seers and Prophets. They are they who saw the mysteries of godliness; they saw the flood before it came; they saw angels ascending and descending upon a ladder that reached from earth to heaven; they saw the stone cut out of the mountain, which filled the whole earth; they saw the Son of God come from the regions of bliss and dwell with men on earth; they saw the deliverer come out of Zion, and turn away ungodliness from Jacob; they saw the glory of the Lord when he showed the transfiguration of the earth on the mount; they saw every mountain laid low and every valley exalted when the Lord was taking vengeance upon the wicked; they saw truth spring out of the earth, and righteousness look down from heaven in the last days, before the Lord came the second time to gather his elect; they saw the end of wickedness on earth, and the Sabbath of creation crowned with peace; they saw the end of the glorious thousand years, when Satan was loosed for a little season; they saw the day of judgment when all men received according to their works, and they saw the heaven and the earth flee away to make room for the city of God, when the righteous receive an inheritance in eternity. And, fellow sojourners upon earth, *it is your privilege to purify yourselves and come up to the same glory, and see for yourselves, and know for yourselves*. Ask, and it shall be given you; seek and ye shall find; knock, and it shall be opened unto you." (*Teachings*, pp. 12-13. Italics added.)

When Will the Son of Man Come?

The time for the Second Coming of Christ is as fixed and certain as was the hour of his birth. It will not vary as much as a single second from the divine decree. He will come at the appointed time. The Millennium will not be ushered in prematurely because men turn to righteousness, nor will it be delayed because iniquity abounds. Nephi was able to state with absolute certainty that the God of Israel would come "in six hundred years from the time my father left Jerusalem." (1 Ne. 19:8.) To a later Nephi the Divine Voice acclaimed: "The time is at hand, and on this night shall the sign be given, and on the morrow come I into the world." (3 Ne. 1:13.)

So shall it be with his return in glory. He knows the set time and so does his Father. Perhaps a latter-day prophet will hear the Divine Voice on the day the veil parts and the heavens roll together as a scroll. But there is this difference between his two comings: The fixed and known time of his triumphal return has not been and will not be revealed until the set hour and the fixed time and the very day arrives. "Jesus Christ never did reveal to any man the precise time that He would come," the Prophet Joseph Smith said. "Go and read the Scriptures, and you cannot find anything that specifies the exact hour He would come; and all that say so are false teachers." (*Teachings*, p. 341.)

The scriptures say he will come as a thief—unexpectedly, without warning, when least expected. This has two meanings, one for the wicked and ungodly and another for the faithful saints. Those who neither believe nor understand will be pursuing their own evil ways—eating as gluttons, drinking as drunkards, and reveling in all the abominations of the world. They will esteem the words of the living apostles and the modern prophets as of no great worth and as the mouthings of religious fanatics. To them the promise of a Second Coming and a millennial era seems but an eschatological echo from unenlightened days long past. And even those who have been born again, who are alive to the things of the Spirit, and who understand the prophetic word—even they shall not know the precise time of his return.

Thus we read that he said to all men, both the righteous and the wicked, that "of that day, and hour, no one knoweth; no, not the angels of God in heaven, but my Father only. . . . And what I say unto one, I say unto all men; watch, therefore, for you know not at what hour your Lord doth come. But know this, if the good man of the house had known in what watch the thief would come, he would have watched, and would not have suffered his house to have been broken up, but would have been ready. Therefore be ye also ready, for in such an hour as ye think not, the Son of Man cometh." (JS-M 1:40, 46-48; Matt. 25:13.) These words were spoken on the Mount of Olives to his ancient disciples; to his modern friends he says of himself: "The Son of Man . . . has taken his power on the right hand of his glory, and now reigneth in the heavens, and will reign till he descends on the earth to put all enemies under his feet, which time is nigh at hand—I, the Lord God, have spoken it; but the hour and the day no man knoweth, neither the angels in heaven, nor shall they know until he comes." (D&C 49:6-7.)

Thus, also, we read that he said to his chosen ones, who had received the ordinances of his holy house, "Behold, I come as a thief. Blessed is he that watcheth, and keepeth his garments, lest he walk naked, and they see his shame." (Rev. 16:15.) These are the saints of the Most High, the ones of whom he said, "And whoso treasureth up my word, shall not be deceived" (JS-M 1:37); even though they can read the signs of the times, they shall not know the precise time of his coming. As Daniel expressed it, "None of the wicked shall understand; but the wise shall understand" (Dan. 12:10), and yet even they, along with the angels of heaven, shall not know the very day and the hour until it arrives.

This brings us to that glorious illustration, devised by Paul, which contrasts the knowledge of the saints and that of worldly people relative to "the coming of the Lord." The ancient apostle says: "The Lord himself shall descend from heaven with a shout, with the voice of the archangel, and with the trump of God." What glories shall attend the day none can tell! "But of the times and the seasons, brethren, ye have no need that I write you," he continues. These words of Paul are for the saints who have treasured up his word; they are for the wise who understand. "For yourselves"—ye favored and blessed ones—"know perfectly that the day of the Lord so cometh as a thief in the night." This is axiomatic; it is assumed in all discussions as to the time of his coming, and no informed person raises questions on this point. "For when they"—those without understanding and who cannot read the signs of the times—"shall say, Peace and safety"—that is, when they shall say, 'We can bring peace on earth through our treaties; we can control our destinies; why should the Lord come to destroy the wicked and usher in the Millennium?'—"then sudden destruction cometh upon them, as travail upon a woman with child; and they shall not escape."

Such is his illustration. The Second Coming is as a woman about to give birth to a child. She and her husband, the midwife at her side, and all who are informed know the birth is near, but they do not know the day and the hour. Even when the pains commence they cannot know what minute the expected one shall arrive. The approximate time, "the times and the seasons," yes—but the precise time, no. "But ye, brethren," Paul continues, "are not in darkness, that that day should overtake you as a thief. Ye are all the children of light, and the children of the day: we are not of the night, nor of darkness."

Then comes the exhortation. Always and everlastingly the prophetic authors use the doctrine of the Second Coming to invite the wicked to repent and to exhort the righteous to keep the commandments. Paul is no exception. "Therefore let us not sleep, as do others; but let us watch and be sober," he says. "For they that sleep sleep in the night; and they that be drunken are drunken in the night. But let us, who are of the day, be sober, putting on the breastplate of faith and love; and for an helmet, the hope of salvation. For God hath not appointed us to wrath, but to obtain salvation by our Lord Jesus Christ." (1 Thes. 4:15-16; 5:1-9.)

In confirmation of Paul's account, the Lord's latter-day word to us is: "The coming of the Lord draweth nigh, and it overtaketh the world as a thief in the night—Therefore, gird up your loins, that you may be the children of light, and that day shall not overtake you as a thief." (D&C 106:4-5.)

In the light of these principles, we are able to understand this statement of the Prophet Joseph Smith: "It is not the design of the Almighty to come upon the earth and crush it and grind it to powder, but he will reveal it to His servants the prophets." (*Teachings*, p. 286.) The Prophet then identifies some events and signs destined to precede the Second Coming, all of which we shall hereafter consider. For our present purposes, it suffices to know that the children of light shall know, not the day or the hour, but the approximate time of our Lord's return.

This approximate time can certainly be narrowed down to a generation. After teaching that desolations would befall the Jews of his day "as a thief in the night," Jesus said: "And it shall come to pass, that this generation of Jews shall not pass away until every desolation which I have told you concerning them shall come to pass." (D&C 45:19-21.) In speaking of the signs of the times in the last days, he said: "Verily, I say unto you, this generation, in which these things shall be shown forth, shall not pass away until all I have told you shall be fulfilled." (JS-M 1:34.) It is on this basis that those who wait for the Second Coming of the Consolation of Israel seek to learn the signs of the times.

The Generation of His Return

Many scriptures attest that "the great and dreadful day of the Lord is near, even at the doors." (D&C 110:16.) In our revelations the Lord says, "The time is soon at hand that I shall come in a cloud with power and great glory" (D&C 34:7), and that "the great day of the Lord is nigh at hand. . . . For in mine own due time will I come upon the earth in judgment" (D&C 43:17, 29). Speaking of his coming, the Lord says in one revelation that it shall be "not many days hence" (D&C 88:87), and in another, that the wars to precede it are "not yet, but by and by" (D&C 63:35). These and like sayings fall into perspective when we hear him say: "These are the things that ye must look for; and, speaking after the manner of the Lord, they are now nigh at hand, and in a time to come, even in the day of the coming of the Son of Man." (D&C 63:53.) We conclude that in the eternal perspective the coming of the Lord is nigh, but that from man's viewpoint many years may yet pass away before that awesome and dreadful day. And we must remind ourselves that he will not come until all that is promised has come to pass.

Time, as measured "after the manner of the Lord," is that which prevails on Kolob. One revolution of that planet is "a day unto the Lord, after his manner of reckoning," such "being one thousand years according to the time appointed" for our earth. (Abr. 3:4.) This earth was created and destined to pass through "seven thousand years of . . . continuance, or . . . temporal existence," with the millennial era becoming its Sabbath of rest. "We are to understand," as it is set forth in the revealed word, "that as God made the world in six days, and on the seventh day he finished his work, and sanctified it, and also formed man out of the dust of the earth, even so, in the beginning of the seventh thousand years will the Lord God sanctify the earth, and complete the salvation of man, and judge all things, and shall redeem all things." Certain named events are then specified to precede his coming. They are "the preparing and finishing of his work, in the beginning of the seventh thousand years—the preparing of the way before the time of his coming." (D&C 77:6, 12.) That is to say, the Lord Jesus Christ is going to come "in the beginning of the seventh thousand years." We, of course, cannot tell with certainty how many years passed from the fall of Adam to the birth of Jesus, nor whether the number of years counted by our present calendar has been tabulated without error. But no one will doubt that we are in the Saturday night of time and that on Sunday morning the Lord will come.

Peter had the Lord's time in mind when he wrote that "there shall come in the last days scoffers," mockers who do not believe the scriptural accounts stating that God created the earth in six days and rested on the seventh. They will say: "Where is the promise of his coming?" They will reject the Second Coming with its millennial era of peace, with its new heaven and new earth wherein death and sorrow cease, because, as they falsely reason: "Since the fathers fell asleep, all things continue as they were from the beginning of the creation." They will say such things as: 'How can there be a millennial era during which men will live to the age of a tree, when everyone knows we are the end product of evolution and that death has always existed on earth?' But Peter says that they "willingly are ignorant" of God's true dealings with reference to the creation, with reference to the flood of Noah, and with reference to the coming day of judgment, a day when "the elements shall melt with fervent heat" and all things shall become new.

To the saints, among whom are we, he says: "But, beloved, be not ignorant of this one thing, that one day is with the Lord as a thousand years, and a thousand years as one day. The Lord is not slack concerning his promise. . . . But the day of the Lord will come as a thief in the night; in the which the heavens shall pass away with a great noise." (2 Pet. 3:3-13.)

Thus, also, we read in latter-day revelation: "Now it is called today until the coming of the Son of Man. . . . For after today cometh the burning—this is speaking after the manner of the Lord." (D&C 64:23-24.)

With reference to that day of which we write, Joseph Smith said: "I was once praying very earnestly to know the time of the coming of the Son of Man, when I heard a voice repeat the following: Joseph, my son, if thou livest until thou art eighty-five years old, thou shalt see the face of the Son of Man; therefore let this suffice, and trouble me no more on this matter. I was left thus, without being able to decide whether this coming referred to the beginning of the millennium or to some previous appearing, or whether I should die and thus see his face. I believe the coming of the Son of Man will not be any sooner than that time." (D&C 130:14-17.) A few days after making this statement the Prophet referred to it in a sermon and said: "I prophesy in the name of the Lord God, and let it be written—the Son of Man will not come in the clouds of heaven till I am eighty-five years old."

It was in this same sermon that he said: "Were I going to prophesy, I would say the end [of the world] would not come in 1844, 5, or 6, or in forty years. There are those of the rising generation who shall not taste death till Christ comes." The rising generation includes all those yet to be born to parents then living. Manifestly many of these are now among us and will be living after the year A.D. 2000 has come and gone.

In this sermon also the Prophet said: "The coming of the Son of Man never will be—never can be till the judgments spoken of for this hour are poured out: which judgments are commenced." (*Teachings*, p. 286.) At this point he alluded to Paul's statements that the saints are the children of light and not of darkness and that the coming day should not overtake them as a thief in the night.

And it is on these points—that he will not come until the signs of the times are fulfilled and that the children of light will recognize the signs—that we shall take our stand as we go forward in our studies.

To all of this we must append this verity: When the day arrives, he will come quickly. The time for repentance and preparation will be passed; the day of judgment will be upon us. His presence "shall kindle a burning like the burning of a fire. . . . And it shall burn and devour his thorns and his briers in one day." (Isa. 10:16-17.)

Hear, then, this counsel, O ye saints: "Be patient in tribulation until I come; and, behold, I come quickly, and my reward is with me, and they who have sought me early shall find rest to their souls." (D&C 54:10.) Also: "Stand ye in holy places, and be not moved, until the day of the Lord come; for behold, it cometh quickly, saith the Lord." (D&C 87:8.)

He Comes in Each Watch of the Night

Few things provide the saints with a more anxious desire to walk uprightly and keep the commandments than does the doctrine of the Second Coming. All those who love the Lord and who seek his face cry out for a place in his kingdom. They know that every corruptible thing will be consumed when he comes, and their hope is to abide the day and then to be with him forever.

Hence, the day when he shall return always has been and always will be a matter of uncertainty. Thus, no matter when they live, all his saints are placed in a position of anxious expectation. All are to await his return as though it were destined for their day. Written in words of fire, they have ever before them the command: Watch and be ready.

As succeeding events occur in the world, there is no question his faithful saints gain a clearer knowledge of when to expect his glorious return. Some of the saints in the meridian of time seem to have thought he would return in their day. Surely many of the Latter-day Saints in the dawning days of this dispensation expected him to come in their lifetimes. We today, as we see the unfolding of his work in all the world, are in the best position of any people up to now to envision correctly the approximate time of his coming. Our children should surpass us in understanding.

Thus it is that his program calls for all the saints, from the day he ascended from Olivet until he comes again to that same holy place, to live as though they would be present to welcome him back! If such be their course, because the Great Judge is no respecter of persons, they will be rewarded as though he had come in their day. And this brings us to one of the great discourses of his mortal ministry, a sermon in which he says he will come again and again, in every watch of the night, as it were.

"Let your loins be girded about and have your lights burning," he says, "That ye yourselves may be like unto men who wait for their Lord, when he will return from the wedding; that, when he cometh and knocketh, they may open unto him immediately. Verily I say unto you, Blessed are those servants"—he is speaking of his saints, of those who have entered into a covenant to serve him and keep his commandments—"whom the Lord when he cometh shall find watching; for he shall gird himself, and make them sit down to meat, and will come forth and serve them." His reward is with him. The faithful who abide the day shall be exalted. They shall be even as he is, and they shall serve each other.

But because all his saints shall not live at the fixed time of his millennial return, he says: "For, behold, he cometh in the first watch of the night, and he shall also come in the second watch, and again he shall come in the third watch." How equitable and just is our God! He shall come to all—not alone to his saints in the final days of the world, but to all his saints who have lived from the first Adam to the last of Adam's race—and all who are waiting in righteousness shall abide the day.

"And verily I say unto you, He hath already come, as it is written of him." He then ministered among them. "And again when he shall come in the second watch, or come in the third watch, blessed are those servants when he cometh, that he shall find so doing; For the Lord of those servants shall gird himself, and make them to sit down to meat, and will come forth and serve them."

Such is the divine plan of the divine being. And in this sense every faithful person lives until the Second Coming of the Son of Man.

"And now, verily I say these things unto you," he continues, "that ye may know this, that the coming of the Lord is as a thief in the night. And it is like unto a man who is an householder, who, if he watcheth not his goods, the thief cometh in an hour of which he is not aware, and taketh his goods, and divideth them among his fellows."

These expressions evoked an immediate and obvious response: "And they said among themselves, If the good man of the house had known what hour the thief would come, he would have watched, and not have suffered his house to be broken through and the loss of his goods."

To this Jesus agreed. "And he said unto them, Verily I say unto you, be ye therefore ready also; for the Son of man cometh at an hour when ye think not." (JST, Luke 12:38-47.)

Let all his people watch and be ready, for he shall surely come in their day, let them live whensoever a divine providence hath decreed.

APOSTASY AND INIQUITY PRECEDE HIS COMING

Gospel Light in Ages Past

In the not far distant future there will be a day of millennial rest, ushered in by the glorious coming of him who is the Son of Man of Holiness. He who came once shall come again. "But before that day the heavens shall be darkened." That is, revelation shall cease, the visions of eternity shall be closed to view, and the voice of God shall no longer be heard. The pure light of heaven shall no longer shine in the hearts of men. "And a veil of darkness shall cover the earth." (Moses 7:61.) Men will no longer penetrate the gloom of ignorance and unbelief, and see and know for themselves the truths of salvation.

After our Lord's first coming and before his dreadful return, there is to be a day of absolute, total, and complete apostasy from the truth. Men are to be left to themselves, wanderers in darkness, without hope and without God in the world. This we shall set forth shortly. But before we can even begin to catch a vision of the enormity of the evil and ignorance that will shroud the earth, we must be reminded of the eternal plan of the Father for all his spirit children. The contrast between the heavenly light of the everlasting gospel and the darkness that covers the earth will be as between the sun at midday and the darkness prevailing at midnight.

The great God, who is the Father of us all, is the Creator of all things. He made the sidereal heavens; the milky way is his; and worlds without number have rolled into existence at his word. Galaxies without end are governed by his will. Endless are the earths inhabited by his spirit children. And as pertaining to them all, he says: "This is my work and my glory—to bring to pass the immortality and eternal life of man." (Moses 1:39.)

Eternal life is the name of the kind of life he lives. Those who so obtain become like him and are as he is. They live in the family unit and bear spirit children of their own; they have all power, all might, and all dominion. They know all things. He ordained and established the plan of salvation to enable them to advance and progress and become like him. It includes, first, an eternity of preparation as spirit beings in a premortal life. Then comes a mortal probation, on one of the earths provided, during which the faithful must remain in communication with their Father. They must receive revelation, see visions, enjoy the gifts of the Spirit, and know God, if they are to be saved. The plan of salvation is the same on all worlds and in all ages.

Here on planet earth the gospel of God, which is the plan of salvation, was revealed first to Adam. It then remained on earth, in whole or in part, without interruption for more than four thousand years. Whole nations and kingdoms fell away from the truth, but there was no period of universal apostasy during the whole so-called pre-Christian era. From age to age, prophets and apostles and preachers of righteousness taught the gospel and performed the ordinances of salvation.

Whenever and wherever men had faith, they saw the face of God, entertained angels, and performed miracles; they healed the sick, raised the dead, and wrought righteousness. Enoch and his whole city so perfected their lives that they were taken up into heaven. A whole generation of Nephites walked so perfectly in the light that every living soul among them was saved. In the meridian of time, Jesus marked the course and charted the way. The apostles after him built up the kingdom as they were guided by the Spirit.

And thus for more than four thousand years there were men who had received revelation, believed the gospel, and walked uprightly before the Lord. He in turn had poured out his Spirit upon them so that they "subdued kingdoms, wrought righteousness, obtained promises, stopped the mouths of lions, quenched the violence of fire, escaped the edge of the sword, out of weakness were made strong, waxed valiant in fight, turned to flight the armies of the aliens." (Heb. 11:33-34.) They had power "to break mountains, to divide the seas, to dry up waters, to turn them out of their course; to put at defiance the armies of nations, to divide the earth, to break every band, to stand in the presence of God; to do all things according to his will, according to his command, subdue principalities and powers; and this by the will of the Son of God which was from before the foundation of the world." (JST, Gen. 14:30-31.)

In the Lord's view, and from his eternal perspective, the course and way of life here set forth is the norm. It is the way men should live. It is the way many—perhaps most—do live on the endless earths that roll through the immensity of space. It is a perfectly normal thing for faithful and righteous people on all earths to raise the dead, to be caught up to the third heaven, to see and hear unspeakable things. It is the way all men will live during the Millennium, when, as we suppose, more people will dwell on earth (perhaps many times more) than have dwelt here during all of the preceding six thousand years.

It is true that there have been apostate nations and peoples from the beginning. But never, never during more than four millennia, was there a day when the Lord was without some legal administrators to preach and teach his word. The day of universal apostasy was reserved for that period between the first and second ministries of the Messiah. It is no wonder that the apostles and prophets use such plain and harsh words to describe the day of apostasy which will usher in our Lord's return. It is an awful thing for millions—nay, billions—of people to be in rebellion and to have turned their souls over to Satan.

Apostasy is to forsake the gospel, and the gospel is the everlasting covenant of salvation that God makes with his people. The fulness of the everlasting gospel is the new and everlasting covenant—a covenant revealed anew from age to age, a covenant that is everlastingly the same, for its terms and conditions are eternal; they never vary. And so Isaiah, speaking of the last days and the Second Coming, says: "The earth mourneth and fadeth away, the world languisheth and fadeth away, the haughty people of the earth do languish." The vineyard is being prepared for the fire.

"The earth also is defiled under the inhabitants thereof." Why? Because of wickedness. What is the nature of the sin? Isaiah answers: "Because they have transgressed the laws, changed the ordinance, broken the everlasting covenant." His answer is complete. Men have forsaken the whole gospel system—its laws, ordinances, and saving truths. A covenant that is everlasting no longer continues; it has been broken by men! They have forsaken their God. For such a course they must pay the penalty. "Therefore hath the curse devoured the earth, and they that dwell therein are desolate"—or, better, 'they that dwell therein are found guilty' —"therefore the inhabitants of the earth are burned, and few men left." (Isa. 24:4-6.) The burning occurs at the Second Coming. In our modern revelations, the Lord says that in that day the wicked "shall be cut off from among the people: For they have strayed from mine ordinances, and have broken mine everlasting covenant." (D&C 1:14-15.)

Darkness Covers the Earth

"I clothe the heavens with blackness" (Isa. 50:3), and there is no more revelation.

"Behold, the darkness shall cover the earth, and gross darkness the people" (Isa. 60:2), so that none in that day shall know the truth.

"I will cause the sun to go down at noon, and I will darken the earth in the clear day." (Amos 8:9.) Men will no longer be enlightened from on high.

Thus saith our God. Such is his promise, spoken prophetically of our day. And here, given in modern times, is his announcement that as he spake, so has it come to pass: "Verily, verily, I say unto you, darkness covereth the earth, and gross darkness the minds of the people, and all flesh has become corrupt before my face." (D&C 112:23.)

It is an evil day, a damnable day. There is no salvation in the teachings or philosophies of men. The Judeo-Christian ethic cannot free men from their sins, and the sects of Christendom have all gone astray. Even those who have a form of godliness are quick to deny the power thereof. The gifts of the Spirit no longer pierce the mists of darkness which cover the earth. It is a day of apostasy, a day when men are ripening in iniquity, a day when the tares are being bound in bundles and made ready for the burning.

These are the days foretold in holy writ. "Behold, the days come, saith the Lord God, that I will send a famine in the land, not a famine of bread, nor a thirst for water, but of hearing the words of the Lord." How dire are these days, days in which men have sunk so low spiritually that they worship, as they suppose, a God who is unknown and unknowable and incomprehensible. But how could it be otherwise when there is no revelation! "And they shall wander from sea to sea, and from the north even to the east, they shall run to and fro to seek the word of the Lord, and shall not find it. In that day shall the fair virgins and young men faint for thirst." (Amos 8:11-13.)

The universal apostasy is one of the signs of the times. It was destined to be before his Second Coming. Paul wrote an epistle to the saints in Thessalonica telling them that as children of light they should know the times and seasons of our Lord's return. Apparently some of them gained the impression he would come in their day. In a second epistle the apostle testified again of the promised return of the Blessed One in flaming fire, and then added words of caution relative to the appointed time.

"Now we beseech you, brethren, by the coming of our Lord Jesus Christ, and by our gathering together unto him," he writes in words of soberness, "That ye be not soon shaken in mind, or be troubled by letter, except ye receive it from us; neither by spirit, nor by word, as that the day of Christ is at hand." 'Do not be deceived by any sermons or epistles which lead you to believe that Christ will come in your day.'

"Let no man deceive you by any means; for there shall come a falling away first, and that man of sin be revealed, the son of perdition." Two conditions are here set forth. Christ shall not come until there is a falling away from the faith once delivered to the saints, until there is a universal apostasy; and further, he will not come until the operations of Lucifer—the man of sin, the son of perdition—are manifest in the world to an extent and degree beyond anything before known.

Of the evil and iniquity destined to cover the earth before the Second Coming, the apostle Paul said: "The mystery of iniquity doth already work"—it has even now commenced—"and he [Lucifer] it is who now worketh, and Christ suffereth him to work"—it is part of the plan that men be tempted of the devil—"until the time is fulfilled that he shall be taken out of the way." That is, Satan shall go to and fro upon the earth, raging in the hearts of men, until he is bound in the millennial day. "And then," when the Millennium comes, "shall that wicked one be revealed, whom the Lord shall consume with the spirit of his mouth, and shall destroy with the brightness of his coming. Yea, the Lord, even Jesus, whose coming is not until after there cometh a falling away, by the working of Satan with all power, and signs and lying wonders." (JST, 2 Thes. 2:1-9.)

Light is of God, darkness of the devil. Gospel truths lead to salvation, false doctrines to damnation. The man Satan—a spirit man, a man of sin, the evil person of whom the scripture asks: "Is this the man that made the earth to tremble, that did shake kingdoms; That made the world as a wilderness, and destroyed the cities thereof; that opened not the house of his prisoners?" (Isa. 14:16-17)—the man Satan brings the apostasy to pass. He and his works have been manifest in all ages. And the worst lies ahead.

Our day of dreadful apostasy and woeful wickedness was known to ancient prophets without number. Nephi, for one, said that "in the last days . . . all the nations of the Gentiles and also the Jews," who dwell "upon all the lands of the earth, . . . will be drunken with iniquity and all manner of abominations." Addressing himself to earth's latter-day inhabitants he cried: "Behold, all ye that doeth iniquity, stay yourselves and wonder, for ye shall cry out, and cry; yea, ye shall be drunken but not with wine, ye shall stagger but not with strong drink. For behold, the Lord hath poured out upon you the spirit of deep sleep."

Drunken with blood and iniquity and evil! Staggering under the weight of false doctrines, false ordinances, and false worship! Spiritually dead—dead as pertaining to the things of righteousness! How awful is the day, and why is it thus? Nephi answers: "Behold, ye have closed your eyes, and ye have rejected the prophets." Without prophets, without apostles, without revelation, the mind and will of the Lord are not known among men. Nephi then tells why these are not present among men: "Your rulers, and the seers hath [the Lord] covered because of your iniquity." (2 Ne. 27:1-5.) "Where there is no vision, the people perish." (Prov. 29:18.)

"Iniquity Shall Abound"

When darkness covers the earth and apostasy is everywhere, then sin and evil rear their ugly heads over all the earth and are everywhere to be found. And the darker the apostate night, the more evil and damning are the sins. The acts of men grow out of their beliefs. When men believe the gospel and are blessed with true religion, their personal conduct conforms to the divine standard; but when they forsake the truth and sink into apostasy, sin takes over in their lives. Thus Jesus, in speaking of the day in which there would be a falling away from his gospel, said: "Iniquity shall abound." (JS-M 1:30.) It could not be otherwise in such an age. Sin and every evil thing always abound when there is apostasy. Their presence today is one of the signs of the times. Without God and true religion in their lives, men sink into unbelievable depths of degradation.

In the golden era of Nephite history when "the people were all converted unto the Lord, upon all the face of the land," "there was no contention in the land, because of the love of God which did dwell in the hearts of the people. And there were no envyings, nor strifes, nor tumults, nor whoredoms, nor lyings, nor murders, nor any manner of lasciviousness; and surely there could not be a happier people among all the people who had been created by the hand of God. There were no robbers, nor murderers, neither were there Lamanites, nor any manner of -ites; but they were in one, the children of Christ, and heirs to the kingdom of God. And how blessed were they!" (4 Ne. 1:2, 15-18.) The existence of all of these evils today is the conclusive and irrefutable proof that apostasy prevails.

On the other hand, and in a passage of superlative insight, Paul tells us what happens in the lives of men when they forsake the truth. He refers to some who once "knew God" but did not remain true to the faith. They "changed the truth of God into a lie," he says. That is, they forsook the gospel, they apostatized, and darkness supplanted the light that once was theirs.

"Wherefore God also gave them up to uncleanness through the lusts of their own hearts, to dishonour their own bodies between themselves." Because they turned away from him, "God gave them up unto vile affections"—think now of homosexuals, and lesbians, and all those in the last days who revel in unclean, unholy, and unnatural sexual perversions—"for even their women did change the natural use into that which is against nature: And likewise also the men, leaving the natural use of the woman, burned in their lust one toward another; men with men working that which is unseemly, and receiving in themselves that recompence of their error which was meet."

Be it known that the sexual perversions sweeping the United States and other nations in this day are not of God. Those who pursue them are evil, degenerate, and depraved. It matters not what these advocates of lewdness and license may believe or say. These things are of the devil and lead to hell.

Speaking of them, Paul continues: "And even as they did not like to retain God in their knowledge, God gave them over to a reprobate mind, to do those things which are not convenient; Being filled with all unrighteousness, fornication, wickedness, covetousness, maliciousness; full of envy, murder, debate, deceit, malignity; whisperers, Backbiters, haters of God, despiteful, proud, boasters, inventors of evil things, disobedient to parents, Without understanding, covenantbreakers, without natural affection, implacable, unmerciful: Who knowing the judgment of God, that they which commit such things are worthy of death, not only do the same, but have pleasure in them that do them." (Rom. 1:21-32.)

Paul also spoke prophetically of our day: "Now the Spirit speaketh expressly," he said, as the message was borne in upon him with power and clarity, "that in the latter times some shall depart from the faith, giving heed to seducing spirits, and doctrines of devils." Doctrines of devils! Harsh language this! Where will such be taught? Is it amiss for us to say plainly that Satan's churches teach Satan's doctrines? And are not his doctrines those which lead men, not to the heavenly kingdom where the righteous dwell, but to that realm where the enemy of all righteousness reigns?

And what of those who give heed to these seducing spirits who whisper their false doctrines into ears attuned to evil? The preaching of those so attuned will consist of "speaking lies in hypocrisy." Knowing full well that their words are false, they will yet send them forth because they are pleasing to the carnal mind. "Having their conscience seared with a hot iron," they will justify their own evil deeds. And to show forth a form of godliness, as it were, they will be "forbidding to marry, and commanding to abstain from meats," and many such like things. (1 Tim. 4:1-3.)

"This know also, that in the last days perilous times shall come," our apostolic authority continues. "For men shall be lovers of their own selves, covetous, boasters, proud, blasphemers, disobedient to parents, unthankful, unholy, without natural affection, trucebreakers, false accusers, incontinent, fierce, despisers of those that are good, traitors, heady, highminded, lovers of pleasures more than lovers of God; having a form of godliness; but denying the power thereof."

The perilous times foretold are here. Every alert person, every day of his life, can identify men of every kind named in the holy word. All these evil persons, taking pleasure in their own unholy deeds, are found in all nations. And there are times when their Gadianton bands are so powerful that whole nations persecute the saints, wage war, and revel in the most abominable practices. Think, for instance, of the utter depravity that caused evil men, having gained political control of a nation, to use their power to murder millions of Jews during World War II.

With reference to the whole assemblage of evil men whom he has named, Paul's counsel is: "From such turn away." Then, in a tone of sadness, he adds: "For of this sort are they which creep into houses, and lead captive silly women laden with sins, led away with divers lusts." It is one of the signs of the times that women shall rebel against the established order of right and decency, and that their course will demean and destroy the sanctity of the home and the blessings of a godly family. And all such, wise as they are in their own conceits, are "ever learning, and never able to come to the knowledge of the truth." (2 Tim. 3:1-7.)

"This generation is as corrupt as the generation of the Jews that crucified Christ," the Prophet Joseph Smith said in 1843, "and if He were here to-day, and should preach the same doctrine He did then, they would put Him to death." (*Teachings*, p. 328.) Social and world conditions are worse now than they were in 1843, and they will continue their downward rush until that great and dreadful day arrives in which a just God will come in flaming fire to take vengeance upon the wicked.

This is indeed a vile and hellish day in which carnality reigns, a day in which men are ripening in iniquity preparatory to the day of burning. In it there is but one ray of hope. The light of the gospel shines in the darkness, and all who will come to that light have power to rid themselves of the curses of carnality and to live as becometh saints.

True it is that sinners cannot be saved in their sins, but He who came to cleanse men from their sins will yet receive all who repent and come unto him. According to the holy word, "the works of the flesh" are "adultery, fornication, uncleanness, lasciviousness, idolatry, witchcraft, hatred, variance, emulations, wrath, strife, seditions, heresies, envyings, murders, drunkenness, revellings, and such like." These works cover the earth today. With reference to them, the scripture says: "They which do such things shall not inherit the kingdom of God." (Gal. 5:19-21.)

But men can repent and be saved. "Know ye not that the unrighteous shall not inherit the kingdom of God?" Paul asks. "Be not deceived," he says, for "neither fornicators, nor idolaters, nor adulterers, nor effeminate, nor abusers of themselves with mankind, nor thieves, nor covetous, nor drunkards, nor revilers, nor extortioners, shall inherit the kingdom of God."

But—and herein lies man's hope!—our ancient friend then says: "And such were some of you"—some of you saints were once partakers of all these evils—"but ye are washed, but ye are sanctified, but ye are justified in the name of the Lord Jesus, and by the Spirit of our God." (1 Cor. 6:9-11.)

Men need not perish, not even in this dire day.

Chapter 5

FALSE WORSHIP ABOUNDS BEFORE HIS COMING

False Christs Precede His Coming

False Christs preceded the destruction of Jerusalem and the temple, both of which occurred in A.D. 70, and they shall be manifest again before the Second Coming. They are, in fact, now here, and their presence is one of the least understood of all the signs of the times.

Jesus told the meridian apostles, as they sat with him on the Mount of Olives, that before the destruction of the temple, which was then but forty years away, "many shall come in my name, saying—I am Christ—and shall deceive many." Then of the period between that destruction and his Second Coming, he said: "If any man shall say unto you, Lo, here is Christ, or there, believe him not; For in those days there shall also arise false Christs, and false prophets, and shall show great signs and wonders, insomuch, that, if possible, they shall deceive the very elect, who are the elect according to the covenant. Behold, I speak these things unto you for the elect's sake." (JS-M 1:6, 21-23.)

False Christs! False Redeemers, false Saviors! Will there actually be men who will claim to fulfill the Messianic prophecies and who will step forth to offer their blood for the sins of the world? Is it possible that some will say, "I am the way, the truth, and the life; come unto me and be ye saved"? Or that others will profess to return in glory bearing the wounds with which the true Christ was wounded in the house of his friends?

True, there may be those deranged persons who suppose they are God, or Christ, or the Holy Ghost, or almost anything. None but the lunatic fringe among men, however, will give them a second serious thought. The promise of false Christs who will deceive, if it were possible, even the very elect, who will lead astray those who have made eternal covenant with the Lord, is a far more subtle and insidious evil.

A false Christ is not a person. It is a false system of worship, a false church, a false cult that says: "Lo, here is salvation; here is the doctrine of Christ. Come and believe thus and so, and ye shall be saved." It is any concept or philosophy that says that redemption, salvation, sanctification, justification, and all of the promised rewards can be gained in any way except that set forth by the apostles and prophets.

We hear the voice of false Christs when we hear the Athanasian Creed proclaim that "whosoever will be saved" must believe that the Father, Son, and Holy Ghost are incomprehensible and uncreated, that they form a Trinity of equals, who are not three Gods but one God, and not one God but three Gods, and that unless we so believe we "cannot be saved," and "shall perish everlastingly." (*Book of Common Prayer*, The Church of England, pp. 68-71.)

We hear the voice of a false Christ when we read such things as these: "There is but one living and true God everlasting, without body, parts, or passions." (*Book of Common Prayer*, Article I.)

"Holy Scripture [meaning the Bible] containeth all things necessary to salvation: so that whatsoever is not read therein, nor may be proved thereby, is not to be required of any man, that it should be believed as an article of Faith, or be thought requisite or necessary to salvation." (Article VI.)

"We are accounted righteous before God, only for the merits of our Lord and Saviour Jesus Christ by Faith, and not for our own works or deservings: Wherefore, that we are justified by Faith only is a most wholesome Doctrine, and very full of comfort." (Article XI.)

"Predestination to Life is the everlasting purpose of God,

whereby (before the foundations of the world were laid) he hath constantly decreed by his counsel secret to us, to deliver from curse and damnation those whom he hath chosen in Christ out of mankind, and to bring them by Christ to everlasting salvation, as vessels made to honour. Wherefore, they which be endued with so excellent a benefit of God be called according to God's purpose by his Spirit working in due season: they through Grace obey the calling: they be justified freely: they be made the sons of God by adoption: they be made like the image of his only-begotten Son Jesus Christ: they walk religiously in good works, and at length, by God's mercy, they attain to everlasting felicity.

"As the godly consideration of Predestination, and our Election in Christ, is full of sweet, pleasant, and unspeakable comfort to godly persons, and such as feel in themselves the workings of the Spirit of Christ, mortifying the works of the flesh, and their earthly members, and drawing up their mind to high and heavenly things, as well because it doth greatly establish and confirm their faith of eternal Salvation to be enjoyed through Christ, as because it doth fervently kindle their love towards God: So, for curious and carnal persons, lacking the Spirit of Christ, to have continually before their eyes the sentence of God's Predestination, is a most dangerous downfall, whereby the Devil doth thrust them either into desperation, or into wretchlessness of most unclean living, no less perilous than desperation." (Article XVII.)

"The Baptism of young Children [infant baptism] is in any wise to be retained in the Church, as most agreeable with the institution of Christ." (Article XXVII.)

We hear the voice of a false Christ when we hear the divines of the day preach that salvation comes by the grace of God, not of works lest any man should boast, but simply by believing in and confessing the Lord Jesus with one's lips; or that signs and gifts and miracles are done away; or that ministers have power to represent the Lord and preach his gospel because they have a feeling in their heart that such is the course they should pursue.

We hear the voice of one false Christ, echoing from the camps of communism, expounding the devil-devised declaration that religion is the opiate of the people. We hear another such voice when races alien to Israel acclaim that the one God has no need for a Son to mediate between himself and fallen man.

We see the works of false Christs when women and homosexuals are ordained to the priesthood, as it is supposed; or when elaborate rituals pervert and twist and add to the sacrament of the Lord's supper; or when sins are forgiven through the doing of penance and the paying of money, as it is supposed.

Indeed, false Christs are everywhere. Joseph Smith named the Methodists, Presbyterians, and Baptists as among "the sects" who were crying "Lo, here!" and "Lo, there!" in that glorious spring of 1820. (JS-H 1:5.) The apostle John referred to false Christs as antichrists. He identified them as apostates, as those who "went out from us," as those who deny "that Jesus is the Christ," or who deny "the Father and the Son," and as those "who confess not that Jesus Christ is come in the flesh." (1 Jn. 2:18-23; 2 Jn. 1:7.)

The Church of the Devil Reigns on Earth

To say there will be false Christs in the last days means there will also be false prophets, false ministers, and false churches. We shall now show that false and evil and abominable churches do and shall exist before the coming of him who offers to all men membership in his one true Church.

We have heard Paul's prophecy announcing there would be a universal apostasy before "the coming of our Lord Jesus Christ." In it our apostolic colleague, speaking of the man of sin—of that evil spirit who acclaims himself as the God of this world—speaking of Lucifer, Paul says: He it is "who opposeth and exalteth himself above all that is called God, or that is worshipped; so that he as God sitteth in the temple of God, shewing himself that he is God." (2 Thes. 2:4.)

When Satan enters the Church of God, replaces Deity in the hearts of men, and commands them to worship him; when men forsake the doctrines of Christ and believe what they hear from false Christs; when they become carnal, sensual, and devilish by nature, and set their hearts upon the things of this world—to whose church do they give allegiance, Christ's or Satan's?

When miracles and gifts and revelations cease; when men teach with their learning and deny the Holy Ghost who giveth utterance; when the love of God and the peace of heaven are replaced with a spirit of lewdness and indecency—whose church is involved, the church of the Lord or the church of the devil?

To gain an understanding of how and why the presence of false churches is one of the signs of the times, let us turn now, with an open heart and mind, to that which is written by the prophets. Our best source material by far comes from the Book of Mormon, whose major pronouncements on the matter we shall consider in their proper settings.

Few men have equaled Nephi in seership and prophetic utterance. He saw in vision the birth, baptism, and ministry of the Holy One. He saw the call of the Twelve, the crucifixion of Christ, and the multitudes of the earth joining to fight against the apostles of the Lamb. He saw apostasy and wickedness sweep through the Gentile nations in the day that darkness covered the earth and gross darkness the minds of the people.

As he viewed this day of darkness, this evil day after the apostolic era, he said: "I saw among the nations of the Gentiles the foundation of a great church." An angel with whom he was then conversing said: "Behold the foundation of a church which is most abominable above all other churches." Note it well: There are degrees of abomination; there are levels of iniquity; one church sinks deeper into the cesspool of sin than any other. The angel then described it as the church "which slayeth the saints of God, yea, and tortureth them and bindeth them down, and yoketh them with a yoke of iron, and bringeth them down into captivity." This is the kind of inspired utterance that is fulfilled over and over again by the same or an equivalent organization. As it happened in the first centuries of the Christian era, so, we may be assured, it has happened and will happen again in our dispensation. The day of persecution and martyrdom has not passed.

"And it came to pass that I beheld this great and abominable church," Nephi said, "and I saw the devil that he was the founder of it." The man of sin is sitting in the temple of God, demanding worship, and proving thereby that he is God. "And I also saw gold, and silver, and silks, and scarlets, and fine-twined linen, and all manner of precious clothing; and I saw many harlots," Nephi continued.

Then from the angel came this word: "Behold the gold, and the silver, and the silks, and the scarlets, and the fine-twined linen, and the precious clothing, and the harlots, are the desires of this great and abominable church. And also for the praise of the world do they destroy the saints of God, and bring them down into captivity." (1 Ne. 13:1-9.)

John the Revelator saw the same vision that was given to Nephi. To John, an angel—perhaps the same one who conversed with Nephi—called the great and abominable church "the great whore that sitteth upon many waters." John saw her sitting "upon a scarlet coloured beast, full of names of blasphemy. . . . And the woman," he said, "was arrayed in purple and scarlet colour, and decked with gold and precious stones and pearls, having a golden cup in her hand full of abominations and filthiness of her fornication: And upon her forehead was a name written, MYSTERY, BABYLON THE GREAT, THE MOTHER OF HARLOTS AND ABOMINATIONS OF THE EARTH. And I saw the woman drunken with the blood of the saints, and with the blood of the martyrs of Jesus." (Rev. 17:1-6.)

This is the church of the devil that came into being after New Testament times. It was founded by Satan, and its interests lay in wealth and worldliness and carnality. This is the church into whose hands the scriptures came. These scriptures, so the angel said to Nephi, came "from the Jews in purity unto the Gentiles." As they were first written, they "contained the plainness of the gospel of the Lord."

But the word of God, recorded in purity and plainness, is as deadly poison to an apostate church. It is far better for such an organization to have them in a partial, twisted, and perverted form. Indeed, it is imperative, from their standpoint, that the scriptures be altered to conform to their practices.

And so, with reference to the scriptures, the angel said to Nephi: "After they go forth by the hand of the twelve apostles of the Lamb, from the Jews unto the Gentiles, thou seest the formation of a great and abominable church, which is most abominable above all other churches; for behold, they have taken away from the gospel of the Lamb many parts which are plain and most precious; and also many covenants of the Lord have they taken away."

Why have they done this terrible thing? The angel yet speaks: "And all this have they done that they might pervert the right ways of the Lord, that they might blind the eyes and harden the hearts of the children of men."

And then, repeating himself for emphasis, for there must be no question about the iniquity of that great church which is not the Lord's church, the angel said: "Wherefore, thou seest that after the book hath gone forth through the hands of the great and abominable church, that there are many plain and precious things taken away from the book, which is the book of the Lamb of God." (1 Ne. 13:24-28.)

The sad picture thus far portrayed is then softened somewhat by the angelic promise of a restoration of the gospel in the latter days; and the "abominable church" is further identified as "the mother of harlots," which accords with what John wrote, and which can only mean that other apostate churches spring from her. (1 Ne. 13:29-42.)

To introduce the promised gospel restoration, Nephi's angelic visitant alludes to the eventual fall of the Babylonish church. He calls it "that great and abominable church, which was founded by the devil and his children, that he might lead away the souls of men down to hell," and says that they whose church it is shall fall into the very pit "which hath been digged for them."

Then comes the glorious word that the Lord "will work a great and marvelous work among the children of men." Revelation, visions, gifts, miracles, all that the ancient saints enjoyed shall commence anew. Those who believe and obey the heavenly word shall gain "peace and life eternal," while the disobedient and rebellious shall be "brought down into captivity, . . . according to the captivity of the devil."

This brings us in point of time to the dispensation of the fulness of times. In this setting Nephi is to see the church of the devil again—to see it in a new perspective and from a different vantage point. He will see that it has matured and grown, that it has come of age, and that it has a power and an influence over nations and kingdoms that exceed anything of the past. "Look, and behold that great and abominable church, which is the mother of abominations, whose founder is the devil." Such is the angelic invitation.

As Nephi looks, the angel says: "Behold there are save two churches only"—at long last the gospel has been restored; universal apostasy is giving way before the light of heaven; there is a true church on earth as well as a false one; "the one is the church of the Lamb of God, and the other is the church of the devil." There is only light and darkness; there is no dusky twilight zone. Either men walk in the light or they cannot be saved. Anything less than salvation is not salvation. It may be better to walk in the twilight or to glimpse the first few rays of a distant dawn than to be enveloped in total darkness, but salvation itself is only for those who step forth into the blazing light of the noonday sun. "Wherefore, whoso belongeth not to the church of the Lamb of God," the angelic prophet proclaims, "belongeth to that great church, which is the mother of abominations; and she is the whore of all the earth."

Nephi tells us what he saw on earth in our day, in the day of restoration, in the day when the gospel was again found among men. "I looked and beheld the whore of all the earth," he says, "and she sat upon many waters." Her influence was everywhere. No land or people were rid of her power; the islands and continents, sitting as they do in the waters of the world, came under her dominion. Then, horrible and woeful as the reality is, Nephi saw that "she had dominion over all the earth, among all nations, kindreds, tongues, and people."

What is the church of the devil in our day, and where is the seat of her power? If we accept the angelic word, if we believe as Nephi believed, and if, the Lord willing, we see what Nephi saw, then we shall accept without question the reality around us. The church of the devil is every evil and worldly organization on earth. It is all of the systems, both Christian and non-Christian, that have perverted the pure and perfect gospel; it is all of the governments and powers that run counter to the divine will; it is the societies and political parties and labor unions that sow strife and reap contention. It is communism; it is Islam; it is Buddhism; it is modern Christianity in all its parts. It is Germany under Hitler, Russia under Stalin, and Italy under Mussolini. It is the man of sin speaking in churches, orating in legislative halls, and commanding the armies of men. And its headquarters are everywhere—in Rome and Moscow, in Paris and London, in Teheran and Washington—everywhere that evil forces, either of church or state or society, can be influenced. The immanent and all-pervading presence of evil in high places is one of the signs of the times.

"And it came to pass that I beheld the church of the Lamb of God"—The Church of Jesus Christ of Latter-day Saints—"and its numbers were few," Nephi continues, "because of the wickedness and abominations of the whore who sat upon many waters; nevertheless, I beheld that the church of the Lamb, who were the saints of God, were also upon all the face of the earth." This pertains to a day yet future. The saints of the Most High are not yet, as a people and with organized congregations, established upon all the face of the earth. When the day comes that they are, they still will not compare in power with the forces of evil. Even then, as Nephi foresaw, "their dominions upon the face of the earth were small, because of the wickedness of the great whore whom I saw."

What follows in Nephi's account lies in the future. It will occur after the saints are established in all nations. Of that coming day Nephi says: "I beheld that the great mother of abominations did gather together multitudes upon the face of all the earth, among all the nations of the Gentiles, to fight against the Lamb of God." Our persecutions and difficulties have scarcely begun. We saw mobbings and murders and martyrdom as the foundations of the work were laid in the United States. These same things, with greater intensity, shall yet fall upon the faithful in all nations.

But as the hour of judgment nears, the Lord will preserve and glorify his people. "And it came to pass that I, Nephi, beheld the power of the Lamb of God, that it descended upon the saints of the church of the Lamb, and upon the covenant people of the Lord, who were scattered upon all the face of the earth; and they were armed with righteousness and with the power of God in great glory." The salvation of the saints, both temporally and spiritually, now and always is grounded upon obedience to the holy covenants they have made.

"And it came to pass that I beheld that the wrath of God was poured out upon the great and abominable church, insomuch that there were wars and rumors of wars among all the nations and kindreds of the earth." Such has been already to some extent, and hereafter will be to a greater degree.

"And as there began to be wars and rumors of wars among all the nations which belonged to the mother of abominations"—note this well: all nations are owned, as it were, by the evil and carnal powers of the world—as Nephi saw these things, the angel said: "Behold, the wrath of God is upon the mother of harlots; and behold, thou seest all these things—And when the day cometh that the wrath of God is poured out upon the mother of harlots, which is the great and abominable church of all the earth, whose founder is the devil, then, at that day, the work of the Father shall commence, in preparing the way for the fulfilling of his covenants, which he hath made to his people who are of the house of Israel." (1 Ne. 14:1-17.) Then shall the kingdom be restored to Israel in all its millennial glory, Zion shall be built up in perfection, and the Lord himself shall reign gloriously over those who are his.

FALSE CHURCHES PRECEDE HIS COMING

"They Are All Wrong"

Let us now walk with Joseph Smith into a grove of trees in Western New York in the spring of 1820. He is troubled in mind and spirit; a great religious revival is sweeping the frontier areas around Palmyra, and he desires to know which church is true. As we walk we hear a faint echo of an apostolic sermon in the distance. It seems to say: "Is Christ divided?" (1 Cor. 1:13), and we, with the Lord's future seer, wonder: how can churches whose beliefs and practices conflict all be true?

We are there when the heavens open. There is a pillar of light. Two Personages, "whose brightness and glory defy all description," stand above the seeking seer-to-be. The Father testifies of his Beloved Son and commands, "*Hear Him!*" Joseph asks which of all the sects is right and which he should join. The word that comes back from the Son of God causes the very pillars of Christendom to totter and sway. Joseph is to "join none of them," for they are "all wrong." Some words are spoken about creeds that are an abomination in the Lord's sight and about professors of religion who are corrupt and whose hearts are far removed from divine standards. (JS-H 1:16-19.) Thus is ushered in the dispensation of the fulness of times; it comes in a day when all churches are false; it is a day in which Satan has power over his own dominions.

Being thus enlightened, and being thus fully aware of how the Lord views all churches, we turn to the Book of Mormon account.

We hear Nephi's words. He is speaking of our day. "The Gentiles are lifted up in the pride of their eyes, and have stumbled," he says, and "they have built up many churches"—not one true church, but many false churches—in which "they put down the power and miracles of God, and preach up unto themselves their own wisdom and their own learning, that they may get gain and grind upon the face of the poor." It is as though he saw the divinity schools of the day where the scriptures are dissected in Greek and Hebrew and where their true and plain meanings are spiritualized away; for how, as they suppose in the schools, can a man preach unless he has been trained for the ministry?

"And there are many churches built up which cause envyings, and strifes, and malice. And there are also secret combinations, even as in times of old, according to the combinations of the devil, for he is the founder of all these things; yea, the founder of murder, and works of darkness; yea, and he leadeth them by the neck with a flaxen cord, until he bindeth them with his strong cords forever." (2 Ne. 26:20-22.)

Nephi then tells of the coming forth of the Book of Mormon and of the restoration of the gospel. "It shall come to pass in that day," he says, "that the churches which are built up, and not unto the Lord, when the one shall say unto the other: Behold, I, I am the Lord's; and the others shall say: I, I am the Lord's; and thus shall every one say that hath built up churches, and not unto the Lord—And they shall contend one with another; and their priests shall contend one with another, and they shall teach with their learning, and deny the Holy Ghost, which giveth utterance." It is as though he saw the religious revivalism that led Joseph Smith to ask which of all the churches was right and which he should join.

"And they deny the power of God, the Holy One of Israel; and they say unto the people: Hearken unto us, and hear ye our precept; for behold there is no God today, for the Lord and the Redeemer hath done his work, and he hath given his power unto men; Behold, hearken ye unto my precept; if they shall say there is a miracle wrought by the hand of the Lord, believe it not; for this day he is not a God of miracles; he hath done his work."

After naming other "false and vain and foolish doctrines"

taught in our day, the inspired account says: "Because of pride, and because of false teachers, and false doctrine, their churches have become corrupted, and their churches are lifted up; because of pride they are puffed up. They rob the poor because of their fine sanctuaries; they rob the poor because of their fine clothing; and they persecute the meek and the poor in heart, because in their pride they are puffed up. They wear stiff necks and high heads; yea, and because of pride, and wickedness, and abominations, and whoredoms, they have all gone astray." These words, as with so many in the Nephite scriptures, are so clear and plain and have such obvious application to conditions known to every observant person in our day that they would only be weakened by further exposition.

Having spoken thus of the false churches of our day; having shown that they love the things of this world more than the things of God; having condemned the ministers who teach for doctrine the commandments of men, who have replaced the pure truths from heaven with the philosophies of men mingled with scripture—having so spoken, Nephi raises a warning voice. It is addressed to the members of "the only true and living church upon the face of the whole earth," with many of whose members the Lord is not "well pleased." (D&C 1:30.)

"They have all gone astray," he says of those who live in the last days, and then adds, "save it be a few, who are the humble followers of Christ." He is speaking of the day, be it remembered, in which the gospel in its everlasting fulness has been restored for the last time. And of the true saints he says: "Nevertheless, they are led, that in many instances they do err because they are taught by the precepts of men." (2 Ne. 28:3-14.)

Even in the true Church in the last days there will be some who do not believe the whole body of revealed truth; some who do not give full allegiance to the Cause of truth and righteousness; some who are members in name only and who continue to live after the manner of the world. This also is one of the signs of the times. It shall be as it was among some of old whom Paul rebuked: "When ye come together in the church," he wrote to the Corinthians, "there be divisions among you." Contention, debate, and false views have no place in the Church and kingdom of our Lord. The doctrines are his, not ours, and our concern should be to gain the mind of Christ and to think what he thinks on every point. But the fact is that there are divisions in the Church, for the very reason Paul now gives: "There must be also heresies among you, that they which are approved may be made manifest among you." (1 Cor. 11:18-19.)

Heresies among the Saints! Sadly it is so. Are there not those among us who believe the theories of men rather than the revealed word relative to the creation of the earth and organic evolution? Do we not still have teachers who say that God is progressing in knowledge and learning new truths; that there will be a second chance for salvation for those who reject the gospel here but accept it in the spirit world; that there will be progression from one kingdom of glory to another in the world to come? And are there not those among us who refuse to follow the Brethren on moral issues, lest their agency and political rights be infringed, as they suppose? Truly, there are heresies among us.

"They Teach for Doctrines the Commandments of Men"

Apostasy and false churches go hand in hand; they aid and abet each other. When men forsake the gospel they find a form of godliness in churches of their own creation, and these churches teach doctrines that sustain men in their apostasy. Moroni, in a great outburst of righteous indignation, speaks of the abominations in the lives of those who worship at the altars of the world. He names the day as the one in which the Book of Mormon shall come forth and be proclaimed to the world.

"It shall come in a day when the power of God shall be denied," he says, "and churches become defiled and be lifted up in the pride of their hearts; yea, even in a day when leaders of churches and teachers shall rise in the pride of their hearts, even to the envying of them who belong to their churches."

To this we add: It shall come forth and go to the world in a day when there are churches for homosexuals, churches that accept adulterers, churches containing murderers, and even churches for those who worship Satan. It shall come in a day when there shall be churches for sinners who imagine their sins are remitted, without any act on their part, simply because Christ died for sinners.

But back to Moroni. "It shall come in a day when there shall be great pollutions upon the face of the earth; there shall be murders, and robbing, and lying, and deceivings, and whoredoms, and all manner of abominations; when there shall be many who will say, Do this, or do that, and it mattereth not, for the Lord will uphold such at the last day. But wo unto such for they are in the gall of bitterness and in the bonds of iniquity." Such is the state of the world when men worship at the altars of the world.

"Yea, it shall come in a day when there shall be churches built up that shall say: Come unto me, and for your money you shall be forgiven of your sins." Viewing our day in vision, our ancient friend then says: "O ye wicked and perverse and stiffnecked people, why have ye built up churches unto yourselves to get gain? Why have ye transfigured the holy word of God, that ye might bring damnation upon your souls? Behold, look ye unto the revelations of God; for behold, the time cometh at that day when all these things must be fulfilled."

These harsh words do not say and do not mean that in the last days all men on earth will choose evil rather than good when the choice is placed before them. There are many who feel instinctively that their creeds are wrong and their doctrines false. There are those who seek truth and desire righteousness. As the inspired word has it: "There are many yet on the earth among all sects, parties, and denominations, who are blinded by the subtle craftiness of men, whereby they lie in wait to deceive, and who are only kept from the truth because they know not where to find it." (D&C 123:12.)

But again let Moroni speak. "Jesus Christ hath shown you unto me, and I know your doing," he says of those who live in this day when the word of the Lord is again coming forth. "And I know that ye do walk in the pride of your hearts; and there are none save a few only who do not lift themselves up in the pride of their hearts, unto the wearing of very fine apparel, unto envying, and strifes, and malice, and persecutions, and all manner of iniquities; and your churches, yea, even every one, have become polluted because of the pride of your hearts. For behold, ye do love money, and your substance, and your fine apparel, and the adorning of your churches, more than ye love the poor and the needy, the sick and the afflicted."

Do men today need prophetic warnings as did those in olden times? Let them hear Moroni's words, spoken as it were with the trump of God. "O ye pollutions, ye hypocrites, ye teachers, who sell yourselves for that which will canker, why have ye polluted the holy church of God?" he cries. How far removed are the rite-laden churches of Christendom from the pure and guileless worship of the primitive saints. How soft and compromising are the ear-tickling sermons of our day as compared to the divine invective of Paul and Peter and Jesus. How sad it is to see worshippers who think only of themselves and who care not a farthing for the widows and the orphans.

To those in the churches of our day Moroni calls: "Why are ye ashamed to take upon you the name of Christ? Why do ye not think that greater is the value of an endless happiness than that misery which never dies—because of the praise of the world? Why do ye adorn yourselves with that which hath no life, and yet suffer the hungry, and the needy, and the naked, and the sick and the afflicted to pass by you, and notice them not?

"Yea, why do ye build up your secret abominations to get gain, and cause that widows should mourn before the Lord, and also orphans to mourn before the Lord, and also the blood of their fathers and their husbands to cry unto the Lord from the ground, for vengeance upon your heads?

"Behold, the sword of vengeance hangeth over you; and the time soon cometh that he avengeth the blood of the saints upon you, for he will not suffer their cries any longer." (Morm. 8:26-41.)

Such is the divine word relative to the great and abominable church, to her harlot daughters, to the many churches in the last days, and to the part they all play in the falling away that precedes the Second Coming. Before recording the final fate—both of that great church which is not the Lord's church, and of all churches founded and nurtured and led by the devil and his children—we must weave into the great tapestry we are making a few words about secret combinations.

Secret Combinations Abound in the Last Days

In some detail and at extended length Ezekiel prophesies of the great premillennial warfare between Israel and those nations prophetically identified as Gog and Magog. He tells of the death and desolation spread by the assembled armies; that all men on earth shall shake at the presence of the returning Lord; and of the destruction of the wicked by divine power. With all these matters we shall deal in depth in their proper settings. For our present purposes we need only record that the Lord will then rain upon Gog "and upon his bands, and upon the many people that are with him, an overflowing rain, and great hailstones, fire, and brimstone," and that he "will send a fire on Magog." (Ezek. 38-39.) This is the promised day of burning when every corruptible thing shall be consumed.

In latter-day revelation the Lord confirms this prophetic word that death and destruction are destined to fall upon men at the day of his coming. He includes some of the specific things named by Ezekiel. Of the decreed consummation of the wars then in progress, the divine word says: "And the great and abominable church, which is the whore of all the earth, shall be cast down by devouring fire, according as it is spoken by the mouth of Ezekiel the prophet, who spoke of these things, which have not come to pass but surely must, as I live, for abominations shall not reign." (D&C 29:21.)

In Ezekiel's account, great nations with their armies of mighty men and their trains of munitions come to do battle. They have their planes and ships and tanks and atomic bombs and are waging such warfare as has never been known before. Then comes the devouring fire from heaven that destroys the armies of Gog and Magog, which armies are identified as the great and abominable church. That is to say, the church of the devil is more than an ecclesiastical organization that teaches false doctrines so as to lead men carefully down to hell. It is more than priests and ministers and places of worship. It is also the political powers that hold in their hands the destinies of nations. It is the churches and their religious doctrines, and it is also the governments and their political philosophies. It is the political doctrines in which men believe and for which they die to satisfy their innate needs to worship. And this brings us to a consideration of the secret combinations that are to be in the last days.

Our Book of Mormon authors speak a great deal about the secret combinations that arose among the Jaredites and among the Nephites and that were destined to arise among the Gentile nations in the last days. They tell us that these secret combinations brought to pass the destruction of the Jaredites and the Nephites and will bring similar destruction on any latter-day nations that permit them to gain an ascendancy. Writing of nations in the last days, Moroni says: "Whatsoever nation shall uphold such secret combinations, to get power and gain, until they shall spread over the nation, behold, they shall be destroyed; for the Lord will not suffer that the blood of his saints, which shall be shed by them, shall always cry unto him from the ground for vengeance upon them and yet he avenge them not." (Ether 8:22.)

What are these secret combinations which have such powers that whole civilizations are destroyed by them? They wear many guises and appear in many forms. They were the Gadianton robbers among the Nephites, and the perpetrators of the Spanish inquisition in the dark ages. Among us they include some secret and oath-bound societies and such Mafia-like groups as engage in organized crime. They include some political parties, some revolutionists who rise up against their governments, and those evil and anarchist groups which steal and kidnap and murder in the name of this or that political objective. They are always groups that seek money and power and freedom from the penalties that should attend their crimes.

Secret combinations are tools of Lucifer to accomplish his purpose and to destroy the works of God. The devil "stirreth up the children of men unto secret combinations of murder and all manner of secret works of darkness." (2 Ne. 9:9.) They keep men from accepting the gospel; they destroy the freedoms and true worship of the saints; and they spread wickedness and abominations everywhere. With reference to the Jaredites, the scripture says: "They did reject all the words of the prophets, because of their secret society and wicked abominations." (Ether 11:22.) Among the Nephites, the Gadianton robbers sought to destroy the rights and privileges of the true church, the way of worship of the saints, "and their freedom and their liberty." (3 Ne. 2:12.)

Shortly before the wicked were destroyed at the time of the crucifixion, the Gadianton robbers obtained "the sole management of the government" among the Nephites, "insomuch that they did trample under their feet and smite and rend and turn their backs upon the poor and the meek, and the humble followers of God." (Hel. 6:39.) Their minions filled "the judgment-seats"; they usurped "the power and authority of the land," laid "aside the commandments of God," flouted justice, condemned "the righteous because of their righteousness," and let "the guilty and the wicked go unpunished because of their money." They sought to "get gain and glory of the world," that they might "more easily commit adultery, and steal, and kill, and do according to their own wills." (Hel. 7:4-5.)

These Nephite descriptions of the secret combinations of their day give us an understanding of what their prophets meant when they spoke of like evil organizations in the last days. Speaking of the coming forth of the Book of Mormon, Moroni, for instance, said: "It shall come in a day when the blood of saints shall cry unto the Lord, because of secret combinations and the works of darkness." (Morm. 8:27.)

Moroni also said that these secret combinations caused the destruction of the Jaredite and Nephite nations and will cause our destruction if we permit them to control our government. Speaking directly to us he said: "It is wisdom in God that these things should be shown unto you, that thereby ye may repent of your sins, and suffer not that these murderous combinations shall get above you, which are built up to get power and gain—and the work, yea, even the work of destruction come upon you, yea, even the sword of the justice of the Eternal God shall fall upon you, to your overthrow and destruction if ye shall suffer these things to be." Any nation that permits a secret combination to gain control of its government shall be destroyed; such is the everlasting decree of a just God.

"Wherefore, the Lord commandeth you," Moroni continues, that "when ye shall see these things come among you that ye shall awake to a sense of your awful situation, because of this secret combination which shall be among you." Moroni here speaks of one particular secret combination and prophesies that it will be among us in our day. Either it will prevail over us or, alternatively, "Wo be unto it, because of the blood of them who have been slain; for their cry from the dust for vengeance upon it, and also upon those who built it up."

Next Moroni turns the key so that all who have ears to hear can understand what the secret combination is and can identify those who build it up. "For it cometh to pass," he says, "that whoso buildeth it up seeketh to overthrow the freedom of all lands, nations, and countries." This is a worldwide conspiracy. It is now entrenched in many nations, and it seeks dominion over all nations. It is Godless, atheistic, and operates by compulsion. It is communism. "And it bringeth to pass the destruction of all people, for it is built up by the devil, who is the father of all lies; even that same liar who beguiled our first parents, yea, even that same liar who hath caused man to commit murder from the beginning; who hath hardened the hearts of men that they have murdered the prophets, and stoned them, and cast them out from the beginning."

The issue is thus squarely put. Good and evil are arrayed in battle line. Good, in all its beauty and fulness, is found only where the gospel flourishes. Evil is everywhere; worldliness fills the world; and false churches and false political philosophies—combined as one in the great and abominable church—hold dominion over the nations. "Wherefore, I, Moroni, am commanded to write these things that evil may be done away, and that the time may come that Satan may have no power upon the hearts of the children of men, but that they may be persuaded to do good continually, that they may come unto the fountain of all righteousness and be saved." (Ether 8:18-26.)

We have read of the predicted fall of the armies of the great and abominable church as they come from Gog and Magog to make war against Israel. Truly, as Nephi said: "That great and abominable church"—in all its parts, be they ecclesiastical or political—

"the whore of all the earth, must tumble to the earth, and great must be the fall thereof. For the kingdom of the devil must shake, and they which belong to it must needs be stirred up unto repentance, or the devil will grasp them with his everlasting chains, and they be stirred up to anger, and perish." (2 Ne. 28:18-19.)

"And the righteous need not fear, for they are those who shall not be confounded," Nephi also says. "But it is the kingdom of the devil, which shall be built up among the children of men, which kingdom is established among them which are in the flesh—For the time speedily shall come that all churches which are built up to get gain, and all those who are built up to get power over the flesh, and those who are built up to become popular in the eyes of the world, and those who seek the lusts of the flesh and the things of the world, and to do all manner of iniquity; yea, in fine, all those who belong to the kingdom of the devil are they who need fear, and tremble, and quake; they are those who must be brought low in the dust; they are those who must be consumed as stubble." (1 Ne. 22:22-23.)

FALSE PROPHETS PRECEDE HIS COMING

True Prophets Reveal True Doctrines

Our attention now turns to what the inspired word has to say about the false teachers, false ministers, and false prophets who shall spew forth their damning doctrines in the days of desolation and sorrow that precede the Second Coming of the true Teacher, the chief Minister, and the presiding Prophet. Their presence is one of the signs of the times, and they shall prophesy and teach so near the truth "that, if possible, they shall deceive the very elect." (JS-M 1:22.)

Lest we be deceived, we must know the differences between true and false prophets. "Beware of false prophets," Jesus said (Matt. 7:15), and we cannot recognize a false prophet unless we know what a true one is.

Our whole system of revealed religion calls for us to believe in true prophets, to cleave unto their counsels, and to conform to the word of the Lord that falls from their lips. Prophets and seers, how great they are! They stand in the place and stead of the Lord Jesus in administering salvation to fallen man. Their vision is endless and their understanding reaches to heaven. What, then, is the nature and mission of a true prophet?

A prophet is a living witness of the divine Sonship of the Lord Jesus Christ. He is one who knows by personal revelation that Jesus is the Lord who worked out the infinite and eternal atonement by which salvation comes. This "testimony of Jesus is the spirit of prophecy" (Rev. 19:10), and one so gifted and so endowed has power, if need be, to "prophesy of all things" (Mosiah 5:3).

A prophet is a legal administrator who has been called of God to represent him in teaching the doctrines of salvation to men on earth. He is one who is empowered to perform the ordinances of salvation so they will be binding on earth and sealed everlastingly in the heavens. He is a teacher of eternal truth; he expounds the plan of salvation. He is a witness of the Lord; he testifies of Christ. He is a minister; he does everything for mortal men that is needed to save and exalt them in the highest heaven. When called to the ministry, he holds the priesthood and is endowed with power from on high. It is his privilege to receive revelation, to see visions, to entertain angels, and to see the face of God.

True prophets are always found in the true Church, and false prophets, as we shall see, are always found in false churches. In setting forth the chief identifying characteristics of the Lord's Church, Paul said: "God hath set some in the church, first apostles, secondarily prophets, thirdly teachers, after that miracles, then gifts of healings, helps, governments, diversities of tongues." (1 Cor. 12:28.) Indeed, the saints and the Church "are built upon the foundation of the apostles and prophets, Jesus Christ himself being the chief corner stone." (Eph. 2:19-20.)

Where there are apostles and prophets, there is the Church and kingdom of God on earth; and where these are not, the true Church and the divine kingdom are not present. How can a church be the Lord's Church unless it receives revelation from him? Who can head up the Lord's work on earth if there are no prophets? Who can preach and teach true doctrines without prophetic insight? Who can perform the ordinances of salvation with binding certainty and sealing surety unless they are legal administrators endowed with power from on high?

And so it is written that Christ "gave some, apostles; and some, prophets; and some, evangelists; and some, pastors and teachers"—all given as "gifts unto men." For what purpose? They are given "for the perfecting of the saints, for the work of the ministry, for the edifying of the body of Christ."

How long are they to remain in the Church? "Till we all come in the unity of the faith"; until that millennial day when every living soul is converted to the truth; until righteous men are prepared to receive their own instructions direct from the Lord.

What blessings come to men because there are apostles and prophets? These are many. The chief are that obedient persons have power to press forward in righteousness, to gain "the knowledge of the Son of God," to perfect their souls, and to become joint-heirs with Christ, than which there are no greater blessings. Further, those who give heed to true prophets and who take apostolic counsel are not "tossed to and fro, and carried about with every wind of doctrine." They know the truth and are not deceived by false prophets and teachers. Those who "lie in wait to deceive" have no power over them. They are not moved "by the sleight of men, and [the] cunning craftiness" of evil and designing persons. (Eph. 4:11-14.)

In this probationary estate we must choose between good and evil, virtue and vice, light and darkness. We must pursue an upward or a downward course; we must get nearer to the Lord or nearer to the devil. God's voice and his counsel come from the light of Christ and by way of his prophets; the devil's enticements are whispered into the minds of men from an evil source and are taught by false prophets who represent him whose word they teach. All men follow either true or false prophets. Those who do not give heed to the divinely sent representatives of the Lord, by virtue of that fact alone, follow those who are not of God.

False Prophets Teach False Doctrines

What are false prophets? They are teachers and preachers who profess to speak for the Lord when, in fact, they have received no such appointment. They are ministers of religion who have not been called of God as was Aaron. They may suppose—often sincerely and with pious devoutness—that it is their right to tell others what they must do to be saved when, in fact, they have received no such commission from on high.

They are teachers of religion who do not receive revelation and have not gained from the Holy Ghost the true testimony of Jesus.

They are ministers of religion who do not hold either the Aaronic or Melchizedek priesthoods, and try as they may it is beyond their power to bind on earth and have their acts sealed eternally in the heavens.

False prophets are false teachers; they teach false doctrine; they neither know nor teach the doctrines of salvation. Rather, they have followed cunningly devised fables that they suppose make up the gospel of Christ, and they preach them as such. They are the ministers who proclaim a false way of salvation, the expounders of doctrines that are not of God, and the proclaimers of every man-made system of religion on earth. They are the political leaders among the communists and the doctrinaires who lead men to accept freedom-destroying systems. They are the philosophers and sages who seek to explain God, existence, right and wrong, agency, immortality, and other religious concepts without reference to revelation. They are all of the political and religious leaders who proclaim philosophies and doctrines that lead men away from God and the salvation he offers to men.

The issue where false prophets are concerned is not one of their attempting to foretell the future and failing. True prophets do on occasions prophesy of that which is to be because they have the testimony of Jesus, which is the spirit of prophecy. But the great commission of prophets is to bear witness of Christ, to teach the doctrines of salvation that he has revealed to them and their associates, and to perform with power and authority those ordinances that he has ordained. When men who are not called and appointed and empowered to do these things nonetheless assume the prerogative of so doing, they are false prophets.

In the Book of Mormon we have an account of the course pursued by a particularly vocal and evil false prophet. His teachings illustrate what many with a like bent are wont to acclaim. The curse and untimely death that fell upon him are symbols of the fate of all who raise their voices against the Divine Voice. It was about 74 B.C. when this antichrist, whose name was Korihor, arose among the Nephites. He taught that there should be no Christ whose atonement would remit their sins; that the Messianic prophecies were the foolish traditions of their fathers, because no man could foretell the future; that men prospered according to their own genius, and conquered according to their own strength, and that whatever they did was no crime. He said there was no life after death, and many, as a consequence, were led to commit whoredoms and to wallow in wickedness.

In a confrontation with Alma, in the typical way of an adulterous and evil priest, Korihor demanded to see a sign. After he was struck dumb by the power of God, he wrote these words: "The devil hath deceived me; for he appeared unto me in the form of an angel, and said unto me: Go and reclaim this people, for they have all gone astray after an unknown God. And he said unto me: There is no God; yea, and he taught me that which I should say. And I have taught his words; and I taught them because they were pleasing unto the carnal mind; and I taught them, even until I had much success, insomuch that I verily believed that they were true; and for this cause I withstood the truth, even until I have brought this great curse upon me." (Alma 30:53.)

Lucifer does not come personally to every false prophet, as he did to Korihor, any more than the Lord comes personally to every true prophet, as he did to Joseph Smith. Such an appearance—either of God on the one hand or of Satan on the other—is, however, the end result of full devotion to the respective causes involved. In each instance an earthly representative, by obedience to the laws that are ordained, may see the face of the master he serves. But in every case the will of the evil one is manifest to his false prophets, just as the will of the Righteous One is manifest to his true prophets. All prophets are spokesmen: true prophets speak for God, and their words lead to life and salvation; false prophets speak for the devil, and their words lead to death and damnation.

False Prophets Minister on Every Hand

There is only one true doctrine: it is the doctrine of Christ; it is the gospel of salvation by conformity to which men may gain peace in this life and eternal life in the world to come. But there are many false doctrines—doctrines of every hue and color, of every size and dimension, of every shape and kind, all of which lead men on the downward course. True prophets speak with one voice, false prophets with as many voices as there are prophets. Most of the false prophets of our day fall into one or more of the following categories:

1. *False prophets serve false Christs and belong to false churches.*

We live in "a crooked and perverse generation" (D&C 34:6); the sects of the day are "the congregations of the wicked" (D&C 60:8), and their ministers are false teachers, meaning false prophets. We have already seen that false Christs are false systems of religion, which proclaim a Christ of this sort or that, and which suppose that salvation comes through their way of worship. Jesus' warning is against "false Christs, and false prophets." He said: "If they"—meaning false prophets—"shall say unto you: Behold, he"—a supposed Christ or system of salvation—"is in the desert; go not forth: Behold, he is in the secret chambers; believe it not." (JS-M 1:22, 25.)

If there are false Christs, there are false witnesses of these Christs. If there are false churches, there are false ministers. It is, "as with the people, so with the priest." (Isa. 24:2.) If true ministers preach in the congregations of the saints, false ministers hold forth in the congregations of the wicked. "Beware of false prophets." (Matt. 7:15.)

2. *False prophets worship false gods and teach others so to do.*

Eternal life comes to those who worship "the only true God, and Jesus Christ," whom he hath sent. (John 17:3.) There is no salvation in worshipping a false god. "Shall a man make gods unto himself, and they are no gods?" Jeremiah asked with reference to the great day of apostasy. (Jer. 16:20.) Isaiah spoke of men worshipping idols, which would be utterly abolished at the Second Coming. (Isa. 2:8-22.) In that graphic imagery which came so naturally to him, John said men in our day would "worship the beast." (Rev. 14:8-11.) And the Lord said of those in our day: "They seek not the Lord to establish his righteousness, but every man walketh in his own way, and after the image of his own God, whose image is in the likeness of the world, and whose substance is that of an idol." (D&C 1:16.)

If men worship a three-in-one spirit essence that fills the immensity of space and is everywhere and nowhere in particular present, are they worshipping a true or a false God? If men are invited to worship false gods in false churches, what must we think of the preachers who issue the invitations and who expound upon the nature of the Deity there adored?

3. *False prophets serve Satan, whose prophets and ministers they are.*

Paul tells us that the great apostasy before the Second Coming would result from "the working of Satan with all power and signs and lying wonders, and with all deceivableness of unrighteousness in them that perish; because they received not the love of the truth, that they might be saved. And for this cause God shall send them"—or, better, allow them to have—"strong delusion, that they should believe a lie: That they all might be damned who believed not the truth, but had pleasure in unrighteousness." (2 Thes. 2:9-12.)

Now, who is to bring this horrible thing to pass? The scripture ascribes it to Satan. But does he do it as a single soul, or does he have an organized corps of workers? The scriptures also teach that the Lord will proclaim his word in every ear, but he does it through his servants. So it is with Satan. He has his servants, and they do his bidding.

If there is a church of the devil, will not Satan also have his ministers to govern its affairs? If the devil sows tares in the fields of the Lord, will he not do it by the mouths of the servants of sin who follow him? How aptly does Moroni say: "A bitter fountain cannot bring forth good water; neither can a good fountain bring forth bitter water; wherefore, a man being a servant of the devil cannot follow Christ; and if he follow Christ he cannot be a servant of the devil." (Moro. 7:11.)

4. *False prophets are all corrupt.*

In that glorious theophany manifest in the spring of 1820, when God once more unveiled his face, the Beloved Son told young Joseph Smith that all the sects were wrong and all their creeds an abomination in his sight. Then came the divine word relative to those who governed the churches and taught the creeds.

The Son of God said "that those professors were all corrupt." (JS-H 1:19.)

Corrupt ministers! Ministers no longer in that state of uprightness, correctness, and truth that becometh the servants of the Lord; ministers who were changed into a bad and some into even a depraved state. How aptly is it written in the holy book that "there should be mockers in the last time, who should walk after their own ungodly lusts"; that "these be they who separate themselves, sensual, having not the Spirit"; and that "these are murmurers, complainers, walking after their own lusts; and their mouth speaketh great swelling words"—how great their sermons are!—"having men's persons in admiration because of advantage." (Jude 1:16-19.)

Speaking of such, Peter has left us some of the most severe and harsh language found in holy writ. He says they "walk after the flesh in the lust of uncleanness, and despise government. Presumptuous are they, selfwilled, they are not afraid to speak evil of dignities." He says they "shall utterly perish in their own corruption; and shall receive the reward of unrighteousness. . . . Spots they are and blemishes, sporting themselves with their own deceivings while they feast with you; having eyes full of adultery, and that cannot cease from sin; beguiling unstable souls: an heart they have exercised with covetous practices; cursed children: which have forsaken the right way, and are gone astray."

How well the Spirit guides him in his choice of words. He continues: "When they speak great swelling words of vanity, they allure through the lusts of the flesh, through much wantonness." That is, men can obey their counsel and still live after the manner of the world. "While they promise them liberty, they themselves are the servants of corruption: for of whom a man is overcome, of the same is he brought in bondage." (2 Pet. 2:10-19.)

5. *False prophets teach false doctrines.*

In the vision that opened our dispensation, we also hear the Divine Voice say with reference to the corrupt professors that "they draw near to me with their lips, but their hearts are far from me; they teach for doctrines the commandments of men." (JS-H

1:19; Isa. 29:13.) Truly this is the day of which Isaiah spoke: "The priest and the prophet have erred, . . . they are out of the way, . . . they err in vision, they stumble in judgment." And then with reference to the spiritual food they offer their congregations, he acclaimed: "All tables are full of vomit and filthiness, so that there is no place clean." (Isa. 28:7-8.)

The scriptures abound in statements relative to the evil teachings of the corrupt professors of religion in the last days. Paul said: "The time will come when they [the people of the world] will not endure sound doctrine; but after their own lusts shall they heap to themselves teachers, having itching ears; and they shall turn away their ears from the truth, and shall be turned unto fables." (2 Tim. 4:3-4.)

And these words of Peter apply: "There were false prophets also among the people, even as there shall be false teachers among you, who privily shall bring in damnable heresies [that is, heresies of perdition], even denying the Lord that bought them, and bring upon themselves swift destruction. And many shall follow their pernicious ways; by reason of whom the way of truth shall be evil spoken of. And through covetousness shall they with feigned words make merchandise of you." (2 Pet. 2:1-3.)

But nowhere do we find plainer preachments about false prophets than in the writings of Nephi. He says of our day: "There shall be many which shall say: Eat, drink, and be merry, for tomorrow we die; and it shall be well with us. And there shall also be many which say: Eat, drink, and be merry; nevertheless, fear God—he will justify in committing a little sin; yea, lie a little, take the advantage of one because of his words, dig a pit for thy neighbor; there is no harm in this; and do all these things, for tomorrow we die; and if it so be that we are guilty, God will beat us with a few stripes, and at last we shall be saved in the kingdom of God. Yea, and there shall be many which shall teach after this manner, false and vain and foolish doctrines, and shall be puffed up in their hearts, and shall seek deep to hide their counsels from the Lord; and their works shall be in the dark." (2 Ne. 28:7-9.)

If there is a great and abominable church, surely its ministers will teach abominable doctrines. If the Lord sends his servants to preach saving truths, should it come as any surprise to find ministers of Satan teaching damning lies? What a terrible thing it is to teach false doctrines that lead men carefully down to hell! Should we be shocked to hear Nephi acclaim: "And all those who preach false doctrines, . . . wo, wo, wo be unto them, saith the Lord God Almighty, for they shall be thrust down to hell!" (2 Ne. 28:15.)

6. *The teachings of false prophets deny God and the Godhead.*

Just as some shall gain eternal life by worshipping the true and living God, so shall others inherit eternal damnation by worshipping false gods. The greatest truths known to man are that God is a personal being in whose image we are made, that he is our Father, and that we have power to become as he is. The greatest heresy found in Christendom is that God is a spirit, an essence that fills immensity, an uncreated force or power having neither body, parts, nor passions.

The heart and core and center of revealed religion is that the Son of God atoned for the sins of the world, that he abolished death so that all shall rise in the resurrection, and that he made salvation available on conditions of obedience. The second greatest heresy in Christendom is that men are saved by grace alone without works, merely by confessing the Lord Jesus with their lips.

The greatest gift men can receive in this life is the gift of the Holy Ghost and the resultant revelation and gifts of the Spirit that thereby come into their lives. And the third greatest heresy in Christendom is the teaching that God is dead, that he has done his work in times past, and that there are not gifts and signs and miracles today.

True prophets teach the true doctrines; false prophets teach heresies.

7. *The teachings of false prophets destroy the family unit and deny the purposes of God.*

Our whole purpose in life, the very reason for our mortal probation, is to enable us to create for ourselves eternal family units patterned after the family of God our Father. Those who so obtain will have eternal life, and it is the very glory of God to lead his children to this high state.

Where among all the ministers of the world are there any who teach such a plan of salvation as this? And if they do not teach the true plan of salvation, what system and plan do they proclaim?

8. *False prophets malign Joseph Smith, fight against the Book of Mormon, and deny the restoration of the gospel.*

Peter said of false prophets: "These, as natural brute beasts, . . . speak evil of the things that they understand not." (2 Pet. 2:12.) Where is this seen better than in the reaction of ministers of religion to the Lord's great latter-day work? Of the coming forth of new revelation, they say: "We have received the word of God, and we need no more of the word of God, for we have enough!" (2 Ne. 28:29.) Of the coming forth of the Book of Mormon, their cry is: "A Bible! A Bible! We have got a Bible, and there cannot be any more Bible." (2 Ne. 29:3.) And their cries of "Delusion, false prophets, Mormon fraud," only fulfill the Lord's promise to Joseph Smith, that "fools shall have thee in derision, and hell shall rage against thee." (D&C 122:1.) Truly, Satan and his ministers sow tares in the fields of the Lord. (D&C 86:3.)

9. *False prophets teach with their learning rather than by the power of the Holy Ghost.*

In the true Church, all faithful people enjoy the gift of the Holy Ghost. The Holy Ghost is a revelator. His appointment is to testify of Christ, to bring all things of God to our remembrance, and to guide men into all truth. "By the power of the Holy Ghost ye may know the truth of all things." (Moro. 10:5.) In the true Church, prophets and preachers speak by the power of the Holy Ghost. So strict is this law that they are told: "If ye receive not the Spirit ye shall not teach." (D&C 42:14.)

It follows that in false churches, where the gifts of the Spirit are not found, men "teach with their learning, and deny the Holy Ghost, which giveth utterance." (2 Ne. 28:4.) In such churches they "preach up unto themselves their own wisdom and their own learning, that they may get gain and grind upon the face of the poor." (2 Ne. 26:20.) Where ministers of religion preach by the power of the Holy Ghost, there is the true Church; where they do not, there the true Church is not.

10. *False prophets teach for hire and divine for money.*

"Thus saith the Lord concerning the prophets that make my

people err, . . . The priests thereof teach for hire, and the prophets thereof divine for money." (Micah 3:5, 11.) "But the laborer in Zion shall labor for Zion; for if they labor for money they shall perish." (2 Ne. 26:31.) Need we say more on this point?

11. *False prophets do not raise the warning voice and cry repentance.*

True prophets preach repentance; they invite men to forsake their sins and be baptized; their voice is a warning voice, one that sets forth the sorrow and desolation reserved for the rebellious. But how can the ministers of Christendom speak thus boldly against sin and evil and iniquity when their livelihood is in the hands of the sinners in their congregation?

Speaking of prophets who have forsaken the Lord to serve another master, Isaiah leaves us this graphic imagery: "His watchmen are blind: they are all ignorant, they are all dumb dogs, they cannot bark; sleeping, lying down, loving to slumber. Yea, they are greedy dogs which can never have enough, and they are shepherds that cannot understand: they all look to their own way, every one for his gain, from his quarter." (Isa. 56:10-11.)

12. *False prophets prophesy falsely.*

The primary sin of false prophets is false teaching—teaching that does not lead men to God and salvation. But when they do attempt to prophesy, in the sense of foretelling the future, their words fail and their prophecies do not come to pass. "A wonderful and horrible thing is committed in the land; The prophets prophesy falsely, and the priests bear rule by their means; and my people love to have it so." (Jer. 5:30-31.)

Professors of religion in our day undertake so-called radio ministries or conduct great televised revivals, all with a view to solving the problems of men and of nations. They speak great swelling words to explain the visions of Daniel and of the Apocalypse. They apply selected scriptures to national and international events and postulate this or that calendar schedule, including oftentimes even the very time of the Second Coming. The great pyramid in Egypt is often woven into their preaching as though it were a book of scripture in stone. By the time one prophecy fails, another takes its place in the minds of their devotees, so that the cycle of mysticism and fablizing goes on in almost one eternal round. It is marvelous what darkened minds will accept in the name of religion!

13. *False prophets perform false ordinances that have no efficacy, virtue, or force in and after the resurrection.*

Think of the rituals and imagery that have supplanted the simple sacrament of the Lord's supper as found among the primitive saints.

Think of the prayers offered to St. Genevieve, St. Barbara, St. Joan, and an endless retinue of canonized persons, all with the thought that they will intercede with the Lord for and on behalf of the petitioners.

Think of baptism by pouring and sprinkling rather than by immersion in similitude of the death, burial, and resurrection of Him whom the ordinance is designed to typify.

Think of infant baptism and be reminded of the Holy Word which says: "It is solemn mockery before God, that ye should baptize little children. . . . He that supposeth that little children need baptism is in the gall of bitterness and in the bonds of iniquity, for he hath neither faith, hope, nor charity; wherefore, should he be cut off while in the thought, he must go down to hell. . . . Wo be unto them that shall pervert the ways of the Lord after this manner, for they shall perish except they repent. . . . And he that saith that little children need baptism denieth the mercies of Christ, and setteth at naught the atonement of him and the power of his redemption. Wo unto such, for they are in danger of death, hell, and an endless torment." (Moro. 8:9-21.)

Think also of Nadab and Abihu, who offered "strange fire"—ordinances of their own devising—upon the altar of the Lord, and wonder if the fire from heaven that devoured them was not a type and a shadow of the spiritual destruction awaiting all who pervert the right ways of the Lord with ordinances of their own. (Lev. 10:1-2.)

14. *False prophets do not receive revelation, see visions, entertain angels, and see the face of God.*

"These are wells without water, clouds that are carried with a tempest; to whom the mist of darkness is reserved for ever." (2

Pet. 2:17.) Wells without water! Prophets who do not prophesy, seers who do not see the future, ministers who receive no revelation, teachers who are lost in a mist of darkness!

They are they of whom the Lord says: "Night shall be unto you, that ye shall not have a vision; and it shall be dark unto you, that ye shall not divine; and the sun shall go down over the prophets, and the day shall be dark over them. Then shall the seers be ashamed, and the diviners confounded: yea, they shall all cover their lips; for there is no answer of God." (Micah 3:6-7.)

This is the day of wonder and amazement. Men rely upon themselves and imagine in their own minds what is to be; they seek not the Lord, to learn from him the providences he hath ordained. "Stay yourselves, and wonder; cry ye out, and cry: they are drunken, but not with wine; they stagger, but not with strong drink. For the Lord hath poured out upon you the spirit of deep sleep, and hath closed your eyes: the prophets and your rulers, the seers hath he covered." (Isa. 29:9-10.)

Oh, if men would but turn unto Him who is the same yesterday, today, and forever, who is no respecter of persons, and who treats all men alike, he would speak unto them as he spoke unto their fathers! Once again his prophets and saints would see his face and converse with their fellowservants beyond the veil.

15. *False prophets deny the gifts of the Spirit and latter-day miracles.*

They "deny the revelations of God, and say that they are done away, that there are no revelations, nor prophecies, nor gifts, nor healing, nor speaking with tongues, and the interpretation of tongues." And among them none of these are found, for they have dwindled in unbelief, and departed from the right way, "and know not the God in whom they should trust." (Morm. 9:7, 20.)

16. *False prophets do not have the testimony of Jesus, which is the spirit of prophecy.*

Joseph Smith said: "According to John, the testimony of Jesus is the spirit of prophecy; therefore, if I profess to be a witness or teacher, and have not the spirit of prophecy, which is the testimony of Jesus, I must be a false witness; but if I be a true teacher and witness, I must possess the spirit of prophecy, and that constitutes a prophet; and any man who says he is a teacher or a preacher of righteousness, and denies the spirit of prophecy, is a liar, and the truth is not in him; and by this key false teachers and impostors may be detected." (*Teachings*, p. 269.)

17. *False prophets promote carnal and evil causes that are not of God.*

"The land is full of adulterers, . . . For both prophet and priest are profane." (Jer. 23:10-11.) And thus it ever is. Adultery and a profane priesthood go hand and hand. Harlots are the desires of the great and abominable church. Every form of sin and evil abounds when spiritual leaders go astray. Lucifer's ministers teach worldly concepts and encourage carnal practices. They ordain homosexuals and women to a priesthood they pretend to hold. They profess to forgive sins for money. They stamp out heresies, as they assume, by an inquisition. Their faith is propagated by the sword. Religious wars sweep through nations and kingdoms. They persecute those who do not believe as they do. The whole history of Christendom from the day the apostles fell asleep to the present hour has been one unending course of war and blood and carnage and plague and immorality and evil, in all of which the spiritual rulers of the people have guided men in their carnal course.

18. *False prophets do not hold priesthood.*

They are not legal administrators with power and authority to bind on earth and seal in heaven. The ordinances they perform have whatever validity man can give them for this life, but they have no efficacy, virtue, or force in the life to come. They have "a form of godliness, but they deny the power thereof." (JS-H 1:19.) Most of them have scarcely heard that there is a Melchizedek Priesthood, or have assumed that Christ alone held such a delegation of divine power. Where are their apostles, high priests, patriarchs, and seventies? As to the Aaronic Priesthood, that, they suppose, ceased when the law of Moses was fulfilled. And as to the keys of the kingdom, well, they are just something to argue and wonder about.

19. *False prophets engage in priestcrafts.*

We look back upon the priest-ridden societies of the past and wonder how whole nations and kingdoms had their wealth and means and power put at the disposal of their religious rulers. And yet, how many there are even in our day who are subject to the same dominion. How great is the number of ministers who engage—openly, blatantly, even proudly—in priestcrafts, for, by definition, "Priestcrafts are that men preach and set themselves up for a light unto the world, that they may get gain and praise of the world; but they seek not the welfare of Zion." (2 Ne. 26:29.)

20. *False prophets work false miracles and engage in sorceries, witchcrafts, and magic.*

We have seen the priests of Pharaoh perform false miracles by the power of the devil. Among the Nephites in their darkest hour "there were sorceries, and witchcrafts, and magics; and the power of the evil one was wrought upon all the face of the land." (Morm. 1:19.) Witchcraft and sorcery and false miracles are not things of the past. Today also there are mediums and wizards who chirp and mutter as they arrange for their devotees to hear from the dead. Today also there are those who pretend to engage in great healing ministries. And what we now see is only the beginning. As the hour of the Second Coming draws nearer, and Satan gains greater power over more of his followers, we shall see even greater outpourings of evil power. Indeed, the day is not far distant when the evil one will make "fire come down from heaven on earth in the sight of men" (Rev. 13:13), and "the spirits of devils, working miracles," will "go forth unto the kings of the earth and of the whole world, to gather them to the battle of that great day of God Almighty" (Rev. 16:14).

21. *False prophets are leaders of apostate groups that have broken away from the true Church.*

Peter climaxes his denunciation of false prophets by speaking of traitors to the truth, deluded persons who are more to be despised and pitied than any of the false prophets of the world. He speaks of apostates who leave the true church to follow their own wayward and ill-conceived courses. "If after they have escaped the pollutions of the world through the knowledge of the Lord and Saviour Jesus Christ," he says, "they are again entangled therein, and overcome, the latter end is worse with them than the beginning. For it had been better for them not to have known the way of righteousness, than, after they have known it, to turn from the holy commandment delivered unto them. But it is happened unto them according to the true proverb, The dog is turned to his own vomit again; and the sow that was washed to her wallowing in the mire." (2 Pet. 2:20-22.)

Would it be amiss for us to conclude this portion of our analysis by applying to the Latter-day Saints the words of the Beloved John, who wrote relative to the former-day saints. "We are of God," he said. "He that knoweth God heareth us; he that is not of God heareth not us. Hereby know we the spirit of truth, and the spirit of error." (1 Jn. 4:6.)

THE TIMES OF RESTITUTION

The Promised Age of Restoration

Shortly after the ascension of the Lord Jesus into heaven, where he now sits on the right hand of God the Father Almighty, Peter took it upon himself to do what he had seen his Master do. Peter healed a man without reference to the faith of the decrepit person. Jesus had opened the eyes of one who was born blind in order to gain a congregation and to set the stage for a glorious proclamation of his own divine Sonship. All this is set forth in the sermon about the Good Shepherd. (John 9-10.) Peter healed "a certain man lame from his mother's womb" for a similar reason.

The man, begging at the gate of the temple, asked for alms from Peter and John. Peter said, "Look on us," which the man did. Then from the lips of the Chief Apostle came these divine words: "Silver and gold have I none; but such as I have give I thee: In the name of Jesus Christ of Nazareth rise up and walk." The man arose, walked, leaped, praised God, and showed himself to all the people in the temple. The people, knowing the man was born lame, "were filled with wonder and amazement," and all ran together in Solomon's porch.

Peter had his congregation. As when Jesus opened the blind eyes, the people could not do other than listen to the one who had wrought so great a miracle in their presence. "Ye men of Israel, why marvel ye at this?" Peter asked. "Or why look ye so earnestly on us, as though by our own power or holiness we had made this man to walk?"

Then came the kind of a sermon that no false prophet would ever preach. Peter's words were not designed to tickle their ears, or to please their vanity, or to encourage them to pay him for preaching. "The God of our fathers, hath glorified his Son Jesus," Peter said, "whom ye delivered up, and denied him in the presence of Pilate, when he was determined to let him go. But ye denied the Holy One and the Just, and desired a murderer to be granted unto you; and killed the Prince of life, whom God hath raised from the dead; whereof we are witnesses."

That is: 'You caused his arrest; you delivered him to Pilate; you denied him. You chose Barabbas, the murderer, to be released; you are guilty of the death of one who was holy and just and innocent. His blood is upon your hands. You are murderers.' These things must be made clear if we are to understand what follows. Peter is speaking to murderers. "I wot [know] that through ignorance ye did it, as did also your rulers," he then added. They did not know that Jesus was their Lord—on that point they were ignorant; but he was a man who had done nothing worthy of death, and they caused his death. Pilate, on their behalf, issued a legal decree that resulted in a judicial murder.

And because "no murderer hath eternal life abiding in him" (1 Jn. 3:15), Peter is not going to ask them to repent and be baptized. Instead he says: "*Repent ye therefore, and be converted*"—'Repent and believe; convert your flinty hearts of stone into hearts of flesh; change from your awful state of disbelief and rebellion to one of glorious faith'—"*that your sins may be blotted out*"—'that you may, in the providences of Him who is merciful to those who repent, gain a forgiveness of your sin of shedding innocent blood'—"*when the times of refreshing shall come from the presence of the Lord*"—'when the earth shall be renewed and receive its paradisiacal glory; when all things shall be made new; when there shall be a new heaven and a new earth; when the millennial era shall commence'—"*And he shall send Jesus Christ, which before was preached unto you*"—'when the Lord shall send his Son again; when Jesus shall return to live and reign with men; when the glorious day of the Second Coming of the Son of Man arrives; when Jesus comes again, even the same Jesus whose gospel we now preach'—"*Whom the heaven must receive until the times of restitution of all things, which God hath spoken by the mouth of all his holy prophets since the world began*"—'Which Jesus must remain in heaven until the age of restoration; until the period of time begins in which the Lord shall restore all things; until God commences the restoration of all things known to and predicted by all the holy prophets from the beginning.' (Acts 3:1-21. Italics added.)

That is to say: Christ came once. He was crucified, died, and rose again. He ascended into heaven where he now is. And he shall come again to usher in the Millennium, to refresh the earth, to make of it a new earth, to restore its paradisiacal glory. But he cannot come, and the promised day will not arrive, until a period of time commences which is named the Age of Restoration.

Peter does not say that all things will be restored before the Lord comes. What he does say is: Christ cannot come until the Age of Restoration has its beginning. That age commenced in the spring of 1820 and is now shedding its light and truth abroad, and it will continue to do so until well into the millennial era. That age will include the events incident to the Second Coming and will continue after that glorious and dread day. Indeed, the great reservoir of revealed truth will not be made available until after the Lord comes and destroys the unbelieving and rebellious. "When the Lord shall come, he shall reveal all things," our scripture recites, "things which have passed, and hidden things which no man knew, things of the earth, by which it was made, and the purpose and the end thereof—things most precious, things that are above, and things that are beneath, things that are in the earth, and upon the earth, and in heaven." (D&C 101:32-34.)

What is it that shall be restored in the times of restitution of all things? What is it that God hath spoken by the mouth of all his holy prophets since the world began?

It is everything pertaining to the salvation and exaltation of his children. God's eternal purposes are to bring to pass the immortality and eternal life of man. He has no others. His plan of salvation is the gospel of God. By obedience to its laws and conditions, men have power to advance and progress and become like him. By such obedience, they have power to gain eternal life, which is the kind of life he lives.

It is everything pertaining to the divine Sonship of the Lord Jesus Christ—how he was chosen and foreordained in the councils of eternity to be the Savior of the world and the Redeemer of men; how he was born as the Son of God, inheriting from his Father the power of immortality; how he took upon himself the sins of all men, beginning in Gethsemane as he sweat great drops of blood from every pore, and continuing on the cross when the sufferings of Gethsemane were renewed; how he abolished death and brought life and immortality to light through the gospel; how he burst the bands of death and brought to pass the resurrection for all men; and how he will come in glorious immortality to live and reign on earth for a thousand years.

It is all of the gifts of the Spirit—the miracles, signs, and wonders of the past. It is revelation and visions and a knowledge of the wonders of eternity. It is the way and the means and the power whereby the Holy Spirit of God can make of man a new creature—can burn dross and evil out of him as though by fire; can bring him forth in a newness of life, free from carnality and sin; and can sanctify his soul and make him a fit companion for Gods and angels.

It is the fulness of the everlasting gospel. It is priesthoods, and keys, and powers, and authorities. It is the truths of salvation as they were taught in wondrous glory in the City of Holiness where Enoch dwelt. It is the covenant God made with Abraham that in him and in his seed all generations should be blessed.

It is the keys of creation as used by Jehovah and Michael in the creation of the earth. It is the keys of presidency over all men as used by Adam and Noah, the fathers of all men from their days onward. It is the keys to gather Israel and lead them from the darkness of their present Egyptian bondage into the light of their promised land. It is the sealing power possessed by a lowly Tishbite who became a mighty prophet. It is the apostolic commission vested in Peter, James, and John, and their fellows. It is every key, power, and authority ever possessed by any prophet and seer in any location and in any age. All are to come again in the dispensation of the fulness of times.

But it is more. It is also governments and kingdoms. It is lands and properties and peoples. The church and kingdom of God on earth is to be set up again. Israel is to be gathered into the church. In due course the political kingdom is to be restored to Israel. The Book of Mormon shall come forth, including the sealed portion. The lost portions of the Bible shall again be read from the housetops. The gospel is to go to the Lamanites, and they shall become again a pure and a delightsome people. Jerusalem of old shall be rebuilt in its old place, and a New Jerusalem shall arise in America. The knowledge of God shall cover the earth as the waters cover the sea, and once again men shall speak a pure language. Men shall be resurrected, and all of the eternal purposes of the Lord shall come to pass.

Was this earth once a garden fair, without thorns, thistles, briers, and noxious weeds? It shall be renewed and receive again its paradisiacal glory. The burning desert shall blossom as the rose and become once again like the garden of the Lord. Was it once blessed with rolling hills, pleasant valleys, and rivers of splendor? In the promised day every mountain shall be made low, every valley shall be exalted, and the rough places shall be made smooth.

Was there a day when the continents were one land and the islands were not separated from them? Such shall come again. The great deep shall be driven back into the north and the land surfaces of the earth shall be one again as they were in the days before they were divided.

Did Enoch's Zion, filled with righteous souls, once grace the earth? So shall it yet be. He and all his city shall return to dwell in peace on earth with those who once again can abide the laws which caused the ancient ones to be translated. Was the earth once new, glorious, and paradisiacal in nature? So shall it be again. The earth shall be renewed. There will be a new heaven and a new earth whereon dwelleth righteousness.

All things pertaining to the creation and peopling and destiny of the earth—these are the things that God hath spoken by the mouth of all his holy prophets. This revealed knowledge shall be restored, and the events of which they spoke shall come to pass, all during that age of the earth known as the times of restitution. Of all these things we shall speak more particularly hereafter in their proper settings.

The Age of Renaissance and Preparation

The times of restitution—the age of restoration—was not born without a long period of gestation. This glorious and wondrous age, in which floods of celestial light were destined to shine again in the hearts of men, did not spring into being full grown. The Age of Restoration did not burst forth unannounced in the midst of the dark ages; there was no sudden flash or blaze of heavenly light in the midnight sky. Its dawning came gradually as rays of light and truth and understanding pierced the eastern sky. The stranglehold of the great and abominable church on the minds and souls of men was not broken with one burst of Sampsonian strength. And even now, in modern times, the iron grasp of evil keeps the masses of men from seeing through the mists of darkness that yet cover the earth.

The times of restitution in which the Lord shall "do his work, his strange work; and bring to pass his act, his strange act" (Isa. 28:21), had its forerunners. As Elias went before Messias, so the Renaissance and then the Reformation prepared the way for the Restoration. Beginning in the 14th century (the 1300s) there was a new birth of learning. An inquiring spirit spread forth among men. Universities sprang up. There were splendid achievements in art and architecture, and scientific discoveries began to shake the creeds of darkness. By about 1450 printing presses were spreading the ideas of the new intellectuals. The Gutenberg Bible came forth in 1456.

"The urge to inquire, to debate, and seek new explanations spread from the field of classical learning into that of religious studies," the astute Winston Churchill tells us. "Greek and even Hebrew texts, as well as Latin, were scrutinised afresh. Inevitably this led to the questioning of accepted religious beliefs. The Renaissance bred the Reformation. In 1517, at the age of thirty-four, Martin Luther, a German priest, denounced the sale of Indulgences, nailed his theses on this and other matters on the door of Wittenberg Castle church, and embarked on his venturesome intellectual foray with the Pope. What began as a protest against Church practices soon became a challenge to Church doctrine. In this struggle Luther displayed qualities of determination and conviction at the peril of the stake which won him his name and fame. He started or gave an impulse to a movement which within a decade swamped the Continent, and proudly bears the general title of the Reformation. It took different forms in different countries, particularly in Switzerland under Zwingli and Calvin. The latter's influence spread from Geneva across France to the Netherlands and Britain, where it was most strongly felt in Scotland. . . .

"Heresies there had always been, and over the centuries feeling against the Church had often run strong in almost every country of Europe. But the schism that had begun with Luther was novel and formidable. All the actors in it, the enemies and the defenders of Rome alike, were still deeply influenced by medieval views. They thought of themselves as restorers of the purer ways of ancient times and of the early Church. But the Reformation added to the confusion and uncertainty of an age in which men and states were tugging unwillingly and unwittingly at the anchors that had so long held Europe. After a period of ecclesiastical strife between the Papacy and the Reformation, Protestantism was established over a great part of the Continent under a variety of sects and schools, of which Lutheranism covered the larger area. The Church in Rome, strengthened by the heart-searching Catholic revival known as the Counter-Reformation and in the more worldly sphere by the activities of the Inquisition, proved able to maintain itself through a long series of religious wars."

Then Churchill, quoting Charles Beard, poses some blunt questions: " 'Was, then, the Reformation, from the intellectual point of view, a failure? Did it break one yoke only to impose another? We are obliged to confess that, especially in Germany, it soon parted company with free learning; that it turned its back upon culture, that it lost itself in a maze of arid theological controversy, that it held out no hand of welcome to awakening science. . . . Even at a later time it has been the divines who have most loudly declared their allegiance to the theology of the Reformation who have also looked most askance at science, and claimed for their statements an entire independence of modern knowledge. I do not know how, on any ordinary theory of the Reformation, it is possible to answer the accusations implied in these facts. The most learned, the profoundest, the most tolerant of modern theologians, would be the most reluctant to accept in their fullness the systems of Melancthon and of Calvin. . . . The fact is, that while the services which the Reformers rendered to truth and liberty by their revolt against the unbroken supremacy of medieval Christianity cannot be over-estimated, it was impossible for them to settle the questions which they raised. Not merely did the necessary knowledge fail them, but they did not even see the scope of the controversies in which they were engaged. It was their part to open the flood-gates; and the stream, in spite of their well-meant efforts to check and confine it, has since rushed impetuously on, now destroying old landmarks, now fertilising new fields, but always bringing with it life and refreshment. To look at the Reformation by itself, to judge it only by its theological and ecclesiastical development, is to pronounce it a failure; to consider it as part of a general movement of European thought, to show its essential connection with ripening scholarship and advancing science, to prove its necessary alliance with liberty, to illustrate its slow growth into toleration, is at once to vindicate its past and to promise it the future.' " (Winston S. Churchill, *A History of the English-Speaking People* [New York: Dodd, Mead & Co., 1956], vol. 2, pp. 4-8.)

As they view things, the scholars of the world know that the Reformers and the Reformation did not solve the problems of an ancient religion or of an awakening science. From our vantage point, we gain a clearer perspective. We know that Christ in his day brought the bright light of the glorious gospel; that thereafter there was darkness; pure truths were twisted into evil heresies; godly conduct degenerated into carnal lewdness. Then came the Renaissance, as the light of Christ refreshed the consciences of men; as art and architecture and learning were born anew; as science and a search for truth outside the creeds found place in the hearts of men. Then came the Reformation; the Catholic yoke was broken; Protestantism arose and commanded the allegiance of peoples and nations. And thus for half a millennium the Lord channeled the thinking of men and prepared them spiritually for the day of revelation and restoration, the day when the bright light would shine again.

America: The Land of Liberty

America was discovered, colonized, and made into a great nation so that the Lord would have a proper place both to restore the gospel and from which to send it forth to all other nations. As a prelude to his coming, and so the promised work of restoration would roll forward, the foundations of the American nation were laid in the days of the Renaissance and the Reformation. "The Spirit of God," meaning the light of Christ, rested upon "a man among the Gentiles," meaning Columbus. He discovered America in 1492. Then other Gentiles, guided from on high in like manner, "went forth out of captivity" to colonize the New World. Then came the Revolutionary War in which "the Gentiles that had gone out of captivity were delivered by the power of God out of the hands of all other nations." (1 Ne. 13:12-19.) Nephi saw all this in vision, and through it the foundations were laid for the establishment of the United States of America.

Be it noted that those who colonized America "went forth out of captivity." That is, they left the Catholic and Protestant nations of Europe in search of religious freedom; they, as pilgrims and separatists, sought a place where they could worship God according to the dictates of their conscience rather than as decreed by the reigning monarchs of the moment.

The Protestant churches of Europe freed themselves from the yoke of Rome, only to create their own state churches, which in turn compelled all nationals to worship as decreed by the particular brand of Protestantism that prevailed in their nation. There was no religious freedom as such, nor could there be as long as the civil law dictated forms and systems of worship.

But in America it was different. No one colony had power to

force all others to worship its way. Out of political necessity the Thirteen Colonies, when they united to form a new nation, were forced to approve religious freedom and to let each church in each colony go its own way. Thus, in the providences of the Lord, freedom of worship was guaranteed in the new nation. And thus, speaking of this and other freedoms, Jesus, after his resurrection, said to the Nephites: "It is wisdom in the Father" that the Gentiles "should be established in this land, and be set up as a free people by the power of the Father," that the Book of Mormon and the gospel might be taken to the Lamanites, "that the covenant of the Father may be fulfilled which he hath covenanted with his people." (3 Ne. 21:4.)

The Constitution of the United States is the political document that guarantees to men their freedom; it is the supreme law of the land; it is the standard by which all laws are measured. "I established the Constitution of this land," the Lord says, "by the hands of wise men whom I raised up unto this very purpose." The Constitution and the laws enacted in harmony therewith "should be maintained for the rights and protection of all flesh, according to just and holy principles." (D&C 101:76-80.) "And that law of the land which is constitutional, supporting that principle of freedom in maintaining rights and privileges," the Lord also says, "belongs to all mankind, and is justifiable before me." (D&C 98:4-10.)

There is, thus, one great nation on earth that exalts and protects freedom and liberty and the right to worship as one chooses. "This land," the land of America, "shall be a land of liberty," saith the Lord, "and there shall be no kings upon the land. . . . For I, the Lord, the king of heaven, will be their king, and I will be a light unto them forever, that hear my words." (2 Ne. 10:10-14.) And further, in Moroni's language: "This is a choice land, and whatsoever nation shall possess it shall be free from bondage, and from captivity, and from all other nations under heaven, if they will but serve the God of the land, who is Jesus Christ." (Ether 2:12.)

This is the land of prophecy and of destiny. Here the gospel was restored; here men are free to worship; here they have the talents and the means to carry the word to other nations. This is the Lord's base of operations in the last days. From here the word of truth shall go forth to prepare a people for the Second Coming of the Son of Man. This land, Isaiah says, "sendeth ambassadors"—the elders of Israel—to all the "inhabitants of the world, and dwellers on the earth." They shall say: "See ye, when he lifteth up an ensign on the mountains; and when he bloweth a trumpet, hear ye." (Isa. 18:1-3.) That call is now going forth.

THE RESTORATION OF THE GLORIOUS GOSPEL

Restoration and the Eternal Plan

In the eternal providences of Him whose work and glory it is to save his children, an immutable decree went forth in the beginning. The Eternal One swore, with his own voice and in his own name—with a certainty that is as firm as the pillars of heaven—that in the last days he would restore the fulness of his everlasting gospel.

This restoration of the glorious gospel of God would prepare a people for the Second Coming of the Son of Man. This restoration of the plan of salvation would make eternal life available to more of his children—more? ten thousand times ten thousand more—than all the preaching and all the labors of all the prophets of all the ages. This restoration of all the truths, and all the powers, and all the graces ever enjoyed and possessed by any people would be the most glorious and wondrous event ever to occur on planet earth, save only the atoning sacrifice of the Son of God. And it was destined to take place in "the times of restitution" and to be part of the promised "restitution of all things, which God hath spoken by the mouth of all his holy prophets since the world began." (Acts 3:21.)

In the beginning when men were few and times were simple, the Lord revealed the fulness of his everlasting gospel. To Adam and his children the command came: "Believe on his Only Begotten Son, even him who he declared should come in the meridian of time, who was prepared from before the foundation of the world." Men thus came to know that salvation is in Christ and that to gain such a great reward they must believe and obey his law. "And thus the Gospel began to be preached, from the beginning, being declared by holy angels sent forth from the presence of God, and by his own voice, and by the gift of the Holy Ghost. And thus all things were confirmed unto Adam, by an holy ordinance, and the Gospel preached, and a decree sent forth, that it should be in the world [in a series of dispensations], until the end thereof." (Moses 5:57-59.)

And thus also was the pattern set for the giving of the gospel to men in whatever age and under whatever circumstances it was destined to come. Three means of divine direction were and are required:

1. Men must hear the voice of God. Those holy beings whom it is life eternal to know must reveal themselves from heaven. God stands revealed or he remains forever unknown. The heavens must rend; revelations must rain forth; and the things of God must be manifest in plainness and purity to those who dwell on earth.

2. Holy angels must minister to mortals. They must confer priesthoods and keys; they must reveal truths and doctrines; they must identify themselves as the fellow servants of the preachers of righteousness who dwell on earth.

3. Men must receive the gift of the Holy Ghost. Thereby revelation comes, for the Holy Ghost is a revelator; he knows all things and gives them freely to all who attune themselves to his eternal broadcasts. Thereby dross and evil is burned out of human souls as though by fire, for the Holy Ghost brings the baptism of fire. Thereby men are born again and their souls sanctified, for the Holy Ghost is a sanctifier. Thereby all of the gifts and signs and miracles are found among the faithful, for the Holy Ghost, who is no respecter of persons, gives to all in accordance with their faith. And by the power of the Spirit—the Holy Spirit of Promise—men are sealed up unto eternal life.

What, then, is the gospel that is dispensed from heaven to

men? It is the great and eternal plan of salvation. It is the way and the means provided by the Father whereby his spirit children—Christ included—can advance and progress and become like him. It is the trials and training of preexistence, the problems and probation of this mortality, and the glory and honor of a future day. It is the atonement of Christ, the ransom from the fall, the plan of redemption. It is "the gospel of God," as Paul said, "Concerning his Son Jesus Christ our Lord, which was made of the seed of David according to the flesh; And declared to be the Son of God with power, according to the spirit of holiness, by the resurrection from the dead. . . . It is the power of God unto salvation." (Rom. 1:1-4, 16.)

And because it is the power of God that saves men, it includes both what the Lord does for us and what we must do for ourselves to be saved. On his part it is the atonement; on our part it is obedience to all that is given us of God. Thus the gospel includes every truth, every principle, every law—all that men must believe and know. Thus it includes every ordinance, every rite, every performance—all that men must do to please their Maker. Thus it includes every priesthood, every key, every power—all that men must receive to have their acts bound on earth and sealed eternally in the heavens.

The fulness of the everlasting gospel, meaning all that is needed to enable men to gain a fulness of everlasting salvation, has been given of God in successive dispensations. The Adamic age set the pattern, and there has been a partial or total restoration in each succeeding dispensation. Jesus thus restored the gospel of the kingdom in his day. He brought back again much of what the ancient prophets and saints had enjoyed in their days. The total apostasy following his day calls for a total restoration in the last days.

This promised, destined, and decreed latter-day restoration is so replete with glory and wonder; it is so infinite and eternal in scope and importance; it is destined to affect so many of the spirit hosts of heaven, all children of the Eternal Father; it does and will mean so much to so many—that all of the holy prophets knew it would come to pass, and almost all who wrote prophetically have had more or less to say about it. "Surely the Lord God will do nothing, but he revealeth his secret unto his servants the prophets." (Amos 3:7.)

Whenever prophets so live as to receive a knowledge of things past, present, and future, such is showered upon them. All that they have said about the gathering of Israel, the return of the Ten Tribes, the coming forth of the Book of Mormon, the establishment of Zion, the building of a New Jerusalem and the restoration of the Old Jerusalem, of the Second Coming of the Lord, and of the millennial era—all these things and more—are part of what is involved in the restoration of the gospel in the last days. We shall consider them all, each in its place and position in the eternal scheme of things. First, however, we shall note a few of the promises, given in general terms, relative to the restoration of the gospel as such.

Moroni and the Other Angelic Ministrants

John, the Beloved Revelator, banished on Patmos for the love of God and the testimony of Jesus, saw in vision the restoration of the glorious gospel in the last days. "And I saw another angel fly in the midst of heaven," he said, "having the everlasting gospel to preach unto them that dwell on the earth, and to every nation, and kindred, and tongue, and people."

How the sects of Christendom must shake in their hollow shells! God Almighty, by the mouth of his prophet, says there is to be revelation in the last days, in a day subsequent to New Testament times, in a day following the great apostasy. An angelic ministrant descends from the courts of glory. What message does he bring? Behold, it is the everlasting gospel, the eternal plan of salvation, the same saving truths had in all dispensations. It is given again to men. The age of restoration sheds forth its brilliant light.

And to whom shall this same gospel, this gospel had of old, this gospel which is everlasting, to whom shall it be preached when the angel comes? To all who dwell upon the earth, to the inhabiters of every nation, to all the kindreds of men, to those who speak every tongue, and to every people on the face of the globe—all are to hear the message. And if it is to be offered to all, do any of them already have it? Truly, John is seeing the heavens rend, revelation is commencing anew, the angels of God are coming again as they did of old; but John is doing more—he is testifying of the absolute, total spiritual darkness that covers the earth. The new gospel, which is the old gospel, which is the everlasting gospel, is being restored for the blessing of all men. None have it; it is coming again for the benefit and blessing of all.

With a loud voice—there is no fear, nothing is hidden, nothing is done in secret—with the trump of God, the angel says: "Fear God, and give glory to him; for the hour of his judgment is come: and worship him that made heaven, and earth, and the sea, and the fountains of waters." Immediately thereafter another angel announces the fall of Babylon, which is the destruction of the great and abominable church. (Rev. 14:6-8.)

Once again men are invited—nay, commanded—to worship the true and living God who is the Creator of all things. The Second Coming is soon to be, and evil Babylon is about to be burned with unquenchable fire. Worship God! "Worship the Father in spirit and in truth; for the Father seeketh such to worship him. For unto such hath God promised his Spirit. And they who worship him, must worship in spirit and in truth." (JST, John 4:25-26.)

No longer does it suffice to rely on the creeds that make of God a spirit essence filling immensity, which has neither body, parts, or passions. To every man who has thus made "gods unto himself, and they are no gods," to all who have thus "inherited lies, vanity, and things wherein there is no profit," to all who will hear his voice, he now acclaims: "Behold, I will this once cause them to know, I will cause them to know mine hand and my might; and they shall know that my name is The Lord." (Jer. 16:19-21.) That this new knowledge of the ancient God was first manifest in the spring of 1820, with the appearance of the Father and the Son to the first prophet of this dispensation, is, of course, known to all the saints.

Truly, as the scripture saith, murder and tyranny and oppression, during the long days of spiritual darkness, have been "supported and urged on and upheld by the influence of that spirit which hath so strongly riveted the creeds of the fathers, who have inherited lies, upon the hearts of the children, and filled the world with confusion, and has been growing stronger and stronger, and is now the very mainspring of all corruption, and the whole earth groans under the weight of its iniquity. It is an iron yoke, it is a strong band; they are the very handcuffs, and chains, and shackles, and fetters of hell." (D&C 123:7-8.)

But thanks be to God, in this age of restoration, the voice of God is heard again. He speaks. His angel descends and the mighty restoration is underway. Moroni, the first great angel of the restoration, came many times. His first appearance was during the night of September 21-22, 1823. He revealed the hiding place of the Nephite scriptures, instructed Joseph Smith relative to their translation, and gave him the care and custody of the gold plates for an appointed season. The Book of Mormon was published to the world in 1830. This volume of holy scripture contains the fulness of the everlasting gospel, meaning that it is a record of God's dealings with a people who had the fulness of the gospel, and in it is an inspired account of what men must do to gain eternal life in our Father's kingdom. It contains the "word" of the gospel.

In November 1831, addressing himself to the "inhabitants of the earth," the Lord said: "I have sent forth mine angel flying through the midst of heaven, having the everlasting gospel, who hath appeared unto some and hath committed it unto man, who shall appear unto many that dwell on the earth." (D&C 133:36.) Up to this point in time, Moroni had come with the Book of Mormon, John the Baptist had restored the Aaronic Priesthood and its keys, and Peter, James, and John had conferred upon mortal men the Melchizedek Priesthood and the keys of the kingdom, and the Church had been organized. Other angels would thereafter bring their keys. The Lord's angels were bringing to pass the promised restoration, a restoration of the "word" of the gospel and a restoration of the "power" of the gospel. (1 Thes. 1:5.) Of the preaching of this gospel in all the world before the Second Coming we shall speak more particularly hereafter.

Elias of the Restoration

In one or many ancient scriptures, none of which have been preserved for us, the word of the Lord, spoken with prophetic fervor, acclaimed that Elias would come and restore all things before the Second Coming of the Lord. Would God that we now had this ancient prophetic word as someday we shall. Whether it is revealed anew to us before or after the Second Coming may well depend upon our spiritual preparation to receive it. But thanks be to Him from whom revelations come, we do have enough scriptural references to it so that we can envision with some clarity the doctrine relative to Elias of the Restoration.

It is perfectly clear that the Jews in the day of Jesus knew that Elias was to come and restore all things. "When the Jews sent priests and Levites from Jerusalem" to Bethabara to inquire of John the Baptist what right he had to baptize, the inquisitors asked: "Who art thou?" They also raised the issue as to whether he was Elias. "And he confessed, and denied not that he was Elias; but confessed, saying; I am not the Christ." Then came the query: "How then art thou Elias?" His answer: "I am not that Elias who was to restore all things." Next came his great pronouncement that he was sent to prepare the way before the Lord as foretold by Isaiah. But his interrogators still persisted. "Why baptizest thou then," they asked, "if thou be not the Christ, nor Elias who was to restore all things?" In answer, John testified that Christ himself was the Elias who was to restore saving truths for their day. "I baptize with water," he said, "but there standeth one among you, whom ye know not; He it is of whom I bear record. He is that prophet, even Elias, who, coming after me, is preferred before me, whose shoe's latchet I am not worthy to unloose, or whose place I am not able to fill; for he shall baptize, not only with water, but with fire, and with the Holy Ghost." (JST, John 1:20-28.)

Peter, James, and John, the chosen three, smitten with wondering awe, saw Moses and Elijah (Elias) minister to their Lord and Friend on the Mount of Transfiguration. Coming down from the heights of Hermon, they pondered how it was that the prophetic word said Elias would come *before* the Messiah to prepare the way, and yet here on the Holy Mount he had come *after*. They asked: "Why then say the scribes that Elias must first come?" Jesus confirmed the verity of the ancient word. He said: "Elias truly shall first come, and restore all things, as the prophets have written." There would be a day of restoration in the last days. Then the ancient word about Elias would be fulfilled.

As pertaining to their day, Jesus then said: "And again I say unto you that Elias has come already, concerning whom it is written, Behold, I will send my messenger, and he shall prepare the way before me; and they knew him not, and have done unto him whatsoever they listed. Likewise shall also the Son of man suffer of them. But I say unto you, Who is Elias? Behold, this is Elias, whom I send to prepare the way before me." Two Eliases are involved, one who went before and another who came after. "Then the disciples understood that he spake unto them of John the Baptist, and also of another who should come and restore all things, as it is written by the prophets." (JST, Matt. 17:9-14.)

There is no valid reason for confusion as to the identity and mission of Elias. There was a man named Elias who came to Joseph Smith and Oliver Cowdery on April 3, 1836, in the Kirtland Temple to restore "the gospel of Abraham." (D&C 110:12.) Whether he was Abraham himself or someone else from his dispensation, we do not know. Elias is one of the names of Gabriel who is Noah, and it was in this capacity that Gabriel visited Zacharias the father of John the Baptist. (D&C 27:6-7.) Elias is the Greek form of the Hebrew Elijah, and in this sense has reference to the prophet from Tishbe. Elias is also the title or name of a forerunner who goes before to prepare the way for someone who is greater; this is the doctrine of Elias, and in this sense John the Baptist was both Elias and an Elias. John came in the way that Gabriel (who is Elias) promised, that is, "in the spirit and power of Elias, . . . to make ready a people prepared for the Lord." (Luke 1:17.) In this sense also, the Aaronic Priesthood is the Priesthood of Elias because it prepares men for the greater priesthood. We shall hereafter speak of Joseph Smith as the Elias who came to prepare the way for the Second Coming.

But, as we have seen, there is also an Elias of the Restoration, meaning that there is also a doctrine of Elias that pertains not to preparation alone, but to restoration. Christ was Elias in his day because he restored the gospel for those then living. In our revelations the Lord says that Gabriel (Noah) is the "Elias, to whom I have committed the keys of bringing to pass the restoration of all things spoken by the mouth of all the holy prophets since the world began, concerning the last days." (D&C 27:6.) The one who holds the keys is the one who directs the work; keys are the right of presidency. Thus Gabriel, who stands next to Michael (Adam) in the heavenly hierarchy, has a great directing and supervising work in connection with the restoration of all things.

John the Revelator not only saw an "angel fly in the midst of heaven, having the everlasting gospel to preach unto them that dwell on the earth" (Rev. 14:6) in the last days, but he also "saw four angels standing on the four corners of the earth, holding the four winds of the earth, that the wind should not blow on the earth, nor on the sea, nor on any tree." (Rev. 7:1.) The mission of these four angels is not as apparent as is the mission of the angelic ministrant who is named as bringing the gospel to all men. That our understanding of the restoration of the gospel might be perfected, however, the Prophet Joseph Smith, writing by the spirit of revelation, said of them: "We are to understand that they are four angels sent forth from God, to whom is given power over the four parts of the earth, to save life and to destroy; these are they who have the everlasting gospel to commit to every nation, kindred, tongue, and people; having power to shut up the heavens, to seal up unto life, or to cast down to the regions of darkness." (D&C 77:8.) Thus there is more than one angel involved in the restoration of the gospel in the last days.

Then John saw yet another heavenly ministrant come forth to play his part in the strange act of the Lord of heaven. "And I saw another angel ascending from the east," he said, "having the seal of the living God: and he cried with a loud voice to the four angels, to whom it was given to hurt the earth and the sea, Saying, Hurt not the earth, neither the sea, nor the trees, till we have sealed the servants of our God in their foreheads." (Rev. 7:2-3.) This refers to sealing the servants of God up unto eternal life so "they shall pass by the angels, and the gods, . . . to their exaltation and glory in all things, as hath been sealed upon their heads, which glory shall be a fulness and a continuation of the seeds forever and ever. Then shall they be gods." (D&C 132:19-20.) And, be it noted, it was Elijah the prophet who restored the sealing power in this dispensation.

Again, so that the divine commission involved might be understood by those who are spiritually literate, the Prophet, as guided by the Spirit, gave this explanation: "We are to understand that the angel ascending from the east is he to whom is given the seal of the living God over the twelve tribes of Israel; wherefore, he crieth unto the four angels having the everlasting gospel, saying: Hurt not the earth, neither the sea, nor the trees, till we have sealed the servants of our God in their foreheads. And, if you will receive it, this is Elias which was to come to gather together the tribes of Israel and restore all things." (D&C 77:9.) Some of this sealing has already occurred—a few of Ephraim and a sprinkling of Manasseh have been sealed up unto eternal life; but the great day of fulfillment, where all Israel is concerned, lies ahead. And again, be it noted, there is more to the labors of Elias of the Restoration than the works of one angel only.

Continuing his inspired exegesis of the hidden truths in the Apocalypse, the Prophet asked: "What are we to understand by the little book which was eaten by John, as mentioned in the 10th chapter of Revelation?" His answer: "We are to understand that it was a mission, and an ordinance, for him to gather the tribes of Israel; behold, this is Elias, who, as it is written, must come and restore all things." (D&C 77:14.) Thus John himself is another of these enigmatic Eliases, all of whose ministries combine to fulfill the ancient word that Elias shall come and restore all things in the times of restitution, which "times" began in the spring of 1820 and shall continue until after the Lord Jesus reigns again among men. We shall have more to say about Elias of the Restoration in chapters 10 and 11.

The Ancient Prophets and the Restored Gospel

We are inclined to believe that all of the ancient prophets knew about the restoration of the gospel in the last days. We know they all had the plan of salvation; they all knew that salvation is in Christ; they all knew he would come to atone for the sins of the world; and they all knew about the Second Coming. Those who were prophets in Israel knew about the latter-day gathering of that chosen people, and some of them knew about the Nephite nation and the coming forth of the Book of Mormon. Implicit in all this is the fact that they must have known about the restoration of that gospel which would gather Israel and prepare a people for the Second Coming of Him in whose name they worshipped the Father.

Our purpose here is simply to sample a few slivers of the prophetic word so as to have the concept before us that the restoration of the gospel in the last days was one of the great wonders toward which the ancients looked with anxious expectation. The Lord's purposes were not hidden from them any more than they are from us. They knew as we know that the day of final triumph and glory for the Lord's people was reserved for the last days.

Joel, for instance, had many things to say about the gathering of Israel, about the wars and desolations of the last days, and about the Second Coming. By his mouth the Lord said: "I will pour out my spirit upon all flesh; and your sons and your daughters shall prophesy, your old men shall dream dreams, your young men shall see visions: And also upon the servants and upon the handmaids in those days will I pour out my spirit." Then, he continues, shall come to pass the wonders in the heavens and on earth, the blood and fire and vapors of smoke, and the sun turning to darkness that shall attend "the great and the terrible day of the Lord." (Joel 2:28-31.) Can there be any doubt that these dreams and visions preceding the Lord's return will come to those who believe and obey the same gospel laws that qualified their forebears to receive like heavenly manifestations? Indeed, when Moroni first came to the Prophet, he quoted these very words from Joel and said they would soon be fulfilled. (JS-H 1:41.)

When Isaiah promised that the Lord would "set up an ensign

for the nations" and gather the dispersed of Israel, the ensign, the standard, the divine flag around which all men should rally was to be the holy gospel. (Isa. 5:26; 11:12.) When the Lord said, as Isaiah records, "Forasmuch as this people draw near me with their mouth, and with their lips do honour me, but have removed their heart far from me, and their fear toward me is taught by the precept of men: Therefore, behold, I will proceed to do a marvellous work among this people, even a marvellous work and a wonder: for the wisdom of their wise men shall perish, and the understanding of their prudent men shall be hid" (Isa. 29:13-14)—when these divine words were uttered, they had reference to the restoration of the gospel in our day. And some of these very words were quoted by the Son of God in the First Vision. (JS-H 1:19.) Many latter-day revelations identify the marvelous work here named as the restored gospel.

When the Lord said, "A law shall proceed from me, and I will make my judgment to rest for a light of the people" (Isa. 51:4); when the call shall go forth, "Arise, shine; for thy light is come, and the glory of the Lord is risen upon thee" (Isa. 60:1); when the pronouncement was made, "The Lord God will cause righteousness and praise to spring forth before all the nations" (Isa. 61:11); when the divine word shall say, "Lift up a standard for the people," and the call shall go forth "unto the end of the world, . . . Behold, thy salvation cometh" (Isa. 62:10-11)—when all these and many like pronouncements were and shall be made, be it known that they all refer to the Lord's great latter-day work of restoration. His purposes were known to his ancient friends.

When the Lord promised to reveal unto scattered Israel "the abundance of peace and truth" (Jer. 33:6), and when he said, "I will give them one heart, and I will put a new spirit within you . . . That they may walk in my statutes, and keep mine ordinances, and do them" (Ezek. 11:17-20)—when all this comes to pass, it will be in and through and because of the restored gospel. His statutes, his laws, and his ordinances make up the gospel. Through them men are born again and receive a new spirit.

Among the Book of Mormon prophets, the word relative to the restoration of the gospel came with that clarity and perfectness for which the Nephite record is renowned. To illustrate: "I will be merciful unto the Gentiles," the Lord told Nephi, for, in the last days, "I will bring forth unto them, in mine own power, much of my gospel, which shall be plain and precious." (1 Ne. 13:34.) Much of the gospel as here used means the fulness of the gospel as we use the term. We have the fulness of the gospel, meaning we have all of the powers and sufficient of the doctrines to enable us to gain a fulness of salvation. We do not have all of the truths and doctrines possessed by the Nephites in their golden era.

One added illustration will suffice. An angel, speaking in the name of the Lord, as prophets on both sides of the veil are wont to do, said to Nephi: "For the time cometh, saith the Lamb of God, that I will work a great and marvelous work among the children of men; a work which shall be everlasting, either on the one hand or on the other—either to the convincing of them unto peace and life eternal, or unto the deliverance of them to the hardness of their hearts and the blindness of their minds unto their being brought down into captivity, and also into destruction, both temporally and spiritually, according to the captivity of the devil." (1 Ne. 14:7.) The gospel saves and the gospel damns. It saves those who believe and obey; it damns those who reject it and continue to walk in carnal ways. It is the standard by which all men, both the great and the small, shall be judged. And thus it is.

THE DISPENSATION OF THE FULNESS OF TIMES

Elias Restores the Truths and Doctrines

Let us reason by way of analogy. Let us personify two of the greatest events of history. Let us thereby show the relationship that exists between the "times of restitution" and "the dispensation of the fulness of times."

The "times of restitution" has, as it were, a close friend, a relative, someone begotten by the same father, carried in the same womb, and born in the same family. His name is "the dispensation of the fulness of times." These two are not identical twins, but they are brothers in a closely knit family. The times of restitution was born first; he came to prepare the way for his younger brother, the dispensation of the fulness of times. With this second son came the greater power and glory. In his hands we find the fulness of the everlasting gospel, which itself is the power of God unto salvation.

These twain were born in the household of faith, and their names were selected by revelation. The times of restitution is so named because he is the age of restoration, the age in which God has promised to restore all things, all truths, all powers, all that he hath spoken by the mouth of all his holy prophets since the world began, all this and more. It is the age in which the Lord designs to restore the earth itself to its primeval and paradisiacal state. The dispensation of the fulness of times gains his divine name because he is the dispensation of the fulness of dispensations, or the time of the fulness of times, or the gospel age in which every truth and every power possessed in any dispensation of the past shall be restored.

The times of restitution is a special friend of Peter. Indeed, we heard the Chief Apostle say that the Lord Jesus, who has all power, must remain in heaven and cannot return in glory to reign mightily among his saints, until after this age of restoration commences. The dispensation of the fulness of times developed an especial fondness for Paul, and the Apostle to the Gentiles prophesied about him. Among other things, he said that "the God and Father of our Lord Jesus Christ" has "made known unto us the mystery of his will, according to his good pleasure which he hath purposed in himself." The "mystery of his will," his strange act, the glorious events reserved by him to take place in the last days are these: "That in the dispensation of the fulness of times he might gather together in one all things in Christ, both which are in heaven, and which are on earth; even in him." (Eph. 1:3, 9-10.)

All things! O how glorious is the promise! Already the heavens have been rent and the saving truths of the gospel are with men. However dark it may be among the cults of men and in the halls where false doctrines are taught, the light of heaven shines in the hearts of the saints. And the promised outpouring of divine truth has scarcely begun. To his saints who have made everlasting covenant with him, to the faithful who have received the gift of the Holy Ghost, to all those who love and serve him "in righteousness and in truth," the promises are infinite and eternal. "To them will I reveal all mysteries, yea, all the hidden mysteries of my kingdom from days of old," the Lord says, "and for ages to come, will I make known unto them the good pleasure of my will concerning all things pertaining to my kingdom." How glorious is this word!

Of them the heavenly Voice acclaims: "Yea, even the wonders of eternity shall they know, and things to come will I show them, even the things of many generations. And their wisdom shall be great, and their understanding reach to heaven; and before them the wisdom of the wise shall perish, and the understanding of the prudent shall come to naught."

How can all this be? The Lord continues: "For by my Spirit will I enlighten them, and by my power will I make known unto them the secrets of my will—yea, even those things which eye has not seen, nor ear heard, nor yet entered into the heart of man." (D&C 76:5-10.) Truly, the things of God are known only by the power of his Spirit!

When shall all this be? To his saints the divine word is: "God shall give unto you knowledge by his Holy Spirit, yea, by the unspeakable gift of the Holy Ghost"—note it well, knowledge "that has not been revealed since the world was until now." It shall be knowledge "which our forefathers have awaited with anxious expectation to be revealed in the last times." It shall be knowledge "which their minds were pointed to by the angels, as held in reserve for the fulness of their glory." It is destined to be revealed in "a time to come in the which nothing shall be withheld, whether there be one God or many gods, they shall be manifest. All thrones and dominions, principalities and powers, shall be revealed and set forth upon all who have endured valiantly for the gospel of Jesus Christ."

Nor is even this all. The divine word continues: "And also, if there be bounds set to the heavens or to the seas, or to the dry land, or to the sun, moon, or stars—All the times of their revolutions, all the appointed days, months, and years, and all their glories, laws, and set times, shall be revealed in the days of the dispensation of the fulness of times—According to that which was ordained in the midst of the Council of the Eternal God of all other gods before this world was, that should be reserved unto the finishing and the end thereof, when every man shall enter into his eternal presence and into his immortal rest." (D&C 121:26-32.)

"And not only this, but those things which never have been revealed from the foundation of the world, but have been kept hid from the wise and prudent, shall be revealed unto babes and sucklings in this, the dispensation of the fulness of times." (D&C 128:18.) "For I deign to reveal unto my church," the Lord says, "things which have been kept hid from before the foundation of the world, things that pertain to the dispensation of the fulness of times." (D&C 124:41.)

The door to the dispensation of the fulness of times was opened in the spring of 1820 when the Father and the Son appeared to Joseph Smith, and it will not be closed until "the Lord shall come" and "reveal all things." (D&C 101:32.) On that glorious spring morning, traditionally believed to be the sixth of April, the Gods of heaven revealed themselves again. "I saw a pillar of light exactly over my head, above the brightness of the sun, which descended gradually until it fell upon me," the Lord's great latter-day prophet tells us. "When the light rested upon me I saw two Personages, whose brightness and glory defy all description, standing above me in the air. One of them spake unto me, calling me by name and said, pointing to the other—*This is My Beloved Son. Hear Him!*"

From them, by the mouth of the Son, the word came that all the churches were wrong; "that all their creeds were an abomination in his sight"; that the ministers of religion "were all corrupt"; and that the worship of the day had "a form of godliness," but not "the power" to save a human soul. (JS-H 1:16-19.)

Thus, as the door of the dispensation opened, revelation commenced anew; the musty creeds of a creaking Christendom were swept aside; the Father and the Son were seen as personal beings in whose image man is made; the fact of universal apostasy was confirmed; and a promise was given that the fulness of the everlasting gospel would soon be restored through Joseph Smith. From that dawning day, the light of truth has grown brighter and brighter, and before the dispensation ends it will be as when the sun shines in its strength.

In due course the Book of Mormon came forth and the unsealed portion was translated and published to bring salvation to all those who will believe it and the testimony it bears of Him by whom salvation comes. Many revelations came through the prophet and seer of our day, of whom the Lord said: "Thou shalt give heed unto all his words and commandments which he shall give unto you as he receiveth them, walking in all holiness before me; for his word ye shall receive, as if from mine own mouth, in all patience and faith." (D&C 21:4-5.)

A portion of the Lord's word that came through Joseph Smith and that has been partially ignored by many Latter-day Saints is found in the revisions he made by the spirit of revelation in the Bible itself. He prepared his New Translation for publication in his day, but the power of evil was so great, and the persecutions and drivings of the saints were so extensive and severe, that the work as then prepared did not come forth in that day. We have since published in the Pearl of Great Price the portions known as the Book of Moses and as the 24th chapter of Matthew. In 1979 the Church also published in the footnotes and appendix of their official Bible many of the major changes. There will, of course, be a future day when added revisions, made with prophetic power, will become part of the Stick of Judah.

In this connection, be it also remembered that the brass plates that Nephi took from Jerusalem contain more of the word of the Lord for the comparable period than does our present Old Testament. They, of course, will also come forth in due time as part of the restoration of all things. Indeed, Lehi prophesied "that these plates of brass should go forth unto all nations, kindreds, tongues, and people who were of his seed. Wherefore, he said that these plates of brass should never perish; neither should they be dimmed any more by time." (1 Ne. 5:18-19.)

Without any question, however, the scripture that is yet to come forth, which will reveal more of the mind and will and purposes of the Lord than any other, is the sealed portion of the Book of Mormon. Moroni says that "there never were greater things made manifest than those which were made manifest unto the brother of Jared." All of these things are recorded in the sealed portion of the book. Of them, the Lord said to Moroni: "They shall not go forth unto the Gentiles until the day that they shall repent of their iniquity, and become clean before the Lord. And in that day that they shall exercise faith in me, saith the Lord, even as the brother of Jared did, that they may become sanctified in me, then will I manifest unto them the things which the brother of Jared saw, even to the unfolding unto them all my revelations, saith Jesus Christ, the Son of God, the Father of the heavens and of the earth, and all things that in them are." (Ether 4:4-7.)

Nephi spoke similarly. He said: "The book shall be sealed; and in the book shall be a revelation from God, from the beginning of the world to the ending thereof. Wherefore, because of the things which are sealed up, the things which are sealed shall not be delivered in the day of the wickedness and abominations of the people. Wherefore the book shall be kept from them."

And further: "The book shall be sealed by the power of God, and the revelation which was sealed shall be kept in the book until the own due time of the Lord, that they may come forth; for behold, they reveal all things from the foundation of the world unto the end thereof." This causes us to ask: How would the worldly-wise react if they learned from the book the falsity of their evolutionary theories and how damning their views are about the creation of the world? How would they react if they found detailed prophecies about Joseph Smith and the dispensation in which we live? What if men found in them the mysteries of the kingdom that are revealed in the temples? Would the Lord thus be casting pearls before swine? Our present revelations do, of course, have many allusions to things that are most assuredly set forth extensively and with clarity in the sealed scriptures.

It seems apparent, under all the circumstances, that the sealed portion of the Book of Mormon will not come forth until after the Lord Jesus comes. Nephi's prophetic word is: "And the day cometh that the words of the book which were sealed shall be read upon the house tops; and they shall be read by the power of Christ; and all things shall be revealed unto the children of men which ever have been among the children of men, and which ever will be even unto the end of the earth." (2 Ne. 27:7-11.)

To those who suppose they believe the Bible but who do not now believe and accept all that the Lord has given to the world, we simply quote what he has to say on the subject: "Wherefore murmur ye, because that ye shall receive more of my word?" (2 Ne. 29:8.) Can men know too much of the mind and will and purposes of their God?

And to those who do not seek for added light and knowledge from on high, our sorrowful word is: From you shall be taken away even that which ye have received.

Elias Restores the Powers and Priesthoods

When the prophetic word calls for the restoration of the fulness of the everlasting gospel in the last days, such includes the restoration of the power and keys and priesthoods that were part and portion of that eternal plan of salvation. The gospel fulness cannot be restored if a vital part is left out.

When the promise is made that Elias must return before the Second Coming and restore all things, that restoration of necessity includes the conferral again upon mortal men of every priesthood held anciently; of every divine and eternal commission ever given to the prophets of old; of the keys of the kingdom, the holy apostleship, and the power to bind on earth and have it sealed everlastingly in the heavens.

If ours is the dispensation in which God has promised to "gather together in one all things in Christ," if this includes "all things . . . which are in heaven, and which are on earth" (Eph. 1:10), and if the priesthood is in heaven and men are on earth, then these two must come together again. Angelic ministrants must bring back the ancient powers.

If "the Holy Priesthood . . . continueth in the church of God in all generations, and is without beginning of days or end of years," and if "this greater priesthood administereth the gospel and holdeth the key of the mysteries of the kingdom" (D&C 84:6, 17-19), then that priesthood must accompany the restoration of the eternal truths comprising the gospel. Otherwise, who would administer the Lord's work on earth, and how would his earthly kingdom be governed? The Lord's house is a house of order and not a house of confusion. Unless there are legal administrators to identify and proclaim his gospel and to govern and control all of his affairs, there would be anarchy.

If, as Paul reasoned, the law of Moses was administered by the lesser priesthood; if the divine word called for Christ and others, coming after Moses and the law, to minister in the greater priesthood; and if, "the priesthood being changed, there is made of necessity a change also of the law" (Heb. 7:12), it follows that the Lord's affairs on earth, in all generations, must be administered by those holding power and authority.

The Aaronic Priesthood administers the law of Moses; the Melchizedek Priesthood, always and everlastingly, administers the gospel. It cannot be otherwise. Thus, if the gospel comes again, the priesthood must come also; otherwise, the revealed system would not be the true gospel, and even if it were, there would be none to administer its affairs on earth.

Thus, none can escape this conclusion: When God Almighty restores the fulness of his everlasting gospel, he restores also the fulness of his everlasting priesthood.

Priesthood is the power and authority of God delegated to man on earth to act in all things for the salvation of men. The keys of the priesthood and of the kingdom are the right of presidency; they are the right to direct the manner in which others use their priesthood; they are the right to preside over and govern all the affairs of the Church, which is the kingdom; they are the right, power, and responsibility to use the priesthood to do all things necessary to save and exalt fallen man, and to carry out all of the purposes of the Lord on earth.

All this being true, we should expect the ancient prophets, as they prophesied of the restoration of the gospel, also to speak of the legal administrators who are destined to administer the Lord's affairs in the last days. And such is the case.

In the last days, when "Zion shall be redeemed with judgment, and her converts with righteousness," the Lord promised Israel: "I will restore thy judges as at the first, and thy counsellers as at the beginning." (Isa. 1:26-27.) Those who serve as bishops are common judges in Israel, and they labor "among the inhabitants of Zion." (D&C 107:74.) "Counsellers" are other priesthood leaders who guide the destinies of the Lord's people.

In the age of restoration the cry shall go forth: "Awake, awake; put on thy strength, O Zion; put on thy beautiful garments, O Jerusalem, the holy city." (Isa. 52:1.) And in answer to the question "What people had Isaiah reference to" in this passage, the Prophet said: "He had reference to those whom God should call in the last days, who should hold the power of priesthood to bring again Zion, and the redemption of Israel; and to put on her strength is to put on the authority of the priesthood, which she, Zion, has a right to by lineage; also to return to that power which she had lost." (D&C 113:7-8.)

These priesthood brethren "shall build the old wastes, they shall raise up the former desolations, and they shall repair the waste cities, the desolations of many generations." Of them the prophetic word acclaims: "Ye shall be named the Priests of the Lord: men shall call you the Ministers of our God." (Isa. 61:4-6.) "They shall declare my glory among the Gentiles," the Lord says. They shall gather Israel, "And I will also take of them for priests and for Levites, saith the Lord." (Isa. 66:19-21.) Through Jeremiah the Lord said of gathered Israel: "And I will set up shepherds over them which shall feed them." (Jer. 23:4.) And the promise is that when the Lord comes, "he shall purify the sons of Levi, and purge them as gold and silver, that they may offer unto the Lord an offering in righteousness." (Mal. 3:3.)

The dispensation of the fulness of times is the greatest of all the dispensations. In it the gospel shall be preached to more people than in all previous dispensations combined. In it the saving ordinances will be performed for the endless hosts of men who lived without a true knowledge of Christ and his saving truths. In it Israel shall be gathered and a people prepared for our Lord's return.

This dispensation of restoration and glory now has all of the power and authority ever possessed by any people in any age. It shall receive in due course all of the light and truth ever revealed. It may be pictured as a great ocean into which all the dispensation-rivers of the past flow. Representatives have come from each of the great biblical dispensations to restore the keys and powers they possessed. It is of them that we shall now speak. Each of them played his part in the restoration of all things, and each, in this sense, came as the Elias of the Restoration.

John the Baptist, our Lord's Elias, came first. On May 15, 1829, he descended from the courts of glory, laid his hands upon

Joseph Smith and Olivery Cowdery, and said: "Upon you my fellow servants, in the name of Messiah I confer the Priesthood of Aaron, which holds the keys of the ministering of angels, and of the gospel of repentance, and of baptism by immersion for the remission of sins; and this shall never be taken again from the earth, until the sons of Levi do offer again an offering unto the Lord in righteousness." (D&C 13.)

Thus mortal men received both the lesser priesthood and the keys that go with it. They received an endowment of heavenly power, together with the right to use it for the benefit and blessing of their fellowmen. They could now begin to preach the gospel; they could baptize for the remission of sins; but they could not confer the gift of the Holy Ghost. In due course, by the authority they then received, the sons of Levi will offer again their sacrificial performances before the Lord, as Malachi promised.

Shortly thereafter the First Presidency of the Church as it existed in the meridian of time also visited Joseph and Oliver and conferred priesthood and keys upon them. In specifying the mission they performed, the Lord says: "Peter, and James, and John, whom I have sent unto you, by whom I have ordained you and confirmed you to be apostles, and especial witnesses of my name, and bear the keys of your ministry and of the same things which I revealed unto them; Unto whom I have committed the keys of my kingdom, and a dispensation of the gospel for the last times; and for the fulness of times, in the which I will gather together in one all things, both which are in heaven, and which are on earth." (D&C 27:12-13.)

Referring to this glorious visitation, Joseph Smith testifies: "Peter, James, and John [came] in the wilderness between Harmony, Susquehanna county, and Colesville, Broome county, on the Susquehanna river, declaring themselves as possessing the keys of the kingdom, and of the dispensation of the fulness of times." (D&C 128:20.)

What did these ancient apostles restore? They brought back the Melchizedek Priesthood, which administers the gospel and governs the Church and includes the holy apostleship. They conferred the keys of the kingdom and the keys of the dispensation of the fulness of times. As a result, the Church was organized again among men on April 6, 1830. They restored the apostolic commission to go into all the world and preach the gospel with signs following those who believe.

Three ancient prophets came on April 3, 1836, to Joseph Smith and Oliver Cowdery in the Kirtland Temple. Moses committed unto them "the keys of the gathering of Israel from the four parts of the earth, and the leading of the ten tribes from the land of the north." Thus the priesthood was to be used for those purposes.

Elias "committed the dispensation of the gospel of Abraham, saying that in us and our seed all generations after us should be blessed." That is, he brought back the authorization to use the priesthood to perfect eternal family units, even as this commission and covenant was had by Abraham and those who followed after him.

Then Elijah came and restored the sealing power, the power that binds on earth and seals in heaven, the power by which all ordinances have efficacy beyond the grave, the power that turns the hearts of children to their fathers and fathers to their children. It is a power that operates for the living and the dead. (D&C 110:11-16.)

Gabriel who is Noah also came. He "committed the keys of bringing to pass the restoration of all things." (D&C 27:6.) We assume that the continents were divided, beginning in his day, and that he also brought back the power by which the great deep will be commanded to return to its own place in the north so that the islands will become one land again. (D&C 133:23.)

Raphael, whom we assume to have been Enoch or someone from his dispensation, came and committed such keys as appertained to that day. No doubt these included the power to use the priesthood to translate men, as will be the state of all those who abide the day of the Second Coming.

Michael who is Adam came. The keys he brought are not named. But we know he was the presiding high priest over all the earth and that he held the keys of creation and participated in the creation of this earth. We suppose these are the rights and powers he restored. The holy priesthood will be used in eternity as well as in time. It is not only the power and authority to save men here and now; it is also the power by which the worlds were made and by which all things are. It also could well be that Adam, who brought mortality and death into the world, was also permitted to restore the power that brings immortality and life to his descendants. Christ, of course, in the ultimate sense holds the keys of the resurrection and of raising souls in immortality, but, as we also know, it is his practice to operate through his servants, and righteous persons will, in due course, participate in calling their loved ones forth in the resurrection.

These holy angels whom we have named, all taken together, are the Elias of the Restoration. It took all of them to bring to pass the restoration of all the keys and powers and authorities needed to save and exalt man. "For it is necessary in the ushering in of the dispensation of the fulness of times, which dispensation is now beginning to usher in," the Prophet Joseph Smith says, "that a whole and complete and perfect union, and welding together of dispensations, and keys, and powers, and glories should take place, and be revealed from the days of Adam even to the present time." (D&C 128:18.)

All of the keys, powers, and authorities conferred by holy angels upon Joseph Smith and others have been given to each person called to the holy apostleship and set apart to serve in the Council of the Twelve of The Church of Jesus Christ of Latter-day Saints. "For unto you, the Twelve, and those, the First Presidency, who are appointed with you to be your counselors and your leaders, is the power of this priesthood given," the Lord says, "for the last days and for the last time, in the which is the dispensation of the fulness of times. Which power you hold, in connection with all those who have received a dispensation at any time from the beginning of the creation; for verily I say unto you, the keys of the dispensation, which ye have received, have come down from the fathers, and last of all, being sent down from heaven unto you." (D&C 112:30-32.)

And thus it is that there are many now on earth—including all who have received the fulness of the priesthood and who are magnifying their callings therein—to whom this word comes from the

Lord: "Ye are lawful heirs, according to the flesh, and have been hid from the world with Christ in God—Therefore your life and the priesthood have remained, and must needs remain through you and your lineage until the restoration of all things spoken by the mouths of all the holy prophets since the world began. Therefore, blessed are ye if ye continue in my goodness, a light unto the Gentiles, and through this priesthood, a savior unto my people Israel. The Lord hath said it." (D&C 86:9-11.)

THE CHURCH IN THE LAST DAYS

The Eternal Church

How little the world knows about the Church, the eternal Church, the Church of the living God! How microscopic is the knowledge of most men as to the Church which administers the gospel, the Church by which salvation comes, the Church through which the Lord Omnipotent regulates all his affairs in all worlds and throughout all eternity!

Even the saints ofttimes see only small struggling congregations—a few faithful souls here and a few there, encompassed by the evils of the world—and they wonder how the Church will survive and what destiny it has. What are even a few million humble followers of the Lamb as compared to billions of unbelievers? How can these few withstand the combined powers and pressures of communism and Islam, of Buddhism and Confucianism, and of all the sects of a worldly Christendom? How can they preserve their integrity and ways of worship in the face of atheism and infidelity and organized crime, and when subject to governmental controls of education and of employment and of families? How will they escape the pestilence and plagues and wars that a wicked world brings upon itself?

If we are to envision what is involved in the Second Coming of the Son of Man, we must know the place and mission of the Church in the eternal scheme of things. We must know why and by what power it has been restored. We must know that there is no single organization that will have as much influence for good upon men and nations in our day as will that church which the Lord has set up anew to be a light to the world and "a standard for the nations." (D&C 115:5.)

The Church on earth is patterned after the Church in heaven, where God himself is its President, Lawgiver, and King. The Church there is the administrative agency through which the Almighty governs the universe. Members of the earthly Church "who overcome by faith" shall be members of "the church of the Firstborn" in the highest heaven of the celestial world. (D&C 76:53-54.) Such persons, however, need not await that celestial day to gain a perfect knowledge of God and his heavenly kingdom. Through "the power and authority of the higher, or Melchizedek Priesthood," they "have the privilege of receiving the mysteries of the kingdom of heaven, to have the heavens opened unto them, to commune with the general assembly and church of the Firstborn, and to enjoy the communion and presence of God the Father, and Jesus the mediator of the new covenant." (D&C 107:18-19.)

Our gracious God gave his church to Adam, the first man of all men. It was an earthly church patterned after its parent in heaven. It was an earthly kingdom designed to prepare men to return to their heavenly home. The Church as we have it is the kingdom of God on earth; those who make themselves worthy of all its blessings here and now will be inheritors of all its blessings in the kingdom of God hereafter.

The Melchizedek Priesthood "continueth in the church of God in all generations" (D&C 84:17), which is to say that whenever and wherever men have the Melchizedek Priesthood, there is the Church and kingdom of God on earth. Conversely, when and where there is no Melchizedek Priesthood, there is no true Church and no earthly kingdom which is the Lord's, and consequently, no way to prepare men to go to the eternal church in heaven. The purpose of the Church on earth is to prepare men for membership in the eternal Church in heaven.

The priesthood is God's power, and it administers the gospel; the gospel is the plan of salvation; the Church is an organized body of believers who have the gospel. The purpose of the Church is to make salvation available to men through the gospel and by the power of the priesthood.

Adam, Seth, Enos, Cainan, Mahalaleel, Jared, Enoch, Methuselah, Lamech, and Noah all held presiding positions in the Church in their days. They were all righteous high priests. So also was it with Shem and Melchizedek—for whom "the church, in ancient days" (D&C 107:4) named the priesthood—and with Abraham, Isaac, and Jacob. The congregations of Israel were the congregations of the Church in their day. Isaiah, Jeremiah, Ezekiel, Daniel, and all the holy prophets prized their membership in the Lord's earthly kingdom and have gone on to receive their inheritances in his heavenly kingdom. Nephi speaks of "the brethren of the church" (1 Ne. 4:26) near the year 600 B.C., and the Church as such was established among the Nephites whenever they were faithful enough to receive it.

Our conclusion: The Church is eternal. Priesthood is eternal. Keys are eternal. Apostolic power is eternal. And all of these have been, are now, and always will be found together whenever the true Church is on earth. With this understanding, we are ready to view the setting up anew of the Church on earth as a prelude to the Second Coming of Him whose witnesses we are.

Elias Restores the Church and Kingdom

When the ancient revelations foretell the restoration of the gospel in that day of darkness preceding the return of the Eternal Light, they are speaking also of the setting up anew among men of the true Church and kingdom of God on earth. The gospel and the priesthood and the Church go together. They are one in spirit and purpose. All that we have said about the restoration of the gospel in the last days and about the giving again of power and keys to mortals applies also to the organizing again of the Church on earth. To all this let us now append a few prophetic words that speak of the restoration of the Church and kingdom as such.

In one of the most abused and misinterpreted passages in the whole Bible, Jesus promised to give Peter certain keys and powers, which would enable the ancient apostle to build up the Church and kingdom in the meridian of time. The apostolic party was near Caesarea Philippi, up north of the Sea of Galilee and near Mount Hermon, at the time. Jesus asked: "Whom do men say that I the Son of man am?" He was told of the various views of Herod Antipas and the priests and the people. "But whom say ye that I am?" he queried. Peter, being moved upon by the Holy Ghost, and receiving utterance by the power of the Spirit, testified: "Thou art the Christ, the Son of the living God."

Jesus commended and blessed Peter for his witness. "Flesh and blood hath not revealed it unto thee, but my Father which is in heaven," he said, "and upon this rock"—the rock of revelation—"I will build my church; and the gates of hell shall not prevail against it." Then came what to the world is an enigmatic promise: "And I will give unto thee the keys of the kingdom of heaven: and whatsoever thou shalt bind on earth shall be bound in heaven: and whatsoever thou shalt loose on earth shall be loosed in heaven." (Matt. 16:13-19.)

These keys, as we are aware, are the right and power to preside over the kingdom which is the Church. They enable the legal administrators who hold them to perform the ordinances of salvation so they will be binding on earth and sealed in heaven. Unless, for instance, a baptism performed on earth has efficacy and force in heaven, it will not admit the penitent person into the eternal heaven, which his soul desires. These sealing keys were, in fact, given to Peter, James, and John about a week later, when they climbed nearby Mount Hermon to meet with Moses and Elijah and to participate in the glory of the Transfiguration. Later they were given to all of the Twelve, so that all had the power to bind and loose both on earth and in heaven. (Matt. 18:18.)

And as we have heretofore recited, Peter, James, and John restored their keys and powers and their apostolic commission to Joseph Smith and Oliver Cowdery, thereby enabling them to organize the same church and kingdom that Peter and the apostles presided over in their day. The initial organization took place on April 6, 1830, with the perfecting of the kingdom coming as added keys were received from heavenly ministrants and as the growth of the work warranted.

There are many false churches, but there can be only one true

Church. There are many false gospels, false prophets, and false Christs, but there can be only one true system of religion, only one gospel that has power to save and exalt fallen man. Christ is not divided; truth is not at variance with itself; conflicting doctrines and ordinances cannot all be right. The Divine Voice in the spring of 1820 said of all the sects of men: 'They are all wrong.' (JS-H 1:19.) After he had restored his own church, "The Church of Jesus Christ of Latter-day Saints" (D&C 115:4), he called it "the only true and living church upon the face of the whole earth." (D&C 1:30.)

His great latter-day proclamation was: "If this generation harden not their hearts, I will establish my church among them." And establish it he did! And how comforting are his words: "Whosoever belongeth to my church need not fear, for such shall inherit the kingdom of heaven," if, of course, they keep the commandments. "But it is they who do not fear me, neither keep my commandments but build up churches unto themselves to get gain, yea, and all those that do wickedly and build up the kingdom of the devil—yea, verily, verily, I say unto you, that it is they that I will disturb, and cause to tremble and shake to the center."

His church will have his gospel. "Behold, this is my doctrine —whosoever repenteth and cometh unto me, the same is my church. Whosoever declareth more or less than this, the same is not of me, but is against me; therefore he is not of my church." Men either come to the true Church and sustain it and all its views and teachings or they are not of God. Only those who are of God and of his church shall be saved.

"And now, behold, whosoever is of my church," saith the Lord, "and endureth of my church to the end, him will I establish upon my rock, and the gates of hell shall not prevail against them." (D&C 10:53-56, 67-69.)

The Lord's rock is his gospel. He commands all those who are established thereon to proclaim his message, saying: "Repent, repent, and prepare ye the way of the Lord, and make his paths straight; for the kingdom of heaven is at hand; yea, repent and be baptized, every one of you, for a remission of your sins; yea, be baptized even by water, and then cometh the baptism of fire and of the Holy Ghost."

Such is his message of salvation to all men. Of it he says, "Behold, verily, verily, I say unto you, this is my gospel; and remember that they shall have faith in me or they can in nowise be saved; and upon this rock I will build my church; yea, upon this rock ye are built, and if ye continue, the gates of hell shall not prevail against you." (D&C 33:10-13.) The true Church is built upon the rock of his gospel, upon the rock of faith in the Lord Jesus Christ, upon the rock of personal revelation, which, coming by the power of the Holy Ghost, reveals that he is the Son of the living God, who was crucified for the sins of the world.

The Latter-day Kingdom of the God of Heaven

There is scarcely a more dramatic account in ancient writ than the interpretation by Daniel the prophet of the dream of Nebuchadnezzar the king. Daniel and the children of Judah were in captivity in Babylon, in bondage to Gentile overlords who were evil and wicked and merciless. So vile and carnal were the Babylonians, so corrupt and evil was their nation, so filled with the power of Satan were their priests and religionists, that from then until now, the very name Babylon has caused the prophetic mind to wince with horror. Indeed, it has become the prophetic symbol for all that is evil and antichrist in the world, and for all that comes from Satan. Babylon is the world; Babylon is the church of the devil; Babylon is all that is evil and degenerate and vile on this benighted globe. And Babylon in that day ruled the world.

And so, it was into this dark hell of hatred, into this place of persecution for the Lord's people, into this realm where naught but evil reigned and where Satan was worshipped, that the Lord Jehovah chose to send a few rays of heavenly light that would ease the burdens of his people. To Nebuchadnezzar there came a dream—call it the dream of dreams, if you will, for it forecast God's dealings with nations and kingdoms for the next two and a half millenniums. Out of it came some surcease from toil and trouble for the Jewish exiles in Babylon, because the king made

Daniel "ruler over the whole province of Babylon, and chief of the governors over all the wise men of Babylon." (Dan. 2:48.)

Nebuchadnezzar first dreamed his dream of awful import—shall we not say it was a vision?—and then the remembrance of the thing was taken from him. Troubled in spirit, he called upon the magicians, astrologers, sorcerers, and Chaldeans to reveal and then interpret his dream. If they could tell him the dream, he would then believe their interpretation. Their failure was predestined, and the king in anger commanded that they and all the wise men of Babylon be cut in pieces and their houses made into a dunghill. When the soldiers came to slay Daniel and his fellows, the prophet persuaded the captain of the king's guard to give him time and he would make the interpretation. The secret was then revealed to Daniel in a night vision.

Taken before the king, Daniel said: "The secret which the king hath demanded cannot the wise men, the astrologers, the magicians, the soothsayers, shew unto the king." Their power was from beneath; they were servants of Satan; their religion was not founded on the rock of revelation; visions and the things of the Spirit were far from them. "But there is a God in heaven that revealeth secrets," Daniel said, "and [he] maketh known to the king Nebuchadnezzar what shall be in the latter days."

The dream and its meaning pertain to our day, "the latter days," the days just preceding the Second Coming of Him who gave the dream. "Thy dream, and the visions of thy head upon thy bed, are these; As for thee, O king," Daniel said, "thy thoughts came into thy mind upon thy bed, what should come to pass hereafter: and he that revealeth secrets maketh known to thee what shall come to pass."

Standing in the most awesome mortal presence then on earth, speaking boldly before all of the imperial court, relying upon prophetic insight and seeric assurance, Daniel then gave forth the divine word: "Thou, O king, sawest, and behold a great image." Doubt is absent; Daniel knows. "This great image, whose brightness was excellent, stood before thee; and the form thereof was terrible." No artist has yet gained the inspiration to paint the terrible form nor the awesome visage of this great image, nor do we suppose that mortal skill could record on canvas what the Lord placed first in the mind of the wicked king and then in the heart of the righteous prophet. Providentially we have a few descriptive words from that prophet, the prophet in whose presence even the roaring lions closed their mouths.

"This image's head was of fine gold," Daniel continued, "his breast and his arms of silver, his belly and his thighs of brass, his legs of iron, his feet part of iron and part of clay." Such was the wondrous image chosen by divine wisdom to represent the successive and great kingdoms of men. Looking back we can identify with ease the respective earthly powers whose periods of supremacy were molded and sculptured into the terrible image.

"Thou, O king, art a king of kings: for the God of heaven hath given thee a kingdom, power, and strength, and glory," Daniel said to Nebuchadnezzar. "And wheresoever the children of men dwell, the beasts of the field and the fowls of the heaven hath he given into thine hand, and hath made thee ruler over them all. Thou art this head of gold." Babylonia was indeed the first world-kingdom. She held sway from about 605 to 538 B.C., with Nebuchadnezzar's prosperous reign lasting from about 606 to 562 B.C. His voice was as the voice of God to the millions who trembled at his word. His armies traversed the earth, conquered kingdoms, and transported whole nations from one land to another by the sharpness of their swords and the piercing power of their spears. On the roof of his vast palace in Babylon were the famous hanging gardens, ranked as one of the Seven Wonders of the World.

"And after thee shall arise another kingdom inferior to thee," Daniel told Nebuchadnezzar, "and another third kingdom of brass, which shall bear rule over all the earth." These kingdoms are the Medo-Persian or second world-kingdoms, whose dominion prevailed from about 538 to 333 B.C. and the Grecian powers that prevailed beginning with the conquest of the Persian Empire by Alexander the Great in 332 B.C.

"And the fourth kingdom shall be strong as iron: forasmuch as iron breaketh in pieces and subdueth all things: and as iron that breaketh all these, shall it break in pieces and bruise." Here we see the powers of Rome, beginning with the Caesars, particularly

Augustus, who ruled when the Lord Jesus was born, and continuing until the first barbarian king ruled in Italy in A.D. 476. The two legs of iron symbolize perfectly the division into an eastern and a western Roman Empire, with Constantine the Great (in whose day the Nicene Creed was written) establishing a new capital at Byzantium and giving it the new name of Constantinople (now Istanbul).

"And whereas thou sawest the feet and toes, part of potters' clay, and part of iron, the kingdom shall be divided; but there shall be in it of the strength of the iron, forasmuch as thou sawest the iron mixed with miry clay. And as the toes of the feet were part of iron, and part of clay, so the kingdom shall be partly strong, and partly broken. And whereas thou sawest iron mixed with miry clay, they shall mingle themselves with the seed of men: but they shall not cleave one to another, even as iron is not mixed with clay." Clearly these are the numerous, divided, warring kingdoms—some strong, others weak—that grew out of the mighty Roman Empire. That they did not "cleave one to another" has resulted in the death and misery of many people during the long ages from the fall of Rome to the day of restoration with which the dream is now prepared to concern itself.

Having thus described the terrible image, Daniel tells the king: "Thou sawest till that a stone was cut out without hands, which smote the image upon his feet that were of iron and clay, and brake them to pieces. Then was the iron, the clay, the brass, the silver, and the gold, broken to pieces together, and became like the chaff of the summer threshingfloor; and the wind carried them away, that no place was found for them: and the stone that smote the image became a great mountain, and filled the whole earth."

By way of interpretation, Daniel's divine word is: "And in the days of these kings"—those of divers sorts, powers, and strengths, which grew out of the Roman Empire—"shall the God of heaven set up a kingdom, which shall never be destroyed: and the kingdom shall not be left to other people, but it shall break in pieces and consume all these kingdoms, and it shall stand for ever. Forasmuch as thou sawest that the stone was cut out of the mountain without hands, and that it brake in pieces the iron, the brass, the clay, the silver, and the gold; the great God hath made known to the king what shall come to pass hereafter: and the dream is certain, and the interpretation thereof sure." (Dan. 2:27-45.)

How wondrous are the ways of the Lord! How glorious are the mysteries of this kingdom! And how sweet is the word he sends by dreams and visions and seeric interpretations! Here we have seen the kingdoms of this world, kingdoms drenched in blood and held together by the arm of flesh, one following another until the set time for the great latter-day restoration of all things. Then a stone is cut out of the mountain without hands and a kingdom is set up by the God of heaven. It is a new kind of kingdom. The arm of flesh plays no part in its creation. It is created without man's hand. It comes from God. It is established by revelation. It is the Church and kingdom of God on earth.

And it grows until it fills the whole earth, until the knowledge of God covers the earth as the waters cover the sea, until every living soul on earth is converted. And what of the other kingdoms? This eternal kingdom, this kingdom which shall never be destroyed, this kingdom which is the new and everlasting kingdom, shall break in pieces and consume all kingdoms. It shall make a full end of all nations; they shall vanish as the chaff before the summer breeze and shall not be found on earth. And the new kingdom shall not be left to any other people; never again will there be a general apostasy; the Church of the God of heaven will be set up on earth to stand forever. Thus saith Daniel. Thus saith the Lord. "And the dream is certain, and the interpretation thereof sure." (Dan. 2:45.)

This kingdom was set up on April 6, 1830, by revelation and commandment from on high. It is "called by a new name, which the mouth of the Lord" has named. (Isa. 62:2.) For, as the prophets foretold, "the Lord God shall . . . call his servants by another name" (Isa. 65:15) in that day when Israel is restored and her people are prepared for his coming. It is The Church of Jesus Christ of Latter-day Saints, and its eternal destiny is assured. For thus saith the Lord: "The keys of the kingdom of God are committed unto man on the earth, and from thence shall the gospel roll forth unto the ends of the earth, as the stone which is cut out of the mountain without hands shall roll forth, until it has filled the whole earth."

And further, by way of invitation, the revealed word says: "Call upon the Lord, that his kingdom may go forth upon the earth, that the inhabitants thereof may receive it, and be prepared for the days to come, in the which the Son of Man shall come down in heaven, clothed in the brightness of his glory, to meet the kingdom of God which is set up on the earth. Wherefore, may the kingdom of God go forth, that the kingdom of heaven may come, that thou, O God, mayest be glorified in heaven so on earth, that thine enemies may be subdued; for thine is the honor, power and glory, forever and ever." (D&C 65:2, 5-6.)

The Mission of the Church and Kingdom

When we say, as say we must with all the power and persuasion at our command, that the Almighty promised to set up his Church and kingdom again on earth before his millennial return; when we speak of the restoration of the everlasting gospel in the last days; and when we testify that the ancient keys and powers must once again be vested in mortal men—such pronouncements mean that everything that appertains to, is connected with, or is part of the gospel shall be restored and shall be administered by the Church. God's Church and kingdom can accomplish its destined mission only if it is restored in all its glory, beauty, and perfection. That mission divides into three parts:

1. *Preaching the gospel to the world.*

The Church must—for that Lord whose church it is has so commanded—the Church must proclaim the fulness of the everlasting gospel in all the world and to every creature, for it is an imperative duty God has laid upon us. All men are children of the Father. They are entitled to hear the warning voice. Israel must be gathered out of Babylon into the earthly kingdom so that all who will may believe and obey and be saved.

2. *Perfecting the saints.*

No unclean thing can enter into the Eternal Presence and final eternal rest. Repentant souls must retain a remission of their sins. They must go from grace to grace until they perfect their souls. It is our privilege to obtain and perfect the attributes of godliness so they may be restored to us again in the resurrection. We are to build up a Zion composed of the pure in heart. We are to prepare a people for the coming of the Sinless One with whom the saints, being themselves free from sin, can then associate.

3. *Saving the dead.*

Thanks be to God for his mercy and grace! How pleasing it is to know that the Merciful One, who desires to see all his children saved, has made provision for the preaching of the gospel in the world of spirits, for the performance for them of vicarious ordinances in holy temples, and for the planting in the hearts of the children the promises made to the fathers.

We shall speak more particularly of all these things, each in its proper place, as we open to view the designs and purposes of the Lord as pertaining to the last days. We mention them here to make it clear to all that the restoration of the gospel and the Church embraces, includes, and was intended to include all that the Church now has or shall hereafter receive. The Church is God's earthly kingdom, and he will continue to do with it whatsoever is pleasing unto himself. And blessed be his holy name for all that he has given and does give and shall give unto his saints.

PREACHING THE EVERLASTING WORD

Preaching in All Nations

Let it be written with a pen of steel on plates of gold. Let the sound go forth with the trump of God so as to shake the earth and cause every ear to tingle. It is the eternal decree of the Great Jehovah. The fulness of the everlasting gospel, as restored by the Prophet Joseph Smith, shall be preached to every nation, and kindred, and tongue, and people. Then, and only then, shall the Lord Jesus Christ descend in the clouds of glory with ten thousand of his saints. But first the everlasting word must and shall go forth. Such is the will of heaven.

Jesus said: "This Gospel of the Kingdom shall be preached in all the world, for a witness unto all nations, and then shall the end come, or the destruction of the wicked." (JS-M 1:31.) What is the gospel of which our Lord speaks?

It is the gospel that he taught, the gospel of Peter, James, and John, the gospel of Paul and the primitive saints—not the gospel of an apostate Christendom.

It is the gospel that God is our Father and we are his children; that we dwelt in his presence in preexistence; that he is a Holy Man, having a body of flesh and bones; that he is a personage of tabernacle in whose image man is made—not the gospel that God is a spirit that fills immensity and is everywhere and nowhere in particular present.

It is the gospel that Christ, as the Lamb slain from the foundation of the world, atoned for the sins of all men on condition of repentance; that he brought life and immortality to light through his gospel; that immortality is a free gift for all men, but that eternal life comes only to those who believe and obey—not the gospel that men are saved by grace alone, without works, simply by confessing the Lord Jesus with their lips.

It is the gospel that men will be punished for their own sins and not for Adam's transgression—not the gospel that infants must be baptized to free them from Adam's sin; not the gospel that chosen souls are predestined to gain salvation through the grace and goodness of God, for reasons known to him alone, without reference to the deeds done in the flesh.

It is the gospel that men must be born again; that the Holy Ghost is a revelator and a sanctifier; that the gifts of the Spirit and miracles of every sort are always poured out upon the faithful—not the gospel that the Lord has done his work and that gifts and miracles ceased with the ancient apostles.

It is the gospel that the heavens are open; that God speaks today; that angels minister as of old; and that holy men can see the face of their Maker in the same way as did their forebears—not the gospel that the heavens are as brass, that revelation is not needed in this scientific age, and that the Bible contains all that is needed for the salvation of man.

It is the everlasting gospel, the gospel of God, the gospel that saved Adam and the ancients, the gospel that can make of man a god and of this earth a heaven—not the gospel of mystery, and of vagaries, and of the philosophies of men.

It is the restored gospel. It is the gospel brought back by angelic ministration, as we have already seen. And now it shall go forth and be offered to all men. Of this gospel, restored by Moroni and other angelic ministrants, the holy word says: "And this gospel shall be preached unto every nation, and kindred, and tongue, and people." This is a prophetic utterance that is not yet fulfilled, but will be in due course. For "the servants of God shall go forth, saying with a loud voice: Fear God and give glory to him, for the hour of his judgment is come; And worship him that made heaven, and earth, and the sea, and the fountains of waters—Calling upon the name of the Lord day and night, saying: O that thou wouldst rend the heavens, that thou wouldst come down, that the mountains might flow down at thy presence." (D&C 133:37-40.)

This restored gospel will reveal the true God and make his laws known. It shall go to all men before the hour of his judgment arrives. It will prepare a people for that dreadful day. And with reference to it, we say, as did Paul of old: "Though we, or an angel from heaven, preach any other gospel unto you than that which we have preached unto you, let him be accursed." (Gal. 1:8.)

When the prophetic word says the gospel shall be preached in every nation, it means every nation. It includes Russia and China and India. When it speaks of every kindred and people, it embraces the people of Islam and the believers in Buddha. When it mentions every tongue, it includes all the confusing dialects of all the sects and parties of men. The gospel is to go to them all. And the Lord will not come until it does.

Manifestly there is an assigned order in which the various nations and peoples shall hear the word. There is a divine timetable known to God and made manifest to his servants, little by little, as their strength and means increase, thus enabling them to go to new and added places. Nations rise and nations fall, kindreds and peoples come and go, the earth is inhabited here and there at one time or another, all according to the divine will.

Paul acclaimed that God "hath made of one blood all nations of men"—all men are brothers, all are the children of Adam—"for to dwell on all the face of the earth"; also, that the Lord "hath determined the times before appointed, and the bounds of their inhabitation." And all of this he hath done, "That they should seek the Lord," and that "haply they might feel after him, and find him." (Acts 17:26-27.) Indeed, the very purpose of life itself is for men to come unto God and to worship him in spirit and in truth. This can be done only when they learn his laws and believe his gospel.

We have commenced the preaching processes in most of the free world; the voice of warning is beginning to go forth; and a few of Ephraim and a sprinkling of Manasseh have begun to gather into the true fold. But the great day of missionary work lies ahead. We must go to all nations and do far more in those nations where the work has begun. In due course the Lord will break down the barriers among men. The iron curtain will rise; the prohibitions against preaching in the Islamic world will fade away; the Jews will be free to believe or not as they choose—and the everlasting word will go forth as He has decreed.

Preaching amid War and Desolation

The preaching of the everlasting word is for the purpose of saving souls. The servants of the Lord, the elders of his kingdom, the missionaries who carry the message are called to labor in his fields. They go forth to reap; they are to gather the wheat into barns and bind up the tares for the day of burning. And as it has always been, the harvest is great and the laborers are few, and we must plead with the Lord of the harvest to send us more witnesses of his holy name. "Behold, the field is white already to harvest," he says, "therefore, whoso desireth to reap, let him thrust in his sickle with his might, and reap while the day lasts, that he may treasure up for his soul everlasting salvation in the kingdom of God. Yea, whosoever will thrust in his sickle and reap, the same is called of God." (D&C 6:3-4.)

Those who labor with their might "shall be laden with many sheaves." (D&C 75:5.) These sheaves are then carried to the threshing floor where the chaff is blown away and the wheat made ready for the granary. These threshing processes are now going on for the last time on earth. The Lord of the harvest has sent laborers into his fields to gather in the wheat before he burns the tares with unquenchable fire. The day is rapidly approaching when every corruptible thing will be consumed and there will be a new heaven and a new earth whereon dwelleth righteousness.

But what is not as well understood among us as it should be is that the harvest is to go forward under increasingly difficult circumstances. It could not be otherwise in a world that is ripening in iniquity. War and pestilence and desolation shall cover the earth before the Lord comes, and the preaching of his holy word must and shall go forward in the midst of these. "I call upon the weak things of the world," the Lord says, "those who are unlearned and despised, to thrash the nations by the power of my Spirit." To thrash is to thresh; they are one and the same.

How and under what circumstances shall this preaching go forward? "Their arm shall be my arm," the Lord says of his servants, "and I will be their shield and their buckler; and I will gird up their loins, and they shall fight manfully for me; and their enemies shall be under their feet; and I will let fall the sword in their behalf, and by the fire of mine indignation will I preserve them." This promise to let the sword fall in behalf of his servants must of necessity mean that the Lord will use the wars that are fomented and fought by the wicked to open nations and kingdoms to the preaching of the gospel. Thus, by the weak and the simple, laboring in the midst of tribulation, "the poor and the meek shall have the gospel preached unto them, and they shall be looking forth for the time of my coming," saith the Lord, "for it is nigh at hand." (D&C 35:13-15.)

Let us, then, look at the prophetic word which associates the preaching of the gospel in the last days with a time of war and desolation. Micah, after saying "the house of the Lord shall be established in the top of the mountains," with Israel gathering thereto, says that "many nations" shall then gather against the Lord's people. "But they know not the thoughts of the Lord," he says, "neither understand they his counsel: for he shall gather them as the sheaves into the floor." That is to say: When nations and peoples gather to oppose us, we must preach the saving truths to them as Ammon and his brethren did to the Lamanites. There is nothing but the gospel that will soften the hearts of men and cause them to turn away from war, and from evil, and from opposition to God.

It is in this setting, then, that the Lord commands: "Arise and thresh, O daughter of Zion"—stand forth, proclaim my word, thrust in your sickles, carry many sheaves to the threshing floor—"for I will make thine horn iron, and I will make thy hoofs brass: and thou shalt beat in pieces many people: and I will consecrate their gain unto the Lord, and their substance unto the Lord of the whole earth." (Micah 4:1, 11-13.) The laborers in the Lord's fields will come off triumphant; they will make many converts whose substance will be used to further the work.

Joseph Smith poured forth these eloquent words relative to the preaching of the gospel in our day: "The servants of God will not have gone over the nations of the Gentiles, with a warning voice, until the destroying angel will commence to waste the inhabitants of the earth, and as the prophet hath said, 'It shall be a vexation to hear the report.' I speak thus because I feel for my fellow men; I do it in the name of the Lord, being moved upon by the Holy Spirit. Oh, that I could snatch them from the vortex of misery, into which I behold them plunging themselves, by their sins; that I might be enabled by the warning voice, to be an instrument of bringing them to unfeigned repentance, that they might have faith to stand in the evil day!" (*Teachings*, p. 87.)

The prophet who spoke of the vexation here mentioned was Isaiah. To vex is to trouble grievously; it is to harass; it is to afflict as with a disease. Vexation is a state of trouble; it is a cause of trouble and of affliction. Speaking of the Lord's latter-day people and of the desolations promised in their day, Isaiah said: "The overflowing scourge shall pass through, then ye shall be trodden down by it. From the time that it goeth forth it shall take you: for morning by morning shall it pass over, by day and by night: and it shall be a vexation only to understand the report." Or, as it is otherwise translated, "It shall be nought but terror to understand the message." Then, Isaiah continues, "the Lord shall rise up . . . that he may do his work, his strange work; and bring to pass his act, his strange act. Now therefore be ye not mockers, lest your bands be made strong: for I have heard from the Lord God of hosts a consumption, even determined upon the whole earth." (Isa. 28:18-22.)

In latter-day revelation, speaking of the day when the times of the Gentiles shall be fulfilled, the Lord says: "There shall be men standing in that generation, that shall not pass until they shall see an overflowing scourge; for a desolating sickness shall cover the land. But my disciples shall stand in holy places, and shall not be moved; but among the wicked, men shall lift up their voices and curse God and die." (D&C 45:31-32.) And through it all, we must and shall continue to preach, morning after morning, day after day, and night after night.

The Lord's Controversy with the Nations

The ancient prophets speak of the Lord Jehovah engaging in a controversy with his people and with all the nations of the earth in the last days. He will discuss with them a controverted matter; he will dispute and debate a controversial issue; and the views of the contending parties will be proclaimed in a setting of strife. The issue at stake will be whether men believe his gospel, repent of their sins, keep his commandments, and gain salvation; or whether they rebel against him, reject the light of truth, walk in darkness, do wickedly, and are damned. It will be the greatest controversy of the ages.

Hosea, speaking of "the Lord and his goodness in the latter days," proclaims: "Hear the word of the Lord, ye children of Israel: for the Lord hath a controversy with the inhabitants of the land, because there is no truth, nor mercy, nor knowledge of God in the land." How aptly he describes the day of apostasy, the day when darkness covers the earth and gross darkness the minds of the people! "By swearing, and lying, and killing, and stealing, and committing adultery, they break out, and blood toucheth blood. Therefore shall the land mourn, and every one that dwelleth therein shall languish." (Hosea 3:5; 4:1-3.) Such is the setting in which the great controversy shall wage.

Micah prophesies of "the remnant of Jacob" that "shall be among the Gentiles" in the last days. (Micah 5:8-15.) His words, in their entirety and with some additions, are quoted by the Risen Lord to the Nephites. (3 Ne. 21:12-19.) Then Jesus says: "For it shall come to pass, saith the Father, that at that day"—the day of restoration and of gathering, the day in which we live—"whosoever will not repent and come unto my Beloved Son, them will I cut off from among my people, O house of Israel; And I will execute vengeance and fury upon them, even as upon the heathen, such as they have not heard. But if they will repent and hearken unto my words, and harden not their hearts, I will establish my church among them, and they shall come in unto the covenant and be numbered among this the remnant of Jacob, unto whom I have given this land for their inheritance." (3 Ne. 21:20-22.) Such shall be the result of the great controversy—men shall save or damn themselves depending upon the part they play in the warfare between truth and error.

And so it is that we hear Micah proclaim: "Hear ye now what the Lord saith; Arise, contend thou before the mountains, and let the hills hear thy voice. Hear ye, O mountains, the Lord's controversy, and ye strong foundations of the earth: for the Lord hath a controversy with his people, and he will plead with Israel." (Micah 6:1-2.)

The Lord's controversy! The Lord pleading with men—pleading by the mouths of his servants—to repent and be saved, and men rejecting the message! And so we turn to the words of Jeremiah to learn what will happen to the nations of men who reject the truth in the last days. In words descriptive of Armageddon-like scenes, Jeremiah says: "I will call for a sword upon all the inhabitants of the earth, saith the Lord of hosts. Therefore prophesy thou against them all these words, and say unto them, The Lord shall roar from on high, and utter his voice from his holy habitation; he shall mightily roar upon his habitation; he shall give a shout, as they that tread the grapes, against all the inhabitants of the earth."

The scene thus depicted is one descriptive of the Second Coming. Having so asserted, the prophetic word continues: "A noise shall come even to the ends of the earth; for the Lord hath a controversy with the nations, he will plead with all flesh; he will give them that are wicked to the sword, saith the Lord. Thus saith the Lord of hosts, Behold, evil shall go forth from nation to nation, and a great whirlwind shall be raised up from the coasts of the earth. And the slain of the Lord shall be at that day from one end of the earth even unto the other end of the earth: they shall not be lamented, neither gathered, nor buried; they shall be dung upon the ground." (Jer. 25:29-33.)

In the midst of his great prophecy about the worldwide war during which the Lord Jesus will return, the prophet Joel inserts these words about offering, even then, the saving word to wicked men. Thus saith the Lord: "Put ye in the sickle, for the harvest is ripe: come, get you down; for the press is full, the fats overflow; for their wickedness is great. Multitudes, multitudes in the valley of decision: for the day of the Lord is near in the valley of decision." (Joel 3:13-14.)

Of the wars and destructions, and of Armageddon itself, we shall speak more particularly hereafter. The issue with which we now wrestle is the one of preaching the everlasting word in the midst of war and desolation and pestilence and evil of every sort. And in the light of all that the prophets have said, some conclusions seem inescapable. The gospel shall be preached. It shall go to every nation, and it shall go in the day of vengeance and of evil. It may be that millions of preachers will be needed to raise the warning voice in every ear. Certainly billions of worldly men will oppose the message. Indeed, all the forces of evil men, all the subtleties of Satan, and all the horrors of hell shall rise to fight the truth. The controversy shall cover the whole earth, and the servants of the Lord will plead with men everywhere to repent and believe the gospel. Knowing these things, we cannot permit opposition, however powerful and severe, to deter us from complying with the divine commission to proclaim the gospel to every creature.

Making Converts in All Nations

What will be the result of the great controversy—the Lord's controversy, the controversy between truth and error, the warfare between the saints and the world—that shall be waged in all nations and among all people before the Second Coming? What choice will men make in the valley of decision? Will they choose to believe in the Only Begotten or go their own way to sorrow and destruction and death? And if but few believe; if all the voices of earth and hell cry out for the destruction of the Lord's people—what then? Will the saints be preserved, and if so, how?

Let there be no mistake on these matters. The gospel shall be preached everywhere; success will attend the labors of those who proclaim the truth; converts by the thousands and the millions will be made in all nations. There is no question about this; none can stay the hand of the Lord or of his servants; the message shall go forth. Comparatively speaking, however, a few only in all nations will believe the restored truth; the masses of men in all nations will mock and scorn the true ministers and their message; the battle lines of the controversy will be tightly drawn.

Then, when the saints have done all that in their power lies, both to preach the everlasting word and to build up the eternal kingdom; when they of themselves can no longer go forward with the decreed success attending their labors; when the wars and desolations and carnality of men are about to overwhelm them—then the Lord will take over. By his own power he will destroy the wicked, complete his strange act, and pour out the consumption decreed.

These things are set forth by Nephi in this manner. He is speaking of the last days. An angel has just shown him "that great and abominable church, which is the mother of abominations, whose foundation is the devil." He has learned that "she is the whore of all the earth," and that in the last days "she sat upon many waters; and she had dominion over all the earth, among all nations, kindreds, tongues, and people." These are the very nations, kindreds, tongues, and peoples to whom the gospel must go; these are the nations where the Lord's controversy shall be waged; these are the peoples who stand in the valley of decision.

In this setting Nephi says: "I beheld the church of the Lamb of God"—The Church of Jesus Christ of Latter-day Saints!—"and its numbers were few, because of the wickedness and abominations of the whore who sat upon many waters." This is the day when "there are save two churches only; the one is the church of the Lamb of God, and the other is the church of the devil." This is the day when "whoso belongeth not to the church of the Lamb of God belongeth to that great church, which is the mother of abominations." The evil forces on earth, which control nations and kingdoms, false religions of all sorts and kinds, the communistic powers, and every worldly organization which opposes the cause of truth and righteousness—all these are gathered under one banner, the banner of Lucifer. All these are united in an evil cause, the cause that opposes the saints of the Lamb.

"Nevertheless," Nephi continues, meaning in spite of all this opposition, "I beheld that the church of the Lamb, who were the saints of God, were also upon all the face of the earth." The Church of Jesus Christ of Latter-day Saints will be established in all nations and among every people before the Lord comes. There will be a few saints everywhere. Success in this sense shall attend the labors of those who go forth to preach the gospel.

However, Nephi continues, "their dominions upon the face of the earth were small, because of the wickedness of the great whore whom I saw." These dominions, comparatively speaking, are small now; they will be small in days to come; great and glorious as the Church shall become before the appointed dreadful day, its rulership and influence in the world will be immeasurably less than that of the combined evil forces of earth and hell that taken together are the church of the devil.

How, then, will the Lord's controversy fare? Nephi says: "I beheld that the great mother of abominations did gather together multitudes upon the face of all the earth, among all the nations of the Gentiles, to fight against the Lamb of God." Those who oppose the Lord's Church oppose him. To reject the apostles and prophets who are sent to preach the gospel is to reject him who sent them. To be in opposition to The Church of Jesus Christ of Latter-day Saints on moral issues is to link arms with Satan and to fight against God. On this point we must speak plainly and bluntly—there is no middle ground; men are either for him or against him, and those who are not for him are against him.

And the Lord will not let his people fail. "I, Nephi, beheld the power of the Lamb of God," the scriptural account continues, "that it descended upon the saints of the church of the Lamb, and upon the covenant people of the Lord, who were scattered upon all the face of the earth; and they were armed with righteousness and with the power of God in great glory. And it came to pass that I beheld that the wrath of God was poured out upon the great and abominable church, insomuch that there were wars and rumors of wars among all the nations and kindreds of the earth."

This is the day in which we live. These wars and rumors of wars have been, now are, and yet will be. The worldwide wars of the recent past, and the never-ending rumors and reports of the present now, in all of which the communications media so delight, are but a type and a shadow of the wars and rumors of wars that soon shall be poured out without measure.

Nephi saw our day. He described it as a day in which "there began to be wars and rumors of wars among all the nations which belonged to the mother of abominations." As he viewed the awful scene, the angelic ministrant who presided over the visions then being given to a mortal man said these solemn words: "Behold, the wrath of God is upon the mother of harlots; and behold, thou seest all these things—And when the day cometh that the wrath of God is poured out upon the mother of harlots, which is the great and abominable church of all the earth, whose foundation is the devil, then, at that day, the work of the Father shall commence, in preparing the way for the fulfilling of his covenants, which he hath made to his people who are of the house of Israel." (1 Ne. 14:9-17.)

This word speaks of us. We are of Israel, and the covenants made with our fathers are now being fulfilled. We are called to preach the everlasting word in all the world that our scattered brethren of the house of Jacob may all hear the message, be gathered into the fold of their Ancient Shepherd, and there find refreshment with all his sheep. And it matters not that the warning voice must go forth in the midst of war and desolation. That it would be thus was foreseen and foreknown from the beginning. So be it.

THE BOOK OF MORMON AND THE SECOND COMING

What Think Ye of the Book of Mormon?

We have some truths to tell and some testimony to bear about a volume of latter-day scripture—the Book of Mormon—which does now and yet shall shake the very foundations of Christendom. We intend to state, with a plainness that defies misunderstanding, how this holy book prepares the way for the Second Coming of the Son of Man; how it makes ready a people for that dread and glorious day; how all men on earth will be saved or damned because they believe or disbelieve its words; and how the ancient prophets foretold that the Lord Jesus would not come in the clouds of glory until this book of books, this American Bible, this voice from the dust, came forth and was offered to all men in all nations.

The coming forth of the Book of Mormon and its publication to the world is one of the signs of the times. It is one of the great events destined to occur before the Second Coming. Prophets and preachers of righteousness spent four thousand years recording the truths it contains. Civilizations rose and fell as they accepted or rejected the teachings on its pages. And the world today will rise or fall, nations will survive or perish, men will gain celestial glory or suffer with the damned in hell, all depending upon their reaction to this volume of holy writ.

This holy book, this Nephite record, this voice of God speaking, as it were, with seven thunders, came forth to bear testimony of the divine Sonship of Christ and to teach the doctrines of salvation to every nation, and kindred, and tongue, and people. It is the very volume of holy scripture that has been prepared by the Lord to take his message of salvation to a wicked world in the last days. Its message is for the Lamanites, and for the whole house of Israel, and for the Gentiles, and for every living soul upon the face of the whole earth.

And no man—great or small, wise or ignorant, theologian or atheist—no man who lives on the earth in the last days can be saved in the kingdom of heaven unless and until he comes to know, by the power of the Holy Ghost, that this holy book is the mind and will and voice of God to the world. And all who reject its message will be damned. This is as plain and blunt a declaration as the one made by the Lord Jesus with reference to the heaven-sent baptism that he commanded his apostles to preach to the world. It is one of the great foundation stones of revealed religion in modern times. Men will stand or fall—eternally—because of what they think of the Book of Mormon.

Before we can identify the time and the season of our Lord's triumphant return, we must learn what part the Book of Mormon has played and yet will play relative to that coming day. The book itself is an inspired history of God's dealings with the ancient inhabitants of the Americas. It was written by prophets and seers upon plates of gold and other metals in their own tongues and languages. The many prophetic records that came into being were condensed, abridged, and quoted by the prophet-historian Mormon as he wrote the book that now bears his name.

The accounts deal primarily with the prophet Lehi and his descendants who lived and labored in the Western Hemisphere for about a thousand years—from shortly after 600 B.C. to almost A.D. 421. There is also a brief abridgment of the history of the Jaredite people who left the Old World at the time of the confusion of tongues at the tower of Babel (about 2247 B.C.), were led to the Americas by the hand of the Lord, and lived as a great people and a mighty nation until their destruction in Nephite times.

But the Book of Mormon is more, far more, than an inspired history. It is a volume of holy scripture comparable in scope, in doctrine, and in literary excellence to that greatest of all books, the holy Bible. Indeed, it is an American Bible, which was written "by the spirit of prophecy and of revelation." (Title page.) It expounds the doctrines of salvation in plainness and perfection. It contains the fulness of the everlasting gospel, meaning that it is a record of God's dealings with a people who had the fulness of the gospel, and meaning also that in it is a divine delineation of the laws and truths and powers by which salvation may be gained. It sets forth the covenants God has made with his people. It was translated by the gift and power of God by the great seer of latter days. And it is now published to the world "to the convincing of the Jew and Gentile that Jesus is the Christ, the Eternal God, manifesting himself unto all nations." (Title page.)

As we inquire into the second coming of that eternal God of whom the Book of Mormon testifies, we must ask and answer such questions as these: What is the relationship between the Book of Mormon and the Second Coming? How is this book involved in the restoration of all things? In what way does it help to prepare a people for millennial peace and righteousness? What effect does it have on the gathering of Israel? Does it, in fact, prove the reality of the restoration and the presence of the glorious gospel among men? What is its relationship to the Bible and the other scriptures that have lighted and will light the way to eternal life? And what docs the prophetic word have to say about its coming forth and the part it will play in the eternal scheme of things?

Let every man who loves truth and cherishes goodness ponder in his heart the great query: *What think ye of the Book of Mormon?* And further: *Whence came it? Is it of God or of man? And if it be of God, what is my responsibility with reference to it?*

"Truth Shall Spring Out of the Earth"

No man can speak too highly of the Holy Bible, that volume of divine writ which came down from heaven to light the path back to those celestial realms. The Bible contains the mind and will and voice of God to all men everywhere; it is a record of his dealings with some of his children during the four thousand years from the first Adam, by whom the fall came, to the Second Adam, by whom the ransom was paid.

In its original and perfect form the Bible was a transcript of those celestial records which the Lord designed, in his infinite wisdom, to reveal to his earthly children. It bears witness of Christ and teaches the doctrines of salvation. It charts the course leading to eternal life. It tells men how and in what way they can attain peace in this life and eternal glory in the realms ahead.

The King James Version of the Bible is by all odds the best and plainest rendition of the original records that the translators of the world have produced. It is the Bible version prepared by the Lord for use by his modern prophet, Joseph Smith, when he translated the Book of Mormon, brought forth the revelations in the Doctrine and Covenants, and laid the foundations of the great work of restoration in the latter days. The Joseph Smith Translation, commonly called the Inspired Version, has added to and perfected much of the King James Version, and someday—we suppose it will be a millennial day—the work of perfecting the Bible will be completed, and men will then have again the scriptural knowledge possessed by their forebears.

All that is said of the Bible applies with equal force to the Book of Mormon. It too is a volume of holy writ; it too is an inspired history of God's dealings with ancient civilizations; it too contains the fulness of the everlasting gospel. The peoples with whom it deals dwelt for some twenty-six hundred years in the Americas, where they developed civilizations and a religious zeal comparable to any of the races and nations of the Old World.

In the Book of Mormon is found a new witness for Christ; in it the doctrines of salvation are set forth with a clarity and plainness that surpass the Bible; and in it is found the proof that God has spoken again in these last days. No man can speak too highly of the Book of Mormon or testify with excessive power of its truth and divinity. It too is a transcript from the eternal records of heaven, and in its original form it contained much more than a wise Father has permitted to be translated and published among us. And in a yet future day—and again we suppose it will be millennial— the fulness of the Book of Mormon accounts will be preached from the housetops.

In the eternal providences of the Lord, known and revealed from the beginning, the Book of Mormon was destined to make its appearance in the last days as part of the glorious restoration of all things. This fact he revealed to many of his ancient prophets—Enoch, Joseph who was sold into Egypt, Isaiah, Ezekiel, Zenos, and no doubt many others whose prophecies are on the brass plates or in other books yet to come forth.

As part of those eternal providences of which we speak, the Lord designed from the beginning to bring the Book of Mormon forth from the ground as a voice from the dust, as truth springing out of the earth. The symbolism and imagery in this are beautiful. As revelation pours down from above to water the earth, so the gospel plant grows out of the earth to bear witness that the heavenly rains contain the life-giving power. Heaven and earth join hands in testifying of the truths of salvation. Their combined voices are the voice of restoration, the voice of glory and honor and eternal life, the voice from heaven, and the voice out of the earth. Such is part of the Lord's act, his strange act, the act in which all who are willing to forsake the world and come unto him with full purpose of heart may play a part. "And out of small things proceedeth that which is great." (D&C 64:33.)

Enoch, whose mortal ministry preceded by five thousand years the coming forth of the Book of Mormon, saw in vision both the Second Coming and the coming forth of the volume of holy scripture that would prepare the way for that glorious day. To him the Lord said: "And righteousness will I send down out of heaven"—that is, revelation shall commence anew and the gospel shall be restored—"and truth will I send forth out of the earth, to bear testimony of mine Only Begotten; his resurrection from the dead; yea, and also the resurrection of all men." (Moses 7:62.) The Book of Mormon shall come forth from American soil, from plates buried in Cumorah, from the soil that supported the people of whom it speaks. The Book of Mormon shall come forth containing the *word* of the gospel which will unite with the *power* of the gospel that comes down from heaven. The Book of Mormon shall come forth to testify of Christ and his resurrection and the resurrection of all men. It was to be the Lord's way of bringing to light anew his saving truths.

David, whose doings preceded by almost three thousand years the coming forth of the Book of Mormon, was led by the Spirit to say: "I will hear what God the Lord will speak"—oh, that all men would open their hearts to hear and believe and obey—"for he will speak peace unto his people, and to his saints." His gospel is a message of peace, peace in this life, and peace everlasting in the kingdom of peace. "Surely his salvation is nigh them that fear him." Salvation is always nigh when the Lord speaks; his voice, coming by revelation or recorded in the scriptures, is the voice of salvation. "Mercy and truth are met together; righteousness and peace have kissed each other. Truth shall spring out of the earth; and righteousness shall look down from heaven. Yea, the Lord shall give that which is good." (Ps. 85:8-12.) Such is the manner in which the restoration shall be brought to pass. Heaven shall reveal her wonders, and earth shall bear an echoing testimony. God shall speak to his prophets, and the Book of Mormon shall proclaim the same words. The same words that flow down from above shall spring forth in the record of a civilization long dead.

Isaiah, whose voice was heard some twenty-six hundred years before the voice spoke from the dust, received these words from the Lord: "Drop down, ye heavens, from above, and let the skies pour down righteousness: let the earth open, and let them bring forth salvation, and let righteousness spring up together; I the Lord have created it." It is the age-old message of heaven and earth uniting to testify of the truth. Having given these words of truth to his great prophet, the Lord then, as a warning to the disbelievers of the last days, acclaims: "Woe unto him that striveth with his Maker!" (Isa. 45:8-9.) Our Maker's words as they come down from heaven and as they spring forth out of the earth must not be treated lightly.

A Voice Speaks from the Dust

Behold what wonders God hath wrought! Truth springs out of the earth; the gold plates are translated by the gift and power of

God; and the voice we hear is one that whispers from the dust. It is the voice of all the Nephis, of Alma and Amulek and Abinadi, of Ether and Mormon and Moroni—of all the Nephite and Jaredite prophets. It is the voice of the Lord Jesus Christ, who ministered among the Nephites, inviting them to feel the prints of the nails in his hands and in his feet and to thrust their hands into his riven side. It is the voice of doctrine and testimony and miracles. It is the voice of God speaking to men through the Book of Mormon.

Knowing beforehand what should come to pass in the last days, the Lord Jehovah spoke by the mouth of Isaiah relative to the Nephite peoples who should "be visited of the Lord of hosts with thunder, and with earthquake, and great noise, with storm and tempest, and the flame of devouring fire." Because they forsook the Lord and fought against Zion, it should be with them "as when an hungry man dreameth, and, behold, he eateth; but he awaketh, and his soul is empty: or as when a thirsty man dreameth, and, behold, he drinketh; but he awaketh, and, behold, he is faint, and his soul hath appetite." Because they rejected the gospel and fought against the truth, they should be destroyed.

But a record would be preserved, and through it the great things revealed to their prophets would be known again. "And thou shalt be brought down," the prophetic word intones, "and shalt speak out of the ground, and thy speech shall be low out of the dust, and thy voice shall be, as of one that hath a familiar spirit, out of the ground, and thy speech shall whisper out of the dust." The spirit and tone and tenor of the message shall be familiar. A like account, one dealing with the same truths, the same laws, and the same ordinances, is found in the Bible.

In this setting Isaiah speaks of the universal apostasy; of the words of a sealed book being delivered to one who is learned, but who confesses that he cannot read a sealed book; of the Lord piercing the spiritual darkness and doing a marvelous work and a wonder among men, which work is the restoration of the gospel; and of the influence the book—the Book of Mormon—will then have in all the world. We shall note some of this shortly. (Isa. 29:1-24.)

Isaiah's words were engraved on the brass plates. Nephi pondered their meaning and learned by revelation that they applied to the descendants of Lehi in their American promised land and also to the Gentiles in the last days. In expounding them, Nephi taught that the seed of Lehi would dwindle in unbelief after the destruction of the Nephites, "after the Lord God shall have camped against them round about, and shall have laid siege against them with a mount, and raised forts against them." Herein is the destruction of the Nephite peoples foretold. "And after they shall have been brought down low in the dust, even that they are not, yet the words of the righteous shall be written, and the prayers of the faithful shall be heard, and all those who have dwindled in unbelief shall not be forgotten." How the faithful had pled with the Lord that the gospel would come again in the last days and go to their seed and to all men!

"For those who shall be destroyed," who are the Nephites, "shall speak unto them out of the ground, and their speech shall be low out of the dust, and their voice shall be as one that hath a familiar spirit; for the Lord God will give unto him power, that he may whisper concerning them, even as it were out of the ground; and their speech shall whisper out of the dust."

The Nephite voice shall never cease. It shall be trumpeted in every ear until the end of time. The whisper from the dust shall build up to a mighty crescendo which shall reverberate from one end of heaven to the other. What began as a whisper will soon sound like roll upon roll of thunder. "For thus saith the Lord God: They shall write the things which shall be done among them, and they shall be written and sealed up in a book, and those who have dwindled in unbelief [the Lamanites in the day of their degeneracy] shall not have them, for they seek to destroy the things of God.

"Wherefore, as those who have been destroyed [the Nephites] have been destroyed speedily; and the multitude of their terrible ones shall be as chaff that passeth away—yea, thus saith the Lord God: It shall be at an instant, suddenly—And it shall come to pass, that those who have dwindled in unbelief shall be smitten by the hand of the Gentiles." That is, the American Indians shall be smitten and driven by the American people. At this point Nephi speaks of the dire apostasy of the last days, of the many false churches and secret combinations, and of the priestcrafts that lead men astray. (2 Ne. 26:1-33.)

"In the last days," Nephi continues, when those in "all the nations" and "upon all the lands of the earth" are "drunken with iniquity and all manner of abominations," then once again shall the wrath of God rest upon them as it did upon the Nephites at the time of their destruction. "And when that day shall come they shall be visited of the Lord of Hosts, with thunder and with earthquake, and with the flame of devouring fire. And all the nations that fight against Zion, and that distress her, shall be as a dream of a night vision."

Nephi continues by quoting the words of Isaiah about the hungry and thirsty who dream their needs are satisfied and who awake to find their bellies gnawing with hunger and their thirst unquenched. He notes Isaiah's words about those—about all men—who are drunken, but not with wine, and who stagger, but not with strong drink, and then he comes to the book, the Book of Mormon.

"And it shall come to pass that the Lord God shall bring forth unto you the words of a book, and they shall be the words of them which have slumbered. And behold the book shall be sealed; and in the book shall be a revelation from God, from the beginning of the world to the ending thereof." Such were the gold plates delivered by Moroni, not to the world, but to a prophet called of God to translate and proclaim a portion of the divine word engraved by the ancients upon the sacred plates. In part the plates were sealed. "Wherefore, because of the things which are sealed up, the things which are sealed shall not be delivered in the day of the wickedness and abominations of the people. Wherefore the book shall be kept from them."

When wickedness ends, when abominations are no more, when the Lord comes and the wicked are destroyed—which is the end of the world—then shall the book itself come forth for the edification of all. "For the book shall be sealed by the power of God, and the revelation which was sealed shall be kept in the book until the own due time of the Lord, that they may come forth; for behold, they reveal all things from the foundation of the world unto the end thereof."

The restoration of all things cannot be completed until all things are restored. As we have seen, the Lord Jesus cannot come until the era of restoration commences, but the full restoration will not occur until after he comes. "And the day cometh that the words of the book which were sealed shall be read upon the house tops; and they shall be read by the power of Christ; and all things shall be revealed unto the children of men which ever have been among the children of men, and which ever will be even unto the end of the earth."

Nephi's account then speaks of the translation of the portion of the book that men in our day are able to receive; of the witnesses who "shall testify to the truth of the book and the things therein"; and of the learned one (Professor Charles Anthon) to whom some of the words were delivered, and who said, "I cannot read a sealed book." (JS-H 1:63-65.)

Next the inspired writing records the commandment given to Joseph Smith: "Touch not the things which are sealed." And also, "When thou hast read the words which I have commanded thee, and obtained the witnesses which I have promised unto thee, then shalt thou seal up the book again, and hide it up unto me, that I may preserve the words which thou hast not read, until I shall see fit in mine own wisdom to reveal all things unto the children of men. For behold, I am God; and I am a God of miracles; and I will show unto the world that I am the same yesterday, today, and forever; and I work not among the children of men save it be according to their faith."

Then there follows the prophecy about a marvelous work and a wonder—the restored gospel—which is to come forth after the Book of Mormon as we have it is translated, followed by the prophetic words relative to the effect our present Book of Mormon shall have upon men when we proclaim its message to the world. (2 Ne. 27:1-35.) We shall speak of this in chapter 14.

Ephraim Holds the Stick of Joseph

Ezekiel, who was carried captive into Babylon and who lived in the days of Lehi, received the divine word that there would be two great books of scripture in the last days—the Bible and the

Book of Mormon. The one should come from the kingdom of Judah and the other should have its source in the kingdom of Ephraim, the two nations that comprised divided Israel anciently.

To this great prophet of Judah, the Lord said: "Take thee one stick, and write upon it, For Judah, and for the children of Israel his companions." The designation and title thus recorded on the stick symbolized the word of the Lord that came to the prophets of Judah, some of whose words are preserved for us in the Bible. The people of Judah, among whom Ezekiel then ministered, knew of such prophetic writings and such seeric sayings as had thus far been received. Their contents were taught in every household.

"Then take another stick, and write upon it, For Joseph, the stick of Ephraim, and for all the house of Israel his companions." The message so inscribed symbolized the divine word that would come through the house of Joseph, that Joseph who was sold into Egypt and whose sons, Ephraim and Manasseh, each held tribal status in Israel. Of these words the people of Judah had no knowledge in that day, for the divine sayings were yet to find utterance through prophetic lips. Ezekiel's hearers could not have done other than wonder what great sayings were yet to come through another people, a people to whom but little of the word of the Lord had thus far been revealed.

Then came the divine injunction: "And join them one to another into one stick; and they shall become one in thine hand." The two sacred books, the two volumes of holy scripture, the word of the Lord as it came to Judah and his fellows on the one hand, and the same word as it came to Joseph and his fellows on the other—these accounts were to become one in Ezekiel's hand.

Each would bear witness of Christ. Each would teach sound doctrine. Each would chart the course to eternal life in the Everlasting Presence. Each would be the mind and will and voice of God to the world. One would be a witness from the Old World, the other from the New World. And they would be one, for there is one God and one Shepherd over all the earth, and he speaks the same words to all who will attune their souls so as to hear his eternal message.

"And when the children of thy people shall speak unto thee,

saying, Wilt thou not shew us what thou meanest by these? Say unto them, Thus saith the Lord God; Behold, I will take the stick of Joseph, which is in the hand of Ephraim, and the tribes of Israel his fellows, and will put them with him, even with the stick of Judah, and make them one stick, and they shall be one in mine hand. And the sticks whereon thou writest shall be in thine hand before their eyes."

Thus the Lord foretold his purposes relative to the written records which would testify of him and of his goodness unto men. Ezekiel was then to use the two sticks that became one as a means of teaching the gathering of Israel, the restoration of the gospel, the building of temples in the last days, and the millennial reign of the Eternal David, concerning all of which we shall have more to say hereafter. (Ezek. 37:15-28.)

The stick of Joseph—the prophetic word that has come through his seed—is now in the hands of Ephraim. Joseph Smith was of Ephraim; we are of Ephraim; and Moroni has given to us "the keys of the record of the stick of Ephraim." (D&C 27:5.) Ephraim receives the blessings of the firstborn, and as such he is gathering first in the last days. The Book of Mormon, which gathers Israel, is in our hands and is one with the Bible in presenting the truths of salvation to the world.

All of these things were known to Lehi; in addition, he knew they would be fulfilled through his seed. "I am a descendant of Joseph who was carried captive into Egypt," Lehi said. "And great were the covenants of the Lord which he made unto Joseph." These covenants are written on the brass plates, from which source Lehi learned them, and they will in due course come forth in their fulness and perfection for all men to read.

"Joseph truly saw our day," the day of the Nephites, Lehi continues. "And he obtained a promise of the Lord, that out of the fruits of his loins the Lord God would raise up a righteous branch unto the house of Israel; not the Messiah"—one of whose titles is the Branch, signifying he would be born as a branch of that olive tree which is Israel—"but a branch which was to be broken off, nevertheless, to be remembered in the covenants of the Lord that the Messiah should be made manifest unto them in the latter days, in the spirit of power, unto the bringing of them out of darkness unto light—yea, out of hidden darkness and out of captivity unto freedom."

To Joseph the Lord said: "The fruit of thy loins shall write; and the fruit of the loins of Judah shall write; and that which shall be written by the fruit of thy loins, and also that which shall be written by the fruit of the loins of Judah, shall grow together, unto the confounding of false doctrines and laying down of contentions, and establishing peace among the fruit of thy loins, and bringing them to the knowledge of their fathers in the latter days, and also to the knowledge of my covenants, saith the Lord."

Also to Joseph of old, but speaking of Joseph Smith, the seer of the latter days, the Lord said: "I will give unto him that he shall write the writing of the fruit of thy loins, unto the fruit of thy loins." That is, Joseph Smith will translate the Book of Mormon and send it forth to the Lamanites, who are the seed of Joseph. "And the words which he shall write shall be the words which are expedient in my wisdom should go forth unto the fruit of thy loins. And it shall be as if the fruit of thy loins had cried unto them from the dust; for I know their faith.

"And they shall cry from the dust; yea, even repentance unto their brethren, even after many generations have gone by them. And it shall come to pass that their cry shall go, even according to the simpleness of their words. Because of their faith their words shall proceed forth out of my mouth unto their brethren who are the fruit of thy loins; and the weakness of their words will I make strong in their faith, unto the remembering of my covenant which I made unto thy fathers." (2 Ne. 3:1-21.)

We are witnesses that all of these things have or shall come to pass, and we testify that the Book of Mormon, both as now constituted and as it shall hereafter be, shall change the whole history of the world.

THE BOOK THAT WELCOMES THE SECOND COMING

The Divine Mission of the Divine Book

Few men on earth, either in or out of the Church, have caught the vision of what the Book of Mormon is all about. Few are they among men who know the part it has played and will yet play in preparing the way for the coming of Him of whom it is a new witness. Few are they who believe its truths and abide by its precepts to such a degree that they would qualify to read the sealed portion of the plates and learn the full account of what the Lord has in store for the people of the world.

Guarding carefully against the use of unwarranted superlatives, let us summarize the divine mission of the Book of Mormon under these headings:

1. *The Book of Mormon bears witness of Christ.*

This holy book, this sacred record, this divine transcript copied from celestial pages which are filed in the libraries above, this book bears solemn witness of Him by whom salvation comes. Above all else it acclaims the divine sonship of the Son of God; it speaks of the Holy Messiah who came to save his people; it tells of his birth, ministry, crucifixion, and resurrection. Having the prints of the nails in his hands and in his feet, and carrying the gashing wound made by a Roman spear in his side, he himself ministered, in love and compassion, to his other sheep in their

American promised land. Christ the Lord stands at the heart and core and center of the book. And the witness it bears of him shall go forth to every nation, and kindred, and tongue, and people, before he comes to rule and reign on earth for a thousand years.

The Bible itself, which recounts much of his life and many of his doings, does not bear a sweeter or purer testimony of his infinite goodness and grace than does this companion volume of holy writ. Why should any who profess to love the Lord and to seek his face have aught but praise for a work that acclaims so perfectly the majesty and glory of the one who is Lord of all?

2. *The Book of Mormon reveals and proclaims the everlasting gospel to the world.*

Salvation is in Christ and in his holy gospel. Moroni, in glorious immortality, flew through the midst of heaven to bring again the everlasting word; Joseph Smith translated the ancient record; and it is now going forth in many languages to all who will receive it. The Book of Mormon contains the fulness of the everlasting gospel. When the revealed word says the gospel restored through Joseph Smith shall be preached in every nation and to every people before the Lord comes, it includes the directive that the Book of Mormon shall go forth to all people and then shall the end come. This book is the way and the means, prepared by the Lord, to preach his gospel in all the world for a witness unto all people.

3. *The Book of Mormon teaches the true doctrines and proclaims the saving truths.*

Truth, diamond truth, pure truth, the truth of heaven, leads men to salvation. True doctrines save; false doctrines damn. In the midst of darkness and apostasy the Book of Mormon came forth to proclaim the doctrines of salvation in plainness and purity, so that all men may know what they must believe to be saved in God's kingdom.

4. *The Book of Mormon sustains and clarifies the Bible.*

The Bible bears true witness of God and his gospel as far as it is translated correctly. Many plain and precious things have been deleted, however; and the Book of Mormon is the means, provided by divine wisdom, to pour forth the gospel word as it was given in perfection to the ancients. It has come to preserve and sustain the Bible, not to destroy or dilute its message.

5. *The Book of Mormon gathers scattered Israel into the true fold and to the appointed places.*

Is the Book of Mormon accomplishing its divine purpose? How else can we account for the fact that those who believe its words forsake all that they have and join with the saints to build up the kingdom? Hundreds of thousands have forsaken lands, homes, families, and the nations of their ancestors to start anew, in poverty and in weakness, with the Lord's people in a desert wasteland. Hundreds of thousands now assemble in stakes of Zion in nation upon nation because they know by the power of the Holy Ghost that the Book of Mormon is true. And endless hosts shall yet place the beauty of its message ahead of the wealth and prestige of the world.

6. *The Book of Mormon proves the truth and divinity of the Lord's great latter-day work.*

If the Book of Mormon is true, then Jesus Christ is the Son of the living God, because that book bears repeated witness of this eternal verity. If the Book of Mormon is true, then Joseph Smith was called of God to usher in the dispensation of the fulness of times and to set up again on earth the Church and kingdom of God. The book proves he was a prophet. If he received the plates from an angel; if he translated them by the gift and power of God; if he received revelations from the Almighty—all of which is a reality if the Book of Mormon is true—who can say he was not a prophet? If the Book of Mormon is true and Joseph Smith is a prophet, who can deny that The Church of Jesus Christ of Latter-day Saints, which he set up by divine direction, is in fact the kingdom of God on earth?

7. *The Book of Mormon came to prepare a people for the second coming of the Son of Man.*

This is implicit in all we have said. It is the restored gospel and the gathering of Israel that prepare men to meet their Lord. It is repentance and right living and keeping the commandments that qualify them to abide the day of his coming. And it is the Book of

Mormon that preaches the gospel and invites men to believe and repent.

8. *The Book of Mormon came to save (or damn) the souls of men.*

Such is the grand conclusion. Men will gain celestial rest or welter with the damned in hell depending on how they view the Nephite record. He that believeth shall be saved! Believeth what? Men must believe the everlasting gospel; they must accept the prophets and legal administrators sent in their day; they must cleave unto the word of truth given of God in the day of their probation. All of this requires that they believe the Lord's word as found in the Book of Mormon—in the Book of Salvation, if you will.

Much of the summary of the power and purpose, the mission and influence, of the Book of Mormon has already been discussed in one connection or another. We shall now expand our bare-bones outline on the remaining points.

The Book of Mormon Perfects the Biblical Message

The Holy Bible has done more to preserve the culture and civilization of Christendom than any other single thing. The invention of printing and the publishing of the Bible did more to lift the shroud of darkness that covered the earth than anything else ever did. The King James Version of the Bible has preserved the English tongue and kept the English-speaking peoples anchored to those standards of decency and morality without which men become animals and nations crumble and decay. And yet neither this Bible nor any Bible has been preserved in sufficient purity to enable men to find the course leading to eternal life and then to walk therein. To gain this end—so devoutly to be desired—the world had to await the coming forth of the Book of Mormon.

Nephi saw in vision both the Bible and the Book of Mormon. As to the Bible he was told by an angel: "When it proceeded forth from the mouth of a Jew it contained the plainness of the gospel of the Lord, of whom the twelve apostles bear record; and . . . these things go forth from the Jews in purity unto the Gentiles." Then came the day of darkness, of apostasy, and of evil.

Then, after the gospel truths went forth "by the hand of the twelve apostles of the Lamb, from the Jews unto the Gentiles," the angel said, "thou seest the foundation of a great and abominable church, which is most abominable above all other churches." This evil church, this church of the devil, this outgrowth of primitive Christianity, was the most wicked and satanic church then on earth. It pretended to make salvation available while following Lucifer rather than the Lord. Of those in this dire church the angel continued: "They have taken away from the gospel of the Lamb many parts which are plain and most precious; and also many covenants of the Lord have they taken away."

Why did they do this evil thing? The angelic answer was: "And all this have they done that they might pervert the right ways of the Lord, that they might blind the eyes and harden the hearts of the children of men." When the scriptures are perverted, it becomes easy to find ways to walk after the manner of the world and revel in ungodliness. The philosophies of men, mingled with scripture, soon replace the pure word as it was once written in the holy record. "Wherefore, thou seest that after the book hath gone forth through the hands of the great and abominable church," the angelic word continues, "that there are many plain and precious things taken away from the book, which is the book of the Lamb of God."

Thus in the earliest days of the apostasy, the church that once was the Lord's forsook him and worshipped and served what its fancy chose. Then Nephi saw the perverted Bible go forth among all the nations of the Gentiles, including the people in America. In this setting the angel said: "Because of the many plain and precious things which have been taken out of the book, which were plain unto the understanding of the children of men, according to the plainness which is in the Lamb of God—because of these things which are taken away out of the gospel of the Lamb, an exceeding great many do stumble, yea, insomuch that Satan hath great power over them."

But through it all a brighter day lay ahead. The Lord God promised that he would not "suffer that the Gentiles shall forever remain in that awful state of blindness, which thou beholdest they are in, because of the plain and most precious parts of the gospel of the Lamb which have been kept back by that abominable church, whose formation thou hast seen."

There was to be a day of restoration; the light of heaven was to pierce the darkness covering the earth; new scripture was to lift the gross darkness enshrouding the hearts of men. For thus saith the Lord: "After the Gentiles do stumble exceedingly, because of the most plain and precious parts of the gospel of the Lamb which have been kept back by that abominable church, which is the mother of harlots, saith the Lamb—I will be merciful unto the Gentiles in that day, insomuch that I will bring forth unto them, in mine own power, much of my gospel, which shall be plain and precious, saith the Lamb."

The promise is then made of the coming forth of the Book of Mormon. Lehi's seed shall keep the record; they shall be destroyed and dwindle in unbelief; and their records shall be hidden in the earth. In due course these records shall "come forth unto the Gentiles, by the gift and power of the Lamb. And in them shall be written my gospel, saith the Lamb, and my rock and my salvation." (1 Ne. 13:20-36.)

And thus, the Lord be praised, we have his eternal promise that the Bible will be added to, clarified, perfected, as it were, by the Nephite scripture—that glorious volume, the Book of Mormon—before the second coming of the Son of Man!

Lucifer Wages War Against the Book of Mormon

Satan guided his servants in taking many plain and precious things, and many of the covenants of the Lord, from the Bible, so that men would stumble and fall and lose their souls. When these truths and doctrines and covenants are restored through the Book of Mormon, what may we expect from Satan and from his servants? Their natural reaction—their craft is in danger!—will be to poison the minds of men against the Nephite scripture, so they will continue to stumble as they rely on the Bible alone.

One obvious approach is for them to write in their creeds, to preach from their pulpits, and to use all their powers of learning and sophistry to proclaim such doctrines as these: revelation has ceased; the gifts of the Spirit are no longer needed; the Bible suffices; it contains all that is needed for salvation; what was good enough for Paul and Peter is good enough for us. To all such who should arise in the last days, and their numbers are many, this word came from the Lord to Nephi: "Wo be unto him that hearkeneth unto the precepts of men, and denieth the power of God, and the gift of the Holy Ghost!" What blessing is there in a religion where the power of God is not manifest and where the gifts of the Spirit are not found? Can a religion without power to heal the sick and raise the dead have power to exalt a mortal soul in celestial glory?

"Yea, wo be unto him that saith: We have received, and we need no more!" How unthinkable it is that man can close the mouth of God! If the Great God is the same yesterday, today, and forever; if he is no respecter of persons and he spoke in times past; if a soul is just as precious in his sight today as it ever was, how dare anyone presume to close the heavens and say, "Our God is dead; his voice is stilled; revelation was for the ancients, not for us"? Are all the problems of the earth solved? Is there no need for divine guidance to direct the affairs of men today?

"Wo unto all those who tremble, and are angry because of the truth of God! For behold, he that is built upon the rock receiveth it with gladness; and he that is built upon a sandy foundation trembleth lest he shall fall." Why should men be angry because God spoke to Joseph Smith? If they do not believe he did so, then why rise up in wrath? If they are right, and there is no revelation, they have nothing to fear. But the devil knows who the Lord's prophets are and where the work of the Almighty is found. And all who are built on false and sandy foundations rise up in fear. Only those who belong to false churches fear and deride the prophets; only those without the light and guidance of heaven rise up to fight the Lord's work.

"Wo be unto him that shall say: We have received the word of God, and we need no more of the word of God, for we have enough!" How devilish and evil it is to say: "We want no new truths; we choose to remain in darkness; we prefer ignorance as a way of life. The light of this candle suffices; let no man discover electricity. We have enough."

The Lord's own condemnation of all such small, bigoted, and prejudiced souls is set forth in these words: "Thus saith the Lord God: I will give unto the children of men line upon line, precept upon precept, here a little and there a little; and blessed are those who hearken unto my precepts, and lend an ear unto my counsel, for they shall learn wisdom; for unto him that receiveth will I give more; and from them that shall say, We have enough, from them shall be taken away even that which they have." How plain and pure is this word! How it accords with all that God has said in all ages! Surely the day shall come when all those who find fault with the revelations given to Joseph Smith and who deny the divine status of the Book of Mormon shall have cause to fear and tremble. Surely their souls shall be in turmoil and their minds filled with anxieties as they stand before the judgment bar.

"Cursed is he that putteth his trust in man," the divine word continues, "or maketh flesh his arm, or shall hearken unto the precepts of men, save their precepts shall be given by the power of the Holy Ghost." Unless the power of God attends the teaching of doctrine, unless the Holy Spirit bears witness of the truths expressed, unless the words spoken have divine approval, they have no saving power. And where there is no salvation, there must of necessity be damnation.

"Wo be unto the Gentiles, saith the Lord God of Hosts! For notwithstanding I shall lengthen out mine arm unto them from day to day, they will deny me." How many things there are on every hand that invite and entice men to believe the word found in modern scripture. One scientific discovery after another bears witness of what God by his prophets has proclaimed to the world. Every jot and tittle of reason and logic and sense combine to show the excellence of the Lord's way as recorded in holy writ. And yet men deny and disbelieve.

"Nevertheless, I will be merciful unto them, saith the Lord God, if they will repent and come unto me; for mine arm is lengthened out all the day long, saith the Lord God of Hosts." (2 Ne. 28:26-32.) Thanks be to God there is hope—even for those who thus far have fought the truth—if they will repent of their false doctrines and false teachings; if they will forsake the master who heretofore has guided their thinking and desires; and if they will worship the Lord and fellowship his saints.

Having laid this foundation, the Lord goes on to a glorious climax. In doing so, he both reasons with men and announces his own views. And who can deny his word or refute the divine logic it sets forth? "My words shall hiss forth unto the ends of the earth," saith the Lord God, "for a standard unto my people, which are of the house of Israel; And because my words shall hiss forth"—note it well, it is one of the signs of the times; one of the things that must and shall occur before the Second Coming; one of the things that lets us know the day is near—"many of the Gentiles shall say: A Bible! A Bible! We have got a Bible, and there cannot be any more Bible." How vain, how foolish, how arrogant for man to tell God what he can and cannot do. Are there no new truths to be revealed? Were the Jews the only people to whom God ever spoke? Who but Satan would teach such a doctrine?

"But thus saith the Lord God: O fools, they shall have a Bible"—strong language this!—"and it shall proceed forth from the Jews, mine ancient covenant people." The Bible is the book of the Jews; salvation is of the Jews; they are the source of Gentile knowledge about God and his laws. "And what thank they the Jews for the Bible which they receive from them? Yea, what do the Gentiles mean? Do they remember the travails, and the labors, and the pains of the Jews, and their diligence unto me, in bringing forth salvation unto the Gentiles?"

Jesus, who was crucified, and Peter, who died in like manner, were Jews. Isaiah, who was sawn asunder, and Jeremiah, who languished in a foul dungeon, were Jews. Daniel, who was cast into a den of lions, and Ezekiel, who was carried captive into Babylon, were Jews. "O ye Gentiles, have ye remembered the Jews, mine ancient covenant people? Nay; but ye have cursed them, and have hated them, and have not sought to recover them. But behold, I will return all these things upon your own heads; for I the Lord have not forgotten my people."

How severe is the condemnation of those who suppose they believe part of the Lord's word, but who openly reject the remainder. "Thou fool, that shall say: A Bible, we have got a Bible, and we need no more Bible. Have ye obtained a Bible save it were by the Jews?" And if the world received its Bible from the Jews, wherein does this differ from receiving the Book of Mormon from the Nephites?

"Know ye not that there are more nations than one? Know ye not that I, the Lord your God, have created all men, and that I remember those who are upon the isles of the sea; and that I rule in the heavens above and in the earth beneath; and I bring forth my word unto the children of men, yea, even upon all the nations of the earth? Wherefore murmur ye, because that ye shall receive more of my word?" (2 Ne. 29:2-8.) And thus it is. Let those who reject the Book of Mormon know that, like their counterparts in Jerusalem who rejected the Lord Jesus when he ministered among them, they are fulfilling the prophetic word and are bringing to pass one of the signs of the times.

THE BOOK THAT PREPARES THE WAY

The Divine Power of the Divine Book

The written word—how great it is! The divine word—how it has shaped the destiny of men and governed the course of nations! The holy scriptures—how they have brought to pass the purposes of the Lord, among both believers and unbelievers!

Nephi, at the peril of his own life, slew Laban and gained the brass plates for himself and his people. Because of them, the Nephites knew and lived the law of Moses; because of them, they preserved their language, their culture, their civilization, and even their religion. The Mulekites, on the other hand, being without the written word, dwindled in unbelief, lost their language and culture and religion, and degenerated to a low and uncivilized state. So also was it with the Lamanites after they destroyed the Nephite nation. They were degenerate, slothful, and without God in the world; they enjoyed none of the gifts of the Spirit and had no hope of eternal life.

Such decency and civilization as prevailed during the dark ages came because a few biblical truths were taught and a handful of people had access to the written word itself. The revival of learning and the breaking of the shackles of ignorance came to pass because the Bible was published to the people. Protestant churches exist because members of the Catholic Church began to read the Bible and compare what they learned with the practices of their church. There were wars and battles and crusades; there were compacts and alliances and treaties; there were nations and kingdoms and peoples—all of which played their part in history because men felt this or that way about the written word. The whole history of the the English-speaking peoples in particular has been one of religious wars and religious conflicts.

Nor has it been nor shall it be any different where the Book of Mormon is concerned. Like the Bible, it is a volume of holy writ that speaks forth the mind and will of the Almighty. Like the Bible, it invites men to forsake the world and live as becometh saints. Like the Bible, it has such an impact upon the hearts of men that they are prepared to die in defense of their beliefs. Already the ten thousands of Ephraim and the thousands of Manasseh have left Babylon and come to Zion with songs of everlasting joy because of it. And before the end of the world, which is the premillennial destruction of the wicked, and before the end of the earth, which shall not occur until after the Millennium, the Book of Mormon shall so affect men that the whole earth and all its peoples will have been influenced and governed by it.

What says the prophetic word with reference to the divine power that shall attend this divine book?

After the Lord told Enoch that in the last days righteousness would come down out of heaven (meaning the gospel would be restored), and that truth would come out of the earth to bear testimony of Christ and his gospel (meaning the Book of Mormon would come forth), then the divine word acclaimed: "And righteousness and truth will I cause to sweep the earth as with a flood." That is to say: The restored gospel and the Book of Mormon will surge forth in a tide that cannot be stayed. As flooding rains and surging rivers sweep bridges and obstacles before them; as houses and lands and even mountains flow down by the power of a flood; as water cleanses and washes away the filth of the world—so shall the divine word go forth. There is no power like the power of a flood; nothing can stay its swirling, surging, sweeping waves. So shall it be with the spread of truth in the last days.

And why shall the flood of truth—the gospel and the Book of Mormon—go forth? "To gather out mine elect from the four quarters of the earth," the Lord says, "unto a place which I shall prepare, an Holy City, that my people may gird up their loins, and be looking forth for the time of my coming; for there shall be my tabernacle, and it shall be called Zion, a New Jerusalem." (Moses 7:62.)

What then is the power of the Book of Mormon? It will proclaim the everlasting gospel; it will gather Israel; it will build the New Jerusalem; it will prepare a people for the Second Coming; it will usher in the Millennium—at least it will play such an important part in all of these that its value and power can scarcely be overstated.

Ezekiel bears a like witness. It is part of his prophecy about the Stick of Judah and the Stick of Joseph. When he was asked, "Wilt thou not shew us what thou meanest by these?" the Lord directed him to answer that even as the Bible and the Book of Mormon became one in his hand, so should the divided kingdoms of Judah and Ephraim become one kingdom in the last days. "Say unto them," he was told, "Thus saith the Lord God; Behold, I will take the children of Israel from among the heathen, whither they be gone, and will gather them on every side, and bring them into their own land: And I will make them one nation in the land upon the mountains of Israel." One nation, one people, one gospel, one set of standard works, one doctrine (that in the Bible and the Book of Mormon)—such shall be their heritage in that day.

"And one king shall be king to them all," and he shall be the Lord Jesus Christ, the Son of David, the King of Israel. "And they shall be no more two nations, neither shall they be divided into two kingdoms any more at all," for those who come unto Christ "are no more strangers and foreigners, but fellowcitizens with the saints, and of the household of God." (Eph. 2:19.) They are members of one kingdom, the kingdom of their King.

"Neither shall they defile themselves any more with their idols, nor with their detestable things, nor with any of their transgressions: but I will save them out of all their dwellingplaces, wherein they have sinned, and will cleanse them: so shall they be my people, and I will be their God." They will believe in Christ, repent of their sins, be cleansed in the waters of baptism, and become the Lord's people.

"And David my servant"—the Eternal David, the Son of David, the one of whom David of old was a type and a shadow—"shall be king over them; and they all shall have one shepherd." This is the day of which the angel said to Nephi: "These last records, which thou hast seen among the Gentiles [the Book of Mormon and other latter-day scripture], shall establish the truth of the first, which are of the twelve apostles of the Lamb [the Bible], and shall make known the plain and precious things which have been taken away from them; and shall make known to all kindreds, tongues, and people, that the Lamb of God is the Son of the Eternal Father, and the Savior of the world; and that all men must come unto him, or they cannot be saved. And they must come according to the words which shall be established by the mouth of the Lamb; and the words of the Lamb shall be made known in the records of thy seed [the Book of Mormon], as well as in the records of the twelve apostles of the Lamb [the Bible]; wherefore they both shall be established in one; for there is one God and one Shepherd over all the earth." (1 Ne. 13:40-41.)

"They shall also walk in my judgments, and observe my statutes, and do them." They shall keep the commandments; they shall live the gospel; they shall walk in the light. They shall dwell in the appointed place, "and my servant David"—the Eternal David—"shall be their prince for ever." Christ will reign among them, and he will be their everlasting King.

"Moreover I will make a covenant of peace with them; it shall be an everlasting covenant with them." They shall have the gospel; it is the covenant of peace; it is the new and everlasting covenant, the covenant of salvation.

"And I will place them, and multiply them, and will set my sanctuary [my temple] in the midst of them for evermore. My tabernacle also shall be with them: yea, I will be their God, and they shall be my people. And the heathen shall know that I the Lord do sanctify Israel, when my sanctuary [temple] shall be in the midst of them for evermore." (Ezek. 37:15-28.)

What is it that shall happen when the Bible and the Book of Mormon become one in the Lord's hand? Israel shall gather both spiritually and temporally. They shall become one people, and division and disunity among them shall cease. "Ephraim shall not envy Judah, and Judah shall not vex Ephraim." (Isa. 11:13.) The Lord himself, the Eternal David, shall be their King and their Shepherd. They will repent and be baptized and keep the commandments. The everlasting gospel shall be their most prized possession, and the Lord's houses of worship and his holy temple will be in their midst.

And how will all this be brought to pass? Not by a dead and dying Christendom; not by a people without power and authority; not by those who do not even know what the Lord's sanctuary is; not by the Bible, from which many plain and precious things and many covenants of the Lord have been lost. These things will come to pass in the day of restoration, when righteousness comes down from heaven and truth springs out of the earth. They will be brought to pass by the power of God, by his holy gospel, by the Book of Mormon, wherein the gospel is recorded, and which is sent forth to testify of Christ, to teach doctrine, and to prove the truth and divinity of the Lord's great latter-day work.

Isaiah's great prophecy about the Book of Mormon and the restoration of the gospel speaks of the destruction of the Nephite nation; of their voice speaking from the dust with a familiar spirit; of the day of apostasy when men are drunken but not with wine, and when they stagger but not with strong drink; of the vision of all being as the words of a book that is sealed; of the Lord restoring the gospel; of their land becoming a fruitful field; and, then, of the Book of Mormon going forth to play its part in the great work of the latter days. "And in that day"—when all these things come to pass—"shall the deaf hear the words of the book, and the eyes of the blind shall see out of obscurity and out of darkness." (2 Ne. 27:29.)

"Bring forth the blind people that have eyes, and the deaf that have ears." (Isa. 43:8.) Bring forth those who are blind to the light of the gospel, who cannot see that which is shown before them in the Bible; bring forth those who are deaf to the voice of the Spirit, who do not hear the voice of the Lord as it speaks from the ancient scriptures. Let them see and hear the words of the Book of Mormon where the precious truths are set forth with such plainness that none need err. Then will their eyes be opened and their ears unstopped, and the deaf shall hear and the blind see.

"And the meek also shall increase, and their joy shall be in the Lord, and the poor among men shall rejoice in the Holy One of Israel." (2 Ne. 27:30.) The meek are the God-fearing and the righteous; they come unto the Lord because of the Book of Mormon; they rejoice in his glorious goodness and shout praises to the Holy One of Israel.

Then the holy word speaks of what shall be at the Second Coming. "For assuredly as the Lord liveth they"—his saints, the meek among men, those who have believed the words of the book—"shall see that the terrible one is brought to naught, and the scorner is consumed, and all that watch for iniquity are cut off," as also will be the case with those "that make a man an offender for a word, and lay a snare for him that reproveth in the gate, and turn aside the just for a thing of naught." (2 Ne. 27:31-32.) This is the day when every corruptible thing shall be consumed. Those who believe the Book of Mormon and turn unto the Lord shall be saved in the day of burning, for the book came to prepare a people to meet their God.

"Therefore thus saith the Lord, who redeemed Abraham, concerning the house of Jacob, Jacob shall not now be ashamed, neither shall his face now wax pale." Those who accept the gospel and live the law no longer fear the day when the wicked shall be consumed. "But when he seeth his children, the work of mine hands, in the midst of him, they shall sanctify my name, and sanctify the Holy One of Jacob, and shall fear the God of Israel." Israel and her children and her children's children shall worship and serve the true and living God.

"They also that erred in spirit shall come to understanding, and they that murmured shall learn doctrine." (Isa. 29:1-24.) Such is the purpose of the Book of Mormon. Members of false churches who err in spirit, who think they have the truth, are brought by the Book of Mormon to the fulness of the gospel. Those who have based their beliefs on isolated verses and obscure passages, and who have wondered and murmured at seeming biblical conflicts, come to learn sound doctrine. No longer do they worry about the atonement, salvation by grace alone, infant baptism, the priesthood, the gifts of the Spirit, the passages about an apostasy, a gospel restoration, and the gathering of Israel. All things fall into place because of this new witness for Christ and his gospel, this witness which bears the name of the prophet Mormon.

Proving the Second Coming

We are mindful of Peter's prophecy that in the last days scoffers shall rise up, "walking after their own lusts, And saying, Where is the promise of his coming?" (2 Pet. 3:3-4.) We are aware that few only among us mortals, including even those who call themselves Christians, believe that he will come, clothed with immortal glory, having a body of flesh and bones, to live and walk and be among men again. This brings us face to face with such questions as these: How do you prove there will be a second coming? How can anyone know he will come again? Are the views of various religionists on this matter simply legend, folklore, and myth?

A special standard of judgment is needed to prove anything in the spiritual realm. No scientific research, no intellectual inquiry, no investigative processes known to mortal man can prove that God is a personal being, that all men will be raised in immortality, and that repentant souls are born of the Spirit. There is no way to perform an experiment in a laboratory that will duplicate the appearance of the Father and the Son in the spring of 1820, or the coming of Moroni or Moses or Elijah to the Prophet Joseph Smith, or the vision of the degrees of glory opened to the view of Joseph Smith and Sidney Rigdon. Spiritual verities can be proven only by spiritual means. The visions of eternity can be duplicated only by those who abide the laws that enable them to attune their souls to the infinite. This is as yet beyond the spiritual capacity of most weak and faltering mortals.

The Lord has given to us all, however, a standard of judgment that is both unique and perfect. By using it we may gain a perfect knowledge as to the Second Coming or any other gospel verity. In the ultimate and final sense of the word, this standard of judgment is to receive the Holy Spirit, whose mission is to reveal and bear witness of the truth. In practice it is something else; it is the Book of Mormon. This book is the volume of divine truth that the Lord has given to the world to prove all else that he has ever said.

How and in what way does the Book of Mormon prove there will be a second coming of Christ? Or, for that matter, how does it give absolute certainty where any great spiritual verity is concerned? In principle, when we are able to determine one spiritual verity with absolute certainty, that determination carries with it an irrefutable witness of many other truths. For instance, if we know there is a Son of God, we of necessity also know there is a God; otherwise he could not have had a Son. If we know that the Holy Messiah redeemed men from the fall of Adam, we also know that there was an Adam and that he brought temporal and spiritual death into the world. If we know that God is the same yesterday, today, and forever, and that he sent angels to minister to men anciently, we also know that under the same circumstances and in like situations he will send angels to minister to men today.

Thus, if we know by revelation from the Holy Ghost that the Book of Mormon is a volume of holy scripture that came forth by the gift and power of God; if we know that it was translated by a man who communed with angels and saw visions; if we know that it is the voice of God to a degenerate world—we thereby know that Joseph Smith was a prophet and that the doctrines taught by the Nephite prophets are true.

These realizations bring us to a consideration of certain revealed concepts that show the position of the Book of Mormon in the eternal scheme of things. After saying that the Book of Mormon persuades men to do good, to believe in Jesus, and to endure to the end, and after saying it speaks harshly against sin, Nephi acclaimed: "No man will be angry at the words which I have written save he shall be of the spirit of the devil." And further: "Believe in Christ. . . . And if ye shall believe in Christ ye will believe in these words, for they are the words of Christ, and he hath given them unto me; and they teach all men that they should do good." (2 Ne. 33:4-5, 10.)

The Lord Jesus spoke these words to Moroni: "He that will

contend against the word of the Lord, let him be accursed; and he that shall deny these things"—the things then spoken, the things written in the Book of Mormon—"let him be accursed; for unto them will I show no greater things. . . . And he that believeth not my words believeth not my disciples. . . . But he that believeth these things which I have spoken"—and which are recorded in the Book of Mormon—"him will I visit with the manifestations of my Spirit, and he shall know and bear record. For because of my Spirit he shall know that these things are true; for it persuadeth men to do good. And whatsoever thing persuadeth men to do good is of me; for good cometh of none save it be of me. I am the same that leadeth men to all good; he that will not believe my words will not believe me—that I am; and he that will not believe me will not believe the Father who sent me." (Ether 4:8-12.)

Mormon addressed these words to the Lamanites living in the last days: "Repent, and be baptized in the name of Jesus, and lay hold upon the gospel of Christ, which shall be set before you, not only in this record [the Book of Mormon] but also in the record which shall come unto the Gentiles from the Jews [the Bible], which record shall come from the Gentiles unto you. For behold, this is written for the intent that ye may believe that; and if ye believe that ye will believe this also; and if ye believe this ye will know concerning your fathers, and also the marvelous works which were wrought by the power of God among them." (Morm. 7:8-9.)

From these passages we reach certain clear conclusions relative to believing in Christ and in his holy word. Among them are these: A belief in Christ and a belief in the Book of Mormon go together; they are locked in each other's arms; they cannot be separated. Like Ezekiel's two sticks, they are one in the hands of the Father. Those who believe in Christ also believe the Book of Mormon because it contains the words of Christ. Those who believe the words of Christ, as given by his disciples and as recorded in the Book of Mormon, believe in Christ. And those who do not believe these words do not believe in him. The Book of Mormon bears witness of Christ and of the Bible; it is written to persuade men to believe in their Lord and in his ancient word. Those who believe the Book of Mormon believe the Bible, and those who believe the Bible believe the Book of Mormon.

Having set forth these concepts from the Book of Mormon itself, we are now prepared to put the capstone on the whole matter by catching the vision of these words of latter-day revelation. They are in the revelation commanding Joseph Smith and his associates to organize again on earth that eternal church which is the kingdom of God on earth. The revealed word says: "God ministered unto him [Joseph Smith] by an holy angel [Moroni], whose countenance was as lightning, and whose garments were pure and white above all other whiteness." God, who is the Lord Jesus Christ, by the hand of Moroni, during the whole night of September 21-22, 1823, revealed to his chosen prophet the hiding place of the ancient record and a knowledge of much that was destined to be in the last days before his glorious return.

And God "gave unto him commandments which inspired him." The word poured forth by the mouth of the angel, by the power of the Spirit, by the opening of the heavens, by the audible voice of God himself—all speaking peace, all giving direction, all laying the foundation for the work that now has commenced.

And God "gave him power from on high, by the means which were before prepared [the Urim and Thummim], to translate the Book of Mormon." Truth must spring out of the earth; a voice must whisper from the dust; the testimony of a people long dead must be heard. Joseph Smith must translate the Book of Mormon, "which contains a record of a fallen people"—it is an inspired history—"and the fulness of the gospel of Jesus Christ to the Gentiles and to the Jews also." Here then is the promised record prepared from ages past, prepared by the unwearying diligence of a whole congregation of prophets, prepared by God himself that his gospel, the plan of salvation, might be known again among men.

The newly called prophet must translate the Book of Mormon, "which was given by inspiration"—to Nephi, Alma, Mormon, and the ancient prophets—"and is confirmed to others by the ministering of angels"—angelic ministrants bore record to their fellow servants on earth that the ancient word was true—"and is declared unto the world by them." Joseph Smith, the Three Witnesses, all who gained the knowledge from heaven-sent messengers then presented the message to the world and testified to all men that it was true.

The Book of Mormon came forth "proving to the world that the holy scriptures [those in the holy Bible] are true, and that God does inspire men and call them to his holy work in this age and generation, as well as in generations of old; thereby showing that he is the same God yesterday, today, and forever." (D&C 20:6-12.) Thus the Nephite record came forth to prove that the Bible is true; it came forth to prove that Joseph Smith, its translator, was and is a prophet; it came forth to prove that God calls men again in this day "to his holy work," which holy work, being the Lord's, is itself eternally and everlastingly true.

In the absolute and eternal sense, the greatest and most important issue in the field of revealed religion in all ages is this: Is there a God in heaven who ordained and established a plan of salvation to enable his children to advance and progress and become like him?

Also in the absolute and eternal sense, because that eternal plan of salvation is based upon and made operative by the atoning sacrifice of God's Son, we can properly say that the heart and center of revealed religion in all ages is: Was Jesus Christ the Son of the living God who was crucified for the sins of the world, did he bring life and immortality to light through the gospel, and is his the only name given under heaven whereby man may come unto God and find that eternal life so devoutly desired by the righteous?

In a nearer and more pointed sense, we can with propriety, in this day and dispensation, say that the great and eternal issue to be resolved is: Was Joseph Smith called of God? For if he was, then the witness he has borne of the Lord Jesus is true, and the church he organized administers the eternal plan of salvation of the Father.

And even more pointedly, let us say that there is no greater issue ever to confront mankind in modern times than this: Is the Book of Mormon the mind and will and voice of God to all men? For if it is, then Joseph Smith was a prophet, the testimony of Jesus he gave is true, and the plan of salvation of the Great God is in full operation.

It is no wonder, then, that we find the Prophet himself saying: "I told the brethren [the modern Twelve Apostles of the Lamb] that the Book of Mormon was the most correct of any book on earth, and the keystone of our religion, and a man would get nearer to God by abiding by its precepts, than by any other book." (*Teachings*, p. 194.)

The keystone is the central stone at the top of an arch which binds the whole structure together. When it is firmly in place, the arch stands; when it is removed, the structure falls. Thus "our religion," the whole system of revealed truth that has come to us by the opening of the heavens, stands or falls depending upon the truth or falsity of the Book of Mormon. This holy volume proves the divinity of the work as a whole and of every part and portion individually.

And so the prophetic word, having set forth the general concept that the Book of Mormon came forth to prove the divinity of the work itself, begins to particularize. "By these things"—the coming forth of a record written anciently by the spirit of prophecy; its translation by the gift and power of God; the confirmation of its truth by angelic ministration—"By these things we know" the verity of all that has been revealed to us. Among the items then and there listed are these: "That there is a God in heaven"; that he created all things; that he revealed his holy truths to man; that Adam fell and men became carnal, sensual, and devilish; that the Only Begotten atoned for the sins of the world; and that those who believe and obey shall be saved. (D&C 20:17-31.) These truths are but illustrations; the application of the principle knows no bounds.

Every accountable person on earth—there is no exception; this principle has universal application; no living soul is exempt—every such person who will read the Book of Mormon, ponder its truths in his heart, and ask God the Eternal Father in the name of Christ, in sincerity and with real intent, "having faith in Christ," shall come to know, "by the power of the Holy Ghost," that the book is true. (Moro. 10:3-5.) All such persons can then, by the same power, testify to the truth of all things pertaining to the glorious restoration now in process. They can say:

We know that the Father and the Son appeared to Joseph Smith because the Book of Mormon is true.

We know that the angelic ministrants conferred priesthoods and keys upon mortals in this day because the Book of Mormon is true.

We know that Joseph Smith is a prophet of God because the Book of Mormon is true.

We know that The Church of Jesus Christ of Latter-day Saints is the kingdom of God on earth, the one place where salvation may be found, because the Book of Mormon is true.

We know that the Lord Jesus Christ will come in the clouds of glory in due course because the Book of Mormon is true.

The truth and divinity of the Book of Mormon is an absolute and unshakable witness that there will be a second coming of Christ!

ISRAEL: THE CHOSEN PEOPLE

The Israel of God

Blessed Israel, the people favored by the Father—who are they and what part do they play in the eternal scheme of things?

For the last four thousand years the whole history of the world—the rise and fall of nations; the discovery of islands and continents; the peopling of all lands and the fates which have befallen all people—for four millenniums the whole earth has been governed and controlled for the benefit of the children of Israel. And now the day of their glory and triumph is at the door.

The concept of a chosen and favored people, a concept scarcely known in the world and but little understood even by the saints of God, is one of the most marvelous systems ever devised for administering salvation to all men in all nations in all ages. Israel, the Lord's chosen people, were a congregation set apart in preexistence. In large measure, the spirit children of the Father who acquired a talent for spirituality, who chose to heed the divine word then given, and who sought, above their fellows, to do good and work righteousness—all these were foreordained to be born in the house of Israel. They were chosen before they were born. This is the doctrine of election. They were true and faithful in the premortal life, and they earned the right to be born as the Lord's people and to have the privilege, on a preferential basis, of believing and obeying the word of truth. Believing blood, the blood of Abraham, flows in their veins. They are the ones of whom Jesus said:

"My sheep hear my voice, and I know them, and they follow me: And I give unto them eternal life; and they shall never perish, neither shall any man pluck them out of my hand." (John 10:27-28.)

Because their numbers were known and the days of their mortal probation were selected in advance, Moses was able to say: "When the most High divided to the nations their inheritance, when he separated the sons of Adam, he set the bounds of the people according to the number of the children of Israel. For the Lord's portion is his people; Jacob is the lot of his inheritance." (Deut. 32:8-9.) And thus Jehovah said to Israel anciently: "If ye will obey my voice indeed, and keep my covenant, then ye shall be a peculiar treasure unto me above all people: for all the earth is mine: And ye shall be unto me a kingdom of priests, and an holy nation." (Ex. 19:5-6.) "For thou art an holy people unto the Lord thy God: the Lord thy God hath chosen thee to be a special people unto himself, above all people that are upon the face of the earth." (Deut. 7:6; 14:2.) And thus Peter said to Israel in his day: "Ye are a chosen generation, a royal priesthood, an holy nation, a peculiar people; that ye should shew forth the praises of him who hath called you out of darkness into his marvellous light." (1 Pet. 2:9.) And as it was in those days, so it is today. Gathered Israel is now and everlastingly shall be a holy nation, a peculiar people, and a kingdom of priests who minister salvation to the peoples of the world.

Israel are the seed of Abraham; they are the children of the prophets; and they associate with the Lord's seers. Israel are the friends of apostles and revelators; they are the children of God by faith; they are the sons and daughters of the Lord Jesus Christ in whose name they worship the Father. Paul acclaims that they are the ones "to whom pertaineth the adoption, and the glory, and the covenants, and the giving of the law, and the service of God, and the promises." They are the nation "of whom as concerning the flesh Christ came."

But "they are not all Israel, which are of Israel: Neither, because they are the seed of Abraham, are they all children: but, In Isaac shall thy seed be called. That is, They which are the children of the flesh, these are not the children of God." And all this, Paul says, was determined of God beforehand, "that the purpose of God according to election might stand, not of works, but of him that calleth." (Rom. 9:4-11.)

Adam came to be the father of all living; Noah succeeded to this high status and became the father of all living from his day onward; and Abraham came to be the father of the faithful, the father of all who believe and obey the gospel from his day onward as long as the earth shall stand. Of this we shall speak more particularly when we set forth the promises made to the fathers, which must be planted in the hearts of the children before the Lord comes. For our present purposes it will suffice to know that the seed of Abraham, and then the seed of Isaac, and then the seed of Jacob (who is Israel) comprise the chosen people, a people who first save themselves and who then offer salvation to all men. Salvation is of Israel; or, as Jesus said of the portion of Israel yet unscattered in his day, "Salvation is of the Jews." (John 4:22.)

Israel, anciently, went down into Egypt to find corn lest they die of hunger; they came out of Egyptian bondage to worship God without the interference of the world, and they then became a mighty people in their promised land. Thereafter, for rebellion, they were scattered in all the nations of the earth. The scriptures abound with prophetic statements relative to them, to their scattering in ancient days and their gathering again in latter days, to their restoration as a people and a kingdom; and to their ultimate glory, honor, and renown among the nations of men. It is of these things that we shall now speak.

Scattering the Chosen Ones

The gathering of Israel, now commenced and now in progress, is one of the signs of the times. It is one of the marvels of the ages, one of the worldwide and earth-shaking occurrences destined to come before and to continue after the Second Coming. It is written that "all Israel shall be saved"—all who return and are faithful—all shall be saved by the Deliverer who shall come out of Zion, for he "shall turn away ungodliness from Jacob," and in the appointed day, he "shall take away their sins." (Rom. 11:26-27.)

No man, in these last days, can be saved unless he gathers with Israel and casts his lot with the chosen people. No man can gather with the elect unless and until he knows who they are and where they reside. Nor can any person identify Israel and fully envision what is involved in the doctrine of the gathering unless he knows how, and why, and in what manner, and where Israel was scattered. The gathering grows out of the scattering, and the reasons for the scattering will reveal how the gathering will be brought to pass.

During the almost two thousand years from the birth of Jacob in 1837 B.C. to the destruction of Jerusalem and the scattering of the Jews in A.D. 71, Israel swung back and forth like a pendulum, manifesting exceedingly great righteousness on the one hand and the most abominable wickedness and perversion on the other. When she was righteous, the Lord Jehovah poured out his gifts and powers upon her and she triumphed over all her enemies. In the days of her rebellion, she was overrun by alien nations; her fair sons and daughters fell by the sword; pestilence and disease swept through her cities; and captive remnants were carried into other nations to serve the gods of men and of devils.

Israel was governed by the law of Moses, which was the preparatory gospel, and at times portions of her people had the fulness of the gospel. The Nephites had both the gospel and the law of Moses as did those, from time to time, who followed the counsels of Elijah and Isaiah and various of the prophets. Thus the people—not always but during periods of especial righteousness—enjoyed the gifts of the Spirit and walked in a pleasing way before their God. And that God, the God of Israel, was the Lord Jehovah who is the Lord Jesus Christ. This we must know if we are to understand the scattering and the gathering.

It was faith in Christ of which Paul spoke when he recited the glories and grandeurs of Israelitish history. It was faith in Christ that parted the Red Sea, broke down the walls of Jericho, put to flight the armies of aliens, raised the dead, and rent the heavens. (Heb. 11:23-40.) Indeed, "all the holy prophets . . . believed in Christ and worshiped the Father in his name." (Jacob 4:4-5.)

Having these things in mind, we are prepared to ask why Israel was scattered and where and in what places the elect and chosen ones found new places of abode. On these points the prophets speak *in extenso*; many passages deal with these issues; there is no dearth of revealed knowledge as to the *why* and the *where* of the scattering. And we must not be deceived on the points at issue.

1. *Why was Israel scattered?*

Israel was scattered from time to time during some fifteen hundred years of her history. Why? It is a sad and sorry tale. But the record is clear; the divine word is specific; the passages giving the reasons are numerous. Israel was rejected, cursed, smitten, and scattered for her sins and because she rebelled against the God of Israel.

Israel, from time to time and on many occasions, sank back into the bondage of Egypt, into the bondage of Babylon, into the bondage of the world, because she forsook the Lord Jehovah and worshipped and lived after the manner of the world. As a people she reveled in all of the abominations of the carnal nations that preceded her in Canaan. She trusted in the arm of flesh as did the Canaanites and Hittites. She found pleasure in the astrology and necromancy of the Amorites and the Perizzites. She looked with favor on the practices of the Hivites and the Jebusites.

Israel was cursed because she partook of all the evils of the world in which she dwelt. Her young men visited the temple prostitutes of Ashtoreth, and her young women defiled themselves as harlots with the heathen. Her priests sacrificed on the altars of Baal, and Solomon himself built an altar to Molech whereon Ahaz and others sacrificed children. Portions and groups of Israel in Palestine sank to the same depths of depravity and evil that prevailed among the Lamanites in that day when murder and adultery and human sacrifices became their way of life.

Israel was scattered because she apostatized; because she broke the Ten Commandments; because she rejected the prophets and seers and turned to wizards that peep and mutter; because she forsook the covenant; because she gave heed to false ministers and joined false churches; because she ceased to be a peculiar people and a kingdom of priests. When she became as the world, the Lord left her to suffer and live and be as the world then was.

"Hath a nation changed their gods?" Jehovah asked his people. Have they accepted gods "which are yet no gods"? he asked. "My people have changed their glory for that which doth not profit," he said. "Be astonished, O ye heavens, at this, and be horribly afraid, be ye very desolate, saith the Lord. For my people have committed two evils; they have forsaken me the fountain of living waters, and hewed them out cisterns, broken cisterns, and that can hold no water." (Jer. 2:11-13.) Israel forsook Jehovah, from whom living waters flow, and worshipped other gods. Israel no longer drank the living water, which, if men drink, they shall never thirst more. Rather she made her own churches, her own cisterns—"broken cisterns," false churches—which can hold none of the waters of life.

Lehi and his family left Jerusalem for their American promised land in 600 B.C. In about 588 B.C. Nebuchadnezzar overran Jerusalem and took the people captive into Babylon. At this time Mulek led another colony to the Americas, where in due course they founded the great city of Zarahemla. Seventy years after the fall of Jerusalem, Cyrus the Persian, having first conquered Babylon, permitted a remnant of the Jews to return to Jerusalem and build again their city and temple. These were the forebears of the Jews of Jesus' day, which Jews were finally scattered to the four winds after the destruction of Jerusalem by Titus in A.D. 70.

All of these historical events, and others of which we have little or no knowledge, came to pass in complete conformity with the prophetic word.

Jacob himself, the father of all Israel, prophesied of one of his sons: "Joseph is a fruitful bough, even a fruitful bough by a well; whose branches run over the wall" (Gen. 49:22), thus foreshadowing the establishment of the Lehite civilization in the Americas. Lehi was of the tribe of Manasseh.

This same Joseph is the one who said: "The Lord hath visited me, and I have obtained a promise of the Lord, that out of the fruit of my loins, the Lord God will raise up a righteous branch out of my loins." He then spoke of the deliverance of Israel from Egyptian bondage. "And it shall come to pass that they shall be scattered again," he said, "and a branch shall be broken off, and shall be carried into a far country; nevertheless they shall be remembered in the covenants of the Lord, when the Messiah cometh." (JST, Gen. 50:24-25.) All of this speaks of Lehi and his seed, a mighty people in the Americas, and of the visit of the Lord Jesus to them after his mortal ministry in Jerusalem.

Moses, speaking to all of the twelve tribes, said: "If thou wilt not hearken unto the voice of the Lord thy God, to observe to do all his commandments and his statutes, . . . [then] shalt [thou] be removed into all the kingdoms of the earth. . . . And ye shall be plucked from off the land whither thou goest to possess it. And the Lord shall scatter thee among all people, from the one end of the earth even unto the other; and there thou shalt serve other gods, which neither thou nor thy fathers have known." (Deut. 28:15, 25, 63-64.)

To Amos the Lord said: "I will sift the house of Israel among all nations, like as corn is sifted in a sieve, yet shall not the least grain fall upon the earth." (Amos 9:9.) Micah recorded the promise that "the remnant of Jacob shall be among the Gentiles in the midst of many people." (Micah 5:8.) And the Lord's word preserved by Zechariah is: "I scattered them with a whirlwind among all the nations whom they knew not." (Zech. 7:14.)

Nephi bears a concurring testimony. "The house of Israel, sooner or later," he says, "will be scattered upon all the face of the earth, and also among all nations." Then speaking of the Ten Tribes he acclaims: "And behold, there are many who are already lost from the knowledge of those who are at Jerusalem. Yea, the more part of all the tribes, have been led away; and they are scattered to and fro upon the isles of the sea; and whither they are none of us knoweth, save that we know that they have been led away."

Then he speaks of the Jews who shall crucify Christ. Because they harden their hearts against the Holy One of Israel, he says, "they shall be scattered among all nations and shall be hated of all men." And then he turns to the scattering of Lehi's seed: "After all the house of Israel have been scattered and confounded, . . . the Lord God will raise up a mighty nation among the Gentiles, yea, even upon the face of this land; and by them shall our seed be scattered." (1 Ne. 22:3-7.)

So speak the scriptures, and what we have written is but a small part of what the prophets have said. And from it all we conclude: Israel—all Israel, every tribe, including the Ten Tribes, who for the moment are lost because we cannot identify them—all Israel is now scattered in all nations and among all peoples. Unless we know this, we cannot catch the vision of the gathering that is to be.

Ephraim—The Wanderer in Israel

Ephraim is the presiding tribe in Israel. He plays the chief role in both the scattering and the gathering of the chosen seed. It is his privilege to lay the foundation for the Second Coming, and the part he is to play has already commenced.

All of the tribes have played and shall play their part in the Lord's strange act. Each has provided and shall provide prophets and seers, and the members of each stand equally before the Lord in seeking and obtaining eternal life. Christ came of Judah as did most of the prophets and apostles of old. Moses and Aaron were of Levi, Paul of Benjamin, and the Nephite prophets of Manasseh. Joseph Smith and the latter-day apostles and prophets are of Ephraim. The Book of Mormon is the Stick of Joseph in the hands of Ephraim. And it is Ephraim who is to guide the destiny of the kingdom in the last days and to bring the blessings of the gospel to the other tribes in the family of Jacob.

Manasseh and Ephraim, born in that order to Joseph, were adopted by their grandfather, Jacob. "And now, of thy two sons, Ephraim and Manasseh," Jacob said to Joseph, "behold, they are mine, and the God of my fathers shall bless them; even as Reuben and Simeon they shall be blessed, for they are mine; wherefore they shall be called after my name. (Therefore they were called Israel.) And thy issue which thou begettest after them, shall be thine, and shall be called after the name of their brethren in their inheritance, in the tribes; therefore they were called the tribes of Manasseh and of Ephraim." Even Joseph's other children were to become the seed of these first two sons.

Then Israel's great patriarch gave Joseph this promise: "The God of thy fathers shall bless thee, and the fruit of thy loins, that they shall be blessed above thy brethren, and above thy father's house"—Manasseh and Ephraim were to take precedence over the other tribes of Israel—"For thou hast prevailed, and thy father's house hath bowed down unto thee, even as it was shown unto thee, before thou wast sold into Egypt by the hands of thy brethren; wherefore thy brethren shall bow down unto thee, from generation to generation, unto the fruit of thy loins forever; For thou shalt be a light unto my people, to deliver them in the days of their captivity, from bondage; and to bring salvation unto them, when they are altogether bowed down under sin." (JST, Gen. 48:5-11.) It is Ephraim and Manasseh who shall administer salvation unto the whole house of Israel in the last days.

Joseph then took Manasseh and Ephraim to Jacob, whose eyes were dim with age, to receive a patriarchal blessing. The young lads were so placed that Jacob's right hand would be placed on Manasseh's head and his left on Ephraim's. But Jacob, "guiding his hands wittingly," reversed the order of precedence. With his right hand on Ephraim and his left on Manasseh, he said: "The Angel which redeemed me from all evil"—meaning the Lord Jehovah, who is the Lord Jesus—"bless the lads; and let my name be named on them, and the name of my fathers Abraham and Isaac; and let them grow into a multitude in the midst of the earth."

Joseph was displeased with the placement of his father's hands. "Not so, my father," he said, "for this is the firstborn; put thy right hand upon his head." Jacob refused. "I know it, my son, I know it," he replied; "he also shall become a people, and he also shall be great: but truly his younger brother shall be greater than he, and his seed shall become a multitude of nations."

Continuing as guided by the Spirit, Jacob "blessed them that day, saying, In thee"—or, better, by thee—"shall Israel bless, saying, God make thee as Ephraim and as Manasseh: and he set Ephraim before Manasseh." (Gen. 48:14-20.)

Reuben, the firstborn, through sin forfeited his right to rule in Israel, and the birthright, by divine direction, passed to Ephraim, an adopted son. Thus, as the Lord promised to gather Israel, he said: "I am a father to Israel, and Ephraim is my firstborn." (Jer.

31:9.) Ephraim shall stand supreme and shall be a guide and a light to his fellows.

In keeping with this concept is the latter-day promise that when the Ten Tribes return, "they shall bring forth their rich treasures unto the children of Ephraim" who are the Lord's "servants." And these other tribes shall "fall down" before Ephraim "and be crowned with glory, even in Zion, by the hands of the servants of the Lord, even the children of Ephraim. . . . Behold, this is the blessing of the everlasting God upon the tribes of Israel, and the richer blessing upon the head of Ephraim and his fellows." (D&C 133:30-34.)

Speaking of the day of gathering and of the people who should bring it to pass, Moses said: "Joseph . . . shall push the people together to the ends of the earth." The tribe of Joseph shall do it! And who is Joseph? Moses continues: "And they are the ten thousands of Ephraim, and they are the thousands of Manasseh." (Deut. 33:16-17.)

Thus, if Israel is to be scattered in all nations upon all the face of the earth; if she is to be gathered by the tribe of Joseph; if Ephraim has the birthright and is the presiding tribe; if the other tribes are to receive their blessings from Ephraim—then Ephraim must also be in all nations upon all the face of the earth, and Ephraim must be the first tribe to gather in the last days. And so it is.

Of the scattering of Ephraim—not alone the Kingdom of Ephraim, but more particularly the tribe itself—the prophetic word says many things, of which these are but a sample: "Ephraim, he hath mixed himself among the people. . . . Strangers have devoured his strength." (Hosea 7:8-9.) "Ephraim hath hired lovers. . . . Because Ephraim hath made many altars to sin, altars shall be unto him to sin." (Hosea 8:9-11.) He has worshipped and served other gods. "Ephraim shall return to Egypt"; he shall leave the true God and return to the worship of the world. "As for Ephraim, their glory shall fly away like a bird. . . . Ephraim is smitten, their root is dried up, they shall bear no fruit. . . . My God will cast them away, because they did not hearken unto him: and they shall be wanderers among the nations." (Hosea 9:3, 11, 16-17.) And there is more, much, much more in similar vein.

Such was the day of scattering. But ours is the day of gathering, a gathering that must commence and has commenced with Ephraim. This is the day when "the rebellious are not of the blood of Ephraim." (D&C 64:36.) This is the day when the cry is going forth:

Come home, ye wanderers; turn to the Lord, ye prodigals; leave the husks and the swine and feast upon the fatted calf! Come home, O Ephraim, and fill thy appointed place in pushing together thy fellows from the ends of the earth!

ISRAEL: GATHERING HIS CHOSEN ONES

God Guarantees the Gathering

Has the Lord Omnipotent, who has all might, all power, and all dominion, spoken with absolute finality with reference to the destiny of his people? Most assuredly he has. Is the decree of the Almighty relative to Israel immutable? Verily it is so. It is his eternal word; it shall come to pass as surely as he lives; it is the decree of his own mouth. Though heaven and earth pass away, not one jot or tittle of his holy word shall fail. Israel shall be gathered; the kingdom shall be restored to the chosen people; Zion shall rise again, for the mouth of the Lord hath spoken it.

It shall be a literal gathering. The seed of Abraham, those in whose veins flows the blood of Jacob, those who are the children of the prophets after the manner of the flesh, shall find their place in the family of their fathers. Though they are separated from their parents by a thousand generations, yet shall they claim their inheritance among the elect. Israel shall be gathered and become one family. In all eternity there is nothing more sure than this. It carries the seal and the guarantee of the Lord God himself.

"For there shall be a day," saith the Lord—and that day is today; it is now; its dawning sun has already risen—"that the watchmen upon the mount Ephraim shall cry, Arise ye, and let us go up to Zion unto the Lord our God." Hear it again, O ye scattered ones, and let it be written in every heart. Ephraim shall bring salvation to you in the last days. Ephraim shall hear the word from the Lord and proclaim it to you. In his hands shall be the Stick of Joseph, which is the Stick of Ephraim, which is the Book of Mormon, which contains the fulness of the everlasting gospel, which is the standard around which all men must either rally or be damned. The call shall come unto you from the mountains of Ephraim. Be wise and give heed.

"For thus saith the Lord; Sing with gladness for Jacob, and shout among the chief of the nations: publish ye, praise ye, and say, O Lord, save thy people, the remnant of Israel." Salvation now goes forth to the scattered remnants in all the nations of their habitation. Publish the word; praise the Lord. Cry Salvation, and Glory, and Honor. The promised day of restoration is here.

"Behold, I will bring them from the north country," saith the Lord—meaning from all the country north of Palestine, north of their original promised land, north of where they were when for their sins they were scattered—"and gather them from the coasts of the earth." Yea, and they shall come not only from the north country, but from all the coasts and regions of the earth, from all the lands where the whirlwind of scattering has carried them. "And with them [are] the blind and the lame, the woman with child and her that travaileth with child together; a great company shall return thither."

So sure is the sound of the trumpet—God does not deal in uncertainties—that even the lame and the blind shall walk with stumbling steps in the caravan of the gathered; even women with children and those travailing in birth shall suffer whatever need be rather than be left behind. Numerous babies were, in fact, born the very night the driven saints, leaving their homes in Nauvoo, crossed the frozen Mississippi River to seek a refuge known only to that God who led their fathers through the Red Sea in ancient days.

"They shall come with weeping, and with supplications, will I lead them." How sweet and tender is the relationship between the Lord and his people. How often the strong weep as they testify of his goodness to them. How he pleads with them to press forward and endure to the end. "I will cause them to walk by the rivers of waters in a straight way, wherein they shall not stumble: for I am a father to Israel, and Ephraim is my firstborn." Let the saints come to Zion, whence streams of living water flow, yea, rivers of water give that refreshment of which, if men drink, they shall never thirst more. The way is straight and the course is narrow, but the Lord shall be a father to all who heed the call of Ephraim and walk therein.

"Hear the word of the Lord, O ye nations, and declare it in the isles afar off, and say, He that scattered Israel will gather him, and keep him, as a shepherd doth his flock. For the Lord hath redeemed Jacob, and ransomed him from the hand of him that was stronger than he. Therefore they shall come and sing in the height of Zion, and shall flow together to the goodness of the Lord." Let all the ends of the earth know that this is the mind and will and purpose of the Almighty; it is his decree, and none can stay his hand.

"Thus saith the Lord, which giveth the sun for a light by day, and the ordinances of the moon and of the stars for a light by night, which divideth the sea when the waves thereof roar; The Lord of hosts is his name: If those ordinances depart from before me, saith the Lord, then the seed of Israel also shall cease from being a nation before me for ever. Thus saith the Lord; If heaven above can be measured, and the foundations of the earth searched out beneath, I will also cast off all the seed of Israel for all that they have done, saith the Lord." (Jer. 31:6-12, 35-37.)

And thus it is. With this principle Isaiah and all the prophets accord, and none can stay the hand that brings it to pass. As there is night and day, as there is heaven and earth, as there is life and death, just so surely will God gather Israel in the last days. Yea, he that scattereth Israel is now gathering her.

Israel Gathers to Jehovah

Jehovah is the God of Israel who led his people out of Egypt and to whom they then gathered in the land of Palestine. Thereafter they were scattered when they forsook him and his laws and worshipped and served false gods. The gathering of Israel—guaranteed as we have seen by Jehovah himself—consists primarily, chiefly, and above all else in the acceptance of and the return to the Lord Jehovah and his laws.

The Lord Jehovah and the Lord Jesus Christ are one and the same person. That person is the Son of God; he is the Savior of men and the Redeemer of the world; he is the Holy One of Israel, the Holy Messiah by whom redemption comes. True religion consists in worshipping the Father, in the name of the Son, by the power of the Holy Ghost. Such was the case with Israel of old in the days of their enlightenment. It was a departure from this course that caused the scattering, and it will be a return to this perfect worship that will bring to pass the gathering.

We have heretofore quoted the word of Jehovah, as given to Jeremiah, that Israel was scattered because they forsook him and worshipped false gods, and that they would continue so to worship in their scattered state in all nations. Then, in this setting, and speaking of the wonders that will attend his great latter-day work—wonders so great that even the parting of the Red Sea will seem insignificant in comparison—in this setting the Lord speaks of the gathering of his people and how and in what way it will be brought to pass.

"Behold, the days come, saith the Lord, that it shall no more be said, The Lord liveth, that brought up the children of Israel out of the land of Egypt; But, The Lord liveth, that brought up the children of Israel from the land of the north, and from all the lands whither he had driven them: and I will bring them again into their land that I gave unto their fathers." This is the promise. Such of the gathering of Israel as has come to pass so far is but the gleam of a star that soon will be hidden by the splendor of the sun in full blaze; truly, the magnitude and grandeur and glory of the gathering is yet to be.

"Behold, I will send for many fishers, saith the Lord, and they shall fish them"—a few here and a few there, in this stream and that, with a large catch occasionally filling the gospel net when it is cast into some favored lake—"and after will I send for many hunters, and they shall hunt them from every mountain, and from every hill, and out of the holes of the rocks." This is the great missionary work of the kingdom. The elders of Ephraim go forth to find the elect of God, hidden as they are from the knowledge of men.

These lost sheep of the fold of Israel shall be found among the Gentiles. Seeing all this in vision, Jeremiah exclaimed: "O Lord, my strength, and my fortress, and my refuge in the day of affliction"—thus using the words and expressing the feelings that would be in the hearts of those who gather—"the Gentiles shall come unto thee from the ends of the earth." That is, those who are not Jews in the sense of being the nationals of the Kingdom of Judah shall be gathered again unto their God.

When they are gathered, they will say: "Surely our fathers have inherited lies, vanity, and things wherein there is no profit. Shall a man make gods unto himself, and they are no gods?" Let that which men worship be made with the axe and saw, with the hammer and chisel, with the furnace and mold; or let it be made in the minds of men and be written in the creeds of apostasy—no matter: men cannot create God. Whatever comes from their hands or springs from their minds is nothing more than a poor, shriveling shadow of the Eternal Reality. God is the Almighty, not an idol made by the hands of man, not a spirit essence dreamed up by fertile brains and described in decadent creeds. God is not what the Christians describe in their creeds; he is not what the Buddhists worship in their temples, nor is he what the heathen bow before in their groves.

God is the Lord Jehovah, and there is none else to whom men must come for salvation.

"Therefore," thus saith Jehovah, "behold, I will this once cause them to know"—'I will identify myself again to men for the last time'—"I will cause them to know mine hand and my might." Once again men will be able to worship Him who made heaven and earth and the sea and the fountains of waters, as he shall be identified by the angelic ministrant who restores the everlasting gospel; once again the true knowledge of God shall be proclaimed in the ears of all living; once again men shall know that God stands revealed or he remains forever unknown.

"And they shall know that my name is The Lord." (Jer. 16:14-21.) 'They shall know that I am Jehovah; that I am the Eternal One; that I am the God of Israel; that I am the God of Abraham, Isaac, and Jacob; that I am the Lord Jesus Christ, the Son of God, the

Redeemer and Savior. And knowing me, they shall of necessity know my word, which is my law, which is my gospel.'

Is it any wonder, then, that the Personage who addressed young Joseph on that spring morning in 1820 commanded him to join none of the sects of the day? Or that the divine lips "said that all their creeds were an abomination in his sight"? (JS-H 1:19.)

Lies, vanity, and things wherein there is no profit! What does it profit a man to worship a cow or a crocodile? The creeds of men and of devils! Can a spirit essence or the laws of nature bring to pass the immortality and eternal life of man? Let uninspired men define God as an incorporeal, uncreated nothingness; let them say he is everywhere and nowhere in particular present; let them prattle about a being who is without body, parts, and passions—so be it: the holy word says these concepts are lies.

Jehovah is the Son; he has a body of flesh and bones as tangible as his Father's. This once, for the final time, to usher in the dispensation of the fulness of times and to prepare gathering Israel for the Second Coming of their ancient God, he has manifest himself and his laws to men on earth. Jehovah be praised!

Israel Gathers to the Gospel

The gathering of Israel—both that which comes *before* and that which comes *after* the Second Coming of the Son of Man—consists of two things. It consists, first, of receiving the restored gospel and of joining The Church of Jesus Christ of Latter-day Saints. Next it consists of assembling to whatever places are appointed for the worship of the Lord and the receipt of the fulness of his blessings.

Thus, the gathering is both spiritual and temporal. The spiritual gathering makes us members of the Church and kingdom of God on earth; it gives us a new birth, a new heart, a new allegiance. Through it we become fellow-citizens with the saints; we forsake the world; we come into the marvelous light of Christ. The temporal gathering consists of assembling physically to an appointed place where we can be strengthened in our determination to serve God and keep his commandments, and where we can receive the ordinances of salvation in their eternal fulness. There was not and could not be a gathering until the gospel was restored; and there is not and cannot be a gathering to specific locations without continuing revelation to name the places and appoint the times of assembly.

The promises to scattered Israel are glorious indeed. "I will gather them out of all countries, whither I have driven them," saith the Lord. "And they shall be my people, and I will be their God"—Jehovah is speaking—"and I will give them one heart, and one way, that they may fear me for ever, for the good of them, and of their children after them: And I will make an everlasting covenant with them." (Jer. 32:37-40.) The gospel is the everlasting covenant, the covenant of salvation that the Lord makes with all who come unto him.

Gathered Israel shall no longer walk in darkness and rebellion as did their fathers. "I will give them one heart," saith the Lord, "and I will put a new spirit within you; and I will take the stony heart out of their flesh, and will give them an heart of flesh." Why? "That they may walk in my statutes, and keep mine ordinances, and do them: and they shall be my people, and I will be their God." (Ezek. 11:19-20.)

And after they keep his commandments, they shall see his face as did the prophets of old. "There"—in your places of gathering—"will I plead with you face to face," he promises. "And I will cause you to pass under the rod, and I will bring you into the bond of the covenant." (Ezek. 20:35-37.) Is not this the promise he has given us? "Every soul who forsaketh his sins and cometh unto me, and calleth on my name, and obeyeth my voice, and keepeth my commandments, shall see my face and know that I am." (D&C 93:1.)

Old Testament prophecies about the gathering use language that means Israel shall gather to their ancient inheritances in Palestine. This, of course, will come to pass, and it is also descriptive of the phase of the gathering that enabled the ancients to envision clearly the literal nature of what was to be. The Book of Mormon prophets speak similarly, although their emphasis is on the Americas—the land of Joseph—as the gathering place for Ephraim and Manasseh. In addition, the Book of Mormon, with repeated emphasis, speaks not of a gathering to one place only, but of a gathering to appointed lands, meaning to all of the appointed places.

"The Lord God will proceed to make bare his arm in the eyes of all the nations, in bringing about his covenants and his gospel unto those who are of the house of Israel," Nephi says. "Wherefore, he will bring them again out of captivity, and they shall be gathered together to the lands of their inheritance; and they shall be brought out of obscurity and out of darkness; and they shall know that the Lord is their Savior and their Redeemer, the Mighty One of Israel." (1 Ne. 22:11-12.)

It is not the *place* of gathering that will save the scattered remnants, but the *message* of salvation that comes to them in their Redeemer's name. When he issues the call—"Assemble yourselves and come; draw near together, ye that are escaped of the nations"—what is important is that men turn to him in whatever nation and place they find themselves. "Look unto me, and be ye saved, all the ends of the earth," he says, "for I am God, and there is none else." Salvation is not in a *place* but in a *person*. It is in Christ; he alone ransoms men from death and redeems them from the grave; he alone grants them eternal life in his Father's kingdom; no man cometh unto the Father but by him. "Unto me every knee shall bow, [and] every tongue shall swear," saith Jehovah who is Christ. (Isa. 45:20-23.)

The Lord "has covenanted with all the house of Israel," Jacob says, in what amounts to a perfect summary of the whole matter, "that they shall be restored to the true church and fold of God; when they shall be gathered home to the lands of their inheritance, and shall be established in all their lands of promise." (2 Ne. 9:1-2.) We shall consider this matter more fully when we set forth that the gathering of Israel consists in coming to Zion or to any of her stakes no matter where they are located. It suffices for the present to know, with certainty and clarity, that the true gathering is to the true gospel that is proclaimed by the true Christ.

"Ye Are My Witnesses"

Who and how and by what means will Israel be gathered in the last days? Who among men can so much as identify a single lost sheep from the fold of the chosen ones? What man is there who would dare say to another: Come, assemble here; leave houses and wives and lands and properties, and come; cast your lot here in this desert wasteland with a handful of pilgrims?

How can anyone learn who Jehovah is? Or which among the religions of the world has the true gospel? And even if he could, where would he get the power to work the miracles and wonders that shall surpass the parting of the Red Sea?

Israel is to be gathered by the power of God, by the authority of the priesthood, by the preaching of the gospel, by the servants of the Lord going forth two by two into all the nations of the earth. The Lord's sheep hear his voice, and they follow him, and another they will not follow. Israel is gathered by the missionaries of the kingdom.

It is not a matter of armies assembling and marching under great banners to an ancient homeland. It is not a matter of earthly kings moving masses of men as Nebuchadnezzar did when Judah went into captivity. It will not be done by kings and parliaments and rulers. The gathering of Israel results from the Holy Spirit of God working in the hearts of contrite souls. "Ye shall be gathered one by one, O ye children of Israel," Isaiah acclaimed. (Isa. 27:12.) Converts come one at a time; people are baptized as individuals; every person must make his own decision.

"Turn, O backsliding children, saith the Lord; for I am married unto you: and I will take you one of a city, and two of a family, and I will bring you to Zion: And I will give you pastors according to mine heart, which shall feed you with knowledge and understanding." Such is the Lord's way for gathering his people. So shall Judah and Israel—the Jews and the Ten Tribes—"come together out of the land of the north." (Jer. 3:14-18.)

Six souls were gathered into the sheepfold of Israel by Jehovah himself on the 6th day of April in 1830. By heaven-sent revelation and divine commandment they set up the new kingdom whose destiny it is to fill the whole earth. These few followers of the true Shepherd were appointed pastors to find others of the lost sheep and to lead them into the fold—one by one, one of a city and two of a family.

These new pastors, the first legal administrators on earth since the meridian of time, became the first elders in the new kingdom. To them and to others who soon joined with them, the Lord gave this commission: "Ye are called to bring to pass the gathering of mine elect; for mine elect hear my voice and harden not their hearts." (D&C 29:7.) He commanded them: "Gather mine elect from the four quarters of the earth, even as many as will believe in me, and hearken unto my voice." (D&C 33:6.) Their instructions were: "Push the people together from the ends of the earth." (D&C 58:45.)

Truly, as the Lord had said of old, "I will save the house of Joseph, . . . And they of Ephraim shall be like a mighty man, and their heart shall rejoice." This is that Ephraim of whom he said: "I will sow them among the people: and they shall remember me in far countries; and they shall live with their children, and turn again," and concerning whom his promise is: "I will hiss for them, and gather them; for I have redeemed them: and they shall increase as they have increased." (Zech. 10:6-9.)

Thus, the ten thousands of Ephraim, and thereafter the thousands of Manasseh, began to return to their ancient God and to live as had their faithful fathers. By the 3rd of April in 1836 many thousands had come out of the Egypt of the world into a promised land of gospel peace. And then the heavens were rent, the Great God sent Moses back to confer keys and powers upon mortals, and the way was prepared for the full gathering that would make the first flight out of Egypt seem as nothing. The millions of our fathers who escaped the bondage of Pharaoh would be but the seed from which a bounteous harvest of billions would be reaped when the final harvest was ripe.

Moses came. He conferred upon Joseph Smith and Oliver Cowdery "the keys of the gathering of Israel from the four parts of the earth, and the leading of the ten tribes from the land of the north." (D&C 110:11.) Keys are the right of presidency; they are divine authorization to use the priesthood for a specified purpose; they empower those who hold them to use the power of God to do the work of Him whose power it is.

How was Israel gathered the first time? In what way came they out of Egypt, free from bondage, carrying the riches of the land with them? Truly it was by the power of God. With a mighty hand and a stretched-out arm and with fury poured out, Jehovah led his ancient people. And he did it by the hand of Moses, his servant, who held the keys of the gathering, the keys and power to use the priesthood to part the Red Sea and do all else that must needs be.

When "the Lord shall set his hand again the second time to recover the remnant of his people" (Isa. 11:11) from all the countries whither he hath driven them, how shall the work be done? It shall be again as it was before. His prophets, holding again the keys and powers possessed by Moses, shall lead Israel out of the bondage of a modern Egypt. Again Jehovah will move among the people with a mighty hand and a stretched-out arm and with fury poured out.

Thus Israel returns at the direction of the president of The Church of Jesus Christ of Latter-day Saints. Thus when the Ten Tribes come forth from the lands of the north to receive their blessings in the temples of God, they will come at the command of the presiding officer in the true Church. When they fall down before Ephraim, as their fathers did before Joseph of old, and when they are blessed by the children of Ephraim, it will be because the one who holds the keys of the kingdom of God on earth turns the key in their behalf. He alone is empowered to use all of the keys in their eternal fulness. There is never but one on earth at a time who can preside over and direct all of the affairs of the Lord among mortals, and this includes the gathering of all Israel as well as all else involved in the heaven-directed work.

Let no one suppose that the Ten Tribes, having been gathered by the elders of Israel so as to return in a body; let no one suppose that because they bring their scriptures with them; let no one suppose that because prophets mingle among them—let no one suppose that any of this shall happen independent of the senior apostle of God on earth who holds the keys of gathering and who is authorized to use them as the Spirit directs. There is one God and one Shepherd over all the earth, and there is one prophet and one presiding officer of the earthly kingdom, and he has rule over all of the Lord's affairs in all the earth.

This brings us to a consideration of how the lost sheep shall come to know that Jehovah is their God; how he will this once cause them to know that his name is The Lord; how they will be led to forsake the lies, vanities, and unprofitable things of their fathers—how they will be led to come unto Christ and believe his gospel in the last days.

The answer is: They will be guided by testimony. Their souls will vibrate—even as one tuning fork does with another that is similarly calibrated—when they hear the witness borne relative to the restoration of eternal truth in the last days. They will respond with glad acclaim to the written testimony in the Book of Mormon and will cry out in joyous tones: "The Stick of Joseph in the hands of Ephraim is the mind and will and voice of the Lord to us and to all Israel and to all men. Come, let us go up to the mountain of the Lord where his house is found and there receive our eternal blessings."

Let us now hear how Isaiah gives the word of the Lord on this matter. "I am the Lord thy God, the Holy One of Israel, thy Saviour," the ancient word acclaims. And it is the Lord Jehovah who is speaking. "I will bring thy seed from the east, and gather thee from the west; I will say to the north, Give up; and to the south, Keep not back: bring my sons from far, and my daughters from the ends of the earth; Even every one that is called by my name." It is the Lord Jesus who is speaking. He is calling his sons and his daughters from the ends of the earth; he is speaking to those who have received his gospel and who have exercised the power thus given them to become the sons of God by faith; he is naming those who have been spiritually born of him. He is speaking to those who have been adopted into his family and have taken upon them his name, which is the name of Christ. He is saying what he said through Hosea: "The number of the children of Israel shall be as the sand of the sea, which cannot be measured nor numbered; and it shall come to pass, that in the place where it was said unto them, Ye are not my people, there it shall be said unto them, Ye are the sons of the living God. Then shall the children of Judah and the children of Israel be gathered together, and appoint themselves one head, and they shall come up out of the land." (Hosea 1:10-11.)

To his sons and daughters thus gathered into his fold in all nations, the Lord acclaims: "Ye are my witnesses, saith the Lord, and my servant whom I have chosen: that ye may know and believe me, and understand that I am he." It is the Lord's servants who proclaim his divinity to the world; they are the ones who testify that salvation is in Christ; it is their witness that brings in converts and is binding on earth and in heaven. "I, even I, am the Lord; and beside me there is no saviour. I have declared, and have saved, and I have shewed, when there was no strange god among you: therefore ye are my witnesses, saith the Lord, that I am God." (Isa. 43:3-12.) He alone is the Saviour; he alone is that Jehovah who this once will cause men to know his name and his might. And the word so affirming shall go forth to all men in the last days by the mouths of his servants the prophets.

Truly, as all the scriptures attest: Faith cometh by hearing the word of God taught by a legal administrator who teaches and testifies by the power of the Holy Ghost. And thus it is that the word is going and shall go forth whereby Israel shall know their God and come again to his eternal truths.

THE LAMANITES AND THE SECOND COMING

The Lehites: A Case Study

We know enough about the Lehite peoples, during the twenty-five hundred years of their existence as an identifiable branch of the house of Israel, to enable us to use them as an ideal case study of the scattering and gathering of Israel. Their days of faith and devotion, their nights of sorrow and darkness, their travels and trials—all these are set forth in the Book of Mormon with sufficient detail to enable us to learn how the Lord Jehovah treats his people when they are righteous and when they are wicked. Knowing what he did with reference to Lehi and his seed and those who joined with them, we can envision how and in what manner he is dealing with all the branches of the olive tree that is Israel.

Lehi was a Jew of Jerusalem, a loyal subject of Zedekiah king of Judah, a member of the house of Joseph and of the tribe of Manasseh. He and his family, along with Ishmael the Jew and his family, and Zoram the Jew, neither of whose tribal affiliations are named but who also may have been of Manasseh, left Jerusalem in about 600 B.C. After some ten years of travel and preparation, climaxed by a long and tempestuous ocean voyage, they landed somewhere on the west coast of South America. They were thus scattered from their original homeland but gathered to their new promised land, the land promised to Joseph and his seed forever.

Mulek, the son of Zedekiah, together with his friends and followers, who also were Jews and who well may have had among them representatives from many tribes, particularly the tribe of Judah, made a similar journey to the Western Hemisphere. In due course they joined with the Nephites and were adopted into and swallowed up by that branch of the Lehite civilization. They also were thus scattered from Jerusalem but gathered to the land of Joseph.

Lehi's seed divided into two nations—the Nephites, who maintained their membership in the true Church and who worshipped the true God, and the Lamanites, who forsook the faith, rejected the gospel, and turned to the worship of false gods. These latter were cursed by the Lord for their rebellion, and he placed a mark upon them—a dark skin—lest the Nephites should intermarry with them and sink into their loathsome and degraded state.

For a thousand years these Lehite peoples alternately flourished and prospered on the one hand, or dwindled in darkness and struggled without civilization and decency on the other. In the main the Nephites were righteous and the Lamanites were wicked, though on occasions this was reversed. Ordinarily when Nephites apostatized and joined the Lamanites, they became Lamanites, but there was one glorious period when the Lamanites were converted, when they joined with and became Nephites, and when they received back skins that were white.

During the Golden Era, after the ministry of the Risen Lord among them, there were no dissenters, neither Lamanites "nor any manner of -ites; but they were in one, the children of Christ, and heirs to the kingdom of God." (4 Ne. 1:17.) When apostasy began again among them, however, the old tribal claims were revived, and the warfare and ways of old prevailed once more.

The Nephites as a people were destroyed by the Lamanites by about A.D. 400. Thereafter the Lamanites—the American Indians—apparently joined by a few wanderers from Asia or elsewhere, broke up into warring factions, continued to degenerate, and became what Columbus and subsequent European Gentiles found in the Americas. These American Indians are descendants primarily of Laman and Lemuel, though they also include some of the seed of Nephi and Ishmael and Zoram and others of the ancient worthies. They are Lamanites because of lineage, and they are Lamanites because of apostasy and disbelief and wayward living.

Providentially the Book of Mormon preserves for us the prophecies and promises made to and about Lehi and his seed and those who were adopted, as it were, into his family. By the simple expedient of studying the Lamanite scattering and gathering, we shall learn the concepts that will enable us to understand, in principle, what is happening to every branch of that nation which sprang from righteous Jacob.

The Lamanite Scattering

The Lamanites were cursed, scattered, and scourged; they became an evil, loathsome, and degenerate people; their skins turned black and their hearts became as flint—all because they forsook the Lord and chose to walk after the manner of the world. They left the Church; they apostatized; they rejected the gospel; they made gods unto themselves which were no gods. They treated the truths of salvation the same way their kindred in Jerusalem were doing in the day the vengeance of Babylon fell upon them.

Nephi was told by his angelic associate that the Lamanites would "dwindle in unbelief." Then he saw in vision that "after they had dwindled in unbelief they became a dark, and loathsome, and a filthy people, full of idleness and all manner of abominations." (1 Ne. 12:22-23.) And the angel said that "the wrath of God" rested upon them. (1 Ne. 13:11.)

Why did such an evil fate befall children born in the house of Israel, children whose inheritance was with the chosen people, children whose right it was to obtain all the blessings of Abraham, Isaac, and Jacob? Nephi gives answer in this way. He says the Lord "caused the cursing to come upon them, yea, even a sore cursing, because of their iniquity. For behold, they had hardened their hearts against him, that they had become like unto a flint; wherefore, as they were white, and exceeding fair and delightsome, that they might not be enticing unto my people the Lord God did cause a skin of blackness to come upon them."

Righteousness brings blessings, and wickedness spawns cursings. "And thus saith the Lord God: I will cause that they shall be loathsome unto thy people, save they shall repent of their iniquities. And cursed shall be the seed of him that mixeth with their seed; for they shall be cursed even with the same cursing." To this Nephi adds, "And the Lord spake it, and it was done." And also: "Because of their cursing which was upon them they did become an idle people, full of mischief and subtlety, and did seek in the wilderness for beasts of prey." (2 Ne. 5:21-24.)

Mormon picks up the same theme, using even stronger language. He speaks of the Lamanite destiny as the final great conflict between them and the Nephites draws near. "For this people shall be scattered," he prophesies, "and shall become a dark, a filthy, and a loathsome people, beyond the description of that which ever hath been amongst us, yea, even that which hath been among the Lamanites, and this because of their unbelief and idolatry. For behold, the Spirit of the Lord hath already ceased to strive with their fathers; and they are without Christ and God in the world; and they are driven about as chaff before the wind. They were once a delightsome people, and they had Christ for their shepherd; yea, they were led even by God the Father. But now, behold, they are led about by Satan, even as chaff is driven before the wind, or as a vessel is tossed about upon the waves, without sail or anchor, or without anything wherewith to steer her; and even as she is, so are they."

Nor is this all. These Lamanites, even in the days of the colonizing and settling of the Americas by the Gentiles, shall continue to be driven and slaughtered. In the United States, in Mexico, in Peru, in Uruguay, and in every place from one end of the Americas to the other, the sword of vengeance has spilled the blood of Father Lehi's children. "And behold, the Lord hath reserved their blessings, which they might have received in the land, for the Gentiles who shall possess the land," Mormon continues. "But behold, it shall come to pass that they shall be driven and scattered by the Gentiles; and after they have been driven and scattered by the Gentiles, behold, then will the Lord remember the covenant which he made unto Abraham and unto all the house of Israel." (Morm. 5:15-20.)

Such is the scattering of the Lamanites. The key words and phrases of holy writ are: unbelief, filthy, idleness, abominations, iniquities, mischief, subtlety, idolatry, without Christ and God in the world, led about by Satan, and the consequent cursings and wrath. And from our case study we are expected to learn that these same things led to the scattering of all branches of the chosen people.

The Lamanite Gathering

Our case study now turns to the day of Lamanite gathering. The long night of apostate darkness that left the remnants of Lehi's seed in their low and fallen and loathsome state is drawing to an end. Already the rays of gospel light are rising in the eastern sky and the day of gathering is dawning. Lamanites in the United States and Canada, in Mexico and Central America, and in the various nations of South America, together with the Lamanites in the islands of the South Pacific, whom we call Polynesians—all these are coming back, one by one as the divine decree requires. And when the day has fully dawned, as soon it must, they will be a glorious people indeed.

Indeed, that day—the day of the Lamanite—shall dawn before the Second Coming. Its arrival will be one of the signs of the times, and all those who can read the promised signs will thereby know that the coming of their Lord is nigh at hand. Pending that day, the Lord's command to his people is: "Be not deceived, but continue in steadfastness, looking forth for the heavens to be shaken, and the earth to tremble and to reel to and fro as a drunken man, and for the valleys to be exalted, and for the mountains to be made low, and for the rough places to become smooth—and all this when the angel shall sound his trumpet."

Having so announced, the Lord then relates all this to the gathering of Israel, including the Lamanite gathering. "But before the great day of the Lord shall come," he says, "Jacob shall flourish in the wilderness, and the Lamanites shall blossom as the rose. Zion shall flourish upon the hills and rejoice upon the mountains, and shall be assembled together unto the place which I have appointed." (D&C 49:23-25.) The physical gathering here alluded to is the assembling of the Latter-day Saints in the tops of the mountains in western America. It is there that Zion shall flourish upon the hills and rejoice upon the mountains. The wilderness referred to is the then-uninhabited areas that were colonized by Brigham Young less than a score of years later. And as to the day when the Lamanites shall blossom as the rose, it has scarcely commenced. They are not yet, except in a beginning degree, the pure and delightsome people of whom the scriptures speak. It is to these promises relative to their gathering that we shall now give attention.

Both the Lamanites and the Nephites were of the tribe of Manasseh, whose father, Joseph, was sold by his brethren into Egyptian slavery. This Joseph, one of the greatest of the ancient seers, saw in vision his Lehite descendants and their civilization in the Western Hemisphere. He saw them as "a branch . . . broken off" from the olive tree of Israel, a branch separated from their kinsmen in the Old World; and he saw that they would "be remembered in the covenants of the Lord." He saw them gathered back to the ancient standards when "the Messiah should be made manifest unto them in the latter days, in the spirit of power, unto the bringing of them out of darkness unto light—yea, out of hidden darkness and out of captivity unto freedom." This restoration, Joseph of old testified, would be brought to pass through a seer—Joseph the seer of latter days—whom the Lord would raise up to commence the restoration of all things and to bring the remnants of Israel "to the knowledge of the covenants" that the Lord made with their fathers. (2 Ne. 3:5-7.)

Lehi and Nephi both had similar spiritual insights relative to that portion of Joseph's seed which inhabited the Americas. "The house of Israel was compared unto an olive-tree, by the Spirit of the Lord which was in our fathers," Nephi said. Then he asked: "Are we not broken off from the house of Israel, and are we not a branch of the house of Israel?" Then, "concerning the grafting in of the natural branches" to the parent tree, Nephi prophesied: It shall be "in the latter days, when our seed shall have dwindled in unbelief." It shall be "many generations after the Messiah shall be manifested in body unto the children of men." When it comes to pass, "then shall the fulness of the gospel of the Messiah come unto the Gentiles, and from the Gentiles unto the remnant of our seed." Thus shall the gospel bring to pass the gathering of Israel.

"And at that day shall the remnant of our seed know that they are of the house of Israel," Nephi continues to prophesy, "and that they are the covenant people of the Lord; and then shall they know and come to the knowledge of their forefathers, and also to the knowledge of the gospel of their Redeemer, which was ministered unto their fathers by him; wherefore, they shall come to the knowledge of their Redeemer and the very points of his doctrine, that they may know how to come unto him and be saved." Such is the prophetic word. How plainly the Book of Mormon prophets speak. Can anyone mistake the true intent and meaning and reality of the Lamanite gathering?

"And then at that day," Nephi continues, "will they not rejoice and give praise unto their everlasting God, their rock and their salvation? Yea, at that day, will they not receive the strength and nourishment from the true vine? Yea, will they not come unto the true fold of God?" In answer the son of Lehi acclaims: "Behold, I say unto you, Yea; they shall be remembered again among the house of Israel; they shall be grafted in, being a natural branch of the olive-tree, into the true olive-tree." (1 Ne. 15:12-16.)

How is the gospel to go to the Lamanites and to all Israel in the latter days? It shall be through Joseph Smith and the Book of Mormon. The angelic word on this point to Nephi was couched in these words: "These last records [the Book of Mormon and the revelations given in the latter days], which thou hast seen among the Gentiles, shall establish the truth of the first [the Bible], which are of the twelve apostles of the Lamb, and shall make known the plain and precious things which have been taken away from them; and shall make known to all kindreds, tongues, and people, that the Lamb of God is the Son of the Eternal Father, and the Savior of the world; and that all men must come unto him, or they cannot be saved." (1 Ne. 13:40.)

Thereafter Nephi prophesies: "For after the book of which I have spoken [the Book of Mormon] shall come forth, and be written unto the Gentiles, and sealed up again unto the Lord [all of which has now transpired], there shall be many which shall believe the words which are written; and they shall carry them forth unto the remnant of our seed." The Book of Mormon is going forth, not only to the seed of Lehi, but to the whole world, as rapidly as our strength and means enable us to place it in the hands of receptive persons.

"And then shall the remnant of our seed know concerning us, how that we came out from Jerusalem, and that they are descendants of the Jews. And the gospel of Jesus Christ shall be declared among them; wherefore, they shall be restored unto the knowledge of their fathers, and also to the knowledge of Jesus Christ, which was had among their fathers. And then shall they rejoice; for they shall know that it is a blessing unto them from the hand of God; and many generations shall not pass away among them, save they shall be a pure and delightsome people." (2 Ne. 30:3-6.) These words are now in process of fulfillment. The scales of darkness have fallen from a few eyes and shall fall from many; and, ere long, the pure and delightsome status shall be attained by this remnant of the covenant people.

Thus we learn that the Lamanites shall come out of apostate darkness into the light of the gospel; they shall escape from the captivity of sin and gain the freedom of the gospel; they shall be grafted in to the natural olive tree again—because they worship the Father in the name of the Son by the power of the Spirit.

Thus we learn that they shall blossom as the rose and become a pure and a delightsome people, because they return unto the Lord their God; because they accept Christ as their Savior; because they glory once again in their Redeemer—the Redeemer of Israel—who has bought them with his blood and whose atoning sacrifice brings immortality to all men and the hope of eternal life to those who believe and obey.

Thus we learn that they shall come into the fold of the Good Shepherd—the Shepherd of Israel—when they believe the Book of Mormon, when they come to a knowledge of the covenants made with their fathers, when they reject the false doctrine of Laman and turn to the true doctrine of Nephi.

The Lamanites—A Pattern for All Israel

Our knowledge of the Lamanite gathering lets us know how and in what manner all Israel will return again to Him who has chosen them as his own. Through it we learn how all the tribes—Ephraim and Manasseh wherever they are; the Jews who are scattered and mocked in all nations; the Ten Tribes who are lost and hidden among all the nations of the Gentiles—thus we learn how and in what manner they too shall be gathered. It is with Ephraim as it is with Manasseh; it is with Joseph as it is with Judah; and it shall be with Reuben and Simeon as with all the other tribes. All are alike unto God. All shall gather on the same terms and conditions.

It is, of course, the most natural thing in the world for the Book of Mormon prophets to take the words spoken by Isaiah and the other prophets—words spoken relative to the whole house of Israel—and show how they are fulfilled in their own seed whom we and they know as the Lamanites. Where better should their interests have been centered than in their own family members? Should we not do the very same thing and make a specific application of the prophetic word to our own children who also are of Israel, though, in fact, they are only a small part of the whole nation?

But the Nephite prophets knew and repeatedly testified that what they said about the Lamanite gathering applied also to the gathering of all Israel. "After our seed is scattered," Nephi said, "the Lord God will proceed to do a marvelous work among the Gentiles, which shall be of great worth unto our seed"—the marvelous work is the restoration of the gospel to the Gentiles, to a people who were not nationals of the kingdom of Judah—"wherefore, it is likened unto their being nourished by the Gentiles and being carried in their arms and upon their shoulders." (1 Ne. 22:8.) The allusion here is to Isaiah's great prophecy—made to all the house of Israel, and which Nephi had previously quoted—that when the Lord raised his standard and restored his gospel to the Gentiles, their kings would be nursing fathers and their queens nursing mothers in bringing the Israelites back to the lands of their inheritance. (1 Ne. 21:22-23.) In applying these words, Nephi's first emphasis is on the Lamanite gathering. It takes precedence, even as our own families are more important to us than are others. Then, as he continues to speak of the gathering in the day of restoration, he broadens the view to include all Israel. "And it shall also be of worth unto the Gentiles; and not only unto the Gentiles but unto all the house of Israel, unto the making known of the covenants of the Father of heaven unto Abraham, saying: In thy seed shall all the kindreds of the earth be blessed." All the house of Israel means all the house of Israel. The words mean what they say and include the Ten Tribes.

Because the house of Israel is scattered in all nations, the gathering must take place on all the surface of the earth. Hence the prophetic word acclaims: "And I would, my brethren, that ye should know that all the kindreds of the earth cannot be blessed unless he shall make bare his arm in the eyes of the nations. Wherefore, the Lord God will proceed to make bare his arm in the eyes of all the nations, in bringing about his covenants and his gospel unto those who are of the house of Israel." The gospel shall go to all Israel in all nations in all the earth. "Wherefore, he will bring them again out of captivity, and they shall be gathered together to the lands of their inheritance"—which lands (a plural word) we shall define and identify more particularly hereafter—"and they shall be brought out of obscurity and out of darkness; and they shall know that the Lord is their Savior and their Redeemer, the Mighty One of Israel." (1 Ne. 22:9-12.)

One other of the many like passages will suffice for our purposes. Our friend Mormon, as he nears the end of his divinely appointed work, that of preserving the everlasting word as it was had among the Nephites, says: "I write unto you, Gentiles, and also unto you, house of Israel, when the work shall commence, that ye shall be about to prepare to return to the land of your inheritance." Then, as though this salutation was not sufficient, and lest any should be confused as to the people to whom the Book of Mormon shall go, Mormon wrote: "Yea, behold, I write unto all the ends of the earth; yea, unto you, [the] twelve tribes of Israel." *The Book of Mormon is written to the twelve tribes of Israel.* And this includes the lost Ten Tribes. For that matter, the New Testament itself is addressed "to the twelve tribes which are scattered abroad." (James 1:1.)

"And these things doth the Spirit manifest unto me; therefore I write unto you all"—all the house of Israel. Why? "That ye may believe the gospel of Jesus Christ, which ye shall have among you; and also that the Jews, the covenant people of the Lord, shall have other witness besides him whom they saw and heard, that Jesus, whom they slew, was the very Christ and the very God. And I would that I could persuade all ye ends of the earth to repent and prepare to stand before the judgment-seat of Christ." (Morm. 3:17-22.) That is to say, all Israel, the Lamanites and the Ten Tribes included, shall be gathered if and when they believe the Book of Mormon. The Ten Tribes shall return after they accept the Book of Mormon; then they shall come to Ephraim to receive their blessings, the blessings of the house of the Lord, the blessings that make them heirs of the covenant God made with their father Abraham.

But, says one, *are they not in a body somewhere in the land of the north?* Answer: They are not; they are scattered in all nations. The north countries of their habitation are all the countries north of their Palestinian home, north of Assyria from whence they escaped, north of the prophets who attempted to describe their habitat. And for that matter, they shall also come from the south and the east and the west and the ends of the earth. Such is the prophetic word.

But, says another, *did not Jesus visit them after he ministered among the Nephites?* Answer: Of course he did, in one or many places as suited his purposes. He assembled them together then in exactly the same way he gathered the Nephites in the land Bountiful so that they too could hear his voice and feel the prints of the nails in his hands and in his feet. Of this there can be no question. And we suppose that he also called twelve apostles and established his kingdom among them even as he did in Jerusalem and in the Americas. Why should he deal any differently with one branch of Israel than with another?

Query: *What happened to the Ten Tribes after the visit of the Savior to them near the end of the thirty-fourth year following his birth?* Answer: The same thing that happened to the Nephites. There was righteousness for a season, and then there was apostasy and wickedness. Be it remembered that darkness was destined to cover the earth—all of it—before the day of the restoration, and that the restored gospel was to go to every nation and kindred and tongue and people upon the face of the whole earth, including the Ten Tribes of Israel.

But, says yet another, *what about their scriptures—will they not bring them when they return?* Answer: Yes, they will bring the Book of Mormon and the Bible, both of which were written to them and must be received by them before they gather. And further, as we devoutly hope, they will also have other records that will give an account of the ministry of the resurrected Lord among them—records that will come forth in a marvelous manner, at the direction of the president of The Church of Jesus Christ of Latter-day Saints, who is a revelator and a translator and who holds the keys of the kingdom of God on earth as pertaining to all men, the Ten Tribes included.

And, finally, says yet another, *will they not come with their prophets and seers?* Answer: There is no other way they or any people can be gathered. Of course they will be led by their prophets, prophets who are subject to and receive instructions from, and prophets who report their labors to the one man on earth who holds and exercises all of the keys of the kingdom in their fulness. Did not Paul say that "the spirits of the prophets are subject to the prophets," and that "God is not the author of confusion"? (1 Cor. 14:32-33.) The Lord's house is a house of order; it has only one head at one time; Christ is not divided. In this day when the head of the Church can communicate with all men on earth, there is no longer any need for one kingdom in Jerusalem and another in Bountiful and others in whatever place or places the Ten Tribes were when Jesus visited them. This is the promised day when there shall be one God, one Shepherd, one prophet, one gospel, one church, and one kingdom for all the earth. This is the day when one man shall direct all of the Lord's work in all the earth; the day when he shall bring all Israel into one fold; the day when one man will give an account of his stewardship over all the earth at Adam-ondi-Ahman just before the great day of the Lord arrives.

Come, Ye Lamanites

Mormon himself issues the great call to the Lamanites of the latter days. It is a call to gather into the sheepfold of their ancient fathers and to receive again the protecting care of the Shepherd of Israel. It is a call to come out of the deserts of sin and find rest in a pleasant land that flows with milk and honey. It is a call to receive again the gifts and blessings of those upon whom the face of the Lord once shone. It is a divine proclamation that sets the pattern for the call that must go forth to all the scattered remnants of the Lord's covenant people. What he says unto one applies to all: all shall return and gain divine approval on the same basis.

Come, ye Lamanites; come, ye Jews; come, ye lost tribes of Israel—come. Come and drink of the waters of life; come feast on the manna from heaven; come bask in the light of the Lord. Return, O backsliding Israel; return unto Him whom your fathers served; return unto the Lord your God. His arm is not shortened that he cannot save; his voice is heard again; the word of salvation, now in the hands of Ephraim and Manasseh, is for all the seed of Jacob.

"Know ye that ye are of the house of Israel." The blood of Abraham, Isaac, and Jacob flows in your veins. Ye are their seed after the manner of the flesh. "Know ye that ye must come unto repentance, or ye cannot be saved." Ye cannot be saved in your sins. Repent, repent; why will ye perish? Ye cannot live after the manner of worldly men and find favor with God.

"Know ye that ye must come to the knowledge of your fathers, and repent of all your sins and iniquities, and believe in Jesus Christ, that he is the Son of God, and that he was slain by the Jews, and by the power of the Father he hath risen again, whereby he hath gained the victory over the grave; and also in him is the sting of death swallowed up." Salvation is in Christ. Beside him there is no Savior. It is now as it was in the days of your fathers. "And he"—Christ the Lord—"bringeth to pass the resurrection of the dead, whereby man must be raised to stand before his judgment-seat. And he hath brought to pass the redemption of the world, whereby he that is found guiltless before him at the judgment day hath it given unto him to dwell in the presence of God in his kingdom, to sing ceaseless praises with the choirs above, unto the Father, and unto the Son, and unto the Holy Ghost, which are one God, in a state of happiness which hath no end."

Jehovah who is Christ scattered his people because they rejected him and his law. Christ who is Jehovah shall gather his people when they return unto him and believe again his holy gospel. "Therefore," ye Lamanites, ye Jews, ye twelve tribes of Israel, "repent, and be baptized in the name of Jesus, and lay hold upon the gospel of Christ, which shall be set before you, not only in this record [the Book of Mormon] but also in the record which shall come unto the Gentiles from the Jews [the Bible], which record shall come from the Gentiles unto you."

Thus we say: Come, all ye house of Israel, all ye scattered sheep, all ye lost and fallen ones; come, ye of every tribe and family; believe the testimony of Joseph Smith and those upon whom his prophetic mantle has fallen. Come out of the world, out of the bondage of Egypt, and join The Church of Jesus Christ of Latter-day Saints, for this church administers the gospel, and the gospel is the plan of salvation. Come to the Lord's house and receive your blessings and inherit thereby the same blessings given to Abraham, Isaac, and Jacob and promised to all of their righteous children. All ye who "are a remnant of the seed of Jacob," know that "ye are numbered among the people of the first covenant; and if it so be that ye believe in Christ, and are baptized, first with water, then with fire and the Holy Ghost, following the example of our Savior, according to that which he hath commanded us, it shall be well with you in the day of judgment. Amen." (Morm. 7:1-10.)

Chapter 19

THE JEWS AND THE SECOND COMING

Who Are the Jews?

When he made flesh his tabernacle, our blessed Lord—Mary's Son, one Jesus by name—came to the Jews of his day. They were his own people when he dwelt among the sons of men. He himself was a Jew. And when he comes again—as the Son of God, as the Incarnate Jehovah—it will be to his own, to the Jews; and he himself will be a Jew, a Jew of the Jews, the Chief Jew of the chosen race.

It was Jewish blood that was shed for the sins of the world. It was Jewish blood that oozed in great gouts from every pore as he suffered beyond compare in Gethsemane. It was Jewish blood that clotted around the nails in his hands, dripped from the wounds in his feet, and gushed from his riven side. It was a Jew who died on a cross that all men might be freed from the agonies of the flesh and the terrors of death. And it will be a Jew—the Rejected Jew, the Chief Jew, the King of the Jews, risen in glorious immortality—who shall come again, in all the glory of his Father's kingdom, as the remnant of that once great nation cries out: 'Blessed be he who cometh in the name of the Lord. Hosanna in the highest. All glory to his everlasting name.'

The second coming of the Son of Man will be a day of Jewish glory and triumph. As they were singled out to see his face and hear his voice when he came to atone for the sins of the world, so—after long centuries of being cursed and scourged and slain—

they will be chosen again to see the wounds in his flesh, to accept the salvation of the cross, and to find at long last their Promised Messiah. They will yet play the role assigned them for that glorious day when he comes to complete the salvation of man and to crown his work before delivering the kingdom spotless to his Father. And even as we study the Jewish religion and the Jewish way of life in order to understand what Jesus did and said in the Palestine of the past, so we must know the part the Jews are to play in his glorious return, if we ourselves are to abide the day and find ourselves numbered with those of the chosen race.

Who, then, are the Jews, and what part shall they yet play in the gathering of Israel and the return of their King? There is a maze of fuzzy thinking and shoddy scholarship, both in the world and in the Church, that seeks to identify the Jews, both ancient and modern, and to expound upon what they have believed and do believe. It is not strange that the divines of the day—not knowing that the kingdom is to be restored to Israel at that glorious day; not having the Book of Mormon and latter-day revelation to guide them—it is not strange that they come up with false and twisted views about the mission and destiny of the Jews. It is a little sad that church members sometimes partake of these false views and of this secular spirit so as to misread the signs of the times.

The term *Jew* is a contraction of the name *Judah*, but the Jews are not the members of the tribe of Judah as such. After the reign of Solomon, the Lord's people divided into the *kingdom of Israel* and the *kingdom of Judah*. Nearly ten tribes served Jeroboam in Israel and two and a half tribes served Rehoboam in Judah. The Levites were scattered among all the tribes. Judah, Simeon, and part of Benjamin comprised the kingdom of Judah. In actual fact, and considering blood lineage only, both kingdoms had in them people from all of the tribes. Lehi, who lived in Judah and was a Jew, was of the tribe of Manasseh. The Jews were nationals of the kingdom of Judah without reference to tribal ancestry. Thus the descendants of Lehi, both the Nephites and the Lamanites, were Jews because they came out from Jerusalem and from the kingdom of Judah. (2 Ne. 33:8.)

The Jews today are also those whose origins stem back to the kingdom of their fathers. Clearly the dominant tribe—dominant, however, only in the sense of political power and rulership—was Judah. As to the bloodlines, who knows whether there are more of Judah or of Simeon or of Benjamin or of some other tribe among the Jews as we know them? Paul, a Jew, was of the tribe of Benjamin. The name *Judea*, now used as a noun, is actually an adjective meaning *Jewish* and is the Greek and Roman designation for the land of Judah.

Since the Ten Tribes were taken into Assyria and lost from the knowledge of their fellows more than a century before the Jews went into Babylonian captivity, the prophets began to speak of Jews and Gentiles and to consider as a Gentile everyone who was not a Jew. This classifies Ephraim and the rest of scattered Israel as Gentiles. Everyone, in this sense, who is not a Jew is a Gentile, a concept that will enable us, in due course, to set forth what is meant by the fulness of the Gentiles.

As to their ancient beliefs, the Jews had either the fulness of the gospel or the preparatory gospel as their religious zeal and devotion of the moment warranted. They were always subject to the law of Moses, but whenever, as among the Nephites, their prophets held the Melchizedek Priesthood, they also had the fulness of the gospel. Both under the gospel and under the law—this latter, at least, in their more righteous days—they had a hope in Christ and understood that salvation would come through his atoning sacrifice. And as our studies will now show, the Jews were scattered when they forsook their Messiah, and they will be gathered when they return to him.

The Jewish Scattering

The Jews, the Lord's ancient covenant people! Would God that today they might be as were their righteous forebears, when David drove the Jebusites from Jerusalem, when Solomon reigned in splendor with great wisdom and compassion, when Isaiah extended the life of Hezekiah! Oh, that once again a Daniel might close the mouths of the lions that roar against them, and a Zerubbabel might arise to build again an holy sanctuary in their own Jerusalem! Oh, that a Peter, James, and John might once more be found among them who could stand on a modern Mount of Transfiguration, converse with Moses and Elias, and hear the voice of God as the divine Shekinah spreads its luminous brilliance over the heights of Hermon!

For three thousand years the history of the Jews—and God's dealings with them—has been the history of mankind. Never in all history has any people been treated, even in small measure, as have these ancient covenant ones. For half the time mortal man has dwelt on earth; for one hundred and fifty generations of fathers and sons; from the day the first David ascended the throne of Israel until the Second David shall come to reign on earth for a thousand years—during all this length of days, the history of the earth has revolved and will revolve around the seed of Abraham to whom the promises were made. In the days of their faith they have climbed one Sinai after another and seen Jehovah face to face. In the days of their rebellion they have suffered the eternal burnings of one Gehenna after another and been subject to that evil spirit who dwells in Sheol. Those who saw the face of their Maker dwelt in the Holy City and have gone on to dwell in the Eternal Presence. Those who loved darkness rather than light, because their deeds were evil, spent their days outside the city walls in the Valley of Hinnom, and they now dwell among the servants of the one whom they listed to obey.

Moses the man of God placed before all Israel heavenly blessings and hellish cursings, the blessings being conditioned upon faith and obedience and righteousness, the curses, upon rebellion and disobedience and wickedness. In the days of their cursings the seed of Jacob were promised desolation and disease and bondage. Wars and plagues and famines would be their common lot. Tender and delicate women would eat their own children in the siege against Jerusalem, and then, finally, speaking particularly of Jewish-Israel, the divine word affirmed: "Ye shall be plucked from off the land whither thou goest to possess it. And the Lord shall scatter thee among all people, from the one end of the earth even unto the other; and there thou shalt serve other gods, which neither thou nor thy fathers have known." How far the ancient people have departed from the pure worship of the Father, in the name of the Son, by the power of the Holy Ghost, which existed among their fathers!

"And among these nations shalt thou find no ease, neither shall the sole of thy foot have rest: but the Lord shall give thee there a trembling heart, and failing of eyes, and sorrow of mind: And thy life shall hang in doubt before thee; and thou shalt fear day and night, and shalt have none assurance of thy life." As the full significance of these words sinks into our souls, our minds turn to Russia and Germany and all the nations that have slain the Jews because they were Jews, by the thousands, and the tens of thousands, and the hundreds of thousands, and by the millions. Truly of these Jews the prophetic word acclaims: "In the morning thou shalt say, Would God it were even! and at even thou shalt say, Would God it were morning! for the fear of thine heart wherewith thou shalt fear, and for the sight of thine eyes which thou shalt see." (Deut. 28:15-68.)

Knowing all these things, and having in mind particularly the siege when human flesh will be all that is left to satisfy the pangs of hunger, we are not surprised to hear Jesus say, on the Mount of Olives, speaking of the then imminent destruction of Jerusalem by Titus in A.D. 70, "Then, in those days, shall be great tribulation on the Jews, and upon the inhabitants of Jerusalem, such as was not before sent upon Israel, of God, since the beginning of their kingdom until this time; no, nor ever shall be sent again upon Israel." And then, as though the famine and blood and death of the Roman siege were not enough, the Voice on Olivet adds: "All things which have befallen them are only the beginning of the sorrows which shall come upon them." (JS-M 1:18-19.)

Why were the Jews scattered and scourged and slain? From the beginning of their kingdom—from the day Rehoboam taxed the people into bondage to the day of Pilate, when they were still rendering unto Caesar the things that are Caesar's—they were scattered because they forsook the Lord Jehovah and his laws. And from the day Pilate said "Take ye him, and crucify him," they were scattered because they crucified their King.

Let this fact be engraved in the eternal records with a pen of steel: the Jews were cursed, and smitten, and cursed anew, because they rejected the gospel, cast out their Messiah, and crucified their King. Let the spiritually illiterate suppose what they may, it was the Jewish denial and rejection of the Holy One of Israel, whom their fathers worshipped in the beauty of holiness, that has made them a hiss and a byword in all nations and that has taken millions of their fair sons and daughters to untimely graves.

What saith the holy word? "They shall be scourged by all people, because they crucify the God of Israel, and turn their hearts aside, rejecting signs and wonders, and the power and glory of the God of Israel. And because they turn their hearts aside, . . . and have despised the Holy One of Israel, they shall wander in the flesh, and perish, and become a hiss and a by-word and be hated among all nations." (1 Ne. 19:13-14; 2 Ne. 6:9-11.) Such is the prophetic word of Nephi. His brother Jacob speaks in like language. "There is none other nation on earth that would crucify their God," he says. "But because of priestcrafts and iniquities, they at Jerusalem will stiffen their necks against him, that he be crucified. Wherefore, because of their iniquities, destructions, famines, pestilences, and bloodshed shall come upon them; and they who shall not be destroyed shall be scattered among all nations." (2 Ne. 10:3-6; 25:12-15.)

The Jewish Gathering

Why and how and in what manner shall the Jews be gathered again in the last days? It shall be with them as it is with the Lamanites, who unbeknown to the world are, in fact, Jews, and as it is with Ephraim and all the house of Israel. The Jews shall be gathered one of a city and two of a family, a favored person here and an elect soul there. They shall come back because they believe the Book of Mormon and when they accept the gospel. They shall return, a few to Palestine, most of them to the folds of their Ancient Shepherd as these are found in all the nations of the earth. They shall come again to the Holy One of Israel, wait no longer for a Messiah who is to come, but accept Christ as their Savior and plead with the Father in the name of the Son for the cleansing power of his blood. They shall return when they join the true Church, The Church of Jesus Christ of Latter-day Saints.

Truly, as Isaiah promised, the cry shall go forth—nay, is even now going forth: "Awake, awake, stand up, O Jerusalem, which hast drunk at the hand of the Lord the cup of his fury; thou hast drunken the dregs of the cup of trembling [staggering], and wrung them out." Thy sons have suffered "desolation, and destruction, and the famine, and the sword. . . . Therefore hear now this, thou afflicted, and drunken, but not with wine: Thus saith thy Lord the Lord, and thy God that pleadeth the cause of his people, Behold, I have taken out of thine hand the cup of trembling [staggering], even the dregs of the cup of my fury; thou shalt no more drink it again." (Isa. 51:17-22.)

Isaiah's poetic imagery is added upon and given anew in plain words by the Book of Mormon prophets. Moroni, who wrote the title page of this volume of holy scripture, said that it was sent forth "to the convincing of the Jew and Gentile that JESUS is the CHRIST, the ETERNAL GOD, manifesting himself unto all nations." His father Mormon said, "These things," meaning the Book of Mormon, "are written unto the remnant of the house of Jacob. . . . And behold, they shall go unto the unbelieving of the Jews; and for this intent shall they go—that they may be persuaded that Jesus is the Christ, the Son of the living God; that the Father may bring about, through his most Beloved, his great and eternal purpose, in restoring the Jews." (Morm. 5:12-14.) The Book of Mormon gathers Israel, including the Jews, who are part of Israel. It "contains the truth and the word of God." It came forth by way of "the Gentile," that "it may go to the Jew, of whom the Lamanites are a remnant, that they may believe the gospel, and look not for a Messiah to come who has already come." (D&C 19:26-27.) Such is the word of the Lord given in this day.

Jacob recounts that after the Jews crucify Christ, "they shall be scattered, and smitten, and hated; nevertheless, the Lord will be merciful unto them, that when they shall come to the knowledge of their Redeemer, they shall be gathered together again to the lands of their inheritance. . . . The Messiah will set himself again the second time to recover them; wherefore, he will manifest himself unto them in power and great glory, unto the destruction of their enemies, when that day cometh when they shall believe in him. . . . For the Mighty God shall deliver his covenant people." (2 Ne. 6:9-17.)

Nephi prophesies of the coming of the Only Begotten of the Father in the flesh; of his rejection by the Jews "because of their iniquities, and the hardness of their hearts, and the stiffness of their necks"; of his crucifixion, resurrection, and the salvation he thus brings; of his resurrected appearances; of the subsequent destruction of Jerusalem; and of the scattering of the Jews "among all nations." Then come these prophetic words: "And after they have been scattered, and the Lord God hath scourged them by other nations for the space of many generations, yea, even down from generation to generation until they shall be persuaded to believe in Christ, the Son of God, and the atonement, which is infinite for all mankind—and when that day shall come that they shall believe in Christ, and worship the Father in his name, with pure hearts and clean hands, and look not forward any more for another Messiah, then, at that time, the day will come that it must needs be expedient that they should believe these things."

How awful has that scourging been! Like the Chief Jew whose flesh was torn by the beads of lead and the sharp bones in the Roman flagellum, as he was scourged for sins that were not his, so a whole nation has cringed beneath the lacerating whip, for their own sins and those of their fathers. And as it has been for generations, so shall it be until they repent and come unto Him whom their fathers slew and hanged on a tree, which faith and repentance shall come to pass when, and only when, they believe the Book of Mormon and turn to Joseph Smith, through whom the gospel has been restored in and for our day.

"And the Lord will set his hand again the second time to restore his people from their lost and fallen state." Once he led them out of Egyptian bondage into a promised land, with a mighty hand and with power poured out; and he will yet again lead them out of the Egypt of the world into the only true and living Church upon the face of the whole earth. "Wherefore, he will proceed to do a marvelous work and a wonder among the children of men. Wherefore, he shall bring forth his words unto them, which words shall judge them at the last day, for they shall be given them for the purpose of convincing them of the true Messiah, who was rejected by them; and unto the convincing of them that they need not look forward any more for a Messiah to come, for there should not any come, save it should be a false Messiah which should deceive the people; for there is save one Messiah spoken of by the prophets, and that Messiah is he who should be rejected of the Jews." (2 Ne. 25:12-18.) When that day comes, they shall, as Jacob said, "be restored to the true church and fold of God." (2 Ne. 9:2.)

The Day of Jewish Conversion

When will Jewish Israel be gathered again into the true Church and fold of their ancient Messiah? When will they accept the Lord Jesus Christ as the Savior of the world and worship the Father in his holy name? When will they believe the Book of Mormon, be cleansed from their sins in the waters of Judah, and come and receive their blessings under the hands of Ephraim, the firstborn? Will these things come to pass before or after their ancient and once rejected King returns in power and great glory to reign gloriously among his saints?

Nephi prophesies that the gospel of Jesus Christ shall be taken to the remnant of Lehi's seed in the last days; that they shall believe and obey and gain anew the knowledge and blessings enjoyed by their fathers; and that "their scales of darkness shall begin to fall from their eyes; and many generations shall not pass away among them, save they shall be a pure and delightsome people." In this setting of Lehite conversion, and of the newness of life that shall be theirs after the Book of Mormon comes forth, our ancient friend prophesies also of the Jews. "And it shall come to pass that the Jews which are scattered also shall begin to believe in Christ; and they shall begin to gather in upon the face of the land; and as many as shall believe in Christ shall also become a delightsome people." Then the prophetic word continues—and the chronological order of events is of great import—then Nephi talks at length about millennial conditions and the triumph and glory of the Lord's people in that blessed day. (2 Ne. 30:3-18.)

That is to say, the Jews "shall begin to believe in Christ" before he comes the second time. Some of them will accept the gospel and forsake the traditions of their fathers; a few will find in Jesus the fulfillment of their ancient Messianic hopes; but their nation as a whole, their people as the distinct body that they now are in all nations, the Jews as a unit shall not, at that time, accept the word of truth. But a beginning will be made; a foundation will be laid; and then Christ will come and usher in the millennial year of his redeemed.

As all the world knows, many Jews are now gathering to Palestine, where they have their own nation and way of worship, all without reference to a belief in Christ or an acceptance of the laws and ordinances of his everlasting gospel. Is this the latter-day gathering of the Jews of which the scriptures speak? No! It is not; let there be no misunderstanding in any discerning mind on this point. This gathering of the Jews to their homeland, and their organization into a nation and a kingdom, is not the gathering promised by the prophets. It does not fulfill the ancient promises. Those who have thus assembled have not gathered into the true Church and fold of their ancient Messiah. They have not received again the saving truths of that very gospel which blessed Moses their lawgiver, and Elijah their prophet, and Peter, James, and John, whom their fathers rejected.

This gathering of the unconverted to Palestine—shall we not call it a political gathering based on such understanding of the ancient word as those without the guidance of the Holy Spirit can attain, or shall we not call it a preliminary gathering brought to pass in the wisdom of him who once was their God?—this gathering, of those whose eyes are yet dimmed by scales of darkness and who have not yet become the delightsome people it is their destiny to be, is nonetheless part of the divine plan. It is Elias going before Messias; it is a preparatory work; it is the setting of the stage for the grand drama soon to be played on Olivet. A remnant of the once-chosen people must be at the proper place, at the appointed time, to fulfill that which aforetime has been promised relative to the return of the Crucified One to the people who once chanted, in a delirious chorus, as Pilate sought to free him at the fourth Passover, "Crucify him, crucify him."

Seated on the Mount of Olives, surrounded by the Twelve, in

the Olivet Discourse Jesus said of his glorious return: "And the remnant"—those Jews who have come out of the nations of the earth to live again in the land of Judah—"shall be gathered unto this place." This place is Palestine; it is Jerusalem; it is the Mount of Olives on the east of the holy city. "And then they shall look for me, and, behold, I will come; and they shall see me in the clouds of heaven, clothed with power and great glory; with all the holy angels." (D&C 45:43-44.) This coming—and there will be many appearances which taken together comprise the second coming of the Son of Man—this coming will be in the midst of war; it will be preceded by the destruction of the wicked; it will be to those Jews "that remain" after the day of burning, as Zechariah so aptly identifies them.

Foretelling and describing that day and that appearance, Jehovah said of olden time: "And I will pour upon the house of David, and upon the inhabitants of Jerusalem"—meaning upon those that remain after the wars, after the burning of the vineyard, after the destruction of the wicked—"the spirit of grace and of supplications: and they shall look upon me whom they have pierced, and they shall mourn for him, as one mourneth for his only son, and shall be in bitterness for him, as one that is in bitterness for his firstborn."

There follows a pronouncement relative to the inconsolable grief of those whose eyes are now open and who now know their fathers have walked in darkness, choosing to lose their souls rather than accept their Savior. Then comes this gladsome word: "In that day there shall be a fountain opened to the house of David and to the inhabitants of Jerusalem for sin and for uncleanness." They shall be baptized and receive the Holy Ghost! Sin and dross and evil will be burned out of them as though by fire. False worship shall cease. It is the millennial day. Their King is among them, and they know it. "And one shall say unto him, What are these wounds in thine hands? Then he shall answer, Those with which I was wounded in the house of my friends." (Zech. 12:10-14; 13:1, 6.)

The holy word that has come to us speaks of that day in these words: "And then shall the Jews look upon me and say: What are these wounds in thine hands and in thy feet? Then shall they know that I am the Lord; for I will say unto them: These wounds are the wounds with which I was wounded in the house of my friends. I am he who was lifted up. I am Jesus that was crucified. I am the Son of God." (D&C 45:51-52.)

And thus cometh the day of the conversion of the Jews. It is a millennial day, a day after the destruction of the wicked, a day when those who remain shall seek the Lord and find his gospel. And, for that matter, so shall it be with reference to the gathering and triumph of all Israel. What we do now in preparation for the Second Coming is but a prelude. The great day of gathering and glory lies ahead. It will be in that age when men beat their swords into plowshares and their spears into pruning hooks, and there is peace in all the earth.

THE GENTILES AND THE SECOND COMING

Who Are the Gentiles?

We have spoken and shall yet speak in glowing terms of Israel and her destiny as we rejoice in the goodness of God to his chosen people. But what of the aliens, what of those in whose veins none of the blood of father Jacob flows, what of the Gentiles? Shall they not play some part in the Lord's strange act, that act which is now being performed on the stage of the world? Have they no part to play in preparing a people for the second coming of the Son of Man?

Would it be amiss to take a Pauline approach to the Israel-Gentile relationship and ask: What? "Is he the God of the Jews only? is he not also of the Gentiles? Yes, of the Gentiles also." (Rom. 3:29.) And does not the Father of us all love all his children? Has he no work for his less-favored seed in that day when the whole earth and the people in every nation must hear the announcement of the return of the God of Israel, who is also the God of the whole earth? Is salvation reserved for the Jews only, or for Israel only? Did no one but Abraham have seed deserving of reward? God forbid. Such cannot be. Salvation is for all men, and there is work enough in the vineyards of the Lord for ministers chosen from every nation. None have more talents than they can use, and none have so few that they cannot perform some service for their King. As it was when Jesus first came, so it is today: the harvest truly is plenteous, but the laborers are few.

Truly, God "hath made of one blood all nations of men for to dwell on all the face of the earth" (Acts 17:26), and hath determined, in his own infinite wisdom, how and when they can best serve him and what they should do to further his interests. In it the Gentiles shall play their part, as we are about to see. But first, who are the Gentiles of whom we shall speak? Where are they found, and what relationship do they have both to Jewish Israel and to all Israel?

We have heretofore identified the Jews as both the nationals of the kingdom of Judah and as their lineal descendants, all this without reference to tribal affiliation. And we have said, within this usage of terms, that all other people are Gentiles, including the lost and scattered remnants of the kingdom of Israel in whose veins the precious blood of him whose name was Israel does in fact flow. Thus Joseph Smith, of the tribe of Ephraim, the chief and foremost tribe of Israel itself, was the Gentile by whose hand the Book of Mormon came forth, and the members of The Church of Jesus Christ of Latter-day Saints, who have the gospel and who are of Israel by blood descent, are the Gentiles who carry salvation to the Lamanites and to the Jews. The Lamanites, having come out from Jerusalem, are in fact Jews, although they are not the Jews of whom we speak when we divide mankind into the two camps of Jews and Gentiles.

There were, of course, Gentiles before there were Jews and before there was a kingdom of Judah. They were simply the aliens, the people of other nations, the citizens of other kingdoms, the worshippers of other gods than the Lord. In that day they were outside the pale of saving grace because they had neither the gospel in its fulness nor the law of Moses. It was proper then, and it is proper now, to refer to the Gentiles as those unbelievers who do not serve the Lord Jehovah (the God of Israel), and to refer to Israel as the believers who accept him as their God and who strive to do his will.

Israel in her scattered state is made up of those who are the literal seed of Jacob, even though they are now serving other gods than the Lord, and the Gentiles are those who have not descended from this ancient patriarchal house. Manifestly Israel and the alien nations have intermarried and many of earth's inhabitants are of mixed blood. With these concepts before us we are prepared to set forth the word of scripture relative to the Gentiles and their great latter-day work.

The Gospel Goes to the Gentiles

To envision why and under what circumstances the gospel was and is destined to go to the Gentiles, in preference to the Jews, we must take a brief overview of the dealings of God with mortals through the ages. We must open to view the hoary facts of antiquity and pierce the prophetic curtain that veils the future. We must come to know that the Father of us all, in his infinite goodness and grace, desires to save all his children; that he offers his saving truths to men under those circumstances in which the greatest possible number will believe and obey; and that he blesses those who seek his face and curses those who choose to walk in worldly ways.

Accordingly, a gracious God first gave his gospel to Adam and commanded him to teach his children—all his children from generation to generation—that salvation is in Christ and comes because of his atoning sacrifice. This our first mortal father did. And soon the pattern for all ages was set. The Abels among men sought the Lord, and the Cains served Satan. Men built cities of holiness wherein Enoch and his converts became pure in heart, and cities of sin in which the wicked and ungodly gratified the lusts of the flesh. There were righteous nations where the saints strengthened each other in the holy faith, and wicked nations in which none of the truths of heaven were found. Truly, the law of agency was and is in active operation in all ages and among all people.

Men are born into mortality with the talents and abilities acquired by obedience to law in their first estate. Above all talents—greater than any other capacities, chief among all endowments—stands the talent for spirituality. Those so endowed find it easy to believe the truth in this life. In large measure they are sent to earth in the households of faith where the gospel is known and taught and where they will have a better chance to gain salvation. In large measure, since the day of Abraham, they have been born in Israel where the Lord's will is known. Even now the scattered and lost sheep of that favored house find it easier to accept the gospel than is the case with the residue of men. True it is that "all mankind"—Jew and Gentile alike—"may be saved, by obedience to the laws and ordinances of the Gospel." (A of F 3.) But the word of truth is sent to some before it goes to others because they earned the right to such preferential treatment in preexistence.

Thus some nations had the gospel before the flood and others did not. In that day "the seed of Cain," for instance, "were black, and had not place" among the people of God. (Moses 7:22.) Converts, however, were sought and made from among the balance of Adam's posterity. Similarly, after the flood, in the days of Abraham, the seed of Ham were "cursed . . . as pertaining to the Priesthood," and thus could not receive the fulness of the ordinances of the house of the Lord. (Abr. 1:26.) But when Abraham and his family left Ur to dwell in Canaan, he says they took with them "the souls that we had won in Haran." (Abr. 2:15.) Then, as now, the servants of the Lord were seeking to save their fellowmen.

From the day Israel was led out of Egypt and established as a nation until the ministry of their Messiah among them, the blessings of salvation were reserved almost exclusively for them. During that entire time the aliens had no claim upon Jehovah and his goodness. He was the God of Israel alone in the true sense of the word. But even then such Gentiles as took the yoke of the law upon them became Israelites by adoption and were blessed equally with the natural seed of Abraham. "The stranger that dwelleth with you shall be unto you as one born among you," the Lord commanded, "and thou shalt love him as thyself." (Lev. 19:34.)

Jesus made himself subject to this same law during his mortal ministry. With minor exceptions he confined his ministerial labors to "the lost sheep of the house of Israel." During a brief stay near Gentile Tyre and Sidon, he withheld his healing goodness from "a woman of Canaan" until she importuned with exceedingly great faith. "It is not meet to take the children's bread, and to cast it to dogs," he said. (Matt. 15:21-28.) During a short visit to the half-Jew, half-Gentile area of Decapolis, he proclaimed the gospel to all who there abode. But the great burden of his labors were with the Jews only. And when he sent the Twelve forth, they were similarly restricted. "Go not into the way of the Gentiles," he said, "But go rather to the lost sheep of the house of Israel." (Matt. 10:5-6.)

But all of this was simply to give the Jews the first opportunity to receive the gospel. Thereafter the divine word was to go to the Gentiles, as the prophetic word so eloquently attests. "I am sought of them that asked not for me," saith the God of Israel; "I am found of them that sought me not: I said, Behold me, behold me, unto a nation that was not called by my name." (Isa. 65:1.) "I will gather all nations and tongues; and they shall come, and see my glory." My ministers "shall declare my glory among the Gentiles. . . . And I will also take of them"—the Gentiles!—"for priests and for Levites, saith the Lord." (Isa. 66:18-21.) "For from the rising of the sun even unto the going down of the same my name shall be great among the Gentiles; . . . my name shall be great among the heathen, saith the Lord of hosts." (Mal. 1:11.)

It was to the Jews that the Messiah came, but he also came to save all men, both Jew and Gentile alike. The Messianic word affirms: "He shall bring forth judgment to the Gentiles," and shall be "a light of the Gentiles." (Isa. 42:1, 6.) Matthew interprets Isaiah's words to mean: "And in his name shall the Gentiles trust." (Matt. 12:21.) And saintly Simeon, in the temple, holding the Christ Child in his arms, was guided by the Spirit to testify that the newly born Messiah had come as "a light to lighten the Gentiles," as well as to be the glory of Israel. (Luke 2:32.)

The ancient word from Israel's God was: "Look unto me, and be ye saved, all the ends of the earth: for I am God, and there is none else." He is the one unto whom "every knee shall bow" and "every tongue shall swear." (Isa. 45:22-23.) And that all men might come unto him and be saved, he, after his resurrection, commanded his ancient apostles, "Go ye into all the world, and preach the gospel to every creature." (Mark 16:15.) At long last the promises to the Gentiles were to be fulfilled. His word, his gospel, his salvation was, eventually, for all men of every race, culture, and creed.

This new course of inviting all men to come and eat at the table of the Lord ushered in a new era of hope and salvation for all the seed of Adam. It was indeed a vision so broad and a concept so glorious that even the ancient Twelve were slow to understand its full import. They were Jews trained in Jewish theology and had seen their Master limit his work to their own kindred. The token of the covenant that set them apart from all nations had been cut into the very flesh of their bodies. They had yet to learn that circumcision, which they had supposed was an eternal and everlasting rite, had been done away in Christ, and that the sun of Jewish separateness was setting.

Hence, God gave Peter the vision of the unclean creatures and commanded: "What God hath cleansed, that call not thou common." Peter was then sent to Cornelius, where that Lord who is no respecter of persons, in the presence of his chief apostle, gave the Holy Ghost to Gentiles even before baptism, to the great astonishment of those "of the circumcision." (Acts 10:1-48.) From that day, the gospel went to both the Jews and the Gentiles, with a lessening emphasis on the Jews and an increasing call to the erstwhile aliens. After Paul and Barnabas had been rejected by the Jews, they said: "It was necessary that the word of God should first have been spoken to you: but seeing ye put it from you, and judge yourselves unworthy of everlasting life, lo, we turn to the Gentiles. For so hath the Lord commanded us, saying, I have set thee"—meaning the God of Israel—"to be a light of the Gentiles, that thou shouldest be for salvation unto the ends of the earth." (Acts 13:46-47.) After the destruction of Jerusalem and the scattering of her people, the *times of the Jews* drew to an end; thereafter the gospel went mainly to the Gentiles.

The Gospel Restored to the Gentiles

There were, in effect, three peoples, three different religious worlds, in the day of Jesus. These were:

1. The Jews, who had the Aaronic Priesthood, the law of Moses, the words of the prophets, and the hope of a messianic deliverer. It was among them that the Lord Jesus ministered as a mortal.

2. The other branches of the house of Israel, meaning (a) the Nephites, who had the Melchizedek Priesthood, the law of Moses, and the fulness of the gospel, and (b) the lost tribes of Israel, whom the Lord centuries before had led away into the lands northward, and who were not then known to have either the priesthood or the divine law. It was among these—the Nephites and the Ten Tribes—that Jesus ministered as a resurrected personage.

3. The Gentiles, meaning all other races of men, who dwelt wherever the nations of men were found. All these were without priesthood and authority and had none of the saving truths. Among them the Lord Jesus did not minister either as a mortal or an immortal, and to them the gospel was destined to go by the power of the Holy Ghost.

Jesus first took the gospel to the Jews, and it was by them rejected. Few indeed were the true believers among them. Then he took the very same truths and the very same powers to the rest of the house of Israel, whom we believe to have been faithful for many years thereafter. We know the Nephites hewed to the line of righteousness for two hundred years as did no other people of whom we know save only those in Enoch's Zion. Then the word of truth went to the Gentiles who were "converted through" the preaching of the Jews. These Gentiles did not "at any time" hear the Lord's voice, and he was not manifest unto them "save it were by the Holy Ghost." (3 Ne. 15:22-23.)

It is to those who are not Jews that the Lord promised to give his gospel first in the last days. "In the latter days, when our seed"—now known as Lamanites—"shall have dwindled in unbelief, yea, for the space of many years," Nephi said, "and many generations after the Messiah shall be manifested in body unto the children of men, then"—and this is to be in the glorious age of restoration in which we now live—"then shall the fulness of the gospel of the Messiah come unto the Gentiles, and from the Gentiles unto the remnant of our seed." This gospel shall come to them "by way of the Gentiles." Why? "That the Lord may show his power unto the Gentiles," Nephi continues, "for the very cause that he shall be rejected of the Jews, or of the house of Israel." (1 Ne. 15:13-17.)

We are those Gentiles of whom Nephi speaks. We have received in this age of restoration the fulness of the everlasting gospel. It is now beginning to go from us to the Lamanites and to the Jews. But the great day of the Lamanites and the great day of the Jews both lie ahead. In the full and true sense of the word, the day of their worldwide glory, the day of the triumph and glory of both the Lamanites and the Jews, in all nations—that day will be millennial.

Jesus spoke many things to the Nephites, for their benefit and for ours, about these things. His words let us know what is to happen relative to the house of Israel both before and after he comes in glory to usher in the great Millennium. Speaking of the Jews, whom he identified as "my people at Jerusalem, they who have seen me and been with me in my ministry"—and they were to be scourged and scattered in all nations—of them Jesus said: "Through the fulness of the Gentiles, the remnant of their seed, . . . may be brought to a knowledge of me, their Redeemer." These dissident and rebellious souls whose fathers had cried: "His blood be on us, and"—God help us!—"on our children" (Matt. 27:25); these Jews who have not yet accepted the Lord Jesus as the Son of God and as their Promised Messiah, these descendants of those with whom God made covenant in olden times —they "shall be scattered forth upon the face of the earth because of their unbelief," Jesus says.

But when they accept Him whom their fathers rejected; when they believe in the one whom they slew and hanged on a tree; when they turn to the very Messiah who was born of Mary in Bethlehem of Judea and accept him as their King—then shall they be heirs of salvation along with faithful Abraham their father. "Then will I gather them in from the four quarters of the earth," Jesus promises, "and then will I fulfill the covenant which the Father hath made unto all the people of the house of Israel." The great day of glory for any people comes after they believe, after they are converted, after they obey the law upon which the receipt of the promised blessings is predicated. As with all Israel, so with the Jews; they shall be blessed after they believe and obey.

"And blessed are the Gentiles," Jesus testifies, "because of their belief in me, in and of the Holy Ghost, which witnesses unto them of me and of the Father." The holy gospel comes to us not because Jesus ministered among us in the days of his flesh, as he did to the Jews; not because he appeared and taught us as a resurrected personage, as he did to the Nephites and the Ten Tribes; rather, the gospel comes to us "in and of the Holy Ghost." We are in a like category with those in Jesus' day of whom he said: "The Gentiles should not at any time hear my voice," and "I should not manifest myself unto them save it were by the Holy Ghost." (3 Ne. 15:23.)

Of the Gentiles in the last days, our Lord continues: "Behold, because of their belief in me, saith the Father, and because of the unbelief of you, O house of Israel, in the latter day shall the truth come unto the Gentiles, that the fulness of these things shall be made known unto them." We shall receive again the gospel; we shall know what the ancients knew; we shall have the words Jesus spoke to the Nephites.

That the Gentiles of our day do not believe in the one and only Savior of mankind is one of the most self-evident truths of history. A few Jews believed when he came to them, but most of them rejected him and his salvation. So it is today. A few Gentiles believe, but the masses of men continue on in their carnal courses as worldly men have in all ages. Hence: "Wo, saith the Father, unto the unbelieving of the Gentiles—for notwithstanding they have come forth upon the face of this land [America], and have scattered my people [the Lamanites] who are of the house of Israel; and my people who are of the house of Israel have been cast out from among them, and have been trodden under feet by them; And because of the mercies of the Father unto the Gentiles, and also the judgments of the Father upon my people who are of the house of Israel, verily, verily, I say unto you, that after all this, and I have caused my people who are of the house of Israel to be smitten, and to be afflicted, and to be slain, and to be cast out from among them, and to become hated by them, and to become a hiss and a byword among them— . . . And then will I remember my covenant which I have made unto my people, O house of Israel, and I will bring my gospel unto them." In the last days the gospel goes first to the Gentiles and then to the Jews and Lamanites.

Why will the Lord take the gospel from the unbelieving Gentiles? Jesus answers: "At that day when the Gentiles shall sin against my gospel"—he is speaking here more particularly of the United States of America, of the nation that has scattered the Lamanites, of the nation that esteems itself greater than any other nation—"and shall be lifted up in the pride of their hearts above all nations, and above all the people of the whole earth, and shall be filled with all manner of lyings, and of deceits, and of mischiefs, and all manner of hypocrisy, and murders, and priestcrafts, and whoredoms, and of secret abominations; and if they shall do all those things, and shall reject the fulness of my gospel, behold, saith the Father, I will bring the fulness of my gospel from among them."

When will the Lord take the gospel from the unbelieving Gentiles? It will be when the fulness of the Gentiles is come in, when he remembers the covenant made with his own people, when the hour for millennial glory has arrived. "And then . . . I will show unto thee, O house of Israel, that the Gentiles shall not have power over you; but I will remember my covenant unto you, O house of Israel, and ye shall come unto the knowledge of the fulness of my gospel. But if the Gentiles will repent and return unto me, saith the Father, behold they shall be numbered among my people, O house of Israel."

The Gentiles as a whole and as a people will not repent and be numbered with the house of Israel. They are ripening in iniquity and the end is near, for the destruction of the wicked, which is the end of the world, shall soon come. But any portion of the Gentiles who do repent will be blessed and will not be destroyed in the coming day. Such shall inherit the blessings next spoken of by Jesus: "And I will not suffer my people, who are of the house of Israel, to go through among them, and tread them down, saith the Father."

Next Jesus speaks of the day when the wicked shall be cut off from among the people, when they will be burned as stubble, when every corruptible thing will be consumed. In doing so he uses some graphic imagery. "But if they will not turn unto me, and hearken unto my voice, I will suffer them, yea, I will suffer my people, O house of Israel, that they shall go through among them, and shall tread them down, and they shall be as salt that hath lost its savor, which is thenceforth good for nothing but to be cast out, and to be trodden under foot of my people, O house of Israel." In the full and true sense, Israel shall triumph over her foes only when the Millennium is ushered in, only when her Messiah comes to deliver them from the aliens, only when the wicked are destroyed and the Lord reigns gloriously among his saints.

It is in this setting—a millennial setting; a day of millennial glory; the day when peace prevails because the wicked have been destroyed—it is in this setting that Jesus says: "Then"—in the day of which we speak—"the words of the prophet Isaiah shall be fulfilled." These are the words: "Thy watchmen shall lift up the voice; with the voice together shall they sing, for they shall see eye to eye when the Lord shall bring again Zion." We are establishing Zion now, but our Zion is only the foundation for that which is to be. We are laying a foundation; the promises relative to the glorious Zion of God which shall yet stand upon the earth shall be fulfilled after the Lord comes. "Break forth into joy, sing together, ye waste places of Jerusalem," Isaiah continues, "for the Lord hath comforted his people, he hath redeemed Jerusalem." The true and full redemption of Jerusalem must await the day of the Lord's return. "The Lord hath made bare his holy arm in the eye of all the nations; and all the ends of the earth shall see the salvation of God." (3 Ne. 16:4-20.) Again, we have made a beginning, but the glorious fulfillment lies ahead.

We shall pick up and amplify these thoughts in the next chapter as we consider the Gentile fulness. At this point, as we speak of the gospel going to the Gentiles before the Second Coming, it but remains for us to bear one added solemn witness.

I was present, together with my Brethren of the Twelve and the counselors in the First Presidency, when the voice of God, speaking from the midst of eternity by the power of the Spirit, revealed a glorious truth to his servant the prophet. The message then confirmed in the heart and soul of President Spencer W. Kimball was that the time, long desired and devoutly sought for, had now come to offer to all men of every race and color, solely on the basis of personal worthiness, the fulness of the blessings of the Holy

Priesthood, including celestial marriage and all of the blessings of the house of the Lord.

All of us then present in the holy temple on that blessed occasion became living witnesses of the reality of the revealed word that then came to the one appointed to receive revelation for the Church and for the world. Each of us received a confirming witness in our souls—the Holy Spirit of God speaking to the spirits within us—so that we can and do testify to the world that the revelation came and that it is the mind and will and voice of the Lord.

The receipt of this revelation is one of the signs of the times. It lets us know that the coming of the Lord Jesus Christ to usher in the great Millennium is not far distant. It opens the door so that we can truly preach the gospel to every nation and kindred and tongue and people. Now there are no restrictions as to where Zion can be established or to the people who can become heirs of full salvation.

Having borne this witness and laid this foundation, we are now ready to build upon the foundations here laid and turn our attention to that rather enigmatic expression "the fulness of the Gentiles," which we shall do in chapter 21.

THE TIMES OF THE GENTILES

The Gentiles and the Abrahamic Covenant

As we rejoice in the goodness of a gracious God to the Gentiles; as we marvel to see him give the blessings of the chosen people to the aliens; as we realize that the gospel blessings are for all men, Jew and Gentile alike—we must yet keep in proper perspective the favored status of blessed Israel. It was to Abraham that the promises came; it was Isaac who inherited all things from Abraham; and it was Jacob upon whom the fulness fell in his day. It is the God of Israel who, having first blessed the chosen seed, became the God of the whole earth and offered his gospel unto all who would believe and obey.

How glorious is the word that the Lord Jehovah chose Abraham, his friend, above all the inhabitants of the earth, to be the father of the faithful for all generations—not the father of the faithful in the house of Israel only, but the father of the faithful in all nations. "In thy seed shall all the nations of the earth be blessed" was the divine decree. (Gen. 22:18.)

How glorious is the word, given to Abraham, "In Isaac shall thy seed be called." (Gen. 21:12.) 'In this Sarah's son shall the promises be fulfilled. He shall inherit the blessings given to thee, Abraham, his father. Through him shall come the chosen and favored seed who shall believe the gospel and worship the true God and be saved in his kingdom.'

How glorious is the word that the God of Israel chose Jacob, who is Israel, to inherit the blessings of his fathers—the blessings of life and salvation through the atonement of the Son of God.

And how glorious is the word that the Gentiles may be adopted into the family of Abraham and receive, inherit, and possess equally with the literal seed. "As many as receive this Gospel shall be called after thy name," the Lord Jehovah promised Abraham, "and shall be accounted thy seed, and shall rise up and bless thee, as their father." And further: "In thy seed after thee (that is to say, the literal seed, or the seed of the body) shall all the families of the earth be blessed, even with the blessings of the Gospel, which are the blessings of salvation, even of life eternal." (Abr. 2:10-11.)

Thus, salvation comes because of the covenant God made with Abraham. It was Jesus himself who said, "Salvation is of the Jews." (John 4:22.) It must go from Israel to others. If the Gentiles are to gain such a blessed boon, they must become Israelites; they must be adopted into the fold of Abraham; they must rise up and bless him as their father. It was to the natural seed of Jacob that Isaiah said these words of the Lord, and they are equally true with reference to the adopted seed: "Hearken to me, ye that follow after righteousness, ye that seek the Lord: look unto the rock whence ye are hewn, and to the hole of the pit whence ye are digged. Look unto Abraham your father, and unto Sarah that bare you: for I called him alone, and blessed him, and increased him." (Isa. 51:1-2.) Abraham alone is the father of us all, speaking after the manner of the flesh, and all who receive the blessings of the gospel are either natural or adopted sons in his everlasting family.

Thus, also, Nephi says: "As many of the Gentiles as will repent are the covenant people of the Lord; and as many of the Jews as will not repent shall be cast off; for the Lord covenanteth with none save it be with them that repent and believe in his Son, who is the Holy One of Israel." (2 Ne. 30:2.) The covenant here involved is the Abrahamic covenant. It is, Nephi says, the "covenant the Lord made to our father Abraham, saying: In thy seed shall all the kindreds of the earth be blessed." And it shall "be fulfilled in the latter days." (1 Ne. 15:18.)

And thus Jesus, ministering among the Nephite portion of Israel, tells them of their favored status. "Ye are the children of the prophets; and ye are of the house of Israel," he says. They were the natural seed of the ancient patriarch, and so he says: "Ye are of the covenant which the Father made with your fathers, saying unto Abraham: And in thy seed shall all the kindreds of the earth be blessed." Because of this favored status, because they were heirs of promise, because they were the literal seed and the blood of Israel flowed in their veins, they had preference over the aliens. Thus Jesus said to them: "The Father having raised me up unto you first, and sent me to bless you in turning away every one of you from his iniquities; and this because ye are the children of the covenant—And after that ye were blessed then fulfilleth the Father the covenant which he made with Abraham, saying: In thy seed shall all the kindreds of the earth be blessed—unto the pouring out of the Holy Ghost through me upon the Gentiles, which blessing upon the Gentiles shall make them mighty above all, unto the scattering of my people, O house of Israel." (3 Ne. 20:25-27.)

It is Israel first and the Gentiles second. It is the chosen seed ahead of the alien nations. The natural sons are already in the family when the adopted sons take upon themselves the name of him whom they choose as their father. But all men, in or out of the house of Israel, are freed from their iniquities in the same way. If they "walk in the light," as God "is in the light," if they have "fellowship one with another," as becometh true saints, then "the blood of Jesus Christ his Son cleanseth [them] from all sin." (1 Jn. 1:7.) There is no other way. All are alike unto God.

Israel's Millennial Gathering and Glory

Knowing that Israel and the aliens shall join in one fold and have one Shepherd, we are prepared to pick up again, as he himself did, the threads of Jesus' preaching to the Nephites about the chosen seed and those who join with them. In 3 Nephi 16, Jesus spoke of the gospel coming to the Gentiles in the latter days; of the gathering of Israel from the four quarters of the earth; of the Gentiles, drenched in wickedness and abominations, sinning against the gospel; and then of the gospel going to others of the house of Israel. He spoke of the triumph of Israel as the Millennium was ushered in, and said that in that millennial day the words in Isaiah

52:8-10 would be fulfilled. All this we considered in chapter 20.

Now, after an interval of teaching on other matters, the Risen Lord returns to his prior theme—the part Israel and the Gentiles are to play in his strange act in the dispensation of the fulness of times. "Ye remember that I spake unto you, and said that when the words of Isaiah should be fulfilled—behold they are written, ye have them before you, therefore search them—And verily, verily, I say unto you, that when they shall be fulfilled then is the fulfilling of the covenant which the Father hath made unto his people, O house of Israel."

With this introduction we are back to the general subject of the latter-day gathering of Israel and to the specific passage in Isaiah that is to find fulfillment in the Millennium. This is Isaiah 52:8-10, which Jesus will soon quote again. But first, in this setting among the Nephites, our Lord says: "And then"—that is, in the millennial day—"shall the remnants, which shall be scattered abroad upon the face of the earth, be gathered in from the east and from the west, and from the south and from the north; and they shall be brought to the knowledge of the Lord their God, who hath redeemed them."

Israel shall be gathered in part before the Millennium, and that gathering is now going forward apace, with particular reference to Ephraim, the firstborn, and Manasseh, his twin. But Israel shall be gathered in full after the Millennium commences, and that gathering will include the Jews and, as we are about to see, the Ten Tribes. What Jesus now says is not all intended to be chronological. He will make interpretive comments as he goes forward, but there is ample explanation to enable us to conclude with some certainty much of what is to precede and what is to follow his millennial return.

"And I say unto you, that if the Gentiles do not repent after the blessing which they shall receive, after they have scattered my people"—our Lord announces by way of introduction to what is to follow. He is saying that if the Gentiles—the non-Jews—to whom the gospel has been restored in the last days do not accept that gospel, then, after they have scattered the Lamanites, as they have now done, certain things will happen. These are:

"Then"—in the day of our Lord's return—"Then shall ye, who are a remnant of the house of Jacob, go forth among them; and ye shall be in the midst of them who shall be many; and ye shall be among them as a lion among the beasts of the forest, and as a young lion among the flocks of sheep, who, if he goeth through both treadeth down and teareth in pieces, and none can deliver. Thy hand shall be lifted up upon thine adversaries, and all thine enemies shall be cut off."

These words of our Lord to the Nephites are quoted from Micah 5:8-9 and have reference to the desolations and ultimate burning that shall destroy the wicked at the Second Coming. Except for a few who are the humble followers of Christ, the Gentiles will not repent. They will revel in their abominations and sin against the restored gospel, and they will be burned by the brightness of our Lord's coming while the righteous—here called the remnant of Jacob—shall abide the day. And then, in the prophetic imagery, it will be as though the remnant of Israel overthrew their enemies as a young lion among the flocks of sheep.

It is in this setting, a setting that has ushered in the Millennium, that the promise is made: "And I will gather my people together as a man gathereth his sheaves into the floor." This is the great gathering destined to occur after our Lord's return. By way of further explanation of the triumphant events involved, Jesus now says: "For I will make my people with whom the Father hath covenanted, yea, I will make thy horn iron, and I will make thy hoofs brass. And thou shalt beat in pieces many people; and I will consecrate their gain unto the Lord, and their substance unto the Lord of the whole earth. And behold, I am he who doeth it." Again the prophetic imagery comes from the Old Testament. It is taken from Micah 4:13.

"And it shall come to pass, saith the Father, that the sword of my justice shall hang over them at that day; and except they repent it shall fall upon them, saith the Father, yea, even upon all the nations of the Gentiles." Again Jesus is speaking of the complete separation of the righteous and the wicked that will take place when he comes. "And it shall come to pass," in that millennial day, "that I will establish my people, O house of Israel." The Millennium is Israel's day.

"And behold, this people"—the Nephites, the Lamanites, the descendants of Lehi—"will I establish in this land [America], unto the fulfilling of the covenant which I made with your father Jacob; and it shall be a New Jerusalem. And the powers of heaven shall be in the midst of this people; yea, even I will be in the midst of you." Christ will reign personally upon the earth in that millennial day when the remnant of Lehi becomes a mighty people in America and when the New Jerusalem is the capital of the kingdom of God on earth.

A little later Jesus speaks of the Gentiles and the Jews and places the Jewish gathering after his Second Coming. Of the Gentiles he says: "When they shall have received the fulness of my gospel, then if they shall harden their hearts against me I will return their iniquities upon their own heads, saith the Father." They will suffer for their own sins; the Lord's blood will not cleanse them because they do not repent. And we repeat, most of the Gentiles will reject the truth and be bundled with the tares to be burned at that great day.

Of the Jews he says: "And I will remember the covenant which I have made with my people; and I have covenanted with them that I would gather them together in mine own due time, that I would give unto them again the land of their fathers for their inheritance, which is the land of Jerusalem, which is the promised land unto them forever, saith the Father." The Jews shall dwell again in Jerusalem of old, and in all Judea, and in all Palestine. "And it shall come to pass that the time cometh, when the fulness of my gospel shall be preached unto them; And they shall believe in me, that I am Jesus Christ, the Son of God, and shall pray unto the Father in my name."

At this point he returns again to Isaiah 52:8-10—which we have heretofore quoted and which we have seen is a passage reserved for millennial fulfillment—quoting it this time as the word of the Father, for "the Father and I are one," he says. "And then"—the time, be it remembered, is millennial—"shall be brought to pass that which is written," Jesus says, quoting three passages, all from this same 52nd chapter of Isaiah, and all relative to the gathering, rejoicing, and triumph of his people. These are Isaiah 52:1-3, 6; Isaiah 52:7; and Isaiah 52:11-15, which the astute student will desire to read and ponder in the setting here given. "Verily, verily, I say unto you, all these things"—those things Jesus has just said and those he has quoted from Isaiah—"shall surely come, even as the Father hath commanded me," Jesus says. "Then shall this covenant which the Father hath covenanted with his people be fulfilled; and then shall Jerusalem be inhabited again with my people, and it shall be the land of their inheritance." (3 Ne. 20:10-46.)

Jesus then gives a sign whereby all men "may know the time" when all these things he has told them about Israel and the Gentiles "shall be about to take place." The sign is the establishment of a free people in the United States of America; it is the restoration of the gospel in the last days; it is the carrying of the gospel to the Lamanites; it is the martyrdom of the Prophet Joseph Smith and his eternal triumph in the kingdom above. After this sign has been given, "it shall come to pass that whosoever will not believe in my words, who am Jesus Christ," he says, "which the Father shall cause him [the latter-day seer] to bring forth unto the Gentiles, and shall give unto him power that he shall bring them forth unto the Gentiles, (it shall be done even as Moses said) they shall be cut off from among the people who are of the covenant."

Then Jesus quotes again Micah's words about the remnant of Jacob being among the Gentiles as a young lion among the flocks of sheep, equating such with the wicked being cut off from among the people as Moses said. But this time he continues the Old Testament quotation to include Micah 5:10-15, which deals with the social and religious changes that will occur at the Second Coming. To the imagery and doctrine of Micah he adds: "It shall come to pass, saith the Father, that at that day"—the day of our Lord's return—"whosoever will not repent and come unto my Beloved Son, them will I cut off from among my people, O house of Israel; And I will execute vengeance and fury upon them, even as upon the heathen, such as they have not heard." This is the great day of burning when the wicked shall be as stubble.

Jesus' next statements seem to be commentary and explanation relative to events that will happen both before and after his coming. It is not always possible for us in our present state of spiritual enlightenment to put every event into an exact category or time frame. We are left to ponder and wonder about many things, perhaps to keep us alert and attentive to the commandments should the Lord come in our day. And some of the prophetic utterances apply to both pre- and post-millennial events; some have an initial and partial fulfillment in our day and shall have a second and grander completion in the days ahead.

And so we now hear Jesus say of the Gentiles: "If they will repent and hearken unto my words, and harden not their hearts, I will establish my church among them, and they shall come in unto the covenant and be numbered among this the remnant of Jacob." There follows an announcement of the building of a New Jerusalem in America and the gathering of the elect into its sacred walls. "And then shall the power of heaven come down among them; and I also will be in the midst." This, of course, is millennial. (3 Ne. 21:1-25.)

Jesus now speaks of the work among all the dispersed of Israel, with particular reference to the Ten Tribes. We are left to wonder whether he means they shall return before or after his own coming in the clouds of glory. The inference is that they will return during the Millennium, which is also the apparent meaning of the recitations in D&C 133:22-35, which we shall hereafter consider. In any event we know that the great day of gathering and glory for Israel and for the believing Gentiles lies ahead. It is reserved for the millennial day when the Lord Jesus dwells and reigns among his covenant people.

The Fulness of the Gentiles

Oh, that the Jews, the Lord's ancient covenant people, had received their Messiah when he came unto his own!

Oh, that they had believed his words and obeyed his law when he taught in their streets and preached in their synagogues!

Oh, that they had believed and obeyed in the day appointed for their salvation, in the day which was the times of the Jews!

Glory and honor and blessing, peace and joy and salvation—for them and for their children—was offered to them, offered without money and without price. They were invited to feast on the good word of God and to drink of the waters of life. But they would not.

They rejected the gospel, gave no heed to the Divine Voice, and crucified their King—all because their deeds were evil. And so God sent upon them sore destructions. Their house—both the temple and the city—was left unto them desolate; they were scourged and slaughtered and slain; they were condemned and cursed and crucified. And a remnant, a few captives of a once great nation, was scattered upon all the face of the earth and among every people.

"These be the days of vengeance," Jesus said. "There shall be great distress in the land, and wrath upon this people. And they shall fall by the edge of the sword, and shall be led away captive into all nations." Well might we ask: How long, how long, O Lord, shall the curse rest upon these Jews? When will they return to the ancient standard and be counted again among the sheep of their once-rejected Shepherd? Jesus answers: "Jerusalem shall be trodden down of the Gentiles, until the times of the Gentiles be fulfilled." (Luke 21:22-24.)

With the destruction of Jerusalem in A.D. 70; with the tearing apart of the temple, stone by stone, as the Romans made its gold and riches their own; with the scattering of the Jews in all nations—the times of the Jews ended. Their day to receive the glad tidings of salvation on a preferential basis was past. At that hour the times of the Gentiles dawned upon the earth. And from that hour the apostles and prophets began to turn to the aliens to find those who would believe in the God of the whole earth, who is Jesus Christ.

For almost two thousand years; for almost two millenniums; for as long a time as from Abraham, who fathered Israel, to Jesus, who came to save the seed of that ancient patriarch—Jerusalem has been and is "trodden down of the Gentiles." In 1917 Field Marshal Edmund Allenby of Great Britain captured the city almost without opposition, and a measure of political freedom thus came to the site where once Melchizedek was king and which David took from the Jebusites. Since then the once holy city, and its environs, and all of Palestine, have been available for the temporal return of the Jews. An initial and preparatory political gathering is now underway. But the city is still a Gentile stronghold, and it is still trodden down by forces alien to those true believers who one day will build anew its walls and erect therein again a holy temple to Jehovah. That many who now gather there are of the loins of Israel is of little moment, "For they are not all Israel, which are of Israel: Neither, because they are the seed of Abraham, are they all children," as Paul said. (Rom. 9:6-7.) And also: "Blindness in part is happened to Israel, until the fulness of the Gentiles be come in." (Rom. 11:25.) The true Israelites and the true Jews believe in the true Messiah and worship his Father in spirit and in truth. And so it is that the times of the Gentiles is not yet fulfilled, and so it is that the city where our Lord was crucified shall be trodden down by Gentile unbelievers until that day of fulfillment dawns upon the earth.

Jesus, on the Mount of Olives, alone with the Twelve, as we suppose, as they gazed upon the glittering brilliance of Herod's Temple in the distance, said: "And now ye behold this temple which is in Jerusalem, which ye call the house of God, and your enemies say that this house shall never fall. But, verily I say unto you, that desolation shall come upon this generation as a thief in the night, and this people shall be destroyed and scattered among all nations. And this temple which ye now see shall be thrown down that there shall not be left one stone upon another." This is the destruction and scattering of the Jews in A.D. 70, which ended the times of the Jews and commenced the times of the Gentiles.

"And it shall come to pass, that this generation of Jews"—those then living who had rejected their Messiah and were ripened in iniquity and ready for destruction—"shall not pass away until every desolation which I have told you concerning them shall come to pass." Their fate was to suffer an overflowing scourge and to feel the intolerable weight of the abomination of desolation, all of which was a type of the scourges and desolations that shall yet precede the Second Coming.

What is the relationship of these events, all now part of the hoary records of antiquity, to the yet future Second Coming? Jesus continues to speak: "Ye say that ye know that the end of the world cometh; ye say also that ye know that the heavens and the earth shall pass away; And in this ye say truly, for so it is; but these things which I have told you shall not pass away until all shall be fulfilled. And this I have told you concerning Jerusalem; and when that day shall come, shall a remnant be scattered among all nations; But they shall be gathered again; but they shall remain until the times of the Gentiles be fulfilled." The true gathering of the Jews to their homeland shall not occur until the day—yet future—when the times of the Gentiles is fulfilled.

"And in that day"—the day when the times of the Gentiles is about to be fulfilled—"shall be heard of wars and rumors of wars, and the whole earth shall be in commotion, and men's hearts shall fail them, and they shall say Christ delayeth his coming until the end of the earth. And the love of men shall wax cold, and iniquity shall abound. And when the times of the Gentiles is come in"—when it begins anew, as it were, for this is the second time the true gospel shall go to the Gentiles (the first was in Paul's day, and the second is in our day, a day in which the same gospel preached by Paul has been restored), and thus—"when the times of the Gentiles is come in, a light shall break forth among them that sit in darkness, and it shall be the fulness of my gospel; But they"—the Gentiles—"receive it not; for they perceive not the light, and they turn their hearts from me because of the precepts of men. And in that generation shall the times of the Gentiles be fulfilled." (D&C 45:18-30.)

When Moroni appeared to Joseph Smith in 1823, he "stated that the fulness of the Gentiles was soon to come in." (JS-H 1:41.) Those who love the Lord and believe his gospel await that day with anxious expectation and ponder the words of the Lord Jesus, also spoken on Olivet: "In the generation in which the times of the Gentiles shall be fulfilled," he said, "there shall be signs in the sun, and in the moon, and in the stars; and upon the earth distress of nations with perplexity, like the sea and the waves roaring. The earth also shall be troubled, and the waters of the great deep; Men's hearts failing them for fear, and for looking after those things which are coming on the earth. For the powers of heaven shall be shaken. And when these things begin to come to pass, then look up and lift up your heads, for the day of your redemption draweth nigh. And then shall they see the Son of man coming in a cloud, with power and great glory." (JST, Luke 21:25-28.)

The Call to the Gentiles

We have now set forth, in weakness and with fumbling phrases, and yet with such clarity and plainness as our weakness permits, the glorious doctrine that the Gentiles also are heirs of the covenant God made with Abraham. Shall we not add to our words a call, coupled with a warning, to the Gentiles everywhere?

We testify that God has in these times, the times of the Gentiles, restored the fulness of his everlasting gospel to prepare a people for the second coming of the Son of Man. The Book of Mormon has now "come unto the Gentiles" as a sign "that the covenant which the Father hath made with the children of Israel . . . is already beginning to be fulfilled."

Therefore, by way of testimony and exhortation, we say to the Gentiles: "Ye may know that the words of the Lord, which have been spoken by the holy prophets, shall all be fulfilled; and ye need not say that the Lord delays his coming unto the children of Israel." Behold, he will come as he hath said, and none can say him nay.

"And ye need not imagine in your hearts that the words which have been spoken are vain, for behold, the Lord will remember his covenant which he hath made unto his people of the house of Israel." And he will also remember all who join with Israel to further his work in this final dispensation. They shall be blessed with the faithful and made heirs of all the promises.

"And when ye shall see these sayings"—the Book of Mormon —"coming forth among you, then ye need not any longer spurn at the doings of the Lord, for the sword of his justice is in his right hand." Truly, the Book of Mormon has come forth in such plainness and perfection that all men are expected to believe its pure truths and to give heed to the wondrous witness it bears. "And behold, at that day"—when the true doctrines of Christ are set forth before men in such a glorious way in the Book of Mormon—"if ye shall spurn at his doings he will cause that it [the sword of his justice] shall soon overtake you."

And so, by way of warning, we say to the Gentiles: "Wo unto him that spurneth at the doings of the Lord; yea, wo unto him that shall deny the Christ and his works!

"Yea, wo unto him that shall deny the revelations of the Lord, and that shall say the Lord no longer worketh by revelation, or by prophecy, or by gifts, or by tongues, or by healings, or by the power of the Holy Ghost!" And oh, how many of the great churches in Christendom, to say nothing of the religious groups who do not even profess to believe in Christ, fall under this condemnation!

"Yea, and wo unto him that shall say at that day"—when, we repeat, all things are so wondrously and clearly set forth, so much so that no person who has arrived at the years of accountability is justified in misunderstanding the terms and conditions of the great plan of redemption that is in Christ—"wo unto him that shall say at that day, to get gain, that there can be no miracle wrought by Jesus Christ; for he that doeth this shall become like unto the son of perdition, for whom there was no mercy, according to the word of Christ!" Those who deny the great miracles of the opening of the heavens, of the appearance of the Great God, of the coming forth of the Book of Mormon, of the ministering of angels to men, of the pouring out of the Holy Ghost upon the faithful, and of an endless retinue of accompanying blessings—those who deny these miracles do so at their peril.

"Yea, and ye need not any longer hiss, nor spurn, nor make game of the Jews"—and oh, how common this has been and is among the self-appointed pious ones of a decadent Christendom!—"nor any of the remnant of the house of Israel; for behold, the Lord remembereth his covenant unto them, and he will do unto them according to that which he hath sworn. Therefore ye need not suppose that ye can turn the right hand of the Lord unto the left, that he may not execute judgment unto the fulfilling of the covenant which he hath made unto the house of Israel." (3 Ne. 29:1-9.)

By way of commandment we say to the Gentiles: "Hearken, O ye Gentiles, and hear the words of Jesus Christ, the Son of the living God, which he hath commanded me [Mormon] that I should speak concerning you, for, behold he commandeth me that I should write, saying:

"Turn, all ye Gentiles, from your wicked ways; and repent of your evil doings, of your lyings and deceivings, and of your whoredoms, and of your secret abominations, and your idolatries, and of your murders, and your priestcrafts, and your envyings, and your strifes, and from all your wickedness and abominations, and come unto me, and be baptized in my name, that ye may receive a remission of your sins, and be filled with the Holy Ghost, that ye may be numbered with my people who are of the house of Israel." (3 Ne. 30:1-2.)

And, finally, by way of invitation and exhortation to the Gentiles and to the house of Israel, we say: "Come unto Christ, and lay hold upon every good gift, and touch not the evil gift, nor the unclean thing.

"And awake, and arise from the dust, O Jerusalem; yea, and put on thy beautiful garments, O daughter of Zion; and strengthen thy stakes and enlarge thy borders forever, that thou mayest no more be confounded, that the covenants of the Eternal Father which he hath made unto thee, O house of Israel, may be fulfilled.

"Yea, come unto Christ, and be perfected in him, and deny yourselves of all ungodliness; and if ye shall deny yourselves of all ungodliness and love God with all your might, mind and strength, then is his grace sufficient for you, that by his grace ye may be perfect in Christ; and if by the grace of God ye are perfect in Christ, ye can in nowise deny the power of God.

"And again, if ye by the grace of God are perfect in Christ, and deny not his power, then are ye sanctified in Christ by the grace of God, through the shedding of the blood of Christ, which is in the covenant of the Father unto the remission of your sins, that ye become holy, without spot." (Moro. 10:30-33.)

Chapter 22

THE PROMISES MADE TO THE FATHERS

The General Promises

Certain promises made by the prophets of the past must come to pass before the return of earth's Chief Prophet. As the children of these ancient prophets, we may well ask: What are the promises made of old to our fathers, and what is their relationship to the Second Coming? Indeed, who are the prophetic fathers, and what was said by them that does or should affect us their children? And what obligations rest upon us with respect to these ancient promises?

Thoughtful analysis and careful study of the prophetic word enable us to put these promises into two categories: general promises relative to the chosen seed as a people, and specific promises centered in those families who, when taken together, form the chosen race. The general promises involve nations and kingdoms and lands and peoples. They include within their bounds the dealings of the Lord with Israel and the Gentiles and the peopling of the lands of the earth. The specific promises bring the blessings of the gospel, and the glories possessed by them of the past, into the souls and lives of the families of the present.

First, then, let us make a brief overview of the general promises of the Lord to the chosen people and to all men. And then we shall see that these general promises were given so that certain specific blessings might come to those who pledged their allegiance to the great worldwide movements that a divine providence is now causing to occur among all the races of men.

On Mount Olivet, eastward from Jerusalem, in the intimate circle of those whom he had chosen to stand as apostolic witnesses of his holy name, the Lord Jesus said: "As ye have asked of me concerning the signs of my coming, in the day when I shall come in my glory in the clouds of heaven, to fulfil the promises that I have made unto your fathers, For as ye have looked upon the long absence of your spirits from your bodies to be a bondage, I will show unto you how the day of redemption shall come, and also the restoration of the scattered Israel." (D&C 45:16-17.) Then followed the great Olivet Discourse on the destructions destined for their day, on the signs of the times of our day, and on his glorious return in the latter days.

But what are "the promises that I"—he, be it remembered, is Jehovah, the God of their fathers—"have made unto your fathers"? Clearly they are the promises relative to his second coming and the worldwide events that shall attend that dreadful day. He names two of them, the day of redemption and the gathering of scattered Israel. Having this perspective, we immediately know what the general promises are; and of them, in this work, we have spoken or yet will speak in detail. To have the Lord's eternal perspective ever before us we shall, at this point, simply allude to some of them.

The promises made to the fathers include the glorious reality that the Messiah of Israel will come again, as the great Deliverer, to save his people from the bondage of Babylon. They include the immutable decree that he will take vengeance on the wicked and slay the ungodly with the breath of his lips, and that his redeemed, whose year it shall be, will find millennial rest for a thousand years and then eternal peace forever. They include the sure word—God's eternal promise—that there will be a day of refreshing, a day of a new heaven and a new earth, a day when the wolf and the lamb will feed together and the lion shall eat straw like the bullock.

The promises made to the fathers include utterances without end of a day of restoration in which all things fore-announced by all the holy prophets of all the ages shall come to pass. There is the promise of dire and evil apostasy between the two comings of the Lord of glory. There are all the promises about false prophets, false churches, false worship, and false gods—all to spread their evil venom in the last days. There are the promises that iniquity shall abound and abominations cover the earth. Men everywhere are to be drunken with blood; war and carnage are to cover the earth; and evil men, led by evil leaders, shall do evil deeds.

The promises made to the fathers are that the Book of Mormon shall come forth; that Israel shall gather to the ancient standard and believe in their ancient God; that in a yet future day the political kingdom shall be restored to Israel, and they shall rule the whole earth; that Zion shall arise and shine; and that the Gentiles shall come to her light. There are the promises that in the days of certain kings the God of heaven shall set up his own eternal kingdom, which will grow and increase until it breaks in pieces all other kingdoms and fills the whole earth. There are the promises about salvation for the dead, that the prisoners shall go free, and that those who did not have the opportunity to receive the gospel in this life shall have that glorious privilege in the spirit world. There is the promise of a New Jerusalem to be built upon the American continent, to be a companion and a sister city to the Old Jerusalem which shall rise again in glory on the ancient site. There are the promises that the earth itself will receive again its paradisiacal glory and become as it was in the days before the fall.

The promises indeed are many. We mention but a few that the concept may be before us. And as pertaining to these promises, those named and unnamed—God himself by his own mouth and in his own name has sworn that they shall surely come to pass. And all these promises—there are no exceptions—have been given with one object and intent in view. That purpose is to enable the Abrahamic promises to live in the lives of those who are the seed of the father of the faithful. It is through the Abrahamic covenant that salvation is made available to Jew and Gentile alike.

The Abrahamic Promises

Christians, Jews, and Moslems—three races and cultures, almost as diverse and varied as the races of men can be—all claim

Abraham as their father, all look upon him as the ancient patriarchal giant among men, all give a certain lip service to the common concept that God made some sort of a covenant with him that somehow blesses his seed after him.

The Jews claim him as their ancestor and suppose that the law of Moses and the word of the prophets have come to them because of their heirship in Abraham's family. But Jesus excoriated them with these cutting words: "If ye were Abraham's children, ye would do the works of Abraham." (John 8:39.) Whatever their natural bloodline was, they had been cut off from the family and house of their ancient progenitor because their lives no longer conformed to the Abrahamic standard.

Christians, whether of Jewish or Gentile blood, suppose they are heirs of Abraham's blessings because Paul said of the ancient saints who believed the true gospel: "Ye are all one in Christ Jesus. And if ye be Christ's, then are ye Abraham's seed, and heirs according to the promise." (Gal. 3:28-29.) They suppose that Israel is now some kind of a spiritual kingdom composed of all the warring and bickering sects of a divided Christendom, to whom by the grace of God, with little or no reference to the works of righteousness, the blessings of salvation shall come. But as with the Jews, so with the Christians: "If ye were Abraham's children, ye would do the works of Abraham." (John 8:39.)

Our brethren of Islam are even farther removed from any vestige of reality. They suppose that the promises came down, not through Isaac as the scriptures say, but through Ishmael, and that he, the son of the bondwoman, was the one Abraham came near to sacrificing on Moriah. And as to their doctrinal beliefs, they are even farther removed from fact and truth than are their views of history. Indeed, they scarcely have any theology that resembles or is patterned after the teachings of the true prophets. One of the chief purposes of their Koran—perhaps, in the eternal perspective, the chief purpose—is to deny affirmatively the divine Sonship of him through whom salvation comes. Their general concept is: 'Allah had no need for a son to redeem men; he has but to speak and it is done.' And so again we are faced with the same test of true Abrahamic descent that applies to apostate Jewry and to that

Christendom which has lost the fulness of the everlasting word. Those who do the works of Abraham, those who believe what he believed and worship as he worshipped, those who have the fulness of the everlasting gospel, those who "are of faith, the same are the children of Abraham." (Gal. 3:7.) None others qualify.

What, then, are the promises made to Abraham for himself and for his seed? And are there now any among men who can qualify as his true seed in the full sense? Brief fragments of truth, a sliver here and a twig there, have come down to us in the records of the past. The accounts in Genesis let us know that the Lord said to Abraham: "I will make of thee a great nation, and I will bless thee, and make thy name great; and thou shalt be a blessing: And I will bless them that bless thee, and curse him that curseth thee: and in thee shall all families of the earth be blessed." (Gen. 12:2-3.) Here indeed is a promise for Abraham and for all the families of the earth whether they sprang from the loins of the great patriarch or not.

Later the Lord said to his friend Abraham: "I will make thy seed as the dust of the earth: so that if a man can number the dust of the earth, then shall thy seed also be numbered." (Gen. 13:16.) And again: "Look now toward heaven, and tell the stars, if thou be able to number them: and he said unto him, So shall thy seed be." (Gen. 15:5.) And yet again: "Thou shalt be a father of many nations." (Gen. 17:4.) And finally: "By myself have I sworn, saith the Lord, . . . That in blessing I will bless thee, and in multiplying I will multiply thy seed as the stars of the heaven, and as the sand which is upon the sea shore; and thy seed shall possess the gate of his enemies; And in thy seed shall all the nations of the earth be blessed." (Gen. 22:16-18.)

All of these are biblical promises. Their full meaning, as there found, is hidden from the spiritually illiterate and can, in fact, be known only by revelation. As we are about to see, they pertain to the continuation of the family unit in the highest heaven of the celestial world. But first, be it noted, the same promises were renewed to Isaac and to Jacob in their days. To Isaac the Lord said: "I will make thy seed to multiply as the stars of heaven, and will give unto thy seed all these countries; and in thy seed shall all the nations of the earth be blessed." (Gen. 26:4.) And to Jacob the promise came in these words: "And thy seed shall be as the dust of the earth, and thou shalt spread abroad to the west, and to the east, and to the north, and to the south: and in thee and in thy seed shall all the families of the earth be blessed." (Gen. 28:14.)

In the providences of the Lord, there has come to us in the Book of Abraham a broader and more carefully delineated account of the Abrahamic covenant, which includes these words: "And I will make of thee a great nation, and I will bless thee above measure, and make thy name great among all nations, and thou shalt be a blessing unto thy seed after thee, that in their hands they shall bear this ministry and Priesthood unto all nations." It is the seed of Abraham who themselves hold the same priesthood held by their noble forebear who will take salvation to all the nations of the earth.

"And I will bless them through thy name; for as many as receive this Gospel shall be called after thy name, and shall be accounted thy seed, and shall rise up and bless thee, as their father." This promise we have considered in connection with the part the Gentiles are playing and shall play incident to the Second Coming. Now the great covenant reaches its climax in these very express words: "And I will bless them that bless thee, and curse them that curse thee; and in thee (that is, in thy Priesthood) and in thy seed (that is, thy Priesthood), for I give unto thee a promise that this right shall continue in thee, and in thy seed after thee (that is to say, the literal seed, or the seed of the body) shall all the families of the earth be blessed, even with the blessings of the Gospel, which are the blessings of salvation, even of life eternal." (Abr. 2:9-11.)

All the families of the earth, Jew and Gentile alike—whether composed of blood descendants or adopted sons—shall receive the blessings of the gospel only when it is taken to them by Abraham's seed. His seed are the ministers of Christ; they hold the holy priesthood; they have received the divine commission to preach the gospel in all the world and to every creature. And what are the blessings they offer mankind? They are salvation and eternal life.

And what is salvation? Joseph Smith's definition is: "Salvation consists in the glory, authority, majesty, power and dominion which Jehovah possesses and in nothing else; and no being can possess it but himself or one like him." (*Lectures on Faith*, lecture 7, para. 9.) And what is eternal life? It is the name of the kind of life God lives. It consists of two things: life in the family unit, and the receipt of the fulness of the Father, meaning the fulness of the power, glory, and dominion of God himself.

What, then, is the promise made to Abraham and to his seed, meaning to that portion of his seed who, rising up and blessing him as their father, in fact do Abraham's works and qualify for the rewards he received? The blessings of Abraham and his seed are the blessings of celestial marriage, which order of matrimony is the gate to exaltation in the mansions on high.

What a wondrous thing it is to behold mortal men—Abraham, Isaac, and Jacob, our patriarchal fathers—receiving the divine word that in them and in their seed all generations shall be blessed, and that their posterity, through the continuation of the eternal family unit, shall be as the dust of the earth in number, as the sands upon the seashore in multitude, as the stars in the sidereal heavens in endless continuance! As we ponder such a glorious thought, may we ask: Is it conceivable that such a mighty seer as Joseph Smith might also have received this promise? As we shall see shortly, he did; it was the same promise given to Abraham, Isaac, and Jacob. Would we dare go further and ask if the president of The Church of Jesus Christ of Latter-day Saints might also be in this category? He is, as are his counselors. And what of the Twelve? They too have been so blessed, as have all the First Quorum of the Seventy. And as the crowning cause for wonderment, that God who is no respecter of persons has given a like promise to every elder in the kingdom who has gone to the holy temple and entered into the blessed order of matrimony there performed. Every person married in the temple for time and for all eternity has sealed upon him, conditioned upon his faithfulness, all of the blessings of the ancient patriarchs, including the crowning promise and assurance of eternal increase, which means, literally, a posterity as numerous as the dust particles of the earth.

That none of these things would or could be known except by revelation scarcely needs to be stated. And the crowning revelation in our day on the promises made to the fathers is couched in these words: "Abraham received all things, whatsoever he received, by revelation and commandment, by my word, saith the Lord, and hath entered into his exaltation and sitteth upon his throne. Abraham received promises concerning his seed, and of the fruit of his loins—from those whose loins ye are, namely, my servant Joseph—which were to continue so long as they were in the world; and as touching Abraham and his seed, out of the world they should continue; both in the world and out of the world should they continue as innumerable as the stars; or, if ye were to count the sand upon the seashore ye could not number them. This promise is yours also, because ye are of Abraham, and the promise was made unto Abraham; and by this law is the continuation of the works of my Father, wherein he glorifieth himself. Go ye, therefore, and do the works of Abraham; enter ye into my law and ye shall be saved." (D&C 132:29-32.)

And thus it is that the restoration of celestial marriage, the Lord's holy and perfect order of matrimony, has come into the world as one of the required events that must occur before the second coming of the Son of Man.

Elias and Elijah Prepare the Way

No tradition was more firmly planted in the hearts of Jewish Israel in Jesus' day than the firm belief that Elijah the prophet would come again to prepare the way before the expected Messiah. Both John and Jesus were assumed by some to be this ancient prophet come again. To this day devout Jews set a vacant chair at their table for Elijah when they celebrate the feast of the Passover. In part, at least, this universal belief grew out of Jehovah's promise given by the mouth of Malachi: "Behold, I will send you Elijah the prophet before the coming of the great and dreadful day of the Lord: And he shall turn the heart of the fathers to the children, and the heart of the children to their fathers, lest I come and smite the earth with a curse." (Mal. 4:5-6.)

Moroni, ministering to Joseph Smith during the whole of the night of September 21-22, 1823, rendered a plainer translation of these words: "Behold, I will reveal unto you the Priesthood, by the hand of Elijah the prophet, before the coming of the great and dreadful day of the Lord. And he shall plant in the hearts of the children the promises made to the fathers, and the hearts of the children shall turn to their fathers. If it were not so, the whole earth would be utterly wasted at his coming." (D&C 2:1-3.)

Both of these translations are correct; both convey the mind and will of the Lord; and both teach sound and true doctrine. Taken together, they give us an expanded and comprehensive view of the mission of Elijah that we would not gain from either of them alone. As a matter of fact, both the Book of Mormon (3 Ne. 25:5-6) and the Doctrine and Covenants (D&C 128:17-18), in scripture given after Moroni's visit, use the less perfect though true translation.

By combining the concepts found in both versions of these prophetic words we learn:

1. Elijah the Tishbite, a strange and unusual prophet, who ministered in Israel more than nine hundred years before the coming of the Lord Jesus Christ in the flesh; Elijah, who called down fire from heaven in the confrontation with the priests of Baal and on other occasions; Elijah, who sealed the heavens that there was no rain in all the land for three and a half years; Elijah, who raised from death the son of the widow of Zarephath; Elijah, at whose word her barrel of meal did not waste nor her cruse of oil fail until the Lord sent again rain on the earth; Elijah, who smote the river Jordan with his mantle to divide the waters and enable him and Elisha to pass over on dry ground; Elijah, who was translated and taken up into heaven in a chariot of fire without tasting death; Elijah, than whom, save Moses only, there was scarcely a greater prophet in all Israel; Elijah, who came again in a body of flesh and bones on the Mount of Transfiguration to join with translated Moses and the mortal Jesus in conferring upon Peter, James, and John the keys of the kingdom; Elijah, than whom few have been greater in all the long history of this earth—Elijah shall come again before the great and dreadful day of the Lord, before the earth burns as an oven, and before all the proud and they who do wickedly shall be as stubble. Elijah shall come again before the second coming of the Son of Man.

2. Elijah will reveal unto men the priesthood. He will bring again the sealing power. He will authorize mortals to use the priesthood to bind on earth and seal everlastingly in the heavens. He will give the same keys to Joseph Smith and Oliver Cowdery that he gave to Peter, James, and John on the holy mount.

3. Elijah shall plant in the hearts of the children the promises made to the fathers. As Joseph Smith expressed it, "He shall reveal the covenants of the fathers in relation to the children, and the covenants of the children in relation to the fathers." (*Teachings*, p. 321.) Who are the fathers? They are Abraham, Isaac, and Jacob, to whom the promises were made. What are the promises? They are the promises of a continuation of the family unit in eternity; of posterity in numbers as the dust of the earth and the stars in the firmament; of eternal increase; and of the consequent glory, and honor, and exaltation, and eternal life inherent in such a way of eternal existence.

4. Elijah shall turn the hearts of the fathers to the children, and the hearts of the children to their fathers. His coming shall unite families, unite them in this life and unite them in eternity. Because he comes, all of the ordinances of salvation and exaltation shall be binding on earth and in heaven, both for the living and for the dead. Because he comes, we can be sealed together as husband and wife in the holy temple so that our marriage union shall endure both in time and throughout all eternity. Because he comes, the living children will seek after their dead fathers, identifying them through genealogical research, so that the sealing ordinances may be performed for them vicariously in the holy temples.

5. Elijah's coming will keep the earth from being smitten with a curse and from being utterly wasted at our Lord's return. "The hearts of the children of men will have to be turned to the fathers, and the fathers to the children, living or dead," the Prophet said, "to prepare them for the coming of the Son of Man. If Elijah did not come, the whole earth would be smitten." (*Teachings*, p. 160.) Because of his coming, men will be saved and exalted. If the sealing power—the power that binds on earth and seals in heaven—was not given to men, there would be no harvest of saved souls when the Lord reaps in his fields. Thus, the vineyard would be

cursed; it would be wasted; it would have failed to serve the useful purpose for which it was created.

But praise God, Elijah has come, as has Elias. On the 3rd day of April in 1836, in the Kirtland Temple, both of these ancient worthies appeared to Joseph Smith and Oliver Cowdery. As the holy account attests: "Elias appeared, and committed the dispensation of the gospel of Abraham"—that is to say, he gave them the great commission given of God to Abraham, which pertained to the family unit and its eternal continuance in the realms ahead—"saying that in us and our seed all generations after us should be blessed." Who Elias was when he dwelt in mortality, we do not know. He may have been Abraham himself. But no matter; what is important is that he brought back the eternal covenant, with all its promises, that Jehovah had given to Abraham, Isaac, and Jacob.

"After this vision had closed," the sacred writing continues, "another great and glorious vision burst upon us; for Elijah the prophet, who was taken to heaven without tasting death"—but who attained his resurrected glory when Jesus rose from the grave—"stood before us, and said: Behold, the time has fully come, which was spoken of by the mouth of Malachi—testifying that he [Elijah] should be sent, before the great and dreadful day of the Lord come—To turn the hearts of the fathers to the children, and the children to the fathers, lest the whole earth be smitten with a curse—Therefore, the keys of this dispensation are committed into your hands; and by this ye may know that the great and dreadful day of the Lord is near, even at the doors." (D&C 110:12-16.)

Elias, who lived, as we suppose, some four thousand years ago, and Elijah, who underwent his mortal probation some three thousand years ago, these two, mighty prophets of old, have come again to play their part in preparing a people for the second coming of him whom they and we accept as our Savior. Line upon line the promised miracles that prepare the way of the Lord in the last days are truly coming to pass.

Salvation for the Dead and the Second Coming

Much might be said about the doctrine of salvation and exaltation for our dead ancestors. It is well known among us that all who do not have the privilege to believe and obey the holy gospel in this life shall have that blessed privilege in the world of spirits as they await the day of the resurrection. All who would have accepted the holy word with all their hearts had they been permitted to hear it in this life, all such shall receive this opportunity in the spirit world; we shall perform the saving ordinances for them vicariously; and together, if we are all true and faithful, we shall attain an inheritance in the Eternal Presence. How glorious is the concept here involved. A gracious God will save all who believe and obey whether they heard the gospel in this life or in the spirit world.

Our present concern, however, is to make it clear—crystal clear so that none can doubt—that the principles of salvation for the dead had to be revealed before the Second Coming as part of the preparation for that great day. We have spoken of the coming of Elijah and know that he came to prepare men to do this very work. Of this infinitely great and glorious work the Prophet said: "The greatest responsibility in this world that God has laid upon us is to seek after our dead." (*Teachings*, p. 356.) It is a work that exceeds in magnitude even the preaching of the gospel in all nations, for it will go forward and be one of the dominant undertakings of the Millennium itself.

We do not know all things pertaining to the purposes and plans of the Lord in the salvation of his children. But this we do know: His system for offering salvation to the dead as well as for the living must go forward to prepare the way for his return.

"And saviours shall come up on mount Zion," Obadiah prophesied, "and the kingdom shall be the Lord's." (Obad. 1:21.) That is to say, 'Saviors shall come up upon Mount Zion to prepare the way for the Lord.' The Lord's counsel on this matter is given by the Prophet Joseph Smith in these words: "The keys are to be delivered, the spirit of Elijah is to come, the Gospel to be established, the Saints of God gathered, Zion built up, and the Saints to come up as saviors on Mount Zion.

"But how are they to become saviors on Mount Zion? By building their temples, erecting their baptismal fonts, and going forth and receiving all the ordinances, baptisms, confirmations, washings, anointings, ordinations and sealing powers upon their heads, in behalf of all their progenitors who are dead, and redeem them that they may come forth in the first resurrection and be exalted to thrones of glory with them; and herein is the chain that binds the hearts of the fathers to the children, and the children to the fathers, which fulfills the mission of Elijah. . . .

"The Saints have not too much time to save and redeem their dead, and gather together their living relatives, that they may be saved also, before the earth will be smitten, and the consumption decreed falls upon the world.

"I would advise all the Saints to go with their might and gather together all their living relatives to this place, that they may be sealed and saved, that they may be prepared against the day that the destroying angel goes forth; and if the whole Church should go to with all their might to save their dead, seal their posterity, and gather their living friends, and spend none of their time in behalf of the world, they would hardly get through before night would come, when no man can work." (*Teachings*, pp. 330-31.)

The promises made to the fathers! How wondrous and great they are! Promises to gather Israel, to restore the gospel, to build up Zion anew! Promises to plant in our hearts the desires to gain the blessings of Abraham himself! And promises that we can turn the key in behalf of our dead ancestors so that we with them may be inheritors of the fulness of our Father's kingdom!

TEMPLES AND THE SECOND COMING

Temples: Their Nature and Use

Holy temples of our God—what are they? What purposes do they serve? Who knows how and in what manner to build them? Who knows the use to which they should be put?

Holy temples of our God—sacred sanctuaries set apart from the world, unique and unusual buildings into which only a favored few may enter—what part shall they play in the second coming of him whose houses they are?

With reference to the not-far-distant day when the Son of Righteousness shall rend the veil and come down to dwell with men again on earth, the ancient word attests: "The Lord, whom ye seek, shall suddenly come to his temple." (Mal. 3:1.) Like witness is borne in the modern word: "I am Jesus Christ, the Son of God," he says, "wherefore, gird up your loins and I will suddenly come to my temple." (D&C 36:8.)

Now, if the Lord is soon to come with unexpected suddenness to his temple, where is that sacred sanctuary? If it is yet to be built, who is to do it, and where is the construction site? How and in what manner shall the work go forward, and what will the glorious edifice look like when it is finished? And how, except by revelation, can any people choose the site, prepare the house, and have it in readiness when the time comes for the Heavenly Visitant to rend the veil and come to that holy of holies which he will accept as his own?

These are vital questions, and if we can find a people who know the answers, we will have identified the true saints on earth. How can any stewards be the Lord's true servants unless they labor in his vineyards, dwell in his house, and are keeping all things in readiness for their Lord's return? True it is that if a people know and practice the true law of temple construction and use, they are the Lord's people, and they have the power of God unto salvation which Paul called the gospel. And true it is also that if a church is without a knowledge of these mysterious matters, it is not composed of the Lord's people, and in it there is no power to save souls.

There is, of course, a sense in which the world itself is the temple to which the Lord will come, although in its low and fallen state it is far from the type of sanctuary fit for a heavenly King. We have, in fact, a rather enigmatic scripture, the full depth and meaning of which we cannot plumb, in which we are commanded: "Prepare for the revelation which is to come, when the veil of the covering of my temple, in my tabernacle, which hideth the earth, shall be taken off, and all flesh shall see me together." (D&C 101:23.) But as will be increasingly clear from the analysis now to be set forth, the Lord will come to his temples in the sense of specific buildings erected and dedicated to his holy name.

A temple is a house of the Lord, literally and in the full sense of the word. He owns it. It is sacred and clean and pure—a fit abode for the Holy One. Where else would he come except to the purest and most sacred places on earth? When he has no houses on earth, he comes to his servants on mountaintops, in groves of trees, or in desert places. But when there is a holy house fit for his presence, such is the place where his servants see his face—all of which is a type of what shall be when he comes to rule and reign on earth. He will appear in many places, chief among which will be the holy houses built and dedicated to him.

Thus, as Haggai records of the latter-day temple to which the True Owner will come: "Thus saith the Lord of hosts; Yet once, it is a little while, and I will shake the heavens, and the earth, and the sea, and the dry land; And I will shake all nations, and the desire of all nations shall come: and I will fill this house with glory, saith the

Lord of hosts. . . . The glory of this latter house shall be greater than of the former, saith the Lord of hosts: and in this place will I give peace, saith the Lord of hosts." (Hag. 2:6-9.) And thus Isaiah, writing of the day when the Lord will come with fire, tells Israel, "He shall appear to your joy," and there shall be "a voice from the temple"—his voice—"a voice of the Lord that rendereth recompence to his enemies." (Isa. 66:5-6.)

A temple is also a sanctuary to which those who are striving with all their hearts to become like the Holy One may come to enter into sacred covenants with him. It is the place where baptisms for the dead are performed; where the faithful are endowed with power from on high; where the sealing power restored by Elijah unites worthy couples in the bonds of eternal matrimony; where the fulness of the priesthood is received; and where those who are true and faithful in all things receive the assurance of eternal life in the Eternal Presence. A temple is a place where the saints make the same covenants made by Abraham and receive for themselves the promises made to the fathers.

Thus, the Lord, as Ezekiel records, said to scattered Israel: "I will take you from among the heathen, and gather you out of all countries, and will bring you into your own land. Then will I sprinkle clean water upon you"—in my holy temples—"and ye shall be clean: from all your filthiness, and from all your idols, will I cleanse you. A new heart also will I give you, and a new spirit will I put within you: and I will take away the stony heart out of your flesh, and I will give you an heart of flesh. And I will put my spirit within you, and cause you to walk in my statutes, and ye shall keep my judgments, and do them." (Ezek. 36:24-27.) Truly, temples prepare a people to meet their God.

The Mountains of the Lord's Houses

Lift up thine eyes, O Israel, lift up thine eyes "unto the hills," whence cometh thy help. (Ps. 121:1.) Gaze not in the valleys below; look not toward the low and the mean; view not what is carnal and evil. Look now to the mountains of Israel; fix thy gaze upon the mount of the Lord; view now those heaven-kissed heights, whence cometh thy help. Lift up thine eyes unto the mountains of the Lord.

The mountains of the Lord! The mountains of the Great Jehovah! The holy places where the soles of his feet have trod! How grand they are! And they are the towering peaks and the cloud-topped summits where the temples of the Lord—all of them—shall be built in the last days.

In all the days of his goodness, mountain heights have been the places chosen by the Lord to commune with his people. The experiences of Enoch, and of Moriancumer, and of Moses show how the Lord deigned to deal with his servants when they lifted themselves temporally and spiritually toward heaven's heights.

"Turn ye, and get ye upon the mount Simeon," was the divine command to Enoch. "And it came to pass that I turned and went up on the mount," he said, "and as I stood upon the mount, I beheld the heavens open, and I was clothed upon with glory; And I saw the Lord; and he stood before my face, and he talked with me, even as a man talketh one with another, face to face." (Moses 7:2-4.)

Jared's brother, Moriancumer, scarcely a whit behind Enoch in faith and righteousness, took sixteen small stones "upon the top of the mount," there to plead with the Lord to touch the stones that they might give light in the Jaredite barges. There followed the grandest and most comprehensive revelation of the Lord Jesus Christ that had ever been given to any man up to that time. The mighty Jaredite prophet then saw the spirit body of Him who would one day take upon himself flesh and blood, that he might redeem his people, and he was shown things that are to this day hidden from us for want of the spiritual capacity to understand them. (Ether 3:1-28.)

Moses, in like manner, "was caught up into an exceedingly high mountain, And he saw God face to face, and he talked with him, and the glory of God was upon Moses," and he saw the wonders of eternity and received the account of the creation and redemption of our planet and of worlds without number. (Moses 1–3.)

And also, in like manner, Nephi received glorious visions on the mountain heights; Peter, James, and John, with their Lord on the Mount of Transfiguration, saw in vision the millennial earth and received from heavenly visitants keys and powers; and Elijah, on Horeb, the mount of God, received some of his great spiritual experiences. On one occasion anciently, "the glory of the Lord abode upon mount Sinai, . . . And the sight of the glory of the Lord was like devouring fire on the top of the mount in the eyes of the children of Israel." (Ex. 24:16-17.)

Is it any wonder, then, that in prophetic imagery the term "mountains of the Lord" has become a symbol to identify the places where spiritual blessings are received? The restored gospel is "a banner upon the high mountain" (Isa. 13:2); when we preach the gospel, we "publish it upon the mountains" (D&C 19:29); and the Lord's promise to Zion is that she "shall flourish upon the hills and rejoice upon the mountains" (D&C 49:25). The highest accolade of praise bestowed upon a preacher of righteousness is the sweet expression: "How beautiful upon the mountains are the feet of him that bringeth good tidings, that publisheth peace; that bringeth good tidings of good, that publisheth salvation; that saith unto Zion, Thy God reigneth!" (Isa. 52:7.)

Singling out the righteous from among men, the Psalmic word asks: "Who shall ascend into the hill of the Lord?" Is not the hill of the Lord the place where salvation is found? "Or who shall stand in his holy place?" (Ps. 24:3.) Is not his holy place his temple on earth and his eternal kingdom hereafter? Indeed, those who gain exaltation in the highest heaven hereafter are said to "come unto Mount Zion." (D&C 76:66.) Truly, the mountains of the Lord are the places of greatest spiritual refreshment in this life and the places of the fulness of spiritual enjoyment in the life to come.

All of this is but prelude to saying that all of the holy temples of our God in the latter days shall be built in the mountains of the Lord, for his mountains—whether the land itself is a hill, a valley, or a plain—are the places where he comes, personally and by the power of his Spirit, to commune with his people. If he has no house on earth, he comes to a mountaintop or other places of his own choosing, but when his people have built him a place "where to lay his head" (Matt. 8:20), as it were, then he comes to that holy house.

Isaiah names the building of latter-day temples as a sign both of the gathering of Israel and of the second coming of Christ. Israel, as we are aware, is to gather to places where there are temples so her municipals may gain the blessings made available in these holy houses, and these blessings prepare their recipients to meet the Lord, who will suddenly come to his temple.

Isaiah introduces his pronouncement relative to temples by saying: "The word that Isaiah, the son of Amoz, saw concerning Judah and Jerusalem." That is, the subject under consideration is the kingdom of Judah and her capital city, Jerusalem. "And it"—what he is about to say concerning Judah and Jerusalem—"shall come to pass in the last days, when the mountain of the Lord's house shall be established in the top of the mountains, and shall be exalted above the hills, and all nations shall flow unto it." The building of a temple in both the mountain of the Lord and the tops of the mountains, unto which the elect of the Lord shall come out of all nations, is the promised sign. This is first and foremost the temple, capped with six spires and crowned with an angelic ministrant sounding the trump of God, that now stands in Salt Lake City in the tops of the mountains of America. All of the temples now built or that may be built in the high mountains of America also do or will fulfill this prophetic word.

"And many people," Isaiah continues, "shall go and say, Come ye, and let us go up to the mountain of the Lord, to the house of the God of Jacob; and he will teach us of his ways, and we will walk in his paths; for out of Zion shall go forth the law, and the word of the Lord from Jerusalem." Then the ancient seer proceeds to speak of the Second Coming and its effect upon Judah and Jerusalem. (2 Ne. 12:1-22; Isa. 2:1-22.) His words about the gathering have received a partial fulfillment in the gathering of Israel from many nations to the American Zion in the tops of the mountains, but their complete realization is for another day and another location, as we shall soon see. And the statement about the law going forth from Zion and the word of the Lord from Jerusalem will come to pass during the Millennium, as we shall also see in due course. At this point our concern is to know with surety that latter-day temples must arise in the mountains of the Lord before the

Second Coming; that none can build such holy houses unless divinely commissioned to do so; and that when they are built—in proof, as it were, of their divine status—all nations will flow unto them.

We shall now turn our attention to the temples yet to be built in Old Jerusalem and in the New Jerusalem, both of which also are to be built in the mountains of the Lord.

Temples in the New and Old Jerusalems

We expect to see the day when temples will dot the earth, each one a house of the Lord; each one built in the mountains of the Lord; each one a sacred sanctuary to which Israel and the Gentiles shall gather to receive the blessings of Abraham, Isaac, and Jacob. Perhaps they will number in the hundreds, or even in the thousands, before the Lord returns. During the Millennium their presence will be everywhere, for the billions of church members will all be entitled to the fulness of the ordinances and blessings of the Lord's holy houses. But there are two great temples in particular, two glorious houses of the Great Jehovah, that must be built by his people before he comes—one in Jerusalem of old, the other in the New Jerusalem.

Old Jerusalem, the ancient holy city, has been and will again be a temple city. On three occasions of which we know, the Lord's own earthly house, as a priceless gem in a heaven-set crown, has graced the ground that is now claimed by the Jews and trodden down of the Gentiles. Solomon built a majestic mansion for the Lord in the day of Israel's glory. Zerubbabel built it anew when the remnant returned from bondage in Babylon. And Herod—a wretched, evil man whose every act bore Satan's stamp—built it for the final time in the day our Lord made flesh his tabernacle. This is the temple—one of the architectural wonders of the world, whose marble blocks were covered with gold, and whose influence upon the people cannot be measured—this is the temple that was torn apart, stone by stone, by Titus and his minions.

Thus Herod's temple became a refuse heap, and with its destruction ancient Judaism died also. Sacrifices ceased; the Jews, as a nation, gave up the ghost; the law of Moses, the man of God, became a curse; and the Jews were driven into every nation, there to struggle and suffer until the voice of their Messiah shall call them home to build anew his holy house in the city of his choice. For "it shall come to pass," according to the holy word, that the Lord shall return them to their ancient soil. "Ye shall be gathered one by one, O ye children of Israel," saith the divine word. Ye shall be gathered when "the great trumpet shall be blown, . . . and shall worship the Lord in the holy mount at Jerusalem." (Isa. 27:12-13.)

As to Herod's Temple, the disciples presented this petition: "Master, show us concerning the buildings of the temple." From Jesus came this answer: "Behold ye these stones of the temple, and all this great work, and buildings of the temple? Verily I say unto you, they shall be thrown down and left unto the Jews desolate. . . . See ye not all these things, and do ye not understand them? Verily I say unto you, There shall not be left here upon this temple, one stone upon another, that shall not be thrown down." (JST, Mark 13:1-5.)

So it was promised, and so it came to pass. And thus ended temple work in Jerusalem, in the old temple with its Mosaic ordinances, in the temple whose work, like the law of Moses of which it was a symbol, was fulfilled. And thus was it to be in Jerusalem until the promised day when a new temple should arise—perhaps on the very site of the old one—in which the gospel ordinances of the new kingdom shall be performed.

This new temple shall be the one of which Ezekiel spoke. "I will make a covenant of peace" with Jewish Israel when they return to the ancient fold, saith the Lord. "It shall be an everlasting covenant with them"—even the fulness of the everlasting gospel, which is the new and the everlasting covenant—"and I will place them, and multiply them, and will set my sanctuary [my temple] in the midst of them for evermore. My tabernacle also shall be with them: yea, I will be their God, and they shall be my people. And the heathen shall know that I the Lord do sanctify Israel, when my sanctuary shall be in the midst of them for evermore." (Ezek. 37:26-28.)

This is the day of which Zechariah spoke: "Thus saith the

Lord; I am returned to Jerusalem with mercies: my house shall be built in it, saith the Lord of hosts. . . . My cities through prosperity shall yet be spread abroad; and the Lord shall yet comfort Zion, and shall yet choose Jerusalem." (Zech. 1:16-17.) And then shall the Millennium be ushered in, for, saith the Lord, "I will bring forth my servant the BRANCH. . . . I will remove the iniquity of that land in one day," the day of burning when every corruptible thing shall be consumed. "In that day, saith the Lord of hosts, shall ye call every man his neighbour under the vine and under the fig tree." (Zech. 3:8-10.)

Who shall build this temple? The Lord himself shall do it by the hands of his servants the prophets. "Behold the man whose name is The BRANCH; . . . he shall build the temple of the Lord"—and, be it remembered, the Branch is one of the Messianic designations by which the Promised Messiah is known—"Even he shall build the temple of the Lord; and he shall bear the glory, and shall sit and rule upon his throne." And whence shall the workmen come to build the sanctuary? "They that are far off shall come and build in the temple of the Lord." (Zech. 6:12-15.)

Who are those "that are far off" who shall come to Jerusalem to build the house of the Lord? Surely they are the Jews who have been scattered afar. By what power and under whose authorization shall the work be done? There is only one place under the whole heavens where the keys of temple building are found. There is only one people who know how to build temples and what to do in them when they are completed. That people is the Latter-day Saints. The temple in Jerusalem will not be built by Jews who have assembled there for political purposes as at present. It will not be built by a people who know nothing whatever about the sealing ordinances and their application to the living and the dead. It will not be built by those who know nothing about Christ and his laws and the mysteries reserved for the saints. But it will be built by Jews who have come unto Christ, who once again are in the true fold of their ancient Shepherd, and who have learned anew about temples because they know that Elijah did come, not to sit in a vacant chair at some Jewish feast of the Passover, but to the Kirtland Temple on April 3, 1836, to Joseph Smith and Oliver

Cowdery. The temple in Jerusalem will be built by The Church of Jesus Christ of Latter-day Saints. "They that are far off," they that come from an American Zion, they who have a temple in Salt Lake City will come to Jerusalem to build there another holy house in the Jerusalem portion of "the mountains of the Lord's house." (D&C 133:13.)

Then "many people and strong nations shall come to seek the Lord of hosts in Jerusalem, and to pray before the Lord." (Zech. 8:22.) "And it shall be in that day, that living waters shall go out from Jerusalem; . . . And the Lord shall be king over all the earth: in that day shall there be one Lord, and his name one." (Zech. 14:8-9.) These are the waters of which the scripture saith: "They shall be healed." (Ezek. 47:9.)

All of this brings us to that inspired statement of the Prophet Joseph Smith relative to the temple in Jerusalem and the Second Coming: "Judah must return," he said, "Jerusalem must be rebuilt, and the temple, and water come out from under the temple, and the waters of the Dead Sea be healed. It will take some time to rebuild the walls of the city and the temple, etc.; and all this must be done before the Son of Man will make His appearance." (*Teachings*, p. 286.)

From the temple in Old Jerusalem we now turn to a consideration of the temple in the New Jerusalem. Neither of the Jerusalems—neither the Old Jerusalem, which shall be built up again, nor the New Jerusalem yet to rise on the American continent—can be a holy city, a city of Zion, until a house of the Lord graces that Mount Zion upon which each is located. The Lord will not reign in or send forth his law from a city in which he has no house of his own. And so, in July 1831 the Prophet Joseph Smith, then in Jackson County, Missouri, importuned the Lord in these words: "When will the wilderness blossom as the rose? When will Zion be built up in her glory, and where will thy Temple stand, unto which all nations shall come in the last days?" (Introductory heading, D&C 57.) In answer the Lord said: "This is the land of promise, and the place for the city of Zion. . . . Behold, the place which is now called Independence is the center place; and a spot for the temple is lying westward, upon a lot which is not far from the court-house." (D&C 57:1-3.)

It is of this city, a city that shall be built before the Second Coming, that the Lord said to Enoch: "I shall prepare, an Holy City, that my people may gird up their loins, and be looking forth for the time of my coming; for there shall be my tabernacle, and it shall be called Zion, a New Jerusalem." (Moses 7:62.) It is in this city, the New Jerusalem in Jackson County, that the house of the Lord unto which all nations shall come in the last days shall be built, "which temple," the Lord said in September 1832, "shall be reared in this generation. For verily this generation shall not all pass away until an house shall be built unto the Lord, and a cloud shall rest upon it, which cloud shall be even the glory of the Lord, which shall fill the house." (D&C 84:1-5.)

Because the saints were "hindered by the hands of their enemies, and by oppression," the Lord withdrew the time limitation (D&C 124:49-54), and the command now in force is: "Zion shall be redeemed in mine own due time." (D&C 136:18.) When that is to be remains to be seen, but that it will surely come to pass, as part of the preparation of the Lord's people for his glorious return, is as certain as that the sun shines or that the Great God is Lord of all. When the appointed time comes, the Lord will reveal it to his servants who preside over his kingdom from Salt Lake City, and then the great work will go forward. They will direct the work; they hold the keys of temple building; the temple will be built by gathered Israel and particularly by Ephraim, for it is unto Ephraim that the other tribes shall come to receive their temple blessings in due course. Some Lamanites may assist and some Gentiles may bring their wealth to adorn the buildings, but the keys are with Ephraim, and it is Ephraim that is now stepping forth and that yet shall step forth to bless the rest of the house of Israel.

Chapter 24

THE HOLY ZION OF GOD

What Is Zion?

Zion, Zion, blessed Zion—Zion concerning whom all of the prophets from the beginning have spoken—what shall we now say of thee? O thou choice and favored one, what part art thou destined to play in the second coming of thy King, the King of Zion?

Shall we not say that thou hast been chosen above all others to prepare a people for earth's true King? Shall we not say that only a pure people will be fit companions for the Holy One who has said he will yet reign in Zion? Shall we not say that the Lord will not come until Zion is built up by his people; that when he comes he will also bring Zion with him; and that then Zion in its fulness shall flourish and prosper beyond any comprehension we now have? And shall we not say that those who gain celestial rest itself shall do so because they come unto Mount Zion, the Heavenly Jerusalem, and to the general assembly and Church of the Firstborn?

What then is Zion, and how is she to be esteemed? Our first contact with the Zion of God comes in the day of Enoch. That seer of seers, whose faith was so great that at his word the earth trembled, mountains fled, and rivers turned out of their courses, converted great hosts to the gospel. These saints of the Most High kept the commandments and attained such unity and perfection that "the Lord came and dwelt with his people, and they dwelt in righteousness." It was then as it shall be when he comes again. In Enoch's day, "The fear of the Lord was upon all nations, so great was the glory of the Lord, which was upon his people." So shall it be with the enemies of God when the great Millennium is ushered in: the fear of the Lord shall be upon all those who fight against his saints. Nor is this all. As to the ancient Zion, the account says: "And the Lord blessed the land, and they were blessed upon the mountains, and upon the high places, and did flourish." And again so shall it be in the latter end of the earth. Again the Lord will bless the land; indeed, so great shall be the blessing that the whole earth shall become as it was in the day of the Garden of Eden.

It is in this setting that the holy word records: "And the Lord called his people ZION, because they were of one heart and one mind, and dwelt in righteousness; and there was no poor among them." And it is from these words that we gain our basic concept of Zion. Zion is those who have overcome the world and who are fit companions for him who said: "Be holy, for I am holy" (Lev. 11:45), and "Ye shall be holy: for I the Lord your God am holy" (Lev. 19:2).

"And Enoch continued his preaching in righteousness unto the people of God. And it came to pass in his days, that he built a city that was called the City of Holiness, even ZION." And so we learn that Zion became also a place. The place where the people named Zion dwelt became the place named Zion. The city bore the title of the people, and of course it was a City of Holiness, for all of its inhabitants were holy. And because they were holy, the Lord preserved them from their enemies, even as he shall do in the latter days. This marvelous manifestation of preserving care caused Enoch to say to the Lord: "Surely Zion shall dwell in safety forever." To this the Lord replied: "Zion have I blessed, but the residue of the people have I cursed," even as it shall also be when Zion comes in the last days. And that his servant might know the state of Zion, "the Lord showed unto Enoch all the inhabitants of the earth; and he beheld, and lo, Zion, in process of time, was taken up into heaven. And the Lord said unto Enoch: Behold mine abode forever." (Moses 7:13-21.)

Later in the scriptural account this general summary is made relative to the saints of ancient days: "And all the days of Zion, in the days of Enoch, were three hundred and sixty-five years."

When the Millennium comes, Zion will continue for a thousand years. "And Enoch and all his people walked with God, and he dwelt in the midst of Zion; and it came to pass that Zion was not, for God received it up into his own bosom; and from thence went forth the saying, ZION IS FLED." (Moses 7:68-69.) Such is the divine word relative to the Zion of old, the original Zion, the first Zion, the Zion of Enoch, the Zion taken by God into his own bosom. Why was she taken? Because all her municipals were fit to dwell with the Lord; because all of them were too pure, too holy to remain longer in this carnal and wicked world. And it shall yet be, when the Lord brings again Zion in her fulness and glory, that all his people will walk with him, and he shall dwell on earth with them for a thousand years. And then it shall be said: The Lord hath brought again Zion, his own city, the City of Holiness, the City of our God.

Zion Through the Ages

After those in the City of Holiness were translated and taken up into heaven without tasting death, so that Zion as a people and a congregation had fled from the battle-scarred surface of the earth, the Lord sought others among men who would serve him. From the days of Enoch to the flood, new converts and true believers, except those needed to carry out the Lord's purposes among mortals, were translated, "and the Holy Ghost fell on many, and they were caught up by the powers of heaven into Zion." (Moses 7:27.) "And men having this faith"—the faith of Enoch and his people—"coming up unto this order of God"—the holy order of priesthood which we call the Melchizedek Priesthood—"were translated and taken up into heaven." (JST, Gen. 14:32.)

After the flood, righteous men, knowing what had been before their day, continued to seek a place in Zion. Of those who lived in the days of Melchizedek it is written: "And now, Melchizedek was a priest of this order; therefore he obtained peace in Salem, and was called the Prince of peace. And his people wrought righteousness, and obtained heaven, and sought for the city of Enoch which God had before taken, separating it from the earth, having reserved it unto the latter days, or the end of the world; And hath said, and sworn with an oath, that the heavens and the earth should come together; and the sons of God should be tried so as by fire." (JST, Gen. 14:33-35.)

But thereafter except in a few isolated instances—those of Moses, Elijah, Alma the son of Alma, John the Beloved, and the Three Nephites are the only ones of which we know—except in these cases, each involving a special purpose, the Lord ceased translating faithful people. Rather, they were permitted to die and go into the spirit world, there to perform the ever-increasing work needed in that sphere. We are led to believe that Abraham, Isaac, and Jacob, and some of the faithful of old continued to seek an inheritance in the City of Enoch. Paul says they "looked for a city which hath foundations, whose builder and maker is God," and that they "confessed . . . they were strangers and pilgrims on the earth. For they . . . declare plainly that they seek a country." (Heb. 11:10, 13-14.)

There has been no perfect Zion on earth since the flood. There have been many righteous congregations of saints upon whom the Lord has poured out rich blessings, but none of these has attained the degree of perfection that would enable the Lord to dwell among the people. These numerous congregations, however, have contained the choicest and most favored of earth's inhabitants. Such congregations have included and do include the faithful among the Jaredites; those who served the Lord in ancient Israel; the believing Lehite congregations; the so-called primitive saints who believed the words of Peter and Paul; certainly some groups of believers among the Ten Tribes, to whom Jesus went after his resurrection; and, of course, the various congregations of Latter-day Saints in our day. All these have sought the Lord, have struggled to perfect their lives, and—knowing they were strangers and pilgrims in a strange land, far from their heavenly home—have looked forward, with an eye of faith, to an inheritance in that city whose builder and maker is God.

Certain of the capital cities and chief places of worship of the saints in various ages have been used to crystallize in the minds of the people the concept that there is a Zion where the pure in heart shall dwell. Foremost among all of these was Jerusalem of old. It was Zion in its day. From it the word of the Lord went forth, and to it every male in Israel was commanded to come three times each year to appear before the Lord and there to worship him in spirit and in truth. Salt Lake City in our day, with its conferences and administrative offices, serves a similar purpose. It is a modern Zion. But none of these compare with the New Jerusalem yet to be built in Missouri, or to the coming millennial Zion with all its grandeur and splendor.

Our Present Zion

Our present Zion is the one whose mission it is to prepare a people for the return of the Lord. We are appointed, in due course, to build the New Jerusalem and to erect therein the holy temple to which he shall come. We are now in process of building up the stakes of Zion and of striving to perfect our lives so we will be able to build Zion itself in the appointed day.

And as we seek to build up Zion we are brought back to the Lord's definition of Zion. Our revelation says: "This is Zion—THE PURE IN HEART." (D&C 97:21.) Again the message comes through loud and clear. Zion is people. Zion is those whose sins are washed away in the waters of baptism. Zion is those out of whose souls dross and evil have been burned as though by fire. Zion is those who have received the baptism of fire so as to stand pure and clean before the Lord. Zion is those who keep the commandments of God.

Zion is the pure in heart. "And blessed are all the pure in heart, for they shall see God." (3 Ne. 12:8.) That is to say: If and when the latter-day Zion becomes like the original Zion, then the Lord will come and dwell with his people as he did in the ancient Zion. That we have not yet attained this high state of righteousness is clear, for few among the saints see the face of the Lord while they are in mortality, to say nothing of the Lord coming and dwelling with the whole body of his people as he did anciently.

Thus, Zion is built up by righteousness and destroyed by wickedness, for Zion is composed of righteous people, and if they cease to keep the commandments, they are no longer Zion. It was of the labors of rebellious Israel in times past that the Lord said: "They build up Zion with blood, and Jerusalem with iniquity. The heads thereof judge for reward, and the priests thereof teach for hire, and the prophets thereof divine for money: yet will they lean upon the Lord, and say, Is not the Lord among us? none evil can come upon us. Therefore shall Zion for your sake be plowed as a field, and Jerusalem shall become heaps, and the mountain of the house as the high places of the forest." (Micah 3:10-12.) And it is of the building of Zion in the last days that the Lord says: "And Zion cannot be built up unless it is by the principles of the law of the celestial kingdom; otherwise I cannot receive her unto myself." (D&C 105:5.)

On August 2, 1833, the Lord gave his saints—his small band of struggling, striving saints—such a promise, relative to the establishment of Zion, as none but he could fulfill. If Zion is true and faithful in all things, he said, "she shall prosper, and spread herself and become very glorious, very great, and very terrible. And the nations of the earth shall honor her, and shall say: Surely Zion is the city of our God, and surely Zion cannot fall, neither be moved out of her place, for God is there, and the hand of the Lord is there; And he hath sworn by the power of his might to be her salvation and her high tower." That is, if Zion in the last days becomes like Zion was in the early days, the same preserving care from on high will rest upon her, the Lord will dwell in her midst, and the wicked of the world will have no power over her.

But Zion did not become again as she once was, for reasons we shall note, and the Lord's promise has been reserved for millennial fulfillment. Indeed, when it was given, the Lord accompanied it with a solemn warning. "Let Zion rejoice," he said, "while all the wicked shall mourn. For behold, and lo, vengeance cometh speedily upon the ungodly as the whirlwind; and who shall escape it? The Lord's scourge shall pass over by night and by day, and the report thereof shall vex all people; yea, it shall not be stayed until the Lord come; For the indignation of the Lord is kindled against their abominations and all their wicked works." Vengeance has rested, is resting, and will rest upon all the nations of the earth. Their inhabitants have been, are now, and yet will be scourged and cursed and driven and slain because of their abominations. Such will not cease until the wicked are destroyed when the Lord comes.

And now, to Zion the Lord gives this warning: "Nevertheless, Zion shall escape if she observe to do all things whatsoever I have commanded her. But if she observe not to do whatsoever I have commanded her, I will visit her according to all her works, with sore affliction, with pestilence, with plague, with sword, with vengeance, with devouring fire." (D&C 97:18-26.) Zion in that day did not keep the commandments and gain the promised blessings, nor have we, their successors in interest, risen to the standard set by them of old. The saints sought to build up Zion in Missouri and failed. Some of the promised scourging fell upon them, and more of it will yet fall upon us if we do not keep the commandments more fully than in the past.

On December 16, 1833, the Lord revealed why our early brethren failed. "At this time the Saints who had gathered in Missouri were suffering great persecution. Mobs had driven them from their homes in Jackson County, and some of the Saints had tried to establish themselves in Van Buren County, but persecution followed them. The main body of the Church was at that time in Clay County, Missouri. Threats of death against individuals of the Church were many. The people had lost household furniture, clothing, livestock and other personal property, and many of their crops had been destroyed." (D&C 101; introductory heading.)

Why, oh why, did the Lord permit these persecutions and drivings? His answer, which contained also an assurance of salvation for those so chastened, came in these words: "I, the Lord, have suffered the affliction to come upon them, wherewith they have been afflicted, in consequence of their transgressions; . . . Behold, I say unto you, there were jarrings, and contentions, and envyings, and strifes, and lustful and covetous desires among them; therefore by these things they polluted their inheritances." (D&C 101:1-9.)

Zion shall be redeemed and built up at the appointed time—a time yet future—and she "shall not be moved out of her place." (D&C 101:17.) The saints are to "wait for a little season"—as the

Lord measures time—"for the redemption of Zion. . . . First let my army become very great," the Lord says, "and let it be sanctified before me. . . . And let those commandments which I have given concerning Zion and her law be executed and fulfilled, after her redemption." (D&C 105:9, 31, 34.) As men measure time, the period of waiting is "many years." (D&C 58:44.) Meanwhile we are appointed to strengthen the stakes and sanctify our souls—all in preparation for the great day ahead.

"And blessed are they who shall seek to bring forth my Zion at that day"—the day in which we live and the day that is yet to be—"for they shall have the gift and the power of the Holy Ghost; and if they endure unto the end they shall be lifted up at the last day, and shall be saved in the everlasting kingdom of the Lamb; and whoso shall publish peace, yea, tidings of great joy, how beautiful upon the mountains shall they be." (1 Ne. 13:37.)

Israel Gathers to Zion

"There shall be a day"—and thanks be to God, that day is now—"that the watchmen upon the mount Ephraim shall cry, Arise, ye, and let us go up to Zion unto the Lord our God." We who are of Ephraim, who have received the fulness of the everlasting gospel by the opening of the heavens, we send forth the cry. We stand on the mount Ephraim and blow the trump of God; our voices mingle with the angels beyond the veil, as we say to all Israel: "Come home; come to Zion; be one with us; wash away your sins in the waters of baptism; be clean; turn to the Lord and serve him as in days of old. Know ye that Zion is the pure in heart." And we know that success will attend our labors and that the scattered ones "shall come and sing in the height of Zion, and shall flow together to the goodness of the Lord." (Jer. 31:6, 12.) As the Lord lives, scattered Israel is coming and shall come to Zion.

Our divine commission to bring Israel to Zion is recorded in our revelations. But it can also be read in the inspired decisions of the living oracles who send forth the elders of Israel, duly and properly instructed, to tell the people in all nations where and under what circumstances they shall gather in their day and situation. One of the greatest of the written calls came in a revelation to the Prophet Joseph Smith on November 3, 1831, a mere nineteen months after the Church and kingdom of God had been set up again on earth in this final gospel dispensation. It is to this wondrous document of superlative worth, and one filled with dynamic expression, that we shall first give our attention. Then we shall note some other revealed statements and weave them all into the inspired procedures ordained by those who hold the keys of gathering and who are thereby empowered to specify the place and direct the manner in which each soul in scattered Israel shall gather.

Speaking to his newly established church, to the little flock gathered into his latter-day sheepfold, to those who already believed his word and sought to learn and do his will, the Lord said: "Prepare ye, prepare ye, O my people; sanctify yourselves; gather ye together, O ye people of my church, upon the land of Zion, all you that have not been commanded to tarry." The Lord always gathers his people. In this wicked world they must come together to strengthen each other in the holy faith. They must assemble in congregations to teach one another the doctrines of the kingdom. They must use their united strength to bear the burdens of each other, to mourn with those who mourn, and to comfort those who stand in need of comfort. They must come where the temples of God stand so as to be endowed with power from on high. Where but among themselves can they worship the Lord in spirit and in truth? Where else can they work out their salvation with fear and trembling before the Lord? Truly, if the Lord's people do not gather, they cannot and will not be saved. Alone in the world, each unprotected sheep would soon be destroyed by the wolves of wickedness.

Hence the Lord says to his saints: "Go ye out from Babylon. Be ye clean that bear the vessels of the Lord." Forsake the world; cleave unto the kingdom; no longer live as other men live. You are a people set apart. "Call your solemn assemblies, and speak often one to another." Teach, train, counsel, instruct, exhort, and testify; join one with another in sacred meetings. "And let every man call upon the name of the Lord." All are alike unto God. All are to believe; all are to pray; all are to preach. Every man is to stand as a minister of Christ. "Yea, verily I say unto you again, the time has come when the voice of the Lord is unto you: Go ye out of Babylon; gather ye out from among the nations, from the four winds, from one end of heaven to the other." Israel was scattered to the four winds; and as was the scattering, so shall the gathering be; the believing remnant must separate themselves from the world in every nation.

"Send forth the elders of my church unto the nations which are afar off; unto the islands of the sea; send forth unto foreign lands; call upon all nations, first upon the Gentiles, and then upon the Jews." This we are now doing to a modest extent; this we shall continue to do to a greater extent until the Lord comes; and even then the voice of the Lord, by the mouths of his servants, shall continue to cry out until every living soul on earth is converted and gathered into the true fold.

"And behold, and lo, this shall be their cry"—in this present world—"and the voice of the Lord unto all people: Go ye forth unto the land of Zion, that the borders of my people may be enlarged, and that her stakes may be strengthened, and that Zion may go forth unto the regions round about." In November 1831, and for many years thereafter, the gathering of Israel was to the United States of America, where Zion and her stakes needed strengthening. The Church was young; its numbers were few; the armies of the Lord yet needed to become very great, very strong, and very powerful. To come off victorious over Babylon, all of the strength of the whole kingdom needed to be centered in one place, centered in the mountain where the Lord's house would be exalted above the hills.

The gathering of Israel to the Zion of God is to prepare them for the Second Coming. And so the divine word continues: "Yea, let the cry go forth among all people: Awake and arise and go forth to meet the Bridegroom; behold and lo, the Bridegroom cometh; go ye out to meet him." Men go forth to meet the Bridegroom when they join the Church and fill their lamps with that Holy Spirit which the world cannot receive, but which is the priceless possession of every true believer. "Prepare yourselves for the great day of the Lord. Watch, therefore, for ye know neither the day nor the hour."

Where, then, shall Israel assemble to prepare for that great day? "Let them, therefore, who are among the Gentiles flee unto Zion." This they began to do as soon as the warning voice was raised in their hearing. "And let them who be of Judah flee unto Jerusalem, unto the mountains of the Lord's house." This is yet future; Judah has yet to begin to believe in such numbers that they can assemble in the land of their fathers to build the destined temple there. This will be one of the final events before the coming again of their Messiah.

But the call now is to all men, Jew and Gentile alike: "Go ye out from among the nations, even from Babylon, from the midst of wickedness, which is spiritual Babylon." There is a great key hidden in these words. The gathering is both temporal and spiritual. Israel gathers spiritually by joining the Church; she gathers temporally by assembling where church congregations are found. The great issue is one of leaving Babylon, leaving the world, leaving wickedness; it is one of becoming pure in heart so as to be part of Zion.

Such a glorious and worldwide movement as the gathering of Israel to Zion must not occur in a haphazard way; it must not be left to chance; the Lord's work always goes forward in an organized and systematized way. And so the Lord cautions—cautions? nay, commands—his saints: "Let not your flight be in haste, but let all things be prepared before you; and he that goeth, let him not look back lest sudden destruction shall come upon him." Is it not written elsewhere, "No man, having put his hand to the plough, and looking back, is fit for the kingdom of God"? (Luke 9:62.)

"Hearken and hear, O ye inhabitants of the earth. Listen, ye elders of my church together, and hear the voice of the Lord; for he calleth upon all men, and he commandeth all men everywhere to repent." (D&C 133:4-16.) This, then, is the message of gathering: Come unto Christ; repent and be baptized; receive the gift of the Holy Ghost and become pure, as pure and untainted from the sins of the world as is a newly born babe. Then assemble with the saints that the sanctifying processes may work in your life and you become a fit subject to stand before the King of Zion when he comes to reign in his glory.

Where Is Zion?

Building on the foundations heretofore laid, we are now ready to inquire: Where shall the temporal gathering of Israel be? Where shall scattered Israel assemble in the last days? Are all converts to the kingdom destined to come to western America? Where is Zion? To all of these, and to all like questions, there are answers from the Lord that no man need misunderstand.

Be it remembered that Zion is people; Zion is the pure in heart; Zion is the saints of the living God. And be it also remembered that the people called Zion build the places called Zion. Thus wherever the saints build an old or a new Jerusalem, wherever they establish cities of holiness, wherever they create stakes of Zion, there is Zion; and where these things are not, Zion is not.

It is clear that the gathered remnants of Judah shall build a holy city, the Jerusalem of old. Here then is Zion—Zion as a capital city—to which, as the prophets foretold, Israel shall return. Will they all live in Jerusalem itself? Obviously not; they did not do so anciently, and they will not do so in the last days. Zion will reach out and embrace the whole land of Palestine.

It is also clear that the gathered remnants of Joseph will build a holy city, a New Jerusalem in Jackson County, Missouri. Here also is Zion—Zion as a capital city—to which, again as the holy word records, Israel shall gather. Once again we ask: Will they all dwell in this Zion itself? Again the answer is clear. This will be a city whence the law goes forth. Gathered Israel shall dwell in various places; one place alone would never be able to contain them all.

These capital cities will be glorious indeed. Of them the psalmic and prophetic word acclaims: "Great is the Lord, and greatly to be praised in the city of our God, in the mountain of his holiness. Beautiful for situation, the joy of the whole earth, is mount Zion, . . . the city of the great King. God is known in her palaces." (Ps. 48:1-3.) And also: "The Lord loveth the gates of

Zion more than all the dwellings of Jacob. Glorious things are spoken of thee, O city of God. . . . And of Zion it shall be said, This and that man was born in her: and the highest himself shall establish her." (Ps. 87:2-5.) But with it all, they are but types and shadows of a much greater Zion that shall have like glory and whose inhabitants shall reap equal praise.

As we are aware, the building of the New Jerusalem lies in the future, at a time yet to be designated by revelation. There is no present call for the saints to purchase land or to live in Jackson County or in any place connected therewith. The revealed word relative to the gathering to Independence and its environs will come through the prophet of God on earth. When it does come—with the consequent return of the saints to that Zion which shall not be moved out of its place—that call will not be for the saints in general to assemble there. The return to Jackson County will be by delegates, as it were. Those whose services are needed there will assemble as appointed. The rest of Israel will remain in their appointed places. The Lord's house is a house of order, and faithful saints do as they are told and go at the bidding of their prophet, for his voice is the voice of the Lord. And as with the New Jerusalem, so with the Jerusalem of old. Those assigned will build up the city. It certainly will not be the abiding place of all converted Jews.

Zion will be built up in many places. Jesus said that "the covenant which the Father hath made with the children of Israel" was one involving "their restoration to the lands of their inheritance" (3 Ne. 29:1)—not one land but many. Speaking of "all the house of Israel," Nephi prophesied, "they shall be gathered together to the lands of their inheritance" (1 Ne. 22:9-12)—not one land but many. Both the house of Israel and the Jews, Jacob promised, "shall be gathered home to the lands of their inheritance, and shall be established in all their lands of promise" (2 Ne. 9:1-2; 10:7)—not in one location, or in several, but in many. In the day of gathering the Lehite remnants of Joseph are to receive the land of America as their inheritance. (3 Ne. 20:13-14.)

The law of gathering as given to us has varied to meet the needs of an ever-growing Church that one day will have dominion over all the earth. In 1830 the saints were commanded to assemble in "one place." (D&C 29:8.) How could it have been otherwise? They were told to "assemble together at the Ohio" (D&C 37:3) and to go forth to Zion in "the western countries" (D&C 45:64). In 1833 they were told to gather in the Zion of Missouri, "Until the day cometh when there is found no more room for them; and then I have other places which I will appoint unto them," saith the Lord, "and they shall be called stakes, for the curtains or the strength of Zion." They were to worship the Lord "in holy places." (D&C 101:21-22.) In the revealed prayer dedicating the Kirtland Temple (1836), the Prophet importuned for the righteous, "that they may come forth to Zion, or to her stakes, the places of thine appointment, with songs of everlasting joy." (D&C 109:39.) In 1838 the Lord spoke of "the gathering together upon the land of Zion, and upon her stakes." (D&C 115:6.) In 1844 the prophetic word acclaimed: "The whole of America is Zion itself from north to south, and is described by the Prophets, who declare that it is the Zion where the mountain of the Lord should be, and that it should be in the center of the land." (*Teachings*, p. 362.)

We now have stakes of Zion in many nations, in Europe and Asia and South America and upon the islands of the sea. Before the Lord comes, there will be stakes in all lands and among all peoples. Any portion of the surface of the earth that is organized into a stake of Zion—a City of Holiness, as it were—becomes a part of Zion. A stake of Zion is a part of Zion—it is just that simple. And every stake becomes the place of gathering for the saints who live in the area involved.

We now have temples at the ends of the earth. Many more will be built before the dread day when the Lord comes to his temple. In these houses of the Lord every priesthood, key, power, endowment, and gospel blessing is available. There is nothing the saints of God can receive in the Salt Lake Temple that is not also available in the Sao Paulo Temple.

How well Isaiah spoke when he said: "He shall cause them that come of Jacob to take root: Israel shall blossom and bud, and fill the face of the world with fruit." (Isa. 27:6.)

Where then is Zion? It is wherever there are congregations of the pure in heart. And where is Israel to gather? Into the stakes of

Zion, there to perfect themselves as they wait patiently for the Lord. How glorious is the word that the God of Israel is the God of the whole earth, and that he who hath chosen Jacob hath also chosen all those who will repent and come unto him and live his laws.

THE TWO JERUSALEMS AND THE SECOND COMING

Jerusalem Falls from Grace

Zion and Jerusalem, as cities, are or should be one and the same. The original Zion was the City of Holiness wherein the pure in heart dwelt. All her inhabitants were of one heart and one mind, and they lived together in love and in righteousness. Anciently Jerusalem was appointed by the Lord to be the *City of Peace*. The name itself apparently derives from the Hebrew *shalom (shalem)* meaning peace. Melchizedek was king of Salem, and like Enoch, whose converts worshipped the Lord in the *City of Holiness*, so the converts of Melchizedek worshipped in the *City of Peace* where Melchizedek reigned as the Prince of peace. (JST, Gen. 14:33.)

But whereas Zion was taken up into heaven, Jerusalem, following a long and tempestuous history in which she both ascended to the heights and sank to the depths, was thrust down to hell, as it were, there to await a future day of restoration and glory. Commonly called the *Holy City*, because the House of the Lord was there and the Son of God ministered in her streets and synagogues, she is now known to the saints as "the great city, which spiritually is called Sodom and Egypt, where also our Lord was crucified." (Rev. 11:8.) She is the one concerning whom the divine decree went forth. Thus saith the Lord, "I will remove Judah also out of my sight, as I have removed Israel, and will cast off this city Jerusalem which I have chosen, and the house of which I said, My name shall be there." (2 Kgs. 23:27.) And as it was promised, so it came to pass. Titus destroyed the city, tore down the temple stone by stone, slew more than a million Jews with the sword, and made slaves of the rest.

Why, why, oh why, did the Holy City become a vile and pestilent hole? Why did the Great Jehovah permit his holy house to be desecrated by the Gentiles and made by them into a dung hill? Why were the chosen people scourged and slain and scattered and made a hiss and a byword in all nations? The answer is clear and certain. It was because they crucified their King. It was because they rejected the God of their fathers. It was because they did not believe the gospel of salvation when it was taught to them by legal administrators sent of God. Truly the Lord said by the mouth of his ancient prophet: "They build up Zion with blood, and Jerusalem with iniquity. The heads thereof judge for reward, and the priests thereof teach for hire, and the prophets thereof divine for money: yet will they lean upon the Lord, and say, Is not the Lord among us? none evil can come upon us. Therefore shall Zion for your sake be plowed as a field, and Jerusalem shall become heaps, and the mountain of the house [the mountain of the temple] as the high places of the forest." (Micah 3:10-12.) And as it was promised, so it came to pass, both in the day of Nebuchadnezzar and again in the meridian of time.

Jerusalem Shall Rise Again

Though there may be many Jerusalems—each a Zion in its own right, because its inhabitants dwell in righteousness—yet there are two in particular that concern us because of the part they are destined to play in the Second Coming of the one who shall yet reign in the Jerusalem of His choice. These two are the Jerusalem now standing in Palestine and the New Jerusalem yet to be built in Jackson County, Missouri. Both will house a holy temple, and each will serve as a world capital during the Millennium. Biblical prophecies relative to the Second Coming make frequent reference to Zion and Jerusalem as two cities, not one. As a prelude to specifying how both Jerusalems, the Old and the New, fit into our Lord's return, we should ponder and interpret at least a few of the relevant passages from the Old Testament.

Isaiah—the great prophet of the restoration, the one who seems to have known as much about our day as we ourselves know—Isaiah cried out: "Oh that thou wouldest rend the heavens, that thou wouldest come down, that the mountains might flow down at thy presence." Then he speaks other words about that glorious day which will usher in the era of righteousness to follow. In them he inserts one of the reasons why the Lord cannot yet come. "Thy holy cities are a wilderness," he says, "Zion is a wilderness, Jerusalem a desolation. Our holy and our beautiful house [the temple], where our fathers praised thee, is burned up with fire: and all our pleasant things are laid waste." (Isa. 64:1-12.) That is, two holy cities must be prepared to receive the Lord when he comes. As long as Zion is a wilderness, where a city is yet to be built, and as long as Jerusalem, having been destroyed, is yet a desolation, the Lord will not rend the heavens and cause the mountains to flow down at his glorious advent.

Both Isaiah and Micah prophesied of the building of temples in the last days, of the gathering of Israel to those holy houses, and of the gospel teaching they would there receive. "For out of Zion shall go forth the law," they both said, "and the word of the Lord from Jerusalem"—thus naming the two great world capitals and indicating the authoritative decrees to go forth from each. Isaiah put his words in a millennial context by saying that "he [Christ] shall [then] judge among the nations, and shall rebuke many people: and they shall beat their swords into plowshares, and their spears into pruninghooks: nation shall not lift up sword against nation, neither shall they learn war any more." Micah says all this and more. He speaks in addition of the millennial gathering of Israel and says, "The Lord shall reign over them in mount Zion from henceforth, even for ever." (Isa. 2:1-5; Micah 4:1-7.)

Joel, whose words were quoted by Moroni to Joseph Smith, told of the "wonders in the heavens and in the earth," and of the "blood, and fire, and pillars of smoke" that would precede the Second Coming. "The sun shall be turned into darkness, and the moon into blood, before the great and the terrible day of the Lord come," he said. When these things fall upon the earth, there will be no security and no salvation except for those who believe and obey the everlasting gospel. "And it shall come to pass, that whosoever shall call on the name of the Lord shall be delivered: for in mount Zion and in Jerusalem shall be deliverance, as the Lord hath said, and in the remnant whom the Lord shall call." (Joel 2:30-32.) Two great cities of deliverance, Zion and Jerusalem; two great world capitals, Jerusalem of the Jews and the New Jerusalem of all Israel! In that day, "The sun and the moon shall be darkened, and the stars shall withdraw their shining. The Lord also shall roar out of Zion, and utter his voice from Jerusalem; and the heavens and the earth shall shake: but the Lord will be the hope of his people, and the strength of the children of Israel." In that day, "Judah shall dwell for ever, and Jerusalem from generation to generation," and it shall be said, "The Lord dwelleth in Zion." (Joel 3:15-16, 20-21.)

Truly, truly shall it be. Jerusalem shall rise again. As she fell from grace because she forsook the living God, so shall she rise again when she once more worships her Eternal King in the beauty of holiness. As she fell because of iniquity, so shall she be restored through righteousness. When the Jews receive the fulness of the everlasting gospel as it has been restored through the Prophet Joseph Smith, they will return to Jerusalem as the Lord's true legal administrators to build up Jerusalem as a Zion and to place again on the ancient site the temple of the new kingdom. And then when the Lord comes, the ancient city will shine forth with a glory and a splendor never before known among mortals.

How gloriously speaks the prophetic word of that day! "Thus saith the Lord; I am returned unto Zion, and will dwell in the midst of Jerusalem" for a thousand years, "and Jerusalem shall be called a city of truth; and the mountain of the Lord of hosts the holy mountain." It shall be the mountain where the temple stands.

And what of the inhabitants of the Holy City? "Thus saith the Lord of hosts; There shall yet old men and old women dwell in the streets of Jerusalem, and every man with his staff in his hand for very age." It is the day when men shall live to the age of a tree and then be changed from mortality to immortality in the twinkling of an eye. "And the streets of the city shall be full of boys and girls playing in the streets thereof." It is the day when the children of the prophets shall grow up without sin unto salvation.

It is also the day of the final great and glorious gathering of Israel. "Thus saith the Lord of hosts; Behold, I will save my people from the east country, and from the west country; And I will bring them, and they shall dwell in the midst of Jerusalem: and they shall be my people, and I will be their God, in truth and in righteousness." And it shall not be with the gathered ones as it was with those who were scattered. "But now I will not be unto the residue of this people as in the former days, saith the Lord of hosts. For the seed shall be prosperous; the vine shall give her fruit, and the ground shall give her increase, and the heavens shall give their dew; and I will cause the remnant of this people to possess all these things." It is the day of the new heaven and of the new earth, when the desert blossoms as the rose and all the earth becomes as the garden of the Lord.

And what manner of conduct shall prevail among men? "These are the things that ye shall do," the holy word affirms: "Speak ye every man the truth to his neighbour; execute the judgment of truth and peace in your gates: And let none of you imagine evil in your hearts against his neighbour; and love no false oath: for all these are things that I hate, saith the Lord." And in that day "many people and strong nations shall come to seek the Lord of hosts in Jerusalem, and to pray before the Lord. Thus saith the Lord of hosts; In those days it shall come to pass, that ten men shall take hold out of all languages of the nations, even shall take hold of the skirt of him that is a Jew, saying, We will go with you: for we have heard that God is with you." (Zech. 8:1-23.)

The New Jerusalem

"We believe . . . that Zion (the New Jerusalem) will be built upon the American continent." So specified the seer of latter days in our tenth Article of Faith. Zion, the New Jerusalem, on American soil! And we hasten to add, so also shall there be Zions in all lands and New Jerusalems in the mountains of the Lord in all the earth. But the American Zion shall be the capital city, the source whence the law shall go forth to govern all the earth. It shall be the city of the Great King. His throne shall be there, and from there he shall reign gloriously over all the earth. And so, let us now drink deeply from some of those passages in holy writ which tell of our American Zion. As we do so we must rightly divide the word of God, as Paul might have cautioned, lest we become confused as to what shall happen before and what after the Second Coming.

To Enoch the Lord swore with an oath in his own name, because, as Paul would say, he could swear by no greater, that he would come a second time "in the last days, in the days of wickedness and vengeance. . . . And the day shall come that the earth shall rest," he said, speaking of the Millennium, "but before that day the heavens shall be darkened, and a veil of darkness shall cover the earth." This is the evil and universal apostasy that has prevailed for nearly two thousand years and that even now covers the earth except where the faithful among the saints are concerned. "And the heavens shall shake, and also the earth," the Lord continues, "and great tribulations shall be among the children of men, but my people will I preserve." Then he speaks of the glorious restoration, of the coming forth of the Book of Mormon, and of righteousness and truth sweeping the earth as with a flood. To what purpose? "To gather out mine elect from the four quarters of the earth, unto a place which I shall prepare, an Holy City, that my people may gird up their loins, and be looking forth for the time of my coming." The Holy City of which he speaks shall be built before the Second Coming. Of this city the Lord says: "There shall be my tabernacle"—the place where my saints shall worship —"and it shall be called Zion, a New Jerusalem."

The saints of the living God, the true believers who worship the God of Enoch, the righteous souls who receive revelation and know how and where and in what manner to build the Holy City—they shall build the New Jerusalem before the Lord comes. "Then"—that is, after the city is built—"Then shalt thou [Enoch] and all thy city meet them there, and we will receive them into our bosom, and they shall see us; and we will fall upon their necks, and they shall fall upon our necks, and we will kiss each other." It is the Lord who is speaking. He continues: "And there"—in the New

Jerusalem—"shall be mine abode, and it shall be Zion, which shall come forth out of all the creations which I have made; and for the space of a thousand years the earth shall rest." (Moses 7:60-64.)

Our Lord, risen in glorious immortality, taught his Nephite saints about the latter-day gathering of all Israel. "I will gather my people together as a man gathereth his sheaves into the floor," he said. "And behold, this people"—the Lehite civilization who were of the house of Joseph—"will I establish in this land [America], unto the fulfilling of the covenant which I made with your father Jacob; and it"—apparently the whole land—"shall be a New Jerusalem. And the powers of heaven shall be in the midst of this people; yea, even I will be in the midst of you." (3 Ne. 20:18, 22.) Clearly Jesus is speaking of the New Jerusalem during its millennial existence, for it is then that he shall dwell on earth among the righteous.

A short while later in the same discourse, still speaking of the latter days, Jesus said the rebellious would be cut off from the house of Israel, but that among the righteous he would establish his church. "And they shall come in unto the covenant and be numbered among this the remnant of Jacob, unto whom I have given this land for their inheritance." It is these righteous people, these believing ones who have made covenant with the Lord, who shall build the New Jerusalem. "And they shall assist my people, the remnant of Jacob, and also as many of the house of Israel as shall come, that they may build a city, which shall be called the New Jerusalem." The gathered elect of Israel shall build the city under the direction of the President of The Church of Jesus Christ of Latter-day Saints. "And then shall they assist my people that they may be gathered in, who are scattered upon all the face of the land, in unto the New Jerusalem." Note it, there is to be a great and glorious day of gathering after the New Jerusalem is built. And after this gathering "shall the power of heaven come down among them; and I also will be in the midst," meaning that the Lord will reign personally upon the earth during the Millennium. (3 Ne. 21:20-25.)

This New Jerusalem is to be built in Jackson County, Missouri, and its glory and power shall be known in all the earth. "And it shall be called the New Jerusalem, a land of peace, a city of refuge, a place of safety for the saints of the Most High God; And the glory of the Lord shall be there, and the terror of the Lord also shall be there, insomuch that the wicked will not come unto it, and it shall be called Zion. And it shall come to pass among the wicked, that every man that will not take his sword against his neighbor must needs flee unto Zion for safety. And there shall be gathered unto it out of every nation under heaven; and it shall be the only people that shall not be at war one with another. And it shall be said among the wicked: Let us not go up to battle against Zion, for the inhabitants of Zion are terrible; wherefore we cannot stand. And it shall come to pass that the righteous shall be gathered out from among all nations, and shall come to Zion, singing with songs of everlasting joy." (D&C 45:66-71.) All this lies in the future. The city has yet to be built, and it will not be built and cannot be built except by a people who are living a celestial law. And after it is built, the fear and dread of the Lord will rest upon the wicked as they see how and in what manner the Lord preserves its righteous inhabitants.

As we might surmise, the sealed portion of the Book of Mormon contains a full and complete account of all things pertaining to the New Jerusalem and the second coming of Christ. From the writings of Ether, preserved in full on those plates, Moroni digested for us a few salient facts that enable us to glimpse what is to be. He tells us the American continent "was the place of the New Jerusalem, which should come down out of heaven, and [the place of] the holy sanctuary [temple] of the Lord." This New Jerusalem is the City of Enoch, which shall return after the Lord comes again. "Behold, Ether saw the days of Christ [the days of his glorious Second Coming], and he spake concerning a New Jerusalem upon this land." This New Jerusalem seems to be the one built by the saints in the latter days to which the New Jerusalem from heaven shall come.

"And he," meaning Ether, Moroni continues, "spake also concerning the house of Israel, and the Jerusalem from whence Lehi should come—after it should be destroyed it should be built up again, a holy city unto the Lord; wherefore, it could not be a new Jerusalem for it had been in a time of old; but it should be built up again, and become a holy city of the Lord; and it should be built unto the house of Israel." Moroni, summarizing Ether, says that "a New Jerusalem should be built upon this land"—the land of America, built up in the same way Old Jerusalem shall be rebuilt, that is, by mortal hands—built up "unto the remnant of the seed of Joseph, for which things," he says, "there has been a type."

The type is then given in these words: "For as Joseph brought his father down into the land of Egypt, even so he died there; wherefore, the Lord brought a remnant of the seed of Joseph out of the land of Jerusalem, that he might be merciful unto the seed of Joseph that they should perish not, even as he was mericful unto the father of Joseph that he should perish not. Wherefore, the remnant of the house of Joseph shall be built upon this land; and it shall be a land of their inheritance; and they shall build up a holy city unto the Lord, like unto the Jerusalem of old; and they shall no more be confounded, until the end come when the earth shall pass away." We who are of Ephraim (and of Manasseh) into whose hands the Church and kingdom has now been given shall build the city in due course, and we and our children after us shall never be confounded or lose the faith; for our dispensation, the promise is that the gospel shall remain with us to prepare a people for the second coming of Him whose servants we are.

And when our Lord returns, Moroni continues, "there shall be a new heaven and a new earth; and they shall be like unto the old save the old have passed away, and all things have become new." These words are descriptive of the millennial earth, the paradisiacal earth, the transfigured earth that shall be again as it was in the days of the Garden of Eden.

"And then"—after there is a new heaven and a new earth—"cometh the New Jerusalem"—in all its millennial glory, joined as it will be with Enoch's city—"and blessed are they who dwell therein, for it is they whose garments are white through the blood of the Lamb; and they are they who are numbered among the remnant of the seed of Joseph, who are of the house of Israel. And then also cometh the Jerusalem of old; and the inhabitants thereof, blessed are they, for they have been washed in the blood of the Lamb; and they are they who were scattered and gathered in from the four quarters of the earth, and from the north countries, and are partakers of the fulfilling of the covenant which God made with their father, Abraham." (Ether 13:3-11.) This glorious destiny for Old Jerusalem is clearly millennial. There will be a beginning before the Lord comes, but the great day shall be when he is here to send forth his word from his ancient holy city.

The millennial setting of the New Jerusalem is nowhere seen better than in the biblical words of the Beloved Disciple. He records: "And I saw a new heaven and a new earth"—he is seeing the millennial earth—"for the first heaven and the first earth were passed away; and there was no more sea." The continents and islands have become one land and are no more divided by the oceans of the earth. "And I John saw the holy city, new Jerusalem [the City of Enoch], coming down from God out of heaven, prepared as a bride adorned for her husband." Christ is the husband, and the robes with which his beloved ones are adorned are the robes of righteousness. "And I heard a great voice out of heaven saying, Behold, the tabernacle of God is with men, and he will dwell with them, and they shall be his people, and God himself shall be with them, and be their God." Christ, who is the Lord God, shall reign on earth. "And God shall wipe away all tears from their eyes; and there shall be no more death, neither sorrow, nor crying, neither shall there be any more pain: for the former things are passed away." (Rev. 21:1-4.) All these things, as we shall see in a later context, are descriptive of life during the Millennium.

This indeed shall be the glorious day when "the graves of the saints shall be opened; and they shall come forth and stand on the right hand of the Lamb, when he shall stand upon Mount Zion, and upon the holy city, the New Jerusalem; and they shall sing the song of the Lamb, day and night forever and ever." (D&C 133:56.) Among other things they shall sing:

The Lord hath brought again Zion;
The Lord hath redeemed his people, Israel,
According to the election of grace,
Which was brought to pass by the faith

And covenant of their fathers.
The Lord hath redeemed his people;
And Satan is bound and time is no longer.
The Lord hath gathered all things in one.
The Lord hath brought down Zion from above.
The Lord hath brought up Zion from beneath.
The earth hath travailed and brought forth her strength;
And truth is established in her bowels;
And the heavens have smiled upon her;
And she is clothed with the glory of her God;
For he stands in the midst of his people.
Glory, and honor, and power, and might,
Be ascribed to our God; for he is full of mercy,
Justice, grace and truth, and peace,
Forever and ever, Amen.
—D&C 84:99-102

The Celestial Jerusalem

When this earth becomes a celestial sphere; when it becomes the eternal heaven for exalted beings; when the Father and the Son abide, as occasion requires, on its resurrected surface—then again shall the holy city come down from God in heaven to be with men on earth. Or, rather, of that day of celestial rest, shall we not say that the whole earth shall be a heavenly Jerusalem?

It is Paul who tells us that the saved saints shall "come unto mount Zion, and unto the city of the living God, the heavenly Jerusalem, and to an innumerable company of angels, . . . and to God the Judge of all." (Heb. 12:22-23.) And our revelations speak of exalted beings as "they who are come unto Mount Zion, and unto the city of the living God, the heavenly place, the holiest of all." (D&C 76:66.) But it is John to whom we turn to read the grand imagery, also literal, that describes that celestial Jerusalem.

John saw "the holy Jerusalem, descending out of heaven from God, having the glory of God." He saw the celestial light that blazed forth in her streets, showing that God himself was there. He saw the great wall with twelve gates, guarded by twelve angels, with the names of the twelve tribes of Israel inscribed thereon, showing that saved Israel and all who are adopted into Abraham's family shall dwell therein. He saw the twelve foundations on which were the names of the twelve apostles of the Lamb, showing that all who dwell in the sacred city have believed the witness and obeyed the counsel of those who testified of Christ. He saw the great size of the city, the enormous length and breadth and height, signifying that it encompassed the whole planet. He saw the jewels and precious stones and gates of pearl and streets of gold, letting him know that those who dwell therein inherit all things and nothing is withheld.

"I saw no temple therein," he said, "for the Lord God Almighty and the Lamb are the temple of it. And the city had no need of the sun, neither of the moon, to shine in it: for the glory of God did lighten it, and the Lamb is the light thereof." This is the day when the earth, as a sea of glass, exists in its sanctified, immortal, and eternal state. "And the nations of them which are saved shall walk in the light of it," John says, "and the kings of the earth do bring their glory and honour into it." Only exalted beings shall reign within its walls. "And the gates of it shall not be shut at all by day: for there shall be no night there. And they shall bring the glory and honour of the nations into it. And there shall in no wise enter into it any thing that defileth, neither whatsoever worketh abomination, or maketh a lie: but they which are written in the Lamb's book of life." (Rev. 21:10-27.)

Truly Zion is the *City of Holiness* and Jerusalem is the *City of Peace*, and in them none but the righteous shall dwell.

Chapter 26

RESTORING THE KINGDOM TO ISRAEL

Israel: Her Kingdom and Power

Jesus ministered among men, taught them the gospel, and appointed pastors to feed his flock, but he did not restore the kingdom to Israel. Our Lord worked out the infinite and eternal atonement in Gethsemane and on Calvary; he rose in glorious immortality from the Arimathean's tomb; and he commanded the Twelve to go into all the world, preach the gospel to every creature, baptize believers, and give them the gift of the Holy Ghost—but he did not restore the kingdom to Israel.

The restoration of the kingdom to Israel—that was the thing uppermost in the minds of Jewish Israel in our Lord's day. They had even tried to take him by force, coronate him with an earthly crown, and put a sword wielded by the arm of flesh into his hands. They sought freedom from Roman bondage with a fanatical passion. Their blood drenched the great altar in Jehovah's house and flowed in rivulets in the streets of the Holy City as a witness that freedom from Gentile rule was worth more to them than life itself.

And so even the Twelve—after spending three years with Jesus in his mortal ministry; after associating with him for forty days as a resurrected being; and after being taught all that it was expedient for them to know to perform the labor that then was theirs—even the apostles sought yet to learn of the fulfillment of the prophetic word concerning Israel the chosen. "When they therefore were come together," at the time appointed for the ascension of Jesus into heaven, to sit down on the right hand of the Majesty on high, "they asked of him, saying, Lord, wilt thou at this time restore again the kingdom to Israel?"

They had received the keys of the kingdom of heaven; they presided over the Church and kingdom of God on earth; they held the holy apostleship, than which there is no higher power and authority on earth. They knew that theirs was an earthwide commission to carry the hope of salvation to all men. But what of the volumes spoken by the prophets of old about the glory and triumph of Israel? When would the scattered remnants of Jacob return? When would Jerusalem become a holy city whence the word of the Lord would go to all people? When would the Gentiles—Rome included!—bow beneath Israel's rod? And when would Israel govern all the earth?

To all this there was an answer, but it was not theirs to learn. Their ears were not to hear the glad tidings that have now been heralded in ours. To them Jesus said: "It is not for you to know the times or the seasons, which the Father hath put in his own power." That knowledge was reserved for another people in a future day. "But ye shall receive power," Jesus told them, "after that the Holy Ghost is come upon you: and ye shall be witnesses unto me both in Jerusalem, and in all Judea, and in Samaria, and unto the uttermost part of the earth." The kingdom was not to be restored to Israel in their day. Let them preach the gospel and save souls before the dire day of darkness that soon would cover the earth. The promised day of restoration, the day of Israel's triumph and glory, the day of millennial glory—all this lay ahead. It was scheduled for the last days. "And when he had spoken these things, while they beheld, he was taken up; and a cloud received him out of their sight." (Acts 1:6-9.) Thus Jesus' last words to his mortal ministers reaffirmed their great commission for the meridian of time, and they refrained from revealing the set time for favoring Israel and putting the ancient kingdom once again in her hands.

In her righteous days Israel prevailed over all opposing powers. Her armies put the aliens to flight; Jehovah fought her battles;

and David reigned on a stable throne. King David, then a man after the Lord's own heart, "executed judgment and justice unto all his people" (2 Sam. 8:15), and they prospered temporally and spiritually. Prophets dwelt among them, the heavens were open to the faithful, and the gifts of the Spirit blessed whole congregations. But in the days when they forsook the Lord and walked after the manner of the world, they were scourged and cursed and scattered. Through it all, however, the prophetic word held forth the hope of a gathering and a day of glory and triumph beyond anything ever known by them. Once again, according to the promises, Israel, as a theocracy, would receive laws from on high and administer them for the blessing of mankind. Once again there would be officers and judges and peace and prosperity.

This kingdom of which the apostles and prophets have spoken has not yet been restored to Israel but soon will be. The age of restoration has commenced, and the ecclesiastical kingdom—which is the Church—has been set up again. For the present there is a separation of church and state; the Church administers salvation and gives laws to its people on moral and spiritual issues, and the state administers civic matters and enacts such laws as are needed to govern in the affairs of men. But when the Lord comes and takes over the governments of the earth, he will place all things, both ecclesiastical and civic, in the hands of his own true kingdom. Then, as it is written, "the saints of the most High shall take the kingdom, and possess the kingdom for ever, even for ever and ever. . . . And the kingdom and dominion, and the greatness of the kingdom under the whole heaven, shall be given to the people of the saints of the most High, whose kingdom is an everlasting kingdom, and all dominions shall serve and obey him [the Lord]." (Dan. 7:18, 27.) Such is the kingdom that shall be restored to Israel in due course.

Gathering the Remainder of the Elect

Much of the prophetic word relative to the gathering of Israel in the last days has a dual fulfillment. It is descriptive of the gathering now in process, which is premillennial, but it has a far greater and more expanded application to the gathering after the ushering in of the Millennium when the earth shall be cleansed by fire. This final gathering will occur after the wicked masses of carnal men have been burned as stubble and after the barriers now separating the nations of the earth have been broken down.

The premillennial gathering is going forward and shall continue to go forward in the midst of war and desolation and persecution. All of the forces of evil do and shall oppose it, for it is of God and they are of the devil. But the gathering destined to come after the Second Coming shall be by power—divine power—and shall take place after Satan is bound and after the wicked have been destroyed. In that day hell will no longer be able to fight against God, and Zion will triumph and flourish to the full.

Few have written as clearly and plainly about these matters as did Nephi. He prophesied that "the Lord God will proceed to make bare his arm in the eyes of all the nations, in bringing about his covenants and his gospel unto those who are of the house of Israel." Israel "shall be gathered," he said, when they come to know "that the Lord is their Savior and their Redeemer, the Mighty One of Israel." That evil powers shall oppose this gathering and fight against Zion is so axiomatic it scarcely needs stating. Evil men always oppose righteous causes. The church of the devil always does the bidding of its master. But over this church, in due course, righteousness shall prevail. "And the blood of that great and abominable church," Nephi says, "which is the whore of all the earth, shall turn upon their own heads; for they shall war among themselves"—as they are even now doing—"and the sword of their own hands shall fall upon their own heads, and they shall be drunken with their own blood." Can anyone with spiritual insight look upon the nations of the earth today, in this day when we are struggling with all our might to gather Israel into the stakes of Zion, and not see a beginning fulfillment of Nephi's words?

"And every nation which shall war against thee, O house of Israel," the inspired word continues, "shall be turned one against another, and they shall fall into the pit which they digged to ensnare the people of the Lord." This is not yet, but soon shall be. "And all that fight against Zion shall be destroyed"—such is their eventual destiny—"and that great whore, who hath perverted the right ways of the Lord, yea, that great and abominable church, shall tumble to the dust and great shall be the fall of it."

When shall this come to pass? "For behold, saith the prophet, the time cometh speedily that Satan shall have no more power over the hearts of the children of men; for the day soon cometh that all the proud and they who do wickedly shall be as stubble; and the day cometh that they must be burned." That day is the great and dreadful day of the Lord. "For the time soon cometh that the fulness of the wrath of God shall be poured out upon all the children of men; for he will not suffer that the wicked shall destroy the righteous."

Of course, Satan will slay some of the righteous that their blood—with the blood of all the martyrs of all the ages—may cry from the ground as a witness against those who fight against God. Yet, as a people the true saints shall prevail. The Lord "will preserve the righteous by his power, even if it so be that the fulness of his wrath must come, and the righteous be preserved, even unto the destruction of their enemies by fire." This refers to the day of burning that shall attend the Second Coming. "Wherefore, the righteous need not fear; for thus saith the prophet, they shall be saved, even if it so be as by fire."

Nephi continues to use language descriptive of the Second Coming; promises that "the time surely must come that all they who fight against Zion shall be cut off"; says that "the righteous need not fear"; and speaks of the destruction of the kingdom of the devil. Then he says: "And the time cometh speedily that the righteous must be led up as calves of the stall, and the Holy One of Israel must reign in dominion, and might, and power, and great glory." Such shall be in the Millennium. In this setting our prophetic friend says: "And he gathereth his children from the four quarters of the earth; and he numbereth his sheep, and they know him; and there shall be one fold and one shepherd; and he shall feed his sheep, and in him they shall find pasture." Do we not see in this a millennial gathering of the elect from the four quarters of the earth?

"And because of the righteousness of his people"—his people are gathered Israel—"Satan has no power; wherefore, he cannot be loosed for the space of many years; for he hath no power over the hearts of the people, for they dwell in righteousness, and the Holy One of Israel reigneth." (1 Ne. 22:11-26.)

Those of Israel who live on earth and are worthy, and who are not gathered before the Lord comes, shall be gathered thereafter. "And they shall see the Son of Man coming in the clouds of heaven, with power and great glory," Jesus said, "and he shall send his angels before him with the great sound of a trumpet, and they shall gather together the remainder of his elect from the four winds, from one end of heaven to the other." (JS-M 1:36-37.) How shall this work be performed, and who shall do the actual gathering in of the lost sheep? As we are aware, the scriptural promise announced that an angel would fly through the midst of heaven having the everlasting gospel to preach unto all men. And as we have seen, this restoration was brought to pass by many angels, as each restored knowledge and keys and priesthood, and then mortal men proclaimed the angelic message to their fellowmen. So shall it be, as we suppose, in this final gathering of the elect by the angels. The message itself shall come from on high, and the Lord, as his custom is, will work through his servants on earth. They will do the work as they are now doing it. The elders of Israel will gather Israel after the Lord comes, on the same basis as at present.

Truly, saith the Psalmist, "Our God shall come, and shall not keep silence: a fire shall devour before him, and it shall be very tempestuous round about him. He shall call to the heavens from above, and to the earth, that he may judge his people." And what shall his call be? He shall say: "Gather my saints together unto me; those that have made a covenant with me by sacrifice." So shall it be in the day of judgment. "And the heavens shall declare his righteousness: for God is judge himself." (Ps. 50:3-6.)

Gathered Israel Governs the Earth

It will serve our purposes well to analyze selected prophetic utterances about the gathering of Israel. We shall choose a few whose chief fulfillment is millennial, and we shall seek to learn from them the governing status of the chosen people in that blessed day. We have already seen that Jesus put chapter 52 of Isaiah in a millennial context. In it is found the cry: "Awake, awake; put on thy strength, O Zion; put on thy beautiful garments, O Jerusalem, the holy city: for henceforth there shall no more come into thee the uncircumcised and the unclean." In the day of which we speak there will be none who are unclean in the telestial sense of the word, for the wicked will be destroyed by the brightness of His coming. And there will be none who are uncircumcised, as it were, for all who seek the blessings of the Holy City will be in harmony with the plans and purposes of Him whose city it is.

"Break forth into joy, sing together, ye waste places of Jerusalem: for the Lord hath comforted his people, he hath redeemed Jerusalem." (Isa. 52:1, 9.) It is the millennial Old Jerusalem, rebuilt in the cause of righteousness, of which the prophet here speaks. It is the same consoling word that the Lord gave by the mouth of Isaiah in these words: "Comfort ye, comfort ye my people, saith your God. Speak ye comfortably to Jerusalem, and cry unto her, that her warfare is accomplished, that her iniquity is pardoned: for she hath received of the Lord's hand double for all her sins." (Isa. 40:1-2.)

It is Isaiah, speaking of the Second Coming, who says: "And the light of Israel shall be for a fire, and his Holy One for a flame: and it shall burn and devour his thorns and his briers in one day." So it is said of the day of burning when the vineyard is cleansed. "And [the fire] shall consume the glory of his forest, and of his fruitful field, both soul and body," the account continues. "And the rest of the trees of his forest shall be few, that a child may write them." The wickedness of men is so widespread, and their evils are so great, that few—comparatively—shall abide the day. "And it shall come to pass in that day"—the day of burning, the day when every corruptible thing is consumed, the day when few men are left—"that the remnant of Israel, and such as are escaped of the house of Jacob, shall no more again stay upon him that smote them; but shall stay upon the Lord, the Holy One of Israel, in truth.

The remnant shall return, even the remnant of Jacob, unto the mighty God." (Isa. 10:17-21.) They shall be gathered after the coming of the Lord.

We also learn from Isaiah that in the millennial day, when "the whole earth is at rest, and is quiet," then Israel shall "break forth into singing." Why? Because "the Lord will have mercy on Jacob, and will yet choose Israel, and set them in their own land: and the strangers shall be joined with them, and they shall cleave to the house of Jacob." Such spiritual blessings as come to the Gentiles shall be theirs because they cleave unto Israel. "And the people"—the Gentiles—"shall take them, and bring them to their place: and the house of Israel shall possess them"—the Gentiles—"in the land of the Lord for servants and handmaids: and they shall take them captives, whose captives they were; and they shall rule over their oppressors." (Isa. 14:1-7.) Israel shall rule; the Gentiles shall serve; the kingdom is the Lord's. His people are the governing ones—such is the meaning of Isaiah's imagery.

When Israel receives her latter-day glory; when she gains again the kingdom that once was hers; when she attains her ultimate supremacy over all the earth—it will be in response to the divine call: "Arise, shine; for thy light is come, and the glory of the Lord is risen upon thee." Christ has come, and his glory is with Israel. And then shall the ancient promise be fulfilled: "The Gentiles shall come to thy light, and kings to the brightness of thy rising." The Gentiles shall bring their wealth and their power. As the sons of Jacob return to the ancient fold, they shall be helped on their way by the great and the good and the mighty of the earth. "And the sons of strangers shall build up thy walls, and their kings shall minister unto thee," saith the holy word. "For the nation and kingdom that will not serve thee shall perish; yea, those nations shall be utterly wasted. . . . The sons also of them that afflicted thee shall come bending unto thee; and all they that despise thee shall bow themselves down at the soles of thy feet; and they shall call thee, The city of the Lord, The Zion of the Holy One of Israel." (Isa. 60:1-22.) What better words could Isaiah have chosen to bear record of the preeminence and power and rulership of Israel in the day of the Lord Jesus Christ?

And yet he has more to say. "They shall build the old wastes, they shall raise up the former desolations, and they shall repair the waste cities, the desolations of many generations," he says. "And the strangers shall stand and feed your flocks, and the sons of the alien shall be your plowmen and your vinedressers. But ye shall be named the Priests of the Lord: men shall call you the Ministers of our God: ye shall eat the riches of the Gentiles, and in their glory shall ye boast yourselves." (Isa. 61:4-6.)

"For, behold, the Lord will come with fire, and with his chariots like a whirlwind, to render his anger with fury, and his rebuke with flames of fire." It is the great and dreadful day of the Lord. "For by fire and by his sword will the Lord plead with all flesh: and the slain of the Lord shall be many." And then what? What comes after his dreadful coming? Why, "I will gather all nations and tongues," he says, "and they shall come, and see my glory." (Isa. 66:15-18.)

Micah prophesies of the Second Coming and describes the millennial era of peace that will then commence. In it, he says, "they shall sit every man under his vine and under his fig tree; and none shall make them afraid: for the mouth of the Lord hath spoken it. For all people will walk every one in the name of his god, and we will walk in the name of the Lord our God for ever and ever." There will be freedom of worship in that day; until all men receive the everlasting gospel, they will continue to worship as they choose. Unbelievers will still need to come to a knowledge of the truth and to gather into the stakes of Zion with the Lord's people. "In that day"—the millennial day—"saith the Lord, will I assemble her that halteth, and I will gather her that is driven out, and her that I have afflicted; And I will make her that halted a remnant, and her that was cast far off a strong nation: and the Lord shall reign over them in mount Zion from henceforth, even for ever." (Micah 4:3-7.)

We need not pursue this course of inquiry further. Isaiah said many other things about it; Jeremiah and Ezekiel and Joel and others of the prophets added their concurring witnesses. We are all under obligation to search the scriptures, to ponder what is found in them, and to gain a correct understanding of all their various parts. It suffices for our present purposes to know that the premillennial gathering of Israel, in which the true believers come to Zion, "one of a city, and two of a family" (Jer. 3:14), shall one day reach such proportions that men will say: "Who hath heard such a thing? who hath seen such things? Shall the earth be made to bring forth in one day? or shall a nation be born at once? for as soon as Zion travailed, she brought forth her children" (Isa. 66:8).

We have before us, then, the doctrine and the witness that the great day of Israel's gathering and glory lies ahead; that the prophetic word can never find complete fulfillment in this wicked world; and that in the better day which lies ahead, all things shall come to pass as the prophets have foretold. In this setting we are now ready to turn our attention to the return of the Ten Tribes and the reign of the Second David.

THE RESTORATION OF THE TEN TRIBES

Why They Shall Come from the North Countries

"We believe in the literal gathering of Israel and in the restoration of the Ten Tribes." (A of F 10.) This inspired language leaves the clear impression that the gathering of Israel is one thing and the restoration of the Ten Tribes is another. Why this distinction? Are not the Ten Tribes a part of Israel? And if Israel is to be gathered, surely in the very nature of things this would include the gathering of the major portion of that ancient and favored people.

An immortal Moses, appearing in resurrected glory on the 3rd day of April, 1836, in the Kirtland Temple, committed unto his mortal fellowservants, Joseph Smith and Oliver Cowdery, "the keys of the gathering of Israel from the four parts of the earth, and the leading of the ten tribes from the land of the north." (D&C 110:11.) Again there is a distinction between Israel as a whole and the Ten Tribes who are the dominant portion of Jacob's seed. All scripture comes by the power of the Holy Ghost and is verily true. When special and unusual language is used, there is a reason. Holy writ is not idle chatter; it is the mind and will of the Lord; it says what he wants said. And so it now behooves us to learn why it is one thing to gather Israel from the four parts of the earth and yet another to lead the Ten Tribes from the land of the north.

We have already seen that all Israel, including specifically and pointedly the Ten Tribes, is scattered in all the nations of the earth, upon all the islands of the sea, and among every people who dwell on this planet. It is absolutely basic and fundamental to know this. We cannot understand the gathering of Israel, we cannot envision what is meant by the restoration of the Ten Tribes, and we cannot properly relate these two things to the Second Coming of our Lord unless we know where Israel and the Ten Tribes now are.

We are also aware that the Ten Tribes were first taken as a body into Assyria; that they went out from Assyria, northward, in a body, under prophetic guidance; and that they were then splintered and driven and scattered into all places and among all peoples. These Ten Tribes, no matter where they are located, are in nations and places known in the days of Isaiah and Jeremiah and the ancient prophets as the north countries. Hence, their return to Palestine at least will be from the land of the north.

The tribe of Ephraim is one of the Ten Tribes; and her people became wanderers in the nations, where they now reside and where they are now being found and gathered, one of a city and two of a family, into the stakes of Zion in those nations. This gathering of Israel is not to an American Zion; it is not to Palestine and the ancient holy land; it is not to any central place or location. Rather, it is to the holy places of safety that are now being set up in all nations as rapidly as our strength and means permit. As we have seen, this gathering of Ephraim falls in the category of the gathering of Israel and not of the leading of the Ten Tribes from the land of the north. This gathering of Ephraim is into the stakes of Zion in all the nations of the earth. There are, of course, isolated and unusual instances of people from the other lost tribes gathering with Ephraim, but these are few and far between. The gathering of these other tribes is not yet, but by and by.

What, then, is meant by the leading of the Ten Tribes from the land of the north? Our answer is: Just what the words say. We are gathering Israel now in all nations and counseling them to stay where they are, there to enlarge the borders of Zion, there to build up stakes of Zion in their own lands and among their own people. But with the Ten Tribes, in part at least, it will be another thing. They are destined to return (at least in large and representative numbers) to the same soil where the feet of their forebears walked during the days of their mortal pilgrimage. They are to return to

Palestine. At least a constituent assembly will congregate there in the very land given of God to Abraham their father. Others will, of course, be in America and in all lands, but the formal return, the return from the north countries, will be to the land of their ancient inheritance.

Why They Shall Return to Palestine

Abraham went into the land of Canaan, where the Lord said unto him: "Unto thy seed will I give this land." (Gen. 12:7.) "For all the land which thou seest, to thee will I give it, and to thy seed for ever. . . . Arise, walk through the land in the length of it and in the breadth of it; for I will give it unto thee." (Gen. 13:15-17.) "Unto thy seed have I given this land, from the river of Egypt unto the great river, the river Euphrates." (Gen. 15:18.) "And I will give unto thee, and to thy seed after thee, the land wherein thou art a stranger, all the land of Canaan, for an everlasting possession; and I will be their God." (Gen. 17:8.) All these promises, made to Abraham, were renewed to Isaac, unto whom the Lord said: "Sojourn in this land, and I will be with thee, and will bless thee; for unto thee, and unto thy seed, I will give all these countries." (Gen. 26:3.) Then to Jacob came the same promise: "The land whereon thou liest, to thee will I give it, and to thy seed." (Gen. 28:13.) "And the land which I gave Abraham and Isaac, to thee I will give it, and to thy seed after thee will I give the land." (Gen. 35:12.) And also: "Behold, I will make thee fruitful, and multiply thee, and I will make of thee a multitude of people; and will give this land to thy seed after thee for an everlasting possession." (Gen. 48:4.)

Paul, pleading before Agrippa, hearkened back to these ancient promises—that Israel, in time and in eternity, as mortal men and as immortal beings, should inherit everlastingly the land of Abraham—and said: "Now I stand and am judged for the hope of the promise made of God unto our fathers: Unto which promise our twelve tribes, instantly serving God day and night, hope to come. For which hope's sake, king Agrippa, I am accused of the Jews." And what was that hope, the hope of the twelve tribes of Israel? It was that even in eternity, as resurrected beings, they should have this blessed soil where once their fathers dwelt. Hence, Paul asked: "Why should it be thought a thing incredible with you, that God should raise the dead?" (Acts 26:6-8.)

It is clear; it is plain; it is certain: God gave ancient Canaan to Abraham, Isaac, and Jacob, and the twelve tribes of Israel, of whom the Ten Tribes are the dominant part. It is their land, in time and in eternity. It is their land now whenever they are worthy to tread its blessed surface. And it shall be theirs again in that everlasting eternity that lies ahead. "It is decreed that the poor and the meek of the earth shall inherit it," in that celestial day when it shall be crowned with the presence of God, even the Father. (D&C 88:17-19.) Where else, then, would we expect to see the Ten Tribes return? Where else would we expect them to assemble to worship the God of their fathers and to be inheritors of the promises made to the ancient ones whose seed they are?

Thus it is that we see why the revelations speak of the gathering of Israel from the four parts of the earth into the Church and kingdom of God on earth, and also of the leading of the Ten Tribes from the land of the north back again to their promised Canaan. The gathering of Israel is one thing, the return of the Ten Tribes to a specified place is another; and Moses gave to men in our day the keys and power to perform both labors. This means that Israel is gathered at the direction and pursuant to the power and authority vested in the legal administrators who preside over The Church of Jesus Christ of Latter-day Saints. And it also means that the Ten Tribes—scattered, lost, unknown, and now in all the nations of the earth—these Ten Tribes, with their prophets, with their scriptures, in faith and desiring righteousness, shall return to blessed Canaan at the direction of these same legal administrators. The President of the Church is the only person on earth at any given time who does or can exercise these or any other priesthood keys in their eternal fulness. He will direct the return of the Ten Tribes. It will not come to pass in any other way.

Before we can envision what is involved in the final gathering of Israel and the return of her King to reign over the house of Jacob and over all men, we must learn (1) where the Ten Tribes now are, and why they are scattered in all nations; (2) the place to which they shall return, and the moving power that will sweep them into old Canaan again; (3) where the keys are vested that will direct such a worldwide movement, and how they came to be held by the President of the Church; and (4) when these lost tribes are appointed to journey back to the land of their fathers, meaning whether it is before or after the coming of Him in whose name they shall then worship the Father. We have set forth the answers to the first three of these matters and shall now turn our attention to the time of the return of the lost tribes of Israel.

The Ten Tribes—Their Millennial Return

We do not say that occasional blood descendants of Reuben or Naphtali or others of the other tribal heads shall not return to their Palestinian Zion, or assemble in an American Zion, or find their way into the stakes of Zion in all nations, all before the Second Coming of Christ. Some shall no doubt return to Canaan as true believers and members of the true Church, with the intent and purpose of fulfilling the scriptures and building up the ancient cities of Israel. This may well happen in some small measure, and to it there can be no objection. Great movements have small beginnings, and floods that sweep forth from bursting dams are first forecast when small rivulets trickle from the pent-up reservoirs. But we do say that the great day of the return of the Ten Tribes, the day when the assembling hosts shall fulfill the prophetic promises, shall come after our Lord's return. In this connection let us turn to the word of scripture.

We have had much to say relative to the teachings of the Risen Lord to the Nephites about the last days. In Third Nephi, chapter 20, he speaks of the millennial gathering of Israel. Then in chapter 21, he tells of the establishment of the United States of America; of the coming forth of the Nephite word in the Book of Mormon; of the restoration of his everlasting gospel; of the triumph of Israel over their Gentile foes when the Millennium is ushered in; and of the end of evil and wickedness in that glorious day of peace and righteousness. Then he speaks of the New Jerusalem in America; of the gathering of people to it before he comes; and of his coming to dwell in the midst of his people. "And then"—after the gathering of Israel to the New Jersualem—"shall the power of heaven come down among them." This refers to the Second Coming. "And I also will be in the midst." He shall reign personally upon the earth. "And then"—after his return and during the Millennium—"shall the work of the Father commence at that day, even when this gospel shall be preached among the remnant of this people." There is to be a millennial gathering of the Lehite people. "Verily I say unto you, at that day"—note it well, the day involved is millennial—"shall the work of the Father commence among all the dispersed of my people, yea, even the tribes which have been lost, which the Father hath led away out of Jerusalem." The Ten Tribes are to return after the Second Coming. Their establishment in their land of promise shall not come to pass until there is a new heaven and a new earth wherein dwelleth righteousness. They were led away in a day of war and wickedness; they shall return in a day of peace and righteousness.

"Yea," and it is in that day that "the work shall commence among all the dispersed of my people, with the Father, to prepare the way whereby they may come unto me, that they may call on the Father in my name." Our present endeavors offer the gospel to all those whom the hunters and fishers can find in the forests and streams of the world. In the coming day the word will go to "all the dispersed," and none shall escape hearing its word of peace and salvation.

"Yea, and then shall the work commence, with the Father, among all nations, in preparing the way whereby his people may be gathered home to the land of their inheritance." This is a specific gathering back to Palestine. "And they shall go out from all nations"—note that his people, including as he said the tribes which have been lost, who are the Ten Tribes, who have been scattered in all nations, shall go out therefrom—"and they shall not go out in haste, nor go by flight, for I will go before them, saith the Father, and I will be their rearward." (3 Ne. 21:1-29.)

Isaiah's Prophecy of Their Millennial Return

We shall now turn to two parallel passages, D&C 133:25-35 and Isaiah 35:1-10, and weave them together into one consecutive account. They both speak of the same events, and each one supplements and enlarges upon the concepts revealed in the other. Their united voice teaches and testifies of what is to be in the coming day when the Ten Tribes of Israel are led back to their ancient homeland.

"And the Lord, even the Savior, shall stand in the midst of his people, and shall reign over all flesh." So proclaims our modern revelation. The setting of what is to follow is thus millennial. Christ is among his people and is King over all the earth. It is the day of the new heaven and the new earth. Thus, of it, Isaiah says: "The wilderness and the solitary place shall be glad for them"—that is, for those who then dwell on earth and who shall possess it from generation to generation—"and the desert shall rejoice, and blossom as the rose. It shall blossom abundantly, and rejoice even with joy and singing: the glory of Lebanon shall be given unto it, the excellency of Carmel and Sharon, they shall see the glory of the Lord, and the excellency of our God." The whole earth shall be as the Garden of Eden, for the earth has been renewed and received its paradisiacal glory. And those who dwell on earth shall see the glory of God, for he shall dwell among them.

In that day, "They who are in the north countries shall come in remembrance before the Lord." The lost tribes of Israel, the Ten Tribes whose members are scattered among the northern nations, shall be remembered. The set time to favor them will have dawned. The work of the Father will then commence among them; converts will be made; they will believe the everlasting gospel taken to them by the elders of Ephraim; and they will be baptized and receive the gift of the Holy Ghost. They will become again the Lord's people. "And their prophets shall hear his voice, and shall no longer stay themselves."

Their prophets! Who are they? Are they to be holy men called from some unknown place and people? Are they prophets unbeknown to the presiding officers of "the only true and living church upon the face of the whole earth"? (D&C 1:30.) Perish the thought! The President of the Church, who holds the keys to lead the Ten Tribes from the nations of the north wherein they now reside, holds also the keys of salvation for all men. There are not two true churches on earth, only one; there are not two gospels or two plans of salvation, only one; there are not two competing organizations, both having divine approval, only one. "Is Christ divided?" (1 Cor. 1:13.) God forbid. Their prophets are members of The Church of Jesus Christ of Latter-day Saints. They are stake presidents and bishops and quorum presidents who are appointed to guide and direct the destinies of their stakes and wards and quorums.

The true Church is or should be made up of prophets without number. "Would God that all the Lord's people were prophets, and that the Lord would put his spirit upon them!" Moses exclaimed to ancient Israel. (Num. 11:29.) "Ye may all prophesy one by one, that all may learn, and all may be comforted," Paul said. Every man should be a prophet for his family and for those over whom he is called to preside in the Church and kingdom of God on earth. But there is to be no diversity of views, no differences of opinion, among the prophets. A prophet is a prophet only because he receives revelation from the Holy Ghost and is in tune with the Spirit of God. Anarchy is foreign to a heaven-sent organization. The Lord's house is a house of order and not a house of confusion. And so "the spirits of the prophets are subject to the prophets." (1 Cor. 14:29-32.)

There is only one presiding prophet on earth at any one time, and he is the President of the Church. All other prophets are subject to him and his direction. There is not now on earth and there shall not be—as long as the earth shall stand or there is one man on the face thereof—a prophet who is not subject to and whose acts are not governed by the presiding prophet. Who, then, shall the prophets be among the Ten Tribes? They shall be the worthy and faithful members of the great latter-day kingdom who serve as all faithful elders now serve. Thus saith the Lord: "It shall not be given to any one to go forth to preach my gospel, or to build up my church, except he be ordained by some one who has authority, and it is known to the church that he has authority and has been regularly ordained by the heads of the church." (D&C 42:11.)

"And they [their prophets] shall smite the rocks, and the ice shall flow down at their presence." Presumably, when our sphere becomes a new earth; when every valley is exalted and every mountain is made low; when the islands become one land, and the great deep is driven back into the north countries—when all these and other changes occur, then there will also be changes in the climate, and the ice masses of the polar areas will no longer be as they now are.

"And an highway shall be cast up in the midst of the great deep." The revelation to Joseph Smith says no more on this point than these words convey. Isaiah gives a somewhat more expansive view in these words: "And an highway shall be there, and a way, and it shall be called The way of holiness; the unclean shall not pass over it; but it shall be for those [who are worthy, and]: the wayfaring men, though fools, shall not err therein. No lion shall be there, nor any ravenous beast shall go up thereon, it shall not be found there; but the redeemed shall walk there." It appears that a way will be provided to assemble the outcasts of Israel again in their promised land. The safe and secure physical arrangements, whatever they may be, will, in fact, be but symbolical of the way of holiness whereon only the righteous can find footing. The way of holiness cannot be other than the strait and narrow path. The wayward tribes, having forsaken the ancient holy way, having been scattered for their wickedness, shall now be gathered because they forsake the world and seek again that whereon the footprints of their fathers are found.

Our revelation says: "Their enemies shall become a prey unto them." Isaiah gives meaning to this assurance by saying: "Strengthen ye the weak hands, and confirm the feeble knees." The people themselves will need the assurance that God is with them and that they will be preserved. "Say to them that are of a fearful heart," the ancient prophet continues, "Be strong, fear not: behold, your God will come with vengeance, even God with a recompence; he will come and save you." Once forsaken, left alone, now they shall be enfolded in the arms of his love. And oh, what blessings await them! "Then the eyes of the blind shall be opened, and the ears of the deaf shall be unstopped. Then shall the lame man leap as an hart, and the tongue of the dumb sing." The miracles of the mortal ministry of the Holy One will be but a type and a shadow of those that shall attend the immortal ministry of the same Holy One.

Isaiah then says: "In the wilderness shall waters break out, and streams in the desert. And the parched ground shall become a pool, and the thirsty land springs of water: in the habitation of dragons, where each lay, shall be grass with reeds and rushes." We do not doubt that this is temporal, for the deserts of this old earth, in its fallen and barren state, shall become the gardens and flowering fields of the new earth in the millennial day. But it is also spiritual, for the latter-day revelation says: "And in the barren deserts there shall come forth pools of living water; and the parched ground shall no longer be a thirsty land." In that day all Israel shall drink from streams of living water, streams that flow direct from the great Fountain Head, streams filled with the words of eternal life of which men may drink and never thirst more.

The climax of Isaiah's prophetic utterances relative to the millennial return of the many tribes of Israel is: "And the ransomed of the Lord shall return, and come to Zion with songs and everlasting joy upon their heads: they shall obtain joy and gladness, and sorrow and sighing shall flee away." The latter-day word tells us: "They shall bring forth their rich treasures unto the children of Ephraim, my servants. And the boundaries of the everlasting hills shall tremble at their presence. And there shall they fall down and be crowned with glory, even in Zion, by the hands of the servants of the Lord, even the children of Ephraim." Thus they will assemble, not alone in their ancient lands—as a representative constituency, at least, must assemble—but in the latter-day Zion where the headquarters of Ephraim is found. And once again we learn that this glorious return is not of a people receiving independent revelation, not of a people with independent prophets, not of a people who are independent of the constituted authorities of the great latter-day kingdom that has already been set up on earth. Ephraim will be their head. They will come to Ephraim, at the direction of Ephraim, and they will receive the blessings of the house of the Lord that are now administered by those of us who are of Ephraim. Indeed, they will come because they believe what is written in the Stick of Ephraim, which is the Book of Mormon.

"And they shall be filled with songs of everlasting joy. Behold, this is the blessing of the everlasting God upon the tribes of Israel, and the richer blessing upon the head of Ephraim and his fellows. And they also of the tribe of Judah, after their pain shall be sanctified in holiness before the Lord, to dwell in his presence day and night, forever and ever." (D&C 133:25-35; Isa. 35:1-10.) Thus the ancient kingdom of Ephraim with its Ten Tribes and the kingdom of Judah with the smaller portion of Israel shall once again become "one nation in the land upon the mountains of Israel; . . . and they shall be no more two nations, neither shall they be divided into two kingdoms any more at all: . . . so shall they be my people, and I will be their God." (Ezek. 37:22-23.)

JOSEPH SMITH AND THE SECOND COMING

Joseph Smith: The Seer of Latter Days

Think now of the concepts set forth so far in our study of the Second Coming of the Desire of All Nations. Think of that wondrous age of restoration in which the Great God has sent down righteousness from heaven and caused truth to spring out of the earth. Remember that once again God's eternal plan of salvation—it is the fulness of the everlasting gospel—is resident with mortal men. Name over in your mind the holy angels who have come from the courts of glory to give power and authority, priesthood and keys, knowledge and intelligence, to fallen man. Look around you and see the hosts of gathered Israel who have come out of Babylon into the latter-day kingdom of Him whom their fathers served.

Rejoice with the saints in the gifts and signs and miracles that are everywhere to be seen in the households of faith. Savor once again that sweet spirit which overshadowed you when you knelt at a holy altar in a sacred sanctuary built in the mountains of Israel. Weep again as you recall the blood of modern martyrs mingled with that of their ancient fellows to cry against the wicked and ungodly.

And as you ponder these verities and recall these scenes, as your feelings are mellowed and awed by the immensity and glory of it all, ask yourself: Who among men has brought all this to pass? To whom was the gospel restored, and to whom were the keys and powers committed? Where is the one for whom the heavens were rent, and who drank in the revealed word as the scorched earth absorbs the gentle rain? Can all these things take place without a living prophet?

Those with spiritual insight know the answer, an answer that comes to them by revelation from the Holy Spirit of God. The man involved is Joseph Smith. He is the mighty restorer, the head of the dispensation of the fulness of times, the seer of latter days. Truly, as it is written: "Joseph Smith, the Prophet and Seer of the Lord, has done more, save Jesus only, for the salvation of men in this world, than any other man that ever lived in it." (D&C 135:3.)

How and in what way did this modern Moses, this latter-day Abraham, this seer among seers, accomplish such a great work for so many of the sons of men? The mighty mission, given of God to our chief modern prophet, falls into two categories:

1. Joseph Smith was the revealer of the knowledge of Christ and of salvation to men on earth, the revealer who brought the ancient truths back again after a long night of spiritual darkness. Unless and until men know and believe the true religion, they cannot be saved. Truth is the rock foundation upon which all progress and ultimate salvation rest.

2. Joseph Smith was a legal administrator who received power and authority from heavenly visitants, by virtue of which he was authorized to preach the gospel and administer all of its ordinances so they would be binding on earth and sealed everlastingly in the heavens. Like Peter, he held the keys of the kingdom of heaven so that whatsoever he bound on earth would be bound in heaven, and whatsoever he loosed on earth would be loosed in heaven.

Viewed from the eternal perspective, Joseph Smith ranks among the dozen or score of the greatest and mightiest souls so far sent to earth. Christ is first, Adam second, and, in the priestly hierarchy, Noah is third. "Adam is the father of the human family, and presides over the spirits of all men," and Noah "stands next in authority to Adam in the Priesthood." (*Teachings*, p. 157.) We have no way of ranking Enoch and Moses and Abraham and the other dispensation heads; we can only say they all were among the noble and great in the councils of eternity, and that the Lord sent the greatest spirits he had to head his gospel dispensations. All of the other apostles and prophets in any dispensation are but echoes and shadows of the one who ushers in the Lord's work for that day and age. It is no wonder, then, that the saints of latter days have received this command from the Lord with reference to Joseph Smith: "Thou shalt give heed unto all his words and commandments which he shall give unto you as he receiveth them, walking in all holiness before me; For his word ye shall receive, as if from mine own mouth, in all patience and faith." (D&C 21:4-5.)

Every prophecy about any of the great and glorious events destined to take place in the dispensation of the fulness of times is in its nature a prophecy about Joseph Smith. If the gospel is to be restored, there must be a living prophet to receive the old yet new message. If Elijah is to come before the great and dreadful day of the Lord, there must be an appointed person to receive his message. If Israel is to be gathered, according to the ancient word, someone must be empowered to identify the chosen people, to name the places of gathering, and to specify when and under what circumstances the children of the prophets shall assemble.

One of the most expressive and pointed prophetic utterances relative to the one chosen to head the dispensation of the fulness of times comes to us from Joseph who was sold into Egypt. "A seer shall the Lord my God raise up, who shall be a choice seer unto the fruit of my loins," he testified. To Joseph of old, the Lord said: "A choice seer will I raise up out of the fruit of thy loins; and he shall be esteemed highly among the fruit of thy loins. And unto him will I give commandment that he shall do a work for the fruit of thy loins, his brethren, which shall be of great worth unto them, even to the bringing of them to the knowledge of the covenants which I have made with thy fathers." In expounding upon this promise, the son of Jacob said: "His name shall be called after me; and it shall be after the name of his father. And he shall be like unto me; for the thing, which the Lord shall bring forth by his hand, by the power of the Lord shall bring my people unto salvation." (2 Ne. 3:6-15.) Joseph Smith was foreordained in the councils of eternity to come to earth in the last days, to set up again on earth the true Church and the Lord's kingdom, and to prepare a people for the second coming of the Lord.

Joseph Smith: The Revelator Who Brings Salvation

Salvation is in Christ. There is no other by whom it comes. He is the Redeemer of men and the Savior of the world. He alone worked out the infinite and eternal atonement whereby all men are raised in immortality while those who believe and obey are raised also unto eternal life. "Salvation was, and is, and is to come, in and through the atoning blood of Christ, the Lord Omnipotent." None other has ever lived on earth, none other now lives among us, and none other will ever breathe the breath of life who can compare with him. None other, among all the billions of our Father's children, will ever deserve such eternal praise as all the hosts of heaven heap upon him. Yea, "There shall be no other name given nor any other way nor means whereby salvation can come unto the children of men, only in and through the name of Christ, the Lord Omnipotent." (Mosiah 3:17-18.)

But Christ and his laws can be known only by revelation. His gospel must come from heaven or remain forever unknown. And his word must go forth by the mouths of his servants the prophets, or the message will never be heard. Christ calls prophets. They represent him. Their voice is his voice; their words are his words; and they say what he would say if he were personally present. "I am the vine, ye are the branches," he says to his legal representatives on earth. "He that abideth in me, and I in him, the same bringeth forth much fruit: for without me ye can do nothing." (John 15:5.)

And thus, for this dispensation of grace, we come to Joseph Smith. He was called of God to reveal anew the doctrines of salvation. He was called of God to stand as the Lord's legal administrator, dispensing salvation to all men—repeat: *all men*—in the last days. Christ is the True Vine; Joseph Smith is the chief branch for our day. Moroni told him that his "name should be had for good and evil among all nations, kindreds, and tongues, or that it should be both good and evil spoken of among all people." (JS-H 1:33.)

And as the Prophet, years later, suffered in the jail at Liberty, Missouri, for the testimony of Jesus and the love of the Lord that was his, the voice of the Lord comforted him with these words: "The ends of the earth shall inquire after thy name, and fools shall have thee in derision, and hell shall rage against thee; While the pure in heart, and the wise, and the noble, and the virtuous, shall seek counsel, and authority, and blessings constantly from under thy hand." (D&C 122:1-2.)

And thus, all men—every living soul who has lived or shall live on earth between the spring of 1820 and that glorious future day when the Son of God shall return to reign personally on earth—all men in the latter days must turn to Joseph Smith to gain salvation. Why? The answer is clear and plain; let it be spoken with seven thunders. He alone can bring them the gospel; he alone can perform for them the ordinances of salvation and exaltation; he stands, as have all the prophets of all the ages in their times and seasons, in the place and stead of the Heavenly One in administering salvation to men on earth.

The Father is the author and originator of the gospel. It is his plan of salvation; he ordained and established its terms and conditions so that his spirit children, Christ included, might advance and progress and become like him. The Son is the Savior and Redeemer who, through his great atoning sacrifice, put all of the provisions of his Father's plan into full operation. It is the atonement of Christ that gives efficacy, virtue, and force to all things in the gospel. They are operative because the Holy Messiah took upon himself the sins of all men on condition of repentance and because he laid down his life to ransom men from eternal death. And it is the Lord's prophets who take the word of salvation to their fellowmen. It was to Joseph Smith that the Lord said: "This generation shall have my word through you." (D&C 5:10.) There is none other who will bring it. Joseph Smith is the man. It is the word of the Lord, but it comes by the mouth of his latter-day prophet.

Every person who is called of God to preach the gospel and build up his kingdom in the latter days is but an echo of Joseph Smith. The latter-day Twelve "are called to go unto all the world" and "to preach my gospel unto every creature," the Lord says.

(D&C 18:28.) What gospel? The everlasting gospel, the same gospel preached by Paul and Peter, the gospel that has been revealed anew to Joseph Smith. And by what power do they preach? By the power of the Holy Ghost and the Holy Priesthood, both of which powers have come to them from the head of our dispensation. Can they bind on earth and seal in heaven as did the ancient apostles? They can! Whence came their power to do so? From Joseph Smith, who received the keys of the kingdom from angelic ministrants. And what of all the elders of Israel and all the ministers of the kingdom? They all preach the same gospel and administer the same ordinances, and are endowed with the same power. To all his servants the Lord says: "You shall"—it is mandatory—"declare the things which have been revealed to my servant, Joseph Smith, Jun." (D&C 31:4.)

We do not pretend to have authority and gospel knowledge because we read in holy writ that those anciently were so endowed. Ours is a modern commission; ours is a present-day power; the message we declare has been revealed anew to us. That it conforms to the ancient word is apparent, for it is the same gospel given again. To all of us the Lord says: "Teach the principles of my gospel, which are in the Bible and the Book of Mormon, in the which is the fulness of the gospel." (D&C 42:12.) We are to "remember the new covenant, even the Book of Mormon." The divine decree to us is: "Remain steadfast in your minds in solemnity and the spirit of prayer, in bearing testimony to all the world of those things which are communicated unto you." (D&C 84:57, 61.) We are to go forth, to proclaim the gospel, and to prune the vineyard; we are not to tarry, but to labor with our might. The Lord tells us to lift up our voices as with the sound of a trump, "proclaiming the truth according to the revelations and commandments" he has given us. (D&C 75:2-4.)

Our message is a living, vibrant, modern message. We speak of the appearance of the Father and the Son to Joseph Smith in our day. We tell of Moroni and the Book of Mormon. We testify that holy angels came from the courts of glory and gave priesthoods and keys to mortals. We bear witness of the truth and divinity of the revelations given to Joseph Smith and his successors. We declare the things that have come to us. Of course, we believe what the ancients believed; of course, we enjoy the same gifts of the Spirit that enriched their lives; of course, we have the same hope of eternal life that filled their souls. Their doctrine is our doctrine. The Bible as well as the Book of Mormon is true: both are the mind and will and voice of the Lord; both are accounts of a people who had the fulness of the gospel. But our commission, our authority, our message for mankind has come to us by the opening of the heavens. And Joseph Smith is the mighty prophet through whom it came.

Joseph Smith: The Messenger Before His Face

Our Blessed Lord did not come unannounced when he made flesh his tabernacle and dwelt as a man among men. Neither will he conceal the day of preparation for his resplendent second coming. He will announce his imminent return. Those with ears to hear will know he is soon to come, clothed in glorious immortality, to rule and reign among the sons of men. John the Baptist, of blessed memory, was his forerunner in the meridian of time. Joseph Smith, the prophet and seer of latter days, whose innocent blood was mingled with that of the Blessed Baptist, is his forerunner in the fulness of times.

There are two great prophecies about the messengers who shall prepare the way before the face of the Lord. One is by Isaiah, the other comes from Malachi. Each of them refers both to the meridian and to the millennial advents, but more especially to the latter. By the mouth of Malachi the Lord said: "Behold, I will send my messenger, and he shall prepare the way before me: and the Lord, whom ye seek, shall suddenly come to his temple, even the messenger of the covenant, whom ye delight in: behold, he shall come, saith the Lord of hosts." (Mal. 3:1.) What follows speaks solely and exclusively of the Second Coming and the day of judgment and burning that will accompany it.

Through Isaiah the Lord speaks of comfort to Jerusalem that shall be fulfilled after the Second Coming. In that setting (as the full and amplified account is quoted in Luke) Isaiah's prophetic words say: "The voice of one crying in the wilderness, Prepare ye the way of the Lord, and make his paths straight. For behold, and lo, he shall come, as it is written in the book of the prophets, to take away the sins of the world, and to bring salvation unto the heathen nations, to gather together those who are lost, who are of the sheepfold of Israel; Yea, even the dispersed and afflicted; and also to prepare the way, and make possible the preaching of the gospel unto the Gentiles; And to be a light unto all who sit in darkness, unto the uttermost parts of the earth; to bring to pass the resurrection from the dead, and to ascend up on high, to dwell on the right hand of the Father, Until the fullness of time, and the law and the testimony shall be sealed, and the keys of the kingdom shall be delivered up again unto the Father; To administer justice unto all; to come down in judgment upon all, and to convince all the ungodly of their ungodly deeds, which they have committed; and all this in the day that he shall come; For it is a day of power; yea, every valley shall be filled, and every mountain and hill shall be brought low; the crooked shall be made straight, and the rough ways made smooth; And all flesh shall see the salvation of God." (JST, Luke 3:4-11.) The next words in the Isaiah account add: "And the glory of the Lord shall be revealed, and all flesh shall see it together: for the mouth of the Lord hath spoken it." (Isa. 40:1-5.)

These two prophetic pronouncements are applied to John the Baptist by the New Testament writers, and truly he came to prepare the way for our Lord's mortal ministry. But each of the inspired accounts has an infinitely greater and grander fulfillment in the last days. John came to prepare the way for the atoning ministry, the ministry of reconciliation, as Paul calls it, the ministry that brought life and immortality to light through the gospel. Joseph Smith came to prepare the way for the triumphal coming, the coming in power and glory with all the hosts of heaven, the coming when the vineyard will be burned and the wicked destroyed, the coming when righteousness and peace shall be established among those who abide the day.

How do messengers prepare the way before the Lord? First, they identify Him whose forerunners they are; they testify of his divine Sonship; they introduce him to the world—all with a view to persuading men to come unto him and be saved. Second, and equally important, they prepare a people to receive him. They qualify a people to abide the day of his coming, to see his face when he arrives, to enjoy his presence, and to dwell with him and enjoy the gifts and graces that are his.

And how is a people prepared to meet their God? What must they do to stand in his presence and hear the blessed word: "Well done, thou good and faithful servant; enter into the joy of thy Lord"? To be so blessed, they must receive the message of the messenger. They must believe in that Lord who sent him. They must accept the gospel and live its laws. They must forsake the world, repent of all their sins, be baptized, and receive the gift of the Holy Ghost. They must become pure in heart, for all the pure in heart shall see God. They must (in our day) join The Church of Jesus Christ of Latter-day Saints and become the saints of the Most High.

There are none in our day to whom the Lord has given the power of language to set forth the goodness and grace of Christ, or the beauty and holiness of his everlasting gospel, or the mighty strength and spiritual stature of the latter-day prophet sent to prepare the way before the Lord. Perhaps these things can be known in full only by the power of the Spirit.

But this we know: The Lord sends men to match the message, and Joseph Smith, as a revealer of Christ and a restorer of eternal truth, has been the instrument in the hands of the Lord of preparing the way before him. Thus, from that Lord who shall soon come, we hear this word: "I have sent mine everlasting covenant into the world, to be a light to the world, and to be a standard for my people, and for the Gentiles to seek to it, and to be a messenger before my face to prepare the way before me." (D&C 45:9.)

The everlasting covenant is the latter-day messenger before the Lord. It is the ancient standard raised anew. It is an ensign upon Mount Zion around which the honest in heart from all nations may rally. The everlasting gospel itself is the messenger. And whereas the gospel came through Joseph Smith, he becomes and is the messenger. He it is who raised the Lord's standard; he it is who raised the ensign to the nations; he it is who waved the banner of truth and righteousness in the sight of all men—all as promised in the ancient word.

What says the ancient word on these points? It says that the Great Jehovah will make an everlasting covenant with his people when he comes to reign gloriously among them. "I will make a new covenant with the house of Israel, and with the house of Judah," saith the Lord. It shall be made with both kingdoms, with all Israel, with the Jews and the Ten Tribes. And "this shall be the covenant that I will make," saith the Lord, "I will put my law in their inward parts, and write it in their hearts; and will be their God, and they shall be my people." (Jer. 31:31-33.) "Behold, I will gather them out of all countries, whither I have driven them in mine anger, and in my fury, and in great wrath; and I will bring them again unto this place, and I will cause them to dwell safely: And they shall be my people, and I will be their God: And I will give them one heart, and one way, that they may fear me for ever, for the good of them, and of their children after them: And I will make an everlasting covenant with them." (Jer. 32:37-40.) "I will bring you into the bond of the covenant." (Ezek. 20:37.) The new covenant, the everlasting covenant, the new and everlasting covenant is the fulness of the everlasting gospel. It is to this that the Lord's people will come in the last days.

"My people are gone into captivity, because they have no knowledge," saith the Lord. Yet they shall return. For "he will lift up an ensign to the nations from far, and will hiss unto them from the end of the earth: and, behold, they shall come with speed swiftly." (Isa. 5:13, 26-30.) Israel shall gather again to the gospel covenant. "And in that day there shall be a root of Jesse, which shall stand for an ensign of the people; to it shall the Gentiles seek: and his rest shall be glorious [or, better, glory shall be his resting place]." (Isa. 11:10.) "What is the root of Jesse spoken of in the 10th verse of the 11th chapter? Behold, thus saith the Lord, it is a descendant of Jesse, as well as of Joseph, unto whom rightly belongs the priesthood, and the keys of the kingdom, for an ensign, and for the gathering of my people in the last days."

Are we amiss in saying that the prophet here mentioned is Joseph Smith, to whom the priesthood came, who received the keys of the kingdom, and who raised the ensign for the gathering of the Lord's people in our dispensation? And is he not also the "servant in the hands of Christ, who is partly a descendant of Jesse as well as of Ephraim, or of the house of Joseph, on whom there is laid much power"? (D&C 113:4-6.) Those whose ears are attuned to the whisperings of the Infinite will know the meaning of these things.

Truly, "the Lord shall set his hand again the second time"—he set it the first time when he led Israel out of Egypt, and also when he brought back a few scattered ones from Babylon—"to recover the remnant of his people," who are in all the nations of the earth and upon "the islands of the sea. And he shall set up an ensign for the nations, and shall assemble the outcasts of Israel, and gather together the dispersed of Judah from the four corners of the earth." (Isa. 11:11-12.) Israel (the Ten Tribes) and Judah (the kingdom of Judah, whose descendants are known as Jews) are now in all the earth, but shall soon return to the lands of their inheritance, as we have already set forth.

How glorious it is to know that there shall be a literal gathering of Israel—all Israel—as the Lord has appointed! Can we not feel the exulting joy and sense of triumph in Isaiah's repeated words about that gathering? Is it not satisfying to know that it is going forward and shall continue to go forward by virtue of the keys given by Moses to Joseph Smith? "All ye inhabitants of the world, and dwellers on the earth, see ye, when he lifteth up an ensign on the mountains; and when he bloweth a trumpet, hear ye." (Isa. 18:3.) That ensign now floats in the cooling breezes of a modern Zion, and that trumpet is now sounding forth the gladsome tidings of glory and salvation to all men.

"Thus saith the Lord God, Behold, I will lift up mine hand to the Gentiles, and set up my standard to the people." (Isa. 49:22.) "I will make an everlasting covenant with them." (Isa. 61:8.) And those of us with whom this covenant has been made have this word from the Lord: "Lift up a standard for the people. Behold, the Lord hath proclaimed unto the end of the world, Say ye to the daughter of Zion, Behold, thy salvation cometh; behold, his reward is with him, and his work before him." Christ the Lord cometh. "And they shall call them, The holy people, The redeemed of the Lord: and thou shalt be called, Sought out, A city not forsaken." (Isa. 62:10-12.) "For thus shall my church be called in the last days, even The Church of Jesus Christ of Latter-day Saints. Verily I say unto you all: Arise and shine forth, that thy light may be a standard for the nations; And that the gathering together upon the land of Zion, and upon her stakes, may be for a defense, and for a refuge from the storm, and from wrath when it shall be poured out without mixture upon the whole earth." (D&C 115:4-6.)

Thank God for the gospel. Thank the Lord for Joseph Smith and the great restoration of eternal truth in our day. Jehovah be praised that his messenger has delivered his message.

Chapter 29

THE PARABLES OF THE SECOND COMING

The Three Great Parables of His Coming

Our Blessed Lord, who spake as none other ever has spoken or shall speak, included in his parables numerous allusions to and pronouncements about his Second Coming. Our present purpose is to extract from these gems of literary excellence the teachings they set forth relative to that great and coming day. The parables involved teach many lessons. Our arrangement of the subject matter is simply to help us put in a proper perspective all things concerning the coming of Him whose parables they are. First, then, we shall consider what are probably the three greatest parables pertaining to the Second Coming.

1. *The Parable of the Wheat and the Tares*

The Lord Jesus, and his holy apostles, and the legal administrators whom they call—all these sow good seeds in all the world. The good seeds are the children of the kingdom, the true saints, those who are faithful and true. They are the wheat. This sowing took place first in the meridian of time and then again "in the last days, even now," when "the Lord is beginning to bring forth the word" anew. (D&C 86:4.)

Lucifer and his ministers oversow the field. Their seeds are the children of the wicked one, the children of disobedience, those who live after the manner of the world. They are the tares. And the tares seek to smother the wheat, lest any should ripen and be harvested and find place in the barns of the householder, for the enemy seeks to destroy the souls of men.

He whose vineyard it is decrees that the tares shall not be rooted up lest the wheat also be destroyed. They are to grow together until the day of harvest. Then the reapers shall gather the wheat unto salvation, the tares shall be bound in bundles, and the field shall be burned. (Matt. 13:24-43; D&C 86:1-11.) And even now, for the day of His coming is at hand, "the angels are waiting the great command to reap down the earth, [and] to gather the tares that they may be burned." (D&C 38:12.)

2. *The Parable of the Ten Virgins.*

In the last days, before the Son of Man comes, his church is likened unto ten virgins, all of whom have accepted the gospel invitation to attend the marriage feast of the Lamb. But the bridegroom delays his coming; the hour for the marriage is uncertain; it is late and darkness covers the earth. Surely he will not come at such an unseemly hour.

Five of the virgins are wise and have taken the Holy Spirit for their guide; their lamps are lighted and they await the coming of Him whose feast it is. But five are foolish; they do not put first in their lives the things of their Lord; other interests consume their attention. Their lamps are without oil, for they have not made the Holy Ghost their constant companion.

At midnight the cry goes forth: "Behold, the bridegroom cometh; go ye out to meet him." While the foolish virgins seek to make themselves worthy—for salvation is a personal matter, and no man can claim the good works of another—the wise virgins enter into eternal reward and the door is shut. And so the Lord counsels his people: "Watch therefore, for ye know neither the day nor the hour wherein the Son of man cometh." (Matt. 25:1-13.)

"At that day, when I shall come in my glory," the Lord

says, "shall the parable be fulfilled which I spake concerning the ten virgins. For they that are wise and have received the truth, and have taken the Holy Spirit for their guide, and have not been deceived—verily I say unto you, they shall not be hewn down and cast into the fire, but shall abide the day." (D&C 45:56-57.) "And until that hour there will be foolish virgins among the wise; and at that hour cometh an entire separation of the righteous and the wicked." (D&C 63:54.) Therefore, "let the cry go forth among all people: Awake and arise and go forth to meet the Bridegroom; behold and lo, the Bridegroom cometh; go ye out to meet him. Prepare yourselves for the great day of the Lord. Watch, therefore, for ye know neither the day nor the hour." (D&C 133:10-11.)

3. *The Parable of the Fig Tree.*

When men see the tender leaves of the fig tree begin to shoot forth, they know that summer is near. In like manner, when the elect see the signs of the times, they know that the Lord's coming "is near, even at the doors." (Matt. 24:32-33.) We live in the day when the signs are coming to pass. This is the day when "the poor and the meek shall have the gospel preached unto them, and they shall be looking forth for the time of my coming," the Lord says, "for it is nigh at hand—And they shall learn the parable of the fig-tree, for even now already summer is nigh." (D&C 35:15-16.) "And it shall come to pass that he that feareth me shall be looking forth for the great day of the Lord to come, even for the signs of the coming of the Son of Man." (D&C 45:39.)

The Parables of Judgment and Vengeance

The Second Coming is a day of judgment, a day of vengeance, a day of burning. "I will come near to you to judgment," is the Messianic promise. (Mal. 3:5.) In that day the wicked shall be destroyed; the righteous shall find eternal peace; and the Great Judge of all the earth shall measure to every man as his works merit. And so we find

Jesus speaking parables that will cause men to ponder these truths, parables that will encourage them to do good and work righteousness so they will be numbered with the true saints in that dread day.

1. *The Parable of the Gospel Net.*

The Church and kingdom of God on earth, which both preaches and administers the holy gospel, is like a great draw net or seine that sweeps through large areas of the sea. Fish of every kind are caught. The good are gathered into vessels and the bad are cast away. And thus it shall be when the Lord Jesus returns in glory to judge and rule. The wicked—though caught in the gospel net, though in the Church, though gathered with the Israel of God—shall be severed from among the just and shall be cast "into the furnace of fire." (Matt. 13:47-53.) Church membership alone is no guarantee of salvation. Only the God-fearing and the righteous shall sit down in the kingdom of God with Abraham, Isaac, and Jacob, and all the holy prophets.

2. *The Parable of the Wicked Husbandmen.*

The Divine Householder plants his earthly vineyard and lets it out to husbandmen. In due season he sends his servants to receive the fruits. They are rejected, beaten, stoned, and slain. Last of all he sends his Son, whom the wicked husbandmen slay—all of which brings forth the promise that the wicked husbandmen will be destroyed and the vineyard let out to other husbandmen who will bring forth fruits in due season. At this point Jesus said: "Did ye never read in the scriptures, The stone which the builders rejected, the same is become the head of the corner: this is the Lord's doing, and it is marvellous in our eyes? . . . And whosoever shall fall on this stone shall be broken: but on whomsoever it shall fall, it will grind him to powder." (Matt. 21:33-46.)

To his disciples, by way of interpretation, Jesus said: "I am the stone, and those wicked ones reject me, and shall be broken. And the kingdom of God shall be taken from them, and shall be given to a nation bringing forth the fruits thereof; (meaning the Gentiles.) Wherefore, on whomsoever this stone shall fall, it shall grind him to powder. And when the Lord therefore of the vineyard cometh, he will destroy those miserable, wicked men, and will let again his vineyard unto other husbandmen, even in the last days, who shall render him the fruits in their seasons. And then understood they the parable which he spake unto them, that the Gentiles should be destroyed also, when the Lord should descend out of heaven to reign in his vineyard, which is the earth and the inhabitants thereof." (JST, Matt. 21:51-56.)

3. *The Parable of the Great Supper.*

According to Jewish tradition, the resurrection of the just, and the subsequent setting up of the kingdom of God, was to be ushered in by a great festival in which all of the chosen people would participate. Hence their saying: "Blessed is he that shall eat bread in the kingdom of God." As a response to this very statement, Jesus tells of a certain man who gives a great supper. The guests who are bidden excuse themselves for frivolous and foolish reasons. Thereupon the master of the house, being angry, turns away from the covenant people, to whom he first offered the good things of his gospel table. Now he invites the Gentiles, in their spiritually halt and lame and blind status, as well as the pagans and foreigners who live at a great distance—he invites all these to come and eat at his table. (Luke 14:12-24.)

And thus it is reaffirmed that the blessings of the gospel profit only those who feast upon the eternal word, and that the alien and the foreigner who feast on the good work of God shall be blessed when the Supper of the Great God is prepared to usher in his millennial reign. It is of that feast of good things that the elders of Israel are now inviting all men to partake.

4. *The Parable of the Marriage of the King's Son.*

A certain king (who is God) prepares a marriage for his son (who is Christ), Jesus says, thus confirming the Jewish tradition that the Messianic kingdom will be ushered in by a great feast in which God and his people will be united, symbolically, in marriage. The wedding is ready, but the invited guests do not come. They make light of the invitation and even slay the servants who bring them the word. Hence, other people (the Gentiles) are invited and the feast goes forward. But when one comes without a wedding garment (the robes of righteousness), the king says: "Bind him hand and foot, and take him away, and cast him into outer darkness; there shall be weeping and gnashing of teeth." (Matt. 22:1-14.)

And so it is, as the millennial day approaches, that the servants of the Lord go forth, inviting all men, Jew and Gentile alike, to come to "the supper of the Lamb," to "make ready for the Bridegroom," to come to "a feast of fat things," and "of wine on the lees well refined," to come to "a supper of the house of the Lord, well prepared, unto which all nations shall be invited." (D&C 58:6-11; 65:3.) And it shall yet come to pass that those who accept the invitation and come to the feast, but who do not wear the approved wedding garments and are not clothed in the robes of righteousness, shall be cast into outer darkness. In that day only the pure and the clean shall feast at the eternal table.

5. *The Parable of the Unjust Judge.*

A certain widow whose cause is just importunes for redress before an unjust judge. He cares nothing for right and justice but grants her petition lest she weary him with her continuing pleas. Thus Jesus teaches that "men ought always to pray, and not to faint. . . . And shall not God avenge his own elect, which cry day and night unto him, though he bear long with them? I tell you that he will come, and when he does come, he will avenge his saints speedily." (Luke 18:1-8; JST, Luke 18:8.)

However the saints are treated in this life, whatever burdens are strapped to their aching backs, whatever wrongs are inflicted upon them by evil men—all will be made right in the coming day of judgment. Let them importune for redress of grievances, here and now. If their pleas go unheeded by unjust men, yet the Great Judge shall render a right decision in his own due time.

It was this very parable that that Judge used to teach his Latter-day Saints to importune at the feet of judges, governors, and presidents for the righting of many wrongs. If these pleas went unheeded—and they did—he promised to "arise and come forth out of his hiding place, and in his fury vex the nation"—which he did, in part at least, in the Civil War—"And in his hot displeasure, and in his fierce anger, in his time, [he] will cut off those wicked, unfaithful, and unjust stewards, and appoint them their portion among hypocrites, and unbelievers; Even in outer darkness, where there is weeping, and wailing, and gnashing of teeth." (D&C 101:81-92.) What an awful burden rests upon governmental officers to enact, administer, and interpret laws—all in harmony with the mind and will of the Eternal Judge.

The Parables of Ministerial Service

If those who bear rule in earthly governments shall give account of their man-delegated stewardships before the Eternal Bar, how much more so shall it be with those stewards who bear rule in the earthly kingdom of him who is Eternal. Shall they not give an account before the Eternal One relative to their heaven-delegated stewardships? Three of the parables bear a solemn witness in this respect.

1. *The Parable of the Laborers in the Vineyard.*

Laborers are called to serve in the vineyards of the Lord—some as the sun rises, others as late as the eleventh hour, when there remains but little daylight. Their promised pay is a penny for the day, and yet each is paid the same. Those who bear the heat and burden of the day receive no more than the new converts who come into the kingdom during their latter years. (Matt. 20:1-16.)

There is no mercenary calculation of payment scales in

the celestial realms. The venerable apostle and the lowly elder each receives all that the Father hath if he magnifies his calling in the Holy Order. The seed of Cain, from whom the blessings of the priesthood and the fulness of the ordinances of the house of the Lord have been withheld for nearly six thousand years, shall now, in the eleventh hour, be paid their penny and enter into the fulness of reward hereafter. In the providences of the Lord, none of his ministers shall receive less than is promised, and none need feel that others of seemingly lesser service have been overpaid. There is no jealousy among those who abide the day of his coming and who sit down with him in his kingdom. "And he makes them equal in power, and in might, and in dominion." (D&C 76:95.)

2. *The Parable of the Pounds.*

A certain nobleman (Christ) goes into a far country (his heavenly home) to receive for himself a kingdom (all power in heaven and on earth) and then to return (the second coming of the Son of Man). He leaves his servants (the apostles and others) to care for his affairs. To each of his ministers he gives a pound to use in his work. His citizens (the wicked and rebellious in general) hate him and send a message after him, saying, "We will not have this man to reign over us."

He returns; he calls his servants; he asks for an accounting. Those in whose hands his affairs were left make their reports. One has multiplied his pound into ten, another into five, and they are commended and given rule over ten and five cities respectively. Another returns only the pound he received. He made no profit; he saved no souls during his ministry. "I feared thee," he said, "because thou art an austere man: thou takest up that thou layedst not down, and reapest that thou didst not sow."

The nobleman sits in judgment upon his slothful servant, classifies him with the wicked, takes from him the original pound, and gives it to the one with ten pounds. The Lord's ministers are all endowed with the same blessings;

all have the gift of the Holy Ghost; all hold the Holy Melchizedek Priesthood; all are promised an inheritance of eternal life; all are to search the same scriptures and learn the same doctrines of salvation; all must live the same laws to be saved; all are commanded to bring souls to Christ. Those who do nothing damn themselves and lose their own salvation.

And what of those who sent a message deriding the claims of the Nobleman? "Those mine enemies, which would not that I should reign over them," he now decrees—it is the Second Coming, when the wicked shall be destroyed—"bring [them] hither, and slay them before me." (Luke 19:11-28.)

3. *The Parable of the Talents.*

Again, as the parabolic account recites, the Lord Jesus is going to travel to his heavenly home; this time the ministers who are left to govern his affairs are endowed with various talents, every man according to his several abilities, and after a long time the Lord is to return and have a reckoning with his servants. No two men are of like talent and ability; none are equal; all have a variety of capacities and aptitudes. And each is appointed to use all his powers in the service of the Master. Each is called to serve him with all his heart, might, mind, and strength. Nothing less will do. The gifts came from God, and they are to be used in his service.

When the Lord returns—it is his Second Coming—each servant who had many talents and who doubled them receives the blessed benediction: "Well done, thou good and faithful servant: thou hast been faithful over a few things, I will make thee ruler over many things: enter thou into the joy of thy lord." But the servant with little ability, who feared the Lord and hid his talent, is adjudged as wicked and slothful. His talent is taken from him and given to one with ten talents, and the Lord decrees: "Cast ye the unprofitable servant into outer darkness: there shall be weeping and gnashing of teeth." (Matt. 25:14-30.) Those who do not use their talents to save souls are damned.

The Parables of Hope

The Second Coming shall be a day of peace and joy and reward for the righteous. They look forward in hope to the day of their Lord's return. No greater joy can come to them than to see his face, dwell in his presence, and be as he is.

1. *The Eagles of Israel Assemble.*

Unto what shall the Lord liken the gathering of Israel in the last days? What figure shall he use to remind all men how and why and under what circumstances the lost and scattered ones will come to their appointed places?

He is seated with the Twelve on Olivet, unfolding before them the mysteries of the kingdom, the hidden things pertaining to his second coming and the triumph of his chosen Israel. "And now I show unto you a parable," he says. "Behold, wheresoever the carcass is, there will the eagles be gathered together; so likewise shall mine elect be gathered from the four quarters of the earth." (JS-M 1:27.)

The soaring, free eagles, the mightiest of the birds of the air, whose choice of domain knows no bounds, these free-spirited ones choose to come to the carcass. Such is our Lord's illustration, chosen with divine insight. It compares in graphic imagery with his sweet words about the lilies of the valley that neither toil nor spin, and yet are more grandly arrayed than even Solomon in all his glory, thus showing the living care of a gracious God over all created things. It is like his saying that the foxes have holes and the birds of the air have nests, but the Son of Man hath not where to lay his head, thus testifying that he had forsaken all worldly things that he might be about his Father's business. It is akin to his likening the full and white heads of barley, crying out for the reaper, to the souls of men, souls also ready to be harvested.

How often the Twelve, and all whose lives have been

blessed with the joys of a pastoral people, had seen the eagles assemble from all directions and descend from their aerial heights to satisfy their pangs of hunger by ripping the flesh from a sheep or a goat that was slain. In our American deserts we see the great vultures of the air seeking food for themselves and their young from the carcasses of animals that have died. In their hunger they fly in great soaring circles around dying and decrepit earthbound forms of life, awaiting the moment when the morsels of flesh shall be theirs.

And so we see the eagles of Israel scattered by the four winds from one end of heaven to the other. We see them flying in the skies of all nations in search of spiritual food, waiting for a day when life-assuring morsels will come into view. They are free, independent thinkers, anxious to escape the darkness of the night and to soar into the dawn of a new day. The creeds of men do not feed their souls. They are not at rest in the lands of their scattering. They yearn for that which their fathers enjoyed in the days of their ancient glory.

Then the food that will feed their souls is made available. The gospel is restored; the Book of Mormon comes forth; the gifts and graces enjoyed by the ancients are again found on earth. It is time for Israel to come home. The eagles are invited to feast upon the good word of God. They seek the food that satisfies the soul. They descend from their lofty heights of worldliness and feast upon those things of which men may eat and never hunger more. The gospel gathers Israel, and where it is, there the eagles of Israel shall be found.

2. *The Parable of Our Lord's Dwelling with His People.*

With reference to the various kingdoms of his creating, to the planets and worlds that roll in their orbits, inhabited as they are with the children of the Father, the Lord in our day has given us this parable:

"Behold, I will liken these kingdoms unto a man having

a field, and he sent forth his servants into the field to dig in the field.'' Thus they went forth to labor in all the kingdoms he had created, some on this earth, others on another. But none of his servants were to be forgotten, none were to be left alone without his guidance and direction. ''And he said unto the first: Go ye and labor in the field, and in the first hour I will come unto you, and ye shall behold the joy of my countenance. And he said unto the second: Go ye also into the field, and in the second hour I will visit you with the joy of my countenance. And also unto the third, saying: I will visit you; And unto the fourth, and so on unto the twelfth.'' There is order and system in all the Lord's doings. He visits in one part of his fields today and in another part tomorrow. All shall see his countenance in due course.

''And the lord of the field went unto the first in the first hour, and tarried with him all that hour, and he was made glad with the light of the countenance of his lord. And then he withdrew from the first that he might visit the second also, and the third, and the fourth, and so on unto the twelfth.'' Such is the course he is now pursuing with our millennial visitation almost at hand.

''And thus they all received the light of the countenance of their lord, every man in his hour, and in his time, and in his season—Beginning at the first, and so on unto the last, and from the last unto the first, and from the first unto the last; Every man in his own order, until his hour was finished, even according as his lord had commanded him, that his lord might be glorified in him, and he in his lord, that they all might be glorified.'' Those who dwell with their lord in the day he visits in their field shall be glorified. They are the meek who shall inherit the earth; they are the God-fearing and the righteous. And they in turn glorify their Lord, for they bring forth much fruit unto him.

''Therefore, unto this parable I will liken all these kingdoms,'' he says, ''and the inhabitants thereof—every kingdom in its hour, and in its time, and in its season, even according to the decree which God hath made.''

What, then, is the application of the parable? "I leave these sayings with you to ponder in your hearts," he says, "with this commandment which I give unto you, that ye shall call upon me while I am near." (D&C 88:51-62.) Truly, the time draws near and the day will soon arrive when he will visit us in our field, and if we are to find joy in his presence and glory in the light of his countenance, we must make ourselves worthy.

THE SIMILITUDES OF THE SECOND COMING

The Earth and Its Five Transformations

From the day of its temporal creation to the day when it becomes a celestial sphere, planet earth has passed or will pass through five transformations. Each of these is or will be of such a magnitude as to change the whole course of the lives of all or of major portions of the inhabitants of the earth. As the future home of mortal man, this earth was created first spiritually and then temporally. In the pristine day, before the fall, before death entered the scheme of things, the earth was in a paradisiacal or Edenic state. It was then a glorious garden and a fit abode for Adam and Eve, whose bodies of flesh and bones had been made from the dust of the earth, even as ours have been.

In order for our first parents—the first man and the first woman—to have children, however, a change had to be made in their bodies. It was decreed that they fall from their then deathless state to a state of mortality; death itself must enter the world. Procreation must needs commence among all created things, and procreation, in the sense of mortal offspring who are born and die, requires mortal bodies. The life of the body is in the blood, and blood must begin to flow in the veins of man and beast.

Being thus reminded of the nature of this earth when it was first brought into temporal existence, and being thus reminded of the immortal existence that then prevailed among all the creations of our gracious God, we are in a position to list the five transformations that have since befallen the earth. We are ready to be made aware of the effect each one has had or will have upon man and all forms of life.

1. This earth was created in a terrestrial state, an Edenic state, a paradisiacal state. It was pronounced very good by its Creator. All of the land masses were in one place and the waters in another. There was no death or sorrow or disease. Then came the fall of Adam, which brought temporal and spiritual death into the world. And the effects of the fall passed upon the earth and all forms of life on its surface. It became a telestial or fallen orb as at present, a world in which death and disease, sorrow and suffering, and all of the ills of the flesh are everywhere to be found. Adam and Eve, earth's sole human inhabitants, became mortal so they could begin the process of providing bodies for the spirit children of the Eternal Father.

2. In the days of Noah came the flood, a universal flood, a flood that immersed the earth and destroyed men and beasts. We suppose that at this time the continents and islands were divided, with the division becoming complete in the days of Peleg.

3. At the time of the crucifixion there was a great earthquake. In the Americas this was of such immeasurable proportions that the whole surface of the continents was changed. Mountain ranges arose, valleys disappeared, cities sank into the sea, and almost a whole civilization was destroyed.

4. When the Millennium is ushered in, there will be a new heaven and a new earth. It will be renewed and will receive again its paradisiacal glory. The islands and continents will come together again, and there will be one land mass, as it was in the days before it was divided. It will become again a terrestrial sphere. As it was baptized in water in the days of Noah, so it shall be baptized by fire in

the day of the Lord Jesus Christ. The entire vineyard will be burned and the wicked will be as stubble.

5. Finally, when all things relative to the salvation of men are completed, it will become a celestial sphere, to be inhabited by saved beings to all eternity.

We are approaching the day of burning when the promised new heaven and new earth will be created. And as we shall now see, the transformation in the days of Noah, and all that attended it, is a similitude and type of that which is to be in the day of burning that is soon to be.

Noah and the Second Coming

"The Son of Man shall come," Jesus said. "But of that day, and hour, no one knoweth; no, not the angels of God in heaven, but my Father only." Then he gave one of the great signs whereby the general time of his return might be known. "But as it was in the days of Noah, so it shall be also at the coming of the Son of Man," he continued, "For it shall be with them, as it was in the days which were before the flood; for until the day that Noah entered into the ark they were eating and drinking, marrying and giving in marriage; and knew not until the flood came, and took them all away; so shall also the coming of the Son of Man be." (JS-M 1:37-43.)

This similitude lets us know that the normal activities of life will continue unabated until the day of cleansing comes, and also that these ordinary activities will be as evil and wicked as they were in that day when men were drowned by the flood lest their evil deeds further offend their Maker.

Wickedness and evil commenced in the days of Adam; it spread and increased until, by the time of the flood, it covered the earth and contaminated every living soul save Noah and his family. When Adam preached the gospel to his seed, Satan came among them and taught false doctrines, "and they loved Satan more than God. And men began from that time forth to be carnal, sensual, and devilish." (Moses 5:13.) As it was then, so it is today. Satan rages in the hearts of men, and wickedness and carnality are almost the norm of life.

As the number of men increased, their evil deeds grew in magnitude. In the days of Seth, "the children of men were numerous upon all the face of the land. And in those days Satan had great dominion among men, and raged in their hearts; and from thenceforth came wars and bloodshed; and a man's hand was against his own brother, in administering death, because of secret works, seeking for power." (Moses 6:15.) And so it is today. The power of Satan is everywhere. "Signs and lying wonders" are poured forth on every hand. (2 Thes. 2:9-12.) Men give heed "to seducing spirits, and doctrines of devils." They speak "lies in hypocrisy; having their conscience seared with a hot iron." (1 Tim. 4:1-2.) War and bloodshed are now a way of life. We expect them; they are the norm.

In the day of these evils, Enoch was sent forth to cry repentance, even as the Lord's servants go forth today. "I am angry with this people," the Lord said, "and my fierce anger is kindled against them; for their hearts have waxed hard, and their ears are dull of hearing, and their eyes cannot see afar off." How like this is the generality of mankind today. "And for these many generations, ever since the day that I created them, have they gone astray, and have denied me, and have sought their own counsels in the dark; and in their own abominations have they devised murder, and have not kept the commandments, which I gave unto their father, Adam." And as Enoch cried repentance and said, "Choose ye this day, to serve the Lord God who made you" (Moses 6:27-33), so we go forth crying, "Repent ye, for the great day of the Lord is come" (D&C 43:22).

And so wickedness spread and iniquity prevailed until the Lord said to Enoch, "They are without affection, and they hate their own blood." And also: "There has not been so great wickedness as among thy brethren," no, not in all the worlds of the Lord's creating. Therefore, saith the Lord, "will I send in the floods upon them, for my fierce anger is kindled against them. . . . Satan shall be their father, and misery shall be their doom; and the whole heavens shall weep over them."

As Enoch felt the weight and the terror of all this evil, he pled for the seed of Noah. "I ask thee, O Lord, in the name of thine Only Begotten, even Jesus Christ," he prayed, "that thou wilt have mercy upon Noah and his seed, that the earth might never more be covered by the floods." Then the Lord covenanted with Enoch that he would stay the floods, and that a remnant of Noah's seed "should always be found among all nations, while the earth should stand."

With continuing pleas, Enoch asked: "When shall the earth rest? . . . Wilt thou not come again [a second time] upon the earth?" The divine reply: "As I live, even so will I come in the last days, in the days of wickedness and vengeance, to fulfill the oath which I have made unto you concerning the children of Noah; And the day shall come that the earth shall rest." (Moses 7:33-61.)

From Adam to Noah, like rolling crashes of thunder, each louder than the one before, evil and carnality and wickedness increased until "every man was lifted up in the imagination of the thoughts of his heart, being only evil continually." In that day, "The earth was corrupt before God, and it was filled with violence. And God looked upon the earth, and, behold, it was corrupt, for all flesh had corrupted its way upon the earth. And God said unto Noah: The end of all flesh is come before me, for the earth is filled with violence, and behold I will destroy all flesh from off the earth." (Moses 8:22-30.)

In like manner, from the days of martyrdom and death when Rome slew the saints and sent the faithful followers of the lowly Nazarene into the gladiatorial arenas, from then until now, and from now until Armageddon, the roaring thunders of evil and the piercing lightnings of iniquity have been and are and will increase. In consequence, at the appointed time the Lord will burn the wicked with unquenchable fire. It will be a day of burning and desolation and death. As the earth was cleansed once by water, so it shall be cleansed a second time by fire.

What was it in Noah's day that caused such an outpouring of evil to cover the earth? Note it and note it well: it was their marriage discipline, their disregard of proper family relations, their gluttony and their drunkenness—all of which led to wars and carnality and corruption. When Noah cried repentance to the people, they said: "Behold, we are the sons of God"—they claimed for themselves the blessings of true religion, though they lived after the manner of the world—"have we not taken unto ourselves the daughters of men?" Men were marrying out of the Church because they preferred a lewd and lascivious way of life rather than the one decreed in proper matrimony. "And are we not eating and drinking, and marrying and giving in marriage?" Theirs was a life of gluttony and drunkenness. "And our wives bear unto us children, and the same are mighty men, which are like unto men of old, men of great renown." (Moses 8:21.)

Is it any different today? Never in the entire history of the world has there ever been such an assault on the family unit as there is now. In some nations women work and the state rears their children. Under the cloak of supposed equal rights, college dormitories and athletic shower rooms are opened to male and female students alike. Women are handed rifles and taught the ways of war, and they are employed alongside men in drudgery and labor that destroys feminine sensitivities. Male homosexuals marry each other. Millions of couples live together in sin. Death-dealing abortions have legal approval. Courses given in public schools encourage and approve immoral practices. Prostitution is legal in some jurisdictions. All this and all else prevailing in our social structure make us wonder how much worse things must become before the burning fires of destruction shall cover the earth.

Truly, "by the word of God," the earth in Noah's day was "overflowed with water," and its inhabitants "perished." And so, "the heavens and the earth, which are now, by the same word are kept in store, reserved unto fire against the day of judgment and perdition of ungodly men." (2 Pet. 3:5-7.) So says the holy word, and so shall it be.

Shadows, Similitudes, and Types of His Coming

Israel's prophets used the current events with which the people were familiar to teach great truths relative to the Second Coming. Their wars and calamities were pointed to as types and shadows of what would be in that great day. The brutality and bloodshed and carnage that wrought havoc in Israel became a similitude of the greater warfare and destructions destined to overrun the earth in the last days. To the extent that we have prophetic insight as to what will transpire when our Lord returns, we can do the same thing with reference to the wars and plagues of our day. Such similitudes as the following are worthy of note:

1. *The Destruction of Sodom and Gomorrah.*

It was Jesus himself, after using the similitude about Noah and the Second Coming, who said: "Likewise also as it was in the days of Lot; they did eat, they drank, they bought, they sold, they planted, they builded; But the same day that Lot went out of Sodom it rained fire and brimstone from heaven, and destroyed them all. Even thus shall it be in the day when the Son of man is revealed. . . . Remember Lot's wife." (Luke 17:28-32.)

In Sodom and Gomorrah there was such lewdness and immorality and perversion and wickedness and evil as is seldom found on earth. All the people were as those who lived in the days of Noah, and all deserved the same fate. When Lot and his loved ones left Sodom, all who remained were carnal, sensual, and devilish; all were ripened in iniquity; all were ready for the burning. Among them there was not the slightest intimation of the destructions that lay ahead. As they continued the normal activities of life reveling in their evil ways, of a sudden, coming as it were from the midst of eternity, fire and brimstone destroyed them and their cities. As for Lot's wife, she looked back; that is, she turned again to the things of the world, and she too was destroyed with the wicked. So also shall it be at the end of the world.

Even now the generality of men love Satan more than God; even now sodomic practices—immorality, homosexuality, and all manner of perversions—are found among great segments of our society; even now the righteous are leaving the world and finding place in the stakes of Zion. And as the residue of men go forward in their normal activities, reveling in their wickedness as did they of old, the day of burning, coming, as it were, from the midst of eternity, shall come upon them. And should any of the saints look back as did Lot's wife, they will be burned with the wicked.

2. *Assyria, the Enemy of Israel.*

What better similitude could Isaiah choose, to show the destructions incident to the last days, than to point to the warlike ways of the neighboring kingdom of Assyria? Assyria was the great world power that invaded the land of Israel and carried the Ten Tribes into captivity and bondage. The slaughter and sorrow, the death and destruction, and the evil religious influences of the Assyrian invasion can scarcely be overstated. When a whole nation is transported to another area of the earth, it is, for them, a day of gloominess and dark despair. When the invasion is, in fact, a holy war against Jehovah and his people; when it is directed by an Assyrian king who acts as regent on earth for the national god Ashur; when the false religion of the pagans overthrows the true kingdom of Jehovah—when these things happen, surely the Lord must come out of his hiding place and fight the battles of his people. And such is the message Isaiah delivers.

Though earth and hell combine to fight against the true believers who have the true gospel; though there is apostasy and darkness and the saints are carried away to a spiritual Assyria; though the cause of Satan triumphs for a season—surely the Lord will come again in the last days to save his people and destroy their enemies. Such is the similitude with which we are dealing.

"And what will ye do in the day of visitation, and in the desolation which shall come from far?" Isaiah asks. "To whom will ye flee for help? and where will ye leave your glory?" In answer the Lord promises to punish Assyria, even as he will punish the wicked enemies of his people in the last days. As the Assyrians conquer nations and kingdoms, with power and might, so that none stand against them, even so shall the Lord send destruction and burning at his coming. "Therefore shall the Lord, the Lord of hosts . . . kindle a burning like the burning of a fire. And the light of Israel shall be for a fire, and his Holy One for a flame: and it shall burn and devour his thorns and his briers in one day." The vineyard shall be burned at his coming, and the latter-day "Assyrian," the one who opposes his people in that great day, shall be burned as are thorns and briers. "And the rest of the trees of his forest shall be few, that a child may write them." (Isa. 10:3-19.) Comparatively few will remain on earth to enjoy the millennial bliss.

3. *Moab: A Type of All Nations.*

When the Lord comes, he will make a full end of all nations; none shall abide the day; all shall be destroyed. There will be no law but his law when he comes. Isaiah's prophecy about the destruction of Moab in the last days taught this to ancient Israel.

In the midst of a prophetic account as to what would happen to Moab, Isaiah uttered these Messianic words: "And in mercy shall the throne be established: and he shall sit upon it in truth in the tabernacle of David, judging, and seeking judgment, and hasting righteousness." (Isa. 16:5.) Later, in the midst of a glorious Messianic sermon about the resurrection and the Second Coming, Isaiah said: "And it shall be said in that day, Lo, this is our God; we have waited for him, and he will save us: this is the Lord; we have waited for him, we will be glad and rejoice in his salvation." Christ shall save his people when he comes again. At this point the scripture says: "For in this mountain shall the hand of the Lord rest, and Moab shall be trodden down under him, even as straw is trodden down for the dunghill." (Isa. 25:9-10.) And as with Moab, so with all nations in the great and coming day.

4. *Egypt: First Smitten, Then Healed.*

In the last days all nations shall be smitten and destroyed and the wicked among them shall be burned. But what of those who remain? They shall turn unto the Lord and be saved with his people Israel. Isaiah made Egypt the illustration of this concept.

After setting forth the woes that would come upon Egypt, Isaiah then promised: "They shall cry unto the Lord because of the oppressors, and he shall send them a saviour, and a great one, and he shall deliver them." Is there deliverance for any people except in and through the Savior of mankind? Are any ever freed from oppression in the full sense until they cleave unto the Lord of hosts? Next Isaiah says: "And the Lord shall be known to Egypt, and the Egyptians shall know the Lord in that day." Such has never yet been the case in Egypt, but it shall soon be. They, along with all nations, shall be opened to the preaching of the gospel, and a foothold will be gained. Then cometh the end, and then shall those who remain rally to the standard set up before them. "And the Lord shall smite Egypt: he shall smite and heal it: and they shall return even to the Lord, and he shall be intreated of them, and shall heal them." Egypt shall have the blessings of the gospel.

And as with Egypt, so with all nations. A residue shall turn unto the Lord and be blessed of him. Then shall be fulfilled that which is written: "Blessed be Egypt my people," saith the Lord, "and Assyria the work of my hands, and Israel mine inheritance." (Isa. 19:20-25.)

5. *Modern Similitudes of His Coming.*

Those who know what lies ahead, and who have prophetic insight as to the future, find it easy to devise similitudes that are as plain and graphic as those used by Isaiah or any of the prophets. They can compare the desolations poured out upon Jerusalem in A.D. 70 with those that will fall upon all men in the last days. They can compare the destructions of the Jaredite and Nephite peoples with the destructions that shall befall the wicked in all nations at that great and dreadful day. They can look to the bloodshed and horrors of two world wars and see in them a type and a shadow of what shall be as the Armageddon of the future rears its ugly head of horror before us. They can speak of atomic holocausts and of hydrogen bombs that will desolate whole nations and peoples. All these things are but types of what is yet to be.

Out of this horrible picture there is only one ray of hope. Those who believe and obey, whether in life or in death, shall have eternal life. The God-fearing and the righteous who remain, together with those who rise from their graves to meet our Lord at his coming, shall have joy everlasting with him in his kingdom. However awesome is the future, the promised reward is worth the price, and the promised glory will swallow up all sorrows. It is the Lord's work, and he will bring it off triumphant.

THE WORLD OF WICKEDNESS IN THE LAST DAYS

Satan Reigns on Earth

These are the days of evil and abominations destined to precede the coming of the Holy One. We have no words at our command, nor do we have the ability to coin phrases descriptive of the wickedness of the modern world, nor would we use such words or coin such phrases if it lay in our power to do so. We do not desire to dwell on devilish and degenerate conduct. Of these our days, Jesus said simply: "And in that day shall be heard of wars and rumors of wars, and the whole earth shall be in commotion, and men's hearts shall fail them, and they shall say that Christ delayeth his coming until the end of the earth. And the love of men shall wax cold, and iniquity shall abound." (D&C 45:26-27.)

Of our present world, a world of carnality and corruption, the holy word attests: "Enoch saw the day of the coming of the Son of Man, in the last days, to dwell on the earth in righteousness for the space of a thousand years; But before that day he saw great tribulations among the wicked; and he also saw the sea, that it was troubled, and men's hearts failing them, looking forth with fear for the judgments of the Almighty God, which should come upon the wicked." (Moses 7:65-66.)

And Nephi bore this testimony: "Behold, in the last

days, . . . all the nations of the Gentiles and also the Jews, both those who shall come upon this land and those who shall be upon other lands, yea, even upon all the lands of the earth, behold, they will be drunken with iniquity and all manner of abominations—And when that day shall come they shall be visited of the Lord of Hosts, with thunder and with earthquake, and with a great noise, and with storm, and with tempest, and with the flame of devouring fire." (2 Ne. 27:1-2.)

Who can deny that these things are now upon us? We shall speak hereafter of the natural disasters and the eventual fire that shall cleanse the earth. But we must first set forth why there is so much evil in all the world. It is one of the signs of the times. It comes because of lust and carnality in the hearts of men. It comes because men love Satan more than God and choose to worship at his altars. We have seen that this was the case before the flood when the earth was cleansed by water, and now we see it in our day when the earth will soon be cleansed by fire.

In the early days of our dispensation, when the Lord was laying the foundations of his great latter-day work, he said: "The day speedily cometh; the hour is not yet, but is nigh at hand, when peace shall be taken from the earth"—that time has now come, and peace has been taken from the earth—"and the devil shall have power over his own dominion." That day also is now with us, and Lucifer reigns in the hearts of his own. "And also the Lord shall have power over his saints"—and thanks be to God, this too is a present reality—"and shall reign in their midst, and shall come down in judgment upon Idumea, or the world." (D&C 1:35-36.) And the day is soon to be when he shall come down in judgment and be in our midst.

How then does Satan reign over men? Where is his kingdom, and what is his dominion? We have already spoken of the apostasy, of the false worship, false prophets, and false churches of the last days. These are his kingdom. There his dominion is found. He is the author of apostasy, the lord of false worship, and the prophet of false churches. He is the founder of secret combinations and the spreader of lies. And so we have this inspired account of the coming forth of the Lord's work in the last days: "It shall come in a day when the blood of saints shall cry unto the Lord, because of secret combinations and the works of darkness." We have seen some of this; Joseph and Hyrum fell in Carthage jail, and thousands of the saints met untimely deaths because of the drivings and persecutions in Missouri and the bitter cold of their snow-impeded journeys to the valleys of the mountains. Their blood cries unto the Lord for vengeance against those who denied them further mortal experience.

"Yea, it shall come in a day when the power of God shall be denied, and churches become defiled and be lifted up in the pride of their hearts; yea, even in a day when leaders of churches and teachers shall rise in the pride of their hearts, even to the envying of them who belong to their churches." These churches are part of that great church which is not the Lord's church, which is abominable and evil and which shall be burned with the tares when the Lord of the vineyard comes.

"Yea, it shall come in a day when there shall be heard of fires, and tempests, and vapors of smoke in foreign lands; And there shall also be heard of wars, rumors of wars, and earthquakes in divers places." These are part of the signs of the times, as we shall hereafter note. Our chief present concern, however, is in these graphic words: "Yea, it shall come in a day when there shall be great pollutions upon the face of the earth; there shall be murders, and robbing, and lying, and deceivings, and whoredoms, and all manner of abominations; when there shall be many who will say, Do this, or do that, and it mattereth not, for the Lord will uphold such at the last day." The account then speaks of the wickedness of the churches that have "transfigured the holy word of God" to the point that their adherents feel comfortable in living godless lives because they suppose, falsely, that they will be saved.

If churches sell indulgences remitting the penalties for sins that will be committed in the future, what incentive is there to live righteously? If they say, "Come unto me, and for your money you shall be forgiven of your sins," why worry about doing good or working righteousness? (Morm. 8:27-33.) If salvation is for sale for a few pence, why should even those who profess to be religious concern themselves with the struggles and labors that will enable them to gain faith like the ancients? If churches can save souls by grace alone, without works, what is to deter men from living after the manner of the world while they suppose their eternal inheritance shall be with God and Christ and holy beings?

If even the professors of religion can live in sin and be saved, what of those who openly rebel against God and his laws? How may we expect to see them live? And if, as the evolutionists suppose, life is all chance and happenstance, without the guidance of a Divine Providence, what is there to worry about? Life will cease with death anyway. And so with the atheists. If there is no God and no eternal judgment, is not a life of greed and sin and lust and murder as acceptable as one of religious privation?

Truly, these last days are days of wickedness and abomination, and they have become such through and because of apostasy from the truth. They have become such because the allegiance of men is pledged to Lucifer. Men choose to believe false doctrines—whether these doctrines bear the name of science or religion—and as a consequence, their way of life is evil. This is how and why they worship as Satan dictates. This is what is meant by loving Satan more than God.

What better illustrations are there than these as to why men must believe the truth in order to live godly lives? False beliefs invite wicked deeds. True beliefs lead to a life of righteousness. "The Messiah will set himself again the second time to recover'' his people, Jacob said. And ''when that day cometh when they shall believe in him''—believe with all the fervor and devotion manifest in ancient days—then ''he will manifest himself unto them in power and great glory, unto the destruction of their enemies.'' This has reference to his second coming. ''And none will he destroy that believe in him.'' They shall abide the day and not be burned with the wicked. ''And they that believe not in him shall be destroyed, both by fire, and by tempest, and by earthquakes, and by bloodsheds, and by pestilence, and by famine.'' (2 Ne. 6:14-15.) These are the judgments of a just God that shall fall upon the world in the last days.

Wars and Rumors of Wars in the Last Days

What is the crowning evil on earth, the one that spreads the greatest suffering, the one that spawns all other evils? Surely it is war. Murder is the most wicked of all sins, and war is mass murder. Millions among men have suffered untimely deaths in the wars of the past; and before the coming desolations are ended, the number will be in the billions. The souls of most of those slain by the sword have gone where Lucifer laughs at their misery and rejoices in their remorse of conscience.

Next to murder in the category of personal sins comes immorality—adultery, homosexuality, fornication, and unchastity in all its forms. After these abominations, in no known order, come all the ills and evils of our day. And all of these grow out of and are multiplied by war. Surely war is the greatest evil that has or can spread its soul-destroying power over all the earth.

Wars have been waged from the beginning. Nations and kingdoms and civilizations have been destroyed. Bloodshed and carnage have made men insensitive to every instinct of decency and refinement. For instance, the Nephites, in the day of their greatest degeneracy, took the daughters of the Lamanites as prisoners, robbed them of their ''chastity and virtue,'' and, then, in Mormon's language, "they did murder them in a most cruel manner, torturing their bodies even unto death; and after they have done this, they devour their flesh like unto wild beasts, because of the hardness of their hearts; and they do it for a token of bravery." (Moro. 9:9-10.)

How do the wars of the past compare with those destined to be fought in the last days? They were but preparation and prologue for the present and the future. The great and dreadful wars have been reserved for the last days, the days after the invention of the machine, the days when the number of wicked persons would swell into the billions. This is the day when a new order of war would be instituted, and that new order began with the Civil War in America. It was then that modern armaments had their birth. Already they have grown into a hideous monster, and the end is nowhere to be seen.

Thus it is that the prophetic word speaks of wars and rumors of wars as being among the signs of the times. Jesus set the stage for our consideration of these matters when, discoursing on Olivet, he said of the gathered ones of Israel in the last days: "And they shall hear of wars, and rumors of wars. Behold I speak for mine elect's sake"—he is speaking of those in our day who will be able to distinguish what the scriptures say about the ancient wars from what they say relative to those of the present; they are the ones who shall catch the vision of a new order of blood and carnage reserved for the last days—"for nation shall rise against nation, and kingdom against kingdom; there shall be famines, and pestilences, and earthquakes, in divers places." (JS-M 1:28-29.) And also: "And there shall be earthquakes also in divers places, and many desolations; yet men will harden their hearts against me, and they will take up the sword, one against another, and they will kill one another." (D&C 45:33.) He is here giving the wars of the last days a place of preeminence and standing among all the wars of the ages.

"I, the Lord, am angry with the wicked," he said to

Joseph Smith. "I am holding my Spirit from the inhabitants of the earth. I have sworn in my wrath, and decreed wars upon the face of the earth, and the wicked shall slay the wicked, and fear shall come upon every man; And the saints also shall hardly escape; nevertheless, I, the Lord, am with them, and will come down in heaven from the presence of my Father and consume the wicked with unquenchable fire. And behold, this is not yet, but by and by." (D&C 63:32-35.) The decreed wars have commenced; they are in progress; but the day of burning is by and by, in the day when he comes again.

These latter-day wars had their beginning in 1861. "I prophesy, in the name of the Lord God, that the commencement of the difficulties which will cause much bloodshed previous to the coming of the Son of Man will be in South Carolina. . . . This a voice declared to me, while I was praying earnestly on the subject, December 25th, 1832." (D&C 130:12-13.) Such is the inspired pronouncement of the seer of our day. Indeed, it was on that very Christmas day in 1832 when he received the revelation and prophecy on war. This revelation specifies: "Verily, thus saith the Lord concerning the wars that will shortly come to pass, beginning at the rebellion of South Carolina, which will eventually terminate in the death and misery of many souls; And the time will come that war will be poured out upon all nations, beginning at this place."

The end of these wars is not yet, far from it. After repeating that "war shall be poured out upon all nations," the revealed word attests: "With the sword and by bloodshed the inhabitants of the earth shall mourn; and with famine, and plague, and earthquake, and the thunder of heaven, and the fierce and vivid lightning also, shall the inhabitants of the earth be made to feel the wrath, and indignation, and chastening hand of an Almighty God, until the consumption decreed hath made a full end of all nations." (D&C 87:1-6.) These wars and plagues and desolations shall continue—and increase—until the kingdoms of this world are destroyed and He reigns whose right it is.

This is quite a different preparatory period than some, even among the elect, have supposed would exist prior to the Second Coming. This coming will not be ushered in by righteousness, but by wickedness. It will not come when the saints have converted the world and prepared men to meet their God. It will not come because the generality of mankind is ready to receive the Second David. Indeed, the great battle of Armageddon itself will be in progress when the Lord comes. And thus we read in the prophetic word: "Proclaim ye this among the Gentiles; Prepare war, wake up the mighty men, let all the men of war draw near; let them come up: Beat your plowshares into swords, and your pruninghooks into spears: let the weak say, I am strong." This is said of the last days; it is the opposite of what shall be in the millennial day when men shall beat their swords into plowshares and their spears into pruning hooks and shall not learn war anymore at all. But for the premillennial period the call is: "Assemble yourselves, and come, all ye heathen, and gather yourselves together round about: thither cause thy mighty ones to come down, O Lord. Let the heathen be wakened, and come up to the valley of Jehoshaphat: for there will I sit to judge all the heathen round about." (Joel 3:9-12.) It is Christ the Lord who thus speaks. He will come in the day of war and desolation; then he will judge all men and divide the sheep from the goats.

Isaiah's great prophecy relative to the fire and desolation that will attend the Second Coming is preserved for us in these words: "For, behold, the Lord will come with fire, and with his chariots like a whirlwind, to render his anger with fury, and his rebuke with flames of fire. For by fire and by his sword will the Lord plead with all flesh: and the slain of the Lord shall be many. . . . And they [those who are left] shall go forth, and look upon the carcases of the men that have transgressed against me," saith the

Lord, "for their worm shall not die, neither shall their fire be quenched; and they shall be an abhorring unto all flesh." (Isa. 66:15-16, 24.)

Truly, in the last days men "shall be drunken with their own blood, as with sweet wine." (Isa. 49:26.) All these things have begun; they are now underway, and they shall increase in intensity and in horror until that dreadful day when the God of battles himself shall descend from heaven with a shout and with the trump of the archangel.

The Earth Itself Cries Repentance

This earth was created for us, to be our abiding place during a mortal probation. It was made in such a way as to best serve our needs. The Lord had power to arrange the earth, the elements, and all created things in the way that would best serve man, his crowning creation. Why did he make provision for natural disasters, acts of God, as they are called in legal parlance? What purpose is served by earthquakes, floods, volcanic eruptions, storms, tempests, heat waves that burn the crops of men, and cold waves that freeze the fruits of the earth? These have all been woven into the continuing existence of our earth, an earth designed to serve us. Why?

It seems clear that we are here in mortality to gain experiences that could not be gained in any other way. We need to combat and overcome the forces of nature. We must face up to the sorrows and vicissitudes of mortality if we are to appreciate the eternal joys of immortality. And in addition, the disasters of earth—controlled as they are in the infinite wisdom of that Lord who knoweth all things—are used by him to temper and train us. He uses natural disasters to bring to us the conscious realization that we are dependent upon a Supreme Being for all things. He uses them as a means of judgment to punish us for evil deeds done in the flesh. He uses them to humble us so that perchance we will repent and live as he would have us live.

"Except the Lord doth chasten his people with many afflictions, yea, except he doth visit them with death and with terror, and with famine and with all manner of pestilence, they will not remember him." (Hel. 12:3.) And all of this has particular application in this day of wickedness when the world is being prepared to receive its rightful King.

There is an account, in the visions and revelations of Enoch, in which our very planet is personified and delivers a message. This method of divine teaching lets us know that the earth itself is used to get men to do what they must do to gain salvation. "Enoch looked upon the earth; and he heard a voice from the bowels thereof, saying: Wo, wo is me, the mother of men; I am pained, I am weary, because of the wickedness of my children. When shall I rest, and be cleansed from the filthiness which is gone forth out of me? When will my Creator sanctify me, that I may rest, and righteousness for a season abide upon my face?" This is a sweet and poignant expression that alludes to the great millennial day when the earth will rest because wickedness ceases among men who were made from the dust of the earth. "And when Enoch heard the earth mourn, he wept, and cried unto the Lord, saying: O Lord, wilt thou not have compassion upon the earth?" (Moses 7:48-49.)

In some of our latter-day scriptures the Lord uses a like teaching technique. "Hearken ye, for, behold, the great day of the Lord is nigh at hand," he says to his servants. Then he commands them: "Lift up your voices and spare not. Call upon the nations to repent, both old and young, both bond and free, saying: Prepare yourselves for the great day of the Lord; For if I, who am a man, do lift up my voice and call upon you to repent, and ye hate me, what will ye say when the day cometh when the thunders shall utter their voices from the ends of the earth, speaking to the ears of all that live, saying—Repent, and prepare for the great day of the Lord? Yea, and again, when the lightnings shall streak forth from the east unto the west, and shall utter forth their voices unto all that live, and make the ears of all tingle that hear, saying these words—Repent ye, for the great day of the Lord is come?" The very elements of the earth echo, as it were, the message of the servants of the Lord.

"And again, the Lord shall utter his voice out of heaven, saying: Hearken, O ye nations of the earth, and hear the words of that God who made you. O, ye nations of the earth, how often would I have gathered you together as a hen gathereth her chickens under her wings, but ye would not!" How beautiful this imagery is. In the literal sense the words will be spoken by the servants of the Lord; in the eternal sense they will be his words, for when his servants speak by the power of his Spirit, their words are his words.

Our Lord's graphic expression continues: "How oft have I called upon you by the mouth of my servants, and by the ministering of angels, and by mine own voice, and by the voice of thunderings, and by the voice of lightnings, and by the voice of tempests, and by the voice of earthquakes, and great hailstorms, and by the voice of famines and pestilences of every kind, and by the great sound of a trump, and by the voice of judgment, and by the voice of mercy all the day long, and by the voice of glory and honor and the riches of eternal life, and would have saved you with an everlasting salvation, but ye would not!" (D&C 43:17-25.)

Can there be any question that the Lord has woven the disasters of nature into his program for a purpose? Can we doubt that he uses them for our benefit and blessing? In the midst of a great revelation concerning his coming, he says to us, the elders of his kingdom: "And after your testimony cometh wrath and indignation upon the people." We shall preach the gospel to the world, and if they do not believe and obey, they will be cursed. "For after your testimony cometh the testimony of earthquakes, that shall cause groanings in the midst of her, and men shall fall upon the ground and shall not be able to stand." There are greater earthquakes ahead than there have ever been in the past. "And also cometh the testimony of the voice of thunderings, and the voice of lightnings, and the voice of tempests, and the voice of the waves of the sea heaving themselves beyond their bounds. And all things shall be in commotion; and surely, men's hearts shall fail them; for fear shall come upon all people."

After the disasters and terrors of the last days, "Angels shall fly through the midst of heaven, crying with a loud voice, sounding the trump of God, saying: Prepare ye, prepare ye, O inhabitants of the earth; for the judgment of our God is come. Behold, and lo, the Bridegroom cometh; go ye out to meet him." (D&C 88:88-92.)

PLAGUES AND PESTILENCE IN THE LAST DAYS

Plagues and Pestilence Prepare the Way of the Lord

Before this earth becomes a fit habitat for the Holy One, it must be cleansed and purified. The wicked must be destroyed; peace must replace war; and the evil imaginations in the hearts of men must give way to desires for righteousness. How shall this be brought to pass? There are two ways: (1) By plagues and pestilence and wars and desolation. The wicked shall slay the wicked, as did the Nephites and the Lamanites in the day of the extinction of the Nephites as a nation. Plagues will sweep the earth, as the Black Death ravaged Asia and Europe in the fourteenth century. The carcasses of the dead will be stacked in uncounted numbers to rot and decay and fill the earth with stench. (2) Then, at his coming, the vineyard will be burned. The residue of the wicked will be consumed. No corruptible thing will remain. And this earth will then become a fit abode for the Prince of Peace.

Thus Jesus on Olivet said: "There shall be famines, and pestilences, and earthquakes, in divers places." (JS-M 1:29.) And the Lord, in March of 1829, said to Joseph Smith: "A desolating scourge shall go forth among the inhabitants of the earth, and shall continue to be poured out from time to time, if they repent not"—and they will not repent, as we know from other revelations—"until the earth is empty, and the inhabitants thereof are consumed away and utterly destroyed by the brightness of my coming. Behold, I tell you these things, even as I also told the people of the destruction of Jerusalem; and my word shall be verified at this time as it hath hitherto been verified." (D&C 5:19-20.) Then in September 1832 this word came from the Lord: "I, the Almighty, have laid my hands upon the nations, to scourge them for their wickedness. And plagues shall go forth, and they shall not be taken from the earth until I have completed my work, which shall be cut short in righteousness—Until all shall know me, who remain." (D&C 84:96-98.)

Thus, all men have a choice. They can repent, or they can suffer. They can believe and obey, or they can reject the truth and live in disobedience. They can prepare themselves to abide the day and to stand when he appeareth, or they can bow in submission to the plagues and pestilences that lie ahead; and, should they escape these, they can then be numbered with the great host who will be burned at his coming.

John Reveals the Signs of the Times

Many prophets speak of the plagues and woes to be poured out without measure upon men in the last days. None do so, however, with such vivid imagery and in such graphic language as did the Beloved John. His divine commission was to see in vision "all things . . . concerning the end of the world" and to write them for the blessing and enlightenment of men. (1 Ne. 14:18-27.)

John's visions are not chronological—deliberately so—and we cannot, with our present knowledge, place on a chronological chart each thing of which he speaks. Some of the woes proclaimed are of such a nature as to have a continuing or a repeated fulfillment. We shall, therefore, consider them in the order in which they are recorded in the book of Revelation, interspersing as we go along such commentary and explanation as seems needed. Many of the specific things to which John alludes are considered in extenso in other contexts in this book.

John saw a book, sealed on the back with seven seals, which "contains the revealed will, mysteries, and the works of God; the hidden things of his economy concerning this earth during the seven thousand years of its continuance, or its temporal existence." Each seal contains the things of a thousand-year period beginning at the time of Adam's fall and continuing until the end of the Millennium. (D&C 77:6-7.)

The Lamb of God opened each seal to show forth the great things of each succeeding thousand years, things that would begin or occur during that period. When he opened the sixth seal—and we are now living near the end of the sixth period of a thousand years—"lo, there was a great earthquake; and the sun became black as sackcloth of hair, and the moon became as blood; And the stars of heaven fell unto the earth, even as a fig tree casteth her untimely figs, when she is shaken of a mighty wind." (Rev. 6:12-13.) There may be more than one occasion when the light of the sun and the moon shall be withheld from men, and when it will seem as though the very stars in the firmament are being hurled from their places. What is here recited could mean that the light of the sun is blotted out by smoke and weather conditions, which would also make the moon appear "as blood." This falling of the stars "unto the earth" could be meteoric showers, as distinguished from the stars, on another occasion, appearing to fall because the earth itself reels to and fro. Perhaps the passage has reference to both types of falling stars. The latter-day revelation that seems to parallel John's words has come to us in this language: "Not many days hence and the earth shall tremble and reel to and fro as a drunken man; and the sun shall hide his face, and shall refuse to give light; and the moon shall be bathed in blood; and the stars shall become exceedingly angry, and shall cast themselves down as a fig that falleth from off a fig-tree." (D&C 88:87.)

Next, in language that may refer to what shall be during the seventh seal, John says: "And the heaven departed as a scroll when it is rolled together; and every mountain and island were moved out of their places." Surely this has reference to the continents becoming one land again. "And the kings of the earth, and the great men, and the rich men, and the chief captains, and the mighty men, and every bondman, and every free man, hid themselves in the dens and in the rocks of the mountains; And said to the mountains and rocks, Fall on us, and hide us from the face of him that sitteth on the throne, and from the wrath of the Lamb: For the great day of his wrath is come; and who shall be able to stand?" (Rev. 6:14-17.) These events must surely be destined to occur during the wars and terrors of the last days and before the day of burning when the wicked are consumed. As to their chronology, they are listed in latter-day revelation as coming after the half hour of silence in heaven (D&C 88:95), which silence is designated in Revelation 8:1 as occurring after the seventh period of one thousand years has commenced.

Plagues Poured Out in the Seventh Seal

We are now living in the Saturday night of time; the millennial morning will soon dawn. This is the end of the sixth seal, and the seventh seal will soon be opened. Our modern revelation tells us plainly that Christ will come sometime after the opening of seventh seal; it will be during the seventh thousand years and after the events listed in the eighth chapter of John's writings. The plagues and woes there recited shall all take place during the seventh seal, and they are "the preparing of the way before the time of his coming." (D&C 77:12.) Will he come ten or fifty or a hundred years after the opening of the seventh seal? Or will his various appearances be interspersed with the signs of the times that are reserved for that future day? Answers to these and like questions have been withheld from us and will be known only as the various events transpire.

And when the Lamb "had opened the seventh seal, there was silence in heaven about the space of half an hour." If the time here mentioned is "the Lord's time" in which one day is a thousand years, the half hour would be some twenty-one of our years. (Abr. 3:4; 2 Pet. 3:8.) Could this be interpreted to mean that such a period will elapse after the commencement of the seventh thousand-year period and before the outpouring of the woes about to be named?

"And I saw the seven angels which stood before God; and to them were given seven trumpets," John continues. "And there were voices, and thunderings, and lightnings, and an earthquake." Would that we knew, as John apparently did, what the voices said. "And [then] the seven angels which had the seven trumpets prepared themselves to sound." And thus the scene is set for the recitation of the plagues and woes and sorrows that are to sweep the earth after the opening of the seventh seal.

1. *The First Angel: Hail and Fire Descend.*

"The first angel sounded, and there followed hail and fire mingled with blood, and they were cast upon the earth: and the third part of trees was burnt up, and all green grass was burnt up." Is this the "overflowing rain, and great hailstones, fire, and brimstone," of which Ezekiel spoke? (Ezek. 38:22.) Could all this be brought to pass through atomic warfare, or will it come by natural disasters, as when God rained fire and brimstone upon Sodom and Gomorrah? Speculatively, most of the plagues and destructions here announced could be brought to pass by men themselves as they use the weapons and armaments they have created.

2. *The Second Angel: The Sea Is Smitten.*

"And the second angel sounded, and as it were a great mountain burning with fire was cast into the sea: and the third part of the sea became blood; And the third part of the creatures which were in the sea, and had life, died; and the third part of the ships were destroyed." We have no way of conceiving what kind of a natural calamity would destroy a third part of the sea life and of all ships. Will it be a volcanic eruption of such magnitude as to involve whole continents? Or will it be a rain of atomic bombs sent forth by warring nations?

3. *The Third Angel: Earth's Waters Are Polluted.*

"And the third angel sounded, and there fell a great star from heaven, burning as it were a lamp, and it fell upon the third part of the rivers, and upon the fountains of waters; And the name of the star is called Wormwood: and the third part of the waters became wormwood; and many men died of the waters, because they were made bitter." Could this result from atomic fallout or pollutions from the factories of the world? Or will it be brought to pass by some law of nature beyond our control?

4. *The Fourth Angel: The Light-Bearing Luminaries Are Smitten.*

"And the fourth angel sounded, and the third part of the sun was smitten, and the third part of the moon, and the third part of the stars; so as the third part of them was darkened, and the day shone not for a third part of it, and night likewise." Perhaps a merciful God withholds from us the ways and the means whereby the very luminaries of heaven will cease to serve their ordained purposes for a third part of the time.

"And I beheld, and heard an angel flying through the midst of heaven," John here interjects, "saying with a loud voice, Woe, woe, woe, to the inhabiters of the earth by reason of the other voices of the trumpet of the three angels, which are yet to sound!" (Rev. 8:1-13.) Four angels have trumpeted their woes upon a wicked world, and it is scarcely a beginning of what is to be.

5. *The Fifth Angel: Modern Warfare Curses the World.* The whole of the ninth chapter of Revelation is a recitation of the woes pronounced by the fifth angel. "They are to be accomplished after the opening of the seventh seal, before the coming of Christ." (D&C 77:13.) They are, thus, perils and destructions that lie ahead, although in small measure some like woes have already befallen large portions of mankind.

"And the fifth angel sounded, and I saw a star fall from heaven unto the earth: and to him was given the key of the bottomless pit [or, better, the pit of the abyss]." Lucifer, who was cast out of heaven, now has his new abode, an endless hell where he holds the keys of power and dominion over his fellow demons and over all mortals who bow before him as their master.

"And he opened the bottomless pit; and there arose a smoke out of the pit, as the smoke of a great furnace; and the sun and the air were darkened by reason of the smoke of the pit." Lucifer opens the doors of hell, and every vile influence ascends from its evil depths as does smoke from a great furnace. So dark is the smoke and so widespread is the evil that the sun and the air are darkened.

"And there came out of the smoke locusts upon the earth: and unto them was given power, as the scorpions of the earth have power." Men as locusts—evil, wicked, guided by Satan and filled with the spirit of the times—begin their warfare.

"And it was commanded them that they should not hurt the grass of the earth, neither any green thing, neither any tree; but only those men which have not the seal of God in their foreheads. And to them it was given that they should not kill them, but that they should be tormented five months: and their torment was as the torment of a scorpion, when he striketh a man. And in those days shall men seek death, and shall not find it; and shall desire to die, and death shall flee from them." We can only speculate as to how this will be fulfilled. The warriors of the world apparently attack men without destroying the fruits of the ground. Only those in Zion who are sealed up unto eternal life have power to withstand the onslaught. Could it be that John is seeing the effects of poisonous gas, or bacteriological warfare, or atomic fallout, which disable but do not kill?

"And the shapes of the locusts were like unto horses prepared unto battle; and on their heads were as it were crowns like gold, and their faces were as the faces of men. And they had hair as the hair of women, and their teeth were as the teeth of lions. And they had breastplates, as it were breastplates of iron; and the sound of their wings was as the sound of chariots of many horses running to battle. And they had tails like unto scorpions, and there were stings in their tails: and their power was to hurt men five months." John is seeing warfare and armaments so foreign to his experience that he has no language to describe to the people of his day the horror and destructive power of it all. We suppose the Lord is showing him machine guns and cannons, tanks and airplanes, flame throwers and airborne missiles, to say nothing of other weapons of which we ourselves have as yet no knowledge.

"And they had a king over them, which is the angel of the bottomless pit, whose name in the Hebrew tongue is Abaddon, but in the Greek tongue hath his name Apollyon. One woe is past; and, behold, there come two woes more hereafter." Satan is king. He rules in the hearts of men. He commands the armies of mortal men who wage these wicked wars among themselves.

6. *The Sixth Angel: Armageddon Spreadeth Destruction.*

"And the sixth angel sounded, and I heard a voice from the four horns of the golden altar which is before God, Saying to the sixth angel which had the trumpet, Loose the four angels which are bound in the great river Euphrates [or, rather, as the Inspired Version has it, in the bottomless pit]. And the four angels were loosed, which were prepared for an hour, and a day, and a month, and a year, for to slay the third part of men." Four angels of the devil, demons from the depths of hell, are given free reign to lead the armies of men in destroying a third of the population of the earth. If, as is not improbable, the earth by then has, say, twelve or fifteen billion inhabitants, then the magnitude of the slaughter in this Armageddon of the future will be such as to destroy more people than now live on earth.

"And the number of the army of the horsemen were two hundred thousand thousand: and I heard the number of them." No such armed forces—two hundred million strong—have ever yet drawn the sword of battle at any one time on earth, nor could that number of armed combatants ever have been assembled until these last days in which we now live.

"And thus I saw the horses in the vision, and them that sat on them, having breastplates of fire, and of jacinth, and brimstone: and the heads of the horses were as the heads of lions; and out of their mouths issued fire and smoke and brimstone. By these three was the third part of men killed, by the fire, and by the smoke, and by the brimstone, which issued out of their mouths. For their power is in their mouth, and in their tails: for their tails were like unto serpents, and had heads, and with them they do hurt." In this divine summary is seen again, as we suppose, an account of guns and armored tanks, of flame throwers and airplanes, and of airborne missiles and the smoke of atomic bombs.

"And the rest of the men which were not killed by these plagues yet repented not of the works of their hands, that they should not worship devils, and idols of gold, and silver, and brass, and stone, and of wood: which neither can see, nor hear, nor walk: Neither repented they of their murders, nor of their sorceries, nor of their fornication, nor of their thefts." (Rev. 9:1-21.) Neither the Nephites nor the Jaredites repented when rivers of blood flowed on their battlefields and millions of their number were slain by the sword. Neither shall these carnal and evil inhabiters of a weary and wicked world repent when the abomination that maketh desolate is poured out upon them.

The war they shall wage is a religious war. It will be against the Lord's covenant people, as we shall hereafter see. It will be waged by men who "worship devils"; they will be in conflict with others whose God is Jehovah. And the blood and carnage and death will not bring the carnal and wicked warriors to repentance. Repentance is a gift of God; it follows faith; and the tares among men, who are being prepared for the burning, are without God in the world and have no faith.

7. The Seventh Angel: Christ Comes and Destroys the Wicked.

Before the sounding of the trump of the seventh angel, John was permitted to see the part he was destined to play in the latter-day restoration of all things (Rev. 10:1-11), and to learn of the two prophets to be slain in Jerusalem just before the battle of Armageddon, of which battle the sixth angel spoke. After recounting the ministry of these two prophets, of whom we shall speak more particularly hereafter, the account says: "The second woe is past; and, behold, the third woe cometh quickly." (Rev. 11:14.)

With reference to these three woes, the present author has written: "After showing John the woes that would befall mankind before the Second Coming (Rev. 6:9-17; 7; 8:1-13), the Lord by an angelic ministrant promised three more woes, which were to attend and usher in the reign of the Great King (Rev. 8:13). The first of these was the unbelievably destructive series of wars leading up to the final great holocaust. (Rev. 9:1-12.) The second was the final great war itself in which one-third of the hosts of men should be slain. (Rev. 9:12-21; 10; 11:1-14.) And now the third woe is to be the destruction of the remainder of the wicked when the vineyard is burned by divine power and the earth changes from its telestial to its terrestrial state. In destructive power and effect this woe is to surpass all others many times over." (*Commentary* 3:511.)

It is in this setting, then, that we read: "And the seventh angel sounded; and there were great voices in heaven, saying, The kingdoms of this world are become the kingdoms of our Lord, and of his Christ; and he shall reign for ever and ever." Christ the Lord reigneth. After the plagues and pestilences, after the destruction of the wicked, after the burning of the vineyard—then cometh the great day. Earth's rightful King reigneth.

"And the four and twenty elders, which sat before God on their seats, fell upon their faces, and worshipped God, Saying, We give thee thanks, O Lord God Almighty, which art, and wast, and art to come; because thou hast taken to thee thy great power, and hast reigned." What a glorious day it is for the saints when their King reigneth. All evil shall then cease, and naught but righteousness and peace shall prevail on all the earth.

"And the nations were angry, and thy wrath is come, and the time of the dead, that they should be judged, and that thou shouldest give reward unto thy servants the prophets, and to the saints, and them that fear thy name, small and great; and shouldest destroy them which destroy the earth. And the temple of God was opened in heaven, and there was seen in his temple the ark of his testament: and there were lightnings, and voices, and thunderings, and an earthquake, and great hail." (Rev. 11:15-19.) When the Lord comes, he will destroy those who destroyed the earth. He is angry with the wicked, and in his wrath he will cleanse his vineyard by fire, and in his mercy he will reward his prophets and his saints. The wicked who remain after the first woe and the second woe shall be destroyed in the third.

Chapter 33

THE SEVEN LAST PLAGUES

The Two Prophets: Martyred in Jerusalem

Our setting for the slaughter of the two prophets in Jerusalem and for the seven last plagues is not only in the seventh seal, but also just before and during the time when the seventh angel is announcing the plague of burning and destruction that will usher in the Second Coming. "In the days of the voice of the seventh angel, when he shall begin to sound," John tells us, "the mystery of God should be finished, as he hath declared to his servants the prophets." (Rev. 10:7.) That is, the great winding-up scene will come to pass during the time the plagues and events pronounced by this angel are occurring. These events are heralded by the ministry and death of the two witnesses in Jerusalem; then the seventh angel will sound his trump to proclaim the outpouring of the seven last plagues, the battle of Armageddon, the fall of Babylon, and the burning of the vineyard with fire.

John is given a reed and told to measure the temple in Jerusalem, but not the court of the Gentiles, which is part of the holy site, "for it is given unto the Gentiles: and the holy city shall they tread under foot forty and two months." That is to say, there will be a day of universal apostasy. It will commence when the apostles and prophets cease to minister among men and will continue until the opening of the heavens again in the spring of 1820. A part of this apostasy calls for Jerusalem to be trodden down of the Gentiles. The detailed application of the period of forty-two months has not as yet been revealed.

In this setting, however, the word that comes from the Lord is: "I will give power unto my two witnesses, and they shall prophesy a thousand two hundred and three score days, clothed in sackcloth." Who are these witnesses, and when will they prophesy? "They are two prophets that are to be raised up to the Jewish nation in the last days, at the time of the restoration, and to prophesy to the Jews after they are gathered and have built the city of Jerusalem in the land of their fathers." (D&C 77:15.) Their ministry will take place after the latter-day temple has been built in Old Jerusalem, after some of the Jews who dwell there have been converted, and just before Armageddon and the return of the Lord Jesus. How long will they minister in Jerusalem and in the Holy Land? For three and a half years, the precise time spent by the Lord in his ministry to the ancient Jews. The Jews, as an assembled people, will hear again the testimony of legal administrators bearing record that salvation is in Christ and in his gospel. Who will these witnesses be? We do not know, except that they will be followers of Joseph Smith; they will hold the holy Melchizedek Priesthood; they will be members of The Church of Jesus Christ of Latter-day Saints. It is reasonable to suppose, knowing how the Lord has always dealt with his people in all ages, that they will be two members of the Council of the Twelve or of the First Presidency of the Church.

How will their witness be received by the people? This we do know. It will be with these two witnesses as it was with their Lord some two millenniums before. The righteous will believe their words, and the wicked will thirst for their blood. "And if any man will hurt them, fire proceedeth out of their mouth, and devoureth their enemies: and if any man will hurt them, he must in this manner be killed. These have power to shut heaven, that it rain not in the days of their prophecy: and have power over waters to turn them to blood, and to smite the earth with all plagues, as often as they will." It will be with them as it was with Elijah, who both called down fire from heaven to consume his enemies and sealed the heavens that there was neither dew nor rain for three and a half years. And it will be with them as it was with Moses, who turned the rivers and waters of Egypt into blood and who smote the Egyptians with many plagues.

"And when they shall have finished their testimony, the beast that ascendeth out of the bottomless pit shall make war against them, and shall overcome them, and kill them." Satan shall slay them by the hands of his ministers, even as he slew their Lord by the hands of the Jews and the Romans who hearkened to his will.

"And their dead bodies shall lie in the street of the great city, which spiritually is called Sodom and Egypt, where also our Lord was crucified. And they of the people and kindreds and tongues and nations shall see their dead bodies three days and an half, and shall not suffer their dead bodies to be put in graves." There will not be so much as a Pilate to authorize a Joseph of Arimathea to take their bodies and place them in a borrowed grave.

"And they that dwell upon the earth shall rejoice over them, and make merry, and shall send gifts one to another; because these two prophets tormented them that dwelt on the earth." The rejoicing of the wicked at the death of the righteous constitutes a witness, written in blood, that the rebels of the world have ripened in iniquity and are fit and ready for the burning.

"And after three days and an half the Spirit of life from God entered into them, and they stood upon their feet; and great fear fell upon them which saw them. And they heard a great voice from heaven saying unto them, Come up hither. And they ascended up to heaven in a cloud; and their enemies beheld them." As with their Lord, whose witnesses they were, the two prophets arise from the dead on the third day and ascend into heaven.

"And the same hour was there a great earthquake, and the tenth part of the city fell, and in the earthquake were slain of men seven thousand: and the remnant were affrighted, and gave glory to the God of heaven." Jerusalem is shaken by a mighty earthquake even as it was at the crucifixion of Christ. This time many of the wicked are slain, while the saints—those Jews who have accepted Christ and his gospel, those who have participated in building the temple, those who have received the ordinances of the house of the Lord and are waiting for his return—they shall give glory to the God of heaven.

"The second woe is past; and, behold, the third woe cometh quickly." (Rev. 11:1-14.) The third woe, the burning of the vineyard, shall soon commence.

Plagues Manifest the Wrath of God

"And I saw another sign in heaven, great and marvelous," our apostolic friend and colleague tells us, "seven angels having the seven last plagues; for in them is filled up the wrath of God." (Rev. 15:1.) These are seven other angels whose plagues shall be poured out in the day of the seventh angel of whom we have been speaking. Their plagues shall fulfill all that has been written and promised that should fall upon the wicked before the war of Armageddon and the day of burning.

At this late date in the history of the world, the warning voice has been raised in every nation and to every people; the gospel has been preached in every tongue and among every kindred. All have been invited—nay, commanded—to come unto Christ, to repent, to believe and obey his gospel, to join with the saints, and to become inheritors of eternal life. The masses of men have rejected the gospel message, have persecuted the saints and slain the prophets, and have continued to walk in worldly paths. They are now ripened in iniquity. The servants of the Lord who have gone forth proclaiming the glad tidings of salvation for the last time have now exercised the power given them "to seal both on earth and in heaven, the unbelieving and rebellious; Yea, verily, to seal them up unto the day when the wrath of God shall be poured out upon the wicked without measure—Unto the day when the Lord shall come to recompense unto every man according to his work, and measure to every man according to the measure which he has measured to his fellow man." (D&C 1:8-10.)

"I looked, and, behold, the temple of the tabernacle of the testimony in heaven was opened," John continues, "And the seven angels came out of the temple, having the seven plagues, clothed in pure and white linen, and having their breasts girded with golden girdles." The ceremonies of the earthly temple with which John was familiar are being reenacted in heaven to teach with great power and eternal impact the marvelous truths involved. "And one of the four beasts gave unto the seven angels seven golden vials full of the wrath of God, who liveth for ever and ever." The vials are bowls or small vessels to hold liquids. "And the temple was filled with smoke from the glory of God, and from his power; and no man was able to enter into the temple, till the seven plagues of the seven angels were fulfilled." (Rev. 15:5-8.)

And so it is that the day has arrived and the hour is at hand. Let the plagues come in their fulness. All the plagues of the past are but a prelude. Now, with the burning just ahead, the wrath of God will be manifest in the greatest plagues of the ages.

What Are the Seven Last Plagues?

"And I heard a great voice out of the temple saying to the seven angels, Go your ways, and pour out the vials of the wrath of God upon the earth." These, then, are the seven last plagues, the plagues that pour out the fulness of the wrath of God upon the wicked, the plagues that usher in the second coming of the Son of Man:

1. *A Noisome and Grievous Sore.*

"And the first went, and poured out his vial upon the earth; and there fell a noisome and grievous sore upon the men which had the mark of the beast, and upon them which worshipped his image." Could this be the same plague of which Zechariah speaks when he says that men's "flesh shall consume away while they stand upon their feet, and their eyes shall consume away in their holes, and their tongue shall consume away in their mouth"? (Zech. 14:12.) Does it have reference to these words of latter-day revelation: "And their flesh shall fall from off their bones, and their eyes from their sockets"? (D&C 29:19.) Is this a plague that will result from atomic fallout? Or from some worldwide pollution of the air we breathe, the food we eat, and the water we drink? It is to come upon those who worship at the altars of evil, leaving the inference that those only will escape who have faith in the Lord and who exercise the power of the priesthood to rebuke the evils that otherwise would afflict them.

2. *The Seas Become Blood and Their Life Dies.*

"And the second angel poured out his vial upon the sea; and it became as the blood of a dead man: and every living soul died in the sea." This will be a plague of unbelievable breadth and depth. When all the oceans of the world are so polluted that all life in them dies, how can anyone measure the effect this will have on mankind?

3. *All Water Turns to Blood and Is Diseased.*

"And the third angel poured out his vial upon the rivers and fountains of waters; and they became blood." The plague that contaminated the great waters of the saline seas is now extended to include the rivers and streams and springs from which thirst is quenched and crops are watered. What an awful thing it is to be cursed by the Almighty!

Perhaps the horror of all this caused John to marvel that the Great Judge of all the earth would deal thus with men.

And yet wherein does it differ in principle from the destruction of man by the flood of Noah or the burning of the world at the Second Coming? In any event, John records: "And I heard the angel of the waters say, Thou art righteous, O Lord, which art, and wast, and shalt be, because thou hast judged thus." The wicked are receiving that which they merit and deserve. "For they have shed the blood of saints and prophets"—two of whom are the martyrs to be slain in Jerusalem—"and thou hast given them blood to drink; for they are worthy. And I heard another out of the altar say, Even so, Lord God Almighty, true and righteous are thy judgments."

4. *The Sun Scorches Men and the Earth.*

"And the fourth angel poured out his vial upon the sun; and power was given unto him to scorch men with fire. And men were scorched with great heat, and blasphemed the name of God, which hath power over these plagues: and they repented not to give him glory." This appears to be a plague of nature, one that the Lord will impose upon the world. Occasional brief heat waves destroy the crops of an area of the earth. What will it be like when the whole earth is afflicted with heat at the same time? Suppose temperatures rose to a hundred and ten, or a hundred and twenty, or a hundred and thirty degrees Fahrenheit—what effect would this have on all forms of life?

5. *Darkness, Pain, and Sores in the Kingdoms of the World.*

"And the fifth angel poured out his vial upon the seat of the beast; and his kingdom was full of darkness; and they gnawed their tongues for pain, and blasphemed the God of heaven because of their pains and their sores, and repented not of their deeds." We have spoken of darkness covering the earth and gross darkness the minds of the people. We see, even now, the grossly wicked ways of men because they believe a lie. We shudder at the abominations on every hand because men love darkness rather than light. We ask:

Can things get worse than they are before a just God will destroy men as he did in the days of Noah? We answer: They can, and they will.

In the day when the fifth angel pours out his vial upon the earth, darkness will increase. The great and abominable church, who is the whore of all the earth, will be full of darkness. Its doctrines will partake more and more of the evils of the world. There will be less and less light and truth, and more and more darkness and error. Hence, sin and evil will increase. And this process will go on until Babylon falls, and when she falls she will have attained a state and a degree of wickedness beyond anything in her long and evil history. The saints can expect to see more cultism, more false doctrines in the world, a greater emphasis in educational fields upon false scientific theories, more evil practices among the ungodly, more abominations among sex-obsessed men, and more of all that is evil everywhere—and then cometh the end of the world. What a horrible plague is the plague of darkness!

6. *False Miracles as the World Prepares for Armageddon.*

"And the sixth angel poured out his vial upon the great river Euphrates; and the water thereof was dried up, that the way of the kings of the east might be prepared. And I saw three unclean spirits like frogs come out of the mouth of the dragon, and out of the mouth of the beast, and out of the mouth of the false prophet. For they are the spirits of devils, working miracles, which go forth unto the kings of the earth and of the whole world, to gather them to the battle of that great day of God Almighty." Devils—of whom the frogs are a type and a shadow—shall work miracles. The world will be so degenerate that men will choose to follow magicians and politicians who deceive and defraud rather than turn to prophets who have power to move mountains and save souls.

And what greater miracle can these evil spirits perform, working as they always have through receptive mortals, than to indoctrinate men in all nations with that hate and lust for power which will cause them to assemble (in an age of atomic warfare!) with a view to the utter destruction of civilization? Then, as that great day of God Almighty arrives, and as the war of wars is being waged, Christ will come. "Behold, I come as a thief. Blessed is he that watcheth, and keepeth his garments, lest he walk naked, and they see his shame." He will come to save his saints, those who have kept their garments, and to destroy the wicked, those whose hearts are only evil continually.

"And he gathered them together into a place called in the Hebrew tongue Armageddon." The center of the battle will be on the mount and in the valley of Megiddo and on the plains of Esdraelon, though, since all nations are involved, it cannot be other than a worldwide conflict.

7. *War, Upheavals of Nature, and the Fall of Babylon.*

"And the seventh angel poured out his vial into the air; and there came a great voice out of the temple of heaven, from the throne, saying, It is done. And there were voices, and thunders, and lightnings; and there was a great earthquake, such as was not since men were upon the earth, so mighty an earthquake, and so great." This is the time when earth's land masses shall unite; when islands and continents shall become one land; when every valley shall be exalted and every mountain shall be made low; when the rugged terrain of today shall level out into a millennial garden; when the great deep shall be driven back into its own place in the north. It is no wonder that the earthquake shall exceed all others in the entire history of the world.

"And the great city was divided into three parts, and the cities of the nations fell: and great Babylon came in remembrance before God, to give unto her the cup of the wine of the fierceness of his wrath. And every island fled away, and the mountains were not found." The cities of the world shall be destroyed. Babylon shall fall, of which we shall speak more particularly hereafter. The wicked shall taste the fulness of the wrath of God.

"And there fell upon men a great hail out of heaven, every stone about the weight of a talent: and men blasphemed God because of the plague of the hail; for the plague thereof was exceeding great." (Rev. 16:1-21.) We shall speak of this hail when we consider Ezekiel's prophecies about the battle of Armageddon. But we should here observe that Armageddon is a holy war. In it men will blaspheme God. They will be in rebellion against Jehovah. The armies that face each other will have opposing philosophies of life. It will be religious instincts that cause them to assemble to the battle. And the plagues poured out upon them will not cause them to repent.

Such—sadly—is the destiny that lies ahead.

And such—providentially—is not right at hand. It is some years away. It shall come to pass by and by.

Chapter 34

THE SIGNS OF THE TIMES

What Are the Signs of the Times?

In the days of his flesh, our blessed Lord preached the gospel, spake as never man spake, and wrought an endless array of miracles. Blind eyes saw, lame men leaped, and deaf ears heard. Lepers became clean, and dead corpses rose from their biers. He walked on a tempestuous sea, silenced a raging storm, and fed thousands with a little fish savory and a few small loaves of barley bread.

Yet those who hated him demanded "that he would shew them a sign from heaven." They wanted to see something that fitted their ideas of what the Promised Messiah would do. Let him rain fire and brimstone on Rome or dry up the Jordan with a wave of the hand. Let him leap from the pinnacle of the temple and be caught by a legion of angels before he crushed his feet on the rocks below. Let him do some spectacular thing that would identify him to their Gentile overlords and send waves of terror through the ranks of the wicked.

In answer Jesus said: "When it is evening, ye say, It will be fair weather: for the sky is red. And in the morning, It will be foul weather to day: for the sky is red and lowring. O ye hypocrites, ye can discern the face of the sky; but can ye not discern the signs of the times?" (Matt. 16:1-3.) The true signs of his divinity were before them. Let them pay attention to the doctrine he preached. Let them ask the lame and the blind and the deaf, who now leaped and saw and heard, let them learn from those whom he had healed whether he was the Son of God or not. Let them view the true signs of the times, not seek for something they had imagined in their evil hearts should be the case. The true signs were before them, and they could be read as easily as the signs foretelling the day's weather.

And so it is today. The Lord has poured and is pouring out the signs of the times on every hand. He is showing forth the very things, promised of old, that are to herald the coming of the Son of Man. And the issue before all men is whether they are able to read the signs of the times or whether they will ignore the divine warnings and continue on their godless course to an assured destruction. The true saints have this promise: "Unto you it shall be given to know the signs of the times, and the signs of the coming of the Son of Man." (D&C 68:11.) What, then, are these signs? Let us consider them under the following headings:

1. *The Preparatory Signs.*

When the apostles fell asleep, save only John who was translated, the gospel sun soon set upon a wicked world. Almost immediately a dark night of apostate darkness covered the earth. Early in the coming dawn, before the gospel sun rose again, certain preparatory work was under way to herald that glorious day. The Lord began to pour out his Spirit—the Light of Christ—upon men everywhere. As guided thereby, an age of renaissance and reformation began. The dark gloom of the long night began to give way before a destined dawn. Printing was discovered, the Bible was published, and learning increased. Columbus discovered America; its colonization followed; and an inspired constitution was adopted for the United States. The King James Version of the Holy Bible was translated to bring the ancient word to the people among whom the gospel would soon be restored. All these things, and many more that were companion to them, constitute the preparatory, initial signs that set the stage for the other and greater signs that were and are to be. These preparatory signs were but prelude to the promised day when young men would see visions and old men would dream dreams and the Lord would pour out his Spirit upon all flesh.

2. *The Signs That Prepare a People for Their Lord.*

This is the group of signs, above all others, that men must see and understand if they are to know the generation of their Lord's return. These signs include the opening of the heavens so that revelation pours forth anew as it did in ancient days; the coming forth of the Book of Mormon, that ancient record which testifies of Christ and his gospel; and the restoration, for the last time, of the fulness of the everlasting gospel, with all its graces, powers, and glories.

These signs include the setting up again on earth of the only true and living Church, the establishment of the Zion of God once more among men, and the preaching of the restored gospel in all the world as a witness unto all nations. They include the restoration of keys and powers and priesthoods, the coming of angelic ministrants from former days to confer upon mortals their rights and prerogatives, and the restitution of all things spoken by the mouths of all the holy prophets since the world began. They include the coming of John the Baptist, and Peter, James, and John; of Moses and Elijah and Elias; of Raphael and Gabriel and Michael; and of divers angels—all bringing back again their ancient powers and glories.

These signs include the sending of a messenger before the face of the Lord to prepare his way; the great and wondrous ministry of Joseph Smith, the prophet and seer of the Lord, who has done more save Jesus only for the salvation of men in this world than any other man who ever lived in it; and the total and complete establishment again on earth of all that appertains to the dispensation of the fulness of times. These, and all that grows out of them, constitute the great and glorious signs of the times. And they have already been shown forth that believing souls might be prepared by righteousness to abide the day of the Lord's coming.

3. *The Signs Involving the Chosen Ones of Israel.*

Surely these are signs that even the wicked and ungodly can discern in the face of the sky, as it were. Many scattered ones in all nations shall forsake families and friends and moneys and lands and gather to the houses of the Lord in the tops of the mountains of Israel. Others shall come together and live as people set apart; they shall make the stakes of Zion in all nations their refuge. The Jews shall go to Jerusalem preparatory to accepting Him whom their fathers crucified. The Ten Tribes—long lost from the knowledge of men—shall take up an abode in their ancient Palestine; the times of the Gentiles shall be fulfilled; and the Lamanites shall blossom as the rose. And accompanying it all, persecution shall be the heritage of the faithful. All who forsake the world and begin to live as becometh true saints shall feel the scourge of Satan, whether they are the seed of Abraham or the children of the aliens. Surely when people assemble in great numbers, when new nations are born in a day, and when whole congregations change their way of life, surely these are signs that can be read by all.

4. *The Temple-centered Signs.*

What ought the world to think when temples begin to dot the earth? When men begin to talk again of salvation for the dead as did Peter? When they begin anew to baptize for the dead as did Paul? Is not the coming of Elijah one of the signs of the times? And does not the fact that genealogical research, for all practical purposes, was born on the 3rd day of April in 1836 prove that he came? Every temple built in the last days, every new wave of genealogical interest and research, every baptism performed for the dead, every vicarious ordinance performed in a house of the Lord—all these are signs of the times, witnesses that the Lord's coming is near, even at the door.

5. *The Signs Involving Present World Conditions.*

How and in what way do worldliness and apostasy and

false worship become signs of the times? The answer is self-evident. The world itself is the social circumstances created by the acts of worldly people; it is the society in which carnal and sensual and devilish people dwell, and the end of the world is the destruction of the wicked. As the end draws near, wickedness and worldliness will increase until all the proud and they who do wickedly shall be ready for the burning.

Thus the signs of the times include the prevailing apostate darkness in the sects of Christendom and in the religious world in general. False churches, false prophets, false worship—breeding as they do a way of life that runs counter to the divine will—all these are signs of the times. As men's consciences are seared with the hot iron of sin, the Spirit of the Lord ceases to strive with them, sorrow and fear increase in their hearts, and they are prone, increasingly, to do that which is evil—all of which things are signs of the times. Robbery, plunder, murder, and violent crimes of all sorts; many of the strikes and labor disputes in the industrial world; much of the litigation that clogs the courts of the nations; drug abuse and indecent and immoral conduct; the spreading plague of evil abortions; the abominations of incest and homosexuality—all these things are signs of the times. Satan is not dead, and his influence is increasing and shall increase in the world until the end comes.

6. *The Signs of Wars and Plagues and Disasters.*

These are the signs toward which men generally look as they try to discern the face of the latter-day skies, and yet these are the lesser signs, those of relatively little moment when compared to the great signs involving the restoration of the saving truths. Nonetheless they are part of the signs of the times, and they are now being shown forth in power and with sorrowful results.

They include wars and rumors of wars. Probably there has been no single moment since South Carolina rebelled in 1861 when there has been peace on earth. We do not anticipate even a scant duration of time in the future when all armed conflict and all bloodshed will cease, until the Great Millennium arrives. Until then there will be wars and desolation and death; until then disease and plagues and pestilence will sweep the earth from time to time; until then there will be famines and hunger and men dying for want of bread. In these last days all things shall be in commotion. The waves of the seas will spread death; the volcanoes in many lands will belch forth their fire and brimstone; and earthquakes will increase in number and intensity. Woes shall rest upon men as the Lord by the voice of the forces of nature calls upon them to repent and be as he would have them be.

7. *The Signs That Lie in the Future.*

In the very nature of things, the signs of the times will not cease until the Lord comes. Those that involve chaos and commotion and distress of nations will continue in the future with even greater destructive force. Men's hearts will fail them for fear in greater degree hereafter than heretofore. Wars will get worse. Moments of armistice and peace will be less stable. Viewed in the perspective of years, all worldly things will degenerate. There will be an increasing polarization of views. There will be more apostasy from the Church, more summer saints and sunshine patriots who will be won over to the cause of the adversary. Those who support the kingdom because of the loaves and the fishes will find other bread to eat. While the faithful saints get better and better, and cleave more firmly to the heaven-sent standards, the world will get worse and worse and will cleave to the policies and views of Lucifer.

Among the specific signs that lie ahead are the building of the New Jerusalem and the rebuilding of the Jerusalem of old. The great conference at Adam-ondi-Ahman must yet be held. The two prophets must minister and be martyred in Jerusalem. The gloom and despair and death of Armageddon must yet cover the earth; Babylon must fall; the vineyard must be burned; and then the earth shall rest and the Lord Jesus shall rule and reign for the space of a thousand years. But before that great day there shall be signs and wonders of a marvelous and miraculous kind shown forth in heaven and on earth. These we shall consider in the next chapter.

Our souls cry out: "God hasten the day of the coming of thy Son," and yet we know that such cannot be. The day is fixed and the hour is set. The signs have been, are now, and will hereafter be shown forth. Our obligation is to discern the signs of the times lest we, with the world, be taken unawares.

Chapter 35

THE PROMISED SIGNS AND WONDERS

Signs and Wonders in Heaven and on Earth

We come now to those great signs of mystery and wonder, the signs that cause even the faithful to marvel and to wonder how and under what circumstances they will come to pass. They are to be shown forth in heaven above and on the earth beneath. They involve forces and powers beyond the control of man, except possibly in a few instances, and they all are in the future. None of them have yet transpired, nor will they for some years. There are, as we shall see, a number of specific things that must precede the manifestation of these signs to men. These signs and wonders of which we speak are indeed the crowning and culminating signs of the times, and their occurrence will be almost or actually concurrent with the great and dreadful day of the Lord.

Various passages of scripture tie these signs together and speak of them in such a way that it seems the course of wisdom for us to follow substantially the same course. The signs of which we speak are:

1. *Manifestations of blood, and fire, and vapors of smoke.*

2. *The sun shall be darkened and the moon turn into blood.*

3. *The stars shall hurl themselves from heaven.*

4. *The rainbow shall cease to appear in the mists and rains of heaven.*

5. *The sign of the Son of Man shall make its appearance.*

6. *A mighty earthquake, beyond anything of the past, shall shake the very foundations of the earth.*

As we consider these coming signs, our concern will be twofold: to identify what is involved so there will be no doubt as to the occurrences themselves, and to place each sign in its relationship to other known events so we can pinpoint, insofar as the revealed word allows, the actual time when it shall come to pass.

These various signs are alluded to, defined, and set forth in many passages of scripture. Each passage gives only a partial view of what is involved, and each adds a perspective not found in any of the others. All of them taken together let us know, insofar as can be, what the realities are. There remains, of course, much that we do not yet know about these signs. It is, however, a moral certainty—perhaps it is even a prophetic certainty—that more will be revealed about them before the time when they are manifest. Certainly, for instance, the two prophets who shall minister in Jerusalem for three and a half years, preaching and prophesying, shall make inspired utterances about that which is to come after their day and before the coming of their Lord. But let us now look to that prophetic word available to us and learn what we can of the mysterious signs and wonders that are yet to be shown forth by divine power in heaven and on earth.

Jesus said, as Luke records it: "And there shall be signs in the sun, and in the moon, and in the stars." The luminaries of the skies, in some marvelous way, shall bear a witness of the Lord's return. "And upon the earth" there shall be "distress of nations, with perplexity." The nations and kingdoms of the world, with all their leadership and power, shall not know where to turn or what to do. Their leaders will be perplexed. Shall they align themselves with these nations or with those? What alliances will best serve their own national interests? Rumors of war are everywhere. What is to be done to find peace and security? Or to add glory and renown to their nation? No human power can give the answers.

And amid it all, natural disasters shall be everywhere, "the sea and the waves roaring"—there shall be no safety upon the waters in the last days—"men's hearts failing them for fear, and for looking after those things which are coming on the earth: for the powers of heaven shall be shaken." Ought not men's hearts to fail them for fear when they see the volcanic eruptions, the earthquakes, the famine, the pestilence, the plagues, and the disease? It is as though the very human race is about to be destroyed. Is this to be the end of the earth and of all life upon its face? "And then shall they see the Son of man coming in a cloud with power and great glory." And among all the inhabitants of the earth, only the Latter-day Saints will have any peace of mind. Jesus' next words are addressed to them: "And when these things begin to come to pass"—and we are seeing some of them now, though the great day of fulfillment lies ahead—"then look up, and lift up your heads; for your redemption draweth nigh." (Luke 21:25-28.)

In revealing to us some of the things he said to the apostles on Olivet, the Lord said: "And it shall come to pass that he that feareth me"—meaning the faithful saints—"shall be looking forth for the great day of the Lord to come, even for the signs of the coming of the Son of Man." With all our hearts we seek to know and understand these signs. "And they shall see signs and wonders, for they shall be shown forth in the heavens above, and in the earth beneath." Some of these signs we have seen; most of them lie in futurity. "And they shall behold blood, and fire, and vapors of smoke." The blood and fire and vapors of smoke could all be man-made. Atomic bombs—dealing death, shedding blood, spreading fire, and rising in great clouds of smoke—could bring this to pass. In full measure it must refer to the fire and brimstone to be rained upon men at Armageddon, but it may be that even this will be the result of man's doings. "And before the day of the Lord shall come, the sun shall be darkened, and the moon be turned into blood, and the stars fall from heaven. . . . And then they shall look for me, and, behold, I will come." (D&C 45:39-44.)

These words are more specific than those in Luke. One, at least, of the "signs in the sun" is that it shall be darkened. It is not hard to envision how this shall come to pass. Samuel the Lamanite gave the Nephites a sign—separated as they were by an ocean from the actual events—whereby they would know of the death of Christ. "In that day that he shall suffer death," was the prophetic word; "the sun shall be darkened and refuse to give his light unto you; and also the moon and the stars; and there shall be no light upon the face of this land, even from the time that he shall suffer death, for the space of three days, to the time that he shall rise again from the dead." (Hel. 14:20.)

The fulfillment of Samuel's prophetic word is recorded in these words of scripture: "There was thick darkness upon all the face of the land, insomuch that the inhabitants thereof who had not fallen could feel the vapor of darkness; And there could be no light, because of the darkness, neither candles, neither torches; neither could there be fire kindled with their fine and exceedingly dry wood, so that there could not be any light at all; And there was not any light seen, neither fire, nor glimmer, neither the sun, nor the moon, nor the stars, for so great were the mists of darkness which were upon the face of the land. And it came to pass that it did last for the space of three days that there was no light seen." (3 Ne. 8:19-23.) This darkness came upon the Americas along with the great destructions that caused the whole continents to become deformed and changed. It is reasonable to suppose that some equivalent thing will cause darkness to cover the earth in the last days.

One, at least, of the signs "in the moon" is that the

moon shall be turned into blood. It is not difficult to envision a scene, amid the fires and burnings that shall ravage the earth, in which the moon, viewed through the smoke and polluted atmospheric conditions, would appear as red as blood. Little previews of this, when conditions are just right, are occasionally seen on earth even now. As to the stars falling from heaven, we shall have more to say shortly.

To what we have already seen about the signs shown forth by the sun, moon, and stars, let us add this verse from an early revelation: "Behold, I say unto you," saith the Lord, "that before this great day"—'my second coming'—"shall come the sun shall be darkened, and the moon shall be turned into blood, and the stars shall fall from heaven, and there shall be greater signs in heaven above and in the earth beneath." (D&C 29:14.) This divine word seems to say that yet unnamed signs—to be shown forth in heaven above and on the earth beneath—shall exceed in magnitude and glory even those of which we have been speaking. What these are remains to be seen.

Both Isaiah and Joel speak of these signs to be shown forth in the sun, moon, and stars, and seem to place the promised events in the midst of war and desolation. Isaiah says: "Behold, the day of the Lord cometh, cruel both with wrath and fierce anger, to lay the land desolate: and he shall destroy the sinners thereof out of it." Truly, it is the great and dreadful day of the Lord, the day of vengeance that was in his heart, the day when the wicked shall be burned. "For the stars of heaven and the constellations thereof shall not give their light: the sun shall be darkened in his going forth, and the moon shall not cause her light to shine." The new emphasis here, for our purposes, is on the moon and the stellar constellations being darkened as well as the sun. Obviously, if the sun is darkened, such will be the case also with the moon, for this lesser light is but a reflection of the greater; and if great darkening mists blot out the nearby brilliance of the sun, they will surely do the same for the twinkling glimmerings of the distant stars. "And I will punish the world for their evil, and the wicked for their iniquity," the holy word continues, thus keeping the heavenly signs in their setting, "and I will cause the arrogancy of the proud to cease, and will lay low the haughtiness of the terrible." (Isa. 13:9-11.)

Joel adds a new dimension by giving the word in this way: "And I will shew wonders in the heavens and in the earth, blood, and fire, and pillars of smoke." All this we have heretofore considered. "The sun shall be turned into darkness, and the moon into blood." This, too, we have duly noted. But then Joel says, with reference to the whole matter, that it shall come to pass "before the great and terrible day of the Lord come." (Joel 2:30-31.) Then, almost immediately, he launches into a prophecy about Armageddon and its dire destructions. This lets us know that although, as Isaiah seems to say, the desolations are in progress when the signs are given, yet the fulness of the day of wrath, meaning the final day of burning and destruction, shall not come until after the signs are shown forth. This accords with and amplifies what we have quoted from latter-day revelation.

Now let us come to the matter of the stars falling or being hurled from heaven. Our latter-day revelation speaks of the coming of the Lord and says that "so great shall be the glory of his presence that the sun shall hide his face in shame, and the moon shall withhold its light, and the stars shall be hurled from their places." (D&C 133:49.) From this account we conclude that the stars shall fall from heaven at the time of his arrival rather than before. In another passage, heretofore quoted in another connection, the Lord says: "Not many days hence and the earth shall tremble and reel to and fro as a drunken man; and the sun shall hide his face, and shall refuse to give light; and the moon shall be bathed in blood; and the stars shall become exceedingly angry, and shall cast themselves down as a fig falleth from off a fig-tree." (D&C 88:87.) Other passages also speak of the earth trembling and reeling to and fro and specify that it shall be when the Lord sets his foot again upon the Mount of Olives. (D&C 45:48.) Employing the strong language and graphic imagery that he alone can use with such power, Isaiah says: "The earth is utterly broken down, the earth is clean dissolved, the earth is moved exceedingly." He is talking of the new heaven and the new earth that shall come into being when the elements melt with fervent heat. "The earth shall reel to and fro like a drunkard, and shall be removed like a cottage; and the transgression thereof shall be heavy upon it." This, we repeat, is in the day of burning. "And it shall come to pass in that day, that the Lord shall punish the host of the high ones that are on high, and the kings of the earth upon the earth." (Isa. 24:19-21.)

Knowing that the earth is to reel to and fro, knowing that the mighty deep shall return to its place in the north, knowing that the continents and islands shall join again, what about the stars and their fall from heaven? Our answer is that it will seem to men on earth as though the stars—those great suns in the sidereal heavens around which other planets revolve—are falling because the earth reels. The great fixed stars will continue in their assigned orbits and spheres. The sun also will continue to give light, but it will appear to men to be darkened; and the moon will remain as she has been since the creation, but it will seem to mortal eyes as though she is bathed in blood.

Many scriptures speak of earthquakes as one of the signs of the times. We have noted this, somewhat repetitiously, as it has been associated with other matters. The clear inference is that for some reason as yet unknown to man, earthquakes have been and are destined to increase both in number and intensity in the last days. Certainly they shall increase in terror and destructive power simply because there are more people and more man-made structures on earth than at any previous time. And clearly the crowning earthquake—the earthquake of earthquakes—is the one that shall occur as the earth reels to and fro and the stars seem to fall from their places in the sidereal heavens.

As we consider the reeling of the earth to and fro and the total realignment of its land masses incident to the Second Coming, and as we consider the burning of the vineyard by fire to destroy the wicked, as they were once destroyed by water in the days of Noah, we are faced with a somewhat difficult problem relative to the rainbow. We say difficult because not all things relative to it have been revealed, and we have only a few slivers of divine truth upon which to build our house of understanding. In the eternal sense nothing is difficult once the whole matter has been revealed to minds prepared and qualified to receive and understand. Let us lay a foundation for the place the rainbow is destined to play in the Second Coming by recounting the circumstances under which it apparently came into being.

Seed time and harvest, in the sense of one season following another, exist because the axis of the earth is tilted twenty-three and a half degrees from the upright. This is the reason we have summer and winter, spring and fall. The first reference in the scriptures to seasons as we know them is in connection with the flood of Noah. There is a presumption that prior to the flood there were no seasons because the axis of the earth was upright, and a similar presumption that when the Millennium comes and the earth returns to its original paradisiacal state, once again the seasons as we know them will cease and that seed time and harvest will go on concurrently at all times. The whole earth at all times will be a garden as it was in the days of Eden.

Whatever the case may be with reference to these things, something apparently happened with reference to the rainbow in Noah's day, and something is certainly going to happen with reference to it in connection with the Lord's return. We are left to speculate relative to some of these matters, which is not all bad as long as any expressed views are clearly identified for what they are. In fact, in our present state of spiritual enlightenment the Lord deliberately leaves us to ponder and wonder about many things connected with his coming; in this way our hearts are centered upon him so that we will qualify in due course to receive absolute and clear revelation on many things.

After the flood Noah offered sacrifices, worshipped the Lord, and said in his heart: "I will call on the name of the Lord, that he will not again curse the ground any more for man's sake, for the imagination of man's heart is evil from his youth; and that he will not again smite any more everything living, as he hath done, while the earth remaineth." Man had been destroyed once, meaning every living soul save the eight who were on the ark. Such a slaughter staggers the imagination. Conceive of cities and nations buried under mountains of water and of millions of dead bodies tossed about by the watery waves. What was more natural than for Noah to plead with his God that such should never come to pass again?

With these thoughts, Noah coupled the sincere and devout prayer "that seed-time and harvest, and cold and heat, and summer and winter, and day and night, may not cease with man." Question: Why this prayer? Answer: If man was to survive in a world provided with days and nights and cold and heat, he must also have summer and winter and their consequent seed time and harvest. The seasons, as then given, must continue so that man might provide for himself food, clothing, and shelter.

In reply God told Noah and his sons: "I will establish my covenant with you, which I made unto your father Enoch, concerning your seed after you." This covenant, as we have seen, was that a remnant of the seed of Noah, after the flood, should inhabit the earth forever. At this point in the account the Lord promises that the various forms of life in the ark shall survive and multiply. And also: "Neither shall all flesh be cut off any more by the waters of a flood; neither shall there any more be a flood to destroy the earth." Thus the Lord granted Noah's petition in part only. He received no promise that man—wicked men—should not thereafter be destroyed, only that there would be no future destruction of all life by a flood.

Truly there was to be another day of death and destruction. But it would be a day of burning, a day when every corruptible thing should be consumed, a day when every living soul, save the few who were righteous, should be destroyed. "And I will establish my covenant with you," the Lord promised, "which I made unto Enoch, concerning the remnants of your posterity." Not all of Noah's seed would be burned. The God-fearing and the righteous would abide the day. A remnant—eight souls, as it were—would enter into the ark of the kingdom, shut the doors against the rain of wickedness in the world, and save themselves from the untoward generation of men among whom they had dwelt.

"And God made a covenant with Noah, and said, This shall be the token of the covenant I make between me and you, and for every living creature with you, for perpetual generations; I will set my bow in the cloud; and it shall be for a token of a covenant between me and the earth." The inference is that the rainbow is being shown forth for the first time and that for some reason unknown to us it had not been manifest before. However this may be, again for reasons unknown to us, the rainbow will soon cease to show its glimmering rays of color in the mists and clouds of the air.

"And it shall come to pass, when I bring a cloud over the earth"—the Lord is continuing to speak to Noah—"that the bow shall be seen in the cloud; and I will remember my covenant, which I have made between me and you, for every living creature of all flesh." This is the testimony the rainbow bears as pertaining to the flood of Noah, a flood that is past.

But that same rainbow also bears a witness about something that lies in the future. "And the bow shall be in the cloud," the divine word continues, "and I will look upon it, that I may remember the everlasting covenant, which I made unto thy father Enoch; that, when men should keep all my commandments, Zion should again come on the earth, the city of Enoch which I have caught up unto myself." The rainbow bears record that God will send again the Zion of Enoch, that the ancient holy city, the ancient City of Holiness, will descend out of heaven and be with men again on earth.

"And this is mine everlasting covenant, that when thy posterity shall embrace the truth"—when remnants of Noah's seed accept the gospel in the last days—"and look upward, then shall Zion look downward, and all the heavens shall shake with gladness, and the earth shall tremble with joy; And the general assembly of the church of the firstborn shall come down out of heaven, and possess the earth, and shall have place until the end come. And this is mine everlasting covenant, which I made with thy father Enoch." All this is part of the Second Coming. We shall build a New Jerusalem in Jackson County, Missouri, and Enoch's city shall descend and join with it.

Having stated these glorious truths, the Lord's very next words are: "And the bow shall be in the cloud, and I will establish my covenant unto thee, which I have made between me and thee, for every living creature of all flesh that shall be upon the earth. And God said unto Noah, This is the token of the covenant which I have established between me and thee; for all flesh that shall be upon the earth." (JST, Gen. 9:6-25.)

It is clear from the foregoing that there is some relationship between the destruction of the world by water in Noah's day, the destruction by fire in the day of the Lord Jesus Christ, and the placing of the rainbow in the heavens as a token of a covenant that involved both the flood and the Second Coming. Joseph Smith, with characteristic spiritual insight, ties the whole matter together by statements made on two different occasions. "The Lord deals with this people as a tender parent with a child," the Prophet said, "communicating light and intelligence and the knowledge of his ways as they can bear it. The inhabitants of the earth are asleep; they know not the day of their visitation. The Lord hath set the bow in the cloud for a sign that while it shall be seen, seed time and harvest, summer and winter shall not fail; but when it shall disappear, woe to that generation, for behold the end cometh quickly." (*Teachings,* p. 305.)

"I have asked of the Lord concerning His coming," the Prophet also said, "and while asking the Lord, He gave a sign and said, 'In the days of Noah I set a bow in the heavens as a sign and token that in any year that the bow should be seen the Lord would not come; but there should be seed time and harvest during that year: but whenever you see the bow withdrawn, it shall be a token that there shall be famine, pestilence, and great distress among the nations, and that the coming of the Messiah is not far distant.' But I will take the responsibility upon myself to prophesy in the name of the Lord, that Christ will not come this year, . . . for we have seen the bow." (*Teachings*, pp. 340-41.)

When shall all these things come to pass? When will the sun and the moon and the stars play their portentous part in the coming of Christ? When will the glimmering beauty of the bow in heaven cease to portray its span of colors to men? When will the sign of the coming of the Son of Man be given? We have already shown that the seven last plagues shall be poured out after the opening of the seventh seal, and thus in the beginning of the seventh thousand years. It is then that Armageddon shall be fought; it is then that Jerusalem shall again reap the fate that once was hers; it is then that the abomination that maketh desolate shall utterly destroy the wicked within her walls. All this, of course, will come after Judah returns, after the Jerusalem temple is built, after the Jews have begun to believe in their true Messiah.

Thus, Jesus on Olivet spoke of the gospel of the kingdom being preached in all the world in the last days and of a second "abomination of desolation" being "fulfilled." Then, using language that establishes a definite time frame and that sets forth an order of chronology, he said: "And immediately after the tribulation of those days"—the plagues and wars and abominable desolation that shall destroy again the city of Jerusalem in the final great war—"the sun shall be darkened, and the moon shall not give her light, and the stars shall fall from heaven, and the powers of heaven shall be shaken." He is speaking thus of the final great signs, the wonders and marvels that are yet to be, the final signs that shall be shown forth in heaven and on earth.

And then comes this word: "And, as I said before, after the tribulation of those days, and the powers of heaven shall be shaken"—with some deliberation and by emphasis born of repetition he is identifying the time frame—"then shall appear the sign of the Son of Man in heaven, and then shall all the tribes of the earth mourn; and they shall see the Son of Man coming in the clouds of heaven, with power and great glory." (JS-M 1:31-36.)

The sign of the coming of the Son of Man—what is it? We do not know. Our revelation says simply: "And immediately there shall appear a great sign in heaven, and all people shall see it together." (D&C 88:93.) In 1843 someone by the name of Redding claimed to have seen this promised sign. In response to this claim, the Prophet Joseph Smith said: "I shall use my right"—his right as a prophet to know and identify the signs of the times—"and declare that, notwithstanding Mr. Redding may have seen a wonderful appearance in the clouds one morning about sunrise (which is nothing very uncommon in the winter season) he has not seen the sign of the Son of Man, as foretold by Jesus; neither has any man, nor will any man, until after the sun shall have been darkened and the moon bathed in blood; for the Lord hath not shown me any such sign." (*Teachings*, p. 280.) Then the Prophet quoted the famous statement from Amos, "Surely the Lord God will do nothing, but he revealeth his secret unto his servants the prophets" (Amos 3:7), indicating that when the sign is given, the Lord's servants the prophets, including all the faithful saints, will know it for what it is, and thus be made aware that the long-expected day has arrived.

On another occasion the Prophet, after reciting that before our Lord returns, Jerusalem and her temple must be built and the waters of the Dead Sea healed, continued by saying: "There will be wars and rumors of wars, signs in the heavens above and on the earth beneath, the sun turned into darkness and the moon to blood, earthquakes in divers places, the seas heaving beyond their bounds; then"—meaning after all these things—"then will appear one grand sign of the Son of Man in heaven. But what will the world do? They will say it is a planet, a comet, etc. But the Son of Man will come as the sign of the coming of the Son of Man, which will be as the light of the morning cometh out of the east." (*Teachings*, pp. 286-87.)

All people shall see it together! It shall spread over all the earth as the morning light! "For as the light of the morning cometh out of the east, and shineth even unto the west, and covereth the whole earth, so shall also the coming of the Son of Man be." (JS-M 1:26.) Surely this is that of which Isaiah said: "And the glory of the Lord shall be revealed, and all flesh shall see it together: for the mouth of the Lord hath spoken it." (Isa. 40:5.) Surely this is that of which our revelation speaks: "Prepare for the revelation which is to come, when the veil of the covering of my temple, in my tabernacle, which hideth the earth, shall be taken off, and all flesh shall see me together." (D&C 101:23.) Surely this is that day of which Zechariah prophesied: "The Lord my God shall come, and all the saints with thee. And it shall come to pass in that day, that the light shall not be clear, nor dark: But it shall be one day which shall be known to the Lord, not day, nor night: but it shall come to pass, that at evening time it shall be light. . . .

And the Lord shall be king over all the earth." (Zech. 14:5-9.)

And thus all the promised signs shall come to pass and the Great God, who is Lord of all, shall come and reign on earth; and for the space of a thousand years the earth shall rest.

Chapter 36

BABYLON: A SIMILITUDE OF THE CHRISTIAN ERA

Babylon of Babylonia

It is our hope now to show how and in what way the fall of Babylon is related to the second coming of Him whose return will burn all those in Babylon. In order to do so, we must have some background information about Babylon herself and the part she played in the history of Israel anciently. Only in this way can we envision fully why she was chosen as a type and a figure for the downfall of evil organizations and the overthrow of worldliness in the last days.

We are so far removed in point of time from ancient Babylon that any impact she has on us and our lives seems to be no greater than that of a dim shadow cast by a passing cloud. We know so little about her evil power and man-made glory that we no longer fear and tremble at the mere mention of her name as did our forebears in ancient Israel. We have ceased to recoil in revulsion at her evil practices, and seldom equate them anymore with the sodomic vices of Gomorrah. We have lost sight of the great underlying reasons why the ancient prophets made Babylon and her fall a similitude for apostate religions, for evil governments, and for the world in general, all of which are destined to fall as Babylon fell.

It was in the days of Isaiah and Jeremiah that the prophetic word began to deal at great length with Babylon of Babylonia and her impact upon the ancient saints in Israel. As Jerusalem was the holy city where Jehovah's word was law, so Babylon was the evil metropolis from which the will of Satan went forth. As Palestine was the holy land where remnants of Israel still dwelt and where prophets still parted the heavenly veil, so Babylonia was a worldly kingdom where the priests of sin sought direction from that master whose servants they were. As Jerusalem was the sacred site of the house of the Lord in which the Jews worshipped their God in the name of Jehovah, so in Babylon there were more than fifty temples in which false gods received the meaningless incantations and worship of apostate peoples. Jerusalem was the capital city of the Lord's earthly kingdom; Babylon held a like status in the earthly kingdom of Lucifer.

Located astride the Euphrates, some fifty miles south of modern Baghdad in Iraq, Babylon was the most splendid city of antiquity. In size and magnitude it was overwhelming. Within its walls, on two hundred square miles of land, in closely spaced buildings, dwelt hosts of the Gentile hordes. During the reign of Nebuchadnezzar, who overran Judah and destroyed Jerusalem, it became the largest and most elaborate city in the ancient world. Also within its walls were the famous hanging gardens, rated by the Greeks as among the seven wonders of the world. Its engineers and artisans both bridged over and tunneled under the great Euphrates, and the city had extensive parks, magnificent buildings, navigable canals, and splendid streets. Chariots could be driven on its dual walls, and its municipals found it easy to believe that the works of their hands had been made by Omnipotence itself.

In the course of a long and stormy history, many other nations and kingdoms were subject to and bowed before Babylon. After Lehi left Jerusalem in 600 B.C., Nebuchadnezzar in successive invasions, in 597, 586, and 581 B.C., overran the kingdom of Judah, destroyed Jerusalem, and took the Jews captive and transported them to Babylon, there to live in bondage. How filled with tears and sorrow are these sad words of the ancient covenant people, serving as slaves to Gentile overlords in Babylon, the center of worldliness: "By the rivers of Babylon, there we sat down, yea, we wept, when we remembered Zion. We hanged our harps upon the willows in the midst thereof. For there they that carried us away captive required of us a song; and they that wasted us required of us mirth, saying, Sing us one of the songs of Zion. How shall we sing the Lord's song in a strange land?" (Ps. 137:1-4.)

Then, in the providences of the Lord, Cyrus the Persian in 539 B.C. conquered Babylon and freed the captive Jews that they might go back to Jerusalem and build anew, as they then did under Zerubabbel, the holy sanctuary of the Great Jehovah. Their temple vessels, taken into Babylon along with their blinded king Zedekiah, were returned. And the Jews began a new life in their homeland, albeit in large part an apostate way of life, which prepared them for what they were when the Lord Jesus came among them.

But with Cyrus the Persian began the decline and fall of Babylon. Never again did it regain the glory and splendor of the days of Nebuchadnezzar, all of which is reminiscent of the statement made by Daniel to that great king, while interpreting for him his dream of the great image: "Thou, O king, art a king of kings: for the God of heaven hath given thee a kingdom, power, and strength, and glory. And wheresoever the children of men dwell, the beasts of the field and the fowls of the heaven hath he given into thine hand, and hath made thee ruler over them all. Thou art this head of gold. And after thee shall arise another kingdom inferior to thee." (Dan. 2:37-39.)

Babylon was also destroyed by Xerxes in 478 B.C. and again after Alexander the Great overran the Persian empire in 330 B.C. A rival city was soon built on the Tigris, and Babylon never recovered. Today the greatest world city of antiquity is a mound of desert earth that will not rise again. Babylon the great has fallen forever.

Ancient Babylon Prefigures Modern Babylon

In prophetic imagery, Babylon is the world with all its carnality and wickedness. Babylon is the degenerate social order created by lustful men who love darkness rather than light because their deeds are evil. Babylon is the almighty governmental power that takes the saints of God into captivity; it is the false churches that build false temples and worship false gods; it is every false philosophy (as, for instance, organic evolution) that leads men away from God and salvation. Babylon is false and degenerate religion in all its forms and branches. Babylon is the communistic system that seeks to destroy the freedom of people in all nations and kingdoms; it is the Mafia and crime syndicates that murder and rob and steal; it is the secret combinations that seek for power and unrighteous dominion over the souls of men. Babylon is the promoter of pornography; it is organized crime and prostitution; it is every evil and wicked and ungodly thing in our whole social structure.

Conditions in the world today are as they were in ancient Babylon. What, then, is more natural than for the prophets, aware of the sins and evils and final destruction of Babylon, to use her as a symbol of that which now is and which shall soon be. The things that happened with reference to the ancient Jews in Babylon of Babylonia were in similitude of what was destined to be with reference to the Lord's people and the spiritual Babylon of the world after the coming of Christ. Let us consider the similitudes involved under four headings.

1. *As the Jews were carried as captives into Babylon, so the Church and kingdom set up by the Lord Jesus has been overcome by the world.*

If the Jews had lived in all respects as becometh saints, walking uprightly before the Lord and keeping his commandments, he would have preserved them in their own land with their own king. Israel was scattered and the Jews went into captivity because of disobedience. Such was the punishment decreed for their rebellion. The Lord pours plagues upon the wicked in consequence of their sins, and so the outpourings of pestilence and sorrow fulfill his purposes.

The Babylonian captivity of the Jews was thus in harmony with the mind and will of the Lord. And so with reference to it, the Lord said to Jeremiah: "I have made the earth, the man and the beast that are upon the ground, by my great power and by my outstretched arm, and have given it unto whom it seemed meet unto me. And now have I given all these lands into the hand of Nebuchadnezzar the king of Babylon, my servant; and the beasts of the field have I given him also to serve him. And all nations shall serve him. . . . And it shall come to pass, that the nation and kingdom which will not serve the same Nebuchadnezzar the king of Babylon, and that will not put their neck under the yoke of the king of Babylon, that nation will I punish, saith the Lord, with the sword, and with the famine, and with the pestilence, until I have consumed them by his hand." (Jer. 27:5-8.)

In like manner the saints in the early days of the Christian era soon forsook the faith. Tares were sown in the gospel fields. And "the apostate, the whore, even Babylon, that maketh all nations to drink of her cup, in whose hearts the enemy, even Satan, sitteth to reign"—even he took over the kingdom. (D&C 86:3.) The apostasy was complete and universal. All nations and kingdoms served the king of Babylon. But in the eternal providences of Him who gives nations and kingdoms to whomsoever he chooses, the ascendancy of Babylon will not last forever. The Jews were in Babylon for seventy years, and Babylon has now ruled the world for nearly two thousand years since the early apostles fell asleep, but her kingdom will soon fall. Thus saith the Lord: "They have strayed from mine ordinances, and have broken mine everlasting covenant; They seek not the Lord to establish his righteousness, but every man walketh in his own way, and after the image of his own God, whose image is in the likeness of the world, and whose substance is that of an idol, which waxeth old and shall perish in Babylon, even Babylon the great, which shall fall." (D&C 1:15-16.)

2. *As false prophets arose in Israel to cry peace and safety and to announce, falsely, that the Jews would soon be free from Babylonian bondage, so false ministers in an apostate Christendom profess to make salvation available to men on terms and conditions of their own.*

False prophets always arise to oppose the truth. There must needs be an opposition in all things. Whenever the Lord sends his true ministers, Satan sends his priests. It appears that almost a whole congregation of false prophets stepped forth to deceive the people relative to the Babylonian captivity. The situation became so serious that the Lord gave this commandment: "Hearken not ye to your prophets, nor to your diviners, nor to your dreamers, nor to your enchanters, nor to your sorcerers, which speak unto you, saying, Ye shall not serve the king of Babylon: For they prophesy a lie unto you, . . . For I have not sent them, saith the Lord, yet they prophesy a lie in my name; . . . that ye might perish, ye, and the prophets that prophesy unto you." (Jer. 27:9-10, 15.)

One of these false prophets was Hananiah, who had a great confrontation with Jeremiah "in the house of the Lord, in the presence of the priests and of all the people." Using the Lord's name, Hananiah prophesied that the yoke of the king of Babylon had been broken and that the vessels of the Lord's house would be returned to Jerusalem within two years. To dramatize his sayings, Hananiah broke a yoke of wood. The word of the Lord that then came through Jeremiah acclaimed that the king of Babylon would "put a yoke of iron upon the neck of all these nations," which could not be broken. As to the false prophet, Jeremiah said: "Hear now, Hananiah; The Lord hath not sent thee; but thou makest this people to trust in a lie. Therefore thus saith the Lord; Behold, I will cast thee from off the face of the earth: this year thou shalt die, because thou hast taught rebellion against the Lord. So Hananiah the prophet died the same year in the seventh month." (Jer. 28:1, 14-17.)

Wherein does this differ from what goes on today in the religious world? False ministers, in their houses of worship, before their fellows, and in the presence of the people, profess to tell what the Lord has said about salvation, when he has said no such thing. They speak, as it were, in his name—on the authority of the Holy Book, as they express it—telling men who live in Babylon to do this or that and be saved. Their doctrines are false; they teach people to trust in a lie. God has not sent them; they are blind guides who lead blind followers into pits of despair.

3. *As the Jews came out of Babylon, freed from captivity, so the call goes forth today to flee from Babylon and the chains of worldliness and to come into that liberty wherewith Christ hath made men free.*

Scriptures that commanded the ancient Jews to arise, leave Babylon, and go back to their homeland, and those scriptures that command modern Israel to leave the world and come to a latter-day Zion, are almost identical in thought content. Ancient Babylon was the world, with all its evil and wickedness, from which the Jews of old must flee to be saved; Jerusalem was their Zion where the faithful must assemble to worship the Lord. And the world, all of it, with its Babylonish carnality, is the spiritual Babylon from which all who love the Lord must flee; they too must come to Zion, a latter-day Zion, there to worship the Lord their God and become heirs of salvation.

The Lord's call to his ancient covenant people to leave Babylon and return to Jerusalem contained such commands and exhortations as these: "Flee and escape out of the land of Babylon, . . . declare in Zion the vengeance of the Lord our God." (Jer. 50:28.) "Flee out of the midst of Babylon, and deliver every man his soul: be not cut off in her iniquity; for this is the time of the Lord's vengeance. . . . Come, and let us declare in Zion the work of the Lord our God. . . . My people, go ye out of the midst of her, and deliver ye every man his soul from the fierce anger of the Lord. . . . Remember the Lord afar off, and let Jerusalem come into your mind." (Jer. 51:6, 10, 45, 50.)

Could we not, with propriety, use these very words in calling upon men to come into the kingdom today? Indeed, some of the words used with reference to the ancient gathering again in Jerusalem seem to have been chosen so as to have a dual application. For instance: "In those days, and in that time, saith the Lord"—and the time and the day, with equal propriety, can be the return from Babylon and the coming out of the world and into the latter-day kingdom—"the children of Israel shall come, they and the children of Judah together, going and weeping: they shall go, and seek the Lord their God. They shall ask the way to Zion with their faces thitherward, saying, Come, and let us join ourselves to the Lord in a perpetual covenant that shall not be forgotten." (Jer. 50:4-5.)

As it was anciently, so it is today. The ancient call is going forth in a modern setting. Those who flee from the Chaldeans, as did their fathers, shall be saved in Zion, as were their fathers. Those who loiter by the way and who remain in whole or in part in Babylon shall be destroyed in the coming day of burning. "Go ye forth of Babylon," Isaiah says to us in the last days, "flee ye from the Chaldeans, with a voice of singing declare ye, tell this, utter it even to the end of the earth; say ye, The Lord hath redeemed his servant Jacob." (Isa. 48:20.) The great day of gathering is at hand.

How joyous is the day! What glories and wonders attend its arrival! It is the dawning of that day of which Isaiah acclaimed: "Break forth into joy, sing together, ye waste places of Jerusalem: for the Lord hath comforted his people, he hath redeemed Jerusalem." This is not yet, but is soon to be. "The Lord hath made bare his holy arm in the eyes of all the nations; and all the ends of the earth shall see the salvation of our God." This also is soon to be. "Depart ye, depart ye, go ye out from thence, touch no unclean thing; go ye out of the midst of her; be ye clean, that bear the vessels of the Lord." (Isa. 52:9-11.)

With these words of poetic majesty calling to us over a span of two and a half millenniums, we hear also the like strains of melody made in our day. To us, the Lord our God—"who shall come down upon the world with a curse to judgment; yea, upon all the nations that forget God, and upon all the ungodly" among his people—the Lord says that "he shall make bare his holy arm in the eyes of all the nations, and all the ends of the earth shall see the salvation of their God." He is confirming the word given anciently through Isaiah. "Wherefore, prepare ye, prepare ye, O my people," the divine voice continues. "Sanctify yourselves; gather ye together, O ye people of my church. . . . Go ye out from Babylon. Be ye clean that bear the vessels of the Lord. . . . Yea, verily I say unto you again, the time has come when the voice of the Lord is unto you: Go ye out of Babylon; gather ye out from among the nations, from the four winds, from one end of heaven to the other. . . . Go ye out from among the nations, even from Babylon, from the midst of wickedness, which is spiritual Babylon." (D&C 133:2-5, 7, 14.)

4. *As Babylon was destroyed with violence, never to rise again, so shall it soon be with spiritual Babylon; she too shall be swept from the earth, and hell will be filled with her municipals.*

Here is a truism that all men should hear: Babylon fell, and her gods with her; and Babylon shall fall, and her gods with her. False gods create an evil society. The world is the world, and Babylon is Babylon, because they worship false gods. When men worship the true God according to gospel standards, their social conditions rival those in Enoch's city; when men worship false gods, they fall into the ways of the world, and their social conditions become as those in Babylon. When we view the fall of Babylon anciently, what we see is the destruction of her idols and ways of worship; and when we shall come to the fall of Babylon in the last days, it will be—oh, blessed day—the destruction of false worship. The Athanasian creed will return to the realms of darkness where it was spawned. The doctrine of salvation by grace alone without works shall be anathema. The great and abominable church shall tumble to the dust. False worship shall cease.

It comes as no surprise, then, to find the accounts of the destruction of ancient Babylon interspersed with expressions about the fate of her false gods. "Declare ye among the nations, and publish, and set up a standard," the Lord said to Jeremiah; "publish, and conceal not: say, Babylon is taken, Bel is confounded, Merodach is broken in pieces; her idols are confounded, her images are broken in pieces." Merodach (Marduk) was king of the gods of Babylon. Bel was one of the principal deities. According to apocryphal sources, it was the image of Bel-Marduk that Daniel and his companions were asked to worship.

Babylon's sins befell her because she was "proud against the Lord, against the Holy One of Israel." Hers was a "land of graven images," and the people were "mad upon their idols." (Jer. 50:2, 29, 38.) Babylonians were wicked because their gods had no power to lift them to righteousness. "Every man is brutish by his knowledge; every founder is confounded by the graven image: for his molten image is falsehood, and there is no breath in them. They are vanity, the work of errors: in the time of their visitation they shall perish." And so the Lord says: "I will punish Bel in Babylon, . . . and the nations shall not flow together any more unto him: yea, the wall of Babylon shall fall. . . . Therefore, behold, the days come, that I will do judgment upon the graven images of Babylon: and her whole land shall be confounded, and all her slain shall fall in the midst of her." (Jer. 51:17-18, 44, 47.) Truly, false worship is the root of all evil.

When John the Revelator wrote the account of his vision of the future fall of Babylon, we suppose he had before him chapters 50 and 51 of Jeremiah, chapter 13 of Isaiah, and other scriptures that tell of the fall of old Babylon. At least John picked up the language and emphasis of the old scriptures and gave them new meanings and impact in the new scripture that flowed from his pen. All of this ancient word is deserving of an in-depth study. For our purposes, however, that we may have a feel at least of what is involved, we select out the following expressions.

Babylon is to be overthrown by "an assembly of great nations from the north country," and she shall become "a wilderness, a dry land, and a desert." And, "Because of the wrath of the Lord it shall not be inhabited, but it shall be wholly desolate: every one that goeth by Babylon shall be astonished, and hiss at all her plagues." Of her it shall be said: "How is the hammer of the whole earth cut asunder and broken! how is Babylon become a desolation among the nations!" What is her destiny? "The wild beasts [wolves, or howling creatures] of the desert with the wild beasts of the islands shall dwell there, and the owls [ostriches] shall dwell therein: and it shall be no more inhabited for ever; neither shall it be dwelt in from generation to generation. As God overthrew Sodom and Gomorrah and the neighbour cities thereof, saith the Lord; so shall no man abide there, neither shall any son of man dwell therein. . . . At the noise of the taking of Babylon the earth is moved, and the cry is heard among the nations." (Jer. 50:9, 12-13, 23, 39-40, 46.)

"Babylon hath been a golden cup in the Lord's hand, that made all the earth drunken: the nations have drunken of her wine; therefore the nations are mad. Babylon is suddenly fallen and destroyed: howl for her. . . . O thou that dwellest upon many waters, abundant in treasures, thine end is come, and the measure of thy covetousness. . . . And Babylon shall become heaps, a dwellingplace for dragons [jackals], an astonishment, and an hissing, without an inhabitant. . . . Thus shall Babylon sink, and shall not rise.'' (Jer. 51:7-8, 13, 37, 64.)

We know of no prophet whose ability to create similitudes and use them to teach great and eternal truths equals that of Isaiah. When he speaks of the fall of Babylon and of the second coming of Him who overthrew Babylon once and will do so again, there is no way of knowing where one account ends and the other begins. Indeed, in his presentation the fall of Babylon becomes the destruction of the wicked in the last days, and ''the day of the Lord'' that overthrew the wicked anciently is the same day that shall crush them into nothingness in the days that lie ahead. The fall of Babylon anciently, with all its blood and horror, becomes and is the similitude whereby those with spiritual insight come to know what will be involved in the future fall of the kingdom of the same name.

There is, Isaiah says, ''a tumultuous noise of the kingdoms of nations gathered together: the Lord of hosts mustereth the host of the battle. They come from a far country, from the end of heaven, even the Lord, and the weapons of his indignation, to destroy the whole land.'' When and in what age shall this occur? The application is to both falls of both Babylons. Having so stated, Isaiah next says: ''Howl ye; for the day of the Lord is at hand; it shall come as a destruction from the Almighty. Therefore shall all hands be faint, and every man's heart shall melt: And they shall be afraid: pangs and sorrows shall take hold of them; they shall be in pain as a woman that travaileth: they shall be amazed one at another; their faces shall be as flames.'' As far as we are concerned, he is speaking of the Second Coming, but the facts and the imagery had their beginning in the ancient destructions.

Then Isaiah speaks of the Lord's wrath, the destruction of the wicked, and the sun being darkened, which we have quoted in other connections, all of which refer to the Second Coming. This is followed by descriptive language that occurred anciently and will be repeated in due course. Then comes the famous passage about the fate of Babylon: "And Babylon, the glory of kingdoms, the beauty of the Chaldees' excellency," the seeric word proclaims, "shall be as when God overthrew Sodom and Gomorrah. It shall never be inhabited, neither shall it be dwelt in from generation to generation: neither shall the Arabian pitch tent there; neither shall the shepherds make their fold there. But wild beasts of the desert shall lie there; and their houses shall be full of doleful creatures; and owls [ostriches] shall dwell there, and satyrs [he-goats] shall dance there. And the wild beasts of the islands shall cry in their desolate houses, and dragons [jackals] in their pleasant palaces: and her time is near to come, and her days shall not be prolonged." (Isa. 13:4-8, 19-22.)

Then come these words, which have a dual meaning: "How hath the oppressor ceased! the golden city ceased! The Lord hath broken the staff of the wicked, and the sceptre of the rulers. He who smote the people in wrath with a continual stroke, he that ruled the nations in anger, is persecuted, and none hindereth. The whole earth is at rest, and is quiet: they break forth into singing." (Isa. 14:4-7.) The whole earth is at rest! It is the Millennium. Truly, "Babylon is fallen, is fallen; and all the graven images of her gods he hath broken unto the ground." (Isa. 21:9.) The Lord is King, and he alone is worshipped.

Chapter 37

THE FALL OF BABYLON

The Time of the Fall of Babylon

When, oh, when will Babylon fall? When will wickedness cease and the earth rest? Must the saints forever face and fight the abominations in this present fallen and carnal world? Every faithful soul cries out: "Thy kingdom come. Thy will be done in earth, as it is in heaven." (Matt. 6:10.) And come it must, and come it will; and it shall be ushered in by the fall of Babylon. There is no concord between Christ and Belial; and when the Lord comes to reign, the world and its wickedness must be cast into the lake of fire.

Our insight into the fall and utter destruction of this great whore of all the earth, who sitteth upon many waters and exerciseth dominion over the kings of the earth, our insight into her death and the burning of her disease-ridden body, comes from the pen of John. And nowhere else in all his writings—not in his Gospel, not in his epistles, not elsewhere in the Apocalypse—nowhere does he delve so deeply and write so plainly and with such incisive particularity as he does in recording the fall and destruction of Babylon. Oh, how he and all the saints have longed for the day when this earth, free from Babylon and her abominations, shall be a fit abode for the King of Peace and Righteousness!

In setting forth what shall soon transpire with reference to false churches, false governments, and false ways of worship, all being part and portion of Babylon, we shall simply follow the recitations of the Beloved John, interspersing them with such explanations as are needed to put them in their relationship to the whole of that strange act which the Lord is performing on the stage of the world. Our first reference follows the announcement of the restoration of the everlasting gospel by an angelic ministrant. This angel—who we have seen was, in fact, many angels, all of whom combined to bring again the doctrines, powers, and keys that taken together comprise the fulness of the everlasting gospel—this angel, who has already come, shall be followed by two more. The next one to come shall issue the great proclamation: "Babylon is fallen, is fallen, that great city, because she made all nations drink of the wine of the wrath of her fornication." Fornication, adultery, and whoredoms, these are the terms the prophets use to describe the false worship, the devil's way of worship, the worship that is not of God. They are the most grievous of all sins save murder only, and they are used to denote the most degenerate of all states that can befall man save only his death and destruction, and that state is to worship false gods and thereby to be cut off from any hope of salvation. Thus Babylon is fallen because she imposed false religion, false worship, and thereby a degenerate way of life upon men in all nations.

False worship brings damnation. And so we hear the next angel say, of those in Babylon: "If any man worship the beast and his image, and receive his mark in his forehead, or in his hand"—whoso readeth let him understand—"The same shall drink of the wine of the wrath of God, which is poured out without mixture into the cup of his indignation; and he shall be tormented with fire and brimstone in the presence of the holy angels, and in the presence of the Lamb: And the smoke of their torment ascendeth up for ever and ever: and they have no rest day nor night, who worship the beast and his image, and whosoever receiveth the mark of his name." (Rev. 14:8-11.)

Babylon shall fall after the gospel has been restored, and those in Babylon shall suffer the fires of eternal torment, the burning anguish of cloudy and seared consciences, in that hell which is prepared for the wicked. Why? Their fate befalls them because they worshipped—not the Father, in the name of the Son, by the power of the Spirit—but the beast and his image. They sacrificed at evil altars. Theirs was a worldly way of life. They did not overcome the world, and put off the natural man, and become saints through the atonement of Christ the Lord. They dwelt in Babylon in the day of her fall, in the day when the sword of vengeance fell upon her.

When will Babylon fall? We have already set forth that which is known about the seven last plagues and shown that they will take place in the beginning of the seventh thousand years. One of these, the sixth, involved "the spirits of devils, working miracles"; it resulted in the gathering together of all nations to "the battle of that great day of God Almighty" at Armageddon. Then, still in the day of the seventh seal, the seventh angel poured out his vial, and there followed the greatest earthquake of the ages, the one in which "every island fled away, and the mountains were not found." It is in this setting that John records: "And the great city was divided into three parts [he is speaking of Jerusalem], and the cities of the nations fell [this is all the great cities in all nations]: and great Babylon came in remembrance before God, to give unto her the cup of the wine of the fierceness of his wrath." Then John speaks of the "great hail out of heaven" that shall destroy those in the battle of Armageddon. (Rev. 16:14-21.)

That is to say, Babylon shall fall during the battle of Armageddon. She shall fall in the very hour when the Lord returns. She shall fall when the vineyard is burned and every corruptible thing is consumed. Until then, Satan shall have power over his own dominion and abominations shall abound. But thanks be to God, when the hour of his judgment is come, the wicked shall be destroyed, millennial rest will commence, and he shall reign gloriously among his saints for the space of a thousand years.

Babylon: The Church of the Devil

Babylon the great has been arraigned before the bar of the Great Jehovah; many witnesses have borne record of her sins; and the blood of the martyred saints has cried out against her. She has been weighed in the balance and found wanting, and the Great God has issued his eternal decree. The penalty is death. Babylon shall be burned with fire. The execution date is set and shall not be delayed.

Our friend John, by divine appointment, is about to see her fall and describe the cleansing fires that shall consume the corruptions within her walls. But first he must see her in all her wickedness and degeneracy. After an angelic ministrant sets forth her sins and shows him the iniquities in which she is ensnared, his voice will join the great chorus that cries, Amen, to the judgment rendered by the Just Judge against all that is evil and carnal and devilish in the world.

"One of the seven angels which had the seven vials," out of which were poured the seven last plagues, said to John: "Come hither; I will shew unto thee the judgment of the great whore that sitteth upon many waters: With whom the kings of the earth have committed fornication, and the inhabitants of the earth have made drunk with the wine of her fornication." What sins must men commit to be found deserving of death? The sins of Babylon—what are they? Why is she to be burned with fire? The angelic reply cries out: Because of her fornication; that is, because of false worship, false religion, and a false plan of salvation, because she guides men to worship false gods. And if the Judge of all the earth, whose judgments are just, decrees the death penalty, who shall question the wisdom of the verdict, or say him nay on the day of the execution?

"So he carried me away in the spirit into the wilderness," John says, "and I saw a woman sit upon a scarlet coloured beast, full of names of blasphemy, having seven heads and ten horns." This woman is the great and abominable church. "The seven heads are seven mountains"—the seven hills of Rome—"on which the woman sitteth." John is seeing that which Nephi saw.

"And the woman was arrayed in purple and scarlet colour, and decked with gold and precious stones and pearls, having a golden cup in her hand full of abominations and filthiness of her fornication." When Nephi saw in vision these same things, an angel—perhaps the same one who appeared to John—said to the American seer: "Look, and behold that great and abominable church, which is the mother of abominations, whose founder is the devil." (1 Ne. 14:9.) "And it came to pass that I beheld this great and abominable church," Nephi said, "and I saw the devil that he was the founder of it. And I also saw gold, and silver, and silks, and scarlets, and fine-twined linen, and all manner of precious clothing; and I saw many harlots. And the angel spake unto me, saying: Behold the gold, and the silver, and the silks, and the scarlets, and the fine-twined linen, and the precious clothing, and the harlots, are the desires of this great and abominable church." (1 Ne. 13:6-8.)

"And upon her forehead," John continues, "was a name written, MYSTERY, BABYLON THE GREAT, THE MOTHER OF HARLOTS AND ABOMINATIONS OF THE EARTH." What a name this is for a church—no, not a church, but rather a particular church—the church of the devil. Names among the Hebrews bore witness of the chief characteristics of those upon whose heads they were placed. This church—glorifying the mysterious and unknown; aping the conduct of those in the great city of Nebuchadnezzar; herself a harlot and also the mother of other apostate churches—this church was the mother of the abominations of the earth. Her theology and her practices fostered sin and encouraged men to walk in a Babylonish path without fear of divine retribution. "Come unto me," she proclaimed, "and for your money you shall be forgiven of your sins." (Morm. 8:32.) Wars were fought at her command and converts were made, not by the sweet voice of persuasion, not by inspired preaching, but by the edge of the sword and the point of the spear. Inquisitions took the lives of her heretics, and religion became an arm of the state so that sovereign lords could enforce religious rites and force men to believe approved doctrines.

"And I saw the woman"—the great and abominable church, the church of the devil—"drunken with the blood of the saints, and with the blood of the martyrs of Jesus: and when I saw her, I wondered with great admiration." Nephi's views were similar. "I saw among the nations of the Gentiles," the American prophet said, "the formation of a great church. And the angel said unto me: Behold the formation of a church which is most abominable above all other churches, which slayeth the saints of God, yea, and tortureth them and bindeth them down, and yoketh them with a yoke of iron, and bringeth them down into captivity. . . . And also for the praise of the world do they destroy the saints of God, and bring them down into captivity." (1 Ne. 13:4-5, 9.)

John's account makes it clear that both church and state are involved in the abominations that shall bring to pass the fall of Babylon. As the angel has already intoned, "the kings of the earth have committed fornication," with "the great whore that sitteth upon many waters." Now in the hidden and half-understood imagery in which the whole concept is couched, the angel speaks of ten kings, symbolical, as we suppose, of all the kings of the earth. "These have one mind, and shall give their power and strength unto the beast. These shall make war with the Lamb, and the Lamb shall overcome them: for he is Lord of lords, and King of kings: and they that are with him are called, and chosen, and faithful. And he saith unto me, The waters which thou sawest, where the whore sitteth, are peoples, and multitudes, and nations, and tongues." In the ultimate sense it is the church and not the state that has responsibility for the abominations of the last days, for the moral standards come from religion. The state is an arm, a tool, a part of Babylon; the state operates on the basis of the low and evil standards of the church.

The nations and parts of Babylon shall war among themselves. These nations "shall hate the whore, and shall make her desolate and naked, and shall eat her flesh, and burn her with fire." So spake the angel to John. "For God hath put in their hearts to fulfill his will, and to agree, and give their kingdom unto the beast, until the words of God shall be fulfilled. And the woman which thou sawest is that great city"—Rome, the capital city of the Babylonish church—"which reigneth over the kings of the earth." (Rev. 17:1-18.)

Our understanding of what John saw and taught is confirmed and clarified by the parallel accounts of the same things written by Nephi. Speaking of this same latter-day period, when the day for the burning of the tares is near, an angel said to Nephi: "Behold there are save two churches only; the one is the church of the Lamb of God, and the other is the church of the devil." At this late date, after the restoration of the gospel, after the setting up again on earth of the church and kingdom of God, after abominations had reigned for centuries—after all this, men are divided into two camps. There is polarization; the righteous are on one hand and the wicked on the other. "Wherefore, whoso belongeth not to the church of the Lamb of God belongeth to that great church, which is the mother of abominations; and she is the whore of all the earth."

Having heard this angelic pronouncement, Nephi then said: "And it came to pass that I looked and beheld the whore of all the earth"—the time frame is now the latter days—"and she sat upon many waters; and she had dominion over all the earth, among all nations, kindreds, tongues, and people." Babylon is everywhere; the evil power controls the world. Worldliness is supreme; carnality reigns in the hearts of people in all nations. It cannot be otherwise, for no standard of righteousness is raised by those who have long since lost the pure and perfect gospel of the lowly Nazarene. In this period there are but few members of "the church of the Lamb of God."

But the downfall of the great and abominable church is at hand. The fall of Babylon is about to come to pass. And thus Nephi sets forth in plain words what John has preserved for us in imagery and figures. "And it came to pass that I beheld that the wrath of God was poured out upon the great and abominable church," Nephi says, "insomuch that there were wars and rumors of wars among all the nations and kindreds of the earth." Surely this is our day, and surely the intensity and horror of what is to be shall increase as the days go by. "And as there began to be wars and rumors of wars among all the nations which belonged to the mother of abominations, the angel spake unto me, saying: Behold, the wrath of God is upon the mother of harlots; and behold, thou seest all these things—And when the day cometh that the wrath of God is poured out upon the mother of harlots, which is the great and abominable church of all the earth, whose founder is the devil, then, at that day, the work of the Father shall commence, in preparing the way for the fulfilling of his covenants, which he hath made to his people who are of the house of Israel." (1 Ne. 14:10-17.)

This is the day in which the Lord "will preserve the righteous by his power, even if it so be that the fulness of his wrath must come, and the righteous be preserved, even unto the destruction of their enemies by fire. Wherefore, the righteous need not fear; for thus saith the prophet, they shall be saved, even if it so be as by fire." (1 Ne. 22:17.) This is the day in which Babylon shall fall, to which fall we shall now turn our attention.

"Babylon Is Fallen, Is Fallen"

Babylon was conceived by Satan, gestated in hell, born in sin, and lives in lust and lewdness. She has grown into a horrible two-headed monster. Hers is an ecclesiastical kingdom, and hers is a political kingdom. We shall now view, through the eyes of John, the fall of the ecclesiastical kingdom; and when we recount what the revelations say about the battle of Armageddon, we shall tell of the fall of the political kingdom. The church of the devil is both an ecclesiastical and a political kingdom; it reigns in the hearts of men by imposing false doctrines upon them, and it uses the power of the state to enforce its hellish decrees. John's account of the fall of Babylon speaks of both kingdoms, but dramatizes the greatness of the fall and the severity of the judgments by speaking particularly of the fall of the ecclesiastical kingdom.

John's account primarily speaks of the same thing Nephi told about in these words: "Behold, that great and abominable church, the whore of all the earth, must tumble to the earth, and great must be the fall thereof. For the kingdom of the devil must shake, and they which belong to it must needs be stirred up unto repentance, or the devil will grasp them with his everlasting chains, and they be stirred up to anger, and perish." (2 Ne. 28:18-19.)

What is it, then, that the ancient apostle has to say about the fall of the great and abominable church? "I saw another angel come down from heaven, having great power," he says, "and the earth was lightened with his glory." The devil's kingdom on earth, which is his church, is "full of darkness." (Rev. 16:10.) How fitting that the angel who comes to announce its fall is of such standing and stature and glory that the whole earth is lightened by his very presence. When Babylon falls, darkness flees and light shines forth.

"And he cried mightily with a strong voice, saying, Babylon the great is fallen, is fallen, and is become the habitation of devils, and the hold of every foul spirit, and a cage of every unclean and hateful bird." What is this declaration but an application of Isaiah's prophecy about ancient Babylon. Wild beasts and doleful creatures, satyrs and dragons, were to take over forever what was once the mightiest and grandest city ever built. So shall it be, the angel said, with spiritual Babylon in the last days.

"For all nations have drunk of the wine of the wrath of her fornication, and the kings of the earth have committed fornication with her, and the merchants of the earth are waxed rich through the abundance of her delicacies." The Babylonish church falls; the church that caused kings and nations to worship false gods—which false worship is spiritual fornication!—lo, she falls. As our latter-day revelation has it: "That great church, the mother of abominations, that made all nations drink of the wine of the wrath of her fornication, that persecuteth the saints of God, that shed their blood—she who sitteth upon many waters, and upon the islands of the sea—behold, she is the tares of the earth; she is bound in bundles; her bands are made strong, no man can loose them; therefore, she is ready to be burned." (D&C 88:94.)

At this point John "heard another voice from heaven, saying, Come out of her, my people, that ye be not partakers of her sins, and that ye receive not of her plagues. For her sins have reached unto heaven, and God hath remembered her iniquities." As it was in the days of Cyrus, so shall it be in the day of Christ. The cry shall go forth: 'Go ye out from Babylon; flee ye from the Chaldeans; forsake the world; turn your face to Zion; come, worship the Lord in his holy mount. Believe the gospel and partake not of the promised plagues.'

And as to Babylon: "Reward her even as she rewarded you, and double unto her double according to her works: in the cup which she hath filled fill to her double. How much she hath glorified herself, and lived deliciously, so much torment and sorrow give her: for she saith in her heart, I sit a queen, and am no widow, and shall see no sorrow." How marvelous to the carnal mind is the religion of the world! Those who worship at its shrines and who mouth its doctrines thereby drink an opiate that dulls the conscience. They are free to live in lust, free to savor deliciously the fleeting fancies of the flesh, and yet to have a hope of salvation as they suppose.

"Therefore shall her plagues come in one day, death, and mourning, and famine; and she shall be utterly burned with fire: for strong is the Lord God who judgeth her." Plagues first, the burning second—and those who escape the disease and pestilence shall be consumed in the fires. For "all the proud and they that do wickedly shall be as stubble; and I will burn them up, for I am the Lord of Hosts; and I will not spare any that remain in Babylon." (D&C 64:24.)

In this setting we hear a great dirge; mournful sounds fill the air; the kings and merchants and great ones of the earth lament and weep over the fall of all those things in which they trusted. "And the kings of the earth, who have committed fornication and lived deliciously with her, shall bewail her, and lament for her, when they shall see the smoke of her burning, Standing afar off for the fear of her torment, saying, Alas, alas, that great city Babylon, that mighty city! for in one hour is thy judgment come." When the religions of men and of devils fail; when the churches of men and of devils are shown forth for what they are; when the ways of men and of devils come to naught—then, oh then, what howling and lamentation shall arise from ten thousand times ten thousand throats!

"And the merchants of the earth shall weep and mourn over her; for no man buyeth their merchandise any more: The merchandise of gold, and silver, and precious stones, and of pearls, and fine linen, and purple, and silk, and scarlet, and all thyine wood, and all manner vessels of ivory, and all manner vessels of most precious wood, and of brass, and iron, and marble, And cinnamon, and odours, and ointments, and frankincense, and wine, and oil, and fine flour, and wheat, and beasts, and sheep, and horses, and chariots, and slaves, and souls of men." The riches of this world—how little value they shall have in eternity. The precious baubles of gold and the granaries filled with corn—of what worth shall they be in that great day? And that great and abominable church, which thrives on merchandising and which sells the souls of men for any price the market will bear—of what profit will it all be to her in the day of burning?

"And the fruits that thy soul lusted after are departed from thee, and all things which were dainty and goodly are departed from thee, and thou shalt find them no more at all. The merchants of these things, which were made rich by her, shall stand afar off for the fear of her torment, weeping and wailing, And saying, Alas, alas, that great city, that was clothed in fine linen, and purple, and scarlet, and decked with gold, and precious stones, and pearls! For in one hour so great riches is come to nought." The city is Babylon; she is the similitude. The city is Rome; but she too is only a type and a figure. The city is all the cities of the world—San Francisco, Chicago, and New York City; London, Paris, and Berlin; Moscow, Tokyo, and Sao Paulo—all of which are subject to the rule and dominion of evil and carnality.

"And every shipmaster, and all the company in ships, and sailors, and as many as trade by sea, stood afar off, And cried when they saw the smoke of her burning, saying, What city is like unto this great city! And they cast dust on their heads, and cried, weeping and wailing, saying, Alas, alas, that great city, wherein were made rich all that had ships in the sea by reason of her costliness! for in one hour is she made desolate." How the commerce of the world will be affected when the hearts of men are no longer centered on the delicacies and merchandise that are carried in ships.

"Rejoice over her, thou heaven, and ye holy apostles and prophets; for God hath avenged you on her." God hath done it; it is the day of his vengeance. No longer need the righteous wear out their lives in the war with worldliness; it is the day of righteousness and peace in which all evil has fled. It is the millennial day.

"And a mighty angel took up a stone like a great millstone, and cast it into the sea, saying, Thus with violence shall that great city Babylon be thrown down, and shall be found no more at all." As Isaiah said: "It shall never be inhabited, neither shall it be dwelt in from generation to generation." (Isa. 13:20.) "And the voice of harpers, and musicians, and of pipers, and trumpeters, shall be heard no more at all in thee; and no craftsman, of whatsoever craft he be, shall be found any more in thee; and the sound of a millstone shall be heard no more at all in thee; And the light of a candle shall shine no more at all in thee; and the voice of the bridegroom and of the bride shall be heard no more at all in thee: for thy merchants were the great men of the earth; for by thy sorceries were all nations deceived." Thy sorceries, thy magic incantations, thy masses and rites and mysterious recitations—thy substitutes for that pure religion, with its simplicity of worship, that was found among the primitive saints—all these have deceived all nations.

"And in her was found the blood of prophets, and of saints, and of all that were slain upon the earth." (Rev. 18:1-24.) Murder, martyrdom, and war, these three, the death-dealing tools of the evil one—all such that have occurred in all the earth are laid at the door of the mother of abominations whose end is soon to be.

"And after these things I heard a great voice of much people in heaven, saying, Alleluia; Salvation, and glory, and honour, and power, unto the Lord our God: For true and righteous are his judgments: for he hath judged the great whore, which did corrupt the earth with her fornication, and hath avenged the blood of his servants at her hand. And again they said, Alleluia. And her smoke rose up for ever and ever." (Rev. 19:1-3.)

And thus it shall be with Babylon, Babylon the great who is fallen, is fallen. And when she falls, God grant that we may join in the heavenly chorus of Alleluia, the chorus of praise and adoration to the Lord our God, who hath wrought her destruction.

Chapter 38

ARMAGEDDON: FORETOLD BY THE PROPHETS

Armageddon: A Day of Blood and Horror and Death

Surely the Lord God who revealeth his secrets unto his servants the prophets, and who maketh known unto them all things which it is expedient for them to know, according to the heed and diligence they give unto him, surely he will tell them of that great Armageddon that lies ahead. Surely, if the God of Battles is destined to return, destroy the wicked, and bring peace on earth, all at the very moment when the greatest war of the ages is in progress, surely he will tell his prophets about that coming war. If he has been at pains to speak of wars and rumors of wars in the last days, surely he will not overlook revealing all we are able to bear about the final great war that will usher in the Millennium. If prophetic voices—rising early, crying out during the heat of the day, and refusing to be silenced when the night comes—if these voices have told us about lesser wars and smaller plagues, surely they will cry out, in advance, about the plague of plagues and the war of wars.

Be it remembered that both Nephi and John saw in vision the evil and dire apostasy and the formation of the great and abominable church in post-apostolic days. Be it remembered that to each of them was shown how this wretched harlot and mother of abominations, this wicked whore of all the earth who was like unto Babylon of old, gained power over the kings of the earth and those who dwelt in all nations. Recall also that they both beheld the restoration of the gospel in the last days, the gathering again of the Lord's ancient covenant people, and the frightful plagues and final war that would usher in the Second Coming. Be it remembered also that the Lord God hath shown all these things unto "others who have been," and that "they have written them; and they are sealed up to come forth in their purity, according to the truth which is in the Lamb, in the own due time of the Lord, unto the house of Israel." (1 Ne. 14:26.)

We have already quoted at some length from Nephi and John and some others on these matters. Let us now, however, pick up a few additional slivers of revealed truth from various of the prophets. Let us drink as deeply as our spiritual thirst permits from the fountains of inspiration and wisdom. When the seventh seal is opened, all these things relative to Armageddon and the great winding-up scene will come to pass in their eternal fulness. Can any of us know too much or envision too fully what lies ahead? Perhaps if our cup of knowledge is full and our obedience runneth over, we shall escape some of the plagues and sorrows that shall fall upon the wicked when the cup of their iniquity is full.

As we search the scriptures for prophetic statements about Armageddon, we must have the promised coming events in their true perspective. Armageddon is the final great battle in a war that covers the earth and involves all nations. We suppose it will be the first and only time, until the armies of Gog and Magog clash for a second time after the Millennium, when no nation in any land will be neutral. This coming conflict will be universal, and out of it will come the final day of destruction and burning. It will exceed in horror, intensity, and scope all prior wars. It is only in the last days that there are enough people on earth to field armies of the required size, and only now do we have the weapons to slay millions at a single blast. What, then, say the prophets about Armageddon?

Approaching this matter, as he so often did in his Messianic utterances, David said: "The Lord trieth the righteous. . . . Upon the wicked he shall rain snares, fire and brimstone, and an horrible tempest." (Ps. 11:5-6.) "He shall judge among the heathen, he shall fill the places with the dead bodies." (Ps. 110:6.) "All nations compassed me about: but in the name of the Lord will I destroy them." (Ps. 118:10.) Fire and brimstone are to be rained upon all nations; all of their ungodly inhabitants shall be destroyed in the name of the Lord; dead bodies will be everywhere; it is a day of judgment.

"Thy men shall fall by the sword, and thy mighty in the war," Isaiah says of a latter-day Zion in which there are some wicked and wanton people. "And her gates shall lament and mourn." (Isa. 3:25-26.) "And I will punish the world for their evil, and the wicked for their iniquity; and I will cause the arrogancy of the proud to cease, and will lay low the haughtiness of the terrible. . . . Every one that is found shall be thrust through; and every one that is joined unto them shall fall by the sword. Their children also shall be dashed to pieces before their eyes; their houses shall be spoiled, and their wives ravished." (Isa. 13:11, 15-16.) These expressions are part of a recitation of what is to be at the Second Coming.

"Come near, ye nations, to hear; and hearken, ye people: let the earth hear, and all that is therein; the world, and all things that come forth of it." Let all men know of the coming wars and desolations; let them know that Armageddon is at the door; let them know that the sword of the Lord's justice hangs heavily over all men. Let not these things be hidden from them. They are entitled to be warned, and God, by the mouth of Isaiah, raises the warning voice.

"For the indignation of the Lord is upon all nations, and his fury upon all their armies: he hath utterly destroyed them, he hath delivered them to the slaughter. Their slain also shall be cast out, and their stink shall come up out of their carcases, and the mountains shall be melted with their blood." How horrible is the day. The destruction of the Jaredites and of the Nephites is as nothing in comparison. The dropping of atomic bombs on Hiroshima and Nagasaki, and the Lord only knows where else, is only the beginning of sorrows, as it were. This coming war shall involve all nations, and the dead shall not be numbered.

When shall all this be? When shall all nations come to the slaughter, when shall the carcasses of their great ones raise such a stench as has never before choked the nostrils of men? It shall be when "all the host of heaven shall be dissolved"—when the elements shall melt with fervent heat—"and the heavens shall be rolled together as a scroll"—one of the great events incident to the Second Coming—"and all their host shall fall down, as the leaf falleth off from the vine, and as a falling fig from the fig tree." The prophetic word is sure; the eventuality is certain; the war is decreed, and the war shall come.

"For my sword shall be bathed in heaven: behold, it shall come down upon Idumea, and upon the people of my curse, to judgment." Of these same things our latter-day revelation says: "Wherefore the voice of the Lord is unto the ends of the earth, that all that will may hear: Prepare ye, prepare ye for that which is to come, for the Lord is nigh; And the anger of the Lord is kindled, and his sword is bathed in heaven, and it shall fall upon the inhabitants of the earth. . . . And also the Lord shall . . . come down in judgment upon Idumea, or the world." (D&C 1:11-13, 36.) And it is just such newly revealed pronouncements as this—picking up and interpreting the very words and phrases of the ancient word as they do—that, among other things, enable us to know with unshakable certainty the true meaning of much that the ancient prophets said.

But back to Isaiah and the great and last war of which he is speaking. "The sword of the Lord is filled with blood, . . . for the Lord hath a sacrifice in Bozrah, and a great slaughter in the land of Idumea. . . . For it is the day of the Lord's vengeance, and the year of recompences for the controversy of Zion. And the streams thereof shall be turned into pitch, and the dust thereof into brimstone, and the land thereof shall become burning pitch. It shall not be quenched night nor day." (Isa. 34:1-10.) After this, Isaiah speaks of the coming of the Lord, of the desert blossoming as the rose, and of the ransomed of the Lord returning to Zion with songs of everlasting joy.

From yet another passage, in which Isaiah is speaking of the Second Coming and the Millennium, we select these words relative to the final great war: "For by fire and by his sword will the Lord plead with all flesh: and the slain of the Lord shall be many. . . . I will gather all nations and tongues. . . . And they shall go forth, and look upon the carcases of the men that have transgressed against me: for their worm shall not die, neither shall their fire be quenched; and they shall be an abhorring unto all flesh." (Isa. 66:16, 18, 24.) Not only shall the dead bodies of the slain pollute the earth, but their spirits shall also be cast into hell, there to suffer the torments of the damned.

By the mouth of Jeremiah, the Lord sent a message to "all the kingdoms of the world, which are upon the face of the earth." The ancient prophet was to "take the wine cup" of the Lord's "fury" and "cause all the nations . . . to drink it." He was to say to them: "Thus saith the Lord of hosts, the God of Israel; Drink ye, and be drunken, and spue, and fall, and rise no more, because of the sword which I will send among you."

It is to the nations of the earth that are and shall be in our day that these dire words are addressed. They shall all fall by the sword, and none shall remain, or rise again, or be a nation or a kingdom thereafter. "For I will call for a sword upon all the inhabitants of the earth, saith the Lord of hosts." Lo, at long last, all men in all nations in all the world are to feel the wrath of the Lord.

"Therefore prophesy thou against them all these words, and say unto them, The Lord shall roar from on high, and utter his voice from his holy habitation; he shall mightily roar upon his habitation; he shall give a shout, as they that tread the grapes, against all the inhabitants of the earth. A noise shall come even to the ends of the earth; for the Lord hath a controversy with the nations, he will plead with all flesh; he will give them that are wicked to the sword, saith the Lord." Almost all men upon all the face of the earth will be wicked; a few only will stand in holy places and find a covert to shield them from the terrible storm. As to the others, the wicked shall slay the wicked until there are few men left. It shall be an awful day.

"Thus saith the Lord of hosts, Behold, evil shall go forth from nation to nation, and a great whirlwind shall be raised up from the coasts of the earth. And the slain of the Lord shall be at that day from one end of the earth even unto the other end of the earth: they shall not be lamented, neither gathered, nor buried; they shall be dung upon the ground." (Jer. 25:14-33.) How many will be slain, and who shall count the number of dead bodies? When we come to the revealed description of the battle itself, we shall see that the slain will be a third of the inhabitants of the earth itself, however many billions of people that may turn out to be.

Armageddon: A Day for Repentance and Hope

So far we have spoken more particularly of the blood and horror and death that shall cover the earth as part of the final great conflict that ushers in the Millennium. Words fail us and prophetic pens shake with palsy as those who see the future seek to record the bestiality and wickedness, the plagues and the sorrows of that coming day. And yet, amid it all, there are a few rays of hope for some of the saints in whose day the great desolations shall come. And there is ultimate triumph and glory and honor—either in life or in death—for all the faithful. For, be it remembered, it is on the mount and in the valley of Meggido, and on the plains of Esdraelon, and on the Mount of Olives—at which places the great battle of Armageddon shall center—that the Millennium will be born.

Let us, then, turn to the prophetic words of Joel, who includes in his inspired writings an added dimension, a dimension of hope and salvation for a favored few, where the final war is concerned. He speaks of the dread and death that shall attend it. But he also issues a call of repentance to Israel, coupled with a promise that some few, through righteousness, may escape the horrors of that dread day. And he restates what all the prophets affirm, that in the millennial day Israel and all the faithful shall finally triumph over all their enemies and ever thereafter live in joy and peace before the Lord.

Joel speaks first of the plagues that have destroyed the fruits of the earth, and then of the armies—"strong, and without number, whose teeth are the teeth of a lion"—that have come against Israel. The land is wasted and their social order is in complete disarray. But the chosen people have a responsibility; the defenders of Jerusalem must do all they can to save themselves; the cause of freedom must still have its champions. And so the prophetic call goes forth: "Gird yourselves, and lament, ye priests: howl, ye ministers of the altar: come, lie all night in sackcloth, ye ministers of my God." There is work to be done; repentance is needed; perhaps the Lord will still hear our cry. If the God of Battles is to come down and fight for Israel as he did in the days of their fathers, he must be importuned. The people must unite in mighty faith. It was by faith that the mouths of lions were closed anciently, and so shall it be again when the teeth of lions afflict the Lord's people.

"Sanctify ye a fast, call a solemn assembly, gather the

elders and all the inhabitants of the land into the house of the Lord your God, and cry unto the Lord, Alas for the day! for the day of the Lord is at hand, and as a destruction from the Almighty shall it come." Surely if there is any hope for any people in that day, it will be in the Lord of Hosts. Who can stay the rain of atomic bombs? How can any be healed from the atomic fallout, except by the power of faith? How can the crops of the earth grow and the beasts of the field survive in the days of the plagues, except by the power of faith?

"How do the beasts groan! the herds of cattle are perplexed, because they have no pasture; yea, the flocks of sheep are made desolate. O Lord, to thee will I cry: for the fire hath devoured the pastures of the wilderness, and the flame hath burned all the trees of the field. The beasts of the field cry also unto thee: for the rivers of waters are dried up, and the fire hath devoured the pastures of the wilderness." (Joel 1:1-20.) Faith and faith alone will prevail in that dread day. For all others there will be naught but sorrow and suffering and death.

As to Armageddon itself, Joel waxes eloquent. He sees in vision our modern warfare and describes it in terms of the weaponry and combatants of his day. "Blow ye the trumpet in Zion, and sound an alarm in my holy mountains," saith the Lord. "Let all the inhabitants of the land tremble: for the day of the Lord cometh, for it is nigh at hand." The Great Jehovah shall return; all men must be warned; the war-of-his-return is at hand; let the trumpet sound the alarm.

Unless men are warned they shall perish, for it is "a day of darkness and of gloominess, a day of clouds and of thick darkness, as the morning spread upon the mountains." Never has there been a day like unto this day. Even in the days of Noah there was not so great wickedness as in this gloomy and mournful hour. Men are prepared for the slaughter, and the armies are assembling. "There hath not been ever the like, neither shall be any more after it, even to the years of many generations." Not until the war of Gog and Magog after the Millennium, plus a little season, will there be another conflict like unto it.

"A fire devoureth before them; and behind them a flame burneth." Are these the flame-throwers, the incendiary bombs, and other means yet to be devised by men that shall be used to burn and destroy? "The land is as the garden of Eden before them, and behind them a desolate wilderness; yea, and nothing shall escape them." It is as when Rome planted Carthage with salt. It is as when the Medes and the Persians put a torch to Babylon. It is as when an atomic bomb fell upon Hiroshima.

How can Joel, who has seen nothing but swords and spears and shields, describe the warriors and their weapons? "The appearance of them is as the appearance of horses; and as horsemen so shall they run." Are these the tanks and trucks and mechanized vehicles used by a modern army? "Like the noise of chariots on the tops of mountains shall they leap, like the noise of a flame of fire that devoureth the stubble, as a strong people set in battle array." Is he seeing airplanes and helicopters and intercontinental ballistic missiles? Or does the vision show weapons and armaments yet to be invented?

"Before their face the people shall be much pained: all faces shall gather blackness." How fearful modern weaponry has become. How horrendous is the slaughter, which no soldier in the ranks can avoid. "They shall run like mighty men; they shall climb the wall like men of war; and they shall march every one on his ways, and they shall not break their ranks: Neither shall one thrust another; they shall walk every one in his path: and when they fall upon the sword, they shall not be wounded. They shall run to and fro in the city; they shall run upon the wall, they shall climb up upon the houses; they shall enter in at the windows like a thief." How disciplined and invincible are the warriors. How safely they stand behind their armor. How rapid is their movement from one scene of conflict to another. Their spies are everywhere. To Joel it is beyond anything he has imagined or supposed in his wildest dreams.

Their thunderous power cannot be resisted. "The earth shall quake before them; the heavens shall tremble: the sun and the moon shall be dark, and the stars shall withdraw their shining." It is the great and dreadful day; it is the day of the Second Coming; and the Lord himself shall descend from heaven with a shout and with the voice of the archangel.

"And the Lord shall utter his voice before his army: for his camp is very great: for he is strong that executeth his word: for the day of the Lord is great and very terrible; and who can abide it?" One host opposes the other. One host is for God and his cause; the other fights against him. Both hosts are comprised of wicked and worldly men, but one is defending freedom, and the other would destroy liberty and enslave men. One defends free institutions, freedom in government, freedom to worship the god of one's choice according to one's own conscience, and the other, Lucifer-like, seeks to overthrow liberty and freedom in all its forms. And the Lord himself is interceding to bring to pass his own purposes.

But if the Lord is to fight the battles of his people, ought they not turn to him and plead for his help? "Therefore also now, saith the Lord, turn ye even to me with all your heart, and with fasting, and with weeping, and with mourning." Armageddon is in progress; the dreadful day has arrived; but still the Lord's arm is not shortened that he will not save the penitent. There is still hope for those who believe and repent and obey. Therefore, let the cry go forth: "Rend your heart, and not your garments, and turn unto the Lord your God: for he is gracious and merciful, slow to anger, and of great kindness, and repenteth him of the evil." With this call comes the quiet assurance couched by Joel in question form: "Who knoweth if he will return and repent, and leave a blessing behind him?" Truly he will do so for those who seek him with all their hearts; truly his saints will be blessed, whether in life or in death, no matter how dire and gloomy the day.

Members of the Church will have a special need to seek the Lord in those days. "Blow the trumpet in Zion," the divine word commands, yea, "sanctify a fast, call a solemn assembly; Gather the people, sanctify the congregation, assemble the elders, gather the children, and those that suck the breasts: let the bridegroom go forth of his chamber, and the bride out of her closet. Let the priests, the ministers of the Lord, weep between the porch and the altar, and let them say, Spare thy people, O Lord, and give not thine heritage to reproach, that the heathen should rule over them: wherefore should they say among the people, Where is their God?" Let the members of The Church of Jesus Christ of Latter-day Saints keep the commandments, stand fast in the day of doom, and prepare for the day of their redemption.

When the Lord has tested their faith to the full, he will give his answer. Then his help will come. For his saints there shall be a great reward. It is millennial peace. Because they sought the Lord with all their hearts in an evil and gloomy day, they in turn shall abide the day of his coming. "Then will the Lord be jealous for his land, and pity his people. Yea, the Lord will answer and say unto his people, Behold, I will send you corn, and wine, and oil, and ye shall be satisfied therewith: and I will no more make you a reproach among the heathen."

In that day those who fight on the Lord's side shall come off victorious. "I will remove far off from you the northern army," saith the Lord, "and will drive him into a land barren and desolate, with his face toward the east sea, and his hinder part toward the utmost [western] sea, and his stink shall come up, and his ill savour shall come up, because he hath done great things." All of these things shall not happen in an hour or a day or, we suppose, a few years. The final war will be long and perilous, with many battles and much bloodshed and continuing horrors. But in the end the proper cause will triumph.

Then will the Lord's word as given through Joel come to pass: "Fear not, O land; be glad and rejoice: for the Lord will do great things. Be not afraid, ye beasts of the field: for the pastures of the wilderness do spring, for the tree beareth her fruit, the fig tree and the vine do yield their strength. Be glad then, ye children of Zion, and rejoice in the Lord your God. . . . And the floors shall be full of wheat, and the fats shall overflow with wine and oil. . . . And ye shall eat in plenty, and be satisfied, and praise the name of the Lord your God, that hath dealt wondrously with you: and my people shall never be ashamed." All this shall come to pass in the millennial day.

"And ye shall know that I am in the midst of Israel, and that I am the Lord your God, and none else: and my people shall never be ashamed." In that day the Lord shall dwell personally upon the earth. "And it shall come to pass, that whosoever shall call on the name of the Lord shall be delivered: for in mount Zion and in Jerusalem shall be deliverance, as the Lord hath said, and in the remnant whom the Lord shall call." (Joel 2:1-32.) O glorious, wondrous day! O blessed millennial day!

By way of summary and recapitulation Joel, speaking in the first person for the Lord, says: "For, behold, in those days, and in that time, when I shall bring again the captivity of Judah and Jerusalem"—when Judah returns to Palestine, and when old Jerusalem is rebuilt by the true saints, and when her promised temple sits again on the ancient sacred site—then "I will also gather all nations, and will bring them down into the valley of Jehoshaphat, and will plead with them there for my people and for my heritage Israel, whom they have scattered among the nations, and parted my land." This is the promised day of Armageddon when all nations are involved in the final war. Jehoshaphat, meaning Jehovah judges, is a valley near Jerusalem.

Then, in that day, the cry shall go forth: "Proclaim ye

this among the Gentiles; Prepare war, wake up the mighty men, let all the men of war draw near; let them come up: Beat your plowshares into swords, and your pruninghooks into spears: let the weak say, I am strong. Assemble yourselves, and come, all ye heathen, and gather yourselves together round about: thither cause thy mighty ones to come down, O Lord." The might of the world and the mighty among men shall be assembled. The day of the war of wars has arrived.

It shall be a day of judgment. "Let the heathen be wakened, and come up to the valley of Jehoshaphat: for there will I sit to judge all the heathen round about." In that day there will be a complete separation between the righteous and the wicked. In that day the great Judge shall issue his decrees. The wicked shall be destroyed and faithful Israel shall be saved.

It shall also be a day of missionary work. Men shall not be judged and found wanting until they have had opportunity to hear the gospel and forsake the world. The voice of warning shall be raised by the elders of Israel. They shall preach the everlasting gospel with a loud voice and with the sound of a trump. The names of Jesus Christ and Joseph Smith shall be trumpeted in every ear. "Put ye in the sickle, for the harvest is ripe: come, get you down; for the press is full, the fats overflow; for their wickedness is great. Multitudes, multitudes in the valley of decision: for the day of the Lord is near in the valley of decision." All men, from one end of the earth to the other, must then decide whether they are for God or against him, whether they will obey his gospel law or continue to live after the manner of the world, whether they will come unto Christ or continue to serve Satan.

Then "the sun and the moon shall be darkened, and the stars shall withdraw their shining." Then "the Lord also shall roar out of Zion, and utter his voice from Jerusalem; and the heavens and the earth shall shake: but the Lord will be the hope of his people, and the strength of the children of Israel." Then shall the great Millennium pour forth its blessings upon all who remain. "So shall ye know that I am the Lord your God dwelling in Zion, my holy mountain," saith the Lord. "Then shall Jerusalem be holy, and there shall no strangers pass through her any more." Only the pure and the clean and the worthy shall walk through her streets in that day.

"And it shall come to pass in that day, that the mountains shall drop down new wine, and the hills shall flow with milk, and all the rivers of Judah shall flow with waters, and a fountain shall come forth of the house of the Lord, and shall water the valley of Shittim." It is the day appointed for the redemption of Zion and for the glory of the chosen people. "Egypt shall be a desolation," however, "and Edom shall be a desolate wilderness, for the violence against the children of Judah, because they have shed innocent blood in their land." Those in Egypt and in Edom who remain, and those in every nation who have not received the gospel and bowed the knee to Him whose gospel it is, shall not as yet receive the fulness of the promised blessings.

"But Judah shall dwell for ever, and Jerusalem from generation to generation. For I will cleanse their blood that I have not cleansed: for the Lord dwelleth in Zion." (Joel 3:1-21.) The great day of redemption and of salvation for the Jews is reserved for the Second Coming. Then, when the Lord dwells among his people—among those who remain—they shall be cleansed by baptism and saved by righteousness.

JERUSALEM AND ARMAGEDDON

Armageddon: Jerusalem Besieged

Jerusalem is the Holy City, the city of David, the city of the Great King. It is the city where Melchizedek, the king of Salem and the prince of peace, reigned in righteousness and with his people served the Lord in spirit and in truth. Jerusalem, captured by David from the Jebusites, became the capital city in Israel and later the capital of the kingdom of Judah.

In her environs the Son of God was born; in her streets the Holy Messiah ministered; and in her temple the witness was borne of his divine Sonship. Outside her walls, in a garden called Gethsemane, suffering in agony beyond compare, he took upon himself the sins of all men on conditions of repentance. Outside her walls at a place called Golgotha, he was nailed to a cross and crucified for the sins of the world. Outside her walls in a quiet garden, he burst the bands of death, arose from the Arimathean's tomb, and brought life and immortality to light.

Jerusalem, in the days of her sorrow, was sacked by Nebuchadnezzar, conquered by Rome, put to the torch by Titus. And now for nearly two millenniums she has been trodden down of the Gentiles, and the end of her sorrow is not yet. In the days ahead some of the faithful will gather again within her walls and shall build the promised temple, a temple whose functions and uses will be patterned after the house of the Lord in Salt Lake City. Thereafter two prophets—valiant, mighty witnesses of the Lord Jesus Christ—will teach and testify and prophesy in her streets for three and a half years, at which time they will be slain, resurrected, and caught up to heaven. In the midst of the great war of Armageddon then in progress, Jerusalem will fall, the Lord will come, and the remnant of Judah that remains will accept the Nazarene as their King.

Jerusalem has ascended to the heights and descended to the depths. The Lord Omnipotent, who was and is from everlasting to everlasting, made the dust of her streets holy because the soles of his feet found footing there. The blood of prophets cries from that same dust for vengeance against godless wretches to whom innocent blood was of no more worth than sour wine. Jerusalem has been and yet again will be destroyed for her iniquities. When Nebuchadnezzar pillaged and burned and slew and carried the Jews into Babylon, it was because they had rejected Jeremiah and Lehi and the prophets. It was because they walked in an evil course. When Titus tore her asunder, slew most of her citizens, and made slaves of the rest, it was a just retribution because she had crucified her King. And when she falls again, amid the horror and brimstone and blood and fire of Armageddon, it will be because she has again slain the prophets and chosen to worship Baal and Bel and Merodach and all the idols of the heathen rather than the Lord Jehovah.

Wars come because of sin. They are born of lust and evil. The great tribulations sent upon the Jews in the days of Titus exceeded anything ever sent of God upon them from the beginning of their kingdom until that time. The tribulations parallel the sins. The Just One was slain, and the unjust murderers paid the penalty. So shall it be at Armageddon. The whole world will be wallowing in wickedness, but Jerusalem will be, as it were, the capital of all the wretched evils of the world. Once again the cup of her iniquity will be full, and she shall fall as she fell before. Then, having been cleansed by blood, she shall rise to become the millennial capital from which the word of the Lord shall go forth to all the earth.

Jehoshaphat, meaning Jehovah judges, is the valley between Jerusalem and the Mount of Olives. It is in this valley that the returning Lord will sit to judge the heathen nations. The Mount of Olives (also, Olivet) is a mountain of modest size on the east of the Holy City. It is there that the Lord will set his foot when this same Jesus who ascended from Olivet returns again.

The valley of Megiddo (once Megiddon), meaning place of troops, is part of the plain of Esdraelon (or plain of Jezreel), which is some twenty miles long and fourteen miles wide. It was on the plain of Esdraelon that Elijah had his confrontation with the priests of Baal. The valley of Megiddo has been a famous battleground through the centuries. It is in Samaria, a few miles south of Nazareth of Galilee. Armageddon is the hill of the valley of Megiddo west of Jordan on the plain of Jezreel. And Armageddon is the place where the final war will be fought, meaning, as we suppose, that it will be the focal point of a worldwide conflict, and also that as a place of ancient warfare, it will be a symbol of the conflict that will be raging in many nations and on many battlefronts.

Having these things in mind, let us turn to the prophetic word relative to Jerusalem and the final great battle during which our Lord will return. "Behold, I will make Jerusalem a cup of trembling unto all the people round about," saith the Lord, "when they shall be in the siege both against Judah and against Jerusalem." Armageddon is in process; all nations are at war; some are attacking Jerusalem and others are defending the once holy city. She is the political prize. Three world religions claim her—Christianity, Islam, and Judaism. Emotion and fanaticism run high; it is a holy war as such have been called through the ages. Men are fighting for their religion. They are in siege against the city of Jerusalem and the land of Judah.

"And in that day will I make Jerusalem a burdensome stone for all people: all that burden themselves with it shall be cut in pieces, though all the people of the earth be gathered together against it." What though all the nations of the earth come up to battle against Jerusalem, yet, in due course, and after the fall of the city and the destruction of the wicked, all shall fail and fall and their venture shall come to naught. "In that day, saith the Lord, I will smite every horse with astonishment, and his rider with madness: and I will open mine eyes upon the house of Judah, and will smite every horse of the people with blindness." (Zech. 12:2-4.) The warring hosts shall be smitten with madness, and a blind rage will overrule all reason. Men will say, "Let us eat and drink; for tomorrow we shall die," and the answering word will be: "Surely this iniquity shall not be purged from you till ye die, saith the Lord God of hosts." (Isa. 22:13-14.)

How will the battle go, and who will come off victorious? What chance for life will any have, considering the destructive power of the weapons then in the hands of the madmen who command the armies? In answer we are told: "And it shall come to pass, that in all the land, saith the Lord, two parts therein shall be cut off and die; but the third shall be left therein." This is Israel of whom he speaks. These are the armies who are defending Jerusalem and whose cause, in the eternal sense, is just. Two-thirds of them shall die.

"And I will bring the third part through the fire, and will refine them as silver is refined, and will try them as gold is tried: they shall call on my name, and I will hear them: I will say, It is my people: and they shall say, The Lord is my God." (Zech. 13:8-9.) We repeat: It is a religious war. The forces of antichrist are seeking to destroy freedom and liberty and right; they seek to deny men the right to worship the Lord; they are the enemies of God. The one-third who remain in the land of Israel are the Lord's people. They believe in Christ and accept Joseph Smith as his prophet and revealer for the last days.

But what of the wicked among the defenders of Jerusalem? They shall be destroyed. "Behold, the day of the Lord cometh, and thy spoil shall be divided in the midst of thee," saith the Lord. "For I will gather all nations against Jerusalem to battle"—remember, this is Armageddon, and all the nations of the earth are at war—"and the city shall be taken, and the houses rifled, and the women ravished; and half of the city shall go forth into captivity, and the residue of the people shall not be cut off from the city." So shall it be with Jerusalem when she falls again.

But what of the fate of those who fought against her? In spite of her fall, Jerusalem shall be victorious. Though she is taken and pillaged and her women ravished, yet in the end she shall be victorious. As to her enemies the account says: "And this shall be the plague wherewith the Lord will smite all the people that have fought against Jerusalem; Their flesh shall consume away while they stand upon their feet, and their eyes shall consume away in their holes, and their tongue shall consume away in their mouth." Already man has created weapons that will have this very effect upon those upon whom the death-dealing powers are sent forth. And lest any assume that the ancient word shall not be fulfilled in the full and literal sense, the Lord in our day acclaims: "I the Lord God will send forth flies upon the face of the earth, which shall take hold of the inhabitants thereof, and shall eat their flesh, and shall cause maggots to come in upon them; And their tongues shall be stayed that they shall not utter against me; and their flesh shall fall from off their bones, and their eyes from their sockets; And it shall come to pass that the beasts of the forest and the fowls of the air shall devour them up." (D&C 29:18-20.)

These things boggle the mind and dull our sensitivities.

We can scarcely conceive the full horror of what is involved, and what we do envision shall be only the beginning of sorrows, as it were. "And it shall come to pass in that day, that a great tumult from the Lord shall be among them; and they shall lay hold every one on the hand of his neighbour, and his hand shall rise up against the hand of his neighbour." It is as though the whole world shall become one great arena of anarchy, with every man wielding his own sword and seeking to betray and slay his brother. "And Judah also shall fight at Jerusalem"—Jerusalem shall be defended manfully—"and the wealth of all the heathen round about shall be gathered together, gold, and silver, and apparel, in great abundance. And so shall be the plague of the horse, of the mule, of the camel, and of the ass, and of all the beasts that shall be in these tents, as this plague." (Zech. 14:1-2, 12-15.) Man and beast alike shall suffer and die, and the whole earth shall be one great Gehenna, where the worms and rats and creeping things feast on the carcasses of the slain.

The Jewish Conversion and Cleansing

Out of Armageddon will come great blessings, in the eternal sense, to those Jews and others who abide the day. "In that day"—when all nations are gathered together against Jerusalem and she has become a cup of trembling unto all the people—"shall the Lord defend the inhabitants of Jerusalem; and he that is feeble among them at that day shall be as David; and the house of David shall be as God, as the angel of the Lord before them." This is the day when two shall put their tens of thousands to flight, when divine intervention will scatter the hosts of the wicked, when in weakness and by faith the Lord's people will wax valiant and put to flight the armies of the aliens.

"And it shall come to pass in that day, that I will seek to destroy all the nations that come against Jerusalem," saith the Lord. (Zech. 12:8-9.) "Then shall the Lord go forth, and fight against those nations, as when he fought in the day of battle." The battles will be fought by the warriors of earth, but the Lord's hand will be in it. It shall be with the defenders of Jerusalem as it was with Gideon and his three hundred soldiers when they put the Midianites to flight. It shall be as when Samson burst the cords with which he was bound, found a new jawbone of an ass, and with it slew a thousand Philistines. It shall be as when Israel prevailed over the armies of Amalek as long as Aaron and Hur held up the hands of Moses. The Lord will fight for Israel as he fought times without number for them during the long years of their sorrow and travail.

And then he shall come in person. The Great God shall appear. "And his feet shall stand in that day upon the mount of Olives, which is before Jerusalem on the east, and the mount of Olives shall cleave in the midst thereof toward the east and toward the west, and there shall be a very great valley; and half of the mountain shall remove toward the north, and half of it toward the south." This shall be part of the upheavals which cause every valley to be exalted and every mountain to be made low. This shall be the immeasurably great earthquake foreseen by John and spoken of by the prophets.

Then, with reference to the people, the account continues: "And ye shall flee to the valley of the mountains; . . . yea, ye shall flee, like as ye fled from before the earthquake in the days of Uzziah king of Judah: and the Lord my God shall come, and all the saints with thee." (Zech. 14:3-5.)

And further, with reference to the people—meaning those who remain, for by this time the wicked will have been destroyed by the plagues and the war and the burning—with reference to the people the Lord says: "And I will pour upon the house of David, and upon the inhabitants of Jerusalem, the spirit of grace and of supplications." Lo, at long last the Jews shall turn to their Messiah and believe in him who was born of Mary in Bethlehem of Judea. They will supplicate the Lord their God, in the name of Christ who is the Deliverer, even as their forebears did, and the Lord will hear their cry. They will pray to the Father in the name of the Son, having faith in Christ, to gain the witness, borne of the Spirit, that the Book of Mormon is the mind and will and voice of the Lord to a fallen world. They will come to know by the revelations of the Holy Spirit of God that the Book of Mormon is a Jewish book that deals with Jews who went out from Jerusalem in the days of Zedekiah king of Judah.

"And they shall look upon me whom they have pierced." (Zech. 12:10.) The pierced one appears; the Prophet of Nazareth of Galilee stands before them; the Carpenter's Son whom they rejected comes in immortal glory. Now they know whether any good thing can come out of Nazareth and whether a true prophet shall arise from Galilee. The riven side of the Son of Man retains the wound whence came blood and water as his dead body hung on the cross of Calvary. "And one shall say unto him, What are these wounds in thine hands? Then he shall answer, Those with which I was wounded in the house of my friends." (Zech. 13:6.)

Oh, what sorrow, what mourning, what wailing shall rise in that day from the lips of all men in all nations, from all who have not made Christ—the true Christ—their King. How the Jews will mourn because they crucified their King. What sorrow will be in the hearts of the Mohammedans because they acclaimed him as one of the prophets and denied his divine Sonship. What tears will water the faces of all those whose fathers bequeathed false forms of worship to them. And how the Christians will wail—wail until it will seem their very souls shall dissolve into nothingness—for they, favored above all the kindreds of the earth, had the Holy Scriptures and could read the words of the ancient prophets and the holy apostles, and yet they did not believe the true gospel of the lowly one by whom salvation came. As Jesus said on Olivet, "Then shall all the tribes of the earth mourn; and they shall see the Son of Man coming in the clouds of heaven, with power and great glory." (JS-M 1:36.)

Zechariah, himself a Jew and writing to the Jews, and speaking of his own nation, said: "They shall mourn for him, as one mourneth for his only son, and shall be in bitterness for him, as one that is in bitterness for his firstborn." How apt is this language. The only Son of God, the Firstborn of the Father, is the one who was slain. If men mourn over the loss of an only son, who is their heir and firstborn, how much more ought they to mourn for the firstborn and heir of the Father, his Only Son, who, having come to bring salvation, was rejected and crucified by his friends.

"In that day shall there be a great mourning in Jerusalem, as the mourning of Hadadrimmon in the valley of Megiddon. And the land shall mourn, every family apart; the family of the house of David apart, and their wives apart; the family of the house of Nathan apart, and their wives apart; The family of the house of Levi apart, and their wives apart; the family of Shimei apart, and their wives apart; All the families that remain, every family apart, and their wives apart." (Zech. 12:10-14.) Then shall be fulfilled that which is written: "Behold, he cometh with clouds; and every eye shall see him, and they also which pierced him: and all kindreds of the earth shall wail because of him." (Rev. 1:7.)

We have received by revelation an amplified account of what the Lord Jesus said in the great Olivet discourse. Of his return to the Jews, which we are here considering, this holy word says: "Then shall the arm of the Lord fall upon the nations. And then shall the Lord set his foot upon this mount [the Mount of Olives], and it shall cleave in twain, and the earth shall tremble, and reel to and fro, and the heavens also shall shake. And the Lord shall utter his voice, and all the ends of the earth shall hear it; and the nations of the earth shall mourn, and they that have laughed shall see their folly. And calamity shall cover the mocker, and the scorner shall be consumed; and they that have watched for iniquity shall be hewn down and cast into the fire. And then shall the Jews look upon me and say: What are these wounds in thine hands and in thy feet? Then shall they know that I am the Lord; for I will say unto them: These wounds are the wounds with which I was wounded in the house of my friends. I am he who was lifted up. I am Jesus that was crucified. I am the Son of God. And then shall they weep because of their iniquities; then shall they lament because they persecuted their king." (D&C 45:47-53.)

"In that day there shall be a fountain opened to the house of David and to the inhabitants of Jerusalem for sin and for uncleanness." (Zech. 13:1.) A fountain, the cleansing fountain, the fountain of the Lord! What is it? It is a baptismal font. The house of David, the inhabitants of Jerusalem, the upright and noble in all nations, good men at the ends of the earth and among every kindred—all shall be baptized for the remission of sins. All shall receive the gift of the Holy Ghost, that baptism of fire which burns dross and evil out of a human soul as though by fire. In that day all men will gather with Israel, all shall come to Zion, all shall dwell in the cities of holiness, all shall see the face of the Lord for they are pure in heart.

Armageddon: The Abomination of Desolation

Daniel speaks of something called "the abomination that maketh desolate" (Dan. 12:11), and specifies that it shall take place when "the sanctuary," which is the temple in Jerusalem, is "trodden under foot" (Dan. 8:13). Speaking of "the buildings of the temple," Jesus said, "They shall be thrown down, and left unto you desolate." Also: "There shall not be left here, upon this temple, one stone upon another that shall not be thrown down."

Then, on Olivet, the disciples asked: "Tell us when shall these things be which thou hast said concerning the destruction of the temple." Our Lord recited various events destined to occur and then said: "When you, therefore, shall see the abomination of desolation, spoken of by Daniel the prophet, concerning the destruction of Jerusalem, then you shall stand in the holy place."

For the saints in that dread and evil day, Jesus counseled: "Then let them who are in Judea flee into the mountains." They are to leave the city and the land and go to a place of safety. "Let him who is on the housetop flee, and not return to take anything out of his house; Neither let him who is in the field return back to take his clothes." Their flight must be in haste. Roman steel will take the life of any who linger. Houses and crops and property are of no moment. If their lives are to be spared, they must forsake the things of this world and assemble with the fleeing saints in holy places, there to prepare themselves for a better world where the riches of eternity are found.

"And wo unto them that are with child, and unto them that give suck in those days." Anything that delays their flight or hinders their escape will seem as burdensome as a great millstone round their necks. "Therefore, pray ye the Lord that your flight be not in the winter, neither on the Sabbath day." The fewer the restrictions and burdens surrounding their flight to freedom, the better. "For then, in those days, shall be great tribulation on the Jews, and upon the inhabitants of Jerusalem, such as was not before sent upon Israel, of God, since the beginning of their kingdom until this time; no, nor ever shall be sent again upon Israel."

Guided by inspiration, the primitive saints withdrew from Jerusalem and Judea before the desolating scourges fell upon the city and the people. The saints left the unholy city and went to a place of safety, a holy place, a place made holy by their presence, for it is not places but people that are holy. Then Titus came with his legions; a spirit of blind fanaticism swept over the whole Jewish nation; and in the war that followed, more than a million Jews in

Jerusalem were slain, every stone in the temple was torn from its place, and the balance of the people were carried away as captives and slaves. And it all came to pass because of sin and iniquity, because the Jewish nation rejected, scourged, and crucified their King. It came to pass because of abominations in the hearts of men, and it was a scourge and an abomination to them.

Then, in the Olivet discourse, when Jesus came to a consideration of the events of the last days, he said: "And again shall the abomination of desolation, spoken of by Daniel the prophet, be fulfilled." That which once happened to Jerusalem and its inhabitants shall happen again. "And immediately after the tribulation of those days, the sun shall be darkened, and the moon shall not give her light, and the stars shall fall from heaven, and the powers of heaven shall be shaken." (JS-M 1:2-33.) Such shall come to pass when the Lord Jesus comes again, when he puts his foot once more upon the Mount of Olives, when the earth reels to and fro.

In Luke's account of the abomination of desolation that took place in A.D. 70, we find these words of the Lord Jesus: "And when ye shall see Jerusalem compassed with armies, then know that the desolation thereof is nigh." So shall it be again; so shall it be shortly after the opening of the seventh seal when all the nations of the earth are gathered at Jerusalem. "Then let them which are in Judea flee to the mountains; and let them which are in the midst of it depart out; and let not them that are in the countries enter thereinto." Is this the way the saints shall be saved in the last days when two-thirds of the inhabitants shall be cut off and die and only one-third be left? If more than a million were put to the sword in A.D. 70, how great shall be the slaughter when atomic bombs are used? "For these be the days of vengeance, that all things which are written may be fulfilled." And again, in another day of vengeance, with even more of the prophetic word to be fulfilled, how great shall be the overflowing of abomination. "But woe unto them that are with child, and to them that give suck, in those days! for there shall be great distress in the land, and wrath upon this people." As it was once, so shall it be again. "And they shall fall by the edge of the sword, and shall be led away captive into all nations: and Jerusalem shall be trodden down of the Gentiles, until the times of the Gentiles be fulfilled." Will the temple be destroyed as it once was? How long shall the forces of evil control the city before the God of Battles comes down in fury and vengeance? These things we do not know. Of this only are we certain: At that day "there shall be signs in the sun, and in the moon, and in the stars; and upon the earth distress of nations, with perplexity." (Luke 21:20-25.) And then the Lord our God shall come in glory.

Pending that day, we are reminded that the Lord has said to us in our day: "A desolating scourge shall go forth among the inhabitants of the earth, and shall continue to be poured out from time to time, if they repent not"—and they will not repent—"until the earth is empty, and the inhabitants thereof are consumed away and utterly destroyed by the brightness of my coming. Behold, I tell you these things, even as I also told the people of the destruction of Jerusalem; and my word shall be verified at this time as it hath hitherto been verified." (D&C 5:19-20.)

And also: "In that generation" when "the times of the Gentiles" is fulfilled, "there shall be men standing in that generation, that shall not pass until they shall see an overflowing scourge; for a desolating sickness shall cover the land. But my disciples shall stand in holy places"—as did the primitive saints—"and shall not be moved; but among the wicked, men shall lift up their voices and curse God and die." (D&C 45:30-32.)

It is for these very reasons, among others, that we are commanded to "go forth among the Gentiles for the last time, as many as the mouth of the Lord shall name, to bind up the law and seal up the testimony, and to prepare the saints for the hour of judgment which is to come; That their souls may escape the wrath of God, the desolation of abomination which awaits the wicked, both in this world and in the world to come." (D&C 88:84-85.) And thus it is.

ARMAGEDDON: GOG AND MAGOG

Armageddon: A Religious War

In the coming day—a dire, dread, damning day—woes without measure will fall upon men. Pestilence, plagues, and death will stalk the earth. The kings of the earth and of the whole world will gather to fight the battle of that great day of God Almighty. Their command center will be at Armageddon, overlooking the valley of Megiddo. All nations will be gathered against Jerusalem. Two hundred thousand thousand warriors and more—two hundred million men of arms and more—shall come forth to conquer or die on the plains of Esdraelon and in all the nations of the earth. At the height of this war, the Lord Jesus will put his foot on the Mount of Olives and save his ancient covenant people. Of all this we are aware.

Now it is our purpose to show that this war will be a religious war, a war in which the servants of Satan assail the servants of the Lord and those allied with them. The great and abominable church will wage war against everything that is decent in the world and will then be thrown down by devouring fire. The two witnesses we shall call to give extended testimony about this coming conflict with Gog and Magog are Daniel and Ezekiel. Their words we shall accept as law. Some of it will come to us in plainness; other portions of what they have to say will be hidden behind strange names and among unknown nations.

Daniel, speaking of that which shall come to pass "in the latter days" (Dan. 10:14), says a king of the south and a king of the north shall each have dominion and power over nations and peoples. Who these kings shall be and what nations shall be subject to them, no man knows. It is sufficient for our present purposes to know that the king of the north shall come with his armies and overrun the "chosen people, . . . and none shall stand before him: and he shall stand in the glorious land, which by his hand shall be consumed." The chosen people are the servants of the Lord with whom he has made the covenant of salvation; and the glorious land is Palestine, the Holy Land, the land promised of God to the seed of Abraham, with whom the covenant of salvation was made in days of old.

After this there will be wars and intrigue, with one king following another. Then again a king will come from the north. "His heart shall be against the holy covenant; and he shall do exploits, and return to his own land." It is a holy war; his armies are fighting a people because of their religion. He shall come again and be repulsed. Again Daniel says he shall "have indignation against the holy covenant." And also, he shall "have intelligence with them that forsake the holy covenant." Traitors to the cause of truth and righteousness will give their support to him.

When he comes again, it will be the occasion of "the abomination that maketh desolate," which we have heretofore seen means the fall of Jerusalem again in the final great war. We do not speculate as to what nations are involved in these wars. It is well known that the United States and Great Britain and the Anglo-Saxon peoples have traditionally been linked together in causes designed to promote freedom and guarantee the rights of man. It is also well known that there are other nations, ruled by a godless communistic power, that have traditionally fought to enslave rather than to free men. It is fruitless to try and name nations and set forth the alliances that are to be. Our purpose in alluding at all to these recitations of Daniel is to show that Armageddon will be a holy war. There will be political overtones, of course. Wars are fought by nations, which are political entities. But the underlying causes and the moving power in the hearts of men will be their views on religious issues. The grand desideratum will be whether they are for Christ and his gospel or against him and his cause.

Having these things in mind, it is instructive to ponder what Daniel has to say about these final great conflicts that usher in the day of millennial peace. After speaking of "the abomination that maketh desolate," Daniel says: "And such as do wickedly against the covenant shall be corrupt by flatteries." Those who oppose the covenant that is the everlasting gospel shall be flattered into joining the godless forces. "But the people that do know their God shall be strong, and do exploits." God is known by revelation; knowledge of him is found in the hearts of the faithful. "And they that understand among the people shall instruct many." The gospel will be taught; the mind and will of the Lord will be proclaimed; those who oppose the cause of truth and righteousness will do so with their eyes open. "Yet they shall fall by the sword, and by flame, by captivity, and by spoil, many days." These events shall go forward over a long period of time; there will be ample opportunity for all nations to choose the course they will pursue; the testing purposes of mortality will be fulfilled.

"And some of them of understanding shall fall, to try them, and to purge, and to make them white, even to the time of the end: because it is yet for a time appointed." Though they fall in this life, they shall rise in eternal glory in the next. Even the saints must be tried and tested to the full; the Lord is determining whether they will abide in his covenant even unto death, and those who do not so abide are not worthy of him.

At this point Daniel describes the anti-gospel, anti-Christ, anti-God nature of the king and his armies from the north. "He shall exalt himself, and magnify himself above every god," the scripture saith, "and shall speak marvellous things against the God of gods, and shall prosper till the indignation be accomplished: for that that is determined shall be done." Already the communistic nations exhibit this spirit. As the polarization between good and evil continues apace in the last days, we may expect to see even more resistance manifest by them toward God and his laws.

"Neither shall he regard the God of his fathers," the account continues, "nor the desire of women, nor regard any god: for he shall magnify himself above all. But in his estate shall he honour the God of forces: and a god whom his fathers knew not shall he honour with gold, and silver, and with precious stones, and pleasant things. Thus shall he do in the most strong holds with a strange god, whom he shall acknowledge and increase with glory: and he shall cause them to rule over many, and shall divide the land for gain." From the perspective of Daniel, in whose day all men worshipped one kind of a god or another, what would be more strange than to worship a god composed of spirit nothingness, or, as atheists do, to worship a philosophy that says there is no god. Clearly the great issues at Armageddon are God and religion and a way of worship. Satan will have done his work well; by then billions of earth's inhabitants (even more so then than now) will be in open rebellion against the gospel and every principle of truth and virtue found therein.

Now Daniel turns to the war itself. "And at the time of the end," he says, "shall the king of the south push at him: and the king of the north shall come against him like a whirlwind, with chariots, and with horsemen, and with many ships; and he shall enter into the countries, and shall overflow and pass over." It is a worldwide conflict. "He shall enter also into the glorious land"—Armageddon and Jerusalem are the central sites—"and many countries shall be overthrown." Some nations shall escape, and "he shall have power over the treasures of gold and of silver, and over all the precious things" of many others. "But tidings out of the east and out of the north shall trouble him: therefore he shall go forth with great fury to destroy, and utterly to make away many. And he shall plant the tabernacles of his palace between the seas in the glorious holy mountain; yet he shall come to his end, and none shall help him." (Dan. 11:15-45.)

As far as Daniel's account is concerned, the conclusion of the whole matter is summed up in these words: "And at that time"—the time of the end—"shall Michael stand up, the great prince which standeth for the children of thy people"—he shall sit at Adam-ondi-Ahman, as we shall hereafter see—"and there shall be a time of trouble, such as never was since there was a nation even to that same time: and at that time thy people shall be delivered, every one that shall be found written in the book." The full impact of Armageddon, of the abomination of desolation, of the final great war of the ages—the full impact shall fall upon the ungodly among men, and only those whose names are written in the Book of Life will find a full measure of security and joy.

Then shall be brought to pass the resurrection that attends the return of our Blessed Lord. "And many of them that sleep in the dust of the earth shall awake, some to everlasting life, and some to shame and everlasting contempt. And they that be wise shall shine as the brightness of the firmament; and they that turn many to righteousness as the stars for ever and ever."

After learning all these things, Daniel asked an angelic ministrant who ministered unto him this question: "How long shall it be to the end of these wonders?" In reply he was told: "The words are closed up and sealed till the time of the end. Many shall be purified, and made white, and tried; but the wicked shall do wickedly: and none of the wicked shall understand; but the wise shall understand." (Dan. 12:1-10.) And thus it is.

Gog and Magog Attack the Covenant People

Ezekiel gives us another view and perspective of what shall be when the armies from the north invade the glorious land. This is the religious war of which Daniel spoke. It is a holy war in which emotion rules and ways of worship are at stake. It is a war between Christ and his gospel, and Lucifer who sought to deny men their agency even before the world was. In it we shall see Christ come to champion the cause of his people, and in it we shall see the fall of the great and abominable church, which is the church of the devil. She shall fall as Babylon of old fell.

Gog and Magog are all the nations of the earth who take up the sword against Israel and Jerusalem in the day of Armageddon. Their identities remain to be revealed when the battle alliances are made. We can assume, however, that the United States, as the defender of freedom in all the world, will head one coalition, and that Russia, whose avowed aim is to destroy freedom in all nations, will head the enemies of God.

Ezekiel's prophetic utterances begin with the divine assurance that Gog and Magog and all their armies shall be defeated. It could not be otherwise. God and his purposes must and shall prevail. To all these nations, combined in one great and evil enterprise against his people, the Lord says: "I will turn thee back, and put hooks into thy jaws, and I will bring thee forth, and all thine army, horses and horsemen, all of them clothed with all sorts of armour, even a great company with bucklers and shields, all of them handling swords." Their weaponry and military prowess and massive strength shall be of no moment in that day. The Lord himself is governing the outcome of the battle. Gog and all his multitudes shall fall and fail, and shall be as when God overthrew Sodom and Gomorrah.

The destined events are these: "In the latter years," Israel shall return to her land, coming out of all the nations of the earth. Old Jerusalem shall be rebuilt and the latter-day temple shall stand within its walls. When the appointed time comes to assemble all nations to fight against Jerusalem, Gog and Magog shall come according to this promise. "Thou shalt ascend and come like a storm, thou shalt be like a cloud to cover the land, thou, and all thy bands, and many people with thee."

Nations that go to war are engaged in either righteous or evil causes. The Lamanite assaults were evil; the Nephite defenses were righteous. Israel's attacks on the Amorites and other inhabitants of Canaan were directed by the Lord and were right. When the Philistines came against David and his people, their cause was evil. It was the will of the Lord that the American colonies free themselves from European domination in the revolutionary war, and so their cause was just. Armageddon will be a war of aggression instituted by Gog and Magog. Theirs will be an evil cause. Those nations that defend Israel and Jerusalem will be doing what the Lord wants done. To them it will be a righteous war.

And so, of Gog and Magog, Ezekiel prophesied: "Thus saith the Lord God; It shall also come to pass, that at the same time shall things come into thy mind, and thou shalt think an evil thought." Is not this also the case with all nations that seek to subjugate and enslave other peoples and nations? "And thou shalt say, I will go up to the land of unwalled villages; I will go to them that are at rest, that dwell safely, all of them dwelling without walls, and having neither bars nor gates." The destructive power of their weapons will be so great that it will be as though the cities of the earth were unwalled villages.

Thus Gog and Magog shall go forth "to take a spoil, and to take a prey; to turn thine hand upon the desolate places that are now inhabited, and upon the people that are gathered out of the nations, which have gotten cattle and goods, that dwell in the midst of the land." Conquerors steal from their victims. Nebuchadnezzar takes the golden vessels from the temple. Hitler makes bare the art galleries of France. Gog and Magog shall confiscate the wealth of Israel, and those who see it shall say, "Art thou come to take a spoil? hast thou gathered thy company to take a prey? to carry away silver and gold, to take away cattle and goods, to take a great spoil?" To the victor belong the spoils; the mere fact that Armageddon is a religious war will not deny Gog his gold.

"Therefore, son of man," the Lord says to Ezekiel, "prophesy and say unto Gog, Thus saith the Lord God; In that day when my people of Israel dwelleth safely, shalt thou not know it? And thou shalt come from thy place out of the north parts, thou, and many people with thee, all of them riding upon horses, a great company, and a mighty army: And thou shalt come up against my people of Israel, as a cloud to cover the land; it shall be in the latter days, and I will bring thee against my land, that the heathen may know me, when I shall be sanctified in thee, O Gog, before their eyes." O Gog, O Magog, how great are thy hosts; how strong is thy armor; how destructive is thy power! When thou falleth, with all thy greatness, all men will know that God alone could defeat such dread and fearsome hosts.

"Thus saith the Lord God; Art thou he of whom I have spoken in old time by my servants the prophets of Israel, which prophesied in those days many years that I would bring thee against them?" We suppose all of the prophets in Israel spoke more or less about the second coming of the King of Israel and about the wars and desolations that would precede and attend that dreadful day. The preserved words of many of them testify of that which is to be in the last days. Isaiah tells us of the fire and blood and desolation that will attend the Second Coming, and that "the slain of the Lord shall be many" in that day. (Isa. 66:16.) Jeremiah says the Lord will "call for a sword upon all the inhabitants of the earth, . . . And the slain of the Lord shall be at that day from one end of the earth even unto the other end of the earth." (Jer. 25:29, 33.) Zechariah sets forth in extenso what shall take place when the Lord gathers "all nations against Jerusalem." (Zech. 12–14.) Zephaniah devotes almost the entire three chapters of his writings to the same thing. So also does Joel. Daniel and Malachi in due course will open their mouths on the same matters. There is nothing hidden or secret about the general course of events that the Lord God shall bring to pass in his own good time, a time that is now not far distant.

"And it shall come to pass at the same time when Gog shall come against the land of Israel, saith the Lord God, that my fury shall come up in my face. For in my jealousy and in the fire of my wrath have I spoken, Surely in that day there shall be a great shaking in the land of Israel"—this is the mighty earthquake when the Mount of Olives cleaves and mountains and valleys and continents change their shapes, as we have so often noted—"So that the fishes of the sea, and the fowls of the heaven, and the beasts of the field, and all creeping things that creep upon the earth, and all the men that are upon the face of the earth, shall shake at my presence, and the mountains shall be thrown down, and the steep places shall fall, and every wall shall fall to the ground." This is the moment of the Lord's return. All things shall shake at his presence. The earthquakes and the tremblings and the distortions of the landmasses of our planct shall all take place when and as he comes to dwell again among men.

What of Gog and all his hosts in that dread day? What of the nations who have come to battle against the chosen people? Ezekiel's accounts are not chronological, and much that he recites will require periods of time to accomplish. But incident to the Second Coming, this word will be fulfilled: "And I will call for a sword against him throughout all my mountains, saith the Lord God: every man's sword shall be against his brother." This, in truth, will be a worldwide conflict; the sword that is wielded in the mountains of Israel will be the same sword that slays men in all nations.

"And I will plead against him with pestilence and with blood; and I will rain upon him, and upon his bands, and upon the many people that are with him, an overflowing rain, and great hailstones, fire, and brimstone." It shall be, in the literal and full sense of the word, as it was with Sodom and Gomorrah. Fire and brimstone will fall upon the armies of the wicked in all nations. That which is going forward in Palestine is but a type and a shadow of that which shall be in all nations and among all peoples. We must remind ourselves that this is a worldwide conflict and that all nations are involved. "Thus will I magnify myself, and sanctify myself; and I will be known in the eyes of many nations, and they shall know that I am the Lord." (Ezek. 38:1-23.) All men will know that no power save the power of God can bring to pass that which has thus been brought to pass.

Gog and Magog: Their Fall and Destruction

We now come to the prophetic word about the destruction of Gog and Magog, and all the nations that have forsaken the Lord, and all the wicked in all the earth. "I am against thee, O Gog," saith the Lord. "And I will turn thee back, and leave but the sixth part of thee." Gog, who came from the "north parts" to do battle "upon the mountains of Israel," shall return to the lands whence she came. But she will leave five dead bodies behind for every one live man who returns. She came, a mighty host, like a storm and like a cloud covering the land; she shall return, few in number, bowed and beaten by the rains of the Almighty.

"And I will smite thy bow out of thy left hand, and will cause thine arrows to fall out of thy right hand." Her weapons of war will not serve their purpose; she will be without oil for her war machines, and her bullets will be defective and not find their marks. "Thou shalt fall upon the mountains of Israel, thou, and all thy bands, and the people that is with thee." Death and destruction shall leave the slain of the Lord in all the earth.

"I will give thee unto the ravenous birds of every sort, and to the beasts of the field to be devoured. Thou shalt fall upon the open field: for I have spoken it, saith the Lord God." Pestilence, plagues, disease shall sweep as a desolating scourge through the ranks of the armed ones. And the weapons of war in the hands of the defenders of Israel shall take their toll. Dead bodies, unburied, will litter the land.

"And I will send a fire on Magog, and among them that dwell carelessly in the isles"—it is the great day of burning—"and they shall know that I am the Lord." None but the Lord himself can cause the elements to melt with fervent heat so that every corruptible thing is consumed. "So will I make my holy name known in the midst of my people Israel; and I will not let them pollute my holy name any more: and the heathen shall know that I am the Lord, the Holy One in Israel." How could it be otherwise? The wicked are destroyed, and the heathen nations—yet to hear the gospel and be converted—shall have all these great wondrous signs before them.

"Behold, it is come, and it is done, saith the Lord God; this is the day whereof I have spoken." This is the day! Oh, blessed day! The Lord reigns; the year of his redeemed has come; this is the day!

At this point in his prophetic utterances—which are not and were not intended to be chronological—Ezekiel tells in graphic language of the aftermath of the defeat of Gog and Magog by the sword. We would be derelict if we did not quote his very words, words written by the power of the Spirit. They are indeed the words of the Lord himself.

"And they that dwell in the cities of Israel shall go forth, and shall set on fire and burn the weapons, both the shields and the bucklers, the bows and the arrows, and the handstaves, and the spears, and they shall burn them with fire seven years: So that they shall take no wood out of the field, neither cut down any out of the forests; for they shall burn the weapons with fire.'' It seems to us as we consider this coming eventuality that almost all of the wealth of the world will have been spent for weapons of war. It is indeed Lucifer's last chance to destroy the souls of men on the field of battle before he is bound and has no power for the space of a thousand years.

''And they shall spoil those that spoiled them, and rob those that robbed them, saith the Lord God.'' From the standpoint of time all this must take place before the cleansing fires prepare the earth for the abode of the Clean One.

''And it shall come to pass in that day, that I will give unto Gog a place there of graves in Israel, the valley of the passengers on the east of the sea: and it shall stop the noses of the passengers: and there shall they bury Gog and all his multitude: and they shall call it The valley of Hamon-gog. And seven months shall the house of Israel be burying of them, that they may cleanse the land.'' Has there ever been such an enterprise as this? Will there ever be such a graveyard as Palestine? There the embalmed bodies of the righteous rest in sacred tombs, awaiting the sound of the trump of God that shall call them forth in the resurrection of life; and there the mangled carcasses of the wicked shall lie in unmarked graves, awaiting the sound of a later trump that will call them forth in the resurrection of damnation.

''Yea, all the people of the land shall bury them,'' the divine word continues, ''and it shall be to them a renown the day that I shall be glorified, saith the Lord God. And they shall sever out men of continual employment, passing through the land to bury with the passengers those that remain upon the face of the earth, to cleanse it: after the end of seven months shall they search. And the passengers that pass through the land, when any seeth a man's bone, then shall he set up a sign by it, till the buriers have buried it in the valley of Hamon-gog. And also the name of the city shall be Hamonah. Thus shall they cleanse the land." (Ezek. 39:1-16.)

As we close this portion of our analysis, we must note that the great war involving Gog and Magog is both premillennial, as we have here set forth, and also postmillennial in the sense that there will be another great conflict with wicked nations just before this globe becomes a celestial sphere. We shall speak of this hereafter. The similarities between the two great conflicts justify calling them by the same name. This John does in these words: "And when the thousand years are expired, Satan shall be loosed out of his prison, And shall go out to deceive the nations which are in the four quarters of the earth, Gog and Magog, to gather them together to battle: the number of whom is as the sand of the sea. And they went up on the breadth of the earth, and compassed the camp of the saints about, and the beloved city: and fire came down from God out of heaven, and devoured them." (Rev. 20:7-9.)

As with some Messianic prophecies that speak of both the first and the second advents of our Lord in the same language, it may be that portions of Ezekiel's great prophecy are subject to dual fulfillment. Our concern is with what lies ahead for us. Postmillennial events will be revealed in full to those who live during the Millennium. The knowledge then given will stand as a warning for those of future generations, even as the words of Ezekiel warn us to live as becometh saints. We speculate that much the same thing that happens in the first war with Gog and Magog will be repeated in the second.

The Supper of the Great God

After the defeat by the sword of the armies of Gog and Magog, and in the day when the slain of the Lord cover the earth and are as dung upon its face, then the fowls and the beasts shall gorge themselves upon the flesh and blood of the dead. This awful happening, attended by all the stench and stink of the rotting corpses, is set forth in both the Old Testament and the New and in latter-day revelation. It will indeed be something to behold.

This word came from the Lord to Ezekiel, saying: "Speak unto every feathered fowl, and to every beast of the field, Assemble yourselves, and come; gather yourselves on every side to my sacrifice upon the mountains of Israel, that ye may eat flesh, and drink blood." The mountains of Israel are but the illustration; the same event will occur in all nations and among all peoples, for Armageddon knows no bounds. "Ye shall eat the flesh of the mighty, and drink the blood of the princes of the earth, of rams, of lambs, and of goats, of bullocks, all of them fatlings of Bashan." In that day the flesh and blood of the great and mighty of the earth shall be of no more worth than that of the animals of the fields. "And ye shall eat fat till ye be full, and drink blood till ye be drunken, of my sacrifice which I have sacrificed for you. Thus ye shall be filled at my table with horses and chariots, with mighty men, and with all men of war, saith the Lord God." There neither has been nor will be any feast like unto this feast. What a blessing it will be for the earth to burn and be cleansed of its corruption and its filth. "And I will set my glory among the heathen, and all the heathen shall see my judgment that I have executed, and my hand that I have laid upon them." (Ezek. 39:17-21.)

John, in his visions of what was to be in the last days, saw "an angel standing in the sun" and heard him cry "to all the fowls that fly in the midst of heaven, Come and gather yourselves together unto the supper of the great God; That ye may eat the flesh of kings, and the flesh of captains, and the flesh of mighty men, and the flesh of horses, and of them that sit on them, and the flesh of all men, both free and bond, both small and great." (Rev. 19:17-18.) And our latter-day revelation, speaking of those who have fallen by the plagues and by the sword in Armageddon, says: "And it shall come to pass that the beasts of the forest and the fowls of the air shall devour them up." (D&C 29:20.)

We have set forth, thus, what the inspired writers say about the blood-soaked scene of gore and corruption that is yet to be. It makes us wonder why it has been revealed in such detail in at least three dispensations. Certainly it will be a literal event in the coming day. But more than this, it surely bears witness of other truths that men should know. It testifies that wickedness shall cover the earth in the last days; that all nations shall take up the sword in the final war of the ages; that men in uncounted numbers will die of plagues and pestilence and by the edge of the sword; and that the dead bodies of all, kings and rulers included, heaped as dung upon the ground, shall, in death, have no more worth than the carcasses of the beasts of the field. Perhaps, above all else, the horror of it all stands as a call to wayward men to repent, to cease their warfare against God, and to seek an inheritance with his people, many of whom will be preserved in that dread day.

Armageddon Ushers in the Millennium

There are three great things that will grow out of and come because of Armageddon. They are:

1. *In the course of this final great conflict the Lord himself shall return, the vineyard shall be burned, and the millennial day will dawn.*

2. *Out of the defeat of Gog and Magog comes the end of all the nations of the earth and the final triumph of Israel as a people and as a nation.*

3. *Out of Armageddon comes the destruction of the political kingdom on earth of Lucifer and the fall of the great and abominable church.*

As to the Second Coming and the millennial day thus commenced, we have heretofore made frequent allusion to these and shall deal more particularly with them hereafter.

As to the coming end of all nations and the final triumph of Israel, we should make a brief comment. Many of the present nations of the earth will be here, flourishing, fighting, struggling for a place in the sun, when the Lord comes. It is our firm conviction as a people that the stars and stripes will be waving triumphantly in the breeze, as a symbol of the greatness and stability of the United States of America, when the Lord comes. This nation was established to be the Lord's base of operations in this final gospel dispensation. From it the gospel is to go to every other nation and people. The greater its influence among the nations of the world, the more rapidly the gospel spreads. But the Lord has told us that all nations, the United States included, shall cease to be when he comes. These are his words: "With the sword and by bloodshed the inhabitants of the earth shall mourn; and with famine, and plague, and earthquake, and the thunder of heaven, and the fierce and vivid lightning also, shall the inhabitants of the earth be made to feel the wrath, and indignation, and chastening hand of an Almighty God, until the consumption decreed hath made a full end of all nations." (D&C 87:6.)

There will be no law but the Lord's law when he comes, and that law will be administered by the nation then set up to rule the world. That nation is Israel. They will possess the political kingdom. Thus the Lord said through Jeremiah: "Fear not thou, O my servant Jacob, and be not dismayed, O Israel: for, behold, I will save thee from afar off, and thy seed from the land of their captivity; and Jacob shall return, and be in rest and at ease, and none shall make him afraid. Fear thou not, O Jacob my servant, saith the Lord: for I am with thee; for I will make a full end of all the nations whither I have driven thee: but I will not make a full end of thee, but correct thee in measure; yet will I not leave thee wholly unpunished." (Jer. 46:27-28.) Also: "Thou art my battle axe and weapons of war," the Lord said to Israel, "for with thee will I break in pieces the nations, and with thee will I destroy kingdoms." (Jer. 51:20.) This we have seen shall be the case at Armageddon.

Now let us return to Ezekiel's prophetic word relative

to Gog and Magog and the Lord's chosen Israel. Based on all that is set forth with reference to this final series of wars, the Lord says: "So the house of Israel shall know that I am the Lord their God from that day and forward." Those who remain will believe in him and recognize his hand in all that has happened to them as individuals and as a nation. "And the heathen shall know that the house of Israel went into captivity for their iniquity: because they trespassed against me, therefore hid I my face from them, and gave them into the hand of their enemies: so fell they all by the sword. According to their uncleanness and according to their transgressions have I done unto them, and hid my face from them." It is the age-old testimony borne by all the prophets of Israel. That people was scattered because they forsook the Lord and his laws and chose to worship other gods. They will be gathered when they come unto Christ, believe his gospel, and worship the Father in his name, as did their fathers.

"Therefore thus saith the Lord God; Now will I bring again the captivity of Jacob, and have mercy upon the whole house of Israel, and will be jealous for my holy name; After that they have borne their shame, and all their trespasses whereby they have trespassed against me, when they dwelt safely in their land, and none made them afraid. When I have brought them again from the people, and gathered them out of their enemies' lands, and am sanctified in them in the sight of many nations; Then shall they know that I am the Lord their God, which caused them to be led into captivity among the heathen: but I have gathered them unto their own land, and have left none of them any more there." Such also is the age-old testimony of all the prophets. Israel, blessed Israel, shall return to her ancient lands and believe again those saving truths which brought joy and peace and eternal reward to her fathers.

Then comes the glorious promise: "Neither will I hide my face any more from them: for I have poured out my spirit upon the house of Israel, saith the Lord God." (Ezek.

39:22-29.) Israel shall remain and rule and be established forever. Hers is the one kingdom that shall prevail, because it is the Lord's kingdom. The Lord will restore again the kingdom to Israel, according to the promises.

As to the destruction of the political kingdom of Lucifer on earth and the fall of the great and abominable church, there are a few additional things that must be said. After reciting some of the plagues and desolations of the last days, and after speaking of the Supper of the Great God as set forth by Ezekiel, our latter-day revelation says: "And the great and abominable church, which is the whore of all the earth, shall be cast down by devouring fire, according as it is spoken by the mouth of Ezekiel the prophet, who spoke of these things, which have not come to pass but surely must, as I live, for abominations shall not reign." (D&C 29:21.)

Now, Ezekiel spoke only of devouring fire—of fire and brimstone—being rained upon Gog and Magog and all the nations that fought against Israel. He made no mention of a great and abominable church being involved, but the Lord here tells us that it was, in fact, the great whore of all the earth who was being destroyed by the fire. That is to say, there is both a political and an ecclesiastical kingdom of Lucifer on earth. It is with his kingdom as it is with the Lord's. There is an ecclesiastical kingdom of God on earth that is The Church of Jesus Christ of Latter-day Saints, and there shall be a political kingdom of God on earth in that day when the kingdom is restored to Israel and the Lord himself reigns. Satan's kingdom is composed of all that is evil and corrupt and carnal and wicked no matter where it is found. He operates through what we call churches, and he operates through what we call governments. Both are part of his kingdom. And in the final great day that lies ahead, the fall of one will be the fall of the other. When Babylon falls, she will take with her the churches of the world and the nations of the world. As the Lord makes a full end of all nations, so he will make a full end of all evil churches. Men will be free to believe as they choose during the Millennium, but the great and abominable church, the whore of all the earth, will no longer be among men, because the wicked portion of mankind will have been burned as stubble.

At Armageddon that great political power which "seeketh to overthrow the freedom of all lands, nations, and countries," and which "bringeth to pass the destruction of all people," and which is itself "built up by the devil" (Ether 8:25)—that very political kingdom, in all its parts, shall be burned with fire. It is the great and abominable church.

And thus out of Armageddon and the burning of the vineyard will come the great millennial blessings for all those who abide the day, the great and dreadful day of the Lord, to which we shall now turn our attention.

THE GREAT AND DREADFUL DAY OF THE LORD

The Great Day of His Wrath

The great and dreadful day of the Lord! What is it, and when will it come? Is it a day of sorrow or of joy? Is it our desire to live when that dread hour arrives, or will we plead for a merciful death lest the devastations and suffering be greater than we can bear? Will it be a day of vengeance and suffering or a day of redemption and peace?

Having spoken of the plagues and pestilence of the last days; having seen men's flesh fall from off their bones and their eyes drop from their sockets as incurable diseases cursed whole nations of men; having viewed with wonder and awe the fall and burning of the great whore of all the earth with whom the masses of men wallowed in evil debauchery; having seen all nations besiege Jerusalem, and having gasped in horror as the two-edged swords made bare the bowels of millions of the wicked wretches of the world, to say nothing of the kings and mighty ones who ruled over them—being aware of all these things, and all that attends them, what more can we possibly say about a day that bears the name "the great and dreadful day of the Lord"?

And yet there is more—much, much more—that

makes us wonder. Is the coming day one for whose coming we should yearn? Or is it a day to be shunned, one we hope will be reserved for some future age? The answers to be given depend upon whose lips phrase the questions. For the faithful saints, the divine word is: Let the day come. The universal plea on every righteous tongue is: "Thy kingdom come. Thy will be done in earth, as it is in heaven." (Matt. 6:10.) In the heart of every true believer is the plea: Come, O thou King of Kings; save us, O our God. We have waited long for thee. Oh, that thou mightest rend the heavens and come down in glory in our day.

But among the wicked it is not and it ought not so to be. To them the divine word acclaims: "Woe unto you that desire the day of the Lord! to what end is it for you? the day of the Lord is darkness, and not light. As if a man did flee from a lion, and a bear met him; or went into the house, and leaned his hand on the wall, and a serpent bit him. Shall not the day of the Lord be darkness, and not light? even very dark, and no brightness in it?" (Amos 5:18-20.) In truth and in reality, except for faithful members of The Church of Jesus Christ of Latter-day Saints; except for other decent and upright people who are living clean and proper lives in spite of the allurements and enticings of the world; except for those who are living either a celestial or a terrestrial law—except for these, the Second Coming will be a day of vengeance and of wrath. As a warning to ourselves and to all men, we shall now turn our attention to the revealed word that identifies that great and dreadful day as a day of wrath and sorrow.

Many revelations speak of the wrath of a just God that shall be poured out upon men and nations in the day of his coming. Some of these we have quoted or shall quote in other connections; let us, however, make brief references or allusions at this point to a few of the more important passages that have bearing on the points involved. "I will punish the world for their evil, and the wicked for their iniquity," the Lord told Isaiah, with reference to his second coming, "and I will cause the arrogancy of the proud to cease, and will lay low the haughtiness of the terrible." Will the Lord be angry with the wicked and manifest his wrath upon men in so doing? He says: "I will shake the heavens, and the earth shall remove out of her place, in the wrath of the Lord of hosts, and in the day of his fierce anger." (Isa. 13:11, 13.) And again: "Behold, the Lord cometh out of his place to punish the inhabitants of the earth for their iniquity." (Isa. 26:21.)

What comfort is there for the wicked in such prophetic words as these preserved for us by Zephaniah? "The great day of the Lord is near, it is near, and hasteth greatly, even the voice of the day of the Lord." He is speaking of our day. We live in the last days, when the day of the Lord is near. "The mighty man shall cry there bitterly." How could it be otherwise as men fall in Armageddon and the other wars that are ordained? "That day is a day of wrath, a day of trouble and distress, a day of wasteness and desolation, a day of darkness and gloominess, a day of clouds and thick darkness, a day of the trumpet and alarm against the fenced cities, and against the high towers." These next words bear an added witness of the fate of unnumbered millions in the final premillennial wars: "And I will bring distress upon men, that they shall walk like blind men, because they have sinned against the Lord: and their blood shall be poured out as dust, and their flesh as the dung." And what of their money and the power it brings—will it save them? "Neither their silver nor their gold shall be able to deliver them in the day of the Lord's wrath; but the whole land"—or, better, the whole earth—"shall be devoured by the fire of his jealousy: for he shall make even a speedy riddance of all them that dwell in the land." (Zeph. 1:14-18.)

By way of counsel to his people who shall live in this day of anger and wrath, the Lord says: "Wait ye upon me, saith the Lord, until the day that I rise up to the prey: for my determination is to gather the nations, that I may assemble the kingdoms"—this, of course, is at Armageddon—"to pour upon them mine indignation, even all my fierce anger: for all the earth shall be devoured with the fire of my jealousy." (Zeph. 3:8.)

Nahum also has somewhat to say about these matters. His words are an added testimony and another view of what is to be in the great and dreadful day. "God is jealous, and the Lord revengeth," he says; "the Lord revengeth, and is furious; the Lord will take vengeance on his adversaries, and he reserveth wrath for his enemies." However much it may be supposed, by those who are wise in their own conceits, that God is a God of mercy and peace and love, in whom no harshness or stern judgment is to be found, the fact is that he is a God of wrath, and anger, and vengeance, and destruction, where the wicked are concerned. Mercy and love and kindness are for the God-fearing and the righteous among men. "The Lord is slow to anger, and great in power, and will not at all acquit the wicked: the Lord hath his way in the whirlwind and in the storm, and the clouds are the dust of his feet. He rebuketh the sea, and maketh it dry, and drieth up all the rivers. . . . The mountains quake at him, and the hills melt, and the earth is burned at his presence, yea, the world, and all that dwell therein." This is Nahum's unique way of foretelling the great day of burning.

Then he asks: "Who can stand before his indignation? and who can abide in the fierceness of his anger? his fury is poured out like fire, and the rocks are thrown down by him." (Nah. 1:2-6.) And to these questions we answer: Those who love and serve him with all their hearts shall never be called upon to stand before his indignation or to abide in the presence of his fierce anger.

Do these utterances of the ancient prophets seem brutal and punitive? Do they project the image of an austere and stern Deity who deals with men in a harsh and iron-fisted way? Does it seem from them that his purpose is to crush and condemn rather than save and exalt? It would seem that the answer in each instance is yes; and if this is so, so be it. That is, the answers are yes, where the wicked and ungodly are concerned. In his love and in his mercy, a gracious God seeks the salvation of all his children. But he cannot save the righteous without damning the wicked; he cannot reward the obedient without condemning the rebellious; he cannot fill the hearts of the righteous with unmeasured blessings without pouring out his wrath upon the wicked. Indeed, how could a just and holy Being who cannot look upon sin with the least degree of allowance do other than send wrath and vengeance upon those who worship Satan and rebel against Him?

And so we find in our latter-day revelations a complete endorsement and approval of all that he said to the ancient prophets about the day of his wrath. These revelations speak of "the day when the wrath of God shall be poured out upon the wicked without measure." (D&C 1:9.) In them he says: "Hear the word of him whose anger is kindled against the wicked and rebellious. . . . Let the wicked take heed, and let the rebellious fear and tremble; and let the unbelieving hold their lips, for the day of wrath shall come upon them as a whirlwind, and all flesh shall know that I am God." (D&C 63:2, 6.) "Behold, the day has come, when the cup of the wrath of mine indignation is full," saith the Lord. (D&C 43:26.) "For behold, mine anger is kindled against the rebellious, and they shall know mine arm and mine indignation, in the day of visitation and of wrath upon the nations." (D&C 56:1.)

It is not a pleasant thing to think of that which lies ahead for worldly people, for those in all nations who walk in carnal paths, for those in the Church who do not keep the commandments. "The time is soon at hand that I shall come in a cloud with power and great glory," saith the Lord. "And it shall be a great day at the time of my coming, for all nations shall tremble." (D&C 34:7-8.) "For when the Lord shall appear he shall be terrible unto them, that fear may seize upon them, and they shall stand afar off and tremble. And all nations shall be afraid because of the terror of the Lord, and the power of his might." (D&C 45:74-75.)

Is it any wonder that men in that day, as Jesus promised, shall say "to the mountains, Fall on us; and to the hills, Cover us"? (Luke 23:30.) Yea, in that day shall be fulfilled that which is written: "And the kings of the earth, and the great men, and the rich men, and the chief captains, and the mighty men, and every bondman, and every free man, hid themselves in the dens and in the rocks of the mountains; and said to the mountains and rocks, Fall on us, and hide us from the face of him that sitteth on the throne, and from the wrath of the Lamb: For the great day of his wrath is come; and who shall be able to stand?" (Rev. 6:15-17.)

The Day of Vengeance

Does it seem strange that the meek and lowly Nazarene is also a God of vengeance? Are modern religionists in the cults of Christendom so imbued with the idea that he is a God of mercy that they forget completely that he is also a God of justice? Can he be a God of rewards without being a God of punishments?

Truly, wrath and vengeance are bedfellows. When the Lord pours out his wrath without measure, the wicked suffer the vengeance of a just God in exactly the same proportion. It is their day of reckoning; they are given measure for measure as their deeds warrant; it is a day of retribution and avengement. It is "the day when the Lord shall come to recompense unto every man according to his work, and measure to every man according to the measure which he has measured to his fellow man." (D&C 1:10.)

What says the holy word as to the vengeance of God in that great and dreadful day of his coming? To Enoch the Lord said: "As I live"—these are the words of an oath, an oath sworn in his own name—"even so will I come in the last days, in the days of wickedness and vengeance." (Moses 7:60.) Through Isaiah this word came to Israel: "Be strong, fear not: behold, your God will come with vengeance, even God with a recompence; he will come and save you." (Isa. 35:4.) "For it is the day of the Lord's vengeance, and the year of recompences for the controversy of Zion." (Isa. 34:8.) Of that day the Lord said to Micah: "And I will execute vengeance in anger and fury upon the heathen, such as they have not heard." (Micah 5:15.)

Paul said to certain of the saints in his day: "It is a righteous thing with God to recompense tribulation to them that trouble you." Vengeance is poured out in righteousness; it comes as a just and proper reward for the deeds done in the flesh; it is the Lord's way of recompensing the wicked for their rejection of his truths and the persecutions they have heaped upon his people. "To you who are troubled," Paul continues, "rest with us, when the Lord Jesus shall be revealed from heaven with his mighty angels, In flaming fire taking vengeance on them that know not God, and that obey not the gospel of our Lord Jesus Christ: Who shall be punished with everlasting destruction from the presence of the Lord, and from the glory of his power; When he shall come to be glorified in his saints, and to be admired in all them that believe . . . in that day." (2 Thes. 1:6-10.) This is not Paul's idea, nor is it ours. He did not originate the concept, nor did we. The law of vengeance comes from God, and what can man do to change it? "Vengeance is mine; I will repay, saith the Lord." (Rom. 12:19.)

In like manner our modern revelations bear a confirming witness of the vengeance that shall come upon the wicked in the last days. "And it shall come to pass, because of the wickedness of the world," the Lord said to Joseph Smith, "that I will take vengeance upon the wicked, for they will not repent; for the cup of mine indignation is full; for behold, my blood shall not cleanse them if they hear me not." (D&C 29:17.) *They will not repent.* It is in their power to do so; all men have it in their power to believe and obey and be saved; all are able to obtain a celestial inheritance by obedience to the laws and ordinances of the gospel. But the reality is, *they will not repent.* Hence, vengeance is their just recompense.

"Behold, vengeance cometh speedily upon the inhabitants of the earth, a day of wrath, a day of burning, a day of desolation, of weeping, of mourning, and of lamentation; and as a whirlwind it shall come upon all the face of the earth, saith the Lord." There is a certain smugness in the Church, a feeling that all these things are for others, not for us. But do not the same hurricanes often destroy the homes of the righteous as well as the wicked? And do not the same drouths often burn the crops of the saints along with those of the Gentiles? Do not the righteous and the wicked often fight side by side in the same wars? And do not atomic bombs fall on all the inhabitants of doomed cities? Where, then, shall the vengeance of the last days be found? The Lord says: "And upon my house shall it begin, and from my house shall it go forth, saith the Lord; First among those among you, saith the Lord, who have professed to know my name and have not known me, and have blasphemed against me in the midst of my house, saith the Lord." (D&C 112:24-26.) Vengeance is for the wicked, in and out of the Church, and only the faithful shall be spared, and many of them only in the eternal perspective of things.

Thus the Lord says to his saints: "Hearken, O ye people of my church, saith the Lord your God, and hear the word of the Lord concerning you—The Lord who shall suddenly come to his temple; the Lord who shall come down upon the world with a curse to judgment; yea, upon all the nations that forget God, and upon all the ungodly among you." (D&C 133:1-2.) The saints in the Church and the Gentiles in the world will both be judged by the same standard—the standard of Christ. How can anyone be judged by any other measuring rod? He hath given a law unto all things, and all things are subject to him.

Isaiah and Joseph Smith join hands to paint a dramatic picture of the vengeance and the love of the Lord at his second coming. To each of them the Lord revealed the same truths, which each recorded in language suited to the understandings of people in his day. Isaiah asked these questions: "Who is this that cometh from Edom, with dyed garments from Bozrah? this that is glorious in his apparel, travelling in the greatness of his strength?" Perhaps there was some such event known to ancient Israel that their prophet chose to use in teaching them of the Second Coming. In any event the revealed answer came: "I that speak in righteousness, mighty to save." The answer comes from their Savior. The next question was: "Wherefore art thou red in thine apparel, and thy garments like him that treadeth in the winefat?" In answer the Lord said: "I have trodden the winepress alone; and of the people there was none with me: for I will tread them in mine anger, and trample them in my fury; and their blood shall be sprinkled upon my garments, and I will stain my raiment."

This picture is a familiar one in Israel. The wine is trampled from the grapes in great vats, staining the garments of the laborers as though with blood. But in this case the second coming of Christ is involved, the one harvesting the crop is the Lord himself, and the winepress is full of the wrath of God. Thus John heard a command given to one of the angels of God in heaven. It was: "Thrust in thy sharp sickle, and gather the clusters of the vine of the earth; for her grapes are fully ripe." It is the day of harvest. "And the angel thrust in his sickle into the earth, and gathered the vine of the earth, and cast it into the great winepress of the wrath of God. And the winepress was trodden without the city, and blood came out of the winepress." (Rev. 14:18-20.)

With this in mind, we hear the rest of the answer as to why the Lord was red in his apparel: "For the day of vengeance is in mine heart, and the year of my redeemed is come." The Lord, coming in the day of vengeance, is pouring out the wrath of God upon the wicked, which is symbolized by the great winepress filled with the red juice of grapes. "And I looked, and there was none to help," the Lord continued, "and I wondered that there was none to uphold: therefore mine own arm brought salvation unto me; and my fury, it upheld me." Christ alone hath brought salvation to Israel and to all men. "And I will tread down the people in mine anger, and make them drunk in my fury, and I will bring down their strength to the earth." (Isa. 63:1-6.) As the grapes are trodden in the winepress of wrath, so shall the wicked be trodden down at the last days.

Joseph Smith's comparable and clarifying revelation says: "And it shall be said: Who is this that cometh down from God in heaven with dyed garments; yea, from the regions which are not known, clothed in his glorious apparel, traveling in the greatness of his strength? And he shall say: I am he who spake in righteousness, mighty to save." All through their ancient history, it was this Lord Jehovah who called upon his people, inviting them to come unto him and live his laws and be saved.

"And the Lord shall be red in his apparel, and his garments like him that treadeth in the wine-vat. . . . And his voice shall be heard: I have trodden the winepress alone, and have brought judgment upon all people; and none were with me; And I have trampled them in my fury, and I did tread upon them in mine anger, and their blood have I sprinkled upon my garments, and stained all my raiment; for this was the day of vengeance which was in my heart." (D&C 133:46-51.) How awful is the scene in this day of vengeance. The blood of the slain at the coming of the Lord will stain his garments as the red wine stains the raiment of those who tread on the grapes. He will tread on them as men trample on the fruit of the vine. Thus it shall be when the Son of Man harvests the earth, and when "he treadeth the winepress of the fierceness and wrath of Almighty God." (Rev. 19:15.)

The Year of the Lord's Redeemed

Is there no hope for anyone in the dreadful day? There is for those who are true and faithful in all things. For them, whether in life or in death, it will be a time of glory and renown. Will they escape the outpouring of divine wrath and avoid the vengeance with which the wicked will be smitten? They will. They are the true Israel who yearn for the restoration to them of the ancient kingdom. They are the ones who shall abide the day and who shall live and reign on earth with their Lord for the space of a thousand years. And blessed are they, for they shall inherit the earth.

Isaiah and Joseph Smith now turn to a consideration of the love and mercy and goodness that shall be showered upon the faithful in Israel in the day of their Lord's return. It shall fall as the gentle rain from heaven upon those who know the Lord and believe his gospel and seek his face. "Oh that thou wouldest rend the heavens," they pray, "that thou wouldest come down, that the mountains might flow down at thy presence, As when the melting fire burneth, [and] the fire causeth the waters to boil." All this is descriptive of what shall be when the elements melt with fervent heat and the valleys and mountains are no more. Why do the faithful yearn for such a day? It is the one in which the yoke of the world will be removed from their shoulders. How proper it is for them to plead with their Lord to come down, "to make thy name known to thine adversaries, that the nations may tremble at thy presence!" Let Israel be free; let the wicked and ungodly be removed. When shall it be? "When thou didst terrible things which we looked not for, thou camest down, the mountains flowed down at thy presence."

Then comes one of the most glorious promises in all holy writ. "For since the beginning of the world men have not heard," the holy account continues, "nor perceived by the ear, neither hath the eye seen, O God, beside thee, what he hath prepared for him that waiteth for him." Then and in that day, for one thing, they will be with their Lord; he will be among them as he was in Enoch's ancient city. Hence they say: "Thou meetest him that rejoiceth and worketh righteousness, those that remember thee in thy ways." (Isa. 64:1-5.)

When shall all these things come to pass? When will the importuning cries ascend to the throne of grace? When, oh when, will there be righteous men on earth who know enough about the Lord and his purposes and plans to plead with him to come down in all the glory of his strength? It should be done in our day. We are the ones who are appointed to make the petitions. Thus our revelation recites that an angel shall fly through the midst of heaven bringing anew the fulness of the everlasting gospel. "And this gospel"—the restored gospel—"shall be preached unto every nation, and kindred, and tongue, and people."

How shall it be preached? "The servants of God shall go forth, saying with a loud voice: Fear God and give glory to him, for the hour of his judgment is come; and worship him that made heaven, and earth, and the sea, and the fountains of waters—Calling upon the name of the Lord day and night, saying: O that thou wouldst rend the heavens, that thou wouldst come down, that the mountains might flow down at thy presence." That is our message. We call upon the world to worship the true God who created all things and to plead with him for the return of his Son that the blessings promised the faithful may be realized.

"And it shall be answered upon their heads"—the Lord will hear their prayers and come down as they have petitioned—"for the presence of the Lord shall be as the melting fire that burneth, and as the fire which causeth the waters to boil." All that is destined to attend his coming shall surely come to pass as the holy word asserts.

Then shall his saints say: "O Lord, thou shalt come

down to make thy name known to thine adversaries, and all nations shall tremble at thy presence—When thou doest terrible things, things they look not for." Who among the wicked and ungodly look for the Lord to pour out plagues, to spread pestilence, to decree wars, to come in burning fire and consume every corruptible thing, to cause such upheavals that mountains and valleys and continents and oceans shall all be rearranged? "Yea, when thou comest down, and the mountains flow down at thy presence, thou shalt meet him who rejoiceth and worketh righteousness, who remembereth thee in thy ways." Truly, it is the true saints, the faithful members of the kingdom, those who have kept themselves unspotted from the world—they are the ones the Lord shall meet and reward and save when he comes. They are the ones who shall receive a fulfillment of the promise: "For since the beginning of the world have not men heard nor perceived by the ear, neither hath any eye seen, O God, besides thee, how great things thou hast prepared for him that waiteth for thee." (D&C 133:37-45.)

For the wicked and ungodly, the Second Coming is a day of vengeance; for the saints of the Most High, it ushers in an era of righteousness and joy and peace. They are then redeemed and freed from all oppression. "Let the wicked perish at the presence of God," saith the scripture. "But let the righteous be glad; let them rejoice before God: yea, let them exceedingly rejoice." (Ps. 68:2-3.)

In that day, as Isaiah expresses it, the righteous shall say: "I will mention the loving kindnesses of the Lord, and the praises of the Lord, according to all that the Lord hath bestowed on us, and the great goodness toward the house of Israel, which he hath bestowed on them according to his mercies, and according to the multitude of his loving kindnesses. For he said, Surely they are my people, children that will not lie: so he was their Saviour." And how sweet and tender this expression is: "In all their affliction he was afflicted." Their sorrows were his; their pains also; he himself bore their afflictions. "And the angel of his presence saved them"—oh, how often it was so—and "in his love and in his pity he redeemed them; and he bare them, and carried them all the days of old." (Isa. 63:7-9.)

And lest we forget, lest we fail to see the full and true meaning of his ancient word given through Isaiah, we find the same Lord saying to Joseph Smith: "And now the year of my redeemed is come"—having reference to his return and the ushering in of the millennial era—"and they shall mention the loving kindness of their Lord, and all that he has bestowed upon them according to his goodness, and according to his loving kindness, forever and ever." Truly he spoke thus in olden times, and truly he spoke in like words in our day. "In all their afflictions he was afflicted. And the angel of his presence saved them; and in his love, and in his pity, he redeemed them, and bore them, and carried them all the days of old." (D&C 133:52-53.)

How comforting it is to know that for the saints the great and dreadful day of the Lord shall be one of loving-kindness and goodness! Thanks be to God for his tender mercies and saving grace!

Chapter 42

THE DAY OF JUDGMENT

The Psalmic Prophecies of the Judgment

Cleopas and Luke, valiant and faithful disciples of the Lord Jesus in their day and generation, walked and conversed with the Risen Lord on the Emmaus Road for some two or three hours. It was the day of the first Easter. Jesus withheld his identity from them; they manifest doubts and anxieties about the reports of his resurrection and triumphal status as the King of Israel. Jesus said to them: "O fools, and slow of heart to believe all that the prophets have spoken: Ought not Christ to have suffered these things, and to enter into his glory? And beginning at Moses and all the prophets, he expounded unto them in all the scriptures the things concerning himself."

That evening in the upper room where many of disciples were eating together and bearing testimony of what various of their number had that day seen and heard and learned about the Risen One, and as Cleopas and Luke told of their conversations on the Emmaus Road, and how the identity of Jesus was made known unto them in the breaking of bread in Emmaus, the Lord Jesus himself stood in their midst. He spoke; he ate; and they felt the nail marks in his hands and feet and thrust their hands into the gaping spear wound in his riven side. Then Jesus said: "These are the words which I spake unto you, while I was yet with you, that all things must be fulfilled, which were written in the law of Moses, and in the prophets, and in the psalms, concerning me." Having so said, "Then opened he their understanding," Luke tells us, "that they might understand the scriptures." (Luke 24:25-27, 44-45.)

The great message coming from the Emmaus Road and the upper room is, of course, that their Lord—Jesus of Nazareth of Galilee, the carpenter's son, the one with whom they had lived and labored for the three years of his mortal ministry—had now risen from the dead; that he had come forth in glorious immortality as the first fruits of them that slept; and that, therefore, he was the Son of God as he had so often testified in the days of his flesh. There are no more glorious truths than these. But another message delivered on these two occasions is that all things pertaining to his birth and ministry and death and glorification—and, we hasten to add, all things pertaining to his return in judgment in the last days—were before taught in the law of Moses and in the Psalms and in the Prophets.

And all things recorded in these holy scriptures must and shall be fulfilled, as pertaining to both his first and his second advents. It is our responsibility to search the holy word, uncover the prophetic utterances, and learn how and when and in what way they shall be fulfilled, lest he say to us, "O fools, and slow of heart to believe all that the prophets have spoken."

With reference to the coming day of judgment, let us turn first to the Psalms, to those inspired poetic gems of rhythmic beauty, which speak in grand words of the return of the Lord Jesus to judge the world. They speak as plainly of this coming day as they do with reference to his first coming, and to his ministry, atoning sacrifice, death, and resurrection. Indeed, it is the divine purpose to set forth in prose, poetry, and song repeated allusions to and truths about the Lord Jesus and all that he has done and yet will do in the eternal scheme of things. It is the divine purpose to keep the hearts of men turned everlastingly to Him by whom all things are, by whom salvation comes, by whom men are resurrected, judged, and awarded their places in the mansions that are prepared.

What then say the Psalms about the coming day of judgment? They say: "The Lord shall endure for ever [or, better, sitteth (as king) for ever]: he hath prepared his throne for judgment. And he shall judge the world in righteousness, he shall minister judgment to the people in uprightness." Jehovah is the Judge; the Lord Jehovah judgeth all men; the Father hath committed all judgment unto the Son. "The Lord is known by the judgment which he executeth: the wicked is snared in the work of his own hands. . . . The wicked shall be turned into hell, and all the nations that forget God." How can a just God do other than send the wicked to hell? If he saves the righteous, he must damn the wicked. He shall make a full end of all nations at his coming, and the wicked among them shall be burned, with their eternal spirits, as a consequence, going to hell. "Arise, O Lord; let not man prevail: let the heathen be judged in thy sight." (Ps. 9:7-8, 16-17, 19.) Such are the inspired words of David the king.

From Asaph the seer, who wrote in words of psalmic rhythm and beauty, we have received this prophetic word: "Our God shall come, and shall not keep silence: a fire shall devour before him, and it shall be very tempestuous round about him. He shall call to the heavens from above, and to the earth, that he may judge his people. Gather my saints together unto me; those that have made a covenant with me by sacrifice. And the heavens shall declare his righteousness: for God is judge himself." (Ps. 50:3-6.) Amid devouring fire, with angelic trumpets heralding the word from one end of heaven to the other, the Great God will come to his saints, to the people prepared to receive him. Angelic choirs—and, be it noted, Asaph, who gave us this word, was the leader of David's choir—shall rend the heavens with songs of praise and adoration. And it is pleasant to suppose that Asaph and other like-seeric musicians shall lead the heavenly choirs that shall sing in that day.

These words also come to us from Asaph: "Thou didst cause judgment to be heard from heaven; the earth feared, and was still, when God arose to judgment, to save all the meek of the earth." (Ps. 76:8-9.) Truly the meek shall inherit the earth in the day of judgment. And yet again: "Arise, O God, judge the earth: for thou shalt inherit all nations." (Ps. 82:8.)

In two other Psalms, whose authors are unknown and who well may have been either Asaph or David, we find these expressions: "Say among the heathen that the Lord reigneth: the world also shall be established that it shall not be moved: he shall judge the people righteously. . . . For he cometh, for he cometh to judge the earth: he shall judge the world with righteousness, and the people with his truth." (Ps. 96:10, 13.) When the Lord comes to reign, all men will be judged "with his truth," which is his gospel. "Let the floods clap their hands: let the hills be joyful together before the Lord; for he cometh to judge the earth: with righteousness shall he judge the world, and the people with equity." (Ps. 98:8-9.)

Isaiahanic Prophecies of the Judgment

Our friend Isaiah—than whom few prophets have been greater—is known in all Christendom as the Messianic prophet. And truly he spake many wondrous things about the coming of the Messiah in the meridian of time. But those of us who hold the key that opens the full and true meaning of his many prophetic utterances know that the burden of his message pertained to the last days. Included in this greater portion of his Spirit-guided sayings, he had much to say about the day of judgment incident to the second coming of the Son of Man. Much that he wrote about the day of vengeance, the fall of Babylon, and the awful Armageddon that lies ahead, we have already considered. Let us now set forth some of that which he recorded relative to the Lord Jesus sitting in judgment when he comes again in all the glory of his Father's kingdom.

In his great prophecy about the gathering of Israel and the building of the temple in the tops of the mountains in the last days, Isaiah says: "And he [Christ] shall judge among the nations, and shall rebuke many people: and they shall beat their swords into plowshares, and their spears into pruninghooks: nation shall not lift up sword against nation, neither shall they learn war any more." (Isa. 2:4.) The setting here is one of judgment followed by millennial peace. The nations are judged, the wicked are rebuked, and the social order destined to prevail on the new heaven and the new earth is ushered in. Micah, in the same prophecy, has him judging "among many people" and rebuking "strong nations afar off" (Micah 4:3), but the thought and intent are the same. The Lord Jesus sits in judgment at his coming.

Then in his insightful prophetic utterance about the Stem of Jesse (who is Christ), Isaiah intones: "He shall not judge after the sight of his eyes, neither reprove after the hearing of his ears." There is more to judgment than seeing and hearing, more than heeding the words of witnesses, more than appears on the surface. There is, in addition, that which is in the heart of those who are judged. And so, "With righteousness shall he judge the poor, and reprove with equity for the meek of the earth." How favored are the faithful poor—poor as pertaining to the things of this world, rich as pertaining to eternity—and how blessed are the meek, for they shall inherit the earth. "And he shall smite the earth with the rod of his mouth, and with the breath of his lips shall he slay the wicked." The vineyard shall be burned and every corruptible thing shall be consumed. "And righteousness shall be the girdle of his loins, and faithfulness the girdle of his reins." (Isa. 11:3-5.) All that he does, both for the righteous and the wicked, shall be just and right. Then the account speaks of the wolf and the lamb dwelling together and various other things that will prevail during the Millennium and after the judgment that precedes it.

Of these same events, in another context, Isaiah says: "And in mercy shall the throne be established: and he [Christ] shall sit upon it in truth in the tabernacle of David, judging, and seeking judgment, and hasting righteousness." (Isa. 16:5.) We hear again the counsel: "Be strong, fear not: behold, your God will come with vengeance, even God with a recompence; he will come and save you" (Isa. 35:4)—meaning he will pour out vengeance upon the enemies of Israel; he will reward them for all their evil deeds and opposition to his covenant people; and he will save Israel with an everlasting salvation.

Speaking of the day when "every valley shall be exalted, and every mountain and hill shall be made low," and the various other things that will accompany the Second Coming, Isaiah says: "Behold, the Lord God will come with strong hand, and his arm shall rule for him: behold, his reward is with him, and his work before him." (Isa. 40:1-10.) Then, speaking of the day when the "standard" of salvation is lifted in the last days, Isaiah gives the Lord's decree to Zion in these words: "Behold, thy salvation cometh; behold, his reward is with him, and his work before him." (Isa. 62:10-11.) He rewards the faithful at his coming; they are judged and found worthy; they abide the day. And then, at long last, after six thousand years during which sin and war and evil have hindered and defeated his eternal purposes, then, in the promised millennial day, the Lord's work will prosper perfectly. So glorious shall be the state of so many for the space of a thousand years that, for the first time, as it were, the Lord's work of bringing to pass the eternal life of man will truly be before him.

Knowing and believing all these things, we are prepared to exult in our hearts and praise the Lord with our lips for his goodness, as we hear a divine voice acclaim: "Hearken unto me, my people," and the Latter-day Saints are the

Lord's people, "and give ear unto me, O my nation: for a law shall proceed from me, and I will make my judgment to rest for a light of the people." Thanks be to God, that law now has come; it is the fulness of his everlasting gospel; by it he will judge the world, and it now stands as a light for all men. "My righteousness is near." The millennial day is almost upon us. "My salvation is gone forth." The gospel is being preached to prepare a people for the coming day. "And mine arms shall judge the people; the isles shall wait upon me, and on mine arm shall they trust." The Lord shall soon come to judge the people. Hence, "Lift up your eyes to the heavens," O ye saints of the Most High, "and look upon the earth beneath." Read the signs of the times, the signs now being shown forth in the heavens above and in the earth beneath. "For the heavens shall vanish away like smoke, and the earth shall wax old like a garment, and they that dwell therein shall die in like manner." This old world shall die; there shall be a new heaven and a new earth; it will be a millennial earth. And "my salvation shall be for ever, and my righteousness shall not be abolished," saith the Lord. (Isa. 51:4-6.)

The New Testament Doctrine of the Judgment

In all ages, from Adam to this hour, the holy prophets have taught the true doctrine of the judgment. They have always set forth those concepts and verities that would encourage men to live in such a manner as to gain the glorious reward of eternal life when their day and time came to stand before the Eternal Bar. The hour of judgment is not the same for every man. Some are judged at one time and others at a different hour. There are, in fact, many days of judgment available, but always the same Judge sits at the same judgment bar, always the same laws govern the procedures, and always a just and right judgment is imposed.

Our birth into mortality is a day of judgment in that it signalizes we were found worthy while in the premortal life to undergo a mortal probation and thus to continue on the course leading to eternal life. There are those who press forward along this course during this mortal probation—with a steadfastness in Christ, having a perfect love of God and of all men, keeping the commandments, and doing only those things that please their Lord—until they are translated and taken up into heaven, or until their calling and election is made sure. Either of these glorious eventualities is in itself a day of judgment. Their celestial inheritance is thus assured, though they have not yet gained bodies of immortal glory. Death also is a day of judgment when the spirits of men go to either paradise or hell as their deeds warrant.

The second coming of Christ is the great day of judgment for all men, both the living and the dead. In it those who qualify come forth in the resurrection of the just and obtain their rewards in the kingdoms established for them. At that time the decree goes forth that the rest of the dead shall remain in their graves to await the resurrection of the unjust and their consequent telestial inheritance. At that time the wicked among men are consumed as stubble, their bodies become dust again, and their spirits are consigned to an eternal hell to await the day of the resurrection of damnation. At that time those mortals who are worthy escape the burning, abide the day, and remain on the new earth with its new heavens in the presence of earth's new King.

Then, in the final day, when all is done and accomplished according to the divine purpose—after all men, the sons of perdition included, have risen from death to life and have become immortal—all men will stand before the bar of God in a final day of judgment. The eventual destiny of all men will have been determined before that day, but then the final and irrevocable decrees will be issued as pertaining to every living soul.

With this perspective before us, it is now our purpose to summarize the New Testament doctrine of the day of judgment as it pertains particularly to the second coming of the great and eternal Judge of quick and dead. We will do so under the following headings:

1. *Christ the Lord Is the Judge of All.*

That Lord—the Lord Jehovah—whom all the ancient prophets identified as the one who should judge the world is the Lord Jesus Christ. The spirit Jehovah became the mortal Christ, and the Lord Jesus, rising in glorious immortality, became the incarnate Jehovah who now sits on the right hand of the Majesty on High. Thus Jesus said: "The Father judgeth no man, but hath committed all judgment unto the Son: That all men should honour the Son, even as they honour the Father." And further: The Father "hath given him authority to execute judgment also, because he is the Son of man." He is the Son of Man of Holiness who is God. "I can of mine own self do nothing," Jesus continued, "as I hear, I judge: and my judgment is just; because I seek not mine own will, but the will of the Father which hath sent me." (John 5:22-23, 27, 30.) Christ is the Eternal Judge, and he does and shall operate in strict conformity to those eternal laws which he and his Father ordained from before the foundations of the world.

In harmony with this concept Jesus said: "For the Son of man shall come in the glory of his Father with his angels; and then he shall reward every man according to his works." (Matt. 16:27.) "Whosoever therefore shall be ashamed of me and of my words in this adulterous and sinful generation; of him also shall the Son of man be ashamed, when he cometh in the glory of his Father with the holy angels." (Mark 8:38.) And speaking of this day, Paul said that God "hath appointed a day, in the which he will judge the world in righteousness by that man [Christ] whom he hath ordained; whereof he hath given assurance unto all men, in that he hath raised him from the dead." (Acts 17:31.)

2. *The Second Coming Is the Day of Judgment.*

On this point Jude tells us: "And Enoch also, the seventh from Adam, prophesied of these, saying, Behold, the

Lord cometh with ten thousands of his saints, To execute judgment upon all, and to convince all that are ungodly among them of all their ungodly deeds which they have ungodly committed, and of all their hard speeches which ungodly sinners have spoken against him." (Jude 1:14-15.) Their words and their deeds, and, we may add, their thoughts, will condemn the ungodly in that dread day.

John describes that day, when the kingdoms of men are destroyed and the Lord comes to reign, in this way: "And the nations were angry, and thy wrath is come, and the time of the dead, that they should be judged, and that thou shouldest give reward unto thy servants the prophets, and to the saints, and them that fear thy name, small and great; and shouldest destroy them which destroy the earth." (Rev. 11:18.) John also records that in the day when "the hour of his judgment is come," Babylon shall fall and the wrath of God shall be "poured out without mixture" upon the wicked. (Rev. 14:7-10.)

3. *All Men Are Judged by Gospel Law.*

How and by what law will men be judged at the Second Coming? They will be judged by Christ and by his law, which is the gospel. Indeed, there is no other law by which they could be judged. He hath given a law unto all things. Those who abide the law are justified; those who break the law are condemned. Murder is murder in and out of the Church; sin is sin by whomsoever it is committed; evil is evil no matter where it is found. The standard and rule of judgment is the gospel; there is no other.

Let us hear what Paul has to say about this. He speaks of "the day of wrath and revelation." He addresses himself to Jew and Gentile, member and nonmember, believer and nonbeliever alike. His subject is "the righteous judgment of God." And he says that God "will render to every man according to his deeds." It matters not who they are, whether they are numbered with the saints or have cast their lot with the wicked and ungodly. Christ will judge all men according to his law, which is his gospel.

To the faithful saints, whom Paul describes as those "who by patient continuance in well doing seek for glory and honour and immortality," the promised reward is "eternal life." But for the wicked and ungodly, whom he describes as those "that are contentious, and do not obey the truth, but obey unrighteousness," there is no promise of eternal life. Instead they receive "indignation and wrath, tribulation and anguish." These are the heritage of "every soul of man that doeth evil." On the other hand, "glory, honour, and peace" are reserved for "every man that worketh good." "For as many as have sinned without law shall also perish without law," Paul says, "and as many as have sinned in the law shall be judged by the law." God, he says, is no respecter of persons, and "in the day when God shall judge the secrets of men by Jesus Christ"—note it—the judgment shall be "according to my gospel." (Rom. 2:5-16.)

Peter promises the faithful who stand fast in the fiery trials of life and who are "partakers of Christ's sufferings; that, when his glory shall be revealed," at His second coming, they shall "be glad also with exceeding joy." (1 Pet. 4:12-13.) And John records of that day: "He that is unjust, let him be unjust still: and he which is filthy, let him be filthy still: and he that is righteous, let him be righteous still: and he that is holy, let him be holy still. And, behold, I come quickly; and my reward is with me, to give every man according as his work shall be." (Rev. 22:11-12.)

One of the grandest expressions in all literature is the sweet yet awesome account Jesus gives of himself, seated on his glorious throne, in the coming day of judgment. He says: "When the Son of man shall come in his glory, and all the holy angels with him"—it is the day of his glorious return attended by legions of exalted beings from ages past—"then shall he sit upon the throne of his glory." The judgment is set and the books are opened, as it were. "And before him shall be gathered all nations: and he shall separate them one from another, as a shepherd divideth his sheep from the goats: And he shall set the sheep on his right hand, but the goats on the left." (Matt. 25:31-33.) The standard by which the assembled hosts will then be judged is whether they have lived Christian lives; whether they have ministered to the needs of their fellowmen; whether they have fed the hungry, clothed the naked, and visited the sick and imprisoned. It will be whether they have lived the laws revealed by him who is the Judge.

4. *The Apostles Shall Sit as Judges at the Second Coming.*

Jesus said to the Twelve who were with him in Jerusalem: "In the regeneration when the Son of man shall sit in the throne of his glory, ye also shall sit upon twelve thrones, judging the twelve tribes of Israel." (Matt. 19:28.) John said: "And I saw thrones, and they sat upon them, and judgment was given unto them: and I saw the souls of them that were beheaded for the witness of Jesus, and for the word of God, and which had not worshipped the beast, neither his image, neither had received his mark upon their foreheads, or in their hands; and they lived and reigned with Christ a thousand years." (Rev. 20:4.) The reality is that there will be a whole hierarchy of judges who, under Christ, shall judge the righteous. He alone shall issue the decrees of damnation for the wicked.

5. *The Final Day of Judgment Comes After the Millennium.*

Life continues during and after the Millennium. The resurrection of the unjust takes place after the Millennium. And the final great day of judgment will take place at the end of the earth. Hence John said: "And I saw a great white throne, and him that sat on it, from whose face the earth and the heaven fled away; and there was found no place for them." Christ sitteth upon the throne in the final day of judgment. "And I saw the dead, small and great, stand before God; and the books were opened: and another book was opened, which is the book of life: and the dead were judged out of those things which were written in the books, according to their works." (Rev. 20:11-12.)

The Day of Judgment Is Near

We have now seen what the ancient prophets and seers had to say about the day of judgment that is to accompany the Second Coming. As far as their prophetic writings reveal, some of the biblical prophets seem to have been concerned with almost nothing else. Their interest in these matters sets a pattern for us. Indeed, of all the people who have ever lived, we are the ones who should have greater anxiety and concern about what is to be in the great and dreadful day than any others. We are the ones who live when the dread events are dawning and when they may come to full fruition.

Providentially, our modern revelations about the day of judgment are often couched in the same language and abound in the same phrases as those used by the ancient prophets. These latter-day renditions of what is in the mind of Deity often amplify, clarify, and put a divine stamp of approval upon what was said anciently. We have, for instance, quoted from Isaiah 11 about the Lord coming to judge the world and usher in the Millennium. Nephi, with these same words before him on the brass plates, paraphrases, interprets, and expands them as follows: "And it shall come to pass that the Lord God shall commence his work among all nations, kindreds, tongues, and people, to bring about the restoration of his people upon the earth." These introductory words name the time in which the day of judgment shall come. It shall be after the restoration of the Lord's people has its beginning, but before it is all accomplished. In this setting Nephi picks up the thought content of Isaiah's inspired writing. "And with righteousness shall the Lord God judge the poor, and reprove with equity for the meek of the earth." The Great Judge shall sit in judgment. "And he shall smite the earth with the rod of his mouth; and with the breath of his lips shall he slay the wicked." So shall it be in the day of burning. "For the time speedily cometh that the Lord God shall cause a great division among the people, and the wicked will he destroy; and he will spare his people, yea, even if it so be that he must destroy the wicked by fire." The polarization that will gather the righteous into one camp and the wicked into another has already commenced, and these processes shall continue until the Lord comes. In that day, "Righteousness shall be the girdle of his loins, and faithfulness the girdle of his reins." (2 Ne. 30:8-11.) His judgments in that day shall be just. Nephi's language, quoted and paraphrased from Isaiah, then goes on to describe millennial conditions.

Similarly, referring repeatedly to various ancient scriptures, the Lord tells us that he "shall come to recompense unto every man according to his work, and measure to every man according to the measure which he has measured to his fellow man"; that "his sword is bathed in heaven, and it shall fall upon the inhabitants of the earth"; and that he "shall come down in judgment upon Idumea, or the world." (D&C 1:10, 13, 36.) In like manner, also to Joseph Smith the Lord said: "Mine apostles, the Twelve which were with me in my ministry at Jerusalem, shall stand at my right hand at the day of my coming in a pillar of fire, being clothed with robes of righteousness, with crowns upon their heads, in glory even as I am, to judge the whole house of Israel, even as many as have loved me and kept my commandments, and none else." (D&C 29:12.)

So also we read: "Be patient in tribulation until I come; and, behold, I come quickly, and my reward is with me, and they who have sought me early shall find rest to their souls." (D&C 54:10.) And also: "Wo unto you rich men, that will not give your substance to the poor, for your riches will canker your souls; and this shall be your lamentation in the day of visitation, and of judgment, and of indignation: The harvest is past, the summer is ended, and my soul is not saved! . . . For behold, the Lord shall come, and his recompense shall be with him, and he shall reward every man, and the poor shall rejoice." (D&C 56:16, 19.)

Need we say that the day of judgment is near, even at our doors? Truly, as the Lord measures time, the coming of the Great Judge is at hand. Elijah the prophet, whose return must be "before the coming of the great and dreadful day of the Lord" (Mal. 4:5), has already come. He appeared to Joseph Smith and Oliver Cowdery in the Kirtland Temple on April 3, 1836. Among other things, he then said: "By this ye may know that the great and dreadful day of the Lord is near, even at the doors." (D&C 110:16.) If such was the case in 1836, how much more so is it today?

Further, the signs of the times, in profuse abundance, all as promised by the prophets of old, are being manifest on every hand. The tender branches of the fig-tree are already covered with leaves. We know that "summer is nigh at hand." And as Jesus said on Olivet, "So likewise, mine elect, when they shall see all these things, they shall know that he is near, even at the doors." (JS-M 1:38-39.) Gospel light has pierced the long night of darkness that covered the earth; the gospel in all its glory, beauty, and perfection now shines forth in celestial splendor; a people once again is being prepared to meet their God. Israel is gathering into the appointed stakes; the walls of Zion are rising in holy places; and the promises made to the fathers have been planted in the hearts of the children. Wars and rumors of wars cover the earth; famines and diseases and an upheaval of the elements are increasing; and we have had a beginning taste of the plagues and pestilences and death and destruction. Armageddon is just around the corner. The hour is near, and the day is at hand.

THE DAY OF BURNING

He Comes—in Flaming Fire

Our Lord—the blessed Jesus, who came once as Mary's son and lived as a mortal among men—shall come again in all the glory of his Father's kingdom. He came once, born as a baby among babies in Bethlehem; he grew up as a child among children in Galilee; and he walked as a man among men, preaching and ministering throughout all Palestine.

Jesus of Nazareth came into this life alone, a single spirit entering mortality at the appointed time. Though angels heralded his presence and heavenly choirs sang of his birth, the earth did not shake, the heavens did not roll together as a scroll, fires and tempests did not testify of his coming. The earth did not reel to and fro as a drunken man, and the mountains and valleys remained as they had been in ages past.

But it shall be otherwise when he comes again. He shall not come in secret. His advent will not be in a caravanserai, near a little village in Judea, among tethered beasts of burden. "The Son of Man cometh not in the form of a woman," as the sect of Shakers supposed, "neither of a man traveling on the earth." (D&C 49:22.) This time all the thunders of heaven will herald his approach and that of those who are with him. "Behold, the Lord cometh with ten thousands of his saints, to execute judgment upon all," as promised by Enoch of old. (Jude 1:14-15.)

This time he shall come in flaming fire, the vineyard shall be burned, and every living soul on earth shall know that a new order, of worldwide dimensions, has been ushered in. Thus saith the holy word: "The Lord Jesus shall be revealed from heaven with his mighty angels, in flaming fire taking vengeance on them that know not God, and that obey not the gospel of our Lord Jesus Christ." (2 Thes. 1:7-8.)

In flaming fire! What kind of fire? Flaming fire is flaming fire. It is actual, literal fire, fire that burns trees, melts ore, and consumes corruption. It is the same kind of fire that burned in the furnace of Nebuchadnezzar when Shadrach, Meshach, and Abednego were cast into its blazing flames. And though the heat and flames of fire "slew those men" whose lot it was to cast the three Hebrews into its flames, yet, miraculously, upon the bodies of these three "the fire had no power, nor was an hair of their head singed, neither were their coats changed, nor the smell of fire had passed on them." (Dan. 3:16-27.) And so shall it be at the Second Coming when the same literal fire burns over all the earth. The wicked shall be consumed and the righteous shall be as though they walked in the furnace of Nebuchadnezzar.

Graphic accounts of the fire and burning that will attend the Second Coming are found in the ancient word. "Our God shall come, and shall not keep silence," acclaims the Psalmist; "a fire shall devour before him, and it shall be very tempestuous round about him." (Ps. 50:3.) And also: "The Lord reigneth. . . . A fire goeth before him, and burneth up his enemies round about. His lightnings enlightened the world: the earth saw, and trembled. The hills melted like wax at the presence of the Lord, at the presence of the Lord of the whole earth." (Ps. 97:1-5.)

None of the prophets excel Isaiah in literary craftsmanship and in the use of grand imagery to teach and testify about the God of Israel and his laws. "The Lord cometh,'' Isaiah says, ''burning with his anger, and . . . his lips are full of indignation, and his tongue as a devouring fire. . . . And the Lord shall cause his glorious voice to be heard, and shall shew the lighting down of his arm, with the indignation of his anger, and with the flame of a devouring fire, with scattering [i.e., with a blast], and tempest, and hailstones.'' And ''the breath of the Lord, like a stream of brimstone,'' shall kindle the fires that destroy false worship. (Isa. 30:27-33.) ''For, behold, the Lord will come with fire, and with his chariots like a whirlwind, to render his anger with fury, and his rebuke with flames of fire. For by fire and by his sword will the Lord plead with all flesh: and the slain of the Lord shall be many.'' (Isa. 66:15-16.)

And, rising to Isaiahanic heights, Habakkuk tells of a vision he saw of the Second Coming. ''God came,'' he says, even ''the Holy One. . . . His glory covered the heavens, and the earth was full of his praise. And his brightness was as the light. . . . Before him went the pestilence, and burning coals [fiery bolts] went forth at his feet. He stood, and measured [shook] the earth: he beheld, and drove asunder the nations; and the everlasting mountains were scattered, the perpetual hills did bow.'' (Hab. 3:3-6.) We shall speak more particularly of the coming of the Lord in flaming fire, as the scriptures do, in connection with the cleansing and burning of the vineyard.

He Comes—and the Elements Melt

When the Lord comes in his glory, in flaming fire, that fire will both cleanse the vineyard and burn the earth. In that day, so intense shall be the heat and so universal the burning, the very elements of which this earth is composed shall melt. The mountains, high and glorious and made of solid rock, shall melt like wax. They shall become molten and flow down into the valleys below. The very earth itself, as now constituted, shall be dissolved. All things shall burn with fervent heat. And out of it all shall come new heavens and a new earth whereon dwelleth righteousness. It is of these things—and they, above all else, show the literal nature of the burning fires that shall attend that dreadful day—it is of them that we must now make mention.

Peter, along with James and John, the other two members of the First Presidency in their day, saw in vision the transfiguration of the earth. These three were then with Jesus on Mount Hermon. It was the occasion when he himself was also transfigured before them. Speaking of this day of transfiguration, this millennial day—ushered in, as it will be, by the day of burning—our revelation says: "The earth shall be transfigured, even according to the pattern which was shown unto mine apostles upon the mount; of which account the fulness ye have not yet received." (D&C 63:20-21.) Thus these holy apostles saw the pattern, the way, and the manner in which the transfiguration of the earth occurred. A part, but not all, of what they saw, we know.

Knowing how this transfiguration was to take place, having seen it all in vision, Peter has left us these graphic words: "The heavens and the earth, which are now," he says, meaning our present earth and the aerial heavens that surround it, are "reserved unto fire against the day of judgment and perdition of ungodly men." Then, recording what he and his brethren had seen on the Mount of Transfiguration, Peter said: "But the day of the Lord will come as a thief in the night; in the which the heavens shall pass away with a great noise, and the elements shall melt with fervent heat, the earth also and the works that are therein shall be burned up."

Fervent heat—what is it? It is hot, glowing heat. The word itself comes from the Latin verb *fervere*, meaning to boil or to glow. It is the heat of which our revelation, alluding to a prophecy of Isaiah (Isa. 64:1-3), says: "The presence of the Lord shall be as the melting fire that burneth, and as the fire which causeth the waters to boil."

(D&C 133:41.) There has as yet been no heat on earth of such extent and intensity that it could melt the very planet itself. Such is reserved for the day of burning.

"Seeing then that all these things shall be dissolved," Peter continues, "what manner of persons ought ye to be in all holy conversation and godliness, looking for and hasting unto the coming of the day of God, wherein the heavens being on fire shall be dissolved, and the elements shall melt with fervent heat?" Work righteousness or be burned! How persuasive is this exhortation to walk uprightly before the Lord! "Nevertheless we, according to his promise, look for new heavens and a new earth, wherein dwelleth righteousness." The transfiguration shall truly come to pass; the wicked shall be burned as stubble, and the Lord will reign in millennial splendor among those that remain. "Wherefore, beloved, seeing that ye look for such things, be diligent that ye may be found of him in peace, without spot, and blameless." (2 Pet. 3:7-14.)

These same things were known to the ancient prophets, and some allusions to them have been preserved for us in their writings. Speaking of the Second Coming, Isaiah says: "The earth is utterly broken down, the earth is clean dissolved, the earth is moved exceedingly." (Isa. 24:19.) Amos says: "And the Lord God of hosts is he that toucheth the land, and it shall melt, and all that dwell therein shall mourn. . . . And all the hills shall melt." (Amos 9:5, 13.) Then he speaks of that portion of the gathering of Israel which is to take place during the Millennium.

Micah leaves us his witness in these words: "The Lord cometh forth out of his place, and will come down, and tread upon the high places of the earth. And the mountains shall be molten under him, and the valleys shall be cleft, as wax before the fire, and as the waters that are poured down a steep place." (Micah 1:3-4.)

And how pointed and express are the words of Nahum: "God is jealous, and the Lord revengeth; the Lord revengeth, and is furious; the Lord will take vengeance on his adversaries, and he reserveth wrath for his enemies." This is the great and dreadful day of the Lord, the day of vengeance that was in his heart, the day of burning in which every corruptible thing shall be consumed. "The Lord is slow to anger, and great in power, and will not at all acquit the wicked: the Lord hath his way in the whirlwind and in the storm, and the clouds are the dust of his feet." Nahum is seeing the desolations of the last days. "The mountains quake at him, and the hills melt, and the earth is burned at his presence, yea, the world, and all that dwell therein." (Nahum 1:2-5.)

Upon all this—all that Peter and the prophets have said about the flaming fires and burning heat that shall attend his coming—the Lord has put his stamp of approval. After saying that every corruptible thing shall be consumed at that dread day, he adds: "And also that of element shall melt with fervent heat; and all things shall become new, that my knowledge and glory may dwell upon all the earth." (D&C 101:25.)

He Comes—to Cleanse His Vineyard

In the full sense of the word, the whole earth is the vineyard of the Lord. In it, from time to time, in one place or another, all according to his good will and pleasure, the Lord of the vineyard plants peoples and nations and kindreds and tongues. Always he gives them such nourishment as they can bear, and some bring forth good fruit, others evil. He plants tame olive trees in choice spots and lets wild trees grow where they will. Branches are grafted back and forth in the hopes of turning the balance in favor of the good so the Lord of the vineyard may reap a rich harvest. "For behold, the field is white already to harvest; and it is the eleventh hour, and the last time that I shall call laborers into my vineyard," he says. "And my vineyard has become corrupted every whit; and there is none which doeth good save it be a few; and they err in many instances because of priestcrafts, all having corrupt minds." (D&C

33:3-4.) Even the good fruit is not as good as it ought to be.

In a more particular and limited sense, "the vineyard of the Lord of hosts is the house of Israel" (Isa. 5:7), and they of Israel are the trees of his planting. They were planted as tame olive trees in Palestine and were given every opportunity to bring forth good fruit. Fruitless branches were cut off and grafted into wild trees in the nethermost part of the vineyard of the world. And even now some of these branches are being brought back from their wild and Gentile state and once again are being given life and sustenance from the roots of the original tame trees.

Laborers are again called to labor in the Church and in the world for the salvation of men. They are going out to prune the vineyard for the last time. And the branches that bear no fruit—whether in the Church or in the world—shall soon be burned. The burning of the earth both is and includes the burning of the vineyard, depending upon what is meant by vineyard. The wicked and ungodly, in and out of the Church, shall be consumed in the fires. And "if the fire can scathe a green tree for the glory of God," our scripture says with reference to that which befalls even the righteous, "how easy it will burn up the dry trees to purify the vineyard of corruption." (D&C 135:6.)

In the allegory of the tame and wild olive trees, the Prophet Zenos, speaking of the final pruning of the vineyard in our day, records these words of the Lord of the vineyard: "And for the last time have I nourished my vineyard, and pruned it, and dug about it, and dunged it"—all of which is now going forward—"wherefore I will lay up unto mine own self of the fruit, for a long time, according to that which I have spoken. And when the time cometh that evil fruit shall again come into my vineyard"—when corruption begins to enter the only true Church and kingdom of God—"then will I cause the good and the bad to be gathered; and the good will I preserve unto myself, and the bad will I cast away into its own place.

And then cometh the season and the end; and my vineyard will I cause to be burned with fire." (Jacob 5:76-77.)

Then, as Isaiah says, "the light of Israel shall be for a fire, and his Holy One for a flame." Then shall the flame "burn and devour his thorns and his briers in one day." Then shall it "consume the glory of his forest, and of his fruitful field, both soul and body. . . . And the rest of the trees of his forest shall be few, that a child may write them." (Isa. 10:17-19.) And what follows speaks of the glory of that portion of Israel destined to gather in the millennial day.

It is of these last days of darkness and delusion that the holy word says: "Behold, the Lord maketh the earth empty, and maketh it waste, and turneth it upside down, and scattereth abroad the inhabitants thereof." Because the fruit is evil and few men stay on the Lord, the earth shall be emptied of its inhabitants—almost. "And it shall be, as with the people, so with the priest; as with the servant, so with his master; as with the maid, so with her mistress; as with the buyer, so with the seller; as with the lender, so with the borrower; as with the taker of usury, so with the giver of usury to him." The evil fruit that grows on the trees of the world will cover the earth. Those in all levels of society, high and low, will bring forth works fit only for the burning.

"The land shall be utterly emptied, and utterly spoiled: for the Lord hath spoken this word. The earth mourneth and fadeth away, the world languisheth and fadeth away, the haughty people of the earth do languish." The time of the end of the world is at hand. "The earth also is defiled under the inhabitants thereof." Why has all this evil come upon the trees of his forest? "Because they have transgressed the laws, changed the ordinance, broken the everlasting covenant." Apostasy reigns supreme; an evil tree cannot bring forth good fruit. Do men gather grapes of thorns or figs of thistles? "Therefore hath the curse devoured the earth, and they that dwell therein are desolate: therefore the inhabitants of the earth are burned, and few men left." (Isa. 24:1-6.) Truly, the vineyard shall be burned of corruption in the coming day!

He Comes—It Is the End of the World

The end of the world—what is it, and when shall it be? It is not the end of the earth. By the world we mean the customs, practices, and interests of men as social beings. We mean the social order that prevails among those who live on the earth. We mean the carnality, sensuality, and devilishness that rules in the lives of the wicked and ungodly. We mean the way of life followed by those who love Satan more than God because their deeds are evil.

Worldly people lie and steal and cheat; they take advantage of their neighbor for a word; and they bear false witness, both with the voice of gossip and on the witness stand when they have sworn to speak only the truth. Worldly people rob and plunder and murder. They accept war as a matter of national policy. They are lewd and lascivious. Sex sin is their friend; pornography walks with them; their conversation is profane and vulgar. They include adulterers and homosexuals and those whose thoughts dwell on low and base and sex-oriented things.

The world is evil, carnal, base. It fights the truth, kills the prophets, slays the saints. Worldly people oppose and fight The Church of Jesus Christ of Latter-day Saints because they belong to another kingdom, the kingdom of the devil. The end of the world is the end of all this: it is the end of wickedness; it is the ushering in of a new world, a new age, a new social order—the order of peace and righteousness.

Jesus said: "I am not of the world." (John 17:16.) "I have overcome the world." (John 16:33.) To his apostles he explained: "If ye were of the world, the world would love his own: but because ye are not of the world, but I have chosen you out of the world, therefore the world hateth you." (John 15:19.) And it was the beloved John who counseled: "Love not the world, neither the things that are in the world. If any man love the world, the love of the Father is not in him. For all that is in the world, the lust of the flesh, and the lust of the eyes, and the pride of life, is not of the Father, but is of the world." And having so taught, he added these words of wondrous comfort: "And the world passeth away, and the lust thereof: but he that doeth the will of God abideth for ever." (1 Jn. 2:15-17.)

One of the questions that the disciples asked Jesus on Olivet was: "What is the sign of thy coming, and of the end of the world, or the destruction of the wicked, which is the end of the world?" His answer included the whole Olivet Discourse. He spoke of the things that must occur before he came again, including the restoration of the gospel in the last days, which restored gospel, he said, "shall be preached in all the world, for a witness unto all nations, and then shall the end come, or the destruction of the wicked."

We are now in process of preaching the gospel to the world. It has not yet been offered to those in every nation in the full and true sense of the word. And the Lord will not return until we have accomplished the work he has given us to do. Up to this point in time we have received the gospel, the kingdom has been established, and the word is going forth as rapidly as our strength and means allow. Many of the Lord's latter-day servants are faithful and true in their attempts to spread the saving truths; others are slothful, seem to care little for the great commission given them, and partake more or less of the spirit of the world. Knowing that such would be the case in our day, Jesus climaxed his Olivet Discourse by telling about the faithful and the unfaithful members of the Church in the last days.

"Who, then, is a faithful and wise servant," he asked, "whom his lord hath made ruler over his household, to give them meat in due season? Blessed is that servant whom his lord, when he cometh, shall find so doing; and verily I say unto you, he shall make him ruler over all his goods." Exaltation consists in receiving, inheriting, and possessing all that the Father hath. Those who so obtain shall rule and reign forever. To say they shall be rulers over all their Lord's goods is but the beginning description of their eventual status.

"But if that evil servant shall say in his heart"—he is speaking now of rebellious church officers in the last days; he is speaking of those who have rulership in his church in the dispensation of the fulness of times; he is speaking of those who live just before the Second Coming—if any such shall say in his heart, "My lord delayeth his coming, and shall begin to smite his fellow-servants, and to eat and drink with the drunken, the lord of that servant shall come in a day when he looketh not for him, and in an hour that he is not aware of, and shall cut him asunder, and shall appoint him his portion with the hypocrites; there shall be weeping and gnashing of teeth. And thus comcth the end of the wicked, according to the prophecy of Moses, saying: They shall be cut off from among the people; but the end of the earth is not yet, but by and by." (JS-M 1:4, 31, 49-55.)

The end of the world is near; it shall soon come; it shall come suddenly, with violence, and amidst burning and desolation. The warning voice, sent forth from God in our day, pleads with all men to prepare themselves so they can abide the day and not be cut off from among the people. "Ye say that ye know that the end of the world cometh," Jesus said to his disciples, and "ye say also that ye know that the heavens and the earth shall pass away," he continued; "and in this ye say truly, for so it is." The end of the world shall come when the heavens and the earth, as now constituted, pass away. It shall come when there are new heavens and a new earth, millennial heavens and a millennial earth. "But these things which I have told you shall not pass away until all shall be fulfilled." That is, the ancient disciples were not to suppose that the end would come in their day. There was to be an apostasy, and a scattering of Israel, and a restoration of the gospel, and a gathering of the elect, and the establishment of Zion anew—all before the end of the world. After all this—"in that day," Jesus continued, there "shall be heard of wars and rumors of wars, and the whole earth shall be in commotion, and men's hearts shall fail them, and they shall say that Christ delayeth his coming until the end of the earth"—then, in that day, the end of the world will come. (D&C 45:22-26.) And we now live in the beginning days of sorrow and war and commotion and disbelief that will usher in the day of burning. World conditions are evil and corrupt. They will continue to degenerate and get worse. Then suddenly, in a not distant day, when all the prophecies have been fulfilled to the uttermost, the end will come and the wicked will be destroyed.

The Second Day of Burning

The end of the world ushers in the millennial era. The end of wickedness brings in the new day of righteousness. This old earth and this old heaven, with all their evil and corruption and worldliness, shall come to an end; and there will be new heavens and a new earth whereon dwelleth righteousness. All this shall come to pass in the great day of burning that is soon to be.

This earth, the very planet on which we live, is being prepared for eternal salvation. As with all things, it was created first as a spirit sphere. Then came the physical creation in which it was made and organized as a terrestrial or paradisiacal planet. In that day there was no death. Then Adam fell and brought death into the world, and the effects of his fall passed upon himself, upon Eve, and upon all forms of life, and upon the earth itself.

This earth, this orb, this planet, fell and became a telestial earth, which it now is. In this fallen state, as with those fallen men who become heirs of salvation, the earth was baptized by immersion; the waters of Noah covered its entire surface, and the corruption on its face was buried in them. When the Lord comes again, our earth will be baptized with fire so that dross and evil will be consumed with fervent heat, even as these are burned out of a human soul through the baptism of the Spirit.

In this day of burning there will be the new heavens and the new earth of which the revelations speak. The earth will become again a paradisiacal or terrestrial sphere. It will be renewed and be as it originally was in the day of the Garden of Eden. Death as we know it, meaning physical death, will cease. Men, for instance, will then live to the age of a hundred years and be changed from their terrestrial mortality to a state of eternal immortality in the twinkling of an eye. Then after the Millennium, plus a little season, which we assume will be a thousand years, the earth will again be burned; it will again be changed; there will again be new heavens and a new earth, but this time it will be a celestial earth. This is also spoken of as the resurrection of our planet.

Speaking of the death of the earth, and in acclaiming the glory of God, the Psalmist says: "Thou laid the foundation of the earth: and the heavens are the work of thy hands. They shall perish, but thou shalt endure: yea, all of them shall wax old like a garment; as a vesture shalt thou change them, and they shall be changed." (Ps. 102:25-26.) To Isaiah the Lord speaks in a like vein: "Lift up your eyes to the heavens, and look upon the earth beneath," the divine voice acclaims, "for the heavens shall vanish away like smoke, and the earth shall wax old like a garment, and they that dwell therein shall die in like manner: but my salvation shall be for ever, and my righteousness shall not be abolished." (Isa. 51:6.) As with men, so with the earth; both shall die and both shall be resurrected.

By revelation in our day the Lord says: "The great Millennium, of which I have spoken by the mouth of my servants, shall come. For Satan shall be bound, and when he is loosed again he shall only reign for a little season, and then cometh the end of the earth." It will, of course, be the end of the world of wickedness that then exists, but it will also be the end of the earth. "And he that liveth in righteousness shall be changed in the twinkling of an eye, and the earth shall pass away so as by fire." (D&C 43:30-32.) This is the second day of burning, the day when planet earth becomes a celestial sphere, an abiding place for the Lord God and the holy men of all ages as their time and circumstances permit. This will complete the salvation of the earth; it will then have become an eternal heaven whereon those who gain eternal life may live forever.

Chapter 44

ABIDING THE DAY

"Who May Abide the Day of His Coming?"

A gracious God, who does all things well and is himself all powerful, all wise, and all knowing, reveals his mind and will to men so they can advance and progress and become like him. He gives his doctrines to men so they will know what to believe and what to do to gain eternal life. All doctrine—all gospel concepts of every sort and nature—all are revealed and preached to prepare men for celestial rest. And we have no better illustration of this than the doctrine of the second coming of the Son of Man. One of the chief reasons this doctrine is revealed is to teach us what we must do, whether in life or in death, to abide the day.

Our prophetic friends in days of old were wont to counsel the saints on the doctrine of abiding the day of the coming of the Lord. Their words have greater import for us, as the day itself draws near, than they did for those in ancient times. We shall note, for our own guidance, what some of our brethren of old had to say about this doctrine. As we do so, it will be impressed upon us anew, with great force and power, that the righteous shall abide the day of his coming and the wicked shall be burned as stubble. It is hoped that this will guide us in choosing which group to join and where we should pledge our personal allegiance.

Let us turn first to some of the pointed and poetic words of Isaiah. "The sinners in Zion are afraid," he said, as he viewed with seeric vision the Zion of God in the last days. "Fearfulness hath surprised the hypocrites," he intoned, as he foresaw that even in the Church and kingdom of God in our dispensation there would be those who did not keep their covenants and walk uprightly before the Lord. Then, speaking of the elect of God in the day of their Lord's return, he cried out: "Who among us"—among the saints of the living God, among the true believers, among those who have forsaken the world and know the course leading to eternal life—"shall dwell with the devouring fire? who among us shall dwell with everlasting burnings?" When the vineyard is burned, who among us shall withstand the flaming fires? When the elements melt with fervent heat and all things become new, who among us shall withstand the searing heat? And, finally, when this earth becomes a celestial sphere—a sphere of everlasting burnings—who among us shall find place thereon?

His answer comes with all the surety that attends pure and perfect prophetic knowledge. "He that walketh righteously, and speaketh uprightly," he says; "he that despiseth the gain of oppressions, that shaketh his hands from holding of bribes, that stoppeth his ears from hearing of blood, and shutteth his eyes from seeing evil." How deep is the meaning of the prophetic word. In the world men amass fortunes by oppressing the poor; their hands are ever grasping after bribes and ill-gotten gain; their spoken words concern blood and war and how they will profit thereby; and they see and rejoice in evil on every hand. With him that is righteous, it is not so. His heart is on the riches of eternity that it is the good pleasure of the Father to give to his saints. And as a result, "He shall dwell on high."

With reference to all those who are able to pass through the devouring fires of the Second Coming, the promise is: "Thine eyes shall see the king in his beauty." Christ shall live and reign among them. "They shall behold the land that is very far off." Theirs shall be a millennial inheritance on the new heavens and the new earth that are to be. (Isa. 33:14-17.)

Joel, one of our ancient friends in whose prophetic renown we rejoice, one who wrote with power and insight of our day and of the second coming of that Lord in whom the saints of all dispensations delight, the prophet Joel said: "And the Lord shall utter his voice before his army: for his camp is very great"—he speaks of the day of Armageddon—"for he is strong that executeth his word: for the day of the Lord is great and very terrible." Of all this we have made ourselves somewhat aware. The great and dreadful day of the Lord is all that the prophets have said and more; mere words cannot describe the horror of the coming holocaust nor the terror that will take hold of the wicked in that day. Having so reminded us, Joel asks: "And who can abide it?"

Who indeed? Who among us shall qualify to remain in the flesh and enjoy the blessings of the new heavens and the new earth that are to be? As all those with sense and knowledge and discernment know, it will be those who believe and obey. "Therefore also now, saith the Lord, turn ye even to me with all your heart, and with fasting, and with weeping, and with mourning." Come, worship the Lord in Spirit and in truth. "And rend your heart, and not your garments." Let the substance be more than ritual. "And turn unto the Lord your God: for he is gracious and merciful, slow to anger, and of great kindness, and repenteth him of the evil." (Joel 2:11-13.) These words are addressed to Israel, to gathered Israel, to Israel of the last days. We are they.

Though "the Lord is slow to anger, and great in power," Nahum tells us, he "will not at all acquit the wicked." When is it that the wicked shall be rewarded for their evil deeds? It is in the day of his coming, for "the mountains quake at him, and the hills melt, and the earth is burned at his presence, yea, the world, and all that dwell therein." It is the end of the world; every corruptible thing is consumed in the fire; the wicked are cut off from among the people.

Then Nahum asks the age-old questions: "Who can stand before his indignation? and who can abide in the fierceness of his anger?" As to the righteous, the answer comes: "The Lord is good, a strong hold in the day of trouble; and he knoweth them that trust in him." As to the wicked, the divine word says: "His fury is poured out like fire, and the rocks are thrown down by him. . . . For while they [the wicked] be folden together as thorns, and while they are drunken as drunkards, they shall be devoured as stubble fully dry." (Nahum 1:3-10.)

"Every Corruptible Thing . . . Shall Be Consumed"

Our revelations tells us that when the Lord comes, "every corruptible thing, both of man, or of the beasts of the field, or of the fowls of the heavens, or of the fish of the sea, that dwells upon all the face of the earth, shall be consumed; and also that of element shall melt with fervent heat." (D&C 101:24-25.) With this concept before us, we are able to envision what Zephaniah meant in the emphatic pronouncements he made along this same line. We shall now digest and quote a few of his words.

"I will utterly consume all things from off the land, saith the Lord." He is speaking of the day of burning that shall attend the Second Coming. "I will consume man and beast; I will consume the fowls of the heaven, and the fishes of the sea, and the stumblingblocks with the wicked; and I will cut off man from off the land, saith the Lord." Nothing that is evil and wicked shall abide the day; all that falls short of the required standard shall be burned in the fires of fervent heat; it shall be as with man, so with the beast. Nothing that is corruptible shall remain.

False worship shall cease. The great and abominable church shall tumble to the dust; Babylon shall fall; the church of the devil, composed of the tares of the earth, shall be burned. "I will cut off the remnant of Baal," the Lord says. It shall be with them as it was with the priests of Baal in the days of Elijah. False priests, "and them that worship the host of heaven upon the housetops; and them that worship . . . and that swear by Malcham [the god of the Ammonites]; and them that are turned back from the Lord [apostates]; and those that have not sought the Lord, nor enquired for him [lukewarm members of the Church, among others]"—all these shall be consumed.

Zephaniah speaks of punishment for those who deal in "violence and deceit," for the drunken who are "settled on their lees," and for those who think the Lord will pour no "evil" upon them in the day of his coming. "That day is a day of wrath," saith the Lord, "a day of trouble and distress, a day of wasteness and desolation, a day of darkness and gloominess, a day of clouds and thick darkness." Can anything but evil befall the wicked in the great and dreadful day? "And I will bring distress upon men, that they shall walk like blind men, because they have sinned against the Lord." Is not this the case today with men and their leaders? "And their blood shall be poured out as dust, and their flesh as the dung." And shall this not come to pass in the great wars of the last days? "Neither their silver nor their gold shall be able to deliver them in the day of the Lord's wrath; but the whole land shall be devoured by the fire of his jealousy: for he shall make even a speedy riddance of all them that dwell in the land." (Zeph. 1:2-18.)

The prophetic word would be incomplete if it did not tell men what they must do to avoid being consumed in the dread day of burning that will attend our Lord's glorious return. "Gather yourselves together" is the divine call to Israel. "Seek ye the Lord, all ye meek of the earth, which have wrought his judgment; seek righteousness, seek meekness: it may be ye shall be hid in the day of the Lord's anger." (Zeph. 2:1-3.) Believe the gospel; join the only true and living Church; keep the commandments—this is the voice of the Lord to all men everywhere. "Therefore wait ye upon me, saith the Lord, until the day that I rise up to the prey: for my determination is to gather the nations, that I may assemble the kingdoms, to pour upon them mine indignation, even all my fierce anger: for all the earth shall be devoured with the fire of my jealousy." (Zeph. 3:8.) He speaks of Armageddon, which in part shall consume the wicked.

Men's Works Tried by Fire

The fierce flames, the fervent heat, the burning fires of the Second Coming that destroy the wicked shall also cleanse the righteous. When we say that the wicked and ungodly shall be consumed; when we say that only the righteous shall abide the day; when we say that there shall be an entire separation between the righteous and the wicked in that day—we must take into account the fact that there are no perfect men. All men fall short of divine standards; none attain the high state of excellence manifest in the life of the Lord Jesus; even the most faithful saints commit sin and live in some degree after the manner of the world. But such worldly works as remain with the righteous shall be burned so that the saints themselves may be saved. Let us take this comforting assurance from the inspired writings of one of our apostolic colleagues of old.

Paul said: "Other foundation can no man lay than that is laid, which is Jesus Christ." Our house of salvation must be built on Christ. He is our Savior. our Redeemer, our Advocate, our Mediator. He brought life and immortality to light through his gospel. He alone makes salvation possible; we are saved by his goodness and grace, provided we keep his commandments.

But not all men build on this one secure foundation, and some who do may yet remain entangled in worldly pursuits that keep them from living as near perfection as the gospel cause enables them to do. And so Paul continued: "Now if any man build upon this foundation"—that is, upon the foundation of Christ—with "gold, silver, precious stones, wood, hay, stubble"—that is, if their hearts are still set somewhat upon the things of this world—yet "every man's work shall be made manifest: for the day shall declare it, because it shall be revealed by fire; and the fire shall try every man's work of what sort it is." In the day of burning, all evil and corruptible works shall be consumed; only good works will remain. "If any man's work abide which he hath built thereupon"—that is, which he has built upon Christ—"he shall receive a reward." Then comes the comforting assurance: "If any man's work shall be burned," because some things in his life are yet worldly, "he shall suffer loss." No one ever gets an unearned blessing. "But he himself shall be saved; yet so as by fire." (1 Cor. 3:11-15.) The Prophet Joseph Smith changed this last sentence to read: "But he himself may be saved; yet so as by fire." (JST, 1 Cor. 3:15.) Thus the burning that destroys every corruptible thing is the same burning that cleanses the righteous. Evil and sin and dross will be burned out of their souls because they qualify to abide the day, even though all their works have not been as those of Enoch and Elijah. If only perfect people were saved, there would be only one saved soul—the Lord Jesus.

We have in holy writ many illustrations of the people and the works that will abide the day, and what works, and of whom, will be burned at His coming. Perhaps no prophet has surpassed Malachi in discoursing on these matters. He announces that the Lord will come in the last days and then asks: "But who may abide the day of his coming? and who shall stand when he appeareth?" The reason some will not abide the day is given in these words: "He is like a refiner's fire, and like fullers' soap: and he shall sit as a refiner and purifier of silver; and he shall purify the sons of Levi, and purge them as gold and silver." Their evil works shall be burned, and they themselves shall be cleansed and saved, as Paul's exposition assures us.

Then Malachi sets forth the words of the Lord Jehovah,

who is the Lord Jesus, as he speaks in the first person. "And I will come near to you to judgment," he says. The Second Coming is the day of judgment. "And I will be a swift witness against the sorcerers, and against the adulterers, and against false swearers, and against those that oppress the hireling in his wages, the widow, and the fatherless, and that turn aside the stranger from his right, and fear not me, saith the Lord of hosts." The works here named, together with those who do them, shall be burned at his coming. None who live in this worldly way shall abide the day. Then comes the promise that the faithful in Israel shall be saved. "Ye sons of Jacob are not consumed," saith the Lord. Those who are not consumed abide the day.

But the unfaithful in gathered Israel have no such promise. They are told: "even from the days of your fathers ye are gone away from mine ordinances, and have not kept them." The Lord's ordinances are his laws and commandments. There are those in the Church who have not walked in the light and kept the covenant made in the waters of baptism. "Return unto me, and I will return unto you, saith the Lord of hosts." There is yet time; the day is not at hand, and the hour has not arrived. There is yet a little season in which men may repent. But the lukewarm members of the Church, assuming in their minds that they have done no great evil, ask: "Wherein shall we return?" What have we done that is so grossly amiss? Have we not shown some measure of devotion? Surely we do not walk in a wicked way; what is our offense?

Then, as though the answer came from the fires and thunders of Sinai, the Lord of Hosts asked: "Will a man rob God?" Some might sink to such a depth as to rob their fellowmen. But who would be so vile, so devoid of all decency and right, so defiantly rebellious as to rob the Great God who created all things and who has poured out his bounties without measure upon men in all nations? Who would rob God? "Yet ye have robbed me," saith the Lord. In seeming unbelief that they could be accused of so gross a crime, even the most rebellious in Israel ask, "Wherein have we robbed thee?" The answer is forthcoming. He whose judgments are just and who does all things well replies: "In tithes and offerings." All Israel has covenanted in the waters of baptism to pay one-tenth of their increase annually into the tithing funds of the Church. That tenth is the Lord's tenth. It no longer belongs to the steward in whose hands it rests for the moment. It is the Lord's. To misappropriate the Lord's property is dishonest. In his sight it is robbery. Hence he says: "Ye are cursed with a curse; for ye have robbed me, even this whole nation." (Mal. 3:1-9.)

What is it that we thus learn from the Lord with reference to those who shall abide the day of his coming? We learn that those in Israel who are refined and purified shall walk unharmed in the furnace of Nebuchadnezzar, as it were, and upon their bodies the millennial fires have no power. Not a hair of their heads shall be singed, and the smell of fire shall not cling to their garments. But as for the sorcerers, the adulterers, the false swearers, those who oppress the poor, and those who rob God—none of these shall abide the day. And as to his own covenant people who choose to rob him of that which is his, the Lord in our day has issued this warning: "Behold, now it is called today until the coming of the Son of Man, and verily it is a day of sacrifice, and a day for the tithing of my people; for he that is tithed shall not be burned at his coming." (D&C 64:23.)

The Wicked Shall Be Burned at His Coming

Sometimes even the saints of the Most High become discouraged in their warfare with the world. Some among them forget for a moment that there will be a day of burning in which the wicked shall be consumed; some wonder if all their service and selflessness and sacrifice are worth the price. Knowing their thoughts and hearing their words, the Lord rebukes them by saying: "Your words have been stout against me." 'You have complained about the hardships of life and forgotten that I have ordained all these things for your ultimate glory and blessing.' To this the Lord's people reply: "What have we spoken so much against thee?" The Lord responds: "Ye have said, It is vain to serve God: and what profit is it that we have kept his ordinance, and that we have walked mournfully before the Lord of hosts?" 'Is it worth it to keep the commandments of God and deny ourselves all these pleasant delicacies and diversions that abound in the lives of other people?' Then the Lord explains: "Now"—in this present world of wickedness; in this day of carnality and evil; in this day when the wicked and ungodly do whatever is right in their own eyes—"Now we call the proud happy; yea, they that work wickedness are set up; yea, they that tempt God are even delivered." It is their world; it is their day; it is the hour of their delight. But soon their world will end; their day will pass away; and what they suppose are the delights of life will turn to ashes in their hands.

But for those who fear the Lord and keep his commandments, it shall be otherwise. They shall abide the coming day. "And they shall be mine, saith the Lord of hosts, in that day when I make up my jewels; and I will spare them, as a man spareth his own son that serveth him." They shall not be burned. "Then shall ye return, and discern between the righteous and the wicked, between him that serveth God and him that serveth him not." (Mal. 3:13-18.) However much the wicked may prevail in their own world; however eminent and great they now are in the eyes of their ilk; however much they may suppose their carnal course is one of happiness—yet in the day of burning (when there shall be a complete separation of the righteous and the wicked), those who serve God shall triumph. The new world will be their world.

"For, behold, the day cometh, that shall burn as an oven; and all the proud, yea, and all that do wickedly, shall be stubble: and the day that cometh shall burn them up, saith the Lord of hosts, that it shall leave them neither root nor branch." (Mal. 4:1.) Moroni's rendition of this statement as given to the Prophet on that September night in 1823 changed a portion of it to say: "For they that come shall burn them, saith the Lord of Hosts." (JS-H 1:37.) And, alluding to and paraphrasing Malachi's words, the Lord said in our day: "For after today cometh the burning—this is, speaking after the manner of the Lord—for verily I say, tomorrow all the proud and they that do wickedly shall be as stubble; and I will burn them up, for I am the Lord of Hosts; and I will not spare any that remain in Babylon. Wherefore, if ye believe me, ye will labor while it is called today." (D&C 64:24-25.)

Let us, then, labor while it is called today. Let us put our hands to the plow and look not back, lest we, like Lot's wife, become entangled again in the web of worldliness and lose our souls. Let us gather to Zion and within her walls rejoice. And thanks be to God for the restoration of the everlasting gospel; thanks be to him for the gathering of Israel and for the standard of righteousness that now waves in the mountains of Israel. Thanks be to his holy name for revealing anew what men must do "to prepare their hearts and be prepared in all things against the day when tribulation and desolation are sent forth upon the wicked."

For thus saith the Lord: "The hour is nigh and the day soon at hand when the earth is ripe; and all the proud and they that do wickedly shall be as stubble; and I will burn them up, saith the Lord of Hosts, that wickedness shall not be upon the earth; For the hour is nigh, and that which was spoken by mine apostles must be fulfilled; for as they spoke so shall it come to pass; For I will reveal myself from heaven with power and great glory, with all the hosts thereof, and dwell in righteousness with men on earth a thousand years, and the wicked shall not stand." (D&C 29:8-11.)

THE DAY OF SEPARATION

This Evil Day

This is an evil day, a day of disease and darkness and death. Our society is sick; our governments lack vision; our educational system takes an amoral and neutral position on the great Christian verities. Even the churches of Christendom, so-called, to say nothing of the non-Christian and pagan ways of worship, are decadent, sin-ridden, and incapable of raising the warning voice. Even in the one true Church, sad and unfortunate as it may be, the wheat and tares together grow.

Crime of every sort is increasing. Murder and rape and robbery are as much a way of life as they were in the days of Noah. Sexual perversions are lauded as an acceptable life-style for a growing portion of the people of our planet. Satan is abroad in the land. He and his fellow demons rage in the hearts of men. He sits in high places and rules in organizations of all sorts. It is his world; he knows it, and he is in command. There is rejoicing in the courts of hell and laughter on the lips of its courtiers as they survey the shambles they have made of our modern social structure.

In this present world of carnality and evil, the righteous and the wicked mingle in the same congregations. And as far as the arm of flesh is concerned, there is no way to stay the surging flood of evil that has been unloosed. The divine purpose allows iniquity to abound and sin to increase. The saints of God do and shall continue to strive with all their power to build dikes of righteousness that will contain the tides of evil that are sweeping over all the earth. But it will be a losing affray; at least it will be a war they will not win until the Man of War who is the God of Battles comes to champion their cause—which is his cause—and to fight their battles and to destroy their enemies.

This is a day in which—ere long!—"the wrath of God shall be poured out upon the wicked without measure." (D&C 1:9.) This is a day, saith the Lord, in which "a desolating scourge shall go forth among the inhabitants of the earth, and shall continue to be poured out from time to time, if they repent not, until the earth is empty, and the inhabitants thereof are consumed away and utterly destroyed by the brightness of my coming." (D&C 5:19.) "For I, the Almighty, have laid my hands upon the nations, to scourge them for their wickedness. And plagues shall go forth, and they shall not be taken from the earth until I have completed my work, which shall be cut short in righteousness—until all shall know me, who remain." (D&C 84:96-98.)

This is a day of which the Lord says: "I, the Lord, am angry with the wicked; I am holding my Spirit from the inhabitants of the earth. I have sworn in my wrath, and decreed wars upon the face of the earth, and the wicked shall slay the wicked, and fear shall come upon every man; and the saints also shall hardly escape; nevertheless, I, the Lord, am with them, and will come down in heaven from the presence of my Father and consume the wicked with unquenchable fire." (D&C 63:32-34.)

As we are acutely aware: "They that are wise and have received the truth, and have taken the Holy Spirit for their guide, and have not been deceived . . . they shall not be hewn down and cast into the fire, but shall abide the day." And conversely: "Calamity shall cover the mocker, and the scorner shall be consumed; and they that have watched for iniquity shall be hewn down and cast into the fire." (D&C 45:50, 57.) Truly, "he that is not purified shall not abide the day." (D&C 38:8.)

The Burning of the Tares

We have made repeated references to the burning of the vineyard, which is the earth, and to the fact that every corruptible thing of every sort, including those portions of all forms of life that do not meet the divine standard, shall be consumed at the Second Coming. This is the cleansing of the earth and its atmospheric heavens that will change it into a new heaven and a new earth. This is also the occasion when the tares shall be burned, and the burning of the tares is the destruction of the wicked at our Lord's return.

As faith precedes the miracle, so wickedness precedes the burning. It was so in Sodom, and so it shall be in the coming day. The law is the Lord's; it is that the wicked of all ages shall burn in hell, and those who live in the day of his coming shall be as stubble. The fires of a just God shall leave them neither root nor branch. And so, as the day of burning nears, we are more deeply concerned than men have ever been as to what is involved in the soon-to-be burning of the tares.

In the parable of the wheat and the tares the kingdom of heaven, meaning the true Church and kingdom of God on earth, was likened unto a man who sowed good seed in his field. The one who sowed the seed was the Lord Jesus; the field was the world; the good seed was the children of the kingdom, the true saints, the believing and obedient souls who accepted the gospel and forsook the world to serve Christ. But while men slept, the Lord's enemy, who is Satan, the devil, the evil one, came and sowed tares among the wheat and went his way. Tares, in the literal sense of the word, are a noxious weed that resembles wheat; they are a "bastard wheat" that is so much like the true wheat that the plants cannot be distinguished from it until the grain begins to ripen. In the parable the tares are the children of the wicked one; they are those in the Church and in the world who live wicked and ungodly lives, who are carnal, sensual, and devilish, and who live after the manner of the world.

"But when the blade was sprung up, and brought forth fruit," the parable continues, "then appeared the tares also." Seeing this, the Lord's servants asked if they should gather up the tares. The answer: "Nay; lest while ye gather up the tares, ye root up also the wheat with them. Let both grow together until the harvest, and in the time of harvest, I will say to the reapers, Gather ye together first the wheat into my barn; and the tares are bound in bundles to be burned."

What then, is the meaning of the parable, and how shall we interpret it? Jesus answers: "The harvest is the end of the world, or the destruction of the wicked." The fulfillment is yet future; the end of the world is not yet, but by and by. "The reapers are the angels, or the messengers sent of heaven." They are the servants of the Lord who go forth to harvest the earth, and to gather the wheat into barns. "As, therefore, the tares are gathered and burned in the fire, so shall it be in the end of this world, or the destruction of the wicked." After a farmer harvests his wheat, he burns the field to destroy the weeds, lest they reseed the field and his land be ruined. "For in that day, before the Son of man shall come, he shall send forth his angels and messengers of heaven." Moroni and the other angels have come and the messengers chosen of heaven are now going forth. "And they shall gather out of his kingdom all things that offend, and them which do iniquity, and shall cast them out among the wicked; and there shall be wailing and gnashing of teeth." The Church must be cleansed before the Lord comes; the tares must be cast out with their like kinds in the world, there to be burned. "For the world shall be burned with fire." (Matt. 13:24-30, 36-43; JST, Matt. 13:29, 39-44.)

That we might catch the full vision and import of this

parable, the Lord gave to it a new and enlarged meaning in our day. He said that "the field was the world, and the apostles were the sowers of the seed," and that Satan, operating through the Babylonish whore, which is the great and abominable church, sowed the tares, which then grew and choked the wheat, and drove the true Church into the wilderness. This is descriptive of the great apostasy. Finally, in the last days, comes the restoration. Good seed is again sown in the field of the Lord; again the blade springs forth in a tender and delicate form. Again it grows among the tares sown by the evil one, and again the angels plead with the Lord of the harvest for permission to go forth and reap down the fields. "But the Lord saith unto them, pluck not up the tares while the blade is yet tender (for verily your faith is weak), lest you destroy the wheat also. Therefore, let the wheat and the tares grow together until the harvest is fully ripe; then ye shall first gather out the wheat from among the tares, and after the gathering of the wheat, behold and lo, the tares are bound in bundles, and the field remaineth to be burned." (D&C 86:1-7.)

Speaking of this parable, the Prophet Joseph Smith, with a wondrous flow of inspired words, tells us: "The harvest and the end of the world have an allusion directly to the human family in the last days." The message of the parable is for us in this day. "As, therefore, the tares are gathered and burned in the fire, so shall it be in the end of the world; that is, as the servants of God go forth warning the nations, both priests and people, and as they [the priests and people] harden their hearts and reject the light of truth, these first being delivered over to the buffetings of Satan, and the law and the testimony being closed up, as it was in the case of the Jews, they are left in darkness, and delivered over unto the day of burning; thus being bound up by their creeds, and their bands being made strong by their priests, [they] are prepared for the fulfilment of the saying of the Savior—'The Son of Man shall send forth His angels, and gather out of His Kingdom all things that offend, and them which do iniquity, and shall cast them into a furnace of fire, there shall be wailing and gnashing of teeth.'

"We understand that the work of gathering of the wheat into barns, or garners, is to take place while the tares are being bound over, and [incident to the] preparing for the day of burning; that after the day of burnings, the righteous shall shine forth like the sun, in the Kingdom of their Father." (*Teachings*, pp. 97-98, 101.)

And so it is that we hear the voice of the Lord saying in our day: "All flesh is corrupted before me; and the powers of darkness prevail upon the earth, among the children of men, in the presence of all the hosts of heaven—Which causeth silence to reign, and all eternity is pained, and the angels are waiting the great command to reap down the earth, to gather the tares that they may be burned; and, behold, the enemy is combined." (D&C 38:11-12.)

And also: "I must gather together my people, according to the parable of the wheat and the tares, that the wheat may be secured in the garners to possess eternal life, and be crowned with celestial glory, when I shall come in the kingdom of my Father to reward every man according as his work shall be; While the tares shall be bound in bundles, and their bands made strong, that they may be burned with unquenchable fire." (D&C 101:65-66.)

"Cut Off from Among the People"

We live in a day when the whole social structure is dividing itself into two camps. This is a day of the polarization of all people. In the Church the faithful members are perfecting their lives and drawing nearer to the Lord and his way of life. In the world wickedness is increasing and the rebellious and carnal among men are sinking to lower levels of evil and depravity than has been the case in any past days. These trends will continue unabated until the Lord comes. When he arrives there will be, on the one hand, a people prepared to meet him, and, on the other hand, there will be greater wickedness and carnality than has ever before been known. As time goes on, fewer and fewer among men will remain aloof from one or the other of these camps.

Then when the Lord comes, he himself will both cause and complete the division among the people. Then there will be a great day of separation in which the wicked will be consumed and the righteous will be rewarded. In discoursing upon the great day of restoration and the millennial conditions that will then be ushered in, Nephi says: "For the time speedily cometh that the Lord God shall cause a great division among the people, and the wicked will he destroy; and he will spare his people, yea, even if it so be that he must destroy the wicked by fire." (2 Ne. 30:10.) This, of course, has reference to the day of burning that will attend the Lord's return. This is the same day of which the Lord said to Zechariah, "I will remove the iniquity of that land in one day." The wicked shall cease to be on earth. But as to the righteous: "In that day, saith the Lord of hosts, shall ye call every man his neighbour under the vine and under the fig tree." (Zech. 3:9-10.) The saints will continue to inherit the earth during the Millennium.

Our latter-day revelations speak with great particularity about what is to transpire with reference to the righteous and the wicked when the Lord comes. "And he that liveth when the Lord shall come, and hath kept the faith, blessed is he; nevertheless, it is appointed to him to die at the age of man. Wherefore, children shall grow up until they become old; old men shall die; but they shall not sleep in the dust, but they shall be changed in the twinkling of an eye. . . . These things are the things that ye must look for; and, speaking after the manner of the Lord, they are now nigh at hand, and in a time to come, even in the day of the coming of the Son of Man. And until that hour there will be foolish virgins among the wise; and at that hour cometh an entire separation of the righteous and the wicked; and in that day will I send mine angels to pluck out the wicked and cast them into unquenchable fire." (D&C 63:50-54.)

This division among the people, this entire separation of the righteous and the wicked, this destruction of the ungodly and the saving of the righteous by fire—all of this was taught in ancient Israel by reference to one of Moses' greatest Messianic prophecies. Moses, the mediator of the old covenant (the law), which prepared men to receive the new covenant (the gospel), of which Christ was the Mediator—Moses proclaimed to Israel of old: "The Lord thy God will raise up unto thee a Prophet from the midst of thee, of thy brethren, like unto me; unto him ye shall hearken." So spake the ancient lawgiver with reference to the Lord Jesus Christ, their Promised Messiah. "And the Lord said unto me," Moses continued, "I will raise them up a Prophet from among their brethren, like unto thee, and will put my words in his mouth; and he shall speak unto them all that I shall command him. And it shall come to pass, that whosoever will not hearken unto my words which he shall speak in my name, I will require it of him." (Deut. 18:15, 17-19.)

There well may have been more to these ancient words than is recorded in Deuteronomy. At least Jesus and all the prophets gave them a more express and expanded meaning than they seem to have in their Old Testament context. Jesus, on Olivet, after speaking of unfaithful servants who ate and drank with the drunken, who forsook the labors of their ministry, and who, accordingly, were cut asunder and appointed their portion with the hypocrites, where there was weeping and gnashing of teeth—Jesus said: "And thus cometh the end of the wicked, according to the prophecy of Moses, saying: They shall be cut off from among the people." To this Jesus added, "But the end of the earth is not yet, but by and by," meaning that the destruction of the wicked is the end of the world but not the end of the earth. (JS-M 1:55.)

Peter quoted Moses' Messianic words, rendering in this way the portion about the Lord requiring men to heed the

Messianic message: "And it shall come to pass, that every soul, which will not hear that prophet, shall be destroyed from among the people." (Acts 3:22-23.) When Moroni came to Joseph Smith, he quoted Peter's words "precisely as they stand in our New Testament. He said that that prophet was Christ; but the day had not yet come when"—and at this point he targums or interprets Peter's words—"when 'they who would not hear his voice should be cut off from among the people,' but soon would come." (JS-H 1:40.)

Our blessed Lord, ministering in glorious immortality among the Nephite Hebrews, testified: "I am he of whom Moses spake, saying: A prophet shall the Lord your God raise up unto you of your brethren, like unto me; him shall ye hear in all things whatsoever he shall say unto you. And it shall come to pass that every soul who will not hear that prophet shall be cut off from among the people." (3 Ne. 20:23.) And further, after having spoken of the restoration of the gospel in our day by one of his appointed servants, the Risen Lord said: "Therefore it shall come to pass that whosoever will not believe in my words, who am Jesus Christ, which the Father shall cause him [the restorer of eternal truth in the last days] to bring forth unto the Gentiles, and shall give unto him power that he shall bring forth unto the Gentiles, (it shall be done even as Moses said) they shall be cut off from among my people who are of the covenant." (3 Ne. 21:10-11.)

In his revealed preface to his book of commandments the Lord says: "And the arm of the Lord shall be revealed; and the day cometh that they who will not hear the voice of the Lord, neither the voice of his servants, neither give heed to the words of the prophets and apostles, shall be cut off from among the people." Why? Because of apostasy; because they do not keep the commandments; because "they have strayed from mine ordinances, and have broken mine everlasting covenant"; because "they seek not the

Lord to establish his righteousness, but every man walketh in his own way"—these are the reasons they shall be cut off from among the people. (D&C 1:14-16.)

How and in what manner will the wicked be cut off in the last days? In two ways: first, by the plagues and desolations that have already commenced and that are yet to be poured out upon the wicked, and then by the burning fires of vengeance that shall attend the Second Coming. Thus Jacob says that the Lord will gather his people again into his holy sheepfold, and that "the Messiah will . . . manifest himself unto them in power and great glory, unto the destruction of their enemies, when that day cometh when they shall believe in him; and none will he destroy that believe in him. And they that believe not in him shall be destroyed, both by fire, and by tempest, and by earthquakes, and by bloodsheds, and by pestilence, and by famine." (2 Ne. 6:13-15.)

Jacob's brother Nephi gives what is perhaps the best analysis in all the scriptures relative to those events which will be consummated by the cutting off of the wicked from among the people. He speaks of the day of gathering in which Israel "shall be brought out of obscurity and out of darkness," a day that has now commenced. Israel is no longer hidden and obscure; her whereabouts are known. She is scattered in all nations, and she is now coming out of the darkness of the ages. The light of heaven is beginning to dwell in her heart. Her children are joining the true Church. It is the day when "they shall know that the Lord is their Savior and their Redeemer, the Mighty One of Israel." It is the day in which "the blood of that great and abominable church, which is the whore of all the earth, shall turn upon their own heads; for they shall war among themselves, and the sword of their own hands shall fall upon their own heads, and they shall be drunken with their own blood." Even now the nations and kingdoms that comprise the great and abominable church are at each other's throats from time to time, and this shall increase until the great day of Armageddon when that evil church shall be utterly destroyed. "And every nation which shall war against thee, O house of Israel, shall be turned one against another, and they shall fall into the pit which they digged to ensnare the people of the Lord." Israel shall come off triumphant; truth will prevail; the Lord's cause shall conquer all. "And all that fight against Zion shall be destroyed, and that great whore, who hath perverted the right ways of the Lord, yea, that great and abominable church, shall tumble to the dust and great shall be the fall of it."

When the church of the devil is destroyed at our Lord's return, who will remain on earth over whom Satan can rule? When his kingdom is destroyed and its municipals are burned, who will be left on earth to do his bidding? Clearly, if Satan has neither a kingdom on earth among mortals nor servants among men who will do his bidding, his reign of blood and horror on earth must cease. And so Nephi says: "The time cometh speedily that Satan shall have no more power over the hearts of the children of men; for the day soon cometh that all the proud and they who do wickedly shall be as stubble; and the day cometh that they must be burned." It is clear from the context that Nephi gained these views from someone whom he identifies simply as "the prophet," and that they are the same views Malachi had before him when he wrote the words of his prophecy.

"For the time soon cometh that the fulness of the wrath of God shall be poured out upon all the children of men; for he will not suffer that the wicked shall destroy the righteous. Wherefore, he will preserve the righteous by his power, even if it so be that the fulness of his wrath must come, and the righteous be preserved, even unto the destruction of their enemies by fire. Wherefore, the righteous need not fear; for thus saith the prophet, they shall be saved, even if it so be as by fire." Whatever desolations and destructions may befall all men, both the righteous and the wicked, prior to the coming of the Lord, in that day the final triumph of the God-fearing and the upright shall be brought to pass.

"Behold, my brethren, I say unto you, that these things must shortly come; yea, even blood, and fire, and vapor of smoke must come; and it must needs be upon the face of this earth; and it cometh unto men according to the flesh if it so be that they will harden their hearts against the Holy One of Israel." Men would be spared the desolations of the last days if they would repent and live the gospel. The Lord does not delight in the destruction of the wicked. His bounteous mercy and grace and goodness are available for all men in all ages, but they are poured out only upon those whose works merit the receipt of such a wondrous boon. "For behold, the righteous shall not perish; for the time surely must come that all they who fight against Zion shall be cut off."

In this setting Nephi comes to the words of Moses that we are considering. "And the Lord will surely prepare a way for his people, unto the fulfilling of the words of Moses, which he spake, saying: A prophet shall the Lord your God raise up unto you, like unto me; him shall ye hear in all things whatsoever he shall say unto you. And it shall come to pass that all those who will not hear that prophet shall be cut off from among the people. And now I, Nephi, declare unto you, that this prophet of whom Moses spake was the Holy One of Israel; wherefore, he shall execute judgment in righteousness. And the righteous need not fear, for they are those who shall not be confounded." (1 Ne. 22:12-22.)

Truly, as Isaiah saith, in the day of his coming "he shall smite the earth with the rod of his mouth, and with the breath of his lips shall he slay the wicked." (Isa. 11:4.) "Then shall be fulfilled that which is written, that in the last days, two shall be in the field, the one shall be taken, and the other left; Two shall be grinding at the mill, the one shall be taken, and the other left." (JS-M 1:44-45.) And as

Jesus also said: "I tell you, in that night there shall be two men in one bed; the one shall be taken, and the other shall be left. Two women shall be grinding together; the one shall be taken, and the other left. Two men shall be in the field; the one shall be taken, and the other left." (Luke 17:34-36.) Truly, there shall be a complete separation of the righteous and the wicked in the day of his coming. What manner of men ought we, therefore, to be?

Chapter 46

HE COMETH IN GLORY

"Prepare to Meet Thy God"

We have woven the doctrine of the Second Coming, including much of the prophetic word relative to that glorious day of promise, into one great tapestry that is as broad as eternity and as beautiful as any of the paintings that hang in celestial galleries. Or, rather, we have pierced the veil as best we could, to let those who seek the face of the Lord gain glimpses of what the Master Weaver has himself woven on the tapestries of eternity.

We have seen threads of ten thousand kinds; we have viewed scenes of every hue and nature; our souls have been thrilled with the divine artistry of it all. And in the center of this glorious work of heavenly art we see the Son of God coming in glory and splendor to be with men again; we see him conferring renown and honor upon his saints; we see him living and reigning in the midst of his beloved Israel for the space of a thousand years. It is this grand consummation, this wondrous and blessed day, toward which all things point.

And how could it be otherwise? The whole purpose of the Father is to save his people. He created the earth, peopled it with his children, and gave them the holy gospel—all to the end that they might believe and obey and be saved. He sent Adam to be the common parent of all men and to bring mortality and procreation and death into being. He sent his Son to ransom men from the fall and to bring to pass the immortality and eternal life of man. And he promised that he would destroy the wicked and bring peace and glory and triumph to his people in the great millennial day.

All things through the ages have pointed to this final day of rest and peace. And throughout this whole work, with inept and faltering fingers, we have sought to weave, page by page, those threads which belong in the Lord's eternal tapestry, and chapter by chapter we have attempted to describe the scenes the Lord has envisioned from the beginning—all to the end that those now living might know what to expect and how to prepare for the coming day.

Now let us gaze in rapture upon this glorious tapestry, which depicts the most majestic event since the very creation of the earth itself. No one prophet has told us all that is to be in that day of glory and wonder. Each has woven a few threads into the grand design; each has added a hue and a dimension to give depth and perspective to the scene; each has borne his appointed witness relative to the coming of the one who is Lord of them all.

As we gaze in awe at the grand picture, we see the Lord Jesus ascending from Olivet as angelic witnesses testify that he shall come again in like manner at that place. From this splendid scene our eyes turn to the dark and dire and devilish days when Satan has dominion over his own. We see false churches, false worship, and false prophets. Iniquity abounds and evil is everywhere. There is universal apostasy; darkness covers the earth and gross darkness the minds of the people; it is the evil night that must precede the dawn of the restoration.

Then—praise God!—the age of restoration arrives. Light shines in the eastern sky. The glorious gospel is restored; the dispensation of the fulness of times is ushered in; and the Church of the living God is given again to the saints of the Most High. The everlasting word goes forth;

the Book of Mormon bears witness of our Lord and his gospel; the name of Joseph Smith is spoken from the housetops in reverential tones. Ancient prophets confer power and authority upon their mortal fellow servants. And Israel begins to gather again. The Lamanites, the Jews, and the Gentiles all play their appointed roles. Temples rise in the tops of the mountains of Israel, the holy Zion of God is built up again, and two world capitals rise in splendor so the law can go forth from Zion and the word of the Lord from Jerusalem.

From these pleasant scenes our eyes are diverted to the world of wickedness of the last days. We are sickened at the sight of sin; we tremble as we see the plagues and pestilence and disasters and wars. In the background, woven with threads of fire, we see Armageddon and burning and destruction. It is with relief that we see the whorish Babylon, with all her evil and sensuality, burned with everlasting fire. Lo, this is the great and dreadful day of the Lord. It is a day of judgment and of fire and of the entire separation of the righteous and the wicked. Also in the background we see the return of the Ten Tribes, the perfecting of Zion, and the descent from heavenly heights of the City of Holiness.

And in the center of all things standeth Christ. Lo, he comes, as it is written of him. Angelic hosts attend; tens of thousands of his saints make up his train; the holy apostles and the prophets of all ages are on his right hand and on his left, having crowns of gold upon their heads. And the tapestry stretches on into eternity. No man can view it all, and we marvel at what we have seen and prepare ourselves to see more. We know that what we have seen is hidden from the world; the view is reserved for those whose spiritual eyes are open. In the world, as Jeremiah foresaw, "both prophet and priest are profane"; the ministers of religion do not take counsel from the Lord; there is darkness and apostasy. But the saints have this prophetic word: "In the latter days ye shall consider it perfectly." (Jer.

23:11, 20.) And so, as we gaze in worshipful wonder at the transcendent tapestry of Him whose servants we are, we cry aloud: "Prepare to meet thy God, O Israel." (Amos 4:12.)

Those who are preparing to meet their God are the Lord's people; all others hearken to the voice of a different shepherd. The true saints can read the signs of the times. They know that the apostasy, the restoration, the gathering of Israel, and the building up of Zion in the last days are all necessary preludes to the glorious return of the Lord Jesus. Their constant prayers ascend to heaven, saying: "Thy kingdom come. Thy will be done in earth, as it is in heaven." (Matt. 6:10.) 'Let the millennial day dawn; let peace and righteousness dwell on earth; let thy people be saved with an everlasting salvation.' "Oh that thou wouldest rend the heavens, that thou wouldest come down, that the mountains might flow down at thy presence." (Isa. 64:1.) They say: "I will wait upon the Lord, that hideth his face from the house of Jacob, and I will look for him." (Isa. 8:17.) Truly, "the people of the Lord are they who wait for him; for they still wait for the coming of the Messiah," and "he will manifest himself unto them in power and great glory, unto the destruction of their enemies." (2 Ne. 6:13-14.)

The Blessed One Cometh

Almost all of the prophets speak of the glory and grandeur of the Second Coming. It is to be a day of wondrous renown in which all Israel and all the saints shall come off triumphant. We have spoken somewhat about this in various places throughout this work. And we shall now sample the prophetic word with a view to gaining a feeling relative to what is to be. So voluminous are the accounts in this field that we shall scarcely allude to a hundredth part of them. By themselves they would constitute a book on the Second Coming, and even then their meaning would be known and their import felt only by those enlightened by the power of the Spirit. Truly, this is a realm in which the things of God can be known only by the power of the Holy Ghost. How can the finite mind, unquickened by a higher power, even conceive how resurrected beings can return and live among men; how mortals can be freed from disease and sorrow; and how they can live, without death, until they are the age of a tree? How can the mortal man envision the return in glorious immortality of one who died upon a cross and was buried in a tomb? How can we comprehend how earthly bodies can stand unharmed in flaming fire as the very elements melt with fervent heat? How can we understand the innate glory of ten thousand times ten thousand things that will attend and follow the return of the Son of Man? As we turn our attention to these things, it will be well worth our while to ponder some portions at least of the prophetic word.

Jesus himself said that at his coming his people would say of him: "Blessed is he who cometh in the name of the Lord, in the clouds of heaven, and all the holy angels with him." Since that primeval day when the Lord "laid the foundations of the earth," and in which "the morning stars sang together, and all the sons of God shouted for joy" (Job 38:4-7), since the day of creation's dawn, has there ever been another time when all the angels of God in heaven have participated in one single event? Of the day of his return, Jesus also said: "They shall see the Son of Man coming in the clouds of heaven, with power and great glory; and whoso treasureth up my word, shall not be deceived, for the Son of Man shall come, and he shall send his angels before him with the great sound of a trumpet, and they shall gather together the remainder of his elect from the four winds, from one end of heaven to the other." (JS-M 1:1, 36-37.) Who else will ever come in the Father's name in the clouds of heaven with great glory shining forth on every hand? Who else will command legions of angels to do his bidding in all parts of the earth?

Hear also these words from Jesus: "When the Son of

man shall come in his glory, and all the holy angels with him"—there is no doubt as to who shall be in attendance—"then shall he sit upon the throne of his glory: And before him shall be gathered all nations: and he shall separate them one from another, as a shepherd divideth his sheep from the goats." (Matt. 25:31-32.) All the holy angels, all the nations of men, one throne, one Supreme Judge, one day of millennial judgment—has there ever been such a scene as this? How aptly Jesus chooses his words to show the incomparable glory of the coming day!

Jude and Enoch, though separated by three thousand years, unite their voices in testifying of the glory and judgment that will attend the Second Coming. In speaking of the condemnation that will befall "ungodly men" in that great day, Jude says: "And Enoch also, the seventh from Adam, prophesied of these, saying, Behold, the Lord cometh with ten thousands of his saints, To execute judgment upon all, and to convince all that are ungodly among them of all their ungodly deeds which they have ungodly committed, and of all their hard speeches which ungodly sinners have spoken against him." (Jude 1:4, 14-15.) The ten thousands of his saints are the holy angels; they are the righteous of ages past who are already resurrected. They shall attend their Lord and shall, by assignment from him, "execute judgment." They are the ones of whom Malachi wrote: "They that come shall burn them, saith the Lord of Hosts, that it shall leave them neither root nor branch." (JS-H 1:37.) The day of judgment, the day of burning, ten thousands of judges—"Do ye not know that the saints shall judge the world?" Paul asked (1 Cor. 6:2)—how majestic and awesome shall this day be!

What saith Isaiah, the Messianic prophet, about the glory and power of that great day when the Lord shall come again? His message is one of fear and dread for the wicked, one of peace and security for the righteous. "O ye wicked ones," he cries, "enter into the rock, and hide thee in the dust, for the fear of the Lord and the glory of his majesty shall smite thee." None can hide from the Lord of Hosts; none can avoid the piercing gaze of the all-seeing eye; none can flee to a place beyond Jehovah's jurisdiction. In that great day the wicked will wish they could become part of the rocks—hidden, obscure, overlooked. They will seek to hide in and be as the dust of the earth, lest they be called before the Eternal Bar to face Him who is judge of all. "And it shall come to pass that the lofty looks of man shall be humbled, and the haughtiness of men shall be bowed down, and the Lord alone shall be exalted in that day." Kings and rulers, the mighty and great, the rich and the proud—all that walk in wickedness—shall be abased. The Lord alone—together with those who have become like him!—shall be exalted in that day.

"For the day of the Lord of Hosts soon cometh upon all nations, yea, upon every one"—none shall escape—"yea, upon the proud and lofty, and upon every one who is lifted up, and he shall be brought low." Both nations and people will be humbled. He will make a full end of all nations, and the wicked who comprise them shall be burned as stubble. Then, using that type of poetic imagery for which he has such great renown, Isaiah continues: "Yea, and the day of the Lord shall come upon all the cedars of Lebanon, for they are high and lifted up; and upon all the oaks of Bashan; and upon all the high mountains, and upon all the hills, and upon all the nations which are lifted up, and upon every people; and upon every high tower, and upon every fenced wall; and upon all the ships of the sea, and upon all the ships of Tarshish, and upon all pleasant pictures." The earth itself and the vegetation that grows from the ground shall be affected. The mountains and hills shall be made low. Every nation and people shall feel the arm of the Almighty. Their defenses, their armaments, their weapons of war shall avail them nothing. Their commerce and wealth shall vanish away, and even the pleasant scenes of this mortal earth shall be no more. When else shall such earthshaking wonders as these even come into mind?

And then, by way of poetic reprise, and with a divine and thunderous emphasis, Israel's poetic prophet acclaims again: "And the loftiness of man shall be bowed down, and the haughtiness of men shall be made low; and the Lord alone shall be exalted in that day." Then he says that "the fear of the Lord shall come upon them, and the glory of his majesty shall smite them, when he ariseth to shake terribly the earth." (2 Ne. 12:10-19.) The earth shall reel to and fro; it shall shake; all things shall change in that day when it becomes a new heaven and a new earth. How glorious and wondrous shall that day be!

Latter-day Israel has these promises, relayed to them by the mouth of Isaiah: "Your God will come with vengeance, even God with a recompence; he will come and save you." (Isa. 35:4.) "And the Redeemer shall come to Zion, and unto them that turn from transgression in Jacob, saith the Lord." (Isa. 59:20.) "He shall appear to your joy. . . . For, behold, the Lord will come with fire, and with his chariots like a whirlwind, to render his anger with fury, and his rebuke with flames of fire." (Isa. 66:5, 15.) Truly, great are the words of Isaiah.

Others of the prophets speak similarly. By the mouth of Zechariah, the Lord promises to be "the glory in the midst" of Jerusalem in the latter days. "Sing and rejoice, O daughter of Zion," he says, "for, lo, I come, and I will dwell in the midst of thee, saith the Lord. And many nations shall be joined to the Lord in that day, and shall be my people: and I will dwell in the midst of thee, and thou shalt know that the Lord of hosts hath sent me unto thee. And the Lord shall inherit Judah his portion in the holy land, and shall choose Jerusalem again." (Zech. 2:4-5, 10-12.) Once again this time in the latter days, the Lord Jesus shall dwell among his people; Jerusalem shall be his abode as it once was.

Haggai records this word from on high: "Thus saith the Lord of hosts: Yet once, it is a little while, and I will shake the heavens, and the earth, and the sea, and the dry land;

and I will shake all nations, and the desire of all nations shall come." (Hag. 2:6-7.) Of the Second Coming Habakkuk testified: "God came. . . . His glory covered the heavens, and the earth was full of his praise. And his brightness was as the light. . . . Before him went the pestilence, and burning coals went forth at his feet. He stood, and measured the earth: he beheld, and drove asunder the nations; and the everlasting mountains were scattered, the perpetual hills did bow: his ways are everlasting." (Hab. 3:3-6.) And of the millennial day, he said: "The Lord is in his holy temple: let all the earth keep silence before him." (Hab. 2:20.) Hosea speaks of "the Holy One in the midst of thee." (Hosea 11:9.) Joel records these words of the Lord: "Ye shall know that I am in the midst of Israel, and that I am the Lord your God, and none else: and my people shall never be ashamed." (Joel 2:27.) "I am the Lord your God dwelling in Zion, my holy mountain: then shall Jerusalem be holy, and there shall be no strangers pass through her any more. . . . For the Lord dwelleth in Zion." (Joel 3:17, 21.) And Zephaniah records this joyful word: "Sing, O daughter of Zion; shout, O Israel; be glad and rejoice with all the heart, O daughter of Jerusalem. The Lord hath taken away thy judgments, he hath cast out thine enemy: the king of Israel, even the Lord, is in the midst of thee: thou shalt not see evil any more. In that day it shall be said to Jerusalem, Fear thou not: and to Zion, let not thine hands be slack. The Lord thy God in the midst of thee is mighty; he will save, he will rejoice over thee with joy; he will rest in his love, he will joy over thee with singing." (Zeph. 3:14-17.) And in the Psalmic word we read: "When the Lord shall build up Zion, he shall appear in his glory." (Ps. 102:16.) The intent and meaning of these and many other passages are evident. We need not say more on this point.

"Prepare Ye the Way of the Lord"

These are the last days; the signs of the times are now being shown forth on every hand; and the coming of the

Lord is not far distant. In the early days of this final gospel dispensation, when his servants were just beginning to lay the foundations of his earthly kingdom, the Lord said: "The voice of the Lord is unto the ends of the earth, that all that will hear may hear: Prepare ye, prepare ye for that which is to come, for the Lord is nigh." (D&C 1:11-12.) Prepare for the pestilence and plagues and sorrows of the last days. Prepare for the second coming of the Son of Man. Prepare to abide the day, to stand when he appeareth, and to live and reign with him on earth for a thousand years. Prepare for the new heaven and the new earth whereon dwelleth righteousness. Prepare to meet thy God.

Speaking of our day, Isaiah said that a voice would cry in the wilderness—that a sweet voice of sound doctrine and true testimony would be heard in the wilderness of sin—and that the voice would say: "Prepare ye the way of the Lord, make straight in the desert a highway for our God. Every valley shall be exalted, and every mountain and hill shall be made low: and the crooked shall be made straight, and the rough places plain: And the glory of the Lord shall be revealed, and all flesh shall see it together: for the mouth of the Lord hath spoken it." The great day of his coming is at hand. The Lord's people must be ready. They must do the things he has commanded, as a people and as individuals, to stand in his presence and receive his approval when he comes.

"O Zion, that bringest good tidings," Isaiah exhorts, "get thee up into the high mountain; O Jerusalem, that bringest good tidings, lift up thy voice with strength; lift it up, be not afraid; say unto the cities of Judah, Behold your God!" Be ready; prepare; believe his word; live his law; do the assigned labors; qualify as his people; send forth the glad tidings that he is near. "Behold, the Lord God will come with strong hand, and his arm shall rule for him: behold, his reward is with him, and his work before him." In that glorious day, far more than when he came before, "He shall feed his flock like a shepherd: he shall gather the lambs with his arm, and carry them in his bosom, and shall gently lead those that are with young." (Isa. 40:3-11.) Then shall be fulfilled that which is written, "The Lord is my shepherd; . . . and I will dwell in the house of the Lord for ever." (Ps. 23:1, 6.)

Prepare ye the way of the Lord! How is it done, and what arrangements must be made? How do we prepare for the coming of him whose we are, him who redeemed us and in whose pastures we feed? What must be done to prepare the way before him? Even as he will not come unattended, so all things must be in readiness when he arrives. And the preparation he requires is specific and personal for individuals; it is general and of universal application for his congregations; and it is fearsome and dreadful where the masses of men are concerned.

As individuals, we prepare to meet our God by keeping his commandments and living his laws. He will receive into his own bosom those only who abide the day of his coming. We prepare the way before his face by being born again, by cleansing and perfecting our souls, by gaining the companionship and sanctifying power of the Holy Spirit in our lives. The gospel in its everlasting fulness, restored as it has been in these last days, is here to prepare a people for the second coming of the Son of Man.

As congregations and as a people, we prepare the way before him by doing the worldwide work he requires at our hands. Before he comes, the gospel must be preached in every nation, to every people, with signs following those who believe. Before he comes, the name of Joseph Smith and the message of the Book of Mormon must be proclaimed from the housetops. Before he comes, many of the lost sheep of Israel must be gathered out of Babylon into the stakes of Zion, stakes now organized and yet to be organized in all nations. Before he comes, Zion must be built up, temples must rise wherever there are stakes, and the promises made to the fathers must be planted in the hearts of the children. Before he comes, his people must forsake the world; they must gather around the ensign raised in these latter days; they must be tried, so as by fire, to see if they will abide in his covenant, even unto death.

And as to the masses of men, as to the wicked and ungodly in general, as to those who esteem the things of this world of greater worth than the riches of Christ—all these are preparing, not to receive the joy of his countenance, but for the great day of burning. For them the Second Coming will be the day of vengeance that has been in the heart of the one to whom every knee shall bow and every tongue confess that he is Lord of all.

How can any people prepare to meet their God, how can any person know what to do in his individual case to prepare the way before his Lord, how can any and all know the course they should pursue except such is revealed to them from on high? The Second Coming is the Lord's doing, not man's. He will bring it to pass with power. He will do all that he has said. And he will require all others to meet his needs and conform to his standards. There must be general revelation to his people directing them in their course; and there must be personal revelation, coming by the power of the Holy Ghost, to each individual saint, directing him in the course he should pursue. The ancient scriptures and the modern scriptures contain much that has been revealed relative to this glorious and dread day. One of the great secrets of understanding what was revealed anciently, which is often hidden in a recitation of local historical circumstances unfamiliar to us, is to learn the same concepts from latter-day revelation. What the Lord has revealed to us ties together and interprets what he revealed to our ancient counterparts. It is appropriate at this point to sample what he has said in our day.

"Be faithful until I come, and ye shall be caught up, that where I am ye shall be also." (D&C 27:18.) "For I will reveal myself from heaven with power and great glory, with all the hosts thereof, and dwell in righteousness with men on earth a thousand years, and the wicked shall not stand."

(D&C 29:11.) "Wherefore, be faithful, praying always, having your lamps trimmed and burning, and oil with you, that you may be ready at the coming of the Bridegroom—For behold, verily, verily, I say unto you, that I come quickly." (D&C 33:17-18.)

To each of his servants in this day, the Lord sends this word: "Lift up your voice as with the sound of a trump, both long and loud, and cry repentance unto a crooked and perverse generation, preparing the way of the Lord for his second coming." And then, that all may understand what lies ahead, he says: "For behold, verily, verily, I say unto you, the time is soon at hand that I shall come in a cloud with power and great glory. And it shall be a great day at the time of my coming, for all nations shall tremble. But before that great day shall come, the sun shall be darkened, and the moon be turned into blood; and the stars shall refuse their shining, and some shall fall, and great destructions await the wicked." The very reason for preaching the gospel to the world is so believing souls may escape the sorrows and desolations that lie ahead. "Wherefore, lift up your voice and spare not, for the Lord God hath spoken; therefore prophesy, and it shall be given by the power of the Holy Ghost. And if you are faithful, behold, I am with you until I come—And verily, verily, I say unto you, I come quickly." (D&C 34:6-12.)

"They shall look for me, and, behold, I will come; and they shall see me in the clouds of heaven, clothed with power and great glory; with all the holy angels; and he that watches not for me shall be cut off." (D&C 45:44.)

"Prepare ye the way of the Lord, prepare ye the supper of the Lamb, make ready for the Bridegroom." (D&C 65:3.)

"Prepare ye, prepare ye, O inhabitants of the earth; for the judgment of our God is come. Behold, and lo, the Bridegroom cometh; go ye out to meet him." (D&C 88:92.)

THE PRIVATE AND PUBLIC APPEARANCES

Our Lord's Many Appearances

The second coming of the Son of Man consists not of one but of many appearances. Our blessed Lord will come—attended by all the hosts of heaven, and in all the glory of his Father's kingdom—not to one but to many places. He will stand on one continent after another, speak to one great assemblage after another, and work his will among succeeding groups of mortals. Allusions to and some explanations concerning these various appearances are found in the ancient word. These, however, might well go unnoticed or remain without proper interpretation if it were not for the clarifying views found in latter-day revelation.

For instance, one of David's psalms calls upon us to "give unto the Lord the glory due unto his name," and then, rather enigmatically, the inspired psalmic word acclaims: "The voice of the Lord is upon the waters: the God of glory thundereth: the Lord is upon many waters. The voice of the Lord is powerful; the voice of the Lord is full of majesty," and a number of similar expressions. Then the millennial setting is shown by prophetic assurance, "The Lord sitteth King for ever. The Lord will give strength unto his people; the Lord will bless his people with peace." (Ps. 29:1-11.) Joel also, in the midst of an extended prophecy about the Second Coming, has this to say about the voice of the Lord in that day: "The Lord also shall roar out of Zion, and utter his voice from Jerusalem; and the heavens and the earth shall shake: but the Lord will be the hope of his people, and the strength of the children of Israel." (Joel 3:16.) Note the two places, Zion and Jerusalem, from which the voice will go forth. We shall set forth shortly how the voice of the Lord will be involved in his coming.

John the Beloved Revelator saw in vision a Lamb standing "on the mount Sion, and with him an hundred and forty and four thousand, having his Father's name written in their foreheads." Thereupon, as he records it, "I heard a voice from heaven, as the voice of many waters, and as the voice of a great thunder." (Rev. 14:1-2.) And Malachi prophesies: "The Lord, whom ye seek, shall suddenly come to his temple, even the messenger of the covenant, whom ye delight in: behold, he shall come, saith the Lord of hosts. But who may abide the day of his coming?" (Mal. 3:1-2.)

Jesus ascended from the Mount of Olives as an angelic voice acclaimed: "This same Jesus, which is taken up from you into heaven, shall so come in like manner as ye have seen him go into heaven" (Acts 1:11), leaving us to suppose that he will return to the same holy spot on that beloved mountain, to the same mountain where the great Olivet Discourse relative to his coming was delivered. And this, as we learn from Zechariah, shall come to pass in the full and literal sense of the word. Speaking of the final great day of Armageddon, the prophetic word recites: "Then shall the Lord go forth, and fight against those nations, as when he fought in the day of battle. And his feet shall stand in that day upon the mount of Olives, which is before Jerusalem on the east. . . . And the Lord my God shall come, and all the saints with thee." (Zech. 14:3-5.)

In revealing to us some of the things he taught his disciples on Olivet, the Lord included these words: "Then shall the arm of the Lord fall upon the nations. And then shall the Lord set his foot upon this mount [the Mount of Olives], and it shall cleave in twain, and the earth shall tremble, and reel to and fro, and the heavens also shall shake. And the Lord shall utter his voice, and all the ends of the earth shall hear it." (D&C 45:47-49.)

And in a divine proclamation also given in our day we are told: "Hearken and hear, O ye inhabitants of the earth. Listen, ye elders of my church together, and hear the voice of the Lord; for he calleth upon all men, and he commandeth all men everywhere to repent. For behold, the Lord God hath sent forth the angel crying through the midst of heaven, saying: Prepare ye the way of the Lord, and make his paths straight, for the hour of his coming is nigh—When the Lamb shall stand upon Mount Zion, and with him a hundred and forty-four thousand, having his Father's name written on their foreheads. Wherefore, prepare ye for the coming of the Bridegroom; go ye, go ye out to meet him. For behold, he shall stand upon the mount of Olivet, and upon the mighty ocean, even the great deep, and upon the islands of the sea, and upon the land of Zion. And he shall utter his voice out of Zion, and he shall speak from Jerusalem, and his voice shall be heard among all people; and it shall be a voice as the voice of many waters, and as the voice of a great thunder, which shall break down the mountains, and the valleys shall not be found." (D&C 133:16-22.)

Where, then, will the Lord come, in what places will he stand, and whence shall his voice be heard? The Lord, whom we seek, shall suddenly come to his temple, meaning that he will come to the earth, which is his temple, and also that he will come to those holy houses which he has commanded us to build unto his blessed name. Indeed, he came suddenly to the Kirtland Temple on the 3rd day of April in 1836; he has also appeared in others of his holy houses; and he will come in due course to the temples in Jackson County and in Jerusalem. And he will come to his American Zion and his Jewish Jerusalem. His voice will roar forth from both world capitals. He will speak personally, angelic ministrants will proclaim his word, and his mortal servants will speak with his voice. His feet will stand on Olivet on the east of Jerusalem, and he will come with the 144,000 high priests to Mount Zion in America. And where else? Upon the oceans and the islands and the continents, in the land of Zion and elsewhere. The clear meaning is that there will be many appearances, in many places, to many people. And when the day is at hand and the hour has arrived, he will come quickly, as the prophetic word, both ancient and modern, so repetitiously attests. "Surely I come quickly," saith the Lord, to which John replies: "Even so, come, Lord Jesus." (Rev. 22:20.) And we echo John's plea.

He Cometh to Adam-ondi-Ahman

We now come to the least known and least understood thing connected with the Second Coming. It might well be termed the best-kept secret set forth in the revealed word. It is something about which the world knows nothing; it is a doctrine that has scarcely dawned on most of the Latter-day Saints themselves; and yet it is set forth in holy writ and in the teachings of the Prophet Joseph Smith with substantially the same clarity as any of the doctrines of the kingdom. It behooves us to make a needed brief commentary about it.

Before the Lord Jesus descends openly and publicly in the clouds of glory, attended by all the hosts of heaven; before the great and dreadful day of the Lord sends terror and destruction from one end of the earth to the other; before he stands on Mount Zion, or sets his feet on Olivet, or utters his voice from an American Zion or a Jewish Jerusalem; before all flesh shall see him together; before any of his appearances, which taken together comprise the second coming of the Son of God—before all these, there is to be a secret appearance to selected members of his Church. He will come in private to his prophet and to the apostles then living. Those who have held keys and powers and authorities in all ages from Adam to the present will also be present. And further, all the faithful members of the Church then living and all the faithful saints of all the ages past will be present. It will be the greatest congregation of faithful saints ever assembled on planet earth. It will be a sacrament meeting. It will be a day of judgment for the faithful of all the ages. And it will take place in Daviess County, Missouri, at a place called Adam-ondi-Ahman.

Adam-ondi-Ahman, of eternal fame, first comes to our attention because of a great conference held there by Father Adam in his day. "Three years previous to the death of Adam, he called Seth, Enos, Cainan, Mahalaleel, Jared, Enoch, and Methuselah, who were all high priests, with the residue of his posterity who were righteous, into the valley of Adam-ondi-Ahman, and there bestowed upon them his last blessing." Nearly a thousand years had then passed since the first man and the first woman had stepped from Eden's garden into the lone and dreary world, there to begin the procreative processes that peopled a planet. We do not know how many million mortals made this earth their home in that day, or how many of them were true and faithful to that Lord whom Adam served. Disease and plagues were not then as common and horrendous as they are now. The physical bodies of earth's inhabitants had not yet degenerated to the disease-ridden, germ-governed shells of their former glory that is now the norm. We can suppose the population of the earth far exceeded that of later ages when the ills of the flesh and a rising infant mortality set a sin-inflicted limit on the numbers of men. And it is not unreasonable to suppose that many righteous spirits were born in that blessed day and that the numbers of the righteous were exceedingly great. We may not be amiss in supposing that many millions responded to the call to come to a general conference in Adam-ondi-Ahman.

This we do know, however: "The Lord appeared unto them"—Jesus Christ their King stood in their midst—"and they rose up and blessed Adam, and called him Michael, the prince, the archangel." How great and glorious is the eternal stature of the first man! "And the Lord administered comfort unto Adam, and said unto him: I have set thee to be at the head; a multitude of nations shall come of thee, and thou art a prince over them forever. And Adam stood up in the midst of the congregation; and, notwithstanding he was bowed down with age, being full of the Holy Ghost, predicted whatsoever should befall his posterity unto the latest generation." Such is an abbreviated account of what happened at Adam-ondi-Ahman in that pristine day. Our revelation that recites these words closes with the statement: "These things were all written in the book of Enoch, and are to be testified of in due time." (D&C 107:53-57.)

When the full account comes to us, we suppose we shall read of the offering of sacrifices in similitude of the sacrifice of the Only Begotten; of the testimonies borne by both men and women; of great doctrinal sermons delivered by the preachers of righteousness who then ministered among them; and of the outpouring of spiritual gifts upon the faithful then assembled. What visions they must have seen; what revelations they must have received; what feelings of rapture must have filled their bosoms as they feasted upon the things of eternity! Did Adam speak of the great latter-day gathering at Adam-ondi-Ahman, and did the faithful see with their spirit eyes what was then to be? These and a thousand other things "are to be testified of in due time." But this we do know: All that happened at Adam-ondi-Ahman in those early days was but a type and a shadow—a similitude, if you will—of what shall happen at the same blessed place in the last days when Adam and Christ and the residue of men who are righteous assemble again in solemn worship.

If we are to understand what shall transpire at Adam-ondi-Ahman in the near future, we must first envision the relationship between the Lord Jehovah, who is Christ our

Savior, and the man Adam. Christ is the Firstborn of the Father, the Only Begotten in the flesh, and the Lamb slain from the foundation of the world. He is the Redeemer of the world and the Savior of men. He is the Son of God and is one with the Father in power, might, and dominion. Adam is the foremost spirit next to the Lord Jehovah. He is the archangel, the captain of the Lord's hosts who led the armies of heaven when Lucifer rebelled; he is Michael, the mightiest of all the spirit host save only the Lord Jesus; and he came to earth as Adam, the first man. His relationship with the God of Israel is set forth in the revelation which says that "the Lord God, the Holy One of Zion, . . . hath established the foundations of Adam-ondi-Ahman," and "hath appointed Michael your prince, and established his feet, and set him upon high, and given unto him the keys of salvation under the counsel and direction of the Holy One, who is without beginning of days or end of life." (D&C 78:15-16.) Thus Adam stands next to the Holy Messiah, receives counsel and direction and power from him, and (under Christ) administers salvation to all men.

The Prophet Joseph Smith instructed the early brethren at great length on these matters. "The Priesthood was first given to Adam," he said; "he obtained the First Presidency, and held the keys of it from generation to generation. He obtained it in the Creation, before the world was formed." Priesthood is the power and authority of God. By it the worlds were made; by it the Lord's agents do everything that is needed for the salvation of men. The keys are the right of presidency; they empower their holders to direct the manner in which others use their priesthood. Presiding officers hold keys and perform whatever labors they are authorized by the Lord to perform. Adam held the priesthood and the keys. "He had dominion given him over every living creature. He is Michael the Archangel, spoken of in the Scriptures. Then to Noah, who is Gabriel: he stands next in authority to Adam in the Priesthood; he was called of God to this office, and was the father of all living in this day, and to him was given the dominion. These men held keys first on earth, and then in heaven.'' Thus Adam is first and Noah is second, among all the inhabitants of the earth, save Jesus only, where both priesthood and keys are concerned.

''The Priesthood is an everlasting principle,'' the Prophet continued, ''and existed with God from eternity, and will to eternity, without beginning of days or end of years. The keys have to be brought from heaven whenever the Gospel is sent. When they are revealed from heaven, it is by Adam's authority.'' Adam, under the direction of the Holy One, holds the keys of salvation for all men. He presides over all dispensations; all the dispensation heads and all the prophets receive direction from him; all report their labors to him. He is the chief person in the hierarchy of God, and he directs all of the affairs of the Lord on earth.

''Daniel in his seventh chapter speaks of the Ancient of Days; he means the oldest man, our Father Adam, Michael, he will call his children together and hold a council with them to prepare them for the coming of the Son of Man.'' By his children is meant the residue of his posterity that are righteous; all of his posterity will not be involved, only those—as it was in the days of the original gathering at Adam-ondi-Ahman—who are worthy. ''He (Adam) is the father of the human family, and presides over the spirits of all men, and all that have had the keys must stand before him in this grand council.'' Every prophet, apostle, president, bishop, elder, or church officer of whatever degree—all who have held keys shall stand before him who holds all of the keys. They will then be called upon to give an account of their stewardships and to report how and in what manner they have used their priesthood and their keys for the salvation of men within the sphere of their appointments.

''This,'' the grand council of Adam-ondi-Ahman, ''may take place before some of us leave this stage of action. The Son of Man stands before him, and there is given him glory and dominion. Adam delivers up his stewardship to Christ, that which was delivered to him as holding the keys of the universe, but retains his standing as head of the human family.'' This explanation is descriptive of the priesthood order of things. Every man is honored in his position; every man is accountable for the manner in which he performs under his divine commission. Adam is at the head, and he supervises all others.

''The Father called all spirits before Him at the creation of man, and organized them.'' This was the grand council in heaven of which we so often speak. ''He (Adam) is the head, and was told to multiply.'' He, under Christ, was at the head in preexistence; and he, under Christ, is at the head so far as all things pertaining to this earth are concerned. ''The keys were first given to him, and by him to others. He will have to give an account of his stewardship, and they to him.'' And as all the spirits of men attended the grand council in preexistence, so all the righteous shall attend a like council at Adam-ondi-Ahman before the winding-up scenes.

''Christ is the Great High Priest; Adam next. Paul speaks of the Church coming to an innumerable company of angels—to God the Judge of all—the spirits of just men made perfect; to Jesus the Mediator of the new covenant. (Hebrews 12:22-24.)'' In this setting, as he speaks of an innumerable company of angels and of the just and great of all ages who have gained membership in the Church of the Firstborn, which is the Church among exalted beings, the Prophet then says: ''I saw Adam in the valley of Adam-ondi-Ahman. He called together his children and blessed them with a patriarchal blessing. The Lord appeared in their midst, and he (Adam) blessed them all, and foretold what should befall them to the latest generation. This is why Adam blessed his posterity; he wanted to bring them into the presence of God.'' (*Teachings*, pp. 157-59.) Thus, we are left to conclude that the ancient gathering of the righteous at Adam-ondi-Ahman involved a great host of people, even as will be the case with the like gathering that is soon to be in the last days.

Daniel's account of the great latter-day council at Adam-ondi-Ahman includes these words: "I beheld till the thrones were cast down, and the Ancient of days did sit, whose garment was white as snow, and the hair of his head like the pure wool: his throne was like the fiery flame, and his wheels as burning fire. A fiery stream issued and came forth from before him: thousand thousands ministered unto him, and ten thousand times ten thousand stood before him: the judgment was set, and the books were opened." (Dan. 7:9-10.) Thrones are cast down: the kingdoms of this world cease; it is the day when the Lord makes a full end of all nations. He alone shall be exalted in that day. The Ancient of Days, the oldest and most ancient of men, Adam our father, sits in judgment over the righteous of his race. Be it remembered that the Twelve Apostles of the Lamb, who were with the Lord in his ministry in Jerusalem, shall judge the whole house of Israel, meaning that portion of Israel who have kept the commandments, "and none else." (D&C 29:12.) There will be a great hierarchy of judges in that great day, of whom Adam, under Christ, will be the chief of all. Those judges will judge the righteous ones under their jurisdiction, but Christ himself, he alone, will juuge the wicked. All this we have heretofore set forth; now we are seeing Adam sitting in his judicial capacity. And the scene is glorious indeed.

Who are the "thousand thousands" who "ministered unto him"? Are not these the millions who have held keys and powers and authorities in all dispensations? Are they not the ones who are called to report their stewardships and to give an accounting of how and in what manner they have exercised the keys of the kingdom in their days? Will not every steward be called upon to tell what he has done with the talents with which he was endowed? Truly, it shall be so; and those who minister unto the Ancient of Days are indeed the ministers of Christ reporting their labors to their immediate superiors, even back to Adam, who holds the keys of salvation over all the earth for all ages.

And who are the "ten thousand times ten thousand" who stand before him? Are not these the one hundred million and more who have been faithful and true in the days of their mortal probations? Are they not the same "ten thousand times ten thousand" who are "kings and priests," and who will live and reign with Christ a thousand years? Are they not the ones who shall sing in that great day the song of the redeemed, saying, "Worthy is the Lamb that was slain to receive power, and riches, and wisdom, and strength, and honour, and glory, and blessing . . . Blessing, and honour, and glory, and power, be unto him that sitteth upon the throne, and unto the Lamb for ever and ever"? (Rev. 5:10-13.) Truly, it is so; this is a part of that great day for which all the righteous have yearned, and the Lord Jesus, in its course, is using and honoring his ministers. Each one is operating within the sphere of his assignment; each is serving in his appointed way. The judgment is set and the books are opened, and the Lord God, who is judge of all, is judging all by the hands of his servants whom he hath appointed. This is that of which John wrote: "And I saw thrones, and they sat upon them, and judgment was given unto them. . . . And they lived and reigned with Christ a thousand years." (Rev. 20:4.)

But Daniel has yet more to say about the great events soon to transpire at Adam-ondi-Ahman. And we need not suppose that all these things shall happen in one single meeting or at one single hour in time. It is proper to hold numerous meetings at a general conference, some for the instruction of leaders, others for edification of all the saints. In some, business is transacted; others are for worship and spiritual refreshment. And so Daniel says: "I saw in the night visions, and, behold, one like the Son of man came with the clouds of heaven, and came to the Ancient of days, and they brought him near before him." Christ comes to Adam, who is sitting in glory. He comes to conform to his own priestal order. He comes to hear the report of Adam for his stewardship. He comes to take back the keys of the earthly kingdom. He comes to be invested with glory and dominion so that he can reign personally upon the earth. As President Joseph Fielding Smith expresses it: "Our Lord will then assume the reigns of government; directions will be given to the Priesthood; and He, whose right it is to rule, will be installed officially by the voice of the Priesthood there assembled." (*The Way to Perfection*, p. 291.) Thus Daniel says: "And there was given him dominion, and glory, and a kingdom, that all people, nations, and languages, should serve him: his dominion is an everlasting dominion, which shall not pass away, and his kingdom that which shall not be destroyed."

Daniel also tells us of the conflict between the kingdoms of this world and the kingdom of God. In spite of the opposition of the world, he says, "the saints of the most High shall take the kingdom, and possess the kingdom for ever, even for ever and ever." And also: "I beheld, and the same horn made war with the saints, and prevailed against them; until the ancient of days came, and judgment was given to the saints of the most High; and the time came that the saints possessed the kingdom." In this present world Lucifer reigns. This is the great day of his power. The kingdoms of men prevail in many ways over the Church and kingdom of God. Evil forces "devour the whole earth, and shall tread it down, and break it in pieces." But Lucifer's day is limited; he shall soon be bound. "The judgment shall sit, and they shall take away his dominion, to consume and to destroy" the Lord's work and his kingdom. "And the kingdom and dominion, and the greatness of the kingdom under the whole heaven, shall be given to the people of the saints of the most High, whose kingdom is an everlasting kingdom, and all dominions shall serve and obey him." (Dan. 7:13-27.)

The worshipful nature of the final gatherings at Adam-ondi-Ahman—and surely such will be patterned after what happened there anciently—the worshipful wonder of it all is seen in the administration of the sacramental emblems that will then take place. These are the emblems that testify of the spilt blood and broken flesh of our Redeeming Lord, even as the shed blood and broken flesh of sacrificial animals bore a like witness in days of old. In the upper room, as he and his disciples kept the Feast of the Passover, Jesus instituted the ordinance of the sacrament. After doing so he said: "But I say unto you, I will not drink henceforth of this fruit of the vine, until that day when I drink it new with you in my Father's kingdom." (Matt. 26:29.)

With reference to the use of sacramental wine in our day, the Lord said to Joseph Smith: "You shall partake of none except it is made new among you; yea, in this my Father's kingdom which shall be built up on the earth." In so stating, he is picking up the language he used in the upper room. Then he says: "The hour cometh that I will drink of the fruit of the vine with you on the earth." Jesus is going to partake of the sacrament again with his mortal disciples on earth. But it will not be with mortals only. He names others who will be present and who will participate in the sacred ordinance. These include Moroni, Elias, John the Baptist, Elijah, Abraham, Isaac, Jacob, Joseph (who was sold into Egypt), Peter, James, and John, "and also with Michael, or Adam, the father of all, the prince of all, the ancient of days." Each of these is named simply by way of illustration. The grand summation of the whole matter comes in these words: "And also with all those whom my Father hath given me out of the world." (D&C 27:4-14.) The sacrament is to be administered in a future day, on this earth, when the Lord Jesus is present, and when all the righteous of all ages are present. This, of course, will be a part of the grand council at Adam-ondi-Ahman.

Adam-ondi-Ahman—meaning the place or land of God where Adam dwelt—is at a place called Spring Hill, Daviess County, Missouri. This site is named by the Lord "Adam-ondi-Ahman, because, said he, it is the place where Adam shall come to visit his people, or the Ancient of Days shall sit, as spoken of by Daniel the prophet." (D&C 116.) There is a great valley there in which the righteous will assemble; and where there are valleys, the surrounding elevations are called mountains. Thus our revelations speak of "the mountains of Adam-ondi-Ahman" and of "the plains of Olaha Shinehah, or the land where Adam dwelt." (D&C 117:8.) Sacred indeed is the whole region for what has taken place and what will take place in its environs.

Adam-ondi-Ahman, the land of God, the dwelling place of Adam—surely it is a blessed and holy place! There Adam our Prince will give an accounting to Christ our King. The Prince serves the King! The King always is supreme, though he honors the Prince by giving him power and dominion over his realms for an appointed season. But when the King returns, the Prince steps aside, and the Supreme Lord of all rules and reigns on earth. And thus, as the Lord lives, has it been and will it be.

THE SON OF DAVID REIGNETH

The Lord Reigns on Earth

How little the world knows of the coming day when Christ, as our tenth Article of Faith says, "will reign personally upon the earth," meaning, as the Prophet tells us, that he will "visit it," from time to time, "when it is necessary to govern it." (*Teachings*, p. 268.) And how little even the saints know of the government that is to be, meaning that their King will reign over Israel, on the throne of David, being himself the Second David, and that, as a prelude thereto, the "Gentiles" will "lick up the dust" of the feet of the chosen people. (Isa. 49:23.) And yet these are profound truths that are spread forth *in extenso* in the revealed word. To understand the Second Coming, we must consider them in their proper relationship to all the events of the latter days.

The holy word, given of old, abounds in such prophetic promises as these: "And the Lord shall be king over all the earth: in that [millennial] day shall there be one Lord, and his name one." (Zech. 14:9.) The promise to Israel in that day is: "The king of Israel, even the Lord, is in the midst of thee: thou shalt not see evil any more. . . . The Lord thy God in the midst of thee is mighty; he will save, he will rejoice over thee with joy. . . . At that time will I bring you again, even in the time that I gather you." This is the millennial gathering! "For I will make you a name and a praise among all people of the earth, when I turn back your captivity before your eyes, saith the Lord." (Zeph. 3:15-20.) "I am the Lord thy God, . . . for there is no saviour beside me. . . . I will be thy king: where is any other that may save thee in all thy cities?" (Hosea 13:4, 10.) And of the sanctuary from which the divine law shall go forth, the prophetic word is: "And the name of the city from that day shall be" Jehovah-shammah, "The Lord is there." (Ezek. 48:35.)

Matthew includes in the interpretation of the parable of the wicked husbandmen the statement that the disciples of that day "understood . . . that the Gentiles should be destroyed also, when the Lord should descend out of heaven to reign in his vineyard, which is the earth and the inhabitants thereof." (JST, Matt. 21:56.) In our dispensation the divine word says: "The Lord shall have power over his saints, and shall reign in their midst, and shall come down in judgment upon Idumea, or the world." (D&C 1:36.) "For I will reveal myself from heaven with power and great glory, with all the hosts thereof, and dwell in righteousness with men on earth a thousand years, and the wicked shall not stand." (D&C 29:11.) "And the Lord, even the Savior, shall stand in the midst of his people, and shall reign over all flesh." (D&C 133:25.) And our friend John, in the visions vouchsafed to him, "heard as it were the voice of a great multitude, and as the voice of many waters, and as the voice of mighty thunderings, saying, Alleluia: for the Lord God omnipotent reigneth." (Rev. 19:6.) The Lord reigneth! How glorious is the day! Hallelujah (praise Jehovah), for Jehovah reigneth! Alleluia (praise Christ), for Christ reigneth! And the Lord Jehovah is the Lord Jesus; they are one and the same.

When the Lord reigns, how will he do it? John says: "He shall rule them with a rod of iron." (Rev. 19:15.) What is the rod of iron? Nephi says: "I beheld that the rod of iron . . . was the word of God, which led to the fountain of living waters, or to the tree of life." (1 Ne. 11:25.) Thus, Christ reigneth in and through and by means of the gospel. There is no other way. Men will be subject to him because they believe the gospel. The gospel is his law. He has no other. And so we read relative to his coming: "And another trump shall sound, which is the fifth trump, which is the fifth angel who committeth the everlasting gospel—flying through the midst of heaven, unto all nations, kindreds, tongues, and people; and this shall be the sound of his trump, saying to all people, both in heaven and in earth, and that are under the earth—for every ear shall hear it, and every knee shall bow, and every tongue shall confess, while they hear the sound of the trump, saying: Fear God, and give glory to him who sitteth upon the throne, forever and ever; for the hour of his judgment is come." (D&C 88:103-104.) Every knee shall bow! The Lord reigneth! He is King over all the earth!

David Prophesies of Christ's Reign

In the days of David, Israel's kingdom was glorious indeed. The Twelve Tribes—"instantly serving God day and night" (Acts 26:7), as Paul expressed it—were united; they were independent of any other earthly power; freedom and power and prestige welled up in the hearts of the chosen seed. A thousand years later, when the Son of David walked among them, Israel had no kingdom. Her municipals were scattered among the nations where most of them served other gods and no longer knew the Lord Jehovah whose people they once were. The remnant in Palestine bowed beneath the Gentile rod and served the Herods and the Caesars whose swords were sharp and whose arms were as iron. Up to that time the prophetic word relative to the glorious restoration of the chosen people in might and power and dominion seemed as distant as it had when Nebuchadnezzar took their fathers into Babylon. The prophetic pronouncements of what was to be in the Messianic day were yet to be fulfilled. Hence we hear the ancient Twelve on Olivet, when the hour for the ascension had arrived, asking Jesus: "Lord, wilt thou at this time restore again the kingdom to Israel?" (Acts 1:6.)

Restore again the kingdom to Israel! When will the Lord's kingdom come? When will it be set up again on earth as it once was—with a king and a court, with laws and judges, with power and magnificence? Such was not for the day of Peter and Paul; it was reserved for our day, and the promised consummation is not far distant. What is more appropriate, then, than to have David himself prophesy of his even greater Son who will one day sit on his father's throne and reign over the house of Israel forever? It is to the words of the sweet singer of Israel that we shall turn first as we consider the coming reign of the Second David. His words relative to the millennial day are comparable to those he spoke about the meridian day. The Spirit revealed to David wondrous truths relative to the two comings of his incomparable Son.

"The Lord most high is terrible," the psalmic word recites; "he is a great King over all the earth. He shall subdue the people under us, and the nations under our feet." All nations shall be subject to Israel in that great day. The Gentiles shall bow beneath the gospel rod. "He shall choose our inheritance for us." The meek shall inherit the earth. "For God is the King of all the earth: sing ye praises with understanding. God reigneth over the heathen: God sitteth upon the throne of his holiness. . . . He is greatly exalted." (Ps. 47:2-9.) "O let the nations be glad and sing for joy: for thou shalt judge the people righteously, and govern the nations upon earth." This is the millennial day. "Then shall the earth yield her increase; and God, even our own God, shall bless us." (Ps. 67:4-6.)

From a prayer of David we extract these words which are clearly Messianic, though some of them, as originally given, applied to contemporary events. It was the prophetic practice among the Hebrews to use local circumstances as similitudes to teach the glories and wonders of the gospel and of the Messiah who would come to save his people. "He shall judge thy people with righteousness, and thy poor with judgment," David said. "He shall judge the poor of the people, he shall save the children of the needy, and shall break in pieces the oppressor. They shall fear thee as long as the sun and moon endure, throughout all generations." The Lord's reign shall be eternal; the saints shall possess the kingdom forever and ever. "He shall come down like rain upon the mown grass: as showers that water the earth." As the dews of heaven, so shall the knowledge of God descend upon those who seek his face. "In his day shall the righteous flourish; and abundance of peace so long as the moon endureth." How glorious shall be that blessed day of righteousness and peace. "He shall have dominion also from sea to sea, and from the river unto the ends of the earth. They that dwell in the wilderness shall bow before him; and his enemies shall lick the dust." Israel truly shall stand triumphant in that day.

"Yea, all kings shall fall down before him: all nations shall serve him." Christ is King of all. "For he shall deliver the needy when he crieth; the poor also, and him that hath no helper. He shall spare the poor and the needy, and shall save the souls of the needy. He shall redeem their soul from deceit and violence: and precious shall their blood be in his sight. . . . His name shall endure for ever: his name shall be continued as long as the sun: and men shall be blessed in him: all nations shall call him blessed. Blessed be the Lord God, the God of Israel, who only doeth wondrous things. And blessed be his glorious name for ever: and let the whole earth be filled with his glory." (Ps. 72:2-19.) Granted that some of the language is figurative and will not find literal fulfillment in the millennial day, yet the concepts taught are truly glorious. In substance and in thought content they all shall surely come to pass.

Other psalmic pronouncements that will find total fulfillment only in the millennial day include: "Arise, O God, judge the earth: for thou shalt inherit all nations."

(Ps. 82:8.) "O worship the Lord in the beauty of holiness: fear before him, all the earth. Say among the heathen that the Lord reigneth. . . . He shall judge the people righteously. . . . He cometh to judge the earth: he shall judge the world with righteousness, and the people with his truth." (Ps. 96:9-13.) "The Lord reigneth; let the earth rejoice. . . . Clouds and darkness are round about him: righteousness and judgment are the habitation of his throne. A fire goeth before him, and burneth up his enemies round about. His lightnings enlightened the world: the earth saw, and trembled. The hills melted like wax at the presence of the Lord, at the presence of the Lord of the whole earth." (Ps. 97:1-5.) "The Lord reigneth; let the people tremble. . . . The Lord is great in Zion." (Ps. 99:1-2.) "All thy works shall praise thee, O Lord; and thy saints shall bless thee. They shall speak of the glory of thy kingdom, and talk of thy power; To make known to the sons of men his mighty acts, and the glorious majesty of his kingdom. Thy kingdom is an everlasting kingdom, and thy dominion endureth throughout all generations." (Ps. 145:10-13.) "The Lord shall reign for ever, even thy God, O Zion, unto all generations. Praise ye the Lord." (Ps. 146:10.) Those with spiritual insight find in the Psalms priceless pearls of wisdom and revelation. Truly, their pleasant words and sweet similitudes open the eyes of our understanding with reference to the coming reign of the Son of David.

Christ Reigns on David's Throne

The Lord Jesus Christ—the King of heaven and the rightful ruler of the earth—set up his earthly kingdom among men on the 6th day of April in 1830. That kingdom, now named The Church of Jesus Christ of Latter-day Saints, is an ecclesiastical kingdom. It is ruled and governed by the priesthood; it administers the gospel; it holds the keys of salvation for all men. It is the only true and living church upon the face of the whole earth and is the one place where salvation may be found. It is, in the true and literal sense of the word, the kingdom of God on earth, and as such it is preparing men to go to the kingdom of God in heaven, which is the celestial kingdom.

When the Lord, in the first instance, in the days of Adam set up his kingdom on earth, it was both an ecclesiastical and a political kingdom. From the day of the first man down to the flood, all of the righteous people in earth were governed, both ecclesiastically and politically, by the same leaders and with the same power—the power and authority of the holy priesthood. Apostate peoples who broke off from the true church, as then officered and organized, created both churches and governments of their own. Often these were united as one, patterning themselves after the true Adamic system; sometimes the two ways of life were separately administered. Such peoples had false religions and, from the true theocratic perspective, false governments also. There is only one true religion, the religion in which God rules by revelation. And, in the full and divine sense, there is only one true government, the government in which God rules. All things are spiritual unto the Lord; from his standpoint there is no such thing as a temporal commandment, and it is his right to rule in all things both temporal and spiritual.

For the time being, however, because men are not prepared and are unwilling to take direction from the Lord; because they love darkness rather than light, their deeds being evil; because they choose to believe false religions and to be governed by political powers that fall short of the perfect and divine standard—because of these conditions, the Lord has ordained a system under which church and state should be separated. In the full and true sense this system of separation of church and state is in active operation only in the United States of America. Some other nations make reasonable attempts to allow freedom of worship, but most of the population of the earth is ruled by governments that also tell them what they must believe, how and what they must worship, and what they must do, as they falsely suppose, to gain salvation. These are corrupt, evil, and apostate systems. As the union of church and state under God is the most perfect form of worship and government, so the union of church and state under man leads to false worship and denies men a hope of full salvation. Whenever in our day the power of the state, with its armies and jails, usurps the prerogatives of the church and proceeds to govern in religious matters, the church of the evil one flourishes. Men are hailed before a Spanish inquisition; they are put to death for forsaking Islam and becoming Christians; they are driven into ghettos and murdered in concentration camps; or they are scourged in synagogues and crucified on crosses. There is nothing more evil, more cruel, more wicked than false religion that can survive only by the sword of Cortez, or the armies of Mohammed, or the gestapo of Hitler.

Both church and state, as the world knows them, will soon cease to be. When the Lord comes again, he will set up anew the political kingdom of God on earth. It will be joined with the ecclesiastical kingdom; church and state will unite; and God will govern in all things. But even then, as we suppose, administrative affairs will be departmentalized, for the law will go forth from Zion (in Jackson County), and the word of the Lord from Jerusalem (in Palestine). But, nonetheless, once again the government of the earth will be theocratic. God will govern. This time he will do it personally as he reigns over all the earth. And all of this presupposes the fall of Babylon, and the death of false religions, and the fall of all earthly governments and nations. And these things, as we are aware, shall surely come to pass.

Thus, when we speak of the Lord returning to reign personally upon the earth, we are talking about a literal return. We have in mind a King ruling on a throne. We mean that laws will come forth from a Lawgiver; that judges will be restored as of old; that there will be a full end of all nations as these now exist; that earth's new King will have dominion and power over all the earth; and that Israel, the chosen people, will possess the kingdom and have everlasting dominion. It is to these things that we shall now turn our attention.

Isaiah, in one of his greatest Messianic utterances, acclaims: "And the government shall be upon [Messiah's] shoulder. . . . Of the increase of his government and peace there shall be no end, upon the throne of David, and upon his kingdom, to order it, and to establish it with judgment and with justice from henceforth even for ever." (Isa. 9:6-7.) Isaiah's words, thus given, are but the foundation for the angelic proclamation of Gabriel to the Virgin of Nazareth of Galilee. Of the child Jesus whom she should bear, the angelic word promised: "He shall be great, and shall be called the Son of the Highest: and the Lord God shall give unto him the throne of his father David: And he shall reign over the house of Jacob for ever; and of his kingdom there shall be no end." (Luke 1:31-33.) Thus, Christ shall provide the government. He shall reign on the throne of David forever. Peace shall prevail, and justice and judgment shall be the order of the day. And it is Israel, the chosen ones, over whom he shall reign in a kingdom that shall never cease. There is nothing figurative about this; it is not something that can be spiritualized away. It is the coming reality; it shall surely come to pass.

Isaiah, speaking of the Second Coming, also says: "Then the moon shall be confounded, and the sun ashamed, when the Lord of hosts"—for such he is!—"shall reign in mount Zion, and in Jerusalem, and before his ancients gloriously." (Isa. 24:23.) His ancients are the prophets and patriarchs of olden times who, as we shall hereafter see, shall reign with him on earth. Isaiah also promises: "Behold, a king shall reign in righteousness, and princes shall rule in judgment." (Isa. 32:1.) And also, speaking of the millennial day when men "shall see the king in his beauty," Isaiah says: "For the Lord is our judge, the

Lord is our lawgiver, the Lord is our king; he will save us." (Isa. 33:17, 22.) In the full and true sense, the Lord will not stand as Judge, or Lawgiver, or King, and will not save men to the full, until the Millennium.

Our latter-day revelations bear a like testimony. "In time ye shall have no king nor ruler, for I will be your king and watch over you," the Lord tells us. "Wherefore, hear my voice and follow me, and you shall be a free people, and ye shall have no laws but my laws when I come, for I am your lawgiver, and what can stay my hand?" (D&C 38:21-22.) And also: "For the Lord shall be in their midst, and his glory shall be upon them, and he will be their king and their lawgiver." (D&C 45:59.) And yet again: "Be subject to the powers that be"—to the governments that now exist—"until he reigns whose right it is to reign, and subdues all enemies under his feet. Behold, the laws which ye have received from my hand are the laws of the church, and in this light ye shall hold them forth." (D&C 58:22-23.) For the present we are subject to the laws of the land; when the true and perfect millennial order prevails, all rule and government, both civil and ecclesiastical, will come from our Eternal Head.

Others of the prophets also have somewhat to say about these things. In a rather remarkable passage Zechariah ties the gathering of Israel and the millennial reign together in these words: "Ho, ho, come forth, and flee from the land of the north, saith the Lord." This is his call to Israel and to Judah, his ancient covenant people, scattered as they are in the lands northward from Palestine. This is the call that has now commenced and will yet go forth with increased sound. "For I have spread you abroad as the four winds of the heaven, saith the Lord." Israel is scattered, and Israel must be gathered. "Deliver thyself, O Zion, that dwellest with the daughter of Babylon." Go ye out from Babylon; flee from the world; turn from your apostate and fallen ways; return unto the God of Israel. And as to those nations and this Babylon (the world) that have wrought so great a havoc upon the chosen seed, the divine word says: "For thus saith the Lord of hosts; After the glory hath he sent me unto the nations which spoiled you: for he that toucheth you toucheth the apple of his eye. For, behold, I will shake mine hand upon them [the nations], and they shall be a spoil to their servants: and ye shall know that the Lord of hosts hath sent me." Israel shall finally prevail over the Gentile nations. Her eternal triumph is assured.

"Sing and rejoice, O daughter of Zion: for, lo, I come, and I will dwell in the midst of thee, saith the Lord." The Lord Jesus Christ shall reign personally upon the earth. "And many nations shall be joined to the Lord in that day, and shall be my people." Gentile nations shall be converted; the blacks shall receive the priesthood; nations long outside the pale of saving grace shall come into the fold and shall rise up and bless Abraham as their father. "And I will dwell in the midst of thee, and thou shalt know that the Lord of hosts hath sent me unto thee. And the Lord shall inherit Judah his portion in the holy land, and shall choose Jerusalem again." How wondrous it shall be. "Be silent, O all flesh, before the Lord: for he is raised up out of his holy habitation." (Zech. 2:6-13.) So shall it be in the coming day.

Zechariah also says: "He shall speak peace unto the heathen: and his dominion shall be from sea even to sea, and from the river even to the ends of the earth." (Zech. 9:10.) Ezekiel saw in vision "the glory of the God of Israel," and "his voice was like a noise of many waters: and the earth shined with his glory." With reference to the Lord's holy sanctuary, the voice said: "Son of man, the place of my throne, and the place of the soles of my feet, where I will dwell in the midst of the children of Israel for ever, and my holy name, shall the house of Israel no more defile. . . . And I will dwell in the midst of them for ever." (Ezek. 43:2-9.) His throne shall be in his holy house; his reign shall be a personal one, even the very soles of his feet again treading the dust of the earth; and Israel shall honor and serve him. Of that day Micah says: "And the Lord shall reign over them in Mount Zion from henceforth, even for ever." (Micah 4:7.) And because the law is to go forth in that day from an American Zion, he himself said to Nephite Israel: "This people will I establish in this land [the Americas], unto the fulfilling of the covenant which I made with your father Jacob; and it shall be a New Jerusalem. And the powers of heaven shall be in the midst of this people; yea, even I will be in the midst of you." (3 Ne. 20:22.)

Nephi speaks of the destruction of the kingdom of the devil in the last days, of the wicked being brought low in the dust, and of their being consumed as stubble. "And the time cometh speedily," when all this is brought to pass, he says, "that the righteous must be led up as calves of the stall, and the Holy One of Israel must reign in dominion, and might, and power, and great glory." (1 Ne. 22:23-24.) Truly, he shall reign whose right it is; he shall make "a full end of all nations" (D&C 87:6), and with his saints he shall possess the kingdom forever and ever. In that day a great voice in heaven shall say: "The kingdoms of this world are become the kingdoms of our Lord, and of his Christ; and he shall reign for ever and ever." (Rev. 11:15.)

The eventual triumph of the Lord's people is assured; there is to be a millennial day of glory and honor and peace; the fulness of the earth shall be theirs in that day, and all nations and kingdoms shall serve and obey them. But all the promised rewards need not be deferred until that day. Even now the saints can begin the process of inheriting the kingdom. They have power to begin to reap some of the millennial rewards. "I have decreed a decree which my people shall realize," the Lord said in the early days of this dispensation, "inasmuch as they hearken from this very hour unto the counsel which I, the Lord their God, shall give unto them. Behold they shall, for I have decreed it, begin to prevail against mine enemies from this very hour. And by hearkening to observe all the words which I, the Lord their God, shall speak unto them, they shall never cease to prevail until the kingdoms of the world are subdued under my feet, and the earth is given unto the saints, to possess it forever and ever.'' (D&C 103:5-7.)

THE SECOND DAVID REIGNETH

The Branch of David Reigneth

David, who slew Goliath, mighty, mighty David, the one king above all others to whom ancient Israel for a thousand long years looked as a symbol of Israelite triumph and glory—mighty David became the similitude for the very Messiah himself. As David slew Goliath and saved Israel from the Philistines, so the Messiah would break the Gentile bands and remove from his people the alien yoke. As David united and ruled over the Twelve Tribes of Israel, so the Messiah would unite the two kingdoms, Judah and Israel, and reign over one people in peace and glory forever. It is a grand and comforting feeling to know that the house of which you are a part—your own kindred and people—shall one day destroy their enemies and rule the world. Blessed Israel had this hope; King David was its symbol, a type and a shadow of what was to be, and the Messiah, Israel's Eternal King, would bring it to full fruition. Thus David the Son of Jesse became the type and figure for yet another, for David the Son of God, for the Messiah who, according to the flesh, would come as the Son of David. Let us, then, hear the prophetic word relative to these things.

Messiah's latter-day reign over the chosen people, his triumphant rule over the Twelve Tribes of Israel, his exercise of kingly power like his father David—all this presupposes the gathering together of scattered Judah and lost Israel. Let Israel gather first and then let Messiah reign. And so we read in holy writ: "I will gather the remnant of my flock out of all countries whither I have driven them, and will bring them again to their folds; and they shall be fruitful and increase." They shall come into the fold of Judah in Jerusalem, into the fold of Joseph in America, into the folds established in the stakes of Zion in all nations. "And I will set up shepherds over them which shall feed them." Once again they shall hear the good word of God; they shall bask in the light of the gospel; they shall rejoice in Jehovah as their Shepherd. "And they shall fear no more, nor be dismayed, neither shall they be lacking, saith the Lord." All their needs will be supplied by the Shepherd of Israel.

Then a glorious thing will happen. The kingdom will be restored to Israel, and they shall gain the political power as well as the ecclesiastical. "Behold, the days come, saith the Lord, that I will raise unto David a righteous Branch, and a King shall reign and prosper, and shall execute judgment and justice in the earth." Jehovah reigneth; Christ reigneth; the Son of David sits on the throne of his father. "In his days Judah shall be saved, and Israel shall dwell safely"—the two ancient kingdoms shall be one again—"and this is his name whereby he shall be called, THE LORD OUR RIGHTEOUSNESS." The King who reigns on David's throne is the Lord.

With Israel gathered again, with the scattered remnants of Jacob rejoicing anew in the very things their fathers possessed, with the Appointed One reigning on the throne of David forever, is it any wonder that the glories of their ancient history shall fade into a comparative insignificance? "Therefore, behold, the days come, saith the Lord, that they shall no more say, The Lord liveth, which brought up the children of Israel out of the land of Egypt; But, The Lord liveth, which brought up and which led the seed of the house of Israel out of the north country, and from all countries whither I had driven them; and they shall dwell in their own land." (Jer. 23:3-8.) What was the deliverance from Egypt, with the plagues and miracles and parting of the Red Sea, in comparison with the assembling of Israel from the ends of the earth to bow before the throne of the Lord Our Righteousness? The Lord Our Righteousness, he who is our Lord when we are righteous—what can compare with his personal reign? The seed of Israel will be more blessed than were their fathers of old; the latter-day glory will exceed that of Sinai and Horeb and Carmel.

Also in the writings of Jeremiah we find the Lord's promise to reveal unto his people in the latter days "the abundance of peace and truth," meaning the gospel, and to gather them "as at the first." Then again he makes the great promise concerning the Seed of David. "In those days, and at that time, will I cause the Branch of righteousness to grow up unto David; and he shall execute judgment and righteousness in the land." Jeremiah's other promise was that the Lord would raise up unto David a righteous branch, a branch that would be the Seed of David. This time the promise is that he will raise up the Branch of righteousness, a Branch that is the Son of Righteousness, meaning the Son of God. In this connection be it remembered that the Book of Mormon uses the name Son of Righteousness as one of the names of Christ. Thus the Branch is to be both the Son of David, after the flesh, and the Son of God, in the eternal sense. Of the days of his reign the account continues: "In those days shall Judah be saved, and Jerusalem shall dwell safely: and this is the name wherewith she shall be called, The Lord our righteousness." That is to say, the Holy City also shall bear the name of the great King who reigns there. "For thus saith the Lord; David shall never want a man to sit upon the throne of the house of Israel." (Jer. 33:6-7, 15-17.) Manifestly this promise to David that he shall have posterity reigning on his throne forever can be fulfilled only in and through Christ, the Eternal King.

Additional knowledge about the Branch of David, who is also the Branch of God, is recorded in Zechariah. "Thus speaketh the Lord of hosts," says Zechariah, "Behold the man whose name is The BRANCH; and he shall grow up out of his place, and he shall build the temple of the Lord: Even he shall build the temple of the Lord; and he shall bear the glory, and shall sit and rule upon his throne; and he shall be a priest upon his throne." (Zech. 6:12-13.) The Reigning One, at whose direction the temples in Jerusalem and elsewhere shall be built in the last days, shall be both a king and a priest. Indeed, he is the Great High Priest, and in the eternal sense, those who rule and reign everlastingly are all both kings and priests. It could not be otherwise, for the power by which they reign is the priestly power of the Almighty.

These words, also in Zechariah, place the reign of the Branch in its true millennial setting. "I will bring forth my servant the BRANCH," saith the Lord, "and I will remove the iniquity of that land in one day," the day of burning in which every corruptible thing shall be consumed. "In that day, saith the Lord of hosts, shall ye call every man his neighbour under the vine and under the fig tree." (Zech. 3:8-10.) These last words contain the prophetic figure of speech that describes life during the Millennium. Micah, for instance, says that during that blessed era of peace, "They shall sit every man under his vine and under his fig tree; and none shall make them afraid." (Micah 4:4.)

David—Our Eternal King

Even as the Book of Mormon (the Stick of Joseph in the hands of Ephraim), and the Bible (the Stick of Judah) become one in the Lord's hands; even as they both contain the fulness of the everlasting gospel; even as men in our day must accept and believe both volumes of holy scripture to be saved—so shall perfect unity return to the divided houses of Israel in the last days. The kingdom of Judah (whence the Bible comes) and the kingdom of Israel (whence, through Joseph, the Book of Mormon comes)—these two kingdoms shall become one in the Lord's hands. Such is the word that the Lord gave to Ezekiel. The Bible and the Book of Mormon, companion volumes of holy scripture, are now one in the Lord's hands; both are published to the world; both contain the mind and will and voice of the Lord to all men. And both are the tools used by the elders of Israel to gather in the long dispersed and widely scattered lost sheep of that ancient house. Indeed, the Book of Mormon, proving as it does the truth and divinity of the Lord's latter-day work, is the message sent to Israel that causes them to gather again into the sheepfold of their fathers.

It is in this setting, then, the setting showing forth the power and influence of the Bible and the Book of Mormon, that the Lord tells Ezekiel of the gathering of Israel and the reign of David over them. "I will take the children of Israel from among the heathen, whither they be gone," saith the Lord, "and will gather them on every side, and bring them into their own land." This gathering is now in process and will continue until the two ancient kingdoms are fully established again. "And I will make them one nation in the land upon the mountains of Israel; and one king shall be king to them all: and they shall be no more two nations, neither shall they be divided into two kingdoms any more at all." The illustration used to teach the unity and oneness of this gathering is perfect. The two nations shall be one as the Bible and the Book of Mormon are one. No one who truly believes the Bible can reject the Book of Mormon, and every person who believes the Book of Mormon believes also the Bible. They speak with one voice. And so shall it be with the two kingdoms of Israel. They will be perfectly united in the last days, believing the same truths, walking in the same paths, worshipping the same Lord, and glorying in the same eternal covenants. "Neither shall they defile themselves any more with their idols, nor with their detestable things, nor with any of their transgressions." False worship shall cease where they are concerned. As their fathers rejected Baal, so they shall forsake the creeds of Christendom that exhort men to worship an incomprehensible spirit nothingness to which the names of Deity have been given. No more will they walk in the ways of the world; no more will they wallow in the mire of Babylon; no more will they delight in the passions and lusts of carnal men. "But I will save them out of all their dwellingplaces, wherein they have sinned," saith the Lord, "and will cleanse them: so shall they be my people, and I will be their God." Their sins will be washed away in the waters of baptism; they will be born again; and they will become the children of Christ, his sons and his daughters.

It is in this setting—a setting of faith and conversion and gathering; a setting of unity and oneness and righteousness; a setting of worthiness and obedience—it is in this setting that the Lord says: "And David my servant shall be king over them." What David? The Eternal David, the Lord Our Righteousness, who shall dwell among his people and reign in power and glory over all the earth. "And they all shall have one shepherd." What Shepherd? The Good Shepherd, the Lord Jehovah, who led their fathers anciently and will now lead them in the same paths. "For there is one God and one Shepherd over all the earth." (1 Ne. 13:41.) And "they shall also walk in my judgments, and observe my statutes, and do them." They shall keep the commandments, even as the people did in the Zion of old, when once before the Lord came and dwelt with his people and they dwelt in righteousness.

"And they shall dwell in the land that I have given unto Jacob my servant, wherein your fathers have dwelt; and they shall dwell therein, even they, and their children, and their children's children for ever." Of course, as we have seen, the ancient tribes shall be established, at least on a representative basis, in the very lands where their forebears dwelt. There was no better or more explicit way for the Lord to teach the glory and beauty and wonder of the gathering and the triumphal reign. But they shall also dwell in all the earth, for the whole world will become one great Zion, one bounteous Garden of Eden. "And my servant David shall be their prince for ever." David reigns forever! He is Christ the Lord, the Son of David, after the manner of the flesh, David's Lord, speaking from the perspective of eternity.

"Moreover I will make a covenant of peace with them," saith the Lord; "it shall be an everlasting covenant with them." The gospel is the new and everlasting covenant. It bringeth peace, and peace will prevail on earth for the space of a thousand years because men live in harmony with its eternal principles. "And I will place them, and multiply them, and will set my sanctuary in the midst of them for evermore." The temples of the Lord will dot the earth during the Millennium. In them the living will receive the ordinances of exaltation, and the work will be wound up for the worthy dead of all ages. "My tabernacle also shall be with them: yea, I will be their God, and they shall be my people." How sweet and lovely is this thought! When the Lord's true tabernacle is with men; when they assemble therein to worship the Father, in the name of the Son, by the power of the Holy Spirit; when their lives at long last conform to the divine will and pattern—then they are his people and he is their God. "And the heathen shall know that I the Lord do sanctify Israel, when my sanctuary shall be in the midst of them for evermore." (Ezek. 37:15-28.) David reigns; how glorious is the day!

The same God who revealed his mind and will concerning Israel and her King to Ezekiel gave a similar message to Jeremiah. That word, as it pertained to the gathering of his people, included these promises: "I will break [the Gentile] yoke from off thy neck, and will burst thy bonds," saith the Lord. "Therefore fear thou not, O my servant Jacob, saith the Lord; neither be dismayed, O Israel: for, lo, I will save thee from afar, and thy seed from the land of their captivity; and Jacob shall return, and shall be in rest, and be quiet, and none shall make him afraid." Truly this is his millennial destiny. "For I am with thee, saith the Lord, to save thee; though I make a full end of all nations whither I have scattered thee, yet will I not make a full end of thee: but I will correct thee in measure, and will not leave thee altogether unpunished." The one nation that shall survive the great and dreadful day is the nation of Israel. And as to them and their nation, the divine word is: "They shall serve the Lord their God, and David their king, whom I will raise up unto them." (Jer. 30:8-11.)

Hosea records his views in these words: "For the children of Israel shall abide many days without a king, and without a prince, and without a sacrifice, and without an image, and without an ephod, and without teraphim." Their heaven-directed government and their God-given religion shall cease. They shall be subject to the powers that be and shall serve other gods than the Lord. Such is the state of most of them at this time. But, "Afterward shall the children of Israel return, and seek the Lord their God, and David their king; and shall fear the Lord and his goodness in the latter days." (Hosea 3:4-5.) They shall respond to the call of the elders of the restoration, who themselves are of Israel, and who send forth the message to their fellows to worship that God who made heaven and earth and the sea and the fountains of waters and, worshipping him, to return thereby to the kingdom of the great King who is the Second David.

To Amos the divine word came, saying: "Behold, the eyes of the Lord God are upon the sinful kingdom"—ancient Israel and her kingdom—"and I will destroy it from off the face of the earth; saving that I will not utterly destroy the house of Jacob, saith the Lord." Their kingdom went the way of the other evil kingdoms of old; their nation became but a memory; and because they sinned, they became subject to other sinners whose arms were stronger and whose swords were sharper. But they remained as individuals; the house of Jacob, as a people, yet had an eternal destiny. "For, lo, I will command, and I will sift the house of Israel among all nations, like as corn is sifted in a sieve, yet shall not the least grain fall upon the earth." Israel shall be scattered, and not one grain shall bring forth fruit unto eternal life until the day of gathering when they repent of their sins and return to the Lord. "All the sinners of my people shall die by the sword," and in plagues and in other ways; they shall be as other men in the world.

But it will not ever be thus. "In that day"—the latter days—"will I raise up the tabernacle of David that is fallen, and close up the breaches thereof; and I will raise up his ruins, and I will build it as in the days of old." Israel shall assemble and worship the true God, and the old kingdom shall then be established anew. Bounteous harvests will grace the earth, and Israel and the Gentiles who join with her "shall build the waste cities, and inhabit them; and they shall plant vineyards, and drink the wine thereof; they shall also make gardens, and eat the fruit of them." Peace will prevail. "And I will plant them upon their land, and they shall no more be pulled up out of their land which I have given them, saith the Lord thy God." (Amos 9:8-15.)

In the day of gathering the Lord promises to save his flock. "And I will set up one shepherd over them," he says, "and he shall feed them, even my servant David; he shall feed them, and he shall be their shepherd. And I the Lord will be their God, and my servant David a prince among them; I the Lord have spoken it." (Ezek. 34:22-24.)

There is, of course, much more. Whole volumes might be written about Israel—her scattering, gathering, and final triumph—but we have confined ourselves here to passages that speak of the King and the Shepherd who is destined to rule and reign on the throne of David in the millennial day. How beauteous the holy word is! How better could the ancient prophets have taught the glory and power of

Christ's millennial reign than to equate it with the image David had in the eyes of the people? And David's greater Son shall soon come as the Second David to rule and reign over Israel and the world forever. Thanks be to God for the hope and joy that come to us because of this assured verity.

THE NEW HEAVEN AND NEW EARTH

The Salvation of the Earth

We are approaching the day when there will be a new heaven and a new earth. By earth we mean this planet, this orb, this abiding place for mortal men; we mean the lands and the seas, the ground whereon we walk, and the pleasant valleys and towering mountains; we mean the great rivers and small streams, the Edenic gardens and the desert waste lands; we mean all of the places where the soles of our feet have trod. By heaven we mean the atmospheric heavens, the layers of air and moisture that surround the earth, the clouds of heaven and the free-moving breezes; we mean the life-giving breath that is breathed into the nostrils of living creatures; we mean the blue skies and the rainbow-hued panoramas of color that attend the rising and setting sun. And when we say the heavens and the earth shall be made new, we have in mind changes so dramatic and alterations of such giant proportion that things as they are now will scarcely be remembered or brought to mind.

In order to understand the doctrine of a new heaven and a new earth, we must have an awareness of the old heaven and the old earth. We must know that they were not always in their present state and that their eventual destiny is to be the home and abiding place of exalted beings. We must know that the earth itself is subject to eternal law and is in process of gaining its salvation. Truly is it written that the earth "must needs be sanctified from all unrighteousness, that it may be prepared for the celestial glory; For after it hath filled the measure of its creation, it shall be crowned with glory, even with the presence of God the Father." And also: "The earth abideth the law of a celestial kingdom, for it filleth the measure of its creation, and transgresseth not the law—Wherefore, it shall be sanctified; yea, notwithstanding it shall die, it shall be quickened again, and shall abide the power by which it is quickened, and the righteous shall inherit it." (D&C 88:18-19, 25-26.)

As to the plan of salvation for men, it includes successive phases of existence and requires certain acts on the part of the candidates for salvation. Men were born as the spirit children of God. The first man, Adam, was placed on earth in an Edenic or paradisiacal or terrestrial state, in which there was neither procreation nor death. Then came the fall, which brought mortality with its consequent procreation and death, and all men are now in a mortal, a fallen, or a telestial state. Those who live on earth during the Millennium will gain a terrestrial state in which there will be no death, in the sense of separation of body and spirit, although they will continue to have children. To gain salvation, men must be baptized in water and of the Spirit; they must obey a celestial law; and they must die and rise again in immortality. The ultimate destiny of saved beings is to dwell in the celestial kingdom.

As to the plan of salvation for the earth, it also calls for successive phases of existence and for whatever else is involved for the earth to abide the law and fill the full measure of its creation. This earth was first created as a spirit planet. Then came the Edenic or paradisiacal or terrestrial creation, during which period all forms of life were placed on its surface, in its waters, or in the atmospheric heavens that surround it. Next came the fall—the fall of man, the fall of all forms of life, and the fall of the earth. The fallen earth became a telestial sphere, which it now is.

In the coming millennial day it will be renewed and receive again its paradisiacal glory and will thus return to its terrestrial or Edenic state. And its final destiny is to become a celestial globe and shine like the sun in the firmament. In the process of abiding a celestial law, the earth was baptized by immersion in the days of Noah; and it will be baptized by fire at the Second Coming. This old earth is also destined to die and to be resurrected in the day of quickening. During the Millennium it will, in effect, be in a translated state, which, as pertaining to men, is the state Enoch and his people and some others attained. Thus, the earth was first a spirit planet and then a terrestrial globe. It is now a telestial earth; during the Millennium it will become terrestrial again; and finally, it will become a celestial earth. With an awareness of all this, we are ready to consider the new heaven and new earth that is soon to be.

The Paradisiacal Earth

"We believe"—it is an official, a formal, a canonized pronouncement—"that the earth will be renewed and receive its paradisiacal glory." (A of F 10.) All things when first created—the earth and all forms of life—were paradisiacal in nature and were pronounced by their Creator as "very good." (Moses 2:31.) There was no sin, no sorrow, and no death in that day. And the Great Creator blessed the earth and all things on its face. Then came the fall, and the earth which God had blessed was cursed. "Cursed shall be the ground for thy sake," he said to Adam; "in sorrow shalt thou eat of it all the days of thy life. Thorns also, and thistles shall it bring forth to thee, and thou shalt eat the herb of the field." (Moses 4:23-24.) To Cain the Lord said: "When thou tillest the ground it shall not henceforth yield unto thee her strength." (Moses 5:37.) And later, with reference to all men, the divine account says: "And God cursed the earth with a sore curse, and was angry with the wicked, with all the sons of men whom he had made." (Moses 5:56.) That curse now prevails; it is in full operation, and it will continue so to be until the millennial day. Then the earth and all things that remain after the day of burning will return to a paradisiacal state, a state in which all things will be blessed and prospered as they were in the primeval day. A thing cannot be renewed unless it was new in the first instance. The earth was paradisiacal once, and it will become so again.

Enoch sought to learn from the Lord when the curse would be removed and when the earth would be blessed again. After he and his city had been translated, "Enoch looked upon the earth; and he heard a voice from the bowels thereof, saying: Wo, wo is me, the mother of men; I am pained, I am weary, because of the wickedness of my children. When shall I rest, and be cleansed from the filthiness which is gone forth out of me? When will my Creator sanctify me, that I may rest, and righteousness for a season abide upon my face?" How graphic and wondrous is this way of teaching—to let the very earth itself cry out for rest and blessings! "And when Enoch heard the earth mourn, he wept, and cried unto the Lord, saying: O Lord, wilt thou not have compassion upon the earth? Wilt thou not bless the children of Noah?" And the Lord did then bless the earth to this extent: he decreed that life on its face should never again be destroyed by a flood. But the basic questions remained unanswered, and so Enoch yet "cried unto the Lord, saying: When the Son of Man cometh in the flesh, shall the earth rest? I pray thee, show me these things." He then saw the crucifixion, the convulsions of nature that attended it, the opening of the prison doors, and the reserving of the wicked "in chains of darkness until the judgment of the great day. And again Enoch wept and cried unto the Lord, saying: When shall the earth rest? And Enoch beheld the Son of Man ascend up unto the Father; and he called unto the Lord, saying: Wilt thou not come again upon the earth? . . . I ask thee if thou wilt not come again on the earth." How great were the pleadings of this holy prophet to know what would be in the last days!

"And the Lord said unto Enoch: As I live, so will I come in the last days, in the days of wickedness and vengeance. . . . And the day shall come that the earth shall rest, but before that day the heavens shall be darkened, and a veil of darkness shall cover the earth; and the heavens shall shake, and also the earth; and great tribulations shall be among the children of men, but my people will I preserve." Then the Lord told Enoch of the restoration of the gospel, the coming forth of the Book of Mormon, the building of the New Jerusalem, and the return of the original Zion, and gave him the promise that "for the space of a thousand years the earth shall rest. And it came to pass that Enoch saw the day of the coming of the Son of Man, in the last days, to dwell on the earth in righteousness for the space of a thousand years." (Moses 7:48-65.)

Isaiah speaks of the latter-day glory and triumph of Israel as a people, of their return from captivity, of the dominion they will have over the nations that oppressed them, and of the fall of Babylon. Then, using the same concept—that of the earth resting in the day of its paradisiacal glory—he says in majestic simplicity: "The whole earth is at rest, and is quiet: they break forth into singing." (Isa. 14:1-8.) How pleasing that day will be! As the Lord worked six days in the creation and rested the seventh, as man is commanded to labor for six days and then rest and worship on the seventh, so the earth itself, after being cursed with the wickedness of her children during six long millenniums, shall soon enjoy a Sabbath of rest for the promised thousand years.

The Day of Transfiguration

This earth as it is now constituted, and the atmospheric heavens as they now are, both of them in their fallen and telestial state shall soon cease to be. They shall die. As with men, so with the earth; death is essential to salvation. A change must take place in the earth; it must go from a lower to a higher state. It is now in a telestial state and must be transformed into one that is terrestrial before it eventually receives its final celestial glory. All this is set forth in the holy word. The inspired Psalmist, for instance, in extolling the greatness of God says: "O my God, . . . thy years are throughout all generations. Of old hast thou laid the foundation of the earth: and the heavens are the work of thy hands. They shall perish, but thou shalt endure: yea, all of them shall wax old like a garment; as a vesture shalt thou change them, and they shall be changed: But thou art the same, and thy years shall have no end." (Ps. 102:24-27.) The earth shall wax old; it shall perish; it shall be changed!

As with so many of the mysteries of the kingdom, Isaiah leaves us a plain and precious witness of the change that is to be in the earth. To him the Lord said: "Lift up your eyes to the heavens, and look upon the earth beneath: for the heavens shall vanish away like smoke, and the earth shall wax old like a garment, and they that dwell therein shall die in like manner: but my salvation shall be for ever, and my righteousness shall not be abolished." (Isa. 51:6.) It is the same message as that delivered by the Psalmist. The heavens and the earth, being old and having served their purpose where men are concerned, shall die. The atmospheric heavens as they now are shall cease to be, and so also will it be with the earth. They shall be changed. "The windows from on high are open, and the foundations of the earth do shake. The earth is utterly broken down, the earth is clean dissolved, the earth is moved exceedingly." Prophets always use the best language at their command to describe what the Lord wants them to say. These words of Isaiah are to be interpreted as meaning exactly what they say. "The earth shall reel to and fro like a drunkard, and shall be removed like a cottage; and the transgression thereof shall be heavy upon it; and it shall fall, and not rise again." (Isa. 24:18-20.) When the Lord comes and the telestial earth ceases to be, when it dies its appointed death, it will not rise again in its old fallen and degenerate state. The day will then have arrived that is referred to in the writings of Isaiah in these words: "For, behold, I create new heavens and a new earth," saith the Lord, "and the former shall not be remembered, nor come into mind." (Isa. 65:17.) So glorious shall the new earth be that men will no longer concern themselves with what once was.

Moroni inserted into his digest of the writings of Ether these words: "The earth shall pass away. And there shall be a new heaven and a new earth; and they shall be like unto the old save the old have passed away, and all things have become new." (Ether 13:8-9.) Life will go on during the Millennium. The earth as a sphere will still be here. And the new earth will be patterned after the old one in the same sense that translated beings are patterned after the mortal men they once were. They are the same persons, but their nature and powers and faculties are so changed that their whole way of life is new. So shall it be as between our present earth and the new earth that is to be.

Peter calls this day when there will be a new heaven and a new earth; this day when the earth shall wax old and die and in which the heavens shall vanish away like smoke; this day in which things on earth will be changed as men change the vestures that clothe them; this day in which the earth will be broken down and dissolved and moved exceedingly; this day in which the earth will be renewed and receive its paradisiacal glory and become again as it originally was in the day of the Garden of Eden—Peter calls this day "the times of refreshing" that "shall come from the presence of the Lord" when "he shall send Jesus Christ, which before was preached" unto the Jews. (Acts 3:19-20.) It will be the day of change needed to make the earth a fit habitation for its true King and the other resurrected beings who will live and reign with him for the appointed thousand years. And well might Peter so speak. He was one of three in the meridian of time, the other two being James and John, who saw in vision the whole glorious renewal of the earth. Alluding to what they saw on the Mount of Transfiguration, our revealed word says: "He that endureth in faith and doeth my will, the same shall overcome, and shall receive an inheritance upon the earth when the day of transfiguration shall come; When the earth shall be transfigured, even according to the pattern which was shown unto mine apostles upon the mount; of which account the fulness ye have not yet received." (D&C 63:20-21.) The new heaven and new earth, the paradisiacal earth, the renewed earth, the refreshed earth, the transfigured earth, the millennial earth—all these are one and the same. How blessed the earth will be in that day!

The Transfigured Earth

What will the transfigured earth be like? Unto what shall we compare it? And how shall we find words to describe the glory and beauty of all things in that day? Providentially the prophetic word gives us glimpses of the future. Using the best language at their command, our inspired forerunners have recorded some of the visions vouchsafed to them relative to the new heaven and the new earth, and they have written down some of the revelations they received about the wonders of the Millennium. In their accounts we read of mountains becoming plains, of valleys ceasing to be, and of the very landmasses of the earth uniting into one grand continent. We read of deserts becoming gardens and of the whole earth yielding her fruit as in Eden of old. The prophetic word, designed as it is to encourage us to prepare to abide the day, is fascinating to the extreme. And it is to this word that we now turn as we seek to weave into the eternal tapestry of the Second Coming those threads which will picture the new heaven and the new earth that are to be. Then, in later chapters, we shall speak of the kind of life men, and all created things, shall live on their newly made paradisiacal planet.

Our course is charted for us with reference to these coming events by this divine word: "Be not deceived, but continue in steadfastness, looking forth for the heavens to be shaken, and the earth to tremble and to reel to and fro as a drunken man, and for the valleys to be exalted, and for the mountains to be made low, and for the rough places to become smooth—and all this when the angel shall sound his trumpet." (D&C 49:23.) And, be it noted, this divine exhortation has the effect of endorsing and approving what the ancient prophets have said about the changes in the earth that will occur as the millennial day dawns.

One of the plainest and most-oft-repeated statements about the ushering in of the Millennium is the promise of a great shaking of the earth, of earthquakes that are everywhere at one and the same time, and of mountains and valleys and seas and landmasses that move. "Yet once, it is a little while," saith the Lord, "and I will shake the heavens, and the earth, and the sea, and the dry land; and I will shake all nations, and the desire of all nations shall come." (Hag. 2:6-7.) Christ, the Desire of all nations, shall come amid the greatest shaking of the earth and of all things that there has ever been or ever will be in the entire history of this planet.

Everything on earth—the historical events then in progress, the beasts and all forms of life, and the inanimate objects that do not act for themselves—everything on earth will be affected by the great shaking. For instance, John tells us that in the midst of Armageddon, there will be "a great earthquake, such as was not since men were upon the earth, so mighty an earthquake, and so great." (Rev. 16:18.) Through Ezekiel the Lord said of that same day: "Surely in that day there shall be a great shaking in the land of Israel; so that the fishes of the sea, and the fowls of the heaven, and the beasts of the field, and all creeping things that creep upon the earth, and all the men that are upon the face of the earth, shall shake at my presence, and the mountains shall be thrown down, and the steep places shall fall, and every wall shall fall to the ground." (Ezek. 38:19-20.) And the Lord shall come. "And his feet shall stand in that day upon the mount of Olives, which is before Jerusalem on the east, and the mount of Olives shall cleave in the midst thereof toward the east and toward the west, and there shall be a very great valley; and half of the mountain shall remove toward the north, and half of it toward the south. And ye shall flee to the valley of the mountains; . . . yea, ye shall flee, like as ye fled from before the earthquake in the days of Uzziah king of Judah: and the Lord my God shall come, and all the saints with thee." (Zech. 14:4-5.) The prophetic word in Joel attests that at the Second Coming "the heavens and the earth shall shake" (Joel 3:16), and our latter-day revelation says "the everlasting hills shall tremble" (D&C 133:31).

We have already quoted the words in Isaiah that say the earth will be dissolved. The Psalmist says the same thing: "The earth and all the inhabitants thereof are dissolved." (Ps. 75:3.) Peter picks up this same theme and explains how it shall come to pass. "The day of the Lord will come," he says, "in the which the heavens shall pass away with a great noise, and the elements shall melt with fervent heat, the earth also and the works that are therein shall be burned up." This we have heretofore considered in other connections. But now note particularly what will happen to the earth. "Seeing then that all these things shall be dissolved," Peter continues, "what manner of persons ought ye to be in all holy conversation and godliness, looking for and hasting unto the coming of the day of God, wherein the heavens being on fire shall be dissolved, and the elements shall melt with fervent heat?" These things, he says, shall come to pass in the day when there are "new heavens and a new earth." (2 Pet. 3:10-13.)

Being aware, thus, that the heavens and the earth, as they now are, shall be dissolved and that the very elements shall melt with fervent heat, we catch a new vision of what is meant by the prophetic word that the mountains shall melt at the Second Coming. Nahum says: "The mountains quake at him, and the hills melt, and the earth is burned at his presence, yea, the world, and all that dwell therein." (Nahum 1:5.) "For, behold, the Lord cometh forth out of his place, and will come down, and tread upon the high places of the earth. And the mountains shall be molten under him, and the valleys shall be cleft, as wax before the fire, and as the waters that are poured down a steep place." (Micah 1:3-4.) Our revelation, echoing the prayer found in chapter 64 of Isaiah, says that the servants of God in the last days will call upon the name of the Lord day and night in these words: "O that thou wouldst rend the heavens, that thou wouldst come down, that the mountains might flow down at thy presence." They are answered that "the presence of the Lord shall be as the melting fire that burneth, and as the fire which causeth the waters to boil." In their prayers the saints will say: "Yea, when thou comest down, and the mountains flow down at thy presence, thou shalt meet him who rejoiceth and worketh righteousness, who remembereth thee in thy ways." (D&C 133:40-44.) And so Isaiah says: "Prepare ye the way of the Lord. . . . Every valley shall be exalted, and every mountain and hill shall be made low: and the crooked shall be made straight, and the rough places plain: And the glory of the Lord shall be revealed, and all flesh shall see it together." (Isa. 40: 3-5.) And so Zechariah says: "And the Lord shall be king over all the earth. . . . All the land shall be turned as a plain. . . . And men shall dwell in it, and there shall be no more utter destruction." (Zech. 14:9-11.)

When the Lord first created this earth, as appears from the revealed account, all of the landmasses were in one place and all of the great waters in another. Continents and islands as we now know them did not exist. "And I, God, said: Let the waters under the heaven be gathered together unto one place, and it was so; and I, God, said: Let there be dry land; and it was so. And I, God, called the dry land Earth; and the gathering together of the waters, called I the Sea; and I, God, saw that all things which I had made were good." (Moses 2:9-10.) Continents and islands, each in their several positions, came into being later, we suppose in large measure as part of the universal flood and the changes then wrought upon the earth. The account in Genesis says the earth was divided in the days of Peleg (Gen. 10:25), meaning, as we suppose, that the division into continents and islands was completed in his day. Peleg was, in fact, the fifth generation from Noah, and his name means division. In any event, there now are continents and islands, which was not always the case.

Now, when the Lord stands upon Olivet and when he utters his voice from Zion and from Jerusalem, it shall be heard among all people. "And it shall be a voice as the voice of many waters, and as the voice of a great thunder, which shall break down the mountains, and the valleys shall not be found. He shall command the great deep, and it shall be driven back into the north countries, and the islands shall become one land; And the land of Jerusalem [the Holy Land] and the land of Zion [America] shall be turned back into their own place, and the earth shall be like as it was in the days before it was divided. And the Lord, even the Savior, shall stand in the midst of his people, and shall reign over all flesh." (D&C 133:20-25.) It is an interesting speculative enterprise to look at a map or a globe of the world and to wonder how, with modest adjustments involving the rising and sinking of various areas of the earth, the continents and islands might fit back together again. There is much to indicate they once were joined and would easily fit back in their former positions.

Knowing as we do from latter-day revelation that the islands and continents were once joined in one landmass and will yet again be joined, we find new meaning in allusions and comments found in the ancient scriptures. As part of a description of the Second Coming, John tells us: "And the heaven departed as a scroll when it is rolled together; and every mountain and island were moved out of their places." (Rev. 6:14.) In connection with the greatest earthquake of the ages, John says: "And every island fled away, and the mountains were not found." (Rev. 16:20.) Also in a Second Coming setting John speaks of the voice of the Lord "as the voice of many waters, and as the voice of a great thunder." (Rev. 14:2.) This is the identical language used by the Lord in telling Joseph Smith that the mountains and valleys shall not be found, that the great deep (apparently the Atlantic Ocean) will be driven back into the north countries, "and the islands shall become one land." (D&C 133:22-23.) The voice of many waters and of a great thunder could well be the thunderous surging of a whole ocean moving half an earth's distance from where it now is. And all of this gives deep meaning to John's account, which says: "And I saw a new heaven and a new earth: for the first heaven and the first earth were passed away; and there was no more sea." (Rev. 21:1.) The apparent meaning of this is that the sea, or ocean, that separates the continents will cease to be, for their great landmasses will be joined together again.

Isaiah, speaking of Zion and Jerusalem in a Second Coming setting, in an apparent reference to the joining of the continents, and using that prophetic imagery for which he has such great renown, says: "Thy land shall be married." (Isa. 62:4.) Also in a setting relative to the Millennium and the gathering of Israel, Isaiah says, "There shall be an highway for the remnant of his people, which shall be left." That is, those who are left because they have abided the day of our Lord's coming shall find a highway to lead them to their appointed gathering places. It shall then be, Isaiah says, "like as it was to Israel in the day that he came up out of the land of Egypt." (Isa. 11:16.) As the Lord provided a highway through the Red Sea for his people anciently, as they traveled to their promised land, so will he provide a way for them to travel in the latter days. Our latter-day revelation, after stating that the great deep shall be driven back into the north countries and that the continents shall become one land, states that "they who are in the north countries," meaning the Ten Tribes, shall return. "And an highway shall be cast up in the midst of the great deep" for them. (D&C 133:23-27.) Would we go too far astray if we were to suggest that the highway is created by the joined landmasses, and that as ancient Israel found a dry path through the Red Sea, so latter-day Israel will find a dry path where the Atlantic Ocean once was? It is at least a thought to ponder, for surely we are expected to seek for interpretations relative to all that has been revealed concerning the Lord and his coming.

After our Lord comes and the new heaven and the new earth are a reality, then the earth will bring forth bounteously to support the billions of our Father's children who shall soon find lodgment on its surface. We do not know what changes will cause this to be. Our knowledge is limited to a few slivers of revealed truth here and there throughout the canonized word. Our revealed description of the millennial return of Israel says: "They shall smite the rocks, and the ice shall flow down at their presence. . . . And in the barren deserts there shall come forth pools of living water; and the parched ground shall no longer be a thirsty land." (D&C 133:26-29.) If the great ice masses shall flow down before them, it presupposes worldwide climatic changes. And if the deserts are freely watered, conditions will be far from what they now are. It could be—we do not know, we can only speculate—it could be that the axis of the earth will become upright and no longer have the twenty-three-and-a-half-degree tilt that causes seasons. It could be—we do not know—that such was the case in the beginning, which might account for the great glacial ages about which scientists speculate. The first mention in the scriptures of "seedtime and harvest, and cold and heat, and summer and winter," as we know them, is found after the flood of Noah. (Gen. 8:22.) At this point, it is wise to state that there is much more that we do not know than that which is known about many things that were anciently and that will be again.

The change in the earth itself is described in Isaiah on this wise: "Thorns and briers" shall prevail in the land, "Until the spirit be poured upon us from on high, and the wilderness be a fruitful field, and the fruitful field be counted for a forest." Then righteousness will prevail, "And my people shall dwell in a peaceable habitation, and in sure dwellings, and in quiet resting places," saith the Lord. (Isa. 32:13-18.) "The wilderness and the solitary place shall be glad for them; and the desert shall rejoice, and blossom as the rose. It shall blossom abundantly, and rejoice even with joy and singing. . . . For in the wilderness shall waters break out, and streams in the desert. And the parched ground shall become a pool, and the thirsty land springs of water." (Isa. 35:1-7.) "I will even make a way in the wilderness, and rivers in the desert," saith the Lord. (Isa. 43:19.) "For the Lord shall comfort Zion: he will comfort all her waste places; and he will make her wilderness like Eden, and her desert like the garden of the Lord; joy and gladness shall be found therein, thanksgiving, and the voice of melody." (Isa. 51:3.)

And to Isaiah's witness, let us add this one prophetic promise from Joel: "And it shall come to pass in that day, that the mountains shall drop down new wine, and the hills shall flow with milk, and all the rivers of Judah shall flow with waters. . . . Judah shall dwell for ever, and Jerusalem from generation to generation. For I will cleanse their blood that I have not cleansed: for the Lord dwelleth in Zion." (Joel 3:18-21.)

So shall it be on the transfigured earth.

THE SECOND COMING AND THE RESURRECTION

The Dead: Their Glorious Rising

Of all the resurrections that ever have been or ever will be upon this earth, the most glorious—the one that transcends all others in power, grandeur, and might—will be the resurrection that attends the return of the Lord Jesus. He will come with ten thousands of his saints, all of them resurrected persons from ages past. He will call forth from their graves and from the watery deep ten thousands of his other saints, all of them righteous persons who have lived since his mortal ministry. Those among his saints on earth who are faithful will be caught up to meet him in the clouds of glory, and they will then return to earth with him to live out their appointed days on the new earth with its new heavens.

Job's ever-recurring question—"If a man die, shall he live again?" (Job 14:14)—has been answered, long since, with all the finality of a divine *ipse dixit*. Man shall live again; nay, man does live again, for the Lord Jesus burst the bands of death and gained the victory over the grave. And with him in his resurrection were all the righteous dead from the day of righteous Abel to that of Zacharias the son of Barachias, as it were, whom they slew between the temple and the altar. In that mighty host was Job himself. Indeed, with Christ in his resurrection were Adam and

Noah and Job; with him were Abraham, Isaac, and Jacob, and all the holy prophets; with him were Enoch and Moses and Elijah and all other translated persons; and with him were all the saints of all prior ages who had been true and faithful in all things—all came forth in glorious immortality when the Lord Jesus turned the key. (D&C 133:54-56.)

And all those who were with Christ in his resurrection, and all others who have since been resurrected, they are the ones who shall return with him in the day of his coming; they are the ones who shall be with him when he calls the sleeping saints to awake and rise from their graves. Thus Job testifies: "I know that my redeemer liveth, and that he shall stand at the latter day upon the earth: And though after my skin worms destroy this body, yet in my flesh shall I see God: Whom I shall see for myself, and mine eyes shall behold, and not another; though my reins be consumed within me." (Job 19:25-27.) And as it is with Job, so shall it be with all the faithful: all shall stand in the latter days upon the earth; all, in their flesh, shall see their God; all shall be with their Risen Lord by whom the resurrection comes.

Those in days past who did not believe and obey the truths of heaven, so as to cleanse and perfect their own souls, shall not be found in the clouds of heaven with the Returning One. And those who do not live the laws of the holy gospel shall not have part in that glorious resurrection which attends his return. Thus we hear Jesus say: "Whosoever shall be ashamed of me, and of my words, in this adulterous and sinful generation, of him also shall the Son of Man be ashamed, when he cometh in the glory of his Father with the holy angels." And what applied in that day applies also in this. Those who do not flee from this present evil world and find gospel refuge and gospel peace with the true saints, of them shall the Lord, whose gospel it is, be ashamed in the dreadful day ahead. "And they shall not have part in that resurrection when he cometh. For verily I say unto you, That he shall come; and he that layeth down his life for my sake and the gospel's, shall come with him, and shall be clothed with his glory in the cloud, on the right hand of the Son of man." (JST, Mark 8:41-43.)

Speaking of all who have died in the faith since the resurrection of Christ, and of all who are true and faithful in the day of his return, Paul gives us these consoling words: "I would not have you to be ignorant, brethren, concerning them which are asleep, that ye sorrow not, even as others which have no hope." Truly, those who believe and obey find peace in this world and have a hope of eternal life in the world to come. "For if we believe that Jesus died and rose again, even so them also which sleep in Jesus will God bring with him." All the dead of all the ages, having risen in glorious immortality, will come with the Lord Jesus to the millennial earth. "For this we say unto you by the word of the Lord, that we which are alive and remain unto the coming of the Lord shall not prevent them which are asleep. For the Lord himself shall descend from heaven with a shout, with the voice of the archangel, and with the trump of God: and the dead in Christ shall rise first." The saints shall come forth from their graves, even before he sets foot on earth. "Then we which are alive and remain shall be caught up together with them in the clouds, to meet the Lord in the air: and so shall we ever be with the Lord." He shall return; the immortal saints will return with him; and those who are yet mortal shall return to continue their lives in his presence on the earth. "Wherefore comfort one another with these words." (1 Thes. 4:13-18.)

Thus Paul says: "Behold, I shew you a mystery"—and how mysterious and strange it is to worldly people, particularly those who have pledged their allegiance to the evolutionary fantasies of Darwinism. "We shall not all sleep, but we shall all be changed, In a moment, in the twinkling of an eye, at the last trump: for the trumpet shall sound, and the dead shall be raised incorruptible, and we shall be changed." (1 Cor. 15:51-52.) Those who abide the day of the Lord's coming will be changed so as to stand the fire and the glory of that dread time; they will be changed when they are caught up to meet the Lord in the air, and they will be changed again when they attain their prescribed age and gain their immortal glory.

Thus also we read in our revelations: "He that endureth in faith and doeth my will, the same shall overcome, and shall receive an inheritance upon the earth when the day of transfiguration shall come. . . . Yea, and blessed are the dead that die in the Lord, from henceforth, when the Lord shall come, and old things shall pass away, and all things become new, they shall rise from the dead and shall not die after, and shall receive an inheritance before the Lord, in the holy city." Both the living and the dead shall be blessed with a millennial inheritance. "And he that liveth when the Lord shall come, and hath kept the faith, blessed is he; nevertheless, it is appointed to him to die at the age of man. Wherefore, children shall grow up until they become old; old men shall die; but they shall not sleep in the dust, but they shall be changed in the twinkling of an eye." Such is the doctrine Paul taught, as did all the prophets and apostles of old. "Wherefore, for this cause preached the apostles unto the world the resurrection of the dead." When shall all these things be? The divine answer affirms: "These things are the things that ye must look for; and, speaking after the manner of the Lord, they are now nigh at hand, and in a time to come, even in the day of the coming of the Son of Man." (D&C 63:20, 49-53.) "And all they who suffer persecution for my name, and endure in faith, though they are called to lay down their lives for my sake yet shall they partake of all this glory." (D&C 101:35.)

When Shall the Dead Rise?

"To every thing there is a season, and a time to every purpose under the heaven." (Eccl. 3:1.) So saith the Preacher. And true it is. There is a time to be born and a time to live, and a time to die and a time to live again. There is a time to put on this mortal clay and gain these mortal experiences and a time to shuffle off this mortal coil with all its troubles and sorrows. There is a time to face the sorrow of death and a time to rise in immortality and lay hold on everlasting life.

And so we ask: When shall the dead rise? When shall the prisoners be freed from their prison house? When shall their bodies and spirits join together inseparably to form immortal souls? We hear the Lord Jehovah, in whom is "everlasting strength," say to the faithful of Israel: "Thy dead men shall live." If a man dies, he shall rise again. But when shall it be ? The Lord Jehovah answers: "Together with my dead body shall they arise." The time shall come for a God to be born, for a God to live among men, for a God to die, and for a God to rise again. Then there shall be a resurrection of the righteous; then they shall come forth; then the cry will go forth: "Awake and sing, ye that dwell in dust." Then "the earth shall cast out the dead." (Isa. 26:4, 19.) Such was the Messianic promise, and as Isaiah testified, so it came to pass. Christ gained the victory over death and hell for himself and for all those who believed in his holy name and who walked as becometh saints. That was the first resurrection.

How resurrections are numbered or how many there are is of no special moment. What matters is the kinds and types of resurrections and who shall come forth in them. Abinadi, who ministered among his American Hebrew brethren a century and a half before the birth of that Lord whose servant he was, prophesied: "The bands of death shall be broken, and the Son reigneth, and hath power over the dead; therefore, he bringeth to pass the resurrection of the dead." The Son is the Lord Jehovah of whom Isaiah spoke. He is the firstfruits of them that slept, and in some way incomprehensible to us, the power of his resurrection passes upon all men so that all shall rise from the dead. The miracle in all this is like the miracle of creation itself.

"And there cometh a resurrection," Abinadi continues, "even a first resurrection." It could not have been other than a first resurrection, for it involved Christ, the firstfruits, and those who came forth along with his dead body. It would be, Abinadi prophesied, "even a resurrection of those that have been, and who are, and who shall be, even until [the time of] the resurrection of Christ—for so shall he be called." To be with Christ in his resurrection—such was the glorious hope of all the saints who lived from the day of the first Adam, by whom mortality came, to the day of the Second Adam, by whom immortality came. Thus, Abinadi continues, "the resurrection of all the prophets, and all those that have believed in their words, or all those that have kept the commandments of God, shall come forth in the first resurrection; therefore, they are the first resurrection."

What is the reward and status of those who were with Christ in his resurrection? "They are raised to dwell with God who has redeemed them; thus they have eternal life through Christ, who has broken the bands of death." (Mosiah 15:20-23.) Theirs is a state of glory and exaltation. Three of them—Abraham, Isaac, and Jacob—are singled out by name and made patterns for all the rest. Of these three the Lord says: "They have entered into their exaltation, according to the promises, and sit upon thrones, and are not angels but are gods." (D&C 132:29, 37.) These are they who were with Christ in his resurrection, who, as Matthew says, "came out of the graves after his resurrection, and went into the holy city, and appeared unto many." (Matt. 27:53.) These are they whom the Lord Jesus will bring with him in the clouds of glory when he comes to rule and reign among men for a thousand years.

The first resurrection that concerned Abinadi, and all the prophets and saints who lived and died before the day of atonement, occurred in the meridian of time. Some others have been resurrected since then. We know of Moroni, John the Baptist, and Peter and James, all of whom had ministerial assignments to be performed among mortals that required angelic messengers who had bodies of flesh and bones. It may be that many others have also burst the bands of death and risen from their graves. But for the generality of the saints, the first resurrection is the one that will attend our Lord's return. All we know with surety as to the time of any individual's resurrection is that "every man" will come forth "in his own order," that "celestial bodies, and bodies terrestrial," and bodies telestial will all come forth, successively, to find their places in kingdoms having the same names. (1 Cor. 15:23-44.)

Those who "keep the commandments of God, and the faith of Jesus," shall come forth in the first resurrection, which is also called the resurrection of life, or the resurrection of the just. It is of them that John wrote: "Blessed are the dead which die in the Lord from henceforth: Yea, saith the Spirit, that they may rest from their labours; and their works do follow them." (Rev. 14:12-13.) It is of them that Jesus says: "At the day of my coming in a pillar of fire, . . . a trump shall sound both long and loud, even as upon Mount Sinai, and all the earth shall quake, and they shall come forth—yea, even the dead which died in me, to receive a crown of righteousness, and to be clothed upon, even as I am, to be with me, that we may be one." (D&C 29:12-13.) And also: "Hearken ye, for, behold, the great day of the Lord is nigh at hand. For the day cometh that the Lord shall utter his voice out of heaven; the heavens shall shake and the earth shall tremble, and the trump of God shall sound both long and loud, and shall say to the sleeping nations: Ye saints arise and live; ye sinners stay and sleep until I shall call again." (D&C 43:17-18.)

In the great Olivet Discourse, Jesus spoke of the signs of his coming, of the redemption of his saints, and of the restoration of scattered Israel. He held up the hope of a glorious resurrection as the greatest triumph any of his saints could achieve in the day of redemption. "For as ye have looked upon the long absence of your spirits from your bodies to be a bondage, I will show unto you how the day of redemption shall come, and also the restoration of the scattered Israel," he said. (And may we here insert that all of the faithful of all of the ages have striven or are now striving so to live that they will come forth from their graves and enter into their immortal rest at the earliest possible time.) And so Jesus told of the signs and wonders that would precede and attend his glorious return, and of the plagues and desolations to be poured out upon the world, and then, by way of promise, said: "But before the arm of the Lord shall fall, an angel shall sound his trump, and the saints that have slept shall come forth to meet me in the cloud." The first resurrection will precede the desolations and horrors to be poured out upon the wicked without measure in the day of our Lord's return. "Wherefore, if ye have slept in peace blessed are you," he continues, "for as you now behold me and know that I am, even so shall ye come unto me and your souls shall live, and your redemption shall be perfected; and the saints shall come forth from the four quarters of the earth." That is to say, the saints who are alive and who are worthy shall be caught up to meet the Lord and the heavenly hosts that accompany him.

Now note the chronology. Jesus' next words are: "Then"—that is, after the saints that sleep have been resurrected, and after the living saints have come forth from the four quarters of the earth—"Then shall the arm of the Lord fall upon the nations. And then shall the Lord set his foot upon this mount, and it shall cleave in twain, and the earth shall tremble, and reel to and fro, and the heavens also shall shake." (D&C 45:16-48.) And then he speaks of the calamities and the burning of the iniquitous and of his appearance to the Jews who remain. Truly the righteous need not fear, for either in life or in death their redemption is assured.

Jesus Comes and the Dead Rise

No matter when they lived, the righteous dead, those destined to gain eternal life in our Father's kingdom, always come forth in the next available resurrection. That resurrection to them is the first resurrection. For us the first resurrection will take place when our Lord returns attended by those who came forth in a previous first resurrection. Then all the righteous dead, all having risen in glorious immortality, will live and reign with him on earth. Let us now see how and in what way all the resurrections that lie ahead relate to the great and dreadful day of his coming.

It is not possible for us, in our present relatively low state of spiritual understanding, to specify the exact chronology of all the events that shall attend the Second Coming. Nearly all of the prophetic word relative to our Lord's return links various events together without reference to the order of their occurrence. Indeed, the same scriptural language is often used to describe similar events that will take place at different times. Thus, in the midst of prophetic pronouncements relative to "the day of the Lord's vengeance," when "the indignation of the Lord" shall fall "upon all nations, and his fury upon all their armies," Isaiah says: "And all the host of heaven shall be dissolved, and the heavens shall be rolled together as a scroll." (Isa. 34:2-8.) In speaking of that which shall transpire during "the sixth seal"—that is, during the sixth one-thousand-year period of the earth's temporal continuance, which is the era in which we now live—John tells us of an earthquake, of the sun and moon being darkened, and of the stars falling upon the earth. Then he says: "And the heaven departed as a scroll when it is rolled together; and every mountain and island were moved out of their places." It is "the great day of his wrath." (Rev. 6:12-17.) Later John says that during "the seventh seal," and thus in a day yet to be, "there was silence in heaven about the space of half an hour." (Rev. 8:1.)

All these things, particularly the hidden and undefined period of silence, are somewhat enigmatic. The Lord has not yet seen fit to tell us their full and complete meanings. But, having them before us, let us see what the Lord has said about them in latter-day revelation, with particular reference to the resurrection. After saying that the great and abominable church "is the tares of the earth," and that "she is ready to be burned," the revealed word affirms: "And there shall be silence in heaven for the space of half an hour; and immediately after shall the curtain of heaven be unfolded, as a scroll is unfolded after it is rolled up, and the face of the Lord shall be unveiled." Then—and these events, of necessity, are chronological—then "the saints that are upon the earth, who are alive, shall be quickened and be caught up to meet him." These are they of whom Paul and others have spoken, as we have heretofore seen. They all shall abide the day and receive an inheritance in the holy city.

"And they"—it is his saints of whom the Lord is speaking—"who have slept in their graves shall come forth, for their graves shall be opened; and they also shall be caught up to meet him in the midst of the pillar of heaven—They are Christ's, the first fruits, they who shall descend with him first, and they who are on the earth and in their graves, who are first caught up to meet him; and all this by the voice of the sounding of the trump of the angel of God." (D&C 88:94-98.)

Christ's, the first fruits—who are they? They are all those who were with him in his resurrection. They are all those of Enoch's city, a righteous people who first were translated and who then gained full immortality when Christ rose from his tomb. They are all those of ages past who have burst the bands of death. They are the living saints who are quickened by the power of God and are caught up to meet their Lord in the air. They are the righteous dead who shall come forth in this, the morning of the first resurrection, to receive an inheritance of eternal life and to be one with their glorious Lord. All these shall have an inheritance of exaltation in the highest heaven of the celestial world. All these shall "behold" their Lord's "face in righteousness," for they shall "awake" with his "likeness." (Ps. 17:15.)

"And after this another angel shall sound, which is the

second trump; and then cometh the redemption of those who are Christ's at his coming"—meaning after his coming—"who have received their part in that prison which is prepared for them, that they might receive the gospel, and be judged according to men in the flesh." These are they who come forth with bodies terrestrial and who shall go to the terrestrial kingdom. "And again, another trump shall sound, which is the third trump; and then come the spirits of men who are to be judged, and are found under condemnation; and these are the rest of the dead; and they live not again until the thousand years are ended, neither again, until the end of the earth." Theirs shall be a telestial inheritance. "And another trump shall sound, which is the fourth trump, saying: There are found among those who are to remain until that great and last day, even the end, who shall remain filthy still." (D&C 88:99-102.) These, of course, are the sons of perdition.

Thus all shall rise from death to life, all shall come forth from the grave, all shall live forever in immortality. But oh, what a difference it makes whether we come forth in the resurrection of the just or that of the unjust, whether we are caught up to meet the Lord in the air or whether we are told to remain asleep in the dust of the earth until he calls again. How expressive are the words of Abinadi: "There is a resurrection, therefore the grave hath no victory, and the sting of death is swallowed up in Christ. . . . Even this mortal shall put on immortality, and this corruption shall put on incorruption, and shall be brought to stand before the bar of God, to be judged of him according to their works whether they be good or whether they be evil—If they be good, to the resurrection of endless life and happiness; and if they be evil, to the resurrection of endless damnation, being delivered up to the devil, who hath subjected them, which is damnation—Having gone according to their own carnal wills and desires; having never called upon the Lord while the arms of mercy were extended towards them; for the arms of mercy were extended towards them, and they would not; they being warned of their iniquities and yet they would not depart from them; and they were commanded to repent and yet they would not repent. And now, ought ye not to tremble and repent of your sins, and remember that only in and through Christ ye can be saved?" (Mosiah 16:8-13.)

Israel: Her Resurrected Glory

Ancient Israel knew that their destiny was to inherit the earth, to receive their promised land again in eternity, and to live and reign forever in the presence of their King. Yea, and not only Israel, but all the righteous saints who preceded them knew also that their final glory and triumph would be in the day of resurrection. Hence the great need so to live as to come forth in the resurrection of life and endless happiness rather than in the resurrection of endless damnation. Thus, "Enoch saw the day of the coming of the Son of Man, in the last days, to dwell on the earth in righteousness for the space of a thousand years; . . . and he saw the day of the righteous, [and] the hour of their redemption." (Moses 7:65-67.) And thus our revelations, paraphrasing Isaiah, say: "And now the year of my redeemed is come; . . . And the graves of the saints shall be opened; and they shall come forth and stand on the right hand of the Lamb, when he shall stand upon Mount Zion, and upon the holy city, the New Jerusalem; and they shall sing the song of the Lamb, day and night forever and ever." (D&C 133:52, 56. See also Isa. 63:4-9.)

In the last days, when all things are in readiness for our Lord's return, "there shall be a time of trouble, such as never was since there was a nation [of Israel] even to that same time: and at that time thy people shall be delivered, every one that shall be found written in the book [meaning in the Lamb's Book of Life]. And many of them that sleep in the dust shall awake, some to everlasting life, and some to shame and everlasting contempt." (Dan. 12:1-2.) So spoke Daniel. Hosea's like witness to that same people acclaimed: "O Israel, thou hast destroyed thyself; but in me is thine help." No matter that you have apostatized and been cursed and peeled and driven, lo, these many years. In the last days thy seed shall return to the ancient sheepfold. And even the worthy dead, of them it is written: "I will ransom them from the power of the grave," saith the Lord. "I will redeem them from death: O death, I will be thy plagues; O grave, I will be thy destruction." (Hosea 13:9-14.)

Ezekiel's grand vision of the valley of dry bones contains in many respects the most insightful description of the resurrection ever to find its way into the canonized accounts. "Can these bones live?" the Lord asked. His answer: "Behold, I will cause breath [spirit] to enter into you, and ye shall live: And I will lay sinews upon you, and will bring up flesh upon you, and cover you with skin." Flesh and bones and sinews and skin and all the organs of the human body are perfected and placed in their glorified state in the resurrected body. That body walks and talks as Jesus did on the Emmaus road; it eats and digests food as he did in the upper room; it is real and literal and tangible. And so the Lord said to Ezekiel: "These bones are the whole house of Israel. . . . Behold, O my people, I will open your graves, and cause you to come up out of your graves, and bring you into the land of Israel. And ye shall know that I am the Lord, when I have opened your graves, O my people, and brought you up out of your graves, And shall put my spirit in you, and ye shall live, and I shall place you in your own land." (Ezek. 37:1-14.)

Knowing thus that immortal men shall dwell on the same earth that once was theirs; knowing that Israel shall inherit even the very parcels of land promised their fathers; and knowing that Christ our King shall reign personally upon the earth during the Millennium—this knowledge puts us in a position to understand the promises that exalted beings shall live and reign with their Lord during the coming blessed period of peace. "In mine own due time will I come upon the earth in judgment," the Lord says, "and my people shall be redeemed and shall reign with me on earth. For the great Millennium, of which I have spoken by the mouth of my servants, shall come." (D&C 43:29-30.) The Beloved John tells us that "Jesus Christ . . . hath made us [the faithful elders of his kingdom] kings and priests unto God and his Father." (Rev. 1:5-6.) And we might add, he hath made the faithful sisters of his kingdom queens and priestesses. And further: He hath "made us unto our God kings and priests: and we shall reign on the earth." (Rev. 5:10.) What is a king without a kingdom? Unless they are given dominion and power over an appointed kingdom, their reign will be shallow and powerless.

If righteous men come up in the resurrection to reign as kings, and if Christ our Lord is their King, then he, as the scriptures say, is a King of kings. In the same sense he becomes a Lord of lords, a Ruler of rulers, and a God of gods. (Rev. 19:16.) Truly, blessed is the Lord, and blessed also are all they who become one with him and who receive all that his Father hath. "And I saw thrones, and they sat upon them," our apocalyptic friend says of exalted men, "and judgment was given unto them: and I saw the souls of them that were beheaded for the witness of Jesus, and for the word of God, . . . and they lived and reigned with Christ a thousand years. . . . Blessed and holy is he that hath part in the first resurrection: on such the second death hath no power, but they shall be priests of God and of Christ, and shall reign with him a thousand years." (Rev. 20:4-6.) Of these things the Prophet Joseph Smith said: "Christ and the resurrected Saints will reign over the earth during the thousand years. They will not probably dwell upon the earth [in the sense of having a permanent residence here], but will visit it when they please, or when it is necessary to govern it." (*Teachings*, p. 268.) Earth's main inhabitants, as we are about to see, will be those who continue to come here from celestial realms to gain their bodies and to prepare themselves for immortal glory.

Chapter 52

MORTAL MAN AFTER THE SECOND COMING

Man: In What Form Is He Found?

What will be the nature of life in all its forms and varieties during the Millennium? Will man and all living things, in their infinite variety, remain as they are now? Are there changes that must take place in man, and in beasts, fowls, fishes, and creeping things, to enable them to dwell on the new earth and to breathe the air of the new heavens that will surround it? And with reference to man in particular, what kind of life will he live when Satan is bound and death and disease and sorrow as we know them are no more?

Our mortal experiences and our finite logic—devoid of divine guidance, and without revelation from on high—would lead us to assume that life has always been as it now is, and that all things will continue everlastingly as they now are. But such is as far from the fact as heaven is from hell. Neither the earth, nor man, nor life of all sorts and kinds, has always been as it now is. Mortality is but a slight and passing phase of existence, a shimmering moonbeam that shines for a moment in the darkness of our earthbound life; it is but a day in an endless eternity; something else came before, and an entirely different way of life will follow after.

Before we can even glimpse the nature of things millennial, we must know something about the great and eternal stages through which our planet has passed and will pass. This earth has not always been as it now is, and it will not long remain in its present state. It has changed in the past, and it will take on a new form in the future. Before we can understand the nature of man and his life on the new earth that is to be, we must know something about the phases of existence through which he may or can pass. He has not always been a benighted, corruptible mortal, subject to disease and death, nor will he always so remain.

We need not suppose, in our smug self-sufficiency, that we know all things about the human race or about the creation and stages of existence of the planet given of God as a home for his children. We can no more understand ourselves than we can comprehend that God who made us. We can no more envision how and in what manner the Lord created the earth, and how he changes it from one type and kind of sphere to another, than we can step forth and duplicate his omnipotent enterprises. But we do possess some slivers of eternal truth, and we have received certain basic truths about ourselves and the earth that enable us to understand the over-all scheme of things. It is this revealed knowledge that enables us to view millennial life in its proper perspective and relationship to all things.

This earth was created first spiritually. It was a spirit earth. Nothing then lived on its face, nor was it designed that anything should. Then came the physical creation, the paradisiacal creation, the creation of the earth in the Edenic day and before the fall of man. After the fall, the earth became telestial in nature; it fell from a terrestrial to a telestial state; it became a fit abode for mortal life. Such is the state in which it now is. When the millennial day dawns, the earth will be renewed and receive its paradisiacal glory; it will return to its Edenic state; it will be (as contrasted with its present state) a new heaven and a new earth. In the process of change the earth will be burned; it will dissolve; the elements will melt with fervent heat, and all things will become new. There will also be a short postmillennial period of which we know very little, and finally the earth will become a celestial sphere and will shine like the sun in the firmament.

In its present telestial state, wickedness prevails on its face and anyone can live here no matter what his life-style. When the earth returns to its terrestrial state, none will be able to live on its surface unless they abide at least a terrestrial law. Hence, every corruptible thing will be consumed when the earth is cleansed at the beginning of the Millennium. That is, all who are worldly, all who are carnal, sensual, and devilish, all who are living a telestial law will be destroyed. Finally, when the earth becomes a celestial sphere, none shall remain on its face except those who are living a celestial law. This earth will then become a celestial kingdom.

Man and all forms of life existed as spirit beings and entities before the foundations of this earth were laid. There were spirit men and spirit beasts, spirit fowls and spirit fishes, spirit plants and spirit trees. Every creeping thing, every herb and shrub, every amoeba and tadpole, every elephant and dinosaur—all things—existed as spirits, as spirit beings, before they were placed naturally upon the earth. Then natural, or earthly, or paradisiacal bodies were provided for spirit men and all forms of life. Our first parents and the original forms of life of every kind and specie were placed on earth in a paradisiacal state. In that state there was no procreation, no death, no mortality (as we know it), and no blood flowing in the veins of man or of the animal kingdom. Then came the fall, the effects of which passed upon all mankind and upon every form of life. Sorrow and disease and death entered the world. Man and all created things were able to procreate and reproduce their kind. Blood began to flow in the veins of man and beast. Their bodies underwent a change and they became mortal. Mortality is the state in which procreation abounds and death prevails. When mortals die, they live again as spirits, except that they do not return to the presence of God, but abide in a place appointed, where they await the day of their resurrection.

Some mortals have been translated. In this state they are not subject to sorrow or to disease or to death. No longer does blood (the life-giving element of our present mortality) flow in their veins. Procreation ceases. If they then had children, their offspring would be denied a mortal probation, which all worthy spirits must receive in due course. They have power to move and live in both a mortal and an unseen sphere. All translated beings undergo another change in their bodies when they gain full immortality. This change is the equivalent of a resurrection. All mortals, after death, are also resurrected. In the resurrected state they are immortal and eternal in nature, and those among them who are privileged to live in the family unit have spirit children. Millennial man will live in a state akin to translation. His body will be changed so that it is no longer subject to disease or death as we know it, although he will be changed in the twinkling of an eye to full immortality when he is a hundred years of age. He will, however, have children, and mortal life of a millennial kind will continue. We shall speak more particularly of all this shortly.

During the Millennium there will, of course, be two kinds of people on earth. There will be those who are mortal, and those who are immortal. There will be those who have been changed or quickened or transfigured or translated (words fail us to describe their state), and those who have gone through a second change, in the twinkling of an eye, so as to become eternal in nature. There will be those who are on probation, for whom earth life is a probationary estate, and who are thus working out their own salvation, and those who have already overcome the world and have entered into a fulness of eternal joy. There will be those who will yet die in the sense of being changed from their quickened state to a state of immortality, and those who, having previously died, are then living in a resurrected state. There will be those who are subject to the kings and priests who rule forever in the house of Israel, and those who, as kings and priests, exercise power and dominion in the everlasting kingdom of Him whose we are. There will be those who, as mortals, provide bodies for the spirit children of the Father, for the spirits whose right it is to come to earth and gain houses for their eternal spirits, and those who, as immortals (Abraham is one), are already begetting spirit children of their own. There will be those for whom the fulness of eternal glory is ahead, and those who, again like Abraham, have already entered into their exaltation and sit upon their thrones and are not angels but are gods forever and ever. We have heretofore summarized such things as we know about the immortal beings who shall dwell, from time to time, on earth during the Millennium. We shall now consider such things as have been revealed with reference to those who are born and who live here during the thousand years of plenty and peace.

Man: His Millennial State

We shall use the word *mortal* to describe those who live on earth during the Millennium and who are not resurrected. They will be mortal in the sense that they have the power of procreation and will beget children. "And the earth shall be given unto them for an inheritance," saith the Lord, "and they shall multiply and wax strong, and their children shall grow up without sin unto salvation." (D&C 45:58.) They are the ones of whom the Lord said: "They shall see the kingdom of God coming in power and great glory; . . . For behold, the Lord shall come, and his recompense shall be with him, and he shall reward every man, and the poor shall rejoice; And their generations"—their posterity, the seed of their bodies, the lives that come into being because of them, their children—"shall inherit the earth from generation to generation, forever and ever." (D&C 56:18-20.)

Men during the Millennium will be mortal because they will die—not as men die now, with the spirit leaving the body and the body returning to the dust whence it came, but they will die according to the pattern and system ordained to occur during that blessed period of the earth's temporal continuance. There will be no graves during the Millennium. Men's bodies will not see corruption, and their spirits will not go to a spirit world, there to await a future resurrection. Rather, "children shall grow up until they become old; old men shall die; but they shall not sleep in the dust, but they shall be changed in the twinkling of an eye." (D&C 63:51.) "In that day an infant shall not die until he is old; and his life shall be as the age of a tree; and when he dies he shall not sleep, that is to say in the earth, but shall be changed in the twinkling of an eye, and shall be caught up, and his rest shall be glorious." (D&C 101:30-31.) Such is the revealed word as it came to Joseph Smith. The same truths, as given to Isaiah, announce: "There shall be no more thence an infant of days, nor an old man that hath not filled his days: for the child shall die an hundred years old; but the sinner being an hundred years old shall be accursed." (Isa. 65:20.) Isaiah's description of life and death during the Millennium seems to preserve the concept that even then—even in that blessed day when Satan is bound and righteousness overflows—even then men are free to come out in open rebellion and, as sinners, suffer the fate reserved for the sons of perdition. Manifestly they, being accursed, would die the death with which we are familiar, for their resurrection is destined to be in that final day when those shall come forth "who shall remain filthy still." (D&C 88:102.)

There are no words in our language that accurately convey to our minds either the nature of man or the type of life he is destined to live during the Millennium. In that day, in process of time at least, the Lord has promised to restore "a pure language," so that all men may "call upon the name of the Lord, to serve him with one consent." (Zeph.

3:9.) For the present, however, conditions in that blessed day are so far outside the realm of our experience that we do not have the language at our command to describe them. Perhaps the best thing we can do is to describe the life and status of translated beings and to say that their life is closely akin to that of millennial man.

Enoch and his city were all translated and taken up into heaven without tasting death. So also were Moses and Elijah and Alma and many others of whom we have no record. Indeed the whole focus of life among the worthy saints from the day of Enoch to the day of Abraham was so to live that they would be caught up and receive an inheritance in that city whose builder and maker was God. All these were with Christ in his resurrection; that is, they received their resurrected and immortal bodies at that time. John the Revelator and the Three Nephites and others whose identity is unknown have been translated since the day of Christ. They are all carrying on their ministries of preaching and prophesying and will do so until the Second Coming, when they will receive their resurrected and immortal bodies. The Lord, for instance, promised John: "Thou shalt tarry until I come in my glory, and shalt prophesy before nations, kindreds, tongues and people." This ministry is among mortals on earth, but John has great powers that mortals do not possess. "I will make him as flaming fire and a ministering angel," the Lord promised, and "he shall minister for those who shall be heirs of salvation who dwell on the earth." (D&C 7:3-6.)

It is from the Book of Mormon account relative to the Three Nephites that we gain our greatest scriptural knowledge about translated beings. Jesus told them: "Ye shall never taste of death; but ye shall live to behold all the doings of the Father unto the children of men, even until all things shall be fulfilled according to the will of the Father, when I shall come in my glory with the powers of heaven. And ye shall never endure the pains of death; but when I shall come in my glory ye shall be changed in the twinkling of an eye from mortality to immortality; and then shall ye be blessed in the kingdom of my Father." Similarly, the faithful saints who are alive when the Lord comes, and who are caught up to meet him in the midst of the pillar of heaven, shall be quickened. Their bodies shall be changed from mortality as we know it to a millennial-type mortality, to the type of mortality possessed by translated beings. Those who are born during the Millennium will enjoy this same quickened state, and all of them, each in his order, will be changed in the twinkling of an eye to his resurrected and immortal state when he becomes one hundred years of age.

"And again, ye shall not have pain while ye shall dwell in the flesh," the Lord Jesus promised them, "neither sorrow save it be for the sins of the world." (3 Ne. 28:7-9.) Similarly, pain and sorrow, tears and weeping, and the anguish and sadness of our day—all these shall cease in the millennial day. Our revelation says simply: "And there shall be no sorrow because there is no death." (D&C 101:29.) Isaiah promised: "He will swallow up death in victory; and the Lord God will wipe away tears from off all faces." (Isa. 25:8.) And to Isaiah the Lord said: "Be ye glad and rejoice for ever in that which I create: for, behold, I create Jerusalem a rejoicing, and her people a joy. And I will rejoice in Jerusalem, and joy in my people: and the voice of weeping shall be no more heard in her, nor the voice of crying." (Isa. 65:18-19.) And from the pen of the Revelator we learn: "And God shall wipe away all tears from their eyes; and there shall be no more death, neither sorrow, nor crying, neither shall there be any more pain: for the former things are passed away." (Rev. 21:4.)

After summarizing many things that happened to the Three Nephites in the course of their ministry among the descendants of Lehi, Mormon said: "And they are as the angels of God, and if they shall pray unto the Father in the name of Jesus they can show themselves unto whatsoever man it seemeth them good." Then, in discussing whether they were mortal or immortal, Mormon gave this exposition: "I have inquired of the Lord, and he hath made it manifest unto me that there must needs be a change wrought upon their bodies, or else it needs be that they must taste of death." It is one thing to die and another to taste of death. All men shall die, but those who receive an instantaneous change from mortality to immortality do not taste of death. And so Mormon continues: "Therefore, that they might not taste of death there was a change wrought upon their bodies, that they might not suffer pain nor sorrow save it were for the sins of the world. Now this change was not equal to that which shall take place at the last day; but there was a change wrought upon them, insomuch that Satan could have no power over them, that he could not tempt them"—and surely this will be the case with men during the Millennium—"and they were sanctified in the flesh, that they were holy, and that the powers of the earth could not hold them. And in this state they were to remain until the judgment day of Christ; and at that day they were to receive a greater change, and to be received into the kingdom of the Father to go no more out, but to dwell with God eternally in the heavens." (3 Ne. 28:30-40.)

The Growing Glory of the Millennium

Our Blessed Lord will come at the appointed time. The great conference at Adam-ondi-Ahman will assemble to worship the King on schedule. There will be an exact moment when his foot first touches the Mount of Olives. He will stand on Mount Zion with the 144,000 high priests at a given point in time. Armageddon will spread its fire and horror and death when and as decreed in the divine timetable. The tares will be burned and the vineyard cleansed of corruption when the Lord Jesus returns. And there will be a day and an hour and a split second that marks the beginning of the Millennium. The seventh of the thousand-year periods can only commence at one single instant in time. As we have seen, many of the events incident to the Second Coming will take place during the close of the sixth seal and others after the opening of the seventh seal. And yet the formal beginning of the Millennium will take place at a fixed and determined and set moment. It cannot be hastened by righteousness nor delayed by wickedness. The old earth will die, and the new heaven and the new earth will be born at as exact an instant as is the case with the birth or death of any form of life. We speak thus so there will be no confusion or misunderstanding when we also say that the full glory and wonder of the millennial day will unfold gradually; that there will be wicked men on earth after the Millennium has commenced; and that the final glory and triumph of Israel will take place gradually after the Millennium itself has been ushered in. Let us now see what the holy word has to say relative to these things.

First, the cleansing of the vineyard, the burning of the earth, and the destruction of the wicked by fire shall all come to pass in a short time, in a single day, as it were. And then there will be but few men left on earth. "I will remove the iniquity of that land in one day," the Lord told Zechariah. (Zech. 3:9.) And in Isaiah we find numerous prophetic expressions phrased in that imagery in which he so excelled. "Many houses shall be desolate, even great and fair, without inhabitant." (Isa. 5:9.) Those sent to raise the warning voice to the world are to do so "until the cities be wasted without inhabitant, and the houses without man, and the land be utterly desolate, and the Lord have removed men far away." (Isa. 6:11-12.) In the day of the Lord's coming, "the light of Israel shall be for a fire, and his Holy One for a flame: and it shall burn and devour his thorns and his briers in one day; and shall consume the glory of his forest, and of his fruitful field, both soul and body: and they shall be as when a standardbearer fainteth. And the rest of the trees of his forest shall be few, that a child may write them." (Isa. 10:17-19.) "Behold, the Lord maketh the earth empty, and maketh it waste, and turneth it upside down, and scattereth abroad the inhabitants thereof. . . . The land shall be utterly emptied, and utterly spoiled. . . . Therefore hath the curse devoured the earth, and they that dwell therein are desolate: therefore the inhabitants of the earth are burned, and few men left." (Isa. 24:1-6.) Who can doubt that there will be but few men left at the beginning of the Millennium?

The prophetic word that sets forth what is to be during the Millennium speaks of "new heavens and a new earth, wherein dwelleth righteousness." (2 Pet. 3:13.) It says that every corruptible thing shall be consumed when the vineyard is burned. And yet the Prophet Joseph Smith said: "There will be wicked men on the earth during the thousand years. The heathen nations who will not come up to worship will be visited with the judgments of God, and must eventually be destroyed from the earth." (*Teachings*, pp. 268-69.) Taken together, these concepts mean that wickedness that is telestial in nature, wickedness that consists of living after the manner of the world, that wickedness which is carnal, sensual, and devilish by nature—all such shall cease. Those who so live will be destroyed. They are the tares of the earth.

But wickedness is a matter of degree, and even those who are upright and decent by worldly standards but who reject the gospel and do not worship the true God are considered to be wicked by gospel standards. They are "under the bondage of sin." They do not accept the message of the restoration and gain a remission of their sins in the waters of baptism. "And by this you may know the righteous from the wicked, and that the whole world groaneth under sin and darkness even now." (D&C 84:49-53.) Thus the divine word, as given by Zechariah, says that "it shall come to pass"—in the millennial day—"that every one that is left [after Armageddon] of all the nations which came against Jerusalem shall even go up from year to year to worship the King, the Lord of hosts, and to keep the feast of tabernacles. And it shall be, that whoso will not come up of all the families of the earth unto Jerusalem to worship the King, the Lord of hosts, even upon them shall be no rain. And if the family of Egypt go not up, and come not, that have no rain; there shall be the plague, wherewith the Lord will smite the heathen that come not to keep the feast of tabernacles. This shall be the punishment of Egypt, and the punishment of all nations that come not up to keep the feast of tabernacles." (Zech. 14:16-19.) Thus there will be many churches on earth when the Millennium begins. False worship will continue among those whose desires are good, "who are honorable men of the earth," but who have been "blinded by the craftiness of men." (D&C 76:75.) Plagues will rest upon them until they repent and believe the gospel or are destroyed, as the Prophet said. It follows that missionary work will continue into the Millennium until all who remain are converted. Then "the earth shall be full of the knowledge of the Lord, as the waters cover the sea." (Isa. 11:9.) Then every living soul on earth will belong to The Church of Jesus Christ of Latter-day Saints.

The Millennial Way of Life

With the concept before us of a growing and glorious Millennium in which every living soul will be converted and come into the sheepfold of Israel, we are ready to view with rejoicing the way of life that will prevail on the new earth. Thanks to our friend Isaiah, we have many pen pictures, inscribed with spiritual insight and poetic genius, that tell us of what is to be in that great day. We cannot do better than to pick from his seeric sayings a few of the highlights, adding a word here and there that has fallen from other prophetic lips.

As we have heretofore seen, the millennial day is one in which the Lord himself will dwell with men. This is a boon of inestimable worth. We can scarcely conceive of the glory and wonder of it all. The Lord Jesus Christ, the King of heaven, our Savior and Redeemer, the Lord God Omnipotent dwelling among men! In our day righteous men strive all their days to see a glimpse of his face and to hear a word from his lips, and few there be with faith sufficient to part the veil and see and hear for themselves. Isaiah himself was one of these. "In the year that king Uzziah died," Isaiah tells us, "I saw also the Lord sitting upon a throne, high and lifted up, and his train filled the temple. . . . Then said I, Woe is me! for I am undone; because I am a man of unclean lips, and I dwell in the midst of a people of unclean lips: for mine eyes have seen the King, the Lord of hosts." (Isa. 6:1, 5.) But in the millennial day the righteous shall see his face and hear his voice; they shall receive light and truth and wisdom as such fall from his lips. His throne shall be set up among them, and they shall hear him preach in their conferences. His voice shall again be heard on a mountain in Galilee as the Sermon on the Mount takes on a new and expanded meaning that none of us ever thought that it had. We shall hear again, in an upper room, as it were, the sermon on love and on the Second Comforter, and feel anew the power and spirit of the Intercessory Prayer. And to these will be added such other sermons as have never entered the heart of man as Jesus expounds the mysteries of eternity. Truly, truly did Isaiah promise: "For since the beginning of the world men have not heard, nor perceived by the ear, neither hath the eye seen, O God, beside thee, what he hath prepared for him that waiteth for him." (Isa. 64:4.)

In that day the Lord Jesus will hear the pleas of his people and answer them with blessings upon their heads. "And it shall come to pass, that before they call, I will answer; and while they are yet speaking, I will hear." (Isa. 65:24.) "And in that day whatsoever any man shall ask, it shall be given unto him." (D&C 101:27.) And "with righteousness" shall the Lord "judge the poor, and reprove with equity for the meek of the earth." Unjust judgments shall cease. That God who is no respecter of persons will weigh every man in the same balance, and all will be judged fairly and equitably. "And righteousness shall be the girdle of his loins, and faithfulness the girdle of his reins." (Isa.

11:4-5.) He shall be clothed in the robes of righteousness! He shall wear the garments of faithfulness! Even the girdles and robes and sandals and garments which cover his body and adorn his feet shall bear witness of his goodness and grace. "In that day shall there be [even] upon the bells of the horses, HOLINESS UNTO THE LORD; and the pots in the Lord's house shall be like the bowls before the altar. Yea, every pot in Jerusalem and in Judah shall be holiness unto the Lord of hosts." (Zech. 14:20-21.) What a glorious day it will be when Christ the Lord reigns and judges his people! How, oh how all the things shall be centered in the Lord and shall bear record of his goodness in that day!

In that day there will be peace on earth; wars will be unknown and unheard of; crime and evil and carnality will vanish away; and the Son of Righteousness shall replace evil with good, for he, as "The Prince of Peace," and the Creator of Righteousness, shall reign "upon the throne of David." (Isa. 9:6-7.) There will be no murders; even if an evil Cain should seek the life of a righteous Abel, he could not slay him. During the Millennium there will be no death because, for one reason, there will be no blood to spill upon the ground. There will be no robbings, nor stealing, nor kidnapping, nor treachery, nor immorality, nor lasciviousness, nor any manner of evil. What would our society be like if these sins and all their ilk were abolished, if there were no prisons for the criminals, no reformatories for the recalcitrant, no lands of banishment for the treasonous? Where there is peace, there is neither crime nor war. And in that day men "shall beat their swords into plowshares, and their spears into pruninghooks: nation shall not lift up sword against nation, neither shall they learn war any more." (Isa. 2:4.) "He maketh wars to cease unto the end of the earth." (Ps. 46:9.) "The whole earth is at rest, and is quiet: they break forth into singing." (Isa. 14:7.) "And the work of righteousness shall be peace; and the effect of righteousness quietness and assurance for ever. And my people," saith the Lord, "shall dwell in a peaceable habitation, and in sure dwellings, and in quiet resting places." (Isa. 32:17-18.)

In that day family units will be perfected according to the plans made in the heavens before the peopling of the earth. Celestial marriage in its highest and most glorious form will bind men and women together in eternal unions, and the resultant families will truly continue forever. One of the most provocative millennial passages forecasts the order of matrimony that will then prevail, saying: "And in that day"—the millennial day—"seven women shall take hold of one man, saying, We will eat our own bread, and wear our own apparel: only let us be called by thy name, to take away our reproach," the reproach of being without a husband, without children, without a family of their own. This shall come to pass after the destruction of the wicked, and it is one of many scriptural intimations that the generality of women are more spiritual than are most men. The inference is that far more women will abide the day of his coming than will be the case with men. And they, being clean and upright, and desiring family units and children and the exaltation that grows out of all these things, will turn to the marriage discipline of Abraham their father so they may be blessed like Sarah of old.

"In that day"—the millennial day, the day in which seven women shall cleave unto one man—"shall the branch of the Lord be beautiful and glorious." He is speaking of those who are left on the olive tree that is Israel. "And the fruit of the earth shall be excellent and comely for them that are escaped of Israel." Only those in Israel who abide the day and escape its burning desolations shall partake of the millennial glory. "And it shall come to pass, that he that is left in Zion, and he that remaineth in Jerusalem, shall be called holy, even every one that is written among the living in Jerusalem: When the Lord shall have washed away the filth of the daughters of Zion, and shall have purged the blood of Jerusalem from the midst thereof by the spirit of judgment, and by the spirit of burning." Only the righteous in Israel shall remain. They shall be holy, for they have not been consumed in the day of burning. "And the Lord will create upon every dwelling place of mount Zion, and upon her assemblies, a cloud and smoke by day, and the shining of a flaming fire by night: for upon all the glory shall be a defence. And there shall be a tabernacle for a shadow in the daytime from the heat, and for a place of refuge, and for a covert from storm and from rain." (Isa. 4:1-6.)

In that day "the eyes of the blind shall be opened, and the ears of the deaf shall be unstopped. Then shall the lame man leap as an hart, and the tongue of the dumb sing." (Isa. 35:5-6.) The miracles of Jesus when he once dwelt among men are but a pattern and a sample of what shall be when he comes again. "He shall feed his flock like a shepherd: he shall gather the lambs with his arm, and carry them in his bosom, and shall gently lead those that are with young." (Isa. 40:11.) The abundance of our Lord's teachings and of his tender care when he was once among us are but a small part of what shall be when he comes again to be with his people.

In that day Israel "shall build the old wastes, they shall raise up the former desolations, and they shall repair the waste cities, the desolations of many generations." (Isa. 61:4.) "And they shall build houses, and inhabit them; and they shall plant vineyards, and eat the fruit of them. They shall not build, and another inhabit; they shall not plant, and another eat: for as the days of a tree are the days of my people, and mine elect shall long enjoy the work of their hands," saith the Lord. "They shall not labour in vain, nor bring forth for trouble; for they are the seed of the blessed of the Lord, and their offspring with them." (Isa. 65:21-23.) Yea, thus saith the Lord unto his people Israel: "In that day shalt thou not be ashamed for all thy doings, wherein thou hast transgressed against me: for then I will take away out of the midst of thee them that rejoice in thy pride, and thou shalt no more be haughty because of my holy mountain." What a change it will be even for the chosen people when only the righteous among them remain in the millennial day. "I will also leave in the midst of thee an afflicted and poor people, and they shall trust in the name of the Lord." These are the poor of this world who are rich in faith. "The remnant of Israel"—those who abide the day—"shall not do iniquity, nor speak lies; neither shall a deceitful tongue be found in their mouth: for they shall feed and lie down, and none shall make them afraid." Their new state shall be far removed from what once prevailed among them.

"Sing, O daughter of Zion; shout, O Israel; be glad and rejoice with all the heart, O daughter of Jerusalem. The Lord hath taken away thy judgments, he hath cast out thine enemy: the king of Israel, even the Lord, is in the midst of thee: thou shalt not see evil any more. In that day it shall be said to Jerusalem, Fear thou not: and to Zion, let not thine hands be slack. The Lord thy God in the midst of thee is mighty; he will save, he will rejoice over thee with joy; he will rest in his love, he will joy over thee with singing." (Zeph. 3:11-17.) Such shall be the promised day, the day of the triumphant gathering of Israel, the day in which the Lord will make his people rulers over all the earth. This is the day in which "their enemies shall become a prey unto them." (D&C 133:28.) This is the day when the Lord will fulfill his promise: "For as the new heavens and the new earth, which I will make, shall remain before me, saith the Lord, so shall your seed and your name remain." (Isa. 66:22.)

We have spoken thus about mankind in general and Israel in particular in setting forth, briefly, their millennial states. But what about other forms of life? Will their life and birth and death be as it now is? Or will they too be changed when the new heavens and the new earth replace this old mortal sphere? It is written: "And he that sat upon the throne said, Behold, I make all things new." (Rev. 21:5.) All things includes all things, and although the scriptures do not speak with particularity about the millennial status of plants and herbs and trees and the vegetable kingdom, we do know that they will go back to that state of existence which was theirs in the Edenic day. But the revealed word does have somewhat to say about the animal kingdom. "In that day," for one thing, "the enmity of man, and the enmity of beasts, yea, the enmity of all flesh, shall cease from before my face," the Lord says. (D&C 101:26.) There will be no wild animals. The coyote will not stalk the deer, and the wolf will not kill the sheep, and all forms of life will be the friends and servants of men.

Isaiah gives us these poetically phrased particulars about animal life during the Millennium. "The wolf and the lamb shall feed together," he says, "and the lion shall eat straw like the bullock." Implicit in this pronouncement is the fact that man and all forms of life will be vegetarians in the coming day; the eating of meat will cease, because, for one thing, death as we know it ceases. There will be no shedding of blood, because man and beast are changed (quickened) and blood no longer flows in their veins. "And dust shall be the serpent's meat," meaning, as we suppose, that they shall no longer eat mice and vermin and animal life. "They shall not hurt nor destroy in all my holy mountain, saith the Lord." (Isa. 65:25.) And further: "The wolf also shall dwell with the lamb, and the leopard shall lie down with the kid; and the calf and the young lion and the fatling together; and a little child shall lead them. And the cow and the bear shall feed; their young ones shall lie down together: and the lion shall eat straw like the ox. And the suckling child shall play on the hole of the asp, and the weaned child shall put his hand on the cockatrice' den [adders' den]. They shall not hurt nor destroy in all my holy mountain." (Isa. 11:6-9.)

Having spoken thus about the millennial state of man and all forms of life, we are ready to consider the great and eternal purpose of the Millennium itself, which is to provide an atmosphere for a way of worship that will lead worthy spirits to eternal life in our Father's kingdom. We shall now turn to the glorious matter of that true and perfect worship destined to cover the earth after it has become a new earth and the wicked have been consumed.

Chapter 53

MILLENNIAL WORSHIP

Why There Is a Millennium

The purpose of the Millennium is to save souls. There can be no doubt about this. It is the Lord's work and his glory to bring to pass the immortality and eternal life of man. This is axiomatic among us. All that he does during all the endless ages of his everlasting existence is designed to save souls. There is no aim or end or purpose in anything that comes from God, except to further the salvation of his children.

The Almighty Elohim is the father of billions of spirit children, all of whom lived for millions (perhaps billions) of years in his eternal presence. He ordained and established the plan and system whereby they might advance and progress and become like him. That plan is the gospel of God, known to us as the gospel of Jesus Christ because he is the one chosen to put all of its terms and conditions into operation.

Our Eternal Father knows all of his spirit children, and in his infinite wisdom, he chooses the very time that each comes to earth to gain a mortal body and undergo a probationary experience. Everything the Lord does is for the benefit and blessing of his children. And each of those children is subjected to the very trials and experiences that Omniscient Wisdom knows he should have. Those who were entitled to an inheritance in Enoch's Zion came to earth in that day. Those whose spiritual stature qualified them for life among the Nephites during that nation's golden era found their inheritance with that people in ancient America. Apostles and prophets are sent to earth to do the work of apostles and prophets at the time and season when their particular talents are needed. All of the elders of Israel were foreordained and sent to earth in the house of Jacob to minister to their kinsmen and to the Gentiles. Indeed, spiritually endowed souls, in large measure, have been born in the house of Israel ever since the day of Father Jacob. We are here now in latter-day Israel, scattered in all the nations of the earth, because that is where the Lord wants us to be, and that is where we need to be for our own development, advancement, and salvation.

Millions of children, from Adamic times to our day, have died before they arrived at the age of accountability, and, because they were alive in Christ and had never died spiritually, they shall have eternal life. It will come to them through the atonement of Christ. They never were called upon to undergo and overcome the trials and temptations that almost overpower us. Billions of spirits will come to earth during the Millennium, when Satan is bound, when there is peace on earth, when there is no sorrow because there is no death, when they will not be confronted with the evil and carnality that face us. They will grow up without sin unto salvation. Thus saith the holy word.

Knowing this, we are obliged to conclude that a millennial inheritance is the kind and type of mortal life that billions of spirits are entitled to receive. Whatever the Lord does is right whether we understand his purposes or not. Without question there are many valiant souls now living who are worthy to receive a millennial birth, but who were sent to earth in this day of wickedness to be lights and guides to other men and to lead many of our Father's children to eternal life. But nonetheless, there will be billions of millennial mortals who will never be tested, as fully as we are, and who will go on to eternal life, as do little children, because an Almighty God in his infinite wisdom arranges that kind of a life for them. The Lord gives each of us what we need. And, we repeat, the whole millennial system has been ordained and established to save souls. There is no other reason for any of the Lord's dealings with his children. He wants them to gain salvation, and he does for them what he knows they need done, in each instance, to hasten them along the way to perfection. We must understand and believe these concepts if we are to envision properly the worship that will prevail on earth during the soon-to-be thousand years of peace and righteousness.

Why False Worship Shall Cease

Because the Millennium is designed to save souls, the whole system of worldly worship that now prevails on earth—in which there is no salvation—will come to an end. The worship of the beast and of his image and of every false god will cease. Because salvation comes only to those who worship the Father, in the name of the Son, by the power of the Holy Ghost, such is the sole and only kind of worship that will be found on earth when full millennial conditions prevail. The worship of other gods than the Lord will fade into the shadows of the past. No longer will men heap adoration upon idols, or pay homage to a spirit essence that fills the immensity of space, or reverence the laws and powers of nature as though they were God himself. No longer will they pray to supposed saints, pleading with them to mediate between them and the Lord.

Because salvation results from rigid adherence to principles of true religion, all forms of false religion will come to an end. False religions will die; heresies will cease; false doctrines will no longer be taught. Because there is and can be only one true Church and kingdom of God on earth, all the churches of men and of devils will go out of existence. The great and abominable church, whose founder and preserver is Lucifer, will be no more. Communism and its system of force and anarchy and compulsion will be overthrown. There is an eternal principle, as eternal and everlasting as God himself, that truth will prevail. And the millennial era is the time appointed for right to prevail and for truth to triumph.

Why, why will all this come to pass? Because neither the world, nor worldliness, nor false churches, nor false religions can lead men to salvation. And the Millennium is designed to save souls. And how, how will it be brought to pass? In two ways: by the destruction of the wicked as the Millennium dawns, and by the labors of the Lord's witnesses during the early years of that blessed era of peace. We have already spoken of both of these eventualities. The vineyard is to be burned; every corruptible thing will be consumed; the proud and all they that do wickedly shall be burned as stubble. The tares, even now, are being bound in bundles preparatory to the great day of burning. The great and abominable church shall soon fall, and its zealots will be destroyed by devouring fire. Then those who remain, of all sects, parties, and denominations, being the upright among men, will be converted to the gospel so that the prophetic word may be fulfilled which says: "For the earth shall be filled with the knowledge of the glory of the Lord, as the waters cover the sea." (Hab. 2:14.)

Looking forward to this great day, the scriptures speak of the blessings to be bestowed upon the saints and the curses that will come upon those who practice false religion and who worship gods other than the Lord. "The Lord reigneth"—it is the millennial day—"let the earth rejoice," saith the Psalmist. "A fire goeth before him, and burneth up his enemies round about." It is the promised day of burning. "The hills melted like wax at the presence of the Lord, at the presence of the Lord of the whole earth." This we have considered in connection with the new earth and the new heavens that are to be. "The heavens declare his righteousness, and all the people see his glory." Blessed be the righteous in that day. And: "Confounded be all they that serve graven images, that boast themselves of idols." (Ps. 97:1-7.) Graven images and idols—these are the signs and symbols of false religions. They identified false worship anciently in the literal sense, and they identify it today in either a literal or a figurative sense, as the case may be.

Isaiah uses a similar approach to the destruction of false worship both at the dawn of and during the Millennium. After speaking of the era of peace in which "nation shall not lift up sword against nation, neither shall they learn war any more," he says: "Their land is also full of idols; they worship the work of their own hands, that which their own fingers have made." Such shall be the state of the masses of men when the Lord comes. Isaiah says that "the fear of the Lord and the glory of his majesty shall smite" the wicked. "For the day of the Lord of Hosts soon cometh upon all nations, yea, upon every one; yea, upon the proud and lofty, and upon every one who is lifted up, and he shall be brought low. . . . And the loftiness of man shall be bowed down, and the haughtiness of men shall be made low; and the Lord alone shall be exalted in that day." All this, in principle, we have heretofore set forth. Now note: "And the idols he shall utterly abolish." False worship shall cease. It will happen in a day, as it were, where Babylon is concerned, but it will take a little longer where those religious systems of lesser evil are concerned.

And what of those who have believed in false systems of salvation? "They shall go into the holes of the rocks, and into the caves of the earth," saith Isaiah, "for the fear of the Lord shall come upon them and the glory of his majesty shall smite them, when he ariseth to shake terribly the earth." But back to the false systems of religion themselves: "In that day a man shall cast his idols of silver, and his idols of gold, which he hath made for himself to worship, to the moles and to the bats." (2 Ne. 12:8-20; Isa. 2:4-20.) Men shall no longer worship gods they themselves have made. It matters not whether they are carved from stone or cast in molds. It matters not whether they are graven with an artificer's tools or described in the creeds of an apostate Christendom. Truly this is what Jeremiah foresaw when he recorded that the converts to the restored gospel in the latter days would say: "Surely our fathers have inherited lies, vanity, and things wherein there is no profit. Shall a man make gods unto himself, and they are no gods?" (Jer. 16:19-20.)

Micah received virtually the same vision of the millennial era that came to Isaiah. After bearing record of the peace that will prevail when nations no longer learn war, Micah tells us of the worship that will then prevail on earth. "For all people will walk every one in the name of his god," he says, "and we will walk in the name of the Lord our God for ever and ever. In that day . . . the Lord shall reign over them in mount Zion from henceforth, even for ever." (Micah 4:5-7.) The Lord then told Micah what would happen to the religions of the world when the Millennium was ushered in. The word so revealed is of such import that Jesus quoted it to the Nephites with a few additional expressions. These are the words of Deity to Israel: "And I will cut off witchcrafts out of thy land, and thou shalt have no more soothsayers; thy graven images I will also cut off, and thy standing images out of the midst of thee, and thou shalt no more worship the works of thy hands; and I will pluck up thy groves out of the midst of thee; so will I destroy thy cities." False worship shall cease; false gods shall be no more; and even the places of false worship, be they groves or cathedrals, shall be plucked up. Religions that are not of God will find no adherents.

And what happens when men reject false worship and turn to the Lord? The Lord gives this answer: "And it shall come to pass that all lyings, and deceivings, and envyings, and strifes, and priestcrafts, and whoredoms, shall be done away." True religion always has caused and always will cause men to forsake all evil and cleave unto the good. But of those, even in the Millennium, who do not turn unto the Lord, Jesus says: "For it shall come to pass, saith the Father, that at that day whosoever will not repent and come unto my Beloved Son, them will I cut off from among my people, O house of Israel; and I will execute vengeance and fury upon them, even as upon the heathen, such as they have not heard." (3 Ne. 21:16-21; Micah 5:12-15.)

Why Satan Shall Be Bound

There is nothing that dramatizes better the difference between us men in this day, and our seed who will live in the millennial day, than the simple fact that then, in that day, Satan will be bound. Today he rages in the hearts of men; today he is the father of lies and the master of sin; today he fosters crime, promotes evil, and stirs up wars. His works, those in which his soul rejoices, are the works of the flesh. And "the works of the flesh," Paul tells us, are these: "Adultery, fornication, uncleanness, lasciviousness, idolatry, witchcraft, hatred, variance, emulations, wrath, strife, seditions, heresies, envyings, murders, drunkenness, revellings, and such like." (Gal. 5:19-21.) But in the coming day all this will cease. The Millennium will be a day of peace and righteousness. "And Satan shall be bound, that he shall have no place in the hearts of the children of men." (D&C 45:55.) Yea, "Satan shall be bound, [even] that old serpent, who is called the devil, and [he] shall not be loosed for the space of a thousand years." (D&C 88:110.)

When the Eternal Father announced his plan of salvation—a plan that called for a mortal probation for all his spirit children; a plan that required a Redeemer to ransom men from the coming fall; a plan that could only operate if mortal men had agency—when the Father announced his plan, when he chose Christ as the Redeemer and rejected Lucifer, then there was war in heaven. That war was a war of words; it was a conflict of ideologies; it was a rebellion against God and his laws. Lucifer sought to dethrone God, to sit himself on the divine throne, and to save all men without reference to their works. He sought to deny men their agency so they could not sin. He offered a mortal life of carnality and sensuality, of evil and crime and murder, following which all men would be saved. His offer was a philosophical impossibility. There must needs be an opposition in all things. Unless there are opposites, there is nothing. There can be no light without darkness, no heat without cold, no virtue without vice, no good without evil, no salvation without damnation.

And so, in the courts of heaven, the war of wars was waged. Christ and Michael and a mighty host of noble and great spirits preached the gospel of God and exhorted their brethren to follow the Father. Lucifer and his lieutenants preached another gospel, a gospel of fear and hate and lasciviousness and compulsion. They sought salvation without keeping the commandments, without overcoming the world, without choosing between opposites. And they "prevailed not; neither was their place found any more in heaven. And the great dragon was cast out, that old serpent, called the Devil, and Satan, which deceiveth the whole world: he was cast out into the earth, and his angels were cast out with him." And his legions, the legions of hell, are everywhere. They are "the third part of the stars of heaven," the one-third of the spirit children of the Father; and they were cast out of their heavenly home because of rebellion. And so the holy word says: "Woe to the inhabiters of the earth and of the sea! for the devil is come down unto you, having great wrath." And he goes forth "to make war" with all men and particularly with those who "keep the commandments of God, and have the testimony of Jesus Christ." (Rev. 12:4-17.) And the war that is now going on among men, the war between good and evil, is but a continuation of the war that began in heaven.

But wickedness shall soon be driven from the face of the earth. "For the great Millennium, of which I have spoken by the mouth of my servants, shall come. For Satan shall be bound, and when he is loosed again he shall only reign for a little season, and then cometh the end of the earth." (D&C 43:30-31.) John's graphic account of the binding of Satan comes to us in these words: "And I saw an angel come down from heaven, having the key of the bottomless pit and a great chain in his hand. And he laid hold on the dragon, that old serpent, which is the Devil, and Satan, and bound him a thousand years, and cast him into the bottomless pit, and shut him up, and set a seal upon him, that he should deceive the nations no more, till the thousand years should be fulfilled: and after that he must be loosed a little season." (Rev. 20:1-3.)

What does it mean to bind Satan? How is he bound? Our revelation says: "And in that day Satan shall not have power to tempt any man." (D&C 101:28.) Does this mean that power is withdrawn from Satan so that he can no longer entice men to do evil? Or does it mean that men no longer succumb to his enticements because their hearts are so set on righteousness that they refuse to forsake that which is good to follow him who is evil? Clearly it means the latter. Satan was not bound in heaven, in the very presence of God, in the sense that he was denied the right and power to preach false doctrine and to invite men to walk away from that God whose children they were; nay, in this sense, he could not have been bound in heaven, for even he must have his agency.

How, then, will Satan be bound during the Millennium? It will be by the righteousness of the people. Thus Nephi says: "The time cometh speedily that Satan shall have no more power over the hearts of the children of men; for the day soon cometh that all the proud and they who do wickedly shall be as stubble; and the day cometh that they must be burned." The destruction of the wicked sets the stage for millennial righteousness. When the wicked are burned, those who are left will not be susceptible to the promptings from beneath. "And the time cometh speedily that the righteous must be led up as calves of the stall, and the Holy

One of Israel must reign in dominion, and might, and power, and great glory." During the Millennium, when the Lord reigns, children will grow up in an environment of righteousness. No longer will the calves of Abraham's herds and the lambs of Jacob's flocks be lost in the deserts of sin; no longer will they forage for food by the wayside and drink water from stagnant pools; no longer will they be pulled down by the evils and designs of conspiring men. In the millennial day, in the household of faith, children will be brought up in the nurture and admonition of the Lord, as calves in the stall, as lambs in the sheepcote.

And in that day, the Holy One of Israel "gathereth his children from the four quarters of the earth; and he numbereth his sheep, and they know him; and there shall be one fold and one shepherd; and he shall feed his sheep, and in him they shall find pasture." It is, then, in this blessed millennial setting that the great proclamation about the binding of Satan is made. "And because of the righteousness of his people, Satan has no power; wherefore, he cannot be loosed for the space of many years; for he hath no power over the hearts of the people, for they dwell in righteousness, and the Holy One of Israel reigneth." (1 Ne. 22:15, 24-26.) Thus Satan is bound because he "shall have power over the hearts of the children of men no more, for a long time." (2 Ne. 30:18.) Thus the probationary nature of man's second estate is preserved even during the Millennium. It is not that men cannot sin, for the power is in them to do so—they have their agency—but it is that they do not sin because Satan is subject to them, and they are not enticed by his evil whisperings.

Come: Worship and Be Saved

The whole purpose of our mortal life is to gain salvation; it is to return to our Father as members of his family; it is to gain an inheritance of eternal life in his everlasting kingdom. Eternal life is made available through the atonement of Christ and comes to those who believe and obey. It is reserved for the faithful who accept the gospel and live its laws. It comes to those who worship the Father in spirit and in truth. Thus all the purposes of life either do or should center in the glorious gospel.

We rejoice in the gospel, which is the plan of salvation, as have our forebears in all past dispensations. We seek to believe the Lord's law in spite of the philosophies of men, as did the faithful before us. We strive to live in harmony with the divine will notwithstanding the enticements of the flesh, as did they of old. And both we and they have looked forward and do look forward to the glorious promised day when the philosophies of men and the enticements of the flesh will no longer lead men away from the truths of salvation. The blessings of the millennial day of peace and righteousness and perfect worship—out of which full salvation comes—have always been known to true believers. Let us dip into the scriptural treasure house and see how those of old felt about the day of millennial worship.

In the day when only a handful of men, the few that were called Israel, worshipped the true God, and when with a mortal eye no man could foresee that the heathen nations would become one with the chosen people, the Spirit caused the Psalmist to acclaim unto the Lord: "All the earth shall worship thee, and shall sing unto thee; they shall sing to thy name." (Ps. 66:4.) "All nations whom thou hast made shall come and worship before thee, O Lord; and shall glorify thy name." (Ps. 86:9.) "O sing unto the Lord a new song," cried the Psalmist, "sing unto the Lord, all the earth. . . . For he cometh to judge the earth: he shall judge the world with righteousness, and the people with his truth." (Ps. 96:1, 13.)

Isaiah looked forward to the day when "the earth shall be full of the knowledge of the Lord, as the waters cover the sea." (Isa. 11:9.) "And in that day"—the millennial day in which all men worship the Father in spirit and in truth—his people shall say: "Behold, God is my salvation; I will trust, and not be afraid: for the Lord JEHOVAH is my strength and my song; he also is become my salvation." How few there were who worshipped at Jehovah's altars in Isaiah's day! How glorious it will be when all men in all nations turn unto him! When they do, this shall be their promise: "With joy shall ye draw water out of the wells of salvation." They shall all drink the living waters. "And in that day shall ye say, Praise the Lord, call upon his name, declare his doings among the people, make mention that his name is exalted. Sing unto the Lord; for he hath done excellent things: this is known in all the earth. Cry out and shout, thou inhabitant of Zion: for great is the Holy One of Israel in the midst of thee." (Isa. 12:1-6.) In that day, the day when "the Lord God will cause righteousness and praise to spring forth before all the nations," each of those who drinks water from the wells of salvation will say: "I will greatly rejoice in the Lord, my soul shall be joyful in my God; for he hath clothed me with the garments of salvation, he hath covered me with the robe of righteousness, as a bridegroom decketh himself with ornaments, and as a bride adorneth herself with her jewels." (Isa. 61:10-11.)

Truly the millennial era is the age of salvation. It has been established by the Lord to save souls. Truly he shall send to earth during that blessed period those who earned the right, by faith and devotion in the premortal life, to receive their mortal probation in a day of peace and righteousness. It is not unreasonable to suppose that more people will live on earth during the millennial era than in all the six millenniums that preceded it combined. And all those who live on the new earth with its new heavens shall be saved. The Lord be praised for his goodness and grace.

THE NATURE OF MILLENNIAL WORSHIP

Worship in the Gospel Way

We say again—the concept must be engraved in our hearts with a pen of iron—we say again: The Millennium is designed to save souls. It has no other purpose. Accordingly, if salvation is gained by those who believe the gospel and obey its laws, and it is, then the gospel must continue during the Millennium. If the Church administers the gospel so as to make salvation possible, and it does, then the Church must endure through the Millennium. If the holy priesthood is the power to seal men up into eternal life, and it is, then this very delegation of power and authority from the Almighty must continue to bestow its beneficent blessings during the Millennium. The gospel in its everlasting fulness, including all of its saving powers, truths, and ordinances; The Church of Jesus Christ of Latter-day Saints, "the only true and living church upon the face of the whole earth" (D&C 1:30), the one place where salvation may be found; the Melchizedek Priesthood, which is "the power of an endless life" (Heb. 7:16), the power to create, to redeem, to save, and to exalt—these three (the gospel, the Church, and the priesthood) must and shall continue during the Millennium.

It may be that the name of the Church will change. Only in our dispensation has it borne its present name. It may become The Church of Jesus Christ of Millennial Saints. No matter, it will always be his church and his kingdom; it will always carry his name. It may be that we shall cease speaking of the Melchizedek Priesthood and call the Holy Order by its ancient name, "the Holy Priesthood, after the Order of the Son of God." (D&C 107:3.) No matter, it will be the same power and the same authority, and it will serve the same purpose. We see no reason why the name of the gospel should change. It was called the gospel of God in the preexistent eternities, meaning it was the plan of salvation ordained and established by God the Father to save his children. It is known to us as the gospel of Jesus Christ because our Lord put all of its terms and conditions into full operation when he bore the sins of men in Gethsemane and laid down his life on the Golgothan cross. No doubt the new dispensation will be called the millennial dispensation rather than the dispensation of the fullness of times, as at present. Again, no matter, for all dispensations have their own names, each indicative of the age of the earth involved, but all are dispensations of the same eternal gospel, given from God in heaven and received by man on earth. As the Adamic dispensation merged into the Enochian, so shall our dispensation grow into the great millennial outpouring of divine grace.

Gospel laws and gospel ordinances are eternal. They are the same in all ages and on all worlds. During the Millennium children will be named and blessed by the elders of the kingdom. When those of the rising generation arrive at the years of accountability, they will be baptized in water and of the Spirit by legal administrators appointed so to act. Priesthood will be conferred upon young and old, and they will be ordained to offices therein as the needs of the ministry and their own salvation require. At the appropriate time each person will receive his patriarchal blessing, we suppose from the natural patriarch who presides in his family, as it was in Adamic days and as it was when Jacob blessed his sons. The saints will receive their endowments in the temples of the Lord, and they will receive the blessings of celestial marriage at their holy altars. And all of the faithful will have their callings and elections made sure and will be sealed up unto that eternal life which will come to them when they reach the age of a tree. We see no reasons why the ordinances of administering to the sick or the dedication of graves should continue, for disease and death shall be no more.

Gospel doctrines also are eternal. The saving truths never vary. They too are the same in all ages and on all earths. And they center in and bear testimony of the Lord Jesus Christ and his infinite and eternal atonement. During the Millennium the sweetness of song and the voice of sermon will unite to testify of all things pertaining to Christ and his goodness and grace. Thus our revelations say that when the year of Christ's redeemed is come, when the millennial era dawns, his saints "shall mention the loving kindness of their Lord, and all that he has bestowed upon them according to his goodness, and according to his loving kindness, forever and ever." And when the graves are opened and the saints "come forth and stand on the right hand of the Lamb, when he shall stand upon Mount Zion, and upon the holy city, the New Jerusalem," then, saith the holy word, "they shall sing the song of the Lamb, day and night forever and ever." (D&C 133:52, 56.)

In song and in sermon, the glad tidings of salvation will be stated and restated. The sermons will be the mind and will and voice of the Lord, and the very power of God unto salvation itself, for they will be spoken by the power of the Holy Ghost. And as to the song of the Lamb, the Lord has revealed to us some at least of the words it contains, words of worship and wonder and beauty. John's account tells us the saints sang "a new song." In praising Christ it acclaims: "For thou wast slain, and hast redeemed us to God by thy blood out of every kindred, and tongue, and people, and nation; and hast made us unto our God kings and priests: and we shall reign on the earth." Then John "heard the voice of many angels, . . . and the number of them was ten thousand times ten thousand, and thousands of thousands; saying with a loud voice, Worthy is the Lamb that was slain to receive power, and riches, and wisdom, and strength, and honour, and glory, and blessing." After this the ancient apostle says: "And every creature which is in heaven, and on the earth, and under the earth, and such as are in the sea, and all that are in them, heard I saying, Blessing, and honour, and glory, and power, be unto him that sitteth upon the throne, and unto the Lamb for ever and ever." (Rev. 5:9-13.) Truly, in our present state we have no way to comprehend or feel the glory and majesty of the worship that will prevail during the Millennium.

The Day of Millennial Revelation

We have the fulness of the everlasting gospel, meaning that we have all that is needed to gain the fulness of salvation. We have every truth, doctrine, and principle, every rite, power, and ordinance—all that is needed—to gain exaltation in the highest heaven of the celestial world. But we do not know all things; there are doctrines in endless array of which we know next to nothing; indeed, there are more things in the darkness of the unknown than there are in the light of the known. We do not even know what the faithful knew in Enoch's Zion, nor among the Nephites when they dwelt in righteousness for generations. We do not know what is on the sealed portion of the plates from which the Book of Mormon came. Ours is a day for drinking milk; the day when we, as a people at least, can partake of the meat of the word is in the future.

That future is millennial. In that day, "all things shall become new," saith the Lord, "that my knowledge and glory may dwell upon all the earth. . . . Yea, verily I say unto you, in that day when the Lord shall come, he shall reveal all things—Things which have passed, and hidden things which no man knew, things of the earth, by which it was made, and the purpose and the end thereof—Things most precious, things that are above, and things that are beneath, things that are in the earth, and upon the earth, and in heaven." (D&C 101:25, 32-34.) As we ponder these heaven-sent words, we are led to exclaim: Thanks be to him who is the Way, the Truth, and the Life, who knows all things and who seeks to pour out his revelations, and all the knowledge of eternity, upon all who will receive them. Ere long the dark veil of ignorance and unbelief that covers the earth and blinds the minds of men shall be pierced. Light and truth will fall from heaven as does rain from the clouds above.

The knowledge of God, the knowledge of those Gods whom it is life eternal to know, shall be in every heart. No longer will theologians suppose that God is a spirit essence that fills immensity while he dwells in the human heart. No longer will philosophers pontificate about some great first cause that inexplicably brought order into a chaotic universe. No longer will Babylonish churches place crucifixes in the hands, or the images of Diana of the Ephesians, as it were, and no longer will they worship the works of their own hands in the great cathedrals of Christendom. The knowledge of God, the truth about God, the fact that he is a Holy Man, will come by revelation into every human heart. The knowledge of God will cover the earth.

All things are to be revealed in the millennial day. The sealed part of the Book of Mormon will come forth; the brass plates will be translated; the writings of Adam and Enoch and Noah and Abraham and prophets without number will be revealed. We shall learn a thousand times more about the earthly ministry of the Lord Jesus than we now know. We shall learn great mysteries of the kingdom that were not even known to those of old who walked and talked with the Eternal One. We shall learn the details of the creation and the origin of man and what fools mortals are to follow the fads of the evolving evolutionary nonsense that litters the textbooks of academia. Nothing in or on or over the earth will be withheld from human ken, for eventually man, if he is to be as his Maker, must know all things.

Hear in this connection these words of Nephi: In that day, "the earth shall be full of the knowledge of the Lord as the waters cover the sea. Wherefore, the things of all nations shall be made known; yea, all things shall be made known unto the children of men. There is nothing which is secret save it shall be revealed; there is no work of darkness save it shall be made manifest in the light; and there is nothing which is sealed upon the earth save it shall be loosed. Wherefore, all things which have been revealed unto the children of men shall at that day be revealed." (2 Ne. 30:15-18.) Surely man could not ask for more than this in the way of light and truth and knowledge, and yet expect to remain in the flesh as a mortal and be in process of working out his salvation. Surely this is the day in which the Lord shall fulfill the promise of holy writ that says: "God shall give unto you knowledge by his Holy Spirit, yea, by the unspeakable gift of the Holy Ghost, [knowledge] that has not been revealed since the world was until now; which our forefathers have awaited with anxious expectation to be revealed in the last times, which their minds were pointed to by the angels, as held in reserve for the fulness of their glory; a time to come in the which nothing shall be withheld, whether there be one God or many gods, they shall be manifest." (D&C 121:26-28.) That this outpouring of divine goodness has already commenced is not open to question. That it will continue, in far greater measure, after our Lord comes again, who can doubt?

The Day of the Second Comforter

There is a divine outpouring of heavenly grace and power that exceeds anything else known to men or angels. There is a Spirit-conferred gift that is greater than anything else of which the human mind can conceive. There is a spiritual endowment so wondrous and great, so beyond comprehension and understanding, so divine and godlike in its nature, that it cannot be described in words. It can only be felt by the power of the Spirit. Those only who are the peers of the prophets and who mingle with seers on equal terms; those only who like Isaiah and Ezekiel and John and Paul have laid their all on the altar and have risen above every carnal desire; those only who are in harmony with the Lord and his Spirit and who keep his commandments as they are kept by the angels of God in heaven—they alone can receive this gift. It is called the Second Comforter.

Our blessed Lord—alone with the Twelve in the upper room a few hours before he went to Gethsemane, where great gouts of blood would drop from every pore as he bore the sins of all men; and a few hours before, on the cross of Calvary, he would cry, "It is finished," and permit his spirit to leave the body—our blessed Lord gave his beloved friends this promise: "I will not leave you comfortless: I will come to you. Yet a little while, and the world seeth me no more; but ye see me: because I live, ye shall live also." Christ after his death will come to them. They will see him, and he will comfort them. Yea, they will both see him and feel the nail marks in his hands and in his feet and thrust their hands into his riven side. He will eat before them, and their sorrow will be turned into joy. And because of his glorious rising from the Arimathean's tomb, they too shall conquer death and break the shackles of the grave.

"At that day ye shall know that I am in my Father, and ye in me, and I in you." They will be one with him as he is one with his Father. "He that hath my commandments, and keepeth them, he it is that loveth me: and he that loveth me shall be loved of my Father, and I will love him, and will manifest myself to him." The promise is not theirs alone—the Twelve are but the pattern; all that they receive will come also to every faithful person who abides the law that entitles him to receive the same gifts and blessings. Jesus, after his death and resurrection, will manifest himself to all who have faith enough to rend the veil and see their Lord.

Jesus was then asked: "Lord, how is it that thou wilt

manifest thyself unto us, and not unto the world?" His reply: "If a man love me, he will keep my words: and my Father will love him, and we will come unto him, and make our abode with him." (John 14:18-23.) Not only will the Lord Jesus appear to the faithful, but he, in his goodness and grace, will also manifest the Father. Mortal man will see the Father and the Son. And that there will be no doubt as to the meaning of our Lord's words, it is written in our revelations: "John 14:23—The appearing of the Father and the Son, in that verse, is a personal appearance; and the idea that the Father and the Son dwell in a man's heart is an old sectarian notion, and is false." (D&C 130:3.)

There are, of course, two Comforters. The Holy Ghost is the Comforter offered the saints in connection with baptism. He is a revelator and a sanctifier; he is the Holy Spirit. The gift of the Holy Ghost is the right to the constant companionship of this member of the Godhead based on faithfulness. "Now what is this other Comforter?" the Prophet Joseph Smith asked. His answer: "It is no more nor less than the Lord Jesus Christ Himself; and this is the sum and substance of the whole matter; that when any man obtains this last Comforter, he will have the personage of Jesus Christ to attend him, or appear unto him from time to time, and even He will manifest the Father unto him, and they will take up their abode with him, and the visions of the heavens will be opened unto him, and the Lord will teach him face to face, and he may have a perfect knowledge of the mysteries of the Kingdom of God; and this is the state and place the ancient Saints arrived at when they had such glorious visions—Isaiah, Ezekiel, John upon the Isle of Patmos, St. Paul in the three heavens, and all the Saints who held communion with the general assembly and Church of the Firstborn." (*Teachings*, pp. 150-51.)

Those who receive the Second Comforter shall see the Lord. He will attend them, appear to them from time to time, and teach them face to face. It was so with the ancient Twelve after Jesus rose from the dead; it will be so with all who attain like spiritual heights, for God is no respecter of persons. Obedience to the same laws always brings the same blessings. Thus the divine word acclaims: "Verily, thus saith the Lord: It shall come to pass that every soul who forsaketh his sins and cometh unto me, and calleth on my name, and obeyeth my voice, and keepeth my commandments, shall see my face and know that I am." (D&C 93:1.)

Those who receive the Second Comforter see the visions of eternity and have a perfect knowledge of the mysteries of the kingdom. "And to them will I reveal all mysteries, yea, all the hidden mysteries of my kingdom from days of old," saith the Lord, "and for ages to come, will I make known unto them the good pleasure of my will concerning all things pertaining to my kingdom. Yea, even the wonders of eternity shall they know, and things to come will I show them, even the things of many generations. And their wisdom shall be great, and their understanding reach to heaven; and before them the wisdom of the wise shall perish, and the understanding of the prudent shall come to naught. For by my Spirit will I enlighten them, and by my power will I make known unto them the secrets of my will—yea, even those things which eye has not seen, nor ear heard, nor yet entered into the heart of man." (D&C 76:7-10.)

Among those who received the Second Comforter are the three Nephites, whom we have been using as a pattern and type of what men will be like in the Millennium. These three American apostles "were caught up into heaven, and saw and heard unspeakable things. And it was forbidden them that they should utter; neither was it given unto them power that they could utter the things which they saw and heard; and whether they were in the body or out of the body, they could not tell; for it did seem unto them like a transfiguration of them, that they were changed from this body of flesh into an immortal state, that they could behold the things of God." (3 Ne. 28:13-15.)

Now, having in mind these concepts about the Second Comforter, and knowing that all those who so obtain have their callings and elections made sure, let us catch the vision, if we can, of one of the great prophetic utterances of Jeremiah. "Behold, the days come, saith the Lord"—and we shall soon show that the days involved are millennial—"that I will make a new covenant with the house of Israel, and with the house of Judah." Hear it and mark it well: it will be a new covenant, a new and an everlasting covenant; it will be the fulness of the everlasting gospel, not in name only, but in fact and in deed, in active operation in the lives of men. It will be "not according to the covenant that I made with their fathers in the day that I took them by the hand to bring them out of the land of Egypt; which my covenant they brake, although I was an husband unto them, saith the Lord." When the Lord brought Israel out of Egypt he offered them the fulness of the gospel. Moses held the Melchizedek Priesthood, and his people could have lived the higher gospel law had they chosen to do so. But they broke not only the gospel covenant but also the Mosaic or lesser covenant, at least in large measure.

"But this shall be the covenant that I will make with the house of Israel; after those days, saith the Lord, I will put my law in their inward parts, and write it in their hearts; and will be their God, and they shall be my people." There will be a day when latter-day Israel will serve the Lord with all their hearts and make themselves worthy of the fulness of his glory. "And they shall teach no more every man his neighbour, and every man his brother, saying, Know the Lord: for they shall all know me, from the least of them unto the greatest of them, saith the Lord: for I will forgive their iniquity, and I will remember their sin no more." (Jer. 31:31-34.)

Joseph Smith tells us that Jeremiah's prophecy will be fulfilled during the Millennium. The Prophet speaks of making one's calling and election sure and of the sealing power whereby "we may be sealed up unto the day of redemption." Then he says: "This principle ought (in its proper place) to be taught, for God hath not revealed anything to Joseph, but what He will make known unto the Twelve, and even the least Saint may know all things as fast as he is able to bear them, for the day must come when no man need say to his neighbor, Know ye the Lord; for all shall know Him (who remain) from the least to the greatest." These are the very words of Jeremiah's prophecy; and they will find their complete fulfillment among those "who remain," those who abide the day, those who gain an inheritance on the new earth when it receives its paradisiacal glory again. "How is this to be done?" the Prophet asks. How shall men come to know the Lord and understand all the hidden mysteries of his kingdom without a teacher? His answer: "It is to be done by this sealing power, and the other Comforter spoken of, which will be manifest by revelation." (*Teachings*, p. 149.)

Men will know God in the millennial day because they see him. He will teach them face to face. They will know the mysteries of his kingdom because they are caught up to the third heaven, as was Paul. They will receive the Second Comforter. The millennial day is the day of the Second Comforter, and whereas but few have been blessed with this divine association in times past, great hosts will be so blessed in times to come.

What, then, will be the nature of worship during the Millennium? It will be pure and perfect, and through it men will become inheritors of eternal life. And in this connection, be it known that it is the privilege of the saints today to separate themselves from the world and to receive millennial blessings in their lives. And any person who today abides the laws that will be kept during the Millennium will receive, here and now, the spirit and blessings of the Millennium in his life, even though he is surrounded by a world of sin and evil. And so we say, in the language of Joseph Smith as he finished the record of the vision of the three degrees of glory: "Great and marvelous are the works of the Lord, and the mysteries of his kingdom which he showed unto us, which surpass all understanding in glory, and in might, and in dominion; Which he commanded us we should not write while we were yet in the Spirit, and are not lawful for man to utter; Neither is man capable to make them known, for they are only to be seen and understood by the power of the Holy Spirit, which God bestows on those who love him, and purify themselves before him; To whom he grants this privilege of seeing and knowing for themselves; That through the power and manifestation of the Spirit, while in the flesh, they may be able to bear his presence in the world of glory. And to God and the Lamb be glory, and honor, and dominion forever and ever. Amen." (D&C 76:114-119.)

WATCH AND BE READY

The Watchmen on Mount Ephraim

Come we now to the climax of all our stumbling and faltering words of exposition, and of exhortation, and of testimony. Come we now to the reason we have written, in weakness and in simplicity, this work. Come we now to the great object and purpose that has led us to expound so many divine doctrines, to proclaim so fervently the reality of the mighty restoration, and to testify with such unbounded zeal of the goodness and grace of that Lord who will soon descend from heaven with the shout of the archangel. That object and purpose is two-pronged:

1. It is to persuade men to believe in the Lord Jesus Christ, who when he first came worked out the infinite and eternal atonement and brought life and immortality to light through the gospel, and who shall soon come again in great glory and with wondrous power to complete the salvation of men and to live and reign on earth with the righteous for a thousand years.

2. It is to encourage those who believe so to live that, whether in life or in death, they shall abide the day of his coming and qualify to be with him forever.

And so we now say to all men everywhere, to men of all sects, parties, and denominations, but more particularly to those who believe: Hear ye the words of the watchmen, and be ye ready for that which is soon to be. "For there shall be a day"—and as the Lord lives, that day is now—"that the watchmen upon the mount Ephraim shall cry, Arise ye, and let us go up to Zion unto the Lord our God." (Jer. 31:6.) Go ye, go ye up to Zion; find refuge in one of her stakes, and be ye one with those who are pure in heart.

The Lord has prepared a feast of good things for all who come to Zion. The word has gone forth: "Prepare the table, watch in the watchtower, eat, drink." (Isa. 21:5.) The table is now loaded with meat and drink. All men are invited to come and feast on the good word of God and to drink of the waters of life, while the watchman in the watchtower stands ready to warn them of the desolations and plagues and sorrows of the last days. The time of restitution has arrived, the fulness of the everlasting gospel is once again on earth, the Book of Mormon bears its witness of Joseph Smith and of Jesus Christ and of the setting up anew of the Church and kingdom of God on earth. Angelic ministrants have conferred priesthood and keys upon men; Elijah and Elias and Moses and many prophets have restored their keys and powers; the mountain where is the Lord's house is now known in all the earth. The Church of Jesus Christ of Latter-day Saints, which administers that gospel whereby salvation comes, is now going forth, "clear as the moon, and fair as the sun, and terrible as an army with banners." (D&C 5:14.) The gospel is now being preached in one nation after another as a witness unto all people so that the end may come at the appointed time. From the spiritual standpoint, all things are in process of fulfillment so that the Lord may come at the time of his choosing.

It is in this setting that the Lord says: "Go, set a watchman, let him declare what he seeth." Let him warn the saints and the world of the wars and desolations that are to be. Let him cry repentance and invite all men to come unto Christ and be saved. Let him proclaim the everlasting gospel to the world. Let him invite men to flee from the abomination of desolation to be poured out upon the wicked in the last days. One of his cries, soon to come forth, will announce: "Babylon is fallen, is fallen."

Let every man find a watchman that he may be warned of the dangers ahead. Let him ask: "Watchman, what of the night?" And the watchman will say: "The morning cometh, and also the night: if ye will enquire, enquire ye: return, come." (Isa. 21:6, 9, 11-12.) The morning breaks, the shadows flee. Those who walk in the light of the gospel are no longer in darkness. But the night also cometh for those who turn from the light. Let all men seek light and prepare for the Second Coming. Let them inquire: Where is the word that was promised to come forth by angelic ministration when the hour of the Lord's judgment was nigh? Let them return to the ancient sheepfold; let them come to Zion, there to worship the Lord our God. Let the watchmen on Mount Ephraim raise the warning voice and let the honest in heart among all people flee to Zion, for the day of desolation is upon us.

Warnings from the Chief Watchman

Jesus himself is more pointed and express in commanding men to live righteously in order to abide the day of his Second Coming than are any of his servants. He, as the Chief Watchman on the towers of Israel, tells us in plain and powerful phrases what our fate will be if we fail to prepare for that dread day, and also of the blessings that await us if we make ourselves ready. His words abound on almost every subject throughout this work. Here we shall consider those that constitute the express commands to watch, pray, and be ready for the coming day.

On Olivet, after giving the parable of the fig tree, after saying no one would know the day or the hour of his coming, after comparing his return to the flood that swept men to a watery grave in the day of Noah, Jesus said: "Then shall be fulfilled that which is written"—he is alluding to some scripture lost to us—"that in the last days, two shall be in the field, the one shall be taken, and the other left; two shall be grinding at the mill, the one shall be taken, and the other left; and what I say unto one, I say unto all men; watch, therefore, for you know not at what hour your Lord doth come." (JS-M 1:44-46.) These words can be used in a dual way. They can be applied to the destruction of the wicked in the day of burning, when only the righteous abide the day, or they can be applied to the gathering of the remainder of the elect by the angels, when they are caught up to meet their Lord, with those who are unworthy of such a quickening being left on earth. Luke makes this latter application to words of the same meaning and then explains: "This he [Jesus] spake, signifying the gathering of his saints; and of angels descending and gathering the remainder unto them; the one from the bed, the other from the grinding, and the other from the field, whithersoever he listeth. For verily there shall be new heavens, and a new earth, wherein dwelleth righteousness. And there shall be no unclean thing; for the earth becoming old, even as a garment, having waxed in corruption, wherefore it vanisheth away, and the footstool remaineth sanctified, cleansed from all sin." (JST, Luke 17:38-40.) No matter which usage is made of the teaching involved, the conclusion is the same: watch, be ready, be worthy; there is safety in no other course.

Then Jesus, continuing the Olivet Discourse, said: "But know this, if the good man of the house had known in what watch the thief would come, he would have watched, and would not have suffered his house to have been broken up, but would have been ready. Therefore be ye also ready, for in such an hour as ye think not, the Son of Man cometh." This illustration is one of great force and power, and it takes on new and deeper meaning as wickedness, including burglary and robbery and stealing, all increase as the day of his coming nears.

Our Lord next gives another illustration with a dual application. It can refer to self-appointed servants (ministers and priests) who serve in an apostate Christendom in the last days, and it can also apply to true ministers in the day of restoration who do not walk as becometh men of Christ. "Who, then, is a faithful and wise servant," he asks, "whom his lord hath made ruler over his household, to give them meat in due season?" The Lord's ministers are appointed to feed the flock of God. "Blessed is that servant whom his lord, when he cometh, shall find so doing; and verily I say unto you, he shall make him ruler over all his goods." In the true sense this could only apply to the elders in latter-day Israel who, in fact, are the only legal administrators on earth, whose authority is traced to the Lord, and whose power and authority come in full measure from him. "But if that evil servant shall say in his heart: My lord delayeth his coming, and shall begin to smite his fellow-servants, and to eat and drink with the drunken, The lord of that servant shall come in a day when he looketh not for him, and in an hour that he is not aware of, and shall cut him asunder, and shall appoint him his portion with the hypocrites; there shall be weeping and gnashing of teeth. And thus cometh the end of the wicked, according to the prophecy of Moses, saying: They shall be cut off from among the people; but the end of the earth is not yet, but by and by." (JS-M 1:47-55.)

Mark alone of our Gospel authors preserves for us these blessed words of counsel, counsel that has double the meaning in this dispensation that it had when spoken some two thousand years ago: "Take ye heed, watch and pray: for ye know not when the time is." How true this is, even today, when we can put almost all of the signs of the times into a reasonably certain chronological order, and when we know that nearly all of them have already been shown forth. "For the Son of man is as a man taking a far journey, who left his house, and gave authority to his servants, and to every man his work, and commanded the porter to watch. Watch ye therefore: for ye know not when the master of the house cometh, at even, or at midnight, or at the cockcrowing, or in the morning: Lest coming suddenly he find you sleeping. And what I say unto you I say unto all, Watch." (Mark 13:33-37.)

As to the world, almost all who dwell therein are asleep. They know not that the promised signs are unfolding on earth and in heaven and are easily discerned by the faithful. They know not that the times of restitution have commenced that the times of refreshing may come. They know not that the Book of Mormon has come forth, according to the ancient promises, and that the everlasting gospel in all its glorious fulness is once more on earth. They know not that the Lord has sent his messenger to prepare the way before his face and that even now voices of legal administrators are crying: Behold, and lo, the Bridegroom cometh; go ye out to meet him. And as to the Church, many in it are drowsy and some sleep. The eyes of many of the saints are heavy with the sleep of the world; long hours of past vigilance have caused them to suppose that the Lord delayeth his coming, and they find it easy to eat and drink with the wicked and to live after the manner of carnal men. They are not awake and alert, watching at even, and at midnight, and at cock-crowing, and in the morning.

Luke alone of our Gospel authors records for our guidance and enlightenment these words directed to all disciples, but more especially to those of us who live at this time when the hour of our Lord's coming is nigh: "Let my disciples therefore take heed to themselves, lest at any time their hearts be overcharged with surfeiting, and drunkenness, and cares of this life, and that day come upon them unawares." Let it come upon the world unawares, as it will, but the saints of God, the children of light, those who know the signs of the times, those who have the gift of the Holy Ghost, God forbid that it take them unawares! "For as a snare shall it come on all them who dwell on the face of the whole earth." The wicked will be caught in the snare and shall not escape; the righteous will be assembled in holy places awaiting the hour when they shall be caught up to meet the Lord in the air. "And what I say unto one, I say unto all, Watch ye therefore, and pray always, and keep my commandments, that ye may be counted worthy to escape all these things which shall come to pass, and to stand before the Son of man when he shall come clothed in the glory of his Father." (JST, Luke 21:34-36.)

So speaks the Lord Jesus to the members of his Church, his Church in all ages, but particularly in these last days when the end is drawing nigh. All men are invited to forsake the world and come into the true kingdom. But the warning is to Church members, to the saints of the Most High, to the elect of God who have made covenant in the waters of baptism to serve their Lord with all their strength. To them, and in a general sense to all men, the Lord's call is: Let not drunkenness lead you to destruction. True saints are sober, reflective, in control of their faculties. Drunkenness is of the devil. Cease from surfeiting. Be not intemperate in indulging in food and drink. Avoid gluttony and winebibbing. Flee from all these things lest your hearts be set on carnal rather than spiritual things. Be not overcome by the cares of this life. It is not temporal pursuits, business dealings, civil and political positions, educational attainments, and such like things, that really matter in life. The cares of this life so often keep even the saints from preparing for the rewards of the life to come.

Watch: in Life or in Death

None of us know whether we will be alive when the Lord comes or not. Life hangs on a thread, and death is only a breath away. Nor does it matter whether we meet the Lord in life or in death if we have watched for his coming and are ready for the meeting. "I testify . . . that the coming of the Son of Man is nigh, even at your doors," the Prophet Joseph Smith said. "If our souls and our bodies are not looking forth for the coming of the Son of Man; and after we are dead, if we are not looking forth, we shall be among those who are calling for the rocks to fall upon them." (*Teachings*, p. 160.) In life or in death it is the same.

If we are prepared to meet him in life, we will be prepared to meet him in death. Hence the call of all the prophets to the saints in their days, no matter what age was involved, has been: Be ye ready now; prepare to meet thy God as though he would come in whatever dispensation is involved.

Echoing the feelings and sentiments of their Lord and writing as guided by the Holy Spirit, they of old counseled the saints in their day (and the saints in ours!) along these lines: Peter, the chief apostle, said: "Gird up the loins of your mind, be sober, and hope to the end for the grace that is to be brought unto you at the revelation of Jesus Christ." (1 Pet. 1:13.) Also: "The end of all things is at hand: be ye therefore sober, and watch unto prayer." (1 Pet. 4:7.) And yet again: "Seeing then that all these things shall be dissolved"—when the Lord comes—"what manner of persons ought ye to be in all holy conversation and godliness, looking for and hasting unto the coming of the day of God, wherein the heavens being on fire shall be dissolved, and the elements shall melt with fervent heat?" His answer: "We, according to his promise, look for new heavens and a new earth, wherein dwelleth righteousness. Wherefore, beloved, seeing that ye look for such things, be diligent that ye may be found of him in peace, without spot, and blameless." (2 Pet. 3:11-14.)

James gives us this counsel: "Be patient therefore, brethren, unto the coming of the Lord. Behold, the husbandman waiteth for the precious fruit of the earth, and hath long patience for it, until he receive the early and latter rain. Be ye also patient; stablish your hearts: for the coming of the Lord draweth nigh. Grudge not one against another, brethren, lest ye be condemned: behold, the judge standeth before the door." (James 5:7-9.) And from Paul we take these words: "Let us not sleep, as do others; but let us watch and be sober." He is speaking to the saints. "For they that sleep sleep in the night; and they that be drunken are drunken in the night. But let us, who are of the day, be sober, putting on the breastplate of faith and love; and for an helmet, the hope of salvation." (1 Thes. 5:6-8.)

In all ages and as part of all dispensations the divine word is the same. In our day, as the end draws near, the Lord says: "Be faithful, praying always, having your lamps trimmed and burning, and oil with you, that you may be ready at the coming of the Bridegroom—For behold, verily, verily, I say unto you, that I come quickly." (D&C 33:17-18.) "Abide ye in the liberty wherewith ye are made free; entangle not yourselves in sin, but let your hands be clean, until the Lord comes." (D&C 88:86.) "The coming of the Lord draweth nigh, and it overtaketh the world as a thief in the night—Therefore, gird up your loins, that you may be the children of light, and that day shall not overtake you as a thief." (D&C 106:4-5.) "Go ye out from Babylon. Be ye clean that bear the vessels of the Lord. Call your solemn assemblies, and speak often one to another. And let every man call upon the name of the Lord. . . . Awake and arise and go forth to meet the Bridegroom; behold and lo, the Bridegroom cometh; go ye out to meet him. Prepare yourselves for the great day of the Lord. Watch, therefore, for ye know neither the day nor the hour." (D&C 133:5-6, 10-11.)

"Behold, I come as a thief. Blessed is he that watcheth, and keepeth his garments." (Rev. 16:15.) He that hath ears to hear, let him hear.

Chapter 56

CELESTIAL REST AND GLORY

The Celestial Earth

After the Millennium—what? Is this great day when there shall be peace on earth and goodwill in the hearts of men—is it an end in itself? Is this the day of rest and righteousness, when there is neither sorrow, disease, nor death—is it the *summum bonum* of all things? When Israel triumphs and wickedness ceases and the Lord Jehovah lives and reigns on earth—will we then reach the great end and goal toward which all things point? Or is the millennial era but a way and a means to prepare most of the spirit hosts of an Almighty Elohim for even greater heights of joy and peace, of glory and exaltation?

We have in this work, if we may borrow a concept from Isaiah, set forth "the word of the Lord . . . precept . . . upon precept, precept upon precept; line upon line, line upon line; here a little, and there a little." Step by step, point by point, doctrine by doctrine, "with stammering lips" and a faltering "tongue," we have built a house for the Millennial Messiah, as it were. In a dark and benighted world where the "tables" of doctrine "are full of vomit and filthiness, so that there is no place clean," we have sought to set forth what the Lord has revealed about his second coming and his reign in glory on the paradisiacal earth. Much that we have said is the milk of the word, but some portions have been meat and can be understood only by those "that are weaned from the milk, and drawn from the breasts." (Isa. 28:8-13.)

But all that we have said, and all that we might say if our insight were greater and our understanding more expanded, all our words are but an attempt to show the way to the eternal destiny far greater than anything millennial. The Millennium is simply a means to an end; it is that portion of the earth's temporal continuance during which billions of our Father's children will so live as to gain eternal life. Out of the millennial era will come, without question, more saved souls than will result from all the rest of the ages combined. And after the Millennium will come celestial rest and glory.

This earth is destined to be a celestial sphere. It is now in a telestial state and will return to its Edenic or terrestrial state during the Millennium. Its final destiny, in John's language, is to be "a sea of glass like unto crystal" (Rev. 4:6), which our revelation identifies as "the earth, in its sanctified, immortal, and eternal state." (D&C 77:1.) The inspired word also says: "The angels do not reside on a planet like this earth; but they reside in the presence of God, on a globe like a sea of glass and fire. . . . The place where God resides is a great Urim and Thummim. This earth, in its sanctified and immortal state, will be made like unto crystal and will be a Urim and Thummim to the inhabitants who dwell thereon." (D&C 130:6-9.)

During the Millennium, Satan is bound. Because of the righteousness of the people, he has no power over them. "And when the thousand years are expired," John tells us, "Satan shall be loosed out of his prison." (Rev. 20:7.) This means that once again men will begin to give heed to his enticements. Satan was bound among the Nephites during their golden era. None of the people were then subject to his wiles; all lived in righteousness, and all were saved. But in A.D. 201, "there began to be among them those who were lifted up in pride, such as the wearing of costly apparel, and all manner of fine pearls, and of the fine things of the world. And from that time forth they did have their goods and their substance no more common among them. And they began to be divided into classes; and they began to build up churches unto themselves to get gain, and began to deny the true church of Christ." (4 Ne. 1:24-26.) Soon there were persecution, crime, murder, and evil of every sort. So shall it be at the end of the Millennium. Men will begin again, gradually, to partake of the things of this world; pride and carnality and crime will commence anew; true believers will be persecuted and false churches will arise. Satan will be loosed because he is no longer bound by the righteousness of the people.

"And when he [Satan] is loosed again he shall only reign for a little season, and then cometh the end of the earth." This "little season" is presumed to be another thousand years. The reasoning is that Christ came in the meridian of time, which means both the high point in time and the middle of time. The millennial era will be the seventh period of one thousand years of this earth's temporal continuance; thus an added thousand-year period is needed to place the meridian of time in the midpoint in history. But be that as it may, "he that liveth in righteousness"—at the time of the actual end of the earth—"shall be changed in the twinkling of an eye, and the earth shall pass away so as by fire." This will be a second day of burning, the day when this earth becomes a celestial globe. "And the wicked shall go away into unquenchable fire, and their end no man knoweth on earth, nor ever shall know, until they come before me in judgment." (D&C 43:31-33.)

"And again, verily, verily, I say unto you," saith the Lord, "that when the thousand years are ended, and men again begin to deny their God, then will I spare the earth but for a little season." The language here bears out the concept that apostasy and its consequent evil way of life will be the key that opens the prison in which Satan is bound. "And the end shall come, and the heaven and the earth shall be consumed and pass away, and there shall be a new heaven and a new earth." There was a new earth and new heavens when the Millennium commenced. This is a second new heaven and new earth; it is the celestial earth and its heaven. The language in each instance is similar, but the meaning is different. In one instance the new earth is the paradisiacal earth; in this case it is the celestial globe. "For all old things shall pass away, and all things shall become new, even the heaven and the earth, and all the fulness thereof, both men and beasts, the fowls of the air, and the fishes of the sea; and not one hair, neither mote, shall be lost, for it is the workmanship of mine hand." (D&C 29:22-25.) All forms of life shall then be immortal; all shall come forth from death and live in a resurrected state forever; the resurrection applies to men and animals and fowls and fishes and creeping things—all shall rise in immortality and live forever in their destined orders and spheres of existence.

The war that began in heaven and has continued on earth will reach its climax during the little season after the Millennium. John says that when Satan is loosed, he "shall go out to deceive the nations which are in the four quarters of the earth, Gog and Magog, to gather them together to battle: the number of whom is as the sand of the sea." Once again war shall cover the earth; it will be Armageddon all over again. "And they"—the armies assembled in the forces of Lucifer—"went up on the breadth of the earth, and compassed the camp of the saints about, and the beloved city: and fire came down from God out of heaven, and devoured them." (Rev. 20:8-9.) Then Satan was cast out into outer darkness forever.

In latter-day revelation the account is given thus: "And Satan shall be bound, that old serpent, who is called the devil, and shall not be loosed for the space of a thousand years. And then he shall be loosed for a little season, that he may gather together his armies." The war in heaven was a war of ideologies; it was a war to determine how men would be saved; and so it is in the warfare of the world today. Lucifer's forces advocate a plan of salvation that is contrary to the Lord's true plan. And in the process, armies assemble and wars are fought, for the devil delights in destruction. And so shall it be after the Millennium. "And Michael, the seventh angel, even the archangel, shall gather together his armies, even the hosts of heaven." The saints of God, those who are in harmony with the divine will, those who are subject to priesthood direction, those who believe in Christ and align themselves in his cause, they shall take direction from Michael, who, under Christ, holds the keys of salvation for all His children. "And the devil shall gather together his armies; even the hosts of hell, and shall come up to battle against Michael and his armies." It is a continuation of the war in heaven. "And then cometh the battle of the great God; and the devil and his armies shall be cast away into their own place, that they shall not have power over the saints any more at all. For Michael shall fight their battles, and shall overcome him who seeketh the throne of him who sitteth upon the throne, even the Lamb. This is the glory of God, and the sanctified; and they shall not any more see death." (D&C 88:110-116.)

The Meek Inherit the Earth

Who shall dwell on the celestial earth? To answer this, we need but inquire who dwells on our present earth, and who shall dwell on the paradisiacal earth that is to be? And as we are aware, any mortal can live on this present low and fallen earth who lives at least a telestial law, because this earth is in a telestial state. Those who abide the day of our Lord's return, and who thus remain to live on the new earth with its new heavens, must live at least a terrestrial law, for the earth will then return to its Edenic or terrestrial state. And in the day of burning when this earth becomes in fact a celestial globe, none will be able to live on its surface unless they live a celestial law.

Telestial law is the law of evil, carnality, and corruption. Those who so live develop telestial bodies, which can stand telestial glory, which is found in a telestial kingdom. Terrestrial law is the law of decency and uprightness from a worldly standpoint. Those who conform to this higher order thereby create for themselves terrestrial bodies, which in turn can stand terrestrial glory and go to a terrestrial kingdom. Celestial law is the law of the gospel; it is the law of Christ. It calls upon men to forsake the world and rise above every carnal and evil thing. It calls upon men to repent and be baptized and receive the sanctifying power of the Holy Spirit of God. It requires that they become new creatures of the Holy Ghost. Only those who so live acquire thereby celestial bodies; only such bodies can stand celestial glory, and this glory is found only in a celestial kingdom. Since the final destiny of this earth is to become a celestial globe, it thereby becomes the ultimate and highest heaven for all the faithful who have lived on its surface.

One of several identifying characteristics of those who live a celestial law and hence will have an eternal inheritance on this earth is to call them the meek of the earth. In the scriptural sense the meek are the God-fearing and the righteous. Jesus said of himself: "I am meek and lowly in heart." (Matt. 11:29.) The meek are those who keep the commandments and are fit persons to associate with Him in whom meekness was perfected. Hence the psalmic word, given of old, "The meek shall inherit the earth; and shall delight themselves in the abundance of peace. . . . The righteous shall inherit the land, and dwell therein for ever." (Ps. 37:11, 29.) And hence the Beatitude, spoken by Jesus in the Sermon on the Mount, "Blessed are the meek: for they shall inherit the earth." (Matt. 5:5.)

All of this brings us to the divine word, revealed in latter days to Joseph Smith, in which the Lord tells his people how to gain an inheritance on the celestial earth. "And the redemption of the soul," saith the Lord, "is through him that quickeneth all things, in whose bosom it is decreed that the poor and meek of the earth shall inherit it.'' This is a modern reaffirmation of the ancient doctrine that the meek shall inherit the earth. Then, of the earth itself, the revelation says: ''Therefore, it must needs be sanctified from all unrighteousness, that it may be prepared for the celestial glory; for after it hath filled the measure of its creation, it shall be crowned with glory, even with the presence of God the Father; that bodies who are of the celestial kingdom may possess it forever and ever; for, for this intent was it made and created, and for this intent are they sanctified.'' It is common among us to say that the Lord's plan is to make of this earth a heaven and of man a God. Earth and man, both sanctified by obedience to gospel law, shall go forward everlastingly together. And whereas Christ the Son will grace the millennial earth with his presence, even God the Father will take up his abode, from time to time, on this earth in its celestial day.

''And again, verily I say unto you,'' the great proclamation continues, ''the earth abideth the law of a celestial kingdom, for it filleth the measure of its creation, and transgresseth not the law—Wherefore, it shall be sanctified; yea, notwithstanding it shall die, it shall be quickened again, and shall abide the power by which it is quickened, and the righteous shall inherit it. For notwithstanding they die, they also shall rise again, a spiritual body.'' (D&C 88:17-27.) God grant that we may be among them! These are they who lived during the Millennium and were changed at the age of a tree from mortality to immortality. And also, as pertaining to men in our day, ''These are they which came out of great tribulation, and have washed their robes, and made them white in the blood of the Lamb. Therefore are they before the throne of God, and serve him day and night in his temple: and he that sitteth on the throne shall dwell among them. They shall hunger no more, neither thirst anymore; neither shall the sun light on them, nor any heat. For the Lamb which is in the midst of the throne shall feed them, and shall lead them unto living fountains of waters: and God shall wipe away all tears from their eyes." (Rev. 7:14-17.)

The Celestial Jerusalem

O Jerusalem, Jerusalem, the Holy City, the City of the Great King, the symbol of Jehovah's rulership over his people, when wilt thou be sanctified and perfected? When wilt thou receive thy eternal glory and be a world capital from which the word of the Lord shall go forth to all nations? Surely it will be during the Millennium, or at least measurably so. As men measure matters of all sorts, the millennial day is the day of the triumph of Israel and of the City of David and of all the Lord's interests on earth. But there shall also be a heavenly Jerusalem, a celestial Jerusalem, a holy city in which both God and Christ will dwell, as occasion requires, and whence their word shall go forth to all the angelic hosts and to all exalted beings.

The heavenly Jerusalem is the capital city on the celestial earth. It is the place from which this celestial sphere will be governed. It is a symbol of God's eternal dominion over his own. In the extended and full sense the whole earth in that day will be a celestial Jerusalem. It was Paul, our friend of days gone by, speaking of those who would ascend the heights and receive eternal exaltation, who said: "Ye are come unto mount Sion, and unto the city of the living God, the heavenly Jerusalem, and to an innumerable company of angels, to the general assembly and church of the firstborn, which are written in heaven, and to God the Judge of all, and to the spirits of just men made perfect, and to Jesus the mediator of the new covenant." (Heb. 12:22-24.) The city of the living God, where saints and angels dwell! The Church of the Firstborn, the Church in heaven, all of whose members are exalted! Just men made perfect through Him who hath redeemed us with his blood! What greater glory can there be than to be one with those who dwell in such a city?

Our friend John, also an apostolic colleague of days gone by, saw in vision the Celestial City in all its glory and perfection, and it was his privilege to record for us as much of what he saw as our spiritual stature permits us to receive. He saw "that great city, the holy Jerusalem, descending out of heaven from God, having the glory of God: and her light was like unto a stone most precious, even like a jasper stone, clear as crystal; and had a wall great and high, and had twelve gates, and at the gates twelve angels, and names written thereon, which are the names of the twelve tribes of the children of Israel: on the east three gates; on the north three gates; on the south three gates; and on the west three gates."

Enoch's city shall return as the Millennium casts her silver rays o'er all the earth. It also is "the holy city, [a] new Jerusalem." But "the holy Jerusalem," the Celestial City, shall come after the Millennium, after the little season, after Michael leads the hosts of heaven against Lucifer, at whose beck the hosts of hell respond, and after the devil and his minions have been cast out into that outer darkness where they shall remain forever. And what better symbolism could the Lord have chosen to show the eternal triumph and glory of his chosen Israel than to place the names of the tribes of Jacob on the gates thereof? Surely the saved of Israel shall enter the Holy City through the gates appointed. And surely all men who are saved from the day of Abraham to the end of time shall belong to the house of Israel, for the faithful, be they Jew or Gentile, shall rise up and bless Abraham as their father. All such shall be adopted into the chosen lineage; all such shall become one with the Lord's people. Every single soul who has lived since Abraham and who gains eternal life shall rule and reign forever in his respective place in one of the tribes of those mighty patriarchs whom Jehovah himself chose to bear his name and after whom he himself has since been called. Truly he is the God of Abraham, Isaac, and Jacob.

"And the wall of the city had twelve foundations, and in them the names of the twelve apostles of the Lamb." (Rev. 21:2, 10-14.) Again the symbolism is perfect. As there are twelve tribes of Israel, who are the Lord's chosen people, so they were ruled by twelve princes—"the princes of Israel, heads of the house of their fathers, who were the princes of the tribes, and were over them." (Num. 7:2.) These princes held the equivalent of the apostolic office and position and were called upon to bear witness of Jehovah and his saving power and to lead their people in paths of truth and righteousness unto that same eternal life which we ourselves now seek. They were leaders in the congregation or church as it existed in Israel.

And as it had been among his people in the days of their birth as a nation, so Jehovah ordained that it should ever be. He organized his congregation or church and called his twelve princes in the meridian of time. It was to the saints in that holy organization that Paul said: "Ye are . . . built upon the foundation of the apostles and prophets, Jesus Christ himself being the chief corner stone." (Eph. 2:19-20.) How fitting that the names of the twelve apostles of the Lamb are in the very foundations of the Celestial City! They are the ones who held the keys of salvation for all men in their days. And there are no inhabitants within the sacred walls except those who believed the apostolic witness and obeyed the heaven-sent counsel of those sent to minister in their day. It is, of course, implicit in the whole presentation, for God is no respecter of persons, that there are other names also in the foundations and walls, names in addition to the Twelve of Jesus' day. Surely the names of the prophets and seers and legal administrators of the ages are all there.

There is no way to describe the Celestial City. In our finite state we cannot comprehend the glory and wonder of it all. There are no words in our language that can convey to our earthbound minds the eternal brilliance and shining brightness that prevail where God is. To give us some glimmer of what is involved, the holy account speaks of a city whose length and breadth and height are beyond understanding. The city is a cube that measures twelve thousand furlongs, close to fifteen hundred miles, in length and breadth and height. The inspired account says that "the city was pure gold, like unto clear glass," and "the foundations of the wall of the city were garnished with all manner of precious stones," which are named as being jasper, sapphire, chalcedony, emerald, sardonyx, sardius, chrysolite, beryl, topaz, chrysoprasus, jacinth, and amethyst. Then the account says: "And the twelve gates were twelve pearls; every several gate was of one pearl: and the street of the city was pure gold, as it were transparent glass." As we have heretofore seen, the celestial earth is described as being like a sea of glass and fire, and as a sphere like unto crystal, none of which we can fully comprehend.

"And I saw no temple therein," John continues, "for the Lord God Almighty and the Lamb are the temple of it." Both God and Christ dwell on the celestial earth and in the Celestial City, and the city and the whole earth (and in the ultimate sense of the word, they are one and the same) are, in fact, a temple. The whole earth in that day will be a Holy of Holies—not a Holy of Holies into which the high priest alone will enter once each year on the day of atonement, there to make atonement for the sins of the people and to pronounce the ineffable name, but a Holy of Holies where all the saints will dwell on all days, and where they, having been redeemed by the blood of the Lamb, will shout praises to God and the Lamb, using all their names, including many we do not even yet know.

"And the city had no need of the sun, neither of the moon, to shine in it: for the glory of God did lighten it, and the Lamb is the light thereof." (Rev. 21:15-23.) Of course there is no need for a sun by day and a moon by night, for the earth will have become a sun. It will be its own sun. Hence Paul's statement, "Our God is a consuming fire."

(Heb. 12:29.) Hence Isaiah's queries: "Who among us shall dwell with the devouring fire? who among us shall dwell with everlasting burnings?" (Isa. 33:14.) Hence Joseph Smith's statement relative to the saints who gain eternal life: "Although the earthly tabernacle is laid down and dissolved, they shall rise again to dwell in everlasting burnings in immortal glory, not to sorrow, suffer, or die any more; but they shall be heirs of God and joint heirs with Jesus Christ." And also: They must be "able to dwell in everlasting burnings, and to sit in glory, as do those who sit enthroned in everlasting power." (*Teachings*, p. 347.)

"And the nations of them which are saved shall walk in the light of it: and the kings of the earth do bring their glory and honour into it." All those who dwell therein have eternal life. "And the gates of it shall not be shut at all by day: for there shall be no night there. And they shall bring the glory and honour of the nations into it. And there shall in no wise enter into it any thing that defileth, neither whatsoever worketh abomination, or maketh a lie: but they which are written in the Lamb's book of life." (Rev. 21:24-27.)

Our apostolic author continues: "And he [the angelic ministrant] shewed me a pure river of water of life, clear as crystal, proceeding out of the throne of God and of the Lamb." These are the waters of which men shall drink and never thirst more. "In the midst of the street of it, and on either side of the river, was there the tree of life, which bare twelve manner of fruits, and yielded her fruit every month: and the leaves of the tree were for the healing of the nations." Adam in his ancient Eden was denied the privilege of partaking of the fruit of the tree of life, lest doing so he should live forever in his sins. But now, all who are freed from sin through the blood of the Lamb shall partake forever of that fruit of which men eat and never hunger more. "And there shall be no more curse: but the throne of God and of the Lamb shall be in it; and his servants shall serve him." Whereas the earth was cursed so that it brought forth thorns, thistles, briers, and noxious weeds, whereas man was required to eat his bread in the sweat of his face; whereas sorrow and death passed upon all men—all this in the beginning—now the ransom has been paid and all things have become new. The curse is gone and the earth is blessed, and all who dwell thereon enjoy peace and joy and life. "And they shall see his face; and his name shall be in their foreheads." All men shall see God, and on the crowns they wear will be his name—the name of God!—for they have exaltation and are themselves gods. "And there shall be no night there; and they need no candle, neither light of the sun; for the Lord God giveth them light: and they shall reign for ever and ever."

And of all of this John says (and what need he say more?): "Blessed are they that do his commandments, that they may have right to the tree of life, and may enter in through the gates into the city." (Rev. 22:1-5, 14.)

Eternal Life and Godhood

Full salvation is eternal life, and there is no other degree of eternal reward that has any special allurement for us. As Joseph Smith taught: "Salvation consists in the glory, authority, majesty, power and dominion which Jehovah possesses and in nothing else; and no being can possess it but himself or one like him." Let this definition weigh heavily upon us. It is the Lord's way of identifying the greatest of all the gifts of God, which is eternal life. Think of its meaning; it speaks of *glory!*, *authority!*, *majesty!*, *power!*, and *dominion!* In each instance they are to be the same characteristics as those possessed by the Lord Jehovah himself.

We are aware that the Eternal Father ordained and established a system of salvation to enable his spirit children to advance and progress and become like him. It was called the gospel of God. Christ was the chief advocate of this great and eternal plan and was chosen to be the Savior and Redeemer through whose good offices all of its terms and conditions have become operative. Hence, it is now called the gospel of Jesus Christ as a witness to all men that salvation is in Christ and in him alone. In his position as the Father's witness, as the chief proponent of the Father's plan, Christ proposed, as the Prophet taught, "to make" all mankind "like unto himself, and he was like the Father, the great prototype of all saved beings; and for any portion of the human family to be assimilated into their likeness is to be saved; and to be unlike them is to be destroyed; and on this hinge turns the door of salvation." (*Lectures on Faith*, lecture 7, paragraph 16.)

Thus those who gain eternal life, which is exaltation, become like God. They believe what he believes, know what he knows, and exercise the same powers he possesses. Like him they become omnipotent, omniscient, and omnipresent. They have advanced and progressed and become like him. They are the ones who receive an inheritance in the Celestial City.

"Thou art God," Enoch said to the Father, and "thou hast made me, and given unto me a right to thy throne." (Moses 7:59.) Man may sit on God's throne. Jesus said to the Three Nephites: "Ye shall have fulness of joy; and ye shall sit down in the kingdom of my Father; yea, your joy shall be full, even as the Father hath given me fulness of joy; and ye shall be even as I am, and I am even as the Father; and the Father and I are one." (3 Ne. 28:10.) Men may be even as Christ is and be one with him and his Father. And Jesus, announcing a principle of universal application, said: "To him that overcometh will I grant to sit with me in my throne, even as I also overcame, and am set down with my Father in his throne." (Rev. 3:21.) The Father, the Son, and all those who gain eternal life—which is the name of the kind of life that God lives—shall sit on the same throne and be one in all things.

Life both here and hereafter is very personal and real. We know what the associations of life are in this sphere and what they will be for the faithful in the realms ahead. Godly and upright living in both realms centers in the family unit.

There is no more sweet or tender or loving relationship known on earth than that which should exist between a man and his wife. And they twain should have like feelings for their children and descendants and for their parents and progenitors. With this in mind, we quote the inspired word that says: "And that same sociality which exists among us here will exist among us there, only it will be coupled with eternal glory, which glory we do not now enjoy." (D&C 130:2.)

And this brings us to the part celestial marriage plays in gaining eternal life. The revealed word acclaims: "In the celestial glory there are three heavens or degrees; and in order to obtain the highest, a man must enter into this order of the priesthood [meaning the new and everlasting covenant of marriage]; and if he does not, he cannot obtain it. He may enter into the other, but that is the end of his kingdom; he cannot have an increase." (D&C 131:1-4.) Eternal life or exaltation grows out of the continuation of the family unit in eternity. Exalted beings—who shall sit with God on his throne and be as he is—shall go to the highest heaven in the celestial world. Such is the sole and only place where the family unit continues. There they will have eternal increase, meaning spirit children in the resurrection forever and ever. Those who go to all lower kingdoms do not and cannot have such an increase.

In the resurrection all shall come forth from their graves. Every living soul will be resurrected; all will gain immortality. Those who believe and obey the fulness of gospel law, having been raised in immortality, will also be raised unto eternal life. The difference between those who have immortality only and those who have both immortality and eternal life is one thing: the continuation of the family unit in eternity. Those who go to the highest heaven in the celestial world will have eternal life because the family unit continues. Those who go to the lower two heavens in that kingdom, or to the terrestrial kingdom, or to the telestial kingdom, will have immortality only. Of them it is written: "For these angels did not abide my law; therefore, they cannot be enlarged, but remain separately and singly, without exaltation, in their saved condition, to all eternity; and from henceforth are not gods, but are angels of God forever and ever." In the resurrection men are raised to be angels or to be gods. Angels have immortality only; gods have both immortality and eternal life.

Of those who enter the Lord's order of matrimony and who keep their covenants and are true and faithful in all things, the Lord says: "They shall pass by the angels, and the gods, which are set there, to their exaltation and glory in all things, as hath been sealed upon their heads, which glory shall be a fulness and a continuation of the seeds forever and ever." That is to say, eternal life consists of two things: (1) the continuation of the family unit in eternity, which means a continuation of the seeds or the everlasting begetting of children; and (2) the receipt of the fulness of the glory of the Father, which is all power in heaven and on earth.

"Then shall they be gods, because they have no end; therefore shall they be from everlasting to everlasting, because they continue; then shall they be above all, because all things are subject unto them. Then shall they be gods, because they have all power, and the angels are subject unto them." (D&C 132:17, 19-20.) What saith the holy word about such glorious ones as these? It saith: "They are they who are the church of the Firstborn." Their membership is in the eternal church in the eternal heavens; the Church of the Firstborn is the church among exalted beings.

"They are they into whose hands the Father has given all things—they are they who are priests and kings, who have received of his fulness, and of his glory." They are the same kings and priests who lived and reigned with Christ on earth during the thousand years. And now they have received the fulness of the glory of the Father; they have all power in heaven and on earth; there is nothing they do not know and no power they do not possess. They "are priests of the Most High, after the order of Melchizedek, which was after the order of Enoch, which was after the order of the Only Begotten Son." They hold the power and authority of God, the very power by which the worlds were made; indeed, now they are creators in their own right; and in due course worlds will come rolling into existence at their word.

"Wherefore, as it is written, they are gods, even the sons of God." Having such high and glorious status, how could they be anything less than gods? "Wherefore, all things are theirs, whether life or death, or things present, or things to come, all are theirs and they are Christ's, and Christ is God's."

Viewing such a glorious destiny, shall we become high and lifted up in our feelings? Shall we let a holier-than-thou spirit enter our hearts? Let us, rather, remember that "they shall overcome all things," and that unless we so achieve, we shall not be numbered among them. "Wherefore, let no man glory in man, but rather let him glory in God, who shall subdue all enemies under his feet." We are not the ones who created these high rewards; we cannot resurrect ourselves; we cannot raise ourselves unto eternal life and place ourselves on the throne of God. All this is his doing; let us rejoice in him.

"These shall dwell in the presence of God and his Christ forever and ever." Theirs is an inheritance in heaven. "These are they whom he shall bring with him, when he shall come in the clouds of heaven to reign on the earth over his people. These are they who shall have part in the first resurrection. These are they who shall come forth in the resurrection of the just." And it is of them that we have spoken as we have recounted how the heavens would roll together as a scroll; how the saints on earth would be caught up to meet the Lord in the air; and how the dead in Christ would rise first.

"These are they who are come unto Mount Zion, and

unto the city of the living God, the heavenly place, the holiest of all." This is the Celestial City of which we have spoken. "These are they who have come to an innumerable company of angels, to the general assembly and church of Enoch, and of the Firstborn." John saw their number as ten thousand times ten thousand and thousands of thousands.

"These are they whose names are written in heaven, where God and Christ are the judge of all." Is he not telling us here that the names of all the exalted are written in the Lamb's Book of Life, and that their names, as well as those of the Twelve Apostles of the Lamb, shall be inscribed in the foundations and pillars, and on the thrones and royal seats, and in all the places of worship in the true Eternal City? "These are they who are just men made perfect through Jesus the mediator of the new covenant, who wrought out this perfect atonement through the shedding of his own blood. These are they whose bodies are celestial, whose glory is that of the sun, even the glory of God, the highest of all, whose glory the sun of the firmament is written of as being typical." All this glory, and all these wonders, and all this exaltation come because of the atoning sacrifice of the Lord Jesus Christ.

"And he makes them equal in power, and in might, and in dominion." (D&C 76:54-70, 95.) "And then shall the angels be crowned with the glory of his might, and the saints shall be filled with his glory, and receive their inheritance and be made equal with him." (D&C 88:107.)

And thus endeth our witness for the present moment. This work is completed. When more light is available and added revelations have been received, others with greater spiritual endowments will enlarge and perfect it. But for the present, according to our best judgment and understanding, we have testified of the coming of the Lord Jesus Christ to rule and reign on earth in the last days.

Our witness is true, and our doctrine is sound. He came once, and he shall come again. And nearly all that must precede that dread day has already transpired. God grant that "when he shall appear, we," according to the promises, "shall be like him" (1 Jn. 3:2), and that we shall find peace and glory with him, first in the New Jerusalem and then in the Holy Jerusalem.

Behold, and lo, the Bridegroom cometh, and that blessed year—the year of his redeemed—is at hand. The kingdoms of this world are falling, and the Lord God Omnipotent reigneth. Praise ye the Lord!

INDEX

Easter morning, first, 17-20
Egypt, 364-65
Elements, melting of, 526-29, 621
Elias: Christ as, 102; title of, applies to many, 103; keys restored by, 119, 268; of Restoration, 120
Elijah, 102, 105, 119; to come before great and dreadful day, 265-66; mission of, 267; appearance of, in Kirtland Temple, 268
Emmaus Road, 509-10
Enoch: Zion of, 89; saw coming forth of Book of Mormon, 150; upon mount Simeon, 274; cried repentance, 358; God's covenant with, 414-15; wept for earth, 615-16
Ensign to nations, 340-41
Ephraim: stick of Joseph in hands of, 156-57; tribe of, presides in last days, 189, 191; received greater blessing than Manasseh; 190; scattering of, 191-92; return of, to God, 202; tribe of, defined as Gentiles, 233; calls Israel to Zion, 289; gathering of, 320; millennial blessings of, 328-29. *See also* Israel
Eternal life: definition of, 37, 264, 705; gaining, 669-70, 706; differentiated from immortality, 707-8
Eternity: seven ages of, 11-23; cycle of, 23
Exaltation: age of, 22; involves becoming like God, 706. *See also* Salvation

Faith: power attending, 37-38; justification by, 48
Fall of Adam, 13, 643
False Christs, 47-48; doctrines of, 48-50; witnesses of, 73. *See also* Churches, false; Doctrines, false; Prophets, false
Family unit: importance of, 77; in Millennium, 655; eternal, 706-7
Fathers: promises made to, 258-60; turning hearts of, to children, 267
Fig tree, parable of, 344
Fire: plagues of, 382, 395, 559-60; and brimstone, 485; attending Second Coming, 525-26; purifying, 543-44; preserving righteous by, 559. *See also* Burning
First fruits of the Lord, 636
First Vision, Joseph Smith's, 57, 112
Flesh: falling of, from bones, 394; of mighty, beasts shall eat, 488-90
Flood, great, 356; as similitude of Second Coming, 357-61
Foreordination, 182, 660-61
Freedom, America is land of, 93-94

Gabriel, 119
Gadianton robbers, 64-65
Gathering of Israel: Moses restored keys of, 119, 202; role of Book of Mormon in, 161, 171-73; is sign of times, 184; God has decreed, 193-95; involves returning to Jehovah, 195; wonders of, will surpass preceding miracles, 196, 603-4; is spiritual and temporal, 198-99, 292; promises attending, 199; to appointed lands, 199-200; requires power and spirit of God, 201, 203; commandments concerning, given to first elders, 202; flight from Egypt was type of, 203; president of Church directs, 203, 322; will be as gathering of Lamanites, 214; must take place over whole earth, 215; Jesus speaks of, to Nephites, 247; to Zion, 290-92; premillennial, 311-12; millennial, 313-14; in preparation for Messiah's reign, 603, 608-10. *See also* Israel
Genealogy, 267, 270; as sign of times, 402
Gentiles: gathering of, into Israel, 197, 316; scattering of Lamanites by, 209; as nursing fathers and mothers to Israel, 214; definition of, 222, 233; offering of gospel to, after Jesus' death, 236-37; restoration of gospel through, 238; majority of, do not believe, 240; unrighteous among, destruction of, 241-42, 247-49; adoption of, into Abraham's family, 245; times of, to be fulfilled, 254-55; warning to, 255-57; to serve Israel in Millennium, 316-17;

Homosexuality, 43
Husbandmen, wicked, parable of, 345-46

Idols, destruction of, 430, 542, 664-65
Immortality: age of, 19-20; of all life forms, 696; differentiated from eternal life, 707-8
Increase, eternal, 707
Indians, American, 207-8. *See also* Lamanites
Iniquity: earth's inhabitants drunken with, 41-42; abundance of, in last days, 42-45, 100-101, 366-67, 549; men may repent of, 45-46; scattering of Israel due to, 186-87, 224-25; in Noah's day, 357-61; world ripened in, 392-93, 455; is sign of times, 403; recompense for, 500-501; increasing division of, from righteousness, 554. *See also* Sin
Intelligence, organizing of, 12
Isaac, 244, 262
Isaiah, 106-7, 513-15
Israel: uniting divided kingdoms of, 171-73, 329, 606; are chosen people, 182-83, 246; salvation is of, 184, 245, 701; vacillation of, between right and wrong, 185; scattering of, because of iniquity, 186-87, 224-25; all twelve tribes of, scriptures are written to, 215; is scattered to all nations, 216; call to, to return to sheepfold, 218-19; gospel went primarily to, before Christ, 235-36; glorious day of, is millennial, 248-49, 251; restoration of kingdom to, 309-11, 491-93; land of Canaan given to, 321-22; eagles of, 351-52; signs of times involving, 402; to champion cause of freedom, 454-55; many armies of, to die defending Jerusalem, 465-66; is the Lord's vineyard, 530; baptism of, 607; hope of, in resurrection, 638-39; shall enjoy fruits of labors, 656; the Lord will make new covenant with, 681. *See also* Gathering of Israel; Jews
Jackson County, Missouri, 280-81, 303-4
Jacob: remnant of, 140-41; blessings inherited by, 244-45, 263
Jehoshaphat, 459-60, 464
Jehovah: Israel must return to, 195; is Jesus Christ, 196; will make himself known, 197-98
Jerusalem: ripening of, in iniquity, 8, 463-64; siege against, 223; trodden down by Gentiles, 252-53, 389-90; temple to be built in, 278-80; as City of Peace, 297; destruction of, due to iniquity, 297-98; to be become great world capital, 299-300; state of, during Millennium, 300-301; rebuilding of, unto house of Israel, 304-5; celestial, 307-8, 700-705; two witnesses in, 390-92; redemption of, 461, 569; heights and depths of, 462-63; battle in, 464-67; the Lord will defend, 467-68. *See also* New Jerusalem
Jesse, root of, 339-40
Jesus Christ: testimony of, 4-6; ascension of, 6-9; life of, 15-17; resurrection of, 19-20; those who seek, shall find rest, 33; comes in all watches of night, 34-35; true prophets bear witness of, 69, 81; testimony of, is spirit of prophecy, 81-82; knowledge of, restored to earth, 88; as Elias, 102; new witness for, Book of Mormon is, 149, 159-60; as Eternal David, 172, 607-8; belief in, implies belief in Book of Mormon, 176-77; faith in, worked Israelite miracles, 185; is Jehovah, 196; witnesses of, 205; visited Ten Tribes after resurrection, 216; was a Jew, 220; Jews shall look upon, and recognize, 230-31, 469-71; three peoples in day of, 237-38; teachings of, to Nephites, 246-47; becoming sanctified in, 257; will suddenly come to temple, 271, 577-78; return of, to reign on earth, 306, 589-90; did not restore kingdom to Israel, 309; salvation comes only through, 333, 543-44; will visit all his people, 353-54; men demanded signs from, 399; shall defend Jerusalem, 467-68; to stand upon Olivet, 468, 576-77; great and dreadful day of, 495; shall be red in apparel, 503-4; loving

Mountains: of the Lord, 274-77; men desire, to fall upon them, 500
Mulek, 187, 206-7
Mysteries of godliness: revealing of, 110, 675-77, 680; are understood only by Spirit, 682-83

Natural disasters, 374-77, 408. *See also* Earthquakes
Nebuchadnezzar, 127-30, 187, 422-23, 463
Nephi: seeric abilities of, 51; saw great and abominable church, 51-56, 438-39
Nephites: golden era of, 42, 207; destruction of, Isaiah foresaw, 152-53; voice of, to speak from dust, 152-54; Jesus ministered among, 159; history of, 207; Jesus' teachings to, 246-47; the Three, 647-49, 680
Net, gospel, parable of, 345
New Jerusalem: Book of Mormon gathers people to, 170-71; building of temple in, 280-81; to be built in America, 302-4; for remnant of Joseph, 305. *See also* Zion
Noah: wickedness in day of, 357-61; prayed for his posterity, 414; God's covenants with, 414-16; stands next to Adam in priesthood, 581-82
North countries, leading of Israel from, 216, 325

Olive tree, Israel likened to, 211-12
Olives, Mount of, 464; cleaving of, 468, 576-77, 620-21
One of a city, gathering of, 201
Opposition in all things, 667
Ordinances: false, 80; binding, on earth and in heaven, 125; vicarious, for dead, 133, 269-70; performed during Millennium, 673-74

Palestine: gathering of Jews to, 229; Ten Tribes to return to, 320-22
Parables: of wheat and tares, 342-43; of ten virgins, 343-44; of fig tree, 344; of gospel net, 345; of wicked husbandmen, 345-46; of great supper, 346; of marriage of king's son, 346-47; of unjust judge, 347-48; of laborers in vineyard, 348-49; of pounds, 349-50; of talents, 350-51; of eagles, 351-52; of the Lord visiting his people, 353-54
Paradisiacal earth, 89, 356, 397, 614-15, 643
Peace: City of, 297; taking of, from earth, 367; millennial, 513, 654; covenant of, 608
Perfecting the saints, Church is for, 132-33
Persian Empire, 129
Pestilence. *See* Plagues
Peter: healed lame man, 85-86; restored Melchizedek Priesthood with James and John, 118; held keys to bind on earth and in heaven, 125; vision of, of unclean creatures, 237
Pilate, Pontius, 18
Plagues: cleansing of earth by, 378-79, 474; seen by John the Revelator, 379-80; unleashed by seven angels, 382-87; last, 393-98; justice of, 395; to smite Babylon, 444-45; to smite enemies of Jerusalem, 466; will continue until Second Coming, 550
Plan of salvation. *See* Salvation, plan of
Political systems, evil, 64; connection of, with ecclesiastical systems, 493
Posterity, blessings of, 262-65
Pounds, parable of, 349-50
Predestination to salvation, 48-49
Preparing the way of the Lord, 25, 34, 336-38; role of temples in, 273; commandments concerning, 571, 574; methods of, 572-74
Pride: of false churches, 60-62; abasing of, at Second Coming, 568
Priestcrafts, 82-83
Priesthood: false prophets do not hold, 82; must accompany restored gospel, 115-16; responsibilities of, 116-17; Aaronic, restoration of, 117-18; Melchizedek, restoration of, 118; extending blessings of, to all races, 242-43; Adam's preeminence in, 581-82

323-24; description of return of, 325-29. *See also* Israel
Ten virgins, parable of, 350-51
Testimony: borne by author, 4-6, 181; guidance of, will gather Israel, 204
Theocracy, 596
Thief in night, Second Coming is as, 27-28, 35, 687
Thousand years, the Lord's day is as, 31-32
Three Nephites, 647-49, 680
Time, Lord's reckoning of, 30-32
Tithing, 545-46
Titus, 463
Transformations, five, undergone by earth, 356-57, 535-36, 613-14, 642-43
Translated beings, 284-85, 644; life of, compared to millennial man, 647; ministries of, 647-49
Trinity, false concept of, 48, 73-74
Truth: is not divided, 126; springing out of earth, 150-51; Book of Mormon teaches, 160; flood of, 170; leads to righteousness, 369; will prevail, 663

Unjust judge, parable of, 347-48
Unprofitable servant, parables concerning, 349-51
Urim and Thummim, 178; earth to become, 694

Vengeance of the Lord: to rest upon nations, 287-88, 498, 500-504; justice of, 501; beginning with his house, 502
Vineyard of the Lord, 529; burning of, 530-32
Virgins, ten, parable of, 343-44
Voice of the Lord, 575-76

War: in heaven, 12, 666-67; missionary work in time of, 137-39; is earth's greatest evil, 370; ancient and modern, 370-71; as sign of times, 371, 403-4; preparing for, 373, 455, 460; ushers in Second Coming, 373-74; third part of men killed in, 386-87; comes because of sin, 463; within great and abominable church, 558-59; ceasing of, in Millennium, 654; final, after Millennium, 696-97. *See also* Armageddon
Warnings: are going forth, 685; given by Jesus, 686-90
Watches of night, Savior comes in all, 34
Watchman: heed words of, 684-86; Chief, 686
Waters: living, 328; smiting of, 383, 394
Wheat and tares: parable of, 342-43, 511-54; grow together in latter days, 549-50
Wicked, slaying of, 140-41, 250-51, 558; by fire, 313, 387-88, 547-48; at Armageddon, 450-53; by wrath of God, 496-500, 550; in one day, 650-51
Wicked husbandmen, parable of, 345-46
Wickedness. *See* Iniquity; Sin
Winepress, analogy of, 503-5
Wisdom, pouring out of, upon saints, 110-11, 675-77
Witchcraft, 83
Witnesses of Christ, 205, 310; two, in Jerusalem, 390-92
Woe, third and final, 387-88
Women: rebellion of, 45; seven, will cleave unto one man, 655
World: definition of, 532; righteous are not of, 532-33; end of, 534-35, 556
Worship, false, to cease, 662-65
Wrath of God: vials filled with, 393; pouring of, upon wicked, 496-500; fulness of, 559

Xerxes, 423

Zion: of Enoch, 89, 282-84; laying foundations of, 242; in Jackson County, Missouri, 280-81, 303-4; various localities called, 285-86, 293; is the pure in heart, 286; scourging of, 288; redemption of, 288-89, 461; gathering of saints to, 290-92; will be built in many places, 293-95; to become great world capital, 299-300; of Enoch, to meet New Jerusalem, 302-3, 416; fleeing unto, for safety, 304; those who fight against, to be destroyed, 559-60. *See also* New Jerusalem